THEOLOGICAL DICTIONARY

OF THE

NEW TESTAMENT

EDITED BY

GERHARD KITTEL

Translator and Editor

GEOFFREY W. BROMILEY, D. LITT., D. D.

Volume II

Δ—H

WM. B. EERDMANS PUBLISHING COMPANY

GRAND RAPIDS, MICHIGAN

Theological Dictionary of the New Testament

Translated from
Theologisches Wörterbuch zum Neuen Testament
Zweiter Band: Δ—H, herausgegeben von Gerhard Kittel
Published by
W. Kohlhammer Verlag
Stuttgart, Germany

First printing, March 1964
Second printing, May 1966
Third printing, October 1968
Fourth printing, May 1971
Fifth printing, August 1973
Sixth printing, May 1974
Seventh printing, May 1976

PHOTOLITHOPRINTED BY CUSHING - MALLOY, INC.
ANN ARBOR, MICHIGAN, UNITED STATES OF AMERICA
1971

Preface

At the conclusion of this second volume we realise that when we undertook the work we underestimated its magnitude. Perhaps it might have been possible pedantically to keep to the projected limits, though whether we could have done so without jeopardising the scholarly value is doubtful. Yet neither the editor nor publishers could resist the demand especially of our fellow-workers that if the work were to be done at all it should be done as thoroughly as possible in order that a true and lasting foundation should be laid for future research. Many remarks of friendly critics and encouraging voices from amongst our readers have confirmed us in our view that we are taking the right course.

We are deeply grateful that it has been possible to carry through the work thus far without any serious outer or inner disturbance. May this task which unites so many New Testament scholars help our Church to the health and true unity which can come only from the New Testament message.

Tübingen, July 1935.   *Kittel*

Editor's Preface

From the publication of the first volume, and during the years of its long and arduous composition, the *Theologisches Wörterbuch zum Neuen Testament*, familiarly known as Kittel or abbreviated as *TWNT*, has secured for itself a solid place in biblical scholarship, not only as a reference work or a starting-point for further research, but also as a formative contribution to theology.

There has, of course, been some misunderstanding of its role. While it is not a simple lexicon, it obviously cannot replace either the full commentary or the biblical theology. Its task is to mediate between ordinary lexicography and the specific task of exposition, more particularly at the theological level. For this reason attention is concentrated on theologically significant terms, and on the theologically significant usage of these terms.

When this is understood, Kittel is safeguarded against the indiscriminate enthusiasm which would make it a sole and absolute authority in lexical and exegetical matters. It is also safeguarded against the resultant criticism that it involves an illegitimate task for which it uses improper means. Its more limited, yet valid and invaluable role, can be appreciated, and its learning and insights incorporated into the great task of New Testament interpretation.

Hitherto access to the great bulk of *TWNT* has been only in the original language. Some of the more important articles have been translated in the *Key Words* series, and by virtue of the significance of the words selected this series has performed a most useful service. Yet even the chosen articles have undergone some abridgment and editorial redaction, quite apart from the fact that the main part of Kittel has not been translated at all.

By contrast, the present rendering aims to present the whole of *TWNT* in a faithful reproduction of the original. At the cost of less felicity, for German scholarship is no guarantee of stylistic elegance, the rendering is more closely tied to the German. Quotations are fully given in the original Hebrew, Greek and Latin, and the references are left as they are apart from essential changes. For scholars who may wish to consult the original, even the pagination is retained except for a slight fluctuating variation of no more than two or three pages either way. The external size of the volumes has been much reduced, however, and costs have been trimmed so as to provide the student with maximum material at minimum price.

It need hardly be said that the translation and publication of Kittel is no necessary endorsement of everything contained in it. Written by many scholars over a long period, Kittel naturally contains articles of unequal value and varying outlook. Indeed, there are internal disagreements as regards basic presuppositions, historical assumptions and specific interpretations. The ultimate worth of the undertaking lies in its fundamental orientation and its objective findings ; for these it is now presented in translation.

In the preparation of the volumes particular thanks are due to Professor F. F. Bruce of the University of Manchester for his many valuable suggestions and corrections in the course of laborious proof-reading. Also deserving of mention in this instance are the publishers for the courage and helpfulness which they have displayed in so monumental an enterprise, and the printers for the skill with which they have handled such difficult material. In spite of every effort, it would be presumptuous to suppose that all errors have been avoided, and the help of readers will be appreciated in detecting and eliminating those that remain.

Pasadena, California, 1964.

G. W. Bromiley

Contents

Contents

CONTRIBUTORS

Editor :

Gerhard Kittel, Tübingen.

Contributors :

Otto Bauernfeind, Tübingen.
Friedrich Baumgärtel, Greifswald.
Johannes Behm, Berlin.
Georg Bertram, Giessen.
Hermann W. Beyer, Greifswald.
Friedrich Büchsel, Rostock.
Rudolf Bultmann, Marburg.
Albert Debrunner, Jena.
Kurt Deissner, Greifswald.
Gerhard Delling, Glauchau.
Werner Foerster, Münster.
Gerhard Friedrich, Tübingen.
Ernst Fuchs, Winzerhausen (Württemberg).
Heinrich Greeven, Greifswald.
Walter Grundmann, Dresden.
Hermann Hanse, Kuhlhausen (Elbe).
Friedrich Hauck, Erlangen.
Johannes Herrmann, Münster.
Joachim Jeremias, Göttingen.
Hermann Kleinknecht, Tübingen.
Karl Georg Kuhn, Tübingen.
Wilhelm Michaelis, Berne.
Hugo Odeberg, Lund.
Albrecht Oepke, Leipzig.
Erik Peterson, Munich.
Herbert Preisker, Breslau.
Otto Procksch, Erlangen.
Gottfried Quell, Rostock.
Gerhard von Rad, Jena.
Karl Heinrich Rengstorf, Tübingen.
Oskar Rühle, Stuttgart.
Hermann Sasse, Erlangen.
Hans Heinrich Schaeder, Berlin.
Heinrich Schlier, Marburg.
Karl Ludwig Schmidt, Basel.
Otto Schmitz, Bethel.
Johannes Schneider, Berlin.
Julius Schniewind, Kiel.
Gottlob Schrenk, Zürich.
Hans Freiherr von Soden, Marburg.
Gustav Stählin, Leipzig and Madras, India.
Ethelbert Stauffer, Bonn.
Hermann Strathmann, Erlangen.
Albrecht Stumpff, Tübingen.
Artur Weiser, Tübingen.
Hans Windisch, Halle.

> δαίμων, δαιμόνιον, δαιμονίζομαι,
> δαιμονιώδης, δεισιδαίμων,
> δεισιδαιμονία

δαίμων, δαιμόνιον.

A. δαίμων in the Greek and Hellenistic World.

1. A basic animism underlies the Greek δαίμων concept. This persisted amongst the Greeks. In the historical period especially it was obviously combatted by educated and especially philosophical circles from which we draw almost all our knowledge of all levels of Gk. thought. Yet even these circles had to orientate themselves by popular ideas and thus give evidence of the common view to varying degrees. Hence we can fully understand the δαίμων concept only against the background of popular animistic beliefs. We may begin with the solid fact that the term δαίμων is used both for deity or minor deity and also in a philosophical sense, and that animistic views underlie the latter usage and thus demand our attention. [1]

δ α ί μ ω ν κτλ. On A.: R. Heinze, *Xenocrates* (1892), 78 ff.; H. Usener, *Götternamen* (1896), 291 ff.; O. Waser, in Pauly-W., IV (1901), 2010-12, *s.v.*, "Daimon"; A. Abt, *Die Apologie des Apuleius von Madaura u. d. antike Zauberei* (1908); J. Tambornino, *De antiquorum daemonismo* (1909); M. Pohlenz, *Vom Zorne Gottes* (1909), 129-56; F. Andres, *Die Engellehre d. griech. Apologeten d. 2. Jhdt.* (1914), 101-58 (quoted as *Engellehre*); in Pauly-W. Suppl. III (1918), 267-322, *s.v.* "Daimon" (quoted as Andres); T. Hopfner, *Griechisch-ägyptischer Offenbarungszauber,* I (1921); P. Friedländer, *Platon,* I (1928), 38-67; F. Pfister in *Bursians Jahresberichte,* Suppl., 229 (1930), 113; E. C. E. Owen, "Δαίμων and Cognate Words," JThSt, 32 (1931), 133-53; U. v. Wilamowitz-Moellendorff, *Der Glaube d. Hellenen,* I (1931), 362 ff. On B.: A. Kohut, *Über d. jüdische Angelologie u. Dämonologie in ihrer Abhängigkeit vom Parsismus* (1866); H. Duhm, *Die bösen Geister im AT* (1904); A. Jirku, *Die Dämonen u. ihre Abwehr im AT* (1912); H. Kaupel, *Die Dämonen im AT* (1930); EJ, VI, 634 ff.; Str.-B., I, 983 f.; III, 412 ff.; IV, 501 ff.; A. Bertholet, *Bibl. Theologie d. AT,* II (1911), 385 ff.; Bousset-Gressm., 331 ff.; Weber, 251 ff.; Schl. Mt., 259 f., 293, 324. On C.: O. Everling, *Die paulinische Angelologie u. Dämonologie* (1888); F. Conybeare, "The Demonology of the NT," JQR, 8/9 (1896/7); M. Dibelius, *Die Geisterwelt im Glauben d. Pls.* (1909); G. Kurze, *Der Engels- u. Teufelsglaube d. Ap. Pls.* (1915); J. Weiss, RE³, IV, 408 ff., *s.v.* "Dämonen" and "Dämonische"; O. Bauernfeind, *Die Worte der Dämonen im MkEv* (1927); H. Weinel, *Die Wirkungen des Geistes u. d. Geister* (1899), 1 ff.; Zn. Mt. on 10:1; Wbg. Mk., 58, n. 57; Kl. Mk.², 17; Hck. Mk., 24 f.; Ltzm. 1 K. on 10:20; Joh. W. 1 K. on 10:20; H. Gressmann, ZNW, 20 (1921), 224-30; Dausch Synpt.⁴, 153 ff. (with addit. bibl.); F. Sickenberger, "Engels- u. Teufelslästerer im Jud- u. 2. Petrbrief," in *Mitteilg. d. schles. Ges. f. Volkskunde,* 13/14 (1911), 621-39; K. Fenner, *Die Krankheit im NT* (1930); G. Sulzer, *Die Besessenheitsheilungen Jesu* (1921); T. K. Oesterreich, *Die Besessenheit* (1921); A. Titius, "Über d. Heilungen v. Dämonischen im NT," in *Theol. Festschr. f. N. Bonwetsch* (1918), 31 ff.

[1] Tambornino, 73 f. and Heinze, 114 view the development differently, assuming that the philosophers (from the time of Plato in the case of Heinze) used demonology for the purposes of theodicy and in conflict against myths, and that in consequence, and also through oriental influence, the doctrine of demons became basically dualistic and was popularised in this form. Against this Andres (267) rightly argues: "The concept and term δαίμων are much older (sc. than Homer), and lead us back to earlier periods of Gk. religion in which it resembles that of primitive peoples." Even in the philosophical development Andres emphasises again and again the connexion with popular belief (290, 294).

The etymology of δαίμων is uncertain. The root ΔΑΙ is basic, and cf. δαίομαι,[2] though the sense is doubtful. W. Porzig[3] is perhaps right in suggesting disruption or rending apart, and therefore in his conception of the δαίμων as that which consumes the body. This would certainly be in keeping with the animistic basis.[4]

Even in Homer the meaning is debated.[5] Certainly in the earliest periods known to us δαίμων is rather less precise than θεός. From its total usage we may perhaps best define it as a "supernatural power."

2. δαίμων as a Term for Gods and Divine Powers.

It is first used a. to denote "gods," and may still be used in this sense in Hellenism.[6] More specifically, it is used b. for "lesser deities." This is Plato's allusion when he defines δαίμονες as θεοί or θεῶν παῖδες νόθοι ἢ ἐκ νυμφῶν ἢ ἔκ τινων ἄλλων (Ap., 27cd), appealing to the popular view: ὧν δὴ καὶ λέγονται.[7] Thus we also read of δαίμονες πρόπολοι in the train of the gods,[8] of a Ἀδρεὺς δαίμων which has his name from the ingathering of fruits,[9] or of a δαίμων ἐπιμύλιος, ἔφορος τῶν ἀλετῶν.[10] These figures may have been gods originally, but the decisive point is that their character had changed at the time of writing.

Since δαίμων is more general than θεός, it is used c. when an"unknown superhuman factor" is at work: Philostr. Vit. Ap., IV, 44: ἐς ἔννοιαν ἀπηνέχθη δαίμονος ... ἔδοξε τῷ Τιγελλίνῳ ταῦτα δαιμόνιά τε εἶναι καὶ πρόσω ἀνθρώπου, καὶ ὥσπερ θεομαχεῖν φυλαττόμενος ...[11] Again, especially in the tragic dramatists, it denotes d. "anything which overtakes man," such as destiny, or death, or any good or evil fortune, Eur. Alc.: τὸν παρόντα δαίμονα,[12] cf. also Epict. Diss., I, 19, 19: κατά τινα δαίμονα == "by chance," and Jos. → 10. It can also be used generally for "fate," as in Soph. Oed. Tyr., 828 f.: ἆρ' οὐκ ἀπ' ὠμοῦ ταῦτα δαίμονός τις ἂν κρίνων ἐπ' ἀνδρὶ τῷδ' ἂν ὀρθοίη λόγον;

From this sense it is only a step to e. that of a "protective deity" watching over a man's life, or certain portions of it. Thus Pindar Olymp., 13, 105 speaks of the δαίμων γενέθλιος, and an unknown writer speaks of a new δαίμων beginning on the wedding night.[13] Menander Fr., 18 is particularly clear: ἅπαντι δαίμων ἀνδρὶ συμπαρίσταται

---

[2] Andres, 267; W. Schmid in Berliner philolog. Wochenschr., 47 (1927), 231.

[3] Indogerm. Forschungen, 41 (1923), 169/73.

[4] Cf. the name מַזִּיקִין in Judaism (→ 12) and Gk. names of demons such as Ἐμπούσα == "Bloodsucker," Λαμία == Devourer, Μορμολύκη == Werewolf and euphemistic names like Ἀλεξίκακοι etc., Hopfner § 27 ff.

[5] Waser, 2010: In Homer θεός means rather "the personality of a god as defined by cultus and mythology, whereas δαίμων denotes his power and activity as brought before us in life and nature." Cf. Andres Engellehre, 102: In Homer a god is called δαίμων when he meets man in his power and activity, whereas θεός is used for the divine personality itself." In the art. in Pauly-W., op. cit., 281 Andres emphasises that already in the Iliad δαίμων has more of a hostile character and that in the Odyssey it sends evil. From images like δαίμονι ἴσος for the onrushing hero Porzig concludes that a feeling of horror is essential to the concept, while Pfister finds the original conception in that of the "impersonal vital and magical power" of man.

[6] For examples, v. Hopfner § 11 and 166, sct. 179 f. (253 f.). Wilcken Ptol., I, 78, 35: πρὸς τὸν δαίμονα Κνῆφιν.

[7] Plat. Phaedr., 246e: Zeus is followed on his winged chariot by στρατιὰ θεῶν τε καὶ δαιμόνων.

[8] Andres, 283 f. Paus., I, 2, 5: δαίμων Ἄκρατος τῶν ἀμφὶ Διόνυσον; Plut. Quaest. Rom., 51 (II, 277a): Λάρητες ἐρινυώδεις ... καὶ ποίνιμοι δαίμονες.

[9] Etym. M., 18, 36.

[10] Eustath. Thessal. Comm. in Od., XX, 106.

[11] Note the θεομαχεῖν. Cf. Andres, 285.

[12] For further examples, Andres, 286.

[13] Andres, 288. Cf. also Usener, Götternamen, 295 ff.

εὐθὺς γενομένῳ μυσταγωγὸς τοῦ βίου ἀγαθός.[14] By the time of the Orphics this had led to the coining of the words εὐδαίμων and κακοδαίμων.[15,16] The thought was then applied in different ways. Heracl. Fr., 119 (I, p. 100, 11, Diels) coined the phrase ἦθος ἀνθρώπῳ δαίμων. Plato worked it out as follows (Resp., X, 617e, cf. 620d): οὐχ ὑμᾶς δαίμων λήξεται, ἀλλ᾽ ὑμεῖς δαίμονα αἱρήσεσθε. In Stoicism δαίμων then became f. a term for the "divinely related element in man": τὸ μὴ κατὰ πᾶν ἔπεσθαι τῷ ἐν αὐτῷ δαίμονι συγγενεῖ τε ὄντι καὶ τὴν ὁμοίαν φύσιν ἔχοντι τῷ τὸν ὅλον κόσμον διοικοῦντι.[17] The reference was to the νοῦς, the divine part in man, as explicitly in M. Ant., V, 27: ὁ δαίμων, ὃν ἑκάστῳ προστάτην καὶ ἡγεμόνα ὁ Ζεὺς ἔδωκεν ἀπόσπασμα ἑαυτοῦ. οὗτος δέ ἐστιν ὁ ἑκάστου νοῦς καὶ λόγος. In Epictetus the term amounts to much the same thing as conscience,[18] Diss., III, 22, 53: βούλευσαι ἐπιμελέστερον, γνῶθι σαυτόν, ἀνάκρινον τὸ δαιμόνιον, δίχα θεοῦ μὴ ἐπιχειρήσῃς. It is along these lines that we have reference to a τιμωρὸς δαίμων or to τιμωροί (Corp. Herm., I, 23; XIII, 7b). In the same context we may mention the use of the word for the interpretation of natural occurrence. It cannot be said with certainty whether the statement of Thales: νοῦν τοῦ κόσμου τὸν θεόν, τὸ δὲ πᾶν ἔμψυχον ἅμα καὶ δαιμόνων πλῆρες,[19] belongs to this category, but there are echoes of the thought in Epict. Diss., III, 13, 15: οὐδεὶς "Αιδης οὐδ᾽ 'Αχέρων ... ἀλλὰ πάντα θεῶν μεστὰ καὶ δαιμόνων. Similarly the stars are called δαίμονες.[20]

3. The Influence of Popular Religion on the Philosophical Systems.

In the above presentation δαίμων is philosophically understood as a general divine power and thus incorporated into the stream of Greek thinking. Yet philosophy could not stop at this. It was unable to carry through with full consistency its understanding of the world as a κόσμος of abstract forces. It also introduced δαίμονες as personal intermediary beings. This was helpful in the attack on myths and in their explanation. Oriental influences were also at work, as was the need for a theodicy. But the formulation of the doctrine of δαίμονες as controlling and disposing forces was mainly determined by the popular belief which we can here see at work and which can be largely reconstructed from the philosophical conceptions.[21] Thus Plutarch refers to the 'Αλάστορες as an example of evil demons (Def. Orac., 14. II, 417d).

A first instance of the influence of popular belief is to be seen in the fact that philosophy, too, sets heroes alongside demons. In popular belief it is hard to separate the two. Perhaps they are one and the same, as some philosophers assume. More specifically, however, the development led to a separate class of ἥρωες. The idea of intermediary beings was more systematically worked out in the course of time, and in the Neo-Platonists we thus find several classes of intermediaries. In philosophy the main task of these beings is to be messengers between the gods and men, i.e., to exercise supervision over men. Thus Hesiod Op., 122 f. already

---

[14] CGF, II, 974, Meineke ; Andres, 288.
[15] Usener, *Götternamen*, 296. Δαίμων can thus mean the evil star as well as the good spirit. Cf. Andres, 286 f.
[16] For more detail, cf. Andres, 289.
[17] Posidonius in Galen, *De Hippocrate et Platone*, 5, 6 (p. 469, Kühn); cf. also E. Zeller, *Philos. d. Griech.*⁴, III, 1 (1876), 328, n. 2; cf. Andres, 299.
[18] H. Osborne, JThSt, 32 (1931), 169 : δαίμων is the one good parallel to conscience in antiquity.
[19] Aëtius, I, 7, 11 in Andres, 290. According to Heinze, 85, δαίμονες here means gods.
[20] Hopfner § 166.
[21] Cf. the thesis of Hopfner that popular views and philosophy go hand in hand at every point (§ 10).

calls them φύλακες θνητῶν ἀνθρώπων. Plato lays down the lines of future development in Symp., 202e : πᾶν τὸ δαιμόνιον μεταξύ ἐστι θεοῦ τε καὶ θνητοῦ... Ἑρμηνεῦον καὶ διαπορθμεῦον θεοῖς τὰ παρ' ἀνθρώπων καὶ ἀνθρώποις τὰ παρὰ θεῶν, τῶν μὲν τὰς δεήσεις καὶ θυσίας, τῶν δὲ τὰς ἐπιτάξεις τε καὶ ἀμοιβὰς τῶν θυσιῶν, ἐν μέσῳ δὲ ὂν ἀμφοτέρων συμπληροῖ, ὥστε τὸ πᾶν αὐτὸ αὑτῷ ξυνδεδέσθαι. διὰ τούτου καὶ ἡ μαντικὴ πᾶσα χωρεῖ καὶ ἡ τῶν ἱερέων τέχνη τῶν τε περὶ τὰς θυσίας καὶ τὰς τελετὰς καὶ τὰς ἐπῳδὰς καὶ τὴν μαγγανείαν πᾶσαν καὶ γοητείαν. The Stoics adopt this view, and Posidonius integrates the demons into the great σύνδεσμος of nature.[22] For Plutarch the demons are mediators (e.g., Def. Orac., 13, II, 416e), and Max. Tyr. gives the following definition in VIII, 8 : εἰσὶ δ' αὐτῷ (sc. θεῷ) φύσεις, ἀθάνατοι δεύτεροι, οἱ καλούμενοι δεύτεροι ἐν μεθορίᾳ γῆς καὶ οὐρανοῦ τεταγμένοι· θεοῦ μὲν ἀσθενέστεροι, ἀνθρώπου δὲ ἰσχυρότεροι· θεῶν μὲν ὑπηρέται, ἀνθρώπων δὲ ἐπιστάται· θεῶν μὲν πλησιώτατοι, ἀνθρώπων δὲ ἐπιμελέστατοι.[23] This leads Porphyrius to the view that everything in nature is controlled by demons.[24]

In the more detailed development of the doctrine that demons are intermediary beings, regard is had to popular belief at three specific points. First, it is noteworthy that demons are brought into special connexion with those parts of the cultus and religion which are closest to animism, i.e., with magic and incantations. We can see this even before Plato in Empedocles,[25] and Xenocrates in particular traces back the apotropaic cult to evil demons,[26] while Stoicism attributes Manticism to demons.[27] This is true of Plutarch, and in Apuleius De Deo Socratis, 6 we read : *cuncta denuntiata et magorum varia miracula omnesque praesagiorum species reguntur* (i.e., by demons). In Xenocrates there emerges already a distinction between the higher forms of religion and the lower and more popular forms with which demons or evil demons are connected. In the developed form of this conception demons are forces which seek to divert from true worship, as in Porphyr. Abst., II, 40 : ἐν γὰρ δὴ καὶ τοῦτο τῆς μεγίστης βλάβης τῆς ἀπὸ τῶν κακοεργῶν δαιμόνων θετέον, ὅτι αὐτοὶ αἴτιοι τῶν περὶ τὴν γῆν παθημάτων, οἷον λοιμῶν, ἀφοριῶν, σεισμῶν, αὐχμῶν καὶ τῶν ὁμοίων, ἀναπείθουσιν ἡμᾶς, ὡς ἄρα τούτων αἴτιοί εἰσιν οἵπερ καὶ τῶν ἐναντιωτάτων, ἑαυτοὺς ἐξαίροντες τῆς αἰτίας... τρέπουσίν τε μετὰ τοῦτο ἐπὶ λιτανείας ἡμᾶς καὶ θυσίας τῶν ἀγαθοεργῶν θεῶν ὡς ὠργισμένων. ταῦτα δὲ καὶ τὰ ὅμοια ποιοῦσιν, μεταστῆσαι ἡμᾶς ἐθέλοντες ἀπὸ τῆς ὀρθῆς ἐννοίας τῶν θεῶν καὶ ἐφ' ἑαυτοὺς ἐπιτρέψαι. At an earlier stage already Apuleius De Deo Socr., 14 had traced back the cults of individual peoples to demons,[28] also ascribing unworthy myths to them (cf. Plutarch).

Secondly, it is to be noted that the demons as rulers of human destiny are specifically connected with misfortune and distress. This hurtful sway of demons is made to serve a positive goal in Corp. Herm., XVI, 10 f. : τὰ δὲ ὑπὸ τῶν θεῶν

---

[22] Diog. L. says of the Stoics in VII, 151: φασὶ δὲ εἶναι καί τινας δαίμονας, ἀνθρώπων συμπάθειαν ἔχοντας, ἐπόπτας τῶν ἀνθρωπείων πραγμάτων· καὶ ἥρωας, τὰς ὑπολελειμμένας τῶν σπουδαίων ψυχάς. On Posidonius, cf. K. Praechter, *Die Philosophie d. Altertums*[12] (1926), 479.

[23] Corp. Herm., XVI, 18 : δαίμονες δὲ θεοῖς ὑποτεταγμένοι ἀνθρώπους διοικοῦσιν.

[24] Andres, 314 f.

[25] Hopfner § 17.

[26] Heinze, 81-83, 94, 110 f.

[27] Andres, 298.

[28] *Ibid.*, 308.

ἐπιταττόμενα ἐνεργοῦσι θυέλλαις καὶ καταιγίσι καὶ πρηστῆρσι καὶ μετα-
βολαῖς πυρὸς καὶ σεισμοῖς, ἔτι δὲ λιμοῖς καὶ πολέμοις ἀμυνόμενοι τὴν ἀσέ-
βειαν... θεῶν μὲν γὰρ τὸ εὖ ποιεῖν, ἀνθρώπων δὲ τὸ εὐσεβεῖν, δαιμόνων δὲ
τὸ ἐπαμύνειν. [29] Similarly Plutarch, appealing to the disciples of Chrysippus, can
say in Quaest. Rom., 51 (II, 276f/277a): οἱ περὶ Χρύσιππον οἴονται φιλόσοφοι
φαῦλα δαιμόνια περινοστεῖν, οἷς οἱ θεοὶ δημίοις χρῶνται κολασταῖς ἐπὶ τοὺς
ἀνοσίους καὶ ἀδίκους ἀνθρώπους.

Thirdly, many philosophical systems have assimilated the doctrine of demons
possessing men. Extraordinary conditions are popularly ascribed to indwelling
deities, especially in the tragic dramatists and e.g. Hippocrates. [30] This was called
δαιμονᾶν or δαιμονίζεσθαι, a view which is developed in Porphyrius Abst., II,
36 ff. [31] to the effect that evil demons clothe themselves with flesh and blood in
the human body to kindle evil desires. But Plutarch already speaks plainly of demons
which undermine virtue in Dio, 2, 3 (I, 958e): οὐκ οἶδα μὴ τῶν πάνυ παλαιῶν ἀτο-
πώτατον ἀναγκασθῶμεν προσδέχεσθαι λόγον, ὡς τὰ φαῦλα δαιμόνια καὶ
βάσκανα προσφθονοῦντα τοῖς ἀγαθοῖς ἀνδράσι καὶ ταῖς πράξεσιν ἐνιστάμενα
ταραχὰς καὶ φόβους ἐπάγει σείοντα καὶ σφάλλοντα τὴν ἀρετήν, ὡς μὴ δια-
μείναντες ἐν τῷ καλῷ καὶ ἀκέραιοι βελτίονος ἐκείνων μοίρας μετὰ τὴν τελευτὴν τύχωσιν. In Corp. Herm., XVI, 15 this view is then linked with astrology. In
an ethical spiritualisation of the doctrine there can then be reference to a δαίμων
τιμωρός, ὅστις τὴν ὀξύτητα τοῦ πυρὸς προσβάλλων τοῦτον (sc. τὸν ἀσεβῆ)
βασανίζει καὶ ἐπ' αὐτὸν πῦρ ἐπὶ τὸ πλέον αὐξάνει καὶ θρώσκει αὐτὸν αἰσθη-
τῶς καὶ μᾶλλον ἐπὶ τὰς ἀνομίας αὐτὸν ὁπλίζει, ἵνα τύχῃ μείζονος τιμωρίας, [32]
and on the other hand it can be argued that falsehood belongs to the very essence
of demons. [33] This development is, however, comparatively late. [34]

Philosophy incorporated these intermediaries into its system and world view by
ascribing πάθη to demons [35] and by giving at least to evil demons a location close
to the earth. The doctrine that demons are ἐμπαθεῖς is old, going back at least as
far as Empedocles. [36] According to Plato [37] it was worked out by Xenocrates, [38]
and was shared by Chrysippus as well as Posidonius, and by Plutarch as well as
Apuleius and the Neo-Platonists. [39] Similarly, we already find the idea of their
location in the air in the Epinomis. [40] This is greatly expanded in connexion with
the πάθη doctrine, [41] and is then incorporated by the Neo-Platonists into a great
system of intermediaries which become the more imperfect and wicked the closer
they approximate to earth. [42] Thus the demons become spatial, and their place in

---

29 Nevertheless, this positive estimation of demons is not maintained throughout the
tractate.
30 Eur. Hipp., 141 ff. (→ 6); Andres, 277.
31 Cf. also Andres, 286.
32 Corp. Herm., I, 23. Cf. XVI, 15.
33 Hopfner § 52, based on Porphyr.
34 Cf. also Celsus (Orig. Cels., VIII, 60), cf. Andres, 310.
35 At this point, we need not touch on the idea of the mortality of demons linked with
that of their πάθη.
36 Hopfner § 17; Andres, 291.
37 Andres, 296; Heinze, 92-94.
38 Heinze, 80 ff., 94 ff.; Andres, 296 f.
39 Andres, 298 f., 301 ff., 307 ff., 311 ff.
40 Andres, 296.
41 Andres, Sctn. II passim.
42 Hopfner § 35 ff.

the great ladder from God to man and spirit to matter is that of beings which are superior to man but still imperfect. Their imperfection does not affect their relative divinity. Their wickedness is not simply that of an implacably and causelessly evil will; it is due to their link with matter, and may thus be regarded as an impulsion by cravings which are only too familiar to man, whether in the form of envy, or a self-seeking desire for honour, or the thirst for blood and the odour of sacrifice. [43] Although this view of the πάθη and location of demons corresponds to the impulse of Greek thinking, it is simply a reflection of the popular view of spirits. In animistic belief spirits are radically incalculable, and their operations are conceived after the analogy of men and their passions; they are easily provoked to wrath and envy.

4. δαίμων in Popular Greek Belief.

So far as concerns popular belief and its animistic basis we may simply say a. that demons are fundamentally the spirits of the departed. [44] In general, poetry and philosophy made a distinction between δαίμονες and ἥρωες, or spoke only of μάκαρες δαίμονες: Eur. Alc., 1002 f.: αὖτα ποτὲ προὔθαν' ἀνδρός, νῦν δ' ἐστὶ μάκαιρα δαίμων. [45] But Lucian gives us a clue to popular belief when he causes Peregrinus Proteus to pronounce through Theagenes that the one burned will appear as δαίμων νυκτόφυλαξ (Pergr. Mort., 27). We find the same idea in a phrase like δαίμονάς τινας εἶναι καὶ φαντάσματα καὶ νεκρῶν ψυχάς, Luc. Philopseudes, 29, or the reference in Hippocrates De Morbo Sacro, 1 (VI, p. 362, Littré): ὁκόσα δὲ δείματα νυκτὸς παρίσταται καὶ φόβοι καὶ παράνοιαι καὶ ἀναπηδήσιες ἐκ τῆς κλίνης καὶ φόβητρα καὶ φεύξιες ἔξω, Ἑκάτης φασὶν εἶναι ἐπιβολὰς ἢ ἡρώων ἐφόδους. The reference in Plinius Hist. Nat., XVIII, 118 is to the same effect, namely, that the Pythagoreans avoid beans because *mortuorum animae* are in them. [46] A particular role is played at this point by the souls of the disinherited or of those who have met violent death [47] — an animistic trait which is also seen in the particular connexion between Hecate and the other deities of the underworld on the one side and belief in demons or especially possession on the other: Eur. Hipp., 141 ff.: σὺ γὰρ ἔνθεος, ὦ κούρα, εἴτ' ἐκ Πανὸς εἴθ' Ἑκάτας ἢ σεμνῶν Κορυβάντων ἢ ματρὸς ὀρείας φοιτᾷς; Porphyr. De Philosophia ex Oraculis Haurienda, III, 164 bc: τοὺς δὲ πονηροὺς δαίμονας οὐκ εἰκῇ ὑπὸ τὸν Σάραπιν ὑποπτεύομεν... ὁ αὐτὸς δὲ τῷ Πλούτωνι ὁ θεός, καὶ διὰ τοῦτο μάλιστα δαιμόνων ἄρχων. [48]

According to popular belief demons are b. "shades" which appear in all kinds of places, especially the lonely, at all possible times, especially at night, and in the most varied forms, especially those of uncanny beasts. Lucian is again our best

---

[43] Porph. Abst., II, 37: ὡς ἄρα καὶ βλάπτοιεν ἂν εἰ χολωθεῖεν ἐπὶ τῷ παρορᾶσθαι καὶ μὴ τυγχάνειν τῆς νενομισμένης θεραπείας. Plut. Dio, 2, 3 (I, 958e) (→ 5).

[44] Contested by K. Latte, *Gnomon*, 3 (1927), 42.

[45] Hes. Op., 121 ff. Xenocrates and Posidonius (Heinze 83 and 98) as well as Apuleius (*ibid.*, 118) called the souls of the departed δαίμονες. Elsewhere, however, the Stoics avoided both terms, → n. 22. Cf. Tambornino, 69.

[46] Tambornino, 7.

[47] Andres, 275 f.; E. Rohde, *Psyche* [9, 10] (1925), 411 f.; Tambornino, 68 ff.

[48] Tambornino, 22; Xenophon, Ephesiaca, 1, 5: μάντεις and ἱερεῖς murmured strange things, ἐξιλάσκεσθαί τινας λέγοντες δαίμονας, καὶ προσεποίουν ὡς εἴη τὸ δεινὸν ἐκ τῶν ὑποχθονίων θεῶν. Δαίμονες πρόπολοι are particularly numerous in the train of the chthonic deities, Andres, 284.

witness when in Asin., 24 he causes the robbers to overtake the pursued maiden at a cross-roads and in mocking to say: ποῖ βαδίζεις ἀωρία, ταλαίπωρε; οὐδὲ τὰ δαιμόνια δέδοικας; or again when he writes in Philopseudes, 17: μόνος γὰρ Ἴων ... τὰ τοιαῦτα εἶδεν, οὐχὶ δὲ καὶ ἄλλοι πολλοὶ δαίμοσιν ἐντετυχήκασιν, οἱ μὲν νύκτωρ, οἱ δὲ μεθ' ἡμέραν ... (ibid., 31) αὐχμηρὸς καὶ κομήτης καὶ μελάντερος τοῦ ζόφου ..., ἄρτι μὲν κύων, ἄρτι δὲ ταῦρος γιγνόμενος ἢ λέων (of a demon). Furthermore, the demons are "spirits" manifested in the most diverse mischances. Happenings are often mysterious until it is recognised that a demon is at work. Thus we read in Dio Chrysostomus that in Olympia the horses shied at one spot on the racecourse, and the narrative continues (Or., 32, 76): ἔδοξεν οὖν τοῖς Ἠλείοις ὡς δαιμονίου τινὸς ὄντος ἱδρύσασθαι βωμόν. καὶ τὸ λοιπόν φασιν ἀπ' ἐκείνου γεγονέναι τὸν τόπον ἀσφαλῆ. The demon simply wanted its sacrifice; it was ἐμπαθής. [49] Other harmful demons have to be countered by the most drastic means, as when Apollonius of Tyana stoned the pest demon. [50] At this point we may recall the many popular names for demons or groups of demons, such as Ἀλεξίκακοι, Ἀλάστορες, Ἐμποῦσα, Λαμία and many others. [51] The belief in possession is also a part of popular belief, this being reflected in the tragic dramatists and spiritualised to some degree by the philosophers. This belief leads us directly to magic. Thus Plutarch tells us in Quaest. Conv., VII, 5, 4 (II, 706d/e): οἱ μάγοι τοὺς δαιμονιζομένους κελεύουσι τὰ Ἐφέσια γράμματα πρὸς αὐτοὺς καταλέγειν καὶ ὀνομάζειν. Philostratus narrates the healing by Apollonius of many who were possessed. [52] Ps.-Plutarch mentions a stone in the Nile which, when held to the nose of the possessed, expels the demon, so that he can say of it (De Fluviorum et Montium Nominibus, 16, 2, II, 1159d): ποιεῖ δὲ πρὸς τοὺς δαιμονιζομένους. Not so common, but no less clear, is the view that illnesses may be traced to demons. [53] Thus we read in Plato Leg., VII, 790d/e that nurses and αἱ περὶ τὰ τῶν Κορυβάντων ἰάματα τελοῦσαι walk around with young children who cannot sleep, and sing, καθάπερ αἱ τῶν ἐκφρόνων βακχειῶν ἰάσεις. Similarly, Plinius Hist. Nat., II, 16 refers to a demon of fever (cf. Philostratus Vit. Ap., IV, 10, 147 f. → n. 50). [54]

This leads us to the magic literature. Here are reflected both the myths and figures of the official cult and also popular ideas. Prescriptions are given against δαιμονῶντες, δαιμονιζόμενοι, δαιμονιόπληκτοι [55] and δαιμονοτάκται. [56] Their main content is the conjuring of a demon, god, κύριος or similar spirit [57] who with the help of magic formulae and practices, or through the power of a higher name, can be impressed into service (Preis. Zaub., V, 164 ff.: ὑπόταξόν μοι πάντα τὰ δαιμόνια, ἵνα μοι ἦν ὑπήκοος πᾶς δαίμων οὐράνιος καὶ αἰθέριος καὶ ἐπίγειος καὶ ὑπόγειος) or warded off (ibid., IV, 2698 ff.: φύλαξόν με ἀπὸ παντὸς δαίμονος ἀερίου καὶ ἐπιγείου καὶ ὑπογείου καὶ παντὸς ἀγγέλου καὶ φαντάσματος καὶ σκιασμοῦ καὶ ἐπιπομπῆς).

---

[49] Paus., VI, 20, 17: βάσκανόν τε εἶναι καὶ οὐκ εὐμενῆ δαίμονα.
[50] Philostr. Vit. Ap., IV, 10, 147 f.
[51] Hopfner §§ 28 ff.
[52] Philostr. Vit. Ap., III, 38, 138; IV, 20, 157 f.
[53] The reference is to what we would call inner sicknesses, i.e., those whose natural causes were not perceptible to the ancient world, as distinct from external wounds etc.
[54] On this pt., cf. Andres with bibl., and Tambornino passim.
[55] A. Dieterich in Jbch. f. Phil. Suppl., 16 (1888), 810 (IX, 1).
[56] Preis. Zaub., IV, 1374 f.
[57] Ibid., 218: Typhon is invoked: κύριε, θεὲ θεῶν, ἄναξ, δαῖμον. Cf. Abt 179 f. (253 f.).

A special role is played here, too, by the spirits of the dead, a νεκύδαιμον being invoked in Preis. Zaub., IV, 361, cf. εἴδωλα τῶν νεκύων in IV, 1474 f. More sophisticated ideas are also found, e.g., in the 8th Book of Moses[58]: οὗ αἱ ἀγαθαὶ ἀπόρροιαι τῶν ἀστέρων εἰσὶν δαίμονες καὶ Τύχαι καὶ Μοῖραι, ἐξ ὧν δίδοται πλοῦτος, εὐκερασία, εὐτεκνία, τύχη, τροφὴ ἀγαθή. The god who rules over life is called δαίμων in Preis. Zaub., XIII, 708 ff.: σὺ δὲ πυνθάνου· δέσποτα, τί μοι εἵμαρται; καὶ ἐρεῖ σοι καὶ περὶ ἄστρου καὶ ποῖός ἐστιν ὁ σὸς δαίμων καὶ ὁ ὡροσκόπος καὶ ποῦ ζήσῃ καὶ ποῦ ἀποθανεῖσαι. There is also invocation of the demons which control the elements in the sense of Neo-Platonic systematisation, e.g., Preis. Zaub., IV, 460 (Horus): δαῖμον ἀκοιμήτου πυρός.[59] Ibid., VII, 579 ff. distinguishes demons from ghosts.

In sum, we may say that in popular Greek belief the δαίμων is a being, often thought of as a spirit of the dead, endowed with supernatural powers, capricious and incalculable, present in unusual places at particular times and at work in terrifying events in nature and human life, but placated, controlled or at least held off by magical means. Philosophy tried to fashion these notions into the conception of the δαίμων as a divine force, but it had to take the popular belief into account, and to varying degrees it thus incorporated demons into its system as intermediary beings, and also found a radical place for popular belief with its doctrine of the πάθη of demons. Fundamentally, the whole Greek and Hellenistic view of demons is marked by the fact that everything demonic is brought into conjunction with the divine. The specific task of the πάθη doctrine is to make it possible to speak of the evil operations of divinely related beings.[60] There can be no thought of an absolute gulf between the divine and the demonic, even the spirits being also sinister powers.[61]

5. Demon Terminology in the Greek and Hellenistic World.

With a view to NT usage our primary concern here is with the difference between δαίμων and δαιμόνιον. The former is the usual term for the whole field; the latter is more limited in time and content. Δαιμόνιον is originally the neuter of the adj. δαιμόνιος. The meaning of the adj. brings out most clearly the distinctive features of the Gk. conception of demons, for it denotes that which lies outside human capacity and is thus to be attributed to the intervention of higher powers, whether for good or evil.[62] Τὸ δαιμόνιον in pre-Christian writers can be used in the sense of the "divine." The context sometimes makes it plain that it is not thought of as a true substantive.[63] This

---

[58] A. Dieterich, Abraxas (1891), 196, 4 ff.

[59] The fact that in magic the demons apparently do not occupy an intermediary spatial position between heaven and earth (Abt, 183 [257]) is linked with the further fact that in the Hellenistic period magic made use of all gods and spirits where they were localised (Abt, 183 [257], 4). Originally the spirits of magic are located in the air and on earth.

[60] Plut. Is. et Os., 25 (II, 360d/e): (τοὺς δαίμονας) ἐρρωμενεστέρους μὲν ἀνθρώπων γεγονέναι λέγουσι καὶ πολλῇ τῇ δυνάμει τὴν φύσιν ὑπερφέροντας ἡμῶν, τὸ δὲ θεῖον οὐκ ἀμιγὲς οὐδ' ἄκρατον ἔχοντας ...

[61] Cf. the striking distinction in Vett. Val., II, 12: ἐν ἱεροῖς τὸν βίον ἕξουσιν — ὑπὸ δαιμονίων καὶ φαντασίας εἰδώλων χρηματισθήσονται. We occasionally find a similar distinction elsewhere, e.g., Plut. Sept. Sap. Conv., 8 (II, 153a/b): τί ὠφελιμώτατον; θεός. Τί βλαβερώτατον; δαίμων; also Corp. Herm., IX, 3.

[62] Plut. Gen. Socr., 20 (II, 589d) speaks of ἱεροὺς καὶ δαιμονίους ἀνθρώπους, Ditt. Or., 383, 175 f.: κατὰ δαιμόνιον βούλησιν, "according to the divine will." Aeschin., 1, 41: περὶ δὲ τὸ πρᾶγμα τοῦτο δαιμονίως ἐσπουδακώς, "fearfully."

[63] Plat. Resp., II, 382e: πάντῃ ἄρα ἀψευδὲς τὸ δαιμόνιόν τε καὶ τὸ θεῖον. The argument in Plat. Ap., 27b/c would be superfluous if δαιμόνια were already regarded as a subst.

use midway between adj. and subst. is closely linked with the application of the term, and is to be interpreted in the light of it. It might be used in indefinite and comprehensive connotation of the divine generally, as in the Delphic inscription : [64] τὰν πᾶσάν τε σπουδὰν ποιούμενος τᾶς εἰς τὸ δαιμόνιον εὐσεβείας; [65] or especially of fate, where the use of the neuter of the adj. may be explained by the haziness of the belief in fate, cf. Demosth., 19, 239 : οἱ θεοὶ δὲ εἴσονται καὶ τὸ δαιμόνιον τὸν μὴ τὰ δίκαια ψηφισάμενον. [66] In Epictetus τὸ δαιμόνιον does not mean only fate, [67] but also the good spirit in man : Diss., III, 22, 53 : ἀνάκρινον τὸ δαιμόνιον, called δαίμων in I, 14, 12 and 14. In the work περὶ ὕψους, 9, 8 δαιμόνιον is, of course, used more generally for the divine, but in 9, 5 the horses of the gods are called δαιμόνια. Plutarch plainly uses δαιμόνια for intermediary beings, more specifically the evil : Quaest. Rom., 51 (II, 276 f./277a → 5); Dio, 2, 3 (I, 958e): τὰ φαῦλα δαιμόνια καὶ βάσκανα προσφθονοῦντα τοῖς ἀγαθοῖς ἀνδράσι; though Max. Tyr. can say [68] that Homer Ἀθηνᾶν καλεῖ τὸ δαιμόνιον. Here τὸ δαιμόνιον has become a subst. In the magic pap. the term is comparatively frequent. This fact has not yet been adequately explained. It is perhaps because the subst. is rooted in popular belief, possibly as a diminutive of δαίμων. [69] As we can see from the LXX (→ 12), the subst. is considerably older than is shown by the literary attestation.

Among other names for intermediary beings in the pre-Christian Gk. world we need refer only to ἥρως, εἴδωλον and ψυχή. Only in the post-Christian era do we find the words πνεῦμα and ἄγγελος, undoubtedly under Judaic influence.

6. δαίμων in Josephus and Philo.

Even terminologically Philo adopts the Gk. view. Thus he uses the adj. δαιμόνιος as special praise, e.g., in Aet. Mund., 64 : τέχνῃ δαιμονίῳ, ibid., 76 : τὸ δ᾽ ἀληθὲς δαιμονίως ἐστὶ καλόν, even linking it with θεῖος, ibid., 47: the stars ἢ θείας ἢ δαιμονίας φύσεις νομίζοντας. Δαίμων also signifies destiny in Omn. Prob. Lib., 130 (in a discussion between Greeks), as also in Flacc. 168 and 179. The word denotes a protective spirit in Omn. Prob. Lib., 39 : εὐμένειαν ὡς παρὰ τύχης καὶ ἀγαθοῦ δαίμονος αἰτεῖσθαι γλίχονται, and minor deities in Decal., 54 : δαίμονας ἐναλίους ὑπάρχους αὐτῷ (Ποσειδῶνι) προσαναπλάττοντες. Finally, the manes of a murdered wife are called δαίμονες (plur.) in Leg. Gaj., 65. The demonology of Philo is characterised by the fact (Gig., 6 and 16 ; Som., I, 141) that he regards the whole cosmos as having soul. He assigns δαίμονες to the air as their abode. For him, angels and demons are beings of the same character, though only some, aloof from what is earthly, are used by God as messengers, while others become men of different kinds. Philo thus stands in the Hellenistic tradition, sharing its terminology as opposed to the biblical and equating angels and demons. He does not refer to popular belief except perhaps when he says that knowledge of the equation of ἄγγελοι, ψυχαί and δαίμονες liberates from the burden of δεισιδαιμονία (Gig., 16). Worth noting is the fact that in Vit. Mos., I, 276 Balak leads Balaam to a hill, ἔνθα καὶ στήλην συνέβαινεν ἱδρῦσθαι δαιμονίου τινός, ἣν (!) οἱ ἐγχώριοι προσεκύνουν (→ 12).

---

[64] BCH, 20 (1896), 624, 13 f. (2nd cent. B.C.).
[65] CIG, 3045 (139a): μάλιστ᾽ ἄν τις στοχάζοιτο ἐκ τῆς συναντωμένης ἡμεῖν εὐμενείας διὰ ταῦτα παρὰ τοῦ δαιμονίου. The δαιμόνιον of Socrates also belongs linguistically to this category.
[66] Plat. Theaet., 151a : ἐνίοις μὲν τὸ γιγνόμενόν μοι δαιμόνιον ἀποκωλύει ξυνεῖναι. Menand. Epit., 527 f.: εὖ μοι κέχρηται ... τὸ δαιμόνιον. So also later Paus., VIII, 33, 1; Appian Hist. Rom., Libyke, 59. The index of Ditt. Syll.³ is also instructive, for there δαιμόνιον never denotes an intermediary being or the spirit of the dead.
[67] Diss., III, 1, 37; IV, 4, 39, Fr. 11 (fate = providence = Zeus).
[68] VIII, 5.
[69] Tert. Apologeticum, 32 (I, p. 237, Oehler): nescitis genios daemonas dici et inde diminutiva voce daemonia?

Josephus, too, moves in the world of Hellenistic usage and conception, but with one striking exception. The adj. δαιμόνιος means "dreadful" : συμφορὰ δαιμόνιος (earthquake) in Bell., 1, 370; superterrestrial : πρὸς ... τὰς δαιμονίους πληγὰς ἀθυμεῖν εἰκὸς ἦν, in Bell., 1, 373; and violent in relation to human acts : δαιμονίῳ ὁρμῇ τινι χρώμενος, a soldier sets fire to the temple, in Bell., 6, 252. Cf. also the common reference to δαιμόνιος πρόνοια, e.g., Ant., 13, 314; Bell., 2, 457; 7, 82 and 318. Only in relation to Saul does he speak of a δαιμόνιον πνεῦμα (Ant., 6, 214), thus approximating to the usage of the Palestinian Rabbis. Τὸ δαιμόνιον is used generally for the divine in Ap., 2, 263 and Bell., 1, 69. Δαίμων can be used for an individual mishap in Vit., 402 : ἐμποδὼν γενομένου δαίμονός τινος, and for fate in Bell., 1, 628 : ἐπεὶ δαίμων τις ἐξερημοῖ τὸν ἐμὸν οἶκον ... κλαύσομαι μὲν ἐγὼ τὴν ἄδικον εἱμαρμένην, cf. also Ant., 13, 415; 14, 291; Bell., 1, 556; 4, 41. Δαίμονες are spirits of the dead, and indeed of the blessed dead, in Bell., 6, 47 — an address of Titus to his soldiers. They are also the ghosts of the dead who seek vengeance in Ant., 13, 317: ψυχὴν ὀφειλομένην ἀδελφοῦ καὶ μητρὸς ... δαίμοσιν. The Roman view of *manes* [70] is borrowed, as also by Philo with his reference to the δαίμονες of a single individual, in Ant., 13, 416 : τοὺς Ἀλεξάνδρου δαίμονας; cf. also Bell., 1, 521, 599 and 607. Δαίμων is used for the protective spirit in Ant., 16, 210 : δαιμόνων ἀγαθῶν ἔτυχεν. Only once does Joseph. call the demons δαίμονες (Ant., 8, 45); elsewhere they are always δαιμόνια. He defines them as πονηρῶν ἀνθρώπων πνεύματα τοῖς ζῶσιν εἰσδυόμενα καὶ κτείνοντα τοὺς βοηθείας μὴ τυγχάνοντας (Bell., 7, 185, → n. 45). He mentions demons in speaking of the depression of Saul, which he attributes to δαιμόνια, Ant., 6, 166, 168 and 211 (they enter into him and evoke the attacks on David). He also mentions them in relation to the continuing magical power of Solomon, which binds the demons dwelling in men and casts them out (Ant., 8, 45-48).

A doubtful passage is Bell., 1, 84 : μηκέτι ταῖς ἐκ τῶν ἐμῶν σπλάγχνων χοαῖς ἐπειρωνευέσθω τὸ δαιμόνιον. In any case, however, Josephus is strikingly consistent in calling evil spirits δαιμόνια, even though he uses δαίμων in the Hellenistic sense.

B. The OT and Later Jewish View of Demons.

1. Belief in Spirits and Demons in the OT.

In the OT there are many traces of a belief similar to the popular Greek belief in spirits. The spirits of the dead to be consulted in witchcraft are called אֱלֹהִים in the invocation of the witch of Endor in 1 S. 28:13 : אֱלֹהִים רָאִיתִי עֹלִים מִן־הָאָרֶץ. We also read in Is. 8:19: הֲלוֹא־עַם אֶל־אֱלֹהָיו יִדְרֹשׁ בְּעַד הַחַיִּים אֶל־הַמֵּתִים.[71] This אֱלֹהִים corresponds exactly to the Gk. δαίμων. It is not certain whether the spirits of the dead are also denoted by אוֹב and יִדְּעֹנִי.[72] It is important, however, that in the days of Saul those who conjured up the dead were driven out of the land. This could hardly have been without precedent. It rests rather on the ancient command stated in Dt. 18:10 : לֹא־יִמָּצֵא בְךָ ... קֹסֵם קְסָמִים מְעוֹנֵן וּמְנַחֵשׁ וּמְכַשֵּׁף.[73] The force of this command is revealed in 1 S. 15:23a : חַטַּאת־קֶסֶם מֶרִי.[74] Balaam describes it as a characteristic of Israel, לֹא־נַחַשׁ בְּיַעֲקֹב וְלֹא־קֶסֶם בְּיִשְׂרָאֵל (Nu. 23:23). It is in keeping with the prohibition of magic that the name רְפָאִים is customary for the dead.[75] This prohibition

---

[70] Cf. Waser, 2011 f. On Jos., cf. A. Schlatter, *Wie sprach Josephus von Gott?* (1910), 41 ff.; *Theologie d. Judt.*, 35 f., 226 f.

[71] Jirku, 1 ff.

[72] Jirku contests this, 5 ff.

[73] Cf. Lv. 19:31; 20:6, 27 and 2 K. 21:6; 23:24.

[74] קסם is used for the conjuring up of a departed spirit in 1 S. 28:8.

[75] If the term is linked with רָפָה, cf. Ges.-Buhl, *s.v.*

is also responsible for the fact that the whole sphere of demonology appears only on the margin in the OT. In many stories (e.g., Jacob at Jabbok) and cultic usages we may suspect an animistic basis, but these things have no great influence on the OT and our conclusions are only tentative. Demonic figures are encountered for certain only in the שֵׁדִים, the שְׂעִירִים, [76] and proper names like לִילִית, עֲזָאזֵל and עֲלוּקָה. On occasion these spirits are mentioned to depict the utter destruction of Babylon or Edom, in the ruins of which all kinds of beasts and שְׂעִירִים find their dens and Lilith a resting place (Is. 34:14; 13:21). The underlying popular beliefs concerning the abodes of demons and the homelessness of Lilith may be easily recognised, but the passages show no less plainly that these beliefs are only used and not accepted. In a few passages there is reference to sacrifices to שֵׁדִים and שְׂעִירִים. Thus in Lv. 17:7: וְלֹא־יִזְבְּחוּ עוֹד אֶת־זִבְחֵיהֶם לַשְּׂעִירִים אֲשֶׁר הֵם זֹנִים אַחֲרֵיהֶם de-notes spirits to whom a portion is offered on the occasion of sacrifice. The other passages refer to Israel's idolatry: Dt. 32:17: יִזְבְּחוּ לַשֵּׁדִים לֹא אֱלֹהַּ אֱלֹהִים לֹא יְדָעוּם; Ps. 106:37: וַיַּעֲמֶד־לוֹ כֹהֲנִים לַבָּמוֹת וְלַשְּׂעִירִים וְלָעֲגָלִים; 2 Ch. 11:15: וַיִּזְבְּחוּ אֶת־בְּנֵיהֶם וְאֶת־בְּנוֹתֵיהֶם לַשֵּׁדִים אֲשֶׁר עָשָׂה. Here it is hard to determine whether שֵׁד and שָׂעִיר are used contemptuously of idols or of real demons. [77] The only passage where there is possible reference to protection against demons is in Ps. 91:6 if we follow the LXX and read מִקֶּטֶב וְשֵׁד צָהֳרָיִם. [78] In general we may say the OT knows no demons with whom one may have dealings in magic even for the purpose of warding them off.

The Gk. δαίμων concept embraced the forces which mediate between God and men. It is characteristic of the OT that a special name was coined describing such powers as God's messengers, i.e., מַלְאָךְ → ἄγγελος. In this way a linguistic and material basis was given for dualism within the spirit world, and the way was thus prepared for later development. It is particularly important to realise that the actual workings of destructive powers, which in the Gk. world are attributed to δαίμονες, are in the OT ascribed to the rule of God. God sends the מַלְאָךְ הַמַּשְׁחִית not merely to avenge Himself on His enemies [79] but also to bring famine and pestilence (2 S. 24:16). To express the same thought רוּחַ רָעָה is also used, [80] this being plainly distinguished from רוּחַ יהוה (1 S. 16:14). OT monotheism is thus maintained, since no power to which man might turn in any matter is outside the one God of Israel.

In the LXX שֵׁד is always translated δαιμόνιον, as is שָׂעִיר in Is. 13:21; 34:14. [81] On the other hand, in Lv. 17:7; 2 Ch. 11:15 (εἴδωλα καὶ) μάταια is used for שָׂעִיר. δαιμόνιον also occurs in ψ 90:6, [82] and in Is. 65:3 we have (θυμιῶσιν) τοῖς δαιμονίοις, ἃ οὐκ ἔστιν. Mention may also be made of Bar. 4:7: παρωξύνατε γὰρ τὸν ποιήσαντα ὑμᾶς θύσαντες δαιμονίοις καὶ οὐ θεῷ. The fact that δαι-

---

[76] Strictly the "hairy ones," cf. W. R. Smith, Die Rel. d. Semiten (1899 G.T.), 84: the jinns are also thought of as hairy.

[77] Perhaps we should also read בָּמוֹת הַשְּׂעִירִים in 2 K. 23:8, and לַשֵּׁדִים for שׂוֹרִים in Hos. 12:11 (12), where the LXX has ἄρχοντες for שָׂרִים.

[78] We hardly need mention the other passages in which there seem to be echoes or primitive conceptions of demons of sickness or tree demons.

[79] Gn. 19:1, 15; Ex. 12:23; 2 K. 19:35; Ps. 35:5 f.; Ez. 9:1 ff.

[80] Ju. 9:23; 1 S. 16:14 ff., 23; 18:10; 19:9; cf. 1 K. 22:21 ff.

[81] Materially similar is Bar. 4:35: κατοικηθήσεται ὑπὸ δαιμονίων.

[82] Ps. 96:5 Mas.: כָּל־אֱלֹהֵי הָעַמִּים אֱלִילִים.

μόνιον can also be used for אֱלִיל (along with βδέλυγμα, εἴδωλον and χειροποίη-τον), and that εἴδωλον and μάταιον occur for שָׂעִיר (along with δαιμόνιον), shows that the LXX takes for granted something which is by no means certain in the Mas., namely, that δαιμόνιον is a contemptuous term for heathen gods. The point of the translation is not simply to express the fact that Israelites must have no more dealings with heathen gods than with demons, but also to show that δαιμόνιον signifies the spirits of popular belief which are so dreadful to man: such beings are the gods of the heathen. The meaning of δαιμόνιον is thus nar-rowed down as compared with the Gk. δαίμων.

Apart from the verse in ψ 90:6 already mentioned, true spirits are found only in Tob. 6:8 ff. Here we read of an evil and envious spirit which attacks and destroys man. This is the first indication of a new development according to which the spirits are brought into connexion with man. It will be our task to trace this development in the sections which follow. At the same time, by its consistent use of δαιμόνια rather than δαίμονες for these spirits, the LXX sets a linguistic pattern. This is followed no less by Joseph. than by the NT. It is a mere hypothesis to explain this choice in terms of the more general character of δαιμόνιον. [83] The more likely explanation is that δαιμόνιον belongs more specifically to popular belief. Thus the LXX probably gives us the oldest examples of a popular usage which is only sparsely attested in the Hellenistic period. Δαίμων is avoided because it is too closely associated with positive religious elements, whereas δαι-μόνιον indicates from the very first the hostile spirits of popular belief. The singular passage in Philo (→ 9) seems to support this. Philo is choosing a word familiar either from the LXX or surrounding popular speech to indicate hostile spirits, and therefore suitable to describe the idols of Balak.

2. Tannaitic Judaism.

In Tannaitic Judaism we find a widespread belief in the existence of spirits, and the important point is that the Rabbis take this into account either positively or negatively. The wealth of name is noteworthy. We find a. individual names like Lilith, Agrath bath Machlath, [84] Bath Chorin [85] and others; b. group names, of which the OT שֵׁד is very common, while שָׂעִיר is seldom found. [86] No less common than שֵׁד is מַזִּיק ("smiter"), an easily understandable name, while פֶּגַע ("assailant") is rare. Particularly common is the simple רוּחַ, or compounds like רוּחַ רָעָה (a different use from that of the OT), or רוּחַ־בִּישׁ, or especially רוּחַ טֻמְאָה. The use of רוּחַ for "spirit" is Jewish, since it is only later and under Jewish influence that we find πνεύματα (cf. ἄγγελοι) in Hellenism.

In Judaism the conception of spirits is based on that of angels. Wings are ascribed to them, and special knowledge, though in respect of sensual needs they resemble men. [87]

As concerns the functions ascribed to demons in Rabbinic Judaism, the OT view is followed that the magician achieves real contact with them. Thus in bSanh., 65b and S. Dt. on 18:12 [88] there is a comparison, attributed to Aqiba in the first source and R. Eleazar in the second, between the one who attains to the position where the רוּח טומאה dwells on him and the rabbis who vainly seek that the רוח הקדש should rest

---

[83] Dibelius, 226 f.
[84] bPes., 112b (Bar.), Str.-B., IV, 514.
[85] bShab., 109a (Bar.), Str.-B., IV, 517.
[86] S. Lv. 17:7 thinks it necessary to explain שְׂיִּרִים by שֵׁדִים, Str.-B., IV, 501.
[87] bChag., 16a (Bar.), Str.-B., IV, 507 f.
[88] Str.-B., I, 492; IV, 503.

upon them. This comparison also shows us that God's Holy Spirit is the direct opposite of the רוח טומאה, there being a complete antithesis and therefore absolute incompatibility between them. This opposition is plainly brought out in the later passage Ex. r., 10, 7 on 8:14, [89] in which מעשה שדים and מעשה אלהים are contrasted. It is not accidental that the name "spirit of uncleanness" or "spirit of defilement" is used here. Uncleanness is contracted at its abodes, especially graves. Horror of these places (→ βδέλυγμα) colours the name, which is used especially for demons in necromancy. [90] In the 2nd century the sense of the demonic and unclean in relation to spirits began to fade, and therefore the name רוח טומאה became less frequent. In bSanh., 101a R. Jose forbids the consultation of שֵׁדִים only on the Sabbath, and even this is not successful. [91]

It is perhaps in reflection of the view that demons are unclean that washing the hands in the morning is connected with demons [92] — a custom which goes back to the time of Jesus. [93] Yet the menace of demons is perhaps more compelling than their uncleanness. Thus in Baraita bPes., 112a [94] a רוח רעה rests on food and drink left under the bed over night, and to drink water over night at midweek and the Sabbath is dangerous on account of the רוח רעה.

The main function of demons in Rabbinic Judaism is to do harm to life and limb. The Rabbis take note of this in many decisions. The man who fears a רוח רעה may extinguish the Sabbath lamp (Shab, 2, 5). On account of the demon Agrath bath Machlath one should not go out alone at night. [95] Because of demons one should not enter ruins, [96] and R. Jonathan says [97] that the מזיקין would kill man if he were not protected by God's Word.

It need hardly surprise us that sickness is attributed to demons in the Tannaitic period. Thus a Baraita bAZ, 12b [98] calls Shabriri the demon of blindness, and bBek., 44b interprets the Mishnah expression רוח קצרית as signifying the בן נפלים. [99] On the other hand, not all sicknesses are traced back to demons.

As we read of demons of sickness, there are also references to seducing demons. In a Baraita bErub., 41b [100] we read : ג' דברים מעבירין את האדם על דעתו ועל דעת קונו אלו הן עובדי כוכבים ורוח רעה ודקדוקי עניות, and a Baraita of the school of R. Ishmael, bSota, 3a, [101] says that a man will only lust after a woman if a רוח has entered into him. This use of רוח is linked, however, with the tendency to ascribe inexplicable happenings to spirits. Thus Erub., 4, 1 takes it that a רוח רעה can cause a man to transgress the Sabbath. The reference is to attacks of madness which also occupy the Rabbis elsewhere.

In assessing the Tannaitic view of demons it is important that the demons are not brought into any firm connexion with Satan either now or later, and that their supreme aim is to do harm to life and limb. There was confidence that God and His angels,

[89] Schl. J. on 10:21.
[90] bNidda, 17a (Simeon b. Jochai), Str.-B., I, 492. The "spirit of the uncleanness of corpses" referred to by Jochanan b. Zakkai, Pesikt., 40a (Str.-B., IV, 524) is mentioned only to make it clear to the Gentiles (v. the continuation).
[91] Str.-B., IV, 525.
[92] bBer., 51a (Bar.), Str.-B., IV, 513; bShab., 108b (Bar.), Str.-B., IV, 517.
[93] To Shammai, bJoma, 77b, Str.-B., IV, 517.
[94] Str.-B., IV, 503.
[95] bPes., 112b (Bar.), Str.-B., IV, 514.
[96] bBer. 3a (Bar.), Str.-B., IV, 516d.
[97] Midr. Ps. 104 § 24, Str.-B., IV, 528.
[98] Str.-B., IV, 532.
[99] Ibid., 525.
[100] Str.-B., IV, 503. Cf. S. Dt., 318 E on 32:17: מה דרכו של שד נכנס לאדם וכופה אותו, and S. Dt., 321 on 32:24, Str.-B., IV, 523.
[101] Str.-B., IV, 504.

and study of the Torah, were able to protect against them, but even in the time of the
Mishnah fear of demons led to all kinds of external precautions against them. [102] This
gives evidence of an obvious weakening of faith in God. Positive dealings with demons
are strictly forbidden in general, as we may see from the name רוח טומאה. But the Rabbis
made some concessions to the witchcraft which was so widespread among the people. [103]
Thus it is reported of R. Jochanan b. Zakkai that he understood the language of
demons! [104] In distinction from the Gks., however, Judaism did not regard demons as
intermediaries between God and men. The spirit world remained sharply divided into
angels and demons, whether in popular belief or among the Rabbis. The שֵׁד never
became a מַלְאָךְ. The hope of Israel was that one day the spirits as well as the nations
would fear Israel. [105]

Only occasionally did the מַלְאָכִים become demons. This was first the case with the
מַלְאֲכֵי חַבָּלָה or מַלְאָכִים מַשְׁחִיתִים, which were partly seen as fulfilling the will of God [106]
and partly as in the service of Satan, while others were quite remote from God. [107]
Already in the Tannaitic period angels could be described as demonic powers hostile to
men. [108] R. Eliezer b. R. Jose ha-Gelili went further and spoke of the angels of Satan
which lead the ungodly. [109] But this does not remove the distinction between angels and
demons. There is simply a linguistic fusion which is to be understood historically.

3. Pseudepigraphical Judaism.

Linguistically and materially pseudepigraphical Judaism stands between the OT and
Rabbinic Judaism in respect of demonology. In particular, there is no parallel to the
Rabbinic name מַזִּיק, although in terms of Gn. 6:1 ff. there is reference to a fall of the
"sons of God," to fallen ἄγγελοι υἱοὶ οὐρανοῦ (Eth. En. 6:2) and therefore to fallen
angels (cf. esp. Eth. En. and Jub. 5:1). In Da. 4:10, 14, 20 we read of a holy עִיר, translated ἄγγελος in the LXX and ἐγρήγορος in ᾽Α and Σ. This name is linked with
the fallen angels in Eth. En. 10:9; 15:9; Jub. 10:5; Damasc. 2:8. [110] Satan's angels are
also called demons in Vit. Ad., 16 (ἡμεῖς); Damasc. 16:5. Most common, however, is
πνεῦμα (Eth. En. 15:8; 19:1; Jub. 10:5; 11:5; Apc. Eliae 23:5). We thus find unclean
spirits in Eth. En. 99:7; evil spirits in Jub. 10:3, 13; 11:4; 12:20; spirits of Beliar in
Damasc. 12:2; spirits of Mastema in Jub. 19:28 and a very common use of πνεῦμα,
πνεῦμα Βελίαρ, πνεῦμα τῆς πλάνης etc. in Test. XII. Demons are referred to with
comparative infrequency. We have δαίμονες in Apc. Adae; [111] Apc. Abr. 26B; [112]
δαιμόνια in Eth. En. 19:1; Gr. Bar. 16:3; unclean demons in Jub. 10:1. The use of πνεῦμα
and δαίμων is parallel in the pseudepigraphical and Rabbinic writings.

Of the view of demons in the pseudepigrapha we should note first that, in contrast
to the Rabbis, we meet only rarely the belief in capricious spirits which seek to harm
man and against which precautions can be taken. Cf. Apc. Adae 10a, p. 141; 1a and 4a,
p. 142, James; [113] Gr. Bar. 16:3 and esp. Eth. En. 15:11: καὶ τὰ πνεύματα τῶν γιγάν-

---

[102] Shab., 8, 3, Str.-B., IV, 529; Shab., 6, 9, Str.-B., IV, 532.
[103] Ab., 2, 7: מרבה נשים מרבה כשפים.
[104] bSukka, 28a, Str.-B., IV, 535.
[105] jBer., 9a, 37, Str.-B., IV, 527; S. Lv., 26, 6, Str.-B., IV, 527.
[106] R. Jose b. Juda, bShab., 119b, Str.-B., III, 416. Cf. Str.-B., III, 412 ff.
[107] Tanch. תזריע 115b, Str.-B., III, 30a.
[108] bPes., 112b, Str.-B., 308.
[109] T. Shab., 17, 2 f., Str.-B., III, 416m.
[110] Read עִירֵי הַשָּׁמַיִם for עִירֵי הַשָּׁמַיִם.
[111] M. R. James, Apocrypha anecdota, Texts and Studies, II, 3 (1893), 139 ff.; I, a, p. 142.
[112] N. Bonwetsch, Apk. Abrahams (1897), 35. Cf. M. Friedländer, Die rel. Bewegungen
(1905), 306 ff.
[113] → n. 111.

τῶν (νεφέλας) ἀδικοῦντα, ἀφανίζοντα καὶ ἐνπίπτοντα καὶ συνπαλαίοντα καὶ συνρίπτοντα ἐπὶ τῆς γῆς, πνεύματα σκληρὰ γιγάντων, καὶ δρόμους ποιοῦντα ... καὶ ἐξαναστήσει ταῦτα εἰς τοὺς υἱοὺς τῶν ἀνθρώπων ... In Jub. 49:2 the hostile forces of Mastema slay the firstborn according to Rabbinic ideas of the מלאכים משחיתים, while Test. L. 3:2 still sets in the lowest heaven πάντα τὰ πνεύματα τῶν ἐπαγωγῶν εἰς ἐκδίκησιν τῶν ἀνθρώπων. In general, however, the work of demons in the pseudepigrapha is to seduce man. They tempt to witchcraft, to idolatry, to war, strife and bloodshed, to prying into hidden mysteries. Even the benefits of culture are Danaic gifts of the demons (Eth. En. 8:1). Only rarely are other functions ascribed to them. In Apc. Eliae we read of a fast which expels them. In the Lives of the Prophets, 16 [114] the madness of Nebuchadnezzar is caused by a demon, and in Jub. 15:31 there is reference to national angels which can make their nations idolatrous. In connexion with idolatry it is also said that the heathen pray to demons (Eth. En. 99:7; Jub. 1:11; 22:17). These demons are differentiated from seducing spirits (Eth. En. 19:1). In S. Bar. 10:8, as in Is. 13:21; 34:14, nighthags (= לילית?), demons and jackals are finally summoned to the ruins of Jerusalem. But the emphasis falls on the demonic work of seduction. In this work they oppose God. The beginning of their demonic existence is a "fall," usually described in relation to Gn. 6. [115] Hence the position of demons is not due to natural ἐμπάθεια. Their fall implies sin and guilt, as expressly stated in Eth. En. If the cause of their fall is desire in the human sense, it constitutes guilt for angels who were once holy. [116] Much space is devoted to depictions of the judgment on these angels. In Eth. En. there is the more detailed view that the fallen angels give birth to monsters which now seduce men while the angels themselves are kept in prison awaiting judgment (15:1-7, 8-12). In Jub. the idea is worked out rather differently. Unclean demons begin to tempt the sons of Noah but are then committed to the place of condemnation in 9 f., and Mastema takes up the work of seduction in fulfilment of his will among men (10:9).

The pseudepigrapha sometimes show more clearly than the Rabbinic works that the demons are connected with, or subordinated to, Satan. They are called the spirits of Mastema, and in Jub. 10:8, 11 it is expressly said that evil spirits are subject to Satan and serve him. The Test. XII are controlled by this view, referring constantly to the distinction between the spirits of Beliar and the Spirit of God. There is here, however, a certain tendency to spiritualise which should not be overlooked, i.e., when we read of the spirits of all vices. Except in the Test. XII there is no clear or basic subjection of demons to Satan. Many groups and leaders are mentioned, a particular role being played by Asmodaios and Shemyaza.

When we survey the whole development from the reserved attitude of the OT to the more or less complete triumph of the popular view by way of the outlook of the pseudepigrapha, we may conclude that the decisive feature in Jewish demonology is that the demons are evil spirits and that the link with the souls of the dead is broken. [117] Again, there is no bridge between evil spirits and good. This helps us to realise to what degree Josephus and Philo are hellenised. Historically there are many links with the Babylonian belief, and the pseudepigrapha give evidence of stimulation by surrounding cultures. Yet the truth remains that

---

[114] P. Riessler, Altjüd. Schrifttum (1928), 871 ff.
[115] For the corresponding Rabbinic ideas, mostly of a later period, v. Str.-B., IV, 505 ff. It is characteristic of the closed system of the Rabbis that the demons are regarded as having been created on the evening of the last day of creation, Str.-B., IV, 506b.
[116] Ch. 15, e.g., v. 4: καὶ ὑμεῖς ἦτε ἅγιοι καὶ πνεύματα ζῶντα, αἰώνια καὶ ἐν αἵματι σαρκὸς ἐγεννήσατε; v. 6: ὑμεῖς δὲ ὑπήρχετε πνεύματα ζῶντα αἰώνια ...
[117] Schl. Mt., 259 f.

Judaism adopted only that for which the ground had been already prepared. When pseudepigraphical writings like Eth. En., Jub. and Test. XII, which chronologically precede the older Rabbinic utterances, emphasise so strongly the seductive power of demons, we can see at what point Judaism was prepared for the adoption of demonology, namely, in its realisation that there is in man a will which resists the attempted fulfilment of the Law and which is thus to be ascribed to demonic influence. It is by inner necessity, therefore, that in these writings the demons are closely linked with Satan, and that in the Rabbinic literature, with its recognition of the possibility of fulfilling the Law, the seductive activity of demons and their link with Satan are far less prominent.

Pseudepigraphical Judaism was also convinced that in the Gentile world and its culture there is at work an evil will, not of individual men, but of demons. From a different angle, therefore, the doctrine of demons was linked with that of the two aeons. A broader basis was thus given to the doctrine, for now, as distinct from the OT, all evil was no longer traced back to the rule of God. To be sure, God might still send angels of punishment. Yet in the doctrine of ill-disposed angels and demons who seek to do harm to life and limb, it became obvious that the present world order, with all its suffering, want and mortality, is in conflict with the will of God.

C. The View of Demons in the NT.

1. The NT usage corresponds to the later Jewish. Only once (Mt. 8:31) do we have δαίμων. Everywhere else δαιμόνιον is used (11 times in Mt., 11 [13] in Mk. and 23 in Lk.). Also common are πνεῦμα (once each in Mt., Mk. and Ac., twice in Lk.), πνεῦμα ἀκάθαρτον (twice in Mt., 11 times in Mk., 5 in Lk. and twice in Ac.), or πνεῦμα πονηρόν (once in Mt. at 12:45, 3 times in Lk. and 4 in Ac.). Peculiar to Mk. is πνεῦμα ἄλαλον or πνεῦμα ἄλαλον καὶ κωφόν (9:17, 25). Cf. also Lk. 13:11: πνεῦμα ἀσθενείας, and Ac. 16:16 : πνεῦμα πύθων. Mk. is thus most faithful to the specifically Jewish usage (πνεῦμα ἀκάθαρτον = רוח טומאה), and Lk. follows, though he can coin an expression like πνεῦμα δαιμονίου ἀκαθάρτου in 4:33, [118] which must have seemed strange and inaccurate to Palestinian ears. John uses δαιμόνιον 6 times. In the Epistles, however, πνεῦμα occurs 3 times (1 Jn. 4:1, 3, 6) and in Rev. we find δαιμόνιον 3 times, πνεῦμα ἀκάθαρτον twice and πνεῦμα once. The Athenians use δαιμόνιον in Ac. 17:18. Paul has δαιμόνιον 4 times in 1 C. 10:20 f. (on the basis of the OT), πνεῦμα and δαιμόνιον once each in 1 Tm. and πνεῦμα in Eph. 2:2. There are a few references to the angels of Satan, i.e., in Mt. 25:41; 2 C. 12:7; Rev. 12:7, or simply to angels in this sense, i.e., 1 C. 6:3; 2 Pt. 2:4; Jd. 6 and Rev. 9:11. The whole usage is typically later Jewish.

2. Basically the NT stands in the OT succession. There is no reference to spirits of the dead; the dead sleep until the resurrection. [119] Δαίμων, with its suggestion of an intermediary between God and man, is avoided. Angels and demons are antithetical. Indeed, it is only in the NT that we have a full and radical distinction.

When we survey the passages mentioned, we note first how comparatively infrequent are the NT references to demons except in the case of the possessed. No trace whatever remains of the belief in ghosts, which is so important in the

---

[118] The West. reading is πνεῦμα δαιμόνιον ἀκάθαρτον.
[119] 1 Th. 4:16; 1 C. 15:23b; Rev. 20:4, 11 ff.

Rabbis. Even when Paul speaks of the hazards of his journeys through lonely places (2 C. 11:23 ff.), he is not speaking of the perils due to demons (→ 13). He attributes to an angel of Satan only the strange physical hindrance and injury of 2 C. 12:7. The decisive point here is that he sees in the suffering an attack on his spiritual and physical life which he can only regard as the work of an angel of Satan. In the great reduction of fear of demons, however, we are to see an effect of the NT faith in God as the Guardian of His people. In the light of this faith all fear of demons necessarily yields to steadfast assurance.

Nevertheless, the fact that demons are mentioned only with relative infrequency in the NT does not mean that their existence and operation are contested or doubted. For Paul witchcraft is meddling with demons.[120] But there can also be intercourse with demons in the normal heathen cultus (1 C. 10:20 f.).[121] While idols are nothing, and the Christian enjoys freedom, demons stand behind paganism. Perhaps the puzzling expression in 1 C. 12:2 : πρὸς τὰ εἴδωλα τὰ ἄφωνα ὡς ἂν ἤγεσθε ἀπαγόμενοι, refers to the activity of demons. In Rev., too, we read of the worship of demons alongside that of blind and deaf εἴδωλα (9:20). In the last time both Paul and Rev. expect a particular activity of demonic powers : 1 Tm. 4:1: τὸ δὲ πνεῦμα ῥητῶς λέγει ὅτι ἐν ὑστέροις καιροῖς ἀποστήσονταί τινες τῆς πίστεως, προσέχοντες πνεύμασιν πλάνοις καὶ διδασκαλίαις δαιμονίων; Rev. 16:13 f.: εἶδον ἐκ τοῦ στόματος τοῦ δράκοντος ... πνεύματα τρία ἀκάθαρτα ὡς βάτραχοι· εἰσὶν γὰρ πνεύματα δαιμονίων ποιοῦντα σημεῖα ... they seduce kings in the last time.

> According to the general interpretation of Rev., we may see in 9:1 ff. either an eschatological event or one which has already occurred. In any case, however, the ascent of the locusts from the abyss denotes an activity of demonic powers under the leadership of a single power, the ἄγγελος τῆς ἀβύσσου (v. 11). Since eschatological events are more specifically dealt with from ch. 12 onwards, we cannot reject out of hand the possibility that ch. 9 depicts the present activity of demonic forces among men.[122]

Paul refers to such activity in other passages. He advises us to be armed for conflict against πνευματικὰ τῆς πονηρίας in Eph. 6:12. James, too, speaks of a wisdom which is δαιμονιώδης in 3:15. We also have the admonition in 1 Jn. 4:1: δοκιμάζετε τὰ πνεύματα εἰ ἐκ θεοῦ ἐστιν, cf. 4:3, 6. It is constantly repeated in the NT that all demonic powers are reserved for judgment : Mt. 25:41: τὸ πῦρ τὸ αἰώνιον τὸ ἡτοιμασμένον τῷ διαβόλῳ καὶ τοῖς ἀγγέλοις αὐτοῦ; Mt. 8:29 : As mouthpieces of the spirits the possessed say to Jesus : ἦλθες ὧδε πρὸ καιροῦ βασανίσαι ἡμᾶς; According to Paul believers will have a part in this judgment, and that not merely as spectators, as in the pseudepigrapha : 1 C. 6:3 : οὐκ οἴδατε ὅτι ἀγγέλους κρινοῦμεν; On the other hand, 2 Pt. 2:4 : εἰ γὰρ ὁ θεὸς ἀγγέλων ἁμαρτησάντων οὐκ ἐφείσατο, ἀλλὰ σιροῖς ζόφου ταρταρώσας παρέδωκεν εἰς κρίσιν τηρουμένους, and Jd. 6 : ἀγγέλους τε τοὺς μὴ τηρήσαντας τὴν ἑαυτῶν ἀρχὴν ἀλλὰ ἀπολιπόντας τὸ ἴδιον οἰκητήριον εἰς κρίσιν μεγάλης ἡμέρας δεσμοῖς ἀϊδίοις ὑπὸ ζόφον τετήρηκεν agree with the pseudepigrapha that judg-

---

[120] For this reason there are many warnings against sorcery in the NT (Gl. 5:20; Rev. 9:21; 18:23; 21:8; 22:15).
[121] This is not so in principle.
[122] W. Foerster, ThStKr, 104 (1932), 279 ff.

ment has already been passed on some angels, so that they are imprisoned until the final judgment. We are reminded of speculations such as those of Eth. En. 10 ff. and Jub. 10:1 ff.

This concludes the NT evidence apart from the stories of possession, for it is only with qualifications that we can adduce Paul's references to ἀρχαί, ἐξουσίαι and δυνάμεις (→ ἐξουσία). The obvious restraint of the NT is due to the fact that it does not have the general interest in the powers of darkness which is so palpable in the pseudepigrapha. It is also due to the fact that there is no relative autonomy of demons as in later Judaism as a whole. In the NT demons are completely subject to Satan, who is called ἄρχων τῆς ἐξουσίας τοῦ ἀέρος (Eph. 2:2), the kingdom of demons being described a parte potiori as that of the air. In the NT there are two kingdoms, the kingdom of the prince of this world and the kingdom of God. Satan fights with all his might against the kingdom of God. There is thus no place for any special interest in the subordinate helpers in this conflict, whether angels on the one side or demons on the other. It is in keeping with this complete subjection of demons to Satan that the NT refers with comparative frequency to the angels of Satan (→ 16). In the pseudepigrapha the name angel is used with reference to the fallen angels of Gn. 6 or to the angels of destruction, as especially in the Rabbis. [123] In the NT, however, the approach is different; the demons are angels and instruments of Satan. That this unconditional subjection of demons to Satan is new may be seen from the Beezebul story (Mk. 3:20 ff. and par.), where the opponents of Jesus refer to a prince of demons, Beezebul (→ Βεεζεβούλ), but Jesus in His reply quietly substitutes Satan for this prince and argues the impossibility of a divided kingdom of Satan. In virtue of this subjection, the activity of demons loses the occasional and relatively innocuous character which it often has especially in the Rabbis. Instead there is mortal conflict.

It is also worth noting that the NT does not speak of individual seducing spirits after the manner of Test. XII. Evil thoughts come from the heart (Mt. 15:19). Because men do not honour God as Creator, He gives them up εἰς ἀδόκιμον νοῦν (R. 1:28). To be sure, sin and the flesh are individual forces. Yet they do not come from without, like demons. They indicate the mode of existence of humanity itself, which is now sinful.

3. When we turn to the many passages in the Synopt. and Acts which refer to those possessed by demons, three points are to be made. First, with respect to demons as the cause of sickness, it should be noted that in the NT not all sicknesses are attributed to demons even in older strata of the Synoptic tradition. Nevertheless, it may be said that the existence of sickness in this world belongs to the character of the αἰὼν οὗτος of which Satan is the prince. It is for this reason that Jesus says of the woman who has a πνεῦμα τῆς ἀσθενείας (Lk. 13:11): ἣν ἔδησεν ὁ σατανᾶς ἰδοὺ δέκα καὶ ὀκτὼ ἔτη (v. 16). Cf. Ac. 10:38: ἰώμενος πάντας τοὺς καταδυναστευομένους ὑπὸ τοῦ διαβόλου. Thus, while not all sicknesses are the work of demons, they may all be seen as the work of Satan. This thought perhaps plays a role in many other stories of the demonic. Secondly, in most of the stories of possession what is at issue is not merely sick-

---

[123] Cf. Pes. r., 36, 161b, Buber (Str.-B., II, 2), where Satan, when he sees the pre-existent Messiah, exclaims: Truly, this is the Messiah, who will one day plunge me and all the angel princes of the nations into Gehenna.

ness but a destruction and distortion of the divine likeness of man according to creation. The centre of personality, the volitional and active ego, is impaired by alien powers which seek to ruin the man and sometimes drive him to self-destruction (Mk. 5:5). The ego is so impaired that the spirits speak through him. Jesus is conscious that He now breaks the power of the devil and his angels because He is the One in whom the dominion of God is present on behalf of humanity (Mt. 12:28 and par.). Thus the healing of the demon-possessed is an essential part of the record in the Synopt. and Acts. The crucial thing is that demons are expelled by a word of command issued in the power of God and not by the invocation of a superior but essentially similar spirit, nor by the use of material media.

Thirdly, the demons, as πνευματικά, possess a certain knowledge which they must express in words in face of Jesus : σὺ εἶ ὁ ἅγιος τοῦ θεοῦ, and which is formulated in terms of their own existence as רוחות טומאה. They also recognise their fate (Mt. 8:29; Jm. 2:19). The confession which Jesus seeks to evoke is not, however, this witness which proceeds from demonic knowledge. Hence He forbids it.

4. In John the people's estimate of Jesus is expressed in the phrase : δαιμόνιον ἔχει (καὶ μαίνεται), 7:20; 8:48, 49, 52; 10:20, 21. If this is in the first instance a kind of popular term of reproach, there lies behind it the fact that on Jewish soil (as distinct from Hellenistic) it contains a most radical rejection on religious grounds. A man who has a δαιμόνιον should not be heard. Hence Jesus resists the accusation : ἐγὼ δαιμόνιον οὐκ ἔχω, ἀλλὰ τιμῶ τὸν πατέρα μου (Jn. 8:49). From the NT standpoint the reproach implies total rejection and dishonouring.

> The charge brought against Paul by the Athenians in Acts 17:18 : ξένων δαιμονίων δοκεῖ καταγγελεὺς εἶναι (not ξένων δαιμόνων), which at first sight seems rather strange in the light of Gk. usage, does not prove that individual gods were already called δαιμόνια in Athens. There is rather an allusion to the charge brought against Socrates. In Rev. 18:2 : Babylon ἐγένετο κατοικητήριον δαιμονίων, both the wording and outlook are OT.

The NT view of demons is consistently opposed to the Gk. divinisation of the demonic. It also dispels the constant fear of evil spirits. Yet it confirms the popular sense of something horrible and sinister in such spirits, bringing out the demonic nature of their activity as an attack on the spiritual and physical life of man in fulfilment of the will of Satan. The NT bears witness to the victory won by Jesus over evil spirits — a victory which is efficacious for the community and will preserve it through the temptations of the last time. The OT view of the demonic, namely, that the concern of Israel is with God alone, is fully maintained. Demonology, however, brings into focus the character of the world as the αἰὼν οὗτος.

δαιμονίζομαι.

"To be possessed by a δαίμων."

Originally in all the senses of δαίμων : Philem. Fr., 181 (CAF, II, 530): ἄλλος κατ' ἄλλην δαιμονίζεται τυχήν, with δαιμονᾶν, to suffer from a δαίμων. The LXX does not use the term (found only in ᾽Α ψ 90:6 : ἀπὸ δηγμοῦ δαιμονίζοντος μεσημβρίας). In Joseph. we find δαιμονᾶν to denote particular excitement (Bell., 1, 347; 2, 259; 7, 389), and δαιμονίζεσθαι is used once in Ant., 8, 47 for possession. Here, too, the relatively more common popular word for possession seems to be sparsely attested in this sense among Greek speaking Jews. It is noteworthy that the Rabbis have no corresponding verb, [1] and in relation to the Synoptic problem it is significant that this verb is comparatively most frequent in Mt.

† δαιμονιώδης.

"Demonic"; occurring in the NT only in Jm. 3:15 (→ 17).

† δεισιδαίμων, † δεισιδαιμονία.

General expression for "piety," the more precise sense varying according to the two constituents δείδω = "to fear" (ἔδεισα) and δαίμων. Thus δεισιδαιμονία may on the one side denote a "pious attitude towards the gods," i.e., "religion," [1] and on the other "excessive fear of them." [2] In general, however, it is not used in the non-Christian world for "superstition," i.e., fear of evil spirits, since the Greeks hardly see the radical distinction between gods and spirits, and could only have a poor sense of any such distinction. Yet there is sometimes present a certain fear of spirits. [3]

It was well suited to be a general and supremely neutral expression for religion or piety because δαίμων is used generally for a supernatural power (→ 2). In the NT it is used in this sense by Festus in Ac. 25:19, and the adj. is used by Paul of the Athenians in Ac. 17:22: ἄνδρες Ἀθηναῖοι, κατὰ πάντα ὡς δεισιδαιμονεστέρους ὑμᾶς θεωρῶ.

Foerster

δάκτυλος

The only significant use in the NT is in Lk. 11:20, where Jesus says of Himself that He drives out demons with the δάκτυλος θεοῦ. The phrase "finger of God" denotes God's direct and concrete intervention.

The term is OT. a. In Ps. 8:3 the heavens are the work of God's fingers, while the finger of God moved over the upper waters acc. to Gn. r., 4 (4a). b. In Ex. 31:18; Dt. 9:10 the tables of the Law γεγραμμέναι (ἐν) τῷ δακτύλῳ τοῦ θεοῦ (בְּאֶצְבַּע אֱלֹהִים). Cf. S. Nu., 61 on 8:4: ... and God showed it to Moses כְּאִלּוּ בְּאֶצְבַּע as though with His finger, i.e., as clearly as if He had pointed His finger. For more recent parallels, cf. M. Ex. on 12:2 and bMen., 29a. Cf. also Da. 5:1 ff.; O. Sol. 23:21, where the heavenly missive is written with the finger of God. c. The finger of God works miracles in

---

δαιμονίζομαι. [1] Schl. Mt., 124.

δεισιδαίμων κτλ. Pr.-Bauer, s.v. δεισιδαιμονία; Zn. Ag. on 17:22; J. E. Harrison, *Prolegomena to the Study of Greek Religion* (1908), 4 ff.; H. Bolkestein, *Theophrastos' Charakter d. Deisidaimonia* (1929); P. J. Koets, Δεισιδαιμονία (Diss. Utrecht, 1929); Schl. *Theol. d. Judt.*, 156 f.

[1] Common as an official term for religion in Joseph., e.g., Ant., 19, 290.

[2] Theophr. Char., 16: ἀμέλει ἡ δεισιδαιμονία δόξειεν ἂν εἶναι δειλία πρὸς τὸ δαιμόνιον.

[3] Philo Gig., 16: ψυχὰς οὖν καὶ δαίμονας καὶ ἀγγέλους ὀνόματα μὲν διαφέροντα, ἓν δὲ καὶ ταὐτὸν ὑποκείμενον διανοηθεὶς ἄχθος βαρύτατον ἀποθήσῃ δεισιδαιμονίαν.

δάκτυλος. J. Löw, *Die Finger in Literatur u. Folklore der Juden. Gedenkbuch zur Erinnerung an D. Kaufmann* (1900), 61-85.

Ex. 8:19. [1] In M. Ex. on 14:38 the appearance of the hand of God at the Red Sea indicates a culmination of His plagues through a single finger. There is mention of a magical finger on an Egypt. ostracon : [2] ἐξορκίζω κατὰ τοῦ δακτύλου τοῦ θεοῦ (Semitic influence ?). Cl. Al. Strom., VI, 16 : δάκτυλος γὰρ θεοῦ δύναμις νοεῖται θεοῦ, δι' ἧς ἡ κτίσις τελειοῦται οὐρανῶν καὶ γῆς, ὧν ἀμφοῖν αἱ πλάκες νοηθήσονται σύμβολα. [3]

Schlier

δέησις → δέομαι.

δεῖ, δέον ἐστί

1. Most common in the 3rd pers. sing. neut. (δεῖ with inf.), or in the form δέον ἐστίν, this word expresses the "character of necessity or compulsion" in an event. The term itself does not denote the authority which imparts this character. It is thus given its precise significance when conjoined with this power.

In most cases the word bears a weakened sense derived from everyday processes. It thus denotes that which in a given moment seems to be necessary or inevitable to a man or group of men, e.g., ἀνέδωκε διαβούλιον, τί δεῖ ποιεῖν (Polyb., VII, 5, 2; cf. 4 Βασ. 4:13 f., where the LXX translator adds his own interpretation to the Mas. מה לעשות לו).

In the language of philosophy the term expresses logical and scientific necessities, e.g., δεῖ δὲ πρῶτον ὑμᾶς μαθεῖν τὴν ἀνθρωπίνην φύσιν καὶ τὰ παθήματα αὐτῆς, Plat. Symp., 189d; εἰ δὲ οὕτως, οὐσίαν εἶναι δεῖ πάσης κινήσεως καὶ γενέσεως ἔρημον (sc. τοῦ θεοῦ), Corp. Herm., VI, 1a.

Ethical or even religious obligations may also be denoted. State law may stand behind these, as when Xenophon says of this law : φράζον ἅ τε δεῖ ποιεῖν καὶ ἃ μή, Mem., I, 2, 42. But so, too, may the law as an expression of the will of God, e.g., in the LXX : ὧν οὐ δεῖ ποιεῖν, Lv. 5:17; ἀποστρέφειν δὲ δεῖ ἀπὸ ὁδοῦ σκολιᾶς καὶ κακῆς, Prv. 22:14a; cf. πᾶσαν ἐνέργειαν μετὰ δικαιοσύνης ἐπιτελεῖν δεῖ, Ep. Ar., 159, or the law which, through insight into the nature of the world, dwells in the heart of man ἠρώτα, πρὸς τίνα δεῖ φιλότιμον εἶναι· ἐκεῖνος δὲ ἔφη· πρὸς τοὺς φιλικῶς ἔχοντας ἡμῖν οἴονται πάντες ὅτι πρὸς τούτους δέον· ἐγὼ δ' ὑπολαμβάνω, πρὸς τοὺς ἀντιδοξοῦντας φιλοτιμίαν δεῖν χαριστικὴν ἔχειν, ἵνα τούτῳ τῷ τρόπῳ μετάγωμεν αὐτοὺς ἐπὶ τὸ καθῆκον καὶ συμφέρον ἑαυτοῖς. δεῖ δὲ τὸν θεὸν λιτανεύειν, ἵνα ταῦτ' ἐπιτελῆται· τὰς γὰρ ἁπάντων διανοίας κρατεῖ, Ep. Ar., 227. In the LXX sense δεῖ can also be used in the NT to express religious and ethical obligation, e.g., Lk. 13:14; 22:7. The will of God known to the Christian community lays duties upon it and upon the individual Christian (1 Thess. 4:1; 1 Tm. 3:2, 7, 15; Tt. 1:7); these then become custom and as such stand under the δεῖ.

---

[1] In a letter to Ashirat-jashur found at Ta'annek, there is reference to the finger of Ashirat, G. Hölscher, *Gesch. d. isr. u. jüd. Rel.* (1922), § 35, 5.
[2] W. E. Crum, *Coptic Ostraca* (1902), 4 f., No. 522; cf. Deissmann LO, 260.
[3] Cf. Tert. Marc., 4, 27 = *virtus creatoris*.

The authority behind the δεῖ may be belief in fate, and it then becomes a term for the "divinely ordained necessities of destiny"; cf. ἔδεε ... κατὰ τὸ θεοπρόπιον πᾶσαν τὴν 'Αττικὴν τὴν ἐν τῇ ἠπείρῳ γενέσθαι ὑπὸ Πέρσῃσι, Hdt., VIII, 53. In a similar sense it may be used for cosmic necessity: πάντα δὲ δεῖ γίνεσθαι καὶ ἀεὶ καὶ καθ' ἕκαστον τόπον, Corp. Herm., XI, 6a.

Finally, the word is used in magic for the "presuppositions essential to the success of magic" — δεῖ προαγνεύειν ἐπὶ ἡμέρας τρεῖς, Preis. Zaub., III, 284; φυλακτήριον ὃ δεῖ σε φορεῖν, IV, 2694, or for the "compulsion of magic," as in a Selene incantation: τὸ δεῖ γενέσθαι, τοῦτ' οὐκ ἔξεστι φυγεῖν· τὸ δεῖ, ποιήσεις, κἂν θέλῃς κἂν μὴ θέλῃς, IV, 2255 ff. (cf. 2299 ff., 2321).

This brief review shows us that the term is at home in Gk. and Hellenistic usage. The case is different in the OT and the Rabbis. There is a reason for this. Behind the term stands the thought of a neutral deity, of an (→) ἀνάγκη deity, which determines the course of the world and thus brings it under the δεῖ. This necessity expressed by the δεῖ affects the thought, volition and action of individuals, so that the word constantly recurs. Even in the weaker everyday usage the underlying thought may still be discerned. The biblical view of God, however, does not express a neutral necessity. It thinks of God in terms of the will which personally summons man and which fashions history according to its plan. This means that the OT uses a personal address where the Gk. world would have δεῖ. In the LXX, Josephus, other Jewish Hellenists and even the NT, however, the Gk. and Hellenistic usage is adopted. Tension is thus introduced by reason of the inadequate concept of God which underlies this usage. A plain example is to be found in Lv. 5:17: where the LXX has ὧν οὐ δεῖ ποιεῖν for the Mas. אֲשֶׁר לֹא תֵעָשֶׂינָה. On the other hand, when the LXX, the Hellenistic Jews and even more so the NT adopt the word, they speak a language understood by those whom they are attempting to reach. And by linking it with, and referring it to, the biblical view of God, they make it plain that it no longer expresses the neutral necessity of fate. Instead, it indicates the will of God declared in the message. This is the standpoint from which it is applied in many different ways.

2. The usage of Luke is important in this connexion. Of the 102 occurrences of δεῖ or δέον ἐστί, 41 are to be found in the Lucan writings. Luke is familiar with the term from his Hellenistic background, and it fits his way of thought. Hence he often turns to it. Yet it is evident that with the alteration of the background from which the term derives, its character has also changed. It is used in different ways. As in the LXX, it sometimes expresses the will of God revealed in the Law (Lk. 11:42; 13:14; 22:7; Ac. 15:5). Jesus clashes with this δεῖ of the Law when in defiance of the Rabbinic halacha He follows the δεῖ of the will of God as He knows it (Lk. 13:16, cf. v. 14). The term may thus be used as a general expression for the will of God, the statement with which it is linked thereby acquiring the significance of a rule of life (Lk. 15:32; 18:1; Ac. 5:29; 20:35). Jesus sees His whole life and activity and passion under this will of God comprehended in a δεῖ. Over Him there stands a δεῖ which is already present in His childhood. This is the δεῖ of the divine lordship (Lk. 2:49). It determines His activity (Lk. 4:43; 13:33; 19:5). It leads Him to suffering and death, but also to glory (Lk. 9:22; 17:25; 24:7, 26; Ac. 1:16; 3:21; 17:3). It has its basis in the will of God concerning Him which is laid down in Scripture and which He unconditionally follows (Lk. 22:37; 24:44). His disciples, apostles and community are also laid under this δεῖ which derives from the will of God. Claimed by the divine will, they are shaped and determined by it down to the smallest details of their lives (Lk. 12:12; Ac. 9:6, 16;

14:22; 19:21; 23:11; 27:24). This usage has similarities to that of Josephus.[1] The δεῖ, which as an expression of the will of God is at all these points an expression of His saving will, finally reveals to man his state of loss and thus demands faith in God's act of salvation (Ac. 4:12; 16:30). The whole of God's will for Christ and for man is thus comprehended in this δεῖ as Luke conceives it. The usage is Hellenistic, but it is determined by knowledge of the personal will of God who is a living person and not a neutral necessity. This will of God claims man in every situation of life and gives goal and direction to life on the basis of its saving purpose.

3. The usage of Luke has the widest implications. It gathers up all the relations within which δεῖ is found in the rest of the NT.

The word δεῖ expresses the necessity of the eschatological event, and is thus an eschatological term in the NT. It is well adapted for this role, since the eschatological event is one which is hidden from man, which can be known only by special revelation, and which sets man before an inconceivable necessity of historical occurrence grounded in the divine will. The tension which results when δεῖ is linked with the biblical doctrine of God applies also to this δεῖ which stands over the great eschatological drama. It is the δεῖ of the mysterious God who pursues His plans for the world in the eschatological event. Not a blind belief in destiny, but faith in God's eternal plans formulates this δεῖ. The δεῖ denotes that God is in Himself committed to these plans. It thus expresses a necessity which lies in the very nature of God and which issues in the execution of His plans in the eschatological event.

The concept is formulated by Daniel as follows: ἔστι θεὸς ἐν οὐρανῷ ἀνακαλύπτων μυστήρια, ὃς ἐδήλωσε τῷ βασιλεῖ Ναβουχοδονοσὸρ ἃ δεῖ γενέσθαι ἐπ' ἐσχάτων τῶν ἡμερῶν (Da. LXX 2:28;[2] cf. 2:29, 45). It is taken up by the Apocalyptist, who begins his work with the words: ἀποκάλυψις Ἰησοῦ Χριστοῦ, ἣν ἔδωκεν αὐτῷ ὁ θεός, δεῖξαι τοῖς δούλοις αὐτοῦ ἃ δεῖ γενέσθαι ἐν τάχει (Rev. 1:1; cf. 4:1; 22:6). The same formulation is found in the Syn. apocalypse. After recounting the events which will come to pass, Jesus says: δεῖ γὰρ <πάντα> γενέσθαι, ἀλλ' οὔπω τὸ τέλος (Mt. 24:6 and par.).[3] It is emphasised as quite essential to the close of the eschatological period and the beginning of the end: εἰς πάντα τὰ ἔθνη πρῶτον δεῖ κηρυχθῆναι τὸ εὐαγγέλιον (Mk. 13:10; cf. Jn. 10:16). The imperative of eschatology is both to judgment and salvation. All the detailed acts of this eschatological occurrence stand under it. To it belongs the Messianic time which opens with the return of Elias, whom Jesus finds in John the Baptist: ἐπηρώτησαν αὐτὸν οἱ μαθηταὶ λέγοντες· τί ⸂οὖν οἱ γραμματεῖς λέγουσιν ὅτι Ἠλίαν δεῖ ἐλθεῖν πρῶτον; ὁ δὲ ἀποκριθεὶς εἶπεν· Ἠλίας μὲν ἔρχεται καὶ ἀποκαταστήσει πάντα· λέγω δὲ ὑμῖν ὅτι Ἠλίας ἤδη ἦλθεν (Mt. 17:10 ff.; Mk. 9:11). The coming of Elias, which the disciples see under this imperative, has already been fulfilled according to these sayings. The eschatological,

---

δεῖ. [1] Cf. Schl. Lk. 54, 587, 652.

[2] In the Mas. this is a future, the reference being prophetic: דִּי לֶהֱוֵא בְּאַחֲרִית יוֹמַיָּא.

[3] It might be that the words used by Joseph. to describe the nature of God come from apocalyptic: ἅτε δεῖ γενέσθαι προλέγει (Ant., 10, 142). They are divested of their eschatological character and made into a simple statement. Cf. Schl. Mt. 698. The same influence is perhaps to be seen in the magic formulation τὸ δεῖ γενέσθαι, τοῦτ' οὐκ ἔξεστι φυγεῖν in Preis. Zaub., IV, 2255.

Messianic age has come. This throws a clear ray of light on the use of δεῖ in Christ's prophecies of His suffering and resurrection. It has a secure place in these according to the Synoptists: δεῖ αὐτὸν εἰς Ἱεροσόλυμα ἀπελθεῖν καὶ πολλὰ παθεῖν ἀπὸ τῶν πρεσβυτέρων καὶ ἀρχιερέων καὶ γραμματέων καὶ ἀποκτανθῆναι καὶ τῇ τρίτῃ ἡμέρᾳ ἐγερθῆναι (Mt. 16:21 and par.; cf. also Lk. 17:25; 24:7, 26; Ac. 3:21; 17:3). The suffering, death and resurrection of Christ are parts of the eschatological drama. Christ is not just the Preacher of eschatology; His history is eschatology. This δεῖ, under which His suffering, death and resurrection, and according to Lk. His ascension, stand, belongs to the mysterious divine work of judgment and salvation in the last time. What Paul and other NT figures say of the suffering, death and resurrection of Christ is the theoretical development of this mysterious δεῖ and therefore the interpretation of the eschatological action of God in His Christ. This is confirmed by the fact that in the NT *kerygma* this history of Christ is declared to be the fulfilment of Scripture: πῶς οὖν πληρωθῶσιν αἱ γραφαὶ ὅτι οὕτως δεῖ γενέσθαι (Mt. 26:54; cf. Lk. 22:37; 24:25 f.). John shares this view with the Synoptists when he interprets the crucifixion as follows: ὑψωθῆναι δεῖ τὸν υἱὸν τοῦ ἀνθρώπου, ἵνα πᾶς ὁ πιστεύων ἐν αὐτῷ ἔχῃ ζωὴν αἰώνιον (3:14; cf. 12:34), or when he refers to Scripture in relation to the resurrection: οὐδέπω γὰρ ᾔδεισαν τὴν γραφήν, ὅτι δεῖ αὐτὸν ἐκ νεκρῶν ἀναστῆναι (20:9). In Paul's use of the term we are confronted by such eschatological necessities as the reign of Christ in the eschatological age up to the end (1 C. 15:25), the judgment (2 C. 5:10) and the resurrection change (1 C. 15:53), which has its basis in the present separation from God in virtue of the divine invisibility (1 C. 8:2).

4. In connexion with the δεῖ which shapes the history of Christ, δεῖ has also a place in the description of God's saving action towards men. This action is in John regeneration, the new birth of man without which he can have no part in the kingdom of God: δεῖ ὑμᾶς γεννηθῆναι ἄνωθεν (Jn. 3:7). In the apostolic *kerygma* we read: καὶ οὐκ ἔστιν ἐν ἄλλῳ οὐδενὶ ἡ σωτηρία· οὔτε γὰρ ὄνομά ἐστιν ἕτερον ὑπὸ τὸν οὐρανὸν τὸ δεδομένον ἐν ἀνθρώποις, ἐν ᾧ δεῖ σωθῆναι ἡμᾶς (Ac. 4:12). The saving action of God towards men reaches its goal in faith in the name of Jesus. When the shaken jailor at Philippi asks what is necessary for salvation: τί με δεῖ ποιεῖν ἵνα σωθῶ, he is given the answer: πίστευσον ἐπὶ τὸν κύριον Ἰησοῦν, καὶ σωθήσῃ σὺ καὶ ὁ οἶκός σου (Ac. 16:30 f.; cf. Hb. 11:6). [4]

5. In connexion with the description of the will of God for human conduct as plainly revealed in the Law and in the actions of Jesus corresponding to God's will as He knew it (→ 22; cf. also δεῖ as an expression of the necessity grounded in the will of God, R. 12:3; 1 Th. 4:1; 2 Th. 3:7; 1 Tm. 3:2, 7; 3:7 etc.), δεῖ can also denote the will of God which calls for definite prayer. [5]

---

[4] δεῖ is linked with the question of salvation, e.g., in the Herm. writings. Here we read of the heavenly journey which requires regeneration: ὁρᾷς, ὦ τέκνον, πόσα ἡμᾶς δεῖ σώματα ... διεξελθεῖν καὶ πόσους χορούς δαιμόνων ... καὶ δρόμους ἀστέρων ἵνα πρὸς τὸν ἕνα καὶ μόνον θεὸν σπεύσωμεν (Corp. Herm., IV, 8b). Or again: πρῶτον δὲ δεῖ περιρρήξασθαι ὃν φορεῖς χιτῶνα, "τὸ σκοτεινὸν περίβολον," τὸ τῆς ἀγνωσίας ὕφασμα, τὸ τῆς κακίας στήριγμα, τὸν τῆς φθορᾶς δεσμόν (VII, 2b). Man's situation separates him from salvation: ... καὶ μυσαρᾶς ἡδονῆς ἐμπλήσας, ἵνα μήτε ἀκούῃς περὶ ὧν ἀκούειν σε δεῖ μήτε βλέπῃς [περὶ ὧν] <ἃ> βλέπειν σε δεῖ (VII, 3).
[5] Cf. Max. Tyr., XI.

Luke interprets the parable of the pleading widow as follows : τὸ δεῖν πάντοτε προσεύχεσθαι καὶ μὴ ἐγκακεῖν (Lk. 18:1). Paul sees the infinite gulf between the will of God and the realisation of the new divine fellowship in the prayer life of the Christian : τὸ γὰρ τί προσευξώμεθα καθὸ δεῖ οὐκ οἴδαμεν (R. 8:26), and he refers to the intercession of the πνεῦμα. John raises the question in the talk between Jesus and the Samaritan woman. She asks concerning the divinely appointed place ὅπου δεῖ προσκυνεῖν, and Jesus in His reply speaks of the divinely appointed manner : πνεῦμα ὁ θεός, καὶ τοὺς προσκυνοῦντας ἐν πνεύματι καὶ ἀληθείᾳ, δεῖ προσκυνεῖν (Jn. 4:20 ff.). In this way, He raises the question concerning Himself, for worship can be in accordance with the will of God only in the God-given πνεῦμα who sets in the ἀλήθεια by bringing into relationship with Christ who is the ἀλήθεια.

Grundmann

> δείκνυμι, ἀναδείκνυμι,
> ἀνάδειξις, δειγματίζω,
> παραδειγματίζω, ὑπόδειγμα

δείκνυμι.

Since the term has no history of meaning, we can only study its various peculiarities and distinctions in the NT in relation to secular usage.

A. The Usage outside John's Gospel.

1. In Mt. 4:8 and par. : καὶ δείκνυσιν (sc. ὁ διάβολος) αὐτῷ πάσας τὰς βασιλείας τοῦ κόσμου it means "to show" in the sense of "to point to something" and thus to draw attention to it. But it is hard to distinguish this from "to show" in the sense of "to exhibit something," e.g., in Lk. 24:40 = Jn. 20:20 : ἔδειξεν αὐτοῖς τὰς χεῖρας. Cf. Hb. 8:5 = LXX Ex. 25:40. Lk. 20:24 : δείξατέ μοι δηνάριον, should probably be mentioned in the same connexion. [1] In Mt. 8:4 and par. : σεαυτὸν δεῖξον τῷ ἱερεῖ means "show thyself, let the priest see thee."

There are naturally many examples of this use outside the NT. On Mt. 4:8, cf. Thuc., I, 87, 2 : ἀναστήτω εἰς ἐκεῖνο τὸ χωρίον, δείξας τι χωρίον αὐτοῖς; Diod. S., II, 22, 4 : καὶ βασίλεια παλαιὰ δεικνύουσι; Epict. Diss., III, 2, 12 : ἄνθρωπος ... δακτύλῳ οὗ δείκνυται ὡς λίθος ... ἀλλ' ὅταν τις τὰ δόγματα αὐτοῦ δείξῃ, τότε αὐτὸν ὡς ἄνθρωπον ἔδειξεν. In the LXX, cf. Nu. 22:41 : ἔδειξεν αὐτῷ ... μέρος τι τοῦ λαοῦ; Ju. 1:24 f.; 4:22 : δεῦρο καὶ δείξω σοι τὸν ἄνδρα ὃν σὺ ζητεῖς; Wis. 10:10. Cf. also 1 Cl. 10, 7; Just. Ap., I, 19, 2; Tat. Or. Graec., 27, 1; 34,1. On Lk. 24:40,

---

δ ε ί κ ν υ μ ι κτλ. J. Gonda, Δείκνυμι. *Semantische Studie over den Indo-Germaanschen Wortel Deik* (1929); Dausch Synpt., 485 f.
[1] Though possibly also "to hand" or "to give." There are many examples of this usage in Gonda, *op. cit.*, 32-38.

cf. Eur. Hel., 548 : ὡς δέμας δείξασα σόν; Plat. Phaedr., 228d/e; Gorg., 469e; Diod. S., I, 67, 6; Jos. Ant., 2, 35; Epict. Diss., II, 8, 25; Sib., 1, 380 : καὶ δείξῃ θνητοῖσι τύπον ("form") καὶ πάντα διδάξῃ. In the LXX, cf. Ex. 25:8, 40; 26:30; Nu. 8:4; 2 Ch. 23:3 : καὶ ἔδειξεν αὐτοῖς τὸν υἱὸν τοῦ βασιλέως. Cf. also Corp. Herm., I, 14 : Ἄνθρωπος, created from Νοῦς, ἔδειξε τῇ κατωφερεῖ φύσει τὴν καλὴν τοῦ θεοῦ μορφήν· ἡ δὲ ἰδοῦσα ... On Mt. 8:4 and par., cf. Hom. Od., 13, 344 : δείξω Ἰθάκης ἔδος; Soph. Ant., 254; Xenoph. Cyrop., VIII, 4, 15; Epict. Diss., I, 18, 14; IV, 7, 25; Plut. Praec. Conjug., 14 (II, 139 f): ὥσπερ ἐσόπτρου ... ὄφελος οὐδέν ἐστιν, εἰ μὴ δείκνυσι τὴν μορφὴν ὁμοίαν. In the LXX, Lv. 13:49; Ex. 33:18 : δεῖξόν μοι τὴν σεαυτοῦ δόξαν (v.l. ἐμφάνισόν μοι σεαυτόν); Dt. 5:24; ψ 58:10. [2] Cf. also 1 Cl., 16, 12 : δεῖξαι αὐτῷ φῶς; Tat. Or. Graec., 16, 2 : τοῖς ἀνθρώποις ἑαυτοὺς ἐκείνων (sc. demons) δεικνύντων; Preis. Zaub., III, 599 : χαίρομεν ὅτι σεαυτὸν ἡμῖν ἔδειξας.

Plat. Crat., 430e : τὸ δὲ δεῖξαι λέγω εἰς τὴν τῶν ὀφθαλμῶν αἴσθησιν καταστῆσαι, might be taken as a general definition of δείκνυμι in this sense.

2. As a second group we may consider such meanings as go beyond the simple sense of "to cause to see." We may think here of the meaning "to point to," sometimes almost in the sense of "to point out," cf. Mk. 14:15 : αὐτὸς ὑμῖν δείξει ἀνάγειον; Ac. 7:3 : δεῦρο εἰς τὴν γῆν, ἣν ἄν σοι δείξω (= Gn. 12:1). 1 Tm. 6:15 : ἣν (ἐπιφάνειαν τοῦ κυρίου ἡμῶν) καιροῖς ἰδίοις δείξει ὁ ... δυνάστης, stands alone, for here δεικνύναι no longer means "to show" but "to bring to pass." Yet the original meaning is still discernible to the extent that Christ's epiphany will be effected by God in such a way as to make Christ visible.

Among secular illustrations of Mk. 14:15 and par., cf. Hom. Od., 6, 178 : ἄστυ δέ μοι δεῖξον; Eur. Rhes., 515 : δείξω δ' ἐγώ σοι χῶρον, ἔνθα χρὴ στρατόν ... νυχεῦσαι; Polyb., V, 85, 12 ; Epict. Diss., III, 2, 11. In the LXX, cf. Dt. 34:1, 4; 4 Βασ. 6:6 : καὶ ἔδειξεν (Heb. ראה hiph.) αὐτῷ τὸν τόπον. General par. to 1 Tm. 6:15 may be found in passages where δείκνυμι means "to create or fashion," and more specific par. in those where it means "to cause to experience" or "to bring to experience." For the former, cf. Eur. Cret. Fr., 3 : δείξας γὰρ ἄστρων τὴν ἐναντίαν ὁδόν; Alexis Fr., 268 (CAF, II, 396): τῶν νήσων ἃς δέδειχεν ἡ φύσις θνητοῖς μεγίστας. Worth noting is LXX Nu. 16:30, where וְאִם־בְּרִיאָה יִבְרָא יְהֹוָה is rendered ἀλλ' ἢ ἐν φάσματι δείξει κύριος. [3] Cf. also Ael. Arist., 13 (I, p. 300, Dindorf): ἡ μὲν ὡς πρώτη τεκοῦσα τὸ τῶν ἀνθρώπων γένος, ἡ δ' ὡς πρώτη δείξασα τοὺς καρπούς. Barn., 5, 6 : αὐτὸς δὲ ἵνα καταργήσῃ τὸν θάνατον καὶ τὴν ἐκ νεκρῶν ἀνάστασιν δείξῃ, ὅτι ἐν σαρκὶ ἔδει αὐτὸν φανερωθῆναι, ὑπέμεινεν. Here, however, δείκνυμι acquires the special sense of "to cause to experience something," which is also common in the LXX, e.g., Dt. 3:24 : σὺ ἤρξω δεῖξαι τῷ σῷ θεράποντι τὴν ἰσχύν σου καὶ τὴν δύναμίν σου καὶ τὴν χεῖρα τὴν κραταιὰν καὶ τὸν βραχίονα τὸν ὑψηλόν; cf. also ψ 59:5(7); 70:20; 77:11; Jer. 18:17; Qoh. 2:24; 3 Macc. 5:13.

3. Alongside δείκνυμι in the sense of "to cause to see," which may become "to cause to experience," we may set a third group in which δείκνυμι denotes "to show" in the sense of "to indicate something verbally," and therefore "to teach, explain or demonstrate." This sense is found already in 1 C. 12:31b : ὁδὸν ὑμῖν

---

[2] Here and in the other LXX passages mentioned δείκνυμι is the transl. of the hiph. of ראה and is thus the causative of ὁρᾶν "to make visible," "to cause to see." In ψ 58:10 δεικνύναι ἐν τοῖς ἐχθροῖς renders the Heb. ראה hiph. with ב.

[3] So Gonda, op. cit., 45. For a different view, v. Deissmann in P. M. Meyer, Griech. Papyrus-Urkunden der Hamburger Stadtbibl. (1911), No. 22, n. 5.

δείκνυμι. It is seen more plainly in Ac. 10:28 : κἀμοὶ ὁ θεὸς ἔδειξεν μηδένα κοινὸν ... λέγειν ἄνθρωπον and Mt. 16:21: ἀπὸ τότε ἤρξατο 'Ιησοῦς Χριστὸς δεικνύειν τοῖς μαθηταῖς αὐτοῦ ὅτι δεῖ αὐτὸν εἰς 'Ιεροσόλυμα ἀπελθεῖν. [4] In the first case it means "to teach" with a slight suggestion of "to prove." In the second it means "to teach or instruct," as shown by the par. διδάσκειν in Mk. 8:31 (Lk. 9:22 has the colourless εἰπὼν ὅτι) with the nuance of "to expound," "to make plain." The sense of "to indicate," "to disclose" or "to prophesy" is possibly present also.

The following secular examples may be noted. For 1 C. 12:31b, Hom. Od., 12, 25; Eur. Herac., 1048; Aeschin., 1, 90 : καὶ δέδεικται φανερὰ ὁδός, δι' ἧς ἀποφεύξονται; Epict. Diss., I, 4, 29; III, 22, 26; Sib., 6, 9. In the LXX, 1 Βασ. 12:23 : καὶ δείξω ὑμῖν τὴν ὁδὸν τὴν ἀγαθὴν καὶ τὴν εὐθεῖαν (ירה hiph.); ψ 49:23; Mi. 4:2; Is. 40:14 : ἢ τίς ἔδειξεν αὐτῷ κρίσιν; ἢ ὁδὸν συνέσεως τίς ἔδειξεν αὐτῷ (למד and ידע); Jdt. 10:13; 4 Esr. 4:4; Herm. s., 5, 6, 3 : ἔδειξεν αὐτοῖς τὰς τρίβους τῆς ζωῆς, δοὺς αὐτοῖς τὸν νόμον ... The sense of "to teach" is found, e.g., in Aesch. Prom., 481 f.: ἐγώ σφισιν ἔδειξα κράσεις ... ἀκεσμάτων; Soph. Ai., 1195; Ant., 300 : πανουργίας δ' ἔδειξεν ἀνθρώποις ἔχειν; Eur. Andr., 707; Plat. Leg., III, 676c; Epict. Diss., I, 4, 32; I, 18, 4. In the LXX, Dt. 4:5 (למד pi); Job 34:32 : σὺ δεῖξόν μοι (ירה hiph) ('Α : δίδαξόν με; Σ : σὺ διασάφησόν με). 4 Esr. 10:33; Dg., 11, 2. There are few examples of the sense "to expound," "to explain" or "to make plain"; cf. Hom. Od., 10, 303 : φύσιν αὐτοῦ ἔδειξεν; Aeschin., 2, 116; Aristot. Pol., IV, 8, p. 1293b, 31; Ditt. Syll.³, 972, 152. Examples of "to disclose," "to reveal," will be found below.

B. The Usage in the Johannine Writings.

In these writings δείκνυμι is of frequent occurrence and the sense emerges from the actual texts.

1. In the Gospel δείκνυμι is primarily found in statements formulated by the Evangelist himself : Jn. 2:18 : τί σημεῖον δεικνύεις ἡμῖν ὅτι ταῦτα ποιεῖς; Jn. 10:32 : πολλὰ ἔργα ἔδειξα ὑμῖν καλὰ ἐκ τοῦ πατρός. He is, of course, ascribing the usage to the speakers, so that the distinction has no practical significance. The σημεῖα οὐκ ἰδεῖν of 6:26 corresponds to the σημεῖον δεικνύειν. On the other hand, σημεῖα ποιεῖν may be used instead of σημεῖα δεικνύειν in 2:11, 23; 3:2 etc. [5] Similarly, in 10:32 we have ἔργα δεικνύειν and in 10:25 ἔργα ποιεῖν. [6] In the action of Jesus the δεικνύειν is a demonstration of works. As the works of Jesus are accomplished, they point to God. They are thus signs, and can be done or shown as such, i.e., manifested in their character as revelation. Thus δεικνύειν acquires the sense of "to reveal," "to disclose."

For examples outside the NT, cf. Hom. Od., 3, 173 f.: ᾐτέομεν δὲ θεὸν φῆναι τέρας· αὐτὰρ ὅ γ' ἡμῖν δεῖξε; Jos. Ant., 18, 211: σημεῖόν τι πρόφαντον αὐτῷ δεῖξαι; 20, 168 : δείξειν ... τέρατα καὶ σημεῖα; Ep. Jer. 66 : σημεῖά τε ἐν ἔθνεσιν ἐν οὐρανῷ οὐ μὴ δείξωσιν; Sib., 2, 189 : ... κακὰ σήματα τρισσὰ κόσμῳ ὅλῳ δείξειεν ἀπολλυμένου βιότοιο; 12 (10), 29; 14, 158; Oracula Chaldaica, 45, Kroll. It

---

[4] The δεικνύειν of Jm. 2:18 corresponds to its frequent use in the diatribe in a sense which hovers between "to indicate" and "to demonstrate." Dib. Jk. ad loc.

[5] Cf. also σημεῖον ἐπιδεῖξαι (v.l. δεῖξαι) in Mt. 16:1.

[6] Cf. also ἔργα τελειοῦν in 4:34; 5:36; 17:4 or ἐργάζεσθαι τὰ ἔργα in 3:21; 6:28; 9:4.

is worth noting that elsewhere one can also say: σημεῖον (σῆμα) φέρειν, πέμπειν, ποιεῖν, διδόναι. [7]

Jn. 14:8 ff. is to be understood in the same way. Philip says to Jesus: κύριε, δεῖξον ἡμῖν τὸν πατέρα. The request is out of order, for "he that hath seen me hath seen the Father." The Father has been manifested to him in the ῥήματα and ἔργα which He does through Jesus (14:10 f.). The δεικνύειν τὸν πατέρα is thus a disclosing of God in the words and works of Jesus. As a visible and audible address to men, it demands on their part ὁρᾶν, γινώσκειν and πιστεύειν.

In John's Gospel δείκνυμι is also used for the disclosure of the Father to the Son. Thus we read in 5:20: ὁ γὰρ πατὴρ φιλεῖ τὸν υἱὸν καὶ πάντα δείκνυσιν αὐτῷ ἃ αὐτὸς ποιεῖ καὶ μείζονα τούτων δείξει αὐτῷ ἔργα ἵνα ὑμεῖς θαυμάζητε. The unity of the Son with the Father consists in the fact that the Son sees and accomplishes the works manifested to Him by the Father. The δείκνυμι is an assignment of the work of the Father to the Son in exhibition of His own action. Hence δίδωμι τὰ ἔργα may be used for δείκνυμι τὰ ἔργα in 5:36; 17:4. [8] The Father's giving of His own works to be fulfilled by the Son (ἵνα τελειώσω or ποιήσω αὐτά) means that they are displayed in such a way that the Son obediently recognises and accomplishes them. To the δεικνύναι of the ἔργα there corresponds a διδάσκειν or λέγειν of the ῥήματα in 8:28; 12:49a and 50b. [9] Hence this δεικνύναι, too, contains the thought of a revelation in action which constitutes a claim. [10]

2. In the Revelation of John the most important passage is 1:1 f.: Ἀποκάλυψις Ἰησοῦ Χριστοῦ, ἣν ἔδωκεν αὐτῷ ὁ θεός, δεῖξαι τοῖς δούλοις αὐτοῦ ἃ δεῖ γενέσθαι ἐν τάχει, καὶ ἐσήμανεν ἀποστείλας διὰ τοῦ ἀγγέλου αὐτοῦ τῷ δούλῳ αὐτοῦ Ἰωάννη, ὃς ἐμαρτύρησεν τὸν λόγον τοῦ θεοῦ καὶ τὴν μαρτυρίαν Ἰησοῦ Χριστοῦ, ὅσα εἶδεν. The λόγοι τῆς προφητείας (v. 3), which are written down, represent a revelation of Jesus Christ in the sense that He reveals Himself in them. This revelation, however, was given to Him by God in order that in Him there should be shown to the righteous the immediate future. This δεικνύειν was accomplished by way of a mediated impartation to John, who saw and attested it. Thus John attests both the Word of God and the self-witness of Jesus Christ. In the witness of John God attests Himself in the self-disclosure of Jesus Christ as the One who controls the imminent future. We thus see that the term δείκνυμι signifies here a. a divine declaration in the form of revelation (cf. the *angelus interpres* of 1:10 f. and the repeated assertion ἐγενόμην ἐν πνεύματι etc. in 1:10; 4:2; 17:3 and 21:10); b. divine revelation in the sense of an anticipation of the future (cf. also 4:1; 22:6); and c. an intermingling of intimation on the one hand and symbolism on the other, as suggested by the relating of δείκνυμι to (→) σημαίνω. The response to the divine revelation is thus an ἰδεῖν (1:2) which is also used with reference to the beings and matters manifested in the revelation (4:1 f.; 17:1, 3; 21:9 f.; 22:1 (22:8).

The general roots of this usage are naturally to be found in the meaning "to cause to see," "to manifest" (*infra*). But examples may be found of a usage much closer to that

---

[7] Cf. Gonda, *op. cit.*, 17.
[8] Cf. ψ 84:7: δεῖξόν ἡμῖν κύριε τὸ ἔλεός σου καὶ τὸ σωτήριόν σου κύριε δῴης ἡμῖν.
[9] Cf. also, however, Nu. 23:3; Jer. 45:21.
[10] Cf. 3 En. 48 C[20] 11:1-3; H. Odeberg, *The Fourth Gospel* (1929), 204: δείκνυσιν = הראה and is to be equated with διδάσκει (הורה) and ἀποκαλύπτει (גלה).

of Revelation. Thus in some typological exegesis the word obviously means "to intimate in advance," e.g., 1 Cl., 26, 1: God δι' ὀρνέου δείκνυσιν ἡμῖν τὸ μεγαλεῖον τῆς ἐπαγγελίας αὐτοῦ; Barn., 13, 3 f.: αἰσθάνεσθαι ὀφείλετε τίς ὁ Ἰσαὰκ καὶ τίς ἡ Ῥεβέκκα καὶ ἐπὶ τίνων δέδειχεν ὅτι μείζων ὁ λαὸς οὗτος ἢ ἐκεῖνος. καὶ ἐν ἄλλῃ προφητείᾳ λέγει φανερώτερον ... Cf. 5, 9; 7, 5 (13, 6); Act. Thom., 121. More important is the use of δείκνυμι where the reference is to the unveiling of a divine secret, and esp. to the seeing of phenomena in a dream or a prophetic vision. This occurs in secular passages. Cf. Aesch. Prom., 170 : ἐμοῦ ... χρείαν ἕξει μακάρων πρύτανις δεῖξαι τὸ νέον βούλημα ...; 175 : τόδ' ἐγὼ καταμηνύσω; Eur. Hipp., 42 : δείξω δὲ Θησεῖ πρᾶγμα, κἀκφανήσεται; Plat. Tim., 41e. But it is more characteristic of the LXX, [11] in which the verb has the theological sense of "to reveal" in 82 of 119 occurrences, and in which the idea of revelation is often imported into the text, the Mas. using very different expressions. Cf., e.g., Gn. 41:25, 39; Ex. 33:5, 18; Dt. 4:5; 5:24; 4 Βασ. 8:10, 13; Hos. 5:9; Am. 7:1: οὕτως ἔδειξέ μοι κύριος ὁ θεός, καὶ ἰδοὺ ... 7:4, 7; 8:1 (= 7:17); Zech. 1:20 : καὶ ἔδειξέ μοι κύριος τέσσαρας τέκτονας; 3:1; Jer. 24:1. The distinctive content is particularly expressed in passages which speak of the showing of the word to the prophet. So, e.g., Nu. 23:3 ff.: καὶ πορεύσομαι εἴ μοι φανεῖται ὁ θεὸς ἐν συναντήσει, καὶ ῥῆμα ὃ ἐάν μοι δείξῃ ἀναγγελῶ σοι ... καὶ ἐνέβαλεν ὁ θεὸς ῥῆμα εἰς τὸ στόμα Βαλαάμ... (24:17); Jer. 45:21; Bar. 5:3; Ez. 11:25; 40:4; Da. LXX 10:1: πρόσταγμα ἐδείχθη τῷ Δανιήλ (Θ : λόγος ἀπεκαλύφθη τῷ Δανιήλ). So far as it is a matter of God's showing, the Heb. equivalent is האר hiph. [12] Parallels to the LXX and ultimate Jewish usage may be found not only in the apocalyptic writings [13] but also in Herm., who often uses δείκνυμι in the sense of "to disclose" or "to reveal." Cf. esp. Herm. v., 3, 1, 2 : νηστεύσας πολλάκις καὶ δεηθεὶς τοῦ κυρίου ἵνα μοι φανερώσῃ τὴν ἀκοκάλυψιν ἥν μοι ἐπηγγείλατο δεῖξαι διὰ τῆς πρεσβυτέρας ἐκείνης; 3, 2, 3; 3, 3, 1 f.; 4, 1, 3 : τὰς ἀποκαλύψεις καὶ τὰ ὁράματα ἅ μοι ἔδειξεν διὰ τῆς ἁγίας Ἐκκλησίας ...; 5, 5; m., 11, 1; s., 3, 1; 4, 1; 5, 3, 2; 5, 4, 2 : κύριε, ὅσα ἄν μοι δείξῃς, καὶ μὴ δηλώσῃς, μάτην ἔσομαι ἑωρακὼς αὐτὰ καὶ μὴ νοῶν τί ἐστιν; 6, 1, 5; 2, 5; 8, 1, 1; 11, 5; 9, 1, 1 and 4; 9, 2, 1 and 7; 9, 10, 5.

The context of these passages makes it plain a. that δείκνυμι can be used synon. with φανεροῦν, ἐμφανίζειν and even ἀποκαλύπτειν (v., 3, 3, 2); b. that it demands a (ἐμ-) βλέπειν or ἰδεῖν leading to a μαθεῖν; and c. that there is also need of a δηλοῦν or ἐπιλῦσαι or even ἀποκαλύπτειν (s., 5, 3, 2). The word is used in relation to continually new symbols, but now, in distinction from Rev., a set form of exposition is also laid down.

As an example of the wide role of the term in apocalyptic literature generally we may refer to the usage in Hippolyt. De Antichristo. Here the term can mean "to prove," as in 15 (p. 12, 12, Achelis); 19 (p. 14, 23); 51 (p. 34, 14): δείξωμεν δι' ἑτέρων ἀποδείξεων. But it also has the sense of a. "to reveal or disclose" (= φαίνειν), as in 6 (p. 8, 4 f.): ἐδείχθη ὁ σωτὴρ ὡς ἀρνίον, καὶ αὐτὸς (sc. ὁ ἀντίχριστος) ὁμοίως φανήσεται ὡς ἀρνίον, ἔνδοθεν λύκος ὤν; cf. 50 (p. 33, 19); b. "to prophesy," as in 19 (p. 14, 23 f.): οὗτος (sc. Δανιήλ) ... ἔδειξεν ἐν ἐσχάτοις καιροῖς καὶ τὴν τοῦ ἀντιχρίστου παρουσίαν καὶ τὴν τοῦ παντὸς κόσμου συντέλειαν; and perhaps also 44 (p. 28, 3 and 16), where δείκνυμι is interchangeable with κηρύσσω (l. 9); and c., in a sense which is difficult to differentiate from b., where the prophecy may also be written, "to refer to mysteriously, viz. in written prophecy" (an exegetical term), as in 8 (p. 10, 1 f.): ἵνα (sc. Δαβίδ) δείξῃ ἐν τῷ ῥητῷ (ψ 3:6) τὴν κοίμησιν καὶ τὴν

---

[11] I owe this to G. Bertram.

[12] The prophet also "shows," e.g., Ez. 40:4; 43:10. The Heb. here is נגד, usually rendered either ἀπ- or ἀναγγέλλειν.

[13] E.g., Apc. Pt. 2:4; 5:15; Slav. En. 32:3, 6.

ἀνάστασιν αὐτοῦ ποτε γεγενημένην. Alternatives for δείκνυμι in this third sense are δηλοῦν in 9 (p. 10, 7 f.), 61 (p. 41, 13); μυστικῶς δηλοῦν in 25 (p. 17, 21 and 24; 18, 3), διδάσκω in 24 (p. 17, 6, 7, 9 and 11); μηνύειν (p. 17, 13); κηρύττειν in 44 (p. 28, 3, 9 and 16); and esp. σημαίνειν in 2 (p. 4, 20 f.); 8 (p. 9, 11); 43 (p. 27, 20 and 24).

ἀναδείκνυμι.

This occurs in two passages, Lk. 10:1: μετὰ δὲ ταῦτα ἀνέδειξεν ὁ κύριος ἑτέρους ἑβδομήκοντα (δύο), and Ac. 1:24: σὺ κύριε ... ἀνάδειξον ὃν ἐξελέξω ἐκ τούτων τῶν δύο ἕνα. The two instances correspond to two different senses attested outside the NT. [1] In the former the meaning is "to appoint," "to institute" or "to proclaim someone," with some vacillation between the idea of "ordaining someone for something" and the more legal "instituting" or "declaring to be instituted."

In Xenoph. Cyrop., VIII, 7, 23 : ἃ (sc. ἔργα) δυνατοὺς ὑμᾶς ἐν πᾶσιν ἀνθρώποις ἀναδείξει, the word means "to make" (cf. Polyb., I, 80, 12). But it is esp. common where there is reference to appointment to a public office or position. Polyb., IV, 48, 3 : βασιλέα ἑαυτὸν ἀναδεδειχώς; IV, 51, 3; τὸν Ἀχαιὸν ἀναδεδειχότα προσφάτως αὐτὸν βασιλέα; Diod S., I, 66, 1; XIII, 75, 5; XIII, 98, 1; Jos. Ant., 20, 227; Plut. De Artaxerxe, 26, 3 (I, 1024e): (Artaxerxes) ἀνέδειξε τὸν Δαρεῖον βασιλέα; De Arato, 3 (I, 1028d); Galb., 14 (I, 1058d) etc. In the LXX it is found in Da. 1:20 Θ : καὶ ἀνέδειξεν αὐτοὺς σοφοὺς παρὰ πάντας; 2 Macc. 9:14 : ἀνέδειξεν (= "declare") πόλιν ἐλευθέραν. More commonly it is a political action. Cf. Da. 1:11 LXX : εἶπεν ... τῷ ἀναδειχθέντι ἀρχιευνούχῳ (Θ: πρὸς Ἀμελσάδ, ὃν κατέστησεν); 2 Macc. 9:23, 25; 10:11; 14:12 : στρατηγὸν ἀναδείξας τῆς Ἰουδαίας (sc. Νικάνορα); 14:26 (Ἀ : ἀπέδειξεν); 1 Esr. 1:32 : ἀνέδειξαν βασιλέα = 2 Ch. 36:1 : κατέστησαν ... εἰς βασιλέα; 1 Esr. 1:35, 41, 44; 2:3; 8:23.

In Lk. 10:1, therefore, the word is taken from the political sphere and the institution of the seventy has the character of a public and official action.

2. In Ac. 1:24, however, the word should be translated "to disclose" or "to reveal." The divine declaration takes place in the lot.

This usage is also, though less frequently, attested outside the NT. [2] Thus we may refer to Xenoph. Hist. Graec., III, 5, 16 : Θρασύβουλος ... ἀποκρινάμενος τὸ ψήφισμα καὶ τοῦτ᾽ ἀνεδείκνυτο (v.l. ἐνεδ.); LXX Hab. 3:2 : ἐν μέσῳ δύο ζῴων γνωσθήσῃ, ἐν τῷ ἐγγίζειν τὰ ἔτη ἐπιγνωσθήσῃ· ἐν τῷ παρεῖναι τὸν καιρὸν ἀναδειχθήσῃ; 2 Macc. 2:8 : καὶ τότε ὁ κύριος ἀναδείξει ταῦτα, καὶ ὀφθήσεται ἡ δόξα τοῦ κυρίου ... καὶ ἡ νεφέλη ὡς καὶ ἐπὶ Μωυσῇ ἐδηλοῦτο; P. Oxy, VIII, 1081, 31: αὐτὴ ἡ ἀπόρροια τῆς εὐνοίας ἀναδείξει ὑμῖν· πῶς ἡ πίστις εὑρετέα. Hipp. De Antichristo, 52 (p. 35, 4 f.): οὗτος (sc. ὁ ἀντίχριστος) ... τοῖς τότε καιροῖς ὑπ᾽ αὐτῶν ἀναδειχθεὶς καὶ κρατήσας ... τῶν τριῶν κεράτων. [3]

ἀ ν α δ ε ί κ ν υ μ ι. [1] On ἀναδείκνυμι in the sense of "to dedicate," cf. E. Peterson, *Festschr. für A. Deissmann* (1926), 320-326. Cf. also Gonda, *op. cit.*, 63 f.

[2] Vett. Val., II, 38, 119, 26 in Pr.-Bauer should not be included acc. to Gonda, 61.

[3] S : "is manifested," "appears"; we should probably read "was manifested," "appeared" (Bonwetsch).

ἀνάδειξις.

The meaning in Lk. 1:80: τὸ δὲ παιδίον ... ἦν ἐν ταῖς ἐρήμοις ἕως ἡμέρας ἀναδείξεως αὐτοῦ πρὸς τὸν 'Ισραήλ, is not quite certain. The usual translation is "installation" with reference to 3:1 ff. and 10:1. This is supported by secular usage,[1] acc. to which ἀνάδειξις signifies the choice, institution or proclamation of officials. On this view the "institution" of the Baptist has a certain public and official character acc. to Lk.

Cf. Plut. Cato Minor, 44 (I, 781b): ὡς δ' ἦκεν ἡ κυρία τῆς ἀναδείξεως; 46 (I, 728a); Mar., 8, 5 (I, 409e); Polyb., XV, 26, 7 etc.

On the other hand, we have also to take into account the possible sense of "appearance" or "manifestation" along the lines of the mid. ἀναδείκνυσθαι. If we take this view, the appearance of the Baptist is presented in Lk. 1:80 as part of revelation.

This usage is attested in Diod. S., I, 85, 4: καὶ διὰ ταῦτα διατελεῖ (sc. Isis) μέχρι τοῦ νῦν ἀεὶ κατὰ τὰς ἀναδείξεις αὐτοῦ (sc. Osiris) μεθισταμένη πρὸς τοὺς μεταγενεστέρους. Otherwise it is found only in Christian writings:[2] Hipp. De Antichristo, 54 (p. 36, 3 ff.): Δεδειγμένων οὖν τῶν ῥητῶν τούτων τῆς τε φυλῆς καὶ τῆς ἀναδείξεως καὶ τῆς ἀναιρέσεως, ... ἴδωμεν καὶ τὴν πρᾶξιν αὐτοῦ; Const. Ap., I, 55, 1: πρὸ μικροῦ τῆς ἀναδείξεως αὐτοῦ τῆς σωματικῆς; ibid., V, 13, 2: ὁ κύριος ἀνάδειξιν ὑμῖν τῆς οἰκείας θεότητος ἐποιήσατο; ibid., VIII, 133, 7; Orig. Comm. in Joh., Fr. 90 on Jn. 12:31 ff.: ἐνέστη καιρὸς ἀναδείξεως τῶν κρινούντων τὸν κόσμον; ibid., 56 on Jn. 4:13; Comm. in Joh., VI, 9, 60.

† δειγματίζω.

This is a rare word meaning "to exhibit," "to make public," "to bring to public notice," esp. that which seeks concealment, so that it almost has the sense of "to expose." P. Greci e Latini, 447, 18: εἰ οὖν σοὶ δοκεῖ καὶ ἐάση<ι>ς με δειγματίσαι πρὸς αὐτούς, Asc. Is. 3:13 (P. Amh., I, col. VIII, 21): ἀπὸ τοῦ δειγματισμοῦ ὅτι ἐδειγμάτισεν τὸν Σαμαήλ; Act. Pt. et Pl., 33: ἔλεγε πρὸς τὸν λαὸν ἵνα ... δειγματίσουσιν αὐτὸν (sc. Simon Magus). The context is as follows: ὥστε πάντας τοὺς εὐλαβεῖς ἄνδρας βδελύττεσθαι Σίμωνα τὸν μάγον καὶ ἀνόσιον αὐτοῦ καταγγέλλειν.[1] For later usage, cf. Athanasius Epistula ad Episcopos Aegypti et Libyae, 11 (MPG, 25, 564a): ἐπειδὴ κρύπτουσιν αὐτοὶ καὶ φοβοῦνται λέγειν, ἀναγκαῖον ἡμᾶς ἀποδῦσαι τὸ κάλυμμα τῆς ἀσεβείας καὶ δειγματίσαι τὴν αἵρεσιν.

In the NT the sense is plain in Mt. 1:19: μὴ θέλων αὐτὴν δειγματίσαι. Joseph did not wish to cite Mary publicly and thus to expose her. There is no evident distinction from παραδειγματίζειν, and in א*GℜÞpl this is the reading. In Col. 2:15: ἀπεκδυσάμενος τὰς ἀρχὰς καὶ τὰς ἐξουσίας καὶ ἐδειγμάτισεν ἐν παρρησίᾳ θριαμβεύσας αὐτοὺς ἐν αὐτῷ, the sense is "to make a public exhibition," not by a proclamation[2] of the Kyrios, but by the public display of the vanquished forces before the cosmos, possibly in a triumphal procession.

ἀνάδειξις. [1] Cf. E. S. Roberts and E. A. Gardner, Intro. to Gk. Epigraph., II (1905), 119.
[2] In the LXX, only at Sir. 43:6 in the sense of "indication" or "exhibition."

δειγματίζω. Liddell-Scott, s.v.; Preisigke Wört., s.v.
[1] As a loan word δεῖγμα (cf. Jd. 7; Dg., 3, 3; 4, 5; 7, 9) passed into the Rabbinic literature. Schl. Mt. 14; δειγματίζειν = ריגמא אשׁי.
[2] Loh. Kol. ad loc., who rightly, in my view, refers ἀπεκδυσάμενος to divestment of dignity rather than despoiling of weapons.

Athanasius Vita St. Antonii, 35 (MPG, 26, 893c) here uses παραδειγματίζειν. Demons fear the sign of the Lord's cross, ἐπειδήπερ ἐν αὐτῷ τούτους ἀποδυσάμενος παρεδειγμάτισεν ὁ σωτήρ.

† παραδειγματίζω.

This derives from παράδειγμα and is more common than δειγματίζω. It is a stronger word, meaning "to expose to public obloquy," often at the pillory, though this is not intrinsic to the meaning. In Hellenistic writings we may note Polyb., II, 60, 7: περιαγόμενον δ' εἰς τὴν Πελοπόννησον καὶ μετὰ τιμωρίας παραδειγματιζόμενον, οὕτως ἐκλιπεῖν τὸ ζῆν; XXIX, 19, 5: ἡ δὲ σύγκλητος ... βουλομένη παραδειγματίσαι τοὺς 'Ροδίους; XXXV, 2, 10; Plut. De Curiositate, 10 (II, 520b): ἑαυτὸν παραδειγματίζων.

In the LXX, cf. Nu. 25:4: λάβε πάντας τοὺς ἀρχηγοὺς τοῦ λαοῦ καὶ παραδειγμάτισον αὐτοὺς τῷ κυρίῳ κατέναντι τοῦ ἡλίου (v.l. λαοῦ). Here παραδειγματίζειν denotes public hanging. The Heb. equivalent is יקע hiph, which indicates a mode of execution involving public exposure. Cf. 2 S. 21:6, 9, where the LXX reads: ἐξηλιάσωμεν αὐτοὺς τῷ κυρίῳ. In Jer. 13:22: διὰ τὸ πλῆθος τῆς ἀδικίας σου ἀνεκαλύφθη τὰ ὀπίσθιά σου, παραδειγματισθῆναι τὰς πτέρνας σου, παραδειγματίζειν is used for חמס niph = "to suffer violence." It may thus be given the sense of "to punish." In Ez. 28:17; Est. C 22 (13:11), however, it means "to pillory," "to put to open shame." Both verb and noun may be used both of the pious suffering of martyrs and of the punishment of the ungodly and profligate. Cf., e.g., 3 Macc. 3:11 and 7:14; and in the former sense Σ ψ 30:20 (LXX: ταραχή).

In the NT the only occurrence apart from Mt. 1:19 א .ℜ pl is in Hb. 6:6: Those who have fallen away cannot be renewed to repentance, ἀνασταυροῦντας ἑαυτοῖς τὸν υἱὸν τοῦ θεοῦ καὶ παραδειγματίζοντας. In the apostasy of the baptised Christ is crucified through them and thus publicly shamed. They expose Christ to public obloquy by their apostasy.

Cf. later Mart. Pt. et Pl., 51: ἡμεῖς αὐτὸν (Simon) οὐ παραδειγματίζομεν ἀλλ' ὁ κύριος ἡμῶν 'Ιησοῦς Χριστός; 52: ἤγγικεν γὰρ ὁ σὸς παραδειγματισμὸς καὶ ἡ ἡμετέρα ἀνάγκλησις; Ep. de Mart. S. Pothini, 16 (MPG, 5, 1448a): τὰ οὖν σώματα τῶν μαρτύρων παντοίως παραδειγματισθέντα καὶ αἰθριασθέντα ἐπὶ ἡμέρας ἕξ, μετέπειτα καέντα.

† ὑπόδειγμα.

This is rejected by the Atticists in favour of παράδειγμα.[1] In Hellenistic Gk. it means an "example" either given or adduced. But it also acquires the sense of a "document," "proof" or even "model." Cf. Xenoph. Eq., II, 2, 2: ταῦτα γὰρ ὑποδείγματα ἔσται τῷ πωλοδάμνῃ, ὧν δεῖ ἐπιμεληθῆναι; Polyb., III, 17, 8: ὑπόδειγμα τῷ πλήθει ποιῶν ἑαυτόν; III, 111, 6: καὶ μεθ' ὑποδειγμάτων ἐγὼ πρὸς ὑμᾶς πολλοὺς διεθέμην λόγους; VI, 54, 6: ὑποδείγματος καὶ πίστεως ἕνεκεν; Plut. De Marcello, 20 (I, 309b): πολιτικῆς ἀρετῆς ὑποδείγματα; Philo Rer. Div. Her., 256; Conf. Ling., 64; Jos. Bell., 1, 374; 6, 103; 2, 397: ὑπόδειγμα (warning example); Cornut. Theol. Graec., 27 etc. The reference in BGU, 1141, 43; P. Fay., 122, 16 is to a sample or pattern.

ὑ π ό δ ε ι γ μ α. Wnd. Hb.², 72; Rgg. Hb.³ on 4:11; 8:5; 9:23; F. Bleek Hb., II, 1 (1836), 554 f.

[1] Cf. Phryn. Ecl., 4, p. 62.

The customary usage is largely followed in the LXX, which often employs ὑπόδειγμα and παράδειγμα as alternatives. Cf. Sir. 44:16; 2 Macc. 6:28, 31; 4 Macc. 17:23 with 3 Macc. 2:5; 4 Macc. 6:19; Nah. 3:6; Jer. 8:2; 9:22; 16:4. Worth noting is Ez. 42:15 : διεμέτρησῃ τὸ ὑπόδειγμα τοῦ οἴκου, the reference being to the prophetic vision of the temple which is a model for the new house of God. Similarly, David gives Solomon a παράδειγμα (תַּבְנִית) of the temple in 1 Ch. 28:11, 12, 18, 19 (LXX). The word (תַּבְנִית) rendered ὁμοίωμα in Dt. 4:17 LXX is translated ὑπόδειγμα in ᾽Α. Thus ὑπόδειγμα may also mean "image" or "copy." More precisely, it denotes what is similar. Thus the picture of an original object may be seen as reflecting it and therefore as a copy, or as indicating what is seen in the spirit and therefore as a representation or model. Cf. also Ez. 8:10, where the LXX has ὁμοίωσις (= ὁμοίωμα) and ᾽Α ὑπόδειγμα. Cf. Ex. 25, where the תַּבְנִית of the tabernacle is rendered παράδειγμα in v. 8 and τύπος in v. 40.

The LXX usage gives us the clue to the meaning of ὑπόδειγμα in Hb. 8:6 : οἵτινες ὑποδείγματι καὶ σκιᾷ λατρεύουσιν τῶν ἐπουρανίων, and Hb. 9:23 f.: ἀνάγκη οὖν τὰ μὲν ὑποδείγματα τῶν ἐν τοῖς οὐρανοῖς τούτοις καθαρίζεσθαι, αὐτὰ δὲ τὰ ἐπουράνια κρείττοσιν θυσίαις παρὰ ταύτας. οὐ γὰρ εἰς χειροποίητα εἰσῆλθεν ἅγια Χριστός, ἀντίτυπα τῶν ἀληθινῶν, ἀλλ᾽ εἰς αὐτὸν τὸν οὐρανόν ... The σκηνή seen by Moses on the mount is the τύπος, the original. The tabernacle of the Jews made by Moses is the copy and reflection.[2] It is the ὑπόδειγμα καὶ σκιά, the shadowy reflection, of the heavenly original. Hence the χειροποίητα, which as ὑποδείγματα are contrasted with the ἐπουράνια, are ἀντίτυπα τῶν ἀληθινῶν, copies or counterparts of the true and original things. But as such they are also, in the sense of Hebrews, models which point to these heavenly things. The word ὑπόδειγμα thus has a double sense which is best brought out by the neutral "image." In virtue of this double sense we can see again that the typical character of the OT cultus only appears when it is seen in the light of Christ. Set in this light, it points to heavenly things. Conversely, it is genuinely seen to be a model only when we accept its character as an image.

The other NT passages use the term in the sense of "example" or "model." In Jm. 5:10 the prophets of God are ὑπόδειγμα ... τῆς κακοπαθίας καὶ μακροθυμίας. In Jn. 13:15 Jesus says that in washing the feet of the disciples He had given them a ὑπόδειγμα of mutual service. This is more than an example. It is a definite prototype. In a typical act they experience the love of Jesus and are to cause others to have the same experience : ὑπόδειγμα ... ἔδωκα ὑμῖν, ἵνα καθὼς ἐγὼ ἐποίησα ὑμῖν καὶ ὑμεῖς ποιῆτε. In 2 Pt. 2:6; Hb. 4:11 ὑπόδειγμα is a warning or bad example. Cf. also 1 Cl., 5, 1; 6, 1; 46, 1; 55, 1; 63, 1; Papias Fr., 3.[3]

Schlier

---

[2] This is a general Jewish idea, cf. Str.-B., III, 702 ff. But in Judaism everything belonging to the σκηνή represented heavenly things essentially. For Christianity, however, the Jewish σκηνή provided only an obscure copy.

[3] Patrum Apost. Opera, ed. Gebhardt, Harnack, Zahn (Ed. min.³ 1900), 73.

† δεῖπνον, δειπνέω

In the everyday sense this means "meal" or "chief meal" (Lk. 14:12) or "feast" [1] (Mk. 12:39 and par.; 6:21; Jn. 12:2; 1 C. 10:27 D).

In the NT the word takes on theological significance 1. by its cultic use in 1 C. 11:20 : → κυριακὸν δεῖπνον, [2] "the meal consecrated to the Lord," "the Lord's Supper." [3] The evening table fellowship of the community constitutes divine service. It is profaned by the separation of individuals to ἴδιον δεῖπνον (v. 21). According to the Pauline tradition (v. 23 ff.), the celebration rests on the institution of Jesus on the night of His betrayal, i.e., after the Last Supper, cf. v. 25 (Lk. 22:20 ℌℜ): μετὰ τὸ δειπνῆσαι [4] (cf. also Jn. 13:2, 4; 21:20). For more general points, → ἀγάπη (I, 55), πάσχα, τράπεζα.

It also takes on theological significance 2. as an eschatological image. The "heavenly banquet of the last time," in which the redeemed will participate, is a meaningful expression for perfect fellowship with God and with Christ in the consummation. Cf. esp. Lk. 14:24, in interpretation of the parable of the Great Supper, v. 16 ff.: οὐδεὶς τῶν ἀνδρῶν ἐκείνων τῶν → κεκλημένων → γεύσεταί μου τοῦ δείπνου, and Rev. 19:9 : → μακάριοι οἱ εἰς τὸ δεῖπνον τοῦ γάμου τοῦ → ἀρνίου κεκλημένοι where the images of the eschatological banquet and the marriage-feast (→ γάμος) merge into one another, as already in Mt. 22:2 ff. Cf. also Mt. 8:11; 26:29; Lk. 22:29 f., 16, 18. [5] The saying of Christ as He knocks at the door in Rev. 3:20 : ἐάν τις ἀκούσῃ τῆς φωνῆς μου καὶ ἀνοίξῃ τὴν θύραν, εἰσελεύσομαι πρὸς αὐτὸν καὶ δειπνήσω μετ' αὐτοῦ καὶ αὐτὸς μετ' ἐμοῦ, also points us, in the context of the Revelation Epistles (cf. 2:5, 16, 25; 3:11), to eschatological union with the Friend who is welcomed in, the Lord of the *parousia*. [6] The dreadful opposite of the final banquet of the blessed is τὸ δεῖπνον τὸ μέγα τοῦ θεοῦ (Rev. 19:17, based on Ez. 39:17 ff.), to which the birds of prey are summoned (cf. Mt. 24:28; Lk. 17:37), the hosts of Antichrist having been overthrown and destroyed.

δεῖπνον is common for a "cultic meal" in the religious speech of Hellenism, [7] e.g., Jos. Ant., 18, 73 : an invitation to the δεῖπνον of Anubis in the temple of Isis in Rome ;

δ ε ῖ π ν ο ν, δ ε ι π ν έ ω. Moult.-Mill., 138 f.; Pr.-Bauer, 270; Liddell-Scott, 375.

[1] On ancient meals and feasts, cf. Pauly-W., IV (1901), 1201 ff.; on Jewish, cf. J. R. Willis, DCG, II, 150 ff.; Str.-B., II, 204 ff.; IV, 611 ff.; I, 914 f.

[2] The phrase δεῖπνον κυριακόν might also be used for the stories of the feedings in Mk. 6:35 ff. and par. and the meal with the seven in Jn. 21:12 ff., although the term δεῖπνον does not actually occur in the Synopt. accounts and ἀριστοῦν is used in Jn. 21. In both these cases the Lord dispenses food, as He also dispenses wine at the marriage in Cana. Hence these stories should be set alongside the institution narrative. They were used as symbols of the Lord's Supper in early Christian art, which avoided any direct representation. Cf. K. Künstle, *Ikonographie der christlichen Kunst*, I (1928), 413, with bibl. [Bertram].

[3] → κλάσις, κλάω and the related discussions of the Lord's Supper in the NT.

[4] Cf. Joh. W., 1 K., 286; Ltzm. K.³, 58; Sickb. K., 53.

[5] On this pt., cf. J. Jeremias, *Jesus als Weltvollender* (1930), 74 ff.

[6] Not to a present experience of individuals (Zn. Apk., I, 316, cf. R. H. Charles, *The Revelation of St. John*, I [1920], 101), nor to the Lord's Supper (Loh., *ad loc*.). Cf. Bss., Had., *ad loc*.; Rohr. Off., 127.

[7] Cf. Ltzm. K.³, 49 ff.; F. Pfister and O. Eissfeldt, RGG², III, 1854 ff.; K. Völker, *Mysterium u. Agape* (1927), 212 ff.; H. Seesemann, *Der Begriff* κοινωνία *im NT* (1933), 52 ff.

an Ephes. inscription (BMI, III, 2, 483 B, 10) refers to ἀνάλωμα τοῦ δείπνου in the cult of Artemis ;[8] an inscription from Notion (BCH, 47 [1923], 375, 6) refers to the δεῖπνον of an Aesculapius fraternity;[9] Plut. Ser. Num. Pun., 13 (II, 557 f.): the invitation of Pindar by a herald to the cultic meal of the Delphic priesthood in the days of Plutarch : Πίνδαρος ἐπὶ τὸ δεῖπνον τῷ θεῷ;[10] similarly Ael. Var. Hist., 9, 95 : the invitation of Homer with Apollo ἐπὶ ξένια in Argos. Cf. also the δεῖπνα τοῦ κλήρου in the circle of the Gnostic Marcus, Iren., I, 13, 4. Original invitations may be consulted in P. Oxy, 1755 : ἐρωτᾷ σε 'Απίων δειπνῆσαι ἐν τῷ οἴκῳ τοῦ Σεραπείου εἰς κλείνην τοῦ κυρίου Σαράπιδος τῇ ιγ ἀπὸ ὥρας θ; P. Oxy., 110; 523; 1484; 1485 : ἐρωτᾷ σαι διπνῆσαι ὁ ἐξηγητὴς ἐν τῷ Δημητρίῳ σήμερον ἥτις ἐστὶν θ ἀπὸ ὥρας ζ. The underlying thought is that of *communio,* of the union of those who eat with the deity. So also in the Gr. church, cf. Chrys. Liturg., p. 396, 5 ff.: τοῦ δείπνου σου τοῦ μυστικοῦ σήμερον υἱὲ θεοῦ κοινωνόν με παράλαβε. On the suspecting of Θυέστεια δεῖπνα or ἀνθρωποφαγία among Christians, cf. Athenag. Suppl., 3, 1; Tat. Or. Graec., 25, 3.

The image of the eschatological feast (of rejoicing or judgment) goes back to the eschatology of Israel. Cf. Is. 34:6 ff.; Jer. 46:10; Zeph. 1:7 and esp. Is. 25:6 (the feast of fat things and wine on the lees prepared by Yahweh on Mount Sion [24:23] for all nations). A grotesque note is first introduced in Ez. 39:17 ff. (→ 34).[11] It is used as an image of fellowship with God in the last days in Eth. En. 62:14 : "The Lord of spirits will dwell over them, and they will eat and lie down and rise up to all eternity with that Son of Man"; Slav. En. 42:5 : "At the last coming he will lead out Adam and the patriarchs and bring them (into the paradise of Eden) that they may rejoice, as when a man invites his friends to eat with him, and they come and speak with one another before the palace, joyously awaiting his feast, the enjoyment of good things, of immeasurable wealth and joy and happiness in light and everlasting life." In Christian apocalyptic cf. 4 (5) Esr. 2:38 : *videte numerum signatorum in convivio Domini ;* Herm. s., 5, 2, 9; 5, 3 (moralised). In Rabb. writings, cf. the parables in bShab, 153a; Midr. Cant. r., 9, 8 ; also Midr. Est., 1, 4 : "The feast of our God, which He will prepare for the righteous, has no end" ;[12] Pesikt. r., 41, where Jacob is invited to the feast of redemption סְעוּדַת גְאוּלָה;[13] cf. Midr. Ps. 14:7: מִזְמָן לַסְעוּדָה.

                                                                                        Behm

---

[8] Cf. on this pt. H. Oppermann, RVV, 19, 3 (1924), 67 f. On the meals and public feasts organised by the priests of Zeus Panamaros, *ibid.,* 78 f.; also BCH, 51 (1927), 95, No. 61, 10 and 98, No. 64, 5.

[9] On sacred feasts in the cult of Mithras, cf. F. Cumont, *Die Mysterien des Mithra*[3] (1923). 124 and 146 f.; Haas, *Bilderatlas,* Lfrg., 15 (1930) (Leipoldt), 18 f., 23 and 46 ; in the cult of Sabazius etc., cf. F. Cumont, *Die orientalischen Religionen im römischen Heidentum*[3] (1931). 56 and 60.

[10] Cf. U. v. Wilamowitz, *Pindaros* (1922), 129, n. 1.

[11] On the mythological and religious background of these conceptions, cf. H. Gressmann, *Der Ursprung d. israel.-jüd. Eschatologie* (1905), 136 ff.; A. Jeremias, *Das AT im Lichte des alten Orients*[4] (1930), 982 f., 733 f.

[12] Str.-B., IV, 1154; I, 878 f., with additional material.

[13] *Ibid.,* IV, 1157. Cf. also Dalman WJ, I, 90 f.

δεισιδαιμονία, δεισιδαίμων → δαίμων.

δέκα

In Israel as in other peoples the importance of the number "ten" is linked with original reckoning by fingers. Thus ten is the basis of the decadic system which arose with the duodecimal in antiquity.

In the OT ten is a favourite round figure, which may be greater or less according to circumstances. Thus, without any speculative signification, the Law of God is given in Ten Commandments (Ex. 20; Dt. 5); the power of God is successively revealed in ten plagues (Ex. 7-11); there are ten patriarchs before the Flood (Gn. 5); the tenth is the sacred offering to God (Gn. 28:22); ten is a prominent number in the measurements of the ark (Gn. 6:15), the tabernacle (Ex. 26 and 27) and the temple (1 K. 6; 7).

The number is also prominent in Judaism. Abraham is brought to perfection in ten temptations (Ab., 5, 3). The world is created by ten divine words (bMeg., 21b). In the cultus true divine service is constituted only by the presence of ten men (Meg., 4, 3), with the consequent presence of the Shekinah (bSan., 7a).[1] The number is so fixed in this respect that the word מִנְיָן (number) may be used for it.[2] In Hillel's third rule of exposition[3] עֵדָה (congregation) and עֲשָׂרָה are equivalents. The provision that at least ten persons must be present at the Passover may be mentioned in the same connexion (T. Pes., 4; Jos. Bell., 6, 423).

The use of the number ten is important in apocalyptic.[4] The division of the total world period into ten epochs expresses the full extent of times, as in the ten weeks apocalypse which goes back to the age of the Maccabees.[5] Here three weeks represent the pre-Israelite period, and the tenth week (the seventh of Israel) is the age of the Messiah.[6]

In later Judaism there is speculation on the meaning of numbers. Cf. esp. Philo,[7] for whom ten is the number of perfection. Vita Mos., I, 96 : τέλειος ἀριθμός; Spec.

δ έ κ α. D. Schenkel, *Bibellexikon,* V (1875), 690 f.; RW, II, 716; BW, 737 f.; ERE, IX, 406 ff.; RE³, 21, 601 and 605; B. Pick, "Der Einfluss der Zehnzahl auf das Judentum," *Allg. Zeitschr. des Judentums Jahrgg.,* 58, 29 ff.; K. Baehr, *Symbolik des mos. Kultus* (1837), I, 175 ff.; E. Wölfflin, "Zur Zahlensymbolik," *Arch. f. lat. Lexikographie,* 9 (1896), 333 ff.; W. Roscher, "Die Zahl 50 im Kultus usw.," ASG (1917), 5; A. Jeremias, *Das AT im Licht des Alten Orients*⁴ (1930), Index, esp. 823; *Handbuch d. altorient. Geisteskultur*² (1929), 265 ff.; G. Kittel, *Rabbinica* (1920), 39 ff.; K. Staehle, *Die Zahlenmystik bei Philo v. Alexandria* (1931).

[1] Jesus' rule in Mt. 18:20 is an amendment also found in Judaism, cf. Str.-B., I, 794 f.

[2] The prescribing of the מִנְיָן seems to have come from Babylon (cf. Soph., 10, 7). It is certainly early. Cf. S. Krauss, *Synagogale Altertümer* (1922), 98 f.; "Minjan" in *Jahresberichte der isr.-theol. Lehranstalt in Wien,* 37-39 (1933), 51-74.

[3] bMeg., 23b; Strack, Einl., 97 f.

[4] Bousset-Gressm., 247 f.; Str.-B., IV, 987 ff.

[5] En. 93:1 ff.; 91:12-17; Da. 9:24; Sib., 4, 47 f. (10 γενεαί); 4 Esr. 14:11 f. (Eth. text, cf. Kautzsch, *Apkr. u. Pseudepigr.,* II, 399 A c). Cf. 10 *saecula* among the Etruscans : Censorin., XVII, 5 (Pauly-W., 2, series I [1920], 1697, *s.v., saeculum*).

[6] Str.-B., I, 43 f. Ten things are renewed in the Messianic age (luminosity of the stars, fertility etc.), Ex. r., 15 in Str.-B., III, 253 f.

[7] In this respect he follows the Greeks, esp. Speusippos, cf. Pauly-W., 2nd series, III (1929), 1658; *ibid.,* II (1896), 1087, 19, *s.v.,* "Arithmetica"; J. Tropfke, *Gesch. d. Elementarmathematik*² (1921), I, 93 ff., 108; Staehle, 4 f.

Leg., II, 201; IV, 105 : τελειότατος ... ἱερώτατός τε καὶ ἅγιος; hence also Congr., 109 : ἡ δεκὰς ... τὸ δικαιοσύνης μνημεῖον.

In the NT, where there is no express symbolism, ten plays a less significant role. It is used as a smaller round number, e.g., in Lk. 19:13; 15:8; Mt. 25:1; Rev. 2:10 (a short period of persecution, Da. 1:12, 14). More important is the proof of Jesus' Messianic power by ten miracles in Mt. (8; 9). The genealogy in Mt. (1:1 ff.) is linked with the schema of world fulfilment in ten weeks. Abraham comes with the fourth and the Messiah with the tenth. [8] In Rev. the ten horns represent a totality of power as in Da. 7:20. [9] Occasionally the number ten serves as a framework for enumeration, e.g., R. 8:38 f., where ten powers are unable to separate the righteous from God, or 1 C. 6:9 f., where ten vices exclude from the kingdom of God.

On Gnostic speculations about the number ten, cf. Iren., I, 17, 1; 18, 3.

Hauck

δεκτός → δέχομαι.

δεξιός

From the stem δεκ-, from which → δέχομαι is also formed, δεξιός means "right," a. as the opposite of ἀριστερός or εὐώνυμος ("left"). In this sense it may be used adj. in conjunction with the most varied subst., e.g., χείρ, ὀφθαλμός, οὖς, κέρας etc. [1] In the form ἡ δεξιά, it may also denote b. the right hand of God as the symbol of divine power. It is common in this sense in poetry, esp. the Psalms. [2] δεξιὰ κυρίου ἐποίησεν δύναμιν, δεξιὰ κυρίου ὕψωσέν με (ψ 117:15; cf. 19:6). With His right hand Yahweh saves the oppressed (16:7), punishes the enemies of the righteous (20:8) and helps His people in all situations (62:8). With His right hand He has given His people the land (43:3) and redeemed them from the Egyptians (Ex. 15:6, 12). With His right hand He helps them in every emergency (59:5). In all these things His power is linked with His righteousness : δικαιοσύνης πλήρης ἡ δεξιά σου (47:10). With His right hand He also accomplished the creation of the world : καὶ ἡ χείρ μου ἐθεμελίωσε τὴν γῆν, καὶ ἡ δεξιά μου ἐστερέωσεν τὸν οὐρανόν (Is. 48:13). As a symbol of divine power ἡ δεξιά is also used outside the Bible. Of the murderers of the Jewish emissaries it is said : οὐ διαφεύξονται τὸν μέγαν ὀφθαλμὸν αὐτοῦ καὶ τὴν ἀνίκητον δεξιάν, Jos. Bell., 1, 378. A magic incantation contains the words : ὁρκίζω χέρα δεξιτερήν, ἣν κόσμῳ ἐπέσχες, Preis. Zaub., I, 306. In another place we have : σῶμα

---

[8] Str.-B., I, 43 f.; K. Bornhäuser, *Die Geburts- u. Kindheitsgesch. Jesu* (1930), 15 f. The three groups of fourteen from the time of Abraham correspond to the six seven week periods of the time of Israel acc. to En. 93:91.

[9] Bss. Apk., 408 explains this in terms of the Parthian satraps linked with Nero redivivus; B. Weiss, *Die Joh. Apk.* (TU, 7, 1 [1891]), 208 n. refers it to the rulers of the ten Roman provinces.

δ ε ξ ι ό ς. Cr.-Kö., 274 f.; Deissmann NB, 78 f.; Str.-B., IV, 452 ff.; F. J. Dölger, *Antike u. Christentum,* I (1929), 236 ff.; Dausch Synpt.⁴, 272; Rohr. Hb.⁴, 11.

[1] Innumerable examples might be given. They may be found in any concordance, lexicon or index. The NT naturally uses the term in this sense. Cf. esp. Aristot. Cael., 2, p. 284b, 6 ff.; Probl., 31, 12 f., p. 958b, 16ff.

[2] In all these instances ἡ δεξιά is the rendering of ימין.

τέλειον ἐμοῦ, διαπεπλασμένον ὑπὸ βραχίονος ἐντίμου καὶ δεξιᾶς χειρὸς ἀφθάρτου, *ibid.*, IV, 498, also IV, 518 : βεβελτιωμένος ὑπὸ κράτους μεγαλοδυνάμου καὶ δεξιᾶς χειρὸς ἀφθάρτου. c. The word δεξιός acquires a particular meaning in virtue of the common linking of it with what is favourable or honourable. When birds are in flight in Greece (as distinct from Rome), it is auspicious if they are on the right side : ἐπεὶ δὲ αὐτοῖς ἀετὸς δεξιὸς φανεὶς προηγεῖτο, προσευξάμενοι θεοῖς καὶ ἥρωσι . . . Xenoph. Cyrop., II, 1, 1. Josephus tells us that of the two stones on the shoulders of the high-priest that on the right side had a particular brilliance (Ant., 3, 215). The Rabbis located man's good impulses on the right side (Nu. r., 22, 9 on 32:1 [Str.-B., III, 94 f.]). Joseph. calls good fortune δεξιὰ τύχη in Bell., 1, 430. The right side is the side of honour. Those who are worthy sit or walk on the right (cf. 3 Βασ. 2:19; ψ 44:9; Str.-B., I, 835). The right side is the one to which one turns in prayer : καταστὰς δεξιός, ἀθανάτοις θεοῖσιν ἐπευχόμενος (δεξιός *pro* ἐπὶ δεξιᾷ), Theogn., 943 f. (cf. Plaut. Curc., I, 1, 70 : *si deos salutas, dextrovorsum censeo*). The right side is the religiously vital one even in the OT and the Rabbis; cf. Nu. r., 22, 9 on 32:1: "The heart of the wise is at his right hand" (Qoh. 10:2). This applies to the righteous, who direct their heart to the Torah, which is at the right hand of God, acc. to Dt. 33:2. [3] "But a fool's heart is at his left" (Qoh. 10:2). This applies to the ungodly, whose heart is set on wealth, which is on the left, as in Prv. 3:16 : "In her left hand are riches." d. δεξιός can thus be used as a synon. of εὔνους, ἀγαθός, ἐπιτήδειος, Suid., *s.v.* (cf. *ibid.*, *s.v.* δεξιά : δεξιὰ ἔλεγον οἱ παλαιοὶ τὰ συνετά, ἀριστερὰ δὲ τὰ μωρά). It is told of the Pythagoreans : τὸ οὖν δεξιὸν καὶ ἄνω καὶ ἔμπροσθεν ἀγαθὸν ἐκάλουν, Simplic. in Aristot. Cael., II, 2, p. 386, 20 f., Heiberg ; . . . ζητῶν δεξιὸς εἶναι . . ., Aristoph. Nu., 429 (cf. Ra., 1370 ; also Plat. Menex., 235c : οἱ ῥήτορες δεξιοί). The same usage occurs in the Rabbis: "The anointed, that is, the most eminent (המיומן, part. pu. of ימן) among the anointed," bHor., 12a. [4] Cf. also the saying : Whoso is occupied with the Torah on the right hand (= profoundly) (למיימינים), to him it is a means of life and salvation ; but whoso is occupied with it on the left (= superficially) (למשמאלים), to him it is a medicine unto death," bShab., 88b. [5] e. Finally, δεξιά (sing.) and δεξιαί (plur.) denote a treaty or compact : ἵνα τηρήσωσι αὐτῶν τὴν δεξιάν, P. Oxy., 533, 18 (2nd. cent. A.D.). Of a violator it is said by Aristot. that he sets aside ὅρκους, δεξιάς, πίστεις, ἐπιγαμίας (Rhet., I, 14, p. 1375a, 10). This usage derives from the custom of giving the right hand at the conclusion of an agreement or alliance : νῦν οὖν δῶμεν δεξιὰν τοῖς ἀνθρώποις τούτοις, καὶ ποιήσωμεν μετ' αὐτῶν εἰρήνην, 1 Macc. 6:58 (cf. Jos. Ant., 18, 328 f.; in the NT Gl. 2:9). The safe conduct given to Joseph. by Vespasian is described by him as follows : δεξιάς τε τῷ Ἰωσήπῳ δοῦναι κελεύσας, Bell., 3, 344 (synon. with πίστεις : πίστεις περὶ σωτηρίας ἐδίδοσαν, *ibid.*, 345). [6]

In biblical usage the term is important from two angles.

1. In the great judgment at the end of the days Jesus divides men. In the picture used He places the sheep, which are the εὐλογημένοι τοῦ πατρός, on the right hand, while the goats, which are the κατηραμένοι, are set on the left (Mt. 25:31 ff.). This follows the conception, already noted, that the right side is the favourable one, the side of bliss and salvation.

There are clear parallels for this image. In Midr. Cant., 1, 9 (90a), [7] there is the following exposition of 1 K. 22:19 : "Some (of the angels) gave their verdict on the right and some

---

[3] The words מימינו אשדת למו in Dt. 33:2 are taken by the Rabbis to mean : "On His right hand a fiery law, i.e., a heavenly Torah written with fire, for them."

[4] Str.-B., I, 980 f.

[5] *Loc. cit.*

[6] Cf. Deissmann NB, 78 f.; O. Eger, *Rechtsgeschichtliches zum NT* (1919), 40 f.

[7] Str.-B., I, 981.

on the left; some weighed down the scale of merit and some that of guilt." In Plato we read of the judges in the hereafter : τοὺς μὲν δικαίους κελεύειν πορεύεσθαι τὴν εἰς δεξιάν τε καὶ ἄνω διὰ τοῦ οὐρανοῦ ... τοὺς δὲ ἀδίκους εἰς ἀριστεράν τε καὶ κάτω (Resp., X, 614c).

2. The term δεξιός takes on its specific NT sense in passages where it is used to express the exaltation of Christ. In his Pentecost sermon in Ac. 2:34 Peter says that the ascension of Christ to the right hand of God is followed by His session there, and He describes this exaltation as a mighty act of God which God has accomplished by His right hand [8] as the final miracle in the story of Jesus — τῇ δεξιᾷ οὖν τοῦ θεοῦ ὑψωθείς (2:33) and τοῦτον ὁ θεὸς ἀρχηγὸν καὶ σωτῆρα ὕψωσεν τῇ δεξιᾷ (δόξῃ ? D) αὐτοῦ ... (Ac. 5:31). This is the fulfilment of the promise of the royal Psalm as Messianically understood in the NT and Jewish tradition. [9] The Psalm reads as follows (ψ 109:1): εἶπεν ὁ κύριος τῷ κυρίῳ μου : κάθου ἐκ δεξιῶν μου ... The fact that it was Messianically understood in the NT and Jewish tradition is proved both by the firmly attested debate in Mt. 22:41 ff. and by the statement of Jesus before the council. In the former, the last of a series in Mt. 21:23 ff. and par., Jesus goes over to the attack. His aim is to show that Davidic sonship does not exhaust His Messiahship, but that it has a higher and more far-reaching significance. "This formula (sc. concerning the Davidic sonship), which is supposed to express the glory of Christ, becomes a riddle in the question of Jesus, since the glory of Christ is so great that beside it the title 'son of David' denotes His humiliation." [10] Davidic sonship implies the restoration of the Davidic throne and the Davidic kingdom. Jesus is not satisfied with this political Messianic goal. "He does not look towards the royal city but towards the throne of God." [11] Jesus claims a place at God's right hand because He does not aim to be a mere Jewish Messiah but the Lord of the world. [12] He explicitly confesses this Messiahship when tried before the council. After the ascension Christians acknowledge Jesus as the Christ exalted to the right hand of God. This may be seen throughout the NT : Ac. 2:34; 5:31; 7:56; R. 8:34; Eph. 1:20; Col. 3:1; Hb. 1:3, 13; 8:1; 10:12; 12:2; 1 Pt. 3:22. This means, however, that in what has taken place after the resurrection they see a fulfilment of the claim of Jesus to His place of honour at the right hand of God. Peter in his sermon at Pentecost says briefly and clearly: κύριον αὐτὸν καὶ χριστὸν ἐποίησεν ὁ θεός, τοῦτον τὸν 'Ιησοῦν ὃν ὑμεῖς ἐσταυρώσατε (Ac. 2:36). By His exaltation to the place of honour alongside God, Jesus of Nazareth has become the Christ and Kyrios of the world. The Messianic Psalm is thus fulfilled ; the Messiah has entered His glory ; the Messianic age has dawned. Jesus in the place of honour

---

[8] → 37. Lk. follows the OT and Jewish usage.

[9] In this Psalm the address is originally to the king of Israel, perhaps at the coronation. "In the first instance the phrase 'at the right hand of Yahweh' is perhaps to be taken quite concretely as indicating that the throne and audience chamber are to the south of the temple, so that the king is enthroned at the right hand of Yahweh, whose throne is in the temple" [v. Rad].

[10] Cf. Schl. Mt., 660; also Zn. Mt., 646 ff.; Hck. Mk., 149 f.

[11] Schl. Mt., 660.

[12] Concerning the place of the debate within the Gospel, which is vital to the interpretation, it should be noted that it is preceded both by Mt. 21:1 ff., which raises the question of Davidic sonship, and also by Mt. 21:33 ff., where with the authority of the Lord of the world Jesus proclaims the judgment and lays down the course of the kingdom of God.

at the right hand of God has a share in the glory and power and deity of God which He exercises by sending the Holy Spirit. Certainty of this is mediated by Pentecost acc. to the account of Lk. [13]

Rather strikingly, the older Synagogue [14] did not refer the Psalm to the Messiah but to Abraham. God took Abraham and set him at His right side (bSanh., 108b). It might also be referred to David : Because of the plenitude of good works found in him, one day (sc. in the eschatological age of salvation) he will sit at the right hand of the Shekinah, as in Ps. 110:1 ... (Seder Elij. r., 18 [90]). Only after 250 A.D. does the Messianic interpretation come to the fore again (as in the NT period acc. to Mt. 22:44 and par.) in typical conflict with the Abrahamic view: "In the future God will cause the king, the Messiah, to sit on His right hand (cf. Ps. 110:1), and Abraham on His left. And Abraham's face will change colour, and he will say to God: My descendant sits on the right hand and I on the left? And God will graciously say to him: Thy descendant on My right hand, and I on thine" (Midr. Ps. 18 § 29 [79a]). The obvious reason why earlier exegesis rejected a Messianic interpretation was to prevent Christians appealing to Scripture.

Another Rabbinic view should be mentioned even though it has no connexion with this Psalm. This sets the Torah at the right hand of God in the earlier age (→ 38), and then in the Messianic age the Christ will occupy the place previously held by the Torah.

Grundmann

δέομαι, δέησις † προσδέομαι	(→ ἐρωτάω, εὔχομαι).

δέομαι, δέησις.

1. The original significance of δέομαι is "to lack," "to be in need of," and of δέησις "lack." [1] This is no longer present, however, in the NT and post-apost. fathers (though cf. the composite → προσδέομαι). Even in the LXX there are only a few traces of it (e.g., Job 17:1; [2] 4 Macc. 2:8; ψ 21:24 ?). Similarly Joseph. Ant., 14, 437; Ap., 2, 12; Ant., 1, 247 (part.). It is common in Philo, e.g., ὁ μὲν γὰρ θεὸς πάντα κεκτημένος οὐδενὸς δεῖται, Vit. Mos., I, 157 (cf. Spec. Leg., I, 271) etc.

2. In the NT δέομαι always has the sense of "to ask" or "to seek" as the context may determine. In the form δέομαί σου at the beginning of direct speech it may sometimes mean no more than "please," as when Paul asks the chiliarch for permission to address the people (Ac. 21:39) or the eunuch asks Philip to explain the passage in Isaiah (Ac. 8:34). The word has a fuller sense in the case of requests to Jesus, whether to be spared, like the demon in the man at Gerasa (Lk. 8:28), or for help and healing (Lk. 5:12; 9:38). Cf. also the moving appeal which, on the basis of his apostolic commission and out of concern for the welfare

---

[13] Cf. H. v. Baer, *Der Heilige Geist in den Lukasschriften* (1926), 84 and 92 ff.
[14] Cf. Str.-B., IV, 452 ff.
δ έ ο μ α ι. [1] Cf. Boisacq, 180.
[2] R. Helbing, *Die Kasussyntax der Verba bei den Septuaginta* (1928), 172.

of his missionary communities, Paul can also use with his earnest admonitions: δεόμεθα ὑπὲρ Χριστοῦ ... (2 C. 5:20; v. also 10:2; Gl. 4:12). In the NT δέομαι is used almost exclusively by Luke and Paul (Mt. 9:38 being the exception). δέησις does not occur at all in the general sense of "wish."

Constr. δέομαί τινος of the person to whom the request is made. This need not be present if it is clear from the context (Ac. 26:3; 2 C. 5:20; 10:2). The obj. of the request is in the acc. (2 C. 8:4) or inf., with once a ἵνα clause. Less frequently, the LXX also uses δεῖσθαι of requests to men: ἐάν σου δέηται ὁ ἐχθρός ... Prv. 26:25; πολλοί σου δεηθήσονται, Job 11:19. In petitions: δέομαι οὖν σου, εἴ σοι δοκεῖ, μὴ περιίδης με ἀδικηθέντα ὑπ' αὐτοῦ, Preisigke Sammelbuch, IV, 7446, 6; ibid., III, 6764; 6989, 11 (all from the Zeno archives, 3rd cent. B.C.). δέησις occurs in the same sense in P. Petr., II, 19, 1a, line 2 (3rd cent. B.C.). Philo Leg. Gaj., 276 and 279; Flacc., 97. Joseph.: (David) ... ἐδεήθη τοῦ βασιλέως, Ant., 6, 321; ... πολλὰς ποιησαμένων δεήσεις ἐλθεῖν εἰς τὸ θέατρον, Bell., 7, 107.

3. It thus comes to be used for requests to God and therefore for "to pray," "prayer," "petition." In this sense it is first used for specific prayer in concrete situations. Thus Jesus prays that Peter's faith may be strengthened (Lk. 22:32; Hb. 5:7 being the only other verse in which it is used of the prayer of Jesus). Again, Paul brings his missionary plans before God with prayer (R. 1:10; 1 Th. 3:10). In Ac. 4:31 δεηθέντων αὐτῶν refers to the preceding prayer (v. 24 ff.). Paul uses δέησις to describe his intercession for his brothers after the flesh (R. 10:1), the word being frequently used for intercession. Yet δέησις can denote prayer as an expression of piety in general (though only in Paul) as well as specific petition. The latter sense is still present in the phrase δέησιν (δεήσεις) ποιεῖσθαι (Lk. 5:33; Phil. 1:4; 1 Tm. 2:1), but it is hard to distinguish the aspect of "petition," since the object of the prayer is not mentioned and the situation provides no clue. In Ac. 10:2 we read of Cornelius: ποιῶν ἐλεημοσύνας πολλὰς τῷ λαῷ καὶ δεόμενος τοῦ θεοῦ διὰ παντός. Equally indeterminate is the content of the δεήσεις in Lk. 2:37; 5:33; 1 Tm. 5:5: προσμένει ταῖς δεήσεσιν καὶ ταῖς προσευχαῖς. [3]

Constr.: δέομαί τινος as above under 2., except that the gen. is now more frequently ommitted. A petition the fulfilment of which is particularly uncertain is presented in an εἰ clause in Ac. 8:22 and R. 1:10. Grammatically the weakening of the original sense and approximation to προσεύχεσθαι is indicated by the constr. δέομαι πρός τινα in Ac. 8:24 (cf. ἡ δέησις πρὸς τὸν θεόν, R. 10:1; Hb. 5:7). The content is mostly given in a ὅπως or ἵνα clause, ὑπέρ τινος or περί τινος denoting intercession. The LXX uses δέησις predominantly, and the NT exclusively, for requests to God. Since the word is common in secular Gk. for requests, it is easy to give it this special sense (cf. Epict. Diss., II, 7, 12; IG, IV, ed. min., 126, 17 [2nd cent. A.D.]). Joseph.: The edict of Darius from the story of Daniel: ... ὅπως μήτ' αὐτῷ (!) τις μήτε τοῖς θεοῖς δεόμενος αὐτῶν καὶ εὐχόμενος εἴη Ant., 10, 253; δέησις δ' ἔστω πρὸς τὸν θεὸν ... (defin.), Ap., 2, 197.

† προσδέομαι.

In his Areopagus address in Ac. 17:22 ff., Paul first links the familiar altar inscription to the OT thought of God, and then speaks of the omnipotent Creator

---

[3] On the distinction from προσεύχεσθαι, προσευχή, as on prayer generally, → εὔχομαι, προσεύχομαι.

προσδέομαι. E. Norden, Agnostos Theos (1913), 13 f.; Pr.-B., 1142.

of all things, whom he brings into effective contrast with the idolatry rampant in Athens : οὐκ ἐν χειροποιήτοις ναοῖς κατοικεῖ οὐδὲ ὑπὸ χειρῶν ἀνθρωπίνων θεραπεύεται προσδεόμενός τινος, αὐτὸς διδοὺς πᾶσιν ζωὴν καὶ πνοὴν καὶ τὰ πάντα (Ac. 17:24 f.). In this passage προσδέομαι means not to be self-sufficient but "to have need of something else." This element of need of something more is amply attested in inscriptions and the pap. (→ infra), but was quickly weakened again (→ infra). This was the more easily possible because the προσ- was not introducing a completely new aspect but simply strengthening the original sense ; for "to need" always contains the thought of something to be added. [1] In the NT, too, the emphasis does not lie on the προσ- ; it is repudiated that God stands in need of anything. This thought is part of the polemic against anthropomorphic conceptions of deity which is found not merely in the Gk. world [2] from the time of Euripides, and especially in Stoicism, [3] but also in the OT. Deutero-Is. pours scorn on the helplessness of idols which are made with hands and which have thus to be secured lest they should totter (40:20; 41:7; 46:7). Similarly, Wis. 13:16 says of the idol : ἵνα μὲν οὖν μὴ καταπέσῃ προενόησεν (sc. the carver) αὐτοῦ, εἰδὼς ὅτι ἀδυνατεῖ ἑαυτῷ βοηθῆσαι, καὶ γάρ ἐστιν εἰκὼν καὶ χρείαν ἔχει βοηθείας. It is part of Philo's concept of God that the One who has made all things stands in need of nothing, Vit. Mos., I, 157; δεῖται γὰρ οὐδενὸς οὔτε ὁ πλήρης θεὸς οὔτε ἡ ἄκρα παντελὴς ἐπιστήμη, Det. Pot. Ins., 54. Paul may be mentioned in the same connexion, for he regards the στοιχεῖα as weak and ineffectual, and demands that the Galatians should not subject themselves to these lords now that they know the true God (Gl. 4:8 f.; cf. also 1 C. 12:2). Of early Christian writings we may refer to the Epistle to Diognetus, which uses similar arguments against the heathen sacrificial cults (2, 1 to 3, 5).

For προσδέομαι with an emphatic προσ- (→ supra), cf. the Philip inscription at Larissa : ἡ ὑμετέρα πόλις διὰ τοὺς πολέμους προσδεῖται πλεόνων οἰκητῶν, IG, IX, 2, 517, line 5 (214 B.C.); also an Aesculapius inscr. in Epidauros (ibid., line 13): αὐτὰ δ' οὐθενὸς φάμεν ἔτι ποιδεῖσθαι, cf. line 18 ; πυνθανομένου αὐτοῦ, εἴ τινος καὶ ἄλλου δέοιτο (ibid., IV, ed. min., 121, 4th cent. B.C.); P. Greci e Latini, VIII, 969 (1st cent. B.C.); Zeno Pap., IV, No. 59648: [4] ἔχομεν γὰρ ξύλα ἱκανὰ ... ὥστε οὐ προσδεησόμεθα. With a weakened προσ-: Ditt. Syll., 313, 11 (4th cent. B.C.); Preisigke Sammelbuch, III, 7172, 13 (3rd cent. B.C.): καὶ τὰ (sc. ἀγάλματα) προσδεόμενα ἐπανορθώσεως ἀνενεώσατο. The LXX uses the word in the sense of "to have need" (Prv. 12:9 : προσδεόμενος ἄρτου; Sir. 42:21), but also in the sense derived analog. from δεῖσθαι and found esp. in Herod., i.e., "to request" (Sir. 4:3; 13:3). Cf. also Jos. Ant., 7, 340 : David tells Solomon of all the costly materials which he has gathered for the building of the temple, and concludes : ἂν δέ τι τούτοις προσδέῃ, σὺ προσθήσεις.

Greeven

---

[1] The correct use of προσδέομαι is as follows : "I need this or that (δέομαι), and more in addition"; → supra [Debrunner].

[2] Norden, op. cit.

[3] E.g., Epict. Diss., III, 13, 7.

[4] Catalogue général des Antiquités égyptiennes du Musée de Caire, 89, ed. C. C. Edgar (1931), 90.

δέος → φόβος.

| δεσμός, δέσμιος | → αἰχμάλωτος.

The "imprisonment" (lit. "fetter") of the "imprisoned" apostle takes on a particular religious significance in phrases like δέσμιος Χριστοῦ Ἰησοῦ (Eph. 3:1; Phlm. 1, 9); δέσμιον αὐτοῦ (2 Tm. 1:8); δέσμιος ἐν κυρίῳ (Eph. 4:1); ἐν τοῖς δεσμοῖς τοῦ εὐαγγελίου (Phlm. 13); also ὥστε τοὺς δεσμούς μου φανεροὺς ἐν Χριστῷ γενέσθαι[1] (Phil. 1:13). There can be no doubt that the actual imprisonment of Paul everywhere underlies the usage. But this real imprisonment is set in relation to Christ and the Gospel. Christ is its author. He is the One for whose sake it is fulfilled and also the One to whom human self-will should be offered in sacrifice.[2] The whole fate of the prisoner is lifted up into the sphere of the κύριος (→ ἐν).

Reitzenstein suspects a dependence of the statements (incl. → κατέχειν in Phlm. 13) on the terminology of the Mysteries. He adduces the κατοχή — the meaning of which is greatly contested (Wilcken) — to which the initiate in Serapeum at Memphis must subject himself prior to his final dedication, and which Reitzenstein also sees in Apul. Met., XI, 15 and Hipp. Ref., I, prooem, 2. Acc. to this view, Paul regards his imprisonment as a preparation for the final Christ mystery of σὺν Χριστῷ εἶναι (Phil. 1:23). A decisive argument against this is that in Phil. (2:24) and Phlm. (22) Paul does not treat his imprisonment as the penultimate stage. The whole complex of conceptions suspected by Reitzenstein would be much more in keeping with συν(αιχμάλωτος) (→ I, 195 f.). There we have a much stricter application of the image of the apostle's subjection to bondage to Christ. It should also be noted that there are links between the statements and ψ 68:33 : τοὺς πεπεδημένους αὐτοῦ (אֲסִירָיו) οὐκ ἐξουδένωσεν; Is. 45:13 : (a saying of Yahweh): "He shall let go my captives (גָּלוּתִי)[3]."[4]

Kittel

δεσμός, δέσμιος. Loh. Phlm., 174 f.; Dib. Gefbr., 78 f.; Meinertz Gefbr.[4], 78, 84, 117; O. Schmitz, *Die Christusgemeinschaft des Pls. im Lichte seines Genetivgebrauchs* (1924); Reitzenstein Hell. Myst.[3], 196 ff., 214 (more explicitly, though more cautiously, than in the 2nd. ed. [1919], 77, 86); Wilcken, Ptol., 52-77.

[1] The analogy of other statements makes the link ἐν Χριστῷ/φανερούς (the knowledge is in the Christian sphere and serves Christ, Dib. Gefbr., 55) less likely than the link ἐν Χριστῷ/δεσμούς (the bonds are in Christ or for His sake), as assumed already in Ps.-Pl. Laodic., 6 : *vincula mea quae patior in Christo,* and as in no way refuted by the order of words (notwithstanding Loh. Phil., 40).

[2] The gramm. formulation demands an interfusion of gen. auct., gen. qual. and gen. poss.

[3] Though we should perhaps follow the LXX (τὴν αἰχμαλωσίαν τοῦ λαοῦ μου) in reading גָּלוּת עַמִּי.

[4] It is worth noting that Rabb. exegesis made no attempt to explain the suffix forms.

| δεσπότης, οἰκοδεσπότης, οἰκοδεσποτέω | (→ κύριος). |

† δεσπότης.

A. δεσπότης outside the NT.

1. Greek Usage.

The word is first found in literature in Pindar with the sense of "owner," "possessor" (e.g., Pyth., 4, 207: δεσπόταν ναῶν; also Pyth., 9, 7: δέσποιναν[1] χθονός). By derivation and basic meaning it belongs to the sphere of domestic rule.[2] This is proved by the etym.; it goes back to the (unattested) Indo-Germ. *demspot-* "the lord of the house," which has a par. in the Sansk. *pátir dán*.[3] The position of the lord of the house in the Indo-Germ. sphere gives it the implication of unlimited authority or power. The transition of the word from the complex of domestic rule to that of political is probably to be attributed to historical developments and events, as with related terms like ἄναξ. In the process the word acquires a specific sense. "It seems to enter the political sphere through the intrusion of an alien people taking the land in possession. In fact the new ruler assumes all the functions native to the δεσπότης as an owner in terms of his own social structure." "Hence, when a ruler is seen in connexion with some such political event, the term δεσπότης is apposite."[4] It is in keeping that δεσπότης is always marked by a notable lack of enthusiasm in relation to rulers. Originally the only feeling in respect of him is that of the subject towards the one whom he must serve. We can thus understand why the older Greeks, in the light of their humane political relationships, regarded δεσπότης and δέσποινα as more suitable to denote the position of barbarian rulers.[5]

If we take note especially of the social history of the term, we can easily see how the word came to have the special meanings associated with it. The δεσπότης is a. the master of the house who normally rules unconditionally his family and household; Aesch. Pers., 169: ὄμμα γὰρ δόμων νομίζω δεσπότου παρουσίαν. b. He is the lord as distinct from the slave: Aristot. Pol., I, 3, p. 1253b, 4 ff.: οἰκία δὲ τέλειος ἐκ δούλων καὶ ἐλευθέρων (sc. συνίσταται) ἐπεὶ δ' ἐν τοῖς ἐλαχίστοις πρῶτον ἕκαστον ζητητέον, πρῶτα δὲ καὶ ἐλάχιστα, μέρη οἰκίας δεσπότης καὶ δοῦλος ... καὶ πατὴρ καὶ τέκνα.[6] c. He is the absolute ruler in the sense of an unlimited possibility of the exercise of power unchecked by any law, as exemplified in the Persian

---

δ ε σ π ό τ η ς. Liddell-Scott, 381; Preisigke Wört., I, 329 f.; Trench, 60 ff.; Schl. Lk., 199; H. Usener, *Götternamen* (1896), 220 ff.; W. W. Graf Baudissin, *Kyrios als Gottesname im Judentum*, II (1929), 140 ff.; 152 ff.; 156 ff.; K. Stegmann von Pritzwald, *Zur Geschichte der Herrscherbezeichnungen von Homer vis Plato* (1930), 83 ff., 102 ff., 129 ff., 148 ff.; Vrede Kath. Br.⁴, 65, 129.

[1] δέσποινα, formed on the model of δεσπότης, is found already in Hom. Od., 14, 127 etc. as the fem. alongside ἄναξ. The reason why δεσπότης is not used in Homer is probably because it creates difficulties in verse. Cf. Stegmann v. Pritzw., 102, n. 308.

[2] *Ibid.*, 83.

[3] Cf. A. Walde and J. Pokorny, *Vergleichendes Wörtb. d. indogerm. Sprache* (1927), I, 787 [A. Debrunner].

[4] Stegmann v. Pritzw., 84, with examples from Tyrtäus.

[5] Pindar in Pyth., 4, 11 calls the barbarian Medea δέσποινα Κόλχων. Cf. also Stegmann v. Pritzw., 85, 149.

[6] Cf. with many other passages Philo Vit. Mos., I, 201: καὶ τὰ τούτου (of the cosmos) μέρη πρὸς ἅπασαν χρείαν ὧν ἂν θέλῃ (sc. God) ὡς δεσπότῃ δοῦλα ὑπηρετήσοντα.

monarch (Isocr., 4, 121, cf. 5, 154; 6, 84). The Gk. protest against this is expressed in the fact that the word is directly linked with τύραννος in Plat. Leg., IX, 859a. The positive application begins with the fact that the King of Macedonia, when he attained to pre-eminence, expressed his absolute superiority by styling himself δεσπότης as well as ἡγεμών (cf. Demosth., 18, 235). [7] d. The word is used esp. for the gods when it is desired to emphasise their power, as in Xenoph. An., III, 2, 13 in a sentence designed to bring out to readers the extent of their freedom in relation to man: οὐδένα γὰρ ἄνθρωπον δεσπότην ἀλλὰ τοὺς θεοὺς προσκυνεῖτε. [8] In prayers the address δέσποτ' ἄναξ etc. is very common, the δέσποτ' serving to emphasise the confession of dependence already present in ἄναξ. If the gods are δεσπότης (as Osiris in Preisigke Sammelbuch, 5103 [3rd cent. B.C.]), the goddesses are δεσπότις (as Isis in P. Oxy., XI, 1380, 231: σὺ καὶ πάντων δεσπότις ἰσαεί) or δέσποινα. [9] e. δεσπότης is naturally used for the Roman emperor (P. Oxy., IX, 1204, 15 [the time of Diocletian]: ... τῶν δεσποτῶν ἡμῶν τῶν Σεβαστῶν καὶ τῶν Καισάρων). [10] This results both from the sense c. and esp. from d. f. Finally, δεσπότης is an astrological term, more common in the expanded form → οἰκοδεσπότης, to denote the planets, inasmuch as these make their influence felt at certain times on the οἶκος which each of them has in a picture of the zodiac (Vett. Val., I, 1, p. 5, 16 etc.).

In all the passages adduced the term expresses a social position or rank of the one thereby described. Yet it is not a delineation of status, as one might at first suppose. All the uses of the word agree in this, and it is for this reason that the Jews found it especially adapted to be linked with the name of God. Philo and Josephus can follow the general Gk. usage without any difficulty, whether they apply it in the civil and judicial sphere [11] or use it to describe the position and power of God. [12, 13] Joseph. is indeed a particularly good witness to the strict meaning of the word when he tells us in Bell., 7, 418 f. that the Jewish rebels would rather face tortures and burning to death than acknowledge (ὁμολογεῖν) and describe (ἐξονομάζειν) the Roman emperor as δεσπότης, i.e., recognise that his power validly binds and claims them too.

The character of the term as an appellative made possible its adoption in the Gk. Bible. Here it serves especially to emphasise the power of God. In the main, however, it is strongly subsidiary to → κύριος. It appears some 56 times, but only 22 times as a subject or in subordinate extension of the subject. No less than 25 times it is an address to God, partly as the simple δέσποτα (in Jos. 5:14 for אֲדֹנָי), [14] partly as δέσποτα κύριε (in Gn. 15:2, 8 for אֲדֹנָי יְהֹוָה) and Jer. 1:6; 4:10; 14:13 (A) for אֲדֹנָי יְהֹוִה, and in many cases in such a way that the κύριε is not

---

[7] Cf. Stegmann v. Pritzw., 150.

[8] Cf. further Eur. Hipp., 88; Plat. Euthyd., 302d; but also Philo Rer. Div. Her., 22 ff.; Jos. Ant., 11, 64.

[9] On this pt., cf. the passages adduced by Kern in Pauly-W., V (1905), 252 ff.

[10] For further material from the pap., cf. Preisigke Wört., I, 329.

[11] Jos. Ant., 3, 314; cf. also Schl. Mt., 343.

[12] → n. 6 and the examples from Philo and Joseph. in Schl., Theol. d. Judt., 25 f.; Wie sprach Josephus von Gott? (1910), 9.

[13] In Joseph. δέσποτα is the most common form of address in prayer (Schl., Theol. d. Judt., 25); for Philo, cf. Baudissin, II, 157 ff.

[14] In Jos. 5:14 we have only an indirect invocation. The δέσποτα (for אֲדֹנִי not אֲדֹנָי) refers to the ἀρχιστρατηγὸς δυνάμεως κυρίου, who encounters Joshua as the messenger of God, and thus corresponds to the style of addressing exalted personages in the East (→ 46). Materially, however, this passage belongs to the context under discussion (→ n. 23); cf. Baudissin, I, 500 f.

defined by the subject, as in Jon. 4:3; Da. 9:15. In the majority of other passages δεσπότης is simply used for God with a clear emphasis on His omnipotence : ὁ πάντων δεσπότης, Wis. 6:7; 8:3 (cf. also 3 Macc. 2:2). This helps us to understand the relation between δεσπότης and → κύριος in the usage of the Gk. Bible. If κύριος is here a name for God, God is κύριος because He is τῶν πάντων δεσπότης. The classical proof of this statement is to be found in Job 5:8 : κύριον δὲ τῶν πάντων δεσπότην ἐπικαλέσομαι, a saying which is followed in v. 9 ff. by reference to the power of God and to the fact that it is unlimited (15 : δυνάστης; 17: παντοκράτωρ). [15]

With the use of the word to denote the omnipotence of God, its use in the human sphere fades into the background. Yet the latter also occurs, thus confirming the formal character of the term as displayed also in the non-biblical usage. The instances of δεσπότης in the Book of Judith constitute a special group. Here the term is applied only to Holofernes except in 9:12, where God is addressed : δέσποτα τῶν οὐρανῶν καὶ τῆς γῆς. In 5:20; 11:10 Holofernes is even addressed δέσποτα κύριε — an expression which elsewhere in the LXX is reserved for God alone (cf. also 5:24; 7:9, 11). Sometimes we find the antithesis δεσπότης/δοῦλος (Wis. 18:11) or δεσπότης/οἰκέτης (Prv. 17:2; 22:7; Παροιμ 24:33; cf. Prv. 6:7), which is familiar in non-biblical Gk. (→ 44) and hardly needs further explanation.

In sum, we find all the various senses in the LXX except a. and f. There is a variant of c. in the fact that the ἀρχιστρατηγός rather than the king is called δεσπότης in Jdt. 5:24 (cf. with some reservations Jos. 5:14, → n. 14). A non-biblical instance of this usage may be found in P. Giess., 17, 3 (2nd cent. A.D.), where a στρατηγός Apollonius is called δέσποτα. The word is also found in the sense of "commander" in 4 Macc. 6:31; 18:2, where it is used of the εὐσεβὴς λογισμός in relation to the πάθη; but this belongs fundamentally to category c.

2. The Reason for the Paucity of δεσπότης in the LXX.

Attention should be paid to the way in which δεσπότης is used in the LXX and its distribution among the various books. They are interconnected. The distribution is particularly striking. In the Torah it is found only in Gn. 15:2, 8 in the formula δέσποτα κύριε. In the history books we find it only in Jos. 5:14, though many occasions arose on which it might have been used. In Is. we find it in 1:24; 3:1; 10:33, always in the formula ὁ δεσπότης κύριος σαβαώθ or κύριος ὁ δεσπότης σαβαώθ (1:24), which is a rendering of הָאָדוֹן יְהוָה צְבָאוֹת. [16] Jeremiah uses it in 1:6; 4:10; 14:13 and 15:11 in address to God ; in the first two cases it occurs in the formula δέσποτα κύριε in translation of אֲדֹנָי יְהוִה. On the other hand, it is found 6 times in Wis., 5 in 2 Macc., 4 in 3 Macc., 4 in Sir. etc. This distribution justifies the conclusion that the term is not really at home in the biblical world and only comes to be more closely linked with it as the years pass. Perhaps its introduction was largely out of the formal concern to distinguish in translation the two terms יְהוָה and אֲדֹנָי. [17] At any rate, it is only in other translations of the canonical books that δεσπότης is more often used for אָדוֹן and אֲדֹנָי, as also occasionally for יְהוָה. [18] This is the more striking when we realise that in the

---

[15] Further Jewish material may be found in Baudissin, II.

[16] This formula is elsewhere found only in Is. 10:16; 19:4. Since no regard is paid to הָאָדוֹן in the translation, it should perhaps be excised from the Mas. Cf. BHK² ad loc. and Baudissin, I, 500; II, 243.

[17] Cf. Baudissin, I, 493.

[18] Cf. ᾽Α : ψ 11:4; 61:12; Σ : ψ 29:8; 34:22, 23; 38:7; 43:23; 54:9; 67:20; 88:49; 109:1 [G. Bertram].

Psalter מָשַׁל is rendered δεσπόζειν in ψ 21:28; 58:13; 65:7; 88:9; 102:19, and מֶמְשָׁלָה is translated δεσποτία in ψ 102:22 and 144:13, in passages where there is most emphatic reference to the omnipotence of God.

The main reason for this paucity of the word can be found only in its abstract character. It did not have this at first, but acquired it in the course of its history. With the disappearance of the original sociological significance, it was progressively reduced to the sense of an absolute right of disposal over persons or things. The full extent of the abstraction emerges when the word is not more closely defined, and especially in the common Gk. usage in connexion with divine names.

On biblical soil, however, the biblical concept of God prevents a similar linking of δεσπότης with God. In distinction from Gk. Hellenistic religion, Judaism has a view of God which is explicitly and exclusively determined by history. God is here the Creator. As such, He is the Lord of all things, yet in such a way that those who believe in Him do not merely hear or read about this but have personal experience of it. Hence, when the authority and omnipotence of God are attested in the OT, there is testimony to His historical acts as known to the people and to righteous individuals. [19] In the OT, therefore, God's omnipotence is a very concrete reality and has nothing whatever to do with abstractions or mere conceptions. For this reason, no specific word is required to express the omnipotence of God; it is implied in His very name. Hence it is understandable that, e.g., אֲדֹנָי יִלְעַג־לָמוֹ in Ps. 2:4 should be rendered καὶ ὁ κύριος ἐκμυκτηριεῖ αὐτούς in the LXX, i.e., that God's name κύριος should be used for אֲדֹנָי. In these circumstances, there is little role for δεσπότης in the transposition of the OT into Gk. Its relative paucity may thus be explained in terms of the biblical view of God.

This also helps us to understand the three distinctive characteristics of δεσπότης when used of God in the LXX. The first is that it is made concrete to some extent by additions like τῶν πάντων (Wis. 6:7; 8:3; cf. Job 5:8), τῶν πατέρων (1 Esr. 4:60), πάσης κτίσεως (3 Macc. 2:2), τῶν οὐρανῶν καὶ τῆς γῆς (Jdt. 9:12), in which the omnipotence of God is presented as knowable and known in creation and history. [20] The second is that the term is much more common in the later books of the OT, [21] and especially that the intrusion of Hellenism [22] accounts for its use here in the absolute, [23] even if only in the form of the common address to the deity in prayer. The third is that in Gn. 15:2, 8 Abraham is appealing to the omnipotence of God in a unique way which is not repeated, so that the word readily suggested itself to the translator. [24] The remaining passages resist any attempt at systematic integration beyond the general con-

---

[19] Cf. already Gn. 15:1 ff., also Nu. 14:11; Ps. 78; 105; 106, but also Ps. 104 and Job 38 ff. The same is basically true of later Judaism and of the attestation of God's omnipotence by the NT (cf. Ac. 7:2 ff. etc., but also 1 C. 15:35 ff.).

[20] Cf. also Joseph. Ant., 1, 272; 4, 40, 46; Schlatter, *Wie sprach Josephus von Gott?* (1910), 9.

[21] Esp. in those originally written in Gk.; cf. Baudissin, II, 160 ff., though his interests are more linguistic than theological.

[22] Σιρ. 31:29; 2 Macc. 5:17, 20; 6:14; 9:13; 3 Macc. 5:12.

[23] Jos. 5:14 (→ n. 14); Da. 9:8 ff. may be cited as examples of the Hellenistic and Oriental manner of approaching the deity as slaves. In distinction from Hellenism, however, the emphasis here lies on the omnipotence of God rather than the impotence of man. If this is so, in both instances we have an attempt to subordinate the Gk. formula to the biblical view of God.

[24] The same concern underlies ψ 11:4 ʼΑ, where the LXX has κύριος, and ψ 109:1 Σ, where the LXX again has κύριος.

clusion that they reveal Hellenistic or Oriental and Hellenistic influence. This is undoubtedly true in large measure of Josephus.

B. δεσπότης in the NT.

1. Secular Usage. In the NT δεσπότης occurs 10 times. We first note the sense of "lord" or "owner" in contrast to slaves (= b.), of which there are 4 instances. In 1 Tm. 6:1 f. there is an admonition to Christian slaves to please God in their conduct towards their masters whether the latter are Christians or not (cf. also Tt. 2:9 and 1 Pt. 2:18). In 2 Tm. 2:21 the word is used either for "master of the house" (= a.) or "owner" in a figure in which true Christians are compared with a σκεῦος εἰς τιμήν, ἡγιασμένον, εὔχρηστον τῷ δεσπότῃ, εἰς πᾶν ἔργον ἀγαθὸν ἡτοιμασμένον.

In 1 Tm. 6:1 f.; Tt. 2:9 we have the antithesis δοῦλοι and δεσπόται; in 1 Pt. 2:18 οἰκέται and δεσπόται. There is here a difference between the Past. and Col. 3:22 and Eph. 6:5, where the antithesis is δοῦλοι/κύριοι. οἰκέται is found with δεσπόται in Jos. Bell., 3, 373 [25] as well as the LXX Jos. 5:14; Prv. 17:2; 22:7; Παροιμ 24:33. These linguistic features are not without a bearing on the interrelations of the different texts, and should certainly be noted.

2. God as δεσπότης. In Lk. 2:29 Simeon, when he prays to God in the temple, addresses Him as δέσποτα (cf. d.). In Ac. 4:24 the group which welcomes back Peter and John after their release uses the same address in its thanksgiving and intercession. We have here the same custom as that attested in Joseph. (→ n. 13).

For this reason, we need not seek an esoteric meaning in the address of Simeon, as though "it lay with God alone to summon him out of this life" (cf. Sir. 23:1: δέσποτα τῆς ζωῆς μου). [26] Neither linguistically nor materially is this possible, the more so as such a formula in the mouth of a Jew is designed to acknowledge God as God and to glorify Him rather than to express a feeling of dependence.

The deduction of δέσποτα from the Palestinian invocation of God as רִבּוֹנִי, whose similarity to δέσποτα is widely illustrated, [27] is contradicted by the fact that δέσποτα is attested much earlier than the Semitic term as a Jewish form of address to God. The Semitic word is not found even in the later portions of the Heb. Bible. It thus seems likely that רִבּוֹנִי is a secondary construction, forming a parallel to δέσποτα, but not a model for it, in the Semitic use of the Jews. [28] God is also intended in the address in Rev. 6:10: ὁ δεσπότης ὁ ἅγιος καὶ ἀληθινός. [29]

3. Jesus as δεσπότης. A completely new feature is the description of Jesus as δεσπότης in Jd. 4: τὴν τοῦ θεοῦ ἡμῶν χάριτα μετατιθέντας εἰς ἀσέλγειαν καὶ τὸν μόνον δεσπότην καὶ κύριον ἡμῶν Ἰησοῦν Χριστὸν ἀρνούμενοι and 2 Pt. 2:1: ψευδοδιδάσκαλοι, οἵτινες παρεισάξουσιν αἱρέσεις ἀπωλείας καὶ τὸν ἀγοράζοντα αὐτοὺς δεσπότην ἀρνούμενοι. In both passages, which are undoubtedly interrelated, the expression is used against errorists. These are distinguished in 2 Pt. 2:1 by their rejection of the δεσπότης, Jesus. In Jd. 4 it is just possible that we have a twofold formula, the monotheistic confession of one δεσπότης and then that of Jesus, [30] who is here rejected. Yet if we interpret Jd. 4

---

[25] Wnd. Pt., ad loc.
[26] Zn. Ag., ad loc.
[27] Cf. the passages in Dalman WJ, I, 147.
[28] This is the view of Schl. Lk., 194, though רִבּוֹנִי is not adduced under the Semitic parallels, ibid., 198.
[29] Cf. Loh. Apk., ad loc. for this expression.
[30] Cf. Kn. Jd., ad loc.

in the light of 2 Pt. 2:1, we cannot accept this view and must see a single construction. We are again surprised by the proximity of ἀγοράζειν and δεσπότης; from Pauline usage we should have expected κύριος. Yet the description of Jesus as δεσπότης is supported by the use of δεσπόσυναι for later members of His family in Eus. Hist. Eccl., I, 7, 14. Perhaps δεσπότης is here used rather than κύριος to suggest the function of Jesus as the One who commands and exercises influence and power. To Him there corresponds an ἀγοράσας which emphasises His right to His own in virtue of His saving act (2 Pt. 2:1; → ἀγοράζω, I, 124). This would fit the context. The errorists' conduct is → ἀσέλγεια, and one of the charges against them is that they do not acknowledge Jesus in practice as the One whose will they must take as their guide. If this is so, we have here a linguistic and material parallel to Jos. Bell., 7, 418 f. (→ 45), although in negative form.

This explanation is more likely than that which assumes from the common usage that δεσπότης sets Jesus alongside God as the Almighty. If this were true, it would imply a strong intrusion of abstract Hellenistic thought into Christology. [31] Tempting though this suggestion may be, we should reject it in view of the context, and also on the basis of the interpretation of Jd. 4 by 2 Pt. 2:1.

† οἰκοδεσπότης, † οἰκοδεσποτέω.

These are not class. words (Phryn. Ecl., 348). Acc. to Poll. Onom., XIV, 4, 21, οἰκοδεσπότης is first found in Alexis (4th cent. B.C.). Both terms are common in astrology in the sense already given → 45 (Plut. De Placitis Philosophorum, V, 18 [II, 908b]; they are common in Vett. Val, cf. Index [Kroll], s.v.), yet are not wholly appropriated by this sphere, but also occur infrequently for the relations of everyday life. [1] The prefix οἰκο-, which is basically present already in the δεσ- (→ 44), shows how far the term has departed from its original sense, the construction of a new word having become necessary. Neither word occurs in the LXX or Josephus. [2]

In the NT οἰκοδεσπότης occurs 12 times, esp. in Mt. (10:25; 13:27, 52; 20:1, 11; 21:33; 24:43 and par.; Lk. 13:25; 14:21; Mk. 14:14 and par.). It denotes the "master of the house" who has control over the οἶκος in the widest sense. In the parables in Mt., which illustrate God's action by that of an οἰκοδεσπότης, there is often the emphatic addition ἄνθρωπος (13:27; 20:1, 11; 21:33; cf. Lk. 14:21). The term has a Semitic parallel, if not a model, in the common בַּעַל הַבַּיִת, [3] which like the NT οἰκοδεσπότης denotes the owner of the house in the most comprehensive sense. In the light of בַּעַל הַבַּיִת, the pleonastic οἰκοδεσπότης τῆς οἰκίας of Lk. 22:11 can hardly be regarded as Semitic. [4]

οἰκοδεσποτέω is found only in 1 Tm. 5:14 : "to rule the house and family." It is one of the terms characteristic of the emphasis on family virtues [5] in the Past.

Rengstorf

---

[31] Found in the post-apost. fathers, e.g., 1 Cl., 33, 1 etc.

οἰκοδεσπότης κτλ. Pr.-Bauer, 882; Schl. Mt., 343.

[1] E.g., Ditt. Syll.³, II, 888, 57 f. (238 A.D.); cf. also οἰκοδέσποινα in Plut. Praec. Conjug., 18 (II, 140c) etc.

[2] Pr.-Bauer, s.v. οἰκοδεσπότης, quotes a passage from Jos. Ap., 2, 128, but this is corrupt (cf. Schl. Mt., 343).

[3] Cf. the small selection of examples in Str.-B., I, 667 f.; Schl. Mt., 343.

[4] Cf. Ditt. Syll.³, III, 985, 53 : φύλαξ καὶ οἰκοδέσποινα τοῦδε τοῦ οἴκου.

[5] Cf. Dib. Past., ad loc. and his excursus on 1 Tm. 2:2.

δέχομαι, δοχή, ἀποδέχομαι, ἀποδοχή,
ἐκ-, ἀπεκ-, εἰσ-, προσδέχομαι, δεκτός,
ἀπό-, εὐπρόσδεκτος

δέχομαι.

The distinction from the common → λαμβάνειν is defined as follows: λαβεῖν μὲν γάρ ἐστι τὸ κείμενόν τι ἀνελέσθαι· δέξασθαι δὲ τὸ διδόμενον ἐκ χειρός, Ps.-Ammon. Adfin. Vocab. Diff., *s.v.* λαβεῖν. The verb thus expresses the "reaction to action on the other side." [1] This special nuance is expressed in the following passage: (Oedipus) πόθεν λαβών; οἰκεῖον ἢ ἐξ ἄλλου τινός; (Servant) ἐμὸν μὲν οὐκ ἔγωγ', ἐδεξάμην δέ του, Soph. Oed. Tyr., 1162 f. Nevertheless, the meanings easily merge into one another: οὐκ ἐδέξαντο οὐδ' ἔλαβον ταῦτα οἱ τῶν Θηβαίων πρέσβεις, Demosth., 19, 139.

A. δέχομαι outside the NT.

a. δέχομαι has the sense of to "receive" or "to accept." The objects received may naturally differ, e.g., gifts (Hom. Il., 23, 647; Soph. El., 443; Gn. 33:10), letters (Jos. Ant., 15, 173 etc.; Ac. 22:5), payments (P. Oxy., 96, 5; 138, 26; 140, 18 etc. — it is, in fact, a tech. term in this sphere [2]), goods (Ditt. Syll.³, 289, 11 f.; Job 2:10). It can even be used of the body receiving the soul (Aristot. An., 3, p. 407b, 21).

It can also be used for the "receiving of prophecy as in the flight of birds": φὰς δέκεσθαι τὸ χρησθέν, Hdt., I, 63; ... τὸν οἰωνὸν ..., Hdt., IX, 91. In religious terminology it is used of the "reception of a sacrifice by the deity": ἀλλ' ὅ γε δέκτο μὲν ἱρά, Hom. Il., 2, 420; σὺ δὲ φρένας ἀμφιγεγηθὼς δέξαι' ἱερὰ καλὰ περικτιόνων ἀνθρώπων, Hom. Hymn. Ap., 274; δέγμενος ἱερὰ καλὰ παρὰ θνητῶν ἀνθρώπων, Hom. Hymn. Cer., 29; spiritualised: δέξαι λογικὰς θυσίας ἁγνάς, Corp. Herm., I, 31. It is used in magical incantations: δέξαι μου τὰ φθέγματα (magical formulae), Preis. Zaub., IV, 1181. The word can take on the subsidiary sense of "to suffer": πᾶν δ ἐὰν ἐπαχθῇ σοι, δέξαι, Sir. 2:4; cf. Hom. Il., 18, 115: κῆρα δ' ἐγὼ τότε δέξομαι, ὁππότε κεν δὴ Ζεὺς ἐθέλῃ τελέσαι.

In the prophetic literature of the OT it is linked with παιδεία (Mas. מוּסָר קְּלַ). The prophet Zephaniah demands of his people that they should accept the divine dealings in punishment and instruction (3:7), and he laments like Jeremiah: οὐκ ἐδέξατο παιδίαν, 3:2; cf. Jer. 2:30; 5:3; 7:28; 17:23, also Σ Jer. 42:13; so also ἐπιδέχεσθαι παιδείαν in Sir. 51:26, where the LXX introduces the formula of itself. HT reads: ומשבם אשה תאשמו, "and may your soul bear its burden (namely, of wisdom)." [3] In Prv. 16:17 the LXX diverges from the Mas.: ὁ δεχόμενος παιδείαν ἐν ἀγαθοῖς

δ έ χ ο μ α ι κτλ. In this series of art. we are indebted to G. Bertram for sections on 50 f., 52, 57, 57-8 and 58-9, also for n. 3-8, 10 and 11 on δέχομαι and n. 2 on προσδέχομαι.

δ έ χ ο μ α ι. [1] Cf. λαμβάνειν *est simpliciter accipere,* δέχεσθαι *autem rogatum aliquid sponte et libenter oblatum accipere, vel cum quadam benevolentiae et alacritatis significatione, vel alterius adiuvandi et sublevandi causa, aliquid accipere* (F. W. Sturz, *Lexicon Xenophonteum,* I [1801], 653, *s.v.* δέχομαι).

[2] Cf. F. Preisigke, *Girowesen im griech. Ägypten* (1910), 241, 251.

[3] R. Smend, *Die Weisheit des Jesus Sirach hebr. u. deutsch* (1906).

ἔσται.[4] In all these passages, as we see esp. from Sir., δέχομαι and its composites have the sense of "accepting a burden." This may consist in the divine dealings in the sorrows and emergencies of life, or the demands of wisdom, i.e., the acceptance of the Word of God. In Jer. 9:20 it is plain that δεξάσθω τὰ ὦτα ὑμῶν λόγους στόματος αὐτοῦ signifies the unavoidable acceptance of a revelation of threat. With this we may compare the necessary acceptance of the revelation of God's wrath, as in Hos. 4:11: καὶ οἶνον καὶ μέθυσμα ἐδέξατο καρδία λαοῦ μου, which the LXX independently of the Mas. formulates in the picture of the cup of wrath. This image is also used in Jer. 32:14, this time in a lit. rendering of the Mas.: לָקַחַת־הַכּוֹס (25:28). Again, in 'Ιωβ 4:12 the reference is to acceptance of the secret and shattering revelation of God. In the light of this, even the acceptance of the words and commands of God as we have it in the Wisdom literature (→ 52) needs to be conceived at a deeper level. Thus in Dt. 33:3 the difficult Mas. is translated in the LXX: ἐδέξατο ἀπὸ τῶν λόγων αὐτοῦ νόμον, signifying the acceptance of a burden, the more so as there stands behind δέχεσθαι a נשׂא. Cf. also Sir. 6:32 f. Perhaps 'Ιωβ 32:11 in Θ is to be taken in the same way.[5] The more common terms ὑπομένειν and ἐκδέχεσθαι[6] denote not merely temporal waiting but patient acceptance or suffering.[7] The same thought is linked with the undertaking of a vow. Hence we can understand why Σ renders the Mas. עָלַי ("upon me") of ψ 55:12 by ἀναδέχομαι.

In the special sense of "to bear away," "to remove," or "to forgive sin," δέχεσθαι is often used for נשׂא. Thus in Gn. 50:17, the brothers' request to Joseph: δέξαι τὴν ἀδικίαν.[8] In this sense ἀναδέξασθαι is also used for נשׂא in an Alius of the Hexapla at Lv. 10:17. Conversely, the Gk. ἐκδέχεσθαι as well as the Heb. נשׂא can mean "to be laden with sin." We see this in an unfamiliar transl. of Lv. 24:15; cf. the acceptance of the revelation of wrath (→ supra). In Is. 40:2 the punishment of sins is expressed by δέχεσθαι (for לקח): ἐδέξατο ... διπλᾶ τὰ ἁμαρτήματα αὐτῆς.

b. δέχομαι "to receive." In this sense it is used for the hospitality which was everywhere honoured and regarded as sacred in the ancient world. τίς δὲ ξένους

---

[4] In Sir. 18:14 ἐκδέχεσθαι is used in the same sense. HT is lacking. In Sir. 35(32):14 HT is very uncertain. ὁ φοβούμενος κύριον ἐκδέξεται παιδίαν corresponds either to דורש אל יקח מוסר or דורש חפץ־אל יקח לקח. In Prv. 19:20 Σ has ἐπιδέξεται παιδείαν for Mas. קבל מוסר.

[5] Acc. to the Mas. Elihu waited (יחל) modestly until the end of the speeches of Job and the three friends. In B the LXX substitutes a demand for attention. A is closer to the Mas. ἤκουσα τοὺς λόγους ὑμῶν; Σ: ὑπέμεινα; Θ: ἐξεδεξάμην τοὺς λόγους ὑμῶν.

[6] Cf. ψ 24:3, Σ: ἀπο- (προσ-)δέχομενοι, LXX: ὑπομένοντες, 'Α, Ε': the same or προσδοκοῦντες, Mas. קוה. Is. 8:17: 'Α: προσδέχομαι, LXX: μενῶ, Θ: ὑπομενῶ, Σ: προσδοκήσω, Mas. חכה; Hab. 2:3: 'Α: προσδέχου, LXX: ὑπόμεινον, Mas. חכה. The meaning in these passages is that of patient and believing expectation.

[7] The compos. ἐπιδέχεσθαι and ἀναδέχεσθαι can denote the bearing of suffering. Thus in 2 Macc. 6:19: τὸν μετ' εὐκλείας θάνατον μᾶλλον ἢ τὸν μετὰ μίσους βίον ἀναδεξάμενος; 7:29: ἐπίδεξαι τὸν θάνατον. Cf. also the painful severity of the ἐπεδέξατο πείσειν τὸν υἱόν; 1 Macc. 1:63: ἐπεδέξαντο ἀποθανεῖν, ἵνα μὴ μιανθῶσιν. In the Gk. transl. there is, of course, an intentional terminological distinction between the receiving of good and of evil at 'Ιωβ 2:10, where the Mas. has קבל pi for both, but the LXX differentiates: εἰ τὰ ἀγαθὰ ἐδεξάμεθα ἐκ χειρὸς κυρίου, τὰ κακὰ οὐχ ὑποίσομεν.

[8] προσδέχεσθαι is used in this way in the request of Moses and Aaron to Pharaoh. Ἐξ. 10:17: προσδέξασθε οὖν μου τὴν ἁμαρτίαν. Cf. also the δεκτόν at Gn. 4:7 in Σ for the difficult שְׂאֵת ('Α: ἀρέσεις). Whether שְׂאֵת is used here in the sense of removing sin or removing the countenance, i.e., gracious acceptance, must always remain doubtful. In favour of the second view, we may point both to the context and also to the fact that προσδέχεσθαι (Gn. 32:20) and ἀναδέχεσθαι ('ΑΣΘ 'Ιωβ 42:8) are both linked with πρόσωπον for the Heb. נשׂא פנים.

ἀφθονώτερον δέχεται, Xenoph. Oec., 5, 8; cf. Hom. Od., 19, 316. It is particularly common in this sense in the NT, partly because Jesus and Paul were compelled to rely a good deal on hospitality by their mode of life, cf. Lk. 9:53; Jn. 4:45; Gl. 4:14; 2 C. 7:15. The high estimation of hospitality in the NT derives in large measure from a similar high estimation in Judaism, which coined the sentence : "Hospitality is greater than the greeting of the Shekinah," bShab., 127a. [9] Beyond the special sense of hospitality, δέχομαι denotes the friendly reception which might be accorded a man more generally, e.g., Ῥώμη μετὰ πολλῆς αὐτὸν (sc. Vespasian) ἐδέξατο προθυμίας, Jos. Bell., 7, 63. [10]

c. δέχομαι "to receive, hear or understand the words of someone." We thus have the common expression λόγον δέχεσθαι, e.g., Eur. Med., 924; Polyb., I, 43, 4; Jos. Ant., 18, 101; Prv. 4:10; Jer. 9:20. Thus Jesus says to the people : εἰ θέλετε δέξασθαι, αὐτός ἐστιν Ἠλίας ὁ μέλλων ἔρχεσθαι (Mt. 11:14). In the OT this sense is particularly common in the Wisdom liter. with regard to the words and commands of God, or to wisdom itself. In all such cases it is used for לקח, e.g., σοφὸς καρδίᾳ δέξεται ἐντολάς, Prv. 10:8 f. etc. In Dt. 30:1 and Is. 57:1 the reference is to pious insight into the ways of God with His people and with righteous individuals, esp. in suffering and death. In Dt. 30:1 we have δέξῃ εἰς τὴν καρδίαν σου for וַהֲשֵׁבֹתָ אֶל־לְבָבֶךָ. In Is. 57:1 the Mas. runs : הַצַּדִּיק אָבָד וְאֵין אִישׁ שָׂם עַל־לֵב וְאַנְשֵׁי חֶסֶד נֶאֱסָפִים בְּאֵין מֵבִין, and the LXX translates : ἴδετε, ὡς ὁ δίκαιος ἀπώλετο, καὶ οὐδεὶς ἐκδέχεται τῇ καρδίᾳ, καὶ ἄνδρες δίκαιοι αἴρονται, καὶ οὐδεὶς κατανοεῖ. Since κατανοεῖ and ἐκδέχεται τῇ καρδίᾳ are interchanged in א, the latter might stand for בִּין hiph., as בִּין is in fact translated καταδέχεσθαι in Dt. 32:29. That we do not have here a purely intellectual notion is shown by the use of καταδεχόμενος τῇ καρδίᾳ for נְדִיב לֵב in Ex. 35:5. There is also a volitional element, even though δέχεσθαι and compos. might have the theoretical meanings of "to learn," "to perceive," "to realise" : 3 Macc. 3:22 ἐκδέχεσθαι; 5:27: ἀποδέχεσθαι; Job 40:19 δέχεσθαι; Prv. 9:9 δέχεσθαι (the LXX here confuses לקח "to take" with לֶקַח "insight"). For the assumptions are again ethical and religious rather than intellectual. These assumptions are expressed by δέχεσθαι and compos. even where they are not plainly stated in the Mas.

δέχεσθαι is used for the acceptance of a wish in Jos. Vit., 193; 2 C. 8:17.

d. In the LXX there is also a special cultic use of δέχομαι in translation of רָצָה, "to find pleasure," "to receive favourably." רצה and רָצוֹן, and the hapax legomenon רָצָא in Ez. 43:27, are commonly rendered in the LXX by δέχεσθαι (6 times), δεκτός (25 times ; → 58), παραδέχεσθαι (once in Prv. 3:12, quoted in Hb. 12:6), → προσδέχεσθαι (14 times → 57), → προσδεκτός (twice, Prv. 11:20; 16:15). Only → εὐδοκεῖν (22 times, of which 11 are in the Psalter) and → εὐδοκία (8 times, 7 in the Psalter, though also 4 in Sir.) are nearly as common and tend to crowd out δέχεσθαι, esp. in

---

[9] Cf. also the saying of R. Jochanan, who reckoned hospitality among the things of which man enjoys the fruits in this life, whereas the main reward is reserved for the life to come (bShab., 127a). Cf. Str.-B., I, 588 ff.; IV, 565 ff.

[10] The concept of hospitality, and of the more general friendly reception of strangers, victors and emissaries, is expressed in the Gk. Bible not merely by the simple form but also by most of the compos., which have more or less the same sense in the Gk. rendering of the Bible even though they may diverge widely with the development of the term in classical and Hell. Gk. "To receive" in this sense may be expressed by δέχεσθαι itself, but also by ἀναδέχεσθαι (Ac. 28:7); ἀποδέχεσθαι (examples s.v.); εἰσδέχεσθαι (Wis. 19:16; cf. δέχεσθαι, 19:14); ἐκδέχεσθαι, 3 Macc. 5:26; ἐπιδέχεσθαι, 1 Macc. 12:43; 3 Jn. 9, 10; παραδέχεσθαι, 2 Macc. 4:22 vl.; cf. Ac. 15:4; προσδέχεσθαι (e.g., 1 Ch. 12:18); ὑποδέχεσθαι (4 times in the LXX and 4 in the NT, always in this sense). Often different MSS may use different compos. at the same text, e.g., ψ 118:122 : LXX ἐκδέχεσθαι or ἐνδέχεσθαι; Σ ἀναδέχεσθαι; Ac. 15:4 : ἀποδέχεσθαι and παραδέχεσθαι; and esp. Jdt. 13:13 : ἀπο-, εἰσ-, ἐπι-, and ὑποδέχομαι.

the Psalter, as a rendering of רצה. In cultic contexts the word is often used with ref. to sacrifice or prayer which God graciously accepts (Dt. 33:11 and Lv. 7:8 [18]; 19:7 etc.) or rejects ('Ιωβ 8:20, where the LXX independently chooses this formulation). [11]

προσδέχεσθαι is also found at Σ ψ 50:19, where the LXX has εὐδοκεῖν (Mas. חפץ). The Heb. רצה and the Gk. are in no sense complete equivalents. The Heb. denotes "to find favour," the Gk. "to accept." The logical subject in the former is man, in the latter God. The theocentric character of the OT tradition thus finds clear expression only in the Gk. That God "receives man" is the thought which is formulated by the LXX with some degree of independence of the Heb. רצה (cf. also → εἰσδέχομαι, 57).

B. δέχομαι in the NT.

In the NT the word is twice used in special connexions.

1. When Jesus sends out His disciples, acc. to Mt. His address to them concludes with the words: ὁ δεχόμενος ὑμᾶς ἐμὲ δέχεται, καὶ ὁ ἐμὲ δεχόμενος δέχεται τὸν ἀποστείλαντά με. ὁ δεχόμενος προφήτην εἰς ὄνομα προφήτου μισθὸν προφήτου λήμψεται, καὶ ὁ δεχόμενος δίκαιον εἰς ὄνομα δικαίου μισθὸν δικαίου λήμψεται. καὶ ὃς ἐὰν ποτίσῃ ἕνα τῶν μικρῶν τούτων ποτήριον ψυχροῦ μόνον εἰς ὄνομα μαθητοῦ, ἀμὴν λέγω ὑμῖν, οὐ μὴ ἀπολέσῃ τὸν μισθὸν αὐτοῦ (Mt. 10:40 ff.). Behind the two sayings there stands a statement which derives from the שליח institution of later Judaism and which has its basis in the Semitic law of the messenger (→ ἀπόστολος, I, 414): "The emissary of a man is as the man himself." This shows us how the passage is to be taken. Those who are sent out are the emissaries or apostles of Jesus (→ I, 426). Their reception, and the hospitality accorded them, imply reception of Jesus [12] and therefore of God. "The disciple is made aware what a great thing he brings to those who receive him. For he mediates to them attachment to Jesus, and this is attachment to God." [13] In the form of the apostles Jesus knocks at the doors of men's hearts. [14] Hence great significance is attached to the sending of the disciples and apostles. For the disciples and apostles are the bearers of Christ. [15] They stand alongside the prophets and righteous men whose reception, because they were such, conferred participation in the reward reserved for them. By associating the disciples and apostles with prophets and righteous men, and by inferring that their reception is the reception of Christ, Jesus indicates the significance of their mission, namely, that Christ is present in them, and of their apostolate, namely, that they should continue the mission of Jesus. The stress is not in the first instance on the hospitality so highly estimated by the Jews (→ 51 f.). Hence we cannot interpret the sayings in terms of humanistic ethics. The emphasis is on the apostolate in virtue of which they bring attachment to Jesus and therefore to God. This helps us to understand the third saying. All the benevolence and love and fellowship expended on them, however insignificant or small it may seem to be, will carry a sure reward

---

[11] Mas. has the verb חזק hiph. "to hold fast": "God does not hold misdoers fast by the hand."

[12] Cf. v. 14: καὶ ὃς ἂν μὴ δέχηται ὑμᾶς μηδὲ ἀκούσῃ τοὺς λόγους ὑμῶν.

[13] Schl. Mt., 351.

[14] Receiving Christ is also equated with believing in Him in Jn. The terms used are → λαμβάνειν, παραλαμβάνειν.

[15] Cf. Corp. Herm., IV, 4: Of those who have come to proclaim the νοῦς, and who are baptised by it, it is said: οὗτοι μετέσχον τῆς γνώσεως, καὶ τέλειοι ἐγένοντο ἄνθρωποι, τὸν νοῦν δεξάμενοι.

in virtue of their apostolate, namely, the βασιλεία τῶν οὐρανῶν. And Christ tells His own that in receiving a child in His name they receive Him : καὶ ὃς ἐὰν δέξηται ἓν παιδίον τοιοῦτο ἐπὶ τῷ ὀνόματί μου, ἐμὲ δέχεται, Mt. 18:5 and par. In the man who suffers distress and needs assistance Christ comes to His own, and what they do for such a man in His name they do for Him. The significance of the illustration of the child derives from the setting of the pericope. "The disciple demonstrates his renunciation of power and greatness when he does not value only the work which enjoys great success. Even the reception of a single child establishes fellowship between Christ and the disciples." [16]

2. With this particular statement should be linked the more general NT references to the reception of the Gospel. δέχεσθαι τὸν λόγον τοῦ θεοῦ is a recurrent phrase in Ac. (8:14; 11:1; 17:11; cf. Jm. 1:21; 1 Th. 1:6; 2:13). Instead of the Gospel as the message, the content of the message may also be mentioned, namely, the βασιλεία τοῦ θεοῦ, which men are to receive with the confiding and simple attitude of the child (Mk. 10:15; Lk. 18:7) because it is only in such an attitude that the offence of Christ is overcome in faith ; or the χάρις τοῦ θεοῦ, which is not received in vain (2 C. 6:1); or the ἀγάπη τῆς ἀληθείας, which is expressed in the Gospel (2 Th. 2:10). The use of δέχομαι in this connexion — it is an equivalent of faith — shows us that in the total NT view man's existence over against God is limited to the reception of His gift. It has no immanent possibilities. In hearing the message, however, man is liberated for decision in relation to it. Thus we read in 1 C. 2:14: ψυχικὸς ἄνθρωπος οὐ δέχεται τὰ τοῦ πνεύματος τοῦ θεοῦ. Only when God speaks His Word and opens the understanding through the Spirit can man also decide. The divine claim of the Gospel sets man in the freedom of decision. This is the theological significance of the term δέχομαι.

† δοχή.

Subst. of δέχομαι as used in the sense of "receiving as a guest" (→ 51 f.), and therefore having the sense of "meal" or "feast," i.e., the meal linked with hospitality. Cf. Plut. Suav. Viv. Epic., 21 (II, 1102b). It is found in the pap. [1] and the LXX, [2] but not in Joseph.

In the NT it occurs only in Lk., and first at 5:29 : καὶ ἐποίησεν δοχὴν μεγάλην Λευὶς αὐτῷ ἐν τῇ οἰκίᾳ αὐτοῦ. [3] Granting hospitality in his house, the new disciple Levi holds a feast which is expressly called "great." It is also found on the lips of Jesus in 14:13, when the poor and maimed and halt and blind are to be invited to a feast : καὶ μακάριος ἔσῃ, ὅτι οὐκ ἔχουσιν ἀνταποδοῦναί σοί· ἀνταποδοθήσεται γάρ σοι ἐν τῇ ἀναστάσει τῶν δικαίων. Jesus Himself does not hesitate to visit the publican in order to bring salvation, and He demands that the will of God should be fulfilled by extending table fellowship to the outcast and needy.

---

[16] Schl. Mt., 546.

δοχή. [1] V. Preisigke Wört., s.v.
[2] Gn. 21:8; 26:30; 1 Esr. 3:1; Est. 1:3; Θ Da. 5:1.
[3] Mt. has : καὶ ἐγένετο αὐτοῦ ἀνακειμένου ἐν τῇ οἰκίᾳ ... (9:10); Mk.: καὶ γίνεται κατακεῖσθαι αὐτὸν ἐν τῇ οἰκίᾳ αὐτοῦ (2:15). δοχή is thus Lucan. The other passage is peculiar to Lk. On 5:29, cf. Schl. Lk., 61.

† **ἀποδέχομαι.**

This comp. of δέχομαι means much the same as the simple form.[1] In classical Gk. it is greatly used for the "reception of spiritual magnitudes," and thus comes to have the nuance of "to approve," "to accede to." It is used in this more precise sense in Joseph., e.g., ὁ θεὸς καὶ τὴν μετάνοιαν ὡς ἀρετὴν ἀποδεχόμενος (Ant., 9, 176); τὴν ἐκείνου παρρησίαν ὅμως ἀπεδέχοντο (Ant., 16, 378). The thing approved may also be in the gen. (after the model of the verbs "to grasp" or "to demand"): ἐλεήσας ὁ θεὸς καὶ τῆς αἰτήσεως ἀποδεξάμενος (Ant., 10, 27). When used of men in Joseph. it means "to have a high regard for": παρ' ἡμῖν οὐκ ἐκείνους ἀποδέχονται τοὺς πολλῶν ἐθνῶν διάλεκτον ἐκμαθόντας (Ant., 20, 264). In the LXX it is found only in the apocr. literature. It denotes either the acceptance and approval of things (1 Macc. 9:71; 4 Macc. 3:20 — though also simple acceptance in 3 Macc. 5:27), or the reception of persons with joy, honour and jubilation (1 Macc. 12:8; 2 Macc. 3:9; 4:22; 13:24 v.l.).

In the NT it occurs only in the Lucan writings and in the general sense of "friendly reception." Thus it is said of Jesus : ... ἀποδεξάμενος αὐτοὺς (sc. the masses which thronged Him) ἐλάλει αὐτοῖς περὶ τῆς βασιλείας τοῦ θεοῦ, καὶ τοὺς χρείαν ἔχοντας θεραπείας ἰᾶτο (Lk. 9:11). Those who seek Him are received by Him with joy, as shown by His declaring to them the message of salvation and His giving them a share in the powers of salvation. But Jesus, too, is awaited and joyfully received by the crowds (Lk. 8:40). The same word is used in relation to the reception of Paul in the churches (Ac. 18:27; 21:17) and his own attitude towards those who come to him (28:30).

The word is used like δέχομαι under B, 2. (→ 54) in Ac. 2:41: οἱ ... ἀποδεξάμενοι τὸν λόγον,[2] though Cod. D has πιστεύσαντες.

† **ἀποδοχή.**

Subst. of ἀποδέχομαι, and thus meaning "acceptance." Apart from a single refer. in Thuc., it is only Hellenistic, and therefore comparatively late. Cf. Joseph. Ant., 18, 274, where Petronius is summoned to convey to the emperor τὸ ἀνήκεστον αὐτῶν πρὸς τὴν ἀποδοχὴν τοῦ ἀνδριάντος ... Like the verb, however, it usually denotes friendly reception and therefore approval or appreciation. There are many instances of this : δίκαιοί εἰσιν κἀκεῖνοι τυγχάνειν ἀποδοχῆς (Jos. Ant., 6, 347); οἵτινες μεγάλης ἀποδοχῆς ... ἔτυχον (Ep. Ar., 308); ἀνὴρ ... πολλῆς τῆς ἀποδοχῆς ἄξιος (Diog. L., V, 64); τοσοῦτον δ' ἀποδοχῆς ἠξιοῦτο (ibid., 37). It is common in the historian Polybius, cf. esp. διὰ τὴν παρ' ἐκείνοις ἀποδοχὴν αὐτοῦ καὶ πίστιν (I, 43, 4); τότ' ἤδη καὶ πᾶς ὁ συνεχὴς λόγος ἀποδοχῆς τυγχάνει παρὰ τοῖς ἀκούουσιν (I, 5, 5); and also X, 19, 7; XXXII, 10, 11. Thus it is no less common in Jewish than Greek Hellenism in this sense, and the way is thereby opened for understanding its use in the NT.

In the NT it occurs twice in 1 Tm. : πιστὸς ὁ λόγος καὶ πάσης ἀποδοχῆς ἄξιος (1:15; 4:9).[1] Probably we have here a kerygmatic expression which is strongly influenced and characterised by Hellenism. The word (sc. of proclamation) is sure and is therefore worthy of approval and high estimation. A brief and clear account is given of the word : Christ has come into the world to save sinners

---

ἀ π ο δ έ χ ο μ α ι. [1] For examples, v. Pass., s.v.

[2] On Ac. 24:3 : πάντῃ τε καὶ πανταχοῦ ἀποδεχόμεθα, in the speech of Tertullus, cf. S. Lösch, "Die Dankesrede des Tertullus" in Theol. Quart., 112 (1931), 315 ff.

ἀ π ο δ ο χ ή. [1] Cf. Dib. Past. on 1 Tm. 1:15.

(1:15), and faith in it is εὐσέβεια ... ἐπαγγελίαν ἔχουσα ζωῆς τῆς νῦν καὶ τῆς μελλούσης (4:8). In this man has a share in the work of Christ. The certainty and worthiness of this word on which man may build his existence without doubt, consists in the fact that θεὸς ζῶν ... σωτὴρ πάντων ἀνθρώπων (4:10) is the One who speaks it.

ἐκ-, † ἀπεκδέχομαι.

ἐκδέχομαι has the two meanings a. "to accept," "to receive" (as δέχομαι) and b. "to await." It is found in the latter sense in Ac. 17:16 : ἐκδεχομένου αὐτοὺς τοῦ Παύλου; cf. Soph. Phil., 123; Polyb., III, 45, 6; also Jos. Ant., 11, 328 : ... τὴν τοῦ βασιλέως παρουσίαν ἐξεδέχετο, and Ant., 6, 49; cf. also 1 C. 11:33; 16:11.

ἀπεκδέχομαι is rare in secular Gk. Hipparch uses it in the sense of "to draw a conclusion," and indeed in the derogatory sense of "to draw an erroneous conclusion" : ὁ δὲ ἀπεκδέχεται ἅπαν ψεῦδος, Arat. Phaen., I, 7, 7 (cf. 6, 11; 7, 18). In Sext. Emp. and the Roman writer Heliodorus it is found in the sense of "to await": ... ἕτερόν τι ἀπεκδεχόμενοι τέλος, Sext. Emp. Math., II, 73; ὅμως ἐσιώπων, τὸ μέλλον ἀπεκδεχόμενος, Heliodor. Aeth., II, 35 (cf. VII, 23). It is not found in the LXX or Josephus.

In the NT ἀπεκδέχομαι, as distinct from ἐκδέχομαι "to wait for someone," is used by Paul to express "expectation of the end." This is a distinctive Pauline usage. Christians stand in this attitude of expectation : καὶ αὐτοὶ τὴν ἀπαρχὴν τοῦ πνεύματος ἔχοντες [ἡμεῖς] καὶ αὐτοὶ ἐν ἑαυτοῖς στενάζομεν, υἱοθεσίαν ἀπεκδεχόμενοι, τὴν ἀπολύτρωσιν τοῦ σώματος ἡμῶν, R. 8:23. In virtue of the reception of the Spirit the Christian attitude is one of burning expectation in conformity with the divine plans, δι' ὑπομονῆς ἀπεκδεχόμεθα (R. 8:25). This expectation is focused on the transformation of the world in which they will receive the public sonship which in faith they already enjoy as adoption (8:14) and which will be visibly fulfilled in the resurrection of the body. This attitude is linked with the whole creation whose form is one of expectation. The expectation of creation has the same goal as that of Christians : ἡ ... ἀποκαραδοκία τῆς κτίσεως τὴν ἀποκάλυψιν τῶν υἱῶν τοῦ θεοῦ ἀπεκδέχεται (R. 8:19). Christ is thus the Consummator. The consummation has already begun secretly in the adoption of Christians in faith. It will reach its climax with the public manifestation of the sonship of Christians when the creation, too, will move from the corruptible form of expectation to the incorruptible form of consummation. This will take place at the return of Jesus Christ, so that the content of expectation may be stated as follows : σωτῆρα ἀπεκδεχόμεθα κύριον Ἰησοῦν (Phil. 3:20; cf. 1 C. 1:7). As the justified, Christians have as the content of expectation the hope of righteousness : ἡμεῖς γὰρ πνεύματι ἐκ πίστεως ἐλπίδα δικαιοσύνης ἀπεκδεχόμεθα (Gl. 5:5). The word ἀπεκδέχεσθαι thus describes the existence of Christians as one which on the basis of reception (→ δέχομαι) awaits the consummation, the cosmos being included in this attitude. The theme of this expectation, i.e., the transformation of the world, gives meaning both to Christian existence and to the being of the cosmos.

To express eschatological expectation in Hb., we find both ἐκδέχεσθαι (Hb. 10:13; also Jm. 5:7) and ἀπεκδέχεσθαι : ἐκ δευτέρου χωρὶς ἁμαρτίας ὀφθήσεται τοῖς αὐτὸν ἀπεκδεχομένοις εἰς σωτηρίαν (Hb. 9:28). This formulation stands plainly under Pauline influence. A similar Pauline influence is not found in 1 Pt. 3:20 : ὅτε ἀπεξεδέχετο ἡ τοῦ θεοῦ μακροθυμία ἐν ἡμέραις Νῶε ..., where there is reference to the divine patience.

† εἰσδέχομαι.

εἰσδέχομαι usually means "to receive someone to a place or into a circle or fellow-ship." [1] In the LXX it has religious overtones in the prophets as a translation of קבץ, signifying the reception of the rejected people into gracious fellowship with God. It thus has a place in the prophetic proclamation of salvation (Hos. 8:10; Mi. 4:6; Zeph. 3:19, 20, which is quoted in 2 C. 6:17, the only use of εἰσδέχομαι in the NT → infra; Zech. 10:8, 10 [ἐξ ᾿Ασσυρίων]; Jer. 23:3 [τοὺς καταλοίπους τοῦ λαοῦ μου ἐπὶ πάσης τῆς γῆς]; Ez. 11:17; [20:34]; 20:41: προσδέξομαι ὑμᾶς ἐν τῷ ἐξαγαγεῖν με ὑμᾶς ἐκ τῶν λαῶν καὶ εἰσδέχεσθαι ὑμᾶς ἐκ τῶν χωρῶν). [2] In accordance with the basic Heb. meaning of "to gather," this reception is also an assembling. The basic Heb. can be related to the divine wrath (Zeph. 3:8; Hab. 2:5; Ez. 22:19, 20 for קבץ qal and the subst. קְבֻצָה). But Ez. 20:34 shows that this revelation of wrath stands in necessary connexion with the revelation of salvation and therefore denotes a reception by God. This re-ception implies not merely the gathering of the people out of the nations but also their purification and judgment.

In the NT the word is found only in the quotation in 2 C. 6:17, which is taken partly from Is. 52:11 and partly from Zeph. 3:20. Its meaning is as follows. In the new covenant the people of God throughout the world are taken up into fellowship with God. The promise of the prophets is thus fulfilled, not with national restriction to Israel, but in the sense of the divine work of salvation towards the cosmos. The people of Israel in the NT is the new humanity in Christ.

† προσδέχομαι.

προσδέχομαι has two main meanings. a. It can be used like the simple form to denote "receiving someone" (e.g., ... τοὺς ἀπὸ Πελοποννήσου προσδέξασθαι συνοίκους, Plat. Leg., IV, 708a; of Jesus in the NT: ἁμαρτωλοὺς προσδέχεται; Lk. 15:2; cf. Phil. 2:29) or "accepting something" in the sense either of active agreement (e.g., Xenoph. Hist. Graec., VII, 4, 2: προσεδέχοντο τὴν τῶν ᾿Αρκάδων συμμαχίαν, Jos. Bell., 2, 412: ἀεὶ προσδεχομένους τὰς ἀπὸ τῶν ἔξωθεν ἐθνῶν δωρεάς; Hb. 11:35: οὐ προσδεξάμενοι τὴν ἀπολύτρωσιν) or of patient endurance (e.g., φθορὰν οὐ προσ-δεχόμενον, Plat. Tim., 52a; τὴν ἁρπαγὴν τῶν ὑπαρχόντων ὑμῶν μετὰ χαρᾶς προσεδέξασθε, Hb. 10:34). προσδέχομαι in the sense of accepting something is used of the gods in connexion with prayer and sacrifice (e.g., πρόσδεξαί μου τὴν λιτανείαν, Preis. Zaub., III, 582; πρόσδεξαί μου τοὺς λόγους ὡς βέλη πυρός, ibid., IV, 1176 f.; εὐμενῶς ... προσδέχεσθαι τὴν θυσίαν παρεκάλει, Jos. Ant., 1, 98; God οὐ προσδέ-ξεται τὰς δεήσεις, ibid., 6, 42; κύριος τὴν προσευχήν μου προσεδέξατο, ψ 6:9; πρόσδεξαι τὴν θυσίαν, 2 Macc. 1:26). In the LXX, προσδέχομαι (like δέχομαι) is used for רצה in cultic connexions, cf. Lv. 22:23. Cf. the rejection of sacrifice in the prophetic literature (Hos. 8:13; Mi. 6:7; Am. 5:22). Cf. also προσεδέξατο αὐτὸν ἡ ψυχή μου in Is. 42:1 (v. Ez. 20:40 f.): God's good-pleasure in man.

προσδέχομαι, however, is also used in the sense of "to await" (e.g., Eur. Alc., 130: νῦν δὲ βίου τίν᾿ ἔτ᾿ ἐλπίδα προσδέχωμαι; ἐδήλωσαν αὐτῷ τὴν κατὰ τὸν ἀδελφὸν τύχην, προσδεχομένῳ μέντοι καὶ αὐτῷ, Jos. Ant., 14, 451; προσδεχόμενος τὴν

εἰσδέχομαι. [1] For examples, v. Pass., s.v. εἰσδέχομαι. Joseph. also uses the term in this way in Ant., 9, 150; 13, 241; Bell., 5, 301.

[2] The simple δέχεσθαι is used in the same sense in the image of the eagle and its young in Dt. 32:11. προσδέχεσθαι is found in this sense in Zeph. 3:10 as well as Ez. 20:41 (cf. Lk. 15:2). ἐνδέχεσθαι or ἐκδέχεσθαι (= ערב, "to stand security") is used in the same way in ψ 118:122. In Mi. 2:12 and Nah. 3:18 ἐκδέχεσθαι is used for קבץ; as elsewhere εἰσδέχεσθαι. Mi. 2:12 should be compared with Jer. 23:3 (→ supra). προσδέχομαι occurs in this sense in Is. 45:4 and 55:12, though with no basis in the Mas.

ἐλπίδα τῆς σωτηρίας μου, Job 2:9a; προσδεχόμενοι τὴν ἀπὸ σοῦ ἐπαγγελίαν, Ac. 23:21). In the LXX it is often used in this sense for יחל: 'Ιωβ 29:23; Σ 'Ιωβ 30:26; for קוה: Σ ψ 24:3; for חכה: Is. 8:17 (Cod. 264); 'A Hab. 2:3; for חמה hitp.: Θ 2 K. 15:28. With no basis in the Mas. it is also found in 'Ιωβ 2:9a : τὴν ἐλπίδα τῆς σωτηρίας μου; 'Ιωβ 2:9d : τὸν ἥλιον; ψ 54:8 : προσδεχόμην τὸν σώζοντά με (Mas. אָחִישָׁה מִפְלָט לִי, "I would hasten away to a place of refuge").[1] ψ 103:11: προσδέξονται ὄναγροι εἰς δίψαν αὐτῶν; Wis. 18:7: προσεδέχθη ... σωτηρία μὲν δικαίων, ἐχθρῶν δὲ ἀπωλία. In Is. 28:10 there is a threat of eschatological tribulation, and Ez. 32:10 is to be understood in the same way. Yet only a few of the passages contain the declaration of eschatological salvation or judgment. It is only in the NT that the word takes on this more precise sense.

In the NT προσδέχομαι is used predominantly in the sense of "to await."[2]

1. It is used of those who wait for the kingdom of God. Thus it is said of Joseph of Arimathea in Mk. 15:43 : καὶ αὐτὸς ἦν προσδεχόμενος τὴν βασιλείαν τοῦ θεοῦ, of Simeon in Lk. 2:25 : προσδεχόμενος παράκλησιν τοῦ 'Ισραήλ, of Anna in Lk. 2:38 : ἐλάλει περὶ αὐτοῦ πᾶσιν τοῖς προσδεχομένοις λύτρωσιν 'Ιερουσαλήμ. The expectation of these people is concentrated on the coming of the Messiah.[3] Their mood is expressed in the words of R. Jonathan (c. 220 A.D.): "May the bones rot of those calculators of the end who say : He has caused the end to arrive without himself coming, therefore he will not come. Be patient, as it is said : 'If he tarry, be patient' " (bSanh., 97b). The kerygma of the Synoptic Gospels is that the expected Messiah has come and the tarrying of Israel is over.

2. προσδέχομαι is also used of the subject of Christian expectation. This is the resurrection of the dead (which Christians look for with the Pharisees, Ac. 24:15), eternal glory at the return of Christ (Tt. 2:13), the mercy of Christ in the judgment (Jd. 21). Jesus tells His disciples that they should be ὅμοιοι ἀνθρώποις προσδεχομένοις τὸν κύριον ἑαυτῶν (Lk. 12:36). In genuinely Pauline contexts we usually have → ἀπεκδέχομαι rather than προσδέχομαι.

† δεκτός, † ἀπό-, † εὐπρόσδεκτος.

The verbal adj. δεκτός, from → δέχομαι, has the basic meaning "what one can accept."[1] In the LXX it is linked with → δέχομαι in transl. of רָצָה "to find pleasure," and means "acceptable" or "pleasing" on the basis of a divine act of will.

ἀπόδεκτος, from → ἀποδέχομαι, has the same meaning, in this case already present in the verb. It is known in Hellenism (cf. Plut. Comm. Not., 6, 2 [II, 1061a]: ποῦ γὰρ αἱρετὸν ἢ πῶς ἀπόδεκτόν, μήτε θαυμάζειν ἄξιόν ἐστιν ..., Aesch. Sept. c. Theb. Schol., 910 : ἐπίχαρις] ἀπόδεκτος τοῖς ἐχθροῖς, Schol., 1007: ... τὸ ταφῆναι αὐτὸν ἀγαπητὸν καὶ ἀπόδεκτον ὑπάρχοντα τῇ γῇ ..., Schol., 1008 : φίλαις κατα- σκαφαῖς Γ ἐντίμοις καὶ πρεπούσαις καὶ ἀποδέκτοις ἐκείνῳ. Cf. Jos. Ant., 18, 274; Stob. Ecl., II, 97, 17 ff.).

εὐπρόσδεκτος corresponds to δεκτός. Like ἀποδεκτός it is known in Hellenism (cf. Plut. Praec. Ger. Reip., 4, 16 [II, 810c]: ὅπως εὐπρόσδεκτος γένηται τοῖς πολ- λοῖς (sc. ὁ λόγος, Aristoph. Pax Schol., 1054: ... εἰ εὐπρόσδεκτος ἡ θυσία).

In the LXX this word group is mostly used for רָצָה. Prv. 10:24 is an exception. Here the LXX formulates an independent thought : ἐπιθυμία δὲ δικαίου δεκτός, Mas. :

π ρ ο σ δ έ χ ο μ α ι. [1] Transl. of H. Gunkel in Die Psalmen (1926) ad loc. The text should not be amended to follow the LXX, as suggested by Buhl in BHK.

[2] Its occurrences in other senses have been already noted.

[3] Cf. Str.-B., II, 124 ff., 141.

δ ε κ τ ό ς. [1] On the form δεκτέος in class. and Hell. Gk., v. the dictionaries.

וְתְ אֶנֵת צַדִּיקִים יֶחֱ. δεκτός is no longer used in the sense of a definite cultic view but expresses an ideal of piety: God stands in covenant with the righteous; His good-pleasure is the only valid norm. δεκτός thus takes on a general and absolute significance and can later be used in ethical connexions apart from the concept of God. The LXX also goes its own way in Sir. 3:17: ἐν πραΰτητι τὰ ἔργα σου διέξαγε, καὶ ὑπὸ ἀνθρώπου δεκτοῦ ἀγαπηθήσῃ. Here ἄνθρωπος δεκτός denotes the righteous man whose judgment we should follow because it is acceptable to God. Cf. Prv. 22:11: δεκτὸν δὲ αὐτῷ πάντες ἄμωμοι; also Job 33:26; Prv. 11:20; 16:15. In Sir. 2:5: ἄνθρωποι δεκτοὶ ἐν καμίνῳ ταπεινώσεως [δοκιμάζονται], the thought of election is linked with that of trial.

1. In the LXX the terms are connected with the sacrificial cultus. It is assumed that sacrifices which are declared to be pleasing to God are infallible, cf. Lv. 1:3; 19:5 vl.; 22:19 f. But when Israel apostatises the prophet says that its sacrifices are no longer acceptable to Yahweh (Jer. 6:20). Only in the last time of conversion will they be acceptable again (Is. 56:7). The cultic idea is spiritualised in the Wisdom literature and is finally abandoned in consequence of this development. Not sacrifices, but the acts and prayers of the righteous, are desired by God and acceptable to Him: δεκταὶ παρὰ κυρίῳ ὁδοὶ ἀνθρώπων δικαίων ... ἀρχὴ ὁδοῦ ἀγαθῆς τὸ ποιεῖν τὰ δίκαια, δεκτὰ δὲ παρὰ θεῷ μᾶλλον ἢ θύειν θυσίας, Prv. 16:7 (cf. 15:8). Men who do these things are δεκτοί: δεκτοὶ δὲ αὐτῷ πάντες ἄμωμοι. Cf. Prv. 22:11; Job 33:26; Prv. 11:20; 16:15 (→ supra).

This spiritualisation of the cultus is both continued in the NT and reorientated to its central message. The ministry of the Philippian community to Paul is described by him as θυσία δεκτή, εὐάρεστος τῷ θεῷ (Phil. 4:18). The task of the community of Christ is defined in 1 Pt. 2:5 as follows: ... ἀνενέγκαι πνευματικὰς θυσίας εὐπροσδέκτους θεῷ διὰ Ἰησοῦ Χριστοῦ. Paul sometimes conceives of his own work from the standpoint of priestly ministry and can thus say of his missionary labours: ... ἵνα γένηται ἡ προσφορὰ τῶν ἐθνῶν εὐπρόσδεκτος, ἡγιασμένη ἐν πνεύματι ἁγίῳ (R. 15:16).

The cultic connexion is completely abandoned in the statement in Ac. 10:35: ὁ φοβούμενος αὐτὸν (sc. τὸν θεὸν) καὶ ἐργαζόμενος δικαιοσύνην δεκτὸς αὐτῷ ἐστιν (cf. 2 C. 8:12). This is so whether we relate the acceptability to men or to a fellowship of men (cf. Lk. 4:24; R. 15:31). The same is true in 1 Tm., where the word is used parallel to καλός in the form: τοῦτο καλὸν καὶ ἀπόδεκτον ἐνώπιον ... θεοῦ (2:3); cf. 5:4, though here most readings do not have καλόν.

2. The word has special significance in Is. 61:2, according to which the prophet has the task: καλέσαι ἐνιαυτὸν κυρίου δεκτόν. This saying is to be understood Messianically. The Messianic age is the acceptable time chosen by Yahweh. It is the time of salvation and of the divine presence (cf. 49:8 ff.; 58:6 ff.). Rabbi Jose (c. 150 A.D.) said of the ἐνιαυτὸς δεκτός: "This is the time ordained to salvation" (bSan., 102a). The NT is full of the realisation that this time has come. At His first appearance in Nazareth Jesus applies these words to Himself: ... σήμερον πεπλήρωται ἡ γραφὴ αὕτη ἐν τοῖς ὠσὶν ὑμῶν (Lk. 4:18 ff.). With Him, the Messiah, there is present the Messianic age, the time of divine election, acceptance and presence. According to the Evangelist, it is present with His coming to earth. Writing to the Corinthians, Paul interprets the event into which they are incorporated as God's hearing and helping, and therefore as the fulfilment of what the prophet promised (Is. 48:8 ff.); he can thus go further and say: ἰδοὺ νῦν καιρὸς εὐπρόσδεκτος (LXX: δεκτός), 2 C. 6:2.

Grundmann

† δέω (λύω)

1. This is common in the NT in the sense of "to bind" or "to bind together" (Mt. 13:30: δήσατε αὐτὰ [τὰ ζιζάνια] εἰς δέσμας); "to bind to" Mk. 11:2, 4, cf. Mt. 21:2; Lk. 19:30); "to wrap up" (Jn. 11:44: δεδεμένος τοὺς πόδας καὶ τὰς χεῖρας κειρίαις; 19:40: ἔδησαν αὐτὸ (τὸ σῶμα) ὀθονίοις; and most frequently "to chain" (Mk. 5:3, 4; Mt. 22:13), which can easily pass over into the sense of imprisonment [1] (Mk. 6:17; cf. Mt. 14:3; Mk. 15:1, 7, Mt. 27:2; Jn. 18:12, 24; Ac. 9:2, 14, 21; 12:6; 21:11, 13; 22:5, 29; 24:27; Col. 4:3; Rev. 19:14; 2 Tm. 2:9, where the Word of God is not bound). Figur. it can be used of the mutual commitment of partners in marriage (R. 7:2; 1 C. 7:26, 39). [2] It is used of supernatural binding in Lk. 13:16: ἣν ἔδησεν ὁ Σατανᾶς, [3] and also in Ac. 20:22: δεδεμένος ἐγὼ τῷ πνεύματι. [4] In Rev. 20:2: καὶ ἐκράτησεν τὸν δράκοντα, ὁ ὄφις ἀρχαῖος, ὅς ἐστιν Διάβολος καὶ ὁ Σατανᾶς, καὶ ἔδησεν αὐτὸν χίλια ἔτη, it is linked with the notion, found among many peoples, [5] of the antigodly monster which will be overcome and chained for a certain period.

2. Behind the δεῖν καὶ λύειν of Mt. 16:19; 18:18, there unquestionably stands the Heb. אָסַר and הִתִּיר or the Aram. אֲסַר and שְׁרָא of the Rabbis. A purely magical binding and loosing such as may be found elsewhere in Gk. and Rabbinic usage is ruled out by the context. Jesus does not give to Peter and the other disciples any power to enchant or to free by magic. [6] The customary meaning of the Rabbinic expressions is equally incontestable, namely, to declare forbidden or permitted, and thus to impose or remove an obligation, by a doctrinal decision. [7] The only question is whether this normal Rabbinic meaning applies here or not. [8] This very

δ έ ω. Pr.-Bauer, s.v.; the Comm. on Mt. 16 of Zn., Wellhausen, Kl., Str.-B., Schl.; Dalman WJ, I, 175-178.

[1] The meanings of δέω here mentioned are all common in non-biblical Gk., cf. Pape, Pass., s.v. The transition from "to chain" to "to take prisoner" or "to imprison" is found already in Plat. Leg., IX, 864e: ἐν δημοσίῳ δεσμῷ δεθείς etc.

[2] Cf. Achill. Tat., I, 11: ἄλλη δέδεμαι παρθένῳ; Iambl. Vit. Pyth., 11, 56: τὴν μὲν ἄγαμον, τὴν δὲ πρὸς ἄνδρα δεδεμένην.

[3] The terms "bind" for the power exercised over someone by a sorcerer, god or spirit, and "loose" for freeing from this power, are very common in the magic of different peoples. Examples: Diod. S., I, 27: ὅσα γὰρ ἐγὼ (Isis) δήσω οὐδεὶς δύναται λῦσαι; bShab., 81b: "Then she spoke something and bound it (the ship); and they spoke something and loosed it" (Str.-B., I, 739a). Cf. Deissmann LO, 254 ff.; M. Lidzbarski, Ephemeris f. semit. Epigr., 1 (1900), 31; R. Wünsch, CIA, Appendix (= IG, III, 2), XXX; A. Dell, ZNW, 15 (1914), 38 ff.

[4] πνεῦμα here is the Spirit of God rather than the spirit of Paul. It is an open question whether formulae from a mythical drama of redemption lie behind the poetic use of δέω in Wis. 17:17: μιᾷ γὰρ ἁλύσει σκότους πάντες ἐδέθησαν (the Egyptian darkness) and the materially related passages in ψ 67:6; 68:33; 78:11; 101:20; 106:10 and 145:7.

[5] Cf. Dib. Th. Exc. on II, 2, 10; J. Kroll, Gott und Hölle (1932).

[6] Dalman WJ, I, 175; Zn. Mt., ad loc.; Wellhausen, ad loc. Definite examples are given in Str.-B., I, 738 ff. Whether there is any definite connexion between this Rabbinic usage and that of magic (→ n. 3) it is hard to say, but the probability is that there is not.

[7] Cf. Schl. Mt., ad loc.

[8] Str.-B., I, 739 adduces b MQ, 16a and Tosafot on b Men, 34b. He also refers incorrectly to the λύειν τε καὶ δεῖν in Jos. Bell., 1, 111, which can only mean "to release and to imprison," since the passage is speaking of the royal jurisdiction which the Pharisees received under Alexandra, and not of the synagogal ban. Niese reads δεσμεῖν. Dalman WJ, I, 178 has tried to show that שְׁרָא "to loose" can mean "to pardon."

Gospel (23:8) rejects any attempt on the part of the disciples to assume the position of rabbis. They are not to use this title, and the position of teacher is reserved for Jesus alone. Indeed, there was no room for rabbis in the congregation, since a legal understanding of the will of God, and therefore casuistry, were set aside by Jesus. On the other hand, it is only rarely that אסר and התיר or שרא mean to impose or remove a ban, to expel from and receive back into the congregation. [9] Nevertheless, this meaning is attested, and must therefore be considered as the true sense of δεῖν καὶ λύειν in Mt. 16:19; 18:18. In the case of Mt. 18:18 this would give us a simple transition from v. 17, which speaks finally of expulsion from the community. It would also enable us to see a parallel in Jn. 20:23 : ἄν τινων ἀφῆτε τὰς ἁμαρτίας, ἀφέωνται αὐτοῖς· ἄν τινων κρατῆτε, κεκράτηνται. Finally, this is the way the fathers almost unanimously understood the passages from Tertullian Pud., 21 and Orig. Comm. in Mt., XII, 14. [10] The neutral ὅ and ὅσα can hardly be adduced to the contrary in the light of Jn. 6:39; 10:29; 17:2, 24. [11] Hence, even if we cannot say more, the weight of probability is definitely in favour of the interpretation : "to impose and remove the ban." [11]

Büchsel

δηλόω

δηλοῦν is common in Gk. (and the pap.) for "to make evident, plain or clear," "to show," "to declare," "to impart," "to demonstrate." In Jewish and Christian writings it is first used in the ordinary secular sense of "to indicate," "to impart," e.g., Jos. 4:7; Tob. 10:8; Joseph. Ant., 4, 105; 1 C. 1:11; Col. 1:8; Ign. Tr., 1, 1; Ign. R., 10, 2. In arguments we often find the phrase δῆλον ὅτι, 1 C. 15:27; Gl. 3:11; 1 Tm. 6:7 (ℵ text); similarly we have δῆλον ποιεῖν (Mt. 26:73), "to make evident," and δῆλον εἶναι (2 Cl., 12, 4), "to be evident." In later Gk. usage δηλοῦν is also used of the communication of cultic mysteries (Paus., IV, 33, 5; IX, 25, 6), and of divine revelation given in dreams or other ways (Diod. S., XVIII, 60, 4; Ael. Arist., 47, 51 and 55; 49, 48).

In the LXX, too, the word is used in this special way for the divine revelation (usually for forms of ידע and interchangeably with γνωρίζειν etc.). God declares His name (Ex. 6:3), His plans (Ex. 33:12), His secrets (ψ 50:6; Da. 2:28 f., 30), His demands (3 Βασ. 8:36; 2 Ch. 6:27; ψ 147:9). It is in keeping that the oracle of the Urim and Thummim is rendered δήλωσις καὶ ἀλήθεια. But δηλόω can also be used to indicate the divine act of revelation in judgment and grace (Jer. 16:21; ψ 24:14; cf. 2 Macc. 2:8 : of the δόξα of God). Philo uses the formula ὡς δηλοῖ τὸ λόγιον (Fug., 157; Migr. Abr., 85; cf. 92) to denote the revelation given in the OT.

In the NT δηλοῦν is less common than → ἀποκαλύπτειν and φανεροῦν, which are used especially for the active and above all the eschatological revelation of

---

[9] Zn. Mt. on 16:19, n. 76.

[10] "The personal passive construction" אָסוּר, מֻתָּר. Str.-B., 740 β shows that in Rabbinic usage persons as well as things can be the object of אסר and התיר (שרא).

[11] With Dalman, Str.-B., Schl. against Zahn, Wellhausen and Klostermann.

God, whether still future or fulfilled and being fulfilled in Christ and the Gospel. δηλοῦν is used for the (future) divine act of revelation only in 1 C. 3:13 : ἑκάστου τὸ ἔργον φανερὸν γενήσεται· ἡ γὰρ ἡμέρα δηλώσει, ὅτι ἐν πυρὶ ἀποκαλύπτεται (cf. the material par. in 4:5 : ὁ κύριος, ὃς ... φανερώσει τὰς βουλὰς τῶν καρδιῶν). δηλοῦν is more commonly used for the instruction given by the divine πνεῦμα (whether in the oldtime prophets, 1 Pt. 1:11 or in the Scriptures, Hb. 9:8; 12:27; cf. Philo → supra), but also by the κύριος Himself (2 Pt. 1:14). Yet it is impossible to make any clearcut distinction from ἀποκαλύπτειν, as may be seen, e.g., from Mt. 11:26 and par.; 1 C. 14:30; 1 Pt. 1:12. As in the 8th Book of Moses (Preis. Zaub., XIII, 614) we find the request to the angel : δήλου μοι πάντα, similarly, δηλοῦν is the office of the angel of revelation in Herm. m., 4, 3, 3; 4, 1; 8, 8 etc. As in the image in Da. δηλοῦν denotes God's manifestation of future events, so it is again in Herm. v., 3, 12, 3. Instruction is in view when Ign. Sm., 7, 2 says that the πάθος of the Lord is revealed (δεδήλωται) in the εὐαγγέλιον; on the other hand, the reference is to the divine act of revelation in R. 1:17: δικαιοσύνη γὰρ θεοῦ ἐν αὐτῷ ἀποκαλύπτεται, or R. 3:21: νυνὶ δὲ ... δικαιοσύνη θεοῦ πεφανέρωται. δηλοῦν can be applied to the ἐντολή in Herm. m., 6, 2, 10, and it can also be used of the instruction given to others in Herm. v., 3, 8, 10 (in this case distinguished from ἀποκαλυφθῆναι by divine revelation).

It corresponds to the essentially rational character of δηλοῦν that the word has the particular sense of "to interpret" or "to explain." As it is used of the allegorical interpretation of the Stoics (Cornut. Theol. Graec., 6, p. 6, 13 f.; 33, p. 71, 4), so in Da. 2:5 ff.; 7:16 LXX it is used of the interpretation of dreams and visions, and in Jos. Ant., 3, 187 of the explanation of the highpriestly dress. In a Stoic sense we read in 1 Cl., 24, 3 : ἡμέρα καὶ νὺξ ἀνάστασιν ἡμῖν δηλοῦσιν. In Barn., 9, 8; 17, 1 δηλοῦν is used of the allegorical interpretation of the OT. In Herm. s., 5, 4, 1 ff.; 8, 1, 4 etc. it denotes the elucidation of puzzling symbols.

Bultmann

† δημιουργός   (→ κτίζω).

Strictly the "one who pursues public affairs," then the "builder" or "artisan," often used in Gk. and in Gnosticism for the "architect" or "creator" of the world. Neither this term nor the verb δημιουργεῖν is ever used of God the Creator in the LXX, but only in the secular sense, as in 2 Macc. 4:1: τῶν κακῶν δημιουργός, and the verb in Wis. 15:13; 2 Macc. 10:2; 4 Macc. 7:8. δημιουργεῖν is never found in the NT, and δημιουργός only in Hb. 11:10 : ἐξεδέχετο γὰρ τὴν τοὺς θεμελίους ἔχουσαν πόλιν, ἧς τεχνίτης καὶ δημιουργὸς ὁ θεός. For more details concerning the relation of δημιουργός to κτίστης, and the reasons for its paucity in biblical usage, → κτίζω.

Foerster

δῆμος, ἐκδημέω, ἐνδημέω,
παρεπίδημος

† δῆμος.

δῆμος means originally a "divided portion," hence a. "district" or "community," i.e., the division of a people or territory; [1] b. "land," "territory" or "dwelling of a people"; c. "the people as inhabitants" of a land or city. In this sense it is everywhere used and attested. It can have the derogatory nuance of the mob as distinct from the aristocracy. But it can also have a proud ring, as in Athens, where it is used for the free and self-governing citizens.

Almost always in the LXX, esp. in Nu. where it is most common, δῆμος is used for מִשְׁפָּחָה and means "race" or "family" (e.g., Ju. 13:2). Only later does it take on the sense of "people," e.g., Da. 8:24; 9:16, where it is used for עַם, usually translated → λαός; cf. also 1 Macc. 8:29; 12:6 etc. This is the sense in which Joseph. uses the term (e.g., Ant., 14, 259; Vit., 309 f.). The NT follows suit; δῆμος signifies people as the population of a city in Ac. 12:22 (Jerusalem), 17:5 (Thessalonica) and 19:30, 33 (Ephesus).

† ἐκδημέω, † ἐνδημέω.

ἐκδημέω has the same meaning as the more common ἀποδημέω, and like it derives from ἔκδημος (ἀπόδημος) = ἐκ (ἀπό) τοῦ δήμου ὤν. It thus has the sense of "to be abroad," the root δῆμ- being used in sense b., though there is a hint of c., since the man who is abroad is also away from his own people. The word is found in class. Gk. (e.g., ὁ μὲν οὖν ἐκδημῶν οὕτω καὶ τοιοῦτος ὢν ἐκδημείτω, Plat. Leg., XII, 952d; οἰκείτω τὸν ἐνιαυτὸν ἐκδημῶν, Plat. Leg., IX, 864e; ἡ ... γοῦν ψυχὴ διὰ φιλοσοφίας λαβοῦσα ἡγεμόνα τὸν νοῦν, ἐπεραιώθη καὶ ἐξεδήμησεν (sc. εἰς τὸν τόπον), Ps.-Aristot. Mund., 1, p. 391a, 11 f.; αὐτῶν τούτων καὶ τῆς θεωρίης ἐκδημήσας ὁ Σόλων εἴνεκεν, Hdt., I, 30: Θεωρὸς ... ἐκδημῶν, Soph. Oed. Tyr., 114), as also in Hellenism (e.g., ἐκδημήσαντος εἰς Δάμασκον Ἐλισσαίου, Jos. Ant., 9, 88 etc.).

ἐνδημέω means "to stay at home or in one's own land," e.g., ... πυνθάνεσθαι εἰ τοὺς Πολύμνιος παῖδας ἐνδημοῦντας εὑρήσει, Plut. Gen. Socr., 6 (II, 578e); ... ξένους τοὺς ἐνδημοῦντας ... Ditt. Syll.[3], 1045, 10 f., cf. 1157, 23 and 80 f.; ... καὶ αὐτοὶ ἐνεδάμησαν ἀξίως καὶ τοῦ θεοῦ καὶ τᾶς πόλιος, 555B, 15 f. [1] The ingress. aor. means "to go home," cf. 2 C. 5:8.

These two terms, which are not found in the LXX, occur in an important context in the NT: θαρροῦντες οὖν πάντοτε καὶ εἰδότες ὅτι ἐνδημοῦντες ἐν τῷ σώματι ἐκδημοῦμεν ἀπὸ τοῦ κυρίου. διὰ πίστεως γὰρ περιπατοῦμεν, οὐ διὰ εἴδους· θαρροῦμεν δὲ καὶ εὐδοκοῦμεν μᾶλλον ἐκδημῆσαι ἐκ τοῦ σώματος καὶ ἐνδημῆσαι πρὸς τὸν κύριον· διὸ καὶ φιλοτιμούμεθα, εἴτε ἐνδημοῦντες, εἴτε ἐκδημοῦντες, εὐάρεστοι αὐτῷ εἶναι (2 C. 5:6 ff.). Two ideas are contained in this statement: 1. bodily existence is absence from the Lord; and 2. full fellowship

---

δ ῆ μ ο ς. [1] Cf. Pass., s.v. δῆμος; Ditt. Syll.[3], Index s.v. δῆμος; numerous examples from Hdt., Thuc., Demosth. etc.

ἐ κ δ η μ έ ω κτλ. Wnd., Bchm., Ltzm. K. on 2 C. 5; Sickb. K.[4], 112; Vrede Kath. Br.[4], 90; R. Kabisch, Die Eschatologie des Paulus (1893), v. Index under 2 C. 5:6 ff.; A. Bonhöffer, Epiktet und das Neue Testament (1911), 112; W. Mundle, "Das Problem des Zwischenzustandes," in Festschr. f. A. Jülicher (1927), 105 ff.; → βαρέω, I, 559 f.

[1] The terms were common in contemporary speech, cf. the examples in Preisigke Wört.

with the Lord is possible only outwith this bodily existence. Two self-contained modes of being are denoted by the words ἐκδημεῖν and ἐνδημεῖν. Paul and Christians generally are in the sphere of corporeality, of somatic being, and they are chained to this sphere. The *Kyrios* is in a being under very different categories. The two spheres of being are separated, and the separation of the spheres implies the separation of those who are in them, i.e., of the *Kyrios* and Christians. This is stated as a fact (εἰδότες, v. 6). Yet the separation is not absolute. This is declared in the statement which underlies the fact of separation : διὰ πίστεως γὰρ περιπατοῦμεν, οὐ διὰ εἴδους. To speak of faith is to mention a reality in human life which overcomes absolute separation. Faith, however, is not the final reality, since it is directed to what is as yet invisible to outward appearance (cf. R. 4:17 ff.). Paul works this out in his life as one who is always given over to death (2 C. 4:7 ff.). This faith is an operation of the Spirit and thus comes from the sphere beyond. This is the basis of θαρρεῖν within the realisation of separation. The desire of the Christian is ἐνδημεῖν πρὸς τὸν κύριον, i.e., to live in communion with Christ in the sphere in which He is. This communion is περιπατεῖν διὰ εἴδους, i.e., a face to face relationship. Hence Paul desires by ἐκδημῆσαι ἐκ τοῦ σώματος to be translated out of the sphere of this world and its corporeality into that of the *Kyrios*. [2] For the existence in this world marked by θαρρεῖν and καὶ εὐδοκεῖν μᾶλλον he gives the direction : εὐάρεστοι αὐτῷ εἶναι, v. 9. [3] Thus the being of Christians is understood as one which has its normative centre in the *Kyrios*, so that from the standpoint of this centre it is separation from the *Kyrios*, yet not an absolute separation, but one which is bridged by the spiritual gift of faith, so that there is θαρρεῖν in the separation. Hence the being of the Christian is one which contains within itself a longing, created by the separation, for translation into the sphere of the *Kyrios*, where there is full communion and perfection in εἶδος. It is a being which finally includes a determination to journey abroad, with the predicate "acceptable to the *Kyrios*."

† παρεπίδημος.

This is a rare word. [1] Polyb., XXXII, 6, 4 : πᾶσι τοῖς Ἕλλησι τοῖς παρεπιδήμοις; also P. Petr., I, 19, 22; III, 7, 15. More common are the subst. παρεπιδημία and the verb παρεπιδημέω, which are not found in the LXX or NT, but are common in the speech of the period. παρεπιδημέω means "to stay in a place as an alien" with the suggestion of transitoriness, cf. P. Oxy., 473, 2 : ἔδοξε τοῖς ἄρχουσι καὶ τῷ δήμῳ καὶ ῾Ρωμαίων καὶ ᾿Αλεξανδρέων τοῖς παρεπιδημοῦσι; cf. also P. Oxy., 1023, 4; BGU, 113, 12; 265, 19; 780, 14; Ditt. Syll.[3], 714, 30; Ep. Ar., 110. παρεπιδημία means "the (temporary) stay of a foreigner in a place" : e.g., τάν τε παρεπιδαμίαν ἐποιήσατο καλὰν καὶ εὐσχήμονα, Ditt. Syll.[3], 772, 2 f.; cf. 734, 10 etc.; Polyb., IV, 4, 2; X, 26, 5 etc. This gives us the meaning of παρεπίδημος, namely, "one who is (temporarily) resident in a place as an alien."

---

[2] Windisch, *ad loc.*, adduces Hellen. par. and concludes that Paul's thinking here is Hellenistic. This is a mistake. He overlooks the following points : 1. that the question of the mode of the ἐνδημεῖν πρὸς τὸν κύριον is not treated ; 2. that there is thus no qualification of the Pauline view elsewhere that in the next life we shall have a bodily existence under different categories from those of the present life ; and 3. that the chief concern is communion with Christ, for which there are no Hellenistic analogies. The par. adduced, therefore, have only formal significance.

[3] On the difficulty of the εἴτε ἐνδημοῦντες εἴτε ἐκδημοῦντες of v. 9, *v.* Wnd., *ad loc.*, also Mundle, 108.

π α ρ ε π ί δ η μ ο ς. [1] Though cf. Deissmann B, 146 f.

In the NT 1 Pt. 1:1: ἐκλεκτοῖς παρεπιδήμοις; 2:11: παρακαλῶ ὡς παροίκους καὶ παρεπιδήμους ἀπέχεσθαι τῶν σαρκικῶν ἐπιθυμιῶν. Christians are presented as men who have no country of their own on this earth ; they are simply temporary residents. For this reason they are not to allow themselves to be shaped by the things which largely determine life on this earth : the σαρκικαὶ ἐπιθυμίαι. Their alien status emerges clearly in the fact that they belong to the διασπορά, the Jewish concept being applied to Christians. Their life in the διασπορά brings clearly into focus their existence as παρεπίδημοι. And the fact that they are called ἐκλεκτοὶ παρεπίδημοι shows that their home is the place from which their election proceeds.

The term παρεπίδημος is found in the LXX. In Gn. 23:4, when Abraham is seeking a place of burial for Sarah, he says : πάροικος καὶ παρεπίδημός εἰμι μεθ' ὑμῶν. Here παρεπίδημος is used in the secular sense for the resident alien. In Hb. 11:13 the word is allegorised and given a religious significance. For this religious use, cf. ψ 38:12 : πάροικος ἐγώ εἰμι ἐν τῇ γῇ καὶ παρεπίδημος καθὼς πάντες οἱ πατέρες μου. [2]

The idea that the life of man is a sojourn and his true home is in heaven is found in Hellenistic philosophy. But here it is shaped by cosmological dualism according to which the soul belongs to another world and is imprisoned in the body. [3]

Grundmann

διά [1]

A. διά with Gen.

1. Spatial : "through," "through ... to," Mt. 7:13 : διὰ τῆς στενῆς πύλης; Mk. 10:25 and par.; Jn. 10:1; R. 15:28; 1 C. 3:15; 2 C. 11:33; Hb. 10:20 etc.

2. Temporal : a. of the whole duration of a period of time : "through" ; b. of part of a period of time : "during" ; c. of distance in time : "after."

---

[2] παρεπίδημος is a translation of תּוֹשָׁב, a "resident without rights of citizenship," Ges.-Buhl. The ἐν τῇ γῇ of the LXX B is added along dualistic lines. The Mas. has עִמָּךְ and AR etc. thus render παρὰ σοί. The appeal to alien status is here introduced in order to support the claim to help from the God who extends special protection to strangers. Cf. G. Rosen and G. Bertram, *Juden und Phönizier* (1929), 46 [Bertram].

[3] For examples, cf. M. Meister, *De Axiocho Dialogo* (Diss. Breslau, 1915), 86-88; cf. also n. 3, and → ξένος, where the whole idea is discussed.

δ ι ά. Bl.-Debr. § 222 f.; διὰ χειρός (χειρῶν), στόματός τινος § 140, 217, 259, 402 f. M. Johannessohn, "Der Gebrauch der Präpositionen in der Septuaginta," in *Mitteilungen des Septuaginta-Unternehmens der Ges. d. Wiss. zu Göttingen*, III, 3 (1926), 235 ff.; H. Ljungvik, *Studien zur Sprache der apokryphen Apostelgeschichten* (1926), 30; W. Kuhring, *De praepositionum Graecarum in chartis Aegyptiis quaestiones selectae* (Diss. Bonn [1906]), 39 f.; J. Käser, *Die Präpositionen bei Dionysius Hal.* (Diss. Erlangen [1915]), 49 f., 54; C. Rossberg, *De praepositionum Graecarum in chartis Aegyptiis Ptolemaeorum aetatis usu* (Diss. Jena [1909]), 37 ff.; O. Gradenwitz, "L'importanza delle preposizioni nel linguaggio giuridico demonstrata dai papiri," *Bolletino dell' Istituto di Diritto Romano*, IX (1896), 98 ff.; A. Berger, *Die Strafklauseln in den Papyrusurkunden* (1911), 60 ff.; B. Laum, *Stiftungen in der griechischen und römischen Antike*, I (1914), 128; E. Norden, *Agnostos Theos* (1913), 240 f. f.; A. Schettler, *Die paulinische Formel "durch Christus"* (1907); G. J. A. Jonker, "De paulin. formule 'door Christus,'" ThSt, 27 (1909), 173-208.

[1] Related to δίς, Lat. *dis-*; cf. also δύο and *tw-* (between) from a by-form with *du-*.

For sense a. cf. δι' ὅλης τῆς νυκτός, Xenoph. An., IV, 2, 4 ; ἱερεὺς διὰ βίου, Preisigke Sammelbuch, 1269, 8; διὰ παντὸς (τοῦ χρόνου), Hdt., IX, 13; σοῦ διὰ παντὸς μνείαν ποιούμενοι, P. Lond., I, 42, 6 (172 B.C.). In the LXX cf. διὰ παντός (for the adverbial and substant. תָּמִיד), Nu. 4:7: οἱ ἄρτοι οἱ διὰ παντός; Nu. 28 f. *passim,* Ez. 46:15 : ἡ ὁλοκαύτωσις ([τὸ] ὁλοκαύτωμα) ἡ ([τὸ]) διὰ παντός; Lv. 6:20 : θυσία διὰ παντός; cf. Ex. 30:8, where we have the double translation θυμίαμα ἐνδελεχισμοῦ διὰ παντός. For sense b., cf. διὰ (τῆς) νυκτός, Palaeph., I, p. 4, 15; IV, p. 12, 11; P. Ryl., 138, 15 (1st cent. A.D.). For sense c., cf. δι' ἐτέων εἴκοσι, Hdt., VI, 118; Ditt. Or., 56, 38 (3rd cent. B.C.); 4 Macc. 13:21. [2]

In the NT we find sense a. in the phrase : δι' ὅλης νυκτός, Lk. 5:5; Ac. 1:3; [3] Hb. 2:15; διὰ παντός, Mt. 18:10; Mk. 5:5; Hb. 9:6 etc.; sense b. in Ac. 5:19; 16:9; 17:10; 23:31; sense c. in Mk. 2:1; Ac. 24:17; Gl. 2:1. The non-classical "within" is found in Mk. 14:58 and par. = ἐν τρισὶν ἡμέραις in Mt. 27:40 and Jn. 2:19.

3. Modal, a. of manner : "through," "in," or "with" ; b. of accompanying circumstance : "with," "among," and sometimes, acc. to the context, "in spite of."

For sense a. cf. διὰ φόβου εἶναι, Thuc., VI, 59 : δι' αἵματος οὐ διὰ μέλανος; Plut. De Solone, 17 (I, 87e). Of the adverbial expressions in which it occurs in the Gk. Bible, reference may be made to διὰ κενῆς, since it is sometimes used in moral and religious connexions, e.g., in ψ 30:6; 1 Macc. 6:12; Sir. 23:11 with reference to the fault of levity or lack of conscience. For sense b. cf. διὰ φιλημάτων ἰέναι, Eur. Andr., 415.

In the NT we find sense a. in διὰ παραβολῆς, Lk. 8:4; Jn. 19:23; R. 8:25; 15:32; διὰ πίστεως/εἴδους, 2 C. 5:7; 5:10; 10:11; Hb. 13:22; 2 Jn. 12. Sense b. occurs in διὰ πολλῶν θλίψεων, Ac. 14:22; ... δακρύων, 2 C. 2:4; R. 2:27 (in spite of); 4:11; 14:20; 1 C. 16:3; 2 C. 6:7 f.; Eph. 6:18; Hb. 9:12. 1 Jn. 5:6 : δι' ὕδατος καὶ αἵματος, should also be mentioned in this connexion. The reference is neither to the baptism and death of Jesus, nor to the Christian sacraments in their interrelationship, but to Christian baptism alone, which may be described as a real sprinkling with the blood of Christ (cf. 1 Pt. 1:2; → βαπτίζω, I, 540). The personal gen. is found in 2 Tm. 2:2 : διὰ πολλῶν μαρτύρων.

4. Instrumental : a. with gen. of cause : "by means of," "with," "through" ; b. with gen. of person : "through the mediation of."

For sense a., cf. δι' ὁσίων χειρῶν θιγών, Soph. Oed. Col., 470; P. Oxy., II, 268, 7 : διὰ χειρός, "from hand to hand," "directly"; though in the LXX, under Hebraic infl., there is approximation to b. "through the mediation of." In Ex. 35:29; 37:19; Nu. 7:8; Is. 37:24; Prv. 26:6 בְּיַד is rendered διά with the gen. of the person who mediates. Cf. 2 Macc. 4:11; 7:30; 3 Macc. 7:10. διὰ χειρός is maintained as a lit. rendering, e.g., Lv. 10:11; Ez. 37:19; 38:17. In Ex. 17:1 עַל־פִּי is rendered διὰ ῥήματος (κυρίου); in Nu. 3:16, 39, 51; 4:37 etc. διὰ φωνῆς (κυρίου); and in 9:23 διὰ προστάγματος (κυρίου). The instrumental use of διά with gen. becomes a formula to describe the mediation of Scripture in 2 Macc. 2:23; 11:15; 4 Macc. 4:24; 1 Esr. 2:2 etc. Yet in the

---

[2] A. Boëthius, *Die Pythais* (1918), 64 f. refers also to Plut. Cim., 8 (I, 483e), IG, II, 2, 1366, cf. 1365, 18 ff. He has in view IG, III, 1, 74, 5 (= Ditt. Syll.[3], III, 1042, 5): διὰ ἑπτὰ ἡμερῶν, cf. *ibid.*, 73, 20 : ἑβδομαίαν. Elucidation may also be found in Corp. Herm., X, 6 : (The beauty of the good) τὴν ὅλην ψυχὴν ἀναλαμβάνει καὶ ἀνέλκει διὰ τοῦ σώματος (away from the body).

[3] Though cf. W. Michaelis, ThBl, 4 (1925), 102 f. He correctly argues with M. Albertz, ZNW, 21 (1922), 259 ff. against Meyer Ursprung, I, 40 that δι' ἡμερῶν τεσσεράκοντα does not denote an unbroken 40 day period of intercourse between the Risen Lord and the disciples, but individual appearances (ἐν πολλοῖς τεκμηρίοις) spread over 40 days.

majority of cases, as elsewhere where one might expect διά, the Hebraic ἐν is found. For sense b. cf. δι' ἑρμηνέως λέγειν, Xenoph. An., II, 3, 17. Of the legal representative on an ostracon from Thebes. [4]

In the NT sense a. is found in διά νόμου, R. 3:27; Gl. 2:19, 21; διά πίστεως, R. 3:22, 25; Gl. 2:16; διά τῆς χάριτος, Ac. 15:11; Gl. 1:15; Mk. 16:20; Jn. 17:20; διά τοῦ θανάτου τοῦ υἱοῦ (θεοῦ), R. 5:10; Col. 1:20, 22; 1 C. 4:15; Tt. 3:5; Hb. 2:10b etc. It is in this light that we can best understand 1 Tm. 2:15 : διά τῆς τεκνογονίας, i.e., by Christian preservation in the most basic vocation of woman (others see sense 3b). [5] On the borderline of b. are such phrases as διά τῶν χειρῶν αὐτοῦ in Mk. 6:2; cf. Ac. 11:30; 14:3; 15:7, 23; also διά τοῦ πνεύματος, Ac. 11:28; 1 C. 2:10; 12:8; 2 Tm. 1:14. On διά τοῦ ὀνόματος ('Ιησοῦ etc.) → ὄνομα. Sense b. occurs in a phrase like διά τοῦ προφήτου, Mt. 1:22; 2:5; Hb. 3:16 etc.; R. 1:2; Jn. 1:17; Ac. 15:12 : ὅσα ἐποίησεν ὁ θεὸς σημεῖα ... δι' αὐτῶν; Gl. 3:19 : δι' ἀγγέλων. [6] The formula "through Christ" (δι' αὐτοῦ, δι' οὖ) is also to be taken more often in the sense that Christ mediates the action of another, [7] i.e., the action of God, namely, creation (Jn. 1:3; 1 C. 8:6; Col. 1:16); the revelation of salvation and reconciliation (Jn. 1:17, par. διά Μωυσέως); 3:17; Ac. 10:36; 2 C. 5:18; Col. 1:20), miracles (Ac. 2:22); judgment (R. 2:16); the consummation of salvation (R. 5:9; 1 C. 15:57); the impartation of the Spirit (Tt. 3:6). Yet the expression can also be used occasionally, though without any causal implication (→ infra), to describe Christ as also the Mediator of man's activity towards God. Indeed, the original sense can sometimes shine through : εἰσελθεῖν, ἔρχεσθαι πρὸς τὸν πατέρα, προσέρχεσθαι τῷ θεῷ, προσαγωγὴν ἔχειν δι' αὐτοῦ (Jn. 10:9; 14:6; Hb. 7:25; R. 5:2). Yet it is never suggested that Christ is interposed as an intermediate authority between God and man which may be set in motion by human acts. The basic assumption is always that God takes the initiative through His action in Christ and thus makes all human achievement superfluous and excludes any intermediate authority. There is an approach to the causal use in the phrase πιστεύειν, πίστις, πιστὸς δι' αὐτοῦ (Jn. 1:7; Ac. 3:16; 1 Pt. 1:21).

5. Causal : a. of the cause : "in consequence of," "on the basis of," "on account of" ; b. of the author : "from," "for the sake of." This gives rise to the most urgent problem from the standpoint of biblical theology. Schettler emphasises this causal use, and explains the formula διά Χριστοῦ exclusively in terms of the pneumatic Christ, whereas Paul surely saw an inseparable unity between the pneumatic Christ and the historical. [8] Yet there are elements of truth in his presentation as compared with the traditional notion that Christ is to be regarded as the Mediator of the religious expressions of man (sense 4b).

---

[4] Deissmann LO, 98, cf. L. Wenger, Die Stellvertretung im Recht der Papyri (1906), 9 ff.

[5] Cf. B. Weiss, ad loc.

[6] If the point of v. 20 is that the Law does not come from a single person, but from many (Ltzm. Gl., ad loc, as opposed to Sieffert and Zn. Gl., ad loc), then the logic of the thought means that we must take the διά in v. 19 causally (→ 5b), as also indicated by ἐν χειρὶ μεσίτου. Yet Pl. does not elsewhere contest the divine origin of the Law (cf. R. 7:14 and also Gl. 3:21), and Jewish sources, too, speak only of a co-operation of angels in the giving of the Law (cf. Ac. 7:53). The idea of angels actually inscribing the Law is first found only in antinomian Gnosticism (Lidz. Joh., 192). Pl. thus verges on a causal understanding of διά to the degree that it fits his argument, but he does not work it out consistently. A. Schweitzer, Die Mystik des Ap. Pls. (1930), 71 ff. lays one-sided stress on the Gnostic element in Paul and yet still hesitates between the renderings "by" and "through."

[7] The view of Schettler, who contests this in favour of 5b, leads to forced exegesis.

[8] There is an excellent criticism in Jonker, op. cit.

Sense a. is rare in secular usage. Cf. τὰ διὰ τῶν χρηματισμῶν ὑπάρχοντα, on the basis of, or acc. to, the books. [9] Sense b. is used of men in 4 Macc. 1:11; 1 Esr. 6:13; of God in Plat. Symp., 186e (Aesculapius); Ael. Arist., 45, 14 (Serapis): πάντα διὰ σοῦ καὶ διὰ σὲ ἡμῖν γίγνεται. A subtle distinction between διά with the gen. and διά with the acc. is also found in Philo Cher., 125 (cf. Hb. 2:10). The gen. construction is also found in a purely causal sense in the widespread triadic formula: ἐν τὸ πᾶν καὶ δι' αὐτοῦ τὸ πᾶν καὶ εἰς αὐτὸ τὸ πᾶν. [10] It is used of the God of Israel in Ep. Ar., 313. Particularly instructive is Philo Leg. All., I, 41: τῶν γινομένων τὰ μὲν καὶ ὑπὸ θεοῦ γίνεται καὶ δι' αὐτοῦ, τὰ δὲ ὑπὸ θεοῦ μέν, οὐ δι' αὐτοῦ δέ (but through the νοῦς which rules in the human soul). A certain distinction of prepositions remains. But διά serves to denote a relatively independent causa secunda.

In the NT we find sense a. in R. 8:3: ἐν ᾧ ἠσθένει διὰ τῆς σαρκός; 2 C. 9:13: they glorify God διὰ τῆς δοκιμῆς τῆς διακονίας. In Hb. 11:4a; R. 5:18; 7:7; 10:17 and 2 Pt. 1:4a there is also a tendency for the instrumental to become causal. It is in such terms that we should understand expressions like διὰ θελήματος θεοῦ 1 C. 1:1; Eph. 1:1; Col. 1:1. Distinctive is παρακαλεῖν διὰ τῶν οἰκτιρμῶν τοῦ θεοῦ in R. 12:1; also διὰ τοῦ κυρίου ἡμῶν 'Ιησοῦ Χριστοῦ καὶ διὰ τῆς ἀγάπης τοῦ πνεύματος in R. 15:30; and διὰ τῆς πραΰτητος καὶ ἐπιεικείας τοῦ Χριστοῦ in 2 C. 10:1. This usage corresponds to that of the causal per in requests or oaths: orare, iurare, obsecrare, dicere per deos, fortunas etc. In Attic one says πρός τινος. Whether the use of διά is a Latinism or developed independently in Hellenistic Gk., is hard to say. In any case it is not instrumental but causal in terms of the religious basis. Cf., however, R. 12:3: λέγω διὰ τῆς χάριτος τῆς δοθείσης μοι, though here again we do not have a purely instrumental use. Sense b., i.e., the causal usage in relation to persons, is undoubtedly found of men (or angels) in Mk. 14:21 and par.; Ac. 12:9; 24:2; R. 5:12, 16; 1 C. 11:12; 15:21; 2 C. 1:11, 19; Hb. 13:11; 1 Pt. 2:14; and of God in R. 11:36 1 C. 1:9; Hb. 2:10. It is in the light of these that we are primarily to understand the distinctive Christian formula "through Christ" in its various nuances. Only in Hb. 2:3 does this refer to the historical Jesus: (σωτηρία) ἀρχὴν λαβοῦσα λαλεῖσθαι διὰ τοῦ κυρίου. Elsewhere it is always used of the exalted, [11] though with no separation from the historical. [12] The whole Christ is the Author of apostolic authority: R. 1:5; Gl. 1:1; 2 C. 3:4; 1 Th. 4:2; of the ethical fruits of believers: Phil. 1:11; of comfort: 2 C. 1:5; of peace with God: R. 5:1; of the triumph of believers: R. 8:37; of God's good-pleasure in them: Hb. 13:21; of the life of the resurrection: 1 C. 15:21; of final deliverance: 1 Th. 5:9. Hence constructions like εὐχαριστεῖν, χάρις θεῷ, δοξάζειν τὸν θεὸν διὰ 'Ιησοῦ Χριστοῦ (R. 1:8; 7:25; 2 C. 1:20; 1 Pt. 4:11; R. 16:27), ἀναφέρειν θυσίαν διὰ 'Ιησοῦ Χριστοῦ (Hb. 13:15; cf. 1 Pt. 2:5), etc. do not mean that Christ interposes as an intermediary between God and man, or, to put it in other words, that "Christ is set in motion by an act of man, but rather that an act of Christ underlies the existence and action of the Christian, the initiative always being with Christ." [13] It is to be noted that the formula "through Christ" is never linked with verbs of

---

[9] Kuhring, 40 f.

[10] The inscription on a magical ring in M. Berthelot, Alchimistes Grecs, I (1887), Introd., 132 f.; cf. also Texte Grec., p. 85, 13 f. (Chemes); II (1888), Texte Grec., p. 143, 21; 169, 9 f. (Zosimus). Norden, op. cit., 248 f.

[11] Rightly stressed by Schettler in opposition to the common restriction to the earthly Jesus.

[12] Jonker against Schettler.

[13] Schettler, op. cit., 61 f.

asking, as one might expect if the traditional view were correct. By contrast, it often occurs with verbs of thinking etc. God undoubtedly stands in the background as the final Author, and therefore it is hard to fix the limits between 5b. and 4b. (cf. Eph. 1:5; 2:18). Nevertheless, the formula "through Christ" gives pregnant expression to the constitutive significance of Christ for the whole of the Christian life. On παρακαλῶ διὰ τοῦ κυρίου ἡμῶν ᾽Ιησοῦ Χριστοῦ (R. 15:30) → 68.

B. διά with Acc.

1. Spatially "through ... to." In classical Gk. it is found only in poetry, but in Hellenistic in prose from the time of Dion. Hal. [14] Sib., 3, 316 : ρομφαία διελεύσεται διὰ μέσον σεῖο. In the light of this Lk. 17:11: διήρχετο διὰ μέσον [15] Σαμαρείας καὶ Γαλιλαίας, seems to be linguistically sound. It can hardly mean, however, "through Samaria and Galilee," since the goal of the journey is Jerusalem, and this would make the reverse order more likely. Perhaps the meaning is "through the border territory of Samaria and Galilee" (i.e., to Perea). If this is the true sense, the expression is rather unusual. Should one prefer another reading ?

2. Modally instead of the correct gen. ↓(→ 66). Gl. 4:13 : You know that I first preached the Gospel to you in bodily infirmity. The translation "on account of bodily infirmity" [16] is linguistically possible, but it is not the only possibility and yields no real sense. The reference is rather to the state in which the preaching took place.

All the older expositors seem to have taken Paul in this way. The Lat. have *per infirmitatem,* and the Syr. *cum essem in miseriis* (Theod. of Mopsuestia). Cf. also the Gk.: μυρίους θανάτους ὑπέμενον κηρύττων ὑμῖν (Chrys.). Comparable is the phrase : διὰ πᾶσαν ἀφορμήν, "on every occasion" (BGU, II, 632, 11). [17]

3. It is usually causal : "on account of," "for the sake of." In this sense it is very common with the acc. of cause, though the acc. of person is also used to denote the author. In conjurations it alternates with the gen. (→ 68). The latter seems to be preferred with verbs of requesting and invoking, the former when there are demands. It can sometimes be used for ἕνεκα, [18] a final element being here introduced.

Hom. Od., 8, 520 : νικῆσαι ... διὰ μεγάθυμον ᾽Αθήνην. Proclus, De Forma Epistolari, No. 12, p. 9 (ed. R. Hercher, Epistolographi Graeci [1873]): μὴ κατοκνήσῃς διὰ τὸν κύριον. Inscript. on an amulet : διαφύλαξον διὰ τὸ ὄνομα τοῦ ὑψίστου θεοῦ. [19] Gn. 12:13 : ὅπως εὖ μοι γένηται διὰ σέ, καὶ ζήσεται ἡ ψυχή μου ἕνεκέν σου. 4 Macc. 16:25 : διὰ τὸν θεὸν ἀποθανόντες. διά is often used in the LXX for עַל and esp. עַל־כֵּן, "on the basis of," διὰ τοῦτο. διὰ τί is also common in the OT for לָמָּה or מַדּוּעַ, In the NT διὰ τοῦτο is especially favoured in the four Gospels. διὰ τό with the inf. or acc. and inf. is often found in the Gk. Bible for many Hebraic expressions. In Is. 53:5 διὰ τὰς ἁμαρτίας ἡμῶν (= מִפְּשָׁעֵינוּ) is purely causal, as shown

---

[14] Käser, 54; Bl.-Debr. § 222.
[15] אBL ; A al διὰ μέσου, D μέσον without διά (Bl.-Debr. § 215, 3).
[16] Zn. Gl., *ad loc.*
[17] Deissmann LO, 150, No. 13, 11. Cf. Ltzm. Gl., *ad loc.*
[18] Johannessohn, *op. cit.,* 242.
[19] S. Eitrem and A. Fridrichsen, *Ein christliches Amulett auf Papier* (1921), 24, 6 f. (4th cent. A.D.).

by the antithesis to 4b. The teleological expansion is given only in v. 5b. In Is. 64:6 : διὰ τὰς ἁμαρτίας ὑμῶν (=בְּיַד־עֲוֹנֵינוּ) "thou gavest us up to the power of our sins," represents a change of imagery in the LXX.

When the personal acc. is used in the NT, it generally denotes "for the sake of" with a certain final element : Mk. 2:27: τὸ σάββατον διὰ τὸν ἄνθρωπον ἐγένετο; 1 C. 8:11: ὁ ἀδελφὸς δι' ὃν ὁ Χριστὸς ἀπέθανεν. Cf. further Jn. 11:42; 12:30; 1 C. 11:9. But the final significance is also found sometimes even with the acc. of thing. Thus Mt. 15:3, 6 : διὰ τὴν παράδοσιν ὑμῶν "for your tradition" (Mk. 7:9 : ἵνα τὴν παράδοσιν ὑμῶν τηρήσητε); 1 C. 9:23 : διὰ τὸ εὐαγγέλιον, ἵνα συγκοινωνὸς αὐτοῦ γένωμαι; Phil. 2:30 : διὰ τὸ ἔργον τοῦ Χριστοῦ μέχρι θανάτου ἤγγισεν.

Some passages stand in need of special elucidation. Exegesis of R. 4:25 : ὃς παρεδόθη διὰ τὰ παραπτώματα ἡμῶν καὶ ἠγέρθη διὰ τὴν → δικαίωσιν ἡμῶν, is confronted by the dilemma that notwithstanding the basic text in Is. 53:5 the parallelism demands a final sense in the first half of the verse, [20] or conversely that the causal interpretation destroys the parallelism. [21] An attractive possibility is to take both parts of the verse causally : "who was delivered because of our sins and raised again because of the justification of humanity made possible by his death." [22] This also avoids the difficulty of seeming to divide Christ's work, even if only for rhetorical purposes, into a negative and positive side. The conception of the death of Christ as the final act of the old aeon and of His resurrection as the first act of the new (cf. 1 C. 15:22) is truly Pauline. The only trouble is that the purely causal sense of διά with the acc. cannot be shown from the *koine*. Comparison should be made with 2 C. 13:10 and 1 Tm. 1:16. In the latter verse especially the διὰ τοῦτο plainly corresponds to the ensuing ἵνα. In R. 4:25 the final connexion between the resurrection of Christ and justification can be emphasised because in the preceding verse justifying faith is characterised as πίστις ἐπὶ τὸν ἐγείραντα 'Ιησοῦν. [23] Already in διὰ τὰ παραπτώματα ἡμῶν, in distinction from the underlying text, there is surely a final element in Paul : "in consequence of our sins and in order to expiate them." Elsewhere the apostle expresses the same thought in terms of → περί or the even more pregnant → ὑπέρ. [24] This gives us a possible interpretation even though there is still a slight interference with the parallelism. R. 11:28 is particularly instructive in this respect : κατὰ μὲν τὸ εὐαγγέλιον ἐχθροὶ δι' ὑμᾶς, κατὰ δὲ τὴν ἐκλογὴν ἀγαπητοὶ διὰ τοὺς πατέρας : "in regard to their attitude to the Gospel they are hated (and thus stand under the wrath of God) for your sakes, i.e., in order that salvation may come to you Gentiles, but in so far as the election is normative they are beloved because of the fathers, i.e., in consequence of their election." For here the parallelism is only rhetorical, and yet no doubts arise as in R. 4:25. The rhetorical character of the statement does not entitle us, however, to make a sharp theological distinction between forgiveness and justification, as did Osiander.

Oepke

---

[20] Philippi, B. Weiss. R., *ad loc.*
[21] Zn., Khl. R., *ad loc.*
[22] Godet, Lipsius R., *ad loc.*
[23] Cf. Khl., Ltzm. R., *ad loc.*
[24] Cf. on the one side R. 8:3 and on the other 1 C. 15:3. In Gl. 1:4 the readings vacillate between the two prepositions.

| διαβάλλω, διάβολος | → Σατανᾶς. |

† διαβάλλω.

Basically διαβάλλω and its deriv. διαβολή, διάβολος have the sense of "separating" : [1] Plat. Symp., 222cd : πάντα τούτου ἕνεκα εἰρηκώς, τοῦ ἐμὲ καὶ ᾿Αγάθωνα διαβάλλειν, οἰόμενος δεῖν ἐμὲ μὲν σοῦ ἐρᾶν καὶ μηδενὸς ἄλλου; Aristot. Pol., V, 11, p. 1313b, 16 ff., where διαβάλλειν ἀλλήλοις is par. τὸ συγκρούειν καὶ φίλους φίλοις καὶ τὸν δῆμον τοῖς γνωρίμοις. In Plutarch we find expressions like διαβάλλειν πρὸς τὴν βρῶσιν (sc. ἰχθύν), Quaest. Conv., VIII, 8, 4 (II, 730 f.) or ἡμᾶς πρὸς ἐκεῖνα τὰ πάθη διαβάλλοντες, ibid., VIII, 7, 2 (II, 727d), "to separate from." Hence the passive : "to be set in opposition to someone," "to hate or to be hated by him" : Hdt., V, 35 : Μεγαβάτῃ διαβεβλημένος; Andoc., 2, 24 : οὐδὲν οὖν ἔτι ὑπολείπεται ὅτῳ ἄν μοι δικαίως διαβεβλῆσθε. This leads quite easily to the sense of "to accuse," as in the orator Antiphon (480-410 B.C.), 2 δ 2 (Thalheim): καινότητα γὰρ δή, εἰ χρὴ καινότητα μᾶλλον ἢ κακουργότητα εἰπεῖν, διαβάλλουσί με. In the first instance, of course, διαβάλλειν does not mean judicial accusation, but the hostile will expressed in complaints and reproaches, and therefore denunciation : Philostrat. Vit. Ap., III, 38 : the demon ὑπισχνεῖτο δέ, εἰ μὴ διαβάλλοιμι αὐτὸν πρὸς ὑμᾶς, δώσειν τῷ παιδὶ πολλὰ ἐσθλά. [2] Often, however, it is hard to distinguish between διαβάλλειν and "to calumniate" : Hdt., VIII, 90 : τῶν τινες Φοινίκων, τῶν αἱ νέες διεφθάρατο, ἐλθόντες παρὰ βασιλέα διέβαλλον τοὺς ῎Ιωνας, ὡς δι᾿ ἐκείνους ἀπολοίατο αἱ νέες. This leads us to many further meanings, e.g., "to repudiate" (Zosimus : [3] ῾Ερμῆς ... διαβάλλει καὶ τὴν μαγείαν), "to misrepresent" (Demosth., 18, 225 : οὐκ ἦν ... τότε δ νυνὶ ποιεῖν, ἐκ ... ψηφισμάτων πολλῶν ἐκλέξαντα ... διαβάλλειν), "to give false information" (Thuc., III, 4, 4 : πέμπουσιν ἐς τὰς ᾿Αθήνας ... τῶν τε διαβαλλόντων ἕνα) and esp. "to deceive" : Hdt., III, 1, where the false princess says to Cambyses : ῏Ω βασιλεῦ, διαβεβλημένος ὑπὸ ᾿Αμάσιος οὐ μανθάνεις, ὅς ἐμὲ ... ἀπέπεμψε, ὡς ἑωυτοῦ θυγατέρα.

In the NT διαβάλλειν is used only in Lk. 16:1 of the unjust steward : ... οἰκονόμον, καὶ οὗτος διεβλήθη αὐτῷ ὡς διασκορπίζων τὰ ὑπάρχοντα αὐτοῦ : "he was accused unto him." There is here no necessary thought of calumniation.

δ ι α β ά λ λ ω, δ ι ά β ο λ ο ς. On A: Liddell-Scott. s.v.; M. Bréal in Revue des Études Grecques, 16 (1903), 495. On B: H. Duhm, Die bösen Geister im AT (1904), 16 ff., 58 ff.; K. Marti, "Der Ursprung des Satans," ThStKr, 65 (1892), 207 ff.; J. W. Rothstein and J. Haenel, Comm. on 1 Ch. (1927), 377 ff. On C: Weber, 218 ff., 251 ff.; Bousset-Gressm., 331 ff.; Moore I, 191, 406 f., 492 f.; Str.-B., I, 136 ff.; Jew. Enc., XI, 68 ff.; Jüd. Lex., V, 117 ff.; P. Volz, Jüdische Eschatologie (1903), 79 ff.; J. Köberle, Sünde und Gnade im rel. Leben d. Volkes Israel (1905), 469 ff., 559 ff.; O. Holtzmann, Nt.liche Zeitgeschichte² (1906), 370 ff. A. Bertholet, Bibl. Theologie d. AT, II (1911), 389 ff.; H. J. Holtzmann, Bibl. Theologie d. NT² (1911), 60 ff.; S. Mowinckel, ZNW, 32 (1933), 103. On D : EB. 4296 ff.; RE³, XIX, 564 ff.; O. Everling, Die paul. Angelologie und Dämonologie (1888); M. Dibelius, Die Geisterwelt im Glauben des Paulus (1909); G. Kurze, Der Engels- u. Teufelsglaube d. Ap. Pls. (1915), 29-71; G. Gloege, Reich Gottes u. Kirche im NT (1929), 123-129; H. D. Wendland, Die Eschatologie d. Reiches Gottes (1931), 26, 48 f.; W. Grundmann, Der Begriff d. Kraft i. d. nt.lichen Gedankenwelt (1932), 49 ff.; Schl. Gesch. d. Chr., 98, 236, 434 f.; Theol. d. Ap., 135 f., 171 ff., 278 f.; Dib. Th. on I, 2:18; Wnd. Pt. on I, 5:8; Dausch Synpt.⁴, 75; Tillm. J.⁴, 151, 184; Rohr Hb.⁴, 18; J. Grill, Untersuchungen über die Entstehung d. 4. Ev., II (1923), 44 ff. On the problem of religious history, Bousset-Gressm., 482, 513 ff.; Meyer Ursprung, II, 106 ff.; Clemen, 112 f.

[1] The concrete meanings "to carry over" etc. are not considered here.
[2] This helps us to understand the equation of ὁ διάβολος with "talebearer."
[3] M. Berthelot, Alchimistes Grecs, II (1888), Texte Grec., p. 230, 2 (in Reitzenstein Poim., 103).

διάβολος.

A. Linguistic.

1. The subst. διαβολή and διάβολος are most commonly used in the sense of complaint (Thuc., I, 131, 2 : ὁ δὲ βουλόμενος ὡς ἥκιστα ὕποπτος εἶναι καὶ πιστεύων χρήμασι διαλύσειν τὴν διαβολήν ...) and esp. calumniation : Thuc., VIII, 91, 3 : ἦν δέ τι καὶ τοιοῦτον ἀπὸ τῶν τὴν κατηγορίαν ἐχόντων, καὶ οὐ πάνυ διαβολὴ μόνον τοῦ λόγου, cf. expressions like ἐπὶ διαβολῇ εἰπεῖν in Hdt., III, 66 or διαβολὰς ἐνδέκεσθαι in Hdt., III, 80. But there are also instances of the various meanings which derive from διαβάλλειν "to separate," e.g., Plut. Cons. ad Apoll., 15 (II, 110a): ἡ πρὸς θάνατον διαβολή; "to see oneself in a mirror as one is," οὐ μικρόν ἐστιν εἰς διαβολὴν τοῦ πάθους Plut. De Cohibenda Ira, 6 (II, 456b). For διάβολος "calumniator," cf. Aristoph. Eq., 44 f.: ἐπρίατο δοῦλον, βυρσοδέψην Παφλαγόνα, πανουργότατον καὶ διαβολώτατόν τινα. In Aristot. Topica, IV, 5, p. 126a, 31 f. we have σοφιστὴν ἢ διάβολον ἢ κλέπτην, and in Plut. Quaest. Conv., VIII, 7, 2 (II, 727d), διάβολος is used as a par. of ψίθυρος. Yet διάβολος is not restricted to this sense. This is shown by its connexion with τυραννικός (Athen., 11, 118) and Athen., 11, 119 : Εὐφραῖος ... παρὰ Περδίκκᾳ ... διατρίβων ... οὐχ ἧττον αὐτοῦ ἐβασίλευε, φαῦλος ὢν καὶ διάβολος, ὃς οὕτω ψυχρῶς συνέταξε τὴν ἑταιρίαν τοῦ βασιλέως, ὥστε οὐκ ἐξῆν τοῦ συσσιτίου μετασχεῖν, εἰ μή τις ἐπίσταιτο τὸ γεωμετρεῖν ἢ τὸ φιλοσοφεῖν (almost in the sense of "unfriendly"). διάβολος means "talebearer" in Corp. Herm., XIII, 13b : (οὐχ) ὑπεμνηματισάμην, ἵνα μὴ ὦμεν διάβολοι τοῦ παντὸς εἰς τοὺς πολλούς, and cf. XIII, 22b.

2. Joseph. does not use either διάβολος or other names for Satan.[4] He uses διαβάλλειν and διαβολή in the sense of "calumniation,"[5] though also "accusation."[6]

3. The LXX used διαβολή mostly in the sense of "calumniation,"[7] though it could denote "enmity" in Sir. 28:9.[8] In Nu. 22:32 (the angel to Balaam): ἐξῆλθον εἰς διαβολήν σου, "in order to resist thee." Διαβάλλειν is once used for "to calumniate,"[9] and once for "to accuse."[10] The compos. ἐνδιαβάλλειν means "to attack."[11] In ψ 108:6 διάβολος is the "accuser" : διάβολος στήτω ἐκ δεξιῶν αὐτοῦ. In Est. 7:4; 8:1, Haman is called διάβολος in the sense of "opponent" or "enemy" (Mas. צָרַר, צֹרֵר). In 1 Macc. 1:36 the acra is called a διάβολος (par. παγίς and ἔνεδρον) in the sense of "obstacle."

The LXX also used διάβολος for שָׂטָן "devil," in the sense of "the one who separates," "the enemy," "the calumniator," "the seducer."[12] Since this is an innovation in the LXX, we can only deduce the meaning from the rendering and from the context. The latter seldom suggests "calumniator," but rather "accuser" or "adversary." This is so in 1 Ch. 21:1 and Job 1 and 2, unless we prefer "seducer." Even in Zech. 3:1 ff.,

---

[4] A. Schlatter, *Wie sprach Josephus von Gott?* (1910), 41, 1; S. Rappaport, *Agada u. Exegese bei Flavius Josephus* (1930), 55. Acc. to Schl. Lk. on 4:2 only διάβολος could lie behind the Lat. text of Ap., 2, 56 : *Apion autem omnium calumniator.*

[5] Jos. Ant., 16, 81; 19, 201; Bell., 1, 633.

[6] Ant., 10, 251; 14, 169 (Ἡρώδην ἐκάλει δικασόμενον ὑπὲρ ὧν διεβάλλετο).

[7] Prv. 6:24; Sir. 19:15; 26:5; 38:17; 51:2, 6; 2 Macc. 14:27; 3 Macc. 6:7.

[8] Ἀνὰ μέσον εἰρηνευόντων ἐκβάλλει διαβολήν.

[9] 4 Macc. 4:1: πάντα τρόπον διαβάλλων. The word denotes false accusation in 2 Macc. 3:11.

[10] Da. 3:8 LXX : ἄνδρες Χαλδαῖοι διέβαλον τοὺς Ἰουδαίους (Θ : διέβαλλον); Da. 6:24 Θ : τοὺς ἄνδρας τοὺς διαβαλόντας τὸν Δανιήλ (LXX: καταμαρτυρήσαντες).

[11] ψ 70:13 : ἐκλιπέτωσαν οἱ ἐνδιαβάλλοντες τὴν ψυχήν μου. Cf. also ψ 37:20; 108:4, 20, 29.

[12] The last is suggested by Bréal.

where he is in fact the accuser, the verb שָׂטַן is rendered ἀντικεῖσθαι : καὶ ὁ διάβολος ἱστήκει ἐκ δεξιῶν αὐτοῦ τοῦ ἀντικεῖσθαι αὐτῷ = וְהַשָּׂטָן עֹמֵד עַל־יְמִינוֹ לְשִׂטְנוֹ. This seems to force us to the conclusion that "accuser" is not the primary meaning. Since the rendering "seducer" does not fit all the contexts, "adversary" is the required translation. The work of the adversary implies always an attempt on the part of the διάβολος to separate God and man. It is an open question whether the verb διαβάλλειν influenced the usage.

Foerster

B. The OT View of Satan.

Whether שָׂטָן belongs to the nouns in וָו,[13] or whether it represents a simple construction קְטָל, is a debated issue, though even in the latter case it is based on the verb שָׂטַן. In the first instance the term denotes a quality rather than a function, and the basic meaning is "enemy" or "adversary."

1. For the most part OT usage does not follow this general line of meaning, though it may be seen, e.g., in 1 S. 29:4 and Ps. 71:13 (cf. also Gn. 26:21). So far as we can see, the word has a special place in the judicial life of Israel. The *satan is the enemy* in a specific sense, i.e., the accuser at law. His place is on the right hand of the accused (Zech. 3:1), and his intervention is described in the terms עָמַד עַל (Zech. 3:1; 1 Ch. 21:1). In the request of one who is prosecuted that the situation might be reversed and that "an adversary should stand at his right hand" (עָמַד עַל, Ps. 109:6; cf. v. 20, 29), all these elements may be discerned. שִׂטְנָה denotes accusation in Ezr. 4:6. Another judicial term for this legal functionary seems to have been מַזְכִּיר עָוֹן, which is used figuratively in Ez. 21:28 f.; 29:16. Similarly the woman of Zarephath sees in Elijah an accuser who has come to call her sin to remembrance (1 K. 17:18). The cup-bearer in the story of Joseph appears before Pharaoh as his own accuser in Gn. 41:9. When Ezekiel calls Nebuchadnezzar or the Egyptians מַזְכִּיר עָוֹן, he does so on the basis of an interesting theology of history. Yahweh has a special function for the enemies of Israel. They are the accusers of Israel and are thus related to the guilt of God's people. This important conception entitles us to see in the satans raised up against Solomon[14] — the Edomite Hadad and the Aramean Rezon — not merely enemies according to the general sense of the term, but adversaries in the specific legal sense. According to the Deuteronomic view of the writer, Solomon has sinned, and it is in relation to his sin that these satans are raised up during his reign. A concrete illustration is thus given of the proposition which underlies the Deuteronomic theology of history, namely, that the history of the people of God is its judgment.

2. Heavenly as well as earthly government has a similar agent, i.e., one to fulfil the function of judicial prosecutor in the court of heaven. A particularly vivid picture of this is given in the prologue to the Book of Job. From this narrative, which has no dogmatic concerns, we may gather that the heavenly beings are received by Yahweh on special days. On such days the court of heaven assembles before the Lord, and the prosecutor is among those present. He is not a demonic being. He is an official prosecutor and may be reckoned among the בְּנֵי הָאֱלֹהִים. He has a special function in this circle. His task is to go through the earth and consider men. In opposition to the favourable view of Yahweh, he

---

[13] H. Bauer and P. Leander, *Historische Grammatik d. hebr. Sprache* (1922), 500.
[14] 1 K. 11:14 ff., cf. 1 K. 5:18.

questions the inward sincerity of the piety of Job. In so doing, however, he is acting in the interests of God. If he decides to proceed against Job, Yahweh must authorise him to do so, and it is thus Yahweh Himself who really puts Job to the test (cf. Job 1:11; 2:4). This view of Satan does, of course, contain implicitly the elements which later produce a more sinister conception. The authorisation which he receives from Yahweh gives him control over such hostile factors as sickness, natural disasters, robbery etc. *De facto*, then, he is more than prosecutor. He has powers which go beyond his purely legal function. It is at this essential point that the analogy to the earthly מַזְכִּיר עָוֹן breaks down.

A similar picture is given in the fourth vision of Zechariah (3:1 ff.). Here again we have a heavenly prosecutor, and this time at an actual trial. Here again the *saṭan* is not an evil power. The accused, Joshua, is in fact guilty, even though the accusation is quashed. The organ of law is confronted by the organ of grace, the מַלְאַךְ יְהוָה, who is always in the OT the protector of the divine covenant of grace (→ ἄγγελος, I, 74 f.).

It is striking how rarely the *saṭan* notion is expressed in the OT. The literary attestation does not justify the conclusion that it is exclusively post-exilic, for, whatever the age of the prologue to Job, there can be no doubt that it rests materially on a very old source. What we may conclude is that in the true religious world of Israel the figure of the heavenly *saṭan* is not of central importance, and that there is thus no rigid consistency in the conception of this figure in different times and circles. Perhaps it may even be that the same heavenly figure is not always denoted by the term, so that fundamentally any בְּנֵי הָאֱלֹהִים may be despatched as an accuser. In Nu. 22:22 the angel of Yahweh is the one who confronts Balaam as *saṭan*. Yet even though there may be a certain fluidity in the concept, it is questionable whether we should identify with this more or less clearly defined figure of a prosecutor the personified spirit who seduced Ahab and his prophets in 1 K. 22:19 ff. The difficulty is that there is no basic similarity between the prosecutor and the seducer. Nevertheless, Micaiah's vision of the heavenly court is very like that of Job 1 f. (→ 73), and it is possible that there was some realisation in Israel of an adversary who in certain circumstances might not merely stand in a *de iure* relation to Israel's sin but also embody the threat to its whole existence.

This leads us quite naturally to the third passage which refers to a heavenly *saṭan*. It is first to be noted that the figure of the *saṭan* does not belong originally to the story recorded in 1 Ch. 21:1, but has been introduced as an amendment into this version. David was tempted by Yahweh to a great sin, i.e., the numbering of the people. The Chronicler felt that this was to put it too baldly, [15] and therefore substituted *saṭan* for Yahweh. This certainly gives us a more exact picture of God, but it does not remove the great paradox inherent in the whole belief in the devil. The fact that no article is used with *saṭan* shows us that some such belief is here present. *Saṭan* is now a proper name rather than a mere designation of office. Nor would there be much sense in the amendment unless there had also been a decisive change in the conception of *saṭan*. The legal element in the concept is still present in the וַיַּעֲמֹד עַל of the Chronicler. But there is a sharp contrast in the וַיָּסֶת, which plainly denotes a harmful and even hostile influence. The original attributing of the act of temptation directly to Yahweh would hardly have been consonant with the highly important relationship of Yahweh to David which is

---

[15] Cf. the similar treatment of Ex. 4:24 in Jub. 48:2 f.

one of the special concerns of the Chronicler. Nevertheless, there is here no meta-physical dualism. The basic theology of the work makes this quite plain. The Chronicler is not trying to remove the event from the divine plan of salvation. He is simply setting it at a greater distance from Yahweh, and to do this there suggests itself the figure of *satan,* to whom all kinds of unmotivated evil had been increasingly assigned in addition to his legitimate legal powers. It is not impossible that new Persian influences to some degree helped to bring about this inner change in the conception of *satan.* Yet the figure of *satan* as such is in no sense borrowed from the Persians. The OT prosecutor and adversary is a figure for whom there are no analogies. [16] In Persian religion there is certainly no parallel to the legal element, and similarly the OT view shows no trace of the dualistic background apart from which one could hardly understand the figure of Angra Mainyus.

The OT *satan* embodies the threat to man from the world of God, whether as the prosecutor of ethical faults or as a demonic and destructive principle firmly anchored in the plan of salvation. [17] The positive and non-dualistic integration into the divine court and the divine government is the distinctive feature of the OT view as compared not merely with Persian ideas but also with those of post-canonical writings. [18] In these we can detect a process towards the complete absolutising of Satan over against God. [19] Satan is the chief of a hostile kingdom, an absolute principle of evil. This development is difficult to explain in detail. The intrusion of dualism into the apocalyptic world-view on the basis of Persian influences is only one of the factors at work. Attention should also be paid to the revival of ancient mythologoumena (the fight with the dragon, the serpent of Paradise, marriages with angels). Deriving from very different contexts, these tend to crystallise around the figure of Satan and thus to contribute an essential broadening of content.

von Rad

C. The Later Jewish View of Satan.

The few OT references initiated further development in pre-NT Judaism, and this finally produced many combinations of the Satan concept with originally very different ideas (e.g., an identification with the evil principle or with the angel of death), and the attributing to Satan of many features which derive from such independent sources as the story of fallen angels, with no original reference to Satan. It should be stressed that the idea of Satan originally had nothing whatever to do with human impulses or with the fallen angels. Four points are to be considered in this regard. a. We learn from Eth. En. 54:6 that there was a definite subjugation of Azazel and his hosts to Satan, and from Jub. 10:8 ff. that Mastema

---

[16] Nor can there be any question of dependence on Babylonian ideas, as often asserted on the basis of KAT, 461, 463. The bêl dabâbi is always a man, according to an oral communication of B. Landsberger.

[17] The story in 1 Ch. 21 culminates in a great act of salvation, the divine authorisation of the cultus in Jerusalem. Even the slaying of Ahab in 1 K. 22:19 ff. takes place within the historical plan chosen by Yahweh.

[18] Azazel confronts Yahweh far more radically as an evil being. Azazel was regarded as a wilderness demon on whom the guilt of Israel could be laid according to the rite of the great day of atonement (Lv. 16). It is worth noting, however, that this figure had no significance in the great context of religion in Israel. It was obviously a pre-Yahwistic element, the relic of a very old cultic action.

[19] Radical dualism was to some degree averted by thinking of Satan as a created but fallen angel.

has nothing to do with the fall of angels or the judgment of fallen angels, though he uses them as his instruments. b. The demons are really autonomous in relation to Satan (→ δαίμων, 13 f.). c. To Satan is attributed only the activity of prosecution.[20] d. A fall of Satan from heaven would make his work impossible. This means that we are not to regard the stories of a fall of angels or of Satan as of first importance in depicting the Jewish conception of Satan.

If a formula is sought to describe the special position of Satan, one is almost impelled to say that Satan is the one who tries to disrupt the relation between God and man, and especially between God and Israel. This takes place in three ways, by temptation to sin, by accusation before God and by trying to thwart the divine plan of salvation. Thus Satan is represented as the tempter of the race and of Israel, e.g., in the case of the fall (→ n. 45), of Cain and Abel,[21] of Noah,[22] of Abraham,[23] of the Exodus,[24] of the golden calf,[25] of David,[26] of the history of Israel,[27] and of many rabbis.[28] There are many general statements concerning his activity as the tempter, esp. in the Test. XII.[29] Satan entices to sin in every form. Comprehensive statements in this regard are particularly common in the Pseudepigrapha. The final aim of temptation is man's destruction. The manner of temptation is varied and often external acc. to the Rabbis.[30] The temptation is often viewed as a ground of mitigation, the Test. XII offering many profound psychological insights into it. Again, the devil seeks to attain his goal by accusing before God[31] and finally by interfering in the history of Israel.[32] In the Pseud-

---

[20] Lv. r., 21 on 16:3 and Cant. r. on 2:1 f. speak of the princes of the nations (שרי אומות העולם) accusing Israel before God.

[21] Apc. Mos., 2 attributes Cain's act to the contention of the enemy.

[22] Jub. 11:5 : Mastema and his spirits deceive the sons of Noah, cf. c. 10.

[23] Jub. 17:16 causes Mastema to tempt Abraham in relation to the offering of Isaac. In Gn. r., 56 on 22:7 Sammael tries to divert Abraham from the way of obedience. For further examples, cf. Str.-B., I, 140. Sarah, too, was tempted by Sammael, Pirqe R. Eliezer, 32 (S. Rappaport, *Agada u. Exegese bei Fl. Joseph.* [1930], 108, No. 105).

[24] Damasc., 5, 18 f.: At the time of Moses and Aaron "Belial raised up Jachne and his brother."

[25] bShab., 89a : Satan tries in every possible way to shake the trust of Israel in Moses when he is up in the mount, finally displaying a bier in the sky as a sign that Moses is dead.

[26] bSanh., 107: Satan in the form of a bird makes an opening in the tent under which Bathsheba sits, so that David sees her. Lives of the Prophets, 21 (P. Riessler, *Altjüd. Schrifttum ausserhalb der Bibel* [1928], 220): Beliar prevents Nathan from warning David prior to the committal of his sin.

[27] Damasc., 4, 12 f.: "During all these years Belial was sent against Israel."

[28] bQid, 91a assembles many such stories, Str.-B., I, 140; III, 109 f.

[29] Test. J. 19:4 : ἐτύφλωσε γάρ με ὁ ἄρχων τῆς πλάνης. Cf. also Test. S. 2:7; D. 1:7; 6:3; B. 6:1; Jub. 10:8; cf. 1:20; 19:28; Gr. Bar. 13:2; Apc. Abr. 14:11 f.

[30] Satan disguises himself, as in Apc. Mos. 17; for further examples, → the stories mentioned in n. 25, n. 26 and n. 28.

[31] Eth. En. 40:7 (several satans as accusers); Jub. 1:20; 48:15, 18; Apc. Zeph. 4:2; 10:5; bBer., 60a : The saying of R. Jose (c. 150 A.D.): "Never should man open his mouth before Satan," is taken to mean that he should not give Satan an opening by mentioning his sins. Ex. r., 43 on 32:11: "When the Israelites had made the calf, Satan rose up and accused them. Moses, however, stood without. What did he do ? He came and expelled Satan and took his place." Later passages are Ex. r., 21 on 14:15, Str.-B., I, 142; *ibid.*, 31 on 22:24, Str.-B., IV, 554. The oldest example of Satan accusing only in the hour of danger is Gn. r., 91 on 42:38 : "R. Eliezer ben Jacob spoke : It thus follows that Satan raises his complaint only in the hour of danger." Cf. also Str. B., I, 142d. Satan accuses those who are secure acc. to Str.-B., I, 143e. He does not do so on the Day of Atonement, *ibid.*, 143 f.

[32] Jub. 48:2, 10 (Satan sought to kill Moses ; he does evil, but nothing beneficial, through

epigrapha he is sometimes depicted simply as the destroyer.[33] The final goal of Satan is classically formulated in Jub. 1:20: "May the spirit of Belchor not dominate them, to accuse them before thee, and to seduce them from all the ways of righteousness, that they may perish far from thy presence."[34] If man yields to temptation, the result may well be a close connexion with the tempter.[35]

These ideas are intersected by others in later Judaism, and are not worked out consistently. This was possible because according to the fundamental legalism of later Judaism man may freely choose either for or against evil and is not therefore constrained by any superior power of the tempter. Indeed, by the merit of his own works or sufferings he may silence the accuser. Thus the figure of Satan becomes dispensable in later Judaism, and may be developed in other ways. Temptation is opposed by the decision for good,[36] the accusation of Satan by human merit,[37] or even by external things,[38] or by Moses, Phanuel, Michael or the angels.[39] In some places, however, it is God Himself who silences Satan,[39] and here it is to be noted that the question how the righteousness of God is maintained is not solved.

It must be particularly emphasised that in later Judaism Satan is not the lord of the world. There are hints in this direction, especially in the sharp dualism between God and Beliar in Test. XII and in the linking of Satan with the evil impulse and with the angel of death, bBB, 16a: Satan יורד ומתעה ועולה ומרגיז ונוטל רשות ונוטל נשמה. But the evil impulse itself is no exact parallel of original sin. It is not a power which wholly enslaves man. The lordship of death has certainly come on all men through the fall, and ceases with the coming of God's dominion, but it is not fundamentally conceived as a hostile power which man cannot throw off. The only passage worth noting is bBB, 16a, in which Job 9:24: אֶרֶץ נִתְּנָה בְיַד־רָשָׁע,

the Egyptian magicians); bSanh., 95a (Satan entices David in the form of a gazelle in the land of the Philistines); cf. Cant. r. on 3:6; Tanch. וישלח, 40b, Str.-B., I, 142c.

[33] Test. B. 3:3 (c β S): ἐὰν τὰ πνεύματα τοῦ Βελίαρ εἰς πᾶσαν πονηρίαν θλίψεως ἐκστήσωσι ὑμᾶς. Cf. Jub. 11:11; 49:2; Ass. Mos. 10:1.

[34] Characteristic is also the view mentioned in → n. 31, namely, that Satan accuses in the hour of danger and that man is thus brought to an unprepared death at a time when he has a debit balance.

[35] Damasc., 12, 2 f.: "The man in whom the spirits of Belial have control and who preaches apostasy"; Gr. Bar. 13:2; Test. XII, R. 4:11; Iss. 6:1: κολληθήσονται τῷ Βελίαρ; D. 4:7; N. 8:6: ὁ διάβολος οἰκειοῦται αὐτὸν ὡς ἴδιον σκεῦος; A. 1:8; B. 3:3; Apc. Abr. 14:6.

[36] Jub. 1:20 (supra); 19:28: "The spirits of Mastema shall not rule over thee or thy seed to keep thee far from God" (a blessing, not a prayer); Damasc., 16, 4 f.: "If a man has resort to the Torah, the angel of Mastema will depart from him"; Apc. Abr. 13 f.; 26:4; Apc. Mos. 10 ff.; cf. also 14 ff. and Test. XII.

[37] bShab, 32a, Str.-B., I, 143: "The advocates (פרקליטין) of man are penitence and good works"; Ex. r., 31 on 22:24: "When a man fulfils the commandments, and is a son of the Torah, and gives alms, Satan comes and accuses him, but his advocates intercede for him and justify him."

[38] bBer., 60a → n. 31; Pesikt., 177b, Str.-B., III, 604c.

[39] For Moses as defender, Ex. r., 43 on 32:11, Str.-B., I, 141 f. → n. 31; for Phanuel, Eth. En. 40:7; for Michael, Ex. r., 18, 5 on 12:29, Str.-B., I, 142b: "R. Jose has said: To whom may we liken Michael and Sammael? To the defending and prosecuting counsel at law ... And Satan comes to speak, but Michael bids him be silent"; for angels, Jub. 48:15 ff.: "They bound Satan on the day when the Israelites took the vessels and clothing of the Egyptians, that he should not accuse them"; for God Himself, Pesikt. r., 45, Str.-B., III, 203: On the Day of Atonement the merits and demerits of Israel are equal. While Satan goes to look for more demerits, God takes some of them from the scales.

is interpreted by R. Eliezer as a blasphemy of Job, while R. Jehoshua says: ‏לא דבר איוב אלא כלפי שטן‎. Perhaps in this as in many other Rabbinic passages one may detect a conflict between two opposing views, the one followed in many Pseudepigrapha, the other (represented by R. Eliezer) achieving dominance in Rabbinic Judaism.

The figure of Satan may be dispensed with altogether. It does not occur in 4 Esr., and hardly at all in Eth. En. In place of Satan the tempter we find ‏יֵצֶר הָרָע‎, with whom he is sometimes identified. [40] As accusers alongside him are angelic witnesses of evil deeds. [41] Sometimes many satans are mentioned instead of one. [42] The reduced position of Satan is perhaps most clearly reflected in the fact that there is no expectation of his destruction in the last time; it is simply stated that in the last time there will be no more Satan. [43]

On the basis of this fairly loose position of Satan in the system of later Judaism, it is quite understandable that legends about demons as well as speculations about the evil impulse should be linked with this figure, and that he should thus come to be regarded as an exalted angel expelled from heaven [44] — a view which is no part of the original conception. The original conception was also weakened by the way in which the motives at work in the temptation of the first human couple were sometimes presented. [45] This reduced Satan to the level of human understanding, and in particular diverted attention from his one goal, i.e., the separation of God and man.

Only when the idea of Satan came to be linked with legends of demons could the impression arise that Satan was connected with certain parts of nature, and

---

[40] bBB, 16a → 77; cf. also Str.-B., I, 139.

[41] bShab., 32a, Bar., Str.-B., I, 143: "Even though 999 (sc. angels, as suggested by the quotation from Job 33:23 f. which follows) assert his guilt against him, One will maintain his merit."

[42] Eth. En. 40:7; Dt. r., 11, 6 on 33:1 (Str.-B., I, 136c): "The angel Sammael, the malefactor, is the head of all satans."

[43] From Rabbinic literature, we can mention only Pesikt. r., 36, and there, too, Sammael is used for the angel of death (Str.-B., II, 2). Cf. also bSukka, 52a (Moore, I, 493): God will one day publicly smite the evil impulse. From the Pseudepigrapha we may mention Apc. Mos. 12 (Seth to the beast): ἀπόστηθι ἀπὸ τῆς εἰκόνος τοῦ θεοῦ ἕως ἡμέρας τῆς κρίσεως; ibid., 39 (God to Adam): καθίσω σε ... ἐπὶ τὸν θρόνον τοῦ ἀπατήσαντός σε· ἐκεῖνος δὲ βληθήσεται εἰς τὸν τόπον τοῦτον; Apoc. Esr. 4:43: "Then said God: The adversary has heard my fearful warning, and is thus hiding; for I will burn up the earth, and with it the adversary of the human race" (acc. to Riessler); Vit. Ad., 39. Cf. also the following passages from Test. XII: Jud. 25:3 acc. to α β S¹: καὶ οὐκ ἔσται ἐκεῖ πνεῦμα πλάνης τοῦ Βελίαρ, ὅτι ἐμβληθήσεται ἐν πυρὶ εἰς τὸν αἰῶνα (Beliar or the spirits ?); L. 18:2: καὶ αὐτὸς (sc. the new priest) ποιήσει κρίσιν ἀληθείας ἐπὶ τῆς γῆς ἐν πλήθει ἡμερῶν; D. 5:10: αὐτὸς γὰρ ποιήσει πρὸς τὸν Βελίαρ πόλεμον. Yet there is the possibility of a good deal of revision in the Test. XII. We certainly cannot adduce Asc. Is. Jub. 23:29; 50:5; Ass. Mos. 10:1 (tunc zabulus finem habebit) simply states that there will be no more evil. Jub. 23:26 shows the specifically legal attitude in this question: Satan disappears with the "reversal."

[44] Pirqe R. Eliezer, 13, 14 and 27, Str.-B., I, 137 f., 139; II, 167.

[45] Wis. 2:24: φθόνῳ δὲ διαβόλου ὁ θάνατος εἰσῆλθεν εἰς τὸν κόσμον. Cf. Gr. Bar. 4:8; Vit. Ad., 12; Apc. Abr. 13; Apc. Mos. 16; Apc. Sedrach 5; Pirqe R. Eliezer → n. 44; bSota, 9b: "Thus we find that the ancient serpent cast its eyes on what was not its due." Gn. r., 18 on 3:1: Acc. to R. Josua b. Qarcha (c. 150 A.D.), Gn. 2:25 ("They were both naked") is written "to show us on account of what sin the evil one (sc. the serpent) came upon them; because he saw that they were occupied in sleeping together, he acquired the desire for it." Cf. Gn. r., 85, 3 on 38:1.

especially with matter, as suggested in Slav. En. 29:4-5. Gnostic trends of this type are no part of the original tradition and are quite alien to Rabbinic Judaism.

When we consider the Jewish names for the devil we find that שׂטן, שׂטנא and διάβολος (Gr. Bar. 4; Apc. Mos. 15 ff.; Apc. Sedrach; Ass. Mos. 10:1 etc.) are all old, and משׂטימא is found as a par. to Satan (Damasc. 16, 5; Jub.). Belial (→ Βελίαρ, I, 607) is also found. A common name in Rabbinic writings and the Pseudepigrapha is סמאל = Σαμμαήλ (Gr. Bar. 4:8). This name is formed like other names of angels and may well bear witness to speculations about Satan such as those mentioned above. The interfusion of speculations concerning Satan and demons is best seen from the figure of Azazel (→ n. 18), esp. in Apc. Abr. [46]

D. The NT View of Satan.

The names. No proper names are found until 2 C. 6:15 (→ Βελίαρ). Along with → Σατανᾶς and διάβολος we find ὁ → κατήγωρ (= Rabb. קטיגור) in Rev. 12:10; ὁ → πονηρός, ὁ → ἐχθρός, ὁ → πειράζων, [47] and (materially impossible in Judaism) ὁ → ἄρχων τοῦ κόσμου τούτου, Jn. 12:31; 14:30; 16:11; ὁ θεὸς τοῦ → αἰῶνος τούτου, 2 C. 4:4; ὁ ἄρχων τῆς → ἐξουσίας τοῦ ἀέρος, Eph. 2, 2; also → δράκων, → ὄφις.

As concerns the alternation between σατανᾶς and διάβολος in the NT, no material distinction may be asserted. Study of the Synopt. and Ac. suggest that Σατανᾶς is closer to Palestinian usage; in the story of the temptation Mk. uses σατανᾶς and the par. have διάβολος, though σατανᾶς is used by Jesus Himself in Mt. 4:10. Cf. Mk. 4:15 and par. In Ac. 10:38; 13:10 διάβολος is used to Gentiles, in contrast to Ac. 5:3; 26:18. There can hardly be any particular reason for the alternation in Jn. and Rev. (cf. Jn. 13:2 and 13:27; Rev. 12:9: ὁ καλούμενος διάβολος καὶ ὁ σατανᾶς). Paul generally has σατανᾶς, though διάβολος is found in Eph. (4:27; 6:11) and (with two exceptions) the Past. The Catholic Epistles also use διάβολος.

The two distinctive features of the NT view of Satan are the absolute antithesis between God and Satan and the presence of the kingdom of God in Christ.

Satan is the prince of this world. He can dispose of its kingdoms according to what he says in Lk. 4:6: (ἡ ἐξουσία αὕτη ἅπασα) ἐμοὶ παραδέδοται καὶ ᾧ ἐὰν θέλω δίδωμι αὐτήν. Paul expresses this in the sharpest possible form in 2 C. 4:4 by calling him ὁ θεὸς τοῦ αἰῶνος τούτου. This means that he arrogates to himself in this world the honour which belongs to God. The dominion of Satan over this world is primarily a dominion over men. He is the strong man armed who guards his goods (Mk. 3:27 and par.). Unredeemed men are in his sphere of lordship (Mt. 6:13: ῥῦσαι ἡμᾶς ἀπὸ τοῦ πονηροῦ; Ac. 26:18; Col. 1:13). A decisive point in the NT view is that man cannot free himself from this yoke. With man's consent, it leads to a connexion with him which Jn. esp. describes in terms which denote a natural interrelation of being, though not according to natural law as in Gnosticism: εἷς διάβολός ἐστιν, Jn. 6:70; ἐκ τοῦ πατρὸς τοῦ διαβόλου ἐστέ, Jn. 8:44; τέκνα τοῦ διαβόλου, 1 Jn. 3:8, 10; υἱὲ διαβόλου, Ac. 13:10; cf. Ac. 5:3; 26:18; Rev. 2:9. Thus the acts of men are ἔργα τοῦ διαβόλου, 1 Jn. 3:8. The goal of Satan's activity is man's destruction in alienation from God. In this

---

[46] Azazel usually appears as the prince of demons, and in Test. Sol. 7:7 is an archangel whom the demons obey. He sometimes assumes the role and position of Satan, but Satan is never conceived of as merely a prince of demons. What is true of Azazel is true also of → Beezebul.

[47] Mt. 4:3; 1 Th. 3:5. It might well be (→ 72) a paraphrase of διάβολος.

sense he is a murderer from the beginning (Jn. 8:44) and his very essence is lying and sin (Jn. 8:44; 1 Jn. 3:8). The destruction which he brings embraces harmful processes of every kind (Mk. 3:23 ff. and par.; Lk. 13:11, 16; 1 C. 5:5; 2 C. 12:7; 1 Tm. 1:20). The demons are subject to him and seek to do bodily and spiritual harm to man in his service. In this connexion he can sometimes be said to have τὸ κράτος τοῦ θανάτου (Hb. 2:14), and although Paul can speak of the dominion of death without mentioning the devil in R. 5, there can be no doubt that the two dominions constitute a single reality. Demons, and finally Satan, lie behind all paganism, and especially behind magic. Thus in Ac. 13:10 the sorcerer is called a child of the devil. In the NT, as in Judaism, Satan is the accuser (Rev. 12:10). Thus all the functions ascribed to Satan in Judaism are found again in the NT. But they now culminate in a single, supernatural power and dominion of Satan to which demons (→ δαίμων, 18) and the whole of this aeon are basically subject.

Christ brings the kingdom of God which puts an end to the kingdom of the devil. He is the One who has bound the strong man and spoiled his goods. Through Him the accuser Satan is cast down from heaven (Rev. 12).[48] In this connexion, reference may be made to Jn. 12:31: νῦν ὁ ἄρχων τοῦ κόσμου τούτου ἐκβληθήσεται ἔξω, and Lk. 10:18 : ἐθεώρουν τὸν σατανᾶν ὡς ἀστραπὴν ἐκ τοῦ οὐρανοῦ πεσόντα. With this fall, Satan loses his right of accusation in respect of all men. Judgment is now committed to Christ. Yet Satan still has a short time on earth (Rev. 12:12). As he contended against Israel in the past (cf. later Judaism), his present battle is against the kingdom of God which has come. He thus appears at the decisive points in the life of Jesus : at the beginning in the temptation (Mt. 4:1 ff. and par.); and at the end (Lk. 22:31: ὁ σατανᾶς ἐξητήσατο ὑμᾶς τοῦ σινιάσαι). He is shown to be active in the treachery of Judas (Lk. 22:3; Jn. 6:70; 13:2, 27; cf. Lk. 4:13 : ἄχρι καιροῦ, with Lk. 22:53 : αὕτη ... ἡ ἐξουσία τοῦ σκότους). In the early days of the community there is similar reference to the activity of the devil (Ac. 5:3), and the Epistles are full of warnings and exhortations in the struggle against Satan (R. 16:20; 1 C. 7:5; 2 C. 2:11; 11:14; 1 Th. 2:18; Eph. 4:27; 6:11, 16; 1 Tm. 3:6 f.; 5:15; 2 Tm. 2:26; Jm. 4:7; 1 Pt. 5:8). Satan is particularly busy to snatch away the seed when it is sown (Mk. 4:15 and par.). The community is delivered from the power of Satan (2 Th. 3:3). It has overcome him (1 Jn. 2:13). It is thus called to fight him with all its might (Eph. 6:10 ff.).

In the last days Satan summons Antichrist to serve him (ἀντίχριστος → χριστός). According to Rev. 13:2 and 2 Th. 2:9 f. Antichrist will arise in the power of Satan and will prevail. Satan will then be bound for the millennial period, will be released for his last assault, and will finally be judged in the lake of fire.[49]

The fact that the community can be overcome by Antichrist brings sharply into focus the tension running through all these statements. The power to act against God is given to Satan by God. καὶ ἐδόθη αὐτῷ is continually said in Rev. 13. The divine assurance of the community is in no way shattered by the power of Satan. Satan can prevent necessary journeys (1 Th. 2:18). He can tempt members of the community (1 Tm. 5:15). He constantly places the community in danger. But in faith the community is in every respect freed from his power, so that even the blows of the angel of Satan (2 C. 12:7) and delivering to Satan (1 C. 5:5; 1 Tm. 1:20) are comprehended in the gracious operation of God.

---

[48] W. Foerster, ThStKr, 104 (1932), 290.
[49] Thus the seat of the devil is not hell, cf. Rev. 12:9, 12 and Schl. Jk., 224 as against Dib. Jk., 184; → γέεννα, I, 658.

In 1 Tm. 3:11: γυναῖκας ... μὴ διαβόλους, and 2 Tm. 3:3 : ἔσονται γὰρ οἱ ἄνθρωποι ... διάβολοι, the word has the predominant Gk. sense of "calumniator." In some other passages the meaning is disputed. Notwithstanding Grill's opposition,[50] the ἐξ ὑμῶν εἷς διάβολός ἐστιν of Jn. 6:70 is undoubtedly to be translated "one of you is a devil," since Jn. especially emphasises the close relation into which men can enter with Satan. There is doubt, however, in the case of Eph. 4:26 f.: ὀργίζεσθε καὶ μὴ ἁμαρτάνετε· ὁ ἥλιος μὴ ἐπιδυέτω ἐπὶ παροργισμῷ ὑμῶν, μηδὲ δίδοτε τόπον τῷ διαβόλῳ. Μηδέ can denote something similar to what precedes, i.e., "do not listen to the calumniator who attacks a brother" ;[51] but the more likely meaning is again : "give the devil no play, no possibility of working." Finally, in 1 Tm. 3:6 f.: δεῖ οὖν τὸν ἐπίσκοπον εἶναι ... μὴ νεόφυτον, ἵνα μὴ τυφωθεὶς εἰς κρίμα ἐμπέσῃ τοῦ διαβόλου. δεῖ δὲ καὶ μαρτυρίαν καλὴν ἔχειν ἀπὸ τῶν ἔξωθεν, ἵνα μὴ εἰς ὀνειδισμὸν ἐμπέσῃ καὶ παγίδα τοῦ διαβόλου, the translation "calumniator" gives good sense. In this case v. 6 points to the danger which is entailed by the office of a newly converted bishop and which might lead to the judging of a calumniator, and v. 7 refers to the traps which the outside world by more or less well-founded arguments tries to set for the one who stands at the head of the community. In both verses, however, the use of the article and of the singular suggest the devil, the more so as τυφωθείς in v. 6 implies an inner danger for the bishop himself. On this rendering, κρίμα denotes the rule of the devil, who seeks through accusations to bring men back under his sphere of influence.

Foerster

διαγγέλλω → ἀγγέλλω, I, 67 ff.

διαγογγύζω → γογγύζω, I, 735.

διαθήκη → διατίθημι, 106 ff.

διαιρέω, διαίρεσις → αἱρέομαι, I, 180 ff.

διακονέω, διακονία, διάκονος

† διακονέω.

The concept of serving is expressed in Gk. by many words which are often hard to differentiate even though each has its own basic emphasis. → δουλεύω means to serve as a slave, with a stress on subjection. → θεραπεύω emphasises willingness for service and the respect and concern thereby expressed (esp. towards God). → λατρεύω means to serve for wages. In NT days it had come to be used predominantly for religious or cultic duties. → λειτουργέω denotes official public service to the people or to the state, being used in the LXX for service in the temple and in Christianity for service in the Church. ὑπηρετέω means at root to steer. In terms of service, it signifies esp. the relation to the master to whom the service is rendered. In Xenoph. → ὑπηρέτης is often used in the sense of adjutant. As distinct from all these terms, διακονέω has the special quality of indicating very personally the service rendered to another. It is thus closest to ὑπηρετέω, but in διακονέω there is a stronger approximation to the concept of a service of love.

---

[50] Grill, *Untersuchungen*, II, 44.
[51] So Ew. Gefbr., *ad loc.*
δ ι α κ ο ν έ ω. Cr.-Kö., 290; Pr. Bauer, 287; Moult.-Mill., 149; Liddell-Scott, 398; W. Brandt, *Dienst und Dienen im Neuen Testament* (1931); G. Uhlhorn, *Die christliche Liebestätigkeit*, I² (1895).

A. διακονέω outside the NT.

1. Fundamental to an understanding of διακονέω in all its uses is the fact that it has an original concrete sense which is still echoed in its figurative meanings. In secular Gk. διακονέω, which is first found in Herodot. and is never too common, means a. "to wait at table": Aristoph. Ach., 1015 ff.: ἤκουσας ὡς μαγειρικῶς κομψῶς τε καὶ δειπνητικῶς αὐτῷ διακονεῖται; Diod. S., V, 28, 4: οἱ δὲ Γαλάται ... δειπνοῦσι δὲ καθήμενοι ... ἐπὶ τῆς γῆς ... διακονοῦνται δ' ὑπὸ τῶν νεωτάτων παίδων; Athen., IX, 21: ὅταν ἐρανισταῖς, Καρίων, διακονῇς; cf. Plut. Virtutem Doceri Posse, 3 (II, 440c). In particular it means "to taste," Ps.-Luc. Asin., 53: καὶ παῖδες ἡμῖν παρειστήκεισαν οἰνοχόοι καλοὶ τὸν οἶνον ἡμῖν χρυσίῳ διακονούμενοι; or "to direct a marriage-feast," Athen., IX, 20: διακονοῦμεν νῦν γάμους; so also Athen., VI, 46; Dio. Chrys. Or., 7, 65. b. Rather more generally it means "to provide or care for," Soph. Phil., 285 ff. In this sense it is often used of the work of women, Plat. Leg., VII, 805e: πότερον ἦν Θρᾷκες ταῖς γυναιξὶν χρῶνται καὶ πολλὰ ἕτερα γένη, γεωργεῖν τε καὶ βουκολεῖν καὶ ποιμαίνειν καὶ διακονεῖν μηδὲν διαφερόντως τῶν δούλων; Plut. Adulat., 22 (II, 63d): ἡ διακονοῦσα πρεσβῦτις. On the basis of these original senses, it has c. the comprehensive meaning "to serve," Hdt., IV, 154: διηκονήσειν ὅ τι ἂν δεηθῇ; Demosth., 9, 43: τῷ δεσπότῃ διακονῶν; P. Oxy., II, 275, 10: διακονοῦντα καὶ ποιοῦντα πάντα τὰ ἐπιτασσόμενα αὐτῷ.

In Greek eyes serving is not very dignified. Ruling and not serving is proper to a man, Plat. Gorg., 492b. The formula of the sophist: "How can a man be happy when he has to serve someone?" expresses the basic Greek attitude (Plat. Gorg., 491e). This attitude is still reflected in Plato's characterisation of the servant as a contemptible flatterer (Gorg., 521ab). In Gorg., 518, shopkeepers, bakers and others, as distinct from physicians and the teachers of gymnastics, pursue activities for the nurture of the body which are described as δουλοπρεπεῖς τε καὶ διακονικὰς καὶ ἀνελευθέρους. Service acquires a higher value only when rendered to the state, Demosth., 50, 2; Plat. Leg., 955cd: τοὺς τῇ πατρίδι διακονοῦντάς τι δώρων χωρὶς χρὴ διακονεῖν. Even the merchant, tradesman or moneylender can in his way render service in the state, Plat. Resp., II, 371a ff. The statesman, however, does so directly, though naturally in terms of an idealistic understanding. For the Greek, the goal of human life is the perfect development of individual personality. This determines the nature of service to others. Logically, the sophist argues, a real man should simply serve his own desires with boldness and cleverness, Plat. Gorg., 492a. Plato contradicts this, but his basic attitude is the same. The only point is that a harmonious individual personality is for him interrelated to the harmonious totality. Gorg., 508a: φασὶ δ' οἱ σοφοί, καὶ οὐρανὸν καὶ γῆν καὶ θεοὺς καὶ ἀνθρώπους τὴν κοινωνίαν συνέχειν καὶ φιλίαν καὶ κοσμιότητα καὶ σωφροσύνην καὶ δικαιότητα, καὶ τὸ ὅλον τοῦτο διὰ ταῦτα κόσμον καλοῦσιν. The form of this κόσμος for social life is πολιτεία. Hence the statesman rules as διάκονος τῆς πόλεως, not for the sake of ruling nor for the sake of his own desires, but for the sake of the service laid upon him, which consists supremely in the education of good citizens. Even this service, however, is determined by the self-understanding of the ego as a microcosm. Thus, even though it demands certain renunciations, it does not entail any true self-emptying for the sake of others. Service is not one of the powers which hold heaven and earth together, and it does not lead to sacrifice.

This view persists in Aristotle and Hellenism. The significance of the πόλις, however, gradually yields before a stronger cosmic awareness in which the wise man has the sense of being a servant of God, Epict. Diss., III, 22, 69; III, 24, 65. As such he is the instrument and witness of God, Diss., III, 26, 28; IV, 7, 20.[1] On the other hand, "if expressions for service become more common in relation to God, they withdraw into the background in relation to one's neighbour."[2] To be sure, realisation of the service to be rendered to God carries with it a certain interrelationship with the totality of creation. But concrete obligations towards one's neighbour almost completely disappear.[3] For the Greek in his freedom and wisdom there can certainly be no question of existing to serve others.

2. Judaism showed a much deeper understanding of the meaning of service. Eastern thinking finds nothing unworthy in serving. The relation of a servant to his master is accepted, especially when he serves a great master. This is supremely true of the relation of man to God. It is noteworthy that the LXX does not use the term διακονεῖν at all, but renders the Heb. equivalents by → δουλεύειν, or, in the cultic sphere, by → λειτουργεῖν and → λατρεύειν. The harsher term δουλεύειν is in no way thought to be unsuitable.

Philo uses διακονεῖν in the general sense of "to serve," with a clear echo of the original meaning "to wait at table," Vit. Cont., 70: διακονοῦνται δὲ οὐχ ὑπ' ἀνδρα-πόδων; cf. also Vit. Cont., 75. From the material understanding of the concept of service one can see how Greek thinking softens the severity of the Jewish view.

In Joseph. διακονεῖν occurs in three senses: [4] "to wait at table," Ant., 11, 163: εὐθὺς ὡς εἶχεν μηδὲ ἀπολουσάμενος διακονήσων ἔσπευσεν τῷ βασιλεῖ τὴν ἐπὶ τοῦ πότου διακονίαν; so also Ant., 6, 52; 11, 166; 11, 188; a woman serves in the night: 18, 74; b. "to serve" with the meaning of "to obey," Ant., 9, 25: βασιλικῷ διακονῶν προστάγματι; cf. also Ant., 17, 140; c. "to render priestly service," Ant., 7, 365: διέ-ταξέ τε μίαν πατριὰν διακονεῖσθαι τῷ θεῷ ἐπὶ ἡμέρας ὀκτὼ ἀπὸ σαββάτου ἐπὶ σάββατον, at the Passover, Ant., 10, 72: τῶν ἱερέων ... διακονουμένων τοῖς ὄχλοις.

Israel had the great heritage of the commandment of Lv. 19:18: "Thou shalt love thy neighbour as thyself." This included full readiness for and commitment to service of one's neighbour. In later Judaism, however, 3 factors tended to obscure it. A sharp distinction came to be made between the righteous and the unrighteous in the antitheses of the Pharisees, and this dissolved the unconditional command of love and service. There arose the attitude lashed by Jesus in the parable of the Good Samaritan. Again, the service was less and less understood as sacrifice for others and more and more as a work of merit before God. Finally, there arose in Judaism the idea, which is so obvious to the natural man, not to accord service, especially service at table, to the unworthy. When Rabban Gamaliel II, the son of the rabbi, served other rabbis reclining at table with him, this caused astonishment. But Rabbi Jehoshua observed (Qid., 32b, cf. M. Ex., 18, 12): "We find that a greater than he served at table. Abraham was greater than he, and he served at table. A third added: God ... spreads the table before all men, and should not Rabban Gamaliel therefore ... stand and serve us?"

---

[1] It is worth noting that Epict. is still aware of the original meaning of διακονεῖν "to wait on," Diss., IV, 7, 37. In a figur. sense the lower capacities of the soul must wait on the higher (διακονεῖν) and serve them (ὑπηρετεῖν), Diss., II, 23, 7, 8 and 11.

[2] Brandt, 37.

[3] Cf. K. Deissner, Das Idealbild des stoischen Weisen (1930), 10 ff.

[4] A. Schlatter, Wie sprach Josephus von Gott? (1910), 13 argues that the transition from the narrower meaning of waiting at table to the more general sense, not found in the LXX, of any work according to the will of God, took place in Josephus under the influence of the equally ambiguous שִׁמֵּשׁ. This is refuted, however, by the fact that the more general sense is found in secular Gk. several centuries before.

B. διακονέω in the NT.

Jesus' view of service grows out of the OT command of love for one's neighbour, which He takes and links with the command of love for God to constitute the substance of the divinely willed ethical conduct of His followers. In so doing, He purifies the concept of service from the distortions which it had suffered in Judaism. Jesus' attitude to service is completely new as compared with the Greek understanding. The decisive point is that He sees in it the thing which makes a man His disciple.

1. In the NT διακονέω is first used in the original sense of "to wait at table" : Lk. 17:8 : ἑτοίμασον τί δειπνήσω, καὶ περιζωσάμενος διακόνει μοι ἕως φάγω καὶ πίω; Jn. 12:2 : ἐποίησαν οὖν αὐτῷ δεῖπνον ἐκεῖ, καὶ ἡ Μάρθα διηκόνει, ὁ δὲ Λάζαρος εἷς ἦν ἐκ τῶν ἀνακειμένων σὺν αὐτῷ. At table there is a palpable distinction between the worthy man reclining on the couch and the girded servant or the attentive woman. It is thus a high honour for the vigilant servants when their returning lord rewards them by girding himself, setting them at table and coming to serve them (Lk. 12:37). The astonishing act of Jesus in the appraisal of service is to reverse in ethical estimation the relation between serving and being served (Lk. 22:26 f.). Among the disciples ὁ ἡγούμενος must be ὡς ὁ διακονῶν. τίς γὰρ μείζων, ὁ ἀνακείμενος ἢ ὁ διακονῶν; οὐχὶ ὁ ἀνακείμενος; ἐγὼ δὲ ἐν μέσῳ ὑμῶν εἰμι ὡς ὁ διακονῶν.

The natural man — and especially the Greek — would see no difficulty in answering the question who is greater, the one who serves or the one who is served. It is obviously the latter. Jesus in His emphatic statement (ἐγὼ δὲ ...) does not oppose to this view the general thought that serving is greater than being served. Instead, He points to the actuality : I am among you as a servant. This is said by the uncontested leader of the disciples, by the Son of Man who knows that He is Lord of the kingdom of God (Lk. 22:29) and who summons the disciples to exercise final judgment on Israel with Him (v. 30). It is thus clear that Jesus is not merely bringing about a radical change in the academic estimation of human existence and action ; He is instituting in fact a new pattern of human relationships. He makes this no less clear in terms of the specific process of waiting at table than by His own action in washing the feet of His disciples.

> There is a variant reading of Lk 22:27 f. in Codex D. This would give the following sense : "Better the leader be servant than the one who sits at table. For I have come among you, not as one who sits at table, but as one who serves. And you have grown through my service." Blass and J. Weiss [5] regard this as the original version. It blunts, however, the sharpness of the antithesis between the current view and that of Jesus, and reduces to mere pedagogy the impressive reference to the manner and conduct of Jesus. It is surely a later softening.

In a rather wider sense διακονεῖν means "to supervise the meal" in Ac. 6:2 : διακονεῖν τραπέζαις. The reference is not merely to the provision of food but to the daily preparation and organisation. H. J. Holtzmann describes the men to whom this task was committed as organisers, dispensers and overseers of meals, τραπεζοποιοί. [6] The διακονεῖν τραπέζαις is brought into emphatic contrast with the διακονία τοῦ λόγου, and embraces practical love rather than the proclamation of the Word.

---

[5] *Schriften d. NT*[3] (1917), ad loc.
[6] H. J. Holtzmann, *Apostelgeschichte*[3] (1901), 51.

It is a debated question how this service, in which the Hellenistic widows felt they were being overlooked, was executed in the period depicted in Ac. 6, whether by the distribution of portions to those in special need [7] or by the arranging of common meals. [8] The latter is more likely. For it means that the overlooking of the Hellenistic widows was probably no mere matter of partiality, and therefore of petty wrangling for the better portions, but a radical difference of opinion on whether they should be admitted to the fellowship and therefore whether they really belonged to the community. Possibly such issues as the attitude to the Law and to the strict Jewish concept of purity were already involved. For the committing of this service to the Hellenistic Seven surely implies rather more than a purely external release of the leaders of the community from administrative duties.

Martha's care for her guest is described as διακονεῖν in Lk. 10:40, the narrower sense being included as in Jn. 12:2. Peter's mother-in-law cares for her guests in the same way in Mk. 1:31 and par. The word also seems to be used in this sense of the angels who ministered to Jesus after the temptation (Mk. 1:13; Mt. 4:11); their ministry consisted in bringing Him food after His period of fasting. [9]

2. The same change in evaluation as we find in respect of waiting at table applies everywhere in the NT to διακονεῖν in the wider sense of "to be serviceable." Sometimes the link with waiting at table may still be discerned, as when it is said of the women who accompany Jesus : αἵτινες διηκόνουν αὐτοῖς (or αὐτῷ) ἐκ τῶν ὑπαρχόντων αὐταῖς (Lk. 8:3). [10] Cf. also Mt. 27:55; Mk. 15:41. In Mt. 25:42-44, however, Jesus comprises under the term διακονεῖν many different activities such as giving food and drink, extending shelter, providing clothes and visiting the sick and prisoners. The term thus comes to have the full sense of active Christian love for the neighbour and as such it is a mark of true discipleship of Jesus. For what the Christian does to even the least of his fellowmen he does to the Lord Himself. [11] Here it is plain that "διακονεῖν is one of those words which presuppose a Thou, and not a Thou towards whom I may order my relationship as I please, but a Thou under whom I have placed myself as a διακονῶν." [12] In exact accord with His own attitude as expressed in Lk. 22:26 f., Jesus draws from this basic insight the demand of Mk. 10:43-45; Mt. 20:26-28 : ὃς ἂν θέλῃ μέγας γενέσθαι ἐν ὑμῖν, ἔσται ὑμῶν διάκονος, καὶ ὃς ἂν θέλῃ ἐν ὑμῖν εἶναι πρῶτος, ἔσται πάντων δοῦλος· καὶ γὰρ ὁ υἱὸς τοῦ ἀνθρώπου οὐκ ἦλθεν διακονηθῆναι ἀλλὰ διακονῆσαι καὶ δοῦναι τὴν ψυχὴν αὐτοῦ λύτρον ἀντὶ πολλῶν. Jesus consciously opposes this command to the natural order whereby the princes of the nations lord it over them and their great ones exercise authority (Mk. 10:42; Mt. 20:25). The aim of Jesus and His disciples is not to set up human orders in this world. Their concern is with the kingdom of God and the age of glory. But the way to this goal leads through suffering and death. This determines at once

---

[7] So J. Felten, *Apostelgeschichte* (1892), 138.

[8] So Wdt. Ag., 131.

[9] So Kl. Mk. on 1:13, also Schniewind NT Deutsch, I (1933), 47, though he would extend the meaning and see an allusion to the Paradise story : "Adam was expelled from Paradise by the angel ; angels are subject to the Messiah" (as in Jn. 1:51).

[10] Pr.-Bauer here translates διακονεῖν "to help someone with one's possessions."

[11] On Mt. 25:42 ff., cf. Plat. Gorg., 517d : ... ἡ πραγματεία ... καὶ περὶ τὸ σῶμα καὶ περὶ τὴν ψυχὴν ... διακονική, ... ᾗ δυνατὸν εἶναι ἐκπορίζειν, ἐὰν μὲν πεινῇ τὰ σώματα ἡμῶν, σιτία, ἐὰν δὲ διψῇ, ποτά, ἐὰν δὲ ῥιγῷ, ἱμάτια, στρώματα, ὑποδήματα, ἀλλ᾽ ὧν ἔρχεται σώματα εἰς ἐπιθυμίαν.

[12] Brandt, 71.

the attitude of all whom God calls to His kingdom. The point of suffering is to be found in the service therein accomplished. This makes it sacrificial. For the Christian, then, there is only one way to greatness. He must become the servant (διάκονος ὑμῶν), indeed, the slave of all (πάντων δοῦλος); cf. Mk. 9:35; 10:44.

This reversal of all human ideas of greatness and rank was accomplished when the Son of Man Himself came, not to be ministered unto (→ 84, in exposition of Lk. 22:26), but to minister. The new feature as compared with Lk. 22:26 is that in Mk. 10:45 and Mt. 20:28 Jesus does not stop at the picture of table service. διακονεῖν is now much more than a comprehensive term for any loving assistance rendered to the neighbour. It is understood as full and perfect sacrifice, as the offering of life which is the very essence of service, of being for others, whether in life or in death. Thus the concept of διακονεῖν achieves its final theological depth. And what is true of Christ Himself is made a command for all His disciples in Jn. 12:26 : ἐὰν ἐμοί τις διακονῇ, ἐμοὶ ἀκολουθείτω, καὶ ὅπου εἰμὶ ἐγώ, ἐκεῖ καὶ ὁ διάκονος ὁ ἐμὸς ἔσται· ἐάν τις ἐμοὶ διακονῇ, τιμήσει αὐτὸν ὁ πατήρ. It can be seen quite irrefutably from v. 25 that discipleship of Jesus Christ demands service even to death. To serve the neighbour, Christ, or God is one and the same thing. The resultant fellowship with the Father is the reward of such service.

3. This gives us at once the meaning of διακονεῖν in the community. According to 1 Pt. 4:10, every *charisma* is a gift entrusted to man with the condition that the man who has been blessed by it should serve as a good steward of the manifold gifts of God. As there is at the beginning of this train of thought (1 Pt. 4:7) an exhortation to prayer and brotherly love, so grateful regard for God and concern for one's neighbour together make the divine gift which each is to receive into a gift which is owed to the neighbour. In 1 Pt. 4:11, as in Ac. 6, the *charismata* are divided into ministry of Word and ministry of act, the latter being specifically described as διακονεῖν. This ministry is to be discharged in the power which God gives and to His glory alone. In true Christian service there can be no thought of the righteousness of works or of religious pride. It takes place both from God and to God.

The Christian has many opportunities of service. Timothy and Erastus are assistants (διακονοῦντες) of Paul in the preaching of the Gospel (Ac. 19:22). Paul would have liked to keep Onesimus with him for similar personal and material service in prison (Phlm. 13). What Onesiphorus did in Ephesus (2 Tm. 1:18) was a free service of love and not the exercise of an official diaconate, [13] in contrast to the normal usage of the Past. The searching and foretelling of the prophets was an advance service to the community (1 Pt. 1:10-12). The apostolic office is a similar service, as we see from Paul's description of the Corinthian church as ἐπιστολὴ Χριστοῦ διακονηθεῖσα ὑφ᾽ ἡμῶν (2 C. 3:3).

4. A particular service which played a great role in the life of Paul was the gathering and transmission of the collection for the saints in Jerusalem (2 C. 8:19 : ἐν τῇ χάριτι ταύτῃ τῇ διακονουμένῃ ὑφ᾽ ἡμῶν; cf. 8:20). When Paul goes to Jerusalem with this gift, he expresses its purpose in the formula : νυνὶ δὲ πορεύ- ομαι εἰς Ἱερουσαλὴμ διακονῶν τοῖς ἁγίοις (R. 15:25). When it is said of the recipients of Hebrews in Hb. 6:10 : διακονήσαντες τοῖς ἁγίοις καὶ διακονοῦντες,

---

[13] 69 al f g vg cl sy Ambst add a μοι to the διηκόνησεν, and thus make it service to Paul, as in Ac. 19:22 and Phlm. 13.

this does not mean that they rendered particular service either to Jerusalem as a whole or to outstanding individuals, e.g., the preachers of the Gospel, [14] but that they discharged the general service of love which Christians evince to one another as saints.

5. In the Past. διακονεῖν means "to discharge the office of a deacon" (→ διάκονος, 89): 1 Tm. 3:10, 13.

† **διακονία.**

διακονία denotes the activity of διακονεῖν. It occurs in the various senses of the latter both in secular Gk. and twice in the LXX : 1 Macc. 11:58 : καὶ ἀπέστειλεν αὐτῷ χρυσώματα καὶ διακονίαν (where we have to render "table vessels of gold" [1]); and Est. 6:3, 5 A : οἱ ἐκ τῆς διακονίας (B : διάκονοι).

In the NT διακονία means 1. "waiting at table," or in a rather wider sense "provision for bodily sustenance." Lk. 10:40 : ἡ δὲ Μάρθα περιεσπᾶτο περὶ πολλὴν διακονίαν. The supervision of the common meals in the early church is called διακονία καθημερινή in Ac. 6:1 (→ 85). [2]

It is also used 2. for any "discharge of service" in genuine love. Thus the house of Stephanas gave itself to the service of the saints (1 C. 16:15). Ministering love is linked with ἔργα, ἀγάπη, πίστις and ὑπομονή in Rev. 2:19. A decisive point for understanding the concept is that early Christianity learned to regard and describe as διακονία all significant activity for the edification of the community (Eph. 4:11 ff.), a distinction being made according to the mode of operation. There were διαιρέσεις διακονιῶν corresponding to the διαιρέσεις χαρισμάτων and ἐνεργημάτων according to 1 C. 12:4 ff. But all these different services were rendered to the one Lord. In each of them the believer serves not only his brother but also Christ. He is responsible for the service committed to him as a gift of grace. In general the → ἀντιλήμψεις mentioned in 1 C. 12:28 must have formed the content of these acts of service, namely, acts of care and assistance on behalf of the community. In R. 12:7 διακονία is placed between προφητεία and διδασκαλία. But even the highest Christian office, the preaching of the Gospel, is described as a ministry of the Word in Ac. 6:4. [3] Probably the original meaning is reflected in this phrase. The Word of God is offered as the bread of life. The true service of the preacher is with a view to the salvation of his brethren, to whom he must render τὴν διακονίαν τῆς καταλλαγῆς by proclaiming to them the Word of reconciliation (2 C. 5:18 f.). In this respect the angels are a model (Hb. 1:14): οὐχὶ πάντες εἰσὶν λειτουργικὰ πνεύματα εἰς διακονίαν ἀποστελλόμενα διὰ τοὺς μέλλοντας κληρονομεῖν σωτηρίαν;

Service is orientated to the Gospel. All effort to keep the Law is διακονία τοῦ θανάτου, διακονία τῆς κατακρίσεως. On the other hand, faith in the glad tidings is διακονία τοῦ πνεύματος, διακονία τῆς δικαιοσύνης (2 C. 3:7-9). These

---

[14] These are the only possibilities considered by R. Asting, *Die Heiligkeit im Urchristentum* (1930), 252.

δ ι α κ ο ν ί α. [1] Kautzsch Apkr. u. Pseudepigr., I, 68.

[2] In D* the term διακονία is repeated in an addition designed to express the view that this was an obligation of the Hebrews alone.

[3] The ministry of the Torah (תּוֹרָה שֶׁל שִׁמּוּשָׁהּ) corresponds formally to the διακονία τοῦ λόγου. This does not refer, however, to preaching, but to learning of the *halacha* through contact with scholars, Str.-B. on Ac. 6:4.

phrases coined by Paul bring out the dialectical tension in the Christian concept of service.

It can also denote 3. the "discharge of certain obligations in the community." The apostolic office is service acc. to R. 11:13; 2 C. 4:1; 6:3 f.; 11:8; Ac. 1:17, 25; 20:24 : τὴν διακονίαν, ἣν ἔλαβον παρὰ τοῦ κυρίου ᾿Ιησοῦ, διαμαρτύρασθαι τὸ εὐαγγέλιον τῆς χάριτος τοῦ θεοῦ; 21:19; 1 Tm. 1:12. So, too, is the office of the evangelist (2 Tm. 4:5), or the activity of Mark, who combines personal service and assistance with missionary work (2 Tm. 4:11). Activity in office is also in view in Col. 4:17 when Paul admonishes Archippus : βλέπε τὴν διακονίαν ἣν παρέλαβες ἐν κυρίῳ, ἵνα αὐτὴν πληροῖς, though it is uncertain whether the reference is to the office of deacon.

In keeping with Paul's use of διακονεῖν, 4. the collection for Jerusalem is described as διακονία. The apostle emphasises that this is not to be regarded merely as an external incident but as a true act of love : R. 15:30 f.; [4] 2 C. 8:1-6; 9:1, 12 f.; cf. also Ac. 11:29 f.; 12:25.

† **διάκονος.**

A. General Uses of διάκονος.

1. "The waiter at a meal," Jn. 2:5, 9.

2. "The servant of a master," Mt. 22:13 : ὁ βασιλεὺς εἶπεν τοῖς διακόνοις. In this sense the Christian is a servant of Christ, Jn. 12:26. It is part of his task, however, to serve his fellows, Mk. 9:35; 10:43; Mt. 20:26; 23:11.

3. In the figurative sense, "the servant of a spiritual power," whether good or evil, 2 C. 11:14 f.: τοῦ σατανᾶ, τῆς δικαιοσύνης; Eph. 3:6 f. and Col. 1:23 : [1] τοῦ εὐαγγελίου; Gl. 2:17: τῆς ἁμαρτίας; R. 15:8 : περιτομῆς; 2 C. 3:6 : καινῆς δια-θήκης. The action of the servant is to the benefit of the magnitude which he serves.

When it is said in R. 15:8 that Christ is a servant of the circumcision, this simply means, of course, that His work is on behalf of Israel.

More difficult is Gl. 2:17: "If, then, we who are accounted righteous in Christ are found to be sinners, is Christ a servant of sin ? By no means." "Servant" here might be

---

[4] BD*G have δωροφορία for διακονία.

δ ι ά κ ο ν ο ς. Cr.-Kö., 289; Pr.-Bauer, 288; H. Achelis in RE³, IV, 600; J. U. Seidl in H. J. Wetzer-B. Welte Kirchenlexikon² (1882 ff.), 3, 1660; J. U. Seidl, Der Diakonat in der kath. Kirche, dessen hieratische Würde und geschichtliche Entwicklung (1884); P. A. Leder, Die Diakonen der Bischöfe und Presbyter (1905); R. Sohm, Kirchenrecht, I (1892); E. Hatch, Die Gesellschaftsverfassung der christlichen Kirche im Altertum, tr. A. Harnack (1883) [The Organisation of the Early Christian Church]; A. Harnack, Entstehung u. Entwicklung der Kirchenverfassung und des Kirchenrechts in den zwei ersten Jahrhunderten (1910); H. Lietzmann, "Zur altchr. Verfassungsgeschichte," in ZwTh, 55 (1914), 97 ff.; W. Brandt, Dienst und Dienen im NT (1931), 155 ff.; L. Zscharnack, Der Dienst der Frau in den ersten Jhdten der christl. Kirche (1902); E. Goltz, Der Dienst der Frau in der christl. Kirche² (1914); A. Kalsbach, "Die altkirchliche Einrichtung der Diakonissen bis zu ihrem Er-löschen," in Röm. Quartalschrift, Suppl. 22 (1926).

[1] It is not quite certain, of course, whether the accompanying clause οὗ ἐγενόμην ἐγὼ Παῦλος διάκονος refers to τὸ εὐαγγέλιον or to the Son of God, who controls the whole line of thought from v. 13. It is worth noting that ℵ and P have κῆρυξ καὶ ἀπόστολος instead of διάκονος, while other MSS combine the expressions.

rendered "promoter." This would give us the following line of argument. In Jewish eyes everyone who does not keep the Law is a sinner (→* ἁμαρτωλός, I, 322; 325); this applies to all Gentiles, with whom Jews may not hold table fellowship. Thus, if Christ causes the Jews who follow Him to renounce the provisions of the Law, He is extending the domain of sin which embraces all the Gentiles. — Yet it is not impossible to keep to the stronger expression "servant of sin." If we do, we must interpret the saying in the light of Gl. 2:20. Christ Himself lives and acts in the man who trusts in Him. If this man is found a sinner, this applies to the Lord Himself dwelling within him, as though He were enslaved to sin. The absurdity of the conclusion naturally illustrates the falsity of the presupposition, namely, the Jewish view of sin. [2]

4. As διάκονος τοῦ εὐαγγελίου the apostle (→ ἀπόστολος, I, 437) is διάκονος Χριστοῦ (2 C. 11:23) and διάκονος θεοῦ in a very special sense, with all the troubles and sufferings and with all the responsibility of this office (2 C. 6:3 ff.). In his description of himself from this standpoint, Paul usually prefers the term δοῦλος (R. 1:1 etc.; Tt. 1:1), which expresses far more clearly the fact that he belongs wholly and utterly to Christ or to God.

5. Timothy is a "servant of God" to the degree that with the preaching of the Gospel he confirms and admonishes the faith of the Thessalonians (1 Th. 3:1-3). [3] Timothy is also called a true servant of Jesus Christ (1 Tm. 4:6). Epaphras is σύνδουλος of the apostles and διάκονος τοῦ Χριστοῦ (Col. 1:7). Tychicus is διάκονος ἐν κυρίῳ (Eph. 6:21; Col. 4:7).

6. Heathen authorities can also be called the servants of God in the discharge of their office, since they are appointed by God and have the task of maintaining God's order in the world (R. 13:1-4).

7. Paul describes himself in Col. 1:25 as a "servant of the Church" (ἐκκλησίας) in virtue of his divinely given commission. Paul and Apollos are no more than servants of both God and the Church as they use their gifts to bring the latter to faith (1 C. 3:5).

B. The Deacon as a Church Official.

1. A distinction may be made between all these general uses and the employment of the term as the "fixed designation for the bearer of a specific office" as διάκονος in the developing constitution of the Church. This is found in passages where the Vulgate has the loan-word *diaconus* instead of the *minister* used elsewhere (cf. Phil. 1:1; 1 Tm. 3:8, 12).

Members of the community who are called deacons in virtue of their regular activity are first found in Phil. 1:1, where Paul sends greetings to all the saints in Philippi σὺν ἐπισκόποις καὶ διακόνοις. Already in this phrase there emerges a decisive point for our understanding of the office, namely, that the deacons are linked with the bishops and mentioned after them. At the time of this epistle there are thus two co-ordinated offices.

We cannot gather with any certainty from this reference what constituted the special work of these officers. It is highly improbable that the reference is to two different

---

[2] Cf. H. W. Beyer in NT Deutsch, II (1933), 453 f.
[3] There are several variants of the phrase διάκονον τοῦ θεοῦ (1 Th. 3:2). D* d e 33 Ambst have σύνεργον τοῦ θεοῦ, B σύνεργον alone, and there are many combinations of διάκονος and σύνεργος. For their interrelationship, cf. Dib. Th., *ad loc.*

aspects of the work of the same men, [4] since this is supported neither by the context nor by 1 Tm. 3:1 ff., 8 ff. Nor can there be any doubt that the description of office has here become a definite designation. [5] Nevertheless, we are not told what the offices involved. Attempts have been made to deduce this from the contents of the epistle. It has often been argued that special thanks are due to the bishops and deacons for the affectionate gift which was sent to Paul in prison and which they collected. [6] This seems to be a very likely reason for the particular mention of ἐπίσκοποι and διάκονοι in this epistle. E. Lohmeyer sets this in the light of the main purpose of the epistle, namely, to strengthen the Philippians in a time of persecution, in which their leaders were in prison. As he sees it, this gives us the main reason for the special greeting to them. [7] There is no proof for this conjecture. The task of the διάκονοι can in fact be deduced only from the actual name of their office and from their later function.

That the diaconate stands in the closest relationship to the episcopate is confirmed by 1 Tm. 3:1 ff. Here an account is first given of the way in which a bishop must conduct himself (vv. 1-7), and this is followed by a list of the requirements for a deacon (vv. 8-13).

Like the bishops, deacons must be blameless and temperate, having only one wife and ruling their houses well. While the bishops must satisfy many other demands, including an aptitude for teaching, deacons are not to be doubletongued or avaricious — qualities necessary in those who have access to many homes and are entrusted with the administration of funds. Yet inward qualities are also demanded of good deacons. They are to hold the mystery of the faith with a clear conscience.

That the primary task of deacons was one of administration and practical service may be deduced a. from the use of the term for table waiters and more generally for servants ; b. from the qualities demanded of them ; c. from their relationship to the bishop ; and d. from what we read elsewhere in the NT concerning the gift and task of διακονία.

Appeal is frequently made to Ac. 6 in explanation of the rise of the diaconate, though the term διάκονος is not actually used. On this view, the deacons undertake practical service as distinct from the ministry of the Word. It is to be noted, however, that the Seven are set alongside the Twelve as representatives of the Hellenists, and that they take their place with the evangelists and apostles in disputing, preaching and baptising. This fact shows (→ 85) that the origin of the diaconate is not to be found in Ac. 6. It is possible, however, that ideas gained from the existing diaconate influenced the author when he gave its present form to his rather puzzling source concerning the relationship of the Seven to the Twelve. If this is so, Ac. 6 may be regarded as indirect evidence concerning the diaconate.

If we ask concerning the origin of the diaconate, we must start with its relationship to the episcopate. It is mentioned with this in the earliest sources, and was never separated from it. The διάκονος is not merely the servant of the church, but also of the bishop. Two problems arise : a. how two integrated offices came into existence ; and b. how the Greek words ἐπίσκοπος and διάκονος came to be used to describe these offices.

---

[4] Haupt Gefbr., ad loc.
[5] As opposed to Loofs, ThStKr, 63 (1890), 628 f.
[6] So finally Brandt, 167 f.
[7] Loh. Phil., 12.

a. There were two offices in the Jewish synagogues. Conduct of worship was entrusted to the רֹאשׁ הַכְּנֶסֶת, the ἀρχισυνάγωγος, who was accompanied by the חַזַּן הַכְּנֶסֶת, always translated ὑπηρέτης and never διάκονος in Greek. If any model is to be sought for the Christian offices of bishop and deacon, this is where we shall find it. It must be remembered, however, that the activity of the ἀρχισυνάγωγος and the ὑπηρέτης is restricted to worship. The direction of the synagogue is in the hands of the elders. There are also collectors of alms (גַּבָּאֵי צְדָקָה) who for their part have no connexion with the conduct of worship. [8] Thus we have in the Jewish community many points of initiation for the Christian offices of bishop and deacon, but neither here nor in paganism are there any exact models which are simply copied. The creative power of the early Church was strong enough to fashion its own offices for the conduct of congregational life and divine worship.

b. The same is true of the terms adopted. These arose in the world of Gentile Christianity, though Jewish Christianity contributed the term πρεσβύτερος. [9] Yet in pre-Christian Greek we never find the words ἐπίσκοπος and διάκονος used in the Christian sense, whether individually or in the distinctive Christian relationship. Early Christianity took over words which were predominantly secular in their current usage and which had not yet been given any sharply defined sense. It linked these words with offices which were being fashioned in the community, and thus gave them a new sense which was so firmly welded with the activity thereby denoted that in all languages they have been adopted as loan-words to describe Christian office-bearers. [10]

The secular sense of διάκονος corresponds to the meanings of διακονέω and διακονία. It denotes one who waits at table, Xenoph. Hier., 4, 1 f.; Demosth., 59, 33; with οἰνοχόος and μάγειρος, Hdt., IV, 71 f.; Athen., X, 17; with ἀγοραστής, Xenoph. Mem., I, 5, 2; or "messenger" with ἄγγελος, κῆρυξ and σπονδοφόρος, Poll. Onom., 8, 137; Soph. Phil., 497; "servant," Aristot. Eth. Nic., VII, 7, p. 1149a, 27; Luc. Alex., 5; τυράννου, Aesch. Prom., 944; "steward," Demosth., 59, 42; Aristoph. Av., 70 ff.; "assistant helmsman," Xen. Oec., 8, 10 and 14; "baker," "cook," "wine-steward" as σωμάτων θεραπευταί, Plat. Gorg., 518bc; "statesman," Plat. Gorg., 518b; of a woman "maid," Demosth., 24, 197; 47, 52. It is rare in the LXX, and occurs only in the secular sense. In Est. 1:10; 2:2; 6:3, 5 it is used for the courtiers and eunuchs of the king (Heb. מְשָׁרֵת). Acc. to Prv. 10:4, the fool shall be the servant of the wise. [11] In 4 Macc. 9:17 a prisoner addresses spearmen who torture him : ὦ μιεροὶ διάκονοι. The word is first used in relation to God by Joseph. on the one side and Epict. on the other. Joseph. also has the customary meanings in Ant., 6, 52; 7, 201 and 224; 11, 188 and 255. The word corresponds here to the new Heb. שַׁמָּשׁ. Elisha ἦν Ἠλίου μαθητὴς καὶ διάκονος, Ant., 8, 354, just as the rabbinic pupil is the servant of his master. But Joseph. can also call himself διάκονος θεοῦ (Bell., 3, 354) or τῆς φωνῆς τοῦ θεοῦ (Bell., 4, 626) on account of the revelation given to him concerning the reign of Vespasian. [12] In Epict. we often find the idea that the cynic is the servant of God. Thus Diogenes is the διά-

---

[8] Schürer, II⁴ (1901), 513 f.; Str.-B., IV, 145 ff.; II, 643.

[9] Cf. H. Lietzmann's basic investigation in ZwTh, 55 (1914), 97 ff.

[10] The extent of Paul's contribution to this terminology is hard to determine. It is certainly found in him ; and it is in his writings that we first find reference both to the official obligations κυβερνήσεις and ἀντιλήμψεις (1 C. 12:28) and to the office-bearers (Phil. 1:1). Yet the varying terminology indicates a state of fluidity rather than fixity. Cf. the equations προϊστάμενοι/ἐπίσκοποι and κοπιῶντες/διάκονοι, 1 Th. 5:12.

[11] Prv. 10:4 a only in the LXX.

[12] Schlatter, Wie sprach Josephus von Gott? (1910), 14.

κονος of Zeus in Diss., III, 24, 65; cf. III, 26, 28; IV, 7, 20. Either in description of calling, or with reference to activities in sacral unions, διάκονος often occurs on inscriptions, mostly in lists of similar titles. Thus in 3rd century (B.C.) Troiza it occurs after ἱαρο]μνάμονες and μάγειρος (IG, IV, 774) or between γραμματεῖς, κᾶρυξ and παῖδες (824). Again, a 1st or 2nd century (B.C.) list of names from Acarnania contains the following : πρύτανις, ἑστία, ὑποπρυτάνιες, μάντις, αὐλητάς, ἱεροφόρος, μάγειρος, διάκονος, ἀρχοινόχους, ἱεροθύτας (IG, IX, 1, 486). And there is a similar list on the pillar of a temple to Apollo dating from at least the time of Christ's birth (IG, IX, 1, 487 and CIG, II, Add., 1793b, p. 982). This is probably how Inscr. Magn., 109 should also run. There can be no doubt that the reference is to cultic actions, sacrifices, consecrations etc. But the work of the διάκονοι obviously remained the same, i.e., the serving of food, since they are always mentioned after the cooks. Thus H. Lietzmann can describe as a cellarer's guild the κοινὸν τῶν διακόνων which acc. to CIG, II, 1800 dedicates an inscription to Egyptian deities. [13] Yet this is obviously a sacral rather than a secular guild, as we can see from the fact that a priest stands at the head. Similarly the inscr. from Metropolis in Lydia (CIG, II, 3037) mentions male and female deacons along with priests and priestesses. According to Inscr. Magn., 217 κομάκτορες, κήρυκες καὶ διάκονοι took part in the dedication of a statue of Hermes. [14]

From these examples we can see that the διάκονος might have a cultic function. But it is a long way from this pagan conception of the deacon to the Christian. If the inscriptions teach us anything, it is that the original meaning of διακονεῖν ("to wait at table") persisted. In accordance with the saying and example of Jesus, early Christianity made this the symbol of all loving care for others. Here is the root of the living connexion between ethical reflection on service in the community and the actual diaconate. Again, the persistent sense of waiting at table is reflected in the fact that the Christian office had its origin in the common meal at the heart of the life of the community, namely, the Lord's Supper. Only in this way can we understand the later history of the diaconate, which has always consisted in assistance at divine service as well as in the external service of the community.

With the episcopate, the diaconate achieved its full stature only with the passing of the first, charismatic group of apostles, prophets and teachers. The capacity for diaconate was also a gift (1 C. 12:28). It is worth noting, however, that ἀντιλήμψεις and κυβερνήσεις are not among the charismata which in the next verse are stated not to be given to all members of the community. To exercise these offices the Christian needs to be elected and called rather than specially endowed by God. The transition from the first group of office-bearers to the second may be seen in 1 Cl., 42, 1 ff. according to the sequence : God, Christ, the apostles and the bishops appointed by them. Clement is obviously conscious of a break in the development at the latter point, and he therefore supports the institution of bishops and deacons by an appeal to the widely divergent text of Is. 60:17: καταστήσω τοὺς ἐπισκόπους αὐτῶν ἐν δικαιοσύνῃ καὶ τοὺς διακόνους αὐτῶν ἐν πίστει. The origin of this rendering, and its significance for the history of the development of the diaconate, have not yet been elucidated. An interesting point is that Cl. derives both episcopate and diaconate from the one root. In Did., 15, 1 the summons to elect bishops and deacons is already self-evident. It is also stated that these succeed to the ministry of prophets and teachers. Cf. also Herm. v., 3, 5, 1; s., 9, 26, 2. The position of deacons naturally changes with the rise of monepiscopacy. They be-

---

[13] ZwTh, 55 (1914), 107.
[14] Cf. also IG, II, 5, 768c; III, 10; XII, 7, 515; Bursians Jahresberichte, 11 (1883), III, 74; C. Michel, Recueil des Inscr., 4 (1901), 1226; P. Flor., 121, 3.

come much more subordinate in relation to the bishop. At the same time, a clear distinction arises between deacons and presbyters. In 1 Cl., 44 presbyter is still an imprecise term for the leaders of the community, but now three distinct offices of bishop, presbyter and deacon emerge in this order (Ign. Mg., 2, 1; 6, 1). Thus deacons are to have in the church an honour similar to that of Christ, bishops to that of God (Tr., 3, 1). This gives us the basis of the later hierarchy, though the development was slow. Deacons are assistants, representatives and often successors of the bishops, e.g., Eleutherus in relation to Anicetus. [15] Shortly before 250 Fabian divided Rome into seven districts, each set under a deacon. [16] Explicit directions concerning the office and consecration of deacons may be found in the Hippol. Canons, the Syrian Didasc. and the Apostol. Constitutions. These bring to an end the development of the diaconate in the early Church.

2. Alongside the deacons there were also deaconesses. Their history begins with R. 16:1 where Paul describes Phoebe as τὴν ἀδελφὴν ἡμῶν, οὖσαν διάκονον τῆς ἐκκλησίας τῆς ἐν Κεγχρεαῖς. It is, of course, an open question whether he is referring to a fixed office or simply to her services on behalf of the community. Similarly, there is no agreement whether 1 Tm. 3:11 refers to the wives of deacons or to deaconesses. It is indisputable, however, that an order of deaconesses did quickly arise in the Church. [17] A particular part was played here by widows who, on the strength of their chaste conduct on the one side and their loving service on the other, already received official recognition in 1 Tm. 5:3 ff.

The relationship between widows and virgins varied in different parts of the ancient world. Both groups had ecclesiastical functions with respect to women members of the Church. In the East the widows were primarily responsible, and though from the time of the Syr. Didasc. there was an independent office of deaconesses, this fell into decay in the early Middle Ages. In the West an independent order of deaconesses never developed in the Roman Church.

Beyer

διακρίνω, διάκρισις → κρίνω.
διαλλάσσω → ἀλλάσσω, I, 253.

| διαλέγομαι, διαλογίζομαι, |
| διαλογισμός |

---

† διαλέγομαι

In classical and Hellenistic Gk. διαλέγομαι is mostly used for "converse" or "discussion": Hom. Il., 11, 407; Hdt., III, 50 f.; Aristoph. Nu., 425; Xenoph. Mem., I, 6, 1; Plato Ap., 19d; 21c etc. In Socrates, Plato and Aristotle there is developed the art of persuasion and demonstration either in the form of question and answer (Socrates), the establishment of the idea by pure thought (Plato), or the investigation of the ultimate foundations of demonstration and knowledge (Aristotle). Because διαλέγεσθαι is the only way in which Greek philosophy can reach the λόγος or idea, it is of central importance. Cf. materially: Plat. Phaed., 99e and linguistically: Plat. Men., 75d; Resp., V, 454a; VII, 537cde; VII, 539c. In Polybius διαλέγομαι is predominantly used for a. "to confer," "to negotiate," e.g., IV, 29, 2; V, 103, 2 etc.; b. for individual speech or

---

[15] Eus. Hist. Eccl., IV, 22, 3.
[16] *Liber pontificalis,* I, 148 (Duchesne).
[17] Cf. H. Kalsbach, *Die kirchliche Einrichtung der Diakonissen* (1926).

representation in such negotiation (IX, 31, 7; XVIII, 9, 4), for the address or speech, e.g., of a general to his soldiers (III, 111, 11; IV, 26, 8; VIII, 31, 3, cf. Diod. S., XVI, 23, 4; c. of the speaking of a language : I, 80, 6 (Punic). In Epict. Diss. διαλέγομαι is customarily used for philosophical dialogue, debate or disputation (I, 5, 6; 9, 23; II, 8, 12; 13, 21; 24, 15; III, 21, 4; 22, 84; IV, 1, 116 and 164; IV, 4, 21) and the results thereby achieved (I, 17, 5; II, 25, 2). It is distinguished from → ἀναγιγνώσκειν, "giving a lecture" (III, 23, 16 and 37). Cf. Polyb., XII, 26c, 2 : ἐν 'Ακαδημείᾳ διαλέγονται. But in Epict., too, it can have the simple meaning of "to speak to someone" (Diss., I, 4, 13; cf. II, 13, 24), and we can see from III, 24, 49 and IV, 1, 157 that he does not restrict the expression to philosophical discourse.

In the LXX, where διαλέγεσθαι is esp. used for דבר pi, the simple meaning a. "to speak or to say to" is predominant, as in 1 Esr. 8:45; Est. D 6:15; Sir. 14:20; Is. 63:1 (of the divine promise). But we also find the sense b. "to treat with someone," as in Ex. 6:27; 2 Macc. 11:20; cf. Ep. Ar., 40. Only very rarely does it mean "to contend with," as in Ju. 8:1: διελέξαντο πρὸς αὐτὸν ἰσχυρῶς, of the charge of the men of Ephraim against Gideon (רִיב). In Joseph. there are 74 occurrences. Of these a. 49 refer to "discussion" (e.g., Ant., 7, 349; 16, 221; Bell., 6, 412 : διελέχθη πρὸς τοὺς φίλους), and 23 of these to official political or military "parleys" (e.g., Ant., 12, 416; Bell., 4, 14, as Polyb. a.). But Joseph. can also use the term διαλέγεσθαι b. for an important and impressive or sometimes obstinate "statement" or "contention" without any particular emphasis on discussion (Ant., 7, 260; 15, 168; Bell., 1, 447), and esp. for the "speech" of a king or general or other important personage to the people (Ant., 8, 111; 15, 126 etc.), or for the solemn "last words" of a dying man (Ant., 7, 383; 12, 285). Related to b. is the use of διαλέγεσθαι c. for the declared purpose of an author "to treat of something" or "to debate with someone" : Ap., 1, 58; cf. Polyb., VII, 11, 1; XVI, 14, 1; Diod. S., XIII, 1, 1; Philo Spec. Leg., II, 1. In only one passage d. does the word specifically mean "disputation," namely, Ant., 7, 278 : πρὸς ἀλλήλους διαλεχθέντων. In Philo there are 25 examples. Of these a. 18 denote "conversation," as in Abr., 223, the term sometimes being used of God speaking with others, e.g., Sacr. AC, 12; Fug., 69. b. There are 6 references to the "speech" of God, of νοῦς, of Scripture, of the Law, without any special emphasis on dialogue, cf. Leg. All., I, 101, 104; III, 118; Fug., 76; Ebr., 101; Spec. Leg., I, 194. c. In one instance the meaning is simply "human speech" : Det. Pot. Ins., 48.

From this review it may be seen that in the Jewish Greek of the Hellenistic period διαλέγεσθαι is used not merely for "conversation" or "negotiation" but quite frequently for "speech" in the sense of an "address," as already in Polybius etc.

In the New Testament there is no instance of the classical use of διαλέγομαι in the philosophical sense. In the sphere of revelation there is no question of reaching the idea through dialectic. What is at issue is the obedient and percipient acceptance of the Word spoken by God, which is not an idea, but the comprehensive declaration of the divine will which sets all life in the light of divine truth. διαλέγομαι occurs in three senses in the NT.

1. In Hb. 12:5 it signifies God's "address" of encouragement (as to sons), for which there are parallels in Is. 63:1 LXX and the instances cited under Philo b. (→ supra).

2. In Ac. διαλέγεσθαι with the dat., or with πρός τινα, or sometimes absol., is used of Paul's addresses in the synagogues (17:2, 17; 18:4, 19), in the temple (24:12), in the school of Tyrannus (19:9), and to the church in Troas (20:7, 9). There is here no reference to "disputation," but to the "delivering of religious lectures or sermons." The only relevant parallels are in Hellenistic Judaism rather than Greek philosophy. What is at issue is the address which any qualified member

of a synagogue might give.[1] Linguistic parallels may be found in Polyb., Diod. S. and Jos., while a material parallel is offered by the διδάσκειν ἐν ταῖς συναγωγαῖς of Mt. 4:23; Mk. 1:21 etc.

3. In Mt. 9:34 the πρὸς ἀλλήλους διελέχθησαν of the disciples on the way indicates "disputing" as in Ju. 8:1 LXX (→ 94) and Jos. Ant., 7, 278 (→ 94), where πρός is also used. In Jd. 9 there is reference to the "disputation" between Michael and the devil about the body of Moses, greater force being given to the term by the addition of διακρινόμενος.

† διαλογίζομαι.

A. διαλογίζομαι in the Greek and Hellenistic World.

In the first instance there are two meanings which treat διαλογίζομαι as a composite of διά and λογίζομαι "to reckon," "to consider."

1. The sense "to balance accounts" (Demosth., 52, 3 with πρός τινα; P. Greci e Latini, V, 510, 10 [3rd cent. B.C.]; pass. Ditt. Syll.[3], 241, C 127 [Delph., 4th cent. B.C.]) is not found in the NT. It is, however, related to the "reckon as" of 2 Βασ. 19:19, except that the word is here used for the λογίζομαι normally found in such a case. In the LXX διαλογίζομαι, like λογίζομαι, is always a translation of חשׁב kal or pi. The word is not found in Joseph.

2. It mostly has the sense of "to ponder," "to consider." Plat. Soph., 231c: πρὸς ἡμᾶς αὐτοὺς διαλογισώμεθα; Polyb., XI, 2, 5; Philo Spec. Leg., I, 213 : διαλογιζόμενος ἐν ἐμαυτῷ ταῦτα. With a philosophical colouring, Ep. Ar., 212: πῶς ἂν τὰ κάλλιστα διαλογίζοιτο; 256 : philosophy is τὸ καλῶς διαλογίζεσθαι πρὸς ἔκαστα τῶν συμβαινόντων. The LXX uses διαλογίζεσθαι for "to reflect on something" : a. in the wholly neutral sense of 2 Βασ. 14:14 A : διαλογιζόμενος λογισμούς, "to consider something" ; ψ 76:5 : ἡμέρας ἀρχαίας, "to consider the days of old" ; ψ 118:59 : "to consider the ways of God"; 4 Macc. 8:11 : "to remember." In 2 Macc. 12:43 V ὑπὲρ ἀναστάσεως διαλογιζομένους means that the sin offering acquires its significance in relation to the resurrection. For the most part, however, the word is used in the LXX b. in the sense of "considering evil or an evil design or stratagem" : ψ 9:22; 20:11; 34:20; 35:4 אAR; 139:8; Prv. 16:30; 17:12: κακά; 1 Macc. 11:8: λογισμοὺς πονηρούς. It is worth noting that in Ἰερ. 27 (50):45 A (B al) διαλογίζεσθαι can be used for God's planning of His judgments.

3. In a third sense διαλογίζεσθαι is used very much like διαλέγεσθαι, with a hint of the derivation from διάλογος. In this case, it means a. "to debate," or sometimes "to engage in philosophical discussion or investigation" : Xenoph. Mem., III, 5, 1: περί τινος, Diog. L., VII, 46 (v. Arnim, II, 39, 35): ὀρθῶς διαλέγεσθαι καὶ διαλογίζεσθαι. Cf. Vett. Val., VI, 1, p. 245, 26 trans. : διαλογίζεσθαι αἱρέσεις, "to discuss something." b. Combining 1. and 3a. the word can thus be used as an official technical term, particularly in Egypt. pap., for "to hold a convention,"[1] over which the governor or his representative presides and which is for the purpose of reviewing the financial or administrative services. After the Roman order for conventions these revisions were also placed in the hands of the convention judge, so that the word took on a judicial as well as an administrative sense, being used specifically for the δικαιοδοσία of conventional activity, with the whole district as the object. This applied even before the time of Diocletian.

δ ι α λ έ γ ο μ α ι. [1] Cf. Schürer, II, 535; J. Hamburger, Real-Enc. für Bibel u. Talmud, II (1883), s.v., "Predigt."

δ ι α λ ο γ ί ζ ο μ α ι. [1] APF, IV, 368 ff.; Preisigke Fachwörter and Wört., s.v.

B. διαλογίζομαι in the NT.

Here two meanings demand consideration.

1. The first is "to ponder," "to consider." This sense emerges most clearly and indisputably in passages in Mk. and Lk. where ἐν ταῖς καρδίαις is added. Mk. 2:6 is an example ; shortly afterwards in Mk. 2:8 we have ἐν ἑαυτοῖς instead, but the use of ἐν ταῖς καρδίαις in the question raised in this verse permits this alternative without misunderstanding. Reference may also be made to Lk. 3:15; 5:22. Only when the sing. διελογίζετο excludes conversation with others, as in Lk. 1:29 with respect to Mary's meditation on the greeting of the angel, or in Lk. 12:17 in relation to the rich fool : διελογίζετο ἐν ἑαυτῷ λέγων, is it unnecessary to add the more precise "in his heart." The reason for the addition is that these two Hellenistic Evangelists are both familiar with the current second sense of "conversation" or "discussion." It is indeed noteworthy that the second meaning is found only in these Evangelists. By contrast, διαλογίζεσθαι ἐν ἑαυτοῖς or παρ' ἑαυτοῖς is used in Mt. 16:7, 8; 21:25 for "to reflect," "to meditate."

2. In a second group of sayings διαλογίζεσθαι is used for "to converse or to discuss with," in the same sense as διαλέγεσθαι but with a greater stress on the element of discussion. These sayings occur only in Mk. and Lk. Mk. 8:16: πρὸς ἀλλήλους; cf. 17; 9:33, where the τί ἐν τῇ ὁδῷ διελογίζεσθε is later explained in v. 34 : πρὸς ἀλλήλους γὰρ διελέχθησαν ἐν τῇ ὁδῷ. The διελογίζοντο πρὸς ἑαυτοὺς λέγοντες of Mk. 11:31 also differs characteristically from the parallel in Mt. 21:25 : ἐν or παρ' ἑαυτοῖς, and undoubtedly denotes discussion among themselves. Similarly, the διελογίζοντο πρὸς ἀλλήλους λέγοντες of Lk. 20:14 with reference to the labourers in the vineyard unquestionably has the sense of discussion, the par. in Mk. 12:7 and Mt. 21:38 simply having εἶπαν (-ον). From what has been said, it seems most likely that the doubtful passage in Lk. 5:21: ἤρξαντο διαλογίζεσθαι λέγοντες denotes both reflection and discussion (cf. λέγοντες), for otherwise Lk. would surely have introduced the restrictive ἐν ταῖς καρδίαις in this verse rather than in v. 22. In v. 22 the One who can read the heart thus traces back the external utterance to the internal source.[2] It is interesting to see in the usage of the Evangelists how those who are closest to Hellenism give evidence of a sharper ear for the ambiguity of διαλογίζεσθαι to Greeks, to whom it might suggest "dialogue" or even the "convention" as well as "reflection."

---

† **διαλογισμός.**

A. διαλογισμός in the Greek and Hellenistic World.

This word is fairly common in Polyb. and the LXX, but does not occur at all in Josephus or Philo. In the LXX it is used for מַחֲשָׁבָה, elsewhere translated λογισμός. In ψ 138:20 it is the rendering of מְזִמָּה, in ψ 138:2 B of רֵעַ, and frequently in Da. Θ of רַעְיוֹן.

1. The sense of "reckoning" is already found in Demosth., 36, 23; cf. Pap. Revenue Laws of Ptolemy Philadelphus (ed. B. Grenfell, 1896), 17, 17 (3rd cent. B.C.); IG, V (I), 1432, 6 (Messene).[1] This usage has obviously influenced Sir. 40:29 א: οὐκ ἔστιν

---

[2] Cf. Zn. Lk., ad loc.

δ ι α λ ο γ ι σ μ ό ς. [1]Cf. Ostraka, I, 494, 622; S. Witkowski, *Epistulae privatae Graecae*² (1911), 52. APF, IV, 368 ff.; for further lit., cf. Preisigke Fachw., *s.v.*

αὐτοῦ ὁ βίος ἐν διαλογισμῷ ζωῆς (AB λογισμῷ): "(his) life is not to be counted (למנות), for a life," but it is not reflected in the NT.

2. The most common sense of the term is a. "deliberation," "reflection" : Ps.-Plat. Ax., 367a : φροντίδες καὶ διαλογισμοί; Strabo, V, 3 and 7; Polyb., III, 61, 6; XVIII, 15, 6; Ep. Ar., 252, 255: πράσσειν μετὰ διαλογισμοῦ; Ju. 5:15 'A. Significant in relation to the NT sense of "questioning" is Sir. 40:2, where there is reference to "apprehension" (together with "fear of heart"). Even more significant is Sir. 36(33):5, where it is said of the fool : ὡς ἄξων στρεφόμενος ὁ διαλογισμὸς αὐτοῦ, "his inconstant thoughts are like a rolling axletree." b. It is also used for "thoughts," in the first instance neutrally for any human thoughts, as in ψ 138:2; Wis. 7:20: the διαλογισμοί of men as that which distinguishes them from other creatures in the universe ; Ep. Ar., 216 : to direct one's thoughts on something ; Sir. 13:26 : troubled thoughts ; Da. 2:29; 4:16 etc. anxious thoughts. Important as par. to the NT are the διαλογισμοί in the καρδία of Galen (v. Arnim, II, 242, 7 and 17; cf. with 241, 30 and 40); Da. Θ 2:30 : οἱ διαλογισμοὶ τῆς καρδίας. For the formula "evil thoughts," cf. ψ 55:5 : πάντες οἱ διαλογισμοὶ αὐτῶν εἰς κακόν; cf. also Is. 59:7; Jer. 4:14; Test. Jud. 14:3 : διαλογισμοὶ ῥυπαροί "filthy (adulterous) thoughts" ; ψ 93:11: διαλογισμοὶ μάταιοι. But the LXX also uses the word for "God's thoughts" : ψ 91:5 (also Σ), Is. 55:8 'Α Σ Θ. c. In Polyb. and the LXX it is also frequently used for "design" or "plan" : Polyb., III, 16, 7; 17, 8; XVIII, 10, 3; "evil project" ψ 145:4; Lam. 3:60 f.; Da. ΘΑ 11:24; 1 Macc. 2:63. It is also used for "God's plans and resolves" in 'Ιερ. 27(50):45 A; ψ 39:5 ABS and Σ.

3. In the sense of "deliberation" or "discussion" (→ διαλογίζεσθαι, 95) it is found in Plut. Apophth. (Alex.), 12 (II, 180c); Epict. Diss., I, 9, 10 : διαλογισμοὺς διαλογίζεσθαι, "to discuss" ; Sir. 9:15 : μετὰ συνετῶν ἔστω ὁ διαλογισμός σου of "instructive conversation."

4. It can also be a technical term for "convention" along the lines of διαλογίζεσθαι (→ 95). BGU, 226, 22 (99 A.D.): τὸν τοῦ νομοῦ διαλογισμόν. P. Oxy., II, 294, 1 (22 A.D.). [2]

5. Finally, it is worth noting that as early as the 2nd cent. B.C. διαλογισμός can be used for judicial investigation and decision : P. Tebt., I, 27, 35; P. Leid. B, I, 13. Thus in Sir. 27:5 : πειρασμὸς ἀνθρώπου ἐν διαλογισμῷ αὐτοῦ, the reference is not to speech, but figuratively to enquiry and examination.

B. διαλογισμός in the NT.

1. The sense of "evil thoughts" is predominant in the NT. Thus in Lk. 2:35 we have reference to the revealing of the thoughts of many hearts in the divine judgment ; or in Mk. 7:21; Mt. 15:19 to the evil thoughts which proceed from the heart ; or in Lk. 5:22; 6:8 to Jesus' perception of the hostile thoughts of the Pharisees ; or in Lk. 9:47 to the ambitious thoughts of the disciples. The ἐματαιώθησαν ἐν τοῖς διαλογισμοῖς αὐτῶν of R. 1:21, as also 1 C. 3:20 (μάταιοι), is taken from ψ 93:11. In view of the more flexible LXX usage, it is striking that the NT uses διαλογισμός only in the negative sense for evil thoughts or anxious reflection. This shows how strong is the conviction that the sinful nature of man extends to his thinking and indeed to his very heart.

2. It can also be used for "anxious reflection" or "doubt." Torturing doubts are denoted in Lk. 24:38. In R. 14:1 : μὴ εἰς διακρίσεις διαλογισμῶν there is to be no disputing about trifles. Similarly, the command in Phil. 2:14 : πάντα ποιεῖτε χωρὶς γογγυσμῶν καὶ διαλογισμῶν, refers to murmuring and doubt. In 1 Tm.

---

[2] Cf. further Preisigke Wört., s.v. and Liddell-Scott, s.v.

2:8 : χωρὶς ὀργῆς καὶ διαλογισμοῦ,[3] the translation "without wrath or disputing"[4] yields good sense, but διαλογισμός does not have to be contention. We thus do better to follow the linguistic instinct of the Greek exegetes[5] and interpret διαλογισμός as doubt or questioning. This also has the advantage of giving a wider range to the admonition.

3. In Lk. 9:46 : εἰσῆλθεν δὲ διαλογισμὸς ἐν αὐτοῖς, the word might be rendered "thought," but it seems better to think in terms of "discussion" when we remember that Lk. likes to add καρδία to διαλογισμός as well as to διαλογίζεσθαι when he is thinking of purely inward deliberation. In v. 47 there is a similar tracing of the outward expression to the inward thought as in Lk. 5:22 compared with v. 21 (→ 96).

4. The κριταὶ διαλογισμῶν πονηρῶν of Jm. 2:4 (→ 97) are judges who reach "bad decisions." The gen. is used Hebraically as an adj. There are many examples to justify us in accepting the more precise "decisions" rather than the linguistically possible "deliberations."

Schrenk

διαμαρτύρομαι → μαρτυρέω.
διανόημα, διάνοια → νοέω.

† διασπορά

This has almost become a loan-word. It refers in the first instance to the Jewish dispersion, i.e., to the scattered Jews (διασπορά from διασπείρειν, "to scatter," used in its general sense in Ac. 8:1, 4; 11:19) living outside Palestine. It has then come to have a rather wider application to any religious or national religious minority living in the territory of another religious or political society. We might thus speak of an Evangelical *diaspora* among Roman Catholic Christians or *vice versa*. Again, we might speak of a *diaspora* of one national group of Evangelicals among others.[1] Yet primarily the term is not linked with history generally but with the history of salvation. Beyond the general religious sense it has a specific biblical and theological meaning.[2]

A. διασπορά outside the NT.

1. Outside the Greek Bible (OT and NT), and Jewish and Christian Greek writings, διασπορά is found only in Plutarch : Suav. Viv. Epic., 27 (II, 1105a), i.e., within a philosophical context; it is said of Epicurus that he τὴν διάλυσιν τῆς ψυχῆς (made the dissolution of the soul) εἰς κενὸν καὶ ἀτόμους διασπορὰν ποιῶν (into a disintegration into empty space and atoms). To the same context belongs one of the "Christian" passages : Cl. Al. Prot., IX, 88, 3 : ἡ δὲ ἐκ πολλῶν ἕνωσις ἐκ πολυφωνίας καὶ διασπορᾶς ἁρμονίαν λαβοῦσα θεϊκὴν μία γίνεται συμφωνία. In this work of

[3] διαλογισμῶν : א c GH 33 424** 1908 Orig Eus Bas Hier.
[4] De Wette, B. Weiss, Dib.
[5] Chrys., Theophylact., Thdrt.
δ ι α σ π ο ρ ά. [1] RGG², *s.v.*
[2] For this reason, it is hard to understand why an expression of such theological importance is not treated in Cr.-Kö.

pedagogy and religious philosophy the author is summoning men to hasten to salvation and new birth in order that "we, the many, should be knit into one body in conformity with the unity of the single essence (i.e., the divine being); let us hasten, and by well-doing attain to a similar unity as we strive towards the good monad." This ethical direction is grounded on the statement already quoted in Greek: "The unity which consists of many moves from multiplicity and dispersion to divine harmony, and thus becomes a single symphony." The Logos is here seen to be the one Leader and Teacher. Something of the same usage is also to be found in Philo, except that he is in some sense influenced at this point by Judaism and should thus be considered only in the light of the specifically Jewish understanding.

2. διασπορά occurs most frequently in the LXX. In all the 12 passages concerned it is a technical term for the "dispersion of the Jews among the Gentiles," and *abstractum pro concreto* for "the Jews as thus scattered." The question of the Heb. equivalent is fairly complicated. In Dt. 30:4 ἡ διασπορά σου is the rendering of נִדַּחֲךָ (נדח niph "expelled, driven out"); and in Neh. 1:9 ἡ διασπορὰ ὑμῶν of נִדַּחֲכֶם. In both these passages, which show some literal agreement, the later restoration to the land of the fathers is contrasted with the present dispersion. In ψ 146:2 τὰς διασπορὰς τοῦ 'Ισραήλ is the equivalent of נִדְחֵי יִשְׂרָאֵל. In all these three passages the Heb. means the same as the Greek, but there is no technical term in the Mas. The same sense is present without any Heb. original in Jdt. 5:19: καὶ νῦν ἐπιστρέψαντες ἐπὶ τὸν Θεὸν αὐτῶν ἀνέβησαν ἐκ τῆς διασπορᾶς οὗ διεσπάρησαν ἐκεῖ; and also 2 Macc. 1:27: ἐπισυνάγαγε τὴν διασπορὰν ἡμῶν. Cf. Ps. Sol. 8:34: συνάγαγε τὴν διασπορὰν 'Ισραήλ. But we also find the same sense with a different Heb. original in Dt. 28:25: ἔσῃ διασπορά (A: ἐν διασπορᾷ) ἐν πάσαις βασιλείαις: Mas. זַעֲוָה, which means "unsettlement," "ill usage," or even "object of terror."[3] Cf. also 'Ιερ. 41:17 (= Jer. 34:17): δώσω ὑμᾶς εἰς διασπορὰν πάσαις ταῖς βασιλείαις τῆς γῆς (= ... לְזַעֲוָה ...);[4] Is. 49:6: τὴν διασπορὰν τοῦ 'Ισραὴλ ἐπιστρέψαι: Mas.: נְצִירֵי יִשְׂרָאֵל (or נְצוּרֵי, נְצִירֵי), which means "the preserved" of Israel. Da. 12:2: (ἀναστήσονται) οἱ δὲ εἰς διασπορὰν καὶ αἰσχύνην αἰώνιον: Mas. חֲרָפוֹת, plur. of חֶרְפָּה "reproach," "ignominy." There is a slight verbal connexion between the LXX and the Mas. in Jer. 15:7, where the διασπερῶ αὐτοὺς ἐν διασπορᾷ corresponds to וָאֶזְרֵם בְּמִזְרֶה ("I will fan them with a fan"). In Jer. 13:14 א* has διασπορᾶς for διαφθορᾶς. It is hard to understand why ἐν τῇ διασπορᾷ should have penetrated into the title of ψ 138 in many texts. — This review makes it plain that there is no Heb. technical term corresponding to the very obvious technical use of the Greek διασπορά.

The Heb. term which corresponds to διασπορά is גּוֹלָה or גָּלוּת, the Aram. גָּלוּ, emphatic גָּלוּתָא.[5] All three words occur in Heb. OT and Rabbinic writings, and in the pregnant sense of the process of "leading away," "deportation," or "exile," or of the state of those "led away," "deported" or "exiled," they find the following equivalents in the LXX : → αἰχμαλωσία (which is also used for שְׁבִי, cf. Eph. 4:8 = ψ 67:18), ἀποικία, ἀποικισμός, μετοικεσία, παροικία (πάροικος, παροικεῖν) (on these → οἶκος).

---

[3] BHK 2,3 suggests וְעֵה on the basis of Is. 28:19. When Luther translates Dt. 28:25: "Thou shalt be scattered among all the nations on earth," he is following the Vulgate (*dispergaris per omnia regna terrae*) as a daughter translation of the LXX.

[4] Luther's rendering of this passage is inexact.

[5] Cf. on this pt. Str.-B., II, 490 on Jn. 7:35; Schl. J., 198 on Jn. 7:35.

3. How did it come about that the Grecian Jews gradually abandoned these pregnant expressions in favour of διασπορά? The pregnant expressions were appropriate in relation to the deportations by Assyrian, Babylonian and to a lesser extent later conquerors, e.g. Pompey. The course of history, however, was always able to heal these severe wounds, and the harsh concrete situation was forgotten. It is also to be remembered that from a very early stage voluntary emigration contributed to the extension of the *diaspora* as well as deportation. Trade relationships and the policies of the princes who were the true heirs of Alexander the Great brought about a considerable intermingling of the peoples. The possible and perhaps even necessary consequence has been well stated by F. Rendtorff : [6] "The Jewish *diaspora* according to the prophetic verdict (Is. 35:8 ; Jer. 23:24 ; Ez. 22:15) is an outworking of the divine judgment and therefore a curse. Only with Hellenistic optimism does a different view develop. We can thus understand how the Septuagint uses the term διασπορά to veil the stark severity of the Hebrew expressions which pitilessly describe the judgment of scattering which God executed on Israel." This estimate is not too assured linguistically, [7] but it is materially sound. Greatness and importance as well as pain and curse did in fact accrue to the Jews through the *diaspora*. Ps. Sol. 9:2 : ἐν παντὶ ἔθνει ἡ διασπορὰ τοῦ Ἰσραὴλ κατὰ τὸ ῥῆμα τοῦ θεοῦ. The Jew living outside Palestine could indeed take unmistakable pride in the fact of the dispersion. It was a benefit in that the Jews could not now be exterminated at a single stroke. [8] The dignity as well as the harsh destiny of Israel as the people of God could be realised when in a circular letter of the Roman Senate on behalf of the Jews the kings of Egypt, Syria, Pergamon, Cappadocia, Parthia and the Greek cities and islands could be mentioned individually and by name (1 Macc. 15:16-24). Jewry could now expand even beyond the original national limits by means of proselytisation (→ προσή-λυτος). In early Christian days there are records of the *diaspora* in 150 places outside Palestine. [9] Πᾶσα δὲ γαῖα σέθεν πλήρης καὶ πᾶσα θάλασσα (Sib. 3, 271). The Jewish historians gladly record the corresponding statements of the Greek geographers. Thus Josephus agrees with Strabo in Ant. 14, 115 : The Jewish people εἰς πᾶσαν πόλιν ἤδη καὶ παρελήλυθεν, καὶ τόπον οὐκ ἔστι ῥᾳδίως εὑρεῖν τῆς οἰκουμένης, ὃς οὐ παραδέδεκται τοῦτο τὸ φῦλον, μηδ' ἐπικρατεῖται ὑπ' αὐτοῦ. The same Josephus speaks in this context of μυριάδες ἄπειροι καὶ ἀριθμῷ γνωσθῆναι μὴ δυνάμεναι (*ibid.*, 11, 133), of πλῆθος (*ibid.*, 15, 14), of the οὐ γὰρ ὀλίγαι μυριάδες τοῦδε τοῦ λαοῦ περὶ τὴν Βαβυλωνίαν (*ibid.*, 15, 39), and he exclaims with obvious pride : οὐ γὰρ ἔστιν ἐπὶ τῆς οἰκουμένης δῆμος ὁ μὴ μοῖραν ἡμετέραν ἔχων (Bell., 2, 398), or τὸ γὰρ Ἰουδαίων γένος πολὺ μὲν κατὰ πᾶσαν τὴν οἰκουμένην παρέσπαρται τοῖς ἐπιχωρίοις (Bell., 7, 43 ; we have here the same verbal stem σπερ- as is also contained in διασπορά). Philo expresses himself similarly (e.g., Leg. Gaj., 36). The same sense of pride may be found even in the NT, e.g., when peoples of all nations come into the community of the Messiah Jesus on the Day of Pentecost (Ac. 2:9-11), or when James speaks of ταῖς δώδεκα φυλαῖς ταῖς ἐν τῇ διασπορᾷ, or 1 Peter of ἐκλεκτοῖς παρεπι-

---

[6] RGG², I, 1918.

[7] "The stark severity of the Hebrew expressions" strictly applies, as we have seen, only to the vocable נדה.

[8] Cf. Str.-B., *op. cit.*

[9] Cf. the map "The World of the Apostle Paul" in A. Deissmann, *Paulus* (1911).

δήμοις διασπορᾶς Πόντου, Γαλατίας, Καππαδοκίας, Ἀσίας καὶ Βιθυνίας. [10]

Yet we must not exaggerate. The destruction of Jerusalem in 70 A.D., and the final extirpation of Palestinian Judaism in Hadrian's war, did much to disturb this pride of the *diaspora*. Prior to 70 A.D. the wounds of earlier expatriations could be healed the more easily because in spite of everything Jerusalem still remained as the holy city and therefore as the focal point not merely of the Holy Land but of the whole *diaspora*. After 70 A.D., however, the *diaspora* became, as it were, completely homeless. A peculiar attitude is found in Josephus. The pride already mentioned is particularly clear in his works. He writes about the *diaspora* as though there had been no destruction of Jerusalem. Apart from his rationalism, and his general desire to secularise Judaism, he is obviously influenced by the specific intention of investing Judaism with an impressive halo in his depiction of the *diaspora*. Nevertheless, the *diaspora* did in fact become something different from what it had been. As in the distant days of the Exile, it now became again in literal truth גּוֹלָה. With this is linked the fact that the generous and sometimes dangerous process of expansion which characterised Greek Judaism (LXX) was now followed by an equally noble and no less dangerous process of contraction (Talmud).

4. A distinctive usage may be seen in Philo, who belongs to the expanding Judaism prior to 70 A.D. In his comprehensive writings the word occurs only once, namely, in Praem. Poen., 115 : ὅθεν εἴρηται πρὸς τοὺς ἐθέλοντας μιμεῖσθαι τὰ σπουδαῖα καὶ θαυμαστὰ κάλλη μὴ ἀπογινώσκειν τὴν ἀμείνω μεταβολὴν μηδὲ τὴν ὥσπερ ἐκ διασπορᾶς ψυχικῆς ἣν εἰργάσατο κακία πρὸς ἀρετὴν καὶ σοφίαν ἐπάνοδον. As already suggested, it may be asked whether the term is here related in any way to the Jewish *diaspora*. It is indeed possible that Philo is not thinking of his own people but using the word like Plutarch before him and Clement of Alexandria after him. Yet it is more likely that he proceeds as in the case of → βασιλεία (τοῦ θεοῦ), taking an expression from the history and existence of his people, divesting it of its eschatological precision and understanding it as a chapter in his ethics (→ I, 574 f.). Thus the historical and eschatological fact of the diaspora is psychologised as διασπορὰ ψυχική. As the migration of Abraham from Ur of the Chaldees to the land of promise is interpreted by Philo as the return of the soul to itself, so history and eschatology are again jettisoned by this Jew who was a Greek philosopher. The fact itself is thus lost to view.

B. διασπορά in the NT.

1. The case is quite otherwise in the NT, which speaks of the διασπορά in OT and then in specifically Christian terms.

The customary usage is found in Jn. 7:35. The Jewish opponents of Jesus Christ put the question : μὴ εἰς τὴν διασπορὰν τῶν Ἑλλήνων μέλλει πορεύεσθαι καὶ διδάσκειν τοὺς Ἕλληνας; There is some doubt who these Ἕλληνες are. They

---

[10] On the history of the Jewish *diaspora*, cf. esp. G. B. Winer, *Biblisches Realwörterbuch* (1847 f.), *s.v.*, *Exil, Zerstreuung* ; cf. also C. Weizsäcker, Art. *Zerstreuung* in D. Schenkel, *Bibellexikon*, V (1875), 712 ff.; T. Mommsen, *Römische Geschichte*, V [10] (1927), 487 ff.; Schürer, II, 1 ff.; III, 537 ff.; J. Juster, *Les Juifs dans l'Empire Romain*, I, II (1914); A. v. Harnack, *Die Mission und Ausbreitung des Christentums in den ersten drei Jahrhunderten*, I[4] (1923), 5 ff.; G. Hölscher, *Geschichte der israelitischen und jüdischen Religion* (1922); Moore, I, II *passim* ; A. Causse, *Les dispersés d'Israël* (1929); G. Rosen, *Juden und Phönizier*, re-edited and expanded by F. Rosen and G. Bertram (1929).

may be Greek speaking Jews, like those of the dispersion, who reside in Jerusalem in territorially organised synagogues and who are elsewhere called Ἑλληνισταί. [11] Such Hellenistic Jews are probably meant in Jn. 12:20 (→ Ἕλληνες); Ac. 11:20 (Ἕλληνας, vl. Ἑλληνιστάς); Ac. 6:1 (Ἑλληνιστῶν); Ac. 9:29 (Ἑλληνιστάς, vl. Ἕλληνας). That non-Greeks could be designated thus may be seen from Mk. 7:26 : ἡ γυνὴ Ἑλληνίς, Συροφοινίκισσα τῷ γένει. On the other hand they may be Greeks in whose territory the Jews live. [12] Ἕλληνες is certainly used in this sense in the NT. No conclusive answer can be given to the question. [13]

2. Jm. 1:1 and 1 Pt. 1:1 are the two other NT passages in which the term occurs, and they are obviously related. If the Epistles are addressed to Jewish Christians, we have the normal usage and the reference is to the Jewish *diaspora*. On the other hand, if they are addressed to Gentile Christians, the word is given a figurative Christian sense. The question is much contested, and is usually dealt with in the various commentaries. A circle is quickly established, which may easily become a vicious one. In traditional exegesis it is assumed that the authors are the Lord's brother James and the apostle Peter, and therefore that the letters are addressed to Jewish Christians, this determining the understanding of the salutation. Or it is assumed that the letter is written to Jewish Christians and this is then used as support for the Jewish Christian thesis. But these points are all contestable. Those who think that the letter is really addressed to Gentile Christians, which cannot be proved in the present article but is simply suggested as possible, will naturally take διασπορά in a figurative sense. This is certainly a possibility.

In Jm. 1:1 the recipients are addressed as αἱ δώδεκα φυλαὶ (→ φυλή) ἐν τῇ διασπορᾷ. Now quite apart from the controversy whether these are Jewish or Gentile Christians, we may expect that, since they are Christians, they will be described as such, especially in the salutation which is the most natural place to do this. [14]

---

[11] This is the view taken in many Comm., but cf. → n. 12.

[12] Cf. Schl. J., *ad loc.* Zn. J., *ad loc.* : "Aram. בְּנֵי גַּלְוּתָא דְיָוָן in distinction from the exiles of Babylon and Media in the third missive of Gamaliel" (G. Dalman, *Aram. Dialektproben*[2] [1927], 3, διασπορὰ Πόντου, 1 Pt. 1:1. Obviously the gen. with διασπορά may well denote the people which lives in this scattered form (Is. 49:6; Ps. 147:2; 2 Macc. 1:27; also Gamaliel, Dalman, *op. cit.* : 'and all the other exile groups of Israel'). But the present gen. can hardly have this force. The Greeks do not live as a dispersed people in alien lands. It is the Jews who live among the Greeks, Romans, Babylonians etc. This essentially Jewish expression was soon misunderstood. A failure to distinguish between the Greek *diaspora* and the Greeks is seen, e.g., in e : *numquit in disparsionem Graecorum incipiet ire et docere eos,* or Ss Sc : "Will he then go to teach the seed (i.e., generation) of the Arameans (i.e., Gentiles)?" Nor can οἱ Ἕλληνες refer to Hellenised Jews any more than to Gentiles, for these are called Ἑλληνισταί in Ac. 6:1; 9:29." These observations of Zn. are weighty and perspicacious; yet the final point can hardly be maintained in face of the interchangeable use of Ἕλληνες and Ἑλληνισταί in the MSS (→ *supra*). Bau. J. takes the same view as Zn. Pr.-Bauer translates "the dispersed among the Gentiles." W. Lock, *A New Commentary on Holy Scripture* (1928) has the rendering "the dispersion among the Greeks." The Vulg. also translates : *in dispersionem Gentium.*

[13] Cf. Bengel, *ad loc.* : *Graecorum sive Judaeorum extra Palaestinam.* A. Tholuck, *Commentar zum Evangelio Johannis*[5] (1837), takes a different view, believing that the Ἕλληνες are real Greeks : Διασπορὰ Ἑλλήνων is normally used *abst. pro concr.* for οἱ διασπαρέντες ἐν τοῖς Ἕλλησιν Ἰουδαῖοι. This can hardly be the case here, as shown by the phrase which follows : διδάσκαλοι τῶν Ἑλλήνων. It thus denotes the place where the διασπαρέντες live."

[14] This is particularly emphasised in Dib. Jk., *ad loc.* : "... there is no mention of the Christian status (of the readers), as is usual in salutations." Cf. also Wnd. Jk., *ad loc.*

If so, the designation of Christians as the twelve tribes puts us on the right track. The → ἐκκλησία (τοῦ θεοῦ) as the OT people of God has now passed from the OT state of promise to the NT state of fulfilment. It is the → ᾿Ισραὴλ κατὰ πνεῦμα, the σπέρμα ᾿Αβραάμ, the ἔθνος ἅγιον, the true περιτομή. There is, of course, no clear support for the equation of αἱ δώδεκα φυλαί with Christians. But if the word δωδεκάφυλον was a current self-designation of the Jews (Ac. 26:7; 1 Cl., 55, 6; Prot. Ev. Jk., 1, 3), it is quite natural that in the process of transition from the OT to the NT the expression should be applied to Christians, whether Jewish or Gentile. The home of Christians is not the earthly Jerusalem, but the Jerusalem which is above (Gl. 4:26), i.e., heaven (Phil. 3:20). [15] In its interrelationship with Judaism early Christianity can see the fact of the *diaspora* in a special light. [16] The phrase δώδεκα φυλαὶ ἐν τῇ διασπορᾷ can be appropriated just as easily as terms like → παρεπίδημος, → πάροικος and → παροικία. [17] The omission of (τοῦ) ᾿Ισραήλ weighs more in favour of a Christian designation than against it. [18] This does not mean that the Gentile Christian hypothesis is proved. It means that Christians as such, whether Jews or Gentiles, do in fact live in dispersion, and therefore the reference may be to Gentile Christians. [19]

What we have said applies implicitly to the use of διασπορά in 1 Pt. 1:1 also. Some difficulty is caused here by the use of the gen. without art. [20] If Jewish Christians are addressed, then this must be understood as a partitive gen. Christian Jews are singled out and addressed from among all the Jews of the dispersion. But the lack of art. still raises a difficulty, even if this is not insuperable in the

---

Yet against the confident exegesis of Dib., there is at least the possibility that we cannot take for granted the link between Jm. 1:1 and 1 Pt. 1:1. The conclusions of Dib. apply with far greater certainty to the fuller expression of 1 Pt. than to the less full of Jm. 1:1, which might be meant quite realistically with no accompanying spiritual sense.

[15] Further examples may be found in Philo ("The negative side of the thought — we are strangers on earth — is expressed already in Philo") and the post-apost. fathers, cf. Dib., *op. cit.*

[16] Cf. K. L. Schmidt, *Die Kirche des Urchristentums*[2] (1932), 269 f.

[17] Harnack, *Mission und Ausbreitung*, I[4] (1923), 421, n. 4: "The Christians' description of themselves as strangers and pilgrims becomes almost technical in the 1st century." Cf. Kn. Pt., 29 f.: "Passages in early Christian literature where the expression διασπορά is used of the dispersed race of Christians cannot, of course, be adduced so freely as those in which παροικεῖν and παρεπιδημεῖν are used. Yet a true exegesis of Jm. 1:1 ... will not think in terms of Jews or Jewish Christians, but of Christians generally, Did., 9, 4 being relevant in this connexion: ὥσπερ ἦν τοῦτο τὸ κλάσμα διεσκορπισμένον ἐπάνω τῶν ὀρέων καὶ συναχθὲν ἐγένετο ἕν, οὕτω συναχθήτω σου ἡ ἐκκλησία ἀπὸ τῶν περάτων τῆς γῆς εἰς τὴν σὴν βασιλείαν. Again, the many OT passages which speak of the return and regathering of the scattered people are naturally applied by Christians to their own γένος, the true and spiritual Israel, so that the thought of διασπορά must have been common amongst them."

[18] This is finely perceived by A. Meyer, *Das Rätsel des Jacobusbriefes* (1930), 123, who points out that "the name Israel is not attached to the twelve tribes, and therefore the tribes are meant to denote the Christian people." Cf. also 78: "No Christian would have applied to the twelve Jewish tribes the expression 'the elect dwellers of the *diaspora*,' which is a title of honour for Christians."

[19] There is thus a certain validity in what is said by Schl. Jk., *ad loc.* — Schl. firmly accepts the Jewish Christian view — concerning the specifically Jewish nature of the phrase in question. Cf. also Hck. Jk., *ad loc.*; M. Meinertz, *Einleitung in das Neue Testament*[4] (1933), 282.

[20] Acc. to Bl.-Debr.[6] § 252 (cf. § 261, 1), the lack of art. is due to the setting of the verse in the salutation.

light of the looser use of the art. in the *koine*. If the reference is to Christians generally, including Gentiles as well as Jews, we may have an epexegetic gen., i.e., the elect residents now present as the *diaspora*, as the people of God scattered in Pontus, Galatia etc. Or perhaps we have an attributive or qualitative gen.: διασπορᾶς = διεσπαρμένοις. But no matter how we take it — and this is the decisive point — in its religious sense διασπορά is now used as a specific term in biblical theology.[21]

The term is not used in the post-apostolic fathers. On the other hand, πάροικος, παροικία and παροικεῖν are common, as already noted. The verb διασπείρειν is found once with reference to the Jewish dispersion, namely, in 1 Cl., 29, 2, quoting Dt. 32:8 : διέσπειρεν υἱοὺς ᾿Αδάμ.

Of the apologists on the limit of the early period, only Justin uses the word, and it is worth noting that he does so in the Dial. with Trypho, where Jewish affairs are prominent. The reference in 117, 2, 4 and 5 is to the Jewish *diaspora*, with a polemic against the Jewish understanding of it. Particularly interesting is 113, 3, where from the fact that Joshua (LXX : ᾿Ιησοῦς) rather than Moses led the people into the Holy Land it is deduced : ᾿Ιησοῦς ὁ Χριστὸς τὴν διασπορὰν τοῦ λαοῦ ἐπιστρέψει.

Karl Ludwig Schmidt

διαστολή → στέλλομαι.

διαστρέφω → στρέφω.

διαταγή, διατάσσω → τάσσω.

διατίθημι, διαθήκη

---

† διατίθημι.

As regards the NT use of the term, we need not consider the act. διατίθημι (= *dispono*, "to set here and there," "to separate," "to distribute," "to establish," "to determine," "to dispose," "to set in a state or position," "to handle"). Our concern is with the med., of whose many meanings ("to set here and there, or to separate, in one's own interests," e.g., "to expose for sale," "to sell" ; "to order one's words," "to expound," "to deliver a lecture or speech"), we need only consider the following : a. "to control according to one's own free desire" either men (Xenoph. Cyrop., V, 2, 7: τὴν θυγατέρα διαθέσθαι ὅπως σὺ ἂν βούλῃ ἐπιτρέπω) or things (Xenoph. Mem., I, 6, 13 : τὴν ὥραν); "to make arrangements or decisions" (Andoc., 4, 30: τὴν ἀποδημίαν) ; more particularly b. as a technical legal term : "to make final testamentary disposition in view of death": e.g., Isaeus 7:1: διέθετο τὴν οὐσίαν ἑτέρῳ; CIG, II, 2448 : τάδε διέθετο ... ᾿Επικτήτα; P. Oxy., 104, 4; Jos. Ant., 13, 407: τὴν βασιλείαν εἰς τὴν ᾿Αλεξάνδραν

---

[21] Cf. Wnd. Pt., *ad loc.*; Kn. Pt., *ad loc.* There are some acute observations in T. Spörri, *Der Gemeindegedanke im ersten Petrusbrief* (1925), 52, n. 2 and 154, n. 1: "There is no necessity to think that the recipients are Jews," and : "The common metaphorical understanding of παρεπίδημοι and διασπορά does not create any tautology because the standpoint of the expressions is different, the one looking to the land in which they are strangers and the other to the land which is their home ..."

δ ι α τ ί θ η μ ι. Cr.-Kö., 1061 f.; Pr.-Bauer, 295 f.; Moult.-Mill., 155 f.; J. Behm, *Der Begriff* διαθήκη *im NT* (1912); E. Lohmeyer, *Diatheke* (1913).

διέθετο. διατίθεσθαι διαθήκην [-ας], or abs. "to make a will," Lys. 19, 39; Aristot. Pol., II, 9, p. 1270a, 27 f.: κἂν ἀποθάνῃ μὴ διαθέμενος (→ διαθήκη, 124); hence ὁ διατιθέμενος "testator," Isaeus, 1:26, 34 f.; BGU, 448; Ditt. Or., 509, 6 and 16; P. Oxy., 99, 9 and 15 etc.; and less frequently, and only in older texts, c. "to come to an arrangement or to order things with others" : Xenoph. Mem., II, 6, 23 : δύνανται καὶ τὴν ἔριν ... ἀλλήλοις διατίθεσθαι ("to settle strife"); Ditt. Syll.³, 205, 10 ff.: τὴν φιλίαν καὶ τὴν συμμαχίαν ... ἣν διέθεντο πρὸς ἀλλήλας αἱ πόλεις ("to establish friendship and covenant relationship"); Plat. Leg., VIII, 834a : διαθεμένους αὖ περὶ τούτων νόμους ("to coordinate laws," cf. shortly before 833e συννομοθετεῖν); Aristoph. Av., 440 f.: ἢν μὴ διάθωνταί γ' οἵδε διαθήκην ἐμοὶ ἥνπερ ὁ πίθηκος τῇ γυναικὶ διέθετο ("to reach agreement," "to conclude a treaty," → διαθήκη); Ditt. Syll.³, 955, 24: ὡμολόγησαν καὶ διέθεντο 'Αρκεσινεῖς ὀφείλειν Πραξικλεῖ ἓξ τάλαντα (3rd cent. B.C.). The emphasis differs, however, from that of συντίθεσθαι, from which διατίθεσθαι is quite distinct. It does not fall on the reciprocal nature of the action. The element of reaching a decision being still strong, it falls rather on the legally binding character of the decision reached either in relation or with respect to others. [1]

In the LXX διατίθεσθαι διαθήκην (→ 126) is consistently used for כָּרַת בְּרִית in the sense of "to take order" or "to reach agreement," e.g., Ex. 24:8; Dt. 4:23; Jos. 9:15 f.; 2 Βασ. 3:13. In Gn. 9:17, however, it is used for הֵקִים בְּרִית, and in Jos. 7:11 for צִוָּה בְּרִית — a sign that the strict sense of "to dispose" or "to determine" was always present to the translators even when they used διατίθεσθαι διαθήκην (cf. ψ 104:9; 2 Ch. 7:18). In 1 Ch. 19:19 διέθεντο μετὰ Δαυίδ (Heb. הִשְׁלִים) means "to make peace with David." Divine disposing is denoted by διατίθεσθαι in Jdt. 5:18: ἀπέστησαν ἀπὸ τῆς ὁδοῦ ἧς διέθετο αὐτοῖς and human self-commitment in Wis. 18:9 : τὸν τῆς θειότητος νόμον ἐν ὁμονοίᾳ διέθεντο ("established as a valid basis").

The mid. alone is found in the NT.

1. The sense "to determine," "to appoint" may be seen in Lk. 22:29 f.: κἀγὼ διατίθεμαι ὑμῖν καθὼς διέθετό μοι ὁ πατήρ μου βασιλείαν, ἵνα ἔσθητε καὶ πίνετε ἐπὶ τῆς τραπέζης μου ἐν τῇ βασιλείᾳ μου, καὶ καθήσεσθε ἐπὶ θρόνων τὰς δώδεκα φυλὰς κρίνοντες τοῦ Ἰσραήλ — an eschatological promise of the parting Jesus to His disciples that as the Father has ordained royal dominion (→ βασιλεία) for Him, so He ordains for the disciples a share in His future reign as those who shall feast (→ τράπεζα) and rule (→ θρόνος, → κρίνω) with Him. Whether we find the obj. of the διατίθεμαι in the βασιλείαν of the subsidiary clause (to give a thought similar to Lk. 12:32), or whether we find it in the ἵνα clause, which is better [2] (cf. Mt. 19:28), διατίθεσθαι obviously has the force of freely ordaining or authoritatively disposing and not of making testamentary disposition ; [3] for the διατίθεσθαι of Jesus corresponds to that of the Father, who is certainly not making His will, and in the context of the sayings of the disciples it has no more connexion with the death of Jesus than the similar sayings in Lk. 12:32 and Mt. 19:28. [4] As the eschatological βασιλεία is ordained for Jesus by the sovereign declaration of the will of God, so it is decided by the sovereign

---

[1] Here it is not possible to take the δια- in the sense of fully or consistently (cf. Lohmeyer, op. cit., 7), since the δια- in διατίθεσθαι signifies "arranging apart from one another" (= dis-ponere) and can hardly have any other sense [Debrunner].

[2] Cf. Behm, op. cit., 65 f.

[3] So Zn. Lk., Kl. Lk.

[4] Behm, op. cit., 66 f.; Lohmeyer, op. cit., 156 f.; K. G. Goetz, Das Abendmahl eine Diatheke Jesu...? (1920), 35 f.

resolve of Jesus that the disciples should reign with Him. [5] On the expression διατίθεσθαι διαθήκην, "to make a covenant," which in the NT, as distinct from the LXX, is used only of the resolves or dispositions of God in salvation history (Ac. 3:25: τῆς διαθήκης ἧς ὁ θεὸς διέθετο πρὸς τοὺς πατέρας ὑμῶν, Hb. 8:10 [= Ἰερ. 38:31]: αὕτη ἡ διαθήκη ἣν διαθήσομαι τῷ οἴκῳ Ἰσραήλ, 10:16: ἡ διαθήκη ἣν διαθήσομαι πρὸς αὐτούς), → διαθήκη, 125.

2. Hb. 9:16 f.: ὁ διαθέμενος, "the testator" in the usual legal sense, → διαθήκη 131.

Behm

† διαθήκη.

A. The OT Term בְּרִית.

1. Equivalents to the LXX διαθήκη.

The LXX διαθήκη is mostly used (270 times, and 5 in Sir.) for the Hebrew בְּרִית (Hex. βριθ, ψ 88:39). Only occasionally is it used for other Heb. words, e.g., for אַחֲוָה "brotherhood" in Zech. 11:14 A; for עֵדוּת "attestation" in the sense of "obligation" in Ex. 27:21; 31:7; 39:15 [35]; Jos. 4:16; for תּוֹרָה "law" in Da. 9:13; for דָּבָר "word" in Dt. 9:5; for כָּתוּב "what is written" in 2 Ch. 25:4. שָׁלֵם hiph can also be rendered διατιθέναι διαθήκην (4 Βασ. 10:19 B). In Sir. διαθήκη is used for חֹק "statute" (10 times, and for חֻקָּה in 47:11). [1] In these cases, however, the free rendering by διαθήκη of related or similar legal terms does not involve any material error, since the conception bound up with בְּרִית-διαθήκη includes legal relationship of all kinds. At any rate, the

---

[5] In the free quotation (from Dt. 4:1, 5) in Barn., 10, 2: διαθήσομαι πρὸς τὸν λαὸν τοῦτον τὰ δικαιώματά μου, we have another instance of διατίθεσθαι in the sense of "to dispose." Cf. 4 Esr. 13:26 vg (of the Son of Man and Messiah): disponet (= διαθήσεται?, "to order"?), qui derelicti sunt, cf. on this verse B. Violet, I, 382 f.; II, 180 and 356.

δ ι α θ ή κ η. On A.: R. Valeton, ZAW, 12 (1892), 1 ff., 224 ff., 13 (1893), 245 ff.; R. Kraetzschmar, Die Bundesvorstellung im AT in ihrer geschichtl. Entwicklung (1896); E. Sellin, Beiträge zur isr.-jüd. Religionsgesch., I: Jahwes Verhältnis zum israelit. Volk u. Individuum (1897); F. Giesebrecht, Die Geschichtlichkeit des Sinaibundes (1899); P. Karge, Gesch. d. Bundesgedankens im AT, 1 (1910); J. Pedersen, Der Eid bei den Semiten in seinem Verhältnis zu verwandten Erscheinungen sowie die Stellung des Eides im Islam (1914); Israel, Its Life and Culture (1926), 263 ff.; M. Buber, Das Kommende, I: Königtum Gottes (1932), 111 ff.; P. Volz, Mose und sein Werk² (1932), 72 ff. Extensive legal material may be found in J. L. Saalschütz, Das mosaische Recht nebst den vervollständigenden talmudisch-rabbinischen Bestimmungen² (1853). On B.-D.: F. Norton, A Lexicographical and Historical Study of διαθήκη (Phil. Diss., Chicago, 1908); E. Riggenbach, "Der Begriff der διαθήκη im Hb.," in Theol. Studien T. Zahn dargebracht (1908), 289 ff.; Hb. ²,³ (1922), 205 ff. etc.; Deissmann LO, 286 f.; F. Dibelius, Das Abendmahl (1911), 76 ff.; J. Behm, Der Begriff διαθήκη im NT (1912); E. Lohmeyer, Diatheke (1913) (on both monographs, cf. G. Vos, Princeton Theol. Review, 11 [1913], 513 ff.; J. Kögel, ThLBl, 35 [1914], 610 ff.; R. Bultmann, ThR, 18 [1915], 264 ff.); H. A. Kennedy, "The Significance and Range of the Covenant-Conception in the NT," Exp., 8, 10 (1915), 385 ff.; Cr.-Kö., 1062 ff.; W. J. Moulton, s.v. "Covenant," DAC, I, 261 ff.; O. Eger, "Rechtswörter und Rechtsbilder i. d. paul. Briefen," ZNW, 18 (1917), 84 ff.; Rechtsgeschichtliches zum NT (1919), 31 ff.; K. G. Goetz, Das Abendmahl eine Diatheke Jesu ...? (1920); Moult.-Mill., 148 f.; G. Dalman, Jesus-Jeschua (1922), 146 ff.; C. Clemen, J. Hempel, O. Schmitz, s.v. "Bund" RGG², I, 1358 ff.; Pr.-Bauer, 285 f.; Liddell-Scott, 394 f.; L. G. da Fonseca, "Διαθήκη — foedus an testamentum?" Biblica, 8 (1927), 31 ff., 161 ff., 290 ff., 418 ff.; 9 (1928), 26 ff., 143 ff.; J. Heller, s.v. "Bund," EJ, I, 1199 ff.; Sickb. K, 103; Rohr Hb., 38 ff.

[1] There is a mistake in 1 K. 20:34 (A): ἐν Δαμασκῷ.

LXX assumes that διαθήκη expresses the essential content of בְּרִית, and, except where there are obvious errors, as in 2 Ch. 23:1 (where we have οἶκος due to confusion of ברית with בית), or Dt. 9:15 AF (μαρτυρίων), the only other occasional renderings are συνθήκη (4 Βασ. 17:15 A) and ἐντολή (3 Βασ. 11:11).[2] It may thus be assumed that where LXX uses διαθήκη the intention is to mediate the sense and usage of בְּרִית.

2. Etymology and Terminology of בְּרִית.

Attempts to derive the meaning of the term from etymology have not led to any very clear or certain conclusions. The only sure fact is that בְּרִית is formed from a root ברה (ברי) by the addition of the feminine ending *t*.[3] To take it as a verbal form, i.e., as the infin. of ברה,[4] in view of the hint of verbal functions in expressions like Lv. 26:42 (בְּרִיתִי יַעֲקוֹב)[5] or Jer. 33:20 (בְּרִיתִי הַיּוֹם) and בְּרִיתִי הַלַּיְלָה), is perhaps linguistically justifiable, but not absolutely necessary seeing the instances are so few and questionable. The decisive argument against this course is the fact that no account is thus taken of the predominant usage, namely, בְּרִית as a *nomen regens* with ensuing gen., and only in Is. 42:6 (וְאֶתֶּנְךָ לִבְרִית עָם) with the prefix ל which is a mark of the infin. The cogency of the cases in which בְּרִית apparently governs an accus., because the preposition אֶת is pointed as *nota accusativi*, is justly debated.[6] Thus בְּרִית is to be regarded as a noun, and in its formation we can detect the influence of femin. nouns which may be traced back to masculines ending in -*i*. Only in terms of this analogy is it possible to explain why we have בְּרִית instead of בְּרִיָה which corresponds to the usual structure of feminines based on ל"י roots. בְּרִיָה occurs in 2 S. 13:5, 7, 10 in the sense of "food," and in 2 S. 13:6, 10; 12:17 the verb ברה means "to eat," and in the hiph in 2 S. 3:35; 13:5 "to give to eat." The sense of "food" may still be instanced for the later בָּרוּת. (Ps. 69:21), which is formed analogously to בְּרִית.[7] Yet in none of the 286 instances of בְּרִית in the Mas. does it have this meaning, nor does it ever seem to have been attached to it. Thus we cannot assume with any certainty that בְּרִית is connected with the root ברה ("to eat") which underlies בְּרִיָה and בָּרוּת. The meaning of the ברה in בְּרִית is indeed the real etymological problem. If we presuppose the identity of this ברה with the ברה in בְּרִיָה, it is worth considering the solution proposed by W. Meyer (and B. Luther),[8] namely, that בְּרִית is the meal or act of eating and בְּרִיָה the food or material of eating. We could then see a similar differentiation to that of שְׁבִיָה and שְׁבִית, from שבה,[9] but with a much more precise distinction between the abstract and concrete. We must also remember that the verbal expressions with which בְּרִית is firmly linked in actual usage[10] never have the sense of meal and cannot be understood in terms of it. We have thus to take into account the possibility that in addition to the root ברה ("to eat") there is another root with the same sound which forms the basis of בְּרִית. There is little support for the view that this is to be found in the verb ברה rather doubtfully attested (cf. BHK)

---

[2] In Gn. 14:13 we have בַּעֲלֵי בְרִית in accord. with the sense.

[3] H. Bauer-P. Leander, *Histor. Gramm. d. hebr. Sprache* (1922) § 76c.

[4] J. Barth, *Nominalbildung* (1889) § 79g; Pedersen Eid, 45.

[5] Syr. קימי דעם יעקוב; cf. BHK³, *ad loc.*

[6] Pedersen Eid, 45, n. 2 on Is. 59:21; Ez. 16:8, 60.

[7] Cf. L. Gulkowitsch, *Die Bildung von Abstraktbegriffen in der hebr. Sprachgeschichte* (1931), 122 f.; Barth, *op. cit.* § 228b.

[8] *Die Israeliten und ihre Nachbarstämme* (1906), 558 n. Cf. also J. Hempel in RGG², I, 1360.

[9] Bauer-Leander § 76c.

[10] Cf. esp. הקים, עָבַר, שמר etc. (lists in Kraetzschmar, *op. cit.*, 247 ff.). כרת, which is the closest, has a different sense.

in 1 S. 17:8 in the sense "to perceive" (E. König, Wörterb., *s.v.*), or "to determine" (Ges.-Buhl, *s.v.*). [11] More likely are hypotheses which find a connexion with the Accadian *barû* in the sense of "to bind" [12] and the related *biritu* in the sense of "binding" or "bond." It is true, of course, that the construction מָסֹרֶת הַבְּרִית (Ez. 20:37), if it really does mean מַאֲסֹרֶת הַבְּ ("binding of the בְּרִית") and "thus contains an ironical reference to the basic meaning of בְּרִית," [13] lends only very doubtful support to this conjecture, nor is there much more to be said for the adducing of the Talmudic בירית, ברית ("knee-band"). [14] Yet alongside the other theories advanced [15] this perhaps demands the most serious consideration. This does not mean, however, that it is of any greater value in interpreting the OT expressions in which בְּרִית occurs, or that it gives us any greater certainty in our attempts at a serviceable translation of the term.

The terminology normally connected with the word is of no greater help since it is itself full of obscurities. This is particularly true of the verb כרת, which is most frequently (86 times) construed predicatively with the accus. בְּ. It means "to cut off," "to cut in two." But in the expression כרת בְּרִית the noun בְּרִית cannot denote the object which is cut in two or cut off. This emerges plainly from the fact that sometimes other accusatives can be put in its place without any basic change in the expression. [16] כרת בְּרִית is thus to be understood as an abbreviated expression in which the direct accus. is suppressed and replaced in terms of *catachresis* by another which denotes the result or goal of the action. [17] That something is cut with the result that a בְּרִית arises is concisely expressed by the formula כרת בְּרִית. An expression like Ps. 50:5 : כֹּרְתֵי בְרִיתִי עֲלֵי־זָבַח ("who 'cut' my בְּרִית at the sacrifice") suggests that the direct object is really an animal whose cutting or slitting [18] was a traditional rite at the conclusion of a בְּרִית. More instructive than the verb with its exclusive reference to the rite are the prepositions normally used to indicate the persons involved. Thus we read that N made

---

[11] Pedersen Eid, 44 f. is strongly in favour of בְּרוּ, though he cannot fix the sense. Does he have in view a denominative of בְּרִית ?

[12] F. Delitzsch, *Assyr. Handwörterb.* (1896), 185a.

[13] Kraetzschmar, *op. cit.*, 246; Karge, *op. cit.*, 229. The combination with אסר is old, cf. Smend Comm., *ad loc.*, but the text can hardly be accepted as it is.

[14] Karge, *op. cit.*, 227 f.; Buber, *op. cit.*, 231 ("constriction"). Acc. to Buber, 113 *"berith,* which only for want of anything better we translate 'covenant,' signifies a relationship which constricts and only secondarily unites two partners, limiting either both or at least one of them." Verbal expressions like בוא בברית, עָמַד give some evidence of a local basic meaning along the lines of Buber's constriction, and הֵפֵר is not opposed to this, but they are linked with the general idea of commitment and have nothing to do with the actual meaning of בְּרִית.

[15] Cf. the enumeration in Pedersen Eid, 45, n. 1; Volz, *op. cit.*, 73, n.

[16] Cf. אָלָה "curse" in Dt. 29:11, or אֲמָנָה "treaty" in Neh. 10:1, or דָּבָר "word" in Hag. 2:5. We can see clearly from 1 S. 22:8, where כרת עִם־פּ׳ is used without object in the sense of "making an alliance with someone," that כרת ברית has become a fixed formula in which the original sense does not matter ; cf. also 1 S. 11:2.

[17] Cf. on this point E. König, *Hist.-krit. Lehrgebäude der hebr. Sprache,* II, 2 (1897), 101 f. (§ 209b).

[18] So Buber, *op. cit.*, 114. On Jer. 34:18; Gn. 15:10, cf. *infra*. Pedersen Eid, 46 assumes a transition of the sense "to cut" into that of "to decide" or "to resolve" after the analogy of Arabic expressions. He does not show convincingly, however, that these analogies compel us to renounce the idea implicit in the original sense. It is true that the Greek ὄρκια τέμνειν, which is often adduced in this connexion, is of no help towards an understanding of Semitic relationships, but it may be that the analogous process of a sacrifice of confirmation (ὄρκια πιστά) underlies this and the Lat. *foedus icere* or *ferire*.

בְּרִית together with (עָם or אֶת) M, or that both did so together (שְׁנֵיהֶם) so that the action was common. There is a stronger emphasis on the initiative of the person named if לְ ("with reference to") is used instead of אֶת or עָם, i.e., N made בְּרִית with reference to M. Yet the change of form does not have to denote a change of content. It may be for the convenience of the author rather than for forensic or dogmatic reasons, though these are not perhaps excluded when it is said that God made בְּרִית with reference to someone. In this case there is no reciprocal action.[19] Of other verbal connexions, בוא "to enter into," עמד "to be in," עבר "to transgress," and הפר "to break" are too colourless to bring out the local sense and thus to help to a reconstruction of the sacral scene.[20] Other expressions like הקים "to establish" or "keep," נתן, שים, "to institute," שמר "to maintain," etc.[21] simply show that בְּרִית is something fixed and valid, as may be seen more plainly from wider considerations than from this purely formal material.

The usual rendering of בְּרִית is "covenant."[22] This is not really a translation but a paraphrase. Hence we must use it with caution if we are to penetrate to the heart of the matter as presented in statements of such widely divergent character.

3. The Concept of the Covenant in the OT.

The OT statements which use the word בְּרִית may be divided into two main groups. To the one belong those in which the concept is understood as the firmly regulated form of a fellowship between God and man or man and God. To the other belong those in which the covenant is presented as the half-legal and half-sacral form of a fellowship between man and man. By way of supplement, note should also be taken of a number of cases in which the word is obviously used poetically and metaphorically to denote a relationship of either God or man to animals or things.[23]

It is tempting to derive from these fairly obvious data the view that there is a secular covenant and a religious, and that these are to be distinguished as fashioned by the will of man on the one side and the will of God on the other.[24] There are certainly good and logical arguments for such a distinction. For it may be assumed from the very outset that it is not indifferent but of the very highest importance whether only men take part in it or whether God Himself is included as a participant. The question arises, however, whether terms like secular and religious really represent the distinction as conceived by the OT authors. For this terminology does not sufficiently bring out the fact that even the so-called secular covenant is usually surrounded by sacral assurances in the form of oaths or sacrifices, so

---

[19] The use of the expression in Ez. and Ch. is probably well attested so far as concerns לְ. This is not so likely, however, in other texts. Even Jos. 24:25 (Joshua with reference to the people) does not constitute any exception (as against Buber, 114, 232).

[20] → n. 14.

[21] Cf. the list in Kraetzschmar, op. cit., 247 ff. Analogous again are such Lat. expressions as foedus frangere, rumpere, violare.

[22] The only danger of error (E. Kautzsch, Bibl. Theol. des AT [1911], 60) is in schematic exegesis. The central meaning of the term is certainly covenant (M. Weber, Religionssoziologie, 3 [1921], 83 n.).

[23] Cf. Is. 28:15, 18 (covenant with death); Job 5:23 (with the stones); 31:1 (with the eyes); 40:28 (with Leviathan). Yahweh has a covenant with day and night: Jer. 33:20, 25; and with the beasts: Ez. 34:25; Hos. 2:20.

[24] Cf. E. Kautzsch, Bibl. Theol. des AT (1911), 60; Kraetzschmar, op. cit., 6.

that it can no longer be called secular. Conversely, the religious covenant is not constructed in a specifically religious way but according to the juridical pattern of legal agreements; it has a basic logical element which is suppressed if it is described as a religious covenant. To see the distinction more clearly, we are thus advised to pay more attention to the purpose of the institution described as a covenant, and to use as a mark of the distinction the degree to which there either is or can be correspondence to the purpose in any given case. When men alone participate, it is obvious that the relationship is legally determined. For when men assemble and formally declare that they belong together under certain conditions, a legal need is met and a valid law established. On the other hand, when God is a participant serious objections arise at once to the introduction of legal ideas, since it is plainly not a normal legal procedure, but one which is at least highly problematic in its practical validity, to declare formally that God enters into a union with certain men under specified conditions. This is a legal transaction for which there is no analogy in the circle of experience. The legal concept of the covenant is given a theological character by the inclusion of a transcendental participant in the relationship, i.e., by the thesis that God Himself is a legal personage with a clearly declared goal. The legal notion is lifted out of the sphere of immanence and used to clarify a religious situation. The concept of the covenant is thus designed to serve a purpose of conceptual clarification. It leads to theological reflection along legal lines. [25] For this reason we prefer to describe this as the theological concept of the covenant in distinction from the purely legal concept which applies to the human covenant with no theological implications. The advantage of this terminology is that it does not dispute but fully recognises the fact that the theological covenant is itself legal in structure, so that a covenant between God and man implies no more, if also no less, than the formal concept of a rightly ordered relationship. To the legal understanding, however, a religious addition is made in the form of a statement about God which is strictly conceptual and therefore theological.

This leads us at once to the main problem of any theological treatment of the concept of the covenant in the OT. It lies in the question concerning the goal of the order according to which God on the one side and man on the other contract a union in covenantal form. Merely to assert the legal order offers no satisfactory explanation unless we are content to expound the customary legal form and then point to naïve views of God which conceive of religion simply in legal terms. Indeed, even if we do describe the concept of the covenant as naïve, as might be said of the introduction of any legal categories into religion and in the last resort of theology generally, this modest insight must not prevent us from recognising in the attempt at theological systematisation a genuine concept of faith, and in this the impelling force behind the development of the most significant and fruitful of all OT concepts. The religious value of the concept may be easily seen from the fact that it strongly demands religious feeling and that it necessarily raises the question of the nature of the asserted legal relationships between God and man, as also of the content in view when a legal concept is introduced to show that there is an established pattern in the dealings between God and man.

---

[25] J. Wellhausen (*Prolegomena*⁶ [1905], 423) rightly describes the covenant as a medium in man's relation to God "which is designed to promote reflection."

Analysis of the covenant concept inevitably leads to the living basis of OT religion because it deals with the problem of man standing before God. It hardly need be demonstrated that this question cannot be fully answered within the framework of a limited investigation of the use and meaning of the word בְּרִית.[26] Yet we should also remember that it is both arbitrary and confusing to regard the concept of the covenant as a kind of common denominator of the history of Israel, which may be used to elucidate statements in which it does not occur. For in certain cases we cannot be sure whether the author views the theory as a binding dogma or gives it his general approval.[27] Our best course is to accept the fact that the concept of the covenant is a self-contained theory of great distinctiveness of structure. For this reason, it is much used by authors who have strong theological interests like Ezekiel or P and D — if we may for once speak of such. On the other hand, it is much less common in writers who do not give such emphasis to these interests, like J and E and the pre-exilic prophets.[28] The reality behind the theory, namely, the divinely instituted fellowship of God with His people, is frequently stated in another way which has little or nothing in common with thinking in the category of the covenant concept. The reason why it is so prominent is not to be sought only in its occurrence at decisive points in the Pentateuchal outline of salvation history as elaborated by the prophets (e.g., the Noachic covenant, the Abrahamic covenant, the Sinai covenant, the covenant of Shechem, the Davidic covenant, the new covenant); it is also to be sought in its simplicity, which is so impressive to legal thinking. This concept is a product of theology, without which no religion can maintain or propagate itself. For religious experiences which cannot be evaluated theologically pass away with time. Ensuing generations, however, have always to reckon with concepts which crystallise out of decisive experiences and preserve the element of truth in them. At any rate, the fact that one is dealing with a formula[29] means that any investigation of the concept must accept the task of explaining the meaning and use of the formula. It will then be necessary to draw wider deductions from the attempted explanation.

4. The Covenant as a Legal Institution.

To understand the legal character of the covenant relationship, we may best begin by concentrating on examples in which human participants alone enter into the בְּרִית status.

---

[26] Cf. F. Baumgärtel, *Die Eigenart der at.lichen Frömmigkeit* (1932), 76 : "Even where the term covenant is not present, the intention behind it may be expressed."

[27] In Amos, e.g., this is more than doubtful in view of 9:7. He uses the term only once in 1:9 and without any reference to God. K. Cramer's exposition of this prophet (*Amos, Versuch einer theologischen Interpretation* [1930]) is in many respects a warning example against over-estimation of the covenant theory. It is certainly not the case that the individual standpoint of the prophet can be ignored simply because the element of truth in the idea of the covenant can be shown to be one of the motifs in the prophetic message. We must not drive the concept to death, finding it even where it is not relevant and wresting it out of ideas which do not contain any theology. It seems to me that W. Eichrodt (*Theologie des AT* [1933], 15 f.) is nearer the truth when he suggests that for certain practical reasons the "classical prophets" could not lay any very great stress on the covenant theory.

[28] Cf. Kraetzschmar, *op. cit.*

[29] A. Weiser, *Glaube und Geschichte im AT* (1931), 59, describes it very aptly as a "formula for the ideology of history." This is shown by the fact that it is already used technically.

The simplest case, i.e., that of the compact of two private individuals, is un-equivocally mentioned only once in the OT, namely, in the accounts of the re-lationship between David and Jonathan.[30] This does not mean, however, that the private covenant was unusual in the normal course of social life. Individual law may well have used the stronger guarantee of the covenant relationship more frequently than the sources suggest.[31] However that may be, the character of the covenant as the ultimate legal form of close interrelationship may be seen particu-larly well from the example of David and Jonathan, since we are expressly told that the two loved one another as their own souls and that it was for this reason that they entered into covenant. When Jonathan entered into covenant with David (לְדָוִד should be rendered "with respect to David" according to the analogy of the usage, 1 S. 18:3) "because he loved him as his own soul" (כְּאַהֲבָתוֹ אֹתוֹ כְנַפְשׁוֹ),[32] he placed under legal guarantee the spontaneous impulse of his heart which seemed to demand a voluntary self-commitment for its definitive confirmation. The legal concept intrinsic to the covenant relationship is thus brought into relation with the strongest sense of fellowship and is thought to be adapted both to support it and indeed to maintain it in every possible crisis. In fact, the legal compact between David and Jonathan seems not to have had any other object than to recognise and confirm the spontaneous feelings on both sides. Nevertheless, the covenant is not identical with the friendship. Even in the brief accounts we have of it, there can be no mistaking its distinctive character as a legal fellowship under sacral guarantees. Jonathan exercised חֶסֶד when he "brought" David and himself into covenant fellowship (1 S. 20:8). This concept חֶסֶד, which the OT often uses in relation to the covenant to express the faithfulness of the covenant partner (→ χάρις),[33] is particularly well adapted to bring out the sober legal character of the relationship established between the two concerned. The participants con-clude a legal compact which defines and confirms the nature and manner of the new state into which they enter. David appeals to this legal compact when he recalls the חֶסֶד of Jonathan and expects of him something corresponding to this חֶסֶד (1 S. 20:8). Both confirm the validity of the compact by concluding it before Yahweh (1 S. 23:18), and therefore presumably in a holy place, and by taking a mutual oath (2 S. 21:7: שְׁבֻעַת יְהוָה אֲשֶׁר בֵּינֹתָם), thus recognising Yahweh's presence as a witness of the transaction. They can thus speak of a "covenant of Yahweh" (1 S. 20:8), for Yahweh protects the legal order. The way in which the relationship was established is described in 1 S. 18:4.[34] By taking the clothes and weapons of Jonathan, David takes a substantial share in his person. Entering into covenant with him, he becomes as the man himself (כְנַפְשׁוֹ). This state which is marked by the exchange of personal powers is itself the covenant.

---

[30] 1 S. 18:3; 20:8; 23:18.

[31] The treaty, e.g., between Solomon and Hiram is a strictly commercial arrangement (1 K. 5:26), but it may be regarded as a subsidiary form of covenant, as may agreements to purchase or exchange more generally. Cf. Hos. 12:1; 1 K. 15:19; Gn. 14:13 for examples of political treaties.

[32] Cf. also 1 S. 18:1: נֶפֶשׁ נִקְשְׁרָה "the soul ... was knit."

[33] Cf. also → I, 236, n. 12.

[34] Jonathan took his robe, another garment, his sword, his bow and his girdle, and gave them to David. According to Arabian analogies, the point of the action seems to be that clothes and other objects of personal use, being impregnated with the living substance of their owner, can mediate his soul to another man to whom they are given. Cf. Pedersen, op. cit., 23 f.; J. Wellhausen, *Reste arabischen Heidentums*[2] (1927), 196.

The covenant between David and Jonathan is certainly exceptional in one respect, namely, that it was by no means the rule that personal attraction should serve as a basis for the legal compact which establishes the covenant. In most cases, therefore, the material strength of the legal conception emerges much more strongly, though with no weakening of the obligation incurred. Indeed, if anything the obligation is usually given even greater emphasis, and accounts of the procedure at the conclusion of a covenant bring out the basis of it in many different ways. Very clear and instructive in this regard are, e.g., the accounts of the covenant made between Jacob and Laban (Gn. 31:44 ff.). This is not a private covenant, since blood relatives have a part in the transaction (cf. vv. 25, 46 and 54) and thus share in the covenant. A first point to notice is that Laban proposes the covenant because of a feeling of legal insecurity on both sides (v. 43 f.). A record of the institution is to be set up as a witness between them. [35] This record consists (v. 45 E) in a stone pillar erected by Jacob, or in a cairn according to the parallel tradition (vv. 46, 48, 52 J). This memorial, if it may be described as such, [36] is also thought of as a watch-tower from which God observes the keeping of the agreement. The content of the agreement is also given in a twofold tradition. [37] On both sides appeal is made to the deity as a witness or judge, Jacob calling on the God of Abraham and the God of Nahor (v. 53 J), and Laban simply on אֱלֹהִים (v. 50 E). It seems that each had in view his own God, and that it is only an impression made by the united narrative that one and the same God is to be witness. On both sides there is also an oath, [38] and then Jacob makes a sacrifice and invites all his brethren to a meal (v. 54 E). These brethren naturally include the relatives of Laban, for the point of the transaction is that all the participants become brethren and stand in the same relationship to one another as though they were blood relatives. In full legal form the families of Jacob and Laban thus enter into covenant. All the essential elements both in the basic legal procedure and in the new status itself are present in the Mosaic account: a. כרת "to cut" is used in summary description of the whole transaction recorded; b. there is a record of the divine attestation and the unalterable validity of the compact; c. more precise details are given of the mutual agreement; d. there is an oath in acknowledgment of the divine guaranteeing of correct intention; e. a sacrifice is offered; and f. the covenant brethren share a common meal. It is obviously the purpose of the narrators to emphasise the fact that this is a fully valid covenant concluded in impeccable manner, and thereby to bring out for the legal expert both the cleverness of Jacob and the stupidity of Laban. We may thus deduce that this was the valid procedure in the conclusion of all covenant relationships. As regards the

---

[35] In the light of vv. 46, 48, 51 f., 31:44 (J) must have contained reference to the setting up of a cairn of witness.

[36] Perhaps the stones are themselves living witnesses who hear what is spoken, cf. Jos. 24:27, since עֵד "witness" is a person. Or possibly J held this view, but it was obliterated by the idea of a watch-tower in E and by the later idea of J in v. 53. Perhaps there is also some influence of the idea of a boundary stone (Babylonian *kudurru*) bearing a curse against those who violate it (Pedersen Eid, 106), though there is nothing of this in the actual wording of the story.

[37] Laban's concern is for the good treatment of his daughters in Jacob's family (v. 50 E), while the legal restrictions and safeguards against aggression seem to be proposed by Jacob in his own interests (v. 52 J).

[38] That it is said of Jacob alone that "he sware by the fear of his father Isaac" (v. 53 E) seems to be due to the condensation of the story on conflation.

formalities, this naturally gives us only the basis. It cannot be proved that the same details were followed in every case. Indeed, we may suppose that a less solemn procedure was often adopted, especially in private agreements. On the other hand, we cannot be sure that accounts of these are always reliable, since the narrators could often condense details which were generally known and therefore self-evident, contenting themselves with a very brief depiction. [39]

As we see it, the legal institution fashioned in the covenant was of decisive importance for the development of the social forms of the life of Israel both as a people and as the community of Yahweh. It was in outworking of this concept that nomadic groups became tribes, the tribes became a group of tribes and power came finally to be concentrated in the monarchy. This concept determines the sociological structure of Israel in small things as well as great, in private life as well as public, in religious as well as commercial. This significance was due to the influence and latent persistence of the nomadic or semi-nomadic organisation displayed by the sons of Israel on their first entry on the stage of history. Like the related Semites who had no sure territory of their own, the Israelites were first composed of tribes resting on the natural blood relationship of families. Blood brotherhood as a natural order constituted a natural legal authority, and a legal authority superior to the bond of blood developed out of an extension of brotherhood by various means. The epitome of this authority is the written covenant, and to establish a covenant is both to enter another bond of blood and also to take the partner into one's own, thus entering into legal fellowship with him. That the covenant seems to be the exclusive and generally recognised and valid order of public law in the period prior to the constitution of the state or nation may be explained by the fact that this legal form is determined by the most important social cement, i.e., that of blood relationship. One might say that the idea of the covenant, or the natural covenant, is the state of fellowship posited among blood brothers and to be observed by them. To shed the blood of one's brother is to fall under a curse (Gn. 4:11). [40] Where the fact of blood relationship is indubitable and incontestable, the covenant is already present and there is no need of legal enforcement, since it is obvious that members of the same sept or clan are one bone and one flesh and are thus brothers (cf. 2 S. 19:13). On the other hand, where this natural connexion is either obscure or completely absent, an analogous legal relationship can be established only by means of a fictional blood relationship. This fiction is the legal covenant which extends the natural. The legal covenant, too, makes the participants brothers [41] of one bone and one flesh, and thus creates the consequent legal situation. It is a totality (שָׁלוֹם), which can be no more broken or altered than the blood relationship itself. This totality, or peace, is the ideal state of fellowship in every relationship; it is an actualisation in law of the thought of brotherhood. Mutually recognising and representing one another as brethren, the participants offer mutual guarantees in their situations and the resultant claims. Their relationship as thus ordered is unalterable, permanent (בְּרִית עוֹלָם) and inviolable, and thus makes supreme demands on the legal sense and responsibility of the participants.

---

[39] Thus the formula "covenant of salt" (Nu. 18:19; 2 Ch. 13:5) refers to a meal ; or again, בַּעֲלֵי שְׁבוּעָה in Neh. 6:18 emphasises the oath of the בַּעֲלֵי בְרִית.

[40] Cf. also Ju. 17:2 : A curse is turned into a blessing once it is seen that it is directed against one's own son and thus violates the compact of blood.

[41] Am. 1:9. Cf. also David's lament for his "brother" Jonathan (2 S. 1:26).

There is no firmer guarantee of legal security, peace or personal loyalty than the covenant. [42] Regard for the institution is made a religious duty by means of the oath taken at its establishment. Those who enter into covenant know that Yahweh Himself keeps strict watch over the sworn fellowship and its order. Violation or depreciation of the accepted duty is recognised to be sin in the strictest possible sense of disregard for the will of Yahweh. To forget the covenant of brethren is to awaken the wrath of Yahweh (Am. 1:9). The covenant thus implies the unconditional validity of law surrounded by sacral assurances. It means legitimate order as opposed to caprice, uncertainty and animosity.

In all probability the establishment of a theoretical or fictional blood relationship is to be regarded as strongly emphasised in the ceremonies of initiation as illustrated in the examples cited. Jacob and Laban held a brotherly feast with their relatives. The special significance of blood in the ritual is sometimes even more strongly emphasised, though we cannot say what is its precise significance. A firmly established expression like "blood of the covenant" (Ex. 24:8; Zech. 9:11) is ambiguous in virtue of its very conciseness. On the other hand, the formal conciseness seems to indicate that blood is regarded as a constitutive element. Unfortunately, however, there is no clue to its significance. Precise and uniform theological value is nowhere ascribed to it. The theoretical incompleteness of unwritten and popular ideas concerning blood as a force or as the substance of life (cf. Dt. 12:23; Lv. 17:14; Gn. 9:4) never yields to a developed and normative conception of the blood ritual in the OT tradition of the covenant. Nor do we find any direct help towards an elucidation of the OT in comparisons with the many traditional Semitic and non-Semitic customs, mostly very unpleasant, which were used outside the Bible as covenant ceremonies, e.g., the sucking or drinking or rubbing of blood. [43] The most that we can say is that this material gives a certain plausibility to the view that even in the custom of Israel we are dealing with blood rites which have nothing to do with sacrifice but which are designed to establish a fellowship of substance between the covenant partners. The only verse which seems to hint at this directly is Ex. 24:8 with its reference to the application of blood to the participants, namely, the altar as the representative of God on the one side and the people on the other. This action takes place after the sacrifice, and it is to be understood in the light of the explanatory words: "This is the blood of the covenant." That is to say, the blood itself is declared to be symbolically or magically the בְּרִית. Both participants are linked with the same blood, and therefore the one is as the other. In this case the rite is a cultic act, for we have here a theological covenant. Yet we may still assume that a similar practice obtained in public law. It should also be recalled that covenantal force is ascribed to the rite of circumcision, which is performed on the body of the covenant partner and in which there is no suggestion of an accompanying sacrifice (Gn. 34:15). [44]

---

[42] The seriousness of the act of Jael is best realised when we remember that accord. to Ju. 4:17b there was peace between the house of her husband and King Jabin. The story must have posed a perplexing problem for every loyal Israelite. If true, it shows that in certain circumstances passionate hatred may be too strong even for the legal guarantee. On the other hand, the case of the Gibeonites in Jos. 9:13 shows that the sworn covenant is respected even when a deception is later disclosed. To have to experience deceit and cunning at the hands of "men of the covenant" who are "men of peace" is a dreadful thing (v. 6 f., 15), and it is enough to make one "to stink among the inhabitants of the land" to abuse the agreed blood ritual which is designed to constitute a single people (v. 22; cf. v. 15 "ye shall be as we"). Cf. Ps. 55:20.

[43] Cf. C. R. Thurnwald, s.v. "Brüderschaft," in M. Ebert, Reallexikon der Vorgeschichte, 2 (1925), 189 ff.; W. Robertson Smith, The Religion of the Semites (G. T., 1899, p. 240 ff.) and the older literature to which he refers.

[44] The case is different in Ex. 4:25 f., where a sacrifice is possible, cf. Wendel, op. cit., 16 ff. Yet there are so many difficulties in the statement that it is not very well adapted

It is hard to understand as sacrifices some of the other bloody rites mentioned in the OT at the conclusion of a covenant (Gn. 15:8 ff. and Jer. 34:18b). The action in Gn. 15:8 ff. [45] is best understood if we set aside all the mythical features in the depiction and take it that the intention of the author is to cause Yahweh to act with Abraham as one man acts with another in the process of making a legal covenant. As in the case of Laban, the motivation here, too, is to be found in the legal insecurity of Abraham. It does not seem to him that Yahweh's promise to give him the land is binding (v. 8 : "Whereby shall I know that I shall inherit it ?"). The legal assurance desired is given in the action which is described as making a covenant in v. 18. Several animals are cut into two halves which are then arranged in rows to make a passage. It is not said that these animals are sacrificed ; they are simply brought by Abraham (v. 10 : וַיִּקַּח־לוֹ; cf. v. 9 : קְחָה לִי) and prepared. [46] The procedure which follows is unusual only in the sense that Abraham's partner is not a man but God. What takes place is in a vision, for Abraham falls into a deep sleep, the state for the reception of revelation (v. 12). In his sleep he seems to see what is described in v. 17. In the darkness there is a fire moving between the animals, its flame shining like a torch. The reader clearly perceives that this represents Yahweh. Covenant fellowship is thus established, and the promise validated. What is depicted is no free invention ; the narrators are giving an exact description of the procedure customarily followed in making a covenant ; the only unique feature is that Yahweh is now made the subject. One can readily understand that fear of reducing too much the distance between God and man prevented a completion of the procedure, so that Abraham did not also pass through as might have been expected. On the other hand, this peculiarity of the theological covenant, namely, the one-sided action of Yahweh, does not justify us in assuming that Abraham offered a sacrifice. [47] For the same custom is attested in Jer. 34:18b in relation to purely human legal procedure. [48] There, too, there is no question of sacrifice ; it is simply noted that the transaction takes place before the Lord as a witness, a refined expression which recalls appealing to God by an oath. The meaning of the action, when taken in connexion with Jer. 34:18a, is thus to be sought in self-cursing, which is the central part of an oath. The men of the covenant are abandoned to a threefold evil because they did not keep the words of the covenant (לֹא הֵקִימוּ אֶת־דִּבְרֵי הַבְּרִית). These words list the obligations and conclude with a curse on those who evade them. The curse stands between the participants (cf. Gn. 26:28 : תְּהִי נָא אָלָה בֵּינוֹתֵינוּ) and is portrayed in the analogous action of the cutting apart of the animals. They see themselves as bloody corpses at the thought

---

to serve as a basis for far-reaching conclusions on the covenant character of marriage. Marriage is not a covenant, but at the very most a covenant sign of clan brotherhood. Mal. 2:14 and Prv. 2:17 use ברית in the sense of Da. 11:28; → n. 72.

[45] The narrative may be divided between J and E, but it is hard to distinguish between them and makes no difference to the sense.

[46] Wendel, op. cit., 114 has again drawn attention to this.

[47] So, e.g., Gunkel, Genesis, 181; Pedersen Eid, 50; Buber, op. cit., 112. The fact that the animals taken were normally used in sacrifice simply shows that they used valuable animals, as was fitting at an official act.

[48] The syntax is irregular, and we may suspect some addition. Yet this does not alter the sense, the only question being whether the passing through the parts of the divided (בתר) calf is on the occasion of a covenant of the men of Jerusalem with King Zedekiah and one another. There can be no doubt that they are following a common legal practice.

of a breach of the covenant. [49] The formula : כֹּה יַעֲשֶׂה יְהֹוָה וְכֹה יוֹסִיף "so will Yahweh do, and more also," probably has its origin in the reference of those who take the oath to the divided carcases through which they pass. [50]

Nevertheless, the whole question whether or not such blood rites involve sacrifice is perhaps an idle one in view of the fact that the tradition does not present any consistent view of the matter. [51] For if Gn. 15 and Jer. 34:18 probably justify us in concluding that the common expression כרת ברית originates in rites which do not include a sacrifice, an instance like Gn. 31:54 shows that a writer like E unthinkingly brings sacrifice at least into proximity to the covenant, thus making it possible to relate כרת ברית to sacrifice. There can be no doubt that the expression is often meant in this sense, and the magical basis of the covenant concept is not always present to the authors to the same degree when the formula is used. The institution moved away increasingly from its natural basis when the tribes of Israel gave up their nomadic ways of life, and especially when they established the state, since it came to be applied more and more to larger and more complicated relationships in which there was little place for the original simple ideas. The sacral and magical features of the covenant become more or less ornamental, the true heart of the matter being found in the transaction.

Thus a covenant with Assyria (Hos. 12:1) is a political treaty. To be sure, the formal aspects might well be much the same as in the case of a covenant of tribes or minor dynasts. [52] But the ideas of brotherhood and peaceful unity were now subsidiary to the necessity imposed by the vital interests of the state. If such fictitious unity with peoples of a stammering speech and domineering displays of force was popular in Israel, it was for very different reasons than those of brotherhood. Such treaties were broken without scruple once reasons of state seemed to demand, no matter what the prophets might say. [53] The broadening out of the older tribal law to international law necessarily entailed some such dissolution or weakening of the original idea to the degree that the sacral guarantee was usually shared between different divine authorities and there thus

---

[49] This explanation of the blood rite in Gn. 15 and Jer. 34:18 seems to be the only possible one, not merely because Ju. 19:29 and 1 S. 11:7 point in the same direction, but also because there are many complete analogies to the whole procedure in the non-biblical world. We may refer especially to a well-known and much quoted record of the treaty between Assur-nirari V and Mati'-ilu of Agusi, in which the former, standing before a ram divided on the occasion of the treaty, pronounces the words: "This head is not the head of the ram, but the head of Mati'-ilu, his sons, his nobles and the people of his land. If Mati'-ilu violates this oath, as the head of this ram is struck off ... so will the head of Mati'-ilu be struck off" (cf. *Mitteilungen der Vorderasiat. Gesellschaft*, 3 [1898] 228; B. Meissner, *Babylonien und Assyrien*, I [1920], 140; II [1925], 83, the slaying as a substitutionary sacrifice; Pedersen Eid, 110 ff.; Wendel, *op. cit.*, 112 f.).

[50] Cf. 1 S. 3:17; 20:13 etc. On these cf. J. P. Valeton, ZAW, 12 (1892), 226. Possibly the linking of the verbs בוא, עבר and עמד with בְּרִית is connected with this rite, cf. the expression "to bring someone into a curse," Ez. 17:13.

[51] It is quite uncertain why animals were given by Abraham to Abimelech in Gn. 21:27 (E). A meal is the occasion in the analogous 26:30 (J). The seven lambs of J (21:30), however, seem to represent a pledge. Does this mean that they are not slain ? Or is the account to be regarded as complete in itself, so that they are to be taken quite simply as a gift ? (Pedersen Eid, 49).

[52] Cf. the examples adduced by Meissner, *Babyl. u. Ass.*

[53] Cf. the threats of Is. in 29:15; 30:1 ff. Yet it is striking how strongly Isaiah seems also to be guided by political insight. Even Jeremiah's opposition to the war party in Judah is not due to any sense of covenant fidelity to the Chaldeans. If one suffers through the violation of the opposite party, Yahweh Himself will avenge this : Is. 33:8 ff. (the historical reference is contested, cf. the Comm., *ad loc.*).

resulted a diminished sense of responsibility on the part of the participants. If the covenant Baal of Shechem (Ju. 9:46) was really the guarantor of the *modus vivendi* of the
Canaanites with the Israelites, one can easily see the dubious aspect of this compromise.
The common prohibition of any covenant with the people of the land may well be based
in part on the experience that it is absolutely impossible to keep any covenant in the
names of such conflicting deities as Yahweh on the one side and Baal on the other. [54]

As the transactional character of the covenant comes to the forefront, it usually
appears that there is an unequal distribution of advantage and disadvantage, of
voluntariness and compulsion, in relation to the participants. This usually arises
quite naturally from the stringent necessities of legal life, from the motives and
goals of the parties concerned, from their desire for a reconciliation of conflicting
interests which cannot be completely fair. Those who are in fact equal hardly
need to enter into a covenant. What produces a covenant is the need to secure
oneself against someone who threatens one's security or to grant security to
someone who is well-disposed and from whom something may be expected. The
linguistic usage itself [55] seems to hint at this unequal distribution when it speaks
of making a covenant "with reference to" someone. This denotes the initiative of
the subject of the action, which may take the form of the imposing of the will of
the active agent on the passive. The point may not seem to be very important.
Indeed, the conclusion drawn probably arises naturally from the circumstances.
Yet we do at least see that in the legal institution of the covenant the parity of
those concerned is neither an essential prerequisite nor a consequence of the
transaction. The covenant as a declaration of will seldom achieves symmetry of
structure, and yet its validity is not thereby impaired. This is something to be
remembered when we discuss the distinctiveness of the so-called theological covenant. This is certainly not to be sought in the disturbance of symmetry between
the two partners, since no significance is ever attached to the question of parity
in the establishment of a covenant.

5. The Theological Covenant.

The introduction of deity as one of the pledged and secured partners in a covenant relationship gives us the theological covenant. God is not here limited to the
position of guarantor of the covenant and its institution, as in a legal covenant.
As a pledge of the common order, He is also subject to it, to the degree that the
question of protective lordship is not left open.

In Yahweh worship this theoretical ordering of the relationship between God and
man is developed into a comprehensive system which finally has universal implications.
Nevertheless, it is not entirely unknown in other oriental religions, though without
undergoing any parallel development. The natural basis of the covenant, the thought of
blood relationship, may be found everywhere in Syro-Palestinian and Arabian cults [56]
where the cultic family treats the deity as its father or establishes brotherhood with the
deity by sacrifice. The same element is expressed rather less intimately and with a

---

[54] The meal to which the inhabitants of the land are invited in Ex. 34:15 seems to be
intended as a covenant meal establishing cultic relationship. This kind of covenant constitutes a constant danger (מוֹקֵשׁ, v. 12), since it is not possible without weakening the
worship of Yahweh. Cf. further Ex. 23:32 f.; Dt. 7:2; Ju. 2:2.

[55] On this point, → 109.

[56] Cf. W. Baudissin, *Adonis und Esmun* (1911), 43 ff.; J. Wellhausen, *Reste arabischen
Heidentums*² (1927), 213 f.

stronger legal emphasis in the appellative designation מֶלֶךְ when applied to a deity.[57] This rests on the tribal organisation and originally denotes the leader of the tribe as one vested with legal prerogatives. It thus presupposes a certain order analogous to the covenant. The actual term "covenant" is used in the phrase בַּעַל בְּרִית "Baal of the covenant," which occurs even in the OT (Ju. 8:33, and אֵל בְּרִית in 9:46) for a Canaanite deity worshipped in Shechem. We do not know, of course, in what relation this deity stood to the covenant, or what kind of covenant it was. It is tempting to see an analogy to the covenant of Yahweh with Israel and thus to conjecture that this deity stood in the same relation to the citizens of Shechem as did Yahweh to Israel. This view cannot be disproved,[58] but it has no more intrinsic probability than other attempts to elucidate this obscure expression.[59] On rather more solid grounds we may compare with the divine covenant of the OT the compact between King Urukagina of Lagaš and the god Ningirsu, which represents an agreement between the two in respect of social legislation,[60] or the covenant renewal which the ancient Arabian prince Karibala-ilu Watar executes in a solemn national act to unite deity and people,[61] or other instances of the theological conception of the covenant in Sabaean religion.[62]

The OT tradition does not show us with any certainty when or by whom the theory was propounded and accepted that Yahweh stands in covenant with Israel. There is every sign, however, that the theory was already present even in the early period prior to the conquest of Canaan, since it agrees with the nomadic or semi-nomadic mode of life of the primitive Israelites and thus seems to offer a key to the consolidation of the nation from a coalition of tribes. On the grounds of the comparatively late origin of the sources underlying the Pentateuch and the records of the Judges, and the paucity of references in the prophets,[63] doubts have been raised whether Moses may be regarded as the author of the theory, or whether he actually acted as the representative of Israel in making the covenant on the mount, as seems to be the view of the Pentateuch. But these doubts are seen to be exaggerated once it is realised that those who propagate them regard a developed monotheistic concept of God in the sense of the prophets and the Law as indispensable to acceptance of an early theological understanding of the covenant in Israel.[64] Many people to-day think that it may be taken for granted that what little we know of the religious views of this early period completely excludes any such developed monotheism either in the invading Israelites or in those portions of the later people already settled in the land. Nevertheless, this does not mean that we must also exclude the possibility that from the time of the redemption from Egypt the confederation which arose under Moses' leadership cherished the idea of a theological covenant with Yahweh and indeed found in the implied sense of

---

[57] Cf. W. Baudissin, *Kyrios* III (1929), 49.

[58] For different reasons it is supported by E. Meyer, *Die Israeliten* (1906), 550; R. Kittel, *Geschichte des Volkes Israel,* II⁶ (1925), 33.

[59] Cf. Karge, *op. cit.,* 334 ff.

[60] The text is given in F. Thureau-Dangin, *Die sumerischen u. akkadischen Königsinschriften* (1907), 52, quoted in Buber, *op. cit.,* 237.

[61] It is the merit of M. Buber, *op. cit.,* 56 f., to have drawn attention to these analogies. The texts may be found in N. Rhodokanakis, *Altsabäische Texte (Sitzungsberichte der Wiener Akademie, phil.-hist. Kl.,* 1930), 19 ff.

[62] Cf. P. Nielsen, *Handbuch der altarab. Altertumskunde,* I (1927), 86 ff.

[63] B. Stade, *Bibl. Theologie des AT,* I (1905), 254 f. thinks that Jeremiah is the earliest representative of the idea of the theological covenant.

[64] Cf. R. Smend, *Lehrbuch der at.lichen Religionsgeschichte*² (1899), 117.

legal obligation the force which enabled them to fulfil their very difficult task.

On such grounds as this we may contend that the divine covenant developed in the modest framework of the tribal covenant. In this connexion we can use the word development only in the sense of recognising a historical seed. The covenant idea could not be proclaimed as a theologoumenon spun out in the void. By its very form it was itself indissolubly bound to history. For if a בְּרִית is in force, it is so only because of its solemn conclusion which determines the whole relationship. Thus, to convince someone of the covenant with Yahweh, appeal had to be made to the history of the reality of the divine commitment asserted. For this reason the Moses stories, the whole tradition of Israel and Judah to the latest periods, and the very structure of the legal concept all presuppose a historical event which established the divine covenant. Indeed, the concept could hardly have attained the significance it did if cherished recollections of the past had not enforced its recognition. The concept implies with the utmost clarity that we are not dealing with a mere idea of God but with an act of God in the remote past. God's will elected the children of Israel, who then for their part elected God, obligating themselves to Him in the covenant. God is the electing God of the elect (→ ἐκλέγω).

Both aspects of this thesis emerge clearly in the tradition concerning the establishment of the covenant with Yahweh. The thought of the electing God is present in the account of the divine covenant made in Shechem under the leadership of Joshua (Jos. 24 JE). Within the total tradition this was added to the accounts of the covenant twice made under Moses (Ex. 24:8 and 34:10), which it expands and ratifies. Yet it must also be regarded as the record of an independent action whose relation to the Moses tradition is a historical problem which we must set aside in this context (→ θεός). Unlike Ex. 19, Jos. 24 attributes the initiative in the whole matter to Joshua as the leader of the people rather than to God. Joshua gathers the heads of the tribes to call for a decision whom they will serve (v. 14 f.). His address shows that only Yahweh has any established claim to be the God of Israel. He brought Abraham from the land beyond the river and separated him from the gods worshipped there. He brought the children of Israel out of Egypt and enabled them to subdue the Amorites. He gave Israel a land which it had not fashioned for itself, cities which it had not built and vineyards and olive groves which it had not planted (v. 13). All this proves that Yahweh took Israel to Himself as opposed to the gods worshipped by its forefathers, and that Israel is thus bound to set aside all other gods and acknowledge Him. This acknowledgment, however, must be responsible and binding: "And if it seem evil unto you to serve the Lord, choose ye this day (בַּחֲרוּ לָכֶם הַיּוֹם) whom ye will serve; whether the gods which your fathers served that were on the other side of the flood, or the gods of the Amorites, in whose land ye dwell" (v. 15). Joshua concludes his address with a confession of Yahweh, who is the only God to whom he and his house consider themselves bound. The assumption is that the tribes addressed are still inclined to serve other gods as well as Yahweh. [65] Possibly individual tribes had their own deities which they were now required to renounce in favour of God, who had proved Himself the Leader of the whole confederation. Those addressed make the acknowledgment: "The Lord is our God" (v. 17), and they

---

[65] Cf. Ju. 5:8.

accept Joshua's proof of this fact. Joshua points out the binding character of their confession (v. 22): עֵדִים אַתֶּם בָּכֶם "ye are witnesses against yourselves"; and he makes a covenant "with reference to the people" (v. 25), the terms of which are written in the book of the divine statutes. The fact that this is a divine covenant is confirmed by the account of the erection of a stone at the sacred tree by the sanctuary, the stone having "heard all the words of the Lord which he spake unto us" (v. 26).

The procedure and significance of this covenant find an analogy in the political act by which royal power is transferred to a man. [66] The theocratic notion that Yahweh is King (cf. Ju. 8:33: יהוה יִמְשֹׁל בָּכֶם) is closely related to the divine cove-nant, so that the covenant made with God may be understood as a royal covenant. This conception has the advantage that it does justice to the historical experiences of Israel which led it to the divine covenant, the process of election being em-phasised. Thus, as a נָגִיד who has proved himself by his acts is appointed מֶלֶךְ by acclamation, so Yahweh is chosen as the supreme court by the act of homage made in concluding the covenant. [67] In this way, not merely is the principle of law and order fully satisfied, but the sober reality of the legal relationship is also invested with the poetry of kingship, and an inspiring doxological motif is heard. Yet there is also implied thereby a warning against any confusion of the principles of the divine covenant and theocracy. If both finally emphasise the same thought that God is the Leader of His people, they do so in different ways and at different points, and the consciousness of legal obligation, together with the thought of the divine initiative, is undoubtedly expressed much more strongly in the conception of the covenant.

This emerges even more plainly in the other accounts to which we have re-ferred, namely, those of the miraculous origin of the covenant of Yahweh with His people at the mount of God. Here transcendental happenings completely dominate the earthly situation. God orders the initiation and execution of a pro-cedure whose ceremonies can hardly be distinguished from those practised at the conclusion of a legal covenant. The narrative reaches its impressive climax in Ex. 24:9-11. Moses and Aaron, Nadab and Abihu, and seventy of the elders of Israel, climb the mount of God and see the God of Israel with their mortal eyes. The reverence of the author prevents him from depicting the theophany itself. As in the accounts of prophetic theophanies, we are only given glimpses of the *entourage* of God, the total impression being that it was so bright that it was not possible to see properly. The representatives of the people held a meal on the mount in the presence of God and therefore obviously with God.

In accordance with the situation, this is a brotherly meal instituting and confirming close fellowship. Doubts have been raised as to the correctness of the words וַיֹּאכְלוּ וַיִּשְׁתּוּ ("they ate and drank") as they have come down in the tradition. The only genuine question, however, is whether there has not been abbreviation of an originally longer account. Statements were perhaps made concerning the meal of brotherhood with Yahweh which proved offensive to the later sense of transcendence and were thus

---

[66] Cf. esp. 1 S. 11 (Saul).
[67] Cf. H. Schultz, *Theol. d. AT*[4] (1889), 407, and also M. Buber, *op. cit.*, chapter 7. On the distinction between נָגִיד and מֶלֶךְ *v.* A. Alt, *Die Staatenbildung der Israeliten in Palästina* (1930), 29 f.

deleted. [68] The words of the covenant are emphasised, the people pledging itself to the terms as read to it (24:7). Thus, although in this composite J E record there is an obvious attempt to lay the main stress on God's side of the covenant and therefore to equate the covenant with the Law according to a widespread OT tradition, on the other hand there is an almost unparalleled appearance of God as a partner and an emphasis on the full validity of the contract by mention of the customary ceremony of brotherhood.

The content of this narrative, which is so affectingly simple in style, is of tremendous force when we recall that God does not stretch out His hand against the leaders of Israel. Those who stood in the grip of the *numen tremendum* were brought to realise that they were dealing with another God than the one normally detected by the anxious heart of man. The words of the narrator give us the impression that Israel had to start relearning everything afresh with this first introduction of the thought of the covenant, and that the recollection that there was here expressed something quite contrary to natural religious experience could never fail to have its effect on future generations in their development of the concept of God.

The basic thought in the message of salvation contained in the covenant theory, namely, that God is willing to set His covenant partner in a *shalom* status, can never be completely forgotten even when it is in danger of being overwhelmed by legal considerations. That there was, of course, a vivid interest in the institution of the legal form of the divine covenant is evidenced by the pedagogic movement which may be seen in the exhortatory conclusion to the delivery of the Law in Deuteronomy (26:17-18). The content of the theological covenant is here conceived in the simplest way to enable every Israelite to see clearly what is at issue in the relationship of Yahweh to Israel and Israel to Yahweh. In a free and only slightly abbreviated rendering the result is as follows : Thou hast caused Yahweh this day to give thee an assurance that He will be thy God on the condition that thou walkest in His ways, keepest His statutes and hearest His voice. On the other hand Yahweh has caused thee this day to declare that thou wilt be His people (עַם סְגֻלָּה) in accordance with what He has said to thee, and that thou wilt keep His commandments, on the understanding that He will make thee the chief of all peoples, and that thou shalt be a holy people for Yahweh thy God, as He has said.

It may be that from the literary standpoint this passage does not constitute a unity, [69] but from the legal standpoint it is one and complete. The reader is introduced to two contracting parties, i.e., God and Israel. Their mutual relations are to be ordered. Both state their conditions and their offers. When the conditions are agreed, each party makes a declaration committing both itself and the other, and this is accepted by the other. Thus no room is left for doubt. Israel knows that as a possession it is just as bound to Yahweh as Yahweh is to Israel. If Israel violates the accepted obligation to keep the Law of Yahweh, Yahweh is no longer bound to act as the God of Israel, i.e., in its favour, and to make it the chief of all peoples. It is easy to see how J's tenderly depicted wonder before God is

---

[68] The same feeling asserts itself in modern interpreters, as may be seen in Buber's attempts to evade this aspect of the matter, cf. *op. cit.*, 227 f. The proposed combination of v. 5 and v. 11 to give a sacrificial meal without Yahweh is an impossible attempt to avoid the conclusion that the narrator conceived of Yahweh as participating in the meal.

[69] Cf. Steuernagel, *Komm. ad loc.*

here completely overlaid by the authoritative assurance of the theological teacher. One can hardly escape the uneasy feeling that this theory is too clear, that it destroys the essential element of mystery in religion and that it thus makes faith superfluous. The weakness of it emerges clearly when we consider that there is nothing to prevent the counterbalancing deduction that if Yahweh fails to fulfil His obligation to act in favour of Israel, as might be easy enough to maintain, then Israel is also freed from its commitment. This is not an agreement between Lord and servant. The parity of the partners is everywhere assumed.

Nevertheless, we do this consistent pedagogue an injustice if we try to foist such a conclusion on him. His popular and instructive presentation of the theological covenant is primarily designed to bring out catechetically the legal obligatoriness of the covenant without any of the complicating qualifications which necessarily result from the God-man relationship. On the other hand, it is this very fact which, while it brings out the theological value of the theory, also exposes its theoretical impracticability, its robust aggressiveness and the danger which it necessarily presents to religion. [70] Its value lies undoubtedly in the sharp and clear emphasis on a knowledge of God which accepts the will of God and knows that this will aims at the establishment of fellowship with Israel. God's dealings are not incalculable. They have a goal which is firmly delineated and can be comprehended by man. All unwholesome terror, all fear of God in the sense of apprehension before His commanding power, all trembling at unknown forces and events, is now banished from religion, and the basis is thus laid for the Gospel, as we might make bold to say. Man is told what God desires of him. The impulse to draw near to God is freed from creaturely paralysis and referred to the norm of the command as an expression of the divine will. The kind of experience reflected in the brief statement in Ju. 6:24: יהוה שָׁלוֹם, "Yahweh means a state of salvation, a fellowship which is both perfect and assured," is echoed in this theory. Such an experience arose early in Israel, and there are no adequate grounds for contradicting the tradition which represents it as that of Moses and those associated with him.

On the other hand, we have to recognise that as developed in Deuteronomy, not merely in this formulation but in principle, the theory is not immune from the weaknesses of any attempt to state in the sober language of theology a knowledge of God won in the glow of experience. The sobriety of a legal concept is no very adequate garment for statements concerning the will and goal of God. This was perceived and stated so quickly in Israel that some have thought that we must deduce from the polemic of the prophets against the foundations of the covenant theory the conclusion that the theory itself was propounded only at a later period. This is not a cogent argument. For if Hosea tried to transfer the theory to the very different legal sphere of marriage in which there is room for both divine and human emotions remote from the law (→ ἀγάπη, I, 31 ff.), or if Amos questioned the election of Israel in the special sense of the covenant theory, [71] the covenant is apparently presupposed and the argument thus falls to the ground. The question

---

[70] It may be that this popularly egocentric view of the covenant contributed to the later tendency on occasion to complain against God for His omissions, e.g., Ez. 18:2; Jer. 31:29 and some of the Psalms.

[71] Am. 5:25.

of date, however, is not the important one. What really matters is that opposition was obviously encountered by the theologico-legal system. This opposition finds its most beautiful expression in the complex of prophetic salvation sayings in Jer. 30 f., the literary origin of which is not quite clear, but which may be attributed with some reservations to the prophet in whose book they appear. The author of 31:31 ff. has the strong feeling that the idea of the theological covenant has out-lived its usefulness and now constitutes a threat. It may well be understood that anxious and sorrowful souls clung to the hope of the covenant. It may also be recognised that the covenant theory deserves much of the praise for saving the religion of Israel in days of grim misfortune. [72] But clinging to God on the ground of legal obligation was still an active force, and religion threatened to succumb to legal claim. The prophet saw this danger, and because of it he broke free from the covenant theory. Yet he did not despise its known and well-loved garment. He thus spoke of the new covenant, though in reality this is no longer a cove-nant. [73] The Law is to be written in the heart (33) and is not therefore a law claiming legal validity. To violate this Law would never occur to anyone. The old covenant is forgotten, and should remain so.

Quell

B. The Greek Term διαθήκη.

διαθήκη is used in class. and Hell. Gk. only in an abstract and figur. sense. [74] 1. It means "order," "institution," Sext. Emp. Math., VII, 136 (Democr.): κατὰ σώματος διαθήκην, "bodily constitution."

2. It is most commonly used for "last will and testament," a techn. term in Gk. jurisprudence in every age, [75] but also found in literary and popular Gk., e.g., Aristoph. Vesp., 584, 589; Plat. Leg., XI, 923e; Epict. Diss., II, 13, 7; BGU, 19, II, 5; P. Lond., 177; Ditt. Or., 753, 8; IG, VII, 3426, 14. On διατίθεσθαι διαθήκην (-ας), and very exceptionally τίθεσθαι διαθήκην, e.g., P. Ryl., II, 116, 9, in the sense of "to make a will," → διατίθημι, 104 f. In the relation of the ancient Gk. will to the *donatio inter vivos*, there is debate whether this is a one-sided or two-sided transaction. In the Hellenistic period the testator normally has full power of dis-position. [76] In literature the word can sometimes be used for a philosophical testa-ment, i.e., the spiritual legacy of a sage (Menipp.: Diog. L, VI, 101; Apollonius:

---

[72] It is worth noting that the use of בְּרִית for Jewish religion in general (Da. 11:28; Mal. 3:1) begins in days of oppression.

[73] The same is true of the "covenant of the people" of Is. 42:6 (→ I, 34, n. 73).

[74] διαθήκη can hardly mean *depositum* in Dinarch., 1, 9 (→ 125), and certainly not in Aetius Amidanus, VII, 113: the κολλύριον ... διαθήκης ἐπικαλούμενον τοῦ χρυσοχόου ὃ κατέλιπεν ἀποθνήσκων is named according to the will of the dying goldsmith (as against Liddell-Scott).

[75] For examples and discussion, in addition to the bibl. in Behm, 6, n. 1 and 11, n. 1, cf. Mitteis-Wilcken, II, 1, 236 ff.; Lohmeyer, 11 ff.; W. D. Ferguson, *The Legal Terms ... common to the Macedonian Greek Inscriptions and the NT* (Phil. Diss., Chicago, 1913), 42 ff.; Eger, *op. cit.*; H. Kreller, *Erbrechtliche Untersuchungen auf Grund der graeco-ägyp-tischen Papyrusurkunden* (1919).

[76] For lit. → n. 75. Even the testaments of the rhetorical age cannot be understood at once as treaties (συμβόλαια), cf. Kreller, *op. cit.*, 297 f. On the sing. and plur. of διαθήκη "testament," cf. Behm, 14 f., and the observation of Thom. Mag., p. 79, 10 (Ritschl): δια-θήκας γράφειν τις λέγεται, οὐ διαθήκην.

Philostr. Vit. App., VII, 35 ; Peregrinus Proteus : Luc. Pergr. Mort., 41). [77] This derives from the legal usage ; it is assumed that the last orders, sayings or admonitions of such a man are particularly binding. Rabbinic Judaism adopted both the word and concept into its own legal language : [78] דייאתיקי, דייתיקי etc., e.g., MQ, 3, 3; BM, 1, 7; bBB, 135b; דייתיקי מבטלת דייתיקי, "a (later) will replaces a (former) will."

3. In the sense of "agreement" or "treaty" it is found only in Aristoph. Av., 440 f.: ἢν μὴ διάθωνταί γ' οἵδε διαθήκην ἐμοὶ ἥνπερ ὁ πίθηκος τῇ γυναικὶ διέθετο (→ διατίθημι, 105). Peisthetairos will lay down his arms only if the birds first make a recognised treaty (461: σπονδαί) with him not to hurt him, solemnly binding themselves by an oath and setting down the terms in writing (445 ff.). This is a treaty between two parties, but binding only on the one according to the terms fixed by the other.

4. A general sense of "ordinance" or "disposition," which arises from the med. of the verb with which διαθήκη is commonly linked, finds literary attestation only in the disputed passage in Dinarch., 1, 9 : τὸ συνέδριον (the Areopagus) ... ὃ φυλάττει τὰς ἀπορρήτους διαθήκας ἐν αἷς τὰ τῆς πόλεως σωτήρια κεῖται, the reference being to mysterious and sacred decrees or statutes which the Areopagus preserves and on which the welfare of the state depends. [79] On the other hand, there are hints that this was a possible and widespread use before the term was given its narrower legal sense and even afterwards. Thus διαθήκη and διάθεσις are closely related (cf. 1.), and if διάθεσις means "order" or "enactment," cf. Plat. Leg., I, 624a : τὴν αἰτίαν τῆς τῶν νόμων διαθέσεως, then the same might be said of διαθήκη. Again, διαθήκη passed into Heb. and Aram. as the loanword דייתיקי in the sense not merely of "testament" (cf. 2.) but also more generally of "ordinance" or "disposition" [80] (e.g., Gn. r., 59, 11 on 24:10 : "Everything of his lord's was in his hand, i.e., the disposition (זו דיאתיקי)"; Lv. r., 19 on 15:25; jSanh., 20c, 50 : "Every ordinance which is partly abrogated is wholly abrogated"; jBer., 9b: "By an ordinance I give it (the dew) to him (Abraham)(בדיאתיקי נתתיו לו)"; jBM, 8a, 57 f.: "Care should be taken not to pervert his ordinances (לפגם דייתיקין שלו)." Since there is nothing to suggest that the Jews themselves gave a new sense to the term, one can only conclude that they were adopting a common Greek sense. "διαθήκη is properly *dispositio*, an 'arrangement' made by one party with plenary power, which the other party may accept or reject, but cannot alter. A 'will' is simply the most conspicuous example of such an instrument, which ultimately monopolised the word just because it suited its differentia so completely." [81] It

---

[77] Cf. the ostensible testament of Orpheus in Theophil., III, 2; Ps.-Just. De Monarchia, 2 etc., and on this pt. Lohmeyer, *op. cit.,* 35 f., who appends a review of testaments in Jewish and Christian literature.

[78] Cf. Str.-B., III, 545 ff.; Dalman, *op. cit.,* 148.

[79] διαθήκας A is to be preferred as *lectio difficilior* to ἀποθήκας N or θήκας (Wolf, Blass). On the question what is meant by διαθῆκαι here, cf. the notes in the editions of Maetzner and Thalheim, also Lohmeyer, 34. The most illuminating explanation is to be found in G. F. Schoemann-J. H. Lipsius, *Griechische Altertümer*[4], I, (1897), 541; cf. MHE, Meier, Allg. LitZtg., Halle (1843), 466 : "The ordinances ... which made the Areopagus the guardian of the national religion, which placed the cultus and the state priests under its special oversight and which gave it power of decision in accusations of ἀσεβείας."

[80] Cf. Str.-B., III, 545.

[81] Moult.-Mill., 148.

remains only to note that the existing examples of the more general sense of "disposition" are all to be found in the religious sphere.

C. The Transition from בְּרִית to διαθήκη in the LXX and Jewish Literature.

1. When the LXX [82] uses διαθήκη for בְּרִית, it is often thinking of a covenant or legal compact, e.g., Gn. 21:27, 32; 1 Βασ. 23:18; 3 Βασ. 15:19; ψ 82:5; Is. 28:15. The common expressions διατίθεσθαι διαθήκην μετά τινος or ἀνὰ μέσον τινὸς καί τινος (elsewhere τινὶ or πρός τινα) refer to the conclusion of a treaty between two partners. The sparse use of the real Greek word for "treaty" (συνθήκη), which is never used for בְּרִית except in 4 Βασ. 17:15 A, shows that διαθήκη was regarded as the equivalent in the LXX, though Aquila, Symmachus and Theodotion later substituted what seemed to them to be the more literal συνθήκη. Even in passages where a single party (God) is the author of the διαθήκη, the linguistic usage (ἀνὰ μέσον, μετά) reminds us of a treaty relationship, e.g., Gn. 9:15, 17; Ju. 2:1; Jer. 14:21; Ez. 16:8: εἰσῆλθον ἐν διαθήκῃ μετὰ σοῦ. On the other hand, it is worth noting that, as διατίθεσθαι διαθήκην is used not only for כָּרַת בְּרִית but also for הֵקִים or צִוָּה בְּרִית (→ διατίθημι, 105), διαθήκη is also used for דָּבָר, עֵדוּת, תּוֹרָה (of God) or כָּתוּב; and also that in both poetic parallelism and lists in prose it is related to such concepts as νόμος, πρόσταγμα, ἐντολαί, δικαιώματα, κρίματα, and to the verbs usually linked with these concepts, e.g., ἐντέλλεσθαι, φυλάττειν, τηρεῖν, παραβαίνειν, παρελθεῖν, ἐμμένειν or πορεύεσθαι. As a synonym of νόμος etc. διαθήκη cannot mean "treaty" or "covenant" but only "ordinance" or "statute." In many other cases, too, the context excludes the idea of the covenant and leads rather to the idea of a one-sided disposition or authoritative ordinance which settles things; e.g., Nu. 25:12 f.: ἰδοὺ ἐγὼ δίδωμι αὐτῷ διαθήκην εἰρήνης ("an ordinance which brings salvation"), καὶ ἔσται αὐτῷ καὶ τῷ σπέρματι αὐτοῦ μετ᾽ αὐτὸν διαθήκη ἱερατείας αἰωνία ("an ordinance which ascribes the priesthood to him and to his successors for ever"); Jos. 24:25: διέθετο Ἰησοῦς διαθήκην πρὸς τὸν λαόν, "Joshua left an ordinance to his people" which bound them according to the preceding transactions (21 ff.). διαθήκη is especially used for the declaration of the divine will at Sinai which is the divine disposition *par excellence* in the OT (Ex. 34:27 f.; Dt. 4:13; 5:2 ff.) and also for its inscription on two tables of stone (Dt. 9:11; Ex. 27:21) which are kept in the κιβωτὸς τῆς διαθήκης κυρίου (Ex. 31:7; 39:35; Dt. 31:25 f.). It is also used for the many ordinances of God which constitute the religious order according to its depiction in the OT (Gn. 6:18; 9:9 ff.; 15:18; 17:2 ff.; Ex. 2:24; 6:4; 31:16; 34:10; Lv. 24:8; 26:9, 11, 45; Dt. 4:23, 31; 8:18; 9:5; 29:1, 12, 14, 25; Jos. 7:11; 23:16; 3 Βασ. 8:21; 4 Βασ. 18:12; Neh. 9:8, and to which, or beyond which, the OT poets and prophets point: 2 Βασ. 23:5; ψ 88:3; 104:8, 10; Is. 59:21; 61:8; Jer. 11:2 f., 6, 10; Ἰερ. 38:31 ff.; 39:40; 41:8; Ez. 34:25; 37:26. The thought of the divine disposition controls at least one part of the passages referred to, in which the expressions διαθήκη μετά τινος or ἀνὰ μέσον ... καὶ ἀνὰ μέσον suggest a treaty relationship, esp. Gn. 9 and 17. Any obscurity is due to the too strict leaning of the translation on the Hebrew original. The remarkable fact that διαθήκη is not an unequivocal concept in the LXX, but hovers between the senses of "covenant" and "disposition," is not based solely on the fact that the Greek term embraces

---

[82] Cf. Riggenbach, *Begriff d.* διαθήκη, 294 ff.; Behm, 21 ff.; Lohmeyer, 78 ff.

both possibilities ; it is to be explained finally in terms of the complex content of the word בְּרִית which the translators were seeking to grasp. In their concern for a suitable rendering of the Hebrew word they must have felt that the originally legal term בְּרִית had come to convey stronger and specifically religious thoughts which went far beyond the idea of a contract between God and man and suggested the idea of a free declaration of the divine will to man's salvation. διαθήκη, too, was a legal term which might comprise different forms of a binding expression of will, e.g., testamentary disposition (which is alien to the OT), a contract between two parties and divine dispositions and sacred ordinances of the most forceful kind. If they thus used διαθήκη for בְּרִית, the one term certainly seemed to be no less rich than the other, but there was a shift of accent through the predominant use of διαθήκη in the religious sense. In other words, the exclusively determinative will of the divine author emerged in clearer focus. The covenant of Yahweh with the patriarchs, Moses, David and the people became freely given ordinances, or dispositions of the sovereign will of God, which declare both His demands and His saving purposes. And in Jer. 31:31 ff., to mention the instance which is most important from the NT standpoint, and which represents both the climax and end of the OT idea of the covenant, the concept καινὴ διαθήκη allows us to conceive of the religion of the age of salvation, to which the gaze of the prophet is directed, only as the free gift of God, as the declaration of His saving will, as the revelation of grace, in relation to which Israel can be only a recipient. "Disposition," "declaration of the divine will," "the divine will self-revealed in history and establishing religion" — this is the religious concept of the διαθήκη in the LXX, and it represents a significant development of the Hebrew term even while preserving its essential content. To try to keep the actual word covenant, [83] which in any case is not really co-extensive with the Hebrew word (→ 109), by adopting such compromises as "covenantal disposition," or "covenanted order or ordinance," [84] or by introducing the alien thought of testament, [85] is only to obscure and pervert the linguistic and historical basis of the διαθήκη idea in the NT.

2. The OT apocrypha and pseudepigrapha [86] present much the same picture as the LXX. In Wis. 18:22 διαθήκη is used as a parallel to ὅρκοι, in Sir. 42:2; 1 Macc. 2:27, 50; Jub. 21:4; 30:21 to νόμος, and in Sir. 45:5 etc. to κρίματα (cf. the expression νόμος διαθήκης in Sir. 39:8; Ps. Sol. 10:5). In Sir. 11:20; 14:12, 17; 16:22; 42:2; 44:20 (with בְּרִית); 45:5, 7, 17; 47:11, it is used to translate pħ. It is also used for the whole Law (βιβλίον διαθήκης, "book of the Law," 1 Macc. 1:57; Sir. 24:23), and for individual commands (1 Macc. 1:15, 63). All this goes to show that the primary thought is that of (God's) "disposition," "order" or "institution," συνθήκη being used for "covenant" or "treaty" in 1 Macc. 10:26; 2 Macc. 12:1; Wis. 1:16 etc. Promise had always been the content of the divine διαθήκη : Sir. 44:20; Wis. 18:22. The hope of future deliverance and salvation rests on the διαθῆκαι τῶν πατέρων as historical declarations of the grace of God in Sir. 44 f. (Moses and David etc. being here numbered among the patriarchs); 1 Macc. 4:10; 2 Macc. 1:2; Ps. Sol. 9:19. God's revealed will is διαθήκη ἁγία, 1 Macc. 1:15, 63, διαθήκη αἰώνιος, Sir. 45:15; a binding norm of conduct, Sir.

---

[83] As favoured by Kennedy, Vos, da Fonseca.

[84] Cr.-Kö., 1068 and Kögel, op. cit., 612.

[85] Dibelius, 85 f. and in part Deissmann, 287.

[86] Lohmeyer, 109 ff.; Cr.-Kö., 1068; on the conception of the new διαθήκη, cf. also A. Frhr. v. Stromberg, Studien zur Theorie und Praxis der Taufe (1913), 65 ff.

39:8; Ps. Sol. 10:5, hence διαθήκη is the epitome of the Jewish religion, 1 Macc. 2:27: πᾶς ὁ ... ἰστῶν διαθήκην ἐξελθέτω ὀπίσω μου (cf. 20, 50); Ps. Sol. 17:17: υἱοὶ τῆς διαθήκης; Jub. 15:26. There is even living hope of the coming of a new divine order in terms of Jer. 31:31 ff., Bar. 2:35: στήσω αὐτοῖς διαθήκην αἰώνιον τοῦ εἶναί με αὐτοῖς εἰς θεὸν καὶ αὐτοὶ ἔσονταί μοι εἰς λαόν (cf. Jub. 1:16 f., 23 ff.; Sir. 18:11 ff. etc.). An extreme development of legalism is combined with eschatological hope in the בְּרִית concept of the Damascus writing. [87] The בְּרִית אֵל in 3:11; 7:5; 13:14 and 14:2 has here the unambiguous character of an "authoritative declaration of will," or "disposition," rather than covenant. The members of the community of the בְּרִית הַחֲדָשָׁה in 6:19; 8:21 pursue their ordered life according to the statutes of the founder. They are to "walk in them in the whole time of iniquity, nor shall they meditate doing anything apart from them until the teacher of righteousness comes at the end of the days," 6:10 f. It is particularly clear at this point that in Judaism the idea of the καινὴ διαθήκη in Jer. 31:31 ff. is linked with Messianic expectations.

3. Philo [88] uses συνθήκη for "treaty," "covenant" (Congr., 78; Leg. Gaj., 37; Qu. on Gn. 26:28 (II, 676, Mangey); he never has διαθήκη. The religious concept διαθήκη θεοῦ (Det. Pot. Ins., 68; Som., II, 224: τὸ δίκαιον ἀδιαφορεῖ διαθήκης θεοῦ) is taken by him from the LXX. He lays the strongest possible stress on the element of the absolute one-sidedness of the expression of the will of the gracious God, Som., II, 223: τὴν πλήρη χαρίτων διαθήκην ἑαυτοῦ — νόμος δ' ἐστὶ καὶ λόγος τῶν ὄντων ὁ πρεσβύτατος — ὡς ἂν ἐπὶ βάσεως τῆς τοῦ δικαίου ψυχῆς ἄγαλμα θεοειδὲς ἱδρύσεσθαι παγίως φησίν. As an allegorist, however, he imports into the LXX concept the current everyday sense of "testament" (Spec. Leg., II, 16). The majesty of the divine διαθῆκαι in the OT is seen by contrast with human testaments, Som., II, 224 on Gn. 9:11: οἱ μὲν ἄλλοι χαρίζονται τὰ διαφέροντα τῶν λαμβανόντων, ὁ δὲ θεὸς οὐ μόνον ταῦτα ἀλλὰ αὐτοὺς ἐκείνους ἑαυτοῖς· ἐμὲ γὰρ ἐμοὶ δεδώρηται καὶ ἕκαστον τῶν ὄντων ἑαυτῷ· τὸ γὰρ "στήσω τὴν διαθήκην μου πρὸς σέ" ἴσον ἐστὶ τῷ "σοὶ δωρήσομαι." Mut. Nom., 52 on Gn. 17:2: διαθῆκαι ἐπ' ὠφελείᾳ γράφονται τῶν δωρεᾶς ἀξίων, ὥστε σύμβολον εἶναι διαθήκην χάριτος, ἣν μέσην ἔθηκεν ὁ θεὸς ἑαυτοῦ τε ὀρέγοντος καὶ ἀνθρώπου λαμβάνοντος· ὑπερβολὴ δὲ εὐεργεσίας τοῦτό ἐστι, μὴ εἶναι θεοῦ καὶ ψυχῆς μέσον, ὅτι μὴ τὴν παρθένον χάριτα. Cf. also ibid., 58 on Gn. 17:4 (also Qu. in Gn., III, 60 on 17:21 [p. 234 f., Aucher]); cf. Sacr. AC, 57 on Dt. 9:5: διαθήκη δ' ἐστὶ θεοῦ συμβολικῶς αἱ χάριτες αὐτοῦ ... ὁλόκληροι καὶ παντελεῖς αἱ τοῦ ἀγενήτου δωρεαὶ πᾶσαι. Philo obviously realised that his figurative interpretation of the divine διαθήκη as a testament differed from the true biblical sense. His knowledge of this sense could in fact be deduced, even if there were no direct evidence, from his hermeneutical principles (the literal and allegorical sense). Even in Philo the firmly developed religious concept of the LXX shines through the enveloping imagery. The term is obviously a formula for the gracious will of God disclosed in history.

4. Rabbinic Judaism [89] maintains the legal side of the בְּרִית conception. M. Ex., 12, 6: "There is no בְּרִית apart from the Law." It considers the multiplicity of covenants in the OT, with Noah, Abraham etc. and three with Israel (at Horeb, in the steppes of

---

[87] Cf. W. Staerk, "Die jüdische Gemeinde des Neuen Bundes in Damaskus," BFTh, 27, 3 (1922); on בְּרִית Lohmeyer, 115 ff.

[88] Cf. Riggenbach, Begriff der διαθήκη, 311 ff.; Behm, 34 ff.; Lohmeyer, 122 ff.; J. Heinemann, Philons griechische und jüdische Bildung (1932), 482 ff., 525. On Joseph., who does not use the religious term διαθήκη = בְּרִית, cf. Riggenbach, op. cit., 295 ff.; O. Schmitz, Die Opferanschauung des späteren Judentums (1910), 210 f., n. 2; Schl., Theol. d. Judt., 47.

[89] Cf. Str.-B., I, 991 f.; II, 279 f., 627 f., 671; III, 262, 704; Dalman, op. cit., 149 ff.; Heller, 1204 f.

Moab and on Mounts Gerizim and Ebal): M. Ex., 23, 19. It also gives thought to the covenants made in each individual commandment (48, or indeed 576 in number): bSota, 37b, Bar; jSota, 21c, 54. It reflects further on the expiatory blood of the covenant at Horeb: Tg. O. Ex., 24, 8; Lv. r., 6, 5 on 5:1. For the most part, however, the בְּרִית is specifically equated with circumcision on the basis of Gn. 17:10 : "This is my בְּרִית between me and thee ... that all thy males should be circumcised." Cf., e.g., הֵפֵר בְּרִית, S. Nu., 112 on 15:31 etc. Cf. also בְּרִית בָּשָׂר, בְּרִית, דַּם בְּרִית ("blood of the covenant"), בְּרִית מִילָה ("the covenant of circumcision with Abraham"), בְּנֵי בְרִית ("sons of the covenant" = Israelites). Cf. also jJeb., 9a, 5 (Str.-B., I, 991 f.); Men., 53b; BQ, 1, 2 f.; Ber., 16b etc. When reference is made to Jer. 31:31 ff., which is only infrequently, emphasis is laid on the future Torah written on the heart as distinct from the ineffective Torah of the world which one learns and forgets, Midr. Qoh., 2, 1; Midr. Cant., 1, 2; Pesikt., 107a. [90] There is a polemic against the early Christian interpretation of this saying in Midr. Cant., 1, 14 (93b). [91]

D. The NT Term διαθήκη.

In the NT [92] διαθήκη occurs 33 times (7 in OT citations). Of these occurrences 9 are in Pl., 17 in Hb., 4 in the Syn. Gospels, 2 in Acts and 1 in Rev.

1. διαθήκη in Paul.

When Paul discusses the relation between the promise and the Law in Gl. 3:15 ff., he introduces an illustration from ordinary human experience and compares the promise of God to Abraham with the διαθήκη of a man, i.e., a "will" : ἀδελφοί, κατὰ ἄνθρωπον λέγω. ὅμως ἀνθρώπου κεκυρωμένην διαθήκην οὐδεὶς ἀθετεῖ ἢ ἐπιδιατάσσεται. τῷ δὲ Ἀβραὰμ ἐρρέθησαν αἱ ἐπαγγελίαι καὶ τῷ σπέρματι αὐτοῦ ... ὅς ἐστιν Χριστός. τοῦτο δὲ λέγω· διαθήκην προκεκυρωμένην ὑπὸ τοῦ θεοῦ ὁ μετὰ τετρακόσια καὶ τριάκοντα ἔτη γεγονὼς νόμος οὐκ ἀκυροῖ, εἰς τὸ καταργῆσαι τὴν ἐπαγγελίαν. The many legal terms used in the passage make it clear that he is here using the word διαθήκη in the sense of Hellenistic law; cf. → κυροῦν, → ἀκυροῦν, → ἀθετεῖν, ἐπιδιατάσσεσθαι etc. [93] This illustration from the legal sphere throws light on God's dealings in salvation history. As a valid will cannot be contested or altered by additions, so the promise of God (→ ἐπαγγελία) which is His original "testament" cannot be invalidated by the Law (→ νόμος) which came later. The point of comparison is simply that of inviolability, unalterability and therefore absolute validity. No regard is paid to the fact that in the case of God's testament the presuppositions of this validity (προκεκυρωμένην) are very different from that of a human will, i.e., the death of the testator. This metaphor of the testament seems to have been worked out by Paul quite spontaneously in accordance with his *penchant* for legal images. [94] If it has certain similarities with the allegorising of Philo (→ 128), it is also distinguished by the predominant use of διαθήκη in the true sense. Paul's religious use of διαθήκη is shaped by the LXX rather than by the current legal sense. In R. 11:27 (quoting Is. 59:21; 27:9; cf. Jer. 31:33 f.): αὕτη αὐτοῖς ἡ παρ' ἐμοῦ διαθήκη, ὅταν

---

[90] Str.-B., III, 89 f., 704.
[91] Transl. Str.-B., II, 279 f.
[92] Behm, 37 ff.; Lohmeyer, 124 ff.
[93] Cf. O. Eger, ZNW, 18 (1917), 88 ff.; Ltzm. Gl.³, 20.
[94] Cf. J. Behm, *Religion und Recht im NT* (1931), 7.

ἀφέλωμαι τὰς ἀμαρτίας αὐτῶν, he takes over an important part of the prophetic idea of the διαθήκη in a form which can only denote the saving disposition of God. In R. 9:4 αἱ διαθῆκαι are numbered among the many advantages of Israel in salvation history which Paul can still value as a Christian, and they obviously mean the declarations of will by which God revealed Himself in the promises and commands of the OT; cf. the διαθῆκαι τῶν πατέρων in later Jewish literature,[95] from which Eph. 2:12 singles out the διαθῆκαι τῆς ἐπαγγελίας, the concrete instances of historical manifestations of the promise of salvation (→ ἐπαγγελία). Paul also follows the traditional biblical understanding in 2 C. 3:6 : ὃς καὶ ἱκάνωσεν ἡμᾶς διακόνους καινῆς διαθήκης οὐ γράμματος, ἀλλὰ πνεύματος, where the new (→ καινός) διαθήκη, whose mark is the Spirit (→ πνεῦμα), in contrast to an old which is characterised by the written letter (→ γράμμα, I, 767), reminds us of Jer. 31:31 ff., of which Paul now sees the fulfilment (in this case positively, while also negatively in R. 11:27, cf. 2 C. 3:6).[96] His ministry relates to the divine order of salvation, to the Gospel, and to the ordering of the relation between God and man as thus determined, i.e., to the Christian religion, not to the Law and the Jewish religion (→ 128; cf. 1 Macc. 2:27 etc.). The παλαιὰ διαθήκη (3:14), which ἐν Χριστῷ καταργεῖται, and at the reading (→ ἀνάγνωσις, I, 344) of which in the synagogue the same veil (→ κάλυμμα, as on the face of Moses, Ex. 34:33 ff.) remains up to the present day in token of the failure of the Jews to see its ineffectiveness,[97] is thus the Mosaic Law as the epitome and basis (so here for the first time) of the old religion. In spite of the sharp dismissal of the old (→ παλαιός) διαθήκη in the whole passage 3:4-18, which reflects Paul's own experience, he still recognises that it is God's διαθήκη, that it has its own → δόξα (v. 7 f.), and that it is a historical declaration of the same God as the God of the new. The only point is that the provisional conditions of the old covenant could not be met and therefore it has been abolished (→ καταργέω), and replaced and transcended by the new covenant which has even greater δόξα (v. 10). When Paul in Gl. 4:24 ff. introduces a typological exposition of the story of Hagar and Sarah, saying of these two women who both bore sons to Abraham : αὖταί εἰσιν δύο διαθῆκαι, the slave Hagar being the Sinai covenant which sets its members in a state of bondage (→ δουλεία) and the free woman Sarah being the heavenly covenant which sets its members in a state of freedom (→ ἐλευθερία),[98] he has in view the same διαθῆκαι as in 2 C. 3, i.e., two orders in the divine history whose essential difference may be seen from the different conditions prevailing in them, Judaism which enslaves on the one side and Christianity which brings the liberty of the sons of God on the other (Gl. 5:1; 4:6 f.; R. 8:15; 2 C. 3:17). In the hands of Paul the OT διαθήκη concept, understood even more sharply and consciously in terms of the sole operation of God and of absolute validity for the recipients, is used as a weapon in the battle for the superiority of Christianity over Judaism, and also as a foundation for the new theology of history. There are two covenants, but there is only one divine will which governs salvation history and

---

[95] On the further development of this idea in the early Church, cf. Behm, 45, n. 3; the Lat. trans. of Iren., III, 11, 8 (MPG, 7, 889) deviates from the Gk. and mentions the declarations to Adam, Noah and Moses.

[96] On the idea of the new διαθήκη in Paul, cf. also v. Stromberg, op. cit., 74 ff.

[97] Cf. Bchm. 2 K.⁴, 165 ff.

[98] On the comparison, v. Zn. Gl.³, 231 f.

which manifests itself definitively in Christ who is both the τέλος νόμου (R. 10:4) and the fulfilment of every promise (2 C. 1:20). The use of ἡ καινὴ διαθήκη in 1 C. 11:25, where it occurs in Paul's account of the sayings of Jesus at the Last Supper, must be discussed in connexion with the Synoptic parallels (→ 3.).

2. διαθήκη in Hebrews.

In Hebrews [99] the situation is much the same as in Paul. It is once used in a general illustration from experience together with other legal terms (ὁ διαθέμενος [106; 105], βέβαιος, ἰσχύειν, φέρεσθαι), the author uses διαθήκη in the popular sense of "testament" : 9:16 f.: ὅπου γὰρ διαθήκη, θάνατον ἀνάγκη φέρεσθαι τοῦ διαθεμένου· διαθήκη γὰρ ἐπὶ νεκροῖς βεβαία, ἐπεὶ μήποτε ἰσχύει ὅτε ζῇ ὁ διαθέμενος, "for where a testament is, there must also of necessity be the death of the testator (in order that it may come into force). For a testament is of force after men are dead ; otherwise it is of no strength at all while the testator liveth." This legal conclusion, however, does not justify us in deducing that the term is used in the sense of "testament" in Hb, [100] or indeed in this particular context. To his depiction of the superiority of the high-priestly ministry of Christ in heaven, which through his sacrificial death accomplished an eternal redemption (9:1-14), the author adds (9:15 ff.) an explanation of the necessity of the death of Christ to salvation. Christ is διαθήκης καινῆς μεσίτης ("guarantor," [101] → μεσίτης), ὅπως θανάτου γενομένου εἰς ἀπολύτρωσιν τῶν ἐπὶ τῇ πρώτῃ διαθήκῃ παραβάσεων τὴν ἐπαγγελίαν λάβωσιν οἱ κεκλημένοι τῆς αἰωνίου κληρονομίας (→ κληρονομία), His death signifying redemption (→ ἀπολύτρωσις) from the transgressions (→ παράβασις) which were committed under the first διαθήκη, so that Christ is the Guarantor of a new διαθήκη, that those called according to the promise (→ ἐπαγγελία) may receive the eternal possession assigned to them, i.e., the promised enjoyment of eternal salvation. [102] In this verse διαθήκη is plainly a religious concept ; the two different and mutually exclusive διαθῆκαι are the same as those referred to in Jeremiah and Paul. But what is the necessary connexion between the death of Christ and the new διαθήκη ? The author answers in v. 16 f., not with a material argument as in v. 11 ff., but with a formal *argumentum ad hominem* (Chrys., ad loc., MPG, 63, 123 : ἐκ περιουσίας). If a διαθήκη is to come into force, death is presupposed. In the light of the external similarity that there is both death and a διαθήκη, he jumps from the religious to the current legal sense of διαθήκη, even at the risk of involving himself in contradictions which show that there is no real parallel. Thus Christ, who is μεσίτης, must act as testator for God, whose will it is, but who does not die. Again, in v. 18 : ὅθεν οὐδὲ ἡ πρώτη χωρὶς αἵματος ἐγκεκαίνισται (v. 19 ff.) a consistent application of the testament metaphor (which is also excluded by → ἐγκαινίζειν) would lead to the absurd idea that in the institution of the first διαθήκη the death of sacrificial

---

[99] Cf. also Riggenbach, *op. cit.*; Behm, 72 ff.; Lohmeyer, 144 ff.; A. Carr, "Covenant or Testament ? A Note on Hb. 9:16 f.," Exp., VII, 7 (1909), 347 ff.; A. Seeberg, *Der Brief an die Hebräer* (1912); v. Stromberg, *op. cit.*, 85 f.; G. Vos, "Hebrews the Epistle of the Diatheke," *Princeton Theol. Rev.*, 14 (1916), 1 ff.; Wnd. Hb.[2] (1931).

[100] Riggenbach esp. favours "testament."

[101] Cf. Behm, 78 ff.; Wnd. Hb.[2], 73.

[102] On κληρονομία in the sense of "apportioned possession" (not "inheritance"), cf. Behm, 89 ff.; Lohmeyer, 97 ff., 140 f., 157 f.

beasts represented that of the testator, i.e., God. Apart from 9:16 f., where play on the popular meaning perhaps complicates as well as helps the line of thought, διαθήκη is everywhere used in Hb. in the sense of a "disposition" (8:6 : νενομο-θέτηται; 9:20 : ἧς ... ἐνετείλατο) of God, which reveals to men His will, and especially His saving will, or it is the order thereby established as a divine institution. The source of this theology of the *diatheke* is — more plainly than in any other Jewish or early Christian writing — Jer. 31:31-34, as shown by the explicit, though abbreviated, references in 8:8-12 and 10:16 f. The central thought is that of the new διαθήκη (9:15 : καινή; 12:24 : νέα). As the second (8:7), this is better (→ ἀγαθός) than the first (7:22). It rests on better promises (8:6). It is more sure (→ ἄμωμος, 8:7). It is eternal (13:20). It thus necessarily (8:7) replaces the old, which is now antiquated and ripe for destruction (8:13; 9:1, 15, 18), being linked to cultic sites and ordinances and vessels [103] (9:14), involving transgressions (9:15) and thus having defects (8:7). God gave the first at Sinai (9:20; Ex. 24:6 ff.). It was consecrated by Moses with a solemn blood ritual (→ αἷμα, 9:18-20): τοῦτο τὸ αἷμα τῆς διαθήκης (v. 20). The security for the second with its gifts of salvation (9:15) is the person of Jesus (→ ἔγγυος, 7:22; → μεσίτης, 8:6; 9:15; 12:24; → 131). His death is its dedication (9:15, 18), accomplishing redemption from the sins committed under the first διαθήκη (9:15). Christ's blood is αἷμα διαθήκης αἰωνίου, 13:20 (Zech. 9:11; Is. 55:3; Ἰερ. 39:40 [= 32:40]; 27:5 [= 50:5]; Bar. 2:35), τὸ αἷμα τῆς διαθήκης, 10:29; the antitype of the blood of Ex. 24:6; holy and making holy (→ ἁγιάζω, I, 112). Unlike Paul and Jeremiah, the author finds the essence of the two διαθῆκαι in the cultic aspect. [104] They are given and ritually ordered with a view to remission, expiation and purification. The new διαθήκη as the *locus* of the heavenly high-priesthood of Christ, who sacrifices Himself, is the true fulfilment of the first, whose earthbound priesthood and sacrifices remained imperfect, σκιὰ τῶν ἐπουρανίων (8:5). The historical understanding, concentrating on the two declarations of the saving will of God in the past and the present, on their interconnexion and distinction, is in danger of ossifying into typological reflection. If there is here a similarity in spirit between the author of Hebrews and Philo, the former has his own conception of the διαθήκη achieved by independent study of Scripture.

3. διαθήκη in the Synoptists.

Of the Synoptists, only Lk. (including Ac.) uses διαθήκη to any extent. In the song of Zacharias in Lk. 1:72, διαθήκη is used of the promise to Abraham : ποιῆσαι ἔλεος μετὰ τῶν πατέρων ἡμῶν καὶ μνησθῆναι διαθήκης ἁγίας αὐτοῦ, ὅρκον ὃν ὤμοσεν πρὸς Ἀβραὰμ τὸν πατέρα ἡμῶν (Ps. 105:8 f.; 106:45; 1 Macc. 4:10; 2 Macc. 1:2; Damasc., 8, 18; 1, 4 etc. [→ 127]. The context here is so fully in line with the OT and Judaism that there can be no doubt that the word is used in the traditional sense of the declaration of the will of God concerning future salvation, promise and self-commitment. That the occurrence of the age of salva-

---

[103] Including ἡ κιβωτὸς τῆς διαθήκης and αἱ πλάκες τῆς διαθήκης (9:4), terms which are taken from the LXX (cf. on the one hand Ex. 31:7; 39:15 and on the other 34:28; Dt. 9:9, 11), though the LXX conception is not found in Hb. Cf. also ἡ κιβωτὸς τῆς διαθήκης αὐτοῦ (sc. τοῦ θεοῦ) in Rev. 11:19 (cf. Nu. 10:33; Dt. 10:8 etc.).

[104] Cf. A. Schlatter, *Die Theologie des NT,* II (1910), 446; H. J. Holtzmann, *Lehrbuch der nt.lichen Theologie*[2], II (1911), 325 f.

tion is understood as God's mercy to the patriarchs and His remembrance of the διαθήκη bears witness to a powerful sense of the saving will of God in its transcendence over time and history. διαθήκη has much the same ring in Peter's address in Ac. 3:25 : ὑμεῖς ἐστε οἱ υἱοὶ τῆς διαθήκης (cf. Ps. Sol. 17:17; Jub. 15:26 → 128), ἧς ὁ θεὸς διέθετο πρὸς τοὺς πατέρας ὑμῶν, λέγων πρὸς Ἀβραάμ ... (followed by the quotation of Gn. 22:18). God's saving will for man as declared previously has now become a present reality in the Messiah Jesus (v. 26). In Ac. 7:8 : ἔδωκεν αὐτῷ διαθήκην περιτομῆς (cf. 1 Macc. 1:15), the reference is to the command of circumcision given to Abraham in Gn. 17:10 (→ περιτομή). Lk. thus follows the conventional Jewish view established by the LXX, though he sees the prophecy and its fulfilment from the Christian standpoint.

The most important Synoptic passage is the saying of Jesus in relation to the cup at the institution of the Lord's Supper, Mk. 14:24 : τουτό ἐστιν τὸ αἷμά μου τῆς διαθήκης τὸ ἐκχυννόμενον ὑπὲρ πολλῶν (Mt. 26:28 : ... τὸ περὶ πολλῶν ἐκχ. εἰς ἄφεσιν ἁμαρτιῶν) and 1 C. 11:25 in a traditional form : τοῦτο τὸ ποτήριον ἡ καινὴ διαθήκη ἐστὶν ἐν τῷ ἐμῷ αἵματι (on which is based Lk. 22:20 ﬡﬡ — ἐστίν, + τὸ ὑπὲρ ὑμῶν ἐκχυννόμενον). Whatever Aramaic expression Jesus used, [105] if He spoke of the διαθήκη (as is very likely in view of the widespread Jewish hope of the διαθήκη of the last days on the basis of Jer. 31:31 ff., → 128), then according to Mk. he described the red wine in the cup as His blood of the διαθήκη (→ αἷμα I, 174), or according to the Pauline tradition He described the cup (→ ποτήριον), i.e., its contents, as the new διαθήκη in virtue of His blood. Age, independence and difficulty suggest that the Pauline form is the older. Mk. has assimilated the saying to that concerning the bread and to Ex. 24:8 : ἰδοὺ τὸ αἷμα τῆς διαθήκης. The saying in the Pauline form is to the effect that the blood (or death) of Jesus establishes the new διαθήκη, and that the wine in the Lord's Supper is thus a representation of the new διαθήκη. Since Jeremiah (with Dt. Is.) was for Jesus the most familiar of all the prophets, we are undoubtedly to relate His saying concerning the new διαθήκη to Jer. 31:31 ff., whose counterpart, the διαθήκη at Sinai after the Exodus, was constituted by blood. It cannot be shown conclusively that there is also a reminiscence of Is. 42:6; 49:8 and the dying Servant of the Lord. [106] Jesus conceived of His Messianic work, fulfilled in His death, from the standpoint of the fulfilment of the prophecy of an eschatological διαθήκη. All the elaborations of the saying in Mk. and Mt. may be understood along these lines. The διαθήκη which He has in view, however, is not His testament [107] — neither in Paul nor Mk. is there any reference to His διαθήκη. [108] As in the OT and Judaism, it is the disposition or institution [109] of God. The task of Jesus

---

[105] If this was not the common loan-word (→ 125) דייתיקי (Zn. Mt.⁴, 697, n. 53 in accord with syˢ syᴾ) or the Heb. בְּרִית adopted from the OT (Lohmeyer, 162, n. 2), it would probably be the Aram. equivalent of בְּרִית, i.e., קְיָם, which is already used for "ordinance" or "statute" in Da. 6:8, cf. Dalman, op. cit., 146 ff.

[106] Dalman, op. cit., 154.

[107] Dibelius, 87 ff.

[108] This idea is never found in the NT and occurs for the first time in Barn. (4, 8; 14, 5 : διαθήκη κυρίου Ἰησοῦ), though without replacing the thought that our concern is with God's διαθήκη.

[109] This is substantially the view of Dalman, op. cit., 146 ff., though he renders קְיָם by the less precise "agreement."

as He sees it is to execute the new decree which God has published to settle the relation between Himself and man. It is to put into effect the eschatological saving will of God. His bloody death, represented by the eucharistic cup, gives life to the new divine order. The καινὴ διαθήκη is a correlative of the → βασιλεία τοῦ θεοῦ. While the latter portrays God as the absolute Lord of the age of salvation, the former seeks to express the overruling divine will which sets the goal. One and the same goal of fulfilment is indicated by both the thought that God reigns and the thought that the new divine order is valid, i.e., the order which finally determines the relation of God to man. The fact that the expression καινὴ διαθήκη occurs only once on the lips of Jesus, though at a decisive point, is no more argument against its central significance that is its infrequent occurrence in the OT apocrypha. [110] In the light of this saying of Jesus we can easily see how Paul and the author of Hb. gave to the concept of the διαθήκη a central position in their theological understanding of history.

In both form and content the NT [111] use of διαθήκη follows that of the OT. The only difference is to be found in the step from prophecy to fulfilment. One can hardly say that the NT takes the same course as the LXX and introduces religious thoughts into the legal word, so that it is "a testament and yet not a testament." [112] Nor can one refer to a transformation of the covenant concept to include that of a testament. [113] Neither "covenant" [114] nor "testament" [115] reproduces the true religious sense of the religious term διαθήκη in the Greek Bible. διαθήκη is from first to last the "disposition" [116] of God, the mighty declaration of the sovereign will of God in history, by which He orders the relation between Himself and men according to His own saving purpose, and which carries with it the authoritative divine ordering, the one order of things which is in accordance with it.

Behm

διαφέρω → φέρω.
διαφθείρω, διαφθορά → φθείρω.

[110] Cf. Lohmeyer, 115 etc.

[111] On the history of the term in the early Church, cf. Seeberg, *Lehrbuch der Dogmengeschichte*, I³ (1922), 144 ff., 176 f., 350, 399 ff. etc.; Behm, 97 ff.; v. Stromberg, *op. cit.*, 87 f.; J. Leipoldt, *Schenute von Atripe* (1903), 106 ff.

[112] Lohmeyer, 164.

[113] O. Procksch, NkZ, 36 (1925), 717.

[114] As suggested by older writers like Kennedy, Vos, da Fonseca, and in places Moult.-Mill., 148, Goetz, 7 ff. and Ltzm. K.³, 111 (cf. also his *Messe und Herrnmahl* [1926], 225), who alternate between "covenant," "disposition" and "testament."

[115] So Cr.-Kö., Deissmann, W. J. Moulton, Dibelius, Lohmeyer (though cf. 139, n. 143 f.).

[116] So Hofmann, A. Seeberg, L. v. Sybel, ThStKr, 95 (1923/24), 120 f.; Pr.-Bauer, Wnd. Hb.², also Ltzm. R.³, 89, 105 (though → n. 114) and O. Schmitz, RGG, I², 1362 ff., who recommends "covenant" for διαθήκη "in accordance with our religious usage, even though we are always dealing with a one-sided disposition of grace."

διδάσκω, διδάσκαλος, νομοδιδάσκαλος,
καλοδιδάσκαλος, ψευδοδιδάσκαλος, διδασκαλία,
ἑτεροδιδασκαλέω, διδαχή, διδακτός,
διδακτικός

διδάσκω.

A. διδάσκω outside the NT.

1. διδάσκειν is commonly attested from the time of Homer. It derives from the root δα(σ), meaning "to teach" (*διδασ-σκω = διδάσκω, Hom. δέδαε "has taught") and "to learn" (Hom. δαῆναι). [1] It denotes "teaching" or "instructing" in the widest sense, whether the point at issue is the imparting of information (cf. Hom. Il., 9, 442 f.: διδασκέμεναι τάδε πάντα, | μύθων τε ῥητῆρ' ἔμεναι πρηκτῆρά τε ἔργων), the passing on of knowledge (cf. Hom. Od., 8, 488, where Odysseus calls to the singer Demodocos: ἤ σέ γε Μοῦσ' ἐδίδαξε, Διὸς παῖς, ἤ σέ γ' Ἀπόλλων), or the acquiring of skills (cf. Plat. Men., 94b: τούτους μέντοι, ὡς οἶσθα καὶ σύ, ἱππέας μὲν ἐδίδαξεν οὐδενὸς χείρους Ἀθηναίων). The word calls attention to two aspects, being applied on the one side to the insight of the one who is to be instructed and on the other to the knowledge presupposed in the teacher. In relation to the second aspect, especially when it is a question of practical arts and crafts, the example of the teacher forms a bridge to the knowledge and ability of the pupil. [2] Thus διδάσκειν is the word used more especially for the impartation of practical or theoretical knowledge when there is continued activity with a view to gradual, systematic and therefore all the more fundamental assimilation. [3] This is very plainly the meaning when it is said of Artemis in Hom. Il., 5, 51 f. that she herself taught men to hunt wild animals (i.e., successfully): δίδαξε γὰρ Ἄρτεμις αὐτὴ | βάλλειν ἄγρια πάντα, or when it is stated in Hdt., III, 81: κῶς γὰρ ἂν γινώσκοι ὃς οὔτ' ἐδιδάχθη οὔτε εἶδε καλὸν οὐδὲν [οὐδ'] οἰκήιον; It is all the more important that copying the example of the teacher is not here regarded as a principle of instruction merely in the sense of imitation. The aim is the highest possible development of the talents of the pupil, but always in such a way that the personal aspect is both maintained and indeed strengthened. [4] There is no trace of any schematism, though the authority of the διδάσκων is in no sense diminished. This is important in relation to the transition of διδάσκειν to Jewish soil.

δ ι δ ά σ κ ω κ τ λ. Thes. Steph., s.v.; Cr.-Kö., 292 ff.; Moult.-Mill., 158; Liddell-Scott, 421 f.; Preisigke Wört., 370 f.; Pr.-Bauer, 298 f.

[1] Cf. A. Walde-J. Pokorny, Vergleichendes Wörterb. d. indogerm. Sprachen, I (1927), 793 (root dens- "high intellectual power, wise counsel"; δήνεα, "clever counsels"); Boisacq, 168, 185 and esp. the bibl. at 1106. The word is not connected with δοκέω, Lat. decet, doceo, as still taught by Walde-Pokorny, I, 784 [A. Debrunner].

[2] "Pupil" is not to be understood here as though the scholar were merely passive ; the relationship is rather sociological.

[3] The duplication and the sk construction point in this direction (cf. W. Porzig, Indogermanische Forschungen, 45 [1927], 152 ff.).

[4] This is not contradicted by the fact that the final goal of Greek education is education for and to the state (cf. P. Barth, Die Geschichte der Erziehung in soziologischer und geistesgeschichtlicher Beziehung² [1916], 103 ff.). On the other hand, the rising individualism of the later classical period found fruitful soil in the customary mode of instruction, as may be seen even in Aristotle when he commends drawing as a skill because it develops an eye for physical beauty (Pol., VIII, 3, p. 1338b, 1 f.; cf. P. Barth, 117).

Only occasionally do we find a use of the term which verges on the religious, as in the Isis hymn of Andros, 39 ff.[5]: ἅδε γονήιων | ἀζομένως τιμᾶν ἔτι νηπιάχως ὑπὸ μαζῶι | κωρισμοῖς ἐδίδαξα μελίφροσι, or the Isis hymn of Kyme, 23[6]: ἐγὼ ἀγάλματα θεῶν τειμᾶν ἐδίδαξα. Both these texts portray the goddess as one who exercises omnipotent concern for a meaningful order in the cosmos and its individual parts, and who thus seeks to promote the cultural and religious development of men. This usage, however, is rare and relatively late.[7] Hermes is sometimes called διδάσκαλος (→ 158), but only in Stoic philosophy and in connexion with the → λόγος. As such (λόγος ὁ ἑρμηνευτικὸς καὶ πάντων διδάσκαλος) Justin compares him with Christ (Apol., I, 21, 2).

How strong is the intellectual and authoritative element in διδάσκειν may be seen from current usage as attested in the pap. and ostraka. In addition to the sense of "to instruct," "to apprise of,"[8] etc., διδάσκειν can also have the sense of "to demonstrate," "to prove," "to show." Thus it can be said in relation to the official reading of an agreement (ἀνάγνωσις τῆς ὁμολογίας) that it "yielded" something definite (ἐδίδαξεν, Mitteis-Wilcken, II, 2, 96, Col. II, 5 [4th cent. A.D.]). On another occasion the word can be used to express the demand that a "valid proof should be adduced": διδαχθήτω (P. Tebt., 72, 453 [2nd cent. A.D.]). In both cases διδάσκειν is closely related in meaning to → δεικνύναι with its objective character.[9]

Simply for the sake of completeness we should also mention a use of διδάσκειν which had already disappeared in Hell. Gk., namely, its use for the chorus instructor whose task it was to train the chorus for great public performances.[10] In this sphere διδάσκειν came to have almost the sense of "to perform," "to execute."[11] And since in the age of the great poetic contests (5th to 4th cent. B.C.) the conductors were usually the authors of the works performed, διδάσκειν can also denote "poetic activity," including the composition of a dithyramb (Hdt., I, 23) as well as a tragedy (Aristoph. Ra., 1026 with reference to Aeschylus; cf. Hdt., VI, 21) or a comedy (Plat. Prot., 327d).

2. In the LXX διδάσκειν occurs about 100 times. In 80 cases there is an original. Among these the root למד figures in 57 instances (לָמַד or לִמֵּד in 55), and is thus predominant. למד is normally the original for διδάσκειν in the Torah (only Dt.), the historical books and the Psalms (apart from ψ 17:34). On the other hand, למד is used only at 21:22 among 14 appearances of διδάσκειν in Job, and only at 5:13 and Παροιμ 24:26 (= 30:3) among 7 in Proverbs. This is the more striking because in the LXX διδάσκειν is the only word for למד except for δεικνύναι in Dt. 4:5; Is. 40:14; 48:17.[12] This can be explained only by assuming that διδάσκειν increasingly comes to have technical significance for the Greek speaking Jews.

In the LXX it is no more possible to restrict διδάσκειν than לָמַד to the religious sphere. In both cases the term can be used for instruction in the use of weapons (2 Βασ.

---

[5] W. Peek, Der Isishymnus von Andros und verwandte Texte (1930, 16.

[6] Peek, op. cit., 122.

[7] The hymn of Andros belongs to the 1st cent. B.C. (P. Roussel, Revue des Études Grecques, 42 [1929], 41, n. 2; cf. Peek, 157), or the Augustan age (Peek, 100 f.); that of Kyme to the 1st or 2nd cent. A.D.

[8] For examples, v. Preisigke Wört.

[9] This sense develops from the theoretical use of the word ("to impart knowledge") which accompanies the practical ("to mediate a skill"), and it leads by way of "to instruct (on the basis of better knowledge)" to "to demonstrate." On the intellectual use of διδάσκειν among the Gks., → 141.

[10] Cf. for what follows E. Reisch in Pauly-W., V, (1905), 402, where other examples are given.

[11] Cf. the passages in Hdt., VI, 21; Plat. Prot., 327d adduced later.

[12] In Dt. 4:5 and Is. 48:17 we have the perf. δέδειχα (not found elsewhere), so that one might ask whether it is used as a substitute for the perf. of διδάσκειν.

22:35 etc. : διδάσκειν χεῖράς τινος εἰς πόλεμον) or practising a song (Dt. 31:19, 22 etc.). The particular object of διδάσκειν, however, is the will of God in its declarations and demands. Thus in ψ 93:10 it is said of God that He teaches men γνῶσις, and in Job 22:2 God is called ὁ διδάσκων σύνεσιν καὶ ἐπιστήμην. διδάσκειν is especially used with reference to the concrete declarations of the divine will as these are present in His δικαιώματα and κρίματα (Dt. 4:1) and ῥήματα (Dt. 4:10), or comprehensively the νόμος (1 Esr. 9:48), and as they lead to the doing of the will of God (ψ 142:10; cf. 50:13). It makes no difference whether the one who gives the instruction is God Himself (Dt. 4:10), the head of the family (Dt. 11:19), or the righteous (ψ 50:13). The term is always marked by the fact that it has a volitional as well as an intellectual reference. The διδάσκειν of the LXX always lays claim to the whole man and not merely to certain parts of him. This is most apparent where it is applied to a will and a way contrary to those of God. In Jer. 12:16 it is the guilt of the nations towards Israel that they ἐδίδαξαν τὸν λαόν μου ὀμνύειν τῇ Βάαλ. The use of διδάσκειν indicates that we are here concerned with an organised and systematic attempt to wean Israel from its God, and that this attempt was crowned with success. The total claim associated with διδάσκειν made it peculiarly fitted to become the word for God's presenting of His will to His people in order to subject the people to this will and to fashion it accordingly.

At this point there emerges a distinction between the secular use and that of the LXX. The idea of a total claim is not to be detected in secular Greek, where the aim is to develop talents and potentialities. In the LXX (OT), on the other hand, the concern is with the whole man and his education in the deepest sense. Nevertheless, this does not mean that there is any final isolation of OT from secular διδάσκειν. There is always the common link that the object of instruction is everywhere envisaged as in some way the goal. It is for this reason that in the OT the prophetic proclamation of the coming salvation is never the object of διδάσκειν; [13] the object is always something which is already there even though it has to be appropriated or developed.

3. In later parts of the OT and on the soil of Rabbinic Judaism we find a fixed usage along the lines indicated in the history of the word among the Jews. Used absolutely, διδάσκειν or the corresponding לִמֵּד denotes the manner in which, by exposition of the Law as the sum of the revealed will of God, instruction is given for the ordering of the relationship between the individual and God on the one side, and the neighbour on the other, according to the divine will.

This usage is found already in 2 Ch. 17:7 ff., where it is told of Jehoshaphat that he caused the people to be taught (לִמֵּד /διδάσκειν) by a number of outstanding men. Incidentally it is mentioned that they had with them the סֵפֶר תּוֹרַת יְהוָה on their journey. The narrator saw no reason to emphasise particularly that it was a matter of instruction in the Law with a view to religious education. This means, however, that לִמֵּד was for him an unambiguous term. [14]

In the Rabbis לִמֵּד is sometimes used in a secular sense. Thus it can be stated that the father is obliged to teach his son a trade (לְלַמֵּד אֻמָּנוּת), and that if he fails to do so this

---

[13] Attention is drawn to this in Cr.-Kö., 292.
[14] Cf. further 2 Ἐσδρ. 8:8 (διδάσκειν); Da. 12:4 Θ (διδάσκειν); Is. 55:12 (ἐν χαρᾷ διδαχθήσεσθε); Sir. 22:7 also belongs here according to the context.

is tantamount to teaching him robbery (לִיסְטוּת, bQid., 30b). [15] In the strict sense, however, לָמַד is now a specialised term for the translation of the Torah into concrete directions for the life of the individual. Sometimes תּוֹרָה etc. can now be added as an object, but the absolute use is also common and quite unambiguous. In Rabbinic exposition of Nu. 3:1 f., the sons of Aaron are also the sons of Moses because, while Aaron begot them, Moses instructed them (לִמֵּד), and for the Rabbis the successful introduction of a man to the Torah means both for the man himself and for God no less than his birth (bSanh., 19b). [16] Since practical instruction in the Law implies exegetical judgment, even when it is not more precisely defined לָמַד can often mean "to reach a scholarly decision," "to pronounce an established scholarly opinion" [17] (Sanh., 11, 2 etc.); when a scribal authority gives a considered judgment in a halachic question, he "teaches" it (Ber., 2, 5 ff. etc.). [18] Thus the word לָמַד carries an unequivocal meaning to the Jewish ear. This is further illustrated by the deriv. תַּלְמוּד, which means the teaching of the Law (→ διδαχή), as also by the formulae בָּא הַכָּתוּב דְּלַמֵּד "Scripture [19] offers instruction" etc. [20] (S. Nu., 70 on 9:13, p. 67, 1, Horovitz) [21] and תַּלְמוּד לוֹמַר 'there is a teaching (of Scripture) in what it says" (Ab., 5, 1; Sota, 5, 4 etc.). [22] This covers the formal aspect; the material, however, will demand separate investigation (→ 142).

B. διδάσκω in the NT.

Of some 95 occurrences in the NT, roughly two thirds are in the Gospels and the first part of Acts. On the other hand, there are only 10 instances in Paul (including Eph.). We can thus see that the emphatic use of the term is among the first followers and in the early Church rather than in the Gentile congregations of Asia Minor or Greece.

As concerns meaning, the term has the unambiguous sense of "to teach," "to instruct." We need hardly discuss the nuances, since these are plain from the various contexts. Thus in Mt. 28:15 the context excludes a religious usage, and in accordance with the history of the word in the LXX the reference is simply to the presence and observance of a direction. On the other hand, it is quite essential to investigate the inner structure of διδάσκειν in the NT.

---

[15] Cf. also Qid., 4, 14 etc.

[16] On this pt. → I, 666.

[17] Developed from this is the use of לָמַד in the formulae לָמַד זְכוּת עַל and לָמַד חוֹבָה עַל "(as an assessor in legal proceedings) to pronounce in favour of or against the accused (after the hearing of witnesses) a decision based on the Law and tradition which is also a verdict in the case at issue, therefore a vote for acquittal or condemnation" (Sanh., 4, 1; 5, 4; 6, 1 etc.). The use of the term לָמַד is an indication of the fact that the witnesses here referred to are not ordinary witnesses but scribal assessors who in their judgment are bound by the Torah and tradition.

[18] Hence the demand addressed to R. Tarfon by his hearers: רַבֵּינוּ לַמְּדֵנוּ, when he made a pronouncement for which they wanted more exact proof (S. Nu., 118 on 18:18, p. 141, 3 f., Horovitz); there are many similar formulae.

[19] Here personified, as often in the Rabbis and occasionally in the NT (e.g., Gl. 3:16, 22).

[20] Also בא הכתוב ללמדך (M. Ex. on 12:4, p. 12, 8, Horovitz-Rabin etc.), בא הכתוב ללמדנו (M. Ex. on 12:11, p. 22, 10 f. etc.), בא הכתוב ללמד (M. Ex. on 22:15, p. 307, 9); cf. W. Bacher, Die exegetische Terminologie der jüd. Traditionsliteratur, I (1899), 95 f.

[21] In all forms of the formula adduced the בא הכתוב may be left out (e.g., we have only ללמד in M. Ex. on 21:14, p. 264, 2; it is never found with the common מלמד, though הכתוב must be supplied as the subject (v. Bacher, 31 f.).

[22] Cf. on this pt. Bacher, 199 ff.

1. The διδάσκειν of Jesus according to the Synoptists.

a. According to the unanimous witness of the Gospels διδάσκειν was one of the most prominent functions of Jesus in His public ministry. Thus in Mt. 4:23, in a comprehensive reference to His wandering ministry in Galilee, we first read that He taught in the synagogues, and only then do we read that He proclaimed the glad tidings of the βασιλεία and healed the sick. Cf. also Mt. 9:35; 11:1. The synagogues are continually mentioned as the places of instruction (Mt. 9:35; 12:9 ff.; 13:54 and par.; Mk. 1:21; Lk. 4:15; Jn. 18:20 etc.), or the temple in Jerusalem (Mk. 12:35; Lk. 21:37; Mt. 26:55 and par., though cf. Jn. 7:14 ff.; 8:20), where there was a special synagogue to which there might well be attached the house of instruction mentioned in T Sukka, 4, 5, [23] since most synagogues provided facilities for instructional purposes (jMeg., 73d, 23). [24] In any case, orderly teaching could be given in the temple. The Evangelists are certainly agreed that a great deal of what has been handed down concerning Jesus consists in teaching material.

b. The form in which Jesus teaches is that of a Jewish teacher of the period. It is true that we are not always told concerning the externalities of the teaching of Jesus. This was hardly necessary, since one part of the Church for which the Gospels were written already knew the customs followed from their own observation, and the other part was not interested in the form but in the all-important content. We do at least have information about what happened in the synagogue at Nazareth (Lk. 4:16 ff.). After the reading of the Scripture portion (Is. 61:1 f.), which took place standing, [25] Jesus seated Himself like other expositors of the time [26] and based His address on the passage just read (Lk. 4:21 ff.). This handling of a text is "teaching" for later Judaism. Hence it is quite apposite that in the brief reference to the incident at Nazareth in Mt. 13:53 ff. and par. the absolute διδάσκειν should be used, though it can be omitted in Lk. 4:16 ff. because the matter is plain enough without it (Mt. 13:54; Mk. 6:2). The same practice of sitting to teach is mentioned by Mt. in 5:1 at the beginning of the Sermon on the Mount, by Mk. in 9:35 when Jesus gave instruction to the Twelve on the occasion of their quarreling for supremacy, and by Lk. in 5:3 at the beginning of the discourse by the lake. [27] It is thus with good reason that Jewish tradition concerning the teaching of Jesus also speaks in terms of לְמַד (bAZ, 17a).

c. If the external form of the teaching of Jesus is within the framework of later Judaism, the same is true of the matter. At Nazareth (Lk. 4:16 ff.) He uses a saying of Isaiah as a basis or starting-point. In other cases we have exposition of the Torah (Mt. 5:21 ff.; 15:3 ff.; 22:37 ff. and par.; cf. also 22:23 ff.). On the other hand, He does not restrict His teaching to exposition of the Law. For one thing, He is against estimation of the Law merely for its own sake. For another, He stands in irreconcilable opposition to the lifeless casuistry which does not start with the situation of the one who needs the counsel of experts in the religious sphere but, irrespective of his own questions, subjects him to its own principle and

---

[23] G. Dalman, *Orte und Wege Jesu*[3] (1924), 317, seems inclined to regard the two as independent.

[24] Cf. Str.-B., II, 150.

[25] *Ibid.*, IV, 161.

[26] *Ibid.*, IV, 185. Cf. Lk. 2:46.

[27] Cf. also Jn. 8:2, where Jesus sits to teach the people.

system,[28] bringing about religious separation from those who for practical reasons[29] or for conscience sake cannot allow themselves to be bound by it.[30] The whole teaching of Jesus is with a view to the ordering of life with reference to God and one's neighbour (Mt. 22:37 ff. and par.; cf. 19:16 ff. and par.). Thus His teaching constantly appeals to the will, calling for a practical decision either for the will of God or against it. He finds a common basis with the Rabbis and the Pharisaic community in the fact that He sees a revelation of the will of God in Scripture and especially in the Law (→ νόμος), so that it is quite impossible for Him to surrender even a single letter (Mt. 5:17 f.). On the other hand, He is distinguished from these groups by the fact that for Him the Law and the whole of Scripture cannot be so restricted in meaning as to be the only way to enter into and to remain in contact with God. For Him the Law and Scripture are rather a confirmation of His own relationship to the Father.[31] Thus the gap between Jesus and the Rabbis in respect of the subject of teaching is to be found, not in the matter itself, but in His own person, i.e., in the fact of His self-awareness as the Son. This is why His teaching, whether in the form of exposition or otherwise, causes astonishment among His hearers (Mt. 7:28; 13:53 and par. etc.): ἦν γὰρ διδάσκων αὐτοὺς ὡς ἐξουσίαν ἔχων, καὶ οὐχ ὡς οἱ γραμματεῖς αὐτῶν (Mt. 7:29; Mk. 1:22).[32]

Yet this is also the point which gives final meaning to the absolute use of διδάσκειν in relation to His teaching, even though Jesus rejects the absolutising of the Law historically presupposed by the word in view of its Semitic equivalent לָמַד. This rejection is to be viewed simply as the repudiation of an aberration. In opposition to it, Jesus resumes the true line of לָמַד in the διδάσκειν attributed to Him. For He is again advancing the claim of God to the whole man in a way which does not allow either contradiction or theoretical reflection. This is a total claim which is not bound to any intermediary authority and which is completely independent of the perception of the one who is claimed. This claim, which has as its goal the education and reformation of man according to the will of God (cf. Mt. 5:48), becomes a reality in the teaching of Jesus. For this reason He is the end of the Law as the Rabbis conceived it, i.e., as the basis and theme of scribal instruction and the way by which man may painfully attain to God (R. 10:4). These are the historico-linguistic reasons why early Christianity spoke of teaching in the absolute when in its tradition it referred to the teaching activity of Jesus among His people. His teaching was for it teaching in the absolute because with

---

[28] To this there belongs the whole complex of oral tradition which as הֲלָכָה לְמֹשֶׁה מִסִּינַי (cf. Strack, Einl., 7) is no less highly estimated than the written Law; this included the handwashings which were by no means generally recognised at the time of Jesus (cf. Mt. 15:2; though cf. also Mk. 7:3) but formed part of the Pharisaic programme of purification (Joachim Jeremias, Jerusalem zur Zeit Jesu, II, B, 1 [1929], 121).

[29] This would include the bulk of the people, who did not have the necessary knowledge of the Law (עַם־הָאָרֶץ).

[30] Like Jesus Himself (Mt. 15:3 ff.).

[31] Cf. Schl. Gesch. d. Chr., 280 f.

[32] This last statement also excludes the possibility that the subject of διδάσκειν is the knowledge of salvation imparted thereby (cf. also Cr.-Kö., 292). This is certainly true of the διδάσκειν of Jesus. In any case, the phrase knowledge of salvation has an accent which contradicts the very essence of לָמַד/διδάσκειν.

every word He brought His hearers into direct confrontation with the will of God as it is revealed in His Word and as it is constantly revealed in history.

It is relevant to the matter that the absol. use of διδάσκειν in this sense [33] dominates not merely the more Palestinian Mt. but all the four Gospels, including Jn., in their statements concerning the teaching of Jesus. We have in Josephus [34] an unimpeachable witness for the fact that an absolute διδάσκειν on the pattern of לִמֵּד would sound strange to Gk. ears. Thus, when Joseph. used the word in this sense, he always [35] added information concerning the subject of the διδάσκειν, either in the acc. [36] or in a ὅτι clause. [37] Yet it is to be noted that even Lk. uses διδάσκειν in the absol. for the teaching of Jesus, even though he is writing for readers outside the Jewish world of thought. This is explicable only on the assumption that the term had acquired for him an absol. sense through its connexion with the person of Jesus, in relation to whom he uses it. The new thing is that Jesus is *teaching,* not that He is teaching in a particular way. [38]

d. A novel feature in this use by the Evangelists is the complete supersession of the intellectual element present in non-biblical usage. The basis of the distinction from the Rabbinic לִמֵּד is also to be sought here. These points have both been referred to earlier (→ 137, 140), but now demand fuller discussion. Our investigation of Gk. usage showed that there was always an intellectual side to διδάσκειν (→ 135). Nor is this limited to the class., the post-class., or even the Gk. Hellenistic writers; it applies no less to the Jew Philo than to Epictetus. A strongly intellectualised use is found in Epictetus. A good example is in Diss., III, 5, 17, where διδάσκειν is set alongside εἰδέναι as its lawful consequence: ταῦτα ἦν, ἃ ᾔδει ὁ Σωκράτης, καὶ ὅμως οὐδέποτε εἶπεν, ὅτι οἶδέν τι ἢ διδάσκει. And elsewhere διδάσκειν mediates instruction which by way of perception exercises a formative influence on the man concerned (Diss., I, 26, 5). For this reason διδάσκειν is for him an essential mark of the philosopher (cf. Diss., I, 29, 9), [39] esp. when it is a matter of attaining to a right understanding of things (cf. Diss., I, 28, 27; IV, 7, 34 f.). The usage of Philo is very much the same. There is in him no trace of the influence of לִמֵּד; everything lies in the sphere of the intellect. [40] Sufficient proof of this may be found in two passages which speak of either Scripture or Moses teaching something, where a more profound usage might be expected. In Rer.

---

[33] Only very occasionally do we find an obj. like τὴν ὁδὸν τοῦ θεοῦ in Mt. 22:16 or πολλά in Mk. 6:34. As a rule it is used without any such explanatory addition. A case apart is Lk. 11:1, where the disciples ask Jesus to teach them to pray; → 144.

[34] Cf. Schl. Mt., 110, 121.

[35] *Ibid.,* 121.

[36] Particularly instructive is Ant., 8, 395: ἐκέλευε ... ἅπαντα τὸν λαὸν ... διδάξαι κατὰ πόλιν τοὺς Μωσείους νόμους καὶ φυλάσσειν τούτους. Joseph. is here telling the story of 2 Ch. 17:7 ff., and in the original he found only the absol. לִמֵּד/διδάσκειν, which is quite unambiguous in the context (→ 137).

[37] Cf. Ant., 3, 91: διδάσκει μὲν οὖν ἡμᾶς ὁ πρῶτος λόγος (i.e., the first commandment), ὅτι θεός ἐστιν εἷς καὶ τοῦτον δεῖ σέβεσθαι μόνον.

[38] Cf. from another angle the statements in P. Feine, *Theologie des NT*[5] (1931), 80; Kittel Probleme, 130.

[39] ὑμεῖς οὖν οἱ φιλόσοφοι διδάσκετε καταφρονεῖν τῶν βασιλέων; μὴ γένοιτο. εἰδέναι (*supra*) as the result of philos. teaching (Diss., IV, 7, 32; cf. also II, 21, 12 ff.).

[40] In the case of some writings this is perhaps saying too much, since the term is at root used in a technical way, e.g., Poster. C., 120, where it is said of corpulence (πιότης): διδάσκει γὰρ ἀφίστασθαι θεοῦ τιμῆς, ἢ πρώτη καὶ ἀρίστη ψυχῆς ἐστι δύναμις. Here we have in διδάσκειν no more than an attempt to establish an observation psychologically.

Div. Her., 243 Scripture is the subject: εἰσηγεῖται δὲ γνώμην ἀληθεστάτην διδάσκων, ὅτι δικαιοσύνη μὲν καὶ πᾶσα ἀρετὴ ψυχῆς, ἀδικία δὲ καὶ πᾶσα κακία σώματος ἐρῶσι, in Rer. Div. Her., 291 Moses : φιλοσοφῶν καὶ διδάσκων ἡμᾶς, τίς ὁ πρὸς ἀλήθειαν εὐγήρως ἐστίν. In both cases the context shows that διδάσκειν is a function of the thinker in which he addresses himself primarily to the thinking powers of his fellows. This is the exact opposite of the διδάσκειν of Jesus with its demands on the will. On the other hand, astonishing though this may seem, it is closely related to the Rabbinic method of teaching.

Linguistically, the usage of Philo and Epictetus resembles that of the Sophists, for whom διδάσκειν and its derivatives are almost slogans in the sense of the intellectual and rational mediation of knowledge and insight. [41] In virtue of this basic attitude, the Sophists are on the one side pioneers in so far as for the first time they make the whole complex of διδάσκειν the theme of systematic investigation. But in raising a total claim for their διδάσκειν they also come into collision with Socrates, who cannot allow that ἀρετή can be taught like other capacities, or in any sense mediated along rational lines ; → 150.

Scribal learning [42] was a reaction by conservative Judaism to the disintegrating force of Hellenism. Its aim was to maintain the faith of the fathers through every peril. It was thus constrained from the very outset to use the methods of its opponents. A closed philosophy and a detailed order of life were needed if, as the Rabbis saw it, Judaism was to be effectively protected against the danger of absorption. This meant that the main emphasis of Rabbinic scholarship came to be put on exegesis, not in the practical religious or ethical sense, but rather in the theoretical. Thus it is understandable that the Rabbis were increasingly characterised by learning as the continually necessary presupposition of teaching, and not so much by exemplary action (→ μανθάνω). The upshot of this imposed development, [43] which is reflected in the attacks of Jesus on the Rabbis in the NT (Lk. 11:46 ff. and par.; 20:46 and par.), is to be found in a resolution proposed by Aqiba, and adopted by the authoritative Rabbis in Lydda during Hadrian's persecution, to the effect that a higher rank is to be conceded to studying the Law than to doing it (S. Dt., 41 on 11:13; bQid., 40b). It can thus be said : "Whosoever is in the Scripture, the Mishnah and the (required) manner of life, will not easily sin, for it is stated : The threefold cord is not so quickly broken (Qoh. 4:12); whosoever is not in the Scripture, the Mishnah and the (required) manner of life, does not belong to that which abides" (Qid., 1, 10). [44] The theological attitude has obviously triumphed in this statement. Basically, however, this is a Greek or Hellenistic attitude rather than a Jewish, since in it the intellectual becomes the predominant principle and there is a falling short of the whole man. For this reason, the Rabbis are finally on the side of Philo and even Epictetus, even though their teaching stands in a different relation to Scripture than that of Philo and finally acquires its meaning only from Scripture. For this reason, too, the figure towards which earlier Jewish history really moves is Jesus, who in contrast to Hellenistic and Rabbinic Judaism gives absolute content to לִמֵּד/ διδάσκειν in His teaching.

---

[41] For examples v. C. P. Gunning, De Sophistis Graeciae praeceptoribus (Diss., Amsterdam, 1915). I owe this reference to H. Kleinknecht.

[42] The teaching office is to be distinguished from Pharisaism in so far as it embraces theology whereas the Pharisees were primarily practical (cf. J. Jeremias, Jerusalem zur Zeit Jesu, II, B, 1 [1929], 122 ff.; Schl. Gesch. d. Chr., 286 ff.; 297 ff.). This did not prevent scribes from usually being Pharisaic leaders (op. cit., 125).

[43] For material on this, cf. Str.-B., III, 85 ff.

[44] Such a man obviously ought not to teach, i.e., to make religious statements, issue religious judgments and claim their acceptance ; if he still does so, amongst other things he must be prepared to be made an → ἀποσυνάγωγος (cf. Jn. 9:22, 34 f.).

2. διδάσκειν in the Johannine Writings.

a. We are concerned only with a limited number of passages (Jn. 6:59; 7:14, 28, 35; 8:20, 28; 9:34; 14:26; 18:20; 1 Jn. 2:27; Rev. 2:14, 20). Some of these at least deserve brief treatment on their own, namely, those which speak more emphatically of teaching by God or by the Spirit. The rest fall essentially under the category of what we have already said concerning the διδάσκειν of Jesus, irrespective of the special content of the teaching of Jesus in them (Jn. 6:59; 7:14, 28, 35; 8:20; 18:20). A special place is occupied by Jn. 9:34, where διδάσκειν is used of the man born blind who, when he was healed, became a witness of Jesus. Indeed, it is used in relation to the opponents of Jesus, who would not accept instruction from him. Also to be numbered apart are the two passages in Rev. which speak of the teaching of Balaam and Jezebel in a way which has its model and presupposition in the OT use of לִמֵּד /διδάσκειν (→ 136). This leaves us with Jn. 8:28; 14:26 and 1 Jn. 2:27.

b. A characteristic of the use of διδάσκειν in Jn. 8:28; 14:26; 1 Jn. 2:27 is that it suggests in the first instance the presence of a direct inspiration or revelation. In Jn. 8:28 Jesus says with reference to His statements concerning Himself : ἀλλὰ καθὼς ἐδίδαξέν με ὁ πατήρ, ταῦτα λαλῶ. In Jn. 14:26 Jesus holds out to the disciples the prospect of the παράκλητος, τὸ πνεῦμα τὸ ἅγιον, and promises : ἐκεῖνος ὑμᾶς διδάξει πάντα καὶ ὑπομνήσει ὑμᾶς πάντα ἃ εἶπον ὑμῖν ἐγώ. In 1 Jn. 2:27 the writer denies that his readers should need anyone to instruct them, because the χρῖσμα which they have received διδάσκει them ... περὶ πάντων καὶ ἀληθές ἐστιν καὶ οὐκ ἔστιν ψεῦδος, καὶ καθὼς ἐδίδαξεν ὑμᾶς, μένετε ἐν αὐτῷ. The → χρῖσμα here is undoubtedly the Holy Spirit, so that this passage should be linked with Jn. 14:26. In any case it denotes the endowment with διδαχή from another world. This is a use of διδάσκειν which we seek in vain in the Synoptists. Hence the question arises whether this is a Hellenistic usage, or one which derives from Hellenistic conceptions, so that it is not to be explained in terms of the usage elsewhere in the Gospel. Thus far, however, no parallel has been adduced which would justify the assumption of borrowing from the outside world.

It is sometimes recalled [45] that Apollonius of Tyana maintains that he is doing only what the gods inspire him to do. But when he calls the gods his counsellors, [46] this is rather different from what Jesus says of Himself, namely, that the Father has taught Him. There is lacking in Apollonius the authoritative element which is so obvious in the context of Jn. 8:28, quite apart from διδάσκειν. Nor does this authoritative element point to Hellenism as the place where an explanation of the striking διδάσκειν is to be found ; it points to לִמֵּד, which is marked, as we have seen, by the unconditional and total claiming of the one who is taught by the one who teaches (→ 137).

We thus do well to explain the διδάσκειν of Jn. 8:28 in the light of לִמֵּד or διδάσκειν as used of Jesus in the Synoptic Gospels. If to the Jewish ear διδάσκειν suggests the successful and total moulding of the will of another by one's own, διδάσκειν expresses the same thought elsewhere stated by John in the phrase ὁ πέμψας με πατήρ, i.e., the thought of the unity of will between Father and Son (→ I, 405). If here διδάσκειν rather than πέμπειν is used for the participation of

---

45 Bau. J.³ on 8:28.
46 Philostr. Vit. Ap., I, 18 : ἐγὼ μὲν θεοὺς συμβούλους πεποίημαι.

God in the work of Jesus, this is because the reference is not to the being of Jesus as the Son, but to His speaking in the name of God. [47]

The position is basically the same in Jn. 14:26 and 1 Jn. 2:27, except that the reference is now to the participation of Jesus in the status of His people. In Jn. 14:26 this is emphasised with reference to the continuation of the work of Jesus by them; [48] in 1 Jn. 2:27 it is asserted in relation to false teachers who raise totalitarian claims on the community and must be radically resisted (οὐ χρείαν ἔχετε, etc.) if the link with Jesus is not to be broken. One of the reasons why διδάσκειν is chosen is because clear goals are set on both sides which cannot be overlooked and which demand the commitment of the whole man. [49]

It cannot be denied that there still remains an ambivalence in the Johannine διδάσκειν; nor does this apply only to these three passages, but to all its occurrences. We can only say, however, that if in Jn. — with the natural exception of Rev. 2:14, 20 — the word continually verges on the sense of "to reveal," this is not due to any special usage but is simply because the subject of διδάσκειν in Jn. and 1 Jn. (including Jn. 9:34) is always Jesus Himself. This distinguishes Johannine from Synoptic usage, but it also shows how in Jn. even sayings which in themselves seem to have no outstanding significance are influenced in content by the central position of Jesus.

This is perhaps the point to append a note on Lk. 11:1. The disciples' request to Jesus: δίδαξον ἡμᾶς προσεύχεσθαι καθὼς καὶ Ἰωάννης ἐδίδαξεν τοὺς μαθητὰς αὐτοῦ, cannot be explained simply in the light of Synoptic usage. It is readily understandable, however, if from the standpoint of Johannine usage we see in the δίδαξον [50] a willingness and readiness of the disciples for unconditional subjection to the direction of Jesus which is affirmed and accepted in the giving of a form of prayer specially designed for them. Understood in this way, the scene loses the episodic character which it first seems to have. The request of the unnamed disciple in Lk. is to be set alongside the confession of the Messiahship of Jesus in Mt. 16:13 ff. and par.; Jn. 6:60 ff., and is thus of central importance in the history of the Church.

3. The διδάσκειν of Early Christianity.

The material presented in Acts and the Epistles may be grouped in three sections. To the first belong the passages which use διδάσκειν after the model of לִמֵּד; to the second those which refer to διδάσκειν about Jesus; to the third those which speak of teaching as a function of the Church. No sharp distinction is possible between the groups, especially in view of the fact that the word is mostly used in the absolute.

a. Already during the life of Jesus and at His command the disciples began to teach (Mk. 6:30), thus making it their own concern to declare the claim of Jesus.

---

[47] It is to be noted, however, that the formula ὁ πέμψας με is twice used in immediate proximity (8:26, 29).

[48] For this reason πέμπειν is again used here of the sending of the Paraclete by God ἐν τῷ ὀνόματί μου.

[49] In spite of Reitzenstein Poim., 246 f. this is something quite different from the use of διδάσκειν illustrated in Corp. Herm., XIII, 2: τοῦτο τὸ γένος, ὦ τέκνον, οὐ διδάσκεται, ἀλλ᾽ ὅταν θέλῃ ὑπὸ τοῦ θεοῦ ἀναμιμνήσκεται, where the aim is intuitive knowledge rather than a clear formation of the will.

[50] Formally there is a link with Rabbinic usage (→ n. 18). This gives us the literary setting. The request for the teaching of a prayer, however, is a new and distinctive feature which can be explained only by the situation.

In Mt. 28:20 the Risen Lord made the continuation of this task the life work of His people. διδάσκειν is here either a presupposition of βαπτίζειν, which for its part implies the μαθητής, or of μαθητεύειν, if the phrase βαπτίζοντες ... πνεύματος (28:19) is regarded as an ancient interpolation.[51] The content of διδάσκειν is πάντα ὅσα ἐνετειλάμην ὑμῖν, and therefore the proclamation of Jesus, His → διδαχή,[52] rather than proclamation concerning Him. This line is pursued in the early Church : the διδάσκειν of the disciples, naturally ἐπὶ τῷ ὀνόματι τοῦ Ἰησοῦ (Ac. 4:18; cf. 5:28, → ἀπόστολος, I, 430 ff.) and their → καταγγέλλειν (→ I, 71) of the resurrection of Jesus accompany one another (Ac. 4:2; cf. 5:42 : οὐκ ἐπαύοντο διδάσκοντες καὶ εὐαγγελιζόμενοι τὸν Χριστὸν Ἰησοῦν; cf. also 15:35) and are not just identical. This does not mean that διδάσκειν is restricted to exegesis of the OT or to instruction in the new interpretation given by Jesus to the Law. Here again the whole complex of Scripture is only a starting-point and background. In the light of it the teaching of the early Church culminates in the call to repentance which is accompanied in the *kerygma* about Jesus by the offer of ἄφεσις ἁμαρτιῶν (cf. Ac. 5:31, but also 20:21).[53] It is thus understandable why offence was given not merely to the Sadducees, who disliked particularly the witness to the resurrection and who included the most prominent priestly families (→ ἀρχιερεύς; Ac. 4:1 ff.; 5:17 f.), but also to more popular religious circles (Ac. 5:34 ff.). This was a call to repentance which demanded justification before it could be accepted. From the standpoint of the history of early Christian proclamation, therefore, there takes place in the διδάσκειν of the early community the unconscious transmission and sifting of traditional sayings, while in the *kerygma* we have the beginning of a collection of the narrative material, both under the comprehensive challenge which stands at the head of the Christian message generally : μετανοεῖτε καὶ πιστεύετε ἐν τῷ εὐαγγελίῳ (Mk. 1:15).

There can be no doubt that the teaching of the early Church followed the external forms of Jewish teaching, since we read of the apostles in Ac. 5:25 : εἰσὶν ἐν τῷ ἱερῷ ἑστῶτες καὶ διδάσκοντες τὸν λαόν. Nor is this any the less important in their case than in that of Jesus, since acceptance of the form denotes similarity of content. That is to say, the teaching consisted primarily in exegesis and exhortation rather than factual instruction in the work of salvation.

There are indeed some passages where διδάσκειν is narrowed down to instruction in the Law, e.g., R. 2:21 and Ac. 15:1, where we are told of the attempt to induce Gentile Christians to accept circumcision by the adducing of Scripture (cf. Gl. 4:21, though διδάσκειν is not used here). Hb. 5:12 should also be mentioned in this connexion : the introduction of Jewish boys to Scripture begins with the διδάσκειν of the alphabet, and a new beginning must now be made, since the learned readers of the epistle are obviously no longer able to "read."

b. Since one of the marks of διδάσκειν is the constant reference to Scripture, it includes proving from Scripture that Jesus is the promised Messiah. This is the

---

[51] Cf. on this pt. Meyer, *Ursprung*, I, 16, n. 1; J. Wellhausen, *Das Ev. Mt.*, ad loc.; F. C. Conybeare, "The Eusebian Form of the Text Mt. 28:19," ZNW, 2 (1901), 275 ff.; E. Riggenbach, "Der trinitarische Taufbefehl," BFTh, 7, 1 (1903). Also Kl. Mt., ad loc.

[52] This verse is also important for an understanding of the word → μαθητής in early Christianity.

[53] In the context Ac. 5:31 is to be taken in this way. Only by the exaltation of Jesus is the justice of His claim demonstrated.

bridge to the use of διδάσκειν in the formula διδάσκειν τὰ περὶ τοῦ Ἰησοῦ (Ac. 18:25) or διδάσκειν τὰ περὶ τοῦ κυρίου Ἰησοῦ Χριστοῦ (Ac. 28:31).[54] There is here an unmistakeable limitation of the content of διδάσκειν. In Ac. 18:25 it takes place in the synagogue, which naturally determines the method (proof from Scripture). In Ac. 28:31 it is expressly mentioned with κηρύσσειν τὴν βασιλείαν τοῦ θεοῦ, with which it is combined to give a comprehensive definition of Paul's preaching in Rome, i.e., to characterise its two aspects (→ 145).[55] Here again one cannot assume that it denotes the impartation of facts; it rather presents these facts in such a way that the only possibility is to accept them or to be betrayed into opposition to Scripture.[56] In this light it is only natural that the attempts in this direction should be described by opponents as a διδάσκειν κατὰ τοῦ νόμου (Ac. 21:28) and a διδάσκειν of ἀποστασία ἀπὸ Μωϋσέως (Ac. 21:21).

The only difficulty is caused by the account in Ac. 18:11 that Paul taught (διδάσκων) the λόγος τοῦ θεοῦ. Though there is here a definiteness never found elsewhere with the possible exception of Ac. 20:20, we are probably right to interpret λόγος τοῦ θεοῦ, not as the word of NT proclamation of salvation in general, but as the proclamation of salvation on the basis of and in the light of Scripture. It is, of course, possible to see in λόγος τοῦ θεοῦ a fixed formula of the early Church; but we should then have to give to διδάσκειν a sense which it does not have elsewhere.

c. The most astonishing aspect of the NT use of διδάσκειν is at a first glance its comparative paucity in Paul.[57] Yet this is easily explained when we realise how closely it is bound to Scripture even in the NT. In a setting where Scripture was not known, διδάσκειν τὰ περὶ τοῦ Ἰησοῦ would be out of place, just as it was very much in place in the early community and in dealings with Jews. Thus Paul speaks of διδάσκειν only with reference to his own instruction of the communities at the time of their foundation (2 Th. 2:15; Col. 2:7; Eph. 4:21)[58] and in the sense of an internal function of Christianity. Even for Gentile congregations proof from Scripture was an indispensable weapon against the attacks of Jews, as shown by the history of the Galatian Church; and it had thus to be given by the apostles. On the other hand, it seems to have had no part in the churches themselves. When Paul in R. 12:7 summons the διδάσκων to serve ἐν τῇ διδασκαλίᾳ of the community, he is not thinking of men who apply the Scriptures to Jesus, but of those who give from Scripture directions for Christian living,[59] and he admonishes them to place their better knowledge wholly in the service of the con-

---

[54] We are here reminded particularly of the attempts of the early community to prove the fulfilment in Jesus of Isaiah's prophecy of the Servant of the Lord; cf. His designation as παῖς (θεοῦ) in Ac. 3:13, 26; 4:27, 30, and on this A. v. Harnack, SAB, 1926, 2, 16 ff.

[55] It is thus in keeping with the use of διδάσκειν, as also of εὐαγγέλιον, when Paul says οὔτε ἐδιδάχθην as well as οὐδὲ παρέλαβον in relation to his Gospel (Gl. 1:12).

[56] This is the alternative which Paul presents to the Galatians on the basis of his christocentric proof from Scripture.

[57] No reference is made here to 1 C. 11:14, since God ultimately stands behind this διδάσκειν, and it thus belongs to the first category.

[58] The last passage is put here because the ἐδιδάχθητε and the accompanying ἠκούσατε point to a mediation of the knowledge that ἀλήθεια is ἐν τῷ Ἰησοῦ, this being the basis of the obligation to walk in purity.

[59] The context demands an interpretation of διδάσκειν in relation to the upbuilding of the life of the community rather than its faith.

gregation. This is the same kind of διδάσκειν with a view to the distinction between good and evil as we have learned to know from the synagogue and the usage of the Gospels.[60]

In Colossians we find διδάσκειν mentioned with νουθετεῖν (1:28; 3:16) in a pastoral and ethical sense as a function of Christians in their mutual dealings. This usage recurs in the Pastorals. In 1 Tm. 4:11 it is linked with παραγγέλλειν, and in 1 Tm. 6:2 with παρακαλεῖν, on both occasions as the privilege and responsibility of Timothy; in 2 Tm. 2:2 it is the task of those who have the necessary personal qualifications, though according to 1 Tm. 2:12 it is forbidden to women.[61] In Tt. 1:11 there is a rejection of those ἐκ τῆς περιτομῆς, διδάσκοντες ἃ μὴ δεῖ αἰσχροῦ κέρδους χάριν. The last passage shows that the historical connexion between Scripture and διδάσκειν is still intact, and also (cf. the ἃ μὴ δεῖ) that it is primarily concerned with ethical directions, or in this case with ethically contestable directions. We thus do well to interpret the other occurrences in the Past. in the light of this reference. The distinction between the Past. and Col. is that what was applied to all Christians in the latter can now be ascribed only to selected Christians, especially the leaders of the congregation. This tallies with the external development of the Church noticeable in a comparison between the Past. and Col.

If this sketch is correct, it confirms the thesis of Harnack that Paul did not give the OT to his congregations as the classical book of edification, at least from the standpoint of moral instruction.[62] In the older epistles R. 12:7 is our only witness that the OT as such was the starting-point for the reconstruction of ethics, and Paul is probably thinking here of Jewish Christians. Of a piece with this is the paucity of διδάσκαλος, διδασκαλία etc. in the older epistles. Only in Col. do we find a reversal,[63] and in the Past. διδάσκειν and other διδασκ- words become prominent again. Should we conclude from this that the OT was now emerging, especially in its legal sections, as the norm of Christian ethics which it became in the ancient Catholic Church? There is perhaps a hint of this in the reminder in 2 Tm. 3:15 that Timothy from a child knew the ἱερὰ γράμματα,[64] τὰ δυνάμενά σε σοφίσαι εἰς σωτηρίαν διὰ πίστεως τῆς ἐν Χριστῷ Ἰησοῦ. Cf. also 1 Tm. 4:13 with its admonition: πρόσεχε τῇ ἀναγνώσει, τῇ παρακλήσει, τῇ διδασκαλίᾳ, and 2 Tm. 3:16: πᾶσα γραφή ... ὠφέλιμος ... πρὸς παιδείαν τὴν ἐν δικαιοσύνῃ.

This does not mean, of course, that the OT was not of great importance for Paul, or that he could dispense with it. Such a thesis is disproved at once by the way in which he uses the OT in his epistles.[65] This applies also to morality, the final basis and goal of which Paul finds in the OT, in the νόμος (cf. R. 3:31). On the other hand, Paul is careful not to make the Law a pitiless taskmaster (cf. Gl. 4:25) for Christianity too. He thus rests his own διδάσκειν on the διδάσκειν of Jesus (cf. Gl. 5:14). Hence, although he speaks highly of the Law (R. 7:12), he builds the new morality on the cross

---

[60] The saying thus indicates the presence of Jewish Christians in Rome.

[61] On this pt., cf. 1 C. 14:34 f. and Str.-B., III, 467 ff.

[62] "Das Alte Testament in den paulinischen Briefen und in den paulinischen Gemeinden," SAB (1928), 124 ff., esp. 128.

[63] In 3:16, of course, διδάσκειν stands in close proximity to the λόγος τοῦ Χριστοῦ. It is thus possible that the reference is to teaching in the sense of Jesus. Even then, however, the passage is of great importance for the history of διδάσκειν within Christianity.

[64] This formula, which in the first instance denotes hieroglyphics, is clearly used for Scripture in Gk. Judaism (Philo Vit. Mos., II, 292; Jos. Ant., 10, 210); cf. Dib. Past., ad loc.

[65] Cf. on this pt. O. Michel, *Paulus und seine Bibel* (1929), 112 ff.

of Jesus, on His ἀγάπη (cf. Phil. 2:1 ff.). In so doing, he prevents early Christianity
from breaking up into different sects which are simply linked with Jesus through a
particular → διδάσκαλος. He thus honours and fulfils the saying of Jesus : ὑμεῖς δὲ
μὴ κληθῆτε ῥαββί· εἷς γάρ ἐστιν ὑμῶν ὁ διδάσκαλος, πάντες δὲ ὑμεῖς ἀδελφοί
ἐστε (Mt. 23:8).

† διδάσκαλος   (→ ῥαββί).

A. The Usage and Character of διδάσκαλος among the Greeks.

1. The Usage.

διδάσκαλος is attested in the sense of "teacher" from the time of the Homeric
hymns [1] and Aeschylus. [2] Indeed, it is occasionally found in the fem. for a "woman
teacher." From the very first it tends to become technical [3] in the sense of "master of
instruction." [4] a. On the one side, this may be the one who imparts instruction, esp. the
"schoolmaster" to whom the young are entrusted for elementary teaching, e.g., in
reading and writing. [5] Thus in Plato εἰς διδασκάλου (sc. οἶκον) φοιτᾶν [6] or εἰς
διδασκάλων φοιτᾶν [7] means "to go to school" and ἐν διδασκάλων "in school." [8] The
word kept this meaning and is found in this sense in Jewish Gk., e.g., Philo [9] and Joseph. [10]

δ ι δ ά σ κ α λ ο ς. S. Herner, "Erziehung und Unterricht in Israel," in *Oriental Studies
dedicated to Paul Haupt* (1926), 58 ff.; E. Ziebarth, *Aus dem griech. Schulwesen*[2] (1914),
where additional lit. may be found ; E. Reisch in Pauly-W., V (1905), 401 ff.; Dalman WJ,
I, 272 ff., 400 f.; S. Krauss, *Talmudische Archäologie,* III (1912), 217 ff.; *Jüd. Lex.,* III
(1929), 1021 ff.; Schürer, III, 372 ff., 491 ff.; Moore, I, 308 ff.; A. Schlatter, "Jochanan ben
Zakkai, der Zeitgenosse der Apostel," BFTh, III, 4 (1899); Cr.-Kö., 293 f.; Bultmann Trad.,
39 ff.; G. Kittel, C. H. Dodd and N. Micklem, Ἰησοῦς ὁ διδάσκαλος καὶ προφήτης,
ThBl, 7 (1928), 249 ff.; C. H. Dodd, "Jesus als Lehrer und Prophet," in *Mysterium Christi*
(1931), 67 ff.; A. v. Harnack, *Die Mission und Ausbreitung des Christentums in den ersten
drei Jahrhunderten*[4], I (1923), 345 ff.; H. Bruders, *Die Verfassung der Kirche von den ersten
Jahrzehnten der apost. Wirksamkeit an bis zum Jahre 175 n. Chr.* (1904), esp. 354 ff.; Schl.,
Gesch. d. erst. Chr., 27; W. Bousset, *Jüdisch-Christlicher Schulbetrieb in Alexandria und
Rom* (1915); J. Wach, *Meister und Jünger* (1925).

[1] Hom. Hymn. Merc., 554 ff.: κατὰ δὲ κρατὸς πεπαλαγμέναι ἄλφιτα λευκά | οἰκία
ναιετάουσιν ὑπὸ πτυχὶ Παρνήσοιο, | μαντείης ἀπάνευθε διδάσκαλοι ἦν ἐπὶ βουσὶ |
παῖς ἔτ' ἐὼν μελέτησα.

[2] Aesch. Prom., 110 f.: ἢ διδάσκαλος τέχνης | πάσης βροτοῖς πέφηνε καὶ μέγας
πόρος.

[3] Being constructed from the present stem as a *nomen agentis,* the word necessarily indicates from the very outset the regular and sustained impartation of knowledge, or instruction in the technical sense [A. Debrunner].

[4] Democr. Fr., 76 (II, 77, 14, Diels): νηπίοισιν οὐ λόγος, ἀλλὰ ξυμφορὴ γίνεται
διδάσκαλος. Cf. further Thuc., III, 82 : πόλεμος βίαιος διδάσκαλος; Lys., 12, 78 : τῷ
καλλίστῳ ὀνόματι χρώμενος δεινοτάτων ἔργων διδάσκαλος καταστάς.

[5] From διδάσκαλος τῶν γραμμάτων (e.g., P. Hal., 1, 260 [3rd cent. B.C.]), there is
constructed the word γραμματοδιδάσκαλος (e.g., Teles, p. 50, 4, Hense ; Ditt. Syll.[3], 578,
9 f. [2nd cent. B.C.]).

[6] Ps.-Plat. Alc., I, 109 d : ἢ ἐμὲ ἔλαθες μανθάνων καὶ φοιτῶν εἰς διδασκάλου ὅς σε
ἐδίδασκε διαγιγνώσκειν τὸ δικαιότερόν τε καὶ ἀδικώτερον.

[7] Plat. Prot., 326c : καὶ οἱ τούτων υἱεῖς πρωαίτατα εἰς διδασκάλων τῆς ἡλικίας
ἀρξάμενοι φοιτᾶν.

[8] Ps.-Plat. Alc., I, 110b : πολλάκις σοῦ ἐν διδασκάλων ἤκουον παιδὸς ὄντος καὶ
ἄλλοθι.

[9] Philo Vit. Mos., I, 21: The νήπιος Moses has διδάσκαλοι of different kinds and
origins ; in Migr. Abr., 116 there is reference to both διδάσκαλοι and παιδαγωγοί.

[10] Jos. Ant., 15, 373 (of Herod): ἔτι παῖδα εἰς διδασκάλου φοιτῶντα.

b. On the other side, in the pre-Alexandrine period it may also denote the "chorus-master," i.e., the one who has charge of the practice of choral poetry for public performance, and who is responsible for its correct performance. [11] Now all the great classical tragedies were intended for public performance rather than private reading, success on the stage being the criterion by which a dramatist received the reputation and crown of a great poet. Hence the Athenian dramatists were all men of the theatre, [12] and it is only natural that they themselves should train the choruses as well as playing specific parts. [13] The word thus came to be used for one who practises his own work with others, and then for the "poet" himself, whether his work be a choral poem, a tragedy or a comedy. Poets might well use it of themselves, as may be seen from Aristoph. Av., 912, where the ποιητής says: οὐκ ἀλλὰ πάντες ἐσμὲν οἱ διδάσκαλοι | Μουσάων θεράποντες ὀτρηροὶ κατὰ τὸν Ὅμηρον. [14] This was, however, a transient use, and the word soon reverted to its original meaning of the "chorus-master," who at a later period was not usually identical with the author; indeed, we sometimes hear of publicly paid χοροδιδάσκαλοι. [15] Yet the usage did not disappear completely, as may be seen from Epict. (Ench., 17): μέμνησο, ὅτι ὑποκριτὴς (actor) εἶ δράματος, οἵου ἂν θέλῃ ὁ διδάσκαλος. [16]

2. The Character of the Word.

Both branches of the usage show clearly how strong the technical and rational element was from the very first, and how it came to the fore with the development of the term. The διδάσκαλος is not just a teacher in general, but a man who teaches definite skills like reading, fighting or music, developing the aptitudes already present. Thus, if the subject of instruction is not clear from the context, it has to be defined more precisely by an indication of the skills in question. This opens up a very wide field. A διδάσκαλος might impart technical ability, the art of strategy (Ditt. Or., 149 [2nd cent. B.C.]), or what is morally reprehensible (κακά), [17] e.g., apostasy (cf. Philo Spec. Leg., I, 56). Because of its factuality, διδάσκαλος can be used quite objectively even in relation to ethical or religious conditions and in statements regarding their origin. The decisive point is that systematic instruction is given; if so, the word is apposite irrespective of the nature of the instruction or of the application of the term either to men or in a more figurative sense.

As this review shows, the usage is consistent. Philo is no exception. For him the priest giving directions about leprosy is a διδάσκαλος (Deus Imm., 134). So, too, is the νόμος φύσεως imparting knowledge (Agric., 66). So is the νόμος itself (Poster. C., 80). So is φύσις, since it points in a certain direction and lays down the right lines of cultic action (Rer. Div. Her., 182). Moses is a διδάσκαλος θείων, ἃ τοῖς ὦτα κεκαθαρμένοις ὑφηγήσεται (Gig., 54); he is ἀληθείας ἐραστὴς καὶ διδάσκαλος (Spec.

---

[11] Cf. Reisch, 401 ff.

[12] U. v. Wilamowitz-Moellendorff, *Griechische Tragödien,* I[9] (1922), 4.

[13] Even Aeschylus was still his own player, though he was also the first to introduce a second player and therefore to train a colleague for the purpose (cf. *ibid.,* IV [1923], 257).

[14] Reisch gives numerous examples of this usage, 402. Cf. also Suid., *s.v.*: ἰδίως διδασκάλους λέγουσι τοὺς ποιητὰς τῶν διθυράμβων ἢ τῶν κωμῳδιῶν ἢ τῶν τραγῳδιῶν.

[15] Cf. Ziebarth, 134 f.

[16] Cf. Philo Flacc., 34.

[17] → also n. 4: Lys., 12, 78.

Leg., I, 59). God Himself is for the σοφοί the ὑφηγητὴς καὶ διδάσκαλος, while the ἀτελέστεροι for their part must be content with the human σοφός (Rer. Div. Her., 19). [18] In all these cases the context betrays a strong intellectualisation. In this respect it is closely parallel to διδάσκειν. In Philo neither term is related to ethics or to moral conduct generally. The stress falls solely and simply on the presence of systematic instruction or on its effects, and this within the philosophical concern of Philo himself.

3. The Consequences of the Character of the Word for the Use of διδάσκαλος. In virtue of the character of the word we can understand the refusal of Socrates to be a διδάσκαλος or to call his mode of teaching διδάσκειν. We call also understand why Epictetus called himself a διδάσκαλος. And we can understand the almost complete absence of the word from the LXX.

a. In Plat. Ap., 33ab Socrates says expressly: ἐγὼ δὲ διδάσκαλος μὲν οὐδενὸς πώποτ᾽ ἐγενόμην ... εἰ δέ τίς φησι παρ᾽ ἐμοῦ πώποτέ τι μαθεῖν ἢ ἀκοῦσαι ἰδίᾳ ὅτι μὴ καὶ οἱ ἄλλοι πάντες, εὖ ἴστε, ὅτι οὐκ ἀληθῆ λέγει. This does not mean only that Socrates refused to found a school or to gather disciples, [19] but no less sharply that he is completely misunderstood if a binding system is made of his statements. Socrates was never a teacher in the sense of trying to instruct and educate the young like the sophistic teachers, or in the sense of advocating an ideal, or particularly in the sense of making himself an example. He never pretended to be a teacher of moral virtue. [20] This would have involved only the contacting and developing of certain impulses. Socrates wanted more ; his aim was to draw the whole man out of an existence which was primarily intellectual and to prepare him for consciously moral action. This did not imply any depreciation of the intellectual. The *ratio* of Sophistry was not constricted by him and his ethos. It was clarified and deepened, as we can see from the philosophy of Plato. He rejects only the merely intellectual, within which ἀρετή becomes one element among others, as with the Sophists. In contrast, Socrates brought back the ethical and the political into essential connexion with the intellectual. It was for this reason that he called his activity ὠφελεῖν rather than διδάσκειν. Furthermore, he sought to render this service to all his fellow-citizens. [21] In this respect, too, his dialectic was opposed to the mere intellectualism of his day, which naturally tended towards the formation of schools and sects. Socrates was differentiating himself at all these points when he refused to be called διδάσκαλος or to allow his methods to be described as διδάσκειν.

b. On the other hand, Epictetus was proud of the titles διδάσκαλος and παιδευτής in relation to his followers (Diss., I, 9, 12). This shows how different he is from Socrates in spite of all the attempts to establish similarity. For him the διδάσκαλος is the most important personage for those who seek perfection, and everything depends on their readiness to take full advantage of what he offers (Diss., II, 21, 10). [22] Already the use of διδάσκαλος shows how strongly schema and system and method replace the living ethos in Epict., as easily confirmed at other points (→ I, 442 f.).

---

[18] God is διδάσκαλος of ἐραστὴς σοφίας (Rer. Div. Her., 102), διδάσκαλος of ἐπιστῆμαι (Sacr. AC., 65), and διδάσκαλος καὶ ὑφηγητής (Congr., 114).
[19] The statement has this sense too, being part of Plato's polemic against Antisthenes, who made out that his own Cynic school was a continuation of the Socratic circle (cf. H.Maier, *Socrates* [1913], 108 f.).
[20] Cf. Plat. La., 200e and the whole context.
[21] This is the reason why his βίος took place publicly and anyone had the chance to speak with him. This is attested by Xenophon (Mem., I, 1, 10) as well as Plato (Ap., 33ab).
[22] ἔρχομαι πρὸς τὸν διδάσκαλον ὡς ἐπὶ τὰ χρηστήρια πείθεσθαι παρεσκευασμένος; To this question the true Cynic had to answer in the affirmative.

c. In the LXX διδάσκαλος occurs only twice, at Est. 6:1 and 2 Macc. 1:10. In the former: καὶ εἶπεν τῷ διδασκάλῳ αὐτοῦ εἰσφέρειν γράμματα μνημόσυνα τῶν ἡμερῶν ἀναγινώσκειν αὐτῷ, the τῷ διδασκάλῳ is added in translation. The context makes it plain that it can have only the sense of "reader" and that it probably denotes the slave who was entrusted with the education of the eunuchs in the broadest sense.[23] In other words, this is the customary Gk. usage. The second passage, however, goes rather beyond this. The Maccabean community is writing to Aristobulus, who belongs to one of the highpriestly families and is to be regarded as the head of the Jews in Egypt.[24] It calls him the διδάσκαλος of King Ptolemy, who must be Ptolemy Philometor. This can hardly mean that he was an adviser to the king.[25] It is not a title conferred by the king, but by the Jews, on the ground that Aristobulus[26] dedicated to the king his ἐξηγήσεις τῆς Μωϋσέως γραφῆς,[27] by which we are to understand a systematic compendium of the total content of the Pentateuch analogous to Philo's De specialibus legibus and with a view to demonstrating that the Μωϋσέως γραφή "already contained all that was later taught by the best Greek philosophers."[28] Aristobulus was called the king's διδάσκαλος because he expounded the Pentateuch in a work dedicated to him. Here, then, we have a use of the term which is dependent on the Jewish use of διδάσκειν in the sense of לִמֵּד[29] and which is thus distinct from ordinary Greek usage. This conclusion has an important bearing on the NT use of the word, since it shows the zeal with which Judaism defended itself against the threat of Hellenistic intellectualisation, and how this found expression linguistically.

Aristobulus could be called a διδάσκαλος in the Jewish sense only because his work served as propaganda for the Jews and was accomplished by him in subordination to this purpose. This means, however, that the word had already been given a specific content. When this happened we do not know. From the fact that it does not occur elsewhere in the LXX, while the part. διδάσκων is often used as a synonym,[30] we may conclude that in the eyes of the translators it was not yet adapted to express what they meant by a "teacher," namely, the man who had to give direction in the way of God according to His Law. If διδάσκαλος has recently been found in a Jerusalem ossuary, this "oldest instance of this title in Jewish epigraphy" shows that it was "in use at the beginning of the Christian era."[31]

It may be that another factor militating against its adoption was the increasing application of the term to the paid and even the publicly appointed or professional teacher. One reason for Socrates' rejection of the title was that he would never take money from his hearers, whether rich or poor (Plat. Ap., 33ab). Similarly, the Jewish teachers of wisdom were not teachers by profession; they gave counsel and direction where it seemed to be needed. For the rest, when mentioned in the LXX they are called σοφός (for חָכָם), so that there is also a linguistic difference from the Gk. διδάσκαλος.

---

[23] Cf. Da. 1:3 'A (?): διδασκάλῳ εὐνούχων (cf. Field, Hexapla, ad loc.).

[24] Cf. C. L. W. Grimm, Kurzgefasstes exegetisches Handbuch zu den Apokryphen des AT, IV (1857), 37.

[25] C. L. W. Grimm is right in rejecting this possibility.

[26] The reference is to the Jewish philosopher Aristobulus of Alexandria, who stands fully in the Gk. philosophical tradition. Cf. concerning him Schürer, III, 512 f.

[27] Chronicon Paschale, I, p. 337, Dindorf.

[28] Schürer, III, 514.

[29] → 137.

[30] Job 21:22; 'Ιωβ 22:2; ψ 118:99 (מְלַמְּדִים: διδάσκοντες); Prv. 5:13 (קוֹל מוֹרַי: φωνὴ παιδεύοντός με καὶ διδάσκοντός με) etc.

[31] Cf. E. L. Sukenik, Jüdische Gräber Jerusalems um Christi Geburt (1931), 17 f. I owe this reference to J. Jeremias.

B. διδάσκαλος in the NT.

1. The Usage.

a. διδάσκαλος occurs 58 times in the NT, and 48 times in the Gospels (not counting Jn. 8:4). In the Gospels it is used 41 times of Jesus, in 29 instances in the direct address διδάσκαλε, with κύριε the most common form of direct address. On 7 occasions it is used of others, twice in Mt. (10:24 f.), 4 times in Lk. (2:46; 3:12; 6:40 twice) and once in Jn. (3:10). In Lk. 3:12 it is used of John the Baptist calling the people to repentance on the banks of the Jordan; in Jn. 3:10 Jesus calls Nicodemus a [32] διδάσκαλος τοῦ Ἰσραήλ; in Lk. 2:46 it is said of the boy Jesus that He sat ἐν τῷ ἱερῷ ἐν μέσῳ τῶν διδασκάλων, listening to them and asking them questions; finally in Mt. 10:24 f.; Lk. 6:40 there is a radical declaration concerning the relationship of the μαθητής to his διδάσκαλος.

To these instances from the Gospels should be added a smaller number from Ac. and the epistles. They are all consistent with one another. The most prominent are those which refer to the διδάσκαλοι as a leading group in the early Christian community (Ac. 13:1; 1 C. 12:28 f.; Eph. 4:11; cf. also Jm. 3:1). In 1 Tm. 2:7; 2 Tm. 1:11 the author calls himself a διδάσκαλος ἐθνῶν or simply a διδάσκαλος. In the three other passages the term acquires a particular meaning from the context (R. 2:20; 2 Tm. 4:3; Hb. 5:12).

b. The first point to emerge clearly from this review of the use of διδάσκαλος in the NT is that the term, and therefore the addressing of Jesus as διδάσκαλε, does not imply any attribution of dignity, like κύριος. The application to John (Lk. 3:12), or to the διδάσκαλοι sitting in the temple (Lk. 2:46), or even to a group of false teachers (2 Tm. 4:3), shows beyond any shadow of doubt that even when used of Jesus διδάσκαλος can denote only an obvious fact; for we naturally cannot suppose that Lk. uses the term in a different sense when it refers to John on the one side and Jesus on the other. What this fact is may be seen quite easily from the passages in the Gospels in which διδάσκαλος is used, and best of all from those in which it is used of others. Jesus Himself (Mt. 10:24 f. and par.) contrasts the μαθητής and the διδάσκαλος; the former is to learn both his goal and his limitations by comparison with the latter. To Jewish listeners this statement was crystal clear, for they could see the relationship concretely before them in that of the Rabbinic pupil to his teacher. Jn. 3:10 is no less plain. When Jesus calls Nicodemus a διδάσκαλος τοῦ Ἰσραήλ, the context makes it evident that He does not have in view particular philosophical capacities; He is honouring him as one to whom the people look as a prominent expositor of the divine will as laid down in the Law and the prophets. Finally, when the publicans in Lk. 3:12 are so shaken by the Baptist's call for repentance that they wish to be baptised, and thus ask John: διδάσκαλε, τί ποιήσωμεν, both the address and the question indicate that on the basis of his knowledge of the will of God he can tell them what they must do to find favour with God. The vaguest reference is to the διδάσκαλοι in Lk. 2:46, though from the nature of Jesus' dealings with them [33]

---

[32] The definite art. does not imply that Nicodemus is the διδάσκαλος of his people in the absolute. It arises out of the pastoral concern of Jesus to show how much he himself needs to learn to hear before he can rightly come before his people with the forceful claim of a teacher to be heard. For the teacher who has not heard brings others into incalculable danger. Cf. Schl., ad loc.

[33] Cf. on this pt. Str.-B., II, 150 f.

we may infer that they were scribes occupied in answering questions which arose out of the Law.

The four or five passages in the Gospels where διδάσκαλος is used of others than Jesus thus display a consistency of usage. The word is directly related to the διδάσκειν of the LXX and the NT, which derives its content from לִמֵּד. In other words, the διδάσκαλος is "one who indicates the way of God from the Torah." [34] This raises two questions, or groups of questions, to which we must now address ourselves. First, we must consider how far the same usage applies when Jesus is described as διδάσκαλος, and therefore what are the theological implications of the term in relation to Him. Then we must ask whether the other NT passages use the word in the same sense as the Gospels.

2. Jesus as διδάσκαλος.

a. That Jesus is addressed as διδάσκαλε presupposes the fact that He outwardly conforms to the Jewish picture of the διδάσκαλος. This is indeed the case. Our investigation of the use of διδάσκειν in the Gospels (→ 139) has already shown us that Jesus may be basically associated with the scribes as regards both the form and content of His teaching. To be a διδάσκαλος and not merely an occasional διδάσκων, however, there was needed the further feature of the presence of disciples gathering around the διδάσκαλος (→ μαθητής). The fact that in the case of both Jesus and John (Jn. 1:35 ff.) certain men had been so gripped by their words that they set themselves in the position of pupils and disciples meant that in the eyes of their contemporaries the final presupposition had been externally fulfilled for granting them the title of διδάσκαλος, for addressing them as διδάσκαλε, [35] and for reckoning them among the teachers of the people.

That the address διδάσκαλε actually has this significance is proved by Jn. 1:38, where Jesus is addressed as ῥαββί by the disciples of Jn., and this is rendered διδάσκαλε for readers not familiar with this form of address (cf. also → ῥαββουνί in Jn. 20:16). Jesus is also addressed as ῥαββί by His disciples in Mt. 26:25; Mk. 9:5; 11:21; Jn. 4:31; 9:2; 11:8; by Nicodemus in Jn. 3:2; by the disciples of John in Jn. 1:49; by the enthusiastic crowd in Jn. 6:25; and by Judas at the arrest in Mt. 26:49; Mk. 14:45. Yet too much significance should not be attached to this, since רַבִּי might be applied to any exalted personage, [36, 37] whereas διδάσκαλε is reserved unequivocally for the teacher.

The Gospels make it clear point by point that the relation between Jesus and the disciples corresponds to that of Rabbinic pupils to their masters and that the

---

[34] This naturally opens up the possibility of using the term for someone who in appearance champions the Law and will of God, but in practice opposes them.

[35] For John the Baptist, cf. Lk. 3:12; cf. also ῥαββί in Jn. 3:26.

[36] רַב originally means "great," and it thus signifes at root one who is exalted, e.g., the prince in relation to the people (for examples cf. Dalman WJ, I, 274), the teacher in relation to the pupil, the master to the slave (cf. Pes., 8, 1), the master craftsman to the apprentice or associate (cf. bAZ, 17b). The Samaritans could even use רַבִּי for God (Dalman WJ, I, 275).

[37] A fine example of the varied use of רַבִּי is given in bBM, 84a, where Resh Laqish (d. before 279 A.D.), who first led the life of a vagrant and was then won for the study of the Law by his later brother-in-law R. Jochanan, can say with reference to his past as לִסְטָא (λῃστής), and then to his present: There (i.e., among the λῃσταί whose leader he was) they called me רַבִּי, and here (i.e., in the school) they call me רַבִּי.

crowd treated Him with the respect accorded to teachers. The description of the disciples as μαθηταί (תַּלְמִידִים)[38] and the use of → ἀκολουθεῖν for their attachment to Him both follow later Jewish terminology. Even the way in which they serve Him is in keeping with current practice. The pupil brings the rabbi's sandals (T. Neg., 8, 2), supports him when needed (bJeb., 42b), prepares the way before him (bKet., 63a),[39] and drives his donkey (T. Chag., 2, 1). A rather later reference (bKet., 96a; R. Joshua b. Levi, c. 250 A.D.) obliges the pupil to do for his teacher all the things a slave would do for his master[40] apart from taking off his sandals.[41] We do not know whether this included washing his feet, since there is no specific reference to this.[42] On the other hand, Jesus included it among the things the disciples owed one another, and He gave them an example by performing this service (Jn. 13:1 ff.), meeting the same kind of opposition from them (13:8) as great rabbis encountered in similar cases (e.g., S. Dt., 38 on 12:30). The disciples of Jesus acted as His boatmen (Mk. 4:35 ff. and par.) and also as distributors of food at the feeding of the multitudes (Mk. 5:37 ff. and par.; 8:6 and par.). They procured the donkey for the entry into Jerusalem (Mk. 11:1 ff.) and also made preparations for the passover (Mt. 26:17 ff.), which included the slaying of the lamb often left to slaves (cf. Pes., 8, 2). All this shows that the position of Jesus among His disciples was really that of the contemporary διδάσκαλος, of the rabbi among his pupils.

Nor is it only by the disciples that He is treated as such, for the crowds also honour Him in this way. In virtue of his handling of the Word of God the people set the teacher even above their own parents unless these also (i.e., the fathers) are teachers. Not only does the teacher precede his own father (BM, 2, 11), but the father stands up in the presence of his son if he is a teacher (bQid., 33b).[43] We know that when Akiba came from the school as a famous man, his father-in-law and his wife reverently kissed his feet (bKet., 63a). We also read that the mother of R. Ishmael (d. c. 135) sought permission from the rabbis to wash the feet of her son when he came from the assemblies, and then to drink the water which she had used; he himself forbade this on the ground of breaking the Fifth Commandment, but she argued that his prohibition was the real breach, since she saw in the action an honouring of herself through her son (jPea 15c, 41 ff.). In the same category we should place the service rendered to Jesus by the mother-in-law of Peter after she was healed (Mt. 8:15), or by the women who followed Him and ministered to Him of their substance (Lk. 8:3; cf. Mt. 27:55 and par.), or by Martha when she περιεσπᾶτο περὶ πολλὴν διακονίαν (Lk. 10:40). This does not

---

[38] In this connexion it is not without interest that Jewish tradition also refers to the תַּלְמִידִים of Jesus (bSanh., 43a Bar.; bAZ, 16b, 17a, Bar.).

[39] On the actual journey he goes behind the teacher (e.g., T. Pes., 1, 27; → I, 212 f.).

[40] שִׁמֵּשׁ (διακονεῖν) can thus be used synon. with הִלֵּךְ אַחֲרֵי (ἀκολουθεῖν); it is one of the marks of the תַּלְמִיד that he serves a specific scholar, i.e., his teacher. This is taken so seriously that a man who studies Scripture and tradition but does not render such service, i.e., attach himself to a scholar, is reckoned as עַם־הָאָרֶץ, or unlearned (bBer., 47, Bar.). Cf. also the way in which T. Ber., 6, 5 refers to a שַׁמָּשׁ who is תַּלְמִיד חָכָם.

[41] This gives concrete significance to the saying of the Baptist in Mk. 1:7; Jn. 1:27.

[42] Cf. Str.-B., II, 557.

[43] This was voluntary, not compulsory; but it is significant that it could even be discussed.

refer only to service at table, though this is naturally prominent (→ διακονία, 87). Mention should also be made of the honouring of the mother of Jesus, for which there are Rabbinic parallels in the case of great rabbis. [44] Along these lines, too, the picture of Jesus the διδάσκαλος conforms to the practice of His day, and the word διδάσκαλος as applied to Jesus in the NT is undeniably linked with the later Jewish רַבִּי.

This is to some extent confirmed by Josephus. [45] His use of the term is important because it presupposes what we have to deduce from the Gospels for want of evidence in the LXX or other writings. Now Joseph. uses διδάσκαλος for the elementary teacher (→ n. 10), but he also uses it for the one who studies the Law, who leads others to study it and who takes from it rules of conduct. This is so in Vit., 274, where Pharisaic emissaries from Jerusalem boast that they are not merely his fellow-citizens but also his διδάσκαλοι. [46] Cf. also Ant., 18, 16, in relation to the Sadducees; when he says of them: πρὸς γὰρ τοὺς διδασκάλους σοφίας, ἣν μετίασιν, ἀμφιλογεῖν ἀρετὴν ἀριθμοῦσιν, and thus distinguishes them from the Pharisees, who preserve the tradition which the rabbi embodies and guarantees, he is following the same usage. [47]

b. If we are to grasp the meaning of the title διδάσκαλος as applied to Jesus, it is essential to realise that He was not in any sense a new phenomenon as διδάσκαλος רַבִּי. On the contrary, the way which He took was a common one when He finally opened the ears and eyes of His people once again to the will of God and its binding power. Nor did He lack recognition. Even in scribal circles it had to be recognised that He was ἀληθής and pointed out the ὁδὸς τοῦ θεοῦ ἐν ἀληθείᾳ (Mt. 22:16 and par.; cf. Mk. 12:32; Jn. 3:2). If there was any objection to His activity as a teacher, it arose from the fact that He had not gone through the prescribed course of instruction or received authorisation from any teaching body (Jn. 7:15; cf. Mt. 13:54 and par.). In itself, then, the teaching of Jesus could not have led to the conflict which brought about His destruction. He might have founded a school like Hillel and Shammai. He might have discussed His differences with the scribes by the usual way of disputation. He might have tried to establish His view along these lines. If so, He would have given offence to some, but could still have been tolerated and recognised. [48] Jesus, however, could not take this path. For He had made His own the cause which God entrusted to Him. In the last resort, therefore, He had made it a human cause in a sense which could never be true of the opinions of Hillel and Shammai.

---

[44] Cf. Str.-B., II, 187 f.

[45] Cf. Schl. Mt., 284; Lk., 90.

[46] Joseph. was himself a Pharisee (Vit., 12) and it is possible that the men concerned had been his teachers.

[47] It need hardly be said that διδάσκαλος denotes a very different type of teacher from the one who gave elementary instruction in ancient Israel (S. Herner, op. cit.). On the other hand, this type did not completely disappear. His work formed the obvious basis for study of the Torah and tradition. Cf. further S. Krauss, *Talmudische Archäologie*, III (1912), 199 ff.

[48] A modern Jew like J. Klausner takes this view. His only charge against the teaching of Jesus is that it is too remote from reality, that it is thus "only an ideal for individuals, an anticipation of the future world," and that in the first instance it cannot serve as an "ethics for the nations and orders of this world" (*Jesus von Nazareth* [1930], 573 f.). It need hardly be shown that this represents a serious misunderstanding of the concern of Jesus from the standpoint of the Pharisee.

Jesus neither could nor would dispute because in so doing He would have surrendered the claim to absoluteness which He raised and which inevitably impressed all who heard and encountered Him. [49] This claim was essential. It could not be separated from His teaching. It emerged in it. This took place at the point where Jesus as διδάσκαλος took up again the line of the OT prophet who goes beyond traditional formulations and proclaims the will of God afresh and directly. Yet He was more than a prophet, for in opposition to the ossified religion and anthropocentric morality of His contemporaries He did not set the כֹּה אָמַר יְהוָה or נְאֻם יְהוָה of the prophets, but His own ἐγὼ δὲ λέγω ὑμῖν, which made it plain to His listeners that He was associating Himself directly with God, not as a mouthpiece, [50] but as the responsible Bearer of His will who is one with Him. [51] In this sense He may describe Himself as the One who fulfils the first direct revelation of God's will in the νόμος both by bringing out the full extent of its claims and also by transcending it to the degree that He offers Himself as the way to the fulfilment of the will of God (Mt. 5:17, 20). [52] Because He is the Son, as John would say, His teaching is different from that of the γραμματεῖς and others, from what theirs could ever be, even though there is a similarity of form and matter.

c. Thus, when the word διδάσκαλος is used of Jesus, His person gives it a tremendous weight which it can never have elsewhere. We might almost dare to say that it stamps Jesus as the new Moses who frees the law from national limitation and offers it to all men. It thus indicates both His authority and His dignity. We may thus understand why the formula ὁ διδάσκαλος λέγει, with no more precise indication who the διδάσκαλος is, is sufficient in the Synoptics to procure the room needed for the Last Supper (Mt. 26:18 and par.). We may also understand why the disciples did not appropriate the name διδάσκαλος after the death of Jesus, [53] although it must have seemed strange that the new leader of a Jewish group so occupied with the study of Scripture as the early Christians should not have been called רַבִּי/διδάσκαλος. Yet the term is never used even of James, the Lord's brother; and if Polycarp later uses διδάσκαλος with a religious accent (Mart. Pol., 12, 2; 16, 2; 19, 1), there is an obvious difference between the teachers of his day and those of the first period. For the latter the unabridged rule of Mt. 23:8 applied. Nor was it merely the letter of the saying which prevented them acknowledging any religious authority alongside or under Jesus; it was the realisation that there is salvation only in Him. For this reason it is a mistake in the NT even to be τοῦ Μωϋσέως μαθητής when the will of God is learned from Him (Jn. 9:28). For Jesus is the absolute διδάσκαλος. He is the One in whom Moses sees himself to be fulfilled (Jn. 5:45 f.). Hence the only possibility for the man

---

[49] Cf. esp., apart from Mt. 7:28 f., the way in which He wins His disciples, no matter whether they attach themselves to Him as though drawn by a magnet (Jn. 1:35 ff.) or whether He summons them to follow Him (Mt. 4:19 and par.). This is something unparalleled in His day, and it is no accident that we have no similar examples.

[50] As against Dodd in *Mysterium Christi*, 82.

[51] Cf. on this pt. Kittel, *op. cit.*, 250.

[52] Cf. also Jn. 1:17.

[53] The only exceptions are 1 Tm. 2:7; 2 Tm. 1:11. But there διδάσκαλος (1 Tm. 2:7: διδάσκαλος ἐθνῶν) is linked with ἀπόστολος, κῆρυξ, so that there can be no appearance of presumption. On this triad, cf. also Herm. s., 9, 15, 4; 16, 5; 25, 2, and Bruders, 354 f.

who seeks salvation is to become a hearer and μαθητής of the διδάσκαλος Jesus.

In the early Christian proclamation of Jesus as we have it in the NT apart from the Gospels, this designation seems to have played no part. This is in keeping with the fact that the crucifixion rather than a collection of sayings stands at the basis of the Christian message. [54] Only with the developing intellectualisation of Christianity do we hear again of Jesus the διδάσκαλος, and the term is not now used in the sense of the רַבִּי which it bore for the first disciples, but in the sense of the founder of a philosophical school, though still with the claim to absoluteness. This may be seen already in the post-apostolic fathers, e.g., when it is said in Barn., 2, 6 that Jesus has brought the καινὸς νόμος, [55] or in 2 Cl. 3, 1 that He is the Mediator of a true knowledge of God. The actual term διδάσκαλος, however, is found only in Ign. Eph., 15, 1, if this applies to Jesus and not to God. [56, 57] Only in the Apologists is He given the place of the διδάσκαλος (cf. Just. Apol., I, 4, 7; 12, 9; 13, 3 etc.). As such He can be compared with Hermes as the πάντων διδάσκαλος [58] (Just. Apol., I, 21, 1 f.), and set at the head of all the "teachers" of syncretism, whether the men concerned (Apollonius of Tyana etc.) [59] bore the term or not. By this time, of course, there is little connexion with the usage of the Gospels, which for its part rests on that of Judaism. [60]

3. The διδάσκαλοι of the Early Christian Community.

When we read of Christian διδάσκαλοι in Ac. (13:1) and the epistles (1 C. 12:28 f.; Eph. 4:11; cf. Jm. 3:1), it is not necessary for our understanding of the term to go outside the early Christian and later Jewish usage, or to seek enlightenment from the Greek world.

a. The situation is clearest in Jm. 3:1 if we can be sure that the epistle is early, or that it derives from the circle of Rabbinic Judaism, [61] for on one or other of these assumptions the word obviously denotes the expositor of the Law who makes possible a right fulfilment. The difficulty lies in the assumptions. On the other hand, there is nothing in the epistle to suggest Greek usage, for the → σοφία of James is practical rather than theoretical, and has thus a distinctively Rabbinic rather than a Greek character.

b. In 1 C. 12:28 f. [62] the διδάσκαλοι come after the ἀπόστολοι and προφῆται in a list of those who discharge specific functions in the community; in Eph. 4:11 they come fourth in a similar list after the ἀπόστολοι, προφῆται and εὐαγγε-

---

[54] The most solid complex within the evangelical tradition is the story of the passion.

[55] Here the Jesus/Moses antithesis is worked out from the standpoint of the lawgiver who is also διδάσκαλος.

[56] Cf. Dg., 9, 6, where God is the Teacher.

[57] The former is more likely, cf. W. Bauer, ad loc.

[58] Hermes bears this name because on the Stoic view he embodies the λόγος, i.e., the reason which derives from God: λόγος ὁ παρὰ θεοῦ ἀγγελτικός (Just. Apol., I, 22, 2). Cf. M. Heinze, Die Lehre vom Logos in der griech. Philosophie (1872), 140 ff.

[59] Cf. on this pt. G. P. Wetter, Der Sohn Gottes (1916), 28 ff.

[60] This is also true of the use of the formula ὁ διδάσκαλος ἡμῶν for Jesus in the Const. Ap. (cf. A. Harnack, "Die Quellen der sog. apost. Kirchenordnung," TU, II, 5 [1886], 25). There is no reason to regard this as a fiction designed to represent the directions as apostolic (A. Harnack, Entstehung und Entwicklung der Kirchenverfassung [1910], 8, n. 1).

[61] Cf. on this pt. the discussion in Kittel Probleme, 58 ff. But v. also F. Spitta, "Der Brief des Jk." (Zur Geschichte und Literatur des Urchristentums, II [1896], 1 ff.); A. Meyer, Das Rätsel des Jacobusbriefes (= Beihefte zur ZNW, 10) (1930), 292 ff.

[62] Cf. also R. 12:7; → 146; 147.

λισταί, being classified with the ποιμένες (τοὺς δὲ ποιμένας καὶ διδασκάλους); in Ac. 13:1 they are mentioned together with the προφῆται. It should be noted that the men mentioned in Ac. 13:1 are all of Jewish origin, and are thus closely connected with the Law. Since the προφῆται and the διδάσκαλοι are obviously not identical, and since the προφῆται are "pneumatics" (1 C. 14:29 ff.), it is likely that the διδάσκαλοι are "non-pneumatics" who edify the congregation by means of their own clearer understanding. [63] This leaves us with the same Jewish and early Christian usage as we have also in the διδάσκειν of the epistles. The same is true as regards 1 C. 12:28 f. And if in Eph. 4:11 the common article makes it plain that the διδάσκαλοι are identical with the ποιμένες, this lies in the nature of the case; for the → ποιμήν is the one who is responsible for the life of the community, and therefore διδάσκειν in the widest sense is part of his office. This is in agreement with Did., 15, 1, where the congregation is summoned to appoint ἐπισκόπους καὶ διακόνους ἀξίους τοῦ κυρίου that these may discharge the λειτουργία τῶν προφητῶν καὶ διδασκάλων; the function of the διδάσκαλος is here, too, a function of divine service. [64] It is self-evident, therefore, that in the first instance the διδάσκαλος does what he teaches (Did., 11, 10; cf. R. 2:21).

We must be on our watch against the idea that there is an order of rank in the lists in 1 C. 12:28 f. and Eph. 4:11. [65] The order is purely material. The activity of the διδάσκαλος is needed only when that of the ἀπόστολος and προφήτης has laid the foundation for the construction of a Christian outlook and manner of life. The διδάσκαλος of the first community is thus linked with the חָכָם or σοφός of later Judaism, whose work lies within the sphere of the community. Thus in Eph. 4:11, at a time when the ἀπόστολοι and the whole first generation are beginning to disappear from the life of the Church, the ποιμένες and διδάσκαλοι are similarly preceded by the εὐαγγελισταί, the new bearers of missionary responsibility. Basically, the situation is much the same as in the first Gospel, where Jesus first appears as the εὐαγγελιστής awakening faith (4:12 ff., 23 ff.) and only then emerges as the διδάσκαλος (5:1 ff.). It is a mark of the insight of the early Church, and especially of Paul, that in the question of edification they did not break free from the example of Jesus at this point.

Once we understand 1 C. 12 and Eph. 4 in this way, 1 Tm. 2:7 and 2 Tm. 1:11 become plain. κῆρυξ takes the place of εὐαγγελιστής and with διδάσκαλος describes the twofold function of the ἀπόστολος. We have here a high sense of mission and an equally strong sense of service typical of Paul. There can be no question either of the Rabbinic claim to rule on the one side or of the Greek claim to knowledge on the other. It is only to show the extent of his ministry that the author calls himself a διδάσκαλος ἐθνῶν in 1 Tm. 2:7. [66]

c. The usage of the early Church must be sharply distinguished from the early Christian use in relation to men also. We are not thinking now of the passages in the Did., but of the usage in the Egyptian Church where the free διδάσκαλος persisted

---

[63] Naturally they need the πνεῦμα too, as may be seen beyond question in 1 C. 12:28 f. (cf. also J. W. 1 C., ad loc.).

[64] Cf. on this pt. A. v. Harnack, Die Lehre der zwölf Apostel (1884), 131 ff.

[65] Pr.-Bauer, 156 calls the apostles of 1 C. 12:28 f. the "incumbents of the highest office in the community"; P. W. Schmiedel (Hand-Comm. z. NT, II, 1² [1892] ad loc.) refers to "a detailed order of rank." Cf. also Bchm., ad loc.; K. Barth, Die Auferstehung der Toten (1924), 49; A. v. Harnack, Mission, 349, n. 3.

[66] R. 2:20; Hb. 5:12 hardly need separate discussion, since in them διδάσκαλος may be understood in terms of the Jewish רַבִּי/διδάσκαλος; → 137 and 145. In 2 Tm. 4:3 διδάσκαλος is almost ironical and gives rise to no problems.

longest. [67] For the Egyptian διδάσκαλος is very different from the teacher of 1 C. 12:28 f. The Church is now invaded by Alexandrian wisdom, and with this it adopts the use of διδάσκαλος for the one who represents and teaches this wisdom, as in Philo. The Alexandrian School is not a continuation of the work of the first Christian teachers, but the introduction of a Greek institution into the Church in Christianised form. [68] Along the same lines the task of the early Apologists and teachers was to "give an orderly presentation and defence of Christianity." [69] It is only natural that among these teachers the intellectualisation of Christianity and faith should reintroduce the very thing against which Jesus and Paul and the early teachers strove with might and main for the sake of God and His undiluted lordship over man.

† νομοδιδάσκαλος (→ νομικός).

This word is not found in secular Gk., nor in the LXX, Josephus [1] or Philo. The only similar construction is νομοδιδάκτης in Plut. Cato Maior, 20 (I, 348b), [2] which is used for those who teach the νόμοι. [3] The linguistic basis of the term is to be found in the formulae τὸν νόμον διδάσκειν (1 Esr. 9:48 etc.) and לִמֵּד תּוֹרָה (Sota, 3, 4) or simply לִמֵּד (→ 137). It can hardly be of Jewish origin, [4] since διδάσκαλος is here equated with רַבִּי. It is rather a Christian construction designed to mark off Jewish from Christian teachers at the decisive point, namely, the absolutising of the νόμος.

It is found three times in the NT : in Ac. 5:34 of Gamaliel as an influential "teacher of the Law" (cf. Ac. 22:3); in Lk. 5:17 (with Φαρισαῖοι) to describe those elsewhere called γραμματεῖς (→ γραμματεύς); and in 1 Tm. 1:7 to denote the legalism of the errorists opposed by the author, but in an ironical sense : they want to be νομοδιδάσκαλοι, but do not really know what the νόμος is all about, and are certainly not called to instruct others in it. [5]

† καλοδιδάσκαλος (→ καλός).

This is nowhere attested outside the NT.

In the NT it is found only predicatively in Tt. 2:3, with a series of adjectives. Being used of the older women, the word is explained by the context. The older women are to keep the younger to their duties, [1] i.e., to every καλὸν ἔργον.

---

[67] Cf. Socrates Hist. Ecclesiastica, V, 22 (MPG, 67, 636), and on this C. Schmidt in *Neutestamentliche Studien, Georg Heinrici ... dargebracht* (= UNT, 6 [1914], 74). In general the διδάσκαλος — and Eph. 4:11 is perhaps a step on the way — quickly becomes one of the office-bearers of the community, particularly the elders. Cf. Barn., 1, 8; 4, 9, where the author emphasises that he is speaking as a well-meaning friend rather than a διδάσκαλος; v. also Bruders, 356, and the formula ἐθελοδιδάσκαλος (Herm. s., 9, 22, 2), which indicates one who has assigned to himself the position of a διδάσκαλος.
[68] Bousset, 314 ff. does not see this clearly enough.
[69] v. Harnack, *Mission*, 373, n. 3.
ν ο μ ο δ ι δ ά σ κ α λ ο ς. Cr.-Kö., 762; for bibl. → διδάσκαλος, 148.
[1] Schl. Lk., 58; Joseph., on the other hand, has the formula ἐξηγηταὶ τῶν πατρίων νόμων (Ant., 17, 149).
[2] Pr.-Bauer, 856.
[3] Naturally this is not the Jewish νόμος.
[4] Cr.-Kö., 762.
[5] Neither the word nor the context justifies the view that for the author of 1 Tm. νομοδιδάσκαλος does not imply "a category of religious history, but a value judgment in the sense of Paul" (Dib. Past., ad loc.). The word could be understood by the readers, and could thus fulfil its purpose, only if the men thus described were in fact occupied with the νόμος.
κ α λ ο δ ι δ ά σ κ α λ ο ς. [1] Dib. Past., ad loc.

κακοδιδασκαλέω (2 Cl., 10, 5) and κακοδιδασκαλία (Ign. Phld., 2, 1) are similar compounds.

† ψευδοδιδάσκαλος.

This is never found outside Christian usage.

In the NT it occurs only in 2 Pt. 2:1, where it is used with ψευδοπροφῆται for false teachers. The ψευδο- suggests both that the claim of the men concerned is false and also that their teaching is erroneous, [1] so that in every respect they are a perversion of the Christian διδάσκαλος, since they reject the claim of Jesus to dominion over their whole lives (→ δεσπότης, 47). [2] We are pointed in the same direction in Pol., 7, 1, where in connexion with ψευδοδιδασκαλίαι it is said of false teachers: ὃς ἂν μεθοδεύῃ τὰ λόγια τοῦ κυρίου πρὸς τὰς ἰδίας ἐπιθυμίας ..., οὗτος πρωτότοκός ἐστι τοῦ Σατανᾶ.

† διδασκαλία.

A. διδασκαλία outside the NT.

1. The word in common in Gk. in the sense of "teaching," including "teaching activity" (e.g., Xenoph. Oec., 19, 15: ἆρα, ἔφην, ὦ Ἰσχόμαχε, ἡ ἐρώτησις διδασκαλία ἐστίν;) as well as the passive sense of "being taught" (e.g., Aristot. Eth. Nic., II, 1, p. 1103a, 15: the διανοητικὴ ἀρετὴ τὸ πλεῖον ἐκ διδασκαλίας ἔχει, ἡ δ' ἠθικὴ ἐξ ἔθους περιγίνεται). Like διδάσκειν and διδάσκαλος, it can be used specifically in relation to drama and the chorus, as in Plat. Gorg., 501e (ἡ τῶν χορῶν διδασκαλία) of the practising of dramatic poems, while in Plut. Cim., 8 (I, 483e) διδασκαλία τοῦ Σοφοκλέους means "a tragedy of Sophocles," and in Plut. Pericl., 5 (I, 155e) τραγικὴ διδασκαλία is used for a whole "dramatic tetralogy" such as every poet had to offer at the games. [1] The word is thus closely linked with διδάσκαλος, from which it derives like φιλία from φίλος etc. It is specially linked with it in its strong reference to the authority of the διδάσκαλος (cf. Xenoph. Cyrop., VIII, 7, 24: καὶ παρὰ τῶν προγεγενημένων μανθάνετε· αὕτη γὰρ ἀρίστη διδασκαλία). It bears an unmistakable intellectual character.

2. Much the same usage is found in Philo. Thus in Jos., 1 he sets in conjunction self-instruction, practice and διδασκαλία as objective teaching. Again, in Deus Imm., 54 he supports a statement on the ground that it is πρὸς τὴν τῶν πολλῶν διδασκαλίαν. Again, in Op. Mund., 79 he believes that in the fact that the first man found everything that he needed for life there lies a διδασκαλία τῶν ἔπειτα to the effect that subsequent generations are guilty of unnecessary luxury if they do not take the first man as their example. In all these cases διδασκαλία suggests the communication or intensification of an insight.

3. In the LXX διδασκαλία occurs four times. In Prv. 2:17 אַלּוּף ("friend") is translated διδασκαλία, [2] and the verse is thus given a place in salvation history, inasmuch

---

ψ ε υ δ ο δ ι δ ά σ κ α λ ο ς. For bibl. → ψευδαπόστολος, I, 445.
[1] Cf. Wnd. 2 Pt., ad loc.
[2] Cf. also Did., 11, 10: Πᾶς δὲ προφήτης διδάσκων τὴν ἀλήθειαν, εἰ ἃ διδάσκει οὐ ποιεῖ, ψευδοπροφήτης ἐστί.
δ ι δ α σ κ α λ ί α. Cr.-Kö., 294 f. E. Reisch in Pauly-W., V (1905), 394 ff.
[1] This leads by a further step to the technical use of the term for the official lists of choral and esp. dramatic performances (cf. Reisch).
[2] There is here a confusion with the root "to teach" אָלַף.

as the imparting of divine instruction at the right time robs the guilty of the possible excuse of ignorance. It is obvious that behind the διδασκαλία νεότητος stands what took place at Sinai. Thus in relation to διδασκαλία we have the same distinction from secular usage, and that of Philo, as in the case of διδάσκειν and διδάσκαλος. In Sir. 24:33 there is an even clearer link with the will of God as revealed in the Law, for here God promises: ἔτι διδασκαλίαν ὡς προφητείαν ἐκχεῶ. This is also true of Sir. 39:8, where it is said of the scribe: αὐτὸς ἐκφαίνει παιδείαν διδασκαλίας αὐτοῦ, καὶ ἐν νόμῳ διαθήκης κυρίου καυχήσεται. In Is. 29:13 God says of Israel: μάτην δὲ σέβονταί με διδάσκοντες ἐντάλματα ἀνθρώπων καὶ διδασκαλίας. The point here is not the use of διδασκαλίαι ἀνθρώπων, for we have seen a similar employment of διδάσκειν etc. when it is a matter of the opposite of what ought to be, but the occurrence of διδασκαλίαι in the plural. Behind this stands a definite conviction that the unequivocal revelation of the will of God is opposed by a plurality of human teachings, so that the latter can raise no claim to absoluteness. This helps us to appreciate why in the LXX διδασκαλία is really a linguistic concession to the world around and is used so rarely. What it expresses is stated far better and far more clearly in νόμος, which also obviates any suspicion that this is simply a matter of human understanding and not of obedient recognition and fulfilment of the will of God.

B. διδασκαλία in the NT.

1. In Mt. 15:9; Mk. 7:7 it occurs in the plur. in a quotation from Is. 29:13 which Jesus uses against the Φαρισαῖοι and γραμματεῖς. In allusion to the same OT verse, it is also used in Col. 2:22 in the formula: ἐντάλματα καὶ διδασκαλίαι τῶν ἀνθρώπων. The only other occurrence in the plur. is in 1 Tm. 4:1, when those led astray are described as προσέχοντες πνεύμασιν πλάνοις καὶ διδασκαλίαις δαιμονίων. We have here a repetition of the LXX use of διδασκαλίαι rather than διδασκαλία for teachings other than the divine.

2. Along the same lines, the singular is always used in the NT when the will of God lies behind διδασκαλία. This is so in R. 12:7, where Paul admonishes the one who teaches to see ἐν τῇ διδασκαλίᾳ a service to the community and to exercise it in relation to the totality. If we have here the active sense of "instructing," in R. 15:4, where in the formula εἰς τὴν ἡμετέραν διδασκαλίαν Paul speaks of the significance of Ps. 69:9 for the community when christologically interpreted, we have the sense of the "instruction" which comes from Scripture.

Finally, Eph. 4:14 should be noted in this connexion: ἵνα μηκέτι ὦμεν ... περιφερόμενοι παντὶ ἀνέμῳ τῆς διδασκαλίας ἐν τῇ κυβείᾳ τῶν ἀνθρώπων. The character of the epistle makes it plain that this cannot refer to special errors against which the author is warning his readers. This is shown also by the fact that πᾶς is added to ἄνεμος rather than διδασκαλία, for this means that the author is thinking of a single διδασκαλία, and this can only be the διδασκαλία pursued in the community. Hence the formula is to be interpreted as follows. In relation to what the community possesses in the historically guaranteed witness concerning Jesus (4:1-11),[3] Paul is warning them against being swayed by each variable wind which comes with the claim of being doctrine and of bringing the will of God as such. This interpretation is in full accord with the use of διδασκαλία as expounded above. The only difference is that it is given a strongly objective colouring in relation to a historical content, whether this consists in a single OT

---

[3] Cf. on this pt. E. Haupt, *Die Gefangenschaftsbriefe* (1897), *ad loc.*

saying as in R. 15:4, or in the general revelation of the will of God in the OT, i.e., in this revelation as seen with the eyes of Jesus and according to His interpretation, as in R. 12:7. [4]

3. The final point is of great significance for an understanding of διδασκαλία in the Past., where the term is very common, 15 of the 21 NT occurrences being found here. The connexion with the historical revelation of God as attested by Scripture and fulfilled in Jesus is often plain from the context, as in 1 Tm. 4:13, where there is exhortation to διδασκαλία as well as to ἀνάγνωσις and παράκλησις, in 2 Tm. 3:16, where it is said of πᾶσα γραφή that it is ὠφέλιμος εἰς διδασκαλίαν, and perhaps in Tt. 2:10 : ἵνα τὴν διδασκαλίαν τὴν τοῦ σωτῆρος ἡμῶν θεοῦ κοσμῶσιν ἐν πᾶσιν (cf. also 1 Tm. 6:3). The formula ὑγιαίνουσα διδασκαλία [5] should also be understood in the light of the historical character of διδασκαλία, recognising as it does that this διδασκαλία is sound and therefore leads to salvation because it comes from God. If διδασκαλία is here used rather than κήρυγμα or some similar word, one reason is that διδασκαλία is particularly well adapted (→ 161) to emphasise the binding character of the historical proclamation, and a second is that it can denote the essential difference between Christian proclamation and the various movements which threaten the community. [6] Hence the use of ἡ καλὴ διδασκαλία, which lays greater stress on the content and practical effect of the διδασκαλία (1 Tm. 4:6), does not denote any real change in usage as compared with ἡ ὑγιαίνουσα διδασκαλία, which emphasises its nature ; nor is there any such change in the other passages (1 Tm. 4:16; 5:17; [7] 6:1; 2 Tm. 3:10; Tt. 2:7).

If διδασκαλία plays so small a role in Judaism and in the NT apart from the Past., and yet is so important in the latter, this is due to the fact that its basic reference is to the διδάσκαλος and his authority. In Judaism and the NT, however, the διδάσκαλος is not the independent bearer of a διδασκαλία as in the Greek world and Philo. He is the one who transmits and mediates a διδασκαλία. This makes the word unsuitable for Judaism and the greater part of the NT. On the other hand, it is very much in place in the Past. For here the author is very conscious of his office as a διδάσκαλος, since his readers have a tendency, not to reject the διδασκαλία which he represents, but to separate themselves from his own person, [8] oblivious of the fact that there can be no dividing the διδάσκαλος and the διδασκαλία, because the commissioned διδάσκαλος alone guarantees the ὑγιαίνουσα διδασκαλία as does the commissioned ἀπόστολος the εὐαγγέλιον τοῦ Χριστοῦ (Gl. 1:6 ff.; → ἑτεροδιδασκαλέω). The word thus offers an instructive example of the way in which new situations in the community

---

[4] The objective and historical character of the word appears in its strict use in the sing. when it relates to God or to the directing of our gaze on Him. It acquires a subjective character only when God is not envisaged as the absolute Subject of all occurrence.

[5] 1 Tm. 1:10; 2 Tm. 4:3; Tt. 1:9; 2:1; → ὑγιαίνω.

[6] The lack of prominence given to → διδαχή in the Past. shows that the concern is not with the teaching of the individual Christian, nor with his particular manner or emphasis in presenting the Gospel, but with the great line of Christian proclamation represented by Paul (1 Tm. 1:10; Tt. 1:3).

[7] Here one might discern in the conjunction of λόγος and διδασκαλία the necessary interrelation between the preaching of faith and instruction in the Christian life, and therefore a specialised use of διδασκαλία which is presupposed and included elsewhere, but not particularly emphasised.

[8] Cf. on this pt. Schl., Gesch. d. erst. Chr., 264 ff.

created a new use of terms even in the early days, a fluidity of thought and expression being thereby manifested.

4. The usage of the early Church corresponds to the change which the word διδάσκαλος had undergone prior to its acceptance into the Church's vocabulary. διδασκαλία now meant the "sum of teaching," and especially of that which had come down from the lips of the apostles. Instead of pastors and advisers of their congregations the apostles had now become teachers of the Church, which was permanently grounded in their teaching, i.e., in their way of proclaiming Jesus (e.g., Cl. Al. Strom., VII, 17, 108 : μία ἡ πάντων γέγονε τῶν ἀποστόλων ὥσπερ διδασκαλία οὕτως δὲ καὶ ἡ παράδοσις). [9] The surprising element which now emerges in the history of the usage is no less than the transformation of the apostolic message into traditional teaching, and therefo.e the incipient ossification of the early Christian kerygma into the dogma of the early Church.

† έτεροδιδασκαλέω.

This word presupposes a έτεροδιδάσκαλος [1] which is not mentioned in the NT, though the persons concerned are often present. The nearest approach to the term is in Paul's description of the "gospel" of the· Galatian Judaisers as ἕτερον εὐαγγέλιον, ὃ οὐκ ἔστιν ἄλλο : the name εὐαγγέλιον is wrongly claimed for their preaching because there is only one εὐαγγέλιον and this is proclaimed by Paul, any other εὐαγγέλιον being no gospel. It is in this light that we are to understand the ἕτερο- in έτεροδιδασκαλεῖν. It carries with it the proclamation of a έτέρα διδασκαλία which is a perversion and is thus to be rejected.

In the NT the word is found only in 1 Tm. 1:3 and 6:3, in both cases with reference to men who disseminate a different teaching from that of the writer and his assistants, making peripheral questions into the main issue (1:4 ff.). Since they are also called νομοδιδάσκαλοι in 1:7, a Judaising stress on the νόμος is what brings their doctrine under the sentence of έτεροδιδασκαλεῖν and distinguishes it from ὑγιαίνουσα διδασκαλία.

έτεροδιδάσκαλος : Eus. Hist. Eccl., III, 32, 8 : διὰ τῆς τῶν έτεροδιδασκάλων ἀπάτης, Ign. Pol., 3, 1: οἱ ... έτεροδιδασκαλοῦντες μή σε καταπλησσέτωσαν.

† διδαχή.

Among the Gks. this is used in the sense of "teaching," "instruction" (Thuc., IV, 126 : διδαχὴν ποιεῖσθαι, "to instruct"; Hdt., III, 134, 4 : ἐκ διδαχῆς λέγειν, "to speak on the basis of instruction"), with a strong tendency to restrict it to the fact, so that διδάσκειν or διδάσκεσθαι can normally be used as an alternative. Philo has the same usage in the one place in which it occurs in his work, [1] namely, Spec. Leg., II, 3 : ... ὑπὲρ ὠφελείας τῶν ἔπειτα καὶ διδαχῆς ἀναγκαίας, ἵνα τοὺς γονεῖς ὃν χρὴ τρόπον τιμῶσι ...

---

[9] Cf. also the expression ὅπως καταξιωθῶμεν ... τῆς μεγαλοφυοῦς διδασκαλίας τῶν εὐαγγελίων τοῦ σωτῆρος ἡμῶν Ἰησοῦ Χριστοῦ in pap. 13415, v. 23 ff. at the Egypt. Museum in Berlin (C. H. Schmidt, "Zwei altchristliche Gebete" in *Neutestamentliche Studien, Georg Heinrici ... dargebracht* [1914], 71, cf. 75).

έ τ ε ρ ο δ ι δ α σ κ α λ έ ω. [1] Bl.-Debr. § 115, 1. "The word is perhaps influenced by έτεροδοξέω (Plato, Philo), έτερόδοξος (Philo etc.), being possibly an early Christian adaptation" [A. Debrunner].

δ ι δ α χ ή. Cr.-Kö., 293; Schl. Mt., 264.
[1] Acc. to Leisegang's index to Philo, *s.v.*

In the LXX it occurs only in the title of ψ 59 in the formula εἰς διδαχήν ("to instruction"), thus corresponding to the Gk. usage and to the original לְלַמֵּד. The same usage is found in Joseph.,[2] as in Ant., 5, 198: οὐδὲν ἐπὶ διδαχῇ τοῦ κρείττονος ἐλάμβανον τῶν προτέρων ἠτυχημένων, or Ant., 17, 159, which speaks of the νόμοι, οὓς Μωσῆς ὑπαγορεύσει καὶ διδαχῇ τοῦ θεοῦ γραψάμενος κατέλιπε. διδαχή is thus synon. with the Rabbinic תַּלְמוּד, which signifies "teaching" in the sense that it might denote according to context either "teaching" or "being taught"; cf. Ab., 6, 2: אֵין לְךָ בֶן־חוֹרִין אֶלָּא מִי שֶׁעָסַק בְּתַלְמוּד תּוֹרָה, "there is none who is truly free except he who is engaged in the study of the Torah," or the common formula מַה־תַּלְמוּד לוֹמַר [8] (= מַה מְלַמֵּד הַכָּתוּב לוֹמַר) "what is taught here ?"

The NT follows this usage fairly closely. When the Synoptists speak of the διδαχή of Jesus, whether with or without mention of its shattering and radical effects upon His hearers (Mt. 7:28; 22:33; Mk. 1:22 and par.; 1:27; 4:2; 11:18; 12:38), they do not mean a particular dogmatics or ethics, but His whole διδάσκειν, His proclamation of the will of God as regards both form and content. In Jn., too, διδαχή comprehends the whole διδάσκειν of Jesus and does not merely denote a compendium of His individual statements (cf. Jn. 7:16 f.;[4] 18:19). Similarly, Mt. 16:12: ἡ διδαχὴ τῶν Φαρισαίων καὶ Σαδδουκαίων, has in view the whole of what the Pharisees or Sadducees διδάσκουσιν, or Ac. 2:42 the whole of what the apostles ἐδίδασκον (cf. Ac. 5:28; 17:19). Paul follows the same usage when he employs διδαχή both for the totality of his διδάσκειν (R. 6:17; 16:17) and for the διδάσκειν that might be necessary in individual cases (1 C. 14:6, 26). The same is true of the Johannine literature, both when it is referring to the διδαχὴ τοῦ Χριστοῦ, to the traditional and familiar way of speaking of Christ[5] (2 Jn. 9 f.), and when it is referring to the διδαχὴ Βαλαάμ (Rev. 2:14), the διδαχὴ τῶν Νικολαϊτῶν (Rev. 2:15) and the διδαχή of Jezebel (Rev. 2:24). The Pastorals (2 Tm. 4:2 = διδάσκειν; Tt. 1:9 διδάσκεσθαι) keep to the same pattern.

The only exceptions are to be found in Hb. 6:2 and 13:9. In the former: βαπτισμῶν διδαχὴν ἐπιθέσεώς τε χειρῶν, διδαχή means an established and formulated doctrine rather than διδάσκειν. In the latter: διδαχαὶ ποικίλαι καὶ ξέναι, the reference is again to definite errors which cause concern to the author and against which he wishes to warn his readers. Here is a usage which is developed further in the post-apostolic fathers (Did., 2, 1; 6, 1; 11, 2 and the title; Barn., 9, 9 etc.), the link with NT usage being dissolved and an approximation made to διδασκαλία.

This review of the use of διδαχή leads to an important conclusion. Especially when it is linked with the name of Jesus, the term enables us to see to what extent the NT or its authors recognised that it is finally God who speaks in the teaching of Jesus and the apostles. This means that there is on the one side both a formal and a material distinction from the Greek concept of teaching, and on the other that the formal

---

[2] Schl. Mt., 264.

[3] Cf. W. Bacher, Die exegetische Terminologie der jüdischen Traditionsliteratur, I (1899), 199 ff.

[4] ἡ ἐμὴ διδαχή does not mean, then, "my own teaching," but "that which I teach" : this understanding gives far more obvious point to the saying with its antithesis.

[5] The formula perhaps came into use in opposition to the διδαχαί of others (cf. Rev. 2:14 ff.). Possibly διδαχὴ τοῦ κυρίου in Ac. 13:12 should be mentioned in this connexion.

similarity to the Rabbinic view brings out all the more sharply the material difference, [6] since the whole consciousness of those who teach in the NT is a consciousness of mission. From the structure of this consciousness it may be seen that Jesus, unlike His messengers, is primarily the One who gives rather than receives (→ ἀποστέλλω, I, 404).

† διδακτός.

This is found in Gk. from the time of Pindar in the sense of a. "taught" (from διδάσκειν τινά); b. "learned" (from διδάσκειν τι, as in Eur. Hipp., 79 of the αἰδώς); and c. "teachable" (as b., so Soph. Trach., 64 : ποῖον; δίδαξον, μῆτερ, εἰ διδακτά μοι). Cf. ¬lso Philo Vit. Mos., I, 76 : τῆς διδακτῆς ... σοφίας κανών, == b.; Leg. All., III, 50 : οὔτε γὰρ ἡ ὅρασις οὔθ᾽ ἡ ἀκοὴ οὔτε τις τῶν ἄλλων αἰσθήσεων διδακτή, == c. Cf. Joseph. Bell., 6, 38 : διδακτὸν ἐν εἰρήνῃ τὸ πολεμεῖν ἔχοντες (== b.). In the LXX it is used in Is. 54:13 for למד: (καὶ θήσω ...) πάντας τοὺς υἱούς σου διδακτοὺς θεοῦ, being here used in the absolute in accordance with the Jewish understanding of διδακτός; on the other hand, in 1 Macc. 4:7: διδακτοὶ πολέμου, it has sense b. as in Jos. Bell., 6, 38. [1]

In the NT we find it in Jn. 6:45 quoting Is. 54:13 LXX, [2] as also in 1 C. 2:13 : ἃ καὶ λαλοῦμεν οὐκ ἐν διδακτοῖς ἀνθρωπίνης σοφίας λόγοις, ἀλλ᾽ ἐν διδακτοῖς πνεύματος. Here the repeated διδακτός (in sense b.) shows that Paul is not insisting on the way in which he has received what he says in contrast to others, but that he knows that he is different from them in virtue of its origin. It is to be noted that the essential point is not that he is διδακτός; it is that he has received his instruction from the right place. Thus the verse finds a natural role in Paul's polemic against the σοφία τοῦ αἰῶνος τούτου.

† διδακτικός.

Outside the NT this is found only in Philo (Congr., 35; Praem. Poen., 27; Mut. Nom., 83 and 88), and he always uses it to describe the ἀρετή of Abraham as "consisting or expressing itself in learning," as compared with Jacob's ἀρετή ἀσκητική.

In the NT it is found in 1 Tm. 3:2; 2 Tm. 2:24 in the sense of "able to teach." This is one of the requirements for a bishop. It belongs to a period when for the sake of spiritual order the free διδάσκαλος is merging with the leader of the community. One of the reasons for this development was that the διδάσκαλοι, or men who claimed to be such (→ ψευδοδιδάσκαλος, 160), were creating difficulties which were threatening the inner and outer life of the Church and which had thus to be overcome.

Rengstorf

---

[6] Jn. 7:16 would be impossible on the lips of a rabbi. The fame of a rabbi rested on his ability to make new pronouncements. It is for this reason that traditional Rabbinic style attaches to a statement the name of the rabbi who coined and established it.

δ ι δ α κ τ ό ς. Schl. J., 177.

[1] Cf. also ᾽Α : Is. 8:16; 29:13; ΣΘ : Is. 29:13.

[2] Also quoted in Ps. Sol. 17:35.

δ ι δ α κ τ ι κ ό ς. Dib. Past. on 1 Tm. 3:2, and excursus after 1 Tm. 3:7; E. Haack, "Die Lehrhaftigkeit des Pfarrers (1 Tm. 3:2)," *Pastoralblätter*, 75 (1933), 364 ff.

δίδωμι, δῶρον, δωρέομαι, δώρημα,
δωρεά, δωρεάν, ἀπο-, ἀνταποδίδωμι,
ἀνταπόδοσις, ἀνταπόδομα, παραδίδωμι,
παράδοσις

δίδωμι.[1]

In accordance with the significance and the realistic character of the thought of love in the NT, i.e., as a gift and not merely a disposition (Jm. 2:16; 1 Jn. 3:17), the word δίδωμι is of frequent occurrence. Particular attention should be paid to its use in John's Gospel. Jesus is what He is by God's gift. Objects of God's giving are the works of Jesus (5:36), His disciples (6:37, 39 etc.), the name of God (17:11), everything (3:35). Jesus' act of love in His death is described as δοῦναι τὴν ψυχήν (Mk. 10:45; cf. Mt. 20:28), ἑαυτόν (Gl. 1:4; 1 Tm. 2:6; Tt. 2:14), τὸ σῶμα (Lk. 22:19). This expression is traditional for the death of martyrs among the Jews and soldiers among the Greeks. 1 Macc. 6:44: Eleazar ἔδωκεν ἑαυτὸν τοῦ σῶσαι τὸν λαὸν αὐτοῦ; 2:50: δότε τὰς ψυχὰς ὑμῶν ὑπὲρ διαθήκης πατέρων. M. Ex., 12, 1: "The fathers and the prophets gave נפשם == τὰς ψυχὰς αὐτῶν for Israel."[2] Thuc., II, 43, 2: τὰ σώματα διδόντες (of the fallen Athenians).[3]

δῶρον, δωρέομαι, δώρημα, δωρεά.

Philo distinguishes between δόμα, δόσις on the one side as less valuable and δῶρον, δωρεά on the other as more valuable (Cher., 84; Leg. All., III, 196; so, too, δίδωμι and δωρέομαι, Decal., 17).[1] So far as concerns δίδωμι and δωρέομαι, this distinction is of no consequence in the NT. δίδωμι is used of the supreme gifts of God, whereas δωρέομαι is rare, though it is the more eminent term. On the other hand, δόμα and δόσις are little used (Mt. 7:11 [Lk. 11:13]; Eph. 4:8; Phil. 4:17; 4:15; Jm. 1:17) and are less significant than δῶρον, δωρεά, δώρημα, though the distinction is fluid, since δόμα is used in Eph. 4:8 for the divine gift.

δῶρον, from δίδωμι, means "gift." It is used of men's gifts to one another in Mt. 2:11; Rev. 11:10; of sacrifices in Mt. 5:23, 24; 8:4; 15:5 (Mk. 7:11 → κορβᾶν); 23:18, 19; Hb. 5:1; 8:3, 4; 9:9; 11:4;[2] of gifts of money in the temple in Lk. 21:1, 4;[3] and of God's gifts to men in Eph. 2:8.

δ ί δ ω μ ι. [1] For a review of the constructions and differentiations of meaning in Pr.-Bauer, cf. Bl.-Debr. § 94 and 95.

[2] Other expressions of the same kind may be found in Schl. Mt., 602.

[3] For examples of διδόναι (ἐπιδιδόναι) ἑαυτόν from the pap. and inscr., v. Nägeli, 56. On Philo → δῶρον, n. 3.

δ ῶ ρ ο ν κτλ. [1] Cf. J. B. Mayor, Epistle of St. James (1913), 53 f.

[2] δῶρά τε καὶ θυσίας in Hb. 5:1; 8:3; 9:9 is probably a formula originating in Hellen. Judaism, cf. Ep. Ar., 234: to worship God οὐ δώροις οὐδὲ θυσίαις. It is a mistake to differentiate between δῶρα and θυσίαι here (cf. Rgg. Hb., 129, n. 27).

[3] δῶρον is used of the gifts of men to the gods in Plat. Euthyphr., 15a: τὰ παρ' ἡμῶν δῶρα τοῖς θεοῖς etc.

δωρέομαι, from δῶρον, means "to give," being found in the mid. (act. in Pindar) in the LXX and often in Philo. In the NT it occurs in Mk. 15:45; 2 Pt. 1:3. It is used of God's giving to man in Plat. Tim., 46e : δι' ὃ θεὸς αὖθ' ἡμῖν δεδώρηται.

δώρημα, "what is given," "gift," is originally found in elevated style. In the LXX it occurs only in the apocryphal writings, Sir. 31(34):18. It occurs in Philo, though less frequently. In the NT it is used for God's gifts to men in R. 5:16 and Jm. 1:17; the latter is perhaps a quotation.

δωρεά, "gift," seems to be more legal than δῶρον and denotes formal endowment. In Attic orators it is used for "state awards" or "bequests"; [4] in the pap. for "fiefs" or "dowries." It is found in the LXX and often in Philo; in the NT it is always used of the gift of God or Christ to men, though it never occurs in the Synopt. (but cf. Jn. 4:10). In Ac. the Spirit is called the δωρεά of God in 2:38; 8:20; 10:45; 11:17; also in Hb. 6:4. Paul uses it more generally for the gifts of God or of Christ in R. 5:15, 17; 2 C. 9:15; Eph. 3:7; 4:7. In the NT it always implies the grace of God.

δωρεάν.

"In vain," an accus. used adverbially, found in the LXX and pap. [1] The basic meaning is "freely," "for nothing," as in Mt. 10:8; R. 3:24; 2 C. 11:7; 2 Th. 3:8; Rev. 21:6; 22:17. Joseph. often uses it in this sense. [2] The Heb. equivalent is חִנָּם, the Aram. עַל מַגָּן, מַגָּן. Other meanings are "without cause" (Jn. 15:25, where the phrase οἱ μισοῦντές με δωρεάν is based on ψ 34:19 and 68:4); "to no effect or purpose" (Gl. 2:21; Ign. Tr., 10). The two derived meanings are never found outside the LXX and NT (including the post-apost. fathers). On the other hand, the LXX often uses δωρεάν for "without cause or guilt," 1 Βασ. 19:5; ψ 34:19; 68:4; and "to no effect," Ez. 6:10. [3] The attachment of these meanings to the Gk. δωρεάν is obviously because it is used for חִנָּם so that we have here a true example of biblical Greek.

ἀποδίδωμι.

1. a. "To give or do something which one should in fulfilment of an obligation or expectation." Mt. 20:8; 2 Tm. 4:8 (a reward); Mt. 21:41 (fruits of the leased vineyard); Mk. 12:17 (Mt. 22:21; Lk. 20:25) (taxes); Mt. 27:58 (the requested body of Jesus); 1 C. 7:3; R. 13:7 (ὀφειλή); Rev. 22:2; Hb. 12:11 (fruit, this formula being also found in the LXX at Lv. 26:4 and in P. Oxy., I, 53, 11); Mt. 5:33 (oath, cf. ψ 50:14; P. Oxy., VII, 1026, 6); Ac. 4:33 (witness); Mt. 12:36; Lk. 16:2; Ac. 19:40; R. 14:12 (vl.); 1 Pt. 4:5 (account). b. More particularly "to repay in the form of reward or punishment" : of the divine retribution, Mt. 6:4, 6, 18; to each according to his works, R. 2:6; 2 Tm. 4:14; Rev. 22:12; cf. ψ 61:12; Prv. 24:12; according to his action, Mt. 16:27 (Sir. 32:24); Rev.

---

[4] Cf. J. Reiskius-T. Mitchell, *Index Graecitatis in singulos oratores Atticos*, I (1828), 263.
δ ω ρ ε ά ν. [1] Cf. Nägeli, 35.
[2] Cf. Schl. Mt. on 10:8.
[3] Cf. Zn. Gl. on 2:21.

18:6. Of human retribution, 1 Tm. 5:4 : ἀμοιβὰς ἀποδιδόναι to parents (a current formula, cf. Dion. Hal. Ant. Rom., VI, 73; P. Oxy., IV, 705, 61 etc.); evil with evil (cf. Prv. 17:13), R. 12:17; 1 Th. 5:15; 1 Pt. 3:9. c. "To give back what has been kept," Lk. 4:20; 9:42; 7:42; 12:59; Mt. 5:26; 18:25-34; Lk. 10:35; 19:8. d. "To sell" (only in the mid., found from the time of Hdt., I, 70, also in the pap. and inscr.), Ac. 5:8; 7:9; Hb. 12:16.

2. The thought of twofold retribution according to works in the last judgment is presupposed in the proclamation of the NT, even in that of Jesus. [1] One of the main purposes of this proclamation is to set men as impressively as possible under the threat and promise which it holds out. In the NT retribution belongs essentially to the future world rather than to the present. The thought of retribution is not a key to the understanding of the experiences of life, but a rule for the expectation of eternity. Retribution is according to love, i.e., works, and not a mere disposition. [2] In concreto, it does not mean only punishment. There is also an emphatic promise for love, even in its most insignificant acts. [3] Thus retribution includes forgiveness.

The thought of retribution cannot be taken out of the message of the NT without destroying it. The relationship between God and man is a personal one in which man the recipient is responsible to God the Giver and is thus subject to His retribution. [4] To do good for good's sake, artlessly and without regard for self, is not the morality of the NT. The morality of the NT is love for God, to whom man is bound by his very existence, and above all as His possession. [5] God and man are not equal partners in their mutual relationship; they are Creator and creature. [6] It thus belongs to the very nature of man to be subject to the divine retribution.

Love and retribution are not opposed. The love of God consists in the fact that He posits a personal creature to whose nature it belongs to be subject to retribution. Only in virtue of sin, i.e., the resisting of this relationship of the creature to the Creator, does retribution work against man. The fact that retribution has its root in the love of God means also that there is no incompatibility between retribution and forgiveness. To assert a tension, a relationship of antinomy or paradox or polarity, between retribution and love, is to be guilty of a profound misunderstanding of the NT message. Love as creation and forgiveness is more than retribution. But the thought of retribution is always enclosed in the NT thought

---

ἀποδίδωμι. [1] On the thought of retribution in the Greek and Roman world, cf. L. Rühl, De Mortuorum Judicio, RVV, 2, 2 (1903); among the Jews, F. K. Karner, Der Vergeltungsgedanke in der Ethik Jesu (1927), 20-44; cf. also H. Braun, Gerichtsgedanke und Rechtfertigungslehre bei Pls. (1930), 2-11.

[2] Jm. 2:17; 1 Jn. 3:17; R. 7:18.

[3] Mt. 18:5; 10:42 etc.

[4] In abstracto, responsibility is possible without retribution, but not in concreto if we are dealing with the responsibility which governs the relatonship, not just transitorily, but eschatologically and therefore definitively. To maintain responsibility while denying retribution is to be betrayed into an abstract and intrinsically impossible idealism.

[5] All morality which insists on autonomy is at least self-deception when measured by the message of the NT.

[6] For this reason God is never the recipient in relation to man, and there is no twosided retribution as in a free agreement which may be revoked at any time.

of love, as it is transcended by it. [7] Neither creation nor forgiveness [8] is conceivable without retribution. How God will conjoin retribution and forgiveness is the secret of His majesty, with which faith may well enjoy fellowship, but only by subjection to its holiness. [9]

ἀνταποδίδωμι, ἀνταπόδοσις, ἀνταπόδομα.

In ἀνταποδίδωμι the thought of recompense in ἀποδίδωμι is strengthened by the prefix ἀντί-. The word is attested from the time of Herodotus, and is common in the LXX and pap. In the NT it is found in 1 Th. 3:9 ("to render thanks"); Lk. 14:14; 2 Th. 1:6 ("to repay" love or trouble); R. 12:19; Hb. 10:30 (quotation from Dt. 32:35: God the One who alone repays); R. 11:35 (quoting Is. 40:14אA: no recompensing God).

The derived subst. ἀνταπόδοσις is attested from the time of Thucydides, but is most common in the post-class. age; [1] it is found in the LXX, pap. and inscr.; in Col. 3:24 it is used of the divine retribution in the last judgment. ἀνταπόδομα also occurs in the LXX; it is found in Lk. 14:12; R. 11:9 (quoting ψ 68:22, which speaks of the retributive punishment of God).

παραδίδωμι.

From the common use of the term, which is often found in the NT as in Gk. generally, we may select the following instances.

1. The word occurs frequently in the passion story, being used for the betrayal of Jesus by Judas (Mk. 14:10 and par. etc.); for His handing over to Pilate by the Sanhedrin (Mk. 15:1 and par.); and for His delivering up by Pilate to the will of the people (Lk. 23:25) or to the soldiers for execution (Mk. 15:15 and par.). [1] The frequent occurrence of the term in this context finds a parallel in the accounts of other trials, e.g., of martyrs (cf. Mt. 10:17; Ac. 12:4 etc.). The Heb. equivalent is מסר.

The formula παραδοῦναι εἰς χεῖράς τινος in Ac. 21:11 (pass. in Mt. 17:22 and par.; Mt. 26:45 and par.; Lk. 24:7; Ac. 28:17) is not found in pure Gk., [2] though it is common in the LXX: Jer. 33:24 f. etc. and occurs in Joseph. Ant., 2, 20 (in the expression: ταῖς χερσὶν αὐτῶν ... παραδοθέντος). There are parallels in the literature of Jewish tradition: ... מוֹסְרָם בְּיַד, S. Dt., 320. [3] In the Gospels and Acts the formula obviously has an OT and Jewish origin.

---

[7] Cf. Hegel's use of "aufgehoben."

[8] Mt. 18:21-35; Mk. 11:25; Mt. 6:12.

[9] Cf. the discussions and bibl. in Braun, op. cit., 14-31.

ἀνταποδίδωμι κτλ. [1] Nägeli, 36.

παραδίδωμι. Pr.-Bauer, s.v. Comm. on the Syn. by Zn., Kl., Hck.; on 1 C. by Joh. W., Ltzm.; Str.-B., II, 714 f.; F. Büchsel, Der Geist Gottes im NT (1926), 346 f.; J. Ranft, Der Ursprung des kath. Traditionsprinzips (1931).

[1] The reference in 1 C. 11:23b is undoubtedly to Judas' treachery. For Jesus was betrayed "in the night" only by Judas (as against Pr.-Bauer, s.v., 981).

[2] But it might well have been used, Bl.-Debr. § 217, 2.

[3] Cf. Schl. Mt., 537 f.

2. The term bears a similar sense in the formula παραδοῦναι ... τῷ σατανᾷ in 1 C. 5:5; 1 Tm. 1:20. Paul uses this only for the case mentioned in 1 C. 5:5, and it had probably become a formula in 1 Tm. 1:20. It is likely enough that Paul adopted it, though it is not found until the 4th cent. A.D. in the literature of Gk. magic [4] or the 3rd in Judaism. [5] Probably it was part of the "legacy of the ancient world," "the only difference between Jewish and pagan devotions consisting in the fact that Satan in the one took the place of the gods of the underworld in the other." [6] That Satan should execute the divine judgment corresponded to Jewish belief. [7] In this handing over to Satan the true agent is not the unwilling community but the spirit of Paul, or rather the power (or name) of our Lord Jesus (cf. v. 4). In OT and Jewish Christian tradition there are several examples of punitive miracles performed by godly individuals from 2 K. 2:23-25 onwards, [8] but no similar miracles are recorded of communities. Pneumatic awareness is more original and powerful among individuals than communities. [9]

3. παραδοῦναι is used of God's judgment on sinners in R. 1:24 ff.; Ac. 7:42 (following Am. 5:25-27). Cf. also Eph. 4:19 : ἑαυτοὺς παρέδωκαν τῇ ἀσελγείᾳ. In R. 6:17: εἰς ὃν παρεδόθητε τύπον διδαχῆς many expositors think in terms of a παραδοῦναι of God; [10] it is more correct, however, to think of a human παραδοῦναι and to take ὃν παρεδόθητε (corresponding to the ὃ ἐπιστεύθην ἐγώ in 1 Tm. 1:11; Tt. 1:3) as ὃς παρεδόθη ὑμῖν. [11]

4. In the expressions παραδοῦναι τὸ πνεῦμα (Jn. 19:30); τὰς ψυχάς (Ac. 25:26); τὸ σῶμα (1 C. 13:3); ἑαυτόν (Gl. 2:20; Eph. 5:25); also παρέδωκεν αὐτόν (R. 8:32 : opp. οὐκ ἐφείσατο) and παρεδόθη (R. 4:25), the main point is willingness to die, or self-sacrificial love. It is striking that we never find εἰς θάνατον in relation to Jesus. It does occur in 2 C. 4:11: ἡμεῖς οἱ ζῶντες εἰς θάνατον παραδιδόμεθα. This is no euphemism; it is more likely an abbreviation explained by the common use of the phrase. παραδίδωμι ἐμαυτόν in the sense of self-sacrifice (cf. παρέχω ἐμαυτόν) is also found in Plat. Euthyd., 285c (→ δίδωμι).

---

[4] R. Wünsch, *Sethianische Verfluchungstafeln* (1898), 14, 16, 3 : παραθίθομε τοῦτον τὸν δυσσεβήν; 15, 16, 38 : ὑμῖν παραδείδουμε τοῦτον τὸν δυσσεβήν, and P. Lond., I, 75 : νεκυδαίμων ... παραδίδωμί σοι τὸν ... The texts in R. Wünsch, *Antike Fluchtafeln*² (1907) do not have παραδιδόναι in this sense.

[5] Ex. r., 21 (84a): God hands over Job to Sammaël (Satan), not to kill Job, but to divert Satan from Israel as it passes through the Red Sea ; cf. Str.-B., III, 358.

[6] Deissmann LO, 256.

[7] Cf. Str.-B., I, 144; IV, 521 ff.; → διάβολος, 79.

[8] Ac. 5:1-10; 13:11 etc.; cf. Ltzm. 1 C. on 5:5 and the Rabbinic stories in Str.-B., II, 714 ff.

[9] We are not to view 1 C. 5:3-5 merely as advice given by Paul (Deissmann LO, 227), or as an ideal and theoretical discussion (M. Dibelius, *Die Geisterwelt im Glauben des Pls.* [1909] 38 ff.); cf. F. Büchsel, *Der Geist Gottes im NT* (1926), 346 f. Paul apparently expects the death of the sinner, perhaps by an accident, or by an illness which will break his defiance of the apostle and bring him to repentance, so that he will be saved on the day of Jesus Christ. It is a mere conjecture that the judgment failed to take effect (E. v. Dobschütz, *Die urchr. Gemeinden* [1902], 40, 269 ff.). On this whole question, → κατάρα and derivatives and the bibl. given there ; cf. esp. I, 449, n. 2; cf. also C. Bruston, "L'abandon du pécheur à Satan," *Revue de Théol. et des Quest. relig.*, 21 (1912), 450-458, and L. Brun, *Segen und Fluch im Urchristentum* (1932), 106 ff.

[10] Cf. Ltzm., *ad loc.*

[11] Cf. Zn. R. on 6:17. Ranft, 259, n. 4 adduces a passage from CIA, III, 1085 : τοὺς δὲ ἐφήβους παρέδωκε εἰς τὸ μητρῷον (the mystery of Cybele), but this is no true parallel.

5. In Mt. 11:27; Lk. 10:22, παραδοῦναι is used in relation to the authoritative position of Jesus as the Messiah or Son of God (cf. also 1 C. 15:24). The widespread view that πάντα μοι παρεδόθη refers to "all secret knowledge" [12] is right only if παρεδόθη is here used of the handing down of teaching from the past. [13] But this is surely excluded by ἀπὸ τοῦ πατρός μου. In τὰ πάντα as such is not the slightest connexion with knowledge. Thus the following statement [14] speaks of the mysterious authority (or nature) of the Son, not of His knowledge of God, and in v. 25-26 that which is hidden from the wise and prudent is this authority or nature of the Son, not His knowledge. The point is substantiated by the Jewish parallels adduced by A. Schlatter, [15] i.e., מוֹסֵר אֶת הַכֹּל (Ex. r., 15, 30) and נָתַן הַכֹּל (Ex. r., 15, 9), which can only refer to world dominion. To deny that Mt. 28:18 offers the closest parallel is an example of "critical" prejudice. [16] In 1 C. 15:24 the reference can only be to the cessation of Christ's dominion. [17]

6. παραδοῦναι is used as a technical term when its object is teaching etc. Thus it is used of the Halachic tradition of the Jews in general in Ac. 6:14, or more specifically of that which goes beyond the Law in Mk. 7:13, or of Christian tradition with no more precise definition of content in R. 6:17; 1 C. 11:2, 23; 15:3, or with such a definition in 2 Pt. 2:21 (ἡ παραδοθεῖσα ... ἐντολή); Jd. 3 (ἡ παραδοθεῖσα τοῖς ἁγίοις πίστις, cf. Pol., 7, 2 : ὁ ἡμῖν παραδοθεὶς [λόγος]). It is also used of the matter of the Gospel in Lk. 1:2, and of the commands (δόγματα) of the apostolic council in Ac. 16:4. This type of παραδοῦναι is verbal rather than written [18] (→ παράδοσις). Similar transmission is found among the Jews and Greeks, and also in the Mysteries. Here, too, the Heb. equivalent is מסר. Teaching tradition is referred to in Plat. Phileb., 16c : οἱ μὲν παλαιοὶ ... ταύτην φήμην παρέδοσαν etc., and the tradition of the Mysteries in Diod. S., V, 48, 4 : μυστηρίων τελετὴ παραδοθεῖσα. In Wis. 14:15, in a description of the worship of idols, we have : παρέδωκεν τοῖς ὑποχειρίοις μυστήρια καὶ τελετάς, for which there are many parallels. [19]

---

[12] Kl., ad loc.

[13] So J. Wellhausen, Das Ev. Matthaei (1904), ad loc.

[14] The introduction of a prior statement concerning the Son's knowledge of God was shown to be incorrect by A. v. Harnack, Sprüche und Reden Jesu (1907), 189 ff. on the ground that it has no support in the MSS and versions. The quotations of the fathers and heretics do not always give us a reliable rendering of the texts which they had. This is proved beyond question in the case of Iren. In IV, 1 he knows that the introduction of the statement concerning the knowledge of the Father by the Son is unwarranted. Nevertheless, he quotes it in IV, 6, 7, and he has a different version in II, 6, 1 and IV, 6, 3.

[15] Schl. Mt., 383.

[16] In opposition to the theory of E. Norden (Agnostos Theos [1913], 288 ff.) that Mt. 11:25-30 derives from theosophical mysticism, cf. Kl. Mt., 101 f.

[17] Cf. the comm. ad loc., and Schl., Theol. d. Ap., 326-328. On παραδιδοῖ, cf. Bl.-Debr. § 95, 2.

[18] παραδιδόναι is, of course, used also with books as object: ταῖς ἱεραῖς βίβλοις ... ἃς ... συνέγραψεν ὑφηγησαμένου θεοῦ καὶ παρέδωκε τοῖς ἀξίοις χρῆσθαι (Philo Vit. Mos., II, 11). Cf. C. A. Lobeck, Aglaophamus I (1829), 39, n.; G. Anrich, Das antike Mysterienwesen (1894), 54, n. 4.

[19] παράδοσις τελετῆς, παραδοῦναι (παραλαβεῖν) τελετάς are tech. terms in the Mysteries (cf. e.g., Theon Smyrnaeus, p. 14 f., Hiller). Cf. Ranft, 181-185, with many examples ; E. Pfister, Philologus, 69 (1915), 415.

7. It is also found in the sense of "to commend or leave to" in Ac. 14:26; 15:40 : χάριτι; 1 Pt. 2:23 : to the divine Judge. It is used in the sense of "to permit" in Mk. 4:29, as also in Hdt., VII, 18 : τοῦ θεοῦ παραδιδόντος; Polyb., XXI, 41, 9 : τῆς ὥρας παραδιδούσης. [20]

παράδοσις.

In the NT this means "tradition" (→ παραδίδωμι, 6.) only in the sense of what is transmitted, not of transmission. In this sense, it does not occur in the LXX, but is found in Philo and Joseph. and in Greek generally, though it less common than in the other sense.

1. In the disputation in Mk. 7 (Mt. 15), Jesus calls Jewish tradition outside the Law the παράδοσις τῶν πρεσβυτέρων, Mk. 7:3, 5 (Mt. 15:2). He also speaks of the παράδοσις τῶν ἀνθρώπων in Mk. 7:8 or ὑμῶν in v. 9, Mt. 15:3, 6. In Joseph. we find such expressions as τὰ ἐκ παραδόσεως τῶν πατέρων (Ant., 13, 297); τὴν πατρῷαν παράδοσιν (Ant., 13, 409); τῇ τῶν πρεσβυτέρων παραδόσει (Ant., 10, 51). [1] In Philo Spec. Leg., IV, 150 we have αὐτῶν (γονέων) ἡ παράδοσις. The Heb. equivalent is מסרה[2] sometimes with the addition הַזְּקֵנִים or in the plural. [3] The Pharisees regarded unwritten tradition as no less binding than the Law. Even Philo claimed piety for such tradition. The Sadducees rejected it (Jos. Ant., 13, 297). [4] So did Jesus. He agreed with the Pharisees that the good demanded of man is obedience to God's commandment. [5] As He saw it, however, men could not add to this commandment, since they were too seriously in conflict with God. Jesus did not argue for freedom in attacking tradition. His service of God, however, was not legalistic, and therefore He would not add to the commands of God. In Gl. 1:14 the πατρικαί μου παραδόσεις are Jewish tradition generally, both written and verbal.

2. For Paul Christian teaching is tradition (1 C. 11:2; 2 Th. 2:15; 3:6; cf. 1 C. 11:23; 15:1-11), and he demands that the churches should keep to it, since salvation depends on it (1 C. 15:2). He sees no antithesis between pneumatic piety and the high estimation of tradition. [6] The essential point for Paul is that it has been handed down (1 C. 15:3), and that it derives from the Lord (11:23). A tradition initiated by himself or others is without validity (Col. 2:8). It is no contradiction that Jesus repudiates tradition and Paul champions it. Paul's tradition agrees with Jesus' rejection, since they are both opposed to human tradition. Paul's use of παράδοσις and παραδοῦναι rests on the Jewish usage, and agrees with that of the Mysteries to the extent that this agrees with Jewish usage. On the other hand,

---

[20] Cf. Kl., ad loc.

παράδοσις. Comm. on Mk. by Kl., Hck.; on Mt. by Zn., Kl., Schl.; on 1 C. by Joh. W., Ltzm.; Ranft (→ παραδίδωμι, 169, Bibl.).

[1] He also uses it for the historical tradition of facts : δεῖ τὸν ἄλλοις παράδοσιν πράξεων ἀληθινῶν ὑπισχνούμενον αὐτὸν ἐπίστασθαι ταύτας, Ap., 1, 53; παράδοσις corresponding to Polyb. XI, 8, 2.

[2] Cf. F. Buhl, Text und Kanon d. AT (1891), 95 f.

[3] Str.-B., I, 691 ff.; Schl. Mt., 477 ff.

[4] Schürer, II[3], 406 ff.

[5] W. Lütgert, Die Liebe im NT (1905), 82 ff.

[6] F. Büchsel, Der Geist Gottes im NT (1926), 275 ff.

Paul does not recognise the sacraments as objects of παραδοῦναι and παράδοσις.[7]

In the days of Paul tradition is in process of acquiring a fixed verbal form.[8] In 1 C. 15:3 ff. we have a fairly settled christological formula, as also in 1 C. 11:23 ff.[9] The same cannot be said, however, of other passages like the lists of vices. The παράδοσις of 1 C. 15:3 ff. is older than Paul and rests on the Jerusalem tradition, even if it does not originate in Jerusalem.[10] The same is probably true of 1 C. 11:23 ff.; the ἀπὸ τοῦ κυρίου implies that the Lord's Supper, its celebration and the appropriate words come from the Lord, not that Paul received the formula in visionary instruction by the ascended Lord.[11]

Büchsel

διερμηνευτής, -νεύω, -νεία → ἑρμηνεύω.

---

[7] We have only partial knowledge of the use of παράδοσις and παραδοῦναι in the Mysteries. It can be shown that τελετή and μυστήριον (and therefore things of a sacramental nature) were objects of παράδοσις and παραδοῦναι (cf. Ranft, 181-185). Teaching occurs less frequently, cf. Norden, *Agnostos Theos,* 290 f.

[8] A. Seeberg, *Der Katechismus der Urchristenheit* (1903); P. Feine, *Die Gestalt des apost. Glaubensbekenntnisses im NT* (1925).

[9] In the case of 1 C. 15:3 ff. this is proved by the distinctiveness of the form, in that of 1 C. 11:23 ff. by the relationship to Mk. and Mt. (though cf. Bchm. 1 K. 15:3).

[10] The witnesses adduced belong to Jerusalem. Heitmüller's suggestion that it derives from Hellen. Christianity (Damascus), ZNW, 13 (1912), 331, is without foundation.

[11] This does not rest merely on the ἀπό (elsewhere Pl. has παρά, Gl. 1:12; 1 Th. 2:13; 4:1; 2 Th. 3:6; cf. Ltzm. on 1 C. 11:23; also Joh. W. 1 K., 283; A. Schweitzer, *Die Mystik d. Ap. Pls.* [1930], 259 f.; Kittel Probleme, 63 f.). A more important point is that nowhere else does Paul appeal to visions for cultic institutions. "1 C. 11:23 ff. rests no less solidly on tradition than 1 C. 15:3 ff." (M. Dibelius, *Formgesch. d. Ev.*[2] [1933], 26, n. 1).

δίκη, δίκαιος, δικαιοσύνη, δικαιόω,
δικαίωμα, δικαίωσις, δικαιοκρισία

The Concept of Law in the OT.

The concept of law exercised so strong an influence on the understanding of all
social relationships that even theological reflection on the fellowship established
between God and man was decisively affected by it. One may say that law is the
basis of the view of God in the OT in so far as it is theologically developed, and
that conversely the endowment of legal concepts with religious meaning contributed to an ethicising of law (→ θεός). This is proved especially by the
usage of the OT. The concept of law is expressed by a series of terms which are
used not merely for the relations of God to man and man to God, but also for the
conduct of both God and man as determined by these relations. If vital religious
relationships and interconnexions are regulated by a religious norm, it is obvious
that this norm is valid for all social relationships, and therefore that law fashions
the ethical norm.

1. The richness of the Heb. usage is in general excellently reproduced in the corresponding LXX words δίκη, δικαιοσύνη, δίκαιος and δικαιοῦν, though a comparison
of the renderings used throughout the LXX shows a strong concern on the part of the
Greek translators to express the vitality of the Hebrew terms by other expressions which
were not always so felicitous. The most important material for our present purpose is
considered in the following review.

δίκη is mostly (9 times) used for ריב (verb and noun), and only once for דִּין
(Ps. 9:4), מִשְׁפָּט (Ps. 139:13) and the rather obscure חָרוּץ (Jl. 4:14 "decision" ?). Its use
4 times (Ex. 21:20; Lv. 26:25; Dt. 32:41, 43) for נקם ("revenge," "to take vengeance")
is a weakening, and its use for דֶּבֶר "pestilence" (Hos. 13:14) is a mistake due to confusion with דָּבָר ("word" or "cause"). It is striking that the LXX uses δίκη so little,
for δίκη best expresses the character of מִשְׁפָּט or צֶדֶק as a norm, and therefore one
might have expected its frequent occurrence. δικαιοσύνη is used 81 times for צֶדֶק,
134 for צְדָקָה and 6 rather freely for the adj. צַדִּיק (Ps. 71:7; Prv. 2:20; 11:21, 30; 15:6;
20:7), cf. also Is. 26:2: גּוֹי־צַדִּיק λαὸς φυλάσσων δικαιοσύνην. There are only 8 instances of חֶסֶד as an equivalent (Gn. 19:19; 20:13; 21:23; 32:10; Ex. 15:13; 34:7; Prv.

δίκη κτλ. In the OT: W. Baudissin, *Kyrios als Gottesname im Judentum u. seine
Stelle in der Religionsgeschichte*, III (1929), 379-428; "Der gerechte Gott in altsemitischer
Religion," *Festgabe für A. Harnack* (1921), 1 ff. (= *Kyrios, op. cit.*, 398 ff.); L. Diestel,
"Die Idee der Gerechtigkeit, vorzüglich im AT, bibl.-theologisch dargestellt," *Jahrbücher für
deutsche Theologie*, 5 (1860), 173 ff.; E. Kautzsch, *Über die Derivate des Stammes* צדק
im at.lichen Sprachgebrauch (1881); H. Fuchs, "Das at.liche Begriffsverhältnis von Gerechtigkeit (צדק) und Gnade (חסד) in Prophetie und Dichtung," *Christentum u. Wissenschaft*,
3 (1927), 101-118; 149-158; K. H. Fahlgren, צְדָקָה *nahestehende und entgegengesetzte Begriffe im AT* (Diss. Uppsala. 1932); H. W. Hertzberg, "Die Entwicklung des Begriffes
מִשְׁפָּט im AT," ZAW, 40 (1922), 256-287; 41 (1923), 16-76; H. Schultz, "Die Beweggründe
zum sittlichen Handeln in dem vorchristlichen Israel," ThStKr, 63 (1890), 1 ff.; J. Hempel,
"Gottesgedanke und Rechtsgestaltung in Altisrael," ZSTh, 10 (1930), 377-395; W. Eichrodt,
Theologie des AT, I (1933), 121-126.

20:22 [28]; Is. 63:7); 6 of אֱמֶת (Gn. 24:49; Jos. 24:14; Is. 38:19; 39:8; Da. 8:12; 9:13).
Other words which are thus rendered are מֵישָׁרִים (1 Ch. 29:17), טוֹב (Ps. 38:21), מָדוֹן
(Prv. 17:14), נִקָּיוֹן (Gn. 20:5), and even פֶּתִי "simplicity" (Prv. 1:22) and זַכוּ "innocence"
(Da. 6:23), and carelessly הַשְׂכִּיל (Prv. 21:16). δίκαιος occurs 189 times for צַדִּיק,
24 times rather freely for צֶדֶק, 5 for צְדָקָה and in Da. 12:3 for הַצְדִּיק. It is also used for
יָשָׁר (Job 1:1, 8; 2:3; Prv. 3:32; 11:4; 14:9; 21:2, 18), for נָקִי (Job 9:23; 17:8 etc.), תָּמִים
(Prv. 28:18). Less aptly and very freely it is used for אֱמֶת, דִּין, חֶסֶד, טָהוֹר, מִשְׁפָּט, נָדִיב, and
נָקָם. δικαιοῦν corresponds to the verb צדק, 8 times in hiph, 4 in pi and once (Gn. 44:16)
in hitp. Yet it also occurs 8 times for the kal, and once even for the noun צֶדֶק (Is. 42:21).
It represents רִיב in Mi. 7:9; Is. 1:17, שׁפט niph in 1 ß. 12:7. In a few instances it is also
used for זכה kal and pi, and for בחן pu. δικαίωμα is used for חֹק (48 times), חֻקָּה (22),
מִצְוָה (Dt. 30:16; 3 Βασ. 2:3), מִשְׁפָּט (38 times), צְדָקָה (2 Βασ. 19:28; Prv. 8:20), רִיב
(Jer. 11:20; 18:19), and erroneously for other terms.

Of the predominant Heb. terms, צדק with its derivatives is thus the only one to be
rendered mainly by δίκη and its derivatives (esp. δικαιοσύνη), while other synon. Heb.
terms are hardly given their proper due. This is particularly so with מִשְׁפָּט, the normative
character of which is not appreciated in the LXX. Only partial justice is done to it by
the renderings κρίμα (182 times) and κρίσις (142), which lay the emphasis on its
active sense as an act of judgment. Another word not to receive its deserts is חֶסֶד.
for which δικαιοσύνη is a particularly good rendering. Instead, the LXX prefers ἔλεος
(172), which introduces an emotional element that hardly does justice to the Heb. In the
same circle as צְדָקָה and מִשְׁפָּט, the root תמם with its derivatives also has a greater
significance than is accorded to it in the LXX.

The most important normative terms for the concept of law as such are מִשְׁפָּט, [1]
צֶדֶק (צְדָקָה), [2] חֶסֶד [3] and חֹק. [4] As in the case of בְּרִית (→ διαθήκη, 110), we may note
both a juridical and a theological use of the terms. The impression is given, though
it cannot be proved directly, that the second developed out of the first. We need

---

[1] מִשְׁפָּט goes through almost all the stages of meaning common to a noun constructed
with the prefix m. It is judging or the creating of law either in the concrete sense of a
sentence which creates law (e.g., 1 K. 20:40; Ps. 17:2) or in the more abstract sense of a
verbal noun (e.g., Lv. 19:15). This leads us to its most commonly attested use as a legal
norm, claim or usage.
[2] There is no discernible shift of meaning as between the masc. and fem. Because of its
brevity צֶדֶק is favoured as a gen. epexegeticus in the sense of צַדִּיק. It means "justness," cf.
מֹאזְנֵי צֶדֶק etc.
[3] חֶסֶד is the natural fairness which orders an agreement in which there is little legal
emphasis, as between the members of an organisation of clans or tribes. It is a mistake to
translate it "love," since it differs from אהב etc. in the fact that it never denotes a personal
feeling, but always a volitional attitude orientated to the concept of law. To exercise חֶסֶד
is to recognise the basis in law and to adopt the corresponding position; to demand חֶסֶד
is to appeal to the sense of law. Love may often be expressed by it, but it does not have
to be, since the attitude denoted by חֶסֶד is required by objective considerations. A more
correct, though not wholly adequate, rendering is "faithfulness." There is a scribal error in
Is. 40:6, where in approximation to later Jewish usage it would have to mean "goodliness."
The etym. is uncertain, cf. T. Nöldeke, Neue Beiträge zur semit. Sprachwissensch. (1910),
93 (→ 112).
[4] Etym. (חקק "to engrave writing on a hard material"), חֹק signifies a written statute,
and like תּוֹרָה etc. (→ νόμος) it is used as a narrower term for law.

not follow this up, however, in an investigation more especially of the theological use. This arises when the terms are used either for the attitude of God or for the specifically religious attitude of man.

2. That God posits law, and that He is bound to it as a just God, is a fundamental tenet in the OT knowledge of faith in all its variations. The element of unity in the faith of all the righteous in Israel, whether prophets, priests, lawgivers, or men of a less distinctive sociological type, is the acknowledgment of God's law ordering all life both great and small and forming a basis for hope. There can be no mistaking the causal connexion between the various ideas of religious law and the historical development of the religion of Yahweh and the form of tribal religion in which God is not merely the Lord of law but also one who is bound by it. Yahweh is the source of all the bodies of law in the OT. [5] Even in the nomadic period the sacred lot (Ex. 28:30) mediated the divine decision not only in civil law but also in political questions; Yahweh's מִשְׁפָּטִים, i.e., His institution of valid law, constitute His direction (תּוֹרָה, Dt. 33:10). In virtue of His quality as chief שֹׁפֵט, His authority as God extends to the concrete relationships of the historical existence of Israel, and the confident question of Abraham (Gn. 18:25 J): הֲשֹׁפֵט כָּל־הָאָרֶץ לֹא יַעֲשֶׂה מִשְׁפָּט. may be a bold challenge, like all attempts to weigh God's actions by human ideas of equity, but as an expression of boundless trust that Yahweh's action, whatever it may be, will correspond to the binding norm of a מִשְׁפָּט, it is a valuable testimony to the subjection to the divine decision which was customary from the very first in the groups which served Yahweh. [6] The law of Yahweh is an order of life which cannot be challenged or changed. It is against nature to despise it (Jer. 8:7). תָּמִים פָּעֳלוֹ, says the Song of Moses (Dt. 32:4). God's action is a perfect whole which stands because all His ways are right. They are right as the dealings which are worthy of acknowledgment, which give to all men their existence, and which assure them in this existence. Yahweh's law is righteous because He is righteous: אֵל אֱמוּנָה וְאֵין עָוֶל צַדִּיק וְיָשָׁר הוּא. One may rely upon it because it is nor crooked or devious; the mind of Yahweh is upright as that of one who is righteous. [7]

In such declarations Yahweh is undoubtedly thought of in terms of His office as Ruler and Judge, as שֹׁפֵט צַדִּיק (Ps. 7:11; Jer. 12:1). At a very early stage in Israel His action was seen from this standpoint even though it had little in common with law in the sense of civil or public law. The Song of Deborah calls the victory of the tribes of Israel צִדְקֹת יהוה (Ju. 5:11): "the righteous rule of Yahweh." If we follow through the implications of this view, we can see how confidence in the judicial qualities of Yahweh advances the concept of God. For if His benefits are considered as righteous judgment even in victories over peoples with other gods, then some place must be found for the view or the belief that the omnipotent rule of the one Yahweh who decides legal disputes extends to other nations. At any rate, the idea of conducting the case of Israel was a means to interpret the order

---

[5] Cf. Dt. 1:17: הַמִּשְׁפָּט לֵאלֹהִים הוּא. This principle is found, of course, in other Semitic religions, cf. Baudissin, *op. cit.*, 382 ff.

[6] On the question of the source of the concept "Judge of the whole earth," → θεός.

[7] Cf. also the statement in Ps. 11:7: צַדִּיק יְהוָה צְדָקוֹת אָהֵב יָשָׁר יֶחֱזוּ פָנֵימוֹ. Here there is room for doubt whether צְדָקוֹת means "just decisions" or "righteous action."

ruling in the world. The dubious feature in this view is that it necessarily separates into parties those who stand under the rule of Yahweh, so that human judgment is far too readily inclined to anticipate the divine. Thus we can see in prayer a tendency to claim the righteousness of God and to ask for the condemnation of opponents (e.g., Ps. 5:8, 10). [8] The concept of righteousness is robbed of its objective power when an attempt is made to force the Judge on the basis of His sense of right. The point may even be reached where the righteousness of God is thought to be operative only for the righteous and innocent (Ps. 18:25 f.). But we hardly do justice to such sayings if we press them theoretically. They rather show how strong religious motifs can arise from a theological mode of viewing the just God, so that it is no longer possible to understand the concept of divine righteousness in purely formal terms. This concept is a legacy of faith, expressing boundless confidence in the moral will of God, in virtue of which what is good endures and what is evil or lawless falls victim to annihilating judgment. From צְדָקָה as the norm for the fulfilled state of שָׁלוֹם there arises צְדָקָה as action, as the conduct which brings about, renews and secures this state.

3. This applies not merely to God's action but also to man's conduct in relation to God and man. The strongly marked love of the authors of the OT for juridical thinking in relation to ethical and religious conduct means that they have continually before them the picture of the righteous as one who seeks justice before the judge, defending and vindicating his cause against those who are full of malice and deceit. This is the way in which to depict the overcoming of the unrest and need of the righteous by faith in the constancy of the saving will of the covenant God. He helps to right (הַצְדִּיק), and the man who is set in the right by His pronouncement is צַדִּיק. Strictly, this picture of the legal process (רִיב) is always present when the OT describes as righteous the pious man who is acknowledged by Yahweh. As the judge decides between two parties, pronouncing in favour of the צַדִּיק and against the רָשָׁע, the wrongdoer, [9] so Yahweh takes action when He intervenes in the confusion of human affairs on behalf of the pious who keep His laws. Thus צַדִּיק comes to have the sense of "the pious," and צְדָקָה, the conduct which is vindicated before a public tribunal and thus leads to pardon, [10] becomes a synonym for "piety" as recognised by the divine pronouncement. [11] It means much the same as אֱמוּנָה, i.e., constancy in executing and fulfilling the commands of God through all uncertainty and conflict. צַדִּיק בֶּאֱמוּנָתוֹ יִחְיֶה (Hab. 2:4): the just lives, i.e., he escapes the sentence of death demanded by his opponents, on the basis of unshakeable fidelity to the command of God. [12] The word אֱמוּנָה excellently describes

---

[8] In the Book of Habakkuk the motifs of individual lamentations are applied to the conflict between Israel and the Chaldeans, e.g., 1:13, and possibly 2:4.

[9] Cf. Dt. 25:1: "If there be a controversy between men, they shall come to the place of judgment (מִשְׁפָּט) that the judges may judge between them (שְׁפָטוּם)": וְהִצְדִּיקוּ אֶת־הַצַּדִּיק וְהִרְשִׁיעוּ אֶת־הָרָשָׁע.

[10] E.g., 1 S. 26:23; 1 K. 8:32.

[11] Dt. 6:25: צְדָקָה תִּהְיֶה לָּנוּ, "if we keep the commandment." Here צדקה almost amounts to a conferred acquittal, cf. Gn. 15:6 (חשׁב) and Ps. 69:27: "The ungodly shall not come בְּצִדְקָתֶךָ"

[12] When אֱמוּנָה as πίστις is given a more general sense in R. 1:17; Gl. 3:11 (Hb. 10:38), this is not wrong but it is certainly a development of the original meaning. ἐκ πίστεώς μου in the LXX is best explained as a misreading. On the other hand, it may be due to a theologising tendency on the part of the translator, since Paul, who was probably quoting freely, also undoubtedly theologises the statement.

the demand made on conduct by faith in God's righteousness and hope of His recognition. The personal misfortune of individuals and the fate of the covenant people often enough seem to justify the view that God's judgment works itself out in the form of condemnation, when misfortune comes on the pious. צֶדֶק does not take here the form of success. [13] In such a situation the thought of righteousness yields to other motifs. Yahweh is a rock to which the righteous finally withdraw for protection against the outside world (Ps. 62:7 etc.). But from this place of refuge it is again possible to make the declaration of faith : לְךָ אֲדֹנָי חָסֶד, "to thee, O Lord, a sense of right is proper ; for thou renderest to every man according to his work" (v. 12). The torture of doubting God's righteousness constitutes the spiritual grief of Job, and the author of the dialogue has tried to depict the experience that when it is a question of confidence in the validity of right between God and man we are dealing with something which we must be able to take for granted. He realises, however, that if the dogma is not to become a hollow phrase it must be projected into a higher sphere than that which is commensurate with human understanding.

Quell

† δίκη.

A. The Idea of Law in the Classical and Hellenistic Greek World. [1]

[2] The basis and centre of early Greek social life from the 8th to the beginning of the 5th century, and then in the philosophical political theory of the 4th century, is the idea of law as a religious, political and ethical magnitude. It is worth noting that the starting-point for the Greeks is not the rational and logical concept of δίκη but the mythical figure of the goddess which bears this name : Hes. Op., 256 ff.

> ἡ δέ τε παρθένος ἐστὶ Δίκη, Διὸς ἐκγεγαυῖα
> κυδρή τ' αἰδοίη τε θεοῖς, οἳ Ὄλυμπον ἔχουσιν.

With increasing rationalisation and intellectual refinement, Hesiod's robust and tangible goddess seated beside the judgment throne of Zeus becomes in Solon the immanent though no less divine principle of law in the world and in civil life (Fr., 1, 8 [I, 17, Diehl]; Fr., 3, 14 ff. [I, 23, Diehl]). [3] For Solon law is not an

---

[13] As in the case of Cyrus' victories in Is. 41:2.

δ ί κ η. R. Hirzel, *Themis, Dike und Verwandtes* (1907), 56-227; P. Kretschmer, *Glotta,* 1 (1907), 381; V. Ehrenberg, *Die Rechtsidee im frühen Griechentum* (1921), 54-102. On the organic historical development of the idea of law in classical Greece, cf. the comprehensive survey in W. Jaeger, *Paideia* (1934), 144 ff., in which we have some pertinent suggestions on the obscure etymology and important observations on the relation of θέμις to δίκη, on the derivation from the sphere of the law of property, and on the most important principles of sharing and equality which are present in the word itself. K. Brugmann, "Δικεῖν als Aor. zu βάλλειν," in *Indogerm. Forsch.,* 39 (1921), 144-49; also P. Kretschmer, *Glotta,* 13 (1924), 267 f.; J. Gonda, Δείκνυμι, *Semantische Studie over den Indo-Germaanschen wortel* deik (Diss. Utrecht, 1929), 224-232; T. Thalheim, *s.v.,* Dike in Pauly-W., V (1905), 574 ff. On Josephus, Schl. *Theol. d. Jdt.,* 40 ff.

[1] Because of the inner connexion, the concept of δίκη is sometimes treated together with that of → δικαιοσύνη, 192 ff.

[2] Apart from the small print, A. is by H. Kleinknecht.

[3] Cf. W. Jaeger, "Solons Eunomie," SAB (1926), 69-85.

invention of man; it is an independent law which, however men may adapt or force it, will always triumph because it is divine. The only difference from Hesiod is that the mode of its divinity is now different. The recognition of δίκη in political life carries with it by analogy its presence as universal law in the cosmos (→ κόσμος). In the only surviving fragment of Anaximander [4] δίκη is an immanent rather than an external force. The movement from a divinity which punishes from without to the immanence of penal retribution leads to the concept of a universal divine norm, [5] as in Heraclitus Fr., 94 (I, 96, Diels): ἥλιος γὰρ οὐχ ὑπερβήσεται μέτρα· εἰ δὲ μή, Ἐρινύες μιν Δίκης ἐπίκουροι ἐξευρήσουσιν.

After Solon the greatest proponent of the concept of law is Theognis, in whose sayings we have the much quoted text: ἐν δὲ δικαιοσύνῃ συλλήβδην πᾶσ' ἀρετή ἐστιν (v. 147 [I, 124, Diehl]). In this early period righteousness is not something inward; it is what is legally (→ νόμος) laid down by the government in relation to society. We can thus understand why the new concept of δικαιοσύνη [6] should include all that is implied by ἀρετή. If for Plato δικαιοσύνη is the basic structure both of the state (Resp., I-IV) and of the human soul (Resp., IV, 443c ff.), we can see here the influence of the underlying religious components of the origin of δίκη. In the ethics of Aristotle too, who devotes a whole book to δικαιοσύνη (Eth. Nic., V), δικαιοσύνη still occupies the place of honour among all virtues (κρατίστη τῶν ἀρετῶν, V, 3, p. 1129b, 27); it is the application of all virtues in human society (ἡ τῆς ὅλης ἀρετῆς χρῆσις πρὸς ἄλλον, V, 5, p. 1130b, 11 f.). Aristotle begins with this general understanding of righteousness as the conjunction of all ethical and political norms. Only secondarily does he distinguish (V, 4, p. 1130a, 14) as one part of virtue the legal righteousness or justice which is concerned with the distribution of honour and money and the regulation of private dealings (V, 4, p. 1130b, 3 ff.; V, 5, p. 1130b, 30 ff.). Purely linguistic investigation confirms this comprehensive usage.

The etymology of δίκη has always been hotly contested. At an earlier stage, when the origin was sought in δείκνυμι, "to show," "to direct," it was argued that the original sense was that of "way or manner or custom," and that the idea of what is right or righteous developed out of this. [7] Now recent research has confirmed the basic point, but it has also shown a crucial mistake in the deductions based upon it. For, while in the Germanic languages such words as Weisung and Weise derive from the adj. weise, wissend (cf. the Engl. "on this wise" and "wise"), δεικνύναι does not mean "to make wise." Other scholars took the opposite path and began with the legal element. δίκη was derived from δικεῖν and a link perceived with the stroke of the judicial staff. [8] But δικεῖν means "to throw" rather than "to strike." δίκη was thus understood by others

---

[4] Fr., 9 (I, 15, Diels): διδόναι γὰρ αὐτὰ (sc. the elements) δίκην καὶ τίσιν ἀλλήλοις τῆς ἀδικίας κατὰ τὴν τοῦ χρόνου τάξιν. The universal process of life is thus a lasting process of legal compensation. In Parmenides too (Fr., 8, 12 f.; cf. Euripides, W. Nestle, Griech. Religiosität, II [1933], 124), δίκη is a power of cosmic order or universal principle, elsewhere called ἀνάγκη or μοῖρα.

[5] On the interpretation of this fragment, cf. Jaeger, Paideia, 217 ff.: "The perception of this norm of natural occurrence has a directly religious meaning. It is not a mere description of facts; it is a justification of the nature of the world" (op. cit., 219).

[6] → δικαιοσύνη, 192.

[7] G. Curtius, Grundzüge d. griech. Etymologie[5] (1879), 134; Cr.-Kö., 296. Cf. also Gonda, 216 f. The derivation from δίχα in Aristot. Eth. Nic., V, 7, p. 1132a, 28 is of value only for the attached discussion.

[8] Hirzel, 60 ff., 94.

as the throw which denotes judgment in the divine court. [9] Yet it is hardly possibly fully to explain δίκη along these lines. Even if δίκη were linked with both δικεῖν and δεικνύναι, [10] or if it were understood in terms of "to stretch out" (the daemon Dike, with the gesture of the outstretched hand, separates the disputants and stretches out the staff in judicial decision), [11] this would give only the sense of right and righteousness, and not of manner and custom, whereas δίκη has always been used for both so far as investigation can tell us. Already in Homer and Hesiod it can sometimes mean judicial sentence, right or righteousness, and sometimes tradition or custom. We have thus to ask whether the two meanings do not derive simultaneously from a common origin, with no question of the priority of the one or the other. And we find that this is so. [12]

The basic meaning of √ deik is "to give direction," "to show," "to indicate," "to posit," "to establish." The visible expression of this is the stretching out of the hand. δίκη thus means both "indicating" or "establishing," and "what is indicated or established" (cf. τιθέναι, θεσμός, statuere, statutum etc.). If we start with this sense of "what is laid down or established," we can explain the development as follows.

1. What is laid down or established becomes an "attitude," a "state," a "mode" or a "manner." a. Thus δίκη ἐστίν can mean "it is customary": Hom. Od., 4, 691; 18, 275; 19, 43. Or Pind. Olymp., 2, 18: ἐν δίκᾳ, παρὰ δίκαν of "what is proper and what is not." The sense of mode or manner is expressed in the accus. δίκην "according to the mode or manner," as in Pind. Pyth., 2, 84: λύκοιο δίκαν. This leads quite naturally to the sense of "tradition" or "custom." LXX: 2 Macc. 8:26 A: ἡ πρὸ τοῦ σαββάτου δίκη. Often in the pap.: P. Flor., 295, 2 (6th cent. A.D.): δίκην βαρβάρων. b. If regard is had to the apportionment of δίκη, we are given the sense of "what is proper to someone," "what is decorous," or "what is right": Hom. Il., 19, 180; Od., 24, 255; Ps.-Hes. Scutum Herculis, 85. Used reciprocally, it signifies "right conduct towards others in which one gives them what is proper," Od., 14, 84; opp., 9, 215. Hence δίκη means "right treatment," Il., 23, 542; Jos. Ant., 14, 28. The word thus becomes an expression for mutual relationship or reciprocity. Cf. Arist. Eth. Nic., V, 7, p. 1131b. From the fact that the philosophers always defined the δίκαιον as τὸ ἴσον (→ δίκαιος, 184), we can see that they felt this reciprocity, just as δίκην διδόναι/δίκην λαμβάνειν expresses reciprocal dealings. c. What is rightly apportioned can be regarded as a necessity of natural law, [13] so that δίκη ἐστίν means "it is laid down," "so it must be," "it is fate": Hom. Od., 11, 218. This meaning "fate" is also found in Sanskrit (dista).

2. When applied specifically in the legal sphere, the word means "what is laid down by law." a. "Law" or "right": Hom. Il., 16, 388; Hes. Op., 219, 279 and 283. In Hes. δίκη is the "right of the oppressed or the weak." Here already we can detect the social sense of the πόλις. δίκη becomes an expression of the will of the πόλις. [14] It can also come to be used quite generally for "right" or "righteousness." Jos. Bell., 5, 2; Philo Spec. Leg., I, 14. b. "Legal case," Hes. Op., 249 and particularly "legal decision or judgment," Hom. Il., 18, 508; 16, 542; Od., 11, 570; Hes. Op., 221 and 225. The narrower forensic sense of a "cause" or "process" or "plea" is predominant (with "custom") in the pap. It is used in the LXX for רִיב (Job 29:16), דִּין (Ps. 9:4) or מִשְׁפָּט (Ps. 140:12 f.) in the sense of "legal cause or dispute." In Jl. 4:14 it is used for חָרוּץ in the sense of "judicial decision." Josephus (e.g., Ant., 4, 268) and Philo give to δίκη both the sense of "punishment" and also of "case," "cause," "plea," "decision," "condemnation" and "fine." In Vit. Mos., I, 46 κτείνει χωρὶς δίκης means "without judicial process." The legal sense is predominant in Epict. Diss. c. In the sphere of law the idea of apportion-

---

[9] Ehrenberg, 76 ff.
[10] Brugmann, 144 ff.
[11] Kretschmer, 268.
[12] Gonda, 228, 230 f.
[13] Ehrenberg, 60.
[14] Ibid., 65 f.

ment is expressed particularly in the use of δίκη for "punishment." We have here a personification in δίκη τιμωρός, Dike as the daughter of Zeus and Themis, the pitilessly avenging "goddess of penal justice," Hes. Theog., 901; Op., 220 ff. and 256 ff.; Orph., 42 and 61. Plato, too, hypostatises: Leg., IX, 872e; Ps.-Plat. Epin., 988e: τιμωρὸς δίκη (ἐπίσκοπος). δίκη pursues the evildoer: Ditt. Syll.³, 1176: δίκη δὲ ἐπικρέματα[ι] τιμωρὸς ἀπελθόν[τι] ἀπειθὴς Νεμέσε[ως]. It seizes him: Soph. El., 528: δίκη νιν εἷλεν. Ant., 538: οὐκ ἐάσει τοῦτό γ' ἡ δίκη. It overtakes him: Jos. Bell., 1, 84; 7, 34: μέτεισι. The evil-doer does not escape it: Ant., 6, 305. [15] It brings everything to light: TGF, p. 934, No. 483, 2. Cf. further Stob. Ecl., I, 62, 21 f.: ἡ δίκη τέτακται τιμωρὸς τῶν ἐπὶ γῆς ἁμαρτανόντων. [16] Even where the sense of mythological connexions is less evident, one can still see the influence of personification: Wis. 11:20: ὑπὸ τῆς δίκης διωχθέντες; 4 Macc. 4:13, 21; 9:9; 12:12; 18:22, where ἡ θεία or οὐράνιος δίκη means "penal justice," while in 8:14, 22 we have a more comprehensive use, i.e., the δίκη which graciously pardons. Philo simply adopts the old tradition of Dike as πάρεδρος Διός (→ supra Hes. and Orph.). As penal justice it sits alongside God (Mut. Nom., 194; Jos., 48) and accompanies Him (Conf. Ling., 118). It is indeed ἔφορος τῶν ἀνθρωπείων πραγμάτων (Jos., 170; Decal., 95). The word can also be used for "punishment" or "retribution" without express personification (Hes. Op., 712; Soph. El., 34). It is used predominantly in this way in the LXX. Verbally, it is used for נקם in Ex. 21:20: δίκη ἐκδικήσεται and Lv. 26:25: ἐκδικεῖν δίκην, "to avenge." It is used for the substant. נקם in Dt. 32:41, 43: ἀποδώσω and ἀνταποδώσω δίκην. The verbal ריב is also translated by it in Am. 7:4: ἐκάλεσεν τὴν δίκην ἐν πυρὶ Κύριος. Cf. 2 Macc. 8:11, 13; 4 Macc. 6:28; Wis. 14:31. Josephus, too, uses δίκη mainly in the sense of "punishment": Ant., 6, 288: λαβεῖν δίκην, "to avenge"; Bell., 7, 450, 453: δίκην ἐπιτιθέναι; Ant., 18, 255: ἐπιτιμᾶν; the measure of punishment: Ant., 13, 294. [17] Cf. Philo Op. Mund., 80 and the pap. [18]

B. δίκη in the NT.

Apart from Ac. 25:15 vl. (→ καταδίκη), δίκη is found only three times, and always in the sense of "penal justice" or "punishment," with no distinctive features. No trace is found of the meaning "custom," "tradition" or "righteousness," or of the narrower legal sense. Popular belief is reflected in Ac. 28:4: διασωθέντα ἐκ τῆς θαλάσσης ἡ Δίκη ζῆν οὐκ εἴασεν. Though Paul has escaped the sea, he is a marked man who is now overtaken by the goddess Dike, "personified justice" (→ 178; supra), through the viper. In the other instances the word conveys the inherited Jewish view of God's eternal judgment, as in 2 Th. 1:9: οἵτινες δίκην τείσουσιν ὄλεθρον αἰώνιον ἀπὸ προσώπου τοῦ κυρίου — the ungodly persecutors of the Church will be visited with destruction as a "punishment."

On δίκην τίνειν, cf. Hdt., IX, 94; Soph. Ai., 113; Plat. Phaedr., 249a and frequently in Plut. [19] Jos. Ant., 14, 293: Μάλιχος δίκην ἐξέτεισεν; Phil. Vit. Mos., I, 245; Deus Imm., 74; Spec. Leg., III, 31: θανάτου δίκην τινέτω; Epict. Diss., III, 24, 4.

---

[15] Schl. Th. d. Jdt., 40 ff. rightly emphasises that Joseph. makes δίκη a hypostasis alongside the divine operation, the most relevant passage being Bell., 7, 34: δίκη with θεοῦ χόλος.

[16] On δίκη in Corp. Herm., cf. J. Kroll, Die Lehren des Herm. Trismeg. (1914), 219 f.

[17] On this pt., cf. Schl., op. cit., 40, n. 3.

[18] Preisigke Wört., 383.

[19] Pr.-Bauer, 309.

Judgment is again the subject in Jd. 7: ὡς Σόδομα καὶ Γόμορρα πρόκεινται δεῖγμα πυρὸς αἰωνίου δίκην ὑπέχουσαι : they lie there as an example, suffering the eternal punishment of fire.

On δίκην ὑπέχειν, cf. Hdt., II, 118; Soph. Oed. Tyr., 552. Polyb. uses the formula for "to bring judgment on oneself" (V, 42, 6) and "to make satisfaction" (XVI, 34, 3); Joseph. for "to suffer punishment" (Ant., 1, 99 etc.) and "to become involved in a judicial process" (Ant., 14, 168).

δίκαιος.

A. δίκαιος in the Greek and Hellenistic World.

1. General Usage and Meaning.

δίκαιος is linked with the stem word δίκη. a. It denotes connexion with tradition or custom, and therefore, applied to a person, indicates "one who conforms, who is civilised, who observes custom" (opp. ὕβρις): Hom. Od., 6, 119 ff. b. It denotes obligations to men and to God, and therefore indicates "one who fulfils obligations towards men," the fulfilment of religious duties being often linked therewith (e.g., by such terms as ὅσιος, εὐσεβής, θεοφιλής, θεοσεβής). Plat. Gorg., 507b and Polyb., XXII, 10, 8 : δίκαια with ὅσια. δικαίως καὶ ὁσίως, Plat. Resp., I, 331a. Joseph. has the same parallelism : Ant., 8, 295, often neut. : Ant., 15, 138. Philo Vit. Mos., II, 108, neut. : Fug., 63. δίκαιος with εὐσεβής, Xenoph. Mem., IV, 8, 11, with express allotment to the relationship to gods and men. Jos. Ant., 7, 384; 9, 236; cf. 15, 376. Joseph. also likes to conjoin δίκαιος and θεοφιλής or θεοσεβής : Ant., 10, 215. [1] There is an early example of this in Aristoph. Pl., 28. Cf. also the LXX : Ex. 18:21. This division, which corresponds to the modern "moral and religious," is usually made, though δίκαιος can include duties to God : Aesch. Sept. c. Theb., 598 : δίκαιος/δυσσεβής; Plat. Euthyphr., 12cde : τὸ ὅσιον as part of δίκαιον. In Joseph., too, δίκαιος can include both the fear of God and good-will to men : Ant., 12, 43. c. δίκαιος and legal norms. δίκαιος is a dominant term in the legal sphere. A man is righteous "who observes legal norms." Aristot. Eth. Nic., V, 2, p. 1129a, 33 : δῆλον ὅτι ὁ δίκαιος ἔσται ὅ τε νόμιμος καὶ ὁ ἴσος. This is true not merely in relation to judicial processes, but also to the δίκη which rules over the whole state, and therefore to civil duties : Demosth., 3, 21: δίκαιος πολίτης. The δίκαιος observes the laws. Hence δίκαιον is linked with νόμιμον : Xenoph. Mem., IV, 4, 13; Philo Spec. Leg., IV, 46.

d. δίκαιος and ethics. In addition to the meanings mentioned, the term has a significance for the whole of life, since life in society demands a plenitude of virtues. Thus τὸ δίκαιον is linked with τὸ καλόν, ἀγαθόν, πρέπον : Epict. Diss., I, 22, 1; II, 17, 6. Hence it becomes a leading term in ethics. In particular the four cardinal virtues, [2] which are possessed by the φρόνιμος, σώφρων, δίκαιος, ἀν-

---

δ ί κ α ι ο ς. Bibl. → δικαιοσύνη. Def. in Aristot. Eth. Nic., V, 2, p. 1129a, 33.

[1] Schl., *Theol. d. Jdt.*, 37 sees here a Pharisaic influence on Joseph., since the parallel underlies the twofold law of love in which Jesus sums up the Law. Yet, as so often in Hellenistic Judaism, we should rather see at this point an interaction of Gk. and OT influences. The usage links Joseph. no less strongly with the Gk. world. He is certainly aware of the all-embracing nature of εὐσέβεια in Judaism, Ap., 2, 171 and 181.

[2] The fourfold division is considerably older than Plato and is first attested in Aesch. Sept. c. Theb., 610 : σώφρων δίκαιος ἀγαθὸς εὐσεβὴς ἀνήρ. Wilamowitz wrongly argued for the excision of this verse as an interpolation of the four Platonic virtues. The fourfold number is probably a comprehensive expression of the early Greek world rather than an invention of Aeschylus.

δίκαιος 183

δρεῖος, are the theme of infinitely varied enumeration. The Stoic interpretation of the term makes it particularly clear that man is here understood statically rather than historically. But even in Plato, for whom righteousness is a distinctively political virtue, it is finally anchored in the soul of man, who inwardly comes to what is proper to himself, to inner order and the harmony of spiritual virtues (Resp., IV, 443c ff.). Thus δίκαιος denotes an existing and controllable habit of the man himself, and in the further development of the concept, in the history of ethics, we are always concerned with an existing state which man expresses. Thus Joseph. does not merely explain δίκαιος in terms of ἀρετή but also uses the significant catchword τὴν φύσιν δίκαιοι to describe the heroes whom he extols: Ant., 7, 110; 9, 216 etc. For him the opposite of δίκαιος is παράβασις τῆς ἀρετῆς: Ant., 6, 93. If δίκαιος hovers between the two senses of "faithful to the law" and "virtuous" (Ant., 1, 158 etc.), his lists of virtues, in which δίκαιος constantly recurs with ἀγαθός, χρηστός, σώφρων etc., display not the slightest difference from current Hellenistic usage (Ant., 9, 260). [3]

Philo makes even more prominent use of δίκαιος in the lists of virtues, often in enumerations of the cardinal virtues (Leg. All., II, 18; Sobr., 38), with a concluding reference to the ἀρετὴ συνόλως ἅπασα (Migr. Abr., 219). His enthusiastic extolling of the δίκαιος gives evidence of the Hellenistic glorification of man. The δίκαιος is a true prop of the human race (Migr. Abr., 121), in which he remains for the healing of sicknesses (ibid., 124), confronting the unrighteous multitude (ibid., 61), even after he himself has attained to all-healing righteousness (Det. Pot. Ins., 123). He seeks τὴν τῶν ὄντων φύσιν (Leg. All., III, 78). πίστις, too, is a δίκαιον in the sense of meritorious virtue (Rer. Div. Her., 94). The merit of virtue is particularly emphasised by the description of the patriarchs (e.g., Abraham in Leg. All., III, 228) as δίκαιοι, and especially Noah, on the basis of erroneous etymology (Det. Pot. Ins., 121). We have here a fusion of the Israelitish usage (צַדִּיק as an epithet for the OT saints) and Hellenistic ethics. Apart from the Hellenistic aspects mentioned, both Joseph. and Philo show a strong connexion with the OT and Jewish tradition.

The use of δίκαιος for the OT saint is common in Joseph.: Ant., 9, 33; 10, 38; 14, 172. Very occasionally he uses δίκαιος as a predicate for God, once in vindication of His judgment (Ant., 2, 108) and twice where he also uses ἀληθινός or ἀληθής in a statement concerning God (Ant., 11, 55; Bell. 7, 323). More generally, he often links ἀλήθεια with δίκαιος (Ant., 7, 269; 8, 23). This helps us to fix his definition of the δίκαιος. He is "the man who is obedient to the commands of God": Ap., 2, 293; Ant., 6, 165; 8, 208: δίκαιος εἶναι πειρῶ καὶ φύλαττε τὰ νόμιμα (cf. Ant., 1, 225). The phrase θέλεις δὲ εἶναι δίκαιος in Ant., 13, 291, which is important for the purpose of comparison with Mt. 1:19, shows that he shares the Pharisaic view of righteousness. This is illustrated by Ant., 18, 18 ("the reward of the righteous"), by the use of δίκαιος in the sense of "worthy" (Ant., 5, 197; 16, 212) and "punctilious" (Ant., 15, 106), and finally by the conviction that one may become righteous through penance (Ant., 6, 21). Philo uses δίκαιος as a predicate of God more frequently than Joseph. God is for him ὁ μόνος δίκαιος θεός (Som., II, 194), ὁ δικαιότατος κριτής (Vit. Mos., II, 279), who is never ἄδικος (Fug., 82).

e. The development of the concept. Except in the NT, all Gk. likes to use the comparative and superlative of δίκαιος for both persons and things: Hom. Il., 13, 6:

---

[3] Josephus often links it with words for goodness, such as εὔνοια (Ant., 1, 318), or ἀγαθός (Ant., 7, 369; 8, 248), or χρηστός (9, 133).

δικαιοτάτων ἀνθρώπων; Epict. Diss., I, 29, 13 of the law of God. [4] A quantitative conception is here transferred to the moral sphere. f. Application to things. There is no par. in the NT for the use of δίκαιος in relation to things in the sense of "good," "right," "legal" and the extended sense of "equal," "even," "exact," "precise" and sometimes "correct" (of weights and measures) [5] or "fertile" of the earth. [6] On the other hand, there are many examples of the NT κρίσις δικαία (Jn. 5:30) [7] or δίκαιαι ὁδοί (Rev. 15:3). [8] If we search Joseph. and Philo for examples of δίκαιος as the predicate of things, it is striking that their common use of it in the sense of "justified," [9] "proper," [10] "fitting" [11] or "established" [12] is never found in the NT.

g. τὸ δίκαιον, τὰ δίκαια. In the NT there are few traces of the neut. use which has an established place in the sphere of law. τὸ δίκαιον means "what is lawful or right." Aristot. Eth. Nic., V, 2, p. 1129a, 34 gives the definition: τὸ μὲν δίκαιον ἄρα τὸ νόμιμον καὶ τὸ ἴσον, τὸ δ' ἄδικον τὸ παράνομον καὶ τὸ ἄνισον. The conjunction of τὸ ἴσον and τὸ ἄδικον reminds us of Col. 4:1. Philo's definition of the δίκαιον (Congr., 90: ἐν ψυχῇ τέλειον καὶ πέρας ὄντως τῶν κατὰ τὸν βίον πράξεων) corresponds to his psychological and ethical peculiarities. The antonyms δίκαιον/ἄδικον are found throughout the Greek speaking world and not in the Bible alone. Epict. Diss., I, 29, 54; II, 1, 5 etc. [13] It is worth noting how the legal view is variously reflected in the definitions of the δίκαιον. [14] In Simonides [15] the δίκαιον is τὸ προσῆκον ἑκάστῳ ἀποδιδόναι, τοῦτο δὲ ὠνόμασεν ὀφειλόμενον. We see here the influence of the law of obligation, i.e., to give to each "what is fitting." In the Pythagoreans it is the talio of the law of punishment and the δίκαιον is "retribution." [16] Plato goes well beyond the narrower legal view with his definition of the central δίκαιον (though in his definitions he always speaks of δικαιοσύνη, of the ἀνὴρ δίκαιος or of the πόλις δικαία) as civil virtue in terms of which each does "what is proper for him." τὸ δίκαιον plays a significant role as law in the specific sense. Hence τὰ δίκαια are "rights," "ordinances," "duties" or "demands." Here the pap. esp. yield a wealth of legal definitions. [17] It is again striking that neither in the sing. or the plur. is this legal use found in the NT, though there are a few examples in the LXX. [18]

---

[4] Stob. Ecl., I, 398, 11: δικαιότεραι of souls. Jos. Ant., 7, 206 (compar.) and Bell., 4, 319 (superl.); Philo Spec. Leg., superl. as predic. of an object (IV, 2).

[5] LXX: Lv. 19:36; Dt. 25:15; Ez. 45:10; Philo Rer. Div. Her., 162; Ditt. Or., 666, 11, the δικαία ἀνάβασις of the Nile (corresponding to demands). Cf. Deissmann B., 113.

[6] Xenoph. Oec., 5, 12; Cyrop., VIII, 3, 38, cf. Cr.-Kö., 296.

[7] LXX: Dt. 16:18 for מִשְׁפַּט־צֶדֶק. Cf. Tg. O. and Jerush. I in Str.-B., II, 466; Eth. En. 60:6; Jos. Ant., 9, 4.

[8] Jos. Ant., 13, 290. αἷμα δίκαιον in Mt. 23:35 belongs to a different context (as also 27:4 B² L Diat Orig Cypr Ambst), since it means "innocently shed blood"; so, too, LXX Jon. 1:14; Prv. 6:17 א c.a A for דָּם־נָקִי.

[9] Jos. Ant., 5, 150: ὀργὴ δικαία; Philo Vit. Mos., I, 244: ἀγανάκτησις δικαία.

[10] Jos. Ant., 2, 272: ἀμοιβὰς δικαίας.

[11] Ibid., 1, 318: εὔνοια δικαία of wives.

[12] Jos. Vit., 93: ὑποψία δικαία.

[13] Both Joseph. and Philo have the antonyms δίκαιος/ἄδικος or ἀσεβής, and they do not just derive them from the OT. Jos. Bell., 2, 139; 5, 407. Philo prefers both in the neut.: Rer. Div. Her., 77; Mut. Nom., 153; Deus Imm., 49.

[14] Hirzel, 186 ff.

[15] Plato Resp., I, 331e; 332a/c; and occasionally Philo: Sobr., 40. For Plato's own definition → 192.

[16] Cf. Aristot. Eth. Nic., V, 8, p. 1132b, 21 ff.: δοκεῖ δέ τισι καὶ τὸ ἀντιπεπονθὸς εἶναι ἁπλῶς δίκαιον.

[17] Preisigke Wört., 379: "right," "title," "legal claim" etc.

[18] Job 8:3; 34:12 A: τὸ δίκαιον = "law or right"; Prv. 18:5: ἐκκλίνειν τὸ δίκαιον ἐν κρίσει, 21:7: πράσσειν τὰ δίκαια "to administer justice"; 16:33: τὰ δίκαια "judgment."

This sense is very common in Polybius, Philo and Joseph. [19] The latter uses it both for the OT Law [20] and for law generally, [21] and he can sometimes mean what is common to all peoples in the legal sphere. [22] He can also speak of natural law. [23] Philo can say that order [24] rules in the relations of the constellations, and like Aristotle he can use this expression in speaking of the difference between positive, conventional law on the one side and natural law on the other. [25] h. δίκαιος linked with verbs. In this respect [26] Joseph. often has such formulae as δίκαιον ἡγεῖσθαι (Ant., 14, 269); τὰ δίκαια πράττειν (Ant., 9, 169); δίκαιον λέγειν (Vit., 194); δίκαια πάσχειν (Ant., 5, 166); δίκαια ἀξιοῦν (Ant., 14, 305). Instead of τὴν δικαιοσύνην ποιεῖν [27] he has τὰ δίκαια ποιεῖν (Ant., 8, 126; 10, 53 etc.). For διώκειν δικαιοσύνην [28] he uses διώκειν τὸ δίκαιον (Ant., 6, 263) He uses δικαιοσύνην for an evaluation of conduct and τὸ δίκαιον for the content of law. Cf. δίκαιον ἡγεῖσθαι in 2 Macc. 10:12 with Jos. Ant., 6, 144 : λογισάμενος οὐκ εἶναι δίκαιον (of God). κρίνειν δίκαιον is found in Ant., 1, 225; 2, 108. i. δίκαιόν ἐστιν. The simple δίκαιόν ἐστιν : "it is right and proper" (also compar. in Jos. Ant., 4, 147 and superl. in Bell., 4, 258) conventionalises the word. Yet alongside the conventionalised use Joseph. can also employ it for the divine Law, as in Ant., 9, 58 : εἶναι δίκαιον, "may it be according to the Law." k. δικαίως can be used to signify both what is "fitting and proper" (Epict. Diss., II, 1, 3) and what is "right or meritorious" (Jos. Ant., 2, 140). On κρίνειν δικαίως, cf. Dt. 1:16; Prv. 24:23; Sir. 32:22. On πάσχειν δικαίως, cf. Wis. 19:13; Test. S. 4:3.

2. δίκαιος in the LXX.

In spite of all the similarities mentioned, the LXX attests a decisive change in the use of the word under the influence of OT motifs. The fundamental belief in God links it firmly to the judgment of God. The concept of virtue is replaced by the basic question how man is to stand before this judgment expressed in the Law as a standard. If in the rest of the Greek world a man is δίκαιος who satisfies ordinary legal norms, fulfilling his civic duties in the most general sense, here the δίκαιος is the man who fulfils his duties towards God and the theocratic society, meeting God's claim in this relationship. It is as he satisfies the demand of God that he has right on his side and therefore a righteous cause before God.

This distinctive religious rootage is even more clearly shown by the antonyms. Over against the δίκαιος as the just and pious man there stands the ἄδικος (Prv. 12:17; 29:27), or the ἁμαρτωλός (ψ 124:3; Tob. 4:17); the ἀσεβής (Gn. 18:23; Prv. 10:28; Wis. 3:10) or the παράνομος (Job 17:8).

In the background is the fact that God Himself is δίκαιος. The fact that in Hellenistic Judaism, too, God can be called δίκαιος, the One who is infallibly consistent in the normative self-determination of His own nature, and who maintains unswerving faithfulness in the fulfilment of His promises and covenant agreements, prepares the ground for the crucial religious importance of the term in the NT. We can see this in 1 Βασ. 2:2 : καὶ οὐκ ἔστι δίκαιος ὡς ὁ θεὸς ἡμῶν; 2 Esr. 9:15; Tob. 3:2. In relation to God,

---

[19] Polyb., III, 21, 10; Jos. Ant., 12, 121.
[20] Ant., 8, 296 : ἱερεὺς τὰ δίκαια χρηματίζων.
[21] Ant., 12, 121: τὰ δίκαια τῆς πολιτείας.
[22] Ant., 16, 176 f.
[23] Bell., 1, 507: τὸ τῆς φύσεως δίκαιον.
[24] Det. Pot. Ins., 88.
[25] Ebr., 34, 64 and 81: θέσει δικαίοις προσέχειν, "to observe conventional law"; λόγος ὀρθός, λόγος τῆς φύσεως, φύσει νόμος, "natural law" (cf. Jos., 29 ff.; Migr. Abr., 95).
[26] Cf. 2 Pt. 1:13: δίκαιον ἡγοῦμαι.
[27] Mt. 6:1.
[28] R. 9:30.

δίκαιος is linked with ὅσιος in Dt. 32:4; ψ 144:17. God is δίκαιος, not merely as the righteous Judge who exercises justice, but also as the One who gives salvation : ψ 114:5 : ἐλεήμων ὁ κύριος καὶ δίκαιος καὶ ὁ θεὸς ἡμῶν ἐλεεῖ (→ δικαιοσύνη, 195).

B. The Righteous in the Synagogue.

1. The Righteous.

The Synagogue inclines to a onesided application of the schema righteous/ungodly which serves the concept of rewards, [29] which logically decides everything and which optimistically reckons with the ability of man to attain to righteousness before God. To the δίκαιος there corresponds the צַדִּיק or יָשָׁר or כָּשֵׁר (Aram. צַדִּיקָא, כְּשָׁרָא, כְּשִׁירָא or זַכָּאי, זַכָּאה). [30] He has kept the Law in all its fulness, [31] and his merits outweigh his transgressions. The ungodly (רָשָׁע for ἀσεβής and πονηρός; Aram. רַשִּׁיעָא, בִּישָׁא) is the one whose transgressions are the heavier. There is, however, a more precise distinction [32] between the wholly righteous (צַדִּיק גָּמוּר), [33] the wholly ungodly (רָשָׁע גָּמוּר), [34] the average (בֵּינוֹנִי) [35] and the penitent (בַּעַל תְּשׁוּבָה). [36] The first have kept the Torah perfectly ; the second have more transgressions than merits ; the third have an equal balance of observance and violation (Hillel and Shammai taking different views of them); [37] the fourth are also the subject of hot debate as to whether they should be ranked above the first. [38] The patriarchs were put in the first category, sometimes as those who had completely overcome the evil impulse. [39] The Synagogue does not give to Abel the prominence which he receives in the NT (→ Ἄβελ, I, 7). Precedence is rather given to Abraham, Isaac, Jacob [40] and others, [41] and in the case of Philo to Noah. [42] (On the merits of the patriarchs → δικαιοσύνη, 197).

Many teachers are specifically numbered among the righteous. Prophets and righteous men are often associated. [43] The prayer of the righteous, which God seeks, [44] turns His thoughts from severity to mercy. [45]

2. The Messiah as the Righteous.

The Messiah is called righteous because His whole nature and action are in conformity with the norm of the divine will. This predicate of the Messiah is common both in the Synagogue and in Apocalyptic. [46] The Synagogue is fond of

---

[29] Str.-B., IV, 484 ff.
[30] Str.-B., III, 222 f.
[31] bAZ, 4a; Midr. Cant., 2, 1 (62a); cf. also Str.-B., I, 816.
[32] bRH, 16b, Bar., Str.-B., I, 50 f.; S. Dt., 307 on 32:4, Str.-B., IV, 1041.
[33] T. Qid., 1, 14 f.; Str.-B., I, 166.
[34] Ab. R. Nat., 40, Str.-B., I, 834.
[35] jRH, 57a, 49, Str.-B., III, 230 f.
[36] bSukka, 53a, Bar., Str.-B., II, 211.
[37] Str.-B., II, 361 f.
[38] bBer., 34b, Str.-B., I, 603.
[39] bBB, 16b/17a, Bar., Str.-B., III, 187; IV, 479.
[40] Pray. of Man., 8.
[41] Cf. Schl. Mt., 688.
[42] Also Sir. 44:17: Νῶε εὑρέθη τέλειος δίκαιος.
[43] Pesikt. r., 40 (167b), Str.-B., III, 124.
[44] bJeb., 64a, bChul., 60b, Str.-B., I, 453.
[45] bSukka, 14a, Str.-B., I, 454. The prayer of the righteous is highly estimated : Eth. En., 47:1, 2, 4; 97:3, 4; Jos. Bell., 5, 403 : δίκαιοι ἱκέται.
[46] H. Dechent, "Der 'Gerechte' — eine Bezeichnung für den Messias," ThStKr, 100 (1927/8), 439 ff. For a parallel in religious history, cf. the δίκαιον πνεῦμα of Apollo, BMI, IV, 1062, and δίκαιος as a name for Isis, P. Roussel, Les Cultes Egyptiens à Delos (1925 f.), 171, 276.

the designation "the Messiah our righteousness." [47] Texts specifically related to the righteous Messiah are Jer. 23:5, [48] 6; [49] 33:15; [50] Zech. 9:9. [51] On the other hand, Is. 53:11b and Da. 12:3 are referred to the saints and to Israel. [52] Only from the 3rd cent. A.D. is the former linked with the Messiah. [53] "The Righteous" is often used as a name for the Messiah in Wis. (e.g., 2:18 : εἰ γάρ ἐστιν ὁ δίκαιος υἱὸς θεοῦ, ἀντιλήμψεται αὐτοῦ; Ps. Sol. 17:35 : καὶ αὐτὸς βασιλεὺς δίκαιος). In Ps. Sol. δικαιοσύνη is often connected with Him (e.g., 17:25, 28, 31, 42; 18:8 f.). In Eth. En. (38:2; 53:6) one of the basic themes is that righteousness is a mark of the Messianic period. Revelation in the coming time of salvation is particularly for the righteous, whose fulfilment of works carries with it the greatest promises. [54]

Hab. 2:4 is interpreted as a comprehensive fulfilment of the commandments in meritorious faithfulness. [55]

C. δίκαιος in the NT.

There is a deep gulf between the NT δίκαιος and the Greek ideal of virtue, which isolates man in independent achievement. The only echoes of the Greek view occur in the Gospels when Jesus is regarded as δίκαιος from the Roman standpoint, and therefore when the emphasis lies on the conventional element in the ethical life. But this involves customary or traditional modes of expression which are not very closely connected with the Greek conception as such. Elsewhere the term obviously follows very strictly the OT understanding, though with a new application to the sphere of salvation as defined in the NT.

1. The Greek and Hellenistic Contacts.

When the wife of Pilate calls Jesus the δίκαιος in Mt. 27:19, this probably means both that He is innocent and that He is morally righteous, unless she is speaking as ἰουδαΐζουσα [56] or Mt. himself is Judaizing the account. The same is true of Pilate's own saying in Mt. 27:24 : ἀθῷός εἰμι ἀπὸ τοῦ αἵματος τοῦ δικαίου τούτου. [57] It is also true of the saying of the centurion at the foot of the cross in Lk. 23:47, as also of Herod's description of John as an ἀνὴρ δίκαιος καὶ ἅγιος (Mk. 6:20). What is meant is a "saint" in the popular sense, though in the first case there is also a suggestion of "innocent." The occurrence of ὅσα δίκαια with ἀληθῆ, σεμνά, ἁγνά, προσφιλῆ in Phil. 4:8 seems to follow the Hellenistic lists of virtues. What we have here is undoubtedly social conduct described in conventional expressions. On the other hand, it is inconceivable that Paul should

---

[47] Pesikt. r., 36 (162a), Str.-B., II, 289; 37 (162b), loc. cit.; 37 (163a), Str.-B., II, 290. Shemone Esre, Petition, 14 (pal. Rec.): "Messiah thy righteousness," Str.-B., IV, 213.

[48] Tg. Str.-B., II, 113.

[49] bBB, 75b; Midr. Cant. on 1:16; Str.-B., I, 66; Midr. Ps. 21 § 2; Str.-B., II, 352; Midr. Prv. 19:21; Str.-B. IV, 784.

[50] Tg. Str.-B., II, 113.

[51] Pesikt. r., 34 (159b), Str.-B., I, 844.

[52] Str.-B., I, 481-485.

[53] bSanh., 98b, Str.-B., I, 481 f.

[54] Str.-B., IV, 799 ff.

[55] Tanch שופטים § 10 (16b, Buber), Str.-B., I, 907; Tg. Hab. 2:4, Str.-B., III, 542.

[56] Act. Pilati (²1876, Tischendorf), 223.

[57] τοῦ δικαίου is not found in BD sy^s. On the other hand, in Act. 14:2 D sy^{hmg} the apostles are called δίκαιοι in respect of their innocence.

not be using δίκαια for action in accordance with the will of God. In Tt. 2:12 : ἵνα σωφρόνως καὶ δικαίως καὶ εὐσεβῶς ζήσωμεν, the mode of expression corresponds to Greek ethics, yet this characteristic of the Past. does not imply material agreement with the Greek view of virtue.

The expressions τὰ δίκαια, τὸ δίκαιον, δικαίως, and the verbal phrases : δίκαιον ἡγεῖσθαι (2 Pt. 1:13 : "I think it fitting, right"), κρίνειν τὸ δίκαιον (Lk. 12:57: "Judge what is right"), all follow normal everyday usage and thus do not reflect any new or distinctive early Christian understanding. If Christian slaves are to render to their masters τὸ δίκαιον καὶ τὴν ἰσότητα (Col. 4:1), this is not very different from the owner of the vineyard allotting to his workers ὃ ἐὰν ᾖ δίκαιον, i.e., what they may claim as fair and just (Mt. 20:4[7]). In Phil. 1:7 καθώς ἐστιν δίκαιον means right and fair in the conventional sense. But already this group of sayings gives evidence of a need to deepen the regard for a central definition orientated on God. This is done in Ac. 4:19 by the addition of ἐνώπιον τοῦ θεοῦ, or in 2 Th. 1:6 by the addition of παρὰ θεῷ and the reference to God's retributive justice. In Eph. 6:1, even though there is no such addition, the phrase τοῦτο γάρ ἐστιν δίκαιον in relation to the obedience of children does not mean only the "right and fitting" of natural law ; it means that which corresponds to the righteous divine order enjoined by the commandment (cf. Jos. Ant., 9, 58; → 185).

2. The Dependence on the OT and Its Supersession.

In content, δίκαιος in the NT is very largely determined by the OT. Our task is to show how the OT view is both adopted and superseded, and how a new emphasis is given to it. a. That God is called the δίκαιος from the standpoint of judgment may be seen particularly clearly in Rev., the language of which is very largely taken from the OT, cf. the δίκαιος εἶ, ὁ ὢν καὶ ὁ ἦν, ὁ ὅσιος in 16:5, and the references to His δίκαιαι κρίσεις in 16:7; 19:2; and δίκαιαι ὁδοί in 15:3 (→ 184). According to 1 Pt. 2:23 Christ committed judgment τῷ κρίνοντι δικαίως (→ 185). The πατὴρ δίκαιε in Jn. 17:25 appeals to the righteous judgment of God which accepts the disciples as distinct from the κόσμος because they have recognised the One whom God sent. If the judicial quality of God is here more deeply confirmed by faith in Christ, in R. 7:12, where the Law is called δικαία, Paul underlines the OT truth that the νόμος as a righteous demand of God bears something of His majesty.

On the other hand — and here we have a new feature — the εἰς τὸ εἶναι αὐτὸν δίκαιον of R. 3:26, whether it explains the ἔνδειξις epexegetically [58] or declares the purpose, [59] in any case expresses the fact that the justice of the One who is absolutely righteous is demonstrated in the atoning sacrifice of Jesus. Similarly, in 1 Jn. 1:9 : πιστός ἐστιν καὶ δίκαιος, ἵνα ἀφῇ ἡμῶν τὰς ἁμαρτίας, God is called δίκαιος in the sense of a righteousness which both judges and saves. In both cases there is an unmistakable influence of δικαιοσύνη (→ δικαιοσύνη, 195) as used in Dt.-Is. and Pl. The new factor is the absolute connection with the atoning death of Christ in which God shows Himself to be δίκαιος.

b. When δίκαιος is applied as a Messianic designation (→ 186 f.), the term is first used quite simply in Ac. 3:13 f.: τὸν ἅγιον καὶ δίκαιον, and Ac. 7:52 : περὶ

---

[58] Lipsius, ad loc.
[59] Zn. R., ad loc.

τῆς ἐλεύσεως τοῦ δικαίου, to describe the piety of Jesus in fulfilment of the will of God. This corresponds to OT usage. Yet in terms of the preaching of the cross in Ac. we can see from the antonyms mentioned in the context (ἀνὴρ φονεύς, προδόται καὶ φονεῖς) that the reference is supremely to the innocent death of Jesus, cf. the αἷμα δίκαιον of Mt. 27:4 vl. on the lips of Judas. Ac. 22:14 refers to the attestation of this innocent Victim in the resurrection. On the other hand, in 1 Jn. 2:29; 3:7 [60] there is advanced against libertinism the fact that those who belong to the δίκαιος, as Jesus is called, must give evidence of righteous conduct. In 1 Pt. 3:18 : δίκαιος ὑπὲρ ἀδίκων, the use of the title for Christ is linked with the thought of substitution and is thus referred to His death. We have the same basic thought in 1 Jn. 2:1, though now transferred to the sphere of His glorification : παράκλητον ἔχομεν πρὸς τὸν πατέρα, Ἰησοῦν Χριστὸν δίκαιον. In all these passages the righteous Christ is the Doer of the will of God in the fullest sense. On the other hand, there is reference to His participation in the righteous judgment of God when Jn. 5:30 speaks eschatologically of Christ's κρίσις δικαία which, in true Johannine fashion, is rooted in His total orientation to the will of Him that sent Him (the opp. is κρίνειν κατ' ὄψιν in Jn. 7:24). Cf. the κύριος as ὁ δίκαιος κριτής in 2 Tm. 4:8.

c. With reference to men who do God's will, δίκαιος is used in the OT sense of the patriarchs (Abel : Mt. 23:35; Hb. 1:14; cf. 1 Jn. 3:12) and saints of the OT (Lot : 2 Pt. 2:7, cf. 8) who stand out from the world with its wicked works. Together with the saints who render full obedience to God, the main representatives of the earlier period are the prophets : Mt. 13:17; 23:29 : προφῆται καὶ δίκαιοι, cf. Mt. 10:41 and the αἷμα δίκαιον of innocent martyrs (Mt. 23:35). At least in narrative passages which describe Jewish relationships, the word δίκαιος always refers here to fidelity to the Law. Sometimes the relationship to God is emphasised, e.g., in Lk. 1:6 with reference to Zacharias and Elisabeth : δίκαιοι ἐναντίον [61] τοῦ θεοῦ; in Lk. 2:25 with reference to Simeon : δίκαιος καὶ εὐλαβής; in Ac. 10:22 with reference to Cornelius : ἀνὴρ δίκαιος καὶ φοβούμενος τὸν θεόν. Joseph's way of treating Mary in Mt. 1:19 corresponds to the basic conception of a righteous man. [62]

A particularly striking fact is that in the Syn. account of the preaching of Jesus the Israelite and Jewish antithesis δίκαιος/ἁμαρτωλός (→ 186) or → ἄδικος is seriously adopted but given an ironical application (Mk. 2:17 and par., cf. Mt. 5:45; Lk. 5:32; 15:7). The Pharisees are the δίκαιοι, the publicans etc. the ἁμαρτωλοί. All are called to conversion, including the righteous; yet the fact that the customary standards are accepted shows that for all the relativity there is an appreciation of the moral distinctions and that the zeal of the righteous finds recognition. [63] In R. 5:7 (cf. v. 6) even Paul, notwithstanding his doctrine of justification, can still describe these relative moral distinctions among men in terms of the usual categories (antith. δίκαιος/ἀσεβής), quite apart from his salvation-centred anthropology. Like ἀγαθός, however, δίκαιος is to be seen as a masc. [64] If the

---

[60] In both cases in expositions of Bultmann's "homiletician" ("Analyse des 1 J.," *Festgabe f. A. Jülicher* [1927], 138-158).

[61] ℵD ἐνώπιον.

[62] Cf. Schl. Mt., 13 as opposed to Str.-B., I, 50 f., where it is presented as the mere fulfilment of a written ordinance.

[63] Schl. Mt., 194, 309; Zn. Mt., ad loc.

[64] Zn. R., 253 f.; Str.-B., III, 222 f.

usual Jewish distinction is not rejected, there is in the Syn. a stern rejection of the hypocrisy of a righteous appearance and of the confidence of the δίκαιος in his own piety (Mt. 23:28; Lk. 20:20; 18:9). This repudiation of the nature of δίκαιος as habit, appearance and self-confidence, and of the associated contempt for others, means that a question-mark is put behind the claim of the righteous (→ δικαιόω, C. 3, 4; Lk. 18:14; 16:15).

The adoption of the Pharisaic belief in the ἀνάστασις τῶν δικαίων (Lk. 14:14, though cf. δικαίων καὶ ἀδίκων in Ac. 24:15) gives further evidence of the persistence of the basic distinctions, which even in Paul are still valid in the last judgment. The context of Lk. 14:14, however, makes it plain that the practice of love constitutes the δίκαιος. [65]

d. δίκαιος can also be used of the disciple or the Christian as the one who truly fulfils the Law or the divine will. It was a common conviction of the apostolic age that the Christian is the one who truly fulfils the Law. Thus the δίκαιος in Mt. 10:41, who is received εἰς ὄνομα δικαίου, is pleasing to God. And the one who receives him out of regard for the fact (ם֑שֵׁל) that he is a righteous man will share his reward. [66] In Mt. 13:49, too, the δίκαιοι from whom the πονηροί will be separated are Christians. The same is true of Da. 12:3 as quoted in Mt. 13:43. [67] According to 13:41 f. they are differentiated from the ποιοῦντες τὴν ἀνομίαν. [68] The δίκαιοι in the last judgment in Mt. 25:37, 46 are those who have attained to true δικαιοσύνη by practising love in unconscious acts of kindness to the Son of Man. The OT colouring of the expression in Lk. 1:17 should not blind us to the fact that here particularly the Messianic time of salvation carries with it the promise that the ἀπειθεῖς will receive the obedient disposition of the δίκαιοι. The Israelite usage is again applied to Christians in Jm. 5:16: δέησις δικαίου, and 5:6: ἐφονεύσατε τὸν δίκαιον. The reference is to the oppression of poor Christians by rich opponents. [69] In 1 Pt. 3:12; 4:18; Hb. 12:23; Rev. 22:11 everything that is elsewhere said of the saints of the OT is transferred to Christians. As δίκαιοι they are contrasted with ἀσεβεῖς and ἁμαρτωλοί. We are not told how they became δίκαιοι. This is the theme of Paul.

e. When we turn to the specifically Pauline use of δίκαιος, we recall (→ 189) that Paul can sometimes accept the distinction between the righteous and the unrighteous apart from the new δικαιοῦσθαι. This is in keeping with the starting-point of his whole new train of thought, namely, that the fulfilment of the divine will is a self-evident demand. Hence he can say in R. 2:13: οὐ γὰρ οἱ ἀκροαταὶ νόμου δίκαιοι παρὰ θεῷ, ἀλλ᾽ οἱ ποιηταὶ νόμου δικαιωθήσονται. This follows directly from the fact of the Law. The δίκαιος is the one who as a doer of the Law will be declared righteous by the divine sentence. On the other hand, we

---

[65] On the question of a general or partial resurrection, cf. Str.-B., IV, 1167 ff.; Bousset-Gressm., 272; Kl. Lk., 151. Joseph. refers only to the resurrection of the righteous, but does not represent the total Pharisaic view, Str.-B., IV, 1188 f. If there is here a certain cleavage in the Lucan tradition, in Lk. 14:14 only the δίκαιοι are mentioned because it is they who gain in the ἀνάστασις.

[66] Schl. Mt., 352; Zn. Mt., ad loc.; Meyer Ursprung, I, 143.

[67] Θ has συνιέντες for δίκαιοι.

[68] Jewish par. to Da. 12:3 may be found in Schl. Mt., 446; Str.-B., I, 673 f.

[69] For par. from the LXX and Apocr., v. Dib. Jk., 221; Hck. Jk., 222.

read in R. 3:10 : οὐκ ἔστιν δίκαιος οὐδὲ εἷς, this being followed by a series of quotations from ψ 14:1-3; Qoh. 7:21, which are designed to show the general sinfulness of all men. Not to be righteous means not to fulfil the Law because one is under sin. Hence one becomes a δίκαιος by receiving in faith the revealed δικαιοσύνη θεοῦ as δύναμις θεοῦ and σωτηρία. The Scripture proof from Hab. 2:4 in both R. 1:17: ὁ δὲ δίκαιος (μου C*) ἐκ πίστεως ζήσεται, and Gl. 3:11: ὅτι ὁ δίκαιος ἐκ πίστεως ζήσεται, omits the μου of the LXX text.[70] The Pauline understanding is in material agreement with the Mas : וְצַדִּיק בֶּאֱמוּנָתוֹ יִחְיֶה, "the just shall live on the basis of his holding fast (to righteousness)." This is the sense irrespective of the suffix î.[71] That only the δίκαιος will attain to life is the ancient truth. The point newly emphasised by Paul is that he cannot have life except by faith.[72] The δίκαιος, then, is that one who is justified by faith, elsewhere called δικαιωθείς by Paul.

Cf. the quotation and understanding of Hab. 2:4 in Hb. 10:38 : ὁ δὲ δίκαιός μου (א A H r vg arm Clem) ἐκ πίστεως ζήσεται.[73] This text, which follows the LXX A, makes it quite impossible to link ἐκ πίστεως with δίκαιος. Here, however, faith has more of an OT colouring as steadfastness in tribulation, and v. 39 gives ζήσεται an eschatological reference.

R. 5:19: διὰ τῆς ὑπακοῆς τοῦ ἑνὸς δίκαιοι κατασταθήσονται οἱ πολλοί, looks to the last judgment, when they will be presented righteous, or made righteous,[74] by God's sentence. The antithetical structure of the section leads Paul to the juxtaposition of ἁμαρτωλοί and δίκαιοι, and he does not say that we are now δίκαιοι. On the other hand, we can see from 1 Th. 2:10 : ὡς ὁσίως καὶ δικαίως ἐγενήθημεν,[75] that Paul can use δίκαιος in relation to the Christian life in the sense of the righteousness which corresponds to divine law.

In the Pauline sphere we should also consider 1 Tm. 1:9 : δικαίῳ νόμος οὐ κεῖται. Against the antinomians, who champion a mixture of νομοδιδασκαλία and libertinism and whose peculiarity is to be found in their attitude to the Law,[76] the true use of the Law is treated in such a way that the Christian is set in antithesis to the lawless as δίκαιος, his freedom from the Law consisting in the fact that he conducts himself according to the divine norm.[77] In Tt. 1:8 it is demanded of a bishop, amongst other things, that he be δίκαιος, and this obviously means that his life should be in accordance with the divine norm, unless the ability to reach just decisions is in view in this list of special episcopal qualities.

---

[70] LXX : ὁ δὲ δίκαιος [+ μου A] ἐκ πίστεώς μου ζήσεται.

[71] Ltzm. R., ad loc. and Khl. R., ad loc. link ἐκ πίστεως with δίκαιος rather than ζήσεται; but this is contrary to both the Mas and the LXX, and is rightly rejected by Zn. R. and Pr.-Bauer.

[72] For Hab. 2:4 in the Rabb. cf. A. Schlatter, Der Glaube im NT⁴ (1927), 609 f.; Str.-B., III, 542 ff.

[73] Rgg. Hb.², 337 f.

[74] E. F. K. Müller, Beobachtungen zur paulin. Rechtfertigungslehre (1905), 15. Zn. R., ad loc. sees here a logical fut. On κατασταθήσονται cf. J. de Zwaan, ThSt, 31 (1913), 85 ff.

[75] Dob. Th., 99. Trench, 208.

[76] H. v. Soden, Komm. zu den Past.² (1893), 160; W. Lütgert, Die Irrlehrer der Past. (1909), 16.

[77] Cf. R. 10:4; 6:14 f.

δικαιοσύνη.

A. Secular and General Religious Usage.

1. δικαιοσύνη in Greek Ethics.

δικαιοσύνη represents the second stage of word construction in relation to δίκη-δίκαιος. Words in -σύνη date from the beginning of abstract thought. This helps us to understand why a term not found in Homer or Hesiod [1] occurs frequently as a virtue in the post-epic period. We can also see a link between this construction and the development of the Greek sense of law. The very close connexion between legal, ethical and religious terminology results from the central position occupied in early Greek thinking by δίκη as right not merely in the legal, but also the political, the ethical and above all the religious sense (→ 178).

Thus δικαιοσύνη occurs a. for the civil virtue of observance of law and fulfilment of duty as early as the 5th cent. Plato inherits this view (→ δίκη, 178). His well-known definition is as follows : τὸ τὰ αὐτοῦ πράττειν καὶ μὴ πολυπραγμονεῖν δικαιοσύνη ἐστίν (Resp., IV, 433a). His utopia is grounded on this concept of δικαιοσύνη. In

δ ι κ α ι ο σ ύ ν η. Def. Aristot. Rhet., I, 9, p. 1366b, 9 ff. Together with text-books of NT theology and Cr.-Kö., v. R. Hirzel, Themis, Dike (→ δίκη, 178, Bibl.); L. Diestel, "Die Idee der Gerechtigkeit," Jahrbücher f. deutsche Theol., 5 (1860), 173 ff.; E. Kautzsch, Über die Derivate des Stammes צדק (1880); C. v. Orelli, "Einige Prämissen zur nt.lichen Versöhnungslehre," ZWL, 5 (1884), 73 ff.; W. Eichrodt, Theologie des AT, I (1933), 121-126; E. Sellin, Theologie des AT (1933), 28 ff., 73 ff.; H. St. J. Thackeray, The Relation of St. Paul to Contemporary Jewish Thought (1900), C. G. Montefiore, Judaism and St. Paul (1914); Bousset-Gressm., 379 ff., 393; Reitzenstein Hell. Myst., 257 ff. Excurs. in comm. on Romans by W. Sanday and A. C. Headlam (on 1:17), Zn. (p. 80 ff.), Ltzm. (on R. 10:3). R. Bultmann, RGG², IV, 1037 f.; E. Vischer, ibid., IV, 1745 ff.; R. A. Lipsius, Die paulin. Rechtfertigungslehre (1853); A. Ritschl, Die christ. Lehre von d. Rechtf. u. Versöhnung, II⁴ (1900); A. Michelsen, "Die δικαιοσύνη θεοῦ im Br. an d. R.," ZWL, 5 (1884), 133 ff.; G. A. Fricke, Der paulin. Grundbegriff d. δικαιοσύνη θεοῦ (1888); H. Beck, "Die δικαιοσύνη θεοῦ bei Pls.," Neue Jahrbücher f. deutsche Theol., 4 (1895), 249 ff.; P. Kölbing, "Studien z. paul. Theologie," ThStKr, 68 (1895), 7 ff.; T. Haering, "δικαιοσύνη θεοῦ bei Pls.," Tübinger Progr. (1896); ThStKr, 69 (1896), 139 ff.; J. A. Beet, "Justification through Faith," Exp., V, 7 (1898), 275 ff.; A. Robertson, "The Righteousness of God," Exp., V, 9 (1899), 187 ff.; H. Cremer, Die paul. Rechtf. Lehre² (1900); J. Denney, "The Theology of the Ep. to the Rom.," Exp., IV, 4 (1901), 81 ff.; J. H. Ropes, "Righteousness in the OT and in St. Paul," JBL, 22 (1903), 211 ff.; E. Kühl, Rechtf. auf Grund d. Glaubens u. Gericht nach d. Werken bei Pls., (1904); J. H. Gerretsen, Rechtvaardigmaking bij Pls. (1905); E. F. K. Müller, Beobachtungen z. paul. Rechtf. Lehre (1905); G. Kittel, "Zur Erklrg. v. R. 3:21 ff.," ThStKr, 80 (1907), 217 ff.; E. Tobac, Le Problème de la Justification dans St. Paul (1908); E. v. Dobschütz, "Die Rechtf. bei Pls., eine Rechtf. d. Pls.," ThStKr, 85 (1912), 38 ff.; G. P. Wetter, Der Vergeltungsgedanke bei Pls. (1912), 161 ff.; W. Macholz, "Zum Verständnis d. paul. Rechtfertigungsgedankens," ThStKr, 88 (1915), 29 ff.; E. Wissmann, Das Verhältnis von πίστις und Christusfrömmigkeit bei Pls. (1926); A. Schlatter, Der Glaube im NT⁴ (1927); W. Michaelis, "Rechtf. aus Glauben bei Pls." in Festgabe f. A. Deissmann (1927); E. Lohmeyer, Grundlagen paulin. Theologie (1929), 52 ff.; K. Mittring, Heilswirklichkeit bei Pls. (1929); K. Oltmanns, "Das Verhältnis v. R. 1:18 - 3:20 zu R. 3:21 ff.," ThBl, 8 (1929), 110-116; H. Braun, Gerichtsgedanke u. Rechtf. bei Pls. (1930); A. Schweitzer, Die Mystik d. Ap. Pls. (1930), 201-221; H. E. Weber, 'Eschatologie' und 'Mystik' im NT (1930), 90 ff.; 109 ff.; O. Zänker, "δικαιοσύνη θεοῦ b. Pls.," ZSTh, 9 (1931), 398-420; K. G. Kuhn, R. 6:7, ZNW, 30 (1931), 305-310; F. V. Filson, St. Paul's Conception of Recompense (1931); A. Schmitt, δικαιοσύνη θεοῦ in Natalicium f. J. Geffcken (1931), 111-131; W. Mundle, Der Glaubensbegriff des Pls. (1932), 82 ff.; W. Grundmann, "Gesetz, Rechtfertigung u. Mystik bei Pls.," ZNW, 32 (1933), 52-65.

[1] R. Hirzel 169 attributes this to the fact that δικαιοσύνη is not in accord with their aristocratic morality. But this is hardly true of Hesiod.

Phaed., 82ab δικαιοσύνη is linked with σωφροσύνη as δημοτικὴ καὶ πολιτικὴ ἀρετή. It is also used b. as a general term for virtue from the time of Theogn., 147 (→ δίκη, 179), quoted by Aristotle in Eth. Nic., V, 3, p. 1129b, 30. Hence in Plato Euthyphr., 12c/e the ὅσιον is a part of the δίκαιον (→ δίκαιος, 182), and in Aristot. De Virtutibus et Vitiis, 5, p. 1250b, 22 f. εὐσέβεια is a part (μέρος) or effect (παρακολουθοῦσα) of δικαιοσύνη c. Already in Plat. Prot., 330b, however, we can see the influential view that δικαιοσύνη should be linked with ὁσιότης (also ἐπιστήμη, ἀνδρεία, σωφροσύνη) as part of virtue in general. Cf. Epict. Diss., III, 26, 32. This is in keeping with the doctrine of the cardinal virtues (→ δίκαιος, 182), of which δικαιοσύνη is one of the most prominent and often the chief. Cf. Plut. De Fortuna, 2 (II, 97e): σωφροσύνη καὶ δικαιοσύνη καὶ ἀνδρεία. d. In mysticism (Corp. Herm., XIII, 18) δικαιοσύνη is set alongside ἐγκράτεια and there is a call for praise. We thus have a mystical conception of virtue. δικαιοσύνη is a δύναμις, a power of virtue with which the regenerate is invested. This corresponds to the use of δικαιόω in Corp. Herm., XIII, 9 (δικαιόω, 212). It is called spiritual harmony or balance (cf. Plato → 183): Stob. Ecl., I, 322, 10. It is rare in the pap., but common in the inscript. Cf. Ditt. Or., 438, 8 (with πίστις, ἀρετή, εὐσέβεια).

Here again it is everywhere true (→ δίκαιος, 183) that according to the basic Greek conception δικαιοσύνη, like all other virtues, is a present ἕξις of man. For ἀρετή as ἕξις, cf. Aristot. Eth. Nic., VI, 13, p. 1144b, 27.

2. The Legal View of the Term.

The close connexion between the legal view and general ethics is plain in the definition of Aristot. Rhet., I, 9, p. 1366b, 9 ff.: ἔστι δὲ δικαιοσύνη μὲν ἀρετὴ δι' ἣν τὰ αὐτῶν ἕκαστοι ἔχουσι, καὶ ὡς ὁ νόμος (opp. ἀδικία). He is here referring to the thought of the judge allotting to each what is his due. Solon's legislation had a considerable influence on the development of the term with its conception of *iustitia distributiva*. The legal influence continues even when ethics broadens the term. For alongside the view of δικαιοσύνη as civil virtue there always lies the use of δικαιοσύνη as a basic legislative principle, e.g., justice, the observance of law and judicial procedure.

Cf. δικαιοσύνη νομοθετική in Plat. Gorg., 464c; δικαιοσύνη δικαστική in Aristot. Pol., IV, 4, p. 1291a, 27; also τὸ νομικὸν δίκαιον in distinction from τὸ πρῶτον δίκαιον in Eth. Nic., V, 12, p. 1136a, 12. Cf., too, Eth. Nic., V, 14, p. 1137a, 31 ff., where legal righteousness is in view in the attempt to establish the relation of ἐπιείκεια to δικαιοσύνη. Thus παρὰ τὴν δικαιοσύνην can mean against the law, Pap. de Théadelphie (ed. P. Jouguet [1911], 23, 9 (4th cent. A.D.).

Very occasionally δικαιοσύνη corresponds to δίκαιος in the sense of correct: Cl. Al. Strom., VI, 4, 36, 2 : τὸν τῆς δικαιοσύνης πῆχυν; a correct yard (cf. LXX Dt. 33:19); ψ 4:5; 50:19 : θυσίαν δικαιοσύνης; ψ 22:3 : τρίβους δικαιοσύνης (always for צֶדֶק).

3. δικαιοσύνη in Josephus and Philo.

a. Since these two writers adopt for the most part the Hellenistic understanding, they may be treated at this point. δικαιοσύνη is rare in Joseph. In only one case is there reference to the δικαιοσύνη of God in the sense of judicial retribution, Ant., 11, 268. In relation to man, the word denotes right conduct in the sense of virtue, Ant., 9, 182; 14, 176; Vit., 7. Statements like those in Ant., 14, 403; 3, 67; 19, 154 may seem to contradict this, but on closer inspection have the same meaning. To be sure, Joseph. maintains a strongly religious definition of the law, viewing the virtues, of which δικαιοσύνη

---

2 On Solon, cf. W. Jaeger, "Solons Eunomie," SAB, 1926, 69-85.

is first, as parts of εὐσέβεια, Ap., 2, 170 f., 291 f. Yet as the first and preeminent quality εὐσέβεια itself opens the list of virtues among whieh δικαιοσύνη is numbered, Ant., 6, 160. The conjoining of·εὐσέβεια and δικαιοσύνη is very common, Ant., 6, 265; 8, 121 etc. In these lists δικαιοσύνη is always ἀρετή, and it usually denotes civil virtue in social life (πρὸς ἀλλήλους), Ant., 18, 117. The linking with εὐσέβεια shows that δικαιοσύνη is referred for the most part to man, though a certain imprecision attaches to it in view of OT influences and reminiscences and the effects of Pharisaism. It can be used as a synon. for observance of the commandments, Ant., 8, 21 and 120 ; 12, 291. Righteousness is merit, Ant. 1, 75 and 99; 18, 117; also the merit of the fathers, Ant., 11, 169. If the concept of God remains, the reference to innate δικαιοσύνη in Ant., 6, 36 (Samuel resists the monarchy διὰ τὴν σύμφυτον δικαιοσύνην) and the link with ethics in Ant. 1, 53 are both Hellenistic. Particular note should be taken of the expression in Ant., 4, 223 : δικαιοσύνη καὶ ἡ ἄλλη ἀρετή, and of the well-known Gk. catena of virtues in Ant., 6, 160 : εὐσέβεια, δικαιοσύνη, ἀνδρεία — this is κάλλος τῆς ψυχῆς. Also linked with δικαιοσύνη are σεμνότης, πρόνοια in Ant., 12, 160; σωφροσύνη in Ant., 11, 217; χρηστότης in Ant., 11, 139; and φιλανθρωπία, καρτερία in Ap. 2, 146.

b. In Philo there is only one passage which deals expressly with the righteousness of God, i.e., Deus Imm., 79. Here δικαιοσύνη is linked with ἐπιστήμη, σοφία, φρόνησις etc. and made a divine attribute in the sense of Stoic ethics, being set over mortals as ἀκραιφνῆ. There is a striking parallel to the ἔνδειξις δικαιοσύνης of R. 3:25 f. in Vit. Mos., II, 237: πρὸς ἐπίδειξιν ἀληθείας καὶ δικαιοσύνης. Naturally the reference here is not to God's saving acts as in Paul, but to the revelation of God when He asks concerning the right. δικαιοσύνη is set in opposition to ἀδικία and other derivatives of ἄδικος in Mut. Nom., 197; Rer. Div. Her., 243; Abr., 104; Op. Mund., 81; Leg. All., III, 77, and it plainly receives its positive significance from the OT Law. It is a main concern of the law-giver in Spec. Leg., IV, 143; Congr., 179 (νομοθετική), πολιτεύεσθαι being also emphasised in Mut. Nom., 240 and κοινωτικόν in Det. Pot. Ins., 72. Philo adopts the Pythagorean definition that δικαιοσύνη distributes impartially to all : Op. Mund., 51: μέτρον δικαιοσύνης καὶ ἰσότητος. This should be the attitude of tℓe judge : Spec. Leg., IV, 56. Hence the connexion of δικαιοσύνη with ἰσότης. This is μήτηρ δικαιοσύνης : Spec. Leg., IV, 231; its origin and source : Spec. Leg., II, 204.

In relation to righteousness Philo has a far more developed ethical conception than Josephus. Noah finds grace with God and is δίκαιος : ἀναπαυόμενον ἐπὶ τῷ καλῷ καὶ δικαιοσύνη συζῶντα (Leg. All., III, 77). δικαιοσύνη is very closely linked with εὐσέβεια, ὁσιότης and θεοσέβεια (Vit. Mos., II, 216 etc.). It emerges from the corresponding definitions, however, that it is a virtue πρὸς ἀνθρώπους (Abr., 208). It is the ἡγεμονίς of the cardinal virtues (Abr., 27) which constitute the καλοκαγαθία (Congr., 31; Abr., 56): φρόνησις, σωφροσύνη, ἀνδρεία, δικαιοσύνη (Leg. All., I, 63 etc.). These are all forms of virtue generally (Sacr. AC, 84). But Philo also has fuller lists. Thus, like Ac. 24:25, he sets ἐγκράτεια alongside δικαιοσύνη in Abr., 103; Jos., 153 (cf. Corp. Herm. → 193). The variations are very large, but statistics show that δικαιοσύνη is always mentioned. An interesting point of style is the great variety, especially in the form of the favourite concluding reference to ἀρετή as a whole (Leg. All., III, 150 etc.). A warm and vibrant religious concern may be detected in Philo in his psychological and mystical discussions within the Platonic and Stoic traditions. We can see this in relation to the origin of δικαιοσύνη in the soul. It comes into being when the three parts of the soul achieve harmony (Leg. All., I, 72 : ὅταν τὰ τρία μέρη τῆς ψυχῆς συμφωνίαν ἔχῃ), when τὸ θυμικόν and τὸ ἐπιθυμητικόν are guided by λογικόν like horses. Cl. Al. Strom., IV, 26, 163, 4 borrowed this idea from Philo. But it comes from Plato Phaedr., 253d; Resp., IV, 443d, and from Posidonius. The work of δικαιοσύνη in the soul is described as healing in Det. Pot. Ins., 123, as peace, ibid., 122, and as joy, Leg. All., III, 247. The main part in relation to it is played by λογισμός (Det. Pot. Ins., 121) and asceticism (ibid., 122). Ethics suggests merit. This seems to be transcended by the idea that God gives virtue (Sacr. AC, 56 f.). But the thought of merit persists, as we may see from the application of the story of Noah in Leg. All., III, 77:

ἀνάγκη τὸν παυόμενον ἀδικημάτων χάριν εὑρεῖν παρὰ τῷ θεῷ. Faith — μεγάλης καὶ ὀλυμπίου ἔργον διανοίας — is a work and achievement of δικαιοσύνη (Rer. Div. Her., 93-95). [3]

B. Righteousness in the LXX.

1. The Righteousness of God. How does the LXX speak of the righteousness of God? Does the translation affect the OT צְדָקָה, צֶדֶק? We have seen that צְדָקָה represents an extraordinarily rich and varied group of concepts. The etymological discussions of Diestel and Kautzsch, who work out thoroughly the idea of the consistent and normative action of God (God Himself being the norm rather than standing under it), bring out something of the meaning of צְדָקָה but hardly exhaust it. It should be emphasised particularly that צְדָקָה implies relationship. A man is righteous when he meets certain claims which another has on him in virtue of relationship. Even the righteousness of God is primarily His covenantal rule in fellowship with His people. [4] The definition of צְדָקָה as a concept of relationship (not, however, an ideal concept) already includes both the forensic elements and the idea of saving action. Diestel and Ritschl unduly suppress the legal element in their reaction against patristic and older Protestant dogmatics, but the concept of judicial righteousness, of God's rule as King and Judge (with retribution, reward and punishment), cannot be divorced from it.

We can see particularly from Dt. Is. (δικαιωθῆναι in 43:9, 26) that the image of the legal dispute is always present. The justice of God vindicates His oppressed people against their conquerors, and as מַצְדִּיק (Is. 50:8 f.) He carries through the cause of righteousness to victory. Hence מִשְׁפָּט can be used as a synon. for צְדָקָה (Is. 58:2). But the mere assertion of the concept of law is inadequate, for the last point shows us that there is implied the positive thought of help or salvation. As the מִשְׁפָּט and צְדָקָה of God intervene judicially for the oppressed, they bring help and salvation. We can see this already in Dt. 32:4, 35 f.; Hos. 2:19 (Mas. 2:21); Mi. 7:9. In Dt. Is. and the Ps. (e.g., ψ 87:11 f.; ψ 102:11, 17, LXX : ἔλεος, ἀλήθεια, δικαιοσύνη), mercy, truth, faithfulness and salvation are closely linked with righteousness. צֶדֶק can thus mean the saving act and covenant faithfulness of God in Jer. 50:7; Is. 41:2, 10; 42:6; 45:8; 51:5. God reveals to His people the saving order of His צְדָקָה. In full accord with the Mas. the LXX uses σωτήρ, σωτηρία, σωτήριον to explain δικαιοσύνη, ψ 64:5; 70:15; 97:2 f.; Is. 46:12 f.; 51:5; 59:17; 61:10 f. Negatively, cf. ψ 68:27; also relevant is Is. 45:23-25. This linking of right and salvation is most deeply grounded in the covenant concept. צְדָקָה is the execution of covenant faithfulness and the covenant promises. God's righteousness as His judicial reign means that in covenant faithfulness to His people He vindicates and saves them.

In the LXX the use of צְדָקָה for God's dispensing of salvation is carried to such a point that δικαιοσύνη can even be used for חֶסֶד (Gn. 19:19; 20:13; 21:23; 24:27; 32:10; Ex. 15:13; 34:7; Prv. 20:22, Mas. 20:28) when ἔλεος is the more usual rendering [5]

---

[3] In detail we may mention the use of δικαιοσύναι for "righteous deeds" in Spec. Leg., IV, 181; cf. LXX Ez. 3:20; Da. 9:18; Sir. 44:10; Tob. 2:14; 2 Cl., 6, 9.

[4] Cf. W. Eichrodt, Theologie des AT (1933), 121 ff. H. Cremer especially insisted on the element of relationship in צְדָקָה.

[5] The use of ἔλεος for חֶסֶד is customary but it is not the most apt rendering. Like צְדָקָה חֶסֶד is an attitude corresponding to a duty or legal obligation. It thus signifies the commitment to an act of loving service which arises within a social relationship (tribe, friendship or covenant). Cf. N. Glueck, "Das Wort hesed im at.lichen Sprachgebrauch," ZAW, 47 (1927).

(ψ 35:10; 39:10 f.; 87:11). It is also used for אֱמֶת, God's covenant faithfulness, in Gn. 24:29; Is. 38:19; 39:8; Da. 8:12. צְדָקָה is rendered ἔλεος in Is. 56:1 and εὐφροσύνη in Is. 61:10, though the forensic implication is not eliminated. In accordance with the Mas. δικαιοσύνη is often linked with κρίσις and κρίμα (both for מִשְׁפָּט) in the LXX, e.g., ψ 93:15; Ez. 45:9, and we even have δικαιοσύνη for מִשְׁפָּט in Is. 61:8; Mal. 2:17 — a proof that even the purely forensic use can be rendered by δικαιοσύνη. Apart from the saving righteousness of God, His justice, linked with the picture of God as Judge, can be frequently expressed by δικαιοσύνη, ψ 9:5; 34:24; 95:13.

2. The δικαιοσύνη of Man. δικαιοσύνη is the observance of the will of God which is well-pleasing to Him (opp. ἀνομία), e.g., Is. 5:7: ἐποίησεν ἀνομίαν καὶ οὐ δικαιοσύνην (of Israel). It is often linked with ἀλήθεια, Tob. 14:7: ἀγαπῶντες τὸν θεὸν ἐν ἀληθείᾳ καὶ δικαιοσύνῃ, and Wis. 5:6, where ὁδὸς ἀληθείας and φῶς δικαιοσύνης are parallels. Test. G. 3. Here the word has the sense uprightness (cf. Eph. 5:9). The parallelism corresponds to the divine image in which צְדָקָה and אֱמֶת are one. Of God: Zech. 8:8; O. Sol. 25:10; Pist. Soph., 69; of man: 3 Βασ. 3:6.

C. Righteousness in the Synagogue.

1. The Righteousness of God. The Synagogue does not speak of the righteousness of God in the sense of R. 3:21. [6] It is typical that צִדְקַת יְהוָה in Dt. 33:21 is referred to Moses, who conferred benefits after the manner of Yahweh, [7] who did what was meritorious before Yahweh, [8] and who exercised righteousness in judgment. [9] Even the LXX did not understand this verse, and made κύριος the subject. On the other hand (→ δίκαιος, 186), under prophetic influence Messiah was often spoken of as the Righteous and as righteousness. Righteousness can have the sense of mercy in Messianic and eschatological expositions. [10]

2. Righteousness as Human Action. צְדָקָה, Aram. צִדְקָה, as human action suffers notable constriction in Rabbinic usage, being used for almsgiving as the most important fulfilment of the Law. [11] ποιεῖν ἐλεημοσύνην in Mt. 6:2 corresponds to the Rabbinic עשה צדקה or עשה מצוה. [12] This private benevolence, usually called צדקה or מצוה, is one of the most meritorious of works. [13] Almsgiving or benevolence is mostly taken to be the sense in exposition of the OT צְדָקָה. [14] Even the LXX frequently has ἐλεημοσύνη for צֶדֶק and צְדָקָה, e.g., for צְדָקָה in Dt. 6:25; 24:13; ψ 23:5; 32:5; 102:6; Is. 1:27; 28:17; 59:16; Da. 4:24; 9:16 Θ; Sir. 3:30: καὶ ἐλεημοσύνη ἐξιλάσεται ἁμαρτίας, cf. 7:10; 16:14: πάσῃ ἐλεημοσύνῃ ποιήσει τόπον. In Prv. 10:2 וּצְדָקָה תַּצִּיל מִמָּוֶת is translated δικαιοσύνη δὲ ῥύεται ἐκ θανάτου in the LXX, while in Tob. 4:10; 12:9 we have ἐλεημοσύνη ἐκ θανάτου ῥύεται. There can be no doubt that in Prv. 10:2 benevolence and almsgiving are also meant. In Tob. 12:9 and 14:11 δικαιοσύνη is twice used in the same context as an explanatory synon. for ἐλεημοσύνη.

---

[6] Str.-B., III, 163.
[7] S. Dt., 355 on 33:21; Str.-B., III, 163.
[8] Tg. O. Dt. 33:21; Str.-B., III, 163.
[9] S. Dt., 355 on 33:21.
[10] jShebiit, 35c, 31; Midr. Ps. 22 § 32 (99a), Str.-B., II, 575.
[11] Str.-B., I, 387 f.
[12] bGit., 7a; Lv. r., 34 on 25:39; Str.-B., I, 388.
[13] Str.-B., IV, 12, 536 ff.
[14] Cf. the exposition of 2 S. 8:15: David acted with justice and benevolence to his people: T. Sanh., 1, 2 ff., Str.-B., III, 210; of Prv. 21:3, 21, bSukka, 49b, Str.-B., I, 500; bBB, 9b, 10b, Str.-B., III, 525; Gn. r., 58 on 24:19, Str.-B., IV, 561c; of Is. 32:17: Ab, 2, 7, Str.-B., I, 387; of Is. 59:17, bBB, 9b, Str.-B., III, 618; of Hos. 10:12, bSukka, 49b, Str.-B., III, 451.

3. The Basis of the Rabbinic View. Some brief indication should be given of the basis of the Rabbinic view discernible even in the LXX. Every fulfilment of the Law: מִצְוָה, carries with it a merit: זְכוּת, which the Israelite earns before God. [15] זְכוּת itself originally means "righteousness," and the verb זכה "to be righteous," "to be worthy," "to merit," "to have merit." [16] The amassing of fulfilments, i.e., of merits, is the goal. [17] Of help are alms, works of charity, the merit of the fathers and other fulfilments of the Law. [18] Standing before God is in exact accordance with the predominance of merits or transgressions. [19] The justifying sentence of God in the last judgment will be for the Israelite if his merits predominate. [20] He will then stand before God as righteous. The purpose of the last judgment is to see whether merit or transgression is the greater. [21] For further details of the Rabbinic doctrine of justification, → δικαιόω, B.

4. The Relation of the Justice of God to His Mercy. In the Ps. Sol. the righteousness and goodness of God are directly related. The divine δικαιοσύνη is God's justice, e.g., 2:16; 3:5; 4:28; 8:29 f., 31; 9:3, 7; cf. 2:12, 19, 36; 3:3; 5:1; 8:27; 10:6; 17:2. [22] Though the relationship is not explained, the goodness or mercy or grace of God is set alongside this judicial function, e.g., 2:40; 5:2, 17; 7:4 f., 8, 9; 8:33 f.; 9:15 f.; 10:8; 11:2, 9. The terms ἔλεος and χάρις, though not δικαιοσύνη, express the concept of salvation. (On the special use of δικαιοῦσθαι with reference to God in Ps. Sol. → δικαιόω, B.) In Jub. there is a similar linking of God's goodness and mercy with His righteousness, which is predominantly conceived as judicial (21:4). [23] Yet, unlike Ps. Sol., Jub. refers to salvation in righteousness (1:15), and it relates mercy and righteousness far more closely (31:25). [24] On the other hand, there is no attempt at equation. In 4 Esr. 8:36, however, we have a statement concerning the merciful righteousness of God which approximates closely to the usage of Paul: "For thereby are thy righteousness and goodness (Lat. Φ: iusticia tua et bonitas tua, p. 238, Violet) manifested, that thou mightest have pity on those who have no treasure of good works." If there is no reference to the act of salvation as in Paul, the idea that God may exercise unmerited mercy in virtue of His righteousness is one which stands on the margin of later Judaism and which would be inconceivable in Ps. Sol.

In the Synagogue law is not צְדָקָה but דִּין. There is much discussion of the relation of God's justice to His mercy. In the first instance, the two are sharply contrasted: מִדַּת הָרַחֲמִים and מִדַּת הַדִּין. [25] But we continually find the statement that the measure of mercy is greater than that of strict justice. [26] There is blessing because mercy restrains His wrath and triumphs over His justice. [27] Thus צְדָקָה in Gn. 18:19 [28] is thought of as mercy, and מִשְׁפָּט as justice (cf. supra, דִּין). The same problem arises in relation to

---

[15] Str.-B., I, 251.
[16] Str.-B., IV, 10. Cf. bBer., 28b; bBB, 10b, Bar., Str.-B., II, 254.
[17] Str.-B., IV, 6.
[18] Loc. cit.
[19] Ibid., I, 251.
[20] Str.-B., IV, 5.
[21] jQid., 61d, 47, Str.-B., IV, 11.
[22] Certainly the παιδεύειν shown to Israel is always linked with mercy (7:3-5; 8:32-35 etc.). When it is said of the Messiah (17:28) that He reigns ἐν δικαιοσύνῃ (opp. ἀδικία), the reference is to the spotlessness of His righteousness before God.
[23] δικαιοσύνη refers to the right conduct of man in 25:1; 30:20.
[24] So also En. 39:5; 71:3.
[25] M. Ex. on 15:2, Str.-B., I, 1042; Gn. r., 12 on 2:4, Str.-B., III, 292; Midr. Cant., 1, 14, Str.-B., II, 279; Gn. r., 65 on 27:1, Str.-B., III, 694.
[26] bSanh., 100a, Bar., Str.-B., I, 444; S. Lv. on 5:17, Str.-B., III, 230; T. Sota, 4, 1. For an appeal to strict justice, cf. Gn. r., 45 on 16:5, Str.-B., III, 301.
[27] bBer., 7a, Bar., Str.-B., II, 79.
[28] E.g., Gn. r., 49 on 18:19, Str.-B., III, 196.

שׁוּרַת הַדִּין and לִפְנִים מִשּׁוּרַת הַדִּין. The one means keeping to the letter of the law, the other a more lenient admission of considerations of clemency. [29] In the customary use of the formula a vital thought is that among men mercy is better than legal rigidity. [30] The same may also be predicated of God. [31] Yet there remains in the Synagogue a final uncertainty and vacillation when the justice and the mercy of God are weighed against one another.

D. δικαιοσύνη in the non-Pauline Writings of the NT.

1. δικαιοσύνη as Just Judgment and Rule.

In the NT δικαιοσύνη occasionally means the just judgment of God exercised by Christ at His return (Ac. 17:31; Rev. 19:11); cf. also the revelation of retributive justice by Christ in Mk. 16 (Freer Logion, 13-15), or 2 Pt. 1:1: the just rule of God in the guidance of the community. We have another isolated example of this use in Hb. 11:33, where ἠργάσαντο δικαιοσύνην (elsewhere δίκην or δίκαιον) refers to the justice of rulers and kings.

There is a most unusual phrase in Hb. 5:13, where ἄπειρος λόγου δικαιοσύνης implies that the infant is incapable of understanding correct, normal speech. [32]

2. δικαιοσύνη as Right Conduct before God.

If we ignore these passages, and postpone for the moment our consideration of the distinctive Pauline formula δικαιοσύνη θεοῦ, we may first maintain that δικαιοσύνη is almost always used in the NT for the right conduct of man which follows the will of God and is pleasing to Him, for rectitude of life before God, for uprightness before His judgment. The fact that the basic relationship to God is always in view, and that it is related to the event of revelation, distinguishes this usage from Greek and Hellenistic ethics and links it firmly with the OT. A brief review of the non-Pauline writings will confirm this.

a. Matthew. It is the consistent usage in Mt. In Mt. 3:15 πληρῶσαι πᾶσαν δικαιοσύνην means that in presenting Himself for baptism Jesus emphasises as His task, not δικαίωμα, the establishment of right, [33] which would be one act, but right conduct which He will fulfil and which will be pleasing to God. [34] According to 5:6 a right state before God is the supreme goal for the πεινῶντες καὶ διψῶντες. We need hardly take this to be the judging and saving δικαιοσύνη θεοῦ in the forensically eschatological sense. [35] On the other hand, in opposition to the Jewish thought of merit, δικαιοσύνη is plainly regarded as a gift which God gives to those who ask for it. [36] In 6:33 ζητεῖτε πρῶτον τὴν βασιλείαν καὶ τὴν δικαιοσύνην αὐτοῦ refers to that which brings the disciple into harmony with the will

---

[29] Str.-B., I, 341; IV, 18.
[30] bBQ, 99b, Str.-B., IV, 19, cf. 15; M. Ex. on 18:20, Str.-B., I, 345.
[31] bBer., 7a, Bar., Str.-B., II, 79; Dt. r., 4 on 10:1, Str.-B., IV, 18.
[32] Rgg. Hb., 144 f. δικαιοσύνη from δίκαιος in the sense of correct (→ 184; 193).
[33] Zn. Mt., 140, cf. Zn. Einl.³, II, 318, n. 10. So also Kl. Mt., ad loc.; Pr.-Bauer, 306.
[34] Schl. Mt., 89 ff. Cf. on Mt. 3:15, A. Friedrichsen in Revue d'Histoire et de Philos. relig., 7 (1927), 245 ff.
[35] Cremer, Paul. Rechtfertigungslehre, 190.
[36] Schl. Mt., 136 f.; Str.-B., I, 201 f.

of God. αὐτοῦ is related to βασιλείαν as well as δικαιοσύνην. Righteousness is here closely linked with God and His kingdom, again as a pure gift from God, like everything connected with the kingdom.

The parallelism to the Pauline doctrine of justification is evident here, as at other points where the Gospel emphasises the merciful salvation of sinners. [37] According to 5:10 right conduct before God brings about persecution. According to 5:20 this δικαιοσύνη must be more abundant than that of the Pharisees. [38] In 6:1 [39] it is a title for exercises and expressions of piety (ποιεῖν δικαιοσύνην). These do not exhaust the concept of righteousness; yet they provide typical illustrations of δικαιοσύνη as action before and for God. When John ἦλθεν ἐν ὁδῷ δικαιοσύνης (21:32), he demanded righteousness of life in accordance with the will of God.

On ὁδὸς τῆς δικαιοσύνης, cf. Job 24:13; Prv. 8:20; 12:28; 16:31; 17:23; 21:16, 21.

b. Luke. The word has the same meaning in Lk. In 1:75 λατρεύειν αὐτῷ ἐν ὁσιότητι καὶ δικαιοσύνῃ ἐνώπιον αὐτοῦ speaks with liturgical power of the Messianic salvation. The linking of ὁσιότης and δικαιοσύνη (Eph. 4:24) is Greek (cf. Wis. 9:3 and LXX Jos. 24:14 A). But the ἐνώπιον αὐτοῦ shows that here, as distinct from the Greek view, δικαιοσύνη is not isolated rectitude limited as ἕξις to man. The distinction between moral and religious action is meaningless. δικαιοσύνη before God is the fulfilment of His will in an action which is pleasing to Him. In Ac. especially it is emphasised that God seeks this even among the heathen : 13:10; 24:25, and that good works done by non-Christians are recognised by God : 10:35 : ἐν παντὶ ἔθνει ὁ φοβούμενος αὐτὸν καὶ ἐργαζόμενος δικαιοσύνην δεκτὸς αὐτῷ ἐστιν. This ἐργάζεσθαι δικαιοσύνην is not, of course, regarded as a sufficient way of salvation ; cf. 10:43 : ἄφεσις ἁμαρτιῶν.

c. Peter. Much the same picture is presented. In 1 Pt. δικαιοσύνη is always the doing of right as acceptable conduct. According to 2:24 liberation from sins by the cross is the presupposition of a life directed by δικαιοσύνη — a motif similar to that of R. 6 (→ 209). In 3:14, as in Mt. 5:10, suffering for the sake of rectitude is mentioned. According to 2 Pt. 2:5 Noah as a herald of δικαιοσύνη is a representative of the right conversation towards the κόσμος ἀσεβῶν which has regard to the command of God. In 2:21 the libertines leave τὴν ὁδὸν τῆς δικαιοσύνης (→ supra), the walk which corresponds to the ἁγία ἐντολή (v. 21). According to 3:13 (→ 187) the new world will be controlled by righteousness.

d. Hebrews. Apart from the peculiar instances mentioned earlier, which give evidence of a sensitiveness to Hellenistic usage but do not essentially change the picture, the same is true of Hb. In 1:9 the ἠγάπησας δικαιοσύνην καὶ ἐμίσησας ἀνομίαν (אA ἀδικίαν) of ψ 44:7 is applied in such a way that the exaltation of Christ is viewed as a reward for His righteousness of life. According to 7:2 Melchisedec is βασιλεὺς δικαιοσύνης, i.e., dedicated to righteousness. As such —

---

[37] Cf. R. Bultmann, "Die Bedeutung des geschichtl. Jesus f. d. Theol. des Pls.," ThBl, 8 (1929), 143.

[38] Acc. to Schl. Mt., 159 ff. the ἐὰν μὴ περισσεύσῃ πλεῖον means that the δικαιοσύνη is to transcend the written Law far more than that of the Pharisees. It is simpler to assume a stronger form of the comp. Cf. ad loc. G. Dalman, Jesus-Jeschua (1922), 62 ff.

[39] The reading ἐλεημοσύνην (EKL etc. many Min, Syr except syˢ) is to be rejected in favour of δικαιοσύνην (א *BD syˢ).

though the allegory is not developed — he is a type of Christ, to whom righteousness is proper. In 11:7 it is said of Noah : τῆς κατὰ πίστιν δικαιοσύνης ἐγένετο κληρονόμος. The word is not used here in a legal sense ; it means an acceptable mode of life corresponding to faith. [40] The statement agrees with Paul to the degree that here, as in Mt., δικαιοσύνη is a gift which man inherits. In 12:11, where the gen. appos. describes the fruit of παιδεία as δικαιοσύνη, what is in view is agreement in character with the will of God.

e. John. The only difference in Jn. is that in his total use of δικαιοσύνη he brings out even more fully what is said in Mt. 3:15 and Hb. concerning the righteousness of Christ by interpreting all righteousness christologically and always linking right action with Christ as the δίκαιος. According to Jn. 16:8, 10 : ἐλέγξει τὸν κόσμον περὶ ἁμαρτίας καὶ περὶ δικαιοσύνης καὶ περὶ κρίσεως, the resurrection and ascension of Jesus declare His righteous being, and in 1 Jn. 2:29 ποιεῖν τὴν δικαιοσύνην is the exercise and demonstration of what Jesus embodies as the δίκαιος, and is therefore a valid sign of being born of God. [41] In 3:7 the antinomianism which would stop at the ἐκεῖνος δίκαιος without drawing the consequences of ποιεῖν τὴν δικαιοσύνην is summoned to right conduct (opp. ἁμαρτία) according to the norm of the true δίκαιος. The main content of this doing of δικαιοσύνη is brotherly love (3:10). With this should be linked the δικαιοσύνην ποιησάτω of Rev. 22:11.

Does this answer the question how there can be righteousness before God ? Mt. plainly tells us that it is a gift of God's kingdom. 1 Pt. 2:24 emphasises that it is made possible by liberation from sins through the cross, and, though the statement is not given dogmatic form, it is very close to the Pauline formulations. Jn., too, stresses the fact that righteousness follows logically from commitment to Christ the δίκαιος, and he thus links true righteousness to the revelation given only in Him. Nevertheless, the Israelite question how man can be צַדִּיק in God's judgment is formally treated only by James and Paul.

3. δικαιοσύνη in James.

The use of δικαιοσύνη θεοῦ in Jm. 1:20 : ὀργὴ ἀνδρὸς δικαιοσύνην θεοῦ οὐκ ἐργάζεται, is not to be identified with the central content of the word as Paul uses it in the light of the saving work of the cross. It undoubtedly means right conduct, the work of righteousness, which is given its distinctive form by God alone, so that it can only be described as the righteousness of God. What man has to do, is the norm and demand of God. Human anger does not achieve this ; it is incompatible with it. Worth noting is the fact that even according to this formula the one who does righteousness is in all respects set in God's righteousness and not his own. To this extent the usage is in keeping with the concern of Paul in R. 10:3 that there should be subjection to the righteousness of God. [42] The saying concerning the fruit of righteousness (cf. Prv. 3:9; 11:30 etc.; Am. 6:12) in 3:18 (gen. of content) views righteousness of life as agreement with the will of God. It is fruit to be gathered, and is thus the end and goal of the whole direction of life.

---

[40] κατά for the gen., cf. Rgg. Hb., 352 f.
[41] On ποιεῖν τὴν δικαιοσύνην, cf. 2 Βασ. 8:15; ψ 105:3; Is. 56:1; 58:2; Ps. Sol. 9:5.
[42] Cf. Schl. Jk., 51, 142.

In these statements Jm. is true to what we have seen to be the dominant line of NT usage. When we come to the much debated passage in 2:23 : καὶ ἐλογίσθη αὐτῷ εἰς δικαιοσύνην, [43] he answers the question in what way man can attain to righteousness before God. This raises the basic question of the way of salvation. We are thus brought close to the concern of Paul in his message of justification.

For the λογίζεσθαι of Gn. 15:6, cf. ψ 105:31 (of Phinehas): ἐλογίσθη αὐτῷ εἰς δικαιοσύνην; also 1 Macc. 2:52; Jub. 14:6 (cf. 31:23); 30:17; 35:2; Philo Rer. Div. Her., 90, 94; Abr., 262.

Characteristic of James' treatment of the subject is his campaign against a dead orthodoxy which speaks of faith but does not take works seriously. Hence he emphasises the union of faith and works. By works he does not understand the works of the Law and precepts as understood by the Synagogue. He means the work of love and obedience, which Paul describes as the fruit of the Spirit and the content of the Christian life. James' whole work proves this. The Jewish idea of merit is no less alien than the Greek conception of virtue. We are simply given a straightforward and non-theological emphasising of the demand that faith should not be distorted by making it a substitute for works. According to 2:23 Abraham was justified before God by the imputation of a faith which found fulfilment in works. It may rightly be said that this view is nearer to the Jewish conception than that of Paul, especially since there is no contrasting of χάρις and ἐργάζεσθαι. It may also be allowed without question that in this section James is referring to a faith which theologically is differently conceived from that of Paul. Yet we should not forget that James does not have in view the Pauline χωρὶς ἔργων νόμου. He is simply engaging in practical argument against the attempt to promote faith without works, and he adopts a popular mode of presentation. Nor should we think that the faith which demons may have is the only faith considered by James. In this respect attention should be paid to the whole attitude of faith which underlies his collection of sayings. This attitude goes rather beyond the faith of mere orthodoxy. On the other hand, it must be admitted that the statement that Abraham was justified on the basis of the demonstrable works associated with his faith represents a view which Paul could hardly have advanced. The crisis through which every work must pass, whether legal or not, is not taken into account by Jm. in this usage. Indeed, his view does not even reach the level of Mt. 6:33 and 1 Pt. 2:24 (→ 198; 199). Nevertheless, the underlying practical motif that the only faith worth considering is one which includes and produces the actual fruit of serious action links his exhortation with the total proclamation of the early Church in spite of the theologically vulnerable formula in 2:23. [44]

---

[43] On Jm. 2:23, cf. Dib. Jk., 168; Wnd., 20 f.; Hck., 124 ff.; Schl., 202 f. On the relationship to Paul, cf. A. Meyer, Rätsel des Jk. (1930), 86 ff.; Schl. Jk., 51-60.

[44] Schl. Jk., 51 ff. attempts to solve the problem by suggesting that Paul's χωρὶς ἔργων νόμου is the older formula which gives rise to the further question whether this means χωρὶς ἔργων? He adduces the libertinism at Corinth by way of comparison. The thesis is suggestive. But there still remains the unresolved tension that λογίζεσθαι is here connected with human works and not with faith alone.

E. δικαιοσύνη in Paul.

1. Origin and Presupposition of the Pauline Message of Justification.

The starting-point for an understanding of what Paul means by the δικαιοσύνη θεοῦ is provided by legal righteousness. According to R. 9:30 the Law is a νόμος δικαιοσύνης because it demands righteousness. Moses himself according to R. 10:5 (אAD*) writes : ὅτι τὴν δικαιοσύνην τὴν ἐκ νόμου ὁ ποιήσας ἄνθρωπος ζήσεται ἐν αὐτῇ.

With δικαιοσύνη ἐκ νόμου we should compare Test. D. 6:10 : κολλήθητε τῇ δι-καιοσύνῃ τοῦ θεοῦ (S¹ add νόμου τοῦ); S. Bar. 63:3 : Hezekiah trusted in his works and built on his righteousness, cf. 67:6, iustitia ex lege; 51:3, qui nunc iustificati sunt in lege mea.

Here, then, δικαιοσύνη ἐκ νόμου is a condition of life. But this refers to a stage in the economy of salvation which is now past. In truth there is now no δικαιοσύνη ἐκ νόμου. To be sure, on the ground of the Law blameless conduct is possible as a relative fulfilment of what is written (Phil. 3:6 : κατὰ δικαιοσύνην τὴν ἐν νόμῳ γενόμενος ἄμεμπτος). But the new knowledge of Paul is that true righteousness before God does not derive from the Law. Thus δικαιοσύνη ἐκ νόμου is denied in Gl. 3:21. The relative and questionable righteousness which derives from the Law (ἡ ἰδία δικαιοσύνη, R. 10:3; Phil. 3:9 : ἐμὴ δικαιοσύνη ἡ ἐκ νόμου, in both cases as self-attained righteousness) is ζημία and σκύβαλα in relation to Christ. Thus δικαιοσύνη cannot be achieved by means of the Law, cf. the εἰ γὰρ διὰ νόμου δικαιοσύνη in Gl. 2:21. The statement in Tt. 3:5 that our deliverance was accomplished κατὰ ἔλεος, οὐκ ἐξ ἔργων τῶν ἐν δικαιοσύνῃ, ἃ ἐποιήσαμεν ἡμεῖς, corresponds materially, though not in detailed wording, to what we have mentioned, inasmuch as ἐν δικαιοσύνῃ denotes the human attainment envisaged in Phil. 3:6, 9. [45]

In his wrestling with the νόμος, Paul attains to the new truth concerning the δικαιοσύνη θεοῦ. One cannot say [46] that the message of justification [47] is one of the things which Paul pronounces as his Gospel, not from original experience, but simply in controversy with Jewish thought, before which he must justify himself. Now there can be no doubt that this is the decisive point at issue in relation to Judaism. Paul speaks very differently to the Corinthians. On the other hand, Paul must first justify himself before his own earlier thinking, and his whole theology is rooted in this radical clarification of the question of the Law. Even what is commonly called the mysticism of Paul cannot be loosed from the new relationship to God achieved by another way than that of the Law. That justification is a militant doctrine and a keypoint in the Christian mission is because there is ex-pressed in it a new insight concerning the relation of the Law and Christ. Paul takes over a sacred Jewish word when he speaks of righteousness, but he turns it against the legal conception of Judaism.

---

[45] On "works of the Law" cf. E. Lohmeyer, "Probleme paulin. Theol., II," ZNW, 28 (1929), 177 ff.

[46] So finally A. Meyer, Rätsel des Jk. (1930), 99 ff., following W. Wrede, Paulus (1904), 72 ff.

[47] On the fact that justification in Paul is always message or word, cf. H. E. Weber, "Eschatologie" u. "Mystik" im NT, 100 f.

The presupposition of his message is the OT concept of God. God is the Judge who demands obedience and who rewards and punishes. Another basic conviction is the sinful bondage of humanity, which is seen to be guilty before God. At this point there is in Paul a far more radical rejection than in Judaism of the optimistic view that fulfilment of the Law is possible. This is linked with the complete collapse of Synagogue piety as he had known it. He still maintains that only the righteous can enjoy true fellowship with God. But the Gospel now adds that it is not man's own work which establishes this fellowship with God. It is God's own sovereign and gracious and decisive intervention for man in Christ.

2. The Meaning of the Pauline Use of δικαιοσύνη θεοῦ and the Main Elements in the Doctrine of Justification.

When the apostle makes his most solemn and weighty pronouncements concerning the establishment of salvation, he uses δικαιοσύνη θεοῦ instead of the simple δικαιοσύνη. There can be no doubt that this is a subj. genitive. The righteousness of God is God's alone; man is taken up into it and set in it. [48] The δικαιοσύνη θεοῦ is God's righteousness as a conjunction of judgment and grace which He enjoys and demonstrates by showing righteousness, by imparting it as His pardoning sentence, but which also draws into His kingdom as new life and thereby pledges to service. It will be fully manifested at the last judgment.

On δικαιοσύνη θεοῦ, cf. Dt. 33:21, where it is said of Gad: צִדְקַת יְהוָה עָשָׂה וּמִשְׁפָּטָיו עִם־יִשְׂרָאֵל, "he fulfilled the righteousness of the Lord and his judgments with Israel," LXX: δικαιοσύνην κύριος ἐποίησεν. Od. Sol. 25:10: "I became mighty in the truth and holy (Copt. purified) in thy righteousness." 4 Esr. 8:36 (→ 197).

a. The Whole of Humanity. This statement does not apply only to the subjective experience of the individual. From the very first it is given the widest possible range (R. 1-3) and embraces all humanity. Hence δικαιοσύνη θεοῦ is not just the experience of the individual. It is supremely the universal divine happening in Christ on behalf of the whole race.

b. The Divine Action. δικαιοσύνη θεοῦ shows God at work. It is not a mere attribute of God in the static Hellenistic sense or in terms of the attributes of older Protestantism. God's δύναμις is involved. Hence it is no less effective than the action of His wrath (cf. the ὀργὴ θεοῦ in R. 1:18), cf. ἀποκαλύπτεται in 1:17, πεφανέρωται in 3:21, ἔνδειξις in 3:25 f. ("demonstration"), and cf. the emphasis on confirmation by the συνίστησιν of 3:5.

c. The Centre in the Cross. This understanding and message are centred in the cross of Christ (R. 3:25 f.; 5:9 f.; cf. 2 C. 5:18; Gl. 3:13), where the saving act

---

[48] This is rightly pointed out by O. Zänker, 399, 418. It may be noted briefly in discussion that A. Ritschl and L. Diestel bring out very well the saving power but neglect the forensic element (cf. more recently A. Schmitt, 129). Zn. identifies the δικαιοσύνη θεοῦ with Christ, but it may be questioned whether general significance should be attached to the unusual statement in 1 C. 1:30. Kühl understands the content rather too formally as the norm which objectively confronts man and which is declared by the Gospel. Lietzmann poses the problem whether we have here a gen. qual.: an attribute of God, or a gen. auct.: imputed righteousness. The most important contributions to the debate are those of Kölbing and Haering, who show a lively appreciation of the twofold character of the concept as embracing both saving action and judicial rule. Yet under the influence of Ritschl even they minimise the saving action in its relationship to the atoning death.

of ἱλαστήριον takes place (→ 218 f.). The νυνὶ δέ of R. 3:21, to be understood temporally, marks the replacing of the way of the Law (3:21 χωρὶς νόμου) by the new way of salvation. The resurrection, however, is always associated with the crucifixion. Hence the δικαιοσύνη θεοῦ is not merely a declaratory act in the world beyond. The closely linked statements have a historical centre, namely, the revealing work of God in the act of the cross. This is what makes possible the statement in 1 C. 1:30 (→ 203, n. 48): Χριστὸς ἐγενήθη δικαιοσύνη, as also ἁγιασμός and ἀπολύτρωσις. δικαιοσύνη, which is obviously basic, has here the same sense as in Gl. and R. [49] A similar personification is to be found in the Χριστὸς εἰς δικαιοσύνην as the τέλος νόμου in R. 10:4.

d. God both is and demonstrates Righteousness. The δικαιοσύνη θεοῦ makes it plain that God is righteous, that righteousness is proper to Him : R. 3:25 f.: εἰς ἔνδειξιν τῆς δικαιοσύνης αὐτοῦ — εἰς τὸ εἶναι αὐτὸν δίκαιον. This statement, however, does not imply a static quality. It is grounded in the demonstration of the ἔνδειξις of His judicial action. δικαιοσύνη is an expression of grace, but of such a kind that the justice of God is also displayed. The ἔνδειξις prevents misunderstanding of the πάρεσις and is thus given concrete form in an act of atonement. [50] Cf. the conjoining of the thought of judgment with the divine action at the cross in Gl. 3:13; 2 C. 5:21; R. 8:3. Nevertheless, the ἔνδειξις is also a declaration of the pardon which brings salvation. [51] We thus have duality, justice and grace being conjoined. Judaism had striven in vain to relate the goodness of God to His justice (→ 197). That God's clemency was greater than His strict equity was only a flickering hope. From the saving act of the cross Paul gathers assurance of faith that the justice and grace of God are here united for all time and on the deepest level. This means that the antinomian misunderstanding of laxity and feeble compromise is unconditionally excluded. Forgiveness is an act of judgment in which the justice of God is fully vindicated. It thus means redemption in sacred purity and with an uncompromising No against evil. If the nomistic Pharisee says that the commanding righteousness of God is revealed in the Law, Paul, the Pharisee who has been apprehended by Christ, goes on to say that the judicial and gracious righteousness of God is declared in the act of salvation.

e. Forensic Justification. The δικαιοσύνη θεοῦ includes justification. Righteousness is forensically ascribed to the believer. It is imparted to him as a new quality before God. The judgment of God achieves the δικαιοσύνη of believers by remission (cf. → δικαιόω, δικαίωμα, δικαίωσις and especially the antonyms κατακρίνειν, R. 8:34; διακονία τῆς κατακρίσεως, opp. διακονία τῆς δικαιοσύνης, 2 C. 3:9; cf. 11:15). Forensically does not mean "as if" he were righteous, since the sovereign sentence of God is genuinely pronounced. Nor does it mean that moral rectitude is attained. What it does mean is that the man who has δικαιοσύνη is right before God. Naturally, the forensic element is only a figure for being righteous before God, and it is not to be pressed in terms of juridical logic. We are not now in the sphere of human jurisprudence. We are dealing with the divine Judge who is also the unlimited King. Hence the symbolical aspect, as with such

---

[49] As against Joh. W. 1 K., 41, and with Schmiedel 1 K., 77.

[50] The πάρεσις cannot (Mundle, Der Glaubensbegriff des Pls., 88) refer to sins before baptism, but stands in the context of salvation history.

[51] In this respect particular note should be taken of the → ὑπόδικος ("subject to penalty") in R. 3:19.

images as καταλλαγή etc., is not to be allowed to predominate by logically pursuing the forensic mode of apprehension. The legal aspect must be transposed at once into a divine key. The *iustificatio iniusti* is against all human standards. The content bursts the forms and an act of grace replaces customary legal procedure. Because this is an incomparable judicial act, our main task is to grasp the basic theme. What is brought out by the legal concept is that God exercises grace which is not capricious but which is in accordance with His holy norms, with the covenant and with true right. The juridical form would be suspect only if the human view of law were to distort the matter, i.e., the holiness of God, as in the Pharisaic idea of a balance-sheet and rewards. The image of the judge is a tenable one because in legal life, however inadequately, imperishable divine norms are expressed. God may thus be described as Judge no less than Father or King, though all these images are drawn from the human sphere. The fact that Paul's message of justification involves a complete paradox helps to prevent any distortion by general human conceptions.

f. The Relationship to the Term → ἄφεσις, the δωρεά now imparted, and the State of Justification. Pardon can sometimes be stated in such words as ἀφιέναι (in the quotation from ψ 31:1 in R. 4:7: ἀφέθησαν αἱ ἀνομίαι) or καταλλάσσειν, καταλλαγή (R. 5:9 f., cf. 2 C. 5:18-20). Yet in general it is important to Paul not merely to speak of forgiveness but by means of δικαιοσύνη to give to forgiveness a precision grounded, enlarged and deepened in divine right. Moreover, the δικαιοσύνη gifted and imparted is more than forgiveness. It is (cf. צְדָקָה in Pl. and Jm.) the helping, saving and efficacious action of God as radical deliverance. The new point in comparison with Judaism is the conviction that δικαιοσύνη is imparted now : R. 3:24-26; 5:1, 9, 17; 8:30; 9:30; 1 C. 6:11, whereas according to the view of the Synagogue justification in terms of merit will come in the ἔσχατον but is not an event revealed in the present. For Paul δικαιοσύνη is δωρεά both imparted and received (R. 5:17: τῆς δωρεᾶς τῆς δικαιοσύνης, gen. appos.). The δικαιοσύνη granted as a gift is also referred to in R. 8:10 : τὸ πνεῦμα ζωὴ διὰ δικαιοσύνην; 9:30 : ἔθνη κατέλαβεν δικαιοσύνην; 10:6. It is because this impartation determines the whole life of faith that one can speak of a state of justification. The continually renewed positing of faith on the ground of imparted δικαιοσύνη is what is meant in Phil. 3:9 : μὴ ἔχων ἐμὴν δικαιοσύνην τὴν ἐκ νόμου, ἀλλὰ τὴν διὰ πίστεως Χριστοῦ, τὴν ἐκ θεοῦ δικαιοσύνην. The question is put : Whence does this arise ? And the answer is : Not from the Law, but from God.

On ἡ ἐκ θεοῦ δικαιοσύνη, cf. צְדָקָה מֵאִתִּי in Is. 54:17; also Bar. 5:2 : περιβαλοῦ τὴν διπλοΐδα τῆς παρὰ τοῦ θεοῦ δικαιοσύνης, and 5:9 : δικαιοσύνη τῇ παρ' αὐτοῦ.

Yet we cannot use this passage to explain the whole complex denoted by Paul's δικαιοσύνη θεοῦ [52] because it treats only of the imparted righteousness of faith and is not therefore, like R. 1:17; 3:21 ff., a solemn description or development of the whole accomplishment of salvation. If the δικαιοσύνη θεοῦ is the righteousness which God enjoys and displays in the act of salvation as well as the righteousness which He constantly imparts on this basis, this multiplicity in the use of the formula is justifiable, since it is always finally and exclusively His righteousness.

---

[52] This is correctly perceived by Haering, Δικαιοσύνη θεοῦ, 6.

The state of justification is not a ἕξις of man, but the δωρεά of righteousness consists in man's being taken up into the righteousness of God.

g. δικαιοσύνη and πίστις. It is by faith that the individual is drawn into the outworking of salvation. Though Paul does not try to localise personal justification, and though his deliberations are not decisively shaped by reflection on a fixed experience, he is not referring to a communal justification [53] but to a justifying action of God which seizes the individual. To be sure, he does not think of individuals in the individualistic sense. When the individual is justified, he becomes a member of the body of Christ as he previously belonged to Israel, the ἔθνη or humanity. Yet the gift of justification determines rather than truncates the personal task of service. It is to be supremely emphasised, however, that beyond all the stress laid on personal experience all that is said remains in the sphere of the objective divine act. This emerges clearly in the fact that in the Pauline communities believers are justified when they are baptised and receive the Spirit: 1 C. 6:11; Gl. 3:6; cf. 3:1-5. [54] On the other hand, this does not mean that justification is magically linked with the sacrament. This is refuted not merely by 1 C. 1:17 but by the whole Pauline concept of faith. Thus in R. 4:11 circumcision is for Abraham a seal τῆς δικαιοσύνης τῆς πίστεως τῆς ἐν τῇ ἀκροβυστίᾳ. δικαιοσύνη is granted prior to the reception of the sacrament. This fact in relation to the father of faith safeguards the view of baptism from sacramental magic (→ δικαιόω, 217, n. 22).

The relation of the subjective attitude to the objective act of salvation demands special treatment. According to R. 10:3 : ἀγνοοῦντες θεοῦ δικαιοσύνην καὶ τὴν ἰδίαν ζητοῦντες στῆσαι, τῇ δικαιοσύνῃ τοῦ θεοῦ οὐχ ὑπετάγησαν, the revelation of pardoning δικαιοσύνη is the ruling power of God to which one must submit. Thus it cannot be regarded only as imparted righteousness in terms of Phil. 3:9. It signifies a divine action which issues a direct summons, which authoritatively binds, which at once draws the believing subject into the act of salvation, which sets him in the power of the righteousness of God. Cf. R. 3:21: δικαιοσύνη θεοῦ διὰ πίστεως Χριστοῦ εἰς πάντας τοὺς πιστεύοντας. [55] δικαιοσύνη is for all who believe. The assertion of faith as a condition is always closely linked with the most objective declarations concerning the δικαιοσύνη θεοῦ: R. 1:17; 3:22-28; 4; 5:1. The achievement and declaration of salvation are never separated from the appropriation of salvation, because the revealing action in question always stands in the I-Thou relationship. The new thing is from the very first and continually related to faith alone. In R. 3:21 διὰ πίστεως is used adverbially to define δικαιοσύνη θεοῦ. In R. 3:26 f., too, this organic connexion between the objective and the subjective is present. The most objective thing that can be said, namely, ἱλαστήριον, is followed at once by διὰ πίστεως, though again not without ἐν τῷ αἵματι, which belongs to ἱλαστήριον rather than πίστεως. Cf. διὰ πίστεως Χριστοῦ and ἐπὶ τῇ πίστει in Phil. 3:9.

The divine objectivity of salvation is thus the objectivity of a saving relationship. But the same is also to be said of faith. Whereas in Philo πίστις is a spiritual σχέσις which may be considered and described in isolation, for Paul it is not an

[53] A. Ritschl, Rechtf. u. Versöhnung, III (1888), 545 f.
[54] Mundle (Der Glaubensbegriff d. Pls., 84 ff., 135 ff.) goes far beyond Paul in his equation of justification with implanting into the sacramental process.
[55] In spite of Zn. R., 176, the Alex. text is to be preferred, cf. Ltzm. R., 46.

isolated phenomenon, because it is referred to the act of salvation. What is accounted for δικαιοσύνη is not faith as a psychic force, or as the work of an Olympian reason or as religious virtue (Philo), but faith with a content of salvation which alone does justice to God, faith as the only way to the disclosure of the one revealed object of faith. The various prepositions used to link δικαιοσύνη and πίστις show even more clearly that it is not a meritorious work. It is striking that we never find δικαιοσύνη διὰ τὴν πίστιν. [56] δικαιοσύνη τῆς πίστεως occurs in R. 4:11; δικαιοσύνη πίστεως in R. 4:13, δικαιοσύνη ἡ ἐκ πίστεως in R. 9:30, the personified [57] ἡ ἐκ πίστεως δικαιοσύνη in R. 10:6, also ἡ (sc. δικαιοσύνη) διὰ πίστεως Χριστοῦ and ἡ ἐκ θεοῦ δικαιοσύνη ἐπὶ τῇ πίστει in Phil. 3:9. The use of λογίζεσθαι (→ 201) confirms these findings. In Gl. 3:6; R. 4:3, 5 f., 9, 11, 22 λογίζεσθαι (חשׁב) means "to take into account," "to reckon," and the term itself might leave the wrong impression of merit. But in fact the doctrine of merit is overthrown by its use in this pointed antithesis. Since πιστεύειν is a divine gift and not a meritorious ἔργον, the ἐλογίσθη brings out the pure grace of the divine giving. What is reckoned is what is established by sovereign grace. Thus the λογίζεσθαι acknowledges that thanks to God there is a full achievement of right in faith.

h. δικαιοσύνη as the Object of Hope. The present salvation carries with it a future salvation. For justification is a grace which implies the dawn of the new aeon and thus bridges time. Hence in the light of the νυνὶ δέ, which has the content of fulfilment, all that happens prior to the end has an interim character. This is the great inversion entailed in justifying faith. In Judaism justification is uncertain and must wait until the day of judgment. Here it is already present and active. It is declared in the light of history and grasped by faith as a present reality. But since the promise of δικαιοσύνη transcends time, and points to the consummation, it gives rise to hope, and at this vital point faith in justification overcomes the hesitation of Jewish eschatology. The justified, who have grasped the Now of forgiveness at the cross, can look forward with confidence to the final sentence. This is not a quietistic dogma. It is a dynamic hope which impels to resolute action. δικαιοσύνη is presented as an object of hope in Gl. 5:5 : ἐλπίδα δικαιοσύνης ἀπεκδεχόμεθα. The context shows that δικαιοσύνη and deliverance are identical in the last judgment. δικαιοσύνης is a gen. appos., and thus means final acquittal. [58] Account should also be taken of the many statements in which δικαιόω is used in the fut.: Gl. 2:16; R. 3:20, 30; 2:13 (though cf. the reservations → δικαιόω, 217). Similarly, in R. 5:19 : δίκαιοι κατασταθήσονται and R. 8:33 : θεὸς ὁ δικαιῶν, there is reference to the last judgment. Again, in R. 10:4-10 (cf. R. 5:17: ἐν ζωῇ βασιλεύσουσιν) what is meant is undoubtedly the imputed δικαιοσύνη which faith receives, but σωθήσῃ in v. 9 and σωτηρία in v. 10, like → ζωή, are eschatological terms which envisage final acquittal for steadfast faith (cf. ζήσεται in v. 5). The linking of δικαιοσύνη and σωτηρία unifies present and future which are distinct. [59] It is not that universal judgment is anticipated in

---

[56] Cf. W. Michaelis, *Rechtfertigung aus Glauben bei Pls.* (1927), 136.
[57] Cf. R. Bultmann, *Der Stil der paulin. Predigt* (1910), 87 f.
[58] Cf. Mk. 16, Freer Logion, 22-24 : τῆς δικαιοσύνης δόξαν, the glory which is to be inherited and which consists in δικαιοσύνη.
[59] Cf. Haering, Δικαιοσύνη θεοῦ, 61.

justification. [60] Rather, this is something both present and future, as are also
ἀπολύτρωσις and υἱοθεσία in Paul. The future form expresses the fact that the
gift is not a passive state but a movement to the τέλος. Like everything given to
us in Christ, this gift stands in the tension of hope.

Paul did not regard the final judgment by works as contradicting justification
by faith. It is still a solid and self-evident part of his preaching. The lasting
significance of judgment brings out the value of the belief in justification as a
totality which embraces present and future. We do not have here a mere relic of
the Jewish view. [61] This is shown beyond any possible doubt by the fact that the
concept of judgment is not an inorganic fossil in Paul, but is given a far greater
depth than in Judaism. [62] The truth is that Paul's concept of the last judgment
emphasises the transcendent divine norm and therefore the radical summons to
fear God. We have seen that the indispensable statement that God is Judge is
the inviolable presupposition of the message of justification. It is true that Paul
never discusses the relation between justification and the last judgment. Yet the
background of judgment remains, and the new assurance is characterised as a
tireless pursuit of the goal, and kept from false confidence, by the seriousness of
judgment. This does not mean that assurance of salvation is either shaken or called
in question. The point is that the thought of judgment serves as a powerful motive
to obedience. The doctrine of justification demands encounter with the unsparing
seriousness of God expressed at the cross. It is only on account of the absolute
norms attested by the last judgment that the understanding of the cross can maintain its validity intact, for only an unceasing acknowledgment of the principle of
final judgment can preserve this understanding from the antinomian perversion
which argues that justification dispenses from any need to do the will of God.
Yet Paul gives impelling motives rather than logical considerations. He has broken
radically with the eschatological omniscience of Judaism. The view of Luther, [63]
that in the act of justification God begins the total renewal of man which He
knows will certainly be brought to completion, is certainly contained in R. 8:30,
but not as an account which satisfies and conforms to reason, since the saving
work of God is always a creative act and therefore a miracle.

i. Justification and Mysticism. Justification and the πνεῦμα are closely linked
in 1 C. 6:11; R. 10:8 f. (πιστεύσῃς ἐν τῇ καρδίᾳ σου); Gl. 5:5. In Gl. 3:2, 5 very
similar expressions are used for the reception of the Spirit as for justification by
faith in R. 3:28. It is also evident that justifying faith and union with Christ in
the sense of identification with His destiny ("mysticism") are closely related:
Gl. 2:16-21 (2:17: δικαιωθῆναι ἐν Χριστῷ); 3:26-29. Even the unusual phrase in
2 C. 5:21: ἵνα ἡμεῖς γενώμεθα δικαιοσύνη θεοῦ ἐν αὐτῷ, shows the close connexion. Because Christ representatively became ἁμαρτία for us, we can become
δικαιοσύνη ἐν αὐτῷ. Here the idea of imputation is transformed into one of being
by the copula γενώμεθα. [64] We are so set in His righteousness and taken up into

---

[60] Cf. P. Kölbing, 8 ff., also Haering, op. cit., 58 f.
[61] The antinomy has often been described as illogical and understood as a legacy of
Judaism, cf. Braun, 24 f.
[62] Cf. Braun, 48, 76, 94.
[63] WA, II, 108, 3 ff., cf. Holl, Ges. Aufs. zur KG, I, "Luther" 2, 3 (1923), 123 ff. Cf. also
H. J. Holtzmann, Lehrbuch der nt.lichen Theol.2, II (1911), 226 ff.; Braun, 31.
[64] Wnd. 2 C., 199 expounds this in terms of mystical perfectionism.

it that we become the righteousness of God in the sense of Jer. 23:6; 33:16 (יְהוָה צִדְקֵנוּ; LXX 40:16 אAQ : κύριος δικαιοσύνη ἡμῶν). This does not mean, of course, that δικαιοσύνη is understood as an attribute in isolation from God. The righteousness is still God's. But the identification is expressed as strongly as possible. In Phil. 3:7-11, too, legal and "mystical" themes are linked. Indeed, throughout Romans it is impossible to separate the state of justification from being in Christ. Now the concepts of justification and faith are not mystical. The basic idea of distance is the inescapable presupposition. We should thus have to assume a theological duality in Paul if we were to find in him the mysticism which unites God and man. The doctrine of justification, however, is a safeguard against any such misunderstanding. The "mystical" terms in Paul are to be taken figuratively, and should not be pressed any more than the legal into a logical scheme which would imply real mysticism. The justification formula is one expression among others. But the linking of legal and mystical images shows that it is only pneumatology which fulfils the work of justification. [65]

k. δικαιοσύνη as the Power of the New Life. Neither in its commencement nor its continuation is the justifying action of God quietistic; it is always teleological. It leads to the royal dominion (βασιλεύειν) of grace : R. 5:12-21, which moves forward victoriously to eternal life. But this is a reign of righteousness : 5:21: ἵνα ἡ χάρις βασιλεύσῃ διὰ δικαιοσύνης εἰς ζωὴν αἰώνιον. Righteousness, then, is not merely found in the beginning; it sustains the whole course. The believer is drawn by it into the movement of the rule of God. Hence the statements concerning justification should not be separated from the lifegiving dominion of Christ (5:21: διὰ Ἰησοῦ Χριστοῦ), from the vivifying of the community. δικαιοσύνη and life are interwoven : R. 5:17, 21. The goal of the living movement initiated by the gift of δικαιοσύνη is ζωὴ αἰώνιος, whereas sin is the movement of death. R. 8:10 : τὸ πνεῦμα ζωὴ διὰ δικαιοσύνην, does not refer to righteousness of life, but to the state of given δικαιοσύνη, "on account of justification." Here we have a pneumatological basis, for the Spirit is for Paul the power of the new life.

In no case should one speak of a closed process of salvation in Paul. [66] Because of justification the new state of service is the distinctive relationship to δικαιοσύνη, and the parallelism with the beginning of justification is consistently drawn (the cross and the resurrection always work together, and faith in δικαιοσύνη is obedience and leads to obedience). According to R. 6:16 there is a ὑπακοὴ εἰς δικαιοσύνην, cf. v. 18 : ἐδουλώθητε τῇ δικαιοσύνῃ. The members become (6:13) ὅπλα δικαιοσύνης, or δοῦλα τῇ δικαιοσύνῃ εἰς ἁγιασμόν (6:19), whereas previously (v. 20) they were ἐλεύθεροι τῇ δικαιοσύνῃ. Thus, without any sense of difficulty or contradiction, the thought of pardoning and forensic righteousness passes over into that of righteousness as the living power which overcomes sin. The righteousness which is given commits the believer to the living power of δικαιοσύνη. It is again δικαιοσύνη which leads to the state of ἁγιασμός. This righteousness as the power which engages the whole life is what overcomes ἀδικία and ἁμαρτία (6:13, 17, 18, 20). In Paul, therefore, δικαιοσύνη can denote both the righteousness which acquits and the living power which breaks the bondage

---

[65] In opposition to the view of O. Pfleiderer, Wrede and A. Schweitzer (*Die Mystik des Ap. Pls.*, 201 ff.) that the doctrine of justification is a subsidiary crater in the main crater of the doctrine of redemption by being in Christ : W. Grundmann, ZNW, 32 (1933), 52 ff.
[66] Windisch in RGG², II, 1204.

of sin. The thought of righteousness of life cannot be separated from it. Righteousness is never equated merely with what is found at the beginning of the Christian life. Our concern is not just with a theory of mission. On the other hand, when used along these lines δικαιοσύνη is not a state of possession. It is a binding, objective power and norm of God. Nevertheless, in analogy with what was said under f., it becomes right action (R. 6:16 : εἰς δικαιοσύνην). Thus in 2 C. 6:7 the ὅπλα τῆς δικαιοσύνης are weapons which are provided by the divine righteousness, subj. gen. [67] In 2 C. 6:14 it is δικαιοσύνη as the opposite of ἀνομία which gives to the Christian life its distinctive character, and in R. 14:17 (the βασιλεία is δικαιοσύνη, εἰρήνη, χαρά) the ethical side is emphasised in the sense of R. 6. In 2 C. 9:9 f., where we twice have δικαιοσύνη in a quotation from the OT (ψ 111:9; Hos. 10:12), the context, which deals with the collection, might well suggest the sense of almsgiving. It is more likely, however, that after the earlier reference to "every good work," what is meant is right conduct worked out in acts of love. In Phil. 1:11 believers are to be πεπληρωμένοι καρπὸν δικαιοσύνης. Whether we take this as gen. appos. : fruit which consists in righteousness, gen. orig. : fruit brought forth by righteousness, or gen. qual. : fruit of righteousness, there can be no doubt that the sense is similar to that of R. 6. If according to Eph. 5:9 the fruit of light consists in δικαιοσύνη, along with ἀγαθωσύνη and ἀλήθεια, this denotes right conduct, yet not in terms of a self-reliant moralism, but in subordination to the divine gift as fruit (cf. Phil. 1:11). In Eph. 6:14 (cf. 5:9): ἐνδυσάμενοι τὴν θώρακα δικαιοσύνης, with truth (from Is. 59:17), there is reference, not so much to the righteousness of faith, but to δικαιοσύνη as a normative living force. According to 2 Tm. 3:16 Scripture serves πρὸς παιδείαν τὴν ἐν δικαιοσύνῃ (cf. Bar. 4:13). The reference here is to right conduct or a godly walk. In 2 Tm. 4:8 : ὁ τῆς δικαιοσύνης στέφανος, the context shows us that what is in view is the crowning of the state of righteousness. "Perfect justification in the last judgment" is a less likely rendering (cf. δίκαιος κριτής). In any case the whole use of δικαιοσύνη in Paul cannot be separated from the conviction that the justifying sentence leads to the righteous state of the new life. Justification mediates subjection to the living power of the creative divine righteousness.

1. The Relation of δικαιοσύνη to ἀρετή in Pauline Writings. The Hellenistic doctrine of virtue is never found. Nowhere in the statements concerning δικαιοσύνη does the Greek ἀρετή occur. Yet one might speak of an incursion of the element of truth in the Hellenistic view into Christianity when we come to the Pastorals. In the Pastorals δικαιοσύνη receives special attention because of the stress on *ethos* as opposed to *gnosis*. In an almost liturgical expression (cf. Lk. 1:75), Eph. 4:24 characterises the Christian state as one of uprightness and piety : the new man is κτισθεὶς ἐν δικαιοσύνῃ καὶ ὁσιότητι τῆς ἀληθείας. But 1 Tm. 6:11 and 2 Tm. 2:22 most remind us of the Greek lists of virtues. In both cases δικαιοσύνη signifies right conduct and is listed with other Christian exercises like εὐσέβεια, πίστις, ἀγάπη, εἰρήνη, ὑπομονή, πραϋπαθία. There is here an influence of the catalogue of virtues. On the other hand, πίστις and ἀγάπη show that the content is different from that of the catenae found in Philo etc.

---

[67] There is no analogy in Pl. for the suggestion of Bchm. 2 K., *ad loc.* : "weapons championing a righteous cause."

† δικαιόω.

A. δικαιόω in Greek and Hellenistic Writings (including Josephus and Philo).

δικαιόω derives from δίκαιος, -ον, and means "to make righteous," or neut. "to establish as right," "to validate" (opp. ἀκυροῦν, "to invalidate," etc.).

1. Pindar, who often coins words, once uses δικαιοῦν in the sense of sovereign validation. The famous Fr., 16, 9 is found in Plato Gorg., 484b : νόμος ὁ πάντων βασιλεὺς | θνατῶν τε καὶ ἀθανάτων | ἄγει δικαιῶν τὸ βιαιότατον | ὑπερτάτᾳ χειρί = "the νόμος makes a δίκαιον, and declares to be right, what would otherwise be supremely arbitrary." [1] According to Plato's exposition, [2] there is thus carried through τὸ τῆς φύσεως δίκαιον. In accordance with nature the law thus gives the character of right to even the most arbitrary act. Natural law culminates in the dominion of the strong. [3] It is in keeping with this nuance in Pindar that the term is often used for divine rule and order in the law : Philo Spec. Leg., I, 67, 109, 140; II, 72, 113; III, 172, 180 etc.; and once Joseph. : Ant., 4, 278. This gives rise to the use of τὸ δικαιωθέν for "what is prescribed": Dion. Hal. Ant. Rom., X, 1, 2; cf. P. Tebt., II, 444 : τὰ διὰ τῆς συνγραφῆς δεδικαιωμένα κεφάλαια, "established amounts."

2. From the legal sphere the word passes into more general use in the sense of "to regard as fair or right," i.e., to formulate for oneself as δίκαιον (cf. ἀξιοῦν, δοκιμοῦν). This is the most common usage : Soph. Oed. Tyr., 6, 575, 640; Oed. Col., 1350, 1642; Hdt., I, 89; Thuc., IV, 122, 5. This is true of Joseph. and Philo. Jos. Ant., 9, 187; 12, 124; cf. Ant., 19, 305. Philo Abr., 142, 171; Migr. Abr., 73; Vit. Mos., I, 44 etc. Joseph., who uses the word ten times, never deviates from Gk. usage. In him the material par. to Paul's δικαιόω is ἀγαπῆσαι τινά τινος. [4] Philo can adduce the δεδικαίωται of Gn. 38:26 (e.g., Mut. Nom., 136), but for the most part he, too, has only this general use. [5] He can thus use it in relation to personal decision in the conduct of life, Ebr., 51; Deus Imm., 9, 159. From the sense "to regard as fair and right," there develops the narrower meaning "to desire" : Thuc., V, 105, 1; "to demand" : Philo Mut. Nom., 19; "to will" : Jos. Ant., 19, 178. Closer to the legal origins are "to judge" (Plut. De Fortuna, 2 [II, 97 f.]; "to grant" : Dio C., 48, 46, 4; 54, 24, 6); "to agree" (Hdt., II, 172); "to permit" (Hdt., III, 118).

3. When the original legal meaning is applied personally, there arises the widespread usage : "to establish τὸ δίκαιον for someone," "to treat someone rightly," "to secure justice for someone." This can also take a negative turn, i.e., "to judge," "to punish" (cf. κακοῦν, "to do wrong," δολοῦν, "to outwit," ζηλοῦν etc.). a. In the general sense, without personal obj., we have "to pronounce sentence" in Thuc., II, 71, 4. With obj., P. Oxy., III, 653. b. "To condemn, to punish someone," Hdt., I, 100; V, 92, 2. Dio C., act.: 38, 11, 3; 52, 24, 4; 54, 19, 2; pass.: 37, 41, 2; 41, 28, 4; 49, 12, 5. c. Esp. of the death sentence (euphemistically): Dio C., 54, 15, 4; 56, 4, 5; 71, 28, 3. Pass.: 37, 12, 2; 43, 24, 4; 55, 14, 3. Of the execution of the death sentence : Plut. Cato Maior, 21 (I, 349a); Jos. Ant., 17, 206; 18, 178; Philo Ebr., 95; Ael. Var. Hist., 5, 18 (with θανάτῳ). Closest

---

δ ι κ α ι ό ω. Bibl. → δικαιοσύνη, 192 n. Cf. also E. Fraenkel, *Griech. Denominativa* (1906), 68, 69, 73, 124.

[1] U. v. Wilamowitz, *Platon,* II (1920), 93, 99, instead of δικαιῶν τὸ βιαιότατον, reads βιαιῶν τὸ δικαιότατον = "doing violence to absolute righteousness," cf. J. Geffcken, *Studien zu Plat. Gorg., Herm.,* 65 (1930), 19. On the other hand A. Busse, *Herm.,* 66 (1931), 126 ff. argues strongly for the older reading.

[2] Cf. Leg., III, 690c; IV, 715a.

[3] Cf. A. Busse, 127 f.

[4] Cf. A. Schlatter, *Wie sprach Josephus von Gott?* (1910), 63.

[5] Epictet. never has δικαιόω.

to the Pauline usage is d. the sense of "to represent the cause of someone," "to secure him justice": Polyb., III, 31, 9. The corresponding pass. usage is found in Aristot. Eth. Nic., V, 10, p. 1136a, 18 ff.: δικαιοῦσθαι "to be treated justly," opp. ἀδικεῖσθαι. Outside the LXX and the NT, however, it is never found in this sense with a pers. obj.: *aliquem iustum reddere.*

4. Particular note should be taken of the mystical use. Corp. Herm., XIII, 9 : χωρὶς γὰρ κρίσεως ἰδὲ πῶς τὴν ἀδικίαν ἐξήλασεν. ἐδικαιώθημεν, ὦ τέκνον, ἀδικίας ἀπούσης. [6] The formula, here perhaps consciously given a Christian reference, definitely means : "we have become sinless." δικαιοσύνη is made over to the mystic as ἀδικία is driven out by the destruction of all evil desires deriving from the body (→ δικαιοσύνη, 193). But the idea of being declared righteous in judgment is rejected, and there is even perhaps a polemic against the Judaeo-Christian concept of δικαιωθῆναι. It may even be that the Egyptian idea of justification by the judgment of the dead is here given a mystical application. [7] According to this conception, the dead are set by Osiris on the scales, are weighed, and are then pronounced righteous because their good works are predominant (though knowledge also counts). Stains are removed by rites of expiation and magic. [8]

B. δικαιόω in the LXX, Apocrypha, Pseudepigrapha and the Synagogue.

In the LXX δικαιοῦν (corresponding to צדק) is a forensic term. Yet it does not have a predominant negative connotation ("to condemn") as in Gk., but is constantly used in the positive sense of "to pronounce righteous," "to justify," "to vindicate." It is almost always linked with the pers. obj., which is true only of the negative sense in secular usage (→ 211). The forensic element is even stronger in the LXX than the Mas. Thus in Is. 45:25 the Mas. בַּיהוָה יִצְדְּקוּ, means that they find righteousness with Yahweh, whereas the LXX ἀπὸ κυρίου δικαιωθήσονται (א*-σεται) means that they are declared righteous by Him. The following uses of δικαιοῦν in the LXX are to be noted.

1. Act. a. For צדק hiph : "to declare someone righteous," "to acquit someone," "to secure justice for him." According to the legal custom of Israel, this δικαιοῦν may not apply for the ἀσεβής : Ex. 23:7; Is. 5:23; Sir. 10:29; 42:2. Only the δίκαιος may be declared righteous : Dt. 25:1 AF; 3 Βασ. 8:32 (δικαιῶσαι δίκαιον), cf. materially Prv. 17:15, and from the religious standpoint ψ 7:9. In the sense of "to help to right" cf. 2 Βασ. 15:4; ψ 81:3; Is. 50:8 (against the opponent at law). Cf. 4 Esr. 4:18 : *aliquem justificare* (opp. *condemnare*), of judicial acquittal. In Sir. 13:22 ἐδικαίωσαν αὐτόν has no legal connotation but simply means "to justify the rich in everyday life" (cf. f. → 213). b. For צדק pi : "to prove to be innocent or righteous." Jer. 3:11: ἐδικαίωσεν τὴν ψυχὴν αὐτοῦ Ἰσραὴλ ἀπὸ τῆς ἀσυνθέτου Ἰούδα (צִדְּקָה נַפְשָׁהּ מִן), "it has shown itself more righteous than." Ez. 16:51 f.: ἐδικαίωσας τὰς ἀδελφάς σου (וַתְּצַדְּקִי אֶת־אֲחוֹתַיִךְ), "thou hast justified thy sisters." c. For רִיב: "to champion someone's cause, to secure justice for him, before the judgment." With acc. of pers.: Is. 1:17 δικαιώσατε χήραν Bab א ΑΓ

---

[6] Reitzenstein Poim., 343; Scott, I, 244. Cf. Reitzenstein Hell. Myst., 258 ff.; C. F. G. Heinrici, *Die Hermes-Mystik u. d. NT* (1918), 37.

[7] Reitzenstein, Hell. Myst., 258 also draws attention to the Persian judgment of the dead and the rather different Mandaean views.

[8] The Egypt. equivalent of δικαιοῦσθαι (cf. J. H. Breasted — H. Ranke, *Gesch. Ägyptens* [1910], 161) is m3ᶜ ḥrw, i.e., "the voice of someone is right," "his statement is found to be right (at law)," "he is vindicated, he triumphs." m3ᶜ as a verb means "to be or to make right," and as an adj. "right, true, genuine, righteous, truthful." Cf. A. Erman-H. Grapow, *Wörterb. d. ägypt. Sprache* (1926/31), II, 12 f., 22, 15; III, 324. ḥrw is "voice," "noise." The idea is that in the judgment of the dead the dead must answer 42 questions relating to his moral conduct in life. The weighing of the heart on the scales of the dead will then show whether he is a "true voice." If so, he is vindicated or triumphant in the judgment of the dead and will thus pass to eternal felicity.

(al : χήρᾳ); Mi. 7:9 : ἕως τοῦ (Α : οὖ) δικαιῶσαι αὐτὸν τὴν δίκην μου, "until he execute judgment for me." d. Occasionally for זכה "to make pure" : ψ 72:13 : ἐδικαίωσα (so also Θ) τὴν καρδίαν μου (זְכִּיתִי) (pass. → 214). זכה pi is often used by the Rabbis for the divine acquittal : 1 Pesikt. r., 40 (169a) (מְזַכֶּה); 2. bErub., 19a (וְיִכַּיתָ); 3. Midr. Ps. 143 § 1 (266b) (לְזַכּוֹת); 4. Tg. Ps. 51:6 (דְּתִזְכֵּי). In these passages⁹ what is meant is 1. acquittal on the Day of Atonement. The man who receives this is a new creature. There is also meant 2. the justification which the dying righteous receives if he is destined for the Gan Eden. A third possibility is justification at the last judgment on the basis of a demonstrable predominance of good works (→ δικαιοσύνη, 197). The multiplicity of related ideas only enhances the uncertainty of the belief in justification. Precedence attaches, of course, to the view that there will be justification only for the righteous on the basis of demonstrable works. ¹⁰ e. Equally rare in the LXX is the use of δικάζω for שפט, "to bring someone to judgment," "to judge," 1 Βασ. 12:7 Α : δικαιώσω ὑμᾶς ἐνώπιον κυρίου (Β δικάσω, אֶשָּׁפְטָה; Εz. 44:24 : τὰ δικαιώματά μου δικαιώσουσιν (בְּמִשְׁפָּטַי וְשֹׁפְטֵהוּ),of the decision of legal statutes. f. In the Ps. Sol. the act. is never related to man in the sense of "to justify someone," "to declare him righteous"; the δικαιοῦν which man pronounces is plainly referred to God. It is always the righteous who vindicates the sentence, judgments and name of God, accepting and acknowledging it to be righteous : 2:16 : ἐγὼ δικαιώσω σε, 3:3, of the righteous : δικαιώσει (Ryle, James read δικαιοῦσιν) τὰ κρίματα τοῦ κυρίου; 3:5; 4:9; 8:7, 27. Cf. 4 Esr. 10:16 : justificare terminum dei, "to accept as righteous the sentence of God" ; also Lk. 7:29 (→ 214). This is in accord with the favourite usage of the Rabbis. bBer., 19a : the sufferer recognises that God's judgment is just (מצדיק); S. Dt., 307 on 32:4 (מְצַדִּיק); jSota, 22c, 41 (צִידֵק) S. Lv. on 10:3 : צָדַק אֶת הַדִּין : "to acknowledge the divine judgment to be righteous."

2. Pass. a. Aor., also fut., for צדק kal. "God is vindicated, is present in righteousness" ψ 50:6 : ὅπως δικαιωθῇς ἐν τοῖς λόγοις σου; Is. 42:21: ἵνα δικαιωθῇ (Σ : ἵνα δικαιώσῃ αὐτόν); Ps. Sol. 8:27: ἐδικαιώθη ἐν τοῖς κρίμασιν αὐτοῦ; 9:3 : ἵνα δικαιωθῇς ἐν τῇ δικαιοσύνῃ σου; Sir. 18:2 : κύριος μόνος δικαιωθήσεται. Cf. O. Sol. 31:5 of Christ : "His appearance was found to be righteous." Of the vindication or right conduct of man (esp. the chosen people) in relation to Yahweh : Is. 43:9 : δικαιωθήτωσαν; v. 26 : ἵνα δικαιωθῇς. Related is the usage in ψ 142:2 : ὅτι οὐ δικαιωθήσεται ἐνώπιόν σου πᾶς ζῶν, where the LXX ("no one can be pronounced righteous [justificabitur] before God's judgment") clearly sharpens the Mas. (לֹא־יִצְדַּק, "nothing living is righteous in thy sight"), so that there is asserted not merely universal sinfulness but the impossibility of justification. Gl. 2:16; R. 3:20 (Pl. always adds : ἐξ ἔργων νόμου) show that this passage had a great influence on the Pauline understanding of justification. Sir., who sets the individual over against the divine judgment, and understands δικαιωθῆναι as forgiveness of sin, usually gives a negative formulation : 23:11: οὐ δικαιωθήσεται (if he has sworn falsely); 34:5: ἀγαπῶν χρυσίον οὐ δικαιωθήσεται (for נקה niph); 9:12 : ἕως ᾅδου οὐ μὴ δικαιωθῶσιν; 1:22 : οὐ δυνήσεται θυμὸς ἄδικος δικαιωθῆναι; 18:22 Β : μὴ μείνῃς ἕως θανάτου δικαιωθῆναι. The μὴ δικαιωθείς is always the one who is laden with sin and who falls victim to divine punishment. Cf. 4 Esr. 12:6 Lat.: si justificatus sum apud te prae multis. ¹¹ The same usage is often found in Job Hex. (always for צדק kal): 9:15 Θ : ὅστις εἰ δικαιωθήσομαι, οὐκ ἀποκριθήσεταί μοι; 10:15 'Α : δικαιωθεὶς οὐκ ἀρῶ κεφαλήν (LXX in both cases ἐὰν ᾦ δίκαιος); 15:14 'Εβρ.: πῶς δικαιωθήσεται γέννημα γυναικός;

---

9 Cf. Str.-B., III, 134 f.; I, 640 f. Cf. also III, 134; Schl. Mt., 375.
10 Cf. Str.-B., III, 134, 186 ff.
11 The pres. in Tob. 6:12 א: σοὶ δικαιοῦται κληρονομῆσαι, refers to civil δίκαιον (cf. 12:4): "Thou wilt be given the right to inherit." Cf. 6:13 א. δεδικαίωταί σοι λαβεῖν αὐτήν, "thou art given the right to take a wife."

ʼΑΘ : καὶ ὅτι δικαιωθήσεται (LXX : ὡς ἐσόμενος δίκαιος); 22:3 Σ : μὴ χρῄζει ἱκανός, ἵνα δικαιωθῇς; 40:3 (Mas. 8) Σ : ἄδικον ποιήσεις με, ἵνα δικαιωθῇς (LXX : ἵνα ἀναφανῇς δίκαιος). b. δικαιωθῆναι as a trans. of צדק pi : Job 33:32 : θέλω δικαιωθῆναί σε (צַדְּקֶךָ) "I will vindicate thee." c. δεδικαιῶσθαι for צדק kal : Gn. 38:26 : δεδικαίωται Θαμάρ ἢ ἐγώ (צָדְקָה מִמֶּנִּי) "she is in the right against me" ψ 18:9 : τὰ κρίματα κυρίου δεδικαιωμένα (צָדְקוּ) "they are righteous" : Ez. 21:13 (Mas. 21:18) : ὅτι δεδικαίωται for pu בְּחַן (the text is corrupt); Prot. Ev. Jk. 5:1 : κατέβη ἐκ ναοῦ κυρίου δεδικαιωμένος, "justified" (after the sacrifice). d. For זכה kal : "to be pure in the legal sense." Mi. 6:11 : εἰ δικαιωθήσεται ἐν ζυγῷ ἄνομος (הַאֶזְכֶּה), cf. ἀπό in the sense of "to be free from" in Sir. 26:29 : οὐ δικαιωθήσεται κάπηλος ἀπὸ ἁμαρτίας; Test. S. 6:1 : ὅπως δικαιωθῶ ἀπὸ τῆς ἁμαρτίας ὑμῶν, "to be innocent of something."

3. Pass. in the intrans. sense : δικαιωθῆναι as a transl. of צדק hitp. : Gn. 44:16 : Judah asks : τί δικαιωθῶμεν (וּמַה־נִּצְטַדָּק) : "How shall we justify ourselves ?" Cf. the pres. use of Sir. 7:5 : μὴ δικαιοῦ ἔναντι κυρίου, "do not set up thyself as righteous"; cf. also the act. in Lk. 16:15 (→ 215).

C. δικαιόω in the NT.

In the NT it is seldom that one cannot detect the legal connexion. δικαιοῦν is never used in the sense of "to regard as fair and right," as in Gk. generally. The LXX, with its legal emphasis, has obviously had the greatest influence on NT usage.

1. "To exercise righteousness." We may first mention the rather unusual application in Rev. 22:11 : καὶ ὁ δίκαιος δικαιωθήτω ἔτι, [12] "the righteous shall continue to exercise righteousness" (opp. ἀδικεῖν).

2. "To vindicate God." The familiar usage of the Ps. Sol. (→ 213), which treats God as the One who is vindicated, is found in Mt., Lk. and the Pauline writings. Act. : Lk. 7:29 : πᾶς ὁ λαὸς καὶ οἱ τελῶναι ἐδικαίωσαν τὸν θεόν, "they justified God by accepting baptism." Pass. : Mt. 11:19 : ἐδικαιώθη ἡ σοφία ἀπὸ τῶν ἔργων αὐτῆς, cf. Lk. 7:35. [13] The ἐδικαιώθη in both these passages should be rendered "demonstrated or acknowledged to be righteous." [14] Cf. also R. 3:4 : ὅπως ἄν

---

[12] Acc. to 38. 79. 2020. vg^cl ep Lugd in Eus. Hist. Eccl., V, 1, 58. Cyprian Testimonia, III, 23 (CSEL, 3, 1, p. 140): justiora faciat. In any case the δικαιωθήτω here simply follows the ἁγιασθήτω. Nestle has : δικαιοσύνην ποιησάτω ἔτι.

[13] τέκνων instead of ἔργων in B²CDEF sy^s c is based on Lk. 7:35, where it occurs in all MSS but ℵ. It is doubtful whether we should follow the suggestion of P. de Lagarde, "Agathangelos," AGG, 35 (1888), 128 that an Aram original עבדיהא might be understood as עֲבְדִיהָא "their servants" or עֲבְדיָהָא "their works" (or עבדיא : עֲבְדַיָא, "servants," עֲבְדַיָא, "works"), since Lk. could hardly have used τέκνα for "servants." If there is any truth in the hypothesis of Schl. Mt., 374 f. that we have to take into account here the different meanings of δικαιοῦσθαι (Hellenistically, "to condemn"), so that the meaning in Lk. is that wisdom is condemned by its children, this would have to be pre-Lucan, since Lk. himself uses the term only in the positive sense. ἀπό with ἔργων means "on account of," "for the sake of," and with τέκνων it has the force of ὑπό (cf. Mt. 16:21; Jm. 1:13). Hence there is no need of the suggestion of M. Dibelius, Joh. d. Täufer (1911), 19, that ἀπό means "far from," or of J. Wellhausen, Das Ev. Mt. (1904), 55, that it is a rendering of the Aram. min q'dâm (Heb. מִפְּנֵי), "before," "over against." The ἔργα are not merely ascetic manifestations but the whole life of the messengers.

[14] Cf. Str.-B., I, 604. Supra (→ 213) in Ps. Sol. and Rabb. Euthymius, ad loc. (MPG, 129, 357c) already expounds δικαία καὶ ἀνέγκλητος ἐλογίσθη. For a similar usage in Joseph., cf. Schl. Mt., 375 f.

δικαιωθῆς (ψ 50:4), which refers to God being justified. Here, of course, Paul follows the Psalm and uses the term in a far more definitely legal sense than in Mt. 11:19 and par., God being represented as one of the parties in a dispute. A similar usage is to be found in the ἐδικαιώθη ἐν πνεύματι of the hymn to Christ in 1 Tm. 3:16, for which "redeemed" is hardly adequate. The idea is that Christ was justified in the sphere of the spirit, i.e., that His claim to be Christ was demonstrated and validated by the resurrection (in contrast to the ἐφανερώθη ἐν σαρκί). Cf. O. Sol. 31:5 (→ 213).

3. "To justify oneself," "to represent oneself as righteous." A weaker sense, which yet betrays its legal origin, is to be found in Lk. 10:29. The νομικός, θέλων δικαιῶσαι ἑαυτόν, wishes to vindicate himself in debate. On the other hand, Lk. 16:15 : ὑμεῖς ἐστε οἱ δικαιοῦντες ἑαυτοὺς ἐνώπιον τῶν ἀνθρώπων, "to declare or to represent oneself as righteous" (pass. → 214) is much closer to the main NT usage. The attitude of the δίκαιος anticipates what God alone can establish by His pronouncement.

4. δικαιωθῆναι in the sense of saving righteousness in the Synoptists. Paul is not the only one to use the term in the strict legal sense. Luke's statement concerning the publican in 18:4 : κατέβη οὗτος δεδικαιωμένος παρ' ἐκεῖνον, can only mean "acquitted," "declared righteous." The saying assumes a present righteousness, [15] though, in distinction from Paul, there is no reference to the saving act of the cross. [16] The reference in Mt. 12:37: ἐκ τῶν λόγων σου δικαιωθήσῃ, opp. καταδικασθήσῃ, [17] is exclusively to the last judgment (→ 217).

5. δικαιόω as used specifically by Paul.

a. The Legal Aspect of the Term. In Paul the legal usage is plain and indisputable. The opposite of δικαιοῦν is κατακρίνειν (R. 8:34). For Paul the word δικαιοῦν does not suggest the infusion of moral qualities, a *justum efficere* in the sense of the creation of right conduct. It implies the justification of the ungodly who believe, on the basis of the justifying action of God in the death and resurrection of Christ. To be sure, the δικαιοῦσθαι is an act of grace rather than of retribution according to works. Yet this act of grace in the cross can be called forensic because in the ἱλαστήριον judgment is executed on all sin in the Substitute. [18] The original Pauline usage envisages δικαιοῦσθαι as an act of God in the saving present, though it is left an open question how this relates to the decision in the last judgment, which is still maintained (→ δικαιοσύνη, 208). The most distinctive use of δικαιοῦν is in R. 4:5 ff. (of Abraham): πιστεύοντι δὲ ἐπὶ

---

15 Str.-B., II, 247 f.

16 The παρ' ἐκεῖνον אB L Or, better than μᾶλλον παρ' D and ἢ γὰρ ἐκεῖνος א, is to be taken in an absolutely exclusive sense, cf. 4 Esr. 12:6 : *prae multis* (→ 213). Hence it has nothing whatever to do with the comp. or superl. use of δίκαιος (→ δίκαιος, 183), nor with an expression like 1 Βασ. 24:18 : δίκαιος σὺ ὑπὲρ ἐμέ, "thou art more righteous than I."

17 Rabb. par. in Schl. Mt., 412.

18 J. T. Beck, *Röm.* (1884), 217-223 (excursus on δικαιοῦσθαι) argues that the forensic concept should be restricted to the principles of the legal norm which applies in the OT (→ 212) and which is linked with the last judgment in R. 2:13. But this contradicts the use of δικαιόω in Paul, whose concern is to clothe the act of grace in legal imagery. Quite logically Beck rejects any thought of judgment at the cross (222), where God acts only as Father and not as Judge (→ δικαιοσύνη, 204).

τὸν δικαιοῦντα τὸν ἀσεβῆ. The opposite is the δικαιῶσαι δίκαιον of civic justice (→ 212). Here the inconceivable factor of an act of grace is consciously contrasted with ordinary legal procedure. This δικαιοῦν is the judicial acquittal which takes place in the saving present. It is neither exclusively objective in the cross nor exclusively subjective in experience. It has rather the objectivity of relationship, enacted at the cross and apprehended in faith (→ δικαιοσύνη, 206). The idea of a judicial act is not applied to the "present process of the religious life," but reserved for the last judgment. Thus δικαιωθῆναι in Gl. 2:16 f. means "to become a righteous man in the eyes of God," the essence of justification being that God helps the sinner to the position and status of one who is righteous in His eyes. [19] This interpretation is valid, though it should be emphasised that the new position and status are the result of a judicial pronouncement.

It may be conceded that the *usus forensis* is not given prominence in every passage by express emphasising of the judicial act. Thus Gl. 5:4 : οἵτινες ἐν νόμῳ δικαιοῦσθε, means quite simply "you who would be righteous by the law." Yet the idea of judgment is everywhere present, as we can see from statements like Gl. 3:11: δικαιωθῆναι παρὰ τῷ θεῷ, or R. 3:20 : δικαιωθῆναι ἐνώπιον αὐτοῦ (quoting ψ 142:2). On the other hand, the main point is obscured if we forget that the *actus forensis* takes place in an act of grace from which it is not to be severed. Only thus do we see the new element as compared with the Rabbinic doctrine of justification, which at root postpones the judicial act until the last judgment. It should also be noted, however, that to think of δικαιοῦσθαι one-sidedly in terms of experience is to imperil the forensic objectivity of the process.

b. Experience and the Act of Salvation. Does the Pauline use of δικαιοῦσθαι make any contribution to the understanding of the related question of experience ? In the following passages there is clear reference in the present tense — which is the mark of the new insight — to the present character of justification : Gl. 3:8 : δικαιοῖ; 3:11: δικαιοῦται, cf. also 2:16 and 3:24; R. 3:24 : δικαιούμενοι δωρεάν; 3:26 : δικαιοῦντα; 3:28 : δικαιοῦσθαι, cf. δικαιοῦται in Ac. 13:39. In addition to the present tenses the preterites (→ 217, n. 22) are no less important, since they treat justification as something which has already happened, as an event. Simply to emphasise the character of justification as an experience, and to reject the view that δικαιοῦσθαι refers to the universal act of salvation accomplished at the cross, [20] ·is to miss the fact that this act is always present as salvation and therefore available for personal apprehension. This is, of course, necessary. When there is reference to δικαιοῦσθαι, πίστις is always included. [21] It is impossible to separate once-for-all justification at the cross and personal justification in faith (→ δικαιοσύνη, 206). R. 5:9 : δικαιωθέντες νῦν ἐν τῷ αἵματι αὐτοῦ, expressly refers to the act of salvation in indication of the Where of justification. This is the effective basis of δικαιοῦσθαι, the invading and self-actualising present of salvation. The δικαιωθέντες οὖν ἐκ πίστεως in R. 5:1 is preceded by διὰ τὴν δικαίωσιν ἡμῶν. One is thus δικαιωθείς in consequence of the δικαίωσις. Here,

---

[19] Zn. Gl., 124 f. Zn. agrees with Beck in limiting the thought of judgment to the last judgment, cf. → n. 18.

[20] Zn. R., 179 f.; 209, n. 17; 258. Zn.'s view is dogmatically determined by the question of the *ordo salutis*.

[21] On nine occasions Paul links πίστις with δικαιόω statements : Gl. 2:16 (twice); 3:8, 11, 24; R. 3:28, 30; 4:5; 5:1.

too, the fact is imperfectly rendered by the mere statement of experience. For the saving act at the cross and personal apprehension belong directly together, so that the one cannot be considered apart from the other. The preterite expresses an accomplished act of grace. [22] Always, however, we have the accompanying ἐκ (Gl. 3:8, 11, 24; R. 3:30; 5:1) or διά (Gl. 2:16) πίστεως to guard against a formulation divorced from experience, relationship to the event of salvation being indissolubly enclosed in πίστις. In R. 8:30 : ἐδικαίωσεν/ἐδόξασεν it is not appropriate to speak of past [23] justification, since here the catena of aorists denotes the certainty of the event from all eternity in the counsel of God. This leads to the decisive point in this view of time. The eternal character of the justifying event of salvation prevents any severing of past and present. The act of salvation is a continuing present.

c. How does the use of δικαιόω reflect the interrelation of present justification and justification at the last judgment? Paul speaks most clearly of δικαιοῦσθαι at the last judgment when he treats of retributive judgment by works, as in 1 C. 4:4 (ἀλλ' οὐκ ἐν τούτῳ δεδικαίωμαι, cf. Mt. 12:37, → 215). In the full sense a man is judicially acquitted and declared righteous only when the retributive sentence of the last judgment has been pronounced in his favour as regards the whole of his life's work. This is clearly a different use of the term from that which we have considered thus far. It shows us that in Paul, too, δικαιωθῆναι is linked with the last judgment. The decision whether the word is used in this sense elsewhere cannot be taken with certainty merely in the light of future forms of δικαιόω. In the denial of justification by works of the Law (→ δικαιοσύνη, 207) in Gl. 2:16 and R. 3:20, the δικαιωθήσεται is taken from ψ 142:2 (→ 213), and as a quotation it hardly provides a definitive answer to the question. What is obvious is that in the light of the understanding of the doctrine in the Synagogue Judaism necessarily referred this future to the last judgment (→ δικαιοσύνη, 197).

The context shows beyond question that the δικαιωθήσονται of R. 2:13 treats of the last judgment (cf. ἀπολοῦνται, κριθήσονται and the continuation in v. 16). But this is a presupposition which must be laid down to convince opponents irrespective of the redemption in Christ. The assumption is that, since the νόμος is of universal validity, only perfect doers can be declared righteous in the last judgment and therefore neither Jew nor Gentile can stand before God. The whole exposition makes it plain that this statement cannot be a final or adequate formula for justification at the last judgment as it may be expected by the believer in Christ, even though the basic principle remains that God judges action in the Last Day.

---

[22] The completed act of grace is meant in 1 C. 6:11 ἐδικαιώθητε with ἀπελούσασθε; R. 4:2 of Abraham : ἐδικαιώθη; R. 5:1, 9; Tt. 3:7: δικαιωθέντες. Dib. Past. on Tt. 3:7 is probably wrong to question the genuine Pauline sense of ἵνα δικαιωθέντες τῇ ἐκείνου χάριτι. Here, as in 1 C. 6:11, baptism is linked with justification. We also have here, as in genuine Pauline writings, the interconnexion of justification, inheritance and the reception of the Spirit (on justification and baptism, → δικαιοσύνη, 206). The attempt of Joh. Weiss to explain 1 C. 6:11 (1 K., 41, 154 f.) by Corp. Herm., XIII, 9 is unconvincing, since there is no question of the setting aside of sin and becoming sinless (for the most energetic defence of this conjecture cf. Reitzenstein Hell. Myst., 259). This view overlooks the connexion between Pauline justification and the OT, and also Paul's conception of a continuing struggle against the σάρξ in the Christian life. On justification and mysticism → δικαιοσύνη, 209. In relation to δικαιόω, the δικαιωθῆναι ἐν Χριστῷ of Gl. 2:17 is important (cf. εὑρεθῶ ἐν αὐτῷ κτλ., Phil. 3:9).

[23] Zn. R., 209.

In R. 5:19: δίκαιοι κατασταθήσονται οἱ πολλοί, as in R. 3:30 (ὃς δικαιώσει), we seem to have a temporal as well as a logical [24] future, for even the fundamentally important and solemn declaration of R. 8:33: θεὸς ὁ δικαιῶν (preceded by the fut. τίς ἐγκαλέσει) obviously refers to the last judgment. Here again (→ δικαιοσύνη, 207) it is thus evident that δικαιοῦν is an eschatological term and that the divine justification which was accomplished at the cross, which is now believed and which is a continuing gift in the present, is to be expected as a consummated and definitive acquittal in the Last Day. This agrees with the fact that for Paul all present redemption is such only because it establishes solid hope: τῇ γὰρ ἐλπίδι ἐσώθημεν (R. 8:24).

d. δικαιωθῆναι ἀπό. The use of ἀπό in connexion with δικαιωθῆναι (→ 214) gives emphatic expression to the thought of redemption. Thus liberation from guilt is meant in Ac. 13:38 f.: καὶ ἀπὸ πάντων ὧν οὐκ ἠδυνήθητε ἐν νόμῳ Μωϋσέως δικαιωθῆναι, ἐν τούτῳ πᾶς ὁ πιστεύων δικαιοῦται. Here again we have legal justification. Only tendentious criticism [25] can think that the ἀπὸ πάντων κτλ. affirms a partial justification by the Law. R. 6:7: ὁ γὰρ ἀποθανὼν δεδικαίωται ἀπὸ τῆς ἁμαρτίας, is an erratic block among the statements of Paul. Here again the ἀπό denotes the liberation of man, this time from the service of sin. Our old man is crucified with Christ that the body of sin might be destroyed and that we should not be able or compelled to serve sin any more; for — and this brings us to the statement — he who dies is (thereby) declared free from sin. The saying thus relates to the man who has died with Christ, and who is thus free from the bondage which chained him to sin.

> The statement is plainly shown to be a Rabbinic one [26] by the parallel in S. Nu., 112 on 15:31, where in relation to Nu. 15:31: "That soul shall utterly be cut off; his iniquity shall be upon him," it is said: כָּל־הַמֵּתִים בְּמִיתָה מִתְכַּפְּרִים[27] = all who die attain expiation through death, but of this man (נֶפֶשׁ from Nu. 15:31) it is true that "his iniquity shall be upon him." Cf. also S. Nu., 4 on 5:8: If a man had to bring a sin offering to make recompense for the embezzling of something entrusted to him (Lv. 5:21 ff., esp. v. 25), but died before he could bring it, the heirs need not offer the sacrifice, for כִּפְּרָה לוֹ נַפְשׁוֹ; "the soul of this man has already atoned for him (namely, by the fact that he has died)." Even apart from these main passages there is other evidence that the basic principle, i.e., that all who die attain expiation by death, is firmly rooted in Jewish thinking (cf. expiation by dying as a martyr, etc.). [28]

The Rabbinic saying that the soul of the dead achieves expiation by death, and the Pauline statement that he who dies is thereby pronounced free from sin, are fully identical in substance. Paul is thus using here a Rabbinic theologoumenon. But the true significance and force of the statement derive from belief in identification with the death of Christ and the consequent pronouncing free from sin. The Rabbinic parallel is also instructive in that it shows us how closely linked are

---

[24] Lips., Zn., Khl. R., ad loc.
[25] Cf. along the lines of F. C. Baur, F. Overbeck, Kurze Erklärung der Ag. (1870), ad loc., and also Pr. Ag., where there is reference to the "ambiguity of the passage."
[26] This was first maintained by K. G. Kuhn, R. 6:7, ZNW, 30 (1931), 305 ff., who argues that the saying was formulated prior to the 2nd cent. A.D. and thus existed in the 1st cent. A.D.
[27] Horovitz (1917), 121, 13.
[28] Cf. Kuhn, op. cit.

justification and atonement in the thinking of Paul. In other words, we have here another confirmation of the significance of the ἱλαστήριον as the basis of justification. [29]

6. δικαιόω in James.

In James the formula ἐξ ἔργων δικαιοῦσθαι occurs three times. The reference is again to present justification. This is ascribed to Abraham and Rahab on the basis of works. From this fact a general deduction is made in respect of belief in justification. While Paul in R. 4:2 (εἰ γὰρ ᾿Αβραὰμ ἐξ ἔργων ἐδικαιώθη) denies that the patriarchs were justified by their works, James in his struggle against non-ethical and purely orthodox monotheism (→ δικαιοσύνη, 201) expressly emphasises that faith unaccompanied by works will not be enough for δικαιωθῆναι. James could hardly accept Paul's definition of Abraham as a πιστεύων ἐπὶ τὸν δικαιοῦντα τὸν ἀσεβῆ (R. 4:5). For him he is a righteous man whose works are recognised. The statements remind us of Paul, e.g., the quotation from Gn. 15:6, δικαιοῦσθαι ἐκ, the problem of ἔργα and πίστις, the χωρὶς ἔργων. But we need not see here a conscious polemic against pseudo-Paulinism or a misunderstanding of Paul. The form of treatment and the use of similar expressions may be explained by their common basis in the tradition of the Synagogue. If there is in this no inner approximation to the Pauline belief and its new insight, there is agreement with the early Christian view that true faith is not idle but active (→ δικαιοσύνη, 201).

δικαίωμα.

A. δικαίωμα outside the NT.

In consequence of the action (words in -μα), the δικαιοῦν which establishes right gives rise to δικαίωμα. This is the fixed form of δίκαιον, whether as a legal claim, a written right (and therefore a legal document), a statute or ordinance, or a judicial sentence, especially of punishment. It also signifies the legal act corresponding to this ordinance or requirement, and therefore the actualisation of justice.

a. "Legal ground or claim." Thuc., I, 41, 1 (cf. VI, 80, 2): δικαιώματα τάδε πρὸς ὑμᾶς ἔχομεν : the established legal claims of allies. Dio C., 37, 51: πρὸς τὰ τοῦ πλήθους δικαιώματα μετέστη (civic rights); Polyb., III, 28, 2 Cod. Augustanus (vl. δίκαια): παρὰ πάντα τὰ δικαιώματα, against all legal claims, the Carthaginians were forced to evacuate Sardinia. This use has left traces in the LXX. Thus in 2 Βασ. 19:28 δικαίωμα (צְדָקָה) means the legal claim of Meribaal with David. In Jer. 11:20 we read of Jeremiah : ὅτι πρὸς σὲ ἀπεκάλυψα τὸ δικαίωμά μου (for רִיב). In Bar. 2:17 it is also said of the dead : οὐχ ... δώσουσιν δόξαν καὶ δικαίωμα τῷ κυρίῳ, though here we can see the influence of the use of δικαιόω for the vindication of God (→ δικαιόω, 213). In the edict of Claudius in Jos. Ant., 19, 285 there is reference to

---

[29] This explanation of R. 6:7 by the Rabb. formula renders superfluous any recourse to magico-mystical motifs in Corp. Herm., XIII, 9, Reitzenstein Hell. Myst., 259 f.

δικαίωμα. In addition to Cr.-Kö., Moult.-Mill., s.v., Zn. R., 278 f.; Sickb. R.⁴, 216; Rohr Hb.⁴, 40. Def.: Aristot. Rhet., I, 13, p. 1373b, 20 ff.; Eth. Nic., V, 10, p. 1135a, 9-14; Ps.-Just. Quaest. et Resp. ad Orth., III, 2, 138c (Otto); Orig. Selecta in Ps. 18 (MPG, 12, 1244c).

the confirmation of earlier legal claims. Ap., 2, 37 refers to the rights granted to the Jews by Caesar. The word is often used for a legal claim in the pap. P. Lond., II, 360, 8 (250 A.D.) δικαίωμα τῆς δούλης, claim on a slave. CPR, 20, 19 (250 A.D.): ἀρκεσθήσομαι ἐν μεγίστῳ δικαιώματι, my greatest claims were met. P. Oxy., VIII, 1119, 15 (254 A.D.): τῶν ἐξαιρέτων τῆς ἡμετέρας πατρίδος δικαιωμάτων. b. "Written proof," "document," "validation," "acts" or other "legal pieces," esp. those which serve to vindicate. The δικαιώματα Ἑλληνίδων πόλεων in Aristot. Fragm., p. 427 (Rose) [1] are written statutes. According to Jos. Ant., 17, 228 Archelaus presents his δικαιώματα to Augustus in a letter. In Jos. Ant., 17, 130 δικαιώματα are proofs in vindication (though not in writing). The term is commonly used in the pap. for supporting documents, acts or titles. [2] It means supporting documents in P. Tor., I, 1, 3, 20 (117 B.C.): παραγινωσκομένων αὐτοῖς ἐξ ὧν παρέκειντο δικαιωμάτων; P. Lille, I, 29, 25 (3rd cent. B.C.); Ditt. Or., I, 13, 13; credentials in BGU, 1, 113, 10 (143 A.D.): παρέθεντο δικαιώματα; ibid., I, 265, 17 (148 A.D.). c. "Statute," "decree" or "ordinance." It is used very frequently in the LXX for pħ and חֻקָּה, being used not for commandments, as in the Decalogue, but for statutes in the wider sense (including cultic and social obligations): Gn. 26:5; Ex. 15:25 f.; Dt. 4:1, 5, 8, 40; 6:1; 7:11; ψ 118:8. It is used for מִשְׁפָּט in Ex. 21:1; Nu. 36:13; Ex. 21:9: δικαίωμα τῶν θυγατέρων; 1 Βασ. 2:12: τοῦ ἱερέως; 8:9 etc.: τοῦ βασιλέως: the law of daughters, of the priests, of the king. Very rarely it is used for מִצְוָה: Dt. 30:16; 3 Βασ. 2:3, ἐντολή being the usual word for this in the LXX. It is used freely for דֶּרֶךְ in Job 34:27. On ἐντολαὶ καὶ δικαιώματα in Lk. 1:6, cf. ˉGn. 26:5; Nu. 36:13; Dt. 4:40; 1 Macc. 2:21: νόμον καὶ δικαιώματα. The LXX usage is followed by Philo with his many references to statutes, Det. Pot. Ins., 67 and 68; Rer. Div. Her., 8; Congr., 163. For duties as τὰ πρὸς ἀνθρώπους δικαιώματα, cf. Decal., 109. Jos. Ant., 17, 108 speaks of τὰ τῆς φύσεως δικαιώματα. It is interesting that in their emphasis on the δικαιώματα τοῦ κυρίου etc. the post-apostolic fathers return to the legal view of the LXX. Here the δικαιώματα are almost always decrees or statutes: 1 Cl., 2, 8 (cf. 58, 2); Barn., 21, 1 (cf. v. 5); so also 2, 1; 4, 11; 10, 2 (quotation); 16, 9: ἡ σοφία τῶν δικαιωμάτων; Herm. m., 12, 6, 4. In spite of its legal flavour, however, the word is meant to denote the NT revelation and amongst other things it can thus be found in the sense of the promulgation of salvation (Barn., 1, 2), which includes the gift of the Spirit. Here there is an obvious reminiscence of צְדָקָה as salvation in the OT (→ δικαιοσύνη, 195). Similarly Prv. 8:20 Hexapla Αλλος has ἐν ὁδοῖς δικαιώματος περιπατῶ (Mas. צֶדֶק, LXX: δικαιοσύνη). d. "Punishment," "sentence." In accordance with the negative use of δικαιόω (→ δικαιόω, 211) in non-biblical Greek, we find a similar use of δικαίωμα in Plato Leg., IX, 864e, where there is reference to other punishments — τῶν δὲ ἄλλων δικαιωμάτων — as well as βλάβη, damages. In 3 Βασ. 3:28 it is used neutrally of Solomon's just judgment in the matter of the infant: τοῦ ποιεῖν δικαίωμα (מִשְׁפָּט). More positively, we have ποιεῖν τὸ δικαίωμα (cf. 2 Ch. 6:35) in 3 Βασ. 8:45, 59 for "to secure right," "to help to right." In the Bible we thus have the same movement towards the positive sphere as in the case of δικαιόω. e. In correspondence with δίκαιον it can mean "right action" (opp. ἀδίκημα). Aristot. Rhet., I, 3, p. 1359a, 24 f.: οἷον τί μεῖζον ἀγαθὸν ἢ ἔλαττον ἢ ἀδίκημα ἢ δικαίωμα. Acc. to Rhet. I, 13, p. 1373b, 20 ff.: διὸ καὶ τἀδικήματα καὶ τὰ δικαιώματα διχῶς ἔστιν ἀδικεῖν καὶ δικαιοπραγεῖν, δικαίωμα = δικαιοπραγεῖν. Again, in Eth. Nic., V, 10, p. 1135a, 9-14 δικαίωμα is set over against ἀδίκημα and explained as follows: καλεῖται δὲ μᾶλλον δικαιοπράγημα τὸ κοινόν δικαίωμα δὲ τὸ ἐπανόρθωμα (restitution) τοῦ ἀδικήματος. What is in view

---

[1] Cf. Aristot. Fr., p. 386 f. (Rose) and the reference in Harpocration: Lexicon in Decem Oratores Atticos (Dindorf, 1853), s.v. δρυμός.

[2] Cf. APF, VI, 1 (1913), 36; Moult.-Mill. and Preisigke Wört., s.v. "Dikaiomata," Auszüge aus alexandr. Gesetzen und Verordnungen, ed. by the Graeca Halensis (1913), 26.

here is restitution for an evil act. Cf. Aristot. Cael., I, 10, p. 279b, 8 f.: προακηκοόσι τὰ τῶν ἀμφισβητούντων λόγων δικαίωματα: setting right. Theodoret on Ps. 118:2 (MPG, 80, 1821b): νόμον καλεῖ ... δικαιώματα, ὡς δικαιοῦν τὸν κατορθοῦντα δυνάμενον. [3] In the LXX it is used for a right act: Bar. 2:19: τὰ δικαιώματα τῶν πατέρων ἡμῶν. Cf. ψ 44:1 'ΑΣ, where the יֶשְׁעִי of the Mas. (= carmina, ποιήματα, LXX: τὰ ἔργα μου) is given an ethical turn by the rendering: τὰ δικαιώματά μου.

B. δικαίωμα in the NT.

1. That the sense of "statute," "requirement" or "ordinance" is the most common in the NT accords with the close link between the language of the NT and that of the LXX. Lk. 1:6 is in full agreement with LXX usage: ἐντολαὶ καὶ δικαιώματα (→ 220). On the other hand, the distinctive use of the term in Paul shows that in such expressions as τὸ δικαίωμα τοῦ θεοῦ or τοῦ νόμου he goes beyond the LXX in his main employment of the word; for in the LXX the plural is preferred, and, even where the singular is used, it normally refers to one of many statutes. The closest parallel to Paul's use is to be found in passages like Prv. 8:20; 19:25. In R. 1:32 (τὸ δικαίωμα τοῦ θεοῦ ἐπιγνόντες) the reference is to the knowledge of God's statutes or ordinances which obtains among men, so that the corruption of worship and sexual life and the general disintegration of society are worthy of death (with perhaps a play on the sense of "punishment" or "sentence," → 220). In Paul's eyes it is important to emphasise that there is for the Gentiles a recognisable divine order which is to be embraced, not as a sum of commands, but (in the sing.) as the one divine will. There is an intentional distinction when in R. 2:26 Paul refers to the statutes of the Law in the plural: τὰ δικαιώματα τοῦ νόμου. Nor is it accidental that in 8:4, which refers to the fulfilment of this demand by walking in the Spirit, the singular is used again to denote the Law in its unity: τὸ δικαίωμα τοῦ νόμου. In Hb. 9:1 δικαιώματα λατρείας means ordinances of divine service or cultic rules; in 9:10 the reference is to the carnal ordinances of precepts concerning meats and purification. Here the LXX plural is adopted (→ 220) and the term is not given the radical significance which it bears in Paul.

2. The next most common use of the word is for a "right act" in fulfilment of legal requirement. In this sense it is used a. of Christ. While δικαίωμα is the opp. of κατάκριμα in R. 5:16 (→ 222), in v. 18 δι' ἑνὸς δικαιώματος is the opp. of δι' ἑνὸς παραπτώματος (παράπτωμα, the fall as a result), and in v. 19 it is replaced or explained by ὑπακοή (opp. παρακοή). The δι' ἑνός, which elsewhere in vv. 12-19 (ten times apart from v. 18, and in every case with incontestable reference to Adam and Christ) is always masc., is best related here, too, to Adam and Christ, so that in 18b as well the reference is to the right action or conduct of Christ. [4] Materially this agrees with other statements of Paul to the effect that Christ, placed under the Law (Gl. 4:4), did not merely fulfil it negatively by having no personal knowledge of sin (2 C. 5:21), but also positively by obedience even to death (Phil. 2:8). In R. 5:18 all this is gathered up in the single statement

---

[3] Used by Suid., s.v. δικαιώματα.
[4] So Hofmann, Zn., Ltzm., ad loc. Althaus, NT Deutsch, ad loc. has the neutr. durch eine Rechttat.

that His total life is δικαίωμα, i.e., a perfect fulfilment of the divine requirement (cf. Mt. 3:15, → δικαιοσύνη, 198). [5]

There is another view that in v. 18, as in v. 16, δικαίωμα should be translated "sentence of justification." [6] This would give a uniform sense throughout the passage. But in the narrower sphere of the antitheses here presented it fails to meet the urgent need to maintain a clear parallelism to παράπτωμα and παρακοή. It has also to take δι' ἑνός as a neut. rather than in the predominant masc., for elsewhere Paul never says that the sentence of justification is pronounced by Christ. [7] The greatest internal difficulty, however, is caused by the ensuing εἰς δικαίωσιν ζωῆς, for if we take this view of δικαιώματος, then we are forced to conclude that Paul distinguishes between the objective sentence and subjective justification. [8] A comprehensive view of the apostle's message, however, shows us (→ δικαιοσύνη, 206; → δικαιόω, 216) that no such distinction is present in Paul, since the justifying act of God (which would be the δικαίωμα of v. 18) is always seen also as an incisive reality in believers.

b. It is also used of God in Rev. 15:4 : ὅτι τὰ δικαιώματά σου ἐφανερώθησαν, "his righteous acts," with emphasis on judgment, and therefore "his righteous judgments" (a combination of A. d. and e., cf. what was said on R. 1:32 → 221).

c. It is used of members of the community in Rev. 19:8 : τὸ βύσσινον τὰ δικαιώματα τῶν ἀγίων, "the righteous deeds of the saints."

3. In R. 5:16 : τὸ μὲν γὰρ κρίμα ἐξ ἑνὸς εἰς κατάκριμα, τὸ δὲ χάρισμα ἐκ πολλῶν παραπτωμάτων εἰς δικαίωμα, the reference is to the sentence of justification (→ 220), [9] since here the antonym is κατάκριμα and δώρημα is a synonym. Materially the meaning is the act of justification, the δικαίωσις. One can see from a comparison of the different meanings of δικαίωσις and δικαίωμα that the two are interchangeable as "punishment," "claim," "demand" and "statute" (→ δικαίωμα, 220), and that in relation to the sense of "just act" (→ δικαίωσις, 223) there are also points of contact, e.g., restitution, or "defence." There can be little question that in R. 5:16 the other -μα words used by Paul inclined him stylistically to this rather uncommon application of the term. [10] Yet Paul is simply following the positive usage of the LXX (→ 220; and cf. the parallel procedure in respect of → δικαιοσύνη, 195; → δικαιόω, 212). The indeterminate meaning of δικαίωμα makes it possible for him to adopt a striking change of meaning in R. 5 (cf. v. 18). In view of the varied usage, we cannot assume a consistent employment of the term even in this section. The antonyms make it plain what is the

---

[5] Cf. Zn., ad loc. Beck's "righteous state of the One" is thus correct. In view of the above parallels there is no cause to think only of the embracing act of the cross. This concentration is undoubtedly Pauline, cf. Phil. 2:8, yet even in this passage Paul says "even" rather than "only" in relation to the cross.

[6] So B. Weiss, Godet, Schl., Khl. and others. The latter prefers "judgment," though, as he formulates it, this is conceived far too formally in relation to the actuality of the process.

[7] Barth, ad loc. attempts the logical translation : "the justification disclosed in the One," but this is not precise enough.

[8] So most clearly Godet and Lipsius (the pronouncement of justification is δικαίωμα in content and δικαίωσις as an actus judicialis), ad loc. But if we consider R. 5:16 (→ supra) we see that in the one sure place where δικαίωμα is used for the sentence of justification the antonym κατάκριμα makes it plain that this sentence is conceived in its full efficacy.

[9] So correctly Fritzsche, Meyer, Philippi, Godet, Barth, ad loc. Beck's reference to righteousness of life is quite impossible.

[10] Ltzm. R., 60; Pr.-Bauer, 308.

meaning at each point. It can also be seen from R. 1:32; 2:26 and 8:4 that Paul could use this many-coloured word in other senses also.

δικαίωσις.

A. δικαίωσις in Greek generally.

δικαίωσις is the act of executing the δίκαιον. It implies the validation of the legal norm in punishment, defence or requirement. But the δίκαιον can also be a personal preference.

The word is rare and is not found in Polyb., Philo [1] or Epict. No traces have been found in the inscr. or pap. a. Its most common sense is that of "condemnation" or "punishment" (→ δικαιόω, 211). Thuc., VIII, 66, 2; [2] Plut. Def. Orac., 21 (II, 421d, vl. [Eusebius]). Plut. De Artaxerxe, 14, 2 (I, 1017 f.); cf. also Plut. Ser. Num. Pun., 22 (II, 565a). [3] Similarly Dio C., 40, 43, 3, and Jos. Ant., 18, 14; 18, 315, this being the only sense in Joseph. b. "Judicial defence and vindication" as an act (→ δικαιόω, 211; 212 f.), the sense adopted by Pl.: Lys., 9, 8. [4] Cf. also ψ 34(35):23 (LXX : δίκη == רִיב; Σ δικαίωσις). This sense is particularly common for more general self-exculpation or the defence of certain actions in daily life. Plut. De Virtute Morali, 9 (II, 449b): "to justify an action sophistically" (opp. ἀπόδρασις). Dio C., 41, 54, 3 : of the advancing of justifying reasons. c. The "claim to a real or apparent right," "legal demand." Thuc., I, 141, 1: δικαίωσις πρὸ δίκης, "demand advanced at law." Dion. Hal. Ant. Rom., I, 87, 1: of resistance to a legal claim, cf. VII, 16, 2. Plut. Demetr., 18 (I, 896e) of demands made on subjects. d. "Arbitrary judgment," "caprice" (cf. the common meaning of δικαιόω, 211: "to regard as fair and right"): Thuc., III, 82, 4 : τὴν εἰωθυῖαν ἀξίωσιν τῶν ὀνομάτων ἐς τὰ ἔργα ἀντήλλαξαν τῇ δικαιώσει : they changed as they saw fit. e. A final meaning is "statute," "law." Lv. 24:22 : δικαίωσις (מִשְׁפָּט) μία ἔσται τῷ προσηλύτῳ καὶ τῷ ἐγχωρίῳ. Plut. De Fortuna, 5 (II, 99c) (as parallels to τέχνη and εὐφημία). Dion. Hal. Ant., Rom., III, 10, 3 : ἀναστρέψασα τὰς ἀνθρωπίνας δικαιώσεις, nature reverses human law.

A comparable Rabbinic phrase is "the judgment of life" : אִיפּוֹפָסִיס שֶׁל חַיִּים (or אִיפּוֹפָסִין) == ἀπόφασις, -σιν; [5] opp. אִיפּוֹפָסִיס שֶׁלָּהֶם לְמִיתָה (or אִיפּוֹפָסִין מִיתָה) jRH, 57a, 49. [6] Cf. also the בְּשָׁלוֹם (in peace), jRH, 59c, 51 [7] and בְּדִימוֹס (with pardon), Pesikt., 155b, [8] both of which are a result of the divine judgment.

B. δικαίωσις in the NT.

In R. 4:25 and 5:18 δικαίωσις is the subst. corresponding to δικαιοῦσθαι and means the act of justification by the divine acquittal (5:18, opp. κατάκριμα) and with reference to the whole existence of man before God.

δ ι κ α ί ω σ ι ς. [1] The vl. δικαίωσις for δεξίωσις in Philo Deus Imm., 79 yields no good sense (the only passage).

[2] δικαίωσις is not to be equated here with δικαιολογία, ἀπολογία (Cr.-Kö., 332). We are rather to prefer the scholiast (Hirzel, Dike, 138, cf. Liddell-Scott, s.v.) who interprets as κόλασις. Cf. Harpocration, Lexicon in Decem Oratores Atticos (Dindorf), s.v. δικαίωσις : ὁ μέντοι Θουκυδίδης πολλάκις τὴν δικαίωσιν ἐπὶ τῆς κολάσεως τάττει.

[3] As opposed to Cr.-Kö., 332.

[4] Cf. Harpocration, op. cit.: Λυσίας ἐν τῷ περὶ τοῦ στρατιώτου, εἰ γνήσιος, καὶ μάλα τὰς δικαιώσεις φησὶν ἀντὶ τοῦ δικαιολογίας.

[5] Cf. S. Krauss, Griech. u. lat. Lehnwörter in Talm. u. Midr., II (1899), 101 f.

[6] Str.-B., III, 230 f.

[7] Ibid., 217 f.

[8] Ibid., 218.

In R. 4:25 : παρεδόθη διὰ τὰ παραπτώματα ἡμῶν καὶ ἠγέρθη διὰ τὴν δικαίωσιν ἡμῶν, the first διά denotes the cause and the second the goal. If we
take [9] the second διά (→ 70) in the sense of "because we are justified," i.e., that
we may be partakers of ζωή αἰώνιος on this basis, this is out of line with the
example of Abraham, whose justification is represented as the result of faith in
God who awakens the dead. Justification is here brought about by the resurrection,
on which the faith of Abraham causes great stress to be laid. If we adopt the
exposition [10] that the resurrection was needed to actualise δικαίωσις, since faith
is kindled only by the resurrection, a corpse being no true object of faith, this is
to substitute the πολλῷ μᾶλλον of R. 5:9 or the μᾶλλον of 8:34 for the kind of
parallel statement which is in fact made here. The death and resurrection of Christ
are closely related for Paul. The Crucified is what He is only because He is also
the Resurrected. Hence Paul can say that we are justified by the death of Jesus,
but also that He was raised for our justification. The form of the statement corresponds to the synthetic parallelism [11] of the matter. It is itself synthetic parallelism. The same thought is here presented in parallel statements, but with an emphasis on the ἠγέρθη in view of the story of Abraham.

In R. 5:18 (εἰς δικαίωσιν ζωῆς) the reference is again to the actualisation of the
divine sentence of justification by the blessing of believers. The attributive ζωῆς
tells us that justification and life are correlative, that the content of δικαίωσις
is life, that it entails life in the full sense, that life is the eternal result and goal,
just as the final end of transgression consists in κατάκριμα. V. 17 and v. 21 show
plainly that ζωή must be understood throughout in an eschatological sense. Paul's
use of ζωή elsewhere (R. 6:4; 8:2, 6, 10) shows also that this life begins now in
the justified. Nevertheless, the phrase δικαίωσις ζωῆς, like the δίκαιοι κατασταθήσονται of v. 19, confirms the view that in Paul justification looks to the consummation in which alone it will attain its τέλος and final establishment (→ δικαιοσύνη, 207; δικαιόω, 217).

† δικαιοκρισία.

δικαιοκρισία is righteous judgment as the quality of a δίκαιος κριτής. [1] The word
is very rare and late. The earliest examples occur in Jewish Hellenistic literature.
a. Test. L. 3:2 : ἐν τῇ δικαιοκρισίᾳ τοῦ θεοῦ; 15:2 : λήψεσθε αἰσχύνην αἰώνιον
παρὰ τῆς δικαιοκρισίας τοῦ θεοῦ; both with reference to the last judgment. Cf.
materially from the same background, En. 27:3; 60:6; 93:14, except that here κρίσις is
not expressly presented as a divine quality, as in δικαιοκρισία. On the other hand,
God is personally called δικαιοκρίτης : 2 Macc. 12:41; Sib., 3, 704. The same word is
found in P. Ryl., 113, 35 (2nd cent. A.D.). b. Hos. 6:5 E [1] (quinta of the Hexapla) (for
מִשְׁפָּט). LXX B τὸ κρίμα μου. [2] c. The remaining examples are from a later period :

---

[9] R. A. Lipsius, Komm. z. R.² (1892), 120.
[10] Zn. R., 241 ad loc.; Khl. R., 155 ff.
[11] J. Weiss, Beiträge z. paul. Rhetorik (1897), 171.

δικαιοκρισία. Apart from Liddell-Scott, Cr.-Kö. and Moult.-Mill., s.v.; cf. Deissmann LO, 72; Nägeli, 48; W. Sanday-A. Headlam on R. 2:5.
[1] The instances in the pap. demand a correction of the definition in Cr.-Kö., namely, a
"judgment which creates law" rather than a "judgment which conforms to law." They
emphasise particularly the character of the judge. Cf. Moult.-Mill., s.v.
[2] δικαιοκρισία is not found in Jos. or Philo, though they have the similar constructions
δικαιολογία and δικαιαρχεία. Cf. δικαιροπτία in Joseph. and δικαιοδοσία and κακο-
κρισία in Polyb.

Hephaestio Astrologus, III, 34 (4th cent. A.D.).³ P. Oxy., I, 71 col. 1, 3 (written request, 303 A.D.): εὔελπις ὢν τῆς ἀπὸ τοῦ σοῦ μεγέθους δικαιοκρισίας τυχεῖν; VI, 904, 2 (petition, 5th cent. A.D.); P. Flor., I, 88, 26 (3rd cent. A.D.).

In the NT R. 2:5: ἐν ἡμέρα ὀργῆς καὶ ἀποκαλύψεως δικαιοκρισίας τοῦ θεοῦ, is to be understood in the strict eschatological sense. The day of wrath reveals the character of God as the Judge who judges righteously. This is contrasted with the moralising of those who condemn heinous evils but do them themselves, so that their judgment is not κατὰ ἀλήθειαν like that of God. 2 Th. 1:5: ἔνδειγμα τῆς δικαίας κρίσεως τοῦ θεοῦ, links δίκαιος with κρίσις but has two separate words.⁴ The statement is to be expounded as follows. The δικαία κρίσις will be revealed in the fact that the persecuted will be accounted worthy of the βασιλεία and their persecutors will receive appropriate retribution.⁵

Schrenk

διόρθωσις → ὀρθός.
διχοστασία → I, 514.

---

† διχοτομέω

In Mt. 24:51: ἥξει ὁ κύριος τοῦ δούλου ἐκείνου ἐν ἡμέρα ᾗ οὐ προσδοκᾷ καὶ ἐν ὥρᾳ ᾗ οὐ γινώσκει, καὶ διχοτομήσει αὐτόν, we can see from the context that the reference of διχοτομεῖν is to punishment, i.e., the ancient punishment of parting asunder with the sword or saw.

In rather different ways this is mentioned, e.g., in Hom. Od., 18, 339; Hdt., II, 139; Epict. Diss., III, 22, 3; 2 Βασ. 12:31; 1 Ch. 20:3; Sus. 55 and 59; Lk. 19:27; Hb. 11:37. διχοτομεῖν itself is cutting or dividing or cleaving or hewing into two parts. a. Plut. De Pyrrho, 24 (I, 399): τὰ μέρη τοῦ σώματος; Polyb., X, 15:5 : τοὺς κύνας δεδιχοτομημένους καὶ τῶν ἄλλων ζῴων μέλη παρακεκομμένα; LXX Ex. 29:17: καὶ τὸν κριὸν διχοτομήσεις κατὰ μέλη καὶ πλυνεῖς τὰ ἐνδόσθια καὶ τοὺς πόδας ὕδατι, καὶ ἐπιθήσεις ἐπὶ τὰ διχοτομήματα σὺν τῇ κεφαλῇ. The Heb. equivalent is נתח pi, which means "to divide," "to cleave," whether of men (Ju. 19:29; 20:6) or animals (Lv. 1:6; 1 Βασ. 11:7), and which is usually rendered μελίζειν. b. Plut. Fac. Lun., 17

---

³ Ed. A. Engelbrecht (1887) in Catalogus Codicum Astrologorum Graecorum.
⁴ For textual material cf. Dob. Th., 242. δικαιοκρισίας in Ephrem, Antiochus, Euthymius shows approximation to R. 2:5.
⁵ Dob. Th. and Wbg. Th., *ad loc.* bring ἔνδειγμα as a predicative noun into the relative clause and take the sufferings as proof that God's judgment is just. But it is better to follow Dib. Th., *ad loc.*, who sees in ἔνδειγμα the start of a new statement and an amplification of ὅ ἐστιν.
δ ι χ ο τ ο μ έ ω. Kl. Mt., *ad loc.*; Dausch Synpt.⁴ 315; Str.-B., I, 969.

(II, 929 f.): ἡ σελήνη διχοτομοῦσα heaven into two parts; Theophr. De Signis Tempestatum, 1, 6 : διχοτομεῖ δὲ τὸν ἐνιαυτὸν Πλειάς τε δυομένη καὶ ἀνατέλλουσα ... ὥστε δίχα τέμνεται ὁ πᾶς χρόνος. c. Logically, Plat. Polit., 302e : τὸ παράνομον καὶ ἔννομον ἑκάστην (sc. πολιτείαν) διχοτομεῖ τούτων; Aristot. Probl., XVI, 4, p. 913b, 31; Part. An., I, 4, p. 644b, 19 etc.

Schlier

διψάω, δίψος

1. "Thirsting" in the strict sense. Jn. 19:28 : ἵνα τελειωθῇ ἡ γραφή, λέγει· διψῶ. The saying expresses realistically the desire of the suffering Jesus for final refreshment before He completes His work in death according to the Scriptures. [1] Mt. 25:35 ff. [2] etc.: "The one who suffers thirst" as an object of active love; R. 12:20 (Prv. 25:21): the "thirsting" enemy; 1 C. 4:11; 2 C. 11:27; "thirst" with hunger (→ πεινάω) as one of the many things which the apostle is called upon to suffer. Rev. 7:16 (Is. 49:10), "thirst" as one of the great needs of the world which the great host of the redeemed has overcome for ever (v. 9). [3]

2. Figuratively, "to desire passionately a spiritual good without which one cannot live," Mt. 5:6 : οἱ → πεινῶντες καὶ διψῶντες τὴν δικαιοσύνην. [4] Esp. "to desire salvation," Jn. 7:37: ἐάν τις διψᾷ, ἐρχέσθω πρός με καὶ πινέτω; Rev. 21:6 : ἐγὼ τῷ διψῶντι δώσω ἐκ τῆς πηγῆς τοῦ ὕδατος τῆς ζωῆς δωρεάν (cf. 22:17). "Not to thirst any more" indicates the satisfaction of longing and therefore perfect felicity as a gift of Christ, Jn. 4:14 : ὃς δ' ἂν πίῃ ἐκ τοῦ ὕδατος οὗ ἐγὼ δώσω αὐτῷ, οὐ μὴ διψήσει εἰς τὸν αἰῶνα, 6:35 : ὁ πιστεύων εἰς ἐμὲ οὐ μὴ διψήσει πώποτε. [5]

According to a common oriental view to give drink to the thirsty was a work of practical assistance pleasing to God. Cf. the Egyptian Book of the Dead, 125 (AOT, I, 12): "I have pleased God by something which He loves; I have given bread to the hungry and water to the thirsty ..."; M. Ex., 14, 19 : [6] "The son was hungry; the father

---

διψάω (δίψος). Moult.-Mill., 165 f.; Liddell-Scott, 440; Pr.-Bauer, 312.

[1] Cf. Zn. J., 660 f. Since the whole content of Scripture is here finally fulfilled (Bau. J.³, 224), we are not thinking of individual sayings like Ps. 22:16 or 69:21.

[2] What Orig. sets on the lips of Jesus in Mt. Tom., XIII, 2 (p. 214, Lommatzsch): ... διὰ τοὺς διψῶντας ἐδίψων, is an exposition of Mt. 25:35 ff. (cf. J. H. Ropes, "Die Sprüche Jesu," TU, 14, 2 [1896] 35) rather than a detached saying (so A. Resch, "Agrapha," ² TU, NF, XV, 3/4 [1906], 132 f.).

[3] Cf. the Roman inscr. in Epigr. Graec., 649, 5 f.: οὐ χειμὼν λυπεῖ σ', οὐ καῦμα, οὐ νοῦσος ἐνοχλεῖ, οὐ πίνη σ', οὐ δίψος ἔχει σ' ...

[4] On the construction, cf. Bl.-Debr. § 171. The opp. of Mt. 5:6 is found in the logion, P. Oxy., I, 1, v. 11 ff.: ἔστην ἐν μέσῳ τοῦ κόσμου καὶ ἐν σαρκεὶ ὤφθην αὐτοῖς καὶ εὗρον πάντας μεθύοντας καὶ οὐδένα εὗρον διψῶντα ἐν αὐτοῖς.

[5] That Jesus as the Bread of life satisfies all thirst as well as hunger is not adequately explained by the formal link between πεινᾶν and διψᾶν (→ supra), but is to be understood in the light of the substance of v. 53 ff. Cf. Zn. and Bau., ad loc.

[6] Cf. in general the excursus "Die altjüdischen Liebeswerke" in Str.-B., IV, 559 ff.

gave him to eat; he was thirsty, and he gave him to drink"; Lidz. Ginza, 18, 5 f.: "If you see someone who is hungry, give him to eat, and if thirsty, give him to drink" (v. 36, 13 f.). Cf. also Ign. Sm., 6, 2: οὐ μέλει αὐτοῖς (the false teachers) ... περὶ πεινῶντος ἢ διψῶντος; the Ps.-Clem. Hom. Epistula Clementis ad Jacobum, 9: διψῶσι παρέχετε ποτόν; ibid., Praedicatio Petri Epitome, III, 69; XI, 4; XII, 32.

Figurative use in the OT. Am. 8:11; Ps. 42:2; 63:1; Is. 55:1; 'Ιερ. 38:25. [7] In Jew. literature, cf. Sir. 24:21; En. 48:1: "In that place I saw the source of righteousness, which was inexhaustible, and around it there were several sources of wisdom, and all the thirsty drank of them and became full of wisdom"; Philo Som., I, 38: τὸ πάντα διψῆν θεοῦ; Fug., 139: τοὺς διψῶντας καὶ πεινῶντας καλοκἀγαθίας (cf. Index); Jos. Bell., 1, 628: διψήσας τοὐμὸν αἷμα; Ab., 1, 4: "Drink in thirstily their words (i.e., of the Rabbis)." [8] Also O. Sol. 6:11 (cf. Pist. Soph., 65): "All the thirsty on earth drank therefrom (from the river of knowledge), and the thirst was satisfied and quenched, since the drink was given by the Most High"; 30:2: "Come, all who thirst, and drink; seek refreshment at the spring of the Lord." In Gk. lit. cf. Pind. Nem., 3, 6: διψῇ δὲ πρᾶγος ἄλλο μὲν ἄλλου; Plat. Resp., VIII, 562c: πόλις ἐλευθερίας διψήσασα; Xenoph. Cyrop., V, 1, 1: οὕτως ἐγὼ ὑμῖν διψῶ χαρίζεσθαι; Plut. Cato Maior, 11 (I, 342e): τοῖς ... διψῶσι τιμῆς καὶ δόξης; cf. Mar., 43, 7 (I, 431b) and De Cohibenda Ira, 11 (II, 460b): τροφῇ μὲν γὰρ ὁ πεινῶν κατὰ φύσιν χρῆται, τιμωρίᾳ δ' ὁ μὴ πεινῶν μηδὲ διψῶν αὐτῆς; Ael. Var. Hist., 14, 22: τῶν ... τὴν μοναρχίαν καταλῦσαι διψώντων; IG, XIV, 1890, 10 f.: ψυχῇ διψώσῃ ψυχρὸν ὕδωρ μετάδ<ο>ς.

Behm

Additional Note: διψάω and Cognates in the LXX.

1. Following the Heb., the Gk. translation formulated the figure of the γῆ διψῶσα. This picture is used in the sense of yearning for salvation in 'Ιωβ 29:23 independently of the Mas.: ὥσπερ γῆ διψῶσα προσδεχομένη τὸν ὑετόν, οὕτως οὗτοι τὴν ἐμὴν λαλίαν. There can be reference here to religious yearning only to the extent that Job's words concern a religious problem and the Hellenistic reader knew and accepted the claim of the book and its constituent parts to be revelation. 'Α coins the figure in ψ 142:6: [ἡ ψυχή μου] ὡς γῆ διψῶσα πρός σέ. In the Mas. the underlying word is עֲיֵפָה, which the LXX translates ἄνυδρος and Σ ἐκλυομένη — expressions which do not carry the thought of yearning but which form the *tertium comparationis* of the image, as in 'Ιωβ 29:23. Is. 53:2 is also to be understood in this sense, though here it is the root [9] which is thirsty rather than the land, cf. passages like Is. 32:2b LXX: [10] ἐν γῇ διψώσῃ (Mas. בְּאֶרֶץ עֲיֵפָה); 35:1 (ἔρημος διψῶσα = מִדְבָּר וְצִיָּה), v. 6 (ἐν γῇ διψώσῃ == בַּעֲרָבָה), v. 7: εἰς τὴν διψῶσαν γῆν (צִמָּאוֹן) πηγὴ ὕδατος ἔσται. The thirsty are men dwelling in a thirsty land or journeying through a thirsty desert. Here again the story of salvation provides the basis of the OT typology, i.e., God's leading of His people through the wilderness after the deliverance from Egypt (Ex. 17:3; Dt. 8:15; Neh. 9:15, 20; ψ106:5; Wis. 11:4, 8, 14). As Yahweh gave water to the people in the desert, as He protected it in the dangers of the thirsty land, so He keeps and saves panting souls, thirsty for salvation, in and from the wilderness of life, ψ 62:1 LXX: ὁ θεός μου ... ἐδίψησέν σοι ἡ ψυχή μου (cf. ψ 41:2), προσαπλῶς σοι ἡ σάρξ μου ἐν γῇ ἐρήμῳ καὶ ἀβάτῳ καὶ ἀνύδρῳ. Only Σ here has a word from the stem διψ-: ὡς ἐν γῇ διψάδι (more in the sense of dry) καὶ ἐκλύσει μὴ ὑπάρχοντος ὕδατος. The Mas. has

---

[7] Cf. R. Smith, *The Religion of the Semites* (1899), 177.
[8] For further material, cf. Str.-B., I, 202 f.; III, 302.
[9] LXX Θ: ὡς ῥίζα ἐν γῇ διψώσῃ; Σ: ἀπὸ γῆς διψώσης.
[10] Is. 32:2a LXX and Θ: ἐν Σειών for Mas. בְּצִיּוֹן; 'Α: ἐν διψαλέῳ; Σ: ἐν ἀνυδρίᾳ.

בְּאֶרֶץ־צִיָּה וְעָיֵף בְּלִי־מָיִם. In the LXX the two stems צִיָּה and עָיֵף are often translated by διψάω. [11] The dry land is the enemy of the thirsty, of creatures which live by water. Cf. also Ez. 19:13 ΄ΑΣ.

2. The religious yearning of men is also expressed directly by the image of thirst in a whole series of passages. In addition to those already mentioned, we may refer to Is. 41:18; 43:20 (א); 44:3; 48:21; 49:9, 10; 55:1; these passages are mostly eschatological, and typologically constitute a transition to sayings in which salvation is depicted as eating and drinking in the kingdom of God (Lk. 22:30, → ποτήριον, δεῖπνον, and the references given there). In ΄Ιερ 38:25 (= 31:24) there is a significant alteration of the Mas. along the lines of Hellenistic mysticism. Jer. 31 treats of the coming salvation, which is depicted in many different ways. Thus the reference in 31:14 Mas. is to the fat with which Yahweh anoints the souls of priests; whether דֶשֶׁן is a gloss or not, the LXX renders the רוה pi of the Mas. by μεθύσκειν "to make drunken," thus applying the concept of intoxication positively along the lines of the Hellenistic oxymoron of sobria ebrietas. The same holds good of 31:25. The Mas. הִרְוֵיתִי נֶפֶשׁ עֲיֵפָה as an expression for the impartation of salvation becomes in the LXX: ἐμέθυσα πᾶσαν ψυχὴν διψῶσαν. [12] This is the more remarkable because elsewhere in the Gk. OT μεθύσκειν is always used negatively of the cup of the wrath of Yahweh. This is shown even more clearly by the passage Dt. 29:19 in the Hexapla ΄ΑΣΘ, which use the same terms, since here the LXX plainly reflects an exegetical understanding of the passage independent of the Mas.: ἵνα μὴ συναπολέσῃ ὁ ἁμαρτωλὸς τὸν ἀναμάρτητον, cf. ΄ΑΣΘ [ἵνα μὴ συναπολέσῃ] ἡ μεθύουσα τὴν διψῶσαν [ψυχήν]. In other words, ἡ μεθύουσα ψυχή is here the ἁμαρτωλός and ἡ διψῶσα ψυχή the ἀναμάρτητος, the concept of the διψῶντες thus taking its distinctive OT form as later used in the NT beatitudes (Mt. 5:6; Lk. 6:21). Similarly in Is. 41:17 the πτωχοί and ἐνδεεῖς etc. are characterised as follows: ἡ γλῶσσα αὐτῶν ἀπὸ τῆς δίψης ἐξηράνθη, and in v. 18 salvation is proclaimed to them: ἐγὼ κύριος ... ποιήσω ... τὴν διψῶσαν γῆν ἐν ὑδραγωγοῖς. In Is. 25:4 it is said of God that He is σκέπη διψώντων, and in v. 5 the thirsty are set in antithesis to the ungodly. In Is. 32:6 the thirsty and fools are no less comprehensively opposed: ὁ γὰρ μωρὸς ... τὰς ψυχὰς τὰς διψώσας κενὰς ποιήσει. In ΄Ιωβ 5:5, too, Σ at least understands the Heb. (Mas. וְשָׁאַף צַמִּים חֵילָם) in the same sense: ἀναρροφῆσαι διψῶν (= δίκαιος, v. 5a) τὴν δύναμιν αὐτῶν (ἀφρόνων, v. 2, 3): "May the thirsty imbibe their power."

3. Finally the image of thirst (and here there can be no doubt as to the reality of the conception) is used in a very different context, i.e., for the torments of hell. In the NT this is assumed in the story of Dives and Lazarus (Lk. 16:24). In the OT thirst and death by thirst are often presented as a divine punishment: Is. 5:13; 50:2; 65:13; Hos.

---

[11] διψάω in the LXX is mostly used for the Heb. stem צמא. But it can often be used for עָיֵף ("weary," "panting"), and for צִיָּה ("dry") in the publication of salvation in Is. 35:1; 41:18; 53:2, where perhaps intentionally the LXX substitutes the thought of thirst for dryness as the presupposition of the publication of salvation. Dryness seemed to be no true presupposition for the revelation of the grace of God! In Is. 25:5 and 32:2 the LXX mistakenly has Σειών for צִיּוֹן, though the parallelism ought to have indicated the true sense. In Is. 25:5 διψῶντες ἐν Σειών offers a double translation of the same Heb. expression. In the main (10 times in the LXX for 16 in the Mas.), צִיָּה is rendered ἄνυδρος. Twice it is translated ἔρημος (΄Ιερ. 27[50]:12; ψ 62:1) and once ξηρός (΄Ιωβ 24:19 [?]). For עָיֵף we either have general expressions for exhaustion like ἐκλύειν (or as vl. κοπιᾶν) and ἐκλείπειν (10 times), or the concrete πεινᾶν and διψᾶν (10 times). For the adj. we have ἄβατος (ψ 62:1) and ἄνυδρος (ψ 142:6).

[12] Cf. H. Lewy, Sobria Ebrietas, Untersuchungen zur Geschichte der antiken Mystik (1929); the assertion on p. 106 needs to be amplified accordingly.

2:3; ψ 106:33; Wis. Sol. 11:14. Many of these passages are of direct significance for the later depiction of the eternal punishment of thirst. There is no reference in canonical Scripture (either OT or NT) to thirst as a penalty in hell. Allusion may be found, however, in 4 Esr. 8:59 : *Sicut enim vos* (the righteous) *suscipient, quae praedicta sunt, sic eos* (the godless inhabitants of the world) *sitis et cruciatus, quae praeparata sunt.*

Bertram

δίψυχος → ψυχή.

διώκω [1]

1. "To impel": a. "to set in rapid motion"; a carriage, Aesch. Pers., 84. Without obj., app. intr. "to journey," "to ride," "to march," "to row," or generally "to hasten": Hom. Il., 23, 344, 424; Od., 5, 332; 12, 182; Xenoph. An., VII, 2, 20; Plut. De Caesare, 17 (I, 715 f.); Chares Hist. Fr., 17 (ed. R. Geier, Alex. M. Hist. Script. [1844], p. 306); LXX Hag. 1:9.

b. "To persecute," "to expel," Hom. Il., 22, 199; LXX Lv. 26:17; Ps. 7:1 etc.; P. Oxy. VIII, 1151, 3 (5th cent. A.D.), amulet: Χ(ριστός) σε διώκει; BGU, III, 954, 7 (6th cent. A.D.): ὅπως διώξης ἀπ' ἐμοῦ ... τὸν δαίμονα. Class. and in pap.: tech. term in law for "to accuse," Aesch. Eum., 583; P. Lond., V, 1708, 25 (Mart. Pol., 7, 1: διωγμῖται = bailiffs). [2]

The Psalms especially present religious persecution as an offence of the persecutors through the use of διώκω or composites with ἐκ and κατά, which in the LXX are almost more common than the simple form. In part the expressions correspond to the Heb., as in ψ 7:2, 6; 30:16; 34:3; 70:11; 108:16; 118:84, 86 etc. (cf. also Jer. 15:15; 20:11; 'Ιωβ 19:28 Σ, not the LXX), but in part the LXX imports the concept independently of the Mas. Thus (ἐκ- or κατα-) διώκω is used for איב in ψ 68:4, and for שפט in ψ 108:31. In ψ 43:17 it is used for נקם hitp (cf. Sir. 39:30), and in ψ 100:5 for צמת hi. In Jer. 20:10 only Θ has this verb for נגד hiph. Qoh. 3:15 in the LXX uses διωκόμενος in the sense of the persecuted righteous, cf. 'Α and even more clearly Σ: ὁ δὲ θεὸς ἐπιζητήσει ὑπὲρ τῶν ἐκδιωκομένων. Conversely, in the Gk. the attitude of the ungodly, too, is described as that of one who is hunted, or who feels that he is hunted: Prv. 12:26 = 13:21; Mi. 2:11 (not the Mas.); Nah. 1:8; Is. 30:28 (not the Mas.); ψ 36:28 A (not the Mas.); Sir. 30:19 (not the Heb.); 39:30 (Heb. נקם). [3]

In the NT we find sense a. in Lk. 17:23 : "Do not run after them," and Phil. 3:12, 14 : "I hasten (towards the goal)" (without obj.). Statistically, however, b. is more

---

δ ι ώ κ ω. [1] On the etymology, cf. Prellwitz, Etym. Wört., *s.v.*; also E. Fraenkel, *Satura Berolinensis* (1924), 20 ff.; P. Kretschmer in *Glotta*, 15 (1926), 189.

[2] A. Schlatter, *Verkanntes Griechisch* (1900), 60 reads דיאקוטטא in Lv. r., 5, 6 on 4:3 and takes this to be διώκτης in the sense of police superintendent. The traditional form דאיקוטטא leads rather to διοικητής, "treasurer." This fits the context at least as well, since there is mention of justice later.

[3] This paragraph is by Bertram.

common (Mt. 23:34; 10:23b, vl. "to drive out"), always in the sense of religious persecution implying guilt on the part of the persecutors (Mt. 10:23; 23:34; Jn. 5:16; 15:20; Ac. 7:52; 9:4; Gl. 1:13 etc., cf. διώκτης in 1 Tm. 1:13; [ἐκ-] διώκω in Lk. 11:49; 1 Th. 2:15), or as a test for the persecuted (Mt. 5:44; Lk. 21:12; R. 12:14; 1 C. 4:12; 2 C. 4:9; Gl. 5:11; 6:12; 2 Tm. 3:12) and therefore as a privilege (Mt. 5:10, 11, 12; cf. 1 Pt. 1:6; 3:14; Jm. 1:2). In Jn. 5:16 the rendering "to bring to judgment" [4] is rather too specialised.

2. "Zealously to follow." a. "to run after a person" (LXX 4 Βασ. 5:21); "to attach oneself to someone" (Xenoph. Mem., II, 8, 6); διώκειν καὶ φιλεῖν τινα (Plat. Theaet., 168a. b. "Earnestly to pursue or promote a cause," τιμάς (Thuc., II, 63); τὸν λ[ι]μ-νασμ[ὸν] δ[ί]οξον τῶν [ἐ]λα[ι]ών[ων], the "irrigation of oliveyards" (P. Fay., 111, 20 (95/96 A.D.). In the LXX it is mostly used for the two-sided רדף, τὸ δίκαιον (Dt. 16:20); εἰρήνην (ψ 33:14; Prv. 15:9; Hos. 6:3; cf. Gr. Sir. 27:8); μάταια (Prv. 12:11; 28:19; Is. 1:23; 5:11; cf. Gr. Sir. 11:10; 29:19; 31[34]:2; 34[31]:5); for חָרֵד adj., 2 Ἐσδρ. 9:4 : λόγον θεοῦ. In the magic pap. δίωκε τὸν λόγον is used for the recitation of magical formulae (P. Lond., I, 46, 394 [4th cent. A.D.]).

In the NT it is used only with material objects (b.) and only by Paul (including the Past.), Hb. and 1 Pt. In R. 9:30, 31 διώκειν (νόμον) δικαιοσύνης refers to that which distinguishes the Jews from the Gentiles yet also leads to their rejection. Elsewhere it always denotes the striving of Christians. The setting of a goal is a feature shared with OT and Rabbinic piety and Hellenistic moralism, but there is here a religious foundation and in consequence a greater intensity and depth. διώκειν δικαιοσύνην, 1 Tm. 6:11; 2 Tm. 2:22; τὸ ἀγαθόν, 1 Th. 5:15; εἰρή-νην, 1 Pt. 3:11 (ψ 33:14); Hb. 12:14; R. 14:19; ἀγάπην, 1 C. 14:1; φιλοξενίαν, R. 12:13.

Oepke

| † δόγμα, † δογματίζω |

The basic meaning of the word is τὰ δεδογμένα (μοι), "what seems to be right." a. "Opinion," esp. in Plato, e.g., Soph., 265c : ἢ τῷ τῶν πολλῶν δόγματι καὶ ῥήματι χρώμενοι. b. The derived meaning "philosophical opinion," "principle" or "doctrine" is rarer in Plato (Resp., VII, 538c : "the principles of the good and the beautiful in which children are instructed"), but is more common in later philosophy from the time of Aristotle ; Plut. Quaest. Platonicae, 1, 4 (II, 1000d): λόγοι ῥητόρων καὶ δόγματα σοφιστῶν (Epict. Diss., IV, 11, 8 : ὥστε ψυχῆς μὲν ἀκαθαρσία δόγματα πονηρά, κάθαρσις δ' ἐμποίησις, οἵων δεῖ δογμάτων; [1] Jos. Ap., 2, 169 : ἀλήθειαν τοῦ δόγματος (i.e., of philosophy); Bell., 2, 142 : the doctrine of the Essenes ; Philo Spec. Leg., I, 269 : σοφία καὶ τὰ σοφίας δόγματα. c. From the basic meaning there also

---

[4] K. Bornhäuser, *Johannesevangelium* (1928), 36, acc. to Schlatter (→ n. 2).
δ ό γ μ α. [1] A. Bonhöffer, *Epiktet und das NT* (RVV, 10 [1910]), 358.

derives the sense of "what is resolved," the "resolution" of an individual or an assembly (→ δοκέω, 2): Plat. Leg., I, 644d, esp. in Xenophon, e.g., An., VI, 4, 11: δόγμα ἐποιήσαντο θανάτῳ αὐτὸν ζημιοῦσθαι. This is used religiously in Preis. Zaub., IV (Paris) 527: [2] κατὰ δόγμα θεοῦ ἀμετάθετον, "according to God's decree." d. Usually the emphasis lies on the fact of "publishing a decree," i.e., "official ordinance or edict": of the ἄρχοντες, Plat. Resp., III, 414b; of the king, Da. Θ 2:13 etc. LXX Est. 4:8 אcamg; 4 Macc. 4:23 ff.; of the emperor, P. Fay., 20, 22; Jos. Bell., 1, 193; of the senate, Jos. Ant., 12, 146. e. Of the Law, 3 Macc. 1, 3: πατρίων δογμάτων; Jos. Ap., 1, 42: αὐτὰ (the Holy Scriptures) θεοῦ δόγματα. It is hardly surprising that this sense intersects with that of "teaching" under b. The Torah becomes a system comparable with the δόγματα of philosophy. It contains the sacred principles of divine philosophy; Jos. Ant., 15, 136: τὰ κάλλιστα τῶν δογμάτων; Philo Leg. All., I, 54 f.: διατήρησις τῶν ἁγίων δογμάτων; Gig., 52.

The verb δογματίζω, not found in older Gk., and in Jos. only in Ant., 14, 249, is in full accord with the meaning of the noun: [3] "to represent and affirm an opinion or tenet": Diog. L., III, 33, 52: "to establish or publish a decree": Diod. S., IV, 83, 7; 2 Macc. 15:36 (resolve of the community); "to proclaim an edict," esp. in the LXX: Da. 2:13; Est. 3:9; 2 Macc. 10:8.

1. In the NT the Lucan writings and Hb. (vl.) use the noun in sense d.: the imperial decree regarding the census in Lk. 2:1; the decree of Pharaoh [4] concerning the killing of children in Hb. 11:23 A; imperial prescripts in Ac. 17:7.

2. Both the noun and the verb are given a special emphasis in Colossians and Ephesians. Col. 2:14: ἐξαλείψας τὸ καθ᾽ ἡμῶν χειρόγραφον τοῖς δόγμασιν ὃ ἦν ὑπεναντίον ἡμῖν; 2:20: τί δογματίζεσθε· μὴ ἅψῃ ...; Eph. 2:15: ἐν τῇ σαρκὶ αὐτοῦ τὸν νόμον τῶν ἐντολῶν ἐν δόγμασιν καταργήσας. In Col. 2:14 δόγμασιν might perhaps be construed grammatically as an instr. dat. belonging to ἐξαλείψας, so that the δόγματα would be the new command or edict of God. [5] On the other hand, the link with 2:20 excludes a strict equation of the noun and the verb, and here the reference is undoubtedly to ordinances of touch and taste. The usage of Hellenistic Judaism (e.) would thus refer [6] the τοῖς δόγμασιν to the Mosaic Law and its demands as the content of the χειρόγραφον and its hostility to man. Hence, as Christ is elsewhere described as the end of the Law, so we are told here that the δόγματα are blotted out by Him and that δογματίζεσθαι is brought to an end. The construction and train of thought are much the same in Eph. 2:15, namely, that the Mosaic νόμος τῶν ἐντολῶν, which consists in δόγματα, is set aside by Christ.

3. As Philo and Josephus appropriated for the divine Law a term used for philosophical principles and imperial edicts, so the Christian community very quickly began to adopt a similar usage. In Ac. 16:4 the word signifies the resolutions and decrees of the early church in Jerusalem which are to be sent out to the cities of the first missionary journey. In the post-apostolic fathers the word comes to be applied to the teachings and prescriptions of Jesus: Ign. Mg., 13, 1; Barn., 1, 6:

---

[2] Mithr.-Liturg, 4, 27.

[3] Liddell-Scott, s.v.

[4] Rgg. Hb., 368, n. 34 suspects an assimilation of the main reading διάταγμα to Lk. 2:1.

[5] Bengel on Col. 2:14: haec sunt decreta gratiae; on Eph. 2:15: per quae proponebatur misericordia in omnes. Cf. already Thdrt., Chrys. Hom. in Eph. 5 (MPG, 62, 39).

[6] As against Loh. Kol., 117, whose exposition in terms of devilish ordinances is hardly likely.

δόγματα τοῦ κυρίου; Did., 11, 3 : τὸ δόγμα τοῦ εὐαγγελίου. In an ancient prayer, dating from the fourth century : ὅπως καταξιωθῶμεν τῶ[ν] εὐαγγελιζομένων δογμάτων τῶν ἁγίων σου ἀποστόλων. [7] Chrys. Hom. in Phil., 6, 2 (MPG, 62, 220) : τὰ τῆς ἐκκλησίας δόγματα; Synesius Ep., 5 (MPG, 66, 1344b) : τὸ δόγμα τὸ θεῖον. From the time of Bas. Spir. Sct., 27 (MPG, 32, 188a) a distinction is drawn between the two parts of Christian teaching : τὰ κηρύγματα and τὰ δόγματα. In the canons of the councils δογματίζω is used in the same sense as ὁρίζω. [8]

Kittel

δοκέω, δόξα, δοξάζω, συνδοξάζω,
ἔνδοξος, ἐνδοξάζω, παράδοξος

The historical problem in relation to this word-group is that in the biblical usage of the LXX and NT the verb δοκέω more or less fully maintains the general Gk. sense with no development in content, whereas there is a significant change in the meaning of the noun, which both loses part of its secular sense in biblical Gk. and also takes on an alien and specifically religious meaning, shared by the verb δοξάζω rather than δοκέω. It is because this substitute verb is present that δοκέω can retain its original meaning. The process is helped by the fact [1] that the formal relationship between δόξα and δοκέω is not too clear and also by the addition to the secular sense of δόξα of a special biblical sense which is not so clear in the case of δοκέω (δόξα in the sense of "reputation" from δοκέω "to count for something"). In any case, δοκέω cannot be used in the sense of furnishing someone with δόξα.

δοκέω.

Everywhere δοκέω has the meaning 1. trans. "to believe," "to think." Mt. 6:7: δοκοῦσιν ὅτι εἰσακουσθήσονται. The only Palestinian usage (under the influence of סבר) is to be found in Mt. 3:9 : μὴ δόξητε λέγειν ἐν ἑαυτοῖς, "do not incline." [2]

2. Intr. "to appear," "to have the appearance," e.g., Ac. 17:18 : δοκεῖ καταγγελεὺς εἶναι, Mt. 17:25 : τί σοι δοκεῖ; Thus δοκεῖ μοι means "it seems good to me," "I decide." It occurs in the NT only in Lk. 1:3 of the individual and in Ac. 15:22 ff. of the assembly, as often in secular Gk.

---

[7] Pap. des Ägypt. Museums Berlin, 13 415; C. Schmidt, "Zwei altchristl. Gebete" in *Nt.liche Studien für G. Heinrici* (1914), 71, 24.

[8] Suic. Thes., I, 935.

δ ο κ έ ω. [1] I owe this to Debrunner.

[2] S. Dt., 322 on 32:28 : לא תהיו סבורים לומר. Cf. Schl. Mt., 73; E. Norden, *Antike Kunstprosa*, II (1909), 487. Cf. also Aesch. Ag., 16 : ὅταν δοκῶ, "if I am pleased (to sing)" [Debrunner].

Acc. to Plato Resp., II, 361b/362a, the antithesis [3] δοκεῖν/εἶναι, which is most important in Gk. thought and ethics of the 5th century, is first formulated for the wider public in Aesch. Sept. c. Theb., 592 (οὐ γὰρ δοκεῖν ἄριστος, ἀλλ' εἶναι θέλει).

It is characteristic that in the Mas. there is no sure equivalent for the δοκέω of the LXX. [4] The OT finds it difficult to express a mere appearance or a purely subjective opinion. In Heb. the person for whom something is thus or thus is often denoted by עַל or בְּעֵינֵי. The distinction between being and appearance, between reality and imagination, finds particular expression in the LXX at 'Ιωβ 15:21 and 20:7, 22 in statements which achieve formal and material parallelism only in the Gk. text. There is no basis for the δοκέω in the Mas. In other passages, too, it is the LXX which emphasises the subjective character of a statement by the introduction of δοκέω. This happens only 3 times in the Torah (Gn. 19:14; 38:15; Jos. 9:31 = 9:25). In Σ we may also refer to ψ 35:2 and Qoh. 9:13. Otherwise it is found only in books for which there is no Heb. original, and esp. 2 and 3 Macc. In all other instances δοκεῖ is used with the dat. of person to express one's will or subjective pleasure (טוֹב עַל, טוֹב בְּעֵינֵי) in the sense of ἀρέσκειν. δοκεῖ μοι, "it seems good to me," "I desire," is also found occasionally for Heb. or Aram. terms which express willingness or readiness. Thus it is used for נדב in Ex. and for צבא in Da. 4 and 5. In detail it is sometimes hard to distinguish between subjective opinion and appearance in the LXX (cf. 'Ιωβ 15:21). The perf. pass. is found in Jdt. 3:8 to express firm will and resolve (vl.: δεδογμένον, ABS: δεδομένον); cf. also Σ 1 Βασ. 20:9 (כְּלָתָה). δοκεῖ is also used for the will of God in 'Ιωβ with no Mas. basis, cf. 'Ιερ. 34:4 (= 27:5); 2 Macc. 1:20. It is used for political will in 1 Macc. 8:26 etc.

3. It is also used intr. for "to count for something," "to be of repute." [5] Mk. 10:42 : οἱ δοκοῦντες ἄρχειν, "those who are accounted rulers." In Gl. 2 it is partly used in the absol. in v. 2, 6b : οἱ δοκοῦντες, and partly defined in v. 6a : οἱ δοκοῦντες εἶναί τι; v. 9 : οἱ δοκοῦντες στῦλοι εἶναι, "those who are of particular repute in the Jerusalem community." Outside the NT the expression can also be used for a reputation which is not merely imaginary but has some substance in it. Cf. Eur. Hec., 295 : κἀκ τῶν δοκούντων αὐτός; Epict. Ench., 33, 12 : οἱ ἐν ὑπεροχῇ δοκοῦντες. Jos. Ant., 19:307: οἱ δοκοῦντες αὐτῶν ἐξέχειν; Bell., 4, 141 and 159. In the light of these passages there is no reason to suspect irony ("those who want to be something"). On the other hand, the abbreviation in v. 2, 6b, and the fourfold repetition, indicate the use of a slogan coined by Paul's opponents. [6]

δόξα.

A. The Greek Use of δόξα.

1. Found already in Homer and Herodotus, this word has in all non-biblical Greek a basic meaning which reflects its link with δοκέω, namely, "what one thinks," "opinion." This takes two forms : a. from δοκέω, "I think," "the opinion

---

[3] W. Schmid, Berliner philol. Wochenschr., 48 (1928), 646 ; A. Fridrichsen, Symbolae Arctoae (Osloenses), I (1922), 45; ThStKr, 94 (1922), 81 f.

[4] This paragraph is by Bertram.

[5] Zn., Ltzm. on Gl. 2.

[6] Comparison with the Talmudic חָשׁוּב (Zn., ad loc.) is possible only in the case of the abbreviated term, but not in v. 6a, 9, since the Talmudic word is used absol. and not with the infin. (cf. Str.-B., III, 537).

δόξα, δοξάζω. J. Schneider, Doxa, eine bedeutungsgeschichtl. Studie (1932); G. Kittel, Religionsgesch. u. Urchrtt. (1932), 82 ff.; H. Kittel, "Die Herrlichkeit Gottes,"

which I have" ; b. from δοκέω, "I count as," "the opinion which others have of me." [1]

a. The subjective sense can be applied in many ways. It may imply "expectation" : παρὰ δόξαν, "against expectation" ; ἀπὸ δόξης : Hom. Il., 10, 324; Od., 11, 344; Xenoph. An., II, 1, 18; ἀπὸ τῆς δόξης πεσεῖν, spe decidere, [2] Hdt., VII, 203; but it may equally well imply the "opinion" or "view which I represent" : ὡς ἐμῇ δόξῃ, Xenoph. Vect., 5, 2 : κατὰ τὴν ἐμὴν δόξαν, Plat. Gorg., 472e. In this sense the term becomes a philosophical catchword [3] for a "philosophical opinion," whether sound or unsound, true or false : δόξαι ἀληθεῖς καὶ ψευδεῖς, Plat. Phileb., 36c; δόξαν μὲν πᾶσαν εἰπεῖν ἀδύνατον, ἐπειδὴ καὶ ψευδής ἐστιν δόξα· κινδυνεύει δὴ ἡ ἀληθὴς δόξα ἐπιστήμη εἶναι, Plat. Theaet., 187b. We read of the loss of a right δόξα when someone is "stolen, bewitched or compelled," Plat. Resp., III, 413a. Counterparts are insight and knowledge (γνώμη, νόησις, ἐπιστήμη), Plat. Resp., V, 476d ff., Tim., 37bc. It stands midway between knowledge and certainty (ἐπίστασθαι and ἀμαθία), Plat. Symp., 202a. From this sense of philosophical opinion it comes to be used for a "philosophical tenet" : κύριαι δόξαι as the title of a philosophical work of Epicurus : Cic. Fin., 2, 7; or for a philosophical axiom : αἱ κοιναὶ δόξαι, Arist. Metaph., II, 2, p. 996b, 28; III, 3, p. 1005b, 29. But the emphasis on the subjective side can be strengthened to give the sense of "mere conjecture," i.e., hazardous statements which are contrary to ἀλήθεια (→ I, 238), and which may even be equivalent to φαντασίαι, dreams, or other products of imagination or illusion : Thuc., I, 32 : δόξης ἁμαρτία; Aesch. Ag., 275 : δόξα βριζούσης φρενός; Philostr. Vit. Ap., I, 23 : δόξα ἐνυπνίου.

b. Since δοκέω usually denotes "good standing," the objective sense is mostly used favourably for "reputation" or "renown" : δόξαν ἀντὶ τοῦ ζῆν ᾑρημένος,

---

Studien zu Geschichte und Wesen eines nt.lichen Begriffes (1934). On A.: F. Astius, *Lexicon Platonicum*, I (1835), 553 ff.; O. Apelt, *Platon-Index²* (1923), 86; R. Marett, "The Meaning of δόξα in Plato," Class. Rev., 17 (1903), 267 f.; K. Schirlitz, *Der Begriff der δόξα in Platons Theaetetos* (Gymnasialprogramm Stargard, 1905); H. Bonitz, *Index Aristotelicus* (1870), 203 f.; A. Deissmann, "Hellenisierung des semit. Monotheismus," NJbch. Kl. Alt., 11 (1903), 165 f.; H. Leisegang, *Index z. Philo* (1926 ff.), 199 f. On C: A. v. Gall, *Die Herrlichkeit Gottes* (1900); W. Caspari, *Die Bdtg. der Wortsippe* כבד *in Hebräischen* (1908); J. Morgenstern, "Biblical Theophanies," Zeitschr. f. Assyriologie, 25 (1911), 139 ff.; 28 (1914), 15 ff.; K. Vollers, ARW, 9 (1906), 180 ff. On D : A. H. Forster, "The Meaning of Δόξα in the Greek Bible," Anglican Theological Review, 12 (1929/30), 311 ff. On D ff.: Schl. Mt., 108, 523, 711; Schl. J., 24 f., 192, 219, 269, 275 f., 288. On E : v. Gall, 66-91; J. Abrahams, *The Glory of God* (1925); Str.-B., I, 752 f., 974 ff.; III, 474; IV, 887, 940 ff., 1138 ff.; On F/G : Joh. W., 1 K., 56 f., 272 f., 371, n. 1; Wnd., 2 K., 115; F. W. Grosheide, Comm. on 1 C. (1932), 98 f., 372; Dob. Th., 102. R. Kabisch, *Eschatologie des Pls.* (1893), 195 ff.; R. B. Lloyd, "The Word 'Glory' in the Fourth Gospel," Exp. T., 43 (1932), 546 ff.; Reitzenstein Hell. Myst., 289, 314 f., 344, 355 ff.; H. Böhlig, *Geisteskultur von Tarsus* (1913), 97 ff.; G. P. Wetter, "Verherrlichung im Joh. Ev.," Beitr. z. Religionswiss., 2 (1915), 32-113; *Phos* (1915), 62 ff., 74 ff.; W. Bousset, *Kyrios Christos²* (1921), 124; E. Krebs, *Der Logos als Heiland* (1910), 162 ff.; Bau. J., 22 f.; Heinrici, 2 K., 168 ff.

[1] This analysis, which recurs in several dictionaries, is based essentially on Liddell-Scott, 444.

[2] It is possible that δόξα should be translated "repute" in this passage, so Schneider, 13, cf. H. v. Herwerden, *Lexicon Graecum²* (1910), s.v. Cf. also J. Schweighaeuser, *Lex Herodoteum*, I (1824), 172 f.

[3] Apelt., 86; Bonitz, 203; also v. Arnim Index. It is immaterial for our purpose whether one can speak of a development of the term in Plato (Marett, *op. cit.*), or even of a change of meaning in one and the same work (Theaetetus, cf. Schirlitz, *op. cit.*). Cf. Schneider, 12 f., and the analysis of the Platonic concept in H. Kittel, 13 ff.

Demosth. Or., 2, 15; δόξαν καταλιπεῖν, Or., 3, 24. But by adding an adjective an evil reputation may easily be denoted: [δόξαν] ἀντὶ καλῆς αἰσχρὰν τῇ πόλει περιάπτειν, Demosth. Or., 20, 10; λαμβάνειν δόξαν φαύλην, Demosth. Ep., 3, 5. In this sense δόξα, with the Homeric κλέος and later τιμή, achieves central significance for the Greeks. Supreme and ideal worth is summed up in the term. A man's worth is measured by his repute. Hence the prayer of Solon to the Muses in 1, 3 f. (Diehl, I, 17): ὄλβον μοι πρὸς θεῶν μακάρων δότε καὶ πρὸς ἁπάντων ἀνθρώπων αἰεὶ δόξαν ἔχειν ἀγαθήν. [4]

> It is in keeping with the nature of the inscript. that the subjective or philosophical meaning is not found in them. The word is here [5] used only in the sense b.: κατ᾽ ἀξίαν τῆς τῶν προγόνων δόξης, Ditt. Syll.[3], II, 796 B, 25; δόξα τε καὶ ἀνδρεία, II, 700, 35; δόξα καὶ τιμή, II, 704 E, 20; in this sense it is also used of the holiness of the deity: εἰς κόσμον [6] καὶ δόξαν τοῦ Βακχείου, III, 1109, 5. On the other hand, both senses are found in the pap., though there are not too many [7] instances: [8] a. ταῦτα προκαλεσαμένη ἅμα τῷ [ἀν]δρὶ δόξαν αὕτη οὐκέτι ἐπὶ τοὺς ὅρκους ἀπήντα, CPR, 232, 27; b. the πρύτανις is the δόξα of his city, P. Oxy., I, 41, 4. In the pap. we can also see clearly the distinctive Judaeo-Christian influence, e.g., the citing of the Lord's Prayer in BGU, III, 954, 24; δόξα πατρὶ καὶ υἱῷ, P. Greci e Latini, VI, 719, 5.

c. A. Deissmann, [9] and then J. Schneider, [10] have advanced the conjecture that in Δόξα as a name for women [11] and for ships [12] we have an original name for light analogous to other names for women. In them, and perhaps in popular speech, there has survived the oldest and most concrete meaning of δόξα, namely, "light" or "radiance"; and this is the meaning which emerges again in the LXX and the NT. Bechtel, however, thinks that the name has an abstract derivation, Δόξα being the one who stands in good repute (δόξα), cf. Ἀξίωμα and ἐν ἀξιώματι. Schneider prefers the analogy to other names deriving from terms for light (Φέγγος, Ζωπύρα, Ἀστήρ, Φωσφόρος, Σελήνη). There would be no objection to this if the basic meaning could be proved. In fact, however, this hypothetical interpretation of the name is the only instance of this sense in the pre-Judaeo-Christian world. Since there are no [13] arguments against the other meaning, which remains

---

[4] I owe this reference to H. Kleinknecht.

[5] Ditt. Syll.[3], IV, Index, 296. In Ditt. Or., II, Index the word does not occur; though cf. 456b, 36 (οὐράνιος δόξα, honouring of the emperor); 90, 2 (μεγαλόδοξος); 168, 56 (δεδοξασμένος); 513, 11 (ἐνδόξως). Cf. Schneider, 18 ff.

[6] Schneider thinks he detects echoes of a concrete meaning in some inscriptions, as here in the parallelism of δόξα and κόσμος ("adornment"). Yet there can be little doubt that the meaning of δόξα here is "repute" rather than "radiance."

[7] According to the indexes, δόξα is not found in the pap. collections of Witkowski ([2]1911), Olsson (1925), Milligan (1912). In P. Masp., 295, 13 δόξα is added.

[8] Preisigke Wört., 393.

[9] Op. cit., 165, n. 5.

[10] Op. cit., 20 f.

[11] Examples may be found in F. Bechtel, Die attischen Frauennamen nach ihrem Systeme dargestellt (1902), 112, 131 f., 138; W. Weissbrodt, Griech. u. lat. Inschr. in der antikarchäologischen Sammlung der Kgl. Akad. z. Braunsberg (1913), 7.

[12] Bechtel, 132.

[13] Deissmann merely suggested the possibility some 30 years ago in a short note. Schneider, however, has subjected it to a broad and comprehensive analysis. It is thus the more instructive that he can express his positive findings only in terms of an "It seems to me ... to be likely" (21). From his excellent treatment and the full review of the materials relevant for a history of δόξα, we can see plainly that there are no instances of the supposed original sense of "glory."

within the sphere of what is known and attested, the hypothesis seems to be both improbable and superfluous. [14]

2. Josephus and Philo follow the customary Gk. usage. In Jos. [15] δόξα means a. "view" [16] e.g., περὶ θεοῦ, Ap., 2, 179, 254 and 256. δόξα can also be erroneous, ματαίαις δόξαις, Ap. 1, 6. In Philo it means a correct or false "opinion" or "philosophical tenet," e.g., of Aristotle or the Pythagoreans, Aet. Mund., 12, of Heracl., Leg. All., III, 7. II, 36: τοῖς δόξαν πρὸ ἀληθείας τετιμηκόσι, Det. Pot. Ins., 161: μὴ πρὸς ἀλήθειαν γεγενῆσθαι, δόξῃ δὲ μόνον ὑπολαμβάνεσθαι. There is here a structural alteration in the meaning of δόξα to the degree that in Plato the δόξα is not measured only by the philosophical measure of what is true or false, but can also be ἄθεος, ἀσεβής, or θεοφιλής, φιλόθεος, ὁσία. In these predicates we can see the influence of the OT world of thought paraphrased by Philo. Poster. C., 42 : ἀσεβῆ καὶ ἄθεον εἰσηγούμενοι δόξαν γένει τῷ Καῒν προσκεκληρώσθωσαν; Leg. All., III, 13 : ἀπὸ τῆς ἀθέου ... δόξης Φαραώ; Praem. Poen., 27: ὁ μὲν οὖν ἡγεμὼν τῆς θεοφιλοῦς δόξης; Det. Pot. Ins., 78 : ἣν μὲν δοκεῖς ἀνῃρηκέναι φιλόθεον δόξαν; Leg. All., III, 126 : πολλάκις συνεισέρχεται μὲν ὁ νοῦς εἰς ἱερὰς καὶ ὁσίους καὶ κεκαθαρμένας δόξας.

b. Yet we also find the term used here for the "honour" or "glory" which accrues to man. Josephus : κόσμον ἑαυτῶν εἶναι τὴν ἐμὴν δόξαν, Vit., 273; εἰς τοῦτο δόξης προελθοῦσι, Ant., 5, 115; τὸ δίκαιον ἀντὶ τοῦ πρὸς δόξαν ἠγαπηκέναι, Ant., 16, 158; δόξα καὶ τιμή, Ant., 2, 268; 6, 200; 11, 217; δόξα αἰώνιος = imperishable fame, Ant., 13, 63; 15, 376. Philo : αἱ δόξης ἢ χρημάτων ἢ ἀρχῆς ἐπιθυμίαι, Op. Mund., 79; χρυσός, ἄργυρος, δόξα, τιμαί, ἀρχαί, Leg. All., II, 107. Even in the verb → δοξάζω, in → ἔνδοξος, and in the derivates δοξομανέω, δοξομανής, and δοξόκοπος ("desirous of fame"), it is hard to see any meaning beyond the two basic senses.

c. In a few passages, however, we can see a transition to the sense of "splendour." The Queen of Sheba came μετὰ πολλῆς δόξης καὶ πλούτου παρασκευῆς, Jos. Ant., 8, 166; cf. also the admiration of the temple κατασκευῆς τε ἕνεκα καὶ μεγέθους ἔτι τε τῆς καθ' ἕκαστον πολυτελείας καὶ τῆς περὶ τὰ ἅγια δόξης, Bell., 6, 267. Here we have a use in which the content of δόξα does not derive from the ideas or opinions of men but from an independent splendour. Yet the author is hardly conscious of the transition, since he is speaking only of objects which arouse the admiration and praise of men and which thus possess δόξα in the usual Gk. sense.

d. The case is rather different with the one exception (among some 250 instances) [17] in Philo's Spec. Leg., I, 45. Moses says to God : "From Thy instructions I am convinced that I cannot receive a clear picture of Thy being. I thus desire to see at least the accompanying δόξα. I believe, however, that the ministering powers around Thee are Thy δόξα; the fact that I have not yet perceived it gives me a great desire to know it." Here there can be no doubt that the context of Ex. 33:18 has given to the term the sense of the divine radiance which Moses saw. The change is obviously due to the impact of biblical usage. It is also evident, however, that this is a foreign body in Philo's total use of the word. The same truth emerges when we study the way in which Jos. and

---

[14] On the theories of Reitzenstein and Wetter, and on the magic pap., → 252.

[15] I owe the Jos. material especially to A. Schlatter.

[16] δόξα can mean "proposition" (i.e., the "view" which becomes a "proposition"), Jos. Ant., 4, 62.

[17] Cf. for what follows Leisegang's Index, 199 f., in which there are some 180 instances of opinio, some 60 of gloria, and 2 of potentia et splendida maiestas divina. For one of these two → supra. The other (Virt., 35) rests on an unfortunate misreading and really belongs to opinio : αἴτιον δὲ τῆς ὁμονοίας τὸ ἀνωτάτω καὶ μέγιστον ἡ περὶ τοῦ ἑνὸς θεοῦ δόξα (= the view of the one God), ἀφ' ἧς οἷα πηγῆς ἐνωτικῇ καὶ ἀδιαλύτῳ φιλίᾳ κέχρηνται πρὸς ἀλλήλους.

Philo handle the story in Ex. 34:30 ff., which tells us how the face of Moses shone (LXX : δεδόξασται) when he returned from Sinai. In Rabbinic exposition (→ 246) and the NT (→ 251) this is taken to imply reflection of the divine כָּבוֹד. Jos., however, ignores the story, and Philo speaks of the inner purity and beauty of Moses (Vit. Mos., II, 69 f.). Equally striking is the way in which Philo deals (Quaest. in Ex., II, 45) with the OT saying about the descent of the δόξα of God on Sinai (Ex. 24:16); he introduces a comparison with the δόξα and δύναμις of an earthly monarch : ἐπεὶ καὶ βασιλέως λέγεται δόξα ἡ στρατιωτικὴ δύναμις. The idea of radiance is obviously quite alien. On the other hand, Jos. can equate δόξα and כָּבוֹד, as in the translation of 'Ιχαβώδης as ἀδοξία in Ant., 5, 360. [18]

In their use of the term the Palestinian Pharisee and the Jewish interpreter of the OT are thus united in following the non-biblical usage as distinct from the biblical. In this respect they are poles apart from the NT authors, whether Jewish and Palestinian Christians or Gentile and Greek.

B. The NT Use of δόξα, I.

Even a cursory survey of the position in the NT reveals a totally different picture. The old meaning a., "opinion," has disappeared completely. There is not a single example in either the NT or the post-apostolic fathers. Other terms like γνώμη in 1 C. 1:10; 7:25, 40, or πρόθεσις in 2 Tm. 3:10, are used instead. The meaning b., "repute" or "honour," is still found : ἔσται σοι δόξα ἐνώπιον πάντων, Lk. 14:10; γυνὴ δὲ ἐὰν κομᾷ, δόξα αὐτῇ ἐστιν, 1 C. 11:15 (opp. ἀτιμία, v. 14; cf. 2 C. 6:8); ζητοῦντες ἐξ ἀνθρώπων δόξαν, 1 Th. 2:6; also Eph. 3:13; 1 Th. 2:20; Phil. 3:19 etc. There has been added the meaning c., "radiance," "glory," which is not found in secular Greek but is already present in Jos. : πάσας τὰς βασιλείας τοῦ κόσμου καὶ τὴν δόξαν αὐτῶν, Mt. 4:8; cf. Lk. 4:6; Σολομὼν ἐν πάσῃ τῇ δόξῃ αὐτοῦ, Mt. 6:29; Lk. 12:27; the δόξα of the kings of the earth, Rev. 21:24, 26; cf. also the quotation from Is. 40:6 in 1 Pt. 1:24 : πᾶσα σὰρξ ... καὶ πᾶσα δόξα αὐτῆς; also the δόξα of the stars in 1 C. 15:40 f. δόξα can also mean "reflection" in the sense of "image" (εἰκών): man is the δόξα θεοῦ and woman the δόξα ἀνδρός, 1 C. 11:7. [19]

In the NT, however, the word is used for the most part in a sense for which there is no Greek analogy whatever and of which there is only an isolated example in Philo. That is to say, it denotes "divine and heavenly radiance," the "loftiness and majesty" of God, and even the "being of God" and His world. How does the word come to have this new significance ? To answer this question it is necessary that we study the OT כָּבוֹד.

Kittel

---

[18] We should not number in this group Jos. Ant., 4, 48 : μεμηνότων κατὰ τῆς σῆς (God's) δόξης, where opposition to God's honour in sense b. is implied.

[19] Cf. the Jewish inscr. from Rome quoted in Ltzm., ad loc. (H. Vogelstein-P. Rieger, Gesch. der Juden in Rom [1895/96], I, no. 56): ἡ δόξα Σωφρονίου Λουκίλλα εὐλογημένη.

C. כָּבוֹד in the OT.

1. כָּבוֹד[20] was always used in a secular sense for "honour." Yet honour was not thought of as a purely ideal quality, but, in accordance with the basic meaning, as something "weighty" in man which gives him "importance." Thus כָּבוֹד could be used for wealth, or for the position of honour conferred by material substance. However natural the transition from wealth to honour, not every כָּבוֹד which is not referred to material possession is to be explained along these lines. Even primarily כָּבוֹד can denote what is weighty in the figurative sense, i.e., what is impressive to men, so that כָּבוֹד approximates to an anthropological term. Nevertheless, one must be on guard against a spiritualisation which runs contrary to the true meaning.

As Abraham is rich (כָּבֵד) in cattle, silver and gold (Gn. 13:2), so the author describes all the movable goods of Jacob as his כָּבוֹד (Gn. 31:1). In Ps. 49:16 the כָּבוֹד of a house is brought into synon. parallelism with wealth, and כָּבוֹד has the same meaning in Na. 2:10. The כָּבוֹד which God will give to Solomon apart from riches, however, does not consist in material possessions, but in importance; and when Joseph's brothers speak of his כָּבוֹד they mean his status as an official (Gn. 45:13). In Is. 5:13 the כָּבוֹד of a people is the nobility. But the word can also be used in another sense. The כָּבוֹד of Moab (Is. 16:14) or of Kedar (Is. 21:16) is more than its material strength; it is its prestige among the nations, i.e., that which gives it standing and importance. In Is. 17:4 כָּבוֹד is an expression for the secret inner might which alone constitutes personified Israel, and in this passage it is significantly linked with the anthropological term "flesh." In the same way the Hebrew can speak of the כָּבוֹד of, e.g., a forest, not in description of its aesthetic or material value, nor as a botanical term,[21] but in definition of its nature. A particularly interesting example (cf. also Is. 35:2; 60:13 etc.) is Is. 10:18: Yahweh will destroy the כָּבוֹד of the forest of Assyria (again personified: מִנֶּפֶשׁ עַד בָּשָׂר). Hence we need not be surprised that כָּבוֹד is used of men as a synon. for נֶפֶשׁ or חַיִּים. Once again כָּבוֹד is something weighty or impressive, a *gravitas* which constitutes man's place in society, and therefore an anthropological term. In all the examples cited attempts have been made to substitute כְּבֵדִי, "my liver" (as the seat of the emotional life); but this is surely incorrect.[22]

2. If in relation to man כָּבוֹד denotes that which makes him impressive and demands recognition, whether in terms of material possessions or striking *gravitas*, in relation to God it implies that which makes God impressive to man, the force of His self-manifestation. As everywhere attested in the OT, God is intrinsically invisible. Nevertheless, when He reveals Himself, or declares Himself, e.g., in

---

[20] The noun כָּבוֹד is a development, in a way which cannot be fixed with linguistic precision, of the root כבד, the basic meaning of which is undoubtedly "to weigh heavily." The subst., however, moved away from the original concrete meaning far more than the part. כָּבֵד.

[21] Caspari, *op. cit.*, 105 f.

[22] Cf. Dillmann in Gn. 49:6. In the Ps., cf. 7:5; 16:9; 30:12; 57:8; 108:1. Here, too, certain exegetes emend according to the Assyrian *kapittu* (liver). Naturally, this secular use might at any time become religious, cf. the fine confession that Yahweh is the כָּבוֹד of a man. The meaning is that whatever constitutes the nature and significance of anyone comes from Yahweh, cf. Ps. 3:3; also Jer. 2:11.

meteorological phenomena, one may rightly speak of the כְּבוֹד יְהוָה, of a manifestation which makes on man a highly significant impression. The more seriously religious reflexion took the idea of Yahweh's invisibility and transcendence, the more this expression for the impressive element in God became an important technical term in OT theology. Our primary concern is with this precise theological term, which is paralleled by a freer use of כְּבוֹד יְהוָה especially in religious poetry.

It is hardly possible to give a history of the word. Though there are undoubtedly variations in the use of כָּבוֹד, these cannot be worked out chronologically. Indeed, it is to be noted that passages which are late from the standpoint of composition are distinguished by poetic archaisms and by conformity to fixed priestly traditions.

a. When we examine passages which describe the כְּבוֹד יְהוָה more precisely, we find traits which point strongly to the phenomenon of a thunderstorm. Thus Ps. 97:1 ff. describes a phenomenon of this nature. There are clouds and lightnings and fire, and the hills melt like wax. According to Ex. 24:15 ff. the כְּבוֹד יְהוָה is like devouring fire in a cloud on the mount. Another passage to which we might refer is Ju. 5:4, for, although the phrase כְּבוֹד יְהוָה does not occur, the reference is to the appearance of Yahweh at the battle on the waters of Megiddo, and the earth quakes, the clouds drop water and the hills quiver. Even in the rather artificial vision on the occasion of the call of Ezekiel (1:1 ff.) the same features recur: storm, cloud, fire, lightning and the noise of rushing water. Finally, in the Thunderstorm Psalm (Ps. 29) the phenomena which accompany the אֶל־הַכָּבוֹד are thunder and flame. It is difficult to say in what sense the concept of כָּבוֹד is expressed in terms of such phenomena. One view is that the oppressiveness of overhanging thunder clouds led to the idea of a כָּבוֹד of Yahweh, as when we read of a עָנָן כָּבֵד on the occasion of the revelation at Sinai (Ex. 19:16).[23] This would mean that in early times Israel actually regarded the thunderstorm as a revelation of Yahweh and called the majestic spectacle of such phenomena the כָּבוֹד of its God. On the other hand, it is striking that the basic thought of weight is no longer present where there is reference to the כְּבוֹד יְהוָה. Hence it is not impossible that כָּבוֹד was used to define that which is intrinsically impressive in the being of God, just as oriental peoples generally use it for light, so that it was only secondarily that traits gathered from the thunderstorm came to be associated with the manifestation of Yahweh.

If ancient Israel sometimes experienced the כָּבוֹד of Yahweh in the thunderstorm, we cannot equate Yahweh with this natural phenomenon as though He were regarded and accepted as a god of thunder, or as though every thunderstorm were a manifestation of the glory of Yahweh as well as every such manifestation a thunderstorm.[24] Indeed, we can see from the beautiful story in Ex. 33:18 ff. that the כְּבוֹד יְהוָה could sometimes be depicted in a very different form from that of the thunderstorm. When Moses expressed a desire to see the כָּבוֹד of Yahweh, we are told that so long as he stands in a cleft of the rock, and Yahweh covers him with His hand, Yahweh will cause all His beauty (כָּל־טוּבִי ?) to pass by him; and when He has passed by, and His hand has been withdrawn, Moses will see Him

---

[23] Cf. Ex. 9:18: בָּרָד כָּבֵד, "severe hail."
[24] As against v. Gall, op. cit., 23.

from behind. There is here only a slight reminiscence of the passing storm. How the close connexion of Yahweh's כָּבוֹד with the phenomenon of the thunderstorm came to be loosened may be seen clearly in authors like Ezekiel and the so-called P for whom the כְּבוֹד יְהוָה is a strictly theological concept.

b. Even an ancient piece like Ps. 19 gives a more precise cosmological delineation which exalts the כָּבוֹד of God (כְּבוֹד אֵל) far above the sphere of natural phenomena (v. 1). One might say that כָּבוֹד is an element which belongs to the higher heavenly regions, which are here plainly distinguished from the firmament (רָקִיעַ) as the sphere of the creaturely. On the other hand, there was little enquiry in Israel into the nature and *locus* of the כְּבוֹד יְהוָה outside the capacity of human comprehension, and therefore the Priestly document sought the more precisely to establish the self-revelation of Yahweh in the earthly.

By way of understanding it should be noted that this document neither stood in the tradition which thought of God as dwelling in the sanctuary, [25] nor shared the Deuteronomic view that God remains in heaven and simply gives His name to the elect people at the cultic centre. For P heaven is certainly the sphere of Yahweh, but He constantly descends to all peoples, e.g., to speak with Moses, to execute judgment etc. The place of supreme encounter is the אֹהֶל מוֹעֵד, the tent of meeting, or more exactly the place which shelters the ark. [26] Thus according to P God has chosen a place where He will maintain His connexion with the people and institute encounter without consuming man through His holiness. Even so, the כְּבוֹד יְהוָה does not come unveiled, but is always surrounded by a cloud. The cloud hovers above Sinai, and it is in the cloud that Moses finds the כְּבוֹד יְהוָה to which he alone comes through the clouds (Ex. 24:15 ff.). The same is true as regards the tent. In the many accounts [27] of the appearance of the כְּבוֹד יְהוָה the clearest is to be found in Ex. 40:34 f., where the cloud covers the tent and the כָּבוֹד fills the interior of it. The nature of the כָּבוֹד itself is to be conceived as a radiant, fiery substance. There proceeds from it fire which consumes the awaiting sacrifice, and after speaking with God Moses has a radiance of countenance which dazzles the Israelites.

If we compare with these accounts the appearance of the כְּבוֹד יְהוָה at the dedication of Solomon's temple, we are struck by the much more concrete conception found in P. On the one side we read indefinitely of a cloud preventing access to the temple, on the other of the clear distinction between the enveloping cloud and the fiery כָּבוֹד. In the case of the latter the כָּבוֹד is not a meteorological phenomen, since the cloud is a covering rather than part of the כָּבוֹד. The כָּבוֹד is a manifestation of the glory of God. [28]

c. Though there are many agreements, Ezekiel belongs to a different tradition from the author of P. It is more than a formal difference that the כְּבוֹד יְהוָה appears to the prophet alone in strange and pregnant visions, in contrast to public revelation

---

[25] The ark is the throne of Yahweh; Yahweh dwells in the temple: 1 K. 8:12; 2 K. 19:14 f.

[26] Technical term וְנוֹעַדְתִּי שָׁם: Ex. 25:22; 29:43 f.; 30:6 etc.

[27] Ex. 16:10; 29:43; Lv. 9:6, 23 f.; Nu. 14:10; 17:7; 20:6.

[28] P does not equate the כְּבוֹד יְהוָה with the pillar of cloud and fire (as against v. Gall, *op. cit.*, 52). There is a free poetic use in Is. 58:8, cf. Caspari, *op. cit.*, 116 f.

to the people as a whole. And the character of these visionary phenomena carries Ezekiel much further than P in the description of the transcendent realities displayed before him. A strange group of winged cherubim flies out of a brooding thunder cloud. Above the surface (רָקִיעַ) of this cosmic picture there is to be seen a throne, and on it something like graphite, a picture like a man, like fire and radiant light : this is the appearance of the כְּבוֹד יְהֹוָה.[29] It is obvious that in Ezekiel the כְּבוֹד יְהֹוָה is separate from the train of cherubim, which may be compared with the protective cloud of P. It leaves it like a carriage, and mounts it again to fly away from the earth on it as on an aeroplane.[30] To this flight of Yahweh from Jerusalem there corresponds His entry into the temple in the great vision of the future (43:1 ff.). Both surprise us by the assumption that the true resting place of the כְּבוֹד יְהֹוָה was and will be again the temple. This is the throne or foot-stool of God. P could never have said this of the tabernacle. The other distinctive feature[31] is that Ezekiel portrays the כְּבוֹד יְהֹוָה in human form, with the strongest possible emphasis on the nature of God as light. It is now evident why so bold a glance at the nature of God cannot belong to the public ministry of a prophet, but only to his rare visionary moments.[32]

d. There are many other references to God's כָּבוֹד in the OT. Nowhere else, however, do they occur in such basic religious statements or in the context of so definite a theological presentation. Most of the others are occasional, with individual and in many cases highly subjective nuances. The above concept of the כְּבוֹד יְהֹוָה could be an urgent concern in Israel only to a few. The many, who were not concerned with lofty theological matters, spoke more freely of Yahweh and His כָּבוֹד, and there was no obstacle to using the term כָּבוֹד in its customary senses. We may now take a brief glance at some of the shades of meaning.

In Ps. 63 the author prays that he may see the כָּבוֹד of God in the sanctuary (v. 2); the conjunction of עֹז and כָּבוֹד makes it plain that he is not thinking in terms of a theophany. In other passages there is approximation to the concept of "honour." The כָּבוֹד of Yahweh is great (Ps. 138:5); Yahweh is מֶלֶךְ הַכָּבוֹד (Ps. 24:8). כָּבוֹד is often linked with שֵׁם when it is desired to magnify the honour or impressiveness of the divine name (Ps. 66:2; 79:9). In such poetic prayers כָּבוֹד often amounts to little more than another word for Yahweh. On the other hand, it can also be used for the external acknowledgment which is either withheld from Yahweh or granted to Him. There is thus a frequent demand to "give" God כָּבוֹד,[33] i.e., to recognise the import of His deity. Indeed, Yahweh Himself can sometimes say that He is not prepared to concede His כָּבוֹד to other gods (Is. 42:8; 48:11). To an extraordinary degree, however, the כָּבוֹד of God is also a theme of religious hope

---

[29] v. Gall rightly argues that Ez. 1:28 ("this was the appearance of the likeness of the כְּבוֹד of Yahweh") does not refer to the vision as a whole, but only to the depiction of the form of God (op. cit., 26 f.).

[30] H. Schmidt, "Kerubenthron und Lade" in Eucharisterion für H. Gunkel (1923), 126.

[31] It cannot be maintained that Ez. shares P's conception of the כְּבוֹד יְהֹוָה (v. Gall, op. cit., 55).

[32] It should be emphasised, however, that in the depiction of his opening vision Ez. weakens his statements, which relate directly to so difficult a subject, by the careful interposition of דְּמוּת and כְּמַרְאֵה (e.g., "a form like the appearance of a man," 1:26, 28).

[33] Jer. 13:16; Ps. 29:1 f.; 96:7 f.; 115:1.

and an established part of eschatological expectation. This is a usage which at an essential point links up with the strict theological usage of P and Ez.; we are here concerned with a manifestation, not so much of the intrinsic nature of God, but of the final actualisation of His claim to rule the world. The poetic exaggeration of Is. that the whole earth is full of the כָּבוֹד of Yahweh (Is. 6:3, cf. Nu. 14:21) is more often formulated as a hope : all lands shall be full of His כָּבוֹד (Ps. 72:19); or, in the refrain, "let thy כָּבוֹד be above all the earth" (Ps. 57:5, 11); then shall all the nations see the כָּבוֹד of Yahweh, and Tubal and Javan shall declare it to the Gentiles (Is. 66:18 f.); indeed, the whole task of Dt.-Is. is to prepare the way that Yahweh's כָּבוֹד may be revealed (Is. 40:5). The saving act to which these eschatological statements refer is finally so embracing that the colours merge into one another and it makes little difference whether it is said that Yahweh will become כָּבוֹד for Israel or that Israel is created for Yahweh's כָּבוֹד (Zech. 2:9; Is. 43:7).

v. Rad

D. δόξα in the LXX and Hellenistic Apocrypha.

In the LXX, as in the NT, we have a very different usage from that which prevailed in the Greek world. The word δόξα is very widely used, some 280 times in the canonical books and some 445 altogether. There are 25 different Hebrew equivalents, although some of these are very rare. [34] On some 180 occasions the Hebrew word is כָּבוֹד, and this is the true and dominant equivalent of the LXX δόξα, the others either having the same, or much the same, meaning as כָּבוֹד. [35] The LXX word receives its distinctive force from the fact that it is used for כָּבוֹד. We find in it the meanings of כָּבוֹד, and we do not find in the LXX term the meanings of the Greek δόξα. It has become identical with כָּבוֹד. This is confirmed by the similar use of → δοξάζω and → ἔνδοξος. In sum, about half of the occurrences in the LXX are renderings of a derivative of כבד. The possible meanings are exactly the same as those of the OT word. [36]

a. Here, and in biblical and biblically influenced Greek as a whole, we hardly ever find δόξα used for opinion. כָּבוֹד cannot bear such a sense, [37] and it is extremely rare for δόξα in the Bible. Other OT words which mean "opinion," like עֵצָה, are rendered βουλή etc., not δόξα.

---

[34] Cf. the figures of Forster, 312 f.

[35] This is true even of so apparently remote a word as בָּשָׂר, which is once translated δόξα in Is. 17:4 : "The fatness of his flesh shall wax lean" ═ τὰ πίονα τῆς δόξης αὐτοῦ σεισθήσεται. בָּשָׂר is here understood as earthly pomp and glory because it disappears. Cf. also Is. 52:14 : ἀδοξήσει ... ἡ δόξα σου (Mas.: תֹּאַרוֹ) ἀπὸ τῶν ἀνθρώπων. The stress on the lowliness of the Servant presupposes that His figure was originally one of glory. Further conclusions cannot be drawn (as against Joh. W. 1 K., 371, n. 1).

[36] ψ 7:5; 29:12; 107:1 are without basic significance. They follow the change in the meaning of כָּבוֹד to "soul" as the seat of human honour and dignity. In Gn. 49:6 the LXX has τὰ ἥπατα (liver).

[37] Qoh. 10:1 (→ 243) is too corrupt in the Mas. to warrant any conclusions regarding a possible use of כָּבוֹד for opinion.

The only passage [38] in the OT Canon in which the Greek translator was perhaps using δόξα for "opinion" is Qoh. 10:1: τίμιον ὁ λόγος σοφίας ὑπὲρ δόξαν ἀφροσύνης μεγάλης. Here the Mas. text is corrupt, and the translator possibly used the stock word δόξα for כָּבוֹד, because it seemed to yield good sense in terms of current Greek usage (→ n. 37).

This sense is no less rare in the Gk. apocrypha and pseudepigrapha than in the OT Canon. In 4 Macc., the most philosophical book in the apocrypha, we find the meaning "opinion" at 5:18 : οὐδὲ οὕτως ἐξὸν ἡμῖν ἦν τὴν ἐπὶ τῇ εὐσεβείᾳ δόξαν ἀκυρῶσαι; cf. also 6:18; and finally Sir. 8:14 : κατὰ δόξαν κρίνειν = כרצון שפט. [39]

b. δόξα, "glory or honour ascribed to someone," "reputation." This is very rare in the OT books. [40] Indeed, δόξα is used less frequently in this sense than כָּבוֹד, for which the only other Greek word which is at all common is τιμή. [41] So strong is the change in the use of δόξα that rather strangely there is very little impulsion to equate כָּבוֹד with δόξα in this original sense of the Greek term. Nevertheless, there are a few instances of this meaning. Indeed, they are fairly common again in Prv., as in Wis., Sir., Macc., Test. XII etc.

πᾶσαν τὴν δόξαν μου (Joseph) τὴν ἐν Αἰγύπτῳ, Gn. 45:13; δόξῃ καὶ τιμῇ ἐστεφάνωσας αὐτόν ψ 8:5; τὴν δόξαν ἀπ' ἐμοῦ ἐξέδυσεν, Job 19:9; τὴν δόξαν αὐτῶν εἰς ἀτιμίαν θήσομαι, Hos. 4:7. γυνὴ εὐχάριστος ἐγείρει ἀνδρὶ δόξαν, Prv. 11:16; δόξα ἀνδρὶ ἀποστρέφεσθαι λοιδορίας, Prv. 20:3; διδόναι ἄφρονι δόξαν, Prv. 26:8; ἔξω δι αὐτὴν (for the sake of wisdom) δόξαν ἐν ὄχλοις, Wis. 8:10; ἡ δόξα ἀνθρώπου ἐκ τιμῆς πατρὸς αὐτοῦ, Sir. 3:11; δόξα καὶ ἀτιμία ἐν λαλιᾷ, Sir. 5:13; δόξα is used for the royal splendour of Simon Maccabeus in 1 Macc. 14:4 f. Cf. δόξα/ἀτιμία in Test. A. 5:2; Test. B. 6:4; διὰ τὴν κοσμικήν μου δόξαν, Test. Jud. 17:8.

c. Since כָּבוֹד can have the sense of "power," "splendour," "human glory," δόξα takes on the same meaning. Yet this does not involve any great transition from the previous sense, since power and splendour usually bring honour and renown. They are often the outward manifestation and even the cause of being honoured. Thus the meanings often merge into one another.

ἔκλειψις δόξης 'Ιακώβ, Is. 17:4 (cf. v. 3); τὸ ἄνθος τὸ ἐκπεσὸν ἐκ τῆς δόξης, Is. 28:1; δόξα τοῦ Λιβάνου, Is. 35:2; εἶδε τὸν οἶκον τοῦτον (the temple) ἐν τῇ δόξῃ αὐτοῦ τῇ ἔμπροσθεν, Hag. 2:3; οἱ βασιλεῖς ἐν δόξῃ μεγάλῃ ... ἐπορεύθη μετὰ δόξης εἰς Πτολεμαΐδα, 1 Macc. 10:58 ff. [42] How strongly the LXX came to sense the thought of God's power in the term δόξα is shown by the fact that it could use δόξα for other Heb. words for power, e.g., עֹז in ψ 67:34; Is. 45:24 : δικαιοσύνη καὶ δόξα (א*: εἰρήνη, Σ: ἰσχύς). An anon. translation has δύναμις τῆς δόξης ('ΑΘ: ἀποκρυφὴ ἰσχύος) [43] for עֻזֹּה חֶבְיוֹן in Hab. 3:4. Again, in Is. 62:8 א seems to have δόξα for

---

[38] Is. 11:3 should not be considered in this connexion (Schneider, 44), since δόξα, like the Mas., plainly indicates facts which are evident, even though deceptive (meaning b. or c.), and not their subjective assessment, whether by the judge or the crowd.

[39] Cf. M. Johannessohn, Der Gebrauch der Präpos. in der LXX (1926), 258.

[40] Only superficially and externally may we consider here the reference to God as One to whom man gives honour; in reality this phrase belongs to the context of the divine δόξα and therefore to another level of the concept. It will thus be treated later under d.

[41] τιμάω, τιμή are used 18 times for the stem כבד. כָּבוֹד is also twice rendered πλοῦτος and once each βάρος, βαρύνω, γλῶσσα, δύναμις, καλός, στρωννύω, χαβώθ.

[42] The rest of the paragraph I owe to Bertram.

[43] Instead of the hapaxlegomenon חֶבְיוֹן, the LXX presupposes a form of חבב rather than חבה.

עֹז, whereas AB have ἰσχύς. The formulation ὤμοσεν κύριος ... κατὰ τῆς δόξης τοῦ βραχίονος αὐτοῦ also seems to suggest might and power, and the same idea is present in the βραχίων τῆς δόξης (תִּפְאֶרֶת) of Is. 63:12. In Is. 40:26 אוֹן is rendered δόξα. Σ and Θ have δύναμις. In content, other passages suggest power, especially the power of God which evokes fear and trembling. Thus Is. 30:30 speaks of δόξα (הוֹד) τῆς φωνῆς αὐτοῦ along with θυμὸς τοῦ βραχίονος αὐτοῦ, and we have δόξα τῆς ἰσχύος αὐτοῦ = הֲדַר גְּאוֹנוֹ in the well-known refrain in Is. 2:10, 19, 21. גָּאוֹן is here rendered ἰσχύς. In many cases this word can also be the original of δόξα, cf. Ex. 15:7; Is. 14:11; 24:14; 26:10 (גֵּאוּת); Mi. 5:4; also Jer. 49:19 (29:20) in ᾽ΑΣ and 50:44 in Θ. Even when תְּמוּנָה is rendered δόξα, as in Nu. 12:8 and ψ 16:14, the idea of power can be present. It was this understanding which in the case of the latter verse made possible the misreading of δόξα as δεξιά in Θ. [44] Cf. 1 Ch. 16:28 : δότε τῷ κυρίῳ δόξαν καὶ ἰσχύν (כָּבוֹד וָעֹז) (v. also v. 27). Cf. also Nu. 23:22 and 24:8, where the Mas. is not very clear and the LXX seems to relate the image of the δόξα μονοκέρωτος to the power of God. The same is true of Ex. 31:18 Θ : ἐν ἰσχύι, ἐν δόξῃ for כְּבָה (read by Θ as בַּכֹּחַ) בִּכְבוֹד. The meaning "terrible power" is especially present in ψ 101:15 and Ex. 33:22. Here δόξα is used for כָּבוֹד.

d. The primary meaning of the LXX word, however, does not emerge except with reference to God. In this sense, of course, it may simply refer to "God's honour" or "power," like כָּבוֹד. But to isolate individual senses can only be a help to understanding. In reality, the term always speaks of one thing. God's power is an expression of the "divine nature," and the honour ascribed to God by man is finally no other than an affirmation of this nature. The δόξα θεοῦ is the "divine glory" which reveals the nature of God in creation and in His acts, which fill both heaven and earth. Again, the "form of the divine manifestation or revelation" of כָּבוֹד, as this controls certain parts of the OT, is for the translator the disclosure or self-revelation of this nature. Thus the "divine radiance" at the giving of the Law, or in the tabernacle or the temple, is very properly to be rendered δόξα. In the LXX and therefore in the Bible generally δόξα acquires its distinctive sense as a term for this divine nature or essence either in its invisible or its perceptible form. God is θεός and βασιλεὺς τῆς δόξης, ψ 28:3; 23:7 ff. As Ez. and P sought to describe the presence of God by telling of the appearance of the כְּבוֹד יְהֹוָה, the δόξα τοῦ κυρίου, so the parallelism of the Psalter can equate what is said about God with what is said about His δόξα : ὑψώθητι ἐπὶ τοὺς οὐρανούς, ὁ θεός, καὶ ἐπὶ πᾶσαν τὴν γῆν ἡ δόξα σου, ψ 56:5.

For "God's honour" with διδόναι, φέρειν, ἀγγέλλειν, διηγεῖσθαι, etc., cf. Is. 48:11; Jer. 13:16; ψ 18:1; 28:1 f.; 95:3, 7 f.; 113:9 etc. διδόναι δόξαν τῷ θεῷ cannot possibly mean giving God something that He does not have. It means acknowledging what is due to Him. This may be seen particularly clearly in Is. 42. The very same δόξα which in v. 8 is no less His possession than His ἀρετή, and which He refuses to surrender, is in v. 12 to be given to Him by those who praise Him, i.e., confirmed and accepted by their conduct. Cf. ψ 28:1 f., 3, 9 : δόξα is brought to the θεὸς τῆς δόξης. In Jer. 13:16 the LXX weakens a relationship very patent in the Mas. : δόξα is brought to the bearer of light who makes light out of darkness. For "God's power and glory," cf. esp. ἐπὶ πᾶσαν τὴν γῆν ἡ δόξα σου, ψ 56:5, 11; 107:5; Is. 6:3; Nu. 14:21. For βασιλεὺς τῆς

---

[44] The opposite interchange in LXX 2 Ch. 30:8 (δόξα for יָד) is to be understood rather as the intrusion of a current doxological formula.

δόξης, also δόξα τῆς βασιλείας σου, cf. ψ 144:11 f.; δόξα τῆς ἁγιωσύνης σου, ψ 144:5, τὸ ὄνομα τῆς δόξης αὐτοῦ, ψ 71:19; θαυμαστὸς ἐν δόξαις, Ex. 15:11. For the "form of God's revelation," cf. ἡ δόξα τοῦ θεοῦ (κυρίου) ὤφθη ἐν νεφέλῃ, Ex. 16:10; Nu. 14:10; κατέβη ἐπὶ τὸ ὄρος, Ex. 24:16; ὤφθη πάσῃ τῇ συναγωγῇ, Nu. 16:19; ἐξῆλθεν ἀπὸ τοῦ οἴκου, Ez. 10:18; ἀνέβη ἐκ μέσης τῆς πόλεως, 11:23; τὸ δὲ εἶδος τῆς δόξης κυρίου ὡσεὶ πῦρ φλέγον, Ex. 24:17. The loss of the ark means the ἀπῴκισται δόξα Ἰσραήλ, 1 Βασ. 4:22.

When the translator of the OT first thought of using δόξα for כָּבוֹד, he initiated a linguistic change of far-reaching significance, giving to the Greek term a distinctiveness of sense which could hardly be surpassed. Taking a word for opinion, which implies all the subjectivity and therefore all the vacillation of human views and conjectures, he made it express something absolutely objective, i.e. the reality of God.

e. From what we have said it is obvious that the Hellenistic apocrypha adopt the LXX usage. Indeed, the sense of opinion is almost completely missing in these works (→ 243). [45] As in Prv., however, there is a certain regression from the reference to God in favour of the sense of human honour or magnificence. Yet the former is also found, e.g., ἀπὸ θρόνου δόξης σου, Wis. 9:10; ἔδειξεν αὐτῷ τῆς δόξης αὐτοῦ, Sir. 45:3; ὀφθήσεται ἡ δόξα τοῦ κυρίου, 2 Macc. 2:8.

E. כָּבוֹד and יְקָרָא in Palestinian Judaism.

1. In the Targums [46] the כָּבוֹד of God is always rendered יְקָרָא, "honour," "worth," "splendour"; e.g., Ex. 16:7; 29:43; 40:34; 1 K. 8:11 etc. The use of יְקָרָא, however, goes rather beyond that of כָּבוֹד in so far as the expression יְקָרָא דַיְיָ — as occasionally δόξα κυρίου in the LXX (e.g., Nu. 12:8) [47] — is often employed to avoid an anthropomorphism in the original. Mas.: "God went up from Abraham" = Tg. O: יְקָרָא דַיְיָ went up from Abraham," Gn. 17:22; Mas.: "God has come" = Tg. O: יְקָרָא דַיְיָ is revealed," Ex. 20:20; Mas.: "They saw the God of Israel" = Tg. O: "They saw יָת יְקַר אֱלָהָא דְיִשְׂרָאֵל," Ex. 24:10. [48] In Tg. J and Tg. Proph. this development is carried even further, so that for "the radiance of Yahweh" we have "the radiance of the shekinah of Yahweh." Tg. O: "When יְקָרִי passes by" = Tg. J I: "When יְקַר שְׁכִינָתִי passes by," Ex. 33:22; Mas.: "My eyes have seen the king, Yahweh Sabaoth" = Tg. Proph.: "My eyes have seen יְקַר שְׁכִינַת מֶלֶךְ עָלְמַיָּא (the radiance of the shekinah of the king of aeons)," Is. 6:5.

2. In Rabb. Judaism כָּבוֹד plays an important role. As in the OT, the word can denote both "divine and human honour," e.g., of the pupil, of the neighbour (Ab., 4, 12), [49] of the woman (bBM, 59a), of the house of Caesar (bJeb., 65b) etc. To the Greek antonyms δόξα/ἀτιμία there correspond דרך כבוד/דרך בזיון, "in honourable and despicable fashion" (bQid., 45b). God recognises justifiable human honour: "God seeks the honour of the despised (בזקריה)," bBer., 19a; "God honoured Abraham with all honour (כל הכבוד)," Tanch. Buber וירא, 25, p. 101. Human honour may be contrasted with divine.

---

[45] Once in Ep. Ar., 139.

[46] v. Gall, 66-81; also Moore, I, 420; Dalman WJ, I², 189.

[47] Mas.: "He saw the form of Yahweh" = LXX: καὶ τὴν δόξαν κυρίου εἶδεν.

[48] LXX: καὶ εἶδον τὸν τόπον οὗ ἱστήκει ὁ θεὸς τοῦ Ἰσραήλ.

[49] "Let the honour (כָּבוֹד) of thy pupil be as dear to thee as the honour of thy neighbour; the honour of thy neighbour as respect (מוֹרָא) for thy teacher; and respect for thy teacher as reverence (מוֹרָא) for heaven." It is striking that the term מוֹרָא (fear) is used instead of כָּבוֹד when the reference is to the teacher and to God.

Thus Saul sought his own honour and neglected the honour of heaven, whereas David did the reverse, Nu. r., 4 on 4:16.

At the same time, כָּבוֹד is used consistently for the divine and heavenly mode of being. "Abraham knew that he should seek and perceive the כָּבוֹד of our Father in heaven," T. Chag., 2, 1. That the *shekinah* and the *kabod* are closely related may be seen from equivalents used in Tg. J. When the *shekinah* comes to Sion, the *kabod* may be seen by all Israel, Tanch. Buber במדבר, 20, p. 18. כבוד התורה is proper to the divine Torah, bSota, 49a. God's throne is the throne of glory (כסא הכבוד); according to Jer. 14:21; 17:12; and as such it is created before the world. [50]

Only occasionally does Rabb. Judaism speak of the participation of man in the *kabod* of God. The example of Moses in Ex. 34:29 ff. is out of the ordinary. Already in S. Nu., 1 on 5:3 [51] his radiance is plainly regarded as parallel to the כְּבוֹד יְהוָה mentioned in Ex. 24:17, and therefore as similar in nature. [52] Cf. also Tg. O : "The radiance of his glory was great"; Tg. J I : "There shone the radiance of his features which had come to him from the light of the glory of the *shekinah* of Yahweh." This connexion was taken for granted by the later Rabbis. [53] Indeed, we even meet the view that at the ordination of Joshua by Moses the laying on of hands by Moses imparted some portion of this radiance which derived from the כבוד of God, so that, "while the face of Moses was as the face of the sun, that of Joshua was as the face of the moon," S. Nu., 140 on 27:20. [54] Similar statements concerning other earthly men are virtually impossible. It can be said that God imparts מכבודו to those who fear Him or to kings (bBer., 58a), but as a rule [55] this does not imply more than power or dignity. The restoration of dominion to Israel can be expressed as follows : "When the Israelites keep the Torah in their midst, God will cause them to possess the throne of glory," Nu. r., 11 on 6:22. But when Aqiba spoke of David sitting on the divine throne, Jose the Galilean accused him of profaning the *shekinah*, bChag., 14a.

On the other hand, we should note the significant view that the first man (→ εἰκών) had a part in God's *kabod* (כבודו עמו) and that this radiance was taken from him after the fall, Gn. r., 11 on 2:3. The unfolding of salvation history aims at restoration. According to R. Samuel b. Nachman (the middle of the 3rd cent. A.D.) God gave to the Israelites at Sinai of the radiance (זיו) of the *shekinah*, Pesikt., 37a. Above all, exposition of Da. 12:3 (also Ju. 5:31) taught that the faces and clothes of the righteous will shine when they are renewed in the coming world. [56] The oldest Rabb. passage which speaks of the eschatological shining of the righteous is probably the saying of R. Simeon b. Jochai concerning the seven joys of the faces of the righteous in the world to come : sun, moon, firmament, stars, lightning, lilies and lights of the temple, S. Dt., 10 on 1:10. There seem to be few depictions in later works, and express statements concerning participation in the glory of God are rare. However tempting, interpretation along these lines is almost always avoided. True blessedness, as in OT eschatology, is contemplation of the glory of the *shekinah*, bBer., 34a (→ 250). On the other hand, it can be said of the Messiah, though only in later passages, that God will spread over Him

---

[50] For examples, cf. Str.-B., I, 974.

[51] K. G. Kuhn, Sifre Nu. (Rabb. Texte, 2nd ser., Vol. 2 [1933], 13).

[52] The word *kabod* does not occur in the original. On the other hand the LXX has ἦν δεδοξασμένη ἡ ὄψις τοῦ χρώματος τοῦ προσώπου αὐτοῦ. On Philo and Joseph. → 236.

[53] Str.-B., III, 514 f. Cf. also *Geniza-Stud.*, ed. S. Schechter (1928), I, 154, Fr. 17, 5a, 4.

[54] I owe this reference to K. G. Kuhn ; cf. 1 C. 15:41. Par : S zutta Nu. 27:20 (p. 321, 14 f., Horovitz).

[55] But cf. Nu. r., 15 on 10:2, → 247.

[56] For examples, cf. Str.-B., IV, 940 ff., 1138.

the radiance of His glory (פורש עליו מזיו כבודו), Pesikt. r., 37 (163a); that He will give Him a share in His *kabod*, and that He will thus invest Him with His own raiment, [57] Nu. r., 15 on 10:2. [58] In and for itself the glory of the Messiah is a self-evident thesis; He it is who with five other things restores the radiance lost by the first man, Gn. r., 12 on 2:4.

3. These ideas play a great part in Apocalyptic. [59] Here, too, it is presupposed that at the fall man was alienated from the glory of God, Apc. Mos. 20 f. Here, too, the blessedness of those who have kept the ways of the Most High is to "contemplate with rapture the glory of the One who receives them," 4 Esr. 7:91. "The radiance of the glory of the Most High" will be visible on the Day of Judgment, 7:42. "Show forth thy glory," is the prayer to God in S. Bar. 21:23. In Eth. En. God is the "Lord of glory," 27:3, 5 etc.; "before his glory no unrighteousness can stand," 50:4; the session of the Messiah on the "throne of glory" is described, 45:3; 51:3; 55:4; 61:8; 62:2 ff.; 69:27 ff. He is the One who comes in glory, S. Bar. 30:1. And in these writings especially there is depicted the shining of the wise and the righteous which is traditional in Apocalyptic from the time of Da. 12:3. "Their countenance shall shine as the sun and resemble the light of the sun," 4 Esr. 7:97. "They shall be changed ... from beauty to splendour, from light to the radiance of glory," S. Bar. 51:10. "Glory will be greater in the righteous than in the angels," 51:11. Eth. En. 38:4 expressly maintains the connexion with the divine glory: "They shall not be able to look on the faces of the righteous because the Lord of spirits shall cause His light to shine on the faces of the saints and the elect righteous"; Sl. En. 22:8 : "Clothe him in the clothes of my glory." In the same connexion we may refer to Ps. Sol. 17:34 f.: ἔρχεσθαι ἔθνη ἀπ' ἄκρου τῆς γῆς ἰδεῖν τὴν δόξαν αὐτοῦ, φέροντες δῶρα τοὺς ἐξησθενηκότας υἱοὺς αὐτῆς, καὶ ἰδεῖν τὴν δόξαν κυρίου ἣν ἐδόξασεν αὐτὴν ὁ θεός.

F. The NT Use of δόξα, II.

1. δόξα as the Divine Mode of Being.

It is obvious that the NT use of δόξα follows the LXX rather than Greek usage. With the senses of "reputation" and "power" already mentioned, the word is also used strictly in the NT to express the "divine mode of being". This is true of all the NT authors. [60] Even writers like Lk. [61] and the author of Hb., who have such a feeling for Greek, are no exception. They use the term as a biblical rather than a Greek term. It is not that they are presenting a particularly inward and spiritualised form of the concept. On the contrary, it is in Lk. that we find the most impressive form of a manifestation of δόξα, Lk. 2:9; 9:31 f.

In the NT, as in the LXX, the meanings "divine honour," "divine splendour," "divine power" and "visible divine radiance" are fluid, and can only be distinguished artificially. In content, however, there is always expressed the divine

---

[57] Just before we read : "To Elijah, too, he imparted מכבודו, and he thus gave life to one who was dead."

[58] There is no Rabb. reference to a session of the Messiah on the throne of glory, cf. Str.-B., I, 978 f. The case is otherwise, however, in Apocalyptic (→ infra).

[59] Cf. v. Gall, 85-91.

[60] The word occurs everywhere except in the Epistles of John, and there is no reason to suppose that there would have been here any radical difference from the Gospel.

[61] Even if Lk. took over many words from his sources, this does not alter the fact that he was using them in a Gospel composed for Hellenistic Gentile Christians.

mode of being, though with varying emphasis on the element of visibility (cf. the Christmas story in Lk. 2:9; the account of the transfiguration in Lk. 9:31 f.; 2 Pt. 1:17; the Damascus experience in Ac. 22:11; the heavenly temple and the heavenly city in Rev. 15:8; 21:23). The NT δόξαν διδόναι, like the ancient phrase (→ 244), does not imply the adding of something not already present; it is rather predication in the sense of active acknowledgment (Ac. 12:23; R. 4:20; Rev. 16:9) or in doxologies as the extolling of what is (Lk. 2:14; 19:38; R. 11:36; 16:27; Eph. 3:21; Phil. 4:20; 1 Tm. 1:17; Rev. 4:9; 7:12 etc.). According to the meaning of the NT authors, therefore, these doxologies presuppose ἐστίν rather than εἴη, as may be seen from Gl. 1:5 (ᾧ ἡ δόξα) and 1 Pt. 4:11 (ᾧ ἐστιν ἡ δόξα). [62] In all these respects we have in the NT term a simple continuation of the Judaeo-Greek usage established in the LXX.

The Johannine usage has certain peculiarities. For here the meanings are abruptly set alongside one another in apparently very strange fashion. Thus on the one side we have reference to the visible δόξα, wholly in the sense of the OT כָּבוֹד: ταῦτα εἶδεν Ἐσαΐας ὅτι εἶδεν τὴν δόξαν αὐτοῦ, 12:41 (cf. also the use of the verb in 12:16, 23, 28); on the other, only two verses later, the word is used in the sense of the human honour or glory which is sometimes given by men and sometimes by God: ἠγάπησαν γὰρ τὴν δόξαν τῶν ἀνθρώπων μᾶλλον ἤπερ τὴν δόξαν τοῦ θεοῦ, 12:43; cf. also 5:41, 44; 7:18; 8:50, 54. In all attempts at translation there is an almost intolerable rift of meanings which the author obviously did not himself feel. His way of using the noun and the verb stands closest to the Palestinian mode of speech which is carried over into the Greek linguistic form. [63]

2. The δόξα of Jesus.

It is to be noted, however, that NT usage itself takes a decisive step by using in relation to Christ a word which was used in relation to God. The relationship can be expressed in many ways, and the whole dynamism of the relationship of God and Christ is reflected in the use of the term. Thus the resurrection of Christ is effected διὰ τῆς δόξης τοῦ πατρός, R. 6:4. Again, the Exalted ἀνελήφθη ἐν δόξῃ, 1 Tm. 3:16. Stephen sees the δόξα of God, and the risen Lord within it, Ac. 7:55. Or again, as 1 Pt. puts it: τὰ εἰς Χριστὸν παθήματα καὶ τὰς μετὰ ταῦτα δόξας, 1:11, and θεὸν τὸν ἐγείραντα αὐτὸν ἐκ νεκρῶν καὶ δόξαν αὐτῷ δόντα, 1:21. The attribution of δόξα to God — δόξα ἐν ὑψίστοις θεῷ, Lk. 2:14; 19:38; Rev. 4:9 — finds parallels in relation to Christ: Hb. 13:21; 1 Pt. 4:11; Rev. 5:12 f. Alongside the θεὸς τῆς δόξης of Ac. 7:2 we may set the κύριος τῆς δόξης of 1 C. 2:8; Jm. 2:1. If OT eschatology implies: ὀφθήσεται ἡ δόξα κυρίου, Is. 40:5, NT eschatology implies: ἐπιφάνεια τῆς δόξης τοῦ μεγάλου θεοῦ καὶ σωτῆρος ἡμῶν Ἰησοῦ Χριστοῦ, Tt. 2:13; ἐν ἀποκαλύψει τῆς δόξης αὐτοῦ (of Christ), 1 Pt. 4:13; 5:1; esp.: ἐρχόμενος ἐν νεφέλαις μετὰ δυνάμεως πολλῆς καὶ δόξης, Mk. 13:26 etc.

All these statements concern the glorification of the risen Lord after Easter. The application of the word to the incarnate Jesus is strictly limited. In Mt. and Mk. it is connected only with the *parousia* (Mk. 8:38; 10:37; 13:26 and par.; Mt. 19:28; 25:31). In Lk. the word is also found in the stories of the birth and the transfiguration. The revelation of δόξα at the birth of Christ (Lk. 2:9), like the

---

[62] Bl.-Debr., 79 § 128, 5.
[63] Cf. the striking par. in Schl. J., 192 f., 219, 247.

appearance of angels, points to His coming from the divine world; it has thus the same force as Jn. 17:5 : δόξη ᾗ εἶχον ... παρὰ σοί. His transfiguration is an eschatological anticipation. [64] Only the word and not the matter is peculiar to Lk. The description of the event in Mk. 9:2 f.; Mt. 17:2; Lk. 9:29 is simply a depiction of what Lk. alone speaks of as ὀφθέντες ἐν δόξῃ and εἶδον τὴν δόξαν.

The picture is rather different in Jn. to the degree that we here find more references to the δόξα of the earthly Jesus. This undoubtedly corresponds to the distinctive Johannine tendency to describe the life of Jesus from the standpoint of the exaltation. It should not be overlooked, however, that the δόξα of the earthly Jesus can be seen only by πίστις : ἐφανέρωσεν τὴν δόξαν αὐτοῦ καὶ ἐπίστευσαν εἰς αὐτὸν οἱ μαθηταὶ αὐτοῦ, 2:11; ὅτι ἐὰν πιστεύσῃς ὄψῃ τὴν δόξαν τοῦ θεοῦ, 11:40; cf. ἵνα δοξασθῇ ὁ υἱὸς τοῦ θεοῦ, 11:4. The statement in 1:14 (ἐθεασάμεθα τὴν δόξαν αὐτοῦ) is not a general statement in the third person but a special declaration of the disciple in the first person (cf. τοῖς πιστεύουσιν, 1:12). In Jn., therefore, the δόξα of Jesus is no more visible in and of itself than in the Synoptists. The mystery of His person must be revealed (Mt. 16:17) and believed. Only in this way can we understand a statement like the οὐδέπω ἐδοξάσθη of 7:39 (cf. 12:16), or the prayer of Jesus in 12-17 for the bestowal of δόξα and δοξασθῆναι (12:23, 28; 13:31; 14:13; 16:14; 17:1, 4, 5). The turning-point, the entry into δόξα, is the cross, the dying of the corn of wheat (12:23 ff.). This emphasis is itself Johannine to the extent that John has a particularly strong sense of the causal connexion between dying and bringing forth fruit, or between the death and the resurrection of Jesus, between the suffering and the glorification of the Son of Man. The δόξα derives from His death. At the same time, what Jesus does in His passion is a process through which ὁ θεὸς ἐδοξάσθη ἐν αὐτῷ (13:31). It is acknowledgment of the divine δόξα in the sense already mentioned, and it carries with it certainty of participation in the same δόξα : ὁ θεὸς δοξάσει αὐτὸν ἐν αὐτῷ (v. 32). In this sense to have regard to the passion is to see δόξα even in the earthly life of Jesus.

3. The Believer and δόξα.

As regards the OT promise, when man is set in a relation of כָּבוֹד, all the emphasis lies on sight. ὀφθήσεται ἐν ὑμῖν ἡ δόξα κυρίου, Lv. 9:6. The story that the face of Moses shone after his speech with Yahweh (Ex. 34:29 f.) is an isolated one (→ 253). It merely tells us that sight is something unheard of and pregnant with consequences. In the case of Isaiah we simply read that he εἶδον τὸν κύριον (Is. 6:1). In eschatology, again, vision is the supreme goal : ὄψεται τὴν δόξαν κυρίου (Is. 35:2); ὄψονται τὴν δόξαν μου (Is. 66:18). Cf. also Ps. Sol. 17:34, 35. In the Midrash the promise of God is that "in the coming aeon, when I have led my *shekinah* to Sion, I will disclose myself in my כָּבוֹד to all Israel, and they shall see and live for ever." [65] For the Rabbis the life of the just in the world to come is that "they sit with their crowns on their heads and are refreshed by the radiance

---

[64] E. Lohmeyer, "Die Verklärung Jesu nach dem Markusevangelium," ZNW, 21 (1922), 183 ff., has an excellent analysis of the character of the scene as an eschatological theophany, but he inclines to a Hellenistic interpretation at this point where the reference is to eschatological δόξα.

[65] Tanch. Buber במדבר 20, p. 18.

of the *shekinah*, for it is written (Ex. 24:11): They see God, and therefore ate and drank."[66]

In the NT this emphasis is weaker as compared with that on participation. This change was to some extent brought about by the development of Jewish eschatology which we described earlier. For here there was eschatological reference to the radiance and transfiguration of the righteous, on the basis of Da. 12:3. In this connexion, we may refer to Mt. 13:43 : τότε οἱ δίκαιοι ἐκλάμψουσιν ὡς ὁ ἥλιος ἐν τῇ βασιλείᾳ τοῦ πατρὸς αὐτῶν. But the decisive influence is to be found elsewhere. Through Christ the σῶμα τῆς ταπεινώσεως is in the resurrection σύμμορφος τῷ σώματι τῆς δόξης αὐτοῦ Phil. 3:21. Believers will have a share in His appearing ἐν δόξῃ : σὺν αὐτῷ φανερωθήσεσθε ἐν δόξῃ, Col. 3:4. We are συγκληρονόμοι Χριστοῦ, and therefore συνδοξασθῶμεν, R. 8:17. He is the ἐλπὶς τῆς δόξης, Col. 1:27. This means that when the NT refers to the eschatological participation of believers in δόξα this is simply part of the general statement of salvation history concerning the connexion and parallelism between the resurrection of Christ and the resurrection and new aeon of believers. Participation in δόξα, whether here in hope or one day in consummation, is participation in Christ. As it is only in the resurrection that God's aim for man is achieved, so His καλεῖν is fulfilled only in the αἰώνιος δόξα which is the true goal (εἰς) of vocation (1 Pt. 5:4, 10; 1 Th. 2:12; 2 Th. 2:14; 2 C. 4:17; 2 Tm. 2:10). Hence it is an object of hope the certainty of which may be a theme of rejoicing (R. 5:2). In apostolic proclamation the promise of Jesus is presented in such forms that those who follow Him may take part ὅταν καθίσῃ ὁ υἱὸς τοῦ ἀνθρώπου ἐπὶ θρόνου δόξης αὐτοῦ (Mt. 19:28).

In this light we may understand a distinctive expression which corresponds to what is everywhere evident in the NT, namely, that a pre-temporal statement accompanies the eschatological and that by way of the πνεῦμα and διακονία, both τοῦ κυρίου, they both shed a new light on the present. In the first instance, it may be affirmed quite simply that the sinner of this aeon displays little of the divine nature according to which, and with a view to which, he was created : ὑστεροῦνται τῆς δόξης τοῦ θεοῦ (R. 3:23). We can only turn our gaze from the στενάζειν of the present to the other aeon. To this there applies the μέλλουσα δόξα ἀποκαλυφθῆναι εἰς ἡμᾶς of R. 8:18 or the ἐλευθερία τῆς δόξης τῶν τέκνων τοῦ θεοῦ of R. 8:21. This means that it is not man of the present, but eschatological man, who shares in the δόξα. σπείρεται ἐν ἀτιμίᾳ, ἐγείρεται ἐν δόξῃ, 1 C. 15:43. Yet along with this forward looking glance there are many remarkable preterites : (σοφίαν) ἣν προώρισεν ὁ θεὸς πρὸ τῶν αἰώνων εἰς δόξαν ἡμῶν, 1 C. 2:7; but above all the ἐδόξασεν in the great series of aorists in R. 8:29 f. Because eschatology consummates the divine action, it has its roots in the divine decree. One might say that if the δόξα of the believer is really the fulfilment and goal of the divine καλεῖν, then in the very nature of the case it has the same origin as the latter.

It is also to be said, however, that for the believer the πνεῦμα is the ἀπαρχή and ἀρραβών of the new thing which brings with it δόξα. Hence, to some degree proleptically, prayer may be made that "according to the riches of His glory God may grant you His Spirit, that ye may become strong in the inner man" (Eph.

---

[66] bBer., 34a.

3:16); and it may also be said ὅτι τὸ τῆς δόξης καὶ τὸ τοῦ θεοῦ πνεῦμα ἐφ' ὑμᾶς ἀναπαύεται (1 Pt. 4:14). In both cases there is to be διὰ τοῦ πνεύματος a full working of eschatological δόξα in the present life of the believer.

This may be seen most clearly in 2 C. 3:7 ff. The key to this whole passage is to be found in the thesis that the believer belongs to the κύριος who is the πνεῦμα (v. 17). We thus have two corresponding trains of thought and series of statements. a. If δόξα was revealed already to Moses, who was concerned only with the διακονία τοῦ θανάτου ἐν γράμμασιν (v. 7), πῶς οὐχὶ μᾶλλον ἡ διακονία τοῦ πνεύματος ἔσται ἐν δόξῃ (v. 8). The δόξα of Moses was small and hardly deserved the name (καὶ γὰρ οὐ δεδόξασται τὸ δεδοξασμένον ἐν τούτῳ τῷ μέρει, v. 10) compared with the new and true δόξα of the Christian (εἵνεκεν τῆς ὑπερβαλλούσης δόξης, v. 10). b. By the δόξα κυρίου, which we see (→ κατοπτριζόμενοι), we ourselves are changed ἀπὸ δόξης εἰς δόξαν (v. 19). This thought is developed in 4:6: ἐν προσώπῳ Χριστοῦ, i.e., in contemplation of the κύριος, there shines in our hearts the light of the knowledge of the δόξα θεοῦ. The whole context, however, stands under the thematic word διακονία. This helps us to understand the comparison with Moses, who as the bearer even of a corruptible διακονία was ἐν δόξῃ. Thus we read in 4:1: διὰ ταῦτα, ἔχοντες τὴν διακονίαν ταύτην. What is described is the δόξα of the office, of proclamation, of κηρύσσομεν (4:5). This proclamation is the message of Christ and therefore of δικαιοσύνη (v. 9); where it takes place, it takes place ἐν δόξῃ. For Paul, however, the δόξα of the office naturally implies the δόξα of the Christian in general (ἡμεῖς πάντες, 3:18). The bridge between the present and eschatology is to be found in the phrase ἀπὸ δόξης εἰς δόξαν. The present is ἐν δόξῃ, but the εἰς points to a coming consummation. In both affirmation and limitation this is in full accord with the ἀπαρχὴ τοῦ πνεύματος. In this prepositional construction, which is to be found elsewhere in Pl. (cf. ἐκ πίστεως εἰς πίστιν, R. 1:17), we have the whole simultaneity of possession and expectation which is the basis of NT piety.

This obviously leads us directly to Jn. 17. Though other words are used, the view is almost completely identical with that presented in 2 C. 3. The disciples see the δόξα of Jesus: θεωρῶσιν τὴν δόξαν τὴν ἐμήν, v. 24. Jesus is glorified in them: δεδόξασμαι ἐν αὐτοῖς (v. 10). He has given them δόξα: τὴν δόξαν ἣν δεδωκάς μοι, δέδωκα αὐτοῖς, 22.

4. The δόξα of the Angels.

In Ezekiel the cherub is the bearer of כָּבוֹד (9:3; 10:4, 18, 22; cf. Sir. 49:8). Similarly in Judaism the concept of divine δόξα can sometimes be transferred to the angelic powers around God. [67] Directly linked with Ez. is Hb. 9:5: Χερουβὶν δόξης. Cf. also Rev. 18:1: ἡ γῆ ἐφωτίσθη ἐκ τῆς δόξης αὐτοῦ (of the angel). A further step is taken in Jd. 8 = 2 Pt. 2:10, where the angelic powers are described as δόξαι. It was by the same process that the divine → δύναμις became a designation for angels. In both Philo and Test. XII both terms were revitalised in this sense. [68]

---

[67] LXX Ex. 15:11: δεδοξασμένος ἐν ἁγίοις, θαυμαστὸς ἐν δόξαις. Test. L. 18:5: οἱ ἄγγελοι τῆς δόξης.
[68] Philo Spec. Leg., I, 45 → 236; cf. also Test. Jud. 25:2: αἱ δυνάμεις τῆς δόξης parallel to ὁ ἄγγελος.

G. Hellenistic Gnosticism.

There is a group of texts in which δόξα is used in the same way as in the LXX and the NT. They belong to the sphere of Hellenistic mysticism and magic literature. Emphatic attempts have been made to show that the OT view of δόξα is to be interpreted in terms of the conception found here. The concept is supposed to have taken shape in Persia, and to have spread with "light" mysticism into Judaism, to Egypt, and especially to the NT.

There is no doubt that in the magic pap. and similar writings [69] we have a use of δόξα not found in ordinary Gk. [70] It hovers between the sense of "power," e.g., as given to the amulet, [71] of "radiance," e.g., that of the sun [72] or especially fire, [73] and of the "divine nature" which as ὑπέρβλητος δόξα belongs to supreme deity (κύριοι τῆς δόξης [74]), [75] which is then passed on τῷ θεῷ πρωτοκτίστῳ, [76] but which is also conferred upon the bodies of those who come from the earth and Hades. [77] The verb can be used in the same way; thus the magician prays to Isis: δόξασόν μοι, ὡς ἐδόξασα τὸ ὄνομα τοῦ υἱοῦ σου "Ωρου. [78]

There can be no question that this usage differs from that of ordinary Greek and is also closely related to the usage of the Bible. "Even though the conception of light as the nature of deity might have arisen independently in different places, the peculiar use of δόξα could not have done so." We are prepared to accept this thesis of Reitzenstein. [79] Yet it is difficult to sustain the supposed priority of the magic pap. Among the texts there is not a single one which can be assigned with any certainty to the pre-Christian era and in relation to which we can exclude Christian or Jewish influence. On the other hand, there can be no doubt as to the distinctive Judaeo-Christian use of δόξα from the time of the LXX. Moreover, all the texts concerned seem to derive from a sphere in close touch with the Judaism of the Dispersion. One has only to look at the magic pap., or at a narrative like that of Ac. 19:13 ff., to see how closely linked to Judaism was the world of magic. Finally, the home of the relevant texts is Egypt, and therefore the land in which the Judaeo-Christian usage also had its origin. It is in every respect likely that the Egyptian *Diaspora* exerted some linguistic influence on its environment. [80] Hence, when we find in these texts a use of δόξα similar to that of Judaism and Christianity, it is not only not impossible but highly probable that there is an actual dependence on Jewish usage. There is, of course, no evidence of a direct Christian influence. The truth is rather that we have in magic an independent development of Jewish usage parallel to the Christian.

A further outworking of either the Jewish or the Christian view is to be found among the Mandaeans and the Manichees. Yet it is possible that here we have the strengthening influence of oriental religious conceptions. Lidz. Ginza, 252, 5: "The Father, the first

---

[69] Test. Sol. belongs to this group; for examples, cf. Schneider, 30 f. On the use of δόξα in astrological fragments and documents, *ibid.*, 34 f.

[70] In Corp. Herm., X, 7 (cf. Reitzenstein Hell. Myst., 289) the sense hardly goes beyond that of "renown" or "honour"; Schneider, 25: "transfiguration" is too strong.

[71] Preis. Zaub., IV (Paris), 1616 ff., 1650.

[72] A. Dieterich, *Abraxas* (1891), 176, 5.

[73] *Ibid.*, 191, 3 f.

[74] Preis. Zaub., VII (London), 713.

[75] *Ibid.*, IV, 1051, 1202 f., cf. 1067 f.

[76] Dieterich, *Abraxas*, 183, 67 ff.

[77] M. P. C. Berthelot, *Collection des Anciens Alchimistes Grecs* (1888), 297, 8 ff.; Reitzenstein Hell. Myst., 314 f.

[78] Preis. Zaub., VII (London), 504; cf. *ibid.*, XXXVI (Oslo), 165.

[79] Reitzenstein Hell. Myst., 289.

[80] Cf. Kittel Probleme, 39, n. 2; A. T. Robertson, *A Grammar of the Gk. NT*[3] (1919), 91.

radiance, commanded and spake it"; 527, 18 : "When I came to the water-brooks, the outflowing of radiance encountered me"; 143, 32 : "There went with him the first great radiance which came forth from the raiment of the Lord of greatness." Cf. the Manichean fragment : "An angel from Paradise has come, a proclaimer of the glories." [81]

There may perhaps be some truth in the thesis that Persian elements underlie the whole biblical concept of δόξα. [82] But if there is such a link, it is to be sought in the history of the distinctive OT view of *kabod*. The perspective is obscured and fore-shortened if in later passages we fabricate unprovable linguistic and conceptual con-nexions by which to explain the NT view of δόξα. This undoubtedly derives directly and uninterruptedly from the OT and Jewish view.

δοξάζω, † συνδοξάζω.

The verb derived from δόξα shares in full its distinctive linguistic history. It always means "to have or to give a share in a δόξα or in the δόξα." In non-biblical Gk. we naturally find reflected the particular senses of the noun a. "to have an opinion," "to believe," "to opine," "to suspect," "to hold"; b. "to give praise," "to laud," "to value," "to honour." The first meaning is common in the tragic dramatists, and is also dominant in Philo. The second is later but quite common : ἐπὶ πλέον τι αὐτὸν δοξάζειν, Thuc., III, 45; τοῦ 'Αβραάμου ἔτι καὶ νῦν ... τὸ ὄνομα δοξάζεται, Jos. Ant., 1, 160; δεδο-ξασμένος = "famous" : Polyb., VI, 53, 10. Even the οὐθεὶς δοξάζεται ἄνευ τῆς ἐμῆς γνώμης of the Isis inscr. from Cyme does not really go beyond this usage, [1] in spite of the essential importance of this and similar inscr. from Ios, Nysa, and esp. the Isis hymn of Andros, for an analysis of the style of later Alexandrian hymns and cultic writings. [2]

As in the case of δόξα, meaning a. is not found at all in the LXX, though there are more thans 100 occurrences. On the other hand, b. is very common, especially for a form of כבד, though sometimes for גדל (Est. 3:1) etc. It is used when honour is shown to men (2 Βασ. 10:3 : δοξάζειν Δαυὶδ τὸν πατέρα σου; Sir. 7:31 : δόξασον τὸν ἱερέα etc.); also in relation to objects, e.g., δοξάσαι τὸ ἱερόν (1 Εσδρ. 8:58 = 8:81), cf. 25 (= 28), 64 (= 67); and especially when God is magnified (Lv. 10:3), honoured and exalted (cf. Ex. 15:1 ff.: ἐνδόξως γὰρ δεδόξασται; v. 11: δεδοξασμένος ἐν ἁγίοις etc.). If this proportion of use reflects already the influence of the biblical concept of δόξα, this influence is paramount in the LXX rendering of Ex. 34:29 f., 35 Mas.: כִּי קָרַן עוֹר פָּנָיו. While Σ and Vg. have "was horned," [3] the LXX has ὅτι δεδόξασται ἡ ὄψις τοῦ χρώματος, which can only denote the "radiant shining" of the skin (as in most translations). The δεδοξάσθαι of Moses is a transfiguration with divine δόξα. By way of transition to this sense we may mention that of "splendour" (→ δόξα, 237): Sir. 50:5 (cf. 46:2): the entry of the high-priest who bears the στολὴ δόξης (בגדי כבוד 50:11; cf. 6:31) is depicted in terms of מה נהדר = ὡς ἐδοξάσθη.

In the NT, too, the sense of "to think" is not found, but that of "to honour," "to extol," is very common, whether in relation to man or to God. Mt. 5:16 : δοξάζουσιν τὸν πατέρα ὑμῶν; 6:2 : ὅπως δοξασθῶσιν ὑπὸ τῶν ἀνθρώπων.

---

[81] F. W. K. Müller, AAB, 1904, 53; E. Peterson, Εἷς Θεός (1926), 227.

[82] So Heinrici 1 K., 168, n. 3; later Wetter, Phos., 73 ff., and esp. Reitzenstein Hell. Myst.
δ ο ξ ά ζ ω. Bibl. → δόξα, 233 f., n.

[1] Schneider, 22, translates "will be glorified," but this seems to be going rather further than the true sense.

[2] Cf. W. Peek, Der Isishymnos von Andros und verwandte Texte (1930); O. Weinreich, DLZ, 51 (1930), 2025 ff.; also Deissmann LO, 108 f.

[3] Hence the idea of the horned Moses. On Ex. 34:29 ff. → 246; 249.

How the verb can also acquire the new biblical sense of "to give and to have a share in the divine δόξα," "to transfigure or to be transfigured," has already appeared in our treatment of δόξα. On Jn. → 251; on R. 8:30 → 250; on R. 8:17 (συνδοξάζομαι) → 250; on 2 C. 3:10 → 251.

† ἔνδοξος, † ἐνδοξάζομαι.

ἔνδοξος in secular Gk. means a. "according to the customary opinion" (δόξα = opinio, opp. παράδοξος); b. "honoured," "esteemed," "renowned" (δόξα = gloria); also of things: "honourable," "magnificent," "extraordinary." Sense a. is not found at all in biblical Gk. On the other hand, sense b. is common in Gk. translations of the OT, esp. of honourable men (1 Βασ. 9:6: ἄνθρωπος ἔνδοξος, etc.), though also of the glories of Jerusalem (1 Εσδρ. 1:53 [= 56]). In relation to God, it is used of His wonderful acts towards Israel (e.g., Ex. 34:10: ποιήσω ἔνδοξα), of the praise offered to Him (Ex. 15:1, 21 in the Song of Miriam: ἐνδόξως γὰρ δεδόξασται), of His honourable name (Is. 24:15; 59:19), but also of Himself as the One who is to be magnified (Is. 60:9: διὰ τὸ τὸν ἅγιον τοῦ Ἰσραὴλ ἔνδοξον εἶναι). These statements concerning God may well owe something to the biblical use of δόξα.

The strong rootage of the word group in the language of the Gk. Bible is shown by the construction of the verb ἐνδοξάζομαι,[1] which is peculiar to the Bible.[2] It can be used of human distinction (4 Βασ. 14:10; Test. S. 6:5 etc.), but for the most part is used of the divine majesty, which is asserted both in good when God is magnified in those who serve Him (Is. 49:3 etc.), and yet also in evil when He shows Himself to be the ἐνδοξαζόμενος in His acts of punishment and retribution towards[3] Pharaoh (Ex. 14:4, 17 f.) or Sidon (Ez. 28:22).

In the NT the adjective is everywhere used in the current[4] sense. This is plain in the Lucan references to the clothes (7:25) and acts of Jesus (13:17), as also in the antithesis ὑμεῖς ἔνδοξοι, ἡμεῖς[5] δὲ ἄτιμοι in 1 C. 4:10. But the same is true of Eph. 5:27. When the Church is described as ἔνδοξος, this refers to its honourable estate, i.e., that it has neither spot nor wrinkle; but the true content of the figure derives from the ἵνα clause: that it should be ἁγία and ἄμωμος. In no case do we have any reminiscence of the divine δόξα in the NT ἔνδοξος.

This connexion appears the more clearly, however, in the only NT use of the verb ἐνδοξάζομαι. 2 Th. 1: v. 10: ὅταν ἔλθῃ (Christ) ἐνδοξασθῆναι ἐν τοῖς ἁγίοις αὐτοῦ; v. 12: ὅπως ἐνδοξασθῇ τὸ ὄνομα τοῦ κυρίου ... ἐν ὑμῖν. OT formulae are hereby adopted and applied to Christ, cf. esp. ψ 88:7: ὁ θεὸς ἐνδοξαζόμενος ἐν βουλῇ ἁγίων, but also Is. 24:15; 59:19 (→ supra). What leads to this application, however, is the use of δόξα in v. 9. For here the δόξα τῆς ἰσχύος αὐτοῦ from[6] which the reprobate fall to destruction is the same as that to which

---

ἔνδοξος κτλ. [1] The only secular example thus far discovered is in Preis. Zaub., XIII (Leiden), 448 f. (cf. A. Dieterich, Abraxas [1891], 182, 6), and this is undoubtedly dependent on biblical usage, as may be seen from the names Ἀδωναί, Βασήμμ, Ἰάω (= Adonai in the name of Yahweh), 453. ἐνδοξάζομαι is not found in either Josephus (Schlatter) or Philo.

[2] The noun ἐνδοξασμός is found only in Σ ψ 45:3; 46:4 and Alius Is. 24:14.

[3] ἐν (Φαραώ etc.) follows the Heb. בְ with כבד niph.

[4] For par. in Joseph., cf. Schl. Lk., 327.

[5] The ὑμεῖς/ἡμεῖς shows particularly clearly how remote from Paul's thinking is any reminiscence of participation in the divine δόξα.

[6] "Away from" or "from"? The stress on ἰσχύς suggests the latter.

the participation [7] of the ἅγιοι (v. 10) and ὑμεῖς (v. 12) in the ἐνδοξασθῆναι of Christ refers. It is characteristic of the basic Pauline understanding that the eschatological statement of v. 10 quite naturally becomes a statement about the present in v. 12.

† παράδοξος.

This word is quite common in secular Gk., Philo, Joseph. [1] and the LXX. It always denotes an "unusual event contrary to belief and expectation" (τὸ παρὰ δόξαν ὄν, cf. the LXX verb παραδοξάζω, "I do something unusual"). In the NT it occurs only in Lk. 5:26, where it is designed to emphasise the unusual aspect of what was seen in Jesus: εἴδον παράδοξα σήμερον.

The word does not have any part in the change of meaning suffered by δόξα in the Bible.

Kittel

> δόκιμος, ἀδόκιμος, δοκιμή, δοκίμιον,
> δοκιμάζω, ἀποδοκιμάζω, δοκιμασία

The stem word is δοκή (δοχή), "watching" (whence δόκιμος, as ἄλκιμος from ἀλκή, μάχιμος from μάχη). δόκιμος as an adj. both of person and object thus denotes [1] a. "tested in battle," "reliable," "trustworthy," b. "a man who is tested, significant, recognised, esteemed, worthy" (e.g., πολίτου δοκίμου ἡ ἀρετὴ εἴναι τὸ δύνασθαι καὶ ἄρχειν καὶ ἄρχεσθαι καλῶς, Aristot. Pol., III, 4, p. 1277a, 26 f.; Λυκούργου, τῶν Σπαρτιατῶν δοκίμου ἀνδρός, Hdt. I, 65: καλέσας δώδεκα τοὺς δοκιμωτάτους, Jos. Vit., 55), or "an object which is tested, genuine or valuable" (τούτους δοκίμοις ἵπποις καὶ ὅπλοις παρεσκευασμένους, Xenoph. Oec., 4, 7); it is particularly used of metals, as consistently in the LXX, Gn. 23:16; 1 Ch. 28:18; 29:4; 2 Ch. 9:17; and finally: πρὸς δαιμονιαζομένους Πιβηχέως δόκιμον, for a reliable means of magic, Preis. Zaub., IV, 3007, cf. I, 246.

ἀδόκιμος, the opp. of δόκιμος, is used of persons (ἀδόκιμοι σοφισταί, of Gk. historians, Jos. Ap., 2, 236; ὡς μὴ ... ἀδόκιμοι παντάπασιν ἐν τῇ πόλει γένοιντο, Xenoph. Resp. Lac., 3, 4) and things (... λόγοις καὶ βουλαῖς καὶ πράξεσιν ἀδοκίμοις ... Philo Conf. Ling., 198, τὸ ἀργύριον ... ἀδόκιμον, Is. 1:22).

δοκιμή. This word is very rare, there being no instances prior to Paul. [2] It means "testing" or "certifying," e.g., τὴν διὰ πυρὸς δοκιμὴν (χρυσίου) ... Eustath. Thessal.

---

[7] Any more exact explanation of the ἐν (for suggestions, cf. Dob. Th., 251) is hardly likely to be in keeping with the thought of Paul when we consider that it is based on the Heb. ‍ב (→ n. 3) and that the statement is so strongly characterised by the OT expression. π α ρ ά δ ο ξ ο ς. [1] Schl. Lk., 60.

δ ό κ ι μ ο ς κτλ. Cr.-Kö., 355 ff.

[1] Acc. to Debrunner; cf. C. Arbenz, *Die Adj. auf* -ιμος (Diss. Zürich, 1933), 38 ff.

[2] Loh. Phil., 117, n. 4.

Opuscula, p. 252, 30 (L. F. Tafel [1832]); Σ ψ 67:30 : ὡς δοκιμὴν ἀργυρίου. Diosc. Mat. Med., IV, 184 only in a few MSS (II, p. 333, n. 9).

δοκίμιον is the neut. of an adj. δοκίμιος, "tested," "genuine," e.g., χρυσὸς δοκίμιος. CPR, 12, 6 f., also 26, 6 etc.;[3] also ψ 11:6. In the subst. form, it has the same meaning as the older (?) τὸ δοκιμεῖον, "means of testing," e.g., Herodian describes soldiers' κάματος as δοκίμιον, II, 10, 12. δεῖ δὲ ὥσπερ κανόνα καὶ στάθμην τινὰ καὶ δοκίμιον ὡρισμένον πρὸς ὃ τις ἀποβλέπειν δυνήσεται τὴν κρίσιν ποιεῖσθαι, Ps.-Dion. Hal. Art. Rhet., 11, 1; δοκίμιον ἀργυρίῳ καὶ χρυσῷ πύρωσις, Prv. 27:21; finally an expression which comes from the more religious East and has a religious colouring : καὶ τῆς πρὸς θεοὺς εὐσεβείας ἔργωι καλλίστωι οὐ μεικρὸν δοκιμεῖον ἀπέλιπεν ... Ditt. Or., 308, 15.

δοκιμάζειν. This verb is found everywhere in the sense of "to test," "to try." The critics of Socrates are challenged : δοκιμαζόντων εἰ ἱκανὸς ἦν βελτίους ποιεῖν τοὺς συνόντας, Xenoph. Mem., I, 4, 1. In the Book of Job we read : ... οὓς λόγους δοκιμάζει, 34:3 LXX. In the NT there is the phrase : ζεύγη βοῶν ἠγόρασα πέντε, καὶ πορεύομαι δοκιμάσαι αὐτά ... Lk. 14:19. In the sense of "to test" it is a techn. term for official testing. Of the Areopagus it is said by Xenoph. : ἡ δὲ ἐν Ἀρείῳ πάγῳ βουλή ... οὐκ ἐκ τῶν δεδοκιμασμένων καθίσταται; Mem., III, 5, 20. In the Leges Plato speaks of the appointment of state officials and envisages δοκιμάζεσθαι for those nominated to office (VI, 754a ff.).[4] With this sense is linked that of "to accept as tested or proved." πάντες ... οὗτοι νόμοι εἰσίν, οὓς τὸ πλῆθος συνελθὸν καὶ δοκιμάσαν ἔγραψε, φράζον ἅ τε δεῖ ποιεῖν καὶ ἃ μή, Xenoph. Mem., I, 2, 42.[5] On an inscr. it is written : ἀνὴρ δεδοκιμασμένος τοῖς θείοις κριτηρίοις τῶν Σεβαστῶν ἐπί τε τῇ τέχνῃ τῆς ἰατρικῆς, Ditt. Syll.[3], 807, 5 — one of the few non-Christian passages where δοκιμάζειν has a religious flavour. With a double accus. it has the sense of "to find someone or something to be ...", e.g., ὃν ἐδοκιμάσαμεν ... σπουδαῖον ὄντα 2 C. 8:22, which may be compared linguistically with, e.g., οὓς δ᾽ ἂν αὐτὸς δοκιμάσῃ πιστοὺς καὶ φίλους, Jos. Ant., 13, 51. Finally, with the infin. it has the sense of "to regard or desire as necessary," e.g., ... μετοικεῖν δοκιμάσας ... Jos. Ant., 1, 157.

ἀποδοκιμάζειν is the opp. of δοκιμάζειν and means "to throw out in the test," "to find unworthy." The one who does not fulfil his pious duties to parents is rejected by the council : ... καὶ ἀποδοκιμάζουσα οὐκ ἐᾷ ἄρχειν τοῦτον ... Xen. Mem., II, 2, 13.

δοκιμασία means "testing."[6] Suid. tells us about official testing s.v. δοκιμασθείς : Λυκοῦργος δὲ γ᾽ δοκιμασίας φησὶ κατὰ τὸν νόμον γίνεσθαι. καὶ γὰρ μία μέν ἐστιν, ἣν οἵ θ᾽ ἄρχοντες δοκιμάζονται· ἄλλη δέ, ἣν οἱ ῥήτορες, τρίτη δέ, ἣν οἱ στρατηγοί. λέγει δὲ ἐν τῷ αὐτῷ λόγῳ καὶ ἱππέων δοκιμασίαν. In the Jewish sphere Joseph. tells us that Moses ἐκάλει τοὺς περὶ ἱερωσύνης ἁμιλλωμένους διὰ τὴν τῶν ἱερέων δοκιμασίαν, Ant., 4, 54.

This whole word group first acquires religious significance in the NT, the ideas of which are shaped by the OT. The reason for this is to be found in the very nature of the subject-matter of the NT, i.e., in the situation of Christian existence.

---

[3] Deissmann NB, 87 f.

[4] In this connexion we also read of the testing of priests according to their lack of physical defects, their blameless birth and the spotless conduct both of themselves and their parents (759). Similar requirements are found among the Jews, where priests and Levites have to undergo a test of this kind. On this point cf. the material in Str.-B., I, 2 f. In 1 Tm. 3:10 there is to be a δοκιμάζεσθαι of deacons, though here the emphasis is on religious and ethical factors.

[5] Cf. the material par. in Joseph., which has a Jewish background : χρώμενοί τε νόμοις οὓς ἀγαθοὺς δοκιμάσας ὁ θεὸς παραδίδωσι ..., Ant., 4, 295.

[6] Cf. Pauly-W., V (1905), 1268 ff.

This situation is determined by received salvation on the one side and impending judgment on the other. The resultant conduct is a striving for attestation, i.e., for the attestation of the salvation already received and for attestation in the test of judgment. This situation and the resultant conduct give the word group its distinctive sense as used in the NT. We are thus brought face to face with ideas which are peculiar to the NT.

1. Human existence stands under the divine testing in which it must prove itself. a. This testing culminates in judgment. Judgment is a testing of human life and achievement: ἑκάστου τὸ ἔργον ὁποῖόν ἐστιν τὸ πῦρ αὐτὸ δοκιμάσει, 1 C. 3:13. [7] The man who has attested himself in life, and whom the testing of judgment shows to be attested, is δόκιμος. It is of the δόκιμος that James writes: ... δόκιμος γενόμενος λήμψεται τὸν στέφανον τῆς ζωῆς, ἣν ἀπηγγείλατο τοῖς ἀγαπῶσιν αὐτόν, 1:12. b. Judgment gathers up the divine testing which takes place in history and by which history is fashioned. In biblical religion God is the δοκιμάζων τὰς καρδίας ἡμῶν, 1 Th. 2:4. [8] Paul expresses his apostolic consciousness as follows ... δεδοκιμάσμεθα ὑπὸ τοῦ θεοῦ πιστευθῆναι τὸ εὐαγγέλιον..., 1 Th. 2:4. The counsel of God, which sifts the hearts, has found them fit for the evangelical office. Their apostolate is grounded in the sifting counsel of God, and in their discharge of it they know that are under His searching eye: ... λαλοῦμεν ... θεῷ δοκιμάζοντι τὰς καρδίας ἡμῶν.

These aspects of NT religion have their origin in the OT. a. The thought of the probing judgment which concludes world history is presupposed in the thesis which underlies the OT view of history, namely, that the history of a people is its judgment. In this connexion Jeremiah especially uses the terms δοκιμάζειν and ἀποδοκιμάζειν [9] in his consideration of the divine background of historical processes. For him, and for pious Israelites generally, God is the Lord "that judgest righteously, that triest the reins and the heart" (11:20). He proclaims to the people the word of Yahweh: "Behold, I have melted them, I have tried them. What shall I do on account of their wickedness?" 9:7. [10] He himself had been appointed by Yahweh to sift the people, a task depicted in the image of the purifier of metals (6:27 ff.). The final judgment on the people can only be that God has rejected and set aside the generation which does such things. In moving terms Jeremiah wrestles with the people for the removal of the rejection which follows his testing: "Hast thou utterly rejected Judah? has thy soul lothed Zion?" 14:19. b. The saints of the OT realise that God tests them. Thus we have in the Ps. the recurrent confession: "Thou hast proved mine heart; thou hast visited me in the night" (Ps. 17:3; cf. 66:10; 139:1). In the changes and chances of life, in hours of visitation and of stillness, the righteous know that God's searching eyes are upon them. These are a proof of the gracious presence of God: ... τούτους μὲν γὰρ ὡς πατὴρ νουθετῶν ἐδοκίμασας ... Wis. 11:10. For this reason they pray to God: "Examine me, O Lord, and prove me; try my reins and my heart," Ps. 26:2; cf. 139:23. The saints wish to live their lives under the eyes of God. Hence the prayer: μή με ἀποδοκιμάσῃς ἐκ παίδων σου, Wis. 9:4.

---

[7] Cf. Test. Abr. 13, where it is said of the angel Pyruel: δοκιμάζει τὰ τῶν ἀνθρώπων ἔργα διὰ πυρός ... εἴ τινος δὲ τὸ ἔργον τὸ πῦρ δοκιμάσει καὶ μὴ ἅψεται αὐτοῦ, οὗτος δικαιοῦται (ed. James, Texts and Studies, II, 2 [1892], 93, 10 ff.).

[8] Cf. Jer. 11:20; v. also Joseph., e.g.: God δοκιμάσαι θέλων αὐτοῦ τὴν διάνοιαν, Ant., 1, 233.

[9] In Jeremiah the terms in the Mas. are בחן (LXX δοκιμάζειν) and מאס (LXX ἀποδοκιμάζειν).

[10] This is how Volz renders it according to his corrected text. The Mas. and LXX differ.

2. The awaiting judgment, and constant submission to the divine scrutiny, fashion a mode of life orientated to testing, and indeed to the testing of assured salvation in the concrete situation of daily life. [11] This explains the concern of the apostle Paul: ... μήπως ἄλλοις κηρύξας αὐτὸς ἀδόκιμος γένωμαι, 1 C. 9:27. a. The question is particularly relevant in the Corinthian letters because of the state of the community and the kind of religion which it had begun to practise. Schlatter has described this type of religion as festive and victorious. [12] It took offence at the unimpressive appearance of Paul, at his anxious and humble attitude. It thus did not see in him an attestation of Christ, which it sought in a visible demonstration of His power ... δοκιμὴν ζητεῖτε τοῦ ἐν ἐμοὶ λαλοῦντος Χριστοῦ ..., 2 C. 13:3. Paul's primary objection to this outlook is to be found in 2 C. 10:18: οὐ γὰρ ὁ ἑαυτὸν συνιστάνων, ἐκεῖνός ἐστιν δόκιμος, ἀλλ' ὃν ὁ κύριος συνίστησιν. Here he lifts the whole question of attestation out of the hands of men and sets it in those of God. God alone decides this issue, which is not subject to human categories of judgment. This means, however, that the question what constitutes true attestation is posed the more urgently.

b. The situation in which it is to be manifested is that of θλῖψις. θλῖψις denotes the earthly situation of the community of Christ. It means being set in a position in which salvation is not yet seen, in which the community is oppressed and persecuted by satanic powers and despised by the world around. In relation to this situation Paul writes: ... ἡ θλῖψις ὑπομονὴν κατεργάζεται, ἡ δὲ ὑπομονὴ δοκιμήν, ἡ δὲ δοκιμὴ ἐλπίδα, R. 5:3 f. [13] The basis of attestation is thus to be found in the patience which keeps the faith and defies circumstances, and in the fruit of this patience in living faith which knows the victory of Christ. Paul thus points the Corinthians to the Macedonians as examples: ... ἐν πολλῇ δοκιμῇ θλίψεως ἡ περισσεία τῆς χαρᾶς αὐτῶν ... ἐπερίσσευσεν, 2 C. 8:2. In θλῖψις they have maintained the joy of Christian faith. The same view is to be found in James: πᾶσαν χαρὰν ἡγήσασθε ..., ὅταν πειρασμοῖς περιπέσητε ποικίλοις, γινώσκοντες ὅτι τὸ δοκίμιον ὑμῶν τῆς πίστεως κατεργάζεται ὑπομονήν, 1:2 f.; and also in Peter: ἐν ᾧ ἀγαλλιᾶσθε, ὀλίγον ἄρτι εἰ δέον λυπηθέντες ἐν ποικίλοις πειρασμοῖς, ἵνα τὸ δοκίμιον ὑμῶν τῆς πίστεως πολυτιμότερον χρυσίου τοῦ ἀπολλυμένου διὰ πυρὸς δὲ δοκιμαζομένου, εὑρεθῇ, 1 Pt. 1:6 f. [14] The thought common to these passages, as also to R. 5:3 f., is that faith is tested in the → πειρασμοί which afflict the community and cause λύπη. [15] Also common to the three passages is the conviction that θλίψεις and πειρασμός are a reason

---

[11] Cf. the term "examination" in S. Kierkegaard, Training in Christianity (E.T., 1941), esp. p. 198: "It is only Christ that can make His life a test for all men. When He ascends up to heaven the examination period begins ... But (and this contributes expressly to define the intervening period as an examination) He is coming again."

[12] Gesch. d. erst. Christ., 215, cf. 205 ff.

[13] On ἡ δὲ ὑπομονὴ δοκιμήν, cf. 4 Macc. 17:12: ἀρετὴ δι' ὑπομονῆς δοκιμάζουσα.

[14] A point which immediately strikes us about this passage is its literary agreement with R. 5:3 f. There can hardly be any question of dependence, and we are perhaps to seek a common source in the exhortation of the first Palestinian community, since the thinking of both Jm. and 1 Pt. seems to point in this direction. Cf. Dib. Jk., 73 ff.; Wnd. Jk., 5 f.

[15] For this idea there are Jewish analogies: ἐν πυρὶ δοκιμάζεται χρυσός, καὶ ἄνθρωποι δεκτοὶ ἐν καμίνῳ ταπεινώσεως, Gr. Sir. 2:5; ἐν βραχεῖ ἀφίσταται εἰς τὸ δοκιμάσαι τῆς ψυχῆς διαβούλιον ἐν δέκα πειρασμοῖς δόκιμον ἀπέδειξέ με ... Test. Jos. 2:6 f.; cf. Jub. 17:17 f.; 19:8.

for joy: R. 5:3: καυχώμεθα; 1 Pt. 1:6: ἀγαλλιᾶσθε; Jm. 1:2: πᾶσαν χαρὰν ἡγήσασθε.

The meaning of τὸ δοκίμιον poses an exegetical problem. In 1 Pt. 1:7 it certainly does not denote a means of testing. It is here a neut. subst. of the adj. δοκίμιος and thus signifies "what is genuine or tested." Deissmann has worked out the possibility of this rendering as follows. [16] The apostle is saying that the genuineness of faith as proved in suffering is more precious than that of gold tried in the fire. But what about Jm. 1:2 f. ? Here there are no obstacles to understanding τὸ δοκίμιον as a means of testing. Suffering is a means of testing faith, and as such leads to patience. The only question is whether the link with 1 Pt. does not incline us to the view that it is what is genuine in faith that works patience, and therefore to the interpretation that we are summoned to joy in temptations because true faith results and attests itself in triumphant patience. If we assume a common basis for the two statements in a fixed form of Christian exhortation, then there is more to be said for this understanding.

Testing thus has its origin in the situation of the community, and it consists in the patient perseverance of faith in Christ to the day of judgment. This is the teaching of Paul to the Corinthians at 1 C. 11:19: δεῖ γὰρ καὶ αἱρέσεις ἐν ὑμῖν εἶναι, ἵνα οἱ δόκιμοι φανεροὶ γένωνται ἐν ὑμῖν. The δόκιμοι are those who, clinging to Christ in faith, do not split up into groups orientated to worldly things. To the attestation of faith in Christ belongs faithfulness in ministry. Paul praises Timothy to the Philippians: τὴν δὲ δοκιμὴν αὐτοῦ γινώσκετε, ὅτι ὡς πατρὶ τέκνον σὺν ἐμοὶ ἐδούλευσεν εἰς τὸ εὐαγγέλιον 2:22. He requires of the Corinthians: διὰ τῆς δοκιμῆς τῆς διακονίας ταύτης δοξάζοντες τὸν θεόν ..., 2 C. 9:13. The Corinthians can give proof of themselves in the collection. Finally, there is attestation in conduct. Paul shows this particularly in 2 C. 13:5 ff., where he takes up with them the question of accreditation and expresses himself to the effect that it matters little to him whether he himself seems to be approved so long as they show themselves to be approved by doing good. [17] The purpose of his writing, as he himself states it, is to see them accredited in the obedience which they show him as an apostle of Jesus Christ (2 C. 2:9). Obedient conduct consists essentially in the demonstration of love. In what he says about the collection Paul's aim is to test the genuineness of love (2 C. 8:8). These thoughts underlie the phrase δόκιμος ἐν Χριστῷ in R. 16:10 and the demand addressed to Timothy: σπούδασον σεαυτὸν δόκιμον παραστῆσαι τῷ θεῷ ..., 2 Tm. 2:15.

c. These statements contain the insight that the attestation which God seeks in the judgment is to be found only in those who believe in Christ, and that there is no such attestation outside this faith. The judgment of Paul on the human race is as follows: ... καθὼς οὐκ ἐδοκίμασαν τὸν θεὸν ἔχειν ἐν ἐπιγνώσει, παρέδωκεν αὐτοὺς ὁ θεὸς εἰς ἀδόκιμον νοῦν, ποιεῖν τὰ μὴ καθήκοντα ..., R. 1:28. The godlessness of man, as the original sin consisting in disregard for God, leads to a determinative outlook which is ἀδόκιμος, i.e., without attestation, in respect of the judgment which tests the race. [18]

---

[16] Cf. Deissmann NB, 86 ff.; Bl.-Debr. § 263, 2; Kn. Pt., 49 ff.; Moult.-Mill., s.v.

[17] On the exegetical problems of this passage, v. Ltzm., Bchm., Wnd. 2 K., ad loc.

[18] There is here a play on words: καθὼς οὐκ ἐδοκίμασαν ... εἰς ἀδόκιμον νοῦν. δοκιμάζειν with the inf. means "to regard as necessary." Cf. τὰ ... ὀνόματα δηλῶσαι τούτων οὐκ ἐδοκίμαζον, Jos. Ant., 2, 176; παραχειμασίαν δὲ ἢ χρήματα πράσσεσθαι οὐ δοκιμάζω, Ant., 14, 195 etc.

3. The life of the Christian is set under the searching eyes of God, and ethics is determined by the concept of accreditation. In this connexion the NT introduces a special use of the verb δοκιμάζειν. Christians are summoned to a twofold testing. a. They are to test or prove what is the will of God. If they are to be approved, they must do the will of God. But to do it, they must know it by testing. In the new positing of human existence in faith, Christians are enabled to know the will of God: μεταμορφοῦσθε τῇ ἀνακαινώσει τοῦ νοός, εἰς τὸ δοκιμάζειν ὑμᾶς τί τὸ θέλημα τοῦ θεοῦ ..., R. 12:2. [19] They thus have a duty to do so. Hence the prayer of Paul: εἰς τὸ δοκιμάζειν ὑμᾶς τὰ διαφέροντα, ἵνα ἦτε εἰλικρινεῖς καὶ ἀπρόσκοποι εἰς ἡμέραν Χριστοῦ, Phil. 1:10. τὰ διαφέροντα is that which is fitting in a given situation. The rule of the Christian life is: ὡς τέκνα φωτὸς περιπατεῖτε ..., δοκιμάζοντες τί ἐστιν εὐάρεστον τῷ κυρίῳ, Eph. 5:9 f. Or again, there is the general rule: πάντα δὲ δοκιμάζετε, τὸ καλὸν κατέχετε, 1 Th. 5:21. This preserves their actions from meaningless caprice and brings them under the seriousness of the will of God. John demands that Christians should test the different phenomena of religious life: δοκιμάζετε τὰ πνεύματα, 1 Jn. 4:1. b. At the same time, however, Christians are summoned to a test of their own accreditation: ἑαυτοὺς δοκιμάζετε, 2 C. 13:5; cf. Gl. 6:4. In virtue of the immediate presence of Christ in the Lord's Supper, the Corinthians who celebrate it in an undisciplined and unworthy manner are challenged: δοκιμαζέτω δὲ ἄνθρωπος ἑαυτόν, καὶ οὕτως ἐκ τοῦ ἄρτου ἐσθιέτω καὶ ἐκ τοῦ ποτηρίου πινέτω, 1 C. 11:28. Christ cannot be approached in a careless and disorderly way. [20] c. In addition, Jesus demands that we should test the times, and He reproaches the Pharisees for not paying regard to the progress of history under the divine direction: τὸ πρόσωπον τῆς γῆς καὶ τοῦ οὐρανοῦ οἴδατε δοκιμάζειν, τὸν καιρὸν δὲ τοῦτον πῶς οὐ δοκιμάζετε; Lk. 12:56.

4. One passage claims special attention. At the conclusion of the parable of the wicked husbandmen, Jesus quotes ψ 117:22 f.: λίθον ὃν ἀπεδοκίμασαν οἱ οἰκοδομοῦντες, οὗτος ἐγενήθη εἰς κεφαλὴν γωνίας, Mt. 21:42 and par. [21] Jesus applies this to Himself. He is the corner-stone which the builders have rejected but which has become the key-stone, cf. Mk. 8:31; Lk. 9:22; 17:25. These sayings are taken up again in 1 Pt. 2:4, 7. The Christian elected by God is subjected to the testing wisdom and insight of men. This is what exposes the final basis of the Corinthian error. This is the basis of the situation of Christians in θλῖψις and of the manner of their attestation. This is what makes it clear that the attestation of Christians is taken out of all the categories of human judgment and is a matter for God alone.

Grundmann

---

[19] The Jew had the possibility of knowing the will of God in the Law. To him Paul says: δοκιμάζεις τὰ διαφέροντα κατηχούμενος ἐκ τοῦ νόμου, R. 2:18. By the endowment of the Spirit the Christian can have direct knowledge of the will of God.

[20] There is an independent use of δόκιμος in R. 14:18: ὁ γὰρ ἐν τούτῳ δουλεύων τῷ Χριστῷ εὐάρεστος τῷ θεῷ καὶ δόκιμος τοῖς ἀνθρώποις. Here δόκιμος is used in relation to men. A good commentary on this passage is to be found in the Rabbinic saying: So do what is good and right in the eyes of Yahweh, i.e., what is good in the eyes of God and what is right in the eyes of men; these are the words of R. Akiba, T. Sheq., 2, 1.

[21] In Rabb. lit. this saying is referred to Abraham (Pirqe R. El., 24), and to David (bPes., 119a; Tg. Ps. 118:22 ff.); only in mediaeval writings is it referred to the Messiah (Rashi on Mi. 5:1). Cf. Str.-B., I, 875 f.

> δοῦλος, σύνδουλος, δούλη, δουλεύω,
> δουλεία, δουλόω, καταδουλόω,
> δουλαγωγέω, ὀφθαλμοδουλία

δοῦλος, σύνδουλος, δούλη, δουλεύω, δουλεία.

All the words in this group serve either to describe the status of a slave or an attitude corresponding to that of a slave. δοῦλος is a "slave," δούλη a "female slave," δουλεύω "to be a slave," "to stand in the relationship of a slave," δουλεία "slavery," σύνδουλος a "fellow-slave," the adj. δοῦλος-η-ον "enslaved" or "performing the service of a slave." The meaning is so unequivocal and self-contained that it is superfluous to give examples of the individual terms or to trace the history of the group. [1] Distinction from synonymous words and groups (→ θεραπεύω, → λατρεύω, → λειτουργέω, → διακονέω [→ 81]) is made possible by the fact that the emphasis here is always on "serving as a slave." [2] Hence we have a service which is not a matter of choice for the one who renders it, which he has to perform whether he likes or not, because he is subject as a slave to an alien will, to the will of his owner. → οἰκέτης is almost exactly synonymous, but in δοῦλος the stress is rather on the slave's dependence on his lord, while οἰκέτης emphasises the position of the slave in relation to the world outside and in human society. [3] This shows us again how strong is the passive element in δοῦλος, and in the whole word group to which it belongs.

A. The Word Group Among the Greeks.

1. The distinctive feature of the self-awareness of the Greek is the thought of freedom. The Greek finds his personal dignity in the fact that he is free. Thus his self-awareness stands out sharply from anything which stands under the concept δουλεύειν. For where there is δουλεύειν human autonomy is set aside and an alien will takes precedence of one's own. This does not mean that there is no place for the thought of service in the Greek world. The Greek city state depended on the service of citizens, and these gave their service with all their powers and even with life itself. What is repudiated is service after the manner of the δοῦλος, who not only has no possibility of evading the tasks laid upon him but who also has no right of personal choice, who must rather do what another will have done, and refrain from doing what another will not have done. In the δοῦλος the free

---

δοῦλος κτλ. Cr.-Kö., 361 ff.; Pr.-Bauer, 319 f.; Deissmann LO, 270 ff.; Trench, 19 ff.; Schl., Theol. d. Jdtm., 49 f.; A. Schlatter, Wie sprach Josephus von Gott? (1910), 12; J. Leipoldt, War Jesus Jude? (1923), 26 ff.; O. Schmitz, Der Freiheitsgedanke bei Epiktet und das Freiheitszeugnis des Paulus (1923); W. Brandt, Dienst und Dienen im Neuen Testament (1931); T. Zahn, Sclaverei und Christenthum in der alten Welt (1879); J. B. Lightfoot, St. Paul's Epistles to the Colossians and to Philemon (1897), 317 ff.; J. J. Koopmans, De servitute antiqua et religione christiana (Diss. Amsterdam, 1920); E. Lohmeyer, Soziale Fragen im Urchristentum (1921).

[1] For the earliest occurrence, v. the dictionaries.
[2] On the interrelationship of the various Gk. words for service, cf. already Athen., VI, 93.
[3] Mutatis mutandis we thus have between δοῦλος and οἰκέτης the same relationship as between libertinus and libertus; cf. E. Klaar, δοῦλος and οἰκέτης, Philol. Wochenschr., 43 (1923), 525 ff.

Greek world always sees its own antitype, and in δουλεύειν it sees the perversion of its own nature. Hence the Greek can only reject and scorn the type of service which in inner or outer structure bears even the slightest resemblance to that of the slave.

This attitude to everything denoted by the term δουλεύειν is reflected in the most various ways both in the Greek world and in Hellenism. The fierceness with which the Greeks fought for political independence finds its explanation here, [4] as does also their scorn for barbarians and especially the Persians (e.g., Plat. Leg., III, 698a) because they were not free but after the manner of δοῦλοι [5] were subject to δεσπόται. [6] It was in accordance with this spirit that Plato in a famous passage depicted the ideal of the Sophists: Πῶς ἂν εὐδαίμων γένοιτο ἄνθρωπος δουλεύων ὁτῳοῦν; ἀλλὰ τοῦτ᾽ ἐστὶν τὸ κατὰ φύσιν καλὸν καὶ δίκαιον, ὃ ἐγώ σοι νῦν παρρησιαζόμενος λέγω, ὅτι δεῖ τὸν ὀρθῶς βιωσόμενον τὰς μὲν ἐπιθυμίας τὰς ἑαυτοῦ ἐᾶν ὡς μεγίστας εἶναι καὶ μὴ κολάζειν, ταύταις δὲ ὡς μεγίσταις οὔσαις ἱκανὸν εἶναι ὑπηρετεῖν δι᾽ ἀνδρείαν καὶ φρόνησιν, καὶ ἀποπιμπλάναι ὧν ἂν ἀεὶ ἡ ἐπιθυμία γίγνηται (Gorg., 491e/492a). Plato himself sharply opposed this view in its positive development in the second part of the statement. [7] Nevertheless, he, too, excluded any δουλεύειν ὁτῳοῦν from his picture of man and his ideal of personality. It makes no difference that in his case the ground of this exclusion lies in the dignity of man, whereas in the case of the Sophists it is to be found in an eudaemonistic outlook. The decisive point is that in both cases we have the same basic attitude which leaves no place for δουλεύειν, no matter what the reason.

For Plato there either is or seems to be only one exception to this rule. This is that he uses the word group in relation to the νόμοι with no sense of anything despicable. For him δουλεῦσαι τοῖς νόμοις is an essential mark of the true citizen (Leg., III, 698c; 700a), just as there can be a solid state only when its ἄρχοντες are δοῦλοι τοῦ νόμου and recognise in the νόμος their δεσπότης (Leg., IV, 715d). Yet it is only in appearance that we have here an exception to the rule that there is no place for δουλεύειν in Plato. This is clear once we consider the nature of Platonic law. [8] In the νόμοι as Plato sees them there is expressed in absolutely binding form that which is posed in man's nature as his goal, no matter whether the πόλις which poses the νόμος owes its decisive perception to a god or to a man who has special gifts of perception at this point (cf. Leg., I, 645b). Because there appears in the νόμος the supra-individual aspect of man, and because this becomes here the basis of ideal human life in the πόλις, [9] the δουλεῦσαι τοῖς νόμοις of Plato does not involve a degrading dependence, but ἐλευθερία as one of the chief possessions of a citizen. It may thus be said that what distinguishes the free man from the slave in the eyes of Plato is that he τοῖς νόμοις δου-

---

[4] Cf. Isocr., 4, 95 etc.

[5] Cf. Eur. Iph. Aul., 1400 f.: Iphigenia: βαρβάρων δ᾽ Ἕλληνας ἄρχειν εἰκός, ἀλλ᾽ οὐ βαρβάρους, | μῆτερ, Ἑλλήνων· τὸ (!) μὲν γὰρ δοῦλον, οἱ δ᾽ ἐλεύθεροι. There could hardly be any sharper distinction between barbarians and Greeks than in terms of δουλεία /ἐλευθερία. For a similar passage, though by no means so sharp, cf. also Isocr., 5, 154.

[6] → already 44 f.

[7] Characteristically, Plato does not speak of a ὑπηρετεῖν ἐπιθυμίαις, ἡδοναῖς etc., like the Sophists, but of a δουλεύειν ἡδονῇ (Phaedr., 238e : with ὑπὸ ἐπιθυμίας ἄρχεσθαι); cf. also Ep., 8, 354e.

[8] For details → νόμος.

[9] Cf. Ep., 8, 354d : τοῖς δὲ δὴ ἐλεύθερα διώκουσιν ἤθη καὶ φεύγουσιν τὸν δούλειον ζυγὸν ὡς ὂν κακόν, εὐλαβεῖσθαι συμβουλεύοιμ᾽ ἂν μή ποτε ἀπληστίᾳ ἐλευθερίας ἀκαίρου τινὸς εἰς τὸ τῶν προγόνων νόσημα ἐμπέσωσιν, ὃ διὰ τὴν ἄγαν ἀναρχίαν οἱ τότε ἔπαθον, ἀμέτρῳ ἐλευθερίας χρώμενοι ἔρωτι. The νόσημα is tyranny.

λεύει because he is one of those who constitute the πόλις and guarantee its solidity. [10] Here, however, Plato finds the goal which is set for man, and therefore he can equate the νόμῳ δουλεία with the θεῷ δουλεία, though without any religious connotation in our sense of the term. [11]

The usage of Aristotle is exactly the same as that of Plato. In Aristotle, too, the word group has a derogatory sense in keeping with its basic meaning. [12] In terms of his thesis that one should not be dependent on men in any way, Aristotle can describe it as δουλικόν if one cannot live without the support of others, even though they be friends. [13] The way in which he speaks of slaves will show us better than any exposition what associations the word has for him: ... φιλία δ' οὐκ ἔστι πρὸς τὰ ἄψυχα οὐδὲ δίκαιον· ἀλλ' οὐδὲ πρὸς ἵππον ἢ βοῦν, οὐδὲ πρὸς δοῦλον ᾗ δοῦλος. οὐδὲν γὰρ κοινόν ἐστιν· ὁ γὰρ δοῦλος ἔμψυχον ὄργανον, τὸ δ' ὄργανον ἄψυχος δοῦλος (Eth. Nic., VIII, 13, p. 1161b, 1 ff.). A similar line is taken in his radical treatment of the δοῦλος problem in the second chapter of the first book of his Politics (p. 1253b, 1 ff.), where we read on p. 1254a, 13 ff.: τίς μὲν οὖν ἡ φύσις τοῦ δούλου καὶ τίς ἡ δύναμις, ἐκ τούτων δῆλον· ὁ γὰρ μὴ αὑτοῦ φύσει ἀλλ' ἄλλου. ἄνθρωπος ὤν, ὃς ἂν κτῆμα ᾖ ἄνθρωπος· κτῆμα δὲ ὄργανον πρακτικὸν καὶ χωριστικόν. From this it is obvious that δοῦλοι have no part in the πόλις or its service, [14] in which the free man finds supreme self-fulfilment. [15]

The Stoics hardly went beyond this view of δοῦλος, δουλεύειν etc., though they had a broader and even universal conception of service. The call to service is issued by Zeus himself: hence the Cynic, though he is free in relation to all, is unconditionally bound to all, and responsible for what they do or leave undone. [16] Committed thus, he is the διάκονος (Epict. Diss., III, 22, 69) and ὑπηρέτης of Zeus (Diss., III, 22, 82 and 95), [17] in exactly the same sense as that in which Plato regarded the work of Socrates as τῷ θεῷ ὑπηρεσία (Ap., 30a). It is worth noting, however, that the formula δοῦλος τοῦ θεοῦ is never used in self-description by the proponent of the Cynic diatribe. It would have been a quite intolerable phrase in its suggestion that the sage has no will or initiative of his own, with all that this implies. The possibility of individual initiative is of the very essence of the Cynic; if it is curtailed, he can no longer be what he claims to be. [18] Thus, for all the emphasis on obligation and service, the stress falls on the dignity of the Cynic's office in relation to men. Perfectly free, [19] he moves among men as the βασιλεὺς καὶ δεσπότης (Epict. Diss., III, 22, 49 etc.). [20] Indeed, he is so free that none can lead him astray in this regard (loc. cit.). He is βασιλεὺς καὶ δεσπότης, however, because he is the sage. In the eyes of Epictetus, therefore, all who do not tread this way are δοῦλοι. For only the sage is free. Those who are not

---

[10] He thus becomes the ὑπηρέτης of the πόλις. In Plato the word ὑπηρέτης is used in the narrower sense for the official servant of the state (e.g., Phaed., 116b).

[11] Ep., 8, 354e: μετρία δὲ ἡ δουλεία, ἄμετρος δὲ ἡ τοῖς ἀνθρώποις· θεὸς δὲ ἀνθρώποις σώφροσιν νόμος, ἄφροσιν δὲ ἡδονή.

[12] Cf. on this pt., Brandt, 30 f.

[13] Eth. Nic., IV, 8, p. 1124b, 31 f.: ... καὶ πρὸς ἄλλον μὴ δύνασθαι ζῆν ἀλλ' ἢ πρὸς φίλον· δουλικὸν γάρ ...

[14] Cf. also Pol., III, 9, p. 1280a, 32 ff.: ... καὶ γὰρ ἂν δούλων καὶ τῶν ἄλλων ζῴων ἦν πόλις· νῦν δ' οὐκ ἔστι διὰ τὸ μὴ μετέχειν εὐδαιμονίας μηδὲ τοῦ ζῆν κατὰ προαιρεσιν.

[15] Cf. the examples in Brandt, 28.

[16] On what follows → I, 410 f.

[17] For further material v. Brandt, 36 f.

[18] → I, 410.

[19] Cf. Schmitz, 11 ff.; K. Deissner, Das Idealbild des stoischen Weisen (1930), 4 f.

[20] The same attitude is found in Seneca (K. Deissner, Paulus und Seneca [1917], 7). Cf. also the examples in J. Kaerst, Geschichte des Hellenismus², II (1926), 111.

wise are slaves, no matter what form their bondage takes (Diss., IV, 1, 7 ff.). [21] Exactly the same outlook may be seen when Plutarch sets δειλία alongside δουλεία (Bruta Animalia Ratione Uti, 4 [II, 987d]).

Philo takes much the same view. For him every ἀστεῖος and σπουδαῖος is free, and every φαῦλος [22] is in the state of the δοῦλος. [23] He thus shares also with Stoicism the tenet that no one is originally a δοῦλος, [24] but that a man makes himself a δοῦλος, whether through κέρδος (Spec. Leg., IV, 3), ὀργή (Conf. Ling., 48), or in some other way (cf. Leg. All., III, 198). For the rest, a certain Jewish influence may be discerned in Philo's use of δοῦλος, since he does not avoid the phrase δοῦλος τοῦ θεοῦ (→ 269).

2. This review of Greek usage of the word group shows us that it has here no connexion with the religious sphere. It is only when the young religions of the Orient press westwards and win hosts of new adherents that the group acquires significance in the religious vocabulary of the Greeks. This is possible, however, only as the Greek view of God, and the resultant relationship of man to the deity, undergoes a powerful and radical change under the influence of eastern religions (→ 269).

There are only a few exceptions to this rule, and on closer inspection even these turn out to be more apparent than real. We have referred already to the phrase ἡ θεῷ δουλεία in Plato (→ 263). There remain only three passages in Euripides. [25] In Eur. Ba., 366 Tiresias maintains : τῷ Βακχίῳ γὰρ τῷ Διὸς δουλευτέον. The saying might be taken to mean that there is advanced for Dionysus a claim to divine honour and service. In the context, however, it seems rather to point to the inevitable necessity of yielding to this powerful god with his demand for obedience. After the failure of friendly advice and an appeal to reason, the phrase is designed to show how great is the danger of resisting the god. There is no question of a positive relationship in the sense of self-sacrifice ; the whole aim is to reject an incorrect attitude as foolish. [26] The second passage is found in Eur. Ion, 309. Here Ion, who remembers only that he has always belonged to the sanctuary of the Delphic oracle, can say : τοῦ θεοῦ καλοῦμαι δοῦλος εἰμί τ', ὦ γύναι. In this passage the phrase δοῦλος τοῦ θεοῦ is synon. with ἱερό-δουλος and seems to conform in every respect to the ordinary usage. Finally, in Eur. Or., 418 Orestes says : δουλεύομεν θεοῖς, ὅ τι ποτ' εἰσὶν οἱ θεοί. He here develops more generally, though also more strongly, his preceding appeal to a command of Apollo for the slaying of his mother (416). There is no thought of confessing absolute dependence on the gods in a religious sense. Nor should it be overlooked that Orestes is seeking to evade responsibility for his act and to attribute it to the god. This is why he emphasises so strongly his dependence on the gods. In this one case the δουλεύειν is adduced in self-exculpation, and it expresses the fact that man is not free in his action. It certainly does not contain any confession of the gods in the sense of a confession of essential dependence on them and full orientation to them.

Within the Gk. concept of God there is in fact no place for this word group as an expression of religious relationship and service. [27] It is a distinctive feature of the Greek attitude to the gods that gods and men may be bound by family relationships. From the

---

[21] Slave and fool are synon. terms in Diss., IV, 1; cf. also Deissner, *Idealbild*, 13.

[22] On related terms of Stoic derivation, → I, 319.

[23] Omn. Prob. Lib., 1 etc.

[24] E.g., Spec. Leg., II, 69 : ἄνθρωπος γὰρ ἐκ φύσεως δοῦλος οὐδείς.

[25] The two first are taken from Ltzm. R. on 1:1; the third I owe to H. Kleinknecht.

[26] The suggestion that the Dionysus cult is in any case alien to Greece (Ltzm. R. on 1:1) is discounted by its high estimation ; indeed, W. F. Otto has recently shown that Dionysus is a Greek god (*Dionysos*, 1933).

[27] Cf. for what follows, J. Leipoldt, *War Jesus Jude?* (1923), 41 ff.

time of Homer, who describes Zeus as the father of the gods and men, this thought runs through the whole history of Greek religion, and even in Christian and post-Christian times it emerges in the idea of the divinity of certain prominent figures such as Apollonius of Tyana, or rulers as κύριοι θεοί. [28] It is in keeping with this that unconditional majesty yields before very human characteristics in the gods of Greece. [29] It is also consistent that there is no place for kneeling, the attitude of the slave before his master, in the ceremonial of Greek religion. [30] There was kneeling only before chthonic deities, [31] and this was not in sign of humility and subjection, nor to denote dependence, but simply for the sake of greater physical proximity. [32] Even in the Mystery religions, with their concern for the deification of devotees, we can still see the influence of the Greek idea of the interrelationship of gods and men. Nor is this idea limited to the Greek world. It is also found to some degree in the religion and religions of the Indo-Germanic peoples. [33]

This is not the place for a systematic appraisal and interpretation of the idea. Its only importance for us is that it enables us to see why the word group in question cannot be used in the terminology of Greek and Hellenistic religion. In view of the interrelationship of gods and men which we find here, there would be little point in describing either service of God, or life under the eyes of God, as δουλεία, or in describing the worshipper as a δοῦλος τοῦ θεοῦ. The worshipper is not so much the δοῦλος as the → φίλος. [34] We can thus understand why the Cynic contemporaries of the apostles do not use the word δοῦλος for their relation to God, but rather describe it as πρὸς θεοὺς ὁμιλία (Epict. Diss., III, 22, 22).

B. The Word Group on Jewish Soil.

When we turn to the Gk. Bible, [35] and investigate its use of the word group, we are struck at once by the degree to which it has crowded out the various synon. (διακονέω, ὑπηρετέω, etc.). Whenever there is reference to service, it is usually expressed by a word from this group. The group is thus freed from the restriction to the service of slaves which marks its use in non-biblical Gk. The reason for this is that it is almost always used for the root עָבַד and its denominatives.

δουλεύω is always used for עבד except in Is. 56:6 (שָׁרַת), Da. 7:14, 27 Θ (פְּלַח); [36] in a few instances where there is in the original no verb for "to serve," it introduces a measure of interpretation into the context (1 Βασ. 2:24; 3 Βασ. 5:6 A). [37] The same is true of δοῦλος (for עֶבֶד with few exceptions), and δουλεία. Only δούλη usually stands

---

[28] Cf. also names like Diogenes (→ I, 410, n. 22) and Hermogenes, which express the same idea (Leipoldt, 43, n. 89).

[29] This is carried to such a point that quite early in the Greek world there could be religious caricature, which was not felt to be irreverent (for details, v. Leipoldt, 49 f.).

[30] Even so pious a man as Plutarch could associate cultic kneeling with the celebration of the Jewish Sabbath and cultic self-defilement, thus drastically expressing his aversion and contempt (Superst., 3 [II, 166a]). On the similar attitude of Diogenes, v. Diog. L., VI, 37. Cf. on this pt. Leipoldt, 44.

[31] For examples → I, 739, s.v. γόνυ, with accompanying bibl.

[32] Leipoldt, 45. Cf. 45 ff. for archaeological data.

[33] The Persians and Romans are to some degree exceptions, cultic kneeling being practised among them (Leipoldt, 46).

[34] E.g., Epict. Diss., III, 22, 95 etc. On the concept φίλος τοῦ θεοῦ in Hellenism, cf. E. Peterson, "Der Gottesfreund," ZKG, 42 (1923), 161 ff.

[35] On what follows, cf. Brandt, 40 ff.

[36] The usual text has λατρεύειν (v. 14) or ὑποτάσσεσθαι (v. 27), which is perhaps a more correct rendering than λατρεύειν.

[37] In ψ 80:6 עבר and עבד are confused by the translator.

for אָמָה or שִׁפְחָה and not for עֶבֶד (exceptions Ex.21:7; Neh. 5:5 B), and this is simply because ancient Heb. did not have any word for a female slave from the main root.

1. From the connexion with עבד it may be seen that in the LXX and Greek Judaism generally the word is used for a slave and his status and situation. It is used quite definitely and emphatically in this way, as shown by its specific use in cases where serving as a slave is not felt to be normal.

In the LXX עֶבֶד is commonly rendered παῖς rather than δοῦλος when the reference is to slaves in the sense of those who from the very first stand at the disposal of another. This is always true in the Pentateuchal legislation concerning slaves. One may thus say that when παῖς is used for עֶבֶד in the sense of slave it denotes a natural relationship which cannot be materially contested, whereas when δοῦλος is used the primary thought is that of the illegality and essential unreason of the service rendered. [38] Thus the word group is used in the LXX for the bondage of the Israelites in Egypt (Ex. 14:5 etc.). Egypt remains always for the Jews the οἶκος δουλείας (Ex. 13:3, 14; 20:2; Lv. 26:45 etc.). When one people falls subject to another, δουλεύειν is the word used to describe the situation, no matter whether the reference is to Israel (Ju. 3:8, 14 etc.; cf. also Jos. Bell., 7, 323 f.) or to another people like the Philistines (1 Βασ. 17:9) or the Egyptians ('Ησ. 19:23). Jacob accepts the state of a δοῦλος when he begins to serve seven years περὶ τῆς 'Ραχήλ (Gn. 29:18), not although, but just because, he is a free man. The whole paradox of the relationship brought about between Jacob and Esau through the deception of the former is brought out when Isaac blesses Esau with the words : τῷ ἀδελφῷ σου δουλεύσεις. [39] The usage is here quite unambiguous.

In view of these findings this is perhaps the place to say a word on the question of the עֶבֶד יְהוָה in Is. 53. It does not really belong to this context, since, in distinction from other עַבְדֵי יְהוָה like Moses, Joshua etc., the LXX does not speak of the δοῦλος but of the → παῖς of God — a usage followed by the NT (Ac. 3:13, 26 etc.). The basis of this rendering is the recognition by the translator of the fact that the עֶבֶד יְהוָה does not render his service within the framework of a relationship to his master which is established for the purpose, but on the basis of an essential position in his οἶκος. It is simply a logical development of the decision taken by the translator of Is. 53 that in 4 Esr. 7:28 f.; 13:32 the ὁ παῖς μου of the LXX has become a filius meus. Yet this is a line of development which leads away from our present word group and which makes it unnecessary to pursue further the question of the עֶבֶד יְהוָה in this context. This is confirmed rather than altered by the fact that in Is. 53:11 his service is described in terms of δουλεύειν.

2. Since the word group is used to denote a relation of dependence or service which may be forced, or sometimes voluntary, but which is always felt to be restrictive, it is the usual linguistic form for the relation of the subject to the king in the despotic monarchies of the ancient Orient.

In this respect the usage of the OT and the LXX simply follows the relations common throughout the ancient East. The king is always the absolute ruler of his subjects, and they are under him like slaves at the whim of their masters. The word group is well adapted to denote this because it always stands in opposition to the thought of freedom. It thus expresses with singular force both the extreme of power demanded and exercised

---

[38] The usage may be defined much more sharply than in Brandt, 41: "The word is used for all possible kinds of service. In the OT, too, it suggests menial service."

[39] In this context it is not necessary to trace the historical meaning of the original. Cf. the comm. ad loc.

on the one side and the extreme of objective subjection and subjective bondage present and experienced on the other.

A few examples will suffice. The courtiers of Saul both call themselves and are called his עֲבָדִים/δοῦλοι like those of any oriental court[40] (1 Βασ. 18:5, 30 A). Among them is David himself (1 Βασ. 19:4 etc.), until he becomes king, and then his captain Joab becomes his δοῦλος (cf. 2 Βασ. 14:19 f.). It is said of the whole people that it δουλεύει the king (3 Βασ. 12:7). There is a fine play on words in 3 Βασ. 12:7 when the πρεσβύτεροι advise the young king Rehoboam to be δοῦλος to the oppressed people, i.e., to relax his claims and to improve its social position, in order the more surely to win its willing and accepted δουλεία. We also get a glimpse of court ceremonial when Abigail, on the visit of David's παῖδες to woo her in his stead (→ I, 416), receives them as David's δούλη and performs the menial task of washing their feet, which she would owe to David as his wife (1 Βασ. 25:40 f.). Again, when Ahaz in 4 Βασ. 16:7 sends a message to the king of Assyria in which he says of himself δοῦλός σου καὶ υἱός σου ἐγώ,[41] he is acknowledging the suzerainty of the Assyrians, exchanging his autonomy for the position of a vassal prince, with all that this entails (cf. 4 Βασ. 24:1 ff.).

An essential point which should not be overlooked in this whole usage is that it is employed only by the subjects or subordinates of a ruler either in description of themselves or in recognition of the similar position of others (e.g., 2 Βασ. 14:19 f.),[42] but that is never used by rulers themselves to describe the relationship of a subject. There is here expressed the fact that in the figurative sense the group always presupposes voluntary or compulsory decision in favour of the powerful claim of another, the degree of power available for the enforcement of the claim obviously being of critical significance.

3. This ceremonial usage of the group is of epoch-making importance because it provides the assumptions on which the words can be adopted into the language of worship. The climax of the historical development is reached when the group comes to describe the relationship of dependence and service in which man stands to God. This also brings us to the point where the Jewish and oriental usage enters into the sharpest possible antithesis to that of the Greek and Hellenistic world.

In the LXX δουλεύειν is the most common term for the service of God, not in the sense of an isolated act,[43] but in that of total commitment to the Godhead. In this light we can understand why the word cannot be used without specifying to whom the service is rendered. The religious terminology of Israel is in many periods affected by the fact that the people offers its δουλεύειν τοῖς Βααλίμ (Ju. 10:6, 10 etc.) or θεοῖς ἑτέροις (Ju. 10:13 etc.),[44] but then again τῷ κυρίῳ. Either is possible, though obviously the only suitable thing for the elect people of the one God is δουλεύειν τῷ

---

[40] For an earlier example, cf. the way in which the royal officials in the Amarna letters always speak of themselves in relation to their lord the king as *ardu* (servants, slaves), J. A. Knudtzon, *Die El-Amarna-Tafeln* (1915), *passim*.

[41] The Semitic original of the expression is very old; cf. the letter of Aziri to Dûdu (Knudtzon, 643 [No. 158, 1 f.]): To Dûdu, my lord, my father, Aziri, thy son, thy servant (ardu-ka), spake as follows ...

[42] Cf. also in the letter of Rib-Addi to the king (Knudtzon, 419 [88, 9 ff.]): Furthermore, what is he, Abdi-asrati, the servant (*ardu*), the dog, that he does as he pleases in the territories of my lord? For further examples, *ibid.,* 1131.

[43] For this → λατρεύειν and → λειτουργεῖν are used.

[44] This is the basis of the Rabb. formula עֲבוֹדָה זָרָה for service rendered to other gods than the God of Israel.

κυρίῳ μόνῳ (Ju. 10:16 etc.). The term always implies the exclusive nature of the relationship, whether we think of the Heb. equivalent עֶבֶד or of the Gk. δοῦλος. This is why the righteous in Israel, e.g., in the Psalms, can use the expression δουλεύειν τῷ κυρίῳ (ψ 2:11; 99:2; 101:22) to express their religious awareness in conscious distinction from the ungodly (→ ἁμαρτωλός, I, 320). [45] It is also the reason why those men in the history of Israel who have satisfied the divine claim on them in an outstanding and exemplary manner are given the honorary title of δοῦλοι e.g., Moses (Jos. 14:7 A; Jos. Ant., 5, 39); [46] Joshua (Jos. 24:29; Ju. 2:8); Abraham (ψ 104:42); [47] David (ψ 88:3 etc.); Isaac (Δα. 3:35); the prophets (4 Βασ. 17:23 etc.); and finally Jacob = Israel as the people of God (Is. 48:20 etc.). [48] This shows us that any other attitude towards God than that of δουλεύειν implies disobedience and betrayal of His cause.

4. The attitude of divine service expressed in the term is shared by the Jewish world with other Semitic peoples and tribes [49] and also with the Egyptians. [50] In every case the conception of God bears the stamp of unconditional majesty and absolute superiority to man. This may be seen from the names of the Semitic deities (Baal, Adon, Adonai/κύριος etc.), which all represent the deity as Lord.

The derivation of this view is irrelevant in the present context. [51] At a later period the conception of God was strongly influenced by ideas bound up with kingship, and the ceremonial of worship with that of the court. [52] The custom of cultic kneeling may be mentioned in the latter connexion. In Jer. 13:10 (θεῷ) δουλεύειν and προσκυνεῖν are used as synon. in poetic parallelism. [53] There is προσκύνησις before God as before the king. This plainly expresses man's complete dependence on God. Again, the sense of commitment to God is reflected in the great number of names which combine the root עבד with a divine name. [54] There is here, whether in Israel or elsewhere, a firm acknowledgment of the claim of the deity to the man concerned. The situation of Israel is unique only to the degree that its whole history is one long revelation of the divine claim both on the people as a whole and on all its individual members. This history, and, of course, the presence within it of the Law as the revelation of the divine will, contain on the one side the constant demand for θεῷ δουλεύειν and on the other the assurance of a singular status in the relationship of service (cf. Jos. Bell., 7, 233 and 418 f.; → 46).

It is at this point that the Jewish world parts company with the oriental mystery religions and also to some extent with Philo so far as concerns the present complex of ideas.

---

[45] Cf. the way in which the righteous man describes himself in the Psalter as δοῦλος θεοῦ (ψ 18:12, 14; 26:9; 30:17 etc.). This should be mentioned here rather than in connexion with the material use discussed under 4.

[46] For further examples, cf. Ltzm. R. on 1:1.

[47] This is the only instance, since Abraham is usually called the → φίλος of God. In Δα. 3:35 Abraham is described as ἠγαπημένος, Isaac as δοῦλος and Jacob as ἅγιος of God.

[48] In Joseph., too, the Jews are sometimes called the δοῦλοι τοῦ θεοῦ (Ant., 11, 90 and 101), though there is here no developed usage (A. Schlatter, Wie sprach Josephus von Gott?, 12). Indeed, Joseph. seems to have serious reservations in regard to the religious use of the term. These are understandable when we remember for whom he was writing.

[49] Cf. on this pt. W. W. Graf Baudissin, Kyrios als Gottesname im Judentum und seine Stelle in der Religionsgeschichte, III (1929), 524 ff.: "Der Verehrer des Gottes als dessen Knecht."

[50] For more details cf. Leipoldt, 36 ff.

[51] Cf. Baudissin, 610 ff.

[52] Cf. Leipoldt, 28 ff.

[53] Brandt, 43.

[54] Cf. the collection of such names in Baudissin, 527 ff.

The mystery religions, too, recognise that man is a slave owned by God and at His bidding, and that he has a special relation to Him as such. But they have no history or universal claim to service such as we find amongst the Jews. Hence one can only enter into service by the way of ritual. One must become a member of the community of Cybele, and therefore her slave, by an act which involves bloody mutilation. [55] In other cases there is religious tattooing corresponding to the branding of slaves, as in the Attis mysteries [56] and also the Dionysus mysteries, where it is done by the burning of an ivy leaf. [57] This rite is in no sense comparable with the Jewish rite of circumcision, which can in certain circumstances be omitted wthout affecting in any way membership of God and His people, [58] whereas omission of the rite of initiation is quite impossible in the Mysteries.

The distinction from Philo in the use of δουλεύειν for divine service is in respect of the way in which he speaks of it. He is at one with the LXX is using the term in this sense, and also in the underlying conception of God as the κύριος. But for him the usage remains essentially figurative. This appears most clearly in his definition of εὐσέβεια: ὥστε ὅταν τὴν εὐσέβειαν λέγωμεν εἶναι θεοῦ θεραπείαν ὑπηρεσίαν τινὰ τοιαύτην φαμέν, ὁποῖον δοῦλοι δεσπόταις τὸ κελευόμενον ἀόκνως ποιεῖν ἐγνωκότες ὑπηρετοῦσι. διοίσει δὲ πάλιν, ὅτι οἱ μὲν δεσπόται ὑπηρεσίας ἐνδεεῖς, ὁ δὲ θεὸς οὐ χρεῖος· ὥστε ἐκείνοις μὲν τὰ ὠφελήσοντα αὐτοὺς ὑπηρετοῦσι, τῷ δ' οὐδὲν ἔξω φιλοδεσπότου γνώμης παρέξουσι· βελτιῶσαι μὲν γὰρ οὐδὲν εὑρήσουσι, τῶν δεσποτικῶν πάντων ἐξ ἀρχῆς ὄντων ἀρίστων, μεγάλα δ' αὐτοὺς ὀνήσουσι γνωρισθῆναι θεῷ προμηθούμενοι (Det. Pot. Ins., 56). In addition to the fact that the idea of the self-sufficiency of God is a typically Greek notion [59] which is alien to the Jewish world, this discussion of Philo is really based on the concept of the φίλος, even though the term δοῦλος is brought in for the sake of clarification. Man is himself exalted in the service of God. The thought of an absolute magnifying and acknowledgment of God retreats into the background. This is very noticeable where Philo uses δουλεύειν positively as a term for divine service. The use is determined by the antithesis. The man who contracts out of the service of God, who is merciful, necessarily become the δοῦλος γενέσεως … τῆς ἀνηλεοῦς. [60] He thus becomes dependent on creation rather than the Creator. He becomes dependent on a creation with which there can be no spiritual relationship. There is thus no possibility or even hope of an ἐλεύθερον εἶναι. [61] For this reason Philo both can and must call θεῷ δουλεύειν οὐκ ἐλευθερίας μόνον ἀλλὰ καὶ βασιλείας ἄμεινον. [62] For the same reason the phrase δοῦλος θεοῦ has for him no significance beyond that of the alternative already mentioned. It is for him a dubious term which does not really describe the relationship of the righteous to God as it is in practice. Thus, although he stands in linguistic affinity with Judaism, so far as concerns the use of this word group he is materially outside it, belonging rather to the Cynic tradition.

---

[55] Catull., 63; Liv., 37, 9, 9; Cic. De Legibus, II, 9, 22 (cf. F. Cumont, *Die orientalischen Religionen im römischen Heidentum*³ [1931], 24 ff.). Possibly something similar is meant when on an inscr. found in Kefr-Hauar (BCH, 21 [1897], 60) a slave (δοῦλος) of the Syrian goddess tells of his successes on begging tours on behalf of his κυρία. It can hardly be supposed than the usual hierodule would be responsible for this kind of inscr.

[56] Prud., 10, 1076 ff.; cf. on this pt. F. J. Dölger, *Antike und Christentum*, 1 (1929), 60 ff.

[57] Dölger, *op. cit.*, 2 (1930), 102 ff.

[58] Str.-B., IV, 26.

[59] Cf. the collection of passages in E. Norden, *Agnostos Theos* (1913), 13 f.

[60] Det. Pot. Ins., 146.

[61] Cf. Leg. All., III, 194 ff.

[62] Spec. Leg., I, 57.

C. The Word Group in the NT.

1. Secular Usage.

a. It is only with some reservation that one can speak of a secular usage of the word group in the NT. In most cases, if one excludes the passages in which it occurs in religious connexions, it is used improperly, i.e., in figures of speech and comparisons, especially in the parables of Jesus. A strict usage is for the most part found only in the epistles, e.g., where there is reference to the attitude of Christian slaves to Christian or non-Christian masters (Col. 3:22 ff. etc.), or the attitude of Christian masters to their slaves (Col. 4:1; Eph. 6:8 f.), or the position of slaves in the community.

These few passages are enough, however, to show that the usage of the NT lies wholly within the framework of that of the time, and cannot be isolated from it. Here again the word group serves to describe a relation of absolute dependence in which the total commitment of the δοῦλος on the one side corresponds to the total claim of the κύριος on the other, being adequately grounded in the mere existence of the κύριος and not needing any particular religious or moral justification beyond this legal basis. [63] The parables of Jesus are extremely restrained as concerns this whole complex of master and slave. He speaks of δοῦλοι when He wishes to emphasise the unconditional nature of human responsibility to God, [64] and also when He wants to make it clear that God in His relationship to man is not constrained by any presuppositions which He must satisfy. [65] The term and concept thus describe a state of affairs which one cannot escape and the consequences of which one must accept if one is not to incur punishment. Alongside the will and commission of the κύριος there is no place for one's own will or initiative. The exclusiveness of the relationship to the κύριος is also affirmed: οὐδεὶς δύναται δυσὶ κυρίοις δουλεύειν ... (Mt. 6:24; Lk. 16:13).

Mt. 6:24 and Lk. 16:13 presuppose the possibility of a slave having two owners with equal shares to him and therefore with equal claims to his services. This is a situation which might and did exist. [66] Indeed, there were slaves who were freed by one master but not the other, so that they were half free and half slave. [67] In such a relationship it was, of course, virtually impossible for a slave to display the same devotion to both, especially as their wishes and interests might vary very widely. Jesus expresses this in the language of His contemporaries and His people by saying that the slave would ἀγαπᾶν the one master and μισεῖν the other, i.e., be less attached to him (→ μισέω). [68] This implies, however, the overthrow of δουλεύειν in the sense of exclusive commitment to one master or the other. What Jesus says about the impossibility of man's attempt to be the δοῦλος of God without severing the connexion with mammon (→ μαμωνᾶς) is simply the logical consequence of a more general factor in man's relationship to God in terms of δουλεύειν. Jesus is not attacking the actual position of a δοῦλος under two masters. [69] He is attacking the man who suffers from the illusion

---

[63] Cf. expressions like ὁ δοῦλος τοῦ ἀρχιερέως, which are in keeping with accepted usage, and esp. Mt. 8:9 and Lk. 7:2 ff.

[64] Cf. Mt. 24:45 ff.; Lk. 12:37 ff.

[65] Cf. Mt. 18:23 ff.; 25:14 ff. and par.; Lk. 17:7 ff.

[66] Cf. Pes., 8, 1: A slave of two masters shall not (on the evening of the Passover) eat of the paschal lamb of both. T. Jeb., 9, 2 mentions the possibility of a slave belonging 99% to a priest and 1% to an ordinary Israelite.

[67] Cf. the examples in Str.-B., I, 433 f.

[68] On the usage cf. Kittel Probleme, 54 f.

[69] So Kl. Mt., ad loc.: Such a relationship ... is impossible.

that he can do what is implied by δουλεύειν without concentrating all his powers on rendering δουλεία in the sense of an exclusive commitment and obligation.

b. It thus follows that in the NT the δοῦλος is the classical picture of bondage and limitation. [70] This being so, it is the more remarkable that he is never spoken of in the disparaging and contemptuous fashion common in the Greek and Hellenistic world. In this respect there is a clear distinction even between the NT and current Judaism. The judgment on the slave is always material, and it remains so even when it is severe. [71] The δοῦλος is never despised or rejected simply because he is a slave.

For Judaism in the time of Jesus, as for the Greek world, the slave was on a lower level of humanity. By law the (Canaanite) [72] slave was classed with immobile goods, [73] had no rights at law and could not own property. [74] Even his family did not belong to him; it was the property of his master, who might give him a favourite slave in marriage. [75] In the cultic sphere this meant that the slave was subject to cultic obligations only to a limited extent. [76] At this point the slave was like a wife, [77] his cultic subordination being thus strongly emphasised (→ I, 787). Above all, however, slaves were ethically inferior, [78] being subject to the law only to a limited degree. [79] They naturally had no genealogies, and therefore there was no possibility of controlling their origin.

Treatment of slaves corresponded to this estimation. Since a slave was a chattel, his master could do with him as he desired; there was none to hinder him. Even mutilation by a master could be followed by the manumission demanded by the Law (Ex. 21:26 f.) only if there were witnesses prepared to give testimony. [80] There must have been a fair number of mutilated slaves to judge from the amount of discussion devoted to them. [81] It is not without significance that even in Rabbinic parables this attitude to slaves finds clear expression. Thus we sometimes read of an angry master throwing a full cup at a slave waiting on him at table, [82] or of a slave having his ears boxed because even with the best intentions he did not fulfil a command in the precise sense intended by his master. [83] In the Rabbis, therefore, the word "slave" constitutes one of the worst insults one man can hurl at another; [84] it was not for nothing than a man might be

---

[70] There is a good example in Gl. 4:1 f.: ἐφ' ὅσον χρόνον ὁ κληρονόμος νήπιός ἐστιν, οὐδὲν διαφέρει δούλου κύριος πάντων ὤν ... ἄχρι τῆς προθεσμίας τοῦ πατρός.

[71] Cf. Mt. 18:32 : δοῦλε πονηρέ; also Mt. 25:26, 30; Lk. 19:22.

[72] I.e., slaves of non-Jewish birth, as distinct from Jewish ("Hebrew") slaves (cf. on this distinction Str.-B., IV, 698). The spontaneous attitude of later Judaism to slaves is expressed only in terms of the former category; that is why we confine our discussion to them.

[73] Str.-B., IV, 719. Cf. on this pt. and on what follows S. Krauss, *Talmudische Archäologie*, II (1911), 91 ff.

[74] Str.-B., IV, 720 f., 722.

[75] Str.-B., I, 803; IV, 721.

[76] Str.-B., IV, 727.

[77] *Loc. cit.*

[78] Cf. Krauss, 92 ff.

[79] In this they resemble the Gentiles (→ I, 324).

[80] Str.-B., IV, 730 f., 736 f.

[81] Cf. Str.-B., IV, 735 ff.; Krauss, I, 247 f.

[82] Sukka, 2, 9; bSukka, 29a.

[83] Str.-B., IV, 734.

[84] Cf. also the proverb : A dog is more honourable (i.e., of greater worth before God) than a slave (M. Ex. on 22:30 [p. 321, 13 Horovitz-Rabin]). On the estimation of dogs as the very lowest of creatures, cf. my comm. on T. Jeb., 3, 4 (*Rabbinische Texte*, 1st Series, Vol. 3 [1933 ff.] 33 f.).

excommunicated for calling his neighbour a slave. [85] If there are several references to particularly good relationships between a master and a slave (Ber., 2, 7), these simply confirm the dark picture presented by the reality at law.

c. The way in which slaves were integrated into the Christian community accords with the manner in which Jesus, and indeed the NT as a whole, thought and spoke of them. If slavery was not rejected from the Christian standpoint, every effort was made to bring it to an end. When a slave had the chance of freedom, he was to seize it joyfully, [86] though recognising that in the last analysis it made no difference whether he was bond or free (1 C. 7:21). More important, indeed, the only important factor, is the active and passive subordination of slaves also to the rule which fashions the life of the community. This is the rule of love, [87] which is rooted in the fact that all members of the community stand in the same relationship to Christ and are thus united on the same level in Him. It is obvious that this must finally lead to the abolition of slavery amongst Christians. [88] Later developments necessarily took this direction, especially when Christian ideas began to acquire normative significance for civilisation generally. [89]

It cannot be emphasised too strongly that the comparative lack of interest shown by the NT [90] in the social fact of slavery is not based on "the remoteness of faith from this world, and the inflexibility of the external orders." [91] In other words, it is not due primarily to the eschatological tension of early Christian life. It is based rather on the redeeming act of Jesus which applies to all men irrespective of their status and origin, because all have equal need of it. The act of Jesus, however, acquires significance for the individual only within the concrete relationships in which he stands and lives, because it is only within these that he commits what the NT calls → ἁμαρτία. In the NT sin always takes the form of concrete disobedience to God, as one may see from the so-called house tables. Hence the goal of NT proclamation is the control of the situation of the individual by the act of Jesus, so that there is produced an attitude and action which in their own time and place are conformable to this act. Hence the primary goal of the slave won for Christ is not the attainment of freedom ; it is that as a slave he should live unto the Lord like all those for whom He died (2 C. 5:15; R. 14:7 ff. etc.).

If, however, the relationships in which Christians live in their very different social classes are subordinated to the gift and task imposed on each individual Christian with his relationship to Christ, the distinction between κύριος and δοῦλος can have only relative significance compared with the fellowship in which both are set by their common participation in Christ. We can thus understand why on the one side Paul is led by his preaching to order the master/slave relationship in terms of a concept taken from

---

[85] Str.-B., IV, 310.

[86] The old question whether Paul is here recommending that the δοῦλος should remain such even if he had the chance to become free (so Ign. Pol., 4, 3, and more recently Joh. W. 1 K., 187 f., ad loc.; H. D. Wendland, Das Neue Testament Deutsch, II [1933], 322 f., ad loc., the contrary view being taken esp. by Lightfoot, 322 f., n. 2; J. C. K. v. Hofmann, Die Heilige Schrift neuen Testaments, II, 2 [1864], 155 ff.; also Schlatter, Erläuterungen zum NT, ad loc. etc.) cannot be pursued in this context. The present reference must suffice.

[87] So also Lohmeyer, 106.

[88] Cf. H. Jacoby, Neutestamentliche Ethik (1899), 362.

[89] Cf. the brief sketch in Zn., 33 ff. It is not unimportant that Origen can see in the δοῦλος of 1 C. 7:21, not a literal δοῦλος, but a figurative description of the γεγαμηκώς (J. A. Cramer, Catenae Graecorum Patrum, V [1844], 140).

[90] One may thus speak in general terms because, in addition to Pl. (incl. the Past.), 1 Pt. presupposes slavery, and orders the master/slave relationship without pressing for a change of status (though the term used in 2:18 is → οἰκέτης).

[91] As against Lohmeyer, 106.

family life (ἀδελφός, Phlm. 16) and why on the other the attitude to God is given precedence over that of the master to the slave or the slave to the master, so that the latter can be seen as representing part of the obligatory relationship of the Christian to God (Eph. 6:5 ff.; Col. 3:22 ff.; 4:1; 1 Tm. 6:1; Tt. 2:9; 1 Pt. 2:18 ff.). We can also see why the NT applies the same rule even when one of the parties concerned is not a Christian, for the obligation to God applies irrespective of human commitments, taking up all such commitments into itself and fashioning them theonomously. Again, we can understand why freedom is never demanded but is to be gratefully received whenever possible. External freedom is valuable. Its value is only relative, however, compared with what communion with Christ brings, compared with freedom from self and all the conditions which spoil life, compared with freedom for God and His will, which is the gift of Christ (cf. 1 C. 7:22). [92]

It should be apparent at once that along these lines the isolation of the δοῦλος as δοῦλος is overcome in a way which differs radically from that of the Cynic diatribe. In the latter, too, the slave can be described as ἐλεύθερος, and as such ranged directly alongside his κύριος. [93] Yet this does not rest on an act which frees the δοῦλος and makes him in all things the ἀδελφός of his master. It rests on perception which makes him inwardly independent of his external situation and either equal or even superior to his master as a man. This final possibility of superiority, which is never even considered in the NT, shows how great is the difference between the NT and Stoicism for all the similarity of terminology. [94] The reason for this is that between them there stands no more and no less than the crucified and risen Christ. [95]

2. Christians as δοῦλοι of God and Christ.

a. The formula δοῦλος θεοῦ is very little used of Christians in the NT, and the same is true of the phrase τῷ θεῷ δουλεύειν. Most references to the δου-λεύειν of Christians speak of it in relation to Christ, on the solid basis of NT Christology. Where we have δοῦλος θεοῦ, it is almost always in connexion with the usage of the righteous of the OT in relation to God, or in quotations. This is always true of δούλη (Lk. 1:38, 48; Ac. 2:18 [quotation]), and cf. esp. Rev. (1:1; 2:20; 7:3; 10:7; 19:2, 5; 22:3, 6), where Moses is given the title of δοῦλος τοῦ θεοῦ in 15:3 (→ 268) and the prophets are called δοῦλοι τοῦ θεοῦ in 10:7 (cf. 19:2), and cf. also Acts (4:29). We have basically the same usage in Ac. 16:17, where the παιδίσκη ἔχουσα πνεῦμα πύθωνα in Philippi describes Paul and his companions as δοῦλοι τοῦ θεοῦ τοῦ ὑψίστου. In 1 Pt. 2:16 it is probably along the same OT lines that the members of Israel are called δοῦλοι of God, this being the more likely in view of the constitutive significance of the thought of the new Israel in this epistle (cf. 1:1 f.; 2:1 ff. etc.).

Particular note should be taken of Jm. 1:1 and Tt. 1:1, where the respective authors describe themselves as θεοῦ ... δοῦλος or δοῦλος θεοῦ. Tt. 1:1 is an exception to the usual Pauline formula (δοῦλος Ἰησοῦ Χριστοῦ), and in any case both go rather beyond the normal Jewish usage, which reserved the phrase either for a few outstanding men or for the whole people. [96] It is difficult to decide whether there is here a conscious adoption of the designation of the prophets as

---

[92] For further details → ἐλευθερία.
[93] Cf. Sen. Ben., III, 22, also the instances from Epictet. in Joh. W. 1 K., 189.
[94] Cf. esp. Joh. W. 1 K., 189 f.
[95] Schmitz, 67 ff., reaches the same result, though he formulates it differently.
[96] Cf. on this pt. Schl. Jk., 87 f.

δοῦλοι τοῦ θεοῦ, and therefore the appropriation of an official or honorary title, or a personal confession of absolute commitment to God. [97]

In the early Church the formula took on a new lease of life, being used increasingly by Christians in self-designation (cf. 2 Cl., 20, 1; Herm. m., 5, 2, 1; 6, 2, 4; 8, 10 etc.). [98] Two considerations accelerated the process. The first was the general acceptance of the idea that Christianity is the true Israel. The second was the conception of Jesus Himself as the Son of God rather than the δοῦλος of God, [99] which prevented any possible rivalry with Him. It lay in the very nature of the case, however, that with this whole development the idea of merit should also come to the fore again in connexion with the formula δοῦλος θεοῦ, [100] the more so as it could be claimed by, or applied to, only those who made a serious attempt to be Christians. For when it is taken seriously this formula presupposes a self-dedication which not all Christians are either prepared or able to accept. [101]

b. Prominent in the theological use of the word group in the NT is the idea that Christians belong to Jesus as His δοῦλοι, and that their lives are thus offered to Him as the risen and exalted Lord. This notion is more comprehensive and far-reaching than the word group itself and thus appropriates many other words and word groups (→ ἐξαγοράζω, I, 126). In the present context, therefore, we can only sketch the main characteristics of this theological usage. The true representative of this whole circle of ideas is Paul.

It is everywhere assumed that men were δοῦλοι before they became believers. This assumption is based on the insight that δουλεία implies obedience to the will of another. In this case, whether voluntarily or compulsorily, ἐλευθερία [102] is lost and the state of dependence reached which constitutes the situation of the δοῦλος: οὐκ οἴδατε ὅτι ᾧ παριστάνετε ἑαυτοὺς δούλους εἰς ὑπακοήν, δοῦλοί ἐστε ᾧ ὑπακούετε; (R. 6:16). The δουλεία in which Paul sees men apart from Christ is to → ἁμαρτία (R. 6:6 ff.), to → ἀκαθαρσία and → ἀνομία (R. 6:19), to → ἐπιθυμία (Tt. 3:3), to the φύσει μὴ ὄντες θεοί (Gl. 4:8), to the στοιχεῖα τοῦ κόσμου (Gl. 4:3, 9) etc., and even to the Jewish → νόμος (R. 7:1 ff. etc.). As Paul sees it, non-Christians are so controlled by these forces that they cannot do anything outside their sphere of influence. That the ὑπακοή has become complete δουλεία is shown by the fact that the life of man in this situation results in καρποφορῆσαι τῷ θανάτῳ (R. 7:5); man himself can no longer determine the results of his life. Basically, this is simply a development of the saying of Jesus in John's Gospel: πᾶς ὁ ποιῶν τὴν ἁμαρτίαν δοῦλός ἐστιν τῆς ἁμαρτίας (Jn. 8:34): he who assents to ἁμαρτία surrenders to it (→ also I, 306).

---

[97] Wnd. Jk., ad loc. thinks that the use of the phrase in Jm. 1:1 is based on its application to the patriarch Jacob in the LXX. On the other hand, the LXX references are always to the people Israel (→ 268).

[98] It thus passed into the liturgical terminology of the Church.

[99] Cf. Schl., Theol. d. Jdt., 50.

[100] I owe this suggestion to K. Holl, Gesammelte Aufsätze zur Kirchengeschichte, II: Der Osten (1928), 107 f.

[101] There is here a decisive break with Jewish usage. The Rabbis and Pharisees did not think of themselves as the slaves of God, nor did they think that on the basis of a special עֲבוֹדָה they would have a place alongside or above others; the עֲבוֹדָה of God is a matter for the whole people and not for individuals (→ 267). The same is true of Josephus, who does not describe the righteous as δοῦλοι θεοῦ. Cf. Schl., Theol. d. Jdt., 49.

[102] We need not take up here the question whether Paul has a concept of free will or not, since it does not affect the present issue.

The status of the Christian, on the other hand, is characterised by the fact that by the death of Jesus he is rescued from the δουλεία of powers which aimed to subjugate him and to separate him from God. Paul describes this liberation in terms of redemption, [103] which in the particular context in which the image is used acquires the character of redemption from the slavery of the νόμος (Gl. 3:13: Χριστὸς ἡμᾶς ἐξηγόρασεν ἐκ τῆς κατάρας τοῦ νόμου; Gl. 4:4 f.: ἐξαπέστειλεν ὁ θεὸς τὸν υἱὸν αὐτοῦ ... ἵνα τοὺς ὑπὸ νόμον ἐξαγοράσῃ). In distinction from their previous δουλεία, the new status in which Christians are set is that of υἱοθεσία (Gl. 4:5 ff.; R. 8:15, 23). This includes the thought of → ἐλευθερία, but only to the degree that this is demanded by contrast with the prior δουλεία. Paul never uses the term to describe the essential nature of the new state. The freedom granted by Christ has the negative import of making him independent of any human authority [104] and of giving him the option of remaining in the old δουλεία or subjecting himself to it again, [105] whereas previously he could not decide against the δουλεία in which he was held (→ δουλόω). Beyond this demarcation from everything connected with his past or a similar future δουλεία, however, the thought of freedom is for Paul of no constitutive significance for the new status of the Christian. The attainment of υἱοθεσία does not mean the attainment of autonomy in every sphere of life, in relation to God as well as to sin. It means establishment in an organic relationship to God through His own intervention, which brings to an end the previous relationship of tension and separation. This relationship finds expression in the demonstration of ὑπακοή towards God by those who are liberated through Christ (→ I, 224). Thus the new state of the Christian comes under the thought of service, though in a very different sense from the earlier usage.

The connexion of those liberated from the δουλεία of the world, sin and death to the One who has liberated them links up with the occasional use of the term for commitment to God. This naturally results from the goal of the redemption, which is obedience rather than autonomy. When Christ undertakes the work of redemption, He makes the redeemed His own possession, giving them directions and goals by which to shape their lives. [106] This commitment is expressed linguistically by calling those who are thus obligated to Christ His δοῦλοι (1 C. 7:22; Eph. 6:6; cf. R. 14:18; 16:18; Col. 3:25). The term shows us that the new state of Christians is fulfilled in → δικαιοσύνη (R. 6:19), in → ἁγιωσύνη (1 Th. 3:13), ἐν καινότητι ζωῆς (R. 6:4), in love and in self-sacrifice — all these things being implied in fellowship with Christ. Especially it makes it clear that there is no path to an orderly relationship with God, or to service which is pleasing to Him, apart from that of unconditional commitment to Him, so that by His work and Word He exercises sovereign rule over the relationship of man to God and

---

103 → I, 124.

104 Cf. simply the one saying in 1 C. 7:23: τιμῆς ἠγοράσθητε· μὴ γίνεσθε δοῦλοι ἀνθρώπων; also Gl. 5:1.

105 Gl. 4:9: ... οἷς πάλιν ἄνωθεν δουλεῦσαι θέλετε.

106 This is the point where the custom of sacral redemption of slaves in antiquity (cf. esp. Deissmann LO, 271 ff.) no longer suffices to explain the NT formula, since it can throw light on manumission through the intervention of Christ, but not on the new commitment of the manumitted to Him. In any case, in sacral redemption it is really the slave who finally purchases his own redemption. Hence we are perhaps better advised to find the basis of Paul's thinking in the ordinary redemption and purchase of slaves (→ I, 125).

God to man, and therefore over man's whole conduct within the ordinary nexus of life.

One point is to be noted. When the NT uses δουλεύειν etc. for the relationship of Christians to Christ, this usage always implies both confession of what has taken place and a readiness to accept at the most personal level the consequences of the given facts. Thus δουλεύειν on man's side corresponds to (ἐξ)αγοράζειν on the side of Christ as a description of the attitude which results from acceptance of His act. What He brings is the freedom which man can know as such only if he binds himself to Him.

Once we grasp this point, we can understand certain statements in John's Gospel, and we see that they are parallel to the sayings of Paul with which they seem at a first glance to be in some contradiction. We think, for example, of Jn. 8:35 f., where Jesus, as the One who brings freedom from sin and therefore a permanent place in the οἰκία of God, [107] is called the Son in order to show how great and secure is that which is granted. But especially we think of Jn. 15:15, in which it must be recalled that Jesus is speaking with reference to His death: οὐκέτι λέγω ὑμᾶς δούλους ..., ὑμᾶς δὲ εἴρηκα φίλους. In this saying, Jesus makes it crystal clear that He is not bringing His own to a state of δουλεία, but to perfect fellowship with Himself. He also makes it clear, however, that fellowship with Him implies that His own should do what He commands them (15:14), and that it is broken if obedience is withheld. But this is the insight of Paul. He and John are firmly agreed in their basic assessment of what is made of disciples by the act of Jesus.

c. The phrase δοῦλος Ἰησοῦ Χριστοῦ occupies a special position when used in self-description, as often in Paul, but also in the salutations of Jm., Jd. and 2 Pt. We might also add Col. 4:12, where Paul describes his fellow-worker Epaphras as a δοῦλος Χριστοῦ.

Even as a self-designation the phrase δοῦλος Ἰησοῦ Χριστοῦ cannot be separated from the understanding of the relationship of Christians to Christ in terms of an interpretation of the work of Christ as redemption. If this is so, then it first suggests the conscious subordination of the one who uses it to the claim of Christ, and therefore his integration into the community. In this sense, it is fully consistent with our picture of Paul as derived independently from other sources. The aim of Paul is not to dominate the Church. He seeks rather to edify it as one who, set in the service of Christ, discharges his office in the place appointed. [108]

Yet this hardly leads us to a full understanding of the phrase δοῦλος Ἰησοῦ Χριστοῦ either in Paul or in the Catholic Epistles. [109] Everywhere the emphasis of the phrase is such that we cannot avoid the fact that it implies, not merely a confession of the saving act of Jesus, but also a description of the specific office of the men who use it. [110] This comes out most plainly in Jm. 1:1, where the author calls himself a θεοῦ καὶ κυρίου Ἰησοῦ Χριστοῦ δοῦλος, and where the

---

[107] Cf. A. Schlatter, *Erläuterungen zum NT, ad loc.*

[108] Cf. the mention of apostles amongst office-bearers in the community (1 C. 12:27 ff.; Eph. 4:11 f.).

[109] It makes little difference in the present context whether these are independent of Paul or dependent (cf. 2 Pt.).

[110] In Paul's case, cf. K. Holl, *Gesammelte Aufsätze*, II (1928), 107.

θεοῦ ... δοῦλος possibly adopts, and it at any rate linked with, the honorary OT title (→ 268). In Gl. 1:10, again, we surely have a description of calling: εἰ ἔτι ἀνθρώποις ἤρεσκον, Χριστοῦ δοῦλος οὐκ ἂν ἤμην. ἀνθρώποις ἀρέσκειν would obviously mean neglect of the only authority which Paul is concerned to please, and therefore a break with it. But this authority is Christ. Hence those who work by His commission, represent His cause and must give account only to Him, are rightly called His δοῦλοι.

Understood thus, the self-designation δοῦλος 'Ιησοῦ Χριστοῦ as used by Paul expands the parallel ἀπόστολος 'Ιησοῦ Χριστοῦ. If the latter describes Paul's office according to its significance and operation towards those without, the former describes it according to the relationship to Christ and therefore its final basis, which consists in the fact that Christ has won Paul from the world and made him His possession.

If in Jm. 1:1 and Jd. 1 we simply have δοῦλος 'Ιησοῦ Χριστοῦ, this is because the men concerned could not be called apostles, whereas there could be no disputing the designation δοῦλος 'Ιησοῦ Χριστοῦ. [111] This correctness in a secondary matter is one of the points which favour the genuineness of the epistles (cf. 2 Pt. 1:1, where we have the combination δοῦλος καὶ ἀπόστολος 'Ιησοῦ Χριστοῦ not elsewhere found in the NT). [112]

3. Jesus Christ as δοῦλος.

a. In this respect we must first consider the foot-washing on the night of the Last Supper (Jn. 13:1 ff.). In this episode Jesus makes it quite clear to His disciples that His office as He sees it consists in His being as a δοῦλος rather than in striving for power or glory.

We do not properly understand the scene, or the intention of Jesus, if we do not realise that washing feet was one of the duties of slaves, and indeed of non-Jewish rather than Jewish slaves (→ 271). [113] In performing this service, Jesus puts Himself in the position of a δοῦλος who must unthinkingly fulfil his office. By thus rendering to the disciples a service which even they did not owe to Him, though the duties of the → μαθητής to his → διδάσκαλος were very much the same as those of a slave to his master (→ 154), He displayed to them the degree of condescension and self-sacrifice which His office entailed. In view of His majesty, only the symbolic position of the slave was adequate to open their eyes and to keep them from illusions in respect of His office.

At the same time, the incident revealed to the disciples the meaning of their own lives as lives in His apostolate. In terms of the rule that the apostle of a man is as the man himself (→ I, 415), He bound them to the same position as that which He adopted. If instead of this principle He has the saying: οὐκ ἔστιν δοῦλος μείζων τοῦ κυρίου αὐτοῦ, οὐδὲ ἀπόστολος μείζων τοῦ πέμψαντος αὐτόν (Jn. 13:16), this is simply expressing the underlying thought formulated in accordance with the situation created by the incident and its significance.

---

111 Paul himself observes this rule in Phil. 1:1, where he describes Timothy and himself as δοῦλοι Χριστοῦ 'Ιησοῦ. Perhaps he is consciously avoiding the name of apostle, to which Timothy has no claim, in order to prevent the community from drawing any distinction between himself and his fellow-worker. They are both δοῦλοι Χριστοῦ 'Ιησοῦ.

112 On the mutual δουλεύειν of Christians → infra.

113 Wives have the same duty (Str.-B., II, 557; → also I, 416), as also sons and daughters towards their father (Str.-B., I, 706; T. Qid, 1, 11).

Obviously the point of the incident is to correct the attitude which He discerns in the disciples. [114] It thus constitutes the permanent basis of the obligation of mutual service, and of service in and for the community, which is laid on all Christians. Thus Paul can exhort the Galatians: διὰ τῆς ἀγάπης δουλεύετε ἀλλήλοις, not in spite of, but on the basis of the fact that they are called to freedom (Gl. 5:13). The freedom received through Christ shows itself to be true and genuine freedom in the fact that in it one is committed to service and humility which are motivated by another rather than oneself, as is, or ought to be, the case with the δοῦλος.

b. In Phil. 2:7 Paul says of Christ: He who was ἐν μορφῇ θεοῦ ὑπάρχων, ἑαυτὸν ἐκένωσεν μορφὴν δούλου λαβών, ἐν ὁμοιώματι ἀνθρώπου γενόμενος. Here the phrase μορφὴ δούλου acquires its significance from the contrast on the one side with the μορφὴ θεοῦ and on the other with the title and dignity of κύριος with which Jesus is invested at the end of the passage. It denotes the entry of Jesus into humanity, or more strictly what this means for Him [115] in relation to the power and glory which He possessed and which He therefore renounced. It thus expresses the greatness of His κένωσις, the object of which is no less than τὸ εἶναι ἴσα θεῷ. According to the use of δοῦλος, μορφὴ δούλου shows the ὁμοίωμα ἀνθρώπου to be the lowest possible point on the way of the κένωσις of Jesus, since there is no term which stands in greater contrast to κύριος or θεός than δοῦλος. In the context, therefore, the expression is obviously a description of what Jesus took upon Himself in becoming man. It is thus in accord with what we found to be the underlying meaning of the foot-washing in Jn. 13:1 ff.

From what has been said, it may be seen that we need not invoke the עֶבֶד יְהוָה of Is. 53 to explain the formula μορφὴ δούλου. [116] Indeed, this is ruled out by the text itself. [117] If there had really been any allusion to the Servant of the Lord of Isaiah, one might have expected a rather more exact description of δούλου which is not only absent but which cannot be supplied from the context. [118] Above all, in the time of Paul παῖς θεοῦ rather than δοῦλος θεοῦ had long since come into vogue as the accepted rendering of עֶבֶד יְהוָה. But this does not occur in this particular context.

It is also to be noted that words like obedience and — with reference to members of the community — humility (ταπεινοφροσύνη, v. 3; ταπεινοῦν, v. 8) [119] are not really adequate to express and to comprehend the content of μορφὴ δούλου. Nor is the term διακονεῖν. [120] As the antitheses show, Paul is not here describing an attitude. He is describing the new situation of Jesus, His new mode of existence, which is inconceivably different from His previous situation. His attitude and conduct in this situation are

---

[114] Neither in matter nor time can one separate Jn. 13:1 ff. from either Lk. 22:24 ff. or Mt. 20:28; Mk. 10:45, although here διακονεῖν is used to describe the service of Jesus rather than δουλεύειν, which is a heightened form of διακονεῖν (Mt. 20:26 f.; Mk. 10:43 f.; cf. Brandt, 79 ff.). The level of δουλεύειν as total self-offering, compared with διακονεῖν as service which does not cancel or even threaten one's own existence, is attained in the δοῦναι τὴν ψυχήν of Mt. 20:28; Mk. 10:45.

[115] The ἐν ὁμοιώματι ἀνθρώπου γενόμενος is the presupposition of Jesus' μορφὴ δούλου.

[116] Loh. Phil., 94.

[117] It is immaterial to this question whether the context in which the phrase occurs derives from Paul or is a pre-Pauline hymn, adopted by him, to Jesus as the Son of Man exalted to be the κύριος (cf. E. Lohmeyer, Kyrios Jesus [1928]).

[118] Renunciation of the εἶναι ἴσα θεῷ does not necessarily imply the δοῦλος θεοῦ, nor even the δοῦλος generally. δοῦλος describes a specific form of the κένωσις of Jesus.

[119] Brandt, 102 f.

[120] Ibid., 104.

described in the next verses, which speak of His obedience μέχρι θανάτου, θανάτου δὲ σταυροῦ (v. 8). We should not miss this distinction, since in so doing we should subjugate the whole passage to the hortatory concern of Paul (vv. 1-5), whereas vv. 6 ff. are in fact purely kerygmatic, and as kerygma of Jesus Christ provide a basis for the introduction of the hortatory material. [121] Naturally, it is Jesus' μορφὴ δούλου which leads to the rejection of the message concerning Him as → σκάνδαλον and → μωρία. Indirectly, this serves to underline the essential nature of the phrase.

δουλόω, καταδουλόω.

Both terms are common from the time of Herodotus and the tragic dramatists and are found in the LXX, where καταδουλόω is to some extent a stronger form of δουλόω. The basic meaning is "to make a slave," "to enslave." The words are used either literally to denote absolute subjection or the loss of autonomy (Hdt., I, 94 and 174; Thuc., I, 98; 1 Macc. 8:10; Epict. Diss., I, 19, 9; = a.), or figuratively (τὰς ψυχάς, Isocr., 12, 78; ἡ τύχη τὸ σῶμα κατεδουλώσατο, Philemo, 95, 8 [CAF, II, 508; 4/3 cent. B.C.]; = b.).

Except in Ac. 7:6, where Gn. 15:13 LXX is quoted and δουλοῦν refers to the enslavement of Israel by the Egyptians (→ 266), the NT always uses the terms in sense b. and therefore figuratively. Two groups may be distinguished, the one in which the words are used in a secular context and the other in which they form part of the religious use of the word group.

In 1 C. 7:15 δουλοῦν expresses total binding by another. When in a mixed marriage the unbelieving partner seeks divorce, οὐ δεδούλευται ὁ ἀδελφὸς ἢ ἡ ἀδελφὴ ἐν τοῖς τοιούτοις. [1] In relation to Jn. 8:34 (→ 274) we have a kind of definition of δοῦλος in 2 Pt. 2:19 : ᾧ γάρ τις ἥττηται, τούτῳ δεδούλωται. Paul adopts a similar use of δοῦλος (→ 277) in 1 C. 9:19 when he says of himself with reference to his office : ἐλεύθερος γὰρ ὢν ἐκ πάντων πᾶσιν ἐμαυτὸν ἐδούλωσα. In this statement he shows himself to be an apostle of Jesus who for the sake of his office is prepared to forego personal rights.

In the other passages δουλοῦν denotes the religious obligation of man to God and His world (R. 6:18, 22) or to His opponents (Gl. 4:3 : στοιχεῖα τοῦ κόσμου). In this respect the Jewish enemies of Paul are helpers of the νόμος, which seeks to bring all men within its grasp (2 C. 11:20; Gl. 2:4). The most important point is that in such contexts δουλοῦν is used in a way which treats man as a mere object of action and occurrence. He stands helplessly between obligation and obligation. The more powerful by contrast is the message that through Christ there is a radical end of δεδουλῶσθαι and its replacement by the reality of a responsible θεῷ δουλεύειν.

† δουλαγωγέω.

"To lead into slavery," "to cause to live the life of a slave." This is a rare word. [1] It is found in Epict. Diss., III, 24, 76 for deprivation of freedom, and in the A.D. period

---

[121] On the history of the understanding of μορφὴ δούλου, cf. F. Loofs, "Das altkirchliche Zeugnis gegen die herrschende Auffassung d. Kenosisstelle (Phil. 2:5-11)," ThStKr, 100 (1927/28), 1-102 passim.

δουλόω, καταδουλόω. Pr.-Bauer, 320, 641; Liddell-Scott, s.v.

[1] Cf. οἴνῳ πολλῷ δεδουλωμέναι in Tt. 2:3, which refers to women who from lovers of wine have become its slaves.

δουλαγωγέω. [1] The instance in Diod. S., XII, 24, 3 is uncertain (Lidd.-Scott, s.v.).

in Longinus, 44, 6 (δουλαγωγοῦσι ... τοὺς βίους) and Chariton, II, 7, 1 (Erotici Scriptores Graeci, II, 38, 5, Hercher). We occasionally find δουλαγωγία (IG, IX [1] 39, 42; P. Oxy., I, 38, 10 [1st cent. A.D.]) and δουλαγωγός (Plut. Contra Voluptatem Fr., 2 [II, 837c]: θηρίον ἐστὶ δουλαγωγὸν ἡδονή). [2]

Paul uses the term along with ὑπωπιάζειν in 1 C. 9:27 to express the fact that his σῶμα, with all that belongs to physical life, is fully and emphatically subordinated to his office, and has a right to existence only in so far as it at least does not hamper him in the discharge of this office.

† ὀφθαλμοδουλία.

There are no examples outside the NT. The basis of the term is ὀφθαλμόδουλος, and even this is found only in post-Christian literature (Const. Ap., IV, 12, 3). [1]

Eph. 6:6 refers to a δουλεία of Christian slaves to their masters which is outwardly correct but which is rendered without dedication and with no sense of inner obligation to the master for the sake of God and of Christ (the deceived ὀφθαλμοί of the master being contrasted with the deceitful ψυχή of the slave). In Col. 3:22 it is used in the plur. for all actions which originate in this dishonest attitude. [2]

Cf. Theodoret on Eph. 6:6 f. (MPG, 82, 552a): ὀφθαλμοδουλείαν δὲ καλεῖ τὴν οὐκ ἐξ εἰλικρινοῦς καρδίας προσφερομένην θεραπείαν, ἀλλὰ τῷ σχήματι κεχρωσμένην.

Rengstorf

δοχή → 54.

---

[2] The quotations are from Liddell-Scott, *s.v.*
ὀ φ θ α λ μ ο δ ο υ λ ί α. Pr.-Bauer, 955.
[1] Bl.-Debr. § 115, 1.
[2] Here the slaves concerned are called ἀνθρωπάρεσκοι, and they lack the ἁπλότης καρδίας which alone can produce acts pleasing to God.

† δράκων (→ ἔχιδνα, ὄφις, Σατανᾶς).

Δράκων, which the ancients derived from δέρκομαι, [1] means "serpent," [2] esp. "dragon" [3] or "sea-monster." [4] In Rev. it is a distinctive term for Satan (12:3, 4, 7, 9, 13, 16, 17; 13:2, 4; 16:13; 20:2).

Of all beasts, the serpent was regarded as demonic in antiquity, thereby revealing the duality of the ancient conception of demons. It plays a great part in Persian, Babylonian and Assyrian, Egyptian and Greek mythology, and in essence this role is always the same ; it is a power of chaos which opposes God either in the beginning or at the end of things, or both. Thus in Parseeism there is the serpent Aži-Dahaka (both at the beginning and at the end), [5] in Babylonia Tiâmat and Labbu with many similar figures, [6] in Egypt Apophis, the main symbol of the Typhon with many others like the crocodile, [7] in Greece the Python which Apollos defeats, the serpent which Kadmos slays and many

---

δ ρ ά κ ω ν. Comm.: Bss. Apk., 336 f., 346 ff.; R. H. Charles, Rev. of St. Jn., I (1920), 298 ff., 310 ff., 317 ff.; Loh. Apk., 94 f.; Had. Apk., 130, 131 f.; Rohr Off.⁴, 107. A. Schlatter, Das AT in d. joh. Apk. (1912), 68, 1; E. Lohmeyer, "Das 12. Kap. der Offenb. Joh.," ThBl, 4 (1925), 285 ff.; A. Jeremias, Babylonisches im NT (1905), 34 ff.; H. Gunkel, Schöpfung u. Chaos (1894); A. Dieterich, Abraxas (1891), 111 ff.; F. Boll, Aus d. Offenb. Joh. (1914), 98 ff.; Clemen, 397 ff.; P. Joüon, "Le grand Dragon," Recherches de Science Religieuse, 17 (1927), 444 ff.; W. Foerster, "Die Bilder in Offenb. 12 f. und 17 f.," ThStKr, 104 (1932), 279 ff.; B. Renz, Der orientalische Schlangendrache (1930).

[1] Pauly-W., s.v. Schlange, 2, Series II (1923), 531.

[2] Schol. on Eur. Or., 479 (Schwartz): γένος μὲν γὰρ ὁ ὄφις, εἶδος δὲ ὁ δράκων καὶ ἔχις καὶ τὰ λοιπὰ τῶν ὄφεων· νῦν δὲ δράκων ἀντὶ τοῦ ἔχις. Servius on Vergil Aen., II, 204 : (Thilo) says that the draco is the serpent which dwells in temples.

[3] G. Daremberg-E. Saglio, Dictionnaire des Antiquités Grecques et Romaines, II (1892), 403 f.; Pauly-W., op. cit., 531 f. Artemid Oneirocr., II, 13 : Δράκων βασιλέα σημαίνει διὰ τὸ δυνατὸν καὶ ἄρχοντα καὶ χρόνον διὰ τὸ μῆκος καὶ διὰ τὸ ἀποδιδύσκεσθαι τὸ γῆρας καὶ πάλιν νεάζειν· ... καὶ πλοῦτον καὶ χρήματα διὰ τὸ ἐπὶ θησαυροὺς ἱδρύεσθαι, καὶ θεοὺς πάντας, οἷς ἐστιν ἱερός. εἰσὶ δὲ οἵδε Ζεὺς Σαβάζιος Ἥλιος Δημήτηρ καὶ Κόρη Ἑκάτη Ἀσκληπιὸς Ἥρωες. These words sum up almost all that the δράκων signifies to the Greeks. Ael. Nat. An., 2, 21: ἥδε ἡ γῆ δρακόντων μήτηρ ἐστὶ μεγέθει μεγίστων· καὶ γάρ τοι καὶ ἐς τριάκοντα ὀργυίας προήκουσι. The δράκων is often said to be μέγιστος etc., but never μικρός.

[4] Esp. instructive is the LXX, which always has ὄφις for תַּנִּין except in Am. 9:3 (and Job 26:13), where the reference is to the תַּנִּין in the sea. It should be emphasised that δράκων does not mean either the poisonous serpent (cf. also Pauly-W., op. cit., 532) or the dragon in our sense. The hell-hound Cerberus is once called δράκων (O. Gruppe, Griech. Mythol. [1906], 408, 5), though it is also represented in the form of a serpent.

[5] = the destroying serpent, SBE, V, Index, s.v. Az-i Dahâk, esp. Yašt, III, 52-60.

[6] Cf. the material assembled in KAT, 502 ff.; M. Jastrow, Die Religion Babyloniens und Assyriens (1905/12), Index, s.v. Schlange, Tiamat ; B. Meissner, Babylon u. Assyrien, II (1925), Index ; A. Jeremias, Das AT im Lichte d. alt. Orients³ (1916), illustrations, p. 16, 21, 57; A. Jeremias, Handbuch d. altorient. Geisteskultur (1913), 14-17, 127, 129, 172-174; ibid. ² (1929). 209a-c; AOT, II, Index of Subj. under Schlange; M. Witzel, "Der Drachenkämpfer Ninib," Keilinschr. Stud. Heft, 2 (1920), with illustrations. For a short summary of all the Babyl. dragon myths, cf. P. Deimel, "Der Drachenkampf bei den Babyl. u. in d. hl. Schrift," Orientalia, Commentarii de rebus Assyr.-Babyl. ... 5 (1922), 26 ff.

[7] H. Brugsch, Rel. u. Mythol. d. alt. Ägypter (1888), Index, esp. p. 709.

mixed figures like Typhoeus/Typhon. [8] There seems to have been a similar general estimation of the red colour ascribed to the serpent in Rev. 12:3. [9] On Greek soil the significance of the fight against the serpent as the original battle of deity against the power of chaos is greatly obscured by the lowering of the stories to the level of sagas. [10] On the other hand, the other aspect of the serpent as a demonic beast emerges more strongly than in Babylon and Egypt, namely, that it is a sacred animal. [11] This dual capacity reveals the dual nature of ancient demonology generally. [12]

The intrinsically impressive view that Rev. is simply borrowing a definite myth breaks down not merely on differences in the conception of the role of Michael [13] but more particularly on the fact that the image of the δράκων does not occur only in the vision of Rev. 12 but is the key image for Satan in the whole book. It is more likely that the serpent has here become, along the lines of the radical depreciation of the demonic in the NT, a demonic animal representing Satan. On the other hand, we should not overlook the link with the story of the serpent in Paradise in Gn. 3. [14] The particular feature mentioned in Rev. 12:15, namely, that a stream of water gushes from the mouth of Satan, is reminiscent of Babylo-

---

[8] Pauly-W., *s.v. Dracon,* V (1905), 1646 f., No. 6 and 7; *s.v. Schlange* (→ n. 1); Daremberg-Saglio, *Dictionnaire,* II, 403/14; Roscher, *s.v.* Python, Kadmos, Typhoeus/ Typhon; T. Schreiber, *Apollon Pythoktonos* (1879); E. Siecke, *Drachenkämpfe* (1907). There is a good review of Gk. conceptions of the serpent in E. Küster, *Die Schlange in d. griech. Rel. u. Kunst* (1913).

[9] A. Jeremias, *Das AT im Lichte des alten Orients*[3] (1916), 15, 2; 315, 4. For Egypt, cf. Brugsch (→ n. 7), 325; for Greece, Eur. Iph. Taur., 1245: οἰνωπὸς δράκων; Plut. Is. et Os., 22 (II, 359e): τὸν δὲ Τύφωνα τῇ χρόᾳ πυρρόν; *ibid.,* 30 (II, 362e).

[10] Cultic depictions of battles between gods and serpents are attested up to a late period. Plut. Def. Orac., 15 (II, 417 f ff.) speaks of examples at Delphi (cf. Luc. Salt., 38); Cyprian tells us in his *Confessio* (*Acta Sanctorum,* Septembr. VII, 222): τῆς ἐν τῇ Ἀκροπόλει Παλλάδος τῷ δράκοντι ἐλειτούργησα, and Greg. Naz. Or. Theol., 5, 31 (MPG, 35, 704c) seems to have something similar in view when he summons Julian: κατάβαλε τοὺς Τριπτολέμους σου καὶ τοὺς Κελεοὺς καὶ τοὺς μυστικοὺς δράκοντας. At the Delphic games the serpent is conceived of as a power hostile to the god; in other passages the context in which the word occurs is uncertain. Typhoeus/Typhon is a power which is hostile not merely to a god but to the gods; it is said of him in Aesch. Prom., 354: Τυφῶνα θοῦρον, πᾶσιν ὃς ἀντέστη θεοῖς. Philodem. writes (De Pietate, LXIb, 1, p. 46 [Gomperz] in Dieterich, *Abraxas* [1891], 113, 3): ἐπιθέσθαι Τυφῶνα εἰρήκα(σι τῇ βασιλείᾳ) Διός, (ὡς Αἰσχύλος) ἐν Προ(μηθεῖ καὶ Ἀ)κουσίλα(ος καὶ Ἐπι)μενίδη(ς καὶ ἄλλοι) πολλοί. Nonnos used the battle with Typhon as an illustration of the conflict of the evil earthly element against the pure heavenly world, V. Stegemann, *Astrologie u. Universalgeschichte* (1930), 111. But Typhon is no δράκων, though it is worth noting that features of the serpent occur in depictions of this monster, *v.* Roscher, *s.v.* Typhoeus/Typhon.

[11] Philo of Byblos (in Fragm. Historicorum Graecorum, III [1849], 572): τὴν μὲν οὖν τοῦ δράκοντος φύσιν καὶ τῶν ὄφεων αὐτὸς ἐξεθείασεν ὁ Τάαυτος, ... πνευματικώτατον γὰρ τὸ ζῷον πάντων τῶν ἑρπετῶν. Plut. De Cleomene, 39 (I, 823e): οἱ τὸ σῶμα τοῦ Κλεομένους ἀνεσταυρωμένον παραφυλάττοντες εἶδον εὐμεγέθη δράκοντα τῇ κεφαλῇ περιπεπλεγμένον ... οἱ δὲ Ἀλεξανδρεῖς ... ἥρωα τὸν Κλεομένη καὶ θεῶν παῖδα προσαγορεύοντες. On the serpent as a sacred animal in Egypt, esp. for Isis and Osiris (Isis as a serpent or with the body of a serpent), and the religious implications of the depictions, cf. J. Berreth, *Studien zum Isisbuch in Apulejus' Metamorphosen* (Diss. Tübingen, 1931). I owe this reference to H. Kleinknecht.

[12] → δαίμων, 8. Syncretism uses the image of the serpent in many different ways as a symbol of the demonic, H. Leisegang, *Die Gnosis* (1924), 110 f.; R. Reitzenstein, "Himmelswanderung u. Drachenkampf," *Festschr. F. C. Andreas* (1916), 33-50; W. Foerster, ThStKr, 104 (1932), 306.

[13] For further arguments, *v.* W. Foerster, ThStKr, 104 (1932), 280/85.

[14] ὁ ὄφις ὁ ἀρχαῖος in Rev. 12:9 denotes the serpent of Paradise.

nian conceptions,[15] of which we have scattered traces in the OT.[16] The Rabbis, too, see connexions between the serpent and the world of the demonic.[17] In Rev. 13:11 (ἄλλο θηρίον ... ἐλάλει ὡς δράκων) δράκων is again an image for the demonic and satanic.

[18] In the Gk. OT. δράκων is used in many verses which owe their imagery to a myth of the conflict between the deity and the dragon of chaos. These are particularly important in this context because Christian views of hell and the devil are to some extent connected with them.[19] Thus in Job 3:8 we read of a monster which is about to swallow up the day-star.[20] The Mas. has לִוְיָתָן; Θ translates δράκων. More often the dragon is a sea-monster, or the sea personified in the dragon of chaos. Cf. 'Ιώβ 7:12 : πότερον θάλασσά εἰμι ἢ δράκων (תַּנִּין), ὅτι κατέταξας ἐπ' ἐμὲ φυλακήν. On ψ 73:13 f., where the Mas. has תַנִּינִים and לִוְיָתָן, Origen comments as follows (Orat., 27, 12): "He who has a part in the dragon is himself none other than the spiritual Ethiopian (the devil), who transforms himself into a serpent by representations of the dragon ... Concerning the body of the dragon which is eaten by the Ethiopians David says : 'Thou has broken the heads of the dragons in the water, thou hast smashed the head of the dragon and given him to be meat to the Ethiopians.' "[21] Here we have the equation of the dragon, the Ethiopian (so Origen, elsewhere the Egyptian) and the devil which determines early Christian interpretation in other passages also, e.g., Ez. 29:3; 32:2; Is. 27:1 [22] — all passages which originally use the animal symbolism politically, as may be seen in the apocalyptic of Daniel. We are to understand ψ 103:25 f.; 148:7; Am. 9:3 etc. along the same lines. Clearest of all is the LXX rendering in 'Ιώβ 26:13 : προστάγματι δὲ ἐθανάτωσεν δράκοντα ἀποστάτην (Mas. נָחָשׁ בָּרִחַ = winged serpent). Gn. 3:15 exerted some influence on the conception, as may be seen in R. 16:20; cf. Test. A. 7: "Peacefully breaking the head of the dragon," and Passio Perpetuae, 4 : draco ... mirae magnitudinis ... calcaui illi caput ; 10: Aegyptius ...[23] calcaui illi caput ... intellexi me ... contra diabolum esse pugnaturam. The equation of the dragon and the devil is also to be found in the expression μίασμα, δράκων found on a Christian amulet.[24] Cf. the Passio Sancti Bonifatii, 13 (p. 289, Ruinart [1713]):[25] "That the filthy, devouring dragon may not hinder me in the way."

Foerster

δρόμος → τρέχω.

---

[15] Tiamat and Labbu are sea-monsters.

[16] W. Foerster (→ n. 13), 304 f.; H. Gunkel, *Schöpfung und Chaos* (1894), 29 ff.; W. Erbt, *Von Jerusalem nach Rom* (1912), 124 ff. → *infra*.

[17] Foerster, 305 f.

[18] This paragraph is by G. Bertram apart from the last sentence.

[19] J. Kroll, *Gott u. Hölle, Der Mythus vom Descensuskampfe* (1932), 316 ff., cf. also Index, *s.v. Drache*.

[20] Cf. C. Steuernagel in Kautzsch, *ad loc.*

[21] F. J. Dölger, *Die Sonne der Gerechtigkeit und der Schwarze* (1919), 52, 54 f.

[22] F. J. Dölger, *Ichthys*, II : *Der heilige Fisch in den antiken Religionen und im Christentum* (1922), 490 f.

[23] The equation of the Egyptian and the devil seems to be assumed in the Leyden magic pap. (Preis. Zaub., XII, 89) when we are told : ἐν δὲ τοῖς πρὸς νότον μέρεσιν δράκων εἶ πτεροειδής.

[24] Epigr. Graec., 1140b (Moult.-Mill., *s.v.*).

[25] F. J. Dölger, *Sol Salutis, Gebet und Gesang im christlichen Altertum* (1925), 380 (the reference here to p. 330 of Ruinart is a mistake).

δύναμαι, δυνατός, δυνατέω, ἀδύνατος,
ἀδυνατέω, δύναμις, δυνάστης,
δυναμόω, ἐνδυναμόω

Words deriving from the stem δυνα- all have the basic meaning of "being able," of "capacity" in virtue of an ability; in contrast to → ἰσχυ-, which stresses the factuality of the ability, the stress falls on being able. Thus far no convincing etymology has been discovered.

δύναμαι a. "to be able," "to be capable of." It is mostly used in a very weak sense. It is common from the time of Homer and examples may be found everywhere. The original sense and the full content may be seen, e.g., in Thuc., IV, 39, where the mighty are called οἱ δυνάμενοι, though here there is a notable development from ability, by way of capacity, to the concept of might or power; or again in instances when δύναμαι is linked with a specific form of power, as in Lys., 6, 48 : πλουτῶν καὶ δυνάμενος τοῖς χρήμασι. b. "to be able," with specific reference to the subjective spiritual or moral attitude which either makes able or not. In this sense it may even mean "to will" or "not to will," e.g., σὲ ... οὐ δύναμαι προλιπεῖν δύστηνον ἐόντα, Hom. Od., 13, 331; cf. Soph. Trach., 546. c. When δύναμαι is applied to things it has the sense of "to be equal to," "to count as," "to signify": ὁ σίγλος δύναται ἑπτὰ ὀβολοὺς καὶ ἡμιοβέλιον, Xenoph. An., I, 5, 6; τοῦτο δύναται ὁ λόγος, Plat. Euthyd., 286c. d. In the LXX δύναμαι is used for a whole list of Heb. words, esp. יָכֹל in Ex. 8:14 ('Εξ. 8:18) and Dt. 22:3, but also הָיָה לֹ in Lv. 26:37; יָסַף hi in Is. 24:20; כָּהֵל in Da. 2:26; 5:8; כּוּל hi in 3 Βασ. 8:64; מָצָא in Job 32:3; עָצַר in 2 Ch. 20:37. In Job 16:14 the part. δυνάμενος is used for גִּבּוֹר; in 1 Βασ. 10:26 A we have υἱοὶ δυνάμενοι for חַיִל (בְּנֵי־הַחַיִל) BHK²); οὐ δύνασθαι for חָדַל in Gn. 41:49; for יָאַל ni in Jer. 5:4; for לָאָה ni in Ex. 7:18; for מָאֵן pi in Job 6:7.

δυνατός, "one who has an ability, a capacity, or power," "one who is powerful." This is a verbal adj. of δύναμαι. The nature of the power may be expressed in different ways: σώμασι καὶ ψυχαῖς, Xenoph. Mem., II, 1, 19; δυνατώτατος λέγειν τε καὶ πράσσειν, Thuc., I, 139. As a neut. adj. it can have the sense of "what is possible," "what can happen," "what is practicable": ὅσον γε δυνατόν, Eur. Iph. Aul., 997. As a subst. τὸ δυνατόν or τὰ δυνατά means power. [1] In the LXX it is used for אַדִּיר in 2 Ch. 23:20; for בָּחוּר in 2 Ch. 13:3, 17; 25:5; and esp. for adjectives which might come under the comprehensive meaning of δυνατός. [2] It is usually a rendering of גִּבּוֹר.

δυνατέω is a verb derived from δυνατός and meaning "to have great ability." It usually occurs in Christian writings, though it is also found in Philodem. De Signis, 11. [3] It is later and less common than → ἀδυνατέω. It is rather superfluous alongside δύνασθαι, whereas ἀδυνατέω has rather a different sense from οὐ δύνασθαι [Debrunner]. Cf. Ju. 5:30 A.

δ ύ ν α μ α ι κτλ. W. Grundmann, *Der Begriff der Kraft in der neutestamentlichen Gedankenwelt* (1932); O. Schmitz, "Der Begriff δύναμις bei Paulus" in *Festschr. f. A. Deissmann* (1927), 139-167. There is an excellent bibl. in Grundmann VII-IX. → n. 15, 22, 23, 28, 55, 63.

[1] Cf. Liddell-Scott, *s.v.*
[2] Cf. Hatch-Redp., *s.v.*
[3] Cf. Liddell-Scott as against Pr.-Bauer, *s.v.*

ἀδύνατος, with ἀ- privativum, is the opp. of δυνατός, i.e., "one who has no ability, capacity or strength," "one who is incapable or incompetent" : e.g., ἀδύνατος χρήμασι, Thuc., VII, 28. ἀδύνατόν ἐστι, "it is impossible." The subst. τὸ ἀδύνατον means "impossibility," Hdt., IX, 60. It is common in the LXX, cf. Job 5:15; 24:4; 29:16 : ἀδύνατος for אֶבְיוֹן; Job 5:16; 20:19; 31:16 : ἀδύνατος for דַּל; for חֵלֶךְ in Jl. 3:10 and for עָנִי in Job 36:15.

ἀδυνατέω derives from ἀδύνατος and means "not to be able." It is found in Plato, Xenoph. etc. It shows us beyond doubt that δυνατέω is not just a Christian word but a current term for which there is accidentally no prior literary attestation. It is often used in the LXX, e.g., Job 42:2 (בָּצַר ni); Job 4:4 (כָּרַע); Is. 8:15 (כָּשַׁל); Lv. 25:35 (מוּט); Gn. 18:14; Dt. 17:8; Zech. 8:6 (פָּלָא ni).

δύναμις, a sing. subst. construction from the root δυνα-, is by far the most important word in the group. The original meaning of "ability" or "capacity" is fully maintained in the natural philosophy of Aristotle. In Arist. Metaph., VIII, 8, p. 1049b, 24 we read : ἀεὶ γὰρ ἐκ τοῦ δυνάμει ὄντος γίγνεται τὸ ἐνεργείᾳ ὂν ὑπὸ ἐνεργείᾳ ὄντος. δύναμις here means potency in contrast to ἐνέργεια or ἐντελέχεια. [4] As potency it is "possibility," "capacity," "ability." In these senses it occurs in the fixed phrases κατὰ δύναμιν, παρὰ δύναμιν, ὑπὲρ δύναμιν. [5] A fine example of this meaning is to be found in Plat. Resp., V, 477cd : φήσομεν δυνάμεις εἶναι γένος τι τῶν ὄντων, αἷς δὴ καὶ ἡμεῖς δυνάμεθα ἃ δυνάμεθα καὶ ἄλλο πᾶν ὅτι περ ἂν δύνηται, οἷον λέγω ὄψιν καὶ ἀκοὴν τῶν δυνάμεων εἶναι ... δυνάμεως γὰρ ἐγὼ οὔτε τινὰ χρόαν ὁρῶ οὔτε σχῆμα οὔτε τι τῶν τοιούτων οἷον καὶ ἄλλων πολλῶν, πρὸς ἃ ἀποβλέπων ἔνια διορίζομαι παρ' ἐμαυτῷ τὰ μὲν ἄλλα εἶναι, τὰ δὲ ἄλλα. δυνάμεως δ' εἰς ἐκεῖνο μόνον βλέπω ἐφ' ᾧ τε ἔστι καὶ ὃ ἀπεργάζεται, καὶ ταύτῃ ἑκάστην αὐτῶν δύναμιν ἐκάλεσα. With its implication of "power," the term δύναμις can be applied over the whole range of life. For physical life, cf. the passage from Plato, in which the powers of hearing and sight are called δυνάμεις. Aristotle has the general statement : πᾶν σῶμα αἰσθητὸν ἔχει δύναμιν ποιητικὴν ἢ παθητικὴν ἢ ἄμφω, Cael., I, 7, p. 275b, 5. Poseidonius has a whole system of physiological powers in which the main concepts are δύναμις θρεπτική and δύναμις σπερματική. Alongside the physical are spiritual and intellectual powers, so that all moral and spiritual and intellectual life may be traced back to the δυνάμεις of man. Human δυνάμεις are only one part of the powers of the cosmos generally. Animals, plants and stars also have their δυνάμεις, [6] and the underlying physical forces of the cosmos, the capacities of subsistence and motion, are also called δύναμις. [7]

In the LXX δύναμις is primarily used for חַיִל, [8] which is the Mas. term in 164 (Cod. B 157) instances of δύναμις. This term has the same meaning as δύναμις, i.e., "ability," "power," "competence," e.g., ψ 83:7 (84:7) etc. In many cases חַיִל Mas. and δύναμις LXX mean "host" or "power of a host" (e.g., Ex. 14:28), which is implied in

---

[4] Cf. the instances in the *Index Aristotelicus* of Bonitz (Akademie ed., Vol. 5), *s.v.* Materially, cf. F. Überweg-K. Praechter, *Die Philosophie des Altertums*¹² (1926), 379 ff.

[5] How firmly established is this generally attested usage may be seen clearly from P. Oxy., XI, 1381, 146, where κατὰ δύναμιν is used within a very different δύναμις concept.

[6] Cf. Xenoph. Cyrop., VIII, 8, 14; Reitzenstein Poim., 259: ... περὶ φυσικῶν δυνάμεων ζῴων τε φυτῶν τε καὶ λίθων. From this point there is a connecting line to medicine and magic. Doctors call the means of healing δύναμις, δυνάμεις, and the magician calls his magical power or powers δύναμις and δυνάμεις. Cf. J. Röhr, *Der okkulte Kraftbegriff im Altertum* (1923), 8 f.; Mithr.-Liturg., 46 A.

[7] Cf. Aristot. Mot. An., 3, p. 699a, 34 : ἔστι γάρ τι πλῆθος ἰσχύος καὶ δυνάμεως καθ' ἣν μένει τὸ μένον ὥσπερ καθ' ἣν κινεῖ τὸ κινοῦν.

[8] The following data are taken from Hatch-Redpath, *s.v.*

the Gk. δύναμις. [9] In 13 instances δύναμις is used for גְּבוּרָה, e.g., Ju. 5:31; 8:21; 1 Ch. 29:11 etc., which is as often rendered ἰσχύς and 33 times δυναστεία. גְּבוּרָה means "power," "strength" in the sense of "superior force" or "dominion." It is for this reason that δυναστεία is preferred in the LXX and that ἰσχύς is used as well as δύναμις. Another word translated δύναμις is כֹּחַ (8 times, e.g., Ex. 9:16 A; 1 Ch. 29:2), though ἰσχύς is more common (98 times), since כֹּחַ denotes the factuality of strength rather than capacity. Note should also be taken of עֹז (21 times as against → ἰσχύς 28 times and → κράτος 6), e.g., 1 Ch. 13:8; and עֱזוּז, אוֹן, אֵל, חֹזֶק, יָד, מָאֹד (once each).

δυνάστης is a *nomen agentis* [10] from the extended stem δυνασ- (first found in Hom.: ἐδυνάσ-θην), and means "the one who can do something." It is connected with δυναστεία, which has the sense of "power," "might," "dominion," e.g., Thuc., III, 62; Soph. Oed. Col., 593. It was used from an early period for "ruler," "the one who is powerful," "the one who exercises authority and rule." God is δυνάστης in Soph. Ant., 608; Sir. 46:5; C. Wessely, *Neue Gr. Zauberpap.* (1893), 665: δυνάστας μεγάλους θεούς. Of the stars it is said in Aesch. Ag., 6: τοὺς φέροντας χεῖμα καὶ θέρος βροτοῖς λαμπροὺς δυνάστας ἀστέρας. It is used of human rulers in Hdt., II, 32. In the LXX it is the translation of 22 different terms, including גִּבּוֹר in 1 Ch. 29:24; גָּדוֹל in Lv. 19:15; חָזָק in Job 5:15; שַׂר in Da. 9:6; 11:5. [11]

δυναμόω and ἐνδυναμόω: The simple and compound both mean "to endue with power," "to make strong," "to strengthen." Apart from the NT, examples are found in the pap., [12] e.g., Preis. Zaub., IV, 197 f., 215 f.; in the LXX, where גבר pi is thus rendered in Qoh. 10:10; גבר hi in Da. Θ 9:27; עָצַם in ψ 51:7; ψ 67:28 and לבשׁ in Ju. 6:34; 1 Ch. 12:18 (A).

A. The Concepts of Power in the Greek and Hellenistic World.

Our review of δύναμις made it plain that the whole of human life and indeed of the life of the cosmos was conceived dynamically. In Greek and Hellenistic reflection concerning the world and its mystery this led increasingly to the acceptance of δύναμις as a cosmic principle. The oldest example is to be found in a larger fragment of the Pythagorean Philolaos: θεωρεῖν δεῖ τὰ ἔργα καὶ τὴν οὐσίαν τῶ ἀριθμῶ καττὰν δύναμιν ἅτις ἐστὶν ἐν τᾶι δεκάδι· μεγάλα γὰρ καὶ παντελὴς καὶ παντοεργὸς καὶ θείω καὶ οὐρανίω βίω καὶ ἀνθρωπίνω ἀρχὰ καὶ ἀγεμὼν κοινωνοῦσα *** δύναμις καὶ τᾶς δεκάδος. ἄνευ δὲ τούτας πάντ' ἄπειρα καὶ ἄδηλα καὶ ἀφανῆ ... ἴδοις δὲ κα οὐ μόνον ἐν τοῖς δαιμονίοις καὶ θείοις πράγμασι τὰν τῶ ἀριθμῶ φύσιν καὶ τὰν δύναμιν ἰσχύουσαν, ἀλλὰ καὶ ἐν τοῖς ἀνθρωπικοῖς ἔργοις καὶ λόγοις πᾶσι παντᾶ καὶ κατὰ τὰς δημιουργίας τὰς τεχνικὰς πάσας καὶ κατὰ τὰν μουσικάν (Fr., 11 [I, 313 f., Diels]). Number is the cosmic principle in genuine Pythagorean teaching, but this is filled with effective force and is thus a dynamic magnitude which fashions all things. Plato on one occasion declares δύναμις to be the absolute mark of being. λέγω δὴ τὸ καὶ ὁποιανοῦν τινα κεκτημένον δύναμιν εἴτ' εἰς τὸ ποιεῖν ἕτερον ὁτιοῦν πεφυκὸς εἴτ' εἰς τὸ παθεῖν καὶ σμικρότατον ὑπὸ τοῦ φαυλοτάτου, κἂν εἰ μόνον εἰσάπαξ, πᾶν τοῦτο ὄντως εἶναι. τίθεμαι γὰρ

---

[9] At this pt. we should mention צָבָא, which is 120 times translated δύναμις in the sense of "hosts" or "forces." In Ch. גְדוּד, עַם, מַחֲנֶה and מִלְחָמָה are either once or more often rendered δύναμις in the same sense.

[10] E. Fraenkel, *Gesch. d. gr. Nomina Agentis*, I (1910), 208 f.

[11] Cf. on δυνάστης K. Stegmann v. Pritzwald, *Zur Gesch. d. Herrscherbez. von Homer bis Plato* (1930), 120 f., 155 f.

[12] Cf. Nägeli, 32; Moult.-Mill., *s.v.*

ὅρον ὁρίζειν τὰ ὄντα ὡς ἔστιν οὐκ ἄλλο τι πλὴν δύναμις (Soph., 247de). [13] Ps.-Aristot. speaks of ἡ διὰ πάντων διήκουσα δύναμις ... τὸν σύμπαντα κόσμον δημιουργήσασα, Mund., 5, p. 396b, 28. Among the Stoics it is the *causa efficiens* of phenomena: ἡ πλειόνων ἐποιστικὴ συμπτωμάτων (Simplicius). [14] The Stoics speak of the invisible force which, self-originating and self-moving, moves the world (II, 112, 39 ff., v. Arnim). The tendency is increasingly to make δύναμις an absolute cosmic principle. The only thing which still lies behind it in Aristotle and Stoicism is the *nous*. Only in Poseidonius does it become a true cosmic principle. [15] In his philosophy there is erected a whole system of powers which fashions the world and operates in it, whether in the macrocosm or the microcosm, and which is based upon the δύναμις ζωτική, the original power of all being, which "inwardly holds the world together." Power is the "vital force which, graded according to the aggregates of matter and the forms of life, makes the cosmos the most perfect of all organisms." This reveals the decisive step which Poseidonius has taken. "Poseidonius is thus an independent philosopher and systematician worthy to be ranked with Aristotle and Chrysippus. The latter teaches that the world is to be explained in terms of concept, the former in terms of reason and Poseidonius in terms of force." [16]

The development of the Greek concept of God is to be sought along these lines. From the philosophical standpoint cosmic principle and God are the same thing. In consequence of this neutral conception of God the Greek philosophers seldom speak of the power of God. [17] This is linked with the old Greek idea of God which was determined by Homer and expressed in terms of idea, and which W. F. Otto has formulated as follows: "Hence the natural itself can stand in the glory of the sublime and the divine. Certainly, the appearance of the Greek gods involves extraordinary and far-reaching events. Yet this does not mean the emergence of a power which knows no limits. It means the emergence of a being which shows a thousandfold its vitality as a great form of being in our world. The first and supreme thing is not the power which produces the act. It is the being revealed in the form. And the most sacred feelings of awe are not induced by the monstrous and illimitably powerful, but proceed from the depths of natural experience." [18] The identity of cosmic principle and deity as the basis of being in phenomena is fully developed by the Stoics, who equate with God the invisible self-originating, self-moving force which moves the world (Sext. Emp., II, 112, 39 ff., v. Arnim). The relationship of cosmic force, which is equated with deity, and cosmic material, which is fashioned by this force, is understood as follows: ἐοίκασι δέ ... εἶδος τῆς ὕλης λέγειν τὸν θεόν· εἰ γὰρ οὕτως ὁ θεὸς μέμικται τῇ ὕλῃ ... ὡς ἐν τοῖς ζῴοις ἡ ψυχὴ τῷ σώματι, καὶ ἡ δύναμις τῆς ὕλης ἐστὶ ὁ θεός (φασὶ γὰρ τὴν ὕλην ποιεῖν τῇ ἐν αὐτῇ δυνάμει) εἶδος <οὔτ>ως ἂν λέγοιεν αὐτῆς τὸν θεόν, ὡς τὴν ψυχὴν τοῦ σώματος καὶ τὴν δύναμιν τοῦ δυνάμει ... (Alex. Aphr., II, 308, 35 ff., v. Arnim). In these fragments deity is a universal pantheistic force, whereas in Platonic and Aristotelian philosophy it was a transcendent being. This

---

[13] In the history of philosophy it is much contested whether this statement is genuine. Powerful arguments for its genuineness are advanced by C. Ritter, *Platon*, II (1923), 126 ff. and 172 ff.

[14] Cf. v. Arnim, III, 49, 12.

[15] This is the picture of Poseidonius given by K. Reinhardt in his *Poseidonius* (1921); *Kosmos und Sympathie* (1926).

[16] Reinhardt, *Poseidonius*, 11.

[17] When Plato, e.g., speaks of a μείζων δύναμις ἢ ἀνθρωπεία (Crat., 438c), or of a θειοτέρα δύναμις ἢ ἡ τῶν ἀνθρώπων (397c), or of the capacities of Apollo (405a), in the first two instances the expression is colourless and in the third he is simply following current usage.

[18] W. F. Otto, *Die Götter Griechenlands* (1929), 10 f. Cf. the common formula in Gk. prayers: δύνασαι γάρ, "Thou canst indeed do this" (also Hom. Od., 10, 306: θεοὶ δέ τε πάντα δύνανται); examples are given in C. Ausfeld, "De Graec. precationibus quaest. select.," *Jbch. f. klass. Phil. Suppl. NT, 28* (1903), 508 ff.

neutral concept of God enters into instructive interaction with the pagan belief in gods at this level of power. The individual gods become δυνάμεις of the universal force. They are personifications of the capacities of a neutral deity. Θεὸν δὲ εἶναι ζῷον ἀθάνατον λογικὸν τέλειον ἢ νοερὸν ἐν εὐδαιμονίᾳ κακοῦ παντὸς ἀνεπίδεκτον, προνοητικὸν κόσμου τε καὶ τῶν ἐν κόσμῳ. μὴ εἶναι μέντοι ἀνθρωπόμορφον· εἶναι δὲ τὸν μὲν δημιουργὸν τῶν ὅλων καὶ ὥσπερ πατέρα πάντων, κοινῶς τε καὶ τὸ μέρος αὐτοῦ τὸ διῆκον διὰ πάντων, ὃς πολλαῖς προσηγορίαις προσονομάζεται κατὰ τὰς δυνάμεις ... (Diog. L., II, 305, 15 ff., v. Arnim). Only after this passage do we have the names of the gods. This method is typical of the philosophical handling of popular polytheism. There is an interesting example of this in Plutarch's De Iside et Osiride. Here the old myths are refashioned into a world picture with the wholly Stoic result: ... οὕτως ἑνὸς λόγου τοῦ ταῦτα κοσμοῦντος καὶ μιᾶς προνοίας ἐπιτροπευούσης καὶ δυνάμεων ὑπουργῶν ἐπὶ πάντας τεταγμένων (67 [II, 377 f.]). The identity of world principle and divine power became complete in the philosophy of Poseidonius, where the original power which gives life to all things, the ζωτικὴ δύναμις, is the deity. [19]

Poseidonius with his philosophy represents an important turn in the development. K. Reinhardt assesses this in the following terms in relation to the one and all principle in Gk. philosophy: "This (principle) becomes the expression of a power, of an explicable, natural, yet secret and mysterious power, whereas in the earlier days of antiquity it was the expression of an evident, natural, yet secret and mysterious order. The old cosmos still stands, but one step further and the forces which on the one side it still unites in itself become its master. Their mystery is no longer dissolved in it; its mystery is dissolved in them. It becomes an indication, a manifestation, a symbol, and the forces become spirits, energies, chains, sources, original forms and emanations of the inexpressible, of the original mystery of existence." [20] This shows us with full clarity how the Greek world became the Hellenistic under the pressure of the spirit of the Orient.

The world is a manifestation of the forces working in and by and on it. All occurrence is comprised in these forces. To do anything, one must participate in them and know them. In view of this conception and basic understanding of the world, which is found both in the philosophical work of Hellenism and also in the popular thinking expressed in magic, one can readily understand the application of the concept. The whole point of magic is participation in the forces of the cosmos. The first presupposition here is to know the means of harnessing these powers. According to the popular view, one is dealing with personified natural forces of a demonic character, and these must be brought under control. As an example of magic, we may cite the well-known passage from the great Paris magic pap., where it is said of the Great Bear: ἀρκτικὴ δύναμις πάντα ποιοῦσα, Preis. Zaub., IV, 1331, and previously: τὴν μεγίστην δύναμιν τὴν ἐν τῷ οὐρανῷ ὑπὸ κυρίου θεοῦ τεταγμένην, IV, 1275 f. These demonic natural and cosmic forces stand under the deity, of which it is still said in the Hellenistic period: τοῦτο γάρ ἐστιν ὁ θεός, τὸ ἀγαθόν· ᾧ πᾶσα δύναμις τοῦ ποιεῖν πάντα, Corp. Herm., XIV, 9. [21] Yet man is nearer to them than to the deity. This is why he seeks to make contact with them. Concerning them we read in Plutarch, who is presumably reproducing the view of the Gk. philosophers Plato, Xenocrates and Chrysippus, who for their part are following the older theologians: ἐρρωμενεστέρους μὲν ἀνθρώπων γεγονέναι λέγουσιν, καὶ πολλῇ τῇ δυνάμει τὴν φύσιν ὑπερφέροντας ἡμῶν, τὸ δὲ θεῖον οὐκ ἀμιγὲς οὐδ' ἄκρατον ἔχοντας, Is. et Os., 25 (II, 360e). In Iambl. Myst. we have an express depiction of these demonic forces. Iambl. describes their origin in the words: λέγω τοίνυν δαίμονας μὲν κατὰ τὰς γεννητικὰς καὶ δημιουρ-

---

[19] Reinhardt, *Poseidonius*, 243 ff.
[20] Reinhardt, *Kosmos und Sympathie*, 249.
[21] Christian influence is perhaps discernible in this passage.

γικὰς τῶν θεῶν δυνάμεις ἐν τῇ πορρωτάτῃ τῆς προόδου ἀποτελευτήσει καὶ τῶν ἐσχάτων διαμερισμῶν παράγεσθαι, and he then defines their powers: δυνάμεις τε τοῖς μὲν δαίμοσι γονίμους, ἐπιστατικάς τε τῆς φύσεως καὶ τοῦ συνδέσμου τῶν ψυχῶν εἰς τὰ σώματα ἀφοριστέον (Myst., II, 1). We are thus dealing with powers in the world which constitute a great nexus of power, a single, supreme power, of which the different demonic powers are emanations.

In the light of this total picture Iambl. portrays the magician, the theurge. He differs from the philosopher by having θεουργικὴ ἕνωσις πρὸς θεούς instead of θεωρητικῶς φιλοσοφοῦντας. This arises as follows: ἡ τῶν ἔργων τῶν ἀρρήτων καὶ ὑπὲρ πᾶσαν νόησιν θεοπρεπῶς ἐνεργουμένων τελεσιουργία ἥ τε τῶν νοουμένων τοῖς θεοῖς μόνοις συμβόλων ἀφθέγκτων δύναμις ἐντίθησι τὴν θεουργικὴν ἕνωσιν (Myst., II, 11). By this ἕνωσις, which is mediated through the δύναμις present in the magic symbols, he surrounds himself with the τῶν θεῶν σχῆμα, and in this attitude ὡς κρείττονας καλεῖ ἀπὸ τοῦ παντὸς δυνάμεις ... καὶ ἐπιτάττει αὐταῖς αὖθις, IV, 2. Thus the magician, knowing the cosmic, divine, demonic forces and their interconnexions, can mediate them for the good or ill of others. To this context belong the prayers and incantations for endowment with power as we have them in the great Paris magic pap. Thus the magician prays: δυνάμωσον, ἱκετῶ, δός τε μοι ταύτην τὴν χάριν ... συνεστάθην σου τῇ ἱερᾷ μορφῇ, ἐδυναμώθην τῷ ἱερῷ σου ὀνόματι (Preis. Zaub., IV, 197 f., 215 f.).

The position of the magician does not exclude the possibility that the gods, who stand alongside the demons or are identified with them, and who still maintain their importance in primitive thinking, might intervene directly with acts of power, especially to help or to heal. In the Greek Hellenistic world Aesculapius esp. is recognised to be a god of healing. The healing miracles of Epidaurus are an example. In the Imuthes-Aesculapius pap., which identifies Imuthes with Aesculapius, the wonderful power of the god is extolled: σύνιτε, ὦ ... ὅσοι θητεύσαντες τὸν θεὸν νόσων ἀπηλλάγητε, ὅσοι τὴν ἰατρικὴν μεταχειρίζεσθε ἐπιστήμην, ὅσοι πονήσετε ζηλωταὶ ἀρετῆς, ὅσοι πολλῷ πλήθει ἐπηυξήθητε ἀγαθῶν, ὅσοι κινδύνους θαλάσσης περιεσώθητε, εἰς πάντα γὰρ τόπον διεπεφοίτηκεν ἡ τοῦ θεοῦ δύναμις σωτήριος. μέλλω γὰρ αὐτοῦ τερατώδεις ἀπαγγέλειν ἐπιφανείας δυνάμεώς τε μεγέθη εὐεργετημάτων [τε] δωρήματα (P. Oxy., XI, 1381, 206 ff.). These miracles of Aesculapius and similar gods are called δυνάμεις, acts of power. Similarly, the acts of punishment in which the gods display their might are given the same name on the Lydian inscr. reproduced by Steinleitner [22] (→ I, 301). [23]

The position of man himself is altered by the dissolution of the unitary cosmos into the forces which rule and affect it. Since these forces are hidden from man, and his knowledge or ignorance determines his being, man stands outside these forces and must attain to participation in them. The question to which the position of man gives rise is sharpened when it is posed as a question of salvation. How can man attain the capacity and power which will lift him above the fate of mortality, or — in Hellenistic terms — will redeem him from the bondage of matter, and thus impart to him immortality? This poses the question of a power of salvation. A comprehensive answer is given to this question in tract. 13 of the Corp. Herm., in the λόγος παλιγγενεσίας. The situation of man is described in the twelve τιμωρίαι: ἄγνοια, λύπη, ἀκρασία, ἐπιθυμία, ἀδικία, πλεονεξία, ἀπάτη, φθόνος, δόλος, ὀργή, προπέτεια, κακία.

---

[22] F. X. Steinleitner, *Die Beicht im Zusammenhang mit der sakralen Rechtspflege in der Antike* (Diss. Munich, 1913). Cf. esp. 79 f., 112, 116.

[23] Instances are P. Oxy., XI, 1381, 42: διηγεῖσθαι δυνάμεις; 90 f.: τὰς αὐτοῦ φρικτὰς δυνάμεις ἀπαγγέλειν. Steinleitner No. 3: ἐνεγράψαμεν τὰς δυνάμεις τοῦ θεοῦ; No. 8: ἐστηλλογράφησα τὰς δυνάμεις ὑμῶν; cf. 9, 18, 21. → ἀρετή, ἀρεταί is more common than δύναμις in these contexts (I, 457 ff.). Cf. A. Kiefer, *Aretalogische Studien* (Diss. Freiburg, 1929), esp. 18-22, and bibl.

In this situation man is lost. This situation, wherein man is controlled by these twelve τιμωρίαι, which are related to the zodiac, poses the question of a power which can liberate and save. This saving power consists in the ten saving forces which enter into man and effect the γένεσις τῆς θεότητος : γνῶσις, χαρά, ἐγκράτεια, καρτερία, δικαιοσύνη, κοινωνία, ἀλήθεια, ἀγαθόν, φῶς, ζωή. These δυνάμεις, which enter into man from without in the mystery, bring about his deification. It is for this reason that the mystagogue greets the initiate : χαῖρε λοιπόν, ὦ τέκνον, ἀνακαθαιρόμενος ταῖς τοῦ θεοῦ δυνάμεσιν εἰς συνάρθρωσιν τοῦ λόγου (Corp. Herm., XIII, 7 f.). [24] The situation is rather different in the well-known Mithras Liturg., which contains the introduction : μύσται τῆς ἡμετέρας δυνάμεως ταύτης ἣν ὁ μέγας θεὸς Ἥλιος Μίθρας ἐκέλευσέν μοι μεταδοθῆναι ... ὅπως ἐγὼ μόνος αἰτητὴς οὐρανὸν βαίνω καὶ κατοπτεύω πάντα (Preis. Zaub., IV, 478 ff.). δύναμις is here the power for the heavenly journey and the vision of God. It is imparted through the initiation. In this sense it thus denotes the initiation which effects deification. [25]

In the first tract. of the Corp. Herm., in Poimandres, there is a different view. Here again the question of salvation is posed by the situation of man. The initiate thus prays : ἐνδυνάμωσόν με (I, 32). Endowed with γνῶσις — for γνῶσις is the saving power — the initiate is ὑπ' αὐτοῦ (sc. λόγου) δυναμωθείς (I, 27). What δυναμοῦν with gnosis accomplishes through the logos, however, is the deification attained by the incorporation of the initiate into the divine system of forces as the δύναμις. [26] After the journey through the girdle of the planets, in which he sets aside the qualities which condition and bring about mortality, he attains ἐπὶ τὴν ὀγδοαδικὴν φύσιν τὴν ἰδίαν δύναμιν ἔχων καὶ ὑμνεῖ σὺν τοῖς οὖσι τὸν πατέρα ... καὶ ὁμοιωθεὶς τοῖς συνοῦσιν ἀκούει καί τινων δυνάμεων ὑπὲρ τὴν ὀγδοαδικὴν φύσιν οὐσῶν φωνῇ τινι ἰδίᾳ ὑμνουσῶν τὸν θεόν. καὶ τότε τάξει ἀνέρχονται πρὸς τὸν πατέρα καὶ αὐτοὶ εἰς δυνάμεις ἑαυτοὺς παραδιδόασι καὶ δυνάμεις γενόμενοι ἐν θεῷ γίνονται. τοῦτο ἔστι τὸ ἀγαθὸν τέλος τοῖς γνῶσιν ἐσχηκόσι, θεωθῆναι (I, 26). The saving process is here taken up into the cosmic system of forces. Behind the whole Greek conception of power as thus far expounded there stands the idea of a natural force which, imparted in different ways, controls, moves and determines the cosmos, and which has its origin in widespread primitive notions of Mana and Orenda. [27]

B. The Idea of Power in the OT.

When we turn from the Greek and Hellenistic world to that of the OT, we enter a different atmosphere. In place of a neutral idea of God we have the personal God. In place of the neutral forces of nature we have the power and might of the personal God, which do not operate in terms of immanent law but which rather carry out the will of God according to His direction. This difference, based upon the whole conception of God, is plainly expressed in the concept of power.

The difference is the more significant because the OT itself contains traces of a natural and neutral idea of power and because this neutral idea, linked with a poly-

---

[24] On this thought → γνῶσις, I, 696, with n. 28, 29; → ἀλήθεια, I, 240.

[25] Cf. Grundmann, 85, n. 3; Mithr.-Liturg., 46 n. There are here references to the origin of this usage in the equation of δύναμις with means of healing, medicine, or means of magic, magic. Cf. also Joh. W. 1 K. on 1:18 ff.

[26] On the relationship of the δυνάμεις of the 1st and 3rd tract., cf. Grundmann, 85, n. 3; 45, n. 8. Here the thesis is advanced that in the δύναμις conception of Poimandres we have an infusion of pseudepigraphical Jewish elements into the mystical Gnostic circles of ideas.

[27] Cf. Grundmann, 26 ff., with bibliography in n. 32.

theistic view of deity, is found in Egypt,[28] from which part of the people of Israel came and where they had obviously been under the influence of prevailing notions. Personalistic elements in the conception of God are conjoined with dynamistic and manistic ideas[29] of a naturalistic character.[30] These are found in great profusion in the Egyptian view of power.[31] It is not surprising that these views, which undoubtedly stand so close to biblical religion, which are the common inheritance of all nature religions, and which are no less present in the religion of the Canaanites, should have left traces in the OT. Even after redaction the stories of the patriarchs give evidence of them. The ark with its singular powers reminds us of mana and similar phenomena. Certain cultic groups, sorcery and the conceptions of blessing and cursing have a manistic character.[32] Everywhere in the OT we see these traces of nature religion and foreign religion. The significant point, however, is that they are only traces, and that they are suppressed and transformed. A distinctive idea predominates. This is the most obvious feature.

The difference between the OT and the surrounding world is grounded in the distinctive relationship of the Godhead to history. As contrasted with the surrounding deities, which are essentially nature gods, the God of the OT is the God of history. The result is that the personalistic character of the idea of God is decisive, and that it absorbs the underlying naturalistic elements. This gives us the further result that the important and predominant feature is not force or power but the will which this power must execute and therefore serve. This is everywhere the decisive feature. But it necessarily brings us into the sphere of history, of which nature is the framework or setting. The reason why this is the decisive feature in religious development is that Israel is determined at the very beginning of its history by a historical event κατ' ἐξοχήν, by the Exodus from Egypt and the deliverance at the Red Sea. The concepts of power constantly recur in this connexion.[33]

A few examples may be given. The oldest is as follows: "Thy right hand, O Lord, is become glorious in power," Ex. 15:6; then v. 13: "With thy hand thou hast led the people which thou hast redeemed; thou has guided them in thy strength unto thy holy habitation." The same theme is introduced in Ex. 32:11. Dt. LXX describes the event in the stereotyped phrase: ἐν τῇ ἰσχύι σου τῇ μεγάλῃ καὶ ἐν τῇ χειρί σου τῇ κραταιᾷ καὶ ἐν τῷ βραχίονί σου τῷ ὑψηλῷ (Dt. 9:26, 29; 26:8; cf. also 4:37).[34] The chain of instances extends to 4 Βασ. 17:36; Bar. 2:11; ψ 76:14, 15.

---

[28] F. Preisigke, *Vom göttlichen Fluidum nach ägyptischer Anschauung* (1920); W. Spiegelberg, "Die ägyptische Gottheit der 'Gotteskraft'" in *Zeitschr. f. ägypt. Sprache*, 57 (1922), 145 f.

[29] Cf. A. Bertholet, *Dynamismus und Personalismus in der Seelenauffassung* (1930).

[30] Cf. Grundmann, 29/30.

[31] For examples, *v.* Preisigke → n. 28.

[32] Cf. A. Bertholet, *Das Dynamistische im AT* (1926), many instances being given. Cf. also J. Hempel, "Die israelitischen Anschauungen von Segen und Fluch," ZDMG, 79 (1925), 20 ff.

[33] In this connexion the Mas. uses כֹּחַ and עֹז, whereas the LXX almost always has → ἰσχύς, which particularly expresses the deployment of power and which is thus preferred in the LXX, δύναμις being very rare. All the same, the incident should be treated here because of its importance for the general context.

[34] As compared with the Mas., the LXX expands the formula into a stereotyped phrase with three members. → χείρ and → βραχίων are symbolic expressions for power, cf. Is. 9:11; 51:5, 9. *V.* also Preis. Zaub., IV, 519, 1279. Cf. O. Weinreich, "Antike Heilungswunder," RVV, 8, 1 (1909).

This happening at the beginning of the history of Israel is also the substance of its religion and leads to its concept of God, which is personalistic and historical. The view of power is interwoven into this concept. Of classical significance in this respect are the words set on the lips of Moses in Dt. 3:24 : κύριε ὁ θεὸς σὺ ἤρξω δεῖξαι τῷ σῷ θεράποντι τὴν ἰσχύν σου καὶ τὴν δύναμίν σου καὶ τὴν χεῖρα τὴν κραταιὰν καὶ τὸν βραχίονα τὸν ὑψηλόν. τίς γάρ ἐστι θεὸς ἐν τῷ οὐρανῷ ἢ ἐπὶ τῆς γῆς, ὅστις ποιήσει καθὰ ἐποίησας σὺ καὶ κατὰ τὴν ἰσχύν σου; When the righteous of the OT are reminded of the power of God, they think of the act of God at the Red Sea which completed the Exodus. The power of God proved itself at a historically decisive hour apart from which there would be no worship of Yahweh and no Israel. The conclusion of the covenant clarifies the resultant obligation. It is a seal attached to the event of the Red Sea. It expresses the fact that Yahweh is Israel's God and Israel the people of Yahweh. Thus a historical event, experienced as the mighty act of God, is explained in terms of its great goal in history. The power of Yahweh, which is unique and incomparable, is to be declared to all nations. Israel is to be the people of Yahweh, and to obey and serve Him. This is the historical awareness of the OT (Jos. 4:23 f.; Ps. 77:15 f.; 145:12; Jer. 16:19 ff.). This awareness, which rests on the act at the beginning of history, includes faith in the further deployment of the power of Yahweh in history. For this reason, there is in the history of Israel continual resort to the power and assistance of Yahweh when needed in times of affliction, e.g., Is. 10:33; Neh. 1:10; Jdt. 9:8; 13:11; 3 Macc. 6:12. According to God's own will and purpose, His power shapes and fashions history. This is the aspect which, notwithstanding points of similarity, distinguishes the concept of God and therefore the concept of power in the OT.

> There is a direct echo of this historical root and of the historical distinctiveness of the OT concept of God in the divine designation יְהֹוָה צְבָאוֹת, which in the LXX is often rendered κύριος τῶν δυνάμεων as well as κύριος σαβαώθ and κύριος παντοκρά-τωρ. Yahweh is hereby represented as a king and lord surrounded by armies. When used for צָבָא, δύναμις means "host." The hosts which are subject to His will represent His power, gain His victories and thus fashion history. An instructive clue to what is meant by these hosts, which are the angels, is to be found in a concept which belongs to the period of Assyrian and Babylonian astrology. The astral deities are linked with the δυνάμεις (2 K. 17:16; 21:3, 5; 23:4 f.). The religion of Israel is distinguished from that of other peoples, according to Dt. 4:19, by its prohibition of worship of astral deities : ἃ ἀπένειμε κύριος ὁ θεός σου αὐτὰ πᾶσι τοῖς ἔθνεσι τοῖς ὑποκάτω τοῦ οὐρανοῦ : Israel prays to the true God, whereas He has allotted to the Gentiles the powers which make up His hosts. Thus OT religion at its best stands in complete contrast with heathenism from the very foundation of its belief in the God of history, as we can see from the continuation in Dt. 4:20 : ὑμᾶς δὲ ἔλαβε ὁ θεὸς καὶ ἐξήγαγεν ὑμᾶς ἐξ Αἰγύπτου ... εἶναι αὐτῷ λαὸν ἔγκληρον ...

The historical character of the view of God and of power determines also the relation to nature. All the gods were originally nature gods. Their powers were natural forces superior to man. Now Yahweh, the God of Israel, has natural features which may be detected in the OT. His appearance is linked with catastrophic volcanic phenomena (→ 239). In the Thunder-storm Psalm (29) His power is revealed in the storm : "The voice of the Lord is powerful ; the voice of the Lord is full of majesty" (v. 4) — this is the rolling of the thunder. On the other hand, the historical character of the worship of Yahweh, which is the distinctive feature, inevitably fashions and determines the natural aspects in a particular way. This is a long process from the standpoint of religious history. [35] The culmination is a belief in the Creator in which nature is essentially the theatre of history and in which it derives from the will and power of the Creator. This belief emerges clearly in the prophecy of Dt. Is. In Is. 40:26 we read: "Lift up your eyes on high, and behold who hath created these things, that bringeth out their host by number: he calleth them all by names by the greatness of his might, for that he is strong in power; not one faileth." God as Creator and Preserver of the world creates and upholds it by His Word, which, as it is the instrument and expression of His will, is also the instrument of His power. [36] This becomes the general OT conception. In the post-exilic sections of Jeremiah we have the saying of Yahweh: "I have made the earth ... by my great power and by my outstretched arm, and I give it unto whom it seems meet unto me" (27:5). A prayer begins with the corresponding words: "Thou, Yahweh, my Lord, hast made the heaven and the earth by thy great power and stretched out arm" (32:17). These passages both stand in historical contexts, and they show plainly that the power of God which fashions history is the same as that which creates and sustains the world.

As this power of Yahweh shapes history and has created and sustains the world, so it affects the individual destinies of human life. A third question alongside that of God and history and God and nature is the question of God and man. The superior power of Yahweh is extolled in Job 12:13, 16: "With him is wisdom and strength; he hath counsel and understanding ... with him is strength and wisdom; he hath understanding and insight." The might and power of Yahweh are revealed in the fact that He holds all things in His hand, effecting all things and doing all things. This is illustrated by examples from history and nature, and from human life. It means that in every national or individual need, crisis or difficulty we should turn to Yahweh and His helping power. God is the One who gives power and strength to His people (Ps. 86:16; cf. Dt. 8:17 f.; Is. 41:10). Of those who fulfil the will of Yahweh revealed in the Law the Psalmist says: "They go from strength to strength" (Ps. 84:7). It may thus be said: "God is our refuge and strength" (Ps. 46:1).

> The concept of power is closely related to other concepts which illustrate the nature of God. His power is not caprice; it is the expression of His will and is thus determined by the content of His will, which consists in righteousness. "Yahweh shall be exalted in judgment, and the holy God in righteousness" (Is. 5:16). Judgment and righteousness correspond in the moral sphere to holiness in the religious. The power of God constitutes the inner energy of holiness and gives it the character of the inaccessible and transcendent. The power constituted of holiness and righteousness is effective as the power of judgment and grace. To the righteousness and holiness of God we should add His glory, [37] the manifestation, recognition, revelation and magnifying of which are effected by His power. "Who is this King of glory? Yahweh, strong and mighty, Yahweh mighty in battle" (Ps. 24:8).

Our review of the concept of power within the totality of the OT view of God leads us to a unique conclusion. The natural basis is completely overcome. The

---

[35] Cf. A. Weiser, *Glaube und Geschichte im AT* (1931), 22 ff.

[36] This form of the belief in the Creator established itself as the distinctive OT form in face of adaptations of primitive cosmogonic myths. Cf. Grundmann, 17, n. 13.

[37] On the interconnexion of these concepts, cf. Grundmann, 20, n. 20.

power of Yahweh is completely different from mana and orenda. This makes possible a development of pure religion. Where the deity is identified with impersonal power, there is introduced into religious life a factor which distorts religion as a living personal relationship to God. This is the factor of magic, cultic ceremony and ritual action. On the other hand, where the idea of God breaks loose from notions of mana and orenda we have the true religious factor of prayer, sacrifice and obedience. In the first case one is dealing with the impersonal mana which can and must be controlled. The presupposition of this control is ritual action, and the means are magical incantations, instruments and ceremonies. Magic is the sum of the matter. In the second case one is dealing with the personal God with whom one may enter into relationship and whose will one must seek to influence. Here again there is a presupposition, i.e., conduct in accordance with God's will, and there are also means, namely, prayer and sacrifice. Religion is the sum of the matter. Only on a personal view of God is the frontier maintained between God and man, Creator and creature. Prayer and sacrifice are aware of this frontier; magic and deification remove it.

The uniqueness of the OT concept of God and of the associated view of power results in doxologies which have their place in the cultus and in prayer, and in epithets which express the power of God. Both of these are common in religious history and there are therefore parallels elsewhere. Yet they are distinguished in the OT by the OT view of power, and thus correspond to the statement in Ps. 145:4 : "One generation shall praise thy works to another, and shall declare thy mighty acts."

Doxologies are to be found in 1 Ch. 29:10-12; Ps. 21:13; 59:16; 68:32 ff.; 2 Ch. 20:6; Jdt. 16:16; Da. 3:37 f.; 4:32. [38] These doxologies are no empty form. In them there is the glow of joy in God, of passion, of experience of God. Epithets are δυνατός in ψ 88:8; Zeph. 3:17; δυνάστης in 2 Macc. 3:24; τῆς ἁπάσης δυνάμεως δυνάστης in 3 Macc. 5:51; θεὸς πάσης δυνάμεως in Jdt. 13:4; πάσης ἐξουσίας δυνάστης in 2 Macc. 3:24. [39] All these predicates are designed to express the might and strength of God.

C. Ideas of Power in Rabbinical and Hellenistic Judaism.

1. a. Awareness of the event at the beginning of the history of Israel as a peculiar demonstration of the power of God persisted in post-biblical Judaism. It was strengthened in the Maccabean wars in which, at a time of national danger, faith was rekindled in the powerful saving act of Yahweh at the commencement of Israel's history, cf. 1 Macc. 4:9-11; 3 Macc. 2:6. In the Rabb. period the great doxology in 1 Ch. 29:11-12, which magnifies the power of Yahweh, is characteristically explained as follows. Rabbi Shela says: "Thine, Yahweh, is the greatness," refers to the work of creation, of which it is said that "he doeth great things past finding out; yea, and wonders without number" (Job 9:10); "and the power," refers to the Exodus from Egypt, of which it is said that "Israel saw the great hand which the Lord displayed against Egypt" (Ex. 14:31), bBer., 58a. In respect of the same passage Akiba refers the greatness to the dividing of

---

[38] Cf. F. Horst, "Die Doxologien im Amosbuch," ZAW, NF, 6 (1929), 45 ff., where it is shown that the doxologies form part of the obligation of sacral law. On the historical aspects cf. E. Norden, Agnostos Theos (1913), 143 ff.; AOT, 13 ff., 241 ff.

[39] Cf. Grundmann, 25 for historical material.

the Red Sea and the power to the killing of the firstborn. The close association between the belief in God and this event emerges most clearly, however, in a Jewish passage in the great Paris magic pap., in which Yahweh is invoked in a way which differs from all similar invocations : "... who was revealed to Israel in a pillar of fire and a cloud by day, who delivered his people from Pharaoh and brought the ten plagues against Pharaoh because he would not hear him ... the great God of Sabaoth, before whom Jordan rolled back, and the Red Sea was parted that Israel might go through," Preis. Zaub., IV, 3033 ff. and 3052 ff. If in post-biblical Judaism the connexion is maintained between belief in Yahweh and history, though with a certain Rabbinic rigidity, the same is true of the connexion between belief in Yahweh and the creation. Indeed, we find here the OT view of the creation of the world by the Word of Yahweh as the instrument of His power. There is a particularly good example of this in Tg. Is., 48:13 with its parallelism of Word and power : "With my Word I have established the earth, and with my power I have suspended the heavens." The characteristic OT association of belief in Yahweh with the view of power is maintained in post-biblical Judaism. The individual can rely on this power of Yahweh. In M. Ex. on 15:2 we read : " 'My power,' that is, thou art a support and strength for all the dwellers upon earth." A significant point here is that we are obviously dealing with the personal power with which Yahweh supports men and sets Himself behind them.

b. At the same time, another line of development becomes noticeable which is particularly important in the NT. This is emphasis on the eschatological deployment of the power of God. There are intimations of this in the OT (Is. 2:19; 40:10; Ez. 20:33 etc.). The experience and insight that many things take place in this world that God does not will, and that by His will He has subjected the world to other powers which are hostile to His purposes, give rise to the hope and longing that God will demonstrate His power in a last great conflict, destroying His opponents and saving those who belong to Him. Thus the righteous wait for God to reveal Himself in His power and definitively to establish His dominion (e.g., Gr. En. 1:4).

Together with this expected demonstration of eschatological power there develops in post-biblical Judaism something which is not so apparent in the OT but which is to be found in the Hellenistic Greek world, namely, an essential belief in the power of demons represented in Judaism by Satan. The eschatological exercise of God's power is basically an overthrow of demonic powers. Between God and humanity there interpose themselves forces which partly fight against God and partly for Him, i.e., the forces of angels and demons. These bear different names, → ἀρχαί, → κυριότητες, → ἐκλεκτοί, → ἐξουσίαι, → θρόνοι, and also δυνάμεις. [40]

How the name δυνάμεις came to be applied to them is not clear. It is first found in Jewish writings [41] as an expression for angels. Its origin is probably to be sought in the title κύριος τῶν δυνάμεων, which we have already discussed above (→ 292). The δυνάμεις, which may be detached from God (cf. the passages mentioned, and also ψ 32:6; Is. 34:4; Da. 8:10), are the heavenly hosts, δυνάμεις being used for צְבָאוֹת. Behind this concept there obviously stands the idea of power. There are terms and notions present in the OT which make possible the assumption of spiritual powers. The term δυνάμεις is designed to express the power of angelic and demonic forces.

What are these δυνάμεις ? Or rather, now that we have shown that they are forces intervening between God and man, what is the nature of their power ? The pseud-

---

[40] Cf. B. Stade-A. Bertholet, *Theologie des AT*, II (1911), 375, with examples.
[41] The only non-Jewish instance is Corp. Herm., I, 26. Cf. Grundmann, 45 f.
[42] Cf. on this pt. O. Everling, *Die paulinische Angelologie u. Dämonologie* (1888), where there is material from the pseudepigraphical apocalypses. Everling tries to explain Paul's statements in the light of this material. Cf. also M. Dibelius, *Die Geisterwelt im Glauben d. Paulus* (1909).

epigraphical writings speak of "powers which are on the dry land and above the water" (En. 61:10); of "powers of heaven which go round in circles" (En. 82:8); of the "powers of motion" (4 Esr. 6:6). The reference is thus to natural forces personified as angels. Thus we read in bPes., 118a that Gabriel is set over fire and Jurqemi over the hail. In En. 40:9 we read of an angel which has precedence of all forces. [43] These powers and forces are intermediate beings between God and man and rule over the realm between heaven and earth. "The air He allotted to winged visible beings, and to other forces (δυνάμεις) which cannot be perceived at all; these are the host of incorporeal spirits ordered according to differences in rank," Philo Plant., 14. [44] Cf. also Spec. Leg., II, 45 : ὅπως αἰθεροβατοῦντες τὰς ἐκεῖ δυνάμεις περιαθρῶσιν. One part of these forces and powers belongs to God and constitutes His host. They share in the heavenly worship of God. "All the powers which were above in heaven received a command and a voice and a light like fire. They magnified him with one voice," En. 61:1; "Thou art the ineffably great power. All spiritual powers bring thee laud and praise," Vit. Ad., 28. The Jewish portion of the Paris magic pap. is influenced by this thought: "... him the whole heavenly force of angels and archangels extols," IV, 3050 f., as also Corp. Herm., I, 26: ... καί τινων δυνάμεων ὑπὲρ τὴν ὀγδοαδικὴν φύσιν οὐσῶν φωνῇ τινι ἰδίᾳ ὑμνουσῶν τὸν θεόν. The other section of these powers belongs to Beliar or Satan, who rules men by means of them. Human existence is the battlefield between angels and demons, between God and Satan.

On this idea cf. Tanch. Mishpaṭim, 19 (Warsaw, p. 106b): "It is said: 'He will charge his angels concerning thee.' And what angels are these? They are those which keep him from evil spirits ... for the whole world is full of spirits and demons." Jub. 10:6: Noah asks Yahweh: "Let them not rule over the spirits of the living, and let them have no dominion over the children of the just from now to all eternity." 10:8: Mastema, Satan, to God: "If none of them remain, I cannot exercise the dominion of my will over the children of men. For they are going to perdition and corruption before my face, for great is the wickedness of the children of men." If these passages do not add anything to the δύναμις idea, they give us a typical illustration of its application in the sphere of the demonic. The δυνάμεις are forces which demonstrate their power in human existence.

The formation of these ideas in Judaism goes back to oriental influences. Here we are on syncretistic territory (→ n. 44). Yet there is a significant distinction as compared with the Hellenistic development of ideas of the demonic (→ I, 288). In Hellenism we have the expression of forces present in the world which constitute a great nexus of

---

[43] Typical of the background of these ideas is Jub. 2:2 f.: "On the first day he created the heavens which are above, and the earth and the waters and all spirits which serve before him, and the angels of the presence, and the angels of holiness, and the angels of the spirit of fire, and the angels of the spirit of wind, and the angels of the spirit of the clouds, of darkness, of hail and of frost, and the angels of the voices of thunder and of lightning, and the angels of cold and heat and winter and spring and harvest and summer, and of all the spirits of all his works in the heavens and the earth and in all the depths of the deep and of darkness and evening and light and dawn and morning, which he hath prepared with the knowledge of his heart." Cf. bBer., 6a: "If the eye were given the ability to see, no one could stand before the mazziqin. Abbaje says: They are more numerous than we; they surround us as does the furrow the plot."

[44] In a typical division, which also shows how open is this field of demonology to syncretistic influences, the passage continues: "Of one part of them it is said that they enter into physical bodies and withdraw again at appointed times; of others, who share the divine constitution, that they have no connexion with the earthly sphere; of the purest that they dwell high above in the ether, being described by the philosophers of the Hellenes as heroes but very fittingly by Moses as the messengers of God, since as emissaries and messengers they intimate the kind gifts of the ruler to the subjects, and the needs of the subjects to the king." Cf. also Gig., 6 f.

power, a supreme power, of which spirits are emanations. Behind this whole conception stands a neutral view of God. In Judaism we are dealing with magnitudes authorised and created by God. Behind this conception stands a theistic view. This distinction applies also to Hellenistic Judaism. The supremacy of God is safeguarded. We have the same outlook on heathenism as in the OT (→ 292), namely, that heathenism worships these intermediate creatures of God and not the living God Himself. Typical is the interpretation of heathenism in Wis. 13:1 ff., where there is also an apology for the Jewish belief in God: μάταιοι μὲν γὰρ πάντες ἄνθρωποι φύσει, οἷς παρῆν θεοῦ ἀγνωσία, καὶ ἐκ τῶν ὁρωμένων ἀγαθῶν οὐκ ἴσχυσαν εἰδέναι τὸν ὄντα, οὔτε τοῖς ἔργοις προσχόντες ἐπέγνωσαν τὸν τεχνίτην. ἀλλ' ἢ πῦρ ἢ πνεῦμα ἢ ταχινὸν ἀέρα ἢ κύκλον ἄστρων ἢ βίαιον ὕδωρ ἢ φωστῆρας οὐρανοῦ πρυτάνεις κόσμου θεοὺς ἐνόμισαν ...; εἰ δὲ δύναμιν καὶ ἐνέργειαν ἐκπλαγέντες, νοησάτωσαν ἀπ' αὐτῶν πόσα ὁ κατασκευάσας αὐτὰ δυνατώτερός ἐστι.

c. The supremacy of God as the Creator and Lord of the world is maintained in Judaism even though angelic and demonic conceptions enter in and to some extent obscure the person of God. And the essence of God is found in His power. As the name of God retreats into the background in Judaism, being replaced by paraphrases, one of these descriptions is "power." Jesus uses this before the Sanhedrin in Jerusalem [45] (Mt. 26:64; Mk. 14:62; though cf. Lk. 22:69, where Lk. explains the expression for his Hellenistic readers, cf. Ev. Pt., 5, 18). When God speaks of Himself in the first person, "power" is again one of the terms used in the Targums, e.g., Tg. O. Dt. 33:26: "And my power is in the highest heaven." Tg. Jer. 16:19b translates the Heb. "to thee" by "to hear thy power." There is here no hypostatisation of the concept of power but a paraphrase of the name of God and the divine I. The fact that the concept of power could be used in this way shows us to what extent the essence of God consists in His power according to the view of Judaism.

The question of saving power was also raised in Judaism and received a typical answer. The Torah is saving power. It is said of it in M. Ex. 15:26: "The words of the Torah which I have given you are salvation and life for you." And the concept of power is associated with it. עֹז and תּוֹרָה are directly equated on the exegetical basis of Ps. 29:11. M. Ex. 15:13: "Thou hast led forth in thy strength" (Ex. 15:13): in the merit of the Torah which they should receive in the future. "Thy strength": this is none other than the Torah, as it is said: "Yahweh giveth strength to his people" (Ps. 29:11). M. Ex. 18:1: "He bringeth neither fire nor flood, but the Holy One, blessed be He! giveth the Torah to his people and his beloved, as it is said: 'Yahweh giveth might to his people' (Ps. 29:11)." Or again, M. Ex. 15:2; S. Nu., 42 on 6:26. It is a firm exegetical principle of the Rabbis that strength and the Torah are one and the same. [46] Cf. also Pesikt., 148a: "... the third vestment (i.e., which God put on) to give the Torah was of power." The Torah is power because it is the cosmic order with which God creates and sustains the world, because by it He directs Israel, because He gives to those who do it sanctification and power, i.e., a share in the coming world. In Jewish existence the Torah becomes saving power as the revelation of the will of God.

2. The concept of power in Philo demands special attention. What Rabbinic Judaism avoided, namely, making power into an independent hypostasis in consequence of the growing emphasis on the divine transcendence and the consequent shunning of the name of Yahweh (→ supra), is found in the Hellenistic Judaism of Philo. [47] If in Rabbinic

---

[45] Cf. Dalman WJ, 164; Str.-B., I, 1006. Ev. Pt., 19: ἡ δύναμίς μου, ἡ δύναμίς μου as the cry of Jesus on the cross.
[46] Cf. W. Grundmann, ZNW, 32 (1933), 53 ff.; also Begriff der Kraft, 86 f.
[47] Cf. E. Bréhier, Les Idées Philosophiques et Religieuses de Philo d'Alexandrie (1926), 136 ff.; H. Windisch, Die Frömmigkeit Philos (1909), 46 ff.; Grundmann, 35 ff.

Judaism God even in His perfect transcendence was still a living person, in the Hellenised Judaism of Philo He is pure being in this perfect transcendence. It was because the Hellenisation of Judaism in Philo had to a large extent Hellenised the concept of God that the power of God could itself become a hypostasis. The same path had been trodden already in the Wisdom literature in relation to wisdom, which became almost the feminine element alongside the deity. Of this wisdom it is said in connexion with the δύναμις of God: ἀτμὶς γάρ ἐστι τῆς τοῦ θεοῦ δυνάμεως καὶ ἀπόρροια τῆς τοῦ παντοκράτορος δόξης εἰλικρινής ... μία δὲ οὖσα πάντα δύναται ..., Wis. 7:25 f. We find a similar relationship between wisdom and power in Philo: ἡ γὰρ ἀκρότομος πέτρα ἡ σοφία τοῦ θεοῦ ἐστιν, ἣν ἄκραν καὶ πρωτίστην ἔτεμεν ἀπὸ τῶν ἑαυτοῦ δυνάμεων, ἐξ ἧς ποτίζει τὰς φιλοθέους ψυχάς, Leg. All., II, 86. In Philo the powers take up a middle role between God and man.

The relationship between God and the powers is defined in such a way that on the one side God in His unity with them is supreme power — this is the Jewish element in Philo's view of God — : θεὸς δ' ἡ ἀνωτάτω καὶ μεγίστη δύναμις ὢν οὐδενός ἐστι χρεῖος, Vit. Mos., I, 111, and yet on the other the powers are independent of God and God withdraws behind them: ... τὸν ἀνωτάτω εἶναι θεόν, ὃς ὑπερκέκυφε τὰς δυνάμεις ἑαυτοῦ καὶ χωρὶς αὐτῶν ὁρώμενος καὶ ἐν αὐταῖς ἐμφαινόμενος, Sacr. AC, 60. The powers distinct from God are linked with the Logos, the ἡνίοχος τῶν δυνάμεων, Fug., 101, which God ἐκπεπλήρωκεν ὅλον δι' ὅλων ἀσωμάτοις δυνάμεσιν, Som., I, 62. As hypostases of God they belong to the eternal world of God, ... ἄφθαρτον ... κλῆρος εἰλήχασι, Cher., 51. The δυνάμεις divide into two main powers, the δύναμις ποιητική and the δύναμις βασιλική, the πρεσβύταται καὶ ἀνωτάτω δύο τοῦ ὄντος δυνάμεις. With these powers are linked the names of God according to their efficacy. According to the ποιητική, καθ' ἣν ἔθηκε καὶ ἐποίησε καὶ διεκόσμησε τόδε τὸ πᾶν, He is called θεός; according to the βασιλική, ᾗ τῶν γενομένων ἄρχει καὶ σὺν δίκῃ βεβαίως ἐπικρατεῖ, He is called κύριος (Vit. Mos., II, 99). The power-hypostases are thus the power which creates and directs the world. As Philo's view of God receives an ethical trait from the biblical conception of God, so, too, does his view of power. Of the κοσμοποιητικὴ δύναμις it is said: πηγὴν ἔχουσα τὸ πρὸς ἀλήθειαν ἀγαθόν (Op. Mund., 21). On the basis of this ethical trait in the view of God and of power, the powers have specific ethical functions: τῶν γὰρ περὶ τὸν θεὸν δυνάμεων ἀρίστων πασῶν μία οὖσα ταῖς ἄλλαις ἰσότιμος ἡ νομοθετική ... διχῇ πέφυκε τέμνεσθαι, τῇ μὲν εἰς εὐεργεσίαν κατορθούντων, τῇ δὲ εἰς κόλασιν ἁμαρτανόντων (Sacr. AC, 131). Their purpose is καθαγιάσαι καὶ καθιερῶσαι (Cher., 106). As νομοθετικὴ δύναμις, power embraces the προστατικὴ τῶν ποιητέων and the ἀπαγορευτικὴ τῶν μὴ ποιητέων (Fug., 104) in one; it is at the same time δύναμις ἵλεως, δύναμις σωτήριος or δύναμις εὐεργέτις — ἀεὶ γάρ ἐστιν ἐπιμελὲς αὐτῷ καὶ ταῖς εὐεργέτισιν αὐτοῦ δυνάμεσι τὸ πλημμελὲς τῆς χείρονος οὐσίας μεταποιεῖν καὶ μεθαρμόζεσθαι πρὸς τὴν ἀμείνω (Spec. Leg., IV, 187), and δύναμις κολαστήριος. ἔστι δὲ καὶ ἡ κόλασις οὐκ ἐπιζήμιον, ἁμαρτημάτων οὖσα κώλυσις καὶ ἐπανόρθωσις (Conf. Ling., 171). The powers thus serve the one goal of overcoming human pollution and they have their source in the holy goodness of God. E. Bréhier finely sums up as follows the distinction from Greek Hellenistic conceptions: "Chez les Stoïciens la puissance a avant tout une signification cosmique. Il s'agit d'une explication physique de la nature. Nous avons vu, au contraire, que les puissances acquièrent ici leur plein sens par le rapport à l'âme humaine." [48]

The roots of the Philonic view of power lie partly in Judaism (the ethical traits and expositions, the thought of a power which creates and directs the world), and partly in the Hellenistic Greek world (the autonomy of the power of God in relation to the powers as hypostases, the severance of the OT concept of power from history). Philo himself draws attention to one of the sources of his teaching. This is the Platonic notion

---

[48] Bréhier, 150.

of ideas: διὰ τούτων τῶν δυνάμεων ὁ ἀσώματος καὶ νοητὸς ἐπάγη κόσμος, τὸ τοῦ φαινομένου τούτου ἀρχέτυπον, ἰδέαις ἀοράτοις συσταθείς, ὥσπερ οὗτος σώμασιν ὁρατοῖς (Conf. Ling., 172); cf. also Spec. Leg., I, 47 f.: τοιαύτας ὑπολ ηπτέον καὶ τὰς περὶ ἐμὲ δυνάμεις περιποιούσας ἀποίοις ποιότητας καὶ μορφὰς ἀμόρφοις καὶ μηδὲν τῆς ἀιδίου φύσεως μήτ' ἀλλαττομένας μήτε μειουμένας. ὀνομάζουσι δ' αὐτὰς ... τινὲς ... ἰδέας. Yet of itself this is inadequate to explain the central position of the powers in Philo and his system. This central position is plain in statements like the following: συνέχεσθαι μὲν τόδε τὸ πᾶν ἀοράτοις δυνάμεσιν, ἃς ἀπὸ γῆς ἐσχάτων ἄχρις οὐρανοῦ περάτων ὁ δημιουργὸς ἀπέτεινε (Migr. Abr., 181)... πανταχοῦ δέ, ὅτι τὰς δυνάμεις αὐτοῦ διὰ γῆς καὶ ὕδατος ἀέρος τε καὶ οὐρανοῦ τείνας μέρος οὐδὲν ἔρημον ἀπολέλοιπε τοῦ κόσμου (Conf. Ling., 136). The world is a great nexus of divine powers which create and sustain its life and being. Behind this teaching, however, stands the philosophy of Poseidonius (→ 288). In Philo's view of power this Hellenistic philosophy unites with the Jewish view of God.

D. The Concept of Power in the NT.

1. The Fact of Christ.

Like all other NT concepts, the concept of power is given its decisive impress by the fact of Christ. This sheds a distinctive light on the use, adoption and development of existing views. We must start, therefore, with the fact of Christ, and see what part is played in it by the concept of power.

There can be no disputing the link with the OT and Jewish picture of the Messiah. Of the OT Messiah Is. says that the spirit of counsel and strength rests upon Him (Is. 11:2). [49] He calls Him a mighty hero (9:5). [50] Micah compares Him with a shepherd and says that He will tend His flock in the strength (ἰσχύς) of the Lord (5:5). [51] In the Royal Psalm 110:2, which was understood Messianically, we read: "The Lord shall send the rod of thy strength out of Zion." [52] The might and power of the Messiah are most explicitly described in Ps. Sol. 17:24, 42 f., 47: "And gird him with might to defeat unrighteous rulers, to purify Jerusalem of the heathen who trample it to destruction ... God has made him strong in the Holy Spirit and wise in counsel with power and righteousness. And the good pleasure of the Lord is with him in strength and he will not be weak ... strong is he in his works and mighty in the fear of God." In all these passages the picture of the Messiah is that of the King. The power granted to Him is victorious power to defeat His enemies. It is the power confessed by the king of Israel: "For who is strong (LXX: ἰσχυρός, Mas.: אֵל) save the Lord? ... the mighty One (LXX: ἰσχυρός, Mas.: אֵל) who maketh me strong (LXX: κραταιῶν, Mas.: מְעוּזִּי) with strength (LXX: δυνάμει, Mas.: חַיִל)ʳ... and maketh me mighty (LXX: ἐνισχύσεις, Mas.: יזר) with strength (LXX: δυνάμει, Mas.: חַיִל) to battle" (2 S. 22:32, 33, 40; cf. Ps. 18:32, 39). The king attributes his success in battle to the power which Yahweh has given him. Messiah is thought of as a king like this, endowed with the strength of Yahweh.

There are also a few traces, however, of a line leading from prophetic power to the Messiah. Prophetic power is that which makes possible testimony to the Lord. Our chief example here is the confession of Micah: "I am full of power (LXX: ἰσχύς, Mas.: כֹּחַ) in the Holy Spirit, full of judgment and of might (LXX: δυναστεία, Mas.: גְּבוּרָה), to declare unto Jacob his transgression, and to Israel his sin," Mi. 3:8. Josephus

---

49 LXX: ἰσχύς, Mas.: גְּבוּרָה.

50 Mas.: אֵל גִּבּוֹר, LXX ℵc.a A: (θεὸς) ἰσχυρὸς ἐξουσιαστής.

51 LXX v. 5: ἰσχύς. Mas.: עֹז.

52 LXX ψ 109:2: δύναμις, Mas.: עֹז.

says of Michaiah ben Imlah: γνώσεσθε δ' εἴπερ ἐστὶν ἀληθὴς καὶ τοῦ θείου πνεύματος ἔχει τὴν δύναμιν, Ant., 8, 408. It is said of Moses in Ac. 7:22 : δυνατὸς ἐν λόγοις
καὶ ἔργοις αὐτοῦ. Along the same lines the NT speaks of John the Baptist in Lk. 1:17:
αὐτὸς προελεύσεται ἐνώπιον αὐτοῦ ἐν πνεύματι καὶ δυνάμει Ἡλίου ἐπιστρέψαι
καρδίας πατέρων ἐπὶ τέκνα καὶ ἀπειθεῖς ἐν φρονήσει δικαίων, ἑτοιμάσαι κυρίῳ
λαὸν κατεσκευασμένον. The infin. define the task for which the power is given as
prophetic. But the prophetic character is also expressed in the ἐν πνεύματι καὶ δυνάμει Ἡλίου. Mal. 3 is fulfilled : Elias has come again. The Messianic age dawns.
δύναμις here is not miraculous power but operative power. [53]

Lk. sees the Messiah in terms of prophetic power. The witness of the two who
went to Emmaus concerning Him is as follows : ἀνὴρ προφήτης δυνατὸς ἐν ἔργῳ
καὶ λόγῳ (cf. Ac. 7:22 of Moses : δυνατὸς ἐν λόγοις καὶ ἔργοις αὐτοῦ)
ἐναντίον τοῦ θεοῦ καὶ παντὸς τοῦ λαοῦ (Lk. 24:19). The royal power which
originally determined the picture of the Messiah is now less evident than the
prophetic. We have here a reflection of the repudiation by Jesus of the royal
ideal of the Messiah in its OT and Jewish form. The verdict of Lk. expressed on
the road to Emmaus rests on historical recollections. Yet Christ is more than a
Prophet endowed with power. He is unique in His existence. His existence is
peculiarly determined by the power of God.

This is the most important feature in the Lucan infancy story, which describes the
conception and birth of Jesus as a miracle of incarnation in the power of God : πνεῦμα
ἅγιον ἐπελεύσεται ἐπὶ σέ, καὶ δύναμις ὑψίστου ἐπισκιάσει σοι· διὸ καὶ τὸ
γεννώμενον ἅγιον κληθήσεται υἱὸς θεοῦ (1:35). Lk. is here describing the conception of Jesus as the miracle of the Virgin Birth. In the parallelisms πνεῦμα ἅγιον/
δύναμις ὑψίστου we have "chastely veiled expressions for the divine miracle which
causes pregnancy." [54] In contrast to similar stories of the birth of divine offspring, [55]
nothing is said concerning the mode of the conception. In the background stands the
biblical conception of the God who begets His Son by a verbal act which cannot be
rationalised, so that the incarnation begins with a conception which transcends the
normal processes of generation. For this reason the Son has a special name not borne by
other men, namely, υἱὸς θεοῦ. [56] The fact that behind the birth story there stands the
biblical concept of God and His verbal act does not prevent the act in question from
having a substantial character. For Lk. δύναμις has the character of a substance. [57]
Hence the Lucan view seems to be that the pregnancy is induced in Mary by her endowment with the substance of power. We may thus say that, while Lk. sees Christ in
terms of the prophetic view of power, he also perceives at the beginning of His existence
a special and unique act of divine power which gives Him the title υἱὸς θεοῦ.

---

[53] Kl. Lk., ad loc.

[54] B. Weiss, Komm. z. Lukasev.[6] (1901), ad loc.

[55] For relevant material cf. E. Norden, Geburt des Kindes (1924); H. Leisegang, Pneuma
Hagion (1922), 24 ff.; K. Bornhäuser, Geburts- und Kindheitsgeschichte Jesu (1931), 81 ff.;
H. v. Baer, Der Heilige Geist in den Lukasschriften (1926), 124 ff., where further lit. is
listed. Cf. also the Comm.

[56] H. v. Baer rightly points out that the Greek Hellenistic element in Lk. is the linking
of the Messianic title "Son of God" with the miracle of conception and birth. Perhaps one
might say, not that He is the Son of God because His birth is miraculous, but that His birth
is miraculous because He is the Son of God. The Lucan story does not read like a Hellenistic cult-legend.

[57] The conception of δύναμις as a substance is in line with manistic notions. This
question is treated esp. by F. Preisigke, Die Gotteskraft der frühchristlichen Zeit (1926).

On the basis of the miraculous beginning of His existence Jesus is equipped with special power and is the Bearer of power. Lk. portrays Him as such: καὶ ὑπέστρεψεν ὁ Ἰησοῦς ἐν τῇ δυνάμει τοῦ πνεύματος εἰς τὴν Γαλιλαίαν (4:14); and: ἐν ἐξουσίᾳ καὶ δυνάμει ἐπιτάσσει τοῖς ἀκαθάρτοις πνεύμασιν (4:36). His activity is the exercise of power in relation to the demonic powers of the world. He has His power in the Holy Spirit, the Spirit and power being indissolubly related for Lk.[58] In His power He expresses His ἐξουσία.[59] The Spirit, who makes it plain that His existence is from God and who unites His existence with God, includes endowment with power in this origin of His existence and union of His existence. As the essence of God is power, so endowment with power is linked with the gift of His Spirit. Endowment with the Spirit gives Him ἐξουσία, a definite personal authority which He has, in substantial terms, the δύναμις to exercise. Relevant in this connexion is the story of the woman with a flux of blood, in which the power of Jesus is represented as the saving power which overcomes the demonic power of sickness.

In the Lucan version, which deviates from the Matthean,[60] it is a good illustration of Luke's conception of power as substance: ... ἐγὼ ... ἔγνων δύναμιν ἐξεληλυθυῖαν ἀπ' ἐμοῦ (8:46).[61] Here is a special application of the general conception of the saving activity of Jesus, of which it is said, characteristically in a Lucan setting: ... καὶ δυνάμις κυρίου ἦν εἰς τὸ ἰᾶσθαι αὐτόν (5:17); ... δύναμις παρ' αὐτοῦ ἐξήρχετο (6:19). Everywhere δύναμις without the article is used for the substance of power which effects salvation. Thus Jesus is for Lk. the Bearer of power in the absolute. The witness of His disciples is: ἔχρισεν αὐτὸν ὁ θεὸς πνεύματι ἁγίῳ καὶ δυνάμει (Ac. 10:38). Jesus Christ is thus a divine miracle, not merely in relation to the beginning of His existence, but in His existence generally.

Alongside this special usage, Lk. also has the general Synoptic usage which describes the miracles of Jesus as δυνάμεις, acts of power.[62] The expression δυνάμεις for acts of power occurs elsewhere and is here applied to the miracles. These are called δυνάμεις or δύναμις in Mt. 11:20 ff. and par. in Jesus' own words to Chorazin, Bethsaida and Capernaum (a saying which attests awareness of the unique character of these miracles); in Mt. 13:58 in relation to the lack of miracles at Nazareth (Mk. 6:2, 5, where 2: καὶ αἱ δυνάμεις τοιαῦται διὰ τῶν χειρῶν αὐτοῦ γινόμεναι ..., indicates the special character of His miracles, and 5 is par. to Mt. 13:58); in Lk. 19:37 in the extolling of His miracles by the crowds; in Ac. 2:22: ... Ἰησοῦν τὸν Ναζωραῖον, ἄνδρα ἀποδεδειγμένον ἀπὸ τοῦ θεοῦ εἰς ὑμᾶς δυνάμεσι καὶ τέρασι καὶ σημείοις ..., where Peter supports his assess-

---

[58] Cf. on this pt. v. Baer.

[59] In the ἐξουσία concept the substantial character of the δύναμις concept, which derives from the personal relationship to God, is limited (→ ἐξουσία). Cf. Grundmann, 57 ff. The term ἐξουσία is particularly common in Mt.

[60] In Mt. the woman is healed by the saying of Jesus: "Thy faith hath saved thee" (Mt. 9:20-22). Cf. Grundmann, 63, n. 10.

[61] The Marcan version runs: ὁ Ἰησοῦς ἐπιγνοὺς ἐν ἑαυτῷ τὴν ἐξ αὐτοῦ δύναμιν ἐξελθοῦσαν (5:30). Preisigke relies on this in the work mentioned in n. 57.

[62] → 289, n. 23. Apart from the Hell. references given there, one should also note the OT ψ 117:16: δεξιὰ κυρίου ἐποίησε δύναμιν (יְמִין יְהוָה עֹשָׂה חָיִל), also Dt. 3:24: גְּבוּרֹתֶךָ (not the LXX), and in Rabb. lit. גְּבוּרֹת, M. Ex. 15:11; S. Dt., 337. There is nothing in Joseph.

ment of Jesus by appeal to His known miracles. The miracles of Jesus are actualisations of the particular power which goes along with His existence.

Jesus is not the only one in His day to work miracles. [63] The Hellenistic and Jewish world is full of miraculous happenings and gods and miracle-workers. The miracles of Jesus are distinguished in three ways from those of the period. a. The NT miracles of Jesus have no connexion with magic, or with magic means and processes, like the majority of miracles outside the NT. [64] The biblical concept of God forbids this. Schlatter notes that Jesus had a view of God which "does not allow His dependence on the means employed by the magician." [65] b. The miracles are evoked by the powerful Word of Jesus, which has nothing to do with magic. On the contrary, He provokes defensive magic [66] against Himself which He overcomes with His Word of power. [67] In all His words He speaks "from the mouth of omnipotence," [68] and thus overcomes the kingdom of demonic powers ruling in sickness, sin and death. This brings us to the heart of the NT view. The miracles of Jesus are part of the invading dominion of God which Jesus brings with His own person in proclamation and act. They are the dominion of God overcoming and expelling the sway of demons and Satan. Like the whole history of Jesus, His miracles are an eschatological event (→ ἁμαρτάνω, I, 304; → δεῖ, 23; → ἰσχυρός). This shows us the decisive difference from all the other miraculous happenings with which they might have superficial resemblances. The history of Jesus is the history of Christ because the kingdom of God comes with Him. c. The miracles presuppose the faith of the One who performs them and also of the one on whom they are performed. They are thus accomplished in a wholly personal relationship. Jesus can do no miracles in Nazareth because faith is lacking (Mt. 13:58 and par.). The disciples cannot heal the boy because they do not have faith (Mk. 9:14 ff.). Hence there is no place for magic. It is not the knowledge of magic media and formulae, but the personal relationship between God and Jesus on the one side and Jesus and men on the other which works the miracle with no magical compulsion. In faith all things are possible and therefore there is all

---

[63] Cf. O. Weinreich, *Antike Heilungswunder* (1909); *Neue Urkunden zur Sarapisreligion* (1918); R. Herzog, *Die Wunderheilungen von Epidauros* (1931); R. Reitzenstein, *Hellenistische Wundererzählungen* (1906); A. Schlatter, *Das Wunder in der Synagoge* (1912); P. Fiebig, *Jüdische Wundergeschichten im neutestamentlichen Zeitalter* (1911). Preis. Zaub., IV, 2445 ff.: Pachrates of Heliopolis before Hadrian ἐπιδεικνύμενος τὴν δύναμιν τῆς θείας αὐτοῦ μαγείας.

[64] Cf. Grundmann, 65 ff. → 289.

[65] Schlatter, *Wunder in der Synagoge*, 84.

[66] Cf. O. Bauernfeind, *Die Worte der Dämonen im Markusevangelium* (1928).

[67] This is also true of miracles which have some of the features of magic (spittle, touch etc.). The substantial conceptions of magic are restrained in their outworking by the dominant outlook. The judgment of F. Fenner is correct: "In the NT the compelling force of the personality of the Healer is the decisive matter. The saving Word of Jesus either bursts or surmounts all inner barriers and thus brings salvation according to the stories of healing in the Gospels" (*Die Krankheit im NT* [1930], 96).

[68] Cf. Pesikt., 125b-126a: "... What is meant by 'before thy fellows'? The Most High, blessed be He! saith to him: All the prophets have prophesied, one prophet from the mouth of another. The Spirit of Elijah rested on Elisha (2 K. 2:15), the spirit of Moses on the 70 elders (Nu. 11:28). But thou shalt prophesy from the mouth of omnipotence: 'The Spirit of the Lord is upon me, because God hath anointed me to bring good tidings to the meek.'" This passage, somewhat abbreviated, is found in Str.-B., I on Mt. 7:29 (ἐξουσία).

power: πάντα δυνατὰ τῷ πιστεύοντι (Mk. 9:23 and par.).[69] In this faith the believer shares in the rule of God and therefore, either actively or passively, experiences miraculous power. Here we have the uniqueness of NT miracles.

Among the people these δυνάμεις evoke astonishment (Mt. 13:54) and praise of God (Lk. 19:37). They give rise to amazement and questioning. In this respect the verdict of Herod Antipas in Mt. 14:2 and Mk. 6:14 is typical. His bad conscience in respect of the execution of John causes him to think that John has risen again in Jesus, thus leading to the judgment: ... διὰ τοῦτο αἱ δυνάμεις ἐνεργοῦσιν ἐν αὐτῷ. This verdict gives an impression of the power of Jesus amongst His enemies. They cannot conceal the fact that unheard of deeds are done by him. But how is this verdict to be understood? Is Dalman right in suggesting that the Gk. is a bad translation of an Aram. original that "mighty deeds are done by him," which is a simple statement of facts?[70] Or are we to see an uneasy conscience disposed to superstition, and, in the light of the attitude of Herod towards Jesus Himself at the trial, when he expected magic to be performed by Him, to conclude that there is here expressed a magical and superstitious conception which implies the rendering that "magical powers are at work in him"?

The picture of Jesus in John is fully in line with that of the Synoptists. It is worth noting that in John δύναμις does not occur either in the sing. or the plur. But the matter itself is present. With → ἐξουσία[71] and → σημεῖον, which give us the Johannine view of power, we also have the verb δύνασθαι. The Synoptic Jesus, too, emphasises His ability as the expression of His capability or power, as when He says to the blind men in Mt. 9:28: πιστεύετε ὅτι δύναμαι τοῦτο ποιῆσαι. In Jn. however, this verb replaces the missing δύναμις in the sense of an act of power, with the emphasis shifting from the objective act to the subjective capacity. Nicodemus greets Jesus with the words: ... οὐδεὶς ... δύναται ταῦτα τὰ σημεῖα ποιεῖν ἃ σὺ ποιεῖς, ἐὰν μὴ ᾖ ὁ θεὸς μετ' αὐτοῦ, Jn. 3:2. The σημεῖα, which in Jn. are the acts of the Messiah, done out of the fulness of Messianic power (→ σημεῖον), are thus conceived as unique and incomparable acts. They express the particular δύναμις of Christ formulated in His δύνασθαι. This δύνασθαι is objectively interpreted by the "unless God were with him." His power is the power of God which He is given in fellowship with the Father who sent Him.

The question of Jesus' δύνασθαι arises in the story of the man born blind, which occurs in the middle of the Johannine *kerygma*. One section of the Pharisees is driven to admit: πῶς δύναται ἄνθρωπος ἁμαρτωλὸς τοιαῦτα σημεῖα ποιεῖν; Jn. 9:16. In the witness of the man himself we have the belief that the δύνασθαι of Jesus comes from God: εἰ μὴ ἦν οὗτος παρὰ θεοῦ, οὐκ ἠδύνατο ποιεῖν οὐδέν, 9:33. Finally, the resistance of the Jews is met by the question: μὴ δαιμόνιον δύναται τυφλῶν ὀφθαλμοὺς ἀνοῖξαι, the attribution of the power of Jesus to demonic powers being

---

[69] Psychologically the utterances of faith on the part of those who come to Jesus for healing have some affinities with the confidence displayed by those who come to Aesculapius (cf. Herzog, *Wunderheilungen von Epidauros*: *Wunder*, 37: ἐόντες εὐέλπιδες, or *Wunder* 75: εἰς δὲ τὸ θεῖον ἐλπίδα πᾶσαν ἔχων, or *Wunder* 3, where the one who at first does not believe is given the name of unbeliever after he has come to do so, or *Wunder* 4, where unbelief is called ignorance). The theological understanding, however, reveals a complete difference in the object to which it refers and in the interpretation which it is given by this reference.

[70] Dalman WJ, 164.

[71] Cf. Grundmann, 80-82.

thus rejected. From the act of Jesus it is presumed that His δύνασθαι is unlimited. At the grave of Lazarus the Jews say : οὐκ ἐδύνατο οὗτος ὁ ἀνοίξας τοὺς ὀφθαλμοὺς τοῦ τυφλοῦ ποιῆσαι ἵνα καὶ οὗτος μὴ ἀποθάνῃ, 11:37. Jesus fulfils the expectation by raising Lazarus, and thus demonstrates again that His δύνασθαι is unlimited. He acknowledges this when He binds the disciples to Him and says to them : χωρὶς ἐμοῦ οὐ δύνασθε ποιεῖν οὐδέν, 15:5. But He also sees clearly the source of His power : οὐ δύναται ὁ υἱὸς ποιεῖν ἀφ᾽ ἑαυτοῦ οὐδέν, ἂν μή τι βλέπῃ τὸν πατέρα ποιοῦντα, 5:19. It derives from the fellowship with the Father given Him by His regard for the work of the Father. For this reason His work is wholly at one with the work of the Father. His δύνασθαι is fully rooted in God : οὐ δύναμαι ἐγὼ ποιεῖν ἀπ᾽ ἐμαυτοῦ οὐδέν, 5:30.

The resultant Johannine portrait of Jesus is in full accord with the Synoptic, but brings out certain new features by making it perfectly clear a. that in the δύνασθαι of Jesus which leads to δυνάμεις we are dealing with the unique Christ event ; b. that the power expressed in this event is the active power of God which initiates the new aeon and which supports Christ in His whole existence.

The power of God which Jesus possessed is particularly demonstrated in the hour and event of His death. The overcoming of death in the resurrection leads Jesus Himself back to the power of God, as may be seen in His debate with the Sadducees, against whom He levels the charge : πλανᾶσθε μὴ εἰδότες τὰς γραφὰς μηδὲ τὴν δύναμιν τοῦ θεοῦ, Mt. 22:29. The demonstration is given. On the Day of Pentecost Peter says of the resurrection of Jesus to the Jews of Jerusalem : ὃν ὁ θεὸς ἀνέστησεν λύσας τὰς ὠδῖνας τοῦ θανάτου, καθότι οὐκ ἦν δυνατὸν κρατεῖσθαι αὐτὸν ὑπ᾽ αὐτοῦ, Ac. 2:24. The interesting point in this formulation [72] is the stating of the impossibility of Christ being held by death. Death could not exercise its dominion over Him. The power of death is thus broken generally by Christ. He has His life by the power of God. As the power of God empowered Him for His acts of power, so it empowered Him for the new life. This is the apostolic testimony after the resurrection. Paul says : τὸν κύριον ἤγειρεν ... διὰ τῆς δυνάμεως αὐτοῦ, 1 C. 6:14; ... ἐσταυρώθη ἐξ ἀσθενείας, ἀλλὰ ζῇ ἐκ δυνάμεως θεοῦ, 2 C. 13:4. In the resurrection of Jesus the power of God breaks through victoriously. If the death of Jesus seemed to be the victory of death even over Christ, so that Paul can speak of a σταυρωθῆναι ἐξ ἀσθενείας, the resurrection is the victory of God and His Christ over the power of death. This leads Paul to the twofold conclusion : ... τοῦ ὁρισθέντος υἱοῦ θεοῦ ἐν δυνάμει κατὰ πνεῦμα ἁγιωσύνης ἐξ ἀναστάσεως νεκρῶν, R. 1:14; and κηρύσσομεν ... Χριστὸν θεοῦ δύναμιν καὶ θεοῦ σοφίαν, 1 C. 1:24. R. 1:4 speaks of the divine sonship of Christ in the fulness of power by the resurrection, by which He also has life in the strict sense of the word. What He has by the resurrection is not divine sonship in general, but divine sonship in the fulness of power, compared with which the kenosis of the incarnation appears to be → ἀσθένεια. In 1 C. 1:24 Christ is called the power of God in the absolute. In His power, which overcomes all the might of darkness and death, He is the power of God. As such He is the theme and content of the Christian *kerygma*.

This passage stands in distinctive contrast to the well-known statement that Simon Magus was called ἡ δύναμις τοῦ θεοῦ ἡ μεγάλη (Ac. 8:10). The sorcerer was

---

[72] Cf. Wdt. Ag., *ad loc.* : "Death (personified as in 1 C. 15:26, 55 f.) is thought of as in travail because it cannot hold the Messiah. When God raises Jesus from the dead, He causes Him to be born to a new life (cf. Col. 1:18), loosing the pains of death."

supposed to be divine as an incarnation of divine power. In 1 C. 1:24 Christ is the δύναμις θεοῦ. The statement rests, as we have seen, on the divine action through Him. In both cases there is an underlying thought form, current at the time, by which concepts like δύναμις and σοφία in 1 C. 1:24, or ζωή, φῶς and ἀλήθεια in Jn., are thought of as personally active. [73] There are various linguistic analogies to the saying concerning Simon Magnus: ἐπικαλοῦμαί σε, τὴν μεγίστην δύναμιν τὴν ἐν τῷ οὐρανῷ, Preis. Zaub., IV, 1275 f.; on a Lydian inscr. the heavenly deity Men is called μεγάλη δύναμις τοῦ ἀθανάτου θεοῦ. [74] The analogies are most interesting linguistically, esp. in respect of the adjectives, and show us to what circles the Magus belonged. On the other hand, they break down materially because they do not illustrate actual identity between a concrete person and the concept. In this respect the statement concerning Simon Magus, who is a living man generally known, is parallel to that concerning Christ, who has traversed this earth and of whom there are still living witnesses, except that in the one case δύναμις is a substantial magical concept and in the other the expression of the power which works triumphantly in history and leads it to its goal, as in the OT and the NT.

Hb. describes the δύναμις of the exalted Christ as a δύναμις ἀκαταλύτου ζωῆς, 7:16, and therefore as a power which, having overcome mortality and corruption, is beyond the reach of mortality and corruption. With this power He is set at the side of God: φέρων τε τὰ πάντα τῷ ῥήματι τῆς δυνάμεως αὐτοῦ, 1:3. At the side of the Father He rules the world by His Word as the Bearer of power. The divine sees Him in His power, which is identical with His glory, in Rev. 1:16: ἡ ὄψις αὐτοῦ ὡς ὁ ἥλιος φαίνει ἐν τῇ δυνάμει αὐτοῦ. [75] To the eye of the divine His δύναμις is as light. [76] The perfected community joins in the hymn of praise: ἄξιός ἐστιν τὸ ἀρνίον τὸ ἐσφαγμένον λαβεῖν τὴν δύναμιν καὶ πλοῦτον καὶ σοφίαν καὶ ἰσχὺν καὶ τιμὴν καὶ δόξαν καὶ εὐλογίαν, Rev. 5:12. In this fulness of power the community on earth awaits His coming again in power, as He Himself envisages when He speaks of the coming of the βασιλεία τοῦ θεοῦ ἐν δυνάμει in Mk. 9:1 — the coming which is to complete the work which He has begun according to the saying: ἐρχόμενον ἐπὶ τῶν νεφελῶν τοῦ οὐρανοῦ μετὰ δυνάμεως καὶ δόξης πολλῆς Mt. 24:30 and par. In the apostolic proclamation Paul speaks of the ἀποκάλυψις Ἰησοῦ ἀπ’ οὐρανοῦ μετ’ ἀγγέλων δυνάμεως αὐτοῦ, 2 Th. 1:7. The return of Christ is the manifestation of the power which He has in His exaltation. It will thus mean the destruction of every hostile force and the perfect establishment of the rule of God κατὰ τὴν ἐνέργειαν τοῦ δύνασθαι αὐτὸν καὶ ὑποτάξαι αὐτῷ τὰ πάντα, Phil. 3:21. What is said here of the perfecting of man in the omnipotence of Christ applies also to the perfecting of the world.

2. The Power of God, Demonic Powers, the Power of Salvation.

The Christ event sheds light on the different connexions in which the concept of power came to be used at an earlier stage and in which it is still used in the NT.

---

[73] O. Bauernfeind, Worte der Dämonen (1928), Einleitung; Reitzenstein Poim., 222 ff.
[74] O. Schmitz, Der Begriff δύναμις bei Paulus (1927), 153.
[75] Cf. Ju. 5:31: Those that "love him are as the sun when he goeth forth in his might."
[76] δύναμις and δόξα (→ 247 f.) are found together in other passages. Cf. R. 6:4: ὥσπερ ἠγέρθη Χριστὸς ἐκ νεκρῶν διὰ τῆς δόξης τοῦ πατρός, and 1 C. 6:15 or 2 C. 13:4, → 304. The same act may be attributed either to the δύναμις or to the δόξα of God.

a. The power of God. We have recognised that there is the closest possible connexion between the power which is given to Christ and the power of God. The power of Christ is the power of God. There is here developed a line of thought already present in the OT in respect of the kingly and prophetic power of the Messiah. Jesus as the Christ is the unique Bearer of divine power. If Lk. conceived of this relationship of divine power and Jesus as its Bearer very largely in terms of endowment with a rather manistic neutral substance of power, in Mt. the ἐξουσία concept (→ 301, n. 59), which is found throughout the Synoptists and which also recurs in Jn., where it is given emphasis by the clear stress on fellowship, causes us to think of power much more personally in the sense of assistance. By personal fellowship Christ shares in the power of God. Even in Lk. the substantial category is intersected by the personal. Thus the power of Christ is always the power of God. As such, it is operative in history, and indeed as an eschatological event. Thus in the NT there is distinctive adoption of the OT view of the power of God active in history, shaping history and setting it its goal. The OT modes of thought and outlook, which centre on the divine action in history and on the setting of a goal for history in an exercise of divine sovereignty, recur in the NT and fashion the fact of Christ. In the Christ event the power of God which shapes history and leads it to its goal is active as an eschatological event.

Compared with this basic fact other statements concerning the power of God are relatively less important. The OT view of God is accepted. God is the Almighty. His omnipotence is revealed, according to the Christ event, in the victory over death : ἐκ νεκρῶν ἐγείρειν δυνατός, Hb. 11:19; cf. R. 4:21; cf. also Mt. 22:29 : πλανᾶσθε μὴ εἰδότες τὰς γραφὰς μήτε τὴν δύναμιν τοῦ θεοῦ. His power is not merely omnipotence but also omnicausality, i.e., a power which relates to the individual and his fate, cf. the Magnificat, where He is called ὁ δυνατός in virtue of this rule, Lk. 1:49; also 2 C. 9:8 : δυνατεῖ δὲ ὁ θεὸς πᾶσαν χάριν περισσεῦσαι εἰς ὑμᾶς, Hb. 2:18 : ... δύναται τοῖς πειραζομένοις βοηθῆσαι. Jesus, who uses the Rabbinic ἡ δύναμις for God (Mt. 26:64 and par.), expresses His omnipotence in the statement : παρὰ δὲ θεῷ πάντα δυνατά (Mt. 19:26 and par.), which is in line with the OT conviction (Gn. 18:14; Job 42:2; Zech. 8:6). In the NT, too, God is the Creator. The world is an expression of His power. Those whose eyes are open will perceive Him : τὰ γὰρ ἀόρατα αὐτοῦ ἀπὸ κτίσεως κόσμου τοῖς ποιήμασιν νοούμενα καθορᾶται, ἥ τε ἀΐδιος αὐτοῦ δύναμις καὶ θειότης (R. 1:20).

In this statement Paul is pursuing a line of thought common in Hellenistic Judaism. Perception of the Godhead and power of the invisible God in the works of creation is referred to in Wis. 13:1 ff. (→ 297), where it is shown that there is real guilt in man's not knowing God (cf. R. 1:20 f.). The same view is also found in Philo : ἀπὸ τοῦ κόσμου καὶ τῶν μερῶν αὐτοῦ καὶ τῶν ἐνυπαρχουσῶν τούτοις δυνάμεων ἀντίληψιν ἐποιησάμεθα τοῦ αἰτίου, Leg. All., III, 97; cf. Spec. Leg., I, 45 ff. and Op. Mund., 7. It is found again in Joseph. Cf. not merely the general passage Ap., 2, 192, but also 2, 167: "He (God) is represented by him (Moses) as uncreated and unchangeable to all eternity ; in beauty he surpasses every corruptible figure, and he is manifest to us through the operation of his power, even though we cannot know him in his essence." Cf. also Ep. Ar., 132.

The OT doxology is thus adopted in the NT and finds a place in early Christian prayer and praise.

At Mt. 6:13 several good MSS have: ὅτι σοῦ ἐστιν ἡ βασιλεία καὶ ἡ δύναμις καὶ ἡ δόξα εἰς τοὺς αἰῶνας. Rev. 4:11: ἄξιος εἶ, ὁ κύριος καὶ ὁ θεὸς ἡμῶν, λαβεῖν τὴν δόξαν καὶ τὴν τιμὴν καὶ τὴν δύναμιν ὅτι σὺ ἔκτισας τὰ πάντα καὶ διὰ τὸ θέλημά σου ἦσαν καὶ ἐκτίσθησαν; 7:12: ἀμήν, ἡ εὐλογία καὶ ἡ δόξα καὶ ἡ σοφία καὶ ἡ εὐχαριστία καὶ ἡ τιμὴ καὶ ἡ δύναμις καὶ ἡ ἰσχὺς τῷ θεῷ ἡμῶν εἰς τοὺς αἰῶνας τῶν αἰώνων. ἀμήν. Cf. 11:17 f.; 12:10 ff.; 19:1 f. These doxologies in Rev. imply acknowledgment and acceptance of the power of God which has an eschatological character, which destroys hostile powers and which brings the world to perfection: ὅτι εἴληφας τὴν δύναμίν σου τὴν μεγάλην καὶ ἐβασίλευσας, 11:17 f.; ἄρτι ἐγένετο ἡ σωτηρία καὶ ἡ δύναμις καὶ ἡ βασιλεία τοῦ θεοῦ ἡμῶν καὶ ἡ ἐξουσία τοῦ χριστοῦ αὐτοῦ, 12:10. This δύναμις, which is eschatological power, is already active in the Christ event. By it Christ has His miraculous existence (Lk. 1:35). It is at work in His activity (→ 300). This eschatological power is the historical power which brings the world and history to their goal.

b. The demonic powers. These are also seen in the light of the Christ event. The NT recognises δυνάμεις (→ 295) and is thus rooted in the Jewish and oriental outlook of the day. Jesus refers to the fact that in the eschatological catastrophe καὶ αἱ δυνάμεις τῶν οὐρανῶν σαλευθήσονται, Mt. 24:49 and par. It is a profitless controversy whether these are angelic or cosmic powers. The context makes it quite clear that they are cosmic. Just before there is reference to the sun and moon and stars being involved in the eschatological catastrophe. On the other hand, there are no cosmic powers which are not spiritual or angelic. These powers will be deprived of their strength with the cosmic catastrophe. Indeed, this has already taken place with the resurrection and exaltation of Jesus Christ. They will be publicly deprived of their strength when Christ publicly takes power at His return. The statements reflect this fact in its duality and tension, [77] which are distinctive of the NT and which give rise to its *kerygma*.

On the one side it is said: ... εἶτα τὸ τέλος, ὅταν παραδιδοῖ τὴν βασιλείαν τῷ θεῷ καὶ πατρί, ὅταν καταργήσῃ πᾶσαν ἀρχὴν καὶ πᾶσαν ἐξουσίαν καὶ δύναμιν, 1 C. 15:24, and on the other: ... ἐγείρας (sc. θεός) αὐτὸν (sc. Ἰησοῦν) ἐκ νεκρῶν καὶ καθίσας ἐν δεξιᾷ αὐτοῦ ἐν τοῖς ἐπουρανίοις ὑπεράνω πάσης ἀρχῆς καὶ ἐξουσίας καὶ δυνάμεως καὶ κυριότητος ..., Eph. 1:20 f., with which we should link 1 Pt. 3:22: ὅς ἐστιν ἐν δεξιᾷ θεοῦ, πορευθεὶς εἰς οὐρανόν, ὑποταγέντων αὐτῷ ἀγγέλων καὶ ἐξουσιῶν καὶ δυνάμεων. The exaltation of Christ implies already the disarming of all cosmic powers. [78] This is one part of the victory of Christ over sin and death and Satan. Here we see the δύναμις of God at work. It is given to Christians to perceive it: τί τὸ ὑπερβάλλον μέγεθος τῆς δυνάμεως αὐτοῦ εἰς ἡμᾶς τοὺς πιστεύοντας, Eph. 1:19. This is said in relation to the exaltation of Christ above all powers. It is a matter of recognising the greatness of the new act of God which underlies the existence of believers. For the existence of those who belong to Christ is newly established by the powerful act of God (δύναμις εἰς ἡμᾶς τοὺς πιστεύοντας). It is removed from the sphere of intermediary powers and set under the dominion of Christ. [79] For this reason the δυνάμεις can have no power over believers: πέπεισμαι γὰρ ὅτι οὔτε θάνατος οὔτε ζωὴ οὔτε ἄγγελοι οὔτε ἀρχαὶ οὔτε ἐνεστῶτα οὔτε μέλλοντα οὔτε δυνάμεις (οὔτε ἐξουσίαι, C 1 pm) οὔτε ὕψωμα οὔτε βάθος οὔτε τις κτίσις

---

[77] Cf. Grundmann, 79 f.

[78] Our statements are limited to δύναμις-δυνάμεις passages. Cf. also → ἀρχή, → ἐξουσία, → θρόνος, → κυριότης, → ἄγγελος. There is rich material esp. in Col. and Eph. → the bibl. in n. 42.

[79] Cf. Grundmann, 48 f., 73 ff., 107 ff.

ἑτέρα δυνήσεται ἡμᾶς χωρίσαι ἀπὸ τῆς ἀγάπης τοῦ θεοῦ τῆς ἐν Χριστῷ ᾿Ιησοῦ τῷ κυρίῳ ἡμῶν, R. 8:38 f.

All powers, cosmic and angelic, are robbed of their power over believers who are newly established in their existence by the ἀγάπη τοῦ θεοῦ. Thus the position of the δυνάμεις in the cosmos acquires a new character in the light of the Christ event.

For Christians the disarming of the powers by Christ leads to opposition in the final eschatological conflict. Revelation gives us the picture of Satan [80] endowing the state with strength and might to wage war on believers: καὶ ἔδωκεν αὐτῷ (the beast which rose up out of the sea) ὁ → δράκων (a symbolical expression for Satan) τὴν δύναμιν αὐτοῦ καὶ τὸν θρόνον αὐτοῦ καὶ ἐξουσίαν μεγάλην ... (Rev. 13:2). In face of his power the question arises: τίς ὅμοιος τῷ θηρίῳ καὶ τίς δύναται πολεμῆσαι μετ᾿ αὐτοῦ (13:4). Paul speaks of the antichrist to whom Satan gives power, depicting his entry as follows: οὗ ἐστιν ἡ παρουσία κατ᾿ ἐνέργειαν τοῦ σατανᾶ ἐν πάσῃ δυνάμει καὶ σημείοις καὶ τέρασιν ψεύδους (2 Th. 2:9). The reference in both cases is to the struggle against the existence of believers.

c. The power of salvation. The fact of Christ answers afresh the question of the power of salvation. τίς ἄρα δύναται σωθῆναι, the disciples ask Jesus in Mt. 19:26, thus raising the question of the ability and power to effect deliverance. The answer given by Jesus is the familiar reference to the omnipotence of God: παρὰ ἀνθρώποις τοῦτο ἀδύνατόν ἐστιν, παρὰ δὲ θεῷ πάντα δυνατά. The answer contains a double insight: first, that no power to save or to deliver is given to man, nor is it possible for man to attain such a power; and second, that such a power is grounded in the omnipotence of God alone, and must proceed from this. This insight is shared by the NT generally.

Paul speaks of the impossibility in R. 8:7: τὸ φρόνημα τῆς σαρκὸς ἔχθρα εἰς θεόν· τῷ γὰρ νόμῳ τοῦ θεοῦ οὐχ ὑποτάσσεται, οὐδὲ γὰρ δύναται· οἱ δὲ ἐν σαρκὶ ὄντες θεῷ ἀρέσαι οὐ δύνανται. In these words there is the sharpest possible criticism of the saving power of Jewish belief, i.e., the saving power of the Torah (→ 297): τῷ γὰρ νόμῳ τοῦ θεοῦ οὐχ ὑποστάσσεται, οὐδὲ γὰρ δύναται. But Paul goes further. Adopting the Jewish expression for the Torah (יהוה עז), he adds the criticism: ἡ δύναμις τῆς ἁμαρτίας ὁ νόμος (1 C. 15:56). By the Torah and its power the indefinite state of sin is actualised as transgression of the Law, and the dominion of death is established as the wages of sin [81] (→ ἁμαρτάνω, I, 310 f.). For this reason Paul calls it the ἀδύνατον τοῦ νόμου (R. 8:3) that it does not overcome sin and death. The Torah has no power of life, and therefore no salvation proceeds from it: εἰ γὰρ ἐδόθη νόμος ὁ δυνάμενος ζωοποιῆσαι, ὄντως ἐκ νόμου ἂν ἦν ἡ δικαιοσύνη (Gl. 3:21). Hb. finds a similar impotence in the Jewish cultus. Even sacrifice has no power to effect salvation. Hb. speaks of sacrifices αἵτινες οὐδέποτε δύνανται περιελεῖν ἁμαρτίας (10:11), and states: ἀδύνατον γὰρ αἷμα ταύρων καὶ τράγων ἀφαιρεῖν ἁμαρτίας (10:4). In relation to the achievement of salvation it is said of sacrifices: οὐδέποτε δύνανται τοὺς προσερχομένους τελειῶσαι (10:1). The general verdict of Jn. is: ἐὰν μή τις γεννηθῇ ἄνωθεν, οὐ δύναται ἰδεῖν τὴν βασιλείαν τοῦ θεοῦ (3:3, also 3:5). There is needed a new creation of man's existence by God. This new creation, which consists in faith in Christ, is wholly the affair of

---

[80] The idea of Satan is not linked with δύναμις in the NT, but with → ἰσχυρός, → ἐνέργεια, → κράτος, → ἐξουσία.

[81] Cf. Grundmann, ZNW, 32 (1933), 55 ff.

God: οὐδεὶς δύναται ἐλθεῖν πρός με ἐὰν μὴ ὁ πατὴρ ὁ πέμψας με ἐλκύσῃ αὐτόν (6:44; also 6:65). Jesus discloses the reason for man's impotence: οὐ δύνασθε ἀκούειν τὸν λόγον τὸν ἐμόν· ὑμεῖς ἐκ τοῦ πατρὸς τοῦ διαβόλου ἐστὲ καὶ τὰς ἐπιθυμίας τοῦ πατρὸς ὑμῶν θέλετε ποιεῖν (8:43 f.). The superiority of demonic and satanic power is the basis of man's inability to save himself.

The power to save and deliver is grounded only in the omnipotence of God and must proceed from it. The disciples who looked to Jesus knew that He brought the saving power of God and that they could attain it in Him. This is the NT and early Christian *kerygma*. The clearest statement is to be found in Paul's confession in R. 1:16: οὐ γὰρ ἐπαισχύνομαι τὸ εὐαγγέλιον τοῦ Χριστοῦ· δύναμις γὰρ θεοῦ ἐστιν εἰς σωτηρίαν παντὶ τῷ πιστεύοντι. Alongside this we may set the statement in 1 C. 1:18: ὁ λόγος γὰρ ὁ τοῦ σταυροῦ τοῖς μὲν ἀπολλυμένοις μωρία ἐστίν, τοῖς δὲ σῳζομένοις ἡμῖν δύναμις θεοῦ ἐστιν. The content is the same, ὁ λόγος ὁ τοῦ σταυροῦ being used instead of εὐαγγέλιον. Each of these is described as the δύναμις θεοῦ.

A. Dieterich [82] and J. Weiss [83] have advanced the thesis that the concept of power is used here as in the Mithras Liturgy (→ 288). In this, according to Dieterich, power means the dedication which mediates strength for the heavenly journey, for the vision of God and for deification. But surely the difference between this and R. 1:16 or 1 C. 1:18 is obvious. On the one side we have a power which, resting on mysterious presuppositions, mediates ecstasy, and on the other the very different power of God which, rooted in a historical act, brings deliverance. Here is also the answer to the even shallower view of J. Weiss, who uses only the first part of the expositions of Dieterich and who says of R. 1:16 that it refers to "an effective and successful direction to salvation" and of 1 C. 1:18 that "the cross of Christ is thought of as a powerful and tested means which God has given to men to liberate them from the power of demons" — it being quite overlooked that the reference is to the λόγος τοῦ σταυροῦ. Appeal to the usage of the Mithras Liturgy is thus of little value. Nor need we seek so far afield for an explanation of the Pauline statements. For in both of them Paul is adopting the well known equation of the Torah and עֹז יהוה (→ 297, 308). The only point is that the Gospel rather than the Torah is עֹז יהוה. The original antithesis leads to the positive assertion that the Gospel is the power of God.

In the message of Christ we thus have the power of God which is the power of salvation. The power of God in the Gospel consists in the fact that it mediates salvation, that by the Gospel God delivers man from the power of darkness and translates him into the kingdom of His dear Son. The δύναμις θεοῦ, which is the Gospel, is not an empty word. It is grounded in the divine act of deliverance in the Christ event, which overcomes the rule of Satan and which works itself out in the continued, factual deliverance accomplished by the preaching of the Gospel. In this context the δύναμις θεοῦ is the power of God, and therefore the power of salvation, which is at work in history, and specifically in the Christ event. It has its origin in a decisive divine act. When the Gospel is called the λόγος ὁ τοῦ σταυροῦ in 1 C. 1:18 (cf. 1:24), [84] this simply brings out the historical character

---

[82] Mithr. Liturg., 46 n.

[83] Joh. W. 1 K., *ad loc.*

[84] Between 1:18 and 1:24 there is a difference of emphasis, the λόγος ὁ τοῦ σταυροῦ being the δύναμις θεοῦ in the one, and Χριστὸς ἐσταυρωμένος in the other (→ 304). This difference, which raises no material problems, shows us clearly that in the proclamation of Christ God is acting through Him as He did through Him on earth.

of the Gospel. The same truth may be seen in Jm. 1:21: δέξασθε τὸν ἔμφυτον λόγον τὸν δυνάμενον σῶσαι τὰς ψυχὰς ὑμῶν. The Gospel is saving power. These statements are determined by the Judaeo-Christian understanding of word and history into which the concept of power is integrated.

On the other hand, in the description of the saving power of the Gospel in 2 Pt. there seems to be a Hellenistic understanding in terms of substance. In 2 Pt. 1:3 f. we read: ὡς τὰ πάντα ἡμῖν τῆς θείας δυνάμεως αὐτοῦ τὰ πρὸς ζωὴν καὶ εὐσέβειαν δεδωρημένης ... ἵνα ... γένησθε θείας κοινωνοὶ φύσεως, ἀποφυγόντες τῆς ἐν τῷ κόσμῳ ἐν ἐπιθυμίᾳ φθορᾶς. The power which is here called divine [85] denotes the necessities for life and piety which are given by the Gospel. And when we ask why they are given we can see the full impact of the Hellenistic conception, for they are given that we might be partakers of the divine nature. The power thus mediates participation in the divine nature. Conceived substantially, as in the Hellenist Luke, and qualified by the adj. "divine," the power mediates a divine substance by which participation in the divine nature is granted. The mediation takes place through the sacrament. We are thus in the sphere where sacramental action takes precedence of the word and faith.

3. The Power of the Disciple.

If the preaching of the Gospel as the δύναμις θεοῦ is the continuation of the saving activity of Jesus Christ, the preachers of the Gospel are logically the continuators of this activity. In fact the apostolate, which is commissioned to preach the Gospel, is grounded in the statement: "The messenger of a man is as the man himself" (→ ἀπόστολος, I, 415; 425). That is to say, the apostles stand in the place of Jesus and are as He is. The risen Lord associates Himself with them and gives them His power, in which they work. In the power of Jesus the apostles stand in the place of Jesus and continue His work.

Jesus already had disciples whom He sent out equipped with His power: ... ἔδωκεν αὐτοῖς δύναμιν καὶ ἐξουσίαν (Lk. 9:1). As the power of Christ, this δύναμις or ἐξουσία is superior to all demonic power: ἰδοὺ δέδωκα ὑμῖν τὴν ἐξουσίαν ... ἐπὶ πᾶσαν τὴν δύναμιν τοῦ ἐχθροῦ ... (Lk. 10:19). As we can see from Ac., [86] Lk. thinks in terms of a manistic endowment, just as He understood the power of Christ along these lines. That the power which the disciples receive is the power of Christ, and that as such it is the power of God, which they possess only in personal faith, is shown by the general Synoptic account of the healing of the epileptic boy in Mk. 9:14 ff. and par. Jesus expressly promises His disciples His own powerful presence in the Spirit: ὑμεῖς μάρτυρες τούτων. καὶ ἰδοὺ ἐγὼ ἐξαποστέλλω τὴν ἐπαγγελίαν τοῦ πατρός μου ἐφ᾽ ὑμᾶς· ὑμεῖς δὲ καθίσατε ἐν τῇ πόλει ἕως οὗ ἐνδύσησθε ἐξ ὕψους δύναμιν (Lk. 24:48 f.); ... λήμψεσθε δύναμιν ἐπελθόντος τοῦ ἁγίου πνεύματος ἐφ᾽ ὑμᾶς καὶ ἔσεσθέ μου μάρτυρες (Ac. 1:8). It is the same power as that which created His own ex-

---

[85] Elsewhere in the NT θεῖος occurs only in the typically Hellenistic Ac. 17:29. The strong dependence on the Hellenistic world of ideas has been strikingly demonstrated in Deissmann B, 227 ff. by reference to the inscr. of Stratonicea, which provides both material and linguistic analogies.

[86] The best commentary on Lk. 10:19 is Ac. 28:3-6. The point here is that the substance of power with which Paul has been endowed is stronger than the poison of the serpent. The same manistic notion is to be seen in Ac. 5:15 and 19:11 ff.

istence [87] and which He possessed during His ministry. He endows His disciples with this power, and they continue His activity in His place (→ I, 433). As Lk. records it, the endowment with power takes place at Pentecost. [88] From this time on the apostles continue the activity of Jesus, both proclaiming the Christian message (καὶ δυνάμει μεγάλῃ ἀπεδίδουν τὸ μαρτύριον οἱ ἀπόστολοι τοῦ κυρίου Ἰησοῦ τῆς ἀναστάσεως, Ac. 4:33) and also working miracles (cf. the healing of the lame man at the gate of the temple, which at once raises the question : ἐν ποίᾳ δυνάμει ἢ ἐν ποίῳ ὀνόματι ἐποιήσατε τοῦτο ὑμεῖς; Ac. 4:7, to which Peter and John, who do not claim to act ἰδίᾳ δυνάμει, Ac. 3:12, give the answer : ἐν τῷ ὀνόματι Ἰησοῦ Χριστοῦ ... οὗτος παρέστηκεν ἐνώπιον ὑμῶν ὑγιής, Ac. 4:10). [89] Lk. gives us a similar picture of Stephen, whom he depicts as πλήρης χάριτος καὶ δυνάμεως in Ac. 6:8. [90] This δύναμις is expressed in proclamation on the one side (6:10) and miracles on the other (6:8).

Paul fits the same pattern. His work is done ἐν δυνάμει σημείων καὶ τεράτων, ἐν δυνάμει πνεύματος, R. 15:19. In the preceding verse this power is attributed directly to Christ. It is in personal union with Christ that his work is done in the power of Christ. This power is expressed on the one side in miracles : ἐν δυνάμει σημείων καὶ τεράτων. There are many references to these in his epistles : τὰ μὲν σημεῖα τοῦ ἀποστόλου κατειργάσθη ἐν ὑμῖν ἐν πάσῃ ὑπομονῇ, σημείοις τε καὶ τέρασιν καὶ δυνάμεσιν, 2 C. 12:12; God ἐνεργῶν δυνάμεις ἐν ὑμῖν, Gl. 3:5; his activity in Thessalonica did not take place ἐν λόγῳ μόνον, ἀλλὰ καὶ ἐν δυνάμει καὶ ἐν πνεύματι ἁγίῳ, 1 Th. 1:5. The marks of an apostle, which show him to be genuinely sent by Christ, are δυνάμεις. He appeals to them in substantiation of his apostolate (→ I, 440). Alongside the power of miracles is the power of proclamation and edification: ἐν δυνάμει πνεύματος. Here we see the connexion between Spirit and power, [91] which we have already seen everywhere in Lk. The Spirit is the One who dispenses and mediates power. The Pauline concept of power is constructed from two different standpoints. On the one side πνεῦμα expresses the mode in which the exalted Lord is present and there is identification with Him. On the other, it expresses the corresponding mode of existence of believers. The unity of the two is to be seen in the synonymous use

---

[87] Lk. 1:35 : δύναμις ὑψίστου; 24:49 : ἐξ ὕψους δύναμις; Ac. 1:8 : δύναμις ἐπελθόντος τοῦ ἁγίου πνεύματος. The connexion between Spirit and power may be seen in all these passages.

[88] Cf. H. v. Baer, *Der Heilige Geist in den Lukasschriften* (1926), 77-108; 182-198. Grundmann, 94 f.

[89] Cf. also Ac. 8:13. The story of Simon Magus gives us a clear picture of the difference between the magical power possessed by Simon and the power of Christ, which comes under other categories. In this as in other passages (e.g., 13:8 ff.; 16:16 ff.) Lk. shows us that powers of magic are present, that they may sometimes be opposed to the power of Christ in the apostles, and that the apostles demonstrate the superiority of the power of Christ. The characteristic differences between the miracles of Jesus and those of the world around, which we delineated on → 302, apply to the miracles of the apostles also. In his individual narratives Lk. shows a clarity which we miss in his more comprehensive statements, e.g., Ac. 5:15; 19:11 ff. Cf. on this pt. Grundmann, 98, n. 7. In this respect Lk. himself offers us the key to historical criticism of his material.

[90] On the relation between χάρις and δύναμις, G. P. Wetter, *Charis* (1913). Wetter's basic thesis is that *charis* is a power concept in the NT. Cf. Grundmann, 96, n. 4.

[91] Cf. Schmitz, *op. cit.*, 145; E. Sokolewski, *Die Begriffe Geist und Leben bei Paulus* (1903), 1 ff.; πνεῦμα καὶ δύναμις, 1 C. 2:4; δύναμις πνεύματος, R. 15:19; πνεῦμα τῆς δυνάμεως, 2 Tm. 1:7. We thus have all three possible connexions.

of ἐν πνεύματι and ἐν Χριστῷ. When we grasp this, it is evident that in the combination of δύναμις and πνεῦμα there is expressed the power with which the risen Lord is present to His people as πνεῦμα. As power and might belong essentially to Christ, the concept of power is linked indissolubly with that of Spirit. In the Spirit Christ is present to the apostle as the Dispenser of power, and in this personal fellowship, granted in and by the πνεῦμα, the apostle is as his Lord. He is not this of himself, but of and by his Lord.

This helps us to understand the important passage in 1 C. 2:1-5 in which Paul speaks of his apostleship. As an apostle he is not a teacher of wisdom; he is a witness of the cross of Christ. Thus his apostleship is discharged οὐκ ἐν πειθοῖς σοφίας λόγοις, ἀλλ' ἐν ἀποδείξει πνεύματος καὶ δυνάμεως, ἵνα ἡ πίστις ὑμῶν μὴ ᾖ ἐν σοφίᾳ ἀνθρώπων ἀλλ' ἐν δυνάμει θεοῦ. The final sentence excludes the understanding of δύναμις as the power of miracles.[92] As a witness of the cross of Christ he establishes his hearers on the δύναμις θεοῦ, not on the σοφία ἀνθρώπων as he would do if he were a teacher of wisdom. This determines the form of his proclamation, which does not consist in dialectical eloquence (ἐν πειθοῖς σοφίας λόγοις) but ἐν ἀποδείξει πνεύματος καὶ δυνάμεως, in demonstration[93] of the Spirit and of power. δύναμις relates to the content of his preaching rather than the form. His preaching has the goal of exhibiting the presence of Christ in the Spirit, and therefore of exhibiting the saving power of God which is identical with Jesus Christ and which is the basis of the existence of believers — ἐν δυνάμει θεοῦ is interchangeable with ἐν πνεύματι or ἐν Χριστῷ. Χριστός, πνεῦμα and δύναμις belong inseparably together.

In the proclamation of Paul Christ is present as πνεῦμα and demonstrates Himself as the δύναμις of God on which is based the new existence of man by faith in this proclamation. As the preacher of Christ he shows forth the saving power of Christ, and through his preaching Christ present in the Spirit establishes believers on this saving power. This event constitutes the Christian community. Thus Paul has become the servant of the Gospel κατὰ τὴν δωρεὰν τῆς χάριτος τοῦ θεοῦ τῆς δοθείσης μοι κατὰ τὴν ἐνέργειαν τῆς δυνάμεως αὐτοῦ, Eph. 3:7 (cf. Col. 1:29).

The use of the concept of power in relation to the incestuous person of 1 C. 5 demands special treatment. Here we read: ἐγὼ μὲν γάρ, ἀπὼν τῷ σώματι, παρὼν δὲ τῷ πνεύματι, ἤδη κέκρικα ὡς παρὼν τὸν οὕτως τοῦτο κατεργασάμενον ἐν τῷ ὀνόματι τοῦ κυρίου ᾽Ιησοῦ συναχθέντων ὑμῶν καὶ τοῦ ἐμοῦ πνεύματος σὺν τῇ δυνάμει τοῦ κυρίου ἡμῶν ᾽Ιησοῦ παραδοῦναι τὸν τοιοῦτον τῷ σατανᾷ εἰς ὄλεθρον τῆς σαρκός, ἵνα τὸ πνεῦμα σωθῇ ἐν τῇ ἡμέρᾳ τοῦ κυρίου, 5:3 ff. The power of Christ is needed to protect the upbuilding of the community, which is threatened by this person and which can be saved only by the extinction of this threat. δύναμις is almost hypostatised, as elsewhere in Paul. But in this respect he is merely adopting Rabbinic usage.[94] The power which Paul exercises in his apostolic activity is the power of Christ, and it is not he, but Christ, who disposes of it. It is necessary that he should co-operate with this power. So far as concerns the effect of the power, Lietzmann is probably right in supposing that we have here something analogous to the story of

[92] E.g., Pr.-Bauer, s.v. ἀπόδειξις: "Proof which lies in possession of the Spirit and the exercise of miraculous power."

[93] ἀποδείκνυμι can mean to prove as well as to demonstrate. ἀπόδειξις as proof is particularly supported by the reading ἐν ἀποκαλύψει in Claromontanus.

[94] → 297, and cf. Grundmann, 104, n. 12.

Ananias and Sapphira in Ac. [95] For the total Pauline view it is important that Satan has no power over the Christian believer. He must be delivered to him. This shows how basic for Paul is the victory of Christ. The reality of the deliverance is shown particularly clearly by the fact that the delivering over to Satan implies only temporary and not definitive destruction. The power of Christ has here the aspect of judicial power.

In the light of the connexion with Christ, and indeed with the Christ who has full power, we can understand the statements which bring out the interrelationship between the Lord and the apostle with reference to the life and apostolate of Paul, which are for him a unity: πάντα ἰσχύω ἐν τῷ ἐνδυναμοῦντί με (Phil. 4:13); χάριν ἔχω τῷ ἐνδυναμώσαντί με Χριστῷ Ἰησοῦ τῷ κυρίῳ ἡμῶν, ὅτι πιστόν με ἡγήσατο θέμενος εἰς διακονίαν (1 Tm. 1:12); ὁ δὲ κύριος μοι παρέστη καὶ ἐνεδυνάμωσέν με, ἵνα δι᾽ ἐμοῦ τὸ κήρυγμα πληροφορηθῇ (2 Tm. 4:17). Paul is aware that he is always sustained in his life as a Christian and an apostle by Christ and His power.

Concerning this use of ἐνδυναμοῦν, "to endow with power," "to furnish with capacity," F. Pfister, who understands the NT˙ concept of power in terms of primitive notions of orenda, tells us that "in the NT, too, ἐνδυναμοῦν implies a strengthening of orenda." [96] For our own part, we do not find such notions anywhere in Paul. He himself gives us a clue to his own understanding of ἐνδυναμοῦν in 2 Tm. 4:17: ὁ δὲ κύριός μοι παρέστη ... Power is operative in the support given by the Dispenser of power. The concept of support [97] expresses the fellowship between Christ and man, and therefore the personal relationship which everywhere predominates in the NT. There is thus no place for orenda notions even in the most primitive strata of the NT.

4. The Community.

The goal of apostolic labour is the community. The place of the existence of the community is determined in the words of Paul in 1 C. 2:1-5 (→ 312): ... ἵνα ἡ πίστις ὑμῶν μὴ ᾖ ἐν σοφίᾳ ἀνθρώπων ἀλλ᾽ ἐν δυνάμει θεοῦ. δύναμις θεοῦ as the saving power of God is the basis of the faith and existence of the community, delivering from the bondage of guilt, demons and Satan, and from the power of death, and translating into the divine kingdom of light and life. In this basic situation of faith the communities are threatened from the place where they had the basis of their previous existence. Thus the close of Eph., which summons to conflict in the hour of peril, begins with the words: τοῦ λοιποῦ, ἐνδυναμοῦσθε ἐν κυρίῳ καὶ ἐν τῷ κράτει τῆς ἰσχύος αὐτοῦ (6:10). [98] The ἐν κυρίῳ describes the place at which they stand. By the reconstitution of their existence they are ἐν κυρίῳ. This place is as it were supplied with the overwhelming power which belongs to Christ. Hence they are summoned: ἐνδυναμοῦσθε. Why they are to do this is described in the verses which follow: ἐνδύσασθε τὴν πανοπλίαν τοῦ θεοῦ πρὸς τὸ δύνασθαι ὑμᾶς στῆναι πρὸς τὰς μεθοδείας τοῦ διαβόλου (6:11, cf. also 12). The community is rescued from the power of Satan and finds itself in a new mode of existence. In this existence, however, it is beset by perils and

---

[95] Ltzm. K., ad loc.
[96] Pauly-W., XI (1922), 2116, s.v. Kultus.
[97] Cf. Grundmann, 102 f.
[98] Cod B, also Origen, read δυναμοῦσθε. For the expression ἐν τῇ κράτει τῆς ἰσχύος αὐτοῦ, → ἰσχύς.

conflicts, and it waits for the final deliverance and the destruction of its enemies. The power of Christ granted to the community is thus by nature a power to protect and preserve. Peter calls believers : τοὺς ἐν δυνάμει θεοῦ φρουρουμένους διὰ πίστεως εἰς σωτηρίαν ἑτοίμην ἀποκαλυφθῆναι ἐν καιρῷ ἐσχάτῳ (1 Pt. 1:5). Paul tells his communities that it is the content of his prayer that they should perceive, καὶ τί τὸ ὑπερβάλλον μέγεθος τῆς δυνάμεως αὐτοῦ εἰς ἡμᾶς τοὺς πιστεύοντας κατὰ τὴν ἐνέργειαν τοῦ κράτους τῆς ἰσχύος αὐτοῦ (Eph. 1:19), [99] that he prays for them : ἵνα ... ἐν πάσῃ δυνάμει δυναμούμενοι κατὰ τὸ κράτος τῆς δόξης αὐτοῦ εἰς πᾶσαν ὑπομονὴν καὶ μακροθυμίαν (Col. 1:11). In the first statement τὸ ὑπερβάλλον μέγεθος τῆς δυνάμεως forms the basis of hope for the content of hope : ὁ πλοῦτος τῆς δόξης τῆς κληρονομίας αὐτοῦ ἐν τοῖς ἁγίοις. The overwhelming power grounded in the resurrection and exaltation of Christ creates for the community, which recognises that it is reconstituted by it, the "hope of calling" and the "riches of his glorious inheritance among the saints." The power which determines the life of Christians in faith should also be the theme of their knowledge by which they can continually appropriate and stand in power, and thus maintain against all appearances to the contrary the hope which they cherish. The purpose of it all is plainly expressed in the Colossians passage. They need the knowledge of power in order that they may be strong εἰς πᾶσαν ὑπομονὴν καὶ μακροθυμίαν. Both of these are necessary under assaults which may easily give rise to sloth, negligence or despondence. ὑπομονή is "perseverance on the basis of the inner victorious sense that all contrary relationships and hostile forces can be overcome." It is "the constancy which proceeds from the inner hope of victory." μακροθυμία is the quality "which does not chide those who unjustly accuse me." [100] This strengthening takes place, as Col. says : αὐξανόμενοι τῇ ἐπιγνώσει τοῦ θεοῦ. In this knowledge there is appropriation of the power to protect and preserve because it brings into fellowship with Christ.

In knowledge, however, the power of the Christian also shows itself to be a power to transform. Paul expresses the wish : ὁ δὲ θεὸς τῆς ἐλπίδος πληρῶσαι ὑμᾶς πάσης χαρᾶς καὶ εἰρήνης ἐν τῷ πιστεύειν εἰς τὸ περισσεύειν ὑμᾶς ἐν τῇ ἐλπίδι ἐν δυνάμει πνεύματος ἁγίου (R. 15:13). In Romans Paul has shown how great and glorious is the hope of the community in Christ. That it is rich in this hope, i.e., that this hope is to it a living reality and power, is due to the operation of the power of the Holy Spirit. The great passage in Eph. 3:14 ff. is highly significant in this regard. Here we read in v. 16 f.: ... ἵνα δῷ ὑμῖν κατὰ τὸ πλοῦτος τῆς δόξης αὐτοῦ δυνάμει κραταιωθῆναι διὰ τοῦ πνεύματος αὐτοῦ κατὰ τὸν ἔσω ἄνθρωπον, κατοικῆσαι τὸν Χριστὸν διὰ τῆς πίστεως ἐν ταῖς καρδίαις ὑμῶν, ἐν ἀγάπῃ ἐρριζωμένοι καὶ τεθεμελιωμένοι. [101] The strengthening with might for which Paul prays takes place through the Spirit of God, i.e., through Christ present in the Spirit to strengthen believers with His power. The goal is the inner man. The result is a true, lasting and indissoluble relationship

---

[99] On κατὰ τὴν ἐνέργειαν τοῦ κράτους τῆς ἰσχύος αὐτοῦ, v. Grundmann, 109 n.; → also ἰσχύς.

[100] Haupt Gefbr., ad loc.

[101] On the construction, loc. cit. There are three petitions. The first of these is formal and seeks endowment with power. The other two show us in what this endowment consists. In relation to the final petition Dib. Gefbr., ad loc., takes the participles in the sense of optatives.

with Christ and attachment to Him [102] — κατοικῆσαι τὸν Χριστὸν διὰ τῆς πίστεως ἐν ταῖς καρδίαις ὑμῶν. But it is also a manner of life and conduct whose basis and theme are love. [103] The final insight that the power of Christ produces Christian love is expressed in 1 Jn. Here we read of the man who is begotten of God : ... οὐ δύναται ἁμαρτάνειν, ὅτι ἐκ τοῦ θεοῦ γεγέννηται (3:9). Being begotten of God gives Christians the possibility of not sinning. [104] If we ask what this means for Jn., we are given the simple answer : πᾶς ὁ ἀγαπῶν ἐκ τοῦ θεοῦ γεγέννηται ... (4:7). The new life finds expression in love for the brethren. This is the goal of the power which has its basis in faith and which overcomes the world. It is in relation to this power for a new manner of life that we are to understand the content of the prayer that "God would make the readers worthy of the vocation" καὶ πληρώσῃ πᾶσαν εὐδοκίαν ἀγαθωσύνης καὶ ἔργον πίστεως ἐν δυνάμει, ὅπως ἐνδοξασθῇ τὸ ὄνομα τοῦ κυρίου ἡμῶν Ἰησοῦ ἐν ὑμῖν (2 Th. 1:11 f.).

That the communities also have a share in the miraculous power of Christ is expressly stated in 1 C. Thus there is reference to ἐνεργήματα δυνάμεων [105] in the enumeration of gifts in 1 C. 12:10. Since the χαρίσματα ἰαμάτων are to be distinguished — for we again have both ἔπειτα δυνάμεις and ἔπειτα χαρίσματα ἰαμάτων in v. 28 — the δυνάμεις are obviously acts of power invading the kingdom of demons. In δυνάμεις demonic forces are resisted and vanquished.

One expression of the power of God is still ahead of the community, namely, the resurrection. The community lives by the resurrection power of Jesus Christ. This fact will finds its consummation in the resurrection of the dead. Paul writes : ... ὃς εἰς ὑμᾶς οὐκ ἀσθενεῖ ἀλλὰ δυνατεῖ ἐν ὑμῖν. καὶ γὰρ ἐσταυρώθη ἐξ ἀσθενείας, ἀλλὰ ζῇ ἐκ δυνάμεως θεοῦ. καὶ γὰρ ἡμεῖς ἀσθενοῦμεν ἐν αὐτῷ ἀλλὰ ζήσομεν σὺν αὐτῷ ἐκ δυνάμεως θεοῦ εἰς ὑμᾶς (2 C. 13:3 f.). The power of Christ in the Christian existence of the Corinthians is grounded in the power of His own life, and thus belongs to the resurrection. The future life of resurrection by the power of God is already latently at work in the Christian life.

This exegesis presupposes a particular decision concerning the ζήσομεν σὺν αὐτῷ ἐκ δυνάμεως θεοῦ εἰς ὑμᾶς. Because of its sound attestation the εἰς ὑμᾶς cannot be omitted as in some simplified readings. Hence we have to ask where it belongs. The parallelism does not allow us to refer it to ζήσομεν, for this means that we shall live (in the resurrection). It is thus to be related to δύναμις θεοῦ, as is possible after the δυνατεῖ ἐν ὑμῖν, the ἐν ὑμῖν being here equivalent to the preceding εἰς ὑμᾶς. Thus the second statement is a further development of the intimation already given that the destiny of Christ is linked with that of believers. Paul is no longer thinking of a visit ; he is formulating a hope. To me it hardly seems possible to relate this to a "demonstration of life and power to be fulfilled in the weighty intervention of which he speaks." [106] Our own suggestion yields good sense. Paul is deducing his hope of the resurrection from the power which has raised Christ and which is already at work in the community to maintain the interrelationship of the destiny of Christ with that of believers.

---

[102] Cf. Gl. 2:20; 4:19.
[103] Cf. Gl. 5:6 etc.
[104] To describe the δύναμις which is superior to sin Jn. uses his own special term δύνασθαι, to which the construction of the sentence gives particular emphasis.
[105] This reading is preferred to ἐνέργεια δυνάμεως, which is found in two MSS.
[106] Bchm. 2 K., ad loc.

The resurrection of believers is based on that of Christ: τὸν κύριον ἤγειρεν καὶ ἡμᾶς ἐξεγερεῖ διὰ τῆς δυνάμεως αὐτοῦ (1 C. 6:14). The power which leads to resurrection is also the power of Christ. The changing of the body of humiliation into a body of glory is a hope grounded in the omnipotence of Christ: κατὰ τὴν ἐνέργειαν τοῦ δύνασθαι αὐτὸν καὶ ὑποτάξαι αὐτῷ τὰ πάντα (Phil. 3:21). The resurrection belongs to the final struggle when hostile forces will be definitively defeated. The Johannine Christ says: κἀγὼ δίδωμι αὐτοῖς ζωὴν αἰώνιον, καὶ οὐ μὴ ἀπόλωνται εἰς τὸν αἰῶνα, καὶ οὐχ ἁρπάσει τις αὐτὰ ἐκ τῆς χειρός μου. ὁ πατήρ μου ὃ δέδωκέν μοι πάντων μεῖζόν ἐστιν, καὶ οὐδεὶς δύναται ἁρπάζειν ἐκ τῆς χειρὸς τοῦ πατρός (Jn. 10:28 f.). [107] Paul confesses that he has given up all things τοῦ γνῶναι αὐτὸν καὶ τὴν δύναμιν τῆς ἀναστάσεως αὐτοῦ (Phil. 3:10), which creates a new and eternal existence. There can be no eternity for human life except on the basis of the resurrection. Paul and the NT never speak of an immortal soul, or of deification by mysteries or magic, or of myths which reflect the hope of eternal life. They speak rather of the sovereign act of power which intervened in the history of Christ and which brought about His resurrection as the only basis of the new existence of Christians and of the eternal hope grounded in this existence in the power of the resurrection of Jesus.

If this view of the NT concept of power is correct, we can understand why Paul writes to the Corinthians: ... γνώσομαι οὐ τὸν λόγον τῶν πεφυσιωμένων ἀλλὰ τὴν δύναμιν· οὐ γὰρ ἐν λόγῳ ἡ βασιλεία τοῦ θεοῦ, ἀλλ' ἐν δυνάμει (1 C. 4:19 f.). [108]

5. Power and Weakness (→ ἀσθένεια). The operation of the power of God, which we have learned to know in the NT as the power of eternity and resurrection, stands under a particular law according to the NT understanding. The place of operation is human and earthly existence which the flesh stamps as weak and corruptible. This is what gives rise to the concealment of the power of God, which is visible only to faith. But this is what also assures us that it really is the power of God and not a human power.

Paul sees this law already in the life and death of Jesus: ... ἐσταυρώθη ἐξ ἀσθενείας, ἀλλὰ ζῇ ἐκ δυνάμεως θεοῦ (2 C. 13:4; cf. R. 1:4). The death of Christ on the cross seems to be a triumph for the devils and Satan. It seems to imply defeat and impotence. In the resurrection, however, the power of God is triumphantly manifested. It was concealed under the flesh in weakness and mortality, and it asserts itself as the power of God. The Gospel comes under this law, of which it may be said: ... τὸ ἀσθενὲς τοῦ θεοῦ ἰσχυρότερον τῶν ἀνθρώπων (1 C. 1:25; → ἰσχυρός).

Paul worked out this law in his activity. He could say of himself: πάντα ἰσχύω ἐν τῷ ἐνδυναμοῦντί με (Phil. 4:13; → 313). He suffered severe physical afflictions and limitations which greatly hindered him in his apostolic work. He wrestled with God for freedom from them. God's answer was in terms of the law which we have mentioned: καὶ εἴρηκέν μοι· ἀρκεῖ σοι ἡ χάρις μου· ἡ γὰρ δύναμις ἐν

---

[107] Following Nestle. The textual difficulties are noted in Nestle, and since they refer to the less crucial middle statement, which is clear in meaning, we need not discuss them here. Cf. the Comm.

[108] Cf. also: ... ἔχοντες μόρφωσιν εὐσεβείας, τὴν δὲ δύναμιν αὐτῆς ἠρνημένοι (2 Tm. 3:5). There is an interesting verbal parallel in Jos. Ant., 13, 409: τὸ οὖν ὄνομα τῆς βασιλείας εἶχεν, τὴν δὲ δύναμιν οἱ Φαρισαῖοι.

ἀσθενείᾳ τελεῖται. And Paul adds: ἥδιστα οὖν μᾶλλον καυχήσομαι ἐν ταῖς ἀσθενείαις, ἵνα ἐπισκηνώσῃ ἐπ' ἐμὲ ἡ δύναμις τοῦ Χριστοῦ ... ὅτε γὰρ ἀσθενῶ, τότε δυνατός εἰμι (2 C. 12:9 f.). He recognised this law in his apostolate: ἔχομεν δὲ τὸν θησαυρὸν τοῦτον ἐν ὀστρακίνοις σκεύεσιν, ἵνα ἡ ὑπερβολὴ τῆς δυνάμεως ᾖ τοῦ θεοῦ καὶ μὴ ἐξ ἡμῶν (2 C. 4:7).[109] And in words which have a thoroughly Pauline ring he wrote out of his own experience: ... ἔδωκεν ἡμῖν ὁ θεὸς πνεῦμα ... δυνάμεως ... μὴ οὖν ἐπαισχυνθῇς τὸ μαρτύριον τοῦ κυρίου ἡμῶν ... ἀλλὰ συγκακοπάθησον τῷ εὐαγγελίῳ κατὰ δύναμιν θεοῦ, τοῦ σώσαντος ἡμᾶς καὶ καλέσαντος κλήσει ἁγίᾳ, 2 Tm. 1:7 ff. In the battle of prayer which raged around his personal destiny Paul experienced the fact that the weakness and limitation of human existence are the necessary presupposition for the operation of the divine power which is made perfect in this weakness and limitation.[110] In his weakness Christ was present to him with His power.[111] In it he was most surely bound to Him. Because weakness was the pledge of the presence of the power of Christ abiding in him, he could boast in it. For in it he found the freedom from self and reliance on Christ which were his destiny. The power found realisation in the accomplishment of his apostolic mission and the attainment of the glory of Christ. When he applied this insight to his apostolate, it became clear that the power concealed in weakness is the power of the resurrection which is hidden in the power of death exercised in the weakness and death of the flesh, and which overcomes the power of death in this concealment.[112] It also became clear that by this law the power of God could be the more abundantly exerted as such. For this reason Paul applied the same law both to individual ministers (2 Tm. 1:7) and to the communities (1 C. 1:26 ff.; → ἰσχυρός). Hence Paul could express the reality of faith by writing both of his apostolate and of Christian existence generally: ἐν δυνάμει θεοῦ (2 C. 6:7).

Grundmann

---

[109] Cf. the antitheses in v. 10 f., 16, which portray the weakness and harassment of the apostle as the dying of Jesus worked out in an interrelationship of destiny, and therefore as a vessel for the divine power which effects salvation, to the end that the life of Jesus may be visible and may be widely manifested as the fact of all-superior power.

[110] This is how we must translate τελεῖται, and not with Ltzm., *ad loc.*: "consumes the body in its operations."

[111] → 311 and n. 94. The meaning is clear and the textual variations are of no consequence.

[112] Here is the basic distinction from all philosophical analogies either in Plato (cf. Wnd. 2 K., on 4:7) or in Philo (*ibid.* on 12:9), or from Rabbinic parallels (*loc. cit.*). Reference may be made to Is. 40:29 ff.: "He giveth strength to the hungry ... they that wait upon the Lord shall renew their strength."

δύω, ἐκδύω, ἀπεκδύω, ἐνδύω,
ἐπενδύω, ἀπέκδυσις

† δύω.

δύω trans. and intr. (the accompanying form δύνω only intr.). Trans. "to submerge," found only in Theophr. De Historia Plantarum, V, 4, 8; intr., also act., "to plunge," "to go down," of the sun in Mk. 1:32; Lk. 4:40; "to draw on," Hom. Il., 18, 416; figur. δύσασθαι ἀλκήν "to arm oneself," Il., 9, 231.

† ἐκδύω.

a. act. "to strip," with acc. of person, P. Magd., 6, 13 (221 B.C.); Mt. 27:28; Lk. 10:30; of object, 1 Βασ. 31:9: ἐξέδυσαν τὰ σκεύη αὐτοῦ. Also with double accus. in Mt. 27:31; Mk. 15:20. b. Mid. "to divest oneself"; with accus. of object: "to take off," τὸν κιθῶνα, Hdt., V, 106; also abs. "to undress," θᾶττον ἐκδυώμεθα, Aristoph. Lys., 686; LXX, so only in Is. 32:11.

In the NT it is used fig. and without object of the putting off of the body in 2 C. 5:4: στενάζομεν βαρούμενοι, ἐφ' ᾧ οὐ θέλομεν ἐκδύσασθαι ἀλλ' ἐπενδύσασθαι (→ 320). The common interpretation[1] that Paul wishes to avoid death and the resultant intermediate state of "nakedness" apart from the body, and that he therefore hopes to live on until the *parousia*, cannot be supported by the unlikely reading ἐκδυσάμενοι in v. 3, "even if we die before the parousia."[2] A strong point against this view is that elsewhere in Paul → στενάζειν means painful but hopeful yearning for final redemption (cf. R. 8:22 f. with 2 C. 5:5). Paul could hardly have described the intermediate state, which is one of fellowship with Christ (Phil. 1:23), as nakedness (→ γυμνός I, 774). The putting off of the body does not refer to the dying of believers prior to the *parousia*, but to the fate of unbelievers who when they die, whether before or at the *parousia*, lose the earthly body without having the heavenly body which believers await according to Paul.[3] The sense is passive (cf. Luther: *entkleidet werden*, → ἐνδύω, 320).

† ἀπεκδύω.

Outside the NT this occurs first in Eustath. Thessal. Comm. in Il., 664, 23 (II, 141).[1] Joseph. has ἀποδύεσθαι in Ant., 11, 223 (figur. 13, 220: ἀπεδύσατο τὴν ὑπόκρισιν, 19, 295, cf. also Porphyr. Abst., I, 31) or μετεκδύεσθαι, Ant., 6, 330 (variant ἀπεκδύς) figur., 6, 264.

In the NT it is found only in Colossians. as a mid. with accus. of object ("fully to put off") in the bold image of 3:9: ἀπεκδυσάμενοι τὸν παλαιὸν ἄνθρωπον. The double compound, if used intentionally, is meant to exclude any possible return

---

ἐκδύω. [1] H. J. Holtzmann, *Nt.liche Theologie*, II² (1911), 220 f.; Bchm., Ltzm. 2 K., *ad loc.*; P. Feine, *Theol. d. NT*⁵ (1931), etc.
[2] D*G it Mcion Chrys, correcting the supposed tautology in the reading ἐνδυσάμενοι.
[3] For bibl. → γυμνός, I, 774.
ἀπεκδύω. [1] Nägeli, 43.

to the old state. The part., loosely linked with what precedes, is meant imperatively. On the meaning of the figure → *infra*. It is used trans. in the sense of act. in Col. 2:15 : ἀπεκδυσάμενος τὰς ἀρχὰς καὶ τὰς ἐξουσίας ... ἐδειγμάτισεν, "disarming the powers and forces, he put them to shame." Attempts to see a middle sense, "to divest himself of," "to put off," are unsatisfactory.[2] As elsewhere in the *koine* (ἐπικαλεῖσθαι = ἐπικαλεῖν, αἰτεῖσθαι with αἰτεῖν in Jm. 4:2 f., συγκαλεῖν and συγκαλεῖσθαι, Lk. 15:6, 9 v.l.), the mid. is used in the active. This is particularly suitable because the usage is figurative and because the One who acts has a personal interest in His action.[3]

ἐνδύω.

a. Act. "to draw on," cf. *induere,* with accus. of object (from the time of Homer, Joseph. Bell., 7, 29 : λευκοὺς ἐνδιδύσκει χιτωνίσκους) or double accus. (Aristoph. Lys., 1021 etc.). Mk. 15:(17)20 and par.; Lk. 15:22; Mt. 22:11; Rev. 15:6 etc. b. Mid. "to put on something," "to clothe oneself with something," "to draw on something," with accus. of object. From the time of Hom.; Joseph. Ant., 8, 185, 362 : σακκίον; 2:90; figur. ἐνδυόμενοι τόλμημα, Aristoph. Eccl., 288; Corp. Herm., X, 18: (τὸ πνεῦμα) ... τὸν ἴδιον ... ἐνεδύσατο χιτῶνα τὸν πύρινον. P. Lond., I, 125, v. 19 : πάλιν θεὸς ἐνδύσεται τὸ ἑαυτῆς κάλλος ὅπερ ἐξεδύσατο. Aristot. An., I, 3, p. 407b, 23 : ἐνδύεσθαι σῶμα (of the soul in the Pythagorean doctrine of transmigration); Sib., 8, 458 : βροτέην ἐνδύσατο μορφήν (of Jesus). Also with personal object : τὸν Ταρκύνιον ἐνδύεσθαι ("to play the role of Tarquin"), Dion. Hal. Ant. Rom., XI, 5; ῥίψας στρατιώτην ἐνέδυ τὸν σοφιστήν, Lib. Ep., 1048, 2.

[1] In the LXX ἐνδύω (ἐνδιδύσκω)[2] is mostly used for לבשׁ and relates to the putting on of clothes. Ιωβ 10:11 is important from the standpoint of biblical anthropology : δέρμα δὲ καὶ κρέα με ἐνέδυσας. A distinctive expression is πνεῦμα (κυρίου, θεοῦ) ἐνέδυσε (v.l. ἐνεδυνάμωσε) τὸν ... in Ju. 6:34; 1 Ch. 12:18; 2 Ch. 24:20. Quite common is the application to investing with ethical and religious qualities of a positive and negative kind, as in some independent statements in the LXX. We find the following expressions: ἐνδύω δικαιοσύνην (Ιωβ 29:14; ψ 131:9; Wis. 5:18; cf. Sir. 27:8); τὴν δήλωσιν καὶ τὴν ἀλήθειαν (1 Εσδρ. 5:40; cf. Ezr. 2:63 [Lv. 8:8] לאורים ולתמים), δύναμιν (ψ 92:1); ἰσχύν (Is. 52:1; 59:17; Prv. 31:25; Sir. 17:3); σωτηρίαν (ψ 131:16, cf. Is. 61:10); δόξαν (1 Macc. 14:9, cf. Sir. 6:31; 27:8); συντέλειαν καυχήματος (Sir. 45:8; 50:11 [ἐνδιδύσκω]); εὐπρέπειαν (ψ 92:1; Prv. 31:25 [= Παρ. 29:44 A]; Bar. 5:1); ἐξομολόγησιν (ψ 103:1); ἐντροπήν (ψ 108:29); αἰσχύνην (Ιωβ 8:22; ψ 34:26; 131:18; 1 Macc. 1:28); ἀφανισμόν (Ez. 7:27); φόβον (Ιωβ 39:19 : רעמה = φόβη, mane ?); κατάραν (ψ 108:18).

1. In the NT it is used literally in Mt. 6:25; Mk. 6:9 (cf. Jos. Ant., 17, 136 : ἐνεδεδύκει δύο χιτῶνας); Ac. 12:21 (cf. Jos. Ant., 19, 344 : Ἀǵrippa στολὴν ἐνδὺς ἐξ ἀργύρου πεποιημένην πᾶσαν); Rev. 19:14 (cf. Da. 10:5) etc.

2. Figuratively it is found a. in the absol. in 2 C. 5:3, where the best authorities have εἴ γε καὶ ἐνδυσάμενοι οὐ γυμνοὶ εὑρεθησόμεθα, "that we might not be

---

[2] Cf. the Comm.

[3] Kühner-Blass-Gerth, II, 1[8], 375, 4; Bl.-Debr.[6] § 316, 1.

ἐ ν δ ύ ω. [1] This paragraph is by G. Bertram.

[2] Bl.-Debr.[6] § 73. ἐν-(ἐκ-)διδύσκω is a Doric construction often found in the NT : Mk. 15:17 (BCDF); Lk. 8:27 (אD); 16:19; Herm. s., 9, 13, 5. Cf. also R. Helbing, *Die Kasussyntax der Verba bei den Septuaginta* (1928), 45 f.

found naked after putting on (i.e., the heavenly body)." Less likely is ἐνδυσάμενοι predicatively and οὐ γυμνοί epexegetically ("that even then [in the case
of the ἐπενδύσασθαι of v. 2] we might be found clothed and not naked"). [3]
ἐνδυσάμενοι takes up again the → ἐπενδύσασθαι of v. 2. The καί is not con-
cessive (as necessarily with the vl. ἐκδυσάμενοι [→ 318]), but εἴ γε καί =
εἴπερ. [4] Paul desires to be clothed with the heavenly body in order that he may
be spared the non-bodily existence of unbelievers (→ γυμνός, I, 774). On the
passive sense of the mid. → infra. b. mid. with accus. of object. Of the Christian
armour in R. 13:12 : τὰ ὅπλα τοῦ φωτός; 1 Th. 5:8 : θώρακα πίστεως; Eph. 6:11:
τὴν (→) πανοπλίαν τοῦ θεοῦ; 6:14 : τὸν θώρακα τῆς δικαιοσύνης. [5] But ἐνδύεσθαι can also be used for the adoption of specific qualities (LXX → 319; also
Herm. v., 3, 12, 2; m., 10, 3, 1): ἐνδύσασθε σπλάγχνα οἰκτιρμοῦ, Col. 3:12. The
mid. can have a passive sense : ἐνδύεσθαι δύναμιν, Lk. 24:49; ἐνδύεσθαι ἀφθαρσίαν, ἀθανασίαν, 1 C. 15:53, 54 : to be invested with power, with incorruptibility,
with immortality. [6]

Much the same sense is given c. by a personal obj. Gl. 3:27: Χριστὸν ἐνεδύ-
σασθε, means that you are clothed upon with Christ, ἐστὲ (→) ἐν Χριστῷ. It can
also be used as an ethical imperative, however, with an active accent in R. 13:14 :
ἐνδύσασθε τὸν κύριον Ἰησοῦν Χριστόν (cf. R. 6:11 with 6:5; Col. 3:5 with 3:3).
The usage of Paul has nothing whatever to do with the donning of the garment [7]
or mask [8] of the god by the initiate. [9] The figurative expressions in Dion. Hal. and
Lib. (→ 319) are the nearest to the imperative usage, though they hardly have the
same content. There are no parallels for Paul's indicative usage. [10] Behind this
stands the eschatological conception of Christ as the second Adam, as anima
generalis. [11] This conception is given a more individual application when Paul
speaks imperatively, though with a strong suggestion of the related indicative in
Col. 2:11, of the putting on of the καινός or νέος ἄνθρωπος (Col. 3:10; Eph.
4:24).

† ἐπενδύω.

"To put on over" (i.e., another garment), act. ἐπὶ τοῦτον ἄλλον κιθῶνα, Hdt.,
I, 195; mid.: ἐπενδυσάμενος χιτῶνα, Jos. Ant., 3, 159; σάκκους ἐπενδύντες ταῖς

---

[3] Bchm. 2 K.; Cr.-Kö., s.v.

[4] Cf. Wnd. 2 K., ad loc.

[5] ἐνδεδυμένος τὴν πανοπλίαν, Jos. Ant., 13, 309; θώρακα ἐνδεδυμένος, Ant., 7, 283;
θώρακα ἐνεδέδυτο; Ant., 6, 171; Is. 59:17.

[6] Cf. Hippocr. De Insomniis, 91: ἐσθῆτα λευκὴν ἐνδεδύσθαι ... ἀγαθόν; Herm. s.,
9, 13, 8. The hardly serviceable pass. aorist forms seem to have been replaced by the middle,
and this is understandable in view of the fact that one usually dresses oneself. Cf. in Eng.
"to don the purple" for "to be invested with rule." Worth noting is the par. ἀλλαγησόμεθα
in 1 C. 15:51 f.

[7] The priestess of Isis clothes herself like the goddess. Cf. the gravestone in Haas,
9/11 Leipoldt, Illustr. 50 with the statues of Isis, and cf. 26 and 27.

[8] F. J. Dölger, Ichthys, I (1916), 116 ff.

[9] Ltzm. Gl., ad loc.; A. Schweitzer, Die Mystik des Apostels Paulus (1930), 135; A.
Oepke, ZNW, 29 (1930), 106 f.

[10] The attempt to explain the indicative also along these lines (Zn. Gl. on 3:27) leads
to the wholly non-Pauline idea that the divine sonship is determined by likeness to Christ.

[11] Symmach. in Victorinus Afer. MPL, 8, 1155b, W. Bousset, Kyrios Christos (1926), 21;
B. Murmelstein, WZKM, 35 (1928), 242 ff.; 36 (1929), 51 ff.

στολαῖς, Ant., 5, 37; σχῆμα ἐνδύτου (v.l. ἐπενδύτου) θώρακος, Bell., 5, 233; synon. μετενδύσασθαι, Ant., 20, 123; Vit., 138. ἐπενδύεσθαι πολλὰ σώματα, Aeneas Gazaeus Theophrastus, 493 (ed. J. F. Boissonade [1836], p. 60).

In the NT it occurs only in 2 C. 5:2, 4 (cf. ἐπενδύτης, Jn. 21:7) for investiture with the heavenly body at the *parousia* in terms of 1 C. 15:51, 53 f. The meaning of the mid. is pass. (as Luther correctly renders it, → ἐνδύω, 320). Since in v. 3 Paul uses the simple ἐνδυσάμενοι, he does not employ ἐπενδύσασθαι to distinguish the change at the *parousia* from that of resurrection, but in the whole passage is simply thinking of the change at the *parousia* (→ γυμνός, I, 774; → ἐνδύω, 319 f.).

† ἀπέκδυσις.

Outside the NT this is first found in Eustath. Thessal. Comm. in Il., 91, 28 (I, 77). [1]

In the NT it is found only in Col. 2:11 in the figurative sense: ἐν τῇ ἀπεκδύσει τοῦ σώματος τῆς σαρκός. Materially relevant is → ἀπεκδύω, 318; cf. R. 6:2 f., 6; Gl. 2:19; 5:24; 6:14.

Oepke

| δώδεκα († ἑκατὸν τεσσεράκοντα τέσσαρες), † δωδέκατος, † δωδεκάφυλον | (→ ἀπόστολος, → Ἰσραήλ). |

From the days of Hom. this is the usual indecl. word for "twelve," and it is adopted by the LXX as such. δώδεκα has no more history of meaning than other numerals, but from an early period it has been highly estimated. Possibly this is due to the division of the year into twelve months, which seems to have originated in Babylon, to have been taken by Caesar by way of Egypt to Rome, and in Rome to have become the basis of the gradually improved chronological system of the West. [1]

With the division of the year into twelve months is linked the *amphictyony*, [2] the primitive federation of several clans or tribes into a sacral union with a common

---

ἀπέκδυσις. [1] Nägeli, 50.

δώδεκα. J. Wellhausen, *Einleitung in die drei ersten Evangelien*[2] (1911), 138 ff.; Meyer Ursprung, I, 291 ff.; III, 255 ff.; Schl. Gesch. d. Chr. 311 ff.; R. Schütz, *Apostel u. Jünger* (1921), 72 ff.; K. Holl, *Gesammelte Aufsätze zur Kirchengeschichte*, II: *Der Osten* (1928), 47 ff., esp. 53, n. 1; Comm. on Rev.

[1] Cf. the brief discussion in RGG², I, 1666 ff. (O. Rühle). The duodecimal system also originated in Babylon.

[2] Cf. for Greece, F. Cauer, *Amphiktyonie*, Pauly-W., I (1894), 1904 ff.; for Italy, where these leagues go back to pre-Roman times, cf. the bibl. in Noth (→ n. 3), 51 ff.

sanctuary as the focal point. Twelve seems to have been a typical number for participants in such unions, whether in Greece or Italy. The reason is that they took it in turns each month to supervise the cultic centre. The institution achieved universal significance to the degree that the system of twelve tribes in Israel perhaps derives from such an early union. [3] The distinctive feature in this case is that even after the decay of the original federation with the disappearance of some members and the fusion of the others into a political society, the system of twelve tribes remained the basis and also the expression of the Hebrew and later the Jewish consciousness of fellowship. [4] To the extent that δώδεκα is used theologically in the NT, its presuppositions are to be found supremely in this fact.

1. The use of δώδεκα as a round number is first found in Mt. 9:20 and par., where it is said of a woman healed by Jesus that she had been ἐν ῥύσει αἵματος δώδεκα ἔτη (Mk. 5:25). We might also mention the twelve baskets of fragments which were left over after the feeding of the five thousand (Mt. 14:20; cf. Mk. 8:19; Jn. 6:13), though in this case it is possible that there is allusion [5] to the number of the participating disciples. [6] We again have a round figure in Ac. 19:7; [7] 24:11.

In all the Synoptic Gospels the story of the woman with an issue of blood is interwoven with that of the raising of Jairus' daughter in a manner which suggests that the combination is earlier than the earliest Gospel. [8] Since Mk. (5:42) and Lk. (8:42) tell us that the girl was twelve years old, it may be that the explanation of the fusion is to be found in the fact that the occurrence of the same number in both stories caused them to be linked [9] — a phenomenon which is frequently to be seen on the soil of Rabb. tradition. [10] On the other hand, the number is only a peripheral feature in the story of the girl in Mk., [11] and the two stories are fused with one another rather than set alongside, as one might have expected if the common number were responsible for their conjunction. Hence we may best conclude that "real recollection is here preserving a historical fact, namely, that the healing of the woman took place on the way to the house of Jairus." [12]

2. In Lk. 2:42 it is at the age of twelve that the boy Jesus first goes to Jerusalem for the Passover with his parents. So far as we can gather from Jewish sources, [13] the purpose of the journey was to familiarise the youngster with the fulfilment of the

---

[3] For references, cf. A. Alt in RGG², III, 438 f.; for an explicit discussion, cf. M. Noth, *Das System der zwölf Stämme Israels* (1930).

[4] Cf. the emphasis on the descent of Jesus from the tribe of Judah (Mt. 1:2 f.; Lk. 3:33 f.), and the stress laid by Paul on his descent from the tribe of Benjamin (Phil. 3:5; R. 11:1); cf. also Lk. 2:36; Ac. 26:7 (δωδεκάφυλον).

[5] Cf. Kl. Mk. on 6:43.

[6] According to Mk. and Lk. the return of the twelve appointed apostles comes immediately before the feeding of the five thousand. Mt. does not specifically report their return (→ I, 427).

[7] For a different view cf. C. Weizsäcker, *Das Apostolische Zeitalter der christl. Kirche*³ (1902), 341: "The fact that there are twelve disciples of John, with its unmistakable allusion to the original apostles, shows us clearly that the whole is an allegory." But cf. Wdt. Ag., *ad loc.*

[8] Bultmann Trad., 228; K. L. Schmidt, *Der Rahmen der Geschichte Jesu* (1919), 148.

[9] This is obviously in the mind of E. Wendling in *Die Entstehung des Marcus-Evangeliums* (1908), 47 f., and esp. n. 1.

[10] E.g., the linking of two traditions by the catchword אַרְבָּעִים שָׁנָה in jJoma, 43c, 68 ff.

[11] It is not found in Mt. at all ; only in Lk. does it receive greater emphasis by being put at the beginning of the story rather than the end (Kl. Lk. on 8:42).

[12] K. L. Schmidt, *op. cit.*

[13] Cf. Str.-B., II, 144 ff.

obligations of the festival. The obligation to observe it strictly began only with the completion of the thirteenth year.[14]

3. The usage of the OT is adopted in Ac. 7:8 (οἱ δώδεκα πατριάρχαι); Mt. 19:28 (αἱ δώδεκα φυλαὶ τοῦ Ἰσραήλ; cf. Lk. 22:30; Rev. 21:12). Formally, at least, we have a similar OT phrase in Jm. 1:1: ταῖς δώδεκα φυλαῖς ταῖς ἐν τῇ διασπορᾷ. The question whether the reference here is to Jews of the Dispersion or to the (Gentile) Christian world understood as the true Israel demands special treatment (→ διασπορά, 102; → Ἰσραήλ).

4. Particular attention should be paid to the use of δώδεκα in Rev. It certainly cannot be separated from the OT view of the twelve tribes as comprising the people of God in the OT. The στέφανος ἀστέρων δώδεκα, which the γυνὴ περιβεβλημένη τὸν ἥλιον (12:1) bears on her head,[15] marks her as a symbolical representation of the θυγάτηρ Σιών, of the Jewish people as such,[16] more particularly in its character as the community of God[17] from which Christ comes (12:5).[18] If the number twelve occurs again in the measurements and arrangements of the new Jerusalem (21:12, 14, 16, 20 f.), this is connected with the fact that in the formula δώδεκα φυλαί it had become "the typical number of completeness, of the inviolable totality of the theocratic people, of the people of possession."[19] Related to the plan of the city of God, this means that in its totality it stands under the divine order and serves the fulfilment of the divine purpose to the degree that this is shown to be actualised in it — the one people of God in the city of God.[20]

For this reason the number δώδεκα is indispensable in relation to the number of the δοῦλοι τοῦ θεοῦ at the end of the days. According to 7:4 ff. (cf. 14:1 ff.)

---

[14] For the Jewish boy the independent keeping of all the commandments of the Torah, including the Passover commandment, begins when he is thirteen and a day (cf. Str.-B., II, 146).

[15] This is often explained in terms of the zodiac, and in the depiction of the woman as thus adorned it is concluded that we have a "reference, easily understood in the first century, to the picture of the heavenly Παρθένος" (F. Boll, Aus der Offenbarung Johannis [1914], 103; cf. the whole context 98 ff.: Regina caeli), which the author of Rev. used to express the unique descent of Jesus from heaven and from a human mother (119 ff.) → n. 16.

[16] The root of the idea is in Gn. 37:9, where the eleven brothers of Joseph appear to him in a dream as ἕνδεκα ἀστέρες. The derivation, common in more recent comm., from Test. N. 5:3 ff. (δώδεκα ἀκτῖνες under the feet of Judah; so Bss. Apk.; Loh. Apk., ad loc. etc.) seems to have little bearing on an understanding of the verse.

[17] Cf. A. Schlatter, Erläuterungen zum NT.

[18] Cf. esp. v. 17: οἱ λοιποὶ τοῦ σπέρματος αὐτῆς. To refer the woman to the Virgin Mary (as often in the early Church, cf. first Method. Symp., VIII, 7) is as little supported by the context as to refer the υἱός to Jewish Christianity of the apostolic period or even to Gentile Christianity (Zn. Apk., 442 f.). The same is true of the attempt to represent the woman as in some sense the Christian Church or a believing Israel of the last time (so Zn. 442). On all these attempts cf. the review by F. Düsterdieck, Kritisch-exegetisches Handbuch über die Offenbarung Johannis (Meyer)² (1865), 419 ff. It would take us too far afield even to discuss briefly the singular and very forced attempt of J. Wellhausen ("Analyse der Offenbarung Johannis," AGG, NF, 9, 4 [1907], 20 f.) to explain the passage as a product of strict Jewish-Pharisaic circles.

[19] R. Kraemer, Die Offenbarung des Johannes (1930), 200.

[20] The author follow Ez.'s vision of the future Jerusalem (Ez. 48:30 ff.; cf. 40:3 ff.), and therefore indirectly Ez.'s models (cf. the Comm., ad loc.). On the other hand, by emphasising the figure twelve as normative in the coming city, he finally lifts this up into the divine sphere and makes it exclusively God's city.

there are δώδεκα χιλιάδες from each tribe[21] and τεσσεράκοντα τέσσαρες χιλιά-δες as a whole (→ σφραγίζω). It is a serious misunderstanding to think that we have here a concrete number, even if it is restricted to "the actual number of Christians of Jewish descent at the time of the Apocalypse,"[22] not to speak of the number of those who are kept in the final tribulation etc. Since the reference is to the sealing of 12,000 from each tribe, it is evident that the number of those sealed is fixed by the decree of God and that the community composed of them bears the mark of absolute perfection. It is also evident, however, that this community is very large.[23] The word δώδεκα is designed to emphasise the divine will, which is here the will to save, and which is revealed as such; the word χιλιάδες lays emphasis on the size of the community; the δώδεκα χιλιάδες from each tribe brings out the orderly nature of the divine action and the perfection of the result; and the number τεσσεράκοντα τέσσαρες χιλιάδες attests the absolute unity of those who are sealed. In sum, we have here a consistent and confident recognition that God is the Lord of His community, and that in it He attains His goal within history. Any other interpretation necessarily leads us astray.

The enumeration of the twelve tribes does not impose an interpretation in terms of Jewish believers, though this has been constantly maintained. Such an interpretation overlooks the fact that in 7:1 ff. there is departure from the customary enumeration.[24] In view of the familiarity of the author with the OT, this cannot possible be of merely archaeological interest. It is rather of radical importance for a true perception of his concern. The Jewish world expected that the time of the Messiah would bring with it a restoration of the Davidic kingdom of the twelve tribes without any restrictions,[25] as we can see clearly from Josephus (Ant., 11, 133).[26] This eschatological scheme, however, is broken in Rev. 7:4 ff., for the tribe of Dan is missing (→ n. 21), and in view of the fervour with which a full restoration was awaited this denotes a breach with the expectation generally, the more so as the appearance of the tribe of Levi gives the list a rather archaic character. The interest of the author is not concentrated on the listing of the tribes as such, but on the truth of salvation history expressed in it and grounded from the very outset in the teleology of the divine way of salvation. In it God remains true to Himself, to His goal, and therefore to His people. Like Paul in similar passages, the author is thus referring to the spiritual Israel actualised in the community of Jesus. His attitude is the same as that of the author of the Fourth Gospel, who could not find in physical descent from Abraham the guarantee of fellowship with God, but who rather saw in a self-conscious insistence on this descent a threat to, and even a destruction of, the historical relationship of the Jews to God (Jn. 8:31 ff.).

---

[21] In the list of tribes Dan is replaced by Manasseh, perhaps because Dan was charged with apostasy (Str.-B., III, 804 f.), or even because Antichrist was expected from Dan (cf. W. Bousset, Der Antichrist [1895], 112 ff.), though this thesis is supported only in early Christian writings (cf. first Iren., V, 30, 2 on Rev. 7:5 ff.).

[22] Zn. Apk., 371 f.

[23] It is in keeping that 7:9 speaks of an ὄχλος πολύς, ὃν ἀριθμῆσαι αὐτὸν οὐδεὶς ἐδύνατο, ἐκ παντὸς ἔθνους καὶ φυλῶν καὶ λαῶν καὶ γλωσσῶν before the throne and the Lamb; "those who are numbered by God cannot be counted, and the number 144,000, which is chosen with reference to Israel, includes a multitude which the human eye cannot measure" (A. Schlatter, Erläuterungen, ad loc.). On the inseparability of 7:9 ff. and 7:1 ff., cf. Loh. Apk., ad loc.

[24] This has been generally noted; → n. 21.

[25] Cf. Str.-B., IV, 799 ff.

[26] Schl., Theol. d. Jdt., 254.

The numbers 12,000 and 144,000 are also found in a cosmic sense among the Mandaeans, the Persians and the Manicheans. [27] Thus the breadth of the earth is 12,000 miles, and the height from the earth to the firmament is 12,000 miles, 12,000 uthras, [28] or 144,000 myriad uthras. [29] Yet we can hardly suppose that the numbers came into Rev. from these sources. [30] If there is a connexion, it is probably the other way round, [31] i.e., that the Mandaeans took the numbers from the Apocalypse. Perhaps this is saying too much. It might well be, however, that the Mandaeans followed both Revelation and also a usage independent of their Jewish background and possibly Persian in origin. [32]

5. The classical use of δώδεκα is in relation to the innermost circle of the disciples of Jesus. In this connexion we have the formulae οἱ δώδεκα μαθηταί (Mt. 10:1 etc.), οἱ δώδεκα ἀπόστολοι (Mt. 10:2; Lk. 22:14), and especially the simple οἱ δώδεκα (Mt. 26:14 etc.). These apply to the same people, but are materially different, since in the Gospels all apostles are μαθηταί, yet not all μαθηταί are apostles (→ I, 424), but only those expressly appointed by Jesus. From Mk. 3:13 f.; Lk. 6:12 f. (cf. Jn. 6:70) it appears that this circle, often referred to simply as οἱ δώδεκα, owes its origin to the choice of twelve from among the adherents of Jesus by a free decision of Jesus Himself, and to the apostolic participation in His office and ministry which He thereby granted to them. If, however, the apostolate is a work of Jesus, there is no reason not to trace back the δώδεκα to a historical act of Jesus, [33] and indeed to an act prior to His resurrection. Rejection of such an act [34] makes quite unintelligible the existence of a group of ἀπόστολοι known as οἱ δώδεκα in the primitive community. Acceptance of it on the basis of the Synoptic records explains at once both their existence and their peculiar position.

An attempt has been made to explain the apostolic college by arguing that in the time between the death of Jesus and the conversion of Paul [35] it developed in Jerusalem as a firm presbyterial group within the larger circle of apostles. [36] But against this theory there is the difficulty of providing any motives for the emergence of these twelve as a normative group when there was not merely a larger body of disciples but they did not even have, [37] and could not claim, [38] any priority in virtue of encounter with the risen Lord. In any case, the fact that the tradition uniformly calls the traitor Judas εἷς τῶν δώδεκα (Mt. 26:14, 47 etc.) shows us that the group goes back to the period prior to

---

[27] Lidz. Joh., II, 8, n. 5; F. Boll, op. cit., 79, n. 3.
[28] Lidz. Joh., II, 8 and 9 ff.
[29] Lidz. Liturg., 18 with n. 2.
[30] Even Loh. is content merely to note the parallel and not to seek a source in Gnosticism.
[31] Esp. now that H. Lietzmann has shown that the Mandaean literature presupposes not merely the NT but a developed Christianity ("Ein Beitrag zur Mandäerfrage," SAB [1930] 596 ff.).
[32] E.g., the 12,000 in Lidz. Joh., II, 8, n. 5.
[33] Tension between the name apostle and the name of the group can be seen only by those who do not perceive the nature of the apostolate and who do not therefore see that the apostolate could not be this in the full sense after the resurrection if it did not go back to the life of Jesus with His disciples (→ I, 424).
[34] This is first found in F. Schleiermacher, Über die Schriften des Lukas (1817), Sämtliche Werke, 1. Zur Theologie, 2 (1836), 63 f.
[35] The terminus ad quem in view of 1 Cor. 15:5.
[36] So yet again Schütz, 76.
[37] 1 C. 15:6 mentions more than 500 brethren who had seen the risen Lord at one time.
[38] Cf. esp. Holl, 53, n. 1; but also Meyer, I, 296 ff.

the crucifixion, [39] and Paul gives similar testimony when he calls the δώδεκα, with Peter, the first witnesses of the resurrection (1 C. 15:5), and thus allots them a place corresponding to their particular link with Jesus in the precrucifixion period. [40] Finally, it should not be overlooked that during the period between the death of Jesus and the election of Matthias (Ac. 1:15 ff.) the tradition speaks of οἱ ἕνδεκα (μαθηταί, ἀπόστολοι, Mt. 28:16; Mk. 16:14; Lk. 24:9, 33; Ac. 1:26); this would have been pointless if the δώδεκα had not been accepted as a group originating in the period prior to the death of Jesus. Indeed, the whole tradition is reduced at this point to a riddle and a legend if we regard the δώδεκα as a product of the first Jerusalem community, [41] not to speak of the fact that this supposed derivation is even more inexplicable.

If the twelve may be traced back to the selection of Jesus, the reason for the limited number is self-evident. The group owes its origin, not to a capricious act of Jesus, but to the goal which is set by the content of the number twelve in salvation history. In the calling of the twelve, Jesus visibly orders both His own and their work in accordance with the divine plan of salvation and in relation to its goal, the preparing of the community of God. As the bond which knits the circle together He thus constitutes common service in one and the same task. Essentially, the twelve are far more than "representatives of the twelve tribes of Israel" [42] or part of the Messianic court of Jesus, even if only in parable. [43] In their selection there is with equal resolution both a backward and a forward look: backward to "the ancient constitution of Israel"; and at the same time forward to "the final form of the Messianic community." [44] In them Jesus made visible to everyone His claim upon Israel, and He did so in such a way that it was evident that He did not merely claim a select group but the whole people in all its divisions. [45] The twelve thus have a place only between Him and His people. They are not a magnitude with any right or possibility of existence apart from this position.

This view of the nature of the twelve is confirmed in many ways. First, we should remember that there is no passage in the NT which makes it plain that the twelve played any special role either in Jerusalem or beyond. [46] All attempts to prove this remain in the sphere of conjecture for lack of evidence. [47] The silence of Paul is particularly noteworthy. He mentions the δώδεκα only in his list of witnesses of the resurrection

---

[39] Cf. also Meyer, I, 297 f.

[40] Loc. cit.

[41] J. Wellhausen was even prepared to go to the length of denying the historicity of the inclusion of Judas with the twelve (144 f.). E. Meyer (I, 296 f.) has pointed out, however, that this involves a denial of the historicity of the appointment of Matthias, since in these circumstances he must either have belonged to the twelve from the very first or must be regarded as a fiction (as in J. Weiss, Das Urchristentum [1917] 34).

[42] So Meyer, I, 299.

[43] Schütz inclines in this direction, 73 f.

[44] Schl. Gesch. d. Chr., 322, where reference is made to Mt. 19:28. On Mt. 19:28 → also 327, 328.

[45] Already in the choice of these men and in the nature of the work allotted to them we may obviously see the renunciation by Jesus of the traditional view of the Messiah. Mt. 26:53 should also be mentioned in this connexion.

[46] On Ac. 6:2 → 327.

[47] This applies also to Holl's discussion of Paul's view of the Church in relation to that of the first community (Ges. Aufs. zur KG, II : Der Osten [1928], 44 ff.) to the extent that he makes the precedence of Jerusalem in the early Church dependent on the fact that it was the residence of the δώδεκα (and of the Lord's brother James).

(1 C. 15:5) in a passage which leaves the impression that in both form and content Paul was making use of a pre-Pauline tradition. [48] If anything is certain about the mention of the twelve in this list, it is that Paul does not speak of them as a constituent part of the organised primitive community, nor as its leaders, but rather as a group among the first witnesses of the resurrection which is of particular importance in virtue of its connexion with Jesus. For the rest, Paul's silence concerning the twelve is strange only for those who try to see in them more than they were, namely, the fellow-labourers of Jesus in His struggle for His own people. Certainly they were not opponents of Paul ; otherwise he could not have ignored them in his controversies with the authorities in Jerusalem. This picture is confirmed by Acts. In Ac. the twelve act as such only on one occasion, namely, the selection of the seven to take charge of the Hellenistic section of the community (Ac. 6:2). Even here, however, they are not rulers. They are rather advisers, and this in relation only to the most restricted circle in the original community.

Secondly, we have to consider that, although Acts tells us of the death of James the son of Zebedee, it does not speak of his place being filled by fresh election as in the case of Judas. This is probably due to the fact that when James was killed the twelve were no longer the unity they had been after the resurrection, whether before or after the addition of Matthias. The emphasis in apostolic work now came to be placed more and more outside the Jewish world, where others played a part with them (cf. Philip in Ac. 8:5 ff., 26 ff.; Peter in Ac. 10:1 ff.). But the most powerful reason for not filling the gap left by the death of James is probably to be sought in the eschatological character of the δώδεκα which makes any replacement impossible, [49] the more so as Jesus had held out the prospect of members of the group dying for Him prior to His return (Mt. 10:16 ff.). [50] As it is true of the work of Jesus that it was accomplished with a demand for historical decision, so it is true of the existence of the δώδεκα that the claim which Jesus made upon His people in them was linked with history and therefore that the possibility of decision thereby granted to the Jewish people was only transitory. Thus, in early Christian tradition, when the δώδεκα were rejected by the Jewish people, they for their part became representatives of the judgment passed on it, and shared increasingly in its outworking. This is surely the meaning of Mt. 19:28 (cf. Lk. 22:30), where in a saying of Jesus they are described as judges of the δώδεκα φυλαὶ τοῦ Ἰσραὴλ ἐν τῇ παλιγγενεσίᾳ, ὅταν καθίσῃ ὁ υἱὸς τοῦ ἀνθρώπου ἐπὶ θρόνου δόξης αὐτοῦ. [51]

It is in keeping with this character of the δώδεκα that the four Evangelists can often describe the narrowest circle around Jesus simply as οἱ δώδεκα, ascribing to it a special task and nature rather than a peculiar dignity or importance. It is also in keeping that the formula is intentional. It is always used in Mt. and Jn., and with two exceptions in Mk. and Lk., [52] when the reference is to the testing of the group (Jn. 6:67 ff., cf. 71), when it is desired to emphasise the close relationship to Jesus (as in

---

[48] Cf. on this pt. A. Seeberg, *Der Katechismus der Urchristenheit* (1903), 45 ff. The attempt to bring the passage under textual suspicion (Joh. W. 1 K., *ad loc.*) can hardly be regarded as successful.

[49] It should not be overlooked that Matthias took the place of the one among the δώδεκα who had forfeited his relationship to Jesus by his conduct (Ac. 1:25). His acceptance into the circle shows us that the claim of Jesus upon His people is still unbroken and unshaken.

[50] Cf. on this pt. K. H. Rengstorf, *Apostolat und Predigtamt* (1934), 22 f.

[51] For our present purpose it makes no difference whether this is an authentic saying of Jesus or one invented by the community (Bultmann Trad., 171). On the basis of an analysis of the formula οἱ δώδεκα I see no reason not to attribute it to Jesus. In any case, we must take the κρίνοντες as it stands, and therefore we cannot take it to indicate the function of the twelve as "rulers of Israel in the last time" (Bultmann Trad., 171).

[52] Mk. 4:10; Lk. 8:1; and even here we might well ask whether the formula is not appropriate.

the story of the Last Supper or the description of Judas, and also Thomas [Jn. 20:24], as εἷς τῶν δώδεκα), or when there is a combination of the two, as in the intimation of the passion (Mt. 20:17 and par.). Even if the selection of the twelve by Jesus had taken place immediately before His death, in all these cases the formula οἱ δώδεκα would be quite correct from the standpoint of the nature of early Christian proclamation, since this is not a chronological representation, but kerygma aiming at decision.

It is also in keeping with the character of the δώδεκα that in Rev. 21:14 the twelve foundation stones of the city bear the names of the twelve apostles of the Lamb. This is the positive side of what is put negatively in Mt. 19:28. If on the one side they are participants in the last judgment, on the other the new community is not conceivable without them. This community is the new Israel assembled from all nations. For a time it might seem as though the twelve had failed in their mission, [53] but with this new understanding of the concept of the people of God they are now highly esteemed again as such and not merely as apostles of special rank; they thus become a decisive factor in determining the Church's awareness of itself. [54]

Rengstorf

δωρεά, δωρεάν, δωρέομαι, δώρημα, δῶρον → δίδωμι, 166 ff.

---

[53] It is worth noting that the formula οἱ δώδεκα (ἀπόστολοι) is not found in the post-apostolic fathers or the Apologists except in the title of the Didache (J. Wagenmann, *Die Stellung des Apostels Paulus neben den Zwölf* [1926], 161 f.).
[54] Cf. on this pt. J. Wagenmann, *op. cit.*, 164 ff.

> † ἐγγύς, † ἐγγίζω,
> † προσεγγίζω

ἐγγίζω "to bring near": Polyb., VIII, 4, 7: τὰς ναῦς τῇ γῇ, mostly intr.: "to approach": Polyb., IV, 62, 5 with gen.; Diod. S., XIII, 77, 3; with dat., Polyb., XVII, 4, 1; Epictet. Diss., III, 10, 14: τῷ διαλυθῆναι τὴν ψυχὴν ἀπὸ τοῦ σώματος; *ibid.,* IV, 11, 3. Rare in the pap., P. Oxy., IX, 1202, 8. With gen., e.g., Pap. de Theadelphie, Pierre Jouguet (1911), 17, 12; with dat.: P. Gen., 74, 17.

ἐγγύς a. "in the vicinity," "close by." Abs. Thuc., III, 55, 1 (ἐγγὺς ὄντες) etc.; with χωρεῖν, Aesch. Sept. c. Theb., 59 f.; with προσέρχεσθαι Soph. Phil., 788; usually with gen.: Hom. Il., 10, 274: ἐγγὺς τῆς ἐκκλησίας; P. Masp., 313, 54. Hence with gen. in the sense of "in the presence of someone": ἐγγὺς τῶν παράρχων, P. Lond., IV, 1660, 21; BGU, III, 814, 30 (ἐγγὺς τοῦ ἀδελφοῦ). More rarely with the dat., as in Hom. Il., 22, 453; Eur. Heracl., 37. b. Temporally "near at hand." Epict. Diss., III, 26, 6: ἐγγὺς ἥκουσιν τῷ μηδ' ἀποθανεῖν δύνασθαι. c. In counting "almost": P. Oxy., III, 472, 34: μετ' ἐνιαυτὸν ἐγγύς; Xenoph. Hist. Graec., II, 4, 32: ἐγγὺς τριάκοντα τῶν ψιλῶν. d. "Similar": Plat. Phaed., 65a: ἐγγύς τι τείνειν τοῦ τεθνάναι; Plat. Gorg., 520a; Epict. Diss., IV, 11, 36. e. "Related": Plat. Resp., III, 391e; Aesch. Suppl., 388; Epict. Diss., III, 1, 20. f. Figur. of a spiritual attitude, Epict. Diss., I, 2, 14; II, 17, 40; IV, 1, 135.

ἐγγίζω is very common in the LXX, though the trans. is rare (Gn. 48:10, 13; Is. 5:8 etc.). Joseph. uses ἐγγίζειν only in the spatial sense (Bell., 5, 408; 6, 16; 1, 617), but קרב in older Heb. is used also for temporal proximity. Spatially, we find ἐγγίζω with ἕως and gen. in Ju. 9:52; 1 Macc. 3:26; with the dat. of person or obj. in Ex. 19:22: κυρίῳ τῷ θεῷ; Dt. 4:7: θεὸς ἐγγίζων αὐτοῖς. Cf. Ιερ. 23:23, where ἐγγίζω is used to denote the nearness rather than the remoteness of God's working (as in the Mas.). With πρός τινα, Gn. 27:22 etc.; with εἰς (B: πρός) and acc., 2 Βασ. 11:20; 19:42; with ἐπί τινα, ψ 26:2. To some extent קרב and נגש acquire technical cultic significance. The pure in the sense of cultic ritual (priests) may draw near to God, e.g., Ex. 3:5; Lv. 21:21 (προσεγγίζω); Ez. 40:46 etc. Elsewhere in the prophets and hagiographa ἐγγίζω is used generally for a pious disposition (with or without τῷ θεῷ or πρὸς τὸν θεόν), Is. 29:13; ψ 31:6; Jdt. 8:27 etc. Temporally it is found in Nu. 24:17; [1] Hab. 3:2; Is. 26:17. In Dt. Is. the approach of the time of salvation is always denoted except in 41:21, e.g., 50:8: ἐγγίζει ὁ δικαιώσας με; 51:5: ἐγγίζει ταχὺ ἡ δικαιοσύνη μου; 56:6: ἤγγικε γὰρ τὸ σωτήριόν μου παραγίνεσθαι. Ez. speaks of the ἐγγίζειν of the day of judgment in 7:7 (= 7:4); 22:4. Cf. כְּשֶׁתִּקְרַב שְׁנַת הַגְּאוּלָה אֲנִי גּוֹאֵל אֶתְכֶם = ὅταν ἐγγίσῃ ὁ ἐνιαυτὸς τῆς λυτρώσεως, ἐγὼ λυτροῦμαι ὑμᾶς, Tanch. בהר 4, 105. Similarly ἐγγύς is a tech. term for the proximity of judgment in OT prophecy, e.g., Jl. 1:15: ἐγγὺς ἡ ἡμέρα κυρίου; 2:1: ἐγγὺς ἡ ἡμέρα σκότους 3(4):14; Ob. 15; Zeph. 1:7; 1:14: ἐγγὺς ἡ ἡμέρα κυρίου ἡ μεγάλη; Is. 13:6; Ez. 30:3. In the LXX ἐγγύς also has the sense of "neighbour," Ex. 32:27 (τὸν ἔγγιστα); ψ 14:3 (τοὺς ἔγγιστα), usually for the Mas. קָרוֹב, but also for אָח in Job 6:15 and רֹאֵי פְּנֵי in Est. 1:14. Often it denotes the relation between God and the righteous: Ps. 33:18: Ἐγγὺς κύριος τοῖς συντετριμμένοις τὴν καρδίαν, ψ 118:151: ἐγγὺς εἶ κύριε; ψ 144:18:

ἐγγύς κτλ. [1] Ἐγγίζω occurs only here in Nu. קרב in the cultic sense is always ⸤tran⸥slated differently, and only once is נגש rendered προσεγγίζειν.

ἑβδομήκοντα → ἑπτά.

ἐγγίζω → ἐγγύς.

Ἐβραῖος → Ἰσραήλ.

ἐγγράφω → I, 769 f.

---

† ἔγγυος

Formed from ἐν and an unattested subst. γύη or γύς (→ hollow hand). This gives us ἐγγυάω, "to pledge," "to engage"; then ἔγγυος and ἐγγύη. Thus ἔγγυος, adj. "offering security," subst. ὁ ἔγγυος "guarantor," i.e., the one who accepts legal obligation (for payment etc.) in a bond. Xenoph. Vect., 4, 20; Aristot. Oec., II, p. 1350a, 19 (καθιστάναι τοὺς ἐγγύους τῶν εἴκοσι ταλάντων); Aeschin. Ep., 11, 12; Plut. De Amatorio Libro, 9 (II, 753d): ἔγγυον ἐπάγεσθαι. Very common in pap., e.g., P. Elephant., 8, 19; P. Hamb., 24, 17. [1] ἔγγυος is also found in the LXX, as in 2 Macc. 10:28. In Sir. 29:15 we see how far the pledge might go: χάριτας ἐγγύου μὴ ἐπιλάθῃ, ἔδωκεν γὰρ τὴν ψυχὴν αὐτοῦ ὑπέρ σου: the ἔγγυος may have to guarantee the other with his life.

This links up with the only NT passage in which the metaphor is used, namely, Hb. 7:22. Like the rest of the NT, Hb. speaks of the present possession of the gifts and powers of the kingdom of God (12:12 ff.). Yet salvation finds fulfilment or completion only in the future (4:1; 6:11 f.; 9:15; 10:36). Hb. emphasises particularly this element of hope in salvation, and thus gives prominence to the promises of God. Promises, however, demand assurances or guarantees. In distinction from the OT, Hb. does not find these in the words or oaths of God (6:17 f.). As in early Christianity generally, present and future are linked to the divine action in Jesus. Thinking in terms of the promises of God, Hb. finds in Jesus the Guarantor. With His life, death and ascension Jesus has given us the assurance (cf. Sir. 29:15) that the beginning of the saving work of God will necessarily be followed by its completion.

Preisker

ἔγγυος. A. Walde-J. Pokorny, *Vergleichendes Wörterbuch d. indog. Sprachen*, I (1927), 636 f.; F. Partsch, *Griech. Bürgschaftsrecht*, I (1909), 113 ff., 228 ff., 281; W. Prellwitz, Homeric ἀμφιγυήεις, "Der Künstler," *Zeitschr. f. vergl. Sprachforschung*, 46 (1914), 169 ff.; J. Behm, *Der Begriff* διαθήκη *im NT* (1912), 77; E. Lohmeyer, *Diatheke* (1913), 145; Mitteis-Wilcken, II, 1, 264 ff.; C. Schwegler, *De Aeschinis quae feruntur epistulis* (1913), 29 ff.

[1] Cf. Preisigke Wört., I, 410; Schwegler, *op. cit.*

ἐγγὺς κύριος πᾶσιν τοῖς ἐπικαλουμένοις αὐτόν. Philo uses ἐγγίζειν as an expression for encounter with God: Leg. All., II, 57 (οἱ ἐγγίσαντες θεῷ, of earthly death leading to the vision of God); Deus Imm., 161 ('Αβραὰμ ἐγγίσας τῷ θεῷ). Joseph. has ἐγγύς without case in Ant., 14, 345: ἐγγὺς γὰρ ἦν ἡ θάλασσα; 7, 284; 8, 340; Bell., 5, 276; with dat.: Ant., 1, 335: ἐγγὺς αὐτῷ γενόμενον; Bell., 2, 138; Ant., 7, 218. More common is the use with the gen.: Ant., 14, 85: ἐγγὺς 'Ιεροσολύμων etc. In the temporal sense Joseph. uses ἐγγύς only in the edict of Caesar in Ant., 14, 193: ἐν τῷ ἔγγιστα ἐν 'Αλεξανδρείᾳ πολέμῳ.

1. The NT usage is based on Dt. Is. In the older writings the distinctive feature of both ἐγγύς and ἐγγίζειν is that they express the characteristic aspect of the early Christian situation, being used of the eschatological fulfilment, of the great turning point in world history, of the coming of the kingdom of God directly into the present as the miracle of God. E.g., Mt. 3:2: ἤγγικεν γὰρ ἡ βασιλεία τῶν οὐρανῶν, cf. Mk. 1:15 and par.; Mt. 10:7; Lk. 10:9, 11; 21:8. Again, we read in Mt. 21:34: ἤγγισεν ὁ καιρὸς τῶν καρπῶν — a similitude for the time of fulfilment; cf. also ἐγγύς in Mk. 13:28 and par.: ἐγγὺς τὸ θέρος, and Mk. 13:29 and par.: ὅτι ἐγγύς ἐστιν ἐπὶ θύραις. [2] Again, ἐγγίζειν is linked with the destiny of the Son of Man, which is simply a sign of the final event (Mt. 26:45; Mk. 14:42 and par.), as is also the coming destruction of Jerusalem (Lk. 21:20) or the approach of the risen Lord to His disciples (Lk. 24:15). Mt. 26:18 refers to Jesus' hour of destiny, which means so much for the ultimate fulfilment. In Lk. 19:11 the ἐγγύς expresses the belief that the journey of Jesus to Jerusalem and the dawn of the kingdom of God coincide. Sometimes Lk. can also use ἐγγίζειν in the strict eschatological sense as a "sacred word" in relation to the mystery of the final fulfilment (10:9, 11; 21:8, 20; 24:15).

Paul uses ἐγγίζειν only to describe the unique aspect of the Christian life. It may indicate the coming of the rule of God in R. 13:12 or the fact that Epaphroditus is placed in danger of martyrdom in Phil. 2:30. He uses ἐγγύς only in the short eschatological message in Phil. 4:5: ὁ κύριος ἐγγύς, and in R. 10:8 in a quotation from Dt. 30:14 which is expounded in terms of eschatological preaching on the basis of the presence of the Messiah. In Eph. 2:13 and 2:17 the Gentiles, who once had no part in the community and were without hope and without God, are described as those who have drawn near in Christ, and therefore in eschatological terms. The Catholic Epistles (Hb. 10:25; Jm. 5:8; 1 Pt. 4:7) also use ἐγγίζειν for a situation of tense eschatological expectation. In Hb., as in OT prophecy, ἐγγύς refers to eschatological judgment. In Hb. 6:8 defection from Christ brings destruction in the imminent judgment. 8:13 speaks of the overthrow of the OT order by the new established in Christ. On the other hand, in Hb. 7:19 and Jm. 4:8 we have the formula ἐγγίζειν τῷ θεῷ from the LXX and Philo, except that the certainty of the actualisation of the drawing near is now stronger and surer and more complete than in the OT and later Judaism. Like the Synpt., Rev. uses ἐγγύς only as a term for the near coming of the kingdom of God. Thus we have ὁ γὰρ καιρὸς ἐγγύς in 1:3; cf. 22:10.

2. A very different use of ἐγγίζειν and ἐγγύς as indications of time and space is also to be found, esp. in Lk. and Jn. 'Εγγίζω is used a. with the dat. to indicate place

---

[2] Lk. 21:31 adds ἡ βασιλεία τοῦ θεοῦ as subj., but it would be simpler to refer it to the *parousia* of the Son of Man, or, with Schl. Mt., *ad loc.*, to the certainty "that the whole promise of Jesus comes to fulfilment and initiates eternal life."

and movement in Lk. 7:12; 15:1, 25; 22:47; Ac. 9:3; 10:9; 22:6, or with εἰς in Mk. 11:1; Mt. 21:1; Lk. 18:35; 19:29; 24:28; with ἐπί τινα in Lk. 10:9 (cf. Lk. 12:33), μέχρι τινός, Phil. 2:30; also in the abs. in Lk. 18:40; 19:37, 41; Ac. 21:33; 23:15. On one occasion Lk. uses it to indicate a festival (22:1); in Ac. 7:17 it denotes the time of promise given to Abraham. b. Temporally, of the hour (Mt. 26:45) or the day (R. 13:12; Hb. 10:25) or an end (Lk. 21:20) etc. In Mt. and Mk. ἐγγίζειν is only once used spatially (Mk. 11:1 and par.), and this in relation to the holy city. ἐγγίζειν does not occur at all in Jn. — a possible sign of the transmutation of eschatological expectation which leaves no place in his vocabulary for the sacred word of the previous period. In Ac. ἐγγύς is used only for place: 1:12: ἐγγὺς Ἰερουσαλήμ; 9:38; 27:8. Ἐγγύς is used temporally in Jn. 2:13; 7:2; 11:55, and it is worth noting that on two occasions this refers to the passover, which elsewhere (2:23; 4:45; 6:4; 11:55) almost certainly has eschatological significance in relation to the paschal lamb (1:29). We thus have here a final eschatological echo, the festival being linked with the death of Jesus with its significance for the last time. Elsewhere in Jn. ἐγγύς is used spatially, e.g., 3:23: ἐγγὺς τοῦ Σαλίμ; 6:19; 6:23: ἐγγὺς τοῦ τόπου, ὅπου; 11:18: Βηθανία ἐγγὺς τῶν Ἰεροσολύμων; 11:54: ἐγγὺς τῆς ἐρήμου; 19:20, 42.

Thus in the early days of Christianity ἐγγύς and ἐγγίζειν are among the words which suggest the sacred awe of all expectation of the *telos*. They express hope of the imminence of the coming world and are therefore sacred words used only in connexion with the great hope of consummation. Only later, when the passion of faith declined, did the usage change, as especially in Lk. and Jn., and they were again used in the secular sense to denote time and place. [3]

Preisker

---

[3] προσεγγίζειν trans. Luc. Amores, 53; often in the LXX, e.g., Gn. 33:6 f.; Jos. 3:4; ψ 118:150. In the NT the text of Mk. 2:4 is contested. אB, and with them Tischendorf, Nestle etc. read προσενέγκαι. On the other hand, AKDit, and with them v. Soden, have προσεγγίσαι for the bringing of the sick of the palsy to Jesus. On the basis of our findings on the use of ἐγγίζειν in Mk., the former is to be preferred; the alteration to προσεγγίσαι is to be regarded as later (cf. what is said on Lk.). The attestation of the term in Ac. 27:27 vl. is very weak.

┌─────────────────────────────────┐
│ ἐγείρω, ἔγερσις, ἐξεγείρω,   │
│ γρηγορέω (ἀγρυπνέω)   │
└─────────────────────────────────┘

ἐγείρω.

1. ἐγείρω in non-biblical Greek. a. trans. "to awaken" from sleep, Hom. Il., 5, 413; cultically : τὸν θεόν; Egypt.: Porphyr. Abst., IV, 9; [1] intr. (pass.) "to wake up," Hom. Il., 2, 41: ἐξ ὕπνου; Jos. Ant., 2, 82 etc.; of watchful states of the soul, Plot. Enn., IV, 8, 1; V, 7, 22. b. trans.: "to arouse," "to stir up," Hom. Il., 5, 208; with impersonal obj.: μάχην, Hom. Il., 13, 778; μῦθον, Plat. Polit., 272d; intr. (pass.): "to stir oneself," Demosth., 19, 305. c. Trans. "to set up," rare in secular Gk. with personal obj. (though cf. d.); "to erect" buildings, posts, images, Luc. Alex., 10; Ditt. Or., 677, 3 (2nd. cent. A.D.); Bito Mechanicus[2], p. 66, 5; Jos. Ant., 15, 391; 298; 328 etc.; cf. Anth. Pal., 9, 236; "to raise up" (Agraphon P. Oxy., 1, 1, recto 6 : ἔγει[ρ]ον τὸν λίθο[ν] κακεῖ εὑρή-

---

ἐγείρω κτλ. Cf. in general the bibl. listed under → ἀνίστημι. E. Fascher, "Die Auferstehung Jesu und ihr Verhältnis zur urchristl. Verkündigung," ZNW, 26 (1927), 1-26; A. D. Nock, "A Note on the Resurrection," in A. Rawlinson, *Essay on the Trinity and Incarnation* (1928), 47-50. S. V. McCasland, *The Resurrection of Jesus* (1932); M. Goguel, *La Résurrection de Jésus dans le Christianisme primitif* (1933). On the raising of the dead by Aesculapius, → I, 369; Pauly-W., II, 1653 f.; R. Herzog, *Die Wunderheilungen von Epidauros* (1931), 142 ; on the raising of the dead by men, O. Weinreich, *Antike Heilungswunder* (1909), 171 ff. On dying and rising gods and the raising of believers with Christ, Chant de la Saussaye, Index *Auferstehung des Gottes* and the individual names of gods ; cf. also Pauly-W. For specialised lit. v. F. Cumont, *Die orientalischen Relig. im röm. Heidentum*[3] (1931). More general studies are J. G. Frazer, *The Golden Bough*[3] (1920-23); O. Pfleiderer, *Das Christusbild d. urchristl. Glaubens* (1903), 55-89; M. Brückner, *Der sterbende und auferstehende Gottheiland in den orientalischen Religionen* (1908); A. Jacoby, *Die antiken Mysterienreligionen und das Christentum* (1910); A. Dieterich, *Eine Mithrasliturgie*[3] (1923); W. Bousset, *Kyrios Christos*[3] (1926), 134 ff.; K. Deissner, *Paulus und die Mystik seiner Zeit*[2] (1921), 124 ff.; A. Oepke, *Die Missionspredigt d. Ap. Pls.* (1920), 138 ff.; A. Kirchner, *Marduk von Babylon und Jesus Christus* (1922); H. Zimmern, *Zum babyl. Neujahrsfest, 2. Beitrag* (1918); J. Leipoldt, *Sterbende und auferstehende Götter* (1923); Kittel Probleme, 82 ff.; *Religionsgesch. u. Urchrtt.* (1932), 125, 128; F. Nötscher, *Altorient. u. at.licher Auferstehungsglaube* (1926); J. Schneider, *Die Passionsmystik des Paulus* (1929); K. Mittring, *Heilswirklichkeit bei Paulus* (1929), 32 ff.; E. Lohmeyer, *Grundlagen paul. Theol.* (1929), 90 ff.; 139 ff.; E. Sommerlath, *Der Ursprung des neuen Lebens nach Pls.*[2] (1927), 63 ff.; H. E. Weber, *Eschatologie und Mystik im NT* (1930), esp. 104 ff.; A. Schweitzer, *Gesch. der paul. Forschung*[2] (1933), 141 ff.; *Die Mystik des Apostels Pls.* (1930), esp. 102 ff.; Khl. and Ltzm. on R. 6; NT theologies by H. J. Holtzmann[2], II (1911), 117 ff.; P. Feine[5] (1931), 193, 199; H. Weinel[4] (1928), 240 ff.; 243; 250; 337 ff.; 443. On the question of the mode of resurrection, Str.-B., esp. I, 887 ff.; III, 474 ff.; IV, 1017 ff.; Weber, 368 ff.; Joh. W., Bchm., Ltzm. on 1 C. 15:35 ff.; Holtzmann, *op. cit.*, 209 ff.; Weinel, *op. cit.*, 324 f.; A. Oepke, "Die Eschatologie des Pls.," *Allg. Ev. Luth. Kirchenz.*, 60 (1927), 458 ff.

[1] Acc. to an inscr. from Rhodes (*Oestr. Jhft.*, 7 [1904], 93), money is to be paid τῷ ὑδραύλῃ ἐγείροντι τὸν θεόν (Bacchus). It seems very doubtful whether this refers to the resurrection of Bacchus (F. Abel, *Rev. Bibl.* NS, 5 [1908], 577). Far more likely it denotes the ἀνακαλεῖσθαι of the god for the sacrifice by music, cf. Plut. Is. et Os., 35 (II, 365a). J. Quasten, *Musik und Gesang in den Kulten der heidnischen Antike und christlichen Frühzeit* (1930), 40. Arnobius, Adversus Nationes, VII, 32 (A. Reiffenscheid in CSEL, IV), says contemptuously : obdormiscunt superi. Cf. 1 K. 18:27. There is a suggestion of new life in the awakening of Dionysus Licnites, who comes back from Persephone ; cf. Otto (→ n. 12), 76 ff.

[2] Ed. C. Wescher, *Poliorcétique des Grecs* (1867) (3rd. or 2nd. cent. B.C.).

σεις με); [3] intr. "to raise oneself," "to rise up," Attic only in the formal intr. act. (→ n. 6) imper. ἔγειρε "up !" (Aristoph. Ra., 340). d. Trans. "to awaken the dead," seldom found in secular Gk. Ps.-Apollodorus Bibliotheca,[4] II, 124 : ὁ δὲ (Heracles in Hades) Θησέα μὲν λαβόμενος τῆς χειρὸς ἤγειρε belongs under c. rather than d., since according to the story Theseus and Peirithoos go down to Hades alive and are chained to a throne. Intr. (pass.) "to rise from the dead"; Epigr. Graec. Praefatio, 646a, 5 : ἐντεῦθεν (from the grave) οὐθὶς ἀποθανὼν ἐγίρε[ται. Although the euphemistic description of death as sleep is common among the Gks. (→ κοιμάω), this use seems to derive from c. rather than a. Preis. Zaub., IV, 195 (in a prayer spoken in the attitude of death): ἔγειρον, ἱκετῶ, τὸν σόν, ἱκνοῦμαι, φίλον; this is followed by a sign of rising again (212 f.).

2. The Biblical Usage.

All these meanings are found in the Bible, but with different nuances and development due to the influence of the Heb. (עוּר, קוּם, עָמַד kal and hiph. etc.) and the distinctive nature of biblical religion. For a. trans. cf. Mk. 4:38; Ac. 12:7, and intr. Gn. 41:4, 7; Mt. 1:24; 25:7; Mk. 4:27, and figur. of the setting aside of carnal assurance in R. 13:11: ὥρα ἤδη ὑμᾶς ἐξ ὕπνου ἐγερθῆναι; Eph. 5:14 : ἔγειρε, ὁ καθεύδων.[5] For b. trans. with impers. obj. cf. Phil. 1:17 (θλῖψιν); with pers. obj. "to cause to appear or to rise up in history" (→ ἀνίστημι, I, 369); Ju. 2:16, 18; 3:9, 15; 3 Βασ. 11:14, 23 (A); Ac. 13:22 (David), 23 (vl.). ἐγεῖραι τέκνα τῷ Ἀβραάμ, Mt. 3:9 and par., cf. Lk. 1:69: ἤγειρεν κέρας σωτηρίας ἡμῖν. Cf. Eka r., 5, 3 on Lam. 5:3 : "The Redeemer, whom I will cause to rise up from among you (שׁאני עתיד להעמיד)"; Shemone-Esre Bab. Recension, 15th Benediction: "Blessed be Thou, O Yahweh, that Thou dost cause to shoot forth the horn of help (מַצְמִיחַ קֶרֶן יְשׁוּעָה)." For b. intr. "to stir oneself," cf. Jer. 6:22; Mk. 13:8 and par., cf. Is. 19:2; "to rise up," of prophets : Mt. 11:11; Lk. 7:16; Jn. 7:52, ψευδόχριστοι; Mt. 24:11, 24; Mk. 13:22, in judgment as an accuser : Mt. 12:42 and par. For c. trans. cf. Gr. Sir. 49:13; 1 Esr. 5:44 (= 43); Jn. 2:19 f., also with pers. obj. "to help to raise," "to set up," an idol in 1 S. 5:3; an animal in Mt. 12:11; τὸν πτωχόν in 1 Βασ. 2:8; ψ 112:7; those who sink to the ground in awe in Da. 8:18; 10:10; cf. 2 Βασ. 12:17; Ac. 10:26; the sick in Mk. 1:31; 9:27; Ac. 3:7; implying "to make well" in Jm. 5:15 (cf. Jos. Ant., 19, 294 : τὸν θεὸν ἐγείρειν τὰ πεπτωκότα). For c. intr. cf. "to rise up strengthened" in Mt. 17:7; Ac. 9:8; "to stand up whole" in Mt. 8:15; 9:6 f.; Mk. 2:12; also gen. "to rise up" : ἐκ τοῦ δείπνου, Jn. 13:4 (cf. Est. 7:7 Heb., solemnly in Nu. 10:35); Mt. 8:26 and par.; in a weakened Semitic sense, marking the beginning of an action, "to commence" (→ ἀνίστημι, I, 368): Ex. 5:8; 1 Ch. 10:12; 22:19; 2 Ch. 21:9; 22:10; Mt. 9:19; Jn. 11:29; often in the imper.: ἐγερθεὶς παράλαβε, Mt. 2:13, 20, or more directly Mk. 14:42 and par.; Jn. 14:31: ἐγείρεσθε, ἄγωμεν ("arise, let us go"); the form ἔγειρε is found not only in Eph. 5:14 (→ supra) but in many passages (Mk. 2:9, 11 and par.; 3:3; Lk. 6:8; Jn. 5:8; Rev. 11:1) with mid. variants (cf. jBik., 65d, 33 : קוּם אתהלך לארעא דישׂראל).[6]

---

[3] Cf. A. Harnack, Über die jüngst. entdeckten Sprüche Jesu (1897); A. Resch, Agrapha[2] TU, NF, XV 3/4 (1906),69, 353; H. G. E. White, The Sayings of Jesus from Oxyrhynchus (1920), LXIII ; Reitzenstein, ZNW, 6 (1905), 203; GGA, 183 (1921), 165 ff. This does not denote blessing in daily work (Harnack) but has a pantheistic sense, perhaps based on Qoh. 10:9.

[4] 2nd. cent. A.D. in Mythographi Graeci, I, ed. R. Wagner (1894).

[5] On the origin of the quotation, cf. Dib. Gefbr., ad loc.; Schürer, III, 362, 365; Clemen, 307. Aristoph. Ra., 340 ff. offers a par. but can hardly be the direct basis. The saying has a genuinely ethical and Christian ring. Materially → 336.

[6] Further instances may be found in Dalman WJ, I, 18 f. קוּם is common for "up !" in Rabbinic writings. Possibly ἔγειρε is an itacist substitution for ἔγειραι, as some later grammarians think. Cf. Reitzenstein GGA, op. cit., 167.

Sense d. "to raise the dead," or pass. "to be raised," "to rise from the dead" (→ ἀνίστημι, I, 369) is found in relation to individual resurrections, negatively in 4 Βασ. 4:31: οὐκ ἠγέρθη τὸ παιδάριον, and positively in Gr. Sir. 48:5; Mt. 9:25; 10:8; 11:5 and par.; Mk. 5:41 and par.; 6:14 and par.; Lk. 7:14; Jn. 5:21; 12:1, 9, 17; Hb. 11:19. In connexion with the person of Jesus these resurrections are signs of the Messianic age and of the coming resurrection of all the dead. Cf. also Mt. 27:52, → ἔγερσις, 337. In relation to the resurrection of Jesus, we find that its significance for the kerygma is intimated already in the prophecy of Jesus (Mt. 16:21; Lk. 9:22; Mt. 17:9, 23; 20:19; Mk. 14:28 and par., ἐγείρειν being a favourite word of Mt.). [7] It is then reflected in the Easter stories (Mk. 16:6[14]; Mt. 28:7; Lk. 24:34; Jn. 21:14), and takes a prominent place in the preaching of the apostles (Ac. 3:15; 4:10; 5:30; 10:40; 13:30, 37; R. 4:24 f.; 6:4, 9; 7:4; 8:11, 34; 10:9; 1 C. 6:14; 15:4, 12 etc.; 2 C. 4:14; 5:15; Gl. 1:1; Eph. 1:20; Col. 2:12; 1 Th. 1:10; 2 Tm. 2:8; 1 Pt. 1:21). God has acknowledged the Crucified by the resurrection, and glorified Him (cf. Ac., also R. 7:4; Phil. 2:9-11; Eph. 1:20 ff.), thus giving force to the redemption (cf. esp. R. 4 [→ 70; 224] and 8; 1 C. 15). If, in distinction from Hellenism (→ I, 368; II, infra), the NT prefers ἐγείρειν and ἐγείρεσθαι to ἀνιστάναι and ἀνίστασθαι (though not, of course, ἔγερσις to ἀνάστασις), this is perhaps because it brings out better the concrete nature of the divine action. The idea of the self-resurrection of Jesus is first found in Johannine theology (Jn. 2:19, 21; 10:17, 18).

Though Paul accepts the empty tomb (ἐτάφη, 1 C. 15:4; [8] ἐτάφημεν, R. 6:4), according to 1 C. 6:13 f.; 15:47, 50; Phil. 2:6, 9 he does not think of the body of the risen Lord in material terms, but as the σῶμα πνευματικόν [9] of the One who is exalted to universal personality in all things, and especially in the Church (Col. 1:18 ff.). On the other hand, apologetic interests incline the evangelical and post-canonical tradition in a more material direction (Lk. 24:39 ff.; Ac. 10:41; Jn. 20:25 ff.; Ev. Naz. in Hier. De Viris Illustribus, 16, MPL, 23, 633b (cf. MPL, 24, 628a = Ign. Sm., 3:2: λάβετε, ψηλαφήσατέ με καὶ ἴδετε, ὅτι οὐκ εἰμὶ δαιμόνιον ἀσώματον. καὶ εὐθὺς αὐτοῦ ἥψαντο καὶ ἐπίστευσαν; Just. De Resurrectione, 9, Copt. Record, Hennecke, 67). Nevertheless, spiritual features are not wanting (Jn. 20:17, 19, 26), and a distinction is perhaps to be made between the immediately risen and the exalted Lord.

The oriental myth of the dying and rising saviour-god (Tammuz, Bel-Marduk, Adonis, Sandan-Heracles of Tarsus, Attis, Osiris, the Cretan Zeus, Dionysus, and cf. the Mithras sacrifice and the double life of Kore) constitutes neither the native soil [10] of the Gospel nor a true parallel to it. ἐγείρειν and ἐγείρεσθαι hardly occur at all in the relevant passages (though we do find ἔγερσις, → 337). It is rather said that the god is delivered (Firm. Mat. Err. Prof. Rel., 22) or that he or the deliverance has come from Hades (Plut. Is. et Os., 19 [II, 358b]; Phot. Bibliotheca, 242 [MPG, 103, 1281a], or that he lives (Ps. Luc. Syr. Dea, 6). Indeed, sometimes the continued life is only partial (Arnobius, Adversus Nationes, V, 7 and 14 [A. Reiffenscheid in CSEL, IV]; Paus.,

---

[7] On the resurrection and parousia in the prior intimation of Jesus, cf. W. Michaelis, Täufer, Jesus, Urgemeinde (1928), 88 f., 99 ff. → I, 370, n. 11.

[8] K. Barth, Die Auferstehung der Toten (1926), 75 ff. gives us a model of ingenious reinterpretation.

[9] A. Schweitzer, Die Mystik des Ap. Pls. (1930), 116 ff.; 262 ff.

[10] On A. Drews, Die Christusmythe (1924), P. Jensen, W. B. Smith, S. Lublinski etc.: A. Schweitzer, Gesch. d. Leben-Jesu-Forschung (1926), 444 ff.

VII, 17, 12), or perhaps even symbolical in the form of budding almonds or figs in the myths or wild jubilation and dramatic representation in the cults. Decomposition may take place (Diod. S., III, 59, 7: ἠφανισμένου τοῦ σώματος διὰ τὸν χρόνον). The resurrection of the god is not original in the Attis cult. [11] Plut. Is. et Os., 11 (II, 355b); 58 (II, 374e) contests the historical character of the myths. Imaginary erotic pictures simply express the unfailing power of nature. The case seems to be rather different when we come to Dionysus. In him the Greeks perceive not so much the successiveness as the identity of life and death. We thus have an advanced identity mysticism of a speculative type. While the spiritual and ethical note is almost completely lacking in the eastern world, it is present here, but in a form very different from that of the NT. In neither case do we find the distinctive eschatological concept, e.g., of R. 6:10. [12] For all the points of contact and mutual influence between the NT and the surrounding world, there is the decisive difference that in the NT the kernel and basis is spiritually and ethically significant history rather than nature myth or speculative myth.

3. The resurrection of believers with Christ is worked out particularly by Paul, but in its main features it forms part of the general teaching of the early Church (R. 6:4-11; Gl. 2:20; Col. 2:12 ff.; Eph. 2:1, 5; 2 C. 4:10 ff.; 1 Pt. 1:3). Naturally, this is not to be thought of as distinct from the life of justification (R. 5:18), whether in terms of a persistent cleavage in the thinking of Paul [13] or with a one-sided emphasis on Christ mysticism. [14] The "mystical" train of thought is based on the juridical (Col. 2:13-15; 2 C. 5:17-21; Gl. 2:20; R. 8:28-39; and the whole context of R. 5 and 6). R. 6 does not describe analogy magic; in the first instance it depicts the new situation of salvation history in which believers are set with Christ (→ σύν). The new life is the — as yet concealed — reality of faith (2 C. 4:7 ff.; 5:7; Col. 3:3), not in the sense that it cannot be grasped psychologically (cf. R. 8:16, 23; Gl. 3:2; 4:6; 2 C. 1:22), but in such a way that it cannot be explained as a magical change, that it is withdrawn from human control, and that it is a divinely posited, eschatological reality which awaits the consummation (R. 8:19 ff.; 2 C. 4:16-18; Phil. 3:11 ff.). [15] Strongly realistic though the thought is, it does not imply that in any strict sense the resurrection of the dead has taken place already (2 Tm. 2:18 describes this view as heretical; and cf. Phil. 3:10 f.; R. 8:11 etc.). There are late analogies to Eph. 5:14 in the Mandaean tradition. [16] A closer examination of all the relevant religio-historical material shows us that these thoughts are partly ethical, partly cultic and partly eschatological. [17] Even in Johannine theology, though there is a strong emphasis on possession (Jn. 11:25; 5:24; 3:18; 1 Jn. 3:6, 9, 14; 5:18), we do not have a complete spiritualising of eschatology (Jn. 21:22; 5:28 f.; 6:39 f., 44; 17:24; 1 Jn. 2:18, 28; 3:2 f.; 4:17; cf. 1:8). → σύν.

---

[11] F. Cumont, Die oriental. Religionen im röm. Heidentum³ (1931), 228, n. 46.

[12] On Dionysus, cf. W. F. Otto, Dionysos, Frankfurter Studien zur Religion und Kultur der Antike, Vol. 4 (1933), 175 ff.

[13] Thus esp. Holtzmann, op. cit. Weinel even sees a threefold way of salvation.

[14] E. Wissmann, Das Verhältnis von ΠΙΣΤΙΣ und Christusfrömmigkeit bei Pls. (1926); A. Schweitzer, Die Mystik des Apostels Pls. (1930).

[15] H. E. Weber, op. cit., 76, n. 1, 92 ff. etc.; K. Mittring, 64 ff.; A. Oepke, ZNW, 24 (1930), 104 ff.

[16] Lidz. Ginza, 382, 7 ff.; 387, 4 ff.; 475, 10 ff.; 550, 6 ff.; 576, 33 ff.; 585, 16 ff.

[17] Cf. Reitzenstein Ir. Erl., 6, 135 etc. Cf. also the three variants in 1 C. 6:14 : ἐξεγείρει, ἐξεγερεῖ, ἐξήγειρεν.

4. On the future resurrection of the dead (Is. 26:19; Da. 12:2 A; Mk. 12:26; Lk. 20:37; Ac. 26:8; 1 C. 15:15-52 *passim*; 2 C. 1:9; 4:14), → ἀνίστημι, I, 371. In the NT the question of the constitution of the resurrection life receives a more unequivocally spiritual answer than in Judaism.

The Jewish hope of resurrection tends to be materialistic. The resurrection occurs at the place of death (Qoh. r., 1 on 1:7, Str.-B., IV, 1025 f.), in clothes (bKet, 111b, Str.-B., III, 475), at the sound of a trumpet 1000 divine ells long, [18] and with any previous characteristics (blind, deaf or dumb, Gn. r., 95, 1 on 46:28), though anything broken is healed (*loc. cit.*). The statement in S. Bar. 50 f. concerning a future change is a compromise between the spiritual and the material. The new is based on an indestructible skeleton (Gn. r., 28, 3 on 6:7 according to a pronouncement of Jehoshua ben Chananya), though it is debated between the schools of Hillel and Shammai whether this takes place in the same order as Ez. 37 or the reverse (Gn. r., 14, 5 on 2:7). The feast of the blessed is depicted at length. [19] Marital intercourse will continue, even if only for the days of the Messiah (to a eunuch in Jos. Ant., 17, 45), although also for the days of the resurrection (cf. bSanh., 92b, Str.-B., I, 888). According to Jalqut, 1 § 111 on Gn. 25:31; bBer., 17a; Ab. R. Nat., 1 etc. (Str.-B., I, 890); Midr. Ps. 146 § 4 (Str.-B., I, 889), however, eating and drinking and commerce and traffic and marital intercourse will also cease. The righteous, who are essentially the Jews, will shine like stars or (seven times more than) the sun (Da. 12:3; Eth. En. 39:7; 51:4 f.; 104:2; 108:11-14; 4 Esr. 7:97, 125; S. Bar. 51:3).

The question of the Sadducees in Mk. 12:23 and par. is malicious, but it corresponds to Rabbinic theology as yet unaffected by spiritualising tendencies. [20] The spiritual conception of Jesus (Mk. 12:25 and par.) is quite new by contrast. Though Jesus speaks of the feast of the blessed, He does not depict it (Mk. 14:25 and par.; Mt. 8:11; Lk. 13:29; cf. also the parables which speak of a banquet). Paul specifically excludes eating as well as sexual intercourse (1 C. 6:13). The σάρξ will be destroyed and the σῶμα changed (1 C. 15:42 ff., 50 ff.; on 15:40 ff. cf. Mt. 13:43 and → *supra*; on v. 37 → γυμνός, I, 774; bKet, 111b, Str.-B., III, 475). Johannine theology avoids any materialistic expressions while presenting a realistic belief in the resurrection.

† ἔγερσις.

This occurs from the time of Empedocles (Fr., 123 [I, 270, 7, Diels]) and Hippocrates (Coacae Praenotiones, 82), though it is not found in Philo. a. Trans. it means the "rousing" or "stimulation" of the spirit (Plat. Tim., 70c; Aristot. Eth. Nic., III, 11, p. 1116b, 30), the "erection" of walls, buildings etc. (Herodian, VIII, 5, 4; 1 Esr. 5:62 [= 59]), the "raising" of a dead man. Preis. Zaub., XIII, 277: ἔγερσις σώματος νεκροῦ (followed by an incantation for the resurrecting of a corpse). b. intr. "awakening" (LXX Ju. 7:19 A), "rising" (ψ 138:2), "recovery" (Aret., II, 11, 5), "rising" from death (Menander Ephesin. in Jos. Ant., 8, 146 = Ap., 1, 119): πρῶτος τοῦ Ἡρακλέους ἔγερσιν ἐποιήσατο ἐν τῷ Περιτίῳ μηνί. [1]

---

[18] Alphabet-Midrash of R. Aqiba, 17c, in Jellinek, Beth ha-Midr., 3, 31, Str.-B., III, 481.
[19] Str.-B., IV, 1146 ff.
[20] Schl. Mt., 650 ff.

ἔγερσις. [1] For the view that πρῶτος is also to be read in Ap., 1, 119, and that the reference is not to the erection of the temple of Heracles but to the feast of the resurrection of Heracles-Adonis, v. F. Abel, *Rev. Bibl.*, NS, 5 (1908), 577 f.

Mt. 27:53: μετὰ τὴν ἔγερσιν αὐτοῦ == "after the awakening or resurrection of Jesus" (→ ἐγείρω, 335). Since the context speaks of signs at the death of Jesus, these words are perhaps a later correction in terms of 1 C. 15:20; Col. 1:18. [2]

† ἐξεγείρω.

From the time of the tragic dramatists and Hdt. to Plut. and Epict. this is found in most of the senses of the simple form, though not of objects. [1] There are only two meanings in the NT: a. "to cause to appear in history," "to call into existence": Zech. 11:16 (== קום hiph); Jos. Ant., 8, 271: βασιλεὺς ἐξεγείρεθ᾽ ὑπ᾽ ἐμοῦ; b. "to awaken (pass. to rise) from the dead": Aesch. Choeph., 495: ἆρ᾽ ἐξεγείρει τοῖσδ᾽ ὀνείδεσιν, πάτερ; cf. R. Wünsch, Antike Fluchtafeln (1912), 5, 21: οἱ δαίμονες ἐξεγερθῶσιν (== the spirits of the dead are raised up by conjuration). In the LXX only Ἰώβ 5:11; Da. 12:2 (Α: ἐγερθήσονται).

1. Sense a. R. 9:17 to Pharaoh: εἰς τοῦτο ἐξήγειρά σε, ὅπως ἐνδείξωμαι ἐν σοὶ τὴν δύναμίν μου. Ex. 9:16: הֶעֱמַדְתִּיךָ, "I have spared thee, [2] LXX διετηρήθης, sharpened by Paul to "called thee into being." The weaker "raised thee from a sick bed" [3] is impossible in spite of Jm. 5:15 (cf. v. 20 ff.). "Provoked thee to opposition" (cf. σκληρύνει in v. 18) [4] is possible in view of 2 Macc. 13:4, but is hardly what Paul can have had in view.

2. Sense b. is found in 1 C. 6:14. There is no particular significance in the alternation between the simple and compound forms.

† γρηγορέω († ἀγρυπνέω).

A later Hellenistic reconstruction of ἐγρήγορα (Pluperfect ἐγρηγόρει understood as ἐποίει). Outside the Bible we find it in Achill. Tat., IV, 17; Jos. Ant., 11, 47 vl.; cf. 7, 48; Bell., 4, 306: "to watch," in the LXX lit. only in Neh. 7:3; 1 Macc. 12:27; Cant. 5:2 (Α, Σ); figur. "to keep zealous watch over," of men and lurking beasts and also of Yahweh: Jer. 5:6; Ἰερ. 38:28; Bar. 2:9; Lam. 1:14; Da. 9:14 Θ; in a religious and ethical sense we have ἀγρυπνέω in Prv. 8:34; Gr. Sir. 36:16.

In the NT 1. literally "to watch": Mk. 14:34 and par., 37 and par.; and in parables with some transition to sense 2: Mt. 24:43; Mk. 13:34; Lk. 12:37, 39.

2. Figur. only of men: "to be vigilant," 1 C. 16:13, esp. in relation to the parousia: Mt. 24:42; 25:13; Mk. 13:35, 37 (Lk. 12:40: γίνεσθε ἕτοιμοι); 1 Th. 5:6; Rev. 3:3; 16:15; with → νήφειν in 1 Th. 5:6, 8; 1 Pt. 5:8, linked with prayer in Mk. 14:38; Mt. 26:41; Col. 4:2; of concern for the salvation of the community,

---

[2] The very weakly attested reading μετὰ τὴν ἔγερσιν αὐτῶν (om syrh) can hardly be considered. Cf. Kl. Mt., ad loc.

ἐ ξ ε γ ε ί ρ ω. [1] Liddell-Scott and Pr.-Bauer, s.v.

[2] So also the Jewish translators and expositors, Str.-B., III, 268 f.

[3] Hofmann, etc.

[4] As occasionally held from the time of Augustine, also Sickb. R., ad loc.; cf. Khl., Zn., Ltzm., ad loc.

γ ρ η γ ο ρ έ ω. Helbing, 82, 84; Thackeray, 263; Bl.-Debr. § 73; Nägeli, 44.

Ac. 20:31; Rev. 3:2. ἀγρυπνέω (only figur.) is found in similar constructions in Mk. 13:33; Lk. 21:36; Eph. 6:18; Hb. 13:17.

3. γρηγορέω is found as the opp. of καθεύδω, "to be alive," only in 1 Th. 5:10.

Oepke

ἐγκαινίζω → καινός.

ἐγκακέω → κακός.

---

† ἐγκομβόομαι

(Act. "to wrap up," κόμβος "band"), "to clothe oneself with …," "to draw on closely" (ἐγκόμβωμα an article of clothing over the naked body). [1] It is not found in the LXX (Θ Is. 3:20: ἐγκόμβωμα).

In the NT we find it only in 1 Pt. 5:5: "to invest oneself with," "to make one's essential[2] characteristic" — whether in relation to brotherly intercourse among Christians or in relation to the attitude to God. In both cases ἐγκομβώσασθε emphasises that → ταπεινοφροσύνη determines decisively the religious attitude and conduct of Christians.

We can divide the sentence before πάντες, in which case ἀλλήλοις is a dat. sociat. meaning "in your dealings with one another," though this is a strange construction. On the other hand, the division may come after ἀλλήλοις, in which case v. 5b should perhaps be linked with what follows and esp. with v. 6 (in which the key word is ταπεινώθητε).

Delling

**† ἐγκράτεια (ἀκρασία),
ἐγκρατής (ἀκρατής),
ἐγκρατεύομαι**

1. The word group ἐγκρατ- takes its sense from the stem κρατ-, which denotes power or lordship, and which expresses the power or lordship which one has either over oneself or over something.

ἐ γ κ ο μ β ό ο μ α ι. [1] Examples may be found in the lex., esp. Thes. Steph.

[2] It is thus stronger than → ἐνδύομαι, though cf. Col. 3:12: ἐνδύσασθε … ταπεινοφροσύνην.

ἐ γ κ ρ ά τ ε ι α κτλ. O. Dittrich, *Geschichte der Ethik* (1926), *v.* Index; G. Delling, *Paulus' Stellung zu Frau und Ehe* (1931), 66, 84; R. Steiger, *Die Dialektik der paulinischen Existenz* (1931), 70 f.

The basic sense is most clearly expressed in the adj. ἐγκρατής. Purely formally this may be derived from ἐν κράτος (ἔχων) with its implication of having power in oneself, or from ἐν κράτει (ὤν) implying a status of power. ἐγκρατής means one who has a status of power or rule, who has power over something, whether this power be factual or spiritual. In the first sense, cf. Hdt., VIII, 49 : τῶν αὐτοὶ χωρέων ἐγκρατέες εἰσί. Plat. Resp., VI, 501e : πρὶν ἂν πόλεως τὸ φιλόσοφον γένος ἐγκρατὲς γένηται; 2 Macc. 8:30 : ὀχυρωμάτων ὑψηλῶν εὖ μάλα ἐγκρατεῖς ἐγένοντο; in the second cf. Plat. Leg., X, 897b of ψυχῆς γένος ἐγκρατὲς οὐρανοῦ καὶ γῆς καὶ πάσης τῆς περιόδου ...; VIII, 839b : εἰ τοῦ νόμου τις τούτου δύναιτο ἐγκρατὴς εἶναι; cf. also ὁ ἐγκρατὴς τοῦ νόμου καταλήμψεται αὐτήν (sc. σοφίαν) (Sir. 15:1). It thus means "to have power or dominion over all things and over oneself," i.e., "to be inwardly strong," cf. Plat. Phaedr., 256b; Plat. Ep., VII, 331d. These meanings favour a derivation from ἐν κράτει ὤν, since ἐν cannot mean "over" in κράτος ἔχων ἐν. Cf. Thuc., II, 29 : βασιλεύς ἐν κράτει, a king with real power. The opp. is ἀκρατής, "one who has no inner strength, who is undisciplined."

ἐγκράτεια thus means the "dominion which one has over oneself or something" in the sense that one may or may not have it, that one can bear it, that one thus controls it, e.g., ἐγκράτεια πρὸς ἐπιθυμίαν βρωτοῦ καὶ ποτοῦ καὶ λαγνείας (desire) καὶ ὕπνου καὶ ῥίγους καὶ θάλπους καὶ πόνου, Xenoph. Mem., II, 1, 1. It may thus mean "endurance" or "steadfastness." Ps.-Plato says of ἐγκράτεια: δύναμις ὑπομενητικὴ λύπης· ἀκολούθησις τῷ ὀρθῷ λογισμῷ, Def., 412b.

For the sense of self-control cf. Plat. Resp., III, 390b; the opp. is ἀκρασία, "lack of control or restraint," e.g., Xenoph. Sym., 8, 27; Jos. Bell., 1, 34.

ἐγκρατεύεσθαι. This word is once used in class. Gk. in Aristot. [1] It is more common in Hellenism. In the LXX we have ἐξελθὼν ἐνεκρατεύσατο in Gn. 43:31 in the sense of "he composed himself."

2. ἐγκράτεια plays an important role in the philosophical ethics of classical Greece and Hellenism.

It is reckoned a cardinal virtue by Socrates : ... ἡγησάμενον τὴν ἐγκράτειαν ἀρετῆς εἶναι κρηπῖδα (foundation) ..., Xenoph. Mem., I, 5, 4. [2] Aristotle devotes a full section to it in Eth. Nic., VII, 1-11, p. 1145 ff., cf. Eth. M., II, 4-6, p. 1200 ff. At the end of the discussion he defines it as follows in distinction from σωφροσύνη : ὁ ἐγκρατής ἐστιν οὐ μόνον ὁ ἐπιθυμιῶν ἐνουσῶν ταύτας κατέχων διὰ τὸν λόγον, ἀλλὰ καὶ ὁ τοιοῦτος ὢν οἷος καὶ μὴ ἐνουσῶν ἐπιθυμιῶν τοιοῦτος εἶναι οἷος εἰ ἐγγένοιντο κατέχειν. ἔστι δὲ σώφρων ὁ μὴ ἔχων ἐπιθυμίας φαύλας τόν τε λόγον τὸν περὶ ταῦτα ὀρθόν ..., ὥστ᾽ ἀκολουθήσει τῷ σώφρονι ὁ ἐγκρατὴς καὶ ἔσται σώφρων· ὁ μὲν γὰρ σώφρων, ὁ μὴ πάσχων, ὁ δ᾽ ἐγκρατὴς ὁ πάσχων καὶ τούτων κρατῶν ἢ οἷός τε ὢν πάσχειν, M., II, 6, p. 1203b, 13 ff. He briefly defines ἐγκράτεια as ἀρετὴ τοῦ ἐπιθυμητικοῦ, καθ᾽ ἣν κατέχουσιν τῷ λογισμῷ τὴν ἐπιθυμίαν ὁρμῶσαν ἐπὶ τὰς φαύλας ἡδονάς, De Virtutibus et Vitiis, 2, p. 1250a, 9 f. Stoicism takes the same view. The most comprehensive Stoic definition is given by Sextus Empiricus : ἐγκράτεια ... ἐστι διάθεσις ἀνυπέρβατος τῶν κατ᾽ ὀρθὸν λόγον γιγνομένων, ἢ ἀρετὴ ὑπεράνω ποιοῦσα ἡμᾶς τῶν δοκούντων εἶναι δυσαποσχέτων, Math., IX, 153 (cf. Stob. Ecl., II, 61, 11 f.; Diog. L., VII, 92). For the Stoics it is a subordinate virtue to σωφροσύνη (Stob. Ecl., II, 60, 20 f.; Diog. L., VII, 92) and belongs to the → ἀγαθά (Plut. Stoic. Rep., 15 [II, 1040 f.]). The concept of ἐγκράτεια, behind which stands the ideal of the free and independent man, of the man who is under no control

---

[1] Cf. Liddell-Scott, s.v.
[2] Cf. Philo Som., I, 124 : ἐγκράτειαν, ὀλιγοδεΐαν, καρτερίαν ὥσπερ κρηπῖδας ὅλου τοῦ βίου καταβεβλημένοι.

but who freely controls all things and who in self-restraint maintains his freedom in face of the φαῦλαι ἡδοναί which would deprive him of it, achieves its ethical significance from the humanistic understanding of life which has freedom as its goal. Polybius gives us a sketch of this in his portrayal of Scipio, to whom a παρθένος is handed as a gift and who — καταπλαγεὶς καὶ θαυμάσας τὸ κάλλος X, 19, 4 — gives her back to her father. The portrait concludes: δι' ὧν καὶ τὰ τῆς ἐγκρατείας αὐτοῦ καὶ τὰ τῆς μετριότητος ἐμφαίνων ..., X, 19, 7.

3. ἐγκράτεια is highly estimated by Philo. For him it means superiority to every desire. This superiority is expressed in restraint. It relates to food, sex and the use of the tongue (Det. Pot. Ins., 101 ff.; Spec. Leg., II, 195). Man must turn ἐκ φιληδονίας εἰς ἐγκράτειαν (Abr., 24); ἐξ ἀκρατείας εἰς ἐγκράτειαν (Virt., 180); ἐξ ἀκρασίας εἰς ἐγκράτειαν (Praem. Poen., 116). This is for him the ὠφελιμωτάτη τῶν ἀρετῶν, and it leads to εὐτέλεια and εὐκολία and ὀλιγοδεΐα, which resist ἀκολασία and πλεονεξία (Spec. Leg., I, 173). He expresses his view of it as follows: ἀντίπαλον δὲ ἐπιθυμίας ἐγκράτεια, ἣν ἀσκητέον καὶ διαπονητέον καὶ σπουδαστέον μηχανῇ πάσῃ περιποιεῖσθαι ὡς μέγιστον ἀγαθὸν καὶ τελειότατον ἰδίᾳ τε καὶ κοινῇ συμφέρον, Spec. Leg., I, 149. It is linked with asceticism, Leg. All., III, 18. It is the presupposition of human felicity: ἀνάντης δὲ ἡ πρὸς ἐγκράτειαν (sc. ὁδὸς) ἐπίπονος μέν, ἐν δὲ τοῖς μάλιστα ὠφέλιμος ... ἡ δ' εἰς οὐρανὸν ἄγει τοὺς μὴ προκαμόντας ἀθανατίζουσα, Spec. Leg., IV, 112. The ascetic attitude of Philo derives from a cosmological dualism in which matter is depreciated. ἐγκράτεια aims at the discarding of all material wants which are not necessary to existence. There is thus a shift of accent as compared with the class. view.

ἐγκράτεια is highly esteemed among the Essenes: οὗτοι τὰς μὲν ἡδονὰς ὡς κακίαν ἀποστρέφονται, τὴν δὲ ἐγκράτειαν καὶ τὸ μὴ τοῖς πάθεσιν ὑποπίπτειν ἀρετὴν ὑπολαμβάνουσιν, Jos. Bell., 2, 120. ἐγκράτεια relates to material conduct, food, sex (... γάμου μὲν παρ' αὐτοῖς ὑπεροψία, ibid., 2, 120). Their life is pure ἄσκησις (ibid., 2, 150). Those wanting to join must give a πεῖρα ἐγκρατείας (2, 138).

ἐγκράτεια is of religious significance in the Hermetic writings, which adopt Gnostic elements. On the rebirth of the initiate ἐγκράτεια rises up in him in the decade of powers. It is hailed: ὦ δύναμις ἡδίστη· προσλάβωμεν, ὦ τέκνον, αὐτὴν ἀσμενέστατα. πῶς ἅμα τῷ παραγενέσθαι ἀπώσατο τὴν ἀκρασίαν, Corp. Herm., XIII, 9.

4. In view of all this, it is striking how small a part is played by the term in biblical religion.

In the LXX it is most common in the Hellenistically influenced Wisdom literature. [3] In the few passages at issue the term implies restraint from sexual and other excesses (Sir. 18:30, cf. Ep. Ar., 278). The knowledge is present: ὅτι οὐκ ἄλλως ἔσομαι ἐγκρατὴς ἐὰν μὴ ὁ θεὸς δῷ (Wis. 8:21). [4] In 4 Macc. 5:34, and therefore in a passage greatly influenced by Hellenism, it is said of ἐγκράτεια: φίλη ἐγκράτεια.

In the NT the word group is not found at all in the Gospels. This is surprising when we remember that later schools have tried to see, e.g., in John the Baptist an Encratite ascetic. On the other hand, Paul compares himself with the athlete:

---

[3] A different translation from the LXX underlies the marginal notes in M. on Lv. 23:21, 28, 29, where ἐγκράτεια or ἐγκρατῶς obviously rests on עצם misunderstood as צום — a substitution more easily possible on the assumption of transcriptions (ασομ in 1 Ch. 4:29 and σωμ in ψ 34:12). In Nu. 6:5, 18 ἐγκράτεια or ἐγκρατής is the rendering of נֵזֶר נִזְרוֹ or הַנָּזִיר. In these passages the reference is to asceticism as a pious achievement [Bertram].

[4] ἐγκρατής usually implies having power over an object. Sir. 6:27; 15:1; Sus. 39.

πᾶς ὁ ἀγωνιζόμενος πάντα ἐγκρατεύεται 1 C. 9:25. Yet ἐγκράτεια here does not denote the asceticism of merit (→ ἀσκέω). It simply tells us that for the sake of the goal towards which he strives, the commission which he has been given and the task which he must fulfil, he refrains from all the things which might offend or hamper. It is not for his own sake, or for the sake of any necessity to salvation, but for the sake of his brethren that he practises ἐγκρατεύεσθαι. This is the fundamental difference from all Greek and Hellenistic conceptions. In the list of virtues in Gl. 5:23 [5] ἐγκράτεια is the opposite of πορνεία, ἀκαθαρσία, ἀσέλγεια ... μέθαι, κῶμοι. The word has been taken over from the surrounding world of Hellenism. Encratite tendencies are perhaps present in view of their open occurrence in 1 C. 7:9: εἰ δὲ οὐκ ἐγκρατεύονται, γαμησάτωσαν· ἐγκρατεύεσθαι refers to sexual restraint, whereas in this context ἀκρασία in v. 5 denotes the sexual impulse and its satisfaction. Marriage is instituted ἵνα μὴ πειράζῃ ὑμᾶς ὁ σατανᾶς διὰ τὴν ἀκρασίαν ὑμῶν. Paul is concerned to protect the new man from sexual defilement even in marital intercourse. [6] Yet in general we are forced to say that restraint in the ascetic sense is "for him finally an alien concept" (Delling). ἐγκράτεια occurs as a virtue in the Greek Hellenistic sense in Ac. 24:25: διαλεγομένου δὲ αὐτοῦ περὶ δικαιοσύνης καὶ ἐγκρατείας; 2 Pt. 1:6: ἐν δὲ τῇ γνώσει τὴν ἐγκράτειαν, ἐν δὲ τῇ ἐγκρατείᾳ τὴν ὑπομονήν, and Tt. 1:8: δεῖ ... τὸν ἐπίσκοπον εἶναι ... ἐγκρατῆ ... In these writings which betray Hellenistic influence there emerges already the Hellenistic doctrine of virtue which plays so strong a part in early Christianity.

The heavy use of the word group in Hermes is typical. Hermes himself is described pragmatically as ὁ ἐγκρατὴς ὁ ἀπερχόμενος πάσης ἐπιθυμίας πονηρᾶς v., 1, 2, 4. ἐγκράτεια occurs in Herm., v., 2, 3, 2 : σώζει σε ... ἡ πολλὴ ἐγκράτεια; 3, 8, 4 : ἡ δὲ ἑτέρα (γυνή), ἡ περιεζωσμένη καὶ ἀνδριζομένη, 'Εγκράτεια καλεῖται· αὕτη θυγάτηρ ἐστὶν τῆς πίστεως. Cf. also m., 6, 1, 1; 8, 1; s., 9, 15, 2; ἐγκρατεύεσθαι : Herm. m., 1, 2; 8, 1 ff.; s., 5, 1, 5.

It is significant that biblical religion finds so little place for the concept of ἐγκράτεια which in the Hellenistic and Greek world is so essentially ethical. The reason for this is that biblical man regarded his life as determined and directed by the command of God. There was thus no place for the self-mastery which had a place in autonomous ethics. Again, belief in creation cut off the way to asceticism. It saw in the world with its gifts the hand of the Creator. Finally, the gift of salvation in Christ left no place for an asceticism which merits salvation.

Grundmann

ἐγκρίνω → κρίνω.

---

[5] ἀκρατής occurs in the list of vices in 2 Tm. 3:3 in the sense of "undisciplined." Jesus accuses the Pharisees of ἀκρασία in Mt. 23:25. The meaning here is not a specifically sexual but a more general "lack of moderation or control," cf. Schl. Mt., 681, with many instances from Joseph.

[6] Cf. Delling, esp. 66-74; 84-86.

ἐγώ

The NT uses ἐγώ in I-formulae which after the Semitic pattern are constructed without copula,[1] esp. in solemn I-proclamations[2] and I-sentences where it is desired to emphasise the subject[3] in distinction from or in opposition to others.[4] The NT ἐγώ acquires religious significance in three respects: first, in proclamations of God, which are important in the Apocalypse; secondly, in the self-witness of Christ, esp. in Jn.; and thirdly in the self-utterances of the Christian (the ἐγώ of R. 7 requiring particular elucidation). One may thus speak of a theological, a christological and an anthropological ἐγώ.

A. The Theological ἐγώ.

1. Divine Proclamations in the Ancient Orient and Hellenism.

The I-style is solidly established in divine proclamations in the ancient East. A self-revelation of Ishtar forms the central part of a Babylonian liturgy.[5] In an Egyptian magic pap. the supreme ruler Rē describes creation and the destruction of the dragon as follows: "I am he who arose as Cheperi ... I created ... I destroyed" etc.; "I" occurs a dozen times.[6] The self-revelation of Ahura Mazda is couched in the same style in the Avesta: "I am Guardian and I am Creator and Protector ... I am called the Saviour ..."[7] Through the centuries this form of self-predication became a common feature in Near Eastern liturgies. Sometimes names and attributes are recounted in this style, sometimes acts, and sometimes both in alternation. In the Hellenistic world Isis is particularly prominent in this form of hymnic predication: "I am Isis ... I am the eldest daughter of Kronos ... I divided earth from heaven ..."[8] In the main part of the Isis hymn of Kyme there are some 28 analogous statements beginning with ἐγώ (εἰμι).[9]

The meaning and purpose of these proclamations is first one of simple self-representation. The reader or hearer is to be acquainted with the person of a particular deity, and there are so many gods. But self-representation becomes self-glorification. The predicates

---

ἐ γ ώ. On A. and B.: G. P. Wetter, "Ich bin das Licht der Welt," *Beitr. z. Relwiss.*, I (1913/14), 166-201; "Ich bin es," ThStKr, 88 (1915), 224-238; *Altchristliche Liturgien*, I, *Das christl. Mysterium* (1921), 116 ff., 145 ff.; K. Zickendraht, Ἐγώ εἰμι, ThStKr, 94 (1922), 162-168; Kittel Probleme, 62; E. L. Dietrich, *Das Selbstbewusstsein in den Rabbinen* (MS). On C.: K. Dick, *Der schriftstellerische Plural bei Paulus* (1900); A. v. Harnack, "Das 'Wir' in den Joh. Schriften" (SAB, 1923), 96-113; E. v. Dobschütz, "Wir und Ich bei Paulus" (ZSTh, 10 [1932]), 251-277; W. G. Kümmel, *Römer 7 und die Bekehrung des Paulus* (1929); R. Bultmann, "Römer 7 und die Anthropologie des Paulus" in *Imago Dei, Festschr. f. G. Krüger* (1932), 53-62; U. Holzmeister, *De plurali categoriae in Novo Testamento et a Patribus adhibito, Biblica* 14 (1933), 68-95.

[1] Rev. 22:13: ἐγὼ ὁ πρῶτος καὶ ὁ ἔσχατος; cf. Is. 44:6.
[2] Jn. 8:12: ἐγώ εἰμι τὸ φῶς τοῦ κόσμου.
[3] Gl. 2:20: ζῶ δὲ οὐκέτι ἐγώ; Lk. 22:32: ἐγὼ δὲ ἐδεήθην; Mt. 21:27: οὐδὲ ἐγώ.
[4] For the most important points concerning usage, forms and syntax, cf. Pr.-Bauer.
[5] Cf. A. Ungnad, *Die Religion der Babylonier u. Assyrer* (1921), 200 ff.
[6] Cf. AOT, 1 ff.
[7] Yašt, 1, 12 ff. in H. Lommel, *Die Yašts des Avesta* (1927), 15; cf. also Yašt, 1, 7; 10, 1.
[8] Deissmann LO, 108 ff., with related texts from Diodor., I, 27; Preis. Zaub., V (London), 145 etc.
[9] W. Peek, *Der Isishymnus von Andros* (1930), 122 ff.; 15 ff. (v. 7, 26, 92, 97, 158). Also "Der Isishymnus von Andros," *Antike* 6 (1930), 325 ff.

claimed by the deity are brought into competition with those of others. Finally, self-glorification serves self-commendation. The deity claims worship and offers help as none other god in heaven. Thus these proclamations are polytheistic in assumption but monotheistic or monolatrous in tendency.

2. Divine Proclamations in the OT and Apocalyptic Judaism.

The I-style acquires a specific ring in the mouth of the true and only God who reveals Himself in Israel. What is only a tendency or beginning in polytheism is here fulfilled.

Thus the divine name יהוה is paraphrased in the monumental formula: "I am who I am" (Ex. 3:14). The Ten Commandments are introduced by a אָנֹכִי which claims all worship for itself and excludes all other cults: "For I, Yahweh, thy God, am a jealous God."[10] This exclusivism is even more powerful in the great revelation of Dt. 32:39 ff.: "See now that I, even I, am he, and there is no god beside me ... neither is there any that can deliver out of my hand ... I ... I ... I ... I ..." It is in Dt. Is., however, that we find the fullest development and that the ἐγώ of God acquires its most pregnant significance. It is used for God as the Subject who can never become an object and before whom all reality, being, happening and volition is object. This ἐγώ of God will not tolerate any second subject, any other god.[11] It has posited the world as an object.[12] The being of God is powerful in relation to that of the world. The will of God is unlimited and independent of any alien influence. God has the first and final word.[13] And the all-powerful being and will of God are manifested in His unwearying and incessant action. This is what gives dynamic character to the I-speeches of Dt. Is. and the whole of the OT.[14] They speak more of what takes place than of what is.[15] Even in relation to man God is the final Subject. Man is what he is always with reference to God.[16] He is lost when God condemns him, pure when God purifies him: "I blot out thy sins for my sake, and do not remember thy transgressions" (Is. 43:25). Not once in the knowledge of God is man the determining subject. God is known rather where He makes Himself known, where He reveals Himself (Is. 41:21 ff.).

The I-style of the OT is continued in Jewish Apocalyptic: "I will lead into bright light those who love my holy name. I will set each on his throne of honour."[17] Self-proclamation is particularly common in theophanies: "I am the God of thy father Abraham ... I am with thee ... I will bless thee" (Jub. 24:22). These I-revelations play the greatest role in the Apocalypse of Abraham: "I am before the aeons and a mighty God ... I am a shield over thee and I am thy Helper."[18] Here we can see clearly the two historico-religious characteristics of Jewish Apocalyptic, namely, the Israelite heritage and oriental influence.

3. I-Speeches of God in the NT.

God is the absolute Subject. This is the final meaning of the ἐγώ in the divine revelations of the OT and Judaism. The NT maintains this concept, but it gives

---

[10] Ex. 20:2 ff. Cf. the I-address of the king at the beginning of the Code of Hammurabi → n. 26.

[11] Is. 45:5, 23; cf. 43:11; 44:6.

[12] Is. 44:24; cf. 43:13.

[13] Is. 44:24; 48:12.

[14] Is. 41:25, 27; 43:1 ff., 15 ff.

[15] Thus in the proem of Dt. 32:39 ff. we read of the essence of God, and in the corpus of His past and future acts.

[16] Is. 41:4, 9 ff.; 42:6.

[17] Eth. En. 108:12. Cf. the great I-speech in Heb. En. 48 C.

[18] Apc. Abr. (Bonwetsch [1897]), 9.

us only a few revelations in I-style, and mostly in quotations. Paul quotes the divine oath of Is. 45:23 in R. 14:11, and he also quotes from Dt. 32 the saying concerning revenge, to which he adds an ἐγώ. [19] Much quoted are the adoption formulae in which God declares the king His son ; these are applied to the sonship of Christ. [20] Rev. refers again to the exposition of the divine name in Ex. 3:14 ('Εγώ ... ὁ ὤν), but adds two new members to the timeless present predication and thus achieves a threefold formula after the manner of the Persian three-tense-schema : ὁ ὢν καὶ ὁ ἦν καὶ ὁ ἐρχόμενος, Rev. 1:8. [21] Alongside this development there are also twofold forms which newly express the divine pro-clamation of Is. 44:6 etc. : [22] ἐγώ εἰμι τὸ ἄλφα καὶ τὸ ὦ, ἡ ἀρχὴ καὶ τὸ τέλος (→ ΑΩ, I, 1 ff.; → εἰμι, 397). Thus Rev. attests the preference for the I-style in apocalyptic generally. [23] But here too, as in the rest of the NT, the speeches of God are far less prominent than those of Christ. It is only in the I-speeches of Christ that ἐγώ takes on its decisive significance in the NT.

B. The Christological ἐγώ.

1. Ruler and Saviour Sayings in the Ancient Orient and Hellenism.

In the ancient Orient we find I-proclamations not merely on the lips of gods but also of kings, deliverers and prophets. Akhnaton says in his hymn to the sun : "Thou art in my heart. None knoweth thee but thy son Akhnaton. Thou hast initiated him into thy plans and thy power." [24] Here the king speaks of himself, or causes himself to be spoken of, in the he-style. [25] In the royal inscriptions of the Euphrates, however, the same I-style predominates as in speeches of the gods. Thus Hammurabi proclaims in the introduction to his Code : "Hammurabi, the shepherd, the called of Ellil, am I ... The prince of kings, who subjugated ..." [26] The Persian kings and their successors adopted this form : "I, Cyrus, the king of the world." But the tone of self-glorification prominent in the Assyrian inscriptions now yields to one of a humbly proud sense of mission which reminds us of Akhnaton. Darius orders the affairs of the nations and ushers in the age of felicity in virtue of his divine installation. There is only one god, namely, Ahura Mazda. Darius is conscious of bearing his commission. He acts in his name and may thus speak in his language. [27]

In the Hellenistic period the Diadochi continue this style. [28] Above all, however, the ἐγώ (εἰμι) becomes a slogan in religious propaganda. The most diverse saviours seek

---

[19] ἐμοὶ ἐκδίκησις, ἐγώ ἀνταποδώσω, R. 12:19 on the basis of Dt. 32:35. Cf. Hb. 10:30.
[20] Ps. 2:7 in Ac. 13:33 and Hb. 5:5; and together with 2 S. 7:14 in Hb. 1:5.
[21] The formula is found without ἐγώ in 1:4; 4:8, and in shortened form in 11:17. On the development of the three-tense-schema, v. Gathas (ed. C. Bartholomae [1905]), 2, 4; 6, 10; 10, 7. Yasna, 39, 2 etc.; Yašt, 13, 154 (F. Wolff, Avesta [1910]).
[22] "The first and the last" is also found in the Gathas, 4, 8; 9, 3 ff.
[23] The liking of the seer for the ἐγώ in divine speech is attested by the continuation of 21:6 : ἐγώ τῷ διψῶντι δώσω. Here a saying of Dt. Is. is handed down in the I-style, cf. Is. 55:1.
[24] AOT, 18.
[25] Cf. AOT, 80 ff. with 339 ff.
[26] AOT, 381 ff. For further details cf. S. Mowinckel, "Die vorderasiatischen Königs- und Fürsteninschriften," in Eucharisterion für H. Gunkel (1923), I, 278 ff. Cf. also W. Baum-gartner, "Zur Form der assyr. Königsinschriften," OLZ, 27 (1924), 313 ff.
[27] F. H. Weissbach, Die Keilinschriften der Achämeniden (1911), 3, 11 ff., 89, 125 ff. Mowinckel, too, emphasises the particular place of these inscriptions, op. cit. (→ n. 26), 281, 320 f.
[28] Cf. the Antiochus inscr. in Weissbach, op. cit.

to win adherents with the claims made in I-proclamations. The Corp. Herm. inclines to the style of divine proclamation: τὸ φῶς ἐκεῖνο, ἔφη, ἐγώ εἰμι νοῦς ὁ σὸς θεός, ὁ πρὸ φύσεως ὑγρᾶς τῆς ἐκ σκότους φανείσης. [29] The redeemer of the Mandaeans speaks more personally: "I am the messenger of light ... I am the true messenger ... I am the messenger of life ..." [30] The influence of this style may still be seen in the Koran. [31] Nor are such addresses confined to writing. Every street-corner prophet or sectarian preacher sought to outbid his predecessors or competitors in impressive self-proclamation. Tricksters imitated the style and used the ancient form as an easy means of making an impression. The people lost confidence, and the educated sneered. Thus Celsus occasionally alludes to propaganda of this kind: Ἐγώ ὁ θεός εἰμι (ἢ θεοῦ παῖς ἢ πνεῦμα θεῖον) ... ἐγὼ δὲ σῶσαι θέλω καὶ ὄψεσθέ με αὖθις μετ᾽ οὐρανίου δυνάμεως ἐπανιόντα. [32] The content shows the influence of Christian modes of thought, but the I-style itself is more ancient and widespread.

2. The I of God's Representatives in the OT and Judaism.

a. The I-style of Near Eastern royal inscr. is also found in the OT. In a long series of I-sentences Nehemiah lists his achievements on behalf of the people of God, [33] with the ultimate purpose of reminding God Himself of his acts and of seeking His mercy. [34] On the other hand, self-predications as god or lord are arrogant and offensive in Jewish eyes, since they violate the honour of the one God. The king of Tyre forgets that he is God's representative, and proudly proclaims: "I am God; I sit on the throne of God, in the midst of the sea." [35] Pompey thinks: "I am Lord over land and sea." [36] God answers such pretension, and by means of frightful catastrophes shows these men their impotence. Alexandrian Judaism, however, was able to give an ethical turn to the oriental glorification of kings, and thus to give a new content to the old form. [37]

The prophets express more purely and forcefully the idea of being God's representatives, as in the Servant Songs of Is. God calls: "Hear me, O Jacob" (Is. 48:12), and in the same style the Servant cries: "Hear me, ye isles; hearken, ye peoples." [38] The I-consciousness of the prophets is God-consciousness, not self-consciousness: "The Spirit of the Lord is upon me" (Is. 61:1 f.). Yet this God-consciousness becomes increasingly rarer in the later period. The prophet with his plenipotentiary power is replaced by the apocalyptist, whose supreme task is to declare the secret revelations of God. [39] The I-saying of the prophet is thus replaced by the authoritative Ἐγὼ Δανιήλ, [40] which becomes a fixed and non-declinable formula: ὅρασις ὤφθη πρὸς μέ, ἐγὼ Δανιήλ. [41]

,b. Meanwhile the I-style of Dt. Is. is adopted and developed in the I-sayings of heavenly wisdom in Prv. 8: "Hear, for I will speak ... whoso findeth me findeth life." But as the king by divine grace is confronted by the despot and the prophet by the

---

[29] Poimandres (Parthey [1854]) 1, 6; cf. 5, 11.
[30] Lidz. Ginz., R. 64 f. (p. 58 f.), 255 (p. 255), 275 ff. (p. 273 ff.); L. 38 ff. (p. 454 ff.).
[31] E. Norden, *Agnostos Theos* (1913), 191.
[32] Orig. Cels., VII, 8 f., cf. Norden, *op. cit.*, 188 ff. → n. 52.
[33] On Neh. 13:8, 25, *v.* Is. 63:5 f. and Mowinckel, *op. cit.* (→ n. 26), 297 ff.
[34] Neh. 5:19; 13:14, 22,, 31.
[35] Ez. 28:2, 9; Syr. Tr. 35:27; cf. Da. 5:20; Is. 47:7 f., 10.
[36] Ps. Sol. 2:33; cf. 2 Macc. 9:8; Ac. 12:21 f.
[37] Cf. the image of the prince in Ep. Ar.; also W. Weber, Herm., 50 (1915), 47-92; *Der Prophet und sein Gott* (1925), 88, 155.
[38] 49:1 ff.; cf. 50:4 ff.
[39] Sl. En. 39:2: "Now ... I do not instruct you with my own mouth, but with the mouth of the Lord."
[40] Da. Θ 7:28; 7:15; 8:5. Cf. Syr. Bar. 13:1 etc.
[41] Da. Θ 8:1.

pseudo-prophet, so wisdom is confronted by folly, which imitates its style and reverses its message (Prv. 9:4 f., 16 f.). The same form is used of wisdom in Sir. (ἐγὼ ἀπὸ στόματος ὑψίστου ἐξῆλθον ... ἐγω ... ἐγώ ..., 24:3 f.) and in the syncretistic Odes of Solomon : "Ye sons of men, turn, and ye daughters, come ... and turn to me ... I will make you wise in the ways of truth." In such I-sayings, however, there are also Gnostic motifs : "I have become strong and mighty, and have taken the world captive." [42]

Wisdom is not the only heavenly being to use solemn I-sayings to men. Angels and other supernatural messengers use the same style. Thus the angel of God in 4 Esr. does not merely speak in the name of God, but can sometimes representatively use the divine I (7:60 f.). In the Apc. Abr., which here again shows its predilection for this form, the angel can even say : "I am Jaoel ... I am he who ordains ... I ... I ... I am sent to thee ..." [43] And in the Test. Abr. death says : ἐγώ εἰμι τὸ πικρὸν ὄνομα· ἐγώ εἰμι κλαυθμός ... [44]

c. Nor is this solemn I-style confined to literature, or to heavenly beings, in later Judaism. On Palestinian soil, too, we find princely figures who feel that they are God's representatives, or who make themselves out to be such. Certainly we do not find such common heathen self-predications as θεός or κύριος. [45] The Damascus Teacher is rather imitating Prv. when he says to his adherents : "Hear me, children, I will open your eyes that you may see." [46] And in relation to John the Baptist, who in many ways resembles the Damascus Teacher, the Synoptists simply have the restricted ἐγὼ ἐβάπτισα ὕδατι. The negative I-saying in Jn. 1:20 f.; 3:28 : ἐγὼ οὐκ εἰμὶ ὁ χριστός, points in the same direction, this being presupposed also in Ac. 13:25. The ἐγώ of Jn. 1:23 is obviously a Johannine trick of style, but it expresses the same basic stand-point as the other I-sayings of the Baptist, since in the restrictive or negative ἐγώ he does not point to himself but past himself. Of Theudas, however, traditions says that he spoke great things of himself, λέγων εἶναί τινα ἑαυτόν, and in Samaria Simon had himself worshipped as → δύναμις τοῦ θεοῦ ἡ καλουμένη ἡ μεγάλη and proclaimed himself εἶναί τινα ἑαυτὸν μέγαν (Ac. 8:9 f.). The schematic way in which Acts reports these phenomena makes it clear that there were many men who could occasionally make such claims in I-formulae. In accord with this is the common use of the question σὺ τίς εἶ. [47] It is a probing question, since it was no easy task to find one's way among all these prophets and pseudo-prophets, these Messianic messengers and false Messiahs (v. Mk. 6:14 ff. etc.). The people ran from one to the other, and apocalyptic circles moved from one hope and disappointment to the next.

d. On the other hand, the Synagogue held aloof from these things. [48] We often find a high sense of office in Rabb. writings. [49] But the Rabbis avoid an exaggerated I-style. [50] It was offensive to them. They had a basic suspicion of the I-proclamations of little prophets and pretended Messiahs. The superior tone and cautious attitude of Gamaliel in Ac. 5:36 f. is typical. [51] And the real or apparent pretension of many I-sayings was

---

[42] Od. Sol. 33:6 ff.; 10:4; cf. Od. 8 f. and 42.

[43] Apc. Abr. (Bonwetsch), 10.

[44] Test. Abr., 13. M. R. James, Texts and Studies, II, 2 (1892), 118.

[45] Cf. Ez. 28:2 and 2 Th. 2:4 : This abomination is charged against Antichrist.

[46] Damasc., 2, 14 (Staerk).

[47] Jn. 1:19 ff.; 8:25; Ac. 21:38; Mk. 14:61; indirectly Mk. 8:27 ff.; 11:27 ff.

[48] V. Str.-B., II, 542; E. L. Dietrich, Das Selbstbewusstsein der Rabbinen (MS).

[49] Sayings like Sl. En. 39:2 (→ n. 39) are handed down similarly by Simon b. Shatach and Rabbi Akiba, Sanh., 19a; jSanh., 18a: "Thou standest before him who spake and the world came into being." Dietrich, op. cit. also draws attention to the tradition in Taan., 23a, according to which the divine utterance in Job 22:28 ff. is transferred to the great man of prayer Choni, who also called himself the "house-fellow" of God, Taan., 3, 8.

[50] So Dietrich, op. cit.

[51] We find the same scepticism in relation to the Baptist and Jesus in Mk. 11:27 ff.

an abomination which they fought against in the name of monotheism. Even the Christology of the Gospels was to many Rabbis simply one heathen heresy among others: "If a man says: I am God — he lies; I am the Son of Man — he will regret it; I ascend to heaven — he will not accomplish it." [52]

3. ᾿Εγώ in the Synoptic Sayings of Jesus.

On the lips of the Synoptic Jesus the emphatic ἐγώ is relatively infrequent. It is found in warnings, promises and commands uttered by Jesus with the sense of His divine power and authority. [53] We find it indirectly in Lk. 4:18 in the introductory sermon in which He quotes Is. 61. On the other hand, we seek it in vain in the Messianic formula [54] ῏Ηλθον πληρῶσαι etc. [55] The more significant, therefore, is the I-style in the Sermon on the Mount, the Cry of Jubilation and the Call of the Saviour.

In Mt. 5:22 ff. there occurs five times the sharp ᾿Εγὼ δὲ λέγω ὑμῖν by which sayings of old time are superseded or opposed. This λέγω ὑμῖν closes an epoch in the history of religion and ethics and creates a new situation. What Jesus is declaring is not simply an explication of old truth; what He is demanding is not simply a new step on the endless way to an eternally valid ideal. The validity of His demand is wholly and utterly linked with acceptance of His person and the authenticity of His mission. The Messiah has come, and with all the authority of God [56] He issues a summons to His people. The ἐγώ alone validates His word.

Jesus Himself speaks of the authority of His office in the Cry of Jubilation in Lk. 10:22: πάντα μοι παρεδόθη ὑπὸ τοῦ πατρός μου. [57] He is on earth the fully authorised representative and executor of God. [58] All God's work is done through Him. He is Mediator for the whole world, and the Mediator of revelation. Alongside the absolute Subject God there comes a second Subject in a unique Thou-relationship, namely, that of the Son who is known by the Father alone and who alone can know the Father. There is no knowledge of God except through the Son.

If the relationship of the Son to the Father is central in this saying, in the Call of the Saviour, which follows the form of the Wisdom literature in Mt., the main point is the relationship of the Son to the human race: δεῦτε πρός με ... [59] The ἐγώ, which represents the place of God in this world, and which opens up access to Him, is necessarily a gathering point for the κοπιῶντες καὶ πεφορτισμένοι. And as in the OT God is the model whom man should follow, so is the Son in this passage: μάθετε ἀπ᾿ ἐμοῦ. The Christ of the NT replaces not only sophia but all the intermediaries of Jewish theology, uniting their offices in one. All historical

---

[52] jTaan., 2, 1 in H. L. Strack, Jesus, die Häretiker und die Christen (1910), 37; Str.-B., I, 486. Cf. Str.-B., II, 465; J. Klausner, Die mess. Vorstell. d. jüd. Volkes i. Zeitalter d. Tannait. (1904) → n. 32.
[53] Mk. 9:25; 14:58. The parallels take a different form.
[54] Cf. Lk. 7:20.
[55] Mt. 5:17; 9:13; 10:34 f.
[56] Cf. the reaction to the Sermon on the Mount among the people (Mt. 7:28 f.).
[57] Cf. Mt. 28:18b.
[58] On Lk. 10:22, cf. Akhnaton's hymn to the sun → n. 24. Cf. E. Norden, Agnostos Theos, 277 ff.; H. Schumacher, Die Selbstoffenbarung Jesu bei Mt. 11:27 (1912). → υἱός.
[59] Mt. 11:28 ff. Cf. Is. 55:1 ff.; Sir. 51:1 f., 23 ff., 31 ff.; 24:28 ff. and the parallels from Prv. and Od. Sol. quoted → 346 f.

and cosmic lines intersect in His ἐγώ. He stands at the heart of the times and in the centre between God and the world.

This position of Christ as Mediator is most clearly expressed when the ἐγώ of Christ is related both to God on the one side and to a circle of men on the other. This is true in the active sense of the threefold relation God-Jesus-the disciples, and in the passive sense of the relation of the weak in the world to Jesus and God. Jesus sends out the disciples with the ἐγώ of divine authority (Mt. 10:16; cf. Lk. 24:49); and He gives the promise: ἰδοὺ ἐγὼ μεθ' ὑμῶν (Mt. 28:20). On the other hand, He intercedes with God for His own: ἐγὼ ἐδεήθην περὶ σοῦ (Lk. 22:32). Above all, however, He sends them out with the words: ὁ ἀκούων ὑμῶν ἐμοῦ ἀκούει, καὶ ὁ ἀθετῶν ὑμᾶς ἐμὲ ἀθετεῖ· ὁ δὲ ἐμὲ ἀθετῶν ἀθετεῖ τὸν ἀποστείλαντά με.[60] The apostles (→ ἀπόστολος) represent Christ as He represents God.[61] In this sense Christ is God, and the apostle is Christ — for the world. Jesus speaks in similar terms[62] of the least of His people, except that now it is a matter of helping men rather than proclaiming God. Christ encounters us in the weak, and in them calls for our help. For the way of God as Jesus treads and indicates it is not that of promoting the strong but of delivering the weak. For this reason what is done to the weak and needy is done to Christ and therefore to God. Always Christ Himself, His ἐγώ, His ὄνομα,[63] stands in the centre. God has made Him the absolute point of intersection of all ages and paths, and the point of division of spirits and destinies. In this sense the christological ἐγώ of the Synoptists expresses *in nuce* the claim of Jesus to absoluteness.

4. 'Εγώ in the Speeches of Christ in John.

The Gospel of John carries this line of thought a stage further.[64] Here the ἐγώ is a characteristic stylistic feature of the revelatory speeches of the Son of God which constitute the major part of the preaching of Jesus. The ἐγώ is often necessary to point a contrast (5:43; 10:10); it is sometimes indispensable (10:25); and it gives to the sayings of Jesus a solemn and almost liturgical ring.[65] We see this when the Son of Man says: εἰς κρίμα ἐγὼ εἰς τὸν κόσμον τοῦτον ἦλθον,[66] ἵνα οἱ μὴ βλέποντες βλέπωσιν καὶ οἱ βλέποντες τυφλοὶ γένωνται, while the blind man who can now see is prostrate in worship before Him (9:39).

In John the ἐγώ takes on greater conceptual fullness and significance. A long series of I-sayings refers to the relationship of the Son to the Father, which John conceives of far more narrowly and strictly than the Synoptists. Some 35 times we have the exclusive ὁ πατήρ μου, and some 25 times the analogous ὁ πέμψας με, the most succinct expression of Jesus' sense of mission. ἐγὼ γὰρ ἐκ θεοῦ ἐξῆλθον καὶ ἥκω· οὐδὲ γὰρ ἀπ' ἐμαυτοῦ ἐλήλυθα, ἀλλ' ἐκεῖνός με ἀπέστειλεν.[67] The Father is with Me, ὅτι ἐγὼ τὰ ἀρεστὰ αὐτῷ ποιῶ πάντοτε (8:29). The Father

---

[60] Lk. 10:16; cf. Mt. 10:40.

[61] Cf. 2 C. 5:20.

[62] Mk. 9:37 and par.; cf. Mt. 10:42; 25:31 ff.

[63] τὸ ὄνομά μου with εἰς, Mt. 18:20; with διά, Mk. 13:13; with ἕνεκεν Lk. 21:12; with ἐπί, Mt. 18:5; with ἐν, Mk. 9:41: ἐν ὀνόματί μου, ὅτι Χριστοῦ ἐστε.

[64] Cf. also F. Büchsel, *Joh. und der hellenist. Synkretismus* (1928), 37 f.

[65] In Jn. the quotation about the one crying in the wilderness becomes an I-saying of the Baptist himself, Jn. 1:23: ἐγὼ φωνὴ βοῶντος. Cf. 3:28. The stylistic influence is plain.

[66] The Synoptists would have written something like: εἰς κρίμα ἦλθον εἰς ...

[67] Jn. 8:42 f.; cf. 5:36; 6:57; 7:29.

is also in Me, κἀγὼ ἐν πατρί. [68] His whole action is to declare the reality of God in world reality. Thus He can say: "He that hath seen me hath seen the Father" (14:9), and even more strongly and comprehensively: ἐγὼ καὶ ὁ πατὴρ ἕν ἐσμεν (10:30). The shortest and most emphatic expression of this unity is the ἡμεῖς of the high-priestly prayer, which in the mouth of anyone else would be blasphemy. Christ seeks to draw the disciples into this fellowship with the Father. This is the great theme of the farewell discourses: ἐγὼ ἐν τῷ πατρί μου [69] κἀγὼ ἐν ὑμῖν καὶ ὑμεῖς ἐν ἐμοί. [70] This fellowship is the presupposition of all true action: χωρὶς ἐμοῦ οὐ δύνασθε ποιεῖν οὐδέν (15:5). The basic datum of this fellowship, however, is → ἀγάπη, and it is actualised in the inclusive relations of which the Johannine Christ continually speaks: ἵνα ἡ ἀγάπη ἣν ἠγάπησάς με ἐν αὐτοῖς ᾖ κἀγὼ ἐν αὐτοῖς (17:26). Nor is the circle of those who are to belong to the Son restricted to the twelve. The Johannine Christ, too, sends out His call to all the people as Saviour: ἐάν τις διψᾷ, ἐρχέσθω πρός με καὶ πινέτω. [71] Indeed, His appearance has significance for the whole world.

This cosmic and decisive reach of the Christ event is expressed by John in I-sayings of a singular character which stylistically go beyond the similar sayings of pretended saviours or even the I-sayings of the Synoptists, and which belong rather to the same category as divine proclamations (→ 343 f.), though even this category is transcended. We refer to statements in which the ἐγώ is linked with an impersonal predicative noun, and often with something abstract, which is always defined by the article. [72] These formulae are particularly common in Jn. 10, but they are found throughout the Gospel. Thus Jesus says: ἐγώ εἰμι τὸ φῶς, ὁ ἄρτος τῆς ζωῆς, ἡ ἄμπελος ἡ ἀληθινή, ἡ θύρα τῶν προβάτων, ἡ ὁδός, and again: ἡ ἀλήθεια, ἡ ἀνάστασις καὶ ἡ ζωή. [73] The logic of these sayings follows its own laws. The definite article with a predicative noun makes it clear that we have here equation rather than subordination. He is light. But He is the true and proper light which alone deserves this name: τὸ φῶς τὸ ἀληθινόν. [74] And in the same sense He is the bread, the life, the truth. He is these things in the supreme and ultimate sense, and He alone. In short, all these concrete or abstract definitions are names which Jesus claims for Himself and denies to any other being or object. John is not speaking of the fact of Christ in abstract speculations. Everything great and significant in the world becomes a name characterising the unique position of this ἐγώ. All creation points beyond itself to Him who transcends it physically, spiritually and ethically. Thus no single name is adequate; and all finally break down before this reality.

But the Johannine Christ speaks of His cosmic being and nature only to introduce His decisive significance for the human race and its action and aspirations. [75] This is adequately shown in each case by the conception or the setting of the I-sayings. Jesus does in fact bring light, bread, wine, physical life etc. These

---

[68] Jn. 10:38; cf. 17:21; 14:20.
[69] Note this μου. The special position of the Mediator is always maintained.
[70] 14:20; cf. 15:7 ff.; 17:22; also 17:18: ἐγὼ ἀπέστειλα.
[71] 7:37; cf. 4:14: ἐγὼ δώσω ὕδωρ (→ 346 f.: Prv. etc., also Is. 55:1).
[72] Occasionally we have a personal noun like ὁ ποιμὴν ὁ καλός in 10:11 → n. 26.
[73] 8:12; 6:35, 48; 15:1, 5; 10:7, 9; 14:6; 11:25. Cf. the influence on R. Ginza, 64 f. (p. 58 f.).
[74] Jn. 1:9; cf. 1 Jn. 2:8 and ἀληθινός in 15:1 and 6:32.
[75] On the teleological orientation of this ἐγώ cf. Jn. 18:37.

are signs revealing to those with eyes to see His supraterrestrial glory and power. The Son delivers His own from the unnatural world of darkness, hunger, thirst and death and sets them in the world of true being, in fellowship with Himself, in vital union with God. This is what He guarantees and promises with His Ἐγώ εἰμι ἡ ὁδὸς καὶ ἡ ἀλήθεια καὶ ἡ ζωή. The christological ἐγώ in John's Gospel is the catchword for a christocentric view of the world.

5. Ἐγώ in the Sayings of Christ in the Apocalypse.

The Apocalypse, too, shows a liking for christological I-sayings which have a twofold solemnity on the lips of the heavenly Son of Man. Ἐγώ Ἰησοῦς ἔπεμψα τὸν ἄγγελόν μου μαρτυρῆσαι ὑμῖν ταῦτα ἐπὶ ταῖς ἐκκλησίαις. Ἐγώ εἰμι ἡ ῥίζα καὶ τὸ γένος Δαυίδ, ὁ ἀστὴρ ὁ λαμπρὸς ὁ πρωϊνός (22:16). While the Johannine Epistles, like the other writings of the NT, occasionally appeal to the Lord and His Word and Spirit, the letters of Revelation claim to be heavenly epistles in which the κρατῶν τοὺς ἑπτὰ ἀστέρας Himself speaks in admonition, warning or promise. The introductory formulae, with their rich liturgical predication, speak of Christ in the third person : τάδε λέγει ὁ ἀμήν. But in the triumphant words at the close Christ often speaks personally, promising τῷ νικῶντι an analogous future or position : δώσω αὐτῷ ἐξουσίαν, ὡς κἀγὼ εἴληφα παρὰ τοῦ πατρός μου καὶ δώσω αὐτῷ τὸν ἀστέρα τὸν πρωϊνόν (2:27 f.). The concluding promise of the whole series is as follows : ὁ νικῶν, δώσω αὐτῷ καθίσαι μετ' ἐμοῦ ἐν τῷ θρόνῳ μου, ὡς κἀγὼ ἐνίκησα καὶ ἐκάθισα μετὰ τοῦ πατρός μου ἐν τῷ θρόνῳ αὐτοῦ (3:21).

The Apocalypse brings out the full analogy of Christ and God even more clearly than the analogical relations between Christ and the disciples which are also recognised in the parting discourses. [76] Thus the proverbial saying concerning God's love and chastisement appears in the final letter as a proclamation of Christ with a preceding ἐγώ. [77] Indeed, the Christ of Rev. often uses the very same I-sayings as are also ascribed to God. In the proem, for instance, God says : ἐγώ εἰμι τὸ ἄλφα καὶ τὸ ὦ, ὁ ὢν καὶ ὁ ἦν καὶ ὁ ἐρχόμενος (1:8), and the Son of Man also says : ἐγώ εἰμι ὁ πρῶτος καὶ ὁ ἔσχατος καὶ ὁ ζῶν (1:17). Here the first two members borrow linguistically from the divine saying in Is. 44:6; there is a material parallel to the → ΑΩ of 1:8; and the whole [78] falls within the three-tense-schema of the divine sayings in Rev. The strongest analogy is at the end of Rev. in 21:6 : ἐγὼ τὸ ἄλφα καὶ τὸ ὦ, ἡ ἀρχὴ καὶ τὸ τέλος, 22:13 : ἐγὼ τὸ ἄλφα καὶ τὸ ὦ, ὁ πρῶτος καὶ ὁ ἔσχατος, ἡ ἀρχὴ καὶ τὸ τέλος. The two I-sayings say exactly the same thing. In the one, however, the speaker is God, and in the other Christ. [79] The Apocalypse could hardly speak of Jesus with greater boldness. Yet neither here not in the NT generally could one speak of a replacement of God by Christ or of an admixture of two magnitudes. Christ is neither another God in the polytheistic sense nor is He in God in the mystical sense. He is instituted by the one God as the authoritative Bearer of the divine office for the whole sphere of this world and its history.

---

[76] V. ὡς and καθώς in Jn. 17:14 etc.

[77] Prv. 3:12; Rev. 3:19 : ἐγὼ ὅσους ἐὰν φιλῶ ἐλέγχω; cf. Is. 55:1 with Jn. 4:14; 7:37. Cf. the reference to Choni → n. 49.

[78] We have the same schema in the ἐγενόμην, ζῶν εἰς αἰῶνας and ἔχω of 1:18.

[79] 21:7 and 22:6, 16.

6. Ἐγώ εἰμι (→ εἰμι).

A separate problem is raised by the occasional use in the Gospels of ἐγώ εἰμι without any predicative definition. It probably derives from the theological "I am he" of the OT and Apocalyptic. This emphatic formula rests ultimately on the "I am that I am" of Ex. 3:14. [80] It takes clearer shape in Dt. 32:39 : "See now that I, even I, am he, and there is no god with me"; and it becomes a fixed formula in the divine proclamations of Dt. Is. "I, even I, am Yahweh; and beside me there is no saviour." [81] "Who hath wrought and done it . . . ? I Yahweh, the first and the last, I am he" (41:4). "Hearken unto me, O Jacob and Israel, my called; I am he; I am the first, I also am the last" (48:12). It is in keeping with the style of the I-saying that the meaning of "I am he" is explained in an accompanying formula, which is usually to the effect that the One who thus speaks is the true and only Subject of all occurrence, the true and only God. [82] The liking for this impressive formula is well brought out in the LXX translation [83] and esp. in Apocalyptic. [84] In the Apc. Abr., which is particularly rich in I-sayings, God says : "Dost thou seek the God of gods ? . . . I am he." [85] And again : "I am he, fear not, for I am before the aeons." [86] The Book of Elijah takes up again the formula of Dt., this time in a purely eschatological sense (8). If the Creator God has revealed the goal of all history, then the knowledge of God will reach its goal and the old saying will be fulfilled : "See now that I, even I, am he." [87] The Christ of the NT speaks in the same style, though not every ἐγώ εἰμι in the Gospels has this full emphatic sense.

In Jn. 9 [88] contention had arisen concerning the identity of the βλέπων with the blind man who was known to the whole neighbourhood. He himself thus said in v. 9 : ἐγώ εἰμι, i.e., I am the man. Similarly, Jesus twice says to the soldiers in Gethsemane : ἐγώ εἰμι, [89] i.e., I am the man. Here we have an ordinary use in relation to the identity of someone who is either known or sought. Similarly, in the darkness in which the disciples can hardly trust their eyes, Jesus says to them : "I am he ; fear not." [90] Yet here, as in the similar formula in Apc. Abr., we should not miss the emphatic overtone. This is strengthened by the continuation, Mk. 6:51f. There is another example of ordinary use in Mk. 14:62, though here the reference is to the claim of Jesus to be the Messiah. To the question : σὺ εἶ ὁ χριστός, ὁ υἱὸς τοῦ εὐλογητοῦ; Jesus answers : ἐγώ εἰμι, "I am." And then, in substantiation of His claim and revelation of His Messiahship, He adds : καὶ ὄψεσθε . . . The I-saying is expounded eschatologically as in the Book of Elijah 8:3 (= Dt. 32:39). Jesus is something which will be manifested only at the end of the days. [91]

---

[80] On the reconstruction of this formula in Rev. → n. 3.

[81] Is. 43:11; cf. 59:16; 63:5 f. and Mowinckel, op. cit. (→ n. 26), 297 ff.

[82] Cf. Dt. 4:35; Is. 43:12 f.; 45:5.

[83] Thus in Job 33:31 God says : ἄκουέ μου, ἐγώ εἰμι λαλήσω for the Heb. וְאָנֹכִי אֲדַבֵּר; cf. Is. 48:12.

[84] "I am he" is used in the ordinary sense in Apc. Mos., 17 and Test. Job, 29, 31 and 36 ; cf. C. Tischendorf, Apk. Apkr. (1866); and M. R. James, Texts and Studies, V, 1 (1897).

[85] Apc. Abr., 8 (Bonwetsch). The predicative noun is to be supplied from what precedes, but there can be no mistaking the emphatic overtone.

[86] Ibid., 9. The continuation in explanatory I-statements corresponds to the form of Dt. Is. and shows that we do not have here a purely pacifying statement.

[87] V. M. Buttenwieser, Die Hebräische Eliasapokalypse (1897).

[88] It is striking that ἐγώ εἰμι occurs in Jn. exactly 7 times. But the use is varied and is not restricted to Jesus. Hence individual exegesis must be our starting-point.

[89] So B, the Old Lat. and the Sin. Syr. in Jn. 18:5, the reference in 18:6 and the repetition in 18:8.

[90] Mk. 6:50; Mt. 14:27; Jn. 6:20.

[91] Mt. 26:64 not incorrectly has σὺ εἶπας for ἐγώ εἰμι (cf. Jn. 18:37), but the πλὴν λέγω weakens the material connexion with the prophecy. Lk. 22:67 ff. is better.

Yet, as Jesus says in Mk. 13:6, at the end of the days many will come ἐπὶ τῷ ὀνόματί μου λέγοντες ὅτι ἐγώ εἰμι, καὶ πολλοὺς πλανήσουσιν. And in 13:21 ff. He gives the warning: καὶ τότε ἐάν τις ... εἴπῃ· ἴδε ὧδε ὁ χριστός, ἴδε ἐκεῖ, μὴ πιστεύετε. ἐγερθήσονται ... ψευδόχριστοι ... ὑμεῖς δὲ βλέπετε· προείρηκα ὑμῖν πάντα. Here the context does not provide any predicate for ἐγώ εἰμι. It is rather a fixed and pregnant formula which applies only to Christ and which is abused by false prophets and pseudo-Messiahs [92] at a time when the final manifestation of Christ is expected and when the question: σὺ εἶ ὁ χριστός, must be asked again of every significant figure. Christ Himself must combat misuse of the I-formula which is proper to Him alone, and He tells His disciples what will happen (cf. Mt. 24:26 f.) in order that they will not give credence to any arrogant "I am he," but wait patiently for the decisive ἐγώ εἰμι from the lips of the exalted Christ. Ἐγώ εἰμι thus becomes here a technical formula for the self-revelation of Christ which has already made a modest beginning in the present and will be completed in the future. [93] This gives the ἐγώ εἰμι of Mk. 13 a particular significance and leads to the Johannine meaning and use of the formula.

The central passage is Jn. 8:24-29. There is a preceding chain of I-predications: ἐγώ εἰμι τὸ φῶς (v. 12), ἐγώ εἰμι ὁ μαρτυρῶν περὶ ἐμαυτοῦ, καὶ μαρτυρεῖ περὶ ἐμαυτοῦ ὁ ... πατήρ (v. 18), ἐγὼ ὑπάγω καὶ ζητήσετέ με, καὶ ἐν τῇ ἁμαρτίᾳ ὑμῶν ἀποθανεῖσθε (v. 21). Life and death decision is decision for or against Christ (v. 24): ἐὰν γὰρ μὴ πιστεύσητε ὅτι ἐγώ εἰμι, ἀποθανεῖσθε ... It is thus plain that the ἐγώ of Jesus is the point where there is the Yes of belief or the No of unbelief. This is the critical point on which the waves of world history break. But ἐγώ εἰμι is still a puzzling predicate. The hearers find it so, and thus ask: σὺ τίς εἶ; But it is to remain puzzling. As in Lk. 22:67 f., Jesus refuses to elaborate: τὴν ἀρχὴν ὅτι καὶ λαλῶ ὑμῖν. He is silent, and lets history speak. As in Mk. 14:62, the future will disclose the meaning and validity of this puzzling saying. The Father will bear witness for Him (cf. 8:18): ὅταν ὑψώσητε τὸν υἱὸν τοῦ ἀνθρώπου, τότε γνώσεσθε ὅτι ἐγώ εἰμι. For the future will display the as yet concealed identity of His work with that of God. (καὶ γνώσεσθε ὅτι) ἀπ' ἐμαυτοῦ ποιῶ οὐδέν, ἀλλὰ καθὼς ἐδίδαξέν με ὁ πατήρ, ταῦτα λαλῶ. The ἐγώ of the Son is linked with the I of the Father in an absolute unity of action: ὁ πέμψας με μετ' ἐμοῦ ἐστιν· οὐκ ἀφῆκέν με μόνον, ὅτι ἐγὼ τὰ ἀρεστὰ αὐτῷ ποιῶ πάντοτε. [94] Jesus is the acting Subject of the history of God. He is this from the beginning (cf. Jn. 1:1 ff. and 1 Jn. 1:1 ff.). πρὶν Ἀβραὰμ γενέσθαι ἐγώ εἰμι. But only now has His action entered its decisive stage (8:58). From now on every step of the history will be a contribution to the revelation and glorification of the Son, to the fulfilment of the meaning of His ἐγώ εἰμι: ἀπ' ἄρτι λέγω ὑμῖν πρὸ τοῦ γενέσθαι, ἵνα πιστεύητε ὅταν γένηται ὅτι ἐγώ εἰμι (Jn. 13:19). This is the final thrust of ἐγώ εἰμι without predicate. The ἐγώ of Christ is the Subject of the history of God, and this history will be nothing but a powerful self-proclamation of Christ. In every victory of the history of God Christ calls to those who hearken: "I am he."

---

[92] Mt. again paraphrases: ἐγώ εἰμι ὁ Χριστός (thus showing how we are to take the ὅτι of Mk. 13:6). This is correct, but robs the formula of its pregnant character.

[93] A different view is taken by E. Norden, *Agnostos Theos*, 194 ff.; G. Klein, *Der älteste christliche Katechismus* ... (1909), 55 ff.

[94] 8:29. Cf. the explanation of the ἐγώ εἰμι in 13:19 f.: ἀμήν ... με.

Attempts have been made to derive the christological I-sayings of the Gospels, and especially of John, from Hellenistic models. This is a shortsighted view. Ultimately the emphatic I-saying goes back, as we have seen, to a twofold root, namely, the ancient oriental tradition which reaches its full flower in syncretism, and OT forms which wither away in the Synagogue. These two traditions come together in Jewish Apocalyptic, and in conjunction influence the contemporary world of Jesus and the Gospels. According to the Synoptists, Jesus adopts the I-formulae, claiming exclusively for Himself the I-sayings of the most diverse representatives of God. In the I-sayings of John He contests the right of the pseudo-saviours and pseudo-gods of the polytheistic world to soteriological I-predications. He Himself transcends them all, and reveals Himself as the definitive Representative of God in the absolute divine formula ἐγώ εἰμι, the purest expression of His unique and immeasurable significance.

It is in keeping with the exclusive character of the I-sayings of Jesus that in post-canonical texts emphatic I-sayings are often used to express pseudo-Christian or anti-Christian pretension. [95] The Apc. of Elijah and Ezra follow Mk. 13 when they cause antichrist to say: "I am the anointed" or "I am the Son of God." [96] In the pseudo-Clementine Homilies the style of Mk. 14:61 and par. is adopted, and Simon is asked: εἰ σὺ εἶ ὁ ἑστώς, to which he replies: ἐγώ εἰμι. [97]

C. The Anthropological ἐγώ.

1. I and We in the Writings of Luke.

In the dedication of Luke's Gospel, after some remarks on his sources and predecessors, we find the words: ἔδοξε κἀμοὶ παρηκολουθηκότι ἄνωθεν πᾶσιν ἀκριβῶς καθεξῆς σοι γράψαι, κράτιστε Θεόφιλε (1:3). This is Greek style. [98] Here for the first time an Evangelist makes personal reference. He has in view a biography which will go beyond the form of previous Gospels [99] as he diligently and artistically shapes the varied testimonies into a βίος of Jesus. This is a Greek ideal. The execution of the project is Greek also in the sense that the great mass of teaching material, which cannot be fitted καθεξῆς into a chronological or biographical scheme, is made into the account of a journey. [100] Similarly, the δεύτερος λόγος, i.e., Acts, opens with a short personal address to the same Theophilus (1:1). Here, too, especially in the second part, accounts of journeys play an important part. The missionary activity of Paul, which obviously comprised several missions, is here compressed into a schema of three or four journeys. Within the accounts the author sometimes uses the We form: ἀναχθέντες δὲ ἀπὸ Τρωάδος εὐθυδρομήσαμεν εἰς Σαμοθρᾴκην etc. [101] It is usually deduced that the author or his informant took part in the events recorded in these sections (cf. 20:5 f.: Οὗτοι δὲ προελθόντες ἔμενον ἡμᾶς ... ἡμεῖς δὲ ἐξεπλεύσαμεν) and that the We passages are thus particularly reliable. Another possibility, however, is that the

---

[95] Cf. also 2 Th. 2:4.

[96] Apc. Eliae, 31 (Steindorff, TU NF, 2 [1899]); Apc. Esr. 4 (Tischendorf, Apc. apocr. [1866]).

[97] Ps.-Clem. Hom., 2, 24 in Bau. J.³ Excurs. on 8:12, with further information on Demon, Pseudomithras, Pseudomessiah. The question (εἰ σύ) and answer (εἰμί, ἐγώ εἰμι) occur frequently in Test. Sol. (McCown), e.g., 2:1 ff.; 25:1 ff. (demon).

[98] Norden, op. cit., p. 316.

[99] M. Dibelius, Formgeschichte des Evangeliums² (1933), 290 f. → εὐαγγέλιον.

[100] The pseudo-historical character of the journey may be seen by comparison with Mt. The general outline of the Gospel is influenced by Mk. and is not the result of new and independent investigation.

[101] Cf. 20:5 ff.; 21:1 ff.; 27:1 ff.

We is a literary device to give vitality and variety to the record, as in similar Hellenistic accounts. [102]

2. We and I in the Johannine Writings.

In eloquent contrast to Luke John's Prologue introduces a We sentence among its cosmic statements concerning the Logos and His incarnation : ἐθεασάμεθα τὴν δόξαν αὐτοῦ, this being followed shortly after by an express ἡμεῖς : ἐκ τοῦ πληρώματος αὐτοῦ ἡμεῖς πάντες ἐλάβομεν. [103] These are words of confession behind which stands a whole circle of witnesses and confessors. As thus introduced, the Gospel is not meant to be a biography. Along the lines of Mark, it is to be a confessional document (cf. 20:31). One is speaking in the name of many [104] with whom he knows that he is united in faith and knowledge, just as Peter speaks in the name of the disciples : ἡμεῖς πεπιστεύκαμεν καὶ ἐγνώκαμεν ὅτι σὺ εἶ ὁ ἅγιος τοῦ θεοῦ (6:69). 1 John has the same Johannine We at the very beginning, in strict parallelism with the Prologue of the Gospel and its conclusion : ταῦτα γράφομεν ἡμεῖς ἵνα ἡ χαρὰ ἡμῶν ᾖ πεπληρωμένη (1 Jn. 1:4; cf. Jn. 20:31).

The same We recurs in the most diverse confessional forms (4:14, 16 etc.). It appears plainly in demarcation from false teachers : ἐξ ἡμῶν ἐξῆλθον, ἀλλ᾽ οὐκ ἦσαν ἐξ ἡμῶν (2:19). This is the certainty of the elect who have surmounted the crisis. But above this faithful ἡμεῖς there stands in hours of temptation the θεός who has elected us, who keeps us, who knows us as we do not know ourselves : ἔμπροσθεν αὐτοῦ πείσομεν τὴν καρδίαν ἡμῶν, ὅτι ἐὰν καταγινώσκῃ ἡμῶν ἡ καρδία, ὅτι μείζων ἐστὶν ὁ θεὸς τῆς καρδίας ἡμῶν καὶ γινώσκει πάντα (3:19 f.). The fact of election is present only before and for God. Behind this binding We, however, there also appears from 2:1 onwards the authoritative I of the writer : τεκνία μου, ταῦτα γράφω ὑμῖν ἵνα μὴ ἁμάρτητε. This is always used when ethical conclusions are drawn from the common theological assumptions (2:7, 12 ff.). It is even more pronounced at the end, taking up again the γράφομεν of 1:4 : ταῦτα ἔγραψα ὑμῖν ἵνα εἰδῆτε ὅτι ζωὴν ἔχετε αἰώνιον (5:13). On the other hand, 2 Jn. begins in the sing., [105] then asserts the unity of the ἐγώ with the fellowship of believers [106] and finally unites the two in a comprehensive ἡμεῖς. 3 Jn. is wholly personal.

The most subtle relationship of We and I is to be found in Rev. : Ἐγὼ Ἰωάννης ὁ ἀδελφὸς ὑμῶν καὶ συγκοινωνὸς ἐν τῇ θλίψει καὶ βασιλείᾳ καὶ ὑπομονῇ (1:9). [107] This John is a brother, a δοῦλος before Christ, a mortal and feeble man (1:17; 5:4; 7:14 f.; 19:10 : κἀγὼ Ἰωάννης ... ὅτε ἤκουσα, ἔπεσα προσκυνῆσαι). But he has seen things to come and has thus received from God a commission which he discharges with prophetic power and with the steadfastness of an apocalyptist. The first ἐγώ in 1:9 stands between the I-sayings of God and Christ, and the final ἐγὼ Ἰησοῦς is followed by a last ἐγώ of John, with a divine curse on those who attack his book (22:18 f.). The self-awareness of the author reaches its climax at this point. But it is by no means self-glorification. It is an awareness of office, and ultimately of God. [108]

---

[102] Cf. Norden, op. cit., 321 ff.

[103] Jn. 1:14, 16.

[104] Jn. 21:24 : οὗτός ἐστιν ὁ μαθητὴς ὁ ... γράψας ταῦτα καὶ οἴδαμεν ὅτι ἀληθὴς αὐτοῦ ἡ μαρτυρία ἐστίν (cf. 19:35; 3 Jn. 12).

[105] With the sender : Ὁ πρεσβύτερος ... τοῖς τέκνοις ... οὓς ἐγὼ ἀγαπῶ.

[106] καὶ οὐκ ἐγὼ μόνος ἀλλὰ καὶ πάντες ...

[107] Cf. ἐγὼ Δανιήλ in Da. 8:1 (→ n. 40 f.). But unlike the Jewish apocalyptists the NT author does not use a great name of the past as pseudonym.

[108] Cf. Sl. En. 39:2, 7 etc.

3. We and I in Paul.

The plur. ἡμεῖς in Paul's letters is essentially stylistic. [109] All the letters begin with the name of Paul as the sender. The most personal of them (Philemon) maintains the sing. to the very end: εὐχαριστῶ τῷ θεῷ μου (v. 4); ἐγὼ Παῦλος ἔγραψα τῇ ἐμῇ χειρί, ἐγὼ ἀποτίσω ... ἐγώ σου ὀναίμην (v. 19 f.). Philippians is also personal, and so, too, is Romans, which is the personal letter, not of a beloved missionary, but of an isolated thinker [110] and controversialist. [111] The We tone is more noticeable in the other letters. It is the style of the cultured man who wishes to keep his person and personal affairs in the background. Where ἡμεῖς is used, it is usually with a special nuance. Sometimes the wider circle gives added authority (1 C. 11:16). Sometimes the reference is to Paul personally as distinct from, or even in opposition to, the recipients of the letter. Thus 2 Corinthians begins: συνυπουργούντων καὶ ὑμῶν ὑπὲρ ἡμῶν τῇ δεήσει. [112] But Paul soon has an ἐβουλόμην (1:15), and from this point on the I and We alternate in swift and irregular succession [113] until a new beginning is solemnly made with the Αὐτὸς δὲ ἐγὼ Παῦλος of 10:1. When Paul wishes to make clear his own position, he mostly uses the sing. and often has the preceding emphatic ἐγώ. Thus the ἐγώ of 1 C. 15:9 refers to his special position in relation to the twelve, which is then relativised again in the Εἴτε οὖν ἐγὼ εἴτε ἐκεῖνοι of 15:11. The ἐγώ of 1 C. 7 has particular significance as the ἐγώ of a pneumatic who constitutes an example and authority, though as such he is clearly distinguished from the κύριος. [114] It is in Galatians that the ἐγώ expresses most clearly opposition to the authority of others and the assertion of Paul's own authority: [115] ἐγὼ γὰρ τὰ στίγματα τοῦ Ἰησοῦ ἐν τῷ σώματί μου βαστάζω (6:17).

The first pers. (sing. and plur.) play an important part in ethical and exhortatory passages in Paul. [116] Paul has a great liking for the cohortative, [117] which exhorts the readers to the moral duty less sharply than the imperative. [118] He thus likes to change from the second person to the first to spare the susceptibilities of his flock. [119] In 1 Th. 5:5 ff. he begins with the assertion: ἐσμέν, and there then follows the cohortative: ἄρα οὖν γρηγορῶμεν. After a gnomic intermediary clause he then draws the same line from the facts to the task in v. 8, and then a third time in v. 9, though not in a cohortative but in a final clause: ἔθετο ἡμᾶς ὁ θεός, ἵνα ... An imperative closes the passage. The negative counterpart is to be found in R. 6:1 ff. Here the conclusion: Ἐπιμένωμεν τῇ ἁμαρτίᾳ is put at the beginning, and Paul expresses it only to reject it. [120] He opposes to it the fact: ἀπεθάνομεν τῇ ἁμαρτίᾳ, and then, in a development of the same motif, συνετάφημεν, ἵνα περιπατήσωμεν. Only after long discussion does he transfer to the second person in v. 11. But the train of thought follows the same line again in v. 15 ff.

---

[109] Cf. the table in Dobschütz, 254.
[110] Cf. 2 Pt. 3:15 f.
[111] 1:8 ff.; 9:1 ff.; 10:1; 11:1 f.; 12:1 ff.; 15:14 ff., 30 f. etc.
[112] 1:11; cf. 1:4 ff., 12 ff.
[113] 1:18 ff. we; 1:23: ἐγὼ δὲ (2:10: καὶ γὰρ ἐγώ); 3:1 ff. we (4:12: ὁ θάνατος ἐν ἡμῖν, ἡ ζωὴ ἐν ὑμῖν; 6:11: τὸ στόμα ἡμῶν; 6:13: ὡς τέκνοις λέγω.
[114] 7:7 f., 10, 12, 25, 40.
[115] 2:6 ff.: ἐμοὶ γὰρ οἱ δοκοῦντες ...; 5:2 ff.: Ἴδε ἐγὼ Παῦλος λέγω ὑμῖν ... Ἐγὼ δέ, ἀδελφοί; 6:11 ff.: Ἴδετε ... τῇ ἐμῇ χειρί.
[116] Cf. v. Dobschütz, 251 ff. and the fine collection in Kümmel, 121.
[117] R. 13:12 f.
[118] Gl. 5:25 f.
[119] 2 C. 7:1; cf. 1 C. 10:8 ff.; R. 14:13.
[120] Cf. R. 3:8; also 1 C. 10:22.

The exhortatory goal served by the cohortative can be attained also by hypothetical I and We sentences [121] which usually have no true reality behind them. [122] Here, too, we have an admixture of assertions and persons. [123] In such contexts the ἐγώ has only exemplary significance, [124] and is more or less equivalent to the indefinite τις or "one." The proper tense of such modes of speech is the present, as in 1 C. 13: "Though I speak with the tongues of men and of angels, and have not charity, I am become as sounding brass, or a tinkling cymbal." Καὶ ἐὰν παραδῶ τὸ σῶμά μου, ἀγάπην δὲ μὴ ἔχω, οὐθέν εἰμι. [125] These are gnomic statements designed to indicate καθ' ὑπερβολὴν ὁδός and having nothing to do with self-confession. [126] This gnomic and timeless sense is maintained even in statements where a general truth is illustrated in the past tense: ὅτε ἤμην νήπιος, ἐλάλουν ὡς νήπιος ... ὅτε γέγονα ἀνήρ, κατήργηκα τὰ τοῦ νηπίου. [127] Only the concluding v. 12 forsakes the gnomic form and refers to the actual situation of the present and state of the future.

The case is rather different in the great argumentative passage in Gl. 2:15 ff., where the style is not so much that of the diatribe as of Rabbinic disputation and debate concerning the Torah. After an introductory σύ, which is addressed to Peter rather than to men generally, Paul continues with a We statement which refers to the historical position: ἡμεῖς φύσει Ἰουδαῖοι καὶ οὐκ ἐξ ἐθνῶν ἁμαρτωλοί. [128] The next sentence speaks of a new situation in salvation history, the significance of which is indirectly supported by a quotation from Scripture. This leads to the practical conclusion: καὶ ἡμεῖς ἐπιστεύσαμεν (v. 16). There follows a fundamental conclusion in the We style (v. 17) and then another in the I style: εἰ γὰρ ἃ κατέλυσα ... συνιστάνω (v. 18). This statement, in the familiar hypothetical form, has a gnomic sense, the ἐγώ having the same meaning as "one." But now Paul goes beyond general discussion of possibilities and truths to the decisive reality: ἐγὼ γὰρ διὰ νόμου νόμῳ ἀπέθανον, ἵνα θεῷ ζήσω. [129] It is the same event as described in v. 16 by ἐπιστεύσαμεν, but now formulated in such a way that the break with the Law is clearly seen to be inevitable. At this point Paul has to use I rather than We because he sees more plainly and acts more consistently than Peter. He thus draws the conclusion in an I sentence: οὐκ ἀθετῶ τὴν χάριν τοῦ θεοῦ. Nevertheless, this is not because we have here his own private concern or personal way. It is rather that he takes seriously the situation of salvation history which must be expressed in his life, [130] and has taken a way which Peter and the rest must also tread. He has made the break and taken the step as a τύπος who summons to μίμησις. [131] The sketch of salvation history in Galatians is

---

121 1 C. 6:12 ff.; 11:31.

122 R. 3:5 ff.; 1 C. 10:29 f.

123 1 C. 14:11 ff.

124 Grotius calls this "metaschematism" in allusion to 1 C. 4:6: μετεσχημάτισα εἰς ἐμαυτόν; cf. Kümmel, 120.

125 1 C. 13:1-3; R. Bultmann ("Paulus," RGG², IV, 1032 f.) compares with this 2 C. 12:15 (ἐγὼ δὲ ἥδιστα ἐκδαπανηθήσομαι) to show that Paul can use ἐγώ in the sense of σῶμα.

126 On the style, v. R. Bultmann, Der Stil der paulinischen Predigt und die stoisch-kynische Diatribe (1910). E. Lehmann and A. Fridrichsen, "1 K. 13, eine stoisch-kynische Diatribe," ThStKr, 94 (1922), 55-95. → ἀγάπη. Kümmel, 126 ff.

127 The I of the picture corresponds to the We of the frame (v. 9: γινώσκομεν; v. 12: βλέπομεν). What appears as past in the picture (ἤμην νήπιος) is in reality present (ἄρτι γινώσκω ἐκ μέρους). On the use of the tenses, cf. also Ps. Sol. 3:5 ff.

128 Even sharper, and with particular relevance for Pl., is Phil. 3:6: κατὰ δικαιοσύνην τὴν ἐν νόμῳ γενόμενος ἄμεμπτος.

129 On the analysis of this statement, v. E. Stauffer, "Vom λόγος τοῦ σταυροῦ und seiner Logik," ThStKr, 103 (1931), 179 ff.

130 Stauffer, op. cit., 186 ff.

131 Cf. τύπος in 2 Th. 3:9; Phil. 3:17; μιμητής and μιμεῖσθαι in 1 C. and 2 Th.; also Gl. 4:12: γίνεσθε ὡς ἐγώ.

further developed by Paul in Romans. Thus we move on methodically from Gal. 2 to R. 7.

4. The I of R. 7.

The autobiographical interpretation of R. 7 has a long history. [132] In v. 9a and 7b expositors have found reminiscences of the innocence of childhood, and in v. 13 ff. confessions of the inner confusion of Paul prior to his so-called conversion. This interpretation is challenged, however, by the brief phrase κατὰ δικαιοσύνην ... ἄμεμπτος which Paul uses to describe his pre-Christian period in Phil. 3:6. [133] The Damascus event is hardly the conversion of a despairing sinner but the calling and overthrow of a self-righteous Pharisee. Thus the autobiographical interpretation of R. 7 has been increasingly replaced by a rhetorically general view, [134] i.e., that here is the same imprecise use as in 1 C. 13, and that the I statements of R. 7 are thus to be taken as a description of man generally under the Law. This interpretation is shattered, however, by the fact that on a closer analysis the I style of R. 7 is not the hypothetical exhortatory of R. 13 but the historically paradigmatic of Gl. 2. Both the autobiographical and rhetorically general interpretations are finally destroyed by the further fact that Romans deals neither with experiences and confessions of the individual soul nor with investigation of the constitution and forms of human existence, but first and last with the progress of salvation history. This is particularly true of R. 7. In R. 1 ff. Paul speaks of the way in which humanity in its various historical groupings is led to its lowest point. In R. 8 he speaks of the saving Christ event. And in between in R. 7 he speaks of the fulfilment of the crisis by the Torah. We have thus to understand the I style of R. 7 in terms of salvation history.

Again and again Romans refers to the three great stages of history. The divine impulsion is turned into its opposite by demonic counterpressure. But everything enterprised against God finally destroys itself and thus leads to the third and final step of history, the accomplishment of the will of God in a final triumph which surpasses every beginning. The decisive third step, however, has now been initiated in the Christ event. It is now being worked out in the destiny and will of man. [135] It is of this turning point in the ages that Paul speaks in R. 7:5 f.: ὅτε γὰρ ἦμεν ἐν τῇ σαρκί, τὰ παθήματα τῶν ἁμαρτιῶν τὰ διὰ τοῦ νόμου ἐνηργεῖτο ἐν τοῖς μέλεσιν ἡμῶν ... νυνὶ δὲ κατηργήθημεν ἀπὸ τοῦ νόμου ... ὥστε δουλεύειν ἡμᾶς ἐν καινότητι πνεύματος. What is expressed in this brief statement is more fully expounded in R. 7:7-8:1 ff., [136] and as in Gl. 2:17 f. there is a transition from the collective ἡμεῖς to the typical ἐγώ.

Having spoken of the end of the Law in 7:6, Paul speaks of its beginnings in 7:7-12. ἐγὼ ... ἔζων χωρὶς νόμου ποτέ. This is the time before Moses, [137] when ἁμαρτία was νεκρά (v. 8). But now the Law enters human history, [138] in itself

---

[132] Among more recent scholars, cf. A. Deissmann, *Paulus* (1911), 64 f.

[133] → n. 128.

[134] A pioneer of this line of interpretation is Bultmann (RGG², IV, 1022 f., and more recently in *Festschr. f. G. Krüger*, 53 ff.). Kümmel goes even further, and E. Fuchs, *Christus und der Geist bei Paulus* (1932) 29 f. goes furthest of all, rather strangely regarding the decisive passages as unreal hypotheses.

[135] R. 3:21 ff.; 5:1 ff.; 6:1 ff., 23.

[136] On Augustine's exegesis of R. 7, cf. H. Jonas, *Augustin und das Paulinische Freiheitsproblem* (1930), 24 ff.

[137] R. 5:12-14.

[138] R. 5:20; Gl. 3:19, 23 f.; R. 3:19 f.

holy and good (v. 12). What in itself is εἰς ζωήν, however, works εἰς θάνατον according to the paradoxical law of the threefold step of v. 10 (cf. 4:15; 1 C. 15:56). The sign of God which demands submission provokes opposition (v. 8a, v. 11a). Where God intervenes, the power of evil rises up against Him. Sin turns the operation of the Law into its opposite : ἐλθούσης δὲ τῆς ἐντολῆς ἡ ἁμαρτία ἀνέζησεν — ἐγὼ δὲ ἀπέθανον (v. 9 f., cf. 11a ἀπέκτεινεν). The time of freedom and continuity has passed (7:7; 3:20); the crisis has come.

Paul begins to speak of this crisis in a second train of thought in vv. 13-20. The Law is in the first instance a radical means to bring into action a dormant sickness. Its aim is to bring sin to its full development and thus to lead the race to its nadir (v. 13). [139] The Law plunges man into an inner conflict of the Ego which tears him. This is the anthropological symptom of the new age. Thus Paul speaks of an ἐγώ (v. 17) which assents to the Law of God (v. 16), which has the will to perform the Law (v. 18; v. 19 f.) and which passionately negates sin (v. 15). But man also confesses : οἶδα ... ὅτι οὐκ οἰκεῖ ἐν ἐμοί, τοῦτ' ἔστιν ἐν τῇ σαρκί μου, ἀγαθόν (v. 18). In him (v. 17, 20), i.e., in his flesh, [140] there dwells sin, which powerfully controls all his actions (v. 16, 18 ff.). In this sense it is true : ἐγὼ σάρκινός εἰμι, πεπραμένος ὑπὸ τὴν ἁμαρτίαν (v. 14b). It is in vain that the true ἐγώ does not acknowledge this sinister I, disclaiming responsibility for its actions : ὃ γὰρ κατεργάζομαι οὐ γινώσκω (v. 15a). Quite without hope is the protest of judgment and will against the terror of ἁμαρτία, this alien usurper and tyrant : οὐκέτι ἐγὼ κατεργάζομαι αὐτὸ ἀλλὰ ἡ ἐνοικοῦσα ἐν ἐμοὶ ἁμαρτία. Nevertheless, man can twice say : This is no longer my Ego (v. 17, 20).

Vv. 21-23, with a concluding ἄρα, give us the result of this analysis : εὑρίσκω ἄρα τὸν νόμον τῷ θέλοντι ἐμοὶ ποιεῖν τὸ καλόν, ὅτι ἐμοὶ τὸ κακὸν παράκειται. A law of corruption reigns over man's existence. Good will gives rise to evil action. The ἔσω ἄνθρωπος (2 C. 4:16) joyfully assents to the νόμος of God. [141] The νοῦς recognises it to be His νόμος. But man stands under the sway of another law which reigns in his members, the νόμος ἁμαρτίας. He is an impotent prisoner.

A passionate cry for redemption from this state which can end only in death, and an anticipatory cry of thanksgiving for the redemptive act of God, [142] now follow in vv. 24, 25a. Then v. 25b gives us the final conclusion with another ἄρα. The various ideas are brought into conjunction and juxtaposition in a last clarification of the state of tension : ἄρα οὖν αὐτὸς ἐγὼ τῷ μὲν νοΐ δουλεύω νόμῳ θεοῦ, τῇ δὲ σαρκὶ νόμῳ ἁμαρτίας (v. 25b). This is how Paul sees the situation of man in the age of the Law. The self of man, one and the same I, stands under a twofold determination. In judgment, it stands under the compelling Law of God; in life under the enforced law of sin. [143]

But this divided state is already overcome. The anthropological account of the twofold corruption of man does not apply to the ἐγώ of the Christian. The crisis

---

[139] R. 5:20b; Gl. 3:19, 24; R. 3:19.

[140] Cf. v. 23 : ἐν τοῖς μέλεσιν. Both denote a potiori the whole man in his determination by the σχῆμα τοῦ κόσμου. Cf. on this pt. R. Bultmann, Paulus, RGG², IV, 1032 f.; Kümmel, 136; Fuchs, 108 f.

[141] Cf. v. 16 : σύμφημι.

[142] Cf. 6:17 (also 6:23) and 1 C. 15:57.

[143] αὐτὸς ἐγώ, not as in 2 C. 10:1, but in the emphatic sense of R. 9:3. Cf. the αὐτός of 1 C. 3:15. Syncretistic examples of αὐτός and its equation with the νοῦς may be found in Reitzenstein Hell. Myst., 403 ff., 408 ff., 413, cf. 338.

of man simply prepares the way for the victory of God. The great age of crisis under the Law is preparatory for the third step of history marked by the Christ event. οὐδὲν ἄρα νῦν κατάκριμα [144] τοῖς ἐν Χριστῷ 'Ιησοῦ. In 8:1 Paul reaches again the historical point of 7:6 at which he was aiming shortly before with his χάρις θεῷ. In c. 8 he describes the situation of the new man whose position [145] is determined by the fact of Jesus. ὁ γὰρ νόμος τοῦ πνεύματος τῆς ζωῆς ἐν Χριστῷ 'Ιησοῦ ἠλευθέρωσέν σε ἀπὸ τοῦ νόμου τῆς ἁμαρτίας καὶ τοῦ θανάτου (8:2). The imprisonment (7:23) is at an end; the cry for liberation (7:24) has been heard (8:10). We are free (cf. 6:22). A new law has entered our existence, [146] superior to the νόμος τοῦ νοός, more powerful than the νόμος τῆς ἁμαρτίας, namely, the νόμος τοῦ πνεύματος, which is posited ἐν Χριστῷ and which aims at ζωή. A new subject has taken possession of our will and action, superseding the νοῦς and resisting ἁμαρτία. This is the *pneuma*.

Τὸ → πνεῦμα is the new concept introduced in c. 8 as compared with c. 7. The pneumatic I is the basic anthropological fact of the new situation after Christ. This pneumatic I is described by Paul in three respects, namely, in relationship to the Christ event, to God and to our somatic being.

When the νόμος lost its power, and history reached its nadir, God intervened, attacking sin in its own most proper sphere of the σάρξ and causing it to destroy itself through the Christ event. What has taken place typically and representatively in the πρωτότοκος, [147] however, seeks expression and execution in the Christian ἵνα τὸ δικαίωμα τοῦ νόμου πληρωθῇ ἐν ἡμῖν. If ἁμαρτία once dwelled in us, Christ now wills to dwell in us, and He does dwell in those who are ἐν Χριστῷ. Here, as in Gl., the reciprocal formula "I in Christ" and "Christ in me" does not refer to a mystical relationship; it describes a historical fact. The Christian is ἐν Χριστῷ in the same sense as the old man is ἐν 'Αδάμ and the Jew ἐν νόμῳ. He is in the situation created by the Christ event. His existence stands under a new sign (8:10, cf. 2 C. 5:17; Phil. 1:21). And to the extent that he takes seriously the new determination of his existence with all its possibilities and tasks, Christ is expressed in him and his action. Once again the act is decisive. It was in action that he came to see his *non posse non peccare*. [148] And it is in action alone that he is now granted the *posse non peccare* (8:4 ff.). The pneumatic I is a reality for man only *in actu*.

Over and in all this, however, God is the absolute Subject in the OT sense. [149] It is His πρόθεσις which is now realised. He has sent Christ into the world and thus brought man to decision, the decision which in any case brings the old situation to an end, whether in the liberation of will and action and therefore in life (8:2 ff.) or in tragic perversion of the will and therefore in death (10:2 ff.). In the last resort man is wholly himself only before God. God's call awakens the deepest self in man, and a cry to God is the first expression of the pneumatic I. [150] In pneumatic converse with God we know the vitality and certainty of the Spirit (8:16; Gl. 4:6). [151] When man himself can find no more words, his pneumatic self speaks in στεναγμοῖς ἀλαλήτοις which God alone

---

[144] Cf. R. 5:18.

[145] Called *conditio* by Augustine in Civ. D., XIII, 14; XXI, 14.

[146] Cf. also E. Fuchs, *op. cit.*, 41.

[147] R. 8:29 : προώρισεν ... ἀδελφοῖς.

[148] R. 8:7: οὐδὲ γὰρ δύναται.

[149] → 344 (also 1 C. 15:10).

[150] 8:15; → βοάω, I, 625.

[151] A different view is taken in bBer., 34b and T. Ber., 3, 3 : "Whose prayer runs smoothly on his lips, to him it is a good sign." Cf. W. Bacher, *Agada der Tannaiten*, I² (1903), 276.

understands. The pneumatic subject can never be an object for us. It cannot be contemplated or controlled. It is accessible only to God. It never exists except in a Thou-relationship to God. Its existence is thus wholly dependent upon God : εἰ θεὸς ὑπὲρ ἡμῶν, τίς καθ' ἡμῶν (8:31; cf. 1 C. 2:10 ff.). It remains in the hands of God even in judgment. [152] It may be determined only by God, and it is manifest only to the ἐρευνῶν τὰς καρδίας (8:27 f.). In the last analysis, therefore, the new anthropological situation exists only ἐνώπιον τοῦ θεοῦ.

In any case, and this is the third point, the new situation does not extend beyond the pneumatic I. Creation still lies in its ancient distress. Even the soma-determined being of the man who has the *pneuma* still bears the mark of the old era (2 C. 4:16). The *pneuma* is only an ἀπαρχή (→ I, 484; 2 C. 1:22; 5:5). Thus the man who before Christ cried out for liberation from the bondage of the σῶμα τοῦ θανάτου now longs for the ἀπολύτρωσις τοῦ σώματος itself. [153] But the *pneuma* is truly an ἀπαρχή which guarantees our future : ὁ ἐγείρας ἐκ νεκρῶν Χριστὸν 'Ιησοῦν ζωοποιήσει καὶ τὰ θνητὰ σώματα ὑμῶν διὰ τοῦ ἐνοικοῦντος αὐτοῦ πνεύματος ἐν ὑμῖν (8:11). Thus the present anthropological situation points forward to a new one in which the pneumatic I has also seized control over the somatic existence of man. And this is a sign of the redemption of creation which through the fall of man fell victim to corruption and which now waits expectantly for the manifestation and liberation of the sons of God. It is thus that the threefold movement of God reaches its goal. Only from this standpoint can we see the tremendous scope of the anthropological situation brought about by Christ. The pneumatic I is the point of departure for a comprehensive renewal of the world which will be revealed only in the final consummation.

The train of thought moves continuously from 7:7 to 8:11. In 8:1, however, Paul suddenly abandons the ἐγώ; in 8:2 he uses a σε [154] instead of the apparently more suitable με, and from 8:4 he alternates between ἡμεῖς and ὑμεῖς. Thus in the plur. pronouns of R. 8 he refers directly to the many who were in view in the ἐγώ of R. 7, the ἡμεῖς making it clear that Paul himself is to be numbered among them. Thus the reference of the ἐγώ of R. 7 to the people of the Law does not exclude a reference to Paul himself ; it rather includes it.

This raises the problem of tension between R. 7 and the κατὰ δικαιοσύνην ἄμεμπτος of Phil. 3:6. There is no escaping this problem, however, by a rhetorically general interpretation. For such an interpretation involves tension with the equation of Gl. 2:15 : φύσει 'Ιουδαῖοι = οὐκ ἐξ ἐθνῶν ἁμαρτωλοί. Since there is tension either way, we must face the problem squarely and try to find a solution. The pre-Christian Paul is in one case described as ἄμεμπτος and in the other as a despairing wrestler. The people of the Torah is in one case described as a morally strict group and in the other as a mass of hopeless sinners. There can be no questioning the validity or the tension of the two statements. Hence their apparent contradiction is to be explained only from the difference in standpoint. In Phil. 3:6

---

[152] Cf. αὐτός in 1 C. 3:15 with the αὐτός in R. 9:3.

[153] καὶ αὐτοὶ τὴν ἀπαρχὴν τοῦ πνεύματος ἔχοντες ἡμεῖς καὶ αὐτοὶ ἐν ἑαυτοῖς στενάζομεν (8:23). Cf. Gl. 5:17.

[154] Formally the same alternation as in 1 C. 14:15 f. (10:9 f.; R. 6:8 ff., 15 f.; 14:13). Thus the best Egypt. (Bℵ) and Old Lat. attestation. But, as shown already by the Sahid. trans., the σε was very early felt to be disruptive, and the smoother με was substituted for it — an alleviation which has made its way into the Western texts. Others went even further and introduced the plur. ἡμᾶς elsewhere dominant in R. 8. Indeed, even in the days of Origen the confusion was so great that many left out the debated pronoun altogether (*v.* critical appar.).

and Gl. 2:15 Paul is speaking from the provisional standpoint of the Jews and in R. 7 from the final standpoint of Christians. Only from the standpoint of those who have become Christians is the situation of pre-Christian Jews seen in all its hopelessness. For now even the previous self-assessment reveals the terrible danger, namely, the danger of self-glory, which is the peculiar sin of the Jew who is zealous for the Law [155] and the most dangerous form of sin generally, though provoked by the Torah. Thus Paul himself rejects the position of Gl. 2:15 in 2:19 and that of Phil. 3:6 in 3:7: ἅτινα ἦν μοι κέρδη, ταῦτα ἥγημαι ... ζημίαν ... καὶ σκύβαλα. The self-assessment of the Jews thus proves to be a dreadful delusion. Only ἐν Χριστῷ can the Jew perceive the delusion and thus recognise the hopelessness of his previous situation. Paul does this in R. 7.

He does this with a sense of unconditional solidarity with his people. [156] But he is not just any Jew. He is "the" Jew. In him there is decisively fulfilled the movement of the people of the Torah from the crisis to Christ. Paul is the ἀπαρχή of his people. [157] This is what gives to the ἐγώ of R. 7 its distinctive sense.

That Paul speaks authoritatively of the situation of the people of the Torah is proved by the Jewish counterpart to R. 7 in 4 Esr. 7. Here, too, we read of the conflict and crisis which are only increased by the Law. [158] Here, too, we are astonished by the self-evident solidarity of the seer and speaker with his people. [159] Here, too, the depiction of the terrible situation culminates in a cry for help. [160] There is a great difference between R. 7 and 4 Esr. 7. But this difference is to be explained by the difference in standpoint, and it thus confirms the interpretation advanced above.

Stauffer

ἑδραῖος, ἑδραίωμα

ἑδραῖος first means in secular Gk. "sitting," "seated," "settled," of men or trades. [1] The pap. call an established domestic employee a ἑδραῖος φαμιλιάριος. [2] ἑδραῖος then comes to denote what is as fixed as a cube (κύβος), "steadfast" or "immovable." The natural philosophers ask which is the ἑδραιότατον στοιχεῖον, the most solid of the four elements, and they answer: ἡ γῆ. Plotinus asks what is τὸ πάντων ἑδραιότατον, and answers: τὸ ὄν. [3] In both cases, the thrust of the question is the same, namely, what is "firm and steadfast by nature." Plotinus, however, looks further afield, seeking that which is absolutely fixed above the relativities of the world of phenomena;

---

[155] R. 10:3.

[156] Cf. R. 9:1 ff.; 10:1; → n. 143.

[157] Cf. R. 11:1; 11:16; 1 C. 16:15; 15:20.

[158] 7:45-48, 72, 128 f.; cf. 3:19 ff.

[159] 7:46 ff.; cf. 8:47 ff.; 12:7. Though Ezra himself is not one of the sinners, or at any rate one of the reprobate, he consciously uses We (e.g., in 7:117 f.) in solidarity with the wicked and rejected. Cf. Apc. Shadrach 5 and esp. 8: οὐ χωρίζομαι ἀπὸ τοῦ γένους ἡμῶν (M. R. James, *Texts and Studies*, II, 3 [1893], 133).

[160] 7:64 ff., 118 f.; cf. 8:35 f.

ἑδραῖος κτλ. [1] ἑδραιόω, "to stabilise"; ἑδραίωσις, "stabilising."

[2] Preisigke Wört., *s.v.*

[3] Heracl. Hom. All., 41 and Plot., VI, 2, 8 (Liddell-Scott, *s.v.*).

and he reaches his answer by a process of speculative abstraction. Behind all becoming and change there must be a being which is permanent by nature.

The OT does not ask concerning natural stability; its concern is with historical persistence. That which is steadfast is what endures in every change and contradiction. But where in the whole world is there anything that can be called steadfast, that has the guarantee of permanence by nature? There is only One who stands fast, namely, He who is in heaven. There is only one thing which persists in the flux of occurrence, namely, His creative and overruling hand. If anything stands fast on earth, it must be established by God, owing its steadfastness, its permanence, its ability to withstand assault, solely to Him.

It is along the lines of this understanding of reality that the Gk. translators of the OT use ἑδραῖος, [4] and more rarely the verb ἑδράζειν and the subst. ἕδρασμα. In the first instance the words refer to God, or rather to the throne of God. This is how ἕδρασμα is used in Ps. 33:14 ʾA and ἑδραῖος in ψ 92:2. As the context shows, the reference is not to the lasting qualities of the material of which the throne is made, but to the permanence and sovereignty of the divine rule. At the same time, there is no attempt to define God's nature. God is not immutable by nature in the Gk. sense. He is the One whose firm hand is perceptible in all occurrence.

This God has established the mountains and so they stand fast. [5] He has set up the throne of David and given a promise to his house, this alone being the guarantee of its stability and future. [6] He must assent to a man's work if it is to stand. [7] He must hold His strong hand over the heart of man if it is to be kept against temptation. Hence a steadfast heart is not a quality or virtue or disposition; it is a determination. It is not possible or certain of itself. There must always be a positing which can come from God alone, and can be assured only by Him. The heart can show itself to be ἑδραῖος only when in need and peril it is orientated to God, as in ψ 56:7 and ψ 111:7. [8] In Sir. 22:17 this reference to God does not have quite the same immediacy; the καρδία ἡδρασμένη is the heart which is filled with the fear of God and with practical wisdom.

In contrast with the heart or work which finds its stability in God is that which seeks it in itself and which will not survive the decisive test. Solomon confidently calls his temple a ἕδρασμα τῆς καθέδρας τοῦ αἰῶνος, but the author, translator and reader of 3 Βασ. 8:13 cannot but reflect that this bold claim was not substantiated in history. The opponents of Ezekiel build a wall and daub it with lime, but God sends a whirlwind to sweep off the lime and to shatter the wall (Ez. 13:10 ff.). Hence in a late Jewish text false teachers and leaders are simply called builders of the wall. [9] If Sir. calls the καρδία ἡδρασμένη a wellbuilt house which will stand in every storm, [10] he compares the heart of the fool to a broken hedge. [11] Nothing can stand that is not established by God.

In the NT the adjective ἑδραῖος occurs only three times (in Paul's letters); ἑδράζειν and ἕδρασμα do not occur at all, nor does ἑδραίωσις. On the other hand, we now have for the first time the subst. ἑδραίωμα [12] in the Pauline corpus. OT ideas are present in the terms, though now referred to the Christ event and

---

[4] ἑδραῖος only in Σ.

[5] ψ 89:2 אˣ : πρὸ τοῦ ὄρη ἑδρασθῆναι.

[6] ἑδραῖος in ψ 88:37.

[7] ἑδραῖος in ψ 89:17.

[8] Cf. Hb. 13:9, → βεβαιόω, I, 600.

[9] Damasc., passim.

[10] In Sir. 22:18 we also have the picture of the wall and plaster.

[11] Sir. 22:17 ff.; cf. Mt. 7:24 f.

[12] ἑδραῖος-ἑδραίωμα on the analogy of → στερεός-στερέωμα.

the situation thereby created. Taken together, the four instances yield a characteristic shift of meaning.

In 1 C. 7:37 [13] ἑδραῖος is used to describe the man who adopts an ascetic life because he can control himself and stand inwardly fast against the assualt of impulse (cf. 7:9, 36, 38). This steadfastness, however, is χάρισμα ἐκ θεοῦ (cf. 7:7). In 1 C. 15:58 Christians are to be ἑδραῖοι and ἀμετακίνητοι. This is possible. For God has overcome death. Hence their life and work, and the earth on which they stand, have a future and are thus of serious import in the present. The presupposition of the steadfastness which is here possible and imperative is a knowledge (εἰδότες) of the historical situation and future of human existence. Cf. 15:19, 57. Acc. to Col. 1:23 those who are reconciled with God must remain τεθεμελιωμένοι καὶ ἑδραῖοι καὶ μὴ μετακινούμενοι ἀπὸ τῆς ἐλπίδος in order that they may stand blameless before Him. God has begun the work. But there is great danger of apostasy. Hence the work of God and the future of His elect are in peril. [14] The anxiety of the world has attacked the Colossians and will drive them, as formerly, from one superstition, cult and ritual to another (cf. 2:7 f.). We must keep to the way on which we are set, remaining steadfast (ἐπιμένετε τῇ πίστει) in the certainty that God alone has the power and that to Christ alone belongs the future in spite of all earthly powers. The power and faithfulness of God are expressed in the steadfastness of our faith. In 1 Tm. 3:15 the ἐκκλησία is called στῦλος καὶ ἑδραίωμα τῆς ἀληθείας. A Church is established which protects and defends the truth against the confusion of myths (→ μῦθος). It gives the faith and thinking of individuals a sure ground in confession (cf. 3:16 etc.). No longer God alone, but also the Church of God, now guarantees the permanence of the ἀλήθεια. The steadfastness of faith has now become loyalty to the Church and the confession. [15]

Stauffer

ἐθελοθρησκεία → θρησκός.

ἔθνος, ἐθνικός   (→ Ἕλλην).

A. People and Peoples in the LXX.

1. In the Heb. OT the main terms for "people" are עַם and גּוֹי. Both denote a group of men or animals associated visibly and according to experience. There is no emphasis on the particular marks or bases of fellowship or relationship, on political or cultural connexions, as in such words as אֶרֶץ, לָשׁוֹן, מִשְׁפָּחָה [1] (Gn. 10:31), which can be used for

---

[13] So with the Hesych. text against the Itala, which omits the word.
[14] Cf. Rev. 2:5 : μνημόνευε οὖν πόθεν πέπτωκας.
[15] In 1 Tm. the Church is the pillar of truth, whereas in Syr. Tr., 44 true doctrine is the basis of the Church.

ἔθνος. [1] Since the Gk. equivalents to the Heb. terms often intersect in the LXX, it is best to treat ἔθνος and λαός together in relation to the LXX ; on the other hand, the NT → λαός will be found at the proper place in the alphabet.

"people" in a more racial, linguistic or geographical sense. Only in the course of the history of Jewish religion did the words גּוֹי and עַם come to be more precisely distinguished. The secular sense retreated into the background. The plur. גּוֹיִם came to be used as a tech. term for the Gentiles, and the sing. עַם for the holy people.

This is reflected in the Gk. translations of the OT. The word δῆμος, [2] which denotes the Gk. community on its political side, is rare in the LXX and is not found at all in later renderings. Indeed, we find it only in Nu., Jos., Ju. and once in Neh., and it is used exclusively for מִשְׁפָּחָה in the sense of smaller clan-like societies within the main group or nation. In the sense of a political nation it is first found in Da. three times for עַם, and more frequently in 1 Macc. In the NT δῆμος is used four times in Ac. for a gathering of the people. The less prominent NT use is in keeping with the more general cultural history of Hellenism. Hellenistic and Roman imperialism destroyed both the Greek *polis* and the δῆμος in the older sense. To some degree, however, the roots are also to be found in the development of OT religion. In spite of the theologoumenon of Abrahamic sonship and the chosen people, Jewry, as distinct from Israel and Judah, was not really a people, but, for proselytes and kindred circles, a religion. [3] This fact naturally affected in large measure the relevant OT terminology taken over from ancient Israel. This is particularly true of the translation of the corresponding terms in the LXX. Here we have in the first instance an extraordinarily clear and uniform picture, ἔθνος being almost always used for גּוֹי and λαός for עַם. In many individual passages, and sometimes in whole books, [4] this purely philological equation determines the translation.

Yet material reasons have also to be considered. As we can see from גּוֹיִם and עַם, and indeed from many deviations in the translation, sometimes to a stronger degree, ἔθνη and λαός also acquire a terminological character in the sense of Gentiles on the one side and the chosen people on the other. How this works out in detail, we may see from a review of the occurrence of עַם and its LXX equivalents, using the Pentateuch as an example. Note should first be taken of the important distinction between the sing. and the plur. [5] In Gn. to Dt. we have עַם in the sing. 362 times and עַמִּים in the plur. 58 times. Of these 420 instances, 351 are rendered by λαός in the sing., which is often used for the plur. ⌈עַמִּים⌉, λαοί for עַמִּים occurs only twice. Elsewhere עַם is rendered ἔθνος 48 times (עַם = ἔθνος 13 times ; עַמִּים = ἔθνος twice ; עַם = ἔθνη three times ; עַמִּים = ἔθνη thirty times). In passages where the reference is to several non-Jewish peoples, there is obviously a tendency to use ἔθνη for עַמִּים. [6] On the other hand, the LXX seems intentionally to avoid the plur. λαοί. The interrelationships are much the same in the other books as in the Pent., whether we take the original or the translation. Of 2000 occurrences of λαός, only some 135 are in the plur. Of these, 35 are in the

---

[2] On the synon. δῆμος, ἔθνος, λαός, cf. Trench, 233 ff.

[3] On the thesis that Jewry is a religion rather than a race, cf. G. Bertram in G. Rosen, *Juden und Phönizier,* revised by F. Rosen and G. Bertram (1929), esp. c. 2 : "Das antike Judentum als Missionsreligion."

[4] It is interesting to compare 1 and 2 Ἐσδρ. The former translates freely ; the latter follows the Heb. original more closely.

[5] We are using the statistics of Mandelkern, who like the LXX does not distinguish between עַם "people" and עַם "relative."

[6] The other transl. of the Hexapla adopt a more purely philological procedure. Thus 'Α uses the plur. λαοί for עַמִּים where the LXX has ἔθνη and where there is a definite sense of "Gentiles," e.g., Gn. 49:10. So, too, do 'ΑΣΘ at Dt. 4:19; 7:19, and Σ at Ex. 19:5. In the sing., too, there is a stronger equation of עַם and λαός in 'Α than in LXX : Dt. 2:21.

Ps.,[7] and often there are purely formal reasons for it, e.g., its use alongside ἔθνη in parallel statements.

2. In a number of passages עַם and גּוֹי/גּוֹיִם or λαός and ἔθνος/ἔθνη are plainly and intentionally differentiated. Thus ἔθνος in Ex. 33:13 is used for "people" in general, whereas λαός denotes the chosen people : λαός σου τὸ ἔθνος τὸ μέγα τοῦτο. λαός θεοῦ is so fixed a notion that it can even be used sometimes for pagan peoples, e.g., in 2 Ch. 32:15 : οὐ μὴ δύνηται ὁ θεὸς παντὸς ἔθνους καὶ βασιλείας τοῦ σῶσαι τὸν λαὸν αὐτοῦ ἐκ χειρός μου. From the standpoint of the god concerned, λαός denotes his people and thus expresses the close relationship between God and people. In this connexion, ἔθνος denotes rather the sphere of dominion. There is a similar use of ἔθνος in the following Hellenistic dedication : τοῖς γῆς καὶ θαλάσσης καὶ παντὸς ἀνθρώπων ἔθνους καὶ γένους δεσπόταις.[8] In Dt. 7:6 the LXX (Mas. עַמִּים, "peoples") sharply distinguishes between ἔθνη, Gentiles, and λαός, the people of God, while in the par. passage in Ex. 19:5, 6 סְגֻלָּה (עַם) = λαός περιούσιος and עַמִּים is rendered ἔθνη, but with philological accuracy גּוֹי קָדוֹשׁ is translated ἔθνος ἅγιον (Dt. 7:6 : עַם קָדוֹשׁ = λαὸς ἅγιος).

The LXX is even more independent in 2 'Εσδρ. 9:11, when it renders עַמֵּי הָאֲרָצוֹת λαοὶ τῶν ἐθνῶν, so that λαοί is used for "peoples" generally and ἔθνη technically for the Gentiles. The corresponding passage in 1 'Εσδρ. 8:80 has ἀλλογενεῖς τῆς γῆς. Hence in 2 'Εσδρ. 9:7, too, ἔθνη is to be taken in the sense of Gentiles. The universalism of LXX piety finds characteristic expression in Da. 9:6, where the Mas. has הַנְּבִיאִים אֲשֶׁר דִּבְּרוּ בְּשִׁמְךָ אֶל מְלָכֵינוּ שָׂרֵינוּ וַאֲבֹתֵינוּ וְאֶל כָּל עַם הָאָרֶץ :... and the LXX translates τῶν προφητῶν, ἃ ἐλάλησαν ἐπὶ τῷ ὀνόματί σου ἐπὶ τοὺς βασιλεῖς ἡμῶν καὶ δυνάστας ἡμῶν καὶ πατέρας ἡμῶν καὶ παντὶ ἔθνει ἐπὶ τῆς γῆς. This means that for the LXX prophetic proclamation is directed to every nation on earth. Θ gives an accurate rendering of the Mas. with its specific reference to the Jewish people in the land of Canaan : ... καὶ πρὸς πάντα τὸν λαὸν τῆς γῆς. Cf. also 2 Βασ. 7:23; 1 Ch. 17:21; 2 Ch. 36:14 = 1 'Εσδρ. 1:47. ἔθνη is obviously used in the sense of "Gentiles" in many religious and ethical contexts also. Thus we often read of the βδελύγματα τῶν ἐθνῶν, cf. 3 Βασ. 14:24; 4 Βασ. 16:3; 21:2 etc., also 4 Βασ. 21:9 = 2 Ch. 33:9; 1 Ch. 16:26.

While גּוֹי, גּוֹיִם is only rarely translated λαός (7 times sing. and 6 plur.)[9] or other Gk. words than ἔθνος, the rendering of עַם is more varied. To establish the content, i.e., the sociological indefiniteness, of all four words גּוֹי, עַם, ἔθνος, λαός, it is instructive to survey the various Gk. words used for גּוֹי and עַם, and the various Heb. words which are the originals of ἔθνος and λαός. A large measure of agreement results. We can best appreciate this by comparing the corresponding LXX and Mas. terms : קָהֵל — συναγωγή; בַּיִת, זֶרַע, מַף, מִשְׁפָּחָה — γενεά, γένος, φυλή; מָקוֹם, אִי, אֶרֶץ — γῆ; דῆμος; לְאֹם, אֻמָּה; ὄχλος, πλῆθος — הָמוֹן; δύναμις; מַחֲנֶה, צָבָא, חַיִל — ἀνήρ, ἄνθρωπος — אָדָם, אֱנוֹשׁ; αὐτόχθων; חָבֵר — πάροικος — זָר, בֶּן־נֵכָר; πολίτης; παῖς, δοῦλος — עֶבֶד; ἡγούμενος — נָשִׂיא; ἐχθρός; צֹאן. If these equations are only occasional compared with the total number of ἔθνος (some 1000) and λαός (some 2000) passages, they show the scope and content of the concept "people," which can

---

[7] The use of ἔθνη for "Gentiles" is very consistent in the Ps. Only once in ψ 105:5 do we have ἔθνος σου as a par. of κληρονομία and ἐκλεκτοί σου. Other parallels between ἔθνος and λαός are to be found only in ψ 32:12 and ψ 42:1 : ἔθνος οὐχ ὅσιον. Of other books, Neh. is marked by philological accuracy, ἔθνη always being used for גּוֹיִם and λαός for עַם.

[8] Cf. Mitteis-Wilcken, I, 2, No. 6, 2.

[9] Sing.: Jos. 3:17; 4:1; Is. 9:3; 26:2; 58:2; Jer. 9:9; 40(33):9; Plur. ψ 66:4 (vl.: ἔθνεσιν); Zech. 14:14; Is. 55:5; 60:5; Ez. 20:41; 28:25.

denote an indefinite group of people, whether in the sense of court circles (Est. 1:3: ἔθνη = עַבְדִּים; cf. 1:16: ἡγούμενοι = עַמִּים) and therefore a narrower stratum, or in the broadest sense the human race, which is the sense of עַם in Is. 42:5 (Yahweh is the God ... who gives breath to the people on earth). To deduce from this passage, which simply refers to the dwellers on earth acc. to their natural determination as עַם, a universal concept of humanity supposedly present in Is. 42:6; 49:6 (διαθήκη γένους, φῶς ἐθνῶν — אוֹר גּוֹיִם, בְּרִית עַם), is going too far. בְּרִית עַם refers to the chosen people. The mission of the Servant of the Lord goes beyond this people to the Gentiles. At least, this is how the passage is understood in the LXX, which presupposes בְּרִית עַם in 49:6 as well. [10] The situation is much the same in ψ 47:10. Even if we accept the reading of the Mas.: נְדִיבֵי עַמִּים נֶאֱסָפוּ עַם אֱלֹהֵי אַבְרָהָם, these princes can hardly be regarded as representatives of the whole race, [11] and we should simply translate: "Princes of the nations gather as the people of the God of Abraham."

3. When the term ἔθνη (גּוֹיִם) is used in the sense of Gentiles, it is often with no sense of a plurality of nations. The word is used non-sociologically to describe all the individuals who do not belong to the chosen people. [12] But God is the King of the peoples (Jer. 10:7; cf. Rev. 15:3). The divine order of the table of nations (Gn. 10) is in accord with this fact. From the first patriarchs there does not descend a single humanity, but a group of nations divided according to clans and differing in language, custom and situation. The attempt to resist this in Gn. 11 has its origin in human pride. God intervenes to re-establish the order imposed by Him. Similarly, in Dt. 32:8 the division of the world into nations is a divine order and not a punishment for human sin: "When the most High divided to the nations their inheritance, when he separated the sons of Adam, he set the bounds of the people according to the number (of the sons of God) ..." [13] The LXX makes the final subsidiary clause into the main clause: ὅτε διεμέριζεν ὁ ὕψιστος ἔθνη, ὡς διέσπειρεν υἱοὺς Ἀδάμ, ἔστησεν ὅρια ἐθνῶν κατὰ ἀριθμὸν ἀγγέλων θεοῦ.

Philo expounded both this passage and Gn. 11 allegorically. As he sees it, the reference here is to ἀρετῆς ἔθνη καὶ εἴδη (Post. C., 91). Gn. 11, however, he understands in terms of the destruction, the διαλύειν, φθείρειν of the συμφωνία κακιῶν. Only in this negative sense can we take διασπείρειν: τὸ δὲ σπείρειν ἀγαθῶν, κακῶν δὲ αἴτιον τὸ διασπείρειν (Conf. Ling., 196). Thus the view, if not of Philo, at least

---

[10] Cf. finally W. Staerk, ZAW, NF 3 (1926), 248 ff.; also the Comm.

[11] Σ and Θ seem to have taken the passage universalistically. Σ: ἄρχοντες λαῶν ἡθροίσθησαν, λαὸς τοῦ θεοῦ Ἀβραάμ. Θ: ἄρχοντες λαῶν συνήχθησαν, λαὸς τοῦ θεοῦ Ἀβραάμ. On the other hand the LXX has: ἄρχοντες λαῶν συνήχθησαν μετὰ τοῦ θεοῦ Ἀβραάμ. Similarly, in ΑΘ Dt. 32:43 the designation as people of God seems to be transferred to the Gentiles. The Heb. is הַרְנִינוּ גוֹיִם עַמּוֹ. For this there are 5 Gk. renderings. The LXX has two next to one another: 1. εὐφράνθητε, ἔθνη, ἄμα αὐτῷ; 2. εὐφράνθητε, ἔθνη, μετὰ τοῦ λαοῦ αὐτοῦ (R. 15:10); 3. Ἀ: αἰνοποιήσατε, ἔθνη, λαὸς αὐτοῦ; 4. Θ: Ἀγαλλιᾶσθε, ἔθνη, λαὸς αὐτοῦ; 5. Ἑβρ: αἰνέσατε, ἔθνη, λαὸν αὐτοῦ.

[12] Cf. the question of גֵּאִים in the Ps. (cf. Ges.-Buhl, s.v. גּוֹי, also ZAW, NF, 3 [1926], 149). The characterisation of the Gentiles here corresponds at least to the idea which the righteous have of the גֵּאִים (Sadducees?). Cf. also the passage quoted above from 2 Ἐσδρ. 9:11.

[13] K. Marti in Kautzsch. The same tradition appears in Heb. Test. N. 8 on Gn. 10:25: "For then (in the days of Peleg) the Holy One came down from his high heaven ... He spoke and commanded each of them that they should teach 70 languages to the 70 races of those who came forth from the loins of Noah ..."; 10: "Hereupon the most High divided the nations, and gave and restricted to each its portion and lot" (Kautzsch). According to § 9 the fall of Gn. 11 is accepted, but it is nations already appointed by God which conspire against Him.

of the underlying tradition concerning the rise of the nations, is marked by the fact that, as an allegorical expositor who has no historical interest, he formulates the question of Dt. 32:8 as follows: ἢ διένειμεν ἔθνη ὁ θεὸς ἢ ἔσπειρεν ἢ ᾤκισεν (Post. C., 90). He thus assumes that a divinely posited good is to be seen in the ordering of the nations. On the other hand, it is due to the influence of Hellenistic imperialism and pacifism in the Roman Empire that these ideas do not appear either in Philo or elsewhere, but rather that on the basis of Gn. 11 the rise of the nations is attributed to human sin, as in Jub. 10:22: "They shall be divided into cities and peoples, and there shall no more be one mind among them until the day of judgment." Nevertheless, in 4 Esr. 3:7, 12 there is no reference to a fall to which the rise of the nations may be traced back. In this passage their existence is to be seen as a natural consequence of the increase of men under the blessing of God. Indeed, in many passages this blessing is related to nations [14] rather than individuals (cf. Gn. 17 and esp. the eschatological blessings in Gn. 18:18; 22:18; 26:4).

The nations play an important part in the prophetic view of history. They are agents of the wrath of God (Hos. 8:10 etc.) towards sinful Israel. They themselves fall victim to this wrath because they do not discharge their mission as a divine task, but in human pride (e.g., Is. 8:9). They are finally the recipients of salvation, which the King of the world will allot to the nations. The kingdoms of the world, which unite in themselves many peoples, languages and cultures (e.g., Da. LXX 4:34b), stand in contrast to the kingdom of God, whose Inaugurator the nations expect as the Messianic Ruler. [15] This is how the LXX and Vg. understand Gn. 49:10: αὐτὸς προσδοκία ἐθνῶν. The Mas. has וְלוֹ יִקְּהַת עַמִּים, which Luther renders: "To him will the peoples cleave" [16] cf. also Ἀ: αὐτῷ σύστημα λαῶν. Many prophetic passages speak of the eschatological salvation which the peoples shall receive, e.g., Is. 2:2-4; Mi. 4:1-3; Is. 25:6-8; 51:4 f.; Zech. 9:16; Jer. 16:19 etc.

If according to these prophetic utterances nation and people as such will maintain their place in the eschatological kingdom of God, there is generally a marked dissolution of the concepts of nation and people in Jewish piety, so that references are to the Gentiles rather than the nations. Apart from the passages mentioned, this is always true when the reference is to the attitude of individuals, e.g., their conversion to Yahweh (Zech. 8:20-23; Is. 44:5 etc.). Even where the union of the Gentiles with the Jews is presupposed, and in all references to the mission and propaganda of Judaism as a religion, which is naturally rather a different matter from divine revelation to the nations, the concept of people is absorbed into that of the Gentiles (e.g., Is. 66:17-21 LXX). Indeed, the term finally comes to be associated with the lower elements in the population (the plebs). Thus Rabbinic Judaism uses the term עַם־הָאָרֶץ in a disparaging sense. In the post-exilic period it came to be used for the Gentiles dwelling in the land (Ezr. 10:2, 11; Neh. 10:31, 32), characterising the inhabitants as Jewish-Gentile mongrels. Increasingly, the term served to express the religious and theological pride of the sects, who tried to draw a strict line of demarcation between themselves and the people, and whose attitude is typically depicted in the NT in the dealings between Pharisees and publicans. In Gk. ὄχλος [17] is used for "people" in this disparaging sense, Jn. 7:49, although according to secular usage either ἔθνος or λαός might have been used equally

---

[14] In the OT God is God and Lord of the nations. Cf. W. Graf Baudissin, *Kyrios*, III (1929), 656 ff.

[15] In the OT Is. 45:1 seems to treat Cyrus as a messiah, and in Jos. Bell., 6, 313 even Vespasian is hailed as such. Cf. Rosen-Bertram, *op. cit.* (→ n. 3), 33 f., 136 f.

[16] In Hag. 2:7 Luther translates חֶמְדַּת כָּל־הַגּוֹיִם "the salvation of the Gentiles," more recently amended to "the good of the Gentiles." This is a christological reconstruction. The Mas. and indeed the LXX both refer to the costly treasures which will adorn the temple in Jerusalem. Cf. G. Bertram, ThBl, 4 (1925), 208 ff.

[17] Cf. Str.-B. on Jn. 7:49, II, 494-519.

well. In the Bible, however, λαός is an established term for the chosen people, and in 4 Macc., for instance, the sing. ἔθνος is regularly used, and occasionally elsewhere, rather after the manner of *populus* for the Roman people. Certainly ἔθνη conveys a negative judgment from the Jewish standpoint. Yet even in the OT this judgment has no final validity in face of the promise of revelation to all peoples, and this is particularly so in the NT in face of the direction of the everlasting Gospel ἐπὶ πᾶν ἔθνος (Rev. 14:6) and the missionary command: μαθητεύσατε πάντα τὰ ἔθνη ("make disciples of all nations," Mt. 28:19).

Bertram

B. ἔθνος in the NT.

1. This word, which is common in Gk. from the very first, probably comes from ἔθος, and means "mass" or "host" or "multitude" bound by the same manners, customs or other distinctive features. Applied to men, it gives us the sense of people; but it can also be used of animals in the sense of "herd" or of insects in the sense of "swarm" (though cf. also ἔθνος μελισσῶν for the race of bees). The original sense may still be seen in the πᾶν ἔθνος ἀνθρώπων of Ac. 17:26.

In most cases ἔθνος is used of men in the sense of a "people." Synon. are → φυλή (people as a national unity of common descent), → λαός (people as a political unity with a common history and constitution) and → γλῶσσα (people as a linguistic unity). ἔθνος is the most general and therefore the weakest of these terms, having simply an ethnographical sense and denoting the natural cohesion of a people in general. [18]

Of some 160 instances in the NT, about 40 are quoted from the OT, and there are many other more or less clear reminiscences or echoes. This relationship to the OT, and esp. to the LXX, does not affect the general sense of ἔθνος, but is of significance from the standpoint of biblical theology in so far as ἔθνη may be given a special sense by the context.

2. There are 64 passages in the NT where we have ἔθνος or ἔθνη without any special sense or characteristics. These occur in all four Gospels (9 in Mt., 4 in Mk., 9 in Lk., 5 in Jn.), in Ac. (16 times), in Pl. (7), in 1 Pt. (1), and in Rev. (13). About 60 refer to a people or peoples in the general sense, and of these the following have in view the Jewish people: Lk. 7:5; 23:2; Jn. 11:48, 50, 51, 52; 18:35; Ac. 10:22; 24:2, 10, 17; 26:4; 28:19; 1 Pt. 2:9. That the Jewish people is meant in the same sense as others, with no particular distinction, may be seen from the various contexts and also from phrases like ἔθνος τῶν Ἰουδαίων in Ac. 10:22 and ἔθνος ἅγιον in 1 Pt. 2:9. In this respect ἔθνος and λαός are used interchangeably (Jn. 11:50; Ac. 4:25, 27; 15:14; R. 15:11). That the expression ἔθνη refers to all nations may be seen from the addition of πάντα in Mt. 24:9, 14; 25:32; 28:19; Mk. 11:17; 13:10; Lk. 21:24; 24:47; R. 15:11; Gl. 3:8.

3. In spite of this addition, however, we sometimes have the feeling — it is hardly more — that the reference is not to all nations including Israel, but to the nations or all nations in distinction from Israel as the גוים. Thus R. 15:11, on the basis of Ps. 117:1, summons all nations to praise God. But this can hardly include Israel, since it is self-evident that Israel should praise God. Again, on the basis of another OT quotation Gl. 3:8 speaks of the blessing of all nations in Abraham. But this surely has in view the nations apart from Israel, since the blessing of

---

[18] In Rev. 5:9; 7:9; 11:9; 13:7; 14:6 we find all four expressions together (cf. also 10:11; 17:15).

Israel in Abraham as its progenitor may be assumed. This raises the possibility of similar references to the Gentiles rather than to all the nations elsewhere, e.g., Mt. 4:15 (Γαλιλαία τῶν ἐθνῶν = גְּלִיל הַגּוֹיִם in Is. 8:23); 20:25 (where ἄρχοντες τῶν ἐθνῶν are more naturally princes of the non-Jewish or Gentile world); Lk. 21:24 ('Ιερουσαλὴμ πατουμένη ὑπὸ ἐθνῶν, the holy city trampled down by the Gentiles); Ac. 4:25 (according to Ps. 2:1 f. the Gentiles rage against the Lord and His Anointed); 7:7 (the same); 13:19 (seven Canaanitish and therefore Gentile peoples); R. 1:5 (Paul is perhaps thinking here of the Gentiles in his mention of all nations); Rev. 10:11; 14:8; 15:3, 4 (where the Jewish or Jewish Christian view of the seer suggests a natural use for Gentiles). There is, of course, no proof that in these passages we have a technical use of ἔθνη in the sense of Gentiles even though the context, often based on the OT, indicates that the Gentiles are meant.

4. There are also many passages in the NT — some 100 as compared with the previous 60 — in which ἔθνη, like the corresponding גּוֹיִם in the OT, is undoubtedly used as a technical term for the Gentiles as distinct from the Jews or Christians: Mt. 6 times; Mk. 1; Lk. 3; Ac. 26 (→ *infra*); R. 23; 1 and 2 C. 5; Gl. 8; Eph. and Col. 6; 1 Th. 2; Past. 2; 1 Pt. 2; 3 Jn. 1; Rev. 10. The concept, though not the term, is found also in John's Gospel (→ 371).

To clarify and establish the sense of Gentiles as distinct from Jews [19] it is enough to mention a few outstanding passages. In Mt. 6:32, for example, Jesus directs His hearers not to pray as the ἔθνη — an ethico-religious contrast between Jews and Gentiles which is based on the special position of Israel in salvation history. The parallel in Lk. 12:30 deliberately emphasises the distinction by the phrase πάντα τὰ ἔθνη τοῦ κόσμου (the → κόσμος to which no true Jew belongs as a member of the people of God). In Mt. 10:5 these ἔθνη are set alongside the despised Samaritans. [20] In Mt. 20:19 (= Mk. 10:33 = Lk. 18:32), in the foretelling of the passion, the Messiah Jesus is to be delivered up to the ἔθνη — the very last people to whom the Messiah of the people of God should be handed over. The same distinction between Gentiles and Jews dominates Acts and the apostolic and post-apostolic letters, and therefore the missionary witness of the primitive community. The ἔθνη as Gentiles go·their own ways and are left to themselves in Ac. 14:16; they are ἀπηλλοτριωμένοι τῆς πολιτείας τοῦ 'Ισραὴλ καὶ ξένοι τῶν διαθηκῶν τῆς ἐπαγγελίας in Eph. 2:12; they are outside revelation, opposed to the Law of God and therefore ἄθεοι ἐν τῷ κόσμῳ in Eph. 2:12. There is a particularly clear distinction between the → 'Ιουδαῖοι and the ἔθνη in 1 C. 1:23, where some MSS have ῞Ελλησι (→ ῞Ελλην) for ἔθνεσιν. Obviously we have here a technical term, though this can easily be lost in the text, as in Eph. 4:17, where some MSS have added the epithet λοιπά. That the ἔθνη, as Gentiles of the

---

[19] It is possible that the word "heathen" comes from ἔθνη. Cf. F. Zorell, *Lex. Graeco-Lat. zum NT*, 2 (1931), *s.v.*: *Sic nomen* (*cum spiritu aspero koines*) *in alias linguas transiit*: copt. nihethnos, arm. hethanosq, *goth.* fem. haithno (Mk. 7:26), *probabiliter angl.* heathen, *germ.* Heiden. If this is correct (cf. A. Walde-J. Pokorny, *Vergleich. Wörterb. d. indogerm. Sprachen*, I [1927], 329), we have here a biblical loan word like *église* (= ἐκκλησία) or *church*, *Kirche* (probably derived from κυριακόν → ἐκκλησία).

[20] Cf. Wilke-Grimm, *s.v.*: τὰ ἔθνη, *ut in VT* הַגּוֹיִם, *gentes exterae a veri dei cultu alienae, pagani, gentiles*. Franz Delitzsch in his Heb. trans. of the NT rightly uses גּוֹיִם for ἔθνη but עַם for ἔθνος (the Jewish people).

world, are riveted to this world or aeon may be seen from Rev. 15:3, where there is a reading αἰώνων for ἐθνῶν. [21]

How fixed and widespread the usage is, is illustrated by the fact that Paul can still call Gentile Christians ἔθνη in R. 11:13 (though there is some doubt as to the exact bearing of ἐθνῶν ἀπόστολος) and Eph. 3:1 (where there is no doubt that Gentile Christians are numbered among the ἔθνη).

It is true that in 1 C. 5:1; 12:2; 1 Th. 4:5; 1 Pt. 2:12; 3 Jn. 7 (ℵ al) and various passages in Rev. the ἔθνη are Gentiles in distinction from Christians, but this usage rests on the fact that Christians are considered true Israelites and the Church as Israel κατὰ πνεῦμα.

It is curious that the Fourth Gospel does not use ἔθνη for Gentiles. The explanation is that in this Gospel the Jews in their obduracy are equated with the κόσμος, the evil world, and are thus themselves to be addressed as ἔθνη. This specifically Johannine conception belongs materially to a common line of thought in the early Church, as we may see from Paul's classifying of Jew and Gentile together from the standpoint of the Gospel.

5. All that we have said may be gathered clearly from the NT itself, though the quotation of a number of OT ἔθνη passages shows the influence of OT usage. The decisive point is the ethico-religious distinction in relation to salvation history. A most succinct and yet also the most comprehensive expression of this is to be found equally in the OT and the NT. Thus τὰ ἔθνη τὰ μὴ εἰδότα τὸν θεόν in 1 Th. 4:5 = ἔθνη τὰ μὴ εἰδότα σε, הַגּוֹיִם אֲשֶׁר לֹא־יְדָעוּךָ in Jer. 10:25.

It is in accord with the relationship of the OT to Rabbinic Judaism on the one side and Hellenistic Judaism on the other that the ἔθνη-גּוֹיִם conception is maintained in the former sphere — this is so obvious that individual instances are unnecessary — and abandoned in the latter. The case is exactly the same as with → βασιλεία (I, 574 ff.). Philo, for example, does not have the distinction which here concerns us. He uses ἔθνος for every people, including the Jewish (ἔθνος → Ἰουδαίων, Spec. Leg., II, 163 etc.). The same is true of Josephus. In his writings the Romans speak of other peoples as ἔξωθεν ἔθνη (e.g., Titus in Bell., 6, 342).

Might it be that there is some trace of Hellenistic influence in the NT equation of ἔθνη with Gentiles? Prior to the Romans, the Greeks described foreigners as ἔθνη in distinction from the → Ἕλληνες. [22] When applied to non-Greek peoples, the word ἔθνος often has a disparaging sense rather like the unambiguous → βάρβαρος. There is at least in ἔθνος the sense of "provincial" in the outer and above all the inner sense. [23] If, then, the Greek Bible of the OT and NT speaks similarly of ἔθνη as the Heb. did of גּוֹיִם, is it not possible that we simply have the same exclusivism of Israel and Judah as is found also amongst the Greeks? [24] The answer is that even at its

---

[21] That we have here a technical term is perhaps also shown by the fact that ἔθνη is sometimes used without art. for "the Gentiles" like the Heb. גּוֹיִם, e.g., Ac. 4:25; R. 15:18. Cf. Bl.-Debr. § 254, 3.

[22] Individual examples may be found in Moult.-Mill., Liddell-Scott, Pr.-Bauer, s.v.

[23] Cf. on this pt. S. Lösch, "Die Dankesrede des Tertullus (Ag. 24:1-4)," Theol. Quart., 112 (1931), 302; also Moult.-Mill., s.v.

[24] This is the view of Moult.-Mill., s.v.: "Hicks in CR (= The Classical Review), 1, p. 42 f. has shown that 'Hellenic life found its normal type in the πόλις, and barbarians who lived κατὰ κώμας or in some less organised form were ἔθνη,' and that similarly in the LXX and NT ἔθνος 'describes the pagan world, outside the Jewish Church,' but occasionally stands for the λαός itself, as in Ac. 10:22; 24:17 al."

greatest what we find in Greece is only analogous to what is seen in Israel in its relationship to all other peoples. Nor does the analogy indicate the true significance or particularity of the ἔθνος statements in the OT.

6. In non-canonical writings of the early Church and in the post-apostolic fathers the specifically biblical view is maintained. A single striking example is the description of the Gentiles as ἄνομα ἔθνη in Mart. Pol., 9, 2. The situation is the same in ancient Church history, cf. Canones Graeci Concilii Laodiceni, 39 : οὐ δεῖ τοῖς ἔθνεσι συνεορτάζειν καὶ κοινωνεῖν τῇ ἀθεότητι αὐτῶν. 25

† ἐθνικός.

This occurs five times in the NT : Mt. 5:47; 6:7; 18:17; 3 Jn. 7; 1 Gl. 2:14 (adv. ἐθνικῶς).

In accordance with what we have said concerning ἔθνος, ἐθνικός means "national," "foreign," "Gentile." In the first two senses it is found only in later Gk. It does not occur at all in the LXX.

The OT and Jewish claim is clearly expressed in Mt. 5:47, where the ἐθνικοί are set in opposition to those who fulfil the Law. If τελῶναι is possible instead of ἐθνικοί, we need hardly be surprised at the combination ὁ ἐθνικὸς καὶ ὁ → τελώνης in Mt. 18:17, with which we may compare the τελῶναι καὶ ἁμαρτωλοί of Lk. 15:1. There is no question here of national distinction, but of the inner mark of a representative of the ἔθνη. This is why → ὑποκριταί is textually possible instead of ἐθνικοί in Mt. 6:7. 2 The phrase ἐθνικῶς καὶ οὐκ Ἰουδαϊκῶς in Gl. 2:14 makes it clear that the distinction from Judaism is always decisive. If Paul the Jew here sets himself on the side of the ἐθνικῶς ζῆν, this merely shows us once more that in the eyes of the apostle mere Ἰουδαῖοι are not ranked above mere ἔθνη, just as the Lord Himself could call the ἁμαρτωλοί, the τελῶναι and therefore also the ἐθνικοί blessed.

In the post-apostolic fathers we find ἐθνικός only once in Herm. m., 10, 1, 4; it is more common in the Apologists (Justin, Aristides).

Karl Ludwig Schmidt

---

† ἔθος

a. "Habit," "use" : Soph. Phil., 894; Thuc., II, 64, 2 (ταῦτα ... ἐν ἔθει τῇδε τῇ πόλει πρότερόν τε ἦν); Plat. Phaed., 82b; Isoc., 8, 91; Epict. Diss., I, 27, 3; III, 12, 6; P. Oxy., I, 155, 7; P. Fay., 125, 5 (ὡς ἔθος ἐστί σοι); 1 Macc. 10:89 (ὡς ἔθος ἐστὶ δίδοσθαι τοῖς συγγενέσι τῶν βασιλέων); 2 Macc. 13:4; Philo Ebr., 195 and 198;

---

25 Cf. Thes. Steph., s.v.

ἐ θ ν ι κ ό ς. 1 → ἔθνος, 371; the reading ἐθνῶν is found as well as ἐθνικῶν.

2 The attempt of E. Nestle (ThStKr, 69 [1896], 102 ff.; cf. his Philologia Sacra [1896], 27 ff.) to make חָבֵר the Heb. or Aram. original of ἐθνικός in Mt. 6:7 (חֲבֵרִים = fellows, i.e., Pharisees) is rightly rejected by Cr.-Kö.

ἔ θ ο ς. Def.: Sext. Emp. Pyrrh. Hyp., I, 146 [Schlatter].

Jos., 83 (Wis. 14:16: ἀσεβὲς ἔθος of the cult of idols). [1] b. "Custom," "cultic ordinance," "law" : Ditt. Syll.[3], 1073, 20 (κατὰ τὸ πάτριον ἔθος); used for Jewish laws in the LXX : 2 Macc. 11:25 (κατὰ τὰ ἐπὶ τῶν προγόνων αὐτῶν ἔθη); 4 Macc. 18:5 (τῶν πατρίων ἐθῶν); Philo Leg. All., III, 30; Virt., 65; Spec. Leg., II, 149 (πάτριον ἔθος); IV, 149 etc. Jos. Ant., 9, 262 (ταῖς ἐξ ἔθους θυσίαις); 9, 263; 20, 100 (τοῖς γὰρ πατρίοις ... ἔθεσιν); 15, 288 (ὑπὲρ τῶν κοινῶν ἐθῶν) with reference to the Jewish sacrifices.

The NT, too, uses ἔθος in these two senses. Lk. alone of the Evangelists records in 22:39 that it was the custom of Jesus to stay on the Mount of Olives. This obviously does not mean that He slept there while staying in Jerusalem, but rather that this was the mountain top on which He followed His custom of prayer when in Jerusalem. Ἔθος is thus used for a religious habit which He did not take over from the cultic community but adopted for Himself. In Ac. 25:16 ἔθος denotes the custom of Roman justice that the accused should be confronted by his accusers and have the chance to defend himself. In Hb. 10:25 there is censure of a bad custom of non-attendance at gatherings which was establishing itself in the community. In Jn. 19:40 ἔθος is used for the burial law of the Jews. This leads on to the use of the term for the cultic laws of the Jews. In this sense it is found only in the Lucan writings. The Jewish cultus is designed to express the faithfulness and constancy of God, to display a dignity and solemnity commensurate with the divine majesty. Hence it has a fixed order and law like every cultus. This is expressed on the one side in the regulation of the priestly office (cf. κατὰ τὸ ἔθος τῆς ἱερατείας, Lk. 1:9) and on the other in an inflexible order, so that the life of the pious is ruled κατὰ τὸ ἔθος τῆς ἑορτῆς (Lk. 2:42). Finally, therefore, ἔθος is used for the whole of the cultic law attributed to Moses (Ac. 6:14; 15:1; 16:21; 21:21; 26:3; 28:17).

Preisker

εἶδον → ὁράω.

---

† εἶδος, † εἰδέα (ἰδέα)

1. "What is visible" (in a man or object): "figure"; [1] "appearance." Lk. 3:22: the πνεῦμα appears σωματικῷ εἴδει ὡς περιστερά; 9:29: ἐγένετο ... τὸ εἶδος [2] τοῦ προσώπου (of Jesus) ἕτερον.

It is common from the time of Homer and Herodotus (e.g., τὸ εἶδος τῆς γυναικὸς ὑπερεπαινέων, Hdt., I, 8); cf. Jos. (Ant., 6, 296; 7, 189) [3] and Philo. [4] In the LXX it is used esp. for מַרְאֶה and תֹּאַר, e.g., εἶδος αὐτοῦ ὡς εἶδος ἀγγέλου (Ju. 13:6), but also καλὴ τῷ εἴδει (Gn. 29:17 etc.). Is. 52:14: ἀδοξήσει ... τὸ εἶδός σου καὶ ἡ δόξα σου ('Α: ὅρασις αὐτοῦ καὶ μορφὴ αὐτοῦ); 53:2: οὐκ ἔστιν αὐτῷ εἶδος (Σ: οὐκ

---

[1] Cf. 2 Macc. 4:11 (παράνομος ἐθισμός); also Sir. 23:14 (= habit); Gn. 31:35 (= דֶּרֶךְ = period, menstruation).

ε ἶ δ ο ς. [1] On the relation to μορφή, cf. Cr.-Kö., 389; Trench, 175.

[2] D Or: ἰδέα; cf. Mt. 28:3: ἦν δὲ ἡ εἰδέα (vl., ἰδέα, the correct reading) αὐτοῦ ὡς ἀστραπή.

[3] Schl. Lk., 44.

[4] H. Leisegang, *Indices* (1926 ff.), 222.

εἶδος αὐτῷ) ... οὐκ εἶχεν εἶδος [5] (Σ: οὐδὲ θεωρία); 53:3 : τὸ εἶδος αὐτοῦ ἄτιμον
(Mas.: נִבְזֶה; Σ: ἐξουδενωμένος). [6]

It can be used of God. Thus LXX translates "Peniel" (Gn. 32:30 f. = 31 f.):
Εἶδος τοῦ θεοῦ. Nu. 12:8 : (God says concerning Moses) στόμα κατὰ στόμα
λαλήσω αὐτῷ, ἐν εἴδει [7] καὶ οὐ δι' αἰνιγμάτων, καὶ τὴν δόξαν Κυρίου εἶδεν
(→ I, 178; I, 217 f.). It is against this background, in the context of hearing and
seeing, that we have the saying in Jn. 5:37: οὔτε φωνὴν αὐτοῦ πώποτε ἀκηκόατε
οὔτε εἶδος αὐτοῦ ἑωράκατε.

Cf. Ex. r., 41, 3 : "Two things Israel asked of God : to see His form (דמותו), and to
hear the words from His mouth." It is most significant for the position of the Rabbinic
exegete that in S. Nu., 103 on 12:8 the explanatory בְּמַרְאָה [8] is not linked with the I of
God contained in the אֲדַבֶּר, but is understood as the seeing of speech : "Thou sayest :
the seeing of speech. Or perhaps of the Shekinah? [9] This is correct, for it is written :
'And he said, Thou canst not see my face : for there shall no man see me, and live'
(Ex. 33:20)."

2. In 2 C. 5:7 the usual rendering [10] of διὰ πίστεως περιπατοῦμεν, οὐ διὰ
εἴδους as "not by sight" does not seem to be very apposite. The presupposed active
use of εἶδος is without a parallel, [11] the word always being used of the fact of
being seen rather than the act of seeing. Elsewhere when Paul indicates by what a
περιπατεῖν is determined he does not use the preposition διά but κατά (R. 8:4;
14:15) or ἐν (2 Cor. 4:2; R. 6:4), or the dative (2 C. 12:18; Gl. 5:16). [12] Here the
διά does not denote the manner of walking, i.e., the circumstance which determines it, [13] but rather the accompanying circumstance (διά, 3b; → 66). Hence the
only possible sense is that we walk in the sphere in which we are referred to faith
and in which there is no visible form.

The only remaining question is what form is at issue. It might be the κύριος [14]
in whom we now believe (cf. the βλέπομεν γὰρ ἄρτι δι' ἐσόπτρου ἐν αἰνίγματι
of 1 Cor. 13:12a) and whose εἶδος we shall see only in the next aeon (cf. the
τότε δὲ πρόσωπον πρὸς πρόσωπον of 1 Cor. 13:12b). This view, however, involves a difficult introduction of the subject of both πίστις and εἶδος, and it
stands in no very strong connection with the general argument of the passage.
Both these objections are overcome if we take the alternative view that the reference is to the form of the Christian [15] which in its full and proper sense belongs

---

[5] Quoted in 1 Cl., 16, 3.
[6] On the text of this verse in the LXX, 'A and Σ, cf. K. F. Euler, *Die Verkündigung vom
leidenden Gottesknecht aus Jes. 53 in der griech. Bibel* = BWANT, 4, 14 (1934), 12 ff.
[7] Mas. וּמַרְאֶה; like the LXX, Samaritanus, Tg. O. and several MSS have בְּמַרְאֶה. So also
S. Nu., 103 *ad loc.* (Kuhn, 269, n. 9) → n. 8. Cf. A. Dillmann, *Comm. on Nu.*² (1886), 66 f.
[8] The Midrash presupposes this reading, → n. 7.
[9] In the Berlin MS of the Midrash אלהים is the seeing of God. Cf. Kuhn, 269, n. 11.
[10] So also Wnd., Ltzm., *ad loc.*; also G. Kittel, *Religionsgesch. u. Urchrtt.* (1932), 103.
[11] Cf. Liddell-Scott, 482; also G. Heinrici, *Das zweite Sendschr. d. Ap. Pls. an die
Korinth.* (1887), 261; *Der zweite Brief an die Kor.* (1900).
[12] Cf. Heinrici, *Der zweite Brief*, 185.
[13] So Wnd., *ad loc.*, 167.
[14] So Heinrici; also A. Schlatter, *Paulus, der Bote Jesu* (1934), 363, 519, 552.
[15] So Cr.-Kö., 390.

only to the period of the ἐνδημῆσαι πρὸς τὸν κύριον (v. 8). In its provisional character the present earthly state is related to the true εἶδος which the believer will enjoy at the last time in exactly the same way as the σκῆνος is to the οἰκία ἀχειροποίητος (v. 1), or the ἐν τῷ σώματι and ἀπὸ τοῦ κυρίου (v. 6) to the πρὸς τὸν κύριον (v. 8). The situation denoted in the verse is just the same as that of 1 Jn. 3:2 : οὔπω ἐφανερώθη τί ἐσόμεθα. [16]

Cf. the Platonic use of εἶδος in the sense of "model," "idea," "essence of a thing" (Symp., 210b; Hi., I, 289d; Phaed., 102b; 103e; Theaet., 148d; Philo Op. Mund., 103; Vit. Mos., II, 76), and perhaps also the use of εἶδος for form as distinct from matter (ὕλη): Aristot. Phys., I, 4, p. 187a, 18; Metaphys., VI, 3, p. 1029a, 29. It is both instructive and self-consistent that the Platonic use does not occur in the NT.

3. εἶδος is often used [17] for manner, [18] and this is the most likely meaning of 1 Th. 5:22 : ἀπὸ παντὸς εἴδους πονηροῦ ἀπέχεσθε, "keep yourselves from every evil manner." [19] The link with v. 21 makes this preferable to the older rendering : "Avoid all appearance of evil." [20] The link is all the stronger if the theory is correct that we have here a quotation of the saying of Jesus concerning the money-changers often referred to in the early Church. [21] This seems very likely in view of the strong verbal similarities and the use of εἶδος for a "mint." [22] In this case v. 21b and v. 22 would be the positive and negative outworking of the main advice in v. 21a : "(As good money-changers) test all things : keep the good and reject the bad."

Kittel

εἴδωλον, εἰδωλόθυτον,
εἰδωλεῖον, κατείδωλος,
εἰδωλολάτρης, εἰδωλολατρία

εἴδωλον.

1. εἴδ-ωλον, from εἰδ-, *videre*, "to see" (cf. → εἶδος, "figure"), means "picture" or "copy," whether artificially made, self-reproduced or simply present. Thus εἴδωλον might mean "figure of a man" in the sense of a copy of the man depicted, but not the

---

[16] Comparison with 1 C. 13:12 is thus no less mistaken than reference to the ἐν εἴδει of Nu. 12:8 LXX. This is particularly true of the latter, since even in 1 C. 13:12 Paul does not seem to be dependent on the Gk. form of the OT verse (→ I, 180).

[17] Cf. Moult.-Mill., 182. Philo, cf. Leisegang, 222 ff.

[18] Partly identical, partly as a sub-division of γένος, as in Aristot. Rhet., II, 20, p. 1393a, 27.

[19] It cannot be fixed with precision whether πονηροῦ is used as an adj. or a subst. ("from evil of every kind"). In the one case cf. Job 1:1, 8 : ἀπεχόμενος ἀπὸ παντὸς πονηροῦ πράγματος, and in the other Jos. Ant., 10, 37: πᾶν εἶδος πονηρίας.

[20] So A. V., cf. Luther, Calvin, Erasmus (*apparentia*); on the other hand cf. Vg (*ab omni specie mala*).

[21] γίνεσθε δόκιμοι τραπεζῖται, τὰ μὲν ἀποδοκιμάζοντες, τὸ δὲ καλὸν κατέχοντες. There is a good analysis of the tradition in A. Resch, *Agrapha*² (1906), 112-128.

[22] Resch, 125.

εἴδωλον. Pape, Pass., Cr.-Kö., Pr.-Bauer, *s.v.* εἴδωλον. Str.-B., III, 51-60, Sickb., 1 K., 38 f.

man himself. [1] It can also be used for images of gods etc. [2] On the other hand, the usual term for the cultic images of the Greeks is ἄγαλμα, while the statues of men are normally called ἀνδριάς and εἰκών. The relevant cultic object as such is not εἴδωλον, but the relation to the deity can be formulated in such a way that it is its εἴδωλον. It helps us to understand the Greek conception and sense of the word that they call reflections in water τὰ ἐν τοῖς ὕδασιν εἴδωλα (Aristot., De Divinatione per Somnum, 2, p. 464b, 9 and 11), and that they also call the shadow εἴδωλον σκιᾶς (Plat. Resp., VII, 532c). εἴδωλον can also be used for shades or apparitions, [3] and is par. to φάσμα. [4] Indeed, the inhabitants of the underworld are called εἴδωλα, [5] though they are no longer the men concerned, but only copies of them. A work of art is called εἴδωλον in the sense of an unconscious and immobile copy quite distinct from the living being in question. [6] εἴδωλον is par. to ψεῦδος in oppos. to → ἀληθές (I, 248). [7] Plato uses εἴδωλα for individual things as the non-real in distinction to ideas or παραδείγματα. [8] εἴδωλον can also denote the image awakened by an object in the soul. [9] It is common in Philo in the sense of what is unreal or deceptive. [10] Though it would be too much to equate it with what is without substance, it certainly denotes "copy" as distinct from the true reality.

---

[1] Hom. Od., 4, 796 : εἴδωλον ποίησε, δέμας ἤϊκτο γυναικί; Hdt., VI, 58, 2 : ὃς δ' ἂν ἐν πολέμῳ τῶν βασιλέων ἀποθάνῃ, τούτῳ δὲ εἴδωλον σκευάσαντες ἐν κλίνῃ εὖ ἐστρωμένῃ ἐκφέρουσιν; I, 51, 3 : γυναικὸς εἴδωλον χρύσεον, τὸ Δελφοὶ τῆς ἀρτοκόπου τῆς Κροίσου εἰκόνα λέγουσιν εἶναι; Polyb., 13, 7, 2 : ἦν γὰρ εἴδωλον γυναικεῖον ... κατὰ δὲ τὴν μορφὴν εἰς ὁμοιότητα τῇ τοῦ Νάβιδος γυναικὶ διαφόρως ἀπειργασμένον; Philo Congr., 65 : εἰδώλων καὶ ἀνδριάντων; Jos. Bell., 5, 513 : παῖδες δὲ καὶ νεανίαι διοιδοῦντες ὥσπερ εἴδωλα κατὰ τὰς ἀγορὰς ἀνειλοῦντο.

[2] Polyb., 31, 3, 13-15 : τὸ δὲ τῶν ἀγαλμάτων πλῆθος οὐ δυνατὸν ἐξηγήσασθαι· πάντων γὰρ τῶν παρ' ἀνθρώποις λεγομένων ἢ νομιζομένων θεῶν καὶ δαιμονίων προσέτι δὴ ἡρώων εἴδωλα διήγετο ... Νυκτὸς εἴδωλον καὶ Ἡμέρας τῆς τε καὶ Οὐρανοῦ, Ἠοῦς καὶ Μεσημβρίας. This is the only established passage in which a pagan Greek uses εἴδωλον for an idol, and it is obviously for the sake of stylistic variation.

[3] Jos. Bell., 7, 452 : ἐβόα βλέπειν εἴδωλα τῶν ὑπ' αὐτοῦ πεφονευμένων ἐφεστηκότα; Vett. Val., II, 12, p. 67, 5 : ὑπὸ δαιμονίων καὶ φαντασίας εἰδώλων χρηματισθήσονται; II, 36, p. 113, 17: τοῦ δὲ Κρόνου ἐν τῷ ὑπογείῳ εὑρεθέντος θεῶν καὶ νεκρῶν εἴδωλα ἐφαντάσθη; Luc. Dial. Mortuorum, 16, 5 : καλῶς ἂν ταῦτα ἔλεγες, εἰ σῶμα ἦσθα, νῦν δὲ ἀσώματον εἴδωλον εἶ.

[4] Plut. Them., 15 (I, 119e): ἕτερα δὲ φάσματα καὶ εἴδωλα καθορᾶν ἔδοξαν ἐνόπλων ἀνδρῶν; Philo Som., II, 133 : εἰδώλων καὶ φασμάτων καὶ ὀνειράτων ἔθνη μυρία; Spec. Leg., I, 26 : εἴδωλα σκιαῖς ἐοικότα καὶ φάσμασιν, οὐδενὸς ἠρτημένα ἰσχυροῦ καὶ βεβαίου; Plut. Superst., 3 (II, 165e): εἴδωλα φρικώδη καὶ τεράστια φάσματα.

[5] Hom. Od., 11, 476 : βροτῶν εἴδωλα καμόντων; 24, 14 : ἔνθα τε ναίουσι ψυχαί, εἴδωλα καμόντων; Soph. Ai., 126 : ὁρῶ γὰρ ἡμᾶς οὐδὲν ὄντας ἄλλο πλὴν | εἴδωλ', ὅσοιπερ ζῶμεν ἢ κούφην σκιάν etc.

[6] Xenoph. Mem., I, 4, 4 : πότερά σοι δοκοῦσιν οἱ ἀπεργαζόμενοι εἴδωλα ἄφρονά τε καὶ ἀκίνητα ἀξιοθαυμαστότεροι εἶναι ἢ οἱ ζῷα ἔμφρονα καὶ ἔνεργα;

[7] Plat. Theaet., 150c : ... βασανίζειν ... πότερον εἴδωλον καὶ ψεῦδος ἀποτίκτει τοῦ νέου ἡ διάνοια ἢ γόνιμόν τε καὶ ἀληθές. Cf. Plat. Soph., 265b : ἢ γάρ που μίμησις ποίησίς τίς ἐστιν, εἰδώλων μέντοι, φαμέν, ἀλλ' οὐκ αὐτῶν ἑκάστων. Cf. Philo Som., II, 162 : ψευδῶν εἰδώλων καὶ ἀβεβαίων φαντασμάτων.

[8] Cf. E. Cassirer, "Eidos und Eidolon" in Vorträge der Bibliothek Warburg, 1922/1923, I (1924), 1-27.

[9] Leucippus, Democritus and Epicurus explained this to mean that εἴδωλα proceed from objects and bring vision to the eyes (II, 8, 33 ff., Diels). Cicero Epistulae, XV, 16, 1 speaks ironically of the εἴδωλα which man should carry in his consciousness.

[10] Cf. Leisegang's Index, and esp. Conf. Ling., 74, where πράγματα ὑφεστηκότα καὶ ὄντως ὑπαρκτά is the opp. of εἴδωλα; Omn. Prob. Lib., 146 : ἄμαυρα εἴδωλα ἀρετῆς ὁρῶντες; Conf. Ling., 69 and 71: σκιάν and εἴδωλον are par.; Praem. Poen., 19 : τῆς ἡδονῆς τὰ εἴδωλα.

2. The LXX uses εἴδωλον for many words meaning images of the gods or heathen deities, namely, עָצָב,[11] פְּסִיל,[12] פֶּסֶל,[13] צֶלֶם,[14] תְּרָפִים,[15] and חַמָּן,[16] which indicate idols as such, גִּלּוּלִים[17] and שִׁקּוּץ,[18] which express contempt and loathing, אֱלִיל[19] and הֶבֶל,[20] which call the gods rather than the images empty, and finally אֵל,[21] אֱלֹהִם,[22] בַּעַל[23] and בָּמָה.[24] A first point to notice is that εἴδωλον rather than ἄγαλμα is used for images of gods. Even more important is that the term is applied to the gods themselves. Behind the usage there is obviously a polemic against paganism. The presence of images as the focus of worship is used to emphasise the unreality of heathen belief and the heathen gods.[25] For the Jews idols and heathen deities are identical, and they prove that the heathen have images but no true God. Thus "copy" (as distinct from the reality) is the word for both images and gods. The word "idol" in its current use does not always convey the precise meaning. Too great an emphasis is often laid on the idea of an object of false worship rather than on that of something without reality which fools have put in the place of the true God. In its strict sense the idol is not merely an alternative god; it is an unreal god, and therefore false as distinct from true and real. Philo and Josephus are both familiar with this use of εἴδωλον.

Thus Philo quotes Lv. 19:4 in Spec. Leg., I, 26, and Gn. 31:35 in Leg. All., II, 46 and Conf. Ling., 74. He uses the other sense of εἴδωλον in his allegorical interpretation. Rachel is αἴσθησις (→ I, 187) and the εἴδωλα on which she sits are the unreal things indicated by the senses (Leg. All., II, 46). Joseph. Ant., 10, 50: Josiah παρῄνει τῆς περὶ τῶν εἰδώλων δόξης ὡς οὐχὶ θεῶν ὄντων ἀποστῆναι; 9, 273: σέβειν τὰ εἴδωλα; 9, 243: βωμοὺς ἀναστήσας καὶ θύων ἐπ' αὐτῶν τοῖς εἰδώλοις; 10, 65: οἱ ἱερεῖς τῶν εἰδώλων. On Ac. 15:20, cf. Joseph. Ant., 9, 273: τὴν πόλιν παντὸς ἐκάθηραν μιάσματος εἰδώλων (cf. also 10, 69 of Josiah: μή τις ἔχοι τι τῶν εἰδώλων ὑπονοῶν).

In pagan Gk. we do not find this usage. The Gks. did not share this view. For either they honour as gods what the Jews call εἴδωλον, or, even if they no longer do so, they have no comprehensive expression for what the Jews call εἴδωλον. The language of the LXX is biblical or Jewish Gk. in this respect. Jewish religion has coined a new expression out of an existing term.

---

11 1 S. 31:9; 1 Ch. 10:9; 2 Ch. 24:18; Ps. 115:4; 135:15; Is. 10:11; 48:5: (עָצָב); Hos. 4:17; 8:4; 13:2; 14:9; Mi. 1:7; Zech. 13:2.
12 2 Ch. 33:22; 34:7; Is. 30:22.
13 Ex. 20:4; Dt. 5:8.
14 Nu. 33:52; 2 Ch. 23:17.
15 Gn. 31:19, 34 f.
16 2 Ch. 14:5 (4); Is. 27:9 (?).
17 Lv. 26:30; Dt. 29:17 (16); 4 Βασ. 17:12; 21:11, 21; 23:24; Ez. 6:4-6, 13; 8:10; 18:12; 23:39; 36:18 (A), 25; 37:23; 44:12.
18 3 Βασ. 11:5, 7.
19 Lv. 19:4; 1 Ch. 16:26; ψ 96:7; Hab. 2:18.
20 Dt. 32:21; Jer. 14:22; 16:19.
21 Is. 57:5.
22 Nu. 25:2; 1 Βασ. 17:43 (A); 3 Βασ. 11:2, 7 (8), 33; Is. 37:19.
23 2 Ch. 17:3.
24 Ez. 16:16.
25 Dt. 4:28; 28:36; 29:16; Is. 2:8, 20; 40:19-20; 44:9-20; 46:1-7; Jer. 10:3-9; Hab. 2:18-19; Ps. 115:4-8; 135:15-18; Wis. 13:10-19; 14:1-14; 15:4-17; Ep. Jer. 4-72; cf. Str.-B., III, 53-60.

Ditt. Or., 201 (cf. n. 8) is a late document under (Jewish?) Christian influence, and therefore its use of εἴδωλα for gods is no evidence of pagan usage prior to the LXX. Catal. Cod. Astr. Graec. (ed. Cumont, Boll, Kroll, Olivieri), VII, 176, 22 : ὁ δὲ μέλλων ἐν Βηθλεὲμ ἐκ τῆς παρθένου γεννᾶσθαι αὐτὸς μέγας διδάσκαλος γενήσεται καὶ τὸ ἀνθρώπινον γένος σώσει καὶ τοὺς εἰδώλων ναοὺς καταλύσει, is so plainly dependent on biblical usage that its use of εἴδωλα for cultic images does not permit us to draw any conclusions as to the normal pagan practice.

3. The NT ι sage rests on that of the LXX or the Jews. In the NT εἴδωλον is used for heathen gods and their images. The word and its derivatives do not occur in the Gospels. They are found only in Ac. 7:41; 15:20; the writings of Paul, R. 2:22; 1 C. 8:4, 7; 10:19; 12:2; 2 C. 6:16; 1 Th. 1:9; and in 1 Jn. 5:21 and Rev. 9:20, derivatives also being found in Eph. and Pt. In relation to Paul's use of εἰδώλων, the question arises how far he regards them as realities. It is evident from 1 Th. 1:9 that they are no gods in comparison with God, and from Gl. 4:8 and R. 1:23 that they are not divine by nature but only products of human sin and folly. But he seems to see demons behind their worship (1 C. 10:19; cf. 8:5), so that we do not have here a purely intellectual dismissal. He gave full weight to Dt. 32:17: ἔθυσαν δαιμονίοις καὶ οὐ θεῷ. In this respect he is wholly Jewish.[26]

In view of the sparseness of the evidence, we cannot say how far he equates idols and demons and how far he distinguishes them. We gather from 1 C. 8:5 that the reality of demons stands behind idols. But demons are not the same as what the heathen believed their gods to be; they deceive men into believing in these gods.[27] See also → θεός; → δαίμων.

† εἰδωλόθυτον.

εἰδωλόθυτον, subst. neuter of the adj. εἰδωλόθυτος, is obviously a Jewish term for → ἱερόθυτον or the rare θεόθυτον.[1] It denotes the meat which derives from heathen sacrifices, though without the intolerable implication of the sanctity of what is offered to heathen gods, or the divinity of these gods (→ κατείδωλος). The heathen in 1 C. 10:28 refers to ἱερόθυτον, while Paul uses εἰδωλόθυτον. The term is first found in 4 Macc. 5:2 : κρεῶν ὑείων καὶ εἰδωλοθύτων ἀναγκάζειν ἀπογεύεσθαι.[2] It does not occur in Josephus. In secular Gk. it is as rare as εἴδωλον in the sense of idol. The Rabbinic words are זִבְחֵי מֵתִים, sacrifice to the dead, and תִּקְרֹבֶת עֲבוֹדַת אֱלִילִים, sacrifice in honour of unreal entities.[3]

Jews were forbidden to eat flesh sacrificed to idols. They were also forbidden to trade in it.[4] It defiled like a corpse if one came into contact with it in an enclosed

---

[26] Str.-B., III, 48-60, esp. 51 f.

[27] Cf. J. Weiss on 1 C. 8:4-6; 10:18-20; K. Barth, Die Auferstehung der Toten (1924), 26.
ε ἰ δ ω λ ό θ υ τ ο ν. Pr.-Bauer, Cr.-Kö., s.v.; Str.-B., III, 54, 377; Joh. W., Bchm., Ltzm. on 1 C. 8-10; M. Rauer, Die Schwachen in Korinth und Rom (1923), 40-52; H. v. Soden, "Sakrament u. Ethik bei Pls.," Marburger theol. Studien, I (1931), 1-40.

[1] Phryn. Ecl., 138, p. 249 : ἱερόθυτον οὐκ ἐρεῖς, ἀλλ' ἀρχαῖον θεόθυτον. Praeparatio Sophistica (ed. Borries, 1911), 74 : θεόθυτα, ἃ οἱ πολλοί ἱερόθυτα καλοῦσιν.

[2] Ps.-Phokylides, 31: αἷμα δὲ μὴ φαγέειν εἰδωλοθύτων δ' ἀπέχεσθαι, is regarded as a later addition by J. Bernays, Gesammelte Abhandlungen (ed. H. Usener), I (1885), 223-226.

[3] Str.-B., III, 54, 377; Ab., 3, 3; bChul., 13b, Bar.; AZ, 2, 3; bAZ, 8a, Bar.; T. Chul., 2, 18 and 20.

[4] AZ, 2, 3.

space.[5] To force a Jew to eat it was to enforce apostasy.[6] The reference was not to the flesh which went into the temple, but to that which came out.[7] The strict prohibition reflects the resolute resistance of Judaism to any kind of religious syncretism.[8] Its basis, namely, that the flesh is offered to the dead or to unreal entities, shows that it is primarily religious. It rests on a strict application of the first commandment and not on superstition, fear of spirits etc.

Paul will allow the enjoyment of εἰδωλόθυτον apart from the cultic act itself (1 C. 10:14-22) and so long as it does not violate the law of love (8:1-13). In this connection he appeals (10:26) to Ps. 24:1. He can take this attitude only because faith has overcome Jewish legalism from within. In the apostolic decree of Ac. 15:29; 21:25, and in Rev. 2:14, 20, we do not have full freedom from legalism. Among the Nicolaitans the desire the eat meat sacrificed to idols is an expression of Libertinism, i.e., of complete renunciation of any commitment to the will of God, as may be seen from their general licentiousness. The same is probably true of Paul's opponents at Corinth.[9]

† εἰδωλεῖον.[1]

This word is found only in the Bible at Da. 1:2; Bel. 10; 1 ᾿Εσδρ. 2:10; 1 Macc. 1:47 (א); 10:83; 1 C. 8:10, and ecclesiastical writers (not Josephus). It derives from εἴδωλον in the sense of idols, and is a scornful term for the heathen temple as a house of idols.

† κατείδωλος.

This occurs only in Ac. 17:16. It is perhaps to be understood by analogy with adjectival constructions like κατάδενδρος ("rich in trees") or κατάλιθος ("rich in stones"),[1] in which case it means "rich in idols." Or it is perhaps a caricature[2] of κατάθεος ("godly" or "pious")[3] in the sense of "idolatrous." The Vulgate *idolatriae deditam* takes the second view, whereas the Peshitta "full of idols"[4] is based on the first. Either is consonant with vv. 22, 23.

εἰδωλολάτρης, εἰδωλολατρία.

εἰδωλολατρία, which in terms of the derivation is more correct than εἰδωλολατρεία, and εἰδωλολατρεῖν come from the subst. εἰδωλολάτρης as γεωμετρία and γεωμετρεῖν come from γεωμέτρης. εἰδωλολατρία is not, therefore, a compound of εἴδωλον and λατρεία. Yet, since the meaning is the same, the reading εἰδωλολατρεία, which is always found in B except at 1 C. 10:14, is quite natural, esp. as the word probably came into use at a time when there was no clear distinction between -εία and -ία.

---

5 bChul., 13b, Bar.
6 4 Macc. 5:2.
7 AZ, 2 and 3.
8 Cf. F. Büchsel, *Joh. u. d. hellenist. Synkretismus* (1928), 10 ff.
9 Cf. F. Büchsel, *Geist Gottes im NT* (1926), 367 ff.
εἰδωλεῖον. 1 According to Bl.-Debr. § 15; § 111, 5, εἰδώλιον is probably a better reading than εἰδωλεῖον.
κατείδωλος. 1 Cf. Wdt. Ag., *ad loc.*
2 Cf. the construction εἰδωλόθυτον for ἱερόθυτον (→ 378).
3 Philo Spec. Leg., II, 256; Poll. Onom., I, 20.
4 Cf. Zn. Ag., 601, n. 46.
εἰδωλολάτρης κτλ. Pr.-Bauer, Cr.-Kö., *s.v.*; Bl.-Debr. § 119, 2.

As λατρεία characterises the Jews (R. 9:4), so εἰδωλολατρία characterises the heathen. The word and the related subst. εἰδωλολάτρης [1] are found only in the NT and dependent Christian writings, and even in the NT they occur only in Paul, 1 Pt. and Rev. The terms are not used by the LXX, Philo, Josephus or other Jews, let alone by pagan authors. However, the word is probably a pre-Christian Jewish term like εἴδωλον in the sense of "idol," and in Rabbinic speech עֲבֹדַת אֱלִילִים [2] gives us a full parallel.

The words denote a gross sin and occur in the lists of vices in 1 C. 5:10, 11; 6:9; 10:7, 14; Gl. 5:20; Col. 3:5; Eph. 5:5; 1 Pt. 4:3; Rev. 21:8; 22:15. Particularly striking is the equation of πλεονεξία and εἰδωλολατρία in Col. 3:5 and Eph. 5:5. Mammon is regarded as an idol in Mt. 6:24. Participation in heathen feasts is εἰδωλολατρία according to 1 Cor. 10:14, 7. [3]

Büchsel

εἰκῆ

This is a dat. fem. used adverbially. [1] By Attic rule it should thus be written with ἰῶτα subscr., though this had already fallen into disuse in the Hellen. period. [2] There are no instances of the adj. εἰκός. [3] The basic meaning is "at random," "with no plan or goal," "for no objective reason." It thus comes to mean "without true right," and the further senses of "in vain," "moderately" and "simply" [4] have also to be taken into account. [5]

In the NT εἰκῆ [6] usually means "in vain" (R. 13:4; 1 C. 15:2; Gl. 3:4; 4:11). It means "without basis" in Col. 2:18.

On Mt. 5:22 cf. the textual discussion in Zn. Justin is no real witness for the omission of εἰκῆ ("without a cause") after πᾶς ὁ ὀργιζόμενος τῷ ἀδελφῷ αὐτοῦ, since he is quoting very freely. Origen, followed by Jerome, Vulgate and Augustine, probably introduced a correction on moral grounds to make all anger reprehensible. ℵ and B are surely dependent on Origen. In the Western and Syrian there is unanimous support for εἰκῆ, and it is probably genuine.

---

[1] In Hermas s., 9, 21, 3; m., 11, 4 we also have the verb εἰδωλολατρέω.
[2] bChul., 13b, Bar.
[3] The attempt made in Cr.-Kö., 394 to find εἰδωλολάτρης in 1 C. 6:9 and ἱερόδουλος (not found in the NT) in 1 Pt. 4:3 and Gl. 5:20 takes the order in these lists too systematically.

ε ἰ κ ῆ. Pape, Pass., Liddell-Scott, *s.v.*
[1] Cf. πῆ, whither, how, why ?, δικῆ, two-fold, κοινῆ, in common etc.
[2] Bl.-Debr. § 26.
[3] Acc. to Liddell-Scott ἑκών ("voluntarily") is prob. linked with εἰκῆ (ἐϝ-εκῆ ?), as also ἕκητι ("by the grace of a god," "for the sake of ..."). But we have also to take into account εἴκω, which gives us the imperf. εἶκε ("it seemed good") in Hom. Il., 18, 520 and the perf. ἔοικα.
[4] Examples may be found in Pape, Pass., Liddell-Scott, Pr.-Bauer.
[5] From εἰκῆ there derives εἰκαῖος, "he who acts without plan or at random or in vain," but also "the average or common man." For examples, cf. Pape etc.
[6] εἰκῆ occurs only once in the LXX at Prv. 28:25, with no Heb. equivalent. It is more common in Σ and ᾽Α. Instead, the LXX usually has → δωρεάν in the more general sense of "in vain."

Both δωρεάν and εἰκῆ came to have a much wider range than their original meaning, esp. δωρεάν, in the usage of the Gk. Bible (→ 166). Both take on the sense of "in vain," and, although they reach it from different standpoints, no distinction of meaning can be seen between them in this regard, at least in the NT.

Büchsel

---

† εἰκών

A. The Prohibition of Images in the OT.

The conviction that Yahweh is not to be depicted in the form of an image is intrinsic to true Yahweh worship. Its basis is to be found in the commandment in Ex. 20:4. [1] In this respect the official cultus presents a uniform picture. Nowhere in the literature do we find any sign either of deviation from or of development to this position. There is thus no reason to contest the Mosaic basis. For it is indisputable that the fundamental teaching of the commandment concerning a jealous God who cannot be made static gives us a firm reason for the prohibition of images. On the other hand, we must not attempt to analyse the motives, for it is only too easy to reduce the work of Moses to the level of popular religious pedagogy. It must also be considered that not all the consequences of the prohibition of images for the faith of Israel were already at work in the first beginnings. Obviously a strong belief in the spiritual nature of Yahweh underlies the Mosaic prohibition. Yet this is not speculative. God is not conceived as essentially remote from matter or from this world. He is rather a God whom man cannot master and control, least of all in the form of a visible, material representation. The literary approach conforms to the cultic. Imagination is not allowed free rein in the description of Yahweh. In both Ex. 24:9 f. and Is. 6:1 ff. we have depiction of what is seen, but reference is made only to the brightness at the feet of God and to the train of His garment.

The oldest known cult of Yahweh was in relation to the ark, and there is no longer any doubt that there were no associated images. [2] However we imagine the ark, and even if it was an empty portable throne, it is linked only to the spiritual presence of Yahweh. David brought the ark to Jerusalem, and Solomon placed it in the temple. Though this involved changes, there is no evidence to suggest that the traditional prohibition of images was abandoned. The dedication

---

εἰκών. On A: R. H. Pfeiffer, "Images of Yahwe," JBL, 45 (1926), 211-222; H. T. Obbink, "Jahwebilder," ZAW, NF, 6 (1929), 264; S. Mowinckel, "Wann wurde der Jahwä-kultus in Jerusalem offiziell bildlos?", *Acta Orientalia,* 8 (1930), 257-279. On Cf.: Moore, I, 446 ff.; Str.-B., IV, 386 ff.; Wnd. 2 K., 137; Ltzm. 1 K. on 15:45; Loh. Kol., 55 f., 140 f.; Dib. Kol., on 1:15 (with excursus). J. Hehn, "Zum Terminus 'Bild Gottes'" in *Festschr. f. E. Sachau* (1915), 36-52; W. Caspari, "Imago Dei" in *Festschr. f. R. Seeberg* (1929), 197-208; P. Bachmann, "Der Mensch als Ebenbild Gottes" in *Das Erbe Luthers, Festschr. f. L. Ihmels* (1928), 273-279; F. K. Schumann, "Imago Dei" in *Festschrift f. G. Krüger* (1932), 167-180.

[1] The prohibition in Dt. 27:15 also goes back to the earliest days.

[2] Gressmann suggested that the ark contained images of a male and female deity (*Die Lade Jahwes* [1920], 44).

of the temple, if we accept as original the fuller LXX version, [3] emphasises the fact that Yahweh dwells in obscurity, and thus denotes His presence apart from images. For in the OT עֲרָפֶל is often used in connection with theophanies, and it refers to the concealment of God. Thus in both Ex. 20:21 and 1 K. 8:12 it is a term for the *deus absconditus*. It is worth noting that the dedication paradoxically links the sun in the firmament with Yahweh in the temple, but emphasises the fact that Yahweh, who is present in non-material form, controls the sun. This reference to the dependence of even the greatest star on Yahweh suggests that from a very early period the prohibition of representations of Yahweh was grounded in the doctrine of creation. There is a similar distinction between Yahweh and the created elements in the appearance of Yahweh to Elijah in Horeb (1 K. 19:11 ff.). Yahweh is not in the storm, the earthquake or the fire. He is paradoxically beyond the natural sphere, as here denoted by the mysterious rustling of a gentle breath. We have to appeal to such passages to understand the prohibition, for the archaeological evidence, i.e., the lack of representations in graves, is not of itself enough, since there is a similar lack of representations of Baal. [4] Obviously there is a great difference between the lack of images of divinised natural forces like Baal and the lack of images of Yahweh.

It may be doubted whether there is in the Mosaic original the hidden connection with the doctrine of creation, but the present form of the commandment (Ex. 20:4; Dt. 5:8) is shaped by this doctrine. For wherever we go in creation — heaven, earth or under the earth — all things are created by Yahweh and subject to Him, so that they cannot be compared with Him. Hence it would be ridiculous to seek a likeness of Yahweh in the created order. When we come to Dt. Is. the rejection of images is based solely upon the doctrine of creation, and we have a clear theological formulation. In Is. 40:12 ff. there is a hymn to the Creator of the world, before whom the nations are as the drop of a bucket and who lifts up the isles like grains of sand; and then the prophet drives home his message against idolatry: "To whom then will ye liken God? or what likeness will ye compare unto him?"

We are not to assume, however, that the reasons for the commandment were always the same. Sometimes the emphasis in attacks on images lies simply on the fact of disobedience and self-will (Am. 5:26; Hos. 8:4 f.; 11:1). The Deuteronomist takes a distinctive path of his own. He bases the prohibition on the fact that Israel at Sinai saw no figure of Yahweh when He spoke to it from the fire (Dt. 4:15 f.).

The older historical and especially prophetic books give clear evidence that the strictness of the commandment was too much for the people. We must remember, however, that the authors were pitiless judges of any departure from the pure worship of Yahweh. Thus modern archaeology has taught us that the golden calf was not really an image or symbol of Yahweh but merely the pedestal of God, [5] and the saying of Jeroboam ("These be thy gods...") may perhaps reproduce the primitive conception of the people (Hos. 13:2) but in fact distorts the original intention. Even where there is reference to foreign gods, [6] the border-line is still difficult to fix, for we can hardly think that there was any complete apostasy

---

[3] 3 Βασ. 8:12: "Jahweh set the sun in heaven (הֵכִין for הֵבִיא), but said that he would dwell in the thick darkness ..."

[4] Cf. J. Hempel, ZAW, 51 (1933), 297.

[5] Obbink, *op. cit.*, 268; W. Eichrodt, *Theologie des AT* (1933), 52.

[6] אֱלֹהֵי הַנֵּכָר, e.g., 2 Ch. 33:15; cf. חַבְלֵי נֵכָר, Jer. 8:19.

from Yahweh except in very rare cases. Thus many Israelites who prayed before images of Hadad most likely had Yahweh in mind. Even the introduction of Assyrian cultic vessels into the temple did not denote any conscious apostasy from Yahweh, who was still the supreme God and Owner of the temple ; the cosmic world and its idols were brought in only as guests. [7] The prophets saw, however, that these images and the sacral traditions linked with them perverted the religion of the worshippers, and their constant protests helped to preserve the full authority of the claim that there must be no images in the worship of Yahweh. Of course, it was only in the pre-exilic period that the prohibition was a burden and that idolatry constituted a temptation. Dt. Is. with his humorous depiction of the making of images made a powerful contribution to the overcoming of the threat (Is. 44:12 ff.).

v. Rad

B. Images of Gods and Men in Judaism and Christianity.

1. The ancient prohibition (Ex. 20:4 f., 23; Lv. 26:1; Dt. 4:16 ff.; 5:8 f.; 27:15) had three practical implications : a. the avoidance and so far as possible the removal of cultic images of alien gods ; b. the lack of images in the native cultus ; and c. the avoidance of representations of men and, partially at least, of other living creatures.

The first implication has been self-evident for Jews and Christians in every age (→ εἴδωλον, 377), and any violation has been regarded as apostasy. The second has also been a strongly emphasised and strongly asserted principle in the Jewish world.

> With regard to a. the pictures of animals and stars on the great curtain of the temple (Jos. Bell., 5, 214) were not regarded as depictions of deities as one might think. They were merely artistic symbols. In the newly discovered synagogue mosaics of Ain ed-Duk and Beth Alpha there is in the middle of the picture of the zodiac a representation of the four-steeded chariot of the sun with Helios [8] as the driver. But even here the Byzantine artists had no thought of depicting the sun-god ; they were simply adopting the traditional form of representing the sun. bAZ, 43b, Bar. forbids pictures of the sun, moon and stars because these are servants of God (ministering angels).
>
> With regard to b. the depiction of the hand of God in the scene of Isaac's sacrifice at Beth Alpha [9] is astonishing for a Jew. There is a similar depiction on one of the newly discovered murals of the synagogue at Dura, which also has a picture of the divine hand lifting Ezekiel by the hair ; both these are several centuries older than the picture at Beth Alpha. [10] On the other hand, these very independent painters of biblical

---

[7] K. Budde, *Auf dem Wege zum Monotheismus* (1910), 10 ff.

[8] For reproductions cf. E. L. Sukenik, *The Ancient Synagogue of Beth Alpha* (1932), Fig. 49; Plate X; Pictures of the zodiac from Kefar Bir' in : Sukenik, Plate 7b; Reconstruction, Fig. 50.

[9] Sukenik, Pl. XIX. In ancient Christian depictions of the sacrifice of Isaac the hand of God is common ; it is thus possible that this mosaic shows the influence of Christian art on 5th and 6th century Judaism.

[10] Plates may be found in C. Hopkins, "Jewish Prototypes of Early Christian Art ?" in *The Illustrated London News*, No. 4919 (July 29, 1933), 188 ff., Fig. 10 (Abraham); 1 and 12 (Ezekiel); cf. also Comte du Mesnil du Buisson, "Les Peintures de la Synagogue de Doura-Europos," *Rev. Bibl.*, 43 (1934), 105-119 (III, 2, Abraham). C. H. Kraeling was so good as to lend me some photographs of these sensational discoveries, and H. Lietzmann (cf. ZNW, 32 [1933], 94 f.) had a great number of photographs which he had been given by excavators.

scenes (→ *infra*) stop short of depicting more than God's hand, the symbol of the divine activity (→ χείρ). We can thus judge how strong was the prohibition.

In relation to the third implication, there were various results in practice. So far as we can see, Jewish art strongly disliked representations of men and therefore scrupulously avoided them. An ancient principle is that "all pictures are permissible except those of men" (bAZ, 42b). The crucial reason was that man is in the likeness of God, as suggested by the prohibition in Ex. 20:23, [11] so that a depiction of man is a depiction of the image of God. For this reason orthodox Jewish art avoids for the most part even biblical scenes, especially those which include men. [12] On the other hand, recent excavations have shown that these restrictions were widely ignored under the influence and after the example of non-Jewish art (→ *infra*).

The great mosaics of Beth Alpha and Ain ed-Duk might be regarded as unusual examples from a later period (5th-6th cent. A.D.). Both have the zodiac and the sun, Beth Alpha has the sacrifice of Isaac [13] and Ain ed-Duk has Daniel in the lions' den. [14] It is probable that in the Byzantine period pious Jews began to depict biblical incidents because the rival Church was appropriating OT scenes which they had regarded as exclusively their own. On the other hand, Hellenistic art seems to have exerted much the same influence in Rome ; thus in the Jewish catacomb of the Vigna Randanini on the Via Appia we find the figure of Nike with Pegasus and other symbols. [15]

The discovery in the synagogue of Dura forces us to the conclusion that in the synagogues of the dispersion there developed to a previously unsuspected degree a depiction of biblical scenes of very high quality. Apart from the sacrifice of Isaac, we can identify either Enoch or Abraham, Moses at the burning bush, the Exodus, the death of the Egyptians in the Red Sea, Aaron with the temple and the ark of the Torah, the miraculous water in the desert (→ 386), the bringing back of the ark of the Torah from the temple of Dagon, Ezekiel, Ezra with the scroll etc. [16] The pictures bear the date of the second year of Philip the Arab, i.e., 245 A.D. At this period in the East there can be no question of a developed Christian art. Although the church in Dura has similar paintings to those of the synagogue, they seem to be much cruder. [17] We have thus to consider the possibility that the murals in the heathen temple, which were particularly significant in Dura, [18] provoked the Jews to rivalry. Like Philo in the

---

[11] Ex. 20:23 : "Ye shall not make beside me" = אִתִּי. R. Joshua (c. 300 A.D.) read אתי as אוֹתִי, "my sign," "my image" (bAZ, 43b). Cf. Str.-B., IV, 391.

[12] In the Jewish catacomb of the Villa Torlonia there are at least two murals which perhaps depict biblical scenes, first, of a meadow in Paradise with animals but no men (cf. H. W. Beyer-H. Lietzmann, *Die jüdische Katakombe der Villa Torlonia in Rom* [1930], 26, Pl. 14b), and secondly, of what seems to be the ark, though again without Noah (cf. K. H. Rengstorf, ZNW, 31 [1932], 42 ff.; on the absence of Noah cf. esp. 44 ff.; for a reproduction, cf. Beyer-Lietzmann, Pl. 5).

[13] Sukenik, Plate XIX.

[14] F. H. Vincent, *Rev. Bibl.*, 28 (1919), 532 ff. (Fig. 535); 30 (1921), 442 f., 577 f. (Plates XV and XVI).

[15] R. Garrucci, *Cimitero degli antichi Ebrei scoperto recentemente in Vigna Randanini* (1862); also E. Cohn-Wiener, *Die jüdische Kunst* (1929), Fig. 77, 78.

[16] For reproductions, cf. C. Hopkins, *op. cit.*

[17] C. Hopkins, "Dura-Europos Discoveries" in *The Ill. London News*, 4869 (August 13, 1932), 239 ff., Fig. 12-16.

[18] Cf. J. H. Breasted, *Oriental Forerunners of Byzantine Painting* (1924); and esp. F. Cumont, *Fouilles de Doura-Europos* (1926); also Kittel, *op. cit.*, Fig. 15 ff.

sphere of philosophy, they could not bear to be inferior to the heathen even in respect of temple decoration. Comparison with the Palmyrene pictures, however, reveals a distinctive synagogue style in form as well as content, as Karl Watzinger has pointed out to me. It may be that Hellenistic artists were brought, possibly from Alexandria, [19] who imported their own form and content with its distinctive Jewish features. [20]

Perhaps in such cases more orthodox Jews later removed human figures. This seems to have happened to the sculptures in Galilean synagogues, [21] and to the mosaics of Ain ed-Duk. [22] Murals could not be removed, and therefore the practice was not to look at them (jAZ, 42b, 58). [23]

In the case of animals, it depends on whether they were regarded as the symbols of a deity or cult. If so, they were just as intolerable as idols, e.g., the eagle on the door of a temple or synagogue, [24] or the dragon. [25] Other animals were mostly accepted as harmless decoration. [26]

Objects used in Jewish worship constituted a privileged group for Jewish art. Thus the scroll [27] and the ark of the Torah were often depicted as symbols of the religion of the Torah. We also find the seven-branched candelabra, the light of the Torah, [28] alongside the ark. Other objects depicted are the palm branches (לוּלָב), pomegranates, citrus fruits (אֶתְרוֹג), of the feast of tabernacles (cf. Lv. 23:40), the horn used at festivals (שׁוֹפָר), the knife of circumcision etc. [29]

---

[19] Watzinger has suggested verbally that the origin of this type of historical painting in Judaism is probably to be found in Jewish Hellenistic illustrations for the OT. At the very earliest it might be connected with the community in Alexandria.

[20] Whether this Jewish art influenced OT Christian art, and if so to what degree, must be determined by future investigation, which now has the materials to discuss the question. Cf. already O. Wulff, Altchr. u. byz. Kunst, I (1913), 69.

[21] Cf. the synagogue at Capernaum, H. Kohl-K. Watzinger, Antike Synagogen in Galiläa (1916), 13, Fig. 18; K. Watzinger, "Die antiken Synagogen Galiläas," in Der Morgen, 6 (1930), 364; G. Kittel, Religionsgesch. u. Urchrtt. (1932), Fig. 35.

[22] Of the Daniel at Ain ed-Duk only the arm outstretched in prayer has survived (→ n. 15). In the pictures of the sun and animals the men and animals have been intentionally scratched out (Sukenik, Pl.1-5 and esp. Fig. 49). The destroyers may well have been orthodox Jews (as in Capernaum, → n. 21) rather than Mohammedans, for the dedicatory inscriptions were intentionally spared, and were therefore read and honoured. For the erasion of animals, cf. Kohl-Watzinger, Fig. 16.

[23] Str.-B., IV, 391k.

[24] For the destruction of the golden eagle placed by Herod above the gate of the temple, cf. Jos. Ant., 17, 151 ff.; for the half-destroyed eagle above the door of the synagogue at Capernaum, cf. Kohl-Watzinger, Fig. 17 f.; Kittel, Fig. 35. Cf. also Kohl-Watzinger, 195 ff.

[25] bAZ, 42b: "All figures are permitted apart from the dragon."

[26] Cf. the dolphins and peacocks in Beyer-Lietzmann, Plate 7b, 9b; Kittel, Fig. 37b. It is debated whether the peacock is purely decorative or has symbolical significance (the resurrection and eternal life), cf. H. Lother, Der Pfau in der altchr. Kunst (1928). Several animals are depicted on the mosaic in the Gerasa synagogue, Sukenik, Plate 7a, XXVI.

[27] Beyer-Lietzmann, Plate 4; Kittel, Fig., 39.

[28] The ark, usually with the candelabra, is found in the Jewish catacombs, cf. Beyer-Lietzmann, Plate 12 f.; N. Müller-N. A. Bees, Die Inschriften der jüd. Katakombe am Monteverde zu Rom (1919), No. 179; Kittel, Fig. 40 f.; on gold vessels, cf. Kittel, Fig. 42 ff.; Sukenik, Fig. 22, 34 f., 38, Plate 1a; on synagogue mosaics, cf. Sukenik, Fig. 27 (Ain ed-Duk), 28 (Jerash), Plate VIII/IX (Beth Alpha); Hopkins, Fig. 14 (Dura). In interpretation of the ark of the Torah, cf. Lietzmann in Beyer-Lietzmann, 21 ff. on the one side and G. Kittel in OLZ, 35 (1932), 459 f. on the other; in interpretation of the seven-branched candlestick, cf. esp. K. H. Rengstorf, ZNW, 31 (1932), 33-60.

[29] Beyer-Lietzmann, Plate 6 (horn); 10 (ethrog); 8, 10, 12 (lulab); 12 (knife of circumcision); 4, 6 (pomegranate). Cf. Kittel, Fig. 39 f.

To determine the content of Jewish art, it is helpful to compare it with the paintings in heathen temples, e.g., at Dura. In the latter we have on the one side the priest or devotee bringing an offering, and on the other the depiction of the deity. [30] There is nothing comparable in the Jewish pictures. Where the heathen has a painting or sculpture of the god, the Jew has the ark of the Torah and the candlestick, the Word of his God. This is his God! And if he is bold and wants to portray the greatness of his God for the proselyte who seeks outward representation, he uses his art to depict the sacred history, i.e., the action of his God. This history and its depiction are genuine history, i.e., the living history of real men with whom and on whom God acts. Here is the difference from depictions of the myths of Mithras, Attis, or Osiris, where we have types of divine action suggested by the myths, but not a real history. The Jew portrays God when he depicts the historical action of God. He does not need a picture of God, of His face and form. At the very most he will introduce the divine hand to show that it is God's work. Moreover, he ignores the worshipper whose pious exercises are painted by the heathen. The great figures of the past whom he depicts are not heroes painted on their own account. Abraham is depicted because God acts on him, Ezekiel because the God who awakens the dead seized him, Moses because he points to the burning bush, the Israelites and Egyptians because God protects the former and smites the latter, Ezra because he reads the Word of God. The real subject is not men, whether devotees of the present or great figures of the past; it is God and His history.

Thus, even though these pictures may be technically influenced from without, they reflect a genuine Judaism. The artists forgot that part of the prohibition which concerns men. But they maintained the more truly the essence of their religion as a historical religion of revelation.

In connection with the picture of water in the wilderness, H. Lietzmann has pointed out to me that the OT passage which refers to twelve springs in the desert is the story of Ex. 15:27 concerning Elim. Rabbinic tradition expounded this story in a peculiar way, as may be seen from the statements in M. Ex., 15, 27 (p. 158 f., Rabin): "(1) The text shows us that the place was more famous than all other places because of the water. [31] (2) You can see that this is so, for there were twelve springs and only seventy palms, but when Israel came and 600,000 men camped there, there was enough for them, not once only but a second time and a third ... (3) R. Eleazar of Modiim said: When the Holy One, blessed be He!, created His world, He created there twelve springs corresponding to the twelve tribes of Jacob and seventy palms corresponding to the seventy elders. (4) And what do we learn from the fact that it is written: 'And they encamped there by the waters'? It tells us that they occupied themselves there with the words of the Torah which were given them in Marah." This shows us how important was the religious interpretation of the miracle at Elim ("more famous than all other places because of the water"), so that we can understand why the painter included this event in the series of sacred events for depiction. As may be seen from the lamps which stand between the tents and above the springs, he paints it primarily because the study

---

[30] Cf. the Dura picture of the sacrifice of the eunuch Otes to the five and of the tribune Julius Terentius to the three Palmyrene deities; Kittel, Fig. 16 f.

[31] The text necessarily became unintelligible when the tradition was lost that this was the most important of all the water miracles; hence the variant מקולל. "meaner than all other places" (Mekilta de-R. Simon bJochai, ed. D. Hoffmann [1905], 74; cf. J. Winter-A. Wünsche, Mechiltha [1909], 151, n. 1).

of the Law is symbolized by the water. Cf. also Megillat Taanit., 8, Str.-B., IV, 346. From this picture we can see how strongly rooted this art is in the exegetical tradition of Judaism, and therefore how genuinely Jewish it is in content, whatever the technical influences.

2. Representations of God were obviously just as objectionable to early Christianity as to Judaism. Yet it must be remembered that, so far as we can see, the question of depicting God or even man or animal never arose at all in the NT, whether from the positive or the negative standpoint. It never entered the head of any early believers to hand down a picture of Jesus or the apostles, let alone to set up a cultic image. The complete lack of interest in this regard marks off the young religion from the syncretistic religions in the surrounding world. The cultic image of Mithras is an integral part of the whole cult; the image of Serapis was created with the rise of this religion; [32] there could be no worship of the emperors without statues. In the religion of the Christians, however, the important thing is not worshipping an image and considering the myth thereby depicted, but listening to the Word (→ ἀκούω, I, 216 ff.). Only in the 1st and 2nd centuries do we have a development in the catacombs, via religious decoration, to the painting of Christian symbols and symbolic figures, especially the Good Shepherd, [33] and then to the depiction of Christ and the apostles and other biblical subjects. [34] A model and impulse for this development might have been provided by the newly discovered, pre-Christian biblical paintings of the Jews, especially in relation to OT scenes. Only gradually do we have the formation of a distinctive content and style determined by Christianity itself and producing Christian art. [35]

As there is little positive interest in the early Christian period, so there is little negative. The absence of inclination towards artistic depiction means also the absence of opposition. There is no prohibition of pictures.

> Only when pictures of Christ began to appear was the question raised whether they are permissible, Iren., I, 25, 6; Act. Jn., 26 ff.; Eus. Hist. Eccl., VII, 18, 36; the canon of the Synod of Elvira (Mansi, II, 264): *placuit picturas in ecclesia esse non debere, ne quod colitur et adoratur in parietibus depingatur.* [36]

3. In the NT itself the question of images arises in the following passages.

a. Mk. 12:16 and par., where the reference is to the image of the emperor. Neither Herod the Great nor the procurators seem to have dared to print images on coins, but Herod's successors, and especially Philip the Tetrarch, introduced their

---

[32] F. Cumont, *Die Mysterien des Mithra*[2] (1911), 200 ff.; *Die orient. Rel. im röm. Heidentum*[3] (1931), 71.

[33] E.g., the catacomb frescoes from the Hypogaeum of Lucina (first half of the 3rd cent.): J. Wilpert, *Die Malereien der Katakomben Roms* (1903), Plates 35 and 66; H. Preuss, *Das Bild Christi im Wandel der Zeiten*[3, 4] (1932), Fig. 1. On the development, cf. K. Koch, *Die altchr. Bilderfrage nach den lit. Quellen* (1917); W. Elliger, *Die Stellung der alten Christen zu den Bildern in den ersten vier Jhrhdten.* (1930); also H. Achelis, RGG[2], I, 251.

[34] For Christ and the apostles, cf. the fresco in the Domitilla catacomb (first half of the 4th cent. A.D.): Wilpert, Plate 148; Preuss, Fig. 6. Other subjects are the raising of Lazarus, the healing of the sick of the palsy, the adoration of the Magi, the feeding of the five thousand etc.

[35] Cf. H. W. Beyer, "Die Eigenart der christl. Kunst im Rahmen der Spätantike," in *Festschr. f. V. Schultze* (1931), 67 ff.

[36] Cf. N. Bonwetsch, RE[3], III, 222.

own images and those of the emperor. [37] These were bound to be offensive to true Jews, partly because they depicted alien rulers, partly because they violated the commandment (→ 384) and partly because images were linked with pagan symbols. [38] Nahum in Tiberias, the "most holy," "never in his life looked at the image on a coin" (jAZ, 42c). [39] Yet for obvious practical reasons there was no actual rejection of the coins (cf. TAZ, 5, 1). [40]

b. ἡ εἰκών τοῦ → θηρίου, "the image of the beast," i.e., the emperor, which is to be worshipped, apostates consenting and the loyal resisting. This is one of the great themes in the second half of Rev. (13:14 f.; 14:9, 11; 15:2; 16:2; 19:20; 20:4).

This kind of clash with the cult of rulers or emperors is not new in Judaism. Obeisance to the divine image of the ruler is the problem in Da. 3:5 ff. The erection of a statue of Caligula in the temple [41] was prevented only by his death (41 A.D., cf. Philo Leg. Gaj., 188; Jos. Ant., 18, 261), while in Alexandria from 38 A.D. the mob, with the connivance of the governor, began to set up images of the emperor in the synagogues (Philo Flacc., 41 ff.), which were removed only under Claudius. [42] Similarly under Pilate there arose the serious struggle about the Καίσαρος εἰκόνες αἳ σημαῖαι καλοῦνται (military standards) which the people resisted so passionately that Pilate finally removed them from Jerusalem (Jos. Bell., 2, 169 ff.; Ant., 18, 55 ff.). We can see from Plin. Ep., X, 96 that worship of the imperial image played a similar role in the persecution of Christians. The presumed life of the image which enables it to speak (Rev. 13:15) reminds us of many priestly devices to make images move. Thus in the Mithras mystery the statue of the god with a lion's head was made to spit out fire by means of a concealed pipe ending in the mouth, [43] and it was said of Simon Magus: ego statuas moveri feci et animavi exanima (Ps.-Clem. Recg., III, 47).

Kittel

C. The Greek Use of εἰκών.

εἰκών (etym. linked with εἴκω, ἔοικα, "to be similar," "to be like," "to appear"), means an image in various senses: a. in the strict sense as an "artistic representation," e.g., a painting, statue or impress on a coin (Hdt., II, 130; Mt. 22:20), the "image of a god" (Ditt. Or., 56, 61; P. Oxy, IX, 1380, 139; Rev. 13:14 f.), or naturally a "reflection" (Eur. Med., 1162) or "apparition" (Plat. Phileb., 396); b. in the metaph. sense of a "mental image," τῆς ψυχῆς (Plat. Tim., 29b), ἀρετῆς (Epigr. Graec., 435, 4), a "similitude" (Plat. Resp., VI, 487e); and finally c. in the sense of a "copy," a "living image," a "likeness," an "embodiment," a "manifestation" (Ditt. Or., 90, 3; cf. the saying of

---

[37] Schürer, I, 430, n. 10; Kittel Probleme, 36, n. 2; P. Thomsen, *Kompendium der pal. Altertumskunde* (1913), 96 (§ 37, IId): coins with the head of Augustus or Tiberius and the inscription: Καίσαρος Σεβαστοῦ or Τιβέριος Σεβαστὸς Καῖσαρ.

[38] The reverse of the coins mentioned in n. 37 shows the temple of Augustus in Paneas (Schürer, I, 430). Cf. F. W. Madden, *Hist. of Jewish Coinage* (1864), 247, where there is a coin with the head of Tiberius and the inscription: Ti(berius) Caesar Divi Au(gusti) F(ilius). The Jews here use Divus of Augustus.

[39] Schl. Mt., 648.

[40] Loc. cit.

[41] Asc. Is., 4, 11: "He will set up his image in all cities." Cf. Dib. Th.², 39.

[42] For imperial temples and statues in Samaria, Paneas and Caesarea, cf. Jos. Bell., 1, 403 f., 413 f. Cf. Kittel Probleme, 36, n. 1.

[43] Cf. F. Cumont, *Textes et Monuments figurés relatifs aux Mystères de Mithra*, II (1896), 196, Fig. 22; Haas, 15 (1930, Leipoldt), Fig. 35/36.

Diogenes of Sinope : τοὺς ἀγαθοὺς ἄνδρας θεῶν εἰκόνας εἶναι, Diog. L., VI, 51; also Luc. Imagines, 28).[44]

1. In Col. 1:15 Christ is described as the εἰκών τοῦ θεοῦ τοῦ ἀοράτου. To modern logic this seems to be a contradiction, for how can there be an image of something which is invisible and without form ?[45] The peculiarity of the expression is related to that of the ancient concept, which does not limit image to a functional representation present to human sense but also thinks of it in terms of an emanation, of a revelation of the being with a substantial participation (μετοχή) in the object.[46] Image is not to be understood as a magnitude which is alien to the reality and present only in the consciousness. It has a share in the reality. Indeed, it is the reality. Thus εἰκών does not imply a weakening or a feeble copy of something. It implies the illumination of its inner core and essence. In the Greek and Hellenistic world this line of thinking took on a strong monistic and optimistic character. We first find it in Plato in the closing words of the Timaeus (92c, where there is almost a direct par. to Col. 1:15): ὅδε ὁ κόσμος οὕτω ζῷον ὁρατὸν τὰ ὁρατὰ περιέχον, εἰκὼν τοῦ νοητοῦ (sa. ζῴου) θεὸς αἰσθητός, μέγιστος καὶ ἄριστος κάλλιστός τε καὶ τελεώτατος γέγονεν εἰς οὐρανὸς ὅδε μονογενὴς ὤν.[47] In Platonic cosmology the world as a whole and not merely man, as in the Christian sphere, is the visible image of the intelligible αὐτοζῷον. The philosophical line leads on from Platonic cosmology to Philo (→ 394). As in Plat. Resp., VI, 509a, Helios is called the εἰκών of the ἰδέα τοῦ ἀγαθοῦ. In Plutarch, too, the sun is the image of God (Ei Delph., 21 [II, 393d]; Stob. Ecl., I, 293, 21), and in the hymn of Proclus (Orph., p. 277) to Helios, in v. 34 the latter is addressed : εἰκὼν παγγενέταο θεοῦ. This concept of images seems to be of systematic importance in the Hermetic conception of the world-organism, the world being the first and man the second image of God (Corp. Herm., VIII, 2, 5 : πρῶτος γὰρ πάντων ὄντως καὶ ἀΐδιος καὶ ἀγέννητος ὁ δημιουργὸς τῶν ὅλων θεός· δεύτερος δὲ ὁ κατ᾽ εἰκόνα αὐτοῦ ὁ κόσμος, ὑπ᾽ αὐτοῦ συνεχόμενος καὶ τρεφόμενος καὶ ἀθανατιζόμενος, ὡς ὑπὸ ἰδίου πατρὸς ἀεὶ ζῶν ὡς ἀθάνατος etc.; Ps.-Apuleius Asclepius, 10).[48] God holds the world together, and the world man. Here, then, we have the basic thought of the harmony which is established by the συμπάθεια τῶν ὅλων of the Stoa.

2. Alongside this cosmological, speculative and philosophical line, there is in the Greek world a no less monistic religious line. We think first of the general religious concept of images. Here the widespread view, constantly assailed, of course, by the philosophers, is that in the image man has the god himself somehow present in his own being. This is confirmed by the miracles and magic associated with the images. The copies have the same powers and the same capacities of

---

[44] In what man's divine likeness consists for the Greeks, apart from the συγγένεια which unites gods and men, we can see from Pindar : ἀλλά τι προσφέρομεν ἔμπαν ἢ μέγαν νόον ἤτοι φύσιν ἀθανάτοις, Nem., 6, 4.

[45] Loh. Kol., ad loc. Cf. Goethe's concept of the basic phenomenon, and his well-known verse which asks what would be either appearance without reality or reality without appearance.

[46] The same relation is present in the case of → μορφή and → νοῦς.

[47] This is the best reading in spite of W. Preuschen, ZNW, 18 (1917/18), 243; cf. A. E. Taylor, A Commentary on Plato's Timaeus (1928), 646 f., where it is suggested that the reading εἰκών τοῦ ποιητοῦ might derive from a Christian reader.

[48] Cf. Dib. Gefbr., Excursus on Col. 1:15.

feeling and action as the originals (Athenag. Suppl., 26 : ἃ γὰρ ἡ εἰκών λέγεται νῦν ἐνεργεῖν). [49] More specifically, if the εἰκών thus expresses the manifestation of the divine in this world, it is not surprising to find the term εἰκὼν τοῦ θεοῦ used as a predicate especially in the Hellenistic cult of the ruler in Egypt, [50] e.g., in the royal style of Philopator : εἰκόνος τοῦ Δι<ός> (Mitteis-Wilcken, I, 2, No. 109, 11, 3rd cent. B.C.). On the Rosetta stone (Ditt. Or., 90, 3) Ptolemy Epiphanes is called εἰκόνος ζώσης τοῦ Διός, υἱὸς τοῦ Ἡλίου. The Hellenistic ruler is supposed to be the god in visible manifestation (ἐπιφανής).

Kleinknecht

D. The Divine Likeness in the OT.

1. The distinctive meaning of the divine likeness in the OT can be understood only when we see it in strict connection with a faith which is basically orientated by the sense of the greatest possible distance from God. The central point in OT anthropology is that man is dust and ashes before God and that he cannot stand before His holiness. Thus the witness to man's divine likeness plays no predominant role in the OT. It stands as it were on the margin of the whole complex. Yet it is highly significant that OT faith adopted this theologoumenon in dealing with the mystery of man's origin.

Whereas in J man is made up of earthly material on the one side (עָפָר מִן הָאֲדָמָה) and the breath of life from God (נִשְׁמַת חַיִּים) on the other, [51] P looks in a different direction from the theological standpoint. [52] The strict sequence of the process of creation is broken after the creation of the animals, and a special resolve on God's part points to something extraordinary which is to follow. It is important that in Gn. 1:1-2:4b the tendency is to separate God from the creature. Instead of direct action, the word of command is enough to call forth the creatures. In the creation of man, however, there is a significant change. In Gn. 1:28 we have the technical term for constructing out of a material (בָּרָא) so that by origin man is brought into a direct relationship with God. To give theological precision to this relationship is the main point of the divine resolve in Gn. 1:26 : "Let us make man in our image, after our likeness."

2. To understand this statement it is necessary to realise that here is no freely ventured theologoumenon but the reconstruction of a myth. In fact many fragments of Mesopotamian literature show to what remote mythological depths the biblical statement finally points us, whether in terms of a divine being which in the creation of man first makes a sketch or picture on a tablet or in terms of the description of this new creature directly as the counterpart or likeness of the deity. [53]

---

[49] Cf. O. Weinreich, "Antike Heilungswunder," RVV, VIII, 1 (1909), 140 ff., and finally and comprehensively J. Geffcken, ARW, 19 (1916/19), 286 ff.

[50] J. Hehn, op. cit., 36 ff. has shown that in the religions of Egypt and Babylon various gods are called the son and image of the supreme god. Similarly Plut. causes the Persian Artabanus to say to Themistocles, who wants to be the great king: ἡμῖν δὲ πολλῶν νόμων καὶ καλῶν ὄντων κάλλιστος οὗτός ἐστι, τιμᾶν βασιλέα καὶ προσκυνεῖσθαι ὡς εἰκόνα θεοῦ τοῦ πάντα σῴζοντος (Plut. Them., 27 [I, 125c]). An interesting point here is the linking of the εἰκών concept with the soteriological aspect.

[51] Gn. 2:7.

[52] Gn. 1:26.

[53] Cf. the Gilgamesh epic, in which Enkidu is created as the likeness of the god Anu, I, 80 ff. (AOT, 151). On material in the ancient Babylonian fragments Ea and Atarchasis (AOT, 205 f.), cf. Hehn, op. cit., 45. In this connection Hehn also draws attention to the distinctive name of Tammuz, "image of Ea," op. cit., 43.

To refer to the mythical background of the biblical statement is not to maintain that this is itself a mythologoumenon. It is simply to show that we are not to interpret the concept of divine likeness in a way which bears no resemblance to ancient oriental thinking. The divine likeness is not to be found either in the personality of man, in his free Ego, in his dignity or in his free use of moral capacity etc. [54] Indeed, we must be careful not to emphasise the differentiation in the twofold statement בְּצַלְמֵנוּ כִּדְמוּתֵנוּ with its distinctive change of prepositions. The author is here wrestling with the expression. He has adopted an ancient formula, and in the terms צֶלֶם and דְּמוּת he is cautiously approaching the mystery that man is an earthly image of God, that he is created in the likeness of Elohim. For this reason the debate whether the divine likeness refers to the spiritual or physical being of man is not very helpful. If we had to think in terms of such an alternative, we should have to decide in favour of a predominantly physical likeness, not in the sense of speculation on God's form or corporeality, but in the sense of a reference to the Elohim nature proper to man. Man is here designated as a creature whose being is not from below but who belongs by nature to the upper region. There are two passages in particular in P which prevent us from interpreting the theologoumenon of the divine likeness in a one-sidedly spiritual sense. In Gn. 5:1 ff. reference is made to the physical progeny of the first man, and it is said of Seth, Adam's son, that he was begotten in the image and likeness of Adam. This statement is most important. It ensures the theological actuality for all generations of the witness to the divine likeness. For in itself the story of a being originally created in the divine likeness would be of no great significance for OT faith. In relation to the particular question, Gn. 5:3 tells us that the transmission of the divine likeness is thought of in terms of the physical sequence of generations and therefore obviously in a physical sense. The second passage is Gn. 9:6, where the prohibition of murder is grounded in the divine likeness. Here the thought is the same. Attack on man's body is violation of God's honour.

Apart from the passages in P, the only OT passage which refers to the divine likeness is Ps. 8:5 f., and this confirms what we have already said, transcending the physical/spiritual alternative. We are here told that man is only a little lower than God and is crowned with glory and honour. It will be seen that the second part of the parallelism develops the first, expounding it in terms of הָדָר and כָּבוֹד. הָדָר undoubtedly refers to the glory of outward appearance, expressing the same naive astonishment as we find in the ancient Babylonian texts. [55] כָּבוֹד, however, has a deeper meaning (→ δόξα, 238). It is the gravitas of man, what is impressive in him, striking the senses but consisting primarily in the inner force which is native to him. [56] This gives us a mysterious point of identity between man and God, for on the OT view כָּבוֹד belongs supremely to Yahweh. When we turn to Jesus Sirach, who is to be treated with caution, we find a basically similar understanding of the divine likeness. [57] The divine likeness consists in the fact that man was invested

---

[54] Cf. the OT theologies of E. Riehm (1889), 170; A. Dillmann (1895), 354; G. Oehler[2] (1882), 221; E. König (1922), 234.

[55] Cf. the Assyr. fragment on the creation of man (AOT, 136): "In the host of the throng he (Ea) made their form glorious" (A. Jeremias, Das AT im Licht des Alten Orients[4] [1930], 46 f.).

[56] Cf. also M. Buber, Königtum Gottes (1932), 214, n. 17: Kabod is the force or dignity of a being which shines out and therefore assumes visible form.

[57] Sir. 17:3 f.

with might at creation. [58] There is no other evidence in the OT as to the proper interpretation of the divine likeness. [59] It is natural that the ineffability of the divine being should help to draw a veil on this Godward side of man.

On the other hand, there are many answers to the question how man is to use his divine likeness and to what it summons him. Thus even in the divine resolve in Gn. 1:26 we are told that man is to be created in the divine image that he may control the whole of creation. This aspect is expressed very strongly in P, [60] which argues that creation is referred to man and needs his dominion as an ordering principle. [61] That man should be furnished with the divine likeness for this purpose is logical enough, for even earthly rulers, when they cannot be present in person, usually set up their images as signs of majesty. [62] Thus man in his sphere of rule as God's vice-gerent is summoned to represent the dominion and majesty of God. It is significant that Ps. 8, which at most is only loosely related to Gn. 1, brings the divinely given task of ruling creation into similar relation to the divine likeness, [63] and the train of thought is the same in Sir. 17:3 f.

3. The OT says nothing about the divine likeness being lost. P emphasises that it was transmitted to Seth. Nevertheless, the steady decline from the long lives of the earliest patriarchs (P) has the theological implication of a degeneration of man's original powers and divinely given *habitus*. And if our explanation of the divine likeness is correct, this degeneration is not unrelated to it.

v. Rad

E. The Divine Likeness in Judaism.

1. Rabbinic theology found the divine image much less of a problem than Philonic exegesis (→ 394) and later Christian theology. Exegetically the main problem in Gn. 1:26 f. was not its relation to Gn. 2:7, [64] as in Philo, but how to understand the "us" in "Let us make man..." How to take this "us" — whether in terms of God's consultation with His own heart, [65] with angels, [66] with the Torah, [67] or with heaven and earth [68] — was a frequently and hotly debated question both in Rabbinic circles and also in debates with heretics. [69]

---

[58] Smend, Ryssel etc. have rightly argued that we should read καθ' ἑαυτόν for καθ' ἑαυτούς in Sir. 17:3.

[59] It may be purely accidental that Ez. 28:13-15, the most highly coloured mythological reminiscence of early man, refers only to man's sinlessness and not to his divine likeness.

[60] Gn. 1:26 : וְיִרְדּוּ; v. 28 : כְּבְשֻׁהָ; cf. also Gn. 9:2.

[61] Bachmann, *op. cit.,* 274 f.

[62] Caspari, *op. cit.,* 208 emphasises this thought.

[63] Cf. the hiphil תַּמְשִׁילֵהוּ.

[64] It is worth noting that this question plays almost no part at all in Rabbinic literature (Str.-B., III, 477 f.), although it seems to invite exegetical discussion. As in many similar cases, the reason is perhaps that the Rabbis avoided an exegesis that might be taken up by Christians for their own exegetical purposes.

[65] Gn. r., 8 on 1:26 (acc. to R. Ammi).

[66] *Loc. cit.,* and also 17 on 2:19 (acc. to R. Acha); cf. Str.-B., III, 681.

[67] Pirqe R. Eliezer, 11 (Str.-B., III, 479).

[68] Gn. r., 8 on 1:26 (R. Josua in the name of R. Levi ; acc. to W. Bacher, *Agada der pal. Amoräer,* I [1892], 184, n. 1. R. Josua is the author of the opinion).

[69] bSanh., 38b; jBer, 12d (cf. Str.-B., III, 543, n. 1). On the Christian side we find the same explanation in Just. Dial., I, 62.

On the other hand, the biblical statement that this man, and indeed this earthly, corporeal, empirical man, was made in God's image, is one that was never doubted or regarded as constituting a problem. [70] Nor do we find that this image, like the *kabod* (→ 246), was thought to be forfeited because of Adam's fall. [71] Among the six things which will be restored, and which have thus been lost, the Rabbis mention radiance (זיו), length of days and an upright figure, but not the divine image. [72] There are certainly statements to the effect that the divine likeness has been diminished or even effaced by reason of sin. But this is not linked with the fall of Adam and a resultant, general, metaphysical sinfulness, but with the individual sin of specific men or groups of men.

b Moed katan, 15b : "Bar Kappara taught : 'My likeness (דמות דיוקני) I had given to them, but through their sin (בעונותיהם, and therefore not Adam's) I changed it'." According to Abba Kohen (Gn. r., 23 on 4:24) the divine likeness (צלם ודמות) ceased after Enoch. Significant, too, is the legend recounted by R. Banaah (bBB, 58a): When he wanted to survey and see the graves of the patriarchs, he was allowed to do so in the case of Abraham but forbidden in that of Adam ; for Abraham is בדמות דיוקני (the likeness of my image), [73] but Adam בדיוקני עצמה (my image itself). This reduction to a second-grade likeness does not apply to Adam himself in spite of the fall. [74]

Since the affecting of the divine likeness is not thought of as a metaphysical principle, there is no radical forfeiture. The same distinction is found in almost the same words in b Chul., 91b, though in relation to the angels who ascended to consider בדמות של מעלה (i.e., God Himself) and then descended to look at בדמות דיוקני של מטה (i.e., man). The divine likeness might still be found in men of the present age, and not merely in outstandingly religious men, but in men generally. When the disciples of Hillel were astonished that he called bathing a good work, he appealed to the divine likeness of his body (אני שנבראתי בצלם ובדמות), which it is meritorious to care for, since it is God's image (Lv. r., 34 on 25:39). To shed blood is to harm the figure of the king, i.e., the likeness of God (M. Ex., 20:17). Whoever despises a man, says R. Tanchuma, should realise that this one whom he despises God made in His image (ברמות אלהים עשה אותו, Gn. r., 24 on 5:1). Thus the famous thesis of Ben Azzai on Gn. 5:1 as the central statement of the Torah [75] is in this respect no exception to the general exegetical tradition of Judaism. And R. Akiba, his opponent in S. Lv., 19, 18, says in Ab., 3, 14 : "Beloved is man, for he is made in the image (בצלם)." [76] It is true, of course, that none of the other Rabbis equalled Ben Azzai in deducing from the OT words the comprehensive thought of humanity and in drawing out the logical implications.

---

[70] On the other hand, the exposition of Gn. 3:22 gives rise to questions ("the man is become as one of us"). Cf. the broad discussion in Gn. r., 21, and esp. the sharp opposition of Akiba in M. Ex., 14, 29 to Pappus' exposition in terms of ministering angels.

[71] Cf. Moore, I, 479.

[72] Gn. r., 12 on 2:4; Tanch. Buber Bereshit, 18. Though the image is not mentioned in 4 Esr. 7:11 f., it remains in Rabbinic tradition.

[73] Cf. R. 1:23 : ὁμοίωμα εἰκόνος; → 395.

[74] We have the same gradation, though applied to Adam too, in Philo, where it expresses dualistic metaphysical speculation on man (→ 394).

[75] S. Lv., 19, 18; jNed., 41c, 31; Gn. r., 24 on 5:1. Cf. W. Bacher, *Agada der Tannaiten*[2] (1903), 417 f.; Str.-B., I, 358.

[76] In Ab. R. Nat., 39, 8 the same statement is attributed to R. Meïr ; cf. Bacher, op. cit., I, 279.

Thus the preservation or loss of the image becomes a matter of personal moral conduct and fulfilment of the Law. According to R. Jacob of Kefar Chanan [77] man will rule if he is our image and likeness (בצלמינו כדמותינו), and fall if he is not: "Let there come then he who is our image and likeness and reign over him who is not" (Gn. r., 8 on 1:27). To be the image is to be worthy. [78] The concept can be taken in this individual ethical sense because there is no inclination to give it a speculative meaning and content [79] and because the concept of sin in this branch of Judaism relates primarily to the sinful individual (→ I, 290).

2. The influence of the Greek spirit, however, introduces the question wherein the divine likeness consists as a metaphysical gift. [80] Wis. 2:23 f. answers: ὁ θεὸς ἔκτισεν τὸν ἄνθρωπον ἐπ' ἀφθαρσίᾳ, and concludes in v. 24 that this gift is taken away by the διάβολος, the obvious reference being to the fall. [81] It is Philo, [82] however, who expounds the εἰκὼν τοῦ θεοῦ in the richest way.

Under Pythagorean influence he links it with the number seven: μόνον οὔτε κινοῦν οὔτε κινούμενον (Op. Mund., 100), but also with the μονάς: ἥτις ἐστίν ἀσώματος θεοῦ εἰκών, ᾧ κατὰ τὴν μόνωσιν ἐξομοιοῦται (Spec. Leg., II, 176). [83] But the οὐράνιος σοφία, too, is ἀρχὴ καὶ εἰκὼν καὶ ὅρασις θεοῦ (as distinct from the ἐπίγειος σοφία: ἀρχέτυπον μίμημα, Leg. All., I, 43). [84] The heavenly νοῦς: κατὰ τὴν εἰκόνα γεγονὼς καὶ τὴν ἰδέαν (sc. θεοῦ), Leg. All., I, 33 and 42. [85] The ἀνθρώπινος νοῦς is sharply distinguished from it: γηγενὴς καὶ φιλοσώματος; though it, too, is θεοειδής, partly because it derives from the breath of God (Gn. 2:7) and partly because it is fashioned after the λόγος as its ἀρχέτυπος ἰδέα. [86] The ψυχὴ ἀθάνατος is formed κατὰ τὴν εἰκόνα τοῦ ὄντος, but this εἰκών is the λόγος. [87] There is often reference to the → λόγος (and the λόγοι) as the εἰκὼν θεοῦ (Conf. Ling., 97 and 147; Fug., 101; Som., I, 115 and 239; II, 45).

In Rer. Div. Her., 230 f. there is a more exact distinction between the ὑπὲρ ἡμᾶς and the καθ' ἡμᾶς ὑπάρχοντα λόγον. The first is ἀρχέτυπος, for Moses calls it εἰκὼν θεοῦ; the second is μίμημα, for of it we read only: κατ' εἰκόνα. Hence it is only τῆς εἰκόνος ἐκμαγεῖον (reflection), at the third stage from the Creator (τρίτον εἶναι τύπον ἀπὸ τοῦ πεποιηκότος), whereas the first is its original (παράδειγμα) and the direct image (ἀπεικόνισμα) of God. This distinction is of the greatest importance for the understanding of man. To be sure, even earthly man, upon whom God breathes (Gn. 2:7; → infra) and whose soul is formed κατὰ τὸν ἀρχέτυπον τοῦ λόγου, is εἰκὼν θεοῦ and not εἰκών τινος τῶν γεγονότων, Plant., 18 f. But this is not true of his body, for God has no human form and the human form has no divine likeness. It applies rather κατὰ τὸν τῆς ψυχῆς ἡγεμόνα νοῦν, Op. Mund., 69. Philo finds his exegetical basis for the distinction in the twofold account of man's creation in Gn. 1:26 f. and Gn. 2:7. This gives rise to the frequently described or assumed distinction, which

---

[77] Ibid., III, 569 f.
[78] Cf. the parallel saying in Gn. r., 8 on 1:27.
[79] Moore, I, 446 f.
[80] Ibid., 448.
[81] Test. N. 2:5 uses the fact that man is created in God's εἰκών to deduce an intimate knowledge of the creature by the Creator.
[82] Cf. Wnd. 2 K., 137; Ltzm. 1 K. on 15:45; → I, 142.
[83] Cf. Rer. Div. Her., 187; Spec. Leg., III, 180.
[84] Cf. Wis. 7:26: (σοφία) εἰκὼν τῆς ἀγαθότητος αὐτοῦ.
[85] Cf. Som., I, 240 f.; Spec. Leg., III, 207.
[86] Leg. All., I, 33; Spec. Leg., III, 207.
[87] Spec. Leg., I, 81, cf. III, 207.

characterises all Philo's theology and anthropology, between the heavenly man who in Gn. 1:26 f. is created as the εἰκὼν θεοῦ and has no part in mortality or earthliness, and the earthly man who according to Gn. 2:7 is fashioned out of dust (Leg. All., I, 31 ff.; → I, 142). [88]

F. The Metaphorical Use of Image in the NT.

1. In the NT the original is always present in the image. What is depicted is here given visible manifestation. Thus εἰκών in Hb. 10:1 [89] is sharply distinguished from mere σκιά: [90] σκιὰν γὰρ ἔχων ὁ νόμος τῶν μελλόντων ἀγαθῶν, οὐκ αὐτὴν τὴν εἰκόνα τῶν πραγμάτων: the Law deals only with the σκιά and not with the essence of things. [91]

This understanding is found throughout the NT. Thus in R. 1:23, though with no particular emphasis, we read that men exchanged the δόξα of the immortal God for the ὁμοίωμα εἰκόνος of mortal man, birds, four-footed beasts and serpents. It is obvious that we have here opposition to the heathen cult of images. The distinctiveness of the expression lies in the juxtaposition of → ὁμοίωμα, which here means the copy, and εἰκών, which is the original copied, i.e., the thing itself and its form. "They exchanged ... for the copy of the figure of men and animals." [92]

Cf. Wis. 13:13 : the woodcarver who makes idols ἀπείκασεν αὐτὸ εἰκόνι ἀνθρώπῳ. Cf. bBB, 58a (→ 393). R. Baanah is visiting the graves of the patriarchs, but when, having seen Abraham, he wants to see Adam, he hears a voice : "Thou hast seen the likeness of my image (בדמות דיוקני), my image itself (דיוקן) thou mayest not see." Other interpretations are to be rejected, e.g., "they exchanged ... for a likeness (ὁμοίωμα) which consists in an image of man," [93] or "for the model (ὁμοίωμα) of an image (εἰκών) in the creation of which men etc. have served as models." [94]

2. Christ as εἰκὼν τοῦ θεοῦ.

When Christ is called the εἰκὼν τοῦ θεοῦ in 2 C. 4:4; Col. 1:15, all the emphasis is on the equality of the εἰκών with the original. Christ is ἐν μορφῇ θεοῦ, in the state of εἶναι ἴσα θεῷ (Phil. 2:6). In Johannine language His being as εἰκών means : ὁ ἑωρακὼς ἐμὲ ἑώρακεν τὸν πατέρα (Jn. 14:9; 12:45). [95] Even if the expression in Col. 1:15 were not accompanied by the parallel υἱὸς τῆς ἀγάπης αὐτοῦ (v. 13), it would still be apparent that the being of Jesus as image is only another way of talking about His being as the Son.

There is, of course, a connection with the divine likeness in the OT. For Paul the εἰκὼν θεοῦ is undoubtedly a magnitude which he owes to Gn. 1:27. [96] If he

---

[88] Cf. also ibid., I, 53, 90 and 94; II, 4; Rer. Div. Her., 57; Conf. Ling., 62 and 146; Op. Mund., 134; Leg. Spec., III, 83 etc.

[89] Cf. Rgg. Hb., 293, esp. n. 93; F. W. Grosheide, De Brief aan de Hebreen (1927), 269.

[90] As against this, in Philo Leg. All., III, 96 the εἰκών itself is equated with the shadow. Like the shadow, it is created directly after the divine original and man after it (and not God Himself).

[91] Already J. J. Wettstein, NT, II (1752), 418, n., referred to Plat. Crat., 306e : καὶ εἶναι εἰκόνας τῶν πραγμάτων.

[92] Ltzm., ad loc.; also A. Schlatter, Erl. z. NT, ad loc.

[93] Hofmann, Zn., ad loc.

[94] Khl., ad loc.

[95] Cf. Wis. 7:26 : (Wisdom is) εἰκὼν τῆς ἀγαθότητος (θεοῦ).

[96] So also Schl. Theol. d. Ap., 299.

here refers it to Christ instead of Adam, it is because he equates Christ with the Adam intended in Gn. 1:27. This is confirmed in 1 C. 15:45 ff., where he speaks of Christ as the second Adam (→ Ἀδάμ, I, 141 ff.). This follows the lines of Philo's connecting of Gn. 1:27 with the heavenly man (→ 394 f.), this man being Christ for Paul and the Logos for Philo. In Paul, however, there is no speculative interest. [97] The most significant things are perhaps in this case what he does not say. He adopts a line of exegesis, and consistently refers certain statements, including that about God's image, to Jesus, not to show "that the Father begat His image in Christ, but that Christ is given us as the image of God by which we may know what God wills and does. This formula does not undermine the personal nature of Christ, as though He were only a divine power or nature." Paul uses "the concept of the image of God also to make clear to the community who Jesus is." [98]

3. Man as Image.

That there is no speculation on Gn. 1:27 behind the thought of Paul is evident from the fact that in 1 C. 11:7 he can unhesitatingly apply the same passage to man, or more precisely to the male, whereas in 1 C. 15:45 (εἰς ψυχὴν ζῶσαν) it would seem that Gn. 2:7 alone applies to man. If the usual exegesis is correct, the expression used in 1 C. 15:49 is even more remarkable. In 1 C. 11:7 Paul had been able to deduce from man's divine likeness certain practical consequences in terms of the concrete life of his day. But only a few chapters later in 1 C. 15:49 he can regard the εἰκὼν τοῦ χοϊκοῦ deduced from Gn. 5:3 as determinative of earthly existence [99] and the εἰκὼν τοῦ ἐπουρανίου of a future. [100]

The main emphasis in Pauline anthropology is on this being of man as εἰκών which is still to be established, or better restored. And this will be done by connection with the being of Christ as εἰκών. In R. 8:29: συμμόρφους τῆς εἰκόνος τοῦ υἱοῦ αὐτοῦ, there is no tautology in μορφή and εἰκών. The general statement that the Christian is to be conformed, or to become the brother (→ I, 145) of the Firstborn, is given its distinctive emphasis by the fact that the Christian will participate in the divine likeness manifested in Christ. The man who is an image of Christ is an image in the specific sense which is the true and original sense for those familiar with the Bible, namely, the sense of Gn. 1:27. This likeness is the goal of the divine προώρισεν and the divine εἰς. As the context shows, it is thus identical with the δόξα, with the divine essentiality which is now present in Christ. The

---

[97] Thus the question whether Paul calls the pre-existent or only the exalted Christ εἰκὼν τοῦ θεοῦ is quite irrelevant.

[98] Schl. Theol. d. Ap., 299; Pls. der Bote Jesu (1934), 528.

[99] The aor. is surely an anticipatory retrospect from the future. G. Heinrici (1880), 542; (1896), 501 takes a different view when he speaks of "the time which is past for the believer — he has already received the Spirit as a pledge." But the context does not support this. It is speaking of the contrast between the earthly, physical σῶμα on the one side and the heavenly, pneumatic on the other. The turning-point between the two halves of v. 49 is not, then, conversion, but death and resurrection.

[100] In spite of strong support for φορέσωμεν, most modern scholars since Beza read φορέσομεν. In fact, o and ω are so often confused in the MSS that the strong attestation of ω should not be regarded as conclusive (cf. ἔχομεν/ἔχωμεν in R. 5:1). In the context (→ n. 99) a cohortative view of the conj. is hardly possible (in spite of Heinrici and others); in this sense even a conj. necessarily approximates very closely to a future. Cf. Joh. W. 1 K., 337.

teaching of 2 C. 3:18 is exactly the same.[101] Those who behold the δόξα κυρίου will attain to a share in it : τὴν αὐτὴν (i.e., that which consists in δόξα) εἰκόνα μεταμορφούμεθα. The emphasis is not on the fact that we shall be like an image manifested in the κάτοπτρον, but that that which is manifested in the κάτοπτρον is the one εἰκών to which the name rightly belongs. The Christian is always concerned to attain to the εἰκών τοῦ ἐπουρανίου which incorporates the divine likeness, and this is the ἔσχατος Ἀδάμ, i.e., Christ (1 C. 15:45 ff.). Or, as we read in Col. 3:10, πάντα καὶ ἐν πᾶσιν Χριστός implies putting on the new man [102] κατ' εἰκόνα τοῦ κτίσαντος αὐτόν. Here it is quite clear that restoration of the divine likeness of creation is identical with the establishment of fellowship with Christ. The Colossian passage also shows us once more how slight is Paul's interest in mythical speculation and how strong is his concern for the supremely concrete ethical consequences of this restoration of the εἰκών, namely, that we should put off fornication, blasphemy and lying (v. 5, 8, 9).

We have here an answer to the question when the restoration of the εἰκών takes place. The position is exactly the same as in all Paul's teaching. It is true that there is an eschatological future in 1 C. 15:49b. It is also true that R. 8:29 points us in the same direction. Nevertheless, in this passage, and even more so in 2 C. 3:18, the eschatological statement is linked to an event which is already present for the Christian.[103] And in Col. 3:10 the restoration of the εἰκών posits a goal of ethical action in this aeon. Like all the gifts in which Christians share, the εἰκών is an ἀπαρχή (→ I, 486). This means that it now is, and yet that it is still to be. It is enjoyed, but not yet enjoyed. Its eschatology is even now at work, and its presence has an eschatological basis.

Kittel

---

† εἰλικρινής, εἰλικρίνεια

εἰλικρινής derives from εἵλη (ἀλέα, ἥλιος), meaning "warmth or light of the sun," and κρίνω, so that the full sense is "tested by the light of the sun," "completely pure," "spotless." The derived subst. εἰλικρίνεια[1] means "purity." The adj. is much more common. There is also a verb εἰλικρινέω, "to purify."[2] The adj. is fairly frequent in Plato[3] and common in Philo.[4] In the LXX it is found only in Wis. 7:25 of wisdom : ἀπόρροια τῆς τοῦ παντοκράτορος δόξης εἰλικρινής (Α : εἰλικρινίας). From the time of Plato it is used in a moral sense.

---

[101] → δόξα, 251; → κατοπρίζομαι.

[102] Along the lines of 1 C. 15:49 we might paraphrase v. 9 : Put off the old man κατ' εἰκόνα τοῦ χοϊκοῦ.

[103] Cf. the discussion of the context of 2 C. 3:7-18 on → 356, and esp. what is said about ἀπὸ δόξης εἰς δόξαν (2 C. 3:18) as a bridge between the present and eschatology (→ 357). Paul might also say : ἀπ' εἰκόνος εἰς εἰκόνα.

εἰλικρινής, εἰλικρίνεια. Cf. Pass., Pape, Cr.-Kö., Pr.-Bauer, *s.v.* Wnd. 2 K., 54; Loh. Phil., 33, n. 5; Sickb. K., 26, 102.

[1] Less accurate forms are εἰλικρινεία and εἰλικρινία; cf. Bl.-Debr. § 119, 4.

[2] Ps. Aristot. Mund., p. 397a, 35; Stob. Ecl., I, 916.

[3] Phileb., 53a, 59c; Phaed., 66a; 81c; Symp., 211e.

[4] 28 times acc. to Leisegang's Index.

In the NT we have εἰλικρινής in Phil. 1:10; 2 Pt. 3:1; εἰλικρίνεια in 1 C. 5:8; 2 C. 1:12; 2:17.[5] The adj. and subst. always denote moral purity.[6]

Büchsel

| εἰμί, [1] ὁ ὤν | → ἐγώ.

1. Already in the LXX the abstract ὁ ὤν is used for God. In Ex. 3:14 the intentionally obscure self-designation אֶהְיֶה אֲשֶׁר אֶהְיֶה or אֶהְיֶה is pregnantly, if with a certain rationalisation, translated ἐγώ εἰμι ὁ ὤν or ὁ ὤν. This leads Greek speaking Jews to use ὁ ὤν as a name for God.[2] Philo employs it frequently, as also the weaker τὸ ὄν;[3] for him ὁ ὤν is the true name of God (Abr., 121), and worship of God as He who is constitutes true piety (Deus Imm., 69). Josephus, too, is familiar with ὁ ὤν as a divine predicate, cf. πεῖσαι δὲ τὸν λαὸν ὅτι μόνος εἴη ὁ θεὸς ὁ ὤν, ὃν ἀπ᾽ ἀρχῆς ἐθρήσκευσαν (Ant., 8, 350). In his rendering of Ex. 3:14 he expressly conceals the name which God gave Himself (Ant., 2, 276).

In the NT ὁ ὤν is a name for God only in Rev. in the forms ὁ ὢν καὶ ὁ ἦν (11:17; 16:5), ὁ ὢν καὶ ὁ ἦν καὶ ὁ ἐρχόμενος (1:4, 8), and ὁ ἦν καὶ ὁ ὢν καὶ ὁ ἐρχόμενος (4:8); → 345; 351. The formulae occur in God's self-predication (1:8), in worship (4:8; 11:17; 16:5), and in salutation (1:4). This explains the non-declinability of ὁ ὤν and the use of ἦν as a kind of participle. Linguistically, this is difficult, but it is not due to negligence. It is designed to preserve the sanctity of the divine self-designation.[4] The formula expresses the supra-temporality, eternity and deity of God. It is thus used with παντοκράτωρ (1:8; 4:8; 11:17), as also with the ἅγιος, ἅγιος, ἅγιος of Is. 6:3.

---

[5] εἰλικρινής is also found in 1 Cl., 2, 5; 2 Cl., 9, 8, and εἰλικρινῶς in 1 Cl., 32, 1. εἰλικρίνεια does not occur in the post-apost. fathers.

[6] Only exceptionally is εἰλικρίνεια used as a pred. for God in the NT (as opposed to Wnd. on 2 C. 1:12).

εἰμι. On 1. Bss., Zn., Loh., on Rev.; O. Weinreich, ARW, 19 (1916/19), 174 ff.; J. Allo, *L'Apocalypse de S. Jean* (1921), Introd. CXLVIII etc. On 2. Zn., Bau., Schl. on Jn.; W. Lütgert, *Joh. Christologie*[2] (1916), 55 ff.; G. P. Wetter, ThStKr, 88 (1915), 224-228; F. Büchsel, *Joh. u. d. hellen. Synkretismus* (1928), 36 ff. On 3. Deissmann LO, 109-112; Bultmann Trad.[2], 161-176; Bau. J.[3], 119; E. Norden, *Agnostos Theos* (1913), 177-239.

[1] On the forms of εἰμί, cf. Bl.-Debr. § 98 and the bibl. given there; on the use of εἰμί in the NT, and its many variations, cf. Pr.-Bauer, *s.v.* Our present concern is only with specific uses which are of theological or religious significance.

[2] This is shown by its penetration into the LXX through a misunderstanding of the Hb. text. In Ἰερ. 1:6; 14:13; 39 (32):17, the אֲהָהּ of the Mas. is to be understood along the lines of Ex. 3:14 as אֶהְיֶה and is to be interpreted accordingly. Cf. W. Graf Baudissin, *Kyrios* (1929), I, 523, 1; III, 699 and 708. The OT designation of God is used as a name for Christ in syncretism too. It is found on a Gnostic cameo along with ΙΧΘΥΣ and ΙΑΩ (cf. F. J. Dölger, *Ichthys* I [1910], 267 ff.). In the Gk. Church it is still found to-day on pictures of Christ, which have the three letters ΟΩΝ on the three ends of the cross within the halo, and also on representations of the Father and the Holy Spirit. It expresses the eternity of God in the LXX sense, being understood by Hellenistic Judaism and Christianity in this way. [Bertram].

[3] Cf. Leisegang's Indexes, 226 ff.

[4] Bl.-Debr., Suppl. to § 143.

We find similar formulae in Jewish tradition. Ex. r. on 3:14 gives the rendering: "I am who I have been, who I now am, and who I will be in the future." Tg. J I Ex. 3:14 :"I am who I was and will be." Tg. J I Dt. 32:39 : "I am who is and who was, and I am who will be, and there is no other God but me." [5] It is interesting that we have here both the triple and the double formula, as in Rev., and that it is used in interpretation of Ex. 3:14. The ἐρχόμενος of Rev. is thus set into all the greater relief. It shows how vital is the expectation of the end in Rev. Cf. the distinctive ἔρχεται in 1:7, the ἔρχου in 22:17, 20 (followed by the μαραναθά), and the ἔρχομαι in 2:5, 16; 3:11; 22:7, 12, 20. In Rev. the formula assumes that salvation history is pressing to its close (ἕως πότε, 6:10). God is not just non-temporal ; He is the Lord of time.

Among the Gks. a three- or two-tense formula [6] is found as early as Homer to denote eternity (ὅς ἤδη [the seer] τά τ᾽ ἐόντα τά τ᾽ ἐσσόμενα πρό τ᾽ ἐόντα, Hom. Il., 1, 70). [7] We also find it in the pre-Socratics : ἦν ἀεὶ καὶ ἔστιν καὶ ἔσται. [8] It recurs in Plato's description of the αἰών (Tim., 37d ff.), on an Eleusinian inscription of the Augustan period (Ditt. Syll.[3], 1125), as a Zeus formula in an oracular saying of Dodona: Ζεὺς ἦν, Ζεὺς ἐστίν, Ζεὺς ἔσσεται, ὦ μεγάλε Ζεῦ (Paus., X, 12, 5), as an Isis formula from Sais : ἐγώ εἰμι πᾶν τὸ γεγονὸς καὶ ὂν καὶ ἐσόμενον (Plut. Is. et Os., 9 [II, 354c]), and as a term for God in the Hermetic writings : *hoc est, hoc fuit, hoc erit semper Asclepius,* 14 (Corp. Herm., 312, 10). [9] It is unlikely that Rev. took the formula from the Gk. tradition and adapted it. On the other hand, the Gk. formula probably passed into the Jewish tradition and thence into Rev. It is possible that a common oriental source stands behind both the Gk. and Jewish traditions, but we cannot assume this, since the formula is found among the Gks. 600 years before it is used by the Jews.

2. ἐγώ εἰμι or ὅτι ἐγώ εἰμι is a self-designation of Jesus in Jn. 8:58 and 8:24, 28; 13:19. In 8:58 it stands in unmistakable contrast to πρὶν ᾿Αβραὰμ γενέσθαι. This is the only passage in the NT where we have the contrast between εἶναι and γενέσθαι. The verse ascribes to Jesus consciousness of eternity or supra-temporality. [10] To the Son who is equal to the Father (5:18 ff.) there is here ascribed what Scripture attributes to the Father ; cf. the אֲנִי הוּא in Is. 43:10 (LXX : ὅτι ἐγώ εἰμι), in which the whole Godhead of God is discerned, i.e., all that distinguishes Him from false gods. The Jewish conception is fully adequate to explain the strong emphasis here laid on εἶναι.

The context is also Jewish. Jesus is compared with Abraham, and He surpasses the glory of Abraham of which the Jews boast. Jewish, too, is the ἐγώ formulation, which does not denote antithesis to other persons, but is to be explained in terms of the Semitic אֲנִי הוּא. [11] The Messianic interpretation of ἐγώ εἰμι, which Zn. advocates for 8:24, 28; 13:19, [12] disrupts the context of 8:58 and the other passages, does not fit in too well

---

[5] Str.-B., III, 750, 788.

[6] Weinreich, *op. cit.,* 178.

[7] The religious meaning of the formula (the seer has divine knowledge) is worth noting, as also the substitution of πρό τ᾽ ἐόντα for the missing part. "having been"; γενόμενα could not be used, at any rate in Homer, for whom τὰ ὄντα are also γενόμενα.

[8] Cf. the passages in Diels according to Kranz' Index, 192.

[9] The formula seems to be of philosophical origin, and to have come into religious usage only later.

[10] Cf. also in 8:24 the contrast between ἐγώ εἰμι and ἀποθανεῖσθε, in 8:28 the exaltation of Jesus (i.e., His triumph over death) as the pre-condition of faith in His being, and in 13:19 the connection with the death of Christ ; the thought of eternal life is always present in the ἐγώ εἰμι, cf. Lütgert, *op. cit.*

[11] Cf. Bl.-Debr. § 277, 1 and 2.

[12] But not for 8:58, cf. Zn. on 8:24 and Büchsel, *op. cit.,* 37, n. 3.

with 8:24, 28; 13:19, and ignores the allusion to Is. 43:10. The rendering "I am He" is also to be rejected. [13] What is at issue is not so much what Jesus is as the fact that He is. The attempt of G. P. Wetter to explain the ὅτι ἐγώ εἰμι in terms of Hellenistic syncretism is quite wide of the mark. [14]

There are interesting examples of ἐγώ εἰμι in the LXX. It occurs as the subject of a following or preceding finite verb and is a translation of אֲנִי or אָנֹכִי: ἐγώ εἰμι καθίσομαι (Ju. 6:18); ἐγώ εἰμι ἐν γαστρὶ ἔχω (2 Βασ. 11:5). [15] Here it is not used as a divine name, since the reference may be to men, and there is insufficient evidence in popular speech for any such usage. We may thus presume that it is simply an emphatic form of the pers. pronoun. This is shown by the fact that at least once in 2 Βασ. 7:29 we find a par. σὺ εἶ with the finite verb. [16]

3. For ἐγώ εἰμι with following nouns of predication (esp. in Jn.), → ἐγώ 352.

Büchsel

εἰρήνη, εἰρηνεύω, εἰρηνικός,
εἰρηνοποιός, εἰρηνοποιέω

εἰρήνη.

A. The Greek Concept of εἰρήνη.

The basic feature of the Gk. concept of εἰρήνη is that the word does not primarily denote a relationship between several people, [1] or an attitude, [2] but a state, i.e., "time

---

[13] Wetter, op. cit.; Bau. J., ad loc.
[14] Cf. Büchsel, op. cit., 37.
[15] There are some 20 passages, cf. Hatch-Redp., I, 367.
[16] Cf. Thackeray, 55, 10, 30; JThSt, 8 (1907), 272.

ε ἰ ρ ή ν η. H. Fuchs, "Augustin und der antike Friedensgedanke," NPhU, 3 (1926), 39-43; 167-223; E. de Witt Burton, To the Galatians (ICC [1921]), 424-426; E. Lohmeyer, ZNW, 26 (1927), 162; J. Heinemann, Philons gr. u. jüd. Bildung (1932), 414; Joh. W. 1 K. on 1:3. On A: B. Keil, "ΕΙΡΗΝΗ," = Berichte über die Verhandlungen der Königl. Sächsischen Gesellschaft, Phil.-hist. Klasse, 68, 4 (1916); G. Herbig, "Friede," Rektorats-rede, Rostock (1919). On B: W. Caspari, "Vorstellung und Wort 'Friede' im AT," BFTh, 14, 4 (1910); Der biblische Friedensgedanke (1916); W. Eichrodt, "Die Hoffnung des ewigen Friedens im alten Israel," BFTh, 25, 3 (1920). On C and D: J. Hempel, ZDMG, 79 (1925), 51 f.; Schn. Euang., 43; Moore, II, 195; A. Meyer, Das Rätsel des Jakobusbriefes (1930), 106; Loh. Kol., 149, n. 1. On E: A. Titius, Die nt.liche Lehre von der Seligkeit, "Der geschichtlichen Darstellung 2. Abt.: Der Paulinismus unter dem Gesichtspunkt der Seligkeit" (1900), 90 f.; B. Weiss, Die bibl. Theologie des NT⁷ (1903) § 83b; K. Mittring, Heilswirklichkeit bei Paulus (1929), 17, n. 2; O. Zänker, ZSTh, 9 (1931/2), 418; A. M. Brouwer, De Bergrede (1930), 242 f.; most of the comm. have brief notes on the relevant passages, esp. Zn. Lk. on 1:79; Bchm. K. on 1 C. 1:3; Joh. W. on 1 C. 7:15; Haupt Gefbr. on Col. 1:2; Dob. Th. on 1 Th. 5:23; Kl. Mk. on 5:34; Kl. Lk. on 10:6.

[1] For this reason the derivation from the stem ΑΡ with ι reduplication, which is advanced by K. Brugmann, ΕΙΡΗΝΗ, Berichte über die Verhandlungen d. Königl. Sächs. Gesell-schaft d. Wissenschaften, Phil.-hist. Klasse, 68, 3 (1916), 13 ff., does not seem very probable; v. Fuchs, 167; cf. A. Debrunner, GGA, 178 (1916), 740, n. 3; E. Hermann, DLZ, 38 (1917), 483-485; P. Kretschmer, Glotta, 10 (1920), 238 f.; F. Stähelin in ΑΝΤΙΔΩΡΟΝ (Festschrift für J. Wackernagel [1923/4], 151. Cf. A. Debrunner in M. Ebert's Reallexikon der Vor-geschichte, IV, 2 (1926), 526.

[2] Brugmann, 2 f. thinks we have examples of the sense of "peaceful nature" in Hom. Od., 24, 485 f.: τοὶ δ᾽ ἀλλήλους φιλεόντων ὡς τὸ πάρος, πλοῦτος δὲ καὶ εἰρήνη ἅλις ἔστω, and also in Hes. Theog., 901 f., where Eirene, Dike and Eunomia are called daughters of Zeus and Themis, but these instances do not give us adequate proof.

of peace" or "state of peace," originally conceived of purely as an interlude in the everlasting state of war. [3] While the Latin *pax* "in the first instance denotes a reciprocal legal relationship between two parties," [4] εἰρήνη is "primarily no more than the passionately asserted, emotionally felt and palpable opposite of πόλεμος." [5] The juxtaposition in the *carmen saeculare* of Horace (v. 57 ff.) characterises the former : *iam Fides et Pax et Honos Pudorque priscus et neglecta redire Virtus audet ;* [6] the latter is defined in Ps.-Plat. Def., 413a : εἰρήνη ἡσυχία ἀπ' ἔχθρας πολεμικῆς. [7] εἰρήνη is often accompanied by ἡσυχία as an explanatory concept, e.g., Plat. Resp., IX, 575b. Typical of the Gk. concept are also the attributes ascribed to the goddess Eirene in poetry, e.g., ὀλβοδότειρα (dispensing riches), πολύολβος, τιθηνήτειρα (nurse) πολήων, and also the way of depicting her in art, e.g., with the small Pluto child, as in Athens, or with the horn of plenty, the herald's staff or the ears of corn, [8] the Roman Pax in contrast being crowned with the laurel. [9] Εἰρήνη is the state of peace from which flow all blessings for both land and people and which is extolled by Philemon as the supreme good : γάμους, ἑορτάς, συγγενεῖς, παῖδας, φίλους, πλοῦτον, ὑγίειαν, σῖτον, οἶνον, ἡδονήν, αὕτη (sc. εἰρήνη) δίδωσι (Fr. 71 [CAF, II] 496 f.).

The sense of "treaty of peace," and therewith the "conclusion of peace" and "conditions of peace," comes in with the βασιλέως εἰρήνη, the Peace of Antalcidas, and replaces the older expressions σπονδαί, συνθῆκαι καὶ ὅρκοι. The oldest example of the use of εἰρήνη in this new sense is Ditt. Syll.[3], 142, 7 (384/3 B.C.): διαφυλάξεν ... τὴν εἰρήνην καὶ τὴν φιλίαν καὶ τὸς ὅρκος καὶ τὰς οὔσας συνθήκας, ἃς ὤμοσεν..." [10]

The basic concept of the "state of rest" also makes possible the linking of εἰρήνη with the gen., e.g., ἡσυχία (Plat. Leg., I, 628b : εἰρήνη τῆς στάσεως, the end of civil war). εἰρήνη can also denote the opposite of disturbance, e.g., laughing (Plat. Symp., 189a/b : γελωτοποιεῖς μέλλων λέγειν, καὶ φύλακά με τοῦ λόγου ἀναγκάζεις γίγνεσθαι τοῦ σεαυτοῦ, ἐάν τι γελοῖον εἴπῃς, ἐξόν σοι ἐν εἰρήνῃ λέγειν).

Εἰρήνη can also signify a "peaceful attitude" (Plat. Leg., I, 628c : τό γε μὴν ἄριστον οὔτε ὁ πόλεμος οὔτε ἡ στάσις ... εἰρήνη δὲ πρὸς ἀλλήλους ἅμα καὶ φιλοφροσύνη ; Epict. Diss., IV, 5, 24 : οὐχὶ ... κηρύσσεις, ὅτι εἰρήνην ἄγεις πρὸς πάντας ἀνθρώπους). But here, too, it is primarily negative. Thus Isoc., 7, 51 brings together πρὸς ἀλλήλους ἡσυχίαν ἔχειν and πρὸς τοὺς ἄλλους εἰρήνην ἄγειν, and in the Epictetus passage the philosopher is thinking more of the absence of hostile feelings than of the presence of kindly feelings to others. The proper expression for a peaceful disposition is φιλία or ὁμόνοια (Epict. Diss., IV, 5, 35 : ταῦτα τὰ δόγματα ἐν οἰκίᾳ φιλίαν ποιεῖ, ἐν πόλει ὁμόνοιαν, ἐν ἔθνεσιν εἰρήνην. Thus εἰρήνη is seldom used for concord between men.

In accordance with its basic sense it was more adapted to denote the state of mind desired by the Stoics. Yet it is not common in Stoic writings. It occurs in Epict., III, 13, 13 : πάντα εἰρήνης μεστά, πάντα ἀταραξίας, but this is because of the contrast with the imperial εἰρήνη. More common is γαλήνη, which is often found in Marc. Aurel. [11] Cf. Plut. Tranq. An., 19 (II, 477a): οὔτε οἰκία πολυτελὴς οὔτε χρυσίου

---

[3] E. Weiss, *Griech. Privatrecht,* I (1923), 171, 18; Keil, 7 ff.

[4] Fuchs, 40. Nevertheless, the Roman concept of *pax* is present in Epict. Diss., III, 13, 9, where the εἰρήνη of Caesar means security against robbers and pirates.

[5] *Op. cit.,* 39.

[6] For another important example from Velleius, *v.* Fuchs, 191.

[7] So Keil, 5, n. 1.

[8] Examples may be found in O. Waser *s.v. Eirene* in Pauly-W., V (1905), 2128 ff.; G. Wissowa *s.v. Pax* in Roscher, III, 2, 1719 ff.

[9] Fuchs, 201.

[10] As found in Keil.

[11] *V.* Index of the *editio maior* of H. Schenkl (1913).

πλῆθος … εὐδίαν παρέχει βίῳ καὶ γαλήνην τοσαύτην, ὅσην ψυχὴ καθαρεύουσα πραγμάτων καὶ βουλευμάτων πονηρῶν. [12]

Special mention must be made of the εἰρήνη which held sway in the Mediterranean world with the government of Augustus. As in this period we have strong echoes of the ancient longing for redemption, so pacification is achieved by the strong hand of the emperor, so that this is hailed as the golden age, e.g., in Vergil's Fourth Eclogue. If we have here the content of the Gk. εἰρήνη, in everyday reality it implies the legal security of the pax Romana : Epict. Diss., III, 22, 55 : ἄν τίς σε δέρῃ, κραύγαζε στὰς ἐν τῷ μέσῳ· ὦ Καῖσαρ, ἐν τῇ σῇ εἰρήνῃ οἷα πάσχω; ἄγωμεν ἐπὶ τὸν ἀνθύπατον.

Foerster

B. שָׁלוֹם in the OT.

1. Seldom do we find in the OT a word which to the same degree as שָׁלוֹם can bear a common use and yet can also be filled with a concentrated religious content far above the level of the average conception. This does not make its investigation easy. If שָׁלוֹם is a general expression of a very comprehensive nature, this means that there is something imprecise about it in almost every instance. In our attempt at a theological enquiry we must keep, therefore, to the passages where the word is not isolated but where it takes on specific meaning from the context or where it is the culmination of a preceding train of thought. Nor should we leave out of account statements where the thought of peace is central even though the term itself is not used.

We constrict the term שָׁלוֹם if we equate it strictly with "peace." At root it means "well-being," with a strong emphasis on the material side. [13] In meetings or letters well-being is wished to others, and in conversations one asks about their well-being. [14] In prayer the good fortune of the ungodly is called שְׁלוֹם רְשָׁעִים. [15] Here and in many other instances שָׁלוֹם really signifies bodily health [16] or well-being and the related satisfaction. [17] More commonly שָׁלוֹם is referred to a group, e.g., a nation enjoying prosperity. This brings us closer to the thought of peace. Thus Hezekiah took Isaiah's prophecy of doom lightly because he expected peace to last in his generation. [18] In this passage there is a curious linking of שָׁלוֹם with אֱמֶת. The conjunction shows that peace implies stability of relationship. Thus in the well-known passage in Eccl. 3 we have the terse antithesis of שָׁלוֹם and מִלְחָמָה. Yet here, too, there are many cases where שָׁלוֹם means something more fundamental than our "peace," as in the expression דְּרַשׁ שָׁלוֹם, i.e., to be concerned for the שָׁלוֹם, the well-being, of a people. [19] This brings us to the great number of passages in which שָׁלוֹם denotes a relationship rather than a state. Thus there is שָׁלוֹם, i.e., a relationship of friendly alliance between Solomon and Hiram. [20] The re-

---

[12] εἰρήνη is used for the harmony and order of the soul in Okellos, Fr. 2, Harder in NPhU, 1 (1926), 27, 1 f.: δικαιοσύνη … ἁρμονία γάρ ἐστι καὶ εἰράνα τᾶς ὅλας ψυχᾶς μετ᾽ εὐρυθμίας.

[13] Ju. 19:20; 1 S. 16:5; 2 S. 18:28 etc. Cf. also Ezr. 5:7.

[14] Gn. 29:6; 43:27; 2 S. 18:29; 20:9 f.

[15] Ps. 73:3; but cf. Is. 48:22.

[16] Cf. the occasional linking of שָׁלוֹם and רְפָא Jer. 6:14; Is. 57:18 f., also Ps. 38:3.

[17] This is particularly common in expressions like "to go in peace" (Gn. 26:29; Ex. 18:23; Is. 55:12 etc.), "to sleep in peace" (Ps. 4:8), or "to be buried in peace" (Gn. 15:15; Jer. 34:5; 2 K. 22:20).

[18] 2 K. 20:19; cf. 2 S. 17:3; 1 K. 2:5.

[19] Dt. 23:7; Jer. 29:7; 38:4.

[20] 1 K. 5:26; cf. also Ju. 4:17; 1 K. 5:4; Gn. 34:21; 1 Ch. 12:18.

lationship may be that of a people. [21] Those who enter into it are called מַלְאֲכֵי שָׁלוֹם. [22] It may naturally exist between individuals too (Zech. 6:13).

Since the Hebrews sometimes use בְּרִית for this kind of alliance, it is not surprising that שָׁלוֹם occurs when there is reference to a covenant. Indeed, the connection between the two words is so strong that in this context שָׁלוֹם seems to have become a kind of official term. The thought may be that the relationship of שָׁלוֹם is sealed by both parties in a covenant. [23] Conversely, it may be that the covenant inaugurates a relationship of שָׁלוֹם. Ezekiel in particular may be cited in favour of the latter. In two passages he tells us that Yahweh makes a בְּרִית שָׁלוֹם for Israel, and in both cases the context makes it clear that the relationship of שָׁלוֹם is the result (Ez. 34:25; 37:26). It must be said that only rarely among its many possibilities of application does the word refer to so spiritual a matter as here. For in these passages שָׁלוֹם does not mean material well-being, but a relationship of peace dependent on the disposition of those who conclude the covenant. It is not surprising that with this emphasis the word could express the final prophetic insights on the interrelation of God and the people of God. Along with the Ezekiel passages which refer to the בְּרִית שָׁלוֹם that Yahweh grants to His people, we may quote especially Is. 54:10: "My kindness shall not depart from thee, neither shall the covenant of my peace (בְּרִית שְׁלוֹמִי) be removed."

2. שָׁלוֹם as the gift of Yahweh. Naturally the goods and values associated with שָׁלוֹם were always referred in Israel to Yahweh, whether in prayer for them, or in recognition that they are His gift when present. This religious use must not be regarded as a deduction or a later development. On the contrary, if we said above that there is a basic material element in שָׁלוֹם, we must acknowledge that when it is used in its full compass שָׁלוֹם is a religious term. In this respect it is more likely that an original religious significance was to some extent lost in the course of time than the reverse.

Gideon had built an altar and gave it the name יְהֹוָה שָׁלוֹם. [24] If it is impossible to give a strict, syntactical exegesis of this very ancient expression, one might venture to say that in its great pregnancy this confession embraces at root all that the pious tried to say later in many different situations, especially as this finds eloquent expression in the prayers of the OT. Yahweh creates שָׁלוֹם in the heavenly spheres, high above all human affairs (Job 25:2). But He is also the pledge of שָׁלוֹם to man. He blesses the people with שָׁלוֹם. Indeed, it may be said that He wills (חָפֵץ) the prosperity of His servants (Ps. 35:27; cf. 147:14). May David and his house experience שָׁלוֹם! (1 K. 2:33). "Pray for the שָׁלוֹם of Jerusalem" (Ps. 122:6).

The belief that שָׁלוֹם truly comes only from Yahweh, but from Him all-sufficiently, is strikingly expressed in Ps. 85. The author in his prayer hears the oracle: "He will speak peace unto his people ... that glory may dwell in our land. Mercy and truth are met together; righteousness and peace have kissed each other." In this train of thought God's disposition to save His people is regarded as the cause

---

[21] Dt. 20:10 קְרָא לְשָׁלוֹם; cf. Ju. 21:13.

[22] Is. 33:7; in the broader sense of a messenger with news of salvation, Nah. 2:1; Is. 52:7 (מַשְׁמִיעַ שָׁלוֹם).

[23] Jos. 9:15; 1 K. 5:26. In Ob. 7 those who are in league (אַנְשֵׁי בְרִית) are also called אַנְשֵׁי שָׁלוֹם in the parallelism.

[24] Ju. 6:24; we must take יְהֹוָה שָׁלוֹם as a nominal statement, cf. Ex. 17:15 (Caspari, op. cit., 141 ff. takes a different view).

of perfect earthly peace. Here we have a climax in the OT use of the term
שָׁלוֹם. [25] In the exhortations of the Holiness Code we find the promise that God
will give His people שָׁלוֹם in the land (Lv. 26:6). The context shows us quite plainly
that a solid blessing is meant, i.e., peace from enemies and wild beasts. Yet this is
a blessing of salvation in the special sense. It is rest and pacification in the land
of promise, and therefore that which Dt. expresses in the distinctive term
מְנוּחָה. [26] We are thus in the immediate proximity of the prophetic promise of שָׁלוֹם.

3. שָׁלוֹם in the prophetic message. From Micaiah the son of Imlah to Ezekiel
there is a minority of prophets of doom who passionately resist the message of
salvation proclaimed by false prophets. In this conflict, continually renewed through
the centuries, the catchword upon which everything turns is שָׁלוֹם. Indeed, even the
technical term יְנַבֵּא לְשָׁלוֹם appears in this connection (Jer. 28:9). שָׁלוֹם seems to have
been the culminating point of the theology of some prophetic circles, and therefore
the term became the centre of bitter controversy between two parties. The issue
may be seen already in the stand of Micaiah against the prophets of salvation,
though the term itself does not occur (1 K. 22:5 ff.). Micah contends against the
same opponents, accusing them of prophesying for gain. Only so long as it is of
profit to them will they proclaim salvation (Mi. 3:5 ff.). Jeremiah flung himself
most deeply into the struggle and was most hotly resisted by these prophets. In
great affliction he asks Yahweh what will be the fate of those who promise Jerusalem eternal salvation (שָׁלוֹם אֱמֶת, Jer. 14:13). "They have healed also the hurt of
the daughter of my people slightly, saying, Peace, peace; when there is no peace"
(Jer. 6:14). In Jer. 28 we have the story of a dramatic encounter between Jeremiah
and these prophets. The point at issue between Jeremiah and Hananiah is שָׁלוֹם
or רָעָה. Finally, Ezekiel makes the same complaint that the false prophets have led
the people astray, seeing visions of salvation (חֲזוֹן שָׁלוֹם) where there is none (Ez.
13:16).

The problem of false prophets goes much beyond the question of שָׁלוֹם and
cannot be pursued in this context. [27] There can be no doubt, however, that the
שָׁלוֹם which they proclaimed was not a final eschatological peace clothed in mythical
conceptions but real political peace for Israel, i.e., the promise that all the serious
political problems would be solved for the best so that Israel could live in a peace
guaranteed by Yahweh. It seems as though Jeremiah originally shared this view
(Jer. 4:10), but he then came to see that Yahweh had "taken away peace from
this people" (16:5). The ψεῦδος of the false prophets was not that they prophesied
שָׁלוֹם, for Jeremiah and Ezekiel could also do this in other situations. It was rather
that they ignored the sin of the people and therefore could not interpret the
darkening political scene in terms of impending judgment. Jeremiah and Ezekiel for
their part coin the counter-slogan אֵין שָׁלוֹם. [28]

If Jeremiah and Ezekiel brought the battle between שָׁלוֹם and אֵין שָׁלוֹם to its
supreme climax, the defeats of 597 and 586 led to a certain relaxation of tension in
this respect, and the promise of שָׁלוֹם in a new and larger sense became one of the

---

[25] Caspari, op. cit., 161.
[26] On this theologoumenon, cf. G. v. Rad, ZdZ, 11 (1933), 104 ff.
[27] Cf. G. v. Rad, "Die falschen Propheten," ZAW, 60 (1933), 109 ff.
[28] Jer. 6:14; 8:11; 12:12; 30:5; Ez. 13:10, 16.

most important elements in their prophecy. Thus Jeremiah can write to the exiles the wonderful statement that Yahweh has for them thoughts of salvation and not of evil (Jer. 29:11). Here we have the basis of the later prophecies of salvation in Jeremiah. Other nations will tremble at the salvation which Yahweh will bring to Jerusalem.[29] The same theme recurs in Ezekiel's culminating announcement of a covenant of peace which God will make with His people (Ez. 34:25; 37:26 ff.). We do not find the conflict over שָׁלוֹם in the later chapters of Isaiah. Here שָׁלוֹם is no longer a catchword which enables us to see an important aspect of the prophetic position. It is simply one of the full and majestic notes characteristic of this prophecy. If Israel had listened to Yahweh, its שָׁלוֹם would have rolled down like a river and its צְדָקָה like waves of the sea (Is. 48:18). The parallelism here shows us that the term is now given a spiritual sense. Similarly, the blessing of salvation promised to the sons of Jerusalem in Is. 54:13 is associated with that of צְדָקָה. The same conjunction of שָׁלוֹם and צְדָקָה is found in the prophetic depiction of the new city of God: "I will also make thine officers peace, and thine exactors righteousness (צְדָקָה)."[30] We are not to gather from this more than the loftiness of the term שָׁלוֹם. In this poetic prophecy there is a concern to sound the richest possible notes, as we can see again from Is. 66:12, where שָׁלוֹם in a rather more material sense is linked with כָּבוֹד. Here, as in the beautiful cry: "Peace, peace to him that is far off, and to him that is near" (Is. 57:19), peace is a term which expresses a wealth of expectation but which is not to be interpreted in terms of a more exact theologoumenon. It has a certain inner impreciseness, so that the translator who has no such many-sided term at his command is often at a loss to know whether in these passages, since שָׁלוֹם is a gift of God's grace to His restored people, he should use the more concrete "well-being," the more obvious "peace," or the theologically more comprehensive "salvation." In Is. 45:7, of course, the last is the only real option: "I am Yahweh ... I accomplish salvation, and create evil."

4. שָׁלוֹם as an element in eschatological expectation. Expectation of a final state of eternal peace is an element in OT eschatology which finds constant expression in the prophets and other writings. The fact of this widespread and many-sided expectation must be mentioned even though the term שָׁלוֹם is not always found in the relevant passages. When we have prophecy of a restoration of the conditions in Paradise,[31] or promise of international peace under divine direction (Is. 2:2 ff.), or expectation of a humble king in the last age who will bring in a time of peace (Zech. 9:9 f.), even though the word שָׁלוֹם is not used in these central eschatological passages, or is used only alongside many others, as in Zech. 9:10, this should not blind us to the fact that we have here a prophetic proclamation of שָׁלוֹם of the widest possible import. Hence we are not to ascribe any greater significance to passages in which the word is actually found. In the names of the Messianic Child in Is. 9:5 the final שַׂר שָׁלוֹם is no more significant than those which precede. The name tells us that as the One who bears God's commission (שַׂר)[32] the Messiah is

---

[29] Jer. 33:9. The authenticity of the saying is disputed by many commentators.

[30] Is. 60:17. According to Is. 32:17 שָׁלוֹם is the result of צְדָקָה.

[31] Is. 11:1 ff.; Hos. 2:20 ff.; Am. 9:13 ff.

[32] W. Caspari, "Echtheit, Hauptbegriff und Gedankengang der messianischen Weissagung Is. 9:1-6," BFTh, 12, 4 (1908), 11 ff.

the Guarantor and Guardian of peace in the coming Messianic kingdom. In v. 6 this is expressed again in the most important statement that to the salvation associated with the throne of David there shall be no end (וּלְשָׁלוֹם אֵין־קֵץ). One might say that the formula of Micah: "This man is peace (or salvation)," sums up the essence of this whole prophecy. The text, however, is somewhat uncertain. [33]

When we consider the rich possibilities of שָׁלוֹם in the OT we are struck by the negative fact that there is no specific text in which it denotes the specifically spiritual attitude of inward peace. There are, indeed, more passages in which it is used of groups rather than individuals. Lam. 3:17 might be taken as a typical example of the latter usage: "And thou hast removed [34] my soul far off from peace: I forgat prosperity." But even here שָׁלוֹם is not something concealed and inward; it manifests itself in the form of external well-being. In the majority of examples, in which the reference is to a group, the term שָׁלוֹם clearly denotes something which may be seen. When we remember the way in which it is linked with צְדָקָה (→ 177), with מִשְׁפָּט (Zech. 8:16) or with פְּקֻדָּה (Is. 60:17), we are forced to say that in its most common use שָׁלוֹם is an emphatically social concept. [35]

v. Rad

C. εἰρήνη in the LXX.

1. If the main sense of the Gk. word εἰρήνη is a state of rest, the Heb. שָׁלוֹם contains the thought of well-being or salvation. Since, then, the LXX uses εἰρήνη for almost all the שָׁלוֹם passages in the OT, and for these alone (for exceptions → 408), it is natural that the content of the Heb. term should have penetrated into the Gk. [36] The usage fashioned by the LXX not merely exerted an influence on the Greek speaking Christian congregations, but caused the word εἰρήνη to be filled out with the sense of the Neo-Hebrew or Aramaic שָׁלוֹם.

2. Common to both שָׁלוֹם and εἰρήνη is the meaning of peace in contrast to war; εἰρήνη is used for שָׁלוֹם in this sense in Prv. 17:1 (שַׁלְוָה) and Is. 14:30 (בֶּטַח). It signifies the time of peace in Is. 14:30: ἐπὶ εἰρήνης ἀναπαύσονται, or peace between nations in Ju. 4:17: εἰρήνη ἦν ἀνὰ μέσον 'Ιαβεὶν ... καὶ ἀνὰ μέσον οἴκου Χάβερ, or the state of peace in 1 Ch. 22:9: εἰρήνην καὶ ἡσυχίαν δώσω ἐπὶ 'Ισραὴλ ἐν ταῖς ἡμέραις αὐτοῦ. Yet for all the apparent identity there are here, too, differences between the Gk. and the LXX, as may be seen in Zech. 8:12: δείξω εἰρήνην· ἡ ἄμπελος δώσει τὸν καρπὸν αὐτῆς, καὶ ἡ γῆ δώσει τὰ γενήματα αὐτῆς, καὶ ὁ οὐρανὸς δώσει τὴν δρόσον αὐτοῦ, where fruitfulness is not a consequence of peace as in the Gk., but is rather the content of divine εἰρήνη. It may be that originally the question of the reason for the coming of someone (ἦ εἰρήνη) was the question of warlike or peaceful intent, as in 4 Βασ. 9:17 ff., yet when Bathsheba receives Adonijah with the words

---

[33] Mi. 5:5. The statement does not fit into the metre, and in any case we cannot be sure whether the demonstr. pronoun refers to what precedes (the Messiah) or what follows (His saving work).

[34] Read hoph וַתִּזְנַח.

[35] Caspari, op. cit., 54.

[36] J. Wackernagel, *Indogerm. Forschungen,* 31 (1912 f.), 263, expresses the opinion that the LXX often "takes a Gk. word whose function is partly co-extensive with the use of the Heb. and uses it to render the Heb. in its other senses, so that many Gk. words are given meanings which are otherwise alien and which they would never have come to have of themselves."

εἰρήνη ἡ εἴσοδός σου; (3 Βασ. 2:13) she is really asking whether his coming means good. In the LXX εἰρήνη does not seem to mean concord instead of personal strife and hatred, [37] nor is it used in the sense of "making peace" or "reconciling." Zech. 8:10 : εἰρήνη ἀπὸ τῆς θλίψεως, is good Gk., even including the prep., which is also found in Epict. Diss., III, 13, 10.

If in these passages the Gk. word εἰρήνη necessarily takes on a broader sense for readers of the LXX, this is even more true in the great number of places where שָׁלוֹם has nothing to do with war but is used in the general sense of well-being in contrast to evil in every possible form. We have first to consider the many passages in which εἰρήνη means the prosperity or salvation of man. This may be in the form of an introductory greeting (εἰρήνη σοι, Ju. 6:23), perhaps in a letter (εἰρήνη ὑμῖν πληθυνθείη, Da. 3:98). It may be in the form of a farewell (πορεύεσθε ἐν εἰρήνῃ, Ju. 18:6; but more commonly ... εἰς εἰρήνην, 1 Βασ. 20:42). It may be an enquiry as to the welfare of someone (εἰρήνη, 2 Βασ. 18:29). It may be reference to a greeting (ἐρωτᾶν τὰ εἰς εἰρήνην, 1 Βασ. 10:4, or simply ἐρωτᾶν εἰς εἰρήνην, Ju. 18:15). It may be a matter of going or returning μετ' εἰρήνης (Gn. 26:29) or ἐν εἰρήνῃ (2 Βασ. 15:27). It may be that the righteous is tempted by seeing the εἰρήνην ἁμαρτωλῶν (ψ 72:3). It may be with reference to the εἰρήνη which the physician brings on the earth (Sir. 38:8). But always the reader of the LXX is given the impression that εἰρήνη has a positive content, that it does not merely mean rest, that it denotes the "whole" state of man which cannot be overthrown by any violence or misfortune. Nowhere is this seen more clearly than in the common expression "to die" and "to be buried" ἐν εἰρήνῃ ('Ιερ. 41:5) or μετ' εἰρήνης (Gn. 15:15), which signifies the opposite of suffering violence, cf. 3 Βασ. 2:6 : σὺ (read οὐ) κατάξεις τὴν πολιὰν αὐτοῦ ἐν εἰρήνῃ εἰς ᾅδου. Also worth noting is Is. 29:24, where, even though the Heb. does not have שָׁלוֹם, we read : αἱ γλῶσσαι αἱ ψελλίζουσαι μαθήσονται λαλεῖν εἰρήνην, and from the context this can hardly mean anything but that they will learn to speak correctly. So common is the use of εἰρήνη for prospering that David can not only ask εἰς εἰρήνην 'Ιωὰβ καὶ εἰς εἰρήνην τοῦ λαοῦ but also εἰς εἰρήνην τοῦ πολέμου (2 Βασ. 11:7), and so firmly established is εἰρήνη as a greeting that it can be shortened : κατέβημεν εἰς εἰρήνην τῶν υἱῶν τοῦ βασιλέως, i.e., "to greet" (4 Βασ. 10:13). It can thus become a cry of salvation (1 Ch. 12:18). [38]

In addition to external prosperity εἰρήνη can denote the total well-being of man, as in ψ 34:27: ἀγαλλιάσαιντο καὶ εὐφρανθείησαν οἱ θέλοντες τὴν δικαιοσύνην μου καὶ εἰπάτωσαν διὰ παντός· Μεγαλυνθείη ὁ κύριος, οἱ θέλοντες τὴν εἰρήνην τοῦ δούλου αὐτοῦ. In ψ 121:8 again we read : ἐλάλουν δὲ εἰρήνην περὶ σοῦ, i.e., on Jerusalem, for which the author has already wished εἰρήνη and εὐθηνία. In other words, the term easily moves from the sense of concrete prosperity to the wider sense of good. Thus in Prv. 3:17, along with αἱ ὁδοὶ αὐτῆς (sc. of wisdom) ὁδοὶ καλαί, we have also πάντες οἱ τρίβοι αὐτῆς ἐν εἰρήνῃ. How far εἰρήνη in this sense can differ from peace more strictly speaking may be seen in 'Ιερ. 45:4, where the war party says to the prophet, who is advising the conclusion of peace : ὁ ἄνθρωπος οὗτος οὐ χρησιμολογεῖ εἰρήνην τῷ λαῷ τούτῳ ἀλλ' ἢ πονηρά, i.e., he is not giving good advice. The term is broadened yet again in the LXX to denote ethical good, e.g., ψ 33:14 : ἔκκλινον ἀπὸ κακοῦ καὶ ποίησον ἀγαθόν, ζήτησον εἰρήνην καὶ δίωξον αὐτήν, and cf. Zech. 8:19; Mal. 2:6; Prv. 12:20; Is. 26:3.

---

[37] The adj. εἰρηνικός is certainly used in this sense (→ 418), and it is worth noting that in almost all the passages where שָׁלוֹם means concord between men εἰρηνικός is used, e.g., 'Ιερ. 45:22; Ob. 7; ψ 34:20; Gn. 37:4; Dt. 2:26; Zech. 6:13, and the free rendering of Jer. 20:10. ψ 40:9 is an exception.
[38] According to the context, the greeting has by oriental custom the actual meaning and content of recognition or homage, e.g., 1 Βασ. 30:21; 2 Βασ. 8:10; 1 Ch. 18:10; cf. also ψ 121:6 (→ 412).

3. This leads on quite naturally to the use of εἰρήνη for the good which comes from God, both in this age and in the age of salvation. It is characteristic of OT piety that the term can signify this divinely given good in any sphere of life. We have the general statement in Is. 45:7: ἐγὼ ... ὁ ποιῶν εἰρήνην καὶ κτίζων κακά, which includes everything from the blessing of the land acc. to Lv. 26:3-6 : ἐὰν τοῖς προστάγμασίν μου πορεύησθε ... δώσω εἰρήνην ἐν τῇ γῇ ὑμῶν ... καὶ ἀπολῶ θηρία πονηρὰ ἐκ τῆς γῆς ὑμῶν, up to the blessing of Nu. 6:26 : ἐπάραι Κύριος τὸ πρόσωπον αὐτοῦ ἐπὶ σὲ καὶ δῴη σοι εἰρήνην. While it is often impossible to give the exact content of εἰρήνη, it is always what is good for man, that wherein his well-being or salvation lies : Jer. 36:11: λογιοῦμαι ἐφ' ὑμᾶς λογισμὸν εἰρήνης καὶ οὐ κακά. The covenant of peace with Phinehas (Nu. 25:12; Sir. 45:24), with Levi (Mal. 2:5) and with David (Ez. 34:25; 37:26) is a covenant of salvation. Thus in ψ 118:165 the great peace of those who love the Law is contrasted with the σκάνδαλον which will not affect them. Peace here brings inner salvation and not destruction. Thus in Sir. 1:18 εἰρήνη, which is nourished by the fear of God, is linked with ὑγίεια ἰάσεως (cf. Is. 9:7[6]). When God glorifies Himself, it means peace, i.e., salvation, εἰρήνη and σωτήριον being linked in ψ 84:8 and 9. This salvation is explicitly called God's salvation in Jer. 16:5. In these passages εἰρήνη does not mean a state of inner peace. Lam. 3:17: ἀπώσατο ἐξ εἰρήνης ψυχήν μου, must be interpreted in terms of the par. ἐπελαθόμην ἀγαθά.

4. As regards the constancy of the rendering of שָׁלוֹם by εἰρήνη, we should note that other terms are selected in a number of passages. These are almost exclusively concerned with external welfare, with greetings, or with coming and going. Attempts have been made to find alternatives more in keeping with Gk. usage, esp. in Gn., e.g., coming and going μετὰ σωτηρίας, Gn. 26:31 ('ΑΣΘ: ἐν εἰρήνῃ); 28:21 ('ΑΣ: ἐν εἰρήνῃ) etc.; and perhaps Gn. 41:16 (σωτήριον, Σ: εἰρήνη); or the use of ὑγιαίνειν, ὑγιής in enquiry as to welfare in Gn. 29:6; 37:14 ('ΑΣ: εἰρήνη); Jos. 10:21; or the greeting in Gn. 43:27: πῶς ἔχετε; or the rendering of שָׁאַל לְשָׁלוֹם by ἀσπάζεσθαι in Ex. 18:7 (cf. 1 Βασ. 25:5 LXX, vl. and Σ). In Gn. 43:23 we have the greeting ἵλεως ὑμῖν ('ΑΣ: εἰρήνη), and Jer. 20:10, instead of the Hebraic ἄνθρωπος τῆς εἰρήνης μου, has ἄνδρες φίλοι αὐτοῦ. Worth noting are Is. 48:22 ('ΑΣΘ: εἰρήνη) and 57:21: οὐκ ἔστιν χαίρειν τοῖς ἀσεβέσιν. Εὐθηνέω occurs for שָׁלוֹם in Job 21:9, and χαρά in Is. 55:12 ('ΑΣΘ: εἰρήνη). This means that the use of εἰρήνη is constant only when it denotes the prosperity which comes to man from God.

In some cases εἰρήνη is used for other words besides שָׁלוֹם: for שֶׁקֶט in 1 Ch. 4:40; for בֶּטַח in Job 11:18 (?); Prv. 3:23; Is. 14:30; Ez. 34:27; 38:8, 11, 14; 39:6, 26; for שַׁלְוָה in Prv. 17:1; Hos. 2:18 Σ. Sometimes there is misreading of the Mas., as in 2 Βασ. 3:24; 2 Ἐσδρ. 4:16; Mi. 2:8; Is. 32:4; (45:24 א*;) Ez. 34:29; Prv. 8:18 'Α.

D. שָׁלוֹם in Rabbinic Writings.

There is an extended use of שָׁלוֹם in Rabbinic literature. We first find the common OT sense of "to greet" in שָׁאַל בְּשָׁלוֹם, pSheq, 2 (Str.-B., I, 382d), also used of dumb greetings by signs, Gn. r., 5 on 1:9, cf. also נָתַן שָׁלוֹם, bBer., 14; Aram. שְׁלָמָא יְהַב, Lam. r. on 1:1. For answering a greeting we have [שָׁלוֹם] הֵשִׁיב, Ber., 2, 1. The Aram. epistolary salutation is שְׁלָמְכוֹן יִסְגֵּא, T. Sanh., 2, 6, [39] or simply (אֵ)שְׁלָם ל, [40] though there are also formulae like רַחֲמָא וּשְׁלָמָא, S. Bar., 78, 2. The oral greeting שָׁלוֹם עֲלָיִךְ occurs in pBer., 2, 4b, 27 (Str.-B., I, 383h), and also ל in bGit., 62a (Str.-B., I, 384o). Customary fare-

---

[39] G. Dalman, Aramäische Dialektproben (1896), 3. On the Rabb. greeting, cf. Str.-B., I, 380-385; II, 584 f.; J. Friedmann, Der gesellschaftliche Verkehr u. die Umgangsformen in talmudischer Zeit (Diss. Würzburg, 1914), 27-38.
[40] bSanh., 96a, Str.-B., II, 94.

wells are לך לשלום and לך בשלום or זיל בשלום. [41] In the Rabbis, too, שָׁלוֹם means well-being. Thus in pBer., 60 it is said that from the 6th to the 9th month of pregnancy there is petition that the child will come out בשלום, and there is also reference to לשלום in coming and going, i.e., to protection from robbers. In Tanch. משפטים, 99a (Str.-B., I, 782) we have the contrast "to go mad" and "to remain at peace." The sense of rest occurs in Lv. r., 5, 1 on 4:3 (שלום מפחד). שָׁלוֹם is also found on Jewish graves in the sense of well-being or salvation. [42]

Like the OT, the Rabbis use שָׁלוֹם for the gift of God to His people. In the Babylonian prayer of 18 petitions, which seek God's blessing on His people, the final petition concludes as follows: ברוך אתה יי המברך את־עמו ישראל בשלום; peace is the portion of the righteous. [43] Here שָׁלוֹם is a par. of בְּרָכָה, [44] and, as in the OT, it sums up the blessings of the Messianic period. Is. 52:7 is usually referred to this, [45] and one of the explanations of the final clause of the Aaronic blessing is that it refers to the peace of the dominion of the house of David. [46] On the other hand, the idea of peace in the Messianic age comes to be limited to concord in Israel, and this shows a strong influence of the new usage which developed after the OT period.

For among the Rabbis שָׁלוֹם is also used for peace as opposed to strife between individuals and not merely nations. Thus we have frequent and emphatic reference to the making of peace (עשה שלום, also הביא ש״) between men. According to Pea., 1, 1 this is one of the things whose fruits are enjoyed already. For Hillel Aaron was a model of one who pursued peace (רדף), Ab., 1, 12. [47] Even though the Gentiles or Israel are guilty of idolatry, so long as they are at peace Satan cannot touch them, S. Nu., 42 on 6:26 (Bar), and in the same great chapter it is explained how even Scripture contradicts itself to maintain peace between men (cf. also Slav. En. 52:11-13). One might almost say that the role which peacemaking assumes among the Rabbis comes nearest to the NT concept of love and takes the place in later Judaism which the requirement of love occupies in the NT. There is, of course, a restriction to the negative side. It is not a matter of seeking the שָׁלוֹם or salvation of one's neighbour, but of seeking שָׁלוֹם in the sense of the end of strife. Perhaps some part was played in this development by the idea that discord was holding up the coming of the Messiah. Thus acc. to Ed. 8:7 Elijah must first establish peace in the world. Nevertheless, the Rabbinic statements evince a strong persuasion that envy, strife and discord are contrary to God's will. On this view the very continuation of the world — and for this there are Gk. par. [48] — depends

---

[41] Acc. to bMQ, 29a לך לשלום is customary in life and לך בשלום at the grave. But acc. to Schl. Lk. on 2:29 this is an overfine distinction not known in Jm. 2:16.

[42] E. Schürer, *Die Gemeindeverfassung der Juden in Rom* (1879), Inscr. No. 31; P. G. Orfali in *Rev. Bibl.*, 32 (1923), 258; H. W. Beyer and H. Lietzmann, *Die jüdische Katakombe der Villa Torlonia in Rom* (1930), 31, No. 18; 37, No. 46. Cf. also G. Bertram, *Crozer Quart.*, 10 (1933), 264. From the Jewish inscr. the wishing of peace passed into early Christian inscr., C. M. Kaufmann, *Die sepulkralen Jenseitsdenkmäler der Antike u. des Urchristentums* (1900), 41 ff.

[43] S. Nu., 42 on 6:26. For further examples of peace as God's gift, v. H. Windisch, ZNW, 24 (1925), 245 f.

[44] J. Hempel, ZDMG, 79 (1925), 51 f. with ref. to bChag, 12b: In the seventh heaven (ערבות) are the treasures of life, peace and blessing: גנזי חיים וגנזי שלום וגנזי ברכה, and Ukzin, 3, 12.

[45] Str.-B., III, 282 f.

[46] S. Nu., 42 on 6:26; cf. also Pesikt., 12 (Schl. J. on 6:45) and Tanch. וישב, 7, 180 (Schlatter). Here we can see the narrowing of the Messianic שָׁלוֹם concept mentioned in the text.

[47] For further examples, cf. Str.-B., I, 217.

[48] Fuchs, 101 ff.

on peace (Ab., 1, 18), though there is also reference, of course, to discord in the "upper family." [49]

This leads to a use of שָׁלוֹם which we do not find in the OT, namely, for the relationship between God and man. Damasc. begins (1, 2) with the fact that God is in conflict (רִיב) with all flesh. This conflict prevails until the making of the tabernacle, which brings peace. [50] Sins like idolatry create enmity between God and Israel, [51] but the stones of the altar cast (מְטִילוֹת) peace between them. [52] Peace and strife between man and God involve a reciprocal relationship in which man is active both positively and negatively.

E. εἰρήνη in the Pseudepigrapha, Josephus and Philo.

In the pseudepigrapha we need consider only the religious and ethical usage. In the Test. XII, as in the imagery of Enoch, we meet with the angel of peace, [53] who according to Test. D. 6:2 is μεσίτης θεοῦ καὶ ἀνθρώπων and ἐπὶ τῆς εἰρήνης τοῦ 'Ισραὴλ κατέναντι τῆς βασιλείας τοῦ θεοῦ στήσεται. Here, as in Test. L. 18:4 and D. 5:9, 11, εἰρήνη means the salvation displayed in the cessation of war (Test. Jud. 22:1 f.), though this does not exhaust it. It is important, however, that in the Test. XII and esp. in Eth. En. its opposite is not the strife between God and Israel or humanity, as in the Rabbis, but the judgment of God. We thus read that for the ungodly there will be οὐκ ἔλεος ... καὶ εἰρήνη (Eth. En. 5:5), and for the fallen guardians of heaven οὐκ εἰρήνη οὔτε ἄφεσις (12:5), while peace is promised to the righteous. For the sake of clarity we should adduce Eth. En. 1:7 f., where, after the announcing of natural catastrophes, we read: πάντα ὅσα ἐστὶν ἐπὶ γῆς ἀπολεῖται, καὶ κρίσις ἔσται κατὰ πάντων· καὶ μετὰ τῶν δικαίων τὴν εἰρήνην ποιήσει, καὶ ἐπὶ τοὺς ἐκλεκτοὺς ἔσται συντήρησις καὶ εἰρήνη, καὶ ἐπ' αὐτοὺς γενήσεται ἔλεος, καὶ ἔσονται πάντες τοῦ θεοῦ καὶ τὴν εὐδοκίαν δώσει αὐτοῖς καὶ πάντας εὐλογήσει καὶ πάντων ἀντιλήμψεται· καὶ βοηθήσει ἡμῖν, καὶ φανήσεται αὐτοῖς φῶς καὶ ποιήσει ἐπ' αὐτοὺς εἰρήνην. Here peace is the non-eruption of judgment, and it is thus linked with pardon (συντήρησις) and with the mercy of the judge (ἔλεος). It can also be linked with φῶς, however, and this means that it is not merely negative, but can also signify salvation. Coupled with this traditional sense of salvation we thus have the meaning "left in peace," as in Eth. En. 5:6: καὶ ἔσται αὐτοῖς (sc. τοῖς ἀναμαρτήτοις) λύσις ἁμαρτιῶν καὶ πᾶν ἔλεος καὶ εἰρήνη καὶ ἐπιείκεια.

Like שָׁלוֹם in the Rabbis, εἰρήνη in the pseudepigrapha can mean peace or concord between men, as in Test. G. 6:3: ἐάν τις ἁμαρτήσει εἰς σέ, εἰπὲ αὐτῷ εἰρήνην.

Josephus follows the OT and Rabbinic usage. In Ant. 1, 179; 8, 405 μετὰ εἰρήνης means prosperous, and in Bell., 2, 135 (the Essenes are εἰρήνης ὑπουργοί) εἰρήνη means concord. There are Hebrew and Greek par. when in Ant., 6, 211 Josephus speaks of the εἰρήνη ἀπ' αὐτῶν, sc. τῶν δαιμονίων, and there are Gk. par. for the linking of εἰρήνη and εὐνομία in Ant., 11, 216. [54]

Both linguistically and materially Philo stands in the Gk. tradition. It is typical of him that in his usage εἰρήνη means both political peace [55] and also the peace of inner

---

[49] For example, cf. Dib. Gefbr. on Col. 1:20; also S. Nu., 42 on 6:26. On this whole subject, v. H. Windisch, ZNW, 24 (1925), 243 and Str.-B., I, 215 ff.

[50] Tanch. Buber נשא § 25; Str.-B., III, 592.

[51] Lv. r., 7 on 6:2; Str.-B., III, 240 f.

[52] M. Ex., 29 = 20, 25 = TBQ, 7, 7; Str.-B., I, 215; cf. also III, 217 f.

[53] C. Kaplan, *Anglican Theol. Review,* 13 (1931), 306-313.

[54] Fuchs, 170.

[55] Heinemann, 413 ff.

rest which, in contrast to the conflict of desire, belongs to God alone [56] and is to be sought only from Him. [57] Thus εἰρήνη is again a mainly negative concept, as in the Gk. use, in Ebr., 97: τὰ περὶ ἡμᾶς τοτὲ μὲν ἠρεμεῖ, τοτὲ δὲ ὁρμαῖς ... χρῆται· καὶ ἔστιν ἡ μὲν ἡσυχία τούτων εἰρήνη βαθεῖα, τὰ δὲ ἐναντία πόλεμος ἄσπονδος. Inward and outward war and peace belong together. Inward war is the worst, [58] and it is the source of all evil, Jos., 57: εἰ δὲ τὰ ἐξ ἀκρασίας στάσεις ἐμφύλιοι καὶ πόλεμοι καὶ κακὰ ἐπὶ κακοῖς ἀμύθητα, δῆλον ὅτι τὰ ἐκ σωφροσύνης εὐστάθεια καὶ εἰρήνη καὶ τελείων κτῆσις ἀγαθῶν καὶ ἀπόλαυσις.

Like Philo, and under the same influence of Gk. philosophy, the Church fathers, too, think of εἰρήνη as the opp. to ἐμφύλιος πόλεμος, [59] as in Ep. Ar., 273 : ἐπηρώτα ... πῶς ἂν κατὰ ψυχὴν καὶ ἐν τοῖς πολέμοις εἰρηνικῶς ἔχοι.

F. εἰρήνη in the NT.

In the NT the meaning of εἰρήνη is much the same as that of the Rabbinic שׁלוֹם. This may be seen first in its use in greetings and similar expressions, where it has the sense of well-being or salvation. We thus have ὕπαγε or πορεύου εἰς εἰρήνην in Mk. 5:34 and par.; Lk. 7:50, and the ὑπάγετε ἐν εἰρήνῃ of Jm. 2:16, as a farewell, and εἰρήνη with the dat. as a greeting on arrival in Lk. 10:5; (24:36;) Jn. 20:19, 21, 26, a translation of the greeting then current in Palestine. In Ac. 16:36 Luke ascribes the greeting πορεύεσθε ἐν εἰρήνῃ to the Roman keeper of the prison, an anachronism which he must have picked up from the LXX and which he no doubt thinks proper on the lips of a new convert. Paul, too, constantly uses the salutation χάρις ὑμῖν καὶ εἰρήνη [60] in his epistles, and we have the same formula in Rev. 1:4. This follows the Hebrew and Aramaic greeting. ἔλεος is added in 1 and 2 Tm., 2 Jn. and Jd. and πληθυνθείη is linked with it in 1 and 2 Pt., Jd., and these bring it even closer to attested Jewish formulae (→ 408 f.). εἰρήνη also occurs sometimes in the closing greeting, 1 Pt. 5:14; 3 Jn. 15; cf. Gl. 6:16. The Gk. form χαίρειν is also found in Ac. 15:23; 23:26; Jm. 1:1; cf. 2 Jn. 10. The final greeting ἔρρωσθε occurs only in Ac. 15:29 (23:30; ἔρρωσο or ἔρρωσθε as vl.). We may compare Ac. 15:33 : ἀπελύθησαν μετ' εἰρήνης, and 1 C. 16:11: προπέμψατε δὲ αὐτὸν ἐν εἰρήνῃ, with the OT expressions "to go ἐν εἰρήνῃ, μετ' εἰρήνης." [61] The saying of Simeon in Lk. 2:29 : νῦν ἀπολύεις τὸν δοῦλόν σου ... ἐν εἰρήνῃ, has the same formal sense. The wider use of εἰρήνη in the sense of security may be seen in Lk. 11:21: ἐν εἰρήνῃ ἐστὶν τὰ ὑπάρχοντα αὐτοῦ (cf. also 1 Th. 5:3). εἰρήνη is the opp. of disorder in 1 C. 14:33 (→ 412) and of persecution in Ac. 14:2 D : ὁ δὲ κύριος ἔδωκεν ταχὺ εἰρήνην.

That it is not the Gk. sense which predominates in the NT is particularly plain when we consider that the principal meaning is salvation in a deeper sense. We are also brought into the Rabbinic sphere by its frequent use for concord between men (Ac. 7:26; Gl. 5:22; Eph. 4:3; Jm. 3:18; cf. 1 Pt. 3:11) and by its link with the word → διώκειν = רדף (→ 409) (R. 14:19; Hb. 12:14; cf. 1 Pt. 3:11). In the NT, as in Rabb. literature,

---

[56] Som., II, 253 : θεὸς μόνος ἡ ἀψευδεστάτη καὶ πρὸς ἀλήθειάν ἐστιν εἰρήνη, ἡ δὲ γενετὴ καὶ φθαρτὴ οὐσία πᾶσα συνεχὴς πόλεμος.

[57] Vit. Mos., I, 304 : φθάνει δὲ χρησμοῖς δωρησάμενος ὁ θεὸς Φινεεεῖ τὸ μέγιστον ἀγαθόν, εἰρήνην, ὃ μηδεὶς ἱκανὸς ἀνθρώπων παρασχεῖν.

[58] Op. Mund., 81.

[59] For examples, cf. Fuchs, 214 ff.

[60] In addition to the comm. v. J. C. T. Otto, Jbcher. f. deutsche Theologie, 12 (1867), 678-697; P. Wendland, Die urchr. Literaturformen (1912), 412 f.; E. v. Dobschütz, Der Ap. Pls., I (1926), 30 f.; J. Wobbe, Der Charisgedanke bei Pls. (1932), 44 f.; O. Roller, Das Formular der paul. Briefe (1933), 61 f. Otto notes the very small influence of the NT greeting.

[61] Joh. W. 1 K., ad loc. suggests an escort in peace and harmony.

there is reference to peace with God. In the parables and narratives εἰρήνη, like שָׁלוֹם,
is used for peace as opposed to war, e.g., Ac. 12:20; 24:2 (state of peace); Mt. 10:34;
Rev. 5:4.

Paul, too, uses εἰρήνη in a sense which undoubtedly approximates to the rarer Gk.
sense of peace of soul, esp. in R. 15:13.

The OT and later Jewish background may also be seen in expressions like εἰρήνην
ποιεῖν, "to make peace," Jm. 3:18 (→ 408), εἰρήνην βαλεῖν = הִטִּיל, Mt. 10:34 (→ 409,
Lk. δοῦναι), εἰρήνην διδόναι = "to give a greeting of peace," Jn. 14:27. [62] There is
perhaps a specific Aramaism in Lk. 14:32, where the king who feels inferior πρεσβείαν
ἀποστείλας ἐρωτᾷ τὰ πρὸς εἰρήνην. This does not mean that he asks for conditions
of peace. It means that he greets the other. In the context, however, this carries the
implication of homage and therefore of unconditional submission. [63]

As regards the material use of the term in the NT three conceptions call for
notice : a. peace as a feeling of peace and rest ; [64] b. peace as a state of reconciliation with God ; [65] and c. peace as the salvation of the whole man in an ultimate
eschatological sense. [66] All three possibilities are present, but the last is the basis.
This confirms the link with OT and Rabbinic usage.

1. εἰρήνη in its widest sense as the normal state of all things.

In 1 C. 14:33 Paul opposes to the confusion caused by prophecy at Corinth the
consideration : οὐ γάρ ἐστιν ἀκαταστασίας ὁ θεὸς ἀλλὰ εἰρήνης. [67] In contrast
to ἀκαταστασία, εἰρήνη is the normal state of things. We need not think of this
in narrowly ethical terms, [68] but along the lines of the Rabbinic use of שָׁלוֹם. But the
fact that in this sense εἰρήνη is linked expressly and emphatically with God
displays the connexion between the inward and the outward noticeable elsewhere
in the NT. The "healthy" or normal state which corresponds to the will of God
is not to be limited to the soul or even to man. It extends basically to the universe
as a whole.

2. εἰρήνη as the eschatological salvation of the whole man.

a. Our starting-point is the OT word שָׁלוֹם in the sense of the salvation which
comes from God, especially the eschatological salvation. Thus we read of the
expected salvation in the song of Zacharias in Lk. 1:79 : προπορεύσῃ γὰρ ἐνώ-

---

[62] → 408 and Schl. J. on 14:27.

[63] We should read ἐρωτᾷ εἰς or πρὸς εἰρήνην, which brings out better the basic Heb.
formula. Cf. H. St. J. Thackeray, JThSt., 14 (1912/13), 389-399, → n. 38.

[64] Cf. Joh. W. 1 K. on 1:3. The Jewish greeting is linked by Paul with "an equable
temperament, so that εἰρήνη is properly the basic religious disposition which the Christian
owes to His God and Lord."

[65] Bchm. K. on I, 7:15 : "εἰρήνη denotes the state of peace which is granted to the
believer when his relationship to God is freed from all tension." Joh. W. 1 K. also thinks
that the reference here is to the harmonious and felicitous disposition of the soul which is
impossible in the misalliance to which Paul refers.

[66] Mostly without express indication of the eschatological element, e.g., Ew. Gefbr. on
Eph. 1:2 : "εἰρήνη is the state of peaceful being unclouded by any tension," the overcoming of a sense of guilt not being the real concern in the desire for εἰρήνη. Cf. Wbg. Pt.
on II, 3:14 (→ 414).

[67] A. Harnack's excision of ὁ θεός (with Marcion and Tertullian), SAB, 1919, 1, 527 ff.,
is hardly necessary. The context plainly shows that Paul does not regard it as necessary to
say that the spirits of the prophets are spirits from the Spirit of God.

[68] Joh. W., ad loc.

πιον κυρίου ... τοῦ κατευθῦναι τοὺς πόδας ἡμῶν εἰς ὁδὸν εἰρήνης.[69] The song of the angels in Lk. 2:14 : δόξα ἐν ὑψίστοις θεῷ καὶ ἐπὶ γῆς εἰρήνη ἐν ἀνθρώποις εὐδοκίας,[70] is not to be taken as a wish, especially in its second part.[71] The reference is not so much to peace among men or with God, but to the salvation which has come to earth. The same is true of Lk. 19:42 : εἰ ἔγνως ἐν τῇ ἡμέρᾳ ταύτῃ καὶ σὺ τὰ πρὸς εἰρήνην,[72] i.e., to thy salvation. The remarkable saying in Lk. 19:38b : ἐν οὐρανῷ εἰρήνη καὶ δόξα ἐν ὑψίστοις, must be taken in the same sense. The closest parallels are Rev. 12:10 : ἄρτι ἐγένετο ἡ σωτηρία ... τοῦ θεοῦ ἡμῶν, and Rev. 19:1: ἡ σωτηρία καὶ ἡ δόξα καὶ ἡ δύναμις τοῦ θεοῦ ἡμῶν, and the meaning is that εἰρήνη (the same as σωτηρία in Rev.) is present and is fashioned in heaven.[73]

Salvation has come as a historical event through Jesus Christ. This is pictured in Rev. 12 and it is intimated in Hb. 13:20 by the linking of ὁ θεὸς τῆς εἰρήνης and ὁ ἀναγαγὼν ἐκ νεκρῶν τὸν ποιμένα τῶν προβάτων τὸν μέγαν. Hb. 7:2 emphasises that Melchisedec as the type of Christ is βασιλεὺς Σαλήμ, ὅ ἐστιν βασιλεὺς εἰρήνης.[74] This salvation is proclaimed in the εὐαγγέλιον τῆς εἰρήνης (Eph. 6:15, cf. Ac. 10:36; Eph. 2:17).[75] It is the salvation of Christ (Jn. 14:27). If Jesus here borrows from the Jewish greeting,[76] this is in itself a warning not to think in terms of inner peace of soul (B. Weiss). The world wishes only שָׁלוֹם; Christ gives the salvation secured by Him. Again in Jn. 16:33 the opposite of εἰρήνη as well-being or security is not anxiety but affliction (θλῖψις).

This was the note heard by the disciples when Jesus used the customary farewell. It is for this reason that it is recorded in the Gospels in Mk. 5:34 par.; Lk. 7:50. Jesus Himself gave the greeting of peace particular significance on the lips of the disciples. The greeting which they give on entering a house is not a wish. It is a gift which is either received or rejected as such. So real is this that if rejected it returns to the disciples, Lk. 10:5 f.; Mt. 10:13.[77] Paul maintained and deepened the usual Jewish greeting along the same lines.[78]

We are admonished to seek this salvation in Hb. 12:14 : εἰρήνην διώκετε μετὰ πάντων, καὶ τὸν ἁγιασμόν, οὗ χωρὶς οὐδεὶς ὄψεται τὸν κύριον. In this context

---

[69] A. Plummer, St. Luke⁴ (ICC, ad loc.) relates this to the peace between God and His people, and Dausch Synpt., ad loc. to true felicity, but we are really to construe it with B. Weiss, Die Ev. des Marcus u. Lucas (1901) and Kl. Lk., ad loc. as Messianic salvation.

[70] It is now generally recognised that the true reading is εὐδοκίας, cf. J. Jeremias, ZNW, 28 (1929), 13 ff.

[71] Cf. also Rev. 12:10 and 19:1 f.: That σωτηρία and δόξα become God's is an event.

[72] This is the true reading, without σου.

[73] Cf. Zn. Lk. and Schl. Lk., ad loc.

[74] For par. from Jos. and Philo, v. Wnd. Hb., ad loc.

[75] In R. 10:15 the koine reading, which adds τῶν εὐαγγελιζομένων εἰρήνην, is secondary.

[76] So B. Weiss, Joh. Ev. (1902); J. H. Bernard, St. John (ICC, 1928); Schl. J.; Bau. J., ad loc.

[77] Mt. rather obscures the point for Greek readers by using ἀσπάζεσθαι instead of "to say, Peace."

[78] Acc. to Roller (→ n. 60), 61 χαίρειν is firmly established in Gk. letters. At the very most we only have occasional infin. like ὑγιαίνειν or εὐπράττειν. It is thus most unlikely that Paul should have been thinking of the Gk. χαίρειν in his χάρις ὑμῖν (καὶ εἰρήνη). This greeting is newly coined by the early Church or perhaps by Paul himself on the formal basis of the Jewish greeting, which allowed other substantives as well as שָׁלוֹם (→ 408 f.).

εἰρήνη μετά cannot mean concord with others, partly because this would demand πρός rather than μετά (→ n. 96) as in R. 5:1, partly because it would not fit the context. After the admonition to make straight paths for our feet that the lame may be healed there follows the injunction to seek salvation in company with all men. This salvation is a power which protects man in Phil. 4:7 [79] and which rules in the heart in Col. 3:15. It is a kingdom in which the believer is protected. Yet it is not identical with man's external affairs and may lead to the experience of bitter enmity (Mt. 10:34 f. par.).

b. In these passages εἰρήνη is materially determined by the fact that it is parallel with ζωή, cf. R. 8:6 : τὸ γὰρ φρόνημα τῆς σαρκὸς θάνατος, τὸ δὲ φρόνημα τοῦ πνεύματος ζωὴ καὶ εἰρήνη. Paul is telling us what the striving of the flesh and the striving of the spirit objectively signify and finally lead to, namely, death on the one side and εἰρήνη on the other. He bases the first part of the verse on v. 7. The striving of the flesh is enmity against God and can only lead to death. [80] He is not thinking in terms either of a harmonious disposition of soul [81] or of peace with God. [82] As ζωή and θάνατος are modes of existence which will be revealed as such eschatologically, so it is with εἰρήνη, the parallel of ζωή. For εἰρήνη (= שָׁלוֹם = salvation) is the state of final fulfilment, the normal state of the new creation. A characteristic parallel is probably to be found in 2 Pt. 3:14 : διό, ἀγαπητοί, ταῦτα προσδοκῶντες σπουδάσατε ἄσπιλοι καὶ ἀμώμητοι αὐτῷ εὑρεθῆναι ἐν εἰρήνῃ. Here, too, εἰρήνη is neither a basic inner disposition [83] nor the grace of God [84] but, as Wohlenberg, ad loc. suggests, the perfect well-being or normality which is inconceivable "apart from a restitution of the psycho-somatic being of his readers after the image of God." [85] In this sense Paul in his closing greetings more often speaks of the θεὸς τῆς εἰρήνης. This designation is firmly linked with what Paul expects of the God of peace. The content of peace may thus be determined from the context. Thus in R. 16:20 : ὁ δὲ θεὸς τῆς εἰρήνης συντρίψει τὸν σατανᾶν ὑπὸ τοὺς πόδας ὑμῶν ἐν τάχει, the destruction of Satan is a part of salvation. The phrase θεὸς τῆς εἰρήνης does not mean, then, that God will dispense peace and blessedness, [86] but that He will destroy Satan. In a material par. to 2 Pt. 3:14, the positive content of salvation and well-being is unfolded in 1 Th. 5:23 : αὐτὸς δὲ ὁ θεὸς τῆς εἰρήνης ἁγιάσαι ὑμᾶς ὁλοτελεῖς, καὶ ὁλόκληρον ὑμῶν τὸ πνεῦμα καὶ ἡ ψυχὴ καὶ τὸ σῶμα ἀμέμπτως ἐν τῇ παρουσίᾳ τοῦ κυρίου ἡμῶν Ἰησοῦ Χριστοῦ τηρηθείη. εἰρήνη is not just "spiritual prosperity" ; [87] it is the salvation of the whole man both body

---

[79] In view of v. 6 we cannot agree with Haupt Gefbr. and Tillm. Gefbr., ad loc. that this means a sense of peace in opp. to anxiety. We are rather to follow Loh. Phil., ad loc., who takes it to mean God's peace in the strict sense. Cf. also O. Schmitz, Die Christusgemeinschaft des Paulus im Lichte seines Genetivgebrauchs (1924), 215 f.

[80] V. B. Weiss (1899) and Zn. R., ad loc.

[81] So Joh. W. 1 K., on 1:3, and to some extent W. Sanday and A. C. Headlam, Romans (→ n. 93), ad loc.

[82] So Sanday-Headlam.

[83] Kn. Pt., ad loc.

[84] Vrede Kath. Br., ad loc.

[85] It is worth noting, and very surprising, that this Hebraic שָׁלוֹם concept occurs in a letter which is otherwise so strongly Greek in feeling as 2 Pt.

[86] Sickb. R., ad loc.

[87] J. E. Frame, Thess. (ICC, 1912, ad loc.).

and soul. Something of the same sense is to be found in Hb. 13:20 f.: ὁ δὲ θεὸς τῆς εἰρήνης ... καταρτίσαι ὑμᾶς ἐν παντὶ ἀγαθῷ. [88] This helps us to understand both "the God of peace" and εἰρήνη generally in other closing greetings. It does not mean the peace of soul which is the result of χάρις, but the salvation of man which comes from God. [89]

On the basis of OT and Rabbinic usage εἰρήνη thus acquires a most profound and comprehensive significance .It indicates the eschatological salvation of the whole man which is already present as the power of God. It denotes the state of the καινὴ κτίσις as the state of definitive fulfilment. In this sense salvation has been revealed in the resurrection of Jesus.

3. εἰρήνη as peace with God.

Only rarely in the NT is εἰρήνη used for the relationship of peace with God. Our first reference is Eph. 2:14-17. [90] Paul is thinking of Is. 57:19, so that the sense of salvation is present. When the term occurs in v. 15, however, expositors are divided whether its opposite → ἔχθρα means the enmity of men against God or the enmity between Jews and Gentiles. We hardly do justice to the passage if we do not perceive that the Law plays a double role, dividing the Gentiles from the commonwealth of Israel and also Israel from God. By the Law there arises both the enmity between Jews and Gentiles [91] and also that of man towards God. Hence in v. 14 αὐτὸς γάρ ἐστιν ἡ εἰρήνη ἡμῶν is to be taken in a comprehensive sense. When Christ abolished the Law, He set aside the twofold disorder of the race both among men and toward God. εἰρήνη means peace with God and within humanity. It thus denotes order, the healing of all relationships. Hence the striking expression ἔχθρα in v. 14 is to be taken generally. Its surprising and almost abrupt position forces us to see a wealth of connections in the saying "the Law which means enmity." In v. 15, too, the disorder of humanity in its twofold sense is denoted by the two adj. εἰς ἕνα καινὸν ἄνθρωπον. ποιῶν εἰρήνην is thus to be taken generally in this verse, as also ἔχθρα in v. 16 : ἀποκτείνας τὴν ἔχθραν ἐν αὐτῷ. We may say that ἔχθρα and εἰρήνη are here objective states which take many different forms in the human race. [92]

If peace with God is part of the sense of εἰρήνη in this passage, it is the sole meaning in R. 5:1, and the verse enables us to consider this more precisely. We need not here decide between the indic. and the conj. Our concern is with the content of εἰρήνη. As the addition πρὸς τὸν θεόν shows, the reference is to a relationship with God. This agrees with the fact that in R. 5:10 men are the

---

[88] J. Moffat, To the Hebrews (ICC, 1924), ad loc.: εἰρήνη has a sense "like the full OT sense of the secure prosperity won by messianic triumph over the hostile powers of evil."

[89] So, e.g., E. de Witt Burton, Galatians (ICC, 1921) on Gl. 1:3 : "εἰρήνη denotes the blessed state of well-being into which men are brought and in which they are kept by the divine χάρις."

[90] Cf. P. Feine, ThStKr, 72 (1899), 540-574; H. J. Holtzmann, Lehrbuch der nt.lichen Theologie, II² (1911), 265 f. and the comm.

[91] In spite of Haupt Gefbr., ad loc. the term ἔχθρα is quite in place. Through the Law and for the sake of it the Jews had to separate themselves from the Gentiles and regard them as enemies, and the Gentiles repaid them with enmity on their side.

[92] The excision of τὴν ἔχθραν in v. 14 (Haupt) and the assumption of a kind of anacoluthon (Feine) in which τὴν ἔχθραν in v. 14 is taken up again in the ἀποκτείνας τὴν ἔχθραν ἐν αὐτῷ of v. 16 are both desperate measures, the latter being ruled out by the fact that Paul could never have let the isolated τὴν ἔχθραν stand in this way.

enemies of God and He has reconciled them (→ καταλλάσσω, I, 255); cf. Eph. 2:16 (→ ἀποκαταλλάσσω, I, 258). Here, then, peace is not a mutual relationship between God and man which man has altered, as among the Rabbis. It is the relationship in which the believer is placed towards God.

The context of vv. 1-11 suggests ἔχομεν. The better attestation of ἔχωμεν is offset by the fact that in R. 14:19 there is better attestation of the impossible indic. διώκομεν instead of the conj., which alone is possible. In manuscript tradition there is an uncontrollable vacillation between the indic. and conj. of the 1st pers. plur.

4. εἰρήνη of men with one another.

In R. 14:17 Paul says : οὐ γάρ ἐστιν ἡ βασιλεία τοῦ θεοῦ βρῶσις καὶ πόσις, ἀλλὰ δικαιοσύνη καὶ εἰρήνη καὶ χαρὰ ἐν πνεύματι ἁγίῳ. Here neither the religious interpretation of Zahn and B. Weiss, the ethical of Sanday-Headlam, [93] nor the mediating of Sickenberger, is really appropriate. Paul is addressing the strong. He tells them that the kingdom of God does not consist, as they think, in bringing others to eat and drink, but in the rule of righteousness, peace and joy among them. χαρά has in view the λυπεῖται of v. 15 ; δικαιοσύνη reminds us that no man's conscience must be violated ; εἰρήνη indicates that in the kingdom of God there will be no kind of sickness, evil or discord. Paul can thus go on to say that those who serve Christ in this sphere (ἐν τούτῳ) are pleasing to God and acceptable to men. He can thus give the final exhortation to follow after τὰ τῆς εἰρήνης καὶ τὰ τῆς οἰκοδομῆς τῆς εἰς ἀλλήλους. Here εἰρήνη is parallel with οἰκοδομή, and it clearly denotes peace with one another. In v. 17, however, there is more to εἰρήνη than this. The building of the kingdom of God implies the creation of something salutary, i.e., εἰρήνη, in the Holy Spirit. Concretely applied in the church at Rome, however, this salutary thing is undoubtedly peace. For peace is salutary. We have something of the same thought in the difficult saying in 1 C. 7:15c : ἐν δὲ εἰρήνῃ κέκληκεν ὑμᾶς (ἡμᾶς) ὁ θεός. Paul seems to be contradicting the saying of the Lord about divorce when he states that if the heathen partner breaks off the marriage the Christian partner is to accept it : οὐ δεδούλωται ὁ ἀδελφὸς ἢ ἡ ἀδελφὴ ἐν τοῖς τοιούτοις. This can refer only to the Lord's saying, to which we are not bound like slaves in such cases. In v. 15c we do not have a restriction but a reason. Only thus can the following verse begin with a γάρ. Hence the δέ has the sense, not of "but," but of "rather." [94] The mention of calling establishes a basis for what precedes, but a basis which, as we may see from the "rather," goes beyond the individual case mentioned and tells us generally that God has called us to peace. [95] εἰρήνη thus means far more than the opposite of strife in a reluctantly maintained marriage. Here, too, it implies the divinely willed and therefore salutary state of all things, the normal state, to the degree that sin is a disruption of the normal. The peace of men with one another is included, however, in this normal state. This content of εἰρήνη, which may take different concrete forms according to the context, is nowhere quite so apparent. Thus 2 Tm. 2:22 certainly does not mean that we are to "foster peace with the inwardly pious," [96] since μετά κτλ. does not refer to εἰρήνη but means "together

[93] To the Romans (ICC⁵, 1907), ad loc.
[94] So Joh. W. and Bchm.
[95] ἐν = εἰς; v. Ltzm., ad loc.
[96] Wbg. Past., ad loc.; also Meinertz Past., ad loc. To express a peaceful relation to

with," and in itself εἰρήνη might well mean "that which brings salvation." On the other hand, it is certainly not said without a glance at the ζητήσεις which gender strifes (v. 23). In a whole list of passages εἰρήνη simply means concord between men. Eph. 4:3 : σπουδάζοντες τηρεῖν τὴν ἑνότητα τοῦ πνεύματος ἐν τῷ συνδέσμῳ τῆς εἰρήνης; also Jm. 3:18 : καρπὸς δὲ δικαιοσύνης ἐν εἰρήνῃ σπείρεται τοῖς ποιοῦσιν εἰρήνην : the seed from which righteousness grows is sown in peace by those who make peace, ζῆλος and ἐριθεία being the opposites of εἰρήνη. [97] It is difficult to say precisely in what sense 1 Pt. 3:11 uses the phrase ζητησάτω εἰρήνην καὶ διωξάτω αὐτήν in the long quotation from Ps. 34, but the meaning is probably "concord" (cf. v. 9).

5. εἰρήνη as peace of soul.

This meaning is undoubtedly present in R. 15:13 : ὁ δὲ θεὸς τῆς ἐλπίδος πληρώσαι ὑμᾶς πάσης χαρᾶς καὶ εἰρήνης ἐν τῷ πιστεύειν. We must remember, however, how the word comes to take on this sense, namely, from its general use in the NT for the normal state. As the phrase θεὸς τῆς εἰρήνης has implications for external life, and as εἰρήνη is used for the normal state of man's total being, so God creates in man the salvation which is the normal state of the soul that is in order — a state inseparable from χαρά. Hence the concept of εἰρήνη differs from the negative γαλήνη of the Stoics (→ 401).

† εἰρηνεύω.

a. "To live in peace," "to be at peace" (as a state). BMI, 894 [1] : εἰρηνεύουσι μὲν γὰρ γῆ καὶ θάλαττα. In this sense it also occurs in the mid. : Polyb., V, 8, 7 : εἰρηνευομένης ἐκ παλαιοῦ τῆς χώρας. In the LXX it is often used for שקט and שלום (2 Ch. 20:30; Job 5:23; 15:21), ישלֵו or שלֵה (Ιωβ 16:13; Da. 4:1), שלה (Job 3:26). In Joseph. it occurs only in the mid. or pass. : Ant., 11, 214 : ἵν' ἀπὸ τούτων εἰρηνευθῇ τῶν κακῶν ἡ βασιλεία; Bell., 6, 300 : τῆς πόλεως εἰρηνευομένης καὶ εὐθηνούσης; cf. also Ant., 20, 49; Vit., 78. This use is not found in the NT, but cf. 1 Cl., 54, 2 : μόνον τὸ ποίμνιον τοῦ Χριστοῦ εἰρηνευέτω; Ign. Pol., 7 etc. b. "to keep peace," "to live at peace with someone" (an attitude). Aristot. Rhet., 1, 4, p. 1359b, 39 : ὅπως πρὸς μὲν τοὺς κρείττους εἰρηνεύηται. In the LXX it is used for שלם hiph and hoph, and in Sir. 6:6 for the phrase אנשי שלומך. Those with whom one is at peace are in the dat.: Sir. 6:6 : οἱ εἰρηνεύοντές σοι ἔστωσαν πολλοί (also Job 5:23), though μετά is also used : 3 Βασ. 22:45. Cf. 1 Cl., 15, 1 and 5 times in Herm. on the basis of 1 Th. 5:13. c. "to make peace," "to reconcile" : Dio C., 77, 12, 1 : τὸν δὲ τῶν Ἀρμενίων βασιλέα διαφερόμενον μετὰ τῶν ἰδίων παίδων ἐκάλεσε μὲν φιλικοῖς γράμμασιν ὡς δὴ εἰρηνεύσων αὐτούς. Cf. in the LXX 1 Macc. 6:60 : ἀπέστειλεν πρὸς αὐτοὺς εἰρηνεῦσαι, "to conclude peace." It is not found in this sense in the NT, though it occurs in Jos. Bell., 2, 367 etc. and in Did., 4, 3; Barn., 19, 12.

In the NT it is used only in the sense of "to keep peace" with ἐν and μετά. In the obscure passage Mk. 9:50 : ἔχετε ἐν ἑαυτοῖς ἅλα καὶ εἰρηνεύετε ἐν ἀλλήλοις, severity in self-discipline is contrasted with peace towards others. In 1 Th.

---

someone the Gk. tongue uses πρός rather than μετά, and in such cases the Heb. uses בין = μεταξύ.

[97] A. Meyer, Das Rätsel des Jk.-Briefes (1930), 263, interprets the passage in a Philonic sense, peaceful implying free from passions as one of the attributes of heavenly wisdom.

εἰρηνεύω. [1] Cf. Wendland Hell. Kult., 410, No. 9.

5:13 external criticism does not enable us to decide between the readings εἰρηνεύετε ἐν ἑαυτοῖς and ... ἐν αὐτοῖς, since the latter might well be αὐτοῖς. We
may best begin by presuming that the three words have no connexion either with
what precedes or with what follows. If we were to link them with what precedes,
i.e., with the leaders, we rob the prior injunction of its force. [2] Hence we should
construe ἑαυτοῖς = αὐτοῖς as ἐν ἀλλήλοις, so that the admonition is to be at
peace with one another. [3] εἰρηνεύειν has the same sense in R. 12:18 : εἰ δυνατόν,
τὸ ἐξ ὑμῶν, μετὰ πάντων ἀνθρώπων εἰρηνεύοντες, and 2 C. 13:11: λοιπόν,
ἀδελφοί, χαίρετε, καταρτίζεσθε, παρακαλεῖσθε, τὸ αὐτὸ φρονεῖτε, εἰρηνεύετε
(in which εἰρηνεύετε is par. to the preceding τὸ αὐτὸ φρονεῖτε).

† εἰρηνικός.

a. "That which relates to peace," Xenoph. Oec., 1, 17 distinguishes πολεμικαὶ and
εἰρηνικαὶ ἐπιστῆμαι, Plut. Sertorius, 6 (I, 571c): ἥμερος μὲν ὢν ἐν ταῖς εἰρηνικαῖς
χρείαις, φοβερὸς δὲ τῇ παρασκευῇ κατὰ τῶν πολεμίων φαινόμενος. b. "peaceful,"
of words and men, also in opp. to war, Isoc., 5, 3 : ὃν δ' ὑπελάμβανον τῶν λόγων
εἰρηνικώτατον εἶναι, Isoc., 2, 24 : πολεμικὸς μὲν ἴσθι ταῖς ἐπιστήμαις καὶ ταῖς
παρασκευαῖς, εἰρηνικὸς δὲ τῷ μηδὲν παρὰ τὸ δίκαιον πλεονεκτεῖν. c. in a wider
sense as the opp. of unrest, Plut. C. Gracch., 10 (I, 839b): οὐχ ὑγιαινούσης οὐδὲ
εἰρηνικῆς ὢν προαιρέσεως. It is difficult to distinguish between εἰρηναῖος and
εἰρηνικός. In Hdt., VI, 57 the ἐμπολέμια γέρεα of the Spartan king are opposed to
the εἰρηναῖα γέρεα (= εἰρηνικός, a.); in Thuc., I, 29, 4 : ὡς δὲ ὁ κῆρύξ τε ἀπήγ-
γειλεν οὐδὲν εἰρηναῖον παρὰ τῶν Κορινθίων (= εἰρηνικός b.); and in Philodem.
Philos. De Oeconomia, ed. Jensen, p. 20 : εἰ δ' ἀναγκαῖόν ἐστι γαμετὴ καὶ λυσιτελὲς
εἰς τὴν φιλόσοφον οἰκονομίαν καὶ καθόλου τὸν εἰρηναῖον βίον (= εἰρηνικός c.).

In the LXX we find only εἰρηνικός, in sense a. as a transl. of שָׁלוֹם (דִּבְרֵי שָׁלוֹם),
Dt. 2:26; 20:11, often in 1 Macc., also 2 Macc. 10:12; Jdt. 3:1; 7:24; in sense b. in 1 Ch.
12:38 : ἐν ψυχῇ εἰρηνικῇ (HT : v. 39 : בְּלֵבָב שָׁלֵם) and in Gn. 42:11-34, where the
question is whether Joseph's brethren are εἰρηνικοί (כֵּנִים) or κατάσκοποι, also in
Gn. 34:21 (שְׁלֵמִים) and 2 Macc. 5:25. εἰρηνικός is frequently used in the LXX to denote
the friendly word of a man in opp. to a divisive rather than a warlike word, the
equivalent being שְׁלֹם (אִישׁ נַפְשׁוֹ הַוַּת in Mi. 7:3 and בְּרִית in Ob. 7), cf. Gn. 37:4; ψ 34:20; 119:7;
Mi. 7:3; Ob. 7; 'Ιερ. 9:8; 45:22. Sometimes one might assume a wider meaning corresponding to that of εἰρήνη in the LXX, cf. Dt. 23:6 : οὐ προσαγορεύσεις εἰρηνικὰ
αὐτοῖς καὶ συμφέροντα αὐτοῖς, where the parallel to συμφέροντα suggests the
sense of saving or salutary. In Sir. 4:8 : κλῖνον πτωχῷ τὸ οὖς σου, καὶ ἀποκρίθητι
αὐτῷ εἰρηνικὰ ἐν πρᾳΰτητι, the meaning is friendly as distinct from hard words. In
ψ 36:37 ἀκακία and εὐθύτης is ἐγκατάλιμμα ἀνθρώπῳ εἰρηνικῷ, in opp. to the
παράνομοι, so that the meaning is almost "righteous." In Zech. 8:16 : ἀλήθειαν καὶ
κρίμα εἰρηνικὸν κρίνατε ἐν ταῖς πύλαις ὑμῶν, the meaning is true, orderly, salutary
judgment.

Philo uses both εἰρηνικός and εἰρηναῖος of the life of the wise who have peace of
soul : Spec. Leg., I, 224 : ἀπολέμῳ καὶ εἰρηνικῷ βίῳ χρώμενος; Spec. Leg., II, 45 :
the wise βίον ἀπόλεμον καὶ εἰρηναῖον ἐζηλωκότες.

---

[2] This is perceived in Dib. Th., ad loc., but the difficulty is not avoided by supposing
that in v. 13a we have the ideal and in v. 13b the practical demand.
[3] This view is supported by the fact that in all the five passage in which Hermas refers
to the saying (v., 3, 6, 3; 3, 9, 2 and 10; 3, 12, 3; s., 8, 7, 2) he is thinking of a mutual relationship of peace among the members of the community. J. E. Frame, To the Thessalonians
(ICC, 1912), ad loc., relates the saying to leaders who under attack did not always defend
themselves too wisely, but this is an artificial interpretation.

In the NT only εἰρηνικός is used, and this only in Hb. 12:11 and Jm. 3:17. In the latter: ἡ δὲ ἄνωθεν σοφία πρῶτον μὲν ἀγνή ἐστιν, ἔπειτα εἰρηνική, ἐπιεικής, εὐπειθής ..., εἰρηνικός is the opp. of ζῆλος πικρός and parallel to ἐριθεία, and means "ready for peace," "peaceful." In Hb. 12:11: πᾶσα μὲν παιδεία ... ὕστερον ... καρπὸν εἰρηνικὸν τοῖς δι᾽ αὐτῆς γεγυμνασμένοις ἀποδίδωσιν δικαιοσύνης, εἰρηνικός is an attribute of δικαιοσύνη and means salutary in the sense of → εἰρήνη F. 2.[1]

† εἰρηνοποιός.

"He who makes peace" in the Gk. sense of the opposite of war: Plut. Nicias, 11 (I, 530c): νέων ἦν καὶ πολεμοποιῶν ἄμιλλα (strife) πρὸς εἰρηνοποιοὺς καὶ πρεσβυτέρους, esp. as a translation of fetiales together with σπονδοφόροι, Plut. Quaest. Rom., 62 (II, 279b). Philo calls God εἰρηνοποιός and εἰρηνοφύλαξ when He protects the people from enemies and natural disasters, Spec. Leg., II, 192.

The word is sometimes used for the strong ruler who establishes peace in the world and who is thus to be respected. Thus Commodus calls himself εἰρηνοποιὸς τῆς οἰκουμένης ἀνίκητος (Dio C., 72, 15, 5). This pacification is by force, so that in the great speech of Antony on the murdered Caesar there is an antithesis of the words γυμνὸς (unarmed) ὁ εἰρηνοποιός to the preceding ἄοπλος ὁ εὐπόλεμος.[1] This forceful pacification is clearly distinguished from that which the Rabbis extol and the term for which (שלום עשה) corresponds to the NT εἰρηνοποιός or -έω.[2] For the Rabbis extol pacification as an act of love, humility and self-denial.

The only NT use is in Mt. 5:9: μακάριοι οἱ εἰρηνοποιοί, ὅτι αὐτοὶ υἱοὶ θεοῦ κληθήσονται. This is to be understood in terms of the Rabb. שלום עשה, which denotes the establishment of peace and concord between men. It is thus a mistake to refer with Dausch to those who promote human happiness and well-being. Nor is it a matter of helping others to peace with God, as Brouwer suggests. The reference is to those who disinterestedly come between two contending parties and try to make peace. These God calls His sons because they are like Him.

† εἰρηνοποιέω.

"To make peace." The mid. is found in Stob. Ecl., I, 409, where it is said of the soul after death: τὸν ἴδιον δρόμον εἰρηνοποιεῖται, it has a peaceful way. In LXX Prv. 10:10 we read: ὁ ἐννεύων ὀφθαλμοῖς μετὰ δόλου συνάγει λύπας, ὁ δὲ ἐλέγχων μετὰ παρρησίας εἰρηνοποιεῖ. In view of the contrast with λύπη this means "promoting well-being" rather than more narrowly "making peace." In Is. 27:5 ᾿ΑΣΘ have εἰρηνοποιήσει instead of the LXX ποιήσωμεν εἰρήνην.

εἰρηνικός. [1] Rgg. Hb., ad loc. makes the unlikely suggestion that εἰρηνικός refers to a feeling of felicity which accompanies the fruit of righteousness in contrast to the preceding lack of joy.

εἰρηνοποιός. Comm. on Mt. 5:9, esp. Schl. Mt.; Zn. Mt.; Dausch Synpt.; H. Windisch, ZNW, 24 (1925), 240 ff.; K. Bornhäuser, Die Bergpredigt² (1927); Fuchs (→ 400 n.), 207; A. M. Brouwer (→ 400 n.), 242 ff.; B. W. Bacon, Exp. T., 41 (1929/30), 58-60.

[1] Dio C., 44, 49, 2. This corresponds to the Roman view of pax, → εἰρήνη, n. 4.

[2] Windisch perceived this distinction, but did not make enough of it.

εἰρηνοποιέω. Comm. on Col. 1:15; H. J. Holtzmann, Lehrbuch der nt.lichen Theologie, II² (1911), 284 f.

In the NT the word occurs only in Col. 1:19 f.: εὐδόκησεν πᾶν τὸ πλήρωμα ... δι' αὐτοῦ ἀποκαταλλάξαι τὰ πάντα εἰς αὐτόν, εἰρηνοποιήσας διὰ τοῦ αἵματος τοῦ σταυροῦ αὐτοῦ, δι' αὐτοῦ εἴτε τὰ ἐπὶ τῆς γῆς εἴτε τὰ ἐν τοῖς οὐρανοῖς. Here, as in the phrase שלום עשה, the reference is to making peace or concord. There is a parallel in Rabbinic statements concerning strife in the upper family (→ 410). As in Eph. 2:14 ff., we are to think of a rift in the terrestrial and supraterrestrial world both in themselves and in relation to God.

Foerster

εἰς

Originally spatial, this word takes on theological significance especially in Paul and John, though also in the Synoptists and Acts. Though weaker and more dependent than the related → ἐν, as may be seen in the phrases εἰς Χριστόν and ἐν Χριστῷ, εἰς has a distinctive sense in the NT.

A. The Spatial Use of εἰς.

1. The Cosmic and Soteriological Sense.

Within the world of NT thought εἰς gives unique expression to the living connection between the separated divine and cosmic realities.

On the Gk. view, the gods belong to the world. Κόσμος is a concept which may be set alongside and even above the divine. The dualism of philosophy makes no radical change. It distinguishes between God and matter, but statically, along the lines of a finally monistic idealism. The κόσμος αἰσθητός and the κόσμος νοητός are interrelated. Hades is truly beyond as another place, but not the world of God. Thus εἰς has no theological significance apart from a few modest beginnings (→ *infra,* 423).

Hom. Il., 19, 128: ἐς Οὔλυμπόν τε καὶ οὐρανὸν ἀστερόεντα ἔρχεσθαι, Heracl. Fr., 30 (I, 84, Diels): κόσμον τόνδε οὔτε τις θεῶν οὔτε ἀνθρώπων ἐποίησεν, ἀλλ' ἦν ἀεὶ καὶ ἔστιν καὶ ἔσται πῦρ. Acc. to Plato things are contained in the ideas. [1] It is hard to find an example of εἰς being used for the transition from the one world

---

εἰς. Liddell-Scott, *s.v.;* Pr.-Bauer, *s.v.;* Preisigke Wört., *s.v.;* F. Preisigke, *Girowesen im griech. Ägypten* (1910), 147 ff.; Moult.-Mill., *s.v.;* Bl.-Debr., esp. § 205-207; 402, 2; Radermacher,[2] esp. 14, 20 f., 122, 128, 140, 145; W. Kuhring, *De praepositionum Graecarum in chartis Aegyptiacis usu* (Diss. Bonn, 1906), 13, 28, 31; J. Käser, *Die Präpositionen bei Dionysius von Halicarnassus* (Diss. Erlangen, 1915), 42 ff.; C. Rossberg, *De praepositionum Graecarum in chartis Aegyptiis Ptolemaeorum aetatis usu* (Diss. Jena, 1909), 17, 30 ff.; M. Johannessohn, "Der Gebrauch der Präpositionen in der Septuaginta" in *Mitteilungen des Septuaginta-Unternehmens der Ges. d. Wiss. zu Göttingen,* III, 3 (1926), 293 ff.; also *Der Gebrauch der Casus u. d. Präpositionen in der Septuaginta,* I (Diss. Berlin, 1910), 4 f.; P. F. Regard, *Contribution à l'Etude des Prépositions dans la Langue du NT* (1919), 156 ff.; 325 ff.; H. Ljungvik, *Studien zur Sprache der apkr. Apostelgeschichten* (Diss. Uppsala, 1926), 30 ff.; G. Rudberg, *Eranos,* 19 (1922), 201; G. N. Hatzidakis, *Einleitung in die neugriechische Grammatik* (1892), 210 f.; A. N. Jannaris, *Historical Greek Grammar* (1897), Index and esp. §§ 1536 ff.; K. Krumbacher, "Studien zu den Legenden des hl. Theodosius," *Sitzungsberichte der Kgl. Bayer. Akademie d. Wiss., phil.-hist. Klasse* (1892), 364 f.; Deissmann B., 113 ff.; NB, 23; LO, 96 f., 138, 147; W. Heitmüller, *Im Namen Jesu* (1903), 99 ff.

[1] E. Zeller, *Philosophie der Griechen*[4], II, 1 (1889), 744 ff.

to the other. [2] ἐξ "Ἀιδου εἰς θεοὺς (= to the upper world?) ἀνελθεῖν is a philosophical fig. of speech (Plat. Resp., VII, 521c). For Antipater of Tyre the world is a ζῷον ἔμψυχον καὶ λογικόν (Diog. L., VII, 139). ὁ ἄνω κόσμος means the earthly world as distinct from the underworld (Iambl. Vit. Pyth., 27, 123). Even μετάρσιον (τῆς ἄνω φύσεως) is an immanent concept (Stob., I, 390, 12). Characteristically monistic is Corp. Herm., XVI, 3: τὸν θεὸν ἐπικαλεσάμενος τὸν τῶν ὅλων δεσπότην καὶ ποιητὴν καὶ πατέρα καὶ περίβολον, τὸν καὶ ἕνα ὄντα <καὶ> τὰ πάντα, οὐ δευτεροῦντος τοῦ ἑνός, ἀλλ' ἀμφοτέρων ἑνὸς ὄντος. The κόσμος νοητός embraces (περιέχων) the κόσμος αἰσθητός (XVI, 12). In spite of OT and Jewish reminiscences Philo continually describes the ascent of the soul without εἰς in the relevant sense (Sacr. A.C., 5: Quaest. in Ex., II, 45 f.). In Vit. Mos., II, 288 εἰς is used, but all the emphasis is on qualitative change. [3] In circles influenced by oriental mythology we find the idea of a journey of the soul, [4] as among the Mandaeans. Yet in the Mithras Liturgy there is no emphatic εἰς, in spite of the stress on certain frontiers between below and above (θύρας ἀποκεκλεισμένας, ἀνοιγμένας, Preis. Zaub., IV, 584 f., 662). The concept ἄνω κόσμος (ibid., 569) is still orientated to pole and compass (cf. εἰς ὕψος = μέσον τοῦ ἀέρος, ibid., 540 f.).

Behind OT piety stand a primitive view of things and an anthropomorphic conception of God. [5] An abstract divine spirituality is quite alien to it. It thus speaks of Yahweh's coming down in a way which would be felt to be purely mythological in other religious settings (Gn. 18:21; Ex. 3:8; Ps. 18:9 etc.). It is worth noting that no goal is given. We have a change of movement within the same circle, not transition from one reality to another (this is especially plain in Gn. 18:21). The frequent references to the God of heaven and earth (Gn. 24:3; cf. 7; Ezr. 5:11, cf. 12; 6:9 f.) and to Yahweh's dwelling in heaven do not in themselves imply the absolute distinction of the Godhead in nature and place, nor the divine transcendence over space and time. They can be taken in a primitive sense, and were so taken (cf. the use of רכב in these contexts, Dt. 33:26; Ps. 18:10; 68:34). The distinctive feature in OT religion is that under cover of the anthropomorphisms and anthropopathisms, which exclude any possibility of dissolution, the specific superiority of God over all creatures is strongly felt and asserted. In this respect passages like Ex. 33:18 ff. and Is. 6 are classic for all time. As the time grew ripe, they led to the conception that heaven and the heaven of heaven cannot contain Him, as in the Deuteronomistic dedication prayer of Solomon in 1 K. 8:27. Hence the dwelling of God can no longer be understood as a natural presence, as alone a natural need, but only as a willed and gracious address of the covenant God (v. 28 ff.). This is vividly depicted in the cultic legend of the Bethel sanctuary in Gn. 28:10 ff. In the fine accounts of the story in J and E the mythological elements are far less extensive than might appear. If the preposition at issue does not here have greater theological significance than it does (cf. v. 12), this is due to contingent factors of style.

Judaism has a strong aversion to mythology and a highly developed understanding of God's transcendence. It replaces the concrete expressions of the OT, which might give rise to mythological misunderstanding, by more abstract statements, and removes God's heaven to the far distance. The transcendence of God is carried so far, as in some Apocalyptic, that the link between God and the world threatens to break. This does not happen. [6] Judaism, esp. Rabbinic, maintains a strong belief in providence. At this

---

[2] F. Ast, Lexicon Platonicum, I (1835), 637 f., s.v. Plat. Soph., 246a : οἱ μὲν (the materialists) εἰς γῆν ἐξ οὐρανοῦ καὶ τοῦ ἀοράτου πάντα ἕλκουσι, is semi-mythological and metaphorical.

[3] E. Bréhier, Les Idées Philosophiques et Religieuses de Philon d'Alexandrie (1908), 240 ff.

[4] Cf. RGG², II, 1898.

[5] Cf. for what follows the account in W. Eichrodt, Die Theologie des AT, I (1933), 104 ff.: "Die Geistigkeit der Gottesvorstellung."

[6] Kittel Probleme, 132 f.; Moore, I, 417, 421, 423 ff.

very time the belief in miracles takes many strange forms. But belief in present manifestations of God is reduced to a mere fragment (Bath qol etc.). For all the magnifying of the covenant and the Torah, there is no consciousness, as in Christianity (cf. Hb. 1:1 etc.), of having experienced a definitive yet ongoing revelation of God. The emphasis in piety is on retrospect of the past and prospect of the future. World reality is thought of statically and dualistically. Two worlds lie alongside one another, or rather the one over the other. They are contemporary, and both equally real.

For Ex. 15:3 : "The Lord is a man of war : the Lord is his name," the LXX has : κύριος συντρίβων πολέμους, κύριος ὄνομα αὐτῷ; and for Ex. 24:10 : "And they saw the God of Israel," it has : καὶ εἶδον τὸν τόπον, οὗ εἱστήκει ὁ θεὸς τοῦ Ἰσραήλ. In the Mishnah we often have paraphrases like the "place," "heaven," "speech," "dwelling," "name." The rendering of the Genesis stories in Jub. is typical. In 3:23, for example, there is evasion of the fact that they heard the Lord God walking in the garden in the cool of the day (cf. Gn. 3:8). In part, Philo's fear of anthropomorphism is philosophical. [7] But even Palestinian Judaism, partly under alien influence, distinguishes God's heaven from the starry heaven and thus comes to have three, four, seven or even ten heavens. [8] The long journeys in the Apocalypses (e.g., Gr. Bar. 4 etc.) are a primitive attempt to portray the transcendence of God's world. Our preposition takes on great theological significance in this context (cf. Jub. 4:15, where the angels, called watchers, come down to earth to teach the children of men and to exercise right and righteousness on earth), and esp. in connexion with apocalyptic vision (Eth. En. 71:1: into heaven ; cf. 2 C. 12:4 : εἰς τὸν παράδεισον; Rev. 8:5 etc.: εἰς τὴν γῆν). Only temporal categories of the scheme of aeons keep the upper hand. Finitum non capax infiniti ; → αἰών, I, 202.

In general the theological significance of the word remains undeveloped in the Jewish world.

The world of NT thought takes over the sharp distinction between the two worlds as a concrete conception with no tendency towards idealistic or pantheistic dissolution. But it bridges the gulf with the help of the concept of fulfilment. Thus eschatology gives rise to the distinctive "mysticism" of the NT, [9] which is not natural mysticism, but spiritual and ethical. There is no identity mysticism in the NT. The unity of the world is present only as it comes into being. But it comes into being through the gracious self-offering of God in Christ. Under these conditions the theological significance of the NT use of εἰς develops as follows.

a. εἰς τὸν → κόσμον in different combinations delimits the earthly creation, with its twofold dependence, from all other reality.

In Jn. 1:9 ἔρχεσθαι εἰς τὸν κόσμον is used of all men. [10] Based on the common Rabb. expression לְעוֹלָם בָּא or אָתָא בְעַלְמָא, [11] it does not imply pre-existence, but the idea of a transcendent background such as we also see in 1 Tm. 6:7: οὐδὲν εἰσηνέγκαμεν

---

[7] Cf. Leg. All., I, 36 (on Gn. 2): μὴ γὰρ τοσαύτης ἀτοπίας ἀναπλησθείημεν, ὥστε νομίσαι θεὸν στόματος ἢ μυκτήρων ὀργάνοις χρῆσθαι πρὸς τὸ ἐμφυῆσαι· ἄποιος γὰρ ὁ θεός, οὐ μόνον οὐκ ἀνθρωπόμορφος. In I, 43 Philo describes anthropomorphic views of God as ἀσέβεια.

[8] For material and bibl. cf. Wnd. 2 K., 371 ff. on 2 C. 12:2 ff.

[9] This was noted at much the same time by both H. E. Weber, "Eschatologie" und "Mystik" im NT (1930) and A. Schweitzer, Die Mystik des Apostels Pls. (1930). Whether we are justified in using the word "mysticism" is another question.

[10] For the combination of ἐρχόμενον κτλ. and πάντα ἄνθρωπον cf. Schl., Wellhausen, ad loc.; a different view is taken by Zn., Bau., Tillm., ad loc.

[11] For examples, v. Str.-B., II, 358 on Jn. 1:9.

εἰς τὸν κόσμον. Sin and death also come into the world of God from without, from a side which is hostile to God, as we read in R. 5:12. Though we have the causal → δι' → ἑνὸς ἀνθρώπου, in view of the story of the fall we cannot rule out the thought of the transcendence of evil. Cf. also 1 Jn. 4:1 and 2 Jn. 7.

The Gk. expresses the same ideas very differently. Anth. Pal. (Palladas), X, 58 : Γῆς ἐπέβην γυμνός, γυμνὸς θ' ὑπὸ γαῖαν ἄπειμι. Plato says with no sense of concrete place : εἰς οὐσίαν ἄγειν (Soph., 219b). Even when traced to demonic influences, evil for the Gks. is within the world. [12]

b. Supraterrestrial love comes into the world to bring salvation. This thought, unheard of for both Jew and Greek, is linked in the NT with the eternal origin of the Son of God, though not always with the same clarity. Eschatological faith looks to the goal rather than the origin.

It attests the soundness of the Synoptic tradition that the soteriological εἰς τὸν κόσμον is alien to it. Even in the Pauline epistles, though these thoughts are present (R. 10:6; Phil. 2:5 ff.; 2 C. 8:9; Gl. 4:4), there is a strong sense of the dualism of the cosmos and therefore the εἰς is not over-significant. [13] Isolated statements may be found in 1 Tm. 1:15; Hb. 1:6; 10:5 etc.

The idea that God sent His only Son into the world that we might live (1 Jn. 4:9) is distinctive of Johannine theology. The related ideas of pre-existence [14] develop almost imperceptibly from the underlying general conception (→ a.).

In Jn. 6:14 : ὁ προφήτης ὁ ἐρχόμενος εἰς τὸν κόσμον, there is a link with 1:9, as also with the → ἔρχεσθαι which is so important from the standpoint of salvation history in the Synoptics. In Jn. 17:18 the mission of mortal men is made par. to that of the Logos into the world. This shows how elastic εἰς still is. But it has a deeper sense in Jn. 3:19 : τὸ φῶς ἐλήλυθεν εἰς τὸν κόσμον. For the context makes it clear whence this light is and who it is. It is He whom the Father sent from Himself (1:1 ff.) into the world (3:17; 10:36) and who as the Logos becoming σάρξ (1:14) came into the world (11:27; 12:46; 16:28; 18:37). Thus even the derived mission of the disciples takes on the quality of eternity.

The Johannine thought of sending finds many par. in Gnosticism, esp. in the Mandaean writings. Lidz. Ginza, p. 58, 17 ff.: "I am the One sent by light, whom the Great One hath sent into this world. I am He who is truly sent, in whom there is no falsehood." [15] In a passage like this it is hardly possible to distinguish with certainty the pre- or extra-Christian element. Its extent has probably been exaggerated. [16] But even though it works with the Johannine presentation of the theme of Christianity, it fails to bring out that on which John lays supreme emphasis, namely, the uniqueness of the person of Jesus, the incomparable ὁ λόγος σάρξ ἐγένετο. On no account must we fail to see the distinction between an ontological and an ethical religion of redemption (→ I, 443).

c. The way of the One who is sent goes through humiliation to the upper world. This thought rather than pre-existence is primary in the NT.

---

[12] K. Latte, "Schuld u. Sünde in der griech. Religion," ARW, 20 (1920/21), 254 ff.

[13] The contesting of pre-existence in Pauline theology by E. Barnikol, Mensch u. Messias (1932) and Philipper, 2 (1932) is not very convincing.

[14] In spite of Harnack, Dogmengesch.⁴, I (1909), 109 f., the significance of the prologue for the whole work may be accepted. Cf. H. J. Holtzmann, Nt.liche Theol.², II (1911), 444 ff.

[15] For rich materials cf. Bau. J., 55.

[16] Cf. H. Lietzmann, "Ein Beitrag zur Mandäerfrage," SAB, 28 (1930), 596 ff.

Whether the accounts of the ascension with their εἰς οὐρανόν (Lk. 24:51[?]; Ac. 1:11 [Mk. 16:19]) are earlier or later, the original proclamation had as its subject the One exalted to heaven, to the glory of God (εἰσελθεῖν εἰς δόξαν, Lk. 24:26; εἰς [τὸν] οὐρανόν, Hb. 9:24; 1 Pt. 3:22; εἰς τοὺς οὐρανούς, Ac. 2:33 f.; εἰς ὕψος, Eph. 4:8 ff.; and materially Ac. 3:21; R. 1:4; Phil. 2:9-11).

That a journey to the lowest regions preceded that to the upper is seldom emphasised in the NT but everywhere presupposed.

The originality of 1 Pt. 3:19; 4:6 is to be found in the description of the accompanying circumstances and in the dogmatic deductions.[18] εἰς is found in a similar connection in R. 10:7; elsewhere we have ἐν (cf. also Mt. 12:40). On the other hand, εἰς τὰ κατώτερα μέρη τῆς γῆς (epexeg. gen.) in Eph. 4:9 is to be understood in the sense of → b. Cf. also Rev. 1:18. Parallels are found not only in 2 K. 2:1 ff. but also in ancient scenes of divinisation esp. in the ruler cults,[19] myths like that of the journey of Ishtar to hell,[20] the general motif of a journey to heaven or hell,[21] and related experiences in the dedications of the Mysteries (Apul. Met., XI, 23 ff.; Plut. in Stob., IV, 1089, 3 ff.). We should not overlook the differences in religious context.

d. The divine act of salvation sets man with full seriousness before the decision where his own path is to lead. εἰς can be used either way.

Disobedience, which includes unbelief (→ ὑπακοή), leads to destruction.

This is shown by a series of partly metaphorical expressions, esp. in the Synoptists, which use verbs of motion with εἰς, e.g., εἰς ἀπώλειαν (Mt. 7:13; Rev. 17:8, 11); εἰς (τὴν) γέενναν (τοῦ πυρός) (Mt. 5:29 f.; Mk. 9:43, 45, 47 and par.; Lk. 12:5); εἰς (τὸ) πῦρ (τὸ αἰώνιον, τὸ ἄσβεστον (Mt. 3:10 and par.; 7:19; 25:41; Mk. 9:43; Jn. 15:6); εἰς τὴν λίμνην (Rev. 19:20; 20:3, 10, 14 f.); εἰς κάμινον (Mt. 13:42, 50); εἰς φυλακήν (Mt. 5:25 and par.); εἰς τὸ σκότος τὸ ἐξώτερον (Mt. 8:12; 22:13; 25:30); εἰς κόλασιν αἰώνιον (Mt. 25:46). The spatial sense must be maintained. What is meant is the place which causes even the demons to tremble (εἰς τὴν ἄβυσσον, Lk. 8:31).

Obedience, which includes faith, leads to life.

εἰς (τὴν) ζωήν (Mt. 7:14; 18:8 f.); εἰς τὴν χαράν (Mt. 25:21, 23); often metaphorically, εἰς τὴν ἀποθήκην (Mt. 3:12 and par.); εἰς τὸν κόλπον 'Αβραάμ (Lk. 16:22); mostly on the assumption of a macrocosmic eschatology, esp. εἰς τὴν βασιλείαν (τοῦ θεοῦ, τῶν οὐρανῶν) with εἰσελθεῖν (Mt. 5:20; 7:21; 18:3; Mk. 9:47; 10:15 [Lk. 18:17]; 10:23, 25; Jn. 3:5); with εἴσοδος (2 Pt. 1:11); with προάγειν (Mt. 21:31); with σώζειν (2 Tm. 4:18); with βιάζεσθαι (Lk. 16:16). The only instance in Jn. seems to be a distant echo from the Synoptists. Paul has the conception (cf. 1 C. 6:10 with Lk. 10:25), but does not use εἰς. This is perhaps a sign of incipient spiritualising (→ 337). The idea occurs esp. in relation to the presence of the kingdom (ἐρρύσατο ἡμᾶς ἐκ τῆς ἐξουσίας τοῦ σκότους καὶ μετέστησεν εἰς τὴν βασιλείαν τοῦ υἱοῦ τῆς ἀγάπης αὐτοῦ, Col. 1:13). This movement into the present is particularly character-

---

[17] Ac. 2:27 should be rendered (in the sense of the author): "Thou wilt not leave my soul in Hades." Cf. Wdt. Ag., ad loc. (→ 433).

[18] Cf. Wnd. Pt., ad loc., where there are materials and bibl.

[19] Cf. the depiction of the apotheosis of Antoninus and Faustina on the base of the Antoninus pillar, now in the Giardino della Pigna of the Vatican. W. Amelung, Skulpturen des Vatikanischen Museums, I (1903), 887 ff., Plate 116; cf. L. Deubner, Röm. Mitteilungen, 27 (1912), 1 ff., cf. Wendland, Hell. Kult., 423, Plate V, 2.

[20] RGG², 1, 711.

[21] RGG², II, 1897 f., 1967 f.

istic of Johannine theology: the believer εἰς κρίσιν οὐκ ἔρχεται ἀλλὰ μεταβέβηκεν ἐκ τοῦ θανάτου εἰς τὴν ζωήν (Jn. 5:24; cf. 1 Jn. 3:14).

The Gk. says εἰς "Αιδου. But the expression μετελθεῖν εἰς τὸν ἀέναον (eternal) κόσμον (Ditt. Or., 56, 48), found on a gravestone in Canopos dating from the 3rd century B.C., is fairly isolated. The joys of the blessed and torments of the damned are vividly portrayed, esp. in the piety of the Mysteries, e.g., the Orphic.[22] There are similar descriptions in Judaism (Eth. En. 24-25; bBB, 74b: The Israelites will enjoy with delight the fabulous beasts prepared for them; cf. Gr. Bar. 4). Yet these are comparatively restrained, esp. on the positive side. In 4 Esr. 7:81 ff. there are some definite beginnings of spiritualisation. More modest, but so much the more impressive, are the NT statements. Only in Rev., and later in the so-called Apc. of Peter,[23] do we have a penetration of sadistic pictures of hell into Christianity.

The use of → ἐν is parallel, though less pregnant.

2. The Psychological Use.

a. εἰς denotes the intrusion of corruptive or salutary influences into the centre of personality.

Demons go into a man (Mt. 9:25; Lk. 8:38; cf. also Mt. 12:44 and par.). Satan puts evil into the heart of a man (Jn. 13:2), or himself comes into him (Lk. 22:3; Jn. 13:27). The former is also true of the avenging God (Rev. 17:17; and materially cf. Is. 6:9, 10; Mk. 4:12; R. 9:18). On the other hand, God sends His Spirit into (the hearts of) believers (1 Th. 4:8; Gl. 4:6). In contrast to unhealthy distraction, return to oneself denotes a restoration of normality. The return of the Prodigal begins when he goes into himself or comes to himself (εἰς ἑαυτὸν ἐλθών, Lk. 15:17).

b. With verbs of sending, speaking, teaching, proclaiming and preaching εἰς denotes address to someone, and is often used for the simple dative.

Jesus is sent to the lost sheep (Mt. 15:24). God reveals Himself to the Jewish people (εἰς ὑμᾶς, Ac. 2:22). The Gospel must be preached εἰς πάντα τὰ ἔθνη (Mk. 13:10; 14:9; Lk. 24:47; cf. εἰς ὑμᾶς, 1 Th. 2:9; εἰς ὑμᾶς πληρῶσαι τὸν λόγον τοῦ θεοῦ, Col. 1:25). The Johannine Christ speaks εἰς τὸν κόσμον (Jn. 8:26). Cf. also πληροῦν τὸν λόγον εἰς τὰς ἀκοὰς τοῦ λαοῦ (Lk. 7:1); εἰς τὰ ὑπερέκεινα ὑμῶν (2 C. 10:16); and for the underlying spatial sense, cf. ἄρτους ἔκλασα εἰς τοὺς πεντακισχιλίους (Mk. 8:19). In 1 Pt. 1:25, however, this is so weak that εἰς is merely used for the dative. When verbs of proclamation are linked with places, εἰς is used for → ἐν.

By its common use of these constructions, which are good Greek but which are also based on Hebrew, Christianity shows itself to be a religion of the word, of speech, of commanding, of hearing and obeying (→ λόγος, εὐαγγέλιον, κηρύσσειν, κήρυγμα, ἀκούειν, ἀκοή, ὑπακοή).

Hom. Il., 1, 402: καλέσασ' ἐς μακρὸν "Ολυμπον; Hdt., VIII, 26: εἰπεῖν ἐς πάντας; Thuc., I, 23: αἱ ἐς τὸ φανερὸν λεγόμεναι αἰτίαι; Plat. Tim., 28c: τὸν ποιητὴν καὶ πατέρα ... τοῦ παντὸς ... εἰς πάντας ἀδύνατον λέγειν. Gn. 24:28: ἀνήγγειλε εἰς τὸν οἶκον = לְבֵית, וַתַּגֵּד, cf. Jer. 5:20. With (ἐξ)αποστέλλω the LXX, like the NT, often uses the good Gk. πρός (Ex. 3:10; Jer. 7:25 etc.), and with κηρύσσειν and

---

[22] On Polygnotus's Delphic Nekyia, cf. Paus., X, 25-31; E. Rohde, Psyche[9, 10], I (1925), 317. There is rich material in the burial art of the Etruscans. Cf. F. Weege, Etruskische Malerei (1921); Photo Alinari, 26096 (the blessed dancing), 26098 (a man and wife at the feast of the blessed), 35838 (Sisyphos and Tityos), etc.

[23] On possible connections with the Orphic Mystery, cf. A. Dieterich, Nekyia[2] (1913).

εὐαγγελίζεσθαι the dative (Is. 61:1). So also Corp. Herm., I, 27: ἤργμαι κηρύσσειν τοῖς ἀνθρώποις τὸ τῆς εὐσεβείας καὶ γνώσεως κάλλος.

3. The use of εἰς to describe a situation.

This use approximates to → D. At root there is often the idea of (compulsory) leading. Not to be led εἰς πειρασμόν is the prayer of the disciples of Jesus (Mt. 6:13 and par.; cf. Mk. 14:38 and par.; 1 Tm. 6:9). God has shut up all in disobedience that He might have mercy on all (R. 11:32). The task of the apostle is to bring every thought captive into the sphere of Christ, to subjugate it to the obedience of Christ (2 C. 10:5).

Perhaps we should explain R. 6:17 along the same lines. Since ὑπακούειν εἰς is not used, we are tempted to read: ὑπηκούσατε τύπῳ διδαχῆς, εἰς ὃν παρεδόθητε. This gives better sense than ὃν παρεδόθητε or ὃς παρεδόθη ὑμῖν. The context suggests the figure of a captive subjected to another power. [24] R. 5:2: προσαγωγὴ ... εἰς τὴν χάριν and Gl. 1:6: μετατίθεσθαι εἰς ἕτερον εὐαγγέλιον may also be mentioned. The Greeks would say: εἰς πόνους καὶ φόβους καὶ λύπας ἐλθεῖν (Plat. Leg., I, 635c).

B. The Temporal Use of εἰς.

1. In a purely temporal sense, when a point of time is given, εἰς means "until," e.g., endure εἰς τέλος, "until the end" (Mt. 10:22; 24:13 and par.), unless there is also a suggestion of → C. "to the utmost." It occurs in other eschatological contexts like 2 Tm. 1:12: God proves faithful εἰς ἐκείνην τὴν ἡμέραν. When a span of time is mentioned it has the sense of "for," e.g., εἰς ἔτη πολλά (Lk. 12:19), esp. in a more formal usage to denote eternity → αἰών, γενεά. On εἰς τὸ → παντελές, cf. → 427. Hom. Il., 14, 86: ἐκ νεότητος ... ἐς γῆρας; Il., 19, 32: εἰς ἐνιαυτόν, "for a year." εἰς τέλος in Hdt., III, 40 simply means "finally," cf. also Lk. 18:5. [25] A Jewish expression underlies 1 Th. 2:16 (cf. ψ 76:9). Job 14:20 = נֶצַח; Test. L. 6:11: ἔφθασε δὲ αὐτοὺς ἡ ὀργὴ τοῦ θεοῦ εἰς τέλος ("for ever"). Cf. Dib. Th., ad loc. In the koine the temporal sense of the formula is not completely obliterated. [26]

2. More common in the NT is the temporal and final use in which an action is performed or a state of affairs is maintained or sought with a view to some appointed end.

μεριμνᾶν, τηρεῖν εἰς τὴν αὔριον, "to care for the next day" (Mt. 6:34; Ac. 4:3; cf. Jn. 12:7; Ac. 25:21); ἡτοιμασμένοι εἰς τὴν ὥραν (Rev. 9:15). The day of Jesus Christ is the goal both of the saving purpose of God and of the expectation of believers. The latter are sealed for the day of redemption by the Spirit (Eph. 4:30). They strive to be without offence, to be approved, to lay a good foundation εἰς ἡμέραν Χριστοῦ,

---

[24] Bl.-Debr. § 294, 5; Zn. R., ad loc.; cf. R. 1:24, 26, 28.

[25] Bl.-Debr., p. 302 suggests the rendering "that she may not completely make an end of me by her continual coming," and elsewhere transition to the modal sense → C. is perceived. But too much stress should not be laid on the present ἐρχομένη (instead of ἐλθοῦσα). A greater effect is achieved if ὑπωπιάζω is taken in its strict sense of "to make black and blue," and the order does not support an exclusive combination of εἰς τέλος with ὑπωπιάζη.

[26] Veröffentlichungen aus der Papyrussammlung der K. Hof- und Staatsbibl. zu München, I. Byzantin. Papyri (ed. A. Heisenberg and L. Wenger, 1914), 13, 70 (6th cent. A.D.): εἰς τέλος συνελάσαι, "to bring to an end" (cf. also Preisigke Wört., s.v. τέλος). Here the formula approximates to the more common εἰς τὸν ἅπαντα χρόνον (P. Oxy., VIII, 1123, 18) and εἰς τὸν ἀεὶ χρόνον (common at the end of letters).

εἰς τὸ μέλλον (Phil. 1:10; 2:16; 1 Tm. 6:19). There is a hardly perceptible line between 2 Pt. 2:4, 9; 3:7 and 1 Pt. 1:5. This sheds a light on the twofold use in Gl. 3:23 : ἐφρου-ρούμεθα συγκλειόμενοι εἰς τὴν μέλλουσαν πίστιν ἀποκαλυφθῆναι and 3:24 : ὁ νόμος ἡμῖν παιδαγωγὸς γέγονεν εἰς Χριστόν, "to faith," "to Christ," and with a view to both according to God's purpose. On the lips of the Johannine Christ there is sometimes an approximation to → D. (Jn. 6:27: ἐργάζεσθε τὴν βρῶσιν τὴν μένουσαν εἰς ζωὴν αἰώνιον, food which remains until and unto eternal life, which extends to eternal life, [27] cf. 4:36).

In secular Gk. this temporal and final usage seems to be common only in connection with a span of time. μισθοδοτεῖν τινας εἰς ἓξ μῆνας, Diod. S., XIX, 15, 5; ἡ εἰς ἐνιαυτὸν κειμένη δαπάνη εἰς τὸν μῆνα δαπανᾶται, the sum of tasks appointed for a year is given out for the month, Xenoph. Oec., 7, 36. On the other hand, it is rare in relation to a fixed point in time. Cf. Plat. Hi., I, 286b : μέλλω ἐπιδεικνύναι εἰς τρίτην ἡμέραν, I will give the address the day after to-morrow; P. Par., 43, 5 : παραγίνεσθαι εἰς τὴν ἡμέραν. But here there is no genuinely final element, as there is in the comparable Ac. 13:42; Lk. 1:20; 13:9. → F. 1.

C. The Modal Use.

In some cases εἰς denotes intensity.

Jn. 13:1: εἰς τέλος ἠγάπησεν. In view of the preceding part. the εἰς is first temporal, but it is also modal : "to the utmost" [28] cf. εἰς τὸ παντελές, Hb. 7:25; [29] cf. also Lk. 13:11. [30] Even plainer is 2 C. 10:15 : μεγαλυνθῆναι ... εἰς περισσείαν, "to find recognition in rich measure." The expression in 2 C. 10:13, 15 distinguishes, qualitatively rather than quantitatively, between unjustified boasting resting on the work of others (ἐν ἀλλοτρίοις κόποις) and justifiable boasting. Pleonastically [31] Paul says in 2 C. 4:17 that the light affliction of the present time works for us καθ' ὑπερβολὴν εἰς ὑπερβολήν ("in excess to excess") an eternal weight of glory. On ἀπὸ δόξης εἰς δόξαν and ἐκ πίστεως εἰς πίστιν, → 430.

εἰς τέλος τουτέστι παντελῶς, Diodorus on Ps. 51:7 (MPG, 33, 1589b); τὴν νίκην ἐς τέλος ἐξειργάσαντο, Appian Rom. Hist. Bell. Mithridaticum, 44 : ἀναβιβάσω σε εἰς τέλος; Gn. 46:4; Jos. 8:24; 2 Ch. 12:12; ψ 73:1; Job 6:9; 2 Macc. 8:29; εἰς τὸ παντελὲς ἀφανισθῆναι, "fully destroyed," Philo Leg. Gaj., 144; Jos. Ant., 1, 267; cf. 3, 264 and 274; 6, 30; 7, 325. On the other hand we have the temporal sense of "for ever" in Ditt. Or., 642, 2 : εἰς τὸ παντελὲς αἰώνιον τειμήν; P. Lond., III, 1164 f., 11. Diog. L., II, 6, 51: φίλος ἦν εἰς ὑπερβολήν; Eur. Hipp., 939 : εἰς ὑπερβολὴν πανοῦργος.

D. εἰς in a Logical Connection.

1. Very occasionally εἰς states the reason.

The transition from a spatial to a causal sense is seen in R. 4:20 : εἰς τὴν ἐπαγγε-λίαν οὐ διεκρίθη, "in view of the promise of God he did not doubt." There is a

---

[27] Cf. Zn. J., ad loc.

[28] Zn., Tillm., ad loc. argue for a purely temporal, Bl.-Debr., p. 302, for a purely modal use (cf. H. Pernot, Etudes sur la Langue des Evangiles [1927], 207; A. Debrunner, Gnomon, IV [1928], 444). Acc. to Bau., ad loc. and Pr.-Bauer, s.v. the two merge into one another.

[29] The immediate context supports a temporal understanding (vg, syr, copt, Wnd. Hb., Rohr Hb., ad loc.), but the modal aspect (armen, Rgg. Hb., ad loc.) cannot be ruled out (cf. v. 11 τελείωσις). The salvation is eternal and therefore perfect.

[30] Purely modal. Either with μὴ δυναμένη, "could not stand upright at all" (vg : nec omnino poterat), or with ἀνακῦψαι, "could not stand upright properly" (Kl. Lk., ad loc.; sys syc allow both meanings). The order and sense support the latter.

[31] Attempts to simplify by excision do not do justice to the thrust of the statement. Cf. Wnd. 2 K., ad loc.

similar use in the phrase εἰς τὸ κήρυγμα (Mt. 12:41; Lk. 11:32), "with a view to the preaching of repentance," as also in εἰς τὰ ἕτοιμα → καυχᾶσθαι (2 C. 10:16), "to boast of what others have done" (→ 427). [32] Similarly the reference in Gl. 6:4 : εἰς ἑαυτὸν μόνον τὸ → καύχημα ἕξει καὶ οὐκ εἰς τὸν ἕτερον, is not merely to open or tacit expressions of self-glory but, as the context shows, to the *materies gloriandi* (v. 4a, 5). Unless honest self-examination shows that there is nothing to boast of, he must find his own justification rather than following the standards of others, thus taking pride only in himself and not in others (= κατὰ τὸν κανόνα ἡμῶν ... οὐκ ἐν ἀλλοτρίῳ κανόνι, 2 C. 10:15 f.). [33]

Cf. P. Giess, I, 66, 9 (2nd cent. A.D.): ἐρωτῶ σε εἰς (Lat. *per*) τὴν τῶν θεῶν εὐσέβειαν "I beseech thee by the fear of the gods" (→ διά, 68 f.).

2. εἰς denotes appointment (Mt. 5:22; 1 C. 11:22; 14:22; Col. 2:22; Jm. 5:3; Rev. 22:2).

In religious contexts there is reference a. to the divine appointment.

The angels are spirits which in the divine service are sent to minister to those who shall inherit salvation (Hb. 1:14). Moses was θεράπων εἰς μαρτύριον τῶν λαληθησομένων, a minister appointed to bear witness to what should be said (Hb. 3:5). What was written in Scripture was written for the instruction of later generations (R. 15:4). Paul is appointed to publish the good news (R. 1:1). His readers are not appointed to wrath but to the winning of salvation (1 Th. 5:9; 2 Th. 2:13), to sonship (Eph. 1:5). God has begotten believers again to a living hope and an incorruptible inheritance (1 Pt. 1:3 f.). In the NT, however, there is an appointment not only to eternal life (Ac. 13:48: τεταγμένοι εἰς ζωὴν αἰώνιον) but also judicially, though not as a *decretum absolutum,* to stumbling in the case of the disobedient (1 Pt. 2:8 : εἰς ὃ [sc. προσκόπτειν] καὶ ἐτέθησαν) → τάσσω, τίθημι. If God does not have the direct purpose, He certainly has the right and the power to appoint vessels to → ἀπώλεια as well as to → δόξα (R. 9:21 ff., and a little less sharply in 2 Tm. 2:20 f.). How to define and to delimit the doctrine of twofold predestination is another question. But it certainly cannot be ruled out altogether.

There is also reference b. to the human appointment which may also be a fulfilment of the divine appointment.

The Spirit demands the separation of missionaries to the work to which He has called them (Ac. 13:2). τοῦτο ποιεῖτε εἰς τὴν ἐμὴν ἀνάμνησιν is how the summons to the Lord's Supper runs. It may be fashioned by Paul, possibly along the lines of Gk. formulae, but it corresponds to the intention of Jesus (1 C. 11:24 f.). Believers should do all things to the glory of God (1 C. 10:31). The distinction from → D. 3. a. is fluid.

This εἰς of appointment may well correspond to the Heb. -לְ (Gn. 3:6 : καλὸν τὸ ξύλον εἰς βρῶσιν = טוֹב ... לְמַאֲכָל), but it is not a Hebraism. In Gk. it often occurs in formal contexts, esp. sacral. Inscr. Priene, 50, 39 (c. 2nd cent. B.C.): ταῦτα δὲ εἶναι εἰς φυλακὴν τῆς πόλεως. Inscr. from the Delphinion at Miletus (ed. G. Kawerau and A. Rehm, 1914), 134, 33 ff. (1st cent. A.D.): ταῦτα δὲ εἶναι εἰς εὐσέβειαν τῶν τε θεῶν καὶ τῶν Σεβαστῶν καὶ διαμονὴν τῆς πόλεως i.e., serving both the pious honouring of gods and Their Majesties and also the security of the city. [34] The will of Epicurus (Diog. L., X, 18) arranges a commemorative meal for the writer and his friend

---

[32] Wnd. 2 C. suggests not very convincingly : εἰς τὰ ἑτερόμετρα (or εἰς τὰ ἑτέροις μερισθέντα) θέλοντες καυχήσασθαι.

[33] Sieffert Gl., *ad loc.*

[34] Deissmann LO., 96 f.

in the words: εἰς τὴν εἰθισμένην ἄγεσθαι γενέθλιον ἡμέραν ... εἰς τὴν ἡμῶν τε καὶ Μητροδώρου μνήμην. [35]

3. Consecutive and final εἰς. The preposition denotes the direction of an action to a specific end. Whether this is incidental or intentional must be deduced from the context and is not always clear.

a. With the subst. or pronomin. acc. it usually has a final sense. This usage, resting on spatial ideas, is linked with → D. 2., as may be seen from a comparison between καλεῖν εἰς μετάνοιαν (Lk. 5:32, also εἰς κοινωνίαν, 1 C. 1:9 and εἰς δόξαν, 1 Pt. 5:10) and βαπτίζειν εἰς μετάνοιαν (Mt. 3:11). The final force of εἰς increases to the degree that the associated prepositional expression becomes an independent adverbial definition.

Cf. the common expression εἰς μαρτύριον αὐτοῖς, Mk. 1:44 and par.; 6:11; Lk. 9:5; cf. Mt. 24:14; Mk. 13:9 (Lk. 21:13 consecut.: ἀποβήσεται ὑμῖν εἰς μαρτύριον); also εἰς μνημόσυνον αὐτῆς, Mk. 14:9 and par. John baptises, and Jesus sheds His blood, for the forgiveness of sins (Mk. 1:4; Lk. 3:3; Mt. 26:28; cf. Ac. 2:38). The Christian message is the power of God to salvation to those who believe (R. 1:16; cf. 10:1, 4). God has set up Christ as a → ἱλαστήριον in His own blood, effective through faith with a view to demonstrating His judicial but especially His gracious righteousness (→ 204): εἰς ἔνδειξιν τῆς δικαιοσύνης αὐτοῦ (R. 3:25). The apostolic mission of Paul is with a view to the obedience of faith among all nations, or among the Gentiles (R. 1:5). In the power of his apostolic authority Paul delivers up the incestuous person at Corinth to Satan for physical destruction, that the spirit may be saved (1 C. 5:5). The eternal life of the blessed, the upbuilding of the body of Christ, and the praise and glory of God, are the aims which are pursued by the saving rule of God and which are thus to be fulfilled through human action (εἰς ζωὴν αἰώνιον, 1 Tm. 1:16; εἰς οἰκοδομὴν τοῦ σώματος τοῦ Χριστοῦ, Eph. 4:12; εἰς ἔπαινον, Eph. 1:6, 14; εἰς δόξαν τοῦ θεοῦ, R. 15:7). A final sense is also present in pronominal combinations like εἰς τί; (Mt. 14:31; Mk. 14:4 and par.; 15:34 [Mt. 27:46: ἱνατί]) and εἰς (αὐτὸ) τοῦτο (Mk. 1:38), with the final clause in Jn. 18:37; Ac. 9:21; 26:16; R. 9:17; 14:9; 2 C. 2:9; Eph. 6:22; Col. 4:8; 1 Pt. 4:6.

Yet in other cases there is an undoubted consecutive use.

1 C. 11:17: οὐκ εἰς τὸ κρεῖσσον ἀλλὰ εἰς τὸ ἧσσον συνέρχεσθε is not so much criticising the purpose as the actual result. Similarly in 11:34 the meaning is not so much that the Corinthians might have aimed at judgment as that their conduct could have the actual result of judgment (ἵνα μὴ εἰς κρίμα συνέρχησθε). Further examples are Rev. 13:3: ἐσφαγμένην εἰς θάνατον; 2 C. 8:2: εἰς τὸ πλοῦτος τῆς ἁπλότητος αὐτῶν, "so that there was a rich access of liberality"; Col. 1:11: δυναμούμενοι εἰς πᾶσαν ὑπομονήν; 2 C. 7:9 f.: ἐλυπήθητε εἰς μετάνοιαν, μετάνοια εἰς σωτηρίαν; R. 10:10: εἰς δικαιοσύνην — εἰς σωτηρίαν; R. 13:4: σοὶ εἰς τὸ ἀγαθόν. The antitheses of R. 5:16, 18, 21; 6:16, 21, which are denoted by the use of εἰς, are goals rather than consequences, and there is a strong final element in R. 6:19. Cf. also R. 3:7; 8:15, 21, 28; 13:14; 2 C. 9:11. In R. 7:10 there is an instructive fusion of both elements.

In many cases the one merges into the other, so that a precise differentiation is impossible.

R. 14:1: μὴ εἰς διακρίσεις, "not to dispute about opinions," or "without giving rise to argumentation." [36] 1 C. 12:13: εἰς ἓν σῶμα ἐβαπτίσθημεν, "in order that there may

---

[35] Joh. W., Ltzm. 1 K. on 11:24.
[36] Cf. the varying translations of Althaus and Jülicher.

be one body," or "with the result that there is one body." Here both are correct. Cf. R. 13:4 : εἰς ὀργήν. Phil. 1:11; Hb. 4:16. This fact should not be used to obscure the final sense where it is present but creates difficulties, e.g., in relation to predestination (→ 428; *infra*).

R. 1:17: ἐκ πίστεως εἰς πίστιν, and 2 C. 3:18 : ἀπὸ δόξης εἰς δόξαν, are not to be understood in terms of OT analogies like ἐκ κακῶν εἰς κακά (Jer. 3:9), ἐκ δυνάμεως εἰς δύναμιν (ψ 83:7) and ἀπὸ τοῦ αἰῶνος ἕως τοῦ αἰῶνος (ψ 89:1), or of χάριν ἀντὶ χάριτος in Jn. 1:16. [37] In R. 1:17 ἐκ πίστεως is a loose addition, like διὰ πίστεως in R. 3:22, to define the phrase δικαιοσύνη θεοῦ (→ 207) [38] in a Pauline sense, whereas εἰς πίστιν is final : The judicial righteousness promised by God (→ 204), as the Jew desires it (δικαιοσύνη θεοῦ = זְכוּת, which in its forensic sense cannot be rendered by δικαιοσύνη alone), is revealed in the Gospel (as a righteousness) from faith with a view to faith. In 2 C. 3:18 ἀπὸ δόξης corresponds to ἀπὸ κυρίου and is thus to be related to the δόξα of Christ, so that εἰς δόξαν is consecutive and predicative (→ also F. 2.). We are transformed from glory to glory (→ 251). [39]

b. With substant. infin. or accus. c. infin: εἰς is predominantly final, though also consecutive.

How the final use develops from the local may be seen in expressions like φρονεῖν εἰς τὸ σωφρονεῖν in R. 12:3 or παραδοῦναι εἰς τὸ ἐμπαῖξαι, σταυρῶσαι, σταυρωθῆναι, θανατῶσαι in Mt. 20:19; 26:2; 27:31 (Mk. 15:20 ἵνα); Mk. 14:55 (Mt. 26:59 ὅπως). Where there is no final concept, we have the autonomously final combination with the infin., as R. 1:11: εἰς τὸ στηριχθῆναι ὑμᾶς; Hb. 2:17: εἰς τὸ ἱλάσκεσθαι; Jm. 1:18: εἰς τὸ εἶναι ἡμᾶς ἀπαρχήν τινα τῶν αὐτοῦ κτισμάτων, "that we may be in some sense the firstfruits of His creatures" etc. Clearly consecutive are such phrases as Hb. 11:3 : κατηρτίσθαι τοὺς αἰῶνας ῥήματι θεοῦ, εἰς τὸ μὴ ἐκ φαινομένων τὸ βλεπόμενον γεγονέναι, "that the worlds were framed by the Word of God, with the result that things which may be seen have proceeded from those which do not appear" ; R. 6:12 : μὴ βασιλευέτω ἡ ἁμαρτία ... εἰς τὸ ὑπακούειν ταῖς ἐπιθυμίαις; 1 C. 8:10 : ἡ συνείδησις ... οἰκοδομηθήσεται εἰς τὸ τὰ εἰδωλόθυτα ἐσθίειν; 2 Th. 2:10 : εἰς τὸ σωθῆναι αὐτούς; R. 7:4 : εἰς τὸ γενέσθαι κτλ. (ἵνα κτλ. is subordinate); 7:5 : εἰς τὸ καρποφορῆσαι κτλ. (v. 6 : ὥστε κτλ. and par.); 12:2 : εἰς τὸ δοκιμάζειν. There is instructive alternation in R. 4:11 ff.: εἰς τὸ εἶναι κτλ. and εἰς τὸ λογισθῆναι, consecutive ; εἰς τὸ εἶναι (v. 16), final ; εἰς τὸ γενέσθαι (v. 18), consecutive again. There are some middle cases where a purpose is present but the emphasis is on the result. An example of this is to be found in 2 C. 4:4 : "Whose unbelieving minds the god of this world has blinded that they do not see the light of the gospel of the glory of Christ." In 2 C. 1:4 Paul speaks of the comfort with which God comforts him that he may comfort others, suggesting that the purpose is achieved in this result. Cf. also R. 3:26 : εἰς τὸ εἶναι αὐτὸν δίκαιον κτλ., where there is obviously a continuation of the εἰς ἔνδειξιν of v. 25, but more particularly the assertion of a result.

The linguistic facts give rise to the theological problem whether in certain statements concerning the guilt of man this is to be understood as an immanent consequence or as the purpose of the divine Judge.

In 1 Th. 2:16 εἰς τὸ ἀναπληρῶσαι αὐτῶν τὰς ἁμαρτίας πάντοτε is dependent on κωλυόντων and cannot be taken consecutively, since this would demand the acc. c. infin.

---

[37] Ltzm. R and 2 K. accepts this interpretation in both passages, Wnd. 2 K. in the former.

[38] Though we cannot adopt his exposition, Khl. R. esp. draws attention to the fact that this phrase needs to be filled out. Cf. ThLBl, 55 (1934), 179 f. Cf. also Sickb. R., *ad loc.*; 2 K. 3:18.

[39] Wnd. 2 K. has renewed this early exegesis.

The simple infin. means "in order that" and strictly implies that the Jews intended to bring their sins to a climax, though probably we have here a less precise and grimly ironical expression for the providential purpose of God, [40] namely, that since they will have it thus, they must now fill up their sins to the limit. In 2 Th. 2:11 εἰς τὸ πιστεῦσαι αὐτοὺς τῷ ψεύδει can be taken consecutively, but this is unlikely in view of the final clause which follows. Here, too, we have a reference to the providential purpose. [41] R. 1:20: εἰς τὸ εἶναι αὐτοὺς ἀναπολογήτους, cannot possibly be final. [42] Certainly the thought that they are to be inexcusable is in line with the thought of the apostle (cf. the threefold παρέδωκεν αὐτούς in vv. 24, 26, 28). But only logically, not grammatically, is God the subject of the sentence. Moreover, the point is to show the ground of the complaint. Hence we should render: "So that they are without excuse." [43]

E. The εἰς of Personal Relationship.

In general the NT makes a correct distinction between εἰς and πρός. εἰς in the sense of "to" (to go to someone etc.) is Homeric. Whether it is also classical is debated. [44] The MSS vary. Later εἰς becomes more common for πρός. In the sense of personal relationship εἰς is not restricted to a specific linguistic circle.

1. εἰς denotes the relationship as such, in the neutral sense. A comparison is made with reference to, or it is valid of, a certain person (1 C. 4:6; Eph. 5:32; cf. Hb. 9:9: παραβολὴ εἰς τὸν καιρὸν τὸν ἐνεστῶτα).

Lk. 12:21: εἰς θεὸν πλουτῶν, hardly fits the preceding parable if it is taken along the lines of R. 10:12 or in the sense that alms are a treasure laid up with God (→ F. 1.). Critical conclusions have been drawn from this. [45] But there are no linguistic reasons (→ infra) why we should not think of being rich in relation to God, so that a wealth which has value in God's eyes, or even God Himself, is the object of possession. The elliptical construction in R. 5:18, which is best taken with ἐγένετο in the first clause and with γενήσεται in the second, works out the parallel neutrally with a changing material content. Through one offence condemnation came with effect upon all, and through one act of obedience life-giving justification came with effect upon all. Though περισσεύειν εἰς is neutral in itself, it has in Paul a predominantly friendly connotation (R. 5:15; 2 C. 1:5; 9:8; Eph. 1:8; → E. 3.). Eur. Or., 542: εὐτυχεῖν ἐς τέκνα, "to be happy with reference to children." Cf. Plato Ap., 35b: οἱ διαφέροντες Ἀθηναίων εἰς ἀρετήν, clearly distinguished from διαφέρειν ἀρετῇ, ibid., 35a.

2. εἰς denotes relationship in a hostile sense. Enmity is directed a. against God, the Son of Man, the Spirit, the emissaries or institutions of God, in the form of sin.

ἥμαρτον εἰς τὸν οὐρανόν (Lk. 15:18, 21). The carnal mind is ἔχθρα εἰς θεόν (R. 8:7). Unloving conduct in matters of conscience is ἁμαρτάνειν εἰς Χριστόν (1 C. 8:12). ἁμαρτάνειν εἰς may sometimes be linked with material objects in such a way as to be finally directed against God (Ac. 25:8; 1 C. 6:18). Blasphemy is a particular form, e.g., βλασφημεῖν, λέγειν λόγον εἰς (Mk. 3:29; Lk. 12:10; Ac. 6:11).

b. It is also directed against men. The NT warns us especially of the hostility of persecutors against the disciples of Jesus (Jn. 15:21; Ac. 9:1; 23:30). Yet it also

---

[40] Dob. Th., ad loc. In R. 7:5 ἐνηργεῖτο makes possible the simple infin.
[41] Dob. Th., ad loc.
[42] Khl. R., ad loc.
[43] Ltzm., Sickb. R., ad loc.
[44] Kühner-Blass-Gerth, II, 1, 468.
[45] Cf. Jülicher Gl. J., II, 614 ff. and Kl. Lk., ad loc.

considers the possibility that one man might sin against another, or even one brother against another (Mt. 18:15, 21; Lk. 17:3, 4; 1 C. 8:12). In such a case it enjoins the necessity of constant readiness to forgive, but it does not ignore the possibility of withdrawal within the limits drawn for believers in Christ. In the same connection Paul can even say of Christ: οὐκ ἀσθενεῖ εἰς ὑμᾶς (2 C. 13:3). The NT does not use εἰς for God's reaction against sin and the sinner. For God is not the enemy of men, nor are men called the → ἐχθροί of God in the passive sense.

Hdt., VI, 65 : ἔχθρη ἔς τινα; I, 86 : λέγειν ἐς . . . ; Aesch. Prom., 945 : ἐξαμαρτεῖν εἰς θεούς; cf. 2 Macc. 7:18; Gn. 20:6 : τοῦ μὴ ἁμαρτεῖν σε εἰς ἐμέ.

3. εἰς denotes friendly relationship a. between man and man.

Mt. 26:10 of the woman of Bethany. In R. 1:27 εἰς is used to show how gross is the perversion of sexual love.

Its specific usage in the NT is for Christian brotherly love : εἰς ἀλλήλους φιλόστοργοι, τὸ αὐτὸ εἰς ἀλλήλους φρονοῦντες, κοπιᾶν εἰς τινα (R. 12:10, 16; 16:6). The εἰς ἀλλήλους of R. 14:19 is much weaker, being little more than an equivalent of the genitive. On the other hand, the εἰς is most significant when Paul speaks of the collection for the poor saints at Jerusalem (R. 15:26; 1 C. 16:3).

The origin and exemplar of this love is the divine love b. of God for man. God reveals His love for those who were enemies in the death of His Son (R. 5:8). The righteousness which God gives reaches out or spreads its wings εἰς πάντας [καὶ ἐπὶ πάντας] τοὺς πιστεύοντας (R. 3:22). [46] What the prophets saw from afar, and what causes the blessed to praise God, is the gift of grace to believers (1 Pt. 1:10; 2 C. 1:11).

It can also denote c. the love of the world and man for God. A basic NT principle is that all things are created for God or to God, or more narrowly for Christ or to Christ (1 C. 8:6; R. 11:36; Col. 1:16). After the fall the original situation was restored by God's reconciling all things to Himself through Christ (Col. 1:20). [47] The practical point of what might otherwise be a lofty theosophical speculation is that divinely sent messengers preach τὴν εἰς θεὸν μετάνοιαν (Ac. 20:21). The positive correlative of this repentance, or more correctly perhaps its positive side, is → πίστις (Ac. 24:24; 26:18; Col. 2:5) or → πιστεύειν εἰς τὸν κύριον Ἰησοῦν, i.e., the faith which is believing in or on the Lord Jesus. This expression is not merely an equivalent of ל הֶאֱמִין, which is rare with reference to God in the OT and which is rendered by the dative in the LXX (Dt. 9:23; Is. 43:10). Nor does it correspond to בְּ הֶאֱמִין (→ 434). It is an original NT construction. The alternation between the substantive and the verbal forms, which recurs in relation to the cognate term "hope" (Ac. 24:15; 1 Pt. 1:21; 2 C. 1:10), is less significant than the full material parallelism and even congruence between εἰς θεὸν and εἰς Χριστὸν πιστεύειν (cf. esp. Jn. 14:1; 1 Pt. 1:21) and the varying distribution of the latter phrase in the NT writings.

---

[46] The fuller reading attested by ﬡ DG and some minusc. etc. is probably due to the combination of an old variant with the original. Cf. Ltzm. R., ad loc.

[47] The debated question whether εἰς αὐτόν refers to God or to Christ need not be discussed here. The former is more probable.

πιστεύειν εἰς in relation to Christ is found in the Synpt. only at Mk. 9:42; Mt. 18:6; in Ac. three times (10:43; 14:23; 19:4), in Pl. three times (R. 10:14; Gl. 2:16; Phil. 1:29), in Jn. over thirty times between 2:11 and 17:20, and in the Johannine Ep. only once (1 Jn. 5:10), ὁμολογεῖν or πιστεύειν ὅτι being much more common.

The concentration of belief in Christ seems to have undergone a development linked with the growing apprehension of what was present in Him from the very first as He is depicted in the Synoptic Gospels. At the end of the process we have expressions like → βαπτίζειν εἰς Χριστόν and βαπτίζειν εἰς τὸ → ὄνομα κτλ. (→ I, 539), which may be compared with technical phrases in Hellenistic finance and which may have been influenced by these terminologically. εἰς Χριστόν never became a formula like → ἐν Χριστῷ. There is hardly the slightest impulse in this direction in an expression like ἀπαρχὴ τῆς 'Ασίας εἰς Χριστόν (R. 16:5).

Thuc., II, 9: φιλία ἐς ἀμφοτέρους. εἰς with proper names is often found in dedications, M. Ant., 4, 23 (to nature): ἐκ σοῦ πάντα, ἐν σοὶ πάντα, εἰς σὲ πάντα. Inscr. on a magic ring (Cod. Marcianus, 11th cent. A.D.): [48] ἓν τὸ πᾶν καὶ δι' αὐτοῦ τὸ πᾶν καὶ εἰς αὐτὸ τὸ πᾶν. P. Amh., 144, 20 (5th cent. A.D.). Egyptian commercial formulae: εἰς Σαραπιάδα (P. Fay., 83, 6 [163 A.D.]); τὰς εἰς τὸν Μάρωνα ... οἰκονομίας, "putting to the account of Maron" (CPR, 1, 11 [83/84 A.D.]); διάστειλον εἰς ὄνο (current abbrev. for ὄνομα) Οὐεστ Σεκοῦδα (Ostrac. Theb., 2nd cent. A.D., Deissmann's collection). [49] The NT εἰς (τὸ) ὄνομα is parallel to the Rabbin. לשׁם only in Mt. 10:41 f.; 18:20 and perhaps Hb. 6.10. [50]

F. Individual Points and the Question of Hebraisms.

1. εἰς often occurs where one might expect ἐν. Staying in a place may be represented as the result of movement towards it.

Thus εἰς occurs with places and place-names together with verbs denoting presence, dwelling etc.: κατῴκησεν εἰς ... Ναζαρέτ, "he settled again in Nazareth" (Mt. 2:23); ἐπέσχεν χρόνον εἰς τὴν 'Ασίαν (Ac. 19:22). Cf. also Mt. 4:13; Lk. 4:23; Ac. 7:12; 8:40; 18:21 vl.; 20:14; 23:11; 25:4; also with a simple subst.: εἰς τὰς συναγωγάς, Mk. 1:39; εἰς συναγωγὰς δαρήσεσθε, Mk. 13:9 (Mt. 10:17 ἐν); [51] cf. Mt. 10:9; Mk. 6:8; 5:14 and par.: τοῦ εὐαγγελίου τοῦ παρόντος εἰς ὑμᾶς (Col. 1:6; 1 Pt. 5:12, if ἐστήκατε is the correct reading). In both Mk. 1:9: βαπτίζειν εἰς τὸν 'Ιορδάνην, and Jn. 9:7: νίπτεσθαι εἰς τὴν κολυμβήθραν, we have the idea of dipping into the water. Cf. also the pregnant combinations βεβαιοῦν, αὐξάνειν εἰς Χριστόν (2 C. 1:21; Eph. 4:15); ἡ μέλλουσα δόξα ἀποκαλυφθῆναι εἰς ἡμᾶς (R. 8:18). On the other hand, in expressions like ὁ ὢν εἰς τὸν κόλπον τοῦ πατρός (Jn. 1:18), εἰς πάντα ὑπήκοοι (2 C. 2:9), or ἐγκαταλείπειν τὴν ψυχὴν εἰς ᾅδην (Ac. 2:27, 31, in the sense of the author), εἰς and ἐν are fully interchangeable. Complete equation is displayed in the use of εἰς in Ac. 7:53 in the sense of the instrumental ἐν: ἐλάβετε τὸν νόμον εἰς διαταγὰς ἀγγέλων = ἐν διαταγαῖς (cf. Mt. 9:34). εἰς is used for the temporal ἐν in Lk. 1:20; 13:9; Ac. 13:42 (with a final suggestion? → 427). The substitution of ἐν for εἰς is rarer (Lk. 9:46; 19:30; R. 5:5; Jn. 5:4, a doubtful verse), but not Lk. 7:17 ("went abroad in"); Mt. 16:28 and Lk. 23:42 [52] ("come with"). On 2 C. 4:6 → λάμπω.

---

[48] M. Berthelot, Collection des Anciens Alchimistes Grecs (1888), Introduction, 132; E. Norden, Agnostos Theos (1913), 240, 249.

[49] Deissmann LO., 96 ff.; Preisigke Girowesen, 147 ff.

[50] Heitmüller, 99 ff.

[51] For many similar instances, cf. Regard, 331 ff.

[52] It is impossible to say with certainty whether εἰς τὴν βασιλείαν (BL lat) is here a poor emendation or ἐν τῇ βασιλείᾳ (אCא pl) is an assimilation to Mt. 16:28.

The interchanging of εἰς and ἐν is not a Hebraism but is Homeric (Il., 13, 628 : ἐν νηυσὶν πῦρ βαλέειν; 19, 121: ἐν φρεσὶ θήσω), classical (Hdt., VI, 1: παρὴν ἐς Σάρδις) and above all Hellen., Act. Thom., 18 (*Texts and Studies*, 5, 1 [1897], James): μὴ δουλεύσει εἰς τὸν ἐμὸν οἶκον. In modern Gk. εἰς has supplanted ἐν. [53] In the NT most of the examples are in Lk., while Mt. and Rev. (though cf. Rev. 11:11) generally distinguish between the two prepositions. In some cases, however, the alternation is to be explained by the difference, or the difference in translation, of Hebrew prefixes (Gn. 16:5 : δέδωκα τὴν παιδίσκην μου εἰς τὸν κόλπον σου = בְּחֵיקֶךָ, otherwise mostly ἐν). Cf. also ὀμνύναι in Mt. 5:34 ff. (= נִשְׁבַּע בְּ, strictly "to swear in common with someone"); εὐδοκεῖν (= חָפֵץ בְּ, 2 Pt. 1:17 εἰς, Synpt. in all par. ἐν); and πιστεύειν (with ἐν in Mk. 1:15; [54] also ἐπί with dat. in R. 9:33 etc., with acc. in R. 4:5; Ac. 9:42 etc. = הֶאֱמִין בְּ, though it is not always to be derived from this (cf. ψ 77:22; Da. 6:23[24] [Θ]; Is. 28:16 [אAQ]; Wis. 12:2). In this connection we should also mention ὕπαγε (πορεύου) εἰς εἰρήνην in Mk. 5:34; Lk. 8:48; 7:50 (= לֵךְ לְשָׁלוֹם, cf. 1 Βασ. 1:17 etc.; Jm. 2:16; Ac. 16:36 and D in both passages in Lk. ἐν).

2. εἰς serves to denote the predicate with verbs like γίγνεσθαι (Mt. 21:42; Mk. 12:10; Jn. 16:21; Ac. 4:11); εἶναι (Mk. 10:8; 1 Jn. 5:8); ἔχειν (Mt. 21:46); ἐγείρειν (Ac. 13:22), or the result with στρέφειν (Rev. 11:6); σχίζεσθαι (Mt. 27:51); συνάγειν (Jn. 11:52); τελειοῦν (Jn. 17:23 etc.). λογίζεσθαι is found in R. 4:3; Gl. 3:6; Jm. 2:23 (1 Macc. 2:52 A nomin., cf. Gn. 15:6 in the original). This usage, again, is not simply a Hebraism. In Theogn., 162 (6th cent. B.C.) we already have : τὸ κακὸν δοκέον γίνεται εἰς ἀγαθόν, and in Heliod. Aeth., VI, 14, where there is no suspicion of Jewish Gk., we read : τὴν πήραν εἰς καθέδραν ποιησαμένη. On the other hand, the influence of ל has strengthened an original tendency. [55]

3. εἰς can also replace the gen. or dat.; 1 Pt. 1:11: τὰ εἰς Χριστὸν παθήματα "the sufferings of Christ"; 1:4 : τετηρημένην ... εἰς ὑμᾶς, "reserved for you"; Eph. 3:16 : κραταιωθῆναι εἰς τὸν ἔσω ἄνθρωπον "to grow strong in the inner man" etc. In the *koine* and in modern Gk. this is common usage. Polyb., I, 7, 12 : τῆς εἰς ἐκείνους τιμωρίας. P. Par. (ed. W. Brunet de Presle, Notices et Extraits des Manuscrits de la Bibliothèque Imperiale, XVIII [1865], 5, II, 2 (114 B.C.): χωρὶς τοῦ ἐς αὐτὴν οἶκον (οἴκου), "outside her house"; *ibid.*, 5, I, 7 (114 B.C.): τὸν εἰς Τάγην οἶκον ᾠκοδομημένον, "the house built for Tage."

                                                                                              Oepke

---

| εἰς | → ἅπαξ, → πρῶτος, → μόνος, → θεός.

1. The Understanding of Uniqueness in the NT.

Only rarely is εἰς used as a digit in the NT (e.g., 2 Pt. 3:8). [1] It usually means "single," "once-for-all," "unique" or "only," or "unitary," "unanimous," or "one of two or many," [2] "only one."

---

[53] Bl.-Debr., 2, n. 1 § 205 f., 218; Hatzidakis, Jannaris, Krumbacher, *op. cit.*

[54] This is an isolated instance. In Jn. 3:15 and Eph. 1:13 πιστεύειν is used in the absol. πίστις ἐν is hardly used in R. 3:25 or Gl. 3:26, where the prepositional expression belongs to the verb. Nor do we have the more pregnant sense of → ἐν, in the sense of πιστεύειν ἐν, in Eph. 1:15; Col. 1:4; or even 1 Tm. 1:14; 3:13; 2 Tm. 1:13; 3:15, as the preceding article shows.

[55] Examples may be found in Johannessohn, I, 4 f. On the question of Hebraisms, cf. Bl.-Debr. § 145 and appendix on p. 298, where older and more recent literature is listed.

εἰς. [1] μία τῶν σαββάτων (Mk. 16:2; Ac. 20:7; 1 C. 16:2) is a Semitism (= אֶחָד בְּשַׁבָּת); v. S. Krauss, *Talmud. Archäol.* II (1911), 422 f.; G. Dalman, *Arbeit u. Sitte in Pal.*, I, 1 (1928), 16, 3; Kl. on Mk. 16:2.

[2] On Mk. 14:10 (ὁ εἰς τῶν δώδεκα), v. Pr.-Bauer, *s.v.*

Its main theological significance is in relation to the formula εἷς θεός. "God is one" is the teaching of the *shema* in Dt. 6:4 : יהוה אחד. There is no God beside Him (Mk. 12:29, 32). His uniqueness is especially significant for His people : ἡμῖν εἷς θεὸς ὁ πατήρ, ἐξ οὗ τὰ πάντα καὶ ἡμεῖς εἰς αὐτόν — καὶ εἷς κύριος Ἰησοῦς Χριστός, δι' οὗ τὰ πάντα καὶ ἡμεῖς δι' αὐτοῦ (1 C. 8:6). In the one God the origin and goal of the world, and in the one Christ history and salvation history, are a unity. [3]

This pregnant εἷς, however, has another significance in early Christianity. It resists all dualism and eliminates any either-or relationship between God and anti-god. Man can serve only one Lord (Mt. 6:24). It denotes the elemental and inviolable union, the *henosis,* of married couples (Ign. Pol., 5, 2), and also points to a higher union with the Lord (1 C. 6:17; Eph. 5:31; → γάμος, I, 649, 651).

A thought particularly expressed by the emphatic εἷς is that everything depends on one thing, that man's whole way and future are decided by one question (Mk. 10:21; Lk. 10:42 vl.). Thus the keeping of the Law stands or falls with one commandment. We all become disobedient with one transgression. The fulness of the divine will is enclosed in the one commandment of love (Mt. 5:18; Jm. 2:10; Gl. 5:14). It is necessary to be vigilant and strong for one hour. Power is given to evil for one hour. In one hour catastrophe descends on all sides and in all forms. [4] Early Christianity has a comprehensive awareness of the astonishing import of the single and unique. The particular is not lost in the vastness of the world and history. The individual bears the whole within it and decides once and for all.

NT thinking is neither individual nor collective, but organic. God's will is directed neither to the isolated soul nor the mass as such, but always to the conditioned and conditioning member of a unit — the house, the people, the race, creation (R. 8:19 ff.). God's action always implies a threefold relation, namely, to God, man and the world (→ ἀγάπη, I, 43; ἐγώ 362). The individual is not solitary before God. He stands in the name of the many, united with them, bound to that which binds them. The questions of their destiny are the questions of his destiny. The one man is not saved or converted for his own sake ; he is called for the sake of the many (Gl. 1:15 ff.; 1 C. 15:9 f.). Personal interest is fulfilled in the sacrifice of what is most individual. The personal expression of the heart before God is realised in intercession for those who are brethren by blood (R. 9:3; 2 C. 1:4 ff.; Col. 1:24). Conversely, the destiny and way of the totality are decided by those of individuals, to whom the divine action is specifically directed (R. 11:1, 14, 16). One for all is the main principle of organic thinking. But this organic thinking is assumed into a higher historical thinking which grows out of the understanding of the unique and its import. The NT does not speak of past events, men and things with a view to reconstructing the past "idiographically" (Windelband). Nor does it speak of them with a view to the attainment of general truth in the "nomothetic" sense. The alternative of contingent facts or eternal rational truths is as little apposite in face of the realities of the NT as is the alternative of the individual or the collective. For the NT, events, men and things are determined by the heritage of the past and the dawning of the future, by the decisive character of the now or never (Gl. 6:7 ff.). The NT speaks of past ages, figures and events which will never recur as such but which are nonetheless mightier than all present

---

[3] The problems of monism and monotheism are dealt with under → θεός.

[4] Mk. 14:37; Rev. 17:12; 18:8 ff. Cf. the late Jewish אַחַת שָׁעָה and on this Schl. Mt., 752 on Mt. 26:40. In the passages quoted the ordinary expression takes on the pregnant sense of Lk. 22:53 : αὕτη ... ἡ ὥρα καὶ ... ἐξουσία τοῦ σκότους.

reality because what is to come is decided in them.[5] Once for all is the main principle of historical thinking.

All these lines of thought, however, converge in a central thought which is specifically characterised by the NT εἷς, namely, the thought that the decision concerning the destiny of creation and the course of history is taken at one point in particular. This idea is worked out in two great complexes, the first that of Adam and the common destiny of the race, the second that of Christ and the unity of the Church.

2. Adam and the Common Destiny of the Race.

a. Already in the Genesis account of the first father Adam and the fall we have the basic conviction that the race is one both in descent and destiny. Later Judaism developed both these aspects (→ I, 291 f.). Alexandrian Judaism did so along the Greek lines of a general destiny of mankind (Ep. Ar., 208; 3 Macc. 4:4), but in Apocalyptic we still have a historical understanding, and therefore the question of the origin of sin is still a live one. Ἥμαρτον, says Eve, καὶ πᾶσα ἁμαρτία δι᾽ ἐμοῦ γέγονεν ἐν τῇ κτίσει.[6] All suffering, even in the animal world, may be traced back to this original event, and especially death (S. Bar. 56:6 ff.; Apc. Mos. 11:28 etc.). But is death the punishment for Adam's sin passed once and for all over the whole race? Or is it the punishment for each individual sin committed by individuals as followers of the first father of the race? Genesis gives the first answer, and it is developed in 4 Esr. with all the basic elements of a doctrine of original sin. When thou didst sin, says the seer to the first father, *non est factum solius tuus casus, sed et nostrum, qui ex te advenimus* (7:118). The *cor malignum* of Adam lives on in his descendants, *et factum est permanens infirmitas* (3:20 ff.). Thus the one seed of evil, once sown, bears a continuing over-luxuriant crop (4:30). With this radically historical anthropology 4 Esr. was consciously opposing the popular dogma of the period which seemed to be demanded both by moral consciousness and by the problem of theodicy, namely, that each individual has chosen his own way *in voluntate sua*.[7] A reply was naturally given, for S. Bar. is a pious correction of 4 Esr. in terms of the popular view that each is his own Adam (54:19). In both cases, however, Adam is the decisive starting-point of history and its woes (S. Bar. 54:15; 56, 6). And according to the apocalyptic view history, which thus stands under the sign of a tragic original event, has as its goal a final event of salvation, the coming of the Son of Man, who as Saviour will renew and surpass the original and decisive office of the first man (→ υἱὸς τοῦ ἀνθρώπου).

Much the same basic views and differences are found in the Synagogue. Here Adam is the first man and the head of all the children of men.[8] But it is debated how his act determines the will and destiny of his progeny. Akiba passionately supported the freedom and responsibility of the individual (bQid., 81a; Ab., 3, 15; cf. M. Ex., 14, 25). Others opposed him (bSanh., 101a; bMak., 24a). Thus God says to Adam: "Do not think of corrupting and destroying my world, for if thou dost corrupt and destroy it there is none to restore it to order"; and to Moses: "Thou diest because of the sin of the first man, for he has brought death on the world." Since the catastrophe of the head, men now come into this world like the children of prisoners — in prison.[9] Therefore

---

[5] → ἅπαξ, I, 381; → ἀπαρχή, I, 486; → καιρός, → πρωτότοκος, → τύπος.

[6] Apc. Mos. 32 (Tischendorf, p. 18). Cf. Sir. 14:17 ff.: ἀπὸ γυναικὸς ἀρχὴ ἁμαρτίας and S. Bar. 48:42.

[7] 4 Esr. 3:8, also Ps. Sol. 9:4 ff.: κρίματα θεοῦ ... ἐν δικαιοσύνῃ ... κατ᾽ ἄνδρα. So, too, Ez. 18:2 ff., as distinct from Ex. 34:7.

[8] Nu. r., 10 on 6:2 in Str.-B., III, 478.

[9] Dt. r., 9 on 31:14; cf. bShab., 55a (both in Str.-B., III, 227 ff.).

"learn from the first man: He was given a command ... and how many deaths hung over him and his descendants." [10] Those who contend for individual retribution, however, put on Adam's lips the words: "In my hand is only one sin" but in yours are many transgressions. Even the death of the righteous is easily explained, for it is the penalty of many venial faults. [11] No less divergent than the answers to this question are the attempts of the Rabbis to draw a connecting line between the original disaster and the corresponding act of deliverance. We hear of the great figure who was created even before Adam in order that some day he might restore what Adam corrupted. This figure, however, is not the son of man, but Abraham (Gn. r., 14 on 2:7). Yet the Messiah also bears a name which refers back to the first man and his fateful significance: ראשׁון = the First. [12] It will be seen how tentative these views are. Only in the NT are the thoughts and problems worked out consistently in a single historical scheme revolving around the figures of the first man and the second.

b. The growth, spread and history of the race start from a single point: ἐποίησέν τε (ὁ θεὸς) ἐξ ἑνὸς πᾶν ἔθνος ἀνθρώπων κατοικεῖν ἐπὶ παντὸς προσώπου τῆς γῆς, ὁρίσας προστεταγμένους καιρούς ... ζητεῖν τὸν θεόν (Ac. 17:26). Nor is it only the physical inheritance which comes from Adam. In addition, there is the heritage of a common destiny ordained by God. Thus the common distress under which the race labours may also be traced back to the original datum of all history, to Adam.

The first man transgressed the commandment of God and thus involved himself in suffering and death. But this one event is not just past history which we may recount or not. Nor is it merely a symbolic representation of general truths concerning sin and its effects. The history of Adam is the history of the origin of sin and of its consequences as these may be seen throughout history: δι' ἑνὸς [13] ἀνθρώπου ἡ ἁμαρτία εἰς τὸν κόσμον εἰσῆλθεν, καὶ διὰ τῆς ἁμαρτίας ὁ θάνατος, καὶ οὕτως εἰς πάντας ἀνθρώπους ὁ θάνατος διῆλθεν (R. 5:12). The once-for-allness of this event is not to be construed in terms of an automatic process or of a law of life or inheritance. It must be understood in terms of time and history. Only because the reality of the world is historical does that which is once and for all become that which is the first of a series, the starting-point of a way. Only because of this does the event of sin become the principle of sin which engulfs all members of the race quite apart from any causal or organic connections.

c. Only those who know the seriousness of the once-for-all can appreciate the historical definiteness and inescapability of the situation in which man now finds himself. He is in a cosmos in which θάνατος is βασιλεύς and all κτίσις is subject to ματαιότης, οὐχ ἑκοῦσα, ἀλλὰ διὰ τὸν ὑποτάξαντα (R. 5:14, 17, 21; 8:20). This is the work of the one. The disposition of the will of man is now such that it impels him to commit sin willingly and thus delivers him up to death — all equally. [14] In this way Paul settles the old and futile debate whether death

---

[10] S. Lv., 120a on 5:17 in Str.-B., III, 230.

[11] Jalkut Simeoni on Nu. 20:24 (§ 764) in Str.-B., III, 229 ff. On the theory of general sinfulness, v. Str.-B., III, 156 f.

[12] Str.-B., I, 65 (→ 'Αδάμ, I, 143, ἄνθρωπος, I, 366).

[13] (δι') ἑνός in R. 5:12-21 is used 8 times of Adam and 4 of Christ.

[14] R. 5:12b: ὁ θάνατος, ἐφ' ᾧ πάντες ἥμαρτον. ἐφ' ᾧ refers back to θάνατος. It thus requires the chiastic correspondence of the four parts of v. 12: "By sin came death" — "to death (ἐπὶ τῷ θανάτῳ) sin led." (Cf. the ἐπί of Gl. 5:13; 1 Th. 4:7; 2 Tm. 2:14.) Sin thus impels towards death. Most commentators are content with the rendering: "On the ground that they all sinned."

is inherited or merited. The fall of Adam created a historical fact which implies not merely external impulsion but also inner corruption of the will, so that the descendants of Adam individually go the way of their progenitor. οὐκ ἔστιν δίκαιος οὐδὲ εἷς, οὐκ ἔστιν ... ὁ ἐκζητῶν τὸν θεόν. Without any exceptions, the race has missed its destiny : [15] οὐκ ἔστιν ἕως ἑνός, R. 3:10 ff. Thus all creation stands under a common lot, and the race of Adam also stands under a common guilt. It is one with the first father in sin and therefore in responsibility for the suffering of the world. None is exempt. All are ἐν ᾿Αδάμ. [16]

3. Christ and the Unity of the Church.

a. Adam is the τύπος τοῦ μέλλοντος, the πρῶτος ἄνθρωπος. He points beyond himself to the δεύτερος ἄνθρωπος, Christ (R. 5:14; 1 C. 15:47). [17] This means : ὥσπερ ἐν τῷ ᾿Αδὰμ πάντες ἀποθνήσκουσιν, οὕτως καὶ ἐν τῷ Χριστῷ πάντες ζωοποιηθήσονται. The validity of this conclusion is established : ἐπειδὴ γὰρ δι' ἀνθρώπου θάνατος, καὶ δι' ἀνθρώπου ἀνάστασις νεκρῶν (1 C. 15:21 f.). In this verse we miss the twofold ἑνός before the twofold ἀνθρώπου, as in R. 5:15. There is a good reason for the omission. The term *Anthropos* is not used here in the generic sense, but as a title which applies to only two figures, Adam and Christ. The mass of those who lived and died between these two κατ' ἐξοχήν does not count beside them. In this full sense Adam is the first man and Christ is literally and truly the second.

In Him, the antitype of Adam, the race is given a new beginning [18] and principle : ὡς δι' ἑνὸς παραπτώματος εἰς πάντας ἀνθρώπους εἰς κατάκριμα, οὕτως καὶ δι' ἑνὸς (→ n. 13) δικαιώματος εἰς πάντας ἀνθρώπους εἰς δικαίωσιν ζωῆς (R. 5:18). As even in Jewish tradition Adam is called the head of the human race (cf. Nu. r., 10), so the εἷς ἄνθρωπος ᾿Ιησοῦς is called the κεφαλή of the new race, πρωτότοκος, ἀπαρχή. [19] Hence with constantly new names and in constantly new forms the relation of the one to the all and yet also the particularity of the one are established.

Christ is man and yet more than man. The One is set in analogy to the many and yet finally He transcends every analogy. He continues the line of humanity, breaks it, and begins a new line. He is more than those who preceded, and yet He is also more than the ἀδελφοί who follow and whose πρωτότοκος He is. He is not only more; He is different, unique.

He is also unique in relation to the first Adam with whom He is compared. He is man and yet more than man (1 C. 15:45 ff.). Nevertheless, He is the positive counterpart of Adam, and, as Paul tries to show in R. 5, [20] the positive influence of the Christ event far transcends in scope the negative of Adam's.

---

[15] → 437: Ac. 17:27: ζητεῖν.
[16] Paul thus goes beyond such ideas as we find in S. Bar. 48:42 f.; 54:19.
[17] δεύτερος (ἄνθρωπος) in v. 47 is hardly a repetition of "the last" in v. 45. For in v. 45 ᾿Αδάμ is the subject, not ἄνθρωπος. The ἄνθρωπος of v. 45a is made necessary by the quotation and disturbs the schematism of v. 45 ff., which is obviously balancing the two contrasts πρῶτος and ἔσχατος ᾿Αδάμ, πρῶτος and δεύτερος ἄνθρωπος. Do ἔσχατος and δεύτερος refer to the same epiphany ? (On πρῶτος, cf. G. Bar. 9:17.)
[18] The one Abraham is the ancestor of the people of God and the startingpoint of its history in Is. 51:1; Ez. 33:24; Mal. 2:15.
[19] Cf. also in Eph. → ἀρχή (I, 483), in Hb. ἀρχηγός (→ I, 488). On πρωτότοκος v. J. B. Frey, *Biblica*, 11 (1930), 373-390.
[20] R. 5:16 : οὐχ ὡς δι' ἑνὸς ἁμαρτήσαντος ... εἰς δικαίωμα; cf. 5:15 : πολλῷ μᾶλλον ἐπερίσσευσεν, and 20 : ὑπερεπερίσσευσεν. On the antithesis εἷς/πολλοί → n. 10.

Jesus is always one of a series, yet He is also a special point in the series. In every series He is the exception which transcends the series. The same principle is often found in the Gospels. He is a prophet and more than a prophet. He is not merely the last in the series of prophets ; He is the ἀγαπητὸς υἱός, unique : ἔτι ἕνα εἶχεν, υἱὸν ἀγαπητόν, Mk. 12:6; cf. Hb. 1:1 f. Again, as the Son He endows us with sonship. Hence we become sons. But He is the Son in a unique sense, μονογενὴς υἱός.

In the NT, however, the uniqueness of Jesus is not established by speculations on His metaphysical essence. It is manifested by His unique historical position. His work is the central point of all occurrence. All previous history moves positively or negatively to the μέλλων, Gl. 3:16; R. 5:14. He brings it to a conclusion and a new beginning : πᾶς μὲν ἱερεὺς ἕστηκεν καθ' ἡμέραν ... τὰς αὐτὰς πολλάκις προσφέρων θυσίας, αἵτινες οὐδέποτε δύνανται περιελεῖν ἁμαρτίας· οὗτος δὲ μίαν ... προσενέγκας θυσίαν εἰς τὸ διηνεκὲς ... μίᾳ ... προσφορᾷ τετελείωκεν ..., Hb. 10:11-14 (→ ἅπαξ, ἐφάπαξ, I, 381). He gives future history its direction and goal, for He has introduced the new as the One for all : ὅτι εἷς ὑπὲρ πάντων ἀπέθανεν· ἄρα οἱ πάντες ἀπέθανον. καὶ ὑπὲρ πάντων ἀπέθανεν, ἵνα οἱ ζῶντες ..., 2 C. 5:14 f. In Jn., too, we read that the εἷς ἄνθρωπος had to die for His people, and not for His people alone. [21] Materially, indeed, the principle of the One for all is to be found in the primitive confession which underlies 1 C. 15:3. It is everywhere plain that the fact of Jesus is not just a particular event of the past which gradually loses its significance. Nor is it a mere example or illustration of an eternal law of life which has a supratemporal meaning. This εἷς is truly singular, and yet it is the point at which all the lines of history intersect. It stands at the heart of history. Hence this εἷς is both unique and all-decisive.

b. The destiny of the race was once decided once and for all in Adam. Similarly in the Christ event the destiny of the new humanity is determined in compendio (Irenaeus). ἐν Χριστῷ implies the unity of the people of God : πάντες γὰρ ὑμεῖς εἷς ἐστε ἐν Χριστῷ 'Ιησοῦ, Gl. 3:28. In R. 12:5 Paul describes the same situation as follows : οἱ πολλοὶ ἓν σῶμά ἐσμεν ἐν Χριστῷ. [22] It is in this historical and in no way mystical sense that Paul calls the Lord the → κεφαλή. Christ is first the κεφαλή πάσης ἀρχῆς καὶ ἐξουσίας. All dominion comes from Him and finds in Him its climax, Col. 2:10. He is then and supremely the κεφαλή to which the ἐκκλησία as σῶμα is subject. [23] All the growth of the Church has its origin in Christ, ἐξ οὗ πᾶν τὸ σῶμα ... αὔξει τὴν αὔξησιν τοῦ θεοῦ, Col. 2:19.

The existence and reality of the Church derive only from the historical fact of Jesus. Its common centre is in the pneuma : διαιρέσεις ... χαρισμάτων ... τὸ δὲ αὐτὸ πνεῦμα (1 C. 12:4, cf. v. 9, 11). Pledges of its continued life are found in the sacramental fellowship, in which each individual acquires a share in one and same living reality enclosed in Christ : εἷς ἄρτος, ἓν σῶμα οἱ πολλοί ἐσμεν· οἱ γὰρ πάντες ἐκ τοῦ ἑνὸς ἄρτου μετέχομεν. [24] Paul continually returns to the image of the σῶμα to bring out the organic unity of the community in all the diversity of its gifts and tasks : ἐν ἑνὶ σώματι πολλὰ μέλη (R. 12:4; cf. 1 C. 12:12 ff.). The Church is a fellowship with a common destiny standing under the νόμος Χριστοῦ. Each must intercede for and suffer

---

[21] Jn. 11:50, 52; 18:14. Cf. Ap. Esrae (Tischendorf), p. 25 : συμφέρει ... μίαν ψυχὴν κολάσασθαι, καὶ μὴ ὅλον τὸν κόσμον εἰς ἀπώλειαν ὑπάγειν.

[22] Cf. Col. 3:15 : ἐκλήθητε ἐν ἑνὶ σώματι.

[23] Col. 1:18 : cf. the thoroughly hierarchical saying in 1 C. 11:3 : ἀνδρὸς κεφαλὴ Χριστὸς ... κεφαλὴ Χριστοῦ ὁ θεός. The two motifs are conjoined in Eph. 5:23.

[24] 1 C. 10:17; cf. 12:12 f.; also Did., 9, 4; Ign. Eph., 20, 2.

with the others. All stand or fall with the one : εἰ ... πάσχει ἓν μέλος, συμπάσχει πάντα τὰ μέλη (1 C. 12:26; cf. Gl. 6:2; 1 C. 4:6).

This thought is particularly pursued and worked out in Ephesians. The unity of history is attained again only in Christ. Only in Him can the history of salvation become universal history. For Christ has destroyed the old order of salvation, ἵνα τοὺς δύο κτίσῃ ἐν αὐτῷ εἰς ἕνα καινὸν ἄνθρωπον ... καὶ ἀποκαταλλάξῃ τοὺς ἀμφοτέρους (Eph. 2:14 f.). Since, however, the Church is to bring unity to men, its own unity is a paramount consideration and it must remember the central guarantees of unity : ἓν σῶμα καὶ ἓν πνεῦμα ... εἷς κύριος, μία πίστις, ἓν βάπτισμα· εἷς θεὸς καὶ πατὴρ πάντων (Eph. 4:4 ff.).

There is a particular interest in unity in John's Gospel. The One died for the many : ἵνα ... τὰ τέκνα τοῦ θεοῦ τὰ διεσκορπισμένα συναγάγῃ εἰς ἕν (11:52). All previous distinctions between men and nations are erased and a new grouping arises with acceptance or rejection of Christ. On the one side are the children of perdition who must perish in hatred and unbelief. [25] On the other side we have the μία ποίμνη gathered around the one Shepherd. [26] Christ Himself stands in unity with the Father and draws His own into the new fellowship, ἵνα ὦσιν τετελειω-μένοι εἰς ἕν (Jn. 17:23; cf. 17:11, 21 f.).

We thus see that Christ is constantly depicted as the starting-point and centre of the new fellowship. He is this in virtue of His hierarchical position as the Mediator. This is particularly clear in Eph. and Jn. This position, however, is based on the historical work which He has accomplished. This is the presupposition. The total view is thus as follows. Within a world which stands under the sign of the fall, or which now decides for this sign in a new fall, there is built up under the sign of the cross the one community of the one Lord. The Church is the new humanity whose author is Christ. It is the καινὸς ἄνθρωπος (Eph. 2:15). The new situation of the world created by the unique Christ event is a positive reality in this aeon only in the form of the Church. Like every divine reality, however, it is attained in the Church only to the degree that the Church takes this reality seriously in faith, thought and action. Thus Eph. demands the ἑνότης of faith, [27] Jn. the fellowship of love (→ ἀγάπη) and Phil. the invincible fellowship of conflict : στήκετε ἐν ἑνὶ πνεύματι, μιᾷ ψυχῇ συναθλοῦντες (Phil. 1:27; cf. 2:2 ff.; R. 12:6). Hence the most significant thing which Ac. can say of the Church in its early development is : τοῦ δὲ πλήθους τῶν πιστευόντων ἦν καρδία καὶ ψυχὴ μία (4:32; cf. 2:42, 46 etc.).

c. This unity of the Church does not imply uniformity. It is organic unity. Within it there are differences between the rich and the poor, [28] freemen and slaves. [29] These are transcended but not removed. Men and women are both members of this organism, but in their own way. [30] It is precisely in the Church that the distinction of sexes

---

[25] They, too, constitute a united block, v. Rev. 17:14, 17; cf. 4 Esr. 13:34 : *colligetur in unum*, and S. Bar. 36:5; 40:1.

[26] Jn. 10:16; cf. 4 Esr. 8:7: *solus enim es et una plasmatio nos sumus;* also S. Bar. 30:2; 85:14; Schᵉmone Esre, 18 (Pal. rec., Str.-B., IV, 214): "Bless us all at all times."

[27] ἑνότης occurs twice in Eph. (4:3, 13) but not elsewhere in the NT, though it is common in Ign. For its secular use, cf. Epicur. Ep., I, 52.

[28] 1 C. 1:26 ff.; 2 C. 8:9 ff.; Gl. 2:10; Ac. 5:4; 6:1 ff. It is in the light of this that we are to understand the "communism" of the early Church. For the post-apost. period, cf. Herm. s., 2, 5 ff.

[29] 1 C. 7:17 ff.; Col. 3:22 ff.; Phlm. 11 ff. These give us the clue to a correct understanding of passages like Gl. 3:28; 1 C. 12:13; Col. 3:11.

[30] In Gl. 3:28 ἄρσεν καὶ θῆλυ stand in unity and distinction ἐν Χριστῷ like δοῦλος and ἐλεύθερος; in 1 C. 11:11 both belong together ἐν κυρίῳ.

acquires its final seriousness from the biological and practical standpoint. Woman is to be silent in the Church, not because she has no gifts or is perhaps too eloquent, but simply because she is woman (1 C. 14:34 f.). The "subjection" of woman to man is established rather than overthrown in the Church. [31] Other differences emerge in the Church. For example, there is the difference between the strong and the weak, which is not effaced but which is to be taken very seriously in theology and ethics. [32] Indeed, the *pneuma* in whom the Church has its unity manifests Himself in a rich plurality of *charismata*: πάντα δὲ ταῦτα ἐνεργεῖ τὸ ἓν καὶ τὸ αὐτὸ πνεῦμα (1 C. 12:11 ff.).

Similarly, national and historical differences are not erased but subsumed in the Church. [33] Paul emphatically calls himself φύσει ᾿Ιουδαῖος. [34] He works and prays ὑπὲρ τῶν συγγενῶν (αὐτοῦ τῶν) κατὰ σάρκα. [35] He becomes a Jew to Jews to win them to Christ. [36] We see here neither the individualistic and cosmopolitan spirit of late antiquity nor the imperialism of the Judaism of Jerusalem. Paul passionately resisted Judaisers who would ground the unity of the Church in the unity of Christianity, proclaiming the absolutism of this Christianity instead of the absolutism of Christ and thus making the cross superfluous. [37] In the service of the one Gospel he was ready to be to those ὑπὸ νόμον ὡς ὑπὸ νόμον and ἄνομος to the ἀνόμοις. [38] He set himself and his message in the world of his hearers in order to show both the offence and the fulfilment which the cross implied for this world. To the theological realism of the Jew it was first an offence but then the power of God. To the philosophical metaphysics of the Greek it was first foolishness but then the wisdom of God. [39] Paul did this work in this way not merely

---

[31] 1 C. 7:36 ff.; 11:3 ff.; 14:34 f.; R. 7:2.

[32] 1 C. 8:7 ff.; 9:22; 10:33; 12:22 ff.; R. 14:1 f.; cf. Herm. s., 2, 5 ff.

[33] Gl. 3:28; 6:15; 1 C. 7:17 ff.; 12:13; R. 10:12; Col. 3:11.

[34] Gl. 2:15; 2 C. 11:22; Phil. 3:5; cf. also R. 11:24b.

[35] R. 9:3 f.; cf. 11:14 : τὴν σάρκα μου.

[36] 1 C. 9:20 : ἐγενόμην τοῖς ᾿Ιουδαίοις ὡς ᾿Ιουδαῖος. There is no μὴ ὢν αὐτὸς ᾿Ιουδαῖος in analogy to the following μὴ ὢν αὐτὸς ὑπὸ νόμον, for Paul is a Jew by race, while in terms of salvation history he is no longer under the Torah. Nor is there any continuation such as ἐγενόμην ῞Ελλησιν ..., for Paul cannot be a fellow countryman to the Greeks as he is to the Jews. Thus in 9:20b and 21 he speaks in theological terms, whereas in 20a he speaks in national categories, as also in Gl. 2:15; R. 9:3 f.; 11:14, 24b; Col. 3:11: ῞Ελλην, ᾿Ιουδαῖος, Σκύθης.

[37] Gl. 2:2-21: ἄρα Χριστὸς δωρεὰν ἀπέθανεν. The so-called apostolic decree (Ac. 15:20; 21:15) shows some Jewish points of style and was perhaps the programme which the Judaisers advanced at the discussion in Gl. 2:9, but were not then able to carry (2:6b). If so, the Judaisers perhaps misrepresented the result of the conference, allowing their proposal to be propagated as an authoritative decision of the church of Jerusalem. On this view its place in Ac. could be accounted for by the fact that the author makes considerable use of traditions from Jerusalem.

[38] 1 C. 9:20 f. It is in this light that we are to understand accounts like those in Ac. 16:1 ff.; 21:24, in spite of F. Overbeck, Ag. (1870), 250, 376 ff. Fulfilment of the Torah does not bring salvation acc. to Gl. 2:16. Yet Paul does not say either that the Torah brings destruction or that its non-observance brings salvation. Fulfilment of the Torah has been finally done away as a means of salvation, hence μὴ ὢν αὐτὸς ὑπὸ νόμον (with all good MSS; omission of this phrase is only for the sake of concealing the antinomianism of Paul and the tensions of the early Church). But observance of the Torah can still be important for Paul as a means of mission — τοῖς ὑπὸ νόμον ὡς ὑπὸ νόμον, ἵνα τοὺς ὑπὸ νόμον κερδήσω. This is the possibility, the task, which Overbeck overlooks.

[39] 1 C. 1:22 ff. On the bearing of the Gospel on the Jewish world, cf. R. 10:4; 3:31; also Ac. 13:14; 18:4 ff.; 28:13 ff., and for its bearing on the Hellenistic world, cf. Col. 2:8 ff.; 1 C. 15:12, 35; and with some reservations Ac. 17:22 ff., 32.

in discharge of the divine task [40] but also on the divine model. [41] He saw how God allowed both Jews and Greeks in their different ways to come to an end of themselves in order to lead them to the goal of salvation. [42] Ac. understands this task along the same lines as the apostle to the Gentiles, and makes this clear in the story of Pentecost. One *pneuma* fills the apostles and from this point they preach the one λόγος θεοῦ in many γλῶσσαι. The nations listen to the Gospel as it comes to them in their own tongue and either accept or reject it. [43] This means that early Christianity knows only one saving event, the cross, and only one Church. But this is neither a national Church nor a universal Church; it is the Church of the nations.

Stauffer

εἰσακούω → ἀκούω, I, 222.

εἰσέρχομαι → ἔρχομαι.

εἴσοδος → ὁδός.

ἑκατὸν τεσσεράκοντα τέσσαρες
→ δώδεκα, 324.

ἐκδέχομαι → δέχομαι, 56.

εἰσδέχομαι → δέχομαι, 57.

εἰσκαλέομαι → καλέω.

εἰσφέρω → φέρω.

ἐκβάλλω → βάλλω, I, 527.

ἐκδημέω → δῆμος, 63.

> ἐκδικέω, ἔκδικος,
> ἐκδίκησις

† ἐκδικέω.

ἐκδικέω, which by assimilation to ἐκδικάζω acquires esp. the sense of "to avenge," "to punish" (ἔκδικος b.), is, like ἔκδικος, developed in this direction only in later Gk., for the Ktesias fragment in Athenaeus (→ 443) is no guarantee of the actual wording of Ktesias (5/4 cent. B.C.).

The bibl. usage develops under the influence of the idea of the absolute holiness of blood among the Jews. Thus in the LXX ἐκδικέω [1] is often used in the specific sense of revenge for נקם and פקד, sometimes, esp. in Ez., for שפט, less frequently for ריב

---

[40] 1 C. 9:16 f., 23 → ἵνα.

[41] The goal in 1 C. 9:22 (ἵνα πάντως τινὰς σώσω) is also stated in R. 11:14: εἴ πως παραζηλώσω μου τὴν σάρκα καὶ σώσω τινὰς ἐξ αὐτῶν. This method of παραζηλοῦν is, however, presecribed for the apostle by the word and will and action of God, R. 10:19; 11:11.

[42] The end of natural theology and ethics, the end of nomistic theology and ethics, the end of human resources, and the saving act of God — this is how Paul develops the ways of God with both Greeks and Jews in R. 1-3.

[43] Ac. 2:11 f.: ἀκούομεν λαλούντων αὐτῶν ταῖς ἡμετέραις γλώσσαις τὰ μεγαλεῖα τοῦ θεοῦ — — γλεύκους μεμεστωμένοι εἰσίν.

ἐ κ δ ι κ έ ω. Anz Subsidia, 364; Nägeli, 33; Moult.-Mill., 192; Preisigke Wört., 442.

[1] Against Cr.-Kö., 340 it may be pointed out that ἐκδικάω is not attested in the LXX. In Lv. 19:18; Dt. 32:43 ἐκδικᾶται is the fut. of ἐκδικάζω, cf. Helbing, 86; Thackeray, I, 229. Similarly in Jdt. 11:10. On the other hand in 2 Macc. 6:15 ἐκδικᾷ can hardly be a fut. in view of ἵνα. In 1 Macc. 9:26 ἐξεδίκα is a poorer reading than ἐξεδίκει (-α acc. to Helbing, 111, Thackeray, 242, cf. ἐκδικᾷ A [-ῇ V]). On ἐκδικᾷ etc. cf. in the NT ἐλεᾷ etc. (Bl.-Debr. § 90).

hiph and דרשׁ. a. Absol. we find it in the pass. "to be punished." ψ 36:28 Low. Egypt. text, 213', Cyr. Alex.: ἄμωμοι ἐκδικήσονται; Sir. 12:8; 23:21; Jos. Ant., 4, 277; 6, 307; also "to be avenged": Gn. 4:24 (cf. v. 15) of Cain: ὅτι ἑπτάκις ἐκδεδίκηται (נקם hoph); Jos. Ant., 7, 285. b. The cause of punishment, or occasion of revenge, is in the acc. [2] φόνον: Ktesias Fr., 37 (C. Müller, 1844, p. 63, 11). θάνατον: Plut. Anton., 67 (I, 947b); Jos. Ant., 7, 386 etc. ἐκδικεῖν τὸ αἷμα, τὰ αἵματα: Ditt. Syll.[3], 1181, 11; the prayer for revenge of Rheneia (2nd/1st cent. B.C.) [3]; 4 Βασ. 9:7: καὶ ἐκδικήσεις (נקם) τὰ αἵματα τῶν δούλων μου τῶν προφητῶν ἐκ χειρὸς ᾽Ιεζάβελ, for "to avenge blood on her and to liberate from her hands" (→ e. and 444), cf. Jos. Ant., 9, 108. In the LXX cf. also Jl. 3:21 A (B: ἐκζητήσω), τὰς ἁμαρτίας, ἀσεβείας, παρανομίας; Am. 3:2, 14 (פקד); Jos. Ant., 15, 156. c. The person avenged is also in the acc. (rarely the dat.): 1 Βασ. 24:13: με (שׁפט); P. Oxy., VI, 937, 7 (3rd cent. A.D.): ἐμαυτόν. τὸν ἀδελφόν, τοὺς ἀδελφούς; Plut. Agidis et Cleomenis cum Gracchis Comparatio, 5 (I, 845e); 1 Macc. 6:22. τὸ ἔθνος: Jos. Ant., 12, 284. τὴν ἀρχήν: Ant., 18, 335. τὸν θεόν: Ant., 20, 116. Dat. Jos. Ant., 18, 347: τοῖς νόμοις, personified. Test. Sol. 20:2: μοι. d. The person punished is normally in the acc., very rarely the dat. ἡμᾶς, ὑμᾶς, σέ: 2 Macc. 6:15; Jdt. 8:27; Is. 57:16 (ריב); Sir. 5:3. Enemies: 1 Βασ. 14:24; 18:25 (נקם). Na. 1:2 (נקם); Sir. 46:1 (2). A people, a district, the earth: Jer. 25:12 (פקד); Ob. 21 (שׁפט); Jdt. 1:12; 2:1. Dat. Ju. 16:28 A (→ c.) τοῖς ἀλλοφύλοις. e. The person to be punished may also be linked with ἐκδικέω by ἐξ or ἐπί, less frequently ἐν or παρά. ἐξ: Nu. 31:2 (→ f.); 4 Βασ. 9:7 (נקם) → b.). ἐπί: Am. 3:2, 14 (פקד); Hos. 2:13 (2:15); 4:9 (פקד); ᾽Ιερ. 23:2 (פקד); 27:15 (נקם); 28:44 (פקד); ἐν: Jer. 5:9 (נקם), 29. παρά: Jos. Ant., 6, 303. εἰς: Ez. 25:12 (→ c.). f. We often find ἐκδικεῖν (τὴν) ἐκδίκησιν or ἐκδικησίαν with the gen. of the person or cause for which revenge is taken. Usually the underlying Heb. is the formula נָקַם נְקָמָה etc. Nu. 31:2; Ju. 16:28 A; Ez. 25:12; cf. 1 Macc. 2:67; 9:42. ἐκδικεῖν δίκην with the gen. is found in Lv. 26:25: to take vengeance for the breaking of a covenant. Cf. also Ez. 16:38; 20:4 (שָׁפַט מִשְׁפָּט); similarly 23:45 (ἐκδικεῖν ἐκδική-σει): "to judge or pronounce sentence," punishment with a wholly negative result being intended. The use in Ez., however, approximates to that of the pap., since the thought of vengeance is replaced by that of judicial process.

The varied use in the pap. reveals a more positive conception linked to the juridical exercise of δίκη. The reference is always to legal action. Thus ἐκδικεῖν means "to decide a case": P. Oxy., VII, 1020, 6 (2nd/3rd cent. A.D.); [4] "to contest at law": Gk. Pap. of the Lib. of Strassburg (ed. Preisigke, 1906 ff.), 79, 7 (1st cent. B.C.). The sense of "to bring someone to judgment" (→ supra on Ez.) is later: P. Gen., 47, 17 (4th cent. A.D.). [5] The commonest use in the pap., comparable with Lk. 18:3, 5; R. 12:19, is for "to fight, to defend, or to plead someone's cause," with an acc. of person or object: Gk. Pap. of the Lib. of Strassburg, 41, 9 (3rd cent. A.D.): ἐκδικῆσαι τὰ τῆς παιδός; P. Amh., 134, 10 (2nd cent. A.D.): ἐρωτῶ σε ἐκδικῆσαι αὐτόν. [6] Later ἐκδικεῖν τινα in the pap. often means "to help someone to justice." [7]

---

[2] On the case with ἐκδικεῖν cf. R. Helbing, Kasussyntax der Verba bei den LXX (1928), 37 f. Cf. Bl.-Debr. § 151 for the alternation of acc. and dat. Cf., too, the class. τιμωρεῖν (ἀμύνειν) τινί, "to help," and the many constructions of τιμωρεῖσθαι and ἀμύνεσθαι [Debrunner].

[3] Deissmann LO, 354 ff.

[4] Moult.-Mill., 192.

[5] The other examples of this usage (Preisigke Wört., s.v.) also come from the 4th cent. We may ignore the senses "to make a legal claim on" (Liddell-Scott, s.v.), cf. P. Ryl., II, 94, 12 (14-37 A.D.); "to defend legal claims" (Moult.-Mill., s.v.); "to raise a complaint" (P. Lips., 33, Col. II, 15, 4th cent. A.D.). These are all connected with the law-courts.

[6] Pap.-Analyses: Moult.-Mill., 192 f. Inscr.: Liddell-Scott, s.v.

[7] Cf. the instances from the 3rd-6th cent. in Preisigke Wört., s.v. ὁ ἐκδικήσας is common on inscr. for "the judge"; cf. Nägeli, 33. On ἐκδικεῖν τὸν τόπον (Ign. Orig., Eus.), cf. Pr.-Bauer, s.v.

In the NT ἐκδικέω occurs 6 times. 1. (→ b.) 2 C. 10:6 : ἐν ἑτοίμῳ ἔχοντες ἐκδικῆσαι πᾶσαν παρακοήν : the apostles are ready to punish all disobedience in the campaign against the fortified strongholds of the enemy. On the other hand, Rev. 6:10 : ἕως πότε, ὁ δεσπότης, οὐ κρίνεις καὶ ἐκδικεῖς τὸ αἷμα, and 19:2 : ἐξεδίκησεν τὸ αἷμα τῶν δούλων αὐτοῦ, follow the LXX pattern with the meaning of revenge. Both passages come under e. in view of the continuation ἐκ τῶν κατοικούντων ἐπὶ τῆς γῆς or ἐκ χειρὸς αὐτῆς. Rev. 19:2 is analogous to 4 Βασ. 9:7 (→ b.).

2. (→ c.) R. 12:19 : μὴ ἑαυτοὺς ἐκδικοῦντες, does not mean "do not procure justice for yourselves" but "avenge not yourselves," for the divine judgment to which we yield replaces revenge.

3. (→ supra). On the other hand Lk. 18:3 : ἐκδίκησόν με ἀπὸ τοῦ ἀντιδίκου (→ ἀντίδικος, I, 375) refers to the justice of the judge, ἀπό — ἐξ is more common — being a pregnant construction expressing the element of liberation (though cf. also → ἐκδίκησις d. : ποιεῖν ἐκδίκησιν ἀπό, Ju. 11:36). In Lk. 18:5 ἐκδικήσω αὐτήν is used in the same sense with the acc. of person.

It is worth noting that Rev. is closest to the OT usage ("to take vengeance"), whereas Lk. the Hellenist, apart from an echo of the LXX in ἀπό, follows the ordinary forensic usage of the time. Paul, too, is more strongly influenced by the OT.

† **ἔκδικος.**

ἔκδικος first means a. ὁ ἐκ (= ἔξω) δίκης ὤν, i.e., "he who by an offence places himself outside the limits of the law." Thus ἔκδικος, -ον means "contrary to the law," "unrighteous." Of persons, Soph. Oed. Col., 920: ἄνδρας ἐκδίκους. Neut., Aesch. Prom., 1093 : ἔκδικα πάσχω; Eur. Hel., 1638 : ἔκδικα (opp. ὅσια). b. The main sense of ἔκδικος and deriv., however, is given by assimilation to ἐκδικάζω. This is made up of ἐξ and δικάζω, and does not derive from ἔκδικος, though ἐκδικέω does : "I am outside the right." ἐκδικάζω means "I decide a legal process," "I avenge." The ἐκδικαστής in Eur. Suppl., 1152 is the "avenger." By assimilation ἔκδικος thus comes to have the sense of "avenger" rather than "outlaw," and ἐκδικέω of "to avenge" rather than "to be without law." Both changes seem to be Hellenistic. Thus ἔκδικος as an adj. means "supporting, defending, avenging the right" in Batrachomyomachia, 97 (ed. T. W. Allen, Homeri Opera): ἔχει θεὸς ἔκδικον ὄμμα, and as a noun "the avenger" who executes a judicial sentence. Plut. De Garrulitate, 14 (II, 509 f.): αἱ ᾿Ιβύκου ἔκδικοι; Herodian, VII, 4, 5 : ἔκδικοι τοῦ γενησομένου ἔργου; II, 14, 6 : ἔκδικος τοῦ Περτίνακος. So also in the LXX : ψ 98:8 Σ : ἔκδικος for ἐκδικῶν (נֹקֵם) ἐπὶ πάντα τὰ ἐπιτηδεύματα αὐτῶν, of God ; Sir. 30:6 : ἐναντίον ἐχθρῶν κατέλιπεν ἔκδικον, the dying father in his child ; 4 Macc. 15:29 : ὦ μήτηρ ἔθνους, ἔκδικε τοῦ νόμου. In Jos. Bell., 5, 377, too, God is ᾿Ιουδαίων ἔκδικος (previously ἄν ἀδικῶνται). But Jos. also uses ἐκδικητής : Ant., 17, 242 of Antipater (cf. LXX ψ 8:2 : τοῦ καταλῦσαι ἐχθρὸν καὶ ἐκδικητήν). c. "Legal officer." This use is early, cf. Inscr. Magn., 93 (2nd cent. B.C.). Cicero Fam., XIII, 56, 1 uses the borrowed word ecdici with legati. Plin. Ep., X, 110, 1: ecdicus Amisenorum civitatis. Ditt. Or., 458, 64; Ditt. Syll.³, II, 679, 16 etc. d. "Advocate" or "legal adviser" — a common use in the inscr. and pap. P. Oxy.,

---

ἔ κ δ ι κ ο ς. Nägeli, 33; Moult.-Mill., 193; Milligan on 1 Th. 4:6; O. Gradenwitz, Einführung in die Papyruskunde, I (1900), 160; Mitteis-Wilcken, I, 1, 80 f.; II, 1, 31; O. Seeck in Pauly-W., IV (1901), 2366 ff.; L. Mitteis, Reichsrecht (1891), 167 ff.; Preisigke Fachwörter, s.v.; Wört., III, 8, s.v. ἔκδικος does not occur in Philo.

II, 261, 14 (55 A.D.); II, 237, Col. VII, 39 (186 A.D.); BGU, I, 136, 4 (2nd. cent. A.D.); later P. Lips., 38, 17 (4th cent. A.D.). e. In the Byzant. period the ἔκδικος τῆς πόλεως is the *defensor civitatis* or *plebis* who is appointed to protect the *humiliores* and who is normally a civic official, Egypt (P. Oxy., I, 6, 901) as early as 336 A.D. P. Oxy., VI, 902, 1 and 10 (465 A.D.) (in Mitteis-Wilcken, II, 2, 72).[1]

In the NT ἔκδικος is found only as a noun in sense b. It is said of God in 1 Th. 4:6 : ἔκδικος κύριος περὶ πάντων τούτων : fraud and similar sins, which are the opposite of ἁγιασμός, will cause the κύριος, as an avenger, to intervene either now or in the final judgment. It is used of the authorities in R. 13:4 : θεοῦ γὰρ διάκονός ἐστι, ἔκδικος εἰς ὀργὴν τῷ τὸ κακὸν πράσσοντι. Their position as avenger, as executor (*vindex*) of divine judgment, is here insisted upon in opposition to revolutionary tendencies in the Roman Church.

† ἐκδίκησις.

a. ἐκδίκησις, "revenge," "punishment," "retribution," is predominantly a Septuagint term. This decides the NT usage. The LXX uses it for the following words : שְׁפָטִים, תּוֹכַחַת, נָקָם, נְקָמָה, פְּקֻדָּה. We also find the plur. in Mi. 7:4; Ez. 16:41; 25:17. A common expression is ἡμέρα or καιρὸς ἐκδικήσεως for יוֹם or עֵת פְּקֻדָּה or נְקָמָה etc. Dt. 32:35 : ἐν ἡμέρᾳ ἐκδικήσεως ἀνταποδώσω in a free translation (Mas. → 446); Hos. 9:7; Ἰερ. 26:10, 21; 27:31;[1] 28:6; 26:10; Sir. 5:7 (9). Josephus has only ἐκδικία, not ἐκδίκησις. He uses it esp. for blood revenge. We find ἐκδικία for a guest and friend in Ant., 1, 208; 19, 20; for a brother in Ant., 2, 107; cf. 137; 13, 19; for all who have been overthrown, murdered or oppressed in 17, 291; Bell., 2, 237; Ant., 7, 294; cf. also Ant., 20, 126, always in the sense of this holy duty of blood revenge or the overhanging threat of divine retribution. In the pap. ἐκδίκησις is used for "punishment": P. Masp., 97, verso D, 51 (6th cent. A.D.); "defence" (P. Lond., V, 1674, 102, 6th cent. A.D.). Here we again have a judicial use (→ ἐκδικέω, 443).[2] The person on whom revenge is taken or punishment executed is in the gen. (ψ 57:10, נָקָם; Ez. 9:1, פְּקֻדּוֹת; Sir. 7:17; Jdt. 8:35; 9:2), or with ἐξ c. gen. (Jer. 11:20, נְקָמָה) or with ἐπί c. acc. (Ez. 25:14, 17). c. The person or cause on whose behalf revenge is taken is also in the gen. This is always so in Jos. (→ *supra*). For Nu. 31:2; 1 Macc. 2:67; 9:42 and the formula ἐκδικεῖν τὴν ἐκδίκησιν, → ἐκδικέω, 443. Cf. also ψ 78:10 : ἡ ἐκδίκησις τοῦ αἵματος (נְקָמָה). d. ποιεῖν ἐκδίκησίν τινι. While in Polyb., III, 8, 10 : τὴν ἐκδίκησιν ποιησάμενος we have the sense of "to make retribution," and in CIG, II, 2826, 15 : ἐκδίκησιν ποιεῖσθαί τινος, the meaning is to demand this from someone, the LXX uses this expression in the sense of "to procure revenge," for עָשָׂה נְקָמָה, etc., cf. Test. Sol. 22:4 (McCown p. 65): ἐὰν τὴν ἐκδίκησιν ταύτην ποιήσεις ἡμῖν, of the execution of punishment. In the LXX the person on whom revenge is taken is usually denoted by ἐν : ψ 149:7 (נְקָמָה); Mi. 5:15 (נָקָם); Ez. 16:41 (שְׁפָטִים עָשָׂה); 25:17 (נְקָמוֹת); 1 Macc. 3:15 etc. Occasionally we have ἀπό, Ju. 11:36 (נְקָמוֹת); cf. Jos. Ant., 6, 211: ἡ ἀπὸ τῶν πολεμίων ἐκδικία; rarely also εἰς : Ez. 25, 11 (שְׁפָטִים). e. διδόναι ἐκδίκησιν or ἐκδικήσεις : Ez. 25:14; 25:17; 2 Βασ. 22:48 (= ψ 17:47), always for נָתַן נְקָמָה. The person punished may be in the gen.: 2 Βασ. 4:8 (נְקָמוֹת), but we never have the dat.

---

[1] The change of meaning in the case of ἔκδικος is very strange. Perhaps there are here two distinct constructions : 1. Attic : "standing outside the law"; and 2. Ionic : "standing outside the judicial process," i.e., as the representative of one of the parties [Debrunner].

ἐκδίκησις. [1] Cf. BHK³, ad loc.

[2] τὰς ἐγδικάσιος, Ditt. Syll.³, 563, 14 = E. Schwyzer, *Dialectorum Graec. Exempla* (1923), 387, 14 (201 B.C. aetol.), comes from ἐκδίκασις (cf. Liddell-Scott), not ἐκδίκησις (Nägeli, 33) [Debrunner].

as elsewhere (cf. 2 Th. 1:8; → infra), though this is used with ἀποδιδόναι: Nu. 31:3 (לָתֵת נִקְמַת יְהֹוָה); Sir. 12:6, and with ἀνταποδιδόναι ἐκδίκησιν: Sir. 32:23.

In the NT, too, ἐκδίκησις means 1. (→ a.) "revenge," "threat," "punishment," usually the last. There is a judicial example, together with ἀπολογία, in 2 C. 7:11. [3] On the other hand, when Dt. 32:35 is quoted in R. 12:19; Hb. 10:30: ἐμοὶ ἐκδίκησις, ἐγὼ ἀνταποδώσω — there is a rather surprising agreement against the LXX (→ 445), — the divine retribution is denoted.

In both cases the quotation follows the Mas. closely (לִי נָקָם וְשִׁלֵם), and also Tg. O. [4] We also find the prophetic ἡμέρα ἐκδικήσεως in the plur. in Lk. 21:22, where it refers to the Last Judgment as the days of divine retribution.

2. (→ b.) 1 Pt. 2:14: ὑποτάγητε ἡγεμόσιν ὡς δι' αὐτοῦ πεμπομένοις εἰς ἐκδίκησιν κακοποιῶν means that the magistrates are sent to punish evildoers.

3. (→ d.) Lk. 18:7 f. twice has ποιεῖν τὴν ἐκδίκησιν, using the gen., which is rare with this expression. Possibly Lk. had in view the use of ἐκδικεῖν τὴν ἐκδίκησιν (→ ἐκδικέω, 443). As concerns the meaning, it is again (→ ἐκδικέω) less influenced by the LXX than by ordinary Hellenistic usage: God will vindicate His elect in the sense of retribution (→ d.). On the other hand, Ac. 7:24: ἐποίησεν ἐκδίκησιν τῷ καταπονουμένῳ, is closer to the LXX ("to procure revenge"), this approximation to OT usage corresponding better to the style of Stephen's address.

4. (→ e.) 2 Th. 1:8: διδόντος ἐκδίκησιν τοῖς μὴ εἰδόσιν θεόν, should be rendered: "to execute revenge." In this passage the dat. is used for the person punished because there is free reference to Is. 66:15: ἀποδοῦναι ἐκδίκησιν αὐτοῦ, and this formula takes the dat. (→ e.).

                                                                                                    Schrenk

ἐκδύω → δύω, 318.   ἐκζητέω → ζητέω.
ἐκκαθαίρω → καθαίρω.

---

† ἐκκεντέω

"To put out" (the eyes), Aristot. Hist. An., II, 17, p. 508b, 6; "to pierce" with a lance or sword, and thus "to kill": Polyb., 5, 56, 12; 15, 33, 4; 24, 7, 6; Polyaen. Strat., V, 3, 8; LXX Nu. 22:29; Ju. 9:54; 1 Ch. 10:4 etc. Often the kind of death fades from view, cf. Jos. 16:10: καὶ τοὺς κατοικοῦντας ἐν Γαζὲρ ἐξεκέντησαν; also 2 Macc. 12:6, so that ἐκκεκεντημένοι in 'Ιερ. 44:10 can mean "severely wounded," and in Lam. 4:9 "smitten." The Heb. equivalent is טען pu in Is. 14:19, הרג qal in Nu. 22:29, otherwise דקר qal and pu. As may be seen from Nu. 25:8, דָּקַר can also be translated ἀποκεντέω.

In the NT the term occurs only in two passages, both based on Zech. 12:10 (12).

---

[3] Cf. Wnd., 2 K., 235.

[4] Str.-B., III, 300, cf. Ltzm., R., 106; Rgg. Hb., 330. H. Vollmer, At.liche Citate bei Pls. (1895), 30 ff., suggests as a basis a Gk. transl. not identical with the LXX; Rgg. suggests Theodotion.

ἐ κ κ ε ν τ έ ω. A. Rahlfs, "Über Theodotions-Lesarten im NT und Aquila-Lesarten bei Justin," in ZNW, 20 (1921), 182-199.

1. Jn. 19:37: καὶ πάλιν ἑτέρα γραφὴ λέγει· ὄψονται εἰς ὃν ἐξεκέντησαν. The basis here is the obscure Heb. of Zech. 12:10 : וְהִבִּיטוּ אֵלַי אֵת אֲשֶׁר דָּקָרוּ "they shall look on ... him whom they have pierced. ʼΑ, Σ and Θ (probably assuming אֲשֶׁר אֵלָי?) take this quite literally. Σ has ἐπεξεκέντησαν instead of ἐξεκέντησαν. But Jn. is not dependent on these, as we can see from his use of ὄψονται instead of the ἐπιβλέψονται of the translations. The LXX has : καὶ ἐπιβλέψονται πρός με, ἀνθʼ ὧν κατωρχήσαντο, which presupposes רָקַד instead of דָּקַר. As Jn. understands it, this verse is torn from its immediate historical context, in which it possibly referred to Onias III, and is treated as a prophecy which "proclaimed the completed reality of the death foreordained for Christ." [1] The OT prophecy of the piercing of the only Son and Firstborn is fulfilled when the spear is thrust into the dead body of Jesus. For Jn. the εἰς ὃν ἐξεκέντησαν denotes the plunging of the spear into the side, and it is not, therefore, to be taken with ὄψονται, which is intrinsically possible. [2]

2. In Jn. there is only a fragmentary application of Zech. 12:10 compared with what we find in Rev. 1:7: ʼΙδοὺ ἔρχεται μετὰ τῶν νεφελῶν, καὶ ὄψεται αὐτὸν πᾶς ὀφθαλμὸς καὶ οἵτινες αὐτὸν ἐξεκέντησαν, καὶ κόψονται ἐπʼ αὐτὸν πᾶσαι αἱ φυλαὶ τῆς γῆς. Here Zech. 12:10 (12) is linked with the early Christian expectation of the return of Christ. The One whom the inhabitants of Jerusalem will bewail as the Beloved (LXX) and Firstborn is the returning Jesus Christ, who will be seen by both Jews and Gentiles as the One who was pierced. Mention of ἐξεκέντησαν serves to emphasise the fact that the One put to death by the world will be manifested at the last as the Lord concerning whom the world in tardy remorse and fear of judgment (both indicated by the κόψονται ἐπʼ αὐτόν) [3] will lament. Closely related to Rev. 1:7 is Mt. 24:30 : καὶ τότε φανήσεται τὸ σημεῖον τοῦ υἱοῦ τοῦ ἀνθρώπου ἐν οὐρανῷ, καὶ τότε κόψονται πᾶσαι αἱ φυλαὶ τῆς γῆς καὶ ὄψονται τὸν υἱὸν τοῦ ἀνθρώπου ἐρχόμενον ἐπὶ τῶν νεφελῶν τοῦ οὐρανοῦ μετὰ δυνάμεως καὶ δόξης πολλῆς. The formulation ὄψονται (instead of ἐπιβλέψονται), and the reference to Zech. in κόψονται πᾶσαι αἱ φυλαὶ τῆς γῆς, as in Rev. 1:7, show that there is a formal interrelationship between the two passages. It is thus probable that they are also related in content, and that the returning, pierced Lord is here presented as the One who appears with the sign of the Son of Man. In Did., 16, 6 the sign of truth, of heavenly declaration, precedes the coming of the Lord on the clouds of heaven. [4] Here the cross seems to be separated from the returning Lord. According to Mt. 24:30 there is to be the shining of this sign in heaven, and the coming Son of Man will then descend. The cross and "power and great glory" belong together. In the Last Day the cross which the world set up in secret will threaten the whole world openly as the victorious sign of the Lord of glory hastening back to it.

The thought of Rev. 1:7, with its free adaptation of Zech. 12:10, is of frequent recurrence. There is, perhaps, a closer approximation to Jn. 19:37 in Barn., 7, 9 : οὐχ οὗτός ἐστιν, ὅν ποτε ἡμεῖς ἐσταυρώσαμεν ἐξουθενήσαντες καὶ κατακεντήσαντες καὶ ἐμπτύσαντες; but cf. with Rev. 1:7 Just. Dial., 32, 2 : ... ἐλέγετο, καὶ δύο παρουσίας αὐτοῦ γενήσεσθαι ἐξηγησάμην, μίαν μὲν ἐν ᾗ ἐξεκεντήθη ὑφʼ ὑμῶν, δευτέραν δὲ ὅτε ἐπιγνώσεσθε εἰς ὃν ἐξεκεντήσατε, καὶ κόψονται αἱ φυλαὶ ὑμῶν ... Cf. also Just. Apol., 52, 12; Dial., 14, 8; 64, 7; 118, 1.

Schlier

---

[1] Schl. J., 355.
[2] Cf. Just. Dial., 14, 8; 32, 2; Apol., 52, 12; as against Bau. J., ad loc.
[3] Cf. Just. Apol., 52, 12; Dial., 32, 2; 64, 7 (?); 118, 1.
[4] Cf. W. Bousset, *Der Antichrist* (1895), 154 ff.

ἐκκλησία → καλέω.   ἐκκόπτω → κόπτω.
ἐκλέγω, ἐκλογή, ἐκλεκτός → λέγω.   ἐκλύω → λύω.
ἐκνήφω → νήφω.   ἐκούσιος → ἑκών.
ἐκπειράζω → πειρασμός.   ἐκπίπτω → πίπτω.
ἐκπληρόω, ἐκπλήρωσις → πληρόω.   ἐκπνέω → πνεῦμα.

---

† ἐκπτύω

"To spit out" [1] — a vulgar *koine* word [2] which occurs in the NT only at Gl. 4:14 : καὶ τὸν πειρασμὸν ὑμῶν ἐν τῇ σαρκί μου οὐκ ἐξουθενήσατε οὐδὲ ἐξεπτύσατε, ἀλλὰ ὡς ἄγγελον θεοῦ ἐδέξασθέ με, ὡς Χριστὸν Ἰησοῦν. It is not used here in the metaphorical sense of "to expose," "to despise," "to reject" etc., [3] but quite literally in the sense of the ancient gesture of spitting out as a defence against sickness and other demonic threats. The Galatians resisted the temptation to see in Paul someone demonically possessed because of his sickness, but received him as an angelic manifestation, indeed, as Christ Jesus Himself.

In relation to ἐκπτύειν (*despuere*) we have to distinguish between the gesture of spitting out or spitting on, and the intention of either warding off the demonic, misfortune or sickness, or of healing by means of spittle. The last two, of course, are often related and even merge into one another. There are several instances of the apotropaic use, which is here our only concern. [4] Plaut. Captivi, 549, speaks of a *morbus qui sputatur,* and Pliny in Hist. Nat., X, 23, 33 of *morbus despui suetus,* meaning epilepsy. In Hist. Nat., XXVIII, 4, 7 Pliny deals with the healing power of spittle ; he incidentally shows how greatly the medicinal use is linked with and even grounded in the apotropaic. We thus read among other things : *Despuimus comitiales morbos, hoc est contagia regerimus, simili modo et fascinationes repercutimus dextraeque clauditatis occursum. Veniam quoque a deis spei alicuius audacioris petimus in sinum spuendo. Eadem ratione terna despuere praedicatione in omni medicina mos est atque ita effectus adiuvare, incipientis furunculos ter praesignare ieiuna saliva.* The *hoc est contagia regerimus* is a rationalistic explanation of something which was originally magical. Cf. Theocr. Idyll., 7, 125 f.: ἁμὶν δ' ἀσυχία τε μέλοι γραῖά τε παρείη, ἅτις ἐπιφθύζοισα τὰ μὴ καλὰ νόσφιν ἐρύκοι; Plaut. Asinaria, I, 1, 25 f.; Catull., 50, 18 ff. Spitting in healing or at incantations naturally has also an apotropaic significance. Cf. Plin. Hist. Nat., XXVI, 9, 69; Tibull., I, 2, 53 f., where Delia pronounces an oracle three times and on each occasion accompanies it by spitting. Theocr. Idyll., 2, 62 : The slave is to spread poison on the threshold of the unfaithful lover καὶ λέγ' ἐπιφθύζοισα· τὰ Δέλφιδος ὀστία μάσσω; Varro De Re Rustica, I, 2. To this defensive gesture against the hostile attacks of gods or demons there also belongs *spuere in sinum.* Cf. Theophr. Char., 15 : ὁ δὲ

ἐ κ π τ ύ ω. Ltzm. Gl., *ad loc.*; Steinmann Gl., 103; M. Krenkel, *Beiträge* (1890), 67 ff.; G. Sittl, *Die Gebärden der Griechen und Römer* (1890), 117 ff.; J. Dölger, *Der Exorzismus im altchristlichen Taufritual* (1909), 135 f.; *Die Sonne der Gerechtigkeit und der Schwarze* (1918), 10 ff.

[1] Liddell-Scott, *s.v.*
[2] Nägeli, 58.
[3] E.g., v. Hofmann Gl.[2], 129; Sieffert Gl.[7], 271 f.; Schäfer Gl. (1890), 317; Burton Gl. (1921), 242.
[4] On the significance of spittle in primitive belief cf. M. Ebert, *Reallexikon der Vorgeschichte* (1924 ff.), XV (Index), 411 *s.v. Speichel.* Cf. also VI, 19. On the use of spittle in healing, cf. Mk. 7:33; 8:23; Jn. 9:6; and Str.-B., II, 15-17.

δεισιδαίμων τοιοῦτός ἐστιν, οἷος ... μαινόμενον δὲ ἰδὼν ἢ ἐπίληπτον, φρίξας εἰς κόλπον πτύσαι; Luc. Apologia pro Mercede Conductis, 6. Among other defensive uses we should also number spitting at someone, as Pliny attests in Hist. Nat., XXVIII, 4, 7: ... cur non et haec credamus rite fieri, extranei interventu, aut si dormiens spectetur infans, a nutrice terna adspui in os. Cf. also Luc. Nec., 7, where the magician spits three times in the face of his client. This is part of his ἐπῳδή. Tyr., 12 : ... καὶ καταπτύσας μου καί· Εἰς τὸν τῶν ἀσεβῶν χῶρον ἄπιθι, ἐπειπὼν ᾤχετο.

This pagan gesture is often found in Christianity. It is true that in Mart. Dasii, 10 (Knopf [3], 94): ἰδοὺ γὰρ καὶ τῶν βασιλέων σου καὶ τῆς δόξης αὐτῶν καταπτύω καὶ βδελύσσομαι αὐτήν, καταπτύειν is used in the figurative sense of "to despise," but earlier in 4 we see that behind this stands the realistic background of the baptismal ceremony : ὁ μακάριος Δάσιος ... κατεπάτησεν τὸν κόσμον σὺν ταῖς ἀπάταις αὐτοῦ καὶ κατέπτυσεν τὸν διάβολον σὺν ταῖς πομπαῖς αὐτοῦ καὶ ὑπέζευξεν ἑαυτὸν τῷ σταυρωθέντι Χριστῷ ... Cf. Pall. Hist. Laus, 15 : καὶ ζήσας (Markos) ἄλλα εἴκοσι πέντε ἔτη ἐν τῷ κελλίῳ ἐκείνῳ χαρίσματος ἠξιώθη καταπτύειν δαιμόνων, ἐντρυφῶν τῇ μονότητι; Eus. Hist. Eccl., X, 4, 16 : ὥστε ἤδη ... τοὺς βασιλέας ... νεκρῶν μὲν εἰδώλων καταπτύειν προσώποις; Tertullian De Idolatria, 11. Probably [5] the oldest instance of the use of sputatio in baptism to drive off the devil is to be found in the church order of the Verona palimpsest published by Hauler. If so, the use goes back to the 3rd and even the 2nd cent. Later the gesture is mentioned after the third baptismal exorcism in the euchologium of the orthodox catholic Church. Here the priest says to the candidate : καὶ ἐμφύσησον καὶ ἔμπτυσον αὐτῷ.

Schlier

ἔκστασις, ἐξίστημι

† ἔκστασις.

a. Literally "change of place," Aristot. An., I, 3, p. 406b, 13 : κίνησις ἔκστασίς ἐστι τοῦ κινουμένου; Hippocr. De Articulis, 56 : faulty position of the thigh. b. Figur. "renunciation of goods" (cessio bonorum), a techn. term in the pap. (BGU, III, 914, 6;

---

[5] Dölger, *Die Sonne der Gerechtigkeit*, 19 ff.

ἔκστασις. For liter. up to 1908, v. RE, XX, 586 f.; for more recent works cf. RGG², II, 95-97, also IV, 1529 ff. The most significant are W. Eichrodt, *Theol. des AT*, I (1933), Index, s.v. "Ekstase," esp. 162 ff., 177 ff.; E. Fascher, Προφήτης (1927), Index, s.v. "Ekstase"; Chant de la Saussaye, Index, s.v. "Ekstase," "Dämonen," "Offenbarung," "Schamanen" etc.; F. R. Lehmann, "Prophetismus in d. Südsee" (*Christentum und Wissenschaft*, 10 [1934], 56 ff.); J. Warneck, *Die Religion der Batak* (1909), 89 ff., 104 ff.; T. Canaan, *Dämonenglaube im Lande der Bibel* (1929); J. Tambornino, "De Antiquorum Daemonismo," RVV, 7, 3 (1909), esp. 62 ff.; E. Rohde, *Psyche*⁹, ¹⁰, ed. O. Weinreich (1925), esp. 14 ff., 58 ff., 94 ff., 349 ff.; Mithr. Liturg.; F. Heiler, *Das Gebet*⁵ (1923), esp. 252 ff., 258 ff., 277 ff., 304 ff., 316 ff., 524 (bibl.); Reitzenstein Hell. Myst.³, esp. 333 ff.; H. Leisegang, *Der Heilige Geist* (1919), 163 ff.; *Pneuma Hagion* (1922); H. Windisch, *Die Frömmigkeit Philos* (1909), 60 ff.; Bousset-Gressm., 394 ff., 449 ff.; P. Volz, *Der Geist Gottes u. die verwandten Erscheinungen im AT u. im anschliessenden Judentum* (1910); F. Häussermann, *Wortempfang u. Symbol in der at. lichen Prophetie* (1932); H. Gunkel, *Die Wirkungen des hl. Geistes nach der populären Anschauung der apost. Zeit u. nach d. Lehre des Apostels Pls.³* (1909); H. Weinel, *Die Wirkungen des Geistes u. der Geister im nachapost. Zeitalter* (1899); F. Büchsel, *Der Geist Gottes im NT* (1926), Index, s.v. "Ekstase"; C. Schneider, *Die Erlebnisechtheit der Apokalypse des Joh.* (1930); J. Leipoldt, *Dionysos* (1931); W. F. Otto, "Dionysos," *Frankfurter Studien zur Relig. u. Kultur der Antike*, 4 (1933), 96 ff., 124 ff.; J. Quasten, *Musik u. Gesang in den Kulten der heidnischen Antike u. christlichen Frühzeit* (1930), 51 ff., 59, 70. → I, 719, → πνεῦμα, προφήτης, ὅραμα, ὅρασις, δαιμονίζομαι, ψυχικός, πνευματικός, θεόπνευστος.

P. Oxy., III, 472, 43); c. Figur. "degeneration"; Theophr. De Causis Plantarum, III, 1, 6 : ἔκστασις τῆς φύσεως, esp. "confusion of spirit," νοῦ, Plot., V, 3, 7 (opp. ἡσυχία); abs. Hippocr. Aphorismi, VII, 5; in astonishment or fear : τὰ μηδὲ προσδοκώμεν' ἔκστασιν φέρει, Menand. Fr., 149 (CAF, III, 44); in envy, Test. S. 4:8; "alienation," ἔκστασις μανική, Aristot. Cat., 8, p. 10a, 1; not always, [1] but often in the sense of almost convulsive, transitory excitement : ἔκστασις φύσεως καὶ εἰκὼν θανάτου, Test. R. 3:1; "transport," Cornut. De Natura Deorum, 30, cf. Philo Ebr., 15 : μέθην, τὴν ἐκστάσεως καὶ παραφροσύνης αἰτίαν. To the extent that the one alienated or transported is full of God, or inspired, or gifted with power, it thus means d. "ecstasy." Plato in Phaedr., 244a speaks of μανία, θείᾳ δόσει διδομένη, and in 256b of θεία μανία. Philo distinguishes 4 senses of ἔκστασις : 1. alienation (cf. Spec. Leg., III, 99, Cher., 69); 2. astonishment and fear (Israel at Sinai); 3. perfect rest, sleep, stupor (Adam in Gn. 2:21, cf. Leg. All., II, 31, Plant., 147); and 4. ἡ δὲ πασῶν ἀρίστη ἔνθεος κατοκωχή (inspiration) τε καὶ μανία, ᾗ τὸ προφητικὸν γένος χρῆται (Abraham, Gn. 15:12), ἐνθουσιῶντος καὶ θεοφορήτου τὸ πάθος (Rer. Div. Her., 258, cf. 264). There is originally no idea of the soul being outside the body for a period. This comes in later, Rer. Div. Her., 69. Cf. Leg. All., III, 40 f.

In the OT we find only c. either in the sense of "illusion" (only Dt. 28:28, where ἔκστασις διανοίας = תִּמְהוֹן לֵבָב) or "fear" or "terror" (צַעַר, מְהוּמָה, פַּחַד, חֲרָדָה etc.), partly for natural causes (Gn. 27:33; 1 Βασ. 14:15a), but partly at the numinous (ψ 30:22; 115:1; Zech. 12:4; Jer. 5:30; Ez. 26:16; 27:35; 32:10; Da. 7:28; 10:7 Θ); often in the phrase ἔκστασις κυρίου, 1 Βασ. 11:7; 14:15b; 2 Ch. 14:14; 15:5; 17:10; 20:29; Zech. 14:13. In Gn. 2:21; 15:12, ἔκστασις is used for תַּרְדֵּמָה, the deep sleep sent by Yahweh. At this point the LXX changes the sense of the original, importing its own theological and anthropological presuppositions. In Nu. 13:33 (32) ἔκστασις is used for דִּבָּה when anxiety is caused by the bad report of the spies. The use of ἔκστασις and the corresponding verb (→ 459) shows that the LXX regards psychologically events and facts which the Mas. views from a very different angle.

In the NT we find c. in the sense of "astonishment" or "terror" at numinous revelations, Lk. 5:26, synon. τρόμος, Mk. 16:8; θάμβος, Ac. 3:10; → ἐξέστησαν ἐκστάσει μεγάλῃ, Mk. 5:42. We also find d. in Ac. It is used of Peter in 10:10 : ἐπέπεσεν ἐπ' αὐτὸν ἔκστασις, and 11:5 : εἶδον ἐν ἐκστάσει ὅραμα, and of Paul in 22:17: γενέσθαι ἐν ἐκστάσει.

Although secondary Hellenistic sources exert no influence on the technical meaning of the word in the OT, and only a weak influence in the NT, the importance of the matter demands a closer examination of ecstasy in the narrower sense, of its nature and its theological significance.

A. Ecstasy outside the NT.

1. The Foundations and Methodical Production of Ecstasy.

Exceptional states of soul attributed to supernatural causes are widespread throughout the whole race. The question whether we have here genuine contacts with divine or demonic power on the one side, or neurotic disturbances and autosuggestion on the other, need not be regarded as posing flat alternatives. Certainly there may be illusion and deception. But even true experience of God cannot be divorced from historical and psychological conditioning, and yet it is not to be discounted for this reason. In ecstasy we have processes which vary widely, so that each instance must be treated on its own merits. Though the boundary between ecstasy and illusion may seem to us to be very

---

[1] A proselyte desires ἔκστασις διανοίας for the disturber of his soul's rest (Ditt. Syll.[3], 1240, 14 f., cf. Dt. 28:28), though as a lasting punishment.

tenuous, the same distinction, as also between ecstasy and possession, was made at an early period. [2] Ecstasy in the narrower sense involves beneficial apprehension and infilling by a higher power which may sometimes be experienced as an impersonal substance and sometimes as a personal being. Indeed, the two may be combined, as when a god puts man in a state of ecstasy, not by entering into him, but by breathing upon him.

Already in the earliest stages there are attempts to induce ecstasy by narcotics, music (esp. by percussion instruments), dancing, rhythmic cries and self-mutilation. [3] Higher forms of mysticism find the goal rather in an absorption associated with visions and auditions. Here, too, we have the development of a definite method which reaches its climax in Yoga, Neo-Platonism and the German Mystics. [4]

2. Ecstasy in the Greek and Hellenistic World. [5]

The Greek, too, classifies illusion and ecstasy together (μάντις from μαίνεσθαι), though without equating them (but cf. 1 C. 14:23 ff.). We do not know how early ecstatic phenomena are amongst the Greeks. Historically known forms are thought to have come from the Orient at the very earliest in the 8th cent. More recently, however, this has been contested in the case of Dionysus. [6] He is known to Homer. [7] But he does not fit into the Olympic system and therefore he is largely ignored in the chivalrous epic. The Anthesteria festival common to the Ionians seems to prove that Dionysus was at home in the Gk. world from at least the end of the second millennium. The location of his grave in Delphi seems to indicate a long tradition. We thus cannot assume a cultic union of two deities in which Apollos sought his own advantage when threatened by a usurper. We are rather dealing with a basic factor in Gk. religion. The distant Olympian and the god of frenzy complement and seek out one another. Together they comprehend the totality of the world as the Gks. experienced it.

The divine human figure of the son of Zeus and Semele comes up from primitive depths. It is not created by a rationalisation of the hunger for life, as the evolutionary theory maintains. It arises from the profoundest sense of the boundlessness of being. In part bewitchingly friendly, in part untameably wild, the god lavishly dispenses his gifts even to the point of the wilful sacrifice of life. The women swarming around him carefuly nourish the wild beasts of the forest and then tear in pieces the young deer and bears, if not their own children. With the same unparalleled impressiveness Dionysus is the distant and hidden god on the one side, the near and manifested on the other. He loves both noise and stillness. His symbol is the mask with its emphasis on presence and yet also its withdrawal from objectivity. The portion of the god no less than his worshippers is drunken desire, wild dancing, creative [8] and prophetic, [9] yet also sinister and destructive [10] frenzy, ecstatic life and life-destroying death. He experiences and suffers himself what he gives and does to others. The profound image of this tragic tension is the vine with its juice which both cheers and liberates and yet also incites

---

[2] Canaan, op. cit., 46 on the distinction, not always maintained, between maǧdûb and maǧnûn → ἕλκω.

[3] So among the Shamans, the dancing and howling dervishes. Cf. also 1 K. 18:26, 28 f.

[4] The stages of absorption are listed in Heiler, 312 f.

[5] In part by H. Kleinknecht.

[6] Otto, op. cit., 51 ff. On this view, Eur. Ba., 13 ff. is not a missionary message but a characterisation of the near and distant god.

[7] Il., 6, 130 ff.; 22, 461; 14, 325; Od., 24, 73 ff.; 11, 325; though cf. U. v. Wilamowitz-Moellendorff, Der Glaube der Hellenen, II (1932), 60 ff.

[8] Otto, 124 ff.

[9] Otto, 134 ff.

[10] Otto, 96 ff.

and bemuses. Wine, the aulos, handclapping,[11] dancing and Bacchic cries are means of producing ecstasy; but here already we have degeneration, an imitative mechanisation, rather than the true root. The basis lies in a religious experience which carries away in its greatness, which terrifies and shatters by its lack of measure or goal.

Ecstasy, like music and tragedy, arises out of these depths characterised finally by death. In its Dionysiac form it is expressed supremely in the swarms of dancing women (maenads). Several descriptions combine to give us a clear picture.[12] The well-known depictions in Eur. Ba., 120 ff., 680-768, 1043-1147, give us the best commentary. Using themes from fairy-stories, they give us a vivid impression of the way in which the world is bewitched for ecstatics, and also of the way in which they feel themselves transported willy-nilly into a union with nature which is partly idyllic and partly wild. The transition to the prophetic is given us in the words of Teiresias (ibid., 298 ff.):

> The god is also seer, for he doth bring us
> Into a frenzy of self-forgetfulness.
> This gives us vision, and when the soul
> Has wholly absorbed the god into itself,
> In depths of rapture it can prophesy.[13]

In the Delphic cult, perhaps with some clever adaptation to that of Apollo, we have the mass ecstasy of the thyiads with their torch dances by night through the wintry landscape of Parnassus. The mantic ecstasy of the individual, on the other hand, is embodied in the Pythia who, on a three-legged seat, intoxicated by scents arising from a vent in the earth, delivers her ambiguous oracles as delivered to her by the προφήτης in a language which is only half-understood. Here is the opportunity for a good deal of priestly deception.[14] The Roman Bacchanalian rite (186 B.C.) offers a picture of ecstasy which corresponds exactly. The only thing is that the masculine element seems to be more prominent in this case. The impulse came from a less cultured Greek of Etruria variously styled sacrificulus and vates.[15] In the nightly gatherings men prophesied like those possessed, with wild convulsions of the body. Women are also mentioned.[16] It was thought that there were raptures to the gods, simulated by machinery according to the rationalistic explanation of Livy.[17]

Similar wild ecstasies are also known in the Attis cult,[18] and to a lesser degree, linked with journeys to Hades, in the cult of Isis.[19] Apparently unconnected with any specific mysteries, but also with no more certain connection with popular religion, we

---

[11] Eur. Ba., 120 ff., 152 ff.

[12] Cf. illustr. in Leipoldt, op. cit., Plate 9; photo Anderson, 23, 709.

[13] Plut. Quaest. Conv., VII, 10, 2 (II, 716b) uses this verse for a not very profound meditation on the theme in vino veritas.

[14] L. B. Holland, "The Mantic Mechanism at Delphi," American Journal of Archaeology, 37 (1933), 201 f., makes the likely suggestion that the three-legged seat of the Pythia, the basis of which has been found, originally contained the oracle, also described as the bones of Dionysus or Python, and that the grave of Dionysus was identical with the rediscovered omphalos situated before the tripod (cf. the illustr., also Haas, 13/14; Rumpf, 19). It is probable that the Pythia herself manufactured the intoxicating scent in the adytum under the oracle, burning barley meal, laurel leaves and hemp seed over a fire. This rose up through a vent in the omphalos and was breathed in. Leisegang's theory that we have here a conception scene (Pneuma Hagion, 32 ff.) is not in keeping with the actual depictions (Leipoldt, Plate III, 5th cent. B.C.). Such ideas seem to have been imported later by those not so conversant with the facts and prepared to put a less favourable construction on them.

[15] Liv., 39, 8, 3.

[16] Liv., 39, 13, 12.

[17] Liv., 39, 13, 13.

[18] Catull., 63.

[19] Apul. Met., XI, 6; 21; 24.

also find in Greece, probably from around the 8th century, certain individual ecstatics both male and female (Bacids and Sibyls). [20] The individual names may perhaps conceal names of types. A particular task is the prophesying of disaster. From the oracles committed to writing there develops a varied form of literature which no longer has anything to do with genuine ecstasy, namely, the Sibylline oracles. These could be consulted for particular purposes, as we know from Rome ; and they were later filled out apologetically in Jewish and Christian pseudepigrapha.

In philosophy, too, ecstasy gained a footing. Heraclitus accepted what the Sibyllines proclaim with frenzied lips. [21] Mystical ecstasy has a secure place in Plato. He borrows from it in his famous description of poetic inspiration : [22] "The poet is an ethereal, easily moved, sacred being, and not able to compose, πρὶν ἂν ἔνθεός τε γένηται καὶ ἔκφρων καὶ ὁ νοῦς μηκέτι ἐν αὐτῷ ἐνῇ ... ἐξαιρούμενος τὸν νοῦν ... ὁ θεὸς αὐτός ἐστιν ὁ λέγων."

The idea that God is in man (χωρεῖν τὸν θεόν, Iambl. Myst., III, 11) alternates with that of the ἔνθεον γίγνεσθαι or ἐνθουσιασμός (Plat. Tim., 71e). The apparent contradiction was not felt in view of the more neutral conception of ἐν and the more fluid and less personal view of god. To both ideas there corresponds a third, that of the temporary separation of the soul from the body. A place must be found for the entering deity. But the soul itself, liberated from the body, can also attain to vision. It may thus be a hindrance to ecstasy, as the body always is. But it may also be an organ.

Different views follow in rapid succession in the Mithras Lit. The ἀνθρωπίνη ψυχικὴ δύναμις must give place for a short time (ὑπεξεστάναι, Preis. Zaub., IV, 523 f.). There follows rapture with a view to the vision of God, primarily in the body divested of the weight of earth (ibid., 538 ff.). Yet cf. 725 f.: ὑπέκλυτος δὲ ἔσει τῇ ψυχῇ καὶ οὐκ ἐν σεαυτῷ ἔσει. (Cf. also 2 C. 12:2 f., → ἀναβαίνω, I, 521). The power of God is mystically portrayed as the true being of man : "First becoming of my becoming, first beginning of my beginning, spirit of the spirit, first of the spirit in me" (488 ff.). But it is also drawn in with the breath : "Breathe in the breath (πνεῦμα) of the rays, drawing in three times to thy fullest extent" (537 ff.; cf. 628 f.: ἕλκε ἀπὸ τοῦ θείου ... εἰς σεαυτὸν τὸ πνεῦμα). It finally confronts the ecstatic in personal and bodily form (635 ff.; 695 ff.). Cic. Divin., I, 50, 114 : Ergo et ii, quorum animi spretis corporibus evolant atque excurrunt foras, ardore aliquo inflammati atque incitati cernunt illa profecto, quae vaticinantes pronuntiant, multisque rebus inflammantur tales animi, qui corporibus non inhaerent, ut ii, qui sono quodam vocum et Phrygiis cantibus excitantur (cf. 51, 115). Chrys. Hom. in Ac. XXII, 1 (MPG, 60, 172): τί ἐστιν ἔκστασις; πνευματική, φησί, θεωρία γέγονεν αὐτῷ· τοῦ σώματος, ὡς ἂν εἴποι τις, ἐξέστη ἡ ψυχή. The word ἔκστασις, originally understood of holy frenzy, seems later to have taken on the sense of rapture. [23]

So far as we know, Philo was the first to use the term in this technical sense. Yet he did not coin the meaning. [24] Rational and mystical-ecstatic knowledge are for him complementary, not identical. But the emphasis is on the latter. On the basis of Gn. 15:12 he gives the following picture of ecstasy (Rer. Div. Her., 263 ff.): "So long as our rational thinking streams around, pouring mid-day light, as it were, into the whole soul, we remain alone and do not experience any divine indwelling (οὐ κατεχόμεθα) ... For when the divine light dawns, the human sets (and vice versa) ... The Νοῦς in us departs (ἐξοικίζεται) at the coming of the divine spirit, and returns (πάλιν εἰσοικί-

---

20 Pauly-W., II (1896), 2801 f.; 2nd series II (1923), 2076.
21 Fr. 92 (I, 96, 7 ff., Diels).
22 Ion, 534b-d.
23 Cf. the word mysticism, originally derived from μύειν, "to close the mouth," and later from μύειν, "to close the eyes." Heiler, op. cit., 248 f.
24 This is proved not only by Philo's artificial classification (→ 450) but also by the independent use in Lk. (→ 450).

ζεται) at His departing. For it is a law that the mortal cannot dwell with the immortal." A higher force controls the tools of language (the ecstatic becomes an ὄργανον θεοῦ ἠχεῖον, κρουόμενον καὶ πληττόμενον ἀοράτως ὑπ' αὐτοῦ, Rer. Div. Her., 259, cf. 68 ff.; Leg. All., III, 40 f., 44, 48, 82, 84; Ebr., 146 ff.; Op. Mund., 71 etc.).

In Hellenism the ecstatic theology of revelation reaches a final climax in Neo-Platonism. The important statements are found in Plot. Enn., IV, 8, 1; VI, 7, 22; 9, 11. Like Plutarch, Iamblichus seeks to support the value of ecstasy and to explain its nature on rational grounds, sometimes almost materialistic.[25] The point is to try to do greater justice to the human factor and yet at the same time to ensure continued interest in ecstasy. Iamblichus, too, calls the ecstatic the ὄργανον of deity (Myst., III, 11).

3. The Significance of Ecstasy for OT Religion.

If we affirm ecstasy in Hellenism, but ignore the analogy in the OT and Jewish field, we bar the way to a truly historical understanding of original Christianity.[26] The analogy must be seen as such, though there are specific differences in detail.

The unusual and eccentric aspect forms the starting-point. Pathological features are not uncommon (Nu. 24:15 ff.; Ez. 3:25 f.; 4:4 ff.). The root נבא seems to have the original sense of "to speak with frenzy." Prophets are repeatedly described as mad (2 K. 9:11; Jer. 29:26; Hos. 9:7), and though this comes from opponents we cannot fail to see the connection.

In the OT, so far as we can see, we have at the beginning the man of God who disposes of supernatural power, and the seer who is gifted with supernatural knowledge, the latter being a seer rather than an ecstatic (Nu. 24:3; 1 S. 2:27; 9:6 ff.; 2 S. 24:11; 1 K. 13:1; 17:18; 2 K. 4:7 etc.). He can pass on his gifts etc. to others (2 K. 6:15 ff.). There are also true ecstatics like Deborah (Ju. 4:4). These are the givers of oracles both for everyday occasions (1 S. 9:6 ff.; 1 K. 14:1 ff.) and for more important, including political (2 S. 24:11), like the soothsayers of the Philistines (1 S. 6:2) and the Aramic חזין of the inscription of King Zakir of Hamath (8th cent. B.C.). This does not exhaust their work, however, for increasingly they come to declare the will of Yahweh and to enforce His ethical demands. Nor are we dealing only with great figures like Samuel (1 S. 15:22) and Nathan (2 S. 12:1 ff.), but also with lesser figures (1 S. 2:27). At the beginning of the monarchy there arises the new phenomenon of group ecstasy.[27] Renouncing everyday life, swarms of nebiim wander through the land to the sound of the harp, cymbal, flute and zither. Unasked, they announce the future, often in the form of judgment and disaster. Their ecstasy is infectious, and grips even those who stand aloof (1 S. 10:5 ff.; 19:20 ff.). Men like Elisha stand out from the rest (2 K. 2:5; 4:38). If there are primitive features and a certain amount of corruption, nebiism cannot simply be interpreted and dismissed as a Canaanitish intrusion into Yahweh religion. The sacred dance of the Yahweh cult left room for it, and in the main the nebiim are opposed to cultural degeneration. They represent the strict ethical majesty of the wilderness God (1 K. 18; 21:17 ff.; 2 K. 5:26 f.; for the connection of Elijah with nebiism, cf. 2 K. 2:5, and of Elisha apart from the passages already mentioned, cf. 2 K. 6:1 ff.; 9:1 ff.). They have a constant sense of the

---

[25] For fuller details cf. Fascher, op. cit., 70 ff.

[26] Reitzenstein and Leisegang in particular are to some extent exposed to this danger.

[27] As yet there is not enough evidence to support a genealogical connection between ecstasy in Palestine and ecstasy in Asia Minor and Greece.

historical leading of the people by Yahweh. It is not improbable that their proclamation also has eschatological features. The feeling of distance in relation to
the Godhead is characteristic. Yahweh Himself does not enter into men ; He works
in them through His Spirit (רוּחַ).

Classical prophecy holds aloof from institutionalised nebiism (Am. 7:14; Is.
28:7 ff.; 29:9 f.; Jer. 23:9 ff.; Ez. 13). Yet this should not prevent us seeing the
points of connection. What is attacked is the corruption of nebiism. Even Amos
allows that the *nebiim* are one of God's valuable gifts to His people (2:11 f.). In
clothes and manner of life, in the whole reception of revelation and even in the
message, there are broad areas of agreement. Many of the prophets accept the
designation *nabi* (Is. 8:3; Hos. 9:7). Some of them come from the prophetic schools,
and ecstatic experiences, visions and auditions are indispensable, especially in
calling (Is. 6:1 ff.; Jer. 1:4 ff.; Ez. 1:1 ff. etc.; Amos 7-9; Zech. 1-6). On the whole,
however, there is an unmistakable decline in the ecstatic element. We no longer
have the attempt to induce ecstasy by artificial means. This comes upon the instrument of Yahweh with irresistible force, causing perhaps more pain than
pleasure to the frail human vessel. Renunciation of ecstatic methodology is characteristic of OT piety from now on. The formula נְאֻם יְהוָה does not normally imply
the reception of the word by ecstatic audition. Visions may be a deception (Is.
28:7 ff.; Jer. 23:9 ff.; Ez. 13). The decisive point is the moral will of Yahweh. The
absolutely indispensable instrument of prophetic proclamation is understandable
speech, i.e., the word.

On the borders of apocalyptic the visionary and ecstatic element seems at a first
glance to resume its importance. This is especially true of Ez., Zech. and Daniel. On
the other hand, the visions here are literary artifices and we do not have to suppose
that they all took place exactly as narrated.

4. Ecstasy in Judaism.

For all the abundance of visions, developed apocalyptic really attests a decline in
ecstatic experiences. The visions of the pseudepigraphical writers are artificial products
of the study. This does not mean, however, that the ecstatic element had completely
vanished. Later Judaism certainly places inspiration in the past and in the Messianic
future (dramatically so in 1 Macc. 4:46; 9:27; 14:41). Yet descriptions of Messianic
experiences show that they still take place (→ I, 724). The apocalyptic writer does not
reject all such experiences as false. Philo continually claims to be an ecstatic, and we
have no reason to distrust his statements. [28] For all his Hellenism, he is a true Jew
in the sense that he does not think of God entering into man, but rather of the injection
of divine powers and intermediaries.

In Rabbinic circles there is frequent reference to visions, fiery appearances [29] and
auditions. [30] Four Rabbis are supposed to have seen Paradise while still in the body, [31]
though it is not certain that this is an ecstatic experience. In general, the Rabbis engaged
in cosmological speculation for which Ez. 1 (cf. jChag., 77b, 8 ff.) provided the basis, as
sometimes in modern Judaism. The fiery phenomena seem to indicate approach to the
spheres in which God dwells. [32] In bChag., 14b Bar. they occur in the story of a dis-

---

[28] For examples v. Büchsel, 89.
[29] Str.-B., II, 603 f. I owe this paragraph to Rengstorf.
[30] On Bath Qol, cf. Str.-B., I, 125 ff.
[31] T. Chag., 2, 3. There is also a fiery appearance and a voice from heaven in the par.
bChag., 14b.
[32] Cf. also the legend in M. Buber, *Der grosse Maggid und seine Nachfolge* (1922), 4 f.

cussion between R. Aqiba and his disciple R. Eleazar b. Arak on the מֶרְכָּבָה of Ez. 1,
and they are here a legendary accretion along with the singing of the trees and the
voice of an angel from the fire. The older but still legendary account is to be found in
jChag., 77a, 51 ff. Often the fiery phenomena have a purely symbolical sense. [33] They
occur in discussions of Scripture, a special role being again played by the מרכבה. It is also
characteristic of the Bath Qol that *ratio* still has its place. Sometimes it denotes a voice
of unknown origin, as in the anecdotes in Jeb., 16, 6; bBer., 3a (a heavenly voice like a
dove and coming from a ruin) etc. [34] One of the earliest examples of ecstasy in Judaism
is the dance of the old rabbis in the forecourt of the temple at the feast of the tabernacles
(Sukka, 5, 4; cf. bSukka, 53a), though here, too, a rational element is discernible.

B. Ecstasy in the NT.

1. Both in external appearance and in his preaching John the Baptist has obvious
and probably conscious links with nebiism. It is all the more significant, therefore,
that such records as we have show no trace either of ecstaticism or of the attempt
to attain it by artificial means. He prays and fasts in the wilderness. But he does
not use any other means. The goal is concentration rather than ecstasy. We
cannot say whether an ecstatic call preceded his work. The NT ascribes to him
neither ecstatic experiences nor miracles. [35] This is a mark of its authenticity. John
is a typical prophet of the word, full of ethical seriousness and glowing with
eschatological passion, but sober and restrained.

2. That Jesus was an ecstatic has been affirmed in some circles. [36] There is
truth in this view as opposed to the conception which, in connection with ecclesiastical or hellenised dogma, ascribes to Him a calm, earthly and more than
earthly equanimity. But it is based on an imprecise definition of ecstasy. [37] Not
everything unusual or exceptional is ecstatic. Not even the eschatological sense
of mission shown by Jesus is *ipso facto* ecstatic. His highly developed life of prayer
and miraculous gifts are better described as pneumatic. [38] The contemporaries of
Jesus often regarded Him as ecstatic in the sense of psychic derangement (Mk.
3:21: ἐξέστη) [39] or even possession (Mk. 3:22 and par.). But these are mis-
judgments due to inadequate knowledge and receptivity. Experiences like the
baptism with its voice from heaven (Mk. 1:10 f. and par.), the temptation (Mt. 4:1
and par.), the cry of jubilation (Mt. 11:25 ff. and par.), and the transfiguration
(Mk. 9:2 ff. and par.) may with greater or lesser justice be described as ecstatic. [40]
But even in these we see a distinction from the sensationalism of current ecstatic-

---

[33] Cf. the passages in Str.-B., II, 603 f.

[34] For the basic factors cf. Dalman, *Bath Kol,* RE³, I (1897), 443 f. Moore, I, 422 : "An
articulate and intelligible sound proceeding from an invisible source." Though cf. L. Blau,
Jew. Enc., s.v.

[35] Jn. 1:32 shows signs of development, by way of Mt. 3:16 f. and Lk. 3:21 f., and is not
therefore to be preferred to Mk. 1:10.

[36] O. Holtzmann, *War Jesus Ekstatiker?* (1903); C. A. Bernoulli, *Jesus wie sie ihn sahen*
(1928), 123 f.

[37] Cf. J. Leipoldt, *Vom Jesusbilde der Gegenwart²* (1925), 129 ff.; also G. Bertram, "Die
Persönlichkeit Jesu. Psychologische Darstellung u. christologischer Gehalt in der evang.
Überlieferung," *Ztschr. f. evangelischen Religions-Unterricht,* 43 (1932), esp. 146 ff.

[38] Cf. F. Büchsel, *op. cit.,* 149 ff., 157 n.

[39] On modern attempts to contest the psychical health of Jesus, cf. J. Leipoldt, *op. cit.,*
133 ff. The best reply is that of A. Schweitzer, *Die psychiatrische Beurteilung Jesu, Darstellung u. Kritik* (1913).

[40] A. Harnack, SAB (1922), 62 ff., esp. 74 f., though more with reference to Peter.

ism. Jesus does not separate Himself from sinners; as the Messiah, He ranges Himself with them along the lines of Deutero-Isaiah. He overcomes the temptations lurking in the Jewish concept of the Messiah. He thanks God for His revelation to the simple. He descends from the Mount of Transfiguration to the need of humanity (cf. Mk. 9:14 ff. and par.). At every point He displays the same normality (cf. also Lk. 10:18-20; Mt. 7:22 f.). [41] The search for parallels in the history of religion contributes less to a true understanding than regard for the context of these experiences in His person and calling. [42] The unique combination of suprahuman characteristics and the greatest simplicity is part of the incomparable richness of this personality. The essence, however, is to be found in the unique relationship to God, the resultant calling and the perfect fulfilment of this calling. But this cannot be described in terms of ecstasy.

3. A powerful, ecstatic element quickly emerges in early Christianity. It is not so much a basis as an accompaniment and mark of the climax. The appearances of the risen Lord are never associated with ecstatic experiences in the NT. [43] Paul puts a completely different construction on his Damascus experience (1 C. 15:8 ff.; Gl. 1:16 → ἐν) and on the experience described in 2 C. 12:1 ff. Later visions of the exalted Christ are described in the colours of ecstasy (Ac. 7:55 f.; cf. 6:15; Ac. 18:9 f.: δι' ὁράματος; 22:17 ff.: ἐν ἐκστάσει), [44] but not the first appearances. At Pentecost (→ I, 724 f.) the concrete historical and eschatological connections in which it is set by the early Church deserve attention. The analogy to Hellenistic ecstasy is expressed by Lk. in a few traits taken from the cult of Dionysus, and especially the "Bacchae" of Euripides. [45] But the ecstatic experiences of the Church rest basically on Jewish soil, as glossolalia belongs to Hellenistic (→ I, 722). The prayer life of the Church also borders on the ecstatic (Ac. 4:24 ff.; 3:9; 16:25 ff.; cf. also the canticles in Lk. 1:46 ff., 68 ff.; 2:28 ff.). Under persecution, in serious emergencies and in face of difficult decisions in missionary work, direction and strength are found in more or less evident ecstatic experiences (Ac. 7:55; 10:10 ff.; 11:5 ff.; 13:2; 16:6 f., 10; 18:9 f.; 22:17 ff.; 27:23 ff.; Gl. 2:1). On the other hand, the Church steadfastly opposes an ecstaticism which is destitute of the fruit of righteousness, of moral discipline, of integrity and love (Ac. 8:9 ff., Simon Magus; 1 C. 12-14).

We know that Paul was an ecstatic, not so much from 2 C. 5:13 (→ 460), but rather from 1 C. 14:18 and 2 C. 12:1 ff. It is possible that his thorn in the flesh [46]

---

[41] This is rightly emphasised by Holtzmann, 114 ff. Medical authorities like Mantegazza, T. J. Hudson and Binswanger tell us that occasional hallucinations are not uncommon in men who are otherwise healthy. Leipoldt, 160, 162; J. Ninck, *Jesus als Charakter*[3] (1925), 284. But the typical ecstatic finds it difficult to return to normal life. He would rather indulge in further ecstasy, and the final result is complete derangement.

[42] "Jesus had also moments of ecstasy when He saw what no eye has seen and heard what no ear has heard, when His inner life made a great leap forward. Such climaxes are harmful only when they have a weakening and disrupting effect. If they inspire to greater activity and focus and increase energy they are a sign of health and a benefit," Ninck, *op. cit.*

[43] It would solve many difficulties to equate the appearance to over 500 brethren at once (1 C. 15:6) with Pentecost (E. v. Dobschütz, *Ostern u. Pfingsten* [1903], 34; K. Holl, SAB [1921], 923), but there are no grounds for so doing in the NT itself.

[44] The identification of these experiences with those recounted in 2 C. 12:2 ff. is rightly rejected by E. Jacquier, *Actes des Apôtres* (1926), 651 *ad loc.*

[45] On these connections cf. F. Smend, *Angelos* 1 (1925), 41 ff.

[46] Cf. on this pt. Wnd. 2 K., excursus on 12:7.

increased the tendency towards ecstatic experiences. But his powerful achievements forbid us to assess him essentially from psychopathic standpoints. In spite of Gl. 2:1 f., the apostle differs from the usual ecstatic by not attributing too great importance to his ecstasies (2 C. 12:1, 11; 1 C. 14:19). Though there are formal analogies to the Hellenistic pneumatic, these do not justify us in regarding him as such. [47] The higher knowledge which Paul claims (1 C. 2:10 ff.) is orientated to salvation history, and for him the break in consciousness does not serve an arrogant pride but humble modesty (2 C. 12:2, 5). [48] He wages a bitter fight against the excesses of orgiastic ecstasy. Regarding the NT prophets → προφήτης.

Similarly, the visions of the Apocalyptist are not sensational but are designed to stir and to strengthen the community in the serious situation of threatened conflict with the world power of imperial despotism in a heightened religious form. They are thus genuine prophecy. Analysis in terms of religious psychology shows us that we have here true ecstatic and visionary experiences, of an emotional but not a pathological kind, which do, of course, undergo further development in reflection and literary presentation. [49]

C. The Ecstatic Element in the Early Church.

The term ἔκστασις is found neither in the post-apostolic fathers nor in the apologists. Nevertheless, the thread of ecstatic experiences does not break off in the post-apostolic and early catholic period. The *Didache* is suspicious of individual self-seekers, not of ecstatics as such (11, 7 ff.). These are still highly regarded. Devotional prayer may lead to visions, though these are not deliberately induced. According to the story of his martyrdom, Polycarp in prayer saw a vision of his pillow in flames three days before his imprisonment, and he then said to those around : "I must be burned alive" (Mart. Pol., 5, 2). In the *Shepherd of Hermas* ecstatic endowment appears within the Church ; in Montanism it breaks away from it.

That oriental prophetism could produce strange fruits well into the second century may be seen from Celsus' well-known description of Christian ecstatics (Orig. Cels., VII, 9): "Many nameless figures who for some casual reason remain inside or outside the temple, partly begging and haunting cities and barracks, make out that they are prophets. Each has the usual saying ready to hand : 'I am God, or God's Son, or the divine Spirit. I have come because the world is perishing and you, O men, are lost because of your wickedness. I will save you, and you will see me come again with the power of heaven. Well for those who have served me in that day ! But on the rest, on cities and countries, I will bring eternal fire ...' And when they have enlarged on this, they add some stupid and unintelligible nonsense which no one of understanding can make out ; for it is without meaning, but it enables any fool or charlatan to interpret it as he will." It is highly probable, of course, that Celsus is here confusing the facts with his own conceptions of Christianity, or generalising from isolated cases. On ecstatic experiences in Gnosticism → I, 723.

In general we may say that, while the Church did not exclude ecstatic revelations, especially in periods of stress, it increasingly recognised and fought against the dangerous and unhealthy features. Thus the ecstatic became more and more heretical. In the Church the orderly ministry assumed control. This might mean impoverishment, but as things stood it brought clarity and security.

---

[47] So esp. Reitzenstein, *op. cit.*
[48] K. Deissner, *Paul. u. die Mystik seiner Zeit*² (1921), 21 ff., 81 ff.
[49] "John is no more pathological than Grünewald or Dürer," Schneider, *op. cit.*, 141.

† ἐξίστημι (ἐξιστάνω).

1. Trans. "to remove from its place," fig. "to alter," πολιτείαν, Plut. De Cicerone, 10 (I, 866b), φύσιν, Timaeus Locrus, 11 (100c; ed. C. F. Hermann [1907]); "to shake," τινὰ φρενῶν, Eur. Ba., 850; τοῦ φρονεῖν, Xenoph. Mem., I, 3, 12; ἀνθρώπους αὐτῶν (synon. κινεῖν), Demosth., 21, 72; with simple acc.: οἶνος ἐξέστησέ με, Stob. Ecl., III, 517, 15, cf. Is. 28:7: "to set in terror" : τὰ ἐξιστάντα καὶ φοβοῦντα τοὺς ἀνθρώπους, Muson. Fr., 8, p. 35, 12 f.; LXX Ju. 8:12; 2 Βασ. 17:2; of Yahweh: ἐκστήσω πάντα τὰ ἔθνη, Ex. 23:27; Jos. 10:10; Ju. 4:15; 2 Βασ. 22:15 etc.

In the NT it is found in Lk. 24:22 : γυναῖκες ἐξέστησαν ἡμᾶς, "to confuse," and in Ac. 8:9 : μαγεύων καὶ ἐξιστάνων τὸ ἔθνος, and v. 11: διὰ τὸ ... ταῖς μαγείαις ἐξεστακέναι αὐτούς, "to bewitch."

2. Intr. (mid. pass. aor. 2, perf. act.): "to remove oneself," used of the loss of capacities in the pap. (P. Ryl., II, 75, 6; 117, 22), and fig. "to lose one's wits" either a. in the sense of "to go out of one's mind" : φρενῶν, Eur. Or., 1021; Jos. Ant., 10, 114; τῶν λογισμῶν, Polyb, 32, 25, 8; Max. Tyr., 27, 5; abs. ἐξίστασθαι καὶ μαίνεσθαι, Aristot. Hist. An., VI, 22, p. 577a, 12; Alciphr. Ep., 3, 2; ἐξίστασθαι καὶ παρανοεῖν, Dio. Chrys. Or., 32, 42; and more rarely b. in the sense of "to be terrified out of one's wits," Philodem. Philos. De Ira, col., 38, 26 f. (ed. C. Wilke [1914]), though the LXX often uses it of fright at natural causes, with an inner object : ἐξέστη Ἰσαὰκ ἔκστασιν μεγάλην, Gn. 27:33, and more generally Gn. 43:33; it usually expresses terror before Yahweh or at His judgments : Jer. 4:9; Ez. 26:16.

In the LXX [1] ἐξίστημι is a techn. psychological term used by the translators to group under a common psychological standpoint things for which different expressions are used in the Mas. Acc. to Hatch-Redpath ἐξίστημι occurs 75 times in the LXX. In 65 passages 30 different Heb. words are rendered (the root חרד 16 times). The more common intrans. usually has the sense of the psychical emotion of terror, anxiety or astonishment, with a strong sense of the numinous. The independence of the LXX in relation to the Mas. may be seen most clearly in the following passages. In Ex. 19:18 the LXX uses "people" instead of "mountain" as the subj. of this verb, and thus makes a human experience out of a natural event. In Hab. 3:2 ecstasy occurs only in the LXX as man's reaction to the revelation of God in word and work. Expressions of joy are also put in terms of numinous experience in Ex. 18:9 and Lv. 9:24 (cf. Hos. 3:5). In textual transmission we sometimes have an alternation between ἐξίστημι (psychological) and ἐξανίστημι (physiological). In Ju. 3:8 the Mas. presupposes a physical movement, whereas parallelism with what follows suggested to the translators the change to an emotional movement. On the other hand, in 3 Βασ. 1:49 the Mas. (חרד) requires an expression of emotion whereas the context seems to favour a physical movement. c. In Philo alone the term is also used for self-alienation in divinely caused rapture (→ ἔκστασις, 450). The Hethites ἑρμηνεύονται ἐξιστάντες, Som., II, 89; the enraptured soul seems μεθύειν καὶ παρανοεῖν καὶ ἐξεστάναι, Ebr., 146. There is perhaps here the additional suggestion, not found elsewhere, of the soul in ecstasy leaving the body, its natural home : σαυτὴν ἀπόδραθι καὶ ἔκστηθι σεαυτῆς Rer. Div. Her., 69. On the nature of ecstasy → ἔκστασις, 453.

In the NT the meaning a. occurs in Mk. 3:21: ὅτι ἐξέστη, "he is beside himself." Mk. is emphasising the extraordinary nature of Jesus. It is unwarranted to suppose that his source was merely intending to say that He "departed." [2] In

---

ἐ ξ ί σ τ η μ ι. [1] This paragraph up to c. is by G. Bertram.
[2] F. Spitta, Zur Geschichte u. Literatur d. Urchristentums, III, 2 (1907), 130 ff. The variants ἐξέσταται αὐτούς ("he escaped from them," D φ it) and ἐξήρτηνται αὐτοῦ ("for they were related to him," or "dependent on him," W 28) are interesting, but simply show how offensive the almost uniformly attested text was felt to be.

2 C. 5:13 ἐξέστημεν is the opp. of σωφρονοῦμεν; if we were beside ourselves, it was for God, and if we are sober, it is for your sakes. So far as we can gather from 1 C. 12-14, the charge that Paul was out of his mind could hardly arise out of his ecstatic experiences — this is also refuted by v. 12. It is probably to be explained in terms of a supposedly "eccentric" assertion of apostolic authority. [3] The word also bears the sense b. when used of astonishment at the revelation of the divine glory, whether in the child Jesus (Lk. 2:47), His miracles (Mt. 12:23; Mk. 2:12; Mt. 9:8 ἐφοβήθησαν; 5:42; Mk. 6:51, Mt. 14:33 προσεκύνησαν; Lk. 8:56), or the wonderful experiences of the early community (Ac. 2:7, synon. θαυμάζω, 12, synon. διαπορέω; 8:13; 9:21; 10:45; 12:16). The term reflects the powerful religious experience of the early Church. The meaning c. is not found in the NT, though cf. → ἔκστασις.

Oepke

ἐκτείνω, ἐκτενής (ἐκτενέστερον),
ἐκτένεια, ὑπερεκτείνω

---

† ἐκτείνω.

In the NT, except in Ac. 27:30, it is used only in the expression "to stretch out the hand" (Lk. 22:53; Jn. 21:18, hands); Mt. 8:3; 12:13, 49; 14:31; 26:51; Mk. 1:41; 3:5; Lk. 5:13; 6:10; Ac. 4:30; 26:1.

1. ἐκτείνω originally means outstretching either as a single movement or as part of a larger complex, and in terms of either extent or tension, cf. someone outstretched in sleep in Xenoph. An., V, 1, 2 : ἐκταθεὶς ... καθεύδων, or the deployment of an army (Xenoph.) or of words for speech, Plat. Leg., X, 887a: οὐ βραχὺς ὁ λόγος ἐκταθεὶς ἂν γίγνοιτο; but also the stretching of the will in eagerness, Hdt., VII, 10, 7: πᾶσαν προθυμίην ἐκτείνειν, and esp. the stretching of a part of the body to introduce or accomplish an action (Aesch. Prom., 323: Οὔκουν ἔμοιγε χρώμενος διδασκάλῳ πρὸς κέντρα κῶλον ἐκτενεῖς), sometimes the hand (Plat. Resp., V, 449b: ἐκτείνας τὴν χεῖρα καὶ λαβόμενος τοῦ ἱματίου), and as a gesture, cf. the outstretching of the hand in friendship (Polyb., II, 47, 2 : τηρεῖν φιλίαν καὶ μὴ φαίνεσθαι πρὸς ἑτέρους ἐκτείνοντες τὰς χεῖρας) or in token of a speech (Quint. Inst. Orat., IX, 3, 84 ff.).

In Ac. 27:30 : ἐκτείνειν ἀγκύρας, we obviously have a technical use, [1] designed to make plain the intention of the sailors. In v. 29 we simply read : ἐκ πρύμνης ῥίψαντες ἀγκύρας τέσσαρας. But then the sailors try to take advantage of their calling. They need the boat to pay out anchors at the front, i.e., to steady the ship. In view of the forward drag, however, this is nonsensical. They cannot achieve the tension indicated by the movement referred to (i.e., paying out the anchor). In other words, there can be no anchoring the ship to the front, and therefore their intention is to flee. [2]

2. ἐκτείνειν τὰς χεῖρας. Since the word has no implied meaning but simply denotes a gesture, it is used in the LXX for many Heb. equivalents whose nuances are not

---

[3] Bchm. 2 K., *ad loc.* Sickb. K., *ad loc.* suggests gifts of tongues or visionary states, Wnd., *ad loc.* a self-seeking and boastful assertion of such special advantages.

ἐ κ τ ε ί ν ω κ τ λ. Pr.-Bauer, *s.v.*; C. Sittl, *Die Gebärden der Griechen u. Römer* (1890), 350 ff. and 50, n. 5; Schl. Mt., 271, 423, 472; Schl. Lk., 56, 433, 436, 646.

[1] Cf. A. Breusing, *Die Nautik der Alten* (1886), 195.

[2] Though cf. R. Knopf in *Schriften des NT, ad loc.*

reproduced by it. This is particularly true in the predominant LXX expression ἐκτείνειν τὰς χεῖρας, which is used especially for the words נטה and שלח (→ I, 400 ff.). It makes no difference whether the one who stretches out the hand is a messenger of God, God Himself, or a man. [3] Nor does it matter for what purpose the hand is outstretched. It may be noted, however, that when there is any grasping at God's property the stronger word ἐπιφέρειν is used instead of ἐκτείνειν (Gn. 37:22; 1 Βασ. 24:7, 11; 26:9; Est. 8:7). In general we may say that ἐκτείνειν τὰς χεῖρας emphasises a graphic element in the story to make it more vivid. Something must always follow the ἐκτείνειν τὰς χεῖρας, whether a gift (Sir. 4:31) or a prayer (1 Ἐσδρ. 8:70; 4 Macc. 4:11). To this extent it often expresses resolve upon a certain act. This gives us a link with NT usage in so far as this has specific features of its own. The usage of Josephus (as distinct from Philo) follows exactly that of the LXX (Ant., 13, 327; 8, 233; 6, 239).

This brings us to a discussion of the use of ἐκτείνειν τὰς χεῖρας in the NT.

When we read in Lk. 22:53 : καθ᾽ ἡμέραν ὄντος μου μεθ᾽ ὑμῶν ἐν τῷ ἱερῷ οὐκ ἐξετείνατε τὰς χεῖρας ἐπ᾽ ἐμέ. ἀλλ᾽ αὕτη ἐστὶν ὑμῶν ἡ ὥρα καὶ ἡ ἐξουσία τοῦ σκότους, Lk. is perhaps emphasising the solemnity of the moment, which the opponents of Jesus do not realise, by using, instead of the common συλλαβεῖν or κρατεῖν of Mt. and Mk., an expression familiar from such passages as Ez. 6:14 ff. Yet there is also the simpler explanation that he wants to make the scene more vivid by bringing before us the hands which want to seize Jesus. The hand is stretched out to attack, as in Mt. 26:51: εἷς τῶν μετὰ Ἰησοῦ ἐκτείνας τὴν χεῖρα ἀπέσπασεν τὴν μάχαιραν αὐτοῦ καὶ πατάξας τὸν δοῦλον τοῦ ἀρχιερέως ἀφεῖλεν αὐτοῦ τὸ ὠτίον. Often this takes place unconsciously. If the action is stressed, it loses its graphic quality. In Lk. 22:51, instead of καὶ ἁψάμενος τοῦ ὠτίου ἰάσατο αὐτόν, the author might have said : καὶ ἐκτείνας τὴν χεῖρα αὐτοῦ ἥψατο τοῦ ὠτίου καὶ ἰάθη. But this would have disturbed the dramatic perspective, which has v. 53 in view.

Mt. 12:49 is also to be understood graphically. Instead of καὶ περιβλεψάμενος τοὺς περὶ αὐτὸν κύκλῳ καθημένους λέγει· ἴδε ἡ μήτηρ μου κτλ. (Mk. 3:34), we have the more emphatic : καὶ ἐκτείνας τὴν χεῖρα ἐπὶ τοὺς μαθητὰς αὐτοῦ εἶπεν· ἰδοὺ ἡ μήτηρ μου κτλ. Instead of a depiction in terms of the gaze of Jesus, as in Mk., Mt. gives us a gesture which lends emphasis to the words which follow. There is here revealed the will of Jesus which is identical with that of His Father in heaven (Mt. 12:50; Mk. says : θέλημα τοῦ θεοῦ). The goal of this will is the μαθητής; it does not express itself in a general truth, as Mk. might suggest. But if the will of Jesus aims at me, I am already apprehended by it. Thus the expression ἐκτείνειν τὰς χεῖρας mediates between a graphic mode of narration and one which carries with it emotional emphasis and even an imperative.

That we should not underestimate the graphic significance appears very plainly in Mt. 14:28-31.

Here the course of the narrative is as follows : 1. As Jesus walks on the water, Peter says to Him : "Lord, if it be Thou, bid me come to thee on the water ;" 2. Jesus says : "Come ;" 3. Peter comes ; 4. Peter is afraid and begins to sink ; 5. Peter calls : "Lord, save me ;" 6. εὐθέως δὲ ὁ Ἰησοῦς ἐκτείνας τὴν χεῖρα ἐπελάβετο αὐτοῦ καὶ λέγει αὐτῷ· ὀλιγόπιστε, εἰς τί ἐδίστασας; 7. They get into the ship, the wind falls and the disciples worship Him : ἀληθῶς θεοῦ υἱὸς εἶ. [4] The scene depicted in Mt. is ob-

---

[3] The thesis argued by Rengstorf in → I, 401, n. 23 needs correction in view of the fact that ἐκτείνειν τὴν χεῖρα in Jer. 1:9 is a rendering of שלח (cf. also Hatch-Redp.).

[4] 14:32 f.; in Mk. ἐγώ εἰμι stands unexplained in the middle of the story, and the scene ends in 6:51 f. with the astonishment of the disciples. Jn. brings the scene to a sudden end with the coming of the ship to land (6:21).

viously viewed from within the ship, as we can see from v. 33. This helps us to understand the grasp of Jesus, for if the others had been pulling Peter back into the boat the same expression would have been used. Yet the important point is not the grasp as such; it is the fact that He always reaches after us. Hence the scene illustrates the statement formulated above, namely, that if the will of Jesus aims at me, I am already apprehended by it.

The miracle in the healing of the withered hand in Mt. 12:9-14 is obviously the restoration of movement. To the command of Jesus: ἔκτεινόν σου τὴν χεῖρα, there thus corresponds the obedience : καὶ ἐξέτεινεν, so that it can be recorded : καὶ ἀπεκατεστάθη ὑγιὴς ὡς ἡ ἄλλη (Mt. 12:13). That this is public may be seen from Mk. 3:3 and Lk. 6:8 (ἔγειρε [καὶ στῆθι] εἰς τὸ μέσον). If Lk. uses only ἐποίησεν instead of ἐξέτεινεν, this underlines the logical sequence. Thus Lk. tells us that there took place what Jesus said, whereas Mt. and Mk. tell us that it happened as Jesus had said. There is no particular stress on the obedience of the man who is healed. We simply see that through His Word the will of Jesus heals a withered arm so that it can be stretched out again. The charm of the narrative is that the same movement which leads to grasping or which serves as a gesture can now illustrate the power of the will of Jesus. [5]

Whereas in this story the graphic element in the gesture depends upon the fact that it may be followed by grasping (cf. Sir. 15:16), [6] in Mt. 8:3 and par. the dramatic effect of the gesture obviously implies that there is no apprehending : καὶ ἐκτείνας τὴν χεῖρα ἥψατο αὐτοῦ λέγων· θέλω, καθαρίσθητι. The contact is not apprehension but a gesture with which, to the appeal of the leper : κύριε, ἐὰν θέλῃς, δύνασαί με καθαρίσαι (Mt. 8:2), Jesus answers : θέλω, καθαρίσθητι. If elsewhere ἅπτεσθαι is one of the techniques of healing in miracle stories, here it is a gesture answering the appeal of the leper and thus manifesting the will of Jesus. The healing itself is then to be shown to the priest, who will certify it to the leper in the regular way (Mt. 8:4). This is not contradicted by the fact that when the 10 are healed in Lk. 17:14 there is no gesture and they are healed as they go, for here the climax of the scene is the return of the Samaritan (v. 15 f.). If we take the gesture and the healing together, we have thus to say that in the outstretching of the hand of Jesus in healing there is revealed the outreach of His will. The will and act of Jesus are to be manifested in their unique unity.

This is true, however, of the general outreach of God's will for which the community prays : δὸς τοῖς δούλοις σου μετὰ παρρησίας πάσης λαλεῖν τὸν λόγον σου ἐν τῷ τὴν χεῖρα ἐκτείνειν σε εἰς ἴασιν καὶ σημεῖα καὶ τέρατα γίνεσθαι διὰ τοῦ ὀνόματος τοῦ ἁγίου παιδός σου Ἰησοῦ (Ac. 4:29 f.). The reference is not to a particular action necessary for the performance of a miracle,

---

[5] Dausch Synpt. on Mt. 12:13 speaks quite wrongly of "an active proof of his decision, the healing of the withered hand ... This was brought about as the sick man stretched it out at the command of Jesus. The outstretching of the hand thus seems to be a condition, a test of faith rather than a sign of healing." More correct is the statement that "the effective cause of healing was a mere act of will on the part of Jesus." On ἐκτείνειν τὴν χεῖρα in miracles of healing, cf. the similar expression, which obviously seems to have been a technical term in medicine too, in the miracles of Epidauros : Ditt. Syll.[3], 1168, 28 : θεὸν ἐφαλέσθαι ἐπὶ τὰν χῆρα καὶ ἐκτεῖναί οὐ τοὺς δακτύλλους. On the tech. term, cf. Hippocr. Epid., V, 23; Diocles. Fr., 141 (p. 178, 3; 183, 2 f. M. Wellmann, Fragmentensammlung der gr. Ärzte 1901). R. Herzog, Die Wunderheilungen von Epidauros (1931), 99; O. Weinreich, Antike Heilungswunder, RVV, 8, 1 (1909).

[6] Cf. R. Knopf on Did., 4, 5 in the Suppl. to Ltzm., Handb. z. NT (1920).

but to a declaration of His will in active self-demonstration. Because we cannot separate the divine act and the divine will, the acts of God are miracles to us. The problem in Ac. 4:30 is not the outstretching of the hand of God, but the meaning of the ἴασις, σημεῖα and τέρατα, which is confused by the miraculous effect of the prayer described in v. 31.

In a technical sense we find ἐκτείνειν τὴν χεῖρα in Ac. 26:1, where Paul introduces his defence before Agrippa with the regular oratorical gesture : ἐκτείνας τὴν χεῖρα ἀπελογεῖτο. This expression, which is good Gk., reminds the exegete that the element common to both the grasp and the gesture is the will which I have in relation to something. Paul is relating himself to Agrippa as an orator. This is to be noted in what follows (the most artistic speech in the NT).

It is open to question whether we have a similar technical use in Jn. 21:18. The structure of the verse is against this view : ἀμὴν ἀμὴν λέγω σοι, ὅτε ἦς νεώτερος, ἐζώννυες σεαυτὸν καὶ περιεπάτεις ὅπου ἤθελες· ὅταν δὲ γηράσῃς, ἐκτενεῖς τὰς χεῖράς σου, καὶ ἄλλος ζώσει σε (v.l., ἄλλοι ζώσουσί σε) καὶ οἴσει (v.l., ἀποίσουσιν — ἀπάγουσίν σε — ποιήσουσίν σοι ὅσα) ὅπου οὐ θέλεις. The variants show that play is here made on the violent death of Peter. The outstretching of the hands can refer to crucifixion, cf. Artemid. Oneirocr., I, 70 : κακοῦργος δὲ ὢν σταυρωθήσεται διὰ τὸ ὕψος καὶ τὴν τῶν χειρῶν ἔκτασιν, [7] and Epictet. Diss., III, 26, 22 : ἐκτείνας σεαυτὸν ὡς οἱ ἐσταυρωμένοι, cf. Barn., 12, 2. On the other hand, the outstretching of the hands here corresponds to the movement of girding. Thus there seems to be no direct allusion to the violent end of Peter. The meaning is that the acknowledged shepherd has finally undergone the most difficult submission of will which man can experience.

In the post-apost. fathers ἐκτείνειν is mostly found in OT quotations. Cf. 1 Cl., 57, 4 with Prv. 1:23 ff.; Barn., 19, 9 and Did., 4, 5 with Sir. 4:31; Barn., 5, 4 with Prv. 1:7; Barn., 12, 2 with Ex. 17:8-13. Herm. v., 4, 1. 9 : ἐκτείνει ἑαυτὸ χαμαί (on the earth), corresponds to Gk. usage. The statement in 1 Cl., 2, 3 : ἐξετείνατε τὰς χεῖρας ὑμῶν πρὸς τὸν παντοκράτορα θεὸν ἱκετεύοντες κτλ., points forward to an increasing future use in liturgical practice (→ 464, n. 3).

† ἐκτενής, ἐκτενέστερον.

Like → ἐκτείνω, from the time of Aesch. and Hdt., and also in Philo, Joseph. and the pap., the word is used of tension of the will and means "tense," "resolute," "eager," cf. Ditt. Or., 339, 20 : τὸ φιλόσπουδον καὶ ἐκτενές; 767, 15 : καὶ τὰ πρὸς θεὸς (sic!) ἐκτενῶς καὶ εὐσεβῶς ἐτέλεσεν; 767, 6 : ἱερατεύσας τε δὶς Καίσαρος τοῦ θεοῦ ἐκτενῶς καὶ φιλοτείμως. In the LXX, where ἐκτενής occurs only 6 times, it is used adv. for the fervour of prayer (3 Macc. 5:9; Jon. 3:8; Jl. 1:14; Jdt. 4:12); cf. 3 Macc. 3:10; 5:29 : Ἡτοίμασται, βασιλεῦ, κατὰ τὴν σὴν ἐκτενῆ πρόθεσιν.

In the NT it is found only at Ac. 12:5; 1 Pt. 1:22; 4:8; Lk. 22:44 (ἐκτενέστερον).

The admonition πρὸ πάντων τὴν εἰς ἑαυτοὺς ἀγάπην ἐκτενῆ ἔχοντες in 1 Pt. 4:8 stands under the declaration πάντων δὲ τὸ τέλος ἤγγικεν in v. 7. The point is, therefore, that Christians should not merely show fervent love to one another (there is also the admonition : σωφρονήσατε οὖν καὶ νήψατε εἰς προσευχάς, in v. 7), but rather that in view of the approaching end they should see to it that their love for one another endures against self-seeking. Only thus can they hope that their love will cover the sins which rend the community (v. 8). For this purpose they will need a will which is pure and which is therefore renewed, so that with the ἐκτενής it seems necessary also to refer to the καρδία

---

[7] Cf. Bau. J., ad loc.

(sc. καθαρά): ἐκ καρδίας ἀλλήλους ἀγαπήσατε ἐκτενῶς ἀναγεγεννημένοι (1 Pt. 1:22).

The word ἐκτενής seems to be most apt in relation to prayer, for here the required concentration of will is produced as it were by a single action (whereas ἀγάπη is always taking different forms). Thus on the occasion of Peter's imprisonment we read of the Jerusalem community: προσευχὴ δὲ ἦν ἐκτενῶς (v.l. ἐκτενὴς) γινομένη ὑπὸ τῆς ἐκκλησίας πρὸς τὸν θεὸν περὶ αὐτοῦ (sc. τοῦ Πέτρου, Ac. 12:5). In view of the great danger of Peter the unceasing prayer made for him by the Church is also fervent, since the Church knows what it is praying for. The tension denoted by ἐκτενής does not apply, therefore, to an action or will which is not certain of its goal.

As a comp. of ἐκτενής we find ἐκτενέστερον in the textually disputed verse Lk. 22:44. Here ἐκτενέστερον refers only to the intensity of the prayer of Jesus. This does not really correspond to the NT sense of ἐκτενής mentioned above, just as vv. 43 f. are generally less clear than v. 42. It is difficult to reconcile an indefiniteness of goal with this intensity. In Gethsemane the concern of the Jesus of the Gospels is not just with dying, as though this were itself a problem. It is with the death related to sin and therefore with the sinners punished by it. Hence Jesus is not a direct example for us in the hour of death, as seems to be suggested in some way in the disputed verse. [1]

When we come to the post-apostolic fathers, it is noteworthy that they no longer use ἐκτενής for Christian action. In 1 Cl., 58, 2 we read: ... ὁ ποιήσας ἐν ταπεινοφροσύνῃ μετ᾽ ἐκτενοῦς ἐπιεικείας ἀμεταμελήτως τὰ ὑπὸ τοῦ θεοῦ δεδομένα δικαιώματα καὶ προστάγματα, οὗτος ἐντεταγμένος ... ἔσται κτλ. The present attitude of the Christian is compared with his definitive being in the future of Jesus Christ, so that the Christian must be constantly aware that he has not yet reached the goal. Instead of a condition of Christian action we thus have an attitude, [2] cf. 1 Cl., 62, 2: You must please God ἐν ἀγάπῃ καὶ εἰρήνῃ μετὰ ἐκτενοῦς ἐπιεικείας. Prayer itself is thus changed into an attitude (1 Cl., 59, 2; 34, 7), so that later ἡ ἐκτενής naturally becomes a liturgical term. [3]

† ἐκτένεια.

Attested from the time of Phryn., [1] this word, like → ἐκτενής, first means "endurance" (LXX Jdt. 4:9; 2 Macc. 14:38; 3 Macc. 6:41), which comes to be thought of as an attitude, 1 Cl., 33, 1: σπεύσωμεν μετὰ ἐκτενείας καὶ προθυμίας πᾶν ἔργον ἀγαθὸν ἐπιτελεῖν, and 37, 1: στρατευσώμεθα οὖν, ἄνδρες ἀδελφοί, μετὰ πάσης ἐκτενείας ἐν τοῖς ἀμώμοις προστάγμασιν αὐτοῦ (sc. τοῦ θεοῦ). In this attitude the Christian is like a soldier who knows his task and his place (1 Cl., 37, 2).

In the NT it occurs only in Ac. 26:7: τὸ δωδεκάφυλον ἡμῶν ἐν ἐκτενείᾳ νύκτα καὶ ἡμέραν λατρεῦον, where it is hoped to attain the promise by persistent service of God both night and day. [2] In place of this Paul points to an event, namely, the revelation of the Lord given him at his conversion (26:13 ff.).

ἐ κ τ ε ν ή ς. [1] Cf. Kl. Lk., ad loc.
[2] Cf. E. Fuchs, *Glaube und Tat in den Mandata des Hermas* (Diss. Marburg, 1931), 45, 56.
[3] Thus in the case of Hermas prayer as an attitude is psychologically the source of his visions. On the relevant usage in Const. Ap., 6, 5; 7, 1, cf. R. Knopf on 1 Cl., 34, 7 (→ ἐκτείνω, n. 6). Cf. also Chrys. Liturg., 373, 3; L. Eisenhofer, *Liturgik,* I (1932), 198; II (1933), 46 ff.; E. A. Sophocles, *Greek Lex.* (1870), *s.v.*

ἐ κ τ έ ν ε ι α. [1] V. Pr.-Bauer, *s.v.*
[2] In the v.l. Ac. 12:5 D: πολλὴ δὲ προσευχὴ ἦν ἐν ἐκτενείᾳ περὶ αὐτοῦ ἀπὸ τῆς ἐκκλησίας, we have an indirect intimation of what later became the common liturgical sense.

† ὑπερεκτείνω.

This is not attested prior to 2 C. 10:14. [1] Cf. Ps.-Demetr., 5. [2] → ἐκτείνω in combination with μέτρον in 4 Βασ. 21:13; Lam. 2:8.

In 2 C. 10:14 [3] the word is used negatively. Paul's opponents arrogantly magnify themselves according to their own standards. Paul is not guilty of exaggeration even when he takes his own achievement as the measure. For he has come where he should, i.e., to Corinth. His journeys are acts by which he is to be measured if a standard is sought for the authenticity of his words or epistles (cf. 1 C. 15:10).

Fuchs

---

† ἔκτρωμα

ἔκτρωμα is not a common word in literature. It comes from ἐκτιτρώσκειν "to cause a miscarriage," "to cast the fruit of the body." In this sense it is found in Hdt., III, 32; Aristot. Hist. An., VII, 4, p. 585a, 22; IX, 3, p. 610b, 35; Plut. Terrestriane an Aquatilia Animalia, 20 (II, 974d); Diod. S., III, 64, 4; IV, 2, 3 (τὸ βρέφος ἐκτρῶσαι). The verb is naturally more common in the works of the Greek physicians (Hippocr., Diosc., etc.). [1] In P. Cairo (ed. E. J. Goodspeed [1902]), 15, 15 (4th cent. A.D.) [2] we get a glimpse into an individual tragedy. Because of blows she had received a woman named Taesis had a miscarriage (τὴν μὲν Τάησιν βαρέαν οὖσαν ἐκ τῶν πληγῶν αὐτῶν ἐξέτρωσεν [1. -αν] [3] τὸ βρέφος). [4] ἔκτρωμα is "untimely birth," "miscarriage," "abortion" (sometimes induced). The reference is always to untimely birth, whether the child lives or not. The decisive feature is the abnormal time of birth [5] and the unfinished form of the one thus born. The word is found in Aristot. Gen. An., IV, 5, p. 773b, 18 (κυήματα ἐκπίπτει παραπλήσια τοῖς καλουμένοις ἐκτρώμασιν). ἐκτρωσμός [6] is used in Preisigke Sammelbuch, 3451, 5 and 10.

The LXX uses ἔκτρωμα only 3 times. In Nu 12:12 it occurs for כַּמֵּת. It here denotes a child which had no life even in the womb and which was thus still-born. The fact that it is used for מוּת gives ἔκτρωμα the sense of still-birth. It is used in the same sense in the other LXX passages. In Job 3:16 and Eccl. 6:3 it is a translation of נֵפֶל, which means miscarriage or untimely birth. 'ΑΣΘ read ἔκτρωμα in ψ 57:8. In Is. 14:19 the translations are all different. For כְּנֵצֶר the LXX has ὡς νεκρός, 'Α ὡς ἰχώρ, Θ ὡς βλαστός, and only Σ has ὡς ἔκτρωμα. ἐκτιτρώσκειν is found in the Gk.

ὑ π ε ρ ε κ τ ε ί ν ω. [1] V. Pr.-Bauer, *s.v.*
[2] E. A. Sophocles, *Gk. Lex.* (1870), *s.v.*
[3] V. Ltzm. K., *ad loc.*

ἔ κ τ ρ ω μ α. [1] For more detailed examples, cf. Rutherford Phryn., p. 288 f.
[2] Preisigke Wört., *s.v.* ἔκτρωμα.
[3] So Moult.-Mill., 200, *s.v.* ἔκτρωμα.
[4] There is a similar case in Ex. 21:22 : "If men strive, and hurt a woman with child, so that her fruit depart from her." At the end of v. 22 we should probably read בְּנֻפְלִים instead of בְּפִלְלִים.
[5] Cf. A. Konstantinides, *Wörtbch. d. griech. Sprache,* II (1902), 80, *s.v.* ἔκτρωμα. ἔκτρωμα = βρέφος προώρως γεννώμενον.
[6] Cf. also Preisigke, *s.v.* ἐκτρωσμός; and on ἔκτρωμα Phryn., p. 208 Lobeck; p. 288 f. Rutherford. Philo Leg. All., I, 76. Hesych., p. 499 Schmidt.

Bible only at Σ Job 21:10: οὐκ ἐξέτρωσε (LXX: οὐκ ὠμοτόκησε, Ἀ: οὐκ ἐξέβαλε). [7]

In the NT ἔκτρωμα occurs only once. Paul in 1 C. 15:8 is stating that he is the last of those who saw the Risen Lord. In this connection he compares himself with an ἔκτρωμα. The meaning of the expression is contested. [8] Since the phrase ὡσπερεὶ τῷ ἐκτρώματι is directly related to the preceding words, in which Paul calls himself ἔσχατον δὲ πάντων, it might be conjectured that ἔκτρωμα denotes one who is born late. But this meaning is not possible. ἔκτρωμα always has the sense of a birth which is too soon. [9] Strictly, then, ἔκτρωμα and ἔσχατον contradict one another. Hence we can take ἔκτρωμα only in a very general sense. Paul is one who from the spiritual point of view was not born at the right time because he had not been a disciple during the lifetime of Jesus. His calling to the apostolic office, which presupposed having seen Christ, could not take place in the normal, orderly, organic sequence. Moreover, his calling is forced as well as abnormal and extraordinary. He is torn from his previous course of life by the powerful intervention of the exalted Christ and set in the kingdom of Christ. He is thus brought to see Christ and to his apostolic calling by a very different route from that of the other apostles. The main emphasis is on the abnormality of the process, which took place when the Risen Lord had ceased to manifest Himself to the disciples. [10]

Since ἔκτρωμα also signifies unfitness for life, Harnack is probably right in his conjecture [11] that Paul is taking a term of abuse hurled at him by his opponents to call in question his apostolic office, and using it to signify that he is truly unworthy of this because, when the other disciples and apostles saw the Lord, he was persecuting Him in His earthly community. Fridrichsen, [12] too, assumes that Paul is adopting a word coined and circulated by his enemies. ἔκτρωμα was a current term of abuse with a religious implication. In relation to the new birth Paul's adversaries called him an ἔκτρωμα. [13] He was "prematurely born in terms of the ἀναγέννησις, an incomplete, deficient, misguided Christian, and therefore quite unable to be an apostle." [14] Paul accepted this judgment, but applied it to his pre-Christian period as a persecutor. It is not a feature of his conversion to Christianity or his apostolate. [15] Prior to his conversion he was an ἔκτρωμα, i.e., "a non-human monster with no true life." [16] This explanation is clever, but there are serious objections to it. In particular, it attributes to

---

[7] In Aram. נְפַל = נְפִילָא, נְפִילָא also שְׁלִילָא, which in the first instance means embryo. In bSota 22a Bar. נְפֵל is paraphrased קטן שלא כלו לו חדשיו "a child whose months (in the womb) are not fulfilled." This is then applied to some students. Cf. Str.-B., III, 471 and 496. In the Mishnah, tract. Keritot, 1, 3-6 treats of different forms of miscarriage and of the appropriate sacrifices.

[8] A full history of the exegesis of ἔκτρωμα may be found in A. Fridrichsen, "Paulus abortivus" (Symbolae Philologicae O. A. Danielsson octogenario dicatae [1932], 79 ff.).

[9] Cf. on this pt. E. Schwartz, NGG (1907), 276, n. 1.

[10] So De Wette, Bengel, v. Hofmann, Strack-Zöckler, J. Weiss, Lietzmann; but not Bachmann, who introduces unnecessary complications.

[11] SAB, 1922, 72.

[12] Op. cit., 80 ff.

[13] Cf. already Bengel: Metaphora inde, unde etiam regeneratio dicitur.

[14] Op. cit., 81.

[15] Op. cit., 79.

[16] Cf. Fridrichsen, 80, where he defines ἔκτρωμα more closely.

Paul's opponents an unlikely conception of regeneration. [17] It also causes Paul to apply the term in a sense which does not seem to agree with what Paul really has in view. Like Fridrichsen, Windisch [18] refers ἔκτρωμα to the pre-Christian attitude of Paul. "It is Paul's judgment of himself in relation to his past."

As Bengel pointed out already, [19] particular stress falls on the article. Paul is the only apostle to have had a basic revelation of Christ in this way, outside the normal order of the apostolic band. This gives him pain, yet is also a source of joy in view of the extraordinary favour shown to him.

Ign. in R. 9, 2 adopted the saying of Paul and applied it to himself. He took it to imply unworthiness (οὐδὲ γὰρ ἄξιός εἰμι, ὢν ἔσχατος αὐτῶν καὶ ἔκτρωμα). In the Apc. Pt., 11 ἐκτιτρώσκειν is used in the sense of "to cast" : αὗται δὲ ἦσαν α[ἱ τὰ βρέφη φθείρο]υσαι καὶ ἐκτρώσασαι. [20] In Eus. Hist. Eccl., V, 1, 45 the Church is figur. described as a virgin mother who has brought forth both living and dead children. Those born dead (οὓς ὡς νεκροὺς ἐξέτρωσε) are Christians who did not confess their faith in times of persecution. [21] In Iren., I, 4, 7 (MPG, 7, 480) ἔκτρωμα is defined as "formless" (ἄμορφος καὶ ἀνείδεος, ὥσπερ ἔκτρωμα). Cf. also Hipp. Ref., VI, 31, 2 (εἰς μόρφωσιν καὶ διαίρεσιν τοῦ ἐκτρώματος). [22]

Schneider

ἐκχέω, ἐκχύν(ν)ω

"To pour out," a. of fluids, also cultically, e.g., Hom. Il., 3, 295 f.: οἶνον ... ἔκχεον; 1 Βασ. 7:6 : ἐξέχεαν ὕδωρ ἐνώπιον κυρίου ἐπὶ τὴν γῆν (drink-offerings for Yahweh, cf. 2 Βασ. 23:16; Nu. 28 f.); Is. 57:6 : κἀκείνοις ἐξέχεας σπονδάς (drink-offerings for false gods, cf. Jer. 7:18; 19:13); Sir. 50:15 : ἔσπεισεν ἐξ αἵματος σταφυλῆς· ἐξέχεεν εἰς θεμέλια θυσιαστηρίου (the libation of wine, Jos. Ant., 3, 234); Sukka, 4, 9 : גִּיס֤וֹף הַמַּיִם, cf. bSukka, 48b; [1] Nu. 19:17; Ex. 30:18 (rites of purification); Did., 7, 3 : ἔκχεον εἰς τὴν κεφαλὴν τρὶς ὕδωρ (baptism by aspersion). αἷμα ἐκχεῖν (ἐκχύν-νειν), like שָׁפַךְ דָּם, means "to shed blood," "to kill," "to murder," → I, 173 f. With other

---

[17] I believe that his suggestion in the closing section (op. cit., 84 f.) that regeneration was regarded as a process in the early Church is unfounded and even incorrect. One can hardly say that "where this process did not come to a successful issue under the mystical power of the sacrament of baptism, a devilish figure emerged." Thus, though his explanation is right in many particulars, it breaks down in its wider implications.

[18] H. Windisch, Paulus und Christus (1934), 144, n. 1. Windisch conjectures that Paul bases his use of the term on Nu. 12:12 (cf. also A. Schlatter, Paulus, der Bote Jesu, 1934, 401). He sees the following parallel : Saul contra the community = Miriam contra Moses.

[19] Bengel, 430 : articulus vim habet.

[20] Cf. also Moult.-Mill., 200.

[21] E. Schwartz, op. cit., thinks that the letter to the Gallic Churches in Eus. Hist. Eccl., V, 1, 45 gives us the only correct explanation of 1 C. 15:8.

[22] Cf. on this pt. E. A. Sophocles, Gk. Lex. (1870), s.v.

ἐκχέω, ἐκχύν(ν)ω. Thes. Steph., III, 644 ff.; Pr.-Bauer, 384; Moult.-Mill., 200. For the Hellenistic χύν(ν)ειν along with χεῖν, cf. Bl.-Debr. § 73.

[1] On cultic libations of water, wine etc., cf. E. Huber, Das Trankopfer im Kulte der Völker (1929); on the drink offering in the OT, cf. E. König, Theologie des AT [3, 4] (1923), 283; J. Benziger, Hebräische Archäologie[3] (1927), 364 etc.; on the libation of water in the Jewish feast of tabernacles, cf. D. Feuchtwang, "Das Wasseropfer u. die damit verbundenen Zeremonien," MGWJ, 54 (1910), 535 ff., 713 ff.; also 55 (1911), 43 ff.; Str.-B., II, 491, 799 ff.; Benzinger, op. cit., 392; Zn. on Jn. 7:37; Schl. J., 199 ff. On the drink offering as an image of martyrdom in Phil. 2:17; 2 Tm. 4:6, cf. O. Schmitz, Die Opferanschauung des späteren Judentums u. d. Opferaussagen des NT (1910), 231 f. and the comm.

objects it can means "to lavish," Ez. 16:36; Tob. 4:17: ἔκχεον τοὺς ἄρτους σου ἐπὶ τὸν τάφον τῶν δικαίων; Sir. 30:18 : ἀγαθὰ ἐκκεχυμένα ἐπὶ στόματι κεκλεισμένῳ; Philo Abr., 157: ἀπ' ἀενάων πηγῶν ἑκάστου τῶν ἀστέρων αὐγὰς ἐκχέοντος, "to pour out," Hom. Od., 22, 3 f.: ταχέας δ' ἐκχεύατ' ὀϊστοὺς αὐτοῦ πρόσθε ποδῶν, Jn. 2:15; 2 Βασ. 20:10; Ac. 1:18.

b. It is also used figur. of spiritual gifts, both helpful and harmful, esp. those which come down lavishly from above, from divine beings : Plat. Epigr., 6 (I, 88 Diehl): σοὶ ... δαίμονες εὐρείας ἐλπίδας ἐξέχεαν, Hos. 5:10 : ἐπ' αὐτοὺς ἐκχεῶ ὡς ὕδωρ τὸ ὅρμημά μου; Ez. 9:8 : ἐν τῷ ἐκχέαι σε τὸν θυμόν σου (cf. Is. 42:25); Lam. 2:4 : ἐξέχεεν ὡς πῦρ τὸν θυμὸν αὐτοῦ (cf. 4:11); Sir. 16:11: ἐκχέων ὀργήν; 18:11: κύριος ... ἐξέχεεν ἐπ' αὐτοὺς τὸ ἔλεος αὐτοῦ; 1:9 (wisdom); Phil. Abr., 76 : τὰς ἀπὸ τοῦ ὄντος ἐκχεομένας αὐγάς.

The following uses are of theological importance in the NT.

1. The expression αἷμα ἐκχύννειν or ἐκχεῖν is used of the violent slaying of OT and NT martyrs in Mt. 23:35 par.; R. 3:15 (= Is. 59:7); Ac. 22:20; Rev. 16:6. It is also referred specifically to the death of Jesus in the saying at the Last Supper in Mk. 14:24; Mt. 26:28; Lk. 22:20 𝔖𝔎. In the saying regarding the cup (Mk.: τοῦτό ἐστιν τὸ → αἷμά μου τῆς → διαθήκης τὸ ἐκχυννόμενον → ὑπὲρ → πολλῶν [Mt.: τὸ → περὶ πολλῶν ἐκχυννόμενον εἰς ἄφεσιν ἁμαρτιῶν]; Lk.: τοῦτο τὸ → ποτήριον ἡ καινὴ διαθήκη ἐν τῷ αἵματί μου, τὸ ὑπὲρ ὑμῶν ἐκχυννόμενον), His violent death takes place for the salvation of man and for the achievement of the new divine order (Jer. 31:31 ff.). But the antitypical relationship of the saying to Ex. 24:8, the story of the solemn sealing of the old διαθήκη by blood at Sinai, does not of itself lead either to the thought of propitiation, which is not present in the OT passage, or to any correspondence between the shedding of the blood of Jesus and the cultic pouring and sprinkling of blood in Ex. 24:6, 8 (→ αἱματεκχυσία, I, 176 f.).[2] The violent death foreseen by Jesus is consciously accepted and thus becomes an act of supreme self-sacrifice superior to all other offerings (→ I, 175).

2. The idea of outpouring, of the streaming down from above of a power hitherto withheld, is also used to describe the impartation of divine gifts or powers in which God imparts Himself. The eschatological prophecy of Jl. 3:1 f., according to which God will pour out the miraculous power of His Spirit like fructifying rain on Israel (cf. 2:23 f.; Is. 32:15), is fulfilled on the early community in the miracle of Pentecost (Ac. 2:16 ff.). The exalted Jesus has fulfilled the will of the Father, ἐξέχεεν τοῦτο ὃ ὑμεῖς καὶ βλέπετε καὶ ἀκούετε (v. 33). In OT prophecy, however, the picture of an outpouring of the Spirit is used not merely for ecstatic inspiration, but also for inner renewal by the Spirit (Ez. 39:29; Zech.

---

[2] On the basis of the complicated text of Lk. 22:20, O. Holtzmann has suggested that after the analogy of Ex. 24:6, 8 a cup was poured out at the Last Supper and one half was emptied out on the ground like the blood at Sinai (Leben Jesu [1901], 363; ZNW, 3 [1902], 359; Das NT ... übersetzt und erklärt, I [1926], 64 f., 206, 321). But this has been refuted by E. Nestle, ZNW, 3 [1902], 252; 7 [1906], 256, and also by H. J. Holtzmann, Lehrbuch der nt.lichen Theologie², I (1911), 366 n. No less satisfactory is the suggestion of A. Spitta, Zur Geschichte u. Literatur d. Urchristentums, I (1893), 268 f., that the ἐκχυννόμενον of Mk. 14:24 refers to the pouring out of the wine-blood into cups for drinking. The further suggestion of K. G. Goetz, Die heutige Abendmahlsfrage² (1907), 188 f., 148 f.; Das Abendmahl eine Diatheke Jesu ...? (1920), 29 ff., that the ἐκχυννόμενον refers to a dedication of the cup, suffers from the fatal weakness of ignoring the basic expression αἷμα ἐκχύννειν ("to kill") which occurs in all the Synoptic accounts.

12:10; cf. Is. 44:3 ff.; Ez. 36:26 f.). Similarly, the early Church uses the same picture both for a fresh outbreak of tongues (Ac. 10:45 → I, 722 ff.) and also for the reception of the Spirit by the Christian in baptism (Tt. 3:5 f.: → πνεύματος ἁγίου, οὗ ἐξέχεεν ἐφ' ἡμᾶς πλουσίως διὰ 'Ιησοῦ Χριστοῦ); cf. Barn., 1, 3: ἐκκεχυμένον ἀπὸ τοῦ πλουσίου τῆς πληγῆς κυρίου πνεῦμα ἐφ' ὑμᾶς; 1 Cl., 46, 6; 2, 2. In indication of the elemental force of this breaking of all previous barriers, Rom. 5:5: ἡ → ἀγάπη τοῦ θεοῦ ἐκκέχυται ἐν ταῖς → καρδίαις ἡμῶν διὰ → πνεύματος ἁγίου τοῦ δοθέντος ἡμῖν, shows that in the death of Christ (v. 6 ff.) there is demonstration of the overflowing wealth of the love of God for sinners giving constant assurance to Christians by the Holy Spirit. [3]

Behm

ἐκψύχω → ψυχή.

| ἑκών (ἄκων), ἑκούσιος |

† ἑκών (ἄκων).

a. "Willing," "intentional," esp. in law, where intentional acts are to be punished more severely. [1] b. "Voluntary," "not under compulsion," the opp. of βία, ἀνάγκη. [2] Ethical and philosophical thought considered under what conditions man acts by free self-determination (→ ἑκούσιος). Aristotle agrees with Plato that the rational will can propose only the good as its goal. Hence the famous statement οὐδένα ἄνθρωπον ἑκόντα ἐξαμαρτάνειν, Plat. Prot., 345d. But in line with common modes of thought Aristotle distinguishes between intentional and unintentional wrongdoing. Unintentional acts are those which arise through external compulsion or in which the goal attained is different from that intended. In such cases there is an element of ignorance involved. Hence Aristotle reduces the degree of culpability and differentiates these from wicked acts. [3] Stoic ethics, too, emphasises that free obedience to the deity is the essence of morality. This free submission to the divine will embraces suffering. [4] The Stoic ideal is that the wise man should willingly accept his divinely imposed lot. In this way he demonstrates his freedom from external fate.

---

[3] Cf. B. Weiss[9], also Bengel, ad loc.; M. J. Lagrange, *Saint Paul Épître aux Romains*[2] (1922), 102. To refer R. 5:5 to the outpouring of the Spirit (as tentatively proposed by Pr.-Bauer, op. cit.; cf. A. Jülicher in *Schriften d. NT*[3], II [1917], 256) is hardly necessary in view of the widespread use of the image in OT and Jewish writings (→ under b., supra).

ἑ κ ώ ν. H. Schmidt, *Synonymik der griech. Sprache,* III (1879), 612 f.

[1] Demosth., 21, 43: ἂν μὲν ἑκὼν βλάψῃ, διπλοῦν· ἂν δ' ἄκων, ἁπλοῦν τὸ βλάβος κελεύουσιν ἐκτίνειν. Sib., 2, 68 (Ps.-Phokyl), opp. ἀγνώς.

[2] Plato Soph., 240c: ἠνάγκακεν ἡμᾶς οὐχ ἑκόντας ὁμολογεῖν, Jos. Bell., 6, 101 and 399. Hom. Il., 4, 43: ἑκὼν ἀέκοντί γε θυμῷ, "voluntarily, though grudgingly."

[3] Aristot. Eth. M., 1, 12, p. 1188a, 6 ff.: οὐδεὶς πράττει ἑκὼν τὰ κακὰ εἰδὼς ὅτι κακά ἐστιν ... κατ' ἐπιθυμίαν γε πράττει· οὐκ ἄρα ἑκὼν ... ἀναγκαζόμενος ἄρα; I, 13, p. 1188a, 17 f.: ὁ ἐγκρατὴς ἑκὼν πράττει τὰ κατὰ τὴν ἐγκράτειαν; I, 34, p. 1195b, 8 ff.; I, 34, p. 1196a, 13 ff.; Eth. Nic., III, 3, p. 1111a, 29. Cf. G. Kafka, *Aristoteles* (1922), 124 f., 135 f.; on the distinction between intentional (ἑκούσιος) and deliberate (προαιρετική) actions, cf. ibid., 130 ff.; on the concept οὐχ ἑκούσιον, cf. O. Kraus, *Die Lehre von Lob, Lohn, Tadel und Strafe bei Aristot.* (1905), 49 ff.

[4] Epict. Diss., IV, 3, 9: ἐλεύθερος γάρ εἰμι καὶ φίλος τοῦ θεοῦ, ἵν' ἑκὼν πείθωμαι αὐτῷ. Fr., 8: ... πείθειν ἑαυτὸν ἑκόντα δέχεσθαι τὰ ἀναγκαῖα; I, 12, 23: ὅπου ... τις ἄκων ἐστίν, ἐκεῖνο φυλακὴ αὐτῷ ἐστιν, καθὸ καὶ Σωκράτης οὐκ ἦν ἐν φυλακῇ, ἑκὼν γὰρ ἦν. Cf. I, 17, 14.

The LXX uses ἑκών only twice. In Ex. 21:13 there is reference to unintentional assault (οὐχ ἑκών, לֹא צָדָה → ἑκούσιος), and it also occurs in Job 36:19. ἄκων is also found twice, in Job 14:17 and 4 Macc. 11:12 ("against one's own will and intention").

In the Talmudic writings ἑκών is used for בְּרָצוֹן or מִדַּעְתִּי in the sense of "with my consent," and ἄκων for בְּאוֹנֶס ("under compulsion") or עַל כָּרְחִי ("against my will"). [5]

In the NT ἑκών means (b.) "willingly" in 1 C. 9:16 f., as opposed to ἀνάγκη (v. 16) or ἄκων (v. 17). In R. 8:20 man sins by his own resolve, whereas nature is subjected to vanity through no will of its own.

† ἑκούσιος.

a. "Willing," "intentional." While → ἑκών is normally used of the person, ἑκούσιος is mostly used of the thing (ἑκούσιος φόνος). [1] Thus acts are done by design or intention. Jos. Ap., 1, 3 ψευδολογία, opp. ἄγνοια. [2] "Not compulsory," Jos. Bell., 2, 209: ἑκούσιος δουλεία; Test. L. 9:7; D 4:6. So also in philosophical usage (→ ἑκών). [3]

In the LXX it is used esp. for cultic acts which are voluntary as distinct from the required sacrifices, Lv. 7:6; 2 Ἐσδρ. 3:5; 8:28. The verb ἑκουσιάζομαι is the counterpart of the Heb. נדב hitp in 2 Ἐσδρ. 2:68; 3:5; 1 Macc. 2:42. The negative ἀκουσίως is used in the LXX of sins which are not done "deliberately" or "with conscious, evil intent": Lv. 4:2, 22, 27; Nu. 15:25; Jos. 20:3, 9, Heb. בִּשְׁגָגָה (opp. בְּיָד רָמָה, Nu. 15:30, "with conscious, evil intent"). [4] A synon. is ἄγνοια in Lv. 5:18; 22:14; Ez. 40:39; 42:13; Qoh. 5:6. Cf. also Philo. [5]

In the NT it is used in sense a. of "intentional and conscious transgressions" whose guilt is heightened by preceding personal experience of saving truth, Hb. 10:26: μετὰ τὸ λαβεῖν τὴν ἐπίγνωσιν τῆς ἀληθείας (→ ἄγνοια). It is also used in sense b. ("not under compulsion") in Phlm. 14: ἵνα μὴ ὡς κατὰ ἀνάγκην τὸ ἀγαθόν σου ᾖ ἀλλὰ κατὰ ἑκούσιον.

Hauck

| † ἔλαιον | (→ ἀλείφω, χρίω).

"Olive oil" (often specified, P. Tebt., 395, 9 and 16: ἐλαίου ἐλαίνου μετρητής; Ez. 27:20: ἔλαιον ἐξ ἐλαίων; Lv. 24:2: ἔλαιον ἐλάϊνον), is found from the time of Hom., also on inscr., in the pap. and in the LXX; in the wider sense it may be used for any oil or fatty fluid: Hippocr. Mul., II, 194: ἔλαιον χήνειον (of the goose);

---

[5] For examples cf. Str.-B., III, 401.

ἑ κ ο ύ σ ι ο ς. [1] H. Schmidt, *Synon. d. griech. Sprache,* III (1879), 612 f.
[2] Antiphon Orator (ed. J. Thalheim [1914]), 1, 26: ἡ μὲν γὰρ ἑκουσίως καὶ βουλεύσασα τὸν θάνατον ἀπέκτεινεν, ὁ δ' ἀκουσίως καὶ βιαίως ἀπέθανε. 5, 92: τὸ μὲν γὰρ ἀκούσιον ἁμάρτημα τῆς τύχης ἐστί, τὸ δ' ἑκούσιον τῆς γνώμης. ἑκούσιον δὲ πῶς ἂν εἴη μᾶλλον, ἢ εἴ τις ὧν βουλὴν ποιοῖτο, ταῦτα παραχρῆμα ἐξεργάζοιτο.
[3] Aristot. Eth. M., I, 12, p. 1187b, 34: ἑκούσιον ... ὃ πράττομεν μὴ ἀναγκαζόμενοι; I, 13, p. 1188a, 30; I, 17, p. 1189b, 1 → ἑκών; M. Ant., 10, 8, 2.
[4] O. Schmitz, *Die Opferanschauungen des späteren Judentums* (1910), 27 f.
[5] Poster. C., 10 f.: ἐν τοῖς ἁμαρτήμασι κουφότερα τῶν ἑκουσίων τὰ ἀκούσια; Deus Imm., 128; Vit. Mos., I, 273: ὑπ' ἀγνοίας, ἀλλ' οὐ καθ' ἑκούσιον.

P. Amh., 2, 93 : ῥαφάνινον (of the radish) ἔλαιον; Hipp. Philos., V, 21: ἔλαιον ... ῥαδινάκη (petroleum). In later Attic it is used for the place where oil is sold : Poll. Onom., IX, 47; Menand. Fr., 896.

In the LXX it is used for שֶׁמֶן, or, together with other products, for יִצְהָר. Along with שֶׁמֶן זַיִת in Ex. 27:20 etc., we once have שֶׁמֶן הַמֹּר, the oil of myrrh (LXX : σμύρνινον ἔλαιον) in Est. 2:12.

The NT teaches us a good deal concerning the widespread significance and use of olive oil in the ancient world.

1. As a form of agrarian produce, ἔλαιον constitutes a part of the productive capacity or mechandise of a country : Rev. 6:6; Lk. 16:6; Rev. 18:13. On oil production cf. inscr. at the time of Hadrian (CIG, I, 355, 2): οἱ τὸ ἔλαιον γεωργοῦντες τὸ τρίτον καταφερέτωσαν; cf. line 64; Ditt. Syll.³, 83, 59 : τοῦ ἐλαίου ἡ ἀπαρχή; Catal. Cod. Astr. Graec., VIII, 3, p. 125, 12 : ἐὰν δὲ βροντήσῃ (in the month of Libra) σίτου ἀπώλειαν δηλοῖ, οἴνου καὶ ἐλαίου πλησμονήν; III, 28, 9. Palestine in particular was rich in oil production : Dt. 8:8 : γῆ ἐλαίας καὶ μέλιτος; Dt. 6:11: δοῦναί σοι ... ἀμπελῶνας καὶ ἐλαιῶνας. Hos. 2:8 (10); Jos. Ant., 2, 591 f. Oil is counted as a possession in Hom. Od., 2, 339 and also 4 Βασ. 20:13; 2 Ch. 32:28; 3 Βασ. 17:12; Jos. Bell., 5, 565; Did., 13, 6; Herm. m., 11, 15, and it is very valuable : Prv. 21:17. In Lydus de Ostentis, 42 : ἔνδεια μὲν ἔσται τῶν ἐπιτηδείων, ἐλαίου δὲ διαφερόντως, it is recognised as one of the essentials of life, as also in Sir. 39:26 : ἀρχὴ πάσης χρείας εἰς ζωὴν ἀνθρώπου, ὕδωρ πῦρ καὶ σίδηρος καὶ ἅλα ... αἷμα σταφυλῆς καὶ ἔλαιον καὶ ἱμάτιον. It is even used for nourishment : Thuc., III, 49; Dt. 12:17; 3 Βασ. 17:12; Ez. 16:13; Act. Thom., 29. Thus oil comes to be used as a symbol of wealth : Dt. 32:13; 33:24; Job 29:6 HT. It is a trading commodity in 3 Βασ. 5:11; Hos. 12:1 (2); Ez. 27:17; 2 Ἐσδρ. 3:7; Jos. Bell., 2, 591; S. Dt. § 355 on 33:24 (148a).

There have been many attempts to explain Rev. 6:6 : καὶ τὸ ἔλαιον καὶ τὸν οἶνον μὴ ἀδικήσῃς. It can hardly be a play on the edict of Domitian in 92 A.D. (Suet. Domitianus, 7), nor a conscious adoption of the astrological notion that in the year of "scales" crops wither but there will be plenty of oil and wine, nor a reference to later Jewish eschatological expectations, nor an admonition to take care of oil and wine as sacramental elements. [1] More likely it is the prophecy of a partial economic crisis and derives from a concrete experience of the divine, which he links with OT warnings. Corn, oil and wine play a distinctive role in the eschatological promises and threats of the OT. Thus we read in Jl. 2:19: Ἰδοὺ ἐγὼ ἐξαποστέλλω ὑμῖν τὸν σῖτον καὶ τὸν οἶνον καὶ τὸ ἔλαιον, καὶ ἐμπιπλησθήσεσθε αὐτῶν ...; cf. v. 24, and Hos. 2:21 f.: καὶ ἔσται ἐν ἐκείνῃ τῇ ἡμέρᾳ, λέγει κύριος, ἐπακούσομαι τῷ οὐρανῷ, καὶ αὐτὸς ἐπακούσεται τῇ γῇ, καὶ ἡ γῆ ἐκακούσεται τὸν σῖτον καὶ τὸν οἶνον καὶ τὸ ἔλαιον, καὶ αὐτὰ ἐπακούσεται τῷ Ἰεζραέλ. On the other hand, Dt. 28:38 ff. speaks of the curse of God which will involve destruction of the corn, oil and wine. V. 40 : ἐλαῖαι ἔσονταί σοι ἐν πᾶσιν τοῖς ὁρίοις σου, καὶ ἔλαιον οὐ χρίσῃ, ὅτι ἐκρυήσεται ἡ ἐλαία σου. Mention should also be made of Mi. 6:15 : σὺ σπερεῖς καὶ οὐ μὴ ἀμήσῃς, σὺ πιέσεις ἐλαίαν καὶ οὐ μὴ ἀλείψῃ ἔλαιον, καὶ οἶνον καὶ οὐ μὴ πίητε, καὶ ἀφανισθήσεται νόμιμα λαοῦ μου. In the OT the reference seems to be to the full curse of God, but in Rev. 6:6, according to the meaning and position of the first four seals, the reference is to a partial judgment (cf. 6:8b). This is expressed in the third seal by saying that corn is so dear that a full day's pay is needed to buy daily bread, but there is no dearth of oil and wine. In the military, political and economic crises and in the high mortality of his own age, the divine finds intimations of the approaching judgment of God. But so far there is no total destruction of vital resources.

ἔλαιον. [1] W. Bousset Apk. (1906), 135 f.; R. H. Charles Apc. (1920), 166 ff.; Loh. Apk., 58 f.; F. Boll, Aus der Offenbarung Johannis (1914), 84 ff.

2. Oil is also used for lamps in Mt. 25:3; cf. Hdt., II, 94; Aristoph. Nu., 56; Plut. Pericl., 16 (I, 162c); Cic. Att., XIII, 28; Ditt. Syll.³, 1042, 10; Ex. 27:20 = Lv. 24:2; Nu. 4:16; Tg. J., I, Ex. 35:28. In Shab., 2, 2 we read of different ways of kindling lamps with oil.

3. Oil is commonly used for various kinds of anointing (→ ἀλείφω, I, 229; → χρίω). In Lk. 7:46: ἐλαίῳ τὴν κεφαλήν μου οὐκ ἤλειψας· αὕτη δὲ μύρῳ ἤλειψεν τοὺς πόδας μου, anointing with myrrh is distinguished from anointing with olive. Here, then, μύρον does not mean ointment as in Mk. 14:3; Jn. 12:3, where the distinguishing νάρδον is added. It means ointment of myrrh, as in Mt. 26:7 (Heb. מוֹר, Aram. מוֹרָא, מֵירָא). μύρον here is the σμύρνινον ἔλαιον of Est. 2:12. The juxtaposition of ἔλαιον and μύρον brings out the contrast between the Pharisee who does not pay the usual honours to his guest, the Messiah, and the sinner who performs this menial office in generous response to the Messiah.

In Hb. 1:9 the passage Ps. 45:7, which the Rabbis interpreted Messianically, [2] is referred to the Son. The quotation is substantially from the LXX: ἠγάπησας δικαιοσύνην καὶ ἐμίσησας ἀνομίαν· διὰ τοῦτο ἔχρισέν σε, ὁ θεός, ὁ θεός σου ἔλαιον ἀγαλλιάσεως παρὰ τοὺς μετόχους σου.

In the original the Ps. speaks of the anointing of the king for the marriage feast. According to the christological interpretation of Hb. the Son is anointed as the Messianic King. In other words, the Son, having loved righteousness, is exalted to Godhead in the sight of all men. He thus becomes the Χριστός. Cf. Just. Dial., 86, 3 : καὶ ὅτι τὸ χρίσμα πᾶν, εἴτε ἐλαίου εἴτε στακτῆς (the oil of myrrh) εἴτε τῶν ἄλλων τῶν τῆς συνθέσεως τοῦ μύρου χρισμάτων, τούτου ἦν, ὁμοίως ἀπεδείξαμεν, καὶ τοῦ λόγου λέγοντος· διὰ τοῦτο ἔχρισέ σε, ὁ θεός ... καὶ γὰρ οἱ βασιλεῖς πάντες καὶ οἱ χριστοὶ ἀπὸ τούτου μετέσχον καὶ βασιλεῖς καλεῖσθαι καὶ χριστοί· ὃν τρόπον καὶ αὐτὸς ἀπὸ τοῦ πατρὸς ἔλαβε τὸ βασιλεὺς καὶ Χριστὸς καὶ ἱερεὺς καὶ ἄγγελος, καὶ ὅσα ἄλλα τοιαῦτα ἔχει ἢ ἔσχεν. It is worth considering whether the author of Hb. does not take strictly the idea of the anointing of the king for marriage, relating it to such thoughts as occur, e.g., in Rev. 19:7 f.; 21:9 f., and thus conceiving of the exaltation of the Son as the marriage of the Messiah with the heavenly community. The term "oil of joy," which recurs in the LXX at Is. 61:3 as ἄλειμμα εὐφροσύνης, arises naturally from the use of oil on joyous and festive occasions. Anointing with oil was not merely a means to strengthen the body and to enhance physical well-being but also to express festive joy: Am. 6:6; Ps. 23:5; Prv. 27:9; Qoh. 9:8. In sorrow, anointing was suspended: 2 S. 12:20; 14:2; Da. 10:3. [3] It is worth noting that the basic asceticism of the Essenes (Jos. Bell., 2, 123) and of the priests described in Porphyr. Abst., IV, 6, 7 forbade anointing, or the use of oil, either in whole or in part.

4. Oil was often used as a means to heal the most divers maladies. With Mk. 6:13 and Jm. 5:14 (→ I, 230), we may also refer to Lk. 10:34 : καὶ προσελθὼν κατέδησεν τὰ τραύματα αὐτοῦ ἐπιχέων ἔλαιον καὶ οἶνον ...

Comparison may be made with Plin. Hist. Nat., XV, 1-8. Here, in a treatise on oil trees, the production of oil and kinds of oil, we read in XV, 4 : Oleo natura tepefacere corpus et contra algores munire, eidem fervores capitis refrigerare; XV, 7: veteri quoque oleo usus est ad quaedam genera morborum. Cf. 23, 34 ff. Vegetius, Digestorum Artis Mulomedicinae Libri, II, 79, 23 (Lommatzsch); Columella, De Re Rustica, VI, 30, 4; VII, 5, 18; Curtius, Historiarum Alexandri Magni, IX, 10, 1: Quippe scabies corpora

---

[2] V. Str.-B., III, 679.
[3] Cf. also the Rabb. examples in Str.-B., I, 426.

invasit, et contagium morbi etiam in alios vulgatum est. Oleum remedio fuit; Dio C., 53, 29, 5 : ἴαμά τε αὐτοῦ οὐδὲν ἦν, χωρὶς ἢ εἴ τις ἔλαιον οἴνῳ μεμιγμένον καὶ ἔπιε καὶ ἠλείψατο. Gal. *De Simplicium Medicamentorum Temperamentis* II, 10 ff.: ἄριστον ἰαμάτων πάντων τοῖς ἐξηραμμένοις καὶ αὐχμώδεσι (dry) σώμασιν. T. Shab., 12, 12; jBer., 3a, 9 : "A sick person may be rubbed on the sabbath with a mixture of oil and wine" (אֲלוּנְתִּית = ἔλαιον οἰνάνθινον). ⁴

Schlier

ἐλέγχω, ἔλεγξις, ἔλεγχος, ἐλεγμός

† ἐλέγχω.

1. Though the NT usage is simple and straightforward, outside the NT it is very complicated. In Hom. ἐλέγχω still means "to scorn," "to bring into contempt." ¹ Later it means a. "to shame" by exposure, opposition, etc.; b. "to blame" ; c. "to expose," "to resist"; then d. "to interpret," "to expound"; and finally e. "to investigate." ²

In the LXX ³ ἐλέγχειν and cognates are used to translate different Heb. stems. When occasionally used for גְּעָרָה (Is. 50:2, v.l. ἀπειλή) or for נָאַץ (Is. 37:3) along with θλῖψις and ὀνειδισμός, it means "to rebuke" or "to shame." It has the same sense when used for מַר in Nu. 5:18 ff. in the fixed formula ὕδωρ τοῦ ἐλεγμοῦ. Indeed, when used for שִׂיחַ in Job 21:4; 23:2 (here only in the LXX), it must be understood similarly. On the other hand, when used for נגע in 2 Ch. 26:20 it means "to punish." In Job 15:6 "condemn" or "convict" is demanded by רשע hi. In Lv. 5:24 (6:5), where אשם means "to atone," ἐλέγχειν introduces the rather different sense of "to convict," while in Prv. 18:17 חקר ("to test," "to examine") is excellently rendered by ἐλέγχειν, which can have this sense. In all other passages in the LXX where there is a Heb. original, it is used for the root יכח and derivatives, and the meaning and use of ἐλέγχειν and cognates in the Gk. Bible is largely determined by this Heb. original. In distinction from → παιδεύειν and יסר, behind which there is always the idea of paternal chastisement, it denotes the disciplining and educating of man by God as a result of His judicial activity. This embraces all aspects of education from the conviction of the sinner to chastisement and punishment, from the instruction of the righteous by severe tests to his direction by teaching and admonition. ⁴ With the general idea of discipline and

---

⁴ Cf. Str.-B., II, 11 f. and the passages quoted in → I, 230, n. 2 and 3.

ἐ λ έ γ χ ω. Pape, Pass., Cr.-Kö., Pr.-Bauer, *s.v.* ἔλεγχος. Zn. Jn., 422, n. 42; Str.-B., I, 787-790; P. Volz, *Jüdische Eschatologie* (1903), 265.

¹ Il., 9, 518; Od., 21, 424; cf. also the use of ἔλεγχος and ἐλέγχης in Homer (Pape).

² Several examples are given in Pape, Pass. It is hard to fix on a basic meaning, cf. Boisacq, *s.v.* ἐλέγχω. Perhaps the underlying sense is "to go into, and to reveal, a sorry matter which brings others into contempt." A. Walde and J. Pokorny, *Vergl. Wörterb. d. indogerm. Sprachen,* I (1927), 436, take it that the basic sense is "to shame" and compare it with Lettish words.

³ This paragraph is by G. Bertram.

⁴ Cf. S. Mowinckel, "Die Vorstellungen des Spätjudentums vom heiligen Geist als Fürsprecher und der johanneische Paraklet," ZNW, 32 (1933), 104 ff.; G. Bertram, "Der Begriff der Erziehung in der griechischen Bibel," in *Imago Dei, Festschr. f. Gustav Krüger* (1932), 46 f.

education, the word group becomes very common in the hagiographa. In the historical and prophetic books it is less common, as also in the NT, where it is more used in exhortation.

2. The use of ἐλέγχω in the NT is restricted. In the act. it is almost always used with the acc. of person, and in the pass. it is used also of persons. It means "to show someone his sin and to summon him to repentance." This may be a private matter between two people, as in Mt. 18:15; Eph. 5:11. But it may also be a congregational affair under the leader, as in the Pastorals : 1 Tm. 5:20; 2 Tm. 4:2; Tt. 1:9, 13; 2:15. [5] It is also the work of the Holy Spirit in the world (Jn. 16:8), [6] of the exalted Christ in the community (Rev. 3:19), and of the Lord in judgment at the *parousia* (Jd. 15). Jesus says that it cannot possibly apply to Him (Jn. 8:46). In relation to sinful persons or acts, ἐλέγχομαι is the experience of the sinner when faced by the prophet who demands repentance (Lk. 3:19; 1 C. 14:24), by conscience (Jn. 8:9 Ral), by the self-revelation of light (Jn. 3:20; Eph. 5:13), by the divine instruction (Hb. 12:5), or by the Law (Jm. 2:9). To indicate the fault περί is used (Lk. 3:19), or, with the pass. ἐλέγχεσθαι, ὡς (Jm. 2:9). Elaboration after περί is introduced by ὅτι (Jn. 16:9-11). [7] The word does not mean only "to blame" or "to reprove," nor "to convince" in the sense of proof, nor "to reveal" or "expose," [8] but "to set right," namely, "to point away from sin to repentance." It implies educative discipline. The corresponding action is ἔλεγξις (2 Pt. 2:16, Balaam's ass in relation to the prophet) and ἐλεγμός (v.l. ἔλεγχος, 2 Tm. 3:16, Scripture in relation to the hearer). The noteworthy and impressive battle against sin which is part of NT Christianity is reflected in the rich use of ἐλέγχω and related words.

3. This battle against sin and the use of ἐλέγχω for it, as we have shown already (→ 473), is based directly upon the OT and Judaism. Correction of evil-doers is demanded in the OT lest hatred develop (Lv. 19:17). For the Rabbis rebuke is an integral part of brotherly love. Both to deliver and to receive it is a duty on the one side and a high moral achievement on the other. [10] The battle against sin in others is part of the very essence of Jewish religion. The idea of God as One who educates by correction (Hb. 12:5) also goes back directly to the OT (Prv. 3:12; Job 5:17 etc.). [11] It is also a traditional part of the Jewish conception of the Last Judgment that the divine Judge should confront sinners with

---

[5] The ἔλεγχε of 2:15 cannot be construed differently from the ἔλεγχε of 1:13 or the ἐλέγχειν of 1:9, even though it is linked with ταῦτα. This is a careless construction, since ταῦτα is correct only with λάλει. Cf. the accus. of object with παρακάλει.

[6] It is hardly appropriate to speak of a judicial office of the Spirit.

[7] To take ὅτι causally (Zn.) is artificial.

[8] This meaning is suitable in Jn. 3:20; Eph. 5:11, 13, where works rather than persons are the subject of ἐλέγχειν. But here, too, the sense is not merely "to display," but "to show to be evil," so that we do best to keep to the rendering "to correct," especially as deeds and doers are closely related.

[9] It is obviously presupposed that the correction is justified and solidly grounded, so that it must be accepted by the one concerned. "ἐλέγχω has more of the sense of *accusare* than *convincere*" (Zn. J., 422, n. 42).

[10] Cf. Str.-B., I, 787-790; also Schl. Mt., 554.

[11] In Wis. 1:8 ἐλέγχειν shows the kindness of wisdom. Thus the book begins with a warning to those who do not take sin with sufficient seriousness (vv. 1-5). Cf. En. 2 ff.

their wickedness (Jd. 15). [12] Josephus uses ἐλέγχειν for both divine and human correction, but also for "to convince," "to make known." [13] Philo uses ἐλέγχειν a good deal. The subject is usually conscience [14] or truth [15] or the Logos, [16] whose rebuke is far more significant than that of men. [17]

In the Gk. philosophers ἐλέγχω, ἔλεγχος, ἐλεγκτικός etc. are very important words. [18] For Plato ἐλέγχειν as the controverting of propositions is essentially the work of the philosopher. [19] In Aristotle ἔλεγχος is the negative conclusion which his theory of logic and rhetoric treats alongside the ἀπόδειξις or demonstration. [20] He devoted a special treatise to the correction of sophistical ἔλεγχοι. [21] In Zeno ἔλεγχος is the title of two treatises. [22] The ἔλεγχος plays an important role in Epictetus. For him ἐλέγχειν is to take from someone his δόγμα, i.e., the basic principle of his life rather than a philosophical theory. [23] He distinguishes the ἐλεγκτικὸς λόγος or χαρακτήρ from the προτρεπτικός and διδακτικός. [24] Socrates is the typical ἐλεγκτικός. [25] It is a duty, but difficult, to accept (ὑποσχεῖν) ἔλεγχος. [26] ἐλέγχειν, ἔλεγχος etc. are here techn. terms in the philosophical cure of souls. [27] The parallel between Epictetus and the NT is instructive, because the usage of Epictetus has a different slant from that of Plato and Aristotle. The undeniable similarity between Jewish and early Christian ἐλέγχειν on the one side, and that of Epictetus on the other, derives from the emphatically ethical application in both cases.

---

[12] Jd. 15 adduces En. 1:9. Cf. S. Bar., 55, 8; 83, 3; 4 Esr. 7:37; 11:37 ff.; 12:31-33; Ps. Sol. 17:25. Cf. also Volz, 265. Volz rightly points out that this rebuke condemns; it is no longer educative. In Jn. 16:8, too, the convincing of the world probably has the sense of condemnation, since there is no question of the repentance of the world.

[13] Of God, Bell., 7, 330: ὁρᾶτε, πῶς ἡμᾶς ἐλέγχει μάταια προσδοκήσαντας κρείττονα τῶν ἐλπίδων ... ἐπαγαγών. Of man, Ant., 8, 325: the widow κατητιᾶτο τὸν προφήτην ὡς ἐλέγξαντα τὰς ἁμαρτίας αὐτῆς, Bell., 7, 447: ὅπως μηδὲ ἀλλαχοῦ τινες τῶν ᾽Ιουδαίων ἐλέγξωσιν αὐτοῦ τὴν ἀδικίαν. In the sense of "to convince," "to show": Vit., 255: ἐλεγχόντων αὐτοὺς τῶν γραμμάτων; Bell., 5, 515: ὁ λιμὸς ἤλεγχε τὰ πάθη; 5, 551: τῆς ἐπινοίας ἐλεγχθείσης; 7, 720: οὐ σφόδρα τὸ σαφὲς ἠλέγχθη; Ap., 1, 3: τὴν ἑκούσιον ἐλέγξαι ψευδολογίαν; 1, 4: τοὺς δὲ βλασφήμως περὶ ἡμῶν καὶ ψευδῶς γεγραφότας αὐτοὺς δι᾽ ἑαυτῶν ἐλεγχομένους παρέξω; 1, 303: εὔηθες ἴσως ἂν εἴη διὰ πλειόνων ἐλέγχειν τοὺς ὑφ᾽ ἑαυτῶν ἐληλεγμένους.

[14] Jos., 48; Spec. Leg., III, 54; IV, 6, 40.

[15] Conf. Ling. 126; Praem. Poen., 4.

[16] Rer. Div. Her., 95; Det. Pot. Ins., 146; Deus Imm., 135, 182; Fug., 118.

[17] Jos., 262; Virt., 206.

[18] Democr. already uses ἐλέγχειν of the exposure of the failings of others in Fr., 60 (II, 75, 16, Diels) and Fr., 222 (II, 105, 12, Diels); he also uses the term in his ethical fragments.

[19] Soph., 241d; 529a; Gorg., 570c; Theaet., 171d; Phaed., 273c.

[20] ἀντιφάσεως συλλογισμός, An. Pri., II, 20, p. 66b, 11, 8; De Sophisticis Elenchis, 9, p. 170b, 1; 10, p. 171a, 2, 4. ἔλεγχος συλλογισμὸς μετ᾽ ἀντιφάσεως τοῦ συμπεράσματος is a conclusion with the refutation of the consequence, 1, p. 165a, 2.

[21] On the relation between the two, cf.: ὅσα ἔστιν ἀποδεῖξαι, ἔστιν καὶ ἐλέγξαι τὸν θέμενον τὴν ἀντίφασιν τοῦ ἀληθοῦς De Sophisticis Elenchis, 9, p. 170a, 24. Aristot. can speak of ἐλεγκτικῶς ἀποδεῖξαι: Metaph., III, 4, p. 1006a, 15. Further material may easily be found with the help of the index of H. Bonitz (1870).

[22] Cf. Zeno Fr., 41 (I, 15, v. Arnim); Diog. L., VII, 4.

[23] Diss., III, 9, 13 (III, 14, 9 οἴησις instead of δόγμα), cf. II, 1, 32; IV, 5, 21.

[24] II, 26, 4; III, 23, 33.

[25] III, 21, 19.

[26] II, 14, 20; I, 26, 17, cf. III, 33, 8.

[27] It is hardly Epict. who makes them this. There is a corresponding usage in the older and middle Stoa. We need only refer to Cynicism: when the "dog" of Diogenes "bites" his friends with a view to improving them, this is ἔλεγχος. Cf. also G. A. Gerhard, Phoinix von Kolophon (1909), 35.

† ἔλεγχος, † ἔλεγξις, † ἐλεγμός.

ἔλεγχος has the senses a. "proof," "means of proof" with a view to convincing and refuting, "convincing," "refutation"; and b. "investigation," "account." [1] The LXX uses it for תּוֹכֵחָה (נוֹכַח‎, הוֹכִיחַ‎), "refutation," "correction." ἔλεγξις is rare and means "persuasion," "refutation." [2]

ἐλεγμός (v.l.: ἔλεγχος) in 2 Tm. 3:16 and ἔλεγξις in 2 Pt. 2:16 mean the rebuking of the sinner, [3] → ἐλέγχω, 474.

In Hb. 11:1, in the well-known characterisation [4] of faith, ἔλεγχος means "proof" or "persuasion" rather than correction. [5] But it cannot be taken in the sense of subjective persuasion, since this does not correspond to the usage. [6] To take πραγμάτων as a subj. gen., so that the facts substantiate themselves to faith in spite of their invisibility, [7] is countered by the fact that ἔλεγχος usually takes an obj. gen. [8] Thus we must take πραγμάτων as an obj. gen. [9] The reference is to the presence of an ἔλεγχος, not to the one who achieves it. By adding ἔλεγχος κτλ. to ἐλπιζομένων ὑπόστασις the inner right of resting on the thing hoped for (→ ὑπόστασις) is established. To find the convincing subject in faith, as most of the older exegetes did, [10] endangers the necessary parallelism of ὑπόστασις and ἔλεγχος, and obscures the inner right of the ὑπόστασις. If we are to name a convincing subject, it can only be God. A faith which of itself contained or offered proof of things unseen would not be the faith of Hb., which stands on the revelation, Word and promise of God and has nothing but what it receives. Thus faith is confidence in what is hoped for, since it is the divinely given conviction of things unseen.

Büchsel

ἔ λ ε γ χ ο ς. Pape, Pass., *s.v.* ἔλεγχος; A. Schlatter, *Der Glaube im NT*[4] (1927), 524 f.; Rgg. Hb. [2], [3] (1922), 340 ff.; Wnd. Hb., 99.

[1] Many examples may be found in Pape.

[2] Cf. Pape. ἔλεγξις is not found in Josephus.

[3] Cf. Joseph. Ant., 8, 252 : ὡς ἐλέγχων τῆς ἐκείνων ἀσελγείας τὴν αὑτῶν σωφροσύνην παραπέμποντες.

[4] One can hardly call it definition, since the author does not try to be exhaustive but leaves much for his readers to fill in. Cf. A. Seeberg Hb. (1912), 120.

[5] So A. Schlatter, *Glaube,* 524 f.; Pr.-Bauer, *s.v.* ἔλεγχος, Windisch, Riggenbach.

[6] Windisch and Riggenb., who both explain it in this way, allow that ἔλεγχος has an obj. rather than a subj. sense (Rgg. Hb., 343).

[7] Schlatter, *op. cit.*

[8] Cf. the examples given by Rgg., 342, n. 70, namely, Epict., III, 10, 11: ἔνθα ὁ ἔλεγχος τοῦ πράγματος, ἡ δοκιμασία τοῦ φιλοσοφοῦντος; Jos. Bell., 4, 337: ἦν οὔτ᾽ ἔλεγχός τις τῶν κατηγορουμένων οὔτε τεκμήριον. Cf. Ant., 17, 110 : ἐρευνητὴς τῶν ἐλέγχων; Ap., 2, 17 : κατ᾽ ἐαυτὸν τὸν ἔλεγχον ἐπισπώμενος. Pape offers only one example of the subj. gen. with ἔλεγχος, Soph. Oed. Col., 1299 : οὔτ᾽ εἰς ἔλεγχον χειρὸς οὔτ᾽ ἔργου μολών.

[9] To see it in the believer, so that he proves to others the reality of unseen things, does not fit in with 11:1, though it might agree with the μαρτύρων of 12:1. For in 11:1 there is no reference to the significance of the believer to others.

[10] Cf. the list in Rgg. Hb., 342, n. 70. Chrys., MPG, 63, 151: ἔλεγχος ... ἐπὶ τῶν λίαν δήλων· ἡ πίστις τοίνυν ἐστὶν ὄψις τῶν ἀδήλων, φησί, καὶ εἰς τὴν αὐτὴν τοῖς ὁρωμένοις φέρει πληροφορίαν τὰ μὴ ὁρώμενα; Oecumenius, MPG, 119, 401d : ἔστι δὲ ἡ πίστις ἔλεγχος καὶ ἀπόδειξις τῶν οὐ βλεπομένων. ἀποδείκνυσι δὲ ὁρατὰ τὰ ἀόρατα· ἡ πίστις πῶς; τῷ νῷ καὶ ταῖς ἐλπίσιν ὁρῶσα τὰ μὴ φαινόμενα. vg : *est autem fides sperandarum substantia rerum, argumentum non apparentium.*

ἔλεος									477

ἔλεος, ἐλεέω, ἐλεήμων,
ἐλεημοσύνη, ἀνέλεος, ἀνελεήμων

ἔλεος, ἐλεέω.

A. The Greek Usage.

In Gk. ἔλεος is a πάθος, i.e., the emotion roused by contact with an affliction which comes undeservedly on someone else. There is in it an element of φόβος that this can happen. Thus we have the definition in Aristot. Rhet., II, 8, p. 1385b, 13 f.: ἔστω δὲ ἔλεος λύπη τις ἐπὶ φαινομένῳ (naturally not "apparent" but "appearing") κακῷ φθαρτικῷ ἢ λυπηρῷ τοῦ ἀναξίου τυγχάνειν, ὃ κἂν αὐτὸς προσδοκήσειεν ἂν παθεῖν. [1] To this extent ἔλεος and φθόνος correspond, for φθόνος is concerned with the welfare of others. [2] νεμεσᾶν also corresponds to ἐλεεῖν as justifiable pain at unmerited prosperity. [3]

In face of the unfortunate this emotion is an ἐλεεῖν which includes the elements of both awe (→ αἰδώς, I, 169) and mercy, so that ἐλεεῖν can be used with both αἰδεῖσθαι [4] and οἰκτίρειν [5] and par. ἔλεος (ἐλεεῖν) in the sense of mercy or sympathy is very common. [6] It is fitting in the noble. [7] The cruel have a νηλεὲς ἦτορ, like

ἔ λ ε ο ς. L. Schmidt, Die Ethik der alten Griechen, II (1882), 290-294; N. Glueck, "Das Wort ḥesed im at.lichen Sprachgebrauche," Beih. ZAW, 47 (1927); W. F. Lofthouse, "Ḥen and Ḥesed in the OT," ZAW, NF, 10 (1933), 29-35; L. Gulkowitsch, D. Entwicklung des Begriffes ḥāsīd im AT (1934).

[1] Cf. Rhet., II, 8, p. 1386a, 27 ff.: ἔλεος is concerned with that in others which we ourselves fear : Poët., 6, p. 1449b, 24 ff.; 13, p. 1452b, 30 ff.; 14, p. 1453b, 1 ff.: tragedy must awaken φόβος and ἔλεος. On the distinction between youth and age in relation to ἔλεος, Rhet., II, 12, p. 1389b, 8 ff.; II, 13, p. 1390a, 19 ff.

[2] Aristot. Rhet., II, 10, p. 1387b, 21 ff.; Epicharmus Fr., 34 (Diels, I, 125, 12); Timocles Fr., 31 (CAF, II, 464). In Stoicism, ἔλεος, like φθόνος, ζῆλος etc., is grouped under λύπη (v. Arnim, III, 96, 9; 99, 38; 100, 7 and 15; 101, 21 etc.; Epict. Diss., III, 22, 13).

[3] Aristot. Rhet., II, 9, p. 1386b, 9 ff.

[4] Hom. Il., 24, 44 : ὡς Ἀχιλεὺς ἔλεον μὲν ἀπώλεσεν, οὐδέ οἱ αἰδώς. The ἱκέτης asks : σὺ δέ μ᾽ αἴδεο καί μ᾽ ἐλέησον (Hom. Il., 21, 74 f.; cf. 22, 123 f.; Od., 3, 96; 22, 312); Antiphon Orator, 1, 26 : ἐλεεῖν corresponding to αἰδοῦς τυγχάνειν. Similarly οἰκτίρειν and αἰδεῖσθαι are linked in Eur. Hec., 286 f.; cf. Tro., 787 f.: ἄνοικτος and ἀναιδείᾳ. In Soph. Oed. Col. the ξένοι αἰδόφρονες (237) are asked : οἰκτίραθ᾽ (242), αἰδοῦς κῦρσαι (247), νεύσατε τὰν ἀδόκητον χάριν (249). Thus the opp. can be ὑβρίζειν (Aristot. Rhet., II, 8, p. 1385b, 20 f.).

[5] E.g., Soph. Phil., 308 f. (ἐλεεῖν and οἰκτίρειν); Eur. Iph. Aul., 491 (ἔλεος par. 478 οἰκτείρειν); Gorg. Fr., 11 (Diels, II, 251, 20 f.); Plat. Euthyd., 288d.

[6] For ἐλεεῖσθαι, "to be pitied," cf. Plat. Resp., I, 336e; for the plur. ἔλεοι for instances in which one is sympathetic, cf. X, 606c; ἔλεον ποιεῖσθαι, Demosth., 24, 111. In Athens ἐλέου βωμός was a place of refuge which later gave rise to the cult of ἔλεος; W. Judeich, "Topographie von Athen" (Handb. d. Altert.-Wiss., III, 2, 2 [1931]), 356 f.; U. v. Wilamowitz, Der Glaube der Hellenen, I (1931), 329. There was an ἐλέου βωμός in Epidauros, Ditt. Syll., 3, 1149.

[7] Demosth., 22, 57: ἀλλ᾽ ἔνεστ᾽ (in the νόμοι and ἔθη) ἔλεος, συγγνώμη, πάνθ᾽ ἃ προσήκει τοῖς ἐλευθέροις. L. Schmidt, op. cit., 290; R. Hirzel, Themis, Dike und Verwandtes (1907), 272 f.

Achilles (Hom. Il., 9, 497) and θάνατος (Hes. Theog., 764 f. → θάνατος, n. 1). The merciful man is called ἐλεήμων [8] (Hom. Od., 5, 191: the θυμός as σιδήρεος or ἐλεήμων, Aristoph. Pax, 425 etc.), the unmerciful νηλεής, later ἀνελεήμων (the adv. is found already in Antiphon Orator, 1, 25) and ἀνηλεής. ἐλεεινός is one who deserves pity. [9] The deity can also be the subject of ἔλεος (ἐλεεῖν); [10] thus God's ἔλεος is displayed in regeneration (Corp. Herm., XIII, 3; 8; 10) and the regenerate is called ἐλεηθεὶς ὑπὸ τοῦ θεοῦ (XIII, 7).

It is typical that the emotion of ἔλεος plays a great part in the administration of justice. The accused must seek to arouse the ἔλεος of the judge; he tries ἐλέου τυχεῖν (Antiphon Orator, 1, 21). Thrasymachos spoke of ἔλεοι (Diels, II, 281, 11 f.) and taught ὡς δεῖ εἰς οἶκτον ἐγεῖραι τὸν δικαστὴν καὶ ἐπισπᾶσθαι ἔλεον (Fr. 6, Diels, 281, 19). For it is possible, in the power of the λόγος, ἔλεον ἐπαυξῆσαι (Gorg. Fr., 11, Diels, II, 251, 26; ibid., 252, 2: ἔλεος πολύδακρυς). Socrates scorns to awaken the ἔλεος of the judges (Plat. Ap., 34c and 35b). As Plato knows ἐλεεινολογίαι (Phaedr., 272a), so Aristot. (Rhet., II, 8, p. 1385b, 11 ff.) discusses the ἔλεος which is one of the πάθη that the orator must know how to kindle. [11] Hence ἔλεος can be related to and conjoined with συγγνώμη. [12] Thus ἔλεος finds its opp. in ὀργή to the degree that this necessarily belongs to δίκη and is thus a legitimate emotion in the judge, whereas ἔλεος makes him partial. [13]

This helps us to see why Stoicism regarded ἔλεος as a sickness of the soul; [14] as πάθος, and even a form of λύπη, it is unworthy of the sage. [15] In this respect we must remember that in Gk. thought ἔλεος is an emotion rather than a moral relationship to others, so that in judicial practice ἔλεος entails partiality. Obviously Stoicism does not inculcate an unmerciful attitude towards others. Our relationship towards them should be determined by the demand for αἰδώς, for ἐπιείκεια, χρηστότης and φιλανθρωπία. [16] ἔλεος is only χρηστότης in appearance (v. Arnim, III, 163, 5 f.), and in any case Epict. and M. Ant. demand ἐλεεῖν in relation to the wicked. [17]

---

[8] ἐλεημοσύνη for pity is first found in Callim. Hymnus in Delum, 152 (par. χάρις); P. Gen., 51, 26; on ἐλεημοσύνη for alms, → 486, n. 4.

[9] E.g., Plat. Leg., V, 731d: ἀλλὰ ἐλεεινὸς μὲν πάντως ὅ γε ἄδικος καὶ ὁ τὰ κακὰ ἔχων, ἐλεεῖν δὲ τὸν μὲν ἰάσιμα ἔχοντα ἐγχωρεῖ ... Cf. also οἰκτρός, Eur. Iph. Aul., 986; Iph. Taur., 227 f.; Hel., 944 f.

[10] For God's ἔλεος, Eur. Or., 333; God's ἐλεεῖν, Menand. Epit., 490; Lib. Or., 64, 112: θεῶν τις ἐλεήσας τὴν τῶν πολλῶν ἀπαιδευσίαν.

[11] Cf. also Ps.-Aristot. Rhet. Al., 35, p. 1439b, 25 ff.; Philodem. Philos. Volumina Rhetorica, Col. XXXV, 16 f. (I, 65, Sudhaus).

[12] Demosth. (→ n. 7) Or., 25, 81 and 83: ἔλεος, συγγνώμη, φιλανθρωπία, the qualities expected in a judge; Or. 21, 100; Aristot. Eth. Nic., 1, p. 1109b, 32; III, 2, p. 1111a, 1 f.; Chrysippus Fr., 641 (v. Arnim, III, 163, 3 f.); Max. Tyr., 33, 3a: ἐλεεινός = σύγγνωστος.

[13] R. Hirzel, op. cit., 416-418; cf. also Plat. Leg., V, 731b-d on the relation between θυμός or ὀργή and ἔλεος. Antiphon Orator, 1, 27 formulates the principle: οὕτω δέ τοι καὶ ἐλεεῖν ἐπὶ τοῖς ἀκουσίοις παθήμασι μᾶλλον προσήκει ἢ τοῖς ἑκουσίοις καὶ ἐκ προνοίας ἀδικήμασι καὶ ἁμαρτήμασι.

[14] v. Arnim, I, 52, 11 ff.; 96, 9 f.; III, 101, 10 etc.; Sen. De Clementia, II, 5, 4 f.

[15] → n. 2, also Epict., II, 17, 26; III, 24, 43; IV, 1, 4; 6, 1; Andronicus, De Passionibus, p. 12, 8 ff. (Kreuttner). Cf. also how ἐλεημοσύνη with φθονερία etc. is numbered among the εὐκαταφορίαι of the ψυχή, v. Arnim, III, 103, 8; the σοφός is not ἐλεήμων, ibid., III, 163, 3; Epict., II, 21, 3 and 5.

[16] Cf. Plut. Tranq. An., 7 (II, p. 468d): ὅπου γὰρ ἔνιοι τῶν φιλοσόφων καὶ τὸν ἔλεον ψέγουσι πρὸς ἀτυχοῦντας ἀνθρώπους γιγνόμενον, ὡς καλοῦ τοῦ βοηθεῖν οὐ τοῦ συναλγεῖν καὶ συνενδιδόναι τοῖς πλησίον ὄντος.

[17] Epict., I, 18, 3 and 9; 28, 9; M. Ant., 7, 26. Cf. the proclamation of Nero to the Gks. in Ditt. Syll.³, 814, 21: οὐ δι' ἔλεον ὑμᾶς, ἀλλὰ δι' εὔνοιαν εὐεργετῶ.

B. The OT and Jewish Usage.

1. In the LXX ἔλεος [18] is normally used for חֶסֶד, and less frequently (6 times) for רַחֲמִים, [19] while ἐλεεῖν occurs mostly for חָנַן, though often for רָחַם pi. [20] In the OT חֶסֶד denotes an attitude of man or God which arises out of a mutual relationship. It is the attitude which the one expects of the other in this relationship, and to which he is pledged in relation to him. Thus the relationship of mutual חֶסֶד arises between relatives and friends, hosts and guests, masters and subjects, or others in covenant relation. [21] חֶסֶד is not primarily a disposition but a helpful act [22] corresponding to a relationship of trust, and faithfulness as the appropriate attitude. [23] The reciprocity of the חֶסֶד obligation is the content of a בְּרִית (1 S. 20:8). Thus the implied demand is a legal one. Both חֶסֶד and מִשְׁפָּט are demanded, [24] as חֶסֶד is also connected with צְדָקָה. [25] As the חֶסֶד of the ruler protects his dominion, [26] so חֶסֶד is what gives security to men in their mutual dealings. [27]

Since on the other side חֶסֶד denotes help or kindness as the grace of a superior, חֶסֶד can also be connected with יְשׁוּעָה, [28] שָׁלוֹם, [29] אַהֲבָה, [30] and esp. רַחֲמִים. [31] As, then, the meaning of חֶסֶד fluctuates between (covenant) faithfulness, obligation and love or grace, so the translation usually has ἔλεος, [32] but occasionally δικαιοσύνη. [33]

If in human relationships the element of obligation may yield before that of favour, [34] so on God's side חֶסֶד particularly comes to denote grace. God's חֶסֶד, too, rests on the בְּרִית by which He has freely bound Himself to the people, [35] so that

---

[18] On τὸ ἔλεος, which is customary in the LXX instead of ὁ ἔλεος, v. Thackeray, 158.

[19] Also for subst. from the stem חנן; for חנן in Ju. 21:22 : ἔλεος ποιεῖν. On חֵן → χάρις.

[20] ἐλεεῖν is also used for חָמַל (6 times), and for נחם ni and pi (5 times); ἐλεήμων is mostly used for חַנּוּן and ἐλεημοσύνη for צְדָקָה. In the LXX we often have πολυέλεος, usually for רַב־חֶסֶד. ἀνέλεος does not occur ; → ἀνελεήμων is found several times. οἰκτίρειν is the normal rendering of חנן and רחם pi (10 or 12 times); οἰκτιρμοί of רַחֲמִים.

[21] V. Glueck, op. cit.

[22] Hence the common plur. (e.g., Is. 63:7; Ps. 25:6; 89:49; Neh. 13:14; LXX alternating between ἔλεος and ἐλέη), and the expression עָשָׂה חֶסֶד. Gn. 24:12; 40:14; 2 S. 3:8; LXX : ποιεῖν ἔλεος, also used for חנן, → n. 19.

[23] Hence the common combination : חֶסֶד וֶאֱמֶת.

[24] Hos. 12:7; Mi. 6:8; Jer. 9:23; Zech. 7:9; Ps. 101:1.

[25] Jer. 9:23; Ps. 36:10; 40:11; 143:11; with צֶדֶק, Ps. 85:10.

[26] Is. 16:5; Prv. 20:28.

[27] Ps. 109:12 and 16; Prv. 11:17; 14:22; 19:22; 21:21.

[28] Ps. 13:5; 85:7; or תְּשׁוּעָה, Ps. 40:10; 119:41; יָשַׁע, Ps. 69:13.

[29] Jer. 16:5; Ps. 85:10.

[30] Jer. 2:2; 31:3.

[31] Is. 63:7; Jer. 16:5; Hos. 2:21; Zech. 7:9; Ps. 25:6; 40:11; 51:1; 69:16 etc.

[32] Also ἐλεημοσύνη, e.g., Gn. 47:29; Prv. 3:3; 16:6 (LXX : 15:27); → n. 20.

[33] Gn. 19:19; 20:13; 21:23; 24:27; Prv. 20:28b (LXX : v. 22).

[34] Est. 2:9 and 17; Ezr. 9:9 (1 Ἐσδρ. 8:77); Da. 1:9, where the LXX always has χάρις (as in Gn. 43:14 for רַחֲמִים), and Ezr. 7:28 (1 Ἐσδρ. 8:26), where the LXX has τιμᾶν.

[35] 1 K. 8:23; Is. 55:3; Ps. 89:49 (cf. v. 28); 106:45. God shows חֶסֶד and אֱמֶת Gn. 24:27; 32:11 (here the LXX has δικαιοσύνη and ἀλήθεια); Ex. 34:6; 2 S. 2:6; Mi. 7:20; Ps. 40:10 f.; 85:10 (here the LXX has ἔλεος and ἀλήθεια); or חֶסֶד and אֱמוּנָה : Ps. 88:11; 89:33; 98:3 (here the LXX has ἔλεος and ἀλήθεια).

the righteous can appeal to God's חֶסֶד [36] assuming that they for their part have
kept their obligations. [37] Those who have made and kept the covenant are the
חֲסִידִים, [38] and they are called the righteous, [39] the upright, [40] and those who fear
God. [41] They confront the רְשָׁעִים, [42] and the prophet bewails the fact that Israel has
forgotten faithfulness. [43] But the righteous can appeal to their חֲסָדִים; [44] God takes
pleasure in such חֶסֶד, [45] and the righteous can also boast of God's חֶסֶד. [46]

In religious usage God's חֶסֶד always means His faithful and merciful help, and
this one-sided understanding is expressed in the use of ἔλεος. We must always
remember, however, that it is the חֶסֶד which God has promised, so that, although
one cannot claim it, one may certainly expect it. In other words, the thought of
חֶסֶד and the thought of the covenant belong together. Yet to the degree that man
is unfaithful, the חֶסֶד for which he hopes takes on the character of pardoning
grace. [47] God keeps to the covenant and promises in spite of man's unfaithfulness,
and from His חֶסֶד there is finally expected definitive redemption from every need.
חֶסֶד thus becomes an eschatological term in salvation history. [48] And it must be
emphasised that חֶסֶד primarily denotes, not a disposition, but the act or demonstration of assisting faithfulness.

In distinction from חֶסֶד, רַחֲמִים originally denotes what we call emotion, or the
seat of a feeling which is felt physically. [49] רַחֲמִים is never πάθος in the Greek sense,
and it has nothing to do with φόβος or λύπη. It is an original sense of oneness
with another, especially between parents and children or brothers and sisters. [50]
Since it is specifically evoked when the other is in trouble, it often amounts to
"pity" or "sympathy," [51] though this is not the precise meaning. [52] "Love" is a
better rendering. It is typical that normally רַחֲמִים and רָחַם, too, denote the act or

---

[36] Ps. 6:4; 25:6 f.; 119:149; 143:12 : "In virtue of thy חֶסֶד cut off mine enemies"; Neh.
13:22; 2 Ch. 6:42.

[37] Ex. 20:6; Dt. 7:12; 1 K. 8:23; Hos. 10:12; Ps. 103:11, 17 etc.

[38] Ps. 50:5; cf. אִישׁ) אַנְשֵׁי חֶסֶד), Is. 57:1; Prv. 20:6. The LXX mostly has ὅσιος for חָסִיד.

[39] Is. 57:1 (הַצַּדִּיק).

[40] Mi. 7:2; Prv. 2:7 f. (יָשָׁר).

[41] Ps. 85:8 f.

[42] Ps. 37:28; 97:10.

[43] Hos. 6:4; Jer. 2:2.

[44] Neh. 13:14.

[45] Hos. 6:6.

[46] Ps. 40:10; 59:10, 16; 63:3; 88:11; 136:1 ff.; Is. 63:7; Ju. 2:20 (LXX always ἔλεος).

[47] For חֶסֶד as the grace of remission, cf. Ex. 34:6 f.; Nu. 14:19; Jer. 3:12 f.; Lam. 3:22 f.

[48] For God's חֶסֶד in salvation history, cf. Is. 54:10; 63:7; Jer. 31:3; Mi. 7:20 (appeal to
the promise); Ps. 25:6 (God is to remember His חֲסָדִים and רַחֲמִים); 106:45. For eschatological
חֶסֶד, cf. Is. 54:8; 55:3; Mi. 7:20; Ps. 85:7; 90:14; 130:7.

[49] Gn. 43:30; 1 K. 3:26; Prv. 12:10; cf. J. Pedersen, Israel (1926), 309 and 525.

[50] Am. 1:11; Hos. 2:19; Is. 63:15 f.; similarly רחם pi denotes this sense and the resultant
concern for others : motherly love in Is. 49:15; fatherly love in Jer. 31:20; Ps. 103:13 (cf.
v. 8); esp. Hos. 1:6 f.; 2:4, 23.

[51] E.g. 1 K. 8:50; Ps. 106:46; Neh. 1:11; 2 Ch. 30:9. For the verb Is. 13:18; Jer. 6:23; 21:7;
42:12 etc.

[52] In all the passages in n. 50 "mercy" or "pity" would be too restricted a rendering.
It is true that the LXX usually has ἔλεος (ἐλεεῖν) or οἰκτιρμοί (οἰκτίρειν), but it is
worth noting that it has ἀγαπᾶν in Hosea 2:23.

expression of love rather than the emotion. One demonstrates love (Zech. 7:9 : עֹשֶׂה, LXX : ποιεῖν), or asks for it (Ps. 69:16), or finds mercy with someone (לִפְנֵי, 1 K. 8:50; Ps. 106:46 etc.). God gives love (Dt. 13:18 : נָתַן; Is. 47:6 : שׂוּם, LXX in both cases διδόναι). As רַחֲמִים is often combined with חֶסֶד (→ n. 31), so it is with רחם and חנן to denote gracious action rather than emotion. [53] Thus רחם can simply mean to bring help (Zech. 10:6). The wrath which is its opp. is the wrath of judgment. [54] Like חֶסֶד, רַחֲמִים may also be the grace of the forgiveness [55] granted to Israel when it repents. [56] Thus רַחֲמִים becomes an eschatological hope. [57]

2. In the language of later Judaism חֶסֶד and רַחֲמִים can hardly be distinguished any more than ἔλεος and οἰκτιρμοί, which are used interchangeably. Both terms may be used, of course, for human kindness and pity. [58] In the Rabbis חֶסֶד is a term for the act of love, [59] and there are frequent exhortations to mercy. [60] But it is used esp. for the mercy of God as the κύριος τοῦ ἐλέους [σου?] (Wis. 9:1). The sense of "faithfulness" is often evident (Sir. 47:22, LXX : ἔλεος). Elsewhere the sense of "mercy" tends to predominate in opp. to the wrath and judgment of God. [61] God acts κατὰ τὸ ἔλεος αὐτοῦ; [62] His ἔλεος applies to Israel, [63] to the ὅσιοι, [64] to those who love Him [65] and fear Him. [66] His ἔλεος is gracious action. [67] He reveals it. [68] It is expected, [69] hoped for, [70] prayed for. [71] It is in keeping that in the LXX ἔλεος is used for various terms which denote the grace of God. [72] Like → ὀργή, it is an eschatological word. χάρις and ἔλεος are shown to the ἐκλεκτοί acc. to Wis. 3:9; 4:15, here linked with → ἐπισκοπή. The age of salvation is the age of ἔλεος (2 Macc. 2:7; 7:29). Thus the victory of the Maccabees can be regarded as the ἀρχὴ ἐλέους (2 Macc. 8:27), the ἡμέρα ἐλέους δικαίων (Ps. Sol. 14:6). [73]

[53] Ex. 33:19; 2 K. 13:23; Ps. 102:13; cf. Ps. 103:8; 116:5.
[54] Dt. 13:18; Am. 1:11; Zech. 1:12; Ps. 77:9.
[55] Ps. 51:1; 79:8; Da. 9:9 (with הַסְּלִחוֹת).
[56] Dt. 30:3; Is. 55:7.
[57] Is. 14:1; 49:13; 54:7; Jer. 12:15; 33:26; Ez. 39:25; Mi. 7:19; Zech. 1:16.
[58] Sir. 28:4; 2 Macc. 4:37; 4 Macc. 9:4; Ep. Ar., 208; Jos. Bell., 1, 352, 560 etc.
[59] גְמִילוּת חֲסָדִים, Ab., 1, 2 etc.; cf. Str.-B., IV, 536, 538 f.
[60] Often with reference to God's mercy : Test. Zeb. 5-8; Str.-B., I, 203; Schl. Mt., 138; Dib. Jk., 138; Wnd. Jk. on 2:13. The Rabbis regard mercy as distinctive of Israel, Str.-B., I, 204 f.
[61] Sir. 5:6; 16:11 f. (רַחֲמִים, LXX ἔλεος, though once οἰκτιρμός in 5:6); Wis. 6:6; 11:9; 12:22; 2 Macc. 6:16; 8:5; Ps. Sol. 18:3 etc.
[62] Tob. 8:16; Sir. 50:22; 51:3; 1 Macc. 13:46; Ps. Sol. 2:40.
[63] Jdt. 13:14; Sir. 32:25 f.; Ps. Sol. 11:9.
[64] Ps. Sol. 2:40; 13:11; the אַנְשֵׁי חֶסֶד (→ n. 38) of Sir. 44:10 are ἄνδρες ἐλέου in the LXX.
[65] Ps. Sol. 4:29; 6:9; 10:4.
[66] Ps. Sol. 2:37; 13:11; 15:15.
[67] ἔλεος takes place (γίνεσθαι) in 1 Ἐσδρ. 8:75; 2 Macc. 2:7; Gr. En. 1:8. God performs it (ποιεῖν ἔλεος) in Tob. 7:11 א; 8:17; this expression is often used of human kindness : Sir. 29:1; 46:7; Tob. 14:7; Test. Zeb. 5:1 (ἐπὶ τὸν πλησίον), 3 f. etc. On divine and human kindness in the Rabbis, cf. Str.-B., II, 184; Schl. Lk., 179 f.
[68] 3 Macc. 2:19; 6:4, 39 (ἐπιφαίνειν).
[69] Sir. 2:7 (ἀναμένειν).
[70] Sir. 2:9.
[71] Ps. Sol. 8:33 f.; 9:16.
[72] Apart from the instances quoted (→ 479), cf. Is. 45:8, where ἔλεος is used for יֶשַׁע, and 60:10, where it is used for רָצוֹן.
[73] Cf. also Ps. Sol. 8:34; 17:51; 18:6 (ἡμέρα ἐλέους par. ἡμέρα ἐκλογῆς), 10; Gr. En. 1:8; 27:4. Cf. H. Braun, Gerichtsgedanke u. Rechtfertigungslehre bei Pls. (1930), 9 and 56.

Philo often speaks of the ἔλεος and ἐλεεῖν of man. ἔλεος is τὸ ἀναγκαιότατον καὶ συγγενέστατον λογικῇ ψυχῇ πάθος. [74] The σοφός cares for the φαῦλος: ἐλέῳ καὶ προμηθείᾳ χρώμενος. [75] Philo sometimes links ἔλεος with οἶκτος [76] and sometimes with φιλανθρωπία; [77] and he stresses the fact that the Law demands ἔλεος. [78] With reference to the Law he speaks in Gk. fashion of the way in which ἔλεος and συγγνώμη are granted ἐπ' ἀτυχημάτων, while there is no ἐλεεῖν for the ἄδικος. [79]

God is ἐλεήμων; [80] of His δυνάμεις the third is the ἴλεως, δι' ἧς ... οἰκτίρει καὶ ἐλεεῖ τὸ ἴδιον ἔργον. [81] God's λόγοι come down to us διὰ φιλανθρωπίαν καὶ ἔλεον; [82] His αὐγαί He sends from heaven δι' ἔλεον τοῦ γένους ἡμῶν. [83] As the merciful God, He is the σωτήρ. [84] Here, however, ἔλεος is understood in Gk. fashion as an emotion. Its object is the frail race of men, [85] and it takes precedence of δίκη. [86] Thus Philo does not speak of the doing of mercy, or of mercy being enacted, though he can say ἔλεον λαμβάνειν. [87] For him ἔλεος has no eschatological significance.

C. ἔλεος/ἐλεέω in the NT.

1. In the NT ἔλεος [88] and ἐλεεῖν [89] are often used for the divinely required attitude of man to man. Indeed, in a few instances ἔλεος has the original OT sense of the kindness which we owe one another in mutual relationships, Hos. 6:6 being alluded to in Mt. 9:13; 12:7: ἔλεος θέλω καὶ οὐ θυσίαν. The word has the same meaning in the accusation against the scribes and Pharisees in Mt. 23:23: ἀφήκατε τὰ βαρύτερα τοῦ νόμου, τὴν κρίσιν καὶ τὸ ἔλεος καὶ τὴν πίστιν; as κρίσις corresponds to מִשְׁפָּט and πίστις to אֱמֶת, so does ἔλεος to חֶסֶד. [90] The

---

[74] Virt., 144.

[75] Sacr. AC, 121. ἔλεος (God's) is also combined with προμήθεια in Fug., 162; cf. God's ἔλεος and πρόνοια in Jos. Ant., 4, 239.

[76] Jos., 227, 230; Spec. Leg., III, 4, 116 etc. This reminds us of the interchangeability of ἔλεος and οἰκτιρμοί in the LXX, though it is Gk. in conception.

[77] Spec. Leg., IV, 72; cf. II, 96 (of God in Som., I, 147).

[78] Spec. Leg., IV, 72; Virt., 141 etc. To repudiate this demand is to put out of action the βωμὸς ἐλέου (→ n. 6), Exsecr., 154.

[79] Spec. Leg., IV, 72, 76 f.; cf. Decal., 69; Poster. C., 9; Jos., 72 etc.

[80] Som., I, 93.

[81] Fug., 95; cf. Sacr. AC, 42: ἐν γὰρ τῷ τοῦ θεοῦ ἐλέῳ τὰ πάντα ὁρμεῖ.

[82] Som., I, 147; cf. Rer. Div. Her., 112: τῆς θείας ἀρετῆς ἀπ' οὐρανοῦ τὴν εἰκόνα (the tent) ἐπὶ γῆν καταπέμψαι δι' ἔλεον τοῦ γένους ἡμῶν.

[83] Som., I, 112.

[84] Fug., 162; Praem. Poen., 39 and 117; ὁ σωτήριος ἔλεος, Deus Imm., 74; Som., II, 149.

[85] → n. 82; 83; cf. also Leg. All., I, 45.

[86] Deus Imm., 74 ff.: ... οὐ μόνον δικάσας ἐλεεῖ, ἀλλὰ καὶ ἐλεήσας δικάζει πρεσβύτερος γὰρ δίκης ὁ ἔλεος παρ' αὐτῷ ἐστιν ...; Leg. Gaj., 367.

[87] Jos., 255 (cf. also Jos. Ant., 4, 269); ἔλεον καὶ οἶκτον λαμβάνειν, Mut. Nom., 133; Vit. Mos., I, 86 f.

[88] In the NT we always have the neut. τὸ ἔλεος → n. 18; Bl.-Debr. § 51, 2; Radermacher², 56 f.

[89] Individual forms are modelled on verbs with -ᾶν, Bl.-Debr. § 90; Radermacher², 89.

[90] Mi. 6:8; Hos. 12:7 demand מִשְׁפָּט and חֶסֶד (LXX: κρίμα and ἔλεος). In Ps. 101:1 the Psalmist extols חֶסֶד and מִשְׁפָּט (LXX: ἔλεος and κρίσις). We read of God's חֶסֶד, מִשְׁפָּט and צְדָקָה in Jer. 9:23 (LXX 24: ἔλεος, κρίμα and δικαιοσύνη). מִשְׁפָּט־אֱמֶת and חֶסֶד וְרַחֲמִים are demanded in Zech. 7:9 (LXX: κρίμα δίκαιον and ἔλεος καὶ οἰκτιρμός); and אֱמֶת and חֶסֶד in Hos. 4:1 (LXX: ἀλήθεια and ἔλεος). On πίστις for אֱמֶת → πίστις. In Lk. 11:42 we simply have ἀγάπη τοῦ θεοῦ instead of ἔλεος and πίστις.

ποιεῖν ἔλεος of the LXX (→ n. 22 and 67) is found in Lk. 10:37 to describe the act of the Samaritan, and in concrete cases it denotes the showing of love and the act of mercy (→ n. 59). ἔλεος has the same sense in Mt. 18:33 : οὐκ ἔδει καὶ σὲ ἐλεῆσαι τὸν σύνδουλόν σου, ὡς κἀγὼ σὲ ἠλέησα; where the demand for mercy is based on the divine mercy, as in Judaism.[91] The only difference is that God's mercy is now thought of as preceding man's. On the other hand, Jm. 2:13 gives us the traditional Jewish formulation : ἡ γὰρ κρίσις ἀνέλεος τῷ μὴ ποιήσαντι ἔλεος (→ n. 67). κατακαυχᾶται ἔλεος κρίσεως.[92] When the Christian tradition adopts such principles, the new feature is not the thought as such, but the knowledge of God in Christ. If in Jm. 3:17 the ἄνωθεν σοφία is characterised as μεστὴ ἐλέους (with εἰρηνική, ἐπιεικής, εὐπειθής), the meaning of ἔλεος should not be restricted to mercy, but can include "loving-kindness" in general. The same is true of R. 12:8 (ὁ ἐλεῶν ἐν ἱλαρότητι). Nevertheless, it is impossible to make a precise distinction, and elsewhere we find the sense of "pity" or "sympathy," as in the οὐκ ἐλεοῦντες πτωχόν of Did., 5, 2 and Barn., 20, 2, which is used to describe those who are on the way of death.[93] If in all these statements the reference is to the kindness or mercy to be shown in cases of earthly need, elsewhere we read of the mercy which is concerned for the eternal welfare of others. This is plain in Just. Apol., 25, 3; 57, 1, as also in Jd. 22 (though here the text is unfortunately not too certain).[94]

2. God's ἔλεος is often thought of in the original OT sense of "faithfulness," i.e., the gracious faithfulness of God, as in the canticles in Lk. 1, which are saturated with OT themes.[95] How the sense of grace can predominate is seen in Lk. 1:58, where it is said of Elisabeth : ἐμεγάλυνεν ὁ κύριος τὸ ἔλεος αὐτοῦ μετ' αὐτῆς. Similarly in Eph. 2:4 God is described as πλούσιος ὢν ἐν ἐλέει, and in 1 Pt. 1:3 He is extolled as ὁ κατὰ τὸ πολὺ αὐτοῦ ἔλεος ἀναγεννήσας ἡμᾶς.[96]

---

[91] → n. 59; esp. Shab., 151 b: "He who has mercy on men, on him will mercy be shown in heaven"; Test. Zeb. 5:3 : ἔχετε οὖν ἔλεος ἐν σπλάγχνοις ὑμῶν, ὅτι εἴ τι ἂν ποίηση τῷ πλησίον αὐτοῦ, οὕτω κύριος ποιήσει μετ' αὐτοῦ; Ep. Ar., ἐπινοῶν οὖν ἕκαστα πρὸς τὸν ἔλεον τραπήσῃ· καὶ γὰρ ὁ θεὸς ἐλεήμων ἐστίν (here the Jewish thought has a Stoic slant).

[92] Cf. Meinertz Kath. Br., 31. This thought is also found in Mt. 5:7: μακάριοι οἱ ἐλεήμονες, ὅτι αὐτοὶ ἐλεηθήσονται, and materially in Mt. 7:1: μὴ κρίνετε, ἵνα μὴ κριθῆτε· ἐν ᾧ γὰρ κρίματι κρίνετε κριθήσεσθε; cf. also 1 Cl., 13, 2, where the tradition of Mt. 7:1 and par. is used : ἐλεᾶτε, ἵνα ἐλεηθῆτε (cf. also Pol., 2, 3).

[93] Cf. also Mart. Pol., 2, 2 : ἐλεεῖν καὶ ὀδύρεσθαι in relation to the sufferings of those who are ill-treated. Here we have the Gk. sense of sympathetic feeling rather than the idea of merciful action.

[94] Cf. the comm.; it is fairly certain that the command ἐλεᾶτε applies in relation to the διακρινόμενοι, i.e., those endangered by false teachers. What is not certain is the οὓς δὲ ἐλεᾶτε ἐν φόβῳ, which refers to those who are hopelessly lost (cf. what follows : μισοῦντες κτλ.). Does this mean that in relation to such the sympathy stirred in the believer should be prevented from expressing itself through φόβος ? Or should we read ἐᾶτε, ἐλάσατε (Wohlenberg), or ἐκβάλατε (Windisch) instead of ἐλεᾶτε ? 1 Cl., 2, 4 is also uncertain : εἰς τὸ σώζεσθαι μετ' ἐλέους καὶ συνειδήσεως τὸν ἀριθμὸν τῶν ἐκλεκτῶν αὐτοῦ. Can we translate : "By your merciful disposition and inward participation" (Knopf)? Or is God's ἔλεος meant (→ infra), συνειδήσεως being an ancient error (A. v. Harnack, Einführung in die alte Kirchengeschichte [1929], 105 f.)?

[95] Lk. 1:50 (on the basis of ψ 102:17), 54 (ψ 97:3), 72 (Mi. 7:20), 78 : διὰ σπλάγχνα ἐλέους θεοῦ ἡμῶν (cf. the formulations in Test. Zeb. 5:3 f. → n. 91, and esp. 7:3; 8:2, 6).

[96] This corresponds to OT expressions like רַב־חֶסֶד in Ex. 34:6; Nu. 14:18; Ps. 86:5, 15 etc. (LXX : πολυέλεος, which is not found in the NT), and רַבִּים רַחֲמִים in 2 S. 24:14; Ps. 119:156; Neh. 9:27; Da. 9:18 etc. (the LXX alternates).

Here there is a plain connection with the history of salvation (→ n. 48), as also in R. 11:30-32: ... οὕτως καὶ αὐτοὶ νῦν ἠπείθησαν τῷ ὑμετέρῳ ἐλέει ἵνα καὶ αὐτοὶ νῦν ἐλεηθῶσιν.[97] It is striking that Paul speaks of God's ἔλεος only in the passages in R. 9; 11; 15 which are concerned with the history of salvation (→ χάρις; on Gl. 6:16 → infra). God's ἔλεος is His eschatological act in salvation history in Christ, as dogmatically formulated in Tt. 3:5: κατὰ τὸ αὐτοῦ ἔλεος ἔσωσεν ἡμᾶς διὰ λουτροῦ παλιγγενεσίας. In this sense Paul also speaks in R. 9:23 of the σκεύη ἐλέους, ἃ προητοίμασεν εἰς δόξαν, where the judicial wrath of God is the opp. (v. 22). The same sense is very plain in R. 15:8 f.: λέγω γὰρ Χριστὸν διάκονον γεγενῆσθαι περιτομῆς ὑπὲρ ἀληθείας θεοῦ, εἰς τὸ βεβαιῶσαι τὰς ἐπαγγελίας τῶν πατέρων, τὰ δὲ ἔθνη ὑπὲρ ἐλέους δοξάσαι τὸν θεόν. God's ἐλεεῖν (and σκληρύνειν) also refers to eschatological salvation in R. 9:15-18, where Ex. 33:19 is used in formulation. This eschatological awareness is expressed in 1 Pt. 2:10 in the referring of Hos. 1:6, 9 to believing Gentiles: οἵ ποτε οὐ λαός, νῦν δὲ λαὸς θεοῦ, οἱ οὐκ ἠλεημένοι, νῦν δὲ ἐλεηθέντες. In the same awareness Ignatius addresses the churches as ἠλεημένη[98] and Act. Andr., 1 characterises God as the ἐλεήσας ἡμᾶς.

Reference may also be made to God's eschatological ἔλεος in relation to the future judgment, as in Judaism. So Mt. 5:7: μακάριοι οἱ ἐλεήμονες, ὅτι αὐτοὶ ἐλεηθήσονται (→ n. 92). So, too, the desire in 2 Tm. 1:18: δῴη αὐτῷ ὁ κύριος εὑρεῖν ἔλεος παρὰ κυρίου ἐν ἐκείνῃ τῇ ἡμέρᾳ. So, too, the admonition in Jd. 21: ἑαυτοὺς ἐν ἀγάπῃ θεοῦ τηρήσατε, προσδεχόμενοι τὸ ἔλεος τοῦ κυρίου ἡμῶν ... Cf. also 1 Cl., 28, 1: ... φοβηθῶμεν αὐτὸν καὶ ἀπολίπωμεν φαύλων ἔργων μιαρὰς ἐπιθυμίας, ἵνα τῷ ἐλέει αὐτοῦ σκεπασθῶμεν ἀπὸ τῶν μελλόντων κριμάτων.[99]

Mention of God's ἔλεος does not always have express reference to the Christ event. It may simply denote the grace of God, with a stronger or weaker suggestion that this grace has come through Christ. This is plain in Gl. 6:16: εἰρήνη ἐπ' αὐτοὺς καὶ ἔλεος, καὶ ἐπὶ τὸν Ἰσραὴλ τοῦ θεοῦ. It is weaker in various salutations[100] which, like that in Gl.6:16, borrow from Jewish greetings.[101] There is

---

[97] Here ἔλεος is obviously God's act in salvation history. It makes no difference to ἔλεος whether we construe τῷ ὑμετέρῳ ἐλέει with ἵνα ... ἐλεηθῶσιν ("that they may know mercy through the mercy shown to you," Zahn) or whether we make it dependent on ἠπείθησαν ("so these have now been disobedient in face of the mercy shown to you, that they also may receive mercy," Lietzmann).

[98] In the introductions to R., Phld., Sm.; the members are called ἠλεημένοι in Eph., 12, 1; cf. the formulae in Tr., 12, 3 and Phld., prooem. God's ἔλεος is understood as the grace of salvation given through Christ in Herm. v., 3, 9, 1; cf. also 2 Cl., 1, 7; 3, 1; Just. Dial., 43, 2; 106, 1; Dg., 9, 2.

[99] The mercy hoped for in the coming judgment is also referred to in Herm. v., 2, 2, 3; 3, 9, 8; s., 4, 2 (ὅταν οὖν ἐπιλάμψῃ τὸ ἔλεος τοῦ κυρίου → n. 68); 2 Cl., 16, 2 (here the ἔλεος of Jesus); Just. Dial. (8, 4 on the lips of the Jew); 18, 3; 96, 3 (ἵνα ἐλεηθῆτε ὑπὸ τοῦ Χριστοῦ); 108, 3 (... εὐχόμεθα κἂν νῦν μετανοήσαντας πάντας ἐλέους τυχεῖν παρὰ τοῦ εὐσπλάγχνου καὶ πολυελέου πατρὸς τῶν ὅλων θεοῦ); 133, 1 (λαβεῖν); 141, 2 (τυχεῖν).

[100] χάρις, ἔλεος, εἰρήνη in the greetings in 1 Tm. 1:2; 2 Tm. 1:2; Tt. 1:4 ﬡ; 2 Jn. 3; so also the concluding greeting in Ign. Sm., 12, 2 (with ὑπομονὴ διὰ παντός); only ἔλεος and εἰρήνη in the introductory greeting in Pol.; ἔλεος, εἰρήνη and ἀγάπη in Jd. 2; Mart. Pol., prooem.

[101] ἔλεος and εἰρήνη correspond to the epistolary greeting in S. Bar. 78:2 and the marriage greeting in Tob. 7:11 ﬡ. For Gl. 6:16, cf. the final greetings in Ps. Sol. 4:29; 6:9; 7:9; 9:20; 11:9; 13:11, and Str.-B., III, 579.

general reference to God's grace, with reminiscences of Jewish expressions, in 1 Cl., 9, 1: ἱκέται γενόμενοι τοῦ ἐλέους καὶ τῆς χρηστότητος αὐτοῦ προσπέσωμεν καὶ ἐπιστρέψωμεν ἐπὶ τοὺς οἰκτιρμοὺς αὐτοῦ (cf. Ps. Sol. 5:17; 8:33 f.); 56, 16 : πατὴρ γὰρ ἀγαθὸς ὢν παιδεύει εἰς τὸ ἐλεηθῆναι ἡμᾶς διὰ τῆς ὁσίας παιδείας αὐτοῦ, cf. Wis. 11:9; 12:22; Ps. Sol. 16:11 ff.; 18:3 ff. Finally, there may be reference to God's goodness and mercy in relation to individual cases of need or specific persons, as when the sick cry to Jesus : ἐλέησόν με. [102] Paul is aware that he is ἠλεημένος ὑπὸ κυρίου (1 C. 7:25; cf. 2 C. 4:1: καθὼς ἠλεήθημεν; 1 Tm. 1:13, 16), though the grace to which he appeals is directly related to the event of salvation. The same is true of Ign. when, imitating Pauline expressions, he sees in martyrdom the ἐλεηθῆναι of which he will be worthy (R., 9, 2; Phld., 5, 1). On the other hand, cf. when it is said to the woman who is healed in Mk. 5:19 : ἠλέησέν σε (sc. ὁ κύριος), or when Paul says of the healing of Epaphroditus in Phil. 2:27: ὁ θεὸς ἠλέησεν αὐτόν, οὐκ αὐτὸν δὲ μόνον, ἀλλὰ καὶ ἐμέ, or when the desire is expressed in 2 Tm. 1:16 : δῴη ἔλεος ὁ κύριος τῷ 'Ονησιφόρου οἴκῳ (distinct from the eschatological ἔλεος of v. 18). So also Hermes v., 1, 3, 2 : ἀλλ' ἡ πολυσπλαγχνία τοῦ κυρίου ἠλέησέν σε καὶ τὸν οἶκόν σου.

† ἐλεήμων.

ἐλεήμων, "sympathetic," "merciful," is an old Gk. word (→ 478) found, e.g., in Stoic writings (→ ἔλεος, n. 15). It is fairly frequent in the LXX (→ ἔλεος, n. 20), mostly with reference to God (Ex. 22:26 or 27; 34:6; ψ 85:14; 102:8 etc.), but sometimes to men (Prv. 11:17; 19:8 or 11; 20:6). In later Judaism it is commonly used of God (e.g., 2 Macc. 1:24; 11:9; Ps. Sol. 5:2; Ep. Ar., 208; Test. Jud. 19:3; Iss. 6:4; Zeb. 9:7; Philo Som., I, 93), [1] occasionally of men (Test. S. 4:4; A. 4:3; Jos. Ant., 10, 41).

God is not called ἐλεήμων in the NT, though the word is thus used in 1 Cl., 60, 1 in a prayer derived from Jewish tradition ; cf. also Just. Dial., 107, 2. It is said of Christ in Hb. 2:17 that He was made like us ἵνα ἐλεήμων γένηται. [2] That man should be ἐλεήμων is part of the command of God in Did., 3, 8; 2 Cl. 4, 3, and Jesus praises the ἐλεήμονες in Mt. 5:7 (→ 484). This is specially demanded of presbyters in Pol., 6, 1.

† ἐλεημοσύνη.

ἐλεημοσύνη for "sympathy" is late in Gk. (→ ἔλεος, n. 8). The LXX usually has the word for צְדָקָה (צֶדֶק). [1] It also uses it with reference to God's צדקה as His relation to His people or to the righteous. God judges by צדקה (Is. 1:27; 59:16; ψ 34:24 v.l.); צדקה is the norm of His conduct (Is. 28:17; ψ 32:5); the man who keeps the Law (Dt. 6:25;

---

[102] Mk. 10:47 f. and par.; Mt. 9:27; 17:15; Lk. 17:13 (to Abraham, Lk. 16:24). The formula is also found in Is. 33:2 (κύριε ἐλέησον ἡμᾶς = חָנֵּנוּ יְ'); CIG, IV, 8528b (εἰς Ζεὺς Σάραπις ἐλέησον); to earthly lords, Jos. Ant., 9, 64 (δέσποτα ...); Epict. Diss., II, 7, 12 (κύριε ...). Cf. W. Lockton, JThSt, 16 (1915), 548-550.

ἐ λ ε ή μ ω ν. [1] Rabb. רחמנא as a divine name, cf. A. Marmorstein, *The Old Rabbinic Doctrine of God*, I (1927), 101 f.

[2] Christian tradition underlies the invocation of Christ as ἐλεήμων ἐν ὥραις βιαίοις in the Leiden magic pap. J., 395, col. VII, 26 (Preis. Zaub., XIII, 290). For Judaism Michael is the merciful, W. Lueken, *Michael* (1898), 143, 2.

ἐ λ ε η μ ο σ ύ ν η. [1] ἐλεημοσύνη is also used in Is. 38:18 for אמת (God's "faithfulness") and Gn. 47:29; Prv. 3:3; 14:22 for חסד (with אמת) to denote human "kindness."

24:13), the innocent man (ψ 23:4) and he who is oppressed (ψ 102:6) will receive צדקה from Him. Since the judgment in which God's צדקה is active will be in favour of His people or of the righteous, we can understand the rendering ἐλεημοσύνη, especially when the cry for צדקה inspires the prayer for deliverance (Da. 9:16 Θ). In Judaism צדקה has not only the sense of "righteousness" as the conduct corresponding to the norm of right, but also of "benevolent activity," as may be seen already in Da. 4:24, and frequently in Rabbinic usage. [2] Greek speaking Jews can use δικαιοσύνη in this sense, [3] but ἐλεημοσύνη is more common. As thus used, it is similar to ἔλεος (→ ἔλεος, n. 67), referring more to benevolent activity, and even almsgiving, [4] than to the emotion of pity. That (God's) ἐλεημοσύνη is the same as (His) ἔλεος may be seen in Ps. Sol. 9:20; 15:15, cf. with 4:29; 11:2 etc.

In the NT ἐλεημοσύνη is found only in the sense of "benevolent activity," and always to the poor ("almsgiving"): Mt. 6:2-4; Lk. 11:41; 12:33; Ac. 3:2 f., 10; 9:36; 10:2, 4, 31; 24:17. So also Did., 1, 6; 15, 4; 2 Cl., 16, 4. [5] The expression ποιεῖν ἐλεημοσύνην, which corresponds to the OT עשׂה צדקה, is common, as in Judaism (Mt. 6:1-4; Ac. 9:36; 10:2; 24:17); so, too, is διδόναι ἐλεημοσύνην, which corresponds to the Rabb. נתן צדקה (Lk. 11:41; 12:33). [6] That almsgiving is a particular exercise of piety for the Jews, along with praying and fasting, [7] is presupposed in Mt. 6; Ac. 10:4, 31. Together with prayer, it is also a Christian exercise in Did., 15, 4; 2 Cl., 16, 4: καλὸν οὖν ἐλεημοσύνη ὡς μετάνοια ἁμαρτίας· κρείσσων νηστεία προσευχῆς, ἐλεημοσύνη δὲ ἀμφοτέρων· ἀγάπη δὲ καλύπτει πλῆθος ἁμαρτιῶν. [8] There is admonition to ἐλεημοσύνη in Lk. 11:41; 12:33, [9] and in Ac. 9:36 Tabitha is lauded as πλήρης ἔργων ἀγαθῶν καὶ ἐλεημοσυνῶν, ὧν ἐποίει, like Cornelius, whose ἐλεημοσύναι are mentioned as a sign of his piety in Ac. 10:2. [10] As Jesus in Mt. 6:2-4 warns against the misuse of almsgiving in the

---

[2] Str.-B., I, 386-388; II, 188 f.; Schl. Mt., 199 f. On Jewish benevolence cf. Excursus 22 in Str.-B., IV, 536-558.

[3] Tob. 2:14; 12:9; 14:11; Bar. 5:9 (always combined with ἐλεημοσύνη); cf. also 2 C. 9:9 f. On the basis of this understanding אMt. 6:1 has τὴν ἐλεημοσύνην instead of τὴν δικαιοσύνην.

[4] It is difficult to distinguish between general benevolence and almsgiving. On the former, cf. Sir. 3:14 (to the father); 3:30; 12:3 (Heb., where extant, צדקה); Tob. 1:3, 16; 2:14; for the latter, cf. Sir. 29:8; Tob. 4:7, 16. The word is not found in Philo or Jos. In Gk. liter. we have one instance of ἐλεημοσύνη (almsgiving) in the apophthegm of Aristot. recorded in Diog. L., V, 17: ὀνειδιζόμενός ποτε, ὅτι πονηρῷ ἀνθρώπῳ ἐλεημοσύνην ἔδωκεν, Οὐ τὸν τρόπον, εἶπεν, ἀλλὰ τὸν ἄνθρωπον ἠλέησα.

[5] In earlier Christian liter. ἐλεημοσύνη is used for the mercy of God only in Just. Dial., 36, 4, quoting ψ 23:5.

[6] For both expressions, cf. Str.-B., II, 188.

[7] Bousset-Gressm., 176 ff.; cf., e.g., Sir. 7:10; Tob. 12:8 f.

[8] 2 Cl., 16, 4 is based on Tob. 12:8 f. Materially, almsgiving (under ἀγάπη) and prayer are also linked in 1 Pt. 4:7 f.

[9] In both cases the underlying tradition is preserved in more original form in Mt. The πλὴν τὰ ἐνόντα δότε ἐλεημοσύνην of Lk. 11:41 translates the general direction of Mt. 23:26 : καθάρισον πρῶτον τὸ ἐντὸς (τοῦ ποτηρίου, an addition of Mt. ?), into a concrete demand. The meaning is not too clear (cf. the comm.). Either : "As concerns your inward life, give alms," or : "Of what you have, give alms" (Wellhausen suggests that Lk. here rests on a misreading of the original Aram.). Lk. 12:33 : πωλήσατε τὰ ὑπάρχοντα ὑμῶν καὶ δότε ἐλεημοσύνην makes the general and negative direction of Mt. 6:19 : μὴ θησαυρίζετε κτλ., both concrete and positive.

[10] On Ac. 10:4 (31): αἱ προσευχαί σου καὶ αἱ ἐλεημοσύναι σου ἀνέβησαν εἰς μνημόσυνον ἔμπροσθεν τοῦ θεοῦ, cf. Sir. 32:8 f.; S. Dt., 277 on 24:13; Gr. Bar. 12 and Str.-B., II, 696.

service of vanity, so Did., 1, 6 warns against imprudent almsgiving ; for this there are parallels in Jewish writings. [11]

† ἀνέλεος.

ἀνέλεος, "unmerciful," is not surely attested outside the NT. [1] It does not occur in the LXX. Taking the place of the Attic νηλεής (and the later ἀνελεήμων and ἀνηλεής → ἔλεος, 478), it is formed after the analogy of πολυέλεος, which is common in the LXX but does not occur in the NT. It is found only in Jm. 2:13 with reference to God's κρίσις on the μὴ ποιήσας ἔλεος (→ 483). Because it is so uncommon, it is replaced by ἀνίλεως or ἀνίλεος in some MSS.

† ἀνελεήμων.

ἀνελεήμων, "unmerciful," is preferred in later liter. [1] It is fairly common in the LXX, [2] but in the NT is found only with ἄστοργος in the list of vices in R. 1:31.

Bultmann

> ## ἐλεύθερος, ἐλευθερόω,
> ## ἐλευθερία, ἀπελεύθερος

A. The Political Concept of Freedom in the Greek World.

Acc. to Ps.-Plat. Def., 415a to be free is to be at one's own disposal : ἐλεύθερον τὸ ἄρχον ἑαυτοῦ. This is also the general sense in Ps.-Plat. Def., 412d : ἐλευθερία ἡγεμονία βίου· αὐτοκράτεια ἐπὶ παντί· ἐξουσία τοῦ καθ᾽ ἑαυτὸν ἐν βίῳ· ἀφειδία ἐν χρήσει καὶ ἐν κτήσει οὐσίας. The popular understanding is expressed in the linguistically untenable [1] etymology : ἐλεύθερος ὁ ἐλεύθων ὅπου ἐρᾷ (Suid.). This underlying formal sense of independence of others persisted in the Greek world.

1. It was partly fashioned by contrast with the bondage of the slave. According to the general Gk. conviction defined in Aristot. Pol., I, 2, p. 1254a, 14 (→ 263): ὃ ... μὴ

---

[11] Sir. 12:1; Sib., 2, 79.

ἀ ν έ λ ε ο ς. [1] Moult.-Mill. quotes ἀνελεῶς from P. Lips., I, 39, 12 (τύψας με [ἀν]-ελεῶς). This derives from the late but well attested ἀνελεής.

ἀ ν ε λ ε ή μ ω ν. [1] → ἔλεος, 478, and Nägeli, 18; M. J. Lagrange, *Epître aux Romains²* (1922), 34.

[2] Mostly for אַכְזָרִי ("unmerciful"), Prv. 5:9; 11:17; 12:10; 17:11; Sir. 13:12; 32:22; 37:11. For אַכְזְרִיּוּת, Prv. 27:4; for אַכְזָר, Job 30:21 (v.l. ἀνελεημόνως). For זוּר: ἀνελεήμων γίνεσθαι. Job 19:13. Cf. also Wis. 12:5; 19:1. The word is not found in Philo or Jos., or in early Christian literature.

ἐ λ ε ύ θ ε ρ ο ς κ τ λ. Liddell-Scott, *s.v.*; Cr.-Kö., 424 ff.; R. Hirzel, *Themis, Dike u. Verwandtes* (1907), 253 ff.; K. Joël, *Der echte und der xenophontische Sokrates*, II, 2 (1901), 561 ff.; J. Weiss, *Die christliche Freiheit nach d. Verkündigung des Ap. Pls.* (1902); A. Bonhöffer, *Epiktet u. d. NT* (1911); O. Schmitz, *Der Freiheitsgedanke bei Epiktet u. d. Freiheitszeugnis des Pls.* (1923); M. Müller, "Freiheit," ZNW, 25 (1926), 177-236; K. Deissner, "Das Idealbild des stoischen Weisen" (= *Greifswalder Universitätsreden*, 24, 1930); H. Jonas, *Augustin u. das paul. Freiheitsproblem* (1930); W. Brandt, *Freiheit im NT* (1932).

[1] O. Schrader, *Reallexikon d. indogerman. Altertumskunde*, II² (1929), 458 ff. derives the word from Indogerm. *leudho-, Gr. *ἐ-λευθο-ς, then, as with φόβος > φοβερός, ἐλεύθερος. This gives the basic sense of "belonging to a people," and therefore "not subject."

αὐτοῦ φύσει ἀλλ᾽ ἄλλου ἄνθρωπος ὤν, the slave is the one who from the first (= by nature) does not belong to himself but to someone else. The formal sense of freedom naturally orientated itself to the political institution of the δοῦλος because in the main this was hardly contested until the time of the Sophists. Here again our witness is Aristotle, not so much because he energetically attacks the Sophist Alcidamas [2] for his discussion of slavery (Pol., I, 3, p. 1253a, 20 ff.), but rather because of the way in which he tries to refute him, namely, with a sober reference to the συμφέρον and δίκαιον of slavery for some and of ἐλευθερία for others (Pol. I, 15, p. 1255a, 1 ff.; I, 21, p. 1255b, 6 ff.). That the abolition of the distinction between slaves and free men would involve serious consequences for the community is the view not merely of the more fiery author of Ps.-Xenoph. Resp. Ath. (1, 12) but also of Plato (Resp., VIII, 563b). The acceptance of the institution of the δοῦλος and therefore of the ἐλεύθερος is a symptom of the fact that the horizon of Greek life and thought was determined by political reality. In the first instance the Greek knew and understood himself within the orders of the state. Thus the question of freedom was decisively determined by the horizon of political experience. Basically, the question is not that of freedom in general. It is the theoretical and practical question of the freedom of the politically free within the polity, i.e., of the freedom of the polity as an association of the free. In the Gk. world ἐλευθερία is primarily a political concept.

2. Acc. to Aristot. Pol., IV, 10, p. 1296b, 17 ff., ἐλευθερία is one of the essentials of a state. With πλοῦτος, παιδεία and εὐγένεια, it is a ποιόν of the πόλις, while ἡ τοῦ πλήθους ὑπεροχή is a ποσόν. The polity can be succinctly described as κοινωνία τῶν ἐλευθέρων, Pol., III, 4, p. 1279a, 21. Cf. Pol., I, 2, p. 1225b, 20 : ἡ δὲ πολιτικὴ ἐλευθέρων καὶ ἴσων ἀρχή. From another standpoint Plato says that a state ἐλευθέραν τε εἶναι δεῖ καὶ ἔμφρονα καὶ ἑαυτῇ φίλην, Leg., III, 693b. If it lacks these three features, it is unlikely to stand, ibid., 693d. Instead of ἐλευθερία, φιλία, φρόνησις, 693c/d, one might also say ἐλευθερία, φιλία, νοῦ κοινωνία, 694b, or τὸ ἐλεύθερον, φίλον, κοινόν, 697c/d. In Thuc., VI, 89, 6, too, the constitution is extolled which guarantees the greatest power and freedom. In the Gk. understanding of the state freedom is an indispensable element. It is for this reason that Pind. Pyth., 1, 61 f. praises Hieron :

> τῷ πόλιν κείναν θεοδμά-
> τῳ σὺν ἐλευθερίᾳ
> Ὑλλίδος στάθμας Ἱέρων ἐν νόμοις ἔ-
> κτισσε·

In these lines the νόμοι are mentioned along with ἐλευθερία. This gives us the limit within which freedom is to be sought and given, namely, the νόμοι and therefore the essence of the νόμος of the polity. [3] The polity, within the confines of which freedom is known, is grounded in and secured by its νόμος, which is simply an embodiment of the vital, elemental claim of the πολιτεία, the citizens. In it, as the principle of the order of the polity (Aristot. Pol., III, 11, p. 1287a, 18 : ἡ ... τάξις νόμος), the citizens recognise and honour their own binding will to live. Hence, so long as νόμος exercises its binding force on individuals, freedom cannot be freedom from or in opposition to the law, but only under the law. Typical is the passage in Hdt., VII, 104, in which Demaratus explains to the Persian king concerning the Lacedaemonians : ἐλεύθεροι γὰρ ἐόντες οὐ πάντα ἐλεύθεροί εἰσι· ἔπεστι γάρ σφι δεσπότης νόμος, τὸν ὑποδειμαίνουσι πολλῷ ἔτι μᾶλλον ἢ οἱ σοὶ σέ. ποιεῦσι γῶν τὰ ἂν ἐκεῖνος ἀνώγῃ· ἀνώγει δὲ τωὐτὸ αἰεί, οὐκ ἐῶν φεύγειν οὐδὲν πλῆθος ἀνθρώπων ἐκ μάχης, ἀλλὰ μένοντας ἐν τῇ τάξι ἐπικρατέειν ἢ ἀπόλλυσθαι. Cf. III, 38; VII, 102. For a similar view cf. also Aristot. Pol., III, 11, p. 1287a, 18 ff.: τὸν ἄρα νόμον ἄρχειν αἱρετώτερον

---

[2] Cf. J. Kaerst, Geschichte des Hellenismus, I³ (1927), 84, n. 1.
[3] Cf. Kaerst, op. cit., 11 ff.

μᾶλλον ἢ τῶν πολιτῶν ἕνα τινά, κατὰ τὸν αὐτὸν δὲ λόγον τοῦτον, κἂν εἴ τινας ἄρχειν βέλτιον, τούτους καταστατέον νομοφύλακας καὶ ὑπηρέτας τοῖς νόμοις. Cf. IV, 4, p. 1292a, 4 ff. Freedom is to be subordinated to the *nomos* of a polity because the latter alone, as the law of the common will, can guarantee freedom against the tyranny of caprice. It is where the *nomos* rules that the inordinate claims either of an individual, the τύραννος, or of the mass, the πλῆθος, can be controlled and curbed, and political freedom can thus be assured to the citizen in virtue of the reason which rules in the *nomos* (Aristot. Pol., III, 11, p. 1287a, 28 ff.). Only εὐνομία can maintain ἐλευθερία. On this connection cf. also Plat. Ep., 8, 354e/f.

Under the *nomos,* however, freedom means alternation of government. If freedom in political life means self-government, and therefore negatively in relation to others : ἐλεύθεροί τε ἀπ᾽ ἀλλήλων (Plat. Leg., VIII, 832d; cf. Resp., VIII, 576a), this is possible in the fellowship of the polity only if those who are to rule as ἐλεύθεροι (Plat. Men., 86d) will ἄρχειν and ἄρχεσθαι alternately. This is clear in Aristot. Pol., VI, 1, p. 1317b, 2 ff. ἐλευθερία has two basic implications : 1. τὸ ἐν μέρει ἄρχεσθαι καὶ ἄρχειν, and 2. τὸ ζῆν ὡς βούλεταί τις. The two are related in such a way that the first proceeds from the second. For it is from the second, which is orientated to the life of the slave (εἴπερ τοῦ δουλεύοντος τὸ ζῆν μὴ ὡς βούλεται), that there develops the striving τὸ μὴ ἄρχεσθαι, μάλιστα μὲν ὑπὸ μηθενός, εἰ δὲ μή, κατὰ μέρος. Cf. also Aristot. Pol., III, 11, p. 1287a, 16 ff. That the thought of freedom became concretely fixed along these lines may be seen also in Eur. Suppl., 404 ff.:

> ... οὐ γὰρ ἄρχεται
> ἑνὸς πρὸς ἀνδρός, ἀλλ᾽ ἐλευθέρα πόλις.
> δῆμος δ᾽ ἀνάσσει διαδοχαῖσιν ἐν μέρει
> ἐνιαυσίαισιν, οὐχὶ τῷ πλούτῳ διδοὺς
> τὸ πλεῖστον, ἀλλὰ χὠ πένης ἔχων ἴσον.

It is the κοινοὶ νόμοι, however, which cause and enable the people to live in freedom and therefore in alternating self-government. Cf. 429 ff.

> οὐδὲν τυράννου δυσμενέστερον πόλει,
> ὅπου τὸ μὲν πρώτιστον οὐκ εἰσὶν νόμοι
> κοινοί, κρατεῖ δ᾽ εἷς τὸν νόμον κεκτημένος
> αὐτὸς παρ᾽ αὑτῷ· καὶ τόδ᾽ οὐκέτ᾽ ἔστ᾽ ἴσον.

The claim of democracy is that it can best realise this kind of freedom. "But what, think you, does it (democracy) define as the good ? Freedom, I said. For in a democratically governed state you will hear that this is the most beautiful thing, so that for a free man it is fitting only to dwell in such a state," Plat. Resp., VIII, 562b f. A state with a democratic constitution is the best guarantee of freedom because fundamentally and in actual political life it allows to all full citizens the same political rights and thus procures that ἄρχειν for the πλῆθος of the people to the fullest possible degree, cf. Aristot. Pol., IV, 4, p. 1291b, 30 ff.; Eth. Nic., V, 10, p. 1134b, 15. The principle of ἰσότης or ἰσονομία — "the most beautiful of all names," Hdt., III, 80 — makes ἐλευθερία possible in democracy, Plat. Resp., VIII, 557a; Plut. De Dione, 37 (I, 974 f.): ὡς ἐλευθερίας ἀρχὴν οὖσαν τὴν ἰσότητα. Thus ἰσότης can be used almost as a synonym of ἐλευθερία, Plat. Resp., VIII, 563b; Aristot. Pol., VI, 1, p. 1318a, 9 f.; IV, 4, p. 1291b, 34 f.; I, 2, p. 1255b, 20; Hdt., VI, 123, where it is said of Harmodios and Aristogeiton that they won ἐλευθερία for Athens, while in Hdt., VI, 131 it is said that they won for it ἰσονομία. The point at issue in ἰσονομία is primarily equality of voice, ἰσοψηφία, of honour and dignity, ἰσοτιμία, of power, ἰσοκρατία, and especially of public speech in official assemblies, ἰσηγορία. Democracy is seen at work, and freedom is given vivid form, in the free speech of the citizen. This is the main target of Ps.-Xenoph. (Resp. Ath., 1, 2): δίκαιον εἶναι πᾶσι τῶν ἀρχῶν (cf. 1, 3; 3, 13) μετεῖναι ἔν τε τῷ νῦν κλήρῳ καὶ τῇ χειροτονίᾳ καὶ λέγειν (cf. 1, 6 and 9 βουλεύειν, λέγειν, ἐκκλησιάζειν) ἐξεῖναι τῷ βουλομένῳ τῶν πολιτῶν. Cf. 1, 12, where we have the term ἰσηγορία. [4] In Hdt., V, 78 freedom is ἰσηγορία as opposed to tyranny. Cf. also ἰσηγορία καὶ ἐλευθερία in Demosth. Or., 21, 124; Polyb., II, 38, 6; VII, 10, 1. Το ἰσηγορία there corresponds → παρρησία, or rather ἰσηγορία is παρρησία from the standpoint of equality. παρρησία, too, is almost synon. with ἐλευθερία. In the citizen's right to say publicly what he thinks there takes concrete form the free self-government of Greek citizens under the common nomos. The democratic state is charac-terised quite simply by the fact that it is "full" of this παρρησία. In a democracy πρῶτον μὲν δὴ ἐλεύθεροι, καὶ ἐλευθερίας ἡ πόλις μεστὴ καὶ παρρησίας γίγνε-ται, καὶ ἐξουσία ἐν αὐτῇ ποιεῖν ὅ τι τις βούλεται, says Plat. Resp., VIII, 557b. Cf. Polyb., IV, 31, 4 : ἐπεὶ τί καὶ θρασύνομεν τὴν ἰσηγορίαν καὶ παρρησίαν καὶ τὸ τῆς ἐλευθερίας ὄνομα πάντες, εἰ μηδὲν ἔσται προυργιαίτερον (more important) τῆς εἰρήνης; Luc. De Piscatore, 17; Luc. Calumniae non temere credendum, 23. Thus παρρησία becomes the test of ἐλευθερία. Materially, this is what is said in Eur. Suppl., 438 ff.:

> τοὐλεύθερον δ' ἐκεῖνο· τίς θέλει πόλει
> χρηστόν τι βούλευμ' ἐς μέσον φέρειν ἔχων;
> καὶ ταῦθ' ὁ χρῄζων λαμπρός ἐσθ', ὁ μὴ θέλων
> σιγᾷ· τί τούτων ἔστ' ἰσαίτερον πόλει;

For the term παρρησία, cf. Democr. Fr., 226 (Diels, II, 106, 7): οἰκήιον ἐλευθερίης παρρησίη, κίνδυνος δὲ ἡ τοῦ καιροῦ διάγνωσις. "Distinctive of freedom is free speech, the only risk being whether one correctly judges the kairos." It can thus be said : οὐδὲν ἂν εἴη τοῖς ἐλευθέροις μεῖζον ἀτύχημα τοῦ στέρεσθαι τῆς παρρη-σίας. "For free citizens there is no greater misfortune than to be deprived of the right of free speech" (Demosth. Fr., 21 [Sauppe, Oratores Attici, 255, 14]). ἐλευθέρα γὰρ γλῶσσα τῶν ἐλευθέρων (TGF, Adespota Fr., 554).

The concept of freedom in Attic democracy, however, had within it elements which contributed to its degeneration. For if on the one side it fosters the life of the polity by the development of the potentialities of the citizens (Hdt., V, 78; III, 80; VII, 103 f.; Aristot. Pol., V, 10, p. 1316b, 24 f.), on the other it threatens the authority of the com-mon nomos by the promoting of the individual. The explanation is as follows. When within the nomos of the polity a man follows the deeper and more radical law of self, with the secret desire to attain the maximum of individual freedom, he can exercise this autonomy to a certain degree and for a certain period, but in the full flush of freedom he is carried along by the force of his realised desire. Thus the law of the polity gives place to that of the enhanced individual. The freedom established by the nomos even-tually comes to be grounded in its own higher law and thus develops into what it is at root, namely, the freedom of its own nomos. Freed now from the protecting nomos, it is understood more and more in terms of the ὅ τι ἂν βούληταί τις ποιεῖν. From the Gk. standpoint despotism, σφόδρα δουλεία τε καὶ δεσποτεία, can overthrow the state, as the example of Persia showed, because it does not allow the individual his natural liberty, Plat. Leg., III, 697c/698a. But "complete freedom, loosed from all author-ity" (Plat. Leg., III, 698a/b), can also damage the state, because finally it does the same thing. Acc. to Plato it arises ultimately from the loss of αἰδώς, and it is characterised by the fact that in all areas of life one will no longer δουλεύειν τοῖς νόμοις (Leg., III, 700a). Νῦν δὲ ἦρξε μὲν ἡμῖν ἐκ μουσικῆς ἡ πάντων εἰς πάντα σοφίας δόξα καὶ παρανομία, ξυνεφέσπετο δὲ ἐλευθερία. ἄφοβοι γὰρ ἐγίγνοντο ὡς εἰδότες, ἡ δὲ ἄδεια ἀναισχυντίαν ἐνέτεκε· τὸ γὰρ τὴν τοῦ βελτίονος δόξαν μὴ φοβεῖσθαι διὰ θράσος, τοῦτ' αὐτό ἐστι σχεδὸν ἡ πονηρὰ ἀναισχυντία διὰ δή τινος ἐλευ-θερίας λίαν ἀποτετολμημένης (Leg., III, 701a/b). "This freedom is followed at once

---

[4] Cf. on this pt. E. Kalinka, Die pseudoxenophontische Ἀθηναίων πολιτεία (1913), 98, n. 3; 135, n. 2.

by that in which one will not obey authority, and this again by the freedom in which one renounces obedience to parents and their instruction. We are near the end when men are concerned not to be subject to the laws, and the end has come when no one cares about oaths or promises or God, but each manifests and imitates again the old titanic nature of the stories, reaching the point where it was, and thus leading a miserable life in unceasing misfortune," Leg., III, 701b/c. Naturally the degeneration of freedom was not always seen in all its ramifications as in Plato (cf. also Resp., VIII, 562 f.). Nevertheless, it was widely recognised and deplored. Its effects were openly displayed in political decline, esp. that of Attic democracy. The exaltation of ψηφίσματα over the νόμος, the suiting of law to the immediate needs of the people, the resultant capricious sway of the πλῆθος, the rise of demagogues leading and led by the mob, were all symptoms of the general ἀνομία which led to the dissolving of distinctions between masters and slaves, men and women, old and young : Aristot. Pol., IV, 4, p. 1292a, 4 ff.; Xenophon Hist. Graec., I, 7, 12; Ps.-Xenoph. Resp. Ath., 1, 8; Demosth., 23, 87; Aeschin., 3, 103; Aristoph. Nu., 1325 ff., 1409 ff. What Callicles says in the Gorgias (492c): τρυφὴ καὶ ἀκολασία καὶ ἐλευθερία, ἐὰν ἐπικουρίαν ἔχη, τοῦτ' ἔστιν ἀρετή τε καὶ εὐδαιμονία, is a common opinion, and no less what Isoc., 7, 20 blames as the result of false instruction : ἡγεῖσθαι τὴν μὲν ἀκολασίαν δημοκρατίαν, τὴν δὲ παρανομίαν ἐλευθερίαν, τὴν δὲ παρρησίαν ἰσονομίαν, τὴν δ' ἐξουσίαν τοῦ ταῦτα ποιεῖν εὐδαιμονίαν. Cf. 12, 131. This degenerate freedom is dangerous to the state and therefore to the citizen from another angle, for it can easily revert to tyranny, which means the rule, not of nomos, but of the whim of an individual. How extreme freedom can turn into extreme slavery may be seen in Plat. Resp., VIII, 563e ff. Here we can quote only a few lines from Ep. 8 which indicate again the true Gk. understanding of political freedom (Ep. 8, 354e): The Sicilians believed they lived happily prior to the rule of Dionysius and Hipparinos, τρυφῶντές τε καὶ ἅμα ἀρχόντων ἄρχοντες ... They deposed the ten generals, ἵνα δὴ δουλεύοιεν μηδενὶ μήτε σὺν δίκη μήτε νόμῳ δεσπότη, ἐλεύθεροι δ' εἶεν πάντη πάντως· ὅθεν αἱ τυραννίδες ἐγένοντο αὐτοῖς. δουλεία γὰρ καὶ ἐλευθερία ὑπερβάλλουσα μὲν ἑκατέρα πάγκακον, ἔμμετρος δὲ οὖσα πανάγαθον· μετρία δὲ ἡ θεῷ δουλεία, ἄμετρος δὲ ἡ τοῖς ἀνθρώποις· | 355a : Θεὸς δὲ ἀνθρώποις σώφροσι νόμος, ἄφροσι δὲ ἡδονή. It is like a distant echo when Dio C., 56, 43, 14 writes : διά τε οὖν ταῦτα, καὶ ὅτι τὴν μοναρχίαν τῇ δημοκρατίᾳ μείξας τό τε ἐλεύθερόν σφισιν ἐτήρησε καὶ τὸ κόσμιον τό τε ἀσφαλὲς προσπαρεσκεύασεν, ὥστ' ἔξω μὲν τοῦ δημοκρατικοῦ θάρσους ἔξω δὲ καὶ τῶν τυραννικῶν ὕβρεων ὄντας ἐν ἐλευθερίᾳ σώφρονι καὶ ἐν μοναρχίᾳ ἀδεεῖ ζῆν, βασιλευομένους τε ἄνευ δουλείας καὶ δημοκρατουμένους ἄνευ διχοστασίας, δεινῶς αὐτὸν ἐπόθουν.

3. Political freedom is an urgent question in Greece from another standpoint. For ἐλευθεροῦν can mean, not only to liberate from a tyrant, as in Hdt., V, 78, but also to liberate from external foes, as in Aesch. Pers., 403; Plat. Menex., 239d; Ep. 8, 355e; Thuc., III, 54; Xenophon Hist. Graec., V, 2, 12; Aeschin., 3, 132; Ditt. Syll.³, 814, 12 ff. etc. In other words, ἐλευθερία includes the concept of the independence of a state in its external relations. In this respect the concept often has an emphatic sense which is grounded in its connection with internal freedom. As we read in Hdt., VII, 135, when the Persian Hydarnes asked the Lacedaemonians why they would not receive their territory from the Persian king as his subjects, they answered that his advice corresponded to only one half of their experience : τὸ μὲν γὰρ δοῦλος εἶναι ἐξεπίστεαι, ἐλευθερίης δὲ οὔκω ἐπειρήθης, οὔτ' εἰ ἔστι γλυκὺ οὔτ' εἰ μή. εἰ γὰρ αὐτῆς πειρήσαιο, οὐκ ἂν δόρασι συμβουλεύοις ἡμῖν περὶ αὐτῆς μάχεσθαι, ἀλλὰ καὶ πελέκεσι. It is the ἐλευθερία of the Gk. citizen who defends his polity and himself along with it, and this against the threat of βάρβαροι, who are to be judged quite simply as δοῦλοι, Plat. Resp., V, 469c; Eur. Iph. Aul., 1400 f. (→ 262, n. 5); Isoc., 5, 154; Xenoph. Hist. Graec., II, 2, 20; III, 1, 21. If the πόλις is attacked by external enemies, it is also threatened by an inner foe, since it lives only in the free citizens. Their free self-government under their own nomos is always at stake. It is thus no accident that

after the Persian War the term ἐλευθερία can be used as a general expression for the autonomy of a state in the interminable internecine wars: Dio C., 9, 31, 7; 48, 13, 6; Ditt. Syll.³, 497, 10; 386, 5 etc. ἐλευθερία thus comes to mean much the same as πολιτεία, e.g., in Dio C., 54, 25. It also means much the same as σωτηρία, and this is even more important in view of the earlier attestation, Xenoph. Hist. Graec., II, 4, 20: ὑπὲρ τῆς κοινῆς ἀμφοτέρων ἡμῶν σωτηρίας τε καὶ ἐλευθερίας. Cf. the oath of the Chersonesians (c. 300/280 B.C.): ὁμονοησῶ ὑπὲρ σωτηρίας καὶ ἐλευθερίας πόλεος καὶ πολιτᾶν καὶ οὐ προδωσῶ Χερσόνασον, Ditt. Syll.³, 360, 5 ff. Cf. ibid., 342, 15 ff.; Dio C., 45, 31, 2: καὶ γάρ τοι διὰ ταῦτα ἐκεῖνοι μὲν ἡμᾶς καὶ ἔσῳζον καὶ ἠλευθέρουν, οὗτος δὲ πᾶσαν μὲν τὴν ἐλευθερίαν ἡμῶν ... ἀφείλετο, πᾶσαν δὲ δημοκρατίαν κατέλυσεν. Though there are material grounds for the use of ἐλευθερία for the existence of a state, it denotes a shift in meaning. And indeed, after the Peloponnesian War the term developed into a political catchword of the small Gk. states, which in their battles were defending not merely their own freedom but the common "freedom" of the states attacked by them or by their opponents. The Lacedaemonians were the first to claim that they were champions of ἐλευθερία. The speech of the Mitylenians in Thuc., III, 9 ff. gives us a good insight into the situation. They had made common cause with Athens towards the end of the Persian War, ξύμμαχοι μέντοι ἐγενόμεθα οὐκ ἐπὶ καταδουλώσει τῶν Ἑλλήνων Ἀθηναίοις, ἀλλ᾽ ἐπ᾽ ἐλευθερώσει ἀπὸ τοῦ Μήδου τοῖς Ἕλλησι. They thus entered the field with the Athenians as αὐτόνομοι ... καὶ ἐλεύθεροι ... But now the Athenians wished to subjugate them as they did their other allies. And for the sake of their freedom and that of the other allies the Lacedaemonians were now to make alliance with them. Cf. also Thuc., II, 8, 4; 72, 1; IV, 85, 1; Xenoph. Hist. Graec., III, 1, 16; V, 2, 12 etc. Naturally the Athenians, too, claimed to be fighting for ἐλευθερία, Plat. Menex., 242a; 243a; IG, II, 1, Add., 52c, 41: ὑπὲρ τῆς ἐλευθερίας τῶν Ἑλλήνων, Thuc., VI, 83, 2 etc. Similarly the Thebans fought for the ἐλευθερία of Boeotia etc., Thuc., III, 62, 5. ἐλευθερία becomes a magical word in Gk. politics. [5] With this generalised sense there is commonly linked the word αὐτονομία, which is materially very close in the domestic political sphere. From the standpoint of civil law the terms overlap to the degree that "the same legal position is indicated by ἐλευθερία from the standpoint of the sovereign power of the citizens and by αὐτονομία from that of their right as a people." [6] Together the two terms describe the full sovereignty of the πόλις. In actual usage, of course, the words are not differentiated with any great precision, and may be used in a way which makes it difficult to decide whether they complement or merely repeat one another, Xenoph. Hist. Graec., III, 1, 20 f.; Polyb., IV, 27, 5; XXI, 19, 9; XX, 7 etc.; IG, II, 5, 65b; Ditt. Syll.³, 330, 24 f.: ἀποστελλόντων τῶν συνέδρων πρέσβεις πρὸς τὸν βασιλέα ὑπὲρ τῆς ἐλευθερίας καὶ αὐτονομίας τῶν πόλεων (306 B.C.); 322, 2 ff.; 323: ἥ τε φρουρά.ἀπῆλθεν ὅ τε δῆμος ἠλευθερώθη καὶ τοὺς πατρίους νόμους καὶ τὴν δημοκρατίαν ἐκομίσατο (308 B.C.); Dio C., 9, 31, 6, partly αὐτόνομος alone, and partly synon. with ἐλευθερία: Xenoph. Hist. Graec., VI, 3, 7-9; Ditt. Syll.³, 409, 35; Dio C., 45, 35, 1. A good example of this whole use of ἐλευθερία and αὐτονομία occurs in the speech of Nero on the freedom of Greece in Ditt. Syll.³, 814, 12 ff. How little importance is attached to the distinction may be seen in Isoc., who in 4, 115 speaks of αὐτονομία alone and in 117 of ἐλευθερία καὶ αὐτονομία (cf. Polyb., IV, 27, 5). In Ditt. Syll.³, 142, 19 ff. we have the text of the treaty of Chios (378/77 B.C.): συμμάχος δὲ ποιεῖσ[θα]ι [Χί]ος ἐπ᾽ ἐλευθ[ε]ρίαι καὶ αὐτονομί[α]ι, μὴ παραβαίνοντας τῶν ἐν ταῖς στήλαις γεγραμμένων περὶ τῆς ἐρήνης μηδέν. In his rendering of the same conditions Diodor. has only πάσας (sc. πόλεις) δ᾽ ὑπάρχειν αὐτονόμους (XV, 28, 4).

---

[5] Cf. M. Pohlenz, Aus Platos Werkstatt (1913), 242 f.; 285 f.; H. Schäfer, Staatsform u. Politik (1932), 173.

[6] T. Mommsen, Staatsrecht, III, 1 (1887), 658; U. Wilcken, SBA, 1929, 292, n. 2; J. Kaerst, op. cit., II³, 80.

B. The Philosophical Concept of Freedom in Hellenism (Stoicism).

1. In Hellenism, and predominantly in Cynic-Stoic philosophy, the extolling of freedom not only does not cease but actually increases. The question of Socrates in Xenoph. Mem., IV, 5, 2 : "Tell me, Euthydemos, do you believe that freedom is a beautiful and glorious good for individuals as well as the state ?" is answered not merely by Euthydemos but by the whole age with an emphatic affirmative. Xenophon himself often praises freedom. It is equal to all earthly treasures, Hist. Graec., IV, 1, 35 f.; it is worth dying for, *ibid.*, IV, 4, 6; cf. An., I, 7, 3; III, 2, 13. But it is even more emphatically praised in the true Cynic tradition. The Cynic is the one who "stands out as ἐλεύθερος, ἐλευθερωτής, ἐλευθεριάζων, who fears no human lord, who is subject only to God, ἐλεύθερος ὑπὸ τὸν Δία (Diogenes Cynicus Ep., 7 [R. Hercher, Epistolographi Graeci, 237]), who not only loves freedom but prefers it to all else (Diog. L., VI, 71). He is a constant enemy and critic of the Macedonian rulers and Dionysus. He does not cease to blame tyrants and to bewail their misery and constant fear, which makes them slaves. He counts them fortunate when they lose their rule and can live ἐλευθέρως in Hellas. He also attacks their parasites, preferring his Attic freedom to all the attractions of court. He extols Harmodios and Aristogeiton, and is proud of living in the city which Hellas liberated from the Medes ... Antisthenes writes περὶ ἐλευθερίας καὶ δουλείας, and the Cynic speaks of these to all men." [7] The Stoic disciples and heirs are no less instant to praise ἐλευθερία as τὸ μέγιστον ἀγαθόν, Epict. Diss., IV, 1, 52, as γενναῖον καὶ ἀξιόλογον, *ibid.*, IV, 1, 54; I, 12, 12, which can be mentioned along with εὐδαιμονία, Epictet. Ench., 1, 4. Freedom is τὸ τῆς ἀρετῆς ὄνομα, Epict. Gnom. Stob., 31. The sentence with which Dio Chrysostomos opens his discussion of δουλεία καὶ ἐλευθερία, Or., 14, 1, repeats the general view : οἱ ἄνθρωποι ἐπιθυμοῦσι μὲν ἐλεύθεροι εἶναι μάλιστα πάντων, καί φασι τὴν ἐλευθερίαν μέγιστον τῶν ἀγαθῶν, τὴν δὲ δουλείαν αἴσχιστον καὶ δυστυχέστατον ὑπάρχειν. He does, of course, go on to say : αὐτὸ δὲ τοῦτο, ὅ τι ἐστὶ τὸ ἐλεύθερον εἶναι ἢ ὅ τι τὸ δουλεύειν, οὐκ ἴσασιν; and this shows us that, in contrast to the Gk. view, the concept of freedom has now become problematical.

2. For the freedom which is now the subject of thought and propaganda is only secondarily and decreasingly the freedom of citizens or the state. It is sensed that there is a much more radical freedom, namely, that of the individual set apart and under the law of his own nature or of human nature generally. The political concept turns into a philosophical. With Sophist enlightenment and the decay of the Greek state man is no longer either theoretically or practically under the self-evident *nomos* of a concrete community. He is directed to his individual nature and to the general cosmos as the guiding lines of his self-understanding and as the horizons of his experience. The question of freedom thus arises in the light of this natural interpretation of existence. If the new concept of freedom is attained in opposition to the political, [8] this is simply a proof that the concept lives on and that it is now involved in new problems. There is full awareness of the change of use. The reinterpretation is naturally understood to a large extent as a discovery of the original meaning. It may be asserted : ... οὕτω δὴ ἀποφαίνει ὁ λόγος οὐ τοὺς φιλοσόφους μεταφέροντας τὰ ὀνόματα, ἀλλὰ τοὺς πολλοὺς τῶν ἀνοήτων ἀνθρώπων διὰ τὴν ἀπειρίαν, Dio Chrys. Or., 15, 32.

The basic formal meaning remains the same. The Gk. tradition of man's self-understanding is not broken. Here, however, is a natural understanding of man in general. Typical is Diog. L., VII, 121: μόνον τε ἐλεύθερον (sc. τὸν σοφόν), τοὺς δὲ φαύλους δούλους. εἶναι γὰρ τὴν ἐλευθερίαν ἐξουσίαν αὐτοπραγίας, τὴν δὲ δουλείαν στέρησιν αὐτοπραγίας. εἶναι δὲ καὶ ἄλλην δουλείαν τὴν ἐν ὑποτάξει, καὶ τρίτην

---

[7] Joël, *op. cit.*, 562 f.
[8] Cf. Dio Chrys. Or., 14 *passim;* Epict. Diss., IV, 1, 6 ff.; Epict. Gnom. Stob., 38 f.; Pisidian inscr., Hermes, 23 (1888), 542 etc.

τὴν ἐν κτήσει τε καὶ ὑποτάξει, ᾗ ἀντιτίθεται ἡ δεσποτεία, φαύλη οὖσα καὶ αὐτή. Cf. Philo Omn. Prob. Lib., 21: οὐδὲν ἄλλο ἄλλῳ συγγενὲς οὕτως, ὡς αὐτοπραγία ἐλευθερίᾳ. The meaning of freedom is more popularly expressed in Epict. Diss., IV, 1, 1: Ἐλεύθερός ἐστιν ὁ ζῶν ὡς βούλεται, ὃν οὔτ' ἀναγκάσαι ἔστιν οὔτε κωλῦσαι οὔτε βιάσασθαι, οὗ αἱ ὁρμαὶ ἀνεμπόδιστοι, αἱ ὀρέξεις ἐπιτευκτικαί, αἱ ἐκκλίσεις ἀπερίπτωτοι. Cf. ibid., I, 12, 9; II, 1, 23; Philo Omn. Prob. Lib., 41. Here, too, freedom is independent self-determination. To seek freedom is to seek and promote this. To enquire into it is to enquire into what makes man free and self-determining, or, as we read in Epict. Diss., IV, 1, 62, into what makes him ἀκώλυτον ... καὶ αὐτεξούσιον. In general terms this is self-knowledge, rational insight into one's own existence, knowledge of life : ἡ ἐπιστήμη τοῦ βιοῦν, ibid., IV, 1, 63. This knowledge must consider in what spheres we may or may not exercise free dominion. It sees from experience that external things, body, possessions, family etc., are not at our disposal — the σῶμα is an ἀλλότριον, ὑπεύθυνον παντὸς τοῦ ἰσχυροτέρου, ibid., IV, 1, 66. On the other hand, it sees that what is inward (τὰ ἔσω, Epict. Diss., II, 13, 11; Ench., 29, 7), the soul, [9] is completely under our control, and with the soul esp. χρῆσις φαντασιῶν and προαίρεσις, "ideas" and "principles." For the former, cf. a good example in Epict. Diss., III, 24, 67 ff.: διὰ τοῦτο ἔλεγεν (sc. Διογένης) ὅτι "ἐξ οὗ μ' Ἀντισθένης ἠλευθέρωσεν, οὐκέτι ἐδούλευσα." πῶς ἠλευθέρωσεν; ἄκουε τί λέγει· "ἐδίδαξέν με τὰ ἐμὰ καὶ τὰ οὐκ ἐμά. κτῆσις οὐκ ἐμή. συγγενεῖς, ... φήμη ... διατριβή, πάντα ταῦτα ὅτι ἀλλότρια· σὸν οὖν τί; χρῆσις φαντασιῶν· ταύτην ἔδειξέν μοι ὅτι ἀκώλυτον ἔχω, ἀνανάγκαστον, οὐδεὶς ἐμποδίσαι δύναται, οὐδεὶς βιάσασθαι ἄλλως χρήσασθαι ἢ ὡς θέλω. τίς οὖν ἔχει μου ἐξουσίαν; Cf. I, 1, 12; Ench., 6. For the latter, cf. Diss., I, 17, 21 ff.: ἄνθρωπε, προαίρεσιν ἔχεις ἀκώλυτον φύσει καὶ ἀνανάγκαστον. Thus no one can prevent you agreeing with the truth. The same applies in relation to impulse, desire and abnegation. Nor can you be forced in respect of the fear of death. Only τὸ σὸν δόγμα exerts compulsion in this case : προαίρεσιν προαίρεσις ... ἐὰν θέλῃς, ἐλεύθερος εἶ· ἐὰν θέλῃς ... πάντα κατὰ γνώμην ἔσται ἅμα τὴν σὴν καὶ τὴν τοῦ θεοῦ. [10]

To attain to freedom, however, knowledge of what I can control (τὰ ἐφ' ἡμῖν) and cannot control (τὰ ἐπ' ἄλλοις, τὰ ἀλλότρια) must be worked out and maintained both theoretically and practically. In pursuit of this basic insight one must free oneself increasingly from false δόγματα in which external existence imposes itself upon me as my reality and seeks to supplant true reality, the προαίρεσις, which I myself am, Epict. Diss., II, 10, 1; III, 1, 40; IV, 5, 12. οὐκ ἐνδέχεται τὸ φύσει ἐλεύθερον ὑπ' ἄλλου τινὸς ταραχθῆναι ἢ κωλυθῆναι πλὴν ὑφ' ἑαυτοῦ. ἀλλὰ τὰ δόγματα αὐτὸν ταράσσει. ὅταν γὰρ ὁ τύραννος εἴπῃ τινὶ "δήσω σου τὸ σκέλος," ὁ μὲν τὸ σκέλος τετιμηκὼς λέγει "μή, ἐλέησον," ὁ δὲ τὴν προαίρεσιν τὴν ἑαυτοῦ λέγει "εἴ σοι λυσιτελέστερον φαίνεται, δῆσον" ... "ἐγώ σοι δείξω ὅτι κύριός εἰμι." "πόθεν σύ; ἐμὲ ὁ Ζεὺς ἐλεύθερον ἀφῆκεν," Epict. Diss., I, 19, 8 f. Cf. Ench., I, 5, 5.

Purification from false δόγματα, however, implies practical withdrawal from human life around. For one thing, this means restriction of desires. Life is a feast. Something is handed to one. ἐκτείνας τὴν χεῖρα κοσμίως μετάλαβε. παρέρχεται· μὴ κάτεχε. οὔπω ἥκει· μὴ ἐπίβαλλε πόρρω τὴν ὄρεξιν, ἀλλὰ περίμενε, μέχρις ἂν γένηται κατὰ σέ. If it satisfies, one is a worthy guest at the table of the gods. "But if of yourself you do not take what is proffered ... you are not merely a worthy guest of the gods ; you will also reign with them," Epict. Ench., 15; cf. Diss., IV, 1, 87. Furthermore, withdrawal from the world means surrender to the pressure of existence, abandonment to circumstances, committal to God. "I have never been thwarted in what I willed or forced in what I did not will. But how is this possible ? I have subjected the course of my life to God. He wills that I have fever ; I also will it. He wills that I seek something ; I also will it. He wills that I desire something ; I also will it. He wills that I attain something ;

---

[9] Cf. Joël, op. cit., 572.
[10] Cf. Epict. Diss., II, 15, 1; IV, 1, 100 ff.; Ench., 9; Philo Deus Imm., 47.

I also will it. He does not will ; I do not will ... Who then can hinder or force me contrary to my resolve ?", Epict. Diss., IV, 1, 89 f. Cf. I, 12, 8 f.; II, 16, 42; 19, 29; 23, 42; Ench., 53, 1; M. Ant., 5, 27; 6, 16. The ardour of the passage betrays the resolution of the philosopher to attain sovereignty over the cosmos in himself, in his inner life. The way of surrender to the cosmos seems to bring about the opposite result. But in fact it is the means to autonomy. For it is only a surrender of what I am not, while what I am remains intact. And with the surrender of what I am, I give up, I let go, that which oppresses me, namely, circumstances. And precisely in so doing I set my inner self free. That surrender to God is meant thus, i.e., that it always implies an attempt to secure the ego, may be seen in an inconsistency in relation to genuine surrender to what the world brings upon us, for it is commanded that in face of too great a pressure of the burdens of existence man should seek escape in death. We have the recurrent image : καπνὸν πεποίηκεν ἐν τῷ οἰκήματι; ἂν μέτριον, μενῶ· ἂν λίαν πολύν, ἐξέρχομαι. τούτου γὰρ <δεῖ> μεμνῆσθαι καὶ κρατεῖν, ὅτι ἡ θύρα ἤνοικται, Epict. Diss., I, 25, 18. [11]

Liberation from the world is only possible, however, if there is in the third place liberation from that which represents the world in us, from that whereby it obviously takes possession of us, namely, from πάθη. In this we abandon ourselves to the impulsion of things. In its neutralisation we withdraw from them. We need not here recount the individual passions, [12] cf. in the Enchiridion of Epict. anxiety in 12, 1, anger in 20, sympathy in 16, astonishment in 19, 2 etc.; but cf. also ἐπιθυμίαι in Xenoph. Ap., 16; Mem., IV, 5, 3 and 6; Philo Rer. Div. Her., 267 ff.; Epict. Gnom. Stob., 38. We may simply affirm that the muffling of passions by recollection of the transitoriness of things [13] finds the eventual liberation of man in the fulfilment of a definite role in life. In ceaseless striving, as we see in the monotonous and plerophoric diatribe of Epictetus, man must learn to despise the things which he cannot control (Epict. Ench., 19, 2), so that he may play well the part which he has to play. "Remember that you are an actor in a role appointed by the author, whether short or long. If He wants you to be a beggar, see that you play the role in a way which is true to life. Your task is to play well the part assigned to you. It is the task of another to select this role," *ibid.*, 17. [14] To be able to play this part well, however, man must free himself from one πάθος in particular, namely, the fear of death. This is the basic πάθος of existence, and it arises most forcefully where man from the very first is conscious of the isolation of individual existence in the vastness of the cosmos. It dominates man in concern for himself, and causes him to try to control what cannot be controlled. Περὶ τίνος γὰρ φοβήσῃ; περὶ τῶν σεαυτοῦ, ὅπου σοι ἡ οὐσία τοῦ ἀγαθοῦ καὶ τοῦ κακοῦ; καὶ τίς τούτων ἐξουσίαν ἔχει; τίς ἀφελέσθαι αὐτὰ δύναται, τίς ἐμποδίσαι; οὐ μᾶλλον ἢ τὸν θεόν, ἀλλ' ὑπὲρ ... τῶν οὐδὲν πρὸς σέ; καὶ τί ἄλλο ἐξ ἀρχῆς ἐμελέτας ἢ διακρίνειν καὶ τὰ σὰ καὶ οὐ σά, τὰ ἐπὶ σοὶ καὶ οὐκ ἐπὶ σοί, τὰ κωλυτὰ καὶ ἀκώλυτα; τίνος δὲ ἔνεκα προσῆλθες τοῖς φιλοσόφοις; ἵνα μηδὲν ἧττον ἀτυχῆς καὶ δυστυχῆς; οὐκοῦν ἄφοβος μὲν οὕτως ἔσει καὶ ἀτάραχος (Epict. Diss., IV, 1, 82 f.). To become free is especially to rid oneself of the fear of death. Every effort is to be made in this direction : ἐπὶ τοῦτον (sc. τὸν τοῦ θανάτου φόβον) οὖν μοι γυμνάζου, ἐνταῦθα νευέτωσαν οἱ λόγοι πάντες, τὰ ἀσκήματα, τὰ ἀναγνώσματα, καὶ εἴσῃ ὅτι οὕτως μόνως ἐλευθεροῦνται ἄνθρωποι (Epict. Diss., III, 26, 39). In the fearless distance of neutralised passion, in which there is voluntary surrender to the ineluctable power of the surrounding world, man takes himself in hand and thus finds freedom.

He does not see, of course, that this violent process of withdrawal from the cosmos and retreat into inwardness has its secret basis in, and brings to expression, that which

---

11 Cf. Schmitz, op. cit., 28.
12 Cf. Joël, op. cit., 608 ff.
13 Cf. Epict. Diss., III, 24, 85 ff.
14 Cf. further examples in Schmitz, op. cit., 26.

is shunned as bondage, namely, the fear of death. The impossibility of this freedom impresses itself upon him most powerfully in the practical form of its unattainability. It is recognised that the demand for this freedom can never be fully satisfied. It is always an ideal even for those who in virtue of their insight and exertion may be called ἐλεύθεροι, the σοφοί, φιλόσοφοι, φρόνιμοι, παιδευόμενοι, σπουδαῖοι, φίλοι τοῦ θεοῦ or whatever else we call them. [15] "You are therefore ... free ? By the gods I hope to be, and desire it, but I cannot yet look the Lord in the face, I still value the body, I give much to keep it unharmed even though it is not unharmed," Epict. Diss., IV, 1, 151. "Show me a man who is sick but still happy, who is in danger but still happy, who is dying but still happy, who is proscribed but still happy, who is the victim of misfortune but still happy; show me such a man. By the gods, I desire to see a Stoic. But you cannot show me one who is perfect ; so show me one who strenuously exerts himself to be so, who strives thereafter. Do me the favour ; do not produce an ancient as the marvel which I have not so far seen," Diss., II, 19, 24 f. Only in isolated figures like Diogenes or Socrates has there been achieved the encouraging example of a truly free man, the possibility of such freedom being thereby demonstrated, Diss., IV, 1, 114 ff.; 123 ff.; 152 ff. etc.

But what is the fruit of this freedom ? Wherein is it enjoyed ? In the peace which is given by attained assurance, and in unshakable rest of soul : οὐκ ἔστιν εὑρεῖν ἀσφαλῆ σύνοδον, πιστόν, ἰσχυρόν, ἀνεπιβούλευτον; οὕτως ἐφίστησιν καὶ ἐννοεῖ, ὅτι, ἐὰν τῷ θεῷ προσκατατάξῃ ἑαυτόν, διελεύσεται ἀσφαλῶς, Epict. Diss., IV, 1, 97 f. Νῦν ἐμοὶ κακὸν οὐδὲν δύναται συμβῆναι, ἐμοὶ λῃστὴς οὐκ ἔστιν, ἐμοὶ σεισμὸς οὐκ ἔστιν, πάντα εἰρήνης μεστά, πάντα ἀταραξίας, Diss., III, 13, 13. Ἐλευθερία and ἀταραξία or ἀπάθεια or even εὔροια are identical in substance. Cf. Epict. Diss., I, 1, 22; 24, 8; II, 1, 21; 16, 41; 18, 28; III, 15, 12; IV, 1, 83 f.; Ench., 29, 7 etc. The man who in the press of the world consciously and deliberately seeks flight in inwardness enjoys the freedom therein attained in the impregnable impassibility of isolated lordship. In so doing he only fulfils what he is, a "part of God," a "son of God," even "God" Himself, Epict. Diss., I, 14, 6 ff.; 19, 9; II, 8, 11 ff.; II, 17, 33 etc.

C. The Concept of Freedom in the NT.

1. In Stoic teaching freedom is man's control over menacing external existence by the conscious and deliberate control of his own soul. The NT, however, realises — generally speaking — that even in the retreat into inwardness man is not free. For in the NT it is evident that freedom is not absent because there is inadequate control of existence but because there is no control of it at all, and therefore no self-dominion. It realises that existence is threatened by itself and not by something outside ; it realises that it is itself deficient, with all that it does. Hence to take oneself in hand is simply to grasp a deficient existence. Self-preservation by retreat into inwardness is merely a way of losing one's true self. In face of lost existence there is only one possibility of coming to oneself, and this is by surrender of one's own will to the will and power of an external force. Man attains to self-control by letting himself be controlled.

More concretely the NT uses ἐλευθερία for freedom from sin (R. 6:18-23; Jn. 8:31-36), from the Law (R. 7:3 f.; 8:2; Gl. 2:4; 4:21-31; 5:1, 13), and from death (R. 6:21 f.; 8:21). Freedom is freedom from an existence which in sin leads through the Law to death. As we may see from R. 6:20 — and so far as possible we shall restrict ourselves to the context of the ἐλευθερία passages quoted — existence in sin is one which is subject to sin : δοῦλοι ... τῆς ἁμαρτίας (R. 6:20, cf. Jn. 8:34). The fulfilment of this relationship is the lawlessness and indiscipline which lead

---

[15] Cf. the Index in Schenkl, *s.v.* or Leisegang on Philo, *s.v.*

to anarchy (R. 6:19b). But lawlessness and indiscipline are surrender to the craving
(→ ἐπιθυμία) of the → σάρξ, to the concupiscent hunger of self-centred earthly
and carnal life. They are the abandonment of man to his intense will to maintain
life. Freedom from sin is necessarily freedom from man's physical desire for life,
for himself.

This desire is unleashed by the Law. In itself the Law is the holy, righteous
and good will of God (R. 7:12). It is appointed for life (R. 7:10), which consists
in living for others, in love (R. 13:9; Gl. 5:14). It is the claim of God made on
all men and given written form in Israel. In it man's history is summoned to fulfilment of God's will. But in the existence of man as it is dominated by sin, by the
self-will of being, it becomes a summons of autonomous existence arbitrarily to
live for itself. The Law brings out the sin of existence in experience (R. 7:7, 13;
3:20 [5:13]). In existence dominated by sin and devoted to self-glory (R. 2:21),
it is experienced as the law of self-preservation, as a call to self-seeking : τὰ
παθήματα τῶν ἁμαρτιῶν τὰ διὰ τοῦ νόμου (R. 7:5), sinful affections being
mediated through the Law. It is "the law of sin in my members" (R. 7:23), the
claim of God misused by the self-seeking love of life to promote itself in my
physical reality. It is an occasion (ἀφορμή, R. 7:8) for the development of my own
"phenomenon" (R. 7:13), not merely when there breaks forth by it the anarchic
impulse referred to in R. 6:17 ff., but also when the nomistic impulse is kindled
thereby. It is of this that the passages speak which refer expressly to freedom
from the Law, especially in Galatians. The freedom "to which Christ has made
us free" [16] (Gl. 5:1), to which "you are called" (Gl. 5:13), which we "have in
Christ Jesus" (Gl. 2:4), is concretely the freedom from the necessity of circumcision for justification before God. And this freedom — as we learn from the
unity of the Law in Gl. 5:3 — is only an example of freedom from the Law in
general as the way to God. It is an acute instance of freedom from the Law which
summons man to meritorious achievements in God's eyes. The Law is in view
when there is reference to freedom from that which stirs man to be his own master,
not by transgressing the Law, but by fulfilling it according to his own interpretation. Here, one might say, we have the Law by which the self-will of existence (i.e., sin) asserts itself in the form of fashioning oneself according to one's
interpretation of the demands of God. In what seems to be honest fulfilment of
the will of God, man still follows his own needs and secretly does his own will
(R. 10:3; Phil. 3:9). Freedom from the Law thus means specifically freedom from
the moralism which awakens hidden self-seeking. It means freedom from the secret
claim which man makes on himself in the form of legal demand. It means freedom
from the meeting of this claim in the form of legal achievement. It means freedom
from self-lordship before God in the guise of serious and obedient responsibility
towards Him.

A further feature of existence in sin under the Law is brought out at a point
which embraces all human existence. To be in sin is to be in deception, i.e., in
falsehood. It is true that this matter is touched on only indirectly in the context of
Jn. 8:32, but it is no less clearly perceived in Jn. than it is in Paul (→ ἀλήθεια,
I, 245; → ψεῦδος). The severing of existence from God means regarding oneself
as God, and this implies concealment of and blindness to one's own true reality in

---

[16] On the textual problems, which do not affect our general understanding, cf. Zn. Gl.,
ad loc.; on the linguistic background of the formulation, cf. the debatable conclusions of
Deissmann LO⁴, 274-281.

which God seeks to declare Himself (R. 2:18 ff.). There is constant self-deception. The truth that life comes from God is suppressed. Falsehood is pursued in the persistent attempt at self-rule. And this attempt is itself concealed from oneself and others in various ways. Freedom from sin and from the Law thus includes essentially freedom from the self-deception of autonomous existence by the disclosure of truth.

The self-seeking existence which goes astray in sin leads finally to death. The wakening of sin in the Law, i.e., of sinful existence by the summons of the Law, means that existence falls victim to death (R. 7:9-11). For the awakening of sinful existence in the claim of the Law implies the surrender of one's being to an existence which is referred to itself and not to God and to life, having separated itself from God and therefore from life. Sin carries death within it. Death is present as that wherein it "lives" and therefore as that wherein its "life" is known (R. 5:21). Death is its power. Living by death (R. 6:23), [17] in separation from God, it promotes its life by death (1 C. 15:56; R. 5:12). In death sin achieves its being in a very real sense. This may be seen in the κτίσις, which is set under the sin which rules man (the φθορά, R. 8:21). Even in nature, which is subordinated to the historical existence of man, the reality of separation from God may be seen in the process of corruption. The absence of God in the life of creation is manifested with pain and sighing in the power of its corruption. More particularly, however, the triumph of death in sin may be seen in the fact that sin continually and in the long run definitively actualises it in the existence of man. Man, who fulfils sin existentially, "abideth not in the house for ever" (Jn. 8:35). By pursuing the separation of his existence from life already accepted by him, he moves to eternal corruption. In the very process of his life he brings about death. This is to be seen in the course of his life. For his works, which are the fruits in which his existence issues, have death as their goal and end. The τέλος of what man does is death (R. 6:21) in the twofold sense that he brings death on himself and also brings it to others in his works. In works sin causes man to grasp his life in relation to the Law and it therefore enables the fatal power of autonomous life to consume himself and others. With respect to this existence which in sin becomes independent through the Law and which is thus impelled towards death, freedom means freedom from self and therefore from an existence given up to death. It is freedom from the law of life which delivers up fallen existence of itself to ruin, i.e., from the "law of sin and death" (R. 8:2).

2. How is freedom attained in existence as thus understood? According to the context, the primary answer is "through the act of Jesus Christ." "To freedom Christ has made us free" (Gl. 5:1). As may be seen from the parallel passages in Gl. 3:13 and 4:4, the reference is to the event of the life of Christ offered up in substitutionary death for others in obedience to the will of God. Our freedom, then, is not an existential return to the basis of individual existence, the soul. It is the event of a historical life radically sacrificed for others. The Son makes us free (Jn. 8:36), the Son who achieves His exaltation in the surrender of His own claim to life.

The second answer to the question how freedom is attained in existence is "through the call which comes to man in the Gospel." For "you are called to

---

[17] One might almost say that death is the account accruing to sin (τὰ γὰρ ὀψώνια τῆς ἁμαρτίας θάνατος).

freedom" (Gl. 5:13). The two answers are not unrelated. The second is linked with the first as follows. In the call of the Gospel men are called to the act of Jesus Christ as the basis of a new life of freedom. We may thus say that in the call of the Gospel there is a real presence of the event of the person of Christ in those who are called. Something of this relationship may be seen in the ἐλευθερία passages. It is said in R. 8:2 that the law of the living and life-giving Spirit in Jesus Christ (ὁ ... νόμος τοῦ πνεύματος τῆς ζωῆς ἐν Χριστῷ Ἰησοῦ) "has made you free from the law of sin and death." We then read in v. 3: "For what the law could not do because of the weakness of carnal (fallen) existence, God has done through the sending of his own Son in sinful flesh, to condemn sin in the flesh." Hence the act of God fulfilled in Jesus Christ must be the basis of the activity of the life-giving Spirit who makes us free, and therefore the basis of our freedom in and under the activity of the Spirit. The claim of the life-giving Spirit in Jesus Christ is thus none other than the claim made on us by the act of God fulfilled in Jesus Christ. That this is so may be seen from v. 4. Here we have the goal of the act fulfilled in Jesus Christ: "That what the Law advances as a just demand may be fulfilled in us who lead our lives according to the measure of the Spirit and not of the flesh." In the claim of the Spirit the act of God fulfilled in Jesus Christ fulfils in us what the Law has in view to the degree that we do not yield to the claim of our own lives but follow the Spirit in whom we stand and who is the Spirit of God or of Christ (R. 8:9). As the Spirit applies the act of God in Jesus Christ, who has overcome us, there is fulfilled in us that which the Law as the will of God demands of us for life. In other words, there has taken place the concrete history of the loving act of Jesus Christ which bears and which therefore covers and remits the sin of others. The love of God as enacted once for all in the death and resurrection of Jesus Christ raises upon us in the Spirit the claim that we should obediently recognise it as what it is, namely, the act of divine life accomplished for us and eternally sustaining us. If we open our lives to this incursion of the Spirit of the act of God in Jesus Christ, there takes place in them the grounding of our lives in the realised love of Jesus Christ. By the Spirit and power of the life of Jesus Christ radically offered up in love, there is brought into being in our lives an existence which is unselfish and self-forgetting because it is dynamically hidden in love and can no longer be self-seeking or self-willed. In the Spirit of the freedom of Jesus Christ, there arises our freedom.

The incursion of the Spirit of the liberating event of the history of Jesus Christ takes place in the call of the Gospel. This call was issued already to Israel in the form of the promise. It created the Jerusalem which is above, the true Israel, to which, as to those who are free, the called of Christ now belong also (Gl. 4:21-31). According to Jn. 8:31 this call is given in Christ's own Word. As the Word in which Jesus Himself speaks (Jn. 8:14), it mediates the truth which is Jesus Himself in His exaltation through suffering (Jn. 14:6). This truth makes free by covering man in its upholding love. As the Spirit of truth the call continually makes the truth known (Jn. 16:13). This takes place concretely in the apostolic Gospel through the activity of those who dispense the life-giving ministry of the Spirit (2 C. 3:6) and therefore the ministry of the κύριος Himself, who is thus the freedom which fashions existence into ever-increasing glory under the impulsion of the Spirit of the κύριος (2 C. 3:17 f.).

The incursion of the Spirit in the event of the Gospel, however, takes place materially and in time, from the standpoint of Christian existence, in baptism. The liberated are the baptised. This may be seen in R. 6:17 f., which is set in the context of the baptismal discussion of 6:1 ff. Bondage under sin is past through ὑπακοῦσαι ... ἐκ καρδίας εἰς ὃν παρεδόθητε τύπον διδαχῆς, i.e., through the fulfilled act of obedience to a formulated doctrine [18] to which one is committed. Liberation from the power of sin thus takes place in an act of obedience to the baptismal teaching which has mastered us. The ὑπηκούσατε ... is then taken up in a second statement : ἐλευθερωθέντες δὲ ἀπὸ τῆς ἁμαρτίας ἐδουλώθητε τῇ δικαιοσύνῃ. The juxtaposition shows us that we are dealing with one and the same thing. The passive formulation ἐλευθερωθέντες δὲ ... ἐδουλώθητε shows us that within the total event there is a fulfilment in which man participates only passively, and that this is the decisive act, as may be seen from its combination with the crucial ἐδουλώθητε. It is by no means difficult to suppose that ἐλευθερωθῆναι indicates the fulfilment of baptism, which accomplishes release from sin in an act of obedience to the formulated Gospel. The sacramental fulfilment of baptism on those who are linked with the Church by the baptismal symbol mediates primarily the freedom which is given us in the act of Jesus Christ. On the basis of the act of baptism in which the Spirit of the love of Jesus Christ is made ours, the claim of this liberating love is made on man. And in view of the incursion of the love of God, which takes place also in the expository form of teaching, man must continually decide for this love which presses in upon him.

3. But how is the freedom of the Spirit of Jesus Christ seized by us as it is brought to us in the Gospel and appropriated to us in baptism ? How does this freedom come to realisation in us ? The decisive answer is in love. It is not in isolation but in life with others that the Christian attains to freedom. In faith in the act of God which, declared in the Gospel and appropriated to us in baptism, sets the life of Jesus Christ at our disposal, man finds his freedom as service rendered to God's righteousness. Taken out of himself by this act of mastery, in faith the man who is summoned thereto by the Spirit in word and sacrament makes the transition from isolation to the practical yielding of his life to the divinely demanded righteousness of love of his neighbour, R. 6:18 ff. Freedom, man's surrender to the will of God, his divinely accomplished transfer from separation to righteousness, is apprehended and declared in righteous work orientated to holiness, R. 6:22. This work can take varied forms, Gl. 5:22. Doing all kinds of good, Christians silence the ignorant lips of fools and show their freedom, amongst other things in obedience to the powers that be, 1 Pt. 2:13 ff. The sons of the heavenly kingdom, who are free, accept civil ordinances for love's sake (ἵνα δὲ μὴ σκανδαλίσωμεν αὐτούς) and pay the usual taxes, even though they do not really apply to them as freemen. This is how they exercise their freedom, Mt. 17:24 ff. In his apostolic work Paul as ἐλεύθερος ἐκ πάντων always addresses himself to the specific natural and historical situation of men. Thus, renouncing his own religious obligations, [19] he is ready to sacrifice his own assurance of life, being enabled to

---

[18] The meaning of τύπος διδαχῆς is much debated in the comm. We take it to be διδαχή given in a τύπος, a fixed form. Cf. E. Norden, Ἄγνωστος θεός (1923), 270 f., who understands it to be a formulary of faith.

[19] This is the only possible meaning of νόμος here. We misunderstand not only this passage but all Paul's teaching if we try to derive from 1 C. 9:19 ff. an adaptation of the apostolic kerygma to the religious insights of the heathen. How could the one who anathematised the Judaising heresy in Gl. 1:9 allow the revealed Gospel to be changed by pagan philosophy ? To him this would not be freedom ; it would be bondage to men and to the reality which conditions them. For it would be an attempt to expound the will of God according to the claims of elemental forces.

do this in the state of freedom attained for him by Jesus Christ, 1 C. 9:19. Again, on the basis of the same freedom he renounces his right as an apostle to have certain basic needs met and especially to earn his keep through the preaching of the Gospel. It is true, of course, that the apostolic → ἐξουσία is at issue in this argument rather than ἐλευθερία. The question: οὐκ εἰμὶ ἐλεύθερος; in 1 C. 9:1, whereby Paul places himself among the ἐλεύθεροι of 1 C. 8, simply introduces a discussion in which the concept of ἐλευθερία is no longer applicable. Materially, however, the line of thinking here is an illustration of the way in which Christian freedom is realised in service which renounces personal claims and is concerned only for the salvation of others (ἵνα μή τινα ἐγκοπὴν δῶμεν τῷ εὐαγγελίῳ τοῦ Χριστοῦ, 1 C. 9:12). The Corinthian Gnostics do not have this genuine freedom which voluntarily seeks the edification of others (1 C. 8:1 ff.). To be sure, they are liberated from εἴδωλα by their knowledge of God, in which they are known by God. But they make this freedom another claim in virtue of which they try to assert themselves among the weak. They bemoan the fact that their freedom must be subject to the criticism of the consciences of others, 1 C. 10:29 f. They want to treat as their own the freedom given them with their knowledge of God. Hence the freedom granted to them, in which all cares and claims are silenced by the love of the Father of Jesus Christ, is not grasped by them in a freedom in which they express the liberation from care and claim appropriated to them by the intervention of Jesus Christ through word and sacrament. They show that their freedom is a semblance by their lack of love. The exercise of freedom in self-giving to others presupposes surrender of the passions and demands in which man ensnares himself (Gl. 5:24). How radical this surrender is may be seen from the command of the apostle in 1 C. 7:20 ff. Here the slave is summoned to care so little about his status that in given circumstances he would prefer to remain a slave than to be free. The basis of the summons is 1. the fact that both slaves and freemen have the same standing before the Lord and are therefore both bound and free, and 2. the danger that in striving after freedom there will be entanglement in claims upon men (even if these are only wishful), and therefore unselfish readiness for others will be impossible. It is for this readiness that the sacrifice of Jesus Christ has freed us. [20]

This surrender of desires in which there is freedom for others is not a self-restricting and therefore a self-asserting ataraxia. This is evident already from both the basis and the fulfilment of Christian freedom. In this context, however, it is made even clearer by the fact that this freedom which crucifies desire and does works of love shows itself to be freedom from the Law. This is to be understood in the light of our previous deliberations on the connection between sin and the Law. The Law provokes us to autonomy against others. The call of the Law must be silenced where the call of the Gospel tells us that we are under the rule of God. In a life which knows that it is provided for in Jesus Christ the Law is no longer needed to assure a life which is unprovided for, and therefore its claim is no longer heard and then either violated or met. On the contrary, the Law is freely fulfilled in its true sense as the will of God. Therefore the works which the

---

[20] There is another exposition of 1 C. 7:21 which sees a concession in 21b. This is hinted at in G, which puts καί before δύνασαι. It overlooks, however, both the general tenor of the passage and also the radical nature of the κλῆσις. The eschatological claim of the cross and resurrection of Jesus Christ kills even social desires and causes us to forget our status (→ 272).

Law is not against, because it is fulfilled in them (Gl. 5:23), are not my own fruits ; they are the fruits of the Spirit. For the Spirit has assigned to me a life in which my own life is taken away, so that I no longer try to provide for it by works done in relation to the Law, but in my works fulfil it as a life for which provision has already been made. The Law does not disappear with its claim, for it is the holy will of God. With its claim, however, it comes to me as a Law which has already been fulfilled by Jesus Christ for me. It is the "law of Christ" (Gl. 6:2). Its claim is that of the accomplished love of Christ. It is thus the "perfect law of liberty" (Jm. 1:25; cf. 2:12). It is the Law of God which is active in the sphere of freedom and which constantly mediates freedom. Hence its fulfilment brings blessedness with it. We may thus say that the proof of freedom from the Law is fulfilment of the law of liberty.

Freedom from sin and the Law culminates in freedom from death. Here, too, we shall consult the ἐλευθερία passages in answer to our question as to the concrete fulfilment of this freedom. Works done in freedom aim intrinsically at ζωὴ αἰώνιος (R. 6:22). As earthly, human works they produce in themselves that which underlies and creates them, namely, the eternity disclosed in the event of the love of Jesus Christ. As they are performed, they thus give knowledge of eternal life. The existence which by the work of the Spirit through word and sacrament is liberated from self-seeking in faith, expresses this freedom in works which make possible for one's neighbour the life which one enjoys oneself, namely, the life which is assured by the love of God in Christ. The man who is no longer fallen, but who rests on the will of God in Christ, brings in the future of God in his works and makes it available to his neighbour in the believing work of love. It is true that this freedom from death is enacted only within an existence which is still given up to death. Existence is still fallen of itself. It knows freedom from death only in the resurrection of Jesus Christ, in which the will of God accomplished this freedom. This freedom, as it is accomplished in the resurrection of Jesus Christ from the dead, has taken place for it in the word of the Gospel, and has been made present to it by the action of the sacrament, as that on the basis of which there can be life in self-forgetful dying. Even in its works existence has it only as that in relation to which it can be. Freedom from death is thus disclosed to it, even in its action, as the future enacted in Jesus Christ. In this ruined existence it will thus be known only as a sign of itself. The works of freedom will manifest eternity as that which is still to come to us in Jesus Christ. But in this way they do manifest it. Thus those who have the Spirit working freedom within them sigh expectantly that they may become the children of God, which will take place only when they are released from the carnal existence which in its bondage seeks to play the lord. Similarly the creation ruined by man cries out with longing that it may be delivered from the deceptive instinct of life and the bondage of death. This liberation will take place with the manifestation of the glory of the children of God revealed in Jesus Christ.

Schlier

ἔλευσις → ἔρχομαι.

† ἕλκω [1]

Our particular concern is with the figur. use in Jn. In Jn. 6:44 Jesus says : οὐδεὶς δύναται ἐλθεῖν πρός με, ἐὰν μὴ ὁ πατὴρ ὁ πέμψας με ἑλκύσῃ αὐτόν, and in 12:32 : κἀγὼ ἐὰν ὑψωθῶ ἐκ τῆς γῆς, πάντας ἑλκύσω πρὸς ἐμαυτόν.

The basic meaning is to "tug" or "draw" (with material obj.: Jn. 18:10; 21:6, 11). In the case of persons (cf. also 3 Macc. 4:7; Ac. 16:19; 21:30; Jm. 2:6) it may mean to "compel" : P. Tebt., 5, 179 (2nd. cent. B.C.): πρὸς ταῖς πραγματείαις ἕλκειν τινάς; P. Masp., 6, 6 (6th cent. A.D.): εἰς τὸ γεωργικὸν λειτούργημα; ibid., 89, 13 : εἰς δουλείαν. It may also mean to "draw" to a place by magic : ποτὶ δῶμα, Theocr., 2, 17. It is used of a magnet, metaph. in Eubulos Fr., 77 (CAF, II, 192): μαγνῆτις γὰρ | λίθος ὡς ἕλκει τοὺς πεινῶντας (drawing the hungry as by a magnet to the Cyprian loaves). Demons feel themselves drawn to the animal life to which they are given up : ὅπου πνεύματος πλείονος ὁλκή ... ἐκεῖ παρουσία τῶν τοιούτων πνευμάτων σοι δηλούσθω (Porphyr. De Philosophia ex oraculis haurienda librorum reliquiae [ed. G. Wolff, 1856], p. 150, 3 f.). Plato has πείθειν καὶ ἕλκειν (Resp., V, 458d); of the inner influencing of the will, Phaedr., 238a : ἐπιθυμίας ἀλόγως ἑλκούσης ἐπὶ ἡδονάς. More comparable with the Johannine usage is that of Porphyr. Marc., 16 : μόνη ἡ ἀρετὴ τὴν ψυχὴν ἄνω ἕλκει καὶ πρὸς τὸ συγγενές. Cf. also Corp. Herm., X, 6 : the beauty of the good τὴν ὅλην ψυχὴν ἀναλαμβάνει καὶ ἀνέλκει. What is in its own way a great comprehensive view of nature and spirit is given us in the statement concerning the demiurge manifesting himself in the sun : ... περὶ αὐτὸν καὶ εἰς αὐτὸν τὰ πάντα ἕλκων, καὶ ἀπὸ ἑαυτοῦ πάντα διδούς· πᾶσι γὰρ τὸ φῶς ἄφθονον χαρίζεται (Corp. Herm., XVI, 5). The word is distinctively Gnostic in such contexts.

In modern Semitic culture we should note the concept of the maǧdûb (as distinct from maǧnûn). "The maǧdûb (from ǧadaba, "to draw") is one who is drawn to God by an irresistible and supernatural force, whereas the maǧnûn is a person indwelt by demons. The former is holy, elected by God and filled with His grace ; the latter is the dwelling-place of a devil or one of his fellows. Notwithstanding, the words are popularly used as synonyms. When a man is suddenly, supernaturally and irresistibly called to God, he often loses the balance of thought (OT par.: 1 S. 10:5; 19:19 ff.; 2 K. 9:11; Jer. 29:26; Hos. 9:7; cf. also Mk. 3:21)." [2] → ἔκστασις, 450.

In the OT ἕλκειν is used of powerful impulse. The obscure εἵλκυσάν σε of Cant. 1:4 is somehow meant to express love. The word is used of mother love in 4 Macc. 14:13; 15:11. We find a beneficent "drawing" of God in Ἱερ. 38:3 : εἵλκυσά σε εἰς οἰκτείρημα. The original refers more to patience. The LXX is thinking, not so much of drawing out in deliverance (Ἱερ. 45:13; 2 Βασ. 22:17), but of drawing to oneself in love. This usage is distinctively developed by Jn., perhaps with some influence of Gnosticism. Force or magic may be discounted, but not the supernatural element. If we take the apparently contradictory statements together, the choice of grace and the universality of grace are both of a gravity and significance to shake the conscience. [3]

ἕ λ κ ω. [1] Fut. ἑλκύσω (Att. ἕλξω); aor. εἵλκυσα.

[2] T. Canaan, Dämonenglaube im Lande der Bibel (1929), 46.

[3] P. M. J. Lagrange, Evang. selon St. Jean² (1925), on 6:44 : "Ne murmurez pas, ne raisonnez pas, comme si vous étiez seuls juges de mon enseignement ; vos facultés naturelles n'y suffiraient pas : il y faut le secours de Dieu, sans lequel personne ne pourrait venir à moi : c'est de lui qu'il s'agit, prenez y garde."

In paganism man "draws" the gods (Menander Fr., 245 [CAF, III, 70 f.]: εἰ γὰρ ἕλκει τὸν θεὸν | τοῖς κυμβάλοις ἄνθρωπος εἰς ὃ βούλεται).

It is debatable whether a beneficent [4] or a violent "drawing" is meant in the agraphon in P. Oxy., IV, 654, 10 and 14 : [τίνες] οἱ ἕλκοντες ἡμᾶς [εἰς τὴν βασιλείαν].

Oepke

| Ἕλλην, Ἑλλάς |
| Ἑλληνικός, Ἑλληνίς |
| Ἑλληνιστής, Ἑλληνιστί |

A. Ἕλληνες in the Greek World.

1. From about 700 B.C. Ἕλληνες [1] was used as a designation for the Greek tribes, cities and states bound by common custom, literature, culture religion, language and nationhood. [2] The term developed and hardened in opposition to → βάρβαροι. The self-awareness induced by contacts with non-Greeks led to a kind of absolutising of Greek language, race and culture. The phenomenon differed, however, from the analogous case of Israel, the chosen people, in relation to *goyim*, by reason of the fact that there was no very prominent religious basis (→ I, 550 f.; → Ἰσραήλ). [3] The finest possession of the Greeks was not a cult, not even that of the Zeus of Olympus, nor the transmission of the epiphany of a god, nor a sacred book, but its → παιδεία as represented in the gymnasium, the theatre, philosophy and art. [4] It is typical that Isoc., 4, 50 (as it seems) restricts the name Ἕλληνες to those Greeks who share in Greek (= Attic) culture. [5] An analogy would be the restriction of the title Jews or Israelites to pious observers of the Law, to the exclusion of עַם־הָאָרֶץ and of apostate Jews who had be-

---

[4] Acc. to the editors. Deissmann LO, 363 ff., however, compares it to Jm. 2:6 (Mt. 10:17; Mk. 13:9). Cf. also E. White, JThSt, 16 (1915), 246 ff.

Ἕλλην κτλ. J. Kaerst, *Geschichte des Hellenismus²*, I (1917), II (1926); J. Jüthner, *Hellenen u. Barbaren* (1923); R. Laqueur, "Hellenismus" in *Schriften d. hessischen Hochschulen* (1925); "Hellenismus" in RGG², II, 1781 ff. (with bibl.); U. Wilcken, "Hellenen u. Barbaren," N.Jbch. Kl. Alt., 17 (1906), 457-471; Wendland Hell. Kult.; A. Bauer, *Vom Griechentum zum Christentum* (1910); E. v. Dobschütz, "Hellenism" in DAC, I, 547 ff. W. Nestle, *Griech. Religiosität*, III (1934), 5 ff.

[1] On the mythical progenitor Ἕλλην, cf. Roscher, I, 2029 f.; a Christian reference is to be found in Aristid. Apol., 8, 1.

[2] Jüthner, 4 ff. Acc. to U. Wilcken, *op. cit.*, 463 the general concept of Ἕλληνες, Πανέλληνες, arose only in the 6th cent. with the colonising movement.

[3] There was perhaps a religious element in the exclusion of barbarians from the Eleusinian mysteries (→ I, 547), as also from the great games (to the degree that ἀγῶνες had also a religious character). The Jewish counterpart is the exclusion of all ἀλλογενεῖς from the temple and feasts (→ n. 44; → I, 266 f.).

[4] W. Jaeger, *Humanismus u. Jugendbildung* (1921); *Antike u. Humanismus* (1925); *Paideia, die Formung des griech. Menschen*, I (1933).

[5] καὶ τὸ Ἑλλήνων ὄνομα πεποίηκε μηκέτι τοῦ γένους ἀλλὰ τῆς διανοίας δοκεῖν εἶναι, καὶ μᾶλλον Ἕλληνας καλεῖσθαι τοὺς τῆς παιδεύσεως τῆς ἡμετέρας ἢ τοὺς τῆς κοινῆς φύσεως μετέχοντας. I am following the exposition of Jüthner (34 f.), though this is contested (cf. Jüthner, n. 92).

comes "Greeks." On the other hand, there was also a tendency to extend the term to barbarians who embraced the Greek language and culture. [6]

2. The process of Hellenising non-Greeks began before the establishment of the Macedonian Greek empire. It was greatly accelerated by this important event. [7] The first result of the conquests of Philip and Alexander was the incorporation of Macedonia and its hinterland into the sphere of Hellenic culture. There followed the superficial Hellenisation of the kingdoms of Asia and Egypt, especially of the existing cities and of the newly established colonial cities, which were under the supervision of Macedonian Greece and the populations of which were partly Hellenised with the adoption of the Greek language and customs. Through mixed marriages there very quickly arose a semi-Greek world. [8] The development took different forms in the different territories. In the kingdom of the Ptolemies the term "Greek" was reserved for the ruling caste which maintained its traditional language, culture and religion in the new land. [9] In Asia, however, there was a wider acceptance of the culture of the ῞Ελληνες by native non-Hellenes. Here the number of new cities was greater, [10] and these became centres for the Hellenisation of the surrounding districts. There was an increasing integration of those born Hellenes with Hellenes of barbarian origin who had accepted ἑλληνισμός, [11] i.e., the Greek language, culture and religion. [12]

Almost as important as the Hellenisation of the East is the spread of Greek culture and language to the West. This began in South Italy and Sicily and moved esp. to

---

[6] Examples are Isoc., op. cit. (?); Plat. Menex., 245d : πολλοὶ φύσει μὲν βάρβαροι ὄντες, νόμῳ δὲ ῞Ελληνες, Aristot. acc. to Klearchos in Jos. Ap., 1, 180 of a Hellenised Jew : ῾Ελληνικὸς ἦν οὐ τῇ διαλέκτῳ μόνον, ἀλλὰ καὶ τῇ ψυχῇ. Cf. Eratosthenes in Strabo, I, 4, 9; also Plut. Alex. Fort. Virt., I, 6 (II, 329c), where we have a picture of the true Hellene who sets aside conditions of external nationality and civilisation and finds the essential marks in outlook and ethos. From the saying of Isoc. quoted in n. 5 we can also deduce that culture is more important than race. There is a Jewish Christian par. in R. 2:26-29, where Paul formulates the concept of a true Jew; cf. Ps.-Clem. Hom., 11, 16 : "A ῞Ελλην is one who, whether Greek or Jew, does not keep the Torah." The racial aspects are immaterial ; the practical attitude to the Torah is the criterion for both terms.

[7] P. Corssen in ZNW, 9 (1908), 84; Laqueur, Der Hellenismus, 18 f.; E. Meyer, Blüte u. Niedergang des Hellenismus in Asien (1925), 7 ff. There is an absolutising of the significance of Alexander in this process esp. in Plut. Alex. Fort. Virt.

[8] E. Meyer, op. cit., 11 f.

[9] Thus from about 300 in Egypt ῞Ελληνες are "citizens of autonomous communities and certain not very numerous groups of settlers," the conditions being Greek extraction and education (Jüthner, 83); W. Schubart, Einführung in die Papyruskunde (1918), 311 f.; Mitteis-Wilcken, I, 1, 12 ff.; instances are found in Moult.-Mill., 204; Preisigke Wört., III, 269. Cf. also the letter of the emperor Claudius to the Alexandrians, Lond. Pap., 1912, in H. I. Bell, Jews and Christians in Egypt (1924), 1 ff.

[10] E. Meyer, op. cit., 21 ff.; T. Mommsen, Röm. Geschichte, V (1885), 295 ff.

[11] For the word ἑλληνισμός, which is not found in the NT, cf. Strabo, XIV, 2, 28 : οἱ βάρβαροι οἱ εἰσαγόμενοι εἰς τὸν ἑλληνισμόν, i.e., acc. to the context, Greek language and civilisation. ἑλληνισμός always signifies what is truly Gk. in speech, culture and religion. Our term "Hellenism," which denotes a development of the classically Greek through the admixture of oriental influences, should not be read into the Greek word. Cf. Laqueur, "Hellenismus" passim. Only the sense of general Greek in contrast to the Attic dialect is attested. P. Oxy., VII, 1012, Fr. 17. Cf. Liddell-Scott, s.v.; E. A. Sophocles, Greek Lexicon (1870), s.v., who adduces two senses : the correct use of the Greek language, and paganism. The verb ἑλληνίζειν, which again does not occur in the NT, means (intrans.) "to speak Greek" (ἑλληνιστί), and then, since language and culture are so closely related, "to think and to live in Gk. fashion," i.e., "in language, disposition or custom to act like a Greek." Pass., s.v.; Liddell-Scott, s.v.; A. Debrunner in Burs. Jahresbericht, 236 (1932), 3, 121.

[12] That the religion of the ῞Ελληνες was accepted with the Hellenisation of the East is emphasised in Plut. Alex. Fort. Virt., I, 5 (II, 328d).

Rome and Central Italy. It was naturally quite independent of the conquests of Alexander, and probably began before his day. [13] In the East the movement persisted even when the Romans put an end to the Greek kingdoms and made the territories provinces of the Roman Empire. Thus the Jew Philo in Leg. Gaj., 147 (→ I, 549) boasts of Augustus that he added to Hellas many Ἑλλάδες, Hellenising barbarian countries in many important respects. [14] Nevertheless, the change led to a revival of eastern cultures, and thus helped forward, though it did not cause, the downfall of Hellenism in Asia.

3. This is the place to consider the fate of the Jewish people in the Hellenistic age. The Jews were naturally caught up in the process of Hellenisation pushed by all the Seleucid rulers, esp. Antiochus IV Epiphanes. Many Jews both at home and of the diaspora learned Greek ; many became Ἕλληνες in the full sense. Everywhere there were Jewish communities which used Greek even in worship and which read the Torah in Greek translation. The attempt of Antiochus Epiphanes to bring about a radical conversion of the Jewish people to ἑλληνισμός (→ n. 11) was frustrated by the loyalty with which most Jews clung to their religion and nationality. Thus a gulf was opened between ἑλληνισμός and Ἰουδαϊσμός. [15] The warding off of the Greek danger by Jews faithful to the Law did not mean, of course, that the Greek world was fully banished from Jewish territory. [16] The tiny state was surrounded by Hellenised cities. Greek culture and language pressed in constantly from without. The last of the Hasmoneans, and then Herod and his sons, posed as Hellenistic rulers, [17] and the incorporation of Judea into the strongly Hellenised Roman Empire strengthened the Hellenising process. Many Jews learned Greek, which in some degree became a second commercial language in Palestine. [18] Thus even in his own land the Jew was brought into contact with Ἕλληνες, whether in Jerusalem, in the half-Hellenised cities of Galilee, or on the roads which crossed the land.

The Jews of the Greek diaspora were even more strongly affected. This is particularly well attested by the rich Hellenistic Jewish literature, whether in the form of translations (LXX etc.) or of original writings, both of which served both the needs of Jews who could not speak any other language but Greek, and also the ends of propaganda among the Greeks. For if the Jews became Greeks, many Greeks became Jews. And Judaism finally maintained itself as such even in the Hellenistic world. [19] Thus the Hellenistic age saw a final development which was a complete perversion from the Gk. standpoint. The term Ἕλλην came to be equated with the idolater or heathen. [20] The presupposition was a shift of accent. The distinguishing mark of the Ἕλληνες is no longer παιδεία imparted by philosophy, but λατρεία, i.e., εἰδωλολατρεία (→ 379). The question arises whether this usage first developed amongst Hellenistic Jews and whether it occurs in the earliest Christian writings, i.e., the NT (→ B. and C.).

In face of the Greek world Hellenistic Judaism makes a distinction. It rejects the mythology, cultus and immorality of the Hellenes, but eclectically appropriates their language, philosophy and external culture. This process is reflected in the Talmud, [21]

---

[13] Jüthner, 60 ff.

[14] On the rare ἀφελληνίσας, cf. Dio Chrys., 37, 26, and Liddell-Scott, s.v., where it is rendered "to hellenise, civilise thoroughly."

[15] Bousset-Gressm., 1 ff.; F. Buhl, "Hellenisten," RE³, VII, 623 ff.; Moore, I, 48 ff.; Schl. Gesch. Isr., 9 ff.; G. Kittel, Die Rel.gesch. u. d. Urchrtt. (1932), 42 ff.

[16] Schürer, II, 1 ff., 57 ff.; Jüd. Lex., II (1928), 1531 ff.

[17] Aristobulus is described by Joseph. (Ant., 13, 318) as a φιλέλλην. Herod felt closer to the Gks. than the Jews (Jos. Ant., 19, 329).

[18] Schürer, II, 84 ff.; G. Dalman, Jesus-Jeschua (1922), 1 ff.; Kittel Probleme, 34 ff.; Zn. Einl., I, 24 ff. The self-testimony of Joseph. is significant (Ant., 20, 262 ff.).

[19] Schürer, III, 24 ff., 420 f.

[20] For examples v. Jüthner, 146, though not all these are valid, since Ἕλλην often means Greek ; also → Ἑλληνιστής 511 ff.

[21] Str.-B., IV, 405 ff.

esp. in the many loan words also found in the Mishnah,[22] in the use of Greek legends and myths,[23] in the recognition of the Greek translation of the Bible, and in the permission to learn Greek, to read Homer and to assimilate Greek wisdom. Even stronger in the Talmud, however, is the counter-movement which begins to exert a particular effect at the beginning of the 2nd century A.D. and which crystallises in the frequently violated prohibition of learning Greek. Here national and political instincts combine with the conviction that the fostering of Gk. culture, which cannot be separated from Gk. idolatry and ungodliness, is incompatible with the service of the Torah.[24]

B. "Ελληνες among the Jews.

The LXX sometimes uses "Ελληνες for יְוָנִים (יָוָן == Ionians), e.g., Da. 8:21; 10:20; 11:2; once at Is. 9:12 for פְּלִשְׁתִּים (τοὺς "Ελληνας ἀφ' ἡλίου δυσμῶν as inhabitants of the islands and lands of the West), and frequently in Macc. The LXX also has 'Ελλάς at Is. 66:19; Ez. 27:13 and 1 Macc. 1:1; 8:9. Of derived words, esp. in the apocr., we have the adj. Ἑλληνικός (Jer., and 2 and 4 Macc.) and Ἑλληνίς (2 Macc. 6:8 A), also the subst. Ἑλληνισμός (2 Macc. 4:13). On the other hand, Ἑλληνιστής and ἑλληνίζειν do not occur. The meaning of "Ελληνες is the customary "Hellenes," esp. those of the colonial territories including Palestine, i.e., the Hellenes in Syria and Egypt.[25]

For the Jews, however, this Greek sphere is a religious rather than a political matter. We owe it to the Seleucid attempts at Hellenisation, and the Jewish resistance, that already in Jewish Greek of the period "Greek" has the accompanying sense of "anti-Jewish" or "hostile to the Jews," and that it thus approximates to the term "Gentile." If this is not so in 1 Macc., it is certainly true in 2 Macc., and therefore perhaps in relation to Jason of Cyrene. Thus in 2 Macc. 4:10 we read of the Hellenistic high-priest Jason: πρὸς τὸν Ἑλληνικὸν χαρακτῆρα τοὺς ὁμοφύλους μετέστησε. In the first instance the reference is to the introduction of Gk. customs (the gymnasium etc.), which also implies the suspension of conflicting Jewish customs required by the Law (4:11). In 4:13 the expression is used: ἀκμὴ τοῦ Ἑλληνισμοῦ καὶ πρόσβασις ἀλλοφυλισμοῦ, i.e., the achievement of Hellenism and transition to an alien existence, with consequent apostasy from the service of the Torah.[26] Here, then, ἑλληνισμός does not mean a fusion of the Hellenic and the Judaic in the modern sense of Hellenism (i.e., with a Judaising or Orientalising of the Hellenic). It means an abandonment of Judaism and apostasy to Hellenism, i.e., to what was then Hellenic. This obviously embraces

---

[22] For bibl. v. Schürer, II, 57 ff.

[23] Str.-B., loc. cit.; Kittel Probleme, 141 ff.

[24] A typical combination, though evoked by special circumstances, is to be found in Bar. BQ, 82b: "Cursed is the man who rears swine, and cursed is the man who teaches his son Greek wisdom."

[25] Alexander earlier ruled ἐπὶ τὴν Ἑλλάδα (1 Macc. 1:1). He, ὁ βασιλεὺς ὁ Μακεδών, was the first who ἐβασίλευσεν τοῖς "Ελλησιν (6:2). The words obviously refer only to European Greece and its inhabitants; cf. 8:9, where the reference is to Greek Macedonians intriguing in Asia Minor. On the other hand, the 137th year of the βασιλεία Ἑλλήνων in 1:10 refers to the era of the Seleucids in Hellenised Syria, and the βασιλεία τῶν Ἑλλήνων in 1 Macc. 8:18, which enslaves Israel and from which the Romans are to liberate it, is the kingdom of the Hellenised Seleucids. Ὁ πικρὸς Ἑλλήνων τύραννος in 4 Macc. 18:20 is the Seleucid Epiphanes. In 2 Macc. 4:36 the "Ελληνες are the Greek inhabitants of Antioch who with the Jews condemn the murder of Onias (cf. 3 Macc. 3:8, where οἱ κατὰ τὴν πόλιν "Ελληνες are the Greek inhabitants of Alexandria). Thus for the Jews of the Maccabean period the Hellenes are the ruling caste in the Seleucid state into which they were for a time incorporated.

[26] W. Grimm in his exegetical handbook to the OT apocrypha, 2 (1857), 83. Cf. also in 4:15 the antithesis between πατρῴας τιμάς and Ἑλληνικὰς δόξας.

the Greek cultus, or Greek idolatry according to Jewish and biblical teaching. According to 6:1-11 the observance of the Sabbath and circumcision are denied to the Jews; the temple is dedicated to Olympian Zeus; a Dionysus festival is introduced; and the neighbouring Gk. cities ('Ελληνίδας πόλεις) are ordered to force the Jews to sacrifice, τοὺς δὲ μὴ προαιρουμένους μεταβαίνειν ἐπὶ τὰ 'Ελληνικὰ κατασφάζειν (6:9). It is still true that τὰ 'Ελληνικά does not mean paganism in general, but Greek culture, custom and religion.

This fact is not obscured by the use of → ἔθνη for non-Jewish peoples or Gentiles [27] — a term which is still found in 2 Macc. (6:4; 14:14 f.) and which is common in 1 Macc., where the reference is simply to the Gentiles (ἔθνη) and not to the "Ελληνες or ἑλληνισμός. In Hellenistic Judaism Hellenism was found to be the most dangerous form of paganism, but as yet there is no simple equation of "Ελληνες and Gentiles. Hellenism is the historically known magnitude of the Greek world with its language, customs and deities.

This is confirmed by Josephus when in Ant., 12, 240 f. he speaks of apostate Jews having 'Ελληνικὴ πολιτεία, i.e., Greek (and not pagan) civilisation, and even wanting to appear unclothed like "Ελληνες; cf. 15, 329, where 'Ελληνικὸς τρόπος means the veneration of images and sculpture (i.e., the Gk. gods). The usage is particularly clear in Jos. Ap., for here he speaks of "Ελληνες in distinction from Αἰγύπτιοι or Χαλδαῖοι (e.g., 1, 14 and 28; 2, 1). Cf. also Vit., 40: οὐκ ἄπειρος ἦν παιδείας τῆς παρ' "Ελλησιν. In this respect Philo, too, is a Greek man of letters. He usually speaks of "Ελληνες in distinction from βάρβαροι or 'Εβραῖοι (usually with reference to the languages) or Χαλδαῖοι. Elsewhere he refers to Gk. philosophers, poets etc. [28] There is no trace of the sense of Gentiles. Indeed, he hardly uses the word ἔθνη in this sense. [29] The same applies to the author of Ep. Ar. when he says of the Greek sculptors and poets that they sought to be τῶν 'Ελλήνων οἱ σοφώτατοι (Gentiles would be quite misleading here); cf. also 121, where he says of the 72 chosen to translate the Torah that they had not only gained competence in 'Ιουδαϊκὰ γράμματα but also had not neglected τῆς τῶν 'Ελληνικῶν κατασκευῆς (the study of Hellenic literature). [30]

There can thus be no suggestion that, in face of the threat of paganism in the form of Gk. culture and religion, Gk. speaking Jews had already begun to use the words "Ελλην, 'Ελληνικός, ἑλληνισμός in the sense of "heathen" or "heathenism," [31] especially as the Gks. were not the only people of non-Jewish descent, language and religion with whom they had dealings.

C. "Ελληνες in the NT.

In the NT 'Ελλάς for Greece in the narrower geographical sense is used only in Ac. 20:2, "Ελλην in Jn., Ac., R., Gl., 1 C. and Col. (not Mt., Mk., Lk.), the fem. form 'Ελληνίς only in Mk. 7:26 and Ac. 17:12, the adj. 'Ελληνικός only in Rev. 9:11: ἐν τῇ 'Ελληνικῇ sc. γλώσσῃ (= ἑλληνιστί in antithesis to → 'Εβραϊστί) and Lk.

---

[27] Strictly, like גּוֹיִם, other nations which do not practise circumcision or live after the Law, and which are thus unclean.

[28] For examples v. H. Leisegang, Index 8 f.

[29] Ibid., 220. ἔθνη is also rare in Joseph. Schl. Theol. d. Judt., 237 cites Ant., 11, 194; 13, 196.

[30] Cf. 38 and the quotation from Ep. Ar., 121 in Philo Vit. Mos., II, 32: τοὺς παρ' αὐτῷ δοκιμωτάτους 'Εβραίων, οἳ πρὸς τῇ πατρίῳ καὶ τὴν 'Ελληνικὴν ἐπεπαίδευντο παιδείαν.

[31] Zn. R., 73. Zn. rightly says that "this is never so in the LXX nor in 1 Macc." But in spite of Zn. the same should be said of 2 Macc. and Jos. too.

23:38 א D ℜ etc. (addition): γράμμασιν ἑλληνικοῖς ῥωμαϊκοῖς ἑβραικοῖς, [32] the adv. ἑλληνιστί (from ἑλληνίζειν) in Jn. 19:20 and Ac. 21:37, and finally the new word 'Ελληνιστής in Ac. 6:1; 9:29 (and 11:20 B [א]ℜ etc.) for the Greek speaking Jew (though → 512). Neither ἑλληνίζειν nor ἑλληνισμός occurs in the NT.

1. The only NT authors who really include the "Ελληνες in their narrative or theology are Luke (Ac.) and Paul. Elsewhere there are only occasional references.

Of the Synoptists, only Mk. says of the woman who came to Jesus on behalf of her daughter that she was a 'Ελληνίς, with the addition Συροφοινίκισσα τῷ γένει (7:26). [33]

The expression is ambiguous. It may denote the non-Jewish, Greek language and civilisation of the locality and of the woman herself. Or is may be a religious term for a Gentile, whether a Greek or a Hellenised Syro-phoenician (*gentilis* vg). [34] In any case, the non-Jewish descent of the woman is emphasised (Mk. 7:27 f.). Since Mk. does not use the term again, it is hard to decide the question. We may simply say that the sense of Gentile is suggested, and if so, this is the oldest example of this specific use. Nevertheless, the ethnographical interpretation is more likely. [35]

Elsewhere in the Synoptic Gospels it is never emphasised that Hellenes came to Jesus, or that a non-Jew with whom He had dealings was a Hellene, e.g., the centurion of Capernaum (Mt. 8:5; Lk. 7:2), or the centurion at the cross (Mk. 15:39). Hence it is hard to decide whether in the saying in Mt. 8:10; Lk. 7:9 : οὐδὲ ἐν τῷ 'Ισραήλ ... we should add in thought "as in this Hellene, or this Σύρος, or this ἐθνικός, or this προσήλυτος." [36] The usual word for Gentile in translation of the sayings of Jesus is → ἐθνικός, not "Ελλην.

With the 'Ελληνίς of Mk. we should group the "Ελληνές τινες ἐκ τῶν ἀναβαινόντων κτλ. who wished to see Jesus in Jn. 12:20 ff.

Half-proselytes of Greek language, [37] φοβούμενοι or σεβόμενοι τὸν θεόν, Greeks or Hellenised Orientals by birth who had attached themselves to the synagogue in their own lands, were described in this way rather than as Gentiles ; the addition ἵνα προσκυνήσωσιν ἐν τῇ ἑορτῇ definitely excludes the sense of Gentiles. Not the conversion of the Gentiles, but that of the Greeks, and its presupposition, the dying of the Son of Man, are illustrated in this scene. It is in keeping that in Jn. 7:35 the Jews misunderstand Jesus to the effect that He proposes to go εἰς τὴν διασπορὰν τῶν 'Ελλήνων and to διδάσκειν τοὺς "Ελληνας. These expressions are to be taken geographically, not religiously. The → διασπορὰ τῶν 'Ελλήνων does not mean 'Ελλάς or γῆ 'Ελλήνων, but Jews dispersed among the Greeks. [38] In fact, however, the reference is probably to

---

[32] Cf. Preisigke Wört., III, 270; Ditt. Or., 56, 74 : ἱεροῖς γράμμασιν καὶ Αἰγυπτίοις καὶ 'Ελληνικοῖς.

[33] Mt. has the archaic Χαναναία in 15:22; cf. Test. Jud. 14:6.

[34] Wbg. Mk.; Jüthner, 90, 143.

[35] Jüthner, *op. cit.* (cf. also Wettstein) compares Luc. Deorum Concilium, 4 : ὁ γάρ τοι γενναιότατος οὗτος Διόνυσος ἡμιάνθρωπος ὤν, οὐδὲ "Ελλην μητρόθεν, ἀλλὰ Συροφοίνικός τινος ἐμπόρου τοῦ Κάδμου θυγατριδοῦς. Such a hybrid might well be called "Ελλην Συροφοίνιξ.

[36] For the latter possibility cf. Lk. 7:5 and the recently discovered inscr. from Stobi with Lietzmann's observations in ZNW, 32 (1933), 93 f.

[37] Str.-B., II, 548; Zn. J., ad loc.; Bau. J., ad loc. takes a different view. Cf. the σεβόμενοι "Ελληνες in Thessal., Ac. 17:4.

[38] Str.-B., II, 490; Zn. J., ad loc. Cf. 1 Pt. 1:1; Paral. Jerem., 16. → διασπορά, 102, esp. n. 12.

the localities, since there is a suggestion that He will teach the Hellenes themselves and not Hellenised, Greek-speaking Jews of the dispersion. [39]

With his two references John is telling us that the idea of offering teaching to the Gentiles twice occurred in the life of Jesus, though it was never realised. The instruction of the Greeks was to come only in the age of the Paraclete. In Jn. it was never enjoined on the disciples during this period (as distinct from preaching to the Samaritans, 4:35 ff.). [40]

2. Acts first tells us of the taking up of the mission to the Hellenes and of their coming into the Christian community. By Ἕλληνες, though with no particular emphasis, it means a. Greeks or Hellenised inhabitants of Syria and Asia Minor, and b. inhabitants of Hellas and Macedonia.

Anonymous Jewish Christians from Cyprus and Cyrene, and therefore baptised Jews of Greek language and civilisation, were the first, in Antioch (11:20), to speak πρὸς τοὺς Ἕλληνας, [41] i.e., to non-Jewish, Greek-speaking inhabitants of this former capital of the Seleucid kingdom [42] and the contemporary capital of the Roman province of Syria, whose population in its upper strata consisted of descendants of true Greeks and Macedonians, and especially of Hellenistic Syrians.

After this beginning of preaching to the Hellenes the author of Ac. often tells us that Paul (and Barnabas) spoke to Ἰουδαῖοι and Ἕλληνες, or that Ἰουδαῖοι and Ἕλληνες believed, as in Iconium in Ac. 14:1 (ὥστε πιστεῦσαι Ἰουδαίων τε καὶ Ἑλλήνων πολὺ πλῆθος); in Thessalonica in 17:4, where τινὲς ἐξ αὐτῶν (sc. Ἰουδαίων) τῶν τε σεβομένων Ἑλλήνων πλῆθος πολύ became adherents; in Berea (17:12), where apart from the Jews (πολλοὶ) τῶν Ἑλληνίδων γυναικῶν τῶν εὐσχημόνων καὶ ἀνδρῶν οὐκ ὀλίγοι became believers, i.e., women and men of the Greek nation who attended the synagogue; in Corinth (18:4), where Paul ἔπειθεν ... Ἰουδαίους καὶ Ἕλληνας; in Ephesus (19:10), where all who lived in Asia, Ἰουδαίους τε καὶ Ἕλληνας, heard the Word, cf. 19:17; cf. also 20:21, where in the account of his missionary work in Ephesus Paul emphasises that he testified repentance and faith Ἰουδαίοις τε καὶ Ἕλλησιν. The Ἕλληνες here are the non-Jewish element in the populations of the cities of Asia Minor, of the province of Asia, and of the Greek towns Corinth and Thessalonica, esp. those who attend the synagogue (cf. 14:1; 18:4; 17:4). From Antioch to Corinth, from Syria to Achaia, Paul constantly meets the same mixture of Jews and Hellenes. The mixture produces mixed marriages. In Lystra Paul meets Timothy, the υἱὸς Ἰουδαίας πιστικῆς, πατρὸς δὲ Ἕλληνος (16:1; cf. 3). Ἕλλην obviously de-

---

[39] In the art. διασπορά (→ 101 f.) a choice is offered between the two possibilities, but the expression "and teach the Hellenes" seems to show what is meant; cf. Schl. J., ad loc.

[40] On the other hand we have the highly singular and possibly spurious statement in Jos. Ant., 18, 63 : καὶ πολλοὺς μὲν Ἰουδαίους, πολλοὺς δὲ καὶ τοῦ Ἑλληνικοῦ ἐπηγάγετο. This would have it that Jesus won many Jews and Hellenes. It goes beyond what is stated in Jn., though it may be based on Synoptic accounts of people coming to Jesus from non-Jewish districts (cf. Mk. 3:8 and par.). Cf. R. Eisler, Ἰησοῦς βασιλεὺς οὐ βασιλεύσας (Religionswissenschaftliche Bibliothek, 9), I (1930), 64 f.; II, 358.

[41] Only AD* have this; BE ℵ and the original of ℵ (with its impossible πρὸς τοὺς εὐαγγελιστάς) have πρὸς τοὺς Ἑλληνιστάς. This reading either attests the interchangeability of Ἕλλην and Ἑλληνιστής (→ 512), or it is based on 6:1, where the distinction is from the Ἑβραῖοι rather than the Ἰουδαῖοι (11:19). Cf. Zn. Ag., 367.

[42] On Antioch in Syria cf. Pr.-Bauer, 118, and, in addition to the bibl. there given, K. Bauer, Antiochia in der ältesten Kirchengeschichte (1919); L. M. Enfrey, Antioche (1930).

notes nationality. [43] The result of this successful missionary activity means that in the Greek-speaking world the communities of the baptised are composed of a few Jews and a greater number of Hellenes (14:1; 18:4; 20:21), and that on his journeys Paul took with him baptised, but not circumcised, Hellenes as companions. It is this fact which underlies the calumnious Jewish accusation that he brought Ἕλληνες into the temple (21:28).

Does Luke think of this Ἰουδαῖοι καὶ Ἕλληνες as equivalent to Jews and Gentiles, so that Ἕλλην means Gentile? This view finds support in the use of ἔθνη immediately after the formula, e.g., in 14:2, where the ἔθνη incited by unbelieving Jews are non-synagogue fellows of the Ἕλληνες mentioned in 14:1 (cf. 14:5, where there is a resultant ὁρμὴ τῶν ἐθνῶν τε καὶ Ἰουδαίων against the apostles), and also in 18:6, where Paul declares that he will now go only εἰς τὰ ἔθνη. The Ἕλληνες thus seem to be Gentiles of Greek descent and language, and in this case the father of Timothy would be a Gentile (16:1) and Paul would in fact have brought Gentiles into the temple (21:28).

Yet though this equation finds support, it is never fully made in Ac. In the first place, the Ἕλληνες are often, as in Jn. 12:20 ff., σεβόμενοι τὸν θεόν (14:1; 17:4), i.e., non-Jews who have already loosed their ties with the goyim. Secondly, the accusation in 21:28 refers to the familiar temple inscription μηθένα ἀλλογενῆ εἰσπορεύεσθαι κτλ. [44] The Ἕλληνες are thus Greek-speaking ἀλλογενεῖς. We may add that acc. to Col. 4:11, 14 the author of Ac. was himself a Ἕλλην by birth. Hence for him the term meant a man of Greek descent, civilisation and speech rather than a Gentile.

3. In addition to Ἕλληνες Ac. uses Ἑλληνισταί in 6:1 and 9:29. [45] This is also a variant of Ἕλληνες at 11:20 in B ℵ E etc., as also in the original of ℵ (in place of the impossible εὐαγγελιστάς). [46] The word seems to be new; it is not found either in Greek or Hellenistic Jewish literature. The meaning is disputed. The dominant view is that the Ἑλληνισταί of Ac. 6:1 (→ 84) are Jewish Christians of Greek language (and possibly culture) as distinct from the → Ἑβραῖοι, i.e., believing Jews of Aramaic language and purely Jewish culture, the former being Jews of the διασπορὰ τῶν Ἑλλήνων who had moved to Jerusalem and the latter native born Jews of Jerusalem. The first community thus consisted of two groups of Jewish Christians distinguished by speech and culture. It is possible that the Ἑλληνισταί also took a less rigid view of the Law, no longer living strictly according to Jewish rites. [47]

Ἑλληνιστής derives from ἑλληνίζειν, as does βαπτιστής from βαπτίζειν and the late and rare Ἰουδαϊστής from → ἰουδαΐζειν. If ἑλληνίζειν means "to speak Greek," but also "to live as a Greek" (cf. ἀττικίζειν, "to speak Attic" and "to have the Attic outlook," or ἰουδαΐζειν "to live as a Jew"), then Ἑλληνιστής includes not only the Greek language but also a Greek or non-Jewish mode of life. This may well fit the Hellenists in Jerusalem. Of course, the Ἑλληνισταί with whom Paul disputed in 9:29,

---

[43] Cf. Eupolemos in Eus. Praep. Ev., IX, 34, 1: Ps.-Suron. Ep. ad Salomon: ἄνθρωπον Τύριον ἐκ μητρὸς Ἰουδαίας.

[44] Ditt. Or., 598; Deissmann LO, 62 f.; → I, 266. Joseph. has ἀλλοεθνῆ for ἀλλογενεῖς in Ant., 15, 417, ἀλλόφυλος in Bell., 5, 194, and Philo τῶν οὐχ ὁμοεθνῶν in Leg. Gaj., 212.

[45] Zn. Ag., 226 ff.; Einl., I, 41 f., 51 f.

[46] The same variant occurs in Test. Sal. 6:8 (McCown UNT, 9): καλεῖται δὲ παρ' Ἑβραίοις Πατικῆ ..., ἔστι δὲ τῶν Ἑλληνιστῶν· Ἐμμανουήλ (variant: παρὰ δὲ Ἕλλησι).

[47] W. Bauer in Festg. f. A. Jülicher (1927), 32 f.; G. P. Wetter, ARW, 21 (1922), 410 ff.

and who tried to destroy him, were fanatical orthodox Jews of the dispersion. Cf. as a parallel the dispute between the Hellenist Stephen and the Λιβερτῖνοι, the Κυρηναῖοι, the ᾿Αλεξανδρεῖς, and the Jews of Cilicia and Asia (possibly including the unconverted Saul), who might all be described as unbelieving ῾Ελληνισταί (6:9). In this sense Paul was a ῾Ελληνιστής, as also the ἀπὸ ᾿Ασίας ᾿Ιουδαῖοι who brought about his arrest in 21:27.

A second view is that the ῾Ελληνισταί are Greeks. [48] The oldest example adduced is ῾Ελληνιστάς for ῞Ελληνας in Ac. 11:20 (opp. ᾿Ιουδαίοις in 11:19). A few later writers called pagan Greeks ῾Ελληνισταί in contrast to Χριστιανοί, e.g., Julian in Sozomenos Historia Ecclesiastica, V, 16; Sozomenos himself in III, 17; VII, 15; Philostorgius MPG, 65, 537 B, 541 A. [49] Here ῾Ελληνισταί is obviously a synon. of ῞Ελληνες; it corresponds to ἑλληνίζειν as used of Greeks in the sense of "to speak Greek," "to live as a Greek," "to be a Greek," and it means "Christians of Greek descent."

In favour of this interpretation in Ac. 6:1 the following points may be made. [50] a. There is no compelling reason why ῾Ελληνισταί should denote Greek-speaking Jews on the one side, ῾Εβραῖοι Hebrew-speaking Jews on the other. [51] ῾Εβραῖοι are in the first instance Jews of pure race. Thus Eusebius calls Philo a ῾Εβραῖος in Hist. Eccl., II, 4, [52] and the Greek-speaking Trypho τὸν τῶν τότε ῾Εβραίων ἐπισημότατον in IV, 18, 6. It may also be asked why a mere difference in language should have caused misunderstanding and disturbance in care for the widows. b. Ac. often refers to Greek-speaking Jews (Aquila in 18:2; Apollos in 18:24 etc.), but never uses the term ῾Ελληνιστής for them. c. The Greek names of the Seven in Ac. 6:5 favour, though they do not prove, the assumption that these were men of Greek descent. The mention of a proselyte (Nicolas of Antioch) shows that believers of Greek descent might at least be included among the ῾Ελληνισταί.

On the other hand, the conclusion that the Jerusalem community consisted of both Jewish and Gentile Christians is out of keeping with the story of Cornelius (Ac. 10 f., esp. 11:17 f.). It might be argued with Cadbury, however, that already according to Ac. 2 the apostolic message of repentance had been addressed to both Jews and Gentiles, so that we may presuppose a mixed community (cf. 2:8 ff., 39). Another objection is that Ac. 9:29 does not make sense on this interpretation, for surely Paul was not disputing with Gentiles in Jerusalem. [53] It must be remembered, however, that in 11:20 ῾Ελληνιστάς is the more difficult and the better attested reading, and here it must mean Greeks or Gentiles, so that 9:29 may be regarded as an anticipation. A final stumbling block is 6:1, and here Cadbury has not found any convincing answer. It may be pointed out, however, that the usual interpretation is not so secure and self-evident as it seems to be in the older exegetical tradition. It is not impossible that ῾Ελληνισταί is an early Christian party name for Christians who did not live according to the Law. [54]

4. Only in 4 Epistles does Paul speak of ῞Ελληνες and their relations to the Gospel, namely, in 1 C., Gl., R. and Col., and always in connection with the

---

[48] H. J. Cadbury, "The Hellenists" in *The Beginnings of Christianity*, Part I, Vol. V (1933), 59-74. Cf. also Vol. IV (1933), 64.

[49] Sophocles, Lexicon, *s.v.*; Cadbury, *op. cit.*, 59. Sophocles uses the passages adduced in favour of the second sense, "defender of paganism," "heathen," to support the interpretation "a Jew whose native language was the Greek" (Ac. 6:1 etc.). Chrys. Hom. Act., 14 (MPG, 60, 113).

[50] Cadbury, 62 ff.

[51] Wnd. 2 K., 351; Dib. Th. u. Phil.², 67 f.

[52] Cadbury, 62 ff. Cf. also W. Bauer, *Rechtgläubigkeit u. Ketzerei im ältesten Christentum* (1934), 55 f.

[53] Cadbury, 70.

[54] Wetter, *op. cit.*

'Ιουδαῖοι, and once or twice with the βάρβαροι. His use of ῞Ελληνες is thus determined by the two formulae 'Ιουδαῖοι καὶ ῞Ελληνες and ῞Ελληνες καὶ βάρβαροι (→ I, 551 f.).[55] For Paul the ῞Ελληνες are thus one great half of the race to whom the Gospel is to be taken.

a. Both formulae have a national sense. Yet the addition πρώτῳ (to 'Ιουδαίῳ) shows that Paul is conscious of the precedence of the Jew on the basis of salvation history. It is worth noting that the formula orientated to salvation history predominates.[56] For Paul ῞Ελληνες is thus the non-Jewish part of the race. The formula is determined by the outlook of the Jew, especially of the Anatolian Jew of the dispersion, of the missionary from Judaism who crosses the borders of the Jewish ghetto into the cultural sphere of the ῞Ελληνες. The presupposition of the formula is the unified culture of the Mediterranean lands as essentially influenced by the Greek tongue and Greek civilisation, and the accompanying fact that Paul as a missionary to the Gentiles does not embrace the whole of the heathen world but confines himself to the ῞Ελληνες in Asia Minor, Macedonia, Illyria, and ancient Hellas. He is not concerned about the Αἰγύπτιοι or Χαλδαῖοι.[57] As he uses it, however, the formula 'Ιουδαῖοι καὶ ῞Ελληνες expresses the universal relevance of the Gospel, especially the Pauline Gospel. ῞Ελληνες are that part of the race which is distinguished from the Jews by language, descent and culture. They are thus the essentially Hellenistic inhabitants of the Roman Empire (apart from the Jews).

Their distinctive characteristic acc. to Paul is wisdom (→ σοφία).[58] This is not a judgment of the student of culture; it is the tragic experience of the missionary. This wisdom possessed or desired by the ῞Ελληνες is the obstacle to their believing reception of the concrete Gospel. The main substance of the Gospel, Χριστὸς ἐσταυρωμένος, is μωρία to these seekers after wisdom, because the wisdom of the Hellenes belongs to different categories from those of the wisdom which God has concealed in His Gospel, 1 C. 1:18 ff.; R. 1:14.

The ῞Ελληνες are characterised very differently in R. 1:18 ff. Here we have a history of the fall of the race as a whole. Yet, although the term ῞Ελληνες does not occur, the reference from 1:16 f. is specifically to the ῞Ελληνες,[59] as may be seen especially from the slogan φάσκοντες εἶναι σοφοὶ ἐμωράνθησαν in 1:22.[60] Their wisdom is evaluated both positively and negatively. Positively, they have really known God from creation (1:21), together with His moral and judicial order (1:32). Negatively, they have fallen into idolatry in spite of this knowledge (1:21 ff.), consciously and joyfully violating the divine order (1:32). Overtaken

---

[55] After Paul, the next Christian author to use the formula ῞Ελληνες/βάρβαροι is Just. Apol., 5, 4; 7, 3; 46, 3; then Tat., 1, 1; 29, 1; 21, 3; 30, 1.

[56] 'Ιουδαῖοι καὶ ῞Ελληνες is obviously a general formula in R. 2:9: ἐπὶ πᾶσαν ψυχὴν ἀνθρώπου ... 'Ιουδαίου τε πρῶτον καὶ ῞Ελληνος. An analogous formula is Πέρσαι τε καὶ ῞Ελληνες, as found in the great inscript. of Antiochos of Commagene (Ditt. Or., 383, 30); cf. also ῞Ελληνες/Αἰγύπτιοι in Preisigke Wört., III, 269.

[57] On the other hand cf. Aristid. Apol., 2, 1, where the polytheists, distinguished from the monotheistic 'Ιουδαῖοι καὶ Χριστιανοί, εἰς τρία διαιροῦνται γένη, Χαλδαίους τε καὶ ῞Ελληνας καὶ Αἰγυπτίους, cf. 12, 1; 13, 1.

[58] Schl. Th. Ap., 296 ff.

[59] Only in 1:23 is one inclined to think also of the Αἰγύπτιοι, though Paul may have seen cultic representations of animals on Gk. soil.

[60] Cf. Aristid. Apol., 8, 2: οἱ οὖν ῞Ελληνες σοφοὶ λέγοντες εἶναι ἐμωράνθησαν χεῖρον τῶν Χαλδαίων; also 13, 7.

by the fearful penalty of God, the "Ελληνες have become a people dominated by sins of unnatural lust and all conceivable wickedness and crime.

As the people of fallen wisdom the "Ελληνες are under judgment and are thus included in the message of salvation. The statements in which Paul formulates this normally use the formula 'Ιουδαίω τε πρῶτον καὶ "Ελληνι (R. 1:16; 2:9; 3:9), which assures to the Jews a temporal precedence in virtue of their relationship to salvation history from their origin (cf. Ac. 13:46), and which puts the "Ελληνες second in accordance with the actual progress of the mission. The declaration of judgment takes the common form of threats of judgment against both the "Ελλην and the Jew who do evil and promises of δόξα καὶ τιμὴ καὶ εἰρήνη to those who do good (R. 2:7-10). As explained in 2:12-16, the reference is to the νόμος written in the heart of the ἔθνη. Thus Paul recognises another type of "Ελλην, i.e., the Greek who has the Law, i.e., the θέλημα τοῦ θεοῦ, in his heart and who fulfils it in his life, namely, the true disciple of the Στοά, as we might say, who really lives according to the teachings of his school. This assessment of the "Ελληνες is reflected again in the admonition in 1 C. 10:32 : ἀπρόσκοποι καὶ 'Ιουδαίοις γίνεσθε καὶ "Ελλησιν καὶ τῇ ἐκκλησίᾳ τοῦ θεοῦ. Here the formula is expanded to include a *tertium genus,* the → ἐκκλησία τοῦ θεοῦ.[61] With the Jews and the ἐκκλησία τοῦ θεοῦ, however, the Hellenes also have a power of moral judgment to which the Corinthian community should have regard. The idea that Christians must take into account the moral judgment of men generally is found elsewhere in the apostle ;[62] here, however, non-Jews and non-Christians are specifically called "Ελληνες. The Hellenes, too, have an organ of moral consciousness. They judge Christians accordingly, and are offended if they do not meet the test. In the enjoyment of this organ they are fully equal with the 'Ιουδαῖοι.

The distinction (διαστολή) which originally separated Jews and Greeks, and which is ultimately expressed in the πρῶτον, is fully resolved in the revelation to both peoples of the God who as the κύριος πάντων lavishes His grace on all who call upon Him (R. 10:12). Thus the apostle declares the crucified Christ as the power of God and the wisdom of God to both Jews and Greeks if they are κλητοί (1 C. 1:24). It is thus demanded that the "Ελληνες as κλητοί should abandon the judgment μωρία (→ 513) and therefore their native σοφία.

The resolution of the distinction implies the fusion of Jews and Greeks into a new unity, the community of God. According to 1 C. 12:13 all of us, εἴτε 'Ιουδαῖοι εἴτε "Ελληνες, are baptised by the Spirit into one body and given to drink of one spirit. The sacrament of the reception of the Spirit makes Hellenes and Jews equal, transforming both into members of the body of Christ and bearers of the Spirit. According to Gl. 3:27 f. baptism, which effects the putting on of Christ, means that there is no more 'Ιουδαῖος or "Ελλην, but that both are absorbed in the unity of the new being which is given us in Christ Jesus. Indeed, Paul is bold to say that by baptism the "Ελλην is incorporated into the seed of Abraham (Gl. 3:29), by which he means a fellowship of promise and inheritance which is open even to the 'Ιουδαῖος only by faith.[63]

---

[61] Cf. A. Harnack, *Mission und Ausbreitung des Christentums,* I⁴ (1924), 262 ff.; Jüthner, 91 f.

[62] 1 Th. 4:12; Col. 4:5.

[63] Cf. as an analogy from the sphere of the σάρξ the curious Jewish assertion of the common descent of Jews and Spartans (ἐκ γένους 'Αβραάμ), 1 Macc. 12:5 ff., 19 ff.

Similarly, we read in Col. 3:9 ff. that in the sphere of the νέος ἄνθρωπος (= Χριστός) put on in baptism the ῞Ελλην καὶ ᾽Ιουδαῖος (the only time they are in this order) no longer exist. Being as a ῞Ελλην belongs to the character of the παλαιὸς ἄνθρωπος which is put off in baptism, i.e., which has vanished or lost its reality.

Paul is the only apostle to be thus interested in the ῞Ελληνες, in their wisdom, their knowledge of God, the law written on their hearts, their life according to this *lex naturalis*, yet also their idolatry, their wickedness, their standing under wrath and judgment, their abandonment to God's penal action, and yet again the revelation of God's salvation to them, and their calling into the body of Christ in which their distinctive Hellenism is dissolved. This interest of Paul is due to the fact that he was specifically the apostle to the ῞Ελληνες. This is also emphasised by him : ῞Ελλησίν τε καὶ βαρβάροις, σοφοῖς τε καὶ ἀνοήτοις ὀφειλέτης εἰμί (R. 1:14), i.e., in virtue of his apostolic calling to the Gentile mission (Gl. 1:16). He is the apostle of the Hellenes (and barbarians), their διδάσκαλος (1 Tm. 2:7). [64] He thus has the tremendous task of accomplishing the deliverance intended for the Hellenes by the preaching of the Gospel, the διδάσκειν τοὺς ῞Ελληνᾶς, and therefore the work which some Jews mistakenly thought that Jesus was proposing to do (Jn. 7:35; → 509). Through him, then, innumerable ῞Ελληνες became believers, and he fought hard that the yoke of Judaism should not be laid on them but that they should have the place appropriate to them according to his Gospel (Gl. 2:5). A concrete example is his companion and helper Titus, who even in Jerusalem, the citadel of Jewish Christians who demanded circumcision, was not forced to be circumcised, thus demonstrating his teaching that through baptism, through the Spirit and in Christ the ῞Ελλην ceases to be a ῞Ελλην, so that he can no longer cause offence to the Jewish Christian, because through baptism the Jew, too, has ceased to be a Jew.

b. For Paul the Hellenes are also Gentiles. This does not mean, however, that the words are equivalent. The sense of Gentiles is certainly not present in the formula ῞Ελληνες καὶ βάρβαροι (cf. Paul's own commentary, σοφοῖς τε καὶ ἀνοήτοις), R. 1:14. Even the other formula, ᾽Ιουδαῖοι καὶ ῞Ελληνες, understands the ῞Ελληνες primarily as men who are distinguished from others by the Greek language and culture. This is particularly clear in Col. 3:11, where βάρβαρος and Σκύθης are used as well as ῞Ελλην καὶ ᾽Ιουδαῖος. National as well as social distinctions are abolished in Christ (→ I, 552). The lists in Gl. 3:28 f. and 1 C. 12:13 are to be evaluated in the same way. The people of the Hellenes is to be fused with the people of the Jews, the Scythians and the barbarians, into a new fellowship by baptism. Again, in Gl. 2:3 the Christian Titus cannot be designated a Gentile by the ῞Ελλην ὤν, even though ῞Ελλην is synonymous with ἀπερίτμητος; what is meant is an uncircumcised non-Jew of Hellenic nationality. Again, in 1 C. 1:22, 25 the ῞Ελληνες are concrete Greeks with their national culture centred on wisdom, not Gentiles. In this passage the Jews themselves are not characterised as the chosen people but as a foolish nation which demands σημεῖα of the preachers of the Gospel. It is in this sense that we are perhaps to take the formula ᾽Ιουδαῖοι καὶ ῞Ελληνες in R. 2:9 f. and 1 C. 10:32.

For Paul there is, of course, a close connection between ῞Ελληνες and ἔθνη. This can be seen from his common use of the parallel ᾽Ιουδαῖοι/ἔθνη, and also from his substitution of ἔθνη for ῞Ελληνες in some passages in which he deals with the ῞Ελληνες. The two phenomena intersect. It might be concluded that ἔθνη is for him a national concept like ῞Ελληνες. But there is an evident distinc-

---

[64] H. Windisch, *Paulus u. Christus* (1934), 143 ff.

tion. A theological idea is present in ἔθνη, namely, the mass of peoples not previously drawn into salvation history (→ 370). The only question is whether this theologoumenon has coloured the term Ἕλληνες. According to R. 3:29 God is a Saviour for both Jews and ἔθνη or περιτομή and ἀκροβυστία. Since the statement sums up the whole discussion from 1:16 ff., we obviously have the equation Ἕλληνες = ἀκροβυστία = ἔθνη. Similarly, the inward νόμος possessed by the ἔθνη applies specifically to the Ἕλληνες (R. 2:14 ff.). It is from them especially that Paul must have deduced the possession of a νόμος by the ἔθνη. The statement does, of course, abolish the Jewish concept of the ἔθνη. The decisive deficiency which makes the non-Jew a Gentile is declared to be abolished. The same is true of R. 2:25-29, where ἀκροβυστία and περιτομή are distinguished, but where finally, in a great transvaluation of values, the circumcised is declared to be uncircumcised (a Gentile) if he is a transgressor, and the uncircumcised is declared to be circumcised (a "Jew") if he keeps the Law. The clearest passage relating the two phenomena of the Ἕλληνες and ἔθνη is 1 C. 1:22-24, where we read Ἰουδαῖοι καὶ Ἕλληνες, then Ἰουδαίοις μὲν ... ἔθνεσιν δέ, [65] and finally Ἰουδαίοις τε καὶ Ἕλλησιν (sc. τοῖς κλητοῖς). Here Ἕλληνες is either fully synonymous with ἔθνη, or the Ἕλληνες are the chief representatives of the ἔθνη. Similarly, in the important discussion in R. 9-11 the statement that there is no διαστολὴ Ἰουδαίου τε καὶ Ἕλληνος in R.10:12 is later followed by the antithesis of Ἰσραήλ (11:7, 25 ff.) and ἔθνη (11:13, 25).

There can thus be no doubt that Paul includes the Ἕλληνες among the ἔθνη and often uses the words interchangeably. Nevertheless, they are not quite identical. This is proved by the use of Ἕλληνες as a national term when the parallel word does not occur. It is also proved by the fact that ἔθνη is more common and is always used in the specific context of direct or indirect theological disputation with the "Jews."

The sense of "Gentile" cannot be proved, then, either from Hellenistic Judaism or the NT. Indeed, we might say that this development could take place only within an assured Christianity on Greek soil, since it presupposes the abolition in principle of all national distinctions (in terms of Gl. 3:28; Col. 3:11 ff.) — something which we do not yet find in Judaism. Nevertheless, Hellenistic Judaism came very near to the equation of the Greek and the Gentile world, and the presuppositions of this equation are all present in Paul.

Windisch

---

† ἐλλογέω

From ἐν λόγῳ (sc. τιθέναι), this means "to lay to account," and is thus a so-called "hypostasis" like ἐγχειρεῖν from ἐν χειρί. [1] It is a technical commercial term for "to charge" in CIG, I, 1732a, 37; CIL, III, p. 836; BGU, I, 40, 31 f.; IV, 1028, 2 etc.; P. Lond., II, 359, 4 (τὰ πλείω ὑπ' αὐτοῦ ἐλλογηθέντα); P. Strassburg (ed. F. Preisigke [1906 ff.]), 32, 10. [2]

---

[65] In ℵ we have the variant Ἕλλησιν.

ἐλλογεῖν. Cf. Moult.-Mill., 204; Deissmann LO, 66.

[1] Cf. Debr. Griech. Wortb. § 149.

[2] Preisigke Wört., I, 471; Deissm. LO, 66; A. Wikenhauser, "Zum Wörterb. des NT," BZ, 8 (1910), 272.

In the NT it occurs twice. It is used in the commercial sense in Phlm. 18. [3] Any loss suffered through the runaway Onesimus is to be charged to the apostle.

In R. 5:13 the ἐλλογεῖσθαι of man's sin by God is to be regarded as given with the revelation of the Law. Adam was confronted by God's Law, and from the days of Moses men have the divine Law. Thus in Adam, and from the days of Moses, sin arises in relation to the divine command (→ ἐντολή) and is revolt against God's will. The Law, however, places under the curse of death those who break it (Gl. 3:10). In the days between Adam and Moses the race had no Law. When men sinned, they did so μὴ ... ἐν τῷ ὁμοιώματι τῆς παραβάσεως Ἀδάμ (R. 5:14; cf. 4:15), i.e., in terms of the total situation created by the fall of Adam and not in conscious enmity against God or rebellion against a given Law (→ ἁμαρτάνω, I, 309 f.). The death which they died was thus a comprehensive destiny posited in Adam, not a punishment. To be sure, God punished sin in this period (R. 2:12 ff.), but not with death. In R. 5:12 ff., however, death is the punishment of sin. Thus, when we read in 5:13: ἁμαρτία δὲ οὐκ ἐλλογεῖται μὴ ὄντος νόμου, it is evident that the ἐλλογεῖσθαι of ἁμαρτία is linked with the Law, and that the ἐλλογεῖσθαι of ἁμαρτία results in death. Where there is a revelation of God's will in the Law, sin is estimated differently. It is not merely participation in the total situation of man; it is transgression of the divinely declared will. Thus sin has very different consequences. It is exclusion from the fellowship of will and life, from the creation of God. In this sense death is no mere destiny; as in the case of Adam and of violators of the Law of Israel (Gl. 3:10; R. 3:19), it is a penalty. Paul thus describes as ἐλλογεῖσθαι the attitude of God to the sinful state of man under the claim of the revelation of the Law. What is meant is that the sin of man as rejection of the revealed will of God is "taken into account" or "charged," so that man is excluded from the divine fellowship of will and creation. [4] Paul denies this in relation to the time between Adam and Moses, but it is the more decisively affirmed of the time after Moses. [5]

Preisker

┌─────────────────────────────┐
│ ἐλπίς, ἐλπίζω,   │
│ ἀπ-, προελπίζω   │
└─────────────────────────────┘

† ἐλπίς, ἐλπίζω.

A. The Greek Concept of Hope.

1. Ἡμεῖς δ' αὖ διὰ παντὸς τοῦ βίου ἀεὶ γέμομεν ἐλπίδων, we read in Plat. Phileb., 39e, in an analysis in which he shows how human existence is determined not

---

[3] Forms like ἐλλόγα in Phlm. 18 are to be explained by the confusion of the types of inflection -ᾶν and -εῖν, cf. Bl.-Debr. § 90.

[4] Cf. Sickb. R.[3] (1923), ad loc.: Pl. "believes that these pre-Mosaic sins ... are not regarded as offences worthy of death like the sins of Adam." Cf. also B. Weiss Komm., ad loc. A. Schaefer, *Die Bücher des NT*, III (1891), ad loc., does not regard death as the consequence of Adam's sin, and therefore he hardly does justice to the passage.

[5] The idea of reckoning goes back to ideas which came into Judaism from the Parsees, who believed that man would be judged acc. to exact records in the heavenly books, cf. A. v. Gall, Βασιλεία τοῦ θεοῦ (1926), 88; Bousset-Gressmann, 258 f.; Str.-B., IV, 1041.

ἐλπίς. Stob., IV, 997-1007 περὶ ἐλπίδος, περὶ τῶν παρ' ἐλπίδα. Th. Birt, *Elpides* (1881); L. Schmidt, *Die Ethik der alten Griechen*, II (1882), 69-74; J. de Guibert, *Recherches*

merely by the αἴσθησις which accepts the present but also by the μνήμη of the past and the expectation of the future, [1] and indeed in such a way that, like recollection of the past, expectation of the future (προχαίρειν and προλυπεῖσθαι 39d) is not an objective assessment but a subjective expectation in fear and hope, whose content arises from what man considers to be his own possibilities. "Man's own being thus determines what he hopes and how he hopes." [2] He whose hopes are ἀληθεῖς is a θεοφιλής. Expectations and hopes are man's own projections of his future.

It is of the nature of man to have ἐλπίδες, [3] i.e., good or bad expectations of the future (ἐλπίς = προσδοκία). [4] What we mean by hope is called ἐλπίς ἀγαθή, [5] though later ἐλπίς is often used for hope in our sense, [6] and this brings out the original etymological significance of ἐλπ- once again. [7]

---

de Science Religieuse, 4 (1913), 565-596; A. Pott, Das Hoffen im NT (1915); F. Wehrli, ΛΑΘΕ ΒΙΩΣΑΣ (1931), 6 ff.; A. Lesky in Gnomon, 9 (1933), 173 ff. On C.: Str.-B., III, 217 ff. Jew. Enc., VI, 459 f.; Moore, II, 287 ff.; Bousset-Gressm., Index under "Hoffnung"; G. Kittel, Die Religionsgeschichte u. d. Urchristentum (1932), 130 ff.; E. Stauffer, "Paulus und Akiba, Der erlösende u. d. tragische Ausgang des Judentums," Saat auf Hoffnung, 69 (1932), 113 ff.; W. Wichmann, Die Leidenstheologie (1930).

[1] There is a similar correspondence between ἐλπίς and μνήμη in Arist. Metaph., XI, 7, p. 1072b, 18; Rhet., II, 8, p. 1386a, 2 f. and 30; De Memoria, 1, p. 449b, 10 ff.: οὔτε γὰρ τὸ μέλλον ἐνδέχεται μνημονεύειν, ἀλλ' ἔστι δοξαστὸν καὶ ἐλπιστόν (εἴη δ' ἂν καὶ ἐπιστήμη τις ἐλπιστική, καθάπερ τινές φασι τὴν μαντικήν), οὔτε τοῦ παρόντος, ἀλλ' αἴσθησις. 27 f.: τοῦ μὲν παρόντος αἴσθησις, τοῦ δὲ μέλλοντος ἐλπίς, τοῦ δὲ γενομένου μνήμη.

[2] H. G. Gadamer, Platos dialektische Ethik (1931), 138; and esp. his interpretation of Phileb., 35a-41b, p. 126-139. In illustration, v. the examples in → n. 8; also n. 13 on the connection between ἐλπίς and ἔρως; cf. also Demosth. Or., 18, 97; Isoc., 1, 39: οἱ γὰρ δίκαιοι τῶν ἀδίκων εἰ μηδὲν ἄλλο πλεονεκτοῦσιν, ἀλλ' οὖν ἐλπίσι γε σπουδαίαις ὑπερέχουσιν.

[3] Stob., V, 1001, 13 f.: Θάλης ἐρωτηθεὶς τί κοινότατον, ἀπεκρίνατο· ἐλπίς· καὶ γὰρ οἷς ἄλλο μηδέν, αὕτη πάρεστιν; Eur. Tro., 632 f.: "Where there is life there is hope"; Plat. Phileb., 39e (→ supra); Theocr., 4, 42: ἐλπίδες ἐν ζωοῖσιν, ἀνέλπιστοι δὲ θανόντες; cf. Birt, op. cit., 6 ff.

[4] This is shown by the examples in n. 1; cf. Plat. Phileb., 36a ff.; ἐλπίς can mean fearful expectation, e.g., Eur. Iph. Aul., 786. Often ἐλπίζειν means "to believe," "to suppose," e.g., Pind. Fr., 61; Emped. Fr., 11 (I, 227, 21, Diels); Heracl. Fr., 27 (I, 83, 5 f., Diels): ἀνθρώπους μένει ἀποθανόντας ἄσσα οὐκ ἔλπονται οὐδὲ δοκέουσιν. Aristoph. Av., 956. Παρ' ἐλπίδα is often used in the same sense as παρὰ γνώμην (→ I, 691, n. 7), cf. Soph. Ant., 330 f.; καὶ νῦν γὰρ ἐκτὸς ἐλπίδος γνώμης τ' ἐμῆς σωθεὶς ὀφείλω τοῖς θεοῖς πολλὴν χάριν. Ἀνέλπιστος means "unexpected," e.g., Eur. Iph. Taur., 1495; Hel., 412 (ἀνελπίστῳ τύχῃ); it means the same as ἀδόκητος in Hel., 656.

[5] Plat. Leg., I, 644c: the δόξαι μελλόντων have the κοινὸν ὄνομα: ἐλπίς, ἴδιον δὲ φόβος μὲν ἡ πρὸ λύπης ἐλπίς, θάρρος δὲ ἡ πρὸ τοῦ ἐναντίου. Ἐλπίς is thus characterised by attributes like ἀγαθή (Pind. Isthm., 8, 15; Plat. Leg., IV, 718a; Aristot. De Virtutibus et Vitiis, 8, p. 1251b, 34 f.; → n. 8; Ael. Arist. Or. Sacr., 48, 28), καλή (Plut. De Bruto, 40 [I, 1002c] → n. 18; Stob., I, 403, 21 → n. 21), γλυκεῖα (Pind. Fr., 214; Plat. Resp., I, 331a), ἱλαρά (Kritias Fr., 6 [II, 315, 11, Diels]), χρηστή (BMI, 894 in Wendland Hell. Kult., 410; often in Philo); and on the other hand κακή (Plat. Resp., I, 330e). The adj. εὔελπις is common (Plat. Ap., 41d; Phaed., 64a); to be εὔελπις is characteristic of youth, Aristot. Rhet., II, 12, p. 1389a, 19 ff. The chief character in Aristoph. Av. is Εὐελπίδης, Good Hope.

[6] Thus in Ps.-Plat. Def., 416a ἐλπίς is defined as προσδοκία ἀγαθοῦ. This usage corresponds to the frequent later distinction of ἐλπίς and φόβος Birt, 6 (and 97, n. 17), 46 f. Later ἐλπίς (ἐλπίζειν) is occasionally used with προσδοκία (προσδοκᾶν), v. Preisigke Wört.

[7] Ελπ- is formed by adding p to the root vel (Lat. vel-le), cf. the Lat. volup (voluptas) and the Gr. ἀλπ- in ἔπαλπνος ("desired"), ἀλπαλέος, ἀρπαλέος, ἄλπιστος, cf. A. Walde-J. Pokorny, Vergleichendes Wört. d. indogerm. Sprachen, I (1930), 295.

How the fact that man hopes is understood at a given time is most significant for the Greek understanding of existence. The twofold value of ἐλπίς is expressed by Soph. Ant., 615 f.:

ἁ γὰρ δὴ πολύπλαγκτος ἐλπὶς πολλοῖς μὲν ὄνησις ἀνδρῶν
πολλοῖς δ' ἀπάτα κουφονόων ἐρώτων.

That man either does or can hope is a comfort for him in a difficult present, cf. Hom. Od., 16, 101 and 19, 84 : ἔτι γὰρ καὶ ἐλπίδος αἶσα. Hope is "golden," Soph. Oed. Tyr., 158, and the θυμός is defeated in which there is no ἐλπίδος φίλον θράσος (Aesch. Ag., 994; cf. 262 : εὐάγγελοι ἐλπίδες).

Pind. Fr., 214 :   γλυκεῖά οἱ καρδίαν ἀτάλλοισα γηροτρόφος συναορεῖ
                (accompany)
                ἐλπίς, ἃ μάλιστα θνατῶν πολύστροφον γνώμαν κυβερνᾶ. [8]

Pind. Isthm., 8, 15 :   χρὴ δ' ἀγαθὰν ἐλπίδ' ἀνδρὶ μέλειν. [9]

Acc. to Thuc., V, 103 ἐλπίς is a κινδύνῳ παραμύθιον. It can comfort the individual in distress : ἀπορίη ξυνὴ τῆς ἑκάστου χαλεπωτέρη· οὐ γὰρ ὑπολείπεται ἐλπὶς ἐπικουρίης (help) (Democr. Fr., 287 [II, 120, 5 f., Diels]). Thus the old fable [10] tells us that Zeus gave man a vessel full of all good things but that man, filled with curiosity, lifted the lid, so that all the good things escaped to the gods and when the lid was put back only ἐλπίς was trapped, man's present comfort. The same motif is found in Aesch. Prom., 248 ff. Prometheus boasts : θνητούς γ' ἔπαυσα μὴ προσδέρκεσθαι μόρον, and to the question τὸ ποῖον εὑρὼν τῆσδε φάρμακον νόσου; he answers : τυφλὰς ἐν αὐτοῖς ἐλπίδας κατῴκισα. The chorus then says : μέγ' ὠφέλημα τοῦτ' ἐδωρήσω βροτοῖς.

But hope is easily deceived [11] and is dangerous. Only a god does not err in his

---

[8] Plato quotes this verse in Resp., I, 331a with the observation : τῷ δὲ μηδὲν ἑαυτῷ ἄδικον ξυνειδότι ἡδεῖα ἐλπὶς ἀεὶ πάρεστι ..., while the wicked lives μετὰ κακῆς ἐλπίδος; cf. Leg., IV, 718a of the good : ἐν ἐλπίσιν ἀγαθαῖς διάγοντες τὸ πλεῖστον τοῦ βίου. Aristot. De Virtutibus et Vitiis, 8, p. 1251b, 33 f.: ἀκολουθεῖ δὲ τῇ ἀρετῇ χρηστότης, ἐπιείκεια, εὐγνωμοσύνη, ἐλπὶς ἀγαθή. Eur. Hel., 1031: ἐν τῷ δικαίῳ δ' ἐλπίδες σωτηρίας. Cf. on the other hand Democr. Fr., 221 (II, 105, 10 f., Diels): ἐλπὶς κακοῦ κέρδεος ἀρχὴ ζημίης. Similarly acc. to Hes. Op., 498 ff. ἐλπίς seduces the indolent into poor projects.

[9] Cf. Soph. Trach., 125 f.; Eur. Herc. Fur., 105 f.

[10] The original point of the fable is preserved in Babrius, 58 (P. Friedländer, *Herakles* [1907], 39 ff.); it is worked over in Hes. Op., 94 ff., and the meaning is disputed (H. Türck, *Pandora u. Eva* [1931], 18 ff.). The same thought occurs in Theogn., 1135 f.: ἐλπὶς ἐν ἀνθρώποις μούνη θεὸς ἐσθλὴ ἔνεστιν, ἄλλοι δ' Οὔλυμπόνδ' ἐκπρολιπόντες ἔβαν, though he knows that hope cuts both ways (637 f.): ἐλπὶς καὶ κίνδυνος ἐν ἀνθρώποισιν ὁμοῖοι· οὗτοι γὰρ χαλεποὶ δαίμονες ἀμφότεροι. From a later period cf. Max. Tyr., 29, 6 b/c : καὶ ἄλλων μυρίων κακῶν ἀνέχονται οἱ ἄνθρωποι δι' οὐδὲν ἄλλο ἢ δι' ἐλπίδα ἀγαθοῦ καὶ ἄγνοιαν. In Heracl. Fr., 18 (I, 81, 16 f., Diels) ἐλπίς seems to be thought of as the suprarational power of ἐξευρεῖν: ἐὰν μὴ ἔλπηται ἀνέλπιστον, οὐκ ἐξευρήσει, ἀνεξερεύνητον ἐὸν καὶ ἄπορον. Acc. to H. Fränkel (in Türck, 6), as against Diels, "he who does not expect what cannot be expected (i.e., what transcends all expectation) will not make the unattainable attainable." On the significance of ἐλπίς as the impelling force in the τέχνη which produces prosperity, cf. Birt, *op. cit.*

[11] εὐπαράγωγος, Plat. Tim., 69d. Ἐλπίς (the θεός) deceives in Eur. Iph. Aul., 392; Iph. Taur., 414 ff.; Suppl., 479 ff.

expectations, [12] and men's ἐλπίδες are uncertain. [13] Man should have regard, not to ἀπεόντα, but to ἐπιχώρια; he should grasp what is παρὰ ποδός. [14] Τὸ ἐλπίς which waits on the uncertain is opposed προμαθέος αἰδώς (Pind. Olymp., 7, 44). In προμάθεια (Pind. Nem., 11, 46) man takes control of the future as he judges and acts on the basis of the present. In Thuc., II, 62 there is a contrast between ἐλπίς, ἧς ἐν τῷ ἀπόρῳ ἡ ἰσχύς and γνώμη ἀπὸ τῶν ὑπαρχόντων, ἧς βεβαιοτέρα ἡ πρόνοια, and in II, 42 between ἐλπίς and ἔργον. It is a mistake for man to go to μαντική and χρησμοί for his ἀφανεῖς ἐλπίδες, V, 103. [15] Acc. to Democr. the ἐλπίδες of fools cannot be fulfilled, but those of the educated and cultured are better than the riches of the uncultured (Fr., 58 [II, 75, 11 f., Diels]; 185 [II, 99, 6 f., Diels]; 292 [II, 120, 20 f., Diels]); for the hope of the wise, which is no longer ἐλπίς in the original sense, is not based on τύχη but on the φύσις which can be scientifically investigated. [16] Here is a typical expression of the distinctive Greek tendency to insure against the future by a conscious integration into the order of the cosmos.

2. Plato, of course, need not renounce the ἔρως which works in ἐλπίς (→ n. 13), for as he sees it this is the impulse to the beautiful and the good. He can thus say of it in Symp., 193d: ἐν τῷ παρόντι ἡμᾶς πλεῖστα ὀνίνησιν εἰς τὸ οἰκεῖον ἄγων, καὶ εἰς τὸ ἔπειτα ἐλπίδας μεγίστας παρέχεται. For Plato himself these εἰς τὸ ἔπειτα ἐλπίδες extend beyond the present life. For if σκότος conceals from man a φίλτερον ἄλλο ζῆν, so that, δυσέρωτες, we are attracted by the dubious glory of earthly life (Eur. Hipp., 189 ff.), the philosopher is εὔελπις in face of death (Plat. Ap., 41c; Phaed., 64a). For him there is πολλὴ ἐλπίς of attaining to the place οὗ ἕνεκα ἡ πολλὴ πραγματεία ἡμῖν ἐν τῷ παρελθόντι βίῳ γέγονεν (Phaed., 67b), and he does not fear death (67c-68b), καλὸν γὰρ τὸ ἆθλον καὶ ἡ ἐλπὶς μεγάλη. Many have indeed died willingly, sustained by the ἐλπίς of seeing their loved ones again in Hades (68a), → θάνατος. The Mysteries which promise initiates a life of bliss after death [17] continually gain in significance (→ ζωή, → ἀθανασία). On the basis of this

---

[12] Pind. Pyth., 2, 49: θεὸς ἅπαν ἐπὶ ἐλπιδέσσι τέκμαρ (goal) ἀνύεται.

[13] Pind., Olymp., 12, 5 f.: αἵ γε μὲν ἀνδρῶν πόλλ' ἄνω, τὰ δ' αὖ κάτω ψεύδη μεταμώνια (vain) τάμνοισαι κυλίνδοντ' ἐλπίδες (cf. 12, 1-13 and Pyth., 10, 59-64; 12, 28-32). Pyth., 3, 19-23: ἀλλά τοι ἤρατο τῶν ἀπεόντων· οἷα καὶ πολλοὶ πάθον. ἔστι δὲ φῦλον ἐν ἀνθρώποισι ματαιότατον, ὅστις αἰσχύνων ἐπιχώρια παπταίνει (look) τὰ πόρσω, μεταμώνια θηρεύων ἀκράντοις ἐλπίσιν. Nem., 11, 42-48: the θνατὸν ἔθνος is guided by μοῖρα, but our members are bound ἀναιδεῖ ἐλπίδι; this has its source in ἔρως or desire (cf. Pyth., 10, 60; Nem., 3, 30; Soph. Ant., 616 → 519, on Plat. Symp., 193d → infra). Around the souls of mortals hang φθονεραὶ ἐλπίδες, Isthm., 2, 43. Solon Fr., 1, 35 f. (Diehl): ἄχρι δὲ τούτου (namely, πρίν τι παθεῖν) χάσκοντες (snap) κούφαις ἐλπίσι τερπόμεθα. These ἐλπίδες are then depicted; then in 63 ff.: μοῖρα δέ τοι θνητοῖσι κακὸν φέρει ἠδὲ καὶ ἐσθλόν. δῶρα δ' ἄφυκτα θεῶν γίγνεται ἀθανάτων. πᾶσι δέ τοι κίνδυνος ἐπ' ἔργμασιν, οὐδέ τις οἶδεν, ᾗ μέλλει σχήσειν χρήματος ἀρχομένου. A hope is seldom fulfilled acc. to Aesch. Ag., 505: πολλῶν ῥαγεισῶν ἐλπίδων μιᾶς τυχών. Cf. Soph. Fr., 205: ἐλπὶς οὐδὲν ὠφελεῖ. Soph. Ai., 477 f.: οὐκ ἂν πριαίμην οὐδενὸς λόγου βροτόν, ὅστις κεναῖσιν ἐλπίσιν θερμαίνεται (κενὴ ἐλπὶς also, e.g., in Hes. Op., 498; M. Ant., 3, 14; Anth. Pal., VII, 376; though cf. πιστὸν ἔλπισμα in Epic. Fr., 68 [Usener], also Plut. Suav. Viv. Epic., 6 [II, 1090d]: πιστὴ ἐλπίς). Antiphon Fr., 38 (II, 303, 2 f., Diels): ἐλπίδες δ' οὐ πανταχοῦ ἀγαθόν· πολλοὺς γὰρ τοιαῦται ἐλπίδες κατέβαλον εἰς ἀνηκέστους (irremediable) συμφοράς. On the connection between hopes and dreams, cf. Birt, 45 ff.

[14] Pind. Pyth., 3, 20; 22; 60; 10, 63; Isthm., 8, 13.

[15] Cf. Aristot. De Memoria, 1, p. 449b, 10 ff. → n. 1.

[16] τύχη μεγαλόδωρος, ἀλλ' ἀβέβαιος, φύσις δὲ αὐτάρκης. διόπερ νικᾷ τῷ ἥσσονι καὶ βεβαίῳ τὸ μεῖζον τῆς ἐλπίδος, Fr., 176 (II, 96, 12 ff., Diels). On the other hand, cf. Heracl. → n. 10).

[17] Isoc., 4, 28; 8, 34; Ael. Arist., 22, 10: περὶ τῆς τελευτῆς ἡδίους ἔχειν τὰς ἐλπίδας ὡς ἄμεινον διάξοντας ... Cic. De Legibus, II, 14, 36: neque solum cum laetitia vivendi rationem accepimus sed etiam cum spe meliore moriendi. Cf. C. A. Lobeck, Aglaophamus (1829), 69 ff.; E. Rohde, Psyche¹⁰, I (1925), 290.

faith Porphyr. Marc., 24 numbers ἐλπίς with πίστις, ἀλήθεια and ἔρως as the four στοιχεῖα which constitute a genuine life ; [18] the τῶν ἐφημέρων ὄρεξις καὶ ἐλπίς must naturally be renounced (ibid., 29). [19]

3. Human earthly hopes obviously have a place in Hellenism as well as hopes of the beyond. [20] As in the Κόρη κόσμου, 28 (Stob., I, 393, 19 ff.), the gift of Zeus to men consists in the fact that he directs wars and gives τύχη, ἐλπίς and εἰρήνη, [21] so Augustus is lauded in the Priene inscr. as the σωτήρ who puts an end to war, fulfils old hopes and kindles new ones. [22] Stoicism had no interest in the phenomenon of hope. In Epict. ἐλπίζειν (ἐλπίς) is used in the older sense of "to expect." [23] He knows : καὶ τοῖς σκέλεσι καὶ ταῖς ἐλπίσι τὸ δυνατὰ δεῖ διαβαίνειν (Fr. 31). He emphasises : οὔτε ναῦν ἐξ ἑνὸς ἀγκυρίου, οὔτε βίον ἐκ μιᾶς ἐλπίδος ὁρμιστέον (Fr. 30). He admonishes, not εἰς ἄλλους ἀφορᾶν, but ἐλπίζειν ἐκ σεαυτοῦ (III, 26, 11). Similarly M. Ant. admonishes : τὰς κενὰς ἐλπίδας ἀφεὶς σαυτῷ βοήθει (3, 14). [24] The statement of Epicurus is typical : μνημονευτέον δ' ὡς τὸ μέλλον οὔθ' ἡμέτερον οὔτε πάντως οὐχ ἡμέτερον, ἵνα μήτε πάντως προσμένωμεν ὡς ἐσόμενον, μήτ' ἀπελπίζωμεν ὡς πάντως οὐκ ἐσόμενον (Diog. L., X, 127). A cynical scepticism is confessed in Anth. Pal., IX, 172, 1: ἐλπίδος οὐδὲ τύχης ἔτι μοι μέλει ... "I ask concerning neither hope nor fortune." [25] Here it is everywhere regarded as self-evident that hope is simply man's projection of the future.

B. The OT View of Hope.

1. Normally the LXX uses ἐλπίζειν (ἐλπίς) [26] for בָּטַח and the derived subst.; [27] though πεποιθέναι (πεποίθησις) is more common for the class בטח (never πιστεύειν). Ἐλπίζειν is also used twice for קָוָה, which is usually rendered ὑπο- (also ἀνα- and περι-) μένειν. תִּקְוָה is most commonly translated ἐλπίς (in Prv. and Job, also Ez. 37:11),

---

[18] → I, 51, n. 147 for bibl. The determination of life by the τέσσαρα στοιχεῖα is described by Porphyr. as follows : πιστεῦσαι γὰρ δεῖ ὅτι μόνη σωτηρία ἡ πρὸς τὸν θεὸν ἐπιστροφή, καὶ πιστεύσαντα ὡς ἔνι μάλιστα σπουδάσαι τἀληθῆ γνῶναι περὶ αὐτοῦ, καὶ γνόντα ἐρασθῆναι τοῦ γνωσθέντος, ἐρασθέντα δὲ ἐλπίσιν ἀγαθαῖς τρέφειν τὴν ψυχὴν διὰ τοῦ βίου. Cf. also Plut. Brut., 40 (I, 1002c): ἐν ἐλπίσι καλαῖς καὶ λογισμοῖς φιλοσόφοις γενόμενος.

[19] Cf. also Jul. Ep., 89, p. 124, 13; 139, 2 f. (μεγάλας ἡμῖν οἱ θεοὶ μετὰ τὴν τελευτὴν ἐλπίδας ἐπαγγέλλονται).

[20] Cf. Birt, 3 f. for the role of ἐλπίς in erotic literature, and Birt, passim for its role in comedy and the Hellenistic and Latin literature influenced by it ; a good example is Luc. De Mercede Conductis. Cf. also Anth. Pal., VI, 330, 1 f. (to Aesculapius): θνητῶν μὲν τέχναις ἀπορούμενος, εἰς δὲ τὸ θεῖον ἐλπίδα πᾶσαν ἔχων. P. Oxy., VII, 1070, 10 f.

[21] Stob., I, 403, 21, the prayer : πλήρωσον κακῶν ἐλπίδων πάντα.

[22] Ditt. Or., II, 458 (in Wendland, op. cit., 409 f.). Cf. also the Halicarnass. inscr. in BMI, 894 → n. 5; Ditt. Syll.³, 797, 5 f. → I, 70; Ditt. Or., 542, 12 (νέαν ἐλπίδα τῆς πατρίδος); 669, 7: ἐλπίζειν in the emperor (Galba); P. Oxy., VII, 1021, 5 ff.: ὁ δὲ τῆς οἰκουμένης καὶ προσδοκηθεὶς καὶ ἐλπισθεὶς Αὐτοκράτωρ ἀποδέδεικται. In the Tomi inscr. published in the Arch.-epigr. Mitteil., 14 (1891), 22-26 (line 3 f.): ὁ δῆμος ἐν τῇ μεγίστῃ καθέστηκεν δυσελπιστίᾳ. Measures are taken (line 34 f.), ἕως τοῦ ἀποκατασταθῆναι τὸν δῆμον εἰς βελτίονας ἐλπίδας.

[23] I, 20, 13; II, 20, 37; 23, 46; Ench., 40.

[24] Cf. also ἐλπίζειν in 9, 29 (μὴ τὴν Πλάτωνος πολιτείαν ἔλπιζε); 10, 36; ἐλπίς in 1, 17 (καὶ μὴ ἀναβαλέσθαι ἐλπίδι τοῦ με ... ὕστερον αὐτὸ πρᾶξαι); 5, 8.

[25] ἐλπίς and τύχη are often linked, Birt, op. cit., 15 (and 100, n. 57); 47; 91 (and 125, n. 213). Spes et fortuna, valete, we read on an epitaph. Carmina Latina Epigraphica (ed. Buecheler), 409, 8.

[26] On the aspiration of ἐλπίς (ἐλπίζειν), v. Thackeray, 124 f.

[27] ἐλπίζειν is used 47 times for בָּטַח and once for בֶּטַח (?); ἐλπίς is used 7 times for בֶּטַח, also 9 times for מִבְטָח, 14 for בֶּטַח and once for בִּטָּחוֹן.

though קוה is rendered πεποιθέναι (Is. 8:17; 33:2), προσδοκᾶν, ἐγγίζειν, ἐπέχειν, and תקוה ὑπόστασις and ὑπομονή. ἐλπίζειν occurs 20 times for חָכָה and 7 for מָחָה, though we also find πεποιθέναι for חסה (9 times) and σκέπη, καταφυγή, βοηθός for מחסה. We find ἐλπίζειν 10 times for the pi of יָחַל and 5 times for the hiph; though here again ὑπομένειν is used. תּוֹחֶלֶת is twice translated ἐλπίς, never ὑπόστασις, though other terms are used. Finally, ἐλπίζειν is used twice for שָׂבַר (προσδοκᾶν twice), and ἐλπίς is used once for שֵׂבֶר (προσδοκία once), once for כֶּסֶל and once for vl. מַבָּט (Zech. 9:5 AQ). We may also add some exceptional cases, e.g., ἐλπίζειν for דָּרַשׁ (Is. 11:10), גָּלַל (ψ 21:9), חָשַׁק (ψ 90:14), שָׁעַן (2 Ch. 13:18), שָׁקַק (Is. 29:8), רָחַץ (Da. 3:28 or 95), נָשָׂא נֶפֶשׁ ('Ιερ. 51:14), etc.; ἐλπίς for חָזוּת (Is. 28:18), חֶסֶד (2 Ch. 35:26), צְבִי (Is. 24:16; 28:4 f.), נָשָׂא נֶפֶשׁ (Dt. 24:15), ἐλπὶς πονηρά for זְוָעָה (Is. 28:19).

2. There is here something characteristic. In the OT there is no neutral concept of expectation. An expectation is either good or bad and therefore it is either hope or fear. Hope itself is thus differentiated linguistically from fear of the future.[28] Hope as expectation of good is closely linked with trust, and expectation is also yearning, in which the element of patient waiting or fleeing for refuge is emphasised.

Hope is thus hope of the good, and so long as there is life there is hope (Qoh. 9:4). But this hope is not a consoling dream of the imagination which causes us to forget our present troubles, nor are we warned of its uncertainty, as in the Greek world. The life of the righteous is grounded in hope. To have hope, to have a future, is a sign that things are well with us.[29] This hope is naturally directed to God.[30] It is naturally referred to most frequently when man is in trouble and hopes that God will deliver and help him. This hope is thus trust, so that we may have קוה and בטח together (ψ 24:1 ff.), or קוה may be used where elsewhere we have בטח in the same sense.[31] This hopeful trust is always demanded,[32] however, even in times of blessing.[33] And when we remember that the Psalms became the prayer-book of the congregation, we can see that the demand is absolute. The righteous are always referred to what God will do, so that hope is not directed

---

[28] It is worth noting that the LXX has ἐλπὶς πονηρά at Is. 28:19, where זְוָעָה means "fear" or "dread."

[29] Prv. 23:18; 24:14; 26:12; Job 11:18. If hope goes, all is lost (Lam. 3:18; Job 6:11; 7:6 etc.); and hope goes with death (Is. 38:18; Ez. 37:11; Job 17:15).

[30] He who trusts in God will be helped (ψ 27:7) and will not be confounded → αἰσχύνω, I, 189 (ψ 24:2 f.; 30:6, 14; 68:6; 118:116; Is. 49:23). The fathers trusted in Him and were not confounded (ψ 21:4). The righteous trusts in God's חֶסֶד (ψ 12:5; 32:18, 22; 51:8), יְשׁוּעָה (Gn. 49:18; ψ 77:22), תְּשׁוּעָה (ψ 118:21, 123 etc.); he waits upon God (ψ 24:20) and His judgment (Is. 26:8); God is his confidence (ψ 9:18; 64:5; 70:5; 90:9 etc.). Salvation is to those who trust in God (Jer. 17:7; ψ 39:4; 90:1 ff.). The righteous should trust in God and wait for Him (ψ 4:5; 26:14; 36:3 etc.; Prv. 20:22 (12); 22:19 etc.); he confesses: "I trust (or trusted) in God" (Is. 12:2; ψ 24:2; 27:7; 30:6, 14; 90:2).

[31] קוה Is. 8:17; 25:9; 26:8; ψ 26:14; 36:9; 68:6 etc.; בטח Is. 30:15; ψ 12:5; 21:4 f. etc. So also חסה (ψ 5:11; 16:7) where elsewhere we have קוה (Is. 40:31; ψ 36:9; 68:6; Lam. 3:25); מחסה (Is. 28:15; ψ 13:5; 60:4 etc.), where elsewhere we have מבטח (ψ 39:4; 64:5). In ψ 70:5 we have both תקוה and מבטח followed by מחסה in v. 7. In the rendering of בטח in Jer. 17:7, and of חסה in ψ 56:1, πεποιθέναι and ἐλπίζειν are used alternately; cf. ἐλπίζειν and ὑπομένειν for קוה in Is. 25:9.

[32] Jer. 17:7; ψ 39:4; 51:8; 90:2; 111:7 etc.

[33] Is. 12:2.

to anything specific, nor does it project its own view of the future, but it consists rather in general confidence in God's protection and help. [34] It may thus be said that God is the hope or confidence of the righteous. [35] This makes quite impossible the Greek contrasting of ἐλπίς with what is παρὰ ποδός, with οἰκεῖον, or with προμήθεια as the foresight which works with controllable factors. Even the present which man thinks he can control is uncertain and incalculable. The difference between hope and trust fades. Trust and certainty are always a hope that the present state will so persist that the factors on which one counts will not change. But where this is not hope in God such confidence is irresponsible security which God will suddenly overthrow and change into fear and anxiety. [36] No man should trust in his riches (ψ 51:7; Job 31:24), his righteousness (Ez. 33:13), men (Jer. 17:5), or his religious inheritance, whether the temple (Jer. 7:4), Bethel (Jer. 48:13) or idols (Hab. 2:18). The deliberations and calculations of men are but wind (ψ 93:11); God brings them to nought (ψ 32:10; Is. 19:3 etc.). "A man's heart deviseth his way: but the Lord directeth his steps" (Prv. 16:9). The nation and its calculating politicians will be confounded if they build on calculable forces and treaties with other countries. [37] Such confidence thinks it can count on controllable factors, but hope is to be directed to Him who cannot be controlled. This trustful hope in God is freed from anxiety (Is. 7:4; 12:2; ψ 45:2; Prv. 28:1). But it must be accompanied by fear of God (Is. 32:11; ψ 32:18; 39:3 etc.; Prv. 14:16, 26; 23:18). For this reason it must be a quiet waiting for God. [38] The opposite is depicted in Job, who will not wait (Job 6:11; 13:15; cf. 2 K. 6:33).

If God's expected help delivers from present distress, [39] it is more specifically thought of as the eschatological help which puts an end to all distress. [40] The attitude of expectant and confident hope increasingly expresses the realisation that everything in the earthly present is provisional, and it thus becomes increasingly hope in the eschatological future.

Bultmann

C. Hope in Rabbinic Judaism.

1. "The Semitic world offers no close parallel to the word ἐλπίς." [41] This statement describes the situation in Palestinian Judaism. There is in fact no word corresponding to ἐλπίς in either form or content. תִּקְוָה had as good as disappeared, [42] and the same is

---

[34] This comes out particularly strongly when it is said that God gives hope rather than help (Jer. 29:11; 31:17; Hos. 2:17), as also when the time of salvation is described as a time of confidence (Is. 32:18; Ez. 28:26; 34:27 f.). It is also expressed in the fact that in declarations of hope what is hoped for is less frequently mentioned than the basis of hope (God, His faithfulness, His name etc.), so that the LXX uses such impossible or rare expressions as ἐλπίζειν (ἐλπίς) ἐπί with dat. or acc., εἰς, ἐν. Good Gk. is ἐλπίζειν with dat., "to rely on" (Thuc., III, 97, 2: τῇ τύχῃ): ἐλπίδες εἰς also occurs in Thuc., III, 14, 1.
[35] Jer. 17:7; ψ 60:4; 70:5.
[36] Am. 6:1; Is. 32:9-11; Zeph. 2:15; Prv. 14:16; "careless" is used in a neutral sense in Ju. 18:7, 10, 27; Jer. 12:5; Job 40:23 of Behemoth.
[37] Hos. 10:13; Is. 31:1; 2 K. 18:24; Is. 36:6, 9; Jer. 2:37; Ez. 29:16.
[38] Is. 30:15; ψ 36:5-7, where הַשְׁקֵט or הִתְחוֹלֵל and דָּמַם are linked with בָּטַח.
[39] ψ 12:5; 32:17, 21; 118:81, 123.
[40] Is. 25:9; 26:8; 30:15; 51:5; Jer. 29:11; 31:16 f.; Mi. 7:7; ψ 45:1.
[41] Schl. Mt., 402.
[42] One of the exceptions is to be found in S. Bar. 78:6, where תִּקְוַת־עוֹלָם is probably the Heb. original (Wichmann, 39, n. 20).

true of others words translated ἐλπίς or ἐλπίζειν in the LXX (→ 521 f.). This is the more surprising since the Rabbinic world was certainly not unfamiliar with the concept of hope. Indeed, it directed its thoughts very much to the future, as may be seen from the existence of the Baruch Apoc. and 4 Esd., which both belong with tolerable certainty to scribal circles in Palestine. More particularly the Messianic hope was an extra-ordinarily strong concern of Palestinian Judaism and its leaders in the 1st and 2nd centuries of our era. If in spite of this preoccupation with the future there was never-theless no word or word group to express it, there must have been very good reasons. These reasons can only be found, however, in the particular form of the expectation of the future in later Rabbinic Judaism. Thus the observation that there is no word or word group corresponding to ἐλπίς, ἐλπίζειν necessarily demands an analysis of the content and goal of this expectation in order to clarify the peculiar linguistic situation.

2. Messianic Expectation.

a. Messianic expectation of the future has both a positive and a negative side. The positive relates to the fulfilment of Jewish hopes, the negative to the expectation of the judgment which at the commencement of the Messianic age will smite the ungodly who as the enemies of God are always the enemies of His people and who in conflict against the Jews will draw down on themselves the wrath and vengeance of God. The two aspects are closely linked, so that we cannot consider them in isolation. In this con-nexion it makes no odds in what order the individual events of the Messianic age were expected, to what degree the circle of ideas was developed, or how it was worked out, especially with the help of scriptural exegesis. [43] We can also ignore the comprehensive complex of signs indicating the beginning of the Messianic era. [44] The essential point is simply the fact that Messianic expectation was not an individual concern but a concern of the whole people and congregation. The individual shared it as a member of the community. For the promises were given to Israel as a totality rather than to Israel as an aggregate of individuals. The people as such received the promise that the future belongs to God. For this reason, non-Jews can participate in the promised blessings only if by circumcision [45] they become fully authorised and fully committed members [46] of the people and congregation. [47] Mere faith in Israel's God is not enough for this. [48] There must also be fulfilment of the statutes of the Law, among which circumcision is both formally the first and materially the presupposition of all other observance. [49]

---

[43] Cf. the Rabb. material in Str.-B., IV, 857 ff.

[44] *Ibid.,* 977 ff.

[45] For circumcision as the basis of the Messianic redemption, *ibid.,* 40, and as the basis of the deliverance of Israel from Gehinnom, III, 264; IV, 1064 ff.

[46] The σεβόμενοι τὸν θεόν (→ σέβομαι) often referred to in the NT accept only some obligations (Sabbath, meats) and receive no privileges, as shown by their relationship to the temple and sacrifices, in which their position is like that of the Gentiles, *ibid.,* II, 548 ff.

[47] The Rabbis seem to have been interested in the σεβόμενοι τὸν θεόν only to the degree that this state held out promise of regular conversion to Judaism ; cf. Juv., 14, 96 ff., and the attitude of the (Pharisaic, Str.-B., I, 926) merchant Eleazar to king Izates of Adiabene : Jos. Ant., 20, 17; 34 ff. (esp. 43 ff.).

[48] Cf. on this pt. what Eleazar says to Izates (Jos. Ant., 20, 44 f.): οὐ γὰρ ἀναγινώσκειν σε δεῖ μόνον αὐτούς (the Mosaic νόμοι) ἀλλὰ καὶ πρότερον τὰ προστασσόμενα ποιεῖν ὑπ' αὐτῶν. μέχρι τίνος ἀπερίτμητος μενεῖς; ἀλλ' εἰ μήπω τὸν περὶ τούτου νόμον ἀνέγνως, ἵν' εἰδῇς τίς ἐστιν ἡ ἀσέβεια, νῦν ἀνάγνωθι.

[49] Cf. Str.-B., IV, 23. If the σεβόμενοι τὸν θεόν are seldom mentioned in Rabb. literature (*ibid.,* II, 716, 719), this may be because the development of pious observance of the Law after the destruction of the temple and cultus led to an increasing rejection of the partial adherence characteristic of this group. The loyal Jew demands full commitment to the Law and if this is lacking speaks of ἀσέβεια even though there is a distinct inclination towards Judaism and evidence of it (→ n. 48).

The Law is decisive in the relationship of the people to God. In it Judaism has the one clear and perfect revelation of the will of God. The work of the Rabbis is simply to unfold it in all its details and to work out all its finer points in order to make possible its concrete fulfilment to the letter. For God has shown His will to the people in the Law in order that it may be done, not in order that it may be made into a philosophical system. [50] Since God's will does not change, because it is His will, and since it is always a saving will, in the expectation of loyal Judaism the coming aeon will have this in common with the present aeon — that the Law will stand over both as the expression of the divine will. The difference between the two aeons is simply that the Law is now entrusted only to the Jews, whereas in the coming aeon it will be kept by the Gentiles too. This is a thought which gained wide acceptance especially in Hellenistic Judaism and which even determined its missionary work. [51] But we find it also in Palestinian Judaism, as may be seen in the expectation that the Messiah would teach the nations the Torah and cause them to serve it. [52] It is obvious, of course, that the Messiah, who can expound the Torah like none other and leave no doubt as to the meaning of passages which are now obscurely or even incorrectly interpreted, [53] will Himself keep the Torah in all its parts, [54] just as God studies the Law and observes its provisions. [55] In this fusion of fulfilment of the Law and Messianic expectation it is also obvious that the Rabbis should make the commencement of the Messianic age dependent on the perfect fulfilment of the Law by Israel. According to a saying of R. Shim'on b. Jochai (c. 150 A.D.), the redemption of Israel will come when Israelites have really kept the Sabbath for two Sabbaths (bShab., 118b).

b. This leads us to a second essential element in Messianic expectation. Its fulfilment is in God's hand, but He has made it dependent on the relationship of His people to Him and His will. Thus the bringing in of the Messianic period and the Messianic redemption is not God's work alone. Man has a share, and to a normative extent in so far as it depends on his achievements when Christ comes and ushers in His kingdom. The coming of the Messiah may thus be arrested or delayed. [56] This means that the Messianic expectation of the Rabbis is cursed by the uncertainty which afflicts future expectation in any religion of works. Though it is certain that the fulfilment will come one day, there is an oppressive sense of being more or less seriously guilty of postponing it. Nor is there any way of measuring how near or far we are from the goal. Only God can decide this, and His assessment is wrapped in impenetrable darkness. The only sure point is that He is strictly just, and will freely give His people nothing. Thus, for all the enthusiastic depictions of the coming One there is a certain note of weariness and especially of uncertainty in Rabbinic expectations of the end. This is expressed both in the theory of the concealment of the Messiah, according to which He is already present and simply waits to manifest Himself, [57] and in the attempts to calculate the

---

[50] The rule that study of the Law takes precedence of fulfilment was formulated only in connection with the Hadrian persecution and the difficulties of observance created by the hostile legislation of the government. For details cf. Str.-B., III, 85 ff.; W. Bacher, Die Agada der Tannaiten, I (1884), 303.

[51] Str.-B., III, 98 ff.

[52] Cf. esp. Tg. Is. 53:11, where the many (→ πολλοί) whom the Messiah causes to serve the Law can only be non-Jewish peoples. The passages in Str.-B., IV, 918 also assume an active teaching ministry of the Messiah to all men. If there is a distinction between Hellen. and Rabb. Judaism, it is simply that the Rabbis, conscious of the election of Israel, essentially restricted their work to the chosen people and tried to prepare for the time of consummation in this sphere.

[53] Str.-B., IV, 1. Jesus takes up this idea of the "new Torah of the Messiah" in His exposition of the Law in the Sermon on the Mount (ibid., IV, 1 ff.).

[54] Ibid., III, 570 f.

[55] Cf. ibid., IV, 1233 f., Index under "Gott."

[56] Ibid., I, 599 ff.

[57] Ibid., III, 315.

time of His appearing. [58] Either way, an effort is made to dispel the uncertainty produced by linking the coming of the Messiah to legal fulfilment. The tension between this fulfilment and the sure and certain plan of God is relaxed. Yet both ways are wrong to the degree that the human *ratio* comes to the forefront.

There is no more astonishing witness to the correctness of this statement than Aqiba, who hailed Bar Cochba as the Messiah and thus led himself, most ot his pupils and finally his people to destruction. [59] We have a full account of his end at the hands of Roman executioners (bBer., 61b). He died confessing the one God of Israel (Dt. 6:4). He thus saw no discord between the confession of God and the acknowledgment of Bar Cochba. In the latter he saw rather the consummation of a life dedicated to the service of God. It may be assumed that Bar Cochba was still alive when Aqiba died. [60] It is thus the more impressive that in the hour of death his concern was only with his personal relationship to God and not with the fate of the movement for which he was dying. The text shows no sign of vacillation. Yet his last words almost sound like a self-vindication. The speaker was dying for God in the service of His Law, not of the Messiah. Once again we see the uncertainty of the Messianic expectation of the Rabbis, this time welling up as it were from the sub-conscious. It emerges with the same clarity in the fact that there is no Rabbinic saying which rejects the regal claim of Bar Cochba as presumptuous and erroneous even after he met his terrible end and dragged down Palestinian Judaism with him. [61] If this fact contains an element of self-accusation, it shows how shaky was the ground of Messianic expectation even for those who were expected to be and who were accepted as experts in the matter.

c. The attitude displayed in this whole sphere is, however, very different from what is meant by hope, quite apart from the Greek word ἐλπίς. There is here calculation, and therefore a calculated attempt to guarantee the expectation. The divine sovereignty is thus abrogated in the sphere of Messianic hope, even if only in theory. It is in keeping that the NT describes the pious circles looking with yearning to the future at the time of Jesus as προσδεχόμενοι (Mk. 15:43 etc., → προσδέχομαι, 58) and not as ἐλπίζοντες. Here is expressed real certainty linked with a sense of right. If man's claim does not stand in the forefront, the emphasis is less on the goodness of God from which the future salvation comes, and which can be grasped only in faith, than on the existing promises which bind God to His people and to the fulfilment of its expectation. The point here is the time rather than the manner. This helps us to see why in terms of the structure of the Messianic expectation of the Rabbis it was inevitable that Jesus and His call for faith should be rejected. To this extent the resurrection of Jesus means for the Jews the destruction of their expectation and their liberation for a hope which is real hope because in every respect it is referred to God alone and not to man.

d. It is grounded in the distinctiveness of Messianic expectation, and in the fact that finally it is no true hope, that in Judaism we increasingly find the accompanying concept of מַלְכוּת שָׁמַיִם, and this as a particular magnitude which finds its peculiar characteristics in its relationship specifically to the individual and in its actualisation. The theoretical separation between the preparatory kingdom of the Messiah and the final reign of God which is already present in germ and which takes effect in the relationship of the individual to God (→ I, 573), as it is assumed in Rabb. apocalyptic [62] and echoed in 1 C. 15:23, has its final basis in the desire to overcome the hopelessness of the individual as a member of his people by making him in person the bearer of his hope. The em-

[58] *Ibid.*, IV, 986 ff.
[59] Cf. A. Schlatter, *Die Tage Trajans und Hadrians* (1897), 50 ff.
[60] A. Schlatter, *op. cit.*, 52.
[61] *Ibid.*, 52 f.
[62] Cf. A. Schweitzer, *Die Mystik d. Apost. Pls.* (1930), 85 ff.

phasis necessarily falls on personal achievement. But this simply shifts rather than solves the problem. Since the whole life of the righteous in the present is determined by consideration of the future, there arises the question of the personal assurance of salvation. The sources show that the Rabbis could not attain this either.

3. The Problem of Assurance of Salvation.

a. Along with the people's expectation of the Messiah is the expectation of the individual. It concerns his personal share in the coming world as this will be decided by God [63] when He separates the righteous from the wicked, assigning the wicked to Gehinnom [64] and the righteous to the joys of the eschatological Garden of Eden. [65] The decision is made in a forensic act. On the basis of the Law and legal attainment God declares who can be accepted as righteous and who cannot be accepted. [66] Thus the thought of attainment determines the life of the righteous in this aeon and determines his eternal destiny in the next.

But this introduces into the individual hope of the Rabbis the same uncertainty which has emerged as the most distinctive mark of its Messianic expectation. It belongs to a religion of works that its adherents cannot have assurance. They cannot know whether they have made the grade, since they do not know the rule to which they are subject. [67] This is strikingly apparent in Judaism as perhaps the classical religion of works. Alongside the assurance that God will give the righteous all conceivable joys is the uncertainty whether one's own attainment is enough to qualify for the blessings of salvation with the righteous, [68] whether the righteous demands of God will finally be met. This lack of personal assurance of salvation [69] cast deep shadows on the last moments of more than one great Jewish teacher. Rabban Jochanan ben Zakkai, the contemporary of the apostles, [70] wept when his pupils cames to his death-bed to receive a final blessing from their dying master. When asked why he wept, he answered: "There are two ways before me, the one to the Garden of Eden, the other to Gehinnom, and I do not know on which they [71] lead me — how can I help weeping?" (bBer., 28b). This is said by the very man whom his disciples described as the "lamp of Israel" and the "strong hammer." It was the same with R. Jochanan (bar Nappacha, who died c. 290 A.D.), the Palestinian Amoraean from whose school came the Jerusalem Talmud. When he died, he asked to be buried neither in white [72] clothes nor black, but in neutral shades, so that he would not be ashamed if he were given a place among the righteous or among sinners (רְשָׁעִים) [73] (jKil., 32b, 8 ff.). [74] In both cases there is the same final uncertainty. "Confidence based on works cannot be assurance, and fear triumphs over faith." [75] This fact is not altered by the confidence of some Rabbis in their last hours. [76] The basic mood of the Rabbis in face of judgment was pessimistic, [77] and it finds clas-

---

63 Str.-B., IV, 1100 ff.
64 Str.-B., IV, 1106 f.
65 *Ibid.,* 1107 f.
66 Cf. jAZ, 2a, 14 ff. (Str.-B., IV, 1203).
67 bQid., 40a, Bar (Str.-B., II, 427).
68 Hence the advice of Hillel: "Do not trust in thyself to thy dying day" (Ab., 2, 4).
69 It is characteristic of all Rabb. Judaism (cf. the passages in Str.-B., III, 218 ff.).
70 A. Schlatter, *Jochanan Ben Zakkai, der Zeitgenosse der Apostel* (1899).
71 The plur. is a cautious way of referring to God, like the δώσουσιν in Lk. 6:38 (cf. Dalman WJ, I, 183 f.).
72 In the Rabb., as in the NT, the robes of the righteous are white.
73 The statement presupposes that man will "come again" as he "goes" — a common view.
74 Cf. Gn. r., 96, 5 on 47:29; also 100, 1 on 49:33.
75 A. Schlatter, *op. cit.,* 73 on the death of Jochanan.
76 Cf. the accounts in Gn. r., 100, 1 on 49:33 and par.
77 Cf. the fact that Aqiba often quoted the Preacher; *v.* Jew. Enc., I, 305.

sical expression in the steady development of casuistry. There is perhaps no more striking proof of this thesis than in the fact that the schools of Hillel and Shammai disputed for more than two years whether it were better for man not to have been created or whether it is good for him to have been created, and that they finally agreed that it were better for him not to have been created (bErub., 13b, Bar). No other view is really possible "under the law."

That there is no universal hope [78] possible under nomism is nowhere more clearly stated than by the Johannine Jesus in Jn. 5:45: ἔστιν ὁ κατηγορῶν ὑμῶν Μωϋσῆς, εἰς ὃν ὑμεῖς ἠλπίκατε. Here the folly of hope in the sphere of legal religion is declared. He who entrusts his eternal future to man will always be accused by God. If any one thinks he can justify himself by the Law, no less a figure than Moses himself will condemn him, because he has not understood that for Moses God alone can bring man to his goal and give him the honour which keeps him from perishing (Jn. 5:44).

b. Recognising the situation, the Rabbis took different steps to try to overcome their uncertainty of salvation. Thus Aqiba hazarded the statement that one can be certain of God's good-pleasure in prayer. [79] A related view [80] was that one may draw conclusions as to the eternal destiny of a man from the manner of his death. [81] The main attempt to overcome the uncertainty, however, was the so-called "theology of suffering." [82] This [83] tries to interpret the suffering of the righteous as a discipline which gives them the opportunity partially or even totally to pay the penalty in this life for the guilt which would otherwise have to be paid for after death. [84] To the forefront is a desire to reduce the number of offences and thus to give increasing preponderance to merits, so that the just God will finally have no option but to justify and to grant access to the Garden of Eden, as He naturally desires. [85] It is worth noting that this view was most fully stated and worked out by Aqiba and his school. [86] According to tradition, [87] he was cheerful at the death-bed of his suffering teacher Eliezer ben Hyrqanos, explaining that he was rejoicing at these sufferings because he saw in them the guarantee that God would be gracious to his teacher. His own attitude at his martyrdom possibly has its root here, especially the interpretation of it as an expression of self-vindication before God (→ 526). But this attempt of the Rabbis to overcome their lack of hope faded into the background relatively quickly. Its last representative was Rabba bar bar Chama, a Babylonian Amoraean of the beginning of the 4th century. [88] The theory

---

[78] In connection with this fact it is interesting that Aqiba used the designation of God as מִקְוֵה יִשְׂרָאֵל in Jer. 17:13 (the "hope of Israel") in the sense of the "plunge-bath of Israel" (Joma, 8, 9): "And it is said: מִקְוֵה יִשְׂרָאֵל is Yahweh. What is meant by the מִקְוֶה? It washes the unclean. So the Holy One, blessed be He, washes Israel." The true sense of the formula would have fitted in very well with the context.

[79] T. Ber., 3, 3.

[80] Aqiba's statement is closely related to that of the famous man of prayer, Choni, who recognised that his prayer was affirmed when it came freely (bBer., 34b, Bar).

[81] Cf. the list in bKet., 103b, also the passages in Wichmann, 3, n. 4.

[82] P. Volz first coined this expression in *Jüdische Eschatologie von Daniel bis Akiba* (1903), 155.

[83] There are examples outside the Rabbis, though it was most common amongst them (Wichmann, 51).

[84] This is not to be confused with the idea of retribution in this world, which is never found within the theology of suffering (Wichmann, 11).

[85] Behind this view is the conviction of God's absolute justice (→ 527). In suffering the righteous is given the chance to atone for unconfessed faults lest he should be rejected on their account. Since God alone decides who will participate in this atoning suffering, the doctrine has a distinct predestinarian character.

[86] Wichmann, 56 ff.

[87] bSanh., 101a; cf. Wichmann, 62 f.

[88] Wichmann, 78.

failed to maintain itself because it could explain the sufferings of the righteous but not their joys. [89] It thus foundered on its own anthropocentricity. This shows us the basis of the lack of assurance amongst the Rabbis, namely, that they could not break free from themselves. Hope arises when man learns to see that he can do nothing for his own salvation, but that God can do everything and that the aim of God is to lead man to salvation, not by the way of attainment, but by a gift *sola gratia*.

Rengstorf

D. The Hope of Hellenistic Judaism.

1. Hellenistic Judaism also realises that hope belongs to life (Sir. 14:2) and that it is extinguished only by death (Ps. Sol. 17:2). The sick man hopes for healing (2 Macc. 9:22 : πολλὴ ἐλπίς). One has hopes for others (Sir. 13:6). Those who are separated hope (or no longer hope) to see one another again (Tob. 10:7; vl. πιστεύειν) etc. Of course, κεναὶ ἐλπίδες καὶ ψευδεῖς ἀσυνέτῳ ἀνδρί (Sir. 31:1, a free rendering of the Heb.). The hope of the ungodly is κενή (Wis. 3:11; cf. 5:14; 16:29) or ἄδηλος (2 Macc. 7:34). When they die, they have no ἐλπίς (Wis. 3:18). The ἐλπίδες of idolaters are ἐν νεκροῖς (Wis. 13:10; cf. 15:6, 10), and it is vain to hope in military strength (Jdt. 9:7). The ἐλπίς of the righteous is fixed on God their σωτήρ. [90] They have καλαὶ ἐλπίδες (Ep. Ar., 261), and so they need not fear (Sir. 31:16; 1 Macc. 2:61 f.). For fear of God is combined with their hope (Sir. 31:14 f.; Ps. Sol. 6:8; and of the Messiah, Ps. Sol. 17:44). God is the ἐλπίς πᾶσιν τοῖς κατέχουσιν τὰς ὁδοὺς αὐτοῦ (Test. Jud. 26:1). Ἐλπίς has the character of trust (Sir. 49:10; Jdt. 13:19; 2 Macc. 15:7: πεποιθὼς μετὰ πάσης ἐλπίδος). The hope of the mighty is in God (Ps. Sol. 17:38), but He is esp. the refuge τοῦ πτωχοῦ καὶ πένητος (Ps. Sol. 5:13; 15:2; 18:3 etc.). If what is hoped for is usually God's protection and help in general, [91] it can also be His assistance in a particular need (2 Macc. 15:7; Jdt. 8:20; Ep. Ar., 18 : μεγάλη ἐλπίς; Jos. Ant., 12, 300 : τὰς ἐλπίδας τῆς νίκης ἔχοντας ἐν τῷ θεῷ). [92] Hope can arise even in the hour of death (2 Macc. 9:20). This hope is denied to the ungodly (Wis. 3:18; cf. 15:10), but the ἐλπίς of the righteous is ἀθανασίας πλήρης (Wis. 3:4). It extends to the resurrection (2 Macc. 7:11, 14, 20). It is the ἐλπίς σωτηρίου παρὰ θεῷ (4 Macc. 11:7). There is also eschatological hope of the restoration of Israel (2 Macc. 2:18; Test. B. 10:11) or of the time of salvation, as attested in Rabb. and esp. apoc. literature. [93]

2. In Philo we see the influence of Gk. psychology. For him ἐλπίς is essentially προσδοκία (Leg. All., II, 43), [94] though he normally follows the later Gk. usage and employs ἐλπίς for the προσδοκία ἀγαθῶν (Abr., 14), so that there is a close link between ἐλπίς and χαρά (Det. Pot. Ins., 140) and he likes to think of ἐλπίς (which

---

[89] *Ibid.*, 77 f.

[90] Sir. 31:14 f.; Ps. Sol. 17:3; cf. 5:16; 8:37; 9:19; 15:1; Sus. 60; Test. A. 7:7 (f.).

[91] Here, too, it can be said that God is ἐλπίς (→ n. 35); contrary to the Heb. text in ψ 13:6; 21:5; cf. also Ps. Sol. 5:13; 15:2.

[92] Joseph. generally follows Gk. usage. Thus ἐλπίς may include expectation of evil : Ant., 2, 211; 6, 215 (δειλαὶ ἐλπίδες); 11, 247 (πονηρὰ ἐλπίς). Expectation of what is desired is ἐλπίς in Ant., 17, 1 (τοῦ αὖθις βίου); Bell., 6, 264 (ἁρπαγῆς); 383 (κέρδους). We often find the Gk. expression παρ' ἐλπίδα(ς), Ant., 7, 179; 198 etc. (also κατ' ἐλπίδα, Ant., 16, 322). Ἐλπὶς σωτηρίας occurs in Ant., 16, 389; Bell., 7, 165; 331 etc.; ἐλπὶς βεβαία in Bell., 7, 413; Ant., 8, 280. While in Ant., 8, 282; 12, 300 we have the OT expression : τὰς ἐλπίδας ἔχειν ἐν τῷ θεῷ, in Bell., 2, 391; 6, 99 we have (θεὸν) σύμμαχον ἐλπίζειν.

[93] Bousset-Gressmann, 202 ff.; Pott, *op. cit.*, 10 ff. Acc. to Eth. En. 40:9 there is an angel "set over the penitence and hope of those who inherit eternal life."

[94] Ἐλπίζειν = "to expect" in Leg. All., III, 87; Cher., 75; Det. Pot. Ins., 160; Fug., 164 etc.

is the antithesis of φόβος in Abr., 14; Mut. Nom., 163) as a preliminary joy. [95] As in the Gk. world, ἐλπίς for him corresponds to μνήμη. [96] Also Gk. is his estimation of ἐλπίς as a consolation in distress (Jos., 20 and 144), for here hope has to do with man's own projection of the future. Without such hope life is not worth living (Praem. Poen., 72).

Nevertheless, when Philo deals more specifically with hope he goes beyond the projection of human and earthly wishes. The object of ἐλπίς is the perfection of man (Rer. Div. Her., 311: ἐλπὶς τελειώσεως), and in this sense ἐλπίς belongs to the essence of the ἄνθρωπος πρὸς ἀλήθειαν, to the λογικὴ φύσις (Det. Pot. Ins., 138 f.). Who does not ἐπὶ θεὸν ἐλπίζῃ is no true man, as shown from the example of Enos ('Ενώς = ἄνθρωπος), who acc. to Gn. 4:26 was the first to hope in God. [97] Enos is the ἐφιέμενος μὲν ἀεὶ τοῦ καλοῦ, μήπω δ' ἐφικέσθαι τούτου δεδυνημένος (Abr., 47). 'Ελπίς should be fixed on God, while ἐπιθυμία refers to the σῶμα (Poster. C., 26). Yet Philo can also speak in the more general OT sense of the hope which is directed to God as the σωτήρ (Leg. Gaj., 196) who gives against and beyond hope, [98] to God's ἵλεως φύσις (Spec. Leg., I, 310; II, 196), or to the ἡμερότης of His φύσις (Fug., 99). In this respect it is esp. hope of forgiveness (Fug., 99; Spec. Leg., II, 196). This ἐλπίς is closely related to πίστις (Leg. All., III, 164). The ἐλπίδες of the wicked are naturally ἀτελεῖς (Exsecr., 142; 149; cf. Praem. Poen., 12). [99] Eschatological hope plays no part in Philo, but Moses has ἐλπὶς τοῦ μέλλειν ἀθανατίζεσθαι (Virt., 67).

E. The Early Christian Concept of Hope.

1. The NT concept of hope is essentially determined by the OT. [100] Only where it is a matter of secular hope do we see the element of expectation characteristic of the Gk. world, and always in such a way that it is expectation of something welcome, with no differentiation between ἀγαθή and πονηρά ἐλπίς.

Thus ἐλπίζειν means expectation with the nuance of counting upon in Lk. 6:34; 1 C. 9:10; 2 C. 8:5; 1 Tm. 3:14; Ac. 16:19; Herm. v., 3, 11, 3. There is a stronger accent on "hoping" in Lk. 23:8; Ac. 24:26; 27:20, and even more clearly in Lk. 24:21; R. 15:24; 1 C. 16:7; Phil. 2:19, 23; Phlm. 22; 2 Jn. 12; 3 Jn. 14; Ign. Eph., 1, 2; 10, 1; R., 1, 1; Barn., 17, 1. Where, however, such expectation relates to persons, we have the trust typical of the OT, e.g., 2 C. 1:13; 5:11; 13:6 and esp. 1:7; 2:15. This may be seen from the interchange with πεποίθησις, which in 1:15 takes up the ἐλπίζειν of v. 13 and in 8:22; 10:2 takes the place of ἐλπίς (cf. 1:7; 10:15). In 1 C. 13:7 hope, like love, is obviously directed to men, though for Paul this attitude rests on the corresponding relationship to God, as shown by the natural transition from the one to the other in v. 13. Since the πάντα ἐλπίζει comes between πάντα πιστεύει and πάντα ὑπομένει, it is evident that the three verbs describe a single attitude.

---

[95] Leg. All., III, 86 f.; Mut. Nom., 161-165; Exsecr., 160. Thus we not infrequently find εὔελπις and εὐελπιστία, v. Leisegang, Index (1926).

[96] Leg. All., II, 42 f., where the third term is αἴσθησις (→ 518); Migr. Abr., 154,. where the third term is ἐνάργεια τῶν παρόντων.

[97] Det. Pot. Ins., 138 f.; Abr., 7-14; Praem. Poen., 11-14.

[98] Leg. All., III, 85; Sacr. AC, 78; Som., I, 71; Decal., 16; Spec. Leg., II, 219; cf. also H. Windisch, Die Frömmigkeit Philos (1909), 53 ff.

[99] ἀτελεῖς ἐλπίδες occurs elsewhere, e.g., Epigr. Graec., 497, 5 : ἀτελεῖς ἐλπίδες of parents whose daughter has died.

[100] Cf. the grammars for grammatical pts. 'Ελπίζειν is used as in the LXX, so that the basis is denoted by ἐπί with the dat. or acc., or by ἐν or εἰς, → n. 34; once with the dat. alone, Mt. 12:21. That ἐλπίς can signify not merely the act or attitude but also rhetorically what is hoped for (R. 8:24; Col. 1:5; Tt. 2:13; Hb. 6:18; in the LXX 2 Macc. 7:14), is in accord with Gk. usage (Aesch. Choeph., 776; → n. 20, and for the interchange between ἐλπίς and ἔλπισμα, Plut. Suav. Viv. Epic., 6 [II, 1090d] → n. 13). The concept of hope is not thereby modified.

2. If hope is fixed on God, it embraces at once the three elements of expectation of the future, trust, and the patience of waiting. Any one of these aspects may be emphasised. The definition of πίστις as ἐλπιζομένων ὑπόστασις in Hb. 11:1 is quite in keeping with the OT interrelating of πιστεύειν and ἐλπίζειν (ψ 77:22) and the usage of the LXX, which has ὑπόστασις [101] as well as ἐλπίς (→ 522) for מִקְוֶה (Ez. 19:5; Ju. 1:12) and תּוֹחֶלֶת (ψ 38:7). The certainty of trust in a divinely given future is underlined, [102] and the added ἔλεγχος [103] πραγμάτων οὐ βλεπομένων emphasises further the paradoxical character of this hoping trust to the degree that it cannot count on controllable factors. [104] This aspect is also stressed by Paul in his definition in R. 8:24 f.: ἐλπὶς δὲ βλεπομένη οὐκ ἔστιν ἐλπίς· ὃ γὰρ βλέπει τις, τί καὶ ἐλπίζει; If in accordance with the context there is here an initial appeal to formal logic, namely, that hope is the only possible attitude to the future if the object is not yet present, the positive meaning for Paul is that ἐλπίς cannot relate to βλεπόμενα because these are πρόσκαιρα (2 C. 4:18); everything visible belongs to the sphere of the → σάρξ on which no hope can be founded. Paul then emphasises the element of patient waiting in ἐλπίς (on 1 C. 13:7 → 530) when he continues: εἰ δὲ ὃ οὐ βλέπομεν ἐλπίζομεν, δι' ὑπομονῆς ἀπεκδεχόμεθα. This trait in hope also gives us the paradox of R. 4:18: ὃς παρ' ἐλπίδα ἐπ' ἐλπίδι ἐπίστευσεν; where we can no longer count on controllable factors. we have to trust in the divine future. The term ἐλπίζειν has the element of sure confidence in 1 C. 15:19; 2 C. 1:10; 3:12; Phil. 1:20; Hb. 3:6; 1 Pt. 1:21 ὥστε τὴν πίστιν ὑμῶν καὶ ἐλπίδα εἶναι εἰς θεόν, [105] while the main stress is on patient endurance in R. 5:4 f.; 15:4; 1 Th. 1:3 (τῆς ὑπομονῆς τῆς ἐλπίδος); 5:8 (ἐλπίδα σωτηρίας, cf. ψ 77:22); Hb. 6:11; 10:23. The only point is that we can never isolate a single element. [106]

If there is no difference from the OT in this aspect of the structure of the concept, the difference is to be found in the situation of him who hopes, as may be seen clearly in 2 C. 3:1-18. The πεποίθησις of which Paul boasts in v. 4 and the ἐλπίς of which he boasts in v. 12 clearly include hopeful confidence in the Corinthians (1:13, 15), but in a much more basic sense they are the apostolic confidence and assurance which he has as a διάκονος of the καινὴ διαθήκη; they are equivalent to the → ἐλευθερία (v. 17) which is freedom from the Law and death, so that παρρησία (v. 12; 7:4) and καύχησις (1:12; 7:4; 10:8 ff.; 11:16 ff.) are

---

[101] For לחי (→ 522) we have ὑποστῆναι in Mi. 5:7 (6), this being also used for חסה (→ 522) in Ju. 9:15.

[102] Cf. in what follows esp. v. 10: ἧς τεχνίτης ... θεός; v. 11: ἐπεὶ πιστὸν ἡγήσατο τὸν ἐπαγγειλάμενον; v. 19: λογισάμενος ὅτι ...; v. 23: οὐκ ἐφοβήθησαν ...; v. 27: μὴ φοβηθεὶς κτλ.

[103] This is mostly used in the LXX for תּוֹכֵחָה (proof).

[104] Cf. again from what follows v. 7: περὶ τῶν μηδέπω βλεπομένων; v. 8: μὴ ἐπιστάμενος ...; v. 19: παραβολῇ ἐκομίσατο; v. 25: μᾶλλον ... ἢ πρόσκαιρον ἔχειν ... ἀπόλαυσιν; v. 27: τὸν ... ἀόρατον ὡς ὁρῶν ἐκαρτέρησεν.

[105] In this passage we may take τὴν πίστιν ὑμῶν and (τὴν) ἐλπίδα as coordinated subj. of εἶναι. In this case both πίστις and ἐλπίς describe the OT concept of believing hope. But we may also take ἐλπίδα as a predicate: "So that your faith is also hope in God." In this case it is emphasised that confident waiting for the divine future is part of faith.

[106] ἐλπίζειν (ἐλπίς) is also used for trust in 1 Cl., 11, 1; 12, 7 (with πιστεύειν); 2 Cl., 17, 7; Barn., 6, 3; Herm. m., 12, 5, 2; 6, 4; Just. Dial., 35, 2. Cf. Jn. 5:45: Μωϋσῆς, εἰς ὃν ὑμεῖς ἠλπίκατε, "in whom your assurance is grounded" (→ 528); cf. also Barn., 16, 1 f.

grounded in it. [107] Thus Christian hope rests on the divine act of salvation accomplished in Christ, and, since this is eschatological, hope itself is an eschatological blessing, i.e., now is the time when we may have confidence. [108] The waiting which is part of ἐλπίς is effected by the Spirit as the gift of the last time, [109] and it rests on πίστις in the act of salvation (Gl. 5:5), just as being in ἐλπίς in R. 8:24 f. is immediately after described as being borne along by the πνεῦμα (v. 26 f.).

With πίστις, ἐλπίς thus constitutes Christian existence. Hence the prayer of R. 15:13; hence also the characterising of Christians as τῇ ἐλπίδι χαίροντες in R. 12:12; hence the characterising of the heathen as μὴ ἔχοντες ἐλπίδα in 1 Th. 4:13, [110] which obviously does not mean that they do not imagine a future after death, but that they can have no well-founded trust in it. Inasmuch as πίστις works in ἀγάπη (Gl. 5:6), πίστις, ἀγάπη and ἐλπίς constitute the being of the Christian as Paul describes it in 1 Th. 1:3, or as he characterises it in 1 C. 13:13 in antithesis to a Gnostic formula. [111] In the light of the OT concept of hope it may also be understood why Paul can say that ἐλπίς endures even though we attain to βλέπειν (v. 12 f.), for hope is not concerned with the realisation of a human dream of the future but with the confidence which, directed away from the world to God, waits patiently for God's gift, and when it is received does not rest in possession but in the assurance that God will maintain what He has given. Even in the consummation Christian existence, in accordance with the concept of God, is inconceivable without ἐλπίς. Prior to the consummation the element of perseverance and patient waiting can be emphasised, as in R. 5:2, 4 f.; 8:20, 24 f.; 1 C. 15:19; Gl. 5:5; 1 Th. 2:19, though this is misunderstood if in the τῇ γὰρ ἐλπίδι ἐσώθημεν (R. 8:24) we do not give force to the ἐσώθημεν, and if παρρησία and καύχησις do not result.

3. Turning from Paul, we find that ἐλπίς is almost completely lacking in Jn. (on Jn. 5:45 → n. 106). As hope directed to the future consummation it occurs only at 1 Jn. 3:3. But what is denoted by ἐλπίς can be included in πίστις, and this is true of Jn. (→ πίστις). The fact that ἐλπίς is not found in Rev. can cause astonishment only if we fail to see that it is here included in the concept of ὑπομονή.

Elsewhere, esp. where the Jewish emphasis is strong, the element of waiting for the eschatological future is prominent; apart from Col. 1:5; 1 Tm. 4:10; Tt. 2:13; 3:7, cf. 1 Pt. 1:3, 13; Hb. 6:18 f.; 7:19, [112] and in Ac., with specific reference to the resurrection, 23:6; 24:15; 26:6 f.; 28:20 and 2:26, which relates ψ 15:9 to the resurrection of Christ. [113] The paradox that Christian ἐλπίς is itself an eschatological blessing because it sees that OT hope is fulfilled in the mission of Jesus appears most clearly in Mt. 12:21, which refers Is. 42:4 to Jesus (cf. R. 15:12), and in

---

[107] Cf. esp. 11:17: ἐν ταύτῃ τῇ ὑποστάσει τῆς καυχήσεως (→ 522), and on the concept → καύχησις R. 5:2: καυχώμεθα ἐπ' ἐλπίδι τῆς δόξης τοῦ θεοῦ, and Hb. 3:6: τὸ καύχημα τῆς ἐλπίδος. In the LXX we have καύχησις, ἐλπίς and ὑπόστασις for תֹּחֶלֶת (Prv. 11:7).

[108] → n. 34. When Paul quotes Is. 11:10 in R. 15:12, for him the promise is already fulfilled.

[109] So also Barn., 11, 11.

[110] So also Eph. 2:12, with the characteristic addition that the heathen are ἄθεοι; 2 Cl., 1, 7.

[111] → n. 18.

[112] Cf. Barn., 8, 5; Just. Dial., 44, 4; Athenag., 33, 1; Sib., 2, 53: δώσει πλούσια δῶρα, αἰώνιον ἐλπίδα.

[113] The reference is also to the resurrection in 1 Cl., 27, 1.

1 Pt. 1:3: (ὁ θεὸς) ὁ ἀναγεννήσας ἡμᾶς εἰς ἐλπίδα ζῶσαν δι' ἀναστάσεως Ἰησοῦ Χριστοῦ ἐκ νεκρῶν. [114] But it may also be seen rather less sharply when Christ is described as our ἐλπίς, [115] when there is reference to the ἐλπίς given to us, [116] and when ἐλπίς, either in connection with other concepts [117] or alone, [118] is presented as the characteristic feature of Christianity. These expressions often have a formal character, as may be seen esp. at Barn., 1, 4 and 6 (→ n. 117) in the fact that πίστις is no longer the basis of ἐλπίς, as in Paul, but rests upon it.

Yet there are still no pictures of the future (except in Rev.), and we may thus see that the character of trust in God's act as a constitutive element of hopeful expectation remains intact, as is sometimes very plain in the formulation. [119] Again, the aspect of patient waiting is sometimes stressed. [120] That ἐλπίς is not isolated in Christian existence, but works itself out in a new attitude to the world, emerges only infrequently in these formal descriptions, though it is occasionally emphasised. [121]

† ἀπελπίζω.

ἀπελπίζειν is first found only in later Gk. literature, in which it is used in the same sense as the earlier ἀπογινώσκειν and ἀπονοεῖσθαι. [1] The meaning is "not to believe or hope" that something will happen. It thus corresponds very largely to the Lat.

---

[114] Ign. Mg., 9, 1: εἰς καινότητα ἐλπίδος; Barn., 16, 8: ἐλπίσαντες ἐπὶ τὸ ὄνομα ἐγενόμεθα καινοί.

[115] Col. 1:27; 1 Tm. 1:1; Ign. Eph., 21, 2; Mg., 11, 1; Tr. prooem.; 2, 2; Phld., 11, 2; → n. 35 and 91; hope in Jesus (ἐπί or εἰς), Barn., 6, 3; 11, 11; Just. Dial., 16, 4; 47, 2 etc.; in His cross, Barn., 11, 8; cf. Just. Dial., 96, 1; 110, 3 in His ὄνομα, Barn., 16, 8 (1 Cl., 59, 3: in God's ὄνομα, Jewish).

[116] 2 Th. 2:16; cf. 1 Cl., 57, 2.

[117] Col. 1:4 f. (ἀκούσαντες τὴν πίστιν ὑμῶν ... καὶ τὴν ἀγάπην, ἣν ἔχετε ... διὰ τὴν ἐλπίδα); Tt. 1:1 f. (ἀπόστολος ... κατὰ πίστιν ἐκλεκτῶν θεοῦ καὶ ἐπίγνωσιν ἀληθείας τῆς κατ' εὐσέβειαν ἐπ' ἐλπίδι ζωῆς αἰωνίου); Hb. 10:22-24; Ign. Mg., 7, 1 (μία ἐλπὶς ἐν ἀγάπῃ); Phld., 11, 2; 1 Cl., 58, 2 (an oath: ζῇ γὰρ ... ἥ τε πίστις καὶ ἡ ἐλπὶς τῶν ἐκλεκτῶν); Barn., 4, 8; 11, 8; Just. Dial., 110, 3; esp. variations on the triad of 1 Cor. 13:13; Barn., 1, 4: ὅτι μεγάλη πίστις καὶ ἀγάπη ἐγκατοικεῖ ὑμῖν ἐπ' ἐλπίδι ζωῆς αὐτοῦ. 1:6: τρία οὖν δόγματά ἐστιν κυρίου· ζωῆς ἐλπίς, ἀρχὴ καὶ τέλος πίστεως ἡμῶν, καὶ δικαιοσύνη κρίσεως ἀρχὴ καὶ τέλος, ἀγάπη εὐφροσύνης καὶ ἀγαλλιάσεως ἔργων δικαιοσύνης μαρτυρία. Pol., 3, 2 f.: ... οἰκοδομεῖσθαι εἰς τὴν δοθεῖσαν ὑμῖν πίστιν· ἥτις ἐστὶν μήτηρ πάντων ἡμῶν, ἐπακολουθούσης τῆς ἐλπίδος, προαγούσης τῆς ἀγάπης ...

[118] Col. 1:23; Eph. 1:18; 4:4; esp. 1 Pt. 3:15 (... λόγον περὶ τῆς ἐν ὑμῖν ἐλπίδος); 1 Cl., 51, 1 (ὀφείλουσιν τὸ κοινὸν τῆς ἐλπίδος σκοπεῖν); Ign. Eph., 1, 2 (ὑπὲρ τοῦ κοινοῦ ὀνόματος καὶ ἐλπίδος); Phld., 5, 2 (ἐν τῷ εὐαγγελίῳ τῆς κοινῆς ἐλπίδος). On the concept κοινὴ ἐλπίς, Thuc., II, 43, 6; Lys., 2, 9.

[119] 1 Pt. 1:3; Tt. 1:2; 2:13 f.; 3:5-7. The link between ἐλπίς and πίστις may be seen in the formulation in Barn., 4, 8: ἵνα ἡ (sc. διαθήκη) τοῦ ἠγαπημένου Ἰησοῦ ἐγκατασφραγισθῇ εἰς τὴν καρδίαν ἡμῶν ἐν ἐλπίδι τῆς πίστεως αὐτοῦ.

[120] Col. 1:23; Hb. 6:18 f.; 10:23; Ign. Phld., 5, 2; Pol., 8, 1; 2 Cl., 11, 5.

[121] 1 Jn. 3:3: πᾶς ὁ ἔχων τὴν ἐλπίδα ταύτην ἐπ' αὐτῷ ἁγνίζει ἑαυτόν ...; Eph., 4:1-4; 1 Tm. 5:5 (though cf. 6:17); Tt. 2:11-14; 1 Pt. 1:13: Ign. Mg., 9, 1; Barn., 11, 11; Athenag., 33, 1. Herm. says repeatedly that hope is lost through sin, v., 1, 1, 9; m., 5, 1, 7; s., 8, 9, 4; 9, 14, 3; 9, 26, 2. But there is the new hope of repentance, s., 6, 2, 4; 8, 6, 5; 8, 7, 2; 8, 10, 2.

ἀπελπίζω. [1] First attested in Hyperides, 5, 35 (p. 88, Jensen) (τῆς πόλεως τὴν σωτηρίαν). Cf. L. Götzeler, De Polybi Elocutione (Diss. Erlangen, 1887), 23; P. Linde, Breslauer philol. Abh., IX, 3 (1906), 31 f.

desperare (and also, as it seems, to *desperare facio*); [2] it takes the acc. and is also found in the pass. Among many possible constructions, [3] its use with sickness or healing is part. common; someone who is given up is ἀπελπισθείς or ἀπηλπισμένος. [4]

In the LXX it occurs in the general sense of "to give up hope" in Sir. 22:21; 27:21 (both times in relation to threatened friendship), and also in 2 Macc. 9:18 in relation to sickness. It is worth noting that in Is. 29:19 אֶבְיוֹנֵי אָדָם is rendered οἱ ἀπηλπισμένοι τῶν ἀνθρώπων; cf. the invocation of God in Jdt. 9:11: ταπεινῶν εἶ θεός, ἐλαττόνων εἶ βοηθός, ἀντιλήμπτωρ ἀσθενούντων, ἀπεγνωσμένων σκεπαστής, ἀπηλπισμένων σωτήρ. [5]

In the NT ἀπηλπικότες occurs in Eph. 4:19 as a vl. (D 257 lat syᵖ) with ἀπηλγηκότες to characterise the heathen; it is in the absol. as in Is. 29:19 and Jdt. 9:11. As in Jdt. 9:11 God is described in 1 Cl., 59, 3 as τῶν ἀπηλπισμένων σωτήρ. In Herm. v., 3, 12, 2 an old man who has lost all hope is described as ἀφηλπικὼς ἑαυτόν. The word is not found in the Apologists.

There is a singular use in Lk. 6:35: δανίζετε μηδὲν ἀπελπίζοντες. For in line with v. 34 (ἐὰν δανίσητε παρ' ὧν ἐλπίζετε λαβεῖν), the only possible meaning is: "Lend without the expectation of receiving again," or, if it is a matter of interest, "without expecting any return." [6]

ἀπελπίζειν is thus used like ἀπαιτεῖν etc. (though this use is attested only from the time of Chrys.), [7] or else there is abbreviation (ἀπελπίζω = ἀπολαμβάνειν ἐλπίζω), as also in the Vg.: *nihil inde sperantes*. The normal use would give us "not despairing" (*nihil desperantes*) in the sense of "hoping for a heavenly return." [8] This is as little in keeping with the context as the sense given by vl. μηδένα ἀπελπίζοντες (א syˢ etc.): "not despairing of any," or trans. "not bringing any to despair." Since it is linguistically possible to accept the first sense, there is no need of the conjecture ἀντελπίζοντες, which would give the same sense.

† προελπίζω.

προελπίζω, "to hope before or first," is attested only by Posidipp. (3rd. cent. B.C.) in Athen., IX, 20 (377c) outside Christian literature.

Acc. to Eph. 1:12 we are elected by the will of God εἰς τὸ εἶναι ἡμᾶς εἰς ἔπαινον δόξης αὐτοῦ, τοὺς προηλπικότας ἐν τῷ Χριστῷ. [1] If the "we" indicates

---

[2] So obviously in Anth. Pal., XI, 114, 6 and also in patristic liter., *v.* Thes. Steph., *s.v.*

[3] Polyb., 23, 13, 2 has the oxymoron ἀπηλπισμέναι ἐλπίδες. Andronicus De Passionibus, p. 14, 14 (Kreuttner) defines ἀθυμία as λύπη ἀπελπίζοντος ὧν ἐπιθυμεῖ τυχεῖν. Nero says in Ditt. Syll.³, 814, 10 f.: μηδὲν παρὰ τῆς ἐμῆς μεγαλοφροσύνης ἀνέλπιστον; → 521.

[4] E.g., Ditt. Syll.³, 1173, 7 and 11: ἀφηλπισμένος ὑπὸ παντὸς ἀνθρώπου. Cf. O. Weinreich, *Antike Heilungswunder* (1909), 195 f.; K. Kerényi, *Die Griech.-orient. Romanliteratur* (1927), 27, n. 11. ἀπογινώσκειν is used in the same sense; though not found in the NT, this occurs in the LXX and Herm. (*v.* Pr.-Bauer).

[5] In Joseph. ἀπελπίζειν is often used in the normal sense of "to give up hope," *v.* Schl. Lk., 249 (on Lk. 6:35). Philo (acc. to Leisegang's Index) never uses ἀπελπίζειν; he has ἀπογινώσκειν, often with τὰς ἐλπίδας as obj. (Leisegang). In the LXX this occurs only at Dt. 33:9 (for לֹא יָדַע); Jdt. 9:11; 2 Macc. 9:22.

[6] In this sense it would find a par. in the much quoted Rabb. saying: "He who does not lend on interest, him God will reckon as having kept all the commandments" (Str.-B., II, 159).

[7] Zn. Lk., *ad loc.*

[8] Zn. Lk., *ad loc.*

π ρ ο ε λ π ί ζ ω. [1] On the construction with ἐν, → ἐλπίς, n. 100.

Jewish Christians as a special group, the meaning is "before the Gentiles" or "prior to the coming of Christ," which would suggest that Christ is the fulfilment of OT hope and would thus be very suitable (→ 531 f.). On the other hand, if the "we" are all Christians, the προ- refers to the present in relation to the eschatological consummation, though this is less likely. The word is not found in the post-apost. fathers or the Apologists.

Bultmann

---

† ἐμβατεύω

a. "To enter," "to go into," Eur. El., 595 (πόλιν); Eur. Heracl., 876 (κλήρους χθονός); Aesch. Pers., 449 (νῆσον); with the gen.: Soph. Oed. Tyr., 825 (πατρίδος); with εἰς and acc.: Demosth., 33, 6 (εἰς τὸ πλοῖον); 44, 16; Jos. Ant., 2, 265. It is mostly used of military invasion in the LXX : 1 Macc. 12:25; 13:20; 14:31; 15:40. In Jos. 19:49, 51 it is used of forceful occupation (the idea of force being introduced by the LXX, since the Mas. נחל and חלק refer to division of the occupied country). In the pap. it often means "to enter into an inheritance."[1] Of gods it means "to come to a holy place when invoked," Soph. Oed. Col., 679 (ἵν᾽ ὁ βακχιώτας Διόνυσος ἐμβατεύει); Eur. Rhes., 225 f. (ναὸν ἐμβατεύων Ἀπόλλον) or "to indwell as daemon",[2] Dion. Hal., I, 77 (ὁ ἐμβατεύων τῷ χωρίῳ δαίμων). b. In the language of the myst.[3] (Ditt. Or., II, 530, 13)[4] it is used inversely to signify the action of those who have just received the mysteries. The texts on the oracle of Apollos of Claros[5] combine ἐμβατεύειν with μυεῖσθαι or παραλαμβάνειν τὰ μυστήρια. Obviously ἐμβατεύειν signifies the further act in the sanctuary which follows παραλαμβάνειν τὰ μυστήρια, i.e., the entering of the inner sanctuary. Thus ἐμβατεύειν is a technical term for the true mystery. The meaning of ἃ ἑώρακεν ἐμβατεύων is that "at initiation he entered into what he had seen." The reference may be to symbols used at ἐμβατεύειν, as suggested by M. Dibelius. Or it may be to visions, i.e., that the initiate first sees the holy places in a vision and then really enters them. Whatever the explanation, our concern is undoubtedly with the continuation of the act of initiation in a cultic chamber, and ἐμβατεύειν is the second and decisive act which carries with it the ἐπιτελεῖν μυστήρια tu which the texts refer. c. "To approach something with a view to examining it." In this sense it denotes intense concern with or enquiry into something, as in 2 Macc. 2:30 : τὸ μὲν ἐμβατεύειν καὶ περίπατον ποιεῖσθαι λόγον καὶ πολυπραγμονεῖν ἐν τοῖς κατὰ μέρος, τῷ τῆς ἱστορίας ἀρχηγενέτῃ καθήκει; Philo Plant., 80 : οἱ προσωτέρω χωροῦντες τῶν ἐπιστημῶν καὶ ἐπὶ πλέον ἐμβατεύοντες.

In the NT the word occurs only at Col. 2:18 in a passage which is much contested exegetically. The senses chiefly favoured are b. and c. Against interpretation in terms of the Mysteries there are two main arguments. First, the inscriptions never use ἐμβατεύειν alone, but always link it with another term (μυεῖσθαι or παραλαμβάνειν τὰ μυστήρια), so that ἐμβατεύειν is the second,

---

ἐμβατεύω. [1] Preisigke Wört., I, 471 f., where we often find ἐμβαδεύω with εἰς and the acc.

[2] E. Fraenkel, *Griech. Denominativa* (1906), 250.

[3] Dib. Gefbr., *ad loc.*; "Die Isisweihe bei Apuleius," SAH, 8 (1917), 4, 30 ff.; W. M. Ramsay, *Athenaeum*, 1913, I, 106 f.; Clemen, 340; M. Maas, "Die antik. Mysterien u. ihre Beziehungen zum Apostel Pls." ThLZ, 38 (1913), 125; Haupt Gefbr., *ad loc.*; Loh. Kol., *ad loc.*; Meinertz Gefbr., *ad loc.*

[4] Dib. refers also to Apul. Met., XI, 23.

[5] T. Macridy in *Oestr. Jhft.*, 15 (1912), 36 ff.; cf. Dib., *op. cit.*, 31 ff.

final and consummating act. Secondly, ἐμβατεύειν takes place in a sanctuary. Neither of these conditions seems to be met in Col. 2:18,[6] so that we can adopt this explanation only if there is no other. Moreover the Gnostic-Jewish philosophy of the Colossian heretics seems to demand the sense c. What they try to achieve by way of ecstasy and asceticism is for Paul opposed to adherence to the exclusiveness of Christ the Head in whom all wisdom and knowledge are given. To keep to Him and thus to participate in divine growth (2:19), there is no need of syncretistic methods of producing visions and therefore knowledge. If we go the way of the false teachers we shall always have to wait for such moments of ecstatic vision, and we shall then have to enter (ἐμβατεύειν) by painful investigation into what has been seen in ecstasy. Paul does not deny the visions; he regards them as a false path because as he sees it all the treasures of wisdom and knowledge are given him in Christ alone (2:3).

The uncertainty of exposition has led to all kinds of unhelpful conjectures. [7]

Preisker

ἐμμένω → μένω.   ἐμφανίζω → φαίνω.

† ἐμφυσάω

ἐμφυσάω is found from the time of Hippocrates in class. Gk., and also in the *koine* and the LXX.[1] Acc. to the latter God "blows" His living breath "into" man[2] or "upon" him by His *pneuma*. The breath of God awakens life in all creation,[3] and when it blows over the place of the dead the dead bones rise up to new life. Thus God will impart His Spirit into Israel that it may come to life again (Ez. 37:5, 14).[4]

The NT has ἐμφυσάω only in Jn. 20:22;[5] it means "to breathe upon or over," though here it is used of Jesus rather than God. Jesus takes the place of God:[6] εἶπεν οὖν αὐτοῖς ὁ Ἰησοῦς πάλιν· εἰρήνη ὑμῖν. καθὼς ἀπέσταλκέν με ὁ πατήρ, κἀγὼ πέμπω ὑμᾶς. καὶ τοῦτο εἰπὼν ἐνεφύσησεν[7] καὶ λέγει αὐτοῖς· λάβετε

---

[6] Cf. also Loh. Kol., *ad loc*. The strongly cultic connection of the word makes it impossible to refer it to the ethical life (cf. Meinertz, *ad loc.*), and thus to translate: "who orders his life according to what he has supposedly seen."

[7] E.g., αἰώρᾳ or ἀέρα (Lightfoot) or ἄμετρα (Hort) κενεμβατεύων. The so-called *koine* tradition has ἃ μὴ ἑώρακεν, and thus introduces a charge which Paul is not bringing in this context (→ *supra*).

ἐ μ φ υ σ ά ω. [1] Pr.-Bauer, *s.v.*

[2] Gn. 2:7; Wis. 15:11 (ἐμφυσήσαντα πνεῦμα ζωτικόν); Vit. Ad., 13; 4 Esr. 3:5. Cf. A. Dieterich, *Abraxas* (1891), 195, 5 f.: ὁ παντοκράτωρ ὁ ἐνφυσήσας πνεῦμα ἀνθρώποις εἰς ζωήν. The raising of the dead in 3 Βασ. 17:21 is fashioned on the quickening of Adam. The Mas. tells us that Elijah stretched himself three times and three times called upon God for the child. The LXX has ἐνεφύσησε τρίς (cf. 4 Βασ. 4:34). But the calling upon God excludes magical conceptions; filled with the spirit, the prophet breathes in the breath of life in the name of God as His representative.

[3] Where God causes His breath to go forth, life springs up; where He withholds it, life perishes (Ps. 104, 29 f.). Cf. also the idea of God's breath of wrath and death (Job 37:10; Ez. 21:31; 22:20 f.; cf. Job 4:21 LXX and 1 Cl., 39, 6: ἐνεφύσησεν).

[4] Ez. 37:9: ἐμφύσησον εἰς τοὺς νεκροὺς τούτους. Cf. also S. Bar. 23:5b.

[5] M. J. Lagrange, *Evangile selon St. Jean* (1925), 516; Bau. J.³, *ad loc.*

[6] Cf. Jn. 20:28 and → ἐγώ 354.

[7] Not inappropriately, D adds an αὐτοῖς, cf. sy.

πνεῦμα ἅγιον ... The Christian continues the work of God in a new form. He who is sent by God now sends the disciples into the world equipped with the Spirit, who is released by the work of Christ and who will complete what has been begun. [8] The Spirit is conveyed as a breath, as in Ps. 104. [9] The bearers of the Spirit, however, receive from Christ [10] the power of loosing and binding: ἅν τινων ἀφῆτε τὰς ἁμαρτίας, ἀφέωνται αὐτοῖς· ἅν τινων κρατῆτε, κεκράτηνται. Here, then, three processes which are separate in the other Evangelists, the giving of the keys, the missionary command and the outpouring of the Spirit, are combined in a single act of creation which denotes the beginning of a new reality of life. [11]

Stauffer

ἔμφυτος → φύω.

ἐν

A. ἐν with the Impersonal Dative.

1. The use of ἐν with the impersonal dat. is of theological significance in the Bible as denoting especially supraterrestrial localities, particularly ἐν τοῖς οὐρανοῖς (ἐν τῷ οὐρανῷ).

ὁ πατήρ μου (or ὑμῶν) ὁ ἐν τοῖς → οὐρανοῖς is peculiar to Mt. (10:32 f.; 12:50; 16:17; 18:10, 19, cf. 5:16, 45; 6:1, [9]; 7:11; 18:14; Mk. 11:26 [25?] and Lk. 11:2 vl. under Matthean influence); κύριος ... ἐν οὐρανοῖς (-νῷ) (Eph. 6:9; Col. 4:1); [1]

---

[8] Jn. 7:39; 16:14 f.
[9] Cf. the double sense of *pneuma* in the LXX and Jn. 3.
[10] Rev. 1:18; Mk. 2:5 ff.
[11] Cf. 1 C. 15:45; 1 Jn. 4:13; Rev. 11:11.

ἐ ν. Bl.-Debr. esp. §§ 4; 164, 1; 179, 2; 187; 195 f.; 198; 219; 220, 1 and 2; Radermacher, Index s.v. ἐν. Cf. the bibl. n. under → διά; P. F. Regard, *Contribution a l'étude des prépositions dans la langue du NT* (1919), 227-376 (though incomplete and not very helpful theologically); P. Barale, "Uso di ἐν instrumentale," *Didaskaleion,* 2 (1913), 423-439. H. Leisegang, *Der Heilige Geist* (1919), esp. 24 ff.; F. Büchsel, *Der Geist Gottes im NT* (1926), Index s.v. "Enthusiasmus." A. Deissmann, *Die nt.liche Formel "in Christo Jesu"* (1892); B., 39, 70, 115 ff.; *Paulus*[2] (1925), esp. 107 ff., 254 ff.; J. Weiss, ThStKr, 69 (1896), 7-33; *Urchristentum,* I (1914), 359-361; B. Weiss, "Der Gebrauch des Artikels bei den Gottesnamen," ThStKr, 84 (1911), 531 ff.; H. Böhlig, Ἐν κυρίῳ, in *Nt.liche Studien für G. Heinrici* (1914), 170-175; W. Bousset, *Kyrios Christos*[3] (1926), 104 ff.; K. Deissner, *Pls. u. d. Mystik seiner Zeit*[2] (1921), 3 f., 66, 71, 115 ff., 135 f.; T. Schmidt, *Der Leib Christi* (1919), esp. 72 ff., 147 ff.; E. Sommerlath, *Der Ursprung des neuen Lebens nach Pls.*[2] (1927), 91-99; E. Wissmann, *Das Verhältnis von* ΠΙΣΤΙΣ *u. Christusfrömmigkeit bei Pls.* (1926), 95 ff., 101, 108; H. E. Weber, "Die Formel 'in Christo Jesu' u. d. paul. Christusmystik," NkZ, 31 (1920), 213 ff.; *Eschatologie u. Mystik im NT* (1930), esp. 50 ff., 81 ff., 94 ff., 103 ff.; W. Weber, *Christusmystik* (1924); L. Brun, "Zur Formel 'in Christus Jesus' im Phil.", *Symbolae Arctoae,* I (1922), 19-37; B. Murmelstein, "Adam, ein Beitrag zur Messiaslehre," WZKM, 35 (1928), 242-275; 36 (1929), 51-86; J. Jeremias, *Jesus als Weltvollender* (1930); A. Schweitzer, *Die Mystik d. Ap. Pls.* (1930), esp. 122 ff.; E. Käsemann, *Leib u. Leib Christi* (1933), 159 ff

[1] In Jn. 3:13 the words ὁ ὢν ἐν τῷ οὐρανῷ (א pl lat sy) are not an addition but are genuine (Zn. Bau. as against Tillm. J.). The meaning is not to be restricted to the pre-existence (Zn.) or the post-existence, but comprehends the whole eternal being of the Logos in heaven (Bau.), cf. 1:18.

ἄγγελοι (Mt. 22:30; Mk. 12:25); χαρά (Lk. 15:7); εἰρήνη (Lk. 19:38); μισθός (Mt. 5:12 and par.); θησαυρός (Mt. 6:20; Mk. 10:21 and par.); πολίτευμα (Phil. 3:20); πατριά (Eph. 3:15) ἐν (τοῖς) οὐρανοῖς or ἐν (τῷ) οὐρανῷ, (τὰ) ἐν τοῖς οὐρανοῖς (ἐν οὐρανῷ) as the opp. of (τὰ) ἐπὶ τῆς → γῆς (Col. 1:16, 20; Eph. 1:10 vl.; Hb. 9:23; Mt. 6:10; 28:18); ἐγγράφεσθαι (Lk. 10:20); τηρεῖσθαι (1 Pt. 1:4) ἐν (τοῖς) οὐρανοῖς. In all these combinations and expressions heaven is thought of as God's dwelling-place (cf. the use with ἀχειροποίητος and αἰώνιος in 2 C. 5:1); but the reference is to the visible heaven in Mk. 13:25 : αἱ δυνάμεις αἱ ἐν τοῖς οὐρανοῖς, and Ac. 2:19 : τέρατα ἐν τῷ οὐρανῷ. The two ideas are very close to one another in Rev. In 12:1, 3; 15:1, and probably 4:1 (cf. 19:11) we are to think of the visible heaven. [2] In 19:14 : τὰ στρατεύματα τὰ ἐν τῷ οὐρανῷ, the angelic hosts are in heaven, though behind this may well be the thought of the stars in heaven, even if the author is no longer aware of the fact. On the other hand, heaven is occasionally thought of as a vault through the openings of which one may with supernatural aid either look or enter into God's heaven. Hence it is of the latter that we are to think in 4:2; 5:3; 8:1; 11:15, 19; 12:7, 8, 10; 14:17; 15:5; 19:1. The standpoint of the divine changes. It is typical of the outlook of Paul that expressions of this kind are less frequent. There are rather more in the Prison Epistles. The terms "heaven" and "earth" do not occur at all in the Pastorals. Cf. ἐν τῷ ᾅδῃ (→ I, 146 ff.), ἐν τοῖς → κόλποις (→ Ἀβραάμ, I, 8), Lk. 16:23; ἐν τῷ → παραδείσῳ, Lk. 23:43. On the spatial conceptions underlying such expressions → εἰς, 420.

ἐν is also used 2. to denote an accompanying state in the sense of "with" : ἔρχεσθαι ἐν ῥάβδῳ (1 C. 4:21); ἐν τῇ δόξῃ (Mt. 25:31); ἐν τῇ βασιλείᾳ αὐτοῦ, "with his kingdom" (Mt. 16:28; on Lk. 23:42 → εἰς, 434); of the accompanying hosts (Lk. 14:31); ἐν (τῷ) αἵματι (1 Jn. 5:6; Hb. 9:25).

3. It also denotes ground or basis : "in virtue of," ἐν τῇ πολυλογίᾳ (Mt. 6:7); ἐν τῷ λόγῳ τούτῳ (Ac. 7:29); καυχᾶσθαι ἐν (R. 2:23; 5:3; Gl. 6:13 f.); ἐν τούτῳ, "on account of" (Jn. 16:30; Ac. 24:16); ἐν ᾧ, "because" (Hb. 2:18); also "therefore" (Hb. 6:17). 4. It may also denote means, "with" or "by," Dt. 22:10; Lv. 8:32; Mt. 5:13 and par.; Mk. 11:28 and par.; Lk. 22:49 : πατάσσειν ἐν μαχαίρῃ, ἐν χειρί, Ac. 7:35 (vl.); Gl. 3:19; esp. ἐν αἵματι (of Christ) with verbs like δικαιοῦν, R. 5:9; καθαρίζειν, Hb. 9:22; λύειν, Rev. 1:5; ἀγοράζειν, Rev. 5:9; also 1 C. 11:25; Eph. 2:13. There is a transition from local to instrumental use in Rev. 7:14; it is purely spatial, however, in R. 3:25 (with προέθετο).

Sense 2. is unusual though not impossible in Gk. (ἐν μαχαίρῃ, -ραις, ἐν ὅπλοις, "to provide with weapons," is found in the pap.,[3] though an accompanying force is classically put in the simple dat.). The same is true of sense 4. (ἐν πυρὶ πρήσαντες, Hom. Il., 7, 429; διαλυόμενοι ἐν τῷ λιμῷ, P. Par., 28, 13, cf. 27, 14 : τῷ λιμῷ; 26:9 : ὑπὸ τῆς λιμοῦ). The classical gen. pret. corresponds to some extent[4] to combinations like ἀγοράζειν ἐν. There are hardly any instances of sense 3. Heb. influence (בְּ) is plain in all three senses. Even ἐν χειρί is a Semitism (בְּיַד). Cf. ἐν → ὀνόματι. On ἐν → σαρκί, ἐν → νόμῳ, ἐν → πίστει, → 542.

B. ἐν with the Personal Dative.

More important and more difficult is the use with the personal dat. We will begin with the simpler cases and move on to the more complicated. The spatial sense is always the starting-point, but we have to ask how far there is an intermingling of other senses, esp. the instrumental. [5]

---

[2] Bss. Apk., ad loc.

[3] Bl.-Debr. § 195, 1, a refers to Moulton, 15 f.; Kuhring, 43 f.; Rossberg, 28.

[4] Cf. the ἐν on a tablet from Hadrumetum (Deissmann B., 25 ff.; 38 f.), line 12.

[5] For constructions in which the verb is central, → ἐλπίζω, → εὐδοκέω, → καυχάομαι, → ὁμολογέω, → πιστεύω, → σκανδαλίζω.

1. ἐν with persons in general.

a. With a name in quotations, ἐν denotes either the book named after an OT character (ἐν τῷ Ἡσαΐᾳ, Ὡσηέ, Mk. 1:2; R. 9:25), or a passage which refers to a character (ἐν Ἠλίᾳ, R. 11:2). [6] b. with the plur. or collective sing. it means "among," R. 1:12, 13; ἐν τοῖς ἔθνεσιν, Gl. 1:16; also for the gen. part. in 1 C. 15:12; Jm. 5:13 etc.; ἐν τῷ συνεδρίῳ, Ac. 5:34. There are class. models for this use. c. It is also used to denote the close connection of a possession, an attribute or an event with the person concerned (Mk. 9:50; R. 9:17; 2 C. 4:12). In expressions which denote knowledge or making known, it is used of the one who makes known (with μανθάνειν, 1 C. 4:6; εἴδετε, ἀκούετε, ἐμάθετε ἐν ἐμοί, Phil. 1:30; 4:9; with ἐνδείκνυμι, R. 9:17; cf. also 2 C. 4:10 f.), but also of the one who knows (φανερόν ἐστιν ἐν αὐτοῖς, R. 1:19; cf. 2 C. 4:3). In the latter case it replaces the simple dat. Thus in Gl. 1:16 : ἀποκαλύψαι τὸν υἱὸν αὐτοῦ ἐν ἐμοί, the translations "in me" and "by me," and speculations on the inwardness of the Damascus experience, [7] have no philological basis.

The popular usage of the apocr. Acts is instructive. Cf. Act. Thom., 20 : [8] εἰσῆλθεν πρὸς τὴν γυναῖκα τοῦ ἄρχοντος καὶ ἀνέγνω ἐν αὐτῇ τὸ εὐαγγέλιον (in the sense of "to" or "with," not "in"); [9] Ep. Abgari, 1: πόλις ἐστὶ βραχυτάτη, ἥτις ἀρκέσει ἐν ἀμφοτέροις. Cf. Act. Thaddaei, 2.

d. In terms of a primitive but persistent psychology, spiritual processes, qualities and possessions in particular are located within man : λέγειν, διαλογίζεσθαι, ἐπιγινώσκειν, εἰδέναι, ἐξίστασθαι, ἐμβριμᾶσθαι, διαπορεῖν, στενάζειν ἐν ἑαυτῷ. Mt. 3:9 and par.; Mk. 2:8; 5:30; 6:51; Mt. 9:3, 21; Lk. 12:17; Jn. 6:61; 11:38; Ac. 10:17; 17:16; R. 8:23; cf. ἐν ταῖς καρδίαις, Mk. 2:6, 8 and par.; ἐν ταῖς συνειδήσεσιν, 2 C.5:11; λόγος ἐν ὑμῖν, Ac. 13:15.

This is particularly true of everything belonging to the religious and ethical sphere : fellowship with God with its effects and reactions : τί ἦν ἐν ἀνθρώπῳ, Jn. 2:25; sin, R. 7:8, 17, 18, 20; the work of Satan, Eph. 2:2, heathen blindness, 2 C. 4:4; Eph. 4:18; the fulfilling of the Law, R. 8:4; the effect of preaching, 1 C. 1:6; Col. 3:16; the word, Jn. 5:38; 8:37; 15:7; the work of God, Phil. 1:6; 2:13; Col. 1:29; τὸ φῶς τὸ ἐν σοί (figurative), Mt. 6:23 and par. (cf. Jn. 11:10; 12:35); δυνάμεις Mk. 6:14 and par.; πηγὴ ὕδατος (figur.), Jn. 4:14; anointing, 1 Jn. 2:27; life, Jn. 6:53; 1 Jn. 3:15; χαρά, Jn. 15:11; πίστις 2 Tm. 1:5; μαρτυρία, 1 Jn. 5:10; ἐλπίς, 1 Pt. 3:15; χάρισμα, 1 Tm. 4:14. So also of Satan, οὐκ ἔστιν ἀλήθεια ἐν αὐτῷ, Jn. 8:44; of God and Christ, ζωὴν ἔχειν ἐν ἑαυτῷ, Jn. 5:26; esp. in Eph. and Col., all the treasures of wisdom, Col. 2:3; the whole fulness of Godhead, 1:19; "hidden in God" as a technical term for the first and last times, Eph. 3:9; Col. 3:3.

e. Sometimes the spatial use passes over into the instrumental : Gn. 9:6 ; ψ 17:30; R. 9:7; Hb. 11:18 : ἐν Ἰσαὰκ κληθήσεταί σοι σπέρμα. Mk. 3:22 and par.: ἐν ... τῷ ἄρχοντι τῶν δαιμονίων ἐκβάλλει τὰ δαιμόνια, cf. Mt. 9:34; 12:27 and par.; ἐν ἀνδρί, Ac. 17:31; of the sanctifying of the heathen partner in a mixed marriage

---

[6] For Rabb. examples, Str.-B., III, 288. Loh. Phil. (cf. Kyrios Jesus [1928], 12 f.) tries to explain Phil. 2:5b along these lines, but intermingles sense c. In this verse the first ἐν surely comes under → 539, 1. b, and the second under → 541, 3. b. Cf. Dib. Gefbr.

[7] Cf. A. Deissmann, Paulus² (1925), 105. O. Kietzig, Die Bekehrung des Paulus (1932), 207 ("the Epistles emphasise the inwardness of experience") is not to be taken in this way. W. G. Kümmel, Römer 7 u. d. Bekehrung des Pls. (1929), 145 rightly comments : ... "a revelation of Christ by God which was ordained for Paul ... neither for nor against a vision."

[8] M. R. James, Texts and Studies, V, 1 (1897), 32, 17 f.

[9] Ljungvik, op. cit. (→ 65, Bibl. n.), 32, where James' conjecture, ἀνέγνωκεν αὐτῇ, is rightly rejected.

by the Christian partner, 1 C. 7:14 (→ ἁγιάζω, I, 112). A borderline case is found in Ac. 17:28 : ἐν αὐτῷ γὰρ ζῶμεν καὶ κινούμεθα καὶ ἐσμέν.

The quotation is from Ps.-Epimenides. [10] The many par., [11] esp. Stoic, suggest partly a local sense (Dio Chrys. Or., 12, 28 : ἅτε γὰρ οὐ μακρὰν οὐδ' ἔξω τοῦ θείου διῳκισμένοι καθ' αὑτούς, ἀλλὰ ἐν αὐτῷ μέσῳ πεφυκότες; Philo Fug., 102 : ἐν αὐτῷ μόνῳ κατοικήσει (the righteous in God), and partly an instrumental (Ps.-Aristot. Mund., 7, p. 401a, 13 : καλοῦμεν αὐτὸν καὶ Ζῆνα καὶ Δία ... ὡς ἂν εἰ λέγοιμεν δι' ὃν ζῶμεν). The instrumental use of ἐν with persons in the NT is largely influenced by בּ, though it is not impossible in Gk. Cf. Dio C., 61, 13 (the words of Nero to his mother): ἐν γὰρ σοὶ καὶ ἐγὼ ζῶ καὶ διὰ σὲ βασιλεύω.

2. ἐν with → πνεῦμα.

a. The thought of the Spirit in man is local. Like evil spirits (Mt. 12:43 ff. and par.; Ac. 19:16), the Spirit of God dwells in man (Nu. 27:18; Ez. 36:27; Jn. 14:17; R. 8:9; 1 C. 3:16; 6:19; Jm. 4:5; cf. R. 5:5 : ἡ ἀγάπη τοῦ θεοῦ ἐκκέχυται ἐν ταῖς καρδίαις ἡμῶν διὰ πνεύματος ἁγίου). [12]

b. The converse that man is in the Spirit (ἐν πνεύματι, Mt. 22:43; Rev. 21:10; ἐν πνεύματι εἶναι, R. 8:9; γενέσθαι, Rev. 1:10; ἐν πνεύματι θεοῦ λαλεῖν, 1 C. 12:3; ἐν πνεύματι προσεύχεσθαι, Eph. 6:18) is also based on a spatial sense. It is debatable whether the Spirit is always thought of as a fluid. [13] Certainly the expression ἐν ἑαυτῷ γενέσθαι in Ac. 12:11 (cf. Xenoph. An., I, 5, 17) — as opp. to → ἐξίστασθαι, 459, cf. 450 — cannot be interpreted along these lines. The ἐν of ἄνθρωπος ἐν πνεύματι ἀκαθάρτῳ (Mk. 5:2) approximates to the idea of a state (cf. A. 2 → 538). This is confirmed by such combinations as ἐν ῥύσει αἵματος εἶναι (Mk. 5:25 and par.), ἐν (τῇ) δυνάμει (τοῦ πνεύματος), ἐν ἐξουσίᾳ (εἶναι), ἐν ἐκστάσει γενέσθαι (Lk. 4:14, 32, 36; Ac. 22:17). Since the conception of the Spirit is itself imprecise, the Spirit may easily be identified with the state produced by Him. The idea is also local, but not fluid, when the two basic orientations of existence, ἐν σαρκί and ἐν πνεύματι, are opposed to one another (R. 8:8 f.). Here there is little trace of the fluid and ecstatic element. The Spirit is the constantly active principle of ethical life. The transition from the ecstatic to the pneumatic is important not merely for the ethical consequences (cf. also R. 9:1; 15:16; ἐν πνεύματι πραΰτητος, Gl. 6:1; 2 C. 6:6 with ἐν γνώσει κτλ.), but also for declarations on the proclamation of the Gospel (1 Th. 1:5, again with material substantives; 1 Pt. 1:12) and prayer (Eph. 6:18; Jd. 20). In what seems to be a most comprehensive way the demand of Jn. 4:23 f. (προσκυνεῖν ἐν πνεύματι καὶ ἀληθείᾳ) emphasises the correspondence between the absolutely boundless and truly personal being of God and the worship which we are to render Him. [14]

---

[10] M. D. Gibson, "The Commentaries of Isho'dad of Merv., IV", Horae Semiticae, X (1913), XII f.

[11] A. Oepke, Die Missionspredigt des Ap. Pls. (1920), with bibl.

[12] On ἐν for εἰς, Bl.-Debr., 2, 1; § 205 f., 218; K. Krumbacher, "Studien zu den Legenden des hl. Theodosius." Sitzungsberichte der Königl. Bayr. Akademie der Wissenschaften, phil.-hist. Kl. (1892), 364 f. → εἰς 433.

[13] Cf. on this pt. H. Leisegang, op. cit. The Gks. certainly say ἐν θεῷ εἶναι, and from this construct the subst. ἐνθουσιασμός (e.g., Plat. Tim., 71e). But it is doubtful whether the ἐν is always to be taken in a fluid sense. Popular oriental belief conceives of demons less mystically and more personally, T. Canaan, Dämonenglaube im Lande der Bibel (1929). The early Christian experience of the Spirit falls into neither category. Cf. F. Büchsel, op. cit.

[14] Büchsel, op. cit., 501 ff.

There is a tendency towards the instrumental use in R. 14:17: δικαιοσύνη καὶ εἰρήνη καὶ χαρὰ ἐν πνεύματι ἁγίῳ; 8:15 : ἐν ᾧ κράζομεν; 1 C. 6:11: ἐδικαιώθητε ἐν τῷ πνεύματι τοῦ θεοῦ; 12:9 : ἐν τῷ αὐτῷ (or ἑνὶ) πνεύματι (v. 8 : διά, κατά, cf. v. 11), and cf. 12:13. While the nuance in Eph. 2:18 (ἐν ἑνὶ πνεύματι) is more local in view of the preceding δι' αὐτοῦ, 3:5 and 4:30 are predominantly instrumental.

3. ἐν Χριστῷ 'Ιησοῦ, ἐν κυρίῳ and Related Formulae.

These formulae are not found prior to Paul and are rare outside the Pauline corpus. They are largely peculiar to Paul, and he is perhaps their author. Even apart from minor distinctions, they can be used in many different ways.

a. In general they denote membership of Christ and the Church, abs. in Phil. 1:13; 3:9; 4:7; with subst. and adj.: ἄνθρωπος, 2 C. 12:2; ἅγιοι, Phil. 1:1; ἀδελφοί, Phil. 1:14; Col. 1:2; νεκροί, 1 Th. 4:16; with an instructive opposite : ἀδελφὸς ... καὶ ἐν σαρκὶ καὶ ἐν κυρίῳ, Phlm. 16; in subst. form : τοῖς ἐν Χριστῷ 'Ιησοῦ, R. 8:1; with verbs : εἶναι, R. 16:11; ἐστίν is to be supplied in 2 C. 5:17; ἐστέ is more natural in 1 C. 1:30 (→ b.): "But of him you have your (true) being in Christ Jesus" (cf. τὰ μὴ ὄντα, v. 28); γίνεσθαι, R. 16:7. b. They may also characterise an activity or state as Christian, θύρα ἀνεῳγμένη, 2 C. 2:12; ἀλήθειαν λέγειν, R. 9:1; μαρτύρεσθαι, Eph. 4:17; πεπεῖσθαι, R. 14:14; Gl. 5:20; Phil. 2:24; 2 Th. 3:4; ἔχειν (τὴν) καύχησιν, R. 15:17; 1 C. 15:31; προσδέχεσθαι, R. 16:2; Phil. 2:29; χαίρειν, Phil. 3:1; 4:4, 10; στήκειν, Phil. 4:1; 1 Th. 3:8; κοπιᾶν, R. 16:12; ἀσπάζεσθαι, R. 16:22; 1 C. 16:19; γεννᾶν, 1 C. 4:15; γαμηθῆναι, 1 C. 7:39; κοιμηθῆναι, 1 C. 15:18; Rev. 14:13; λαλεῖν, 2 C. 2:17; 12:19; ὑπακούειν, Eph. 6:1 (vl.); ἐνδυναμοῦσθαι, Eph. 6:10; παρρησιάζεσθαι, Eph. 6:20; Phlm. 8; περισσεύειν, Phil. 1:26; τὸ αὐτὸ φρονεῖν, Phil. 4:2; παρακαλεῖν, 1 Th. 4:1; 2 Th. 3:12; περιπατεῖν, Col. 2:6; διακονίαν παραλαμβάνειν, Col. 4:17; προίστασθαι, 1 Th. 5:12. Also with subst.: ὁδοί, 1 C. 4:17; συνεργός, R. 16:3, 9; διάκονος, Eph. 6:21; δέσμιος, Eph. 4:1; συναιχμάλωτος, Phlm. 23; πιστός (believing), Eph. 1:1; πίστις (καὶ ἀγάπη), Col. 1:4; 1 Tm. 1:14; 3:13; 2 Tm. 1:13; 3:15; ἀναστροφή, 1 Pt. 3:16. c. They can also be value judgments circumscribing the sphere of reference, δόκιμος, R. 16:10; ἐκλεκτός, R. 16:13; νήπιος, 1 C. 3:1; φρόνιμος, 1 C. 4:10; ἀγαπητός, R. 16:8; τέκνον ἀγαπητὸν καὶ πιστόν, 1 C. 4:17; τέλειος, Col. 1:28; τὸ ἔργον, ἡ σφραγίς μου, 1 C. 9:1, 2; οὐ κενός, 1 C. 15:58; οὔτε περιτομή τι ἰσχύει οὔτε ἀκροβυστία, Gl. 5:6; ἀνῆκεν, εὐάρεστον, Col. 3:18, 20. d. They sometimes denote the objective basis of fellowship with God, with χάρις, 2 Tm. 2:1; σωτηρία, 2 Tm. 2:10; ἀπολύτρωσις, R. 3:24; cf. 8:2; Eph. 1:7; Col. 1:14; ζωὴ αἰώνιος, R. 6:23; Jn. 16:33; θριαμβεύειν, 2 C. 2:14; Col. 2:15; ἐνεργεῖν, Eph. 1:20; καταργεῖν, 2 C. 3:14; κτίζειν, Eph. 2:10; καταλλάσσειν, 2 C. 5:19; χαριτοῦν, Eph. 1:6; 4:32; κληροῦσθαι, Eph. 1:11, 13; 2:6, 13; πάντα ἰσχύειν, Phil. 4:13; παρρησίαν ἔχειν, Eph. 3:12; φῶς εἶναι, Eph. 5:8; Col. 2:10 f. e. Comprehensively it denotes the gathering of the many into one, ἐν σῶμά ἐσμεν, R. 12:5; εἷς ἐστε, Gl. 3:28; Eph. 2:21 f.; ἐκκλησία(ι), Gl. 1:22; 1 Th. 1:1; 2:14; of creation, Col. 1:16 f.; of the summing up of the whole cosmos, Eph. 1:10; also with reference back to eternal election, Eph. 1:4, 9; 3:11 (in this sense it is peculiar to Eph.).

This rich usage cannot be explained as a Hebraism based on the LXX equation of ἐν and בְּ. [15] Nor is it to be wholly explained in terms of a mystically local

---

[15] As rightly pointed out by Deissmann.

conception of "dwelling in a *pneuma* element comparable to the air" (i.e., the exalted Christ). [16, 17] At root is the view of Christ as a universal personality. [18] This is to be construed cosmically and eschatologically rather than mystically in the current Hellenistic sense. Cf. 1 C. 15:22, 45-49; R. 5:12-21. The first and the second Adam (→ I, 141 f.) are progenitors initiating two races of men. Each implies a whole world, an order of life or death (→ 437). Each includes his adherents in and under himself. The NT view is distinguished from oriental speculations about the first man, even in their Jewish form, by the two facts, first, that it never equates the first Adam and the Redeemer, but sees them as two opposite poles, and secondly, that it thinks of the Author of the second creation as historically present, so that this new creation has already been inaugurated. By baptism (→ I, 540) believers are removed from the sphere of the first Adam, which is that of sin and death, into the sphere of the second Adam, which is that of righteousness and life (→ ἐνδύω, 320). This underlying spatial concept gives us the clue to the true significance of the formula ἐν Χριστῷ 'Ιησοῦ and its parallels. Yet here, too, there is both a local and an instrumental element, the former esp. in a.-c., the latter in d. and e. One of the main difficulties arises in this respect. ἐν (τῇ) σαρκί, R. 7:18; 8:3; 2 C. 10:3; Gl. 2:20, in the particular sense of → σάρξ and as a counterformula to ἐν πνεύματι (R. 8:8 f.), denotes a state (= σάρκινοι). When used of persons, ἐν νόμῳ in R. 2:12; 3:19 (= ὑπὸ νόμον, R. 6:14; Gl. 4:4 f., 21; 5:18) suggests a state so strongly that the opposite is ἄνομος (1 C. 9:20 f.; R. 2:12). The same is true of ἐν Χριστῷ. It is no further removed from ἐν πίστει than Χριστὸς ἐν ὑμῖν (2 C. 13:5; Gl. 2:20), but it is more objective. ἐν νόμῳ δικαιοῦσθαι (Gl. 3:11; 5:4) is instrumental (= ἐξ ἔργων νόμου, Gl. 2:16). So, too, is the counterformula ἐν Χριστῷ δικαιοῦσθαι (Gl. 2:17, = διά, ἐκ πίστεως, v. 16). Yet there are still glimpses of a spatial conception (Gl. 3:27). The distinction is not so sharp in Greek.

4. Christ in Believers. The related but less frequent phrase "Christ in believers" is also essentially Pauline. As Adam lives in natural men, so the Inaugurator of the new aeon, Christ, lives in believers (R. 8:10; Gl. 2:20; Col. 1:27). [19] But this means that Christ must be formed in them (Gl. 4:19). This involves travail (→ ὠδῖνες). The sufferings of believers are Christ's sufferings, for in terms of His body, the community, Christ is not yet fully clear of this aeon of sin and death (2 C. 1:5; 4:10; Col. 1:24). In every stress, however, the life of Christ is manifested in our mortal bodies, although it is concealed until at the *parousia*, whether by transformation or resurrection, it bursts through the outer shell and shines forth in glory. Apprehensible for the moment only in imperfect form, it is now — though not only for this reason (1 C. 13:13) — mediated through faith (Gl. 2:20; 2 C. 4:18; 5:7; 2 C. 13:5; R. 4). It is thus an elementary misunderstanding to oppose faith and

---

[16] Deissmann, *op. cit.*, 98.

[17] J. Weiss and Böhlig fail to see any specifically mystical elements in Paul and demand a sharper distinction. Brun emphasises the fact that Pauline piety is not cultic. H. E. Weber thinks that a place must be found for the historical Christ (→ διά, 67), and finds the point of unity in the conscious reality of faith.

[18] Murmelstein, 261 ff.: "The sum of all souls," *anima generalis*; A. Schweitzer speaks of the mystical body of Christ. The latter is closer to Pauline usage, but the two cannot be separated.

[19] Deissmann, *op. cit.*, 92 suggests a parallel in the expression "man in the air" and "the air in man," but this is no real analogy because it does not have the Pauline reference to cosmic history.

the life of Christ in Paul, or even to separate them as though they were unrelated (Eph. 3:17).

5. The ἐν of Fellowship in John. Exclusively in John's Gospel and 1 Jn. (some 15 + 12 times) we have a distinctive ἐν of religious fellowship. As a predicate there is often added εἶναι (Jn. 10:38; 14:10a, 11, 20; 17:21, 23, 26; 1 Jn. 2:5b; 5:20), or more commonly → μένειν (Jn. 6:56; 14:10b; 15:4, 5, 6, 7; 1 Jn. 2:6, 24, 28; 3:6, 24; 4:12, 13, 15, 16). Often the reciprocity of the relationship is emphasised (Jn. 6:56; 10:38; 14:10, 11, 20; 15:4, 5; 17:21, 23, 26; 1 Jn. 3:24; 4:13, 15, 16). In distinction from Paul the Father (though not the Spirit) is brought into the relationship, whether with Jesus (Jn. 10:38; 14:10, 11) or with men (1 Jn. 4:12 f., 15, 16). We thus have a triangle, of which the disciples form the third side (Jn. 14:20; 17:21, 23, 26; cf. 1 Jn. 2:24). The formulae are neither ecstatic nor eschatological. According to Jn. 6:56; 14:23; 15:1 ff. we might call them mystical in the broader sense. But there is reference always to a personal and ethical fellowship of will (κοινωνίαν ἔχειν, 1 Jn. 1:3, 6, 7; and analogous constructions with ἀγάπη and λόγος, Jn. 15:10; 1 Jn. 2:14; 3:17).

This type of expression has nothing to do with ἱερός → γάμος. There are no real parallels in Hellenistic mysticism or Gnosticism. Cf. O. Sol. 5:15 : "The Lord is with me and I with him." Murmelstein translates 17:13 : [20] "I transform them into myself."

Oepke

ἐνδημέω → δῆμος, 63.　　　　　　　ἐνδοξάζομαι, ἔνδοξος → δόξα, 254.

ἐνδυναμόω → δύναμις, 286.　　　　　ἐνδύω → δύω, 319.

ἐνέργεια, ἐνεργέω, ἐνέργημα,

　　ἐνεργής → ἔργον.　　　　　　　　ἐνευλογέω → εὐλογέω.

ἐνθυμέομαι, ἐνθύμησις → θυμός.

---

† ἐνίστημι

The only significant form in the NT is the intr. med. with perf. act. This is mostly used a. in a purely temporal sense, "to enter," τοῦ θέρους ἐνισταμένου with the entry of summer, Theophr. Historia Plantarum, IX, 8, 2; τοῦ ἐνιαυτοῦ at the beginning of the year, 3 Βασ. 12:24; τοῦ ἔαρος, Jos. Ant. 14:38; ἐνστάντος τοῦ ἑβδόμου μηνός, 1 Ἐσδρ. 5:46 (47); 1 Macc. 8:24; 2 Macc. 4:43; 3 Macc. 3:24. In the perf. it means "to have entered," and therefore "to be present," Jos. Ant., 15, 7 : The sabbatical year ἐνεστήκει τότε, Bell., 6, 109; the 11th year of Hiram, Ant., 8, 62. The part., often used as adj., means "present," τοῦ πολέμου πρὸς Φίλιππον ὑμῖν ἐνεστηκότος, Aeschin. Or., 2, 58; τὴν [περὶ] τῶν ἐνεστηκότων ἀπόρων ἀπαλλαγήν, Jos. Ant., 3, 24; Ant., 1, 5; the decree of Augustus : οὐ μόνον ἐν τῷ ἐνεστῶτι καιρῷ ἀλλὰ καὶ ἐν τῷ προγεγενημένῳ, Ant., 16, 162; 20, 267; Vit., 161; 1 Macc. 12:44; 2 Macc. 6:9; 12:3; 3 Macc. 1:16; 1 Ἐσδρ. 9:6 : τρέμοντες διὰ τὸν ἐνεστῶτα χειμῶνα, cf. with Ezr. 10:9 and 2 Ἐσδρ. 10:9. διὰ τὴν ἐνεστῶσαν κακίαν, P. Petr., II, 19, 2, 5 (3rd cent. B.C.); οἱ ἐνεστηκότες ταμίαι, Supplementum Epigraphicum Graecum, ed. J. E. Hondius etc., II (1924), No. 580, 27 and 28 : ἡ ἐνεστῶσα (ἡμέρα), P. Ryl., 77, 39; τοῦ ἐνεστῶτος ἔτους, ibid., 86, 6; both ibid., 88, 14, 15; τοῦ ἐνεστῶτος μηνός, ibid., 141, 8 f. Subst.: ὁ ἐνεστώς (sc. χρόνος), among grammarians a technical term for the

---

[20] Op. cit., 268.

present, Dion. Thr., 638, 22; neut.: τὰ ἐνεστῶτα, "the present," Polyb., 2, 26, 3; opp.: τὰ μέλλοντα, Jos. Ant., 7, 391; 13, 428; 14, 58. b. Less frequently it is used in a hostile sense : "to intervene," of the veto of the people's tribunes, Polyb., 6, 16, 4; Plut. Tib. Gracch., 10 (I, 828e), etc.; of hostile nations ἐνστήσονται καὶ πολλὰ πραγματεύσονται, Jos. Ant., 11, 170. Yet there is no instance of the sense "to menace," at least with the perf. [1] Sense a. fits in better with Hdt., I, 83 (τοιούτων ... ἐνεστεώτων πρηγμάτων), Isoc., 5, 2 (τὸν πόλεμον τὸν ἐνστάντα), and esp. Barn., 17, 2 (περὶ τῶν ἐνεστώτων ἢ μελλόντων).

We have sense a. in 2 Th. 2:2 : ὡς ὅτι ἐνέστηκεν ἡ ἡμέρα τοῦ κυρίου, [2] R. 8:38; 1 C. 3:22 : ἐνεστῶτα — μέλλοντα; Gl. 1:4 : ὁ αἰὼν ὁ ἐνεστὼς πονηρός (= ὁ αἰὼν οὗτος) and with reference to the NT time of salvation in Hb. 9:9 : ὁ καιρὸς ὁ ἐνεστηκώς. In 1 C. 7:26: διὰ τὴν ἐνεστῶσαν ἀνάγκην, the sense of "to threaten" or "to impend," which is not attested elsewhere, is both linguistically and materially improbable. Paul is convinced that we already stand in the sufferings of the new aeon (R. 8:22). [3] The only possible instance of sense b. is 2 Tm. 3:1: ἐνστήσονται καιροὶ χαλεποί ("difficult days will break upon us"), and even here sense a. fits well enough : "difficult days shall come."

Oepke

ἐνκαινίζω → καινός.   ἐνκακέω → κακός.

ἐνκρίνω → κρίνω.   ἐνόπτης → ὁράω.

ἔννοια → νοῦς.   ἔννομος → νόμος.

ἔνοχος → ἔχω.

┌─────────────────────┐
│ ἐντέλλομαι, ἐντολή │
└─────────────────────┘

† ἐντέλλομαι.

ἐντέλλομαι, "to command," "to commission," predominantly med., seldom active : Pind. Olymp., 7, 40 : ἔντειλεν, of the command of the δαίμων Ὑπεριονίδας. Here then (→ ἐντολή, 545) it is used of the deity, though mostly it refers to the commission of a king or ruler, e.g., Hdt., I, 47 and 53, of Croesus to the Lydians ; I, 123, of Astyages ; Xenoph. Cyrop., V, 5, 3, of Cyrus ; Plat. Resp., III, 393e, of Agamemnon. But also Hdt., I, 60, cf. V, 73 : τὰ ἐντεταλμένα, of commissions through heralds or emissaries, cf. Polyb., XVIII, 2, 1: ἐντεταλμένοι, commissioned representatives, or Plat. Prot., 325d

---

ἐνίστημι. [1] Pr.-Bauer, and to some extent Liddell-Scott, s.v. ἐνίστημι, should be corrected along the lines of Cr.-Kö., s.v.

[2] Since there is no question of a spiritualising error, the present perf. has a fut. significance : "in process of coming" (Bl.-Debr., § 323, 3; Dob. Th., ad loc.).

[3] Rightly Bchm., Sick. K., ad loc., also Liddell-Scott, J. Weiss, Ltzm. K., ad loc., and P. Tischleder, Theologie u. Glaube, 12 (1920), 225 ff., are correct in giving an eschatological interpretation, but wrong linguistically. Polyb., 1, 71, 4, ἐνίστατο, is no proof to the contrary. There is an exact linguistic, though not material, par. in Mithr.-Liturg., 4, 9 = Preis. Zaub., IV, 503 : μετὰ τὴν ἐνεστῶσαν καὶ σφόδρα κατεπείγουσαν χρείην "according to the present distress, which afflicts me sorely." Cf. 14, 5 f. = Preis. Zaub., IV, 687: ἐν ταῖς ἐνεστώσαις τῆς σήμερον ἡμέρας ἀγαθαῖς ὥραις. On the other hand, we find sense b. in Preis. Zaub., IV, 692 : ὅταν δὲ ἐνστῶσιν ἔνθα καὶ ἔνθα τῇ τάξει, "when they stand there threatening on both sides in ordered ranks."

ἐντέλλομαι. L. Wenger, Die Stellvertretung im Rechte der Papyri (1906); Mitteis-Wilcken, II, 261; Preisigke Fachwörter, s.v.; Moult.-Mill., s.v.

for what is demanded from the teacher. The word is found some 400 times in the LXX. It is used some 350 times for צוה pi and pu (occasionally for אמר, אצר hi, דבר etc.). It is regularly used for the command of the king, Gn. 12:20, 2 Βασ. 18:5, or of Moses, Lv. 9:5, but esp. the divine ordering: Gn. 2:16. In the pap. ἐντέλλομαι is "to give a commission," An Alexandrian Erotic Fragment (ed. B. Grenfell, 1896), 30 (2nd cent. B.C.), and it thus comes to be used technically of the power of legal representation: P. Lips., 38, 5 and 6 (4th cent. A.D.) → ἐντολή, 546.

In the NT the following senses are to be distinguished.

1. "To give a commission or direction" in general, and not specifically in the religious sense: Mt. 17:9; Mk. 11:6 ΑΧΓΠΣΦ lat syp h; Mk. 13:34; Hb. 11:22.

2. The ἐντέλλεσθαι of God is found mostly in LXX quotations: Mt. 4:6; Lk. 4:10 (ψ 90:11); Hb. 9:20: τὸ αἷμα τῆς διαθήκης ἧς ἐνετείλατο πρὸς ὑμᾶς ὁ θεός, of the ordaining of the covenant, though here the LXX has διέθετο (כרת, Ex. 24:8). Hence also Mt. 15:4 א*C ℜ: ὁ γὰρ θεὸς ἐνετείλατο λέγων, of the 5th commandment, which is seen in antithesis to παράδοσις. In Ac. 13:47 it is used of the missionary command acc. to Is. 49:6. On Jn. 14:31, of the ἐντέλλεσθαι of the Father in relation to the Son, → ἐντολή, 553.

3. We find the ἐνλέλλεσθαι of Moses in Mt. 19:7; Mk. 10:3 (the bill of divorce); Jn. 8:5 (stoning on the occasion of adultery).

4. ἐντέλλεσθαι in the basic religious sense, of the proclamation of Jesus to the disciples, is found in the Synoptists only at Mt. 28:20: διδάσκοντες αὐτοὺς τηρεῖν πάντα ὅσα ἐνετειλάμην. Here the content of all that Jesus has said to the disciples is described as ἐντολή, with no singling out of the commandment of love as in Jn. In their missionary work the disciples are to teach what Jesus has commanded (cf. the formula: τηρεῖν τὰς ἐντολάς). But since it is the present Christ who charges the community to do this, and since it is the baptised who are to render this obedience, it is hardly possible to think of this τηρεῖν of what is commanded in legalistic isolation from Christ Himself in His effective rule among His believing people. In this context the word ἐντέλλεσθαι simply expresses the unconditional obligation to obedience which, grounded christologically, is the obedience of faith. On the other hand, ἐντειλάμενος διὰ πνεύματος in Ac. 1:2 refers to the commands of Jesus to the apostles prior to His ascension. On the ἐντέλλεσθαι of Jesus in Jn. 15:14, 17 as a comprehensive expression for the commandment of love, → ἐντολή, 553 f.

† ἐντολή.

A. ἐντολή outside the NT.

1. ἐντολή in the General Usage of the Greek and Hellenistic World.

ἐντολή, often in the plur., means "order," "commission," "command." Neither in tragedy nor in Attic prose is it common. The usual sense is a. the command of a king, official or general. Hdt., I, 22: of the king to a herald; III, 147: of Darius to a general;

ἐ ν τ ο λ ή. Preisigke Fachwörter, s.v. L. Mitteis, Röm. Privatrecht, I (1908), 230, n. 89. Mitteis-Wilcken, II, 1, 261 and 269. On Joseph., Schl. Theol. d. Judt., 62 f. On Philo's conception of the Law, J. Heinemann, Philons gr. u. jüd. Bildung (1932), 445 ff.; v. Arnim, III, 519-523. On Paul, W. G. Kümmel, R. 7 u. die Bekehrung des Pls. (1929), 55 f.; R. Bultmann, "R. 7 u. d. Anthropologie des Pls." in Imago Dei, f. G. Krüger (1932), 53-62; G. Kuhlmann, Theologia naturalis bei Philon u. bei Pls. (1930), 92-109.

Xenoph. Cyrop., II, 4, 30 : ἐντολὴ τοῦ Κύρου; Diod. S., 4, 2 : of the command of the king (plur.); Luc. Pro Lapsu inter Salutandum, 13 : of orders in the letter of the emperor (with παράγγελμα). So, too, in the LXX : 2 Ch. 29:25; 35:10, 16; Ἰερ. 42:16, 18; Da. 3:12; 1 Macc. 2:31 A; plur.: 2 Macc. 3:13; 4:25; 4 Macc. 4:6. This is also the main usage in Joseph. (63 times), e.g., Ant., 8, 365; 11, 229. It is commonly used in the pap. of orders of the king : P. Tebt., I, 6, 10 (2nd cent. B.C.), concerning the temple. It refers to imperial orders in P. Giess., 7, 22 (2nd cent. A.D.): ἐκ τῶν κυρίου ἐντολῶν; ibid., 62, 11 (2nd cent. A.D.): ταῖς ἐντολαῖς τοῦ κρατίστου ἡγεμόνος. Worth noting because of the addition of ταῖς θείαις to ἐντολαῖς is the inscr. of Skaptopare (Bulgaria): Ditt. Syll.³, 888, 51 (238 A.D.). For commands to an official, cf. P. Giess., 62, 11 (2nd cent. A.D.). Cf. the ἐντέλλεσθαι in Mk. 13:34; Mt. 17:9; Ac. 1:2. In the same sense, for ἐντολή is not an expressly religious term, there is early reference to the divine command : Aesch. Prom., 12 : ἐντολὴ Διός. Joseph. uses ἐντολή with other words for specific ordinances of God in the history of Israel, sometimes through men of God. For the most part, however, these are not the ordinances of the Torah : Ant., 2, 274; 6, 101; 10, 28; 4, 13 (→ infra). The term has also the sense b. of "pedagogic instruction" : Pind. Fr., 167 (ed. Boeckh [1811 f.]: Χείρωνος ἐντολάς, which the Centaur gave to Achilles (the title of a poem). Cf. also Plat. Charm., 157c : directions in relation to incantations. It is used again c. of various other forms of "commission" : Soph. Ai., 567, the last commission of Ajax. Luc. Pro Imaginibus, 16 : the commission of a woman in relation to the poet. In the NT it is used of an everyday command in Ac. 17:15; Col. 4:10; Hb. 11:22 (ἐντέλλεσθαι). This sense remains in modern Gk. d. In the pap. the term also has the sense of "authorisation," e.g., at law (cf. ἐντέλλεσθαι), P. Lips., 38, 3 etc. (4th cent. A.D.); cf. 33, Col., II, 3 (4th cent. A.D.); it is also used for "instruction" : P. Lille, 13, 55 (to the oil merchants); and for the "mandate" to instal an official : New Classical Fragments (ed. B. Grenfell and A. Hunt, 1897), 37, 6 (2nd cent. B.C.), of installation as the supervisor of a village. 1 Tm. 6:14 is probably to be taken in this way, → 555.

2. The Specifically Religious Reference to the ἐντολαί of the Torah in the LXX and Hellenistic Judaism.

The term ἐντολαί (more rarely ἐντολή) first receives its solemn religious character (though cf. Aesch. supra) in the LXX, where it is used 50 times for מִצְוָה (23 times ἐντολαί, 27 ἐντολή), 18 times in the Ps. for פִּקּוּדִים, and occasionally for תּוֹרָה, חֹק, דָּבָר, חֻקָּה. In 11 passages מִצְוָה is translated differently, 5 times by πρόσταγμα or προστάσσειν, once each by νόμοι, λεγόμενα, ἐντάλματα, and 3 times without an equivalent. It means the individual requirements of the OT Law, and is often used with προστάγματα, 2 Ἐσδρ. 7:11; δικαιώματα, Ex. 15:26; Dt. 4:10; 10:13; 27:10; 4 Βασ. 17:13 etc., cf. Test. L. 14:4; Jud. 13:1. In the NT, cf. Lk. 1:6 (of Zacharias and Elisabeth). Cf. also Barn., 4, 11. With μαρτυρία, 4 Βασ. 23:3; κρίματα, 1 Ch. 28:7. The frequent use of ἐντέλλομαι at the same time (Dt. 30:8; Ju. 3:4; 1 Βασ. 13:13 B) shows that ἐντολή refers to what is commanded by God. Cf. ἐντολαὶ τοῦ θεοῦ : Test. L. 14:2, sing.; Test. Jud. 14:6; 16:3 f.; Ass. Mos. 12:10 : mandata dei ; 4 Esr. 7:21 ff.; Ign. Sm., 8, 1. Κυρίου, Test. L. 14:6; Test. Iss. 4:6 etc. τοῦ ὑψίστου, Test. A. 5:4. A favourite expression is φυλάσσειν τὰς ἐντολάς (שָׁמַר); Dt. 8:1, 2, 6, 11; 26:18; 3 Βασ. 8:58; Test. D. 5:1; Test. B. 10:3 f.; Barn., 4, 11. ποιεῖν τὰς ἐντολάς, Test. A. 2:8; Barn., 6, 1 (sing.). That the reference is to specific demands of the Torah is shown by the conjunction of νόμος and ἐντολαί (תּוֹרָה and מִצְוָה) in Ex. 16:18; 24:12; Jos. 22:5; Sir. 35:24; 45:5; Da. 3:30 LXX ; cf. Test. B. 10:3 f.; Test. D. 5:1.

Jewish writers influenced by the prevailing literary taste of Hellenism are less affected by the usage of the LXX. Thus Joseph. seldom uses ἐντολαί, preferring νόμος, νόμοι or τὰ νόμιμα, τὰ ἔθη, θεοῦ δόγματα. Only 9 times (cf. under 1. supra) does he use it of God's command, twice generally in Ant., 7, 342; 8, 337; of the command in Paradise in 1, 43; of the prescriptions of the Mosaic Law 5 times, e.g., 7, 338; 8, 94 and 120. Similarly Philo, except in Praem. Poen., 2, follows the distinctive LXX usage only 5 times, and always in quoted passages which refer to the ἐντολαί (-ή), Spec. Leg., I, 300; Rer. Div. Her., 8; Praem. Poen., 79 and 101; Som., II, 175.

3. The Stoic Truncation of the ἐντολή Concept in Philo.

The striking restriction of the use of ἐντολή in Philo is undoubtedly due to the fact that the word appears to him to be too official and historical, and not sufficiently speculative. This is in keeping with the noteworthy fact that the idea of the covenant is not found in his works. Like Joseph., he prefers νόμος, τὰ νόμιμα, τὸ νόμιμον (cf. νομοθετεῖν, or λόγια, χρησμοί, ἔθη, θεσμός, words which allow of an inner interpretation and philosophical establishment of the meaning and value of law) (Spec. Leg., I, 299). He is less concerned with the realistic content and more with the ethical substance of laws, their agreement with natural law, their reflection of cosmic law. This explains his aversion to ἐντολή, which derives from Stoic ethics. For Stoicism did not conceive of νόμος in the sense of customary legality or elementary moral law, but as λόγος ὀρθός in the sense of supreme moral principles. It thus linked ἐντολή with a primitive form of morality. The voluntary act is higher than the commanded: Leg. All., III, 144. In Leg. All., III, 90-95 Philo commented on the command in Paradise and the expression ἐνετείλατο. The command was not given to the heavenly man, but to the earthly and corruptible Adam. The former is the σοφός or τέλειος who possesses virtue from his own knowledge and who practises it without command. Only the προκόπτων needs the πρόσταξις (command). The prohibition (ἀπαγόρευσις) is for the φαῦλος. The ἐντολή or παραίνεσις concerns the μέσος, νήπιος. Philo tolerates the commandment because the immature and uneducated need admonition. His philosophy thus introduces a tension into the conception of the Law as ἐντολή.

B. The Synoptic Witness endorses the elementary ἐντολή and emphasises its central Unity.

In the Synoptists the use of the term is affected by the debate with Pharisaism.

Acc. to Synagogue teaching there are in the Torah 613 מִצְוֺת, 365 מִצְוֺת לֹא תַעֲשֶׂה, i.e., prohibitions, and 248 מִצְוֺת עֲשֵׂה, i.e., positive commands. [1] Judaism is thus confronted by a plethora of commands which make it difficult to apprehend the unity of the divine will. This situation is illuminated by the pointed question of the young man in Mt. 19:18 : "ποίας which?" It is also attested by the question as to the ἐντολή πρώτη πάντων in Mk. 12:28 or μεγάλη [2] ἐν τῷ νόμῳ in Mt. 22:36. In spite of its atomistic ethics, [3] broken up into individual demands and individual acts, the Synagogue shows definite signs of trying to attain to a unitary conception of the commandments by tracing them back to basic principles. [4] Yet this does not affect the practical position in relation to the many ἐντολαί, and there are many warnings against overlooking any detailed points by reason of such an approach. [5] As concerns fulfilment, the claim of the elder brother in Lk. 15:29 : "I never transgressed thine ἐντολή," finely reproduces the feeling of the Pharisees that they were really fulfilling the commandments. Judaism optimistically

---

[1] Str.-B., I, 814 ff.; 900; IV, 4, 7, 9.
[2] μεγάλη is the Semitic form of the Gk. compar., cf. Schl. Mt., *ad loc.*
[3] Cf. Weber, 277-312; Str.-B., IV, 3-19; 490-500; 1041-1042, No. 3 g.
[4] Cf. Str.-B., I, 907, II, 87 f., III, 543. Moore, II, 87 f. In prophecy (cf. Mi. 6:8) we already find the possible achievements of men reduced to certain rudimentary commandments (in this case three). In Qoh. 12:13 we can see the same process at work in the Wisdom literature. Here, too, is a compendium which gathers up the many detailed provisions (v. Rad).
[5] Cf. esp. S. Dt., 12, 28 § 79 (91a), Str.-B., I, 903d : "A light commandment should be as highly estimated by thee as a heavy." In result, all commandments are equally important. 4 Macc. 5:20 : τὸ γὰρ ἐν μικροῖς καὶ ἐν μεγάλοις παρανομεῖν ἰσοδύναμόν ἐστιν.

reckons with the possibility of doing this. Even in the Gospel, it is allowed that there may be relative fulfilment.

In the Synoptics (cf. Lk. 23:56 on the Sabbath commandment as well as the passages already cited), ἐντολή is used not only of the Decalogue but of other Mosaic provisions : Mk. 10:5 (of the bill of divorcement, cf. Mt. 19:7 with ἐνετείλατο). Mt. 15:4 : אּ C אּ: ὁ γὰρ θεὸς ἐνετείλατο λέγων, is followed by the fifth commandment and another Mosaic command : Ex. 21:17. Cf. Jn. 8:5, where the stoning of the adulteress is described as a Mosaic command. Cf. also Barn., 7, 3 of the law of fasting (Lv. 23:29) and Barn., 9, 5 of the law of circumcision.

In this matter of the content of the witness of Jesus in relation to ἐντολή religion, we should first note His unconditional acceptance of the demands of the Decalogue. He tells the rich man (Mk. 10:17 ff.; Mt. 19:20 νεανίσκος; Lk. 18:18 ἄρχων) that to enter into life (Mt. 19:17) he must keep the commandments, which are obviously a well-known norm. [6] The commandments concerned are those of the second table, amplified in Mt. by the positive command to love one's neighbour which in Lv. 19:18 indicates even to the very simplest what is the elementary will of God. It is true that what follows in the story (εἰ θέλεις τέλειος εἶναι, Mt. 19:20 f.) shows that only by attending to the personal course of action prescribed by this general law can justice be done to the ἐντολή. For the direction to sell all and to give to the poor is a hint as to the specific individual form of fulfilling the commandment of love.

We may also refer to Mt. 5:19. Here even the smallest commandments are endorsed. They must be kept and taught. One's place in the kingdom of heaven is dependent on their fulfilment. Since the Rabbis speak of light and heavy or less and more important commandments rather than of smallest and greatest, [7] the reference here is to the Ten Commandments as those which occupy least space in the scroll of Scripture. [8] Once again Jesus endorses the two tables as an elementary basis. If we compare this with the antitheses which follow in Mt. 5:21 ff., we shall see that the only righteousness which counts is one which does not sink below the Decalogue but which transcends this nationally accepted Law in fulfilment of the authoritative Messianic demands of Jesus. [9]

In Mt. 5:19 there is no suggestion of rank in the true sense. [10] According to the Jewish view, a man who broke one of the Ten Commandments (e.g., an adulterer) would not be ἐλάχιστος ἐν τῇ βασιλείᾳ in the sense of rank. He would not be in the kingdom at all. The point is that a Rabbinic form of expression is adopted to emphasise how seriously one's future destiny depends on one's decision in relation to even the smallest commands. It may be asked, however, whether the reference to the smallest commands is not to be linked with the preceding saying about the ἰῶτα and κεραία (v. 18), so that we are to think of the least important parts of Scripture, of the least significant requirements of the Torah. The answer is that Mt. 5:18, which comes from Q (cf. Lk. 16:17) and thus demands particular attention, does not have for Mt. the Rabbinic sense [11] that the whole Torah will maintain its literal validity in this aeon. For in this

---

[6] Mk. 10:19 and Lk. 18:20 : "Thou knowest the commandments."

[7] Cf. Str.-B., I, 901 ff., 249; G. Dalman, Jesus-Jeschua (1922), 60; I. Abrahams, Studies in Pharisaism and the Gospels, I (1917), 18 ff.; A. E. J. Rawlinson, St. Mark (1925), 170 f.

[8] So already J. A. Bengel, Gnomon (1742), ad loc.; F. Dibelius, ZNW, 11 (1910), 188 ff.; Schl. Mt., ad loc., 157-160.

[9] Cf. Schl. Mt., ad loc.

[10] Cf. the Rabb. doctrine : Str.-B., IV, 1016 ff., esp. 1138-1142; I, 249 f., 774; Dalman WJ, I, 93; Jesus-Jeschua (1929), 61.

[11] Str.-B., I, 244; Moore, I, 269 f.; II, 9.

case Mt. would be contradicting the antitheses which follow. In the context we have here a saying which emphasises in Jewish terms the inviolable authority of Scripture. It is intentionally put at the head of this passage in order that the transcending of the Decalogue by Jesus should not be construed as its dissolution.

Similarly, in the great accusation against the Pharisees that they falsely use the παράδοσις τῶν ἀνθρώπων [12] to overthrow the commandment of God, the basic antithesis is brought out in terms of the Decalogue. Jesus is not really opposing the idea of tradition as such, in this case Corban. He attacks the Halacha because casuistry has become an opponent of the will of God. Under cover of interpretation hatred and irreligion violate the ἐντολή of veneration of parents, and the elementary divine command is overturned. [13] At a period when one could no longer see the wood for the trees because of the detailed rulings, this teaching came with liberating force. Yet Jesus does not lay claim to specific religious originality. His prophetic witness to the truth brings to light again the true basis and meaning of the divine will.

Even when Jesus expounds *in nuce* the main theme of the divine ἐντολή and thus simplifies the ἐντολή concept, [14] giving to it in this concentrated form a dominant place which it never had in the Synagogue, He only brings the more clearly to light that which is already present and known. When tested by the question which is the chief commandment (Mt. 22:36), He unites the first, i.e., the love of God which claims all one's powers and gifts, with the second, i.e., love of one's neighbour. Here love of one's neighbour is both organically rooted in love of God and also seen as an opportunity to practise love of God, and therefore as an act of obedience and gratitude (Lk. 10:27 ff.). To the question which is the most important commandment, Jesus thus answers: There are two (Mk. 12:31) which constitute an inner unity, and Mt. adds that on these two hang all the Law and the prophets (Mt. 22:40). If research into the sources of this story discloses two traditions, the one preserved in Mk. and the other in the special Lucan source, there is reflected in this very duality the conviction of the community that in any case we are dealing with something which is in the Torah, so that Jesus Himself can say it according to the one form and the scribe according to the other. The point is that the scribe has to affirm an answer taken from the Torah. It is to be noted, however, that the definition is from the Torah itself and not from a gloss. Nevertheless, the first part is linked with the daily Sch^ema with its confession of εἷς θεός, and the second reproduces the common Rabbinic compendium of the second table in terms of Lv. 19:18. If the Jew is to find a perspective from which to take the Law to heart, Jesus can only welcome this question. He does not believe, however, that His answer is a new creative act; it is simply a unitary and central conception of the ἐντολή taken directly from the Law.

---

[12] On παράδοσις (→ 172), cf. Gl. 1:14; Col. 2:8; Str.-B., I, 619 ff. Objectively, it is always in the Synopt. παράδοσις πρεσβυτέρων, Mk. 7:3, 5; Mt. 15:2; cf. 15:6. This phrase is used even by opponents. Polemically, the formula is παράδοσις τῶν ἀνθρώπων, Mk. 7:8, or ὑμῶν, Mk. 7:9, 13; Mt. 15:3. Tt. 1:14 speaks of ἐντολαὶ ἀνθρώπων (Halacha) and Ἰουδαϊκοὶ μῦθοι (Haggada), cf. Test. A. 7:5, where we have νόμος θεοῦ and ἐντολαὶ ἀνθρώπων.

[13] There are many different forms of the accusation: "to abandon," Mk. 7:9; "to invalidate," Mk. 7:13; Mt. 15:6; "to transgress," Mt. 15:3.

[14] In Mk. 7:13; Mt. 15:6, we have λόγος τοῦ θεοῦ for ἐντολή. Hence this equation occurs in the Synopt. as well as Jn. (→ 554).

This may be seen most clearly in Lk. 10:27, where the scribe himself answers. Lk. also brings out most strongly the organic structure of the twofold command which is really one. In Mk. 12:32 f., however, the γραμματεύς gives immediate consent, quoting 1 S. 15:22, where obedience is preferred to sacrifice, to show that this twofold love takes precedence of the cultus. This answer makes it plain that he is not far from the kingdom of God (v. 34). The kingdom thus means that we really take the unity of God seriously in love of God and our neighbour. The context of Dt. 6:4 f. is particularly emphatic in Mk., where the endorsement by the scribe in v. 32 introduces more explicit citations from Deuteronomic sayings.

Nevertheless, we cannot but regard this presentation of the twofold command as "distinctive of Jesus."[15] In its very emphasis we may discern a conscious correction of the Pharisaic conception of the dogma of the unity of God, for elsewhere the criticisms of Jesus make it plain that this dogma is bound up with a false isolation of the service of God and a depreciation of love of one's neighbour. On the other hand, it is surely accidental that we do not occasionally find similar combinations of the two commandments among the Rabb. It is frequently found in the Test. XII, and is almost a fixed formula in Iss. 5:2; B. 33, and esp. in a discussion of the OT passages which is strongly reminiscent of the Synopt. formulation, Iss. 7:6 β S¹; D. 5:3. In addition, we have the express par. in Philo Spec. Leg., II, 63 : ἔστι δ' ὡς ἔπος εἰπεῖν τῶν κατὰ μέρος ἀμυθήτων λόγων καὶ δογμάτων δύο τὰ ἀνωτάτω κεφάλαια, τό τε πρὸς θεὸν δι᾽ εὐσεβείας καὶ ὁσιότητος καὶ τὸ πρὸς ἀνθρώπους διὰ φιλανθρωπίας καὶ δικαιοσύνης. Elsewhere there are no instances of the combination. But we do have the commandments individually. For an emphasis on the Schᵉma, cf. esp. the story of the martyrdom of R. Aqiba, Ber., 61b.[16] For the underlining of Lv. 19:18, cf. Aqiba in S. Lv. on 19:18 (Weiss, 89b): "This is a great, general (comprehensive) principle in the Torah,"[17] cf. Shab., 31a, Hillel : "What you would not have done to you, do not to another, this is the whole Torah, and the rest is exposition." On the divine likeness as "an even greater general principle" than Lv. 19:18, cf. Ben Azzai (c. 110 A.D.).[18]

C. The Evaluation of ἐντολή in Terms of the History of Revelation in Paul and Hebrews.

1. Paul gives his own interpretation of ἐντολή in R. 7. For all the reminiscences of the story of the fall, the reference here is not to the prohibition in Paradise.[19]

This is shown a. by the equation throughout the passage of νόμος and ἐντολή. The relationship is that the νόμος becomes acute through the ἐντολή. This is a concrete form of the Mosaic Torah. The main catchword : οὐκ ἐπιθυμήσεις, is not found in Gn. 3, but in the Decalogue. The character of the ἐντολή is described in terms of the tenth commandment because this brings out the most inward form of sin. The decisive drama is inward, not outward. The same relationship between ἐντολή and the Mosaic Law is shown b. by the wider context. The problem of the whole passage is that of the Law and sin. Paul has shown that these are related, and that Christ brings liberation from the Law. He has now to show that this repudiation of the Law does not imply

---

[15] Schl. Mt., ad loc.

[16] Cf. Str.-B., I, 905 ff.

[17] Str.-B., I, 357 f., 907. For expositions, cf. I, 363 f.

[18] Ibid., 358.

[19] This is the view of Theodore and Theodoret, A. Jülicher in Schriften des NT ; Ltzm., ad loc.; A. Meyer, Rätsel d. Jk. (1930), 297; A. M. H. Lagrange, Romains³ (1931), 399. But Chrysostom already takes a different view, cf. W. G. Kümmel, 55 f., with bibl. On the Adamic commands in the Synagogue, Str.-B., III, 37, 41 f. In 4 Macc. 2:23 the νόμος given at creation is the rational knowledge which leads to virtue, cf. 11:5. Cf. J. Heinemann, "Die Lehre vom ungeschriebenen Gesetz im jüdischen Schrifttum," in Hbr. Un. Coll., IV (1927), 149-171.

antinomianism, that the Law itself is not at fault, that it is not itself sin. He ends his exposition with a rejection of sin and an affirmation of the Law (→ *infra*). That ἐντολή is here the concrete Mosaic Law is also shown c. by the historical presentation given us in R. 5.[20] This is indispensable as a key to R. 7. We are told that in the period from Adam to Moses sin is present before the Law is given. It is imputed, however, only through the Law (→ *infra*). For through the Law, as we read in R. 3:20, there is ἐπίγνωσις ἁμαρτίας (cf. R. 7:7). For Paul, however, the Law is linked with Moses. We see from R. 5:13 f. (→ 437) that it is only by transgressing the Law that man comes to full participation in the sin of Adam. It is this very fact that there is a parallel between transgression of the command in Paradise and transgression of the Mosaic command, which explains why aspects of the story of the fall can be used in R. 7 to illustrate our encounter with the ἐντολή of the Law.[21] According to R. 5 the only possible way of explaining these connections is by seeing that it is precisely the Mosaic Law which constitutes the full analogy to the transgression of Adam. By the fact that the ἐντολή of the Torah stamps the race as a host of real sinners there is repeated the same process as in Paradise.

This process, which is presented in terms of universal history in R. 5, is depicted in terms of individual history in R. 7 (→ 358). We are not to take it autobiographically; it is something which continually takes place afresh in the life of man. The main emphasis is on the fact that it is active sin which grasps the opportunity afforded by the ἐντολή (cf. the διά of v. 11).[22] Sin comes to life through the commandment (v. 9 f.), and by the way of deception it brings about in man the consequence of death, which is here understood eschatologically.

The ἐντολή certainly makes possible the fullest influence and development of the power of sin (→ 497). For the commandment gives a consciousness of the power of sin in our desires, and thus gives us a knowledge of sin. In following it, we are plunged into death,[23] for now with open eyes we offend against the known truth of God.[24] Thus true guilt arises out of the already existent ἁμαρτία. Yet the process described in this way gives us the insight (v. 10: εὑρέθη) that reflection on this event must result in a clear-cut distinction between sin and the Law. Guilt alone is in the same category as ἁμαρτία. It can thus be concluded in v. 12 that the Law as a whole, and the ἐντολή as the individual commandment, is holy, just and good. The command as a just requirement of God retains its goodness and majesty. It does not itself constitute the deceptive and wicked adversary. Evil is characteristic only of ἁμαρτία. There is, however, an overriding divine teleology (ἵνα, v. 13). Through the ἐντολή (the good), this seeks to make sin sinful. By means of the command, the divine overruling brings sin out of its obscurity into the light. The unmasking of sin is a necessary prelude to the redemption of the justified. Paul can bring the ἐντολή and ἁμαρτία into this close association only because he no longer expects salvation from the νόμος (ἐντολή).

---

[20] Cf. G. Schrenk, "Die Geschichtsanschauung d. Pls.", *Jbch. d. Theol. Schule Bethel,* 3 (1932), 80, n. 113; "Der Römerbrief als Missionsdokument" in *Aus Theol. u. Gesch. d. reformierten Kirche, Festgabe f. E. F. K. Müller* (1933), 55 f.

[21] Gn. 2:16, cf. 3:3: "If thou eatest, thou must die." On ἐξαπατᾶν cf. Gn. 3:13 (and 2 C. 11:3). On sin as a personal power, cf. the figure of the serpent.

[22] A great deal depends on the act. understanding of ἀφορμὴν λαβοῦσα in v. 8, 11. Cf. Kümmel, 44.

[23] The ἐγὼ δὲ ἔζων χωρὶς νόμου ποτέ of R. 7:9 cannot mean life in the full religious sense (Kümmel, 52), for according to R. 5 the dominion of sin is already present before the νόμος becomes acute. It is relative life in comparison with the death described in v. 10 f.

[24] This is not merely psychological awareness, though we can see from the ἐπιθυμίαν οὐκ ᾔδειν in R. 7:7 that the knowledge includes such awareness.

If he had not found the completed solution in justifying faith, his exposition would have been fatal for all his ethical care in analysis. It would have led ineluctably to antinomianism. [25]

For Paul, then, the ἐντολή is both the concrete Mosaic Law and the characteristic mark of the Law, i.e., its character as command. This is in no sense reprehensible. It is a true expression of God's holy requirement of righteousness. The point of the exposition, however, is the negative one that the νόμος as mere ἐντολή is inadequate and impotent to attain the goal of salvation. If this element of inadequacy is not overcome by the fact that what is commanded is the unconditional will of God, it is also not overcome by the fact that God uses what is insufficient of itself to attain a preparatory goal.

The matter is again viewed in the light of the history of revelation in Eph. 2:14 f. Christ has become peace between Jews and Gentiles by breaking down the hostile barrier, namely, τὸν νόμον τῶν ἐντολῶν ἐν δόγμασιν. The new thing here as compared with R. 7 is that the ἐντολή is the fixed statute or ordinance. Thus the ἐντολαί as individual requirements of the Torah are transitory. Nor can the δόγμα (→ 231) bring any relief. It simply brings the accusation to light (Col. 2:14).

2. If the transitory nature of the ἐντολή is thus pitilessly revealed in Paulinism, the τήρησις ἐντολῶν θεοῦ is still required in relation to the Christian life. In 1 C. 7:19, [26] of course, this denotes the permanent element when the distinction between circumcision and uncircumcision has been removed. If we compare this with the material parallels in G. 5:6; 6:15, we may fill out from Paul himself the content of this τήρησις, namely, the fulfilment in the new being of the spirit, on the basis of faith, of the law of love (Gl. 5:6), which is not grounded in nature but is given as a new creation through Christ (Gl. 6:15). [27] This is wholly in line with the meaning of the καινὴ ἐντολή according to the Johannine view (→ 553). All else that Paul says concerning ἐντολή is in full agreement with the Synoptic evaluation of the concept (→ 547). In R. 13:9, where he states that all the commandments of the second table — καὶ εἴ τις ἑτέρα ἐντολή — are summed up in the law of love, ἐντολή means everything in the Law which relates to one's neighbour. Paul impresses this upon the Christian community. The law of love still has something decisive to say to it. The same holds good of Eph. 6:2, where the community is referred to the fifth commandment: ἥτις ἐστὶν ἐντολὴ πρώτη ἐν ἐπαγγελίᾳ. This can hardly mean that it is the first commandment with a promise (cf. Ex. 20:5 f.), nor that it is the first of the second table with a promise, but that it has a special significance by reason of the promise annexed. [28]

---

[25] On Bultmann's thesis (R. 7 u. d. Anthropologie des Pls., 56) that in R. 7 θέλειν is not a movement of the will in the sphere of subjectivity, → θέλειν. Here we may refer to his view that this θέλειν does not relate to the fulfilling of the ἐντολαί, 57. But vv. 19 and 21 (cf. 18b) give us the clear statements that θέλειν aims at the ἀγαθόν as opp. to the κακόν, at ποιεῖν τὸ καλόν. As we cannot separate the latter from θέλειν, so we cannot separate ἐντολή and ζωή. θέλειν thus relates to the ἐντολή to the degree that this is given with a view to life (v. 10). On the latter pt. cf. Lk. 10:28; Str.-B., III, 129.

[26] Joh. W. 1 K., ad loc. conjectures that the Apocr. Mos., which acc. to Euthalius (A. L. Zacagni, Collectanea monumentorum veterum, I [1698], 561) is reflected in Gl. 6:15, emerges even more clearly in 1 C. 7:19. But Euthalius had in view the formula καινὴ κτίσις, which is commonly attested as a Jewish expression, cf. Str.-B., II, 421 f.; III, 519; Ltzm., ad loc.

[27] The fact that ἐντολῶν has here no art. (cf. R. 7:8-13; Eph. 2:15) means that the reference is to keeping the will of God rather than ordinances.

[28] Cf. Ep. Ar., 228, where the same commandment is called μεγίστη.

In 1 C. 14:37 BₓA 17 it is described as an ἐντολὴ κυρίου that women should keep silence in church gatherings. But the original is surely ὅτι κυρίου ἐστίν DGLatt. [29] Hence ἐντολή is always used of OT commandments in the Pauline corpus, except in 1 Tm. 6:14 (→ 555).

3. In Hb. ἐντολή is used only of the Torah. In 7:5, 16, 18 it refers to the priestly law and in 9:19 to the institution of the covenant. [30] It should be noted, however, that the commandment is always linked with the more comprehensive term νόμος, cf. κατὰ (τὸν) νόμον, 7:5, 16; 9:19. [31] Here again the ἐντολή is the individual ordinance and the νόμος is the sum of the ἐντολαί. Hb. always refers to the authoritative basis of the νόμος because it deals with the radical question of the cultus and priesthood. The fundamental conviction is that the revelation in Christ has shown the old ἐντολή to be a σαρκίνη (7:16) which is external and transitory. The earlier commandment has been authoritatively annulled (7:18) because of its weakness and uselessness, for it has not led to any fulfilment. Its validity as a code has been overthrown as imperfect and outdated.

D. The Christian Message as ἐντολή in the Conflict against Gnosticism and Libertinism (the Johannine Writings and 2 Peter).

In Jn. (apart from Jn. 11:57: διδόναι ἐντολάς, of the command of the rulers) ἐντολή has the following senses.

1. In Jn. 10:18 the Father's ἐντολή to the Son is that in virtue of the ἐξουσία with which He is invested the Son should freely give His life to take it again. In Jn. 12:49, however, the ἐντολή relates to the establishment of the Word by Jesus. If the aim of His work, the mediation of eternal life, is emphasised in 12:50, and the final goal, that the love of the Father and the Son should be made known to the cosmos, in 14:31 (here ἐντέλλεσθαι), this makes it all the clearer that what is meant is the task connected with the sending of the Son, not as an imposed and imperative duty, but as an ordination and authorisation which derives from the love of the Father and is voluntarily accepted by the Son. Cf. also the plural in 15:10 (→ infra).

2. The new ἐντολή of Jesus to His disciples is the command of love. It is given its deepest basis in Jn. 13:34. The new factor is not the law of love as such, nor a new degree of love, but its new christological foundation. They are to love one another as those who are loved by Jesus. They are to actualise the basic love of Jesus. Thus the loving self-giving of Jesus is the root and power of the new ἀγαπᾶν. The same basis (without καινή) is to be seen in 15:12, cf. 15:17 (ἐντέλλεσθαι). Here ἐντολή always means commandment. The imperative remains. But the absolute determination of ἀγαπᾶν by Christ, its rootage in the love of Jesus, causes it to transcend all nomistic moralism and all mysticism, which is excluded by the demand for a definitive decision for the Son.

3. Keeping the ἐντολαί [32] of Jesus is a mark of love for Him. The expression in Jn. 14:15, 21 refers to the action of the disciples according to the will of Jesus.

[29] Cf. Ltzm., ad loc.

[30] Cf. ἐντέλλεσθαι in relation to the ordaining of the covenant, Hb. 9:20 (Mas. כָּרַת).

[31] This consistent use is present in 7:16 in spite of B. Weiss (Brief an d. Heb. [1897]) and Rgg., who here translate "norm": F. Delitzsch, Comm. zum Brief an d. Hebr. (1857).

[32] τηρεῖν τὰς ἐντολάς (cf. Mt. 28:20): Jn. 15:10; 14:15; 1 Jn. 3:22, 24; 5:3. ἔχειν καὶ τηρεῖν: Jn. 14:21; 1 Jn. 2:3 f.; ποιεῖν τὰς ἐντολάς (cf. Test. A. 2:8); 1 Jn. 5:2. περιπατεῖν κατὰ τὰς ἐντολὰς αὐτοῦ, 2 Jn. 6. τηρεῖν τὸν λόγον: Jn. 8:51 f., 55; 14:23; 15:20; 17:6; 1 Jn. 2:5. τοὺς λόγους Jn. 14:24. On Rev. → n. 37.

Love for Jesus is the motivating power, v. 21. ἔχειν as the inner possession of the commandments and τηρεῖν are both regarded as signs of love for Him. The love of the Father and the revelation of the Son find a response in the inner life of disciples (cf. 15:14: ἐντέλλομαι). If the plur. ἐντολαί is not avoided, this does not imply any surrender to legalism. [33] The motivation prevents this, as does also the fact that the plur. is simply a development of John's favourite concept of unity, the τηρεῖν τὰς ἐντολάς leading back intentionally to the λόγον τηρεῖν (cf. Jn. 14:15, 21 with 14:23 f.; 15:10 with 15:20; for 1 Jn. → infra). The ἐντολαί, always summed up in the one command of love, do not imply a Jewish multiplicity of ordinances, but the radiating of the one ἐντολή out into the manifoldness of the obedient life. Since the basis is also the basic quality in observance of the commandments, there need be no further elaboration. In this whole matter Johannine "mysticism" proves to be most unmystical. It is not ecstasy, nor meditation, but fulfilment of the commandments as the one commandment grounded in Jesus.

In the light of Jn. 15:10 it might be asked whether the translation "task" or "commission" is not better under 2. and 3. as well as 1. In this well-known combination what is said in the sing. of the Son is then expressed in the plur. and equated with the keeping of the commandments by the disciples. On the other hand τηρεῖν τὰς ἐντολάς cannot mean "to fulfil a commission." The inner parallel with the mission of the Son shows rather how radically the attitude of faith, which underlies the term ἐντολή, excludes all thought of the Law. If the keeping of the commandments by the disciples and the fulfilment by the Son of the tasks which the Father has given both imply the same abiding in the same love, it is again asserted that the legal requirement of the Law has yielded to the personal fellowship of a relationship of love. The goal of the fulfilled joy of salvation in 15:11 also serves to mark off this keeping of the ἐντολαί from any legal understanding. It is thus apparent that the nomistic view of ἐντολή is quite impossible in Jn.

4. The distinctive features of the use of ἐντολή in the Epistles of Jn. are as follows. a. There is never any discussion of the ἐντολαί without reference to the ἐντολή (in the reverse order in 1 Jn. 4:21 ff.). This arrangement, which is an established characteristic, makes it clear that the law of love, the ἐντολή κατ' ἐξοχήν, is the true content of the ἐντολαί. Comparison with the Gospel suggests reflection on the relation between ἐντολή and ἐντολαί as it is there presented. The exposition is certainly influenced by the sharper conflict with Gnosticism (→ 555). b. This conflict also leads to a stronger emphasis on keeping the commandments of God: 1 Jn. 2:3 (cf. ἀγάπη τοῦ θεοῦ v. 5); 3:22; 5:3; 2 Jn. 4 (of the Father). The Gnostic movement necessitates a stress on the elementary. If it boasts of its mystical union with God (1 Jn. 2:6: ὁ λέγων), the true understanding of love for God must be emphasised in opposition to it. This stress on the elementary is most pronounced in 1 Jn. 4:20 f., where the commandment of love is *the* divine commandment and it is argued along the lines of Mt. 22:37 ff. that love for God cannot be separated from love for one's brother. It is not that there is no connection of the ἐντολή of love with Christ, [34] but it is striking that the profound christological basis of loving as He loved, which is so prominent in the Gospel

---

[33] Cf., as opp. to Bau., Schl. J., *ad loc.*

[34] Cf. 1 Jn. 2:8: "True in him." The fact that Jesus gave the ἐντολή (1 Jn. 3:23), and the links with faith in Christ (1 Jn. 3:23; 4:9; 5:1), with assurance of salvation and the joy of prayer (1 Jn. 3:19 ff., cf. the victory of faith over the κόσμος in 5:4), with the gift of the Spirit (1 Jn. 3:24) and with the birth from God (1 Jn. 5:1), make it clear that the command of love applies wholly and exclusively to the new life.

(Jn. 13:34; 15:12), is not stated here. c. The descriptions of the ἐντολή as "old" and "new" (1 Jn. 2:7 f.; 2 Jn. 5) [35] sound like a meditation on Jn. 13:34 and are presumably directed against the Gnostic love of novelty. The meaning of "old" [36] is "from the beginning of the Christian life" (the "old" ἐντολή being the word which has been heard, 1 Jn. 2:7). It is beyond dispute that the "new" ἐντολή is the command of love (1 Jn. 2:9 ff.). But the christological foundation which distinguishes Jn. 13:34 is again missing. d. Another distinctive view is the definition of ἐντολή not merely as the command of love but also as the union of faith in Christ and love (1 Jn. 3:23). Also new is the addition: "His commandments are not grievous" (1 Jn. 5:3 → βαρύς, I, 557). The first point is again directed against the Gnostics, who are deficient in both respects. The ἐντολή character of faith is in specific opposition to those who deny that Christ has come in the flesh (cf. 2 Jn. 7).

The problem posed by the OT Law is no longer a live issue in the Epistles of Jn. The relationship of faith and Law is not discussed. Nor are cultic or sacramental questions. The term νόμος does not occur (cf. Jn. 1:17 etc.). The basic question of Paul how we are to keep the Law is now irrelevant, for the ἐντολή is bound up from the very first with faith in Christ. The conflict here is with antinomian Gnosticism. It is because this neglects the simplest and most basic duty of Christians (cf. 1 Jn. 2:6) that there is such emphasis on the keeping of the commandments. There can be no true *gnosis* without ἐντολή (1 Jn. 2:3 f.). What is self-evidently valid for Paul as the good and holy and righteous will of God is here summed up in the rule τηρεῖν τὰς ἐντολάς, i.e., the doing of God's will in its most elementary forms as the content of Christianity. But here, too, there are no ἐντολαί apart from the ἐντολή linked with Jesus. Here, too, there is the movement from ἐντολαί to λόγος (cf. 1 Jn. 2:4 with 5), though the formula τηρεῖν τὰς ἐντολάς is predominant in the Ep. as distinct from τηρεῖν τὸν λόγον in the Gospel. It is perhaps easier to see a nomistic view (cf. the καινὸς νόμος of Barn., 2, 6) in an utterance like 1 Jn. 3:23, but in the Epistles as in the Gospel this would be a misunderstanding.

In Rev. [37] the commands of God, esp. in passages directed against idolatry, are again linked with references to faith in Jesus or witness to Him, so that once more we see the Johannine peculiarity of never speaking of the ἐντολαί without mentioning Jesus. Cf. 12:17; 14:12; 22:14 א 046 gig sy Tert Cypr Tycon.

In 2 Peter the polemic against a destructive Libertinism makes it understandable that Christian teaching should twice be described as ἐντολή. Acc. to 2:21 the heretics turn away ἐκ τῆς παραδοθείσης αὐτοῖς ἁγίας ἐντολῆς. Acc. to 3:2 this ἐντολή is described as that τοῦ κυρίου καὶ σωτῆρος. It is mediated through the apostles. In distinction from Jn., there seems to be here more of a movement towards the *nova lex* of the post-apost. fathers.

This is hardly true of 1 Tm. 6:14. The ἐντολή which Tm. is to keep inviolate until the appearing of the *Kyrios* is the charge committed to him (→ 546). [38]

---

[35] The text in v. 6 is, of course, corrupt.
[36] On "old" and "new" cf. Rabb. par., Wnd. Kath. Br., *ad loc.*
[37] On τηρεῖν τὸν λόγον in Rev., cf. 3:8, 10; 22:7, 9 (λόγους). On τηρεῖν τὰς ἐντολάς cf. Rev. 12:17; 14:12.
[38] As rightly perceived by Calvin (*mandatum*), K. Knoke, *Prakt.-Theol. Komm. z. d. Past.* (1887 ff.), *ad loc.*; Dib., *ad loc.* The adjs. go with ἐντολή. It is taken to mean *nova lex* by J. T. Beck, Pr.-Bauer, Meinertz ("Christian teaching").

In the post-apost. fathers there is a mounting emphasis on ἐντολή in the older legal sense. Subjection to the commandments of God is described as the content of the Christian life, Barn., 4, 11; Ign. Tr., 13, 2; Sm., 8, 1; Herm. v., 3, 5, 3 (cf. the commandments of the angel of repentance in Herm. v., 5, 5; s., 10, 3, 4, and the *mandata* of the whole second section). It is also stated of Christ Himself that He fulfilled the commandment of God (Barn., 6, 1: ἐποίησεν τὴν ἐντολήν), but not in the Johannine sense. The Christian ἐντολή plays an important role, though again not in the pneumatic, unitary sense of the Johannine writings (Ign. R. prooem : πᾶσα ἐντολὴ αὐτοῦ). Jesus is the Legislator for Christians [39] (Ign. Eph., 9, 2; Pol., 2, 2; 1 Cl., 13, 3, of a saying in the Sermon on the Mount, together with παραγγέλματα; 2 Cl., 3, 4; 6, 7; 4, 5, μὴ ποιεῖτε τὰς ἐντολάς μου [an apocr. saying of Jesus]; 8, 4; 17, 3, with its Stoic phrase προκόπτειν ἐν ταῖς ἐντολαῖς τοῦ κυρίου). For the Christian Law, cf. 2 Cl., 17, 1: εἰ γὰρ ἐντολὰς ἔχομεν. For Christ as the Legislator of the *nova lex,* cf. also Just. Dial., 12, 2 f.; 116, 2 : ἐὰν πράξωμεν αὐτοῦ τὰς ἐντολάς, of Christ. Test. of the 40 Martyrs of Sebaste (N. Bonwetsch, *Studien z. Gesch. d. Theol. u. Kirche,* I [1897]), 77, 14 f.; 78, 14 f.: αἱ ἐντολαὶ τοῦ Χριστοῦ.

Schrenk

ἔντευξις → τυγχάνω.

ἐντολή → 545 ff.

ἐντυγχάνω → τυγχάνω.

---

† Ἐνώχ   → υἱὸς τοῦ ἀνθρώπου.

A. Enoch in Judaism.

In Judaism the name Enoch comprehends a whole group of ideas which are often very different from one another. Thus the title "Book of Enoch" usually refers neither to a book by Enoch nor to a book about him, but to the kind of material found in the work. This material is naturally linked with the ideas gathered up in the name Enoch. It is rather as though we might use the title "Book of Darwin" for any presentations of the theory of evolution.

There are no sources available to explain the origin and historical development of these ideas. It is obvious that they could not possibly be built up and elaborated merely on the brief record in Gn. 5:21-24. This record simply provided the occasion for linking these ideas with the person of Enoch. Indeed, the record itself gives evidence of the fact that for the priestly author the name aleady stood at the centre of definite speculations. We may assume that at the time of writing various traditions in Judaism were already united with the name Enoch. We can only guess at the character and content of these traditions. The following features are significant : that Enoch was the seventh after Adam; that he walked with God; that he lived 365 years; and that God took him. The walk with God denotes familiarity, or the possession of divine secrets. His position as seventh is obviously designed; it is not something which is noted and interpreted later. This position gives him special prominence along with Adam (the first), Enos (the third) and Noah (the tenth, and the first of the new race). There may be hints here of the myth of the original man. Enoch has a specific relationship to the original man, like Adam (who is perhaps this man), Noah and Enos (the man). May it be that we can speak of representatives of the original man, or bearers of his power, in the various ages of humanity ? Certainly, Enoch is not merely the possessor of divine

---

[39] On κυρίου ἐντολή in 1 C. 14:37 B → 553.

secrets; he is also the particular bearer and guardian of these secrets in his generation. The years of his life (365) may finally denote (in the tradition preserved in P) the interaction of these secrets with those of astronomy. [1]

The record in Gn. 5:21-24 is the oldest known fragment of Jewish tradition linked with the name Enoch. It is also the only such fragment in the OT Canon. This is because the Enoch traditions had become suspect to orthodox Judaism at the time of the fixing of the Jewish Canon (at Jamnia c. 90 A.D.). They were thus carefully excluded from the sacred Scriptures. They were rightly felt to be not truly Jewish. On the other hand, we have clear traces of these traditions in non-canonical writings. It is important that these writings which later became non-canonical were still reckoned among the sacred writings in the early days of Christianity.

In Sir. 44:16 Enoch is mentioned as the first of the great fathers of the primitive period, and it is said of him (in the Heb. original): "Enoch (was found righteous and) walked with Yahweh and was taken, as a miracle of (divine) knowledge for all generations." This statement obviously alludes to Gn. 5, but it does not derive exclusively from this passage. It goes back to independent and amplified traditions. In Sir. 49:14 ff. the roll of the just is as follows: "Enoch, Joseph, Seth, Shem, Enos and Adam," and it is said of Enoch: "Few were created in the earth like Enoch, for he was taken up suddenly (or: into heaven)." In v. 16 it is said of Adam: "The fame of Adam surpasses all who lived on the earth." We may perhaps see behind this statement a basic conception according to which Enoch played a role in the myth of the first man. In the Gk. translation of Sir. 49:14 the original "walked with Yahweh" is rendered εὐηρέστησεν ... τῷ θεῷ, as in Gn. 5:24 LXX. [2] The passage is also quoted in this form in Philo Mut. Nom., 34 and Abr., 17. Cf. Wis. 4:10 f. [3]

The Book of Jubilees must now be mentioned, even though it is later, at least as part of Eth. En., which we shall have to consider next. Jubilees gives us information on contemporary Enoch traditions in 4:17-25; 7:38; 10:17; 19:24-27; 21:10. a. Enoch is the recipient of divine secrets and the guardian of these secrets who passes them on to future generations. He is supposed to have received them in a vision. They include the correct reckoning of time [4] and apocalyptic knowledge of all "that has been and will be ... until the day of judgment" (4:19). They were written down and preserved by him in books. b. He is the lofty ecstatic who dwells in the land of Eden. c. He is a divinely appointed author and witness for and against men and against the fallen angels. d. In the traditions on which Jubilees depends he is also the heavenly high-priest who offers burnt offerings [5] in the sanctuary. [6] In the sources known to us this tradition is only expressed later in post-Christian Jewish mysticism. It also penetrated into later Rabbinic writings (Midr. Nu. 12:15; cf. 2 Leg. Mart., [7] Shi'ur Koma, [8] etc.). e. Enoch's exaltation is linked with his outstanding righteousness (10:17). In this respect he is mentioned along with Adam, Seth, Enos, Noah, etc., as in Sir. Alongside the other

---

'Ε ν ώ χ. [1] Cf. H. Gunkel, Gn. (1917), *ad loc.*

[2] LXX Gn. 5:24: καὶ εὐηρέστησεν 'Ενὼχ τῷ θεῷ καὶ οὐχ εὑρίσκετο, ὅτι μετέθηκεν αὐτὸν ὁ θεός. Sir. 44:16: 'Ενὼχ εὐηρέστησε κυρίῳ θεῷ, καὶ μετετέθη ὑπόδειγμα μετανοίας (or μεγανοίας) ταῖς γενεαῖς. Sir. 49:14 (16): οὐδεὶς ἐκτίσθη τοιοῦτος ἐπὶ τῆς γῆς, οἷος 'Ενὼχ, καὶ γὰρ ἀνελήφθη ἀπὸ τῆς γῆς.

[3] Wis. 4:11 is not disposed to emphasise too strongly Enoch's elevation. His rapture took place merely in order that "wickedness should not alter his disposition or subtlety corrupt his soul." Acc. to Philo Abr., 17 his rapture was away from a former evil life. Similarly, ha had been a wicked man in Rabbinic tradition (Midr. Gn., *ad loc.*).

[4] In acc. with the special concern of Jub., and deriving from the astronomical tradition from which it borrows.

[5] Only once in Jub.

[6] Originally the heavenly sanctuary.

[7] The text may be found in A. Jellinek, *Bet ha Midrasch,* VI (1877), 22.

[8] For the text cf. *Sefer Raziel* (ed. Warschau, 1913, fol. 31a/b). Cf. Heb. En., 15 B.

functions of Enoch, this quality seems to be a Jewish addition taken up into the idea of the bearer of the spiritual divine potency of the first man present in every age.

The Enoch traditions found in Jubilees almost all recur in Eth. En. Nevertheless, we cannot say with certainty that Jub. takes them exclusively from this work. The only certain point is that it rests on the same traditional material and that it incorporates part of the Eth. En. as we now know it. One characteristic of the Eth. En. is its hesitation to lay too much stress on Enoch's elevation. The author or redactor of this work attributes his possession of secrets mainly to visions. He could not entirely suppress the idea of elevation, but he gave it only a minor place. Thus in Eth. En. 71 Enoch's final ascension is linked with his nomination as the son of man. But this exaltation is depicted with striking restraint. Nor does the chapter fit in with the true teaching of the present Eth. En. In this the heavenly figure of the son of man or the first man is not Enoch ; it is equated with the Messiah. Enoch is only the visionary who is granted to see this son of man (48). Hence one might see in Eth. En. an attempt on the part of orthodox Judaism to correct and to Judaize the Enoch traditions. This might explain why Eth. En. could for a period be reckoned among the sacred writings.

The content of the secrets revealed to Enoch in a vision includes a. angelology, and esp. the fall of the angels (the "watchers") and their divine punishment ; b. the different spheres and localities of heaven and the underworld ; c. astronomy ; d. the last time, with suitable exhortations. These different themes are obviously common to the circles which put Enoch at the centre of their speculations on the first man and the son of man. They were usually represented by such circles as the "knowledge of Enoch" or the "secrets of Enoch." Hence the title "Book of Enoch," which was little more than a catchword, as already mentioned.

In accordance with their Jewish origin, these Enoch traditions must have circulated in Jewish circles which, although suspected and opposed by orthodox Judaism at the time of our sources, were not without considerable influence. We may be certain that the underlying mythical conceptions did not really originate in Judaism. We cannot track down the ideas and traditions to their ultimate sources since we have no materials to work with. The most that we can say is that in the sources available, as already noted at various points, we may see traces of the original conceptions, or of conceptions closer to the original material.

The penetration of these traditions, cultivated and propagated in heterodox circles, into normative and orthodox Judaism, is not finally restricted to the correction undertaken by the compiler of Eth. En. As already noted, Jub. makes the exaltation a main part of the tradition. It is true that Test. XII, 4 Esr., S. Bar. and Ass. Mos. are wholly dependent on Eth. En. But the case is different with Slav. En. The author of this work knows Eth. En., but he also finds a place for independent traditions. For him the secrets are not primarily revelations through visions during the earthly life of Enoch ; the revelations imparted to and communicated by him are incorporated into the story of his rapture and final exaltation. The exaltation is his institution as the second highest archangel, as a heavenly figure alongside the throne of God (Slav. En. 22:4-10). The exalted Enoch is an angel of the divine presence or countenance (cf. Heb. En. 10:3 f.; 48c). The destiny of Enoch acc. to Slav. En. reminds us mainly of the ascension of Christ as depicted, e.g., by Paul in Phil. 2. Slav. En. also attests the existence of a whole range of Enoch literature. [9]

The fixing of the Canon meant that all heterodox Enoch traditions, and the books containing them which had previously been regarded as sacred, were excluded from the sphere of orthodox Judaism. But this exclusion did not take place all at once or completely. In the 2nd century individual Rabbis, some quite prominent, engaged in speculations connected with the Enoch tradition. [10] And in Heb. En. we meet a redactor who,

---

[9] Slav. En. 23:6; 33:8 f.; 47:2; 48:6; 54; 68:2.
[10] Heb. En., ed. H. Odeberg (1928), Introduction, 39, 84 ff.

trained in Rabbinic schools, attempts to integrate quite radical Enoch speculations into Rabbinic thought, and to secure their acceptance. [11]

B. Enoch Traditions in Early Christianity.

Since works like Eth. En., Jub. etc. were among the sacred writings in the early days of Christianity, it need hardly surprise us that there are occasional references to them in the NT. The NT contains no independent Enoch traditions, although it is probable that among the sacred writings accepted in early Christianity there were some "Books of Enoch" not known to us (→ 558).

Enoch is mentioned three times in the NT, at Lk. 3:37; Hb. 11:5 and Jd. 14. Lk. 3:37 is based on Gn. 5:21 ff. Heb. 11:5 repeats ideas often found in Eth. En. as well as in Jub. 10:17. [12] Jd. 14 is a literal quotation from Eth. En. 60:8. It is also possible that there are many allusions to Eth. En. in the NT, or that reminiscences of it have affected the modes of expression of NT authors. It is fairly certain that Eth. En. is quoted more than once in Jd. 4-15 (Jd. 4 : Eth. En. 48:10; Jd. 6 : 12:4; 10:4-6, 11 f.; Jd. 14 : 60:8; Jd. 14 f.: 1:9). Charles has pointed to a great number of passages which he regards as dependent on Eth. En. Close examination shows, however, that there are no exact quotations apart from those mentioned. [13] It is incontestable that Rev. makes use of the same expressions and develops the same ideas as those found in Eth. En. and similar works. How far it is directly influenced by them, however, cannot be stated with certainty. From what we know of the formation of Jewish tradition, the fact that we find similar expressions or formulae in two different books does not prove that one is quoting the other. As concerns the Epistles of Paul, apocryphal and apocalyptic works are quoted as sacred writings, and we may thus conclude that there are occasional allusions to the Books of Enoch, or that they have had some influence. In relation to angelology and cosmology there is probably a similarity between the ideas of Eth. En. and those of Col. and Eph. The author of Jn. knows the beliefs not only of orthodox Judaism but also of Jewish apocalyptic and mystical circles. He consciously opposes both. But he seems to detect traces of truth in the latter rather than the former. He is most severe in his rejection of Rabbinism. Jn. 3:13 is primarily directed against such ideas as that of the ascension of Enoch and his exaltation as son of man, i.e., against Enoch traditions as they are assimilated into orthodox Judaism, e.g., in Eth. En. According to Jn. only the pre-existent can be the exalted. It is not impossible that this was the original conception in the heterodox Jewish circles to which we have referred. We can gather this with some degree of probability from traces present in Heb. En. [14] 2 Pt., which is admittedly dependent on Jd., seems not to accept the traditions used by Jd. This does not mean, however, that at the time of 2 Pt. there had been a general movement

---

[11] Ibid., 39.

[12] Jub. 10:17 (Kautzsch): "... he (Noah), who in his life on earth excelled in righteousness, in which he was perfect, all the children of earth apart from Enoch. For Enoch was raised up to be a witness to the generations of the world."

[13] 1 Enoch, ed. Charles (1912), Introd. § 19. "Verbal echoes" of Eth. En. are found (e.g., J. Moffatt, Introd. to the Lit. of the NT³ [1927], 25) in Hb. 4:13 (Eth. En. 9:5; cf. 11:5); Mt. 19:28 (Eth. En. 62:5); 26:24 (Eth. En. 38:2); Lk. 16:9 (Eth. En. 63:10); Jn. 5:22 (Eth. En. 69:27); 1 Th. 5:3 (Eth. En. 62:4); 1 Pt. 3:19 f. (Eth. En. 10:4 f., 12 f.); Rev. passim.

[14] Heb. En., Introd., 83.

against Eth. En. and similar writings in the Church. For confident use is made of Eth. En. in Christian writings later than 2 Pt. [15]

We meet the Enoch traditions in extra-canonical early Christian literature. 1 Cl., 9, 2 f.: Enoch, a righteous man taken up because of his righteousness, is among the righteous patriarchs. In Asc. Is. 9:6 ff. there is an interesting correction of the Enoch traditions. Enoch is taken up and exalted, but only virtually. The actuality will not take place until Christ shall have come (a prophetic fut.). This means that there is no exaltation independent of Christ, as also assumed in Jn. 3:13. But Enoch (like those "who are with him") is destined to bear a crown of righteousness and to sit on a throne (cf. Heb. En. 10:1; 12:3). Cf. also 5 Esr. 1:39. Justin Mart. is perhaps dependent on Eth. En. in Apol., 2, 5. In Barn., 16, 5 there is a quotation from Eth. En. 89:56 ff. The reference in Barn., 4, 3 is to a Book of Enoch unknown to us. [16]

Odeberg

ἐξαγγέλλω → I, 69   ἐξαγοράζω → I, 126 ff.
ἐξαιτέω → I, 194   ἐξακολουθέω → I, 215
ἐξαποστέλλω → I, 406   ἐξαπατάω → I, 384 f.
ἐξανάστασις, ἐξανίστημι → I, 368 ff. ἐξαρτίζω → I, 475 f.
ἐξεγείρω → 338   ἐξέρχομαι → ἔρχομαι.

+-------------------------------------+
| ἔξεστιν, ἐξουσία, |
| ἐξουσιάζω, κατεξουσιάζω |
+-------------------------------------+

† ἔξεστιν.

ἔξεστιν, "it is free" (with the dat.), denotes a. that an action is possible in the sense that there are no hindrances or that the opportunity for it occurs, i.e., "to have the possibility," "to be able." Xenoph. An., VII, 1, 21: νῦν σοι ἔξεστιν, ὦ Ξενοφῶν, ἀνδρὶ γενέσθαι. Epict. Diss., III, 24, 6: ravens and crows, οἷς ἔξεστιν ἵπτασθαι ὅπου θέλουσιν, not that they have the power, but that they have unlimited opportunity (i.e., not δύνανται). Similarly, Epict. often uses ἔξεστιν to denote something which we cannot prevent another from doing because it is in his "power" to do it: Diss., I, 1, 21: τί ἐμὸν καὶ τί οὐκ ἐμὸν καὶ τί μοι ἔξεστιν καὶ τί μοι οὐκ ἔξεστιν; It occurs in this sense in LXX only at 4 Macc. 1:12: περὶ τούτου νῦν αὐτίκα δὴ λέγειν ἐξέσται, and not at all in the NT, though cf. Mart. Pol., 12, 2: ὁ δὲ ἔφη, μὴ εἶναι ἐξὸν αὐτῷ (sc. "to throw Polycarp to the lions"), ἐπειδὴ πεπληρώκει τὰ κυνηγέσια.

b. It also means that an action is not prevented by a higher norm or court, that "it may be done or is not forbidden." Epict. Diss., I, 26, 8: ταῦτα ἐκείνῳ μόνῳ λέγειν ἔξεστι τῷ τοιαύτην ἐπιβολὴν ἐνηνοχότι ("has the moral right"). So Ac. 2:29: ἐξὸν εἰπεῖν μετὰ παρρησίας. In law esp. it denotes something which the law requires or forbids, Plat. Crito, 51d: Laws προαγορεύομεν τῷ ἐξουσίαν πεποιηκέναι Ἀθηναίων τῷ βουλομένῳ ... ἐξεῖναι λαβόντα τὰ αὐτοῦ ἀπιέναι. Thus often in the pap. it means to have "the right, authority, or permission to do or not to do something." Occasionally it is used also of religious and cultic commandments, Hdt., I, 183: ἐπὶ γὰρ τοῦ χρυσέου βωμοῦ οὐκ ἔξεστι θύειν, ὅτι μὴ γαλαθηνὰ μοῦνα. Also in the magic pap.: Preis. Zaub., IV, 2255 f.: τὸ δεῖ γενέσθαι, τοῦτ' οὐκ ἔξεστι φυγεῖν. But in this sense it is relatively rare (→ infra). In the LXX 2 Ἔσδρ. 4:14 (= לָא אֲרִיךְ, "not seem-

---

[15] E.g., Iren., Tert. (cf. 1 En., ed. Charles, Introd. § 18).
[16] τὸ τέλειον σκάνδαλον ἤγγικεν, περὶ οὗ γέγραπται, ὡς Ἐνώχ λέγει. The passage to which allusion is made is not found in any Enoch lit. known to us.
ἔ ξ ε σ τ ι ν. Schl. Mt. on 9:6; 22:16; Theol. d. Judt., 133.

ly"); Est. 4:2; 1 Macc. 14:44; in the NT Jn. 18:31; Ac. 22:25; 2 C. 12:4; [1] also Ac. 16:21; [2] non-juridically Mt. 20:15; Ac. 21:37. It is used esp. to denote the prohibitions of the Jewish Law in the later LXX writings : 3 Macc. 1:11 (add ἐξεῖναι); 4 Macc. 5:18; 17:17; and in the NT in all other passages : Mk. 2:24 and par., 26 and par.; 10:2 and par.; 12:14 and par.; Mt. 12:10, 12; 27:6; [3] Lk. 14:3; Jn. 5:10; 1 C. 6:12; 10:23 (on both the last passages → ἐξουσία C. 5).

c. In Epict. it often means that there are no psychic or ethical obstacles to an action : "to have the (inner) power to do it" : Diss., II, 16, 37: ᾧ γὰρ ἔξεστιν ἐξελθεῖν, ὅταν θέλῃ, τοῦ συμποσίου. It is not used in the NT or the LXX in this sense, though cf. Philo Omn. Prob. Lib., 59.

In the NT ἔξεστιν relates most commonly to the Law and will of God. For the Greek what does not correspond, or corresponds, to the will of the gods is usually (οὐ) θεμιτόν, θέμις, ὅσιόν ἐστιν, as most MSS have at Tob. 2:13 (as distinct from א : οὐ γὰρ ἐξουσίαν ἔχομεν). Plat. Tim., 30a : θέμις δὲ οὔτ' ἦν οὔτ' ἔστι τῷ ἀρίστῳ δρᾶν ἄλλο πλὴν τὸ κάλλιστον, Ps.-Luc. Syr. Dea, 53 and 55 οὐχ ὅσιον, of ritual ordinances. Even Zeus stands under this themis, Max. Tyr., 38, 7: οὐ γὰρ θέμις Διῒ βούλεσθαι ἄλλο τι ἢ τὸ κάλλιστον. These expressions measure actions by an abstract norm, whereas in the NT (οὐκ) ἔξεστιν presupposes a will which makes concrete demands. The term is used in relation to the Jewish Law and the exposition of the Pharisees, and the use of this legal formula is typical of Jewish legalism. The NT itself does not ask εἰ ἔξεστιν, but admonishes us to test τί ἐστιν εὐάρεστον τῷ κυρίῳ (Eph. 5:10). There is a Gk. formulation at Ac. 10:28 : ἀθέμιτόν ἐστιν ἀνδρὶ Ἰουδαίῳ κολλᾶσθαι ... ἀλλοφύλῳ, cf. 1 Pt. 4:3 : ἀθέμιτοι εἰδωλολατρίαι.

Joseph., too, uses ἔξεστιν of legal definitions : Ant., 8, 404; 13, 252, 373; 15, 203, 419; 20, 268 (προήρημαι δὲ συγγράψαι ... περὶ τῶν νόμων, διὰ τί κατ' αὐτοὺς τὰ μὲν ἔξεστιν ἡμῖν ποιεῖν, τὰ δὲ κεκώλυται); Bell., 6, 426. On the other hand, in Philo we have the Gk. θέμις and θεσμός, superior to the Law in dignity : Omn. Prob. Lib., 3 : ὅσοι δὲ φιλοσοφίαν γνησίως ἠσπάσαντο, καταπειθεῖς γενόμενοι τῷ προστάγματι νόμον αὐτὸ μᾶλλον δὲ θεσμὸν ἰσούμενον χρησμῷ ὑπετόπησαν, cf. also, e.g., Op. Mund., 17 (οὐ θεμιτόν) and 144 (θέμις).

The use of ἔξεστιν for what is commanded or forbidden by the Law corresponds to the Rabb. רְשׁוּת :"I, the Lord, have ordained it, and thou hast no leave (וְאֵין לְךָ רְשׁוּת) to question," bJoma, 67b. Certain injunctions are expressed in the Mishnah by the imperf. and prohibitions by לֹא, Shab., 1, 2 : "One should not (לֹא יֵשֵׁב) sit before the barber near the time of the evening sacrifice until one has prayed"; but elsewhere רְשׁוּת is common. There is a linguistic parallel in Joseph. Ant., 18, 90 : καθότι καὶ πρότερον ἦν αὐτοῖς ἐξουσία (subst. with ἐστίν instead of ἐξουσίαν ἔχειν or ἔξεστιν [= לְ רְשׁוּת] as elsewhere).

---

[1] Most expositors take οὐκ ἐξόν to mean "forbidden" in sense b., though they are undecided whether to relate ἀνθρώπῳ to ἐξόν or to λαλῆσαι (for the former, Bchm. K., ad loc.; for the latter Wnd. 2 K., ad loc. and Reitzenstein Hell. Myst., 369). They also refer the ἄρρητα ῥήματα to the mysteries, for which there are no exact parallels. As against this, I prefer to give to ἐξόν sense a. "which it is not possible for a man to utter." We are to think of the praise of angels which in its supraterrestrial glory surpasses every possibility of human expression. This denotes the glory of the Paradise into which Paul was caught up. This view is confirmed by the fact that the statement ἃ οὐκ ἐξὸν ἀνθρώπῳ λαλῆσαι finds literal parallels in many relatively old Rabb. expressions in which it is said with reference to the wonderful way in which God speaks : מַה שֶּׁאֵי אֶפְשָׁר לְאָדָם לֶאֱמֹר כֵּן "what is not possible for man thus to speak," M. Ex., 20, 8; cf. S. Nu., 42 on 6:26; K. G. Kuhn, Sifre zu Nu. (1933), 138, n. 71 (Kuhn).

[2] Cf. Wdt. Ag., ad loc.

[3] Acc. to Kl. Mt., ad loc. the high-priests are thinking of the prohibition in Dt. 23:18.

ἐξουσία.

A. Ordinary Greek Usage.

1. From about the time of Eur., [1] ἐξουσία, derived from ἔξεστιν, denotes "ability to perform an action" to the extent that there are no hindrances in the way, as distinct from δύναμις in the sense of intrinsic ability [2] (cf. ἔξεστιν a.). There seems to be early attestation for it in this sense : Antiphon Orator (ed. Thalheim), 1, 6 : ἐν οἷς μὲν γὰρ αὐτῷ ἐξουσία ἦν σαφῶς εἰδέναι ... οὐκ ἠθέλησεν· ἐν οἷς δ' οὐκ ἦν πυθέσθαι ...; it does not occur, however, in the LXX or NT.

2. ἐξουσία is also the possibility granted by a higher norm or court, and therefore "the right to do something or the right over something," with the inf. and gen., [3] also abs., the right being, acc. to context, "authority," "permission," "freedom" (= ἔξεστιν b.). It is used esp. a. of the possibility of action given authoritatively by the king, government or laws of a state and conferring authority, permission or freedom on corporations or in many instances, esp. in legal matters, on individuals. Translations express different sides of the one term which in itself denotes only the possibility of action. [4] It is then used b. of any right (permission, freedom etc.) in the various relationships similar to and guaranteed by national institutions, e.g., the rights of parents in relation to children, [5] of masters in relation to slaves, [6] of owners in relation to property, [7] and of individuals in respect of personal liberty. [8]

ἐ ξ ο υ σ ί α. On A. and B.: R. Hirzel, *Themis, Dike und Verwandtes* (1907), 129, 1. Bau. J. on 1:12. On C.: Comment. and Theol., esp. Schl. Mt. on 21:23; 28:18; Hck. Mk. on 1:22; Ltzm. 1 K. on 6:12; Joh. W. 1 K. on 6:12; W. Grundmann, *Der Begriff d. Kraft in d. nt.lichen Gedankenwelt* (1932); J. Starr in *The Harvard Theol. Review*, 23 (1930), 302-305; H. Windisch in *Studies in Early Christianity, presented to F. C. Porter and B. W. Bacon*, ed. S. J. Case (1928), 225-227; Reitzenstein Hell. Myst., 363-365; Poim., 48, n. 3; Ir. Erl., 131, n. 3; E. Norden, *Agnostos Theos* (1913), 111, n. 1. On C. 6 : Loh. Kol. on 1:16; 2:15; O. Everling, *Die paul. Angelologie u. Dämonologie* (1888); M. Dibelius, *Die Geisterwelt im Glauben des Pls.* (1909); G. Kurze, *Der Engels- u. Teufelsglaube d. Ap. Pls.* (1915); W. Grundmann, *supra* ; H. Schlier, "Mächte u. Gewalten im NT," ThBl, 9 (1930), 289-297; F. Prat in *Recherches de Science Religieuse*, 3 (1912), 201-229; E. de Los Rios in *Verbum Domini*, 9 (1929), 289-297. On C. 7: Comm.; Everling, Dibelius, Kurze, *op. cit.*; P. Ewald, NkZ, 11 (1910), 507-513; R. Perdelwitz, ThStKr, 86 (1913), 611-613; G. Kittel, *Rabbinica* (1920), 17-31; A. Jirku in NkZ, 32 (1921), 710 f.; P. Tischleder, *Wesen u. Stellung d. Frau* (1923), 156-163; K. Bornhäuser in NkZ, 41 (1930), 475-488; J. Mezzacasa in *Verbum Domini*, 11 (1931), 39-42; W. Foerster in ZNW, 30 (1931), 185 f.; G. Delling, *Pls.' Stellung z. Frau u. Ehe* (1931), 96-105; K. Rösch, *Theologie u. Glaube*, 24 (1932), 361-363; M. Ginsburger in *Revue de Religion et de Philosophie Religieuse*, 12 (1932), 248; Reitzenstein Poim., 230 n.

[1] U. v. Wilamowitz-Moellendorff, Euripides Herakles, II (1889), on v. 337.

[2] Grundmann, 3 f.

[3] Sometimes, although it is not genuinely class., with prep. With κατά → n. 6; with ἐπί, Epict. Diss., I, 9, 15 : οἱ καλούμενοι τύραννοι δοκοῦντες ἔχειν τινὰ ἐφ' ἡμῖν ἐξουσίαν.

[4] Ps.-Plat. Def., 415b : ἐξουσία ἐπιτροπὴ νόμου; Plat. Symp., 182e : ἐξουσίαν ὁ νόμος δέδωκε τῷ ἐραστῇ ... (the possibility). P. Oxy., II, 237, col. VI, 17 (186 A.D.): τοῦ νόμου διδόντος μοι ἐξουσίαν (right). P. Amh., 92, 23 ff. (162/3 A.D.): ἐξουσίας σοι οὔσης ἑτέροις μεταμισθοῦν, ὁπότε ἐὰν αἱρῇ, ἐὰν φαίνηται μισθῶσαι (authority, freedom, right).

[5] P. Oxy., II, 237, col. VIII, p. 162, 3 f.: Διονυσία ὑπὸ τοῦ πατρὸς ἐκδοθεῖσα πρὸς γάμον ἐν τῇ τοῦ πατρὸς ἐξουσίᾳ οὐκέτι γείνεται.

[6] P. Oxy., VIII, 1120, 17 f. of one who illegally takes a female slave : μὴ ἔχων κατ' αὐτῆς ἐξουσίαν (3rd cent. A.D.).

[7] Ditt. Syll.³, 1234, 4 : δίδωμι τὴν τοῦ ... μνημείου ἐξουσίαν.

[8] Ps.-Plat. Def., 412d : ἐλευθερία ἡγεμονία βίου· αὐτοκράτεια ἐπὶ παντί· ἐξουσία τοῦ καθ' ἑαυτὸν ἐν βίῳ· ἀφειδία ἐν χρήσει καὶ ἐν κτήσει οὐσίας. Democr. Fr., 245 (II, 109, 16 Diels): οὐκ ἂν ἐκώλυον οἱ νόμοι ζῆν ἕκαστον κατ' ἰδίην ἐξουσίην (self-determination).

3. The authority mentioned under 2. is illusory unless backed by real power. Behind legal authority stands the power of the state to give it validity, and the rights mentioned under 2. b. are supported by the law and by the power of the state. Thus it is not always possible to separate between authority and power, between ἐξουσία and δύναμις. Occasionally ἐξουσία as authority is set in antithesis to real power or force. Perhaps the basic sense of "possibility of action" is too strongly present here, though cf. P. Oxy., VIII, 1120, 17 f.: μὴ ἔχων κατ' αὐτῆς ἐξουσίαν (3rd cent. A.D.). The ἐξουσία of the king, government or deity is power. [9] Nevertheless, the distinction remains. δύναμις, κράτος etc. denote external power, whereas ἐξουσία is the power displayed in the fact that a command is obeyed, i.e., the power to pronounce it. In this respect, we may refer to the usage of Epict. in his contrast between external things over which others have control (ἐξουσίαν ἔχειν and the inner disposition which we ourselves control : Ench., 14, 2 : κύριος ἑκάστου ἐστὶν ὁ τῶν ὑπ' ἐκείνου θελομένων ἢ μὴ θελομένων ἔχων τὴν ἐξουσίαν εἰς τὸ περιποιῆσαι ἢ ἀφελέσθαι. [10] In relation to the Stoic himself it can also denote moral power (→ 561), Diss., III, 22, 94 : τοῖς βασιλεῦσι ... τὰ ὅπλα παρεῖχε τὸ ἐπιτιμᾶν τισιν ... τῷ κυνικῷ τὸ συνειδὸς τὴν ἐξουσίαν ταύτην παραδίδωσιν, and Diog. L., VII, 121: Only the wise man is free εἶναι γὰρ τὴν ἐλευθερίαν ἐξουσίαν αὐτοπραγίας (Zeno). Only occasionally does ἐξουσία approximate more closely to δύναμις and denote, e.g., the power of a passion. [11]

4. The term ἐξουσία can also be used in antithesis to law in the sense of self-asserted freedom (ἐξουσία ποιητική, poetic freedom), [12] or caprice. At this point it is a parallel to → ὕβρις. [13] It is often used in this way in Joseph., Ant., 20, 180 : ὡς ἐν ἀπροστατήτῳ πόλει ταῦτ' ἐπράσσετο μετ' ἐξουσίας; Ant., 10, 103 : ὁ πᾶς ὄχλος ἐπ' ἐξουσίας ὕβριζεν ἃ ἤθελεν. But this does not alter the fact that ἐξουσία is mostly used in the context of legal order. This is shown by its frequent occurrence with → κύριος, e.g., Diog. Oenoandensis Fr., 57 (ed. Williams 1907), where we have the two together in much the same way as in Epict. (→ n. 10), [14] and Ditt. Syll.³, 1234, 4 f.: δίδωμι τὴν τοῦ προδεδηλουμένου μνημείου ἐξουσίαν Ξένωνι ... ὥστε αὐτὸν εἶναι κύριον τῆς εἰς αὐτὸν ἐνταφῆς καὶ ἐχέτω ἐξουσίαν συγχωρεῖν ...

5. Derived meanings are a. "authoritative position," or "office of state," [15] and more concretely b. "office-bearers" or "rulers," [16] often in the plur., and later c. "laudatory address to office-bearers." [17] The government as such never seems to be denoted by this term. We need hardly consider the final senses of d. "crowd" [18] and e. "pomp." [19]

---

[9] Dio Chrys. Or., 1, 46 : of the king who transgresses the command of Zeus: οὐδὲν ἀπώνατο τῆς πολλῆς ἐξουσίας καὶ δυνάμεως. Poll. Onom., VIII, 86 : κοινῇ μὲν ἔχουσιν ἐξουσίαν θανάτου (the archontes). Sextus Pythagoreus Sententiae, 310 : ἀνθρώπῳ σοφῷ θεὸς θεοῦ δίδωσιν ἐξουσίαν (not κράτος or δύναμις).
[10] The combination of κύριος and ἐξουσία, which denotes the element of law or right in ἐξουσία, is often found : Epict. Diss., II, 2, 26; IV, 1, 59 f.; 12, 8.
[11] Plut. Dio, 11 (I, 962d): νέας ψυχῆς ἐξουσίᾳ μεγάλῃ καὶ δυνάμει παραφερομένης.
[12] Liddell-Scott, s.v.
[13] Preis. Zaub., IV, 1192 f.: διαφύλαξόν με τόνδε ἀπὸ πάσης ὑπεροχῆς ἐξουσίας καὶ πάσης ὕβρεως.
[14] τὸ κεφάλαιον τῆς εὐδαιμονίας ἡ διάθεσις, ἧς ἡμεῖς κύριοι ... τί οὖν μεταδιώκομεν πρᾶγμα τοιοῦτον, οὗ τὴν ἐξουσίαν ἔχουσιν ἄλλοι;
[15] Aristot. Eth. Nic., I, 3, p. 1095b, 21: πολλοὺς τῶν ἐν ταῖς ἐξουσίαις. Dion. Hal. Ant. Rom., VIII, 77, 1: τὴν ταμιευτικὴν ἔχοντες ἐξουσίαν (quaestoria potestas).
[16] Ps.-Plat. Alc., I, 135 a/b : οὐκοῦν ... ἐν πόλει τε καὶ πάσαις ἀρχαῖς καὶ ἐξουσίαις ἀπολειπομέναις ἀρετῆς ἕπεται τὸ κακῶς πράττειν; P. Oxy., II, 261, 15 : ἐπί τε πάσης (!) ἐξουσίας καὶ παντὸς κριτηρίου (55 A.D.).
[17] P. Flor., 86, 19 f.: προῆλθον ἐπὶ τῆς σῆς ἐξουσίας (1st cent. A.D.), shows the transition ; for later cf. P. Oxy., IX, 1103, 3 (360 A.D.).
[18] P. Tebt., 409, 8 f. (5th cent. A.D.): ἐξουσίαν αὐτῶν ἔχει ("plenty of them").
[19] For an example, v. Liddell-Scott.

B. The Jewish and NT Usage.

1. The usage of Joseph. is par. to the Gk. With the gen. or inf. it means "permission" (Ant., 20, 193 : παρεκάλεσαν ἐξουσίαν αὐτοῖς δοῦναι πρεσβεῦσαι περὶ τούτου πρὸς Νέρωνα), "authority" (Vit., 72 : καὶ τὴν ἐξουσίαν τῶν ἐκεῖ πραγμάτων αὐτὸς παρὰ τοῦ κοινοῦ τῶν Ἱεροσολυμιτῶν πεπιστεῦσθαι), "right" given or protected by the law (Ant., 4, 247: ἡ κόρη ... συνοικείτω τῷ κατηγορήσαντι μηδεμίαν ἐξουσίαν ἔχοντος ἐκείνου ἀποπέμπεσθαι αὐτήν) and actual "power of disposal" (Vit., 348 : τοῦ ... ἱεροῦ κινδυνεύοντος ἐν τῇ τῶν πολεμίων ἐξουσίᾳ γενέσθαι). ἐξουσία is also used of God's power (Ant., 5, 109 : ἀποδρᾶναι τὴν ἐξουσίαν αὐτοῦ καὶ τὴν ἀπὸ ταύτης δίκην ἀδύνατον), as also of the power of the king (Vit., 112 : δύο μεγιστᾶνες τῶν ὑπὸ τὴν ἐξουσίαν τοῦ βασιλέως), and it is once used of the real power of the king in distinction from his outward position (Ant., 14, 302 : πρόσχημα μὲν εἶναι λέγοντες τῆς βασιλείας Ὑρκανόν, τούτους δὲ τὴν πᾶσαν ἔχειν ἐξουσίαν). It is once used for the possibility of influence (Vit., 80 : ἐξουσίας ὄντα μεγάλης). The authorities are called ἐξουσίαι (plur.) in Bell., 2, 350, and the sing. seems to be used once for the government as such (→ 566).

Philo, too, follows ordinary Gk. usage.[20] He uses the word particularly for absolute power, whether of the king (αὐτοκρατὴς ἐξουσία, Leg. Gaj., 26; 54; 190), of the governor (Op. Mund., 17), of the people (δεσποτικὴ ἐξουσία, Jos., 67), or of God, to whose absolute ἐξουσία he often refers. It is important that Philo links God's absolute power with His creative activity : Cher., 27: ἔλεγε δέ μοι κατὰ τὸν ἕνα ὄντως ὄντα θεὸν δύο τὰς ἀνωτάτω εἶναι καὶ πρώτας δυνάμεις ἀγαθότητα καὶ ἐξουσίαν, καὶ ἀγαθότητι μὲν τὸ πᾶν γεγεννηκέναι, ἐξουσίᾳ δὲ τοῦ γεννηθέντος ἄρχειν. Contrasted with His loving-kindness, this power is that of punishment : Leg. All., I, 95: ἡ δὲ παραίνεσις γίνεται δι' ἀμφοτέρων τῶν κλήσεων ... καὶ τοῦ θεοῦ ... ἵνα, εἰ μὲν πείθοιτο ταῖς παραινέσεσιν, ὑπὸ τοῦ θεοῦ εὐεργεσιῶν ἀξιωθείη, εἰ δὲ ἀφηνιάζοι, ὑπὸ τοῦ κυρίου ὡς δεσπότου καὶ ἐξουσίαν ἔχοντος σκορακίζοιτο. The soul should contemplate both the lovingkindness and the power : Sacr. A.C., 60 : ἵνα ... δέξηται (sc. ἡ ψυχή) χαρακτῆρας ἐξουσίας τε καὶ εὐεργεσίας αὐτοῦ.

2. In the LXX ἐξουσία first means right, authority, permission or freedom in the legal or political sense, and it is then used for the right or permission given by God (Tob. 7:10 א: The angel says : καὶ ἐγὼ οὐκ ἔχω ἐξουσίαν δοῦναι αὐτὴν ἑτέρῳ ἀνδρὶ πλὴν σοῦ), or for the permission granted or withheld by the Jewish Law (Tob. 2:13 א : οὐ γὰρ ἐξουσίαν ἔχομεν ἡμεῖς φαγεῖν οὐδὲν κλεψιμαῖον). In later writings, esp. Da. and Macc., it then denotes the power of the king or of God, the power which decides in other authoritarian relationships of everyday life, or the authorities : 1 Macc. 10:38 : τοὺς τρεῖς νομοὺς ... προστεθήτω τῇ Ἰουδαίᾳ ... τοῦ μὴ ὑπακοῦσαι ἄλλης ἐξουσίας (א V : dat.) ἀλλ' ἢ τοῦ ἀρχιερέως.

Where there is a Heb. original it is מֶמְשָׁלָה (also rendered ἀρχή, δυναστεία, στρατιά, οἰκονομία) or a derivative of the stem שׁלט (esp. in Da., though also in Sir. 9:13; Qoh. 8:8), for which again there are other translations. In 4 Βασ. 20:13; Is. 39:2 Qmg; ψ 113:2; Sir. 24:11; 1 Macc. 6:11 it borrows from the Heb. מֶמְשָׁלָה the sense of "kingdom" or "sphere of power." This usage recurs in the NT (→ 565), Act. Thom., 10 (Χριστὲ ... ἡ φωνὴ ἡ ἀκουσθεῖσα τοῖς ἄρχουσιν, ἡ σαλεύσασα τὰς ἐξουσίας αὐτῶν ἁπάσας), and Gnostic prayers (Orig. Cels., VI, 31), but it is limited to the Semitic world and is probably influenced by the range of meaning of the Rabb. equivalent (→ 566).

---

[20] Ἐξουσία is used for rights over slaves, Spec. Leg., III, 137; legal authority, permission, Spec. Leg., II, 24 : Moses αὐτοῖς ἀνέθηκε τὴν ἐξουσίαν τοῦ τὰ ὁμοσθέντα φυλάττειν ἢ τοὐναντίον; right, Spec. Leg., III, 70 : the seducer of a maiden μήτε ἀναδύεσθαι τὴν ἐξουσίαν ἐχέτω μήτε παραιτεῖσθαι; office, Leg. Gaj., 71: πατέρες ἰδιῶται γενομένων ἐν ἀρχαῖς μεγάλαις καὶ ἐξουσίαις υἱῶν ὑποστέλλουσιν.

By using ἐξουσία for the Aram. שְׁלֵט when the reference is to God's power, the LXX introduced a term which was adapted far better than such expressions of physical power as ἰσχύς, κράτος, δύναμις, to express the unrestricted sovereignty of God as the One who has the say, whose Word is power : Da. 4:14 : ἕως ἂν γνῷ τὸν κύριον τοῦ οὐρανοῦ ἐξουσίαν ἔχειν πάντων τῶν ἐν τῷ οὐρανῷ καὶ τῶν ἐπὶ τῆς γῆς, καὶ ὅσα ἂν θέλῃ ποιεῖν ποιεῖ ἐν αὐτοῖς, cf. Δα. 3:100; 4:28, 37c; 5:4; Sir. 10:4. That ἐξουσία comes rather late in the LXX in this sense (or any other) is linked with the fact that older writings use the figurative expression "to be in the hands of someone" for this concept, and that the LXX translates this literally : 2 Βασ. 24:14; 1 Ch. 29:12; 2 Ch. 20:6; Job 10:7 etc. (→ χείρ).

Special note should be taken of ψ 135:8 f.: τὸν ἥλιον εἰς ἐξουσίαν τῆς ἡμέρας, where ἐξουσία = τὸ ἐξουσιάζειν, and 2 Macc. 3:24 : ὁ τῶν πνευμάτων καὶ πάσης ἐξουσίας δυνάστης ἐπιφανίαν μεγάλην ἐποίησεν, where it is just possible that ἐξουσία means an angelic power. [21]

3. Formally the usage of the NT is closest to that of the LXX. In the NT ἐξουσία denotes the power of God in nature and the spiritual world (→ C. 2), the power which Satan exercises and imparts (→ C. 3), and especially the power or freedom which is given to Jesus, and by Him to His disciples (→ C. 4, 5), and which includes, e.g., the right to support (→ 570). Similarly in political relationships : Lk. 19:17: ἴσθι ἐξουσίαν ἔχων ἐπάνω δέκα πόλεων; Mk. 13:34 : δοὺς τοῖς δούλοις αὐτοῦ τὴν ἐξουσίαν; of the authority of the Sanhedrin : Ac. 9:14; 26:10, 12; of Pilate : Lk. 20:20; Jn. 19:10; and of freedom of self-determination, Ac. 5:4; 1 C. 7:37. Of the power of kings, Rev. 17:12, 13. It is also used, often in the plur., for the authorities, Lk. 12:11; R. 13:1; Tt. 3:1. Here the sing. tends to assume the more general sense of "government," borrowing from the Rabb. רְשׁוּת, R. 13:2 f.; Mt. 8:9 and par. (→ infra). As in the LXX, it can also mean a sphere of dominion, e.g., the state (Lk. 23:7), the domain of spirits (Eph. 2:2; Col. 1:13 → 567). A new use of the term is for spiritual powers, 1 C. 15:24; Eph. 1:21; 3:10; 6:12; Col. 1:16; 2:10, 15; 1 Pt. 3:22 (→ C. 6).

4. It undoubtedly contributed to the range of meaning of the term in the NT that there existed in רְשׁוּת a Rabb. par. which exerted an unmistakeable influence on the Gk. word. At all essential points רְשׁוּת is co-extensive with ἐξουσία, but it goes beyond it in the very matters in which the NT does so. As a legal term, it has the general sense [22] of power of disposal, but in detail it means the right of possession to something, [23] or the authority or commission, [24] the right, [25] or the freedom, to do something. [26] In the sing. it then denotes government as such (not an individual government), [27] and in this

---

[21] → also n. 63.

[22] Cf. Kassovsky, s.v.

[23] המעות שאינן ברשותו MS, 1, 2. → n. 25.

[24] Qid., 4, 9 : מי שנתן רשות לשלוחו.

[25] יורשיה והבאים ברשותה: heirs and descendants at law (the wife), Ket., 9, 5. A divorced woman : יצאת לרשות עצמה, Ned., 10, 3; the married תכנס לרשותו (with reference to the husband), Ned., 10, 4.

[26] Ab., 3, 15 : הרשות נתונה. Cf. the Rabb. distinction between what is commanded and what is voluntary, e.g., Shebu., 3, 6 : שבועת שבועת מצוה שבועת הרשות, Cf. Schl. Mt. on 9:6.

[27] In this sense also vocalised רָשׁוּת, Dalman Wört.², s.v.

sense it is used for the absolute monarchical power of God.[28] In this respect its influence is reflected in the NT in the use of ἐξουσία for government, for which there are no par. in ordinary Gk., though it is worth noting that there is an instance in Joseph. Ant., 15, 295 : ἀεί τι πρὸς ἀσφάλειαν ἐπεξευρίσκων (sc. Herod) καὶ διαλαμβάνων φυλακαῖς τὸ πᾶν ἔθνος, ὡς ἥκιστα μὲν ἀπ᾽ ἐξουσίας εἰς ταραχὰς προπίπτειν. רְשׁוּת also means the sphere over which one disposes, and then simply sphere or kingdom.[29] If almost all the NT passages where ἐξουσία occurs can be construed with the help of רְשׁוּת, derivatives from the stems מָשַׁל and שָׁלַט may also be taken into consideration.

5. As regards construction, the gen. is classical. It is still the ordinary use in NT times. Thus Epict. has ἐπί with the dat. only once, and the gen. 19 times. The LXX has the gen. 14 times, and prepos. 5 (Tob. 1:21 א; Sir. 30:28, ἐπί with the acc.; Da. 3:97, with the gen.; 3 Macc. 7:21, ἐν; 4 Macc. 4:5, περί). Joseph. seems to use only the gen., Philo the gen. once and once also κατά with the gen. In the NT Paul has the gen. (1 C. 9:12; R. 9:21). There is a different point in the use of ἐν in 1 C. 9:18. In 1 C. 7:37 we have περί. Mk. (6:7) and Mt. (10:1) use only the gen. Lk. 10:19 has the gen. and ἐπί, 9:1 ἐπί with the acc. and 19:17 ἐπάνω. Jn. has the gen. at 17:2, and κατά with the gen. at 19:11. Rev. does not use the gen.; it has ἐπί with the gen. at 2:26; 11:6; 14:18; 20:6, and ἐπί with the acc. at 6:8; 13:7; 16:9; 22:14, this being a Semitism. On the whole question, cf. Radermacher[2], 129 ff.

C. The NT Concept ἐξουσία.

The specific role played by ἐξουσία in the NT world of thought rests on three foundations. First, unlike expressions for indwelling, objective, physical or spiritual power (→ κράτος, → ἰσχύς, → δύναμις), it denotes the power which decides, so that it is particularly well adapted to express the invisible power of God whose Word is creative power. The ἐξουσία of Jesus and the apostles is of the same character. Secondly, this power of decision is active in a legally ordered whole, especially in the state and in all the authoritarian relationships supported by it. All these relationships are the reflection of the lordship of God in a fallen world where nothing takes place apart from His ἐξουσία or authority. They are based upon this lordship. Thus the word ἐξουσία can refer to the fact that God's will is done in heaven. It can also denote the fact that His will prevails in the sphere of nature as an ordered totality (→ ἔργον). Indeed, ἐξουσία is given to Antichrist for his final activity, so that nothing takes place apart from the ἐξουσία or will of God. Especially in the community the word is indispensable to express the fact that we cannot take anything, but that it has to be given to us. Thus ἐξουσία describes the position of Jesus as the Head of the Church to whom all power is given and who gives it to His disciples. This ἐξουσία which is operative in ordered relationships, this authority to act, cannot be separated from its continuous exercise, and therefore thirdly ἐξουσία can denote the freedom which is given to the community.

1. In the first instance, then, ἐξουσία signifies the absolute possibility of action which is proper to God, who cannot be asked concerning the relationship of power

---

[28] In jSanh., 23d there is a contrast between רשות של מעלה and רשות של מטן, Schl. Jm., 163, 1. Cf. the sharp rejection of the idea that two רְשׁוּיוֹת might have created the world (→ n. 63). Gn. r., 1, 10 on 1:1: "No creature can say that two 'powers' have created the world."

[29] It often plays a role in legal definitions, whether we have בִּרְשׁוּת הָרַבִּים or בִּרְשׁוּת הַיָּחִיד e.g., AZ, 4, 11.

and legality in this ἐξουσία, since He is the source of both. Thus the word ἐξουσία arises in two passages which speak directly of God's incontrovertible freedom to act: Lk. 12:5: φοβήθητε τὸν μετὰ τὸ ἀποκτεῖναι ἔχοντα ἐξουσίαν ἐμβαλεῖν εἰς τὴν γέενναν, [30] and Ac. 1:7: οὐχ ὑμῶν ἐστιν γνῶναι χρόνους ἢ καιροὺς οὓς ὁ πατὴρ ἔθετο ἐν τῇ ἰδίᾳ ἐξουσίᾳ. Cf. also Jd. 25: μόνῳ θεῷ σωτῆρι ἡμῶν ... δόξα μεγαλωσύνη κράτος καὶ ἐξουσία πρὸ παντὸς τοῦ αἰῶνος καὶ νῦν καὶ εἰς πάντας τοὺς αἰῶνας (sc. ἐστίν), where ἐξουσία occupies an important place alongside κράτος. This ἐξουσία is that of the Creator. This is expressed by Paul in the metaphor of R. 9:21: οὐκ ἔχει ἐξουσίαν ὁ κεραμεὺς τοῦ πηλοῦ ἐκ τοῦ αὐτοῦ φυράματος ποιῆσαι ὃ μὲν εἰς τιμὴν σκεῦος, ὃ δὲ εἰς ἀτιμίαν; [31] While Philo traces back creation to the ἀγαθότης of God, and dominion over what is created to the ἐξουσία, for Paul the process of creation itself is an exercise of the absolute power of God and its supreme expression, since what is created owes its being to the Creator and thus bears witness in its very existence to the ἐξουσία of the Creator.

2. The ἐξουσία and power of God are variously displayed in the sphere of nature. The frequent use of the term in this context shows that nature is regarded as an ordered totality. Rev. 14:18 speaks of an angel ἔχων ἐξουσίαν ἐπὶ τοῦ πυρός. It is, however, particularly in the eschatological interpretation of world history in Rev. that we read of the ἐξουσία which God has given to the forces of destruction in nature and history: Rev. 6:8: ἐδόθη αὐτοῖς ἐξουσία ἐπὶ τὸ τέταρτον τῆς γῆς ἀποκτεῖναι; 9:3: ἀκρίδες ... ἐδόθη αὐτοῖς ἐξουσία ὡς ἔχουσιν ἐξουσίαν οἱ σκορπίοι τῆς γῆς; 9:10: καὶ ἐν ταῖς οὐραῖς αὐτῶν ἡ ἐξουσία αὐτῶν ἀδικῆσαι τοὺς ἀνθρώπους; 9:19: ἡ γὰρ ἐξουσία τῶν ἵππων ἐν τῷ στόματι αὐτῶν ἐστιν καὶ ἐν ταῖς οὐραῖς αὐτῶν. In these passages ἐξουσία means more than power or ability. It implies that even the power of the scorpion to hurt is lent to it by God. God has final ἐξουσία over the plagues, Rev. 16:9: ἐβλασφήμησαν τὸ ὄνομα τοῦ θεοῦ τοῦ ἔχοντος τὴν ἐξουσίαν ἐπὶ τὰς πληγὰς ταύτας. Angels have an ἐξουσία with which they are invested by God, Rev. 18:1: εἶδον ἄλλον ἄγγελον καταβαίνοντα ἐκ τοῦ οὐρανοῦ, ἔχοντα ἐξουσίαν μεγάλην, καὶ ἡ γῆ ἐφωτίσθη ἐκ τῆς δόξης αὐτοῦ. [32]

3. Also encompassed by the will of God is the ἐξουσία which is Satan's sphere of dominion. Neither in Ac. 26:18: ἀνοῖξαι ὀφθαλμοὺς αὐτῶν, τοῦ ἐπιστρέψαι ἀπὸ σκότους εἰς φῶς καὶ τῆς ἐξουσίας τοῦ σατανᾶ ἐπὶ τὸν θεόν nor in Col. 1:13: ὃς ἐρρύσατο ἡμᾶς ἐκ τῆς ἐξουσίας τοῦ σκότους καὶ μετέστησεν εἰς τὴν βασιλείαν τοῦ υἱοῦ τῆς ἀγάπης αὐτοῦ, can we separate between "power" and "sphere of power," while in Eph. 2:2 ἐξουσία τοῦ ἀέρος is the kingdom of the air. If there is in these expressions a reflection of the Rabb. custom of using a passive to avoid mentioning God, it is also materially necessary to say only that power "is given" to Satan. For the final mystery is not the power of evil itself. It is the fact that the power of evil, which is radically hostile to God, may be exercised as such and yet encompassed by the divine overruling. Thus we read in Lk. 4:6: καὶ εἶπεν αὐτῷ ὁ διάβολος· σοὶ δώσω τὴν ἐξουσίαν ταύτην ἅπασαν

---

[30] Mt. 10:28 has: τὸν δυνάμενον ...

[31] τοῦ πηλοῦ belongs to ἐξουσίαν, since it is superfluous with κεραμεύς. With the OT יֹצֵר there is not usually any explanatory gen., though cf. Jer. 19:1.

[32] Here it might seem that the most obvious meaning is actual power, but ἐξουσία signifies the position of the angel and thus prepares the way for the mention of δόξα in what follows.

καὶ τὴν δόξαν αὐτῶν, ὅτι ἐμοὶ παραδέδοται καὶ ᾧ ἐὰν θέλω δίδωμι αὐτήν. [33] And though it is said of Antichrist that the dragon has given him his power (δύναμις), his position (θρόνος), and therefore ἐξουσίαν μεγάλην ("say," almost "influence"), Rev. 13:2 (cf. 13:4 : προσεκύνησαν τῷ δράκοντι, ὅτι ἔδωκεν τὴν ἐξουσίαν τῷ θηρίῳ), nevertheless the further statements in v. 5 and v. 7: καὶ ἐδόθη ... καὶ ἐδόθη αὐτῷ ἐξουσία ποιῆσαι ("he was given authority to act") ... καὶ ἐδόθη αὐτῷ ἐξουσία ἐπὶ πᾶσαν φυλὴν καὶ λαὸν καὶ γλῶσσαν καὶ ἔθνος, imply that the time when Antichrist is given a free hand with the removal of the κατέχων is decided by God, so that even the rule of Antichrist does not take place apart from the will of God. [34] The same confidence is found in the words of Jesus in Lk. 22 :53: αὕτη ἐστὶν ὑμῶν ἡ ὥρα καὶ ἡ ἐξουσία τοῦ σκότους, [35] and it is for this reason that there is here no self-contradiction. We find ἐξουσία in the same connection in Mk. 16:14 (W text): πεπλήρωται ὁ ὅρος τῶν ἐτῶν τῆς ἐξουσίας τοῦ σατανᾶ and Rev. 13:12: (εἶδον ἄλλο θηρίον ...) καὶ τὴν ἐξουσίαν τοῦ πρώτου θηρίου πᾶσαν ποιεῖ ἐνώπιον αὐτοῦ.

4. The word ἐξουσία is important in understanding the person and work of Christ. It denotes His divinely given power and authority to act. If He is the Son, this authority is not a restricted commission. It is His own rule in free agreement with the Father. ἐξουσία is well adapted to denote this freedom too, as in Jn. 10:18 : ἐξουσίαν ἔχω θεῖναι αὐτήν, καὶ ἐξουσίαν ἔχω πάλιν λαβεῖν αὐτήν, where freedom is implied as well as power. [36] Jesus speaks of the power with which He is invested in Mt. 28:18: ἐδόθη μοι πᾶσα ἐξουσία ἐν οὐρανῷ καὶ ἐπὶ γῆς. This means that Jesus is exalted to be Χριστός and κύριος in the βασιλεία τοῦ θεοῦ. [37] In Rev. 12:1 ff. the divine sees this in a vision, and he hears the heavenly voice in v. 10: ἄρτι ἐγένετο ἡ σωτηρία καὶ ἡ δύναμις καὶ ἡ βασιλεία τοῦ θεοῦ ὑμῶν καὶ ἡ ἐξουσία τοῦ χριστοῦ αὐτοῦ, ὅτι ἐβλήθη ὁ κατήγωρ τῶν ἀδελφῶν ἡμῶν ... As the first part of chapter 12 speaks of the overthrow of Satan with the fulfilment of the work of Jesus on earth, so the hymn proclaims that God has the power and His Anointed the authority to act. According to the NT the κυριότης or ἐξουσία of Jesus is universal, but it applies particularly to men, Jn. 17:2: καθὼς ἔδωκας αὐτῷ ἐξουσίαν πάσης σαρκός, cf. Mt. 11:27 and Jn. 1:12. It also includes the place of Jesus in the coming judgment, Jn. 5:27: καὶ ἐξουσίαν ἔδωκεν αὐτῷ κρίσιν ποιεῖν, ὅτι υἱὸς ἀνθρώπου ἐστίν. [38]

The historical Jesus claims the same ἐξουσία (cf. Mt. 11:27 with 28:18), but within the limits of His earthly calling and commission. The accounts refer to His authority to forgive sins (Mk. 2:10 and par.). The scribes ask concerning the power to forgive (δύναται), though this cannot be separated from the right. In His answer Jesus uses ἐξουσία, which comprises both right and power. [39] There

---

[33] B. Weiss, *Die vier Evang.* (1900) and Zn. Mt., *ad loc.* translate "sphere of power," while Grundmann, 50 prefers "power" in view of the δόξαν αὐτῶν. The difficulty of the αὐτῶν remains in both cases.

[34] On this whole pt. cf. W. Foerster, ThStKr, 104 (1932), 279 ff. On the passive construction, *v.* Grundmann, 53, 21.

[35] ἐξουσία here means that darkness is given freedom to work. Zn. Lk., *ad loc.* wrongly links it with the time and place (Gethsemane at night).

[36] Cf. Zn. J., *ad loc.*; Grundmann, 81.

[37] Ac. 2:36.

[38] Cf. 2 C. 5:10.

[39] The accent is on ἐπὶ γῆς, as previously on the present ἀφίενται; hence ἐξουσία is not the right to proclaim the forgiveness of sins, which constantly takes place ἐπὶ γῆς, but the right and power to effect it.

is also reference to the έξουσία to expel demons (Mk. 3:15; 6:7 and par.; Lk. 10:19), and it is assumed that Jesus has this. In this respect the use of έξουσία for the power which decides, and for authority based on a commissioning force, agrees with the actual mode of exorcism by a word of command. Finally, the word έξουσία is used by the Evangelists (Mt. 7:29) and the Jewish people to describe the impression made by Jesus, and especially by His teaching. The Sanhedrin asks (Mk. 11:28): έν ποίᾳ έξουσίᾳ ταῦτα ποιεῖς; ἢ τίς σοι ἔδωκεν τὴν έξουσίαν ταύτην, ἵνα ταῦτα ποιῆς; By what right does He cleanse the temple, [40] hy a right deriving from His own authority (e.g., as a prophet), or by one grounded in the commission given Him by another? Is the answer of Jesus rather along the lines of Mk. 2:10? Again, the people often refers to the έξουσία of Jesus, especially in the formulation in Mt. 9:8: οἱ ὄχλοι ... έδόξασαν τὸν θεὸν τὸν δόντα έξουσίαν τοιαύτην τοῖς ἀνθρώποις. Cf. also Mk. 1:22 and par.: έξεπλήσσοντο έπὶ τῇ διδαχῇ αὐτοῦ· ἦν γὰρ διδάσκων αὐτοὺς ὡς έξουσίαν ἔχων, καὶ οὐχ ὡς οἱ γραμματεῖς. Mk. 1:27: καὶ έθαμβήθησαν ἅπαντες ὥστε συζητεῖν αὐτοὺς λέγοντας· τί έστιν τοῦτο; διδαχὴ καινὴ κατ᾽ έξουσίαν· καὶ τοῖς πνεύμασι τοῖς ἀκαθάρτοις έπιτάσσει, καὶ ὑπακούουσιν αὐτῷ. [41] Lk. 4:36: έν έξουσίᾳ καὶ δυνάμει έπιτάσσει τοῖς ἀκαθάρτοις πνεύμασιν καὶ έξέρχονται. This is to be understood in the light of the current feeling that there were no longer any prophets. Rabbinic exposition was simply exposition and not prophecy, i.e., it did not speak with direct authority, with έξουσία. [42] Ἐξουσία (== רְשׁוּ) presupposes a divine commission and authorisation which is also power, and the special feature in this έξουσία is that it is inseparable from the proclamation that the kingdom of God is near. With the presence of the Bearer of this authority, of this power to heal and to forgive sins, the kingdom is also present. Hence the formula of Reitzenstein: [43] "A combination of supernatural knowledge with supernatural power," is hardly adequate to convey all that is meant by the text.

5. In the varied use of έξουσία for the authority imparted to the community the outstanding characteristic is that the Church owes its existence and nature to Christ. It needs "enablement" even to enter the kingdom of God: ἔδωκεν αὐτοῖς έξουσίαν τέκνα θεοῦ γενέσθαι (Jn. 1:12). The same thought is figuratively expressed in Rev. 22:14: μακάριοι οἱ πλύνοντες τὰς στολὰς αὐτῶν, ἵνα ἔσται ἡ έξουσία αὐτῶν έπὶ τὸ ξύλον τῆς ζωῆς, and negatively in Hb. 13:10: ἔχομεν θυσιαστήριον έξ οὗ φαγεῖν οὐκ ἔχουσιν έξουσίαν οἱ τῇ σκηνῇ λατρεύοντες. The concept is also indispensable in relation to apostolic action, with the emphasis on power. 2 C. 10:8: έάν τε γὰρ περισσότερόν τι καυχήσωμαι περὶ τῆς έξουσίας ἡμῶν, ἧς ἔδωκεν ὁ κύριος εἰς οἰκοδομὴν καὶ οὐκ εἰς καθαίρεσιν ὑμῶν, οὐκ αἰσχυνθήσομαι; 2 C. 13:10: γράφω, ἵνα παρὼν μὴ ἀποτόμως χρήσωμαι

---

[40] So Hck. Mk., ad loc. But the question may refer to the entry (Schl. Mt., ad loc.) or to the whole activity of Jesus (Grundmann, 73).

[41] On the construction in Mk. 1:27, v. Kl. Mk. and Hck. Mk., ad loc.

[42] Cf. 1 Macc. 4:46: ἀπέθεντο τοὺς λίθους ... έν τόπῳ έπιτηδείῳ, μέχρι τοῦ παραγενηθῆναι προφήτην τοῦ ἀποκριθῆναι περὶ αὐτῶν.

[43] Poim., 48, 3; cf. Hck. Mk., ad loc. and Grundmann, 58. Windisch (→ Bibl.), 225-227, has pointed out that this is the έξουσία of a prophet, cf. Paulus u. Christus (1934), 151 ff.; also Dodd in Mysterium Christi (1931), 73; H. J. Holtzmann, Nt.liche Theologie, I² (1911), 296. J. Klausner, Jesus von Nazareth² (1934), 360 f. finds the expression ὡς έξουσίαν ἔχων "difficult to understand," and mentions a thesis of H. P. Chajes that ὡς έξουσίαν ἔχων rests on a confusion of the two stems מְשֹׁל, "to speak in parables," and מְשֹׁל, "to rule."

κατὰ τὴν ἐξουσίαν ἣν ὁ κύριος ἔδωκέν μοι εἰς οἰκοδομὴν καὶ οὐκ εἰς καθαίρεσιν, Ac. 8:19 : δότε κἀμοὶ τὴν ἐξουσίαν ταύτην ἵνα ᾧ ἐὰν ἐπιθῶ τὰς χεῖρας λαμβάνῃ πνεῦμα ἅγιον. Cf. also Rev. 11:6. This power cannot be used arbitrarily; in its application the apostle is bound to his Lord : εἰς οἰκοδομήν, cf. also Rev. 2:26-28. On the other hand, ἐξουσία presupposes responsible use, as Jesus assumes in the parable in Mk. 13:34 : ὡς ἄνθρωπος ἀπόδημος ἀφεὶς τὴν οἰκίαν αὐτοῦ καὶ δοὺς τοῖς δούλοις αὐτοῦ τὴν ἐξουσίαν, ἑκάστῳ τὸ ἔργον αὐτοῦ, and as Paul demonstrates in his refusal of support. In this connection ἐξουσία denotes the right, e.g., to be supported by the community, 1 C. 9:4-6, 12, 18; 2 Th. 3:9.

More particularly ἐξουσία means the freedom given to the community. This is the subject of Paul's quarrel with the Corinthians ; cf. 1 C. 6:12 : πάντα μοι ἔξεστιν, ἀλλ᾽ οὐ πάντα συμφέρει. πάντα μοι ἔξεστιν, ἀλλ᾽ οὐκ ἐγὼ ἐξουσιασθήσομαι ὑπό τινος. 1 C. 8:9 : βλέπετε δὲ μή πως ἡ ἐξουσία ὑμῶν αὕτη πρόσκομμα γένηται τοῖς ἀσθενέσιν. 1 C. 10:23 : πάντα ἔξεστιν, ἀλλ᾽ οὐ πάντα συμφέρει· πάντα ἔξεστιν, ἀλλ᾽ οὐ πάντα οἰκοδομεῖ.

The ἐξουσία which was a Corinthian slogan may be interpreted either Gnostically as power [44] or as freedom in respect of law. [45] Either way the basis is Paul's own teaching on freedom from the Law (→ 501), and the slogan itself may well be Pauline. It reminds us of the saying in R. 14:14 : οἶδα καὶ πέπεισμαι ἐν κυρίῳ ᾽Ιησοῦ ὅτι οὐδὲν κοινὸν δι᾽ ἑαυτοῦ, which perhaps derives from Mk. 7:15, and which Paul develops in rather a different way in his attack on asceticism in 1 Tm. 4:4 : πᾶν κτίσμα θεοῦ καλόν. These statements are not general truths ; they are valid only for faith. In the first instance they are addressed to Jewish Christians. They dissolve the Rabb. distinction between מִצְוָה and רְשׁוּת [46] and in their concrete application they show what freedom from the Law means. Many Jewish Christians in Paul's congregations, however, were still bound in their consciences to the Law of their people. This was not because they opposed Paul's teaching in principle. It was rather because many things connected with pagan cults raised for them the question whether freedom would not bring them into the sphere of the unclean and even involve them indirectly in a certain participation in paganism for which they could not assume responsibility. This explains the scruples regarding meats and drinks in Rome and Corinth. On the other hand, the declaration of freedom from the Law perhaps led others to vivid and startling demonstrations of this freedom. It is along these lines that Schlatter understands 1 C. 5:1 ff. The inclination to treat sexual questions in the same way as meats might well be linked with the Jewish origin of those concerned. While radically upholding the ἐξουσία of Christians, the πάντα μοι ἔξεστιν, Paul opposes to these tendencies two principles, the principle of what is fitting, of the συμφέρον, and the principle of what is edifying. The first has the man himself in view, and it points to the fact that there is no freedom without danger, for there always lurks the peril of a new bondage, an ἐξουσιασθῆναι. The second considers the neighbour and asks what is helpful to him.

This enables us to see the difference from other types of autonomy. The ἐξουσία of which Poimandres speaks in a prominent passage : εὐλόγητος εἶ, πάτερ· ὁ σὸς ἄνθρωπος συναγιάζειν σοι βούλεται, καθὼς παρέδωκας αὐτῷ τὴν πᾶσαν ἐξουσίαν, [47] the opposite of the ἐναρμόνιος δοῦλος, is the freedom of the inner man from

---

[44] Joh. W. 1 K. on 6:12 : ἐξουσία in Epict. is moral power (→ 561; 563); cf. the picture of the Gnostic Paul in Reitzenstein Hell. Myst., Beigabe XVI.

[45] A. Schlatter, Die korinthische Theologie (1914), passim ; also Paulus, der Bote Jesu (1934), 36 f., and comm., ad loc. Acc. to W. Lütgert, Freiheitspredigt und Schwarmgeister (1908), 119 ff. freedom is grounded in gnosis.

[46] → n. 26.

[47] Corp. Herm., I, 32.

fate and from the influences of the planets. [48] The ἐξουσία of Epictetus is the same apart from the dualistic and cosmological background. Common to both is the idea that this autonomy is grounded in the being of man and is thus intrinsic. In Paul man as a totality is taken up by Christ into the sphere of the βασιλεία θεοῦ, and he is thus liberated from all powers, not by nature, but in faith, which does not disregard the power given to Satan and his forces in this world, but which knows that it is not abandoned to them.

Among Christian Gnostics the term ἐξουσία (= potestas) plays a relatively minor role. But the thing itself is there, and it is a development of the movement already present in Corinth. We can see clearly the reaction against Jewish (and ecclesiastical?) legalism in the accusation of Irenaeus that the Gnostics are always the first at pagan feasts. [49]

Another divergence from NT ἐξουσία is found in the apocryphal Acts, with parallels in the magic pap., in which the word itself is infrequent. [50] In the NT ἐξουσία is sought from God in faith and He gives it freely in Christ. But here it is wrested from higher powers by means of magic. Again, in the NT it is devoted to the service of God. But here it is used for one's own ends.

These non-Christian ideas of ἐξουσία simply represent so many human questions in antique form, namely, the questions of freedom from destiny, of freedom for action, of real power and of authority to act; and it is to these questions that the NT seeks to give an answer.

6. A special use of ἐξουσία in the NT is for supernatural powers, usually together with → ἀρχαί, → δυνάμεις, → κυριότητες.

The expressions ἀρχαί and ἐξουσίαι are not found in Hellenism or pagan Gnosticism in this sense. Even where they might have been used, [51] they do not occur. On the other hand they are found in the Asc. Is. 1:4; 2:2 etc.; [52] Test. L. 3:8, with θρόνοι, in an account of the seven heavens which is obviously not a unity; also in Slav. En. (the longer recension) 20, which locates them in the seventh heaven with archangels, powers, principalities (ἀρχαί), dominions (κυριότητες), cherubim and seraphim etc.; Eth. En. 61:10: "all angels of power, all angels of dominions"; Treasury (ed. C. Bezold, 1883), 1, 3: Angels and archangels, thrones, princes, dominions, lords, cherubs and seraphs. κύριοι, which reminds us of the plur. κυριότητες, are mentioned as belonging to the fifth heaven in Apc. Sophonias. [53] The clearest and most explicit passage is in Test. Sol., 20:14 ff., where the demons as such, who cannot attain to the heavenly regions, are separated from the ἀρχαί, ἐξουσίαι and δυνάμεις which belong there.

The Christian Gnostics and the apocr. Acts also speak of ἀρχαί and ἐξουσίαι. In Simon Magus they are creators. [54] In Basilides, who often speaks of ἀρχαί and less frequently of ἐξουσίαι (potestates), these and others are names for cosmic magnitudes,

---

[48] Cf. Corp. Herm., I, 15. This power and freedom is based on γνῶσις, on knowledge, as rightly pointed out by Reitzenstein (Poim., 48, 3) and also E. Norden, Agnostos Theos (1913), 293, n. 1.

[49] Iren., I, 6, 3 = Epiph. Haer., 31, 21, 2. On the revolutionary character of Gnosticism as revealed in this counter-movement, cf. H. Jonas, Gnosis u. spätantiker Geist, I (1934), 233 ff.

[50] It is common in Test. Sol. (ed. McCown, 1922), cf. McCown's Index (1922).

[51] Cf. Corp. Herm., I, 9; 12 ff.; 25, where there is reference to the ἁρμονία and its ζῶναι, and to the διοικηταί.

[52] At any rate there might be an original ἐξουσία behind the word which A. Dillmann renders potestas (exercitus).

[53] Cl. Al. Strom., V, 11, 77, 2.

[54] Iren., I, 23, 2 f.: Ennoiam ... generare angelos et potestates, a quibus et mundum hunc factum dixit ... Ennoiam ... detentam ab iis, quae ab ea emissae essent potestates et angeli ... descendisse eum (sc. Simonem) ... assimilatum virtutibus et potestatibus et angelis (from the handy edition of W. Völker, Quellen zur Geschichte der christl. Gnosis [1932], 2).

and indeed for forces which are hostile to the Gospel and the Gnostics. [55] In Valentinus, too, we have both terms, [56] as also in the Marcosites, [57] where the reference is probably to planetary spheres under the Demiurge. [58] The apocr. Acts display much the same usage, [59] though here there is a distinctive linking of demons with the powers, [60] and at one point the connection of the ἐξουσίαι with the ἀήρ, [61] which sets them in immediate proximity to demons. On the other hand, in two passages we may perhaps discern a sense of the abstract significance of ἐξουσία. [62]

It is obvious that the idea of "powers" developed on Jewish soil, and that here, too, it finds a parallel in רָשׁוּת [63] as may be seen in Col. [64] Linguistically ἐξουσία is abstract, like the related θρόνος and κυριότης. We also learn from the parallels

---

[55] Iren., I, 24, 6 : *qui haec didicerit ... invisibilem et incomprehensibilem eum angelis et potestatibus universis fieri* (Völker, 45). Hipp. Ref., VII, 25, 5 : ἦλθε τὸ εὐαγγέλιον εἰς τὸν κόσμον καὶ διῆλθε διὰ πάσης ἀρχῆς καὶ ἐξουσίας καὶ κυριότητος καὶ παντὸς ὀνόματος ὀνομαζομένου (*op. cit.*, 52).

[56] Epiph. Haer., 31, 5, 2 : ... μνείαν ποιοῦμαι μυστηρίων πρὸς ὑμᾶς, οὔτε ἀρχαῖς οὔτε ἐξουσίαις οὔτε ὑποταγαῖς οὔτε πάσῃ συγχύσει περινοηθῆναι δυναμένων (*op. cit.*, 60).

[57] Iren., I, 21, 5 : *alii sunt, qui mortuos redimunt ... ut incomprehensibiles et invisibiles principibus et potestatibus fiant ... et praecipiunt eis venientibus ad potestates haec dicere* ... καὶ ταῦτα εἰπόντα διαφεύγειν τὰς ἐξουσίας, ἔρχεσθαι δὲ ἐπὶ τοὺς περὶ τὸν Δημιουργόν (*op. cit.*, 140).

[58] In the Pistis Sophia there are in the lower heavens ἀρχαί, ἐξουσίαι and archangels. There is also a personal force with the name Paraplex, a kind of angel of punishment. But no general conclusions can be drawn from this late production.

[59] V. the index of Lipsius and Bonnet.

[60] Act. Jn., 98 : σοφία δὲ οὖσα ἐν ἁρμονίᾳ ὑπάρχουσιν δεξιοὶ καὶ ἀριστεροί, δυνάμεις, ἐξουσίαι, ἀρχαὶ καὶ δαίμονες, ἐνέργειαι, ἀπειλαί, θυμοί, διάβολοι, Σατανᾶς καὶ ἡ κατωτικὴ ῥίζα.

[61] Act. Phil., 144 (Lipsius and Bonnet, II, 2, p. 85, 4; 86, 1 ff.) : ἐλθὲ νῦν 'Ιησοῦ καὶ δός μοι τὸν στέφανον τῆς νίκης αἰώνιον κατὰ πάσης ἐναντίας ἀρχῆς καὶ ἐξουσίας, καὶ μὴ καλυψάτω με ὁ σκοτεινὸς αὐτῶν ἀήρ.

[62] *Ibid.*, 132 (II, 2, p. 63, 7) : σὲ τρέμουσιν ἀρχαὶ καὶ ἐξουσίαι τῶν ἐπουρανίων (→ 564).

[63] In Rabb. literature there is in a series of passages a polemic against the assumption of two or more רָשׁוּיוֹת. The error combatted is that of the Minim. Its more exact form cannot be fixed with certainty. According to jMeg., 4, 10 the saying : "May he bless thee with good," refers to (belief in) two powers (יברכו טובים שתי רשיות). Since the underlying idea is that only good comes from God and evil from another power, we are obviously to think of a dualistic and possibly a Gnostic teaching. Similarly, the battle against the doctrine that two powers (רשיות) made the world (Gn. r., 1, 10 on 1:1; cf. T. Sanh., 8, 7; bSanh., 38a : "God had no partner [שותף] in the work of creation, as the Minim say) might well be directed against Gnostic δημιουργός-speculations. But the story of how Elisha b. Abuja (Acher) erred, namely, by seeing Metatron seated alongside God (bChag., 15a; Heb. En. 16:3), reminds us rather of the conflict with Christianity. None of this has anything to do with the ἐξουσίαι of Paul, which are subordinate and very numerous beings. Speculation on such beings is perhaps presupposed in Gn. r., 8, 8 on 1:26, where the Minim try to derive the existence of more than one God from the plur. אֱלֹהִים and נַעֲשׂוּ though it is not precisely stated that the reference here is to more than two. In Gn. r., 1, 5 on 1:1, however, it is plainly denied that Michael created the south of heaven, Gabriel the north and God the centre ; and in Sanh., 4, 5; bSanh., 38a it is said that man was created single in order that the Minim should not say that there are many powers in heaven (הרבה רשיות בשמים). It may be noted at this point that when the LXX translates Gn. 1:16 : καὶ ἐποίησεν ὁ θεὸς ... τὸν φωστῆρα τὸν μέγαν εἰς ἀρχὰς (לְמֶמְשֶׁלֶת) τῆς ἡμέρας, it is perhaps thinking of powers like the ἀρχαί of the NT.

[64] Cf. F. Prat, 201-229.

that ἐξουσίαι (like ἀρχαί) are to be distinguished from δαίμονες, whose region does not extend beyond the ἀήρ, and that they are cosmic powers.

It is not possible to distinguish between ἐξουσίαι and ἀρχαί, and to assign to them the different functions of two groups of powers, since neither the NT nor parallels give any indications in this direction. They are different expressions for much the same thing. It might well be that the θρόνοι and κυριότητες stand in the immediate presence of God and are thus to be distinguished from the ἀρχαί and ἐξουσίαι, which are linked with earthly things, [65] but as to this there can be no certainty. Again, it is hardly possible to regard the ἀρχαί and ἐξουσίαι as groups of angels in some contexts and groups of demons in others. [66] Though certain passages seem to point in different directions, cf. 1 C. 15:24 : ὅταν καταργήσῃ πᾶσαν ἀρχὴν καὶ πᾶσαν ἐξουσίαν καὶ δύναμιν, and Eph. 3:10 : ἵνα γνωρισθῇ νῦν ταῖς ἀρχαῖς καὶ ταῖς ἐξουσίαις ἐν τοῖς ἐπουρανίοις διὰ τῆς ἐκκλησίας ἡ πολυποίκιλος σοφία τοῦ θεοῦ, they refer to the same powers. The twofold aspect is the main problem. According to Jewish belief the heavens are the home of different powers which rule nature, and of that which they control, the stars no less than snow and hail. [67] This view is fundamentally different from the Gk. conception of οὐρανός. But Paul has combined with this Jewish foundation the Hellenistic idea of a nexus of destiny embracing the whole κόσμος.

This leads to a conception of several cosmic powers with whose government human life is connected in many ways, and which mediate between God and man. As powers of the created world, they share its twofold character. On the one side they represent the carnal side of fallen creation with the powers which seduce and enslave man. On the other, they belong to the creation which is created ἐν Χριστῷ and εἰς Χριστόν (Col. 1:15 f.). This twofold aspect is the distinctive feature of the relevant NT statements. Neither Judaism nor the Greek world recognises this tension, and Gnosticism presses on to a dualism which separates the created world from God altogether. The decisive point for Paul is that in no regard, whether as fate, or nature, or intermediate beings, or servants of God, can these powers either separate the Christian·from Christ or lead him to Him. [68]

7. The meaning of 1 C. 11:10 : διὰ τοῦτο ὀφείλει ἡ γυνὴ ἐξουσίαν ἔχειν ἐπὶ τῆς κεφαλῆς διὰ τοὺς ἀγγέλους, is much contested. But two points make the meaning clear.

As concerns the context first of all, there is no shift until v. 13, and therefore v. 10 forms part of the discussion of veiling from the one main standpoint, namely, that of the relation of woman to man. That this is still true in v. 10 is made evident by the πλήν of v. 11, which introduces a concluding limitation of the declared subordination of woman to man. Thus v. 10, as may be seen already from the διὰ τοῦτο with which it opens, [69] presents no other standpoint than that of the preceding and the two following

---

[65] Cf. the distinction between the angels of nature and the שרי מלכות שבמרום ערבות רקיע in Heb. En. 14:1.

[66] So G. Kurze, passim and p. 156; also E. de Los Rios in Verbum Domini, 9 (1929), 289-297.

[67] E.g., Eth. En., 17 f. and bChag., 12b.

[68] Loh. Kol., 119 suggests that the powers and forces "signify in a mythical view no other than the natural determination of the world which also engulfs man." Cf. G. Wohlenberg, NkZ, 23 (1912), 241. On this whole pt. cf. also H. Jonas (→ n. 49), passim ; esp. p. 99 : In Gnosticism the demon powers are both personal and spatial concepts. This explains why Gnosticism could also use ἐξουσία in the sense of a sphere of power, → 564; also p. 193 : The cosmic powers (ἐξουσίαι) and the powers which work in man (δαίμονες) have the same unity as that of being and action ; cf. the occasional equation of the ἐξουσίαι with demons mentioned under → n. 60 and 61.

[69] Cf. Dibelius and Kurze.

verses. Secondly, regard should be had to the choice of the verb ὀφείλει, for in Paul this does not imply external compulsion but obligation (except in 1 C. 5:1, and perhaps 7:36). It is thus very probable that in this verse Paul is referring to the moral duty of a woman and not to any kind of imposed constraint. But the various expositions which refer to the concupiscence of angels, [70] or to regard for the leaders of the community, [71] are incompatible with these two points. The only alternative is that the veil is a sign of woman's subordination to man, i.e., that man is the κεφαλὴ τῆς γυναικός. For this there are Rabbinic parallels which treat the veil as a sign of the married woman. [72] In this case, διὰ τοὺς ἀγγέλους refers to the angels as guardian angels or watchers over the natural order. [73] The term ἐξουσία is used materially for the veil. The only question is why it is here used in this way. As such it does not mean a sign of dominion. [74] Possibly Paul is using this bold image to drive home his point, namely, that the veil signifies the dominion to which woman is subject. If we do not accept this view, there remains only the suggestion of G. Kittel [75] that ἐξουσία rests on an Aram. שלטוניה which is once used in the sense of veil, and that the underlying stem שלט, meaning "to conceal" (still to be disclosed) has been linked with the very similar שלט, "to rule," to produce ἐξουσία either as a mistranslation or as popular etymology. In favour of this conjecture there can be no denying the possibility of one speech influencing another in this way; the range of meaning of ἐξουσία in the NT is evidence enough. On the other hand, it must be remembered that it is no more than a conjecture.

† ἐξουσιάζω.

With inf. and gen. (LXX also prep.): "to have and to exercise ἐξουσία" in its various senses. Hence a. "to have the possibility," [1] b. "to have the right," [2] ond c. "to have the power." [3] It is not found in Joseph. In the LXX (act and med.) it occurs at 2 Ἔσδρ. 7:24: οὐκ ἐξουσιάσεις καταδουλοῦσθαι αὐτούς (b.). It is particularly common in Qoh. with reference to the power of rulers and its misuse (e.g., 8:9: τὰ ὅσα ἐξουσιάσατο ὁ ἄνθρωπος ἐν ἀνθρώπῳ τοῦ κακῶσαι αὐτόν) and limitation (9:17: λόγοι σοφῶν ἐν ἀναπαύσει ἀκούονται ὑπὲρ κραυγὴν ἐξουσιαζόντων ἐν ἀφροσύναις) (c.).

In the NT it is found at 1 C. 7:4: ἡ γυνὴ τοῦ ἰδίου σώματος οὐκ ἐξουσιάζει ἀλλὰ ὁ ἀνήρ· ὁμοίως δὲ καὶ ὁ ἀνὴρ τοῦ ἰδίου σώματος οὐκ ἐξουσιάζει ἀλλὰ ἡ γυνή. Paul is not saying here that each partner has a right to the body of the

---

[70] Everling suggests the power exercised by woman through the veil to restrain demons, cf. Dibelius, and A. Jeremias, Babylonisches im NT (1905), 114 f.; also Der Schleier von Sumer bis heute (1931), 36 f. Cf. E. Fehrle, Die kultische Keuschheit im Altertum = RVV, 6 (1910), 38, n. 4.

[71] So Bornhäuser, op. cit.

[72] Str.-B., III, 423-440; A. Schlatter, "Die korinthische Theologie" in BFTh, 18, 2 (1914), 23 f., 54 ff.; Paulus, der Bote Jesu (1934), 309; Jirku, op. cit. The point of the par. from bShabb., 156b adduced by Foerster, op. cit., is that the covering of the head (by the man) denotes subjection to God, whereas the opposite implies rebellion and the rule of evil impulse. Acc. to Act. Thom., 56 γυμνοκέφαλοι are shameless women.

[73] J. Mezzacasa and K. Rösch suggests that the angels veil themselves before God and are thus an example to women.

[74] As suggested by Tischleder, 156 f., following some of the fathers.

[75] Op. cit. Ginsburger, op. cit. advances the same thesis in apparent independence of Kittel's work.

ἐξουσιάζω. [1] Philodem. Philos., Volumina Rhetor., I, col. III, 12 ff. (ed. Sudhaus, I, 6): παρακειμένων δὲ καὶ τοιούτων ἐξουσιάσει παραπλάττεσθαι χαρακτῆρα μοχθηρότατον (on the text, cf. the Suppl.).

[2] CIG, III, 4584: θυγατέρα αὐτῶν μὴ ἐξουσιάζειν τοῦ μνήματος.

[3] Dion. Hal. Ant. Rom., IX, 44, 6: ὡς ἐν ... μὴ βεβαίοις ἔχουσι τὴν ἐλευθερίαν ἐξουσιάζων ... πικρὰς ... ἐποιήσατο κατηγορίας.

other, but that each foregoes the right freely to dispose of his own body (c.). He is thus enjoining those who are married not to rule over one another but mutually to serve one another even in marital questions. The one gives rights to the other. Against the background of ancient conceptions it is important to see with what care Paul assigns the right to respect and the duty to serve equally to both partners. In Lk. 22:25 : οἱ ἐξουσιάζοντες αὐτῶν εὐεργέται καλοῦνται (c.), there is allusion to Qoh. In 1 C. 6:12 : πάντα μοι ἔξεστιν, ἀλλ᾽ οὐκ ἐγὼ ἐξουσιασθήσομαι ὑπό τινος, Paul constructs a pass. along the lines of πάντα μοι ἔξεστιν and with the sense that "I will allow nothing to win power over me." This is a general statement designed to show that there is no freedom without danger, but Paul may also have been thinking more specifically of the fact that πορνεία makes into a μέλος τῆς πόρνης and thus brings under her "power." [4]

† κατεξουσιάζω.

In Jul. Gal., 100c : προσήκει τοίνυν τὸν τῶν ῾Εβραίων θεὸν οὐχὶ δὴ παντὸς κόσμου γενεσιουργὸν ὑπάρχειν οἴεσθαι καὶ κατεξουσιάζειν τῶν ὅλων, [1] this word means, not the misuse of power, but its "possession and exercise." It is not found elsewhere in secular Gk., nor in the LXX, Joseph. or Philo.

In the NT it occurs only at Mk. 10:42 and par.: οἴδατε ὅτι οἱ δοκοῦντες ἄρχειν τῶν ἐθνῶν κατακυριεύουσιν αὐτῶν καὶ οἱ μεγάλοι αὐτῶν κατεξουσιάζουσιν αὐτῶν. Here its primary sense is that they "exercise power over them." There is no earthly government without the use of force. But if the reference in οἱ μεγάλοι is not merely to the authorities, it is likely that the word implies the tendency towards compulsion or oppression which is immanent in all earthly power, and not merely in political. The word also seems to be used in this sense in Act. Thom. [2]

Foerster

ἐξηγέομαι → ἡγέομαι.   ἐξίστημι, ἐξιστάνω → 459 f.

ἐξομολογέω → ὁμολογέω.   ἐξορκίζω, ἐξορκιστής → ὁρκίζω.

ἐξουσία, ἐξουσιάζω → 562 ff.

ἔξω

οἱ ἔξω, "those who are without, who stand outside," 2 Macc. 1:16; also οἱ ἔξωθεν, Hdt., IX, 5. Figur. "foreigners," Thuc., V, 14, 3; Jos. Ant., 15, 314 : τοὺς ἔξω τῆς ἀρχῆς, cf. 316 : παρὰ τῶν ἔξωθεν, "those who are banished," Thuc., IV, 66, 2; Sir. Prolog.: οἱ ἐκτός, "the laity" (in distinction from the scribes). In Rabb. lit. we sometimes find הַחִיצוֹנִים for "those who are without," i.e., for "those condemned as heretics," "who do not accept the halaka of the scribes," [1] so Meg., 4, 8 (cf. bSanh., 100, Bar.). Sanh.,

---

[4] Bchm. K., ad loc.
κατεξουσιάζω. Schl. Mt. on 20:25.
[1] Ed. C. I. Neumann (1880), 178.
[2] Act. Thom., 45 (ed. Lipsius-Bonnet), II, 2, p. 162, app. on line 24 : σὺ δὲ βούλει ὑπὲρ τὸ δέον καὶ τὸ δεδομένον σοι ἡμᾶς κατεξουσιάσαι. Ibid., 98 : ῥῦσαί με ἀπὸ τῆς ἀναισχυντίας Χαρισίου, ὥστε μὴ κατεξουσιάσῃ μου ἡ τούτου μιαρότης.
ἔξω. Pass., I, 993; Liddell-Scott, 600; Pr.-Bauer, 433 f.; Moult-Mill., 226.
[1] P. Billerbeck, Nathanael, 33 (1917), 129. Cf. J. Rabbinowitz, Mishnah Megillah (1931), 130; E. Baneth, Mischnajot, II (1927), 454, n. 53 (referring to the Essenes ?).

10, 1: הַסְּפָרִים הַחִיצוֹנִים "outside books which are not recognised by the Synagogue."[2] ἔξω in the attrib. instead of an adj. means "outside, external," Plat. Phaedr., 248a: εἰς τὸν ἔξω τόπον; BGU, IV, 1114, 5: ἐν τοῖς ἔξω τόποις; P. Oxy., VI, 903, 20: τὰς ἔξω θύρας; Ac. 26:11: ἐδίωκον ἕως καὶ εἰς τὰς ἔξω πόλεις ("alien, i.e., non-Jewish cities"); Herm. v., 2, 4, 3. For Philo[3] the thought is characteristic that there is nothing outside the κόσμος (Plant., 5, 6 etc.). Only of God is the antinomy true: ἔξω τοῦ δημιουργηθέντος ὢν οὐδὲν ἧττον πεπλήρωκε τὸν κόσμον ἑαυτοῦ (Poster. C., 14). Philo speaks of the liberation of the νοῦς from all earthly hindrances in his exposition of Gn. 15:5: τὸν νοῦν εἰς τὸ ἐξώτατον ἐξήγαγε (Leg. All., III, 41).

Mk. 4:11: οἱ ἔξω, "the broad mass of the people not amongst the disciples of Jesus"; 1 C. 5:12 f.; 1 Th. 4:12; Col. 4:5; "non-Christians," esp. "pagans." So, too, οἱ ἔξωθεν at 1 Tm. 3:7 or οἱ ἔξω ἄνθρωποι at 2 Cl., 13, 1. On the anthropological term ὁ ἔξω ἄνθρωπος in 2 C. 4:16: "the outward man," or "man as a corruptible earthly being" (opp. ὁ ἔσω ἄνθρωπος),[4] → ἔσω, → ἄνθρωπος, I, 365.

Behm

ἐπαγγέλλω, ἐπαγγελλία, ἐπάγγελμα,
προεπαγγέλλομαι

ἐπαγγέλλω, ἐπαγγελία.

A. ἐπαγγέλλω, ἐπαγγελία with the Greeks.

a. ἐπαγγέλλω[1] and ἐπαγγελία are originally synon. with other words constructed with ἀγγελ-,[2] and therefore the first sense is "to indicate" or "to declare" (Hom. Od., 4, 755), or "declaration," "report." This must be the starting-point for our discussion of the history of the term. It is from this that the ensuing variations develop. Dio C., 56, 29, 3: βουλῆς τε ἐπὶ τῇ νόσῳ αὐτοῦ ἐπαγγελθείσης ἵν᾽ εὐχὰς ποιήσονται; Thuc., V, 49, σπονδαί are published. πόλεμον ἐπαγγέλλειν in Plat. Leg., III, 702d means "to declare war on someone." b. If it is publicly declared by the state that something must be done, this takes on the character of an order (Thuc., V, 47). In Thuc., VII, 17 στρατιὰν ἐπαγγέλλειν "to order mobilisation." Similarly κατὰ τὴν ἐπαγγελίαν in Polyb., IX, 38, 2 means "according to order." c. ἐπαγγελία becomes

---

[2] Cf. Str.-B., II, 7; III, 362; Elieser ben Jehuda, *Thesaurus totius Hebraitatis*, III (1912), 1536 f. Something of the same in seen in the ecclesiastical language of Syria, cf. *Reliquiae Juris Ecclesiastici Antiquissimae*, ed. A. P. de Lagarde (1856), 60, 4; *Mittheilungen*, I (1884), 228.

[3] According to Bertram.

[4] There is here no exact equation between τὸ ἔξω and σῶμα (or τὸ ἔσω and ψυχή), 2 Cl., 12, 4, → ἔσω.

ἐ π α γ γ έ λ λ ω κτλ. In regard to ἐπαγγέλλω, this art. uses materials prepared by Schniewind, while the preliminary work on ἐπαγγελία and ἐπάγγελμα, also on προεπαγγέλλομαι, was done by Gerhard Friedrich. Bibl.: Pape, Pass., Liddell-Scott; Preisigke Wört., Fachwörter; Moult.-Mill.; E. A. Sophocles, *Greek Lexicon* (1870); H. v. Herwerden, *Lexicon Graecum²* (1910); Pr.-Bauer; Cr.-Kö.; P. Volz, *Die jüdische Eschatologie von Daniel bis Akiba* (1903), Index; Str.-B., III, 207-209.

[1] Both act. and med. are found, thought the med. is more common later. In the NT the med. alone occurs, though the pass. is used; cf. Pr.-Bauer, *s.v.*; Kühner-Blass-Gerth, I, 120; 2 Macc. 4:27; Gl. 3:19; 1 Cl., 35, 4. The fine distinction of Thomas Magister adduced by Pape is, like many statements of ancient grammarians, an artificial one which is not supported by actual usage.

[2] Hence we often have the readings ἀγγελ-, ἀπαγγελ- or εἰσαγγελ- for ἐπαγγελ-. Cf. E. Ziebarth, *Aus dem gr. Schulwesen²* (1914), 11 and Lyc., 14; Stob., I, 387, 15; Ez. 7:26; 1 Jn. 1:5; 3:11, → I, 59.

a technical term at law for the "declaration of a complaint or accusation," "delivery of a judgment." Aeschin. 1, 64 (cf. 81): τὴν ἐν τῷ δήμῳ ἠπείλησεν ἐπαγγελίαν ἐπαγγελεῖν. Against orators who have lost the right of public speech through some fault an accusation is stated for δοκιμασία before the Thesmothetes. Cf. Demosth. Or., 22, 29. [3] Another example of legal use is found in Preisigke Sammelbuch, 4434, 18: ἐξεῖναι αὐτῷ χωρὶς διαστολῆς καὶ ἐπανγελείας [χρήσασθαι] τοῖς νόμοις τῶν ὑποθήκων, "without previous intimation of the charge." d. ἐπαγγέλλομαι then comes to be used in the sense of "to make known something about oneself," "to declare an achievement," "to show one's mastery in something," "to profess a subject." Plat. Prot., 319a: ἐπάγγελμα ἐπαγγέλλεσθαι; Xenoph. Mem., I, 2, 7: τὴν ἀρετὴν ἐπαγγέλλεσθαι, "to specialise in education in virtue; σοφίαν, Diog. L. prooem., 12; ἄσκησιν, Luc. Vit. Auct., 7; παιδεύειν, Demosth. Or., 35, 41. [4] In this respect we might also quote Epict. Diss., I, 4, 3: εἰ δ' ἡ ἀρετὴ ταύτην ἔχει τὴν ἐπαγγελίαν εὐδαιμονίαν ποιῆσαι ... and Epict. Diss., IV, 8, 6. But here there is already a transition to the next meaning. e. An important sense of ἐπαγγέλλεσθαι is "to offer to do something," "to promise," [5] "to vow." "To make promises" is the meaning of ἐπαγγελίας ποιεῖσθαι in Polyb., I, 72, 6, and "to accept the offer" is the sense of ἐπαγγελίαν ἀποδέχεσθαι in Demosth. Or., 21, 14. Cf. Aesch. Choeph., 213: εὐχὰς ἐπαγγέλλεσθαι. Promises are easily made under stress (Polyb., I, 66, 12). But one must guard against the ὑπερβολὴ τῶν ἐπαγγελιῶν (Aeschin., 2, 34). In virtue of ἡ περὶ τὰς ἐπαγγελίας εὐχέρεια (Plut. Adulat., 23 [II, 64b]) great caution is needed in relation to promises, Plut. Adulat., 22 (II, 62e): οὐ μὴν ἀλλὰ δεῖ πρῶτον ἐν ταῖς ἐπαγγελίαις σκοπεῖν τὴν διαφοράν. Promises are often unfulfilled, Polyb., XVIII, 21, 1: ἐν ἐπαγγελίᾳ καταλείπειν and τὴν ἐπαγγελίαν ἐπὶ τέλος ἀγαγεῖν (ibid., XVIII, 28, 1). [6] In respect of promises there is often tension between word and deed (→ ἔργον). He who has been given a promise would like to see it fulfilled. [7] In Polyb., III, 111, 10 we read: διόπερ οὐκέτι λόγων ἀλλ' ἔργων ἐστὶν ἡ χρεία. θεῶν γὰρ βουλομένων ὅσον οὔπω βεβαιώσειν ὑμῖν πέπεισμαι τὰς ἐπαγγελίας. In general promises are comparatively worthless, for they are so seldom kept. Thus ἐπαγγελτικός comes to be used for a man who is always promising but never performs. [8] f. ἐπαγγελία and ἐπαγγέλλεσθαι are often used for promising money: ἐπηγγέλμαθα τῶι ὑπομνη[ματο]γρ[άφωι] ἀργυ[ρίου] [δραχμάς]. [9] ἐπαγγέλλομαι thus comes to have the meaning: "I promise or designate money. [10] This may be in the sense of a "liturgy," i.e., a public service. [11] The sur-

---

[3] Cf. Pauly-W., V (1905), 2707, s.v.

[4] φιλοσοφεῖν ἐπαγγέλλεσθαι, Plut. Quomodo quis suos in Virtute sentiat Profectus, 1 (II, 75c).

[5] There is a transition from d. to e. in Epict. Diss., I, 10, 2: κατατρέχων τοῦ προτέρου ... βίου καὶ περὶ τῶν ἑξῆς ἐπαγγελ<λ>όμενος, ὅτι ἄλλο οὐδὲν ... σπουδάσει ἢ ἐν ἡσυχίᾳ καὶ ἀταραξίᾳ διεξαγαγεῖν τὸ λοιπὸν τοῦ βίου. The statement of Pape (cf. also Cr.-Kö.) that in contrast to ὑπισχνέομαι it denotes an unsolicited promise to be responsible for something is very true of ἐπαγγέλλομαι (→ what follows), though the relationship to ὑπισχνέομαι is fluid. In BCH, 11 (1887), 29 f., No. 42, 5 f. ἐπαγγέλλεσθαι means the same as ὑπόσχεσις, cf. the note of the editors C. H. Diehl and G. Cousin, p. 38.

[6] For another side of the matter, cf. the καταλειπομένη ἐπαγγελία of Hb. 4:1. Aristot. Eth. Nic., IX, 1, p. 1164a, 28: μηθὲν ποιοῦντες ὧν ἔφασαν διὰ τὰς ὑπερβολὰς τῶν ἐπαγγελιῶν. Cf. also Polyb., I, 67, 1: ... μὴ οἷον τὰς ἐπαγγελίας ἐκπλήρουν, ἀλλὰ τοὐναντίον ...

[7] Cf. Aeschin., 1, 169: ἐὰν δ' ὁ αὐτὸς πρὸς ἡμᾶς ἐν τοῖς ἔργοις γένηται οἷος νῦν ἐστιν ἐν τοῖς → ἐπαγγέλμασι.

[8] Plut. Aem., 8 (I, 258e): ἐπεκλήθη δὲ δώσων ὡς ἐπαγγελτικὸς οὐ τελεσιουργὸς δὲ τῶν ὑποσχέσεων.

[9] S. Witkowski, Epistulae Privatae² (1911), 56, 32.

[10] GDI, IV, 690, No. 36, 10: ἀργύριον ἐπαγγέλλεσθαι. Cf. ibid., IV, Rhodes, Index (ed. O. Hoffmann).

[11] P. Oxy., VI, 904, 3 etc. in pap.; cf. GDI, 3624a, 8 (Cos), a subscription list; ibid., 5228, col. I, 21 (Sicily), contributions to a σιτώνιον (probably some kind of fund). Ditt.

prising thing is that throughout the Hellenistic East the word does not merely signify a promise to pay money but is also used as a techn. term for a voluntary payment or donation or subscription. [12] The gifts offered to the emperor on his accession are called ἐπαγγελτικὸν ἀργύριον. [13] In a list of candidates for a state liturgy in the year 119/120 the ἐπαγγελία is set out by villages (P. Giess., I, 59, col. IV, 12 f.). In this case ὁ ἐπαγγειλάμενος is the subscriber. [14] Priests seeking an office promise gifts prior to their accession in order to support their candidature, and in inscriptions this is expressed by ἐξ ἐπαγγελίας, or verbally ἐπαγγειλάμενος. [15] Acc. to Inscr. Priene, 123, 5 ff. anyone entering on an office promises a gift in writing : ἐπηνγείλατο μὲν ἐγγράφ[ω]ς [ἐν τῇ ἐ]κκλησίᾳ κρεαδοτήσειν τοὺς ἀλειψαμένους. We thus read : ἐβεβαίωσεν δὲ τὴν ἐπαγγελίαν παραστή[σ]ας μὲν τοῖς ἐντεμενίοις θεοῖς τὴν θυσίαν. ἐπαγγελία may also be, e.g., a contribution to an association for the worship of deceased ancestors. The assembly resolves to receive the bequest in the words : δεδόχθαι τάν τε ἐπαγγελίαν ἀποδέξασθαι. [16] Since ἐπαγγελίαι were frequently offered to temples, cults and deities, [17] the term is lifted out of the sphere of the secular. It already receives at this point a sacral significance. [18] g. During the early Hellenistic period (340 B.C. to 40 B.C.) it acquired a distinctively sacral use in Asia Minor. [19] ἐπαγγελία is a term for the proclamation of a festival. This might be occasioned by an accession, the epiphany of a god, or an oracle. [20] Legations "declare the festival of a saviour god." [21] They bring the invitation to the βουλή and ἐκκλησία of another city. We have a particularly good example in the case of Artemis Leukophrygene of Magnesia : The 'epiphany' of Artemis will be celebrated. [22]

In all these examples there is reference to man's promises to a god, but never to ἐπαγγελίαι θεοῦ. In an ancient tablet the ἀμοιβαί of the god are naively ex-

---

Syll.³, 577, 10 κατὰ τὴν ἐπαγγελίαν an educational foundation. On → λειτουργία, cf. in this context P. Giess., I, on No. 59, p. 13 ff.

[12] P. Giess., I, on No. 59, p. 16.

[13] Loc. cit.; W. Weber, Untersuchungen z. Geschichte d. Kaisers Hadrianus (1907), 69 f.; Ditt. Syll.³, 832, 6 f.

[14] In the plur. GDI, 3624a, 11 (Cos).

[15] Herwerden; BCH, 5 (1881), 185 ff., 189 ff., and 11 (1887), 12-38; 373-391.

[16] IG, XII, 3, 330, 126 f. Cf. E. Ziebarth, Griechisches Vereinswesen (1896), 7. IG, XII, 3, 329, 6 refers to a cultic fellowship in honour of Anthister which receives an endowment and invests it.

[17] Cf. GDI, 3119c (a very old Corinthian clay tablet): ἐπαγγείλας to the god from whom help is expected ; 3722, 1, a list of subscriptions εἰς τὰν κατασκευὰν τοῦ Ἀφροδισίου ; 4262, 1 f. (Rhodes, 3rd. cent. B.C.): ὑπὲρ τὸν ναὸν τοῦ Διονύ[σου] ; 5342, 2 f. (Euboea c. 100 B.C.): εἰς τὴν ἐπανόρθωσιν τοῦ ἱεροῦ τῆς Ἀρτέμιδος. Ditt. Syll.³, 1116, 8 : to a cultic society etc.

[18] Cf. also at the vow of a κάτοχος in P. Lond., I, 21, 11 f. (162 B.C.): οὐ βουλομενος παραβῆναι τι των ἐν τωι ἱερωι ἐπηγγελμενων. On the term κατοχή, v. 2 → συνέχομαι. Cf. Reitzenstein Hell. Myst., Index. In relation to the imperial cult, Dio C., 59, 20, 1 (deposition of archontes): ὅτι τε ἐς τὰ γενέθλια (→ εὐαγγέλιον) αὐτοῦ ἱερομηνίαν (→ εὐαγγέλιον) οὐκ ἐπήγγειλαν. Stob., I, 387, 15; cf. Windisch 2 K. on 1:20 and G. Heinrici, Die Hermes-Mystik u. das NT (1918), 102 : "The ἐπαγγελία in sacred books is comparable with the way in which the NT constantly speaks of the revelations of God." But cf. W. Scott, Corp. Herm., p. 460, 10, → n. 2.

[19] P. Boesch, Θεωρός, Untersuchungen zur Epangelie gr. Feste (Diss. Zürich, 1908). θεωρός is originally the "spectator," then the "official visitor," then the "one who proclaims a feast."

[20] Ibid., 17 f., cf. 39. Ditt. Syll.³, 1158, 5 ff.

[21] οἱ ᾑρημένοι ... περὶ τῆς ἐπαγγελίας τοῦ ἀγῶνος, Ditt. Syll.³, 561, 9 f., or οἱ ἀποσταλέντες ἐπὶ τὰν ἐπαγγελίαν, ibid., 604, 4. Cf. Boesch, 29 and 62. Synon. : πρεσβευταί, παρακαλεῖν, cf. 2 C. 5:20 and Wnd. 2 K., ad loc.

[22] Boesch, 11 f., 139. Ditt. Syll.³, 559, 13; 558, 7. Ael. Arist., 45, 31 vl. We naturally find σωτηρία in the inscr., and this reminds us of the synon. use in the NT.

pected. There is only one known example of the promise of a god : ἐπηνγείλατο δ' ἐμοὶ ὁ θεὸς κατὰ τὸν ὕπνον ὅτι νικήσομεν (in the "Delic Sarapis Aretalogy").[23] The expression can hardly have been common. Material parallels to sacral ἐπαγγέλλεσθαι may be found already in Hellenism in the use of εὐαγγελ-. In the NT, too, the concept of declaration finds its centre in the thought of the Good News.

B. ἐπαγγελία and ἐπαγγέλλεσθαι in the Jewish World.

1. This word has no preliminary history in the OT.[24] This is the more striking because on the basis of Paul's teaching we tend to consider the OT from the standpoint of promise. But where our Bible uses promise in the OT, various words are used in the Mas. and LXX. These suggest the "Word of God" but do not refer specifically to the divine pledge or promise. For Paul, on the other hand, ἐπαγγελία is a complement of → εὐαγγέλιον. Seeing the OT from the standpoint of ἐπαγγέλλεσθαι, he develops in the light of the goal the idea of a single divine history, though this is never brought under the concept of expectant ἐπαγγέλλεσθαι in the OT itself.

Luther uses "to promise" for the Mas. דבר, and the LXX λαλεῖν, as at Gn. 18:19. With εἰπεῖν, too, דבר is rendered "promise," e.g., Dt. 1:21. In Jl. 3:5 (2:32) the Mas. has אמר, the LXX εἰπεῖν and Luther "promise." In Jer. 18:10 the LXX again has λαλεῖν for אמר. In the Ps. the Luther Bible often has "promise" where the Mas. has צוה and the LXX ἐντέλλεσθαι, e.g., 133:3 (132:3), and even where there is no corresponding word in the Mas. or LXX, e.g., 106:4.

Linguistically both Judaism and the NT follow Hellenistic usage. Thus we find a. (cf. d.): ἐπαγγελίαν ἔχειν, 1 Tm. 4:8;[25] ἐπαγγέλλεται γνῶσιν ἔχειν θεοῦ, Wis. 2:13 : ἐπαγγέλλεσθαι γνῶσιν, 1 Tm. 6:21; θεοσέβειαν, 1 Tm. 2:10; θεοσέβειαν, Philo Virt., 54; πίστιν and ἐπαγγέλλεσθαι Χριστοῦ εἶναι Ign. Eph., 14, 2 : "to profess"; b. (cf. e.): "to make a secular promise," Prv. 13:12;[26] Est. 4:7 (Mas. אמר); Sir. 20:23; esp. of money: 1 Macc. 11:28; 2 Macc. 4:8; Mk. 14:11 etc.

2. The idea of the promise of God was developed in Judaism prior to Paul.

In 3 Macc. 2:10 God promises to hear prayers. In Ps. Sol. 12:8 : ὅσιοι Κυρίου κληρονομήσαισαν ἐπαγγελίας. Test. Jos. 20 : ὁ θεὸς ... ἐπάξει ὑμᾶς εἰς τὰς ἐπαγγελίας τῶν πατέρων, where ἐπαγγελίαι is more than the word of promise, since it also denotes the promised benefit. Joseph., too, speaks of the ἐπαγγελίαι θεοῦ in Ant., 2, 219.[27]

Even before Paul, Abraham, promise and Law are interrelated : S. Bar. 57:2 : "For at that time (the days of Abraham) the Law was known without being written, and the works of the commandments were fulfilled ... and the promise of future life was planted." Ibid., 59:2 : "At that time the light of the eternal Law lightened all who sat in darkness, to declare to believers the promise of their reward." ἀποδοὺς τὴν κληρονομίαν αὐτοῦ πᾶσι καὶ τὸ βασίλειον καὶ τὸ ἱεράτευμα καὶ τὸν ἁγιασμὸν καθὼς ἐπηγγείλατο

---

[23] The title given by O. Weinreich, *Neue Urkunden zur Sarapis-Religion* (1919), 31; Ditt. Syll.³, 663, 25 ff.; NT synon. ἀξίως τοῦ θεοῦ, ἐπαινεῖν.

[24] On the few occasions when ἐπαγγελία and ἐπαγγέλλεσθαι are used in the LXX they have no bearing on the understanding of the words. Sometimes they rest on a misunderstanding of the Heb.

[25] Cf. Dib. Past., *ad loc.*

[26] The Mas. is shorter.

[27] Schl. Theol. d. Judt. (1932), 66. Jos. Ant., 3, 77 uses ἐπαγγελία of the promises of Moses and 5, 307 of the promises of the Philistines to Delilah. Cf. Pr.-Bauer, *s.v.*

διὰ τοῦ νόμου, 2 Macc. 2:17. The attainment of the promises is made dependent on the keeping of the Law. [28] This entails uncertainty as to the fulfilment of the ἐπαγγελίαι. God keeps to what He says. But am I among those who will inherit the promises if I do not keep the Law ? [29]

The same thought occurs in the Rabbis. The very word used for the divine promises, i.e., הַבְטָחָה [30] implies that they are certain and reliable. This is plainly stated : Shebu., 35b : "R. Eliezer (c. 90) said to him : How can He have promised and not fulfilled ? R. Jehoshua (c. 90) answered him : What He has promised, He has done." Or Pesikt. r., 42 (178a): "What He has promised me, He has at once performed." Recipients of promises are Jacob, [31] Abraham, [32] Sarah, [33] David, [34] the Jewish people. [35] Nevertheless, there is an element of dubiety among the Rabbis too. Gn. r., 76 (49a): "R. Judan (c. 350) has said : Hereby we know that there is for the righteous no assurance (no absolutely sure rest in the promises of God) in this world." Are the promises valid for me ? This is the question for the Jew. It is here that the uncertainty of Judaism appears (→ 527). Ber., 4a : "In the name of R. Jose (c. 150) it is taught : David said : Lord of the world, I may confidently hold fast to Thee ... that Thou wilt reward the righteous in the future ; but I do not know whether my portion will be among them or not."

That the promises of God have taken on a distinctively eschatological character may be seen from the apocalypses and from Rabbinic writings. 4 Esr. 4:27: [36] the saeculum cannot sustain quae in temporibus (καιροῖς ?) iustis repromissa sunt ; [37] 4 Esr. 5:40 : finem caritatis, [38] quem populo meo promisi ; 4 Esr. 7:60 : "the judgment (?) promised by me"; [39] 4 Esr. 7:119 : promissum nobis immortale tempus (αἰών !). S. Bar. 14:13 : [40] "to receive the world which thou hast promised to them"; S. Bar. 21:25 : "Do not postpone what Thou hast promised"; S. Bar. 51:3 : "The immortal world (4 Esr. 7:119) which is then [41] promised to them" (opp.: "they have now satisfied my Law," cf. 2 Macc. 2:18). The constant subject of the promise is the "future world." The same is true in the Rabbis. [42] The pass. part. מֻבְטָח from הִבְטִיחַ, "to promise," is often used to denote "confidence that one will be a son (or daughter) of the world to come." [43] The verbum

---

[28] S. Bar. 46:6 : "If you do this, there will come to you the promises which I have already given you."

[29] 4 Esr. 7:119 : quid enim nobis prodest, si promissum est nobis immortale tempus, nos vero mortalia opera egimus.

[30] Cf. Str.-B., III, 207.

[31] Schl. Lk., 459 and Str.-B., III, 207 f.: בִּשְׁבִיל הַבְטָחָה שֶׁהִבְטַחְתִּי לְיַעֲקֹב אֲבִיכֶם, cf. 1 Jn. 2:25 : ἐπαγγελίαν ἐπαγγέλλεσθαι.

[32] Gn. r., 41 on 12:17 (25a); Nu. r., 2 on 2:32 (137c).

[33] Pesikt. r., 42 (178a).

[34] B. Ber., 4a.

[35] Midr. Est. 4:15 (98a). We read of God's promises to proselytes in Ex. r., 19 on 12:43 (81b): "Aqilas, the proselyte (c. 110), asked our teachers (R. Eliezer and R. Jehoshua c. 90) and said to them : What does it mean when it is written : He who loves the stranger to give him food and clothing, Dt. 10:18 ? Are these all the promises given to the proselyte, that he should give him food and clothing ?"

[36] At Gr. En. 25:7 J. Fleming translates εἰπεῖν "to promise"; so, too, G. Beer in Kautzsch Apk. u. Pseudepigr.

[37] The doubts expressed in Violet, II, 16 do not concern our word.

[38] The only doubts relate to caritas (Violet, II, 38).

[39] Lat. creatura : κτίσις instead of κρίσις. But the whole sentence is doubtful (Violet, II, 83).

[40] Following the text acc. to Violet. It agrees substantially with that of Ryssel.

[41] The "then" refers, not to the time of the promise, but to the attainment.

[42] The following section is based on material in Str.-B., III, 207-209.

[43] B. Ber., 4b, Str.-B., III, 208 f.: Eleazar b. Abina (c. 340); Ket., 111a, Abbahu (c. 300); R. Jirmeja b. Abba (c. 250), Tradition of Jochanan b. Nappacha (Strack, Einl., 137). Without dates, b. Meg., 28b and the five examples not in print, Str.-B., III, 209. Eschatological,

finitum activum is often used with the subst. (הַבְטִיחַ הַבְּטָחָה‎, [44] ἐπαγγελίαν ἐπαγγέλ-λεσθαι, → n. 31); thus there is a 1st century debate on the proposition : "What God has promised, He has kept"; [45] cf. ὃ ἐπήγγελται δυνατός ἐστιν καὶ ποιῆσαι in R. 4:21; the verb is also used (more commonly than the subst.) of the Abrahamic promise. [46]

C. ἐπαγγέλλω in the NT.

1. When God is called ὁ ἐπαγγειλάμενος in Hb. 10:23; 11:11, this is perhaps reminiscent of the distinctive substantival use ; [47] in this case it would refer to Him as the Giver (→ 578). On the other hand, there is no analogy for the πιστός which occurs in both texts, and a verbal construction is quite possible (10:23 : κατέχωμεν τὴν ὁμολογίαν τῆς ἐλπίδος ἀκλινῆ, πιστὸς γὰρ ὁ ἐπαγγειλάμενος [sc. τὴν ἐλπίδα]; 11:11: Σάρρα δύναμιν ... ἔλαβεν ... ἐπεὶ πιστὸν ἡγήσατο τὸν ἐπαγγειλάμενον [sc. τὴν δύναμιν]). In content there are Rabbinic parallels. The reference in 10:23 is to eschatological hope and in 11:11 to the promise to Abraham. The same is true in 12:26 : νῦν δὲ ἐπήγγελται λέγων : "Yet once more I will shake ... earth and heaven" ; and on the other side 6:13 : τῷ γὰρ ᾿Αβραὰμ ἐπαγγειλάμενος ὁ θεὸς ... ὤμοσεν.

2. Of the eschaton. There is a Jewish ring about Jm. 1:12 : στέφανον τῆς ζωῆς, ὃν ἐπηγγείλατο (note that mention of God is avoided) τοῖς ἀγαπῶσιν αὐτόν. θεὸν ἀγαπᾶν is a Jewish and not an exclusively Christian formula ; cf. also 2:5 : κληρονόμους τῆς βασιλείας [48] ἧς ἐπηγγείλατο τοῖς ἀγαπῶσιν αὐτόν. The expression ζωή, which is given a Jewish ring by the addition of αἰώνιος, occurs also in 1 Jn. 2:25 : αὕτη ἐστὶν ἡ ἐπαγγελία ἣν αὐτὸς ἐπηγγείλατο ἡμῖν, τὴν ζωὴν τὴν αἰώνιον and Tt. 1:2 : ἐπ᾿ ἐλπίδι ζωῆς αἰωνίου ἣν ἐπηγγείλατο ὁ ἀψευδὴς θεὸς (Hellenistic) [49] πρὸ χρόνων αἰωνίων. Is it an accident that in all these passages we have "eternal life" rather than the Jewish "future world" ? It can hardly be a Hellenism, since αἰών is common in Hellenism and ζωή (αἰώνιος) is also common in Jewish writings.

3. Of the Abrahamic promise. Ac. 7:5 : οὐκ ἔδωκεν αὐτῷ κληρονομίαν ... καὶ ἐπηγγείλατο δοῦναι αὐτῷ εἰς κατάσχεσιν αὐτὴν (the land) καὶ τῷ σπέρ-ματι αὐτοῦ.

4. Paul links the promise to Abraham with the promise of life in R. 4 and Gl. 3. The statement confirmed to Abraham in R. 4:21: ὃ ἐπήγγελται δυνατός ἐστιν καὶ ποιῆσαι — to bring life from the dead, R. 4:15, 17 — was fulfilled in Christ and to Christians (R. 4:24, 25). In Gl. 3:19 Christ is τὸ σπέρμα ᾧ ἐπήγγελ-ται, and what is promised is κληρονομία (Gl. 3:18, 19), i.e., citizenship of the ἄνω ᾿Ιερουσαλήμ (4: 28, 26).

D. ἐπαγγελία in the NT.

1. ἐπαγγελία in Luke. Except in Ac. 23:21, where the Jews in their attempt to kill Paul on the way to the council wait for the promise of the chiliarchs, the

---

too, is the anonymous proverb in b. Erub., 43b, Str.-B., III, 208. The later dating hardly seems necessary. The NT and apoc. confirm the early origin of the idea, and this is even clearer in the subst.

[44] Four examples are given in Str.-B., III, 208.

[45] The debate is between Eliezer and Jehoshua c. 90 (Strack, Einl., 123), Str.-B., III, 208.

[46] Pesikt. r., 42 (178a): (anonym.).

[47] Pr.-Bauer, *s.v.*

[48] ἐπαγγελίας א A is certainly wrong (from Hb. 6:17 ?).

[49] Cf. Wnd. 1 J., *ad loc.*

reference is always to the ἐπαγγελία θεοῦ. This usage is so fixed that θεοῦ can be left out and ἐπαγγελία alone mentioned, for it always implies the promise of God. By way of Judaism ἐπαγγελία has become a specific term for the word of divine revelation in salvation history. It is a word which expresses not merely the promise but also the fulfilment of what is promised.[50] Abraham is a recipient of the promise in Ac. 7:17: καθὼς δὲ ἤγγιζεν ὁ χρόνος τῆς ἐπαγγελίας ἧς ὡμολό-γησεν ὁ θεὸς τῷ Ἀβραάμ, ηὔξησεν ὁ λαὸς καὶ ἐπληθύνθη ἐν Αἰγύπτῳ. The ἐπαγγελία given to the fathers is a Messianic promise, εἰς ἣν τὸ δωδεκάφυλον ἡμῶν ἐν ἐκτενείᾳ νύκτα καὶ ἡμέραν λατρεῦον ἐλπίζει καταντῆσαι, Ac. 26:6 f. The fulfilment has come in Jesus Christ. κατ᾽ ἐπαγγελίαν the σωτήρ has come of the seed of David, Ac. 13:23. εὐαγγελιζόμεθα τὴν πρὸς τοὺς πατέρας ἐπαγ-γελίαν γενομένην, ὅτι ταύτην ὁ θεὸς ἐκπεπλήρωκεν τοῖς τέκνοις ἡμῶν ἀνα-στήσας Ἰησοῦν, Ac. 13:32 f.[51] The Messiah is the Bearer and the Distributor of the Spirit. The πνεῦμα is already promised in the OT (Ac. 2:16 ff.). The disciples have learned of this promise from Jesus Himself (Ac. 1:4). At Pentecost Jesus receives the Spirit from the Father and sends Him to earth (Lk. 24:49; Ac. 2:33). λήμψεσθε τὴν δωρεὰν τοῦ ἁγίου πνεύματος. ὑμῖν γάρ ἐστιν ἡ ἐπαγγελία καὶ τοῖς τέκνοις ὑμῶν καὶ πᾶσιν τοῖς εἰς μακράν (Ac. 2:38 f.). Christians live in the time of fulfilment. The word of promise becomes actuality. There is attainment of the remission of sins and the Holy Spirit.[52]

2. ἐπαγγελία in Paul.

a. Law and promise. Paul asks concerning the relationship between → νόμος and ἐπαγγελία, between human action and divine grace (R. 4), between the demanding will of God and His will to give (Gl. 3). Like the Rabbis, Paul is sure that God keeps His promises. He can execute what He has promised (R. 4:21). He has the power even to raise the dead and to create out of nothing (R. 4:17). Not to believe that His promises will be fulfilled is to do despite to His → δόξα, to doubt His veracity (R. 15:8), and to suspect His faithfulness and omnipotence (R. 4:20). If the promises are to be actualised, they must be loosed from all the human action to which Judaism had related the fulfilment, and made dependent on God alone. διὰ τοῦτο ἐκ πίστεως, ἵνα κατὰ χάριν, εἰς τὸ εἶναι (→ I, 610) βεβαίαν τὴν ἐπαγγελίαν παντὶ τῷ σπέρματι (R. 4:16). The promise presupposes the gracious will of the Giver. But if God's promise is tied to the Law, it is in-validated by the wrath of God which punishes all who violate the Law.[53] Οὐ γὰρ διὰ νόμου ἡ ἐπαγγελία τῷ Ἀβραὰμ ἢ τῷ σπέρματι αὐτοῦ ..., ἀλλὰ διὰ δικαιοσύνης πίστεως (R. 4:13). The words of the apostle are even sharper in Gl. 3. The Law and the promise are mutually exclusive. The promise is no longer promise if it has anything to do with the Law. εἰ γὰρ ἐκ νόμου ἡ κληρονομία, οὐκέτι ἐξ ἐπαγγελίας· τῷ δὲ Ἀβραὰμ δι᾽ ἐπαγγελίας κεχάρισται ὁ θεός (Gl. 3:18). If one tries to attain the → κληρονομία by fulfilment of the Law, one forfeits the promised inheritance; for God showed Himself gracious to Abraham δι᾽ ἐπαγγελίας. The promise is a testamentary disposition which is not altered

---

[50] Cf. Cr.-Kö., s.v.: ἐπαγγελία assumes "such a prominent place in the divine economy that the benefits as well as the members are characterised by it."

[51] On the linking of ἐπαγγελία with → εὐαγγέλιον, cf. R. 1:1 f.; Eph. 3:6; though cf. Hb. 4:1 f.

[52] Cf. Zn. Ag., ad loc.

[53] Cf. B. Weiss, Lehrbuch der bibl. Theol. des NT⁷ (1903), 269 ff.; Brief an die Römer (1899), ad loc.

by the later Law (→ 579). The Law cannot compete with the promises since it does not have the power of the → ζωοποιῆσαι (Gl. 3:21). It serves the preliminary purpose of leading sinful man from works to faith : ἵνα ἡ ἐπαγγελία ἐκ πίστεως Ἰησοῦ Χριστοῦ δοθῇ τοῖς πιστεύουσιν (Gl. 3:22). There is no contradiction in 2 C. 7:1:[54] ταύτας οὖν ἔχοντες τὰς ἐπαγγελίας, ἀγαπητοί, καθαρίσωμεν ἑαυτοὺς ἀπὸ παντὸς μολυσμοῦ σαρκὸς καὶ πνεύματος. The reference here is not to conditions on which the fulfilment of the ἐπαγγελίαι depends ;[55] the passage deals with the involved problem of the indicative and imperative, as in R. 6; Phil. 2:12; 1 C. 6:9 ff.: "Do not be fornicators ; you are sanctified ; you have the promises ; purify yourselves." The greatness of the divine promises and the certainty of the divine pledge are to shape the life of Christians.[56] The fulfilment of the ἐπαγγελίαι is not determined by the conduct of the recipients ; the ἐπαγγελίαι determine this conduct.[57]

b. The recipients of the promise are Abraham and his seed (R. 4:13): τῷ σπέρματι οὐ τῷ ἐκ τοῦ νόμου μόνον ἀλλὰ καὶ τῷ ἐκ πίστεως Ἀβραάμ (R. 4:16). Thus the Jews in NT salvation history have received the various promises of Messianic salvation (R. 9:4), while the Gentiles are ξένοι τῶν (→ n. 35 and p. 130) διαθηκῶν τῆς ἐπαγγελίας (Eph. 2:12).[58] Since the Messiah was to come of Israel, Jesus had to become a Jew ὑπὲρ ἀληθείας θεοῦ, εἰς τὸ βεβαιῶσαι τὰς ἐπαγγελίας τῶν πατέρων (R. 15:8). In the first instance the promises apply to the Jews. It is from them that salvation is to go out to the nations. But the sons of Abraham include those who believe like him and not merely physical descendants. Hence the Gentiles are τὰ ἔθνη ... συμμέτοχα τῆς ἐπαγγελίας ἐν Χριστῷ Ἰησοῦ διὰ τοῦ εὐαγγελίου (Eph. 3:6). What was once promised to Israel is now made available to the Gentiles. The Gospel mediates to them the benefits of salvation. In Gl. 3:16 ff. Paul uses τῷ σπέρματι in a different sense from that of R. 4 (→ supra). He does not now refer it to physical descendants, nor even to those ἐκ πίστεως. On the basis of the singular he relates it to the one seed of Abraham, namely, Christ. He is the true Heir of the promise, of the universal inheritance, and He determines the fellow-heirs. He who has put on Christ (Gl. 3:27), who is in Christ Jesus (3:28), who belongs to Christ, is the seed of Abraham, κατ᾽ ἐπαγγελίαν κληρονόμοι (3:29).

c. The content of the promises, of the promised benefit,[59] whether it be → κληρονομία (R. 4:13; Gl. 3:18, 29), or → ζωή (Gl. 3:21; R. 4:17), or → δικαιοσύνη (Gl. 3:21), or → πνεῦμα (Gl. 3:14; Eph. 1:13), or → υἱοθεσία (Gl. 4:22 ff. and R. 9:8), is always Messianic salvation.[60] Hence it is possible to speak both

---

[54] On the Pauline authorship of the passage, cf. A. Schlatter, *Paulus, der Bote Jesu Christi* (1934), ad loc.

[55] Ltzm. K., *ad loc.*: "These promises of God stated in v. 17b-18 are linked with the conditions laid down in v. 16-17a; if the latter are fulfilled, the former will be appropriated to you." Or Wnd. 2 K., *ad loc.*: "The promises of God demand serious effort on the part of the righteous for their fulfilment."

[56] Cf. A. Schlatter, *op. cit.* on 2 K. 1:20.

[57] There is, of course, another understanding of ἐπαγγελία in Eph. 6:2 ("commandment with promise"), and in the Past. → 579.

[58] Here, as in Gl. 3:16, ἐπαγγελία is closely linked to διαθήκη in meaning.

[59] There can be no clearcut distinction between the word of promise and the promised benefits as attempted in some dictionaries. Both are contained in the term ἐπαγγελία (→ 578).

[60] R. 9:4; 15:8; 2 C. 1:20; 7:1.

of ἐπαγγελίαι in the plural and also of ἐπαγγελία. [61] The promises have been fulfilled in Christ (R. 15:8 → βεβαιόω, I, 602 and → 577 f.). He is the Yea of the promises of God, the fulfilment of salvation in person. By the fact that He has come to earth God has owned His promises; for they are all fulfilled in Him (2 C. 1:20). He has averted the curse of Law, ἵνα τὴν ἐπαγγελίαν (vl. εὐλογίαν) τοῦ πνεύματος λάβωμεν διὰ τῆς πίστεως (Gl. 3:14). In the gift of the → πνεῦμα every Christian has the fulfilment of the promise. This is → ἀπαρχή (R. 8:23) and → ἀρραβών (2 C. 1:22; 5:5) of the final fulfilment ... πιστεύσαντες ἐσφραγίσθητε τῷ πνεύματι τῆς ἐπαγγελίας τῷ ἁγίῳ, ὅς ἐστιν ἀρραβὼν τῆς κληρονομίας ἡμῶν (Eph. 1:13 f.). The Spirit, promised in the OT and then again through Christ, is a mark of completed realisation. He is the seal of the initiated fulfilment and a pledge of the consummation which is still awaited. [62]

3. ἐπαγγελία in Hebrews. The author of Hb. is guided by a different interest when he speaks of the promises. The differences are to be explained by the situation of the readers and the concern of the author, who compares the OT and NT revelation and seeks to encourage wavering Christians to perseverance.

ἐπαγγελίαι were received by Abraham (Hb. 6:12 ff.; 7:6), Isaac and Jacob (11:9); Sarah (11:11), the patriarchs and prophets (11:33), and the Jewish people (4:1 ff.). These were assured of the land of Canaan (11:9), of → κατάπαυσις (4:1), of a posterity (6:14; 11:11), and of αἰώνιος κληρονομία (9:15). They saw the fulfilment of individual promises, [63] though not of the promise in the absolute. [64] All the promises of God converge on the great Messianic salvation whose final consummation has still to come. Abraham dwelt in the land promised to him. But he knew the incompleteness of the fulfilment. Thus he did not settle down there permanently. He lived as a stranger on earth. He awaited the final fulfilment of the city of God which he saw contained in the promise given to him (Hb. 11:7 f.). The fathers of faith ἀπέθανον ... πάντες, μὴ κομισάμενοι τὰς ἐπαγγελίας, ἀλλὰ πόρρωθεν αὐτὰς ἰδόντες καὶ ἀσπασάμενοι, καὶ ὁμολογήσαντες ὅτι ξένοι καὶ παρεπίδημοί εἰσιν ἐπὶ τῆς γῆς. From afar they see the fulfilment of the promise and as pilgrims they hail their home city (Hb. 11:13). [65]

The new διαθήκη (→ 127), established by Christ, ἐπὶ κρείττοσιν ἐπαγγελίαις νενομοθέτηται (Hb. 8:6). In what these promises consist, we are not told. Quoted in Hb. 8:8 ff. are the promises of God in Jer. 31: the Law written upon the heart, perfect knowledge of God and fellowship with Him, and the full remission of sins. These are not new promises. They are promises whose fulfilment is not hampered by any further transgressions. The main deficiency in the old covenant was that it could not accomplish forgiveness. Hence the new promises are better. For here is the complete fulfilment sought but never attained in the old order. [66] διὰ τοῦτο διαθήκης καινῆς μεσίτης ἐστίν, ὅπως θανάτου γενομένου εἰς ἀπολύτρωσιν τῶν ἐπὶ τῇ πρώτῃ διαθήκῃ παραβάσεων τὴν ἐπαγγελίαν λάβωσιν οἱ κεκλημένοι τῆς αἰωνίου κληρονομίας (Hb. 9:15). The death of Christ brings

---

[61] Cf. R. 9:4; 15:8; 2 C. 1:20; 7:1 with Eph. 2:12; 3:6, and Gl. 3:16 with 3:17 ff.

[62] J. T. Beck, Erklärung des Briefes Pauli an die Eph. (1891), ad loc.

[63] Hb. 6:12: τὰς ἐπαγγελίας κληρονομεῖν; 6:15: τῆς ἐπαγγελίας (cf. 11:33: ἐπαγγελιῶν) ἐπιτυγχάνειν.

[64] Hb. 11:13: τὰς ἐπαγγελίας (cf. 11:39: τὴν ἐπαγγελίαν) κομίζεσθαι.

[65] One can hardly refer the plur. ἐπαγγελίαι to individual earthly promises and the sing. to the promise of salvation. The sing. and plur. are used in much the same way, cf. n. 63 and 64, the plur. in Hb. 7:6 with 8:6, and Rgg. Hb. on 6:15.

[66] Cf. B. Weiss, Lehrbuch der bibl. Theol. des NT⁷ (1903), 479.

about the fulfilment. It gives to those who are called the promised eternal inheritance which the expectant believer will receive at the *parousia* which is still to come. The final consummation is still ahead (Hb. 10:36). It will take place soon (Hb. 10:25, 37), for we are already living in the ἔσχατον (Hb. 1:2), in the συντέτεια (Hb. 9:26). Christians are in the tension between what is already and what is not yet (Hb. 6:5). They are beginning to tire and therefore to doubt the consummation. Possession of the divine word of promise does not guarantee reception of the promised benefit. Israel is a terrible example of the possibility of shutting oneself off from the promise through unbelief. φοβηθῶμεν οὖν μήποτε καταλειπομένης ἐπαγγελίας εἰσελθεῖν εἰς τὴν κατάπαυσιν αὐτοῦ δοκῇ τις ἐξ ὑμῶν ὑστερηκέναι· καὶ γάρ ἐσμεν εὐηγγελισμένοι καθάπερ κἀκεῖνοι (Hb. 4:1 f.). [67]

God's will to accomplish His promises is unalterable. With the absolute reliability of an oath He has guaranteed the fulfilment of the promise. This should strengthen the faith and patience of Christians as it once encouraged Abraham, especially as the fulfilment of the promise has already begun for them (Hb. 6:12 ff.). [68] ὑπομονῆς γὰρ ἔχετε χρείαν ἵνα τὸ θέλημα τοῦ θεοῦ ποιήσαντες κομίσησθε τὴν ἐπαγγελίαν (Hb. 10:36). [69]

4. ἐπαγγελία in 2 Peter. The situation in Hb. has now deteriorated. The fathers have now fallen asleep and nothing has happened. The delay in the promised *parousia* [70] has thus raised up scoffers: ποῦ ἐστιν ἡ ἐπαγγελία τῆς παρουσίας αὐτοῦ; (2 Pt. 3:4). The answer is: οὐ βραδύνει κύριος τῆς ἐπαγγελίας, ὥς τινες βραδύτητα ἡγοῦνται, ἀλλὰ μακροθυμεῖ εἰς ὑμᾶς, μὴ βουλόμενός τινας ἀπολέσθαι ἀλλὰ πάντας εἰς μετάνοιαν χωρῆσαι (2 Pt. 3:9). The prophetic word of Scripture is reliable (2 Pt. 1:19 ff.). (→ ἐπάγγελμα.)

ἐπάγγελμα.

ἐπάγγελμα has the meanings of ἐπαγγελία, though it is not so common or so varied. It has the general sense of "declaration," and is then used for "order," [1] "profession" (→ 577), [2] "promise" (→ 577). [3] Philo prefers it to ἐπαγγελία. So Virt., 64:

---

[67] Cf. Wnd. Hb. and Rgg. Hb., *ad loc.*: Jews have received an εὐαγγέλιον as well as Christians. For Jews the ἐπαγγελίαι now fulfilled in Christ are the Gospel, and the NT Gospel is simply a proclamation of the old promises. The two words mean the same thing. There is no substance in the usual distinction which refers ἐπαγγελίαι to salvation still to come and εὐαγγέλιον to salvation already come. Cf. n. 50.

[68] The note in Wnd. Hb. on 6:15: "The reception of the promise was the reward for his μακροθυμία," is hardly appropriate. A. Seeberg, *Der Brief an die Hb.* (1912), has correctly interpreted the verse in its context. There is no question of a condition for the fulfilment of the promise. It is rather shown "that Abraham's patience had its basis in the promise which God has sworn by Himself out of regard for men." On εἰς βεβαίωσιν ὁ ὅρκος → 578; I, 603.

[69] It is obvious that there is in Hb. no tension between the promise and the righteousness of works. Nevertheless, we are not to take → ὑπομονή as an achievement which can claim from God the fulfilment of the promise, but as an attitude corresponding to the → θέλημα θεοῦ. Cf. Rgg. Hb., *ad loc.*

[70] Cf. Mk. 13:30 and par.; Mt. 10:23.

ἐπάγγελμα. [1] Leontius Monachus, MPG, 98, 693a; cf. E. A. Sophocles, *Greek Lex.* (1870), *s.v.*

[2] τὸ ἐπάγγελμα τῆς ἀρτοποιΐας, M. Ant., 3, 2.

[3] Cf. also Liddell-Scott, *s.v.*: Plat. Euthyd., 274a: ὑπὸ γὰρ τοῦ μεγέθους τοῦ ἐπαγγέλματος οὐδὲν θαυμαστὸν ἀπιστεῖν and Aristot. Rhet., II, 24, p. 1402a, 25: καὶ ἐντεῦθεν δικαίως ἐδυσχέραινον οἱ ἄνθρωποι τὸ Πρωταγόρου ἐπάγγελμα· ψεῦδός τε γάρ ἐστιν, καὶ οὐκ ἀληθὲς ἀλλὰ φαινόμενον. Also Demosth. Or., 19, 178: ὑπόσχεσις and ἐπάγγελμα.

ἐπάγγελμα ἐπαγγέλλεσθαι (→ 577). He often uses it in this sense of "office," "profession," "task."

In the NT it occurs only twice in 2 Pt. It means the same as ἐπαγγελία (→ supra). 2 Pt. 3:13: καινοὺς δὲ οὐρανοὺς καὶ γῆν καινὴν κατὰ τὸ ἐπάγγελμα αὐτοῦ προσδοκῶμεν.[4] In opposition to heretics and despisers (2 Pt. 3:4), the greatness and value of the promise are emphasised: ... τὰ τίμια καὶ μέγιστα ἡμῖν ἐπαγγέλματα δεδώρηται (2 Pt. 1:4). The content of the promise is given in 2 Pt. 1:4b, 11; 3:4, 13.

προεπαγγέλλομαι.

προεπαγγέλλομαι is naturally rare, since there is already a πρό in ἐπαγγέλλομαι. It means[1] a. "to announce beforehand." Dio C., 38, 13, 5 act.; also act. Dio C., 40, 32, 3: "publicly to make known the plundering beforehand"; b. "to exert oneself beforehand (earlier) about an office," προεπαγγέλλειν, Dio C., 39, 31, 1; c. "to promise beforehand," med. Dio C., 42, 32, 3: πρότερον προεπαγγέλλεσθαι; pass. Dio C., 46, 40, 2. Inscr. Priene, 113, 71: τὰ προεπηγγελμένα, in the pass. of benefits for the people.

In the NT it is found only twice. In 2 C. 9:5 (pass.) it means "to announce in advance": ἡ προεπηγγελμένη → εὐλογία ὑμῶν. It means the εὐλογία which you have announced in advance, not which I have promised to you in advance. R. 1:2 (med.): "to promise beforehand": → εὐαγγέλιον θεοῦ, ὃ προεπηγγείλατο διὰ τῶν προφητῶν αὐτοῦ ἐν γραφαῖς ἁγίαις.

Schniewind/Friedrich

ἐπαγωνίζομαι → I, 135 f.

† ἔπαινος

ἔπαινος, "praise," "approval," "applause," is a characteristic goal in antiquity,[1] whether on the part of Greeks in the classical period or of later philosophical ethics. It is used with εἰς and the acc., ἐπί and the dat., κατά and the acc., περί, πρός τι, ὑπέρ and the gen. It is apportioned by gods and men: κλέος τε καὶ ἔπαινος πρὸς ἀνθρώπων τε καὶ θεῶν Plat. Leg., II, 663a. In Soph. Ant., 817 it means "approval" of the whole life on descent into the underworld. In Soph. Ant., 669 ἐπαίνου τοῦτον ἐξ ἐμοῦ τυχεῖν is used of the appraisal of king Creon. Soph. Ai., 527 uses it of Ajax' agreement with the words of his beloved. In Soph. Oed. Col., 1411 the reference is to recognition by the public, as also in Plat. Leg., VIII, 841e (τῶν ἐν τῇ πόλει ἐπαίνων), Plat. Polit., 287a, Leg., VI, 762e, La., 181b etc. Epict. Diss., I, 18, 22; II, 13, 4 (ὄχλου ἔπαινος); II, 16, 6; III, 23, 7 (παρὰ τῶν πολλῶν ἐπαίνου); IV, 7, 29 etc. In Plat. Leg., 917c ἔπαινος means the "evaluation of goods." A common antonym is ψόγος ("depreciation"), Plat. Polit., 287a, Leg., VI, 762c. ἔπαινος may be used for the praise both of the individual and of the whole city (Soph. Oed. Col., 720 of Athens: ὦ πλεῖστ' ἐπαίνοις εὐλογούμενον πέδον). Stoic moralism is concerned to free the individual

---

[4] Is. 65:17; 66:22, and often in apoc. V. Wnd. Kath. Br., ad loc.
προεπαγγέλλομαι. [1] Cf. Pass. and Moult.-Mill., s.v.
ἔπαινος. Cf. A. Fridrichsen, "Der wahre Jude und sein Lob" in Symbolae Arctoae, I, ed. Societas Philologica Christianensis (1922), 39-49; E. Hofmann, Qua Ratione ΕΠΟΣ, ΜΥΘΟΣ, ΑΙΝΟΣ, ΛΟΓΟΣ ... adhibita sint? (Diss. Göttingen, 1922), 58 ff., 63 ff.
[1] In relation to the Greeks Hegel speaks of "the restless urge of individuals to display themselves, to show what they can make of themselves, and then to enjoy their standing with their fellows" (acc. to Fridrichsen, op. cit., 47; cf. K. Leese, Die Geschichtsphilosophie Hegels [1922], 195 f.).

from the judgment of men, whether it be ἔπαινος or ψόγος (Epict. Diss., II, 1, 34 ff.; III, 23, 19; M. Ant., 4, 20), but in so doing it simply proves how great value the ancient world laid on ἔπαινος either by individuals or by the public.

For the righteous of the old covenant, God and the congregation are the only norms. Thus in the LXX ἔπαινος is the recognition or praise which the righteous is given by the community, Sir. 39:10; 44:8, 15. But it is naturally the divine approval which really counts. Those from whom this is withheld are judged, like Jehoram in 2 Ch. 21:20 (Mas. חֶמְדָּה) and the makers of images in Wis. 15:19. In Philo, as in the OT, ἔπαινος is approval by God (Rer. Div. Her., 90 and 129; Leg. All., III, 77; Abr., 262) or by the great prophet Moses (Vit. Mos., I, 154; Abr., 275); it may also signify public recognition or applause in the Greek sense (Poster. C., 71; 72; 141: τῶν πολλῶν ἔπαινος; Abr., 186), though in Philo, too, public applause is not the decisive thing for Abraham (Abr., 190).

Frequently in the LXX ἔπαινος may be used for the community's attitude of praise and worship in relation to God, as in hymns. Thus in ψ 34:27 the congregation extols the greatness of Yahweh (Mas. תְּהִלָּה), and in ψ 21:3, 25 (Mas. תְּהִלָּה) it magnifies His great acts of assistance. The throne of God is thought of as surrounded by → δόξα and ἔπαινος (1 Ch. 16:27, Mas. הָדָר). Only in the more Stoic 4 Macc. is ἔπαινος related to insight as the supreme virtue (1:2).

1. The use of ἔπαινος in the NT is similar to that of the LXX. The only value of ἔπαινος is when it does not represent a general human judgment or popular evaluation but when it is the approval of man by God (R. 2:29; 1 C. 4:5). We do not have here the Jewish thought of ἔπαινος as a special reward, but rather the idea that at the last judgment the conduct of believers, in contrast to that of the wicked, will be approved and vindicated by God as the One who is not limited in His judgments as we are, but who searches the human heart in all its depth and hiddenness (cf. also Mt. 25:21, 34 ff.). ἔπαινος thus signifies the acceptance or approval of the righteous by God alone in the last judgment. It is the definitively saving sentence of God in the last time, at the revelation of Jesus Christ (1 Pt. 1:7).[2]

2. For this reason Christians are not concerned about the coveted recognition of men in this life. The only human approval which counts is the approval of those who hold the divine commission. Thus ἔπαινος may be accorded only by a. the Christian community as the body, i.e., the visible manifestation, of the exalted and otherwise invisible Lord. In the delicate and difficult matter of the collection at Corinth only a brother who has been approved in the communities may assist (2 C. 8:18). With the community, the other divinely commissioned body which may award ἔπαινος is the government (R. 13:3; 1 Pt. 2:14). This may fittingly apportion ἔπαινος as the servant of God (R. 13:4), as an order[3] appointed by God in His final will and purpose, "for the Lord's sake" (1 Pt. 2:13). Thus it is one of the functions of those who bear the divine commission to pronounce ἔπαινος; and only such ἔπαινος has any value. ἔπαινος is thus an exercise of the prerogative of those who are divinely commissioned,[4] of the community and the authorities.

Only once in the NT is ἔπαινος used in the classical sense, namely, in Phil. 4:8. Here it implies general human recognition. It is a concept of civic life, like the other terms in this whole passage.

---

[2] Cf. ἐπαινέω, Lk. 16:8. In the LXX ἐπαινέω occurs only 4 times; αἰνεῖν is more common (R. Helbing, Die Kasussyntax der Verba bei den Septuaginta [1928], 15-17).

[3] H. Preisker, Geist und Leben (1933), 80-88.

[4] Hence ἐπαινέω is also used by the apostle in R. 15:11; 1 C. 11:2, 17, 22.

3. Also parallel to LXX usage is the use of ἔπαινος in the NT hymn. The beginning of Eph. (1:3 ff.) has a hymnic character and perhaps uses an old cultic song. [5] Similarly, the intercession of the apostle in Phil. takes hymnic form. Hence in Phil. 1:11 and Eph. 1:6 ἔπαινος denotes the praise and worship of the community in its confession. In both cases we have the combination of → δόξα and ἔπαινος already found in 1 Ch. 16:27. The community does not have to wait for the time of fulfilment to confess God's δόξα and ἔπαινος (Phil. 1:11). It can do this already because it has already experienced salvation (Eph. 1:6). [6] Thus ἔπαινος is the community's attitude of praise on the basis of the salvation which God has already given to it.

Preisker

ἐπαίρω → I, 185 f.

ἐπακολουθέω → I, 215

ἐπαναπαύω → I, 350

ἐπάρατος → I, 451

ἐπέρχομαι → ἔρχομαι.

ἐπιβάλλω → I, 526 f.

ἐπιγινώσκω, ἐπίγνωσις → I, 689 ff.

ἐπαισχύνομαι → I, 189 ff.

ἐπακούω → I, 222

ἐπανόρθωσις → ὀρθός.

ἐπενδύω → 320 f.

ἐπερωτάω, ἐπερώτημα → ἐρωτάω.

ἐπίγειος → I, 677 f.

---

† ἐπιείκεια
† ἐπιεικής

ἐπιεικής means in the first instance "that which is the general conception of life," and therefore "what is fitting, right, or equitable" = aequus, cf. Hom. Il., 23, 246. Thus the neut. ὡς ἐπιεικές is often used for "as is fitting," ibid., 19, 147 etc. It is used for the works of the gods, ibid., 19, 21. Cf. Aristoph. Nu., 1438 : τἀπιεικῆ συγχωρεῖν τινι, "to agree to what is right." It thus takes on in Plat. Leg., I, 650b the further sense of "what is serviceable"; Leg., V, 741d (ἔμπειρός τε καὶ ἐπιεικής), the man of experience and "of an equable temperament," Leg., XII, 597a, the "seasoned" man, Thuc., VIII, 93, 2; Xenoph. Hist. Graec., I, 1, 30, the "reasonable" man who stays within the limits of what is moderate and orderly. Plut. Quaest. Conv., I, 1, 5 (II, 614e): οὐδὲν ἄν ... ἐπιεικέστεροι πρὸς κοινωνίαν, "so little adapted to society ..."; Plut. Suav. Viv. Epic., 13 (II, 1096a): πρὸς δὲ ἡδέως ζῆν ἐπιεικέστερον. So also P. Masp., III, 295, p. 1, 21: πρὸς τὸ μὴ βλαβῆναι τοὺς ἐπιεικεῖς in the sense of "orderly" people ; cf. also the sense of "serviceable" in P. Tebt., II, 484. Hence the combination ἐπιεικῶς καὶ σπουδαίως, P. Masp., II, 151, 236. We thus read in Plat. Ap., 22a : ἐπιεικέστεροι ἄνδρες πρὸς τὸ φρονίμως ἔχειν. Moderation at law then comes to mean, along with εἴκω ("to yield"), "mildness" in the sense of not insisting on the letter of the law in a given case, Aristot. Eth. Nic., V, 14, p. 1137a, 31 ff.; Thuc., IV, 19, 2; Plat. Leg., VI, 757e (moderation in relation to what is just or what is ordered). We thus have the expression ἐπιεικῶς ἔχειν πρός τινα (Isoc., 15, 4) in the sense of "to be moderate or gentle." So also Epict. Diss., III, 20, 11; 23, 4. Epict. Fr., 5, 10 brings ἐπιεικής into opp. with ὑβριστής (what is violent). In Soph. Oed. Col., 1127 ἐπιεικής expresses modera-

---

[5] J. Lohmeyer, *Das Proömium des Eph.*; ThBl, 5 (1926), 120 ff.

[6] In these two passages, too, it may be seen that Paul is thinking in eschatological terms. In Eph. he does so in the light of the community established on earth.

ἐπιείκεια. Cf. A. v. Harnack, "Sanftmut, Huld und Demut," in *Festgabe f. J. Kaftan* (1920), 113 ff. The etym. is difficult. Cf. L. Meyer, *Handbuch der gr. Etymologie*, II (1901), 23 (here put with ἀεικής, μενοεικής, etc.).

tion or kindness towards men and is a parallel to εὐσεβής towards the gods. It occurs with πράως in Plut. De Pyrrho, 23 (I, 389c).

In the LXX this group of words is found only in the later literature apart from 1 Βασ. 12:22; 4 Βασ. 6:3; ψ 85:5. It is mostly used for God's disposition as a Ruler, i.e., for the "kindness" or "goodness" which He can display as King, ψ 85:5; [1] 1 Βασ. 12:22; [2] Wis. 12:18; Bar. 2:27; Da. 3:42; 4:24; 2 Macc. 2:22; 10:4. It can thus be used also of earthly kings (Est. 3:13; 8:13; 2 Macc. 9:27; 3 Macc. 3:15; 7:6, and of men who are close to God and who should thus be holy as He is, namely, the prophet Elisha (4 Βασ. 6:3), or the righteous as the son of God (Wis. 2:19). God in His heavenly greatness as Ruler, the king who should be His earthly reflection, all who have God's gift and commission, have this disposition of mildness just because they exercise sovereign sway.

Joseph. uses ἐπιεικής of the king in Ant., 10, 83 (Joachaz μήτε πρὸς θεὸν ὅσιος μήτε πρὸς ἀνθρώπους ἐπιεικής); 15:14 (the treatment of Hyrcanus by the Parthian king is ἐπιεικέστερον, "of particular kindness"); 15, 182 (Hyrcanus is ἐπιεικὴς καὶ μέτριος); cf. 15, 177. In Ant., 6, 92 Samuel is described as χρηστός and ἐπιεικής, protecting the people from the wrath of God. In Ap., 2, 29 the great lawgiver is represented as a man of ἐπιείκεια who demands ἐπιείκεια even in relation to aliens (Ap., 2, 209). Thus Joseph. uses ἐπιείκεια of the king, the lawgiver and the prophet. Philo, too, uses ἐπιεικής of Moses in Virt., 81, 125, 140, 148; cf. Spec. Leg., IV, 23; Leg. Gaj., 119 (διὰ τὸ σὺν ἐπιεικείᾳ καὶ μετὰ νόμων ἄρχειν). Or he uses it for the mildness of the ruler, Som., II, 295, or for the goodness of God, Spec. Leg., I, 97. Hence he often has combinations like ἐπιείκεια and χρηστότης, Exsecr., 166; ἐπιείκεια and ἡμερότης, Spec. Leg., II, 93; Virt., 134; ἐπιείκεια and πραότης, Op. Mund., 103; ἐπιείκεια and φιλανθρωπία, Spec. Leg., II, 110; ἐπιεικής and φιλάνθρωπος, Flacc., 61; Leg. Gaj., 352; ἐπιεικής and ἥμερος, Virt., 81, 125; ἐπιεικῶς and ἵλεως, Spec. Leg., I, 97.

In Ps.-Plat. Def., 412b (ἐπιείκεια δικαίων καὶ συμφερόντων ἐλάττωσις) and Aristot. Eth. Nic., V, 14, p. 1137a, 31 ff., ἐπιείκεια is thus "the mitigation of strict legal claims out of regard for special circumstances in individual cases." In opposition to strictness in law, Isoc., 18, 34 speaks of κατ' ἐπιείκειαν ψηφίσασθαι; cf. 4, 63. Thus ἐπιείκεια is "clemency" or "leniency." Plat. Leg., V, 735a; Ep., VII, 325b. It is often used with πραότης, Plut. Pericl., 39 (I, 173c); De Caesare, 57 (I, 734d); with οἶκτος, Thuc., III, 40, 2; 48, 1. In the pap. it expresses a moderate disposition or considerate leniency, Pap. Greci e Latini, I, 86, 10; P. Lond., II, 231, 10; P. Masp., II, 151, 188 etc. In the broadest sense it can also mean a "temperate mode of life" as distinct from ἀκολασία, Lys., 16, 11.

In 2 C. 10:1 ἐπιεικείας τοῦ Χριστοῦ refers to the meekness of Christ as a model for Paul and the community. Christ is an example as the Revealer of divine and royal majesty. As the heavenly King (Phil. 2:5 ff.) He is gentle as only one who has full power can be. ἐπιείκεια is thus a complement of heavenly majesty. The weak are always anxiously trying to defend their power and dignity. He who has heavenly authority can display saving, forgiving and redeeming clemency even to His personal enemies. But Paul and the community have also a heavenly calling (Phil. 3:20). They are thus associated with the divine δόξα. For this reason they, too, must display ἐπιείκεια. [3] Even in the most difficult situations the ἐπιείκεια τοῦ Χριστοῦ must determine the relations of Paul and the community. Members of the community must be loyal to the apostle in face of all hostile calumniators (2 C. 10:6). Trusting in the atonement, they must humbly seek ἐπιείκεια, so that

---

[1] Mas. חלס = Ps. 86:5.

[2] Mas. הואיל. The term ἐπιεικής reflects a moral ideal alien to the OT, and therefore there is no fixed Heb. basis (thus יאל hiph is used very differently in Ju. 19:6).

[3] Cf. V. Weber, "Erklärung von 2 C. 10:1-6" in BZ, 1 (1903), 68; Wnd. 2 K., ad loc.

he, too, may exercise his apostolic authority (2 C. 10:8) simply in the sense of the κύριος as ἐπιείκεια. Thus in ἐπιείκεια there is given to Paul and the community a sign of their supraterrestrial possession.

This is even clearer in the use of ἐπιεικής in Phil. 4:5. Because the κύριος is at hand, and the final δόξα promised to Christians will soon be a manifest reality, they can be ἐπιεικεῖς towards all men in spite of every persecution. Faith in their hidden, heavenly plenitude of light and power and life produces a saving gentleness. It is the earthly counterpart of the heavenly glory. Hence it is not weakness or sentimentality. It is the earthly outworking of an eschatological possession (cf. Phil. 2:15-16). As the governor, Felix, ought to manifest a clemency corresponding to his high office (Ac. 24:4), so Christians can be ἐπιεικεῖς in virtue of their heavenly calling given to them by God.

In Jm. 3:17 wisdom as a heavenly creature is given the attributes of rule, [4] and therefore here, too, the early Christian sense of an expression of royal or heavenly majesty is apposite. In 1 Tm. 3:3 ἐπιεικής occurs in an adapted Hellenistic catalogue of duties. Yet the reference is to the bishop of the community who is endowed with authority and who acts as the representative of the community with eschatological assurance and in virtue of eschatological possession. Hence ἐπιεικής is again to be taken in its specific early Christian sense.

On the other hand, in 1 Pt. 2:18 the word is used of masters in their dealings with slaves. There is thus a shift from the LXX use, and the distinctively Christian accent is lacking, since the reference is not merely to Christian masters. There is even less of the specific Christian emphasis, or of that of the LXX, in Tt. 3:2. The literary character of the list, and the schematism of the concepts borrowed from Hellenism, suggest that here, as often enough later, [5] ἐπιεικής bears the general sense of "meek" customary from Attic times. ἐπιεικής is often combined with πραΰς, [6] ταπεινός, [7] φιλανθρωπία, [8] etc.

Preisker

ἐπιζητέω → ζητέω.	ἐπιθυμέω, ἐπιθυμητής, ἐπιθυμία → θυμός.
ἐπικαλέω → καλέω.	ἐπικατάρατος → I, 451
ἐπιλαμβάνομαι → λαμβάνω.	ἐπιλύω, ἐπίλυσις → λύω.
ἐπιμαρτυρέω → μαρτυρέω.	ἐπιορκέω, ἐπίορκος → ὀρκίζω.

---

† ἐπιούσιος

In the NT it occurs only in the Lord's Prayer in Mt. 6:11: τὸν ἄρτον ἡμῶν τὸν ἐπιούσιον δὸς ἡμῖν σήμερον, Lk. 11:3: τὸν ἄρτον ἡμῶν τὸν ἐπιούσιον δίδου ἡμῖν τὸ καθ' ἡμέραν. In Christian writings it is found only in connection with the Lord's Prayer, commencing with Did., 8, 2. Elsewhere it is found only in one

---

[4] At any rate ἡ δὲ ἄνωθεν σοφία is a christological phrase, and the attributes mentioned all refer to Christ as depicted in the Gospels, so that there seems to be good ground for the above interpretation.

[5] Cf. 1 Cl., 30, 8; 56, 1; 58, 2; 62, 2; 21, 7; 13, 1; Ign. Eph., 10, 3. In the biblical sense: 1 Cl., 29, 1; Ign. Phld., 1, 1 f.; Dg., 7, 3; Herm. m., 12, 4, 2.

[6] 2 C. 10:1; Tt. 3:2; 1 Cl., 21, 7; 30, 8; Dg., 7, 3 (→ 589).

[7] 2 C. 10:1; 1 Cl., 30, 8; 56, 1; 58, 2; 62, 2.

[8] 3 Macc. 3:15; 2 Macc. 9:27; Athenag. Suppl., 12 (→ 589).

ἐπιούσιος. Bibl. in Pr.-Bauer, *s.v.* and Symbolae Osloenses, 2 (1924), 31 f. and 9 (1930), 62. Where a definite meaning is offered, the author's name is given with the place where this may be found.

papyrus (a list of expenses) [1] among expenses for chick-peas, straw etc., and for material (δαπάνης) [2] and personal [3] ends an expenditure of ½ obol for επιουσι . . ., which should probably be completed to give ἐπιουσίων. [4] There are no other examples. Linguistically it is difficult to fix the meaning with any precision.

1. The Linguistic Derivation.

Origen said that he did not know the term either in academic or popular speech. The older translations vary widely, [5] as do also the fathers. [6] The first linguistic suggestion is a derivation from ἐπιέναι. The participial stem gives one possible clue, ἐπ + ιοντ + ιος becoming ἐπιούσιος on the analogy of (ἑκών)/ἑκόντιος* > ἑκούσιος etc. [7] This would give the meaning "future," [8] "regular," [9] "second in goodness," [10] "coming

---

[1] Preisigke Sammelbuch, I, 5224. A. Debrunner was the first to draw attention to this example in ThLZ, 50 (1925), 119, but it was independently noted also by M. Dibelius, ThBl., 4 (1925), 267 and H. J. Cadbury, JBL, 45 (1925), 215.

[2] Ibid., line 37a.

[3] Ibid., line 56a.

[4] Sergius Malea in Jerusalem, 1773, retranslated three Armenian codices into Greek at 2 Macc. 1:8 : καὶ προσεθήκαμεν ἡμεῖς τοὺς ἄρτους ἐπιουσίους τῷ κυρίῳ. The Armenian original is not known. The reference is to the showbread. לֶחֶם הַתָּמִיד is used for this at Nu. 4:7; Sys+c used אמינא (corresponding to תָּמִיד) for the ἐπιούσιος of the Lord's Prayer. Perhaps this is the basis of the translation of Sergius Malea. For fuller information, cf. E. Nestle (→ n. 55), 251; J. Haussleiter (→ n. 8), 440; P. W. Schmiedel, PrM, 18 (1914), 360-362; 19 (1915), 23 f.; ThR, 19 (1916), 9 f.; Zn. Mt.⁴, (1922), 278, n. 83.

[5] Ev. Hebr. acc. to Jer.: mahar (מְחָר); Hieros.: דעותרא = "abundant"; Sys+c אמינא; SyrP דסונקנן = "what we need"; Sa.: venientem ; Cop.: crastinum ; It.: cot(t)idianum ; Vg. Mt.: supersubstantialem. The most ancient Georgic Hadishi MS discovered in 1904 has a word constructed with mara in which מְחָר perhaps occurs, S. Kauchtschischwili, Philol. Wochenschr., 50 (1930), 1166-1168. On the transl. cf. esp. C. Tischendorf, NT⁸ on Mt. 6:11; A. Meyer, Jesu Muttersprache (1896), 108; E. Nestle (→ n. 55); Zn. Mt., ad loc.; Dalman WJ, I, 322; F. Hauck (→ n. 24).

[6] On patristic exegesis, cf. esp. F. H. Chase, The Lord's Prayer in the Early Church (1891), 42-53; O. Dibelius, Das Vaterunser (1903), 61 f.; G. Loeschke, Die Vaterunser-erklärung des Theophilus v. Antiochien (1908); J. Haussleiter (→ n. 8), 439; J. P. Bock, Die Brotbitte des Vaterunsers (1911); G. Walter, Untersuchungen z. Geschichte der gr. Vaterunserexegese (1914); Zn. Mt., ad loc.

[7] The only linguistic objections to this derivation have been stated by L. Meyer, NGG, 1886, 247: that constructions in → ούσιος from participial forms in -οντ- are rare in Gk. and cease in the later period (cf. Meyer, Zeitschr. f. vergleich. Sprachforschung, 7 [1858], 424), and by Cr.-Kö., 408 : that there are no other instances of composites in -ούσιος from ἰέναι. Neither of these is decisive.

[8] Cf. τὸ ἐπιόν, "the future." So also H. Grotius. J. Haussleiter, RE³, XX, 439 f.: "for the coming time" = "so long as we live on this earth"; A. Seeberg, "Vaterunser u. Abendmahl" (Nt.liche Studien f. G. Heinrici, 1914), 108-114; Die vierte Bitte d. Vaterunsers (1914), where p. 10 f. he sees a reference to the future bread of the person of Christ, relating the phrase to baptism and the Lord's Supper, between which the Lord's Prayer is set. G. Kuhn, Schweizerische Theol. Zeitschr., 36 (1919), 191-198 : our bread coming for the day = עתידא ליומא = ἐπιούσιος τῇ ἡμέρᾳ, τῇ ἡμέρᾳ having been erroneously separated from ἐπιούσιος, which derives from ἐπὶ + εἶναι. Whatever the merits of the understanding, it is precarious to count on errors. The interpretation "future" is opposed by Cr.-Kö., 408 on the ground that the σήμερον of Mt. cannot mean the future in general but only to-morrow, cf. also Zn. Mt.⁴ (1922), 279, n. 84.

[9] D. Völter, PrM, 18 (1914), 274-276: "the portion of bread which is necessary daily and which returns regularly." The basis of this understanding is found in the older Syr. and Lat. versions, whose "regular" or "daily" goes back to the Heb. תָּמִיד: ἐπιούσιος, from ἐπιέναι, means "that which recurs in regular sequence." Völter also appeals to Sergius Malea. A discussion followed between Völter and P. W. Schmiedel, PrM, 18 (1914), 358-364; 19 (1915). 20-23, 23-26. Neither the appeal to Sergius Malea nor the Gk. derivation

to us daily," [11] or "as is appropriate to us." [12] Linguistically, however, this derivation is not so free from objections as that from the expression ἡ ἐπιοῦσα, sc. ἡμέρα, against which there is no linguistic objection. [13] ἡ ἐπιοῦσα means the day which follows, the next day, [14] the day which is before us. [15] Hence the meaning is that to-day already, or acc. to Lk. daily, we should pray for bread for the next day. This interpretation fits both Mt. and Lk., and it does not render anything superfluous in either. It is also supported by the Ev. Hebr., which acc. to Jerome has *mahar*, "to-morrow." Thus the rendering "for the following day" is now the most widely accepted. [16] Few commentators,

---

is convincing. The Heb. תָּמִיד hardly bears the meanings suggested, and it would be better to go back to the Aram. תְּדִירָא, which can denote "something which happens daily and which is thus regular," Dalman WJ, I, 327.

[10] H. Kothe, *Neue Jahrbücher f. Philologie u. Pädagogik*, 142 (1890), 586 f.: ἐπιέναι = *sequi*, ἐπιούσιος ἄρτος = *panis secundarius* = barley bread, the Palestinian equivalent of the German black bread. But below this is still bran bread, and C. Cron, *ibid.*, 144 (1891), 297 f. asks Kothe whether people who eat the latter are likely to ask for the former.

[11] K. Holzinger, *Philol. Wochenschr.*, 51 (1931), 826-830, 857-863 : ἐπιούσιος "calculated to come," i.e., this day, which may be supplied from the ἡμέρα present in σήμερον. Cf. the objection of A. Debrunner, *ibid.*, 1277 f. and the reply of Holzinger, *ibid.*, 52 (1932), 383 f.

[12] E. Bischoff, *Jesus und die Rabbinen* (1905), 77 f. ὁ ἐπιών, "he who encounters one by the way," and ἄρτος ἐπιούσιος, "nourishment as it comes to us," לֶחֶם צְרָכֵנוּ. A. Pallis, *Notes on St. Mk. and St. Mt.* (1932), 68 f.: ἐπιούσιος = ἐπιβάλλων, "which falls to our share," since in the intr. the words are often synon. Cf. also Kretschmer and Vannutelli in n. 72.

[13] Linguistic objections have been raised by Bolliger (→ n. 24), 279 : that there is no example of an adj. from a fem. part., and Holzinger (→ n. 11), 827: that there are lacking in ἐπιούσιος the two decisive things which give ἡ ἐπιοῦσα ἡμέρα its meaning, namely, the article and ἡμέρα, since ἐπιέναι alone simply means "to come." But these are not very cogent objections. Cf. τεταρταῖος in Jn. 11:39 from ἡ τετάρτη ἡμέρα, P. W. Schmiedel, *Schweiz. Theol. Zeitschr.*, 31 (1914), 42.

[14] Ac. 7:26 (+ ἡμέρα); 16:11; 20:15; 21:18; 23:11 (+ νύξ). It is common in Joseph. (Schl. Mt., 211).

[15] Xenoph. An., I, 7, 1, where ἡ ἐπιοῦσα ἕως is said at midnight. In Plat. Crito, 44a, τῆς ἐπιούσης ἡμέρας is said when it was ὄρθρος βαθύς. Jos. Ant., 10, 169 f.: νυκτὸς ... φονεύει ... τῇ δ' ἐπιούσῃ ... ἧκον. The possibility of such an understanding is not ruled out by Poll. Onom., I, 65 : τὸ δ' εἰς τὴν ἐπιοῦσαν μὴ μένον ἐφήμερον (A. Debrunner, ThBl, 8 [1929], 213).

[16] This view is strongly defended by P. W. Schmiedel, *Schweiz. Theol. Zeitschr.*, 30 (1913), 204-220; 31 (1914), 42-69; *Philol. Wochenschr.*, 48 (1928), 1530-1536. Cf. also Pape, *s.v.*; H. J. Holtzmann, *Die Synoptiker* (1901), 63 ; A. Harnack, SAB, 1904, 208; *Erforschtes und Erlebtes* (1923), 24 f.; A. Plummer, *St. Luke*⁴ (1906), 295 f.; Zahn Kan., 710, n. 1; Einl., II, 319; Mt.⁴ (1922), 280 f. (ἐπιούσιος means "for the day which follows"; Mt. is a not very good rendering of the Aram. which should give τὸν εἰς τὴν αὔριον); Bock (→ n. 6), 14-22 (also referred to the Eucharist); A. Deissmann, *Nt. liche Studien f. G. Heinrici* (1914), 115-119; *Festschr. f. R. Seeberg*, I (1929), 299-306 (where a distinction is made between the "usual" meaning, "something appointed for the following day," and the "occasional," "the bread which is appointed for to-morrow as a reward"); J. Hensler, *Das Vaterunser* (1914), 9-13; J. Weiss in *Die Schriften des NT*³ (1917), on Mt. 6:11; A. T. Robertson, *A Grammar of the Greek NT*³ (1919), 159; Moult.-Mill., *s.v.*; A. Steinmann, *Die Bergpredigt* (1926), 104 f.; Kl. Mt. on 6:11; Schl. Mt., 211-213; K. Bornhäuser, *Die Bergpredigt*² (1927), 157 f. (here, as in Schl., it is stressed that the Rabbis apparently referred to prayer for the morrow's bread, but this is not very certain); J. H. Moulton and W. F. Howard, *A Grammar of NT Greek*, II (1929), 313; Gerlach, *Deutsches Pfarrerblatt*, 34 (1930), 647-648; T. Innitzer, *Komm. zum Ev. d. hl. Mt.*⁴ (1932), 129 f.; H. Greeven, *Gebet und Eschatologie* (1931), 87-90; F. Stiebitz, *Philol. Wochenschr.*, 47 (1927), 889-892 (ἐπιούσια in the pap. first means *diaria* or "portion for the following day," but then there is a strong suggestion of meagre quantity and poor quality). Cf. F. Stiebitz in *Listy Filologické*, 35 (1926), 71-84; 208-219; 58 (1931), 115-122, 254-261; A. Bischoff (→ n. 57), who

however, refer it to the coming aeon. [17] With the same derivation from ἡ ἐπιοῦσα, the word may also refer, of course, to the day which is "already breaking." In this case, we should have a morning prayer in which bread is requested for the day now dawning. It might also be pointed out that in the ancient world the day began the evening before, so that even later in the day it might well refer to the new "day" which was shortly to begin. [18]

The other derivations start with the prep. ἐπί and a form of the verb εἶναι. They all suffer from the objection that the ι is not elided. To overcome this it is no longer necessary to plead the deficient linguistic sense of the author who is supposed to have coined the word, possibly a Jewish Christian. [19] Nor does one need to refer to περιούσιος as a parallel construction which often served the same end. [20] For recent koine research has revealed a growing tendency in the koine to keep the constituent parts of composite words. [21] The only trouble is that in this case it would produce the very

derives ἐπιούσιος from ἡ ἐπιοῦσα, but thinks there is an error in translation ; A. Debrunner, Glotta, 4 (1913), 249, who accepts the derivation from ἡ ἐπιοῦσα as possible, cf. ibid., 13 (1924), 170. E. Gaar, Βιβλίον Ἑλληνικόν B (Vienna, 1931), 155 suggests ὁ εἰς τὴν ἐπιοῦσαν ἡμέραν ἄρτος, following T. Innitzer, supra, and also G. Kroening in Gymnasium, 22 (1904), 165-168 : "reaching to the coming day." J. K. Zenner, Zeitschr. f. kath. Theol., 17 (1893), 173 f., sees in the request for bread only for the next day an expression of modesty, following Hilgenfeld's reading of Ps. Sol. 5:15 : ἡ χρηστότης ἀνθρώπου ἐν φίλῳ καὶ ἐπ᾽ αὔριον, "extends only to friends and only till the morrow."

[17] R. Eisler, ZNW, 24 (1925), 190-192 ; J. Schousboe, Revue de l'Histoire des Religions, 48 (96) (1927), 233-237; A. Schweitzer, Die Mystik d. Ap. Pls. (1930), 233-235; J. Jeremias, Jesus als Weltvollender (1930), 52. This view is opposed by Greeven, op. cit., 88 f.; H. Huber, Die Bergpredigt (1932), 123-125 and others.

[18] In favour of the dawning day, cf. Warth-Löckle, ThStKr, 57 (1884), 769-777; C. Cron, NJbch. f. Philol. u. Pädagogik, 140 (1889), 109-113; 144 (1891), 288-299; A. Kappeler, Schweiz. Theol. Zeitschr., 31 (1914), 147-156 : a morning and evening cultic prayer ; the discussion between Schmiedel and Kappeler in Schweiz. Theol. Zeitschr., 31 (1914), 192 f.; 32 (1915), 118-122; 131-133; F. Nägelsbach, Der Schlüssel z. Verständnis d. Bergpredigt (1916), 40-44 (the word has crept into the Lord's Prayer by error from a morning prayer); M. J. Lagrange, Evangile selon St. Matthieu² (1923), 129 f.; Evang. selon St. Luc² (1921), 323; Liddell-Scott, s.v. for preference ; C. G. Montefiore, The Synoptic Gospels, II² (1927), 101 f. (ἐπιούσιος in an evening prayer means for the coming day and in a morning prayer for the day just beginning); Huber, op. cit.; Dausch, Synpt. on Mt. 6:11. Cf. also Fridrichsen (→ n. 52). Materially R. Wimmerer, Glotta, 12 (1923), 68-82, by an analysis of ἐπιέναι, reaches the sense of "the current day" from "the day just dawning." An opposite view is taken by A. Debrunner, Glotta, 13 (1924), 167-171.

[19] As suggested by Hönnicke (→ n. 24), 177; Bolliger (→ n. 24), 283; Debrunner (→ n. 20), who abandoned this view because of the example in the pap., ThLZ, 50 [1925], 119. Deissmann, Studien f. G. Heinrici (→ n. 16), 118 f., had already seen in the word an instance of popular construction.

[20] Meyer → n. 29; A. Kamphausen, Das Gebet d. Herrn (1866), 86; Debrunner, Glotta, 4 (1913), 251; Schweiz. Theol. Zeitschr., 31 (1914), 38 : περιούσιος provides a word very similar in sound to ἐπιούσιος. A material contrast to περιούσιος is assumed by Münscher → n. 29; Bolliger (→ n. 24), 281 f. : περιούσιος means "what is beyond the need" and ἐπιούσιος "what satisfies it"; but this is rightly rejected by Schmiedel (→ n. 13), 50 f., since οὐσία does not have the sense of "need" in περιούσιος. B. Weiss (→ n. 23), 135 n., and Sickenberger (→ n. 24) agree with Bolliger. Rönsch (→ n. 24) thinks that περιούσιος and ἐπιούσιος are almost synon. (referring to Jerome), but that the former was avoided because it also meant "abundant."

[21] Debrunner, Glotta, 4 (1913), 251. The history of the hiatus question is interesting. At first examples of the non-avoidance of the hiatus were given, like ἐπιεικής, ἐπιορκεῖν, where we have to reckon, of course, with factors in linguistic history. Then with the rise of koine research it was realised that the koine was less precise in this matter. Thus Debrunner could point to the pap. word ἐπιημερινός, P. Oxy., VI, 924, or to ἐπιετής with ἐπέτειος in Polyb., III, 55, 1, or to ἀξιοεπίτευκτος and ἀξιόαγνος in Ign. R., prooem. (→ n. 24), 169; in the same passage one might also point to ἀξιέπαινος as a sign of freedom in this regard. Those who do not think the hiatus question a decisive argument

opposite of the result intended, causing confusion rather than clarity in relation to the composition of the term. [22] Derivation from ἐπεῖναι holds out no greater promise, since the verb was familiar in the elided form. [23] A so-called hypostatisation has been suggested, i.e., a construction comparable to the form ἐπιμήνιος. An older explanation is that ἐπιούσιος is formed from ἐπὶ τὴν οὐσίαν in the sense of "belonging to existence or to life." [24] But οὐσία is not used popularly in the sense of "existence." [25] The related constructions ἀνούσιος, ἐνούσιος, ἐξούσιος, περιούσιος, ὑπερούσιος do not display this meaning. A newer derivation from ἐπὶ τὴν οὖσαν, sc. ἡμέραν, "for the present day," [26] has found much acceptance, but against it there is still the fact that ἡ οὖσα is not attested without ἡμέρα. [27] Less probable are the assumptions that ἐπιούσιος is constructed in contrast to περιούσιος and means "not exceeding our need" as opposed to "exceeding our need," [28] or that it means "what is ἐπί," i.e., "what is for a

---

against derivation from ἐπί + εἶναι will be found in n. 23 to n. 28. Special attention may be drawn to the judgment of philologists. Brugmann/Thumb, Liddell-Scott, Holzinger, Debrunner, Rogge and Moulton/Howard (→ n. 11; 16; 18; 26; 31) are not swayed by the hiatus. A different view is taken by Robertson (→ n. 16); Wimmerer (→ n. 18) and G. Rudberg, *Symbolae Osloenses,* 2 (1924), 42.

[22] This has been advanced by Schmiedel (*Schweiz. Theol. Zeitschr.,* 30 [1913], 214; 31 [1914], 49; ThBl, 8 [1929], 258), Wimmerer and Nägelsbach (→ n. 18), and also Holzinger (→ n. 11), as an argument against derivation from εἶναι. The objection still has force.

[23] So Hönnicke (→ n. 24). The assumption of a new construction from ἐπί and a form of εἶναι lightens the difficulty of the hiatus acc. to Debrunner (→ n. 26). B. Weiss, *Das Mt.-Ev.*[9] (1910), 135 f. derives ἐπιούσιος from ἐπεῖναι, "to belong to."

[24] So already Origen. The main proponent is Cr.-Kö., *s.v.* Cf. also H. Rönsch, ZwTh, 27 (1884), 385-393; E. A. Sophocles, *Greek Lexicon of the Roman and Byzantine Periods* (1888), *s.v.*; A. Bolliger, *Schweiz. Theol. Zeitschr.,* 30 (1913), 276-285, with a reply by Schmiedel, *ibid.,* 31 (1914), 42-69; Dalman WJ, I, 321-334; T. Innitzer, *Komm. z. Evang. d. hl. Lk.*[3] (1922), 256; J. Sickenberger, *Unser ausreichendes Brot gib uns heute* (1923); F. Hauck, ZNW, 33 (1934), 199-202; probably also G. Hönnicke, NkZ, 17 (1906), 176-178. A. Debrunner, *Glotta,* 13 (1924), 170 thinks this a possible derivation, though he himself does not adopt it.

[25] Examples are given in Cr.-Kö., *s.v.* and B. Weiss (→ n. 23). Wimmerer regards these as convincing (→ n. 18). Meyer (→ n. 29), Cron (→ n. 18), Schmiedel, Robertson, Schlatter (→ n. 16) accept οὐσία in the sense of "existence" as a philosophical term, but not a popular. Moult.-Mill., *s.v.* ἐπιούσιος and οὐσία. οὐσία in the pap. means "ability," and it is used abstractly only in the magic pap. The whole matter is very uncertain acc. to A. Debrunner, *Der Kirchenfreund* (→ n. 26).

[26] This has been advanced by A. Debrunner, *Glotta,* 4 (1913), 249-253, and defended by him against Schmiedel (*Schweiz. Theol. Zeitschr.,* 31 [1914], 38-41), Wimmerer (→ n. 18), Holzinger (→ n. 11) and Bonnacorsi (*Indogerm. Forschungen,* 52 [1934], 172, n. 1). Cf. also Debrunner, *Der Kirchenfreund,* 59 (1925), 246-248; ThBl, 8 (1929), 212 f., with Schmiedel's rejoinder, *ibid.,* 258 f. and Debrunner's reply, *ibid.,* 259 f. Further opposition to Debrunner may be seen in G. Rudberg, *Symbolae Osloenses,* 2 (1924), 42; 3 (1925), 76 f., and Gerlach (→ n. 16). Ἡ οὖσα ἡμέρα is found in Soph., a similar expression in the pap., and a related use of the part. ὤν in Ac. 13:1; 14:13 D. The form of the construction is supported by ἐπιμήνιος, ἐπιδέξιος etc. There are instances of the omission of ἡμέρα at least with ἡ ἐπιοῦσα, if not with ἡ οὖσα. With increasing definiteness Debrunner then shows that the new construction (ἐφ-, καθ-) ἡμερούσιος instead of ἡμερήσιος can be explained only in terms of the related ἐπιούσιος. He is supported by K. Brugmann-A. Thumb, *Griech. Gramm.*[4] (1913), 675; Liddell-Scott for preference, and to some extent Moulton/Howard (→ n. 16). Cf. also A. Klotz, *Philol. Wochenschr.,* 45 (1925), 86; J. Coppens, *Ephemerides Theologicae Lovanienses,* 7 (1930), 297 f. Cf. P. Kretschmer, *Glotta,* 17 (1929), 215.

[27] So Schmiedel (→ n. 59), 211; Deissmann, *Studien f. G. Heinrici* (→ n. 16); Schmid (→ n. 46), 28; Moult.-Mill., *s.v.*; Rudberg (→ n. 21); for further considerations, cf. the discussion between Debrunner and Holzinger (→ n. 11).

[28] → n. 20.

purpose," or "what is above." [29] A combination of both derivations, i.e., from ἰέναι and from εἶναι, is the view that a word originally derived from ἰέναι was later thought to be connected with οὐσία. [30] Even the biopsychological way of Rogge, [31] though fundamentally correct, does not lead to an incontestable result, since the series of constructions in which ἐπιούσιος is to be placed is not beyond question.

2. The Meaning of ἐπιούσιος.

a. The review of linguistic possibilities has shown that there can be no linguistic objections to its derivation from ἐπιέναι and esp. from ἡ ἐπιοῦσα. It is worth noting that even Debrunner, who takes another course, regards this as possible. [32] There is strong support for it in Ev. Heb. which acc. to Jerome has *mahar*. For many this is the decisive reason for translating ἐπιούσιος "for the morrow." [33] The convincing element is not the antiquity of Ev. Heb., but that it is in Aram., so that even if it is retranslated from the Gk., [34] which is not established, it will naturally give the Lord's Prayer in the form common to Aramaic speaking Jewish Christian circles in Palestine, and this form will be as near the *ipsissima verba domini* as we can get. [35] On the other hand, the Ev. Heb. is not uncontested, nor is its nature wholly clear. [36] The parts of it known to us do not exclude the influence of alien ideas. On the present state of our knowledge of this Gospel we cannot rule out the possibility that the bread for the morrow of Ev. Heb. indicates a spiritual understanding of the request. This was common in the early Church and led to the complete suppression of the request for bread, e.g., in the Greek text of the Act. Thom. [37] This does not mean that we should set aside the testimony of Ev. Heb. What it does mean is that the remark of Jerome on the text of the petition in Ev. Heb. does not lead to the original text with such certainty that all further discussion must cease. [38]

This discussion takes various turns. An important part is played by the question whether this interpretation is compatible with what Jesus says about anxiety, esp. in Mt. 6:34 : μὴ οὖν μεριμνήσητε εἰς τὴν αὔριον. It is not merely a question of whether prayer for things of the morrow is anxiety. [39] Schmiedel and others have rightly argued

---

[29] L. Meyer, *Zeitschr. f. vgl. Sprachforschung,* 7 (1858), 410-430 : "what is ἐπί = for something, i.e., for life"; *Über d. 4. Bitte d. Vaterunsers* (1886); NGG, 1886, 245-259 : "what is ἐπί = above" (abandoning the earlier view), contested in 1891 by Cron (→ n. 18). Cf. B. Weiss (→ n. 23): "which is for us." Kamphausen (→ n. 20), 72-102, adopted Meyer's first view, and he again was followed by F. W. Münscher, *Neue Jahrbücher f. Philol. u. Pädagogik,* 142 (1890), 112-115.

[30] Kappeler (→ n. 18); Rogge (→ n. 31).

[31] C. Rogge, *Philol. Wochenschr.,* 47 (1927), 1129-1133 : ἐπιούσιος is grouped linguistically with ἐπιτήδειος, ἐφόδια, ἐπιμήνια etc., in which the ἐπί denotes "meeting a need." The example of the last word soon led to its use with οὐσία on the basis of ἡ ἐπιοῦσα and with the sense of "meeting the need of the day." This view is countered by P. W. Schmiedel, *ibid.,* 48 (1928), 1530-1536.

[32] → n. 16.

[33] So Bock, Schmiedel, Hensler, Zahn, Steinmann, Innitzer Mt., Greeven (→ n. 16); esp. Schmiedel (→ n. 13), 52 ff. Even A. Seeberg (*Die 4. Bitte* [→ n. 8], 4) agrees that the Ev. Heb. strongly supports the sense of "for to-morrow," though he himself, with Haussleiter (→ n. 8), takes *mahar* to mean "future."

[34] So Völter (→ n. 9), Bolliger (→ n. 24), Debrunner (→ n. 26).

[35] This is constantly emphasised by Schmiedel (→ n. 16), as also by Zahn (→ n. 16).

[36] W. Bauer, RGG², II, 1673; IV, 473; M. J. Lagrange, *Rev. Bib.,* 31 (1922), 328. G. Kuhn (*Schweiz. Theol. Zeitschr.,* 31 [1914], 35) also rejects the appeal to Ev. Heb. Cf. E. v. Dobschütz, *The Harvard Theological Review,* 7 (1914), 313 f., and J. Wellhausen, *Einleitung in die drei ersten Evangelien²* (1911), 116 f.

[37] Cap. 144.

[38] In any case, the history of Jewish Christianity is fairly obscure.

[39] So Schweitzer (→ n. 17), 233 f.

that prayer is the best antidote to anxiety. [40] The problem is whether I can seek tomorrow's bread for to-day. [41] "What I pray for in advance for the time when I need it, I should not pray to have given me, or to receive, in advance." [42] This leads to further problems. Thus it is surprising to find reference to two times in so short a sentence. [43] Again, on this view the whole petition seems "neither natural nor modest" [44] — an impression given even when no discrepancy is seen with Mt. 6:34. [45] This objection would not be convincing if it were a matter of praying for the bare minimum of food for the morrow. [46] In this case, the request for bread for the morrow would be a request to be kept from having to beg, [47] a request which sets the disciple in the normal course of life and work, [48] a request "for honest food and shelter." [49] But this assumption is unfounded. For wages in Palestine were not given to day-workers the night before. [50] Such workers were given the usual meals during the working day. [51] Nor could the disciples pray in this way any more than daily workers. For they were sent out without bread or money (Mk. 6:8; money according to Mt. and Lk.) because the labourer is worthy of his hire and they were to eat what was set before them in the house (Lk. 10:7). [52] Furthermore, the petition is not concerned whether, when or how the means of livelihood are attained; they are simply sought and received at the hands of God.

---

[40] Schmiedel, Prot. Monatshefte, 18 (1914), 364: "Prayer is the best antidote to this anxiety." Cf. also Deissmann, Innitzer Mt., Montefiore and Schmiedel (→ n. 16 and n. 18).
[41] So Warth and Löckle (→ n. 18), 774; Rönsch (→ n. 24), 386; J. K. Edwards (→ n. 57); Völter, PrM, 19 (1915), 22 f.; W. C. Allen (→ n. 72), 59; Bolliger (→ n. 24); Nägelsbach (→ n. 18); Sickenberger (→ n. 24); Wimmerer (→ n. 18); Cr.-Kö. (→ n. 42).
[42] Cr.-Kö., 407.
[43] Bischoff (→ n. 57), 269.
[44] Völter (→ n. 9), 275; similarly Wimmerer (→ n. 18), 69.
[45] Hönnicke (→ n. 24) takes the view that our bread for the morrow is compatible with Mt. 6:34, but he says on p. 177: "The petition hardly seems natural if we construe it: 'Give us daily our bread for the morrow.' And it certainly seems in this case to express anxiety that we do not know what we shall be eating to-morrow." The question raised by Meyer, Kamphausen, Hönnicke, Haussleiter, Wellhausen, Völter, Seeberg (→ n. 8; 9; 24; 29; 36) and others, namely, why [τὸν ἄρτον] τὸν εἰς τὴν αὔριον is not used for "for the morrow" as in Mt. 6:34, is not decisive, but it has a certain weight. This is shown by the many attempts at explanation found in A. Bischoff, Schmiedel, Deissmann, Moult.-Mill., Fridrichsen (→ n. 16; 57; 72).
[46] Deissmann, Studien (→ n. 16), 117 f., refers to the proverbial saying: "Those who have no bread in the house overnight," as an expression of the deepest poverty. W. Schmid, Glotta, 6 (1915), 28 f., tries to find an ancient equivalent in Dio Chrys., but this is contested by Wimmerer (→ n. 18), 73 f.
[47] Zn. Mt.[4] (1922), 282: "The petition is to the effect that at the right time, i.e., to-day, God will give us the food which we shall need to-morrow. Even the poorest beggar ... may pray thus; though in his case the petition will take on the sense that the heavenly Father should deliver him from this sorry situation of ἀτροφεῖν πρὸς τοὐπιόν ..." Schl. Jk., 189 f.: "We pray to God for the bread necessary for the coming day; if we do not have the ἐφήμερος τροφή, we are forced to ask men too."
[48] Schl. Mt., 211 f.: "The fact that the disciple should ask his food from God in the confidence that he will receive it does not mean that he is lifted out of the natural order and that his life is grounded on a recurrent miracle."
[49] Schl. Mt., 212; Zn. Mt.[4], 281: "The daily worker, who receives his wages in the evening, works to-day in order that he may eat to-morrow"; so, too, Meyer (→ n. 29), Steinmann and Bornhäuser (→ n. 16). W. Crönert, Gnomon, 4 (1928), 89, n. 1 and 576, adduces some examples from antiquity to support the view of Stiebitz that ἐπιούσια corresponds to diaria (→ n. 16). On the other hand, P. Wahrmann, Glotta, 17 (1929), 215 raises the question: "Why must food be measured out beforehand for the following day?"
[50] Dalman, WJ, I, 325: "There is no indication in Jewish literature that the day's portion was given out the day before."
[51] Ibid., 324.
[52] This view is also found in Nägelsbach (→ n. 18) and A. Fridrichsen, Symbolae Oslo-enses, 2 (1924), 31-42.

And it is of the very nature of faith, from which the request springs, that it expects God's help and counts on it for the very time when it is needed, and not before.[53] The same attitude of faith may be seen in the story of the manna in Ex. 16. Nor is it false allegorising to adduce this,[54] for the unity of the OT and the NT comes out strongly at this very point. Thus ἐπιούσιος in the sense of "for the morrow" is hardly conceivable in the concrete situation in which the Lord's Prayer is given, and it leads in fact to an attitude very different from the attitude of faith found in the OT and the NT.

b. Interpretations which remain in the context of time, but point in a very different direction, are the eschatological and the spiritual. The former makes of the fourth petition a repetition of the second. The latter is so closely linked by A. Seeberg with baptism and the Lord's Supper that it loses all probability, and the supporting exposition of the fathers and ancient versions[55] is of more historical than linguistic value. The main objection to both interpretations is that "bread for the morrow" would be an unusual image quite out of keeping with the simple diction of the Lord's Prayer. The argument that the three last petitions are linked by καί and that they thus constitute a unity is no more convincing than the claim that all the others are concerned with the kingdom of God, and that therefore this must apply to the fourth petition too. For the four petitions are united in the fact that they embrace our needs.[56]

c. It is also impossible to sustain the theories that the reference is to panis secundarius, or to what is ἐπί, or to the opposite of περιούσιος, i.e., "sufficient" rather than "super-abounding."[57]

d. The truth seems to be that ἐπιούσιος is not an indication of time but of measure, which is not sufficiently clearly expressed in the suffix, of which Aram. makes a rich use, or in ἡμῶν. The fact that, although there is no objection to the derivation from ἡ ἐπιοῦσα, philologists have sought other derivations, is just as striking as is the further fact that this search all tends in the one direction, namely, that ἐπιούσιος defines the amount of bread.

---

[53] It is worth noting that Schmiedel (→ n. 13), 66 f. can overcome the difficulty posed by σήμερον only by construing "Give us to-day" as "Give us in some way the certainty that we shall receive what we are asking for at the right time."

[54] So Schmiedel, Schweiz. Theol. Zeitschr., 30 (1913), 217; 31 (1914), 63 f. The story of the manna is rightly recalled by Bolliger (→ n. 24) and 'Cr.-Kö., 408: "This is as it were the basis of the petition in salvation history." Similarly Eisler (→ n. 17) and Sickenberger (→ n. 24) refer to Ex. 16.

[55] E. Nestle, ZNW, 1 (1900), 250-252, though he does not decide for any one meaning, thinks it striking that "regular" has found such wide acceptance; in this respect Schmiedel (→ n. 40) points to Jn. 6:27.

[56] As against Seeberg (→ n. 8) and Schweitzer (→ n. 17). The justification of praying for something material is contested by Meyer (→ n. 29). Though Cron (→ n. 18), 291, 296 rejects this interpretation, he sees support for it in its closer agreement with the whole attitude of the prayer. It cannot be supported by Marcion's version of Lk. 11:3 (τὸν ἄρτον σου instead of ἡμῶν), which is undoubtedly an alteration of the original.

[57] → n. 20. We need hardly mention the view once propounded and later abandoned by G. Kuhn, Schweiz. Theol. Zeitschr., 31 (1914), 33-38; (→ n. 8), that ἐπιούσιος is a translation of לחמנא הלכה; "our current bread," since הלכה in the Rabb. writings denotes movement rather than what is customary (דרך). Again, we have only a brilliant conjecture in the theory of A. Bischoff (ZNW, 7 [1906], 266-271) that a defective מָחָר gave rise to ἐπιούσιος = מָחָר and that the real meaning is "the bread which we have earned." The same is true of the suggestion of F. H. Chase (→ n. 6), supported by E. Goltz, Das Gebet in der ältesten Christenheit (1901), 49, that ἐπιούσιος like σήμερον and τὸ καθ᾽ ἡμέραν rests on the single דיומא. Again, the attempt of I. K. Edwards, ZwTh, 29 (1886), 371-378 to go back to the Targumic expression סעיד לחמא (bread which endures) does not lead us any further.

This may happen in two ways. On the one hand, ἐπιούσιος may mean "for to-day." In this case, Jesus is teaching us in prayer to direct our attention to this day and its needs, and daily to ask and to receive our sustenance from God's hand. Linguistically ἐπιούσιος may then be explained again in two ways : from ἡ ἐπιοῦσα in the sense of "the dawning day," or from ἐπὶ τὴν οὖσαν, sc. ἡμέραν. If we take the first course, we must regard the prayer as a morning prayer.[58] For, although the Jewish Sabbath began in the evening, this mode of reckoning applied only in cultic things,[59] and there would be no sense in praying for "this day's bread" in the afternoon, shortly before the commencement of the new "day." A possible Heb. equivalent is לֶחֶם הַיּוֹם, cf. Prv. 27:1, where αὔριον = יוֹם מָחָר is distinguished from ἡ ἐπιοῦσα = יוֹם.[60] We may well ask with Schlatter, however, whether the Lord's Prayer is to be tied in this way to a particular time.[61] There is also another difficulty. The addition τὸ καθ' ἡμέραν (בכל־יום) or σήμερον (יומא דין) serves the purpose of keeping our attention fixed on the one current day. In the short and simple formulation of the Lord's Prayer, the addition of a further definition serving the same purpose surely seems to be tautological.[62] If we accept this objection, we are forced to give up all temporal understanding of the word ἐπιούσιος.[63] The example in the pap. (→ 590 f.) points in the same direction. For if we assume that no more than -ων is to be added to ἐπιουσι-, and that there is nothing else between this and the sum of ½ obol,[64] the sense of a daily ration (diaria), whether we think of ἐπὶ τὴν οὖσαν (ἡμέραν) or ἡ ἐπιοῦσα, is hardly probable in view of the smallness of the amount.[65] More likely is the mention of something necessary or something additional.[66]

e. This leads us to the second way in which the word may define the amount of bread. This rests mainly, though not exclusively, on the interpretation ἐπὶ τὴν οὐσίαν, which gives us the sense of "necessary." We are reminded of the story of the manna, the point of which is that those who gathered too much had no superfluity, and those who gathered too little had no lack.[67] We are also reminded of the saying in Prv. 30:8

---

[58] The idea of a morning prayer is accepted by Cron, Nägelsbach (→ n. 18), and P. Fiebig, Das Vaterunser (1927), 79-83, though the latter construes ἐπιούσιος as "what we need." Montefiore and Kappeler suggest a morning and evening prayer (→ n. 18), and Cron agrees in respect of later use (→ n. 18).

[59] In ordinary things the Jew reckons from the morning, Dalman WJ, I, 332; Arbeit u. Sitte in Palästina, I (1928), 596 f. Thus Schmiedel's argument against the sense of "the dawning" day (Schweiz. Theol. Zeitschr., 30 [1913], 207) loses its point. The fact that the Gk. day began in the evening (Wimmerer [→ n. 18], 75) did not affect Palestine.

[60] Lagrange Mt. (→ n. 18).

[61] Schl. Mt., 212.

[62] As against A. Debrunner, Schweiz. Theol. Zeitschr., 31 (1914), 41; Glotta, 13 (1924), 170 f. Cf. Deissmann, Stud. f. G. Heinrici (→ n. 16), 115 f. Doubt is also thrown on Fridrichsen's hypothesis (→ n. 18) that an original disciples' prayer for bread for the present day has become a family prayer for bread for the coming day, which the family usually keeps in the house. Even recently in country districts in Palestine bread was freshly baked every morning acc. to G. Jentzsch, Neueste Nachrichten aus dem Morgenlande, 78 (1934), 18.

[63] Opponents of a temporal understanding are Münscher (→ n. 29), 113 (on account of the pleonasm), Kothe (→ n. 10), 586 ("Every temporal explanation contains a pleonasm"), and Kamphausen (→ n. 20), 91 f.

[64] F. Zorell, Biblica, 6 (1925), 321 f. suggests ἐπιουσίας δαπάνης. Unfortunately the pap. is not available, so that no fuller investigation of the original is possible, cf. Deissmann in R. Seeberg-Festschrift (→ n. 16), 303.

[65] While Debrunner first suggested "small change" (→ n. 1), he later settled with Stiebitz and Deissmann (→ n. 16) for diaria, Stiebitz in the specific sense of the bare necessity, the minimum quantity and quality. In view of the smallness of the sum Holzinger suggests (→ n. 11) extras or expenses.

[66] Holzinger (→ n. 65).

[67] Ex. 16:18.

which is often adduced in this connection : רְאֵשׁ וָעֹשֶׁר אַל־תִּתֶּן־לִי הַטְרִיפֵנִי לֶחֶם חֻקִּי. Here the קֹח denotes the amount appropriate to the individual. [68] At 24:31 the LXX has for לֶחֶם חֻקִּי τὰ δέοντα καὶ τὰ αὐτάρκη. חסרנון or צרכינן would correspond in Aram. [69] What the Lord has in view is not the space of a day but what is needed by Him and the host of disciples associated with Him. There are many Rabb. parallels for this understanding. [70] If it is true, it expresses confidence that God will give us as we have need. Ἐπιούσιος is not superfluous in this case, and it fits both the Matthean and Lukan versions. This view can also be harmonised easily with the instance in the pap., and the choice of so unusual a word is explained by the difficulty of finding a real Gk. equivalent for the Heb. and Aram. concept — a difficulty which is apparent in the LXX rendering of Prv. 30:8 as well.

As things stand, we cannot say with precision what is the exact derivation of ἐπιούσιος, what was its original sense, or what "occasional" meanings it might have. [71] But in view of the foregoing discussion there can be little doubt that its force is adequately brought out in the rendering : "The bread which we need, give us to-day (day by day)." [72, 73]

Foerster

> ### ἐπισκέπτομαι, ἐπισκοπέω,
> ### ἐπισκοπή, ἐπίσκοπος,
> ### ἀλλοτριεπίσκοπος

† ἐπισκέπτομαι, † ἐπισκοπέω.

The two words form one paradigm. The Attic σκοπέω is a present stem from which only the present and imperf. were formed, and other forms only in the koine. In classical

---

[68] For examples, cf. J. Herrmann, "Der at.liche Urgrund des Vaterunsers" in *Festschr. f. O. Procksch* (1934), 87 f.

[69] Dalman WJ, I, 327; *Jesus-Jeschua* (1922), 124.

[70] Dalman WJ, I, 327, 329 ff.; Str.-B. on Mt. 6:11; K. Bornhäuser, *Der Geisteskampf d. Gegenwart,* 64 (1928), 241-244 and Hauck (→ n. 24) also give Rabbinic material.

[71] For this distinction, cf. Deissmann (→ n. 16).

[72] Many scholars preserve this caution in respect of the linguistic derivation and yet come with remarkable unanimity to the same material explanation. Klotz (→ n. 26), who follows Debrunner, and Wahrmann (→ n. 49) state that not all the linguistic difficulties have been overcome. A. Fridrichsen, who took a definite position in 1924 (→ n. 62), came to the final conclusion in 1930 (*Symbolae Osloenses,* 9 [1930], 62-68): "The most that we can say is that in ἐπιούσιος we probably have a popular term for a small or modest quantity (a 'ration'). The linguistic background and the semasiological development are an open question." Cf. also G. Bonaccorsi, *Primi Saggi di Filologia neotestamentaria,* I (1933), 61-63, 533-539. Our interpretation agrees with that of A. Meyer (→ n. 5) (= לַחְמָא דְמִיסַתְנָא); W. C. Allen, ICC, Vol. 25, Mt.² [1925], 59; E. v. Dobschütz (→ n. 36). Not very different are the views of P. Kretschmer in *Glotta,* 22 (1934), 260 ("necessary" [?] from τὰ ἐπιόντα, "what comes upon one"), and P. Vannutelli in *Athenaeum* (1918), 204 ff. (quoted by Bonaccorsi, 533) (from εἰς τὸ ἐπιόν, "sufficient," Epict. Diss., II, 21, 9 [Debrunner]).

[73] Only when it was too late to use them was the author's attention directed to P. Joüon in *Recherches de Science religieuse,* 17 (1927), 210-229 (cf. BZ, 18 [1929], 365) and E. C. E. Owen in JThSt, 35 (1934), 376 ff.

ἐπισκέπτομαι, ἐπισκοπέω. Cr.-Kö., 998 ff.; Liddell-Scott, I, 657; Moult.-Mill., 243 f.

Gk. these were derived from the root σκεπ-. The present σκέπτομαι is very rare in Attic, though found in Ionic from the time of Homer. [1]

σκοπέω is an iterative and intensive construction from the root σκεπ-, and is thus well adapted as a pres. Thus, e.g., ἐσκόπει denotes continuing or careful scrutiny, whereas ἐσκέψατο refers to the single act. The same is true of ἐπισκοπέω and ἐπισκέπτομαι. [2]

A. ἐπισκέπτομαι, ἐπισκοπέω outside the NT.

1. In secular Gk. ἐπισκέπτομαι is used in the following senses.

a. "To look upon, to consider, to have regard to, something or someone." Soph. Ai., 584: ὦ θάνατε, νῦν μ' ἐπίσκεψαι μολών; Hdt., II, 109: ἔπεμπε τοὺς ἐπισκεψομένους καὶ ἀναμετρήσοντας ὅσῳ ἐλάσσων ὁ χῶρος γέγονε; Xenoph. Cyrop., VI, 3, 21: ἐπισκέψασθε τὰ ὅπλα; VII, 1, 8: ἐπισκέψομαι ἕκαστα πῶς ἡμῖν ἔχει. In the same sense ἐπισκοπέω means "to inspect," Xenoph. An., II, 3, 2: τὰς τάξεις ἐπισκοπῶν. In Oec., 4, 6 it is used of the activity of the king: τοὺς μὲν ἀμφὶ τὴν ἑαυτοῦ οἴκησιν αὐτὸς ἐφορᾷ, τοὺς δὲ πρόσω ἀποικοῦντας πιστοὺς πέμπει ἐπισκοπεῖν. In Plat. Resp., VI, 506b a state is in good order when an informed supervisor watches over it; Epict. Diss., III, 22, 97: (στρατηγός) ... ὅταν τοὺς στρατιώτας ἐπισκοπῇ. It is used in much the same sense of the Cynic: ὅταν τὰ ἀνθρώπινα ἐπισκοπῇ. In pap. letters it is often used at the end in an expression which signifies: "Have a care for yourself," Mitteis-Wilcken, I, 2, 10 (2nd. cent. B.C.): ἐπισκοποῦ δὲ καὶ τὰς ἀδελφάς, P. Oxy., II, 294, 31 (1st cent. A.D.): ἐπισκωποῦ Δημητροῦ[ν] καὶ Δωρίωνα [τὸν πατ]έρα; P. Giess., I, 12, 7: ἐπισκοποῦμαι τὴν σὴν σύνβιον καὶ τοὺς φιλοῦντάς σε πάντας. If the intensive sense as compared with ἐπισκέπτομαι is already apparent in this usage, it comes out quite clearly when the word has a religious significance. As an activity of deities, ἐπισκοπεῖν means "graciously to look down upon ...," [3] "to care for ...," "to watch over ..." It is used of Bacchus in Soph. Ant., 1136: Θηβαίας ἐπισκοποῦντ' ἀγυιάς; of Poseidon in Eur. Iph. Taur., 1414: Ἰλιόν τ' ἐπισκοπεῖ σεμνός; of Pallas Athene in Aristoph. Eq., 1173: ὦ Δῆμ', ἐναργῶς ἡ θεός σ' ἐπισκοπεῖ, "in bodily form the goddess watches over thee"; ibid., 1186: ἐπισκοπεῖ γὰρ περιφανῶς τὸ ναυτικόν, "she manifestly protects the fleet." In acc. with the iterative character of ἐπισκοπέω we do not have here a single action but the expression of an attitude or disposition proper to the gods. The protective blessing of a deity rules or watches over men or things. b. "To reflect on something, to examine it, to submit it to investigation." ἐπισκοπεῖν is used when the action is demanded as something absolutely necessary: Isoc. πρὸς Δημόνικον, 1, 41: πᾶν ὅ τι ἂν μέλλῃς ἐρεῖν, πρότερον ἐπισκόπει τῇ γνώμῃ; Xenoph. Mem., IV, 2, 24: ἐπεχείρησας σαυτὸν ἐπισκοπεῖν ὅστις εἴης; Epict. Diss., I, 11, 38: οὐδὲν ἄλλο ἐπισκοπήσομεν ... ἀλλὰ τὰ δόγματα. On the other hand, ἐπισκέπτομαι is used in cases of a single, specific examination. Thus Plato prefers it in dialogue, e.g., Phaed., 87b: πρὸς δὴ τοῦτο τόδε ἐπίσκεψαι, εἴ τι λέγω; Prot., 348d: Socrates wants to talk with Protagoras because he is convinced that he will best enquire into (ἐπισκέψασθαι) virtue as into other questions which occupy a worthy man. Xenoph. Mem., I, 6, 4: ἐπισκεψώμεθα τί χαλεπὸν ᾔσθησαι τοῦ ἐμοῦ βίου; IV, 2, 25: ἑαυτὸν ἐπισκεψάμενος, ὁποῖός ἐστι. In this sense the term is very common in the pap., e.g., P. Hamb., 25, 2: γράφεις μοι ἐπισκεψάμενον περὶ ὧν ἐγκαλεῖ Διομέδων ... BGU, III, 1004, 6 (3rd cent. B.C.): ἐπισκεψάμενος περὶ τῶν δεδηλωμένων πρόσταξον. Specifically it can mean "to look up a document": Preisigke Sammelbuch, 5232, 32 (1st cent. A.D.): τὴν πρᾶσιν ἐπισκέψασθαι ἐν τῇ βυβλιοθήκῃ; P. Oxy., III, 533, 20 (2nd/3rd cent. A.D.):

---

[1] Kühner-Blass-Gerth, II, 537; W. Veitch, *Greek Verbs Irregular and Defective* (Oxford, 1871), *s.v.* σκέπτομαι; Bl.-Debr.[6] § 101, *s.v.* σκοπεῖν.

[2] I owe this to A. Debrunner, who has also taught me to understand ἐπισκοπέω and ἐπισκέπτομαι in the light of this grammatical fact.

[3] Suid., *s.v.* equates ἐπισκοπέω with καθοράω.

ἐπισκέψασθε ἐκ τοῦ λογιστηρίου τοῦ στρατηγοῦ ἐπιστολὴν τοῦ διοικητοῦ. [4] c. "To visit" : P. Lille, I, 6, 5 (3rd cent. B.C.): διαβάντος μου ἐκ Τεβέτνου εἰς Κορφοτοῦν ἐπισκέψασθαι τὴν ἀδελφήν. In this sense it is esp. used of sick visiting, whether on the part of ministering friends : Plut. De Tuenda Sanitate Praecepta, 15 (II, 129c): τοὺς φίλους ἐπισκεπτόμενον ἀσθενοῦντας; Xenoph. Mem., III, 11, 10 : ἀρρωστήσαντός γε φίλου φροντιστικῶς ἐπισκέψασθαι, or more officially of the doctor : Luc. Philopseudes seu Incredulus, 25 : ἐπεσκόπει δέ με καὶ ἐθεράπευεν Ἀντίγονος; Herodian Hist., IV, 2, 4 : ἰατροί τε εἰσιόντες ἑκάστοτε προσίασι τῇ κλίνῃ καὶ δῆθεν ἐπισκεψάμενοι τὸν νοσοῦντα χαλεπώτερον ἔχειν ἀπαγγέλλουσιν ἑκάστοτε.

2. The LXX gives to the common word ἐπισκέπτομαι a whole series of new meanings. Following up the occasional suggestion given when used of the looking down of the gods, it took on a profound religious sense. In general it was used for the Heb. פָּקַד and took on its many different meanings. It was also used sometimes for בָּקַר, [5] and in isolated cases for דָּרַשׁ, תּוּר, נָחַם, בָּקַשׁ and בָּחַן. Along the lines of the last sense of ἐπισκέπτομαι in secular Gk., the term is used in the LXX, too, for a. "to visit." Ju. 15:1: ἐπεσκέψατο Σαμψὼν τὴν γυναῖκα αὐτοῦ; Sir. 7:35: μὴ ὄκνει ἐπισκέπτεσθαι ἀρρώστον. [6] Also similar to secular usage is sense b. "to look on," ψ 26:4, where we have ἐπισκέπτεσθαι with θεωρεῖν; 4 Βασ. 9:34. A more distinctive meaning is c. "to investigate," "to search," 1 Ἔσδρ. 2:16 (21): ὅπως ... ἐπισκεφθῇ ἐν τοῖς ἀπὸ τῶν πάτερων σου βιβλίοις (for similar usage in the pap. → 600); 2:21 (26); 6:20 (21); 6:22 (23); 2 Ἔσδρ. 4:15, 19; 5:17; 6:1; 7:14; ψ 16:3; as a translation of בָּקַר, Lv. 13:36; of דָּרַשׁ, 1 Ch. 26:31. From this there developed the deeper sense d. "to be concerned about something," "to care for something." In this sense the LXX uses it of the shepherd and his sheep, Jer. 23:2; Zech. 11:16; [7] Ez. 34:11, 12; [8] 2 Ch. 24:6, with the sense of "to keep to ..."; Sir. 7:22 : "If thou hast cattle, be on guard." So also Sir. 49:15 (18). In 2 Ch. 34:12 ἐπισκοπέω is used of the work of ἐπίσκοποι and means "to take oversight" (Heb. נָצַח). [9] Related to c. is e. "to find out about something," 1 Βασ. 17:18 (A); [10] Nu. 14:34; [11] Jdt. 7:7: ἐπεσκέψατο τὰς ἀναβάσεις τῆς πόλεως αὐτῶν. [12] In much the same way ἐπισκοπέω is used for יָדַע in Est. 2:11. The word is often used in the LXX for f. "to muster," Ex. 30:12; in this sense it occurs 43 times in Nu. 1-4. It is variously translated by Luther "to number" or "to order" (A.V. "to take the sum," "to number"), and in one case he simply renders οἱ ἐπεσκεμμένοι "together" for the sum total. Cf. also Nu. 26 passim; Jos. 8:10; Ju. 20 passim; 21; 1 Βασ. 11:8; 13:15; 14:17; 15:4; 2 Βασ. 18:1; 24:2, 4; 3 Βασ. 21 (20):15, 26, 27; 4 Βασ. 3:6; Sir. 17:32. Connected with this usage is the thought of detecting who are absent, and this gives us the sense g. "to miss," pass. "to be missed," "to be absent" 1 Βασ. 20:6 : ἐὰν ἐπισκεπτόμενος ἐπισκέψηταί με ὁ πατήρ σου, "if thy father miss me at the muster."

---

[4] For further examples from the pap. cf. Moult.-Mill., 243 f.; Preisigke Wört.

[5] In Nu. 16:5, however, the translator has obviously confused בֹּקֶר ("morning") with a verbal form of בָּקַר. Again, there is no Heb. equivalent for ἐπεσκέπησαν in Neh. 12:42, and it obviously rests on a misunderstanding of the text.

[6] In Ju. 2:11 ἐπισκέπτομαι is used for נָחַם, the piel of which has the stronger sense of "to comfort."

[7] In א* vid we have ἐπισκέψηται for ζητήσῃ.

[8] Only A.

[9] In Prv. 19:20 (23) there is an obvious misunderstanding of the Heb. original, the confusion of רָע and רֵעַ altering the whole sense.

[10] Luther has besuchen, "to visit."

[11] Only Bab.

[12] Cf. also Jdt. 5:20 (24), where ἐπισκέπτομαι means "to perceive, to realise that ..."

Cf. also 1 Βασ. 20:19, 25, 27; 2 Βασ. 2:30; 4 Βασ. 10:19; Jer. 3:16; Ju. 21:3; 2 Βασ. 2:30 : ἐπισκοπέω for niphal of פָּקַד.

The term ἐπισκέπτομαι has a religious content in the LXX only when God is the Subject of the action. On one occasion ἐπισκοπεῖν is used in a sense similar to the secular idea of the gracious care of the gods for a territory under their protection. In Dt. 11:12 Canaan is described as a land ἣν Κύριος ὁ θεός σου ἐπισκοπεῖται, "upon which God looks down in grace," upon which His eyes rest from the beginning of the year to the end, and which is therefore very fruitful. ἐπισκοπέω is here used for דָּרַשׁ. It denotes an unchanging attitude on God's part. The word ἐπισκέπτομαι actualises this attitude. It is mostly used where we have the rendering "to visit." It combines the various senses of "to visit, to look upon, to investigate, to inspect, to test, to be concerned about, to care for," in description of the act in which the Lord in a special incursion into the course of life of individuals or of a people, mostly Israel, makes known to them His will either in judgment or in grace. It is worth noting that this sense does not occur in secular Greek but only in the context of the OT history of salvation, from which it passes into the NT. This visitation takes place when God draws near to His people in its sin and distress, and shows Himself to be the Lord of history. It may entail the judgment executed by Him. But it may also consist in an act of mercy. The point is that He manifestly enters history. The word "to visit" may signify a visitation of both judgment and grace in the same sentence. Thus we read in Zech. 10:3 : "Mine anger is kindled against the shepherds, and I will punish (visit) the goats ; for the Lord of hosts is gracious to (will visit) his flock the house of Judah." [13]

ἐπισκέπτομαι can thus mean h. "to punish," "to sit in judgment" : Ex. 32:34 : ἦ δ' ἂν ἡμέρᾳ ἐπισκέπτωμαι; Job 35:15 : ὅτι οὐκ ἔστιν ἐπισκεπτόμενος ὀργὴν αὐτοῦ; ψ 58:5 : πρόσχες τοῦ ἐπισκέψασθαι πάντα τὰ ἔθνη; Sir. 2:14(17); Hos. 4:14; Jer. 5:9, 29; Ἰερ. 9:9, 25; Jer. 11:22; 13:21; acc. to Ἰερ. 36(29):32 the judgment will be on individuals ; 37(30):20; 43(36):31; 51(44):29 : ἐπισκέψομαι ἐγὼ ἐφ' ὑμᾶς εἰς πονηρά; Lam. 4:22; God will execute the punishment with a rod : ψ 88:32 : ἐπισκέψομαι ἐν ῥάβδῳ ἀνομίας αὐτῶν, or with famine and sword : Ἰερ. 34:6 (27:8): ἐν μαχαίρᾳ καὶ ἐν λιμῷ; 51(44):13 : ἐν ῥομφαίᾳ καὶ ἐν λιμῷ. But the visitation may be one of blessing, and this gives us sense i. "graciously to accept a man or a people." Gn. 21:1 : "The Lord visited Sarah as he had said ... and Sarah conceived." This does not imply only that God gave an unexpected blessing to a single woman, but also that He enacted part of the history of salvation. Gn. 50:24, 25 : ἐπισκοπῇ δὲ ἐπισκέψεται (פָּקֹד יִפְקֹד) ὑμᾶς ὁ θεός; Ex. 4:31; 13:19; Ju. 1:6; 1 Βασ. 2:21; Jdt. 4:15; 8:33 : ἐπισκέψεται κύριος τὸν Ἰσραὴλ ἐν χειρί μου, says Judith. Ps. 8:4 (in parallelism): ὅτι μιμνήσκῃ αὐτοῦ ... ὅτι ἐπισκέπτῃ αὐτόν (Luther : "that thou acceptest him"). ψ 64:9 : ἐπεσκέψω τὴν γῆν, where God accomplishes the visitation in His creative action in nature, but here, too, with a view to man ; ψ 79:14; 105:4; Sir. 46:14(17); Zeph. 2:7; Jer. 15:15; Ἰερ. 36(29):10; 39(32):41; [14] Ez. 20:40. [15]

j. Finally ἐπισκέπτομαι is used in the sense of "to appoint, to commission, to instal someone" : Nu. 4:27, 32; 2 Ἐσδρ. 1:2 in relation to building the temple ; Neh. 7:1: καὶ ἐπεσκέπησαν οἱ πυλωροί. An important passage is Nu. 27:16 :

[13] A different grammatical construction is used for gracious visitation as compared with judicial. In the former case, the person visited by God is in the acc., while in the latter the thing which causes the visitation is in the acc. and for the person we usually have ἐπί with the acc. Cf. Cr.-Kö., 999 f.

[14] Here ἐπισκέπτομαι is a free rendering of שִׂישׂ.

[15] For דָּרַשׁ. A.V.: "There will I accept them."

ἐπισκεψάσθω Κύριος ὁ θεὸς ... ἄνθρωπον ἐπὶ τῆς συναγωγῆς ταύτης, "Let God the Lord ... set a man over the congregation ... that the congregation of the Lord be not as sheep which have no shepherd." This saying may well have played a part in the installation of leaders in the early Christian Church, and possibly in the selection of the title ἐπίσκοπος for the leaders of the congregation. Cf. also Ac. 6:3.

Outside the Gk. Bible ἐπισκέπτομαι has no religious significance. Philo and Josephus use it only in the secular sense. For Philo it always means "to investigate," as for Plato, and he often puts it at the head of the various trains of thought (ἐπισκεπτέον, ἐπισκεψώμεθα) in his academic writings, e.g., Op. Mund., 92, 101; Leg. All., III, 236; Cher., 21; Congr., 22; Fug., 188 etc. He uses ἐπισκοπέω in the sense of "to contemplate," e.g., celestial phenomena, Mut. Nom., 67; Ebr., 136; "to perceive," Spec. Leg., I, 19; "to test," Decal., 98. In Joseph. ἐπισκέπτομαι is also used of sick visitation, Ant., 9, 179. Only in exposition of biblical visitations does Philo use the word in a deeper sense. [16]

The Rabbis added nothing to the development of the thought of divine visitation. On the other hand, visitation, esp. of the sick, is important in Rabb. ethics. It is one of the works of love which it is the religious duty of every Jew to perform. The visitation of the sick, the sheltering of strangers, the helping of the newly married poor, the comforting of the sorrowing and attendance at funerals are all cultic duties acc. to one Rabbinic opinion (Shab., 127a). Clothing the naked, visiting the sick, comforting the sorrowing and burying the dead are mentioned in Sota, 14a. But visitation of the sick comes first : "Be not negligent to visit the sick, for by such conduct thou wilt reap love," we read already in Sir. 7:35(39). R. Aqiba is more severe : "If any will not visit the sick, it is as though he shed blood," Ned., 40a. "Whoso visits a sick man, lifts a sixtieth part of his burden," Ned., 39b. The point of this visitation is not merely to show sympathy or to convey wishes for recovery, but above all to pray for the sick man.

B. ἐπισκέπτομαι/ἐπισκοπέω in the NT.

1. Jesus undoubtedly knew of the high estimation of the visiting of the sick in Rabbinic ethics. He is adapting formulae such as we find in Sota, 14a when he says that at the Last Judgment the Son of Man will give the kingdom to those to whom He can say : "I was ... sick, and ye visited me : I was in prison, and ye came unto me" (Mt. 25:35 f., 42 f.). Jesus is obviously thinking of the Jewish works of love, but He places the men of all nations (v. 32) under the same command and judges them according to the measure of their fulfilment. Yet in two respects He takes a deeper view. It is not a question of isolated acts, but of a fundamental attitude. Man has to realise that he does not exist of and for himself, but of and for the other. This is to be expressed in his actions. But God is present in this existence with and for others. Jesus makes this clear when He says that what is done or not done to the least of His brethren is done or not done to Him.

---

[16] Cf. his exposition of the visitation of Sarah by God in Cher., 45. Philo understands the wives of the patriarchs allegorically as virtues. But, as pointed out by G. Bertram, he maintains the virgin birth of men of God, and appeals in proof to Gn. 21:1: God causes Sarah to conceive by looking upon her in her loneliness. He uses ἐπισκοπεῖ instead of the LXX ἐπεσκέψατο. There is, of course, no question of divine sonship in the strict sense in spite of the ᾿Ισαὰκ ἐγέννησεν ὁ κύριος in Leg. All., III, 219. For Philo continues : αὐτὸς γὰρ πατήρ ἐστι τῆς τελείας φύσεως, σπείρων ἐν ταῖς ψυχαῖς καὶ γεννῶν τὸ εὐδαιμονεῖν. Cf. also Lk. 1:48 (1 Βασ. 1:11): ἐπέβλεψεν (κύριος) ἐπὶ τὴν ταπείνωσιν τῆς δούλης αὐτοῦ. Cf. on this pt. Clemen, 121; H. v. Baer, Der heilige Geist in den Lukasschr. (1926), 120 f.; J. Heinemann, "Die Lehre vom heiligen Geiste im Judentum und in den Evangelien," MGWJ, 66 (1922), 274 ff. On what follows, cf. the excursus in Str.-B., IV, 559 ff.

James adopts both the best tradition in Jewish ethics and the demand of Jesus for practical love to our neighbours when he says in 1:27: "Pure religion before God and the Father is this, To visit the fatherless and widows in their affliction." [17]

2. Even when ἐπισκέπτεσθαι means "to seek out someone" in the NT, it never implies merely "to visit" them in the usual sense, or for selfish ends, but always "to be concerned" about them, with a sense of responsibility for others. Thus Stephen shows in Ac. 7:23 how there arose in the heart of Moses, learned in all the wisdom of the Egyptians, a desire to go to his brothers, his fellow-countrymen. He seeks them out because he belongs to them and shares responsibility for their destiny. The saying of Paul to Barnabas in Ac. 15:36 is both verbally and materially similar: "Let us go again and visit our brethren in every city ... and see how they do." The visit which they plan to the churches founded by them has the character of a visitation executed in virtue of their apostolic office and commission.

In the same connection we should mention the two passages in the NT in which we have the present stem ἐπισκοπέω. In Hb. 12:14 f. we read: εἰρήνην διώκετε μετὰ πάντων ... ἐπισκοποῦντες μή τις ὑστερῶν ἀπὸ τῆς χάριτος τοῦ θεοῦ. A literal translation is "seeing to it that ..." The sense is thus rather like that of ἐπισκέπτομαι in the LXX when used to describe the work of the good shepherd. It is worth noting that ἐπισκοπεῖν here expresses an attitude which displays the responsibility of the community for the eternal salvation of all its members, and that what later became the specific task of the one, of the leader, is thus represented as a matter for the whole congregation. The congregation as a whole is understood to have as such an essential episcopal ministry and office.

> At 1 Pt. 5:2, AKLP al pler, vg, syrP, copt, arm, eth, interpose ἐπισκοποῦντες before the comma in the sentence: ποιμάνατε τὸ ἐν ὑμῖν ποίμνιον τοῦ θεοῦ, μὴ ἀναγκαστῶς ἀλλὰ ἑκουσίως ... The verse comes in a context which includes the admonition to the elders to care for the flock of God entrusted to them, not of constraint but willingly and joyfully, not for filthy lucre but out of love, not as lords over the community but as examples to the flock. The interposition is obviously to be explained in terms of 2:25 (→ 615), where we read: ἦτε γὰρ ὡς πρόβατα πλανώμενοι, ἀλλὰ ἐπεστράφητε νῦν ἐπὶ τὸν ποιμένα καὶ ἐπίσκοπον τῶν ψυχῶν ὑμῶν. Here the terms ποιμήν and ἐπίσκοπος are brought into close interconnection, and this is repeated in MSS A etc. at 5:2. The official work of presbyters, who are obviously the same as the ἐπίσκοποι καὶ διάκονοι of communities in the Gk. world (→ 615 f.), is thus to follow the pattern of the ποιμήν καὶ ἐπίσκοπος Jesus Christ, consisting in ποιμαίνειν and ἐπισκοπεῖν, in feeding the community and in responsible care for it, in watching over its eternal welfare. The comparison of this responsibility of the elders in the individual church with the work of Jesus Christ in relation to the universal Church conveys to us the dignity of the office as it was understood by early Christianity. Luther says concerning this passage: "To be an episcopus or bishop is to give good heed, to be honest, to watch diligently." [18]

3. If in the sense explained ἐπισκοπέω denotes official activity, [19] according to the LXX ἐπισκέπτομαι can also mean "to look out someone," "to appoint

---

[17] Cf. also Herm. m., 8, 10; s., 1, 8.

[18] *Von den Konziliis und Kirchen*, WA, 50, 574, 20 f.

[19] In the post-apost. fathers ἐπισκοπέω can simply mean "to be a bishop." Thus in Ign. R., 9, 1 we read that "Jesus alone will be her bishop (i.e., of the Syrian church)" when her earthly bishop is taken from her. Ign. greets Polycarp as "the bishop who has God and Jesus Christ as bishop over him," Ign. Pol., prooem. ἐπισκοπεῖν is the activity of the ἐπίσκοπος in Herm. v., 3, 5, 1.

him to an office." Cf. Nu. 27:16; Neh. 7:1 (→ 602 f.). Ac. 6:3 has the term in this sense when the Twelve enjoin the community: ἐπισκέψασθε ἄνδρας ... οὓς καταστήσομεν ἐπὶ τῆς χρείας ταύτης. The process described is of decisive significance in the history of Christian organisation, since here for the first time we have an appointment, not through a call of the incarnate or risen Lord, nor through the self-attestation of the charismatic Spirit in a Christian, but by the election of the members of the congregation. Even when the circle of the Twelve was completed after the elimination of Judas the final decision had still been left with the divine lot. It is assumed, of course, that in the election of the Seven the community will consider only men πλήρεις πνεύματος καὶ σοφίας.

4. The concept of God's visitation, and especially of His gracious visitation of men and nations, passed over from the Heb. Bible and the LXX into the NT. Thus Hb. 2:6 quotes Ps. 8:4 LXX: "Or the son of man, that thou visitest him?" The author expounds this saying christologically. He does not refer it to God's blessing of man as a lowly part of creation, which is the original sense; he relates it to the Son of Man, Jesus Christ.

Again, in Lk. 7:16 we have the insight, impressively attested in the LXX, that God in His gracious intervention in earthly life shows Himself to be the Lord. When the young man at Nain has been raised by Jesus, astonishment falls on the people, καὶ ἐδόξαζον τὸν θεὸν λέγοντες ὅτι προφήτης μέγας ἠγέρθη ἐν ἡμῖν καὶ ὅτι ἐπεσκέψατο ὁ θεὸς τὸν λαὸν αὐτοῦ.

Some MSS add εἰς ἀγαθόν to ἐπεσκέψατο. Their intention is to make it even more clear that this is a visitation of blessing and not of judgment.

Dependence on the OT is also clear in the two passages in the song of Zacharias in which the word ἐπισκέπτομαι occurs: Lk. 1:68: εὐλογητὸς κύριος ὁ θεὸς τοῦ Ἰσραήλ, ὅτι ἐπεσκέψατο καὶ ἐποίησεν λύτρωσιν τῷ λαῷ αὐτοῦ; Lk. 1:78: διὰ σπλάγχνα ἐλέους θεοῦ ἡμῶν, ἐν οἷς ἐπισκέψεται ἡμᾶς ἀνατολὴ ἐξ ὕψους. In both cases the term indicates that God has drawn near to His people and has dealt with it, or will deal with it, in grace. [20] The new feature is that, in association with λύτρωσις, σωτηρία and ἀνατολὴ ἐξ ὕψους, ἐπισκέπτομαι has now become a Messianic concept. In the second saying ἐπισκέπτομαι is related directly to the coming of Christ (→ I, 352).

If the gracious visitation of God applied first to the chosen people, the NT shows how it extends to the Gentiles also. James says in Ac. 15:14: Συμεὼν ἐξηγήσατο καθὼς πρῶτον ὁ θεὸς ἐπεσκέψατο λαβεῖν ἐξ ἐθνῶν λαὸν τῷ ὀνόματι αὐτοῦ. With the refusal of Israel, God creates for Himself a new people out of the Gentile world. We may follow a literal translation: "How God looked to ...," but behind it there stands the whole content of the word ἐπισκέπτομαι in salvation history, and therefore the A.V. could rightly adopt the rendering "visit" (cf. Luther: heimsuchen).

---

[20] At Lk. 1:78 א* BL copt etc. have ἐπισκέψεται, א cACD and many others ἐπεσκέψατο. Schl. Lk., 181 tries to explain the material distinction between the two readings. The fut. suggests that Christ's saving work will take place only when He has grown to manhood, whereas ἐπεσκέψατο expresses the fact that Christ's entry into the world is seen as His own act whereby the Eternal One who lives in God makes Himself the Servant of the divine mercy. It is probable, however, that there is no intended material distinction, but that the fut. is the older reading within the prophecy of vv. 76-79, while the aorist arose by assimilation to the eschatological style of vv. 68-75. Cf. Kl. Lk., ad loc.

† ἐπισκοπή.

1. The word ἐπικοπή first came into common use, and received its distinctive sense, in the LXX. [1] In secular Gk. it is found only once in Luc. Dialogi Deorum, 20, 6, where it means "visit." The urge to find a subst. for the substantive constructions of פָּקַד obviously led to the more extended use of the term in the LXX. Its meaning is closely linked with that of ἐπισκέπτομαι. [2]

Sometimes the subst. is used merely for emphasis. Thus at Gn. 50:24 = Ex. 13:19 we have ἐπισκοπῇ δὲ ἐπισκέψεται ὑμᾶς ὁ θεός along the lines of the Heb. וֵאלֹהִים פָּקֹד יִפְקֹד אֶתְכֶם. Cf. also Gn. 50:25 and Ex. 3:16. ἐπισκοπή never bears the meaning a. "visit" which it has in Luc. and which is common to ἐπισκέπτομαι. On the other hand, it is often used for b. "look," "glance," "contemplation" : Sir. 16:18 : Heaven and earth shake under the divine glance. This rendering is supported by the fact that ἐπισκοπή is a par. of ἐπιβλέπειν in the following verse. The word has a similar sense in Job 5:23 vl. A. More common is the meaning c. "care," "protection." Job 10:12 : "Thy protection hath preserved my spirit." Cf. also Job 29:4; Prv. 29:13; 3 Macc. 5:42. It is God who grants man His gracious care and protection, Wis. 2:20. Man is directed to it. But God is free in respect of it. He may withdraw it. Hence Job's bitter complaint at 6:14 : ἐπισκοπὴ δὲ κυρίου ὑπερεῖδέν με. [3] While ἐπισκοπή in the sense of visitation denotes more commonly the one gracious or judicial intervention of God in human affairs, in these passages it also expresses the grace of the divine preservation of creation. Like ἐπισκέπτομαι, ἐπισκοπή can also have the sense d. "enquiry," "investigation," "examination." Job 31:14 : "When God conducts an examination, what shall I answer him ?" Wis. 3:13 speaks of a testing of souls, as does also Job 7:18, where the parallel is κρίνειν. We may also refer to the technical sense e. "muster" : Ex. 30:12; Nu. 1:21; 7:2; 14:29; 26:18(22), 47(43). On the other hand, there is no equivalent for the verb f. "to miss," pass. "to be missing."

g. The true theological sense of ἐπισκοπή is as the translation of פְּקֻדָּה, "visitation." Again, this takes a twofold form. In the prophets the visitation is usually one of judgment and punishment. This aspect came to predominate so strongly that Hesych. in his lexicon (5th cent. A.D.) gives only ἐκδίκησις as an equivalent. In a much weaker sense the term is used for "scourging" in the sense of judicial discipline in Lv. 19:20. For the most part, however, ἐπισκοπή is not executed by men. It is a destiny which comes on earthly creatures with more than human force. The common fate of men, i.e., the death to which all are subject, is described as ἐπισκοπή in Nu. 16:29. But the Lord who fulfils the visitation is God. Dt. 28:25 : δῴη σε κύριος ἐπισκοπὴν ἐναντίον τῶν ἐχθρῶν. [4]

Judgment will fall on the images of the heathen, Wis. 14:11. The children of the adulteress stand under a curse which will visit them, Sir. 23:24. According to the conceptions of the prophets, there can be no doubt that judgment will come on nations which are not obedient to God. Hence in the language of their eschatology the

---

ἐ π ι σ κ ο π ή. [1] Linguistically the word belongs to a common *koine* type as a *nomen actionis*, like οἰκοδομή in relation to οἰκοδομέω, or παρασκευή to παρασκευάζω. Cf. Bl.-Debr.[6], § 109, 7; P. Tebt., I, 5, 189 (118 B.C.) has ἐπισκοπεία in the sense of "inspection," "revision," "review."

[2] Sometimes the Heb. original is obscure, e.g., Ez. 7:22; Job 34:9; 1 Ἔσδρ. 6:5. On Job 34:9 cf. F. Baumgärtel, *Der Hiobdialog* (1933), 22.

[3] Behind this transl. of Job 6:14 there is obviously a different text from the contested Mas. Cf. F. Wutz, *Transkriptionen* (1933), 342. F. Baumgärtel, *op. cit.*, reconstructs it from the LXX as follows : ורצון שי יעזבני, and translates : "Why has the favour of the Almighty abandoned me ?"

[4] So vl. B*A.

time at which this visitation will come looms with terrifying power. They speak of the καιρὸς ἐπισκοπῆς (Jer. 6:15; 10:15) when the ridiculous idols of human worship will be shattered, or of the ἡμέρα τῆς ἐπισκοπῆς (Is. 10:3), the יוֹם פְּקֻדָּה, which is a reflection of the terrible day of the Lord, if there is not an even closer connection between the two concepts. Sir. 18:20 speaks of a ὥρα ἐπισκοπῆς, Jer. 11:23 of a year of visitation, when the Lord will bring the hosts of evil on the men of Anathoth. [5] God will visit the whole circle of the earth and its kings before establishing His rule on Mount Zion, Is. 24:22. This visitation will be accompanied by thunder and earthquake, Is. 29:6. Thus the thought of approaching ἐπισκοπή takes on apocalyptic colours.

h. While in many instances the day of judgment is simply equated with that of condemnation and punishment, it is also possible for the ἐπισκοπή to include pardon and remission. "Before that judgment comes, try thyself, that thou mayest attain remission in the day of visitation," Sir. 18:20. Hence divine visitation may carry with it a wonderful experience of grace.

This is so in Gn. 50:24 f. (→ 606). According to the prophecy of Joseph God will be gracious to His people Israel and lead it out of Egypt into the promised land. Acc. to Is. 23:16 God will look graciously on Tyre and help it to profitable trade. In Wis. 3:7 it is evident that the καιρὸς ἐπισκοπῆς can be a time of gracious visitation when the righteous will shine as gold in the refinery. In Wis. 4:15 ἐπισκοπή is linked with χάρις and ἔλεος and will be the portion of the righteous. [6] Dreams can be sent by God εἰς ἐπισκοπήν, Sir. 31(34):6.

i. No less notable from the standpoint of the history of the term are the two passages where it has the sense of "office."

The first is Nu. 4:16, where we read of the ἐπισκοπὴ ὅλης τῆς σκηνῆς which is committed to Eleazar, the son of Aaron. Here we can see clearly how the Heb. פְּקֻדָּה and the Gk. ἐπισκοπή lead from the literal sense of oversight to that of official responsibility. More doubtful is the sense of פְּקֻדָּה in the Psalmus Ischarioticus ψ 108:8, where the cursing of the adversary takes the following form in the LXX: τὴν ἐπισκοπὴν αὐτοῦ λάβοι ἕτερος. פְּקֻדָּה may denote either possessions or office (after the model of Nu. 3:32 and 4:16). The LXX assumes the latter sense, though we are not told what the office was. The verse is given the same meaning in Ac. 1:20.

2. a. The NT took over the LXX eschatological concepts καιρὸς τῆς ἐπισκοπῆς and ἡμέρα ἐπισκοπῆς. Jesus Himself refers to the former at Lk. 19:44, and relates it to His own coming to Jerusalem. The day of His entry inaugurates on Mt. Zion the day of gracious visitation for the city. The people receives Him with rejoicing. But Jesus weeps when He sees the city, crying out that it has not known the day of its visitation. The result is not merely the forfeiture of salvation but historical destruction. Thus the visitation becomes a judgment. Once again we can see the great power of the καιρὸς ἐπισκοπῆς to shape history. "The day of visitation" is a phrase used in 1 Pt. 2:12 on the basis of Is. 10:3. The author is warning Christians to live good lives among the heathen. These now calumniate Christians as evil-doers because of their conduct. But if they come to see the truth through their good works, they will glorify God in the day of visitation. This day may be understood as that on which God gives these calumniators at their conversion a true insight into Christian morality. If this is so, the ἐπισκοπή is a personal experience of grace in which Christ becomes Lord over a man. [7]

---

5 Most MSS, of course, have ἐπισκέψεως instead of ἐπισκοπῆς.

6 From Wis. 4:15 the phrase καὶ ἐπισκοπὴ ἐν τοῖς ὁσίοις (or ἐκλεκτοῖς) αὐτοῦ passed into the vl. of Codices A and א at Wis. 3:9.

7 So H. Gunkel in Die Schriften des NT,³ III (1917), ad loc.: The author of the epistle

But the day of visitation may also be understood eschatologically as the great day of judgment when everything will be made manifest and the heathen will have cause to praise God for Christians. [8]

On the basis of 1 Pt. 2:12, or more directly of the LXX, MSS AP and some minusc. and versions add ἐπισκοπῆς to 1 Pt. 5:6 : ταπεινώθητε οὖν ὑπὸ τὴν κραταιὰν χεῖρα τοῦ θεοῦ, ἵνα ὑμᾶς ὑψώσῃ ἐν καιρῷ. On this reading, the visitation denotes the act by which God changes the time of humiliation and suffering into one of exaltation and joy.

b. The NT uses ἐπισκοπή in the sense of "office" as well as "visitation." According to Ac. 1:16 ff. Peter saw in the fate of Judas the fulfilment of OT prophecy. He grounded the need to choose a substitute on ψ 108:8 : "His office let another take" (→ 607). Here, then, the apostolic office is described as ἐπισκοπή. When we know that in 1 Tm. 3:1 the Christian office of bishop (→ 617) is also called ἐπισκοπή, we are tempted to see connections and with their help to explain the development of Christian titles. It should be noted, however, that the term is used for the apostolic office in Ac. 1:16 ff. only because the selection of a replacement was seen to be a fulfilment of the prophecy in ψ 108:8. We cannot deduce from this any closer relationship between the apostolate and the episcopate. On the contrary, early Christianity had a clear sense of the distinction between the two. The term ἐπισκοπή in 1 Tm. 3:1 does not derive from Ac. 1:20 or its OT original. It is newly coined on the basis of the title ἐπίσκοπος which had meantime established itself in the early Church. This is the more easily possible, of course, because ἐπισκοπή is already used for "office" in the language of the LXX. [9]

† ἐπίσκοπος.

A. ἐπίσκοπος in non-biblical Greek.

The word ἐπίσκοπος is best rendered "overseer" or "watch." From this original sense there develops a twofold use which only reunites in a stronger form on Christian soil.

"hopes for a day of visitation when God opens the eyes of the heathen and gives faith in the truth." Cf. also F. Hauck in Das NT Deutsch, ad loc.

[8] Wnd. Kath. Br., ad loc., regards this view as possible and refers to 4 Esr. 7:80 ff.

[9] ἐπισκοπή then established itself as a term for the office of bishop. Cf. already 1 Cl., 44, 1 and 4.

ἐπίσκοπος. Cr.-Kö., 1000 f.; Moult.-Mill., 244 f.; Preisigke Wört., I, 572; III, 114, 400; F. C. Baur, Der Ursprung des Episkopats (1838); J. B. Lightfoot, "The Christian Ministry" in Comm. on Phil.[7] (1883); T. Zahn, Ignatius von Antiochen (1873), 295 ff.; E. Hatch, Die Gesellschaftsverfassung der christlichen Kirchen im Altertum (1883), 17 ff.; 79 ff.; 229 ff.; A. Harnack, Lehre der zwölf Apostel (1884), 140 ff.; E. Loening, Die Gemeindeverfassung des Urchristentums (1888), 47 ff.; 115 ff.; F. Loofs, "Die urchristliche Gemeindeverfassung," ThStKr, 63 (1890), 619 ff.; R. Sohm, Kirchenrecht, I (1892), 81 f.; 157 ff.; J. Réville, Les Origines de l'Épiscopat (1894); Michiels, L'Origine de l'Épiscopat (1900); S. v. Dunin-Borkowski SJ, Die neueren Forschungen über die Anfänge des Episkopats (1900); C. Weizsäcker, Das Apostolische Zeitalter[3] (1902), 613 ff.; Haupt Gefbr. (1902) on Phil. 1:1; H. Bruders SJ, Die Verfassung der Kirche (1904), 105 ff.; 360 ff.; R. Knopf, Das nachapostolische Zeitalter (1905), 147 ff.; A. Harnack RE[3], 20 (1908), 508 ff.; Entstehung u. Entwickelung der Kirchenverfassung (1910), 40 ff.; 60 ff.; P. Batiffol, Urkirche und Katholizismus (1910), 101 ff.; O. Scheel, "Zum urchristlichen Kirchen- und Verfassungsproblem," ThStKr, 85 (1912), 403 ff.; H. Lietzmann, "Zur altchristlichen Verfassungsgeschichte," ZwTh, 55 (1914), 97 ff.; M. d'Herbigny, Theologia de Ecclesia, II (1921), 263 ff.; K. Müller, "Beiträge zur Geschichte der Verfassung der alten Kirche" in AAB (1922), No. 3; Dib. Gefbr. on Phil. 1:1; E. Jacquier, Les Actes des Apôtres (1926), 612 ff.; Loh. Phil. on 1:1; K. Müller, RGG[2], III (1929), 968 ff.; N. Holzmeister, "Si quis

In Gk. ἐπίσκοπος is first used a. with a free understanding of the "onlooker" as "watcher," "protector," "patron." His activity then takes the form of the different senses of ἐπισκέπτομαι, and esp. ἐπισκοπέω, in a gracious looking down upon the one protected and in care for him. Therewith the word ἐπίσκοπος comes to be used b. as a title to denote various offices. The official activities thus described vary, and are usually not too important. In this sense, the word has no religious significance, but is used almost exclusively for very secular appointments with technical and financial responsibilities. On the other hand, behind the sense of "watcher" or "protector" is a religious conception expressed in the fact that it is usually gods who bear this designation.

1. Gods as ἐπίσκοποι.

Where the Greek detected a superhuman force, he assumed a god. The Gk. gods are personified forces, [1] participant in the original force which rules over all. They are thus related to those parts of the creaturely world which are nearest to them and which stand under their protection, whether individuals accepted by them, classes, cities, peoples, places, springs, groves etc. The deity watches over men or things committed to its protection. It cares for them and even fights for them against other gods or powers. The spheres of social life receive their sanctity and their binding seriousness from the fact that deities rule over them. In this quality and activity of a patron the god can be called ἐπίσκοπος. For this word expresses the heart of the relationship, namely, that the god gives particular attention to the object of his patronage. He rules as watcher over the orders which stand under his protection.

Thus in Hom. Il., 22, 254 f. the gods are called watchers over treaties sanctifying their inviolability : μάρτυροι ἔσσονται καὶ ἐπίσκοποι ἁρμονιάων. The same combination of two concepts which later played so great a role in the Christian Church is found also in Herodian Hist., VII, 10, 3, where Zeus is called μάρτυς καὶ ἐπίσκοπος τῶν πραττομένων. In Pind. Olymp., 14, 5 the Charites, the goddesses of Orchomenos, are extolled as protectors of the Minyans, the inhabitants of the city. Aesch. Sept. c. Theb., 271 f. describes the gods as protectors of the market as well as patrons of the city or country : χώρας τοῖς πολισσούχοις θεοῖς πεδιονόμοις τε κἀγορᾶς ἐπισκό-ποις ... That the gods are not merely guardians but also avengers who punish wrong may be seen from the prayer of Electra in Aesch. Choeph., 124 ff., whether we read πατρώιων αἱμάτων ἐπισκόπους with Wilamowitz-Moellendorff or πατρώιων δ' ὀμ-μάτων (or δωμάτων) ἐπισκόπους with Ahrens. Electra trusts that the gods will take up the cause of the murdered father and be gracious to the avenger. Nemesis, the messenger of Dike, is appointed ἐπίσκοπος to take note of the offences of children against their parents: Plat. Leg., IV, 717d. Similarly, on an inscr. of the 2nd cent. A.D. the violator of graves is threatened with the Furies as ἐπίσκοποι, but the wish is expressed in relation to the well-disposed : ἐπισκοποίη δὲ Χάρις καὶ Ὑγεία, IG, XII, 9, 1179, 30 ff. (2nd cent. A.D.). Cf. also IG, XII, 9, 955, 10 ff. The δαιμόνιον can also assume the role of ἐπίσκοπος, P. Par., 63, col. IX, 47 ff. (2nd cent. B.C.). Bacchus is called νυχίων φθεγμάτων ἐπίσκοπος in Soph. Ant., 1148. Pallas Athene holds out her hands over the city as ἐπίσκοπος, Demosth. Or., 421 (ed. J. Bekker, 1854). Callimachus in Hymn., III, 39 calls Artemis ἀγυιαῖς καὶ λιμένεσσιν ἐπίσκοπος. [2] The latter term is conjoined with λιμενόσκοπος in III, 259. Artemis is also called ἐπίσκοπος in Plut. Quaest. Graec., 47 (II, 302c). Acc. to Anth. Pal., IX, 22 pregnant women stand under her protection.

Episcopatum desiderat, bonum Opus desiderat," *Biblica,* 12 (1931), 41 ff.; Meinertz Past. (1931), 47 ff.; Buchberger, LexThK, II (1931), *s.v. Bischof;* J. Jeremias in *Das NT Deutsch,* III (1934), on 1 Tm. 3:1 ff.; H. W. Beyer, "Das Bischofsamt im NT" in *Deutsche Theologie,* 1 (1934), 201 ff.

[1] O. Gruppe, *Griechische Mythologie u. Religionsgeschichte,* II (1906), 1059; U. v. Wila-mowitz-Moellendorff, *Der Glaube der Hellenen,* I (1931), 18 f.

[2] Cf. on this pt. E. Spanhemii *in Callimachi hymnos observationes* (1697), 158.

In a very comprehensive way Plut. in De Camillo, 5 (I, 131 f.) calls Zeus and the gods watchers over all evil and good deeds, so that Thes. Steph. thought the term could best be explained by reference to Hes. Op., 267: πάντα ἰδὼν Διὸς ὀφθαλμὸς καὶ πάντα νοήσας. In fact, in the description of a deity as ἐπίσκοπος we can see the ancient idea of the eye of God scrutinising the acts of men even to the hidden details. In Sext. Emp. Math., IX, 54 we have the corresponding tradition according to which ancient legislators thought of the deity as a watcher (ἐπίσκοπος) over the good works and sins of men, so that none can do ill to his neighbour secretly but must always fear the punishment of the gods. Cf. also Plut. De Fato, 9 (II, 573a).

There is in Cornut. a consistent outworking of the conception that each god has his own sphere of oversight, protection and retribution. Here Zeus and Pallas Athene are the patrons of cities, Theol. Graec. (ed. C. Lang, 1881), 20 (p. 38, 1, Lang), while Pan (27, p. 50, 11), Poseidon (22, p. 44, 2), Apollo (32, p. 68, 4), Dionysus (30, p. 57, 17), and Hermes (16, p. 25, 3) are protective lords over different spheres, and Erato (14, p. 16, 18) is the protectress of the power of dialectical debate.

2. Men as Overseers, Watchers, Scouts.

With the same basic meaning as it has when used of the gods, ἐπίσκοπος can also be applied to the activity of men. But here the sense is not so definite, and can be worked out in many different connections. Protective care, however, is still the heart of the activity which men pursue as ἐπίσκοποι, so that Thes. Steph., s.v. can give the general definition : qui rei alicui curandae praefectus est.

On the border between the human and the divine stands the fabulous creature Argos, who is appointed a watcher acc. to Hes. Fr., 188 (Rzach), and who looks around in all directions with his four eyes. Watchers guard a corpse in Soph. Ant., 217. A dragon is the watcher over Dirce, Eur. Phoen., 932. Plato demands that the νομοφύλακες should be ἐπίσκοποι who see to it that there are no transgressions, Leg., VI, 762d. He describes righteousness itself as a watcher, Leg., IX, 872e. Solon acc. to Plut. De Solone, 19 (I, 88d) appointed an assembly as ἐπίσκοπον πάντων καὶ φύλακα τῶν νόμων.

ἐπίσκοπος is also used in the sense of an "overseer" over goods as the work of a ship's captain or merchant in Hom. Od., 8, 163. Women should be overseers over young married couples, Plat. Leg., VI, 784a. Cf. also VII, 795d. Market overseers have to rule as ἐπίσκοποι σωφροσύνης τε καὶ ὕβρεως, as those who are called to judge what is fair dealing and what is improper, VIII, 849a. Phidias is an overseer over the Periclean buildings, Plut. Pericl., 13 (I, 159e) (→ 613).

The δωμάτων ἐπίσκοπος rules as master of the house, Aesch. Eum., 740.

Hector fell as protector of Troy, Hom. Il., 24, 729 f.

Finally, ἐπίσκοπος can mean a "scout" or "spy," Hom. Il., 10, 38; 342; Soph. Oed. Col., 112.

3. The Cynic as ἐπισκοπῶν and ἐπίσκοπος.

The terms ἐπισκοπῶν and ἐπίσκοπος are used in a special sense in Cynic philosophy. [3] If we are to understand them correctly, we must consider how the forms derived from ἐπισκεπ- relate to the linguistically connected but materially different κατάσκοπος. This is the main word for the Cynic in Epict. Epict. does not think of himself as a philosopher in the sense of quiet reflection on the riddles of the universe, but rather in the sense of having a divine mission in the world as a prophet and preacher of repentance who intervenes in the lives of his fellows and is thus passionately involved in this life. This mission finds linguistic expression in the designations ἄγγελος καὶ κατάσκοπος καὶ κῆρυξ τῶν θεῶν, Epict. Diss., III, 22, 69, or ἄγγελος καὶ κατάσκοπος, ibid., 22, 38. He is the messenger of the gods to the extent that he is conscious

---

[3] Cf. E. Norden, Jbch. f. Phil. Supplementband, XIX (1893), 378 with many examples; Wendland Hell. Kult.², 82; and esp. → I, 409 ff.

of being sent by them. [4] He is their herald and proclaimer because he declares the divine judgment on men. And between these two designations he is also the κατάσκοπος τῶν θεῶν. This has two senses, both of which rest on the literal meaning "spy." In the first place, the Cynic investigates "what is friendly to man and what is hostile," III, 22, 24. He thus strives for perception of the truth as the basis of moral and rational conduct. "When he has accurately discerned this, he must return and declare what is true," III, 22, 25. Secondly, it is the task of the Cynic preacher to test men, whether their lives conform to the truth which has been perceived.

For this testing activity of the Cynic the word ἐπισκοπεῖν is occasionally used instead of κατασκέπτεσθαι, III, 22, 72; 77; 97. It consists in the fact that the wandering preacher so far as he is able considers and tests all men, what they do, how they conduct their lives, what they are concerned about, where they fail in the fulfilment of their duty. "In this manner he goes to all; in this manner he cares for all." In the same sense we are told in Dio Chrys. Or., 9, 1 that Diogenes went to the Isthmian games, not to compete, ἀλλ' ἐπισκοπῶν οἶμαι τοὺς ἀνθρώπους καὶ τὴν ἄνοιαν αὐτῶν. Acc. to Luc. Dialogi Mortuorum, 10, 2, Hermes says to Menippus: ἔμβαινε (in the ferry-boat of Charon) ... καὶ τὴν προεδρίαν παρὰ τὸν κυβερνήτην ἔχε ἐφ' ὑψηλοῦ, ὡς ἐπισκοπῆς ἅπαντας. The significant point is, however, that neither Epict. nor others in his day used the term ἐπίσκοπος to describe this activity. The word κατάσκοπος is always employed. The reason may well be that ἐπίσκοπος generally denoted the watcher over an existing and well-defined sphere. Only in the 3rd cent. A.D., and on the basis of later ideas is ἐπίσκοπος once used in the same way as Epict. uses κατάσκοπος (→ I, 409, n. 19). The Cynic Menedemus, acc. to the account in Diog. L., VI, 102, disguised himself as a Fury and announced that he was an investigator of men's sins (ἐπίσκοπος) who had been sent from Hades and who had to return to the gods of Hades with a report on what he had seen. But this is an isolated case. [5] This use of ἐπίσκοπος and ἐπισκοπῶν had no historical influence.

4. ἐπίσκοπος as a Designation of Office.

In ancient Greece the word ἐπίσκοπος was used in many different ways to describe those who held various official positions in respect of their office and work.

a. In Athens in the 4th and 5th cent. ἐπίσκοπος is a title for state officials. We know this especially from Aristophanes, who in Av., 1022 f. tells of the arrival of an ἐπίσκοπος in the bird kingdom Cloud Cuckoo Land. That he is alluding to real historical models is proved by glosses on his poetry and by inscriptions on which the office appears as depicted by Aristophanes. Acc. to Harpocration, s.v. [6] the ἐπίσκοποι were supervisors sent by the Athenians to the cities of subject members of the Attic League. They were chosen by lot from Athenian candidates and then sent to their respective cities, where they were in some sense governors, though there is uncertainty as to the exact scope of their office. [7] Their main concern was for public order and for the avoidance of friction with Athens. It is likely that they also had some judicial powers. [8] They were maintained by the city in which they officiated. That they were not loved may be gathered from the caricature in Aristophanes. An instance of their work may

---

[4] Epict. Diss., III, 22, 2: ἄγγελος ἀπὸ τοῦ Διός; III, 22, 23; III, 1, 37.

[5] We must keep to the sober distinction between κατάσκοπος and ἐπίσκοπος as drawn by E. Norden, 378 (→ n. 3) and more fully by Rengstorf (→ I, 409). The activity of the κατάσκοπος as ἐπισκοπῶν is to all men. Cf. K. Deissner, ZSTh, 7 (1929/30), 783.

[6] Harpocrationis Lexicon in decem Oratores Atticos, ed. W. Dindorf (1853). Cf. also Suid., s.v.; Anecd. Graec., I, 254: ἄρχοντες ἐπισκεπτόμενοι τοὺς ὑπηκόους καὶ τὰ τούτων πράγματα.

[7] G. Busolt, Griechische Geschichte bis zur Schlacht bei Chaironeia (1885/1904), III, 1, 225 and 590. U. v. Wilamowitz-Moellendorff, Philologische Untersuchungen, I (1880), 16 and 75 f.

[8] C. Daremberg-E. Saglio, Dictionnaire des Antiquités Grecques et Romaines (1877-1919), II, 698 f.; P. Guiraud, La Condition des Alliés pendant la première Confédération Athénienne: Annales de la Faculté des Lettres de Bordeaux, V (1883), 194.

be seen on inscriptions from Erythrae, IG, I, 10 and 11.[9] In 465 B.C. a new constitution was being set up there,[10] and officials from Athens, the *phrurarch* as the military commander and the ἐπίσκοποι as civil officials, played a part in the arrangements, appointing the first assembly of the new order, for which the retiring assembly and the *phrurarch* were later responsible. This does not mean, however, that the ἐπίσκοποι were sent only for a short time. We know that they were permanent officials in Mytilene :[11] Ditt. Syll.³, 76 (427/6 B.C.).

b. We also read of such state officials elsewhere. Thus Appian Rom. Hist., Mithridateios, 48 tells us that Mithridates appointed Philopoimen ἐπίσκοπον Ἐφεσίων. According to Arrian Hist. Indica, 12, 5 there were also ἐπίσκοποι in different parts of India, their responsibilities being those of a secret police. The pap. tell us that there were ἐπίσκοποι in Egypt too. Thus in P. Petr., III, No. 36a, 17 (3rd cent. B.C.) we read : δίκαιον δώσουσιν καὶ λήμψονται ἐπὶ τῶν ἀποδεδειγμένων ἐπισκόπων οἷς ἂν ὁ διοικητὴς συντάσσῃ. Here the ἐπίσκοποι seem to have discharged, or supervised, judicial functions. There is also reference to ἐπίσκοποι in P. Freiburg, 8, 11 (J. Partsch, *Mitt. aus der Freiburger Papyrussammlung,* 2 [SAH, 1916, Abh. 10], 195/6 A.D.). Cf. also P. Oxy., II, 237, Col. IV, 10 (186 A.D.). In one instance the officer in charge of the Ephesian mint is called ἐπίσκοπος on a coin from the time of Claudius, with the addition that he is occupying the post for the fourth time ; elsewhere he is described as ἄρχων or γραμματεύς.[12]

c. More commonly the ἐπίσκοποι are local officials or the officers of societies. Theological research has shown more interest in this usage, since it is felt that here we have the basis of the Christian use, especially when the responsibilities concerned are related to the cultus. In this case, however, while the term is undoubtedly used, and it relates to a work of supervision or control, there is no strict definition of what is involved and the term is never used with precision.

The jurist Charisius (c. 340 A.D.) lists among municipal officials the *episcopi, qui praesunt pani et ceteris venalibus rebus, quae civitatum populis ad cotidianum victum usui sunt.*[13] In other words, they supervise the poor relief of the city. In Megalopolis (IG, V, 2, 1st/2nd cent. A.D.) there is reference to an ἐπίσκοπος καὶ φύλαξ τῆς τῶν πολειτῶν σωφροσύνης, though here we cannot be sure whether an official is meant or an apostle of morality after the manner of the Cynics. From Rhodes (2nd cent. B.C.) we have two different lists of officials similar to those on which διάκονος occurs as an official designation (→ 91 f.). On one of these there is reference to the πρυτάνιες (president), στραταγοί (*praetor,* an honorary title), ταμίαι (treasurer), γραμματεῖς (secretary), ἐπίσκοποι, a γραμματεὺς βουλᾶς, a ὑπογραμματεύς, ἐπιμεληταὶ τῶν ξένων, a ἀγεμὼν ἐπὶ Καύνου (IG, XII, 1, 49, 42 ff. = Ditt. Syll.³, 619; 50, 34 ff.). The reference is obviously to civic officials, though it is not clear how the duties of the prytanes, praetors, treasurers, secretaries and overseers are to be differentiated. On the one list there are five ἐπίσκοποι and on the other three. It is worth noting that διάκονοι and ἐπίσκοποι are never mentioned in the same context.

On the sources thus far adduced there is no sign of any religious connection. In IG, XII, 1, 731, however, we obviously have a list of the officials of a society for the maintenance of the sanctuary of Apollo at Rhodes. This refers to three ἐπιστάται (presidents), a γραμματεὺς ἱεροφυλάκων (secretary of the keepers of the temple),

---

[9] That we are right to read τοὺς ἐπισκόπους καὶ τὸν φρούραρχον on inscr. IG, I, 10, where the word ἐπισκόπους is defective, is proved by IG, I, 11, where we again have ἐπίσκοπος and φρούραρχος together. Cf. also GGA, 165 (1903), 772.

[10] G. Busolt, *Griechische Staatskunde*³ (1926), 1355.

[11] *Ibid.,* n. 4.

[12] F. Imhoof-Blumer, *Kleinasiatische Münzen,* I (1901), 59; J. Friedländer, *Zeitschr. f. Numismatik,* 6 (1879), 15; H. Lietzmann, ZwTh, 55 (1914), 105.

[13] *Digesta Iustiniani Augusti,* 50, 4, 18, 7 (ed. T. Mommsen, II [1870], 914); also W. Liebenam, *Städteverwaltung im röm. Kaiserreiche* (1900), 370.

an ἐπίσκοπος, [14] six ἱεροποιοί (inspectors of the sacrifices), a ταμίας and a ὑπογραμματεὺς ἱεροφυλάκων. Most of them have no direct cultic responsibilities. Indeed, this can be said only of the ἱεροποιοί, who must watch over the sacrifices. On the other hand, they fulfil the temporal tasks which underlie the cultic activity of a society. This is made quite clear by the inscr. IG, XII, 3, 329 (2nd cent. B.C.). A cultic society to honour Anthister on the island of Thera resolves to accept a benefaction and instructs the two *episcopi* Dion and Melehippus to invest the money. These are obviously in charge of financial transactions. Subordinate cultic obligations are discharged by the ἐπίσκοπος on another inscr. of the Roman period found in Dolistovo in Bulgaria. [15] Here we read: Οἴκῳ θείῳ κὲ τοῖς 'Ολυμπίοις θεοῖς οἱ ἱερῖς ... there then follow ten names ... 'Απολλῶνις οἴκουρος (keeper of the house), 'Ορφεὺς μακελλάρις (*macellarius,* in charge of the sacrificial meat), 'Επτέξενις ἐπίσκοπος, Μεστίκενθος κάπηλος (dealer, probably in idols). It is evident that the ἐπίσκοπος is not one of the priests, but one of those who have purely external duties in the cultic society. The same is true when the society of the Alexichites in Myconos instructs its ἐπίσκοπος, who seems to have been a kind of secretary, to proclaim a festival which it has resolved to celebrate. [16] In sum, we may say with E. Ziebarth: [17] "One of the distinctive features of the terminology of Greek societies is that there is no definition of the designations used. The ἐπίσκοποι, like the ἐπιμεληταί, are simply officers who exercise supervision and control."

In Plut. De Numa, 9 (I, 66b) we read that the Roman pontifex was τῶν παρθένων ἱερῶν ἐπίσκοπος. Obviously this does not denote an office, particularly of a cultic nature. It simply describes his task in relation to the Vestal Virgins. Even in pagan times the word *episcopus* was borrowed in Latin, being used sometimes to describe supervisory officials of state. [18]

d. Finally, there is a usage of ἐπίσκοπος for an official which is particularly attested in Syria. An inscr. in Canata (253 A.D.) runs as follows: [19] ὑπὲρ σωτηρίας τῶν κυρίων, ἐπισκοπούντων 'Ανέμου Σαβίνου καὶ Βαυλάνης 'Οδενίθου καὶ Πασίφιλος Καμασάνου, ἐκτίσθη ὁ οἶκος ἐκ φιλοτιμίας τῆς κώμης ἐξ ὧν ἔδωκεν 'Ιουλιανὸς Διονυσίου. The last named has given an endowment to his community. With the money the village is erecting a public building (the stone may still be seen in the ruins of a mosque), which in proof of loyalty is to be dedicated to the two ruling emperors. The other three mentioned constitute a building commission. [20] Their duties appear more clearly on an inscr. in Der'at. [21] There a distinction is drawn between the part played by the Roman legates who initiate the building (προνοίᾳ Στατιλίου ...), an imperial equerry who perhaps takes the chair (ἐφεστῶτος 'Ιουλίου ...) in the society which undertakes the building, the architect Verus who is really in charge of the construction (ὑφηγουμένου Οὐήρου ἀρχιτέκτονος) and three others who supervise the building (ἐπισκοπῇ Αἰλίου Βάσσου ...). [22] From this it may be seen that the ἐπισκοπή does not involve any constructional responsibility but merely supervision of

---

[14] Deissmann NB, 57 emphasises that there is only one. Literally we have ἐπίσκοποι (though the last syllable could perhaps be amended) Τεισίας Διαγόρα καθ' υἱοθεσίαν δὲ 'Αριστοφάνευς. Deissmann favours the reading ἐπίσκοπος, but this is not essential. Cf. H. Lietzmann, ZwTh, 55 (1914), 102. Deissmann adds: "I refrain from any conjectures as to the functions of this ἐπίσκοπος. The mere fact that the word is used in a technical sacral sense in pre-Christian times is significant enough of itself."

[15] *Archäologisch-epigraphische Mitteilungen aus Österreich,* XVIII (1895), 108.

[16] E. Ziebarth in *Rheinisches Museum NF, 55* (1900), 506 ff. (2nd cent. B.C.).

[17] *Das griechische Vereinswesen* (1896), 131. Cf. also F. Poland, *Geschichte des griechischen Vereinswesens* (1909), 337 ff.; on ἐπίσκοπος, *ibid.,* 377.

[18] Cf. CIL, V, 2, 7914 and 7870. Cf. Mommsen, p. 916b.

[19] W. H. Waddington, *Inscriptions Grecques et Latines de la Syrie* (1870), 2412 f.

[20] H. Lietzmann, ZwTh, 55 (1914), 102.

[21] Ditt. Or., II, 614.

[22] There is also reference to προεδρίᾳ Μάγνου Βάσσου. Whether this activity relates directly to the building and the building commission is open to question.

the course of the work in the interests of the builders, and possibly control of the money allocated to the task. It is along these lines that we are to explain the activity of all the other ἐπίσκοποι who are mentioned in the same connection on Syrian building inscr.: Waddington (→ n. 19), 1911, 1989, 1990 (4 ἐπίσκοποι, who obviously control the temple funds), 2298, 2308 (referring to the building of an aqueduct and a temple of Athene, the ἐπισκοπή being exercised, not by specific individuals, but by the magistrate of a particular quarter of the city); also 2309, 2310, 2412e; cf. also Syria, *Publications of the Princeton Univ. Archaeological Expeditions to Syria* in 1904/1905 and 1909, Divolumen, III, Section A, 37, 220 (better completed ἐπιμελομένους ἐπισκόπους than τοὺς τοῦ τεμένους), 222 (with the form ἐπισκοπία), Sect. B, 1003, 1187, 1199. Naturally, the Christian bishops often mentioned on building inscr. after the 4th cent. are not to be confused with these overseers.[23] Ditt. Or., II, 611 tells us that a certain Μεννέας was ἐπίσκοπος πάντων τῶν ἐνθάδε γεγονότων ἔργων (→ also 610).

B. ἐπίσκοπος in Judaism.

1. God as ἐπίσκοπος.

The LXX uses ἐπίσκοπος in the same twofold way as secular Greek. On the one hand it denotes God, and on the other it has the general sense of supervisors in different fields. If in polytheistic belief each deity acts as ἐπίσκοπος over certain men and things, the one God does this far more comprehensively. He is the absolute ἐπίσκοπος who sees all things.

Thus at Job 20:29 the LXX renders the Heb. אֵל by ἐπίσκοπος. As such God is Judge of the ungodly. The term is here brought into relation to κύριος. Philo has the same line of thought. He calls God ἔφορος καὶ ἐπίσκοπος in Mut. Nom., 39, 216. The combination μάρτυς καὶ ἐπίσκοπος, already used by Homer, is also found in Philo at Leg. All., III, 43. In this capacity God is the One from whom no wickedness can be hidden. ὁ τῶν ὅλων ἐπίσκοπος is the Omniscient, Som., I, 91. Thus on Philo's view Moses finely introduces God in the first chapter of the Bible as "the Father of all and the Contemplator of all that has come into being." This judgment rests on the statement that "God saw everything that he had made, and, behold, it was very good," Migr. Abr., 135. In Jewish thought this profound understanding of God as the One who sees all things produced the term πανεπίσκοπος, which occurs more than once in the Sibyllines: 1, 152: πάντα γὰρ οἶδεν ἀθάνατος σωτὴρ πανεπίσκοπος;[24] 2, 177: ὕψιστος πάντων πανεπίσκοπος; 5, 352: θεὸς πανεπίσκοπος οὐρανόθι.

In particular, God sees into the human heart. In this respect the LXX links μάρτυς and ἐπίσκοπος at Wis. 1:6: τῶν νεφρῶν αὐτοῦ (of the ungodly) μάρτυς ὁ θεὸς καὶ τῆς καρδίας αὐτοῦ ἐπίσκοπος ἀληθὴς καὶ τῆς γλώσσης ἀκουστής. Cf. Ac. 1:24, where God is called καρδιογνώστης. God sees what is concealed in the soul of man, says Philo Migr. Abr., 115. God alone perceives the ἐνθυμήματα of man, Migr. Abr., 81.

2. Men as ἐπίσκοποι.

There is no closely defined office bearing the title ἐπίσκοπος in the LXX. But the term "overseer" is freely used in many different ways.

Antiochus appoints ἐπίσκοποι as governors over Israel, 1 Macc. 1:51. Abimelech appoints an "officer" in Ju. 9:28. Is. 60:17 mentions ἐπίσκοποι parallel to ἄρχοντες, though in misunderstanding of the original. "Officers" are called ἐπίσκοποι τῆς δυνάμεως at Nu. 31:14; 4 Βασ. 11:15. There is a good counterpart to, and commentary on the Syrian building inscr. in 4 Βασ. 12:11(12); 2 Ch. 34:12, 17. Here we are told how

---

[23] E.g., *Publications of the Princeton Univ. Expeditions*, III, B, 1003, 1187, 1199 etc.

[24] Cf. J. Geffcken, who is sure the passage is of Jewish origin and who places it at the beginning of the 3rd cent. A.D.: TU, XXIII (NF, VIII), 1 (1902), 48 f., 52.

the money was raised for necessary repairs of the temple, and how it was placed in the hands of the *episcopi* as supervisors who paid it out to the various workmen and labourers. A more strongly cultic use occurs in the great list in Neh. 11:9, 14, 22 where it refers to the "overseers" of the men of Benjamin and of the priests and Levites. In 4 Βασ. 11:18 it is used for "overseers" in the temple. In Nu. 4:16 we have reference to an office directly related to the cultus, though not itself priestly in the strict sense, when Eleazar is made "overseer" of the oil for light, the sweet incense, the daily meat offering, the anointing oil, the whole tabernacle, and everything in the holy vessels within it. Symmachus has ἐπίσκοπος at Gn. 41:34, where the LXX has τοπάρχης.

In Philo Rer. Div. Her., Moses is described as ὁ ἐπίσκοπος in the sense of "the one who knows souls." In Som., II, 186 Eleazar and Ithamar are called ἐπίσκοποι καὶ ἔφοροι, as in Ex. 28:1.

The term is also found in Joseph., who uses it with κριτής in the sense of a "guardian of morals and law," Ant., 10, 4, 1. Cf. 12, 5, 4 : a police official.

C. ἐπίσκοπος in the NT.

Although the word had such a rich background, and was to enjoy an even richer development on Christian soil, it occurs only five times in the NT.

1. In 1 Pt. 2:25 Christ Himself is called ἐπίσκοπος: ἦτε γὰρ ὡς πρόβατα πλανώμενοι, ἀλλὰ ἐπεστράφητε νῦν ἐπὶ τὸν ποιμένα καὶ ἐπίσκοπον τῶν ψυχῶν ὑμῶν. At a first glance it would seem that ἐπίσκοπος here merely strengthens ποιμήν, and thus denotes one who keeps watch over the flock. In general, the terms ποιμαίνειν and ἐπισκοπεῖν were closely linked in describing the work of the shepherd; apart from this passage cf. Ac. 20:28; 1 Pt. 5:2; perhaps also Nu. 27:16; → 601. On the other hand, there is a further meaning for those familiar with the richness of the term. Christ is He who has the fullest knowledge of souls. He knows every inner secret, as is said of God in Wis. 1:6 and the passages quoted from Philo (→ 614). He is also the One who gives Himself most self-sacrificingly to care for the souls of the faithful (cf. ἐπισκοπέω in Hb. 12:15). It is for this reason that ποιμήν and ἐπίσκοπος are so closely related. The phrase "shepherd and bishop of your souls" carries within it all that is said by Greek speaking Gentiles and Jews about God as ἐπίσκοπος. As suggested by the context, which points us to the deepest mysteries of salvation history, ἐπίσκοπος is thus a title of majesty ascribed to Jesus in His work in relation to the community.

The A.V., adapting the alien term, brings out the implications of the passage for Christian history with its suggestion of the ministerial titles "pastor" and "bishop" (cf. Luther's "dem Hirten und Bischof euerer Seelen"). The influence of the terminology is in fact to be seen already in 1 Peter, for in 5:2 ff. the elders are exhorted to feed the flock of Christ, and this led a copyist to enjoin ἐπισκοπεῖν upon the elders (→ 604).

2. In the other passages men are called ἐπίσκοποι as leaders of the Church. This raises two important questions in the history of Church government : a. Who is called ἐπίσκοπος ? and b. From what period does ἐπίσκοπος cease to be a description of the free action of members of the community and become the designation of bearers of a specific office to which they and they alone are called ?

a. In answer to the first question we may note that the wandering, charismatic preachers of the Gospel, the apostles, prophets and teachers, are never called ἐπίσκοποι. This title arises only where there are settled local congregations in which regular acts are performed. For these fixed leaders of congregational life the designations → πρεσβύτεροι or ἐπίσκοποι (καὶ διάκονοι) quickly established themselves. In the first instance — we may postpone for the moment our consideration of later development — the two words πρεσβύτεροι and ἐπίσκοποι did not imply any distinction, let alone antithesis. This may be seen from Paul's speech to the Ephesian elders (Ac. 20:28). Since Luke was himself present and recorded it in his account of the journey, and since its thoroughly Pauline character emerges on close examination, we may accept this as very early testimony. [25]

In Luke's introduction the Ephesian leaders are called πρεσβύτεροι. But Paul says to them: "Take heed therefore unto yourselves, and to all the flock, over which the Holy Ghost hath made you overseers (bishops), to feed the church of God, which he hath purchased with his own blood." It is significant 1. that all the πρεσβύτεροι without exception are called ἐπίσκοποι. They are elders in status (not in virtue of their age but in virtue of their position and accreditation), and they are bishops in responsibility. It is also significant 2. that this responsibility is described in terms of ποιμαίνειν, as in 1 Pt. 2:25 and 5:2 ff., though ἐπίσκοπος is preferred to ποιμήν. It is significant again 3. that there are several ἐπίσκοποι in the one congregation, none of which takes precedence. It is to be noted 4. that their calling to be bishops comes from the Holy Spirit. This does not exclude either election (cf. Ac. 1:21 ff.; 6:3 ff.) or appointment by an apostle, possibly Paul himself (Ac. 14:23). The decisive point, however, is the work of the Holy Spirit on which the sending and authority of their episcopate rest. Finally, it is important 5. that according to the context their task consists in a watchful and solicitous (both ideas are contained in ἐπισκοπεῖν) direction of the congregation on the basis of the redeeming work of Christ to which alone the community owes its existence.

b. In reply to the second basic question in the history of the episcopate, namely, when the description of free activity became a designation of office, it may be said that there was from the very first a necessary impulse in this direction. To be sure, Paul in Ac. 20:28 is simply depicting the work and task of responsible men in the congregation. But he is already directing his words to a definite circle whose members may be called πρεσβύτεροι or ἐπίσκοποι in distinction from others. And these men know that they are called. The office is already present in substance. It has not yet been given a permanent name. But this will soon come.

When Paul in Phil., 1:1 sends greetings πᾶσιν τοῖς ἁγίοις ἐν Χριστῷ Ἰησοῦ τοῖς οὖσιν ἐν Φιλίπποις σὺν ἐπισκόποις καὶ διακόνοις, in the final phrase he has in view individual members of the congregation who are unequivocally characterised by the designation (→ 89). Otherwise the addition has no meaning. [26] It is impossible to argue that he is simply referring here to an activity, e.g., the sending of gifts to Paul, 4:10 ff., and not to an office. [27] If Paul were intending merely to greet those who had collected and sent the love-offering, he would have said so, and not used two words commonly employed by the Greeks as titles. As the words stand, they refer to those whose responsibility is that of ἐπισκοπεῖν and διακονεῖν, though we cannot deduce the exact nature of these tasks from this passage. [28]

---

[25] If this speech can be understood merely as a *vaticinium ex eventu*, then no man has ever taken leave of close friends with a full heart on undertaking a perilous journey and with thoughts of the possibility of his death (cf. v. 22).

[26] To read συνεπισκόποις as a single word is not grammatically possible.

[27] F. Loofs, ThStKr, 63 (1890), 628 f., distinguishes sharply between the name of an office and the description of an office, and he sees only the latter at the period of Philippians. I cannot accept this sharp distinction. Certainly no one was addressed as "Lord Bishop" in Philippi c. 60 A.D. But an unequivocal description of office by means of an accepted term elsewhere used to denote office inevitably becomes a designation of the office.

[28] On the pt. that we cannot equate the ἐπίσκοποι and διάκονοι, as attempted by Haupt Gefbr., ad loc., → 89 f. Cf. also what is said there on the conjecture of Loh. Phil. that the addition σὺν (!) ἐπισκόποις καὶ διακόνοις is to be explained by the fact that these leaders of the community had been in prison, as also on the impossibility of describing their official activity in the light of Phil. 1:1.

c. The Pastorals carry the development a stage further. In 1 Tm. 3:1 ἐπισκοπή is a distinct office which one may seek. To attain it, certain qualifications must be met. It is to be noted that the passage simply outlines the qualifications and not the duties. The author has clear rules by which the congregation must be guided in its selection. The sobriety with which the requirements are stated, some of them being assumed as self-evident, and the fact that in regard to endowment for the episcopal office there is no further reference to the Holy Spirit but simply to essential human qualifications, show how strongly the development is already affected by everyday needs.

There is still a recognition of the greatness of the episcopal office. With pastoral wisdom 1 Tm. lists the requirements to be sought in those who bear it. [29] First comes moral reliability. No particular ascetic attainment is demanded. The leader of a Christian community is also exposed to very human temptations. But he must lead an honourable and exemplary life, avoiding excess. This is what is meant when it is said that he must not be intemperate or quarrelsome or avaricious. Secondly, he must give proof in his own home of his ability to direct the life of the congregation. In this respect, Roman Catholic celibacy stands in direct contradiction to the Bible. The Bible assumes monogamous marriage for the bishop, and places high value on the blessing of a well-conducted, hospitable manse or vicarage in which children are brought up to be obedient and honourable. Ability in domestic rule is a test of ability to guide the congregation. Thirdly, the bishop should be a skilled teacher and therefore an able preacher. Fourthly, he must be a mature Christian so that he will not succumb to the temptation to pride through which the servants of God so easily fall victim to the devil. Nor do the qualifications relate only to the inner life of the community. For fifthly, the bishop for his work's sake must be blameless according to the standards of the non-Christian world, and therefore as far as possible protected against scandal.

There is a parallel passage in Tt. 1:5-9. Titus had the task of appointing elders in the cities of Crete as Paul had done in Asia Minor according to Ac. 14:23. This was the way to ensure the continued life of the churches once the missionaries had gone.

The qualifications of presbyters here are like those of the bishops in 1 Tm. 3:2 ff. In fact, there is an alternation of terms in Tt. 1:7, where we suddenly have ἐπίσκοπος instead of πρεσβύτερος. This is another proof that the two terms originally referred to the same thing, namely, the guidance and representation of the congregation and the work of preaching and conducting worship when there was no apostle, prophet or teacher present. Perhaps an early distinction is to be seen in 1 Tm. 5:17, where some presbyters are singled out and declared worthy of double honour because they have proved to be good προεστῶτες πρεσβύτεροι and have shown special zeal in the preaching of the word and in teaching. They are thus links in the chain of development which produced the primacy of the episcopate.

If 1 Tm. 3:2 and Tt. 1:7 speak of the bishop in the sing. and with the art., the reference is to the bishop as a type and not to the number of bishops in a given place. There is no reference to monarchical episcopate. On the contrary, the evidence of the NT is clearly to the effect that originally several ἐπίσκοποι took charge of the communities in brotherly comity. It is also plain that the point of the office was service, and service alone. A sober and disciplined outlook was required. The bishop, too, received brotherly admonition. His power and authority came only from the Holy Ghost.

The question has been raised whether the ἄγγελοι τῶν ἐκκλησιῶν in Rev. (1:20; 2 f.) are not bishops of the churches, but this is hardly likely (→ I, 86).

---

[29] Cf. J. Jeremias in *NT Deutsch*, III (1934), 14.

D. The Origin and Original Form of the Episcopate.

As in the matter of the diaconate, which is closely linked with the episcopate (→ 90), we must begin here, too, with a distinction between the origin of the episcopal office and that of the designation ἐπίσκοπος, which finally triumphed over such other NT terms as πρεσβύτεροι, ἡγούμενοι, προϊστάμενοι, ποιμένες.

None of the offices denoted by ἐπίσκοπος in the Greek speaking world has so much in common with the Christian office of bishop as to enable us to affirm the possibility of a historical connection. The various national and municipal officials, the supervisors of provisions and coinage, the building commissaries and business managers of cultic unions who were called ἐπίσκοποι, cannot possibly have been models for the leaders of Christian congregations. Nor are we helped further by what we know of the order in the societies of the Hellenistic Mysteries. The wandering Cynic preachers perhaps constitute an instructive parallel to the apostles, but not to bishops. Perhaps we are to turn rather to Jewish models. K. G. Goetz has strongly advocated the view that the ἀρχισυνάγωγος and ὑπηρέτης of the synagogue are the models for the ἐπίσκοπος and διάκονος. [30] From the close connection between these two Christian offices from the very earliest period, it is obvious that the model is to be found only in a corresponding twofold office. As there are similarities between synagogue and early Christian worship, so there are in fact many material parallels between Jewish and Christian cultic offices. The leader of the synagogue conducts divine service, supervises external order and looks after the building ; "whether there was only one ruler of the synagogue or many is not clear from the sources." [31] With the ἀρχισυνάγωγοι there were also πρεσβύτεροι. On the other hand, important differences are to be noted. The chief of these is that so far as our information goes the leader of the synagogue had hardly anything to do with the guidance of the congregation as a fellowship of faith and love.

This is far more true of the leaders of the community of the new covenant in Damascus, in which J. Jeremias finds the model for Christian bishops. [32] This Pharisaic society was divided into camps at the head of which was always a מבקר למחנה (Damasc., 13, 7; perhaps also 9, 11; 18 f.; 22; 13, 6), as there was also a מבקר אשר לכל המחנות over the camps as a whole (14, 8 f.). It is uncertain whether the מבקר אשר לרבים of 15, 8 refers to the latter or to the camp leaders. It is also uncertain whether the priest charged with ἐπισκέπτεσθαι in 14, 6 is to be equated with the מבקר. This designation is the part. piel of בקר, "to investigate," "to have regard to." The מבקר has charge of admissions and expulsions. He is a teacher and preacher. He should deal kindly with the community "as a father with his children," he should pardon their waywardness, and like a shepherd with the sheep — the familiar image — he should loose the chains which bind them. [33] He has judicial responsibilities and authority in many external things. He convenes and directs the assemblies of the community and receives and distributes the offerings. Now in the LXX the Heb. בקר is sometimes rendered ἐπισκέπτομαι (→ 601), for which פקד is the normal Heb. equivalent. Hence we might well translate מבקר by ἐπίσκοπος. [34] Jeremias claims that the position and official duties of the מבקר tally at all points with those of the bishop in the Syrian Didascalia. He thus deduces that "the office of leader

---

[30] K. G. Goetz, Petrus als Gründer und Oberhaupt der Kirche und Schauer von Gesichten (1927), 49 ff.

[31] J. Elbogen, Der jüdische Gottesdienst in seiner geschichtlichen Entwicklung² (1924), 483; Str.-B., IV, 1, 145 ff.

[32] J. Jeremias, Jerusalem zur Zeit Jesu, II, 1 (1929), 130 ff. Goetz defended his thesis against Jeremias in ZNW, 30 (1931), 89 ff. Jeremias then pursued his researches and reached essentially the same standpoint as that of the present article. The author is grateful to him for friendly advice.

[33] Damasc., 13, 7 ff. (Schechter, 1910). There is a new edition by L. Rost in Kl. Texte (ed. H. Lietzmann), No. 167 (1933). For a transl. cf. W. Staerk, BFTh, 27, 3 (1922), 287 f.

[34] Staerk : ephoros.

of the Pharisaic community according to what we know of the מבקר from the Damascus document — and as it was exercised elsewhere among the Pharisees — was a model for the Christian episcopate." There can be no doubt that Jeremias has drawn attention to a notable parallel to the bishop. At the same time, certain questions remain open. Jeremias himself realises that the small community in Damascus could not be a direct model for the Christian Church. And the מבקר bears stronger monarchical features than the older form of the Christian episcopate. He is closer to the 3rd century than to what we know of the earlier ἐπίσκοποι. Another weakness is the lack of any connection with the διάκονος. In any case, we know too little [35] of the Pharisaic leaders in Damascus to come to any solid conclusions either way. There is here no easy solution to the problem.

Nor do we need any such solution. Familiar forms of synagogue and Pharisaic order were no doubt before the eyes of the first Christians. But their community, based on the great commission to preach the Gospel and to live according to it in the most inward of all societies, was something new and distinctive, so that for the fulfilment of its mission new offices had to be created, or to develop out of the matter itself.

The impulse to create fixed offices lay in the nature of the matter. Jesus had called and sent out the Twelve to preach in His name. They were to help Him, and above all to be the bearers of His message after His death. The risen Lord revealed to them, and to others whom He called in His resurrection appearances, their mission. This apostolate was linked to direct commissioning by Christ. Hence it was not transferable. The prophets and teachers, who like the apostles had received from the Spirit the gifts and authority to establish and build up communities through the power of the divinely given word, also died off. They had fulfilled their mission in a wandering ministry. But where churches had been formed, there had to be men who could constitute the focal points when no apostle, prophet or teacher was present. These men had to assume responsibility for the direction and order without which there can be no common life. For these κυβερνήσεις, too, a χάρισμα was necessary (1 C. 12:28). What originally seemed to be an external concern soon showed itself to be a highly responsible ministry of pastoral direction in the outer and inner conflicts of the congregation. The task of conducting worship and preaching was also added. This was the content of the office as we see it when it is recorded of Paul and Barnabas (Ac. 14:23) that already on their first missionary journey they appointed elders, when the apostle refers to προϊστάμενοι in Thessalonica (1 Th. 5:12) and Rome (Rom. 12:8), and when he assumes in Gl. 6:6-10 that there are in the Galatian churches teachers of the Gospel who may claim to be supported for their work. [36] These leaders of the congregations are called ἐπίσκοποι and διάκονοι in Philippi (Phil. 1:1). Their office remained when the special ministry of the apostles, prophets and teachers had ceased. More and more they became the backbone of congregational life.

The title derives from the matter itself in the same way as the office. For Jewish Christians πρεσβύτερος was an obvious term. But Greek Christianity introduced ἐπίσκοποι and διάκονοι, as at Ephesus and Philippi. These were simple, widely known titles, yet not precisely defined and therefore in their very breadth of meaning capable of a new and specific use. It is worth noting that the Christians chose modest words which did not of themselves raise any spiritual claims. The

---

[35] Cf. Jeremias, op. cit., 121, n. 4.
[36] NT Deutsch, II (1933), 478 f.

ἐπίσκοποι and διάκονοι were far behind the apostles and prophets. Nevertheless, the terms were not without content. The διάκονος was sanctified by what Jesus had said about ministering as the heart of discipleship (→ 85). Into the term ἐπίσκοπος was interwoven the whole rich history which from the time of Homer had applied it to divine being and action until Jesus Himself had come as ἐπίσκοπος. There thus combined in the terms a lack of assumption in external form and a deep inward significance, as in the symbol of the fish or the sacrament of the Lord's Supper.

It is true that in the course of two thousand years the lack of assumption has been transformed into the supreme claim which a man can raise in virtue of his office, namely, the claim to publish *ex cathedra* infallible truth in matters of faith and morals. In the present context we cannot even outline the history of this development. It began with the distinction, first apparent in 1 Tm. 5:17, between the καλῶς προεστῶτες and the rest of the πρεσβύτεροι, and with the claim of the former to double honour and reward. In 1 Cl., 42-44 there is still an equation of the ἐπίσκοπος (and διάκονοι) with the πρεσβύτεροι. Nevertheless, Clement helps forward the development in two ways.

First, he advances the doctrine that the bishops and deacons were instituted by the apostles, thus giving the hierarchical ladder God—Christ—apostles—bishops—deacons. Secondly, he provides scriptural proof for the two latter offices in his own version of Is. 60:17: καταστήσω τοὺς ἐπισκόπους αὐτῶν ἐν δικαιοσύνῃ καὶ τοὺς διακόνους αὐτῶν ἐν πίστει, which diverges from both the Mas. and the LXX: καὶ δώσω τοὺς ἄρχοντάς σου ἐν εἰρήνῃ καὶ τοὺς ἐπισκόπους σου ἐν δικαιοσύνῃ.

The *Didache* gives us a better insight into the actual state of affairs. The congregational leaders came into their own when the missionary charismatics either moved on or died. Then ἐπίσκοποι and διάκονοι had to continue their work. This is the point described in Did., 15, 1, where we read: "They (i.e., bishops and deacons), too, render to you the ministry of prophets and teachers. Wherefore do not despise them. For they are your leaders with the prophets and teachers." The latter had no successors. Thus the importance of the elected offices constantly increases. Among them that of bishop begins to take precedence of presbyters and deacons. In Syria and Asia Minor at the beginning of the 2nd century the college of bishops which had originally led the churches had disappeared, being replaced by the monarchical bishop. This is a process which we cannot here describe in detail. We can only reduce it to the formula that the fact of leadership triumphed in virtue of its inherent force. Ignatius, himself a true leader, bears testimony to this in all his epistles. In the ecclesiastical sphere, however, this organised leadership entails the great danger of advancing a claim to be not merely a joint expression of the will of the society but to possess full authority to decide what is eternal truth and what is not. No human power can control the truth. Even the episcopate can only serve it.

† ἀλλοτρι(ο)επίσκοπος.

The word ἀλλοτρι(ο)επίσκοπος occurs only at 1 Pt. 4:15.

ἀ λ λ ο τ ρ ι(ο)ε π ί σ κ ο π ο ς. Cr.-Kö., 1001 f.; Pr.-Bauer, 62; Bengel, *ad loc.*, Kn. Pt., *ad loc.*; Wnd. Pt., *ad loc.*; A. Hilgenfeld, ZwTh, 16 (1873); *Hist.-krit. Einl. in d. NT* (1875), 630. E. Zeller, SAB (1893), I, 129 ff. = *Kleine Schriften*, II (1910), 41 ff.; A. Haus-rath, *Jesus und d. nt.lichen Schriftsteller*, II (1909), 216, 219; Zahn Einl., II, 39 f.; A. Bischoff, ZNW, 7 (1906), 271 ff.; 9 (1908), 171; P. Schmidt, ZwTh, 50 (1908), 28; K. Erbes, ZNW, 19 (1919), 39 ff.; 20 (1921), 249; K. Bornhäuser, *Monatsschrift f. Pastoraltheologie*, 18 (1922), 101.

It is a simple composite like κακο-ποιός (κακὸν ποιῶν), which comes immediately before it. [1] The *koine* keeps the hiatus for the sake of etymological clarity. [2] Most of the MSS, however, have the shorter form, and only KLP al pler ἀλλοτριοεπίσκοπος. [3] Similar constructions with ἀλλοτριο- are found elsewhere in Gk. ἀλλοτριόγνωμος means one who has something else in mind; [4] ἀλλοτριοπράγμων one who meddles in other matters which do not concern him; [5] and ἀλλοτριοφάγος one who eats alien bread. [6] There are other examples, esp. in the temporal sphere. ἀλλοτριονομέω means to put in a strange or alien place, [7] or to live according to foreign customs; [8] ἀλλοτριοπραγέω to pursue matters which do not concern one; [9] ἀλλοτριοφθονέω to envy the goods of others; [10] ἀλλοτριοφρονέω to have another, i.e., a hostile mind. [11] ἀλλοτρι(ο)επίσκοπος is a construction like these, except that we have the noun ἐπίσκοπος instead of the pres. part. of ἐπισκοπέω. Whenever ἀλλότριος is used, it always denotes an activity which is foreign to the doer, or which is not his concern. It is in this light that we are to understand ἀλλοτριεπίσκοπος.

Since the word is not found in Gk. except in the NT, [12] we can deduce its meaning only from the context of 1 Pt., and this does not yield us a wholly unambiguous answer. The author is admonishing his readers to bear cheerfully the sufferings which they must undergo because of their faith. He presupposes that members of the Christian community are persecuted at law for the fact that they are Christians. There is no shame in this. But they must be sure that it is only their Christianity and not something else which is the occasion of their clash with the law. All misuse of the concept of martyrdom is excluded. Within this train of thought we read: μὴ γάρ τις ὑμῶν πασχέτω ὡς φονεὺς ἢ κλέπτης ἢ κακοποιὸς ἢ ὡς ἀλλοτριεπίσκοπος· εἰ δὲ ὡς Χριστιανός, μὴ αἰσχυνέσθω. Like the other three terms in the list ἀλλοτριεπίσκοπος must obviously denote someone who is guilty of conduct which justly involves him in shame and punishment.

It is an open question whether the ἢ ὡς before ἀλλοτριεπίσκοπος can be taken to signify a differentiation from the other three, and therefore, as an extension of the *gradatio ad minus* evident in them, translated by "or merely as." [13] What is not open to question is that the Christian is in no case to be an ἀλλοτριεπίσκοπος.

If we combine this with parallel constructions, the following interpretations are possible.

a. "One who has his eye on others' possessions." In this case ἀλλοτριεπίσκοπος would bear the same relation to κλέπτης as the tenth commandment to the eighth. [14]

There is a material parallel on a pap. from Fayyum in the 2nd cent. A.D., BGU,

---

[1] Bl.-Debr.⁶ § 119, 1.
[2] *Ibid.,* § 124.
[3] A 31 ἀλλότριος ἐπίσκοπος; 40 ἀλλοτρίως ἐπίσκοπος.
[4] Anecd. Graec., I, 385 from the comedian Cratinos.
[5] *Ibid.,* I, 81.
[6] Soph. Fr., 309 in Athen., IV, 164a.
[7] Plat. Theaet., 195a.
[8] Dio C., 52, 36.
[9] Polyb., V, 41, 8.
[10] Hom. Od., 18, 18.
[11] Diod. S., 17, 4, 5.
[12] Dionys. Areop. Ep., 8; MPG, 3, 1089c is influenced by the NT. It reads: ἐκκήρυκτος τῇ θεολογίᾳ πᾶς ὁ ἀλλοτριεπίσκοπος καὶ ἕκαστος ἐν τῇ τάξει τῆς λειτουργίας αὐτοῦ ἔσται, and obviously refers to a bishop intruding into an alien sphere of office.
[13] Cf. Kn. Pt. and Wbg. Pt., *ad loc.*
[14] Cf. the μὴ ἀποστερήσῃς in the list of commandments in Mk. 10:19.

II, 531, col. II, 22 : οὔτε εἰμὶ ἄδικος οὔτε ἀλλοτρίων ἐπιθυμητής. [15] Cf. also Herm. s., 1, 11: μηδὲ τοῦ ἀλλοτρίου ἅψησθε μηδὲ ἐπιθυμεῖτε.

b. "The unfaithful guardian of goods committed to him." In the above examples of words with ἀλλότριος we found that they frequently express an action which is the opposite of what ought to be. Thus the ἀλλοτριόγνωμος is one who has in his mind something different from what he ought to have. In popular etymology, therefore, the ἀλλοτριεπίσκοπος might well be the false guardian who either does not keep, or even misappropriates, that which is committed to him. [16]

c. "The one who meddles in things which do not concern him," "the busybody." [17] The A.V. takes it in this sense ("busybody in other men's matters"); cf. Luther : "One who interferes in the work of another."

E. Zeller has tried to explain this in relation to the work of the Cynics, who because of their activity as κατάσκοποι (→ I, 409) were often accused of *aliena negotia curare* : Horat. Sat., II, 3, 19; Epict. Diss., III, 22, 97. Bengel, too, sees in the *alienarum rerum inspector* a man who interferes in public or private, religious or secular matters which do not concern him. Such a man may easily get himself into trouble, though he is hardly likely to incur judicial punishment.

d. He is more likely to be punished at law if, instead of a mere meddler, he becomes a "calumniator" and "informer."

Nerva attacked informers, [18] and Trajan ordered severe penalties against them. [19] Thus this sense would do justice to the context. On the other hand, it is straining matters too far to render ἀλλοτριεπίσκοπος as *novarum rerum cupidus* and therefore to find in it a guarded expression for revolutionary or traitor. [20]

Beyer

ἐπισκηνόω → σκῆνος.
ἐπισκιάζω → σκιά.

---

† ἐπιστάτης

In the sense of the "master," this occurs in the NT only in the vocative. It is peculiar to the third Gospel (Lk. 5:5; 8:24, 45; 9:33, 49; 17:13) as a translation of

---

[15] Deissmann NB, 51, n. 5 points out that the linking of ἄδικος and ἀλλοτρίων ἐπιθυμητής corresponds to that of κακοποιός and ἀλλοτριεπίσκοπος.

[16] K. Erbes, ZNW, 19 (1919), 39 ff. and 20 (1921), 249 translates "defaulters." He refers to the false shepherds described as ἀλλότριος in Jn. 10:1 ff. and also to Vergil Buc. Ecl., III, 5 f.: *Hic alienus ovis custos bis mulget in hora : et sucus pecori et lac subducitur agnis.* Though from a very unlikely starting-point, much the same practical result is reached by K. Bornhäuser, *op. cit.*, 18 (1922), 101 ff. On the ground of the hiphil of פקד "to commit for safe-keeping," he gives to ἐπίσκοπος the sense of "trustee" and to ἀλλοτριεπίσκοπος that of a "trustee of someone else's property." Thus 1 Pt. 4:15 means : "Let no one suffer as a trustee," i.e., self-evidently, according to Bornhäuser, "as an unfaithful trustee."

[17] Thus in Plat. Phaedr., 230a τὰ ἀλλότρια σκοπεῖν means "to concern oneself with alien and unprofitable things" instead of self-knowledge. Cf. also Xenoph. Mem., III, 7, 9.

[18] Dio C., 68, 1.

[19] Plin. (the Younger) Panegyricus, 34 f.

[20] So esp. A. Bischoff, ZNW, 9 (1908), 171. Similarly, it is hardly justifiable to regard ἐπίσκοπος here as the title of a Christian office and thus to understand ἀλλοτριεπίσκοπος as a bishop who discharges his office in a novel and improper way.

ἐ π ι σ τ ά τ η ς. Preisigke Fachwörter, 89 f.; W. Liebenam, *Städteverwaltung im römischen Kaiserreiche* (1900), 295; J. Rouffiac, *Recherches sur les Caractères du Grec dans le*

the Heb. Aram. רַבִּי. Except in the last instance, it is used only by the disciples. The transcription ῥαββί used by the other Evangelists is avoided by the Hellenist Luke. He also uses διδάσκαλε and κύριε, but does not seem to feel that they are true equivalents. In Mk. 4:38 and par. we have the three terms διδάσκαλε, κύριε and ἐπιστάτα in the Synoptics. Also instructive are Mk. 9:5 and par., 38 and par. (Mk. ῥαββί or διδάσκαλε, Mt. κύριε and Lk. ἐπιστάτα). In some cases (Mk. 11:3 and par.; Lk. 5:8; Mt. 7:21 and par.?), מָר or מָרִי, מָרְנָא may be the original of κύριος, but this can hardly be true of ἐπιστάτα. Nor is מוֹרֶה[1] a likely original.

In secular Gk. there is a rich and varied usage. ἐπιστάτης means one who watches over herds in Soph. Ai., 27; the driver of an elephant in Polyb., I, 40, 11; an Egyptian task master in Ex. 1:11; 5:14;[2] Philo Poster. C., 54; an inspector of public works in Aeschin. Orationes, 3, 14 etc.; 3 Βασ. 5:16; one of the leaders of an athletic society in BMI, IV, 1, 794, 7; the leader of a temple, IG, I, 32, 18 f.; P. Par., 26, 22; Prinz-Joachim-Ostraka (ed. F. Preisigke and W. Spiegelberg, Schriften der Wissenschaftlichen Gesellschaft in Strassburg, 19 [1914]), 60 ff.; cf. No. 2, 6; 18, 5; a music teacher or the leader of a musical competition in APF, 8 (1927), 73; the president of the Athenian college of prytanes in Aristot. Respublica Atheniensium, 44, 1 (ed. Blass, Thalheim, Oppermann [1928]); a high official in 4 Βασ. 25:19; P. Ryl., II, 68, 2; 125, 1; 152, 2; a magistrate or the governor of a city in CIG, III, 4149, 4 (Amastris); IG, XII, 3, 320, 7 (Thera, 3rd cent. B.C.); BGU, III, 1006, 6;[3] even a protective deity in Soph. Oed. Col., 889. The nearest to Lucan usage is in IG, XII, 1, 43, 22 (Rhodes): ἐπιστάτης τῶν παίδων; Inscr. Priene, 112, 73 ff. (1st cent. B.C.): ... ἔτι δὲ σφαίρας καὶ ὅπλα καὶ τὸν ἐπιστάτην τὸν τῶν ἐφήβων τοῖς ἐκ φιλολογίας γραμματικόν, δι᾽ ὦν μὲν τὸ σῶμα βουλόμενος ἄοκνον τυγχάνειν, δι᾽ ὦν δὲ τὰς ψυχὰς πρὸς ἀρετὴν καὶ πάθος ἀνθρώπινον προάγεσθαι. The title was hardly ever used of heads of philosophical schools.[4] We have no knowledge whether or not it was a common form of address.

Oepke

ἐπιστρέφω, ἐπιστροφή → στρέφω.   ἐπισυναγωγή → συναγωγή.
ἐπιταγή → τάσσω.   ἐπιτελέω → τελέω.

ἐπιτιμάω, ἐπιτιμία

† ἐπιτιμάω.

ἐπιτιμάω corresponds to the twofold sense of τιμάω,[1] to accord "honour" on the one side, "blame" or "punishment" on the other. In the latter sense the word comes to mean "to blame," "to reprove," both in class. and Hellenistic Gk.[2] It takes on a special

---

NT d'après les Inscriptions de Priène (1911), 56 f. (with bibl.); W. Foerster, Herr ist Jesus (1924), 209 ff.

[1] F. Delitzsch in his Heb. transl. of the NT.

[2] In the LXX (12 times) and Σ (3 times) ἐπιστάτης is used for 8 different Heb. words. Obviously the LXX has only very general ideas of the offices concerned.

[3] The combination of epistates and strategos is distinctively Parthian: BCH, 57 (1933), 25 ff., esp. 28 ff.; Röm. Mitt., 49 (1934), 197, n. 3.

[4] Though cf. Iambl. Vit. Pyth., 21, 99 (ed. A. Nauck [1884]): ἔθος δ᾽ ἦν τὸν μὲν νεώτατον ἀναγινώσκειν, τὸν δὲ πρεσβύτατον ἐπιστατεῖν δ δεῖ ἀναγινώσκειν καὶ ὡς δεῖ ("to decide the matter and form of the lectures").

ἐπιτιμάω κτλ. G. A. Barton, "The Use of ἐπιτιμᾶν in Mk. 8:30; 3:12," JBL, 41 (1922), 233-236.

[1] → τιμάω, "to evaluate and to measure out punishment," "to estimate highly," "to honour."

[2] V. Pass., Preisigke Wört., s.v.

emphasis in the LXX in terms of the OT thought of the Word of God which evokes the works of God, whether creative or destructive. Thus the creative Word of God (cf. Is. 55:10 f.) which brings forth life (ברא) is contrasted with the reproving Word which calls down destruction (גער).[3] ἐπιτιμάω becomes a technical term for the powerful divine word of rebuke and threat.

God's rebuke shakes heaven (Job 26:11) and moves the earth and the sea (2 Βασ. 22:16; ψ 17:15; 103:7). He threatens the Red Sea and it dries up to let the people of God pass over (ψ 105:9; cf. Is. 50:2 Σ). His Word of command whips up the storm so that men cry to heaven in their distress; His Word of rebuke stills it again so that the waves subside and the cries of distress cease (ψ 106:29 אᵃᶜ). In Syr. Baruch there is still a fine sense of this twofold character of the Word of God: "With threat and reproof thou commandest the flames ... and summonest what is not into being by a Word" (S. Bar. 48:8). Acc. to Zech. 3:2 the threatening Word of God keeps even Satan within bounds: ἐπιτιμήσαι Κύριος ἐν σοί, διάβολε, καὶ ἐπιτιμήσαι Κύριος ἐν σοί. The Apoc. of Ezra (which was, of course, under Christian influence) gives cosmic and eschatological stature to this soundly Jewish motif (cf. S. Bar. 21:23) when it describes how God will one day hurl back Antichrist with a dreadful Word of rebuke (φοβερὰ ἀπειλή).[4] But for the most part God's reproof is directed against men, against the high and mighty until horse and rider are bemused (ψ 75:6; 118:21), against the enemies of God and His people whose raging is like that of the sea (Is. 17:13 'A; ψ 9:5; 79:16), but also against the apostate people itself, so that it wastes and perishes.[5] The last judgment itself will be one of rebuke, for then the divine rebuke will fall like a consuming fire (Is. 66:15 'ΑΣΘ).

It is only with restriction that ἐπιτιμᾶν is used of human threats and reproofs. Thus when Jacob rebukes Joseph because of his presumptuous dreams (Gn. 37:10), we soon see that the rebuke is not justified. 3 Macc. 2:24 (etc.) tells us how dreadfully Ptolemy must expiate (ἐπιτιμηθείς) his insolent threats (ἀπειλή). Only in irony is it said in Is. 30:17 ('ΑΣΘ) that 1000 will flee at the threat of one. The servants of Boaz in Ruth 2:16 are tempted to reprove the foreign gleaner, but their master forbids it. Similarly Akiba warns his disciples in Ket., 63a: "A simple woman falls at the feet of a renowned teacher of the Torah. His disciples wish to drive her away. But he says: Leave her alone; all that we have we owe to her. It was his own wife."[6] Again and again human threatening and reproof is shown to be presumptuous and overhasty. ἐπιτιμάω is not for man, but for God.[7] Thus Baruch prays to God: "Do thou threaten the angel of death" (S. Bar. 21:23). Hence Seth says to the demonic serpent after the manner of Zech. 3:2:[8] "The Lord God rebuke thee."[9] Among the Rabbis a common adjuration is the indirect: "May God rebuke Satan."[10] Only to selected individuals is authority given to utter an effective word of threat according to Jewish tradition. Such authority is given to Abraham in the early period (Jub. 11:19), to men like Enoch and Elijah[11] in the last days, and finally to the Messiah of the lineage of David. He will drive out the demon whom David once tamed when he played the harp for Saul and sang his song

---

[3] Cf. the creative and destructive character of the breath or Spirit of God, → ἐμφυσάω, 536, n. 3.

[4] Apc. Esdrae (C. Tischendorf, Apocal. Apcryph. [1866], p. 29).

[5] Dt. 28:20 'A; Mal. 2:3 'A; Is. 51:20 Θ; though cf. Is. 54:9 'ΑΣΘ.

[6] Cf. Ned., 50a and Str.-B., I, 808.

[7] Satan arrogates to himself divine rights in order to disrupt the divine plan when acc. to Gn. r., 56 on 22:7 he "rebukes" Abraham, arguing that he should spare Isaac. V. Str.-B., I, 747.

[8] Cf. also ψ 67:30 (θηρίοις).

[9] Vit. Ad., 39, with refer. to the day of judgment.

[10] bQid., 81b; v. Str.-B., I, 140.

[11] Apc. Elias 34 f., threatening speeches of Tabitha, Enoch and Elijah against Antichrist, v. G. Steindorff, TU, NF, II, 3a (1899).

of exorcism. [12] Seth adjures the serpent in the name of God, and David the demon in the name of the coming Messiah.

If men have any right of ἐπιτιμᾶν among themselves, it can only be in terms of judicial, paternal or fraternal correction. Thus the Wisdom literature warns us to make good proof of a matter before sentence is passed (Sir. 11:7). On the other hand, we should take to heart the reproofs of the wise (Qoh. 7:6; Prv. 17:10 'ΑΘ). The Damascus document regulates the forms of brotherly correction even to the minutest details (Damasc., 7, 2; 9, 2 ff.). And the Synagogue laid the greatest value on the preservation and codification of reproofs. [13]

The NT maintains the same tradition by 1. forbidding rebuke except as brotherly correction, and 2. treating effective threatening and reproof as the prerogative of God and His Christ alone.

1. ἐπετίμησαν is used for rebuke in Mk. 10:13 and par., when the disciples drive the mothers away with severe words. But their action is overhasty, for Jesus declares like Akiba (→ 624): ἄφετε — μὴ κωλύετε (10:14). It is also used for threatening in Mk. 10:48, when the crowd takes up a hostile attitude to the blind man who cries to Jesus for help. But the blind man continues to cry, and Jesus hears him. Again the ἐπιτιμᾶν is presumptuous and unfounded. It is used for personal scolding in Mk. 8:32, where Peter takes Jesus aside and with heated words tries to turn Him from His path as Satan tried to do with Abraham (→ n. 7); cf. Mt. 16:22: ἵλεώς σοι, κύριε· οὐ μὴ ἔσται σοι τοῦτο. But Jesus resists him with His own ἐπιτιμᾶν: [14] ἐπιτιμᾶν is the prerogative of the Lord.

Only once is a spontaneous ἐπιτιμᾶν on the lips of men allowed to pass unchallenged. This is the rebuke of the one dying thief by the other in Lk. 23:40: ὁ ἕτερος ἐπιτιμῶν αὐτῷ ἔφη. But in this case the rebuke is not from a superior position, but from the standpoint of penitence. Hence humilitas speaks rather than superbia (Lk. 23:41).

Similarly, the early Church recognises only one situation when a formal ἐπιτιμᾶν is in keeping for man. This is the brotherly correction of a fallen brother: Προσέχετε ἑαυτοῖς· ἐὰν ἁμάρτῃ ὁ ἀδελφός σου, ἐπιτίμησον αὐτῷ, καὶ ἐὰν μετανοήσῃ, ἄφες αὐτῷ (Lk. 17:3). Reproof should be accompanied by the awareness of common guilt before God and therefore by a spirit of unconditional forgiveness. The further development of congregational practice may be seen clearly in the injunction in 2 Tm. 4:2 (with the parallel Mt. 18:15): ἔλεγξον, ἐπιτίμησον, παρακάλεσον, ἐν πάσῃ μακροθυμίᾳ καὶ διδαχῇ. In the first instance, however, this congregational discipline is a duty and prerogative of the leaders of the church.

2. ἐπιτιμᾶν is a prerogative of lordship. Primarily, therefore, it belongs to God. When the devil strives with the archangel Michael in Jd. 9, it is said of the latter: οὐκ ἐτόλμησεν κρίσιν ἐπενεγκεῖν βλασφημίας, ἀλλὰ εἶπεν· ἐπιτιμήσαι σοι κύριος. Here we have the favourite indirect formula from Zech. 3:2. [15] Along the same lines, ἐπιτιμᾶν is a prerogative of Jesus in the Gospels. It is a right which declares His position as the Lord.

---

[12] Ps.-Philo, Ant. Bibl., 60, ἐλέγξουσι in M. R. James, Apocrypha Anecdota, Texts and Studies, 2, 3 (1893), 185. Cf. ἔλεγξον in Mt. 18:15; 2 Tm. 4:2.

[13] Cf. Str.-B., I, 787 ff.

[14] This nicety is lost in Mt. 16:23.

[15] The scene is taken from an apocryphal writing and does not appear, or is rephrased, in the par. 2 Pt. 2:11. Acc. to early tradition the reference is to the Assumptio Mosis. Cf. J. Felten, Die Briefe des Petrus und Judas (1929), 265.

Jesus is the διδάσκαλος who rebukes Peter or the self-seeking Sons of Thunder (Mk. 8:33; Lk. 9:55). This is His right. But He is also so truly the Lord that He reserves the right to Himself. When the Pharisees appeal to Him: διδάσκαλε, ἐπιτίμησον τοῖς μαθηταῖς σου, this draws from Him a clear reproof (Lk. 19:39 f.; cf. Mk. 2:23 ff.).

'Επιτιμᾶν is a warning to keep silence on the lips of Jesus when He is acknowledged by His disciples to be the Messiah: καὶ ἐπετίμησεν αὐτοῖς, ἵνα μηδενὶ λέγωσιν περὶ αὐτοῦ (Mk. 8:30).

The construction is toned down in Lk. 9:21, and in Mt. 16:20 the καὶ ἐπετίμησεν is replaced by the hieratic expression τότε διεστείλατο (אC.ℵpl), so that the living directness is lost. This makes it the more dramatically clear that Mark's is the original and the more realistic account, in spite of the brilliant but untenable theory of Wrede that the command to keep silence is a fiction of the early Church. [16] It originates rather in the basic conviction of Jesus that there is a time for decision which is not to be hastened (cf. Lk. 13:13 f.). Thus the manifestation of what He is can come only a step at a time, and will be completed only with the τέλος.

The same command in the same sense is addressed by Jesus, when He heals, to the demons which recognise Him and call out His true name: καὶ πολλὰ ἐπετίμα αὐτοῖς, ἵνα μὴ αὐτὸν φανερὸν ποιήσωσιν. [17] Jesus is not merely the reproving and commanding Lord in the circle of disciples; He is also Lord over the demons and bends them to His will. He is the Stronger who penetrates into the house of the strong man and drives out demons with the finger of God. [18] A threatening word of power is addressed to them with His lordly ἐπιτιμᾶν. Mark graphically depicts the way in which Jesus, proclaimed by God as the Son, takes up the struggle against the demon: ἐπετίμησεν τῷ πνεύματι τῷ ἀκαθάρτῳ λέγων αὐτῷ· τὸ ἄλαλον καὶ κωφὸν πνεῦμα, ἐγὼ ἐπιτάσσω σοι, ἔξελθε. The demonic spirit rears up: καὶ κράξας καὶ πολλὰ σπαράξας ἐξῆλθεν (Mk. 9:25 f.). [19] But the Word triumphs. It is not a magical incantation such as we have in the accounts of marvels. It is the powerful Word of the Son (→ n. 4; → ἐγώ, 348). According to Lk. 4:39 He uses the same mighty weapon against other sicknesses and personal opponents: καὶ ἐπιστὰς ἐπάνω αὐτῆς ἐπετίμησεν τῷ πυρετῷ, καὶ ἀφῆκεν αὐτήν.

Nor is it only the demons, pursuing their unnatural work in men, who recoil before His threatening Word. Jesus also knows and tames the powers which rage in the elemental forces of nature. Καὶ διεγερθεὶς ἐπετίμησεν τῷ ἀνέμῳ καὶ εἶπεν τῇ θαλάσσῃ· σιώπα, πεφίμωσο (→ 624). The elements have found their Master: καὶ ἐκόπασεν ὁ ἄνεμος, καὶ ἐγένετο γαλήνη μεγάλη (Mk. 4:39). This man is more powerful than the forces of nature. Τίς ἄρα οὗτός ἐστιν, ὅτι καὶ ὁ ἄνεμος καὶ ἡ θάλασσα ὑπακούει αὐτῷ; (Mk. 4:41). Christ is the One who commands nature as its Lord and King. [20] Thus the unconditional lordship of Jesus is powerfully revealed in this ἐπιτιμᾶν. [21]

---

[16] W. Wrede, *Das Messiasgeheimnis in den Ev.* (1901), 33 ff.

[17] Mk. 3:12; Barton, *op. cit.* sees a par. in P. Oxy., X, 1295, 5. Here again Lk. tones down and Mt. stylises (Lk. 4:41; Mt. 12:16 ff.).

[18] The word of command and the word of exorcism are combined in ἐπιτιμάω in Mk. 1:25 (Lk. 4:35): ἐπετίμησεν αὐτῷ ὁ 'Ιησοῦς· φιμώθητι καὶ ἔξελθε.

[19] Lk. and esp. Mt. give a far less graphic rendering (Lk. 9:42 f.; Mt. 17:18).

[20] Cf. Gn. 1:28; Mk. 1:13; 11:23.

[21] Cf. also 2 Th. 2:8; Rev. 19:11 ff. and → n. 3, 11.

† ἐπιτιμία.

In class. Gk. and the LXX "punishment." [1] It occurs in the NT only at 2 C. 2:6 as a technical term in congregational discipline for the censure of the church : ἡ ἐπιτιμία αὕτη ἡ ὑπὸ τῶν πλειόνων → ἐπιτιμάω, 625.

Stauffer

ἐπιφαίνω, ἐπιφάνεια, ἐπιφανής → φῶς.　　ἐπιφαύσκω → φῶς.
ἐποικοδομέω → οἰκοδομέω.　　　　　　　　　ἐπουράνιος → οὐρανός.

ἑπτά, † ἑπτάκις, † ἑπτακισχίλιοι,
ἕβδομος, ἑβδομήκοντα,
† ἑβδομηκοντάκις

A. The Background in Religious History.

1. The predominant position of the number seven, esp. in Semitic culture and the Bible, but also among the Germans, the Greeks, [1] the Egyptians etc., [2] is almost certainly due, not to the existence of seven planets, but to observation of the four phases of the moon in seven-day periods, unless, of course, there is no rational explanation.

Against its derivation from observation of the planets is its almost universal character, the fact that seven was highly valued in Greece long before Pythagoras fixed the number of planets at seven (in dependence, as it seems, on Asiatic astronomy and astrology), [3] and the further fact that in some places the number is important even though the number of planets was not established so far as we know. [4] Even in Babylon, where interest in the seven planets seems to have begun, the number seven played a role in myth and the cultus prior to study of the seven planets ; indeed, it seems likely that the Babylonians took over seven as a sacred number from the Sumerians. [5] On the other hand, the phases of the moon could be observed everywhere and were the primitive basis of the reckoning and division of time. [6] The Babylonian creation epic, like the creation story of the OT, makes it clear than the moon played a considerable part in the measuring of time, [7] so that almost of itself seven emerged as a number of great

---

ἐπιτιμία. [1] Preisigke Wört. also notes Ditt. Or., 669, II, 43; P. Lond., I, 77, 53; P. Masp., 4, 12. In the LXX cf. Sir. 11:7 (ἐπιτιμάω as a penal measure); Wis. 12:26 (ἐπιτίμησις as a warning punishment which precedes the κρίσις θεοῦ); 3:10 : οἱ ... ἀσεβεῖς ... ἕξουσιν ἐπιτιμίαν (of God).

ἑπτά. W. H. Roscher, "Die enneadischen und hebdomadischen Fristen und Wochen der ältesten Griechen," ASG, 21, 4 (1903); "Die Sieben- und Neunzahl in Kultus und Mythus der Griechen," *ibid.*, 24, 1 (1904); "Die Hebdomadenlehren der griech. Philosophen und Ärzte," *ibid.*, 24, 6 (1906); RE³, 18 (1906), 310 ff.; 24 (1913), 513 (E. v. Dobschütz); J. Hehn, "Siebenzahl und Sabbat bei den Babyloniern und im AT," *Leipziger semitistische Studien*, II, 5 (1907); F. Boll, *Aus der Offenbarung Johannis, ΣΤΟΙΧΕΙΑ, 1 (1914), 21 ff. and Index, s.v. Siebenzahl* ; J. H. Graf, *Die Zahl Sieben* (1917); J. Hehn, "Zur Bedeutung der Siebenzahl" in *Festschrift für K. Marti (Beihefte z. ZAW, 41 [1925])*, 128 ff.; Comm. on Rev.; RGG², V (1931), 2068.

[1] The part played by the number among the Romans seems to be due to Gk. influence ; cf. E. Wölfflin, *Archiv f. lat. Lexikographie u. Grammatik*, 9 (1896), 343 ff.; but also Roscher, "Sieben- und Neunzahl," 72.

[2] Cf. the materials in Roscher, "Fristen," 28 ff.

[3] Cf. Roscher, "Fristen," 41 ff.; "Sieben- und Neunzahl," 75, n. 165.

[4] Cf. Roscher, "Fristen," 34 f. with n. 117.

[5] Hehn, "Siebenzahl und Sabbat," 45 ff.

[6] Cf. esp. Roscher, "Fristen," 29 f. and Hehn, *op. cit.*, 57 ff.

[7] Cf. the references in Hehn, *op. cit.*, 59 ff.

significance in the cosmos and its order. Added lustre was given to it when the presence
of seven planets was later established. [8] Thus its religious use was made possible and
prepared; [9] and in the same light we can understand the esteem accorded to it both
within and, as we must add, outside the circle of Semitic culture, including Israel and
its religion.

2. If we ask further concerning the cosmic significance of seven according to its
concrete sense in the OT world of thought, a basic point is the equation VII = kiššatu
= "fulness," "totality," which is found among the Babylonians. [10] As has been shown
by J. Hehn, [11] the same equation is true of the Hebrew שֶׁבַע, so that we have here a
common Semitic phenomenon. The true foundation of the equation is the above-men-
tioned observation that time runs in periods of seven days. This leads to the linking of
seven with a completed period, and from here it is only a step to the equation of the
abstract number seven with the concept of what is total or complete. Seven represents
a complete whole and is thus the given magnitude by which to give short and pregnant
expression to such a totality. [12] The number seven thus bears the character of totality,
i.e., of the totality desired and ordained by God.

Naturally, the original clarity of this character was not always maintained. Precisely
where the sacral element predominated, there was a tendency to use seven very widely
as a round number. Among the Babylonians as well as in Israel, seven came to play a
dominant part in ritual, especially in expiations and cleansings, but also in prayers and
the ceremonial of sacrifice. [13] When we find a hand with seven fingers in Babylonian
art, this can only signify the perfect power and might proper to deity alone. [14] On
Israelite soil, we think especially in this connection of the Sabbath as the seventh day
devoted to God, [15] but also of the whole sacred year of Israel and Judaism with its
hebdomadal feasts, the aim in both cases being to order the relationship to God in its
totality, and in such a way that as a totality it is orientated to God. We may also
mention the sabbatical year (Ex. 23:10 f.; Lv. 25:1 ff.; Dt. 15:1 ff.; 31:10 ff.), noting that
only at a later period did it take on social aspects.

These examples are enough to bring out the nature of seven in the OT, the more so
as they may easily be duplicated. It should be noted, of course, that in the early days
of Israelite literature the conception was not complete, especially as concerns the
hebdomadal cycle of Hebrew festivals. This does not alter the fact, however, that it is
part of the cultural heritage of the ancient Semitic world, which certainly includes the
special significance attached to the number seven.

3. Philo stands apart from OT and Jewish usage to the degree that he develops
a definite mysticism of numbers [16] in which seven naturally plays an important part [17]

---

[8] That the planets have a regulative influence on each day of the week is a view which
is first found for certain only in Hellenistic Egypt in the 1st century B.C. It is still an open
question whether there are connections with Babylon and its astrology. E. Schürer thinks it
possible that belief in the planets first took distinctive shape only in Hellenism (ZNW, 6
[1905], 16 ff.). If this is true, a definite planet cultus was first developed in Egypt (cf.
Hehn, op. cit., 51 f.).

[9] For the Gks. cf. Roscher, op. cit., passim and esp. 71, where he argues the dependence
of the Gk. hebdomadal festivals on the cycle of the moon and independence of Babylon and
esp. of a Babylonian planet cultus.

[10] Cf. Hehn, op. cit., 4 f., 52 ff., and "Bedeutung der Siebenzahl," 130.

[11] Cf. esp. "Bedeutung der Siebenzahl," 151 ff.

[12] Cf. Hehn, "Siebenzahl und Sabbat," 62.

[13] Cf. the references assembled in Hehn, op. cit., 34 ff.

[14] D. Nielsen, Die altarabische Mondreligion und die mosaische Überlieferung (1904),
155; Hehn, "Siebenzahl und Sabbat," 17.

[15] On the relation of the Jewish Sabbath to the Babyl. šabbattu, which is not yet fully
clear, cf. the short discussion by O. Eissfeldt, RGG², II, 553 f.

[16] Cf. K. Staehle, Die Zahlenmystik bei Philon von Alexandreia (Diss. Tübingen, 1931).

[17] V. the references in Staehle, 34 ff.

(cf. esp. Op. Mund., 90 ff.). Obvious here is belief in the influence of the seven planets on the cosmos and its inhabitants (Op. Mund., 113). [18] We also find in him repeatedly the view that seven determines the rhythm of human life, and that even the body is subject to its law, [19] since human life goes in seven-year cycles (Op. Mund., 103 ff.). At this point Philo is dependent on Greek tradition, at the beginning of which stands Solon's doctrine of ten weeks of years in the life of man; he himself cites Solon as an authority (Op. Mund., 104). Philo also seems to know the teaching of Ps.-Hippocrates concerning the seven ages of life (Op. Mund., 105). In relation to Solon this is a simplification rather than a new conception, since it starts with the idea of weeks of years in human life. [20]

Particular interest attaches at this point to Philo's relation to his Jewish contemporaries. In its second form the idea of the ages of life is found also in Rabb. Judaism, but only in the later Midrashim, whose dependence on Hellenistic tradition is easy to prove in this respect. [21] The same is true of the conviction that a seven month child may live, but not an eight month. This is found in both Philo and the Rabbis. In Philo it is stated as a fact, with no direct speculative impact, within his discussion of the nature and significance of the number seven. But it has a more speculative bearing in Rabbinic tradition. Thus, in a conversation with Gk. enquirers, R. Abbahu (c. 300 A.D.) says concerning this supposed fact: [22] "From your own lips I will answer you: זיטא איטא אפטא איטא אוכטא." What he means is that the letters which serve to indicate the numbers ἑπτά and ὀκτώ shows how it stands with seven month and eight month babies, for ζ points to ζῆν and η to ἰέναι or ἰτός (jJeb., 5d, 5 ff. — the text is corrupt; Gn. r. 14 on 2:7 etc.). [23] It may be said that by the very appearance of the Gk. words the thought expressed, which in no sense proves the truth of the disputed statement, is given a non-Jewish flavour. This is supported by the fact that it is comparatively late and belongs to a time when Judaism was engaged in lively apologetic interaction with the non-Jewish world around. Here again, then, the speculation linked with seven is secondary. This confirms the fact that Philo and older Palestinian Judaism really go different ways in this respect.

B. The NT Usage.

1. The influence of the OT may be seen in R. 11:4, where Paul quotes 1 K. 19:18. [24] In God's word to Elijah that He had kept 7,000 faithful to Himself in the time of apostasy, Paul finds a testimony to God's saving will for His people in every age as this is manifested in his own day in the existence of at least a small Christian Israel (11:5). We cannot be sure from the context whether Paul connected with the OT number the thought of the totality of the true Israel which is certainly present in 1 K. 19:18.

R. 11:4 is the only passage in Paul, and with Hb. 11:30 in all the NT Epistles, where the number seven occurs. This is perhaps an indication that the special meaning of the

---

[18] *Ibid.,* 41 f.

[19] *Ibid.,* 44 ff.

[20] W. H. Roscher, *Die hippokratische Schrift von der Siebenzahl in ihrer vierfachen Überlieferung = Studien zur Geschichte und Kultur des Altertums,* VI, 3-4 (1913), 9 f., cf. 136.

[21] Cf. also G. A. Kohut, Jew. Enc., I (1901), 233 ff.

[22] A part of Jewish marriage law rests on this, e.g., the provision that a widowed or divorced woman must wait three months before remarrying in order that there should be no doubt whether children are of the first or second marriage (cf. Jeb., 4, 10 etc.).

[23] EJ, I (1928), 118 transcribes ζῆτα—ζήτω; ἦτα—ἴτω.

[24] Paul is using the original here; the LXX has the second person. The change from the original future to κατέλιπον is easily explained by the fact that Paul has before him the fulfilled promise.

number was present to the authors, and that they therefore avoided it where its understanding was difficult or concealed. There is also in the avoidance, however, an element of opposition to contemporary speculation. This was unnecessary because the Christian message was esssentially different from Gnosticism.

Other OT passages to which reference is made are those which speak of the seven days of the siege of Jericho (Hb. 11:30; cf. Jos. 6:1 ff.) and of the seven races which inhabited Canaan prior to the conquest (Ac. 13:19; cf. Dt. 7:1). But these are simply mentioned as historical facts with no attempt at speculation.

2. "Seven days" is a term for week in Ac. 20:6; 21:4, 27; 28:14; and the "seventh day" (Sabbath) is mentioned in Hb. 4:4.

3. Seven is a round number with no hidden sense in the account of the feeding of the four thousand with seven loaves and two fishes; the number of loaves is the same as that of the baskets of fragments (Mt. 15:32 ff.; Mk. 8:1 ff.; cf. Mt. 16:10; Mk. 8:20).

The context suggests no reason why a deeper sense should be sought for the number here, for, although Mt. seems to like seven as a principle in the arrangement of his material, [25] Mk. has the same figure. There are no analogous incidents either in the Rabb. or the Hellenistic sphere, so that no explanation is possible in terms of either usage. [26] Seven is sometimes used for an indefinite magnitude, cf. Test. N. 6: "And again after seven days (months?) I saw our father Jacob ..." with Test. N. Heb. 4: "But no long period passed before another vision was granted to me. We all stood with our father Jacob on the shore of the great sea ..."

4. In some passages in the Gospels older ideas of the significance of the number are linked with its use. a. The Sadducees refer to seven brothers who each married the same wife, six in fulfilment of the appropriate law (Mt. 22:23 ff.; cf. Dt. 25:5 ff.). The implication is that they have in view an infinite series.

Cf. the saying of Aqiba (d. c. 135) to his friends at the grave of his (only) son Simon: "I am comforted, even though I had buried seven sons (and not just one)" (Semachot, 8; bMQ, 21b). [27] We might also mention as a parallel the seven martyred brothers in 4 Macc., who embody the whole people, their mother being addressed in 15:29 as μήτηρ ἔθνους (cf. also 17:2 ff., esp. 6).

If this conception of seven is correct, it is self-evident [28] that the question of the Sadducees does not relate to a real situation. It is a hypothetical case artificially invented to bring into ridicule the Pharisees' hope of the resurrection and their casuistical methods, and also to embarrass Jesus. The answer of Jesus shatters this aspect of the question too by pointing to God as the One before whom all human reckoning comes to an end because He is the Creator and the Almighty.

b. In Mt. 12:45; Lk. 11:26, it is said of the backslider that with the exorcised spirit seven worse spirits return into him. It is also said of Mary Magdalene that δαιμόνια ἑπτά were driven out of her (Lk. 8:2; cf. Mk. 16:9). In both cases the occurrence of the number seven points to the fact that there could be no worse

---

[25] Cf. the seven beatitudes in Mt. 5:3 ff. and the seven parables in Mt. 13; cf. Bultmann Trad., 382. On seven as a stylistic motif, → 633.

[26] In Babylonian texts (Hehn, "Siebenzahl und Sabbat," 38 f.) there are occasional references to seven loaves, e.g., in conjurations. But this has no bearing on the present question.

[27] On the transmission of the sayings of Aqiba, cf. W. Bacher, Die Agada der Tannaiten, I (1884), 305, n. 3.

[28] An important point, though it is contested, is that the Levirate law was no longer kept at the time of Jesus (cf. K. H. Rengstorf, Jebamot [1929], 30 ff.).

state of corruption : καὶ γίνεται τὰ ἔσχατα τοῦ ἀνθρώπου ἐκείνου χείρονα τῶν πρώτων (Mt. 12:45; Lk. 11:26).

There is a certain parallel in 2 K. 4:35. When Elisha lay on the son of the Shunammite to call him back to life, the boy sneezed seven times. This proves that he is really alive again (cf. 4:36). The sevenfold sneeze indicates that life has fully returned as it was before.

c. Particularly important are the passages which speak of sinning seven times and forgiving seven times (Mt. 18:21 f.; Lk. 17:4). In Mt. Peter is asking whether there is not a limit on the duty to forgive if another continually offends, whether we should not stop at seven times, and he receives the answer : οὐ λέγω σοι ἕως ἑπτάκις, ἀλλὰ ἕως ἑβδομηκοντάκις ἑπτά. In Lk. we do not have Peter's question ; Jesus simply says that sevenfold offence must be met by sevenfold forgiveness if there is μετάνοια. Laying aside critical questions concerning the interrelation of the two passages, [29] we need have no doubts as to the meaning of the saying. According to the will of Jesus there is no limit to forgiveness [30] whether the measure of readiness therefor corresponds to the measure of incurred guilt (Lk.) or whether it transcends it (Mt.), since both amount in fact to the same thing.

Already in ancient Babylon seven is linked with confession of sin and with readiness to expiate and to forgive (→ 628). In one penitential psalm [31] the penitent even calls his sins seventy times seven in order to show how immeasurably great they are (cf. ἑβδομηκοντάκις ἑπτά, Mt. 18:22). In another penitential psalm [32] there is a corresponding sevenfold request for forgiveness, with an express desire for sevenfold, i.e., perfect forgiveness. In the sphere of Israel and Judah the great Day of Atonement sees a sevenfold sprinkling of the blood of the sin offering by the high-priest in atonement for the sins of the whole people (Lv. 16:15 ff.; cf. Joma, 5, 4), and this is preceded by a sevenfold sprinkling with the blood of a special sin offering in atonement for himself and his family (Lv. 16:11 ff.; Joma, 5, 3). Here, too, the reference is in both instances to the perfect removal of sin and the attainment of full remission. Finally, we may refer to 2 Βασ. 12:6. The original follows the provisions of the Law (Ex. 21:37) and speaks of fourfold satisfaction for the stolen sheep, while in the LXX we read : καὶ τὴν ἀμνάδα ἀποτίσει ἑπταπλασίονα. This strangely moving translation is clear once we see that it is intended to denote full satisfaction of guilt. This idea is present in the אַרְבַּעְתָּיִם of the original. But here it can be appreciated only in relation to the provision of the Law, while it is more directly indicated in the LXX by mention of the number seven. [33]

Special reference should be made to the ἑβδομηκοντάκις ἑπτά of Mt. 18:22.

In Gn. 4:24 the sevenfold avenging of Cain (cf. also 4:15) [34] is surpassed by that of Lamech שִׁבְעִים וְשִׁבְעָה — a formula which is rendered ἑβδομηκοντάκις ἑπτά in the

---

[29] Lk. 17:4 seems to be older than Mt. 18:21 f. (cf. Bultmann Trad., 151); but it may be that we have two different sayings of Jesus in the two Gospels.

[30] This is the view of the Rabbis. It is true that there are no direct references, but we can learn the Rabbinic view of the human duty of forgiveness quite adequately from passages which tell us that even the divine forgiveness is restricted (T. Joma, 5, 13 [Schl. Mt., 559]; bJoma, 86b Bar. [Str.-B., I, 796]).

[31] Hehn, "Siebenzahl und Sabbat," 34 f.

[32] Ibid., 35.

[33] As a par. cf. the sevenfold (septem ordines) joy which the righteous may expect after death acc. to 4 Esr. 7:88 ff., and the sevenfold torment which will come upon the ungodly (7:79 ff.).

[34] Perhaps a proverbial saying, cf. H. Holzinger in Kautzsch, ad loc.

LXX (so also Test. B. 7). Perhaps this translation is the immediate linguistic pattern for Mt. 18:22. On the other hand, we do not know how the translator understood the formula, and the same is true of the saying of Jesus. It may be that Jesus used שִׁבְעִים וְשִׁבְעָה or a corresponding Aram. expression such as שַׁבְעִין וְשִׁבְעָה] (Tg. O. Gn. 4:24). [35] On the other hand, it makes no material difference whether He is thinking of 490 times or 77, since the figure means that there must be no limits to forgiveness.

d. Finally, it should be noted that the genealogies of Jesus in Mt. and Lk. (Mt. 1:1 ff.; Lk. 3:23 ff.) are basically constructed according to the principle of seven. In this schema, which seems to have been taken over, there is expressed in Mt. and Lk., for all the differences in detail, the same thought that Jesus is shown to be the expected Messiah by His place in the lineage of David as the last in the ninth (Mt.) or eleventh (Lk.) group of seven. [36] The thesis is certainly worth considering in the light of certain distinctive aspects of Jewish tradition.

5. Particularly dominated by the number seven is the Revelation of John. There are seven churches in Asia and seven ἄγγελοι (1:4 ff.). Seven candlesticks (1:13 ff.) and seven stars (1:16 ff.) are linked with the appearance of ὅμοιος υἱὸς ἀνθρώπου. There are seven spirits before the throne of God (1:4; 4:5) and seven seals (5:1 ff.). The Lamb has seven horns and seven eyes (5:6). Seven trumpets are in the hands of seven angels (8:2 ff.). There are seven thunders (10:3 f.). The → δράκων has seven heads and on them seven crowns (12:3; cf. 13:1; 17:3 ff.); and there are seven plagues (15:1 ff.). This prominence of seven is no accident, especially as there are other instances of it in apocalyptic. [37] On the other hand, the attempt to make seven the formal principle of Revelation [38] cannot be carried through consistently. We are thus advised to dwell only on the material significance of seven in Revelation. Here, too, it is certainly the number of perfection, and essentially in the sense that it carries within it "the perfection of the divine work." [39] In this sense it pervades the whole book. [40] Yet it is also used to describe the full development of the forces hostile to God, esp. the beast with seven heads (12:3 etc.). It is worth remembering that this description is designed to bring out the fact that these hostile forces are anti-Christian, just as we read elsewhere that Antichrist imitates the divine manner (cf. 2 Th. 2:4; 2 C. 11:14). We are certainly to put the reference in the context of the whole book (cf. also what follows).

So far as concerns the individual references to seven, these are naturally influenced by the different motifs suggested to the author by apocalyptic tradition and the historical situation. Thus Babylonian myth speaks of a dragon with seven heads, [41] and when bQid., 29b tells of a demon in the form of a dragon with seven heads this shows us that

---

[35] Thus Delitzsch has עַד־שִׁבְעִים וְשֶׁבַע (sc. פְּעָמִים) in his Heb. NT.

[36] Cf. on this whole question K. Bornhäuser, *Die Geburts- und Kindheitsgeschichte Jesu* (1930), 14 ff.

[37] Cf. the references in Loh. Apk., 181 f.

[38] So Loh. Apk., cf. esp. 182 ff.; and before him Boll, 59. There can be no disputing that seven is sometimes a principle of composition in early Christianity. We need only think of the seven parables of Mt. 13 (→ n. 25) or the seven petitions of the Lord's Prayer, which are not without models (→ 628) and which also exerted their own influence, e.g., on the form of the first *sura* of the Koran (cf. H. Winkler, "Fātiḥa und Vaterunser," *Zeitschrift f. Semitistik,* 6 ([1928], 238 ff.).

[39] A. Schlatter, *Erläuterungen zum NT,* on Rev. 1:4 f.

[40] Cf. 3½ as an indication of time (11:9 ff.; cf. 12:14 : καιρὸν καὶ καιροὺς καὶ ἥμισυ καιροῦ, from Da. 7:25; 42 months : 11:2; 13:5; 1260 days : 11:3; 12:6). On the significance of 3½, v. Kittel, *Rabbinica* (1920), 31 ff.

[41] Loh. Apk., 97 on 12:3; → δράκων, 281 ff.

the notion persisted through the centuries. [42] In 17:9 the author himself explains that the seven heads are ἑπτὰ ὄρη, thus pointing his contemporaries unmistakeably to Rome with its seven hills. He also introduces the thought of seven kings, which his readers must have understood but which will always be something of a riddle for us even if we adopt the most obvious suggestion that he has in view seven emperors. [43] When he specifies seven churches, he is no doubt referring to the whole of Asiatic Christianity according to the usage of the book, but it is also worth considering that the seven cities were the provincial centres of the imperial cult. [44] The seven stars, apart from the interpretation in 1:20, [45] contain a conscious or unconscious reference to the linking of the seven planets with Mithras, as we know from many depictions of the god, [46] or even to their linking with the images of the emperors on coins, [47] which might have been a secondary consideration. From the fact that they are ἑπτὰ ἀθάνατοι θεοὶ τοῦ κόσμου (Mithr. Liturg., 10, 15 f.), we can see that they are a symbol of world dominion. In the context of Rev., however, they simply mean that Jesus is the unconditional Lord of the seven churches. The seven thunders (10:3 f.) are best seen in the light of ψ 28:3-9, where there are seven references to the φωνὴ κυρίου and its effects. We do not mean, of course, that the author simply borrowed the thunders and that they had no part in his own visionary experience. [48] The seven λαμπάδες πυρός (4:5) are based on the seven-branched candelabra of the temple, though not restricted to its symbolism as a "pledge of the divine presence" (S. Lv., 24, 3; Str.-B., III, 717). The seven seals (5:1 ff.) relate to the Roman custom of sealing a will with seven seals. [49] On the seven horns (5:6) as a symbol of full power, → κέρας, and on the seven eyes cf. Zech. 4:10 (the "seven eyes" of God).

The number seven does also influence the form of Revelation to a very large extent, [50] but not merely in the sense of an apocalyptic number, as E. Lohmeyer supposes. In this respect Rev. may be compared with Mt. (→ n. 25), and both are grounded in the ancient religious use of seven to express the divine plenitude and totality — a use which is particularly characteristic of the Semites. The number also appears as a formal religious principle outside the Jewish and NT sphere (cf. the seven images in Vergil's 4th Eclogue), but most of the references are from within Judaism. It thus seems likely that, while the author of Rev. did not adopt a specific apocalyptic form, he simply took over the use of seven from the Judaism of his day and combined it with his employment of seven as a principle of arrangement in religious contexts. [51]

Cf. the series of seven related proverbs which yet form a connected whole in S. Nu. § 40 on 6:24; § 42 on 6:26 (four series of seven each); § 84 on 10:35 (two of seven); M. Ex., 15, 7 (two of seven) etc. Similarly, the great Messianic psalm in the Ps. Sol. (17) contains only seven-lined strophes, of which there are seven in the first part and five in the second.

---

[42] There is no need to see a reference to astral conceptions (Boll, 101 f.).

[43] Cf. the comm., ad loc.; rejection of any attempt at contemporary explanation in favour of mythological, such as we see in Loh. Apk., ad loc., simply adds to the obscurity.

[44] Loh. Apk., 14.

[45] There are seven angels around the throne acc. to Jewish tradition (Str.-B., III, 805 f.).

[46] Cf. F. J. Dölger, Antike u. Christentum, 3 (1933), 64 f.

[47] Loh. Apk., 16.

[48] Had. Apk., 115, ad loc.

[49] Cf. W. Sattler, ZNW, 21 (1922), 51 ff.

[50] Cf. the detailed references in Loh. Apk., 181 ff.

[51] The passages which follow I owe to K. G. Kuhn. Cf. also Kuhn's Sifre zu Numeri (Rabbinische Texte, 2nd Ser., Vol. 2 [1933 f.]), 131, n. 27; and on the structure of Ps. Sol. 17 "Die syrische Übersetzung der Psalmen Sal." in BWANT, 4, 17 (1935).

6. In Ac. 6:2 ff. seven men, πλήρεις πνεύματος καὶ σοφίας, are charged with διακονεῖν τραπέζαις (→ 84) by the Church. Here the choice of seven is linked with the fact that there were usually seven leaders in a Jewish community.[52] That this custom was followed[53] shows us how little the Twelve (→ 325) were thought to be a ruling and guiding college. If it had been otherwise, we might have expected twelve διάκονοι as their colleagues or subordinates. But this did not happen. Seven men thus became the first officials of the Church with responsibility for material affairs.

7. According to Lk. 10:1 ff. Jesus did not merely send out the Twelve, but also on a later occasion another ἑβδομήκοντα,[54] thus giving to them, too, a share in His work (→ I, 427). The choice of these seventy as apostles indicates the universalism of Jesus and His goal. At least we can say that it was significant to Luke in this regard, so that from his own distinctive source he brought the account into his gospel even at the risk of a certain conflict with the tradition concerning the mission of the Twelve.

A possible model for the seventy disciples is to be found in the seventy elders who were appointed by Moses (Nu. 11:16) and who also provided the model for the constitution of the great Sanhedrin with its 71 members (Sanh., 1, 6; bSanh., 16b). We find the number elsewhere, and always on the same basis. Thus Josephus as commander-in-chief in Galilee appointed seventy elders to rule the territory (Bell., 2, 570 f.). Similarly, when the Zealots took control in Jerusalem they set up a court with seventy members (Bell., 4, 335 and 341). Again, the Jewish community in Alexandria had seventy elders (jSukka, 55a, 72 ff.),[55] as had also the colony of Babylonian Jews in Batanaea acc. to Joseph. (Bell., 2, 482; Vit., 56). The objection to this basis is that in all these instances we have colleges with technical administrative duties, and this hardly leads us in the direction of discipleship and apostleship as instituted by Jesus.

The alternative is to think of the seventy nations of the world, which was a common conception in later Judaism (apart from Gn. 10 cf. already Dt. 32:8 with Ex. 1:5; also Eth. En. 89:59 f.; Tg. J, I on Gn. 11:7 f.).[56] Since the Rabbis were firmly convinced that the Torah had been offered to all nations before Israel became the one people of the Law, there was a widespread view that it was given to the human race in seventy languages (Sota, 7, 5; T. Sota, 8, 6 etc.). The co-operation of angels in the giving of the Law (→ I, 83) implies according to Pesikt. r., 21[57] that the angel princes, of which each nation has one, received the Torah first for their respective peoples and then passed it on to them.

When, therefore, Jesus sends out seventy messengers with His Word and in His power, against the background of the ideas of the time this raises the symbolical claim to hearing and obedience not merely on the part of Israel but of all humanity, the mission of the Twelve having been restricted expressly to Israel (cf. Mt. 10:5). We thus have a reversal of what took place at the giving of the Law. There God offered the Torah to all peoples and only Israel accepted it. Now Israel rejects the new revelation of the divine will which is first made to it

---

[52] Cf. Str.-B., II, 641.

[53] We are to think of leaders of the Hellenistic section of the congregation and not of a college serving the whole Church (cf. Meyer, Ursprung, III, 155, n. 5).

[54] Some texts have ἑβδομήκοντα δύο (BD pc lat syˢᶜ), but this is probably an assimilation to the fact that the LXX has seventy-two nations rather than seventy in the table in Gn. 10.

[55] In bSukka, 51b Bar. the tradition is not so clear.

[56] For other passages cf. Str.-B., II, 360; III, 48 f.

[57] Ibid., III, 554.

as the people of the divine will, and so it is taken to the whole of the non-Jewish world (cf. Mt. 21:43).

8. On the answer of Jesus to Peter in Mt. 18:22 : ἕως ἑβδομηκοντάκις ἑπτά, → 631 f.

Rengstorf

ἔργον, ἐργάζομαι, ἐργάτης, ἐργασία,
ἐνεργής, ἐνέργεια, ἐνεργέω, ἐνέργημα,
εὐεργεσία, εὐεργετέω, εὐεργέτης

ἔργον, ἐργάζομαι.

A. General Usage.

1. The Greek Usage.

῎Εργον, which derives from the same Indo-Germanic stem [1] and has the same meaning as the English "work" (German *Werk*), and the verbal derivative ἐργάζεσθαι, were both in common use from the time of Homer and Hesiod, and many concepts came to be associated with them, though none specifically. They both denote action or active zeal in contrast to idleness (ἀεργία [ἀργία]), or useful activity in contrast to useless busy-ness (περιεργάζεσθαι, 2 Th. 3:11; cf. περίεργος, Ac. 19:19; 1 Tm. 5:13; also the charge against Socrates, Plat. Ap., 19b), or any kind of active work. The words may be used of agriculture and agricultural economy, but also of the pursuit of various trades, of all kinds of occupations, of commercial undertakings, of trade, shipping and fishing (Rev. 18:17), of the chase, and of art, sculpture and poetry. They may also be applied to working in various materials (metal, wood, stone, clay), or the fashioning or erection of various objects such as vessels or buildings, or all kinds of technical or cultural works, including the winning of natural products. For these varied possibilities there are several examples in the Gk. Bible. The terms also denote work in the social or ethical sense either as a burden laid on man or as a necessary means of life and support. They are applied no less to the domestic tasks of woman than to the public work of men. They refer to works of peace and services in the public welfare, but also to heroic acts of war. As they are thus used in the sphere of moral action, various adjectives are ascribed to them to denote their worth (ἔργα καλά, ἀγαθά, θαυμαστά, ἄδικα, κακά, ἀείκεα; [2] σωφροσύνη, ἀρετὴν ἐργάζεσθαι [Isoc., 13, 6], also ἔργα ἀρετῆς [Xenoph. Cyrop., I, 5, 8]). The cultural significance of work, which is also the divinely willed plan for human life, is especially emphasised in Hes. Op., 307 ff.: ἐξ ἔργων δ' ἄνδρες πολύμηλοί τ' ἀφνειοί τε· | καὶ ἐργαζόμενοι πολὺ φίλτεροι ἀθανάτοισιν. | ἔργον δ' οὐδὲν ὄνειδος, ἀεργίη δέ τ' ὄνειδος. The life of Heracles as one of laborious action in the service of humanity is an exemplary fulfilment of

---

ἔ ρ γ ο ν κ τ λ. Preisigke Wört., 596 f.; Moult.-Mill., 253; Pr.-Bauer, 478 ff.; H. Müller, ""Εργον und ἐργάζεσθαι," *Zeitschrift f. lutherische Theologie u. Kirche*, 37 (1877), 456 ff. On the problem of the righteousness of works → 192, Bibl.; cf. also E. Lohmeyer, "Gesetzeswerke," ZNW, 28 (1929), 177 ff.; "Von Baum und Frucht," ZSTh, 9 (1931), 377 ff.; V. Kirchner, *Der 'Lohn' in der alten Philosophie, im bürgerlichen Recht, besonders im NT* (1908); E. Hauck, *Die Stellung des Urchristentums zu Arbeit und Geld* (1921); E. Troeltsch, *Die Soziallehren der christlichen Kirchen und Gruppen* (1923), 45 ff.; 66 f.

[1] A. Walde and J. Pokorny, *Vergleichendes Wörterbuch der indogermanischen Sprachen*, I (1927), 290 f.

[2] This human evaluation is at issue when, e.g., Philo speaks of ἔργα καλά (Sacr. AC, 78) or Joseph. of θαυμαστὰ καὶ παράδοξα ἔργα (Ant., 9, 182) which are worthy of μνήμη.

human destiny as depicted in popular Cynic philosophy, which regards it as an ideal. [3]
The Hellenistic period thus appropriates at root the ethos of work which dominates the
Works and Days of Hesiod. Honest work is the basis and meaning of life. Naturally,
then, a man is judged by his works, his achievements, his deeds, his total conduct. A
similar formula ἐκ τῶν ἔργων γιγνώσκειν is often found, e.g., in Xenophon. There
is a comparable estimation of man by his works in the Mystery cults on the basis of
natural morality. Thus in the inscription on an altar of the Attis-Cybele cult, found in
Rome in 1919, we read: ἔργα, νόον, πρῆξιν, βίον ἔξοχον ἐσθλὰ προπάντα ...
τοῦτο φέρω τὸ θῦμα. [4] Outside the Bible there is no specifically religious use of ἔργον
and ἐργάζεσθαι, though ἔργα ἀθανάτων is often used of the rule and works of the
gods (Hom. Il., 16, 120; 19, 22). On the other hand, ἔργον is a philosophical term, esp.
in Platonic and Aristotelian philosophy. [5] In Plato the term is linked with τέχνη (Gorg.,
517c). There is a firm relation between ἀρετή and ἔργον (Resp., I, 352d). The word
ἔργον comes from the sphere of civilisation, not of organic nature. For man the ἔργον
ψυχῆς is central (Resp., I, 353a-e). Aristotle developed the concept systematically. It
is found at the beginning of the Nic. Ethics (I, 1, p. 1094a, 3 ff.). Ἔργα are by nature
of more value and more worth seeking than ἐνέργειαι. The ἀρετή of every creature,
e.g., the eye or the race-horse, consists in fulfilling properly its specific ἔργον, i.e.,
seeing or running. Aristotle thus consistently applies the concept of the organic (ἔργον!)
to the whole of nature (An., II, 1, p. 412a, 1 ff.). For him ἐνέργεια or ἔργον is the
form of things, the fulfilment of the disposition inherent in matter. The state of fulfilment
implies true and effective activity.

The passive use of ἔργον is also widespread. In this sense it means what is wrought,
the result of work or the product of the process of work (e.g., a work of sculpture or
architecture or literature or art, also defensive or offensive works; in the OT it is
sometimes found for כְּלִי Nu. 4:16 or יוֹשֶׁר Sir. 9:17, and also for the fruit of the soil,
e.g., Jer. 14:4), or for the reward of work either as wages or as gain. Finally, the
thought of achievement sometimes retreats into the background and we simply have
the weak sense of a "matter" or "thing."

2. The Linguistic Usage of the Greek Bible.

In the Gk. translation of the OT the breadth of meaning is apparent at once in the
great number of different Heb. terms which may be rendered ἔργον or ἐργάζεσθαι.
Thus the verb is often used for such activities as "plowing" (Is. 28:24), "weaving"
(Is. 19:9, 10), "smelting" (Ex. 27:19) or "hewing wood" (2 Ch. 2:10). A particular form
of work is indicated when the term ἔργον is used for words like סְבָלָה (Ex. 1 and 5),
מַס (Ex. 1:11) or מַשָּׂא (Nu. 4:27 B), which denote obligatory or even forced labour.
The same is true when it is used for פְּקֻדָּה, "the regular ministry of sacrifice or of
watching" (2 Ch. 23:18; vl. ἐπισκοπή), יְגִיעַ and עֶסֶק (Job 10:3; 39:11b; Sir. 7:25),
"laborious work," "difficult business or enterprise." Ἔργον and ἐργάζεσθαι appear
most commonly for עָשָׂה, פָּעַל, עָבַד, מְלָאכָה or their derivatives. These words denote an
"action," "work" or "achievement," and more or less cover the various senses of the
Gk. term. Apart from ποιεῖν, ποίημα, which are never used for מְלָאכָה, the only synonyms occasionally found for ἔργον in the OT are πρᾶξις, πρᾶγμα, πράσσειν. [6]

---

[3] J. Kroll, *Gott und Hölle* (1932), 410 f. The average view of Hellenistic philosophy is
also found in Epict. (Diss., II, 4 and 5; III, 26). The decisive words in Epict. are responsibility and self-esteem.
[4] M. J. Lagrange, *Rev. Bibl.*, 36 (1927), 561 ff.
[5] According to H. Kleinknecht. Cf. also F. Kirchner-C. Michaelis, *Wörterbuch der philosophischen Grundbegriffe*[5] (1907), *s.v. Energie*; H. Bonitz, *Index Aristotelicus*, s.v. ἔργον.
[6] δρᾶν is found only once for פָּעַל at ψ 10:3 Σ.

Otherwise the Gk. uses other terms for the Heb. roots mentioned only to bring out a particular sense, which may on occasion be important for a theological understanding of ἔργον in the OT. Thus renderings like δουλεία, λατρεία, πόνος, μόχθος, μισθός obviously display the same social and ethical understanding of the group of concepts to which we are referred already by the Heb. originals. On the other hand, words like αἴνεσις, ἀναφορά, ἐφημερία, λειτουργία reveal a specific cultic use which goes beyond the ordinary sense of the word group. In association with ἀδικία in Ἰωβ 33:17; ἀδικεῖν in Prv. 24:44; and κακόν in Is. 57:12 there is an adverse judgment, while κτίσμα, τέχνη, ἐνέργημα, κατασκευή presuppose different conceptions of the one at work. All this is possible with ἔργον. The particular sense may be determined by the accompanying terms, as by the various Heb. originals. Particularly important are the individual cases where the terms are used for Heb. originals from the ethical and religious sphere. Thus in the Gk. translation many words which denote conduct in general are brought under the concept of work, e.g., דֶּרֶךְ in Job 34:21: αὐτὸς γὰρ ὁρατής ἐστιν ἔργων ἀνθρώπων; 36:23 : τίς δέ ἐστιν ὁ ἐτάζων αὐτοῦ (God's) τὰ ἔργα; Prv. 16:5(7): πάντα τὰ ἔργα τοῦ ταπεινοῦ φανερὰ παρὰ τῷ θεῷ; Sir. 10:6 : ἔργον ὕβρεως = דרך גאוה; 11:21: ἐν ἔργοις ἁμαρτωλοῦ = בַּ[ד]רכי ר[ע]; אֹרַח : Job 13:27: ἐφύλαξας δέ μου πάντα τὰ ἔργα (cf. 33:11); התהלך in Sir. 3:17: ἔργα διεξάγειν.

B. The Divine Work and Action.

1. The divine work of creation.

The verb ἐργάζεσθαι is relatively infrequent in the LXX with the subject God. Thus in ψ 43:1 we have ὁ θεός, ... οἱ πατέρες ἀνήγγειλαν ἡμῖν, ἔργον δ εἰργάσω ἐν ταῖς ἡμέραις αὐτῶν with reference to the past, and in ψ 30:19 Σ (LXX : ἐξειργάσω); 73:12; Job 33:29 with reference to His works among men. There is also a reference to His historical presence and work in the Mas. and LXX of Hab. 1:5, though Σ seems to have in view God's work in the eschatological period. We are to understand Is. 28:21 ΣΘ : ἐργάσασθαι τὴν ἐργασίαν, in the same way. In the NT the ἐργάζεσθαι of God is expressly emphasised in Jn. 5:17. Naturally the Jewish conception of God is decisively influenced by the idea of the divine activity.

This is seen first in the OT in the creation of the world. Thus in Gn. 2:2, 3 we have ἔργον three times for מְלָאכָה. What is meant is the creative work from which God rests. The OT uses ἔργον innumerable times for the work of creation (Mas. usually מַעֲשֶׂה), even where the Heb. has other expressions. The plastic formulation ἔργον κτίσεως may be assumed in S. Bar. 14:17.[7] In 4 Esr. 6:38, 43 : "Thy word created the work," "Thy word went forth and the work was done," stress is laid on the creation of the world and the individual works by the Word. There are other places where the LXX, when it speaks of creation, does not think of the creative activity or labour of God but rather of nature and man as works of God which as such stand to Him in a particular relationship of dependence, obedience and obligation. By this means, which sometimes involves no more than the use of ἔργον for words like מְלָאכָה (Gn. 2) and יְגִיעַ (Job 10:3), the LXX, in keeping with the spirit of Hellenistic Judaism, avoids anthropopathic ideas of God. In so doing, it runs the risk of a deistic conception, which seems to have influenced, e.g., Sir. 16:27. Nevertheless, there was little danger of such a conception taking root on the soil of the biblical belief in God.

Obviously the Bible regards all creation in all its parts as the work of God. Yet when there is mention of the works of God, the reference is usually to a specific group of works. Thus the powerful phenomena of nature in heaven and on earth glorify the honour and might of God. The earth and its creatures, which

---

[7] In the Baruch Apc. and 4 Esr. we follow B. Violet.

are subject to man, and man himself both in his dignity as the image of God and also in his lowliness as a poor instrument of his Maker, all bear witness to the providence of God and His gracious and merciful overruling of His creatures. In the Psalms and the Wisdom literature the thought of the works of creation is highly particularised. We are often told that the incomprehensibly high works of God are a testimony to His greatness. Thus we read in ψ 8:3 : ὄψομαι τοὺς οὐρανούς, ἔργα τῶν δακτύλων σου ... According to ψ 18:1 the works themselves proclaim that they are created by God. [8] With this poetic expression of belief in the Creator we sometimes have proof of God on the ground of creation. [9] Thus in S. Bar. 54:18 the accusation is brought against the wicked : "His works have not taught you, nor has the excellence of his eternal creation convinced you." Wis. 13:1 ff. chides man for his inability to see the Creator in contemplation of His works. Similarly we read in Philo : [10] διὰ τῶν ἔργων τὸν τεχνίτην κατανοοῦντες. In Ps. 90:16 the Mas. refers to the rule of God in human life as manifest to believers : יֵרָאֶה אֶל־עֲבָדֶיךָ פָעֳלֶךָ (Σ : φανήτω παρὰ τοὺς δούλους σου τὰ ἔργα σου). But the LXX (89:16) speaks of believers as the creatures of God upon whom He looks down in blessing : ἴδε ἐπὶ τοὺς δούλους σου καὶ ἐπὶ τὰ ἔργα σου. Similarly, God's pity is claimed for His works in ψ 137:8; 144:9. In Ἰωβ 14:15 there is a petition for protection : τὰ δὲ ἔργα τῶν χειρῶν σου μὴ ἀποποιοῦ. [11] The Mas. reads : "Thou wilt long for the work of thine hands" — which Hellenistic Jews found to be out of keeping with their more refined concept of God. God shows longsuffering even to sinners because they are His works (4 Esr. 7:134). He naturally has full control over the death and life (resurrection) of His creatures (4 Esr. 8:13; cf. 8:7). In Ἰωβ 10:3, as in 14:15, it is presupposed that man holds a special position as one of God's creatures. God will not destroy what He has so laboriously made, [12] is the sense of the Mas. But the ἔργα χειρῶν of the LXX stresses the close connection between Creator and creature concerning which we read in ψ 8:6 : κατέστησας αὐτὸν ἐπὶ τὰ ἔργα τῶν χειρῶν σου. [13] In Is. the expression ἔργα χειρῶν is used of the descendants of Jacob in 29:23 Mas. and Σ, though here the reference is not so much to the creative work of God as to His historical action in raising up the seed of Jacob in order to fulfil His promises to them. The LXX does not make the children of Jacob the work of God ; they are those who see the works of God. In Is. 60:21, too, the reference is to the historical or eschatological rule of Yahweh. On the other hand, Is. 64:8 : ἔργα τῶν χειρῶν σου πάντες ἡμεῖς, appeals again to the pity of the Creator for His creatures. At Is. 45:11 the LXX sees a reference to men as the creatures of God, while the Mas. has in view the acts of God.

---

[8] Σ : τὰ ἔργα τῶν χειρῶν αὐτοῦ, LXX : ποίησιν δὲ χειρῶν αὐτοῦ.

[9] In Jewish and Christian tradition the radiance of the sun, which dazzles man even though it is only that of a creature, is often contrasted with the *doxa* of God or of Christ, cf. Barn., 5, 10, and H. Windisch in *Handbuch z. NT,* Suppl. (1920), *ad loc.,* with further references. On the praise of God by creation cf. also ψ 101:26; 102:22; 103:13, 24 (par. κτίσις), 31; 138:14; 144:10; Da. 3:57 LXX Θ; Sir. 39:14; Tob. 3:11.

[10] Leg. All., III, 99.

[11] At Sir. 47:22 the Gk. translation imports the idea. The meaning of the Heb. is that God will not allow any of His words to fall (unfruitfully) to the ground. The Gk. translates דְּבָרִים ἔργα (both words can mean "matter"), and thus gives us : ὁ δὲ κύριος ... οὐ μὴ διαφθαρῇ ἀπὸ τῶν ἔργων αὐτοῦ.

[12] Cf. E. Steuernagel in Kautzsch, *ad loc.*

[13] Cf. S. Bar. 14:18; 4 Esr. 6:54; also Wis. 14:5; S. Bar. 24:4.

Unique is O. Sol. 8:19 f. Here man in his new being as redeemed is a work of truth, which has the same role as the wisdom of God in Prv. 8:22, i.e., that of mediating creation (in the Mas. wisdom itself is the first work of God; cf. also Wis. 8:4, 5, 6; 9:9; Sir. 1:9). In O. Sol. 8:19 f. truth says: "I have pleasure in them and am not ashamed of them; for they are my work and the power of my thoughts. Who, then, will rise up against my work? and who will not be subject to them?" [14] Here the thought of the creation of man is applied to the new creation of believers in redemption, and it thus becomes "an emotional formula" [15] of saving faith which is in keeping with the religious outlook of the Odes and which is found also in references made in them to the works of God. Cf. 11:9; 12:4, 7; 16:7, 10, 13.

The wonderful nature of God's works is emphasised in Prv. 20:15(12): οὖς ἀκούει καὶ ὀφθαλμὸς ὁρᾷ κυρίου ἔργα καὶ ἀμφότερα. In Sir. 11:4b the reference is not to the wonderful works by which God can punish pride, but to the works which are concealed from those who look only on the external. In the context attention is drawn to the contrast between the modesty of the bee and its usefulness. It is along the same lines that we are to understand Sir. 43:32 and 16:21 LXX: τὰ δὲ πλείονα τῶν ἔργων αὐτοῦ ἐν ἀποκρύφοις, although the following verse brings out the connection between the creative works of God and His present activity in revelation and judgment. The LXX is here dependent on the Heb., which speaks of the hidden sinful or righteous conduct of man. The LXX has made the anthropological statement of the Heb. into a theological. References to God's works as Creator may also be seen in Sir. 16:26, 27. Cf. also Sir. 17:8, 9; 36(33):15; 39:16, 33; 42:15, 16, 22; 43:2, 25, 28. In Sir. 17:19 א*A have ἔργα αὐτοῦ in the sense of creatures of God whose doings as such are manifest to God, while B (there is no Heb.) has ἔργα αὐτῶν and thus introduces the works of men directly. In 18:4 it is an open question whether the reference is to the works of God in creation or to His glorious acts in the course of universal history. If v. 4 points more to the former, the continuation with ἐλέη in v. 5 at least indicates the inner connection between the two. The LXX in general thinks more of God's works than His activity. Again in Prv. 21:8 it makes a theological statement out of an anthropological: ἀγνὰ γὰρ καὶ ὀρθὰ τὰ ἔργα αὐτοῦ (θεοῦ). Here God is subject, while in the Mas. the reference is to right conduct on the part of man. At Job 37:15 the LXX imports the thought of creation independently in the form of a confession: οἴδαμεν ὅτι ὁ θεὸς ἔθετο ἔργα αὐτοῦ. At Qoh. 8:17 stress is laid on the fact that God's works are un-fathomable to man; Σ has ἔργον and the LXX [16] ποίημα; cf. Bar. 2:9; 1 Ἐσδρ. 4:36. The less Jewish piety is determined by the people and the more by the ideas of a universal religion, so much the more the contemplation of God's works comes into the forefront as the expression of a universalistic belief in the Creator. Faith is no longer directed exclusively to the God who has chosen His people and whose sons are the children of Israel; it looks rather to the God who has made the world and whose handi-work is man, each one of us individually.

2. God's activity in the world.

a. In general even Hellenistic Judaism does not regard God's creative activity as a completed work of the past. We can see this, e.g., from the eschatological interpretation of the six days of work (Barn., 15, 3). Faith looks rather to God's rule in history, to his wonderful work of judgment and redemption in the present and the future. At this point, however, Hellenistic and Rabbinic Judaism see a difficulty, raising the question how the omnicausality of God can be reconciled with His Sabbath rest. In this state of un-certainty may be seen the influence of Hellenism, in which the antithesis between the Godhead at work in the world and exalted above it was of great importance in the

---

[14] G. Diettrich, Die Oden Salomos (1911), ad loc.
[15] An expression coined by A. Warburg. Cf. J. Kroll (→ n. 3), op. cit., 528 ff.
[16] Unless we have here a translation after the manner of Aquila.

development of the philosophical concept of God. The view: *Deum nihil habere ipsum negotii* (Cic. Off., III, 28, 102) is confronted by the opposite: *Qui deos esse concedunt, iis fatendum est, eos aliquid agere* (Cic. Nat. Deor., II, 30, 76). The Corp Herm., VI, 1 ff. speaks of the στατικὴ ἐνέργεια, of the constant causality of the Godhead, and it maintains: οὐκ ἀργὸς ὁ θεός (XI, 5). Similarly we read in Max. Tyr., 15, 6: οὐδὲ γὰρ ὁ Ζεὺς σχολὴν ἄγει. In the light of this we can understand Philo, who in Leg. All., I, 3 notes concerning Gn. 2:2: παύεται γὰρ οὐδέποτε ποιῶν ὁ θεός. In Gn. r., 11 on Gn. 2:3 we have a statement of R. Hosha'ja (handed down by R. Pinehas) on the question of God's Sabbath rest which is significant both for its rejection of Deism and its resolution of the problem: "If thou sayest also that on this day God rested from all his work, he certainly rested from his work on the world, but he did not rest from his work on the ungodly and his work on the righteous, but he still works with both." [17]

In all these statements it is assumed that God is active by nature. The same is true of Jn. 5:17: ὁ πατήρ μου ἕως ἄρτι (continually) ἐργάζεται. That God is a living, active, creative God is a basic conception independent of specific views of this activity. The peculiarity of the biblical tradition is to make very concrete individual statements which reveal God's activity in the here and now of the historical situation of the people or the righteous individual. It is the history of the elect people which is attested as the work of God, and individual events which are proclaimed as the acts of God: Ex. 34:10; Dt. 3:24 (vl.); 11:3 (vl.), 7; Jos. 24:31; Ju. 2:7, 10. In these passages the acts of God are seen partly in military successes which made possible the conquest of Canaan and partly in the wonderful events in the wilderness. Here ἔργα sometimes has the sense of miracles. [18] The supreme events are naturally the redemption out of Egypt with its accompanying mighty acts and the crossing of the Red Sea: ψ 65, 3, 5; 76:12. The mythologising emotional motif [19] of the conflict against the powers of chaos is used in the depiction of these events. Nevertheless, the act of God is thought of not merely as something wonderful, astonishing and unique, but also as the divine action which accompanies and determines the history of Israel, which is visible to and recognisable by individual believers, and which causes them to give thanks to God. It is to be noted that the saving history of God's acts belongs to the past; a generation arises which knows nothing of it (Ju. 2:10). The concept of God's act seems to be limited to the extraordinary. It is the redemptive work which establishes Israel's faith in Yahweh. It is the beginning of Israel as the people of God. It is the miracle of the commencement to which one looks back. Faith is not always strong enough to see the present also in the light of the activity of Yahweh.

b. This faith in the present activity of God, in His acts as the direct experience of the individual present, is proclaimed by the prophets. But the less perceptive mass of the people does not see the intervention of God in judgment and redemption. For the prophets themselves the events of history are the acts of God which God fashions with His own hands: Is. 5:12 (cf. the Mas.), 19; 22:11; 28:21; 29:23. For the recalcitrant people these imply judgment. Thus we read in Is. 28:21: μετὰ θυμοῦ ποιήσει τὰ ἔργα αὐτοῦ, πικρίας ἔργον. ὁ δὲ θυμὸς αὐτοῦ ἀλλοτρίως χρήσεται καὶ ἡ σαπρία (vl.: πικρία) αὐτοῦ ἀλλοτρία.

---

[17] Str.-B., II, 461; Clemen, *ad loc.*, 272; G. Heinrici, *Die Hermesmystik und das NT* (1918), 46; Bau. J., *ad loc.*; Zn. J., *ad loc.*, 292.

[18] At Dt. 11:3 B has τέρατα; cf. Sir. 48:14: ἔργα with τέρατα referring to the miracles of Elijah.

[19] J. Kroll (→ n. 3), *op. cit.*, 468.

In this verse ΣΘ even have : ... ἐργάσασθαι τὴν ἐργασίαν αὐτοῦ, ἁμαρτία (cj : ἀλλοτρία) ἡ ἐργασία αὐτοῦ. Here, then, ἁμαρτία, i.e., the fact of sin in the world (e.g., resistance to the prophetic message), and the judgment which necessarily follows, are conceived of as the *opus alienum Dei*. But the *opus alienum* is simply the reverse side of the *opus proprium*, of the *vivificare*, of the work of salvation. This may be seen, e.g., in Ac. 13:41 (on the basis of Hab. 1:5) : ἔργον ἐγὼ ἐργάζομαι ἐν ταῖς ἡμέραις ὑμῶν, ὃ οὐ μὴ πιστεύσητε ἐάν τις ἐκδιηγῆται. The proclamation of salvation determines the threat of judgment. On the other hand, the use of the OT saying in Acts presupposes a change in the conception of God's work. For, while the reference in Hab. is to God's acts in the history of the nations (cf. also 3:2), here the point at issue is the judgment which is the reverse side of the universalistic divine work of mission and salvation. It corresponds to the development of Jewish and early Christian religion under the pressure of political history that NT proclamation, too, should find God's mighty historical work less in the life of the nations than in the upbuilding of the community. The more significant, then, is Rev. 15:3 : μεγάλα καὶ θαυμαστὰ τὰ ἔργα σου ... ὁ βασιλεὺς τῶν ἐθνῶν ... ὅτι πάντα τὰ ἔθνη ἥξουσιν καὶ προσκυνήσουσιν ἐνώπιόν σου. In the NT, too, the divine activity is not to be thought of as merely soteriological. The believer also finds it in everyday events. The understanding of life as a work of God is the result and content of faith in the living God who, e.g., in the Psalms, is proclaimed as the God who restores life to the mortally sick and vindicates the righteous against their enemies. With this concept of the ἔργα θεοῦ it is only natural that the underlying point at issue should not be expressed merely in certain words. It is also present wherever there is reference to God's dealings with man, e.g., in the Book of Tobit. The private life of man can even take on typical or immediate significance in saving history, as may be seen in the marriage of the prophet Hosea or the story of Jonah. What is done to me by my wife, children, friends or enemies, the good or evil done me by men, God Himself does. He acts towards me as men act. No one has seen this with greater perception of faith than Paul, [20] who understands his own life in terms of salvation history (cf. esp. Col. 1:24, also 2 C. 12:7 ff.) and who according to the familiar traditional interpretation of 2 Th. 2:6, 7 (τὸ → κατέχον and ὁ → κατέχων) integrates the historical data of this world into his total eschatological understanding.

It is especially in Dt. Is. and Jer. that God's activity is seen essentially in the course of the history of Israel and the nations. This may be seen in Is. 41:4, where the LXX has ἐνεργέω, but ᾽ΑΣΘ ἐργάζομαι. The most far-reaching verse in this connection, however, is Is. 45:11 Mas. Here Cyrus, the Persian king, is proclaimed as Yahweh's shepherd and anointed. The Creator God is the Lord of history who deals with the nations according to His will. World history is the work of His hands. [21]

There is also reference to God's work in ᾽Ιερ. 28(51):10; 27(50):25 and 31(48):10. In the last of these passages ἔργον is used in the sense of task, and indeed in 31:10 of the task set by God (Mas. מְלָאכָה). In Is. 66:19 א introduces on its own a reference to God's acts, though the context suggests not so much God's rule in history as His saving work for Israel as this affects the nations. The use of ἔργα in Is. 64:4 LXX

---

[20] Cf. H. Windisch, *Paulus und Christus* (1934), esp. 252 ff.
[21] Here, too, the LXX refers ἔργα τῶν χειρῶν to men as the creatures of God, described as ἔργα θεοῦ and also as υἱοὶ θεοῦ.

suggests a similar missionary sense : ... οὐδὲ οἱ ὀφθαλμοὶ ἡμῶν εἶδον θεὸν πλὴν σοῦ καὶ τὰ ἔργα σου ἃ ποιήσεις τοῖς ὑπομένουσιν ἔλεον. A vl. is as follows : τὰ ἔργα σου ἀληθινὰ καὶ ποιήσεις τοῖς ὑπομένουσίν σε ἔλεον. This gives us an independent statement, and the thought of ἔργα ἀληθινά is also introduced. Different words are used in the Mas.: Dt. 32:4 תָּמִים; Da. 4:34 קְשֹׁט (Θ : ἀληθινά); Ps. 111:7 אֱמֶת; cf. also Da. 3:27; Tob. 3:2. That these are acts of the true God, and true divine acts, is the meaning of this formula in missionary propaganda, which is directed against idols and false gods from the standpoint of true faith. We are to understand in the same way, at least in the LXX, the numerous passages which describe the works of God as μεγάλα, θαυμαστά, ἁγνὰ καὶ ὀρθά, ἐν πίστει, μετὰ δικαιοσύνης etc.[22] (ψ 32:4; Prv. 16:9; 18:10 vl. LXX [not the Mas. and ᾽ΑΘ]; 21:8; Job 36:24; Tob. 12:22). There are also many statements in the Psalms and elsewhere which refer to the declaration of the works of God by the righteous. Even where the Heb. thinks only of the praising of God within the congregation, the LXX has in view the missionary task of the righteous : Tob. 12:6, 7. Other statements on God's activity, e.g., in the Wisdom literature, are to be understood as the attestation and proclamation of the power of God which necessarily take on a missionary sense wherever Judaism meets the surrounding world. This is particularly true of LXX Judaism in the Hellenistic Roman period. The attestation of God's activity always takes place with full reference to the present. It is His righteous and gracious work to be manifested in judgment on the ungodly, in the destruction of the heathen and in mercy on the righteous and their redemption from sin and affliction : ψ 27:5; 45:8; 63:9; 91:4, 5; 94:9; 106:22, 24; 117:17; 144:4 ff., 14, 17 etc. Often the reference to God's activity in history, esp. in prayer, is simply an expression of the expectation that God's power and will are ready to deliver and redeem the righteous and to overthrow the ungodly Est. (13:8) C 1; 3 Macc. 2:8; ψ 42:1; 85:8; 105:13; 110:2 ff.; 138:14; 142:5.

c. It is only in the NT, however, that along with the reference to the wonderful works of God we have a clear awareness of His saving work and activity on the basis of the divine will to redeem which is consistently attested in all the individual works. If the concept of the ἔργα θεοῦ corresponds to a comprehensive view of the work of salvation, it is not surprising that it is for the most part lacking in the Synoptic tradition. Only in Mt. 11:2 do we read that John the Baptist in prison hears of the acts of Jesus (so D etc. in accordance with the situation). The Baptist cannot evaluate them as acts of Christ (as in most of the MSS from the standpoint of the Christian readers and possibly the author), and therefore he cannot regard them as the work of salvation.

On the other hand, the concept of God's saving acts through Christ is common in John's Gospel : 5:20, 36; 7:3, 21; 9:3, 4; 10:25, 32, 37, 38; 14:10, 11, 12; 15:24. These statements relate to individual works done by Jesus. As miracles, they bear witness to Jesus and to the salvation which He brings : 5:36 : αὐτὰ τὰ ἔργα ἃ ποιῶ μαρτυρεῖ περὶ ἐμοῦ; cf. 10:25; 14:11; 15:24. But it is not merely the thought of miracles, or of the *doxa* transparent in them, which determines these passages, for in Jn. the thought of καλὰ ἔργα is inseparably linked therewith (10:32). In this christological context, therefore, we are brought up against the problem of works in the NT, and we can at once state that καλὰ ἔργα are a demonstration of God's working in Jesus and therefore in believers. They are testimony to the divine work in man. It is in keeping with the christological outlook of Jn. that miracles can be described directly as God's works, partly in the sense of God's working in Jesus and partly in the sense of the activity which He laid upon Jesus. The thought of the unity of the work of salvation is always there in the back-

---

[22] There are several deviations in the Mas.

ground; thus 9:3: ἵνα φανερωθῇ τὰ ἔργα τοῦ θεοῦ, refers to God's saving activity as a whole, this being manifested in individual miracles by way of example. In many instances, then, the sing. is used in Jn. in this sense, as at 4:34: ἐμὸν βρῶμά ἐστιν ἵνα ποιῶ τὸ θέλημα τοῦ πέμψαντός με καὶ τελειώσω αὐτοῦ τὸ ἔργον; 17:4: ἐγώ σε ἐδόξασα ἐπὶ τῆς γῆς, τὸ ἔργον τελειώσας ὃ δέδωκάς μοι ἵνα ποιήσω. There is an even more comprehensive use in Jn. 6:29, where, to the question: τί ποιῶμεν ἵνα ἐργαζώμεθα τὰ ἔργα τοῦ θεοῦ; the answer is given: τοῦτό ἐστιν τὸ ἔργον τοῦ θεοῦ, ἵνα πιστεύητε ... Active participation in the work of salvation does not consist, therefore, in an action, but in divinely given faith. The gen. τὸ ἔργον τοῦ θεοῦ is a gen. auctoris. The works of God performed through Christ and those performed through believers cannot be separated from one another. They are the one work of God.

This is no less clear in Paul. The ἔργον τοῦ θεοῦ in R. 14:20 is the οἰκοδομή of the community. An agricultural image is used as well as an architectural (γεώργιον, 1 C. 3:9). This activity of God is through the Spirit. It is apparent in the missionary work of the apostle, 1 C. 9:1: τὸ ἔργον μου ὑμεῖς ἐστε ἐν κυρίῳ. The founding of the Christian Church corresponds to the creation of the world. In both cases we have a work of God through the Word or Spirit. The apostle is not alone in doing the work of God. His helpers also do this work, 1 C. 16:10; Phil. 2:30. Even the most secular action in the interest of the Christian work of mission may be regarded as ἔργον κυρίου, and it is thus understandable that in the active expression of faith Paul can see both work for the Lord and the work of the Lord. Thus his admonition in 1 C. 15:58 runs as follows: ἑδραῖοι γίνεσθε, ἀμετακίνητοι, περισσεύοντες ἐν τῷ ἔργῳ τοῦ κυρίου πάντοτε (cf. Rev. 2:26: τηρῶν ... τὰ ἔργα μου), and in Eph. 4:12 the diaconate is described as a work in this sense. That we are always to think of God's working is most evident in Phil. 1:6: ὁ ἐναρξάμενος ἐν ὑμῖν ἔργον ἀγαθόν (θεός). The usage in Ac. is similar; cf. 5:38 and esp. 13:2: ἀφορίσατε ... εἰς ἔργον; 14:26: παραδεδομένοι τῇ χάριτι τοῦ θεοῦ εἰς τὸ ἔργον; also 15:38. Ἔργον means the work of salvation in the widest sense in Ac. 15:18 AD etc.: γνωστὸν ἀπ᾽ αἰῶνός ἐστιν τῷ κυρίῳ τὸ ἔργον αὐτοῦ. ℵ; πάντα τὰ ἔργα αὐτοῦ. For Christians life has meaning to the degree that in it the divine work goes forward (καρπὸς ἔργου, Phil. 1:22). Here again there is in Paul no thought of individual achievement and its results. [23]

C. Human Labour and the Work of Man.

1. Human labour as a curse.

In so far as biblical theology links work with the story of the fall, it regards it as a curse in its necessity for the maintenance of life. This view was almost completely dominant in Hellenistic Judaism.

Thus Gn. 3:17 in the Gk. is ἐπικατάρατος ἡ γῆ ἐν τοῖς ἔργοις σου. Here LXX ΣΘ make the Mas. בַּעֲבוּרֶךָ (᾽Α ἕνεκέν σου) a form of עבד, as also in Gn. 8:21. [24] Thus

---

[23] The LXX distinguishes between the divine work and prophetic action in the story of Elijah in 3 Βασ. 18:36: διὰ σὲ (God) πεποίηκα τὰ ἔργα ταῦτα. Yet in Hellen. Gk. διὰ σέ can also mean "through thee." Mas. בִּדְבָרֶיךָ.

[24] And often in passages of lesser import. The confusion of ד and ר might well have taken place in earlier copies of the Heb. text. It is also possible in Gk. (ΔΛ). Cf. also F. Wutz, Transkriptionen (1933), 192 ff.

the negative attitude of Hellen. Judaism to work decisively affects the text. It is open to doubt whether ἔργα in the LXX refers to the laborious toil of man (so Σ: ἐν τῇ ἐργασίᾳ σου), or to the sinful works of man (so Θ: ἐν τῇ παραβάσει [i.e., transgression of the prohibition] and LXX Gn. 8:21: διὰ τὰ ἔργα τῶν ἀνθρώπων). There can be no doubt however — as may be seen from the context of vv. 17-19 — that from now on all human labour stands under the curse, and therefore takes on the aspect of toil and constraint. By introducing the term ἔργα the LXX and Σ expressed a thought of their own age which is materially present in the Heb. but which is now transferred to the term ἔργον, thus laying upon it the divine curse. It is thus that we are to understand Gn. 5:29: διαναπαύσει ἡμᾶς ἀπὸ τῶν ἔργων ἡμῶν καὶ ἀπὸ τῶν λυπῶν (עִצְּבוֹן) τῶν χειρῶν ἡμῶν καὶ ἀπὸ τῆς γῆς ἧς κατηράσατο κύριος ὁ θεός. Is. 65:22 LXX is to be taken in the same sense. Here the Mas. speaks of the fruit of earthly toil, but the LXX has: τὰ γὰρ ἔργα τῶν πόνων αὐτῶν παλαιώσουσιν. Cf. also κόπος and πόνος in ψ 89:10 (Mas. עָמָל וָאָוֶן). To this conception belongs the expectation in S. Bar. 74:1 that in the eschatological age work will be done without human exertion. That Judaism of the Hell. period could never speak of ἔργον without disparagement may be seen, e.g., in Sir. 30:33 (33:25): χορτάσματα καὶ ῥάβδος καὶ φορτία ὄνῳ, ἄρτος καὶ παιδεία καὶ ἔργον οἰκέτῃ; cf. 30:38 (33:30): εἰς ἔργα κατάστησον καθὼς πρέπει αὐτῷ. A similar passage is Prv. 29:33 (31:15), where the LXX presupposes that work will be the task of female slaves, whereas Θ and Σ rightly translate the Heb. רֹה σύνταξις or πρόσταγμα. In Ex. and elsewhere the idea of forced labour is simply rendered "labour" in the translation. [25] This makes it perfectly plain that the Hell. Jew had a complete aversion for work, which he could not but regard as an imposition, a curse, a matter for slaves. Work, i.e., the need to earn one's livelihood by toil (Test. Iss. 5), is a punishment for sin.

2. Man's work as sin and vanity.

For the Hellenistic Jew, however, the curse of Gn. 3:17 [26] has even deeper implications. Everything called ἔργον in the life of man is sin. When the actions of man are measured by the final criterion, they are shown to be sin.

Thus the Gk. Bible often uses ἔργα *in malam partem* when the reference is to human work. The same is true of the verb, which is frequently linked with an object of negative moral character in such a way as to become almost a single concept: ἀδικίαν, ἀνομίαν, κακά, ψεῦδος, ὑπερηφανίαν ἐργάζεσθαι. In the Psalter particularly we meet with the expression פֹּעֲלֵי אָוֶן [27] ἐργαζόμενοι τὴν ἀνομίαν. In the NT this influences Mt. 7:23; Lk. 13:27. The wickedness of all human action is stated as a principle in many formulations. A Hell. Jewish text to this effect is 1 Ἐσδρ. 4:37: ἄδικα πάντα τὰ ἔργα (τῶν ἀνθρώπων). In many cases Heb. terms like רָעָה, Jer. 44(51):9 A (B א: κακῶν; Ἀ: μῆνις; Σ: ὀργή), תּוֹעֵבָה, Prv. 13:19; תַּזְנוּת, Ez. 23:43 are simply rendered ἔργον. When לֶקַח ("teaching") in Job 11:4 and עֵצָה ("counsel") in Job 21:16 are translated ἔργον, this simply expresses the general thought that all man's action is wicked and corrupt: Job 11:4: μὴ γὰρ λέγε, καθαρός εἰμι τοῖς ἔργοις καὶ ἄμεμπτος ἐναντίον αὐτοῦ, and 21:16: ἔργα δὲ ἀσεβῶν οὐκ ἐφορᾷ. Job 11:4 is closely related to 4:17. Here, too, it is the LXX which introduces the thought of ἔργον. The Mas. runs: הַאֱנוֹשׁ מֵאֱלוֹהַ יִצְדָּק אִם־מֵעֹשֵׂהוּ יִטְהַר־גָּבֶר, but the LXX translates: μὴ καθαρὸς ἔσται βροτὸς ἐναντίον τοῦ κυρίου ἢ ἀπὸ τῶν ἔργων αὐτοῦ ἄμεμπτος ἀνήρ; The LXX thus poses the question of the righteousness of works, and gives a negative answer. Again

---

[25] For detailed proofs → 636. Hell. Judaism does also show respect for faithful daily work; cf. the examples in Deissmann LO, 265 f. → κόπος, κοπιᾶν.

[26] Esp. Θ → *supra*; cf. 8:21 LXX.

[27] On the religious bearing of the Heb. concept on certain practices, esp. magic, cf. S. Mowinckel, *Psalmenstudien*, I (1921), esp. Chapter 1.

in Job 22:3; 33:9 A τοῖς ἔργοις is an addition to ἄμεμπτος or ἁμαρτάνειν which is typical of the reserved attitude of the LXX to the righteousness of works. On Job 21:16 cf. the independent LXX statements in 11:11: αὐτὸς γὰρ οἶδεν ἔργα ἀνόμων and 24:14 : γνοὺς δὲ αὐτῶν τὰ ἔργα παρέδωκεν αὐτοὺς εἰς σκότος. Cf. also Job 36:9; 34:25. At Is. 57:12 the LXX translates מַעֲשֶׂה κακόν, thus correctly rendering as a formulation the ironic words of the Mas. In Jer. 31(48):30 ἔργον is obviously based on a misreading of עֶבְרָה as עֲבֹדָה. The material connection with the sin of pride is maintained, however, as also in Jl. 2:20 : ἐμεγάλυνεν τὰ ἔργα αὐτοῦ. In many instances, of course, the Heb. מַעֲשֶׂה or synonyms are already to be understood *in malam partem*, e.g., Gn. 18:21 Σ; 20:9; Ex. 23:24; 3 Βασ. 16:7; 4 Βασ. 22:17; 1 ᾿Εσδρ. 8:83 (cf. 2 ᾿Εσδρ. 9:13); Is. 3:11, 24; 29:15; 41:29 Qmg; 59:6 LXX Θ; 65:7; 66:18; Jer. 7:13; 25:6; Ez. 16:30; Am. 8:7; Mi. 6:16; Hag. 2:14, 17; Na. 2:14; cf. also the Psalms and hagiographa. Throughout the OT and on into the NT ἔργα χειρῶν ἀνθρώπων is also an established term for idols : Dt. 4:28; 4 Βασ. 19:18; Is. 2:8; Jer. 1:16; ψ 113:12; Wis. 13:10; Rev. 9:20; 2 Cl., 1, 6 etc. A widespread conviction of later Judaism is thus expressed in 4 Esr. 7:119 : "What doth it profit us that we are promised the immortal world when we have done mortal works?" Cf. also 4 Esr. 1:8; S. Bar. 48:38; 54:2a.

This negative assessment of human action, which in the Greek OT is undoubtedly influenced by Hellenistic scepticism and pessimism, first takes on a radically theological character in the NT. Here ἔργον often denotes human work in the sense of vanity and sinfulness : R. 13:12 : τὰ ἔργα τοῦ σκότους, cf. Eph. 5:11; Gl. 5:19 : τὰ ἔργα τῆς σαρκός; Jn. 3:19; 7:7; 1 Jn. 3:12; 2 Jn. 11; 2 Tm. 4:18; Col. 1:21; Barn., 4, 10 : ἔργα πονηρά; 1 Jn. 3:8, cf. Jn. 8:41: τὰ ἔργα τοῦ διαβόλου; Jd. 15 : ἔργα ἀσεβείας; 2 Pt. 2:8; Barn., 4, 1: ἔργα ἄνομα; Hb. 6:1; 9:14 : ἔργα νεκρά. In many cases the term is given a negative connotation by a specific context, as in Mt. 23:3; Lk. 11:48; Jn. 8:41; Tt. 1:16. The decisive question of the righteousness of works is not consciously raised in these passages.

3. The righteousness of works in later Judaism.

The fact that ἔργα is used disparagingly in Pauline theology for an untenable righteousness of works cannot really be explained by the unfavourable view of human actions found in Hellenistic Judaism. For the Pauline verdict refers even to ἔργα which were generally acceptable in the sense of Jewish piety. We think, for example, of the common use of ἔργα for cultic practices. Thus the Greek translation of the OT often has ἔργον, for the Heb. עֲבֹדָה and מְלָאכָה, both of which were used for the direct or indirect service of the temple, of sacrifice, of watching, or even of constructing the temple or tabernacle. It also employs ἐργάζεσθαι in the same sense. The Jewish limitation of the negative appraisal of human action also extends to certain acts outside the cultus if they are understood to be commanded by God. The fulfilling of the Law is naturally a holy work for the Jews. By this man can raise himself up and establish his righteousness.

It is thus that we are to understand the פֹּעֵל צֶדֶק = ἐργαζόμενος δικαιοσύνην of ψ 14:2, or the ἐργάζεσθε κρίμα of Zeph. 2:3, or other OT passages which assume a righteousness of works on which saving faith may rest : Ps. 7:4 f.; 17:3 ff.; 18:20 ff., 25. Cf. also Da. 4:24; Neh. 13:14 (חֲסָדַי), 31; there is a typical interpretation in S. Bar. 63:3 : "Then Hezekiah trusted in his works ... and the Almighty heard him." This self-righteousness so prominent in the memoirs of Nehemiah is opposed by the OT revelation itself (cf. Is. 58:2 f.; 64:5). Nevertheless, the righteousness of casuistically ordered cultic and legal action is the decisive content of later Jewish piety. That the requirement of works is not found only in Rabb. Judaism may be seen from the LXX with its orientation to a righteousness of works as this finds expression in many different passages where the idea of works occurs, e.g., Jos. 4:24 : ἵνα ὑμεῖς σέβησθε κύριον τὸν θεὸν ἡμῶν ἐν παντὶ ἔργῳ (לְמַעַן יְרָאתֶם אֶת־יְהוָה אֱלֹהֵיכֶם כָּל־הַיָּמִים). It is true that in some passages there is to be seen a deeper concept of morality which seems to contradict the legal casuistry and to presuppose a total moral attitude : Sir. 24:22 : οἱ ἐργαζόμενοι ἐν ἐμοὶ (σοφία is speaking) οὐχ ἁμαρτήσουσιν; Sir. 27:9(10): ἀλήθεια πρὸς τοὺς ἐργαζομένους αὐτὴν ἐπανήξει; Prv. 10:16 : ἔργα δικαίων ζωὴν ποιεῖ; Is. 32:17: ἔσται τὰ ἔργα τῆς δικαιοσύνης εἰρήνη. But these isolated impulses — and further examples could be given — are not able to overcome the casuistry necessarily entailed by a righteousness of works. On the contrary, this casuistry constantly expands its dominion and is even able to penetrate into early Christianity. The natural man always looks to his own achievement even in the moral life. He tries to define as precisely as possible the sphere of virtues and vices (cf. the tables found even in the NT).[28] He is always inclined to split the total moral attitude into individual works. 2 Cl., 4, 3 is typical : ὥστε οὖν, ἀδελφοί, ἐν τοῖς ἔργοις αὐτὸν ὁμολογῶμεν, ἐν τῷ ἀγαπᾶν ἑαυτούς, ἐν τῷ μὴ μοιχᾶσθαι μηδὲ καταλαλεῖν ἀλλήλων μηδὲ ζηλοῦν, ἀλλ᾽ ἐγκρατεῖς εἶναι, ἐλεήμονας, ἀγαθούς, καὶ συμπάσχειν ἀλλήλοις ὀφείλομεν καὶ μὴ φιλαργυρεῖν. In its concern for the righteousness of works Judaism often appeals to examples in Scripture. Legends concerning the patriarchs Adam, Enoch, Abraham etc. afford instances of the works demanded by God.[29] Thus we find in Jn. 8:39 the formula : τὰ ἔργα τοῦ ᾽Αβραάμ.[30] The assumption is that the patriarchs knew the Law even though it was not written down, and that they fully performed the works of the commandments. The works of the commandments (מַעֲשֵׂי מִצְוֹת), often simply called מַעֲשִׂים by the Rabbis, correspond to what Paul calls the ἔργα νόμου.[31] Their fulfilment is fulfilment of the will of God, and the eschatological expectation is that arduous study of the Torah will no longer have to precede knowledge and fulfilment of the Law, but that God Himself will write the ἔργα νόμου[32] on the fleshy tables of the heart (Jer. 31:33). Paul applied this thought to the Gentiles and their natural knowledge of God (R. 2:15). In Judaism the works of the Law are the works required by God. The Jews ask concerning these in Jn. 6:28, obviously in the light of their own understanding that there are many such works. In contrast to these works of God or works of the Law are the works which originate in human self-will. According to the belief of Hell. Judaism man is free to choose these : Ps. Sol. 9:7: τὰ ἔργα ἡμῶν ἐν ἐκλογῇ καὶ ἐξουσίᾳ τῆς ψυχῆς ἡμῶν τοῦ ποιῆσαι δικαιοσύνην καὶ ἀδικίαν (ἐν) ἔργοις χειρῶν ἡμῶν. Cf. also Test. N. 2 : "As is his (man's) power, so is also his work ; as is his understanding, so is also his work ; and as is his precept, so is also his action ... either a law of the Lord or a law of Beliar." Between these two possibilities, or ways, man has to decide. His own works are ἀδικία, works of Beliar, in contrast to the works of the Law or works of God. Thus in Bar. 2:9 his own evil thoughts are opposed to the works of the Law required by God. S. Bar. 48:38 f. says the same with the threat of judgment : "Because in all these times they went astray, each in his own works, and did not regard the law of the Almighty, therefore fire consumes their thoughts ..." ῎Εργα as human works are evil, as the works of God good. The former proceed from man's will, the latter from the Law of God.

Even in Jewish piety it is recognised, of course, that fulfilment of the works of the Law is not possible for sinners. It is the privilege of the righteous, among whom are numbered especially the pious of past days and an occasional indefinite group of pneumatics and Gnostics such as we find in the Odes of Solomon. This cleavage between a special class of saints and the ordinary mass of the pious is found especially in S. Bar.

---

[28] For material, cf. Ltzm. R. on 1:31.
[29] G. Bertram in G. Rosen-G. Bertram, *Juden u. Phönizier* (1929), 58 ff.
[30] Str.-B., II, 524 enumerates them, and shows the formula to be Rabbinic.
[31] Str.-B., III, 160 ff.; IV, 559 ff.
[32] *Ibid.,* III, 89 ff.

Thus we read in 2:2 : "Your works (i.e., those of Jeremiah and his followers) are like a strong pillar for the city and your prayers like a solid wall." The difference between saints and average believers is particularly clear in 14:12 ff.: "For the righteous may look forward to the end, and go out of this life without fear ; for with thee they have a store of works laid up in the treasuries . . . But woe to us !" Cf. also 69:4; 51:7. In 85:2, as in 2:2, we read of a substitutionary intercession of the righteous, prophets and saints (?) on behalf of the people : "And these helped us when we sinned, and made intercession for us with him who made us, because they trusted in their works ; and the Almighty heard their prayer and pardoned us." This refers, of course, only to the past. A similar view is found in 4 Esr. Acc. to this work the pious assemble a treasure of good works (Mt. 6:20; Lk. 12:33; 1 Tm. 6:19) on the ground of which salvation will be granted to them : 7:77; 8:33; 9:7, 8 (works or faith); 13:23 (works and faith). But here, too, the reference is only to a select group. Of the mass it is said in 8:36 : "But thy goodness, O Lord, will be shown if thou hast pity on those who have no treasure of works." It is true that in S. Bar. and 4 Esr. works are not merely fulfilment of the Law but מַעֲשִׂים טוֹבִים, i.e., ἔργα καλά, which are certainly demanded in Scripture but do not have the strict character of commandments. The reference, then, is to meritorious works, and esp. the so-called works of love (גְּמִילוּת חֲסָדִים), i.e., almsgiving, peacemaking, the raising of sons to study the Law etc. [33] These works are thought of as a following of God. Acc. to Sota, 14a, R. Simlai says : "The Torah contains works of love at its beginning and at its end. At its beginning, as it is written : Yahweh-Elohim made coats for Adam and for Eve his wife, Gn. 3:21; and at its end, as it is written : He buried (Moses) in the valley, Dt. 34:6."

4. The righteousness of works and the thought of reward.

In later Judaism the developed doctrine of the righteousness of works merged with the thought of reward which in itself is natural to man. [34] A plain conviction of all biblical piety is that God recompenses man according to his works. Yet in the Bible the decisive point is not the anthropocentric thought of reward but the theological concept of God's power and justice. God knows all the acts of men : ψ 32:15 : ὁ συνιεὶς πάντα τὰ ἔργα; Sir. 15:19 : αὐτὸς ἐπιγνώσεται πᾶν ἔργον ἀνθρώπου; Sir. 39:19 : ἔργα πάσης σαρκὸς ἐνώπιον αὐτοῦ. This gives the assurance : ἔστιν μισθὸς τοῖς σοῖς ἔργοις ('Ιερ. 38[31]16) and : ἐν συντελείᾳ ἀνθρώπου ἀποκάλυψις ἔργων αὐτοῦ (Sir. 11:27). The thought of recompense is based on the fact that God recompenses to each according to his works. [35] On the other hand, it seems to destroy the thought of God if one must affirm : "There be just men, unto whom it happeneth according to the work of the wicked ; again, there be wicked men, to whom it happeneth according to the work of the righteous" (Qoh. 8:14). [36]

In practice, however, the problem of theodicy obviously yields to the moralistic thought of reward. By appeal to the hereafter it was hoped to rescue the idea of retribution from the eudaemonistic perspective of mere utility. Acc. to R. Jonathan (c. 220) death came also on the righteous "in order that the ungodly should not make a false show of repentance, and in order that the ungodly should not say : The righteous remain alive

---

[33] Str.-B., IV, 559 ff. The works of love in the special sense are almsgiving, visiting the sick and burying the dead ; loc. cit.

[34] Deissmann LO, 267 has rightly pointed out that the thought of reward in popular piety is not to be measured by the categories of a philosophical ethic.

[35] Jer. 25:14 'ΑΘ; Lam. 3:64; ψ 61:12; Prv. 24:12; Sir. 32(35):24; (Is. 3:10;) Mt. 16:27; 4 Esr. 7:34.

[36] Cf. K. Budde in Kautzsch.

only because they heap up fulfilments of the law and good works, therefore let us heap up fulfilments of the law and good works ; and so their action is not found to be such as took place for its own sake (but such as took place for selfish motives)," [37] Gn. r., 9 on 1:31. The act of judgment naturally produces reward or punishment : [38] "For him who heaps up fulfilments of the law and good works, Gan Eden is there ; but for him who does not heap up fulfilments of the law and good works, Gehinnom is there" (R. Ze'ira, c. 300), Gn. r., 9 on 1:31. According to a saying of Aqiba (Ab., 3, 15), the preponderance of good or evil works will decide. [39] Finally, the ancient idea is present that good works are advocates for us in the judgment, whether they follow us in death (Rev. 14:13) or whether they precede us. [40]

5. The work of man as a divinely given task.

The concept of reward and punishment presupposes that the biblical revelation views the ἔργα of man as performed by divine commission. Thus we read in the story of Eden in Gn. 2:15 : καὶ ἔλαβεν κύριος ὁ θεὸς τὸν ἄνθρωπον ὃν ἔπλασεν καὶ ἔθετο αὐτὸν ἐν τῷ παραδείσῳ, ἐργάζεσθαι αὐτόν. This corresponds to the לְעָבְדָהּ of the Mas. and to the negative statement in 2:5, which presupposes that man is given the charge : ἐργάζεσθαι τὴν γῆν : לַעֲבֹד אֶת־הָאֲדָמָה. How the land is tilled, God teaches man according to Is. 28:23-29. [41]

This brings us into the sphere of what have been called invention sagas, [42] which trace back all man's work of civilisation to God as Instructor. This applies also to the inventions recorded in Gn. 4:20 ff. [43] Philo Byblius interpreted these sagas euhemeristically, and partly on this ground Hellenistic Judaism maintained the cultural priority of the OT tradition. Thus, for example, Moses is the inventor of the Phoenician alphabet acc. to the Jewish historian Eupolemus. [44] Behind these rationalising and historicising reinterpretations, however, stands the fact that in Hellenistic Judaism at least human work is traced back fundamentally to a divine commission. If Gn. 2:15 in J hardly gives us a basis for work in the OT revelation, and if the joy in work in Gn. 1 does not really mean a consecration of labour in P (cf. also Ps. 8:6-8; Sir. 17:1 ff.), yet Hellenistic Judaism traced back its own positive attitude to the OT revelation. This may be seen also in the connection of the thought of man's divinely willed self-expression in work with the mystical concept of redemption as this emerges, e.g., in the Odes of Solomon. Here the planting of man in Paradise, understood as redemption, restores him to his true activity according to creation : "Behold, all are thine excellent labourers who do good works ..." O. Sol. 11:17). [45] This planting in Paradise is obviously not a reward for good works already done ; it is the presupposition of good works. These are just as natural to redeemed man as they were to divinely created man prior to the fall. It need occasion no surprise that the image of God's workman should lead us from the thought of tilling the garden to the moral sphere.

In the same way, later Judaism in spite of everything preserves an ethos of work which finds expression in many Rabbinic utterances. Thus we read in bBer., 32b Bar.: "For four things man needs constancy, and these are : the Torah, good works, prayer and one's earthly avocation." That this earthly avocation stands under God's blessing

---

[37] That the Law should be fulfilled and good works done for the sake of God is clearly expressed also in the Rabbin. saying quoted in Str.-B. on Tt. 2:14.

[38] Str.-B., IV, 11.

[39] Ibid., III, 78; also III, 529 on Jn. 9:4.

[40] Ibid., III, 655, 817.

[41] So the Mas. The LXX understands the ἐργάζεσθαι τὴν γῆν figuratively.

[42] This description fits only the later euhemeristic interpretation in the Hellenistic period.

[43] W. Baudissin, Kyrios, III (1929), 448 ff.

[44] G. Rosen-G. Bertram, op. cit., 18 f., 128 f.

[45] A. Harnack-J. Flemming, Ein jüdisch-christliches Psalmbuch (1910), ad loc.

may be seen esp. in the recurrent formula of Dt.: εὐλογήσει σε κύριος ὁ θεός σου ἐν πᾶσιν τοῖς ἔργοις (τῶν χειρῶν σου). [46] The high estimation of manual work among the Rabbis is well-known. [47] Thus we read in Ber., 8a: "R. Chijja (c. 280) has said: "Greater is he who enjoys of his labour (i.e., supports himself by it), than he who fears God. For lo! it is written of him who fears God: Blessed is the man who fears Yahweh, Ps. 112:1; and lo! it is written of the man who enjoys of his labour: For thou shalt eat the labour of thine hands: happy shalt thou be, and it shall be well with thee, Ps. 128:2; happy shalt thou be in this world, and it shall be well with thee in the next. But 'it shall be well with thee' is not written of him who fears God." Acc. to Ab., 2, 2, Rabban Gamaliel (III, c. 220), the son of the patriarch Jehuda (I), said: "Beautiful is the study of the Torah in conjunction with a worldly occupation (such as manual work or trade); for concern for both causes one to forget sin (so as not to serve it). But all study of the Torah with which one does not combine gainful activity finally ceases and brings sin with it." Yet there are also critical voices arguing that the two are incompatible. Typical is Sir. 38:24 (25) — 39:11: "Of scribes as distinct from those of practical occupation." [48] Here the introduction runs: σοφία γραμματέως ἐν εὐκαιρίᾳ σχολῆς καὶ ὁ ἐλασσούμενος πράξει αὐτοῦ σοφισθήσεται. There then follows a supercilious description of the work of the farmer: τί σοφισθήσεται ὁ κρατῶν ἀρότρου ... βόας ἐλαύνων καὶ ἀναστρεφόμενος ἐν ἔργοις αὐτῶν; But the depiction of various trades which follows breathes a different spirit. In v. 31 it is recognised: ἕκαστος ἐν τῷ ἔργῳ αὐτοῦ σοφίζεται, and according to v. 34 their work serves to maintain creation: ἀλλὰ κτίσμα αἰῶνος τηρήσουσιν καὶ ἡ δέησις αὐτῶν ἐν ἐργασίᾳ τέχνης. Hence it is not surprising that in v. 24 a vl. interpolates οὐ before σοφισθήσεται, approval thus being given to the Rabbinic combination of study of the Torah and practical work.

The criterion of ἔργα and ἐργάζεσθαι applies also in the NT. The practical requirement is soberly addressed to Christians: ἐργάζεσθαι ταῖς ἰδίαις χερσίν, 1 Th. 4:11; 2 Th. 3:10-12; Eph. 4:28. These passages stand under the same ethico-religious sign as the declarations of the apostle Paul concerning his own labour in self-support. This work is sacred to the degree that at least indirectly it serves the Christian community as the σῶμα Χριστοῦ in respect of its good repute in the world. There can indeed be no final distinction between work in temporal avocation and direct work in the service of the community. All ἔργον in the Christian community (and not merely in the organized Church) is finally God's work through men. With this insight of faith the problem of work is solved in the NT. For Paul and for all believers all work is the fruit of faith. This faith is πίστις δι᾽ ἀγάπης ἐνεργουμένη (Gl. 5:6). Thus ἔργον τῆς πίστεως, κόπος τῆς ἀγάπης and ὑπομονὴ τῆς ἐλπίδος are grouped together in the NT (1 Th. 1:3), and the same terms are again closely linked with ἔργον πίστεως in 2 Th. 1:11. Cf. ὑπομονὴ ἔργου ἀγαθοῦ in R. 2:7. A unitary character is thus given to Christian action evoked by God and proceeding from faith. For this reason this action can and must be for Paul the standard by which man is judged (R. 2:6). Nor is this self-evident basis of judgment ever challenged in the NT. This aspect of ἔργα is sharply emphasised in John's Gospel. It embraces "the whole conduct of a man in so far as he falls under the antithesis of good and evil ... with no distinction between more or less good or evil actions" ... "and including the hidden motions of the will, whether in relation to God, to the world or to other men." [49] Even if

---

[46] Dt. 2:7; 14:29; 15:10; 16:15; Job 1:10; ψ 89:17; Test. Jud. 2 (both in the field and in the house); cf. also 2 Ch. 31:21: ἐν παντὶ ἔργῳ ... εὐοδώθη; 32:30; 1 Ἐσδρ. 1:21 etc.

[47] Str.-B., II, 10, 745; III, 338, 604, 641, where other examples are given.

[48] This is the heading given by V. Ryssel in Kautzsch.

[49] Zn. J. on 3:19 and Zn. R. on 2:6.

no logical agreement is possible in relation to the responsibility of man, it is still recognised that αὐτοῦ τὰ ἔργα ... ἐν θεῷ ἐστιν εἰργασμένα (Jn. 3:21) applies to him that does truth. In Ac. 26:20, too, the required works or fruits point to the responsibility of man in his action. Yet this action has no value in itself, but only as a response to the revelation of repentance.[50]

It is thus only κατὰ ἄνθρωπον that one can speak of the works of men. This human manner of speaking can easily lead, of course, to nomistic ideas. We sometimes see the influence of these on the fringe of the NT itself, and esp. in the post-apostolic fathers. Cf. Ign. Eph., 1, 1; Sm., 11, 2; R., 2, 1; Pol., 6, 2 (though Ign. has a good grasp of the matter: Pol., 8, 1: δοξασθῆτε αἰωνίῳ ἔργῳ; 7, 3: ἔργον θεοῦ καὶ ὑμῶν); cf. also Barn., 1, 6: ἀγάπη ... ἔργων δικαιοσύνης μαρτυρία; 19, 1; 2 Cl., 6, 9; 11, 6; 12, 4; 16, 3; 17, 4. The view found in these passages corresponds to the view of good works common in later Judaism. In 1 Cl., 33, 1 false deductions from the Pauline doctrine of justification by faith are repudiated: ἀργήσωμεν ἀπὸ τῆς ἀγαθοποιίας; ... ἀλλὰ σπεύσωμεν ... πᾶν ἔργον ἀγαθὸν ἐπιτελεῖν. The basis of good works is consciously theological: (2) αὐτὸς γὰρ ὁ δημιουργὸς καὶ δεσπότης τῶν ἁπάντων ἐπὶ τοῖς ἔργοις αὐτοῦ ἀγάλλεται. Cf. also 33, 7: ἐν ἔργοις ἀγαθοῖς πάντες ἐκοσμήθησαν οἱ δίκαιοι καὶ αὐτὸς δὲ ὁ κύριος ἔργοις ἀγαθοῖς ἑαυτὸν κοσμήσας ἐχάρη. This leads to 33, 8: ἐξ ὅλης τῆς ἰσχύος ἡμῶν ἐργασώμεθα ἔργον δικαιοσύνης. Hermas is the first Roman Catholic in the sphere of good works, though his views correspond to the popular human mode of understanding. Cf. Herm. s., 8, 11, 1.

6. Word and act, faith and works.

The tension between word and act is naturally expressed everywhere in the Gk. tongue. Thus in Homer ἔπος and ἔργον stand in antithesis. In Attic it is usually λόγος/ἔργον. The relation between the two is a basic question in the philosophy of Plato and Aristotle. Πολιτεύεσθαι καθ' ἡμᾶς ἔργῳ, ἀλλ' οὐ λόγῳ, is the self-evidently recognised requirement of state laws.[51] In Ps.-Pythagoras, Carmen Aureum, 13, the interconnection of the two is presupposed: εἶτα δικαιοσύνην ἄσκει ἔργῳ τε λόγῳ τε.[52] For Philo, too, their relationship is a logical and ethical postulate, so that contradiction between them necessarily rests on sophistry (Poster. C., 86; cf. 87 and 88).[53] In the Hermetic tractates we sometimes find the distinctive, emphatic claim to be in possession of the active word: ἡμεῖς δὲ οὐ λόγοις χρώμεθα ἀλλὰ φωναῖς μεσταῖς τῶν ἔργων (Corp. Herm., XVI, 2).

In the biblical tradition the harmony of word and work is regarded as self-evident so far as revelation is concerned. The LXX formulates the concept, e.g., at Jl. 2:11: ἰσχυρὰ ἔργα λόγων αὐτοῦ (כִּי עָצוּם עֹשֵׂה דְבָרוֹ = Σ ὅτι ἰσχυροὶ οἱ ποιοῦντες τὸν λόγον αὐτοῦ). It is also present in ψ 32:4: εὐθὴς ὁ λόγος τοῦ κυρίου καὶ πάντα τὰ ἔργα αὐτοῦ ἐν πίστει (= Mas.). The presupposed, demanded or stated unity of human conduct is often enough present in the corresponding formulae[54] (cf. βουλή/πρᾶξις, Lk. 23:51;[55] Ac. 5:38; 2 C. 10:11; 1 Jn. 3:18). It is here, however, that there arises the problem which takes on such far-reaching material significance in the NT.

---

[50] E. Lohmeyer, Das Urchristentum, I (1933), 105 ff. Cf. also Eph. 2:10; → ἕτοιμος.
[51] Plat. Crito, 52d; cf. 46d ff. Cf. also Heracl. Fr., 1; 48; Demosth. Or. 8, 73.
[52] Dib. Past. on 1 Tm. 6:11.
[53] Cf. also Mut. Nom., 243: λόγος γὰρ ἔργου σκιά; though cf. Som., II, 302: ὁ μὲν γὰρ τοῦ σπουδαίου βίος ἐν ἔργοις, ἐν λόγοις δὲ ὁ τοῦ φαύλου θεωρεῖται.
[54] For the Rabbis, too, learning is a presupposition of action. Hence the cursing of those without the Law. Cf. Str.-B. on Jn. 7:49, esp. II, 496, 518.
[55] Cf. Cl. Al. Strom., II, 6, 127, 9 f.: τὸ μὲν βούλεσθαι ψυχῆς, τὸ πράττειν δὲ οὐκ ἄνευ σώματος.

Already in Rabbinic tradition there is awareness of a tension between teaching and life which can never be completely overcome, and this becomes the occasion for a reproach against the scribes in Mt. 23:3. The Rabb. conviction is that he who has learned the Torah and yet acts contrary to it blasphemes God.⁵⁶ Christianity, however, demands a preaching of action : Ign. Eph., 10, 1: ἐκ τῶν ἔργων ὑμῖν μαθητευθῆναι (cf. Tr., 3, 2; 1 Pt. 3:1), and contradiction between word and act is a denial of Christ : 2 Cl., 13, 3 : τὰ ἔθνη ... καταμαθόντα τὰ ἔργα ἡμῶν ὅτι οὐκ ἔστιν ἄξια τῶν ῥημάτων ...; Tt. 1:16 : θεὸν ὁμολογοῦσιν εἰδέναι, τοῖς δὲ ἔργοις ἀρνοῦνται. Cf. 2 Cl., 17, 7: ἀρνησάμενος διὰ τῶν λόγων ἢ διὰ τῶν ἔργων τὸν Ἰησοῦν. Herm. s., 9, 21, 2 : τὰ ῥήματα αὐτῶν μόνα ζῶσιν, τὰ δὲ ἔργα αὐτῶν νεκρά ἐστιν.

Such contradiction is obviously assumed in Jm. 1:25 : οὐκ ἀκροατὴς ἐπιλησμονῆς γενόμενος ἀλλὰ ποιητὴς ἔργου, and 2:17: ἡ πίστις, ἐὰν μὴ ἔχῃ ἔργα, νεκρά ἐστιν καθ' ἑαυτήν. Against the Jewish stress on works, to which there corresponds an intellectualistic misunderstanding of faith (faith is monotheism), the author maintains that the two belong together in the relative human sense indicated.⁵⁷ Hebrews goes beyond this relative mode of conception with its designation of works as ἔργα νεκρά (cf. 4 Esr. 7:119). What are meant here are works which lead to death. These are not just mortal sins ; they are all works which do not lead to life, i.e., all which are not of God, which are not the works of God. The contrast with πίστις εἰς θεόν in 6:1 and with λατρεύειν θεῷ ζῶντι in 9:14 demands a radical understanding of ἔργα νεκρά from the standpoint of faith. All works which do not proceed from faith are dead, for they lead to death. Everything which does not take place in the service of the living God is dead.

This gives us the Pauline understanding of the contrast between faith and works. The ἔργα νόμου which are at issue for Paul have become a means of self-righteousness for the Jews. Hence they are no longer an expression of the absolute requirement of God — the Law is this for Paul in Gl. 5:3 — but they spring from man's arrogant striving after self-righteousness. In opposition to them we can only point to the act of God which creates faith in us. All thought of works retreats behind this, and can emerge again only within the community in relation to the working of the Spirit of God in the apostle and in believers, since it is God who works all in all (1 C. 12:6). It thus comes about that the word ἔργον, already suspect in the OT, acquires in Paul a completely negative sense whenever it is a matter of human achievement. For the work of man cannot stand before the exclusive operation of grace.⁵⁸ If nevertheless there is reference to good works in the message of the whole of the NT, and this not merely after a human manner of speaking, it is in virtue of a return to the legitimate use of the term in revelation. It is true of fallen humanity that its works are evil. But the time of salvation restores the situation as it was by creation. All man's work is God's work through man. Thus the ἔργα τοῦ νόμου, the misunderstood and depreciated legal works of the old covenant, are confronted by the ἔργα τοῦ θεοῦ of the new covenant, or rather by the one work of faith active in love (Gl. 5:6; Jn. 6:29).

⁵⁶ Str.-B., I, 910, 239; II, 273, with further examples.
⁵⁷ So H. Preisker, ThBl, 4 (1925), 16 f.
⁵⁸ R. 3:20, 27; 4:2, 6; 9:12, 32; 11:6; Gl. 2-3. The Pauline understanding of the absolute operation of God is also found in 2 Tm. 1:9; Tt. 3:5; also Pol., 1, 3 (cf. Paul Eph. 2:8, 9) and 1 Cl., 32, 3 and 4. Judaism and Rabbinism can naturally give to faith only a relative importance alongside works. Cf. the material in Str.-B., III, 186-201. And even so faith is regarded as a human achievement. The fact of God's omnicausality, which is naturally present in the OT revelation but weakened in Judaism, is first proclaimed again in its purity in the Gospel as the message of salvation.

The natural man cannot of himself perceive this divine work of salvation. The resurrection of Jesus is an inconceivable event which is perceptible only to disciples, to believers. The same is true of all the miracles of the OT and the NT. The unbeliever understands them either simply in terms of earthly goals, as with the Jews and the feeding of the five thousand (Jn. 6:26b), or as the work of demons, as did the scribes the expulsion of devils (Mk. 3:22), or as a tempting of God, like Ahaz when he was told to ask for a sign (Is. 7:12). Only the believer finds the true borderline in this respect in Christ (Mt. 4:7). Only to him is the work of God manifest. For him the ambiguity is removed which clings, humanly speaking, to every ἔργον θεοῦ, whether in His overruling of history as Creator or in His activity in salvation history as Deliverer, so that one and the same event or word, according to the will of God, can produce faith in those who are called and unbelief and obduracy in those who are rejected. For believing Christians the καλὰ ἔργα which meet them in life are never just the work of man; they are the work of God through human hands. Everything which, according to a judgment purified by Holy Scripture, serves the promotion of life, is regarded as καλὸν ἔργον, as ἔργον θεοῦ. Man may abuse the works of the Creator, but earthly goods, family, state, nation, Law (R. 7:12, 13) are still the good work of God as tutors to bring us to Christ.

† ἐνεργέω, † ἐνέργεια, † ἐνέργημα, † ἐνεργής.

The subst. ἐνεργία, ἐνέργεια is found in the sense of "activity" or "energy" from the pre-Socratic period. It denotes activity as distinct from πάθος. The verb ἐνεργεῖν is used in the same way. It derives from ἐνεργός (which itself derives from ἐν ἔργῳ εἶναι), and denotes intr. "to be at work," "to act or start to act," and trans. "to set at work," "to effect." ἐνέργημα means "what is effected," the "act" or "action." ἐνεργής (from the time of Aristotle) means "active."

In Hellenism, [1] as in Philo, [2] the word group is used of cosmic or physical forces [3] at work in man or the world around. In the OT and NT ἐνέργεια, and in the NT the verb ἐνεργεῖν, are used almost exclusively for the work of divine or demonic powers, so that we almost have a technical use. In the OT ἐνέργεια occurs only in Wis. and 2 and 3 Macc. There is thus no Heb. original. In Wis. 7:17 the reference is to the ἐνέργεια στοιχείων. The part. is used in the same sense in 1 Cl., 60, 1: σὺ τὴν ἀέναον τοῦ κόσμου σύστασιν διὰ τῶν ἐνεργουμένων ἐφανεροποίησας. In Wis. 13:4 the term is used of cosmic powers. If in this passage the δύναμις and ἐνέργεια of cosmic phenomena awaken numinous terror, these phenomena are obviously regarded as κοσμοκράτορες (Eph. 6:12), and it is only a step to the view that the ἐνέργειαι themselves are cosmic beings. They are mentioned as such in a list in Act. Jn., 98 which includes them with ἀρχαί, ἐξουσίαι, δυνάμεις (cf. Eph. 1:21; 3:10 etc.), δαίμονες, [4] διάβολοι, Σατανᾶς. In Wis. 18:22 we have ὅπλων ἐνέργεια. Otherwise the reference is always to the ἐνέργεια τοῦ θεοῦ, Wis. 7:26; 3 Macc. 5:28; θεία,

---

ἐνεργέω κτλ. Moult.-Mill., 214; Bl.-Debr.⁶ § 148, 1; § 316, 1; Zn. Gl. on 2:8; Wbg. Th. on I, 2:13 and II, 2:7.

[1] In the pap. it often denotes magical power with no obvious distinction from δύναμις, e.g., Preis. Zaub., IV, 160, 1718. Cf. J. Röhr, "Der okkulte Kraftbegriff im Altertum," *Philol. Suppl.*, 17, 1 (1924), 15-19; A. D. Nock, "Greek Magical Papyri," *Journal of Egypt. Archaeol.*, 15 (1929), 219-235. The philosophical usage (e.g., Aristotle → 636) is of little relevance to the NT.

[2] There are several examples in J. Leisegang, *Indices* (1926), 250 f.

[3] Cf. Corp. Herm., XVI, 4: ἀγαθαὶ ἐνέργειαι (ἡλίου); 13: δαίμονος γὰρ οὐσία ἐνέργεια.

[4] Cf. the passage quoted from Corp. Herm., XVI, 13.

2 Macc. 3:29; τοῦ δεσπότου, 3 Macc. 5:12; τῆς προνοίας, 3 Macc. 4:21. This denotes either His activity as Creator and Sustainer of the world in general (Wis. 7:26) or His active direct intervention in the course of events through miracles, as in the passages adduced from 2 and 3 Macc. In a concealed form we meet the same view in Act. Thom., 51, where the miracle of punishment at the Lord's Supper is attributed to God: οὐ χωρὶς ἐνεργείας τινὸς γέγονεν. A pious outlook which sees God in the everyday gives rise to the saying in Ep. Ar., 266, which attributes the ultimate success of human oratory to God: θεοῦ δὲ ἐνεργείᾳ κατευθύνεται πειθώ. A similar attitude underlies the pious expression in Barn., 19, 6: τὰ συμβαίνοντά σοι ἐνεργήματα ὡς ἀγαθὰ προσδέξῃ, εἰδὼς ὅτι ἄνευ θεοῦ οὐδὲν γίνεται. The verb ἐνεργάζεσθαι also occurs once in the LXX at 2 Macc. 14:40 as a vl. for the simple form and with the same sense. The adj. ἐνεργός occurs at Ez. 46:1 with ἡμέρα in translation of מַעֲשֶׂה, and it gives the sense of a work-day. The verb ἐνεργεῖν is often used in the OT with no particular emphasis, as in Nu. 8:24 as vl. for λειτουργεῖν, or in 1 Ἐσδρ. 2:16(20) in a Gk. addition concerning the rebuilding of the temple, or in Prv. 21:6 for פֹּעַל and 29:30 (31:12) with the dat. ethicus for גָּמַל. The verb is to be taken in the intensive in Wis. 15:11 with its reference to the ψυχὴ ἐνεργοῦσα, i.e., the living and active soul which God breathes into man, and in Wis. 16:17 with its reference to fire. In Is. 41:4 the verb is used for פֹּעַל and with ποιεῖν denotes the operation of God.

In the NT this theological or demonological usage is predominant. Only in Phil. 2:13 does the active ἐνεργεῖν refer to human activity. In Eph. 2:2 the verb is used of the ἄρχων τῆς ἐξουσίας τοῦ ἀέρος. The med. is similarly used in 2 Th. 2:7: τὸ γὰρ μυστήριον ἤδη ἐνεργεῖται τῆς ἀνομίας, and in 2:9 we read of the ἐνέργεια τοῦ Σατανᾶ, who on the appearing of the man of sin will be seen at work in all kinds of deceptive miracles. But finally even his activity is to be traced back to God (v. 11): "God gives to the lying satanic miracles of Antichrist the power to lead astray." [5, 6] In other texts the act. of the verb is used of God and divine powers, e.g., of the operation of the Spirit in 1 C. 12:6, 11. The reference is either to χάρισμα in general (12:6) or to a specific group of divine powers, δυνάμεις (12:10; cf. Mk. 6:14 [7] = Mt. 14:2: δυνάμεις ἐνεργοῦσιν ἐν αὐτῷ). In Gl. 2:8 the apostolic office of Peter and Paul is the purpose and goal of the divine operation. In Gl. 3:5 the reference is to the miraculous demonstrations of power with which God gives force to missionary preaching; cf. Eph. 3:7; Col. 1:29. The difficult expression θύρα ... ἐνεργής in 1 C. 16:9 also refers to the divinely effected possibilities of missionary work. In Hb. 4:12 λόγος ... ἐνεργής is to be understood of the effective Word of God in the sense of the biblical revelation. [8] Phlm. 6 uses the same adj. of the power of the community of faith to create knowledge. Here, too, God is the One who is ultimately at work. He is the One who works all things. Phil. 2:13: ὁ ἐνεργῶν ἐν ὑμῖν τὸ θέλειν καὶ τὸ ἐνεργεῖν ὑπὲρ τῆς εὐδοκίας; [9] Eph. 1:11; Phil. 3:21. But especially He effects the δύναμις τῆς ἀναστάσεως, Eph. 1:19, 20; Col. 2:12; cf. also Mk. 6:14; Mt. 14:2 (where the διὰ τοῦτο refers to the supposed resurrection of John the Baptist). [10]

---

[5] Dob. Th., ad loc.
[6] Cf. Barn., 2, 1 and Act. Joh., 75 (ἐνέργεια κατωτική).
[7] "Angelic powers" (?), cf. Wbg. Mk., ad loc.
[8] Cf. Barn., 1, 7, where ἐνεργεῖν is used of the fulfilment of the promises and prophecies of the prophets and of the Lord.
[9] On the significance of the prepositional phrase, cf. Haupt and Ew. Gefbr., ad loc.
[10] Theophylactus, MPG, 123, 513, in Kl. Mk., ad loc.

In the NT the med. ἐνεργεῖσθαι is found only in Paul and Jm. 5:16, and it is always in the intr. [11] It is not used of God. In 1 Th. 2:13 λόγος is the subject of the relative clause ὅς καὶ ἐνεργεῖται ἐν ὑμῖν τοῖς πιστεύουσιν, and therefore materially this text is to be grouped with Hb. 4:12. According to 2 C. 1:6 the comfort which Paul has for the congregation works itself out ἐν ὑπομονῇ τῶν αὐτῶν παθημάτων, in the patient bearing of sufferings. In Gl. 5:6 it is faith which is active in love. [12] The synergistic misunderstanding of this verse was already rejected by Luther : *opera fieri dicit ex fide per caritatem, non iustificari hominem per caritatem*, Comm., ad loc. (1535). In Eph. 3:20 the reference is to the divine power working in the apostle, and in Jm. 5:16 to the effectiveness of prayer. Only once can the term ἐνέργεια be related to Christ. According to Eph. 4:16 it is He who grants the power of growth to each member of the σῶμα Χριστοῦ. In other passages hostile powers are the logical subject of ἐνεργεῖσθαι, e.g., passions in R. 7:5; death in 2 C. 4:12; τὸ μυστήριον τῆς ἀνομίας in 2 Th. 2:7. Behind these concepts Paul and his readers see demonic powers. In the NT, then, the word group is used of irrational operations, whether divine or demonic.

† εὐεργετέω, † εὐεργέτης, † εὐεργεσία.

This word group is found from the time of Homer, Pindar and the tragic dramatists. εὐεργεσία can indicate an individual benefit or favour, or general benevolence. In the Hellenistic period it is very common in inscr. and the pap. in the sense of a title publicly conferred and generally acknowledged. There are instances of this from the 5th century B.C. to the 2nd cent. A.D. [1] In the Roman period the title *euergetes* is usually combined with others. [2] The manifold use of benefactor and benefit is linked with the civilised outlook of Hellenism. Gods and heroes, kings and statesmen, philosophers, inventors and physicians are hailed as benefactors because of their contributions to the development of the race. [3] As in invention sagas, the difference between gods and men is here dissolved in an euhemeristic sense. If the formal use of the title in public life derives to a large extent from its philosophical significance, the Augustan renaissance makes it one of the basic religio-political concepts of the Golden Age of the Roman Empire. [4] The emperors are divine saviours and benefactors of humanity, [5] for they establish the *pax romana* and with it the presupposition of all human culture.

In the OT we are often told that God is beneficent to His people, but the Gk. translations generally avoid the word group. Only in Σ do we find εὐεργετεῖν for יטב at 1 Βασ. 2:32 and ψ 50:18 and for עשה טוב at ψ 118:65. If the word group is also introduced for עֲלִילָה at ψ 77:11 (LXX), for גמר [6] at ψ 56:2 (LXX), for גמל at ψ 12:6;

---

[11] Cf. Bl.-Debr.[6] § 148, 1; § 316, 1.
[12] → 649.

εὐεργετέω κτλ. Pr.-Bauer, 498 f.; Moult.-Mill., 260 f.; Preisigke Wört., 610 f.; Deissmann LO, 214 ff.; Wendland Hell. Kult., Index, *s.v.* εὐεργέτης; R. Knopf on 1 Cl., 19, 2 in *Handb. z. NT* (1920); E. Skard, "Zwei religiös-politische Begriffe : *Euergetes-Concordia*" (*Norske Videskaps Akademi i Oslo, Avhandlinger*, 1932).
[1] J. Öhler in Pauly-W., VI (1909), *s.v. Euergetes.*
[2] For examples, *v.* D. Magie, *De Romanorum iuris publici sacrique vocabulis sollemnibus in Graecum sermonem conversis* (1905), 67 f.
[3] So esp. Heracles, who in Eur. Heracl., 1252 is called εὐεργέτης βροτοῖσι καὶ μέγας φίλος. Cf. also Diod. S., III, 56, 5; III, 57, 2; III, 60, 3 and 5. Cf. J. Kroll, *Gott und Hölle* (1932), esp. 399 ff.; also Socrates in Plat. Ap., 36d.
[4] Cf. Skard, *op. cit.,* 6-66, where there is a discussion of the earlier history of the concept in the Greek sphere.
[5] Cf. Magie, *op. cit.,* 67 f.
[6] Possibly through confusion with גמל, cf. F. Wutz, *Die Psalmen* (1925), ad loc.

114:7 (LXX) and ψ 141:7; Prv. 11:17; Is. 63:7 (Σ), and for גמול at ψ 102:2 (Σ), this estimation of benefits is really introduced by the translators. Except in Prv. 11:7 the benefactor is always God. It is only of God's benefits that the OT revelation can properly speak. [7] Even in Wis. and 2 Macc. this reference to God is directly or indirectly maintained. [8] In the other Hellenistic books men are benefactors, usually princes. [9] *Euergetes* is never used of God, and it normally has the distinctive Gk. sense. Cf. the additions to Est. 8:12 E 3, 13 (16:3, 13): τόν τε ἡμέτερον σωτῆρα καὶ διὰ παντὸς εὐεργέτην; 2 Macc. 4:2 : τὸν εὐεργέτην τῆς πόλεως 3 Macc. 3:19; 6:24. Even more strongly Hellenistic is the usage of Philo. He can apply the title equally to God or the emperor. Gratitude for benefits received is the essence of this *sapiens pietas.* [10]

In the NT the word group occurs only 4 times. In Ac. 4:9 the miraculous healing of the sick is regarded as a benefit displayed by God through the apostles. In Ac. 10:38 the activity of the Saviour Himself is described from the anthropocentric Hellenistic standpoint of benefit. The same standpoint is seen in 1 Tm. 6:2. Christian slaves should not despise their Christian masters because they are now brothers. They should serve them the more diligently because these masters now have the honourable title of believers loved by God. That they are now concerned for the welfare of their slaves is an outworking of the divine love which they have experienced, and should not be abused. [11] In contrast to this positive use is the rejection of the title of *euergetes* in Lk. 22:25. This is to be taken in the sense of Mt. 23:7 ff.: Be not called Rabbi, master, or doctor, for these titles belong to One alone. Only Christ can really be called *euergetes* (Ac. 10:38). All human benefits may be traced back to Him, or to God. [12] We find the same view in 1 Cl., where the philosophical and religious concept of the divine benefit has a special sense. [13] In the NT the proper position of men as mediators of the divine benefits is that of servants (Mt. 23:11; Lk. 22:26). And what God does through Christ according to the NT revelation does not in the first instance stand under the human standpoint of εὐεργεσία, which seems to promise fulfilment of what man might desire, but under the theological standpoint of the δύναμις εἰς σωτηρίαν (R. 1:16).

Bertram

---

† **ἐρευνάω, † ἐξερευνάω**

ἐρευν- is the older form of the stem. [1] The first literary use of ἐραυν- is in the LXX. [2] A non-literary use of ἐρευν- is still found in 113 B.C. (P. Tebt., I, 38, 19),

---

[7] The concept of God's benefits implies, of course, an anthropocentric development of the biblical understanding of God such as we find in Hell. Judaism and the LXX. The occurrence of the word group in the Bible indicates the introduction of such ideas.

[8] Wis. 3:5; 7:22; 11:5, 13; 16:2, 11, 24; 2 Macc. 5:20; 6:13; 10:38.

[9] Cf. additions to Est. 8:12 E 2 (16:2); 2 Macc. 9:26; 4 Macc. 8:6, 17.

[10] Op. Mund., 169; Leg. All., II, 56; Leg. Gaj., 20 and 149; Vit. Mos., II, 198 : ἐπεὶ δὲ καὶ τῷ μὴ σέβειν θεὸν ἕπεται τὸ μήτε γονεῖς μήτε πατρίδα μήτ' εὐεργέτας τιμᾶν.

[11] A different view is taken in Wbg. Past. on 1 Tm. 6:2. On the history of the interpretation of this disputed passage, cf. B. Weiss, *Erkl. der Past.*[7] (1902), *ad loc.*

[12] There is a confusion of concepts in Act. Joh., 27: "If alongside this God we may call those men gods who are our benefactors ..."

[13] Cf. 19, 2; 20, 11; 21, 1; 23, 1: εὐεργετικὸς πατήρ; 38, 3; 59, 3.

ἐ ρ ε υ ν ά ω κ τ λ. → ἀνεξερεύνητος, I, 357; Pr.-Bauer, *s.v.* (on the correct reading cf. E. Nachmanson in *Eranos,* 11 [1911], 239).

[1] We do not achieve the oldest sense if we link it with the question of ἐρέω in Homer (on whether to put F after ερ or ερε, *v.* Boisacq, *s.v.* ἐρέω).

[2] Then also in Philo and Joseph. (Mayser, I, 113), though the reading may be arbitrarily determined by the various copyists.

while ἐραυν- first appears in P. Oxy., II, 294, 10 in pap. (22 A.D.), though found on inscr. in the 2nd quarter of the 1st cent. B.C., IG, XII, 5, 653, 21. In the NT the MSS mostly have ἐρευν-, though it cannot be said for certain what criteria led to the selection. ³ Nor are there any obvious reasons for the usage in the LXX. Thus in ψ 63:6, where the root occurs three times, א has ευ once and αυ twice. Usually ευ is predominantly or exclusively attested. Only twice does א clearly have αυ instead of the more general ευ. The most that we can say, then, is that αυ and ευ are not to be clearly differentiated even in the same MSS and the same verses.

The general meaning of ἐρευνάω is to "search after," both literally and figur. It is first used a. of animals in the sense of "to sniff out" with the nose, cf. Hom. Od., 19, 436, Emped. Fr., 101 (I, 260, 19, Diels). It is then used b. of men in the sense of "to search" (esp. of houses or possessions, e.g., Aristot. Oec., II, p. 1351b, 27), so also P. Oxy., II, 294, 10 : ὁ ἐμὸς οἶκος ἠραύνηται, and therefore sometimes synon. with φωρᾶν in the sense of investigating a robbery (Plat. Leg., XII, 954b). It then comes to mean c. "to investigate a matter," esp. in the legal sense, though also in the more general sense of enquiry (e.g., Hom. Hymn. Merc., 176). Cf. the NT context of the occurrence of ἀνεξερεύνητος, → I, 357. d. This gives us the further sense of "to test" or "fully to examine" a statement, more particularly from the academic standpoint. Soph. Fr., 80 (TGF, p. 147): μὴ πάντ' ἐρεύνα· πολλὰ καὶ λαθεῖν καλόν. In religious usage it means "to seek," Pindar Fr., 61: οὐ γὰρ ἔσθ' ὅπως τὰ θεῶν βουλεύματ' ἐρευνάσει βροτέᾳ φρενί, because of his limitations man cannot discover the will of God, though he searches diligently: ὃν γὰρ ἂν θεὸς χρείαν ἐρευνᾷ ... (Soph. Oed. Tyr., 725). Cf. Philo Fug., 165 : It is impossible to penetrate to the innermost being of God (ἐρευνᾶν); in the relative sense : ὁ ... νοῦς ... ἐρευνᾷ τὸ θεῖον καὶ τὴν τούτου φύσιν, Leg. All., III, 84. In the sense of γνῶθι σαυτόν, Migr. Abr., 185 (cf. 138); Agric., 72; Som., I, 54.

Esp. in Plato (synon. with ζητῶ, ἐξετάζω) and Philo it is used of academic, scientific, philological (Philo Cher., 105) and philosophical investigations. In Philo it is sometimes used of acute enquiry into the linguistic and other background, e.g., Deus Imm., 167. Thus we often have in Philo the summons ἐρευνήσωμεν, ἐρεύνησον, ἐρευνητέον. The verb often takes αἰτίαν(ς) as object (cf. Plat. Leg., VII, 821a). Philo also uses it for the study of Scripture (of the OT, Det. Pot. Ins., 13), perhaps as a technical term for the work of the scribes (Cher., 14, cf. Det. Pot. Ins., 57 [cf. 141]: τὰ δ' ἐξῆς ἐρευνήσωμεν).

In the LXX we find both ἐρευνάω and ἐξερευνάω ⁴ (on the pure form → supra) in the various senses b.-d., e.g., "to investigate," "to search," or "to seek out" (the ἄνομοι, 1 Macc. 3:5; cf. 9:26), "to find out by questioning" (Jdt. 8:34), even "to discover" or "to invent" (ψ 63:6), "to test" (one's conduct preparatory to repentance, Lam. 3:40). Also important from the religious standpoint is the sense of "to appropriate by search the revelation of God in His commandments" ⁵ (ψ 118:2 : τὰ μαρτύρια αὐτοῦ, cf. v. 129; v. 34 vl.: τὸν νόμον σου; v. 69 : τὰς ἐντολάς σου, cf. v. 115). God "searches" the heart of man in Prv. 20:27, but the question πῶς τὸν θεὸν ἐρευνήσετε; (i.e., His plan for His people) is intended in the negative in Jdt. 8:14.

In the NT ἐρευνάω has the common sense of "thorough investigation," though only in the broader sense of d.

---

³ א always has αυ except in Rev. 2:23, and B except in R. 8:27; Rev. 2:23. Cf. the αυ readings in W. Bousset, Textkritische Studien z. NT (TU, 11, 4 [1894]), 104. Cf. also W. Bousset on Rev. 2:23. Against Bousset's thesis that αυ is Alexandrian, v. R. Helbing, Grammatik der LXX (1907), 7. Thackeray I, 79 thinks that there is at least a possible link with Egypt.

⁴ The following examples cover both.

⁵ That the reference here is not to mere theoretical study of the Torah is shown esp. by the expression μαρτύρια in v. 2.

1. It is used of searching the Scriptures (only in Jn.), as in the LXX (and sometimes perhaps in Philo, though with a predominant scholastic and academic sense), in the sense of "seeking the divine revelation" in Holy Scripture (the OT), which is the actual locus of the living divine revelation (μαρτυροῦσαι, Jn. 5:39).[6] In Jn. 7:52 on the lips of leaders of the Jewish religion it is used of Rabbinic study, which believes itself to be in possession of revelation, but which fails to perceive true revelation because of its bondage to the letter.

2. It can also mean "to look into," being thus used in 1 Pt. 1:11 (cf. v. 10: † ἐξηρεύνησαν) of the activity of the classical prophets of Israel. To them is obviously attributed the function of later Jewish apocalyptists,[7] i.e., that of diligent search for the moment of the appearance of the Messiah, or at least for the conditions by which this moment will be very largely determined.

3. In the NT, too, it is emphasised that God in His innermost reality is inaccessible to man; but while the non-biblical world relates this to God's essence the NT relates it to His action (→ I, 517). Deeper understanding of this is first made possible for the Christian by the Holy Spirit (1 C. 2:10).[8] The probing insight of God into the heart of man is manifested on the one hand in the willing reception of the prayers of the Spirit by the gracious God (R. 8:27) and on the other in preparatory testing by the God of judgment (Rev. 2:23).

Delling

> ἔρημος, ἐρημία
> ἐρημόω, ἐρήμωσις

ἔρημος, † ἐρημία, ἐρημόω.

The adj. ἔρημος (usually τόπος in the NT) and the subst. ἡ ἔρημος refer to "abandonment," whether of a person (πατρὸς ἔρημαι, Soph. Oed. Col., 1717; ἔρημα κλαίω, Eur. Suppl., 775; cf. Gl. 4:27: ἡ ἔρημος, "the abandoned wife"), or a cause (ἐσθὴς ἔρημος ἐοῦσα ὅπλων, Hdt., IX, 63), or a locality. The latter does not have to be a desert. It is a place "without inhabitants," "empty," e.g., an "abandoned city" or a "thinly populated district" (Hdt., IV, 17 f.; VI, 23; VIII, 65: κώμη ἔρημος διὰ τὸ πλείω χρόνον μὴ βεβρέχθαι; P. Lille, I, 26, 3 [3rd cent. B.C.], cf. Mt. 23:38 vl.; Lk. 13:35; Ac. 1:20). It can naturally mean "waste" in the strict sense, e.g., an unprofitable "waste of stone or sand" (e.g., Hdt., III, 102: κατὰ γὰρ τοῦτό ἐστιν ἐρημίη διὰ τὴν ψάμμον), and it can thus be used for a "lonely" heath (e.g., Lk. 15:4, where the shepherd leaves the 99 sheep ἐν τῇ ἐρήμῳ).

The NT puts ἐρημ- to varied use.

1. It can signify a "lonely place" where there are no men, where the demoniac wanders (Lk. 8:29) and where there are many dangers to the body (2 C. 11:26; Hb. 11:38; cf. Lk. 10:30) and also to the soul.[1] It is also a refuge for the persecuted (1 K.

---

[6] ἐρευνᾶτε is indic., v. Schl. J., Zn. J., ad loc.

[7] And not merely of those, or the manner of those, whose writings have come down to us.

[8] On βάθη, cf. also Jdt. 8:14: βάθος καρδίας ἀνθρώπου οὐχ εὑρήσετε, → supra.

ἔρημος κτλ. A. Schlatter, Das AT u. d. joh. Apk. (1922), 77 f.; Schl. Mt., 54 f.; Zn. Ag., 748 f.; Str.-B., II, 284 f., 298, III, 812.

[1] Acc. to traditional Jewish belief demons are particularly found in lonely places and ruins (→ 13); cf. Str.-B., IV, 516; Kl. Mk., also Mt. 12:43: δι' ἀνύδρων τόπων (cf. bSukka, 52b with an exposition of Jl. 2:20).

19:3 f.) [2] or for rebels (Ac. 21:38), though other motifs are present in the latter case (→ 3.).

2. For Jesus the "place without inhabitants" is one where nothing separates Him from God and which He therefore seeks when He wants to escape the crowds (Mt. 14:13; Mk. 1:45; Lk. 4:42; cf. Jn. 11:54) or when He tries to find a place of quiet for His disciples (Mk. 6:31 ff.), but to which the masses often follow Him (Mt. 15:33; Mk. 8:4). What He primarily seeks there — cf. the ταμιεῖον of Mt. 6:6 — is the stillness of prayer (Mk. 1:35; Lk. 5:16). This is surely the point of His forty days in the wilderness which the tradition places after His baptism and which it links with His temptation. In Mk. 1:12 f. and par. the beginning (νηστεύσας, Mt. 4:2) and the end (οἱ ἄγγελοι διηκόνουν αὐτῷ, Mk. 1:13) of the story show that He has in view a period alone with God (under the impulsion of the πνεῦμα, Mk. 1:12) which the tempter tries to disturb.

There are no serious reasons for making the common connection of the forty days with the forty years of Israel in the wilderness (Dt. 8:2). [3] Forty years are not forty days and nights, and recollection of the forty years is not primarily linked with Dt. 8:2 (the temptation and testing of Israel) [4] but with Israel's disobedience on the one side and the time of divine salvation on the other. More apposite are the forty-day fast of Moses in Ex. 34:28; Dt. 9:9, 18 (though the details are different) and the forty-day fast of Elijah, preceded by angelic ministry, in 1 K. 19:5, 8, though here the context is very different from that of the Gospel story, since the wilderness is a place of refuge for Elijah in his flight from the queen (1 K. 19:3 f.), and this aspect does not occur in the story of the temptation.

3. Particular significance attaches to the "wilderness wandering" of Israel in the two senses already indicated. On the one hand, it is marked by the disobedience (Hb. 3:8 f.; Ac. 7:41 ff.; cf. ψ 77:17, 40) which caused a whole generation to perish (1 C. 10:5; Hb. 3:17), this happening τυπικῶς and being written πρὸς νουθεσίαν ἡμῶν (1 C. 10:11). On the other hand, it is a time of grace when God did special signs and wonders for His people (Ac. 7:36; 13:18; cf. Jn. 3:14, the serpent; Jn. 6:31, 49, the manna) and spoke to it in a special way (Ac. 7:38, 44). Here again the recollection serves the present age either by direct description of God's gracious action or by its comparison with the far greater presence of God in the Christ event (cf. esp. Jn. 3:14 f.; 6:31 ff., 49).

Emphasis on the saving aspect of the wilderness period creates in Judaism a tendency to ascribe to it everything great and glorious. The characteristics of the last time, e.g., that the Israelites see God, that the angel of death has no power etc., [5] are carried back into it, and its special features are also linked with the Messianic age, e.g., the blessing of the manna. [6] There thus arises the belief that the last and decisive age of salvation will begin in the ἔρημος, and that here the Messiah will appear. This belief led revolutionary Messianic movements to make for the ἔρημος (Ac. 21:38). It also explains Mt. 24:26 : ἐὰν οὖν εἴπωσιν ὑμῖν·

---

[2] Cf. New Classical Fragments and other Greek and Latin Papyri (ed. Grenfell and Hunt [1897]), 84, 4 (5th/6th cent. A.D.): υἱὸς τὸν εἴδιον πατέρα φωνεύσας καὶ τοὺς νόμους φοβηθεὶς ἔφυγεν εἰς ἐρημίαν.

[3] Cf. D. Strauss, Leben Jesu, I (1835), 422.

[4] In Hb. 3:8 the reference is to the πειρασμός to which God is exposed by His people, and not vice versa.

[5] Str.-B., IV, 939 f.

[6] Ibid., 954.

ἰδοὺ ἐν τῇ ἐρήμῳ ἐστίν, μὴ ἐξέλθητε, and the flight or rapture of the woman into the ἔρημος in Rev. 12:6, 14. The community of Christ is to remain hidden in the wilderness until Christ comes again and ends the assault of Satan.

According to Palestinian expectation as seen not merely in Rabbinic theory but in many incidents recounted by Josephus, flight into the ἔρημος immediately before the last event has a solid place in the eschatological schema. In Rabbinic statements considerable influence was exerted by various OT passages as well as the analogy of Sinai, e.g., Hos. 2:14 : "Therefore, behold, I will allure her, and bring her into the wilderness"; 12:9 : "I . . . will yet make thee to dwell in tents, as in the days of the solemn feast"; Job 30:4 : "Who cut up mallows by the bushes, and juniper roots for their meat." Tanch. עָרַץ 7b : "(The Messiah) drives them forth, and brings them into the wilderness, and causes them to eat saltwort and juniper." Leqach tob Nu. 24:17 (II, 129b): "(The fight with Gog and Magog) . . . but Israel flees and is delivered. Then Israel goes into the wilderness to feed on saltwort and juniper roots for 45 days, and the clouds of glory surround it." It was disputed whether the wilderness was that to the south east (Judah) or to the east (Sihon and Og, or Transjordan).[7] In Joseph. it is esp. the different branches of the Zealot movement which espouse these hopes, like the Egyptian of Ac. 21:38 who assembled his hosts in the ἐρημία and led them against Jerusalem (Bell., 2, 261). In the same context there is mention of the πλάνοι ἄνθρωποι (Bell., 2, 259) who led the people εἰς τὴν ἐρημίαν, ὡς ἐκεῖ τοῦ θεοῦ δείξοντος αὐτοῖς σημεῖα ἐλευθερίας. Similarly in Bell., 7, 438 the weaver Jonathas led his followers in Cyrene εἰς τὴν ἔρημον, σημεῖα καὶ φάσματα δείξειν ὑπισχνούμενος. But the most dramatic scene is at the end of the siege of Jerusalem on the bridge between the upper city and the temple (Bell., 6, 351). The temple has already been destroyed in flames, and the Jews make a final request that with their wives and children they might be allowed to go εἰς τὴν ἔρημον, there to await — although they do not say it — the final act of divine deliverance.

4. There are perhaps many reasons why John the Baptist arose and did his work in the desert. Bannus, who was like him in many ways, also lived in the ἐρημία (Jos. Vit., 11). Along with other signs at his coming, it is surely significant that he gathers the people to him in the wilderness and declares to them (→ 3.) "the glory of God and the coming of Christ."[8] In any case, the Christian tradition saw particular significance in this manner of his appearing, for on this ground — with an existing modification of the meaning of the Heb.[9] — it perceived in him the βοῶν ἐν τῇ ἐρήμῳ of Is. 40:3.[10]

5. That a city or country is ἔρημος or ἠρημωμένη[11] ("devastated") is the natural result of the destructive attack of enemies (Mt. 12:25: ἐρημοῦται, → ἐρήμωσις). It may also be, as in many prophetic sayings of the OT (Is. 6:11; Lam. 5:18; Ez. 6:6 etc.), the consequence of the divine wrath (Mt. 23:38 vl. and par.; Rev. 17:16). Conversely, according to the OT, it can sometimes be a promise of divine grace, for the desert is to become a field (Is. 32:15 f.) or a fruitful and watered land (Is. 35:1 ff.; 41:18 f. etc.) → διψάω, 227.

---

[7] Pesikt., 49b; Str.-B., II, 285.

[8] Schl. Mt., 55.

[9] Heb. "The voice of one who cries : Prepare the way of Yahweh in the desert"; LXX : φωνὴ βοῶντος ἐν τῇ ἐρήμῳ· ἑτοιμάσατε τὴν ὁδὸν τοῦ Κυρίου. On Tg. Proph., which is doubtful, cf. F. Delitzsch, Jesaja⁴ (1899), 410; Zn. Mt., 128, n. 30. Rabb. quotations which include Is. 40:3 may be found in Str.-B., I, 96; II, 154.

[10] Mt. 3:3 = Lk. 3:4, in the story of the Baptist ; Mk. 1:3, prior to it ; Jn. 1:23, a saying of the Baptist himself.

[11] ἐρημόω, of course, has the primary meaning of "to make desolate" rather than "to destroy."

† ἐρήμωσις.

Mt. 24:15; Mk. 13:14; Lk. 21:20 (on the basis of Da. 9:27 [τῶν ἐρημώσεων]; 11:31; 12:11; 8:13 [ἁμαρτία τῆς ἐρημώσεως]; cf. 1 Macc. 1:54): βδέλυγμα τῆς ἐρημώσεως. The nature of the sanctuary is to be used by those who come to worship God there. The βδέλυγμα (→ I, 600) does not destroy it; it makes it desolate by causing pious worshippers to avoid it because of the abomination, and by thus depriving it of any meaning or purpose.

Kittel

---

† ἐριθεία

1. ἐριθεία comes from ἐριθεύω, "to work as a day-labourer," "to conduct oneself as such," "to work for daily hire," [1] and this again comes from ἔριθος, a "day-labourer." [2] ἐριθεία thus means the "work," then the "manner, attitude or disposition of the day-labourer." There are no examples to prove this, but it must be assumed because it corresponds to the sense of ἔριθος and explains the use of ἐριθεία when it occurs. It is because the term is so rare that we cannot demonstrate its sense.

2. Aristot. Pol., V, 3, p. 1303a, 13 ff.: μεταβάλλουσι δ' αἱ πολιτεῖαι καὶ ἄνευ στάσεως διά τε τὰς ἐριθείας, ὥσπερ ἐν Ἡραίᾳ (ἐξ αἱρετῶν γὰρ διὰ τοῦτο ἐποίησαν κληρωτάς, ὅτι ᾑροῦντο τοὺς ἐριθευομένους), καὶ δι' ὀλιγωρίαν. ἐριθευόμενοι here are those who procure office by illegal manipulation, and therefore ἐριθεία is their attitude, i.e., not so much *ambitus* as action, but the personal manner connected with it (cf. the parallel ὀλιγωρίαν). [3] The adj. is used in the same sense in the civic oath of the Itanians: [4] ... οὐδὲ δίκαν ἐ[παξέ]ω ξ[ε]νικὰ[ν] τῶν πολιτᾶν [οὐδὲ]νὶ ἐριθεο[τὰ]ν (ἐριθευτὴν, Attic) παρεορέσι οὐ[δεμι]ᾷι, "I will not on any pretext bring a charge of failure to keep civic law against any citizen for personal reasons." ἐριθεοτάν, the crucial point of the oath, defines such charges as unobjective and self-seeking. Cf. also Polyb., X, 22:9 : οἱ δὲ τῆς στρατηγίας ὀρεγόμενοι διὰ ταύτης τῆς ἀρχῆς ἐξεριθεύονται τοὺς νέους καὶ παρασκευάζουσιν εὔνους συναγωνιστὰς εἰς τὸ μέλλον. Here, too, ἐξεριθεύονται denotes an attempt to influence others in one's own interests. Philo uses ἀνερίθευτος in the same way in Leg. Gaj., 68 : ἡγεμονία δὲ ἀφιλόνεικος καὶ ἀνερίθευτος ὀρθὴ μόνη. He thus demands that leaders should be non-contentious and without personal ambition. Symmachus in his translation of Ez. 23:5, 12 has ἐριθεύεσθαι, in v. 9, προσεριθεύεσθαι (LXX: ἐπιτίθεσθαι), and in v. 11 ἐριθεία (LXX: ἐπίθεσις), of the harlot who offers herself to a man or who entices him. ἐριθεία is thus the attitude of self-seekers, harlots etc., i.e., those who, demeaning themselves and their cause, are busy and active in their own interests, seeking their own gain or advantage. That the honest ἔριθος should have lent his name to this contemptible conduct is a parallel instance to the development of such terms as βάναυσος, originally a worker by or with fire, [5] or *proletarius,* the younger son who has no inheritance and must earn his own living. The aristocratic scorn of the man of property

---

ἐρήμωσις. For bibl. → I, 600, n. 9.

ἐριθεία. B. Weiss, *Erkl. des R.*[9] (1899), 109, n. 2; Zn. R., 113, n. 21; Ltzm. R.[3] on 2:8; Cr.-Kö., 443; M. Lagrange, *Epître aux Romains*[2] (1922), 46.

[1] Heliodor. Aeth., I, 5 : αἱ γυναῖκες ἐριθεύουσιν; Tob. 2:11: ἠριθεύετο ἐν τοῖς ἔργοις τοῖς γυναικείοις.

[2] Frequently attested from the time of Homer; cf. Zn. R., 113, n. 21. ἔριθος as a fem. is mostly used for a spinner or worker in wool (ἔριον) cf. the wrong interpretation of Gregory under 3.

[3] ἐριθεία is again used with ὀλιγωρία in Pol., V, 2, p. 1302b, 4.

[4] Ditt. Syll.[3], 526, n. 8 (3rd cent. B.C.).

[5] Cf. Pape, Pass., *s.v.* βάναυσος, βαναυσία.

and culture for the daily wage-earner is responsible for this change in the meaning of ἐριθεία and ἐριθεύομαι. It regards the ἔριθος as suspect from the very first in view of his concern for gain and his readiness to do things only for profit. [6]

3. Later non-Greeks who came on the word as translators and expositors of the NT often failed to understand it. It is worth noting that Gregory of Nyssa [7] interprets ἐριθεία as τὴν περὶ τὰ ἔρια (wool) σπουδήν, and maintains that Paul, who often permits himself the liberty of innovations, departs from the customary usage and uses the term for ἐριστικὴ καὶ ἀμυντικὴ φιλονεικία. Jerome [8] equates ἐριθεία with φιλονεικία and rixa. [9] Chrysostom, too, has φιλονεικία for ἐριθεία. [10] The Vulgate translates R. 2:8: ex contentione, Peshitto "those who are contentious." Lietzmann thinks it likely that Paul derives ἐριθεία from ἔρις, and he translates it "strife," "contention." [11]

4. A first point to note is that an opprobious epithet of this kind has no fixed meaning but is a complex term in everyday usage. [12] Even at an early stage different people gave the word different senses in the absence of any control of the meaning by derivation. For many it probably had no more than the general sense of baseness, self-interest, ambition, contention etc. But in R. 2:8 contention or strife is rather too specialised, [13] and we do best to see a reference to the despicable nature of those who do not strive after glory, honour and immortality by perseverance in good works (v. 7), but who think only of immediate gain. This meaning is equally applicable in 2 C. 12:20; Gl. 5:20; Phil. 1:17; 2:3; Jm. 3:14, 16; Ign. Phld., 8, 2 : παρακαλῶ δὲ ὑμᾶς, μηδὲν κατ' ἐριθείαν πράσσειν, ἀλλὰ κατὰ χριστομαθίαν. It is better than strife or contention in Phil. 2:3. [14] For this reason, it is best to understand ἐριθεία as "base self-seeking," or simply as "baseness", the nature of those who cannot lift their gaze to higher things.

Büchsel

ἑρμηνεύω, ἑρμηνεία,
ἑρμηνευτής, διερμηνεύω,
διερμηνεία, διερμηνευτής

A. Linguistic.

The basic word means a. "to interpret," "to expound," "to explain" : Soph. Oed. Col., 398 : ὅπως τί δράσῃ ... ἑρμήνευέ μοι; Plat. Resp., V, 453c : τὸν ὑπὲρ ἡμῶν λόγον,

---

[6] The LXX does not have ἐριθεία. It is of no significance that the word does not occur in the Hell. period except in early Christianity, since Polybius and Philo have composites of the verb.

[7] MPG, 44, 1324c.

[8] On Gl. 5:20 (MPL, 26, 416).

[9] Theodoret's "those who exert themselves in wickedness" (MPG, 82, 69) is not an explanation of τοῖς δὲ ἐξ ἐριθείας but of R. 2:8 as a whole (τοῖς δὲ ἐξ ἐριθείας καὶ ἀπειθοῦσι μὲν τῇ ἀληθείᾳ, πειθομένοις δὲ τῇ ἀδικίᾳ).

[10] MPG, 60, 425. Hesych., s.v. suggests εἰργάζετο for ἠριθεύετο, πεφιλοτιμημένων for ἠριθευμένων and μισθωτοί for ἔριθοι, and derives it from ἔρα = γῆ. Suid., s.v. : ἡ διὰ λόγων φιλονεικία (R. 2:8), λέγεται δὲ καὶ ἡ μισθαρνία.

[11] Before Lietzmann J. G. Reiche, Versuch einer ausführlichen Erklärung des Briefes Pauli an die Römer (1833), 34. Ltzm. on R. 2:8; also Dib. Jk. on 3:14; Loh. Phil. on 2:3.

[12] Cf. the complex character of βάναυσος or "proletarian," which can include boorishness, insolence and physical and moral uncleanness, and cannot be rendered by any other single word.

[13] With whom are οἱ ἐξ ἐριθείας striving ?

[14] The admonitions of Phil. 2:3, 4 are against self-seeking and vanity.

ἑ ρ μ η ν ε ύ ω κτλ. On A : Pr.-Bauer, 482, 302 f.; Poll. Onom., V, 154; Pass., I, 1174;

ὅστις ποτ' ἐστίν, ἑρμηνεῦσαι; Philyllius, 11 (CAF, I, 785): ἐκ τᾶς πινακίδος δ' ἀμπερέως, ὅ τι καὶ λέγει τὰ γράμμαθ', ἑρμήνευε, BGU, I, 140, 18 ff.: τὸ αὐστηρότερον ὑπὸ τῶν πρὸ ἐμοῦ αὐτοκρατόρων σταθὲν φιλανθρωπότερον ἑρμηνεύω; Lk. 24:27 D; Ign. Phld., 6, 1: ἐὰν δέ τις 'Ιουδαϊσμὸν ἑρμηνεύῃ ὑμῖν ("propounds Judaism on the basis of the exposition of Scripture"); [1] cf. ἑρμηνεία, "exposition," "explanation" : Plat. Resp., VII, 524b : αὗταί γε … ἄτοποι τῇ ψυχῇ αἱ ἑρμηνεῖαι καὶ ἐπισκέψεως δεόμεναι; Theaet., 209a : λόγος … ἡ τῆς σῆς διαφορότητος ἑρμηνεία; Sir. 47:17: ἐν ᾠδαῖς καὶ παροιμίαις καὶ παραβολαῖς καὶ ἐν ἑρμηνίαις ([obscure] interpretations : Heb. מְלִיצָה[2]) ἀπεθαύμασάν σε χῶραι; Phil. Det. Pot. Ins., 68 : δικαιωμάτων καὶ νόμων ἑρμηνεὺς καὶ ὑφηγητὴς ἄριστος … τῆς … ἑρμηνείας διὰ συγγενικοῦ ὀργάνου, τοῦ φωνητηρίου δήπου, συνισταμένης …; 1 C. 12:10; 14:26; Papias (Eus. Hist. Eccl., III, 39, 3): συντάξαι ταῖς ἑρμηνείαις ("expositions" sc. "oracles of the Lord"); ἑρμηνεύς or ἑρμηνευτής, "expositor," "interpreter": Plat. Leg., X, 907d : λόγος … τῶν νόμων ἑρμηνεύς; Polit. 290c : ἑρμηνευταὶ … παρὰ θεῶν ἀνθρώποις; Jos. Ant., 2, 72 : (Joseph) ἐβούλετ' ἂν ἀγαθῶν ἑρμηνευτὴς αὐτῷ γεγονέναι καὶ οὐχ οἵων τὸ ὄναρ αὐτῷ δηλοῖ; 1 C. 14:28 vl.; Aristid. Apol., 10, 3 : τὸν Ἑρμῆν … λόγων ἑρμηνευτήν; cf. Just. Apol., 21, 2 : Ἑρμῆν …, λόγον τὸν ἑρμηνευτικὸν καὶ πάντων διδάσκαλον (cf. Plat. Crat., 407e). It also means b. "to indicate," "to express one's thoughts in words," "to express" : Thuc., II, 60, 5 : γνῶναί τε τὰ δέοντα καὶ ἑρμηνεῦσαι ταῦτα; Plat. Leg., XII, 966b : λόγῳ τε ἱκανοὺς ἑρμηνεύειν εἶναι; Hermogenes De Methodo Gravitatis, 30 (Rhet. Graec., II, 451): ὅταν μέρος εἰπὼν τοῦ ἔπους παρ' αὐτοῦ τὸ λοιπὸν πεζῶς ἑρμηνεύσῃ, Dion. Hal. De Thucydidis Charactere ac reliquis eius Proprietatibus, 42 : τοῖς ἐνθυμήμασιν ἡρμηνευμένον δαιμονίως; cf. ἑρμηνεία, "expression" : Diogenes of Apollonia, 1 (I, 423, 21 f., Diels): τὴν δὲ ἑρμηνείαν ἁπλῆν καὶ σεμνήν; Aristot. Part. An., III, 17, p. 660a, 35 : χρῶνται τῇ γλώττῃ καὶ πρὸς ἑρμηνείαν; Philo Det. Pot. Ins., 79 : κάλλος ἑρμηνείας; Cher., 105 : ῥητορικὴ … πᾶσιν τὴν πρέπουσαν ἑρμηνείαν ἐφαρμόζουσα. A further meaning is c. "to transfer from a foreign language into a familiar," "to translate" : Xenoph. An., V, 4, 4 : ἔλεξε Ξενοφῶν, ἡρμήνευε δὲ Τιμησίθεος; Plat. Symp., 202e : (πᾶν τὸ δαιμόνιον) ἑρμηνεῦον καὶ διαπορθμεῦον θεοῖς τὰ παρ' ἀνθρώπων καὶ ἀνθρώποις τὰ παρὰ θεῶν; 2 Ἐσδρ. 4:7: γραφὴν Συριστὶ καὶ ἡρμηνευμένην (Heb. מְתֻרְגָּם); Job 42:17b; Jn. 1:42; cf. 38 vl.; 9:7; Hb. 7:2; P. Ryl., 62, 30 : ἑρμήνευσα ἀπὸ 'Ρωμαικῶν; cf. ἑρμηνεία, "translation": Syr. Prolog., line 12 (Swete): τῶν κατὰ τὴν ἑρμηνείαν πεφιλοπονημένων; Ep. Ar., 3 : τὴν ἑρμηνείαν τοῦ θείου νόμου (cf. 11); Philo Plant., 38 : Ἐδέμ — ἑρμηνεύεται δὲ τρυφή; Jos. Ant., 12, 87: τὴν ἑρμηνείαν τῶν νόμων; BGU, I, 326, Col. I, 1: ἑρμηνία διαθήκης; cf. Col. II, 15; P. Oxy., IX, 1201, 12: ἑρμηνεία τῶν 'Ρωμαικῶν; ἑρμηνεύς and ἑρμηνευτής, "interpreter," "translator" : Xenoph. An., I, 2, 17: πέμψας Πίγρητα τὸν ἑρμηνέα παρὰ τοὺς στρατηγοὺς τῶν Ἑλλήνων; Gn. 42:23 : ὁ γὰρ ἑρμηνευτὴς

Pape, I, 1032 f.; G. Heinrici, RE³, VII, 719; Liddell-Scott, 690, 425; Moult.-Mill., 254, 160; Preisigke Wört., I, 599 f., 376; E. v. Dobschütz, Vom Auslegen des NT² (1927), esp. 16, n. 33; F. Torm, Hermeneutik des NT (1930), 1. On B : Kl. Lk., 237; Schl. Lk., 455; C. F. G. Heinrici, Das erste Sendschreiben des Ap. Paulus an die Korinthier (1880), 388 ff.; Der erste Brief an die Korinthier (1896), 372 ff.; Bchm. 1 K.³, 381 ff., 416, 423; Ltzm. K., 68 f., 74; Joh. W. 1 K., 327, 340; Sickb. K. on I, 12:10 and I, 14:23; H. Leisegang, Der heilige Geist, I, 1 (1919), 126 ff., 152 ff.; E. Fascher, Προφήτης (1927), 66 ff., 152 ff., 185; T. Hopfner, "Mantik" in Pauly-W., XIV, 1 (1928), 1261 ff.

[1] Cf. T. Zahn, Ignatius von Antiochien (1873), 368 ff.; J. B. Lightfoot, The Apostolic Fathers, II, 2, 1 (1885), 263; W. Bauer in H. Lietzmann, Handbuch zum NT, Suppl. (1923), 258.

[2] Cf. Prv. 1:6, where 'A and Θ also render מְלִיצָה as ἑρμηνεία, whereas the LXX has σκοτεινὸς λόγος and Σ πρόβλημα. The only other occurrence of מְלִיצָה in the OT is at Hab. 2:6, where the LXX has πρόβλημα and Σ αἴνιγμα. At Is. 43:27 ἑρμηνεύς in 'A and Σ for מֵלִיץ has the sense of "speaker."

(Heb. ריק) ἀνὰ μέσον αὐτῶν ἦν; records from the royal bank at Thebes, 9, 1 (AAB, 1886, *Anh., phil.-hist. Abhandlungen,* I, 18): Ἀπολλώνιος ἑρμηνεὺς τῶν Τρωγοδυτῶν, Papias (Eus. Hist. Eccl., III, 39, 15): Μάρκος ἑρμηνευτὴς Πέτρου γενόμενος. [3]

διερμηνεύω in post-classical Gk. is also used in the senses a. "to expound or explain" : Philodem. Philos., Volumina Rhetorica, I, 84 (ed. Sudhaus, 1892 ff.): ἀγροῖκος ἄνθρωπος καὶ γραμμάτων ἁπλῶς ἀνεπιστήμων οὐ ῥητορικῆς μόνον ἐμπειρίας ἔξω καθεστηκὼς ἱκανὸς ἐξευρεῖν τὰ δήμοις συμφέροντα καὶ διερμηνεῖσθαι σαφῶς; Philo Op. Mund., 31: τὸ ... φῶς ... θείου λόγου γέγονεν εἰκὼν τοῦ διερμηνεύσαντος τὴν γένεσιν αὐτοῦ; Lk. 24:27; 1 C. 12:30; 14:5, 13, 27; cf. διερμηνεία, "exposition," "interpretation" : 1 C. 12:10 vl. (cf. Iambl. Myst., V, 5 : δυσβάτου καὶ μακρᾶς δεόμενον διερμηνεύσεως); διερμηνευτής, "expositor," "interpreter," only in 1 C. 14:28 and Eustath. Thessal. Comm. in II, I, p. 89, 7: ὑποβολεῖς οἱ διερμηνευταί; and b. "to translate": Polyb., III, 22, 3 : ἃς (sc. τὰς συνθήκας) καθ' ὅσον ἦν δυνατὸν ἀκριβέστατα διερμηνεύσαντες ἡμεῖς ὑπογεγράφαμεν, 2 Macc. 1:36; Ep. Ar., 15 : τῆς γὰρ νομοθεσίας ..., ἣν ἡμεῖς οὐ μόνον μεταγράψαι ἐπινοοῦμεν ἀλλὰ καὶ διερμηνεῦσαι (cf. 308, 310); Philo Vit. Mos., II, 31: τοὺς τὸν νόμον διερμηνεύσοντας; in the NT Ac. 9:36.

B. Material.

1. In the OT we sometimes have the thought that the ordinary man can make nothing of dreams even though they come from Yahweh. In Gn. 40:8; 41:16; Da. 2:27 f., 30 the view is advanced that the interpretation must also come from Yahweh in so far as the recipient does not possess a prophetic *charisma.*

2. On the Gk. view one of the gifts proper to man along with perception and reason is the creative gift of ἑρμηνεία, δι' ἧς πάντων τῶν ἀγαθῶν μεταδίδομέν τε ἀλλήλοις διδάσκοντες καὶ κοινωνοῦμεν καὶ νόμους τιθέμεθα καὶ πολιτευόμεθα (Xenoph. Mem., IV, 3, 12). To a special degree, as Plato says in Ion, it is proper to the poet, to whom it is given ἔνθεος καὶ ἔκφρων (Ion, 534b) to create his poems, which are not the work of man but come from the gods, *ibid.,* 534e : οὐκ ἀνθρώπινά ἐστιν τὰ καλὰ ταῦτα ποιήματα οὐδὲ ἀνθρώπων ἀλλὰ θεῖα καὶ θεῶν; 534d : οὐχ οὗτοί εἰσιν οἱ ταῦτα λέγοντες οὕτω πολλοῦ ἄξια, οἷς νοῦς μὴ πάρεστιν, ἀλλ' ὁ θεὸς αὐτός ἐστιν ὁ λέγων, διὰ τούτων δὲ φθέγγεται πρὸς ἡμᾶς. The poet is simply an interpreter of deity (534e: οἱ δὲ ποιηταὶ οὐδὲν ἄλλ' ἢ ἑρμηνῆς εἰσιν τῶν θεῶν, κατεχόμενοι ἐξ ὅτου ἂν ἕκαστος κατέχηται; 535a : καί μοι δοκοῦσι θείᾳ μοίρᾳ ἡμῖν παρὰ τῶν θεῶν ταῦτα οἱ ἀγαθοὶ ποιηταὶ ἑρμηνεύειν). What the poet brings forth by divine power, the rhapsodist passes on and interprets (530c : τὸν γὰρ ῥαψῳδὸν ἑρμηνέα δεῖ τοῦ ποιητοῦ τῆς διανοίας γίγνεσθαι τοῖς ἀκούουσι; 535a : the rhapsodists are thus ἑρμηνέων ἑρμηνῆς). [4] Related to the poet is the divinely inspired seer who, lifted above νοῦς, speaks by higher inspiration (Ion, 534c : ὁ θεὸς ἐξαιρούμενος τούτων τὸν νοῦν τούτοις χρῆται ὑπηρέταις καὶ τοῖς χρησμῳ-

---

[3] This can hardly be "translator" in the strict sense (so esp. A. Link, "Die Dolmetscher des Petrus," ThStKr, 69 [1896], 407 ff., and more recently Meyer Ursprung, I, 157 ff.) but in a looser sense (cf. Zn. Kan., I, 878 ff.; Einl., II, 211 ff. etc.) as the "middleman" who transmits the content of the preaching of the apostle. Cf. the position of Aaron as the one who conveys the thought of Moses — a position explained by Philo Migr. Abr., 81 as οἷον διερμηνεύσει τὰ σά on the basis of Ex. 4:16 : "He will speak for thee." Cf. also the view of Joseph. that he "translates" his Antiquities "from the Holy Scriptures," i.e., that he takes his materials from this source (Jos. Ap., I, 54 : τὴν ... ἀρχαιολογίαν ... ἐκ τῶν ἱερῶν γραμμάτων μεθηρμήνευκα). Cf. *ad loc.* J. G. Müller, *Des Flavius Josephus Schrift gegen den Apion* (1877), 109 f.

[4] On ἑρμηνεία in music, cf. Plut. De Musica, e.g., 32 (II, 1142d): τῆς ἑρμηνείας τῆς τὰ πεποιημένα παραδιδούσης; 36 (II, 1144d): τῶν ποιημάτων ἕκαστον, οἷον τὸ ἀδόμενον, ἢ αὐλούμενον, ἢ κιθαριζόμενον, ἢ ἡ ἑκάστου αὐτοῦ ἑρμηνεία; *ibid.* (II, 1144e): τὸ τῆς ἑρμηνείας ἦθος, εἰ οἰκεῖον ἀποδίδοται τῷ παραποιηθέντι ποιήματι, ὃ μεταχειρίσασθαι καὶ ἑρμηνεῦσαι ὁ ἐνεργῶν βεβούληται, etc.

δοις καὶ τοῖς μάντεσι τοῖς θείοις; cf. Tim.; 71e; Phaedr., 244a ff.). The μάντις (e.g., the Pythia) can be in such a state of rapture as to stammer out obscure and unintelligible words and to be incapable of assessing what he sees and says; to do this is the business of a σώφρων who stands at his side, Tim., 72a: τοῦ δὲ μανέντος ἔτι τε ἐν τούτῳ μένοντος οὐκ ἔργον τὰ φανέντα καὶ φωνηθέντα ὑφ' ἑαυτοῦ κρίνειν, ἀλλ' εὖ καὶ πάλαι λέγεται τὸ πράττειν καὶ γνῶναι τά τε αὑτοῦ καὶ ἑαυτὸν σώφρονι μόνῳ προσήκειν, of the prophet (ibid.: ὅθεν δὴ καὶ τὸ τῶν προφητῶν γένος ἐπὶ ταῖς ἐνθέοις μαντείαις κριτὰς ἐπικαθιστάναι νόμος) who can give the ἑρμηνεία or ἐξήγησις of the pronouncements and visions of the seer (cf. Poll. Onom., VIII, 124: ἐξηγηταὶ δ' ἐκαλοῦντο οἱ τὰ περὶ τῶν διοσημειῶν καὶ τὰ τῶν ἄλλων ἱερῶν διδάσκοντες. → ἐξηγέομαι.

3. The inspiration mysticism of Plato reappears in Philo in speculations on the prophets as the interpreters of God. Moses, the most perfect of the prophets, God filled with the spirit of God and made the ἑρμηνεὺς τῶν χρησμῳδουμένων (Decal., 175; cf. Mut. Nom., 125 f.). [5] Apart from the revelation of the Ten Commandments, which ἄνευ προφήτου καὶ ἑρμηνέως took place miraculously through God Himself (Spec. Leg., III, 7; cf. Praem. Poen., 2; Vit. Mos., II, 213), the words of God are revealed through Moses (Vit. Mos., II, 188; Poster. C., 1) [6] ὡσανεὶ δι' ἑρμηνέως (Vit. Mos., II, 191). Other prophets are mediators of revelation in the same way, e.g., Balaam (Vit. Mos., I, 277: ὥσπερ ἑρμηνεὺς ὑποβάλλοντος ἑτέρου θεσπίζει) and even the Gk. messenger of the gods, Hermes (Leg. Gaj., 99: τὸν ἑρμηνέα καὶ προφήτην τῶν θείων, ἀφ' οὗ καὶ Ἑρμῆς ὠνόμασται, τὰ ἀγαθὰ διαγγέλλοντα). [7] The same is true of the interpreters of dreams (Jos., 95). The prophetic office of interpretation (Migr. Abr., 84: τὸ γὰρ ἑρμηνεῦον τὰ θεοῦ προφητικόν ἐστι γένος ἐνθέῳ κατοκωχῇ [inspiration] τε καὶ μανίᾳ χρώμενον) rests on divine inspiration in the strictest sense, cf. Praem. Poen., 55: ἑρμηνεὺς γάρ ἐστιν ὁ προφήτης ἔνδοθεν ὑπηχοῦντος τὰ λεκτέα τοῦ θεοῦ; Spec. Leg., I, 65: the prophets are ἑρμηνεῖς ... θεοῦ καταχρωμένου τοῖς ἐκείνων ὀργάνοις πρὸς δήλωσιν ὧν ἂν ἐθελήσῃ; Rer. Div. Her., 259: προφήτης γὰρ ἴδιον μὲν οὐδὲν ἀποφθέγγεται, ἀλλότρια δὲ πάντα ὑπηχοῦντος ἑτέρου· φαύλῳ δ' οὐ θέμις ἑρμηνεῖ γενέσθαι θεοῦ, cf. Spec. Leg., IV, 49; Vit. Mos., I, 286. [8] Philo also follows Plato in that he can set alongside the enraptured mediator of revelation a sober interpreter who can clearly grasp and convey that which is given by the Spirit. He turns to Aaron and Moses in Ex. 4:16; 7:1 for an example. God showed to Moses in his conflict with the Egyptian sophists all the thoughts ministering to ἑρμηνεία, and gave them perfectly διὰ τῆς Ἀαρὼν χειροτονίας, ὃν ἀδελφὸν Μωυσέως ὄντα "στόμα" καὶ ἑρμηνέα ... εἴωθε καλεῖν (Det. Pot. Ins., 39; cf. Migr. Abr., 81 [→ n. 3]: "It is most emphatically stressed (Ex. 4:16) that 'he will speak for thee,' οἷον διερμηνεύσει τὰ σά, and that 'he will be thy mouth,' διὰ γὰρ γλώττης καὶ στόματος φερόμενον τὸ τοῦ λόγου νᾶμα συνεκφέρει τὰ νοήματα," 84). The relationship of Aaron to Moses is an allegory of that of λόγος (προφορικός) to διάνοια; the word is a brother of the power of thought, καὶ ἑρμηνεύς ἐστιν ὧν ἐν τῷ ἑαυτῆς βουλευτηρίῳ βεβούλευκεν, πηγὴ γὰρ λόγων διάνοια καὶ στόμιον αὐτῆς λόγος (Det. Pot. Ins., 40). The word is the best interpreter

---

[5] Joseph., too, calls Moses the ἑρμηνεύς of God (Ant., 3, 87). Cf. Schl. Theol. d. Judt., 57 ff.

[6] Cf. L. Cohn-J. Heinemann, Schriften der jüdisch-hellenistischen Literatur, 4 (1923), 4, n. 2.

[7] In pagan Hellenism we have the same teaching, e.g., in the preaching of the Naassenes acc. to Hipp. Ref., V, 7, 29: Ἑρμῆς ἐστι λόγος. < ὃς > ἑρμηνεὺς ὢν καὶ δημιουργὸς τῶν γεγονότων ὁμοῦ καὶ γινομένων καὶ ἐσομένων, or in Porphyry acc. to Eus. Praep. Ev., III, 11, 42: τοῦ λόγου τοῦ πάντων ποιητικοῦ τε καὶ ἑρμηνευτικοῦ ὁ Ἑρμῆς παραστατικός.

[8] On the distinction between ἑρμηνεύς and προφήτης in Vit. Mos., II, 187 ff., cf. L. Treitel, Gesamte Theologie und Philosophie Philos v. Alexandria (1923), 32 f.; Fascher, op. cit., 156 f.

(*ibid.,* 129), ἑρμηνεὺς δογμάτων θείων (*ibid.,* 133), ἑρμηνεὺς διανοίας πρὸς ἀνθρώπους (Migr. Abr., 81). Under the influence of the Platonic doctrine of ideas, Philo develops further his thoughts concerning the name of God (= λόγος), by which alone one may swear (not by God Himself), as His ἑρμηνεύς (Leg. All., III, 207), or concerning human speech as a not altogether reliable interpreter of the thoughts of the νοῦς (Migr. Abr., 72 and 78) [9] or even of things (Spec. Leg., IV, 60, cf. Migr. Abr., 12 : σκιᾷ μὲν δὴ καὶ μιμήματι ἔοικεν ἑρμηνεία, σώμασι δὲ καὶ ἀρχετύποις αἱ τῶν διερμηνευομένων φύσεις πραγμάτων). [10]

4. The ἑρμηνεία γλωσσῶν to which Paul refers along with γένη γλωσσῶν in the list of → χαρίσματα in 1 C. 12:10 (cf. 30) can hardly be translation of the language of the ecstatic in view of the nature of speaking with tongues (→ I, 722; 726). It is rather the conversion of what is unintelligible into what is intelligible and therefore an explanation of the spiritual movement which fills the ecstatic. The διερμηνευτής (1 C. 14:28) does not correspond to the translator (מְתֻרְגְּמָן) who in the course of synagogue worship put the Scripture readings into Aramaic and also communicated out loud to the congregation the softly spoken sermons, [11] but rather to the interpreter of divine oracles in Plato and Philo (→ 664). Yet, while the reference in Plato and Philo was to the exposition of distinct oracles or revelations, here it is a matter of interpreting in the interests of general edification (1 C. 14:5, 26 ff.) ecstatics who are speaking to God (v. 2, 28). The gift of ἑρμηνεία can be given to the one who speaks with tongues (v. 13), but also to another Christian (v. 27). If this *charisma* is not present in a congregation, then there should be no speaking with tongues (v. 28), which by itself is of religious value only for the isolated ecstatic and does not serve any useful purpose for the church as a whole (v. 2, 4). It is hardly possible to gather from 1 C. 12 and 14 any more precise understanding of the Spirit-given arts of projecting oneself into the trance-like state of him who speaks with tongues and of making accessible and fruitful to the whole congregation that which he speaks ecstatically (v. 2). The principle enunciated by Paul, namely, that there must be no speaking with tongues without disciplined ἑρμηνεία (14:26 ff.), means in fact the controlling of the wild torrent of spiritual outbursts in the channel of the clear and disciplined but no less genuine and profound operation of the Spirit through the Word.

5. Lk. 24:27 presents the risen Jesus to those who walked to Emmaus as the expounder of the OT prophecies of His passion and exaltation (cf. v. 25 f.): ἀρξάμενος ἀπὸ Μωυσέως καὶ ἀπὸ πάντων τῶν προφητῶν διηρμήνευσεν αὐτοῖς ἐν πάσαις ταῖς γραφαῖς τὰ περὶ ἑαυτοῦ. The Messianic understanding of the OT which is here indicated only in brief (but cf. Lk. 22:37; Ac. 8:32 f.; Mk. 14:27, 62 etc.) is thus established by Jesus and developed by early Christianity. It rests on an exposition of Scripture which is new in content, though not in method. [12]

---

[9] Cf. Sir. 17:5 (Cod. 248, 70): λόγον τὸν ἑρμηνέα τῶν ἐνεργημάτων αὐτοῦ; less clear is Plut. De Placitis Philosophorum, 20 (II, 908 f.), where τὸν λεγόμενον τοῦ νοῦ ἑρμηνέα seems to presuppose λόγον τὸν ἐνεργητικόν (or προφορικόν) as a connecting phrase in what precedes.

[10] On the Stoic view of the sage as ὁ τῶν τῆς φύσεως ἑρμηνεὺς πραγμάτων in Rer. Div. Her., 213, cf. L. Cohn-J. Heinemann, *op. cit.,* 5 (1929), 271, n. 1.

[11] Cf. Str.-B., III, 465 ff.; IV, 161 ff., 185 ff.; I, 579.

[12] Cf. J. Hänel, *Der Schriftbegriff Jesu* (1919), 197 ff. etc.; O. Michel, *Paulus und seine Bibel* (1929), 188; A. Freiherr v. Ungern-Sternberg, *Der traditionelle at.liche Schriftbeweis de Christo* ... (1913), 275 ff., esp. 287; H. Schlier, "Weissagung und Erfüllung," RGG², V, 1813 f.; and in a few points K. Weidel, "Studien über den Einfluss des Weissagungsbeweises auf die evangelische Geschichte," ThStKr, 83 (1910), 88 ff., 96 f., and F. K.

In the light of their fulfilment, OT sayings are claimed to be prophecies of Christ (→ I, 758), and therefore a radically new meaning is seen in the OT on the basis of the NT revelation.

Behm

ἔρχομαι, ἔλευσις, ἀπ-, δι-, εἰς-,
ἐξ-, ἐπ-, παρ-, παρεισ-, περι-,
προσ-, συνέρχομαι

ἔρχομαι.

A. The General Use of ἔρχομαι.

1. The stem of the word ἐρχ- stands in "suppletive" connection with ἐλθ-, ἐλυθ- (and ἰέναι). In class. Gk. the word has the senses of "to come" and "to go." It is used both of persons and of inanimate objects. Special relationships or nuances are given by prepositions or the context, e.g., "to come to or towards," "to go away," "to return," "to sail" (of ships). The word is used of the occurrence of natural events or fateful happenings, or of the rise of states of mind. In the pap. [1] it is also used for receipt of letters, for transferring, e.g., property by inheritance or purchase, for making an agreement or for undertaking other enterprises. In R. Heberdey-A. Wilhelm, *Reisen in Kilikien* (1896) 154, Inscr. No. 260, 4 f. a patriot concerned about and acquainted with affairs of state is called ἄνδρα φιλόπατριν διὰ πάσης πολιτίας ἐληλυθότα.

2. Of particular significance is the cultic use of the word. [2] In ancient forms of prayer the coming of the deity is besought in the typical formula ἐλθέ or ἐλθέ μοι. The address to the god then follows in the vocative; either his name is mentioned, or his nature and activity are depicted in a list of subst. and adj. In any case, he is described precisely in his divine manifestation. By the invocation ἐλθέ μοι the god is brought down in order to fulfil what are usually the very egotistic desires of man. The formula ἐλθέ or ἐλθέ μοι is particularly common in the prayers of the magic pap. (Preis. Zaub., I, 214, 296; III, 51, 338 f.; IV, 2746, 2786, 2868; V, 249; VIII, 2 ff., 14 f.; esp. striking is II, 83 f.: ἐλθὲ τάχος δ' ἐπὶ γαῖαν ἀπ' οὐρανόθεν <μοι> ὁμιλῶν, "Come down quickly from heaven to earth to speak with me." Along with ἐλθέ we have ἔρχου, δεῦρο and εἴσελθε. Very typical is IV, 1023 f., 1031, 1041, 1045: εἴσελθε, φάνηθί μοι, κύριε; also εἰσερχέσθω ὁ θρόνος τοῦ θεοῦ ... εἰσενεχθήτω ὁ θρόνος, V, 32, 35. In some passages assurance is given that invocation of the deity by magical formulae will be successful: εἰσελεύσεται θεός, XII, 159; τοῦ θεοῦ εἰσελθόντος, IV, 1047; cf. XIII, 12, or ἐπὰν εἰσέλθῃ οὖν ὁ θεός, XIII, 564 f.). [3]

In this connection we are esp. reminded of the Orphic hymns, which often end with a petition for the coming of the god or gods in question. The prayers introduced by ἐλθέ (or ἔρχεο, ἔλθοις, ἔλθοιτ') are normally of 1-3 lines in which the subst. which depict the nature of the god are ranged alongside one another in the vocat. [4] In the

---

Feigel, "Der Einfluss des Weissagungsbeweises und andere Motive auf die Leidensgeschichte" (1910), 27 etc. Parallel to διηρμήνευσεν in Lk. 24:27 is διήνοιγεν τὰς γραφάς in v. 32 (cf. Ac. 17:3); cf. the Rabb. פתח, I, 752, n. 9.

ἔρχομαι. [1] Cf. Preisigke Wört., *s.v.*

[2] On the whole section, C. Ausfeld, "De Graecorum precationibus quaestiones," *Jbch. f. klassische Philol., Suppl.-Bd.,* 28 (1903), 505 ff.; K. Ziegler, *De precationum apud Graecos formis quaestiones selectae* (1905).

[3] Cf. Reitzenstein Poim., 15 ff., 20 f., 27.

[4] The ἐλθέ formula is found in almost every hymn. The texts edited by Abel yield many examples.

Homeric hymns [5] the ἐλθέ formula is rare ; Cer., 360 : ἔρχεο Περσεφόνη ; Ad Hestiam, 4 f.: ἔρχεο τόνδ' ἀνὰ οἶκον, ἔν' ἔρχεο θυμὸν ἔχουσα, σὺν Διὶ μητιόεντι. Cf. Hom. Il., 23, 770 : κλῦθι, θεά, ἀγαθή μοι ἐπίρροθος ἐλθὲ ποδοίιν. Impressive and typical is Plat. Leg., IV, 712b: θεὸν ἐπικαλώμεθα· ὁ δὲ ... ἀκούσας ἵλεως εὐμενής τε ἡμῖν ἔλθοι. Hellen. influence may be seen in two prayers in Joseph. which have the same introductory formula : Ant., 4, 46 : ἐλθέ, δέσποτα τῶν ὅλων, δικαστής μου καὶ μάρτυς ἀδωροδόκητος; 20, 90 : ἐλθὲ σύμμαχος. The cultic use is also attested in IG, XIV, 966; the god gives a man the direction ἐλθεῖν ἐπ[ὶ τὸ] ἱερὸν βῆμα καὶ προσκυνῆσαι, εἶ[τ]α ἀπὸ τοῦ δεξιοῦ ἐλθεῖν ἐπὶ τὸ ἀριστερὸν καὶ θεῖναι τοὺς πέντε δακτύλους ἐπάνω τοῦ βήματος ... V. also Preisigke Sammelbuch, 1142 : Μηνόφιλος ἐλθών (ἐλθών is here used like ἥκων, of coming to worship the deity). For the coming or manifestation of the deity, Eur. Fr., 353 (TGF): ὀλολύζετ', ὦ γυναῖκες, ὡς ἔλθῃ θεὰ χρυσῆν ἔχουσα Γοργόν' ἐπίκουρος πόλει. BCH, 30 (1906), 141, the statement of Eros : ἐλήλυθα ἀγγελῶν τοιοῦτο πρᾶγμά τι· πρᾶγμ[ά τι] τοιοῦτο [ἀγ]γελῶν [ἐλ]ήλυθα. [6] In the same connection we should mention Reitzenstein Poim., 342, 19 f.: ἦλθεν ἡμῖν γνῶσις θεοῦ and ἦλθεν ἡμῖν γνῶσις χαρᾶς.

3. In the Septuagint it is used for 35 Heb. words (mostly for בוא). Its meaning is predominantly local, but it also occurs in cultic statements, either generally for coming to divine service or with προσκυνεῖν, λατρεύειν, θύειν for coming to the house of God, to the sanctuary or to Jerusalem. It is used of prayer which comes to God in 2 Ch. 30:27; cf. ψ 101:1; 118:41, 77, prayer for the coming of the divine mercy. The word is also used with reference to the coming of God, of His Word, of His angels and prophets to men. It is used esp. of the coming of the Messiah (Da. 7:13 : καὶ ἰδοὺ ἐπὶ τῶν νεφελῶν τοῦ οὐρανοῦ ὡς υἱὸς ἀνθρώπου ἤρχετο [Θ ἐρχόμενος]). [7] The Messiah is ὁ ἐρχόμενος ἐν ὀνόματι κυρίου, ψ 117:26. It is also used of the coming of Satan (Job 2:1). Another use is for the coming and going of ages (2 Ch. 21:19) or generations (Qoh. 1:4); γενεὰ ἡ ἐρχομένη is the coming generation in ψ 21:31 etc. A very common use in the Psalms and prophets is for the coming of eschatologically decisive days (the days of salvation and judgment). A universalistic eschatological statement occurs in ψ 78:1: Nations will come to the inheritance of God. In Is. 32:15 there is a promise of salvation which is related to the coming of the Spirit. In the Psalms, Job and elsewhere it is strongly emphasised that evil, misfortune, suffering, tribulation and death come over men. But so, too, does good (cf. Bar. 4:36 : ἡ εὐφροσύνη [joy] ἡ παρὰ τοῦ θεοῦ). Yet the statements that evil and bad things come on men predominate.

In Jos.: ἔρχεσθαι εἰς τὴν ἑορτήν, Bell., 1, 73; 6, 300 (cf. Jn. 4:45); στρατιᾶς, μεθ' ὅσης ἐπὶ πόλεμόν τις, ἀλλ' οὐκ ἐπ' εἰρήνην ἔρχεται; Ant., 12, 395 (cf. Lk. 12:49); ἐλθοῦσαν τὴν βασιλείαν, Ant., 17, 66 (cf. Mt. 6:10; Lk. 11:2); μηνῶν ὁδὸν τεσσάρων ἐλθόντες, Ant., 3, 318 (cf. Lk. 2:44).

Test. XII : "to come," "to come with hostile intent," "to appear" (Jud. 22:2); A. 7:3, of the eschatological coming of God.

4. In the NT, as elsewhere in Gk. literature, the term has the basic sense of "coming" and "going." It is used indifferently of persons and things. The coming often has the sense of appearing, of coming forward publicly, of coming on the scene. It is often used of decisive events, of happenings, of natural phenomena, also of conditions etc. (e.g., τὰ σκάνδαλα, τὰ ἀγαθά). ἔρχεσθαι ἐπί τινα is used in a hostile sense in Lk. 14:31 ("to go against someone in battle"). Both meanings occur, then, in both a literal and a figurative sense.

---

[5] These hymns usually close with χαῖρε, which ıs in some sense a formal par. to the concluding ἐλθέ lines of the Orphic hymns.

[6] For a similar combination of ἐλθεῖν and ἀπαγγέλλειν, cf. Joseph. Ant., 9, 49; 10, 62.

[7] Cf. Asc. Is. 11:1, where the reference is to the coming of the heavenly Son of Man to earth. Cf. also Eus. Hist. Eccl., IV, 6, 2 : ὡς δὴ ἐξ οὐρανοῦ φωστὴρ αὐτοῖς κατεληλυθώς. On this whole question, v. Bousset-Gressm., 264 ff.

The following prepositional combinations should be noted: εἰς τὸ χεῖρον ἐλθεῖν, [8] Mk. 5:26 (in the sense of getting constantly worse); εἰς ἀπελεγμὸν ἐλθεῖν, Ac. 19:27 (to come into disrepute); [9] εἰς ἑαυτὸν ἐλθεῖν, Lk. 15:17 (to come to oneself, to a sensible frame of mind). [10] Once in the NT we have the common Gk. phrase ἐλθεῖν εἴς τι in the sense of moving on to a new subject. Paul writes in 2 C. 12:1: ἐλεύσομαι δὲ εἰς ὀπτασίας καὶ ἀποκαλύψεις κυρίου ("I will now go on to speak of visions and revelations of the Lord"). [11]

B. The Specific Use of ἔρχομαι in the NT.

1. The Synoptics.

a. The coming of Jesus to men. The statements characterised by ἔρχεσθαι in the figurative sense lead us to the very heart of the early Christian message of salvation. They speak of Jesus the Messiah, of the nature of His appearing, of the position of men in relation to Him and of the decision to proclaim Him. The word belongs to the circle of ideas connected with the divine epiphany (→ ἐπιφάνεια).

Of particular significance for the Messianic task of Jesus are the sayings in which He speaks of His coming in the first person. They open either with the negative οὐκ ἦλθον or the positive ἦλθον. They can be grouped under the title of ἦλθον sayings. [12] In them we see Jesus' certainty of mission. Some of the sayings were perhaps given their final form by the community, but we should not be so sceptical as to say that they have no connection with Jesus and to call them "secondary constructions at a later stage." [13] They derive from the Messianic self-awareness of Jesus and are to be explained thereby. In these sayings Jesus gives succinct formulations of His task. He has come to proclaim the kingdom of God (Mk. 1:38 and par.); to call sinners to repentance (Mk. 2:17; Lk. 5:32); to establish a new order of life (Mt. 5:17); to kindle a fire on earth (Lk. 12:49); to work in such a way that by His message men are divided into two groups (Mt. 10:34 ff.; Lk. 12:51 ff.).

At Lk. 22:27 D has: ἐγὼ γὰρ ἐν μέσῳ ὑμῶν ἦλθον (instead of εἰμί) οὐχ ὡς ὁ ἀνακείμενος ἀλλ' ὡς ὁ διακονῶν. There are two ἦλθον sayings in the apocr. tradition. In the Gosp. of the Egypt. (cited in Cl. Al. Strom., III, 9, 63, 2) we have: ἦλθον καταλῦσαι τὰ ἔργα τῆς θηλείας, [14] and in the Gosp. of the Hebrews: ἦλθον καταλῦσαι τὰς θυσίας (v. Epiph. Haer., XXX, 16, p. 140b). [15]

We should also group the ἀπεστάλην sayings with the ἦλθον sayings, → I, 404.

Along with the statements of Jesus concerning His mission we are to consider the Son of Man sayings introduced by the formula: ἦλθεν ὁ υἱὸς τοῦ ἀνθρώ-

---

[8] V. also Witkowski No. 36, line 11 f.: τοῦ παιδίου σου εἰς τὰ ἔσχατα ἐληλυθότος. There are similar formulations in P. Lond., I, 42, 17: εἰς πᾶν τι ἐληλυθυῖα; and P. Flor., II, 212, 3: εἰς τοσαύτην ἀτυχίαν ἦλθες.

[9] There is no instance of ἀπελεγμός in non-Christian usage (v. Pr.-Bauer, s.v. ἔρχομαι).

[10] So also in Diod. S., XIII, 95, 2; Epict. Diss., III, 1, 15. Cf. Preisigke Sammelbuch, 5763, 35.

[11] Cf. on this whole section Pr.-Bauer, s.v. ἔρχομαι, where detailed examples are given.

[12] So H. Windisch, Paulus und Christus (1934), 156.

[13] So Bultmann Trad., 165 ff. On the whole question v. A. v. Harnack, "Ich bin gekommen," ZThK, 22 (1912), 1 ff. Cf. also L. v. Sybel, "Die Ich-Worte Jesu bei den Synoptikern," ThStKr, 100 (1927/28), 382 f.; W. Wrede, Das Messiasgeheimnis (1901), 222, n. 2.

[14] So A. Resch, "Agrapha," TU, V, 4 (1889), 373, who points out that the saying in Mt. 5:17 is corrupted to convey encratistic error.

[15] Resch, loc. cit. The καταλῦσαι of Mt. 5:17 is used to give the strongest possible expression to the vegetarian antithesis to the bloody sacrifices of Judaism.

που. [16] As the Messiah, Jesus realises that He is sent to seek and to save that which is lost (Lk. 19:10; Lk. 9:56 𝔎 al lat syᶜ; [17] Mt. 18:11 𝔎 D pm lat syᶜ). His office is to minister and to give His life a ransom for many (Mk. 10:45; Mt. 20:28). The manner in which He fulfils His life's work is described by Jesus in Mt. 11:18 f.; Lk. 7:33 f. as one of openness to the good things of this world as distinct from the asceticism of the Baptist.

In the same context we should finally refer to the sayings of the demons who know who He is and who in direct address to Jesus define the purpose of His coming as their own destruction (Mk. 1:24; Lk. 4:34; cf. Mt. 8:29).

b. The coming of men to Jesus. In Mk. and Lk. we often have descriptions of the coming of great crowds of men to Jesus. But the outward coming does not mean much. Coming to Jesus must include a cultic action. ἔρχεσθαι must be followed by the → προσκυνεῖν which befits the Messianic dignity of Jesus. This προσκυνεῖν and προσπίπτειν is expressly mentioned of certain individuals who come into close contact with Jesus (cf. Mt. 8:2; 9:18; 14:33; 15:25; Mk. 5:33). There is also an example of this reverent cultic action in the infancy story in Mt., where the wise men from the east confess: ἤλθομεν προσκυνῆσαι (Mt. 2:2).

Even the coming which takes cultic form does not meet the final demands of Jesus. The decisive requirement is discipleship, or ὀπίσω ἔρχεσθαι. [18] This ὀπίσω ἔρχεσθαι implies full surrender to Jesus. It presupposes a simple but joyful and willing coming to Jesus which rests on a clear resolve of the will (εἴ τις θέλει ὀπίσω μου ἐλθεῖν, Mt. 16:24; Mk. 8:34). It embraces hearing the words of Jesus, fulfilling them, and denying oneself (Lk. 6:47; 9:23; 14:27). In the parable of the great supper the summons goes out to all who are invited to the marriage feast of the Messiah: ἔρχεσθε, ὅτι ἤδη ἕτοιμα (Lk. 14:17). But this summons is not heeded by all. The invitation is refused by some in the form: οὐ δύναμαι ἐλθεῖν (Lk. 14:20). In the parable of the royal marriage in Mt. 22 the sad experience which Jesus continually meets with is expressed in the words: οὐκ ἤθελον ἐλθεῖν (v. 3). The decisive moment in a human life, however, is for a man to find his way home to God, his Father, out of the situation of lostness (Lk. 15:20, 30).

When Jesus laid high estimation on the fact that children came to Him, He showed Himself to be the Herald and Dispenser of salvation to them too (Mt. 19:14 and par.).

c. The eschatological coming of the kingdom of God. In the prayer which the Master taught them, the disciples of Jesus pray for the coming of the kingdom of God (Mt. 6:10; Lk. 11:2). [19] On the entry of Jesus into Jerusalem, the praise of the people according to Mk. (11:10) is for the coming Messiah and the coming kingdom, which they understand as a restoration of the kingdom of David along

---

[16] Cf. on this pt. W. Bousset, *Kyrios Christos*² (1921), 6. Bousset claims that the formula ἦλθεν ὁ υἱὸς τοῦ ἀνθρώπου makes the impression of a hieratic stylisation.

[17] Cf. on this pt. W. Wrede, *loc. cit.* Wrede asks concerning Lk. 9:56: "Do we have here retrospective glances at the life of Jesus?"

[18] The coming of men to Jesus which issues in discipleship finds a par. in the Rabbinic world, where the pupil comes (בוֹא) to a rabbi when he becomes his pupil and where he also comes (S. Nu., 118 on 18:18) to serve the scribes (cf. K. G. Kuhn, *Sifre zu Nu.* [1933 ff.], 397, n. 115 and 116). According to Kuhn, the coming to a rabbi or to the rabbis, i.e., entry into the teacher-pupil relationship, necessarily entails ὀπίσω ἔρχεσθαι (הלך אחרי → I, 213) and personal service to the rabbis.

[19] In Rabb. literature the reference is not to the coming (בוֹא) but to the manifestation of the מַלְכוּת שָׁמַיִם (→ I, 571).

the lines of ancient Jewish tradition. When God's kingdom comes, it comes ἐν δυνάμει (Mk. 9:1). The future βασιλεία is identical with the coming aeon in which eternal life will be given to those who leave everything in this life and follow Jesus (Mk. 10:30; Lk. 18:30). βασιλεία θεοῦ, ὁ αἰὼν ὁ ἐρχόμενος (= עוֹלָם הַבָּא) and ζωὴ αἰώνιος are two different expressions for the one actuality of salvation. The special Lucan tradition raises the question (17:20 f.) of the time of the coming of God's kingdom. [20] In Lk. 22:18 there is reference to the future coming of the kingdom of God. Jesus speaks of the Paschal feast in the coming kingdom. Lk. 23:42 ℵ AC al rests on the certainty that the coming of the kingdom of God is linked with the *parousia* of Christ. The kingdom of God is the kingdom of the Messiah. Jesus comes in and with His kingdom (Mt. 16:28; Lk. 23:42 ℵ AC al).

d. The eschatological coming of the Messiah. In the Messianic dogma of Judaism the Messiah is the coming One (ὁ ἐρχόμενος) [21] who with His coming inaugurates the time of salvation. [22] In the Syn. Gospels we find many expressions of the popular belief that the coming of the Messiah must be preceded by the return of Elijah (Mt. 11:14; 17:10, 12; 27:49; cf. Mk. 9:12 f.; also Mk. 15:35). The doubts of the Baptist concerning Jesus are stated in the question: σὺ εἶ ὁ ἐρχόμενος; (Mt. 11:3; Lk. 7:19, 20). The crowd which hails Jesus as the Messiah on His entry into Jerusalem extols Him in the words of ψ 117:25 f.: ὁ ἐρχόμενος ἐν ὀνόματι κυρίου (Mt. 21:9 and par.; [23] Lk. 19:38: ὁ ἐρχόμενος ὁ βασιλεὺς ἐν ὀνόματι κυρίου).

In references to the coming of Jesus in His Messianic glory the early Christian tradition borrows from Apocalyptic. Jesus is the promised Messiah who at the end of the days will come in great power and glory (Mt. 16:27; 25:31 and par.) on the clouds of heaven (Mt. 24:30; 26:64 and par.). To the question when the *parousia* of Christ will take place the answer is given that no fixed time can be laid down (Mt. 24:42 ff. and par.). The only sure thing is that He will come suddenly (Mk. 13:36). The coming of Christ in His second *parousia* will be preceded by the coming of false prophets raising Messianic claims in the name of the Messiah (Mt. 24:5 and par.).

e. The eschatological coming of God to judgment. There is reference to God's coming to judgment in the parables of Jesus. [24] In the parable of the wicked husbandmen God is the lord of the vineyard who comes to exercise terrible retribution on the husbandmen for their maltreatment of his servants and his son (Mt. 21:40 and par.). In the parable of the fig-tree He is the owner who looks for

---

[20] Cf. on this pt. H. J. Allen, "The Apocalyptic Discourse in St. Luke 17," Exp. 9th Series, IV (1925), 59 ff.

[21] On the Rabb. view of the coming of the Messiah, v. Str.-B., IV, 872 ff. The Rabbis see two possible forms of coming, in glory and in humility.

[22] On different conceptions of the coming Messianic age of salvation in the Apcr. and Pseudepigr. on the one side and the Rabb. on the other, cf. *ibid.*, 799 ff. (Excurs. 29: "This world, the days of the Messiah and the future world"). On the Rabb. view the days of the Messiah precede the consummation in a completely new aeon (816 ff.). In the Rabb. הָעוֹלָם הַבָּא "the future world," is either the final aeon beyond the days of the Messiah or the heavenly world of souls to which the righteous go at the moment of death (968 ff.). הֶעָתִיד לָבוֹא is 1. the eschatological 'Olam ha-ba; 2. the days of the Messiah; 3. the world of souls (the hereafter) (833 ff.).

[23] Cf. on Mt. 21:9, Str.-B., I, 850. Acc. to Str.-B. the Rabbis refer the saying either to David (bPes., 119a) or to the final redemption (Midr. Ps. 118, § 22, 244a).

[24] On God's coming for the last judgment in Rabb. lit. v. Str.-B., IV, 1199 ff.

fruit, and, when he does not find it at his coming into the vineyard, orders the destruction of the fig-tree (Lk. 13:6 f.). In the parable of the talents He is the master who comes to reckon with his servants (Mt. 25:19; Lk. 19:13 ff.).

f. The coming of days of decision. In this connection we are to think of a whole series of sayings introduced by the stereotyped formula ἐλεύσονται ἡμέραι [25] and found for the most part in Lk. (17:22; 21:6; 23:29; cf. also Mt. 9:15).

> More than a mere indication of time is found in the saying in the Lucan account (22:7): ἦλθεν δὲ ἡ ἡμέρα τῶν ἀζύμων. This is a day or feast in which something decisive will happen for Jesus and the disciples. Mk. 14:41 brings this out even more clearly : ἦλθεν ἡ ὥρα, i.e., the hour when the passion of Jesus begins.
> Lk. 2:27 implies a divinely appointed hour (Simeon's coming into the temple under the impulsion of the Spirit).

2. The Johannine Writings.

In John's Gospel the theological content of ἔρχεσθαι sayings is even more pronounced than in the Synoptics. The significance of Jesus and the nature of His mission are brought out in sayings concerning His coming. The special character of Jn. means that the local use of ἔρχεσθαι is far less prominent than in the Synoptics, and the figurative far more common. The Johannine conception of Christ gives to sayings about coming a very different form and shape.

a. The coming of Jesus in John's Gospel. The self-attestations of Jesus are more numerous than in the Synoptic tradition. In keeping with the distinctive view of Christ, they also bear a different character from those found in the Synoptists. In the I-sayings (→ 349), especially in statements negated, they almost always have a polemical ring. In them the Evangelist opposes to false views of Jesus the true view which is attested by Jesus Himself and which is therefore authoritative. The Johannine formula for the self-witness of Jesus is ἐγὼ ἦλθον or ἐγὼ ἐλήλυθα.

In conflict with the Jews who will not recognise His Messianic dignity because His earthly origin is not in accord with their Messianic dogma, the Johannine Christ maintains : ἀπ᾽ ἐμαυτοῦ οὐκ ἐλήλυθα (7:28; 8:42). The basis of His Messianic claim is the certainty : οἶδα πόθεν ἦλθον καὶ ποῦ ὑπάγω (8:14). His coming rests on His divine mission (8:42). Here is the foundation of His claim (→ I, 444 f.). He does not come in His own name, but in the name of the Father (5:43). Since He is light and life by nature, the purpose of His coming is accordingly to bring light and life into the dark and dead world (10:10; 12:46). The coming of the Johannine Christ has a single goal, namely, the deliverance of the cosmos from the destruction of alienation from God (12:47). He has not come to condemn the world (12:47). Yet, though He Himself does not judge the world, His coming and existence imply judgment. This helps us to understand the paradoxical saying in 9:39: εἰς κρίμα ἐγὼ εἰς τὸν κόσμον τοῦτον ἦλθον. Men are divided by Him. How this "crisis" is accomplished is plainly stated in 3:19. Light has come into the world, but men love darkness more than light. In 18:37 Jesus defines His task as follows : He has come into the world to bear witness to the truth. His office is to reveal God's nature. The Revealer alone gives true knowledge of God.

The Messianic claim of Jesus is directed against the thesis that His earthly origin is known whereas the Jewish doctrine of the Messiah includes the belief : ὁ δὲ χριστὸς ὅταν ἔρχηται, οὐδεὶς γινώσκει πόθεν ἐστιν (7:27). But it is also

---

[25] In Lk. 23:29 we have ἔρχονται ἡμέραι, but D reads ἐλεύσονται ἡμέραι. This is probably an assimilation to the form found in the other sayings.

directed against the thesis that the Messiah comes only in the future and that He then brings full revelation, even in respect of the right cultus (4:25). The point at issue between Jesus and His opponents is not Messianic theology as such; it is simply whether Jesus is the Messiah. John's Gospel is designed to demonstrate the contention of Jesus that the Messiah of God has come in Him.

The Messianic claim of Jesus is supported by the witness of the Baptist, of whom it is expressly stated: ἦλθεν εἰς μαρτυρίαν ἵνα μαρτυρήσῃ περὶ τοῦ φωτός (1:7). This statement also shows us the place of the Baptist in salvation history. From the standpoint of the Baptist Jesus is ὁ ὀπίσω μου ἐρχόμενος (1:15, 27; cf. v. 30), but still ὁ ἐρχόμενος in the full sense of this traditional Messianic title. The coming of the Baptist is only to prepare the way for the Messiah (1:31). The baptism of John as an eschatological event is interpreted by him as a reference to the manifestation of the Messiah. In John's Gospel a decisive role attaches to the Baptist only as the forerunner of Jesus. On all others who came before Him (ὅσοι ἦλθον πρὸ ἐμοῦ) there is passed the severe and difficult sentence that they were thieves and murderers (10:8).

b. The coming of men to Jesus in John's Gospel. In John, as in the Synoptists, there are general sayings about the coming of men to Jesus. There are, of course, many different gradations (πάντες, 3:26; πολὺς ὄχλος, 6:5; πολλοί, 10:41; the inhabitants of the city of Sychar, 4:30, 40; Nicodemus, 3:2).

> Jesus Himself turns with a gracious invitation to all who come to Him seeking salvation. He reveals Himself to men as the source of eternal life (7:37). The man who follows up the invitation of Jesus is one who comes to Him in a special sense (6:35). This coming is the same as inner readiness to become His disciple (1:47). It bears the character of decision. The summons to come to Jesus can also be issued by those who are already disciples. The call of the witness which they bear is: ἔρχεσθε καὶ ἴδετε. [26] It can be individual, as in the case of Nathanael (1:46). The result is described in the equally terse but very distinctive words: ἦλθαν οὖν καὶ εἶδαν (1:39). He who comes to Jesus is not rejected (6:37). On the contrary, he receives the gift of Christ, namely, everlasting life (6:35).

For the coming of men to Christ, however, the final authority is not the will of man but God. According to John, the answer to the question who come to Jesus is those who are taught by God (6:45). If we then ask how they come, the answer is that none can come unless the Father draw him. Coming to Jesus is a coming effected by God. The apparently free decision of man is a decision ordained by God. Behind the Johannine statements stands the thought of divine election (cf. 6:65).

Those who thus come to Jesus believe in Him. As believers, they are already delivered from judgment (5:24). They come to a full confession of Christ which in 11:27 is formulated as follows: πεπίστευκα ὅτι σὺ εἶ ὁ Χριστὸς ὁ υἱὸς τοῦ θεοῦ ὁ εἰς τὸν κόσμον ἐρχόμενος. The man who comes to Jesus is the man who is born of the Spirit or born again, and whose origin is thus mysterious (3:8).

> The opposite of coming to Jesus is refusal to do so. This is based on a firm resolve to continue in sin (3:19 f.). A clear recognition of this situation underlies the saying of Jesus to the Jews: οὐ θέλετε ἐλθεῖν πρός με (5:40). The result is exclusion from eternal life.

c. The coming of the risen Lord in John's Gospel. The Johannine accounts of the resurrection appearances are introduced by the words ἔρχεται and ἦλθεν.

---

[26] Cf. on this pt. Str.-B., II, 371.

The author of the Fourth Gospel records a threefold mysterious coming of the risen Lord to the disciples : 1. to the disciples apart from Thomas (20:19); 2. to the disciples including Thomas, whose doubts are dissipated by the pneumatic reality of the risen Lord (20:26); and 3. to the disciples at the sea of Tiberias, when the sacred meal was sanctified by His presence (21:13).

d. The coming again of Christ in John's Gospel. John can speak of Christ's coming again wholly along the lines of early Christian tradition. The Johannine form of the early Christian witness is the self-witness of Jesus : πάλιν ἔρχομαι (14:3). In 21:22 f. the reference is to the coming of Jesus in the sense of the eschatological return of Christ. But between the first and second comings of Jesus lies the coming of the Paraclete (→ παράκλητος). In the form of the Spirit there is a continual coming of Christ. This is the so-called realised eschatology of John. [27] As Jesus was sent by God and came to earth, so the Paraclete is sent by the exalted Christ and comes to His community. The coming of the Paraclete implies an unbroken continuity of the coming of Jesus. The only point is that the form of coming has changed, the personal coming being replaced by a pneumatic. Three times Jesus raised the point that men cannot of themselves come to Him, twice to the Jews (7:34, 36; 8:21 f.) and once to the disciples (13:33). [28] This inability makes the sending of the Spirit-Paraclete an absolute necessity for the disciples.

e. The coming of the hour in John's Gospel. In this Gospel an important part is played by sayings concerning a specific point in time whose coming is of decisive significance. They are introduced by the fixed Johannine formula : ἔρχε-ται → ὥρα. In 4:21 ὥρα is the future time of salvation. It is distinctive of the basic outlook of John's Gospel, however, that Jesus does not destroy eschatological certainty; by adding the words καὶ νῦν ἐστιν to ἔρχεται ὥρα (v. 23) He expresses the fact that the Messianic time of salvation has already dawned. The situation is the same in 5:25, where the saying concerning the hour of the resurrection is retained in its eschatological sense, but where the addition of καὶ νῦν ἐστιν reinterprets the statement along the lines of realised eschatology, namely, that the resurrection is already present when men in faith have passed from death to life.

The most significant statements in this regard refer to the hour of the passion and death of Jesus, which for John coincides with the hour of glorification. The ὥρα is God's appointed hour before whose coming no one can take any decisive steps against Jesus. Fundamentally, it is not the hour of earthly human history, but the hour of divine salvation history. In John's Gospel there are two statements of this kind. The first maintains that the hour of Jesus has not yet come (7:30; 8:20); the second maintains that it has come (12:23; 13:1; 17:1).

In the Parting Discourses there is also reference to an hour of the disciples. Jesus is speaking of the time of martyrdom which will bring for them persecution and death (16:2, 4). This period begins already with the hour of His own arrest (16:32).

---

[27] Cf. R. Bultmann, "Die Eschatologie des Joh.-Ev.," Z. d. Z., 6 (1928), 4 ff. Also K. Kundsin, "Die Wiederkunft Jesu in den Abschiedsreden des Joh.-Ev.," ZNW, 33 (1934), 210 ff.

[28] Does this threefold reference to the perfecting and glorifying of Jesus in Jn. take the place of the threefold intimation of His passion in the Syn. ? This is quite possible in the light of John's conception of the passion.

f. The Epistles of John. These speak of the coming of Christ and also of the coming of Antichrist. The latter coming is a sign of the last hour (1 Jn. 2:18; cf. 4:3). In relation to the former, the whole emphasis lies on the fact that Jesus Christ has come in the flesh. The basic confession in the conflict with Docetism is: Ἰησοῦς Χριστὸς ἐν σαρκὶ ἐληλυθώς (1 Jn. 4:2; 2 Jn. 7). In 1 Jn. 5:6 it is stressed that Jesus Christ has come δι' ὕδατος καὶ αἵματος — a statement which may well refer to the sacraments of baptism and the Lord's Supper instituted by Jesus. [29]

g. Revelation. In describing the nature of God, and especially His eternity, Rev. uses the phrase: ὁ ὢν καὶ ὁ ἦν καὶ ὁ ἐρχόμενος (1:4, 8; 4:8; cf. also 11:17).

The author expects the speedy return of Christ. The exalted Lord says to the churches: ἔρχομαί σοι (2:5; ταχύ, 2:16; 22:20). [30] The Church of Christ lives in yearning expectation of His coming again (22:17, 20). The prayer for the coming of Christ is strengthened by the words: ἀμήν, ἔρχου κύριε Ἰησοῦ (22:20). [31] As regards the manner of the coming, the divine follows early Christian tradition. Christ comes as a thief (16:15) and with the clouds (1:7).

For the rest, the ἔρχεσθαι sayings describe the eschatological situation, namely, the coming of judgment on the one hand (6:17; 11:18; 14:7, 15; 18:10) and on the other the coming of the Messianic age of joy in all the glory of its consummation (19:7), this being preceded by the Messianic tribulation (3:10; cf. 7:14).

3. Paul.

In the Pauline Epistles statements concerning the eschatological coming of Christ are far more numerous than those concerning his first coming, which are found only at 1 Tm. 1:15 and Eph. 2:17.

The eschatological statements concerning Christ's coming are wholly within the framework of early Christian tradition. Paul lives in expectation of the imminent coming again of Christ (1 C. 4:5). Distinctive is the Aramaic petition μαράνα θά (1 C. 16:22). The Pauline account of the Lord's Supper contains a reference to Christ's return (1 C. 11:26). The death of Christ is to be proclaimed ἄχρι οὗ ἔλθῃ. [32] Christ will come suddenly like a thief in the night (1 Th. 5:2). But He will come in all His Messianic glory (2 Th. 1:10). The time of salvation is the time which brings in what is perfect and does away what is in part (1 C. 13:10). The wrath of God will fall on unbelievers (Col. 3:6; Eph. 5:6). The appearing of Christ will be preceded by apostasy and the manifestation of the man of sin (2 Th. 2:3).

Paul also uses ἔρχεσθαι to denote the occurrence of significant events in salvation history. He refers to a time in his own life when the Law took on validity for him (ἐλθούσης δὲ τῆς ἐντολῆς, R. 7:9 → 551). The decisive point in salvation history is the coming of faith, i.e., of the time which is a time of faith, characterised by πίστις rather than by νόμος (Gl. 3:23). This time has completely set aside the dominion of

[29] V. F. Büchsel, Die Johannesbriefe (1933), 81 f. Cf. also J. Schneider, Die Passionsmystik des Paulus (1929), 120.

[30] For the construction cf. the class. par. ἀλλ' ἦλθεν αὐτῷ Ζηνὸς ἄγρυπνον βέλος in Aesch. Prom., 374 (cf. Moult.-Mill., III, 255, s.v. ἔρχομαι).

[31] There is a radical difference between this petition and the formulae common in ancient prayers (ἐλθέ (μοι), κύριε, → 666), which are supposed to force the deity. The early Christian prayer is full of humility and hopeful expectation. Nor it is the individual who speaks (ἐλθέ μοι), but the community.

[32] Cf. the grammatical par. in P. Tebt., II, 416, 18-20: ποίησον αὐτῆς τὴν χρίαν ἕως ἔλθω. Cf. also LXX Is. 32:15.

the Law (Gl. 3:25; cf. also 3:19 : ἄχρις ἂν ἔλθῃ τὸ σπέρμα; 4:4 : ὅτε δὲ ἦλθεν τὸ πλήρωμα τοῦ χρόνου).

Also characteristic of Paul are statements in which he shows how he came to the churches. He did so with the full blessing of the Gospel of Christ (R. 15:29), with joy (R. 15:32), not with lofty words or wisdom but in demonstration of the Spirit and power of God (1 C. 2:1). His coming always had one goal : εἰς τὸ εὐαγγέλιον τοῦ Χριστοῦ (2 C. 2:12). In Phil. 1:12 Paul confesses that his imprisonment has helped to further the message of salvation (εἰς προκοπὴν τοῦ εὐαγγελίου ἐλήλυθεν). Paul desires to come to his churches with love and meekness (1 C. 4:21). On his coming he hopes to find them in a right frame of mind which is worthy of the Gospel (2 C. 12:21). He is troubled if he has to come with sorrow (2 C. 2:1, 3) or even to punish (ἐν ῥάβδῳ, 1 C. 4:21). He is not prepared to suffer humiliations at his coming (2 C. 12:21). We can see that these descriptions of his ἔρχεσθαι give us intimate glimpses into the soul of Paul.

4. The Other NT Writings.

In the other NT writings the eschatological use is predominant. In Ac. there is reference to the coming of the great day of judgment (2:20), to the coming again of Christ (1:11), and to the coming of the accompanying time of salvation (3:20). Taking up the Messianic prophecies of the OT, Hb. 8:8 and 10:37 refer to the coming time of salvation. Ac. 19:6 shows that the age of salvation has already dawned; the Holy Spirit comes on the believers in Ephesus by the laying on of the hands of Paul. 2 Pt. 3:3 speaks of the ungodly mockers who will come in the last days.

ἔλευσις. [1]

"Coming." This is rare outside the Bible. It occurs in Dion. Hal. Ant. Rom., III, 59. It is the normal abstract of ἐλεύσομαι, which is common in Ionic and Hellenistic Gk. as well as in the NT. The LXX has ἐλευστέον once (δι' ὀλίγων δ' ἐλευστέον ἐπὶ τὴν διήγησιν, "after this short digression we must return to the story," 2 Macc. 6:17).

The word occurs only once in the NT. Ac. 7:52 speaks of the ἔλευσις τοῦ δικαίου which was proclaimed by the prophets. Here ἔλευσις has the same sense as "appearing" and ὁ δίκαιος is in Judaism the title of the Messianic Judge of the world (→ 186 f.). Hence we are to take the saying as a statement concerning the parousia of the Messiah, Jesus, who will judge the world.

D has ἔλευσις in Lk. 21:7 and Lk. 23:42. That ἔλευσις is the same as παρουσία is shown by the par. to Lk. 21:7 D (σημεῖον τῆς σῆς ἐλεύσεως) in Mt. 24:3 : τὸ σημεῖον τῆς σῆς παρουσίας. In the Lucan passages in D we undoubtedly have a later emendation to make the text smoother.

Like Ac. 7:52, Pol., 6, 3 : ἔλευσις τοῦ κυρίου ἡμῶν, and 1 Cl., 17, 1 : ἡ ἔλευσις τοῦ Χριστοῦ, refer to the first coming of Christ. On the other hand, in Act. Thom., 28 ἔλευσις is the second coming. The term is used for both comings in Iren., I, 10, 1.

ἀπέρχομαι. [1]

ὀπίσω ἀπέρχεσθαι[2] is often used in the Syn. for discipleship. The sharpest

---

ἔ λ ε υ σ ι ς. [1] ἐπέλευσις → 680, n. 1.

ἀ π έ ρ χ ο μ α ι. [1] ἀπέρχεσθαι means "to go away from." Later, however, attention is diverted from the starting-point (ἀπό) to the goal to be reached by ἀπέρχεσθαι, and it thus acquires the sense of "to come to" (= ἀφικνέομαι). So H. Usener, *Legenden der hl. Pelagia* (1879), 49. Cf. also 7, 3 : ἀπήλθαμεν ἐν τῇ μεγάλῃ ἐκκλησίᾳ, "we came into the great church" (also 10, 3; 12, 15 etc.). Cf. BGU, III, 814, 30 (3rd cent. A.D.). The word is occasionally used in this sense in the NT (cf. Mt. 4:24; Jn. 4:47).

[2] ὀπίσω ἀπέρχεσθαι, "to go after someone," in the LXX at Job 21:33. The Hb. הָלַךְ אַחֲרֵי, esp. in Dt., means "to go behind a god in a procession," figur. "to serve a god."

antithesis is an expression like ἀπελθεῖν ὀπίσω σαρκὸς ἑτέρας in Jd. 7, which denotes licentious living. The seriousness of decision for the kingdom of God is expressed in Mk. 9:43; Mt. 5:30. If in relation to the kingdom of God we do not make a radical break with everything that hinders entry into it, we shall go to hell (ἀπελθεῖν εἰς γέενναν). At the end of the apocalyptic vision of John the word is used of the end of the first and fallen creation (21:4 : τὰ πρῶτα ἀπῆλθαν).

διέρχομαι.

In R. 5:12 (→ 437), in a discussion of the origin of sin and death, Paul maintains that death has extended to all men.[1] In Hb. 4:14 we have a statement which is most important for the theology of Hb., namely, that Christ our High-Priest has passed through heaven into the heavenly sanctuary.

εἰσέρχομαι.

"To go or come into." It is often used for "to enter" (e.g., of a chorus, Plat. Resp., IX, 580b). In the commercial world it is used of the movement of money and goods. In legal Attic it denotes going to court. It can then mean "to take up an office." Figur., courage, hunger or desire can "come into" or "upon" men.

In the pap.,[1] apart from the commercial use, it can mean "to make demands on someone" (B. P. Grenfell, *An Alexandrian Erotic Fragment* [1896], 27, Col. III, 2); in relation to time it is used for the "coming" time (P. Oxy., II, 243, 41; IX, 1187, 5; X, 1278, 17).

Cultically, it is found in ancient prayers for invocation of the deity : εἴσελθε, Preis. Zaub., IV, 1001, 1006, 1015, 1019, 1023, 1031, 1041, 1045; εἰσερχέσθω ὁ θρόνος τοῦ θεοῦ, V, 32. For the certainty grounded in magic, cf. εἰσελεύσεται ὁ θεός, XII, 159; εἰσελθόντος δὲ τοῦ θεοῦ, XIII, 704; ἐπὰν εἰσέλθῃ οὖν ὁ θεός, XIII, 564 f. (→ ἔρχομαι, 666).[2] It is also used of men : εἰσιέναι εἰς τὸν ναόν, Ditt. Syll.³, 982, 3. Cf. also P. Tor., I, 8, 19.

In the Septuagint it is used for 19 Heb. words. The sexual use is common as well as the local : εἰσέρχεσθαι πρὸς γυναῖκα, πρὸς ἄνδρα³ (Heb. בוא).[4] But the most significant use is the cultic and sacral. a. God comes to men (e.g., Gn. 20:3; Dt. 4:34); God's glory comes into the temple (Ez. 43:4); the divine Spirit of life comes into the dead in Ez.'s vision (37:10). b. Men go into the sanctuary, εἰσέρχεσθαι being particularly used of the cultic ministry of the high-priest and priests. In such expressions it may be used in the abs. (e.g., Ex. 24:3, 18; 2 Ch. 29:16). The requirement for entry into the place dedicated to God is cultic purity and holiness. In ψ 117:20 and Is. 26:2 righteousness is demanded for entry through the gates of the holy city. c. Men bring their prayers to God with the words : εἰσελθέτω ἐνώπιόν σου ἡ προσευχή μου (ψ 87:2); εἰσελθάτω ἐνώπιόν σου ὁ στεναγμός (ψ 78:11); cf. ψ 118:170 : εἰσέλθοι τὸ ἀξίωμά μου ἐνώπιόν σου. d. Particularly important in relation to the preaching of Jesus, which speaks of entry into the kingdom of God, is the similar expression concerning the entry of the people of Israel into the promised land (εἰσέρχεσθαι εἰς τὴν γῆν, Ex., Lv., Nu., Dt.), often together with κληρονομεῖν (εἰσελθεῖν καὶ κληρονομεῖν, e.g., Dt. 6:18). The same conception underlies the phrase εἰσέρχεσθαι εἰς τὴν κατάπαυσιν, "into the rest of God," in ψ 94:11. The opposite is found in statements concerning the op-

---

διέρχομαι. [1] Cf. Ez. 5:17 (LXX): θάνατος καὶ αἷμα διελεύσονται ἐπὶ σέ.

εἰσέρχομαι. [1] For details cf. Preisigke Wört., s.v.

[2] On εἴσελθε cf. also Reitzenstein Poim., 27.

[3] This use of εἰσέρχεσθαι is reflected in the use of ἔρχεσθαι in Preis. Zaub., XXXVI, 113 : ἕως ἂν ἔλθῃ (until sexual union is achieved).

[4] The word is used in the same sense in Arab. (*daḫala*), in Syr. ('al) and in Aram. (עלל).

ponents of God and His people : εἰσελθεῖν (Β : ἐλθεῖν) εἰς τὸ σκότος, Tob. 4:10 (11); εἰς τὰ κατώτατα τῆς γῆς, ψ 62:9.

In the NT the word is always used in the local sense.

1. The cultic use is fairly common : εἰσέρχεσθαι εἰς τὸ ἱερόν (Ac. 3:8 etc.); εἰς τὸν ναόν (Lk. 1:9; Rev. 15:8); εἰς τὸν οἶκον τοῦ θεοῦ (Mt. 12:4; Lk. 6:4); εἰς τὴν συναγωγήν (Mk. 1:21; 3:1; Lk. 4:16; Ac. 13:14 𝔎 Dpl; 14:1); εἰς Ἱεροσόλυμα (Mk. 11:11). It is used of a solemn act of divine grace in Lk. 1:28 : εἰσελθὼν ὁ ἄγγελος πρὸς αὐτήν (Mary).

2. The most significant statements theologically are when the word is used with εἰς. Among these we turn first to the sayings concerning entry into the kingdom of God (→ I, 581 ff.) in the Synoptists. These are to be ranked with the prophetic and apocalyptic sayings of the Gospels, and are of great seriousness. Entry into God's kingdom is linked with certain conditions, namely, to be converted and become as little children (Mk. 10:15 and par.), to keep the commandments (Mt. 19:17), to do the will of God (Mt. 7:21). There is required a basic religious attitude (δικαιοσύνη) which can be attained only by a radically new beginning (Mt. 5:20). This unconditional orientation to the coming kingdom demands sacrifice, namely, a clean break with everything that would hinder or prejudice the newly established existence of man before God (cf. the sayings about offences in Mt. 18:8 f.). To this new basic attitude belongs constant readiness for the moment when the kingdom of God will come in all its glory and power (Mt. 25:10). There also belongs steadfast piety and faithfulness (Mt. 25:21 ff.). Those who do not fulfil these requirements must be prepared to be rejected at the decisive moment (Mt. 22:12). The task of Jesus and His disciples is to summon men to this kingdom and to win them for it. Hence the demand that men should enter in at the strait gate (Mt. 7:13) and that the disciples should exercise salutary constraint on men by proclaiming their message (Lk. 24:23 : ἀνάγκασον εἰσελθεῖν). Jesus knows that for many the things and values of this world are a hindrance to entry into the kingdom of God. In particular wealth (Mk. 10:23 and par.; Mk. 10:24, trust in riches) is a serious obstacle. The hard saying is applicable to many that they will want to enter in but will not be able (Lk. 13:24). Among those to whom access is barred by their own guilt are to be numbered not only the rich, the indolent and the half-hearted, but especially the Pharisees and scribes. Jesus brings against them the serious charge that by their religious practice they also prevent others from entering the kingdom who desire to do so (Lk. 11:52).

Equivalent expressions to εἰσελθεῖν εἰς τὴν βασιλείαν are εἰσελθεῖν εἰς τὴν ζωήν and εἰσελθεῖν εἰς τὴν χαράν. [6]

---

[5] V. esp. H. Windisch, "Die Sprüche vom Eingehen in das Reich Gottes," ZNW, 27 (1928), 163 ff. Windisch also discusses the synon., p. 166 ff.

[6] On these sayings in the apostolic and post-apostolic period, v. H. Windisch, ZNW, 27 (1928), 171. In post-apostolic literature variants of the Syn. sayings are most common in Herm. (s., 9, 12, 5-8; 9, 14, 1 f.; 9, 15, 2; 9, 20, 2 f.); cf. also 1 Cl., 48, 2-4; 2 Cl., 6, 9. Also worth noting in relation to the Church's formulation is Ps. Clem. Hom., 13, 21: δόγμα θεοῦ κεῖται, ἀβάπτιστον εἰς τὴν αὐτοῦ βασιλείαν μὴ εἰσελθεῖν. An apocryphal saying of the Lord in Act. Phil., 140 (34) runs as follows : ἐὰν μὴ ποιήσητε ὑμῶν τὰ κάτω εἰς τὰ ἄνω καὶ τὰ ἀριστερὰ εἰς τὰ δεξιά, οὐ μὴ εἰσέλθητε εἰς τὴν βασιλείαν μου. Windisch (172 ff.) finds Jewish par. a. in the later Jewish apocalypses (e.g., 4 Esr. 7:14), and b. in the Talmud, where the corresponding expressions are בּוֹא לְעוֹלָם הַבָּא, "ב חֵלֶק, 'ל זָכָה נָחַל, יֵרַשׁ. In respect of the origin of sayings about entry into the kingdom of God Windisch (177 f.) points 1. to the exhortations of Dt., a type being perceived in the entry (LXX : εἰσελθεῖν)

John's Gospel emphasises not merely the religious and ethical requirements but also the sacramental presupposition. None can enter the kingdom of God without regeneration by water and the Spirit (3:5). Faith and the sacrament ensure access into the kingdom. This also means, however, that access is bound up with the mediatorship of Christ (διὰ τῆς θύρας, Jn. 10:2; δι' ἐμοῦ, 10:9). Only those who enter in this way can have a part in salvation. It will be seen that John is more "ecclesiastical" in his thinking than the Synoptists.

According to the witness of Acts (14:22) early Christian proclamation shared the view of Jewish apocalyptic that the final tribulation would precede entry into the kingdom of God.

3. General religious usage. In the Syn. it is used a. of the actions of Jesus: the earthly Jesus comes to sinners (Lk. 19:7), the risen Jesus to the disciples (e.g., the two of Emmaus, Lk. 24:29) to hold fellowship with them. According to Lk. the ascension to God after the completion of the work of salvation is an entry into His glory (Lk. 24:26). It is also used b. of the activity of satanic and demonic forces: Satan enters into Judas (Lk. 22:3; cf. Jn. 13:27). Demons take possession of men. In contrast the Messianic action of Jesus is to drive out demons and to order them: μηκέτι εἰσέλθῃς εἰς αὐτόν (Mk. 9:25). It is used c. of the actions of the disciples, who should be on the watch and should therefore pray that they do not enter into temptation (Mk. 14:38 vl. and par.). For prayer, they are told: εἴσελθε εἰς τὸ ταμιεῖον (Mt. 6:6).

Paul uses εἰσέρχεσθαι only 4 times. Twice he uses it of the coming of unbelievers or non-members into Christian gatherings (1 C. 14:23 f.; cf. also Jm. 2:2: εἰς τὴν συναγωγήν). In R. 5:12 (→ 437), discussing the origin of sin and death in the world, Paul teaches that sin came through man, and had death as its consequence. In his eschatological consideration of the destiny of Israel (R. 11:25) Paul is certain that the fulness of the Gentiles will first come in and that then all Israel will be saved.

Hb. uses εἰσέρχεσθαι a. of the entry of the earthly high-priest into the Holy of Holies (9:25) and of the entry of the heavenly High-Priest into the heavenly sanctuary (6:19; 9:12, 24; 6:20, as a Forerunner for us). It also uses it b. of the coming of Christ into the world to make the all-sufficient sacrifice of His life (10:5). It finally uses it eschatologically c. of the entry of Christians into eternal rest (3:11, 18; 4:1 ff.). Here ψ 94:11 is applied typologically to the Christian situation.

Rev. uses the term predominantly in eschatological statements and contexts. Only those whose names are written in the Book of Life can enter into the holy city of the eternal world; everything unclean and common will be excluded from the city of God (21:27; cf. 22:14). There is almost a mystical ring about the saying of the exalted Christ (3:20) to those who open the door for Him to enter: εἰσελεύσομαι πρὸς αὐτὸν καὶ δειπνήσω μετ' αὐτοῦ καὶ αὐτὸς μετ' ἐμοῦ.

In 2 Jn. 7 𝔎 33 pm it is said of heretics: πλάνοι εἰσῆλθον εἰς τὸν κόσμον. Jm. 5:4 is a word of comfort in social distress: the cries of the economically oppressed go up to God.

ἐξέρχομαι.

"To go out," with ἐκ of the gen. or place; also abs., used also of inanimate things, e.g., words which "go out" of a man, Theaet., 161b; sicknesses which "leave" a man (Hippocr., e.g., Morb., 2, 13); time which "passes." It also has the figur. sense of "to issue": either "to come to fulfilment" (ἐξέρχεσθαι ἐς τέλος, Hes. Op., 218), or "to

---

of the Israelites into Canaan (Dt. 4:1; 6:18; 16:20 the combination of εἰσελθεῖν and κληρο-νομεῖν); and 2. to the temple liturgies (ψ 14 and 23; 117) and the related regulations concerning admission to the cultic community, the central concept being that of δικαιοσύνη (as in Mt.). Finally Windisch draws attention to 2 Hellenistic parallels to the entry sayings (189 ff.), namely, the table of Cebes and Luc. Hermot.

issue from" (a number issues forth, Xenoph. Hist. Graec., VI, 1, 5). In the pap. [1] we also have the senses "to come up" (BGU, I, 93, 30 : οὐδέπω δὲ ἐξῆλθεν ἡ ὑπογραφή, the decision on my request has not yet come up, and in the legal world "to leave," of a court officer leaving the court to carry out an order. [2] An unusual sense is "to stand out" in P. Tebt., II, 283, 9 : ἐξελήλυθεν ἐπὶ τὴν ... μητέρα μου. The word is also used sometimes for "to depart life," "to die," as in Lib. Or., 20, 31 (ἐξέρχομαι τοῦ βίου); Jos. Ant., 1, 223 (ἐξελθεῖν τοῦ ζῆν). In Philo the term is used to describe the mystical and ecstatic process. To come to God, the soul must go out of itself (Leg. All., III, 47; cf. III, 44 : ἐξελθοῦσα τῆς ψυχῆς πόλιν διάνοια).

In the Septuagint it is used for 16 Heb. words. Apart from the local significance, it is used figur. a. of fruit "coming forth" out of the earth, and b. of what man "produces," whether the fruit of the body or of the lips. It is used esp. of the operations which "proceed" from God : νόμος, Is. 51:4; σωτήριον, 51:5; ὀργή, Nu. 16:46; πρόσταγμα, Gn. 24:50 A.; τέρατα, Is. 28:29; His Word Is. 55:11 etc.; His righteousness Is. 45:23. In Sir. 24:3 wisdom says : ἐγὼ ἀπὸ στόματος ὑψίστου ἐξῆλθον. It can also mean "to go out" in the sense of "to end," "to vanish" (e.g., the breath of man in Wis. 16:14; cf. ψ 145:4). The word is particularly significant in its cultic and sacral use, esp. when it expresses the divine epiphany (→ ἐπιφάνεια): Is. 42:13 : κύριος ὁ θεὸς τῶν δυνάμεων ἐξελεύσεται; Zech. 14:3 : ἐξελεύσεται κύριος. Cf. also Zech. 5:5 : ἐξῆλθεν ὁ ἄγγελος; v. also 14:8 : ἐξελεύσεται ὕδωρ ζῶν ἐξ 'Ιερουσαλήμ; and frequently ἐξέρχεσθαι ἐκ τοῦ ἁγίου. It is used for "to come to prayer" in Jdt. 12:6 : ἐξελθεῖν ἐπὶ προσευχήν. It is also used in the sexual sphere in Test. XII, cf. εἰσέρχεσθαι πρὸς γυναῖκα (R. 3:14).

The main sense in the NT is local. It serves especially to denote resurrection (Jn. 11:31: ἀνέστη καὶ ἐξῆλθεν; v. 44 : ἐξῆλθεν ὁ τεθνηκώς; cf. Mt. 27:53).

With the inf. it means "to go forth" to do something according to a prearranged plan (e.g., to preach the Gospel, Mk. 6:12; 16:20; or to pray, Lk. 6:12). Conversely, it can also be said that something "comes forth" from man (e.g., ἐξῆλθεν δόγμα [→ 231] παρὰ Καίσαρος, Lk. 2:1). Rumours "go out" from men (φήμη, Mt. 9:26; ἀκοή, Mk. 1:28; Lk. 4:14; λόγος, Lk. 7:17; cf. Jn. 21:23). Different kinds of utterances (blessing and cursing) proceed from the lips of men (Jm. 3:10). Evil thoughts come out of the heart (Mt. 15:19). But these negative statements are balanced by positive declarations concerning the Word of God and faith. God's Word goes out from authorised apostles (1 C. 14:36), and news of the faith of a community (the Thessalonian) goes out to all places (1 Th. 1:8).

In a particularly distinctive and concrete sense the word can mean "to derive from the vital force of a man." Thus the Jews are ἐκ τῆς ὀσφύος 'Αβραὰμ ἐξεληλυθότες (Hb. 7:5). The word can also be used more generally for "to go out from a fellowship"; "to leave" it as a spiritual home (of the heretics in 1 Jn. 2:19). Without specifically mentioning the point of origin it is used of false prophets in 1 Jn. 4:1 and of various deceivers in 2 Jn. 7. It means going out on missionary work in 3 Jn. 7. In Rev. it refers to the rise of mysterious and sinister figures (6:2, 4), or to angels going forth to inaugurate apocalyptic events (14:15 ff.; 15:6), or to Satan and his work of destruction (20:8).

In the Syn. ἐξέρχεσθαι is the characteristic word for the "going forth" of demons from those possessed by them (Mk. 1:26 and par.; cf. also Ac. 8:7; 16:18). Jesus' command to demons is : ἔξελθε ἐξ αὐτοῦ (Mk. 1:25 etc.). [3]

But the imper. ἔξελθε can also be a request to Jesus. Peter, overwhelmed by the majesty of Jesus, says : ἔξελθε ἀπ' ἐμοῦ (Lk. 5:8). In Mk. 1:38 Jesus says that it is His task to preach the Gospel of the kingdom of God, and He adds : εἰς τοῦτο γὰρ

ἐξέρχομαι. [1] For details v. Preisigke Wört., s.v.

[2] Cf. Preisigke Fachwörter, 79.

[3] Cf. Preis. Zaub., IV, 1243 f.: ἔξελθε δαῖμον ... καὶ ἀπόστηθι ἀπὸ τοῦ δεῖνα. On the construction with ἀπό, cf. P. Oxy., III, 472, 1; 528, 7.

ἐξῆλθον. In Jesus there is unheard of δύναμις (→ 299). When He heals, He perceives that virtue is gone out of Him (Mk. 5:30 and par.).

In Jn. the Messianic self-witness of Jesus can take the form: ἐκ τοῦ θεοῦ ἐξῆλθον (Jn. 8:42; 16:27 f.; 17:8; cf. 13:3). The aim of this self-witness is achieved when the disciples reply to it with the confession: πιστεύομεν ὅτι ἀπὸ θεοῦ ἐξῆλθες (Jn. 16:30). Jesus confirms this confession in the high-priestly prayer: ἔγνωσαν ἀληθῶς ὅτι παρὰ σοῦ ἐξῆλθον (17:8). In the spiritual sense Jesus is the door through which the disciples go in and out and find pasture (Jn. 10:9). [4]

There is a pathetic ring about the saying in Jn. 13:30 f., which tells us that Judas went out, and not merely in the local sense, but also in the sense that he broke off fellowship with Jesus. The same deeper meaning is contained in the statement that Jesus went out of Jerusalem to the place of crucifixion (Jn. 19:17). This is more than a topographical note. It marks a crucial moment not only for Jesus but also for the Jewish people and esp. for Jerusalem. In Hb. the same event, so important in the history of salvation, is shown to have also exemplary significance for Christians. The demand ἐξερχώμεθα πρὸς αὐτὸν ἔξω τῆς παρεμβολῆς (Hb. 13:13) is meant in the sense of identification with the suffering Christ.

In Hb. 11:8 Abraham's departure from his home is regarded as an act of faith. On the other hand, the Pauline view is that Christians should not leave the world (1 C. 5:10). [5] The world is their concrete sphere of operation.

Light is shed on the eschatological situation by Mt. 13:49, where it is said of the angels that they will go forth and separate the wicked from the righteous.

ἐπέρχομαι.

a. "To come to," "to draw near" (with acc. of place). It may be used abs., esp. of the coming forward of the speaker. It is also used of the coming of a time. Figur. certain events (sleep, sickness) come on men. ἐπέρχεταί μοι and με means "it comes upon me" (with nom. of object or inf.); cf. also Corp. Herm., XI, 1b: ὡς δέ μοι ἐπῆλθεν εἰπεῖν οὐκ ὀκνήσω. b. "To come with hostile intent," "to attack," also "to accuse"; figur. "to take up something," "to undertake."

In the pap. [1] it has the senses a. "to approach"; b. "to proceed with force against someone" (P. Lips., 40, col. II, 2; ὁ ἐπελθών, "the aggressor"); c. "to enter illegally"; d. "to be due" (of achievements); e. "to contest the validity of a report"; f. "to oppress someone with demands," "to make claims on someone" (BGU, I, 159, 9 [ὁ δεῖνα] ἐπῆλθέν μοι ἐκπράσσων, "to press for arrears in taxes").

In the LXX it is used for 24 Heb. words. It refers mostly to things, events, or conditions which come on men, including natural events. It is used esp. of the obscure and oppressive evils which come on men. Less frequently it refers to events or conditions which bring salvation, e.g., in Is. 32:15 vl. of the Spirit coming down on men from above. In relation to the eschatological future we have τὰ ἔσχατα καὶ τὰ ἐπερχόμενα (Is. 41:22), τὰ ἐπερχόμενα ἐπ' ἐσχάτου (Is. 41:23), τὰ ἐπερχόμενα (Is. 42:23 etc.), ἐν τῇ ἡμέρᾳ τῇ ἐπερχομένῃ (Jer. 29:4). In the Test. XII it is normally used to denote hostile attack (Jud. 6:3; 9:2; Iss. 4:5; 5:8; Zeb. 2:6). Eschatologically δόξα κυρίου ἐπερχομένου is the glory of the coming Lord (L. 8:11). In Jos. Ant., 6, 305 it is used temporally: ἡ ἐπερχομένη ἡμέρα, "the coming day."

---

[4] Cf. (e.g., on Jn. 19:34) J. Schneider, Passionsmystik des Paulus (1929), 120. Cf. on ἐξελθεῖν as used of blood Rev. 14:20. On Jn. 19:34 cf. Schl. J., 353. Zn. J., 666, sees here only a reference to the reality of the death of Jesus.

[5] ἐξέρχεσθαι ἐκ τοῦ κόσμου for "to die" is already a euphemism among the Jews, אֲזַל מִן עָלְמָא, Tg. Qoh. 1:8; cf. Dalman WJ, I, 141; cf. also 1 K. 2:2. With 1 C. 5:10 cf. also 2 Cl., 5, 1; 8, 3.

ἐπέρχομαι. [1] V. Preisigke Wört., s.v. In the pap. we also have the subst. ἐπέλευσις (P. Oxy., I, 69, 15; XII, 1562, 22; P. Fay., 26, 14) and ἐπελευστικός (P. Oxy., VIII, 1120, 10).

With two exceptions (Eph. 2:7 and Jm. 5:1) the word is used in the NT only in the Lucan writings. Figuratively it means to come on someone; thus a stronger comes on the weaker in Lk. 11:22.[2] This helps us to understand the religious and theological use. The Holy Spirit, represented as the power of God, comes on men who are blessed by God. Twice there is reference to the promise of the Holy Spirit coming on chosen persons, in Lk. 1:35 to Mary, and in Ac. 1:8 to the disciples on the ascension of Jesus. The other passages in Lk. (Lk. 21:26, 35; Ac. 8:24; 13:40) refer to future destruction, and esp. to the catastrophe of coming judgment. The same is true of Jm. 5:1. In Eph. 2:7 we have the eschatological expression αἰῶνες οἱ ἐπερχόμενοι; it refers to the indescribable generosity of the grace of God which will be shown to the Church in Christ Jesus in the ages to come.

Outside the NT the eschatological use is particularly common in Herm. (ὁ αἰὼν ὁ ἐπερχόμενος, v., 4, 3, 5; of the coming terrible events of the last time, v., 3, 9, 5; 4, 1, 1; s., 7, 4; 9, 5, 5).

παρέρχομαι.

a. "To go by," often in the sense of "to miss"; also "to flow past," "to pass by" (of time),[1] e.g., Isoc., 4, 167: ἱκανὸς γὰρ ὁ παρεληλυθώς, ἐν ᾧ τί τῶν δεινῶν οὐ γέγονεν. Then more generally "to pass away" in the sense of "to come to an end," "to perish" (e.g., Theocr. Idyll., 27, 10: τάχα γάρ σε παρέρχεται ὡς ὄναρ ἥβα). b. "To outstrip," "to overtake," to surpass someone in speed," also "to excel in cunning" and therefore "to deceive." c. "To pass over," "to disregard," also "to miss," "to remain unnoticed" (e.g., Demosth. Or. 21, 110: τουτὶ γὰρ αὖ μικροῦ παρῆλθέ μ' εἰπεῖν, "I almost forgot to say this"; cf. also Theogn., 419: πολλά με καὶ συνιέντα παρέρχεται). Also "to go beyond something," "to transgress a command (or law)": νόμον παρέρχεσθαι (Lys., 6, 52 [p. 69, 12, Thalheim[2], 1913]; Hes. Theog., 613; Dion. Hal. Ant. Rom., I, 58; Demosth. Or., 37, 37). d. "To come to," "to arrive at," and specifically "to come forward as a speaker" (e.g., παρελθὼν δὲ ἔλεξε τοιάδε, Thuc. II, 59 etc. and the rhetoricians), "to attain to power," "to enter into an inheritance." In the pap.[2] it means a. "to pass by," "to journey through," "to come together," of ships "to sail past" (P. Giess., I, 54, 11). It also means "to arrive," P. Gen., I, 72, 4: εὐθέως οὖν ἀρ[γ]ύριον ἑτοίμασον, ἵνα παρερχόμενος εὕρω πρ[ὸ] ἐμοῦ; b. of time, "to pass" (e.g., P. Magd., 25, 3: παρεληλυθότος τοῦ χρόν[ο]υ; also P. Fay., 20, 6: ἐκ τοῦ παρελθόντος χρόνου). c. παρέρχεσθαι ἐπὶ τὴν ἀρχήν, "to take up rule" (P. Fay., 20, 1, 12); "to fight a cause" (P. Oxy., I, 38, 11: π[α]ρῆλθον ἐπὶ τοῦ στρατηγοῦ, "I fought my case before the strategos"). In a special sense, Preisigke Sammelbuch, 4489, 1; 3; 8 "to be guilty of breaking a treaty"; BGU, I, 361, Col. III, "to circumvent" (ὁ ἀντίδικος παρέρχεται, the opponent seeks to circumvent the matter).

It is used in the Septuagint for 17 words. The sense is often local. Temporally, it denotes passing (Wis. 2:4, of the life of man); Sir. 42:19: τὰ παρεληλυθότα, "what is past." The immortality of the divine commandment is contrasted with human mortality: ψ 148:6: πρόσταγμα ἔθετο καὶ οὐ παρελεύσεται; Da. 6:12 Θ: τὸ δόγμα Μήδων καὶ Περσῶν οὐ παρελεύσεται. In relation to Mt. 5:18; 24:35 we may think not only of ψ 148:6 but also of the addition to Est. F. 2: περὶ τῶν λόγων τούτων, οὐδὲ γὰρ παρῆλθεν ἀπ' αὐτῶν λόγος. παρέρχεσθαι is particularly important in the sense of "to transgress." This is mainly transgression of the divine statutes: παρελθεῖν τὴν διαθήκην (θεοῦ) (Dt. 17:2), τὸν νόμον (θεοῦ) (Is. 24:5); also τὰς ἐντολὰς τοῦ βασιλέως (2 Ch. 8:15). A similar meaning is "to deviate" (e.g., 1 Macc. 2:22: παρελθεῖν τὴν λατρείαν, "to deviate from our religion"). Theologically, the term is most important in relation to theophanies (Gn. 32:31 [32]: παρῆλθεν τὸ εἶδος τοῦ θεοῦ;

---

[2] Cf. ad loc. Dausch Synpt., 430 f.

π α ρ έ ρ χ ο μ α ι. [1] In grammar ὁ παρεληλυθὼς χρόνος is the past.
[2] For examples v. Preisigke Wört., s.v.

Ex. 33:19 : ἐγὼ παρελεύσομαι πρότερός σου τῇ δόξῃ μου, v. 22 : ἡνίκα δ᾽ ἂν παρέλθῃ μου ἡ δόξα; 2 Βασ. 23:4 : κύριος παρῆλθεν ἐκ φέγγους; 3 Βασ. 19:11: ἰδοὺ παρελεύσεται κύριος). παρέρχεσθαι is also a technical term for the appearance of divine figures (Da. 12:1 LXX, where the appearance of Michael is introduced by the words : κατὰ τὴν χώραν ἐκείνην παρελεύσεται Μιχαὴλ ὁ ἄγγελος ὁ μέγας).

In the NT the brief observation in Lk. 18:37 that "Jesus of Nazareth passes by" might well be a mere topographical note with no deeper significance. [3] On the other hand, there might be more to it. It could denote an epiphany story, and in this case we should have to understand it as a sign of epiphany which reveals the Messianic power and majesty of Jesus in what seems to be an incidental moment. [4]

The word also serves to disclose human guilt. Jesus lashes as culpable both the inward attitude which in unrepentant complacency maintains that it has "left" no commandment "unfulfilled" (Lk. 15:29) and also the religious practice which concentrates on unimportant aspects of the Law but "overlooks" the essential things, the judgment and the love of God (Lk. 11:42).

In some passages the word takes on the more acute sense of passing by in the sense of passing away, or coming to an end, or perishing. Thus in 1 Pt. 4:3 it is used of a particular time in the life of Christians, the time before conversion, which is now definitively over (ὁ παρεληλυθὼς χρόνος). The word is used generally to denote the mortality of all created things (cf. Jm. 1:10). Often it has in this sense an eschatological note. Heaven and earth will pass away (Mt. 5:18; 24:35; Mk. 13:31; Lk. 16:17; 21:33). Even the Law, which maintains its validity to the end of this age, will fall victim to mortality at the conclusion of this age and will therefore lose its validity (Mt. 5:18). Only the words of Jesus are not subject to mortality (Mt. 24:35 and par.). [5] A testimony to early Christian expectation of the end is the saying which speaks of the coming of eschatological events in this generation, namely, that living in the days of Jesus (Mk. 13:30 and par.).

Paul uses the term only at 2 C. 5:17. It comes in the statement of jubilant Christian certainty : τὰ ἀρχαῖα παρῆλθεν, ἰδοὺ γέγονεν καινά.

παρεισέρχομαι.

παρεισέρχεσθαι is of great significance in Paul. [1] In R. 5:20 he says of the Law that it does not play a chief role in the plan of God [2] but has "entered in alongside." Since its effect is unfortunately to increase sin, it can have no decisive significance in the divine plan. [3] In Gl. 2:4 Paul calls the Judaizers παρείσακτοι ψευδάδελφοι, and he declares that they have dishonestly slipped into the churches founded by him to spy out the ground and to turn the churches against him.

περιέρχομαι.

1 Tm. 5:13 is a warning against the danger of idle younger widows going about from house to house and creating trouble in the congregation. In Hb. 11:37 περι-

---

[3] So K. L. Schmidt → I, 129, s.v. παράγω.

[4] So E. Lohmeyer, "En Hij Wilde Hen Voorbijgaan" in Nieuw Theologisch Tijdschrift, 23 (1934), 206-224. Cf. also H. Windisch on Mk. 6:48, ibid. 9 (1920), 298-308; G. A. v. d. Bergh, "De Geestelijk Geladen Christus," ibid., 15 (1926), 221-229.

[5] What Jesus says of His Word the Rabbis maintain of the Torah, namely, that it will last for ever. Cf. Str.-B., I, 244 ff., 961. A noteworthy saying in post-biblical literature is 1 Cl., 27, 5 : οὐδὲν μὴ παρέλθῃ τῶν δεδογματισμένων ὑπ᾽ αὐτοῦ.

π α ρ ε ι σ έ ρ χ ο μ α ι. [1] In Philo Op. Mund., 150 and Abr., 96 it has the weaker sense of "to creep in" (of anxieties).

[2] So also Ltzm. R., ad loc.

[3] Ltzm.: "It acted merely as a subsidiary factor."

ἔρχεσθαι ("to wander about") refers to the suffering of Christian heroes of faith. [1]

προσέρχομαι. [1]

"To come to," "to go to," "to approach," also in a hostile sense. Figur. προσῆλθεν ἐλπίς Eur. Or., 859 etc. "To apply oneself to something" (Diod. S., I, 95 : τοῖς νόμοις; Pluto Cato Minor, 12 [I, 764c]: πολιτείᾳ; Epict. Diss., IV, 11, 24 : φιλοσοφίᾳ; Philo Migr. Abr.: ἀρετῇ; v. also Philo Agric., 123 : προσέρχεσθαι πρός τινα, "to turn to someone"). Of income, "to come in"; sexually, "to go in" to a woman (Xenoph. Sym., IV, 38); generally, "to have dealings with someone" (Demosth. Or., 24, 176; cf. 22, 69).

In the pap. [2] it means "to be concerned about someone," "to take up a matter," esp. "to go to work," "to go to market," "to take up an enterprise," "to act as buyer or bidder," "to appear before a judge," "to take up an inheritance," "to proceed against someone," "to accrue to," of a field in the sphere of agriculture, "to be assigned" to another class (P. Tebt., I, 67, 93). In a pap. letter (a commendatory letter, 16 A.D., B. H. Olsson, Papyrusbriefe aus der frühesten Römerzeit [1925], 63, No. 16) we have προσέρχεσθαι in the sense of "to ask." [3] It also means "to appear" in P. Oxy., I, 40, 4. A special sense is "to appear before a tribunal" in P. Oxy., VIII, 1119, 8.

There are many instances of the cultic use in the sense of "to come before the deity": Dio C., 56, 9, 2 : τοῖς θεοῖς προσερχώμεθα; Porphyr. Abst., II, 47: προσέρχεσθαι τῷ θεῷ; P. Giess., 20, 24 : ἵνα ἀξίως σου καὶ τῶν θεῶν ἀόκνως προσέλθῃ. Philo, too, knows the word in the cultic sense : τῷ θεῷ προσέρχεσθαι (Deus Imm., 8; Sacr. AC, 12).

In the Septuagint it is used for 12 Heb. words. Its use is predominantly local. Like εἰσέρχεσθαι, προσέρχεσθαι γυναικί is also used in the sexual sense (Ex. 19:15 etc.). Hostile intent is denoted in 4 Macc. 4:6. There is a common cultic use for "to come before God," "to come to sacrifice" or "to worship." In Nu. 18:4 no one unqualified is to draw near in the cultic sense. In Jer. 7:16 it means to come before God in intercession. In Sir. 4:15 it means respectfully to approach wisdom, which in Sir. 24:19 (26) cries : προσέλθετε πρός μέ. It is dangerous to draw near to sin (Sir. 21:2). In ψ 90:10 the promise is given : οὐ προσελεύσεται πρὸς σὲ κακά. "To appear in court" is the sense in Dt. 25:1. Figur. it is also used for "to be occupied in a matter," Sir. 4:15 (16); 6:19, 26 (27).

It is common in Joseph. (Ant., 7, 164; 8, 213; 321; 390; 12, 19), always with the sense of "to come to" or "to come before" (8, 390; 12, 19 : προσελθεῖν τῷ βασιλεῖ).

In the NT it is mostly used by Mt. among the Synoptists. In the Johannine writings it occurs only once in the Gospel (Jn. 12:21). It is not found in Paul except at 1 Tm. 6:3 (in the sense of "to devote oneself to"). [4]

In Mt. the statements in which προσέρχεσθαι is used give us a vivid picture of the men surrounding Jesus. The circle of powers, men, groups and classes which came to Jesus with differing concerns is brought out with astonishing clarity. On the one side are the supraterrestrial forces, angels (Mt. 4:11) and the tempter (4:3). On the other side are men : a. those who believe and are loyal, e.g., His disciples (Mt. 5:1; 8:25 etc.; also Mk. 6:35; Lk. 8:24), and after the resurrection the women on their encounter with the risen Lord (Mt. 28:9), and above all Peter with his special question (Mt. 18:21); b. the crowd which seeks His help (Mt. 15:30), the sick (a leper in Mt. 8:2; the blind

---

περιέρχομαι. [1] Cf. Wnd. Hb., ad loc.

προσέρχομαι. [1] Cf. also → προσήλυτος.

[2] For details cf. Preisigke Wört., s.v.

[3] προσέρχεσθαι in the sense of "to ask" is a Latinism.

[4] א* has προσέχεται. Cf. on this pt. C. v. Tischendorf, NT Graece⁸, II (1872) 860 : atque sic olim R. Bentley coniecit. Cf. Dib. Past., ad loc. (52): "The reading προσέχεται is based on 1:4."

in 9:28; 21:14; the woman with an issue of blood in 9:20, cf. Lk. 8:44 : προσελθοῦσα ὄπισθεν; relatives of the sick in 8:5; 17:14); c. men with inner concerns such as the rich young ruler in 19:16, the ambitious mother of the sons of Zebedee in 20:20, the woman of Bethany who anointed Him in 26:7, the disciples of John in 9:14; d. a special group of opponents, e.g., the scribes, Pharisees, Sadducees, high-priests and elders, 8:19; cf. 15:1; 16:1; 19:3 etc.; Judas with his treachery, 26:49, cf. Mk. 14:45; those sent by the Sanhedrin to arrest Him, 26:50; the false witnesses at the hearing before the high-priest, 26:60; the soldiers at the cross, Lk. 23:36.

The word προσέρχεσθαι is seldom used of Jesus coming to men or to His disciples. Where it is, it is usually the first step in His Messianic action, e.g., in the healing of the sick in Mk. 1:31, the raising of the dead in Lk. 7:14, the expulsion of demons in Lk. 9:42 and the giving of the great commission in Mt. 28:18.

In Ac. προσέρχεσθαι denotes certain events of great importance in the early Christian mission. By delivering the Christian message to Cornelius Peter breaks through the Jewish prohibition: μὴ προσέρχεσθαι ἀλλοφύλῳ (Ac. 10:28). The command of the Spirit: πρόσελθε, impels Philip in his missionary service (8:29). Important events in the life of Paul, e.g., his pre-Christian period in 9:1; his imprisonment in 24:23 ℵ 614 pm, and his significant meeting with Aquila and Priscilla in 18:2, stand under the sign of προσέρχεσθαι.

In Hb. and 1 Pt. the word is used in a purely cultic sense. The offering of sacrifices is by προσερχόμενοι (Hb. 10:1). Christians have drawn near to God through faith (Hb. 11:6), through Christ (7:25). They have come to Mount Sion (12:18, 22). But they are also admonished to come to the throne of grace (4:16) or to Christ the High-Priest (10:22). In 1 Pt. 2:3 the Christian decision of faith is called a προσέρχεσθαι πρὸς τὸν κύριον.

συνέρχομαι.

In Ac. 15:38 συνέρχεσθαι εἰς τὸ ἔργον means "to journey with someone" on a common missionary enterprise. [1] 1 C. 11:17 ff. is theologically important. Here the word is a technical term for the coming together of the Christian congregation, especially to administer the Lord's Supper. Paul attacks scandals in Christian gatherings, e.g., divisions, the lack of order and discipline at the Lord's Supper. In 1 C. 14:23, 26 Paul takes up again the question of Christian gatherings and in his directions on spiritual gifts speaks of the task, position and legitimacy of speaking with tongues. [2]

· Schneider

συνέρχομαι. Bl.-Debr.[6] § 202.

[1] Cf. Tob. 5:10 (ℵ), 21; in Tob. 12:1 ὁ συνελθών is the companion on a journey. In Prv. 5:20 and Wis. 7:2 συνέρχεσθαι is an expression for sexual intercourse. In the pap. the word is very common (esp. in marriage contracts) for "to marry" (mostly in the form συνέρχεσθαι πρὸς γάμον); v. the examples in Preisigke Wört., s.v. συνέρχομαι. In 1 C. 7, 5 ℵ pm lat sy συνέρχεσθαι ἐπὶ τὸ αὐτὸ relates to sexual intercourse in marriage. In Mt. 1:18 the phrase πρὶν ἢ συνελθεῖν αὐτούς (Mary and Joseph) has in view the establishment of the marriage relationship.

[2] Ign. speaks of the proper manner of Christian assembly in his Eph., 20, 2. For him the decisive point is συνέρχεσθαι ἐν μιᾷ πίστει.

ἐρωτάω, ἐπερωτάω, ἐπερώτημα	(→ αἰτέω, I, 191; δέομαι, 40; εὔχομαι).

ἐρωτάω.

1. As in secular Gk., ἐρωτάω in the NT first means "to ask," "to enquire," "to seek information." Cf. Lk. 22:68 : ἐὰν δὲ ἐρωτήσω, οὐ μὴ ἀποκριθῆτε. Jesus says to the rich young ruler : τί με ἐρωτᾷς περὶ τοῦ ἀγαθοῦ (Mt. 19:17). Jesus Himself asks His disciples concerning the number of loaves available (Mk. 8:5) and concerning men's views of Him (Mt. 16:13). To the cunning question of His opponents concerning His ἐξουσία (→ 569) He replies with the crushing counter-question — ἐρωτήσω ὑμᾶς κἀγὼ λόγον ἕνα — as to the ἐξουσία of John the Baptist. As though they were ready to be convinced by the words of Jesus Himself and were not seeking ways and means to destroy Him, they seek an explanation ; but His counter-question [1] forces them to give an evasive answer and thus to admit that His claim is no more likely to convince them than that of the Baptist had done (Mt. 21:24; Lk. 20:3). The disciples ask Jesus the meaning of His parables (Mk. 4:10). They also ask Him when the kingdom of God will be set up (Ac. 1:6; cf. also Lk. 9:45). In all these passages, however, → ἐπερωτάω might be used as well ; the Syn. parallels and the textual variants show that the simple and compound forms are used in much the same way.

There is a significant theological usage in John, in whom almost half of the occurrences are found. In the Parting Discourses the question of asking takes on particular importance in the relations between Jesus and His disciples. According to Jn. 16:23 part of the future salvation is that the disciples will not need to ask Him anything further. [2] In a theology in which knowledge and perception are so central, asking can only imply imperfection. The only way to overcome this is by ultimate fellowship with Christ at the deepest level. Thus Jn. 16:30 is not said to glorify Jesus as the One who knows the hearts and who therefore knows the questions of His people even before they are uttered (in spite of Jn. 2:25). [3] It refers to the insight into the meaning of His way of suffering which is newly given to the disciples in a deepened fellowship of knowledge and understanding with their Lord which does not need to ask any more questions. We have here another instance of the present of salvation standing immediately alongside the future, as so often in Jn. (cf. 16:23a). Asking is, of course, the way to attain to full fellowship with the Son and the Father. The necessity of this way is emphasised (Jn. 16:5). But it is to lead to a goal beyond itself. In the light of all this, it is perhaps no accident that ἐρωτάω is almost never used of the disciples in Jn. outside the Parting Discourses (the exception is Jn. 9:2), whereas it is frequently used of the probing, doubting, contentious questions of the Jewish opponents.

ἐ ρ ω τ ά ω. Cr. Kö., 452; Pr.-Bauer, 485 f.; R. Helbing, *Die Kasussyntax d. Verba bei d. LXX* (1928), 40 f.; Bl.-Debr.⁶ § 392, 1c; Bau. Jn. on 16:23. Def.: Philo Rer. Div. Her., 18; Det. Pot. Ins., 57 f.

[1] Cf. also the counter-question in Rabb. literature, Str.-B., I, 861 f.

[2] Against the sense of "to request" we may refer not merely to what precedes but also to the fact that in what follows, esp. in v. 24a, there is not the slightest reference to v. 23a, whereas "to ask" fits v. 25 and v. 29 f. very well. The opposite view is taken by B. Weiss (Meyer *Komm.*⁶ [1880]), *ad loc.; Das Johannesevangelium* (1912), 296.

[3] So Zn. Jn., *ad loc.*

The LXX knows ἐρωτάω generally only as "to ask" (→ infra). It often denotes oracular questions put to God, as frequently attested for secular Gk. on inscriptions (Inscr. Magn., 17, 12 f.: πέμ[πονται εἰς Δελ]φοὺς ἐρωτήσοντες περὶ ..., Ditt. Syll.³, III, 1163, 1165: an oracular tablet of Dodona). Cf. also Jos. Ant., 6, 328: τὸν θεὸν διὰ τῶν προφητῶν ἐρωτᾷ περὶ τῆς μάχης καὶ τοῦ περὶ ταύτην ἐσομένου τέλους προειπεῖν. But it is also used for ordinary asking in Ant., 6, 298: ἐρωτήσας γὰρ αὐτούς, τίς ἐστι Δαυίδης ... Cf. also Philo → 685, Bibl., ἐρωτάω.

2. "To request," "to demand," of any kind of request. Outside the Gospels this is the predominant meaning, the only exception being Ac. 1:6. It can denote both the request of the disciples to Jesus (Mt. 15:23; Lk. 4:38) and that of the Jews to Pilate (Jn. 19:31). Lk. uses it especially for invitation to a meal (Lk. 7:36; 11:37; cf. also Ac. 10:48: ἠρώτησαν αὐτὸν ἐπιμεῖναι; cf. also Ac. 18:20). Like δέομαι (→ 40), which is in many respects parallel, ἐρωτῶ σε can also have the weakened sense of "please" (Lk. 14:18 f.). In distinction from αἰτέω (→ I, 191 ff.), which often suggests a claim or passion (→ προσεύχομαι), ἐρωτάω denotes a genuine request which is humble or courteous.

John uses the term especially for requests made to God and therefore with the sense of "to pray." [4] But in this respect we should note a distinctive nuance, for the word is used almost exclusively of the prayer of Jesus, the one exception being 1 Jn.5:16. Jesus alone has such inward fellowship with the Father that the word can be used both for the disciples' requests to Him (e.g., Jn. 4:31) and for His own petitionary or intercessory prayer to the Father (so also Jn. 16:26 in spite of 23a and 30, → 685). [5]

It is arguable whether the use of ἐρωτάω for "to pray" is a Semitism. [6] It is true that the LXX consistently distinguishes between "to ask" and "to pray" by using ἐρωτάω for the one and αἰτέω for the other in its translation of שׁאל. [7] Yet this does not prevent Semitic influences in the period after the rise of the LXX. Indeed, the LXX itself moves towards the sense of "to request" where the Heb. original is שָׁאַל לְשָׁלוֹם. For the distinctive feature of the term is that it hovers between "to ask" and "to request," as Greeks, too, may see from the context (e.g., 2 Βασ. 8:10). In 'Ιερ. 44:17 ἐρωτᾶν might mean "to request." Cf. also Lk. 14:32; [8] Test. Jud. 9:7; 1 Βασ. 30:21 AB. There are several instances [9] of this use in secular Gk. in the pre-Christian period, and not merely in Egypt (Ditt. Syll.³, 705, 56; 741, 5). The transition from "to ask" to "to request" is particularly easy in the cultic sphere, since a question put to the deity is almost aways bound up with sacrifice which is supposed to carry with it a gracious answer. The priest often reads the answer in the sacrificial animal. Jos. Ant., 5, 42: ἐπὶ στόμα πεσὼν ἠρώτα τὸν θεόν; 7, 164: ἠρώτα φράσαι τὴν αἰτίαν αὐτῷ. The rhetorician Hermogenes (b. c. 160 A.D. in Tarsus) knows ἐρωτάω in the sense of "to request," but rejects it as linguistically false, De Methodo Gravitatis, 3 (ed. H. Rabe [1913], 415 f.). [10]

Constr. ἐρωτάω τινά. The object of the question or request can be in the acc., Mt. 21:24 and par.: λόγον ἕνα; Mk. 4:10: τὰς παραβολάς; Jn. 16:23: οὐδέν; Lk. 14:32: τὰ πρὸς εἰρήνην. In verbal form, the obj. is expressed in sense 1. by an in-

---

[4] On prayer in the NT and synonyms, → εὔχομαι.

[5] → I, 192.

[6] Cf. Cr.-Kö., 452; Deissmann B, 45; NB, 23 f.; LO, 134, 147 f., 160. There is the rather remoter possibility of a Latinism, since rogare can mean both "to ask" and "to request" [Debrunner].

[7] Cf. Deissmann B, 45.

[8] Cf. Kl. Lk., ad loc.

[9] Pr.-Bauer, s.v. No. 2.

[10] Cf. E. A. Sophocles, Greek Lexicon of the Roman and Byzantine Periods (1914), s.v.

direct question in Jn. 9:15 : πῶς ἀνέβλεψεν; Jn. 18:21: τί ἐλάλησα αὐτοῖς (though there usually follows a direct question), and in sense 2. by the infin. (acc. c. infin. with εἰς) or sentences with ἵνα or ὅπως : Jn. 4:40 : ἠρώτων αὐτὸν μεῖναι παρ' αὐτοῖς; 2 Th. 2:1 f.: ἐρωτῶμεν δὲ ὑμᾶς ... εἰς τὸ μὴ ταχέως σαλευθῆναι ὑμᾶς; Lk. 7:36 : ἵνα φάγῃ μετ' αὐτοῦ; cf. Lk. 11:37. περί denotes the direction in which the question or request (or intercession) lies.

ἐπερωτάω.

"To ask," "to question," "to enquire," "to put a question." This is a favourite word of Mk., not usually followed by the other Synoptists. [1] In the first instance it means the same as → ἐρωτάω, with which it is frequently interchanged in the Syn. parallels and the MSS. Sometimes it seems to suggest a more pressing question (Jn. 18:7). It is used for judicial examination (Mk. 14:60 f. etc.), as also for investigation or counter-question (Mk. 15:44; Ac. 23:34). [2] A special use is for the request for a decision in a disputed issue. [3] Thus ἐπερωτάω is the standing expression for the probing and cunning questions of the Pharisees and Sadducees (Mk. 10:2; 12:18 and par.; 12:28 and par.; 12:34 and par.; Lk. 17:20; 20:21). Jesus, too, gives His opponents questions to examine and to decide (Lk. 6:9; Mt. 22:41; Mk. 11:29, par. ἐρωτάω). This sense of the term makes it possible that the decision was not sought in the form of a question but by a statement which expounded the point at issue (Mk. 9:11, 28, though cf. the par.). In face of this usage it may be asked whether the καὶ ἀκούοντα αὐτῶν καὶ ἐπερωτῶντα αὐτούς of Lk. 2:46 denotes, not so much the questioning curiosity of the boy, but rather His successful disputing. V. 47 would fit in well with the latter view. If it is correct, Jesus already commences in His boyhood the conflict in which His opponents will finally have to surrender : οὐκέτι γὰρ ἐτόλμων ἐπερωτᾶν αὐτὸν οὐδέν (Lk. 20:40). In Mt. 16:1 ἐπερωτάω seems to have the meaning "to request." It is to be noted, however, that this is not a true request. It is a demand rather along the lines of the cunning questions of the Pharisees (πειράζοντες).

Paul uses the term, though not very frequently. Wives are to ask their husbands at home, i.e., to be taught by them, if they want to know anything (1 C. 14:35). The other Pauline passage : ἐμφανὴς ἐγενόμην τοῖς ἐμὲ μὴ ἐπερωτῶσιν (R. 10:20), a quotation from Is. (65:1), brings out a new aspect of ἐπερωτάω, since the failure of the prophets or priests to ask of God is here a general indication of an unconverted life. In Paul the original meaning of שׁאל is weakened, and we have to translate : "Who do not ask after me" (cf. 'Ιερ. 37:14 : πάντες οἱ φίλοι σου ἐπελάθοντό σου, οὐ μὴ ἐπερωτήσουσιν).

The constr. is like ἐρωτάω 1., the infin. being used only at Mt. 16:1. The word is found in secular Gk. from the time of Hdt. [4] In Gk. records it becomes a technical diplomatic term from the last third of the 2nd cent. A.D. : ἐπερωτηθεὶς ὡμολόγησα is "to accept the terms of a treaty," "to ratify." [5] The LXX uses the term in the normal

---

ἐ π ε ρ ω τ ά ω. Cr.-Kö., 453; Pr.-Bauer, 442 f.; Moult.-Mill., 231.
[1] Cf. Mk. 7:5, 17; 8:29; 9:28; 10, 2, 17; 12:28; 13:3; 14:60 f., 15:4, with corresponding par.
[2] Cf. Gn. 38:21 LXX.
[3] Cf. on this pt. the Epicurean sentence (Wiener Studien, 10 [1888], 197, 71): πρὸς πάσας τὰς ἐπιθυμίας προσακτέον τὸ ἐπερώτημα τοῦτο· τί μοι γενήσεται ἂν τελεσθῇ τὸ κατὰ τὴν ἐπιθυμίαν ἐπιζητούμενον, καὶ τί ἐὰν μὴ τελεσθῇ; [Peterson].
[4] Liddell-Scott, 618.
[5] For details cf. Preisigke Wört., 537 f.; Pauly-W., 2nd Series, III, 2 (1929), s.v. stipulatio; Corpus Juris Civilis, ed. P. Krüger, T. Mommsen etc., II⁹ (1915), 105 (Cod. Justinianus, II, 12, 27, 2); III⁴ (1912), 469 (Novellae, 97 prooem).

way, esp. for questions put to God (→ 686) or His prophets. Cf. Inscr. Magn., 17, 26 and 36; Ditt. Syll.³, III, 1160. Jos. Ant., 9, 34 : ἐπηρώτων τὸ μέλλον ἐπὶ τῆς στρατιᾶς, though also generally ἐπηρώτα τὴν γνώμην ἑκάστου, Bell., 1, 540; ἕκαστον αὐτῶν λόγους ἐπηρώτα φυσικούς, Ant., 12, 99; cf. Mk. 11:29.

† ἐπερώτημα.

From the time of Hdt. this has been used for "question." From the 2nd century it took on the same diplomatic sense as → ἐπερωτάω. ¹ In the Gk. OT it is found only ² at Da. Θ 4:14, where it seems fairly obviously to be trying to give to the Aram. שְׁאֵלְתָּא ("matter," "affair") ³ the sense of "judgment" or "decision." ⁴ It is not found in Jos., though cf. Ant., 3, 32 (Schlatter). Herm. m., 11, 2 has the word in the sense of "question."

The usage outside the NT throws little light on the one place in the NT where ἐπερώτημα occurs, namely, 1 Pt. 3:21: ... βάπτισμα (→ I, 545), οὐ σαρκὸς ἀπόθεσις ῥύπου ἀλλὰ συνειδήσεως ἀγαθῆς ἐπερώτημα εἰς θεόν. At a first glance it seems likely that in the antitheses used to define baptism, ἀπόθεσις and ῥύπου on the one side correspond to ἐπερώτημα and ἀγαθῆς on the other. Since, however, the putting away of filth and the establishment of good point in the same direction, the true distinction surely lies in σαρκός and συνειδήσεως. It is thus best to keep the parallelism and in accordance with the obj. gen. συνειδήσεως ἀγαθῆς to make σαρκός dependent on ῥύπου and the whole on ἀπόθεσις. The point of the genitives is then to indicate the very different spheres in which the two processes operate. To determine the sense of ἐπερώτημα we do best to turn to its use in the LXX, where it very commonly has the sense of an oracular question addressed to God (cf. εἰς θεόν). ⁵ It is true that the sense of "to pray" is not found in the LXX, ⁶ but a movement in this direction is materially natural and is also fostered by the double sense of ἐρωτάω. In Mt. 16:1 ἐπερωτάω is already well on the way to the sense of "to request." Hence we may translate 1 Pt. 3:21: "Not the putting away of outward filth, but prayer to God for a good conscience." ⁷

In view of v. 21 we should expect the ἀλλά to be followed by a cleansing in the spiritual sense. Thus the request for a good conscience (→ συνείδησις) is to be construed as a prayer for the remission of sins. We cannot be sure that there is here any thought of a specific liturgical prayer. ⁸ Remission of sins is closely related to baptism from the very outset (Mk. 1:4 and par.; Ac. 2:38). Perhaps the author avoided an expression like "the cleansing of the heart from sins" in order to avoid a magical conception of the operation of baptism and in order to stress the fact that the new purity is a gift of God's grace. There is plenty of scope for the technical associations of ἐπερώτημα (→ supra) within this line of thought. ⁹ The baptised enter into a covenant

---

ἐπερώτημα. Cr.-Kö., 454 f.; Pr.-Bauer, 443; Moult.-Mill., 231 f.; Wnd. Pt., Exc. on 1 Pt. 3:21; Kn. Pt., on 1 Pt. 3:21; Wbg. Pt. on 1 Pt. 3:21.

¹ F. Preisigke, Griech. Urkunden des Ägypt. Mus. zu Cairo (Schriften d. Wiss. Ges. in Strassburg, 8 [1911]) No. 1, 16.

² In Sir. 36:3 ἐπερώτημα occurs in Cod. א as a variant for ἐρώτημα and in the same sense.

³ Ges.-Buhl, s.v.

⁴ For later examples of this sense, cf. Moult.-Mill., s.v. and Cr.-Kö., s.v.

⁵ The LXX often has ἐν or διά c. gen. in such cases. Perhaps εἰς is used in 1 Pt. 3:21 because of the shift of meaning in the direction of "prayer."

⁶ As opposed to Kn. Pt., ad loc., who not very cogently adduces ψ 136:3 א (corr) ART.

⁷ So Kn. Pt. and Wnd. Pt., ad loc.; J. Felten, Die 2 Briefe des hl. Petrus u. d. Judasbrief (1929), 112 f. Vrede Kath. Br., ad loc.: Gelöbnis ("vow").

⁸ So, e.g., Wnd. Pt., ad loc.; cf. also Kn. Pt., ad loc.

⁹ Cf. also Cr.-Kö., 455.

with God on the basis of the fact that God "ratifies" the forgiveness of their sins. The figure breaks down, of course, because we do not have here two equal covenant-partners. It has also to be considered that if the term implies a question addressed to God, or a stipulation on which assurance is requested, God is the One who is asked, and this modification of the concept links up with the thought of prayerful questioning which is prominent in the LXX. A comparison suggests itself with the Pauline concept of → δικαιοῦν, which elucidates very much the same situation by means of another legal metaphor.

Greeven

| ἐσθίω | (→ τρώγω).

A. ἐσθίω outside the NT.

1. "To eat and drink," a stock expression of antiquity for the basic functions of natural human self-preservation, Hom. Od., 2, 305; 21, 69; Gn. 24:54; Ju. 19:4; Zech. 7:6 etc.; the distress of having no bread to eat, Dt. 29:6 (5); BGU, III, 949, 6 ff.: σπούδασον, ... δελφάκιον ἀποστῖλαι ἡμῖ[ν ...] ... ἵνα εὕρω[μεν ...] φαγεῖν. The righteous, and esp. scribes, do not need to concern themselves about eating and drinking, M. Ex., 16, 4. [1] It is a rule of life that the sick need to eat, jBer. 9d. [2] Work gives a right to eat and indolence forfeits it, Hom. Od., 19, 27 f.: οὐ γὰρ ἀεργὸν ἀνέξομαι, ὅς κεν ἐμῆς γε χοίνικος ἅπτηται, καὶ τηλόθεν εἰληλουθώς; Hes. Op., 311: ἔργον δ' οὐδὲν ὄνειδος, ἀεργίη δέ τ' ὄνειδος; *ibid.*, 398; Xenoph. Mem., II, 1, 28; Gn. 3:19; Prv. 29:45 (31:27); Sir. 30:26 f. [3] To give the hungry to eat is a work of benevolence in Is. 58:7; Ez. 18:7; Tob. 4:16 (17); Slav. En. 9 : "To give bread to the hungry." ἄρτον ἐσθίειν (a semitism) "to take nourishment," "to have a meal," Heb. אָכַל לֶחֶם, Gn. 37:25; Ex. 2:20; Jer. 41:1; 52:33 etc. (→ I, 477), Aram. אֲכַל לַחְמָא, e.g., bBer., 42b : "We will go and have a meal there and there." [4] For eating and drinking as a mark of this-worldly enjoyment, of passing satisfaction, of licence and pleasure-seeking, cf. the Gilgamesh epic, Ancient Babylonian Recension, Fr. C, II, 6 ff.: [5] "Fill thy body, enjoy thyself day and night ; Make a feast by day, leap and dance both day and night." Cf. also the burial inscr. of Sardanapalos (Suid., *s.v.* Σαρδανάπαλος): ἔσθιε πῖνε ὄχευε, ὡς τά γε ἄλλα οὐδὲ τούτου ἐστὶν ἄξια; Epigr. Graec., 344, 3 : γνῶθι τέλος βιότου· διὸ παῖζε τρυφῶν ἐπὶ κόσμῳ; 3 Βασ. 4:20 Α; Is. 22:13; Qoh. 8:15; Tob. 7:10; Sir. 11:19; Wis. 2:6 f.: δεῦτε οὖν καὶ ἀπολαύσωμεν τῶν ὄντων ἀγαθῶν ..., οἴνου πολυτελοῦς ... πλησθῶμεν; Philo Leg. All., II, 29 : ἐὰν ὁ λόγος ἰσχύσῃ ἀνακαθᾶραι τὸ πάθος, οὔτε πίνοντες μεθυσκόμεθα οὔτε ἐσθίοντες ἐξυβρίζομεν διὰ κόρον, ἀλλὰ δίχα τοῦ ληρεῖν νηφάλια σιτούμεθα; Det. Pot. Ins., 113 : ἄνθρωπος ἐσθίων μὲν ἢ πίνων ἀεί, ἐμπιπλάμενος μηδέποτε ἢ ταῖς μετὰ γαστέρα χρώμενος ἡδοναῖς ἐπαλλήλοις; Gn. r., on 11:2 : "Everywhere where thou findest eating and drinking, Satan brought accusation"; [6] bTaan., 11a: "A man should not say, 'I will go and eat and drink in my house, and peace be on thee, my soul.' " [7] To eat with someone, to hold

---

ἐ σ θ ί ω. Bl.-Debr.⁶ § 101; Pr.-Bauer, 486 ff.; Liddell-Scott, 696; Moult.-Mill., 256; Preisigke Wört., I, 602 f.; J. Haussleiter, Ἐσθίω, τρώγω, *Archiv f. lat. Lexikographie*, 9 (1896), 300 ff.; D. Schenkel, *Bibel-Lexikon,* IV (1872), 86 ff.; HW, I, 940 ff.; RE³, XII, 76 ff.; DCG, I, 504.

[1] Str.-B., I, 421, 435.
[2] *Ibid.,* II, 10.
[3] For further Jewish materials, cf. Dib. Th., 47; Str.-B., III, 641 f.; cf. 379 ff.
[4] Cf. Str.-B., I, 704; II, 6 f.; Dalman WJ, I, 92.
[5] AOT, 194.
[6] Str.-B., I, 143.
[7] *Ibid.,* II, 190. Cf. also Wettstein on 1 C. 15:32; E. Maass, *Orpheus* (1895), 209 ff.; Kl. Lk., 135 f.; Schl. Lk., 317.

table-fellowship, denotes close association, e.g., 1 Βασ. 9:19; jPea, 21b: "He was accustomed to eat with him every day."[8]

2. There are cultic and ritual regulations concerning eating, esp. in the OT and the Jewish world. They apply, e.g., to the portion of the priests at sacrifices, Lv. 2:3; 5:13; 6:9 ff., 7:9, 29 ff.; 10:12 f., etc. to clean and unclean meats, Lv. 11; Dt. 14:3 ff.; to the eating of flesh sacrificed to idols, AZ, 2, 3; T. Chul., 2, 20; to washing the hands before eating, Ber., 8, 2 ff.; Chag., 2, 5 f.; Ed., 3, 2; Jad., 1, 1 ff.; 2, 3; to table fellowship which makes unclean, bSanh., 104a; bBer., 43b etc.;[9] cf. Da. 1:8, 12; 2 Macc. 5:27. Refraining from eating and drinking as a form of asceticism,[10] or fasting (→ βρῶμα, I, 643, n. 6; → γεύομαι, I, 675; → νηστεύω), has a place in OT and Jewish religion, e.g., Ex. 34:28; Dt. 9:9; Zech. 7:5 f.; Jon. 3:7; Est. 4:16; Da. 10:3; 4 Esr. 10:4; S. Bar. 20:5; 21:1; Chul., 8, 1: "Honour to all who eat no flesh"; bBB, 60b; jAZ, 40a;[11] though cf. Mandaism, Lidz. Ginza, 18, 23 f.: "Fast the great fast which is not a fast from worldly eating and drinking;" 450, 10 ff.: "Men and women who fast a fast of iniquity ... who are hungry for bread and do not eat, who thirst for water and do not drink." Religious vegetarianism, which is widespread in religions of all ages, is in the days of the NT rarer in Judaism (cf. Jos. Vit., 11; 4 Esr. 9:24 ff.; 12:51; Test. R. 1:10; Test. Jud. 15:4)[12] than in the Gk. world, where it is found in Orphic religion, in Neo-Pythagoreanism, in Neo-Platonism and in the Oriental Mysteries,[13] e.g., Diog. L., VIII, 38 on the Neo-Pythagoreans: ἐσθίουσί τε λάχανά τε καὶ πίνουσιν ἐπὶ τούτοις ὕδωρ; Philo Vit. Cont., 37 on the Therapeutae: σιτοῦνται ... ἄρτον εὐτελῆ, καὶ ὄψον ἅλες, οὓς οἱ ἁβροδίαιτοι παραρτύουσιν ὑσσώπῳ, ποτὸν δὲ ὕδωρ ναματιαῖον αὐτοῖς ἐστιν· ἃς γὰρ ἡ φύσις ἐπέστησε τῷ θνητῷ γένει δεσποίνας, πεῖνάν τε καὶ δίψαν, ἀπομειλίσσονται, τῶν εἰς κολακείαν ἐπιφέροντες οὐδέν, ἀλλ' αὐτὰ τὰ χρήσιμα, ὧν ἄνευ ζῆν οὐκ ἔστι· διὰ τοῦτο ἐσθίουσι μέν, ὥστε μὴ πεινῆν, πίνουσι δέ, ὥστε μὴ διψῆν, πλησμονὴν ὡς ἐχθρόν τε καὶ ἐπίβουλον ψυχῆς τε καὶ σώματος ἐκτρεπόμενοι; from the Isis mysteries, Apul. Met., XI, 23 : decem continuis illis diebus cibarias voluptates cohercerem neque ullum animal essem et invinius essem, cf. 21; 28; 30. From ancient Egyptian religion (lament for a king), Diod. S., I, 72, 2 : τροφὴν δ' οὔτε τὴν ἀπὸ τῶν ἐμψύχων οὔτε τὴν ἀπὸ τοῦ πυρὸς προσεφέροντο, τοῦ τε οἴνου καὶ πάσης πολυτελείας ἀπείχοντο.

3. Eating and drinking are often linked with the vision of God, e.g., in the OT at Ex. 24:11; Gn. 3:5 f.; Ps. 34:9;[14] cf. also bBer., 17a : "In the future world there will be neither eating nor drinking ... The righteous will rather sit with crowns on their heads and feed on the radiance of the Godhead, for it is written 'They saw God and ate and drank' (Ex. 24:11)." The eating or drinking of deity, or of divine essence, which plays a role in the religion of many peoples,[15] is found in NT times in the cultic meals of the

---

[8] Cf. Schl. Lk., 265; Schl. Mt., 306.

[9] Cf. J. Benzinger, Hebräische Archäologie³ (1927), 395 ff.; RE³, XVI, 564 ff., XXIV, 382 ff.; Bousset-Gressm., 127; Jüd. Lex., V (1930), 539 ff.; Str.-B., I, 695 ff., 498 f., III, 377, 420 f., IV, 376 ff.

[10] Cf. H. Strathmann, Geschichte der frühchristlichen Askese, I (1914), passim.

[11] Str.-B., II, 767, cf. III, 307 f.; Schl. Mt., 373; Schl. Lk., 496; H. Strathmann, op. cit., 34 ff., 64 ff. etc. On fasting in Gk. religion and philosophy, ibid., 215 ff., 282 ff., 305 ff.; cf. → I, 643, n. 6.

[12] On vegetarianism among the Essenes cf. H. Strathmann, op. cit., 87; Bousset-Gressm., 465.

[13] Cf. H. Strathmann, op. cit., 215 ff.; 243 ff.; 254 ff.; 283 ff.; 305 ff.; 333 ff.; Zn. R. and Ltzm. R. on 14:1 ff.

[14] J. Jeremias, Der Gottesberg (1919), 18 f.; A. Jeremias, Das AT im Lichte des alten Orients⁴ (1930), 8 f., 418.

[15] Cf. A. E. Crawley, Art. "Eating the God" in ERE, V (1912), 136 ff.; W. Heitmüller, Taufe und Abendmahl bei Paulus (1903), 40 ff.; E. Reuterskiöld, Die Entstehung der Speisesakramente (1912); Chant de la Saussaye, I, 57, 64, 160, 223; II, 571, 617, 620, 633; RGG², III, 1854 ff.; G. van der Leeuw, Phänomenologie der Religion (1933), 339 f., 341 ff.

Mystery religions.[16] The mysteries of Dionysos Zagreus: Schol. on Cl. Al. Prot. (I, p. 318, 5, Stählin): ὠμὰ γὰρ ἤσθιον κρέα οἱ μυούμενοι Διονύσῳ, δεῖγμα τοῦτο τελούμενοι τοῦ σπαραγμοῦ, ὃν ὑπέστη Διόνυσος ὑπὸ τῶν Μαινάδων, cf. for the Thracian Dionysos cult Plut. Quaest. Rom., 112 (II, 291a): αἱ γὰρ ἔνοχοι τοῖς βακχικοῖς πάθεσι γυναῖκες εὐθὺς ἐπὶ τὸν κιττὸν φέρονται καὶ σπαράττουσι δραττόμεναι ταῖς χερσὶ καὶ διεσθίουσαι τοῖς στόμασιν, Paus., I, 31, 6.[17] For the Eleusinian mysteries, Cl. Al. Prot., II, 21, 2: τὸ σύνθημα 'Ελευσινίων μυστηρίων' ἐνήστευσα, ἔπιον τὸν κυκεῶνα, ἔλαβον ἐκ κίστης, ἐργασάμενος ἀπεθέμην εἰς κάλαθον καὶ ἐκ καλάθου εἰς κίστην, cf. also Arnobius Adversus Nationes, V, 26 (ed. A. Reifferscheid, 1875 in CSEL, IV). The Phrygian mysteries, the σύμβολα τῆς μύησεως ταύτης in Cl. Al. Prot., II, 15, 3 (v. Firm. Mat. Err. Prof. Rel., 18): ἐκ τυμπάνου ἔφαγον· ἐκ κυμβάλου ἔπιον· ἐκερνοφόρησα· ὑπὸ τὸν παστὸν ὑπέδυν, perhaps also the Abercius inscript., line 12 ff. (H. Hepding, Attis [1903], 85): πίστις ... παρέθηκε τροφὴν πάντῃ ἰχθὺν ἀπὸ πηγῆς πανμεγέθη καθαρόν, ὃν ἐδράξατο παρθένος ἁγνὴ καὶ τοῦτον ἐπέδωκε φίλοις ἔσθειν διὰ παντὸς οἶνον χρηστὸν ἔχουσα κέρασμα διδοῦσα μετ' ἄρτου. The initiate tells of his reception into the Isis mysteries in Apul. Met., XI, 24: exhinc festissimum celebravi natalem sacrorum et suaves epulae et faceta convivia. dies etiam tertius pari caerimoniarum ritu celebratus et jentaculum religiosum et teletae legitima consummatio. The Mithra mysteries, Just. Apol., I, 66, 4: ἄρτος καὶ ποτήριον ὕδατος τίθεται ἐν ταῖς τοῦ μυουμένου τελεταῖς μετ' ἐπιλόγων τινῶν, cf. Tert. Praescr. Haer., 40, 4: (Mithra) celebrat et panis oblationem, also the archaeological source material.[18] The Sabazius mysteries, a fresco in the praet. catacomb.[19] On the meaning of the action, cf. Ael. Arist. In Sarapin (I, 93 f. Dindorf): καὶ τοίνυν καὶ θυσιῶν μόνῳ τούτῳ θεῷ διαφερόντως κοινωνοῦσιν ἄνθρωποι τὴν ἀκριβῆ κοινωνίαν, καλοῦντές τε ἐφ' ἑστίαν καὶ προϊστάμενοι δαιτυμόνα αὐτὸν καὶ ἑστιάτορα and Servius Grammaticus Commentarius in Vergili Aen., I, 79 (p. 44, Thilo): 'Tu das epulis accumbere divum' hoc est, tu me deum facis; duplici enim ratione divinos honores meremur, dearum coniugio et convivio deorum.

4. Eating and drinking in fellowship with God belongs also to the Jewish expectation of the eschatological banquet of God;[20] for examples → δεῖπνον 35; also Lk. 14:15;[21] Ex. r., 25 on 16:4: "They will recline at table and eat in Gan Eden."[22] The food of the blessed is manna, S. Bar. 29:8: "At that time supplies of manna will again fall from above; and they will eat thereof in those years because they have lived through the end of the ages"; Sib. Fr., 3, 46 ff. (p. 232, ed. J. Geffcken [1902]): οἱ δὲ θεὸν τιμῶντες ἀληθινὸν ἀέναόν τε ζωὴν κληρονομοῦσι ... δαινύμενοι γλυκὺν ἄρτον ἀπ' οὐρανοῦ ἀστερόεντος; or the fruit of the tree of life, Eth. En. 25:5: "Its fruit will be life to the elect, and it will be planted for food in the sanctuary in the house of God, the King of eternity"; 4 Esr. 8:52; Vit. Ad., 28: "Lord, give me to eat of the tree of life ... At the time of the resurrection ... the fruit of the tree of life will be given to thee that thou mayest be immortal in eternity"; Test. L. 18:11: δώσει τοῖς ἁγίοις φαγεῖν ἐκ τοῦ ξύλου τῆς ζωῆς; but also the flesh of the primeval monsters Behemoth and Leviathan, Eth. En. 60:24; 4 Esr. 6:52; S. Bar. 29:4.[23]

---

[16] Cf. Mithr. Liturg., 100 ff., 213 ff.; O. Gruppe, Griechische Mythologie (1906), 1618 ff., 732 ff.; W. Heitmüller, op. cit., 41 ff.; Clemen, 184 ff.; F. Cumont, Die orientalischen Religionen im römischen Heidentum³ (1931), 56, 60, 63 f., 220, n. 43; Die Mysterien des Mithra³ (1923), 124, 146 f.; Haas, 15 (1930), Leipoldt, Fig. 18 f., 23, 46; H. Gressmann, Die orientalischen Religionen im hellenistisch-römischen Zeitalter (1930), 105 ff., 120 ff., 154; K. Völker, Mysterium u. Agape (1927), 212 ff.

[17] On this pt. v. E. Rohde, Psyche⁴, II (1907), 14 ff.; O. Gruppe, op. cit., 732 ff.

[18] Cumont, op. cit., 146 f. and Haas, op. cit.

[19] Cumont, op. cit., Plate I, 4 (on p. 60).

[20] As in the Sabazius cult, Cumont, loc. cit.

[21] Cf. Schl. Lk., 335 f.

[22] Str.-B., IV, 1148.

[23] For Rabb. par., v. Str.-B., IV, 1156 ff.; Bousset-Gressm., 285.

5. Figur. it means a. "to enjoy," Job 21:25 : οὐ φαγὼν οὐθὲν ἀγαθόν, "to partake of wisdom," Prv. 9:5 (→ I, 643 f.); Sir. 24:21: οἱ ἐσθίοντές με ἔτι πεινάσουσι καὶ οἱ πίνοντές με ἔτι διψήσουσιν. To eat as a spiritual function, Philo Leg. All., I, 97 (on Gn. 2:16): προτρέπει τὴν τοῦ ἀνθρώπου ψυχὴν μὴ ἀφ᾽ ἑνὸς ξύλου μηδ᾽ ἀπὸ μιᾶς ἀρετῆς ἀλλ᾽ ἀπὸ πασῶν τῶν ἀρετῶν ὠφελεῖσθαι· τὸ γὰρ φαγεῖν σύμβολόν ἐστι τροφῆς ψυχικῆς· τρέφεται δὲ ἡ ψυχὴ ἀναλήψει τῶν καλῶν καὶ πράξει τῶν κατορθωμάτων (for a further allegorical interpretation of the Gn. passage, cf. 98 ff.). Allegorising is also found in Qoh. r. on 2:24 : "Wherever there is mention of eating and drinking in this scroll (Qoh.), the Scripture speaks of the study of the Torah and good works." [24]

b. In the OT אָכַל (usually κατεσθίειν in the LXX) is used of the consuming of the sword (2 S. 2:26), of fire (Nu. 16:35; 26:10; Ps. 21:9), of heat (Gn. 31:40), of hunger and sickness (Ez. 7:15; Job 18:13), of the divine wrath (Amos 5:6; cf. Is. 30:27: ἡ ὀργὴ τοῦ θυμοῦ ὡς πῦρ ἔδεται; 26:11: ζῆλος λήψεται λαὸν ἀπαίδευτον καὶ νῦν πῦρ τοὺς ὑπεναντίους ἔδεται; cf. also in Gk. literature Hom. Il., 23, 182 : τοὺς ἅμα σοὶ πάντας πῦρ ἐσθίει; Aesch. Fr., 253 (TGF, 81): φαγέδαιν᾽ ἀεί μου σάρκας ἐσθίει ποδός.

c. In the prophetic warnings of the OT, and also in the laments of the righteous, we have such typical meanings [25] as "to destroy" (of the destruction of the righteous by the ungodly), Ἰερ. 37:16 AB (א: ἐχθροί); ψ 13:4 = 52:4 : τὸν λαόν μου; 26:2 : τὰς σάρκας μου; Prv. 24:37 (30:14): τοὺς ταπεινούς etc., "to eat upon, or at the cost of," Hos. 4:8 : ἁμαρτίας λαοῦ μου; 10:13 : καρπὸν ψευδῆ (the Mas. has the sense of "to bear the consequences of"); 11:6 : ἐκ τῶν διαβουλίων αὐτῶν (here again the Mas. has a different sense, i.e., "the sword shall consume, supra); "to bear the consequences of," Prv. 1:31: τῆς ἑαυτῶν ὁδοῦ τοὺς καρπούς; Is. 3:10 : τὰ γενήματα τῶν ἔργων αὐτῶν etc.

B. ἐσθίω in the NT.

1. Eating is a necessary means of sustaining life (→ ψυχή), Mt. 6:25 and par. One of the most pressing concerns of man is thus to have something to eat, cf. also Mk. 6:36 ff. and par. One of the troubles of Jesus and the disciples in their busy ministry is that they do not have time to eat, Mk. 3:20; 6:31 (on φαγεῖν ἄρτον in Mk. 3:20 etc. → 689 and I, 477). "Eating and drinking" (→ πίνω) is a formal expression for meeting the most vital needs, for satisfying hunger and thirst (on this established combination → 226), Mt. 6:31 and par.; 25:35 ff.; 1 C. 11:22. It has the same meaning as "to take a meal" in Lk. 17:8; 1 C. 11:21 f. That someone raised from the dead is really alive is shown by the fact that he eats, Mk. 5:43 and par.; Lk. 24:41 ff. [26] In accordance with the common rule that the worker is worth his meat, that he should receive sustenance as his wages (Mt. 10:10 and par.; 2 Th. 3:12; Did., 12, 3), that the vineyard should support those who work in it and the flock those who keep it (1 C. 9:7), the wandering missionaries of early Christianity can claim support from the places where they labour, Mt. 10:8 ff. and par.; 1 C. 9:4 : ἐξουσίαν φαγεῖν καὶ πεῖν. Conversely, Christians who devote themselves to indolent enthusiasm are brought under the principle of self-support (→ 689), which Paul elevates to an ethical imperative in 2 Th. 3:10 : εἴ τις οὐ θέλει ἐργάζεσθαι, μηδὲ ἐσθιέτω. To give the hungry to eat is one of the most elementary duties of love for whose fulfilment the Judge will look at the last judgment, Mt. 25:34 ff. The self-evident duty of slaves to prepare a meal for their

---

[24] Str.-B., II, 485.
[25] The concluding lines of this paragraph are by G. Bertram.
[26] Ign. Tr., 9, 1: eating and drinking are a sign of the full humanity of Jesus.

masters on return from their daily work before they themselves can think of eating or drinking [27] is a similitude of the non-selfseeking service which the disciple must render to God, Lk. 17:7 ff. Eating, drinking etc. are a mark of festive joy, Lk. 15:23, but also of a sensual life which is wasted on earthly enjoyment and which is thus doomed to perish, Lk. 12:19; 17:27 f. and par.; Mt. 24:49 and par.; 1 C. 15:32 (Is. 22:13); Jesus Himself, as One who eats and drinks, a gluttonous man and a winebibber, seems to the Jews to be far too worldly for a man of God (Mt. 11:19 and par.). To eat with someone (ἐσθίειν μετά τινος, συνεσθίειν etc.) (to drink) is an indication of close acquaintance and fellowship (Mk. 14:18; Ac. 10:41; Ign. Sm., 3, 3; though cf. Lk. 13:26). The forbidding of συνεσθίειν expresses repudiation of fellowship, 1 C. 5:11.

2. In relation to religion, the natural function of eating is mostly used in the NT, apart from the references to the eating of manna in Jn. 6:31, 49, 58; 1 C. 10:3, in connection with the historical rootage of Jesus and of early Christianity in Judaism, which enforces the OT customs and ritual ordinances regarding eating with casuistical severity. At this point, though the Gospel does not set aside the historical authority of the OT, it transcends the Law. Paul, seeking scriptural support for NT concepts, appeals to the historical precedent of the priests partaking of the sacrifices in 1 C. 9:13, cf. 10:18. Jesus quotes David who ate the showbread in defiance of the sacred privileges of the priests, and He sees here a model for the transgression of the Sabbath by the companions of the Messiah, the disciples, Mk. 2:26 and par. He manifests a similar freedom in relation to the ritual cleansings of the Jews, which amongst other things do not allow eating with unwashed hands, Mk. 7:1 ff.; Mt. 15:1 f., 20. Peter takes a different line in Ac. 10:14 : οὐδέποτε ἔφαγον πᾶν → κοινὸν καὶ → ἀκάθαρτον. But Jesus, in spite of the criticisms of the rabbis, is not afraid to hold table-fellowship which carries with it the risk of defilement (Mk. 2:16 and par.; Lk. 15:2). In the course of the Gentile mission early Christianity, too, learns to overcome Jewish prejudice, Ac. 11:3; Gl. 2:12. In the difficult Hb. 13:10 : ἔχομεν → θυσιαστήριον ἐξ οὗ φαγεῖν οὐκ ἔχουσιν ἐξουσίαν οἱ τῇ → σκηνῇ → λατρεύοντες, it is at least clear that the priests of the OT order of atonement have lost their ancient right to partake of the sacrifices in the NT order ; probably all kinds of sacrificial meals are declared to be incompatible with the NT order. [28] We find abstinence from eating and drinking, or fasting (νηστεύω), as a ritual Jewish custom on the occasion of vows (Ac. 23:12, cf. v. 14 [29] → I, 676), as an ascetic practice which characterises John the Baptist (Mt. 11:18 and par.; cf. Mk. 1:6 and par.; Lk. 1:15), [30] and as an expression of Paul's penitence and sorrow after the Damascus experience, Ac. 9:9. φαγεῖν τὸ → πάσχα is used for "to eat the Paschal lamb (or the passover)" [31] in Mk. 14:12, 14 and par.; Lk. 22:15; Jn. 18:28.

The eating of idol-meats (→ εἰδωλόθυτον, 378 f.) became a problem of early Christian conduct in Corinth (1 C. 8:10) quite independently of the regulations of

[27] Cf. on this pt. Str.-B., II, 235; IV, 713.

[28] Cf. Rgg. Hb. ², ³, 273, 441 f.; Wnd. Hb., 118 f.

[29] Cf. Fr. from Ev. Hebr. (Hier. De Viris Illustribus, 2): *iuraverat ... Jacobus se non comesurum panem ..., donec videret eum resurgentem a dormientibus.*

[30] Cf. Kl. Mk., 8; Hck. Mk., 12.

[31] As in 2 Ἐσδρ. 6:21; 2 Ch. 30:18. Cf. E. Schürer, Über φαγεῖν τὸ πάσχα (1883); G. Dalman, *Jesus-Jeschua* (1922), 80 ff.; Str.-B., II, 837 ff.; Schl. Mt., 739; Bau. J.³, 214, as against Zn. Einl., II³ (1907), 523, 534 ff.; Zn. J. ⁵, ⁶, 632.

OT Law and Jewish tradition (as distinct from Rev. 2:14, 20; 1 C. 10:7). [32] In the conflict between the Gnostics in the congregation who thought themselves above any doubts as to participation in sacrifices, and the "weak" who, as in their heathen past, regarded this eating as a cultic act and therefore found it difficult to eat with a good conscience, Paul decides in 1 C. 8:1, 7 ff. that fellowship with God does not depend on eating or not eating, but that to assert Gnostic freedom to the violation of the duty of love and the wounding of the conscience (→ συνεί-δησις) of other brethren is sin (v. 11 f.), so that it is better to renounce one's own freedom of action rather than to hurt one's brethren (v. 13; → σκανδαλίζω). The same basic thought recurs in the discussion in 1 C. 10:23 ff. There should be no scruples concerning the enjoyment of meat bought in the market or set on the table in a private house, for it is all the gift of God; nevertheless, regard for the conscience of others and the required separation from the pagan cultus may well be reasons for Christians not eating flesh which they learn is idol-meat. In the conflict between the weak and the strong in R. 14:15, which centres primarily on enjoyment of or abstinence from flesh and wine (→ οἶνος), [33] the decisive point in the judgment of the apostle, who personally is on the side of the strong (14:14, 19 ff.; 15:1 ff.), is regard for the weaker brethren and the readiness to forego for the sake of love, peace and mutual edification (14:15, 19; 15:2). The Christian may choose either freedom or asceticism. In God's sight the one is as good as the other (14:2 ff.). But the responsibility of one brother for another demands: μὴ τιθέναι → πρόσκομμα τῷ ἀδελφῷ ἤ → σκάνδαλον (v. 13). Therefore it is better to eat no flesh and drink no wine if it causes others to stumble. This is the true way to exercise a maturer faith (v. 20 ff.). The tendency towards vegetarianism and abstinence on religious grounds, which arises for the first time in Christian history in R. 14, corresponds to a widespread ascetic disposition in later antiquity (→ 690), though there is a Jewish impulse among the weak in Rome, since the οὐδὲν → κοινὸν δι' ἑαυτοῦ which Paul advances against them in v. 14, and the πάντα μὲν → καθαρά which is the slogan of the strong in v. 20, show that the debate finally concerns what is clean or unclean (→ 690; 693); cf. the observance of weekly days of fasting (v. 5: → ἡμέρα) on the Jewish pattern. The standpoint of the apostle in the Corinthian and Roman disputes (→ I, 643) leads beyond both a casuistical legalism on the one side and an individualistic libertinism on the other to the freedom of the Christian who is united to his brethren in God (1 C. 10:31 f.): εἴτε οὖν ἐσθίετε εἴτε πίνετε εἴτε τι ποιεῖτε, πάντα εἰς δόξαν θεοῦ ποιεῖτε· ἀπρόσκοποι ... γίνεσθε.

3. In Corinth assembling to eat has the character of divine service (1 C. 11:33). The reference is to the administration of the Lord's Supper (→ κλάω, κλάσις), v. 20: κυριακὸν δεῖπνον (→ 34) φαγεῖν (cf. φαγεῖν ἀπὸ τῆς → εὐχαριστίας,

---

[32] Cf. apart from the comm. E. v. Dobschütz, *Die urchristlichen Gemeinden* (1902), 26 ff.; W. Lütgert, "Freiheitspredigt und Schwarmgeister in Korinth," BFTh, 12, 3 (1908), 119 ff.; A. Schlatter, "Die korinthische Theologie," BFTh, 18, 2 (1914), 15 f., 45 ff.; M. Rauer, "Die Schwachen in Korinth und Rom," BSt, 21, 2/3 (1923), 5 ff.; H. v. Soden, *Sakrament und Ethik bei Paulus, Marburger Theologische Studien*, I (1931), 2 ff.

[33] Cf. E. Riggenbach, "Die Starken und Schwachen in der römischen Gemeinde," ThStKr, 66 (1893), 649 ff.; E. v. Dobschütz, *op. cit.*, 92 ff., 274 ff.; W. Lütgert, "Der Römerbrief als historisches Problem," BFTh, 17, 2 (1913), 90 ff.; M. Rauer, *op. cit.*, 94 ff. and the comm. The Lord's brother, James, practised abstinence acc. to Hegesipp. in Eus. Hist. Eccl., II, 23, 5: οἶνον καὶ σίκερα οὐκ ἔπιεν οὐδὲ ἔμψυχον ἔφαγεν, as did Peter acc. to Ps.-Clem. Hom., 12, 6: ἄρτῳ μόνῳ καὶ ἐλαίαις χρῶμαι καὶ σπανίως λαχάνοις; cf. 15, 7.

Did., 9, 5). In face of the disorders which make a true communion impossible because the wealthy who come first eat the supper they have brought with them without waiting for the poor and sharing with them (v. 20 ff., 33 f.), Paul lays serious emphasis on the cultic character of the Lord's Supper, showing that this is quite incompatible with profane and selfish eating (v. 22, 34). The eating of the bread and drinking of the wine in accordance with the tradition of the Last Supper (v. 24, cf. Mk. 14:22 and par.) are a sacred action which demands restraint on the part of all participants (v. 26 ff.; → I, 380). According to 1 C. 10:3 there is an OT type in the eating of the manna in the wilderness (→ I, 643).[34] John, too, draws the same parallel, though as he sees it eternal life is mediated, not through partaking of the manna (6:49, 58), but only by eating the true bread from heaven (→ I, 477), which is Jesus and which Jesus gives (v. 50 f.). On the Johannine demand for the actuality of sacramental eating in the paradoxical form of φαγεῖν or τρώγειν τὴν → σάρκα (v. 53 ff.), cf. the discussion of the Lord's Supper in the NT (→ κλάω, κλάσις).

4. To the image of the Messianic meal of the last time (→ 34) there corresponds the eschatological conception of eating and drinking at the table of the heavenly King.[35] In Lk. 14:15 this is expressed by a Pharisee along the lines of Jewish expectation (→ 691). In Lk. 22:30 (→ 105) it is newly applied by Jesus Himself in prospect of His future rule and the part of the disciples in it. Jesus also expects to eat the fulfilled passover in the kingdom of God in Lk. 22:16 (→ πάσχα, → πληρόω).[36] To eat of the tree of life in Rev. 2:7 is to participate in the life of the last time of salvation, in the divine gift of eternal life (→ 691). On the eschatological feast at which the birds will eat the flesh of the hosts of Antichrist (Rev. 19:17 f.), → 34.

5. In Rev. 10:9 (cf. Ez. 2:8-3:3; Jer. 15:16 Mas.), the divine in his vision is to eat a roll of a book. This is a dramatic representation of the process of inspiration by which he is inwardly filled with the revelation imparted to him, with the divine Word of prophecy which he is to proclaim (cf. Jer. 1:9; Is. 6:7 f.).

6. "To eat," "to enjoy" in the figur. sense. This may be used a. of the eating of spiritual food in Jn. 4:32, where Jesus, when asked by the disciples to eat of the provisions which they have bought (v. 31; cf. v. 8), replies: ἐγὼ βρῶσιν ἔχω φαγεῖν ἣν ὑμεῖς οὐκ οἴδατε, cf. v. 34 → I, 644.[37]

It is also used b. of "consuming" by destructive natural forces whose operation reflects the divine judgment, e.g., fire in Hb. 10:27; cf. Rev. 11:5; and rust (which is compared with fire in its effects) in Jm. 5:3.

Behm

---

[34] For φάγε μάννα as an inscr. on an early Christian communion vessel, v. Preisigke Sammelbuch, 5977.

[35] J. Jeremias, "Jesus als Weltvollender," BFTh, 33, 4 (1930), 74 ff.

[36] On the analogous drinking of the fruit of the vine in v. 18; Mk. 14:25; Mt. 26:29, → πίνω.

[37] V. the comm. esp. Charles (1920) and Had., ad loc.; C. Schneider, *Die Erlebnisechtheit der Apokalypse des Johannes* (1930), 79.

ἔσοπτρον, κατοπτρίζομαι

† ἔσοπτρον.

The image in Jm. 1:23 needs no profound[1] interpretation. It simply describes the natural process to which the fleeting nature of a reflection seen in a mirror gives rise. This is a similitude of the man who is a hearer only and not a doer. On 1 C. 13:12 → αἴνιγμα, I, 178.

† κατοπτρίζομαι.

κάτοπτρον[1] means "mirror," figur. in Aesch. Ag., 839, of the magic mirror in Paus., VII, 21, 12; Artemid. Oneirocr., II, 7. It does not occur in the NT. κατοπτρίζομαι means a. act. "to show in a mirror," "to reflect": Ps.-Plut., De Placitis Philosophorum, 5 (II, 894 f.): τοῦ κατοπτρίζοντος (τὴν ἶριν) ἀστέρος, pass. "to be reflected": P. Oxy., XIII, 1609, 19; b. med., "to see oneself in a mirror," Diog. L., III, 26, 39: the drunkard should κατοπτρίζεσθαι etc.; c. "to see something in a mirror," Phil. Leg. All., III, 101: μηδὲ κατοπτρισαίμην ἐν ἄλλῳ τινὶ τὴν σὴν ἰδέαν ἢ ἐν σοὶ τῷ θεῷ.

In the NT it occurs only at 2 C. 3:18: ἡμεῖς δὲ πάντες ἀνακεκαλυμμένῳ προσώπῳ τὴν δόξαν κυρίου κατοπτριζόμενοι. Sense c. gives an interpretation agreeable to the context (→ n. 4), namely, that "with uncovered head, without being blinded like the Israelites, we see the δόξα of the Lord visible as in a κάτοπτρον. It is to be noted that the image is not based on recollection of an ordinary mirror in which one sees what is physically before the mirror, but on the idea of a miraculous mirror in which what is invisible is made visible to prophets and pneumatics (→ αἴνιγμα, I, 178 on 1 C. 13:12). It is only along these lines that we can understand the passage from Philo mentioned under c.[2] The Pauline text thus means that by the πνεῦμα we are those who see. The thought is the same as in 1 C. 13:12. The two statements together show the twofold nature of the Pauline πνεῦμα which is ἀπαρχή (→ I, 485 f.), namely, fulfilment already present (2 C. 3:18) and fulfilment about to come (1 C. 13:12). Both aspects are contained in the figure of the mirror. Moreover, in the context this looking into the divine κάτοπτρον has the wonderful result that those who look are changed

---

ἔσοπτρον. On Jm. 1:23, Dib., 109; Hck., 81; J. B. Mayor, The Epistle of St. James (1913), 71. For further lit., → αἴνιγμα; esp. J. Behm in R. Seeberg Festschr., I (1929), 326-335.

[1] As opposed to R. Reitzenstein, Historia Monachorum (1916), 248 f., who in this passage too (→ κατοπτρίζομαι) assumes, even if in less vivid form, the view of the πνεῦμα as the magical mirror of the soul. For a criticism of this interpretation, cf. Dib., loc. cit.

κατοπτρίζομαι. On 2 C. 3:18: Meyer[5], 91 f.; Bchm.[4], 175 f.; Heinr. Sendschr., II, 189 ff.; Wnd., 127 f. R. Reitzenstein, Historia Monachorum (1916), 243-251; P. Corssen, ZNW, 19 (1920), 2-10; A. E. Brooke, JThSt, 24 (1922), 98; J. Behm in R. Seeberg Festschr., I (1929), 316-322, 326-336.

[1] On the relation between ἔσοπτρον and κάτοπτρον, cf. Bl.-Debr.[6] § 30, 3.

[2] Cf. esp. the arguments of Reitzenstein, which might fit 2 C. 3:18 but not the ἔσοπτρον of Jm. 1:23. Cf. also the same image in a rather different form in Wis. 7:26 (of wisdom) and 1 Cl., 36, 2 (of Christ as the mirror of God). Reitzenstein lays great stress on the quotation from Porphyr. Ad Marcellam, 13, but cf. the penetrating textual and material criticism of Corssen, 3 f. and also W. Bousset, Kyrios Christos[2] (1921), 109, n. 1. As they see it, the meaning of this quotation is that human virtue is the reflection of God (ἐνοπτριζόμενος τῇ ὁμοιώσει θεόν [not θεοῦ]). But this makes crystal clear the radical distinction between the philosophical and the biblical view.

into the likeness of what they see (→ μεταμορφόομαι), i.e., they themselves acquire a share in the δόξα (→ 251). [3]

This understanding is along the lines of most of the early translations, it vg *speculantes,* Marcion (Tert. Marc., V, 11) *contemplantes,* Pel. *contemplamur,* syP *tanquam in speculo videmus,* bo *in speculo videmus.* Cf. also Calvin, [4] *in speculo conspicientes,* Hofmann, Meyer, Heinrici, and most scholars since Reitzenstein (apart from Corssen). The Gk. fathers sometimes try to construe in terms of "to reflect," but there are no examples of this usage of the med., and such exegesis arises less from the living tongue than from attempts at exposition. [5] Thdrt., *ad loc.* (MPG, 82, 397): ἡ καθαρὰ καρδία τῆς θείας δόξης ... κάτοπτρον γίνεται (cf. also Chrys.). So also Erasmus, Luther ("as the mirror takes a picture, so our heart takes the knowledge of Christ") and also Bengel (*dominus ... splendorem faciei suae in corda nostra tanquam in specula inmittens*).

Kittel

---

† ἔσχατος

1. The general use of the term for something which is last either materially (Mt. 5:26; Lk. 12:59) or in space (Ac. 1:8; 13:47: ἕως ἐσχάτου τῆς γῆς) or time (Mt. 12:45; 20:8 ff.; 27:64; Mk. 12:6, 22; Lk. 11:26; Jn. 7:37; 2 Pt. 2:20; Rev. 2:19), becomes theologically significant, at least indirectly, in 1 C. 15:8, in the ἔσχατον [1] of the final resurrection appearance to Paul. The association of littleness with the last (→ 698) gives to this Pauline experience its character as ἔκτρωμα (→ 465 f.). At the same time, ἔσχατον suggests the closing of a series, so that from the time of this ἔσχατον there can be no similar or equivalent events.

2. The eschatological use (→ τέλος) derives from the sense of what is last in time. The formal multiplicity of resultant expressions is to be explained partly by the LXX rendering of the OT בְּאַחֲרִית הַיָּמִים and partly by the influence of the prophetic "day of Yahweh" (→ ἡμέρα). In content, its use reflects the fluidity of early Christian eschatology.

The end began with the coming of Jesus, Hb. 1:2; 1 Pt. 1:20: ἐπ᾽ ἐσχάτου τῶν ἡμερῶν. But the early Christian writings also see their own present as the last time, demonstrated on the one hand by the outpouring of the Spirit (Ac. 2:17: ἐν ταῖς ἐσχάταις ἡμέραις) and on the other by evil times, by scoffers, by the coming of Antichrist etc. (2 Tm. 3:1; Jm. 5:3: ἐν ἐσχάταις ἡμέραις; 2 Pt. 3:3: ἐπ᾽ ἐσχάτων τῶν ἡμερῶν; Jd. 18: ἐπ᾽ ἐσχάτου τοῦ χρόνου (vl. ἐν ἐσχάτῳ χρόνῳ); 1 Jn. 2:18: ἐσχάτη ὥρα). At the same time, there is also expectation of the coming last day which brings with it the last plagues (Rev. 15:1; 21:9), the overcoming of the ἔσχατος ἐχθρός (1 C. 15:26) and, proclaimed by the ἐσχάτη σάλπιγξ (1 C. 15:52), the resurrection of the dead, judgment and salvation (Jn. 6:39 f., 44, 54; 11:24; 12:48: ἐν τῇ ἐσχάτῃ ἡμέρᾳ; 1 Pt. 1:5: ἐν καιρῷ ἐσχάτῳ).

---

[3] O. Sol. 13:1: "Our mirror is the Lord," is no true par., since here man sees himself in God's mirror (v. 2: "See how your countenance looks").

[4] So Calvin, *ad loc.,* who weighs the two early interpretations and decides according to the *praesenti loco melius quadrare.*

[5] How uncommon the use is with ἐνοπτρίζειν too, may be seen from the editorial alteration of the Porphyr. quotation to which Corssen draws attention, 3 f.

ἔ σ χ α τ ο ς. [1] Adv. ἔσχατον as in Mk. 12:6, 22. The adv. combination ἐσχάτως ἔχειν in Mk. 5:23: "to lie on the point of death," is used elsewhere, but is condemned by the Atticists; cf. Pr.-Bauer, 489.

In the Septuagint the eschatological בְּאַחֲרִית הַיָּמִים is usually rendered ἔσχατα (ἐπ' ἐσχάτων), Gn. 49:1; Mi. 4:1 or ἐπ' ἐσχάτου τῶν ἡμερῶν, Nu. 24:14, occasionally also ἐν ἐσχάταις ἡμέραις, Is. 2:2. On the other hand ἐν ἐσχάτῃ ἡμέρᾳ is avoided for לְיוֹם אַחֲרוֹן Is. 30:8 : ὅτι ἔσται εἰς ἡμέρας ταῦτα καιρῷ, Prv. 29:44 (31:26): ἐν ἡμέραις ἐσχάταις. In the Targums [2] we either have בְּסוֹף יוֹמַיָּא "at the end of the days," Tg. O., Gn. 49:1; Tg. O., Nu. 24:14; Tg. J. I., Gn. 49:1; Tg. Mi. 4:1, or בְּסוֹף עֲקַב יוֹמַיָּא "at the end of the course of the days," i.e., at the final end of the days, Tg. J. I., Nu. 24:14. In Rabb. lit. we mostly have קֵץ "end" (Gn. r., 98 on 49:1: OT quotation: בְּאַחֲרִית הַיָּמִים, Rabbinic exposition קֵץ). Rarely, although already in the Tannait. Midrash, הַיּוֹם הָאַחֲרוֹן S. Dt., 357 on 34:2 ("day on which the dead live"); [3] Ex. r., 52 on 39:32 (day of the rewarding of the righteous, based on Prv. 31:25); cf. Tg. J. I., Dt. 34:2. In Apocalyptic writings we often have "last times," 4 Esdr. 6:34; S. Bar. 6:8; Test. N. 8:1 etc., and sometimes also "last days" (plur.), 4 Esr. 10:59; Test. D. 5:4 etc.

On 1 C. 15:45 ff.: πρῶτος/ἔσχατος Ἀδάμ → I, 142; on Rev. 1:17; 2:8; 22:13 : ἐγώ εἰμι ὁ πρῶτος καὶ ὁ ἔσχατος → I, 1 ff.

3. Figur, it means the last in rank, usually to denote what is mean and poor, as the opp. of → πρῶτος. Hence 1 C. 4:9 : ὁ θεὸς ἡμᾶς τοὺς ἀποστόλους ἐσχάτους ἀπέδειξεν. Corresponding to a πρῶτος, Mk. 9:35 : εἴ τις θέλει πρῶτος εἶναι, ἔσται πάντων ἔσχατος (cf. Mk. 10:44 and par.); Mk. 10:31; Lk. 13:30; Mt. 19:30; 20:16 : ἔσονται πρῶτοι ἔσχατοι καὶ ἔσχατοι πρῶτοι. It is used of the last place as the least honourable in Lk. 14:9 f.

Linguistically cf. Dio C., 42, 5, 5 : Πομπήιος ... καθάπερ τις καὶ αὐτῶν τῶν Αἰγυπτίων ἔσχατος, "as one of the meanest of Egyptians." Jos. Vit., 9 : τῶν ἀρχιερέων καὶ τῶν τῆς πόλεως πρώτων. Materially cf. bBB, 10b : "I saw (in rapture — in the hereafter) an inverted world in which the top are bottom and the bottom top."

Kittel

ἔσω [1]

1. οἱ ἔσω in 1 C. 5:12 means those who are within the community, i.e., Christians as distinct from the surrounding pagans (οἱ ἔξω → 576). This is an expression which receives its peculiar content from the distinction. It reflects Paul's awareness of the → ἐκκλησία as a new and closed fellowship separated from the rest of men (cf. 1 C. 10:32).

2. The anthropological term ὁ ἔσω ἄνθρωπος [2] in R. 7:22, alternating with → ἐγώ (v. 17 f., 20) (→ 359) and → νοῦς (v. 23, 25), also related to → καρδία,

---

[2] Str.-B., III, 658, 671.

[3] A. Schlatter, *Die Sprache und Heimat des vierten Evangelisten* (1902), 78; Schl. J., 175. ἔσω. Pass., I, 1196, cf. 814 f.; Liddell-Scott, 700, cf. 498; Pr.-Bauer, 489; Moult.-Mill., 256.

[1] In NT Gk., as in the *koine* generally, we have ἔσω instead of the Attic εἴσω, cf. Bl.-Debr.[6] § 30, 3.

[2] → I, 365; cf. Cr.-Kö., 147 f.; W. G. Kümmel, *Römer 7 und die Bekehrung des Paulus* (1929), 62 f., 134 ff.; R. Bultmann, "Römer 7 und die Anthropologie des Paulus," in *Imago Dei* (1932), 53 ff.; E. Käsemann, *Leib u. Leib Christi* (1933), 122, 147 f. and the comm. on R. 7:22; 2 C. 4:16; Eph. 3:16. ἔσω in the anthropological sense is also found in the interpretation which 2 Cl., 12, 4 gives to an agraphon from Egypt (Eg.-Ev. ?): τὴν ψυχὴν λέγει "τὸ ἔσω," "τὸ" δὲ "ἔξω" τὸ σῶμα λέγει. Cf. Ign. R., 3, 2 : δύναμιν ... ἔσωθέν τε καὶ ἔξωθεν, "power of soul and body."

→ συνείδησις (2:15) and → πνεῦμα (1:9), denotes the spiritual side of man, or man himself in so far as he enjoys self-awareness, as he thinks and wills and feels. As such, as the subject of the power of moral judgment, he is accessible to the divine revelation, can be conditioned by it and is open to its claim (συνήδομαι τῷ νόμῳ τοῦ θεοῦ κατὰ τὸν ἔσω ἄνθρωπον); yet the contradictory practical conduct which is determined by sin brings out the plight of man in the dualism of his existence. The term bears an even stronger religious content in 2 C. 4:16. Here Paul, proved to be an apostle by suffering, distinguishes in himself the ἔξω ἄνθρωπος (→ I, 365), the earthly being in his creaturely mortality (cf. v. 10 ff.), and the ἔσω ἄνθρωπος, the man determined by God, the "Christ coming into being in Christians"[3] (Gl. 2:20; 4:19), who is a καινὴ κτίσις (2 C. 5:17) and who experiences daily renewal in virtue of the divine gift of the ἀρραβὼν τοῦ πνεύματος (2 C. 5:5; → I, 475). In the petition in Eph. 3:16: ἵνα δῷ ὑμῖν ... δυνάμει κραταιωθῆναι διὰ τοῦ πνεύματος αὐτοῦ εἰς τὸν ἔσω ἄνθρωπον, the term is also to be understood of man as the object of God's working or of the place in man at which the power of the Spirit meets and determines him. As used by Paul, the word always carries with it a suggestion, like the parallel ὁ κρυπτὸς τῆς καρδίας ἄνθρωπος in 1 Pt. 3:4, of something which is concealed, and which works in concealment, in the innermost part of man.

Materially what Paul calls the inner man corresponds to the לֵב (→ καρδία) of the OT, and there are formal parallels in the sayings of Jesus in Mk. 7:21: ἔσωθεν ἐκ τῆς καρδίας τῶν ἀνθρώπων οἱ διαλογισμοὶ οἱ κακοὶ ἐκπορεύονται and Lk. 11:39: τὸ ἔσωθεν ὑμῶν γέμει ἁρπαγῆς καὶ πονηρίας, cf. Mt. 23:28. Cf. also bJoma, 72b: "Raba said: A scribe whose inner man does not correspond to the outer is no scribe."[4] But the expression ὁ ἔσω ἄνθρωπος and the antitheses ὁ ἔσω ἄνθρωπος — ὁ ἔξω ἄνθρωπος are of non-biblical origin. They derive from a terminology of Hellenistic mysticism and Gnosticism disseminated by Platonic philosophy (→ I, 365).[5] Nevertheless, even though Paul adopts the language, he uses it to express his Christian anthropology with its soteriological and eschatological orientation.

Behm

---

† ἑταῖρος

From the time of Homer this has been used for "one who is associated with another," the specific sense being determined by the context. Thus it may be a. a "companion," e.g., Philo Som., II, 245: τὶς τῶν ἑταίρων Μωϋσέως, often in a figur. sense, e.g., Plut. Convivalium Disputationum, I, 4 (II, 622b): γέλωτα ... ὕβρεων ... ἑταῖρον ...; or b. a "fellow-soldier," Hom. Il., 1, 345 (cf. Epict. Diss., I, 11, 31), but also Jos. Bell., 3, 362 (address of Josephus to the Jewish soldiers trapped with him in the cave of Jotapata); Ant., 12, 302 (address of Judas Maccabaeus to his army before the battle); c. a "member of the same party," Lys., 12, 43; d. a "member of the same religious society," Ditt. Or., II, 573, 1 f.: Ἔδοξε τοῖς ἑταίροις καὶ Σαββατισταῖς θεοῦ ... e. a "pupil" in the sense of the adherent of specific teachings or of a particular philo-

---

[3] Ltzm., *ad loc.*
[4] Cf. Str.-B., I, 465.
[5] For further material cf. C. F. G. Heinrici, *Das zweite Sendschreiben des Apostels Paulus an die Korinthier* (1887), 233 f.; A. Bonhöffer, "Epiktet u. das NT," RVV, 10 (1911), 115 ff. and Wnd. 2 K. on 4:16.
ἑταῖρος. Pr.-Bauer, 490; Liddell-Scott, 700; Jew. Enc., VI, 421 ff., *s.v. Haber ;* Schl. Mt., 590.

sopher, Aristot. Metaph., I, 4, p. 985b, 4 : Λεύκιππος καὶ ὁ ἑταῖρος αὐτοῦ Δημόκριτος; Xenoph. Mem., II, 8, 1: an ἀρχαῖος ἑταῖρος of Socrates ; [1] f. a "friend" in the good sense, Philo Leg. All., II, 10 : ἐν ταῖς φιλίαις οἱ κόλακες ἀντὶ ἑταίρων ἐχθροί, cf. III, 182, but also in the bad "boon companion," 3 Macc. 2:25 : ἑταῖρος with συνπότης; g. a "colleague," Jos. Ant., 11, 101: Ἀναβασσάρου τοῦ ἐπάρχου καὶ ... ἡγεμόνος καὶ τῶν ἑταίρων αὐτοῦ (here it almost means a subordinate official).

It is not common in the Septuagint, being mostly used for רֵעַ etc., though also for חָבֵר: ἑταῖρος τοῦ βασιλέως [2] (וְרֵעֶה הַמֶּלֶךְ) 3 Βασ. 4:5 (= f.); ... μή ποτε γένωμαι ὡς περιβαλλομένη ἐπ᾽ ἀγέλας ἑταίρων σου (עַל עֶדְרֵי חֲבֵרֶיךָ), Cant. 1:7 (= g.); μὴ ἴσθι ἑταῖρος ἀνδρὶ θυμώδει (... אֶל־תִּתְרַע) Prv. 22:24 (= a.). The word is more common in the other Gk. translations of the OT, esp. for πλησίον in the LXX, e.g., 1 Βασ. 15:28 ΑΣ for πλησίον in the LXX (Mas. רֵעַ); 20:41 Ἀ for πλησίον LXX and ἀδελφός Θ (Mas. רֵעַ); Job 42:7 Σ for φίλος LXX Θ (Mas. רֵעַ); 31:32 Θ for ξένος LXX and προσήλυτος Ἀ (גֵּר). [3] From this review we may perhaps come to the cautious conclusion that it was only gradually that ἑταῖρος won its place in the Gk. Bible.

In later Judaism ἑταῖρος (for חָבֵר) is commonly used for one part of the scribal body. It refers to those who were qualified to be religious teachers and judges, but who had not yet received ordination, so that acknowledgment of their pronouncements depended on recognition of their persons by the parties to which they belonged, not on the assured validity of their position. [4] Since ordination could usually be received only at the age of 40, [5] the number of those who were qualified scribes but who could be counted only personally and not officially as rabbis [6] was not small ; indeed, in times of persecution ordination was sometimes impossible and therefore many never attained to official recognition. These men who are qualified but who do not belong to the official rank of teachers are often called חַבְרַיָּא/ἑταῖροι in the Jerus. Talmud. [7] The word was also used more widely for those who in a particular way sought to live according to the Law, and esp. its requirements of ritual cleanness. [8] In the form of religious societies there thus arose in marked distinction from laxer circles, the ʿAm haʾareṣ, a kind of order of tertiaries. We may rightly ask whether Hellenistic influences are not discernible in this respect. In the texts, חָבֵר is primarily used, of course, in the general secular sense of colleague or associate, female as well as male, [9] but for our purposes this is less important than the special usage to which we have referred. [10]

---

[1] When Iren., V, 33, 4 calls Papias Ἰωάννου μὲν ἀκουστής, Πολυκάρπου δὲ ἑταῖρος, we have a usage similar to that in Aristot. and Xenoph., and also found in Epictet. (Diss., II, 15, 4; II, 22, 29; III, 26, 3). i.e., united by common association with one and the same teacher.

[2] Cf. Epict. Diss., IV, 1, 97: the ἑταῖρος of the emperor.

[3] The three different renderings also reflect the history of the exegesis of גֵּר; → προσήλυτος.

[4] Cf. bSanh., 5a; Str.-B., I, 497.

[5] bSota, 22b; cf. also J. Jeremias, ZNW, 25 (1926), 311.

[6] Here, perhaps, is the root of the description of those who are not yet ordained as תַּלְמִידֵי־חֲכָם. The term denotes those who are between the חָכָם, the ordained, and the תַּלְמִיד, those still under instruction. Cf. Str.-B., I, 496.

[7] Cf. Str.-B., I, 496 .

[8] Cf., e.g., Dem., 2, 3 and the material in Str.-B., II, 500-519.

[9] For examples cf. Levy Wört., II, 8 f.

[10] This is certainly present in the formula תַּלְמִיד וְחָבֵר, e.g., jSheq, 47b, 30 : בֶּן עַזַּאי תַּלְמִיד וְהָבֵר הָוָה דְרַבִּי עֲקִיבָה. Here and in similar cases חָבֵר with תַּלְמִיד implies the presence of ultimate trust and fellowship between the accredited pupil and his teacher, which was naturally of the greatest importance both for himself and his office.

1. Matthew is the only NT writer to use ἑταῖρος. He does so three times, and always in the form of an address : ἑταῖρε. It occurs on the lips of the owner of the vineyard when he answers the spokesman for the workers who grumbled at the wage given to those who started later (20:13), on the lips of the king addressing the man without a wedding-garment (22:12), and on the lips of Jesus when Judas came to betray Him (26:50). Though we should not read too much into the term, we may say that in all three cases it is more than a mere form. It always denotes a mutually binding relation between the speaker and the hearer which the latter has disregarded and scorned. There is a relation of this kind between the owner of the vineyard and the worker hired according to right and custom. [11] A similar relation exists between the king and his guest and between Jesus and His disciple. In all three cases the hearer is guilty of regarding the mutual obligation egotistically, as though it committed only the other party. This is brought out in the final reference to the generosity of the master in 20:13. It is also implicit in 22:12, since the guest had no claim to participate in the wedding but owed his presence solely to the generosity of the king (v. 8 ff.). In the final case the position is obvious. [12]

> If we can see from the ἑταῖρε of the two parables that the generosity is on the side of the speaker, then, unlikely though it may seem, the term shows us that the speaker is God, or that God's action is reflected in his action. This generosity is in no sense negated by the exclusion of the guest in the second parable. The exclusion is simply a necessary result of its abuse. Comparable Rabb. parallels (bShab., 152b; 153a Bar.) suggest that the guest either scorned or defiled the proffered garment and therefore incurred the legitimate wrath of his host. There is no support for a *praedestinatio ad malum* in this parable.

2. Almost more important than the occurrences of ἑταῖρος in the NT are the implications of the fact that it is not found in many passages where one might have expected it. Thus the disciples of Jesus are never called His ἑταῖροι. Indeed, the longer they are connected with Him, the more clearly they realise their distinction from Him. The recognition that He spoke and acted with authority prevents the kind of development to a similar stature which is natural in the case of Rabbinic pupils and their teachers. The only meaningful way in which they can describe their relationship to Him is by self-description as the → δοῦλος of Jesus Christ. On the other hand, Christians in their relationship to one another regarded and described themselves, not as ἑταῖροι, but as → ἀδελφοί. The use of this term shows that they received and accepted their fellowship as something given, as something which was independent of their own desire or volition, and as something which bound them all the closer for this reason. Though we may perhaps see here the influence of Jewish usage (→ I, 145), the fact remains that this designation indicates the divine invasion of the world of human egoism, and that it thus expresses something which ἑταῖρος could never express. We can thus understand why from the very first members of Christian orders described themselves as ἀδελφοί (*fratres*) and not as ἑταῖροι. In so doing, they also gave outward recognition to their common relatedness to the one Lord.

Rengstorf

ἑτερόγλωσσος → I, 726   ἑτεροδιδασκαλέω → 163
ἑτεροζυγέω → ζυγός.

---

[11] Cf. 20:2, 13 f. and on this Str.-B., I, 830 f.
[12] On the ἐφ' ὃ πάρει → πάρειμι.

ἕτερος

In the NT ἕτερος is used in much the same way as ἄλλος (→ I, 264). [1] It is striking, however, that it does not occur in the genuine Mk., is found in Jn. only at 19:37, and is not used in Col., 1 and 2 Th., Tt., Phlm., 1 and 2 Pt., 1 and 2 and 3 Jn. or Rev. Nor has it passed into modern Gk.

As an indefinite number, ἕτερος denotes the new member of a series distinct from those which preceded and either carrying the series forward, e.g., Lk. 14:18 ff.: ὁ πρῶτος ... καὶ ἕτερος ... καὶ ἕτερος; 1 C. 12:8 f.: ᾧ μὲν ... ἄλλῳ δὲ ... ἑτέρῳ ... ἄλλῳ δὲ ... ἄλλῳ δὲ ... ἑτέρῳ ... ἄλλῳ δὲ, or concluding it, Ac. 15:35 : Παῦλος δὲ καὶ Βαρναβᾶς διέτριβον ἐν Ἀντιοχείᾳ ... εὐαγγελιζόμενοι μετὰ καὶ ἑτέρων πολλῶν. It often comprises other men or concepts of the same kind, e.g., "and others" in Ac. 17:34 : τινὲς δὲ ἄνδρες ... αὐτῷ ἐπίστευσαν, ἐν οἷς καὶ Διονύσιος ... καὶ ... Δάμαρις καὶ ἕτεροι σὺν αὐτοῖς, or "the others" in Lk. 4:34 : καὶ ταῖς ἑτέραις πόλεσιν εὐαγγελίσασθαι. It should be noted, however, that ἕτερος may also be used to introduce another kind, [2] e.g., Lk. 23:32 : ἤγοντο δὲ καὶ ἕτεροι κακοῦργοι δύο σὺν αὐτῷ. As a definite number it is used when two specific things or groups are compared or contrasted, e.g., Ac. 23:6 : τὸ ἓν μέρος ἐστὶν Σαδδουκαίων τὸ δὲ ἕτερον Φαρισαίων. In Ac. 20:15; 27:3 it is used for the "next" day. As a distinguishing adj. or adv. it denotes something which is not identical with what has been referred to previously. This may involve a more or less pronounced qualitative distinction, in which case the term acquires theological significance.

Mt. 11:3 : σὺ εἶ ὁ ἐρχόμενος, ἢ ἕτερον προσδοκῶμεν; the qualities which Jewish expectation attributed to the Messiah might better fit another than Jesus.

Mk. 16:12 : Jesus ἐφανερώθη ἐν ἑτέρᾳ μορφῇ, i.e., not in the transfigured corporeality of the risen Lord as one might naturally suppose, nor in the form of a gardener in which He had appeared to Mary Magdalene, but in the form of a traveller.

At the transfiguration of Jesus in Lk. 9:29, ἐγένετο τὸ εἶδος τοῦ προσώπου αὐτοῦ ἕτερον. His face was changed by the glory in which it appeared.

Ac. 2:4 : The disciples ἤρξαντο λαλεῖν ἑτέραις γλώσσαις (→ I, 726). This decisive statement in the miracle of Pentecost can be expounded in two ways. It may express the fact that the disciples spoke in tongues, as explicitly described in 10:46; 19:6 and 1 C. 12:10, 30; 14:1 ff. Against this is the formal objection that it leaves ἑτέραις untranslated, since the phrase γλώσσαις λαλεῖν, as the other passages show, is quite adequate in itself to denote plainly the process of speaking in tongues. [3] There is also the material objection that according to 1 C. 14:2 ff. the distinctive feature of tongues is unintelligibility, and therefore the very opposite of what constitutes the miracle of Pentecost. Hence, if we accept this interpretation, we must find the true miracle of Pentecost in the fact that the hearers were given the gift of hearing and understanding these tongues in their own languages without any interpretation. [4] This view finds some support in Ac. 2:6 and 2:11: ἤκουον

ἕ τ ε ρ ο ς. Bl.-Debr.[6] § 306; Radermacher[2], 77.

[1] Hence in many passages, e.g., Mt. 10:23; Lk. 8:6 ff.; 11:26, many MSS have ἕτερος where others have ἄλλος.

[2] So already in class. Gk., e.g., Thuc., IV, 67, 2 : Πλαταιῆς τε ψιλοὶ καὶ ἕτεροι περίπολοι.

[3] 1 C. 14:21 is no argument against this. The expression ἐν ἑτερογλώσσοις λαλήσω in this verse is a quotation from the Gk. OT (Is. 28:11), though it agrees with ʼA rather than the LXX. In its original sense this certainly refers to men of foreign tongues (→ I, 726 f.) rather than to speaking with tongues, but except in this amended quotation Paul always speaks of γλώσσαις λαλεῖν.

[4] So finally K. Bornhäuser, Studien zur Apostelgeschichte (1934), 22 ff.

εἷς ἕκαστος τῇ ἰδίᾳ διαλέκτῳ λαλούντων αὐτῶν, but it is not very convincing. The other possibility is to take it that λαλεῖν ἑτέραις γλώσσαις means speaking in various languages which were different from the mother tongue of the speakers and which were previously unknown to them. This view alone does full justice to the later ἤκουον εἷς ἕκαστος τῇ ἰδίᾳ διαλέκτῳ λαλούντων αὐτῶν and to the enumeration of the various tongues. On the other hand, it does not explain the contemptuous statement in v. 13, which would seem to be appropriate only to speaking in unintelligible tongues. This leads many scholars to the view that in its present form Ac. 2 unites two different accounts of which one narrates the commencement of speaking with tongues in the early Church and the other a miracle of speaking in foreign languages. If this is true, the expression ἑτέραις γλώσσαις λαλεῖν is the link used by the author to join the two concepts.

Ac. 17:7: καὶ οὗτοι πάντες ἀπέναντι τῶν δογμάτων Καίσαρος πράσσουσιν, βασιλέα ἕτερον λέγοντες εἶναι 'Ιησοῦν. The charge is brought against Paul and his companions in Thessalonica that they were preaching a rival king who would contest the sole authority of the Roman emperor.

R. 7:23: βλέπω δὲ ἕτερον νόμον ἐν τοῖς μέλεσίν μου. This "other law" (→ 355) is distinguished from the Law of God which is "holy, just and good" (v. 12) and from the "law of reason" which consents to it. The other law is the instrument, effective in the flesh of the individual man, of the "law of sin" which is a power ruling over man and which binds him with the help of this ἕτερος νόμος.

In 1 C. 15:40 it is emphasised that the δόξα of heavenly bodies is essentially different from that of earthly.

In Eph. 3:5 the νῦν of the time of salvation is contrasted with ἑτέραις γενεαῖς, with all previous generations.

The ἑτέρως φρονεῖν of Phil. 3:15 can be taken in different ways. It can be expounded in terms of the verses which immediately precede (12-14). In this case those who think otherwise are those who have not yet attained to the deep insight that one can never be, but can only be in process of becoming, a perfect Christian. On the other hand, it may be referred more generally to views divergent from those of Paul, e.g., on the prior question of the religious value of Judaism, or to any imperfect ideas which can be corrected only by divine revelation.

In Hb. 7:11 ff. Jesus is the other priest who is compared with Μελχισεδέκ and it is shown in detail wherein the difference consists which both transcends and fulfils.

This idea of otherness, which occurs in so many forms, is central to the NT as the story of the fulfilment of the promise of God. The new which has come in Jesus Christ is something quite different from what preceded to the degree that it excludes everything else as a way of salvation. There is no other God but one, 1 C. 8:4. [5] And there is no other name under heaven given among men whereby they may be saved but the name of Jesus Christ, Ac. 4:12. This is why the message of the Gospel demands decision.

Gl. 1:6: θαυμάζω ὅτι ... μετατίθεσθε ... εἰς ἕτερον εὐαγγέλιον, ὃ οὐκ ἔστιν ἄλλο is to be taken in the same way. The expression: "You have fallen away to another Gospel," which is hardly a slogan of his opponents but which Paul lets slip in his agitation, is revoked at once by the apostle. There is no other Gospel; there is only the one Gospel of justification by Christ in faith. Thus the teaching

---

[5] ἕτερος is added to οὐδείς in ℵ* KL al pl syr.

of the Judaizers is not another Gospel, let alone a better. It is no Gospel at all.
Cf. also 2 C. 11:4.

Similarly ἑτεροδιδασκαλέω (→ 163) means "to teach something false," "wrongly
to proclaim as the Gospel," and ἑτεροδοξέω means "to hold a wrong view," Ign. Sm.,
6, 2 (ἑτεροδοξία is "error" in Ign. Mg., 8, 1).

As a principal word ὁ ἕτερος is used in the sense of ὁ → πλησίον for one's
"neighbour." The other is the Thou as distinct from the I (ὁ αὐτός). We find
this use already in Demosth. Or., 34, 12 : ἕτερος ἤδη ἦν καὶ οὐχ ὁ αὐτός. In
R. 2:1: ἐν ᾧ γὰρ κρίνεις τὸν ἕτερον, σεαυτὸν κατακρίνεις. The "law of Christ"
can be stated in the formula : μηδεὶς τὸ ἑαυτοῦ ζητείτω ἀλλὰ τὸ τοῦ ἑτέρου
(1 C. 10:24). Complete renunciation of self-love and complete self-giving to others
is the fulfilment of the Law, R. 13:8. In this respect the "neighbour" is not a
collective concept, but the man who in a concrete situation is brought across my
path by God. The Christian must have continual regard to the conscience and
edification of this neighbour, 1 C. 10:29; 14:17.

Beyer

┌─────────────────────────────┐
│   ἕτοιμος, ἑτοιμάζω,   │
│   ἑτοιμασία, προετοιμάζω   │
└─────────────────────────────┘

The clear meaning of this word group is preparation both in the active sense of
"making ready" and in the passive of "readiness," "ability" or "resolution." [1]

The group takes on religious significance only in biblical Gk., [2] i.e., in the LXX,
where it is mainly used for כּוּן whose various senses [3] it assimilates (and sometimes for
בָּרָא, עָשָׂה, and a series of other verbs), [4] and in the NT.

1. The terms are used for the divine creation and preservation, a. in nature
and history. They reflect the pulsating, living quality of the biblical concept of
God. The divine ἑτοιμάζειν relates to heaven and earth : ἡτοίμασεν δὲ οὐρανούς,
Prv. 3:19; 8:27; ἑτοιμάζων οἰκουμένην ἐν τῇ σοφίᾳ αὐτοῦ, Ἰερ. 28:15; ἑτοιμάζων ὄρη ἐν τῇ ἰσχύι σου, ψ 64:6. It relates to specific natural processes : ... τῷ
ἑτοιμάζοντι τῇ γῇ ὑετόν, ψ 146:8; τίς δὲ ἡτοίμασεν ὑετῷ λάβρῳ ῥύσιν, Job
38:25. [5] It relates to individual men : αἱ χεῖρές σου ... ἡτοίμασάν με, ψ 118:73;
νῦν ζῇ κύριος, ὃς ἡτοίμασέν με, 3 Βασ. 2:24, to their needs : ἡτοίμασας τὴν τροφὴν αὐτῶν, ὅτι οὕτως ἡ ἑτοιμασία σου, ψ 64:9, and to their destiny : ταύτην
ἡτοίμασας τῷ παιδί σου Ἰσαάκ, Gn. 24:14, 44, with reference to the bride
Rebekah, ordained for Isaac. It refers to God's eternal being and nature : κύριος

ἕτοιμος κτλ. [1] For detailed distinctions and examples v. Pass., s.v.
[2] Cf. esp. Ael. Arist. Or., 8, 22 : Sarapis μόνος δὲ καὶ ἕτοιμος τῷ τινος δεομένῳ
τοῦτ' ἐπιτελεῖν. ἑτοιμάζειν is worth noting in connection with the sacrificial cultus :
ἱερὸν ἑτοιμάζειν, Hom. Il., 10, 571; ἑτοιμάζειν ταύρους, Od., 13, 184, cf. in the LXX
2 Ch. 35:12 (ὁλοκαύτωσις), 16 (λειτουργία κυρίου).
[3] Meanings of כון are "to arise," "to create," "to found," "to set up," "to prepare,"
"to establish" (mainly niph'al and hiph'il).
[4] Cf. Hatch-Redpath, s.v.
[5] Here in translation of פֶּלֶג.

ἐν τῷ οὐρανῷ ἡτοίμασεν τὸν θρόνον αὐτοῦ, ψ 102:19; ἕτοιμος ὁ θρόνος σου ἀπὸ τότε, ψ 92:2; δικαιοσύνη καὶ κρίμα ἑτοιμασία τοῦ θρόνου σου, ψ 88:14; ἐν τοῖς οὐρανοῖς ἑτοιμασθήσεται ἡ ἀλήθειά σου, ψ 88:2. [6] It relates finally to the people of Israel concerning whose history it is written : ἡτοίμασας σεαυτῷ τὸν λαόν σου 'Ισραὴλ λαὸν ἕως αἰῶνος (2 Βασ. 7:24; cf. ψ 88:4; Sir. 49:12), and which in its history constantly experiences the divine protection, e.g., in its guidance through the wilderness (ψ 77:19 f.), in the conquest : ... εἰς τὴν γῆν, ἣν ἡτοίμασά σοι, Ex. 23:20 (cf. Ex. 15:17; Ez. 20:8), or in the history of the kings, where it is said of Saul : νῦν ἡτοίμασεν κύριος τὴν βασιλείαν σου ἕως αἰῶνος ἐπὶ 'Ισραὴλ [7] (1 Βασ. 13:13) and of David : ... ἡτοίμασεν αὐτὸν κύριος εἰς βασιλέα ἐπὶ 'Ισραήλ (2 Βασ. 5:12; cf. 1 Ch. 14:2).

It relates finally to the judgment which terminates the history : ἡτοίμακε κύριος τὴν θυσίαν αὐτοῦ, Zeph. 1:7. The point is that the word ἑτοιμάζειν and its derivatives are regarded by the LXX translators as suitable for expressing God's whole creative action in every age and at every moment in nature and history. All world-occurrence is the sphere of God's creative work.

b. These expressions are also used for what God prepares and accomplishes soteriologically, mainly in terms of salvation and perdition. God accomplishes salvation : ἃ ὀφθαλμὸς οὐκ εἶδεν καὶ οὖς οὐκ ἤκουσεν καὶ ἐπὶ καρδίαν ἀνθρώπου οὐκ ἀνέβη, ὅσα ἡτοίμασεν ὁ θεὸς τοῖς ἀγαπῶσιν αὐτόν (1 C. 2:9). The inconceivable salvation which God has prepared for those who love Him is at the centre of the NT *kerygma*. On the one side it is fully present and on the other fully future, as Jesus Christ, who is the content of this salvation, is present as the object of faith, and future as the object of hope. It is fully present, for Simeon, holding the infant Jesus in his hands, confesses : εἶδον οἱ ὀφθαλμοί μου τὸ σωτήριόν σου, ὃ ἡτοίμασας κατὰ πρόσωπον πάντων τῶν λαῶν (Lk. 2:30 f.). Again, the fact that salvation is present is implied in the parables of Jesus, e.g., when He says that the wedding feast or the great banquet — both are symbolical images of the Messianic period — is prepared (Mt. 22:4, 8; Lk. 14:17). What now takes place is invitation to the feast. On the other hand, it is fully future. At the last judgment the Son of Man will say to His own : κληρονομήσατε τὴν ἡτοιμασμένην ὑμῖν βασιλείαν ἀπὸ καταβολῆς κόσμου (Mt. 25:34). The Johannine Christ says : ... πορεύομαι ἑτοιμάσαι τόπον ὑμῖν· καὶ ἐὰν πορευθῶ καὶ ἑτοιμάσω τόπον ὑμῖν, πάλιν ἔρχομαι καὶ παραλήμψομαι ὑμᾶς πρὸς ἐμαυτόν, ἵνα ὅπου εἰμὶ ἐγὼ καὶ ὑμεῖς ἦτε, Jn. 14:2 f. The death and resurrection of Christ prepare eternal salvation for His people. [8] Peter writes to his congregation concerning the σωτηρία ἑτοίμη ἀποκαλυφθῆναι ἐν καιρῷ ἐσχάτῳ, 1 Pt. 1:5. To God's preparation in relation to salvation belongs the fact that those who love God are prepared for it by Him (σκεύη ἐλέους, ἃ προητοίμασεν εἰς δόξαν, R. 9:23). There also belongs the fact that what they achieve in this life is previously prepared by God (ἐπὶ ἔργοις ἀγαθοῖς, οἷς προητοίμασεν ὁ θεός, ἵνα ἐν αὐτοῖς περιπατήσωμεν, Eph. 2:10). But God also prepares destruction. At the last judgment the Son of Man says : πορεύεσθε ἀπ' ἐμοῦ κατηραμένοι εἰς τὸ πῦρ τὸ αἰώνιον τὸ ἡτοιμασμένον τῷ διαβόλῳ καὶ τοῖς ἀγγέλοις αὐτοῦ, Mt. 25:41.

---

[6] In the two last quotations the sense is not so much preparation in the act. sense as being prepared or established. The statements are grounded in God's eternal nature which comprises both eternal rest and eternal creating.

[7] Here, too, ἑτοιμάζειν has the sense of establishing.

[8] Cf. the verbal par. in Rev. 12:6 : ... ἔχει (sc. ἡ γυνή) ἐκεῖ τόπον ἡτοιμασμένον ἀπὸ τοῦ θεοῦ.

Rev. 9:15 refers to the conclusion of the last time which precedes the last judgment and which is now in process of fulfilment: ἄγγελοι οἱ ἡτοιμασμένοι εἰς τὴν ὥραν καὶ ἡμέραν καὶ μῆνα καὶ ἐνιαυτόν, ἵνα ἀποκτείνωσιν τὸ τρίτον τῶν ἀνθρώπων. The salvation and perdition prepared from the foundation of the world — an expression which brings out the ineluctable certainty and eternity of salvation and ,perdition — correspond, like the prepared good works of Eph. 2:10, to Rabbinic speculations on things which were ready from the beginning of the world: "Ten things were created in the twilight on the night before the Sabbath: the mouth of the earth, the opening of the well, the mouth of the ass, the rainbow, the manna, the rod, the shamir, the Scripture, the means of writing and the tables. Many say: Also the demons, the grave of Moses and the ram of our father Abraham" (Ab., 6, 5). [9] In another list we have "the Torah, repentance, Gan Eden, Gehinnom, the throne of glory, the heavenly sanctuary and the name of the Messiah" (Pesikt., 54a). [10]

2. To God's creation and preparation correspond a human preparation and preparedness in relation to God. At the beginning of the NT history stands John the Baptist with the prophetic task: ἑτοιμάσατε τὴν ὁδὸν κυρίου, Mt. 3:3 and par., or, as Luke puts it, ἑτοιμάσαι κυρίῳ λαὸν κατεσκευασμένον, Lk. 1:17. The Synoptists see in the work of the Baptist a fulfilment of the divine requirement declared by Dt. Is. (Is. 40:3).

Alongside the prophetic task is the ethical and religious task given to individuals to prepare for fellowship with God.

The Psalmist prays: ἑτοίμη ἡ καρδία μου, ὁ θεός, ἑτοίμη ἡ καρδία μου, ψ 56:7 (cf. ψ 107:1). The preparation of the heart is a specific ethical task in the Wisdom literature: οἱ φοβούμενοι κύριον ἑτοιμάσουσι καρδίας αὐτῶν, Sir. 2:17 (cf. Sir. 18:23; 2:1; Prv. 23:12); ἑτοίμη ἡ καρδία αὐτοῦ ἐλπίζειν ἐπὶ τὸν κύριον, ψ 111:7. Philo uses the terms to denote resolution in an intellectual or gnostic connection (e.g., Agric., 16; Det. Pot. Ins., 10; Som., I, 76; Migr. Abr., 14). The prophet Amos summons the people of Israel: ἑτοιμάζου τοῦ ἐπικαλεῖσθαι τὸν θεόν σου (Am. 4:12). According to the LXX Micah reckons among what is καλόν and what God requires: ἕτοιμον εἶναι τοῦ πορεύεσθαι μετὰ κυρίου (Mi. 6:8). From Israel as from Moses there is demanded readiness to receive the revelation of God. This readiness has a ceremonial and cultic character with taboo-like features (Ex. 19:11-15; 34:2; cf. Nu. 16:16).

In the NT readiness is demanded in three respects: readiness for good works: ... πρὸς πᾶν ἔργον ἀγαθὸν ἑτοίμους, Tt. 3:1; cf. 2 Tm. 2:21; readiness to bear witness to the Gospel: ... ἕτοιμοι ἀεὶ πρὸς ἀπολογίαν παντὶ τῷ αἰτοῦντι ὑμᾶς λόγον περὶ τῆς ἐν ὑμῖν ἐλπίδος, 1 Pt. 3:15; ... ὑποδησάμενοι τοὺς πόδας ἐν ἑτοιμασίᾳ τοῦ εὐαγγελίου τῆς εἰρήνης, Eph. 6:15; and readiness for the return of the Lord. The last requirement Jesus put to His disciples with particular urgency: διὰ τοῦτο καὶ ὑμεῖς γίνεσθε ἕτοιμοι, ὅτι ᾗ οὐ δοκεῖτε ὥρᾳ ὁ υἱὸς τοῦ ἀνθρώπου ἔρχεται, Mt. 24:44; Lk. 12:40. It is illustrated in the parable of the Ten Virgins. In virtue of it the life of Christians becomes a life of conscious and vigilant expectation of a goal which brings salvation and of openness to the possibilities of action determined by this goal. This readiness gives the Christian life a distinctive dynamic character.

Grundmann

[9] For details, cf. K. Marti-G. Beer, 'Abôt (1927), 127 ff.
[10] Cf. Str.-B., I, 974 f., 981 f.

εὐαγγελίζομαι, εὐαγγέλιον,
προευαγγελίζομαι, εὐαγγελιστής

εὐαγγελίζομαι.

A. בָּשַׂר in the OT.

בָּשַׂר in the OT has the general sense of "proclaiming good news" (1 K. 1:42), e.g., the birth of a son (Jer. 20:15). In view of 1 S. 4:17, where the מְבַשֵּׂר proclaims the defeat of Israel, the loss of the ark and the death of the sons of Eli, and of 1 K. 1:42 and Is. 52:7, where the news is characterised as good only by the addition of טוֹב,[1] it has been conjectured[2] that the basic sense is simply to deliver a message, and that the content of the בְּשֹׂרָה is shown to be glad or sad only by the adj. טוֹבָה or רָעָה. This is not so. In all Semitic languages, in Accadian, Ethiopic and Arabic, the sense of "joy" is contained in the stem.[3] The realistic conception of the "word" in Semitic languages is shown by the fact that they have a special stem for declaring something good, whereas Latin and modern languages do not,[4] and Gk. takes a middle course by constructing the composite εὐαγγέλιον, εὐαγγελίζεσθαι.[5] The addition טוֹב in the OT is simply a strengthening of something already present in the stem. בָּשַׂר is often used in the sense of "bringing news of victory" or "declaring a victory." A messenger comes from the place of battle and declares victory over enemies or the death of the opponent.[6] This messenger regards himself as a bearer of good tidings (2 S. 4:10), and he is regarded

---

ε ὐ α γ γ ε λ ί ζ ο μ α ι (N.B. For important reasons Schniewind, who had undertaken this article, could not have it ready in time. With his consent it was thus taken over by his pupil, Gerhard Friedrich, like some parts of the art. ἐπαγγελ-. Friedrich was able to use in MS the unprinted portions of Schniewind's book *Euangelion*, but in conception and construction the art. is his own work.)

In general: Cr.-Kö.; Pr.-Bauer; Liddell-Scott, *s.v.*; Schn. Euang.; P. Zondervan, "Het Woord 'Evangelium'," *Theol. Tijdschrift*, 48 (1914), 187-213; M. Burrows, "The Origin of the Term 'Gospel'," JBL, 44 (1925), 21-33; G. Gillet, *Evangelium, Studien zur urchr. Missionssprache*, Diss. Heidelberg (1924, not in print); E. Molland, *Das Paulinische Euangelion, Avhandlger utgitt av Det Norske Videnskaps Akademi i Oslo, 2 Hist.-Filos. Klasse* (1934), No. 3. On D.: Str.-B., III, 4-11; Dalman WJ, I, 84-86; Schl. Mt., 115, 122, 361; Schl. Lk., 159; A. Schlatter, *Nt.liche Theologie*, I (1909), 583. On E.: Dob. Th., 86; Kl. Mk., 4; Hck. Mk., 12; Zahn. Einl., 169 f., 225, 228, 240 f.; J. Wellhausen, *Einleitung in die drei ersten Ev.²* (1911), 98-104; 147-153; J. Weiss, *Das älteste Ev.* (1903), 24 ff.; A. Seeberg, *Das Ev. Christi* (1905); Schl. Gesch. d. Chr., 53, 135 ff., 169; A. Harnack, *Entstehung und Entwickelung der Kirchenverfassung u. des Kirchenrechts in den 2 ersten Jhdt.* (1910), 199-239; M. Werner, "Der Einfluss paul. Theologie im Mk.," Beih. ZNW, 1 (1923), 98-106; O. Moe, *Paulus u. d. ev. Geschichte* (1912); P. Feine, *Jesus Christus u. Paulus* (1902), 18 f.; J. Weiss, *Das Urchristentum* (1917), 537; C. Holsten, *Die drei ursprünglichen, noch ungeschriebenen Ev.* (1883); C. F. Nösgen, *Geschichte der nt.lichen Offenbarung*, II (1893), 300 f.; J. Müller, *Das persönliche Christentum der paul. Gemeinden*, I (1898); A. Fridrichsen, "Τὸ εὐαγγέλιον hos Paulus," *Norsk. Teologisk. Tidsskrift*, 13 (1912), 153-170, 209-256; J. Schniewind, *Die Begriffe Wort u. Evangelium bei Pls.* (1910), 64-117; A. Oepke, *Die Missionspredigt des Ap. Pls.* (1920), 50 ff.; O. Schmitz, *Die Christusgemeinschaft des Pls. im Lichte seines Genetivgebrauchs* (1924), 45-88; W. Förster, *Herr ist Jesus* (1924), 144; L. Baudimant, *L'Evangile de Saint Paul* (1925).

[1] Cf. also 2 S. 18:27: בְּשׂוֹרָה טוֹבָה.
[2] P. de Lagarde, *Mittheilungen,* I (1884), 216-218; cf. Dalman WJ, I, 84 f.; Str.-B., III, 5.
[3] Schn. Euang., 30.
[4] Cic. Att., II, 12, 1; II, 3, 1; XIII, 40, 1 has the foreign word εὐαγγέλια.
[5] Schn. Euang., 31.
[6] 1 S. 31:9 = 1 Ch. 10:9; 2 S. 1:20; 18:19, 20, 31.

by others as such (2 S. 18:26). By extension, every messenger from a battlefield came to be called מְבַשֵּׂר, even though in some cases he might bear evil tidings.

Transition from a secular to a religious use may be seen in 1 S. 31:9. The Philistines have triumphed, Saul has fallen. The signs of victory, the head of the enemy and his weapons, are displayed in the land. The glad message is proclaimed to idols and people. This declaration has a solemn character. It is a cultic act. Ps. 68:11 is to be taken in the same way. News of Israel's victory over its enemies has come. Yahweh Himself orders a song of victory ; it does not have to be published to Him as to the idols in 1 S. 31:9 — and הַמְבַשְּׂרוֹת צָבָא רָב,[7] "there is a great company of women proclaiming the good news." In the Yahweh cult the women proclaim the victory in a song given by God Himself. בשׂר is again used as a religious term in Ps. 40:10. The man delivered out of his distress declares Yahweh's צֶדֶק in the great congregation. Like a herald of God, he extols in a loud voice His great and wonderful acts.[8] Yahweh has put a new song on his lips (v. 4).

Most significant for an understanding of the NT concept *euangelion* is Dt. Is. and the literature influenced by it. Ps. 40:10 and 68:11 speak only of the isolated acts of Yahweh which are to be declared. Dt. Is., however, expects the great victory of Yahweh, His accession, His kingly rule, the dawn of the new age. In this connection the מְבַשֵּׂר is of the greatest importance.

He is the herald who precedes the people on its return from Babylon to Sion. All Jerusalem stands on the towers and walls expecting the train of returning exiles. Then they see the messenger, the מְבַשֵּׂר, on the top of the hill מַשְׁמִיעַ שָׁלוֹם מְבַשֵּׂר טוֹב מַשְׁמִיעַ יְשׁוּעָה...מֶלֶךְ אֱלֹהָיִךְ: "Peace and salvation, Yahweh is King," he cries to them (Is. 52:7).[9] He proclaims the victory of Yahweh over the whole world. Yahweh is now returning to Sion to rule .The messenger publishes it, and the new age begins. He does not declare that the rule of God will soon commence ; he proclaims it, he publishes it, and it comes into effect. Salvation comes with the word of proclamation. By the fact that he declares the restoration of Israel, the new creation of the world, the inauguration of the eschatological age, he brings them to pass. For the word is not just breath and sound ; it is effective power.[10] Yahweh puts His words on lips of His messengers. He it is who speaks through them. With

---

[7] H. Gunkel, *Die Psalmen* (1926), does not think that "there is a great company of women proclaiming the good news" makes sense in the context. He thus changes מְבַשְּׂרוֹת צָבָא to מִבְּשָׂר אֶת צָבָא, "of flesh the great host." But this conjecture is unnecessary. On the other hand, O. Procksch, AELKZ, 58 (1925), 741 and H. Schmidt, *Gott und das Leid im AT* (1926), 35, 47, read מְבַשְּׂרִי instead of מִבְּשָׂרִי at Job 19:26. Procksch translates : "And when my eyes are opened, I see him as my messenger of good news"; and Schmidt : "After my anguish, when the olive-tree was smitten, he, God, will be my messenger of good news." There are several examples of playing on the word בשׂר in the Rabbis (cf. R. Eisler, ZNW, 24 [1925], 186 f. and Str.-B., III, 6d), e.g., Nu. r., 14 on 7:48 : Much study is a weariness of the body (יְגִעַת בָּשָׂר, Qoh. 12:12). If you exert yourself (יגעת) to study the words of scholars, God will proclaim good news to you — this is the meaning of בָּשָׂר in Qoh. 12:12. V. Schn. Euang., 58, n. 1.

[8] Cf. Gunkel, *ad loc.*

[9] Na. 1:15 is like Is. 52:7, but it does not have the decisive "Yahweh is King." Instead we read : "Keep thy feasts, O Judah." Acc. to E. Sellin, *Das Zwölf-Propheten-Buch* (1922), *ad loc.*, this is not a repudiation of Is., though it is possibly a misunderstanding.

[10] On the significance of the "word" cf. P. Heinisch, "Das Wort im AT und im alten Orient," in *Biblische Zeitfragen*, X, 7, 8 (1922) and O. Grether, "Name und Wort Gottes im AT," *Beih.* ZAW, 64 (1934). On Dt. Is.: S. Mowinckel, *Der Knecht Jahwäs* (1921), 13 ff.; Schn. Euang., 41 f.

His Word He creates the world, He shapes history, He rules the world.[11] The watchers on the walls hear the word and repeat it with rejoicing. It rings through the city and messengers carry it through the land : "Yahweh is King" ; "Behold, your God."[12] A new era begins also for the nations. For Yahweh is a God of the Gentiles as well as Israel.[13] In Ps. 96:2 ff., which belongs to the same world of thought as Dt. Is.,[14] we read : בַּשְּׂרוּ מִיּוֹם־לְיוֹם יְשׁוּעָתוֹ, "Proclaim from day to day his salvation, declare his glory among the heathen, his wonderful acts among all nations ... say among the heathen, The Lord is king." The great eschatological hour has come. The message of Yahweh's acts of power now goes out to the whole world. Daily the glad tidings are to ring out among the heathen. Indeed, according to Is. 60:6 the heathen themselves come to Sion and proclaim the praises of the Lord.[15]

In Dt. Is. the subst. participle, which is already found in a secular sense in 2 S. 4:10 and in a cultic in Ps. 68:11, is a distinctively religious term. The מְבַשֵּׂר is the messenger of God who proclaims the royal dominion of God and who with his effective word ushers in the eschatological period. The verb, too, shares in the religious significance of the subst. part. We can see this in Is. 52:7 and 61:1. In 52:7 the first מְבַשֵּׂר is a subst. part., but the second is to be taken verbally like מַשְׁמִיעַ. In 61:1 the prophet is one who brings good tidings : לְבַשֵּׂר עֲנָוִים שְׁלָחַנִי. The part. does not occur here, but the view is the same as in 52:7.[16] The prophet is sent to proclaim the good news to the poor, and the effect of the proclamation is their liberation.

The close connection between this whole circle of thought and the NT is evident. The eschatological expectation, the proclamation of the βασιλεία τοῦ θεοῦ (we keep the Gk. here for the sake of clarity), the introduction of the Gentiles into salvation history, the rejection of the ordinary religion of cult and

---

[11] Cf. Is. 51:16. In Is. 41:27 P. Volz (*Jesaja,* II [1932], *ad loc.*) cuts out "one that bringeth good tidings to Sion" as out of harmony with the context. The text is corrupt. E. Sellin in NkZ, 41 (1930), 149 proposes אֲמָרַי for רִאשׁוֹן; "My words to Sion, Behold, behold, there they are, and I gave to Jerusalem one that bringeth good tidings." Acc. to K. Elliger, "Deuterojesaja und sein Verhältnis zu Tritojesaja," BWANT, 63 (1933), 229, n. 2, this conjecture "gives a firm place in the text" to the bearer of good news. Whether we accept this conjecture or not, there can be no doubt that the whole song deals with the effective Word of Yahweh. When this comes to Jerusalem, the bringer of good tidings is present.

[12] Is. 52:7; 41:27; 40:9 obviously belong together. It is plain that the same situation is described in 52:7 and 40:9. Cf. Schn. Euang., 37, n. 5 : the mountains, the watchmen who repeat the call = those who publish good tidings ; Yahweh is King = Behold, your God. On 40:9 : מְבַשֶּׂרֶת צִיּוֹן, i.e., whether the *status constructus* is to be taken as an appositional or a strict gen. and מְבַשֶּׂרֶת collectively (the host of those who publish good tidings), cf. Schn. Euang., 35 f. It makes no material difference.

[13] Attention has often been drawn to the conjunction and interconnection of universal and national hopes in Dt. Is. Cf. G. Hölscher, *Profeten* (1914), 326-330. On universalism cf. Is. 40:5; 45:23-25; 49:1, 6; 51:4.

[14] R. Kittel, *Die Psalmen*³ (1922), *ad loc.*; Schn. Euang., 53, n. 2.

[15] The construction in 60:6 is not very clear. Who is the subject of יְבַשֵּׂרוּ? Cf. P. Volz, *Jesaja,* II (1932), *ad loc.* Acc. to Budde in Kautzsch, it is the camels which proclaim the wonderful acts of God by their coming. More apt is the suggestion that it is all nations and not merely the kings (K. Marti, *Jesaja* [1900]).

[16] Schn. Euang., 44 f.

Law (Ps. 40), the link with the terms δικαιοσύνη (Ps. 40:9), σωτηρία (Is. 52:7; Ps. 95:1), and εἰρήνη (Is. 52:7) — all point us to the NT. [17]

B. εὐαγγελίζομαι with the Greeks.

The verb is attested from the time of Aristophanes, [18] and derives from εὐάγγελος. [19] Yet we do not have εὐαγγέλλειν, [20] like ἀγγέλλειν from ἄγγελος, but εὐαγγελίζεσθαι. It is either [21] one of the "sound words" in -ίζειν whose history we cannot trace, [22] in which case it means "to speak as an εὐάγγελος," or it is one of the verbs in -ίζειν which denote a state, [23] so that the sense is "to act like an εὐάγγελος." [24] Either way our concern is with the εὐάγγελος.

The normal use is in the med., though the act. [25] and pass. [26] also occur. [27] It is construed both with the dat. [28] and the acc. [29] of person. The content of the message can be introduced by περί. [30] Sometimes a preposition is also used to denote the recipient of the message. [31]

As in the OT (→ 707), so among the Gks. the term is used for the proclamation of news of victory. [32] The εὐάγγελος [33] comes from the field of battle by ship (Plut. Pomp., 66 [I, 654b]), by horse (Heliodor. Aeth., X, 1), or as ἡμεροδρομήσας, as a swift runner, [34] and proclaims to the anxiously awaiting city the victory of the army, and the death or capture of the enemy (Paus., IV, 19, 5). Often the news is sent in a letter. [35] εὐαγγελίζεσθαι may also be used of political or private communications which

---

[17] The suggestion of Burrows, 22, that it is hardly too much to say that in Dt. Is. εὐαγγελίζεσθαι is a Messianic expression, is not quite accurate. We may rightly say that the early Christians regarded it as such.

[18] Eq., 643.

[19] F. Specht in Schn. Euang., 125.

[20] Phot. Lex., s.v. has εὐαγγελεῖν and also κακαγγελεῖν from κακάγγελος (as an adj. in Aesch. Ag., 636). We find κακαγγέλλω in Eur. Herc. Fur., 1136 and Demosth. Or., 18, 267. On the other hand, we are to read εὖ ἀγγέλλω rather than εὐαγγέλλω in Plat. Resp., IV, 432d and Theaet., 144b. In Luc. Philopseudes, 31 C. Jacobitz notes the reading εὐαγγέλλων for εὐαγγελιζόμενος. Cf. Phryn. Ecl., 335 and Schn. Euang., 126, n. 3.

[21] F. Specht in Schn. Euang., 125.

[22] Debr. Gr. Wortb. § 260.

[23] *Ibid.*, § 266 f.

[24] Schn. Euang., 125, n. 2.

[25] Dio C., 61, 13, 4 MS; Polyaen. Strat. V, 7 MS; P. Amh., 2, 16; P. Giess., I, 27, 6 = Mitteis-Wilcken, I, 2, 17, 5; 1 S. 31:9; 2 S. 18:19 f.; Rev. 10:7; 14:6; Ac. 16:17 in D*.

[26] *Amer. Journ. of Archaeol.*, 2nd Series, 18 (1914), 323, 14; 2 S. 18:31; Mt. 11:5; Lk. 7:22; 16:16; Gl. 1:11; Hb. 4:2, 6; 1 Pt. 1:25; 4:6.

[27] Cf. Bl.-Debr.[6] § 69, 4.

[28] Aristoph. Eq., 643; Demosth. Or., 18, 323; Heliodor. Aeth., X, 1 etc. In the NT, Lk. 1:19; 2:10; 4:18, 43; Ac. 8:35; R. 1:15 vl.; 1 C. 15:1, 2; 2 C. 11:7; Gl. 1:8 vl.; 4:13; Eph. 2:17; 3:8 vl.; 1 Th. 3:6.

[29] Joseph. Ant., 18, 228; Alciphr. Ep., II, 9, 2 MS; Heliodor. Aeth., II, 10; Lk. 3:18; Ac. 8:25, 40; 13:32; 14:15 vl., 21; 16:10; Gl. 1:9; 1 Pt. 1:12.

[30] Jos. Ant., 15, 209; Ac. 8:12; cf. R. 1:3 εὐαγγέλιον περί ... Deissmann LO, 314: εὐανγελ[ίο]υ περὶ τοῦ ἀνηγορεῦσθαι. On εὐαγγελίζεσθαι τὰ περί *v.* Schn. Euang., 101, n. 4.

[31] πρός σε, Menand. Georg., 83; ἐπὶ τούς ..., Rev. 14:6 (א only acc.); ἐν ... Gl. 1:16; R. 1:15 D*; Eph. 3:8 אDG.

[32] Cf. Schn. Euang., 130, n. 2.

[33] The subst. and adj. are not very common; cf. Schn. Euang., 124, n. 2.

[34] Luc. Pro Lapsu inter Salutandum, 3. Here we have the weaker ἀγγέλλειν, but the conception of the news of victory is the same as in the νίκην εὐαγγελίζεσθαι which follows. χαίρετε νικῶμεν, cries the messenger of Marathon, Philippides, καὶ τοῦτο εἰπὼν συναποθανεῖν τῇ ἀγγελίᾳ καὶ τῷ χαίρειν συνεκπνεῦσαι.

[35] Heliodor. Aeth., X, 1 f. Acc. to Luc. Pro Lapsu inter Salutandum, the Athenian δημαγωγός Cleon εὐαγγελιζόμενος τὴν νίκην τὴν ἐκεῖθεν καὶ τὴν τῶν Σπαρτιατῶν ἅλωσιν was the first to put the word χαίρειν at the beginning of the letter.

bring joy. Marius is told by two horsemen that he has been elected consul for the fifth time. [36] Others are gladdened by the birth of a son, [37] by news of an approaching wedding, [38] or of the death of someone, [39] or by other communications. [40] In such cases εὐαγγελίζεσθαι has a more general sense and is more or less synon. with ἀγγέλλειν. [41]

Often the news does not correspond to the facts (Plut. Pomp., 66 [I, 654b]). In time of war esp. false stories of victory are circulated to boost the morale of tired soldiers. [42] News comes to be treated with suspicion and the term loses its value, so that it can be consciously used in an ironical inversion. [43] Nero wanted his mother killed and she was able to save herself and thus to send him the good news of her deliverance. [44] Again, the orator Lycurgus (6, 18) says of the criminal and fugitive that he should declare the τῆς πατρίδος ἀτυχία, i.e., the spoliation of the city, ὥσπερ τῇ πατρίδι μεγάλας εὐτυχίας εὐαγγελιζόμενος.

We often find σωτηρία and εὐτύχημα, εὐτυχία combined with εὐαγγελίζομαι. [45] Victory over enemies is the salvation of the city. In Luc. Philopseudes, 31 a magician tells of the freeing of the house from a ghost. [46] In Lyc., 6, 18 εὐτυχίας εὐαγγελίζεσθαι and σωτηρίαν προσαγορεύειν are almost synon. In the NT εὐαγγέλιον is often linked with σωτηρία, [47] but the idea of εὐτυχία, τύχη does not occur. There is no such thing as chance or fortune in the NT. Faith in God forbids it. The combination is all the more significant for the Gks. (Demosth. Or., 18, 323). Heliodor. Aeth., X, 1 f. is particularly important. Hydaspes communicates to the θειοτάτῳ συνεδρίῳ of gymnosophists his victory over the Persians. He owes the success to τύχη. He now fears the envy of the gods: τὸ γὰρ ὀξύρροπον τῆς τύχης ἱλάσκομαι. He tries to protect himself against this by the prophetic power of the gymnosophists. To the goddess Tyche he opposes the θειότατον συνέδριον of the gymnosophists and their προφητεία. His news of victory is news of the fulfilment of their prophecy. [48] The word εὐαγγελίζεσθαι has here a religious significance. [49]

The εὐάγγελος can be a sacral messenger, one who declares an oracle. [50] This gives us the sense of "to promise." This usage is found only in the Hellenistic period, and mostly in writings under Neo-Pythagorean influence. [51] In Luc. Icaromenippus, 34 the destruction of the philosophers is declared to them on the commission of Zeus. The

---

36 Plut. Mar., 22 (I, 418b): εὐαγγελιζόμενοι τὸ πέμπτον αὐτὸν ὕπατον ᾑρῆσθαι καὶ γράμματα περὶ τούτων ἀπέδοσαν. Luc. Tyrannicida, 9: τὴν ἐλευθερίαν εὐαγγελίζεσθαι (the tyrant is overthrown and democracy restored).

37 Theophr. Char., 17, 7: εὐαγγελιζόμενον, ὅτι υἱός σοι γέγονεν.

38 Longus, III, 33, 1: τὸν γάμον εὐηγγελίζετο; cf. Menand. Georg., 83.

39 Heliodor. Aeth., II, 10: πρῶτα μὲν εὐαγγελίζομαί σε τὴν Δημαινέτης τελευτήν.

40 Aristoph. Eq., 642: The sausage merchant bursts into the council meeting: ὦ βουλή, λόγους ἀγαθοὺς φέρων εὐαγγελίσασθαι πρῶτος ὑμῖν βούλομαι, anchovies have never been so cheap.

41 Alciphr. Ep., II, 9, 2.

42 Polyaen. Strat., V, 7: The left wing of the army is beaten. But the leader εὐηγγέλιζε τοῖς Συρακουσίοις, ὡς τῶν Ἰταλιωτῶν κατὰ τὴν εὐώνυμον τάξιν νενικηκότων ... ὑπολαβόντες οἱ Συρακούσιοι τὸν στρατηγὸν ἀληθῆ λέγειν.

43 Schn. Euang., 102 f., 177 f.

44 Dio C., 61, 13, 4: Agrippina acts as if things had come about κατὰ τύχην. Nero is so incensed at the news that he kills the messenger as though he had come to assassinate him.

45 Cf. Schn. Euang., 145-151.

46 For the σωτηρία of Agrippina, cf. Dio C., 61, 13, 4; → n. 44.

47 Cf. Harnack, Kirchenverfassung, 214, n. 1.

48 Cf. the relationship between ἐπαγγέλλεσθαι and εὐαγγέλλεσθαι in the NT, → 582, n. 51 and 585, n. 67.

49 On the exposition of the passage, cf. Schn. Euang., 149 and c. IX.

50 For examples and discussion, ibid., 185-196.

51 Ibid., c. IX.

εὐαγγέλιον is almost a threat (→ 711). The resolve of the council of the gods is not executed at once because it is a festive season. The reference of εὐαγγελίζεσθαι is thus to the future. This is also true in Luc. Philopseudes, 31. The magician promises that the house will be free of evil spirits in the future.[52] In Soranus, De Muliebribus Affectionibus, 21 the midwife should encourage the pregnant woman : εὐαγγελιζομένη ... τὴν εὐτοκίαν. In Longus, III, 33, 1 τὸν γάμον εὐαγγελίζεσθαι is almost synon. with τοὺς γάμους θύσειν ἐπαγγέλλεσθαι, III, 32, 3. In all these passages there is no question of proclaiming something present, but of referring to something future.

The passages which use εὐαγγελίζεσθαι in connection with a θεῖος ἄνθρωπος deserve particular attention. Philostr. Vit. Ap., I, 28 refers to the appearing of Apollonius.[53] Apollonius is of divine nature (VII, 38). He is honoured by prostration (I, 19). He brings σωτηρία to men by his miracles (VII, 21). He is given the honour of a theophany, i.e., his presence is sought with the solemnity of a divine epiphany (IV, 31).[54] He refuses prostration as a greeting before the image of the king in Babylon. The arrival of this divine man is quickly and joyously proclaimed in the royal palace : εὐαγγελιζόμενοι πᾶσιν. Thales (Iambl. Vit. Pyth., 2, 12) instructs the young Pythagoras and then sends him to the Egyptian priests : εὐηγγελίζετο ... θειότατον αὐτὸν καὶ σοφώτατον ὑπὲρ ἅπαντας ἔσεσθαι ἀνθρώπους.

Surveying the Greek use of εὐαγγελίζομαι, we find many points of contact with the NT. Liberation from enemies and deliverance from the demonic powers which frighten men are occasions for εὐαγγελίζεσθαι. But the link with τύχη, εὐτυχία shows the difference from the NT. The εὐαγγέλιον also treats of divine men. But this is no parallel to the NT. In the NT Jesus Himself is the εὐαγγελιζόμενος.[55] He Himself is the content of His message. Elsewhere this is true only in the imperial cult. On εὐαγγελίζεσθαι in this cult → εὐαγγέλιον.[56] In the sense of "to promise" or "to reveal," εὐαγγελίζεσθαι follows a different usage from that of the Bible. The Word ceases to be active, creative and effective. It reveals, instructs and intimates the future.[57] The "actuality of pronouncement"[58] is thus lost.

C. Septuagint, Philo, Josephus.

1. The Septuagint usually has εὐαγγελίζεσθαι[59] or εὐαγγελίζειν[60] for בשׂר. At 1 Βασ. 4:17 it has παιδάριον for the messenger with bad news from the battlefield, and at Is. 41:27 παρακαλεῖν and 1 Ch. 16:23 ἀναγγέλλεσθαι. The מְבַשֵּׂר corresponds to the Gk. εὐάγγελος. The LXX never uses εὐάγγελος for one who brings good news, but always εὐαγγελιζόμενος. Among the Gks. there is no instance of the part. being used as a subst. εὐαγγελιζόμενος in the LXX is to be regarded as a literal translation of מְבַשֵּׂר.[61] At the decisive points where מְבַשֵּׂר occurs (Is. 40:9; 41:27; 52:7;

---

[52] εὐαγγελιζόμενος αὐτῷ ὅτι καθαρὰν (αὐτῷ) καὶ ἀδείμαντον (without fear) ἤδη ἕξει τὴν οἰκίαν οἰκεῖν.
[53] So Wendland Hell. Kult., 258, n. 2. Though ἐπιφάνεια does not occur, the substance is the same.
[54] Cf. J. Hempel, Untersuchungen zur Überlieferung von Apollonius von Tyana (1920), 63 ff.; H. Windisch, "Paulus und Christus," UNT, 24 (1934), 59 ff., 70 ff.
[55] Schn. Euang., c. IX.
[56] εὐαγγελίζεσθαι is also found in this cult acc. to the American Journ. of Arch., 2 Series, 18 (1914), 323, 14.
[57] R. Bultmann, "Der Begriff des Wortes Gottes im NT" in Glauben und Verstehen (1933), 275.
[58] F. Ebner, Das Wort u. die geistigen Realitäten (1921), 18 ff.
[59] 2 S. 1:10; 4:10; 18:26; 18:31; 1 K. 1:42; 1 Ch. 10:9; ψ 39:9; 67:11; 95:2; Na. 1:15; Is. 40:9; 52:7; 60:6; 61:1; Jer. 20:15.
[60] 1 S. 31:9; 2 S. 18:19 f.
[61] Schn. Euang., 136.

ψ 67:11) the LXX alters the text. In Is. 40:9 and ψ 67:11 it changes the feminine into a masculine. This denotes a weakening rather than a strengthening of the conception. The concept is generalised. At Is. 52:6 f. the LXX gives a completely different sense : πάρειμι ὡς ὥρα ἐπὶ τῶν ὀρέων, ὡς πόδες εὐαγγελιζομένου ἀκοὴν εἰρήνης, ὡς εὐαγγελιζόμενος ἀγαθά. The reference here is to God. He is compared with the time of the year and with one who brings good tidings. [62] This makes it plain that the LXX does not understand what Dt. Is. meant by the messenger. The efficacy of the Word is minimised and the idea of the dawn of the divine rule is lost. In Is. 52:7 מֶלֶךְ אֱלֹהָיִךְ is changed into βασιλεύσει σου ὁ θεός. The inauguration of the dominion of God does not come with the act of proclamation. [63]

We may also refer to Jer. 28:10 (51:10), where the Mas. ספד is rendered εὐαγγελίζεσθαι in ʼA, while the LXX has ἀναγγέλλειν. Jl. 2:32 (3:5) is more important. [64] The text of the Mas. is corrupt. The LXX replaces שְׂרִידִים by εὐαγγελιζόμενοι : ἐν ʼΙερουσαλὴμ ἔσται ἀνασῳζόμενος καθότι εἶπεν κύριος καὶ εὐαγγελιζόμενοι (א : εὐαγγελιζόμενος) οὓς κύριος προσκέκληται. Perhaps we may see here the old conception of the one who brings good news.

In the LXX the combination of εὐαγγελίζεσθαι with σωτηρία is more common than in the Mas. (→ 710); Jl. 2:32 : ἀνασῳζόμενος, and Is. 60:6 : σωτήριον. Is. 60:6 deserves particular note in this regard, for this is the only passage where תְּהִלָּה is rendered σωτήριον. Elsewhere the equivalents are δόξα (Ex. 15:11), ἀρετή (Is. 42:12), ἔπαινος (Ps. 22[21]:3) and αἴνεσις (Ps. 106[105]:47). Perhaps the influence of εὐαγγελίζομαι is responsible for the translation σωτήριον.

In general we may conclude that the LXX does not lead us much further forward in understanding εὐαγγελίζεσθαι.

2. Philo belongs to the world of Gk. thought. He has the verb 9 times (→ προευαγγελίζεσθαι). Three times he uses it of good news generally when telling OT stories. [65] Poetically he causes the Pleiades to announce a good harvest in Op. Mund., 115 and the early almond tree a good crop of nuts in Vit. Mos., II, 186. In these two passages, as in Exsecr., 161 with reference to ἐλπίς and Som., II, 281 with reference to God in an allegory on Ex. 14:30, the verb has the sense of "to promise," which is not found in the OT. How far Philo is from the OT may be seen from Leg. Gaj. Here (99) the emperor is compared with Hermes who is the ἑρμηνεὺς καὶ προφήτης τῶν θείων. ποδωκέστατον (swift of foot) ... εἶναι ... ἐπειδὴ τὰ λυσιτελῆ φθάνοντας εὐαγγελίζεσθαι προσήκει ... κηρύκειον (the herald's staff) ἀναλαμβάνει δεῖγμα συμβατηρίων σπονδῶν (of reconciliation). πόλεμοι γὰρ ἀνοχὰς καὶ διαλύσεις λαμβάνουσιν διὰ κηρύκων εἰρήνην καθισταμένων ... Γάιος δὲ πρὸς τίνα χρείαν πέδιλα (shoes) ἀνελάμβανεν; He does not bring any messages of peace or joy, but only misfortune. We also find the terminology of the emperor cult (→ εὐαγγέλιον) in Leg. Gaj., 231. Before the enthronement of Gaius the ambassadors say : ἀπὸ τῆς ἡμετέρας πόλεως εὐαγγελιουμένη πρὸς τὰς ἄλλας ἔδραμεν ἡ φήμη. Intentionally in this work, which deals with the embassy of the Jews of Alexandria to the emperor on the occasion of honouring the emperor, Philo uses a term customary in the sacral terminology of the imperial cult. [66]

---

[62] Ibid., 68.

[63] Ibid., 73 f.

[64] Ibid., 51, n. 3 and 67, where a copyist's error is seen, though in O. Procksch, "Die kleinen prophetischen Schriften nach dem Exil," in Erläuterungen zum AT, 6 (1916), 85, 122, n. 2, the LXX is regarded as the original.

[65] Jos., 245 : Joseph will εὐαγγελίσασθαι to his father τὰ περὶ τῆς ἐμῆς εὑρέσεως; Jos., 250 : εὐηγγελίζοντο τῷ βασιλεῖ, that Joseph has found his brethren. Virt., 41: Midianite women seduce the young soldiers of Israel : τοῦτο διαπραξάμεναι τοῖς ἀνδράσιν εὐαγγελίζονται.

[66] Schn. Euang., 85-94.

3. Josephus displays the same Gk. usage as Philo. He employs εὐαγγελίζομαι for news of victories [67] and for political communications. [68] He often has the word in biblical narratives [69] even where it is not found in the LXX. [70] This does not indicate any preference for the OT בשׂר, it implies rather a weakening and secularisation. That Joseph. does not think in OT terms may be seen from the fact that he uses the word for "to promise." Ant., 5, 24 : Joshua τὴν ἅλωσιν αὐτοῖς τῆς πόλεως εὐηγγελίζετο. It might seem that here Joshua is a messenger of God proclaiming the fall of Jericho with a word of power. [71] The reference, however, is not to the effective word exercising its force in virtue of its pronouncement. Joshua is simply revealing to the people that Jericho will fall. This is even clearer in Ant., 5, 277 in the story of the birth of a son to Manoah and his wife from Ju. 13. Here εὐαγγελίζομαι is synon. with δηλόω and μηνύω. [72] Other indications of a Gk. background are the linking of εὐαγγελίζομαι with the Stoic concept of πρόνοια and with τύχη (→ 711 f.), [73] and the distrust shown towards messengers (→ εὐαγγέλιον). [74]

Neither in Philo nor Josephus do we find the same conception of the one who brings glad tidings as in Dt. Is. [75] This is not surprising. They have no understanding of history. They do not know salvation history. They have no true eschatology. In place of the great history of God they put the experiences of individuals which are not bound to any age and which may be constantly repeated. [76] The result for the NT is quite negative. Yet the enquiry is not superfluous, since it helps us to see how Jewish writers think and speak under the influence of Hellenism. [77] The NT maintained its independence of Hellenism.

D. Palestinian Judaism.

בשׂר usually means "to proclaim good news," though it may sometimes be used for sad news. In Tg. J. I on Gn. 41:26 f., [78] in the interpretation of the dream, מבשרן is used both of the good cows and ears and also of the bad ones. In the one case it is a good message and in the other a bad. Mostly, however, בשׂר denotes the proclamation of good news, and there is no need to add טוב. [79] In many cases the news refers to events yet to

---

[67] Ant., 7, 245, 250. νίκην εὐαγγελίζεσθαι is pure Gk. Ant., 5, 24 : the fall of Jericho ; Bell., 3, 503 : the taking of Tarichaea.

[68] Ant., 18, 228 : the news of the death of Tiberius ; Bell., 1, 607: the return of Antipater, and Ant., 15, 209 of Herod, to Palestine.

[69] Ant., 5, 24, the capture of Jericho. Ant., 5, 277: the announcing to Manoah and his wife by an angel of the birth of a son. Ant., 7, 56 : Saul is told that the asses are found. Ant., 7, 245-250 : the version of the mission of Ahimaaz from 2 S. 18. In this story the LXX uses the verb 5 times and the subst. forms (→ εὐαγγέλιον) 4 times, but Joseph. has the verb only twice and elsewhere the neutral ἀγγέλλειν or combinations of the word group ἀγγελ- with καλός and ἀγαθός. Ant., 11, 65 : the return of the Jews from Babylon.

[70] Ant., 5, 24, 277; 7, 56; 11, 65.

[71] On the meaning of the word in Joseph. v. also Schlatter, "Wie sprach Josephus von Gott ?," BFTh, 14, 1 (1910), 68; Schl. Mt., Index.

[72] Cf. also Ant., 7, 245 f.

[73] Ant., 7, 245 : ὅτι τῆς παρὰ τοῦ θεοῦ βοηθείας ἔτυχε καὶ προνοίας εὐαγγελίσασθαι. Cf. also 5, 277.

[74] Ant., 18, 228 f.: ... μόνον ἀληθῆ τὰ λεγόμενα εἴη. As Agrippa here does not really believe his slave, so Manoah does not believe the message of the angel in Ant., 5, 277.

[75] Not even in the proclamation of the return from Babylon in Ant., 11, 65. Ant., 11, 64 f.: τυχὼν οὖν τούτων παρὰ τοῦ βασιλέως Ζοροβάβηλος ... εὐχαριστεῖν ἤρξατο τῷ θεῷ τῆς σοφίας καὶ τῆς ἐπ' αὐτῇ νίκης ... τοῖς ὁμοφύλοις εὐηγγελίσατο τὰ παρὰ τοῦ βασιλέως.

[76] Schl. Theol. d. Judt., 259; H. Windisch, Die Frömmigkeit Philos (1909), 99, 108.

[77] Schn. Euang., 111.

[78] Str.-B., III, 6b.

[79] For examples, ibid., 6c.

take place, [80] so that we may render "to promise." [81] We can thus understand why מבושר in jBer., 9d, 25 : "When the lips of man (in prayer) execute the movement (of themselves), then the good news is brought that his prayer is heard," is the equivalent of מובטח ("he may be assured") [82] in the par. Lv. r., 16 on 14:5 (→ 580). בשר is a religious term. [83] God, [84] the Holy Spirit through Scripture, [85] the heavenly voice, [86] angels [87] proclaim to men a joyful message whose content is the forgiveness of sins and the hearing of prayer [88] or a share in the life of the world to come. [89]

It is of great significance that in Palestinian Judaism we still find the same conception of the one who brings good tidings as in Dt. Is. The מבשר comes, and the Messianic age dawns. He proclaims the redemption of Israel and brings peace and salvation into the world.

The tradition concerning the messenger is not uniform. Ps. Sol. 11:2 : κηρύξατε ἐν Ἰερουσαλὴμ φωνὴν εὐαγγελιζομένου· ὅτι ἠλέησεν ὁ θεὸς Ἰσραὴλ ἐν τῇ ἐπισκοπῇ αὐτῶν. [90] Tanch. במדבר Nu. 2:2 : "When one comes bringing glad tidings, it will first be told to Judah"; Na. 2:1: "On the mountains the feet of one who brings good tidings, who publishes peace." [91] Both passages refer to the מבשר. His name is not given. It does not greatly matter who he is. His proclamation is what counts. The decisive thing is that he publishes peace, for peace comes with the act of proclamation. In Midr. Ps. on 147:1 [92] there is a whole host of messengers : "Isaiah said : How beautiful on the

---

[80] Tg. J. I. on Gn. 21:7 (Str.-B., III, 6c): "How worthy of credence was the messenger who brought to Abraham the (good) news (מְבַשְׂרָא דְּבַשַּׂר) and said : "Sarah will one day give suck to children." Or S. Dt., 307 on 32:4 (Str.-B., III, 6d): "Thou hast brought me a good message (וּבִשַּׂרְתַּנִי בְּשׂוֹרָה טוֹבָה), to-morrow my portion shall be with those in the world to come."

[81] For examples, v. Dalman WJ, I, 84 f. and Str.-B., III, 7 f. jSheq., 47c, 62 (Str.-B., III, 7 f.): "Whoso keeps to the land of Israel (i.e., continues to dwell there), and speaks the sacred language, and enjoys its fruits in purity, and recites the schᵉma morning and evening, to him the good news will be brought (יְהֵא מְבוּשָּׂר) that he is a son of the world to come." The par. in jShab. 3c, 23 has "He may be assured (מוּבְטָח לוֹ) that he belongs to the life of the world to come." Cf. also Str.-B., III, 206 ff.

[82] Str.-B., III, 7 f.

[83] Not exclusively, bPes., 3b (Str.-B., III, 6c): Ironically, "Has the corn turned out well? He answered then, The barley has turned out well. Then he was told : Go and bring the (good) news (בשר) to the horses and asses."

[84] Tanch. שמות 64b (Str.-B., III, 7e); Ex. r., 46 on 34:1 (Str.-B., III, 7 and 8).

[85] Sota, 9, 6; bSota, 11a in Str.-B., II, 136; Dalman WJ, I, 85.

[86] jKet., 35a, 26 (Str.-B., III, 7 f.).

[87] Str.-B., III, 7 f. (Tg. Ruth 1:6); II, 96i (bBM, 86b): Michael is to bring the good news (לבשר את שרה) to Sarah.

[88] Ibid., III, 8 (Ex. r., 46 on 34:1): "The good news be brought thee (אתה מבושר) that I have forgiven thee thy sins." Cf. also jBer., 9d, 25 (→ supra).

[89] Ibid., III, 7 for examples.

[90] εὐαγγελίζεσθαι and κηρύσσειν as in Lk. 4:43 f.; 8:1; Ac. 8:1; Mk. 1:14; Mt. 4:23; 9:35; Mk. 13:10 = Mt. 24:14; Mk. 14:9 = Mt. 26:13; Mk. 16:15; Gl. 2:2; Col. 1:23; 1 Th. 2:9; 2 Tm. 1:11; Cant. r. 2:12 : "The voice of the turtle-dove is heard in our land. Who is that ? It is the voice of the anointed king who proclaims and declares (המכריז ואומר): How beautiful on the mountains are the feet of him who proclaims good news, Is. 52:7." כרז = אֶ-ρύσσειν. Schl. Mt., 115 on 4:17; Schlatter Theologie, I, 583; Schn. Euang., XIII.

[91] Cf. Schn. Euang., XIII n., using G. Kittel's translation. Cf. Schl. Mt., 361 on 11:5; Schlatter Theologie, I, 583. Schn. Euang. also refers to Eka r. on 1:21, which in the course of eschatological words of comfort quotes Is. 52:7, but does not mention the name of the messenger.

[92] For the text cf. Schn. Euang., XIII.

mountains are the feet of the מבשר. When the Holy One, blessed be He, will be King, they will all be messengers bearing good news, as it is said, He who declares good things causes peace to be heard ... The Holy One, blessed be He, is King ; it is fitting to praise Him. Why ? Because they are for the dominion (מלכות) of the Holy One, blessed be He. In that hour they all rejoice and exult and praise, for they see that He is King. Hence it is written : He who says to Sion, Thy God is King. And what follows ? The voices of thy watchmen, they lift up their voice and rejoice together, Is. 52:8." They all become messengers publishing glad tidings. The message of the מלכות is carried further by the watchmen. In many cases Elijah is the expected messenger, as in Pesikt. r., 35 (161a): [93] "Three days before Messiah comes, comes Elijah and stands on the mountains of Israel and weeps and mourns over them and says : See, O land of Israel, how long will you stand in barrenness and dryness and desolation ? And his voice will be heard from one end of the world to the other. Then he will say to them, Peace has come into the world, for it is written, Behold on the mountains the feet of those who bring glad tidings, who publish peace, Na. 2:1. When the ungodly hear this, they will all rejoice and say to one another, Peace has come to us. On the second day he will come and stand on the mountains of Israel and say, Good has come into the world, for it is said : Who publisheth good things, Is. 52:7. On the third day he will come and say, Salvation has come into the world, for it is said, Who proclaimeth salvation, Is. 52:7. When he will then see the ungodly, as they themselves say, he will say, Thy God has become King for Sion. This will teach thee that salvation has come for Sion and its children but not for the ungodly. In that hour God will cause His glory and lordship (מלכותו) to appear to all who come into the world, and He will redeem Israel." The one who brings glad tidings can also be the Messiah himself. "R. Jose the Galilean (c. 110 A.D.) said : Great is peace, for when the king, Messiah, will reveal himself (נגלה) to Israel, he will begin only with peace, for it is written, How beautiful on the mountains are the feet of him who bringeth glad tidings (רגלי מבשר), who publisheth peace (Is. 52:7)." [94]

The OT expectation of the מבשר was still alive in the time of Jesus. The examples given bracket the period of early Christianity, Ps. Sol. in the 1st cent. B.C. and R. Jose c. 110 A.D. [95] The passages from the prophets which give us this view of the one who brings good news, Is. 40:9, [96] 41:27, [97] 52:7, [98] 61:1, [99] and Na. 2:1, [100] constantly recur in Rabbinic writings. The parallel with the NT is obvious. The one who brings glad tidings comes. He may be Messiah. But he does not have to be. He may be anonymous. Sometimes it is Messiah, sometimes Elijah, sometimes we are not told who it is. He appears and preaches, and all who hear and receive his message become מבשרים. [101] The מלך יהוה of the OT has become

---

[93] Str.-B., III, 9, where further instances are given.

[94] The concluding chapter of Derekh Erez Zuta (in Str.-B., III, 9c). Str.-B. and Schn. Euang. give other examples. V. also Schl. Theologie, I, 583; Schl. Mt., 115 on 4:17 and 122 on 4:23.

[95] Cf. the exact dating of the Rabbinic tradition in Schn. Euang., XIII.

[96] Tanch. תולדות 16 and 135 (Schl. Mt., 122 on 4:23).

[97] Pesikt., 28e : "I bring you the first, this is the Messiah of whom it is written (Is. 41:27): He is the first at Sion, lo, there they are ! and for Jerusalem I give the one who brings glad tidings," cf. Schn. Euang., XIII and Schl. Theologie, I, 583.

[98] Is. 52:7 is constantly quoted.

[99] Pesikt. r., 36 (162a) (Str.-B., III, 9c): "Ye oppressed (עניים), the time of your redemption has come."

[100] Pesikt. r., 35 (161a) and Tanch. במדבר on Nu. 2:2 → supra.

[101] R. 10:15; Eph. 6:15; Schn. Euang., 70 f. and XIII B.

מלכות שמים (→ I, 571). "Salvation has drawn near (קרבה ישוע)," [102] "the time of God's dominion (מלכות שמים) has come" [103] proclaims the messenger. Nor is the message only for Israel; it is also for the Gentiles (as regards the OT → 709). It is always addressed to Israel. Israel will be restored. Deliverance and redemption will come for it. Yet there is always a connection with the Gentiles too — Israel first and then the Gentiles. They, too, participate in the Messianic salvation. They come to Sion and see the glory of Yahweh. The מלכות שמים applies to them too. For Yahweh is not merely the God of Israel; He is the Lord of the world. [104] This will be proclaimed to the dead as well as the living. Even those who have fallen asleep will receive the message. All men from Adam on hear the voice of the one who brings glad tidings — the news that salvation has come, [105] that the new age, the age of joy, has commenced.

E. εὐαγγελίζομαι in the NT.

The varying occurrence of εὐαγγελίζομαι and → εὐαγγέλιον in the different writings of the NT is worth noting. εὐαγγελίζομαι occurs only once in Mt. at 11:5; 10 times in Lk. (or 11 acc. to 1:28 in 565 it); 15 times in Ac. (or 16 acc. to 16:17 in D*); in Pl. 21 times (or 22 acc. to R. 10:15 in אDG lat sy Ir); twice in Hb.; three times in 1 Pt.; and εὐαγγελίζειν twice in Rev. The verb is not found at all in Mk., John's Gospel and Ep., Jm., 2 Pt. or Jd. It is particularly striking that neither verb nor subst. is found in the Johannine writings. There must be some reason for this. [106] The omission of εὐαγγελίζομαι is probably in keeping with the whole character of John's Gospel. The dramatic, dynamic proclamation of the time of salvation as this takes place by εὐαγγελίζεσθαι does not fit the realised eschatology of the Gospel. [107] In εὐαγγελίζομαι the Messianic secret is kept (→ 716). John's Gospel reflects the calm of fulfilment. In this connection we may also mention the polemic against John the Baptist (→ 719), which seems to make it advisable to avoid using εὐαγγελίζεσθαι on the lips of Jesus.

---

[102] Pirqe Mashiach (Beth ha-Midrash, 3, 73, 17) in Str.-B., III, 10c.

[103] Pesikt. r., 51a in Str.-B., III, 9b.

[104] This is particularly plain in Pesikt. r., 36 (162a) (Str.-B., III, 9c). To be sure, this has בשר, rather than השמיע. But both Schn. Euang. and Str.-B. reckon this among the מבשר-passages, and in content it belongs to them: "He will proclaim to them, the Israelites, and say to them: Ye oppressed, the time of your redemption has come. And if you will not believe, then behold my light streaming over you, for it is written, Arise, shine ... Is. 60:1. On you alone it shines, not on the nations of the earth, for it is written, Behold, darkness covers the earth, and thick darkness the people, but Yahweh will shine over you and His glory will be manifested upon you. Is. 60:2. In that hour God will cause the light of the king, the Messiah, and of Israel to shine, and all peoples of the world are in darkness; and they will all go to the light of the Messiah and Israel, for it is said, And the Gentiles (Gojim) will go to thy light, and kings to the brightness of thy rising, Is. 60:3."

[105] Pirqe Mashiach (Beth ha-Midrash, 3, 73, 17) in Str.-B., III, 10c: "In that hour he will draw near and bring good news (ומבשר) to those who sleep in the twofold grave, and will say to them: Abraham, Isaac and Jacob, arise, you have slept enough. And they will answer him and say: Who is it who has taken off the dust (of the grave) from us? And he will say to them: I am the Messiah of Yahweh, salvation has drawn near, the hour has come. And they will answer him, If this is truly so, then go and bring the good news to the first man, that he may arise first ... Then the first man will arise at once, and his whole generation, and Abraham, Isaac and Jacob, and all the righteous, and all the patriarchs and all generations from one end of the earth to the other, and they will raise the voice of joy and singing, for it is said, How beautiful on the mountains are the feet of him that bringeth glad tidings, Is. 52:7."

[106] Harnack, Kirchenverfassung und -recht, 211, n. 1; also → I, 59.

[107] G. Stählin, "Zum Problem der joh. Eschatologie," ZNW, 33 (1934), 225 ff.

1. Jesus.

Jesus is the One who brings the good news of the expected last time. To the
question of the Baptist He replies in Mt. 11:5 (= Lk. 7:22): [108] τυφλοὶ ἀναβλέ-
πουσιν καὶ χωλοὶ περιπατοῦσιν, λεπροὶ καθαρίζονται καὶ κωφοὶ ἀκούουσιν,
καὶ νεκροὶ ἐγείρονται καὶ πτωχοὶ εὐαγγελίζονται. [109] The whole sentence finds
its climax in the πτωχοὶ εὐαγγελίζονται. The message actualises the new time
and makes possible the signs of Messianic fulfilment. The Word brings in the
divine rule. This is no longer understood in some MSS. Thus Θφ syᶜ rate the
resurrection of the dead higher than the proclamation of the Gospel and therefore
they change the order. [110] The answer which Jesus gives to the Baptist is that the
longed for time is now dawning, that the eschatological good news expected from
the days of Dt. Is. is now being proclaimed, and that the Word has power and
brings into effect what is spoken. Word and miracle, the proclamation of the glad
tidings and the resurrection of the dead (→ 717; 720), are signs of the Messianic
age. εὐαγγελίζεσθαι is also found on the lips of Jesus in Lk. 4:18, 43 and 16:16.
According to Lk. 4:18 Jesus in His sermon at Nazareth applied Is. 61:1 to Himself. Lk. 16:16: ἡ βασιλεία τοῦ θεοῦ εὐαγγελίζεται (→ 719), may not be
authentic in this form, since it is hard to put it back into Aram., [111] the pass. of
בשר meaning "to receive news" rather than "to be proclaimed." On the other hand,
if Lk. is responsible, he shows an accurate perception. The task of Jesus was to
proclaim the → βασιλεία τοῦ θεοῦ. This was His mission, His sacred duty (Lk.
4:43; cf. 1 C. 1:17; 9:16 ff. → 719). The presence of the kingdom of God means joy.

Synonymous with εὐαγγελίζεσθαι is → κηρύσσειν (Lk. 4:43 f. compared with
Mk. 1:38; Lk. 8:1; v. Lk. 20:1: διδάσκειν and εὐαγγελίζεσθαι). The phrase κηρύσσων καὶ εὐαγγελιζόμενος τὴν βασιλείαν τοῦ θεοῦ (Lk. 8:1) gives us a
comprehensive picture of the whole activity of Jesus. His whole life was proclamation of the Gospel. Hence His birth is an εὐαγγέλιον, Lk. 2:10 (→ 721).
Eph. 2:17: καὶ ἐλθὼν εὐηγγελίσατο εἰρήνην ὑμῖν τοῖς μακρὰν καὶ εἰρήνην τοῖς
ἐγγύς. The coming of Jesus to earth, His life and death, were the great message
of peace, the great proclamation of peace. His manifestation, not merely His
preaching but His whole work, is described in terms of εὐαγγελίζεσθαι. The
context shows this. In v. 16 the reference is to His death. In v. 14 He is peace,
and His manifestation is the proclamation of peace. He makes peace between God
and man and between man and man (→ 415 f.). On Ac. 10:36 → 721. Since in

---

[108] On the genuineness of this verse v. Bultmann Trad., 22, 115, 163.

[109] Mt. 11:5 is a quotation from Is. 35:5 and 61:1 with the additions "the lepers are
cleansed" and "the dead are raised." There are similar quotations in Apc. Elias 33:1 ff.
(TU, NF, 2, 2 [1899], 89); Lidz. Joh., 76 (II, 243); Lidz. Ginza r., I, 201 (p. 30); II, 1, 136
(p. 48); Slav. Jos. Bell., 1, 364 ff. But the decisive word εὐαγγελίζεσθαι does not occur.
Thus Slav. Jos. Bell., 1, 364 ff. has instead : Among the anointed it was determined "to make
the rich poor," in addition to making the lame to walk and the blind to see ; Lidz. Ginza r.,
I, 201 (p. 30) has : "He converts the Jews," and ibid., II, 1, 136 (p. 48): "He wins believers
among the Jews," which might perhaps correspond to εὐαγγελίζεσθαι. Cf. R. Reitzenstein,
"Das mandäische Buch des Herrn der Grösse und die Ev-Überlieferung" (SAH, 1919, 12),
61; H. Schaeder, in R. Reitzenstein and H. Schaeder, Studien zum antiken Synkretismus
(1926), 333. Mt. 11:5 can hardly be dependent on the Mandaean writings. R. Reitzenstein,
Das iranische Erlösungsmysterium (1921), 111, n. 1; ZNW, 26 (1927), 51, 55 f.; A. Allgeier,
Theologische Revue, 20 (1921), 181; H. Gressmann, ZKG, NF, 3 (1922), 188; M. Goguel,
Jean Baptiste (1928), 125 f.; H. Lietzmann, SAB, 1930, 596 ff.; Bultmann Trad., 22, n. 2;
H. Schlier, ThR, NF, 5 (1933), 9 ff., 69.

[110] Schn. Euang., XII A.
[111] Dalman WJ, I, 84.

1 Pt. 3:19 it is said of Jesus : καὶ τοῖς ἐν φυλακῇ πνεύμασιν πορευθεὶς ἐκήρυξεν, we must refer the νεκροῖς εὐηγγελίσθη of 1 Pt. 4:6 to Jesus. Even to the dead the good news is brought (→ 717, n. 105) that they might be saved and live.

2. John the Baptist.

Of the activity of John the Baptist it is said in Lk. 3:18 : πολλὰ μὲν οὖν καὶ ἕτερα παρακαλῶν εὐηγγελίζετο τὸν λαόν. He, Elijah (→ 716) (Lk. 1:17; Mt. 11:14; 17:12), is the evangelist. He proclaims the imminence of the kingdom of God. Is he the forerunner of the Messiah or is he more ? In Lk. 16:16 he is the boundary between the old and the new. He still belongs to the Law and the prophets (→ I, 612) even though he is more than a prophet according to Mt. 11:9 : ὁ νόμος καὶ οἱ προφῆται μέχρι Ἰωάννου. ἀπὸ τότε ἡ βασιλεία τοῦ θεοῦ εὐαγγελίζεται. These sayings combat an overestimation of the Baptist which regards him as the One who has come. His birth is announced by the angel (Lk. 1:19 εὐαγγελίζεσθαι) like that of Jesus. This is an intimation of the Messianic salvation. According to Lk. 1:15-17; 68-79 he prepares the way, not for the Messiah, but for God. He is the one who brings glad tidings and therefore the longed for eschatological salvation. His message, then, is good news. Even as a precursor of the Messiah he is an evangelist. His story is the beginning of the Gospel (Mk. 1:1; Ac. 10:36 f.). [112]

3. The host of witnesses, disciples, apostles, evangelists.

R. 10:15 : πῶς δὲ κηρύξωσιν ἐὰν μὴ ἀποσταλῶσιν; καθάπερ γέγραπται· ὡς ὡραῖοι οἱ πόδες τῶν εὐαγγελιζομένων ἀγαθά. Here Is. 52:7 is not referred to the Messiah but to the messengers of the Gospel. The plur. is attested neither in the LXX nor the Mas. Both Ac. 10:36 and Eph. 2:17 quote Is. 52:7 in the sing. Paul is following the tradition of Palestinian Judaism (→ 716) that the watchers on the walls in Dt. Is., the witnesses of Yahweh's coming, become evangelists. [113] Already during the lifetime of Jesus the Twelve go through the land εὐαγγελιζό-μενοι καὶ θεραπεύοντες (Lk. 9:1-6), proclaiming the kingdom of God and working signs like Jesus Himself. The missionary activity of the apostles begins after Pentecost. Ac. 5:42 : πᾶσάν τε ἡμέραν ἐν τῷ ἱερῷ καὶ κατ᾽ οἶκον οὐκ ἐπαύοντο διδάσκοντες καὶ εὐαγγελιζόμενοι τὸν χριστὸν Ἰησοῦν. As a result of persecu-tion in Jerusalem the Gospel is taken further afield. Philip especially, one of the 'deacons,' preaches the Word (Ac. 8:12, 35, 40 → εὐαγγελιστής).

The message is first taken to the Jews, but then also to the Greeks (Ac. 11:20). Paul becomes the evangelist to the Gentiles (Ac. 14:7, 15, 21; 16:10; 17:18; R. 15:20; 1 C. 15:1, 2; 2 C. 10:16; 11:7; Gl. 1:8, 11; 4:13). He is called to bring the Gospel to the Gentiles (Gl. 1:16). This is his → χάρις (Eph. 3:8). He can use εὐαγγελί-ζεσθαι to describe his whole activity as an apostle (1 C. 1:17). Like the prophets (Jer. 1; 20:9; Am. 3:8; Ez. 3:17 ff.), he stands under a divine constraint, so that he must preach. [114] This is his mission (→ 718). 1 C. 9:16 : ἀνάγκη γάρ μοι ἐπίκειται· οὐαὶ γάρ μοί ἐστιν ἐὰν μὴ εὐαγγελίσωμαι. εὐαγγελίζομαι is a missionary term. Ac. 14:15 : εὐαγγελιζόμενοι ὑμᾶς ἀπὸ τούτων τῶν ματαίων ἐπιστρέφειν ἐπὶ θεὸν ζῶντα, ὃς ἐποίησεν τὸν οὐρανὸν καὶ τὴν γῆν ... But the

---

112 E. Lohmeyer, *Das Urchristentum*, I : *Johannes der Täufer* (1932), 3, 5, 11, 15, 20, 23 f., 46, 69. Lk. 1:15 is hardly an allusion to Is. 61:1.
113 Schn. Euang., 70 f.
114 Schniewind, *Wort und Evgl. bei Pls.*, 70.

message is also addressed to Christians (R. 1:15, cf. 11; [115] 1 C. 9:12-18; Gl. 4:13; 2 Tm. 4:5, cf. 2). The same Gospel is proclaimed in both missionary and congregational preaching. Paul makes no distinction. God Himself speaks in preaching, and He does not speak to Christians or to heathen, but to man as such, revealing Himself to him in grace and judgment through the Word (→ εὐαγγέλιον).

The preacher proclaims αὐτόν (Gl. 1:16), namely, τὸν Ἰησοῦν (Ac. 8:35; 17:18), τὸν χριστὸν Ἰησοῦν (Ac. 5:42), τὸν κύριον Ἰησοῦν (Ac. 11:20), περὶ τοῦ ὀνόματος Ἰησοῦ Χριστοῦ (Ac. 8:12), τὸ ἀνεξιχνίαστον πλοῦτος τοῦ Χριστοῦ (Eph. 3:8). Rather more specifically, one may also say παθήματα and δόξα (1 Pt. 1:11 ff.), ἀνάστασις (Ac. 17:18), or βασιλεία τοῦ θεοῦ (Ac. 8:12). Christ is the βασιλεία in person, the αὐτοβασιλεία (→ I, 589). Scripture treats of Him (1 Pt. 1:11 ff.), and therefore the preaching of the Gospel has the OT as its content (Ac. 8:35). καὶ ἡμεῖς ὑμᾶς εὐαγγελιζόμεθα τὴν πρὸς τοὺς πατέρας ἐπαγγελίαν γενομένην, ὅτι ταύτην ὁ θεὸς ἐκπεπλήρωκεν τοῖς τέκνοις ἡμῶν ἀναστήσας Ἰησοῦν (Ac. 13:32 f. → 582). εὐαγγελίζεσθαι is also linked with λόγος (Ac. 8:4), λόγος τοῦ κυρίου (Ac. 15:35), ῥῆμα (1 Pt. 1:25), πίστις (Gl. 1:23), → εὐαγγέλιον (1 C. 15:1; 2 C. 11:7; Gl. 1:11). εὐαγγελίζεσθαι is also closely related to → κηρύσσειν (Ac. 8:4 f.), → διδάσκειν (Ac. 5:42; 15:35), → λαλεῖν (Ac. 8:25; 11:19, 20), → διαμαρτύρεσθαι (Ac. 8:25), → μαθητεύειν (Ac. 14:21), → ἀναγγέλλειν (1 Pt. 1:12), καταγγέλλειν (Ac. 16:17, cf. Cod. D).

εὐαγγελίζεσθαι is not just speaking and preaching; it is proclamation with full authority and power. Signs and wonders accompany the evangelical message. They belong together, for the Word is powerful and effective. The proclamation of the age of grace, of the rule of God, creates a healthy state in every respect. Bodily disorders are healed and man's relation to God is set right (Mt. 4:23; 9:35; 11:5; Lk. 9:6; Ac. 8:4-8; 10:36 ff.; 14:8-18; 16:17 ff.; R. 15:16-20; 2 C. 12:12; Gl. 3:5). [116] Joy reigns where this Word is proclaimed (Ac. 8:8). It brings σωτηρία (1 C. 15:1 f. → εὐαγγέλιον). It is the ὁδὸς σωτηρίας (Ac. 16:17 D*). It effects regeneration (1 Pt. 1:23-25). It is not a word of man, but the living, eternal Word of God. The Holy Spirit, who was sought for the day of salvation, attests Himself now in the time of fulfilment when the glad tidings are proclaimed (1 Pt. 1:12). Hence εὐαγγελίζεσθαι is to offer salvation. It is the powerful proclamation of the good news, the impartation of σωτηρία. This would be missed if εὐαγγελίζεσθαι were to take place in human fashion ἐν σοφίᾳ λόγου (1 C. 1:17). [117]

In 1 Th. 3:6 and Hb. 4:2, 6 there is some variation from the passages thus far discussed. In 1 Th. 3:6, [118] while we do not have a secular use, the faith and love of the Thessalonians are the subject of proclamation rather than Christ. Paul is bringing good news from the field where he has been working as a missionary. In Hb. 4:2, 6 εὐαγγελίζεσθαι is used of OT as well as NT proclamation. The εὐαγγέλιον of the Jews is to be found in the promises (→ 585, n. 67).

---

[115] Ibid., 71. To avoid this exposition, Zn. R., ad loc. prefers the reading καὶ ἐν ὑμῖν attested in the Western text (D* g vg).

[116] Schniewind, Mk., NT Deutsch, I (1933), 56.

[117] Schniewind, Wort u. Evgl. bei Pls., 69.

[118] Rather surprisingly, the Vulgate has annuntiare here instead of evangelizare. But we should not stress this, since it follows the same rule in Ac. 10:36; 11:20; 13:32; 14:15; 17:18. Cf. Hb. 4:2 nuntiare; 4:6 annuntiare; R. 15:20; 1 C. 9:18 evangelium praedicare; but 2 C. 11:7 evangelium evangelizare. Cf. W. Matzkow, De Vocabulis quibusdam Italae et Vulgatae Christianis (Diss., 1933), 26 ff.

4. God.

In two NT passages God is the One who proclaims the good news. In Ac. 10:36 God causes εἰρήνην to be proclaimed through Christ. The Word of the proclamation of peace is τὸ γενόμενον ῥῆμα. It is the story of Jesus, of His life, death and resurrection. This story is God's good news of peace and joy (→ 718), first to the Jews, then to all men, for Christ is πάντων κύριος. In Rev. 10:7 God has revealed His plan of salvation to His servants the prophets of the OT and the NT. It is good news because it proclaims the coming of the Messiah, of the βασιλεία τοῦ θεοῦ, after the overthrow of the dominion of Antichrist.

5. Angels.

Gabriel proclaims to Zacharias (Lk. 1:19) the birth of John the Baptist (→ 719). An angel tells the shepherds of the birth of the σωτήρ (Lk. 2:10 → 718). [119] In both cases the message is an evangel because the desired last time, the coming of Messianic salvation, is proclaimed. χαρὰ μεγάλη rules in the time of salvation (Lk. 1:14 → I, 20). On Rev. 14:6 → εὐαγγέλιον.

εὐαγγέλιον.

A. εὐαγγέλιον outside the NT.

1. בְּשׂרָה in the OT.

The subst. is far less common than the verb. It is found only 6 times in the OT and has the two senses of 1. "good news" (2 S. 18:20, 25, 27; 2 K. 7:9) and 2. the "reward for good news" (2 S. 4:10; 18:22). [1] This twofold meaning of בְּשׂרָה helps us to see the effective power of the word (→ 708). [2] The spoken word is equated with its content. [3] Bad news brings sorrow, and good news causes joy, for the word carries power and effects what it proclaims. Hence the bearer of bad news is guilty of the misfortune which he announces. He is punished for his message and sometimes he is even put to death (2 S. 1:15 f.). In 2 S. 4:10 someone brings David news of the death of Saul. He thinks he is bringing good news, but David has him put to death. This was the בְּשׂרָה, his reward for the good news which he told. It is because the messenger is the bearer of the good fortune or misfortune which he narrates that Joab tries to keep back Ahimaaz from running, for his בְּשׂרָה contains news of the death of the king's son (2 S. 18:20). Ahimaaz runs, but he avoids telling the king of the death of Absalom: "I saw a great tumult, but I knew not what it was." The bearer of good news is rewarded for his message, for he is the cause of joy through his declaration. Good fortune is contained in good news, and therefore he deserves a reward.

In the OT בְּשׂרָה is used only in a secular sense. There is no religious use of the subst. whatever.

2. εὐαγγέλιον among the Greeks.

a. εὐαγγέλιον is an adj. used as subst. Like εὐαγγελίζεσθαι (→ 710), it derives from εὐάγγελος. [4] It means that which is proper to an εὐάγγελος. This gives εὐ-

---

[119] On the relation of this passage to the LXX v. G. Erdmann, *Die Vorgeschichte des Lk.- u. Mt. Ev.* (1932), 17 f.

εὐαγγέλιον. For bibl. → 707 n.

[1] Ges.-Buhl would bring 2 S. 18:22 under 1. R. Kittel in Kautzsch, also W. Nowak (1902), K. Budde (1902), W. Caspari (1926) in the comm., *ad loc.,* all favour 2. (i.e., the messenger's "reward").

[2] On what follows cf. Schn. Euang., 31 f.

[3] דבר can mean "thing," "history," "event," as well as "word."

[4] F. Specht in Schn. Euang., 116.

ἀγγέλιον a twofold sense. For those to whom an εὐάγγελος comes, what is proper to him is good news ; but for the εὐάγγελος himself, what is proper is his reward. In the oldest known example in Hom. Od., 14, 152 f., 166 f. εὐαγγέλιον means "reward for good news." The sense of "good news" is attested only from the time of Cic. Att., II, 3, 1. Yet both meanings are equally sound. Thus εὐαγγέλια θύειν, known from the time of Aristoph. Eq., 656, plainly presupposes εὐαγγέλιον in the sense of good news, for it means "to celebrate good news by sacrifices." [5]

εὐαγγέλιον is a technical term for "news of victory." The messenger appears, raises his right hand in greeting and calls out with a loud voice : χαῖρε ... νικῶμεν. [6] By his appearance it is known already that he brings good news. [7] His face shines, [8] his spear is decked with laurel, [9] his head is crowned, [10] he swings a branch of palms, joy fills the city, εὐαγγέλια are offered, the temples are garlanded, [11] an *agon* is held, [12] crowns are put on for the sacrifices [13] and the one to whom the message is owed is honoured with a wreath. [14] Political and private reports can also be εὐαγγέλια. [15] For them, too, sacrificial feasts are held. [16] But εὐαγγέλιον is closely linked with the thought of victory in battle. This may be seen from the misunderstanding of which we read in Philostr. Vit. Ap., V, 8. Nero had been successful in the games and he ordered εὐαγγέλια to be offered. But some cities believed that he had been victorious in war and had taken some Olympians captive. εὐαγγέλια ἐπάγειν or θύειν is something so familiar that it can be used for comparison or illustration. [17] There is a caricature in Aristophanes. [18]

Good fortune is contained in the words. Aristoph. Pl., 646 ff.: ὡς ἀγαθὰ συλλήβδην ἅπαντά σοι φέρω. καὶ ποῦ 'στιν; ἐν τοῖς λεγομένοις· εἴσει τάχα. πέραινε τοίνυν ὅ τι λέγεις ἀνύσας ποτέ. For this reason the message is rewarded. [19] It is intrinsically

---

[5] Schn. Euang., 120; Aeschin., 3, 160 : εἰς αἰτίαν εὐαγγελίων θυσίας, excludes any possibility of translating εὐαγγέλια θύειν "to offer to the gods the reward for good news"; in this context it can only mean a sacrifice for good news.

[6] Plut. Demetr., 17 (I, 896c).

[7] Heliodor. Aeth., X, 3 : τὴν νίκην καὶ μόνῳ τῷ σχήματι δημοσιεύοντες.

[8] Philostr. Vit. Soph., II, 5, 3.

[9] Plut. Pomp., 41 (I, 640).

[10] Plut. Demetr., 11 (I, 893 f.); Xenoph. Hist. Graec., I, 6, 37.

[11] Heliodor. Aeth., X, 3 : ἀλλὰ τὴν πόλιν ἐπιόντες τῶν εὐαγγελίων ἐμπλήσατε· καὶ οἳ μὲν πρόδρομοι τὸ προστεταγμένον ἔπραττον ... ἐμπέπληστο γοῦν αὐτίκα χαρᾶς ἡ Μερόη, νύκτωρ τε καὶ μεθ' ἡμέραν χορούς καὶ θυσίας ... τοῖς θεοῖς ἀναγόντων καὶ τὰ τεμένη καταστρεφόντων.

[12] Ditt. Or., I, 6, 20 f.

[13] Plut. Apophth. Antiochus Hierax (II, 184a); Plut. Ages., 17 (I, 605c).

[14] Plut. Demosthenes, 22 (I, 855e).

[15] Cic. Att., II, 3, 1 εὐαγγέλια, *Valerius absolutus est*; Heliodor. Aeth., I, 14, the death of the wicked stepmother ; Cic. Att., XIII, 40, 1, the good news that Caesar will join the true friends of the fatherland. For further instances *v.* Schn. Euang., 152.

[16] Plut. Apophth. Antiochus Hierax (II, 184a): πυθόμενος τὸν ἀδελφὸν σώζεσθαι εὐαγγέλια τοῖς θεοῖς ἔθυσε. Diod. S., 15, 74, 2 : Dionysius offers thank-offerings to the gods on the news of his triumph in the games as a poet. Menand. Peric., 413 ff.

[17] Philostr. Vit. Soph., II, 5, 3 : The orator springs up φαιδρῷ τῷ προσώπῳ καθάπερ εὐαγγέλια ἐπάγων τοῖς ἀκροωμένοις ὧν εἰπεῖν ἔχοι.

[18] Aristoph. Eq., 656 εὐαγγέλια θύειν ἑκατὸν βοῦς τῇ θεῷ for the news that anchovies have become cheaper. In Aristoph. Pl., 764 the messenger is given for his good news a cord of cracknels wound round his head.

[19] Aristoph. Pl., 764. The reward naturally differs. Aristoph. Eq., 647; Philostr. Vit. Soph., I, 18, 1, a crown. The Lacedaemonians give to the messenger (Plut. Ages., 33 [I, 614 f.]) who announces the victory of Mantinea only a piece of meat from the common table. Sometimes we hear of dissatisfaction with the reward. Plut. Artaxerxes, 14 (I, 1018b): οὐκ ἠξίου τὰ δοθέντα μισθὸν εὐαγγελίων ἔχειν. For further instances, *v.* Schn. Euang., 140, n. 1.

valuable. It does not merely declare salvation ; it effects it. Because of the importance of the message, the messenger exerts himself to be first. [20] If another arrives before him, his reward is less. [21] A slow messenger can be punished for his dilatoriness, [22] for he deprives the recipients of their good fortune. So far as possible bad news is suppressed. [23] Good news is a gift of the gods. This is why it is celebrated with sacrificial feasts. [24]

It is to be noted that where εὐαγγέλιον is used as a religious term we do not find εὐαγγέλια θύειν. [25] This is surprising, but it is no accident. Either through mis-information or for psychological or political reasons reports were often circulated and festivities held when there was really no cause. Indeed, the truth might sometimes be the very opposite of that for which the festivities were celebrated. [26] Hence scepticism arose, and rewards came to be paid only when the news was verified. [27] As a result of sorry experiences, it was found necessary to make a new distinction between news and event. Thus in Ditt. Or., I, 4, 42 we find both εὐαγγέλια and σωτήρια θύειν. Offerings are made both for the news and for the deliverance. We can understand, therefore, that the misused and suspect expression εὐαγγέλια θύειν was avoided when it was a matter of religious messages concerning the correctness and factuality of which there was no doubt, and why expressions like τὰς εὐχαριστηρίους τῶν ἐπινικίων θυσίας (Heliodor. Aeth., X, 2), τὰς χαριστηρίους εὐχὰς ὑπὲρ τῆς νίκης καὶ σωτηρίας (ibid., X, 6) and τοῖς θεοῖς τὰς ὀφειλομένα[ς] σπονδὰς ἀποδιδόναι (P. Giess., I, 27, 6 ff.) were used instead (→ n. 37). In religious usage the message is again so highly valued that it is equated with the actuality. On the occasion of these messages sacrifice is offered not merely for the message (εὐαγγέλια θύειν) but for the event proclaimed. εὐαγγέλιον is thus estimated as a fact in the oracles and the imperial cult.

Like εὐαγγελίζεσθαι (→ 711), εὐαγγέλιον can be an oracular saying. In Plut. Sertorius, 11 (I, 573d) it is said of a hind, a gift of Artemis, that it reveals many hidden things. When messengers declare a victory, these are declared, τὴν δὲ ἔλαφον ἐστε-φανωμένην ἐπ᾽ εὐαγγελίοις προῆγεν εὐθυμεῖσθαι παρακαλῶν καὶ τοῖς θεοῖς θύειν ὡς ἀγαθόν τι πευσομένους. Thankofferings are made to the gods for supposed oracles. Apollonius (Philostr. Vit. Ap., VIII, 26 f.) sees in spirit the murder of Domitian, and describes how the Logos disseminates itself and causes great joy. The Ephesians do not believe. They ought to offer sacrifice, since Apollonius believes he is the pro-claimer of the εὐαγγέλιον, but he orders them to postpone the sacrifice until the ῥῆμα has taken place. ἔτ᾽ ἀπιστουμένων τούτων ἦλθον οἱ τῶν εὐαγγελίων δρόμοι μάρτυρες τῆς σοφίας τοῦ ἀνδρός. εὐαγγέλιον is the ratification of the promise. The good news of the seer has proved to be true.

On the relations of εὐαγγέλιον to σωτηρία [28] and τύχη [29] → 711.

---

[20] Aristoph. Eq., 642 f.; Plut. Ages., 33 (I, 614 f.).
[21] Plut. Artaxerxes, 14 (I, 1018b): σοὶ ταῦτα δίδωσιν ὁ βασιλεὺς εὐαγγελίων δευτε-ρεῖα· πρῶτος γὰρ ...
[22] Plut. Demetr., 17 (I, 896c).
[23] Heliodor. Aeth., I, 14.
[24] Plut. Phoc., 23 (I, 752b); Diod. S., 15, 74, 2; Plut. Apophth. Antiochus Hierax (II, 184a).
[25] Cf. Schn. Euang., 168-183.
[26] Plut. Demetr., 11 (I, 893 f.). Vauntingly Stratocles strides through the city crowned and proclaims victory. εὐαγγέλια θύειν ἔγραψε. Plut. Ages., 17 (I, 605c): ὅπως δὲ μὴ τοῖς στρατιώταις ἐπὶ μάχην βαδίζουσιν ἀθυμία καὶ φόβος ἐμπέση, τἀναντία λέγειν ἐκέλευσε τοὺς ἀπὸ θαλάττης ἥκοντας, ὅτι νικῶσι τῇ ναυμαχίᾳ· καὶ προελθὼν αὐτὸς ἐστεφανωμένος ἔθυσεν εὐαγγέλια. Isoc. Areop., 10 : ἐπὶ τοιαύταις πράξεσιν εὐαγγέλια μὲν δὶς ἤδη τεθύκαμεν, whereupon misfortune after misfortune strikes us. For further examples v. Schn. Euang., 179.
[27] This lack of confidence in the message is to be seen already in the oldest instance of εὐαγγέλιον ("reward") in Hom. Od., 14, 152 f.
[28] Cf. also Plut. Apophth. Antiochus Hierax (II, 184a): πυθόμενος τὸν ἀδελφὸν σώ-ζεσθαι εὐαγγέλια τοῖς θεοῖς ἔθυσε.
[29] Ps.-Luc. Asin., 26; Menand. Peric., 414 ff. Cf. Schn. Euang., 145-152.

b. εὐαγγέλιον in the imperial cult. This is the most important usage for our purpose. Note must be taken of what is said concerning the θεῖος ἄνθρωπος (→ 712), τύχη and σωτηρία. The emperor unites all these in his own person. This is what gives εὐαγγέλιον its significance and power. The ruler is divine by nature. [30] His power extends to men, to animals, to the earth and to the sea. Nature belongs to him; wind and waves are subject to him. [31] He works miracles and heals men. [32] He is the saviour of the world who also redeems individuals from their difficulties (→ σωτήρ). τύχη is linked up with his person; he is himself τύχη. [33] He has appeared on earth as a deity in human form. He is the protective god of the state. His appearance is the cause of good fortune to the whole kingdom. Extraordinary signs accompany the course of his life. They proclaim the birth of the ruler of the world. A comet appears at his accession, and at his death signs in heaven declare his assumption into the ranks of the gods. [34] Because the emperor is more than a common man, his ordinances are glad messages and his commands are sacred writings. What he says is a divine act and implies good and salvation for men. He proclaims εὐαγγέλια through his appearance, and these εὐαγγέλια treat of him (→ 713). The first evangelium is the news of his birth: ἦρξεν δὲ τῶι κόσμωι τῶν δι' αὐτὸν εὐανγελί[ων ἡ γενέθλιος] τοῦ θεοῦ. [35] "The birthday of the god was for the world the beginning of the joyful messages which have gone forth because of him." [36] Other εὐαγγέλια follow, e.g., the news of his coming of age [37]

---

[30] O. Weinreich, "Antikes Gottmenschentum," *N. Jbch. Wiss. u. Jugendbildung*, 2 (1926), 633-651.

[31] Plut. De Fortuna Romanorum, 6 (II, 319c d): τόλμα καὶ δέδιθι μηδέν, ἀλλὰ ἐπιδίδου τῇ τύχῃ τὰ ἰστία καὶ δέχου τὸ πνεῦμα, τῷ πνέοντι πιστεύων, ὅτι Καίσαρα φέρεις καὶ τὴν Καίσαρος τύχην. οὕτως ἐπέπειστο τὴν Τύχην αὐτῷ συμπλεῖν, συναποδημεῖν, συστρατεύεσθαι, συστρατηγεῖν· ἢ ἔργον ἦν γαλήνην μὲν ἐπιτάξαι θαλάττῃ, θέρος δὲ χειμῶνι, τάχος δὲ τοῖς βραδυτάτοις, ἀλκὴν δὲ τοῖς ἀθυμοτάτοις.

[32] O. Weinreich, "Antike Heilungswunder," RVV, 8 (1909), 65-75.

[33] → n. 31. In P. Giess., I, 3, 3 ff. ἀρετή and τύχη are ascribed to the emperor. The son establishes his might on the ἀρετή and τύχη of the father. In Ditt. Or., I, 229, 62 the τύχη of the king is mentioned along with other gods. Antiochus of Commagene regards himself as τυχή in Ditt. Or., I, 383, 60 ff. Cf. O. Puchstein in *Reisen in Kleinasien und Nordsyrien* (1890) by K. Humann and O. Puchstein, 336 ff.

[34] E. Norden in *Die Geburt des Kindes* (1924), 157 ff.; G. Herzog-Hauser, "Kaiserkult," Pauly-W., Suppl. IV (1924), 819; in P. Giess., I, 3 the emperor is borne aloft on a chariot with white horses.

[35] Inscr. Priene, 105, 40 has been much quoted and discussed: Deissmann LO, 313; Wendland Hell. Kult., 410; Ditt. Or., II, 458, 40; T. Mommsen and U. v. Wilamowitz-Möllendorff, "Die Einführung des asianischen Kalenders" in *Ath. Mitt.*, 24 (1899), 275-293; H. Lietzmann, ThStKr, 82 (1909), 161; P. Wendland, ZNW, 5 (1904), 335 ff.; W. Soltau, *Die Geburtsgeschichte Jesu Chr.* (1902), 34; H. Lietzmann, *Der Weltheiland* (1909), 14; E. Norden, *Die Geburt des Kindes* (1924), 157; E. Petersen, *Die wunderbare Geburt, Religionsgeschichtliche Volksbücher*, I, 17 (1909), 23, 41 f.; A. v. Harnack, "Als die Zeit erfüllet war," *Reden und Aufsätze*[2] (1906), 301-306; A. Bauer, *Vom Griechentum zum Christentum* (1910), 89 f.; E. Lohmeyer, *Christuskult und Kaiserkult* (1919), 27; Zondervan, 188 ff.; Gillet, 35; Molland, 24; Schn. Euang., 87.

[36] For an exposition, cf. Schn. Euang., 83, n. 3; 87, n. 7. With E. Norden, *Geburt des Kindes*, 157 (cf. Norden in Deissmann LO, 447) we may refer εὐαγγέλια to oracular sayings. But this would not fit the other instances of εὐαγγέλιον in the imperial cult.

[37] *American Journal of Archaeology*, 2 Series, 18 (1914), 323: ἐπεὶ Γάϊος Ἰούλιος Καῖσαρ ὁ πρεσβύτατος τῶν τοῦ Σεβαστοῦ παίδων τὴν εὐκταιοτάτην ἐκ περιπορφύρου λαμπρὰν τῶ παντὶ κό[σ]μω ἀνείληφε τήβεννον, ἥδονταί τε πάντες ἄνθρωποι συνδιεγειρομένας ὁρῶντες τῶ Σεβαστῶ τὰς ὑπὲρ τῶν παίδων εὐχάς, ἥ τε ἡμετέρα πόλις ἐπὶ τῇ τοσαύτη εὐτυχία τὴν ἡμέραν τὴν ἐκ παιδὸς ἄνδρα τελησοῦσα[ν] αὐτὸν ἱερὰν ἔκρινεν εἶναι, ἐν ᾗ κατ' ἐνιαυτὸν ἐν λαμπραῖς (ἐ)σθῆσιν στεφανηφορεῖν ἅπαντας, θ[υ]σίας τε παριστάν(αι) τοῖς θεοῖς τοὺς κατ' ἐνιαυτὸν στρατηγοὺς καὶ κατευχὰς ποιεῖσθαι διὰ τῶν ἱεροκηρύκων ὑπὲρ τῆς σωτηρίας αὐτοῦ, συνκαθιερῶσαί τε ἄγαλμα αὐτοῦ τῶ τοῦ πατρὸς ἐνιδρύοντας ναῶι, ἐν ᾗ τε εὐανγελίσθη ἡ πόλις ἡμέρα καὶ τὸ ψήφισμα ἐκυρώθη καὶ ταύτην στεφ(αν)ηφορῆσαι τὴν ἡμέραν καὶ θυσίας τοῖς θεοῖς ἐκπρεπεστάτας ἐπιτελέσαι ...

and esp. his accession: ἐπεὶ γν[ώ]στ[ης ἐγενόμην τοῦ] εὐαγγελ[ίο]υ περὶ τοῦ ἀνηγορεῦσθαι Καίσαρα τὸν τοῦ θεοφιλεστάτου κυρίου ἡμῶν ...[38] Joy and rejoicing come with the news. Humanity, sighing under a heaven burden of guilt, wistfully longs for peace. Doom is feared because the gods have withdrawn from earth. [39] Then suddenly there rings out the news that the σωτήρ is born, that he has mounted the throne, that a new era dawns for the whole world. This εὐαγγέλιον is celebrated with offerings and yearly festivals. All cherished hopes are exceeded. The world has taken on a new appearance.

The imperial cult and the Bible share the view that accession to the throne, which introduces a new era and brings peace to the world, is a gospel for men. We can explain this only by supposing a common source. This is generally oriental. [40] To the many messages, however, the NT opposes the one Gospel, to the many accessions the one proclamation of the → βασιλεία τοῦ θεοῦ. The NT speaks the language of its day. It is a popular and realistic proclamation. It knows human waiting for and hope of the εὐαγγέλια, and it replies with the εὐαγγέλιον, but with an evangel of which some might be ashamed, since it is a σκάνδαλον (Mt. 11:5 f.; R. 1:16; 1 C. 1:17, 23; 2 Tm. 1:8; Mk. 8:35). The Gospel means for men σωτηρία, but σωτηρία through → μετάνοια and judgment (→ 728 f., 732). For many this Gospel may be ironical when they hear it (cf. Ac. 17:32). But it is real joy; for penitence brings joy, and judgment grace and salvation. Caesar and Christ, the emperor on the throne and the despised rabbi on the cross, confront one another. Both are evangel to men. They have much in common. But they belong to different worlds. [41]

3. Septuagint, Josephus.

a. In the Sept. εὐαγγέλιον does not occur in the sing. In the plur. it is found only at 2 S. 4:10 and means the "reward for good news." בְּשׂרָה in the sense of "good news" in 2 S. 18:20, 22, 25, 27; 2 K. 7:9, is rendered ἡ εὐαγγελία. [42] Elsewhere the fem. subst. is very rare, being found only in Jewish and Christian writers. [43] In the Sept., then, there is a distinction between ἡ εὐαγγελία ("good news") and τὰ εὐαγγέλια ("the reward for good news"). This distinction is not found in any other work.

The NT use of εὐαγγέλιον does not derive from the LXX. There is no religious use of either εὐαγγέλιον or εὐαγγελία in the LXX. The plur. τὰ εὐαγγέλια is not found in the NT, nor do we have the sense of "reward for good news" in the NT. The prior history of the NT concept is not to be sought in the LXX.

b. The subst. is not found in Philo's vocabulary. In Josephus, however, we find ἡ εὐαγγέλια (Ant., 18, 229), τὸ εὐαγγέλιον (Bell., 2, 420) and τὰ εὐαγγέλια (Bell., 4, 656) in the sense of glad tidings. Like the verb εὐαγγελίζομαι (→ 714), the subst.

---

[38] Acc. to Deissmann LO, 314, where other instances are given. Cf. also Molland, 25, Schn. Euang., 89 f.

[39] Cf. Wendland Hell. Kult., 142 ff.: "Die Stimmung der augustischen Zeit." Cf. also Inscr. Priene., Halicarnassus, decree from Assos (Wendland, 410).

[40] Lohmeyer, 24; also Zondervan, 203 f.

[41] Melito tried to link together the imperial and Christian cults in his apology to the emperor (Eus. Hist. Eccl., IV, 26, 7 f.): "According to this bishop the world has had two saviours, who appeared together, Augustus and Christ," Harnack, op. cit., 305 f.

[42] In 2 S. 18:22 בְּשׂורָה means "reward for good news" (→ n. 1). H. B. Swete and A. Rahlfs (1935) have εὐαγγελία instead of εὐαγγέλια in their editions of the LXX. But Schn. Euang., 64 reads εὐαγγέλια; for the meaning of the verse and the Heb. demand the translation "reward for a message." Schniewind's emendation is not really necessary, since the LXX paraphrase εὐαγγελία εἰς ὠφελίαν corresponds to the sense of "reward."

[43] Schn. Euang., 65.

εὐαγγέλιον reveals the connection between Joseph. and the Hellen. world. When he refers to a δεινὸν εὐαγγέλιον (Bell., 2, 420), this reminds us of the ironical usage noted among the Gks. (→ 711), but not exclusive to them, since it is found among the Rabbis too (→ 715). More important are the instances which bring us into the context of the imperial cult. In Bell., 4, 618 Vespasian tells the procurator of Egypt that he has taken over the government. τάχιον δ' ἐπινοίας διήγγελλον αἱ φῆμαι τὸν ἐπὶ τῆς ἀνατολῆς αὐτοκράτορα, καὶ πᾶσα μὲν πόλις ἑώρταζεν εὐαγγέλια [δὲ] καὶ θυσίας ὑπὲρ αὐτοῦ ἐπετέλει. The content of the glad message, which is solemnly celebrated, is the elevation of Vespasian to the imperial throne. In Bell., 4, 656 Vespasian receives the εὐαγγέλιον of his proclamation as role ruler : εἰς δὲ τὴν Ἀλεξάνδρειαν ἀφιγμένῳ τῷ Οὐεσπασιανῷ τὰ ἀπὸ τῆς Ῥώμης εὐαγγέλια ἧκε καὶ πρέσβεις ἐκ πάσης τῆς ἰδίας οἰκουμένης συνηδόμενοι.

4. Rabbinic Judaism.

Judaism proved a great help in fixing the development of εὐαγγελίζεσθαι, but it does not seem to lead us much further with regard to the subst. The Rabbis certainly know the word בשרה, and the corresponding בשר (→ 714). They use it for "good news" even without the addition טובה, [44] though occasionally it may be used for "sad news," as in Gn. r., 81 on 35:8 : "While Jacob was still mourning for Deborah, he received the sad news בשורתא that his mother had died." [45] The term is also used in the religious sense. There are no new features, however, as compared with the OT. [46]

We certainly find no echoes of the use of בשרה for the eschatological good news. This is no accident. A new message is not expected with the dawn of God's kingdom. What will be proclaimed has been known from the time of Dt. Is. The longing is that it should be proclaimed. Hence the messenger and the act of proclamation are more important than the בשרה. The new feature is not the message, but the eschatological act. The message brings the new thing, the מלכות שמים. Because all the emphasis is on the action, on the proclamation, on the utterance of the Word which ushers in the new age, בשורה is less prominent than מבשר or בשר. [47]

The interrelations of verb and subst. (בשר בשרה → n. 46) show that the NT εὐαγγέλιον comes from the Jewish and not the Greek world. If the origin of εὐαγγελίζομαι is plain, the same source is naturally to be sought for εὐαγγέλιον. The use of εὐαγγέλιον in the NT shows that this is correct (→ 729). The subst. does not merely denote a specific content ; it also expresses the act of proclamation. The verb בשר is carried over into εὐαγγέλιον, and this points us plainly to Palestine rather than Greece. In Gk. it is most unusual that εὐαγγέλιον should be used for an action.

This seems to be contradicted by the fact that εὐαγγέλιον appears to be a loan-word introduced into Judaism to describe the NT Gospel. In Sheb., 116a [48] we have the malicious conversion of gospel (אונגליון) into אָוֶן גִּלְיוֹן, gloss of destruction, or עָוֺן גִּלְיוֹן, gloss of sins : "R. Meir (c. 150) called it (the book of the Minim, i.e., of Jewish Christians, and therefore the Gospels) Aven-Gillajon, gloss or writing of destruction, and R. Jochanan (d. 279) called it Avon-Gillajon, gloss or writing of sins." From this passage we may conclude that the Jewish Christians had adopted the Gk. εὐαγγέλιον,

---

[44] bKet., 16b (Levy Wört., s.v.) calls the vessel of wine brought to the bride on her wedding-day a בְּשׂוֹרָה that she is a virgin.

[45] Str.-B., III, 5b.

[46] Gn. r., 50 on 19:1 (Schl. Mt., 122 on 4:23), where Michael declares a message : אמר בשורתו; Nu. r., 14 on 7:48 (Str.-B., III, 6d), where God Himself is the proclaimer of glad tidings : מבשרך בשורות טובות.

[47] Schn. Euang., XIV.

[48] Str.-B., III, 11. גִּלְיוֹן originally means a clean role of parchment or a space for notes.

since there is no real equivalent in Aram. The pun is possible only in respect of the Gk. On the other hand, the passage does not prove what has been deduced from it. [49] Palestinian Judaism was bilingual. [50] Aram. might be spoken, but Gk. was understood. It was known that בשורה would be εὐαγγέλιον in Gk. The Rabbinic propensity for puns enabled them to seize on the Gk. word for בשורה and to bring it into disrepute, thus making the hated heretics ridiculous. We are not justified in seeing in גליונים alone a mutilation of evangelium. [51]

B. εὐαγγέλιον in the NT.

While Mk. avoids the verb completely (→ 717), he favours the subst., using it 8 times (including Mk. 1:1 [52] and the non-Markan ending 16:15) as compared with 4 times in Mt. and none at all in Lk. Lk. seems to be fond of εὐαγγελίζεσθαι, but does not have the subst. This has been frequently noted but never explained. We cannot say that Lk. rejects the noun, since it occurs in Ac. twice. All that we can say is that he prefers the verb. [53] In this respect Lk. is more loyal to the original tradition. As noted at other points, [54] he keeps more strictly than the others to the Aram., which would surely have בשר more frequently than בְּשׂוֹרָה. The subst. is also found 60 times in Pl. (including 4 times in Eph. and 4 times in the Past.), [55] and once each in 1 Pt. and Rev.

1. The Synoptists.

If we set aside the use in the title in Mk. 1:1 and the general saying concerning the teaching of Jesus in Mk. 1:14, Mk. uses εὐαγγέλιον consistently in sayings of Jesus. A comparison of Mk. 1:15 with the parallel Mt. 4:17 and Lk. 4:15, of Mk. 8:35 with Mt. 16:25; 10:39; Lk. 9:24; of Mk. 10:29 with Mt. 19:29; Lk. 18:29 — Mk. 16:15 may be left out of account — shows that εὐαγγέλιον was not present in these passages in the original Mk., i.e., in the earliest stratum of the tradition. This leaves only Mk. 13:10 = Mt. 24:14 and Mk. 14:9 = Mt. 26:13. Are these genuine sayings of Jesus? Mk. 13:10 : εἰς πάντα τὰ ἔθνη πρῶτον δεῖ κηρυχθῆναι τὸ εὐαγγέλιον, seems to be incompatible with Mk. 7:27 = Mt. 15:24, 26 and Mt. 10:5, where Jesus disclaims any preaching to non-Jews either by Himself or His disciples (→ 729). This leads us to suspect that Mk. 13:10 was later interpolated into the eschatological discourse as a result of successful Gentile missions. [56] There are similar doubts in relation to Mk. 14:9. The composition of the story in Mk. 14:3-9 does not seem to be uniform. Vv. 8 and 9 look like additions. [57] It is thus doubtful whether the sayings are original and whether Jesus ever spoke of εὐαγγέλιον. This cannot be decided, however, by source criticism. The Gospels are not a stenographic reproduction of the preaching of Jesus. Nor are they an official record of His activity as a teacher. In their original form they are oral tradition. We have to ask, therefore, whether Jesus could have used the term

---

[49] So Wellhausen, Einleitung (1905), 109; less clearly in the 2nd ed., 98.

[50] Kittel Probleme, 36 ff.

[51] Schürer, II⁴, 445, where further lit. may be found. For a different view, cf. Str.-B., III, 11; Schn. Euang., XIV. M. Friedländer, Der vorchristliche Gnostizismus (1898), 81, calls the equation of Giljonim with evangelium a witticism.

[52] ἀρχὴ τοῦ εὐαγγελίου is perhaps a later addition. Tatian and Evangeliarium Hierosolymitanum begin at v. 2: "As it is written." Cf. P. Feine, Einleitung in das NT⁵ (1930), 50. For recent literature on this point, cf. Molland, 34.

[53] Burrows, 29.

[54] Kittel Probleme, 52 ff. On this whole question, cf. Schn. Euang., XIV.

[55] We do not count R. 15:29 because τοῦ εὐαγγελίου is too poorly attested.

[56] Bultmann Trad., 129.

[57] Bultmann Trad., 283, 64.

Gospel. Is it true to the matter itself? Now there can be no doubt that materially the proclamation of Jesus was good news and that He was One who proclaimed good news (→ 718). To the extent that fulfilment of the expectation implies something new, the preaching of the βασιλεία τοῦ θεοῦ brings something new, and transition from the verb to the noun results. If the Messianic secret is kept with εὐαγγελίζεσθαι, it is also kept with εὐαγγέλιον τῆς βασιλείας, since Jewish expectation of the מלכות שמים can be abstracted from the person of the Messiah (→ I, 574). [58] The form εὐαγγέλιον τῆς βασιλείας, however, is not found in the earliest tradition in sayings of Jesus. In Mk. 1:15 the Gospel of the nearness of the kingdom could be proclaimed by an unknown messenger (→ 716). But as formulated the verse undoubtedly derives from Mk. In Mk. 13:10 it is uncertain whether the reference is to the Gospel which treats of Christ or to the Gospel which Jesus proclaimed. On the other hand, in Mk. 14:9 the death and passion of Jesus are undoubtedly the content of the Gospel. [59] The last saying gives the impression of originality, since it is not easy to see why there should be recollection of this unknown woman unless there were something true in the saying. Remembrance of the risen Lord could not erase the thought of this woman, so that the striking phrase λαληθήσεται εἰς μνημόσυνον αὐτῆς has persisted.

The question whether or not Jesus used the word εὐαγγέλιον is finally a question of His Messianic consciousness. If He realised that He was the Son of God who must die and rise again, then He also realised that He was Himself the content of the message of His disciples. In this case His Gospel is not a new teaching; He brings Himself. What is given with His person constitutes the content of the Gospel. Hence τὸ εὐαγγέλιον implies for the disciples the disclosure of the Messianic secret. If both verb and noun are used by Jesus, the verb will be the more common, and Lk. is thus more faithful to the sources. [60] Mk. with his more common use of εὐαγγέλιον implies a direct continuation of the proclamation of Jesus. It is the preaching of the community along the lines of Jesus.

If this is recognised, the question whether we have an authentic saying of Jesus or a construct of the community is of secondary importance. There is also no need to decide between εὐαγγέλιον τῆς βασιλείας and εὐαγγέλιον ᾽Ιησοῦ, and the question whether we have a subjective or objective genitive in Mk. 1:1: ἀρχὴ τοῦ εὐαγγελίου ᾽Ιησοῦ Χριστοῦ, loses its significance. Jesus brings in the βασιλεία. It is actualised in His Word. Hence the message which He proclaims refers also to Him. In Mk. 1:14 Jesus is the Herald (κηρύσσων) of the Gospel which God declares to the world: εὐαγγέλιον τοῦ θεοῦ. Its content is the fulfilment of the time and the imminence of the βασιλεία τοῦ θεοῦ (→ 717). This message demands faith. It is different from Greek and Jewish expectation. It is contrary to appearances. As One who proclaims glad tidings, He cries: μετανοεῖτε, for

---

[58] Werner, 99 f.

[59] Harnack, *Kirchenverfassung*, 203, begins his exposition at Mk. 1:15 and in the light of it expounds all the εὐαγγέλιον passages, including Mk. 14:9, in terms of the Gospel of the kingdom. Unless the variant of Mk. 1:14 is counted, εὐαγγέλιον τῆς βασιλείας does not actually occur in Mk. But acc. to Harnack, 207 Mt. has a right understanding of Mk., and correctly defines the content of the εὐαγγέλιον of Mk. 1:14, 15; 9:35 and 13:10 by the addition τῆς βασιλείας in Mt. 4:17, 23 and 24:14. εὐαγγέλιον τῆς βασιλείας corresponds to the εὐαγγελίζεσθαι τὴν βασιλείαν of Lk. 4:43; 8:1 and 16:16, and therefore to the earlier development of the term in the OT and the Rabbinic writings (→ 709). It is wrong to suggest that βασιλεία is added to εὐαγγέλιον to make the non-Jewish εὐαγγέλιον more probable on the lips of Jesus. Zondervan, 205 f.

[60] Schn. Euang., XIV.

repentance is joy and gives joy. [61] In Mk. 8:35 and 10:29 εὐαγγέλιον does not refer to the missionary activity. [62] The Gospel is equated with Christ, with His ὄνομα (Mt. 19:29), and with the βασιλεία τοῦ θεοῦ (Lk. 18:29). [63] The equivocal attitude of the OT and of Judaism to the Gentiles — their exclusion from the Messianic kingdom and yet their participation in salvation — is resolved by Jesus. He Himself limits Himself to Israel, and during His lifetime He does not allow His disciples to carry the message beyond the borders of their own land. But in the Messianic age all the nations come (Mt. 8:11; Lk. 13:29). How can they come if they are not told? It is when Jesus is exalted from lowliness by His resurrection, when He becomes the κύριος, that the age of salvation begins for the whole world. The proclamation of the Gospel is an eschatological event. Mk. 13:10: εἰς πάντα τὰ ἔθνη πρῶτον δεῖ κηρυχθῆναι τὸ εὐαγγέλιον, is given in Mt. 24:14 the form: κηρυχθήσεται τοῦτο τὸ εὐαγγέλιον τῆς βασιλείας ἐν ὅλῃ τῇ οἰκουμένῃ εἰς μαρτύριον πᾶσιν τοῖς ἔθνεσιν. τοῦτο τὸ εὐαγγέλιον does not mean the Gospel written in Mt.; [64] it means that this Gospel of the kingdom which is now preached to Israel will be declared to the whole world. Similarly, the τοῦτο of Mt. 26:13 is to be understood in terms of the situation. The Gospel is the salvation of those who believe, Mk. 16:15.

2. Paul.

a. Most of the NT εὐαγγέλιον passages are in Paul (→ 727). How firm a magnitude the concept is for him may be seen from the fact that in almost half of the passages he speaks of τὸ εὐαγγέλιον in the absolute. [65] He does not need any noun or adj. to define it. The readers know what it is. Hence explanation is unnecessary. Nevertheless, for us εὐαγγέλιον is not a consistent and clearly definable term which we can express in a brief formula. It is in keeping with the derivation of the word from OT and Rabbinic usage (→ 726) that the substantive is a *nomen actionis*. It describes the act of proclamation: 2 C. 8:18, praise at the preaching of the Gospel; Phil. 4:15: the beginning of activity as an evangelist; 2 C. 2:12: Paul comes to Troas to preach the Gospel; Phil. 4:3, a reference to those who help the apostle in the work of evangelisation. We can see the direct presence of two different senses alongside one another in 1 C. 9:14, where ἐκ τοῦ εὐαγγελίου ζῆν means "to live by the preaching of the Gospel" but καταγγέλλειν τὸ εὐαγγέλιον can only refer to the content of the Gospel. Cf. also 1 C. 9:18b, where Paul makes no use of the ἐξουσία ἐν τῷ εὐαγγελίῳ, of his rights as an evangelist, and 1 C. 9:18a: ἀδάπανον θήσω τὸ εὐαγγέλιον, where he does not merely offer the content of the Gospel without charge, but the salvation itself is free. The twofold sense of the term is particularly clear in R. 1:1: Παῦλος ... ἀφωρισμένος εἰς εὐαγγέλιον θεοῦ, he is "separated to proclaim the Gospel of Christ." The relative clause which is immediately appended: ὃ προεπηγγείλατο

---

[61] Schn. Euang., 4; Schl. Gesch. d. Chr., 53, 137, 169.

[62] J. Weiss, *Urchristentum*, 537.

[63] Acc. to Harnack, *op. cit.*, 204 the Gospel is the message of the kingdom which Christ proclaimed but cannot be the message about Christ Himself since otherwise ἕνεκεν ἐμοῦ καὶ ἕνεκεν τοῦ εὐαγγελίου would be tautological. This was felt by MSS D 28 it sys at Mk. 8:35, as may be seen from the fact that they leave out ἐμοῦ καὶ and simply read ἕνεκεν τοῦ εὐαγγελίου.

[64] Kl. Mt., *ad loc.*; Dibelius, *Die Formgeschichte des Ev.*² (1933), 264, n. 1.

[65] On a strict count, including 2 Tm. 1:8, we have 23 instances of this in Pl.: R. 1:16; 10:16; 11:28; 1 C. 4:15; 9:14 (twice); 9:18 (twice); 9:23; 2 C. 8:18; Gl. 2:5; 2:14; Phil. 1:5, 7, 12, 16, 27; 2:22; 4:3, 15; 1 Th. 2:4; 2 Tm. 1:8; Phlm. 13.

διὰ τῶν προφητῶν αὐτοῦ ἐν γραφαῖς ἁγίαις, does not refer to the activity of proclamation, but to the Gospel itself, i.e., to its content.

b. That a specific content is to be declared with εὐαγγέλιον is clear from the fact that it is combined with different verbs of speaking and hearing.[66] The Gospel is proclaimed: εὐαγγελίζεσθαι τὸ εὐαγγέλιον, 1 C. 15:1; 2 C. 11:7; Gl. 1:11; καταγγέλλειν τὸ εὐαγγέλιον; 1 C. 9:14; κηρύσσειν τὸ εὐαγγέλιον; Gl. 2:2; Col. 1:23; 1 Th. 2:9; cf. 2 Tm. 1:11; λαλεῖν τὸ εὐαγγέλιον, 1 Th. 2:2; γνωρίζειν τὸ εὐαγγέλιον, 1 C. 15:1, cf. Eph. 6:19; διδάσκειν τὸ εὐαγγέλιον, Gl. 1:12, cf. 2 Tm. 1:11; ἀνατίθεσθαι τὸ εὐαγγέλιον, to present the Gospel for discussion, Gl. 2:2. The Gospel as thus proclaimed is heard: ἀκούειν τὸ εὐαγγέλιον, Col. 1:23; προακούειν ἐν τῷ λόγῳ τῆς ἀληθείας τοῦ εὐαγγελίου, Col. 1:5; cf. also παραλαμβάνειν τὸ εὐαγγέλιον, 1 C. 15:1; Gl. 1:12, and δέχεσθαι τὸ εὐαγγέλιον 2 C. 11:4.

That in Paul we never have βασιλεία τοῦ θεοῦ as the content, as in Mt. or Lk.,[67] is purely accidental, since he knows the concept and very seldom defines any specific content. Two passages seem to give a brief summary of the evangelical message, namely, R. 1:1 ff. and 1 C. 15:1 ff. We may also add R. 2:16; 16:25 and 2 Tm. 2:8 (on 1 Tm. 1:11 → 733). The most explicit of these is R. 1:3-4:[68] the pre-existent υἱὸς θεοῦ becomes man, is as such the expected Messiah of the house of David, is raised from the dead and is exalted to be the κύριος. In 1 C. 15:1 the Gospel formerly preached is summed up in terms of the death, burial, resurrection and resurrection appearances of the risen Lord. Neither passage is meant to be a full statement of what Paul understood by the Gospel. We can see this from the fact that the death of Jesus is not mentioned in R. 1:1 ff. nor the incarnation in 1 C. 15:1 ff. For Paul the heart of the good news is the story of Jesus and His suffering, death and resurrection. Everything connected with this may be preaching of the Gospel. It has the right to be so in virtue of its connection with Christ. In Eph. 6:15 the εὐαγγέλιον speaks of peace, and this message of peace brings peace (→ 718). According to R. 2:16 judgment, too, is part of the content of the Gospel. The preaching of the eschatological day of judgment is a message of salvation since Christ, the Saviour of the world, is the Judge. The proclamation of judgment and the message of joy belong together like repentance and joy (→ 728 f.). More generally the content of the κατὰ τὸ εὐαγγέλιόν μου of R. 16:25 is that God can strengthen you in your life of faith as I proclaim it to you non-Jews in my universal preaching of salvation, which is the revelation of the divine counsel to save and which concurs with the proclamation of Jesus. This proclamation is the strengthening of the community. The Gospel implies no break with the OT; it is the fulfilment of the promise. In R. 1:1 ff., 1 C. 15:1 ff. and R. 16:25 ff. Paul appeals to the OT. In it the fact of the preaching of the Gospel is promised,[69] but so, too, is the message itself: 1 C. 15:3 f.: ὅτι Χριστὸς ἀπέθανεν ὑπὲρ τῶν ἁμαρτιῶν ἡμῶν κατὰ τὰς γραφάς ... ὅτι ἐγήγερται τῇ ἡμέρᾳ τῇ τρίτῃ κατὰ τὰς γραφάς. Paul relates the story of the passion to the OT. For him the OT belongs to the Gospel, for it bears witness to Christ. Hence the OT also serves to spread abroad the Gospel among the Gentiles and to bring them to faith (R. 16:25 f.). The Gospel is no new teaching. What is new is what is and will be

---

[66] Molland, 11 f., 41 f.
[67] Harnack, *Kirchenverfassung,* 212 f.
[68] Molland, 67 ff.
[69] Zn. R. on 1:1.

effected through the message. If we were to sum up the content of the Gospel in a single word, it would be Jesus the Christ.

This does not mean that εὐαγγέλιον τοῦ Χριστοῦ in R. 15:19; 1 C. 9:12; 2 C. 2:12; 9:13; 10:14; Gl. 1:7; Phil. 1:27; 1 Th. 3:2; R. 1:16 vl.; R. 15:29 vl.; 1 C. 9:18 vl., εὐαγγέλιον τοῦ κυρίου ἡμῶν 'Ιησοῦ in 2 Th. 1:8 and εὐαγγέλιον τοῦ υἱοῦ in R. 1:9 are an obj. gen. The problem whether we have a subj. gen. [70] or an obj. gen. [71] is not so important as it used to be. No decision is possible on purely formal, grammatical grounds. [72] Materially Christ is for Paul both the object [73] and the author [74] of the proclamation, and He is the author both in His earthly manifestation (R. 16:25) [75] and in His exaltation (R. 15:18; 2 C. 5:20; 2 C. 13:3). [76] The distinctions which we usually make are of no significance to Paul. Christ is both the subject and object of preaching, and the Incarnate and the Exalted are one. It is thus unnecessary to fix the type of gen. in εὐαγγέλιον τοῦ Χριστοῦ. Materially, it includes both, sometimes with a stronger emphasis on the one and sometimes on the other. [77]

c. The Gospel does not merely bear witness to a historical event, for what it recounts, namely, resurrection and exaltation, is beyond the scope of historical judgment and transcends history. Nor does it consist only of narratives and sayings concerning Jesus which every Christian must know, and it certainly does not consist in a dogmatic formula alien to the world. On the contrary, it is related to human reality and proves itself to be living power. 1 C. 15:3 : ὅτι Χριστὸς ἀπέθανεν ὑπὲρ τῶν ἁμαρτιῶν ἡμῶν. This "for our sins" makes the preaching of the death of Jesus into a message of judgment and joy. [78] The proclamation ἐξ ἀναστάσεως νεκρῶν in R. 1:4 does not present the resurrection as an incidental or isolated event but as the beginning of the general resurrection. The Gospel does not merely bear witness to salvation history; it is itself salvation history. It breaks into the life of man, refashions it and creates communities. It cannot be generally perceived (2 C. 4:3); in it there takes place a divine revelation. Through the Gospel God calls men to salvation. The preacher is the mouthpiece of God (2 Th. 2:14). Since the Gospel is God's address, εὐαγγέλιον θεοῦ (1 Th. 2:2, 9), to men, it demands decision and imposes obedience (R. 10:16; 2 C. 9:13). The attitude to the Gospel will be the basis of decision at the last judgment (2 Th. 1:8; cf. 1 Pt. 4:17). The Gospel is not an empty word; it is effective power which brings to pass what it says because God is its author (R. 1:1; 15:16; 2 C. 11:7; 1 Th. 2:2, 8, 9; cf. 1 Pt. 4:17; 1 Th. 1:5 vl.): τὸ εὐαγγέλιον ἡμῶν οὐκ ἐγενήθη εἰς ὑμᾶς ἐν λόγῳ μόνον,

---

[70] So Zahn Einl., II, 169 f.; T. Zahn, *Skizzen aus dem Leben der Alten Kirche*² (1898): *Die Anbetung Jesu*, 299, 388, n. 40; Harnack, *op. cit.*, 215 ff.; Fridrichsen, 229 ff.; A. Seeberg, 45 ff.; Moe, 58 ff.; Schniewind, *Wort u. Ev.*, 107 ff.; Molland, 100.

[71] So Wellhausen, *Einleitung*, 99 f.; Dob. Th., 86; J. Weiss, *Das älteste Ev.*, 26; Müller, 91; Förster, 144; Feine, *Jesus Christus u. Pls.*, 18; Gillet, 89 and most comm.

[72] The Gk. genit. are not too precise. They cannot be too easily forced into the systematisations of grammarians. The sense has to be determined from the context. Cf. Kühner-Blass-Gerth, II, 333 f.

[73] This is also evident in Harnack, 235 f.; Zahn, 169; Schniewind, *op. cit.*, 109, n. 1; cf. also A. v. Harnack, "Das doppelte Ev. im NT" in *Aus Wissenschaft und Leben*, II (1911), 215 ff.

[74] So also E. v. Dobschütz, "Gibt es ein doppeltes Ev. im NT?" ThStKr, 85 (1912), 359, 364 f.

[75] Zahn Einl., II, 169 f.

[76] Schniewind, *op. cit.*, 109.

[77] Cr.-Kö.; Schmitz, *op. cit.*; W. Mundle, *Der Glaubensbegriff des Pls.* (1932), 14.

[78] Molland, 63 ff., does not regard the doctrine of justification as the content of the Gospel but as its theological consequence. Paul knows no such distinction between the Gospel and its "extension" (62). For him the effect of the Gospel is part of its substance, cf. O. Michel, ThLZ, 60 (1935), 141 f.

ἀλλὰ καὶ ἐν δυνάμει καὶ ἐν πνεύματι ἁγίῳ καὶ πληροφορίᾳ πολλῇ (1 Th. 1:5). It is everywhere at work: ἐν παντὶ τῷ κόσμῳ ἐστὶν καρποφορούμενον καὶ αὐξανόμενον (Col. 1:5). By the preaching of the Gospel the Gentiles come to share in the promise. The Gospel unites Jews and Gentiles, mediating salvation to both (Eph. 3:6). Because εὐαγγέλιον includes the dissemination, content and power of the message, in ἵνα μή τινα ἐγκοπὴν δῶμεν τῷ εὐαγγελίῳ τοῦ Χριστοῦ (1 C. 9:12) the phrase ἐγκοπὴ τῷ εὐαγγελίῳ does not mean only hindrance to proclamation. Paul is thinking rather that there should be no hindrance to its operation. He renounces his right for the sake of the Gospel, i.e., that others may be saved. Again, R. 15:19: ὥστε με ἀπὸ Ἰερουσαλὴμ καὶ κύκλῳ μέχρι τοῦ Ἰλλυρικοῦ πεπληρωκέναι τὸ εὐαγγέλιον τοῦ Χριστοῦ does not mean that Paul has concluded his missionary work, but that the Gospel is fulfilled when it has taken full effect. In the preaching of Paul Christ has shown Himself effective in word and sign and miracle (v. 18). Hence the Gospel has been brought to fulfilment from Jerusalem to Illyricum and Christ is named in the communities (v. 20).

The Gospel brings σωτηρία (Eph. 1:13; cf. 1 C. 15:2: δι' οὗ καὶ σῴζεσθε). [79] It is δύναμις εἰς σωτηρίαν (R. 1:16). In its proclamation there is revealed the → δικαιοσύνη τοῦ θεοῦ. The judgment exercised on men in the Gospel brings deliverance and justifies the sinner. Hence τὸ εὐαγγέλιον is the divine act of revelation. [80] Judgment and grace are combined. Judgment is joy, for it destroys sin. In R. 1:16 f. faith is the condition of the efficacy of the Gospel and yet the Gospel also effects faith. So in Phil. 1:27 faith arises through the Gospel and is again directed to it. Faith is present with the Gospel. The message demands and creates πίστις. It contains and imparts εἰρήνη (Eph. 6:15). It effects regeneration and gives new life (1 C. 4:15; cf. 1 Pt. 1:23; Jm. 1:18). By death and resurrection Christ has overcome death and brought life. The life already present in concealment becomes actuality through proclamation. The Gospel gives effect to the act of Christ in the world. It gives life to men (2 Tm. 1:10). The Gospel mediates the presence of something future (Col. 1:5). It is an eschatological event, bringing the fulfilment of ἐλπίς. The hope, ἀποκειμένη ὑμῖν ἐν τοῖς οὐρανοῖς, is already imparted to Christians through the message concerning it (cf. Col. 1:23). εὐαγγέλιον does not merely denote the power of operation. Since the Word effects what it proclaims, εὐαγγέλιον is also an expression for the salvation itself. Thus εὐαγγέλιον τοῦ θεοῦ μεταδιδόναι in 1 Th. 2:8 means to impart the blessing of salvation. Similarly, when Paul speaks of the κοινωνία of the Philippians εἰς τὸ εὐαγγέλιον, he is not thinking merely of their personal activity in spreading the Gospel, nor of their financial support, but of their fellowship in the Gospel itself. From the first day the Gospel has brought forth fruit and God has shown Himself mighty, so that they have become partakers of salvation. For ἡ βασιλεία τοῦ θεοῦ in 1 C. 4:20 [81] we might just as well have τὸ εὐαγγέλιον, cf. 1 C. 2:4 ὁ λόγος and τὸ κήρυγμα. In 2 C. 4:4 ὁ φωτισμὸς τοῦ εὐαγγελίου τῆς δόξης τοῦ Χριστοῦ means that the glory of Christ shines forth in the Gospel of Paul. The Gospel is the manifestation of divine glory in history. It is the form in which the δόξα τοῦ Χριστοῦ appears on earth. It is the presence of Christ. Hence Paul can say, not merely ἀξίως τοῦ θεοῦ περιπατεῖν in 1 Th. 2:12 and ἀξίως τοῦ κυρίου in Col. 1:10, but also ἀξίως τοῦ εὐαγγελίου τοῦ Χριστοῦ πολιτεύεσθαι in Phil. 1:27.

---

[79] Cf. Harnack, Kirchenverfassung, 214, n. 1 on εὐαγγέλιον and σωτηρία.
[80] Schniewind, Wort und Evangelium, 83.
[81] Harnack, op. cit., 213, n. 1.

As Paul is imprisoned for Christ's sake as δέσμιος Χριστοῦ 'Ιησοῦ in Phlm. 9 (→ 43), so he bears chains for the Gospel's sake in Phlm. 13. The Gospel and its content are one. The Gospel becomes a personal magnitude. 2 C. 10:14 : ἄχρι γὰρ καὶ ὑμῶν ἐφθάσαμεν ἐν τῷ εὐαγγελίῳ τοῦ Χριστοῦ. The selection of a sphere of missionary work is not according to the whim of the preacher. It is forced on Paul in the Gospel in connection with the power in whose service he stands (Col. 1:23). Paul calls himself συγκοινωνὸς τοῦ εὐαγγελίου in 1 C. 9:23, namely, a fellow of the Gospel. The Gospel goes through the world (cf. 2 Th. 3:1; 2 Tm. 2:9). It wins men for itself. But its fellow-workers cannot be sure that they will attain to what they promote and declare : πάντα δὲ ποιῶ διὰ τὸ εὐαγγέλιον ἵνα συγκοινωνὸς αὐτοῦ γένωμαι. In R. 15:16 the Gospel is a cultic foundation where Paul renders priestly service that the Gentiles may be an acceptable sacrifice. In R. 11:28, however, it is an order of salvation contrasted with the ἐκλογή. The two, i.e., εὐαγγέλιον and ἐκλογή, are united in the βάθος πλούτου καὶ σοφίας καὶ γνώσεως θεοῦ, R. 11:33. In Eph. 6:19 the Gospel is a μυστήριον which is declared.

d. In the Pauline epistles we often find the formula εὐαγγέλιον ἡμῶν, 2 C. 4:3; 1 Th. 1:5; 2 Th. 2:14; εὐαγγέλιόν μου, R. 2:16; 16:25; 2 Tm. 2:8. With these we may list expressions like τὸ εὐαγγέλιον ὃ εὐαγγελισάμην ὑμῖν, 1 C. 15:1; τὸ εὐαγγέλιον τὸ εὐαγγελισθέν ὑπ' ἐμοῦ, Gl. 1:11: τὸ εὐαγγέλιον ὃ κηρύσσω ἐν τοῖς ἔθνεσιν, Gl. 2:2; cf. also Gl. 1:8 : εὐαγγελίζεσθαι παρ' ὃ εὐηγγελισάμεθα ὑμῖν. Paul does not preach a special Gospel compared with the other apostles. For him there is only one Gospel (Gl. 1:6), the Gospel of Christ, and he shares this with the original apostles (→ 734). If he calls the Gospel his own, it is because he as an apostle is entrusted with its declaration. It is put in his trust like a costly possession (1 Th. 2:4; 1 Tm. 1:11; Gl. 2:7). He is called κῆρυξ καὶ ἀπόστολος καὶ διδάσκαλος of the Gospel in 2 Tm. 1:10. His calling as an apostle is a commission to take the message to the Gentiles (Gl. 1:16). His vocation (κλητός) is to preach the Gospel (R. 1:1; cf. 1 C. 1:17; 9:16). He served God even as a Pharisee. In his new life he serves Him as an evangelist of His Son (R. 1:9). As an apostle he is thus a partner of the Gospel (1 C. 9:23), a priest (R. 15:16), διάκονος κατὰ τὴν δωρεὰν τῆς χάριτος τοῦ θεοῦ τῆς δοθείσης μοι κατὰ τὴν ἐνέργειαν τῆς δυνάμεως αὐτοῦ (Eph. 3:7; cf. Col. 1:23). The apostolate and the Gospel are most closely related (2 C. 10:14). Suffering with Paul is suffering with the Gospel (2 Tm. 1:8). But if the apostle is in bonds, the Gospel is not bound (2 Tm. 2:8 ff.). It goes forth and works and produces fruit. Paul's imprisonment is a defence and confirmation of the Gospel (Phil. 1:16). For this reason he can speak of his imprisonment as a χάρις (Phil. 1:7). What happens to him cannot be considered apart from his task as a preacher of the Gospel. When he speaks of himself in Phil. 1:12, he writes of the προκοπὴ τοῦ εὐαγγελίου. What has befallen him has served to advance the Gospel. The personal ministry of Timothy is for Paul service of the Gospel (Phil. 2:22). Instead of saying : "Like a child the father, so has he served me," he says : "Like a child the father, so has he served the Gospel — which gives life (1 C. 4:15) — with me."

e. According to 1 Tm. 1:11 the Gospel contains teaching on the right use of the Law ; it reveals the δόξα of God (→ 732). The Law has no validity for Christians, but it has validity for non-Christians on account of sins. In R. and Gl. there is no direct connection or antithesis between Law and Gospel. The antithesis is there, for R. 1:16 ff. implies a devaluation of the Law, which is for the Jews a δύναμις εἰς σωτηρίαν bringing life and health (→ 297). Nevertheless, the question of Law and Gospel is never raised. The discussion is rather between → ἐπαγγελία and νόμος. The opponents of Paul in Galatia called their preaching εὐαγγέλιον too. They, too, proclaimed to the Gentiles the presence of the Messianic age brought in by the coming of Jesus. But for them Jesus was the expected Jewish Messiah and Christianity was a fulfilment of Judaism. The Gentiles had to be circumcised and become Jews if they were to share in salvation. They must come to Sion, as was written in the OT. Hence their Gospel became a proclamation of Law. νόμος and εὐαγγέλιον were for them δύναμις εἰς σωτηρίαν. When Paul carries back the conflict between Law and Gospel into the OT by opposing Law and promise, he meets his opponents on their own ground. He shows that the antithesis is already present in the OT and that in accordance with God's will Law and promise have different parts to play in salvation history. The Gospel does not entail any new assessment of men by God, as though justification were previously by the Law and now by the Gospel. The antithesis is grounded in the divine plan of salvation. Perhaps there was once a question of promise or Law. But now that salvation history has reached its goal in Christ, the superiority of the Gospel over Law is evident. Between Paul and the apostles there are no differences. They proclaim the same Gospel. What is revealed to Paul (Gl. 1:11) agrees with the Gospel delivered by the apostles (1 C. 15:1). Because it is revealed, it has the same origin as the Gospel of the apostles. [82] The risen Lord is the *auctor evangelii*. He opens the eyes of men to understanding of the OT and to Messianic events (Lk. 24:19 ff., 45). Since Paul through the appearance of the risen Lord received the task of taking the Gospel to the Gentiles, it was with him that the problem of Law and Gospel arose in a form unknown to the first community. The original Christians kept the νόμος as part of their way of life. But they did not attribute to it any soteriological significance. This made them inwardly free from the Law. In the section on the Gospel in 1 C. 9:20 Paul can say : τοῖς ὑπὸ νόμον ὡς ὑπὸ νόμον μὴ ὢν αὐτὸς ὑπὸ νόμον, ἵνα τοὺς ὑπὸ νόμον κερδήσω. For the sake of the Gospel he is prepared to place himself under the Law. For he knows that Christ alone is salvation. He strives after a similar unity in Gl. 2. The εὐαγγέλιον τῆς ἀκροβυστίας and εὐαγγέλιον τῆς περιτομῆς of v. 7 are not two distinct Gospels. The one unchanging and unabbreviated εὐαγγέλιον τοῦ Χριστοῦ belongs to both Jews and Gentiles. In both cases it is the same Gospel in which God shows Himself to be at work. We can no longer know for certain what was the ἕτερον εὐαγγέλιον of the false teachers of Corinth (2 C. 11:4; cf. 4:3). For the Libertines the Gospel of Paul was dark and hidden. They proclaimed a radiant Gospel of enlightenment. With fine words they sought to make up what they lacked in divine power. If the Gospel transcends the Law, this does not mean license. As the divine address, the Gospel demands obedience when preached to non-Christians (→ 719, 731) and it also requires obedience of Christians. [83] The Gospel is not just missionary proclamation : Col. 1:5 : τὸ εὐαγγέλιον πάρεστιν; 1 C. 15:1: ἑστάναι ἐν τῷ εὐαγγελίῳ. It does not merely found the community; it also edifies it. In Phil. 1:27 it is the criterion of conduct. Confession of the Gospel is subjection to it (2 C. 9:13). We are obedient to the Gospel and meet its demands when we are active in the ministry of love. This active love is the obedience of the confession of the Gospel. It is not a merit but the δωρεά and χάρις of God (2 C. 9:14, 15).

---

[82] Mundle, 53; cf. also F. Sieffert (1899), on Gl. 1:12.
[83] The → ἀγγελία of 1 Jn. 1:5 is also εὐαγγέλιον. In 1 Jn. 3:11 (cf. with 1 Jn. 2:7) it is the ἐντολή whose fulfilment is given with Christ.

3. Revelation.

Rev. 14:6 f. is in many respects striking. [84] An angel is the proclaimer of the Gospel, the Gospel is αἰώνιον, and there is no definite article. Since the content of the Gospel seems to be judgment, it is sometimes argued that this is not τὸ εὐαγγέλιον τοῦ Χριστοῦ but a very different one, one of many which in contrast to the many is eternal. The fact that an angel proclaims it is in keeping with the situation. It is the last time and there is no time to lose. Hence an angel is charged to take the message ἐπὶ τοὺς καθημένους ἐπὶ τῆς γῆς καὶ ἐπὶ πᾶν ἔθνος καὶ φυλὴν καὶ γλῶσσαν καὶ λαόν according to the saying of Jesus that before the end the Gospel must be proclaimed to the whole world (→ 729). The preaching of the Gospel is a sign of the end. The word αἰώνιος expresses the unity, immutability and permanent validity of the divine decree (→ 730, 734). The content of the Gospel is not really judgment, though this would not be out of place (R. 2:16), but the demand for fear of the Lord (cf. Mk. 1:14 f.) and worship of the Creator (Ac. 14:15; 1 Th. 1:5, 9).

C. The Transition of the Word εὐαγγέλιον to Designation of a Book in the Early Church. [85]

In the NT εὐαγγέλιον is oral preaching. Neither epistles nor gospels are called εὐαγγέλιον. The separation of the evangel from actual utterance may be seen already in Paul. For his epistles are at times a repetition of missionary preaching and in 1 C. 15:1 he even says that he will share with the Corinthians in his letter the Gospel which he has proclaimed to them. The basic meaning is that εὐαγγέλιον is the preached word. Iren., III, 1 (MPG, 7, 845a): καὶ Λουκᾶς δὲ ὁ ἀκόλουθος Παύλου τὸ ὑπ' ἐκείνου κηρυσσόμενον Εὐαγγέλιον ἐν βιβλίῳ κατέθετο. Since the preaching bears witness to Christ and His words and acts, and since these constitute the essence of the Gospel, the writings which contain the life and words of Jesus come to be given the name "gospel." The early Christian missionaries pursue both a verbal and a written mission. The written and the spoken word complement one another. Eus. Hist. Eccl., III, 37, 2 : The evangelists τοῖς ἔτι πάμπαν ἀνηκόοις τοῦ τῆς πίστεως λόγου κηρύττειν φιλοτιμούμενοι καὶ τὴν τῶν θείων εὐαγγελίων παραδιδόναι γραφήν. In most cases there is no great difference between the written and the spoken Gospel for those who receive it, since the written Gospel is read out to them. The reader εὐαγγελιστῶν τόπον ἐργάζεται. [86] εὐαγγέλιον still has a greater breadth of meaning in Ignatius. He is certainly acquainted with books which contain the substance of the Gospel. But εὐαγγέλιον is for him a more living concept used, e.g., for the centre and goal of salvation history and for the realisation of the promise (Phld., 9, 2). The preaching of the Gospel is the presence of the incarnate σωτήρ : προσφυγὼν τῷ εὐαγγελίῳ, ὡς σαρκὶ Ἰησοῦ (ibid., 5, 1). From the alternation of εἰς εὐαγγέλιον καταγγέλλειν and εἰς αὐτὸν ἐλπίζειν it may be seen that for him the Gospel is equivalent to

---

[84] It is perverse to see in Rev. 14:6 the starting point for an understanding of the Gospel in terms of religious history, as does Zondervan, 200 f. Similarly, when Dieterich (Mithr. Liturg., 49) characterises εὐαγγέλιον as the revelation of an angelic message and therefore deduces the idea of angelic contemplation, he misses the essential point in both the NT and indeed the Gk. view of evangelium. Again, it is quite impossible to agree with O. Gruppe, Griech. Mythologie (1906), 1323 f., in explaining εὐαγγέλιον in terms of Hermes, the Euangelos. Hermes is very seldom called εὐάγγελος, and evangelium in the NT is not the "good news of the redemption of souls." Cf. Schn. Euang., 201, 240 f.

[85] Cf. Harnack, op. cit., 222 ff.; Zahn Kan., I, 150 ff., 471 ff., 840 ff. G. Heinrici, Beiträge zur Geschichte und Erklärung des NT, I (1894): "Das Urchristentum in der Kirchenge-schichte des Euseb.," 47 ff.

[86] Die allgemeine Kirchenordnung, I, 19 (ed. T. Schermann in Studien zur Geschichte und Kultur des Altertums, Suppl. Vol., III, 1 [1914]).

Christ. In the Did. εὐαγγέλιον is a fixed and definite magnitude of tradition to which appeal may be made (15, 3; 4). It contains the Lord's Prayer (8, 3) and directions concerning the conduct of apostles and prophets (11, 3). The fathers often use the term not merely for the NT Gospels but for the whole of the NT as distinct from the OT. Iren., II, 27, 2 (MPG, 7, 803b): *universae Scripturae et Prophetiae et Evangelia*. All Scripture may be divided into the Prophets and Gospels, i.e., the OT and the NT. The epistles of the NT are also counted as Gospels. [87] It is doubtful, however, whether there is reference to the Pauline corpus in 1 Cl., 47: ἀναλάβετε τὴν ἐπιστολὴν τοῦ μακαρίου Παύλου τοῦ ἀποστόλου. τί πρῶτον ὑμῖν ἐν ἀρχῇ τοῦ εὐαγγελίου ἔγραψεν; [88] the author probably has in view the beginning of Paul's missionary work (cf. Phil. 4:15). The plur. τὰ εὐαγγέλια naturally does not signify different messages, as in the imperial cult. The apostles who preached the Gospel and then transmitted it in writing *omnes pariter et singuli eorum habentes Evangelium Dei*, Iren., III, 1 (MPG, 7, 844b). In the different Gospels the one Gospel of God is declared. ἔδωκεν ἡμῖν τετράμορφον τὸ Εὐαγγέλιον, ἐνὶ δὲ πνεύματι συνεχόμενον, Iren., III, 11, 8 (MPG, 7, 885b). The sing. and plur. alternate with no distinction of sense (cf. esp. Iren., III, 11, 8 f. [MPG, 7, 885 ff.]). τὸ εὐαγγέλιον can denote both the collection of Gospels (Eus. Hist. Eccl., V, 24, 6) and each individual Gospel (Iren., IV, 20, 6 [MPG, 7, 1037a]). To make it clear which Gospel is meant there is added the name, *secundum Matthaeum* (Iren., III, 11, 7 [MPG, 7, 884]). One can also say ἐν τοῖς εὐαγγελίοις (e.g., Cl. Al. Strom., I, 21, 136, 1) even when quoting a saying which in found in only one Gospel, just as we refer to the infancy stories in the Gospels when we are really thinking of Lk. Gospel has become a term for the evangelical writings. The true proclamation of the glad tidings, however, is through the word of the preacher. [89]

εὐαγγελιστής.

Except in ecclesiastical literature this is a rare word. In a non-Christian sense it is attested only on a poorly preserved inscr. from Rhodes, IG, XII, 1, 675, 6, where it means "one who proclaims oracular sayings." [1]

---

[87] For further instances cf. Zahn Kan., I, 101, n. 2.

[88] W. Hartke, *Die Sammlung u. d. ältesten Ausgaben der Paulusbriefe* (1917), 55.

[89] Luther, WA, X, 1, 1, 625 f. "Now what is the star? It is nothing other than the new light, preaching and Gospel orally and publicly proclaimed ... for in the NT the preaching should be publicly declared with the living voice ... For this reason Christ Himself did not write down His teaching as Moses did, but preached it by word of mouth, and ordered it to be preached by word of mouth, giving no command to write it down. Furthermore, the apostles wrote very little ... and before they wrote they had first preached to the people and converted them with their physical voice, which was their true apostolic and NT work." WA, XII, 259: "The Gospel simply means the preaching and declaration of the grace and mercy of God merited and won for us by the Lord Christ through His death. It is not really that which stands in books and is comprised in letters; it is rather an oral preaching and living word; it is a voice which rings out through the whole world and which is publicly uplifted so that it can be heard everywhere," cf. K. Holl, *Gesammelte Aufsätze*, I[6] (1932), 562.

εὐαγγελιστής. Cr.-Kö.; Schn. Euang., 189-194; H. Achelis, "Spuren des Urchristentums auf den griech. Inseln?" ZNW, 1 (1900), 87-100; A. Dieterich, εὐαγγελιστής, ZNW, 1 (1900), 336-338; J. A. Robinson, EB, II (1901), 1430; J. Massie, *Dict. of the Bible*, I (1898), 795 ff.; W. Patrick, DCG, I (1923), 549; R. Sohm, *Kirchenrecht*, I (1923), 42 f.; A. Harnack, TU, II, 1 and 2 (1884), *Die Lehre der zwölf Apostel*, 40, *Prolegomena*, 111 ff.; *Die Mission u. Ausbreitung des Chr.*[4], I (1924), 334, n. 6, 348, n. 2, 350, 352, 359; Zahn Einl.[3], I, 361; T. Zahn, *Skizzen aus dem Leben der Alten Kirche*[2] (1898), *Missionsmethoden im Zeitalter der Apostel*, 87, 344, n. 42; O. Zöckler, *Biblische und kirchenhistorische Studien*, II (1893), 63 ff.; F. Haase, *Apostel u. Evangelist in den orientalischen Überlieferungen*, *Nt.liche Abhandlungen*, IX (1922).

[1] On the text and exposition of the inscr., cf. Schn. Euang., 189 ff.; acc. to Achelis εὐαγγελιστής has a Christian sense even here, but Dieterich (*op. cit.*) rightly raises objections.

It occurs only 3 times in the NT : at Ac. 21:8 of Philip (cf. 8:4 f., 12, 35, 40); at Eph. 4:11 of evangelists along with apostles, prophets, pastors and teachers; and at 2 Tm. 4:5 of Timothy (cf. 1 Th. 3:2; Phil. 2:22). The number of evangelists must have been greater than one might suppose from the number of occurrences in the NT (Phil. 4:3; 2 C. 8:18; Col. 1:7; 4:12). The NT evangelist is not one who declares oracles as among the Greeks. He is the מְבַשֵּׂר, the one who proclaims the glad tidings, the εὐαγγέλιον (R. 10:15 → 719). εὐαγγελιστής originally denotes a function rather than an office, and there can have been little difference between an apostle and an evangelist, all the apostles being evangelists (→ 733). On the other hand, not all evangelists were apostles, for direct calling by the risen Lord was an essential aspect of the apostolate. In all three NT passages the evangelists are subordinate to the apostles. Philip is a supervisor of alms (Ac. 6), not an apostle. In his missionary work in Samaria he preaches and baptises, but the baptised receive the Spirit only through the prayer of the apostles Peter and John (Ac. 8:14 f.). In Eph. 4:11 the evangelists are mentioned only after the apostles. Timothy is called a σύνεργος τοῦ θεοῦ ἐν τῷ εὐαγγελίῳ τοῦ Χριστοῦ in Th. 3:2, but he is a pupil of the apostles rather than an apostle (→ 733). The evangelists continue the work of the apostles. They are not just missionaries, for, as εὐαγγέλιον is congregational as well as missionary preaching (→ 734), so the leader of the community can also be called εὐαγγελιστής (2 Tm. 4:5). His task is κηρύσσειν τὸν λόγον (2 Tm. 4:2).

In the early Church the evangelists were regarded as successors of the apostles. Eus. Hist. Eccl., V, 10, 2 : ἦσαν εἰς ἔτι τότε πλείους εὐαγγελισταὶ τοῦ λόγου, ἔνθεον ζῆλον ἀποστολικοῦ μιμήματος συνεισφέρειν ἐπ' αὐξήσει καὶ οἰκοδομῇ τοῦ θείου λόγου προμηθούμενοι. They lay θεμελίους τῆς πίστεως and the → ποιμένες appointed by them continue the work in the respective congregations, Eus. Hist. Eccl., III, 37, 2 f. In accordance with the development of εὐαγγέλιον (→ 735), εὐαγγελιστής has also the sense of "author of a Gospel," Hipp. De Antichristo, 56; Tertullian Adversus Praxean, 21, 23. The two senses are found alongside one another.

προευαγγελίζομαι.

This is not found in class. Gk. It occurs in Philo Op. Mund., 34; Mut. Nom., 158; Abr., 153. It is also found in Schol. Soph. Trach., 335 (P. N. Papageorgius [1888], 299 f.); Photius, MPG, 101, 1011b; Johannes Climacus, MPG, 88, 670c; Marcus Eugenicus, Imagines 2 (ed. Kayser Philostr. De Gymnastica [1840], 141).

In Gl. 3:8 the → ἐπαγγελία (R. 4:13 ff. and Gl. 3:15 ff.) that in Abraham all nations will be blessed is a προ-ευαγγέλιον. When the blessing came to the nations in Christ, the seed of Abraham (Gl. 3:16), the promise was fulfilled. The prophecy of Scripture that God would justify the Gentiles by faith became a reality and the προ-ευαγγέλιον became the εὐαγγέλιον: R. 1:1 ff.; 1 C. 15:1 ff.: Christ; R. 1:16 f.: justification; R. 16:25ff.; Eph. 3:6; Gl. 1:16; 2:7: the Gentiles.

Friedrich

εὐαρεστέω, εὐάρεστος → I, 456

---

2 Cf. J. Massie, *op. cit.*

π ρ ο ε υ α γ γ ε λ ί ζ ο μ α ι. Schn. Euang., 82, 135, n. 4.

εὐδοκέω, εὐδοκία

† εὐδοκέω.

A. εὐδοκέω outside the NT.

εὐδοκέω developed from the impersonal εὖ δοκεῖ τινί τι, [1] which is not attested but which is to be derived from an ideal εὔδοκος belonging to δέχεσθαι. [2] This does not exclude the fact that in many constructions there is assimilation to δοκεῖ μοι, Polyb., 20, 5, 10; Philodem. Philos. Volumina Rhetorica Supplementum, p. 54 (ed. S. Sudhaus [1895]). εὐδοκέω is a popular Hellen. word adopted by the LXX and other Jewish Gk. writings. But it is older than the LXX. It is found in pap. from the 3rd cent. B.C. and on inscr. from the 2nd. It also occurs in Polyb., Diod. S., Dion. Hal., Philodem. Philos. The many different attempts at Latin translation show the difficulties caused by the term.

In the LXX we very occasionally have the abs. as in ψ 76:7 and Sir. 45:19. In many cases we have εὐδοκεῖν with ἐν and the dat., esp. of person, yet also of object, though more often without ἐν. The acc. of obj. is also common, less frequently of person. The acc. with εὐδοκεῖν is translation Gk. influenced by the Heb. It is not found in Polyb. Occasionally εὐδοκεῖν is used with ἐπί τινι of pers. and obj., and very rarely with εἰς or περί. The construction with the inf. or acc. and inf. is common. The pass. and med. are comparatively limited. In the LXX it is used for רצה qal with בְּ or acc., or for חָפֵץ בְּ or צָלַח hiphil. Synon. for חפץ and רצה (much more frequently) is → θέλειν, and for חפץ and אבה → βούλεσθαι (→ I, 630). רצה is also rendered δέχομαι or προσδέχομαι (→ 50), the latter mostly in a cultic sense (cf. Is. 42:1; Ez. 20:40 f.; Hos. 8:13).

a. The usual meaning of εὐδοκεῖν is "to take pleasure or delight in," "to be glad in." Of God's gracious pleasure in His people as His possession we have εὐδοκεῖν ἐν in ψ 43:3; 149:4; Is. 62:4 B and ΣΘ. Righteous individuals are included in this favour: 2 Βασ. 22:20. Cf. also ψ 17:19. With the acc. of person: Is. 38:17 Σ. Mentioned as the basis and condition of this good pleasure are the fear of God, the right way and good works ψ 146:11; ψ 36:23 Σ; Dt. 33:11 'Α. On the other hand, Yahweh takes no delight in evil or in a faithless people: Mal. 2:17; 'Ιερ. 14:10 אA. Test. Jos. 4:6 (par θέλει). It is often used of the gracious acceptance of sacrifice, with a special emphasis on the prophetic demand for righteousness rather than sacrifice: Lv. 7:18 "Αλλ; ψ 50:16 ff.; 'Ιερ. 14:12; Sir. 31:23 (34:23); pass.: Lv. 19:7 Σ; Mal. 2:13 Σ. The result of missing God's good pleasure can give to οὐκ εὐδοκεῖν the sense of having no good fortune in Is. 54:17 A. We often find this רְצָה בְ in the Rabb. writings, e.g., Cant. r., on 1:5. The term is also used for human favour, e.g., in 1 Βασ. 18:22 Θ of the favour of the king and in Jer. 2:36 א* of Israel's delight in Egypt. With the dat. alone, Diod. S., XVII, 47, 2; with the acc. of person, Gn. 33:10. Pass., 1 Ch. 29:23. To have pleasure in something, ψ 48:13 Σ; Is. 13:17 A; Job 14:6. Often with the dat. of object in Polyb.: 4, 22, 7; 8, 12, 8. Of joy in the sanctuary, 1 Ch. 29:3; ψ 101:14; in the Sabbath, Lv. 26:34; in the works of truth, 1 Ἐσδρ. 4:39. In a bad sense, 1 Macc. 1:43: in the religion of Antiochus. The construction varies, alternating between dat. of obj. and ἐν with the dat. or acc. of obj.

ε ὐ δ ο κ έ ω. Lit.: Bl.-Debr.[6] § 119, 1; 148, 2; 196; 206, 2; 392, 3; Anz Subsidia, 358; Cr.-Kö., Moult.-Mill., Pr.-Bauer, s.v.; Zn. Mt.[4], 147, n. 66; 440, n. 45. On the fuller form εὐδόκησα or ηὐδόκησα, which is a common alternative in the NT even in the same MSS, cf. Winer (Schmiedel), § 12, 5b; Bl.-Debr.[6] § 67, 1; Kühner-Blass-Gerth, II, 11, 33. εὐδοκεῖν in the LXX: R. Helbing, Die Kasussyntax der Verba bei den Septuaginta (1928), 262-265, which also deals with the construction in Polyb. etc. and the inscr.
[1] J. H. Moulton-W. F. Howard, A Grammar of NT Greek, II (1929), § 109.
[2] Bl.-Debr.[6] § 119, 1.

b. "To decide for" in the sense of "to select." 1 Macc. 10:47 אR in the choice between Alexander and Demetrius: εὐδόκησαν ἐν 'Αλεξάνδρῳ. ψ 151:5 of the brethren not appointed to royal dignity: οὐκ εὐδόκησεν ἐν αὐτοῖς κύριος. Thus the thought of election is often linked with εὐδοκεῖν. What is elected is often added in the inf., 1 Macc. 14:41; Polyb., 7, 4, 5. The choice may relate to a material obj. ψ 67:16; 2 Macc. 14:35. εὐδοκεῖν with the infin. and ἤ denotes choice between two possibilities: Sir. 25:16 (23); Polyb., 21, 23, 8: μᾶλλον ἤ "to prefer something." The sense of "to elect" is also found in Is. 42:1 Θ, which underlies the baptismal epiphany of the NT, where, however, we have ἐν with the dat. The εὐδοκεῖν with εἰς of person in Mt. 12:18; 2 Pt. 1:17 seems to be without par., though in Test. Jos. 17:3 we have εἰς with the acc. of obj. Related to this εὐδοκεῖν in the sense of elective resolve is ἐκλέγεσθαι (commonly for בחר): Nu. 16:5, 7; Dt. 12:5, 14; 1 Βασ. 16:8; ψ 32:11, and also αἱρετίζειν (→ I, 184, for בחר but also for חפץ), which can mean "to adopt": 1 Ch. 28:6; 29:1; Hag. 2:23; Mal. 3:17. Similarly οὐκ εὐδοκεῖν with ἐν can mean "to reject," Hab. 2:4 (→ 741). In the Tg. on Is. 43:10 בחר is given the sense "to elect": דְּאָתְרְעֵיתִי בֵיהּ.[3] Cf. the Syrian transl. of Sir. 37:28: καὶ οὐ πᾶσα ψυχὴ ἐν παντὶ εὐδοκεῖ (Heb. לֹא תִבְחַר or תִּבְחַר), which runs: בקליל מתרעיא: "the soul has delight in little." In Sir. 9:12 and 37:28 we again have εὐδοκεῖν with ἐν and the dat. of obj. Here, too, the underlying בחר denotes the element of selectivity.

c. What has been said shows that εὐδοκεῖν implies volition, though with an emotional element. Hence we may often render "to want or desire something": Sir. 15:17. Cf. "to grant somebody (acc.) something (gen.)": P. Lond., I, 3, 6 (2nd. cent. B.C.): a collection for the mummies. In the case of εὐδοκεῖν with the inf. the basic thought is "to will," "to be willing to do something." This is used primarily of a human resolve: Ju. 17:11 "Αλλ; 19:10, 25; 20:13; cf. 1 Macc. 6:23; "to be ready to do something": Polyb., 1, 78, 8; 18, 52, 4; "to have a good will for something":B. P. Grenfell, An Alexandrian Erotic Fragment (1896), I, col. 1, 17 (2nd. cent. B.C.). It may also be used of the divine will, ψ 39:13. Here the usage follows רצה with ל and the inf.

d. The social aspect comes out more strongly in the common sense of "to agree," "to find acceptable," "to consent," "to acquiesce."[4] Here the abs. is much favoured. Gn. 24:26, 48; 1 Macc. 11:29; negat. Ju. 11:17. Of God: Sir. 45:19. Cf. also Polyb., 4, 31, 2; 14, 2, 11 and Diod. S., XI, 47, 2. It occurs very often in the pap., P. Tebt., II, 382, 3 (30 B.C. to 1st cent. A.D.) ἐξ εὐδοκούντων, "with consent"; P. Oxy., III, 496, 8 (2nd. cent. A.D.); εὐδοκῶ as subscription to a document, P. Ryl., II, 120, 24 (2nd cent. A.D.); Ditt. Syll.³, 683, 59 (c. 140 B.C.); P. Lond., III, 1168, 15 (18 A.D.); BGU, I, 300 (2nd cent. A.D.). Hence it often has the sense of "to agree," "to consent to": Tob. 5:17 AB; Polyb., 18, 52, 5. It is often used in Polyb. for consent to a treaty. For "to concede," "to comply," cf. Sir. 18:31 A. What is agreed to is in the dat.: Polyb., 3, 8, 7; Diod. S., IV, 23, 2. In declarations in the pap.: ἐπὶ τούτοις: P. Oxy., I, 94, 15 (83 A.D.); P. Tebt., II, 317, 33 (2nd cent. A.D.). With acc. and inf., Test. Jos. 9:1. The social aspect is even plainer in συνευδοκεῖν, 1 Macc. 1:57; Diod. S., IV, 24, 1; Polyb., 7, 1, 3; P. Lips., 8, 4 (3rd cent. A.D.). In the NT cf. Ac. 8:1; 22:20. For applauding an unrighteous act, which is even worse than the act itself, cf. R. 1:32.[5]

e. Outside the Bible we often find εὐδοκεῖν for "to be satisfied or happy": Polyb., 1, 83, 8; in the negative, 2, 49, 2; or "to be content," Polyb., 29, 12, 8. Med. "to be satisfied with," often in Polyb. and Diod. S. περί τινος, Philodem. Philos. Volumina Rhetorica, II, 52 (ed. S. Sudhaus, Supplementum [1895], p. 44). Polyb. is fond of the abs. εὐδοκεῖν with part. for "to do something gladly," "to find joy in something,"

---

[3] Cf. Dalman WJ, I, 227.

[4] Cf. the def. in Anecd. Graec., I, 260, 21: εὐδοκούμενος ὁ συγκατατιθέμενος καὶ μὴ ἀντιλέγων.

[5] For further information on συνευδοκεῖν, Pr.-Bauer, s.v.

15, 36, 6; 38, 12, 8. We also have ποιεῖν εὐδοκεῖν, "to satisfy": 36, 3, 2. When Philodemus Philosophus, the pupil of Zeno, De Deis, 1, 13 f.; 12, 19 (ed. H. Diels, AAB, 1915, 7) defines the goal of Epicurean philosophy as εὐδοκεῖν, he means the satisfaction which is rationally induced. Thus ἡ εὐδοκουμένη ζωή, the life with which one is satisfied (pass.), is an ethical term : Philodem. Philos. De Morte, 30, 42 (ed. D. Bassi, Papiri Ercolanesi, I [1914], p. 53).

B. εὐδοκέω in the NT.

In the NT we find the abs. εὐδοκεῖν only once at R. 15:27. It is preceded in v. 26 by the construction with the acc. and inf. Syntactically we have the following groups : 1. εὐδοκεῖν ἐν with the dat. of person, or εἴς τινα or τινα, and the opp. οὐκ εὐδοκεῖν ἐν with dat. of person ; 2. εὐδοκεῖν with the acc. or dat. of object, the latter with or without ἐν; 3. εὐδοκεῖν with the inf. or acc. and inf., and sometimes with μᾶλλον.

1. εὐδοκεῖν ἐν with the dat. of person is found in the baptismal declaration in Mt. 3:17: ἐν ᾧ εὐδόκησα, and at the transfiguration in Mt. 17:5 (assimilated to 3:17). Mk. 1:11 and Lk. 3:22 in the Alexandrian text have ἐν σοὶ εὐδόκησα (Lk. ηὐδόκησα). What is meant is God's decree of election, namely, the election of the Son, which includes His mission and His appointment to the kingly office of Messiah. [6] As υἱὸς ὁ ἀγαπητός Jesus is the Recipient of this elective good-pleasure. [7] And He receives this saying as a seal of His obedience in identification with the sinful world as expressed in His baptism.

We find the same conception in the Gospel of the Ebionites in Epiph. Haer., 30, 13, 7. Instead Mt. 12:18, in a free quotation of Is. 42:1, in [b] C² EGKL etc. has : ὁ ἀγαπητός μου, εἰς ὃν εὐδόκησεν ἡ ψυχή μου. [8] Here, as in Is. 42:1, there is a preceding and parallel indication of election : [9] ἰδοὺ ὁ παῖς μου ὃν ᾑρέτισα. We have a similar εἰς ὃν εὐδόκησα, referred to the ὁ υἱός μου ὁ ἀγαπητός at baptism, in 2 Pt. 1:17. In this εἰς ὄν we may simply see the connection, [10] or we may translate "on whom I have set my good-pleasure." [11] The parallel Test. Jos. 17:3 (acc. of obj.) (→ 739) perhaps supports the idea of the direction which the election has taken. The thought of election, most clearly expressed in the αἱρετίζειν and ἐκλέγεσθαι, is also found, again par. with Is. 42:1, in the ὁ υἱός μου ὁ ἐκλελεγμένος of Lk. 9:35 א B syrˢ arm lat aeth memph sah [12] and in the ὁ ἐκλεκτὸς τοῦ θεοῦ of Jn. 1:34 א* syrˢᶜ, P. Oxy., II, 208, fol. 1, recto 7. [13]

Of all the terms for election (αἱρετίζειν, ἐκλέγεσθαι, προσδέχεσθαι, θέλειν), εὐδοκεῖν brings out most strongly the emotional side of the love of Him who

---

[6] Is. 42:1-4 is also referred to the Messiah by the Tg.: "Mine elect, in whom my memra is well-pleased," Str.-B., I, 630.

[7] The ἀγαπητός with υἱός has the sense of only son, cf. Mk. 9:7 with 12:5 f. On this whole question cf. C. H. Turner, JThSt, 27 (1926), 113-129. Mt. 3:17 syrˢᶜ has "my son and my beloved." The original of Lk. 3:22 D it Justin Clem Ambst Tycon Aug, which has been overborne by Mk. 1:11 and par., is ἐγὼ σήμερον γεγέννηκά σε.

[8] ὃν א* B 115, 244. Euseb. has both ὃν and εἰς ὅν. ἐν ᾧ C* Lat D.

[9] Is. 42:1 LXX B : ᾽Ισραὴλ ὁ ἐκλεκτός μου, προσεδέξατο αὐτὸν ἡ ψυχή μου (רָצָה בְ). The προσδέχεσθαι (→ 57), which is very common (for רצה) in cultic connections, is here applied to man. But in Qᵐᵍ we have ὁ ἐκλεκτός μου ὃν εὐδόκησεν ἡ ψυχή μου.

[10] Wbg. Pt., ad loc.

[11] Wnd. Pt., ad loc.

[12] On the fact that ἀγαπητός syrᵖ ᵖʰⁱˡᵒˣ is here secondary cf. A. Merx, Die Evangelien des Mk. u. Lk. (1905), 266; Zn. Lk., ad loc.

[13] Alexand. text : ὁ υἱὸς τοῦ θεοῦ. Cf. on the ἐκλεκτός, which is to be preferred with Blass, Zn., Merx, Harnack, the electus filius in a b.

elects. The question whether the election of Jesus as Son comes only at baptism or is already present before is not answered by the term in spite of the aor. εὐδόκησα. Nevertheless, the expression "beloved or only Son" indicates the uniqueness of the relationship of Father and Son. In view of the total presentation in Mt. and Lk. we can hardly read into the baptism an adoptionist deduction from Is. 42:1.

This use of εὐδοκεῖν in the sense of election is sometimes hardened by the sense of οὐκ εὐδοκεῖν ἐν to the degree that this can only imply rejection (→ 739). We see this in 1 C. 10:5. It is also present in Hb. 10:38, where in terms of Hab.2:4 (→ 739) the οὐκ εὐδοκεῖν applies to cowardly surrender as opposed to the πίστις of the just. [14]

2. The second group has εὐδοκεῖν τι with object, and is said of God. It is found only in the LXX quotation in Hb. 10:6, 8. [15] Cf. 1 Cl., 18, 16. Cf. also ψ 50:16 and 39:6, where θέλειν and εὐδοκεῖν are synonyms as in Hb. 10:6, 8. Elsewhere the object takes the dative or ἐν, i.e., twice in Paul with reference to man's delight in something, 2 Th. 2:12: εὐδοκήσαντες τῇ ἀδικίᾳ (cf. the corresponding ἀγαπᾶν in 2 Pt. 2:15, of δικαιοσύνη in Hb. 1:9), and 2 C. 12:10, where the εὐδοκῶ ἐν ἀσθενείαις implies that the warring aspects of the apostolic life can be a source of gratification because everything takes place ὑπὲρ Χριστοῦ.

3. When εὐδοκεῖν is used with the inf. or acc. and inf. there is a clear hint of choice, resolve or decree. The εὐδοκοῦμεν μᾶλλον of 2 C. 5:8 expresses "what is preferred as better." In 1 Th. 3:1 the reference is to a human decision, Ambst. rightly translating optimum duximus and Theodore of Mopsuestia (ad loc., H. B. Swete [1882]) complacuimus. In R. 15:26 f. there is again reference to free decision. 1 Th. 2:8 refers to a lasting willingness or readiness (impf.). In Lk. 12:32 the reference is to the divine counsel of grace which is free and independent of any human influence and which has as its goal the accomplishment of salvation, the revelation of grace and the deliverance of the community in the βασιλεία. Here, too, we should note the opposite in human hostility. There is a sovereign ring about εὐδοκεῖν in Gl. 1:15, the apostle being set in a dependence on God which makes him independent of men. Similarly in 1 C. 1:21 the εὐδοκεῖν stands in antithesis to the human aberration of cosmic wisdom. In Col. 1:19 it is necessary to take θεός as the subject. [16] Here, too, there is an acc. with inf. The point is that God has resolved that the whole πλήρωμα should dwell in Christ and that the whole through Him (Christ) should be reconciled to Himself (God). The expression repudiates the cosmic faith of Hellenistic astrology. It maintains that in place of faith in the powers of the universe we should set Christ alone as the sum of the divine revelation.

[14] On the reading εὐδοκήσει (assimilation to what precedes), cf. Rgg. Hb., ad loc.

[15] On the correspondence between the quotation in Hb. 10 and the Pap. Fr. L of the Psalms, cf. Rgg. Hb. [2], [3], 300.

[16] With Chrys., J. B. Lightfoot[3] (1904), A. Klöpper (1882), Haupt Gefbr., ad loc. The ἐν αὐτῷ refers to the Son. The view that the Son is also the subj. of εὐδόκησε (Tertullian, J. C. K. Hofmann [1870] ad loc.) makes the whole passage very difficult both materially and formally. It is best to make ὁ θεός alone the subj. Against the view of Ewald Gefbr., ad loc. that the constr. with acc. and inf. is rare, cf. not only → 738, 741, but esp. ψ 67:16. The view that πᾶν τὸ πλήρωμα is the subj. (H. v. Soden[2] [1892], B. Weiss, Das NT, II[2] [1902], T. K. Abbott in ICC [1922], Ew. Dib. Gefbr., ad loc., Pr.-Bauer, s.v. εὐδοκέω) runs counter to the very personal Christology of Col., in which the neutral definitions (cf. 2:2 f.) are simply statements about Christ and elucidate what He is and what God does through Him. There is also the difficulty that πᾶν τὸ πλήρωμα would then have to be the subj. of ἀποκαταλλάξαι as well. The δι' αὐτοῦ (Christ) and εἰς αὐτόν (God) are given their full force only if here, too, God is the subj.

Does εὐδοκεῖν imply an eternal decree of pre-temporal resolution or an intervention of God in the course of temporal affairs? In Gl. 1:15 it is explicitly linked with the intervening ἀποκαλύψαι, and the ἀφορίσας and καλέσας precede in time. Here, then, εὐδοκεῖν is not emphasised as an eternal basis. It is the divine resolve which is contemporary with the historical revelation. Similarly in 1 C. 1:21 the εὐδόκησεν which is orientated to the folly of preaching for the salvation of those who believe is interposed only when it is displayed that the κόσμος by its wisdom does not know God in His divine wisdom. While the question is generally justified, however, it does not arise in respect of Lk. 12:32 and Col. 1:19. Here the reference is to God's supra-temporal decree, though the context does not fix it at any particular point.

† εὐδοκία.

εὐδοκία is not a classical word. It is almost completely restricted to Jewish and Christian literature, and occurs for the first time in the Greek Bible.

It is not even found in the Hellenistic koine. Origen found it only in the LXX, and regarded it as its creation. [1] It arose out of the need for a term corresponding to רצן;

εὐδοκία. Def.: Suidas acc. to Thdrt. on Ps. 5:13 (MPG, 80, 901 A): τὸ ἀγαθὸν θέλημα. Theodore of Mopsuestia, II, 294 (MPG, 66, 973): εὐδοκία δὲ λέγεται ἡ ἀρίστη καὶ καλλίστη θέλησις τοῦ θεοῦ, ἣν ἂν ποιήσηται ἀρεσθεὶς τοῖς ἀνακεῖσθαι αὐτῷ ἐσπουδακόσιν ἀπὸ τοῦ εὖ καὶ καλὰ δοκεῖν αὐτῷ περὶ αὐτῶν. Similarly Etym. M., s.v. εὐδοκῶ: ἡ ἀρίστη καὶ καλλίστη τοῦ θεοῦ ἑκούσιος θέλησις. Lit.: Suic. Thes., s.v.; Cr.-Kö., Moult.-Mill., Pr.-Bauer, s.v. C. F. A. Fritzsche, Pauli ad Rom. Epistola, II (1839), 369-372; Ltzm. R. on 10:1; T. Zahn, "Altes und Neues zum Verständnis des Phil.," Zeitschr. f. kirchl. Wiss. u. kirchl. Leben, 6 (1885), 288 f. (on Phil. 2:13); Ew. Gefbr. on Phil. 2:13; E. Schäder, "Der Gedankeninhalt v. Phil. 2:12 f.," in Greifswalder Studien f. H. Cremer (1895), 245 ff.; A. Deissmann, Pls.² (1925), 167, n. 1. For a different view, cf. E. Schwartz, GGA, 173 (1911), 659. R. Liechtenhan, Die göttliche Vorherbestimmung bei Pls. u. in d. Posidonianischen Philosophie (1922), 39. Dalman WJ, I, 173, 227; Str.-B., I, 476 ff.; II, 118. On Jesus Sir.: R. Smend, Die Weisheit des Jes. Sir. hbr. und deutsch (1906); Griech.-syr.-hbr. Index zur Weisheit des Jes. Sir. (1907); N. Peters, Das Buch Jes. Sir. (1913). On Lk. 2:14: The comm. of A. Plummer (1900); Zn.; Kl.; M. J. Lagrange (1921); Schl., ad loc. F. H. A. Scrivener, A Plain Introduction to the Criticism of the NT, II (1894), 344-347; B. F. Westcott-F. J. A. Hort, The NT, II, Appendix on Lk. 2:14; A. Thenn, "Locus Lk. 2:8-16 ab Origene Graece Explanatus," ZwTh, 34 (1891), 483-487; A. Resch, "Das Kindheits-evgl. nach Lk. u. Mt.," TU, X, 5 (1897), 127; F. Field, Otium Norvicense, III² (1899), 48 f.; A. Hilgenfeld, "Die Geburts- und Kindheitsgeschichte Jesu Lk. 1:5-2:52," ZwTh, 44 (1901), 225 f.; A. Merx, Die Evangelien d. Mk. u. Lk. (1905), 198-202; A. Pott, Der Text d. NT (1906), 66 f.; F. Spitta, Theol. Abhdlgen, Festgabe f. H. J. Holtzmann (1902), 63 ff.; "Die chronolog. Notizen u. die Hymnen in Lk. 1 und 2," ZNW, 7 (1906), 304 ff.; G. Aicher, "Zum Gloria (Lk. 2:14)," BZ, 5 (1907), 381-391; J. Sickenberger, "Zu Lk. 2:14," BZ, 5 (1907), 402 f.; F. Zorell, "Sprachliche Randnoten z. NT," BZ, 9 (1911), 161-163; A. Merk, "Der Engelgesang Lk. 2:14 bei den Syrern," Zeitschr. f. kathol. Theologie, 49 (1925), 625-628; A. v. Harnack, "Über den Spruch 'Ehre sei Gott in der Höhe' und das Wort 'Eudokia'," SAB, 1915, 854-875 (also in Harnack's Studien z. Gesch. d. NT u. d. Alten Kirche, I: Zur nt.lichen Textkritik [1931], 153-179); J. H. Ropes, "Good Will toward Men," Harvard Theol. Review, 10 (1917), 52-56; A. Meyer, Gnomon, 10 (1934), 89 f. E. Hirsch, Luthers deutsche Bibel (1928), 103-105; J. Jeremias, "'Ἄνθρωποι εὐδοκίας (Lk. 2:14)". ZNW, 28 (1929), 13-20; G. v. Rad, "Nocheinmal Lk. 2:14 'Ἄνθρωποι εὐδοκίας," ZNW, 29 (1930), 111-115; M. Dibelius, "Jungfrauensohn und Krippenkind," SAH, 1931/2, 4. Abh., 65 f.; F. Herklotz, "Zu Lk. 2:14," Zeitschr. f. kathol. Theol., 58 (1934), 113 f.; J. Wobbe, "Das Gloria in Lk. 2:14," BZ, 22 (1934), 118 ff.; E. Böklen, "Eudokia in Lk. 2:14," Deutsches Pfarrerblatt, 36 (1932), 309 f.; E. R. Smothers, Ἐν ἀνθρώποις εὐδοκίας, in Recherches de Science Religieuses, 24, 1 (1934), 86-93.

[1] Orig. on Eph. 1:5 (J. A. Cramer, Catenae, VI [1844], 107). Like Theodore of Mopsuestia (supra) he regards the word as made up from τὸ εὖ καὶ τὸ δοκεῖν. Jerome (MPL, 26, 449) copied him. He, too, regarded it as a construct of the LXX, rebus novis nova verba fingentes, and translated εὐδοκία placitum, beneplacitum.

It is not found at all in Joseph. or Philo. [2] The εὐδοξία derived from εὔδοξος ("renowned," "glorious") perhaps helped to fix its specific meaning (Dio C., 53, 3, 3). In modern Gk. both Εὐδοξία and Εὐδοκία are used as proper names with the sense of "Beloved," "Well-pleasing." The construction εὐδόκησις from εὐδοκέω is less in keeping with classical sensitivity. Polyb., Dion. Hal. and Diod. S. have it instead of εὐδοκία. For the most part the latter is restricted to the Jewish sphere.

εὐδόκησις means a. "consent or agreement," Diod. S., XV, 6, 4; Ditt. Syll.³, 685, 108 (2nd cent. B.C.); Orig. Princ., III, 1, 4. It is used of "applause" in Polyb., 16, 20, 4; Dion. Hal., III, 13. It also means "human good-pleasure," Polyb., 27, 10, 4. It is used of the royal will in Ditt. Or., I, 335, 122 (2nd cent. B.C.) and of the divine good-pleasure in 1 Cl., 40, 3. εὐδοκία does not occur in the post-apost. fathers or the Apologists, but reappears in the ecclesiastical writings of the 4th and 5th centuries (→ 750 f.).

A. רצון in the OT.

We must turn first to the OT רצון. It occurs 56 times. 1. It is used predominantly for the pleasure, grace or will of God. In only 16 (as opposed to some 40) cases is it used to describe a human emotion or action.

It occurs a. for a "sacrifice which is pleasing to God" : Lv. 19:5; 22:19 ff.; Is. 56:7; Jer. 6:20; Ps. 19:14. In the sense of what is well-pleasing, as a concrete expression, cf. Mal. 2:13. This use occurs in Prv. as רְצוֹנוֹ: 11:1, 20; 12:22; 15:8, except that here the reference is to uprightness, faithfulness, prayer. Though there is no precise reference, Prv. 10:32 and 11:27 also speak of God. More generally b. רצון implies the "divine grace and favour," Ps. 5:12; 30:5, 7; 51:18; 106:4; Is. 60:10; Prv. 8:35; 12:2; 18:22. This grace can also be thought of as "blessing" or "benefit" : Dt. 33:23, synon. בְּרָכַּת. In Ps. 145:16, too, the reference is to the divine benefits. Worth noting in view of Lk. 2:14 is the occurrence of רָצוֹן as a dependent nom. in Ps. 69:13; Is. 49:8 : עֵת רָצוֹן; Is. 58:5 : יוֹם רָצוֹן; Is. 61:2 : שְׁנַת־רָצוֹן. It is used c. for the "divine will" in Ps. 40:8 and 103:21.

2. In the 16 passages in which man is the subject the reference is to an emotion, disposition or attitude. It may be a. "caprice," "arrogance" or "partiality," being used predominantly in a bad sense for "despotic power" in Da.; cf. Gn. 49:6; Est. 1:8; 9:5; Neh. 9:24, 37; Da. 8:4; 11:3, 16, 36. But it may also have b. a good sense as the "favour of a king," Prv. 14:35; 16:15; 19:12. Concretely, it is that which is pleasing to the king (anal. to 1. a. supra). Prv. 16:13. It may also be used for "reciprocal favour," e.g., cordial agreement among the upright in Prv. 14:9. c. It denotes the direction of the will of the righteous towards God in Ps. 145:19 (the desire of those who fear Him) and in 2 Ch. 15:15 (the seeking of Him with all one's will).

B. רָצוֹן and εὐδοκία in Jesus Sirach.

It is in Jesus Sirach that the word is most fully developed. It is found here 23 times if we add to the רצון passages of the Heb. the occurrences of εὐδοκία where there is no corresponding Hebrew text.

1. The Heb. passages which are not rendered εὐδοκία in Gk. Sir. show a similar usage to that of the OT. The word bears the sense of a. "God's grace or favour" : 4:12; 36:22; 50:22, more generally b. of "God's will" : 48:5, and finally c. of the "caprice, preference or self-opinion of man" : 8:14; 35(32):11.

---

[2] The Pharisee Joseph. does strongly emphasise both human and divine volition, cf. A. Schlatter, Wie sprach Josephus von Gott? (1910), 26 f.; Schl. Theol. d. Judt., 4. But for the latter he uses βούλησις, προαίρεσις, ὅ τι τῷ θεῷ δοκεῖ, βούλεσθαι, θέλειν, though only in Ant. In Bell. there is less emphasis on the divine will. The only possible passage in Philo is the reading of Cod. A at Som., II, 40, and here εὐδικίας is undoubtedly the correct reading.

2. A second group is formed by passages which either translate רצון by εὐδοκία or which only exist in Gk. and use εὐδοκία. In Gk. Sir. the predominant sense is a. the "divine good-pleasure": 1:27 (no Heb.);[3] 11:17 (רצון); 15:15 (רצון).[4] On 31(34):22 (no Heb.) cf. the לרצון of Lv. There is also a cultic reference in 32(35):5: εὐδοκία κυρίου (no Heb.). 32:20, where the Heb. should read תַּמְרוּרֵי רָצֵץ, the complaints of the oppressed. Cf. 35:14 (32:18). b. In Gk. Sir., in a striking development of the Heb., we also have the sense b. of the "divine ordination or resolve":[5] 36:13 (33:14) (no Heb.). This passage, based on Jer. 18:6, was decisive in R. 9.[6] Here, too, the Gk. text points to the divine choice as the determinative counsel, cf. the par. κατὰ τὴν κρίσιν. Another reference to the divine will and ordination is to be found in 39:18(23): ἐν προστάγματι αὐτοῦ πᾶσα ἡ εὐδοκία (Heb. תחתו רצונו יצליח), Note should be taken of the par. σωτήριον in which the will reaches its goal. The divine ordination is also meant in 41:4(6), cf. the preceding κρίμα. In 42:15 א ca (Heb. ופועל רצונו לחקו) the reference is to creation, which exists according to His ordination and good-pleasure. In the corrupt 43:26 A[7] the Gk. reading points us to the divine will reaching its goal. On this sense cf. Eth. En. 49:4; Test. Sol. D, VIII, 4 (McCown [1922], 97*).

But Gk. Sir. also uses εὐδοκία with man as subj. c. as "human will" in 18:31: "When you do the will of your soul, you grant what desire wills" (no Heb.), cf. 9:12(17),[8] and d. as "satisfaction": 29:23: εὐδοκίαν ἔχε (no Heb.): "Be satisfied." Cf. Philodem. Philos. De Pietate, 25 (ed. T. Gomperz, Herkulanische Studien, II [1866], 145, 5).

C. εὐδοκία in the Septuagint and Hexapla.

In distinction from this ampler use in Sir., the LXX has little to offer. Here, too, εὐδοκία is used for רצון, though the latter is more often translated δεκτός, προσδεκτός, εἰσδεκτός (24 times) and θέλημα, θέλησις, θέλειν, βούλεσθαι (12 times). In contrast, εὐδοκία is found only 8 times, and occasionally we have ἀρεστὸν ἐνώπιόν τινος, χάρις, χάρις ἀγαθή, ἔλεος, ἱλαρόν, ἱλαρότης, σωτήριον, ἐπιθυμία. If we do not count Ps. Sol. and Sir., εὐδοκία occurs in the LXX only 10 times, 8 times for רצון and in Cant. 6:3(4) for the hiphil of רצה.

It denotes a. the "divine grace or favour," or the consequent "blessing" in ψ 5:12; 50:18; 88:17; 105:4. In ψ 144:6 also it is not what is desired[9] but the favour of God which is the blessing (→ 743). In Ps. Sol. 8:39, too, εὐδοκία is divine grace (opp. κρίμα). It also signifies b. the "divine good-pleasure": 1 Ch. 16:10; ψ 18:14; 68:13; Ps. Sol. 3:4, which does not treat of man's good will[10] but of the good-pleasure of the Lord.[11] It is used of man in ψ 140:4 LXX Θ, where εὐδοκίαι means evil will.[12] Special note should be taken of Cant. 6:3(4) where the proper name Thirza is rendered εὐδοκία

---

[3] No Heb. means that the Heb. text is not extant.

[4] καὶ πίστιν ποιῆσαι εὐδοκίας, following Peters instead of Smend's ποιῆσαι: "To exercise faithfulness is a matter of good-pleasure." This makes it unnecessary to assume a hyperbaton (Harnack, op. cit., 864, 867 = 165, 168): "Show the fidelity of a good will."

[5] As against Harnack, 867 (= 168).

[6] Vg rightly has: omnes viae eius secundum dispositionem eius. The original text acc. to Cod. 70 (cf. Syr.) is: πλάσαι αὐτὸ κατὰ τὴν εὐδοκίαν αὐτοῦ. The copyist's πᾶσαι for πλάσαι gives us πᾶσαι αἱ ὁδοὶ αὐτοῦ.

[7] Cf. A. Schlatter, Das neu gefundene hbr. Stück des Sir. (1897), and Peters, ad loc.

[8] It is also worth considering whether the translator does not have in view the sense of satisfaction.

[9] Liddell-Scott, Pr.-Bauer, s.v. There is a par. in the dedication to Priapus of Lampsacus, CIG, XIV, 102*: εὐεργεσίας καὶ εὐδοκίας χάριν, though the authenticity is in doubt.

[10] Zahn, Harnack.

[11] Cf. R. Kittel in Kautzsch, Apokr. u. Pseudepigr. und die rabb. Formel (→ 745).

[12] Cf. Harnack, 866 (= 167). But far-reaching deductions should not be drawn from ψ 140:4. The Mas. בְּרָעוֹתֵיהֶם adversus mala eorum, is erroneously read as ברצוניהם.

in LXX 'A. [13] Ps. Sol. 16:12 refers to the satisfaction of the soul. It has been rightly observed that the word is mostly used poetically in the LXX. [14]

There are no particular nuances in the later translators. There is simply a fuller use. In the sense of God's grace, favour or good-pleasure 'A uses it 12 times, Σ 6 times and Θ 5 times more than the LXX. 'A uses it 4 times, Σ 2 and Θ 3 for royal favour and Σ uses it once for cordial agreement among men.

D. Rabbinic Examples of εὐδοκία.

The Rabbis use רָצוֹן mainly for the "divine good-pleasure." Sch. E. (b), 17, benediction. [15] More generally it can also refer to the "will of God," as in Ex. r., 46 on 34:1, [16] cf. the common formula עָשָׂה רְצוֹנוֹ שֶׁל מָקוֹם or עָשָׂה רְצוֹנוֹ [17] to do the will of God : Midr. Qoh., 5, 11 etc. Particularly common is the expression "favour before God." This is not to be explained in terms of a fear of anthropomorphism. [18] It is a courtly mode of address taken over by later Judaism from the courtly language of the Near East. This לְפָנֶיךָ etc. in Ket., 104a; Ber., 32b; Taan., 3, 8 [19] corresponds, therefore, to the idea of the glory of the divine throne. It is often used in prayer : יְהִי רָצוֹן מִלְּפָנֶיךָ, "May it be pleasing to Thee, may it be Thy will" : Ber., 19a, Bar ; 16b; 17a; [20] S. Nu., 89 on 11:9; Tanch. אַחֲרֵי 4, 59. More rarely we have the simple יְהִי רָצוֹן: Ber., 28b (R. Jochanan at his death). [21] The Targums have for רצון: רְעוּתָא, st. abs. רַעֲוָא: Tg. O. on Gn. 28:17; [22] Nu. 14:8; Tg. on Ju. 13:23. This "it is the will before Yahweh" corresponds exactly to the θέλημα ἔμπροσθεν τοῦ πατρὸς ὑμῶν of Mt. 18:14 or the εὐδοκία ἔμπροσθέν σου of Mt. 11:26. [23]

As concerns ἄνθρωποι εὐδοκίας in Lk. 2:14 it is worth noting that the Rabbis make considerable use of בֶּן or בְּנֵי with a following abstract, e.g., בְּנֵי עֲלִיָּה sons of majesty (those honoured in the hereafter); bSukka, 45b; bSanh., 97b. [24] There is an anal. use in Sir. 44:23 B; 44:10 : אִישׁ, אַנְשֵׁי חֶסֶד: ἀνήρ, ἄνδρες ἐλέους. The actual expression in Lk. 2:14 is used only in a figur. sense when an atoning offering is called בַּר הַרְצָאָה, the son of good-pleasure, in bRH, 5b. Yet as in the OT (→ 743) we often find the gen. רצון together with a noun, e.g., Tanch. אַחֲרֵי 4, 59 : שְׁנַת רָצוֹן, under the influence of Is. 61:2; Taan., 3, 8 : לֹא כָךְ שָׁאַלְתִּי אֶלָּא גִּשְׁמֵי רָצוֹן "not this have I desired, but the rain of good-pleasure, i.e., fruitful rain which God sends in His favour ; not destructive torrents." Cf. M. Ex. on 15:14 : כַּעַס שָׁאֵין בּוֹ רָצוֹן.

Human good-pleasure is expressed in phrases like ברצון, (opp. באונס) for "free" as distinct from "forced," cf. T. Nasir, 4, 4; bKet., 9a; Tanch. נשא 19 and 35. On R. 10:1: ἡ εὐδοκία τῆς ἐμῆς καρδίας, cf. בְּרָצוֹן לִבִּי, Eka r. Introd. Apart from the suffix בְּ, לְ and כְּ are particularly common. לרצון opp. שלא לרצון means "intentional/unintentional" : Maksh., VI, 8 or "willingly/unwillingly," ibid., I, 1. For כרצון, "acc. to one's good-pleasure," cf. Eka r., Introd. [25]

---

[13] Though cf. Σ, which has εὐδοκητός, "well-pleasing," "acceptable"; cf. also ψ 67:31 Σ. On this pt., Diog. L., II, 87. For the adv. εὐδοκητῶς, Vita Philonidis Epicurei in P. Herculanensis, 1044 (W. Crönert, SAB, 1900, 950, Fr. 19, line 4).

[14] Harnack, 865 (= 166); 868 (= 169).

[15] Str.-B., II, 118.

[16] Cf. A. Schlatter, Wie sprach Josephus von Gott? (1910), 27.

[17] Str.-B., I, 467, 653, cf. 219, 220, 664.

[18] Ibid., I, 785.

[19] Ibid., II, 190.

[20] Ibid., I, 455 p, cf. I, 607, 786.

[21] Ibid., I, 581. → 527.

[22] Dalman WJ, I, 173.

[23] Cf. Dalman WJ, I, 173, Schl. Mt. on 11:26.

[24] There are many par. in Str.-B., I, 476 ff.

[25] On the Syr. translation of εὐδοκία → 748, n. 40.

E. εὐδοκία in the NT.

1. εὐδοκία in Paul.

In the NT the reference to human will is even less prominent as compared with the sense of God's good-pleasure or will. It occurs only twice. Thus in R. 10:1 it is used of the will of the heart which becomes petition to God. [26] In Phil. 1:15 we can hardly translate "of good intention or sincere purpose," since this, as the opposite of insincerity, lays the emphasis on ethical validity, which owes more to the implied antithesis to διὰ φθόνον καὶ ἔριν than to the normal use of εὐδοκία. Along with the preceding contrast we should rather bring out the element of inclination contained in εὐδοκία. Our rendering should thus be : "of a good mind in the sense of good will." [27] There can be no distinguishing between εὐδοκία orientated to Paul and εὐδοκία orientated to the Gospel. The apostle is identified with his charismatic mission. εὐδοκία thus means good will in respect of the εὐαγγέλιον and its apostolic dissemination. [28]

All the other passages probably refer to the divine good-pleasure and counsel, though there is dispute concerning 2 Th. 1:11 and Phil. 2:13. Paul's request for the Thessalonians is : ἵνα ὑμᾶς ἀξιώσῃ τῆς κλήσεως ὁ θεὸς ἡμῶν καὶ πληρώσῃ πᾶσαν εὐδοκίαν ἀγαθωσύνης καὶ ἔργον πίστεως ἐν δυνάμει.

If we relate this to human good will or human orientation to the good the ἀγαθωσύνης may be either an objective genitive, [29] that God should fulfil every desire for the good and the work of faith, or a subjective genitive, [30] that which pleases the inclination for the good. But the Rabb. use of רָצוֹן, where often there is no express reference to God, makes it likely (cf. the עֵל־רְצוֹן of Is. 60:7 in the OT) that Paul is simply speaking of God's good-pleasure in a concise formula. This is in keeping with the liturgical flavour of 2 Th. 1. This εὐδοκία is orientated to the well-doing of Christians. [31] Paul prays that this will of God should be realised. The meaning of Phil. 2:13 [32] is that the operation of God, which evokes the will and work of believers, takes place in the interests of the divine counsel,

---

[26] The usual rendering "heart's desire" is close, but εὐδοκέω hardly means "to desire," and in respect of εὐδοκία we can adduce only Sir. 18:31. Harnack, op. cit., 869 (= 170), suggests "loving will."

[27] Cf. v. 16 f.: ἐξ ἀγάπης.

[28] "Good and sincere purpose," Pr.-Bauer, s.v., Loh. "Kindly disposition in the sense of good will," Cr.-Kö., s.v., for Paul (Ew., Haupt), for the cause of the Gospel (Dib.), or for both (A. Klöpper [1893]). "God's good-pleasure" (Schl. Erl., cf. Rabb. [→ 745]) is hardly likely in view of the antitheses in v. 15 and in the light of v. 16.

[29] The Lat. favours the obj. gen.: voluntas bonitatis (d e vg Vigilius Fulgentius); Syr. will for the good. J. B. Lightfoot[3] (1873), G. Milligan (1908), Dibelius, Harnack and others emphasise the fact that we have work (ἔργον) along with will (εὐδοκία).

[30] For the subj. gen. cf. Sir. 18:31 (εὐδοκία ἐπιθυμίας) and 9:12. From the context it may be argued that ἔργον, too, is the fruit of faith. Theodor. (Swete, II [1882], 47): et impleat omne placitum bonitatis. Pr.-Bauer, s.v. εὐδοκία: "good will of uprightness," but εὐδοκία does not mean "good" will in this sense (→ 744 f.; cf. 750). Schl. Erl.: "resolve of goodness."

[31] Acc. to Euthymios, Oikumenios, Ambst., Theod. of Mopsuestia, Zwingli, Calvin, Beza, Bengel, ἀγαθωσύνη refers to the good will and counsel of God. But Dob. Th., Oepke (NT Deutsch), ad loc., together with Theophylact., Grotius, rightly refer εὐδοκία to God and ἀγαθωσύνη to man, → ἀγαθωσύνη, I, 18.

[32] For ὑπέρ in the sense of "in the interests of" cf. 2 C. 12:8, 19; R. 1:5; 15:8. Bl.-Debr.[6] § 231, 2, with J. C. K. Hofmann (1871), relates the ὑπὲρ εὐδοκίας to the following sentence. But its position at the end of the sentence quoted emphasises the θεὸς γάρ ἐστιν.

i.e., fulfils the ordination therein foreseen. [33] In Eph. 1:5, 9, 11 we have the synonyms εὐδοκία, θέλημα (will), πρόθεσις (purpose) and βουλή (counsel). To give a fuller characterisation of what is said Eph. often uses cumulative, synonymous genitives (cf. 1:19; 2:14, 15; 3:7). It is thus that the divine will is described as εὐδοκία in v. 5. The term cannot be separated from the βουλή (→ I, 635) which in the προορίζειν (1:5, 11), προτίθεσθαι (1:9) and πρόθεσις (1:11) is described as a pre-temporal purpose. But the aim of this cumulative description demands that εὐδοκία should be seen as expressing a special side of this pre-temporal resolve of the divine will. What is brought out is not merely the προαίρεσις. It is more than the determinate will and counsel as such. It is the content of this counsel as the free good-pleasure [34] which, grounded in God alone and influenced by none else, is His gracious resolution to save. In 1:9 also the κατὰ τὴν εὐδοκίαν αὐτοῦ makes the τὸ μυστήριον τοῦ θελήματος αὐτοῦ into His free good-pleasure. In the general sketch of the goals of salvation in vv. 4-12 the element of free and merciful grace stands at the centre. In all the descriptions of the divine will (→ θέλημα), the strongest expression is found in εὐδοκία.

2. εὐδοκία in the Synoptists.

a. The prayer of Jesus (from Q) in Mt. 11:26; Lk. 10:21 [35] describes as the sovereign divine decree [36] (cf. Sir. → 744) the fact that God has hidden the knowledge of the Son from the wise and revealed it to babes. Jesus rests in this basic will of the Father. This is the conclusion and limit of His thinking as it passes into adoration.

b. The Christmas saying. In relation to 2:14 textual clarification is essential before there can be any attempt at exposition.

The song of the angels is preserved in two forms. The first is a distich:

δόξα ἐν ὑψίστοις θεῷ
καὶ ἐπὶ γῆς εἰρήνη ἐν ἀνθρώποις εὐδοκίας. [37]

---

[33] By using *alacritas* for πληροφορία (Swete, I [1880], 225), Theodore of Mopsuestia refers the εὐδοκία to the will of man. syᴾ, Victorinus, lat, vg have in view the good will brought about by God: *pro bona voluntate*. Erasmus is uncertain. Zahn, Ewald and Pr.-Bauer follow the Lat. For Zahn's argument that otherwise the reference to God should be stated (C adds αὐτοῦ), cf. 2 Th. 1:11 (→ *supra*) and the omission of αὐτοῦ in R. 2:18; 6:4; 12:19; → Lk. 2:14. In Phil. 2:13 further mention of man's will after θέλειν and ἐνεργεῖν would be tautological. Here, as in Lk. 2:14, the Lat. betrays unfamiliarity with the Palestinian use of the formula. Thus Chrys. (ἵνα τὰ δοκοῦντα αὐτῷ γένηται), Theodoret (ἀγαθὸν τοῦ θεοῦ θέλημα), the Reformers and the majority of modern commentators favour a reference to God. The argument from Rabbinic modes of speaking is more important than the appeal to the ὑπὲρ εὐχαριστίας of Egyptian inscr. of the imperial period: A. Deissmann, Pls.² (1925), 167, n. 1. The suggestion of Loh. Phil., *ad loc.* (martyrdom) is artificial.

[34] On Eph. 1:5 cf. Theodor., Chrys., Thdrt.; Cramer Cat., VI, 108, 111. Luther in his Lectures on Romans of 1515/1516 (Ficker, I, 85, 18-21) has the fine statement: *quia sic voluit ac placuit ab eterno, et voluntatis eius nulla est lex nullumque debitum omnino. Voluntas libera, que nulli subjacet* etc. *Ibid.,* I, 136:19-22: *Hoc verbum "placuit" vel "probaverunt" proprie significat bene, spontanee, hilariter placuit.*

[35] On ἔμπροσθέν σου cf. לפני with the Rabbis, → 745. Here, too, there is thought of a council before the throne, → 745; cf. Zn., Schl., *ad loc.* On ἔμπροσθεν Mt. 18:14; Lk. 12:8; ἐνώπιον: Lk. 12:6; 15:10; Rev. 16:19.

[36] Cf. Cramer Cat., I, 88: ὅτι ἤρεσέ σοι.

[37] Found in ℵ *AB*D it vg got; not in C. There is vacillation concerning the ἐν before ἀνθρώποις. It occurs in ℵ *B*AD sa ("of his desire"), got (*in mannam godis viljins*), Orig. Comm. on Jn. 1:12 and Cels., I, 60, gdδ vgᵖᵃʳᵗ, but not in abcef ff² lqr aur vgᵖᵃʳᵗ Irˡᵃᵗ Orˡᵃᵗ, the Lat. fathers Hilarius, with a distinctive order Optatus and Priscillian, Ambr.,

In respect of the gen. εὐδοκίας the older Gk. tradition agrees with the Lat., which manifests a close unity as regards the words: *et in terra pax hominibus bonae voluntatis.* The textus Africanus presupposes εὐδοκίας. It is relatively uncertain whether Iren. and Orig. read εὐδοκία or εὐδοκίας. But their expositions make it clear that they did not think of man's good will, like the Lat., but of the divine will to save.[38] The second form is that of a tristich:

δόξα ἐν ὑψίστοις θεῷ
καὶ ἐπὶ γῆς εἰρήνη
ἐν ἀνθρώποις εὐδοκία.[39]

This is the ℵ text which is also found in older Palestinian attestations (038 Gr. ℵ c, Euseb.) and apart from minor variations in all the Syr.[40] Although both readings can be traced back into the 2nd cent. and the second is certainly pre-Syrian, our decision must be in favour of the first, since the Syr. alone cannot outweigh the older Egyptian tradition and the whole of the Lat. The advantage of the version with the gen., which we must accept as the older,[41] is that it maintains a consistent parallelism:[42] δόξα —

Aug., Orosius etc. It is not present in the old Syr. or Ps.-Athanasius (Montfaucon [1707], II, 53). Thus the ἐν is doubtful, though this does not affect the sense.

[38] Iren. has: *in terra pax hominibus bonae voluntatis,* at III, 10, 4, but this may have been added by the transl., since in the paraphrase he speaks of God as the One *qui suo plasmati, hoc est, hominibus, suam benignitatem salutis de caelo misit.* He thus equates εὐδοκία with *benignitas salutis.* In Orig. Hom., 13 on Lk. 2:8-16 (Thenn → 742 n.; ZwTh, 34 [1891], 483 ff., esp. 485 f.) we have ἐν ἀνθρώποις εὐδοκία three times, as also in Comm. on Jn. 1:12 and Cels., I, 60, though in the exposition (Thenn, 486) a hyperbaton is assumed and the gen. εὐδοκίας is related to εἰρήνη. It is not certain whether we have here a true reading or an interpretative paraphrase which involves comparison with Mt. 10:34.

[39] So 17 uncials esp. of the K I type, Origpart, the Gk. fathers from Gregory Thaumaturgus and Euseb. to Chrys., Theodot. of Ancyra, Proclus, the Const. Ap. and Psalteries which add the *gloria,* arm aeth, all the syr, also sypal. The only variations here are in respect of the καί in the 3rd line and the ἐν before ἀνθρώποις. In Aphraat, too, Lk. 2:14 is a tristich.

[40] There are various renderings of εὐδοκία in the sy. 1. sys has ארעותא לבני אנשא "good-pleasure," which is found in the Tg. but not elsewhere in Syr (Aram. רְעוּת). It is not used by sys at Mt. 11:26 or Lk. 10:21, and is never used by syp for εὐδοκία. 2. Worth noting is the rendering סברא טבא: *spes* or *opinio bona.* This may have come already with Tat. So syp Aphraatsyr Tatarab, cf. also *spes* in Ephr. In Ephrarm we are to understand *spes bonorum.* This most common sy rendering is simply a mechanically literal transl., for to סברא corresponds not only *spes, fiducia, imaginatio,* but also *opinio, cogitatio* = δόκησις, φροντίς, and the verb סבר corresponds to δοκεῖν (ἔδοξεν), as is shown esp. by Aphraat. To סברא (*spes, opinio,* δόκησις) there is simply added טבא as a transl. of εὐ-. To be sure, this main syr reading is related to the Lat. *bonae voluntatis.* Yet *spes* denotes the direction of man's view to God. The nom. instead of the gen. (in all sy) makes impossible the misunderstanding of εὐδοκία as a human quality. It is evident that we have here a Palestinian reaction against the legal conception of εὐδοκία among the Westerns. 3. syh pal have צבינא = θέλημα, "will," "choice," "good-pleasure." It corresponds in Sirsy (R. Smend, Index, *s.v.* εὐδοκία) to the Gk. εὐδοκία, 2:16; 11:17; 18:31; 32:5; 39:18. For the equation of the Heb. רצון and צבינא: cf. Sir. 4:12; 11:17; 36:22; 39:18; 42:15. In Ps. Sol. εὐδοκία occurs 3 times in the Gk. text, and צבינא 4 times in the Syr. צבינא is εὐδοκία (Heb. original רצון) at 3:4; 8:33; 16:12, and צבינא is θέλημα at 7:8. Cf. K. G. Kuhn, *Die syr. Übersetzung der PsSal* = BWANT, IV, 17 (1935). In syh צבינא is as often used for θέλημα as for εὐδοκία. In sys pal p it is elsewhere used for εὐδοκία consistently in the sense of "will," cf. Mt. 11:26; Lk. 10:21.

[41] So in almost all more recent textual criticism since Lachmann. For εὐδοκία cf. McNeile, Scrivener, Field, Cr.-Kö., Ropes. It is usually argued that it is more difficult and therefore earlier. But textual history shows that ἄνθρωποι εὐδοκίας has usually been found more difficult.

[42] This is disturbed by Harnack's reading: δόξα ἐν ὑψίστοις θεῷ καὶ ἐπὶ γῆς. / εἰρήνη

εἰρήνη, ἐν ὑψίστοις — ἐπὶ γῆς, θεῷ — ἐν ἀνθρώποις εὐδοκίας. The first verse has to do with heaven, the second with earth. The second reading could develop from the first as the understanding of Semitic forms was lost. These offended the Gk. sense of language. The practical co-ordination of lines 2 and 3 without καί is non-Semitic. This καί, [43] which is indispensable for three lines, cannot have been lost. Why, then, was it not added? The only reason is that it was not in the original. The reading εὐδοκία could arise from the use of ἐν and reminiscence of εὐδοκεῖν ἐν. But the triumph of the tristich probably owes most to liturgical use. The nominative was suitable for recitation. These considerations demand investigation of a Hebrew original, esp. as there are in the NT no Hebraic passages like those of Lk. 1 and 2 except in Rev. That Luke deliberately adopted a Heb. style (Harnack) is no adequate explanation. Jeremias takes the view that the Lucan birth narrative had already been given Heb. literary form by the primitive Aramaic speaking community, the Baptist groups being interested in the content of Lk. 1. This would give us an original Heb. resting on oral Aram. tradition. But here, too, something from the Hebrew-Jewish sphere might well have passed into the Christian. [44] ἄνθρωποι εὐδοκίας is in any case a Semitic construction. It reminds us of the various combinations of ἀνήρ, ἄνθρωπος, υἱός, τέκνον and their plurals with abstract nouns which are so common in the OT, LXX and NT. Cf. Sir. 44:10: ἄνδρες ἐλέους (אנשי חסד), righteous men; sing. 44:23 B (27); ψ 40:9: ὁ ἄνθρωπος τῆς εἰρήνης μου; in the NT Mt. 8:12; 13:38: υἱοὶ τῆς βασιλείας; Eph. 2:3: τέκνα ὀργῆς. "Man of good-pleasure" is not found elsewhere, but cf. רצון as a dependent nom. → 743 and its figur. use in the Rabbis → 745. Related, too, is Da. 10:11, 19: אִישׁ חֲמֻדוֹת, though "beloved man" (God's favourite) hardly gives us the serious sense of רצון, as used of the divine decree. [45] The root here is אַנְשֵׁי רָצוֹן. [46]

The meaning of the saying. [47] The Messianic acclamation of the angels' song is not a wish (εἴη) but proclamation of the divine event (ἐστίν). God is glorified in heaven with the sending of Christ. This event works itself out on earth in εἰρήνη = שָׁלוֹם, salvation (→ 412 f.). This salvation takes place for men of good-pleasure. Thus the heavenly corresponds to the earthly. It is not as though the δόξα ἐν ὑψίστοις stood in antithesis to an as yet incomplete revelation on earth. [48] According to Lk. 2:9 the δόξα encircles the shepherds too. This is the sign of the new event,

---

ἀνθρώποις εὐδοκίας. Two hyperbata in so short a saying are intolerable, and the second, εἰρήνη εὐδοκίας acc. to Origen's exposition, is unthinkable if there is a Semitic basis. The καὶ ἐπὶ γῆς at the end of a line is disruptive, and the two unrelated sentences are both non-Semitic and difficult even in Gk. Ropes objects to the first version that it gives us an irregular distich. In Gk. this is a real difficulty but it loses its cogency if we suppose an original Heb. structure.

[43] Only sys p h Tatarab have καί (interposed out of stylistic necessity), but not sypal.

[44] Spitta conjectures an influence of Maccab. psalms. In Lk. 19:38, which is also in two parts, we perhaps have an adaptation of the same acclamation, as we should call it rather than hymn. It makes no difference to the question of origin whether we regard it as the verse of a hymn or as liturgical acclamation (E. Peterson, Εἷς θεός [1926], 316).

[45] G. v. Rad: Da. 10:11, 19 forms a model for ἄνθρωποι εὐδοκίας, or better a parallel for the usage.

[46] Merx (→ 742, n.), 201 proposes the following version of the distich:

כָּבוֹד לֵאלֹהִים בַּמְּרוֹמִים

וּבְאֶרֶץ שָׁלוֹם לְאַנְשֵׁי רָצוֹן.

Cf. Jeremias, though he has בְּאַנְשֵׁי. Cfr also Schl. Lk., ad loc. F. Delitzsch, too, translates the first version בְּאַנְשֵׁי רְצֹנוֹ. On Gressmann's conjecture (Kl. Lk. on 2:14), which starts with the Aram. and follows sys, cf. Jeremias, 15.

[47] Cf. the most important discussion in Jeremias, 19 f.

[48] Zn. Lk., ad loc.

that δόξα (→ 247 f.) in heaven is united with εἰρήνη on earth. [49] It is rightly perceived that eschatology in the sense of the great turning-point of the worlds determines the praise, and that the dawn of self-consummating redemption is proclaimed. In the hymns of Rev. 12:10; 11:15; 19:1, 6 the final attainment of this goal is celebrated. [50]

But who are these ἄνθρωποι εὐδοκίας (→ I, 364)? The understanding of the Latin church, namely, men who are of good will, implies legalism if a good will is regarded as decisive for salvation. Hence this rendering has often been taken to mean [51] that the act of salvation is only for those who open themselves to it and willingly accept the grace of God. There are many instances of the use of εὐδοκεῖν for "to agree," "to consent" (→ 739) and of εὐδόκησις in the sense of "agreement" or "assent" (→ 743). On the other hand, εὐδοκία never bears this meaning in Sir., the LXX or the Rabbis. For this reason, we can hardly expect it here. Only later, in Cl. Al. Strom., IV, 15, 97, 3, do we find this sense when we are told that the apostolic decree was published σὺν τῇ εὐδοκίᾳ τοῦ ἁγίου πνεύματος. Another possibility is that it refers to those who give pleasure to God. Now in the OT רצון is often ascribed to God as a response to human conduct, whether in the form of sacrifice, prayer or uprightness. But in these instances the accompanying senses of "favour," "grace" and the "divine will and counsel" prevent exclusive concentration on the idea of man awakening the divine pleasure. Even the acceptance of a sacrifice is an act of divine grace. And in the Gospel the idea that what man does can bring about the fulfilment of divine grace is completely rejected. Even from the purely linguistic standpoint the Lat. translation is incorrect. As used of men (OT, Sir.), εὐδοκία does not mean "good" will, but volition. But this would give an even more serious contradiction to the thought of grace. The evidence in relation to εὐδοκία points so overwhelmingly to the sense of the sovereign will of God that in a passage like this, which speaks of the accomplishment of salvation, there can be no place for reflection on the will of man. We have thus to understand by εὐδοκία the unfathomably gracious and sovereign good-pleasure of God in the sense of His decree as a decree of free grace and favour.

But who are the ἄνθρωποι? The whole race, Israel, or those specifically predestinated? We cannot possibly expound the text in such a way as to involve contradiction between Lk. 2:10 and 2:14. [52] Hence the statement is neither particularistic nor is it universalistic in detachment from salvation history. It refers eschatologically to the elect and redeemed people of God.

Thus εὐδοκία in the angels' song refers to God's gracious counsel addressed in free and incomprehensible favour to the people of His elect.

εὐδοκία plays an important role in Gnosticism. [53] In terms of Col. 1:19 the Valen-

---

[49] Cf. Jeremias, 20 for the correspondence of heaven and earth as a basic concept in the ancient oriental view of the world, cf. Mt. 6:9 f.: "in heaven and on earth."

[50] Loc. cit.

[51] Zn. Lk., ad loc.

[52] Wettstein, ad loc. sees a contradiction between the elect and παντὶ τῷ λαῷ in v. 10. Hilgenfeld, who understands ἄνθρωποι εὐδοκίας universalistically, suggests a Pauline redactor, since elsewhere Lk. 1 f. speaks only of Israel. Merx, 197, 201 f. assumes that the universalistic concept has altered an originally particularistic text and that the final act is to be found in sys P Tatarab, which have "the whole world" for λαός at Lk. 2:10. Jeremias, 19 and Dibelius, Krippenkind, 66 have set aside this question.

[53] Cf. for what follows Harnack, 809 (= 171 ff.). He rightly says (872 = 174) that there is no history of the meaning or development of εὐδοκία in the strict sense.

tinians call the *Soter* εὐδοκία or Εὐδόκητος : [54] Iren., I, 12, 4; Cl. Al. Exc., Theod., 31, 1; *ibid.*, 23, 2. Hence Orig. Comm. in Jn., p. 485, 6 f. (Preuschen [1903]) has the distinctive statement that the pre-existent divine σοφία created the world as εὐδοκία θεοῦ. Cf. Ps.-Clem. Hom., 13, 21 (p. 186, 5). The word is more common in the ecclesiastical literature of the 4th and 5th centuries. It is constantly explained, for difficulty was found with its meaning. Though a few Pauline passages demand another sense, it is usually referred to God, the Logos, or the Spirit, not to the will of man. Particularly common are paraphrases in terms of the divine θέλημα : τὸ ἀγαθὸν θέλημα, τὸ σφοδρὸν θέλημα, τὸ μετ' ἐπιθυμίας θέλημα, ἡ ἐπ' εὐεργεσίᾳ βούλησις, or τὸ σφοδρῶς θελῆσαι, ἡ σφόδρα ἐπιθυμία, or simply ἀρεσκεία, προθυμία, πληροφορία, the last even in Pauline passages wich demand reference to the will of man. The definitions are strikingly varied and give clear evidence of continuing uncertainty, for εὐδοκία is always a foreign term to the Gks. The word plays some part in the Christological conflicts with regard to the will of God, the Logos or the Spirit : Apollonius of Laodicaea De Trinitate, TU, VII, 3 (1892), p. 361, 35; Epiph. Ancoratus, 32, 9; 94, 2; Haer., 23, 3, 5; 23, 5, 1; 27, 7, 2; 30, 31, 4. Cf. the Antiochenes, esp. Theod. of Mopsuestia (Def. → 742, n.).

Schrenk

εὐεργεσία, εὐεργετέω, εὐεργέτης → 654   εὔκαιρος → καιρός.

> εὐλαβής, εὐλαβεῖσθαι,
> εὐλάβεια

A. The non-Christian Usage.

a. The word group εὐλαβής, εὐλαβεῖσθαι, εὐλάβεια (not attested in Hom. and Hes.) denotes in Gk. the attitude of "caution" or "circumspection" in many different nuances. It may mean careful regard for the καιρός (Bias, 17 [II, 217, 8, Diels]; Ps.-Agathon [Diehl, I, 78]; Eur. Or., 699), or "anxious fear," "vigilance," "provision against" (Aristoph. Av., 377; Aristot. Pol., II, 8, p. 1269a, 14; V, 11, p. 1315a, 17: personified in Eur. Phoen., 782), or "concern in the interest of" (Aristoph. Ach., 955; Plat. Leg., III, 691b; XI, 927c), or "conscientiousness" (Plat. Polit., 311a b; Demosth. Or., 21, 61 and 81). In the last sense εὐλάβεια is very close to → αἰδώς (Aristot. De Virtutibus et Vitiis, 4, p. 1250b, 12), and εὐλαβής takes on almost a religious sense, since it is a matter of scrupulous regard for what is right, as seen by the combination of εὐλαβῶς and εὐσεβῶς (Demosth. Or., 21, 61). But the word group can also be used for "religious awe" (Plat. Leg., IX, 879e; Aristoph. Lys., 1277; cf. Eur. Hipp., 100). This sense becomes more pronounced in Hellenism, so that Plut. can use ἡ πρὸς (or περὶ) τὸ θεῖον εὐλάβεια for the Lat. *religio* (De Numa, 22 [I, 75a b]; [1] De Camillo, 21 [I, 139d]; Aem., 3 [I, 256c]). This can also be used for the religious scrupulosity of the Platonists (Plut. Ser. Num. Pun., 4 [I, 549e]), and Diod. S., XIII, 12, 7 uses it of the religious condition of Nikias, whom he also calls → δεισιδαίμων. In this sense we have εὐλάβεια alone in Wilcken Ptol., 42, 22, and in modern Gk. εὐλάβεια has become the term for piety.

---

[54] εὐδοκία and εὐδόκητος are also interchangeable in ψ 67:30 Σ and Cant. 6:3 Σ, as distinct from LXX and 'A.

ε ὐ λ α β ή ς κ τ λ. Trench, 25 f., 105 ff.; W. Naumann, *Untersuchungen zum apokryphen Jeremiasbrief* (*Beih. z. ZAW*, 25 [1913], 38 f.); K. Kerényi, *Byzant.-Neugriech. Jahrbücher*, 8 (1929/30), 306 ff.; E. Jacquier, *Les Actes des Apôtres* (1926), 650; J. C. A. van Herten, Θρησκεία Εὐλάβεια Ἱκέτης. *Bijdrage tot de kennis der religieuse terminologie in het Grieksch*, with a summary in English (Diss. Utrecht, 1934).

[1] Here εὐλάβεια περὶ τὸ θεῖον is equated with εὐσέβεια and contrasted with δεισιδαιμονία.

Yet there is also a development of the sense of "caution" or "restraint" into "fear" or "anxiety" (e.g., εὐλαβεῖσθαι with μή in Polyb., 1, 16, 7; 3, 111, 1; εὐλαβηθείς, "set in anxiety," Diod. S., XVI, 22, 2), from which it is expressly distinguished, e.g., in Demosth. Or., 19, 206; Aristot. Eth. Nic., IV, p. 1121b, 24 ff. Acc. to Moeris (Harpocration et Moeris, ed. I. Bekker [1833], p. 196, 2 f.) εὐλαβεῖσθαι has the sense of φυλάττεσθαι in Attic and φοβεῖσθαι in Hellenistic. The Stoics, of course, seek to distinguish εὐλάβεια as εὔλογος ἔκκλισις from φόβος as ἄλογος ἔκκλισις. They call εὐλάβεια, of which only the sage is capable, one of the three εὐπάθειαι along with → χαρά and βούλησις, and within it they perceive → αἰδώς (as εὐλάβεια ὀρθοῦ ψόγου) and ἁγνεία (as εὐλάβεια τῶν περὶ θεῶν ἁμαρτημάτων), v. Arnim, III, 105, 16 ff. and cf. Index. Epictet. Diss., II, 1 defends the Stoic paradox that true εὐλαβεῖσθαι and θαρρεῖν constitute a unity.

b. In the Septuagint the verb εὐλαβεῖσθαι is found most, though rarely in the older sense of "to be on guard" (Sir. 18:27; 22:22[27]; 26:5; Ep. Jer. 4). It usually means "to fear," being used for various Heb. words, e.g., with acc. Dt. 2:4 (שָׁמַר niph); Sir. 41:3(5) (פָּחַד); Wis. 12:11; 2 Macc. 8:16 (par. καταπλαγῆναι); 9:29. With ἀπό 1 Βασ. 18:15 (גּוּר). 29 (יָרֵא). Absol. Is. 57:11 (דָּאַג); Sir. 31(34):16 (par. δειλιᾶν). With inf. Ex. 3:6 (יָרֵא); 1 Ἐσδρ. 4:28. With μή 1 Macc. 3:30; 12:40. It is hard to differentiate from φοβεῖσθαι and is often used together with it (Dt. 2:4; Is. 57:11; Jer. 5:22; Mal. 3:16; Sir. 7:29[31]; 31[34]:16 f.) or with φόβος (Da. 4:2, where Θ has ἐφοβέρισέν με instead of εὐλαβήθην). It occurs as a vl. with φοβεῖσθαι at Is. 51:12; Job 3:25.

Above all εὐλαβεῖσθαι (often with ἀπό) means the "fear of God," being used in this sense for יָרֵא (Ex. 3:6) and the interjection הַס (Zeph. 1:7; Zech. 2:13[17]; Hab. 2:20), but also for חָסָה (Prv. 24:28 [30:5]; Na. 1:7; Zeph. 3:12 etc.); cf. also Sir. 7:29 (31) (פָּחַד); 18:27; 23:18(26). At Prv. 2:8 חָסִיד is rendered εὐλαβούμενος (αὐτόν) and at 4 Macc. 4:13 εὐλαβηθείς means "one who is filled with religious scruples." εὐλαβῶς ἔχειν at 2 Macc. 6:11 means "to have religious awe."

The εὐλαβής (found only 3 times) is "one who keeps careful watch (against becoming unclean)" in Lv. 15:31 and "the pious" in Mi. 7:2 (חָסִיד); Sir. 11:17 (in both cases vl. εὐσεβής).

εὐλάβεια (used only 3 times) means "concern" or "anxiety" at Jos. 22:24; Wis. 17:8 and "religious awe" at Prv. 28:14.

c. The word group does not occur in the Ps. Sol., the Test. XII or Ep. Ar.

In Jos. Ant., 11, 239, εὐλάβεια is used for the "nervousness" of Esther before the king, and in Ant., 6, 259 τὸ θεῖον εὐλαβούμενοι means the fear of God.

Philo uses εὐλαβής essentially in the older Gk. sense for "fearful" (Vit. Mos., I, 83), "watchful," "cautious" (Leg. Gaj., 182, esp. Som., II, 80, opp. αὐθάδης). εὐλαβῶς ἔχειν is "to be on guard" (Leg. Gaj., 159), "to fear" (Jos., 245; Praem. Poen., 89), and in the sense of religious awe, Rer. Div. Her., 22. εὐλαβεῖσθαι seems to be used always in the sense of "to fear," abs. Abr., 206; Spec. Leg., IV, 6 etc.; with the acc. Flacc., 145; Vit. Mos., I, 215 etc.; mostly with a material obj., but with parents as obj. in Spec. Leg., II, 3 and 234 (differentiated from τιμᾶν or αἰδεῖσθαι) and the high-priests in III, 132. God is the obj., though εὐλαβεῖσθαι does not here have the specific sense of religious awe, in Gig., 47, where it is differentiated from αἰδεῖσθαι. With περί Jos., 255; Virt., 67. Followed by μή Fug., 131; Vit. Mos., I, 236 etc. εὐλαβεῖσθαι occurs in the sense of religious awe in Rer. Div. Her., 29; Mut. Nom., 134; Spec. Leg., II, 54. εὐλάβεια is found in the sense of "nervousness" or "prudence" in Det. Pot. Ins., 45 (cf. Eur. Phoen., 782; Aristoph. Av., 377); Leg. All., III, 113; Virt., 24; it probably has a religious sense in Op. Mund., 156; Spec. Leg., III, 23, and certainly in Rer. Div. Her., 22 and 29; Som., II, 82 and 141 (cf. Leg. Gaj., 236, a respectful attitude before the emperor). On the other hand εὐλάβεια means fear of God rather than awe or reverence in Cher., 29; Spec. Leg., I, 270 and 330. It means reverence before God in Mut. Nom., 201 and before the emperor in Leg. Gaj., 252, and in both cases it is linked with αἰδώς. The Stoic paradox (→ supra) concerning the interrelationship of εὐλάβεια and θάρσος is adapted by Philo in Rer. Div. Her., 22 and 29 to describe a truly pious attitude before God.

B. Early Christian Usage.

The word group is rare in early Christian literature. At Lk. 2:25 εὐλαβής is used with δίκαιος (→ 189) to describe Simeon. At Ac. 2:5 the Jews of the dispersion dwelling at Jerusalem are called ἄνδρες εὐλαβεῖς, and the ἄνδρες εὐλαβεῖς who bury Stephen at 8:2 are again Jews. Ananias is called an ἀνὴρ εὐλαβὴς κατὰ τὸν νόμον at Ac. 22:12. εὐλαβής always means "pious" or "devout" as in the LXX (→ 752), and it is no accident that the piety thus characterised is that which consists in scrupulous observance of the Law, as may be seen in Ac. 22:12 (→ 751). The vg uses timoratus at Lk. 2:25; Ac. 8:2, religiosus at Ac. 2:5 and vir secundum legem at 22:12. In Mart. Pol., 2, 1 we have the sense of reverent fear of God, and in Just. Dial., 79, 2 the term is used for shocked feelings at blasphemous utterance.

The vl. εὐλαβεῖσθαι at Ac. 23:10 has the sense of "to fear," the true reading being φοβεῖσθαι. This sense is perhaps present also at Hb. 11:7: (Νῶε) εὐλαβηθεὶς κατεσκεύασεν κιβωτόν (vg metuens), though it may simply imply reverent awe. "To fear" is certainly the meaning in 1 Cl., 44, 5; Just. Dial., 7, 1 and 123, 3 (where God's ὀργή is the obj.).

εὐλάβεια occurs at Hb. 5:7; 12:28. In the second passage (... ἔχωμεν χάριν, δι' ἧς λατρεύωμεν εὐαρέστως τῷ θεῷ μετὰ εὐλαβείας καὶ δέους [vl. αἰδοῦς]), εὐλάβεια in conjunction with δέος has the sense of "anxiety," so that the combination corresponds to the μετὰ φόβου καὶ τρόμου of Phil. 2:12. The copyist, however, obviously understood it in the sense of "pious reverence" (→ 751 f.), since he amended the δέους to αἰδοῦς; the vg translates cum metu et reverentia. Much disputed is Hb. 5:7: (Jesus) ὃς ... δεήσεις τε καὶ ἱκετηρίας πρὸς τὸν δυνάμενον σῴζειν αὐτὸν ἐκ θανάτου ... προσενέγκας καὶ εἰσακουσθεὶς ἀπὸ τῆς εὐλαβείας, καίπερ ὢν υἱός, ἔμαθεν ἀφ' ὧν ἔπαθεν τὴν ὑπακοήν. If we understand by εὐλάβεια the fear of God or piety, then ἀπό must have the sense of "by reason of," [2] and the meaning is that He was heard because of His piety. This explanation seems to be excluded, however, by the fact that the hearing could then consist only in His deliverance from death. On the other hand, if we give to εὐλάβεια the sense of "fear" or "anxiety," then the meaning is that He was heard out of His anxiety, so that He was liberated from anxiety (if not from death). But this is not satisfactory in the context; in particular it does not do justice to the καίπερ ὢν υἱός. Full justice is done to this only if we assume that the text is corrupt and that there ought to be an οὐκ before εἰσακουσθείς which was understandably cut out on religious grounds. [3]

εὐλάβεια occurs again at Pol., 6, 3: οὕτως οὖν δουλεύσωμεν αὐτῷ (sc. τῷ Χριστῷ) μετὰ φόβου καὶ πάσης εὐλαβείας. Here it might well mean "reverence" before God.

Why is the word group so rare in the religious sense in early Christian literature? And why, when a word was needed for the concept of religion, was

---

[2] For ἀπό in this sense cf. Ps.-Bauer, 137 on ἀπό, V, 1.

[3] So A. v. Harnack, SAB, 1929, 62 ff.; Bl.-Debr.[6] § 211 takes ἀπὸ τῆς εὐλαβείας in the sense of "of his piety," but links it with ἔμαθεν rather than εἰσακουσθείς, and then continues: ἀφ' ὧν <τ'> ἔπαθεν τὴν ὑπακοήν. This is, however, very artificial, and in particular it does not give full weight to καίπερ ὢν υἱός. For other suggestions v. Wnd. Hb.

εὐλάβεια not selected instead of → θρησκεία (Ac. 26:5, vg *religio*), seeing εὐλάβεια seemed to have been marked out for this role by its Hellenistic usage ? One
reason is perhaps that εὐλάβεια does not include cultic piety as does θρησκεία.
But apart from this the main reason is that the decisive element in εὐλάβεια is
the negative aspect of nervous caution, as may be seen from the connection between
εὐλάβεια and δεισιδαιμονία (→ 751). It is thus natural that Jews should be called
εὐλαβεῖς when their piety consists in watchful vigilance against transgressing the
Law. It is also natural that εὐλάβεια should come to be used for the *homo religiosus* in the Eastern Church and in monasticism. Here εὐλαβής and εὐλαβέστατος
become spiritual titles, and ἡ σὴ εὐλάβεια a form of address. [4] It is also natural
that in modern Greece, where religion consists essentially in δεισιδαιμονία, εὐλάβεια should be the common word for piety.

Bultmann

| εὐλογέω, εὐλογητός, |
| εὐλογία, ἐνευλογέω |

† εὐλογέω, † εὐλογία.

Of few words in the NT is it so plain as of εὐλογέω and εὐλογία that they
do not take their meaning from secular Greek but from the fact that they are the
renderings of Hebrew words which acquired their religious significance in the OT
and other Jewish writings.

A. εὐλογέω and εὐλογία in Greek Literature.

Literally εὖ λέγειν means (both in form and content) "to speak well," either in the
sense of "to speak finely" or "to speak well of someone." The first meaning occurs
with the noun. Thus Plat. Resp., III, 400d links εὐλογία, i.e., "fine or noble speech,"
with εὐαρμοστία ("good nature"), εὐσχημοσύνη ("grace of manner") and εὐρυθμία
("proportion") to express a genuinely moral disposition. In Luc. Lexiphanes, 1 the fine
speaker says : σκόπει ..., ὅπως διαπεραίνομαι ... τὸν λόγον, εἰ εὔαρχός τέ ἐστι
καὶ πολλὴν τὴν εὐλογίαν ἐπιδεικνύμενος καὶ εὔλεξις, ἔτι δὲ εὐώνυμος. This
passage shows already that there can also be something unwelcome about fine speaking.
The second meaning, "to praise," "to extol," "to eulogise," is more common along with
the corresponding nouns, though it is almost never found in prose : Aesch. Ag., 580 :
εὐλογεῖν πόλιν καὶ τοὺς στρατηγούς; Soph. Oed. Col., 720 : ἐπαίνοις εὐλογεῖσθαι;
Aristoph. Eq., 565 : εὐλογῆσαι βουλόμεθα τοὺς πατέρας ἡμῶν; *ibid.*, 596 : ἄξιοι
δ' εἰσ' εὐλογεῖσθαι, Eccl., 454 : ἕτερά τε πλεῖστα τὰς γυναῖκας εὐλόγει; Isoc.,
6, 105 : τοὺς βουλομένους εὐλογεῖν ἡμᾶς ἀπορεῖν ποιήσομεν, ὅτι τῶν πεπραγμέ-
νων ἡμῖν ἄξιον ἐροῦσιν; Pind. Nem., 4, 5 : εὐλογία φόρμιγγι συνάορος; Eur. Herc.

---

[4] K. Kerényi, *op. cit.*, 311; A. Zehetmair, *De appellationibus honorificis in papyris obviis*
(Diss. Marburg, 1911), 52 f.; O. Hornickel, *Ehren- und Rangprädikate in den Papyrusurkunden* (Diss. Giessen, 1930), 13 f.

ε ὐ λ ο γ έ ω κτλ. Cr.-Kö., 684 ff.; RE³, XVIII, 148 ff.; RGG², V, 388 ff.; M. Ebert,
Reallexikon der Vorgeschichte, III (1925), 391; XII (1928), 5 ff.; B. Landsberger, "Das gute
Wort" in *B. Meissner-Festschrift*, II = *Mitteilungen der Altorientalischen Gesellschaft*, IV
(1929), 294 ff.; J. Pedersen, *Israel* I/II (Danish 1920; Eng. 1926); S. Mowinckel, *Psalmenstudien*, V : "Segen und Fluch in Israels Kult und Psalmdichtung" (= *Videnskapsselskapets
Skrifter*, II : *Hist.-Filos. Klasse*, 1923, No. 3); J. Hempel, "Die israelitischen Anschauungen
von Segen und Fluch im Lichte altorientalischer Parallelen," ZDMG, NF 4 (1925), 20 ff.;
J. Elbogen, *Der jüd. Gottesdienst in seiner geschichtlichen Entwicklung²* (1924), 4 f.; E. Norden, *Agnostos Theos* (1913), 149 ff.

Fur., 356 : ὑμνῆσαι δι᾽ εὐλογίας θέλω. On the pap. it also comes to means "advocacy": P. Oxy., I, 65, 4 (3rd/4th cent. A.D.): εἰ δὲ ἔχετε εὐλογίαν τινὰ πρὸς αὐτὸν ἀνέρχεσθε ἅμα αὐτῷ. The opp. is κακολογεῖν, κατηγορεῖν (Ps.-Plat. Min., 320e) or ψέγειν (Polyb., 1, 14, 4). On one single occasion we have the εὐλογεῖν of a man by gods : Eur. Suppl., 925 : καὶ μὴν τὸν Οἰκλέους γε γενναῖον τόκον θεοὶ ... εὐλογοῦσιν ἐμφανῶς, the gods honour a man and grant him benefits. But man also extols the god, e.g., Pan : CIG, III, p. 1190, No. 4705b, 2 or Isis, 4705c, 2. The concept of "blessing" plays a surprisingly meagre role in the classical world. There is no specific terminology for it. The content of what the gods lavish on men is denoted by the word ὄλβος, which implies good fortune and all that is necessary to well-being : Hom. Od., 6, 188 f.: Ζεὺς δ᾽ αὐτὸς νέμει ὄλβον Ὀλύμπιος ἀνθρώποισιν, ἐσθλοῖς ἠδὲ κακοῖσιν, ὅπως ἐθέλησιν, ἑκάστῳ. We may also think of Aesch. Eum., 997 ff.: χαίρετ᾽ ἀστικὸς λεώς, ἵκταρ ἥμενοι Διός, παρθένου φίλας φίλοι, σωφρονοῦντες ἐν χρόνῳ. Παλλάδος δ᾽ ὑπὸ πτεροῖς ὄντος ἅζεται πατήρ. The gods are men's helpers and defenders even though they also chide and punish them. But there are no specific acts of blessing. When the expression θεοῦ εὐλογία occurs on an inscr. of the 3rd cent. B.C. (Ditt. Or., I, 74, 1), the reference is to a Jew : Θεύδοτος Ἰουδαῖος σωθεὶς ἐκ πελάγους. Cf. also Ditt. Or., I, 73, 1.

B. Blessing in the OT.

The concept of blessing adopted in the NT is most important in the oriental world and takes on a particular significance in Judaism. This may be seen from the fact that the word εὐλογέω occurs more than 400 times in the LXX.

Blessing, like cursing, is an object of belief in primitive religion.[1] It is one of the oldest religious conceptions that there are beings and forces from which good and life and power derive, as well as those from which evil comes. The transfer is made by actions (gestures or contacts), and especially by words, which may imply either blessing or cursing. According to primitive belief something material comes with the blessing. Once set in motion, as when a father blesses his child, the operation is irresistible unless thwarted by equally strong opposing forces. Men and things which are blessed are as it were endowed with this power and can transmit it, affecting everything with which they come in contact. What has been said applies to the fullest possible degree when the blessing comes directly from the deity. In this case it is a "supernatural furtherance of man's action and course which proceeds from the deity."[2]

Many elements deriving from this religious background may still be found in the terms בֶּרֶךְ and בְּרָכָה which the Israelites use for blessing and which are translated εὐλογέω and εὐλογία in the LXX.[3] "The Heb. בְּרָכָה does not merely signify 'blessing' or 'a blessing,' but also 'being blessed' or 'being filled with blessing,' as well as the concrete blessings which ensue, e.g., good fortune, power, etc."[4]

---

[1] Cf. Reallexikon der Vorgeschichte, III, 391; XII, 5 ff. On what follows cf. esp. Pedersen, 135 ff. The concept of blessing was already well developed in the Babylonian world, as B. Landsberger, op. cit. has shown. It is worth nothing that here already may be perceived a development according to which the blessing comes not merely by gesture and act but decisively by word (313 f.), and that the term karabu denotes the blessing given by the deity as well as man's adoration (294 f.).

[2] R. Kittel, RE³, XVIII, 148; Mowinckel, Psalmenstudien, V (1924), 5 ff.

[3] On a few occasions εὐλογέω is also used for other Heb. words, e.g., הָדַר, Da. 5:23; הָלַל, Is. 38:18; 64:11 (10); יָדָה, Is. 12:1; 38:19; יָרֵא, Is. 25:3; יָתַר, Dt. 30:9; כָּבֵד, Is. 25:3; 43:20; נָגַן, Is. 38:20; רָנַן, Job 29:13; רָצָה, 2 Βασ. 24:23; ψ 48:13; 118:108; שְׁבַח, Da. 5:4.

[4] Mowinckel, 5.

1. Man carries within him a power to bless which he can transmit, usually to his heirs. The content of the blessing is originally the mastery which the father gives to the son before his death. He can give this only once, and the action is irrevocable.

This belief helps us to understand the story of Jacob's deception of Isaac in Gn. 27:1 ff. Jacob himself blesses Joseph in Gn. 48:15; 49:25 f., and also his two sons, putting his right hand on the head of the younger and thus allotting to him the more powerful blessing. There is thus a regular transmission of the blessing as an inheritance. Gn. 49:26: "The blessings granted to thy father excelled the blessing of the everlasting hills, the splendour of the eternal mountains. May they now come on the head of Joseph." The specific content of the blessing are a long and successful life and numerous children, best summed up in the word שָׁלוֹם.[5] The saying in Sir. 3:11 is a moralistic echo of this belief: "The blessing of the father builds the children's houses."

2. But even when Jacob blesses his son Joseph, he does so in the form of prayer to God: "May he bless thee with the blessings of heaven above," Gn. 49:25. The One who possesses and dispenses all blessings is God the Lord. This is the sacred knowledge underlying all OT statements concerning blessing. God, however, is personal will and not impersonal force. Hence even the sayings in which there are echoes of primitive religion acquire a new significance.

There is no longer any connection between blessing and a *mana*. Blessing does not work in the form of a magical power overflowing man. It is not a psychical power which makes its possessor a "lucky fellow" and endows him with special ability.[6] The blessing of Yahweh is the gracious divine gift which He dispenses in sovereign freedom, granting His favour to individuals or to a people and causing the work of their hands to succeed (Dt. 28:12; 8:9-17). Thus there are several passages in which God Himself imparts the blessing: Gn. 1:22, 28; 2:3; 5:2; 9:1; 14:9; 24:19: Κύριος εὐλόγησεν τὸν Ἀβραὰμ κατὰ πάντα; 39:5: ἐγενήθη εὐλογία κυρίου ἐπὶ πᾶσιν; ψ 44:2; 66:6; 128:8; Prv. 10:6 and many others. God can also change a curse into a blessing, Dt. 23:5 (6); Neh. 13:2.

God's blessing rules over creation. As soon as God had created living creatures which did not come forth out of the earth like the plants and beasts of the earth, He blessed them: "Be fruitful, and multiply" (Gn. 1:22). Fishes and birds need this blessing, but especially man.

---

[5] Hempel, 51. In ancient Syrian sources, too, long and effective life and many children are the content of blessing, e.g., inscr. of Assuruballit, I, clay tablet in the Brit. Museum, 96,947, in E. Ebeling, B. Meissner, E. F. Weidner, *Die Inschriften der altassyrischen Könige* (1926), 41. Cf. for the 7th and 6th cent. M. Jastrow, *Die Religion Babyloniens und Assyriens*, I (1905), 416. Here the blessing derives its true character from the *mana*.

[6] R. Kittel (RE, XVIII, 148 ff.), J. Pedersen (*Israel* I/II, 135 ff.) and S. Mowinckel (*Psalmenstudien*, V, 5 ff.) have performed the service of bringing to light the religio-historical roots of Israelite ideas of blessing and cursing. In relation to their work the only task, finely executed by J. Hempel (ZDMG, NF, 4 [1925], 95 ff.; RGG², V, 391 ff.), is to emphasise the fact that, although there are in the OT traces of primitive ideas "which betray their origin in primitive magic in spite of every sublimation," nevertheless the OT transcends these relics and has learned and teaches us a completely new understanding of the blessing of the Almighty in both form and content. Mowinckel's theory that the concept of blessing develops from an "original union of the soul with deity conceived in purely mystical terms" (V, 7 f.) to the more rational conception that Yahweh is the Giver of blessing, suffers from the defects 1. that the essential development takes place prior to the OT, and 2. that it is not quite accurately stated. It may be questioned whether God was ever thought of in Israel as the great primitive force with whom one may have mystical union of soul. And the conception of blessing adopted in Israel was not achieved by way of rationalisation but simply by way of a serious acceptance of the insight that Yahweh is the Lord.

The first thing God does in relation to man is to bless him (Gn. 1:28). The gifts given to him are fruitfulness and dominion. The promise of numerous progeny is the content of many blessings, e.g., Gn. 12:2; 13:16 etc.; also Ruth 4:11 f.; 2 Βασ. 7:11-16; Tob. 10:11 f. God also sustains His work by causing showers of blessing to fall (Ez. 34:26). Fruitfulness of field and cattle, and multiplication of possessions, are promised, cf. Dt. 28:1-13. [7] Ordinances like the Sabbath are blessed as well as man (Gn. 2:3; Ex. 20:11). Cattle and sheep, corn and wine, basket and store all stand under the blessing of Yahweh.

This blessing comes particularly on man as one who is active in history. Adam, Noah, the patriarchs and Moses are all blessed by God. The simplest and fullest expression of this is to be found in the promise of God in Gn. 26:3 : "I will be with thee," [8] or Gn. 17:7 f.: "I will be a God unto thee, and to thy seed after thee." This blessing pronounced over Abraham and all that he has is the promise of God fulfilled in Jesus Christ. Between Abraham and Christ it rests on the people of Israel.

In the dramatic events on mounts Ebal and Gerizim (Dt. 27:9 ff.) the people is shown that its whole history stands under the operation of blessing and cursing (Dt. 11:26 ff.; 30:1 ff., 15 ff.; cf. also Lv. 26:3 ff.). God has left the choice between the two to the people. [9] It is a choice between the wrath of God and the grace of God, between life and death, faith and unbelief, obedience and disobedience. It is in relation to the First Commandment that the decision is made. For the transgressor it becomes a curse ; for him who fears and loves God alone it is a most mighty confirmation of the promise once given to Abraham (Dt. 30:16).

There is also the possibility, of course, that there will be a division between blessing and cursing within the people. Originally blessing is for Israel and cursing for all its enemies. But it is increasingly realised that the blessings are only for those who keep God's commandments, for the righteous. With the development of a righteousness of works there even arises a claim to blessing : ψ 23:4 : "He that hath clean hands, and a pure heart ; who hath not lifted up his soul unto vanity, nor sworn deceitfully. He shall receive the blessing from the Lord, and a righteous reward from the God of his salvation." [10] Behind this there stands, however, the great decision of Jer. 17:5, 7: "Cursed be the man that trusteth in man, and maketh flesh his arm ... Blessed is the man that trusteth in the Lord, and whose hope the Lord is."

3. It is natural that the constant reminder of God's promised blessing should take cultic forms. Indeed, it may be that the cultus is the source of Israelite conceptions of blessing. In it the Israelite asks for life (cf. Amos 5:4 ff.), and this life is granted to him through the divine oracle, through the word of the priest (cf.

---

[7] εὐλογεῖν is linked with μεγαλύνειν in Gn. 12:2, with πληθύνειν in 22:17, with αὐξάνειν in 28:3, with σώζειν, ποιμαίνειν, ἐπαίρειν in ψ 27:9, and with οἰκτείρειν in ψ 66:1.

[8] So also Gn. 39:2-5 : God the Lord was with Joseph. If the blessing which for Joseph's sake came on Potiphar and his house was really automatic according to the primitive conception, i.e., if it was transferred magically from the "lucky fellow" Joseph to the Egyptians (Mowinckel, V, 8), it is significant that this view of the matter was suppressed in the written account. What works in Joseph according to the record is not an independent force. The favour, the gracious will, "of him that dwelt in the bush" came upon the head of Joseph, as is later said of his tribe in Dt. 33:16, and this good-pleasure was extended to those with whom he came in contact.

[9] Hempel, 22, n. 3.

[10] LXX : οὗτος λήμψεται εὐλογίαν παρὰ κυρίου καὶ ἐλεημοσύνην παρὰ θεοῦ σωτῆρος αὐτοῦ.

1 S. 1:17). He is convinced that the substance of the power of blessing must be as it were filled up by certain sacral actions. The decisive point is the desire of the people for constant awareness of blessing. Hence certain specially called men must proclaim blessing in the divine name and by the divine commission, or ask Yahweh for blessing in cultic prayer.

Examples are the blessing pronounced by Melchizedek over Abraham in Gn. 14:19, the great parting blessing of the twelve tribes by Moses in Dt. 33:1 ff. and the blessings of Joshua in 14:13; 22:6, 7, of the high-priest Eli in 1 S. 2:20 and of others. In particular, it is a right of the king to dispense blessing in solemn cultic form. When the ark is brought to Jerusalem and sacrifice has been offered, David blesses the people in the name of the Lord of hosts (2 S. 6:18). When the temple is consecrated Solomon blesses the standing congregation at the beginning and the end (1 K. 8:14, 55). Particular significance has been attached to the fact that Samuel in 1 S. 9:13 blesses a sacrifice, since the original *mana* conception of blessing may be detected in this sacramental act. But the reference is only an isolated one in the OT.

Only gradually does it become a prerogative of the priest to bless. The basis is to be found in Nu. 6:22-27, where the Aaronic blessing is fixed as a formula of priestly blessing.

Aaron blesses in Lv. 9:22 f. The Levites, with other priestly duties, then assume that of blessing, Dt. 10:8; 21:5; 1 Ch. 23:13. From this time onwards blessing plays an increasing role in the cultus. "Prayer for blessing receives the festal procession before the gates of the temple or in the temple court ; in the festal songs blessing is used as a greeting and there is also petition for blessing answered in the solemn tones of the priests ; the whole content of the feast is finally summed up in the majestic blessing of the priest from the altar, and then in the song of thanksgiving the blessing is given back in the form of praise of Yahweh extolling the might and glory of the Godhead." [11] The prayer of Ps. 3:8 is constantly echoed : "Thy blessing be upon thy people."

4. Reference to the cultic praise of Yahweh introduces us to a special use of בֵּרֵךְ and εὐλογεῖν which plays an important part in both the OT and the NT. Not only do we have the blessing of men by God, or by the priests in God's name ; we also have the blessing of God by men.

E.g., Gn. 24:48; Dt. 8:10; Ju. 5:2, 9; Tob. 12:6 : ἀγαθὸν τὸ εὐλογεῖν τὸν θεὸν καὶ ὑψοῦν τὸ ὄνομα αὐτοῦ; ψ 15:7; 33:1; 67:26; Da. 3:57 ff. (32 times). Most common is the formula εὐλογητός or εὐλογημένος ὁ θεός (→ 764). How this may be is explained by religio-historical investigation from the same facts as those hitherto adduced in relation to the origins of blessing. The deity has the power to bless and this power can be lessened by curses or strengthened by blessings.

Again there are hardly any traces of this primitive conception in the OT. But εὐλογεῖν θεόν is an established part of religious life. "The praising of the name of Yahweh is the most distinctive expression of the practice of religion by the congregation." [12] The Israelite who knows that his whole life is in the hands of the Creator cannot find any better expression for his faith and gratitude and hope than by giving God the glory.

---

[11] Mowinckel, V, 130. Mowinckel has well brought out the part played by blessing and cursing in the cultic psalms. On the inner relationship between the blessing of the priest and the hymn of the congregation, as finely expressed in Sir. 50:22, cf. J. Hempel, *Die althebräische Literatur* (1930), 32 f., 70.

[12] B. Duhm, *Das Buch Hiob* (1897), 12. The role of doxology in penal law is pointed out by F. Horst, ZAW, 47 (1929), 50 ff. in relation to Jos. 7:19 and other passages.

This is the precise sense of בֵּרֵךְ and εὐλογεῖν in this connection. The praise of God takes the form of prayer, whether public or domestic. Along with the formula εὐλογητὸς ὁ κύριος (→ 764) the content of this prayer is a declaration of God's works to His glory (Tob. 12:6) which can be applied according to the individual occasion for which one wishes to glorify God.

5. The verb בֵּרֵךְ can often be used for blessing in a more general sense. Originally any greeting between men was a blessing. Thus בֵּרֵךְ can mean "to greet," e.g., 1 S. 13:10, where Saul goes out to meet Samuel in order to salute him. Similarly בְּרָכָה and εὐλογία can be used for the gift with which one greets someone higher in rank, Gn. 33:11; 1 S. 25:27 etc.

6. Finally, בֵּרֵךְ is often used euphemistically where we should really have קָלֵל, "to curse." This use is connected with the ancient fear of cursing and its evil effects even when inadvertently pronounced. Care is taken never to use the name of God and the word for cursing together. Cf. 1 K. 21:10, 13; Ps. 10:3; Job 1:11; 2:5, 9 as distinct from the true sense in 1:21. The whole prologue of Job is built on this twofold sense.

7. We must ask in conclusion whether the rendering of בֵּרֵךְ by εὐλογεῖν in the LXX does not in some sense give a new turn to the concept. Our answer can only be that already in the history of the Hebrew term there takes place the decisive development from primitive dealings with mysterious powers to the expression of man's spiritual relationship to God whose gracious disposition he constantly experiences from creation onwards, giving the response of praise and thanksgiving. The clear Greek word εὐλογεῖν, which means "to praise" in secular Greek (→ 754), simply sets the seal on this development, excluding completely any magical or mystical understanding.

C. Blessing in Judaism at the Time of Jesus.

1. The word εὐλογέω is common in the works of Philo, mostly in expositions of the biblical passages in which it occurs. In a special passage in Praem. Poen. which is now partially lost he treats specifically of the content of blessing in connection with the closing chapter of Dt. Here there is a consistent development of the thought of reward for those who are faithful to the Law. To them all material good fortune is promised. Elsewhere in Philo the concept is strongly rationalised. Migr. Abr., 70 calls blessing the "third gift" of God along with hope of a *vita contemplativa* and "growth to the multiplicity and greatness of the beautiful." It assures the continuance of the other two. Philo also indulges in word play when he divides εὐλογέω into its constituent parts in Abr. Migr., 70, or when he relates εὐλογεῖν ("to bless") and εὐλόγιστος ("rational") and explains the blessing of the Sabbath: αἰτία δ' ἡ δι' ἣν εὐλόγιστός (an intentional ambiguity: "rational" and "blessed") τε καὶ ἅγιος γέγονεν ὁ κατὰ τὸ ἕβδομον καὶ τέλειον φῶς ἄγων ἑαυτόν, Leg. All., I, 18. The εὐλογεῖν τὸν θεόν is now given a strongly rational basis: "Of all the right actions which we may produce, the best and most perfect product is the hymn to the Father of all things," Plant., 135; "It is fitting that the man who has God as his portion should praise and magnify Him," Sobr., 58. Philo enquires as to the true ethos behind this action, and he concludes that unspoken thoughts rather than words are the true norm, Migr. Abr., 117. Joseph. speaks constantly of εὐλογεῖν τὸν θεόν, Ant., 4, 318; 7, 380 f.; 8, 111 and 119; 9, 15; 11, 80, but he does not add to our understanding. He, too, depicts the parting blessing of Moses in Ant., 4, 302, and he speaks of the commandments to which the law-giver annexed blessings in Bell., 5, 401.

2. More significant is the development of the term בְּרָכָה among the Rabbis. Blessing is now imparted according to specific rules which were basically worked out well before the time of Jesus.

a. The Aaronic blessing is firmly established in the temple cultus.

At the daily morning service, between the incense offering and the burnt offering, five priests engaged in the sanctuary come on to the steps before the temple and with up-lifted hands pronounce the blessing (Nu. 6:22 ff.) over the people, the name of Yahweh, though only in the temple at Jerusalem, being openly used rather than a substitute. [13]

b. Only a priest may pronounce the Aaronic blessing in the synagogue.

The congregation answers Amen. If no priest is present, a member of the congregation may utter the blessing in the form of a petition. [14]

c. All forms of prayer which begin with praise of God (בָּרוּךְ = εὐλογητός) are called בְּרָכָה.

These are dealt with in the Mishnah, Tosefta and Talmud tractates Berakoth. [15] Thus the Sch^emone Esre, the chief prayer of Judaism, which every member of the people must recite three times a day, consists of 18 or 19 benedictions. [16] Each of these contains the formula "Blessed be Thou, O Lord" with a different reason.

d. The Jew makes abundant use of ascriptions of praise (Berachot) in other contexts.

Thus they occur at many points in worship. Eight blessings are pronounced on the day of atonement: on the Torah, the service of the temple, the forgiveness of sins, the temple, Israel, Jerusalem, the priests and other prayers. [17] A beracha is also prescribed before and after the great prayers, at the study of the Torah etc.

In particular the Jew uses a blessing at meals. It is a stringent rule that he should eat nothing before a blessing is pronounced. [18] "It is forbidden to man to enjoy anything belonging to this world without a blessing; he who enjoys anything of this world without a blessing commits a violation." [19]

Behind this rule is the lofty view that this whole world belongs to God. Only he who takes with thanksgiving truly receives from God; he who does not robs God. The sayings: "The earth is the Lord's, and the fulness thereof" (Ps. 24:1), and: "The earth hath he given to the children of men" (Ps. 115:16), are not a contradiction. The one applies prior to blessing and the other after. [20] Scriptural proof was found by the Rabbis in Lv. 19:24 and Dt. 8:10. All benedictions begin with the words: "Blessed (בָּרוּךְ, εὐλογητός) be Thou, Yahweh our God, King of the world." The continuation varies. Before bread it runs: "who hast caused bread to come forth out of the earth," and before wine: "who hast created the fruit of the vine." If a man eats alone, he says the blessing to himself. In common meals the main part is opened with a blessing usually pronounced by the head of the house with a piece of bread in his hand. The others confirm it with an Amen. After this the head of the house breaks the bread and dis-tributes to those who sit at table with him. He himself eats first. [21] There is no question of blessing the food and transforming it into something different. He rather praises the Creator who controls the fruits of the earth. [22] At the conclusion of the meal there is a

---

[13] Schürer, II⁴, 355, 535, n. 134.

[14] Ibid., 535 f.; Bousset-Gressm., 175.

[15] Acc. to Elbogen, 4 ff. the fact that the basic form of Jewish prayer is called ברכה may be traced back to 2 Ch. 20:26. He first finds the technical sense in Neh. 9:5.

[16] Schürer, II⁴, 539 ff.

[17] Joma, 7, 11.

[18] Tos. Ber., 4, 1; jBer., 10a.

[19] bBer., 35a.

[20] Ibid., 35ab.

[21] Str.-B., IV, 616 ff.

[22] G. Dalman, Jesus-Jeschua (1922), 123.

common thanksgiving or praise for the food. Usually the head of the house asks the chief guest to pronounce this. After saying "Let us pronounce the blessing," this guest takes the cup of blessing (τὸ ποτήριον τῆς εὐλογίας) and with his eyes on it pronounces a blessing which consists of four benedictions. [24] Thus the whole meal becomes εὐλογία for those who thankfully receive it as a gift from God. [25]

e. The table blessings naturally play an important part in the passover meal.

The preliminaries are opened with festival blessings and blessings of the cup. The main meal is introduced by prayer over the unleavened bread and the accompanying breaking of bread. [26] The cup of wine handed round after the eating of the Paschal lamb, the third in the whole order, is the cup of blessing over which thanksgiving is pronounced. [27]

D. εὐλογέω and εὐλογία in the NT.

1. The NT takes over much of the OT concept of blessing. Hb. 7:1 tells us that Melchisedec blessed Abraham (Gn. 14:19 f.) and it deduces from this (7:6 f.) his great dignity, since it is incontrovertible that the greater blesses the less. Hb. 11:20 f. tells us that Isaac blessed Jacob (Gn. 27:28 f.) and Jacob the sons of Joseph (Gn. 48:15 f.), and that they did so in faith. The NT author cannot but think that the transmission of the blessing from the ancestor to the descendant took place in unshakable confidence in the great promise of God to Abraham. The one who blesses confidently gives those blessed by him into God's protection. Esau is rejected even though he seeks a blessing because he had wickedly despised his right as firstborn (Hb. 12:17).

2. The NT also recognises man's duty to bless God. Zacharias is a true Israelite who, when he can speak again, at once praises the God whose overruling he has so evidently perceived (Lk. 1:64). When Simeon takes the child Jesus into his arms, he can only praise God for the grace which has been given him to see

---

[23] jBer., 11 c f; bBer., 51b.

[24] Str.-B., IV, 627 ff.

[25] It is in this light that we are to understand the inscr. on the golden glass in the Vatican Library (ZNW, 31 [1932], 48 ff., 57): ΟΙΚΟΣ ΙΡΗ(νη)C ΛΑΒΕ ΕΥΛΟΓΙΑ(ν), and on the margin : πίε ζήσαις μετὰ τῶν ΣΩΝ ΠΑΝΤΩΝ. (Cf. G. Loeschcke, ZwTh, 54 [1912], 202; H. W. Beyer and H. Lietzmann, Die jüd. Katakombe der Villa Torlonia in Rom [1930], 23). The inscr. is encircled by a Torah ark (or temple ?) below which are a seven-branched candelabra and cultic vessels. Another golden glass (R. Garrucci, Storia della arte cristiana [1880], VI, 490, 3) bears the mutilated inscr. ... CI BIBAS CVM EVLOGIA COMP ... Finally the word εὐλογία is found on an inscr. of the Monteverde catacomb above a Torah ark between two lamps (N. Müller and N. A. Bees, Die Inschriften der jüd. Katakombe am Monteverde zu Rom [1919], No. 173). These inscr. would be "of the highest interest" for the history of the term εὐλογία (K. H. Rengstorf, ZNW, 31 [1932], 58, n. 3) if only we could interpret them with certainty. But this is not so. In the last two, though this is unlikely, we might have a proper name as on the inscr. N. Müller-N. A. Bees, No. 119. The first is obviously a demand to receive the blessing in a meal eaten after benediction. If the ark of the Torah has a part to play, it is in the sense that only he who keeps the Law will partake of the blessing. (Another explanation is given by Rengstorf, op. cit. Cf. also J. Jeremias, Die Abendmahlsworte Jesu [1935], 58, where the λάβε εὐλογίαν is taken to be a summons on the handing round of the bread of blessing and the cup of blessing. Cyril of Jerusalem and others later use εὐλογία to denote the consecrated wine or cup. Cf. G. Loeschcke, op. cit.)

[26] That this was the sequence at the passover has been shown by J. Jeremias, ZNW, 33 (1934), 203 f.

[27] Str.-B., IV, 54 ff.; G. Dalman, op. cit., 122 ff.; J. Jeremias, Die Abendmahlsworte Jesu (1935), 40.

the Saviour (Lk. 2:28). He himself has entered the kingdom of blessing which flows from Christ. Thus the old man can also bless the parents of the child (2:34).

3. Mary is already within this circle. If every wife in Israel could see the hand of God in the blessing of her body, the mother of the Messiah is especially "blessed among women" acc. to Lk. 1:28, 42 : χαῖρε, κεχαριτωμένη, ὁ κύριος μετὰ σοῦ (the ancient content of the blessing remains the same), εὐλογημένη σὺ ἐν γυναιξίν.

On Lk. 1:42 cf. Jdt. 13:18; 15:12; Dt. 28:3 f.; Ju. 5:24.

Most blessed of all, however, is the Messiah Himself. The people welcomes Him with jubilant cries on His entry into Sion in Mk. 11:9 f.; Mt. 21:9; Lk. 19:38; Jn. 12:13 (the only εὐλογεῖν in John): εὐλογημένος ὁ ἐρχόμενος ἐν ὀνόματι κυρίου, εὐλογημένη ἡ ἐρχομένη βασιλεία τοῦ πατρὸς ἡμῶν Δαυίδ. There is here a twofold sense. He who comes and His kingdom are blessed by God to whom they belong. But they are also greeted by the people which subjects itself to them.

The form of the greeting derives from ψ 117:26, which is related to the Messianic redemption : Midr. Ps. 118 § 22 (244a). Jesus referred the same Psalm to the day of His parousia in Mt. 23:39; Lk. 13:35.

4. When the Messiah appears in earthly form, He goes about among His people as a man of piety. He adopts its customs, and especially its religious practices. When He sits at table, e.g., when He feeds the 4,000 or 5,000, He acts like a normal Jewish host or head of the house. He follows faithfully the accepted form (→ 760). He takes the bread in His hands, pronounces the blessing, breaks the bread and distributes it (Mk. 6:41 and par.; 8:7 and par.).

The only new feature is that in the prayer He does not look downwards as prescribed, [28] but looks up to heaven. Perhaps the point of this is that these are not ordinary meals but miracles, and that He is seeking the help of God. But it is also possible that in virtue of His sense of mission and the inner freedom which this gives He is infusing into the rigid formulae of dealings with God something of what made His own relationship to the Father so vital. Perhaps He also rendered the benedictions (→ 760) in a freer form approximating, e.g., to the Lord's Prayer. [29] He must certainly have fused something of His own into the simple, everyday process of blessing and breaking bread, since otherwise the two on the way to Emmaus would not have recognised Him by this action (Lk. 24:30). If → εὐχαριστεῖν is sometimes used for εὐλογεῖν (and the two together at Mk. 8:6, 7), this does not denote any distinction of sense. εὐχαριστέω, too, is used for בֵּרֵךְ. On the other hand, it is a Gk. misunderstanding of the Aram. original that many MSS [30] add an acc. object (αὐτά or ταῦτα) at Mk. 8:7. If this suggests the idea that Jesus blessed the bread and thus made possible its miraculous increase, we have a relapse into a conception long since left behind in Israel. Similarly at Lk. 9:16 only a few MSS have the abs. and the majority add αὐτούς, a few ἐπ' αὐτούς. [31]

At the Lord's Supper (→ 761), too, Jesus takes the unleavened bread, pronounces the blessing, breaks it and hands it round (Mk. 14:22; Mt. 26:26), as He

---

[28] Str.-B., II, 246.

[29] G. Dalman, op. cit., 124 suggests a formula like : "Blessed be Thou, our Father in Heaven, who dost give us to-day our necessary bread."

[30] αὐτά after εὐλογήσας ℵ BCL etc.; αὐτά before εὐλογήσας, MNWᵈ it (apart from q), vg syᵘᵗʳ go arm; ταῦτα before εὐλογήσας, AFK etc.; without obj. EGH al pl ; D q, which have εὐχαριστήσας instead of εὐλογήσας.

[31] Without obj. ℵ sys.c.h arm aeth; αὐτούς ABC al c e f vg syᵖ ; ἐπ' αὐτούς D a b al Marc Epiph.

does also with the cup of blessing. [32] Here He adds the words of interpretation. [33] That the cup of blessing was still maintained in the early Christian Church may be seen from 1 C. 10:16. Paul here uses the common Jewish expression τὸ ποτήριον τῆς εὐλογίας.

> The only new element is the addition ὃ εὐλογοῦμεν. "This serves to distinguish the cup of which Paul speaks from every other cup ... The thanksgiving applies to the cup because through it the congregation is blessed." By it, it "participates in the blood of Christ." [34]

5. Jesus also blessed people directly, like the children in Mk. 10:16 [35] or the disciples at the ascension (Lk. 24:50 ff.), who reply by praising God. Thus Peter can sum up the whole of Christ's work in the statement that God has sent Him to bless. Paul, too, can journey to the Romans in the fulness of the blessing brought by Christ (R. 15:29). The blessings are one long blessing. The great division in the revealed will of God of which there is evidence in the OT (→ 757) will come to fulfilment at the last day when the Lord will separate the blessed of the Father from the cursed (Mt. 25:34). While the curse brings eternal death, the blessed will enjoy life and entry into the kingdom of God.

> They will know the fulness of the blessing once given to Abraham (Gl. 3:8 f., 14; Hb. 6:14), except that this is now understood wholly as εὐλογία πνευματική (Eph. 1:3).

6. A new law applies to those who are blessed. Cf. Hb. 6:7 f. Called to inherit the earth (1 Pt. 3:9), they are not to repay evil with evil. The natural man finds it just as easy to curse as to bless (Jm. 3:9 f.). The righteous of the OT had a natural fear of cursing like the Greeks. They were also aware that they ought not to curse (→ κατάρα). [36] This is finely expressed in Job 31:30. But it is rather another matter when Jesus gives to His disciples the command which completely overcomes cursing : "Bless them which curse you" (Lk. 6:28; Mt. 5:44). [37] This command made a deep impression on primitive Christianity (R. 12:14; 1 C. 4:12).

7. Because it springs from such unconditional love, εὐλογία can also be used, as in the OT (→ 759), for the gift which Paul seeks as a collection for Jerusalem (2 C. 9:5 f.).

8. In 1 C. 14:16 εὐλογεῖν is used in the sense of a cultic action to express ecstatic praise of God. As distinct from the curse ἀνάθεμα ᾽Ιησοῦς, the confession κύριος ᾽Ιησοῦς, inspired by the Holy Spirit, is the true Christian εὐλογία (1 C. 12:3).

9. It is tempting to interpret in the light of secular Gk. usage (→ 754) the χρηστο-λογία and εὐλογία with which false teachers seduced the hearts of the Romans (R. 16:18). On the other hand, there is perhaps a Palestinian element — the flattering ring of promise through which they carry conviction. [38]

10. The author of Revelation realises that the eternal world of the last time includes the praising and glorifying of Him who sits on the throne and of the Lamb (Rev. 5:12, 13; 7:12).

---

[32] Mk and Mt have εὐλογεῖν of the bread and εὐχαριστεῖν of the cup, Lk. εὐχαριστεῖν of both.
[33] For a summary of recent research cf. J. Jeremias, *Die Abendmahlsworte Jesu*, esp. p. 41.
[34] A. Schlatter, *Paulus der Bote Jesu* (1934), 295 f.
[35] Most MSS (apart from ADE al) have here the rare κατευλογέω.
[36] Cf. J. Hempel, 104 ff.
[37] Mt. 5:44 only in some MSS.
[38] So Cr.-Kö., *ad loc.* and A. Schlatter, *Gottes Gerechtigkeit* (1935), 401 f.

† εὐλογητός.

εὐλογητός is a fixed term in rendering בָּרוּךְ. It is used with εὐλογημένος as בָּרוּךְ is with מְבוֹרָךְ. In the LXX we still have γένοιτο εὐλογημένος in 3 Βασ. 10:9 and εἴη τὸ ὄνομα κυρίου εὐλογημένον in Job 1:21, but in the NT εὐλογητός has an exclusively indicative signification. [1]

The word arose out of the Heb. notion that God needs blessing, later modified to the insight that faith in God means giving Him the glory (→ 758). [2]

1. In the OT men, too, are called εὐλογητοὶ ὑπὸ κυρίου, Gn. 12:2; 26:29; 43:28, and more often with the dat. τῷ θεῷ, Dt. 28:6; Ju. 17:2; Rt. 2:20; Tob. 13:12; Judt. 13:18. More common, however, is the formula εὐλογητὸς κύριος ὁ θεός, Gn. 9:26; 14:20; 1 Βασ. 25:32; 2 Βασ. 18:28; 3 Βασ. 1:48; 8:15; 2 Ch. 2:11; 1 Ἐσδρ. 8:25: εὐλογητὸς μόνος ὁ κύριος, Tob. 3:11; 8:5; ψ 40:13; 67:19; Zech. 11:5. In Melchizedek's blessing in Gn. 14:19 f. we have the two together:

εὐλογημένος Ἀβρὰμ τῷ θεῷ τῷ ὑψίστῳ,
ὃς ἔκτισεν τὸν οὐρανὸν καὶ τὴν γῆν.
καὶ εὐλογητὸς ὁ θεὸς ὁ ὕψιστος,
ὃς παρέδωκεν τοὺς ἐχθρούς σου ὑποχειρίους σοι.

In the Heb. בָּרוּךְ is used in both formulae.

2. The formula of prayer is found in Jewish writings outside the OT. In the Hermetic writings (Reitzenstein Poim., 338) we have εὐλογητὸς εἶ πάτερ, and in Eth. En. 77:1 we find "He who is eternally praised" along with "the Most High." Cf. also Heb. Test. N. 4 and 9; Jub. 22:27. [3] In Palmyra God is called "He whose name is to be praised to eternity." [4] Philo makes a material distinction between εὐλογημένος and εὐλογητός in Migr. Abr., 106 f. The one is the judgment of the crowd, the other presupposes real worth. In the Rabbinic writings הַקָּדוֹשׁ בָּרוּךְ הוּא is one of the commonest combinations. [5]

3. In the NT εὐλογητός is never used of men. Its use is exclusively doxological, Lk. 1:68; R. 1:25; 9:5; 2 C. 1:3; 11:31: ὁ (θεὸς) ὢν εὐλογητὸς εἰς τοὺς αἰῶνας; Eph. 1:3; 1 Pt. 1:3. Probably a liturgical formula arose at a very early stage similar to that of the synagogue (→ 760). [6] We best bring out its religious significance along the lines of Luther that God is praised in Himself but that we pray here that He may be praised among us.

In Mk. 14:61 Christ is called ὁ υἱὸς τοῦ εὐλογητοῦ — an echo of the Jewish concern to paraphrase the name of God.

The formula εὐλογητὸς ὁ κύριος is found in the Gk. Liturgy of Chrysostom. [7] It entered the Roman Mass as the Benedictus [8] and is still found in Luther's Formula Missae of 1523, [9] though not in the German Mass of 1526.

εὐλογητός. [1] Bl.-Debr.[6] § 128, 5.
[2] Cf. J. Hempel, 90 f., where it is pointed out that even alien peoples are summoned to praise Yahweh (Ps. 66[67]:5; cf. Ex. 18:10; 1 K. 5:21).
[3] Cf. Bousset-Gressm., 313, n. 3.
[4] M. de Vogüé, Syrie Centrale, I (1868), Inscr. 74 (111 A.D.) etc.
[5] Cf. G. Dalman WJ, I, 163 f.
[6] W. Bousset, Jesus der Herr (1916), 36.
[7] F. E. Brightman, Liturgies Eastern and Western (1896), 353.
[8] In the recitation of ψ 117:26 and in the active form of the Gloria: benedicimus te.
[9] W.A., XII, 212, 27.

† ἐνευλογέω.

This compound term is first found in Gn. 12:3 [1] and 18:18 where it is designed to stress the fact that the blessing of Abraham embraces all races and peoples: ἐνευλογηθήσονται ἐν σοὶ πάντα τὰ ἔθνη. The word is found again in the quotation in Gl. 3:8. Rather more freely Ac. 3:25 follows the same model and Gn. 22:18: ἐν τῷ σπέρματί σου ἐνευλογηθήσονται πᾶσαι αἱ πατριαὶ τῆς γῆς. [2]

Beyer

εὐνοέω, εὔνοια → νοῦς.

---

† εὐνοῦχος, † εὐνουχίζω

---

1. In the NT this word occurs only at Mt. 19:12 and Ac. 8:27 ff. The LXX has εὐνοῦχος but not εὐνουχίζειν.

Outside the NT [1] εὐνοῦχος (εὐνή, ἔχω) is used not only of men but of castrated animals [2] and of fruits and plants which have no kernel or seed. [3] In Soph. Fr., 721 (TGF, 301) εὐνοῦχα ὄμματα is used of "sleepless, wakeful or even watchful eyes." The verb [4] is often found in both act. [5] and pass. [6] and metaphor. with the obj. γῆν, Philostr. Vit. Ap., VI, 42 or with the obj. φάρμακον, Oribasius, Collectionum Medicarum Reliquiae, VIII, 2, 8 (ed. J. Raeder [1928] in Corpus Medicorum Graecorum, VI, 1, 1).

2. To the Gks. the castration of living creatures is fundamentally alien. It is first found in the Orient. There eunuchs are the servants and overseers of women and later the confidants of nobles and princes, often rising to high positions of state. It is through oriental influence that eunuchs appear in the Gk. world. This influence is particularly clear in the cults of Asia Minor, esp. in the cult of Cybele, then of Attis and the Ephesian Artemis. Here depriving of manhood plays a role as a cultic act, and eunuch priests occupy a prominent place. It is rare outside Asia Minor. Castrated priests are called βάκηλοι or γάλλοι. The term εὐνοῦχος ἱερεύς is found in Vett. Val., 86, 34. Of the various theories [7] as to the origin and meaning of self-emasculation and a priesthood of eunuchs the most probable is that which supposes that is is based on the desire to be like the godhead physically as well as spiritually. The crucial point is transformation into the mode of being of deity. Hence a realistic striving after *mystica unio* must be regarded as the essential root of cultic self-castration. He who has become similar to the deity is taken from the world. By the new relationship to the godhead he has become a new being. It is thus natural that the life of the emasculated should be dedicated to the deity. Their own act of heroic greatness, of a power which overcomes themselves and destroys their previous being, makes them ἁγνοί. They acquire the character of sanctity, have certain functions to perform at cultic festivals and enjoy

---

ἐ ν ε υ λ ο γ έ ω. [1] Here only Cod D[sil] E.
[2] So א A² DEP; ἐπευλογηθήσονται C; εὐλογηθήσονται A*B min.
ε ὐ ν ο ῦ χ ο ς κ τ λ. [1] V. the individual instances in Liddell-Scott, 724 *s.v.* εὐνοῦχος. In the pap. P. Lond., IV, 1447, 171 (8th cent.); also BGU, III, 725, 14 and 29 (7th cent.). Cf. Preisigke Wört., *s.v.*
[2] Cf. P. Masp., II, 141, Fol. VII, Recto line 4 (6th cent.); Philostr. Heroic., I, 3. The verbal adj. εὐνουχιστέον (τοὺς μόσχους), Geoponica (H. Beckh, 1895), XVII, 8, 2.
[3] Among the Pythag. εὐνοῦχος is the name for θρῖδαξ (salad), Athen., II, 80 (p. 69e). Cf. also *ibid.*, XIV, 66 (p. 652 a).
[4] V. Liddell-Scott, 724, *s.v.* εὐνουχίζω.
[5] Luc. Cronosolon, 12.
[6] Gal. De Semine, I, 15 (IV, p. 750, Kühn); Dio C., 68, 2.
[7] V. the express treatment of this question by L. H. Gray in ERE, V, 579, *s.v.* "Eunuch."

public honour and recognition. [8] εὐνουχία and παρθενία are regarded as equivalent in Athenag. Suppl., 33. [9]

3. In the OT the castration of both men and animals is forbidden; it contradicts the divine will in creation. There were thus no eunuchs in Israel itself. The royal courts were an exception. Strict legal forces opposed the practice. They rejected it as a symptom of disintegration incompatible with the exclusiveness of the chosen people of Yahweh. They were ultimately concerned to ward off alien internationalising tendencies. Clear evidence is to be found in Dt. (e.g., Dt. 17:16 ff.). In Dt. 23:2-9 it is laid down that no eunuch is to be received into the congregation of Yahweh. It is hard to decide how far the rejection of the practice is for theological reasons, i.e., because the divinely created and natural state of sexual potency is destroyed, and how far it is due to a desire to maintain a natural, healthy patriarchal cultic order. Both impulses were probably operative.

There is a different emphasis in the prophets. In the third part of Isaiah a universalist tendency present in earlier prophecy finds challenging expression in the statement that eunuchs will be allowed to enter the congregation (Is. 56:3-5). There is, of course, no question of a new cultic norm. A particularly difficult case is selected to show the boundless nature of the loving-kindness of Yahweh.

The strictly legal view determined the practice at least from the time of Ezra.

The eunuch is called סָרִיס in the OT. This word also has another meaning in the OT. In 2 K. 25:19 the סָרִיס is a man with a military commission. Jensen [10] and Zimmern [11] think that the origin of סָרִיס is to be found in an Assyrian ša rēši, ša rīši, strictly the captain at the head. סָרִיס thus denotes military rank as well as a eunuch. The סָרִיס does not have to be a eunuch. In Gn. 39:1 Potiphar is called a סָרִיס of Pharaoh. Acc. to Gunkel [12] סָרִיס in Gn. 39:1 is to be regarded as an addition of the redactor.

The Septuagint [13] translates סָרִיס 31 times as εὐνοῦχος, 7 times in Da. as ἀρχιευνοῦχος (רַב־סָרִיס) and twice as σπάδων. רַב־סָרִיס in Jer. 39:13 is taken to be a proper name (Ραβσαρίς) by Θ ('Ιερ. 46:13). At 'Ιερ. 45:7 = Jer. 38:7 all the transl. except the LXX have ἀνὴρ εὐνοῦχος for אִישׁ סָרִיס. At 'Ιερ. 41:19 = Jer. 34:19 the LXX has δυνάστης for סָרִיס. [14] This emendation leads us to suspect that the LXX abides by the regulation of Dt. which excludes those who are mutilated from the cultus. [15] The εὐνοῦχος of the LXX is often used, like εὐνοῦχος and סָרִיס elsewhere, for high military and political officials; it does not have to imply emasculation. [16] Thus in 'Ιερ. 52:25 the εὐνοῦχος is an ἐπιστάτης τῶν ἀνδρῶν τῶν πολεμιστῶν. In 2 'Εσδρ. 11:11 (Neh. 1:11) εὐνοῦχος is a vl. for οἰνοχόος. In Est. 1:21 the word is used where one ought to have a proper name. In Est. and Da. it always denotes officers of the household of the king or queen.

At the time of Jesus strong Hellenistic influences gave strength to the more liberal view alongside the legal and traditional. Joseph. tells us in Bell., 1, 488 that the three

---

[8] BCH, 44 (1920), 84, No. 16 (Inscr. from Lagina): οἱ σεμνότατοι τῆς Θεᾶς εὐνοῦχοι; BGU, III, 725, 29: εἰς τὸν εὐδοκιμ[ώτατον] ἄπα ῎Ολ εὐνοῦχον. Cf. A. D. Nock, "Eunuchs in Ancient Religion," ARW, 23 (1925), 25-33.

[9] On this whole section cf. also E. Fehrle, Die kultische Keuschheit im Altertum (1910), esp. 104 ff.

[10] Zeitschr. f. Assyriologie, 7 (1892), 174, n. 1.

[11] ZDMG, 53 (1899), 116, n. 2.

[12] Komm. z. Gn. (1901), 379.

[13] In the section on the LXX I am much indebted to G. Bertram.

[14] 'Α and ῎Αλλ: εὐνοῦχος.

[15] Cf. S. Mowinckel, Zu Deuteronomium, 23, 2-9, Acta Orientalia, I (1923), 82 ff.

[16] Cf. also Sir. 20:4 (though not Sir. 30:20).

chamberlains of Herod were eunuchs; and Joseph. himself had a δοῦλος εὐνοῦχος as the teacher and mentor of his boy (Ant., 6, 492).

4. Rabbinic Judaism thinks basically in terms of creation. The Rabbis teach unanimously that it is the duty of every Israelite to have children. He who does not sins against a divine command (Gn. 1:28 : פְּרוּ וּרְבוּ). In S. Lv. on 22:24 [17] the Lv. passage, which in this first instance forbids only the offering of castrated animals, is taken to be a general prohibition of castration. For Rabb. Judaism the castration of men or animals is thus transgression of an express command of God.

In Jeb., 8, 4-6 there is a distinction between the סְרִיס אָדָם, the one emasculated by men, [18] and the סְרִיס חַמָּה, the one emasculated by nature. [19] In Nidda, 5, 9 a twenty-year old youth to whom nature has denied all sexual potency is called a סְרִיס. [20]

For the Rabbis marriage was an unconditional duty. There is only one known instance of a celibate Rabbi. In T. Jeb., 8, 4 we are told that Ben 'Azzai remained unmarried. He justified his attitude in the words : "My soul cleaves to the Torah ; there is no time for marriage ; may the world be maintained by others." He was sharply blamed by other Rabbis. [21] In bSota, 4b it is assumed that he was divorced, and acc. to bKet., 63a he had relations with the daughter of 'Akiba. The point of these statements is obviously to take from his unmarried state something of the blame which attached to it acc. to the Rabbinic view. The same Ben 'Azzai did, of course, proclaim the duty of marrying as a command, thus accepting theoretically the uniform line of Rabb. teaching. In T. Jeb., 8, 4 he says : "He who does not see to the continuation and propagation of the race (as commanded in Gn. 1:28), may he be accounted by Scripture as if he diminished the (divine) image."

In this connection we may again refer to S. Nu. § 99 and § 103 (on Nu. 12:1, 8). [22] Miriam and Aaron complain that Moses has had no intercourse with his wife Zipporah and that he has thus violated a duty. But God justifies the conduct of Moses on the ground that He has required continence from him for the sake of his mission. Thus God can in certain special instances and at particular times dispense from the command of Gn. 1:28 which is otherwise binding on men. Normally the divine will in creation, which seeks the perpetuation and increase of the race, is to be fulfilled.

J. Jeremias [23] concludes from the unanimous teaching of the Rabbis that Paul, who at his conversion was an "ordained scholar," must have been a widower rather than a bachelor. It is open to question whether this thesis can be brought into harmony with 1 C. 7, where Paul describes celibacy as a χάρισμα (→ I, 652). The personal confession of Paul in 1 C. 7:7 is best understood if we assume that he had never married. [24] But there is not sufficient evidence on which to base a firm decision.

5. Jesus Himself transcends the Rabbinic view. In Mt. 19:12 he differentiates three categories of εὐνοῦχοι : 1. those who are so from birth ; 2. those who are mutilated ; and 3. those who have emasculated themselves διὰ τὴν βασιλείαν τῶν

---

[17] Cf. Str.-B., I, 807.
[18] This is one who after birth loses the power to reproduce through human action. V. K. H. Rengstorf, *Jebamot* (1929), 106. Cf. Mt. 19:12 : εὐνοῦχοι ὑπὸ ἀνθρώπων.
[19] This is one who lacks the power to reproduce by nature. V. Rengstorf, *op. cit.*, 107 and cf. Mt. 19:12 : εὐνοῦχοι ἐκ κοιλίας μητρός.
[20] Cf. E. Munk, *Nichtjuden im jüdischen Religionsrecht* (1932), 91.
[21] Cf. Str.-B., I, 807.
[22] I owe this reference to K. G. Kuhn.
[23] J. Jeremias, "War Paulus Witwer?" ZNW, 25 (1926), 310 ff.; also under the same title ZNW, 28 (1929), 321 ff.
[24] Cf. on this pt. E. Fascher, "Zur Witwerschaft des Paulus und der Auslegung von 1 C. 7," ZNW, 28 (1929), 62 ff.; H. Windisch, *Paulus und Christus* (1934), 129.

οὐρανῶν. The only problem is whether the third group have made themselves εὐνοῦχοι literally or figuratively. Now one may hardly assume that Jesus had any contact with circles exposed to Hellenistic influences. Hence He cannot have had in view literal physical castration. He would have a horror of this like all true Jews. He is thinking rather of those who for the sake of the kingdom of God voluntarily renounce the sexual life and marriage. These men concentrate their energies on a goal which lies beyond the tasks posed by natural factors. The same idea is present as with the εὐνοῦχος ἱερεύς, but the practice is quite different. The goal to be attained is the establishment of the kingdom of God on earth. In this saying Jesus is thinking primarily of Himself, and perhaps of the Baptist. The pronouncement makes it plain that the early Church could renounce natural goods as well as enjoy them. [25] The order of creation is affirmed by the Gospel, but it can also be denied for the sake of the kingdom, whose new order transcends the old order of creation.

6. In Ac. 8:27 ff. we read of the eunuch of Queen Candace who comes to faith and is baptised. Here the prophetic saying in Is. 56:3, 4 finds its true and complete fulfilment. The eunuch is no longer shut out from the kingdom of God and the Christian community. [26]

7. Mt. 19:12 had a strong influence on the early Church. [27] Cl. Al. (Strom., III, 7, 59) takes εὐνουχίζειν figuratively, speaking of a εὐνουχίζειν ἑαυτὸν πάσης ἐπιθυμίας. [28] Origen took the saying quite literally and emasculated himself, though later he repented of his act. [29] The saying is often given a literal sense in early exegesis. [30]

In the matter of admitting those mutilated to the ministry, the early Church followed Jewish tradition. It accepted the principle that only those without physical blemish should serve at the altar. Any who were castrated through no fault of their own might be admitted, but those who emasculated themselves were excluded. [31] Canons 21-24 of Const. Ap. (VIII, 47, 21-24) give clear directions in this matter. They run as follows :

εὐνοῦχος εἰ μὲν ἐξ ἐπηρείας ἀνθρώπων ἐγένετό τις ἢ ἐν διωγμῷ ἀφηρέθη τὰ ἀνδρῶν ἢ οὕτος ἔφυ, καὶ ἔστιν ἄξιος ἐπισκοπῆς, γινέσθω (sc. ἐπίσκοπος).

ὁ ἀκρωτηριάσας ἑαυτὸν μὴ γινέσθω κληρικός· αὐτοφονευτὴς γάρ ἐστιν ἑαυτοῦ καὶ τῆς τοῦ θεοῦ δημιουργίας ἐχθρός.

εἴ τις κληρικὸς ὢν ἑαυτὸν ἀκρωτηριάσει, καθαιρείσθω· φονεὺς γάρ ἐστιν ἑαυτοῦ.

λαϊκὸς ἑαυτὸν ἀκρωτηριάσας ἀφοριζέσθω ἔτη τρία· ἐπίβουλος γάρ ἐστι τῆς ἑαυτοῦ ζωῆς.

Schneider

εὐπρόσδεκτος → 58   εὐπροσωπέω → πρόσωπον.

---

[25] Cf. Schl. Mt., 574.

[26] This important official of Queen Candace is not a proselyte (→ προσήλυτος) in the specific sense of one who is circumcised and has undertaken to observe the whole Mosaic Law. It can hardly be argued from Is. 56:3 ff. that he is a real proselyte. For here we have a prophetic vision and demand which can hardly be fulfilled at this point in Judaism. He obviously belongs to the group of adherents of the faith of the God of Israel whom Lk. in Ac. calls σεβόμενοι or φοβούμενοι τὸν θεόν. (Cf. on this pt. H. W. Beyer, *NT Deutsch*, V, 37; Zn. Ag., 313.) It is remarkable, however, that he has a copy of Isaiah, since non-Jews had difficulty in procuring such books.

[27] Cf. the discussion by W. Bauer in "Matth. 19:12 und die alten Christen" in *Nt.liche Studien G. Heinrici dargebracht* [1914], 235 ff.

[28] V. also Strom., III, 15, 99, 4 : οἱ μὲν εὐνουχίσαντες ἑαυτοὺς ἀπὸ πάσης ἁμαρτίας.

[29] Cf. Eus. Hist. Eccl., VI, 8. He had changed his mind concerning the exegesis of Mt. 19:12.

[30] For examples cf. W. Bauer, *loc. cit.*

[31] For details cf. L. H. Gray, *op. cit.* (ERE, V, 583).

εὑρίσκω

εὑρίσκω, "to find." a. "To find after search," Aesch. Prom., 59; Sept. c. Theb., 191 (μηχανήν σωτηρίας); Epict. Diss., I, 24, 15; III, 6, 4 etc.; P. Oxy., VIII, 1153, 18; Gn. 31:35; 1 Βασ. 10:21 etc. b. "To find accidentally," "to come across something," Hom. Il., 1, 498; Od., 24, 462; BGU, II, 380, 18; P. Gen., 54, 31; Gn. 4:14 f.; 18:28 f.; 1 Βασ. 10:2 etc.; med.: κακόν εὕρετο, "drew evil upon himself," Hom. Od., 21, 304; Aesch. Prom., 267 (αὐτός εὑρόμην πόνους); pass. "to be struck by," "to find oneself." Eur. Hec., 274 (ἀδικοῦσα εὑρέθη); Soph. Phil., 452; Epict. Diss., III, 6, 2; III, 5:8 etc.; Dt. 20:11; 4 Βασ. 14:14 etc. c. Of goods "to fetch (money)": Xenoph. Hist. Graec., III, 4, 24; Aeschin., 1, 96; at auctions "to get": F. Preisigke, *Berichtigungsliste der Griech. Papyrusurkunden aus Ägypten,* I (1922), 86 on BGU, III, 992, Col., 2, 4; P. Oxy., I, 94, 13 (ἧς ἄν εὕρη τιμῆς); d. "to procure," "to obtain," often in the med. "to get for oneself": Pind. Pyth., 2, 64 (δόξαν); 1, 48 (τιμάν); 3, 111 (κλέος); Thuc., I, 31, 2 (ὠφελίαν); Gn. 18:3; Ex. 33:13; Nu. 11:11 (χάριν); Gn. 19:19; Ju. 6:17 (ἔλεος); Prv. 21:21 (ζωήν); Jer. 6:16 (ἁγνισμόν); Sir. 11:19 (ἀνάπαυσιν). e. Figur. of "spiritual or intellectual discovery, perception, insight, understanding, on the basis of deliberations, investigations or demonstration": Hom. Od., 12, 392; Aesch. Prom., 59 (εὑρεῖν κᾆ ἀμηχάνων πόρον); Soph. Oed. Col., 1188; Hdt., I, 5; P. Oxy., VI, 918, col. 11, 5; I, 131, 14 (τούς μάρτυρας τούς εὑρεθέντας); Epict. Diss., I, 18, 15; II, 11, 13; III, 17, 3 etc.; Wis. 3:5; Da. 1:20. In the LXX it is used very commonly of finding God: Is. 55:6; 65:1; Ἰερ. 36:13; Prv. 8:17; Wis. 13:6; σοφίαν: Job 28:12; 32:13; Wis. 6:13; Prv. 14:6; (καρδίαν) 2 Βασ. 7:27; ὁδόν: Is. 48:17. Pass. often in the sense of moral and religious judgment which is first made by men (Da. 1:19) but behind which God may stand (Is. 53:9; ψ 16:3; Da. 6:22). Cf. also Gn. 44:16; Neh. 9:8, where God is the subject of εὑρίσκειν concerning the result of a religious and moral test. Philo Fug., 43; Leg. All., 47 (εἰ δέ ζητοῦσα εὑρήσεις θεόν); χάριν, Leg. All., III, 77 f. Pass. in the sense of "to show oneself," "to appear," "to prove oneself," "to be found as": Jos. Bell., 3, 114; Ditt. Syll.³, 736, 51; 972, 65; 1109, 73; P. Oxy., IV, 743, 25.

Linguistically, the NT uses εὑρίσκειν in all the above senses apart from c. The term may sometimes apply to ordinary earthly and possibly contingent facts, but its reference is predominantly to the surprising discovery and mysterious understanding of human existence and historical occurrence in their hidden relationships as seen from the standpoint of and with an ultimate view to the kingdom of God. There is thus reference to a numinous fact in Mt. 1:18 [1] (e.); 12:44 (b.); Lk. 1:30 (d.); 9:36 (b.); 24:2 (b.); 24:3 (a.); 24:23 f. (a.); Ac. 5:10 (b.); 8:40 (b.); R. 7:10 (e.); 7:21 (e.); Gl. 2:17 (e.); Phil. 2:7 (e.); Rev. 9:6 (a.). It occurs in relation to miracles: Mt. 17:27 (b.); Mk. 7:30 (b.); Lk. 8:35 (b.); Jn. 21:6 (a.); Ac. 5:22 f. (b.), faith: Mt. 8:10 (b.); Lk. 18:8 (a.), supernatural gifts: Mt. 7:7 f. = Lk. 11:9 f. (a.); Mt. 7:14 (e.); 10:39 (d.); 11:29 (d.), the unexpected gift of the kingdom of God: Mt. 13:44 (b.), 46 (b.), or encounter with Jesus Himself: Mk. 1:37 (a.); Lk. 2:12 (a.); Jn. 1:41 (b.), 45 (b.); 6:25 (a.); 7:34 f. (a.). It may refer to experience of God: Lk. 4:17 (b.); Ac. 17:27 (e.); R. 10:20 (e.), or to any gift of salvation: Jn. 10:9 (a.): νομήν; Ac. 7:46 (d.): χάριν; R. 4:1 (d.); [2] 2 C. 5:3 (e.); 2 Tm. 1:18 (d.): ἔλεος; Hb. 4:16 (d.): χάριν; 9:12 (d.): λύτρωσιν, or to being miraculously called and saved by God: Mt. 18:13 (a.); 20:6 (b.); 22:9 f. (a.); 24:46 (b.); Lk. 15:5 f. (a.), 8 f. (a.), 24 (b.), 32 (b.). But as it suggests endowment, so it also suggests responsibility: Lk. 13:6 f. (a.); 17:18 (b.); Ac. 5:39 (e.); 1 C. 15:15 (e.); 1 Pt. 1:7 (e.); Rev. 2:2

εὑρίσκω. [1] Here in obvious dependence on Jewish usage, e.g., Jeb., 4, 1 etc. (= נ "to establish").

[2] On εὑρηκέναι in this passage cf. Ltzm. R., *ad loc.*

(e.); 3:2 (e.); 5:4 (e); 14:5 (b.), and the whole seriousness of judgment : Mt. 24:46 = Lk. 12:43 (b.); 2 Pt. 3:14 (e.); Rev. 12:8 (b.); 16:20 (b.); 18:14 (b.), 21 f. (b.), 24 (b.); 20:15 (b.).

Preisker

εὐσέβεια, εὐσεβέω, εὐσεβής → σέβομαι.

---

† εὔσημος

εὔσημος (also ἄσημος in Ac. 21:39 : οὐκ ἄσημος πόλις) is a compound of σῆμα (→ σημεῖον), like ἄναιμος of αἷμα, ἄσπερμος of σπέρμα, ἀνώνυμος of ὄνομα.[1] It means a. "something which gives good signs," and therefore "favourable," e.g., οὐδ' ὄρνις εὐσήμους ἀπορροιβδεῖ βοάς, Soph. Ant., 1021; εὐσήμόν γε φάσμα ναυβάταις; Eur. Iph. Aul., 252. Cf. also ψ 80:3, though vg has *insignis* ;[2] the full moon is a favourable time. Also Prv. 7:20 Θ and "Αλλ; 'Α has πανσέληνος; the LXX takes a different line. b. "something which gives clear sign" (opp. ἄ-σημος, "without clear signs" or "not clearly"), and therefore "clear," "evident," "plain," e.g., ἀλλά ἐστι χρηστῶν καὶ πονηρῶν εὔσημος ... διάκρισις, Plut. Quaest. Conv., VIII, 2, 2 (II, 719b); φωνὴν ... συνέχεσθαι καὶ διαμένειν εὔσημον, *ibid.,* VIII, 3, 1 (II, 720d); ... σαφέσι καὶ εὐσήμοις γράμμασι, Ditt. Or., II, 665, 12; of a plainly recognisable fault, P. Petr., I, 19, 14; P. Flor., 51, 11; Da. 2:19 : ... ἐν ὁράματι ἐν αὐτῇ τῇ νυκτὶ τὸ μυστήριον τοῦ βασιλέως ἐξεφάνθη εὐσήμως.

In the NT it occurs only at 1 C. 14:8 f.: καὶ γὰρ ἐὰν ἄδηλον σάλπιγξ φωνὴν δῷ, τίς παρασκευάσεται εἰς πόλεμον; οὕτως καὶ ὑμεῖς διὰ τῆς γλώσσης, ἐὰν μὴ εὔσημον λόγον δῶτε, πῶς γνωσθήσεται τὸ λαλούμενον; ἔσεσθε γὰρ εἰς ἀέρα λαλοῦντες. In face of the esoteric and ecstatic forms of Corinthian worship Paul demands clarity and plainness in proclamation (= b.), since it is in the divine service of the congregation that decisions are made regarding the declared judgment and salvation within the situation of human conflict between life and death.

Grundmann

εὔσπλαγχνος → σπλαγχνίζομαι.

---

† εὐσχήμων

1. "Honest," "orderly," "becoming." The word is found in this sense only in exhortatory passages in the Pauline Epistles. Presupposing and recognising the knowledge of ethical norms among the heathen (R. 2), the apostle does not hesitate to use for blameless conduct an expression which is generally current in the world around him (→ *infra*). It is true that in basis and power the new life of the Christian differs radically from non-Christian morality. Nevertheless, as concerns εὔσχημον there is agreement with non-Christians who might criticise Christian conduct.[1] This is how we are to understand Paul's statement in 1 Th. 4:12 : ἵνα

εὔσημος.   [1] Cf. Debr. Griech. Wortb. § 143.

[2] Probably we have here a mistranslation of the Heb. כֶּסֶה ("full moon").

εὐσχήμων.   Pr.-Bauer, 510; cf. also s.v. εὐσχημόνως; Liddell-Scott, 734; Moult.-Mill., 266 (cf. -όνως); Deissmann LO, 277; Preisigke Fachwörter, 96.

[1] Cf. on this pt. A. Juncker, *Die Ethik des Ap. Pls.,* I (1904), 188.

περιπατῆτε εὐσχημόνως πρὸς τοὺς ἔξω. It is not as though it were a mere matter of appearance, for the element of appearance[2] has disappeared from the word completely.[3] The point is that those without are capable of justifiable criticism of the εὐσχημοσύνη of Christians. And to give offence to those who are to be won might be fatal. In R. 13:13 εὐσχημόνως with περιπατεῖν, as elsewhere (cf. 1 C. 7:35; 14:40), must refer to honest conduct; the preceding image hardly justifies the restricted sense of "suitably clad."[4] The distinctive feature of the term in this context is that it contains within itself both of these possible senses and thus forms an almost imperceptible transition from the image to the reality. εὐσχήμων denotes the external aspect of the Christian life. This is of decisive significance (1 Th. 4:12; cf. Mt. 5:16). But from this point there is only a slight shift to another sense, from judgment on conduct to the designation of things which have little to do with the ethical and which are more concerned with the aesthetic. This was an easy transition for those who thought in Greek terms. We find it in Paul at 1 C. 12:23 f., where he distinguishes between μέλη ἀσχήμονα and εὐσχήμονα. There is here no distinction of moral value either in the image or the reality. The distinction is purely aesthetic.

Secular Gk. uses εὐσχήμων from the time of Eur. It has the literal meaning: "Of good external appearance" (→ σχῆμα), and it is then applied to the whole external and internal conduct and attitude. The word is often found in inscr. of the 2nd and 1st century with reference to the good administration of public officials, usually along with καλός: Inscr. Magn., 101, 14 f.: ἐποιήσαντο δὲ· καὶ τὴν παρεπιδημίαν καλὴν καὶ εὐσχήμονα καὶ ἀξίαν ἀμφοτέρων τῶν πόλεων (the end of the 2nd cent. B.C.). Inscr. Priene, 55, 13 f.: πρῶτον μὲν τὴν θυσίαν συνετέλεσεν καλὴν καὶ εὐσχήμονα (at the very earliest 128/7 B.C.).[5] Epict. uses the word for what is seemly (Diss., IV, 1, 163; IV, 12, 6). The LXX has εὐσχήμων only once at Prv. 11:25 for right conduct (cf. also 4 Macc. 6:2, where εὐσχημοσύνη is used expressly of the righteous: ἐγκοσμούμενος τῇ περὶ τὴν εὐσέβειαν εὐσχημοσύνῃ [Bertram]). It does not occur at all in the post-apostolic fathers.

2. "Noble," "honourable," "excellent," "prominent." In Mk. 15:43 Joseph of Arimathea is called εὐσχήμων βουλευτής. Mt. 27:57 rather narrows the sense by using πλούσιος, while in Lk. 23:50 f. it seems to be given the sense of moral quality: ἀνὴρ ἀγαθὸς καὶ δίκαιος· οὗτος οὐκ ἦν συγκατατεθειμένος τῇ βουλῇ καὶ τῇ πράξει αὐτῶν. This is remarkable, since Lk. himself uses the word in another sense (Ac. 13:50; 17:12). It is surely a misunderstanding, since every reader would give it the sense of "honourable" when used with βουλευτής (→ infra). This is undoubtedly the sense in Ac. 13:50, where it is used of proselytes who are stirred up against Paul and Barnabas. The same is true of Ac. 17:12, where the reference is to the background of newly won Christians and εὐσχήμων can hardly denote anything other than the higher circles of society.

This external and later almost titular use is predominant in the pap. (though cf. Inscr. Magn., 164, 3). It embraces all the marks of prominent position. Rabel[6] thinks that it is used esp. of wealthy landowners. But from the same period (the end of the 2nd cent. A.D.) cf. the evidence of Phryn. (ed. Rutherford, CCCIX, p. 417): εὐσχήμων· τοῦτο μὲν οἱ ἀμαθεῖς ἐπὶ τοῦ πλουσίου καὶ ἐν ἀξιώματι ὄντος τάττουσιν· οἱ δ' ἀρχαῖοι

---

[2] Still found in Eur.; Liddell-Scott, s.v.
[3] An opp. view is taken in Heinr. Sendschr., I on 7:35.
[4] So Zn. R., ad loc.
[5] Rich comparative material may be found in Pr.-Bauer, s.v. εὐσχήμων and -όνως.
[6] AGG, NF, 16 (1917), No. 3, p. 13.

ἐπὶ τοῦ καλοῦ καὶ συμμέτρου. It thus seems that the term may be used of any prominent person. [7]

Greeven

---

† εὐφραίνω, † εὐφροσύνη

1. εὐφραίνω, a word used from a very early period in Gk., [1] means "to gladden," "to cheer," and in the med. or pass. "to be glad," "to rejoice." The subst. εὐφροσύνη means "joy." In distinction from ἀγαλλιᾶσθαι (→ I, 19) it denotes the mood of joy. That joy involves an inner process is expressed in the fact that the subject is often θυμός or νόημα, φρήν or νοῦς or κῆρ. The objects of joy may be things or events which affect outward physical well-being, and esp. situations which give rise to a mood of common cheerfulness. Thus εὐφροσύνη and εὐφραίνεσθαι are from an early period used of the joy of feasts and festivals. But the facts and processes of the intellectual or spiritual life are also objects of εὐφροσύνη (Plat. Menex, 237a : δι' ἀρετήν). Indeed, εὐφραίνεσθαι is later used specifically for this kind of joy. Thus Plato makes the distinction in Prot., 337c : εὐφραίνεσθαι μὲν γὰρ ἔστιν μανθάνοντά τι καὶ φρονήσεως μεταλαμβάνοντα αὐτῇ τῇ διανοίᾳ, ἥδεσθαι δὲ ἐσθίοντά τι ἢ ἄλλο ἡδὺ πάσχοντα αὐτῷ τῷ σώματι, [2] though this is not in keeping with normal usage. [3] These distinctions were adopted and developed by Stoicism. This defines εὐφροσύνη as an εἶδος χαρᾶς, which for its part is an εἶδος εὐπαθείας, [4] an εὔλογος ἔπαρσις, while ἡδονή is an ἄλογος ἔπαρσις ψυχῆς [5] or a πάθος. [6] εὐφροσύνη is not, of course, an ἀρετή, [7] but an ἐπιγέννημα ἀρετῆς; [8] it is no ἀναγκαῖον πρὸς εὐδαιμονίαν. [9] It is also not possessed by every φρόνιμος or ἀεί like ἀρετή. [10] In content it is defined as χαρὰ ἐπὶ τοῖς τοῦ σώφρονος ἔργοις, [11] as ἡδονὴ διὰ λόγων. [12] The concrete fulfilment of εὐφραίνεσθαι is finely depicted in certain passages in M. Ant. [13]

---

[7] Cf. also BGU, VII, 1713, comm.

ε ὐ φ ρ α ί ν ω κ τ λ. For bibl. → χαρά.

[1] εὐφραίνω to εὔφρων as τεκταίνω to τέκτων, πιαίνω to πίων etc. εὐφροσύνη to εὔφρων as ἀπημοσύνη to ἀπήμων, ἐλεημοσύνη to ἐλεήμων etc.

[2] Cf. also the distinction between the ἡδονή of the ἄφρονες and the εὐφροσύνη of the ἔμφρονες (Plat. Tim., 80b).

[3] Cf., e.g., Soph. Ai., 280 with 273; Aristoph. Ach., 4 f.

[4] v. Arnim, III, 105, 35 ff.

[5] v. Arnim, III, 105, 17 f.; 95, 21; 98, 30.

[6] Ibid., I, 51, 32 ff.; III, 92, 11 ff. etc.

[7] Ibid., III, 23, 24 ff. εὐφραίνεσθαι is reckoned among the κατορθώματα, III, 136, 20 f.; εὐφροσύνη belongs only to the τελικὰ ἀγαθά (opp. ποιητικὰ ἀγαθά), III, 25, 26 and 38, while the ἀρεταί are both τελικὰ and ποιητικὰ ἀγαθά. It belongs to the ἀγαθά found ἐν κινήσει, not ἐν σχέσει, beyond which are the ἀρεταί, as ἐν ἕξει, III, 26, 28.

[8] Ibid., III, 19, 29 f.

[9] III, 27, 14.

[10] III, 25, 2 f.

[11] III, 105, 37.

[12] III, 106, 10.

[13] M. Ant., VI, 48; VII, 13; esp. VIII, 26 : εὐφροσύνη ἀνθρώπου ποιεῖν τὰ ἴδια ἀνθρώπου. ἴδιον δὲ ἀνθρώπου εὔνοια πρὸς τὸ ὁμόφυλον, ὑπερόρασις τῶν αἰσθητικῶν κινήσεων, διάκρισις τῶν πιθανῶν φαντασιῶν, ἐπιθεώρησις τῆς τῶν ὅλων φύσεως καὶ τῶν κατ' αὐτὴν γινομένων; VIII, 43 : εὐφραίνει ἄλλον ἄλλο· ἐμὲ δέ, ἐὰν ὑγιὲς ἔχω τὸ ἡγεμονικόν, μὴ ἀποστρεφόμενον μήτε ἄνθρωπόν τινα μήτε ‹τι› τῶν ἀνθρώποις συμβαινόντων, ἀλλὰ πᾶν εὐμενέσιν ὀφθαλμοῖς ὁρῶν τε καὶ δεχόμενον καὶ χρώμενον ἑκάστῳ κατ' ἀξίαν.

2. The Septuagint consistently uses εὐφραίνεσθαι in the Psalms for שָׂמַח, often par. to or combined with → ἀγαλλιᾶσθαι; in Dt. Is. it is mostly used for רָנַן, normally rendered ἀγαλλιᾶσθαι in the Ps., while ἀγαλλιᾶσθαι, frequently linked with εὐφραίνεσθαι in Dt. Is., is there used for גִּיל, for which it is also used in the Ps. But εὐφραίνεσθαι can also be the rendering of שָׂמַח, גִּיל and שׂוּשׂ in Dt. Is. [14] εὐφραίνεσθαι is also used for the verbs mentioned, esp. שָׂמַח, in other parts of the OT, as also for some others. In the Ps. εὐφροσύνη is consistently the rendering of שִׂמְחָה; in Dt. Is. it occurs for שִׂמְחָה and also for מָשׂוֹשׂ, שָׂשׂוֹן (or שׂוּשׂ) or רִנָּה (or רָנַן); elsewhere it is almost always used for שִׂמְחָה.

The alternation in translation and the combination with other verbs shows that εὐφραίνεσθαι (εὐφροσύνη) does not have a specific meaning sharply differentiated from other expressions for joy such as ἀγαλλιᾶσθαι, χαίρειν etc. It may denote both the individual mood of joy at God's protection and help in time of need (esp. in the Ps.) and also the jubilation expressed in cultic gatherings (also in the Ps.). Since the joy of the last time is often depicted as the joy of cultic celebration, εὐφραίνεσθαι (εὐφροσύνη), like ἀγαλλιᾶσθαι (→ I, 20), becomes an eschatological term, as already in ψ 95:11; 96:1, where heaven and earth share this joy, and esp. in the pictures of the future in Dt. Is. This εὐφρανθῆναι may even be ascribed to God (Is. 65:19). [15] Naturally εὐφραίνεσθαι and εὐφροσύνη are also used of secular joy, but there is a contrast to this in ψ 18:8, where the δικαιώματα κυρίου are described as εὐφραίνοντα καρδίαν.

3. Judaism uses εὐφραίνεσθαι and εὐφροσύνη to denote cultic [16] and eschatological [17] joy. Since obedience to the Law takes on more and more a cultic character, even the φόβος κυρίου can be described as εὐφροσύνη. [18] In secular usage the primary sense is festive joy. [19] The words play a particular role in Philo. [20] He adopts both the special sense of festive joy on the one side [21] and the Stoic view of εὐφροσύνη on the other. The opp. of εὐφραίνεσθαι is to be found in λύπη, [22] but esp. in ἡδονή [23] and ἀφροσύνη. [24] Philo likes to contrast genuine and false festive joy, [25] and he interprets

---

[14] For the stem שׂוּשׂ, εὐφραίνεσθαι is also used of God in Dt. 28:63; Is. 62:5.

[15] The case is rather different when εὐφρανθῆναι is used of God (for שׂוּשׂ) in Dt. 28:63; 30:9, for it here signifies to have pleasure in doing something, with a more secular sense. On the other hand, we find that joy is a feature of the heavenly sphere in the depiction of wisdom as the playful companion of God at creation in Prv. 8:30 f. The LXX here has εὐφραίνεσθαι for the Heb. שָׂחַק.

[16] εὐφραίνεσθαι for cultic joy, 1 Ἐσδρ. 7:14; 9:54; εὐφροσύνη, 1 Macc. 4:56, 59; 2 Macc. 10:6; 3 Macc. 7:16.

[17] εὐφραίνεσθαι for eschatological joy, Tob. 13:14; Test. L. 18:5 (subj. the νεφέλαι); 18:13 (subj. the κύριος); Test. Zeb. 10:2; Test. D. 5:12; εὐφροσύνη, Test. S. 6:7; Ps. Sol. 10:7; 14:6; 17:40.

[18] Sir. 1:11 f.; cf. the later name "joy of the Law" for the 23rd Tishri, when the yearly cycle of Pentateuch readings ended, Str.-B., IV, 154.

[19] εὐφροσύνη as festive joy, Jdt. 12:13, 17; Wis. 2:9; 3 Macc. 5:17, 36 etc.; in Ep. Ar., 202, 274, 294 we can see the influence of Gk. symposium lit. But the Jewish use is not very different. In Judaism joy also denotes festive joy at social functions and esp. weddings, Str.-B., I, 972 f. On εὐφροσύνη in Joseph., v. Schl. Lk., 603; εὐφραίνεσθαι is not found in Joseph., though he has the active, Schl. Lk., 319.

[20] On joy in Philo cf. H. Windisch, Die Frömmigkeit Philos (1909), 56-60.

[21] Spec. Leg., I, 191: ἑορτὴ καιρὸς εὐφροσύνης; cf. Migr. Abr., 92: ἡ ἑορτὴ σύμβολον ψυχικῆς εὐφροσύνης.

[22] Mut. Nom., 168; Vit. Mos., I, 247.

[23] Sacr. AC, 33.

[24] Som., II, 200; Spec. Leg., II, 49, 214; εὐφροσύνη is explained in terms of εὖ φρονεῖν, Som., II, 174.

[25] Spec. Leg., I, 191-193; II, 193-199; Som., II, 167 ff.; Plant., 161 ff.; Ebr., 4.

the fasting required in the Law as πρὸς ἀλήθειαν εὐφροσύνη. [26] φρόνησις is ἀψευδὴς καὶ πρὸς ἀλήθειαν εὐφροσύνη. [27] The φαῦλος does not truly celebrate, [28] for ἑορτὴ ... ψυχῆς ἡ ἐν ἀρεταῖς εὐφροσύνη τελείαις. [29] At a banquet of ἀρετή the soul becomes merry in dancing and song with the ἀρεταί. [30] Seeking after God brings εὐφροσύνη. [31] God causes joys to stream forth from heaven. [32] The Logos gives it. [33] The κόσμος as God's πόλις has eternal εὐφροσύνη. [34] Joy characterises the sphere of God. Thus σοφία is full of χαρᾶς καὶ εὐφροσύνης καὶ τῶν ἄλλων ἀγαθῶν. [35] Strictly, only God has real joy, μόνος εὐφραίνεται. [36] In His relationship to men His εὐφροσύνη (opp. ὀργή) is the supreme blessing, for He rejoices (Dt. 30:9 f.) in those who by reason of their virtues are worthy of His gifts. [37]

4. In the NT εὐφραίνεσθαι and εὐφροσύνη do not play any great part. Theologically they are overshadowed by the far more significant χαρά. We shall have to treat of this separately and must therefore confine ourselves to εὐφραίνεσθαι (εὐφροσύνη). εὐφραίνεσθαι is often used for purely secular joy, and sometimes for the joy of the festive meal. In Lk. 12:19; 16:19 to eat, drink and be merry is the most to which the worldling who forgets God can aspire, hoping to secure it by his possessions. [38] On the other hand, the jollity of the feast may be the expression of a deeper joy, whether it is the jubilation of the inhabitants of earth at the death of the two witnesses in Rev. 11:10, the joy of the father at the son who is found in Lk. 15:23 f., 32, or social jollity in the company of friends in Lk. 15:29. This εὐφροσύνη can also be gratefully understood as the gift of God by which even the heathen may discern His providential rule, Ac. 14:17. The secular sense, not of festive joy, but of joy in mutual fellowship, may also be seen in the εὐφραίνειν of 2 C. 2:2: εἰ γὰρ ἐγὼ λυπῶ ὑμᾶς, καὶ τίς ὁ εὐφραίνων με εἰ μὴ ὁ λυπούμενος ἐξ ἐμοῦ; Εὐφραίνεσθαι as a description of cultic joy is a presupposition in the account of the conduct of Israel around the golden calf at Ac. 7:41: εὐφραίνοντο ἐν τοῖς ἔργοις τῶν χειρῶν αὐτῶν.

In Rev. 12:12 and 18:20 there are echoes of the OT demand for jubilation at God's eschatological acts of judgment, and as in ψ 95:11; Dt. 32:43; Is. 44:23; 49:13 the heavens are also summoned to εὐφρανθῆναι. If the divine is here looking into the future, Paul sees this eschatological εὐφρανθῆναι, to which the ἔθνη are also called according to Dt. 32:43, already fulfilled in the present with the bringing

---

[26] Spec. Leg., II, 194; cf. Migr. Abr., 204.

[27] Spec. Leg., I, 191; Som., II, 248 f.: the ψυχή of the σοφός receives it.

[28] Spec. Leg., II, 49.

[29] Sacr. AC, 111; cf. Abr., 207: τὴν δὲ τῶν σοφῶν (ψυχὴν) ... εὐφραίνεσθαι τοῖς τοῦ κόσμου θεωρήμασιν (→ n. 13); Leg. All., I, 72: δικαιοσύνη cheers the διάνοια; Mut. Nom., 168: the aspect of the σπουδαῖος gives joy to the διάνοια.

[30] Sacr. AC, 33: εὐφροσύνη is the result of κτῆσις and χρῆσις ἀρετῆς, Ebr., 6 (cf. Deus Imm., 96 and 154), of the θεωρητικὸς βίος, Fug., 176.

[31] Spec. Leg., I, 36; Fug., 141; cf. Congr., 162 (ψυχῆς δὲ ἑορτὴ ζῆλος ὁ τῶν ἀρίστων καὶ τελεσφορούμενος πόνος), 167.

[32] Rer. Div. Her., 76; cf. Deus Imm., 81; Leg. All., III, 81.

[33] Som., II, 249.

[34] Ibid., 248.

[35] Rer. Div. Her., 315.

[36] Cher., 86. It may also be pointed out that in P. Oxy., XI, 1380, 19 f., 31 f. Isis is invoked as εὐφροσύνη.

[37] Som., II, 175-179.

[38] On Lk. 12:19 cf. Rabb. par. for the usage in Schl. Lk., 317; Str.-B., II, 190. The religio-historical par. to the morality of φάγε, πίε, εὐφραίνου in Kl. Lk., ad loc. differ from Lk. 12:19 to the degree that in them there is admonition to enjoy life in face of impending death, as in Qoh. 8:15 f.; 9:7 f. Cf. also the burial epigram in Epigr. Graec., 621, 4, that the dead man προλέγει θνατοῖς εὐφροσύνης μετέχειν.

of the message of God's saving act in Christ to the nations, R. 15:10. He also finds the εὐφράνθητι addressed to unfruitful Jerusalem in Is. 54:1 fulfilled in the Christian community, Gl. 4:27. In some sense connected with this insight is the interpretation of ψ 15 in Ac. 2:26, 28, for if in ψ 15:9, 11 the joy is that of the righteous in God's protection, in Ac. it is referred to the risen Christ.

The Christian lit. influenced by the NT naturally uses εὐφραίνεσθαι in the secular sense. [39] Cultic joy is found in Barn., 15, 9 : διὸ καὶ ἄγομεν τὴν ἡμέραν τὴν ὀγδόην εἰς εὐφροσύνην, and there is a noteworthy use in Dg., 12, 9 : διδάσκων ἁγίους ὁ λόγος εὐφραίνεται, where the word preached at divine service is itself the subj. of joy. More common is the application found already in the OT and Judaism (→ 773, 774), namely, that cultic joy is joy in God's commandments and in doctrine. [40] There are several references to future eschatological joy in OT quotations, esp. in Justin. [41] That this joy is already present is expressed in the address τέκνα εὐφροσύνης in Barn., 7, 1. That this is a foretaste of joy is stated by Just. when in Ap., 42, 4 he speaks of the εὐφροσύνη awakened by preaching : προσδοκώντων τὴν κατηγγελμένην ὑπ' αὐτοῦ ἀφθαρσίαν. [42]

Bultmann

εὐχαριστέω, εὐχαριστία, εὐχάριστος →.χάρις.

| εὔχομαι, εὐχή, προσεύχομαι, προσευχή | (→ αἰτέω, δέομαι, ἐπικαλέω, ἐρωτάω, εὐλογέω, εὐχαριστέω, προσκυνέω) |

† εὔχομαι, † εὐχή.

A. The Usage of εὔχομαι, εὐχή.

In non-biblical Gk. the simple εὔχομαι, εὐχή is the most comprehensive term for invocation of the deity. In the earliest period the sense of "to vow" is present as well

---

[39] Barn., 10, 11; Herm. s., 9, 11, 8 (of festive joy, but metaphorically).

[40] Barn., 1, 8; 4, 11 (ἐν τοῖς δικαιώμασιν αὐτοῦ); 10, 11 (μελέτη in the δικαιώματα of the Lord is an ἔργον εὐφροσύνης); 21, 9; among the three δόγματα κυρίου in 1, 6 (→ ἐλπίς, n. 117) the third is as follows : ἀγάπη εὐφροσύνης καὶ ἀγαλλιάσεως ἔργων δικαιοσύνης μαρτυρία ("love which is united with or characterised by," not 'love in merry and joyful works"); Herm. m., 12, 3, 4; s., 5, 7, 1; 9, 11, 8.

[41] For Just. cf. Dial., 80, 1; 130, 1 and 4; cf. 2 Cl., 19, 4 (the righteous once ἀναβιώσας εὐφρανθήσεται εἰς τὸν ἀλύπητον αἰῶνα); Herm. v., 3, 4, 2 (the joy of angels when the building of the tower is completed) s., 9, 18, 4 (the joy of the Son of God at the establishment of the Church).

[42] Cf. the provisional nature of the joy mentioned in → n. 40 at Barn., 1, 8 (δι' ὧν ἐν τοῖς παροῦσιν εὐφρανθήσεσθε).

ε ὔ χ ο μ α ι κ τ λ. On A. : Cr.-Kö., 457 f.; Moult.-Mill., 268; Trench, 115 ff.; R. Helbing, *Die Kasussyntax der Verba bei den Septuaginta* (1928), 224. Def.: Plat. Euthyphr., 14c; Philo Deus Imm., 87; Agric., 99; Som., I, 252; Orig. et Eus. in Psalmos XXI in I. B. Pitra, *Analecta Sacra*, III (1883), 420. On B. : F. Heiler, *Das Gebet⁵* (1923); RGG², II, 869 ff.; E. Rohde, *Die Religion der Griechen, Kleine Schriften*, II (1901), 314 ff.; U. v. Wilamowitz-Moellendorff, *Der Glaube der Hellenen* (1931/2), esp. I, 30 ff., 284 ff., 301; II, 513 ff.; J. Burckhardt, *Griechische Kulturgesch.*, II (1930), 1 ff.; *Religion u. Kultus*; E. Bickel, *Platonisches Gebetsleben, Archiv f. Gesch. der Philosophie*, XXI (1908), 535 ff.; G. Wissowa, *Religion u. Kultus d. Römer²* (1912), 389, 396 ff., 423 ff.; J. Kroll, *Die Lehren des Hermes Trismegistos* (1914), 328 f. On the form of Gk. prayers, cf. E. Norden, *Agnostos Theos* (1913), 143 ff.; K. Ziegler, *De Precationum apud Graecos Formis* (Diss. Breslau, 1905). On C. : Theel, "Das Gebet im AT im Lichte des Neuen betrachtet," in *Theologische Studien u. Skizzen aus Ostpreussen* (1889); E. Caldesaigues, *La Prière dans la Religion de Jéhovah, ses Antécédents, son Histoire* (Thèse Montauban, 1899); J. Köberle, "Die Motive

as the more common "to ask," "to pray." [1] In the LXX this word is almost always used for נדר and often for נזר, but here, and even more so in the NT statistics show a severe loss to προσεύχομαι, προσευχή, which becomes the main word for prayer. There are only a few relics of the simple form in the NT.

εὔχεσθαι πρός τινα in the LXX is normally used in sense 1. (though cf. Job 22:27; 2 Macc. 9:13), but in the NT it occurs only at 2 C. 13:7. εὔχεσθαί τινι in the LXX mostly has sense 2. (Sir. 38:9 is an exception), but the use in Ac. 26:29 is different. What is prayed for is in the acc. with inf. in Ac. 26:29; 27:29; 3 Jn. 2, in the nom. with inf. in R. 9:3, and expressed by a ὅπως clause in Jm. 5:16. There is a simple trans. in 2 C. 13:9.

1. "To pray," "to ask," "to beseech," "prayer," "petitionary prayer," or general "invocation of God." The noun as well as the verb is used in this sense as in Jm. 5:15 f.: [2] ἡ εὐχὴ τῆς πίστεως σώσει τὸν κάμνοντα, "believing prayer will save the sick" (v. 15). This excludes any magical operation of the oil with which the sick is to be anointed by the elders (→ I, 231). It is open to question whether the petition in the following verse is also for forgiveness of sins. [3] In 2 C. 13:7 Paul expressly mentions God, to whom he prays that the Corinthians may do no evil. [4] We should understand v. 9 also of intercessory prayer rather than as a mere wish (cf. Herm. s., 5, 2, 10; 5, 3, 7). In Ac. 26:29 Paul added an immediate τῷ θεῷ to the εὐξαίμην ἄν which for the Greek would be no more than a courteous and respectful wish. [5] The conversion of King Agrippa and the other hearers is for him a subject of earnest prayer; only God can accomplish it. [6]

---

des Glaubens an die Gebetserhörung im AT," *Festschr. d. Univers. Erlangen zum 80. Geburtstag des Prinz-Regenten Luitpold* (1901); M. Kegel, *Das Gebet im AT* (1908); J. Döller, "Das Gebet in religionsgesch. Beleuchtung," in *Theol. Studien der Österreichischen Leo-Gesellschaft,* 21 (1914); A. Greiff, *Das Gebet im AT = At.liche Abhandlungen,* V, 3 (1915); J. Hempel, *Gebet u. Frömmigkeit im AT* (1922); A. Scheuerpflug, *Das Gebet im AT* (unpubl. Diss., Heidelberg, 1923); H. Schmidt, *Das Gebet des Angeklagten im AT* (1928); A. Wendel, *Das freie Laiengebet im vorexilischen Israel = Ex Oriente Lux,* V/VII (1931); F. Delitzsch, HW², I (1893), 484 ff.; F. Buhl, RE³, VI, 393 f.; T. K. Cheyne, *s.v.* "Prayer," EB, III (1902), 3823 ff.; E. R. Bernard, *s.v.* "Prayer," HDB, IV (1902), 28 ff.; H. Lesêtre, *s.v.* "Prière" in F. Vigouroux, *Dictionnaire de la Bible,* V (1912), 663 ff.; H. Schmidt, RGG², II, 875-879; A. Horodetzky, *s.v.* "Gebet," EJ, VII (1931), 121 ff.; Text-books of OT theology and archaeology; Comm. on the Ps. by F. Delitzsch, R. Kittel, W. Staerk and H. Gunkel, and Gunkel's Introduction to the Ps. (completed by J. Begrich, 1933). On D.: W. Staerk, *Altjüdische liturgische Gebete,* Kl. T., 58² (1930); J. Elbogen, *Der jüdische Gottesdienst²* (1924); E. Schwaab, "Historische Einführung in das Achtzehngebet," BFTh, 17 (1913), 246 ff.; Str.-B., IV, 189 ff., 208 ff.; Schürer, II, 497 ff.; Dalman WJ, I, 283 ff.; Bousset-Gressm., 171 ff.; 358 ff. On E.: E. Goltz, *Das Gebet in der ältesten Christenheit* (1901); J. Jeremias, "Das Gebetsleben Jesu," ZNW, 25 (1926), 123 ff.; E. Orphal, *Das Paulusgebet* (1933); P. Christ, *Die Lehre vom Gebet* (1886); A. Klawek, *Das Gebet zu Jesus* (1921); J. Horst, *Proskynein* (1932); H. Greeven, *Gebet u. Eschatologie im NT* (1931); O. Dibelius, *Das Vaterunser* (1903), 1 ff.; Cr.-Kö., 458 f.; Trench, 115 ff.; Pr.-Bauer, 1144 f.

[1] So already in Hom., *v.* Pr.-Bauer, Liddell-Scott, *s.v.* The last meaning seems to go back to the Indo-Germ., Lat. *voveo* (A. Ernout-A. Meillet, *Dictionnaire Etymologique de la Langue Latine* [1932], 1092). The basic meaning acc. to Boisacq, *s.v.* is "*élever solennellement la voix,*" and acc. to Prellwitz Etym. Wört., *s.v.* and Walde-Pokorny, I, 110 "to vow" (so also Debrunner). Cf. also Liddell-Scott, *s.v.*

[2] P al emend Jm. 5:15 to προσευχή and AB 73 emend Jm. 5:16 to προσεύχεσθε under the influence of the more common compound found also in v. 13 f. and v. 17 f.

[3] Cf. Dib. Jk., 235 f.; Wnd. Jk., 33; Hck. Jk., 235 f.; Schl. Jk., 283 f.

[4] A different view is taken in Ltzm. K., 161 f.

[5] Cf. Bl.-Debr.⁶ § 385, 1. Philo Poster. C., 82.

[6] Bengel, *ad loc.*

εὔχομαι, εὐχή in the sense of "to pray," "prayer" are rare in the LXX, e.g., Dt. 9:26; 4 Βασ. 20:2; Da. 6:11, 13 etc. Jos. Ant., 1, 245 (Eliezer prays God that Rebekah might be among the damsels who come); 14, 22 and 24; 1, 270 ff., of the blessing of Isaac, a similar change of meaning from asking to what is prayed for as in 1 Βασ. 2:8. Cf. also Jos. Bell., 7, 155. Philo, too, uses the word in the sense of prayer. It is noteworthy that he takes Dt. 23:21: ἐὰν εὔξῃ εὐχήν, μὴ χρονίσῃς ἀποδοῦναι αὐτήν (as he renders it), quite plainly in the sense of petition and thanksgiving, Sacr. AC, 53 f. [7] Cf. also Leg. All., III, 104; → 775, bibl., Def. From secular lit., [8] the inscr. and pap., attention may be drawn to the Antiochus inscr. of Commagene (1st cent. B.C., Ditt. Or., I, 383), which uses εὔχομαι and εὐχή for intercession, lines 227 and 233.

2. "To vow," "to dedicate," "vow." It is not always possible to distinguish this sense sharply from 1. [9] It appears twice in the NT at Ac. 18:18; 21:23, [10] the noun alone being used. Since the reference is to Jews, [11] and to the shaving of the hair of the head, it must refer to the Nazirite vow. Two different details in 21:23 ff. make this conclusion unavoidable (cf. Str.-B., II, 80 ff., 747 ff., 755 ff.). [12]

The construction εὐχὴν ἔχοντες ἐφ' ἑαυτῶν at 21:23 is influenced by the LXX (Nu. 6:7; 30:7; Mal. 1:14) and also by the view that in his long hair the Nazirite bears on his head a sacrificial gift dedicated to God (Nu. 6:9, 19 etc.). The particularly common expressions εὔχεσθαι εὐχήν and ἀποδιδόναι εὐχήν show us how strong was the impulse to transfer εὐχή to the dedicated gift itself, e.g., Lv. 22:23; 23:38. So also on inscr., Ditt. Syll.[3], 1142 (1/2nd cent. A.D.), Ditt. Or., II, 716 (3rd cent. A.D.), Milet., I, 7 (1924), No. 304 (late) (εὐχὴν ἀνέθηκεν or ἀνέστησεν). Often εὐχήν means "as the gift of dedication, as the sacrifice at a vow" (cf. LXX Lv. 7:6; Ditt. Or., II, 655, 7 [24 B.C.]; Annales du Service des Antiquités de l'Égypte, 20 [1920], 238 f., Theadelphia, 2nd cent. B.C.). [13] Mostly κατ' εὐχήν and (late) ὑπὲρ εὐχῆς signify "in virtue of a vow" (Preisigke Sammelbuch, IV, 7287 [23 B.C.]; Ditt. Or., I, 418, 3 [41 A.D.]; IG, XII, 1, 902 and 911 f.; Publications of the Princeton Univ. Archaeol. Expeditions to Syria in 1904/1905 and 1909, III B (1922) 925, late. Nazirite, Jos. Ant., 4, 72; Bell., 2, 313; Philo Spec. Leg., I, 247 ff. εὐχ- for "to vow" or "vow" is rare in Philo.

3. The original cultic connection became weaker with time, so that εὔχομαι can take on the sense of "to wish" or "to ask" (as already in Pindar). [14] Naturally the border-line is fluid. The special mention of God in Ac. 26:29; 2 C. 13:7 (→ 776) is perhaps an indication that a fully secular understanding is possible and natural. Ancient epistolary style, as seen in 3 Jn. 2: περὶ πάντων εὔχομαί σε εὐοδοῦσθαι καὶ ὑγιαίνειν, shows how indeterminate the term has become. Along with the express mention of a deity (P. Lond., I, 42 [168 B.C.]; [15] Preisigke Sammelbuch, I, 5747, pagan) we may have εὔχομαι alone, so that there is no need to assume

---

[7] Though cf. the emendations of H. Leisegang in L. Cohn, Die Werke Philos von Alexandria in deutscher Übers., III (1919), 236, n. 3.
[8] For further examples cf. Liddell-Scott, Preisigke Wört., s.v.
[9] Cf. W. M. Ramsay, Exp. T., 10 (1898/99), 13.
[10] εὐχή is used for "vow" in the post-apost. fathers only in allusion to the OT (1 Cl., 41, 2; 52, 3) and εὔχεσθαι is never used for "to vow."
[11] The order in Ac. 18:18, in comparison with 17:34 (Lk. 24:1 ADsy), points to Akylas as the subj. of κειράμενος. D (προσευχήν) and d (orationem) are poor attempts to emend what is not properly understood.
[12] For a different view cf. G. Hoennicke, Die Apostelgeschichte (1913), 96 and E. Jacquier, Les Actes des Apôtres (1926), 556 f. Strictly εἶχεν represents a pluperfect.
[13] Cf. Publications of the Princeton Univ. Archaeol. Expeditions to Syria in 1904/05 and 1909, III A (1921), 250.
[14] Cf. Pass., s.v.
[15] S. Witkowski, Epistulae Privatae Graecae (1911), No. 35.

a religious connection even though this is possible (BGU, VI, 1301 [1/2nd cent. B.C.]; Preisigke Sammelbuch, III, 6265 [1st cent. A.D.]). [16] The normal expression which desires above all personal welfare : πρὸ πάντων εὔχομαι ... (BGU, I, 38 [1st cent. A.D.]; P. Oxy., II, 292 [c. 25 A.D.]) [17] is here altered, [18] since the Christian already has the chief thing, namely, divine health of soul (→ ὑγιής, ὑγιαίνω). Paul uses ηὐχόμην for his wish to trade the best thing that he has, his new life ἐν Χριστῷ, for the bringing of his fellow-countrymen to salvation (R. 9:3). This wish is restricted by the fact that the grace of God cannot be exchanged. Paul is simply using a strong expression to show how much he suffers from the disobedience of his own people. We read of those who were shipwrecked in Ac. 27:29 : ηὔχοντο ἡμέραν γενέσθαι, but we are not told that longing for daylight was expressed in prayers or vows.

εὔχεσθαι is used for "to wish" in the LXX only at Jer. 22:27, being the trans. of (שׁׁׁׁׁׁׁׁׁׁׁ) נֵּבֶת־אֵשׁ like ἐλπίζειν at ᾿Ιερ. 51:14. It is common, however, in the post-apost. fathers. The noun εὐχή is used for "wish" [19] neither in the LXX, the NT, nor the post-apost. fathers. But v. Jos. Bell., 5, 255; Vit., 292. Both noun and verb are common in Philo in this sense, e.g., Deus Imm., 164; Fug., 154. εὔχεσθαι in the sense of "to boast" (from the time of Homer) is not found at all in biblical Gk.

B. Prayer in the Greek World.

1. Greek prayer is determined by the particular position of this people in religious history generally. [20] It is true that many Gk. gods bear in their names or attributes the signs of origination in nature, in wood or hill, in the weather or the cycle of the year. Yet belief in God nowhere remained on the level of animism or fetichism. The Gks. everywhere saw in their gods the forces of destiny whose sphere of operation was limited neither materially nor topographically. In keeping with this is their worship, which fundamentally has no place for images. [21] In terms of prayer, this means that magical oracles and petitions and incantations are secondary, the primary feature being a type of prayer which springs from a more independent and profound piety. In this prayer man draws near with his requests to the force which can determine his whole destiny. Also in keeping with the comprehensive power of the deity is the fact that for the Gk. there is no sphere of life which should not be accompanied in all its manifestations by sacrifices and prayers to the gods.

a. For the early period we are dependent on deductions from the belief in God in respect of prayers. The first prayers are found in Homer. Though prayers are often stylistic devices in Homer, they give us a vivid picture of the significance, impulses and themes of prayer. [22]

The heroes of Homer are fully conscious of their dependence on the gods, and they naturally ascribe to them human emotions and impulses of will. They thus approach them as they would powerful princes. Prayer usually arises out of a concrete need and is related to the attainment of specific and palpable goals. Thus sacrifice and prayer are

---

[16] On this whole pt. cf. Wendland Hell. Kult., 414.

[17] A collection of basic material may be found in F. Ziemann, *De Epistularum Graecarum Formulis Solemnibus Quaestiones Selectae* (Diss. Halle, 1911), 317 ff. περὶ πάντων ... seems also to occur in BGU, III, 885 (2nd cent. A.D.), though the text is incomplete.

[18] Cf. χαίρειν > χάρις in Pl.

[19] Found from the time of Plat., Liddell-Scott, *s.v.*

[20] Cf. Heiler, *op. cit.*, 191.

[21] Cf. on this whole pt. Wilamowitz, I, 15 ff.

[22] Particularly valuable for our present study and for the materials collected, are the two works by C. F. Nägelsbach, *Homerische Theologie²* (1861), esp. 211 ff. on prayer ; and *Die nachhomerische Theologie d. griech. Volksglaubens* (1857), 211 f.

offered for preservation in an approaching battle. [23] Achilles intercedes with prayers and offerings for his friend Patroclus, asking Zeus that he may conquer and return safely. [24] Almost always there is requested some gracious overruling which will bring deliverance from a particular emergency or fulfil a specific need. [25] In the main the action of the gods is related only to the fortunes of war, to the determining of the issues of life and death. Only rarely is there prayer for the operation of the deity on men's hearts. [26] A unique climax in Homer is when Hector prays to the gods that his young son may enjoy the might and renown of a hero. [27]

The distinctive nature of the blessings sought shows us that the power of the gods over human destiny is not understood in terms of a fatalistic belief in providence which restricts the sphere of prayer to the inward man. There are rather points in life where man himself can no longer exercise any influence. It is here that the gods rule in the first instance. And since the gods may be swayed, man may seek his salvation with prayer and sacrifice. As all life is increasingly brought under the thought of fate, the more resolutely does εἰμαρμένη bring pressure on the Olympians with their delight in sacrifice. The Homeric heroes confidently seek to win the friendship of the gods. Prayer is usually accompanied by an offering. This offering may be regarded as constituting an obligation. Thus Agamemnon reminds Zeus expressly of his offerings and points to the poor return. [28] Zeus himself may occasionally admit the obligation. [29] But this cannot give any mechanical assurance of being heard. On the contrary, Ajax fears that the prayer of his friends for victory may cause his enemies to pray also and to do so more successfully. Thus it is better — at least in the first instance — to pray softly. [30] If he at once amends this, "for we really fear no one," it is more defiance of the gods than assurance of their help. As sacrifices are offered to win the favour of the gods, so promises are sometimes used to sway them, offerings being vowed in case of a favourable answer. [31] This arrangement is ultimately linked with the fact that the deities are not swayed, or hardly ever swayed, by moral considerations. Odysseus has reason to fear that the prayers of Leiodes, the unfaithful spectator at sacrifice, are partly responsible for his long journey. [32] Naïvely human is also the notion that Athene finds pleasure in her preferences. [33] There is some movement towards a more moral view in the thought that those who pray should satisfy certain demands. Along with the purely cultic requirement that he who prays and sacrifices should have clean hands [34] we also find the demand that he should not be guilty of blood [35] and that no disobedience against the gods should dwell in him. [36]

The basic aspects of Gk. prayer as they are already found in Homer persist into the period which follows. Upright, with head erect and hands outstretched, [37] the Greek calls upon his gods, the constant companions of his whole life, whom he approaches not so much with fear and trembling as with a certain intimacy. "The relationship of the

---

[23] E.g., Il., 2, 400 ff.
[24] Il., 16, 233 ff.
[25] Cf. Nägelsbach, *Homerische Theologie*, 213.
[26] Od., 7, 331 ff. In Il. 16, 514 ff., as we see from v. 529, Glaucos seems to have prayed that his courage might be strengthened.
[27] Il., 6, 476 ff.
[28] Il., 8, 236 ff.
[29] Il., 4, 48 ff.
[30] Il., 7, 194 ff.
[31] E.g., Il., 6, 308 ff.; Od., 17, 50 f. Hence the threefold meaning of εὔχομαι, "ask," "wish," "vow."
[32] Od., 22, 321 ff.
[33] Il., 17, 568.
[34] Il., 6, 266 f.; 16, 230.
[35] Od., 14, 406.
[36] Il., 1, 218.
[37] With invocation of the dead we find new gestures such as stamping and beating on the ground, Aesch. Pers., 683; Eur. Tro., 1305 f.

Greeks to God as expressed in prayer seems to be one of friendship. The Hellenes were masters of friendship; the dominant characteristic of their social relationships is reflected in their dealings with the godhead." [38]

b. The three great tragic dramatists give us a rich picture of the prayer of the Gks. in the classical period. Here, too, it must be noted that prayer is often a poetic instrument, a welcome form of self-depiction. Yet at least in Aeschylus, where it is almost the only form of personal expression, it bears everywhere the freshness of originality. Only in Euripides does it become a mere artistic medium, so that religious scepticism is expressed in it. [39] For the rest, as in Homer, even the artificial prayer still reflects in some sense what was possible and customary for the poet and his age in this respect. Thus invocation of the dead, [40] which is not yet found in Homer, can hardly be an artistic invention of the poet contradictory to current religious practice.

In tragedy there are some differences from the prayers of Homeric figures, esp. as regards content. It is still true that in every situation men can turn to the gods for help. But there is now a greater concern for spiritual and moral blessings. Thus Electra prays that she may be more virtuous than her mother. [41] The chorus of women in the Medea of Euripides describes σωφροσύνη as the finest gift of the gods and prays for protection from the tormenting passion of jealousy. [42] The prayer of the Danaids for hospitable Argos mentions not merely peace and prosperity but also honesty and the fear of God among the divine gifts which are the subject of prayer. [43] There can still be prayer for revenge, [44] but it is always for just and merited retribution. The wrongdoer has no hope of being heard. [45] On the other hand, the pious appeal to the faithful fulfilment of cultic obligations. [46] The words of Hippolytus breathe intimacy with the gods:

σοὶ καὶ ξύνειμι καὶ λόγοις ἀμείβομαι,
κλύων μὲν αὐδήν, ὄμμα δ' οὐχ ὁρῶν τὸ σόν. [47]

There is also trust and confidence in the words of comfort and admonition addressed by the Mycenaean women to the sorrowing Electra: Sighs and tears do not help, but only prayer to the gods. [48] There is a penetrating and yet highly characteristic testimony to Gk. prayer at the end of the Suppliants. The tragedy ends with uncertainty and anxiety concerning the outcome of the expected war with the sons of Aegyptus. In the alternating song of the chorus the inscrutability of the will of the gods is balanced against the summons: μέτριον νῦν ἔπος εὔχου. — τίνα καιρόν με διδάσκεις; τὰ θεῶν μηδὲν ἀγάζειν. [49] In this confident self-restraint Gk. prayer finds its most inwardly consistent characteristic. Even in dealings between man and deity the final culmination is μετρίως ἔχειν. [50]

c. Further testimony to prayer is found in lyric poetry and philosophy. [51] Here, too, we find at first the same indifferent conjunction of naïvely eudaemonistic and ethically

---

[38] Heiler, op. cit., 200.
[39] Cf. on prayer in the tragic dramatists W. Schadewaldt, "Monolog u. Selbstgespräch," NPhU, 2 (1926), 38, 52 f., 96 ff., 101 ff.; → n. 64.
[40] E.g., Aesch. Choeph., 129 ff.
[41] Ibid., 140 f.
[42] Eur. Med., 635 ff.
[43] Aesch. Suppl., 625 ff.
[44] E.g., Aesch. Choeph., 306 ff., 394 ff.; Soph. Phil., 1040 ff.
[45] Aesch. Ag., 396.
[46] Aesch. Choeph., 255 ff.; Soph. El., 1376 ff.; Eur. El., 199 f.
[47] Eur. Hipp., 85 f.
[48] Eur. El., 193 ff.
[49] Aesch. Suppl., 1059 ff.
[50] Cf. Plat. Phaedr., 279c.
[51] There is a good review of the estimation of prayer in Gk. philosophy by H. Schmidt in his Veteres Philosophi quomodo iudicaverint de Precibus, RVV, IV (1907), 1 ff. We may also refer to this work for the Hellenistic literature περὶ εὐχῆς.

purer concerns. The prayer of Solon to the Muses [52] sees in fortune and prosperity, in the trust of friends and the fear of enemies, in rightly acquired wealth, the gifts which may be sought from the grace of the gods ; but there is also prayer for protection against the worst of human failings, namely, ὕβρις. In Xenophon, too, a good name is an object of prayer as well as the usual gifts of fortune. [53] It is assumed by the pious Gk. that nothing should be attempted without prayer to the gods. [54] On the other hand, in philosophical prayer there is an evident effort to set aside an eudaemonistic approach to prayer. [55] It is true that in consequence prayer loses its vitality and spontaneity. It becomes insipid and finally leads to self-exaltation. [56] Nevertheless, in the first instance this development of moral depth and inwardness leads to the supreme culmination of Gk. prayer as it is reached in Plato : ὦ φίλε Πάν τε καὶ ἄλλοι ὅσοι τῇδε θεοί, δοίητέ μοί καλῷ γενέσθαι τἄνδοθεν· ἔξωθεν δὲ ὅσα ἔχω, τοῖς ἐντὸς εἶναί μοι φίλια. πλούσιον δὲ νομίζοιμι τὸν σοφόν· τὸ δὲ χρυσοῦ πλῆθος εἴη μοι ὅσον μήτε φέρειν μήτε ἄγειν δύναιτο ἄλλος ἢ ὁ σώφρων. [57] According to Xenophon, Socrates too is familiar with prayer for the remission of guilt and commends it to the σώφρων. [58] Pindar asks Zeus for uprightness of life. [59] But prayer becomes more general as well as more inward. There is much advice to pray simply for the good. [60] With this is linked the consideration that fulfilment of this desire necessarily implies the non-fulfilment of other, foolish wishes. [61] Pythagoras describes it as the task of the wise to pray for good on behalf of fools who do not recognise it. [62] But by this time we have long since moved out of vital prayer into the colder sphere of philosophical meditation concerning prayer. This brings us into the sphere of scepticism, present continually from the time of Xenophanes. Sometimes scepticism is expressed in the prayers of Euripides. Thus Odysseus in Cyc. prays to Zeus for deliverance. If this is not granted, Zeus is impotent and not the god he is thought to be. [63] Similarly, certain prayers in the Ion betray both in tone and content an attitude which makes true prayer impossible. [64]

2. In the Hellenistic period prayer is affected both by the heritage of Gk. philosophy with its criticism and ideal of prayer and also by the penetration into the Gk. world of the oriental mystery religions whose cultus gives particular features to prayer. Philosophy continues on the course adopted, [65] and is popularised in the new Stoa and related schools. To an even greater degree than in the classical period one may say that the image presented by literature is also true of popular religion.

a. The first great religious and philosophical stream in Hellenism is the popular philosophical enlightenment as this may be clearly seen in the Stoic-Cynic diatribe. Here the ancient belief in the gods is a thing of the past, and a practical monotheism has been attained which is strengthened rather than obscured by the continuing existence of many local cults, since the one supreme God is everywhere worshipped in the many deities. Prayer is certainly offered to various gods, but these represent God and are in no way differentiated. [66] The prayer of philosophers is addressed to this one deity. The nature of the thought of God lays its impress upon prayer. Since the conception of God

[52] Diehl, I, 17 ff.
[53] Xenoph. Oec., 11, 8.
[54] Theogn. Diehl, I, 125, lines 171 f.; Plat. Tim., 27c; Xenoph. Oec., 6, 1.
[55] On other reasons for this development cf. Bickel, op. cit., 538 ff.
[56] Cf. Heiler, op. cit., 202 ff.
[57] Plat. Phaedr., 279b c, cf. Bickel, op. cit., 536 ff.
[58] Xenoph. Mem., II, 2, 14.
[59] Nem., 8, 35.
[60] Xenoph. Mem., I, 3, 2; Ps.-Plat. Alc., II, 148c; Diod. S., X, 9, 8.
[61] Ps.-Plat. Alc., II, 143a.
[62] Diod. S., X, 9, 7.
[63] Eur. Cyc., 353 ff.
[64] E.g., Eur. Ion, 384 ff.; 436 ff.; 907 ff.; cf. Schadewaldt, 102, 118 ff., 130 ff.
[65] → n. 51.
[66] Sen. Ben., V, 25, 4. Omnipresence and omniscience are ascribed to the gods.

is basically impersonal, [67] we do not find in prayer those features which presuppose a personal being to whom it is offered. Above all, there can be no true petition in Stoic prayer. It is true that requests for health of soul, for liberation from desires, for "divine gifts which have nothing to do with carnal and earthly lusts," [68] have the appearance of petitions. But they are not really subjects of prayer ; they simply reflect the ideal which man should seek. He is to become one whose request is only for blessings of this kind. That this is not true petition may be seen from a statement of Seneca : It is foolish to pray for a right disposition when one can attain it of oneself. What need is there to lift up one's hand to heaven or to approach the statues of the gods ? "God is near thee, with thee, in thee." [69] Such statements justify us in wondering whether prayer is seriously meant. [70] Not only is there no serious prayer ; there is also no certainty of being heard. [71] The common request for physical health is repudiated, [72] since we should not ask the gods for things which they do not give. [73] Prayer is thus attacked at the root. Its only remaining content is an expression of resolution in face of destiny. We should not be misled, therefore, by well-known verse of Cleanthes warmly and frequently commended by Epictetus : [74]

ἄγου δέ μ', ὦ Ζεῦ, καὶ σύ γ' ἡ Πεπρωμένη,
ὅποι ποθ' ὑμῖν εἰμι διατεταγμένος.

This Zeus is in fact no more than fate, and the inflexibility (ἀπάθεια, ἀταραξία) of the wise not only separates him by a great gulf from his fellows but also makes it impossible for him to invoke God. [75] Lifted into the icy regions of philosophical speculation, prayer withers and dies. At a later period there is some reaction against this. Marcus Aurelius in his Meditations says : [76] "ὅσον ὅσον, ὦ φίλε Ζεῦ, κατὰ τῆς ἀρούρας τῆς Ἀθηναίων καὶ τῶν πεδίων." ἤτοι οὐ δεῖ εὔχεσθαι ἢ οὕτως· ἁπλῶς καὶ ἐλευθέρως. To be sure the simplicity and freedom of this prayer consist more in the avoidance of a wordy epiclesis or the absence of recollections of past sacrifices or the promises of new ones. In any case he is not expressing a confident petition for rain at a time of drought. The true aspect of his prayer may be seen from another passage [77] in which he rejects this type of concrete petition and extols prayer for inner development as the only kind appropriate to the wise. Certainly we cannot see any evident signs of a warm confidence in God.

b. The second great religious trend in Hellenism is the piety of the Mysteries. Though shaped by cultic forms and rituals, this rests on a basis of individual religious life. The redemption sought in the Mysteries presupposes individual religion. The cultic fellowship is a group of seekers or initiates gathered from every class and nation and united only by the consecrating rites. It is here that prayer takes on its full significance. In the great prayers of the Isis dedication of Apuleius, [78] in the prayer of the Hermes mystery, [79] in the stuttering and stammering of the Paris magic papyri, the individual everywhere experiences with awe the proximity of the deity whose possession he has become by the sacred rites of dedication, whose hands control his destiny and from whom he expects

---

[67] Cf. the regular alternation of *di* and *natura* in Sen., e.g., Ben., IV, 4.
[68] Epict. Gnom. Stob. D., 2; 3; 4 (p. 479, Schenkl); Sen. Ep., 10, 4.
[69] Sen. Ep., 41, 1. The impossibility of getting anything through prayer is plainly stated in De Naturalibus Quaestionibus, II, 35 ff.
[70] Cf. Bickel, *op. cit.*, 549.
[71] Sen. Ep., 10, 4 : *audacter deum roga : nihil illum de alieno rogaturus es*, presupposes that the friend to whom these words are addressed is making right requests.
[72] Epict. Gnom. Stob. D., 2 (p. 479, Schenkl).
[73] Epict. Fr., 17; cf. Diss., II, 7, 12 ff.
[74] Epict. Diss., II, 23, 42; III, 22, 95; IV, 1, 131 etc.
[75] The wise even stands over God, Sen. Ep., 73, 14.
[76] M. Ant., V, 7.
[77] M. Ant., IX, 40; cf. XII, 1.
[78] Apul. Met., XI, 2 and 25.
[79] Reitzenstein Poim., 338.

salvation. Yet prayer is only a penultimate thing for the initiate. The ultimate climax of religious experience is reached in the vision of God, in *adoratio de proxumo*, [80] in ἀτενίζειν τῷ θεῷ. [81] For this mystical vision prayer is simply scaffolding. It forms as it were the bridge from the limited possibilities of human will and work to the sphere of undisturbed, ecstatic and blessed divine vision where silence is the highest form of worship, [82] where words are heard which man cannot utter. [83] It is thus natural that the content of prayer should be secondary and that the whole straining should be towards this visionary experience. Pre-eminence is given to eloquent hymns of adoring worship adorned with every rhetorical device. [84] Then come songs of thanksgiving for the knowledge granted in visions [85] or more generally for the gracious rule of the deity. [86] Prayers for mundane things are rare and they are of minor significance. [87] Intercession for others is usually concerned with their ἄγνοια. [88] We never have a concrete need which gives rise to a cry for help, whether in the form of an external difficulty or a troubled conscience. At most it is general human frailty and finitude which the one who prays seeks to escape in periods of ecstasy and finally for ever. But these things are natural facts rather than moral. How far removed the piety of the Mysteries is from Christian prayer may be seen with especial clarity in Paul. He knows mystical ecstasy (2 C. 12:1 ff.), but in prayer he wins through to the assurance that ὀπτασίαι do not really count, that the grace of God must suffice, and that God's power is supremely operative in weakness (2 C. 12:7 ff.). [89]

c. A rather different picture is presented where Hellenistic piety meets and unites with Judaism as in Philo and the Wisdom of Solomon. So far as prayer is concerned, the Jewish elements are by far the more powerful. To Philo, who even advances new arguments to establish the provisions of the Law concerning vows, [90] it is self-evident that the righteous, the ἀσκητής, should turn to God in prayer. [91] Only of a man who prays can it be said that he lives. [92] What constitutes the greatness of a people is that God is near to it and answers its prayers. [93] The supreme task of the high-priest is to come before God with prayer and intercession for his people, for all humanity and indeed for the whole of creation. [94] One who truly prays has for God the value of a whole people. [95] One should approach God in prayer with purity and penitence, [96] prepared to make confession. [97] One should do so voluntarily. If we pray only when

---

[80] Apul. Met., XI, 23.

[81] Mithr. Liturg., 14, 26.

[82] Reitzenstein Poim., 338 (σιωπῇ φωνούμενε); Mithr. Liturg., 6, 21 f.; 8, 12; 10, 18 (σιγή); Kroll, 335 f. Mysticism usually finds prayer expressed in words inadequate; Heiler, 288 ff.

[83] Apul. Met., XI, 23; Mithr. Liturg., 10, 6 ff.; Jul. Or., 5, 172d.

[84] Apul. Met., XI, 2 and 25. Reitzenstein Poim., 338; Mithr. Liturg., 2, 10 ff.; 8, 16 ff.; 10, 31 ff.; 14, 27 ff.; Preis. Zaub., XIII, 762 ff.; cf. Reitzenstein Poim., 15 ff.

[85] Reitzenstein Poim., 337 f. § 29 and 32; Corp. Herm., XIII, 18 ff.

[86] Apul. Met., XI, 25.

[87] Apul. Met., XI, 2. This prayer is "pre-mystical" and is thus to be adduced with caution. Mithr. Liturg., 14, 3 ff. is not really a request. Where there is petition for earthly blessings, there is retreat from the higher plane and gross eudaemonism quickly develops; v. Preis. Zaub., XIII, 802 ff.

[88] Reitzenstein Poim., 338.

[89] Cf. Greeven, 182 ff.

[90] Spec. Leg., I, 247 ff.

[91] Only on one occasion do we find the idea that an archangel (the oldest Logos = Moses) intercedes for men before God, Rer. Div. Her., 205, cf. Tob. 12:15.

[92] Fug., 56.

[93] Praem. Poen., 84.

[94] Spec. Leg., I, 97; cf. I, 168; II, 167.

[95] This is the exegesis of Dt. 26:17 f. in Philo Virt., 185.

[96] Deus Imm., 8; Virt., 79.

[97] Fug., 80; Det. Pot. Ins., 95.

driven by necessity, we have as little prospect of being heard as the unrighteous. Enforced prayer is worthless. [98] Penitent prayer for mercy [99] is sure of being heard, for God loves to forgive rather than to punish, [100] and goes far beyond our asking. [101] On the other hand He answers only to the degree that it is profitable for us. [102] Philo is most clearly the Hellenist in relation to the subjects of prayer. Only very rarely are these external blessings. Prayer for wealth is rejected. [103] One should pray for a display of God's love rather than His might. [104] The blessings which Philo regards as supremely worthy of prayer to God are increase in virtue, peace, deliverance from anger and other passions, the proper orientation of life, and wisdom (cf. Wis. 7:7 and Solomon's great prayer for wisdom in c. 9). [105] It is prayer which gives the soul true freedom. [106] Man should thus turn to God without delay ; He will not spurn him. [107] Above all one should not forget to give thanks for the gifts which God gives. [108] Even the most poverty-stricken who have nothing more to expect of life have received from God so many and glorious gifts that they should not cease to give thanks. [109] In sum, it may be seen that the OT concept of God is strong enough in Philo to keep prayer in the ethical sphere and to prevent it from evaporating into philosophical speculation. On the other hand, there is in the subjects of his petitionary prayer a tendency which, consistently followed, would necessarily lead to the saying of Seneca that it is foolish to pray for things which one can attain of oneself (→ 782).

As compared with literature, inscr. make only a secondary contribution to our knowledge of Gk. prayer. Worth noting are the public prayers ordered in a council resolution from Magnesia (2nd cent. B.C.), [110] namely, that on a festival dedicated to Artemis Leucophryene all the inhabitants are to come to the goddess in prayer with appropriate sacrifices and to beseech health and fortune for the present and future generations. There are also many and varied accounts of healing and thanksgivings at the shrines of Aesculapius. [111] In Cos in the 2nd cent. B.C. (?) a school officer brings dedicatory offerings to Zeus and Athene for the ὑγεία and εὐταξία of those entrusted to him. [112] We may finally refer to prayer-like hymns and aretalogies which in I or he-style extol the dignity and acts of the deity. [113] The cursing tablets and magic papyri lead us to the lower depths of religion as with their formulae and to some extent with accompanying actions they purport to utilise the powers of deity for the various purposes of exorcism, medicine and eroticism. [114]

Greeven

---

[98] Sacr. AC, 71; Vit. Mos., II, 107.

[99] Vit. Mos., II, 147; Spec. Leg., II, 196; Som., II, 299.

[100] Praem. Poen., 166; Leg. All., III, 213 ff.

[101] Mut. Nom., 253.

[102] Spec. Leg., I, 43.

[103] *Ibid.,* 24.

[104] Plant., 90; Som., I, 163. In both cases Gn. 28:21 is the basis.

[105] Congr., 7; Omn. Prob. Lib., 64; Spec. Leg., II, 17; Abr., 6; Leg. All., III, 104; Vit. Cont., 27 and 89.

[106] Rer. Div. Her., 124; 186; 273.

[107] Sacr. AC, 70.

[108] Spec. Leg., I, 224; Mut. Nom., 220 ff.

[109] Mut. Nom., 222 f.

[110] Ditt. Syll.³, 695, 43 ff.

[111] Cf. the examples in H. Kleinknecht, Πάνθειον, *Religiöse Texte d. Griechentums* (1929), 64 ff.

[112] GDI, No. 3648; cf. also 3480.

[113] Cf. Kleinknecht, *op. cit.,* 68 ff.; also W. Peek, *Der Isishymnus v. Andros und ver-vandte Texte* (1930).

[114] Collected in Preis. Zaub.; cf. also T. Schermann, *Spätgriech. Zauber- und Volksgebete* (Diss. München, 1919).

C. Prayer in the OT.

1. OT Usage.

If we consult the lexicon of Gesenius-Buhl we find that for "to pray" the only Heb. word is the not very common עתר (Aram. צלא). Reference might also be made to פלל, but in fact the OT very seldom uses a verb for prayer. On the other hand, several words belong to the sphere of prayer, and these must all be taken into account if we are to present all the OT material.

a. Proper verbs. For עתר Arab. attests the sense of "to sacrifice." It is tempting to draw from this conclusions as to the original meaning of the Heb. But Heb. usage is against it. It is true that in Ez. 8:11 the subst. st. c. עֲתַר is rendered "smoke of sacrifice" in older versions, but עתר never suggests "to sacrifice" and is never connected with sacrifices. עתר in the qal and hiphil means "to pray (to God)," "to ask (God)," usually in the sense of petition. [115] In the niphal it means "to let oneself be asked (by someone)." The other proper verb for "to pray" is פלל hithpael. The conjecture of Wellhausen [116] that the original meaning is "to make rents, incisions," has found much support. But OT usage provides no material in favour of this historico-religious derivation of the present meaning, and other conjectures based on פלל piel, "to decide," "to judge," [117] seem to be better grounded. The fairly extensive OT evidence (over 60 occurrences) gives the word the uniform sense of "to pray," and often "to ask for someone" (25 times). With פלל is linked the common תְּפִלָּה, "prayer." תפלה denotes both cultic and non-cultic prayer, both sung and spoken prayer. Thus it is often a par. for שִׁיר in the Psalter; [118] Ps. 17, 86, 90, 102 and 142 are called תפלה in the titles, and at the end of Ps. 72 (72:20) the whole collection thus far is called תְּפִלּוֹת דָּוִד.

b. Along with the proper verbs note should be taken of several other words. Of verbs signifying "to wish" שׁאל is often used for "to ask something from God," though relatively infrequently in comparison with its total use. [119] It can sometimes denote sinful asking (Ps. 78:18).

All prayer seeks to awaken God's favour and thus to turn His goodness, grace and mercy to the petitioner. Hence חנן hithpael, "to present oneself acceptably before someone," [120] can mean "to ask God in prayer for favour, grace and mercy." [121] The derived nouns תַּחֲנוּנִים and תְּחִנָּה denote particularly urgent prayer, loud [122] or tearful "supplication" (Jer. 3:21). Hence the expression "my supplication casts itself before God," or "to cast one's supplication before God" (נפל hiphil, Da. 9:18). That prayer is meant to invoke God's friendship, [123] esp. against those who have angered Him, gives us anthropomorphically [124] the expression חִלָּה פְּנֵי יהוה. Acc. to the Arab. par. the original sense is probably "to stroke the face of God," which Marti [125] and others derive from

---

[115] So Gn. 25:21; Ex. 8:26; 10:18; Ju. 13:8 qal; Ex. 8:4, 5, 24, 25; 9:28; 10:17 hiphil.
[116] *Israelitische u. jüdische Geschichte*⁵ (1904), 107; *Reste arabischen Heidentums*² (1897), 126.
[117] E.g., E. König in his *Wörterbuch*.
[118] Ps. 54:2; 55:1; 61:1; 84:8; 86:6; 102:1; 143:1.
[119] Dt. 18:16; 1 K. 3:5, 10, 11; Is. 7:11, 12; Zech. 10:1; Ps. 2:8; 21:4; 27:4; 105:40; Prv. 30:7; 1 Ch. 4:10.
[120] E. König.
[121] Dt. 3:23; 1 K. 8:33, 47, 59; 9:3; Ps. 30:8; 142:1; Job 8:5; 9:15.
[122] Ps. 28:2, 6; 31:22; 116:1; 130:2; 140:6.
[123] נפל לפני Jer. 36:7; 37:20; 38:26; 42:2, 9; Da. 9:20.
[124] Dillmann³ (1897) on Ex. 32:11.
[125] K. Marti, *Geschichte d. israelitischen Religion*⁵ (1907), 41, with a reference to J. Wellhausen, *Skizzen u. Vorarbeiten*, III (1887), 105.

the elsewhere attested "to stroke the image of God," [126] a possible though by no means necessary derivation. [127] In the OT the expression means "to induce God's favour," or "to seek to induce God's favour," namely, through prayer, [128] as also through sacrifice (1 S. 13:12; Mal. 1:9), fasting (Zech. 7:2), the cultus in general (Zech. 8:21, 22) and acceptable conduct (Ps. 119:58; Da. 9:13).

The various words for speaking can also be used, of course, for prayer. The petitioner uses "my words" or "the words of my mouth" for "my prayer." [129] In the Ps. esp., though also elsewhere, prayer is described as calling (קרא), and open prayer seems to have been so much the rule that the silent prayer of Hannah in 1 S. 1 was obviously strange to Eli the priest. In so far as God is called upon by name in prayer, we often have the expression קָרָא בְּשֵׁם יהוה, which in passages like Gn. 12:8; 13:4 etc. can simply mean "to engage in worship" (at a cultic centre). [130] Partic. in the Ps., though elsewhere too, more fervent petition is often expressed by the use of crying, not in the sense that it is accompanied by crying, but that the prayer itself is crying. Thus we have שׁוע piel, "to cry for help in prayer" (e.g., Ps. 31:22; 88:13), and the subst. שַׁוְעָה (e.g., **Ps. 39:12 as a par. to** תְּפִלָּה), also זעק [131] and צעק (e.g., Ex. 14:10; 17:4) "to cry."

The one who prays often points to the sighing or groaning which precedes or accompanies his prayer, [132] and prayer itself is often called "sighing" or "groaning." The words used are אנח niphal "to sigh" (e.g., Ex. 2:23; Lam. 1:21) and the subst. אֲנָחָה "sighing"; [133] המה, "to sigh," "to groan" (Ps. 55:17; 77:3); subst. הָגִיג "sighing" (Ps. 5:2; 39:3, par "my words"); שְׁאָגָה "roaring" (Ps. 22:1 "the words of my roaring," Ps. 32:3). This prayer finally becomes "weeping." Thus in Ps. 6:8 we have weeping (בְּכִי) as a par. to (v. 9) תְּחִנָּה and תְּפִלָּה; Ps. 39:12 "tears" (דִּמְעָה) as a par. to תְּפִלָּה and שַׁוְעָה; cf. also דלף "to weep" in Job 16:20; Ps. 119:28. At its supreme point of fervour, prayer is "to pour out one's soul (1 S. 1:15; Ps. 42:5) or heart (Ps. 62:8; Lam. 2:19) or grief (Ps. 142:2; 102:1) before God" (שׁפך).

c. Extremely common are prayers of praise and thanksgiving. Among the verbs for "to praise," "to extol," "to glorify," we may first mention הלל. [134] Piel: men should "magnify" or "praise" (almost always) either God or His name (Ps. 113:1; Jl. 2:26) or word (Ps. 56:4). It is to this group that there belongs the liturgical formula Hallelujah in Ps. 104:35 and elsewhere. The part. pual describes God as "worthy of praise." [135] It is again a matter of grateful praise when the righteous "boasts" (hithpael) in God [136] or His name. [137] To הלל belongs תְּהִלָּה, the "praise" or "praiseworthiness" of God, whence the plur. the "praiseworthy" acts of God; the rather different plur. (with a masc. ending) in the title of the Psalter expresses the fine belief that all Psalms ultimately minister to the praise of God. ידה hiphil means "to confess," "to confess with praise," "to praise," occasionally of men but mostly of God [138] or His name. [139] In this connec-

---

[126] This is naturally adduced as evidence of earlier images of Yahweh.
[127] For other possibilities cf. E. König and Ges.-Buhl, s.v.
[128] Ex. 32:11; 1 K. 13:6; 2 K. 13:4; 2 Ch. 33:12.
[129] So, e.g., with אָמַר, which except in Jos. 24:27 is used only poetically (Ps. 5:1; 19:14; 54:2).
[130] Cf. also Gn. 4:26.
[131] E.g., Ju. 3:9, 15; 6:6, 7; 1 S. 7:9; Ps. 22:5.
[132] So Ps. 6:6; 31:10; 38:9; 102:5; Lam. 1:22.
[133] Ps. 6:6; 31:10; 38:9; 102:5; Lam. 1:22.
[134] For different views as to the original meaning v. Ges.-Buhl and König.
[135] 2 S. 22:4; Ps. 18:3 etc.; 1 Ch. 16:25.
[136] Ps. 34:3; Is. 41:16; 45:25.
[137] Ps. 105:3.
[138] E.g., Ps. 7:17; 30:12; Ps. 6:5; 75:1; 107:8.
[139] E.g., Ps. 54:7; 106:47.

tion we should also mention תּוֹדָה for "praise"[140] or a "chorus of those who praise," Neh. 12:31, 38, 40. שׁבח piel, hithpael means "to praise," i.e., God[141] or His works (Ps. 145:4) or name (Ps. 106:47). In 1 Ch. 16:4 זכר hiphil is used with הלל piel and ידה hiphil to denote the calling of the families of Levi to this ministry, the most famous being the sons of Asaph; cf. לְהַזְכִּיר in the titles of Ps. 38 and 70. In Is. 63:7 and Ps. 71:16 the meaning is "to name or mention with praise the divine acts of grace or salvation." God has ordained for His works this remembrance with praise (subst. זֵכֶר), Ps. 111:4; the recollection of His goodness should be proclaimed with praise (נבע hiphil), Ps. 145:7. ידע hiphil[142] and נגד hiphil (Ps. 9:11; 71:17; 92:2) are also used for this public praising of the acts, the mighty acts, the miracles, the faithfulness and loving-kindness of God. גדל piel means "to magnify God's name,"[143] and רום polel "to exalt God"[144] or "His name" (Ps. 34:3). "To perform one's vows to God," שׁלם piel used figur. with נֶדֶר, means "to give God the grateful praise which is His due" (Ps. 61:8 and also Ps. 116:14, 18; 22:25; Jn. 2:10). In the OT, too, the sense of "to praise God" is linked with the expression "to bless God," בּרך piel, whether because "to bless God or His name" implies prayer or because it constitutes the content of the prayer of praise and thanksgiving. Thus "to bless God's name" is a par. of "to sing to God" (Ps. 96:2), "to praise Him" (Ps. 100:4), and "to bless God" is a par. of "to lift up one's hands in His name" (Ps. 63:4), "to cause His praise to be heard" (Ps. 66:8) or "to have His praise in one's mouth" (Ps. 34:1). Cf. also 1 Ch. 29:20 and Psalms like 103 (vv. 1-2, 22) and 104 (vv. 1 and 35).

Among the verbs for praise we may also note two which denote religious reflection and meditation but which may also be used for "to speak or to declare with praise," the context making it plain that what is in view is not silent praise, as one might expect, but that which is expressed. These verbs are הגה, "to hum," "to murmur," "to meditate," and שׂיח "to reflect." Both are used poetically for "to talk," the former in Ps. 35:28; 71:24 and the latter in Ps. 105:2; 145:5; Ju. 5:10. שׂיח can also be used of the prayer of complaint, e.g., Job 7:11 and also Ps. 55:2; 77:3.

There are several expressions for "to rejoice," "to exult," "to make merry," not merely in the form of mere interjections but in emphatic praises and songs of praise, as may often be seen from the par. Thus we have גיל,[145] עלז,[146] עלץ,[147] צהל ("to roar" and then "to rejoice"),[148] רוע hiphil ("to cry aloud," then "to exult"),[149] רנן piel ("to cry," then "to rejoice"),[150] פצח, originally "to be bright," then "to be cheerful or merry," "to make merry," either as a par. of רנן or with רִנָּה as an inner obj.[151] שׂמח, "to be joyful," is also used with רנן (Zech. 2:14), עלז,[152] or גיל[153] of joy which is expressed; cf. also Neh. 12:43.

d. To the verbs of praise we must also add those of music and singing, for the praises of God are often said to be sung to the accompaniment of instruments, while

---

140 Ps. 26:7; 42 etc.
141 Ps. 63:3; 117:1; 147:12.
142 Is. 12:4; Ps. 89:1; 105:1; 145:12.
143 Ps. 34:4; 69:30.
144 Ex. 15:2; Ps. 30:1; 99:5, 9; 107:32; 118:28; 145:1.
145 Ps. 9:14; 14:7; 89:16 etc.
146 E.g., Ps. 28:7; 68:4; Zeph. 3:14.
147 1 S. 2:1; Ps. 5:11; 9:2; 68:3.
148 Is. 12:6; 24:14; 54:1; Jer. 31:7.
149 Is. 44:23; Zeph. 3:14; Zech. 9:9; Job 38:7; Ps. 47:1 etc.
150 Is. 26:19; 35:2; 52:8, 9; Jer. 31:12; Ps. 5:11 etc.
151 Is. 52:9; Ps. 98:4; Is. 14:7; 44:23; 49:13; 54:1; 55:12.
152 2 S. 1:20; Jer. 50:11; Zeph. 3:14.
153 Jl. 2:21; Ps. 14:7.

we very seldom hear [154] that Psalms of complaint or petition are sung and accompanied.

שיר "to sing," almost always has the character of joy or praise or thanksgiving, as also the related subst. שִׁיר "song" (including the Lord's song or the song of Sion, Ps. 137:3, 4), which appears in the title of many Psalms, though this does not justify us in classifying these as a particular genre. Thus Miriam in Ex. 15:1, 21 sings the song of the Red Sea, a song of praise, and Deborah and Barak in Ju. 5:1 sing a song of victory in which there is a summons to praise Yahweh. For the most part there is emphasis on the element of praise and thanksgiving in these songs. [155] A musical accompaniment is clearly envisaged in the Psalms. [156] The Levitical temple singers, who are mentioned along with the keepers of the doors in Ezr., Neh. and Ch., play on different instruments. [157] Along with שיר, ענה means "to sing," perhaps as an independent verb, perhaps deriving from ענה "to answer," and having the sense of "to strike up," "to lead," [158] "to lead antiphonal singing." [159]

For the "playing" of instruments in accompaniment of songs of praise and thanksgiving we have זמר piel. This verb, common in the Ps. but rare elsewhere, is mostly linked with זמר, which in Lv. 25:3, 4; Is. 5:6 is used of the pruning of vines and thus means "to pluck off," "to pluck," signifying in music the plucking of strings. On the other hand, attention has been drawn to corresponding words in modern Heb., as also in Aram. and Accadian, which have the sense of "to sing." Yet OT usage favours the former view, for זמֵּר has primarily the sense of "to play" (on an instrument) and not "to sing." [160] In parallelism with various words for to praise or to rejoice or to sing, זמר is mostly used with ידה hiphil and שיר, both found some 10 times in the Psalms. Where used alone, it may have the wider sense of "to play and to sing." [161] The subst., too, has the primary sense of "playing" (on an instrument), [162] though possibly it has the wider sense of playing and singing in Ps. 118:14. From what has been said, it would seem that the term in the title of many Psalms indicates a song accompanied by stringed instruments, unless it simply means "playing on strings" and is a purely musical term. [163] In the present context we need not go into the question of the musical terms שמע hiphil, [164] נגן qal and piel ("to play on strings"), נצח ("to make liturgical music") and למנצח, found in the titles of 55 Psalms and in Hab. 3:19, or שכל hiphil ("to make music") in 2 Ch. 30:21.

e. The word השתחוה. Of the verbs of prayer we have still to mention in conclusion one of the most important. This should be treated separately because in the first instance it seems to relate only to the external attitude of prayer, and yet it very significantly characterises the inner disposition of the prayer of Israel. We refer to שחה hithpael. The meaning is "respectfully to bow down oneself," but the rich usage goes far beyond the gesture of reverence, expressive though this may be. In itself השתחוה does not denote the attitude of prayer, but the gesture of respectful greeting shown to those whom one would or should honour as masters and therefore especially, though not exclusively, to

---

[154] Ps. 7:1; 2 Ch. 35:25.
[155] E.g., Jer. 20:13; Is. 42:10; Job 33:27 and very often in the Ps., e.g., Ps. 13:6; 27:6; 57:7; 65:13 etc.
[156] → infra on זמר.
[157] Neh. 12:28, 29, 42; cf. 1 Ch. 15:16, 19; 2 Ch. 5:12, 13; 23:13.
[158] Ex. 15:21; Ps. 119:172.
[159] For the cultic singing of Psalms antiphonally cf. Ezr. 3:11 and probably Ps. 147:7 and Ex. 15:21.
[160] E.g., Ps. 71:22, 23; 21:13; 27:6.
[161] E.g., Ps. 47:6; 61:8; 66:2, 4.
[162] Am. 5:23; Is. 51:3; Ps. 81:2; 98:5.
[163] We cannot pursue this question here.
[164] We have vocal music in Neh. 12:42, instrumental in 1 Ch. 15:16, 19, 28; 16:5, 42, and the two together in 2 Ch. 5:13.

rulers. [165] The meaning of the gesture is obvious. The Gk. → προσκυνεῖν corresponds to the Heb. השתחוה. One bows down before God esp. when approaching Him in the sanctuary, so that השתחוה comes to denote the performance of cultic actions at a holy place. Thus Abraham, when about to offer up Isaac at the place appointed by God, [166] tells his young men that he will "bow down himself," [167] Gn. 22:5. But there is no need of the sanctuary to do obeisance followed by prayer. Thus in Gn. 24:26, 48 the servant of Abraham prostrates himself before Yahweh in prayer and thanksgiving in the land of Haran, though there is no proper verb for "to pray." We can see how naturally obeisance precedes cultic acts from the passages where השתחוה comes either before [168] or after [169] עבד. But no cultic act need follow prostration. It is in itself a significant and concrete expression for the inner attitude of worship even where there is no reference to formulated prayer. [170] How השתחוה takes on the sense of worshipping God even when used alone to express this may be seen in passages like Lv. 26:1; Ju. 2:12, 17, 19; 2 K. 5:18; Is. 2:20; Jer. 7:2; Ez. 46:2, 3, 9 etc. It is only relatively infrequently [171] that prayer is said to follow obeisance. Thus we have prayer of praise and thanksgiving in Gn. 24:26, 48; prayer for forgiveness in Ex. 34:8; the grateful song of Hannah in 1 S. 1:28; the magnifying of God in Ps. 29:2; praise of the name of Yahweh in Ps. 66:4; 138:1, 2; and magnifying of God in Ps. 99:5. It seems that there can be no prayer wtihout prostration. So far as concerns the act at great festivals, there are many instructive examples, e.g., 1 Ch. 29:20; 2 Ch. 7:3; 20:18; 29:27-30; Neh. 8:6; 9:3. If, as we have seen, there are comparatively few places where there is a proper verb for "to pray," this is partly because, when prayer is intended, the reader knows this from the use of השתחוה, which has itself acquired the necessary content. That השתחוה did not signify merely the external gesture of bowing down oneself, but very quickly came to be used for the inward religious attitude, may be seen from the many passages where we have קדד before השתחוה. For קדד, too, denotes bowing down oneself with one's face touching the earth. [172] Again, נפל is sometimes used for "to prostrate oneself" before [173] השתחוה. Note should also be taken of the fact that סגד ("to bow down to idols") in the Aram. portions of Da. [174] occurs as a loan-word in Dt. Is., [175] where it is used along with השתחוה. [176] It is clear from Is. 44:17 and 46:6, however, that it is not a full synon. of השתחוה, which has a much richer meaning. [177] If we review all the passages in which השתחוה occurs it seems likely that the reference is usually to the worship or prayer preceded and accompanied by obeisance, so that "to worship" or "to pray" is often a materially suitable rendering. Thus E. König suggests the two senses, 1. "to bow down oneself," and 2. metonymically including what follows, "to worship." [178] Kneeling is mentioned as a similar attitude of prayer, ברך qal, [179] כרע (with בִּרְכַּיִם or עַל־בִּרְכַּיִם). [180]

---

[165] E.g., Gn. 23:7, 12; 27:29; 33:3, 6, 7; 37:7, 9, 10; 42:6; 43:26, 28; 49:8 etc.

[166] There is no reference to any accompanying prayer in Gn. 22:7 ff.

[167] This is typical even though it might be objected that in this particular situation he would not have spoken of sacrifice, for the details of the narrative make it clear that those with him must have known that they had come to sacrifice.

[168] E.g., Ex. 20:5; 23:24 etc.

[169] E.g., Dt. 8:19; 11:16; 17:3 etc.

[170] E.g., Ex. 4:31; 12:27; 24:1; 33:10; Nu. 22:31 etc.

[171] In comparison with the very common use of השתחוה in general.

[172] Ex. 34:8; 1 S. 24:9; 28:14; 1 K. 1:31.

[173] Jos. 5:14; Job 1:20.

[174] Da. 2:46; 3 passim.

[175] Is. 44:15, 17, 19; 46:6.

[176] Except in Is. 44:19.

[177] Cf. esp. Is. 46:6 : "They fall down (סגד), yea, they worship (השתחוה)."

[178] Wörterbuch, s.v.

[179] E.g., Ps. 95:6; 2 Ch. 6:13.

[180] 1 K. 8:54; Ezr. 9:5 etc.

There is also reference to standing for prayer in 1 S. 1:26; 1 K. 8:22; Jer. 18:20. [181] In many cases the hands are stretched out to God [182] or to heaven [183] in prayer, also abs., [184] Heb. פָּרַשׂ qal or piel. It is natural that the hands should be lifted up (נָשָׂא). [185] Since emphasis is laid on the fact that the palms are outstretched, the gesture gives us a position in which gifts may be received from the deity.

This concludes our survey of the Heb. words [186] belonging to the sphere of prayer. The review presents a rich and varied picture. For our present purpose we have restricted ourselves to the stricter domain of prayer. We have not considered vows, sacrifices, fasts, blessings or cursings, incantations or magic. If there are closer or more distant connections with these religious forms or phenomena, they all of them contain basic elements which differentiate them from prayer.

2. The Main Features of OT Prayer.

To write a history of prayer in Israel would be to write a history of the religion of Israel in general. If the one is a difficult task which can only be fulfilled in part in the light of the source material found in the OT, this is naturally even more true of the other. A supreme temptation to be avoided is that of trying to discern an evolutionary scheme. We cannot hope to press back to the origins of Israelitish prayer for the simple reason that we cannot press back to the origins of the religion of Israel or of the tribes of which this people was composed. Even the older written sources which we think we have in the OT present us with a life and type of prayer which are by no means primitive. One need only think of Gn. 24. It is true that the later material, esp. from the time of Jeremiah, is much richer. It is also self-evident that prayer developed in Israel with the unfolding of the religion of revelation. We might say a good deal more than is now possible concerning the earlier preexilic period if only we could say for certain which Psalms belonged to the earlier centuries.

a. Prayer and faith in Yahweh. Our primary task is to portray the most essential features of OT prayer as they derive from the religion of Israel and are illustrated in the available materials. The religion of Israel demanded exclusive worship of Yahweh, and therefore all prayer in Israel was necessarily addressed to the one God. It is obvious that this was of decisive importance. The one God is the God of Israel who established the covenant of Sinai, made Israel His people and established this relationship on the obedience of the people to His will. In this relationship Israel is conscious of the might and wisdom, the goodness and faithfulness of Yahweh, but also of His moral holiness and righteousness and therefore of a requirement which, so far as we can see, is moral from the very first. On the basis of these presuppositions the piety of the individual Israelite is always embedded in his awareness of belonging to the covenant people. The individual with his individual faith shares in the faith of the religious and national fellowship. As a member of this fellowship he has a personal share in the relationship with God granted to his people. In the OT, therefore, we constantly

---

[181] Acc. to the Talmud the attitude of the slave before his master.
[182] Ex. 9:29, 33; 1 K. 8:22; Ps. 44:20; 63:4 etc.
[183] 1 K. 8:54; 2 Ch. 6:12.
[184] Is. 1:15; Jer. 4:31; Ps. 143:6.
[185] E.g., Ps. 28:2; Lam. 2:19; 3:41.
[186] From the religious language of Israel one might also refer, e.g., to the expression "to seek (the face of) God" in 2 S. 21:1; Hos. 5:15; Ps. 24:6; 27:8; 105:4; Dt. 4:29; 2 S. 12:16; Jer. 29:13; Hos. 5:6; Zeph. 2:3; Ps. 40:16; 69:6; 105:3; Ezr. 8:22; 2 Ch. 20:4; Ps. 83:16 (the name of God). Only in Ps. 27:8 and 2 Ch. 20:4, also 2 S. 12:16, is it quite clear that this seeking implies prayer, though this is probably the underlying thought in other passages.

see that the individual is praying as a member of the people of Yahweh. The life of prayer, like the whole life of faith, is determined not so much by the relationship "man to God and God to man" as by the relationship "Israelite to Yahweh and Yahweh to Israelite," which for its part is posited by the relationship "Israel to Yahweh and Yahweh to Israel" (→ 524). It is the final relationship which gives the Israelite the confidence which is the ultimate presupposition of all prayer but which can here have a strength that would not be possible apart from this starting-point. In other words, the prayer of the Israelite is directed, not to a God of whom one does not finally know what to expect, but to the God who has made Himself the God of Israel and who has made Israel His people. In prayer the Israelite knows that the God to whom he prays displays a basic goodness and faithfulness towards His people. This is also of fundamental significance for the form of OT prayer. It means that in the religious consciousness of the one who prays an important part is played by the history of his people as the history of the constant and continuing action of the gracious and merciful and holy and righteous God towards Israel. It also means, as may be finely seen in the Psalms, that the experiences of his fellow-countrymen in prayer are of great importance for him and that his experiences are no less important for all others who pray in Israel. Nor is God's action towards His people to cease in the present. Nourished by the divinely given words of the prophets, faith is also expectation and hope of awaited future salvation for Israel. The coming of this salvation is thus a theme of prayer and longing in the Psalms, whether in relation to the whole community of God or to the destiny of the individual.

Faith in God, however, means more for him who prays than that Yahweh is the God of Israel. This faith reaches its true dimensions only as faith that this Yahweh — and this brings us back to our starting-point — is not just the God of Israel but also the one true God who is the Creator and Sustainer of the whole world. We need not go into the question when and how this strictly monotheistic belief established itself in fulness and purity. So far as we can see, it is certainly present in germ from the very outset, and it is fully developed in the prophets (at least after Elijah). This aspect of faith in God is naturally of great significance for the praying Israelite. Of particular importance is the fact that it does not crowd out the other aspect. The Creator and Lord of the world is still the God of Israel, and the God of Israel is the Creator and Lord of the world.

We should not fail to see, of course, that the praying Israelite is much concerned about the hearing of prayer, that he earnestly seeks to be heard, that by complaint and confession of confidence, by appeal to the experiences of His people and of individuals, by remembrance of the goodness and faithfulness and righteousness of God, by reference to his own righteousness, he tries to support his petition, that he may sometimes doubt the goodness and faithfulness and even the righteousness of God, that he does not seem to be too sure of God. This is linked among other things with the fact that for the pious Israelite God is almost always a living and vital person who does not merely have "qualities" but who is very much alive in love or in wrath, so that for all the distance between them the one who prays confronts Him person to person as One who knows all that one thinks, who sees all that one does, who hears when one calls upon Him but who is still the sovereign Lord. That this Lord is not a theological construct but a wholly personal reality is what makes prayer in Israel so vital. But it is also what makes it a matter which is suspended always on the personal decision of the divine Lord.

b. What can the Israelite ask of Yahweh, the God of Israel who is the Creator and Sustainer of the whole world ? The answer is everything. For as he may look to Yahweh for every good gift, so he may also look to the Creator. And he may also thank Him for every benefit. In both cases physical and material blessings seem to be more prominent than spiritual. Even the Psalmist prays more for deliverance from evils than for the forgiveness of sins. Indeed, the latter petition is comparatively rare in the Psalter, though it occurs in prayers of astonishing profundity. [187] First place is taken by the things of the body, of ordinary life. Yet it must be remembered that the Psalmist does not enjoy the light of the Christian belief in eternity, apart from a few early glimmers, and that his hope of the future is not yet hope of the hereafter. It may also be said on the other side that in the OT generally man's existence is seen as a unity, so that physical and spiritual needs are closely related for the praying Israelite. Moreover, there are prayers in the Psalter in which ordinary benefits give place to the supreme good of joy in God and the bliss of fellowship with Him. [188] An important concern in OT prayer is the presence of enemies. It is a particular offence to the Christian reader that the praying Psalmist does not pray for his enemies but against them. Often, though not always, the offence is diminished by the fact that the pious Israelite sees in his own enemies the enemies of Yahweh. Prayer in the Psalms is much affected by the classification of men into two antithetical groups, the "righteous" on the one side and the "ungodly" on the other. [189] Here, too, the faith of the individual is embedded in his consciousness of the community, in his awareness of belonging to the people of the covenant. Nor should it be overlooked that the human reaction against threats and ill-treatment has an influence. This may be seen, e.g., in Ps. 54:5, 7; 58:6 ff. and especially in the terrible imprecations of Ps. 109. But it is also true of Psalms in which the reference is not to enemies of the pious individual within his own people but to the external enemies of Israel, the Gentiles. [190] In these cases, too, we must be careful not to call good what is bad. On the other hand, we must not allow a Pharisaic attitude to prevent us at least from understanding that, in Ps. 149, e.g., we have the "cry for vengeance against the nations of a people which was oppressed and downtrodden for centuries," [191] and that the dreadful desire for revenge in Ps. 137 follows the expression of passionate longing and unshakable loyalty which link the exiles with Sion. Certainly there is no question of the personal revenge of individuals. It should also give us food for thought that in Ps. 17 v. 13 f. is followed at once by v. 15, where fervent longing for God breaks through the limit of traditional belief.

c. Prayer and the cultus. In a cultic religion, religious thought and feeling are closely related to the sanctuaries. This is also true of the prayer of the Israelites, which Isaiah, e.g., mentions along with sacrifices, feasts and solemn days (Is. 1:15). It is obvious that there is calling on the name of Yahweh at the altars, as Israel in its tradition narrates already of Abraham in Gn. 12:8 etc. For at the sanctuaries one may hope to draw near to God and to reach Him in prayer. Thus in the time before the kings Hannah uses the occasion of the annual pilgrimage to Shiloh

---

[187] Ps. 32; 51; 103; 130.
[188] Ps. 4:7; 16:11; 17:15; 23; 27:4; 36:9; 63:1 ff.; 73:25 f.; 131.
[189] Ps. 17:13 ff.; 28; 37:32 ff.; 69:23-29; 94:23.
[190] Ps. 79:10, 12; 129:5-8; 137:7-9; 149.
[191] R. Kittel, *Die Psalmen*[5/6] (1929), 438.

with her husband Elkanah to bring her personal problem to God in urgent prayer (1 S. 1). In particular the temple at Jerusalem is increasingly realised to be the place where Yahweh has chosen to cause His name to dwell (Dt. 12:11 etc.), so that it finally becomes the place which Tr. Is. can call a "house of prayer for all peoples" (56:7). In the verse from Isaiah quoted earlier (1:15) the temple is the place where many prayers are offered. The temple at Jerusalem is the place to which hands are stretched out in prayer [192] as they are stretched out to heaven. [193] In both cases the meaning is that they are stretched out to God, for the ideas that Yahweh dwells in heaven and also on earth in the temple of Sion do not rule out one another but exist together. If one is in the temple court, prayer is uttered towards the temple itself; [194] if one is outside Jerusalem, one faces towards the holy city in prayer. [195] The stronger the religious joy in dwelling in the temple, the more inward the need to pray there. Yet neither in earlier nor later periods is prayer tied to the sanctuary in Israel. The faithful servant of Abraham prays to the God of his master Abraham in the land of Haran [196] at the well of the city of Nahor. Abraham himself [197] prays to Yahweh in the land of the Philistines (Gn. 21:32), as does also Samson. [198] Elijah prays in Phoenicia in the house of the widow of Zarephath. [199] One can also pray at home, as did Isaac [200] or King Hezekiah [201] or Ezra. [202] At a later period an undisturbed upper room was often used (Tob. 3:12; Jdt. 8:5); thus Daniel (Da. 6:11) in exile opened the window of his upper room and prayed three times a day towards Jerusalem. There is perhaps evidence in Ps. 55:17 of the three times of prayer, namely, morning, noon and evening, but we do not find any other mention in the OT. Ps. 4 is an evening prayer and Ps. 5 a morning prayer. [203] The prayers collected in the Psalter show how little prayer in Israel is tied to the sanctuary or to the cultic actions performed there. Considering the orientation of the Psalter, the number of Psalms with no particular relation to the temple or its worship is very remarkable.

In this regard we should consider the question of the relationship between prayer and sacrifice. In a sacrificial religion like that of Israel it is naturally customary to show one's reverence for the deity, not by mere words, but by bringing gifts and offerings. [204] But this can become purely external observance. Sometimes prayer is stated to be of more value than sacrifice. Thus Ps. 50 advances some highly individual arguments against the sacrificial cult and raises the demand that one should rather offer the sacrifices of thankful praise and call upon God in time of need: [205] "Whoso offereth praise glorifieth me" (Ps. 50:23). Similarly in Ps. 69 the Psalmist says: "I will praise the name of God with a song, and will magnify him with thanksgiving. This also shall please the Lord better than an ox or bullock

---

[192] Ps. 28:2; 134:2.
[193] Ex. 9:29; 17:11; 1 K. 8:22, 54; Is. 1:15; Ezr. 9:5; Lam. 2:19.
[194] Ps. 5:7; 28:2; 134:2.
[195] 1 K. 8:38; 2 Ch. 6:34; Da. 6:11.
[196] Gn. 24:12 ff., 28 ff. J.
[197] Gn. 20:17 E.
[198] Ju. 16:28.
[199] 1 K. 17:20.
[200] Gn. 25:21.
[201] 2 K. 20:2.
[202] Ezr. 9:5 ff.
[203] For historical material on these two times of prayer, v. Heiler, Index.
[204] C. v. Orelli, RE³, XIV, 386.
[205] Ps. 50:14, 15.

that hath horns and hoofs." [206] The same is true of petitionary prayer. [207] Though
there is no actual antithesis, Ps. 107:22 and 27:6 speak of spiritual sacrifices of
thanksgiving and praise which do not consist in actual offerings but in songs, and
along the same lines Ps. 141:2 substitutes prayer for sacrifice. But how are sacrifice
and prayer related? We have seen already that Abraham set up altars where he
called on the name of God (Gn. 12:8 etc.). We also have forms of prayer for the
offering of firstfruits (Dt. 26:5 ff.) and the paying of the third year tithes (Dt.
26:13 ff.), though there is no mention of prayer at all in the Leviticus ritual, and
in Dt. it is never mentioned with sacrifice. [208] In the ancient account in 2 S. 6 of
the solemn bringing up of the ark by David there is also no mention of prayer
along with the sacrifices. [209] In prayers in the Psalter we often read of the vowing
of sacrifices. We are also told that songs of thanksgiving were sung when these
sacrifices were offered. [210] They might well have preceded the sacrifice as a
general rule, [211] though possibly they were sung by participants in the feast which
accompanied the sacrifice (Ps. 22:25 f.). In Ps. 66 we have a song of thanksgiving
declaring and preceding a sacrifice of thanksgiving. [212] We are also told in Neh. 12
that songs of jubilation sung by the whole congregation accompanied the sacrifices
offered on the dedication of the wall. [213] Cf. also 2 Ch. 29:27-30; 30:21 f. But we
also have examples of anxious prayer on the occasion of sacrifice. Thus Ps. 54
presupposes that the one who prays is concerned about the preparation of his
sacrifice. [214] In general, it is obvious that the connection between sacrifice and
prayer is comparatively rare in the Psalter. The prayers collected in the Psalter
derive for the most part from a piety in which the prayer or song of thanksgiving
has taken the place of sacrifice. [215]

Since fasting [216] in the OT is predominantly a performance by which man hopes
to ensure that his prayer is heard by God, it is obvious that there should be a
link between them. Thus Jer. 14:12 presupposes the connection between fasting
and supplication. When Nehemiah hears of the sorry state of affairs in Jerusalem,
he fasts and prays (Neh. 1:4). Ezra orders the returning exiles to fast and pray
that they might have a successful journey (Ezr. 8:23). At an hour of crisis Joel
summons the congregation to common prayer and fasting; penitent conversion is
to be expressed in fasting, weeping and lamentation. [217] We learn specifically from
Neh. 9:1 ff. that the penitent prayer linked with fasting contains a confession of
sin. [218]

That prayer is often linked with a vow we have mentioned above in relation to
the vowing of sacrifices. It may be pointed out, however, that in the Psalter the

---

[206] Ps. 69:30, 31.
[207] Ps. 40:6 ff.; 51:16 ff.
[208] E.g., Dt. 12:5 ff.
[209] The Chronicler mentions a psalm of thanksgiving in 1 Ch. 16, but like the processional
singing in 2 S. 6 it is not organically related to the sacrifice.
[210] Ps. 22:25; 54:6; 61:8; 116:17 f.; Jon. 2:10.
[211] Ps. 116:17 f.; Jon. 2:10.
[212] H. Gunkel-J. Begrich, *Einleitung in die Psalmen* (1933), 273.
[213] *Ibid.,* 315.
[214] *Ibid.,* 177.
[215] *Ibid.,* 277 ff.
[216] Cf. F. Buhl, RE³, V, 768-770.
[217] Jl. 1:14; 2:12, 15, 17.
[218] Cf. also 1 S. 7:6; the only place in the Law where fasting is prescribed is in the ritual
of the great Day of Atonement in Lv. 16:29, 31; 23:27 ff.; Nu. 29:7, and this is the great day
of confession of sin.

righteous often vow a song of praise rather than a material offering. There are also examples of a mother making vows in prayer for a son. [219] Hannah, the mother of Samuel, vows that in thanksgiving she will dedicate to God the son for whom she is praying. It is not always said that the vow is accompanied by prayer. [220] But the close connection between them may be seen from passages like Ps. 61:5 : "Thou hearest my vows, thou fulfillest <the desire> of those who fear thy name," and Job 22:27: "Thou shalt make thy prayer unto him, and he shall hear thee, and thou shalt pay thy vows."

d. Finally a word should be said about prayer and magic. We cannot go into the wider question how far there is magic in the religion of Yahweh or how far magical customs and beliefs may be found among the Israelites as those who profess this religion. But there are one or two passages which are so relevant to this theme and which offer such illuminating insights on the distinctiveness of Yahwism that we should not overlook them. In Ex. 17:11, according to v. 9, the reference is to the magical power of the divine rod. But for this purpose Moses did not need to hold up both hands, and in v. 12 it is expressly said that Hur and Aaron held up both arms so that he could keep them up until sunset. The meaning of the gesture obviously has nothing to do with the magic rod. Already in the Targum it is related to prayer. More recent expositors [221] do not agree, but H. Holzinger makes the acute observation [222] that "the original idea that Moses stretched out his miraculous rod against the foes has been changed into the thought of holding on in prayer." Again, in the well-known saying by which Joshua arrests the sun and moon in their courses in Jos. 10:12, 13 the sun and moon are addressed rather than Yahweh, so that we seem to have an incantation rather than petition. But the present text supplies the introductory words : "Then spake Joshua to the Lord." Again, the action of Elisha at the raising of the son of the Shunammite in 2 K. 4:34, like that of Elijah at the raising of the son of the widow of Zarephath (1 K. 17:21), is in itself a magical action. But in our present texts both actions are now preceded (2 K. 4:33; 1 K. 17:20) by prayer to Yahweh, so that the actions are divested of their magical character. The verb גהר, which is used in relation to the action in 2 K. 4:34, 35, is also found in 1 K. 18:42 to describe an attitude which may well have been one of magic rather than of prayer, since we are not actually told that Elijah prayed for rain in v. 40 ff. But the author of James takes it that prayer is implied (Jm. 5:18). Obviously in Yahweh religion there is a force at work to crowd out the magic which had penetrated from primitive religion, and to replace it by prayer.

3. Review of Prayer in the OT.

a. Prayer in the History Books. If we consider the narrative sections of the Pentateuch (or Hexateuch), we see that here, as in the later historical works, the author was not concerned to adorn his accounts with prayers, and that there are not too many express references to the various characters praying. Thus there is no reference to prayer at all in the Joseph stories, nor is there prayer in such characteristic Genesis passages as Gn. 21; 22; 28; 32:25-33. On the other hand, it is undoubtedly true that prayer is often assumed without being mentioned, as, e.g., in

---

[219] 1 S. 1:11; Prv. 31:2.
[220] Not, e.g., in Gn. 28:20 ff.; 31:13; Ju. 11:30 ff.; 2 S. 15:8; Nah. 2:1; Ps. 66:13, 14.
[221] Cf. Dillmann³ (1897), Baentsch (1903), *ad loc.*; Gressmann, *Mose und seine Zeit* (1913), 156.
[222] In Kautzsch⁴, *ad loc.*

Gn. 30:6, 17, 22. Fine examples of prayer usually attributed to J. are to be found in the prayers of the faithful and unselfish servant of Abraham in Gn. 24, perhaps the finest narrative chapter in the whole of the OT. [223] Beautiful, too, is the prayer of the returning Jacob in Gn. 32:10-13, also attributed to J. [224] Moses is always presented as a great man of prayer and especially a great intercessor, whether in the requested prayer for Pharaoh [225] or in requested or unrequested intercession for Israel. In this connection particular emphasis is laid on his intercessions in Ex. 32:11-14, 31 f.; 34:8-9; Nu. 14:13-19, [226] in which he intercedes for his people even to the point of representative self-offering. [227] Like the similar intercession of Joshua, these are ascribed to the later portions of J. There are older prayers for Judah and Levi in the so-called blessing of Moses in Dt. 33 (vv. 7-11).

In the heroic stories of Judges there are few prayers (Gideon in 6:36-40; Manoah in 13:8; Samson in 15:18 and 16:28). The short prayers of the powerful Samson are forceful and fervent, though in 16:28 he prays for the destruction of his enemies, the enemies of his people and of Yahweh.

At the beginning of Samuel is the pious Hannah (1 S. 1:10 ff.) who pours out her heart before God in quiet inaudible prayer. We may suspect that a later redactor has added as her prayer the psalm in 1 S. 2:1-10. If this does not belong to the concrete situation of Hannah, but speaks more generally of the triumph of the righteous and overthrow of the ungodly, looking forward to a (Messianic) king, this is typical of the way in which a psalm of this kind can be used as the prayer of individuals, as also of the fact that the personal piety of individuals in prayer is nourished by the public piety of the nation as a whole. In the David stories we find in the later strata an explicit prayer of David which breathes the prophetic or Deuteronomic spirit and which is one of the finest prayers in the OT (2 S. 7:18-29). On the occasion of the ceremonial bringing up of the ark in 2 S. 6 there is no mention of prayer along with the sacrifices offered by David and the blessing given by him, [228] but we read of the singing [229] and playing [230] of a song of praise by the festive crowd during the preceding procession led by David.

In the story of Solomon in Kings there is the truly royal prayer of Solomon at Gibeon (1 K. 3:6-9) and also Solomon's prayer of dedication in 1 K. 8:23-53, which seems to be greatly expanded and which is attributed to a Deuteronomist.

In the Elijah stories [231] the powerful prophet with his prayer (1 K. 18:36, 37), which finely presents the spiritual religion of Yahweh in opposition to sensual nature religion, gains a great victory over the incensed host of Baal's prophets, whose god is no less contemptible to Elijah than their mode of praying (vv. 26-28).

In the depiction of the history of the kings of Judah in Chronicles, the Chronicler constantly manifests his concern to introduce cultic songs of praise. Thus in his

---

[223] Gn. 24:12-14, cf. 42 ff.; vv. 26-27, cf. 48.
[224] The point, of course, is not so much the grateful confession at the beginning as the petition which follows.
[225] Ex. 8:25, 26; 9:29, 33; 10:8.
[226] Cf. Dt. 9:26-29.
[227] Cf. also David's prayer in 2 S. 24:17.
[228] Cf. what is said above about prayer and sacrifice, → 794 f.
[229] This presupposes v. 21, cf. v. 15.
[230] The Psalm, said to be Davidic in 2 S. 22 (Ps. 18), is thought by, e.g., R. Kittel[5-6] 1929, to belong at the very earliest to the time of Jeremiah or Dt., except for the ancient section vv. 8-16, which might well be Davidic.
[231] Cf. what was said about prayer and magic in relation to 1 K. 17:20, 21; 18:41 ff., → 795.

description of the bringing up of the ark (1 Ch. 16) David appoints Levites to minister at the ark and their cultic and liturgical commission is denoted by הַלֵּל, הוֹדוֹת, הַזְכִּיר (v. 4).[232] He also mentions specifically that David in the first instance entrusted Asaph and his brethren with the singing of the "Praise Yahweh."[233] As the song of praise then used, he gives us a psalm composed of Ps. 105:1-15; 96:1b-13a; 106:1, 47-48a. The people gives the final response[234] "Amen" and "Hallelujah" (1 Ch. 16:8-36).[235] These accounts give us valuable information concerning practices at the time of the author. In other passages, too, we learn more about habits of prayer from the Chronicler than from the older history books. In Kings the only instance of a ruler praying after Solomon is that of Hezekiah,[236] but in Chronicles we read also of the prayers of the righteous kings Asa[237] and Jehoshaphat[238] and even of the ungodly Manasseh after his humiliation.[239] David on one occasion praises God in the presence of the whole congregation (kahal) in a beautiful prose prayer, and he then summons the congregation to a final choral response and to proskynesis.[240] Nehemiah is also a man of serious and fervent prayer both in and outside his own memoirs.[241] On a day of penitence the whole congregation sings a song of praise concluding with supplication (Neh. 9). In the account of Ezra's dissolution of mixed marriages a great impression is made (Ezr. 10:1 ff.) by his public prayer of penitence (9:6-15).

b. When we turn to the Wisdom literature, we find that in Job prayer, and especially prayer for forgiveness and deliverance in humble self-abasement, is so important that all three friends[242] recommend such prayer to Job as the only way out of his distress.[243] It is natural that Job himself, the man of perfect piety, should also be faithful in prayer.[244] In his bitter affliction and complaint, however, we sometimes find some very critical utterances in his prayers.[245] When his speeches in discussion with the friends become prayer-like addresses to God[246] we get very unusual prayers marked by the same boldness as the speeches. But when God Himself addresses him, there is a return to the prayer of humble self-abasement (42:2-6). In Proverbs there is a fine saying concerning the blessing of penitential prayer accompanied by confession of sins (28:13). In general God hears the prayer of the righteous (15:29). This is of greater value than the sacrifice of the ungodly, which is an offence to Him (15:8). The Preacher has many remarkable sayings from the standpoint of OT piety, and among these is an admonition against wordiness in prayer which almost adopts a critical position in relation to prayer generally (Qoh. 5:4).

---

232 → 786 f.
233 הוֹדוּ לי׳; this is obviously intended in v. 7.
234 Cf. Ps. 106:48b.
235 Cf. also 2 Ch. 5:13; 7:3; 20:21, also 23:13 and esp. 29:27-30, and Ezr. 3:10 ff.; Neh. 8:6; 9:5.
236 2 K. 19:15-19; 20:2-3.
237 2 Ch. 14:10.
238 2 Ch. 20:6-12.
239 2 Ch. 33:12-13; cf. v. 18, 19.
240 1 Ch. 29:10-19, 20.
241 Neh. 1:4, 5-11; 2:4; 3:36-37; 5:19; 6:14; 8:6; 13:14, 22, 31.
242 Eliphaz in 5:8; Bildad in 8:5; Zophar in 11:13 ff.
243 Cf. also 22:27.
244 Cf. 12:4; 16:17, 20, 21.
245 9:16; 19:7.
246 7:7-21; 10:2-22; 13:20-14:22; 17:2 ff.; 30:20-23.

c. Prayer in the prophets. In the prophetic writings we find comparatively much less material than might have been expected. This is particularly true of the 8th century prophets. Isaiah in 1:15 lists prayer among many other cultic actions which weary God because of the sins of the people, and he coins the saying quoted by Jesus in Mt. 15:8 f. concerning the sinful praying with the lips of those whose heart is far from God and whose fear of Him is taught by human precept (29:13). It is evident that these sayings are not directed against prayer as such. They reflect the distinctive character of the prophetic demand. Amos, too, has to say that God has no time for the noise of the cultic songs of those who show nothing of the righteousness which He demands. [247] But we are also told how Amos brings himself to pray to God in the vision for the forgiveness of his people, and how God hears this prayer (7:1-6). Micah tells the unjust rulers who oppress and exploit the people that in the time of judgment they will cry to God in vain (3:4). Hosea summons the people to conversion with penitent prayer for forgiveness (14:2-4). If we have few examples of the prayers of the prophets themselves in their writings, this is undoubtedly linked with the fact that their religious life is developed within their awareness of prophetic calling. In speaking to God they are in a different position from most people inasmuch as God Himself speaks to them and through them. But it is also connected with the individual nature of the prophetic personality of Jeremiah that his personal life of prayer constantly breaks into his prophetic utterance. We thus have his sacrificial intercessions for his people [248] and the painful experience of being forbidden by God to pray any more for a people so sunk in sin. [249] There are also the many prayers against his enemies with which he storms Yahweh, the righteous Judge, [250] and which become more noble petitions for the judgment of God. [251] From Jeremiah, too, we have the magnificent saying: "And ye shall seek me, and find me, when ye shall search for me with all your heart" (29:13 f.). Alongside this may be placed the summons of Dt. Is. in 55:6, the promise of Tr. Is. in 58:9 and the even richer promise in 65:24. But this leads us to the post-exilic prophetic writings. More than once we have the promise that all peoples will call on the name of Yahweh. [252] Joel summons the people to a day of fasting and repentance on which it will pray God to turn aside the catastrophic destruction which has overtaken it (1:14-20). The priests are to weep and to pray for mercy between the porch and the altar (2:17). Jonah, too, calls the people of Nineveh to the penitential prayer which will bring deliverance (3:8). The psalm uttered by Jonah when saved from imminent death (2:3 ff.) shows [253] how psalms can be used as prayers. [254] His discouraged prayer for death in 4:2-3, repeated in 4:8, is not in keeping with the general spirit of Hebrew prayer, and indeed the little book generally has several features unusual in Yahwism.

d. The Psalter is the treasure-house of OT prayers of imperishable worth. The lyric poetry [255] of Israel assembled here is for the most part poetic prayer, and

---

[247] This is what is meant in Am. 5:23, 24; cf. 8:10.
[248] Jer. 10:23-25; 14:7-9; 14:19-22.
[249] Jer. 7:16; 11:14; 14:11 f.
[250] Jer. 11:20; 12:1-3; 15:15-18.
[251] Jer. 17:12-18; 18:19-23; 20:7-13.
[252] Zeph. 3:9; Zech. 14:16, 17; cf. also Zech. 10:1; Is. 19:22.
[253] Cf. 1 S. 2.
[254] → 796 on 1 S. 2.
[255] Though not all the poetry in the Psalter is lyric, most of it is.

the collection is so comprehensive and significant that all the other prose or poetic prayers of the OT pale in comparison with it. Presentation of this material [256] presupposes wide formal and material investigation; its religious and theological evaluation is far more difficult that can be measured by the ordinary reader who finds in the Psalter nourishment for the soul. The language of the religious lyric of Israel is always impressive, and sometimes of unparalleled power, in the simplicity of its sentence construction and the wealth of its plastic images. But the poetry is not wholly expressed in words; with its simplicity of construction, its undeveloped tenses and its sparing use of particles it leaves much to the reader if it is to be properly understood. Above all, understanding of the content is linked with insight into the distinctive nature and history of the forms of this lyrical poetry. [257]

General considerations make it likely that it, too, had its origin in worship and that it was first linked with cultic activity. More detailed observations confirm this assumption, so that in individual songs we must be prepared to try to detect marks of their cultic use. If they had a setting in cultic life, to establish this is most important for a true understanding, since it sheds light both on the structure and on individual expressions. This is linked, of course, with the different literary genres, in the distinction of which other formal and material points must be taken into account. In biblical religion, the community, which is both a cultic and a national community, is of basic importance in the shaping of religious life and faith. This fact may be expected to reflect itself in the lyric poetry of the Psalms, the more so as this has its origin in the cultus. Yet the prayers of the community are far less numerous than those of the individual. This may be explained not only by the fact that the individual could always accompany his cultic actions with prayers but also by the unusually strong development of personal piety attested in the Psalms. In this respect it is worth noting that at every point the faith of the individual is shown to be embedded in the collective awareness of belonging to the congregation of Yahweh. We are not mistaken, then, if we think we can see how this greatly strengthened the personal life of faith. This may be noted in some of the greatest prayers in the Psalter.

Some of these prayers, whether individual or congregational, may be fairly easily put in their cultic setting. The majority, however, give little indication of their specific cultic use. We thus have a piety which at root is no longer closely bound up with cultic observance. Yet here, too, it is significant how often, even in the most inward and spiritual prayers, we can see evidence of the ultimate origin of the piety in public worship. We may thus say, e.g., that the love of the pious heart for the sacred dwelling-places of the Most High in Sion by no means limits the attainment of truly spiritual piety as modern western man might suppose. In this connection it should be remembered that possibly only a minority of the prayers collected in the Psalter are pre-exilic. Most of them come after the writing prophets, whose powerful message is rarely repeated in all its purity, but who have obviously had a rich fructifying influence on the piety here expressed. It is the

<hr/>

256 In relation to what follows, cf. all that has been said already concerning the prayers of the Psalms.
257 Cf. esp. the researches of Gunkel: H. Gunkel (-J. Begrich), *Einleitung in die Psalmen: Die Gattungen der religiösen Lyrik Israels* (1933), where there is reference to the earlier important work done by Gunkel; and H. Gunkel, *Die Psalmen* (1926). Cf. also W. Staerk, *Die Schriften des AT*, III, 1² (1920); R. Kittel, *Die Psalmen*⁵, ⁶ (1929); O. Eissfeldt, *Einleitung in das AT* (1934), 114-137.

nature of religious poetry to preserve what is old. For the most part, however, the prayers of the Psalter express the religion of the exilic and post-exilic period. This explains certain essential features. There is a predominance of complaint, grief and earnest supplication on the part of men who are oppressed, who seek help, deliverance, consolation and strengthening and who find them — this is perfectly plain — in the very fact that they may pray. From complaint there arises hope, indeed, certainty, which is faith in the sense of Hb. 11:1. Almost always the one who prays finds his way, both in thanksgiving and also in petition, to the praise of God comprehensively denoted by the later title, תְּהִלִּים. There is always prayer and confidence that God will finally and definitively glorify Himself before the whole world, not merely in His people, but in the individual also.

Many Psalms have more or less the character of spiritual songs. It is worth noting in this regard that their style is not merely that of general edification. On Bible readers of every age they have made the impression of individual experience. In fact, they are probably not quite so individual as they seem. We have to remember that these are poems and therefore developed literary forms which the individual uses and which are marked by specific types of construction and expression. In many respects what we find in the Psalms is confirmed and illuminated by corresponding forms of Babylonian poetry, with which the poetry of Israel probably has some connections. The expositor who is concerned to bring out the distinctive and individual features of particular Psalms must investigate all these forms. He will find much that is not individual, much that is indeed conventional and almost stereotyped. This is particularly true of the imagery, which in many cases does not give us a clear picture of the real situation of the author of the prayer.

Yet experience in every age confirms the fact that there is in the prayers of the Psalter a supreme religious force which can only derive from the God of the Psalmist who is the Father of Jesus Christ. "A remarkable experience in missionary work is that the Gentile world learns to pray from the Psalter. No book of Scripture has become the universal possession of Christian congregations in this way. With terrible realism the young convert from paganism appropriates the prayers and cries of the fathers, seeing himself persecuted with them, hoping for the kingdom of God in terms of these songs, prostrating himself in the penitential Psalms and giving thanks in the songs of praise, magnifying the greatness of God and finding a new relation to creation: 'Lord, how great and manifold are thy works.' It is impressive to see how natives of the Gold Coast, taught by the Psalms, pour out their needs freely before God, ask Him for direction and light, give thanks that they are heard, and set themselves in the divine salvation history which through the Psalms goes out into the world and reaches them too." [258]

Herrmann

D. Prayer in the Synagogue.

The Babylonian exile and the related separation from the temple, which made the sacrificial cultus impossible, brought prayer into the very centre of Jewish piety. Later, perhaps, a strong accent was placed on teaching, on the knowledge and fulfilment of

---

[258] K. Hartenstein, "Das AT in der Äusseren Mission," in *Mission und Pfarramt*, 27 (1934), 80.

the Law. [259] Yet prayer remained the sanctuary in which the pious Jew came before his God with petition and thanksgiving, with confession and praise. It is true that the forced surrender of the sacrificial cult during the exile gave to prayer a specific orientation. Only regular prayer could take the place of regular worship. It was thus inevitable that forms of prayer should arise. This posed the danger of making prayer superficial and opened up the way which would finally lead to the doctrine of the meritoriousness of prayer before God. [260] These distortions, however, were neither necessary nor universal. The distinctive elements in the history of Jewish prayer saw to it that among the Jews the gestures, times and formulas of prayer were far less highly estimated by Jews than by the other peoples and religions of antiquity. How vigorous a life pulsated through the rigid forms is strikingly illustrated in the story of the execution of Aqiba (c. 135). His pupils try to prevent him from keeping the hour and reciting the schema even in death. But he answers: "My whole life long I have been concerned about the verse, 'With all thy soul' (Dt. 6:5); I said, When shall I be able to fulfil it? And now that this is possible, shall I not fulfil it?" [261]

Regular prayer, two or three times a day, is attested fairly early. [262] It is presupposed in Ac. 3:1; 10:9, and indirectly in Mt. 6:5. [263] Josephus (b. 37/38 A.D.) in Ant., 4, 212 refers to the thanksgiving which goes up to God twice a day and he appeals to Moses, so that the habit must have been common in the first Christian century. [264] The content shows that the reference can only be to the schema, probably in its present form. [265] The schema is a confession of faith in form, but is usually regarded as a prayer. [266] It consists of three passages from the Torah (Dt. 6:4-9; 11:13-21; Nu. 15:37-41), and it is Israel's confession of the one God who has not abandoned His people since the exodus, who rewards its obedience with rich gifts and whose commandments the Jew must always keep in mind. The schema is one of the oldest elements in synagogue worship [267] and within the setting of various prayers it is also recited morning and evening. [268] It is highly probably that Jesus grew up with this daily confession. [269]

Strictly, the chief prayer of the Jews, called תְּפִלָּה, "the prayer," for short, is the schemone-Esre. [270] The redaction of 18 benedictions of which it consists goes back to the time of Gamaliel II (c. 100). [271] But only the 12th benediction against apostates is added at this time. The rest of the prayer (apart from the 14th, which refers to the rebuilding of Jerusalem) [272] is a good deal older. [273] This prayer begins with threefold praise (benedictions 1-3). Then follow the petitions proper, which embrace all the concrete individual concerns on the heart of the pious Jew. Prayer is made to God for knowledge, for a penitent heart, for the liberation and regathering of the Jewish people, for the restoration of theocracy, (the rejection of apostates,) the reception of proselytes, (the rebuilding of Jerusalem and the temple,) the hearing of prayer, the acceptance of sacrifice (later, the renewal of sacrificial worship) (benedictions 4-16). Finally, there

---

259 Bousset-Gressm., 126; Kittel Probleme, 9, n. 1.
260 Str.-B., IV, 203 ff., 629e.
261 bBer., 61b; cf. Kittel Probleme, 93, n. 3.
262 Da. 6:10 f., 13; cf. also Ps. 55:17 and Jos. Ant., 4, 212. There are further references in Str.-B., II, 696; on the gestures cf. also → προσκυνέω.
263 Those censured allow themselves to be surprised on the street at the times of prayer.
264 Str.-B., IV, 191; Kittel Probleme, 9.
265 Cf. Schürer, II, 538, n. 150; Elbogen, 25.
266 Str.-B., IV, 189, though note that one "recites" rather than "prays" the schema.
267 Ibid., 153.
268 Ber., 1, 1 and 2.
269 Cf. Jeremias, 127.
270 The text is in Dalman WJ, I¹ (1898), 299 ff.; Staerk, 11 ff. Cf. Str.-B., IV, 211 ff. We need not go into the question of the two recensions, the Palestinian and the Babylonian.
271 Cf. Schwaab, op. cit., 21 ff.
272 A different view is taken in Schwaab, 87 f.
273 Str.-B., I, 406 f.; IV, 218; Schwaab, op. cit., 75, 168.

follows a thanksgiving for the rule of God's love and a concluding prayer for peace (17 and 18). It is worth noting that the whole prayer takes the We-form (cf. the Lord's Prayer). Israel is still conscious of being a community in relation to its God. Since the three first and three last benedictions were the subject of debate between the schools of Hillel and Shammai, we may see in them the oldest parts of the prayer and find their origins in the pre-Christian period. [274] As regards the times of prayer, custom varied between the use of the 18 benedictions two or three times a day. [275] The habit of using a shorter form instead is early, since it led to controversies between scholars c. 90 A.D. [276] It is only from a later period that we have examples of shorter forms. [277] Yet there must have been several prior to the final redaction of the Schᵉmone-Esre, and it is with them that we should probably compare the Lord's Prayer.

Prayers at table probably go back to the pre-Christian period also. The Mishnah [278] records acute controversies concerning these between the schools of Hillel and Shammai, and these presuppose detailed construction. The custom of thanking and praising [279] the Creator before eating does not imply in Jesus any claim to be advancing a new form of piety. We cannot say whether the first Christians brought in any fixed forms of grace at meals. [280]

It is only with reservations that we presuppose other fixed forms of Jewish prayer in the earliest Christian period. We may perhaps date the Qaddish, which has some slight relations to the Lord's Prayer, [281] and also the Abinu malkenu in the first century A.D. [282] In content, the latter adds nothing to the Schᵉmone-Esre. The age of the Musaph prayers and the Habdala is uncertain. [283]

Along with this wealth of liturgical prayer which covers the whole day of the pious Jew, there is plenty of scope for independent extempore prayer. Even at the time of the redaction of the Schᵉmone-Esre it was debated where individual petitions should be included ; that there should be such was taken for granted. [284] The two who go up to the temple to pray, and who pray so differently (Lk. 18:10 ff.), represent an everyday situation. When Jesus accedes to the request of His disciples for guidance in true prayer (Lk. 11:1), this does not mean that He is rejecting the set forms of Judaism. Indeed, the strict regulation of prayer seems to have helped to stimulate and nourish a zeal in prayer which needs possibilities of individual expression alongside the required prayers.

The dangers of set prayer certainly led to misunderstandings, and the tension between the praying individual and the objective forms sometimes found expression in curious psychological and casuistical discussions. [285] The rigid prescriptions regarding the phylacteries and tassels opened the way to magical conceptions. [286] There is rational criticism when it is called foolish to pray that a pregnant woman may have a boy or to pray that it may not be in one's own house if cries are heard on returning home. [287] But it should be stated that these are only low points between the heights. Jesus prayed at meals like the Jews. There is hardly a clause in the Lord's Prayer which either does not or could not stand in Jewish prayers. If Jesus censures Jewish prayer, it is only when He finds

---

[274] Str.-B., I, 406 f.; Schwaab, op. cit., 55 ff.
[275] Cf. Str.-B., II, 696 ff.
[276] Ber., 4, 3; Str.-B., IV, 219, 221.
[277] Staerk, 20.
[278] Ber., 8, 1-8a.
[279] εὐλογεῖν, Mk. 6:41; Mt. 14:19, cf. בֵּרַךְ Ber., 7, 3.
[280] Str.-B., IV, 628.
[281] This is strongly emphasised by Elbogen, 93, who argues that "the first three petitions ... are in full agreement," but cf. Greeven, 82 f. V. also P. Fiebig, Jesu Bergpredigt (1924), 106, No. 302.
[282] Str.-B., I, 408; Fiebig, op. cit., 106, No. 302; Staerk, 28.
[283] Elbogen, 46 f., 116, 122; Str.-B., IV, 192c, 236; Staerk, 21 and 26.
[284] Str.-B., IV, 233.
[285] Ibid., 230e, 231 f.
[286] Ibid., 250 ff., 277 ff.; cf. also 275 and 292 p.
[287] Ber., 9, 3.

in it impure motives (Mt. 6:5), or when He sees it to be a pious mask for moral depravity (Mk. 12:40), or when He detects in it an impenitent heart (Lk. 18:10 ff.). On the one occasion when Jesus attacks "much speaking," He is not referring to the Jews but to the Gentiles (Mt. 6:7). [288] If the first disciples of Jesus had not been Jews, nourished in the rich prayer life of their people and permeated by the significance and power of constant prayer, it is doubtful whether the tradition of effectual, all-embracing, exemplary prayer which we may in essentials ascribe to the Lord would ever have come down to us.

E. Prayer in the NT.

1. Review, Presuppositions and Content.

The prayer of primitive Christianity finds its starting-point and centre in the prayer of Jesus. In prayer the believer experienced the powers of the new world whose imminence Jesus proclaimed, the new and childlike hiddenness in God by which Jesus lived and which He granted. The Lord Himself drew these powers from continuous and unwearying intercourse with the Father in heaven. This recollection of the first Christians is indissolubly connected with what are undoubtedly the most authentic parts of the tradition, namely, with the human agony in the Garden of Gethsemane and with the cry of dereliction on the cross; both these show us Jesus as a man of prayer. There is much evidence, especially in Lk., that He liked to be alone to pray, and although the third Evangelist often goes his own way in this respect there are no grounds for suspecting purely literary considerations. [289] Jesus maintains the Jewish custom of grace at meals (→ 802; εὐλογέω, εὐχαριστέω); His healings and exorcisms are often accompanied by a prayer, a glance towards heaven, or a sigh. [290] In prayer He finds assurance that God acknowledges Himself and His message (Mt. 11:25 and par.). He prays for the loyalty and resolution of His disciples (Lk. 22:31 f.), and even in His agony and dereliction He is calling on God for help and deliverance. For the fourth Evangelist the unity of will between the Father and the Son, and the deity of Jesus, are so palpable that the prayer of Jesus before the raising of Lazarus (11:41 f.), which presupposes a twofold will, namely, that of Him who prays and that of Him who grants, has for him the significance of convincing those around of the divine mission of the Son. But the high-priestly prayer shows that there is no dogmatic rigidity in the conception of Christ. The prayer of Jesus is so much an attitude that the individual acts are secondary; yet the Christ who is in such constant touch with God can also turn to the Father in petition and intercession and intercede for His own. The uniqueness of the relationship of Jesus to His Father is confirmed by the fact that the prayer of Jesus is never mentioned along with or put on the same level as that of the disciples. The only exception is in the conversation with the Samaritan woman (4:22) when speaking of the worship of the Jews and Samaritans prior to the declaration of His own dignity.

The distinctive feature of early Christian prayer is the certainty of being heard. This derives directly from faith in the fatherly love of God, and it is continually strengthened by the references of Jesus to this loving will which infinitely surpasses all earthly goodwill or readiness to help. In primitive Christianity there is no room for the question what one should or should not pray for. Jesus says expressly: πάντα ὅσα προσεύχεσθε καὶ αἰτεῖσθε, πιστεύετε ὅτι ἐλάβετε, καὶ

---

[288] But acc. to Schl. Mt., *ad loc.* censure of the Jews is included.

[289] Greeven, 12 f., 22 f.

[290] V. d. Goltz, 8 f.; Horst, 177.

ἔσται ὑμῖν (Mk. 11:24). [291] The evident presupposition is the unshakable confidence of faith. In the heart of a man who is full of confidence and faith in God there is nothing that he cannot bring to the Father in prayer. Even the most trivial things are worthy of prayer, since everything is of importance in this human life which belongs wholly to God. We may also assume that the early Church had experience of being heard beyond its asking or comprehension (cf. Paul in 2 C. 12:7 ff.). If there are no express instances it is because we do not have the presupposition of unavailing prayer, namely, doubt, feeble faith or distrust. [292] It should not be overlooked, of course, that God is still the Holy One whose judgment will shortly break over this aeon and destroy all that is not of God.

It is the unconditional certainty of being heard which makes it plain that the address to God in the Lord's Prayer has for the disciples a completely new content as compared with the addressing of God as Father customary among the Jews, so that like Jesus they can use the familiar form of the name (ἀββᾶ) which the Jews carefully avoided. [293] The first part of the prayer is grouped around the request: "Thy kingdom come." The first three petitions in Mt., like the request for the Spirit in Lk., are to be understood as the reflection in prayer of the early Christian expectation of the end with its experience in the present and hope of the future. This future of salvation is so close to life that along with it one may freely ask for things necessary to life (→ ἐπιούσιος). The Christian needs not only remission of sins but also deliverance from temptation. This excludes all perfectionism. The new filial relationship to God is not a secure possession. It is under threat and must be constantly attained, or rather given, afresh. This is why Jesus so frequently summons His disciples to turn to God in confident prayer. The question whether Jesus meant the Lord's Prayer to be a formula has often been given exaggerated significance. On the one side, to restrict freedom in prayer is not in keeping with Jesus' estimate of it. Nevertheless, the texts of the Lord's Prayer preserved in Mt. and Lk. obviously lay some claim to be normative. That this claim is justified is supported by the consideration that sooner or later Jesus' criticisms of the excesses of Jewish practices (Mt. 6:1 ff.) must have led the disciples to ask what should be their own attitude in prayer, so that the situation in Lk. 11:1 is not merely conceivable but historically extremely likely, except, perhaps, for the presence of John's disciples in the background. Moreover, there is in Jesus no polemic against the use of formal prayer. There seems to be acceptance of the need to guide those who pray. This is surely the purpose of the Lord's Prayer, which summarises in short sentences all that can and should come from the heart of a Christian in prayer before God.

It is a presupposition of all prayer that man should recognise the divine requirement, abandoning, e.g., all thought of vengeance if he himself seeks forgiveness. Self-seeking desires separate from God. When expressed in prayer, they cannot expect to be heard (Jm. 4:2 ff.). The Christian should be sober in prayer. That is, he should take seriously the fact that the days of this aeon are numbered and cleave to Him who gives true life (1 Pt. 4:7, cf. Pol., 7, 2). Prayer can be hindered by not giving honour to fellow-heirs of life, namely, wives (1 Pt. 3:7). Anything

---

[291] ὅτι ἐλάβετε, "that they are already given you therewith."

[292] There is perhaps a hint of these in Mk. 11:24; cf. Mt. 6:8. Kl. Mk., 133.

[293] Cf. the Lord's Prayer: Dalman WJ, I, 150 ff., 296 ff.; G. Kittel, *Die Religionsgeschichte und das Urchristentum* (1932), 92-95; → ἀββᾶ. Attempts at a reconstruction of the original form may be found in Harnack SAB, 1904, 195 ff.; Greeven, 72 ff. In what is said above we take the latter as a basis.

important to the believer may be the object of petition. External things can be important and can find a place in prayer, as may be seen from the request that the *parousia* should not be in winter (Mk. 13:18 and par.) or Paul's desire that he should some day be able to visit Rome (R. 1:10). As Jesus intercedes for His own before God, and continues to do so after His exaltation according to the fourth Evangelist (cf. Hb. 7:25), so intercession has a place in early Christian prayer. Intercession may be sometimes for "eudaemonistic" blessings. Thus prayer is made for the recovery of the sick (Jm. 5:14 ff.) or the liberation of prisoners (Ac. 12:5). The epistles of the NT make it obvious how the bond of brotherly love is vital and strong in prayer. To crown the conquest of self Jesus even demands that we should pray for our enemies, and according to Lk. He sets an example on the cross. The Stoic in prayer attains clarity concerning his own nature ; nothing which comes from without can affect him. The mystic withdraws from all things ; his soul experiences the delights of mystical vision. But when the Christian comes before God in prayer, he brings with him that which grieves him most, namely, unjust suffering, and before the face of God it is transfigured into intercession for his persecutors. Finally, early Christian prayer includes the prayer of thanksgiving. To be sure, there do not seem to be instances in the earliest sources. The Lord's Prayer contains only petitions. But grace at meals is thanksgiving. Those who witness miracles give God the glory. The story of the ten lepers teaches thanksgiving clearly enough (Lk. 17:11 ff.). Paul in almost all his epistles follows the ancient epistolary custom of a thanksgiving to the gods after the opening salutation, [294] thus showing the churches how grateful he must be to God for all that has been done among them. When in R. 7 he depicts the fruitless effort and striving of the unredeemed, and finally utters the despairing cry : "O wretched man that I am ! who shall deliver me from the body of this death ?" there immediately follows in answer a solemn thanksgiving in confession of redemption through Jesus Christ.

In the world of Pauline thinking prayer takes on a special significance to the degree that it is effected by the Spirit and can thus attest to our spirits through the address ἀββᾶ that we are the children of God (R. 8:15; cf. Gl. 4:6). Paul also experiences the suprapersonal power given by prayer when the Spirit intercedes with wordless sighing for those who cannot pray as they ought. It is an open question whether the reference is to glossolalia. [295] Certainly Paul sees in prayer an intimation and assurance of coming glory.

There was no specific gesture of prayer. Sometimes it might be kneeling as in the case of Jesus in Gethsemane or Paul on the shore at Troas (Ac. 21:5). Sometimes it might be standing (Mk. 11:25), cf. the Pharisee and publican in the temple. According to the earliest sources common prayer seems to have been the order of the day (1 C. 14:13 ff.). The saying about the closet is not directed against common prayer but against showing off in prayer. The common meals of the disciples, who can hardly have given up at once the form of communal life, demanded public prayer. Indeed, according to the saying in Mt. 18:19 a special power of intercession was promised to the praying community, which is what is meant by the "two or three," cf. v. 20.

Like the prayer of Jesus, that of the early Church was first directed to God. But faith in the exalted Lord, together with recollection of His unique intimacy

---

294 Wendland Hell. Kult., 413 f.
295 Cf. Greeven, 153 f.

with God, made possible prayer to Jesus also. [296] The application of the → κύριος of the LXX to the exalted Jesus made the process almost irresistible. Yet it is hard to detect when and in what circumstances it first appeared in detail. On the one side is the obstacle of the unchanged monotheistic belief in God, and on the other the impulse of the fact that the new Christian state and therewith the new possibility of prayer was inseparably linked with the person of Him who was known as the living and effective Head of the community. There are many intervening stages and transitions from calling on Jesus in prayer to God to direct prayer to Jesus for intercession with God. Historical apprehension of this movement will always be to some degree impossible. Yet it is important that, apart from the isolated exceptions in Rev. (5:8, 14), προσεύχεσθαι and προσκυνεῖν are never used with reference to prayer to the exalted Lord.

2. The Words Used.

In accordance with the various acts and experiences which constitute the total life of prayer, prayer itself is described by several terms taken from the dealings between man and man. In detail there are certain fairly clearcut differentiations. αἰτέω, "to want something," is never used of the prayer of Jesus (→ I, 192) but is constantly used when Jesus summons His followers to glad and fervent asking. ἐρωτάω is used for a petition to God only in John, who emphasises the fact that inner fellowship between God and His people is achieved through the One whom He sent. Here, too, it is used only once of men (1 Jn. 5:16) and elsewhere exclusively of the prayer of Jesus. Like ἐρωτάω, παρακαλέω seems to posit a diminished distance between the one who speaks and the One addressed. The demon in Mk. 5:10 shares a supernatural existence with the Son of God. Paul calls on his Lord, by whom he knows that since Damascus he has been called to preach and constantly guided, to restore to him his full powers (2 C. 12:8). Jesus could summon 12 legions of angels from His Father (Mt. 26:53). The word for grace at meals (→ εὐλογέω in the abs.) follows Jewish usage. εὐχαριστέω needs no explanation. By using κράζειν in R. 8:15; Gl. 4:6 Paul expresses the fervour of prayer, but also the fact that prayer can be uttered by men in the power of the Spirit. [297] ἐπικαλέομαι, often used in combination with ὄνομα, serves to emphasise the element of confession in Christian prayer (Ac. 9:14; 22:16; 1 C. 1:2). But since vital prayer always includes petition (cf. the Lord's Prayer), these terms are all far less common than δέομαι, δέησις. δέομαι can also be used in the NT in a secular sense, but the noun is exclusively religious and has much the same meaning as the English "prayer." When δέομαι is used for "to pray," there is almost always a petition (the exception is Ac. 10:2), but this specific sense is not so evident in the case of δέησις (e.g., Lk. 5:33; Phil. 4:6).

Along with all these ordinary terms applied to prayer, there is another word group which from the very first belongs exclusively to the religious sphere and which thus gives us the main words for prayer in the NT. To this we must now turn.

---

[296] On the worship of Jesus cf. v. d. Goltz, 95 ff.; Horst, 186 ff.; and the bibl. in A. Klawek, *Das Gebet zu Jesus* (1919), 2 ff.

[297] Cf. H. Schlier, *Religionsgeschichtliche Untersuchungen zu den Ignatiusbriefen* (1929), 144.

προσεύχομαι, προσευχή.

Constr. προσεύχεσθαί τινι, Mt. 6:6; 1 C. 11:13. The object of prayer is very occasionally in the acc. (e.g., Lk. 18:11; R. 8:26), but mostly in verbal form with ἵνα, ἵνα μή, ὅπως inf. (simple or in the gen., Jm. 5:17);[1] often with ὑπέρ, περί τινος: "intercession." In most cases προσεύχεσθαι is not more closely defined. We have the stronger προσευχῇ προσεύχεσθαι in Jm. 5:17. The gen. with προσευχή usually refers to the one praying, but once to the One addressed (Lk. 6:12; cf. πρὸς τὸν θεόν R. 15:30).

1. "To pray," "to pray to," "to ask," "prayer," "petitionary prayer." We best understand the term by differentiating it from the synonymous δέομαι, δέησις. The distinction is that δεῖσθαι almost always means real asking whereas προσεύχεσθαι is preferred if the fact of prayer is to be denoted with no narrower indication of its content (cf. the solitary prayer of Jesus). More rarely, προσεύχεσθαι can also signify petition (Jesus in Gethsemane; Col. 1:3; 2 Th. 1:11). From the very first προσεύχεσθαι means calling on God, whereas it is not always clear to whom the request is directed when δεῖσθαι is used. To distinguish the nouns is more difficult.[2] Both can mean prayer or petitionary prayer as a regular habit: Ac. 6:4: τῇ προσευχῇ ... προσκαρτερήσομεν (cf. Ac. 2:42); Eph. 6:18: ἐν πάσῃ προσκαρτερήσει καὶ δεήσει; Col. 4:2: τῇ προσευχῇ προσκαρτερεῖτε (δέησις is used in this sense only in Paul). But both can also be used for a single and complete act of prayer, Lk. 22:45: ἀναστὰς ἀπὸ τῆς προσευχῆς; Phil. 1:4: ἐν πάσῃ δεήσει ... τὴν δέησιν ποιούμενος. This is also shown by the common use of the plural, R. 1:10: ἐπὶ τῶν προσευχῶν μου; Lk. 5:33: οἱ μαθηταὶ Ἰωάννου ... δεήσεις ποιοῦνται. Thus the distinction between δέησις and προσευχή is not to be sought in the persistence or inwardness or similar features of the prayer, but solely in the content. And in spite of the interchangeability[3] there are traces of a conscious distinction in this respect. Thus εἰσηκούσθη ἡ δέησίς σου is used in Lk. 1:13 for the concrete request, implied though not expressly stated, which Zacharias makes for a son, while the pious conversation of the centurion Cornelius is described as follows: εἰσηκούσθη σου ἡ προσευχὴ καὶ αἱ ἐλεημοσύναι σου ἐμνήσθησαν ἐνώπιον τοῦ θεοῦ (Ac. 10:31). In the non-Pauline sections of the NT δέησις always means a single, concrete act, never prayer as a phenomenon of the religious life. But when we read in 1 Tm. 2:1 (cf. Jer. 11:14 LXX): ποιεῖσθαι δεήσεις. προσευχάς, ἐντεύξεις, εὐχαριστίας ὑπὲρ πάντων ἀνθρώπων ..., it is evident that the author is thinking of the whole range of prayer rather than of the distinction of individual aspects,[4] and he presents it as a ministry of intercession, though strictly εὐχαριστίας does not seem to fit this conception. Hence it is only with great reserve that we may distinguish and say that προσευχή denotes prayer comprehensively while δέησις can also have the specific sense of petitionary prayer and thus comes to have a particular nuance.

προσεύχεσθαι is found here and there in secular lit. from the time of Aesch.,[5] and with the same twofold sense as εὔχεσθαι, "to pray" and "to perform a vow." Preisigke Sammelbuch, III, 6713, 10 f. (257 B.C.): προσευξάμενος δ[ὲ] αὐ[τῶι, ἐ]ά[μ με] ὑγιάσῃι, διότι ὑπομενῶ ..., and therefore clearly a vow (completed acc. to Edgar).

π ρ ο σ ε ύ χ ο μ α ι κτλ. [1] Bl.-Debr.[6] § 400, 7.
[2] → 41. Cf. Trench, 115 ff., where there are references to older definitions. Cf. also Haupt Gefbr. on Eph. 6:18; Phil. 4:6; Loh. Phil., 170.
[3] → 806.
[4] Cf. Dib. Past., ad loc.
[5] Liddell-Scott, 1511.

Examples on inscr. occur only later, *ibid.,* I, 3740. Already in the LXX προσεύχεσθαι, which is almost always used for הִתְפַּלֵּל, occurring 69 times and εὔχεσθαι only 8, begins to replace the profanely more common εὔχεσθαι (cf. Da. LXX 6:11 with Da. Θ 6:10). The sense "to vow" found in secular Gk. drops away completely in the LXX, being restricted to εὔχεσθαι, εὐχή. This is perhaps why the NT definitely prefers προσευχ-. [6] The post-apost. fathers easily prefer προσεύχεσθαι to the much weaker εὔχεσθαι (→ 778) when speaking of prayer. Jos. uses προσεύχεσθαι only in the story of Daniel [7] (Ant., 10, 252 and 256). Philo uses it for "to pray," though only in Som., II, 139; Spec. Leg., I, 24).

2. Along with an individual act of prayer or prayer as an expression of piety, προσευχή can also be a "place of prayer," [8] especially the Jewish synagogue. [9] According to Ac. 16:13 ff. there was a synagogue at Philippi which Paul visited with his companions to preach the Gospel there to the Jews. It stood by a river, and the Christian missionaries expected to find it there. This is understandable, since it has been noted that synagogues were often built by water, presumably to make the prescribed washings easier (Jos. Ant., 14, 258; [10] P. Tebt., I, 86, 17; 29). [11]

προσευχή is rare in secular Gk., and was thought to occur only in Jewish texts or texts under Jewish influence. [12] In its Doric form, however, it has now been found on an inscr. in the temple of Aesculapius in Epidaurus (IG, IV, 1, *editio minor,* 106, line 27, 4th cent. B.C.): τᾶς ποτευχᾶς (= τῆς προσευχῆς) καὶ τοῦ βωμοῦ. Jewish influence is unlikely. The use with βωμός indicates a concrete sense, i.e., a "place of prayer." Philo uses the word only in this sense. In Jos. it can also mean "prayer," e.g., Bell., 5, 388; Ap., II, 10 (a quotation). The canonical books of the LXX, like the post-apostolic fathers, use προσευχή only for prayer (almost always for תְּפִלָּה); though cf. 3 Macc. 7:20.

Greeven

---

† εὐωδία

In secular Gk. this always bears the literal sense (from εὐώδης, "sweet-smelling" [Homer, e.g., Od., 5, 64]) of "sweet smell," the "scent" of a person or thing which is

---

[6] Cf. W. M. Ramsay, Exp. T., 10 (1898/99), 13: "Was εὐχή felt to be too much connected with the idea of a vow and a gift promised to God?"

[7] For an exhaustive discussion of the usage in Jos. cf. A. Schlatter, "Wie sprach Jos. von Gott?" BFTh, 14 (1910), 73 ff.

[8] On the change of meaning cf. προσβολή "harbour" or συναγωγή "place of assembly." P. Glaue, *Die Vorlesung hl. Schriften im Gottesdienste* (1907), 5, conjectures that προσ-ευχή is a simpler type of συναγωγή, cf. also Zn. Ag., 571 f. and for a different view S. Zarb, "De Iudaeorum προσευχῇ in Act. 16:13, 16," *Angelicum,* 5 (1928), 91 ff., 105 ff.

[9] Pr. Ag. on 16:13; Schürer, II, 499 f., 517 ff.; Deissmann NB, 49 f.; Jacquier, *op. cit.,* 487 f.

[10] Here, however, the meaning is disputed (Schlatter: "Perhaps to hold prayers rather than to build a synagogue").

[11] Ignorance of this fact has produced all kinds of alterations of the text of Ac. 16:13.

[12] Cr.-Kö., 459; examples in Schürer, II, 499, n. 4. The much mutilated inscr. of Olbia on the Black Sea (CIG, II, 2079), which is adduced in Schürer, II, 517, n. 59, yields no certain results and may well be under Jewish influence.

εὐωδία. Apart from the comm. on 2 C. 2:14 f. cf. E. Lohmeyer, "Vom göttlichen Wohlgeruch," SAH, 10 (1919), 9; E. Nestle, ZNW, 4 (1903), 272; 7 (1906), 95 f.; H. Vorwahl, ARW, 31 (1934), 400 f.; Reitzenstein Ir. Erl., 34; Hell. Myst., 82; 393 ff.; A. Harnack, ZKG, 2 (1878), 291 ff.

found to be pleasant (often in the plur.): Aristot. Rhet., I, 11, p. 1370a, 24; Xenoph. Sym., 2, 3. Of plants and fruits, Aristot. Περὶ θαυμασίων ἀκουσμάτων, 82, p. 836b, 17; 113, p. 841a, 13; Plut. Quaest. Nat., 23 (II, 917 f.); Quaest. Conv., III, 1, 1 (II, 645 f.); V, 8, 1 (II, 683c); of wine, Plut. Quaest. Conv., V, 3, 1 (II, 676c); of a healing ointment, Ael. Arist., 49, 22; of the atmosphere (e.g., in the dwelling-place of the deity), Plut. Fac. Lun., 26 (II, 941 f.); in the place of the oracle, Plut. Def. Orac., 50 (II, 437c); in the land of Lethe, Plut. Ser. Num. Pun., 27 (II, 565 f.), and finally for man's breath in speaking, Plut. Def. Orac., 21 (II, 421b); Alex., 4, 2 (I, 666bc). εὐωδία is also used in relation to cultic incense, Diod. S., I, 84, 6; cf. Ostraka, I, § 53.

In the Septuagint it is usually found in the phrase ὀσμὴ εὐωδίας for רֵיחַ (הַ)נִּיחֹחַ (of the prophets only Ezekiel uses the expression). As in Gn. 8:21 the reference is mostly to the sweet smell of the burnt offering, cf. esp. Lv. and Nu. 15; 28; 29 where the thought is of the acceptability of the sacrifice to God. While the Rabbis changed רֵיחַ (הַ)נִּיחֹחַ to נַחַת רוּחַ, "good-pleasure" (e.g., S. Nu. § 107 on 15:7; § 118 on 18:17; § 143 on 28:8), [1] the LXX took no offence at the anthropomorphism of the OT expression. Its rendering of רֵיחַ (ה)נִיחֹחַ has the stem ὀδ- twice, as distinct from the Heb. original. [2] It also shows that no attention was paid in the translation to a dogmatically significant understanding of נִיחֹחַ (i.e., "satisfying," in the sense of "appeasing" the wrath of God). [3] The literal sense merges into a figurative, [4] e.g., in Sir. 24:15, where personified wisdom says of itself: ὡς κιννάμωμον (cinnamon) καὶ ἀσπάλαθος (spiced shrub) ἀρωμάτων δέδωκα ὀσμήν, καὶ ὡς σμύρνα ἐκλεκτὴ διέδωκα εὐωδίαν. [5]

Philo, along with the literal (e.g., Leg. All., I, 42; Op. Mund., 165), has a similar figur. use: καθάπερ ... τὰ ἐκθυμιώμενα τῶν ἀρωμάτων εὐωδίας τοὺς πλησιάζοντας ἀναπίμπλησι, τὸν αὐτὸν τρόπον ὅσοι γείτονες καὶ ὅμοροι σοφοῦ, τῆς ἀπ' αὐτοῦ σπῶντες αὔρας ὅτι μήκιστον χεομένης βελτιοῦνται τὰ ἤθη, Som. I, 178; the influence for good which the wise exert on their environment is compared to the invisible yet irresistible outflowing of a sweet scent.

1. In the NT there are two or three passages in which the sense of εὐωδία is both linguistically (ὀσμὴ εὐωδίας) and materially connected with the sacrificial context well known from the OT. In Eph. 5:2 the sacrifice of Christ and in Phil. 4:18 the loving gift of the congregation to Paul are described as ὀσμὴ εὐωδίας, in both cases with the material though not the grammatical object τῷ θεῷ. In Phil. the parallel expressions θυσία δεκτή and εὐάρεστος τῷ θεῷ reinforce a sense corresponding to OT usage, the sweet savour being that which induces the good-pleasure of God. What is directly perceptible in the OT system is here applied in a close material parallel to that which is no longer within the limits of the prescribed ritual. [6]

2. The meaning is not quite so clear in 2 C. 2:14 f. According to what precedes, Paul begins by magnifying the apostolic office: τῷ δὲ θεῷ χάρις τῷ πάντοτε θριαμβεύοντι ἡμᾶς ἐν τῷ Χριστῷ καὶ τὴν ὀσμὴν τῆς γνώσεως αὐτοῦ φανεροῦντι δι' ἡμῶν ἐν παντὶ τόπῳ· ὅτι Χριστοῦ εὐωδία ἐσμὲν τῷ θεῷ ἐν τοῖς

---

[1] I owe this reference to K. G. Kuhn.

[2] Perhaps to be explained simply by the similarity of sound.

[3] O. Procksch, Die Genesis[2, 3] (1924), 69 on Gn. 8:21.

[4] On religio-historical interconnections cf. Lohmeyer, op. cit., passim.

[5] Here we have a figurative intermingling of the old idea that Paradise (= the garden) is full of fragrance with the association of sweet fragrance with the self-declaration of the Godhead. On both ideas cf. Lohmeyer, op. cit., passim.

[6] Cf. on this pt. Athenag. Suppl., 13, 1: ὁ τοῦδε τοῦ παντὸς δημιουργὸς καὶ πατὴρ οὐ δεῖται αἵματος οὐδὲ κνίσης (fat of sacrifice) οὐδὲ τῆς ἀπὸ τῶν ἀνθῶν καὶ θυμιαμάτων εὐωδίας, αὐτὸς ὢν ἡ τελεία εὐωδία, ἀνενδεὴς καὶ ἀπροσδεής. The rejection of the whole circle of religious ideas linked with εὐωδία leads to the assertion that God Himself is perfect τελεία εὐωδία [I owe this reference to G. Bertram].

σωζομένοις καὶ ἐν τοῖς ἀπολλυμένοις, οἷς μὲν ὀσμὴ ἐκ θανάτου εἰς θάνατον, οἷς δὲ ὀσμὴ ἐκ ζωῆς εἰς ζωήν. The frequently [7] asserted connection between the apostolic declaration Χριστοῦ εὐωδία ἐσμέν and the sweet savours which accompanied the ancient triumphal procession [8] has the disadvantage that it makes the expression purely metaphorical and dispenses with any concrete or material sense. Furthermore, it does not adequately explain the plainly stated power of the εὐωδία to salvation or perdition. For the same reasons the idea that the εὐωδία refers to an anointing of the apostle (cf. 2 C. 1:21) [9] is not of itself adequate. [10]

According to the two passages discussed under 1. an interpretation which connects the image with the thought of sacrifice is in keeping with Pauline usage. The peculiar expression in which the apostle calls himself εὐωδία (in distinction from 14b) is also explained if we take it [11] that Paul is applying the thought of sacrifice to himself and therefore, as in R. 15:16, describing himself and his apostolic calling in terms of a living sacrifice offered to God. On this interpretation, of course, we lose the inner connection of the image with that of the ὀσμὴ τῆς γνώσεως which precedes, and no explanation is advanced of the element of decision so plainly asserted of the savour in v. 15b.

Nevertheless, if in terms of the whole context we see in the personal statement a material parallel to v. 14, so that here, as in v. 15b, the εὐωδία has the Gospel proclaimed by Paul as its material background, [12] we are given the clear picture, found in Judaism also [13] under the same image of "savour," of the power for death or destruction of the Word proclaimed by divine commission. In this passage the word εὐωδία is clearly determined in content by the appositive or explicative gen. [14] τοῦ Χριστοῦ.

If the obj. τῷ θεῷ basically rules out the non-Jewish idea that εὐωδία might be a direct term for the approach or manifestation of God, [15] it is still true that in the religious speech and thinking not merely of the world outside the OT but also of the Christian religion [16] the sweet smell is one of the constant perceptible marks of the invasion of the terrestrial world by the supraterrestrial.   *Stumpff*

---

[7] Cf. *ad loc.* P. W. Schmiedel (1891); Heinr. Sendschr., II and 2 K.; Wnd. 2 K.; W. Bousset in Schr. NT, II; also Schl. K., 495 f.

[8] For examples, cf. Ltzm. K., *ad loc.*

[9] For later examples cf. Wnd. 2 K. *ad loc.*; also Lohmeyer, *op. cit.*, 33 f.

[10] The suggestion in Heinr. Sendschr., II and 2 K., *ad loc.* that the *tertium comparationis* is to be found in the pervasive and irresistible character of the scent (cf. also Bchm. K., *ad loc.*) is tempting, but there is no real support for it, not even in Plat. Resp., IX, 584b.

[11] Schl. K., 495 f.

[12] τὸ κήρυγμα οὐράνιόν ἐστιν μύρον is also the early exposition as found in Cram. Cat. on 2 C. 2:14 [G. Bertram].

[13] R. Jehoshua' b Levi (3rd cent. A.D.) says (Joma, 72b): וזאת התורה אשר שם משה. ‏(Dt. 4:44) :‏ זכה נעשית לו כם חיים לא זכה נעשית לו סם מיתה. והיינו דאמר רבא: דאומן לה סמא דחייא דלא אומן לה סמא דמותא "It is said: And this is the law which Moses laid down; if he has made himself worthy, it is for him a mixture of life, and if not it is for him a mixture of death. This is what the Raba said: For him who rightly devotes himself to it, it is a mixture of life; for him who does not rightly devote himself to it, it is a mixture of death." Lohmeyer, *op. cit.*, 33, n. 1 uses "balsam" for the same word ס‏ם in Taan., 7a.

[14] A fragrance wafted or filled by Christ: P. W. Schmiedel (1891), Heinr. Sendschr., II and 2 K., Bchm. K., *ad loc.*

[15] For examples of this use of the image outside the OT cf. Lohmeyer, 4 ff. → n. 6.

[16] Thus, e.g., the terms "perfume," "knowledge" and "life" are normative in early interpretation of the story of the anointing in Mk. 14:3 ff., cf. Cl. Al. Paed., II, 8, 61 and as early as Ign. Eph., 17, 1 [G. Bertram]. Cf. esp. the significance of the sweet scent in the death of martyrs — a new form of the old idea of sacrifice (Harnack, *op. cit.*, passim).

ἐφάπαξ → I, 383

| ἐχθρός, ἔχθρα | → μισέω. |

Of the related word groups μῖσος, ἔχθρα, πόλεμος, μῖσος denotes the inner disposition from which hostility arises, i.e., "hatred," ἔχθρα means "hostility" as such, irrespective of the underlying disposition or of its manifestation or otherwise in visible form,
and πόλεμος means "war" as the expression of hostility between states and govern-
ments. In the case of μῖσος the only other form is the verb μισέω, while ἔχθρα yields
the common adj./subst. ἐχθρός and the less common verbs ἐχθαίρω, ἐχθρεύω and
ἐχθραίνω, and πόλεμος the adj./subst. πολέμιος and the verb πολεμέω.

The Hebrew usage is much the same. For μῖσος and μισέω we have שָׂנֵא and שִׂנְאָה,
though the part. שֹׂנֵא can also be used as a subst. (LXX μισῶν). The verb אָיַב is rare
apart from the part. אֹיֵב, but אוֹיֵב, used as a subst., denotes both the personal and the
national enemy and thus embraces both πολέμιος and ἐχθρός. אֵיבָה corresponds to
ἔχθρα. For πολεμεῖν we have נִלְחַם, and for the subst. מִלְחָמָה. In keeping with Heb. and
the predominant usage of the LXX the NT does not have πολέμιος or a verb of the
stem εχθ-.

† ἐχθρός.

A. ἐχθρός outside the NT.

In secular Gk. Hom. has only the pass. "hated." The act. first occurs in Hes. and
Pind.: [1] "the hater," "the enemy," "the opponent." In general the active sense predominates, as does also the reference to personal enmity, yet the pass. and the application to
national foes are still found at the time of the NT. With some restriction for his own
purposes, Plut. defines (Superst., 11 [II, 170d/e]): τοὺς κακῶς ἡμᾶς λέγοντας ἐχθροὺς νομίζομεν, ὡς καὶ ἀπίστους καὶ κακῶς φρονοῦντας, and also: μισῶν δὲ
θεοὺς καὶ φοβούμενος ἐχθρός ἐστι. In his work Πῶς ἄν τις ὑπ' ἐχθρῶν ὠφελοῖτο
(II, 86 ff.) Plut. refers only to personal enmity. Yet impersonal hostility cannot always
be separated from it, e.g., Plut.Apophth., Pompeius, 3 (II, 203d): τοῦτον (the guilty)
δὲ αὐτὸν εἶναι τοὺς μὲν φίλους πείσαντα, τοὺς δὲ ἐχθροὺς βιασάμενον ἑλέσθαι
τὰ Μαρίου. ἐχθρός is used for the enemy in war, e.g., Plut. Apophth. Lac., Lycurg., 24
(II, 228d): ὅπως πλείω τοὺς ἐχθροὺς βλάπτοιμεν.

In the LXX ἐχθρός is almost always used for אוֹיֵב, though sometimes for צַר [צֹרֵר]. [2]
Conversely, אוֹיֵב is almost always rendered ἐχθρός, though with other derivatives of
εχθ- we also have ὑπεναντίος 8 times and once each πολέμιος (Est. 9:16), ἀντικεί-
μενος (Is. 66:6), ἀπειθῶν (Is. 66:14). It is striking how often πολέμιος is avoided. In
the canonical books it is found only at Est. 9:16 for אֹיֵב, 1 Ch. 18:10 (ἀνὴρ πολέμιος for
אִישׁ מִלְחָמוֹת), and, with ἐχθρός, 2 Ἐσδρ. 8:31 for אוֹיֵב. Yet it is common in the
apocryphal writings, e.g., Sir. 46:3 for מִלְחָמָה [?]. ἐχθρός is found 13 times in 1 Macc.
and πολέμιος 3 (4) times. In 2 Macc. we have ἐχθρός once, πολέμιος 16 times; in
3 Macc. ἐχθρός 6 times and πολέμιος twice; in 4 Macc. ἐχθρός 3 times and πολέμιος 9. In other apocryphal books we always have ἐχθρός up to Sir. 46:3. Probably

---

ἐ χ θ ρ ό ς. A. Bertholet, *Biblische Theologie des AT*, II : *Die jüd. Religion von der Zeit
Esras bis zum Zeitalter Christi* (1911), 188, 247; B. Weiss, *Lehrbuch der bibl. Theol. des
NT* (1903), 307 f.; H. Weinel, *Biblische Theologie des NT*⁴ (1928), 226; Cr.-Kö., 459 f.

[1] For examples v. Liddell-Scott, s.v.

[2] It is also used for ארב ,אֵיבָה (twice), גּוֹי (ψ 105:41, only in some MSS), זָר, מת ,צמת ,צר ,צמת
hi.

there lies behind this shift an alteration in the Heb., which in later writings adopts אִישׁ מִלְחָמָה and other expressions instead of אוֹיֵב.

While the Heb. אוֹיֵב denotes both personal and national enemies, ἐχθρός has more of the sense of personal hostility. The word is used in the LXX for a. enemies in war among the Gentiles, e.g., 1 Βασ. 29:8; Na. 3:11, 13, and personal enemies in daily life, Ex. 23:4; Nu. 35:23; b. the nations, i.e., the Gentiles, around Israel who are opponents of Israel or its king; c. the enemies of the righteous; d. the enemies of God. The root of the usage is to be found in the fact that the relation between Israel and the Gentiles is not a purely political relation which may change from friendship to war and *vice versa*, so that the Gentiles are πολέμιοι only in times of war and φίλοι in days of peace; the relation is one of constant opposition which can express itself only in wars and other forms of enmity. Thus the enemy of Israel is the enemy of God, Ex. 23:22. Defeat of Israel brings dishonour to God, Jos. 7:8. David's adultery gives cause for the enemies of the Lord [3] to blaspheme, 2 Βασ. 12:14. God's attitude to Israel is reflected in victory or defeat, Ju. 2:14, 18 etc. In Is. 1:24 we have the transition from an enmity which is partly religious and partly national to one which is purely religious, the reference being to God's enemies within Israel. This trend is developed further in the piety of the Psalter, where the opposition is between the righteous and the ungodly, ψ 6:10 f.; 54:3 f. (ἐταράχθην ἀπὸ φωνῆς ἐχθροῦ καὶ ἀπὸ θλίψεως ἁμαρτωλοῦ), and the ungodly is the enemy of God, ψ 36:20. Liberation from enemies and their destruction are thus an expression of hope: Μειχ. 5:9; Is. 62:8; Nu. 24:18; ψ 109:1 f.; 131:18. If the LXX desired a single term for the Heb. אוֹיֵב, the one adapted for the purpose was ἐχθρός, since it denotes hostility as such.

In the Rabbis the stem איב is far less common than שׂנא. The old religious and national opposition is naturally still present, S. Dt., 171 on 18:10 = jSanh., 26b: "He who marries a Syrian begets an enemy of God" (אויב למקום) [4] When something unfavourable has to be said about Israel, recourse is had to the euphemism שׂונאי ישראל, e.g., bShab., 33. Elsewhere "hatred" is declared against idolaters and the עמי הארץ, [5] and Test. XII prophesies concerning the ἐχθροί who will oppress and lead away the disobedient people. [6] Highly relevant are the expositions of Ex. 23:4, where Rabbis refer the expression אֹיֵב to idolaters (national opposition on the religious side), to apostate proselytes, to renegade Israelites and finally to the Israelites themselves, M. Ex. on 23:4. [7] The last interpretation is also found in bPes., 113b on the ground that if one sees something shameful in an Israelite one must "hate" him (acc. to Prv. 8:13). This brings us to enmities within the people. Hatred, or more exactly unjustifiable hatred, is forbidden. It corrupts the people, leads to the destruction of Herod's temple, and produces idolatry, licentiousness and bloodshed. [8] Yet the very expression "unjustifiable hatred" (שׂנאת חנם) shows that there is another kind, as may be seen in Ab. R. Nat., 16, [9] where we read of legitimate hatred of Epicureans, of seducers and of traitors (on the basis of Ps. 139:21), i.e., of enemies

---

[3] The reference, of course, is not simply to the Ammonites with whom David was then at war but to the Gentiles as standing enemies of Israel and of God.

[4] Schl. Theol. d. Judt., 40, n. 2.

[5] Str.-B., I, 359 ff., 366 f.

[6] Test. L. 13:8; Jud. 23:3; Iss. 6:2; Zeb. 9:6; N. 4:2; A. 7:2.

[7] Str.-B., I, 368 f.

[8] Ab., 2, 11; S. Dt., 186 f. on 19:11; Ab. R. Nat., 12; bShab., 32b/33a (Str.-B., I, 364 f.), bJoma, 9a.

[9] Str.-B., I, 365.

in the OT religious sense. We are not, therefore, surprised to find such contradictory statements as that in Derekh Erez (R. Eliezer, 90 A.D.): "He who hates his brother is to be reckoned among those who shed blood," and bJoma, 22b : "A rabbinic scholar who does not bear hatred is no rabbinic scholar." [10] איב and שנא are applied to the relationship between Israel and God, e.g., bShab., 116a : [11] The books of the Minim bring קנאה ואיבה ותחרות between Israel and their Father in heaven. Often, as in this passage, it is a single individual or group which disturbs the relationship between the whole people and God. [12]

Joseph. gives evidence of Rabbinic influence when he opposes ὁμόφυλος and ἐχθρός in Vit., 128. But when in Ant., 9, 282 he says that Jeroboam εἰς τὸ θεῖον ἐξαμαρτὼν ἐχθρὸν αὐτοῖς τοῦτο ἐποίησε μιμησαμένοις τὴν ἐκείνου παρανομίαν (cf. Ant., 4, 190; 6, 156), he sets aside the Rabbinic formulation of enmity between God and Israel with its suggestion of disturbance of the covenant relationship, and he substitutes for it the notion current among the Gks. The Gks. often spoke of men being the enemies of God, both in the act. and the pass. Thus Plut. Superst., 11 (II, 170d) says of the superstitious : μισῶν δὲ θεοὺς καὶ φοβούμενος ἐχθρός ἐστι, "he is the enemy of the gods"; and the common θεοῖς ἐχθρός is a sharp reproach with its sense of "hated by the gods" : Epict. Diss., III, 22, 91: "When anyone asks Diogenes whether he believes in the gods, he receives the answer : καὶ πῶς ... σὲ θεοῖς ἐχθρὸν νομίζων;" Cf. also Plut. Comm. Not., 12, 5 (II, 1064e): ἄδικοι καὶ παράνομοι καὶ θεοῖς ἐχθροὶ καὶ κακοδαίμονες. Of κακία we also read in Plut., ibid., 14 (II, 1065e) that it is θεοῖς ἐχθρὸν καὶ θεομισές. There is a similar expression in Philo Mut. Nom., 30 : ἐχθρὸν γὰρ θεῷ κακία, but Philo uses ἐχθρός specifically to denote the incompatibility of virtue and vice, Fug., 14 : ὄντως ἐστὶν ἐχθρὸν φύσει παιδεία ἀπαιδευσίᾳ καὶ φιλοπονία ἀμελετησίᾳ.

In the Pseudepigrapha ἐχθρός often means the devil. [13] The Rabbis took the enemy of Prv. 25:21 f. to be "evil impulse." [14]

B. ἐχθρός in the NT.

In the NT ἐχθρός is used for personal enemies in the various relationships of everyday life (R. 12:20, a quotation ; Gl. 4:16). More important is the use which follows the OT and the LXX. Thus ἐχθρός can be used for the foes of Israel. In the song of Zacharias in Lk. 1:71, 74 it is expected that the time of salvation will bring deliverance from enemies who now prevent us from serving God "without fear." The same sense is found in a different connection, namely, in the prophecy of the destruction of Jerusalem, in Lk. 19:43. Rev. speaks of the enemies of the NT witnesses to God in 11:5, 12, and ἐχθρός is used in the same way in the saying concerning family division in the days of final decision (Mt. 10:36). [15] ἐχθρός is particularly used, however, for what is hostile to God and His Christ, as in Lk. 19:27: τοὺς ἐχθρούς μου τούτους τοὺς μὴ θελήσαντάς με βασιλεῦσαι ἐπ᾽ αὐτοὺς ἀγάγετε ὧδε; Phil. 3:18 : τοὺς ἐχθροὺς τοῦ σταυροῦ τοῦ Χριστοῦ;

---

[10] Both passages are quoted in Str.-B., I, 365.
[11] R. Ismael, 2nd generation of the Tannaites.
[12] Though cf. Pesikt. § 125 : When Israel said, This is thy god, O Israel (Ex. 32:4), they became the enemies of God (נעשׂו שׂונאים להקב״ה).
[13] Test. D. 6:3 f.; Apc. Mos. 2; 7; 25; 28; Vit. Ad., 17; Gr. Bar. 13:2. V. Ryssel in Kautzsch Apkr. u. Pseudepigr., ad loc., refers Sir. 25:15 : οὐκ ἔστιν κεφαλή (for ראשׁ "poison") ὑπὲρ κεφαλὴν ὄφεως, καὶ οὐκ ἔστιν θυμὸς ὑπὲρ θυμὸν ἐχθροῦ, to the fall, cf. Sir. 25:24. In this case we should have a 2nd century instance of ἐχθρός for the devil. But this interpretation is open to question.
[14] For examples cf. Str.-B., III, 302.
[15] Quoted from Mi. 7:6; cf. Sota, 9, 15.

Ac. 13:10 : ἐχθρὲ πάσης δικαιοσύνης. In this connection we should also mention the many passages which quote Ps. 110:1, e.g., Mk. 12:36 par.; Ac. 2:34 f.; 1 C. 15:25; Hb. 1:13; 10:13. Paul in 1 C. 15:25 (adding πάντας), 26 refers the passage explicitly to all the powers hostile to God, including death.

It is with this reference to enemies of God and His people that ἐχθρός is used in Mt. 5:43 f. par.: ἠκούσατε ὅτι ἐρρέθη· ἀγαπήσεις τὸν πλησίον σου καὶ μισήσεις τὸν ἐχθρόν σου. ἐγὼ δὲ λέγω ὑμῖν, ἀγαπᾶτε τοὺς ἐχθροὺς ὑμῶν καὶ προσεύχεσθε ὑπὲρ τῶν διωκόντων ὑμᾶς. The enemy here is obviously parallel to the persecutor, and ἐχθρός is set in antithesis to the πλησίον, the fellow-countryman and fellow-believer. Moreover, there are many commands to hate national enemies in the OT, e.g., the command to exterminate the Canaanites, [16] as well as passages like Ps. 31:6a HT; 139:21 f.: תַּכְלִית שִׂנְאָה שְׂנֵאתִים לְאֹיְבִים הָיוּ לִי. It is the widespread view of Rabbinic Judaism that the enemy, i.e., the ungodly, the Epicurean or whoever else it might be, is to be hated, and this is in keeping with OT teaching. Possibly we find the same view reflected in 2 Th. 3:15 : καὶ μὴ ὡς ἐχθρὸν ἡγεῖσθε, ἀλλὰ νουθετεῖτε ὡς ἀδελφόν. Here the ἐχθρός is not a personal enemy but the enemy of the community as distinct from the ἀδελφός. Paul's order to avoid the disobedient might otherwise be wrongly taken to mean that he is to be regarded as an enemy.

ἐχθρός is also used to describe the relationship of the natural man to God. R. 5:10 : ἐχθροὶ ὄντες κατηλλάγημεν τῷ θεῷ; Col. 1:21: ὑμᾶς ποτε ὄντας ἀπηλλοτριωμένους καὶ ἐχθροὺς τῇ διανοίᾳ ἐν τοῖς ἔργοις τοῖς πονηροῖς ... ἀποκατήλλαξεν; R. 11:28 : κατὰ μὲν τὸ εὐαγγέλιον ἐχθροὶ δι' ὑμᾶς, κατὰ δὲ τὴν ἐκλογὴν ἀγαπητοὶ διὰ τοὺς πατέρας; Jm. 4:4 : ὃς ἐὰν οὖν βουληθῇ φίλος εἶναι τοῦ κόσμου, ἐχθρὸς τοῦ θεοῦ καθίσταται. On closer inspection, however, we find that the usage varies. In R. 11 ἐχθρός is pass. This is shown not merely by the pass. ἀγαπητοί but also by the δι' ὑμᾶς. The Jews are not "hinderers of the spread of the Gospel" [17] for the sake of the Gentiles. In the whole passage Paul is considering the τέλος of the rejection of Israel. He has in view the attitude of God rather than man. [18] Yet this passage does not decide the others. In these ἐχθρός is act. For Paul's intention in R. 5 is to show the greatness of the divine grace of forgiveness manifested towards those who in their conduct are the enemies of God. A similar result is established by the τῇ διανοίᾳ ("in their mind") of Col. 1:21, and we obviously have an act. in Jm. 4:4, since the antithetical φιλία τοῦ κόσμου clearly means love of the world rather than the friendship shown by the world.

ἐχθρός is finally used for the devil in the parable of the wheat and the tares in Mt. 13:24 ff. and in Lk. 10:19 : δέδωκα ὑμῖν τὴν ἐξουσίαν ... ἐπὶ πᾶσαν τὴν δύναμιν τοῦ ἐχθροῦ. [19] There are parallels for this usage in the Pseudepigrapha, → 813. The devil is the enemy in the absolute sense. He is the enemy both of men and also of God and His kingdom.

---

[16] Schl. Mt., ad loc.; cf. W. C. Allen, St. Mt. in ICC³ (1922), ad loc. We cannot follow Zn. Mt., who argues that in this whole section of the Sermon on the Mount Jesus is contending against the truncation of the OT command by the maxims of the fathers. Cf. P. Fiebig, ThStKr, 91 (1918), 30-64.

[17] So Zn. R., ad loc. In Cr.-Kö., too, ἐχθρός is here taken in the act., but a different view is to be found in A. Schlatter, Gottes Gerechtigkeit (1935), 328.

[18] Though the ἀπιστία of the Jews is not overlooked.

[19] This usage is vigorously taken up in the apocryphal acts, cf. the Index to the ed. of Lipsius and Bonnet.

† ἔχθρα.

"Hatred," "hostility," as an inner disposition, as objective opposition and as actual conflict between nations, groups and individuals. Thuc., II, 68, 2 : ἔχθρα δὲ πρὸς τοὺς Ἀργείους ἀπὸ τοῦδε αὐτοῖς ἤρξατο πρῶτον γενέσθαι; Hdt., 5, 81: Αἰγινῆται ... ἔχθρης παλαιῆς ἀναμνησθέντες ἐχούσης ἐς Ἀθηναίους; Thuc., III, 10, 4 : ἑωρῶμεν αὐτοὺς τὴν μὲν τοῦ Μήδου ἔχθραν ἀνιέντας; Aristoph. Pax, 133 : ἦλθεν κατ' ἔχθραν ἀετοῦ πάλαι ποτέ.

It is not common in the LXX. In the canonical books it is mostly used for hatred and enmity between individuals, in the apocryphal books for hatred and enmity between nations. 1 Macc. 13:6 : συνήχθησαν πάντα τὰ ἔθνη ἐκτρῖψαι ἡμᾶς ἔχθρας χάριν; of the disposition, 4 Macc. 2:13 : καὶ ἔχθραν ὁ λογισμὸς ἐπικρατεῖν δύναται; of God's enmity against the sinful people, Is. 63:10 : ἐστράφη αὐτοῖς εἰς ἔχθραν. The pass. means embroilment in enmity, Prv. 25:10 : ἡ δὲ μάχη σου καὶ ἡ ἔχθρα οὐκ ἀπέσται, ἀλλ' ἔσται σοι ἴση θανάτῳ.

In the Rabbis שנאת הבריות is hatred of men, Ab., 2, 11; one who hates is one who for three days does not speak with someone באיבה, Sanh., 3, 5. For enmity between God and man → ἐχθρός.

In the NT ἔχθρα (in the plur. instances of ἔχθρα) as enmity between men is one of the works of the flesh along with ἔρις, ζῆλος, θυμοί (Gl. 5:20); cf. also Herod and Pilate in Lk. 23:12. In particular cf. Eph. 2:14 : τὸ μεσότοιχον τοῦ φραγμοῦ λύσας, τὴν ἔχθραν, and v. 16 : ἀποκτείνας τὴν ἔχθραν ἐν αὐτῷ. [1] The Law means enmity for man, i.e., enmity between men and enmity against God (not God's enmity against us as in Gl. 3:10, but ours against God as in R. 8:7). Cf. R. 8:7: τὸ φρόνημα τῆς σαρκὸς ἔχθρα εἰς θεόν, "is enmity against God." Jm. 4:4 : ἡ φιλία τοῦ κόσμου ἔχθρα τοῦ θεοῦ ἐστιν, "is hatred of God."

Foerster

---

† ἔχιδνα

"Poisonous serpent" (adder or viper). ἐχίδνης ἰός, Soph. Trach., 771. Its poisonous and dreadful character is presupposed, e.g., Hdt., III, 109; Demosth. Or., 25, 52 and 96 (ἔχις), and is often emphasised by the addition of δεινός (Hes. Theog., 299; Aesch. Choeph., 249; Soph. Trach., 1099).

In the NT it occurs only at Ac. 28:3 : ἔχιδνα ... καθῆψεν τῆς χειρός : "it fastened on his hand," [1] and in addresses to the Pharisees, Mt. 3:7 Lk. par.; Mt. 12:34; 23:33. It does not occur in the LXX, though we find it for אֶפְעֶה, in 'A Is. 59:5, and the related ἔχις is used for פֶּתֶן in Sir. 39:30. Since the current ὄφις is avoided and ἔχιδνα is constant in its use, the poison of the snake is an essential element in the metaphor. It is of the nature of the serpent [2] to be evil and destructive, hence the questions : πῶς δύνασθε ἀγαθὰ λαλεῖν πονηροὶ ὄντες; (Mt. 12:34); πῶς φύγητε ἀπὸ τῆς κρίσεως τῆς γεέννης; (Mt. 23:33), or τίς ὑπέδειξεν ὑμῖν φυγεῖν ...; (Mt. 3:7 par. Lk. 3:7).

ἔ χ θ ρ α. For bibl. → ἐχθρός.
[1] → εἰρήνη, 415.
ἔ χ ι δ ν α. The comm.; E. Nestle, ZNW, 14 (1913), 267 f.
[1] On καθάπτω v. Pr.-Bauer, s.v.
[2] γεννήματα emphasises the fact that this manner is part of their nature ; it is in their blood as in that of their fathers. Cf. Schl. Mt. and Zn. Mt. on 3:7.

In view of the plur. we are not to think of the serpent of Paradise, though of the many ideas associated with the poisonous snake there may be some influence of the fact that it is repulsive [3] and that it is to be radically opposed and destroyed. [4] On the other hand, there is little suggestion of the contrast between the outer smoothness and the inner malignity of the serpent, [5] nor of its cleverness and cunning, [6] nor is any particular part played by the general propensity of snakes to conceal themselves.

Foerster

ἔχω, ἀντέχομαι, ἀπέχω, ἐνέχω, ἔνοχος, κατέχω, μετέχω, μετοχή, μέτοχος, νουνεχῶς, συμμέτοχος [1]   → ἀνέχω, ἀνεκτός, ἀνοχή, σχῆμα, ἕξις.

ἔχω († νουνεχῶς).

A. ἔχειν in Secular Usage.

A glance at the dictionaries shows the astonishing range of meaning possessed by the Greek word ἔχειν. [2] This wealth is for the most part reflected in the NT.

The oldest depiction of it we owe to Aristotle. For him "having" was one of his 10 categories, and he thus examined the word thoroughly in Metaph., IV, 23, p. 1023a, 8 ff., and listed the various meanings. He did not arrange the material logically, but simply gave a list. The same is true of the parallel description in Cat., 15, p. 15b, 17 ff. [3] The many meanings follow two main directions, the first spatial and the second legal, denoting possession. In the first case, we have the sense "to have in, on, around, with

---

[3] Schl. Mt. on 3:7.

[4] Hence the question how they can escape the judgment of hell.

[5] H. J. Holtzmann, *Die Synoptiker*[3] (1901) on Mt. 3:7.

[6] Str.-B., I, 574: Cant. r. on 2:14: "cunning as serpents (כנחשים = ὄφεις). This interpretation is a common one.

ἔ χ ω. The following art. is based on the author's dissertation *Gott haben. Eine religions- und begriffsgeschichtliche Untersuchung zu 1 Jn. 2:23 und 2 Jn. 9*, where the instances are given in full and there is more extended discussion of detailed points.

[1] Apart from the compounds treated there are many others in the NT, but these are of less importance theologically. There are compounds with almost every preposition (cf. the similar series with λαμβάνειν). In the NT there is usually a development of one of the possible meanings, e.g., ἐπέχειν (also προσέχειν), "to direct one's attention to"; παρέχειν, "to put forward" (further developed to "to prepare"); περιέχειν, in a sense which is rare elsewhere, "to contain," of a vessel and its contents, also cosmically, though in Lk. 5:9 we have κατέχειν (1 Pt. 2:6, and Ac. 8:32 περιοχή, the technical term for a quotation); προέχεσθαι (only R. 3:9), "to have before," i.e., "to have shown or to know beforehand," a remarkable med.; συνέχειν, "to oppress," also "to torment," though lit. in Ac. 7:57 "to hold to(gether)," and cf. Ac. 18:5, "to be filled or pressed by"; συνοχή, "distress," "anguish"; ὑπερέχειν, "to have power" and "to surpass," hence ὑπεροχή, "power" and "superiority." It is remarkable how often we get the sense of "to hold fast to the word," Phil. 2:16; 1 Tm. 4:16 (ἐπέχειν); 2 Pt. 1:19 (προσέχειν); → 828 on Tt. 1:9 (ἀντεχόμενον) and → 829 on κατέχειν.

[2] An old Indo-Germ. word with the sense "to hold fast," aor. "to lay hold of," "to get in one's power." In Gk. it already has also the meaning "to have." The German *Sieg* is a related word [Debrunner].

[3] Mentioned here are "to have a quality or moderation," "spatially to have around, on or in one," "to own," and "to have" for sexual intercourse.

or over one," and in the second "to own," "to enjoy," "to have at one's disposal." [4] This leads to much the same results as the English "to have" and "to possess." Even special instances such as ἔχειν with the inf. or the med. ἔχεσθαι can be understood along these lines, though the intr. use of the act. must be treated separately. For the most part the word undoubtedly occurs with a concrete object.

Our present concern must be with the theologically significant uses of the term. In this connection, as in Greek philosophy, ἔχειν is predominantly used with abstract terms. Thus one has, i.e., one bears and disposes of qualities, spiritual gifts and powers of the higher world. Above all, one has fellowship with persons. [5]

A fine example here is the lament of the solitary Zeus at the moment of the world's destruction (Epict. Diss., III, 13, 4): τάλας ἐγώ, οὔτε τὴν "Ηραν ἔχω οὔτε τὴν ᾿Αθηνᾶν οὔτε τὸν Απόλλωνα οὔτε ὅλως ἢ ἀδελφὸν ἢ υἱὸν ἢ ἔγγονον ἢ συγγενῆ. Cf. also the two phrases from private letters : [6] οὐδένα ἔχω μετὰ τὸν θεὸν εἰ μὴ σέ, P. Giess., I, 69, 9 (2nd cent. A.D.), and : μετὰ τὸν θεὸν ἄλλον ἀδελφὸν οὐκ ἔχω, P. Lond., III, 1244, 5 (4th cent. A.D.) .

Spiritual powers and qualities point beyond themselves and raise the question of man's relationship to God (1 C. 4:7). Moreover, personal fellowship may be had not merely with other men but also with gods and demons, and for Christians with Christ and even God. This point will be treated in detail in relation to the NT usage.

B. ἔχειν in the Septuagint.

Hebrew, like other Semitic languages, has no word for "to have." Other words and expressions are available to denote possession and temporal connection, [7] but there is no equivalent for the Gk. ἔχειν. This is evident in the LXX. As compared with non-biblical literature, or even with the NT, ἔχειν is comparatively rare in the LXX. In sum, it occurs only about 500 times. In these instances it is independently suggested by feeling for the Gk. language and is not consistently used for any particular Heb. word. Indeed, in most cases there either is no original or the Heb. has no expression of which ἔχειν is the translation. Hatch-Redp. find Heb. equivalents in only 164 instances, and they need no less than 78 sigla to discuss these. This brief statistical observation shows decisively that the translators do not follow any fixed rule in their use of ἔχειν.

The senses in which ἔχειν is employed cover the whole range of meanings found in classical and hellenistic Gk. Many uses of the term and its combinations which are common in the NT are also prominent in the LXX, e.g., ἐξουσίαν, πνεῦμα, ἐλπίδα, χρείαν ἔχειν. Particularly common is the possession of gifts of the Spirit, of virtues, of spiritual infusions. But ἔχειν is also used quite often of fellowship with persons, and in the later sections of fellowship with God (→ C. 4).

---

[4] The very word "to possess" (cf. the German *besitzen*) suggests that the two meanings have a common root. Possession of a piece of land implies session on it. The possessed has something alien in himself and is the possession of this other power instead of being his own lord.

[5] In the expressions γυναῖκα ἔχειν and ἄνδρα ἔχειν, ἔχειν implies more than a legal relationship, but for the most part it is used, not for personal fellowship, but as a technical term for sexual intercourse ; even outside marriage one may "have" a woman or a man (Aristot. Cat., 15, p. 15b, 28-30 = συνοικεῖν; cf. esp. Ex. 2:1 A F); 5 times in the LXX, in the NT Mt. 14:4; 22:28 = Mk. 6:18; 12:23 = Lk. 20:28, 33; Jn. 4:17 f.; 1 C. 5:1; 7:2, 29; Gl. 4:27 (a quotation).

[6] Cf. Preisigke Wört., *s.v.* θεός.

[7] Esp. "mine is," which is also found in Gk.

Rather surprising, though of little importance to us, is the number of passages where we have the med. ἔχεσθαι (86 times, twice in Da. Θ), usually in the sense of "to attach oneself" (spatially or temporally), "to cling to," or in the sense of εἶναι. [8] In 77 instances it is a part., mostly for various Heb. prepositions. It should also be noted that sometimes ἔχειν is used without obj. in the sense of "to have possessions," "not to be without means." The common secular expression that a condition "has" a man, i.e., controls or has a hold on him, is very rare, and is found mainly in Job. It is impossible to point with certainty to essential deviations from NT usage.

C. ἔχειν in the NT.

1. We may begin with some statistical and comparative data on the occurrence of the term in the NT. It is common in the NT, but is not evenly distributed. Thus it is not found at all in the first two chapters of Lk., this being in keeping with the Semitic colouring of the infancy stories. If it does not occur in Luke's Sermon on the Mount, this is hardly surprising, since it does not figure in the Matthean par. [9] Of the Synoptists only Mk. has more than average use. He uses it frequently, whereas Lk. avoids it. [10] In such cases Mt. usually follows Mk., though Mk. has it in many passages which are fuller than Mt. It is much less common in the epistles, being more suited to narrative style. The Johannine writings use it most. It is very common in Rev. and 1 Jn. has the highest percentage of any book. In Rev. it is often used in a rather bald and stereotyped way to describe what is seen. The things seen all "have" something. They do not "bear" things, nor are they "furnished" or "adorned" with them; they have them. Apart from this, we might almost speak of a distinctive Johannine "having," esp. in relation to the First Epistle. It is in keeping with the theology, with the understanding of the Gospel, which we find in John or the Johannine school that the Christian state is understood as a "having," a possession of salvation. This point demands separate treatment.

From the other passages we can only single out in groups the various points of importance. It is beyond our purpose to enumerate all the possible meanings and occurrences. Almost every meaning found in Gk. is found in the NT too, and there are no meanings that cannot be attested elsewhere. Only the statistics are, of course, peculiar to the NT.

2. Spiritual Possession.

So far as concerns religion and the spirit, the Gk. world speaks mainly of the possession of → νοῦς and → λόγος. The possession of soul (→ ψυχή) links man with other living creatures, [11] but the possession of spirit differentiates him from all others. ψυχὴν ἔχειν has the basic sense of "to have life within oneself," "to be alive"; [τὸν] νοῦν or λόγον ἔχειν means primarily "to have understanding," "to possess the power of thought," "to be rational" (e.g., Isoc. → I, 386). But this usage becomes less prominent with the development of the philosophical concept of spirit [12] according to which a single world spirit pervades the whole and the understanding of the individual is simply a part or emanation or manifestation of this one spirit. Instead of being said to have νοῦς or λόγος, man is now said to have a part (→ μετέχειν) in them. A distinction is also made between the universal spirit and the individual; [13] man has the latter, he has a part

---

[8] Cf. Helbing, Kasussyntax, 129 f. ἔχειν and ἔχεσθαι are almost like two different words for the Gks. [Debrunner].

[9] The exception is Mt. 5:46, cf. Lk. 6:32.

[10] E.g., 2:19 = Lk. 5:34; 3:1 = Lk. 6:6; 5:3 = Lk. 8:27.

[11] For fuller details on ψυχή and its later extension cf. E. Rohde, Psyche[9], [10] (1925).

[12] On what follows cf. M. Heinze, Die Lehre vom Logos (1872); A. Aall, Der Logos, I (1896), II (1899).

[13] κοινός, Dor. ξυνὸς λόγος in Heracl. Fr., 2 (I, 77, 12 ff. Diels); also Sext. Emp. Math., VII, 127; 131; Aristot., e.g., An., II, 3, p. 414b, 23; and the Stoics. The counterpart is ἴδιος λόγος; θεῖος or θεὸς λόγος, in Philo and Christian writers. κοινὸς νοῦς is also common, Epict. Diss., III, 6, 8; Plot.; also νοῦς without the art.

in the former. In this case some thinkers call the universal spirit λόγος and use νοῦς of the individual spirit, e.g., Heracl., Aristot.,[14] the Stoics,[15] Philo,[16] and, under the influence of John's Gospel (→ λόγος), Christian theologians, including the great Alexandrians.[17] Others, however, adopt a reverse procedure, and among these may be mentioned Anaxag.,[18] Plat.,[19] Epict.,[20] Plut.,[21] the Hermetics,[22] Neo-Platonism, and esp. Plotinus.[23] In the last two there is with the participation a pure "having" which is here understood in terms of a mystical fellowship, so that the problem of the relationship of the universal and the individual spirit is distinctively solved. In Plot. there is thus a possession not merely of the νοῦς but also in wholly mystical fashion of the one original spirit variously called ἕν, ὄν, πᾶν, ἀγαθόν, or ζωή. For him ἔχειν as a technical term for the *unio mystica* is almost an equivalent of εἶναι.

When we turn to the NT, we find both similarity and difference. ψυχὴν ἔχειν is used once (Rev. 8:9) of sea creatures, and νοῦν ἔχειν is found in its original sense of "to have understanding" in Rev. 13:18 (cf. the par. expression in 17:9); cf. νουνεχῶς in Mk. 12:34.

Early Christianity regards man as a trichotomy.[24] He consists of body, soul and spirit. Sometimes, however, πνεῦμα is used for spirit and this gives rise to misunderstanding. Not all men have πνεῦμα, but only individuals endowed with the Spirit in the old covenant[25] and Christians who receive the πνεῦμα as a first instalment of eternal salvation. Though the terms differ, the thought is the same as we find in the Hermetics. In the Hermetics all men have λόγος, but only some have fellowship with νοῦς; in the NT all men have νοῦς, but only Christians have πνεῦμα, or, more strictly, have a share in the one Spirit of God and of Christ. This possession of the Spirit by Christians is sometimes understood in ecstatic terms as in the OT. The Spirit of God at certain times comes down on the righteous and inspires them. Yet there is another view advanced by Paul and worked out by John whereby the Spirit comes once and for all into the Christian, renews him and constantly indwells and rules him. This gives a different relationship to the νοῦς.

When we remember how very common is the word πνεῦμα and the thought of possessing the Spirit, it is astonishing how seldom we find the phrase πνεῦμα ἔχειν. This is linked with the fact that the individual does not receive his own πνεῦμα as he has his own νοῦς, but has a share in the one divine Spirit, so that we naturally find the term μέτοχος in Hb. (→ 831 f.). In R. 8:9 the ἔχειν πνεῦμα Χριστοῦ stands among formulae which have a ring of mystical enthusiasm (οἰκεῖν

---

[14] Followed (Eth. M., I, 1, p. 1182a, 23 ff.) by Plato, who knows both; cf. also Pol., VII, 13, p. 1332b, 3 ff.; we often have the opp. ἄλογος, but → n. 19.

[15] Cleanthes in Plut. De Sollertia Animalium, 11 (II, 967e); Ar. Did. Epitome in Eus. Praep. Ev., XV, 15, 5 (MPG, 21, 1344a b); Epict. Diss., I, 3, 3; Sen. Ep., 76, 9; note the Stoic doctrine of the λόγοι σπερματικοί.

[16] Cf. L. Cohn, "Zur Lehre vom Logos bei Philo" in *Judaïca, Festschrift zu H. Cohens 70. Geburtstage* (1912), 303 ff. Note esp. the passages where we have ὀρθὸν λόγον ἔχειν or μετέχειν.

[17] Just. Apol., 46, 1 ff.; 53, 5 f.; Cl. Al. Paed., III, 7, 39, 4; Orig. Hom. in Jer. IX, 1, p. 63 f. etc.

[18] Fr., 12 (I, 404, 6 ff. Diels).

[19] With ἔχειν and μετέχειν we also have σμικρόν, βραχύ τι ἔχειν etc., but → n. 14.

[20] Diss., I, 16, 15; II, 22, 27.

[21] Is. et Os., 1 (II, 351d).

[22] Corp. Herm., XII, 6 and 7 etc., with numerous par. expressions (→ I, 51).

[23] Enn., I, 1, 8; III, 8, 8; V, 1, 12; V, 2, 2; VI, 7, 20 etc.

[24] Dob. Th. on 1 Th. 5:23; cf. also Hb. 4:12.

[25] πνεῦμα [θεοῦ, ἅγιον] ἐν ἑαυτῷ ἔχειν, Gn. 41:38; Nu. 27:18; Da. Θ 4:5; 4:6 A; cf. Test. S. 4.

ἐν . . ., Χριστὸς ἐν . . .), but in the context there is a strong ethical note. The opp. is φρόνημα τῆς σαρκός, and for "Spirit" of Christ we might almost substitute "mind" of Christ.[26] In v. 11 the Spirit is a pledge of the redemption of the body and therefore an eschatological advance (cf. R. 8:23 : τὴν ἀπαρχὴν τοῦ πνεύματος ἔχοντες, also 2 C. 1:22; 5:5).[27] The situation is much the same in 1 C. 6:19. The image of the temple is used mystically by Philo, but here it is obvious from the ethical context that the possession of the Spirit is not intended mystically. Having the spirit of faith in 2 C. 4:13 has nothing whatever to do with mysticism; the concern is again with eschatological expectation. The slightly ironical "I think also that I have the Spirit of God" in 1 C. 7:40 raises no special problem in this context. He who has the Spirit knows what is God's will and what is in place before Him.

The statement is usually taken to be a vindication against other opinions. But in the light of 1 C. 7:10, 12, 25 it is evident that Paul is again setting himself alongside Christ as a bearer of the Spirit κατ' ἐξοχήν. It is not that he is trying to maintain a different view from that of Christ.[28] He is rather arguing that, if he has no saying of the Lord in support of his advice in v. 40a, his own view carries weight as that of one who has the Spirit.

Outside Paul we also find πνεῦμα ἔχειν in Jd. 19. There is here an echo of the Gnostic distinction between the psychics and the pneumatics, though Paul, too, distinguishes between the psychic and the pneumatic. Possibly the author is arguing against Gnostic opponents and turning their own slogan against them.

To the πνεῦμα passages we should also add 1 C. 2:16 : "But we have the νοῦς of Christ." The statement concludes a section in which the reference is consistently to πνεῦμα, and therefore one might have expected πνεῦμα. But Paul is influenced by the preceding quotation from Is. and therefore, equating κύριος and Christ, he writes νοῦς. As elsewhere, and as is often true of πνεῦμα, νοῦς here means "mind" or "disposition." There is no suggestion of the νοῦς concept of the Gks. and of later Hermetic mysticism.[29]

λόγον ἔχειν is found only occasionally in the NT in a varied use which is quite different from that of secular authors. Logos in the NT always means "word" (basically at least), and never ratio. Even the Logos concept in the Prologue to John must be understood along these lines. In Ac. 19:38 λόγον ἔχειν means "to have something to bring forward" (the Heb. דָּבָר often means a cause or matter). In Ac. 20:24 it can hardly be the correct reading. In Col. 2:23 it means "to have the call of something," "to stand at the call of something." In 2 Pt. 1:19 all the emphasis is on βεβαιότερον : "to hold the prophetic word the more firmly" (→ I, 602). A special sense is to be found in Jn. 5:38 : "And ye have not his word abiding in you :[30] for whom he hath sent, him ye believe not." If the saying is a

---

[26] 1 C. 6:17: "He that is joined unto the Lord is one spirit with him," sounds mystical, but the context is one of practical ethics.

[27] To speak of "eschatological mysticism" (A. Schweitzer, Die Mystik des Ap. Paulus [1930]) is quite misleading. Only in terminology and not in content is Paul mystical. Cf. H. E. Weber, Eschatologie u. Mystik (1930).

[28] In this sense it would be intolerable presumption.

[29] As against Reitzenstein Hell. Myst., 338.

[30] Here, as in 1 Jn. 3:15, μένων qualifies ἔχειν. The emphasis is on indwelling rather than on remaining (cf. μονή, "a place to stay in"). We may legitimately think of Col. 3:16 : "Let the word of Christ dwell in you richly," where ἐν ὑμῖν is often taken in the sense of "among you," i.e., that it may be proclaimed and living and pregnant among you.

development of that which immediately precedes (οὔτε φωνὴν αὐτοῦ πώποτε ἀκηκόατε), then it bears the sense of the Prologue : Jesus is not simply speaking God's Word (cf. 6:68); He is God's Word. Hence we have not only to hear and receive His word (in the sense of the parable of the sower or of 1 Th. 2:13); we have to believe His person as the personal revelation of God. To have God's Logos is to possess a part of Him in His Son. This does not mean, of course, that we can find at this point relationships with the λόγον ἔχειν of Greek philosophy.

3. Demonic Possession.

With the idea of spiritual possession already discussed, there is also in Gk. religion and philosophy another trend which seeks to explain the mystery of man by postulating a daemon active within him, i.e., a personal, superhuman being. This is a development of the thought of possession. [31] Our present concern is with the linguistic aspect. There is in this respect an important distinction. If the daemon is for good, it is the man who possesses it, [32] whereas he is passive in relation to evil spirits and they possess him. [33] This demonic possession plays a great role in the magic pap. In part on the basis of the primitive view that one may have the deity and its blessings by means of fetishes, [34] these texts suggests means and practices whereby good and helpful daemons may be secured. [35] The final point is usually to have the name or names, i.e., to know how to force and conjure the being. [36] In many Gnostic trends we can still see traces of this view and the accompanying practices. [37]

This demonic possession finds its counterpart in the NT. As in paganism, it rests here on a polydemonistic view of the world which is particularly evident in the Synoptic Gospels. It is used *sensu bono* in Rev. 3:1: Christ has the seven spirits of God (cf. 1:4; 4:5; 5:6). These seven spirits are thought of as autonomous beings (Rev. also mentions the one πνεῦμα), and they are to be equated with the seven angels which stand before God (Rev. 8 ff. and 15 ff.), just as Philo equates the λόγοι and the ἄγγελοι. In 5:6 they are called messengers who are sent out. What does it mean that Christ "has" them? It obviously means that He has authority over them, that He can command them, just as He rules the sword (2:12) and has the power of the keys (3:7). In all other cases [38] demonic possession is used *sensu malo*. ἔχειν does not mean "to have in one's power" or "to possess." [39] It

---

[31] H. Usener, *Götternamen* (1896), 294 ff. speaks of "gods of the moment." Hom. attributes extraordinary deeds to the temporary indwelling of a god, Il., 5, 185; 9, 49; Od., 15, 530; though he does not use ἔχειν. With reference to the daemon of life we find both : Plat. Resp., X, 617e, 620d (→ 3); though in Polit., 274b it is the daemon which has possession (κεκτημένος). Plot. speaks of possession by the daemon, Enn., I, 2, 6; II, 3, 13; III, 4, 3 etc. He also speaks of the daemon redeeming us, III, 4, 3 (note the title of Enn., III, 4).

[32] Dio Chrys. Or., 69, 4 : τυγχάνειν. Cf. esp. the etymology of εὐδαίμων : Plat. Tim., 90c; Iambl. Protr., 5; Cl. Al. Strom., II, 22, 131, 4; also Aristot. Eth. Eud., IV (η), 14, p. 1247a, 25 ff.

[33] Theocr. Idyll., 4, 40. TGF, Fr. 17 and 92. Cf. also συνέχειν, Preis. Zaub., V, 126.

[34] *V.* the statement on the cuneiform script in AOT, p. 287, line 21; here we are to think of wearing an amulet. Having is also used for possession of an image in Apc. Abr. 2:6; Ep. Jer., 72.

[35] Preis. Zaub., I, 88 and 190; IV, 1948 ff. With ἔχειν we also have verbs of receiving and taking : *ibid.*, I, 54; IV, 2436 and 2999; V, 419 f.; XIII, 345 f. The numen is even sometimes denoted by θεός.

[36] Preis. Zaub., IV, 216 f.; XIII, 790 etc. Cf. Reitzenstein Poim., 17, n. 6; Mithr. Liturg., 112.

[37] *V.* Iren., I, 13, 3 on the Gnostic Marcos.

[38] Possession of the Holy Spirit as treated under 2. is not included here.

[39] If we look for synon. expressions for the NT idea of possession (e.g., λαμβάνειν), we shall find phrases which bring out the passivity of man (e.g., Lk. 9:39).

expresses a spatial relationship and means "to bear in oneself." When Mt. 11:18,
par. Lk. 7:33 and in the plur. Lk. 8:27 speak of having a demon, δαιμόνιον has
completely lost the good sense it has in Socrates and means an evil and ungodly
spirit. In the light of biblical monotheism every aspect of pagan religion is depreciated. In Jn. δαιμόνιον ἔχειν has the weaker sense of "to be out of one's
mind" : Jn. 7:20; 8:48 f., 52. It is a parallel of μαίνεσθαι in 10:20. There is no
longer any idea of possession here ; Jn. does not record a single exorcism. In this
connection one might also refer to the many devilish spirits or spirits of sickness
triumphantly opposed by Jesus and the apostles, Mk. 3:22, 30; 5:15; 7:25; 9:17;
Lk. 4:33; 13:11; Ac. 8:7; 16:16; 19:13. In a broader sense we might also mention
at this point the possession of various ills and afflictions to the extent that this
is regarded as demonic possession. Reference should be made especially to Mk.
3:22 : Βεελζεβοὺλ ἔχει. Jesus so far towers above others by His extraordinary
works that He can be regarded as possessed only by the prince of demons. The
concept of demonic ἔχειν is here extended. Yet Beelzebul is still no more than the
chief demon. He is not the opponent of God or the Messiah. Of real significance
would be a phrase like ἔχειν τὸν σατανᾶν or τὸν ἀντίχριστον. 1 C. 2:12 points
in this direction : ἡμεῖς δὲ οὐ τὸ πνεῦμα τοῦ κόσμου ἐλάβομεν.

4. To have God.

As we have seen, both spiritual possession and demon possession point beyond
themselves. The two lines converge in the thought of "having" God. This phrase
is rare in the NT, but it is distinctively Christian, even though it naturally has a
pre-Christian history.

　　In the Gk. world it is unusual to describe fellowship with the great gods in terms of
"having." [40] More common are the ideas of being the possession of the gods (→ κατέχεσθαι) or of participation in them (→ μετέχειν). Various other expressions of an
enthusiastic type are also found. In the Christian age only Epict. calls for notice. He
uses τὸν θεὸν ἔχειν as a fixed formula, Diss., II, 8, 17. He thinks that we "have" God
in the things of nature, for God is enclosed in all things. Cf. also I, 9, 7; I, 13, 3; IV, 1, 145
(→ 823). It should be noted, however, that not merely in Jewish and Christian, but also
in classical texts, ἔχειν is often used to link the names or designations of the gods with
predicative nouns or adjectives. [41] The most common expressions are : "To have the
deity as a covenant-partner" and ˙— these are particularly noteworthy — "to have the
deity gracious, [42] or ungracious or wrathful." [43] It will be seen where the centre of
interest lies. Reference has already been made to the pantheistically mystical possession
of the original whole. Plot. never uses θεός for this, and therefore we never find in him
θεὸν ἔχειν.

More relevant is Jewish literature. In the OT there is a relationship of possession between God and the people ("thy," "your" God ; the first commandment).
God is Israel's possession in ψ 32:12; 143:15 etc.; Jer. 10:16 (possibly Jdt. 9:12;

---

[40] In Plut. Is. et Os., 25 (II, 360e) τὸ θεῖον is not the deity but the divine nature or
mode of being (= θεότης). In Aristot. Metaph., XI, 7, p. 1072b, 23 θεῖον is an adj.
(= divine).

[41] As one may have a friend (Lk. 11:5), partner (Phlm. 17), father and instructor (1 C.
4:15; Hb. 12:9) or bride (Jn. 3:29), so one may have God as Father, Creator, Leader, Friend,
Protector and Witness (as elsewhere λόγος, or νοῦς, or a daemon, or many gods ; with
"to have" we also have "to attain" and "to use").

[42] ἵλεω or εὐμενῆ ἔχειν, esp. in inscr., but also in the works of Plat., Luc., Philo,
Josephus.

[43] δυσμενῆ or κεχολωμένον, esp. in burial curses.

Sir. 23:12). God is also the inheritance of the Levites who have no land, Dt. 10:9; 18:2 (נַחֲלָה, LXX κλῆρος); Nu. 18:20 (חֵלֶק וְנַחֲלָה, LXX μερὶς καὶ κληρονομία); Ez. 44:28 (נַחֲלָה, LXX κληρονομία, and אֲחֻזָּה, LXX κατάσχεσις), and, with a more general reference, Sir. 45:22. Both expressions are applied to righteous individuals at a later period, and we find numerous expressions of this kind in the Psalter. Thus God is "my" God, heritage, rock, refuge, consolation, light, salvation, helper and deliverer, joy and delight. This thought is particularly prominent in ψ 15 and 72:25 f., where Luther has the insurpassable *wenn ich nur dich habe* for "beside thee" (עִמְּךָ).

If we take a further step, we find in Jewish writings composed in Gk.[44] the phrase we seek, i.e., "to have God."

In the addition of the Septuagint at Est. 4:17 (C. 14 [14:3]), Esther prays κύριέ μου, ὁ βασιλεὺς ἡμῶν, σὺ εἶ μόνος· βοήθησόν μοι τῇ μόνῃ καὶ μὴ ἐχούσῃ βοηθὸν εἰ μὴ σέ, cf. also later in the same prayer, though without βοηθόν. 2 Macc. 8:36 : ὑπέρμαχον ἔχειν τὸν θεόν, and 11:10 : τὸν ἀπ' οὐρανοῦ σύμμαχον ἔχοντες. Note should be taken of the terms "helper" and "covenant partner" already mentioned. 3 Macc. 7:16 : αὐτοὶ δὲ οἱ μέχρι θανάτου τὸν θεὸν ἐσχηκότες. Also Test. XII, e.g., Test. D. 5 : ἔχοντες τὸν θεὸν τῆς εἰρήνης, and Test. Iss. 7: ἔχοντες μεθ' ἑαυτῶν θεὸν τοῦ οὐρανοῦ. Joseph. describes Daniel as ἔχων τὸ θεῖον (= the deity) in Ant., 10, 250, while in Ant., 8, 227 τὸν θεὸν ἔχειν is not used of a man but of every place (and therefore in the sense of Epict. → 822). In relation to the Levite passages Philo constructs the formula τὸν θεὸν κλῆρον ἔχειν, which he uses distinctly on 5 occasions (also twice with "to attain") and of which there are frequent echoes.

There are only a few passages in the NT.

When the Jews in Jn. 8:41 say of themselves that they have only one (spiritual) father, namely, God (formally cf. 19:15), the emphasis is on having a father, and ἔχειν does not therefore express a relationship to God. In R. 1:28 the construction is ἔχειν ἐν ἐπιγνώσει[45] rather than τὸν θεὸν ἔχειν. This is a development of the γνόντες τὸν θεόν of v. 21 and is to be compared with ἐπιγινώσκειν in v. 32 (→ I, 707). They saw little value in really knowing God, in attaining to Him with their knowledge. Col. 4:1 goes somewhat further with its "knowing that ye also have a Master in heaven," but here, too, there is little stress on ἔχειν, the point being to recognise that there is such a Master. Cf. the passage in which Epict. describes his pupils as οἱ τὸν κύριον τὸν μέγαν ἔχοντες καὶ πρὸς τὸ ἐκείνου νεῦμα καὶ κίνημα ζῶντες (Diss., IV, 1, 145 → 822).

ἔχειν is used to express a distinct relation to God only in 1 Jn. 2:23 and 2 Jn. 9. These two verses are almost identical and are certainly related. Both make the having of God as Father dependent on confession of Christ as the Son of God and the Messiah in the flesh. Having the Father includes having the Son. There is reference to having the Son in 1 Jn. 5:12 also. Here the ἔχειν has a highly individual sense. One may believe in God, speak of Him and think one knows Him, yet still not have Him, i.e., not reach Him in prayer, not share His blessings, His forgiveness and eternal grace, not enjoy living personal fellowship with Him.[46]

---

[44] Though cf. also ἡγούμενον [οὐκ] ἔχειν, Hab. 1:14; 2 Ch. 18:16 A ᵃ B and ἔχεσθαι τοῦ θεοῦ, Dt. 30:20.

[45] The comm. adduce par. constructions.

[46] Thus W. Flex in *Zwölf Bismarcks* causes the warrior Frederick the Great to complain to his theological brother : "Wolff in Halle and other humbugs taught me five proofs for the existence of God — is it my fault that I have no God ?"

Only the Christian can understand and accept the fact that this fellowship with God may be had only by way of fellowship with Christ. What it means to have the Son, however, may be seen from many parallels (→ μετέχειν, κερδαίνειν, [κατα-]λαμβάνειν, κοινωνία), and especially from the expressions παράκλητον ἔχειν in 1 Jn. 2:1 and the similar ἀρχιερέα ἔχειν in Hb. 4:14 f.; 8:1; 10:21 (the high-priest of Hb. is primarily an intercessor). Fellowship with the exalted Lord [47] is what gives Paul his power and what is reflected in all his utterances. It is not by chance, however, that we find "to have God" only in Jn. This is part of what we call "Johannine having." Another point which calls for notice is that these sayings of Jn. are in polemical sections. It is at least probable that the author takes the formula from the lips of his Gnostic opponents and uses it against them. They speak a good deal of having, but in his view wrongly.

Similarly 2 Cl., 2, 3 (on the basis of Is. 54:1) contrasts Christians, supposedly abandoned by God, with those who think they have God (τῶν δοκούντων ἔχειν θεόν). [48] And Plot. in opposition to the Gnostics (Enn., II, 9, 9) speaks of those who know they do not have but maintain they do, who persuade themselves they have when they do not, who even pretend they are the only ones who have when they are the only ones who do not. We hardly have any original texts from the early days of Gnosticism, but from the extracts in the fathers we can see that ἔχειν was in common use among them to express metaphysical fellowship. It is in keeping with this that the having of God and Christ (in a wholly mystical sense, as proved by par. expressions) is particularly common in Cl. Al. and Orig., and esp. in the apocr. Acts. It later becomes an integral part of the language of Christian mysticism, though it is certainly not meant in a mystical sense in the NT.

5. Having Hope.

Light is cast on the basic temper of early Christianity when we consider how big a place is occupied by the having of hope in NT statements about salvation. The thoughts of the first Christians are directed always to the end and to eternity. We can see this from some of the phrases used.

First there is the common ἐλπίδα ἔχειν, "to have hope," Ac. 24:15; R. 15:4; 2 C. 3:12; Eph. 2:12; 1 Th. 4:13; 1 Jn. 3:3. [49] Christians have a solid hope, while the heathen are without hope. It is a hope grounded in Christ's redeeming act. This act makes possible a new confidence before God. Christians have a good conscience (ἀγαθὴν (etc.) συνείδησιν ἔχειν), Hb. 10:2; 1 Pt. 3:16; and from a more human angle, Ac. 24:16; 1 Tm. 1:19; Hb. 13:18. They have boldness (παρρησίαν ἔχειν), Eph. 3:12; Hb. 10:19; 1 Jn. 2:28; 4:17 (cf. Phlm. 8; 1 Jn. 3:21; 5:14). They have comfort (παράκλησιν ἔχειν), i.e., they

---

[47] Cf. M. Dibelius, "Glaube u. Mystik bei Paulus" (N. Jbch. Wiss. u. Jugendbildung, 7 [1931], 683 ff.), 696. Mt. 26:11 = Mk. 14:7 = Jn. 12:8 (also Mk. 2:19) reject the idea that the disciples have Jesus constantly : "Me ye have not always." But the reference here is to concrete, spatial presence (μεθ᾽ ἑαυτοῦ). One cannot anoint the exalted Lord, but one may have Him with one in a different way (Mt. 28:20). We need not be disturbed by this saying of Syn. origin within the Johannine writings.
[48] "To have God or Christ" is also found in the post-apost. fathers, 1 Cl., 46, 6; 2 Cl., 16, 1; Ign. Mg., 12, 1; R., 6, 3; Herm. m., 12, 4, 3. Cf. also "to attain God or Christ" (τυγχάνειν, ἐπιτυγχάνειν) in Ign. Eph., 10, 1; 12, 2; Mg., 1, 2; 14; Tr., 12, 2 f.; 13, 3; Sm., 9, 2; 11, 1; R., 1, 2; 2, 1; 4, 1; 5, 3; 8, 3; Pol., 2, 3; 7, 1. This is for Ign. an expression of the heavenly fellowship with God and Christ which is attained in death, and esp. martyrdom. It is thus an eschatological and martyrological concept.
[49] 2 C. 10:15 refers to human things. It is not immediately clear what hope is in the context of R. 15:4. That it is effected by ὑπομονή is also stated in 5:4. The ultimate context is that only those who have hope will bring the required sacrifice.

are comforted, Hb. 6:18, while the rich have had their consolation (Lk. 6:24 → ἀπέχειν). For Christians have their Advocate or Comforter (→ 824). Through Him they have redemption (ἀπολύτρωσιν ἔχειν), Col. 1:14 par. Eph. 1:7, and therefore they have access to God (προσαγωγὴν ἔχειν), Eph. 2:18; 3:12 (R. 5:2).

In relation to all these statements it may be said that Paul (on Jn. → 6.) regards the Christian state as the great blessing of salvation and that he does not locate it only in the future. The present possession of Christians (e.g., the possession of the → πνεῦμα, R. 8:23; 2 C. 1:22; 5:5; Eph. 1:13) is a foretaste of eternal salvation.[50]

If the possession of the Christian is primarily hope and confidence, one may already speak of having the eternal blessing of salvation. This expresses the absolute assurance of hope. In this connection we may also mention μισθὸν ἔχειν, "to have a reward," Mt. 5:46; 6:1; Hb. 10:35 : μισθαποδοσίαν (again invested with an eschatological meaning by Pl. in 1 C. 9:17). "To have a treasure (θησαυρόν) in heaven," Mt. 19:21 par. κληρονομίαν (inheritance) ἔχειν, Eph. 5:5. κρείσσονα καὶ μένουσαν ὕπαρξιν ἔχειν, Hb. 10:34. This possession is already enjoyed by the Christian and lasts into eternal life.

But the chief expression in this regard is [τὴν] ζωὴν [αἰώνιον] ἔχειν (→ also κληρονομεῖν), "to have eternal life," Mt. 19:16; Jn. 3:15, 16, 36; 5:24, 39, 40; 6:40, 47, 53, 54; 10:10; 20:31; 1 Jn. 3:15; 5:12, 13. In R. 6:22 Paul describes this as the "fruit" of the life which Christ has freed from sin.

Eternal life is not immortality. This is possessed by God alone, 1 Tm. 6:16. It is the overcoming of death by resurrection. Yet the term has another meaning in Jn. For Jn. eternal life is already present and may be discerned on this side of the grave. It has already dawned, as though he were already in heaven, cf. Jn. 5:24; 6:53 (ἐν ἑαυτῷ); 1 Jn. 3:15; 5:12. There is a negative counterpart in Rev. 3:1: "Thou hast a name that thou livest, and art dead." God has this eternal or divine life in Himself. The Son has it from Him, and His own receive it through Him (Jn. 5:26). In this connection we may also refer to 1 Tm. 4:8 : "Godliness has promise of the life that now is, and of that which is to come."

We may finally mention 2 C. 5:1: "If our earthly house of this tabernacle were dissolved, we have (ἔχομεν) a building of God."

This present again expresses the absolute certainty of hope. The dwelling is already ready. Materially this is a development of the hope of the resurrection inasmuch as those who bear the spirit (v. 5) are at once invested with the heavenly body at death, and do not have to sleep until the resurrection. It can hardly be otherwise if eternal life is already present and discernible in their present life.

6. Johannine Having.

We have already said of Jn. that he divests the concept of eternal life of its eschatological character and uses it to express the richness of the Christian life.[51] This is characteristic of his whole approach. For him Christianity is not so much life in hope; it is full possession of salvation, a "having." He takes the various expressions used in religion for salvation and claims them for Christianity. And where other apostles expect these blessings in eternity or constantly seek them afresh for their congregations, he always speaks consciously of a "having": τὴν

---

[50] A. Schweitzer finely presents this irruption of the future aeon into the life of the Christian, though unfortunately he uses "Pauline mysticism" as his leading concept. A better formulation is to be found in H. E. Weber, op. cit. Cf. also M. Dibelius, op. cit., 688, 696.

[51] Cf. the παρρησία passages (→ 824).

ἀγάπην τοῦ θεοῦ ἔχειν (5:42), [52] τὴν εἰρήνην ἔχειν (16:33), [53] τὴν χαρὰν ἔχειν (17:13); [54] τὸ φῶς ἔχειν (8:12; 12:35, 36); [55] cf. → 825 for τὴν ζωὴν ἔχειν. It is along the same lines that Ign. hopes to attain God. But John says that Christians already have Him (→ 823). Similarly, he speaks of having fellowship with God (1 Jn. 1:6), whereas Paul simply says that we are called to fellowship with Christ (1 C. 1:9), and that God is faithful and will thus fulfil this calling.

The various blessings of salvation are also seen from another angle in Jn. In several passages they are distinctively related to Christ. Sometimes Christ is an equivalent of the specific term, and sometimes He is the Mediator of the blessing. Thus one has God's Word (5:38), God's love, peace, joy, light and life, fellowship with God, and even God Himself, in Christ. This is Johannine "having."

7. Christianity as Having.

If we consider the NT as a whole, it is evident that Christianity is a religion of having as distinct from other religions of seeking and expecting. Even the wealth of OT piety is far surpassed in this regard. The Jews have their Law, on which they insist (Jn. 19:7). They thus have apparent [56] knowledge of the truth (R. 2:20). In this possession they are superior to the Gentiles (R. 2:14 : τὰ μὴ νόμον ἔχοντα; cf. also 3:2 : ἐπιστεύθησαν κτλ.). They have a zeal of God (R. 10:2). [57] But Christians have a better righteousness, i.e., that of faith (Phil. 3:9). Having faith [58] and fellowship with Christ, they have a share in the accomplished redemption (→ 825), in the resurrection of Christ (→ 825). They also have the Holy Spirit (→ 819) and other gifts of grace (1 C. 7:7; 14:26), peace, joy, sure hope and confidence towards God (→ 824). Furthermore, they have fellowship with God (→ 823) and true *gnosis* (1 C. 8:1, 10 — cf. the opposite in 15:34). [59] We can understand how Paul may formulate the pregnant saying that "the poor in truth can make many rich, [60] and those who have nothing yet possess all things" (2 C. 6:10).

---

[52] ἀγάπην ἔχειν is also used in Jn. 13:35; 15:13; 1 C. 13:1-3; 2 C. 2:4; Phil. 2:2; Phlm. 5; 1 Pt. 4:8; 1 Jn. 4:16, but in these passages it means "to have love to show," "to cherish love," in Jn. "to enjoy God's love."

[53] This is also used in Ac. 9:31 of human peace. Jn. means a higher peace (cf. Jn. 14:27), peace of soul. The MSS leave it an open question whether we should read ἔχομεν or ἔχωμεν in R. 5:1. The more difficult reading is usually to be preferred in such cases, and this would be ἔχωμεν. But what would the conjunctive mean? We should have to assume a special meaning for εἰρήνην ἔχειν in this case. It seems more likely that ω came in quite early as an accidental error. The parallels in vv. 9-10 (δικαιωθέντες in both cases, εἰρήνην ἔχομεν = κατηλλάγημεν) definitely support the indic.

[54] χαρὰν ἔχειν is also used of specific rejoicing on various accounts, 2 C. 1:15 (B); Phlm. 7; 3 Jn. 4; Jn. "my joy."

[55] This is not found elsewhere. In 8:12 it has the sense of finding the way to life. In 12:35 f., as in v. 8, ἔχειν means "to have in spatial proximity, to have accessible." The connection with the person of Christ is particularly clear at this point.

[56] μόρφωσιν ἔχειν is also found in 2 Tm. 3:5 in the sense of "to have the appearance of something," "to possess something only in appearance."

[57] There is a rather different ζῆλον ἔχειν in Jm. 3:14.

[58] πίστιν ἔχειν, 4 Macc. 16:22; Mt. 17:20 par. Lk. 17:6; Mt. 21:21 par. Mk. 11:22; Ac. 14:9; R. 14:22; 1 C. 13:2; 1 Tm. 1:19 (cf. also 3:9); Phlm. 5; Jm. 2:1, 14, 18. The last verse hardly makes sense in its present form in spite of various hypotheses. We are almost forced to assume some textual corruption. It is evident that Jm. has in view someone who is insisting on the necessity of correct belief.

[59] γνῶσιν θεοῦ ἔχειν is found in the LXX only at Wis. 2:13, where it is scornfully used of the righteous by their opponents.

[60] Cf. Ac. 3:6 : "Such as I have give I thee." Peter is poor, yet he can make others rich through his strength of faith.

This sense of wealth is everywhere present in early Christianity (cf. Jm. 2:5 etc. → πλοῦτος). Particularly striking is the parenthetical note in Rev. 2:9. The saying in Paul is formally based on Prv. 13:7, but what a difference ! For there the poor pretends to be rich in order to be able to play an important role or to acquire renown. Here, however, there is assumed a transvaluation of all values. All human possession pales before the wealth we have in God. This does not mean, of course, that it pales before the *unio mystica*. [61] In the words of Cl. Al. Paed., III, 6, 36, 3 : "He possesses many things, yea, all things, who has the eternal good, who has God. For it is written that to him who asketh it is given, to him who knocketh it is opened. If God refuses nothing, then all things belong to the righteous" (cf. 1 Tm. 6:17; cf. also v. 7).

Yet Christian having is not a merit on which one may build ; it is all a gift (1 C. 4:7). Even faith and love and the power of sanctification are continually sought and granted anew by God.

ἔχειν as a merit, meaning "to have something to show," is found in Rev. 2:6, and also 2:25 and 3:11. What is it that these two churches are to have and to hold ? The merits mentioned in 2:19 and 3:10. These and similar acknowledgments in the other letters are to be understood in the light of the militant mood of the book, and are balanced by even stronger censures and warnings.

The thought of individual possession, of a supreme disposition which man has to show, is often seen in the Synoptic saying : "He that hath, to him shall be given" (Mt. 13:12 = Mk. 4:25 = Lk. 8:18; Mt. 25:29 = Lk. 19:26); but this is a mistaken interpretation. The saying is expressing proverbially a fact of daily experience. If it is a proverb, it may have been used on several occasions in different contexts and with different applications. In Mt. 13:12 only the few have thus far understood Him or had an ear for Him (v. 9). Only they will be led into deeper understanding by the parables. [62] Things will remain obscure to the rest. There is, however, no sense of a quality or disposition. In Mk. 4:25 par. Lk. 8:18 the Word is uttered to be transmitted (v. 21 ff.). If the disciples have understood it in such a way that they spread it abroad, they have truly received it and will do so more and more. Otherwise what they have heard loses its value, and becomes only an apparent possession (Lk.). [63] This is perhaps the original sense in the discourse on parables, at the end of the parable of the Sower (esp. v. 20); but Mt. unfortunately misplaced it. The use of the saying in the parable of the talents (or pounds) fits this interpretation, Mt. 25:29 par. Lk. 19:26. All are given the same gift, but not all put it to such good use. The Word does not bring forth fruit in all.

† ἀντέχω (-ομαι).

In sec. Gk. this often occurs in the act. in the sense of "to hold against." In the med. it means to do this in one's own interest, i.e., protectively, and then "to cleave to." It is always used in the med. in the LXX, usually with the gen. and in the above senses, also "to take up," "to concern oneself with," and most frequently "to hold fast."

The NT use is like that of the LXX. Only the med. is used, though with more concern for the interest of others than one's own, 1 Th. 5:14. When used of the relation of the servant to the master (Mt. 6:24 par. Lk. 16:13), it expresses the mutual trust and interdependence reflected in many parables (it occurs along with

---

[61] So Sebastian Franck, *Paradoxa, Traktat,* 91 (ed. H. Ziegler, 1909).

[62] In the two Mt. passages → περισσεύειν has much the same sense as περισσὸν ἔχειν (Jn. 10:10).

[63] On this kind of possession → 824, also Herm. m., 11, 12.

ἀ ν τ έ χ ε σ θ α ι. Apart from the dict., cf. the catena in W. Lock, ICC, 38 (1924) on Tt. 1:9. Cf. also Helbing, *Kasussyntax,* 130.

ἀγαπᾶν). With a material obj. in Tt. 1:9 it means "to be concerned"[1] to keep preaching faithful to the received doctrine,[2] i.e., "to hold fast."

ἀπέχω.

Class. a. "to hold off," "to keep off," b. "to have received (what is owed)," c. "to be distant"; med. "to keep away or to abstain from." In the LXX a. is not found at all, b. twice, and c. and the med. frequently.

NT usage is like that of the LXX. a. does not occur, b. occurs five times, c. six and the med. six. Phlm. 15: "to receive back," is a special use of b., which is normally used for receipts (Phil. 4:18). In the eschatological context of the Sermon on the Mount (Mt. 6:2, 5, 16; Lk. 6:24), the idea of having fully received is theologically important. The disciples of Jesus await a heavenly possession (→ ἔχειν, 825) with which earthly possession cannot compare (→ ἔχειν, 827). A verse apart is Mk. 14:41. For this there are no parallels and we have to decide as best we can. The Western gloss τὸ τέλος is no help, nor is the vg sufficit (for what suffices?). Perhaps the meaning is: "It is not in place."

† ἐνέχω, ἔνοχος.

Class. "to hold fast to something" (an emotion, a state etc.), ἔνοχος, "held fast," "guilty," "subject to" (with dat. of the law which is against one, of the offence or of the merited punishment, sometimes the gen. of offence, or abs.). It is esp. common in burial curses,[1] also with the dat. of the avenging deity. LXX, "to pursue" (by ellipse [τὸν χόλον etc.] or a meaning of independent origin?), med. "to strive after," "to be entangled;" ἔνοχος, "guilty," often abs. or with gen. of guilt.

NT like the LXX, act. "to pursue, press upon," Mk. 6:19; Lk. 11:53. Pass. "to let oneself be entangled," "to subject oneself" (Gl. 5:1), "to be subject" (2 Th. 1:4 vl.). ἔνοχος, a. "subject" (Hb. 2:15); b. "legally subject," "guilty," with gen. of guilt (Mk. 3:29);[2] gen. of the law or value against which one has transgressed (1 C. 11:27; Jm. 2:10, supply τῶν ἐντολῶν); and gen. of the deserved punishment (Mt. 26:66 par. Mk. 14:64). The use of the gen. of guilt and punishment finds a counterpart in the Rabb. חַיָּב (or מתחייב), which is, however, most common in the sense of "engaged or committed to something."[3] Highly singular is Mt. 5:21 f. Here we have the dat. of the local court of judgment, the thought being that a higher court can pass a severer sentence. In the third clause the expression is changed and the actual place of punishment is mentioned (supply τοῦ βληθῆναι). For the first offence one comes before the local court, for the second before the supreme court, and for the third into hell.[4]

---

[1] Cf. 1 Tm. 5:17: κοπιῶντες; 2 Tm. 4:2: κήρυξον.

[2] πιστὸς λόγος is often found in the Past., but with no fixed sense.

ἀ π έ χ ε ι ν. Helbing, Kasussyntax, 179; Deissmann LO, 88 ff.

ἐ ν έ χ ω. Bl.-Debr.[6] § 308.

[1] Ditt. Syll.[3], Indexes, s.v. ἔνοχος.

[2] Cf. Philo Vit. Mos., II, 203: ἁμαρτίας ἔνοχος ἔστω. Here Philo gives a better rendering of the Heb. נְשָׂא חֶטְאוֹ than the LXX with its ἁμαρτίαν λήψεται (Lv. 24:15). Elsewhere Philo has the dat. of guilt or punishment, or a part. construction denoting the guilt.

[3] I owe this reference to K. G. Kuhn.

[4] On this saying cf. the comm., also A. Fridrichsen, "Exegetisches zum NT" in Symbolae Osloenses, 13 (1934), 38 f.

† κατέχω.

This is a more emphatic form of ἔχειν. It means 1. "to hold fast," "to hold back;" 2. (spatially) "to occupy;" 3. (juridically) "to occupy," "to hold in possession." It is also used in various ways intr., e.g., as a technical nautical term for "to make for," "to steer towards," "to land at."

Of the many special meanings the following have religious significance. a. κατέχεσθαι can mean "to be possessed or inspired," also κατοχή, "possession," "inspiration," "ecstasy," κάτοχος and κατόχιμος, "possessed," "inspired," "enraptured." This usage derives from the Thracian worship of Dionysus [1] with its ecstatic character. In the class. period it gradually comes to be used of other deities, esp. those related to Dionysus like the Phrygian Sabazios. In relation to Apollo and the Muses it is figuratively used for artistic inspiration or ecstasy, and in this sense it is an important term in Plato, particularly in the dialogue Ion. Along with other ecstatic terms like μαίνεσθαι or ἔνθεος, the word expresses the passivity of man in relation to daemonic or divine possession (→ ἔχειν 3. and 4.). Underlying the figure is perhaps the thought of the spatial entry of the numen into man and man's being in the power of the other (→ 817, n. 4). b. A very different use is that of κάτοχος and κατοχή for the "prisoner of God" and "imprisonment in God's service," e.g., in the worship of Serapis. [2] The reference is to communal ascetic life in the temple precincts, a distant parallel to the monastic life.

In the LXX κατέχειν occurs 50 times in all portions, and it is always trans. The predominant meaning is 1. "to hold fast." It is worth noting that in a few instances it is used of states which possess man. In this connection we find single occurrences of κάτοχος and κατόχιμος for possession by evil spirits.

In the NT, too, sense 1. ("to hold fast") is predominant. [3] It is used a. of one man holding another, Lk. 4:42; Phlm. 13.

It is also used b. of holding fast spiritual values, instruction received or a course or attitude begun (in the good sense): Lk. 8:15; 1 C. 11:2; 15:2 ("if to this day you have kept (in memory) and still keep (in your hearts) the word which I once declared to you as good news"); 1 Th. 5:21; Hb. 3:6, 14; 10:23.

Maintaining the blessings of salvation received is here again, as in the simple form, regarded as a particularly important Christian virtue. We can understand this in the light of the early Christian situation. The Christian state is one of blissful possession and yet also of a long struggle for survival and recognition in a world which views things so very differently. Only by this holding fast can present possession become eternal and heavenly possession. In the last resort this is true of the Church in every age.

It is also used in a bad sense c. of "holding illegally," "holding in prison" (with ἐν) in R. 1:18; 7:6.

Rather along the same lines it means d. "to prevent an evil person or power from breaking out" (as one imprisons criminals to protect society against them), 2 Th. 2:6, 7.

This mysterious apocalyptic passage with its reference first to a neutral and then to a masculine restraint which holds back the last great outbreak of ungodly forces has

---

κ α τ έ χ ω. [1] Cf. E. Rohde, Psyche [9], [10] (1925), II, 11, n. 1, 14-21, 414.

[2] Cf. W. Otto, Priester und Tempel im hellenistischen Ägypten (1905 ff.), 119-125; Reitzenstein Hell. Myst.[1] (1910), 80; [3] (1927), 197-215; Pauly-W., X (1919), s.v. Katochos; RGG[2], IV, 133 f.; W. Bousset, "Das Mönchtum der sketischen Wüste," ZKG, NF, 5 (1923), 20 ff.; Wilcken Ptol., I (1923), 52 ff., 293 f.; F. v. Woess, Das Asylwesen Ägyptens in der Ptolemäerzeit (1923), 113 ff., 237 ff.; cf. also for additional bibl. E. Schlesinger, Die griechische Asylie (1933), III f. Cf. also → I, 532 for an example from the pap.

[3] Here, too, we find the intr. nautical use of κατέχειν (Ac. 27:40).

been much discussed. [4] In spite of N. F. Freese [5] we must regard the two as identical. αὐτόν (v. 6) refers to the man of sin (v. 3). More recently it has been seen that the concepts have a mythological background. [6] This may explain the combination of the neuter and masc. The mysterious ungodly force which will be let loose just before the end, the mystery of iniquity (v. 7), takes concrete shape in an ἄνθρωπος (v. 3), and therefore the κατέχων (who does not have to be a historical magnitude and might be an angel) is a concrete manifestation of the principle of restraint (τὸ κατέχον). A more exact interpretation is hardly possible. The favourite reference to the *pax romana* hardly fits the personal ὁ κατέχων. May it be that the → νῦν (v. 6) suggests allusion to events or a person who came into view only after Paul's stay in Thessalonica (v. 5)? [7]

2. The sense of "to occupy a place" is found only at Lk. 14:9.

3. "To possess" is the sense in 1 C. 7:30. [8] In 2 C. 6:10 (→ ἔχειν, 826) we have the thought that the wealthy is as free as the poor and the poor as rich as the lord of the whole world. The pass. is used for possession by sickness (with something of all the various senses) in Jn. 5:4.

† μετέχω, μετοχή, μέτοχος, συμμέτοχος.

μετέχειν always means "to have a share in" and the obj. is always in the gen. (*gen. partitivus*, Debrunner). The expression sometimes merges with the equivalent μοῖραν or μέρος ἔχειν μετά etc. to produce μοῖραν or μέρος μετέχειν τινός. μετοχή means "participation," μέτοχος "participant," and συμμετέχειν "to share with." συμμέτοχος does not occur in secular writings.

Two points are of theological significance. a. Plat. [1] describes the relation of the individual thing to the idea as μετοχή or μέθεξις. [2] Aristot. equates this Platonic conception with the μίμησις of the Pythagoreans. [3] Here is the root of a usage which is present in all Gk. philosophy, the relation of the individual spirit and the universal, of the lower and the higher, being called a participation (→ ἔχω, 818). At the end of this development stands Plotinus with his comprehensive spiritual hierarchy in which the lower participates in the higher (μετέχειν or μεταλαμβάνειν) and the higher embraces the lower (περιέχειν or περιλαμβάνειν). Thus μετέχειν is the term used to express the connection with the supraterrestrial world. b. Along the same lines, the relation of man to the gods is also defined as participation; this μετοχή is expressed in the spiritual life (Xenoph. Mem., IV, 3, 14; Aristot. Part. An., II, 10, p. 656a, 1 ff.), in the capacity for religious inspiration (Plat. Phaedr., 253a) and knowledge (Plat. Prot., 322a). But it can also be used for fellowship with God after death (Epigr. Graec., 654, 5). Sometimes this communion is extended to the whole cosmos (Max. Tyr., 11, 11b); Plot., e.g., Enn., II, 9, 16; Iambl. Myst., III, 9). Orig. sometimes speaks of Christians having a part in Christ and God (cf. Ign. Eph., 4, 2; Pol., 6, 1; Iren., IV, 20, 5 [MPG, 7, 1035 f.]). A peculiarity of Orig. is that he postulates a group of intermediaries who participate in

---

[4] Cf. the excursus in W. Bornemann in the Meyer Comm. [5, 6] (1894).

[5] "τὸ κατέχον und ὁ κατέχων," ThStKr, 93 (1920/21), 73-77.

[6] E.g., the description of Horus as κατέχων δράκοντα in P. Leid. W. (Reitzenstein Poim., 27). There are many instances in Dib. Th., *ad loc.*

[7] Cf. 1 Th. 3:4: ὅτε πρὸς ὑμᾶς ἦμεν . . . οἴδατε (sc. now).

[8] οὐ κατέχειν, not "to make no use of," but "even with earthly possessions to be free for God as though there were none" (Schlatter, *Erläuterungen, ad loc.*: "ready for any sacrifice and alert for every nod by which the Lord calls them aside"). Here we can again see the sense of holding fast, restraining; cf. the par. μὴ καταχρώμενοι, "not ready to pay to the uttermost."

μετέχω κτλ. [1] Cf. E. Hoffmann, "Methexis u. Metaxy bei Platon" in *Sokrates, NF*, 7 (1919), *Jahresberichte des Philologischen Vereins zu Berlin*, 48.

[2] Both forms occur in accordance with the simple ἕξις and other composites in -οχή.

[3] Metaph., I, 6, p. 987b, 10 ff.

God in a special sense so that they can even be called θεοί. He links this thought with ψ 44:7 (→ infra).

The word is not common in the LXX and occurs mostly in the later sections. Worth noting is its frequent use in an ethical sense for "to participate in a good or evil deed." μετοχή is found only in ψ 121:3, where it is *abstractum pro concreto* for οἱ μέτοχοι. μέτοχος is mostly used as a subst. for "friend," "companion" (cf. κοινωνός in Phlm. 17), "he who holds fellowship with someone." In Prv. 29:10 it means "participant in, guilty of the blood of another" (cf. Herm. m., 4, 1, 9, "of sin").

There is nothing unusual in the NT use of μετέχειν. The passages in which it occurs can all bear the basic meaning of "to share" : 1 C. 9:10 : to partake of the fruits ; 10:17: the one bread is shared among many ; v. 21: to sit at a table and eat various things and thus to have fellowship with the demons behind idolatrous sacrifices ; cf. on κοινωνούς Hos. 4:17: μέτοχος; v. 30 : Pl. enjoys his share with thanksgiving. In Hb. 2:14 He who comes from the divine world shares flesh with men (note that it is here fully synon. with κοινωνεῖν); 5:13 : children feed on milk and therefore all have one nourishment, sharing in the same stage of development ; 7:13 : Christ is a member of the race of Israel, and, belonging to it, He has a part therein. In 1 C. 9:12 one might have expected ἔχουσιν, for others have power over the community and may legitimately claim to be supported by it. But Pl. is already dominated by the thought that they do not have ἐξουσία alone ; they must share it with him ; hence he uses μετέχουσιν.

We never find μετέχειν Χριστοῦ or θεοῦ in the NT. Yet there is a hint of it in the οὐκ ἔχεις μέρος μετ᾽ ἐμοῦ of Jn. 13:8. [4] Here the reference is to participation in Christ, and this fits in well with John's Gospel. He who is so proud that he will not let Jesus do him service cannot stand in the personal fellowship with Him based upon the cross and remission. If baptism is typified in the footwashing, the saying is to be understood against the background of early Christian thought. By baptism one is incorporated into the body of Christ, into the community. μέρος ἔχειν is also used for this fellowship with Christ. Jn. 14:30 : ἐν ἐμοὶ οὐκ ἔχει οὐδέν, might bear the same sense of having no fellowship with Me, though the context suggests having no power over Me. Jesus is saying farewell (v. 28 f.). He is about to take the final path (v. 31). His disciples are not to think, however, that the prince of the world has power over Him (v. 30). He dies simply in obedience to the Father (v. 31).

μετοχή is used in 2 C. 6:14 not so much in the sense of participation as in that of fellowship (cf. μέτοχος in the OT). It is thus a synonym of → κοινωνία, though elsewhere there is a distinction of meaning, since it is common participation in a third which establishes mutual fellowship (κοινωνία).

μέτοχος is used in Lk. 5:7 in the LXX sense of a partner or colleague (subst.). It is found elsewhere only in Hb., but this is not surprising, since it is a select and almost philosophical term. [5] Except in Hb. 12:8 [6] one might almost detect contact with Platonic modes of expression by way of Philo. Thus in Hb. 1:9 the quotation from ψ 44:7 is related to Christ and the reference is to His μέτοχοι, and if in

---

[4] μέρος ἔχειν also occurs in Rev. 20:6 : "To have a part in the first resurrection."

[5] συμμέτοχος is if anything even more select and it is thus in place in Eph. In Eph. 3:6 the συν- is emphasised; the Gentiles share with the Jews the promise, i.e., the salvation which is already given here and which will be consummated hereafter (cf. 1 Cl., 34, 7). In Eph. 5:7 the reference is to common guilt (as in Prv. 29:10 → supra).

[6] The same combination is found in Sir. 51:28. It is a par. to the μεταλαβεῖν τῆς ἁγιό-τητος αὐτοῦ two verses later.

Hb. 3:14 Christians are called μέτοχοι τοῦ Χριστοῦ (→ I, 601), we have an echo of participation in God which later Christianity brings out more plainly (→ 830). Yet what a difference! The good which Christians share is in Hb. heavenly calling (3:1) and therefore eschatological. Thus fellowship with Christ is consummated only after faithful perseverance (3:14, → κατέχειν, 829). It is now only at its commencement. It is a partaking of the Spirit of Christ (6:4), the preliminary eschatological gift according to the early Christian view. This participation in Christ is brought into the period between the aeons. The partakers of Christ are strictly the angels (1:9), but the divine and angelic world invades this aeon and summons individuals to participation.

Hanse

ζάω, ζωή (βιόω, βίος),
ἀναζάω, ζῷον,
ζωογονέω, ζωοποιέω

ζάω, ζωή (βιόω, βίος) (→ θάνατος).

A. ζωή in Greek Usage.

1. Classical Usage.

a. ζωή (ζῆν) [1] denotes in Greek the physical vitality of organic beings, animals, men and also plants. [2] Life is understood, not as a thing, but as vitality, as the nature or manner which characterises all living creatures as such. [3] Hence ζωή

ζ ά ω, ζ ω ή. E. Rohde, *Psyche*[4] (1907); C. F. Nägelsbach, *Die homerische Theologie* (1840), 308-350; *Die nachhomerische Theologie* (1857), 371-423; P. Kleinert, "Zur Idee des Lebens im AT," ThStKr, 68 (1895), 693-732; W. W. Graf Baudissin, "At.liches hajjim 'Leben' in der Bdtg. von Glück," in *Festschr. E. Sachau* (1915), 143-161; L. Dürr, *Die Wertung des Lebens im AT und im antiken Orient* (1926); O. Procksch, "Der Lebensgedanke im AT," in Chrtt. Wiss., 4 (1928), 145-158, 193-206; A. Bertholet, *Die israelitischen Vorstellungen vom Zustand nach dem Tode*[2] (1914); E. Sellin, "Die at.liche Hoffnung auf Auferstehung und ewiges Leben," NkZ, 30 (1919), 232-289; A. Schulz, *Der Sinn des Todes im AT* (lectures to the Academy of Braunsberg, 1919); F. Nötscher, *Altorientalischer u. at.licher Auferstehungsglaube* (1926); G. Quell, *Die Auffassung des Todes in Israel* (1925); W. Caspari, "Tod u. Auferstehung nach der Enderwartung des späteren Judentumes," *Journal of the Society of Oriental Research*, 10 (1926), 1 ff.; E. v. Schrenck, *Die joh. Anschauung vom Leben* (1898); J. Lindblom, *Das ewige Leben* (1914); J. B. Frey, "Le Concept de 'Vie' dans l'Evangile de Saint Jean," *Biblica* I (1920), 37-58, 211-239.

[1] From an early period the verb can be linked with lengths of time, "to live so many years long." It can also mean "to continue in life." It can be used along with adv. describing life as easy or difficult. Since physical life needs means of life, we may have the phrase ζῆν ἀπό or ἐκ. On all these pts. cf. the lexicons.

[2] Aristot. Eth. Nic., I, 6, p. 1097b, 33 f.: τὸ μὲν γὰρ ζῆν κοινὸν εἶναι φαίνεται καὶ τοῖς φυτοῖς. Cf. An., II, 2, p. 413a, 25 f.

[3] Since ζωή is the self-evident being of man in which he always finds himself, and not something which establishes or encounters him or alternates, ζωή is never hypostatised or deified, cf. φύσις, → θάνατος, ὑγίεια. In Gk. there is no figurative representation of Ζωή. The later theological reflection of the Orphics (Kern Orph. Fr., 298) and the Stoics (v. Arnim, II, 305, 20 f.; 312, 21 f.; 315, 5; Cornut. Theol. Graec., 2, p. 3, 5 ff. [ed. C. Lang, 1881]) certainly derived the name Ζεύς etymologically from ζῆν (Cornutus, the ψυχή of the κόσμος: καλεῖται Ζεύς, πρώτως καὶ διὰ παντὸς ζῶσα καὶ αἰτία οὖσα τοῖς ζῶσι τοῦ ζῆν), but it did not produce any image of ζωή.

cannot be used in the plur. ζωή is expressed in the fact that living creatures rise up and move and have their distinctive ἔργον. Figuratively, therefore, one may speak of the life of, e.g., valid νόμιμα (Soph. Ant., 457), and Plato can describe as a ζῶντα καὶ ἔμψυχον the λόγος τοῦ εἰδότος which is efficacious (Phaedr., 276a). [4] The whole κόσμος as ἔμψυχος can be called a ζῷον. [5] Aristot. in An., II, 2, p. 413a, 22 ff. says that we can speak of ζῆν where there are νοῦς, αἴσθησις, κίνησις καὶ στάσις ἡ κατὰ τόπον, ἔτι κίνησις ἡ κατὰ τροφὴν καὶ φθίσις τε καὶ αὔξησις, or where one of these δυνάμεις is present. ζωή is most commonly defined as movement in the broadest sense, i.e., not merely as spatial movement but also as ἀλλοίωσις. It is self-movement as distinct from mechanical movement. [6]

It thus belongs to physics, and, in so far as this seeks causes, the cause of ζωή is found in the → ψυχή. [7] We may accept as ζῷα all beings ὅσσα ψυχὴν ἔχει (Democr. Fr., 278, II, 117, 8 ff., Diels). [8] Thus in Plat. Phaedr., 105c ff. the immortality of the soul is maintained in view of the fact that ψυχή and ζωή belong essentially together (cf. Phaedr., 245c ff.; Soph., 248e ff.). According to Aristot. An., II, 1, p. 412a, 27 ff. the ψυχή is the ἐντελέχεια ἡ πρώτη σώματος φυσικοῦ δυνάμει ζωὴν ἔχοντος or σώματος φυσικοῦ ὀργανικοῦ (cf. p. 412a, 19 ff.; p. 413a, 20 ff.). It is in keeping that in true Gk. thought, and expressly in Aristot., only σώματα can be regarded as living, since the ψυχή exists only in the σῶμα (An., II, 1, p. 412b, 7 ff.; p. 413a, 3 ff.). Even human ζωή is understood as a natural phenomenon. It does not differ from that of plants and animals by the mere fact that it is my individual life. Death, too, is regarded as a natural phenomenon. It is the antithesis of life (e.g., Plat. Phaed., 71d, 105c ff.) and yet it also belongs to it as its natural end. [9]

ζωή can also be posited of the godhead to the extent that the gods, which are regarded as ἀθάνατοι both in philosophy and in popular superstition, are still classified as ζῷα having a σῶμα and ψυχή, the only point being that this σύστασις is never dissolved. Thus Plato distinguishes between ἀθάνατα and θνητὰ ζῷα (Phaedr., 246d ff.; Tim., 38c ff.). [10] Of course, the gods which are accepted as ἀθάνατοι (the constellations) are not supreme being or supreme deity. Their immortality is simply unending duration in time, whereas non-temporal eternity is ascribed to supreme deity, so that ζωή cannot properly be assigned to it. In Phaed., 106d Plato links together as immortal God and the εἶδος of ζωή (ὁ δέ γε θεός ... καὶ αὐτὸ τὸ τῆς ζωῆς εἶδος καὶ εἴ τι ἄλλο ἀθάνατόν ἐστιν). For him the cosmos is a ζῷον ἔμψυχον, but it is the son of God and not supreme deity itself (Tim., 30b; 34b, 37c, 92b). On the other hand, in Soph., 248e κίνησις, ζωή, ψυχή and φρόνησις are ascribed to the παντελῶς ὄν as well. For Aristot. the deity is incorporeal and unmoved as πρῶτον κινοῦν, but it is

---

[4] There is a late example in Ditt. Syll.³, 1173, 5 : ζῶσαι ἀρεταί (the miracles of Aesculapius).

[5] Plat. Tim., 30b; Albinus, Isagoge, 14, p. 169 (C. F. Hermann, Platonis Dialogi, VI [1870]); v. Arnim, II, 169, 15; 191, 34; 192, 7 etc.

[6] Plat. Phaedr., 245c ff.; Leg., X, 895c ff.; Aristot. An., II, 2, p. 412b, 16 f.; p. 413a, 22 ff.

[7] A materialistic philosophy has naturally to probe further and to derive ζωή from matter. Thus acc. to Diogenes of Apollonia the ψυχή of all ζῷα is the same, namely, ἀήρ, Fr., 5 (I, 425, 19 f., Diels), while acc. to Alexander Polyhistor the Pythagoreans regard θερμόν as ζωῆς αἴτιον, so that it may be said of the radiance of the sun : ζωοποιεῖν πάντα (Diog. L., VIII, 27). For the Stoics πνεῦμα is the basic thing to which all life may be traced, Xenophanes being the first to interpret the ψυχή as πνεῦμα (I, 42, 26, Diels).

[8] In popular and poetical language ψυχή and ζωή can be used interchangeably, cf. Rohde, I, 47; II, 141, n. 1; for ψυχή as the vital force in Ionic philosophy, ibid., II, 139 ff.

[9] Aristot. An., II, 1, p. 412a, 14 f.: ζωὴν δὲ λέγομεν τὴν δι' αὑτοῦ τροφήν τε καὶ αὔξησιν καὶ φθίσιν, → θάνατος.

[10] J. Stenzel, "Über zwei Begriffe der platonischen Mystik : Ζῷον und Κίνησις" (Beilage z. Jahresbericht des Johannes-Gymnasiums zu Breslau, 1914). On the term ζῷον cf. H. Diels, Doxographi Graeci (1879), 432.

still a ζῷον, its ζωή being eternal. [11] Inasmuch as the deity is pantheistically understood as the total κόσμος, the ζῷον ἔμψυχον, we naturally find the scientific concept of ζωή as the vitality of the whole taking individual shape in the specific phenomena of organic life as they rise and change and fall. [12] Yet in Aristot. the deity stands outside the κόσμος as pure νοῦς. The ἐνέργεια of νοῦς is ζωή, but the ἐνέργεια of the divine νοῦς is ζωὴ ἀρίστη καὶ ἀΐδιος (Metaph., XI, 7, p. 1072b, 26 ff.).

b. It may be seen from this usage that Greek thought originally understands by ζωή something rather more than and other than what is expressed by the scientific term ζωή with its fundamentally similar reference to man, animals and plants. If the ζωή of the deity is described as νοεῖν, as θεωρία, and characterised as ἀρίστη, as μακαριότης, then ζωή is defined in terms of what man himself regards as his supreme and characteristic possibility, namely, θεωρία. To the degree that νοεῖν or θεωρεῖν is understood only as a δύναμις present in a natural phenomenon, like αἴσθησις and κίνησις (Aristot. An., II, p. 413a, 23 ff.), it can still be regarded as an expression of ζωή as itself a natural phenomenon. But in fact the understanding of νοῦς goes beyond this. It can be described as something different from vital ζωή which has come into the soul θύραθεν (Gen. An., II, 736b, 27 f.; 744b, 21) and which is the divine in man. [13] If life in the νοῦς, θεωρία, is really man's supreme possibility, and if this θεωρία can never be fulfilled in man except in the greatest separation from the σῶμα, though not apart from it, this means that fundamentally true human ζωή is not the ζωή in virtue of which a being becomes a ζῷον by the unity of σῶμα and ψυχή. In the Greek concept of ζωή there are thus two motifs, as in the concept of ψυχή. On the one side ψυχή is the principle of vital life in matter, and on the other it is the specifically human principle of self-awareness, so that in one trend in Greek philosophy ψυχή can be dualistically opposed to → σῶμα as an eternal and pre-existent stranger within it. [14] Similarly, ζωή is not merely life as a natural phenomenon but also specifically human life which man does not enjoy merely in virtue of the fact that he is a ζῷον.

No clear linguistic distinction is made at this point. Yet it is obvious that specifically human life must be differentiated from natural ζωή. Nor is this a mere question of the differentiation of ζωή in the ζῷα, since not all organisms are equally rich and complicated. [15] Human life is specifically distinct from all other in virtue of the fact that its possibilities are not fulfilled in factuality like those of organic nature. An indication of this is the fact that man's life can be a life for

---

[11] Metaph., XI, 7, p. 1072b, 28 ff.: φαμὲν δὲ τὸν θεὸν εἶναι ζῷον ἀΐδιον ἄριστον, ὥστε ζωὴ καὶ αἰὼν συνεχὴς καὶ ἀΐδιος ὑπάρχει τῷ θεῷ· τοῦτο γὰρ ὁ θεός, Cael., I, 9, p. 279a, 20 ff.; of the θεῖον τὸ πρῶτον καὶ ἀκρότατον : ἀναλλοίωτα καὶ ἀπαθῆ τὴν ἀρίστην ἔχοντα ζωὴν καὶ τὴν αὐταρκεστάτην διατελεῖ τὸν ἅπαντα αἰῶνα. Cael., II, 3, p. 286a, 9 : θεοῦ δ᾽ ἐνέργεια ἀθανασία· τοῦτο δ᾽ ἔστι ζωὴ ἀΐδιος.

[12] Cf. Heracl. Fr., 62 : ἀθάνατοι θνητοί, θνητοὶ ἀθάνατοι, ζῶντες τὸν ἐκείνων θάνατον, τὸν δὲ ἐκείνων βίον τεθνεῶτες (I, 89, 14 f., Diels) and cf. how Anaxim. understands the relation of the γένεσις and φθορά of individual phenomena to the ἄπειρον which is a θεῖον and ἀθάνατον (I, 15, 22 ff.; 17, 29 ff., Diels), and also how Stoicism conceives of the origin of individual life (→ infra).

[13] E. Rohde, II³ (1903), 303, n. 2.

[14] Cf. the mythological tradition which is so significant in the Orphics, the Pythagoreans and Empedocles and which is reconstructed by Plato, → ψυχή.

[15] Aristot. An., II, 2, p. 413a, 20 ff.; cf. μᾶλλον μετέχειν τῆς ζωῆς, Hist. An., VIII, 1, p. 588b, 8.

something, [16] whereas the meaning of natural life is simply the continuation of the individual ζῶον or species. Above all, man's life is not a state but a being in unfulfilled or only partially fulfilled possibilities, while the life of deity is always fulfilled. [17] In the case of man what matters is his true life, and usually this is not identical with his factual life. This may be seen in the fact that Homer calls the gods ῥεῖα (effortlessly) ζώοντες (Il., 6, 138) and distinguishes heroes from men οἷοι νῦν βροτοί εἰσιν. It may also be seen in the fact that human life can be characterised as ἀγαθή (Plat. Resp., 521a), ἀρίστη (Aristot. Metaph., XI, 7, p. 1072b, 28), μακαρία (Plat. Leg., IV, 713c), λυσιτελεστάτη (Plat. Resp., 344e), or αἰσχρά (Plat. Leg., XII, 944c). It may be seen above all in adverbial phrases like εὖ ζῆν, [18] ζῆν κάλλιον καὶ ὀρθότερον (Plat. Menex., 248d), ἄριστα ζῆν (ibid., 248a, cf. Gorg., 512e), κοσμίως ζῆν, [19] κατὰ λόγον ζῆν (Plat. Leg., III, 689d). From this we may gather that human life is more than a natural process of τροφή, αὔξησις and φθίσις (→ 833). It includes an individual and appropriate fate in terms of which it may be regarded as happy or unhappy. Above all it knows its possibilities and thus stands under the question of what is proper to it (the εὖ), [20] whether it is true or perverted. As one may speak of ζῆν κατὰ λόγον, so it may be said that one understands how to live; Xenoph. Mem., III, 3, 11: ἦ οὐκ ἐντεθύμησαι, ὅτι, ὅσα τε νόμῳ μεμαθήκαμεν κάλλιστα ὄντα, δι' ὧν γε ζῆν ἐπιστάμεθα, ταῦτα πάντα διὰ λόγου ἐμάθομεν; Doubt may also arise whether the life we live really deserves the name:

> τίς οἶδεν, εἰ τὸ ζῆν μέν ἐστι κατθανεῖν,
> τὸ κατθανεῖν δὲ ζῆν κάτω νομίζεται (Eur. Fr. [TGF] → θάνατος).

c. This conception is finally facilitated by the co-existence of βίος (βιοῦν) along with ζωή (ζῆν). [21] Factual human life always takes shape in an individual βίος in which it may succeed or fail, and the question arises in what βίος human ζωή is truly manifested. βίος denotes manner of life or character, and it is closely related to ἦθος. [22] βίος can also be used of animals [23] or the gods (Plat. Phaedr., 247e), but here the reference is to species, whereas the βίοι of men (the plur. can

---

[16] ζῆν with dat., e.g., πατρίδι, Demosth. Or., 7, 17, cf. 11, 18; πατρί, Dion. Hal., 3, 17, 3; Menand. Fr., 507 (CAF, III, 145 : τοῦτ' ἔστι τὸ ζῆν, οὐχ ἑαυτῷ ζῆν μόνον.

[17] Aristot. Metaph., XI, 7, p. 1072b, 24 f.: εἰ οὖν οὕτως εὖ ἔχει, ὡς ἡμεῖς ποτέ, ὁ θεὸς ἀεί ...

[18] Plat. Crito, 48b: ὅτι οὐ τὸ ζῆν περὶ πλείστου ποιητέον, ἀλλὰ τὸ εὖ ζῆν; Resp., 354a : ὅ γε εὖ ζῶν μακάριός τε καὶ εὐδαίμων; 387d: αὐτάρκης πρὸς τὸ εὖ ζῆν. Aristot. Part. An., II, 10, p. 656a, 5 ff.: ὅσων μὴ μόνον τοῦ ζῆν ἀλλὰ καὶ τοῦ εὖ ζῆν ἡ φύσις μετείληφεν. τοῦτο δ' ἐστὶ τὸ τῶν ἀνθρώπων γένος. Aristot. coins the term εὐζωία, Eth. Nic., I, 8, p. 1098b, 21, cf. I, 6, p. 1098a, 12 ff.

[19] Plat. Leg., VII, 806e; cf. Ditt. Syll.³, 889, 13 ff.: κοσμίως τε καὶ μεγαλοφρόνως.

[20] Plat. Resp., 329a : The aged say in respect of their youth : τότε μὲν εὖ ζῶντες, νῦν δὲ οὐδὲ ζῶντες. Used emphatically ζῆν means "truly to live" in the burial inscr. in Dio C., 69, 19 : βιοὺς μέν ἔτη τόσα, ζήσας δὲ ἔτη ἑπτά. Plat. Resp., 490b : the ὄντως φιλομαθής strives for comprehension of the ὄντως ὄν that he γνοίη τε καὶ ἀληθῶς ζώη καὶ τρέφοιτο.

[21] βίος and ζωή (ζῆν) are etymologically related; cf. Walde-Pokorny, I, 668 f., 670. This is why their meanings converge. But formally they are so far apart that the sense of their common origin is lost. Hence later ζῆν—ζήσομαι—ἔζησα instead of ζῆν—βιώσομαι—ἐβίων.

[22] The βιολόγος — or ἠθολόγος — is not the biologist but the student of character, the spectator.

[23] Plat. Phileb., 21c of life in ἡδονή : ζῆν δὲ οὐκ ἀνθρώπου βίον ἀλλὰ τινος πλεύμονος (a kind of mollusk).

be used) are their individual forms of life, though always on the specific Greek presupposition that there are only limited possibilities of βίος and that in a true βιός the βίος of the human species is purely expressed. [24] Hence βίος can also become a technical term for the writing of a life (biography). [25] As the individual life, βίος can also mean the time or duration of life. [26] One may speak of βίον ζῆν. Thus ζῆν and βιοῦν can be used synonymously, but also ζωή and βίος. [27] In the sense of leading one's life βίος can also be used in the external sense for calling, trade or even means of support or means, [28] though the reference is to the individual life which is implicated in choice [29] and which stands under the question of its true nature as expressed in the question of the βίος βιωτός, [30] of the → σωτηρία τοῦ βίου (Plat. Prot., 356d e), of the τέλειος βίος. [31] The question is answered, e.g., in statements that βίος is worth living only in the πόλις. [32] For this reason νόμος rules the βίος of men (Democr. Fr., 248 [II, 110, 3 ff., Diels]; Plat. Leg., II, 663a; VII, 803a), and education is needed : πᾶς γὰρ ὁ βίος τοῦ ἀνθρώπου εὐρυθμίας τε καὶ εὐαρμοστίας δεῖται (Plat. Prot., 326b). He who is without the τροφὴ παιδεύσεως : χωλὴν τοῦ βίου διαπορευθεὶς ζωὴν ἀτελὴς καὶ ἀνόητος εἰς Ἅιδου πάλιν ἔρχεται (Plat. Tim., 44c). According to idealistic philosophy, ·life is truly fulfilled as life in the νοῦς, in θεωρία, as the life of the philosopher. [33] If Plat. Phileb., 22a distinguishes τρεῖς βίοι as the basic possibilities given to men, so from the time of Aristot. (Eth. Nic., I, 3, p. 1095b, 14 ff.) there is a customary threefold division of βίοι into the ἀπολαυστικός, πρακτικός (πολιτι-

---

[24] For the ancient concept of βίος as the form of life, cf. esp. W. Jaeger, "Über Ursprung und Kreislauf des philosophischen Lebensideals," SAB, 1928, 390 ff.

[25] Cf. the βίοι of Plut., distinguished from the χαρακτῆρες of Theophr. by the fact that they describe the paradigmatic possibilities of human lives through historical examples, whereas the latter describe typical forms of life suggested by daily observation ; cf. τὰ τῶν βίων παραδείγματα, Plat. Resp., 618a.

[26] We often find expressions like διὰ παντὸς τοῦ βίου, Plat. Symp., 203d, ἅπαντα τὸν βίον, Plat. Leg., VII, 802a; Symp., 181d, διὰ βίου Plat. Phaed., 75d, cf. τὸν βίον τελευτᾶν, Hdt., I, 32, ἐν δυσμαῖς τοῦ βίου, Plat. Leg., VI, 770a.

[27] Heracl. → n. 12; Aristot. Eth. Eud., I, 1, p. 1215a, 4 etc.

[28] Hence βιωτικός, "belonging to everyday life, corresponding to everyday life," Polyb., 4, 73, 8 : χρεῖαι βιωτικαί, Dion. Hal. Compos. Verb., 3 (ed. H. Usener-L. Radermacher, II [1904 ff.], p. 10, 5 f.): πράγματι' ἄττα βιωτικά. Acc. to Phryn. Epitome one should not say βιωτικόν but χρήσιμον ἐν τῷ βίῳ. Dion. Thr. Art. Gramm., 6, 9 : One should present comedy βιωτικῶς and tragedy ἡρωϊκῶς.

[29] Plat. Phileb., 21d : ἆρ' οὖν αἱρετὸς ἡμῖν βίος ὁ τοιοῦτος; cf. 22d; Resp., 617d ff.; Leg., II, 663 : πρὸς τό τινα ἐθέλειν ζῆν τὸν ὅσιον καὶ δίκαιον βίον. Eur. Iph. Aul., 923.

[30] Plat. Ap., 38a : ὁ δὲ ἀνεξέταστος βίος οὐ βιωτὸς ἀνθρώπῳ; Symp., 216a : οὕτω διετέθην, ὥστε μοι δόξαι μὴ βιωτὸν εἶναι ἔχοντι ὡς ἔχω; Gorg. Pal., 20 f. (II, 259, 22 ff., Diels), Xenoph. Mem., IV, 8, 8 : βίος ἀβίωτος. Cf. Plat. Phileb., 62c : εἴπερ γε ἡμῶν ὁ βίος ἔσται καὶ ὁπωσοῦν ποτε βίος.

[31] Aristot. Eth. Nic., I, 6, p. 1098a, 18; cf. also Plat. Leg., VII, 803a f.: τὰ τῶν βίων πειρώμενος σχήματα διαστήσασθαι κατὰ τρόπους τοὺς τῶν ψυχῶν..., ποία μηχανῇ καὶ τίσιν ποτὲ τρόποις συνόντες τὸν βίον ἄριστα διὰ τοῦ πλοῦ τούτου τῆς ζωῆς διακομισθησόμεθα.

[32] Tyrtaeus, 6, 3 ff. (Diehl, p. 10, 2 ff.); Plat. Ap., 37d; Eur. Herc. Fur., 1281 ff.; 1301 f.: τί κέρδος ἔξομεν βίον γ' ἀχρεῖον ἀνόσιον κεκτημένοι; cf. Soph. Phil., 1018 ; v. E. Wolff, "Platons Apologie" in NPhU, 6 (1929), 62 f. Cf. also Anth. Pal., IX, 9 :

οἶκος καὶ πάτηρ βιότου χάρις· αἱ δὲ περισσαί,
φροντίδες ἀνθρώποις οὐ βίος, ἀλλὰ πόνος.

[33] Plat. Resp., 495c of the philosophers who are untrue to philosophy : βίον οὐ προσήκοντα οὐδ' ἀληθῆ ζῶσι. That the reference is to the true nature of life is also plain in the expression that a life which is lived for δικαιοσύνη is such ὅθεν τοῦ ἀνθρώπου ὁ ἐντὸς ἄνθρωπος ἔσται ἐγκρατέστερος, ibid., 589a.

κός) and θεωρητικός. [34] The third is the highest, for it is divine (Aristot. Eth. Nic., X, 8, p. 1178b, 20 ff.; Metaph., XI, 9, p. 1074b, 25 f.).

If, then, it belongs to the ζωή of man that it is a βίος, human life is always regarded as mine. Yet this thought is not carried through radically. The various βίοι are not regarded as unique and unrepeatable; they are classified and graded in self-repeating types. A leading question is that of the normal βίος. It is not the historical moment, or the claim of the Thou addressed to man in it, which gives man the possibility of true being. What he has to actualise in his individual existence is the supratemporal and general, whether as the νόμος of the πόλις or as the λόγος. This is the basis of the Greek view of education. Nevertheless, both as a natural phenomenon and as a (Platonic) ἀληθῶς ζῆν realised in the individual βίος, ζωή belongs to this world. As natural vitality it certainly transcends the individual, but it does not belong to the other world in the religious sense; and as the ζωή which is fulfilled in the individual life as τέλειος βίος it is a human possibility which is not eschatological except perhaps that the μακαρία ζωή is constantly achieved only in the godhead and only intermittently by us (Aristot. → n. 17), since our φύσις is not ἁπλῆ and is thus subject to μεταβολή (Aristot. Eth. Nic., VII, 15, p. 1154b, 21 ff.).

2. Hellenistic Usage.

a. Stoicism. Stoicism is controlled by the ζωή concept of scientific tradition. ζωή, understood as κίνησις in the broadest sense, [35] is physical life expressed in all organic creatures.

> In contrast to Arist. the whole κόσμος is regarded as a unity of the psycho-physical organism, so that the distinction between the ζῷα which have a ψυχή and the λίθοι and ξύλα is relativised (v. Arnim, III, 90, 12 ff.); and the κόσμος as ζῷον ἔμψυχον is regarded as identical with deity (ibid., II, 191, 34 ff.; 305, 15 ff.). Man is thus a part of the κόσμος, a cosmic phenomenon. His birth is a μεταβολή τοῦ πνεύματος εἰς ζωήν. In him the general vital force of the κόσμος, the πνεῦμα, takes individualised form. [36] As life is a natural phenomenon, so is death (→ θάνατος).

It is quite evident, however, that the actual fulfilment of life is not a natural process, that the κατὰ φύσιν or ὁμολογουμένως or ἀκολούθως τῇ φύσει ζῆν (cf. v. Arnim, Index) is not achieved of itself, but has to be undertaken and realised by an intelligent resolve.

> κατὰ φύσιν ζῆν is equivalent to εὖ ζῆν, κατὰ λόγον or κατ' ἀρετὴν ζῆν (v. Arnim, Index). One may thus speak of a βιωτική (sc. τέχνη) (M. Ant., VII, 61). Man must be reminded that he is not just a ζῷον but primarily an ἄνθρωπος; just as Epict. speaks of the ἐξαίρετον which makes man truly man (Diss., III, 1, 25 f.; IV, 11, 3, 27), so M. Ant. speaks of the ἄνθρωπος, καθὸ ἄνθρωπός ἐστιν (V, 15; IX, 2). If man's ζῆν κατὰ φύσιν is realised only in the ζῆν κατὰ λόγον, [37] it is plain that here again life is seen to stand under the question whether it is true life or not. In Stoic parlance, it stands under the question of its τέλος [38] or its σωτηρία. [39] A man who does not

---

[34] F. Boll, "Vita contemplativa" (SAH, 1920, 8).
[35] E. Norden, Agnostos Theos (1913), 19-22; cf. v. Arnim, II, 285, 26 ff.; 287, 33 ff.
[36] v. Arnim, I, 111, 8 f.; II, 134, 25 ff.; 191, 38 ff.; 217, 17.
[37] For animals the κατὰ φύσιν is identical with the κατὰ τὴν ὁρμήν, v. Arnim, III, 43, 16 ff.
[38] v. Arnim, I, 91, 24 ff.; III, 6, 7 ff.; M. Ant., II, 16; V, 15, the τέλος concept is already Platonic.
[39] Epict. Diss., II, 9, 7 f.; IV, 1, 165: Socrates ἀποθνῄσκων σῴζεται. M. Ant., X, 1.

achieve true humanity is described as "dead."[40] In contrast to this true life,[41] natural ζωή is an ἀδιάφορον which has relative value in the fact that its presence is the presupposition for the attainment of the ideal of virtue.[42] True life does not belong to the other world. It is attained in the χρῆσις οἵα δεῖ φαντασιῶν under the direction of the free ἡγεμονικόν. Its attainment is ἐφ᾽ ἡμῖν.[43]

ζωή κατὰ φύσιν can also be called βίος κατὰ φύσιν (v. Arnim, III, 16, 28 f.), and the life of λογικὰ ζῷα can be distinguished from the life of ἄλογα as βίος.[44] The question of the ὀρθὸς βίος is a live one (v. Arnim, I, 86, 27), and in varying dependence on Aristot. three βίοι are distinguished (ibid., III, 173, 4 f., v. Index). The less importance the πόλις comes to have for the sage, the more the normal βίος of the sage becomes a schematic picture for the Stoic. Attainment is achieved in the contemplation and nurture of the inner life with the goal of making oneself independent of the world and destiny in ἀπέχεσθαι and ἀνέχεσθαι, of reducing the significance of the concrete moment to the general requirement of inner freedom, and of thus annihilating it.[45] Nevertheless, it may be seen, æ.g., from M. Ant., that the dogma does not necessarily blind to the claim of the moment (→ θάνατος).

b. Neo-Platonism. Along with the new influences of oriental dualism, the tradition of anthropological dualism (→ 834), which in Plato had been made to serve an idealistic conception of soul and body, again asserted itself in Neo-Platonism, though not at the price of the idealistic concept of ζωή.

On the one side Plotinus maintains the scientific view of ζωή. ζωή belongs essentially to ψυχή, which pervades the κόσμος as a ζῷον ἔμψυχον and distributes itself in the individual souls indwelling σώματα.[46] Yet through this monistic conception runs a dualistic, as may be seen in the fact that for all his polemic against Gnosticism Plot. regards the human ψυχή as a stranger in the σῶμα. It has come down from above and is to seek again its heavenly home by aversion from the earthly. Thus the individual soul survives death (the migration of souls). Hence a tension arises in the understanding of ζωή. ζωή and ψυχή derive from the νοῦς, which is true being. Above this, beyond the νοῦς and οὐσία, is the ἕν, which has no ζωή but is ζωῆς αἴτιον and πηγὴ ζωῆς.[47] To the degree that Plot. views the world and man from the standpoint of descent or emanation, he sets himself in opposition to the Gk. view of ζωή, since ζωή always occupies a lower rung on the ladder of totality, so that Plot. can use the plur. ζωαί. True ζωή belongs to the νοερὰ φύσις; cf. Enn., I, 4, 3 (p. 66, 26 ff.): ὅτι δ᾽ ἡ τελεία ζωὴ καὶ ἡ ἀληθινὴ καὶ ὄντως ἐν ἐκείνῃ τῇ νοερᾷ φύσει, καὶ ὅτι αἱ ἄλλαι ἀτελεῖς καὶ ἰνδάλματα ζωῆς καὶ οὐ τελείως οὐδὲ καθαρῶς καὶ οὐ μᾶλλον ζωαὶ ἢ τοὐναντίον.[48] It is particularly clear, however, that if man is seen from the standpoint of a return from the earthly and ἐπιστροφή to the νοῦς, true life is not a natural process,

---

[40] Epict. Diss., I, 9, 19; I, 13, 5; III, 23, 28; cf. Sen. De Tranquillitate Animi, V, 5: ultimum malorum est e vivorum numero exire, antequam moriaris → θάνατος.

[41] On one occasion M. Ant. calls it, in distinction from the primary life of man, a βίος ἕτερος, X, 8.

[42] E. Benz, Das Todesproblem in der stoischen Philosophie (1929), 50 ff.

[43] R. Bultmann, ZNW, 13 (1912), 100.

[44] v. Arnim, I, 55, 13 ff.: though βίος (βιοῦν) and ζωή (ζῆν) are often used interchangeably.

[45] R. Bultmann, op. cit., 100 ff.; H. Jonas, Augustin u. das paul. Freiheitsproblem (1930), 8 ff.

[46] Enn., V, 1, 2 (p. 162, 19 ff., Volkmann) of the ψυχή: ζῷα ἐποίησε πάντα ἐμπνεύσασα αὐτοῖς ζωήν. IV, 2, 2 (p. 8, 19): ... ζωὴν χορηγοῦσα τοῖς μέρεσι πᾶσι. P. O. Kristeller, Der Begriff der Seele in der Ethik des Plotin (1929), 73: "ζωή is in Plotinus a synonym of energeia and denotes actuality generally." W. Theiler, "Die Vorbereitung des Neuplatonismus" (Problemata, 1 [1930], 67 f.).

[47] Enn., I, 6, 7 (p. 93, 9); VI, 9, 9 (p. 520, 16 f.); cf. how, acc. to Jul. Or., V (p. 219, 16 f., Hertlein), the mother of the gods is προγονικὴ καὶ ζωογόνος θεός.

[48] Cf. also Enn., I, 4, 10 (p. 75, 9 f.): when αἴσθησις is silent, there is a μᾶλλον ζῆν.

but has to be attained by man. True being is not given to the ψυχή, but set as a task. [49] Man has true ζωή, not ἐνεργείᾳ, but δυνάμει. Over against his natural ζῆν, ᾧ θάνατος μέμικται (Enn., VI, 7, 29 [p. 461, 5]), stands the τελεία ζωή (I, 4, 3 f. [p. 66, 20; 23; 27; and 67, 3; 9]), the ἀληθινὴ ζωή (I, 4, 3 [p. 66, 27]; VI, 9, 9 [p. 522, 7]), the ἀληθῶς ζῆν. [50] The way to this is by turning from the σῶμα, χωρισμός, κάθαρσις. [51] This is grasped in contemplation, in which man becomes οὐσία καὶ νοῦς καὶ ζῷον παντελές (VI, 7, 36 [p. 470, 1]), in which he not only has but is ζωή. [52] In θέα man stands in purely passive relation to the ἕν, being fashioned by it and becoming one with it (VI, 7, 31 [p. 463, 21 ff.]): ἔνθα δὴ εἶδε μὲν [the ψυχή] καλὰ πάντα καὶ ἀληθῆ ὄντα, καὶ ἐπερρώσθη πλέον τῆς τοῦ ὄντος ζωῆς πληρωθεῖσα, καὶ ὄντως ὂν καὶ αὐτὴ γενομένη. This ἀληθινὴ ζωή can be described as belonging to the other world, and Plot. calls it an ἄλλη ζωή (VI, 9, 9 [p. 522, 4]). The way to it is, of course, philosophy (VI, 9, 3), though it no longer rests on πολιτικαὶ ἀρεταί but on μείζονες (I, 2; 3-7), and such a man no longer lives the βίος of an ἀγαθὸς ἄνθρωπος, but the βίος τῶν θεῶν. [53] If, then, the ἀληθινὴ ζωή is no longer accomplished in the historicity of human existence but interrupts history as the moment of vision [54] and thus reduces history to a mere theatre (III, 2, 15), yet in contrast to Gnosticism Plot. seeks to understand true ζωή as a determination of actual man to the degree that his life is a constant striving for the ἀγαθόν under the control of ἔρως, so that the illusion of possession is a sign of non-possession (II, 9, 9 [p. 195, 20 ff.]). [55]

c. Gnosticism. In Plot. true divine life is always characterised by attributes like ἀληθινή. [56] In Gnosticism, however, ζωή without attribute denotes the divine life. Again, in Plot., for all the inconsistency, there is a linguistic connection with Greek tradition inasmuch as he distinguishes true life from natural vitality as the specific life of man which is consciously grasped and achieved in spiritual processes. But this connection is abandoned in Gnosticism. In the context of Gnostic dualism life belongs definitely to the divine side. [57] But this means that life has lost the sense of strictly human life. It is understood as a physical phenomenon, yet not as the vitality of cosmic being, but as indestructible duration and also as the underlying force which triumphs over all obstacles. ζωή is regarded as something which is already present in the divine world. It flows down from this world like a mysterious fluid. It can be present as a "something" in man and things (→ δύναμις). Its true bearer is no longer the ψυχή as natural vitality, but the πνεῦμα, [58] the divine breath of life. [59]

---

[49] Kristeller, op. cit., 13.
[50] VI, 7, 29 (p. 461, 6); VI, 9, 9 (p. 521, 1); Plot. also used the older εὖ ζῆν, also εὐζωία, and ἀγαθή and ἀρίστη ζωή.
[51] Kristeller, op. cit., 16-18; 51-53.
[52] I, 4, 4 (p. 67, 18 f.): ὃς δὴ καὶ ἐνεργείᾳ ἐστὶ τοῦτο καὶ μεταβέβηκε πρὸς τὸ αὐτὸ εἶναι τοῦτο.
[53] I, 2, 7 (p. 57, 20 ff.); cf. V, 1, 4 (p. 165, 19 f.): τὸν ὡς ἀληθῶς ἐπὶ Κρόνου βίον. VI, 9, 11 (p. 524, 29 ff.): καὶ οὗτος θεῶν καὶ ἀνθρώπων θείων καὶ εὐδαιμόνων βίος, ἀπαλλαγὴ τῶν ἄλλων τῶν τῇδε, βίος ἀνήδονος τῶν τῇδε, φυγὴ μόνου πρὸς μόνον. Cf. Porphyr. Abst., II, 52: the philosopher receives from God περὶ τοῦ αἰωνίου βίου τὰς ὑποθήκας.
[54] Since εὐδαιμονία or the ἀγαθὴ ζωή cannot be a temporal phenomenon, I, 5.
[55] Kristeller, op. cit., 63 f.
[56] αἰώνιος ζωή is found in Plut. Is. et Os., 1 (II, 351d/e); Porphyr. Abst., II, 52 → n. 53; Max. Tyr., 6, 1 (p. 65, 13 f., Hobein) (the ζωή of man ἐφήμερος, that of God αἰώνιος).
[57] Cf. Hipp. Ref., IV, 43 (p. 66, 26 ff.); IV, 44 (p. 67, 10 ff.).
[58] Under the influence of the Gk. tradition a philosophical writer can replace πνεῦμα by ψυχή, cf. Sallust Περὶ θεῶν, 16: αἱ μὲν χωρὶς θυσιῶν εὐχαὶ λόγοι μόνον εἰσίν, αἱ δὲ μετὰ θυσιῶν ἔμψυχοι λόγοι, τοῦ μὲν λόγου τὴν ζωὴν δυναμοῦντος, τῆς δὲ ζωῆς τὸν λόγον ψυχούσης. Cf. Reitzenstein Hell. Myst., 317 ff., 330.
[59] Instead of the breath (πνεῦμα) the scent can also be the bearer of life (→ ὀσμή),

Behind this lies a primitive view of vital force which the Greek world had long since outgrown but which revives in Hellenism under alien influences, esp. Egyptian. [60] In Egypt life is the divine fluid which flows down from the Godhead on earthly beings and gives them life. The supposedly divine king receives from the Godhead life which is indestructible and which fills him like a fluid. [61]

If this idea is adopted in Gk. Hellenistic writings, it is not primarily in the context of a systematically dualistic philosophy. ζωή is understood as the divine vitality which rules in every living thing and which is sought for man in prayer and wish and esp. in magic. [62] Above all man seeks the φάρμακον τῆς ζωῆς which guarantees immortality and which is assured in the mysteries. [63]

---

e.g., Iren., I, 4, 1: ἔχουσά (σοφία) τινα ὀδμὴν ἀφθαρσίας, ἐγκαταλειφθεῖσαν αὐτὴν τοῦ Χριστοῦ καὶ τοῦ ἁγίου Πνεύματος, → n. 201.

[60] L. Troje, "ΑΔΑΜ u. ΖΩΗ," SAH, 1916, 17; E. Norden, Die Geburt des Kindes (1924), 119-121. For the connection between life (ζωή) and breath (πνεῦμα), v. F. Preisigke, Vom göttl. Fluidum nach ägypt. Anschauung (1920); Die Gotteskraft der frühchristl. Zeit (1922). Persian influences have also to be taken into account. In Persia eternal duration belongs to life from the very first. This emerges in the name of the first man, Gayomard, "mortal life." His myth is designed to explain how living men can die. The history of any one of the terms which in Hellenism are used more or less as equivalents for the power of mana, e.g., ζωή, → πνεῦμα, → δύναμις, → δόξα, → φῶς, → χάρις etc., is not to be sought, of course, in isolation from the rest.

[61] In the titles of Gk. and Egypt. kings we often have the predicate αἰωνόβιος, or else the king is called the εἰκὼν ζῶσα τοῦ Διός (Ditt. Or., I, 90, 3); cf. Norden, op. cit., 120; Preisigke, Gotteskraft, 7.

[62] The Godhead disposes of ζωή and is invoked as κύριος τῆς ζωῆς (Preis. Zaub., XII, 255 f.) or ὁ ζῶν θεός (ibid., IV, 959 f.; XII, 79, and cf. E. Peterson, Εἷς Θεός [1926], 42 f., 309). Cf. also Preis. Zaub., XII, 238: δεῦρό μοι ὁ ἐκ τῶν τεσσάρων ἀνέμων, ὁ παντοκράτωρ, ὁ ἐνφυσήσας πνεῦμα ἀνθρώποις εἰς ζωήν; ibid., XII, 173 f.: εὐχαριστῶ σοι, ὅτι με ἔλυσεν τὸ ἅγιον πνεῦμα, τὸ μονογενές, τὸ ζῶν. If there is Jewish and Christian influence in this sphere, the basis is the generally Hellenistic and syncretistic conception of ζωή. A particular mark of orient. influence is the fact that ζωή is often numbered with ὑγίεια, σωτηρία etc., and simply, means salvation; so in magic, Preis. Zaub., III, 576; T. Schermann, "Griech. Zauberpapyri" (TU, 34, 2b [1909], 41-44; Pap. Osloenses, I [ed. S. Eitrem, 1925], 88). For life in the sense of salvation in acclamations and wishes (also in burial inscr.), cf. Baudissin, Festschr. f. E. Sachau, 156; E. Peterson, op. cit., 26 f., 175 f., 310; F. J. Dölger, Antike u. Christentum, I (1929), 313. It certainly rests on orient. influence (in the first instance of piety) that life and victory are almost equivalent and are combined; cf. Schermann, op. cit., 45; Peterson, op. cit., 159 f., 314; Loh. Apk. on Rev. 2:7; → νικάω.

[63] On φάρμακον τῆς ζωῆς, cf. Reitzenstein Hell. Myst., 314. In magic and the mysteries we can see the influence of older mythological notions of miraculous means of countering death (cf. A. Ungnad-H. Gressmann, Das Gilgamesch-Epos [1911], 147 ff. → ἀθανασία). The conception is widespread of a tree in Paradise whose fruits give immortality (cf. H. Gunkel in his Comm.⁵ [1922] on Gn. 9:2). In Persian it is the Haoma tree; in Hellenistic tradition, perhaps under the infl. of the magical significance of oil in Egypt, it is the olive tree (cf. Bousset-Gressmann, 488; L. Troje, op. cit., 83-88). Hence the significance of a-nointing in the mysteries as a means of conferring immortality, cf. Orig. Cels., VI, 27, p. 97, 5 (P. Koetschau, 1899): κέχρισμαι χρίσματι λευκῷ ἐκ ξύλου ζωῆς, → ἀλείφω, I, 230, 9 ff.; also W. Bousset, ZNW, 18 (1917/18), 16-18; R. Reitzenstein, Die Vorgeschichte der christl. Taufe (1929), 171-175; Wnd. Jk. on 5:14 → 472. Belief in the divine power of flowing water, which derives from (Semitic) nature religion, led to the idea of a fount of life in the heavenly world and also to belief in the lifegiving power of sacramental water, whether as a drink dispensing immortality or as baptism (cf. W. Bousset, Hauptprobleme der Gnosis [1907], 278-296; Reitzenstein, op. cit., 189-200; F. Cumont, Die oriental. Religionen im röm. Heidentum³ [1931], 250 f.; Bau. J. on 4:14; → ὕδωρ). But above all the concept of the water of life is used figuratively for revelation in general, as in the Od. Sol. On the figur. use of the tree of life in Judaism, esp. in Philo, → infra.

In Gnostic dualism life is regarded as an absolutely otherworldly divine power or as the ἀφθαρσία established by it, so that this ζωή cannot be received in the earthly world and its apparent life. [64]

Cf. Valentinus in Cl. Al. Strom., IV, 13, 89, 6 : ὁπόσον ἐλάττων ἡ εἰκὼν τοῦ ζῶντος προσώπου, τοσοῦτον ἥσσων ὁ κόσμος τοῦ ζῶντος αἰῶνος (i.e., of God). Among the Mandaeans God is always called the "life" (distinguished as the first, second and third life), and in contrast to the world this is spoken of as an "alien" or "hidden" life. "Living" or "... of life" is used to denote relationship to the divine world (e.g., messenger, emissary, word, call, way, scent, treasure, water, garment, planting, stem or fruits of life). [65] Acc. to the strata of Gnostic piety the divine power of ζωή is regarded quite materialistically as a something which flows into the believer or there is striving to experience ζωή in the manner of life. Both are reflected in the common combination of ζωή with φῶς. [66] → φῶς, too, denotes the power of the divine world, cf. Hipp. Ref., IV, 43, p. 66, 27: προσῳκείωται ... τῷ μὲν φωτὶ κατὰ φύσιν ἡ ζωή (cf. IV, 44, p. 67, 12). The mystery formula of the Marcosites invokes God as <τὸν> φῶς ὀνομαζόμενον καὶ πνεῦμα ἀγαθὸν καὶ ζωή (Iren., I, 21, 3). In the Teaching of Queen Cleopatra ζωή and φῶς denote the divine being. [67] As "light" and "life" are used for salvation in the Od. Sol. (cf. "immortality" in 8:23; 9:4; 15:8; 40:6 etc.), so in the Coptic Gnostic writings God is light and life (Griech. Christl. Schriftsteller, VIII, 1 [1905], 344, 12; 352, 32; 361, 16 f., C. Schmidt), and what He gives is light or life or the light of life (ibid., p. 103, 10 ff.; 258, 28 ff.). In the Mandaeans light is regularly used for God along with life. [68] This combination is particularly characteristic of one group of Hermetic writings. As Ptolemaios in Epiph. Haer., 33, 7, 7 defines the οὐσία of God as ἀφθαρσία τε καὶ φῶς αὐτὸ ὄν, ἁπλοῦν τε καὶ μονοειδές, so in Corp. Herm., I, 12 the πάντων πατήρ is called ζωή καὶ φῶς. [69] ζωή and φῶς may also be used of the being of true man, i.e., of the original man, who fell into matter and whose divine being intermingled with φύσις, so that man is now διπλοῦς, namely, θνητὸς μὲν διὰ τὸ σῶμα, ἀθάνατος δὲ διὰ τὸν οὐσιώδη ἄνθρωπον (Corp. Herm., I, 15, cf. Scott, I, p. 296, 28 ff.; 300, 10 ff. and Fr., 15, ibid., p. 538). In this common combination (Corp. Herm., I, 9, 12, 17, 21, 32; XIII, 9 and 18 f.) it may be seen that ζωή does not imply mere duration but more particularly the vital force which effects this. That it is understood physically even

---

[64] In the pantheistic parts of the Herm. lit. the ζωή of the Godhead and the cosmos is naturally depicted along the lines of ancient Egyptian piety (cf. Akhenaton's hymn to the sun, G. Roeder, Urkunden zur Religion des alten Ägypten² [1923], 62-65; A. Erman, Die Literatur der Ägypter [1923], 358-362; AOT, 15-18) and the Stoic tradition (cf. J. Kroll, Die Lehren des Hermes Trismegistos [1914], 43-51; ibid., 117 ff. on the world soul in the Hermetics, 158 ff. on the κόσμος as ζῷον). God is ζωή (Corp. Herm., XI, 15 f.); the κόσμος as the son of the supreme God, as His εἰκών and as ἡνωμένος ἐκείνῳ, is the πλήρωμα τῆς ζωῆς (XII, 15; cf. XIV, 10 : οὕτω καὶ ὁ θεὸς ἐν μὲν οὐρανῷ ἀθανασίαν σπείρει, ἐν δὲ γῇ μεταβολήν, ἐν δὲ τῷ παντὶ ζωὴν καὶ κίνησιν).
[65] Cf. the Indexes in Lidzbarski.
[66] Cf. Bau. J. on 1:4; G. P. Wetter, Phōs (1915), 50-56; W. Bousset, Kyrios Christos² (1921), 175 f. Cf. also the Gnostic description of the soul of man as σπινθήρ (spark) τῆς ζωῆς, Hipp. Ref., VII, 28, p. 209, 1 ff.; Iren., I, 24, 2. When a father calls his son γλυκύτερον φωτὸς καὶ ζόης on a Christian inscr. in Rome (W. M. Ramsay, Luke the Physician [1908], 375), this is no true par. → φῶς. On the other hand, the Palestinian inscr. elucidated by E. Peterson, Εἷς Θεός (1926), 37-43, in which φῶς and ζωή are genii to lead the soul to heaven, is relevant in this connection, as is also the common combination of φῶς and ζωή along with the sign of the cross in Christian epigraphy (Peterson, op. cit., 39; F. J. Dölger, op. cit., 12 and 48). In Syria esp. there is a liking for φῶς and ζωή linked in the form of a cross, F. J. Dölger, Ichthys, I (1910), 247 $\left(\begin{matrix} & \Phi & \\ Z & \Omega & H \\ & \Sigma & \end{matrix} \right)$.
[67] Reitzenstein Hell. Myst., 314 f.
[68] Cf. the Indexes in Lidzbarski.
[69] Cf. I, 9 and 21 and the characterisation of God in Fr., 23 and 24 in W. Scott, Hermetica, I (1924), 540, 542.

though it is divine may be seen from the differentiation between ζωή as the power of ψυχή and ζωή as the power of νοῦς (ibid., I, 17); yet here ψυχή is regarded as divine rather than earthly or natural vitality (as μετέχουσα τῆς τοῦ δημιουργικοῦ δυνά- μεως, Fr. 16, Scott, I, p. 538). [70] As a thing rather than a manner of life like βίος, ζωή is contained in man. But it is hampered by the σῶμα, so that man must be taught concerning his true being by revelation in order to liberate himself from the σῶμα [71] and to return to ζωή and φῶς (Corp. Herm., I, 21 and 32). The ἔνωσις of the inner and true man with God implies ζωή for him (I, 6). It is also clear that this is under- stood as a thing, as a divine vitality, as physical force, for the ascent to God can be called the new birth (→ παλιγγενεσία, I, 687) which gives an ἀθάνατον σῶμα (XIII, 3), and this new birth can be described as endowment with divine δυνάμεις, with the last of which, ἀλήθεια (→ I, 240), ζωή and φῶς are associated (XIII, 9, cf. 12). The ἔνωσις thereby attained is indicated by the fact that the divine powers in the regenerate praise God : ... ζωή καὶ φῶς, ἀφ' ὑμῶν εἰς ὑμᾶς χωρεῖ ἡ εὐλογία (XIII, 18), and the regenerate prays : τὸ πᾶν τὸ ἐν ἡμῖν σῶζε ζωή, φώτιζε φῶς (XIII, 19). Cf. also the concluding prayer of the λόγος τέλειος : ἐγνωρίσαμέν <σε>, ὦ <ζωή> τῆς ἀνθρωπίνης ζωῆς. [72]

If ζωή is a physical phenomenon which can simply be called → ἀθανασία (Corp. Herm., I, 28), there is naturally a good deal more in the term, as may be seen from the fact that this ζωή can already be experienced in ecstatic vision and that it can be described as a state of blessedness in which the redeemed sees God and praises him in the dance of heavenly δυνάμεις. [73] In fact, therefore, ζωή is experienced as a definite physical state, and yet it is also awaited in the future. It must be described as other- worldly and eschatological inasmuch as man, even though he has it within him in terms of speculation concerning the first man, [74] does not really have it and cannot truly con- ceive of it as he now is, but must attain to it through a new self-understanding given by divine revelation, through relapsing into contemplation (→ γνῶσις) and through an ascetic manner of life.

It thus appears that the term ζωή implies a concept of true life hereafter which must have the character of individuality and which already has this to the degree that ζωή includes a definite self-understanding and experience. But since man is severed from his historical particularity when the true man is loosed from the σῶμα through which he first receives the concrete possibilities of historical life, freedom from death really means freedom from the specific possibilities of human existence ; when guided by the myth of the first man, the self-understanding of man as knowledge of his whence and whither loses the sense of knowledge of my whence and whither and becomes mere general speculation. Inasmuch as it is thought of non-historically, ζωή can in fact be regarded only as physical vitality ; and to the degree that this ζωή is always my ζωή it can be regarded only as a psychical state. Negatively, this means that its actualisation can be achieved at root only in negations. [75]

---

[70] Cf. the distinction between the two ψυχαί, ibid. and Iambl. Myst., VIII, 6.

[71] Corp. Herm., VII, 2b: τὸ τῆς ἀγνωσίας ὕφασμα, τὸ τῆς κακίας στήριγμα, τὸν τῆς φθορᾶς δεσμόν, ... τὸν ζῶντα θάνατον, τὸν αἰσθητ<ικ>ὸν νεκρόν, τὸν περι- φόρητον τάφον.

[72] Reitzenstein Hell. Myst., 286; Scott, I, p. 376.

[73] Corp. Herm., I, 26 and 30 f.; XIII, 15-21; on the vision of God cf. also IV, 5; X, 4-6.

[74] On competing motifs in Hermetic anthropology, cf. W. Bousset, GGA, 1914, 724-732.

[75] In this sphere Ζωή can be hypostatised as a divine figure (→ n. 3), as may be seen in epigraphy (→ n. 66). When in the Valentinian ogdoad we find the aions-Syzygy Λόγος-Ζωή (W. Bousset, Die Hauptprobleme des Gnosis [1907], 163, 340), this may be due to the influence of Jn. 1:4, but it is possible only on the basis of the Gnostic view of ζωή. In the depiction of Paradise on an Egyptian Christian fresco the first pair are called

There is more than this in the Od. Sol., in which life has also the sense of incorruptibility (11:12; cf. 8:23; 15:8; 22:10 f.; 40:6). But here life and light are actual in the
revelation given in the word (10:1; 12:7; 32:1 f.) by which man understands himself
both in creation and redemption (6:18; 7:12; 13:1 f.). Thus life in the concrete existence
of the believer is fulfilled as the knowledge of God (8:10-12), as joy (15:1 f. etc.) and
as love (8:13; 40:4; 41:6).

Bultmann

B. Life and Death in the OT.

The views of life and death recorded in the writings of the OT are naturally
related to general oriental conceptions. Indeed, at many points they are directly
dependent on ideas which arose in the great cultural centres and which went out
from these to surrounding territories as developed conceptions. It is true, of course,
that faith in Yahweh had resources which enabled it to refashion what was adopted,
to give to it new emphases and to subject it to its own specific heritage. Our task,
however, is not simply to bring out the differences in a process of subtraction.
It is rather to discuss the distinctive OT findings in relation to the familiarity of
Israelite thinking with common oriental conceptions. Only thus can theology
arrive at the required understanding of the relevant statements.

1. Life in the OT.

The OT חַיִּים [76] does not cover all that we mean by life. It indicates only physical,
organic life, and this for the most part as the epitome of the interrelated forces
and phenomena. [77] Yet for the Hebrews the term implies far more than objective
assertion of a natural fact. It also includes an emphatic value judgment. It is not
merely that life is the initial presupposition of all goods and all striving. The possession of life is throughout the OT an intrinsic good which cannot be relativised.
It is indeed the supreme good. Wisdom offers riches and honour in the left hand,
but long life in the right (Prv. 3:16). "All that a man hath will he give for his life"
(Job 2:4). Only on the outer edge of despair can the Israelite be moved to surrender life, [78] for a living dog is always better than a dead lion (Qoh. 9:4). Life in
the OT is often used for fortune. [79] This supreme estimation of immanent life is
also predominant is Egypt and Babylon. In Israel the mere prolongation of physical
life to ripe old age [80] when a man dies old and full of years [81] is regarded as a
special grace, and Dt. sometimes holds out long life as the only reward for

---

'Αδάμ and Ζωή. L. Troje, *op. cit.* conjectures that this is to be interpreted in terms of
Gnostic mythology, so that 'Αδάμ = Φῶς. The fact that many wives of Byzantine emperors were called Ζωή may be traced to the use of ζωή (like κεφαλή) as an endearment,
cf. Juv., 6, 195.

[76] In Phoenician חים; M. Lidzbarski, *Handbuch der nordsemitischen Epigraphik* (1908),
273; perhaps an abstract construction.

[77] F. Delitzsch, *Biblische Psychologie*[2] (1861), 82; the verb חָיָה does not include the full
concept like the abstract form. Baudissin, *op. cit.*, 158. נֶפֶשׁ, too, is often used for life.
Originally it means a light breath, but as the characteristic sign of life it also acquires the
sense of life. J. Köberle, *Natur u. Geist nach der Auffassung des AT* (1901), 180.

[78] Job 3:17 ff.; Sir. 41:2.

[79] Baudissin, *op. cit.*, 159.

[80] Gn. 15:15; Ju. 8:32 etc.

[81] Gn. 25:8; 35:29; Job 42:17 etc.

fulfilment of the divine commandments. [82] Similarly the infinitely varied pursuit of wisdom simply has life or length of life as its goal.

That the presence of vitality is to be attributed to a creative act of the Deity is a common oriental conception. Rather strangely, however, Israel showed little concern about the details of this divine origin of life. The only statement which goes beyond a mere declaration that life comes from God is in J when he says that God breathed into the nostrils of lifeless man the breath of life (Gn. 2:7). The author of the P code obviously avoids any direct formulation of the divine origin of life in man; he carefully steers his way past the climax of all creation stories, the impartation of life. [83] For him, as for the Hebrews generally, the centre of life is in the blood. [84] The two theologians who have given us the earliest OT stories, however, both accept the view that after creation life was affected by a serious disturbance. The author of P brings this out by the steady falling off in the ages of the patriarchs (Gn. 5). Something fails in man the further he moves from his creation. J sees in this shortening of life a form of divine punishment (Gn. 6:3). It is thus brought into close connection with human sin. The important question arises whether according to the view of J life was first given a fixed span at the fall. This must be answered in the negative. No sentence of death is pronounced. [85] The curse is not death, but the making of life bitter. Hence the OT does not teach that death as such is the penalty of sin. Only an early or dishonourable or unusual death is regarded as a punishment. Yet the fall brings two changes for the worse according to J, namely, the pangs of birth and sexual shame. It is to be noted, however, that in this as in other respects J is an isolated voice in the chorus of OT witnesses. The same applies to his interweaving into the stories of Paradise and the fall (→ I, 281 ff.) of the parallel story of the tree of life [86] whose fruits would have endowed man with immortality had not God driven him out of the Garden. The connection with mythical material common to the ancient Orient is incontestable at this point. Elsewhere in the OT there are echoes of similar elements which were originally mythical. Yet when we read of the fountain of life or water of life the use is purely figurative. The mythical background is completely forgotten. It has been crowded out by the theologically significant view of a very different dependence and relationship of life.

In Israel generally there was little religious interest in the origins of life. The ultimate source was known, [87] but far more important for the individual was the actual absolute relationship of his life to God. God is the Lord of life and death. [88]

---

[82] E.g., Dt. 5:16; 16:20; 30:19.

[83] Though creation by the word is so important for him, he does not assert the creation of life by the word. In this respect he was still subject to older ideas. In the case of plants and animals there is an echo of the idea of mother earth (תּוֹצֵא הָאָרֶץ), but nothing is said about man.

[84] Gn. 9:4; Lv. 17:14. There seems to be some contradiction between this and the other conception which regards breath as the constitutive element of life.

[85] We find mention of death only in the subsidiary statement in v. 19b. If the curse imposed death on those who were previously immortal, this would be the main point and it could hardly be relegated to a subsidiary position. In any case, it would there apply only to the man. Gn. 2:17 is a threat which was not carried out; it implies instant death (בְּיוֹם אֲכָלְךָ).

[86] The main story deals with the tree of knowledge; for the interwoven story of the tree of life, cf. the comm.

[87] Ps. 36:9; 139:13 ff.

[88] Nu. 27:16; Job 12:10; Dt. 32:39.

He controls the book of life. [89] And since He was for Israel the One who had given it His covenant and direction, it naturally followed that the preservation or loss of life is decided by the attitude to His Word. This belief embraces the most important specific elements in the OT view of life. The Israelite does not build his view of life on a developed mythology. He does not seek to link himself with creative life by magical rites or mysteries. [90] The Word of God sets him in the decision between life and death. And this belief is so strongly developed that the primitive story and its statements regarding the impartation of life are almost emptied of significance. For the implanting of life at creation is far less important for those who know that its actual attainment or loss depends solely on the Word of God, so that there is constant need of the blessing of life. In the promulgation of Deuteronomy Moses lays before Israel life and death (Dt. 30:15-20), and Israel is to choose life, "for this word is not a vain thing for you; because it is your life" (Dt. 32:47). Thus Dt. with its variations on this theme reaches the paradoxical conclusion that man's life does not depend on bread alone but on the Word of God (Dt. 8:3). Nor is this view peculiar to Dt. Amos considers the possibility that hunger for the Word of God will bring disruption and overthrow (Am. 8:11 ff.). The sharpest development of this line of thought, however, is to be found in Ezekiel. In broad doctrinaire discussions he frees life from all false supports and obligations and relates it wholly and utterly to the Word of God. [91] The obedient chooses life, the disobedient death, and the expositions all lead to the sombre reflection that the just does not receive any special blessings but does remain alive, whereas the disobedient must die. Ez. seems to expect the speedy death of the sinner. This is the culmination of the relationship between the natural process of life and the Word of God. The theological deduction from this belief is obviously that Israel is to understand elemental life quite radically in terms of grace. This life is not merely an aspect but the very foundation of the state of salvation. Only by faith, i.e., by cleaving to the God of salvation, will the righteous have life. [92] It is obvious that life is here understood as a gift. Indeed, in a new development of the ancient oriental estimation, it is understood as enjoyment [93] both of real goods regarded as the blessing of Yahweh on the one hand and of living fellowship with God, whose unshakable certainty gives joy to the righteous, on the other. [94]

In all its varied forms OT wisdom has only the one goal of offering man life, or, in its own words, of leading him on the way of life. [95] Here, too, the possession of life and

---

[89] The idea of the book of life is worked out in two ways. Acc. to the one view it is a book of destiny in heaven, Ex. 32:32; Mal. 3:16; Ps. 69:28, with a strong predestinarian emphasis. Acc. to the other it is a list of citizens in the historical or eschatological community, Is. 4:3.

[90] Cf. the examples of rites for the reviving of the sick, E. Ebeling, *Tod und Leben nach den Vorstellungen der Babylonier* (1931), 65 ff.; on the Osiris mysteries in Egypt, cf. H. Kees, *Totenglauben und Jenseitsvorstellungen der alten Ägypter* (1926), 348 ff.

[91] Ez. 3:18 ff.; 14:13 ff.; 18:1 ff.; 20:1 ff.; 33:1 ff.

[92] Hab. 2:4, cf. Am. 5:4, 14; Jer. 38:20.

[93] Kleinert, *op. cit.*, 720 ff. This helps us to understand 1 K. 3:5 ff. What is praised is not that Solomon objectively estimates wisdom above long life but that he unselfishly renounces so great an individual blessing in the interests of the people over whom he is to rule.

[94] Occasionally the righteous of the OT makes statements with something of a mystical colouring, cf. esp. Ps. 36:8 f.; 73:25; 16:11.

[95] Prv. 2:19; 5:6; 6:23; 10:17; 15:24. There is sometimes a faint resemblance to the concept (cf. Jer. 21:8) in ancient oriental lit.; two examples are given in A. Jirku, *Altorientalischer Komm. zum AT* (1923), 205 (on Jer. 21:8). More important is the fact that Egyptian wisdom aims at this attaining of life, cf. the teaching of Amen-em-ope, AOT, I, 38 ff.

continuation in it cannot be regarded as self-evident or taken for granted. They are linked with a religious and spiritual order. According to this order decision is made concerning the possession or loss of life. Nevertheless, we see here an important theological shift which weakens the stricter OT concept of revelation. It is no longer God or His Word or Law which gives life ; it is wisdom, [96] or even the words of the wise, [97] or discipline. [98] Similarly, the ways of folly lead to death. [99] While the Psalmist glorifies Yahweh as the source of life (Ps. 36:9), this originally mythical image is now applied to wisdom. [100] The difference from the way in which Dt. or the prophets understand the dependence of life is plain. It is linked with the theologising of wisdom, which as an intermediary vessel of revelation interposes itself between God and man.

Both Ezekiel, with his ruthlessly consistent development of the prophetic view of the relation of life to God, and the teachers of wisdom with their theory, involve themselves in no little contradiction with sober reality and everyday experience. This very fact shows us how inalienable were the concerns underlying their belief. The contradiction was felt, however, [101] and it could not be resolved until Israel ceased to regard death as in all circumstances the irrevocable end of all life.

2. Death in the OT.

Whereas the view of Yahweh's relation to life is rich and theologically varied in the OT, the estimation of death in Yahweh religion remains unitary and constant even through many centuries of vigorous religious development. The termination of life by a normal death in old age is accepted as something regrettable but natural [102] against which no protest is made. The OT righteous meet the absolutely irrevocable [103] fact of death with complete resignation. The state expected — a cheerless shadowy existence — is in no respect to be compared with even the most miserable life on earth. Not once does the idea of reunion enliven the gloominess of this prospect. [104] The grave is the dwelling-place of the dead. It is of illimitable duration. For those who survive, the later removing of the remains of the dead from the bier into the pit, where they intermingle with the bones of other corpses, implies surrender of the ultimate individuality and particularity of the dead. With no attempt at harmonisation, we also find alongside this the idea of a world of the dead in the cosmic depths, i.e., in *sheol*, the general gathering place of all the dead. This no less sombre view is of a different origin from that of a shadowy existence in the burial chamber. In the OT it is particularly found in poetic passages.

In this context we need hardly speak of the different notions underlying the various burial rites and customs. In mourning rites etc. we usually find very early and varied elements which unite, change and receive new content, so that the original meaning is

---

[96] Prv. 3:10, 18; 8:35; 9:11.

[97] Prv. 3:2; 4:4, 10, 22; 13:14; 19:16.

[98] Prv. 4:13; 6:23; 10:17; 23:14.

[99] How far life and death are to be taken spiritually in these statements, and whether we may thus see in them an inkling that there is a death without physical death (Sellin, *op. cit.*, 270), are open questions. Great caution is needed in this area.

[100] Prv. 13:14; 16:22; Sir. 21:13.

[101] Ps. 49:7 ff.; 73:2 ff.; 92:8 f.; Job 21:7.

[102] "For we must needs die, and are as water spilt on the ground, which cannot be gathered up again," 2 S. 14:14.

[103] Job 7:9; Ps. 89:48. Even the pre-apocalyptic eschatological outlook does not envisage the conquest of death but a relative prolongation of the span of life, Is. 65:20; Zech. 8:4.

[104] Quell, *op. cit.*, 31.

hard to grasp. The most important point is that where they are still pregnant with religious force they are usually sharply contested by the religion of Yahweh. [105] If one may still perceive in Israel a certain numinous awe nourished by earlier forms of religion, in the sphere of authorised religion all positive sacral quality is denied to the grave, to corpses or to the dead. [106] The dead are unclean, and they make unclean. [107] This expresses the strongest cultic disqualification. If we may see here an obvious contesting of the possession of any independent numinous significance by the dead or the grave, the question of the relation of Yahweh to the dead and their kingdom leads to a very remarkable proposition.

The complaint in various passages that the dead are excluded from the praise of Yahweh leads us to the very heart of the dominant view. "The earth hath Yahweh given to the children of men, but the dead praise not Yahweh." [108] After death, then, the righteous are outside the infinitely important sphere of life in which cultic relationship with God is maintained. In another prayer the consequence is even more plainly drawn (Is. 38:18): "Sheol doth not praise thee: they that go down into the pit wait not for thy faithfulness." Yahweh's grace (אֱמֶת) has no further relevance to the dead. They are cut off from His hand. [109] And this is for centuries the real sting of death in OT religion. Yahweh is the God of life in a wholly exclusive sense. And the sharp antithesis to the view of Yahweh's relation to life is equally plain. We have seen above, not only that life is physically given by God, but that its maintenance is recognised in an act of decision to be dependent on God. In the one case the relation of life to God is complete. Here, however, there is no such relation. Death and its kingdom are outside the stream of power which has subjected all the kingdoms of life to itself. The lack of a point of theological orientation for views as to the state of death means that in Yahweh religion these are held without the definition and integration otherwise characteristic of the OT. It may be assumed either that the dead are with their fathers in the family sepulchre (e.g., Gn. 50:13; Jos. 24:32; 1 K. 2:10; 11:43) or that they are in *sheol* among princes, classes and nations (Is. 14:9 ff.; Ez. 32:21 ff.). Belief in Yahweh provides no reason for bringing these and other variations into harmony.

The religio-historical explanation of this remarkable finding is to be sought in the fact that of all non-Yahwistic cultic spheres that of death was the slowest to be integrated into authorised religion. So long as the religious powers of Israel were engaged in such obstinate battle with the cult of the dead, i.e., so long as this sphere was rated so unfavourably from the religious standpoint, so long it resisted positive integration into the religion of Yahweh. Of course, this religion might have adopted a different attitude at this difficult point if it had not had an important religious equivalent in its hands from the very first. In the thought of the covenant the continuation and persistence of the nation was guaranteed in spite of the corruptibility of the individual, and the powerful

---

[105] Lv. 19:31; 20:6, 27; Dt. 18:11; 26:14; 14:1.

[106] The customs still practised in the religion of Israel (e.g., tearing clothes or shaving the hair) are divested of their original cultic meaning.

[107] Nu. 19:16; Dt. 21:23.

[108] Ps. 115:16 f.; Is. 38:11; Ps. 6:5; 30:10; 88:11 ff.; Sir. 17:27.

[109] Ps. 88:5. Only twice in the OT do we find exceptions to this established view. In Am. 9:2 and Ps. 139:8 *sheol*, too, is regarded as within Yahweh's sphere of influence. But these passages do not represent the common view. They are conclusions drawn from bold individual faith in the omnipotence of Yahweh. On the other hand, the thought of rapture is popular. Yet it does not imply an invasion of *sheol* by Yahweh. The rapture takes place immediately after life comes to an end.

vision of Ez. 37 shows how this belief could always hope for a restoration of the people even out of the most hopeless state of death. [110]

3. The OT Conquest of Death. It remains to show at what point the spell of death over individual life was broken. If the relevant passages do not arise out of the central religious concern, it is the more important to recognise by what forces this ultimate deduction is nourished. That God rules over higher spheres of life into which He may in special instances snatch up (tech. term. לָקַח) chosen individuals is a common idea in Israel. [111] Yet there does not develop out of it a speculative conception of resurrection and eternal life. It is rather that individual believers whose faith is under particular strain have recourse to this as one of the possibilities which may be expected from Yahweh. The particular point at issue was the righteousness of Yahweh, and therefore the definitive fulfilment of His covenant promise which had to come after death. In Ps. 16 the reference is neither to resurrection nor to rapture, but holding fast to the grace of Yahweh plainly leads to the conclusion : "Therefore my heart is glad ... for thou wilt not abandon me to sheol nor suffer that thine holy one should see the pit" (v. 9 f.). The author of Ps. 49 expresses his hope even more boldly and clearly : "God will redeem my soul from sheol, for he takes me to himself" (v. 16). Here, too, the hope is made necessary by the problem of theodicy. Yahweh's promise cannot fail. He is the פֹּדֶה, the liberating Deliverer, who will come to the rescue of those who are in need. Job 19:25 points in the same direction. Here God is the גֹּאֵל from whose intervention Job expects the solution (though only after death). [112] There is a remarkably plain expression of this certainty that the relationship of grace will persist, that the fellowship initiated by God cannot be destroyed, in Ps. 73 : "I am continually with thee ... thou guidest me according to thy counsel, and afterward receivest me in glory. Whom have I in heaven but thee ? Though my flesh and my heart fail, God remains my portion for ever" (v. 23 ff.). One may say that here the OT belief in the hereafter finds its purest formulation. This expectation is neither magical nor mythical nor speculative nor mystical. It is a certainty which is produced in the righteous by the concept of grace alone.

Though it does not express the same individual expectation, the assurance given to Israel in the Isaiah apocalypse : "Thy dead men shall live, thy dead bodies shall rise again" (26:19), is still a proclamation of pure grace. Yet it belongs to a different religious stream. For here we have an assurance which suddenly opens up a new perspective within the great context of the eschatology of Israel. A different prospect is offered at the end of the Book of Daniel : "And many of them that sleep in the dust of the earth shall awake, some to everlasting life, and some to shame and everlasting contempt" (12:2). The new thing here is the resurrection not merely of those who are still to receive the grace of Yahweh but also of the rejected to judgment. We are thus confronted by a completely different conception. Surviving death is not just a certainty for those who do not abandon Yahweh. It is now one of many elements in a comprehensive eschatology which is presented in all its essential features as a fully developed scheme. This implies a final abandonment both of the classical Heb. view of life in this world with its unparalleled religious requirement due to the lack of any hope of the hereafter,

---

[110] Cf. Hos. 6:2; 13:14; on the allusion to the Adonis ıcult, cf. Sellin, *op. cit.*, 247 f. Cf. also the hope of maintaining one's name through physical descendants, Is. 66:22; Ps. 72:17.
[111] Enoch in Gn. 5:21 ff., Elijah in 2 K. 2:9 f. and the *Ebed* in Is. 53:8.
[112] Acc. to most exegetes. For Yahweh as גֹּאֵל cf. Gn. 48:16; Jer. 50:34; Ps. 119:154; Prv. 23:11.

and also of the solution of the problem of death in an individual venture of faith such as we occasionally find in the Psalms.

v. Rad

4. The Concept of Life in the OT.

The OT understanding of life cannot be deduced simply from the use of חַיִּים (חָיָה), though this points us to a typical aspect of this understanding. The phenomenon of natural life, whose primary subject is man, is not made the object of scientific observation and reflection in the OT, nor is it primarily regarded as a phenomenon of nature. It is the being which is man himself. This means that in the first instance it is temporal being. "Life" and "days (of life)" can be used synonymously, and the seeking, desiring or promising of life applies primarily to the continuation of existence. [113] Even when the concept of life is conceived in relation to death as its opposite there can be no doubt that it has temporal extension whose end is death, and that death itself is not a natural process but simply the end. The idea that life and death can be regarded in a dialectical unity (→ 834) is quite alien. To this extent חַיִּים corresponds more to the Greek βίος (when used for the span of life rather than the manner, → 836) than to the Greek ζωή. To ζωή corresponds the OT נֶפֶשׁ (→ ψυχή) in so far as נפש denotes the potency on which life rests. [114] This is the true subject of life and death. [115] Thus everything living can be described as כָּל־הַנֶּפֶשׁ. [116] Life and soul can be parallels, [117] and נֶפֶשׁ can be used for the I or self (Ju. 16:30; 1 S. 18:3); it is this I that lives. [118]

As the term חַיִּים denotes the temporal span of life, so the essence of this living existence is seen in the expressions of life whose subject is נֶפֶשׁ. These are such vital expressions as hunger and thirst, desires and wishes, love and hate. [119] Unlike the Greek ψυχή, נֶפֶשׁ is not also the subject of the intellectual life (→ καρδία, → νοῦς). This is expressed in the fact that the concept of life is linked with that of the flesh. [120] בָּשָׂר is that which lives, [121] and all men or living creatures can be called כָּל־בָּשָׂר. [122] Soul and flesh can be used as parallels or combined, [123] and sometimes בָּשָׂר too, can almost have the sense of "I." [124]

---

[113] Cf. E. v. Schrenck, *op. cit.*, 3-11; J. Lindblom, *op. cit.*, 1-47; and esp. L. Dürr, *op. cit.*, 2-11. In this connection we may also refer to passages in which the national community may be the subject both of life and of continuation in life. Acc. to F. C. Burkitt, ZNW, 12 (1911), 228-230 the plur. חַיִּים is to be explained in terms of life as a series of moments in time.

[114] It is true, of course, that נֶפֶשׁ often corresponds rather to the Gk. ζῷον (Gn. 2:7 etc.) and is often used in a collective sense (J. Pedersen, *Israel, Its Life and Culture* [1926], 99-181). The individual living creatures stand as such in a relationship, though this is historical rather than cosmic, cf. esp. the relationship of the family, the nation (*ibid.*, 255-259, 474-476) and the covenant (*ibid.*, 308 f.).

[115] Gn. 35:18; Ju. 16:30; 2 S. 1:9; Ez. 13:19.

[116] Jos. 10:28 ff.; with the addition חַיָּה, Gn. 1:21, 24; 9:10 ff.; Lv. 11:10.

[117] Ps. 78:50; 88:4; 143:3; Job 33:18, 22, 28; 36:14. Cf. Pedersen, *op. cit.* 151-156.

[118] Cf. the oath in 1 S. 1:26; 17:55.

[119] Cf. B. Stade, *Biblische Theologie des AT*, I (1905), 181; Pedersen, *op. cit.*, 100 f., 147.

[120] Pedersen, *op. cit.*, 176-179. The OT does not distinguish between organic and inorganic nature. All natural being is regarded as living, *ibid.*, 155, 479-482.

[121] Ez. 11:19; 36:26.

[122] Gn. 6:12 f., 19; 7:16, 21.

[123] Ps. 16:9 f.; 63:1; 84:2; Job 13:14.

[124] Prv. 14:30; Qoh. 4:5; 5:5; 11:10; 12:12.

If נֶפֶשׁ is sometimes regarded as a something in man or in his blood, [125] this is not a matter of empirical investigation. Though it rests on primitive observation, it expresses the idea that life is transcendent and not subject to control. We find this idea particularly in passages which state that man lives because God has given to him the breath of life (נִשְׁמַת חַיִּים) [126] or because there dwells in him the רוּחַ which is subject only to God's control, [127] so that flesh as human and spirit as divine can be brought into antithesis (Is. 31:3; cf. Ps. 78:39). [128] Man has life, therefore, only as something which is lent to him. [129] God is Lord of life. [130] He is the living God (Dt. 5:23; 2 K. 19:4; Ps. 42:2). [131] He is the source of life (Ps. 36:9). He kills and makes alive (Dt. 32:39). He has life in Himself, whereas man must sustain it by nourishment or by toil [132] unless God sustains it for him miraculously (Dt. 8:3). Man is mortal. [133]

That life has temporal extension and that it is fulfilled in vital expressions belong to a unitary view of life. In general, life implies movement. [134] More precisely, it involves possibility, orientation, the desire and ability to achieve something. [135] As hunger and thirst, desires, wishes etc. are expressions of נֶפֶשׁ, so desiring, striving and hoping are characteristic of life. [136] Mere existence is not life any more than shadowy continuation in *sheol* (Qoh. 9:4). A life whose possibilities are cut off is no life. Sickness is as bad as death (Job 27:15). Healing and reviving are equivalent to life. [137] God's life, too, is expressed in activity and creation. [138] Life implies a happy life as well as a long one. [139] Life is the clue to fortune. [140] He who is alive can still hope and desire, and therefore life is the supreme good. [141] Death is welcome only to the desperate (Job 3:11-26). The worst suffering is suffering "unto death" (Jon. 4:9). Like suicide, the possibility of understanding death as an act and therefore as an extreme fulfilment of life (→ θάνατος) does not arise. Death is seen only as the impending or actual end of life. It is the state of death rather than the act of dying.

Life means self-knowledge (Qoh. 9:5). It is part of life that man understands himself in his world. Hence the interconnection of light and life [142] (→ φῶς). [143]

---

[125] Gn. 9:4; Lv. 17:11, 14; Dt. 12:23.
[126] Gn. 2:7; cf. Nu. 27:16; Job 12:10.
[127] Gn. 6:3, 17; 7:15, 22; Nu. 16:22; Ps. 104:29 f.; Job 34:14 f.
[128] This is not meant dualistically; cf. Pedersen, 146; on body and soul, 170-179.
[129] Hence חיים is very rarely used with the gen. of the possessor; Baudissin, *op. cit.*, 157, n. 1.
[130] Cf. esp. Ps. 104:29 f.; Job 34:14 f.
[131] Kleinert, *op. cit.*, 693 ff.
[132] Dt. 8:3; 2 K. 4:7; Gn. 27:40; life for the maintenance of life in Prv. 27:27.
[133] Gn. 3:19; 2 S. 14:14; Is. 40:6; Ps. 78:39; 89:48; 90.
[134] Gn. 7:21; cf. 1:28; 8:19; Ps. 69:34; running water is living water.
[135] Pedersen, *op. cit.*, 147, 152 f.
[136] Job 33:20; 38:39; Qoh. 9:4, 6, 10.
[137] Baudissin, *op. cit.*, 152. To the degree that life is fulfilled in vital expressions, death is not a mere end. It is the end, but as a power which constantly threatens and hampers, Pedersen, 153, 180 f., 466-470.
[138] Jos. 3:10 f.; 1 S. 17:26; 2 K. 19:4; Jer. 10:10-16.
[139] Cf. the wish in Ps. 69:32; 22:26.
[140] Baudissin, 143 ff.; Pedersen, 154 f.
[141] 1 K. 3:11; Prv. 3:16; Job 2:4.
[142] Ps. 27:1; 36:9; Job 3:20; 33:28, 30; Qoh. 11:7 f.
[143] Pedersen, 313, 464-466. Cf. also Akhenaton's hymn to the sun in A. Erman, *Die Literatur der Ägypter* (1923), 358-362; G. Roeder, *Urkunden zur Religion des alten Ägypten* (1923), 62-65; AOT, 15-18.

Death is darkness (Qoh. 11:8). It makes everything obscure (Qoh. 2:14 ff.). Life is always my own. [144] As such, it differs from every other life. Death equalises everything (Job 3:19). Life is my own from the very first, and not just by the way I conduct it. Hence there is in the OT no development of the Greek thought of βίος, of its norm and typical possibilities (→ 835). For the same reason, one may speak of a happy or unhappy life (Ps. 90:10), but one cannot speak of living happily or unhappily, well or badly. [145] Thus, although the fact that life is my own implies particularity, there is no thought of a particularity which has to be attained and which persists beyond the empirical realisation of life. For this reason, death finally poses the question whether all life with its joys and sorrows and in spite of its variety is not in vain, since in the long run all share a common fate, all must die. [146] In general, death can also be regarded as a well-earned rest, as sleep (Job 3:17 f. etc.), and man is content when he dies old and full of days, when he has had a long and happy life and is then gathered to his fathers. [147] There is no idea of this not being life in the true and proper sense. In the OT there is no reference to "life" either in the idealistic or the dualistic sense. As temporal, physical life, life is true life if it is long and happy. [148] And this possibility is in the hands of men to the extent that by their obedience to the Law of God or the commands of wisdom they can fashion a long and happy life, or by their disobedience they can choose death, [149] so that there is for them a choice between the way of life and the way of death. [150]

Bultmann

C. ζωή and βίος in the Septuagint.

In the LXX the terms ζῆν, ζωή are used in almost every case for the Heb. originals חיה, חַיִּים. The subst. חַיִּים occurs 147 times in the Mas., and חַיִּין twice in Da. In these 149 instances the LXX uses ζωή 130 times and ζῆν 10 times. Of the other 9, 3 do not occur in the LXX, so that in only 6 cases do we have a different and mostly free rendering. βίος is found only once for יְמֵי חַיִּים at Prv. 31:12. 'ΑΣΘ have here the literal ἡμέραι τῆς ζωῆς. The LXX has maintained the ancient distinction between ζωή as *vita qua vivimus* and βίος as *vita quam vivimus* [151] at least to the extent that βίος is used 11 times in Job and twice in Prv. 3:2, 16 for יָמִים in the sense of length of life, while ζωή is used for חַיִּים in these books as in the rest of the OT. [152] βίος never occurs in the Law and the prophets. In the Hellenistic portions of the OT (Wis., 2 and 3 Macc.) βίος agains denotes length of life. Only in 4 Macc. does the word acquire an ethical

---

[144] Pedersen, 100-103 : the soul always has an individual character.
[145] Baudissin, 157 f.
[146] Qoh. 2:14-17; 3:19-21; 8:10; 9:2 f.
[147] Pedersen, 327 f., 495 f.
[148] *Ibid.*, 147 f.: the soul seeks to be filled or satisfied. To life belongs essential power, joy, salvation, long duration, 230, 313-316, 327-329.
[149] Dt. 30:15-20; 32:47; Ez. 3:18 ff.; 18:1 ff. etc. Cf. Dürr, *op. cit.*, 5-11. Wisdom is the tree of life in Prv. 3:18.
[150] Ps. 16:11; Prv. 5:6; 6:23; 10:17; 14:12.
[151] Trench, 55 ff.
[152] Though cf. Sir. 40:29. Prv. 4:10c repeats 10b. The verb βιοῦν occurs only 5 times as a transl., and twice each in Wis. and 4 Macc. without Heb. original. In 3 cases it is used for חיה (Prv. 7:2; 'ΑΣΘ ζῆν; 9:6 [only A א²; B has βασιλεύειν, 'ΑΣΘ ζῆν]; Sir. 40:28). יָמִים is only once rendered ζωή at Job 7:1, where it is obviously introduced as a par. to the βίος of v. 1a LXX.

sense with ὀρθός or νόμιμος βίος. ζωή occurs 278 times in the LXX, and 191 times in the Heb. canon. In 141 instances it is the trans. of the Heb. חַיִּים, [153] and in 21 it corresponds to a form of חיה. Of the other 29 instances the LXX introduces it 10 times without a Mas. original, and in the other 19 it is either a free rendering or based on misunderstandings or errors of the copyist or translator.

It is only in the hagiographa and apocrypha that the word really becomes a moral and religious term. [154] Like the Heb. חַיִּים, ζωή in the Gk. Bible always has a purely quantitative sense, though in some passages the Gk. term arbitrarily carries with it an estimation of life which goes beyond the ancient Heb. ideal of long life. As renderings of the stem חיה, ζωή and ζῆν in the LXX first mean length of life and vitality as distinct from death and sickness. Thus we read of σάρξ ζῶσα (Gn. 8:21; Lv. 13:10) and ψυχὴ ζῶσα (Gn. 2:7, 19 etc., ᾽ΑΣ also Gn. 1:30, LXX ψυχὴ ζωῆς). All creatures are bearers of ψυχὴ ζωῆς (Gn. 1:30; Σ 1 Βασ. 1:26; cf. 2 Βασ. 15:21), πνοὴ ζωῆς (Gn. 2:7; 7:22), [155] πνεῦμα ζωῆς (Gn. 6:17; 7:15; Jdt. 10:13). It is not possible to make a sharp differentiation between these expressions. [156] But in so far as this animal vitality is a gift of God, ζωή acquires distinctive meaning as a value concept. When we read in Dt. 32:39: ἐγὼ ἀκοκτεννῶ καὶ ζῆν ποιήσω (cf. Da. 4:34a), God is regarded as the Lord of life and death along the lines of the belief in creation. He is the Lord of history who smites but also heals His people. This is at least the historical meaning of the text. In later Judaism, however, the divine gift of life, which has here primarily a natural sense, is understood as the saving gift of eternal life in terms of an eschatological religion of redemption. Thus 4 Macc. 18:18 is adduced with Ez. 37 and Prv. 3:18 (ξύλον ζωῆς) as proof of the resurrection and eternal life. This is linked with the traditional desire for long life, as is evident in 4 Macc. 17:12: ἀφθαρσία ἐν ζωῇ πολυχρονίῳ, and 18:19: αὕτη ἡ ζωὴ ὑμῶν καὶ ἡ μακρότης (א) τῶν ἡμερῶν, which is distinctively altered to μακαριότης in A. Cf. also 15:3: τὴν εὐσέβειαν ... τὴν σῴζουσαν εἰς αἰώνιον ζωὴν κατὰ θεόν; 16:25: διὰ τὸν θεὸν ἀποθανόντες ζῶσιν τῷ θεῷ (cf. 7:19). Rabbinic tradition takes the same view of Dt. 32:39 as the Hellenistic 4 Macc., using it with other passages taken in the same sense [157] to prove the resurrection of the dead. From the time of the Maccabees belief in the hereafter, the resurrection and eternal life, was wholeheartedly accepted in many circles in Jewish theology, [158] though it was not so widespread among the people either then or even in the early Christian period. Thus on the oldest Jewish burial inscr., which are important witnesses to popular Jewish religion in the Roman period, there is little evidence of belief in the world to come. When βιοῦν and ζῆν are used on burial inscr., they refer to the duration and nature of earthly life. [159]

---

[153] Of these 130 compare with the 147 adduced by Mandelkern under חַיִּים and 11 with those adduced by Mandelkern under חַי.

[154] ζωή occurs in the historical books only 54 times and in the prophetic 43, but it is found 94 times in the hagiographa including Da., and 87 times in the apocr.

[155] Cf. also ἐμπνέον ζωῆς in Jos. 10:40.

[156] Philo Leg. All., III, 161 and Det. Pot. Ins., 80 have πνοή for πνεῦμα at Gn. 2:7.

[157] Cf. Str.-B., I, 894 and S. Krauss, Sanhedrin-Makkōt (1933), 267 (Giess. Mishnah, IV, 4/5).

[158] Cf. Da. 12:2 LXX Θ: ζωὴ αἰώνιος = חַיֵּי עוֹלָם; 2 Macc. 7:9: εἰς αἰώνιον ἀναβίωσιν ζωῆς; 7:14: ἀνάστασις εἰς ζωήν; 7:23: τὸ πνεῦμα καὶ τὴν ζωὴν ὑμῖν πάλιν ἀποδίδωσιν μετ᾽ ἐλέους, 7:36: πόνον ἀενάου ζωῆς.

[159] There is no obvious linguistic distinction between the terms on the inscr., though, in formulae like καλῶς βιώσας, βιοῦν is more often used for the moral quality of life, cf., e.g., N. Müller-N. A. Bees, Die Inschriften der jüd. Katakombe am Monteverde zu Rom (1919), No. 30, 34 (though cf. καλῶς ἔζησεν, No. 66, 112), and H. W. Beyer-H. Lietzmann, Die jüd. Katakombe der Villa Torlonia in Rom (1930), No. 6, 25, 42. διὰ βίου on these inscr. refers to longevity (Müller-Bees, No. 109, 175). ζῆν is mostly used to introduce the age: ἔζησεν ἐτῶν ... (several instances).

Yet occasionally on burial inscr. we do find a text from the OT used to support belief in the after life. The image of the bundle of life (צְרוֹר הַחַיִּים, δεσμὸς τῆς ζωῆς) used by Abigail at 1 S. 25:29 increasingly became the great Jewish confession at burial from the Middle Ages onwards. [160] This text is first found on a Heb. burial inscr. in the Christian cemetery at Antinoe in Egypt in the 2nd cent., but it may be confidently quoted in relation to the developing Jewish belief in the resurrection and the popular Jewish understanding of Scripture in the early Christian period, since the same text is used by the Rabbis in similar contexts. They intend thereby to prove the survival of the souls of the righteous in the immediate presence of God (bChag., 12b). [161] Judaism here understood the δεσμὸς τῆς ζωῆς as in some sense a φάρμακον ζωῆς (Sir. 6:16: צְרוֹר החיים). [162] A similar φάρμακον or mysterious agent of life is also found, of course, in the ξύλον ζωῆς of Gn. 3:22 ff.; Is. 65:22; Prv. 3:18; 4 Macc. 18:16. The ξύλον, δι' οὗ γίνεται δικαιοσύνη of Wis. 14:7 belongs to the same group. It is the means, φάρμακον, of the preservation of life for the world, and δικαιοσύνη corresponds to the saving benefit of life. Sometimes ζωή can be used where the Mas. indicates the saving benefit in another way. Thus in Hos. 10:12 ζωή is used for חֶסֶד: σπείρατε ἑαυτοῖς εἰς δικαιοσύνην, τρυγήσατε εἰς καρπὸν ζωῆς, φωτίσατε ἑαυτοῖς φῶς γνώσεως. The terms φῶς and γνῶσις come into the LXX through misunderstanding, so that here, as often in later Judaism, we have ζωή, φῶς and γνῶσις together. There is a similar reference to the knowledge of life in Prv. 22:19 'ΑΣ : γνωστὴν ἐποίησά σοι ζωήν; Mas. הוֹדַעְתִּיךָ הַיּוֹם אַף־אָתָּה, LXX : καὶ γνωρίσῃ σοι τὴν ὁδόν σου. The formulation φῶς ζωῆς is found in Prv. 16:15 in a verse which is readily understandable but which no longer satisfies true religious need : בְּאוֹר־פְּנֵי־מֶלֶךְ חַיִּים. This is rightly translated by 'ΑΣΘΕ' : ἐν φωτὶ προσώπου βασιλέως ζωή, while the LXX has : ἐν φωτὶ ζωῆς υἱὸς βασιλέως. אוֹר הַחַיִּים and אֶרֶץ חַיִּים are obviously stock terms for the sphere of human life, and they may be rendered quite literally in Gk. without any difficulty. This is true of ψ 55:13, where the Mas. לְהִתְהַלֵּךְ לִפְנֵי אֱלֹהִים בְּאוֹר הַחַיִּים is literally translated by the LXX : τοῦ εὐαρεστῆσαι ἐνώπιον τοῦ θεοῦ ἐν φωτὶ ζώντων. Σ, however, has : ὥστε ὁδεύειν ἔμπροσθεν τοῦ θεοῦ διὰ φωτὸς τῆς ζωῆς, so that φῶς τῆς ζωῆς has to be the gracious gift by which the walk before God is possible. At Is. 53:8 both Σ and Θ have ἐκ (ἀπὸ) γῆς ζώντων for מֵאֶרֶץ חַיִּים, while the LXX separates γῆ and ζωή, and thus gives us the sense of the removing of the life of the Servant of the Lord from the earth : αἴρεται ἀπὸ τῆς γῆς ἡ ζωὴ αὐτοῦ. [163] אוֹר הַחַיִּים in the above sense is also found at Job 33:30 in the Mas. Here Θ has a rendering with a strong this-worldly emphasis : τοῦ ἐπιστρέψαι ψυχὴν αὐτοῦ ἐκ διαφθορᾶς, τοῦ φωτίσαι αὐτῷ ἐν φωτὶ ζώντων, but the expression chosen in the LXX allows an exposition in terms of belief in the after life and may itself presuppose such an understanding : ἀλλ' ἐρύσατο τὴν ψυχήν μου ἐκ θανάτου, ἵνα ἡ ζωή (Αא² ψυχή) μου ἐν φωτὶ αἰνῇ αὐτόν. This corresponds to the statement in 33:28 : ἡ ζωή (א² ψυχή) μου φῶς ὄψεται. At Job 11:17, where the LXX agrees with the Mas. apart from the σοι, we have a similar understanding : ἐκ δὲ μεσημβρίας ἀνατελεῖ σοι ζωή. [164]

---

[160] The abbrev. תנצבה is particularly common, cf. G. Bertram, "The Problem of Death in Popular Judaeo-Hellenistic Piety," Crozer Quart., 10 (1933), 286.

[161] Str.-B., III, 532.

[162] A. Marmorstein, ZAW, NF, 2 (1925), 119-124.

[163] K. F. Euler, "Die Verkündigung vom leidenden Gottesknecht aus Js. 53 in der griech. Bibel," BWANT, IV, 14 (1934), 26, 71, 128 f. The LXX version possibly refers to the assumption of Is.

[164] ζωή = חֶלֶד; חֶלֶד, Ps. 39:5; 89:48 = ὑπόστασις, "living creature ;" though cf. Ju. 6:4 : מִחְיָה = ὑπόστασις ζωῆς, "sustenance." Elsewhere חֶלֶד is found only at Ps. 17:14 (γῆ) and 49:1 (οἰκουμένη). For the south as the side of life, cf. Lact. Inst., II, 9, CSEL, 19, 143, lines 19-21; cf. also F. J. Dölger, Die Sonne der Gerechtigkeit und der Schwarze (1919), 44.

That life in the LXX can be taken to mean eternal life is most evident in the transl. of the famous verse Job 19:25, where the LXX has ἀέναος ("eternal") for the Heb. חַי ("living"): גֹּאֲלִי חָי וְאַחֲרוֹן עַל־עָפָר יָקוּם, ἀέναός ἐστιν ὁ ἐκλύειν με μέλλων ἐπὶ γῆς. [165] Θ is more literal : ὁ ἀγχιστεύς (kinsman) μου ζῇ καὶ ἔσχατον ἐπὶ χώματος ἀναστήσει. There is a similar interpretation along the lines of the eschatological gift of salvation in the εἰς τὸν αἰῶνα βασιλεύσητε of Prv. 9:6, where 'ΑΣΘ have ζήσεσθε. The resurrection passages in the Mas. — in addition to those mentioned we should also refer especially in this context to Is. 26:19, יִחְיוּ מֵתֶיךָ, where the LXX has ἀναστήσονται but 'ΑΣΘ ζήσονται — constitute to some degree the starting-point for the understanding of ζωή in the Gk. Bible. Even where the translator is not thinking of the transcendent blessing of salvation, the beliefs of his readers and hearers would often lead them to substitute an eschatological interpretation for a purely this-worldly understanding, the faith and life of the righteous in the present being regarded as a precondition and even as a foretaste of eternal life. Circles which accepted belief in the resurrection interpreted in this sense the corresponding promises in the Law and the prophets : Lv. 18:5; Am. 5:4, 14; Is. 55:3; Ez. 18:32 (A) etc. Along the same lines they also interpret the images found in OT wisdom : ὁδὸς ζωῆς ψ 15:11; Prv. 4:23 (ἔξοδοι); 5:6; 6:23; 8:35; [166] 10:17; 15:24; 16:17; cf. Jer. 21:8; φῶς ζωῆς, ψ 55:13 Σ; δένδρον ζωῆς, Prv. 11:30 ('ΑΣΘ ξύλον ζωῆς, → supra); 13:12; 15:4; πηγὴ ζωῆς, Prv. 13:14; 14:27; 16:22; 18:4 (Mas. חָכְמָה, 'ΑΣΘ σοφίας); Sir. 21:13; cf. Jer. 2:13; 17:13, and also Bar. 3:9 ἐντολαὶ ζωῆς; Ez. 33:15 πρόσταγμα ζωῆς. Wisdom brings life not merely in the sphere of the happiness or longevity of natural life but also as a saving benefit which extends beyond the earthly sphere, i.e., life in the eschatological and also the mystical (gnostic) sense. This may be assumed also in many Psalms. Cf., e.g., the constant repetition of ζῆσόν με in ψ 118. In ψ 48:9 one may see how the thought of eternal life emerges with varying degrees of clarity in the Gk. translations, though it is always introduced into the original. Thus in the Mas. Ps. 49:7b, 9 runs as follows : "He cannot give his ransom to God ... that he should live on and not see corruption." [167] The LXX translates : καὶ ζήσεται εἰς τέλος, ὅτι οὐκ ὄψεται καταφθοράν; 'Α : καὶ ἐπαύσατο εἰς αἰῶνα καὶ ζήσεται εἰς νῖκος; while the clearest expression of belief in the resurrection and eternal life is in Σ : ἀλλὰ παυσάμενος τῷ αἰῶνι τούτῳ, ζῶν εἰς αἰῶνα διατελέσει.

Bertram

---

[165] The treatment of this passage by F. X. Wutz, *Die Transkriptionen von der Septuaginta bis zu Hieronymus* (1933), 331, hardly does justice to the distinctiveness of the LXX. Cf. also the rendering of חַי by θνητός, where it is used of men as mortal creatures : Job 30:23 : οἰκία γὰρ παντὶ θνητῷ γῆ. In corresponding instances the rendering of the root חיה by ζωή or ζῆν is avoided, and instead we have ἄνθρωπος, ψυχή (cf. Job 7:15 A where ζωή = נֶפֶשׁ), ζῷον, θήρ, θηρίον etc. Perhaps at Ez. 32:23, 24, 26, 32 the replacement of γῆς by τῆς in some MSS is almost instinctive, since the combination of γῆ and true ζωή seems to be impossible. At any rate ζωή is also used in a depreciatory sense of earthly life : Qoh. 9:9 : ζωὴ ματαιότητος; Wis. 1:12 : πλάνη ζωῆς; 12:23 : ἀφροσύνη ζωῆς; 15:12 : ζωή—παίγνιον. Cf. also ψ 55:8, where the hapaxlegomenon נוד, uncertain life, is rendered ζωή, and ζωή thus seems to suggest the lowly and miserable nature of life. ζωή is often used for the means of life, as in Prv. 5:9 for הוֹד and 23:3 and 27:27 for לֶחֶם. In the last of these verses, however, the LXX plainly gives a more religious turn to the phrase. While the Mas. is speaking of goats' milk as nourishment, the LXX takes the verse to be the conclusion of the admonition and it thus relates the εἰς ζωήν to the fulfilment of it : υἱέ, παρ' ἐμοῦ ἔχεις ῥήσεις ἰσχυρὰς εἰς τὴν ζωήν σου καὶ εἰς τὴν ζωὴν τῶν (א) σῶν θεραπόντων. Here, too, the attempt of Wutz, *op. cit.*, 244 f. to expound the LXX merely philologically with the aid of the transcription hypothesis seems to be mistaken.

[166] Here the LXX takes its own way. 'ΑΣΘ are closer to the Mas.: ὁ γὰρ εὑρών με εὑρήσει ζωήν (wisdom is speaking).

[167] Acc. to F. Baethgen [2](1897); the emendations of A. Bertholet in Kautzsch, *ad loc.* hardly reproduce the original. H. Gunkel in his translation keeps the negative sense of the saying.

D. The Concept of Life in Judaism.

1. Palestinian Judaism.

a. Life and death. The OT concept of life is consistently maintained in Palestinian Judaism.[168] Men, who are the primary subjects of life, may be simply called the living.[169] Life is extension of natural existence, and "days of life" often mean "life."[170] That life depends on nourishment is self-evident, Sir. 29:21; 39:26 etc., as is also the fact that God is the Lord of life and death, Sir. 11:14; Wis. 16:13; 4 Macc. 18:18. God is invoked as the Father and God of my life, Sir. 23:1, 4. He gives life.[171] He has put the spirit of life in men.[172] He is the living God.[173]

Life is a blessing (Sir. 31:20; Tob. 8:17; 12:9 f.; Bar. 3:14), and, as life is desired in the call for salvation,[174] "to live" means "to be or to become healthy," or "to be delivered."[175] Long life is the reward for good conduct; wickedness shortens life.[176] But death is better than a miserable life.[177] Where it is presupposed that death is the end of everything,[178] this thought admonishes to a wise use of life. God's commandments are commandments of life,[179] His words are words of life,[180] and the Torah is the tree or medicine of life.[181] The metaphor of the ways of life and death is often repeated.[182]

---

[168] Not all the sources can be unequivocally assigned to Palestinian or Hellenistic Judaism. In Gk. Sir., Wis., Test. XII and other works there is an admixture of Pal. and Hell. motifs, so that these writings are mentioned both in this section and in that which follows.

[169] Tob. 12:6; Sir. 7:33 etc.; cf. Da. 2:30 LXX: τοὺς ἀνθρώπους, Θ: τοὺς ζῶντας following the Aram. חַיָּיא.

[170] E.g., Tob. 1:3; 4:3; Jdt. 10:3; 16:22; Sir. Heb. 3:12; more common in the Test. XII; "my days" = "my life," e.g., Test. Iss. 7:5; Zeb. 1:4; D. 1:1. Sir. 50:1 Gr. ζωή and ἡμέραι as par., Heb. דּוֹר and יָמִים. Cf. also Sir. 37:25 Heb.: "The life of a man lasts for days which can be numbered, but the life of Jeshurun for days which cannot be numbered."

[171] 2 Macc. 7:22 f.; 14:46; Schl. J., 173 on 6:33.

[172] Tg. J., I on Gn. 2:7 (ZNW, 12 [1911], 229 f.); Ex. r., 5 on 5:2 (Str.-B., III, 44); Tanch. ויהי, 6 (p. 214); T. Git., 2, 4. For the Spirit of God as a life-giving force, Jdt. 16:14; S. Bar. 21:4; Str.-B., I, 48; III, 240. God's work "lives and endures to eternity," Sir. 42:23.

[173] Ex. r., 5 on 5:2; Lv. r., 6 on 5:1 (Str.-B., III, 44 and 54); Schl. Mt., 504 on 16:16. God as He who lives eternally, Str.-B., II, 674; III, 790; → αἰώνιος. Used of the king, Jdt. 2:12 (ζῶν ἐγώ); cf. Jdt. 11:7; 12:4.

[174] Da. 2:4; 3:9 etc.

[175] Sir. 31:14; Da. 6:20 f.; Jdt. 7:27; 11:3; 1 Macc. 2:33; Ber., 5, 5 (Schl. Mt., 317 on 9:18). Death is enumerated among other afflictions in Sir. 39:29; 40:9; Ps. Sol. 13:2; 15:8. "Sorrow unto death" as an extreme form of sorrow, Sir. 37:2; Ps. Sol. 16:2; Test. Jos. 3:9 (sickness ἕως θανάτου, Test. R. 1:8).

[176] Sir. 4:12; 37:17 f.; Meg., 27b; Taan., 20b; Men., 44a (Str.-B., II, 692 on Ac. 9:13; IV, 267, 275); Ber., 55a (Str.-B., IV, 629).

[177] Sir. 29:24; 30:17; 40:28 f. (of the life of the beggar: "His life cannot be regarded as life"; the LXX differentiates: οὐκ ἔστιν αὐτοῦ ὁ βίος ἐν λογισμῷ ζωῆς; on this pt. v. R. Smend, Die Weisheit des Jesus Sir. [1906], 380 ad loc.); Tob. 3:6, 15; 1 Macc. 4:35; 2 Macc. 6:19; Beça, 33b (Str.-B., I, 566, 819 on Mt. 10:10; 19:22): "The life of the poor is no life . . ." Once suicide is considered as a possibility, Tob. 3:10.

[178] Sir. 10:11; 17:27 f. (the dead do not praise God); 22:11 (light goes out for the dead). The old idea of sheol is maintained (→ ᾅδης).

[179] Bar. 3:9: ἐντολαὶ ζωῆς; cf. 4:1.

[180] At Sinai God spoke "words of life," Ex. r., 29 on 20:2 (Str.-B., I, 464 and Schl. J., 183 on 6:68; cf. 182 on Jn. 6:63). Also Str.-B., II, 681 on Ac. 7:38; III, 129 on R. 3:1 f.

[181] Str.-B., III, 498 on 2 C. 2:16. For the Torah as the tree of life, ibid., II, 483 on Jn. 6:35; III, 792 on Rev. 2:7; as the water of life, II, 435, 483, 752.

[182] Man has the choice between life and death, Sir. 15:17; 36:14; 37:18. On the metaphor of the two ways, Dalman WJ, I, 130 f.; Str.-B., I, 460-463; Bousset-Gressm., 276; → ὁδός. In all these cases (n. 179-182) it is often hard to decide whether life is used in the older sense for a long and happy life on earth or in the sense of eternal life.

Death is the common lot of men. [183] The day of death is concealed, [184] but death does not tarry, [185] and therefore *memento mori*. [186] The fear of death is common to all men. [187] Death may be regarded as rest, [188] and, bitter though it is, it may sometimes be desired, [189] yet the conviction steadily gains ground that it is a punishment of sin. [190] It has come into the world through Eve (or Adam). [191] All men have become sinners and all are worthy of death. [192] This thought may also take the form, however, that death does not come from God but that it was brought into the world through the devil. [193] The angel of death is a devilish figure. [194]

b. Life after death. The greater the concentration on individual life, the more death becomes a burden which makes life vain, and the stronger the sense that real life demands the prolongation of life. Death does not belong to life. It is its contradiction. True life must be eternal. This is how we are to understand the fact that after the time of the Maccabees the expectation of (eternal) life after death constantly gains ground. Nor is this life grounded in the original power of the soul. [195] It is created anew by God through the resurrection from the dead (→ ἀνάστασις). [196] It is the חַיֵּי עוֹלָם (LXX: ζωὴ αἰώνιος, first found at Da. 12:2), which corresponds to eternal damnation. [197] There is hesitation whether all men or only the righteous will be raised, whether the

---

[183] Sir. 14:17; 41:3 f.; Str.-B., I, 754, 815. On the discussions whether there are exceptions (Enoch → 556, → Ἠλείας etc.): Str.-B., I, 753 f.; III, 744 f.; IV, 766. For dying we have such expression as "to see death" (Jdt. 7:27) or "to taste of death" (Str.-B., I, 751 f.).

[184] Sir. 11:19; 14:12; Str.-B., II, 126, 412; III, 473.

[185] Sir. 14:12.

[186] Sir. 28:6; Schab., 153a (Str.-B., I, 878).

[187] Sir. 40:5.

[188] Wis. 4:7.

[189] Sir. 22:11; 41:1 f. Dying is easy for a father who has a good son, Sir. 30:4 f.

[190] Str.-B., I, 815, III, 155-157, 228 f.; Bousset-Gressm., 399 ff. On discussions why the righteous must also die, Str.-B., I, 815 f.; III, 228.

[191] Sin and death are attributed to Eve in Sir. 25:24; Str.-B., I, 137 f.; III, 646. Cf. Vit. Ad. → Ἀδάμ, I, 141. Sin and death came into the world through Adam, 4 Esr. 3:7, 21 f.; 7:118; S. Bar. 17:3; 23:4 etc. Str.-B., I, 815 f.; III, 227 f.; Bousset-Gressm., 406 ff.; Ltzm. R. on 5:12.

[192] 4 Esr. 7:21 ff., 46, 68; 8:31, 35; S. Bar. 54:15 ff.; Str.-B., III, 155-157, 228 f.; → ἁμαρτία. There is some discussion whether there is also death without sin, Str.-B., I, 815 f. ἁμαρτία εἰς θάνατον, Test. Iss. 7:1 vl.

[193] Wis. 1:13; 2:24; Vit. Ad.; Bousset-Gressm., 408 f.; → σατανᾶς, → n. 194.

[194] Str.-B., I, 144-149, 596.

[195] The idea of the immortality of the soul is adopted in Hell. Judaism (→ 859).

[196] God makes the dead alive and is praised as this God in prayers, Dalman WJ, I, 128; Schl. J., 148 on 5:21 (the Spirit makes alive, *ibid.*, 181 on Jn. 6:63). For this reason the dead can be described as living for God in anticipation of the resurrection, Str.-B., I, 892; cf. 4 Macc. 7:19; 16:25. Death and the angel of death will be destroyed, *ibid.*, III, 481-483; IV, 887 f. The conception of *sheol* changes with the hope of the resurrection, → ᾅδης.

[197] There are distinctions of terminology. Alongside חַיֵּי עוֹלָם (opp. חַיֵּי שָׁעָה) = ζωὴ αἰώνιος we also find חַיֵּי עוֹלָם הַבָּא (opp. חַיֵּי עוֹלָם הַזֶּה) and instead of the latter we may simply have עוֹלָם הבא: Str.-B., I, 808 f., 829; II, 726 f.; Dalman WJ, I, 127-129; Schl. J., 158 f. But חַיִּים (ζωή) alone can also be used, Str.-B., I, 464, 808 f., 829; Dalman WJ, I, 129-131, esp. in expressions like "to inherit, to attain to," or "to enter into life," Str.-B., I, 464, 808 f., 829; Dalman WJ, I, 129, 131; Bousset-Gressm., 275 f. We also find the simple verbal form "the dead shall live," Schl. J., 151. Thus in all the types of usage in n. 179-182 life may be eschatological life, as also in the expression "the book of life" in which all those destined for eternal life are written, Str.-B., II, 169 f. (also 170-176 on the different ideas of heavenly books); III, 840; Bousset-Gressm., 258; → βίβλος.

resurrection takes place in stages, and what form the resurrection life will take. [198] Belief in the resurrection partly takes a different course from older expectations of an age of salvation and is partly combined with them. [199] It becomes an academic issue and is defended by the Pharisees against the Sadducees. It is taken for granted in apocalyptic. [200]

The vital question, however, is how far belief in life after death involves modification of the concept of life as such. Is eschatological life really life in a new sense? To a large extent this is undoubtedly not so. The fact that life is regarded as everlasting does not alter the concept. If eschatological life is naturally a life without suffering or restriction, [201] in the OT this is proper to life as such. There is some modification, however, in the fact that the eschatological life is regarded as a life without sin, [202] and that it is also to some extent thought of as a life which is no longer subject to present conditions and vital expressions. Thus Ber., 17a preserves the Rabb. saying: "In the future world there is no eating and drinking, no conceiving and propagating, no trade or travel, no envy, er.nity or strife; but the righteous sit there with their crowns on their heads and bathe in the radiance of the shekinah." [203] If in later Judaism (apart from the Hellenistic sphere) we do not find any idealistic or dualistic notions of life in the hereafter, nevertheless there are certain tendencies towards the emphasising of the otherworldly aspect of eschatological life. These take for the most part the form of a mythological depiction of the mode of heavenly being. [204]

2. Hellenistic Judaism.

a. We may first give a brief sketch of the linguistic usage of Hell. Judaism. The verb ζῆν is normally used of natural life, esp. in common expressions like "to be (still) alive" (e.g., Jos. Ant., 4, 316 etc.; Test. XII, etc.); "to escape with one's life" (Jos. Bell., 6, 189 etc.), "to be well (again)" (Jos. Vit., 421 etc.). It is worth noting that in the LXX ζῆν is also used in the causative for the hiphil of חיה, though → ζωοποιεῖν may also be

---

[198] Str.-B., IV, 1166-1198 on general or partial resurrection. On ideas of the future world, ibid., IV, 799-976, and on sheol, gehinnom and Gan Eden, ibid., 1016-1165. Cf. also Index. On proofs of the resurrection, ibid., I, 893-897; II, 542 f.; IV, 943 f. Cf. also Schürer, II, 638-648; Bousset-Gressm., 269-280; Ltzm. K. on 1 C. 15:37 f., 54; 2 C. 5:1. Where it is assumed that there is only the resurrection of the righteous, the leaving of the wicked in their graves is the second death, though this expression can also be used of appointment to eternal damnation, Str.-B., III, 830 f.

[199] Str.-B., IV, 799-976; Bousset-Gressm., 286-289.

[200] Str.-B., I, 885 f.; Bousset-Gressm., 269-274.

[201] All afflictions (sickness etc.) cease at death, Str.-B., I, 208 f.; III, 253 f.; Bousset-Gressm., 276. The tree of life is important here, though in a different sense from that of → n. 181. Its fruits (and perfume → n. 59) dispense life and health, Str.-B., I, 593 f.; IV, 1123 f., 1152; Bousset-Gressm., 284, → n. 63. Wonderful properties also belong to the water which flows in the age of salvation (Str.-B., II, 436; III, 805), cf. Str.-B., III, 854-857; IV, 934 f.; Bousset-Gressm., 284, → n. 63, → ὕδωρ.

[202] The evil impulse, extinguished by death (Str.-B., IV, 479 f.), will be destroyed by God in the Messianic age (ibid., IV, 482 f.). God will be with the blessed; His Spirit will be poured out etc. (Bousset-Gressm., 279 f.). This corresponds to the idea of judgment, which does not yet occur in this sense in the OT.

[203] For other examples cf. Str.-B., I, 890.

[204] For depictions of an angelic type of existence with mythological traits, cf. Str.-B., I, 209-212; Bousset-Gressm., 276-278. The idea of the heavenly vesture is particularly important, Bousset-Gressm., 277 f.; Wnd. 2 K., 164 f.; also the idea of crowns or wreaths carried by the blessed, Ber., 17a etc. in Str.-B., I, 210, 890; III, 404; IV, 1143, which originally, as attributes of stellar deities, are a sign of the divine mode of being, but which also show some influence of the Gk. idea of the wreath of victory: Asc. Is., 9; S. Bar. 15:8; Test. B. 4:1 (στεφάνους δόξης); cf. Bousset-Gressm., 278; Joh. W. 1 K., 248, 1; Dib. Jk., 86 f.; Dib. Herm. on s., 8, 2, 2 f.; → στέφανος.

employed for this. [205] Distinction may be made between ζωή and βίος (e.g., Sir. 29:21 f.; 40:29), but the words are often used without distinction. Thus they are par. at Wis. 15:12. βίος is used for lifetime in Ep. Ar., 209, 260 (διεξάγειν); Jos. Ant., 11, 219 (διάγειν); 19, 221 (διὰ βίου τοῦ παντός, though cf. δι' ὅλου τοῦ ζῆν in Ep. Ar., 130 etc.). Both ζῆν (Jos. Ant., 9, 165) and βιοῦν (ibid., 1, 346 etc.) may be used with an indic. of time, and one may both βίον ζῆν (4 Macc. 6:18) and ζωὴν βιοῦν (Sir. 40:28). Both βίος (Ep. Ar., 273; Jos. Ant., 1, 326 etc.) and ζωή (Sir. 4:1; 31:25? Test. L. 2:12?) may be used for sustenance. [206]

b. The understanding of life and death. The understanding of life is for the most part Jewish, though with some Hell. modification. God is naturally the living God (2 Macc. 7:33; 15:4; 3 Macc. 6:28), the Lord of life and death (Wis. 16:13; 4 Macc. 18:18). He gives life, though when He is described as χορηγὸς τῆς ζωῆς (Jos. Bell., 2, 131) this is Hell. terminology. [207] And as we read in Jos. Ant., 12, 22 : τὸν γὰρ ἅπαντα συστησάμενον θεὸν καὶ οὗτοι καὶ ἡμεῖς σεβόμεθα, Ζῆνα καλοῦντες αὐτὸν ἐτύμως, ἀπὸ τοῦ πᾶσιν ἐμφύειν τὸ ζῆν τὴν ἐπίκλησιν αὐτοῦ θέντες so in Ep. Ar., 16 the Zeus etymology of Stoicism is used to described God as Creator. Again, as ζωή and σύστασις are combined in Ep. Ar., 154, so acc. to Test. R. 2:4 the first of the seven πνεύματα given to man at creation is the πνεῦμα ζωῆς, μεθ' ἧς ἡ σύστασις (vl. κίνησις) κτίζεται. The result is that the soul, the bearer of the cosmic force of life, is regarded as immortal (→ 859).

Hellenistic influence may also be seen in the fact that both ζωή (ζῆν) and βίος (βιοῦν) are used of the "leading of life." We now find the expressions καλῶς ζῆν (Ep. Ar., 127; Jos. Bell., 7, 341) or καλῶς βιοῦν (Ep. Ar., 32; 39; Jos. Vit., 257), νομίμως βιοῦν (Jos. Ap., 2, 217), ἀδίκως ζῆν (Wis. 14:28; cf. 12:23), ἀσώτως ζῆν (Jos. Ant., 12, 203), κατὰ τοὺς Ἰουδαίων νόμους ζῆν (Jos. Ant., 13, 318; cf. 4 Macc. 11:5), κατὰ τὰ πάτρια ἔθη ζῆν (ibid., 11, 339), μετὰ ἀταραξίας ζῆν (4 Macc. 8:26). Enquiry is made into the βίῳ σύμφορον καὶ καθῆκον (Ep. Ar., 284) and the βίος νόμιμος (4 Macc. 7:15), and there is also reference to the κυβερνᾶν κατορθοῦν of the βίος (Ep. Ar., 147 and 251) and to the σῴζεσθαι of the βίοι τῶν ἀνθρώπων (ibid., 240). In the expression πρὸς ἀλήθειαν ζῆν τὸν ... βίον (4 Macc. 6:18) we see the idea that true life is attained when life corresponds to a transcendent norm. In keeping with this is the genuinely Hellenistic thought of the relative value of the lifetime (Wis. 4:8 f.). Also in keeping is a modified conception of death. We still find the old view in the common description of death as a sleep (ὕπνος αἰώνιος, Test. Iss. 7:9; D. 7:1; ὕπνος καλός, Test. Zeb. 10:1; A. 8:1 etc., κοιμᾶσθαι, Test. S. 8:1; Jud. 26:4 etc.). [208] But the thought is Greek when we read in Jos. Bell., 7, 341 that there is for the ἀνὴρ ἀγαθός the choice : ζῆν καλῶς ἢ τεθνάναι. The time of persecution and martyrdom teaches that death may be an act. The act itself — faithfulness μέχρι θανάτου (3 Macc. 7:16; 4 Macc. 6:21, 30; 7:8, 16 etc.), the choice of a θάνατος τῆς εὐσεβείας (4 Macc. 15:12) rather than transgression of the Law and violation of the nation and sanctuary (4 Macc. 9:1, 4; 16:24 etc.; 1 Macc. 3:59; 3 Macc. 1:29) — the Jew naturally did not have to learn from the Greek. But the understanding of the act is affected by Hellenistic ideas. [209] This may be seen in the fact that ἀποθνήσκειν is often characterised as a meaningful

---

[205] Thackeray, 269.

[206] Jos. uses ἀναβιοῦν (Ant., 18, 14) and ἀναβιῶσαι (Ant., 8, 327; 11, 9) instead of ἀναζῆν; βιοτεύειν is found in Ant., 13, 415; Ap., 1, 68 for "to lead his life." Βιωτικά and βίωσις are not found in Jos., though we have βιώσιμος, "worthy of life," at Ant., 2, 154.

[207] Cf. the combination of OT (Gn. 2:7) and Stoic terminology in Wis. 15:11 (ἠγνόησεν) τὸν ἐμπνεύσαντα αὐτῷ ψυχὴν ἐνεργοῦσαν καὶ ἐμφυσήσαντα πνεῦμα ζωτικόν.

[208] The idea that ὕπνος is an εἰκὼν τοῦ θανάτου in Test. R. 3:1 is Gk., cf. Jos. Bell., 7, 349.

[209] The glorification of martyrs is first found in Hell. Judaism, cf. A. Schlatter, Der Märtyrer in den Anfängen der Kirche (1915), 13 ff.; in the true Jewish view the days of martyrdoms are days of misfortune, ibid., 61 f.

act by prepositional phrases : ἀποθνήσκειν ὑπὲρ τῶν νόμων καὶ τῆς πατρίδος, 2 Macc. 8:21; cf. 7:9; δοῦναι τὰς ψυχὰς ὑπὲρ διαθήκης πατέρων ἡμῶν, 1 Macc. 2:50; more strongly Greek : ἀποθνήσκειν ὑπὲρ ἀρετῆς, 4 Macc. 1:8; ὑπὲρ τῆς καλοκάγα-θίας, 4 Macc. 1:10. Also ἀποθνήσκειν διὰ τὸν νόμον, 4 Macc. 6:27; διὰ τὸν θεόν, 16:25; διὰ τὴν εὐσέβειαν, 9:6; περὶ τοῦ νόμου, 13:9, cf. 2 Macc. 7:37; χάριν τῶν ἀδελφῶν ἡμῶν, 1 Macc. 9:10. [210] This kind of death is called καλός (Jos. Bell., 7, 337), ἀοίδιμος (glorious) (4 Macc. 10:1), μακάριος (4 Macc. 10:15). There is also reference to ἀνδρεία or εὐγενῶς ἀποθανεῖν (1 Macc. 9:10; 2 Macc. 14:42). The death of martyrs is a ὑπόδειγμα γενναιότητος καὶ μνημόσυνον ἀρετῆς (2 Macc. 6:31, cf. Jos. Bell., 7, 351). In particular the great speech of Eleazar in Jos. Bell., 7, 341-388 is full of the ideas of later Stoicism concerning life and death. [211] In the battle ὑπὲρ τῆς ἐλευθερίας death is to be regarded as a καλόν (337, 341), for life rather than death is a συμφορά. Death is a liberation of the soul chained to the θνητὸν σῶμα, whose life in the σῶμα is in truth a τεθνηκέναι (344-358). [212] Thus there is no fear of death, but ἑτοιμότης πρὸς θάνατον (350 f.).

c. The expectation of an eternal life after death is widespread in Hell. Judaism. This is contrasted with the παρὸν ζῆν of 2 Macc. 7:9 and the νῦν βίος of 4 Macc. 12:19 as ζωὴ αἰώνιος (4 Macc. 15:3; Ps. Sol. 3:16; Test. A. 5:2 etc., cf. Ps. Sol. 13:9 : ἡ γὰρ ζωὴ τῶν δικαίων εἰς τὸν αἰῶνα; Wis. 5:15 : δίκαιοι δὲ εἰς τὸν αἰῶνα ζῶσιν) or ἀέναος ζωή (2 Macc. 7:36) or often just ζωή (Test. Jud. 25:1 [v. 4 like 24:4 a Christian addition ?]) or ζῆν (Ps. Sol. 15:15). We also find ἀθανασία (Wis. 3:4; 15:3 : εἰδέναι σου τὸ κράτος ῥίζα ἀθανασίας, though cf. 4:1). The idea of heavenly being is the same as in Palestinian Judaism, [213] which does not adopt the ideas of Gk. philosophy like Jos. Bell., 7, 344, 346 : the soul freed from the burden of earth μακαρίας ἰσχύος καὶ πανταχόθεν ἀκωλύτου μετέχει δυνάμεως. On the other hand the Palestinian idea of resurrection is only partly adopted by Hell. Judaism. [214] It is usually replaced by the idea of the immortality of the soul — a result of the influence of dualistic Hellenistic anthropology. [215] In this connection the older idea of sheol is abandoned in favour of a retribution which follows immediately at death. [216]

d. Philo. In Philo's concept of ζωή we can see the powerful influence of the different Hellenistic traditions. [217] He once uses ζωή in the Gk. and specifically Stoic sense of

[210] On the other hand, the linking of martyrs with the thought of vicarious suffering is Jewish : 2 Macc. 7:37; 4 Macc. 6:28 f.; 17:22 (ἱλαστήριος θάνατος), cf. O. Schmitz, Die Opferanschauung des späteren Judentums (1910), 99 f., 129-132, → ἱλαστήριον. The statement concerning Levi in Test. R. 6:12 : ἀποθνήσκειν ὑπὲρ ὑμῶν ἐν πολέμοις ὁρατοῖς καὶ ἀοράτοις, is not very clear. ὁ ἀναμάρτητος ὑπὲρ ἀσεβῶν ἀποθανεῖται in Test. B. 3:8 is a Christian addition.
[211] W. Morel, Rheinisches Museum NF, 75 (1926), 106-114 links the speech with the ideas of Poseidonius.
[212] Cf. Ep. Ar., 212 : τὴν ἀδικίαν τοῦ ζῆν στέρησιν εἶναι.
[213] → 857 and Bousset-Gressm., 277 f., where Palestinian and Hell. materials are adduced alongside one another. The characteristic combination of φῶς and ζωή (→ 841) is also found in Sib., II, 316, where angels will conduct the souls of the righteous εἰς φῶς ... καὶ εἰς ζωὴν ἀμέριμνον. In the same way we have the idea of the attainment of everlasting life as a victory in 4 Macc. 7:3; 17:15; Wis. 4:2 (→ 840, n. 62).
[214] 2 Macc. 7:14 : ἀνάστασις εἰς ζωήν; ἀναστῆναι εἰς ζωήν, Ps. Sol. 3:16; Test. Jud. 25:1 (25:4 : ἐξυπνισθῆναι εἰς ζωήν a Christian addition ?); cf. 2 Macc. 7:9 : God εἰς αἰώνιον ἀναβίωσιν ζωῆς ἡμᾶς ἀναστήσει; 7:23 : τὸ πνεῦμα καὶ τὴν ζωὴν ὑμῖν πάλιν ἀποδίδωσιν.
[215] We find a dualistic anthropology in Wis. 8:19 f.; 9:15; cf. Bousset-Gressm., 400-402, → ψυχή. The soul is immortal in Jos. Bell., 7, 347 f. (cf. A. Schlatter, Wie sprach Joseph. von Gott? [1910], 47-49); and in Philo → 861. The ψυχή of the righteous is also ἀθάνατος in 4 Macc. 14:6; 18:23.
[216] For judgment immediately after death, cf. Wis. 3:1 ff.; Bousset-Gressm., 294 f., 296 f.
[217] Apart from the Philo literature, cf. J. Grill, Untersuchungen über die Entstehung des vierten Ev., I (1902), 206-211; E. v. Schrenck, op. cit., 17-31.

the vital force which is active in the ψυχή and which is common to all ζῷα, [218] and along the lines of Aristot. he distinguishes the λογικὴ δύναμις from the ζωτική. Man alone has the former, since God breathed into him the πνεῦμα (acc. to Gn. 2:7). [219] If the physical life is a θνητὴ ζωή, [220] God's πνεῦμα has given to νοῦς the δύναμις ἀληθινῆς ζωῆς, so that man (acc. to Gn. 2:7) has become εἰς ψυχὴν ... νοερὰν καὶ ζῶσαν ὄντως. [221]

Along the lines of Gk. and esp. Stoic tradition, the concept of ἀληθινὴ ζωή [222] is regarded as a manner of life, as a mode of βίος. [223] It is the leading of life in ἀρετή, [224] in σωφροσύνη, [225] in the knowledge of God. [226] Thus ὄντως ζῆν is contrasted with κατ' αἴσθησιν ζωή, [227] as μετὰ σώματος ζωή is with the τέλειος βίος. [228] Hence Philo can give the definition : τὸ μὲν ἀγαθὸν καὶ ἡ ἀρετή ἐστιν ζωή, τὸ δὲ κακὸν καὶ ἡ κακία ὁ θάνατος (Fug., 58), and he can thus vary the saying of Heraclites (Fr., 62 [I, 89, 14, Diels] → 834, n. 12) along these lines : ὅτι καὶ ζῶντες ἔνιοι τεθνή-κασι καὶ τεθνηκότες ζῶσι (Fug., 55; Leg. All., I, 108). If there logically results a διττὸν εἶδος ἀνθρώπων (Rer. Div. Her., 57), Philo distinguishes three kinds of ζωή in Rer. Div. Her., 45 f.: ζωῆς δὲ τριττὸν γένος, τὸ μὲν πρὸς θεόν, τὸ δὲ πρὸς γένεσιν, τὸ δὲ μεθόριον (borderland), μικτὸν ἀμφοῖν. [229]

For Philo life in the σῶμα is not merely of lesser value when ruled by → ἡδοναί. It is bad as such, and is a hindrance to the soul. In this connection he uses the Orphic and Platonic pictures of the body as → δεσμός [230] and of the σῆμα, [231] and the σῶμα is the συμφυὴς νεκρὸς ἡμῶν. [232] For this reason Philo can also speak of the souls

---

[218] Spec. Leg., IV, 123; cf. Leisegang, Index.

[219] Det. Pot. Ins., 80; 84. In Op. Mund., 73 Philo distinguishes not only ζῷα ἄλογα and man but also ζῷα νοερά, the stars ; cf. Plant., 12. In Gig., 7 f. the ἀήρ, too, is filled with invisible ζῷα (the ψυχαί), cf. Som., I, 135-7.

[220] Fug., 39 and 59; Virt., 53 and 76.

[221] Leg. All., I, 32 and 35; Rer. Div. Her., 56; Spec. Leg., IV, 123.

[222] Other phrases are ἀληθὴς ζωή (of the σπουδαῖος) in Poster. C., 45; Migr. Abr., 21; Mut. Nom., 213; ἀληθὴς βίος in Leg. All., II, 93. ἡ πρὸς ἀλήθειαν ζωή, Congr., 87; ἡ ἀψευδεστάτη ζωή, Mut. Nom., 213; Rer. Div. Her., 201: ζῆν ἀψευδῶς; θεῷ ζῆν in Mut. Nom., 213; Rer. Div. Her., 111; ἡ θεοῦ or κατὰ θεὸν ζωή in Poster. C., 69.

[223] Philo can use ζωή and βίος or ζῆν and βιοῦν without differentiation (βίος in the Gk. sense, e.g., Vit. Mos., I, 29). He also speaks of the ἀθάνατος or θνητός) and ἄφθαρ-τος βίος of the wise in Det. Pot. Ins., 49; Ebr., 152; Fug., 58 f.; Spec. Leg., I, 345 etc. The θνητὸς βίος is οὐ βίος ἀλλὰ χρόνος, Op. Mund., 156; on ἀβίωτος βίος cf. Leisegang, Index.

[224] Leg. All., I, 35; III, 52 : the μετουσία ἀρετῆς is the εὐδαιμονία ἀληθινῆς ζωῆς. Mut. Nom., 213 : τοῦ μὲν γὰρ κατ' ἀρετὴν βίου, ὅς ἐστιν ἀψευδεστάτη ζωή. Thus the ξύλον τῆς ζωῆς (Gn. 2:9) is ἀρετή, Op. Mund., 154 etc.

[225] Leg. All., II, 93.

[226] Spec. Leg., I, 345.

[227] Rer. Div. Her., 52-62; here two kinds of ψυχή are distinguished as in Spec. Leg., IV, 123. Philo also distinguishes between the πνεῦμα θεοῦ as a physical life-force (ὁ ῥέων ἀὴρ ἀπὸ γῆς) and the divine πνεῦμα as ἀκήρατος (undisturbed) ἐπιστήμη, Gig., 22-27.

[228] Abr., 271; that for the τέλειος βίος it is not a matter of length of life (cf. also Fug., 56 f.) is a Stoic topos, cf. E. Benz, Das Todesproblem in der stoischen Philosophie (1929), 103 ff.

[229] Cf. Gig., 60 f.; Som., I, 150-152; II, 234.

[230] Leg. All., II, 57; III, 51; Det. Pot. Ins., 158; Ebr., 152; Rer. Div. Her., 68. Cf. δεσμω-τήριον, Leg. All., III, 21; Ebr., 101; Migr. Abr., 9; Rer. Div. Her., 85; Som., I, 139.

[231] Leg. All., I, 108; Spec. Leg., IV, 188; cf. τύμβος, Deus Imm., 150; Som., I, 139.

[232] Gig., 15. Cf. Leg. All., III, 69 : τὸν γὰρ δερμάτινον ὄγκον ἡμῶν τὸ σῶμα ... πονηρόν τε καὶ ἐπίβουλον τῆς ψυχῆς οὐκ ἀγνοεῖ (sc. ὁ θεός) καὶ νεκρὸν καὶ τεθνηκὸς ἀεί. μὴ γὰρ ἄλλο τι νοήσῃς ἕκαστον ἡμῶν ποιεῖν ἢ νεκροφορεῖν (bury), τὸ νεκρὸν ἐξ ἑαυτοῦ σῶμα ἐγειρούσης καὶ ἀμοχθὶ (without trouble) φερούσης τῆς ψυχῆς. Ibid., 72: ὁ δὲ φιλόσοφος, ἐραστὴς ὢν τοῦ καλοῦ, τοῦ ζῶντος ἐν ἑαυτῷ κήδεται, ψυχῆς, τοῦ δὲ νεκροῦ ὄντως σώματος ἀλογεῖ. Cf. τὸ νεκροφορούμενον

of philosophers as follows : ἐξ ἀρχῆς ἄχρι τέλους μελετῶσαι τὸν μετὰ σωμάτων ἀποθνήσκειν βίον, ἵνα τῆς ἀσωμάτου καὶ ἀφθάρτου παρὰ τῷ ἀγενήτῳ καὶ ἀφθάρτῳ ζωῆς μεταλάχωσιν (Gig., 14). The wise : ψυχῆ ... ἐπόθει μόνη ζῆν, οὐ σώματι (Vit. Mos., I, 29). As a result of this dualistic conception true ζωή is not the leading of a virtuous life but a life apart from the body, with the idea either of a life after physical death or of ecstatic experiences of the vision of God. But these ideas are not clearly distinguished, and there is no sharp linguistic differentiation. 1. The ἀστεῖοι, who lead the βίος μετ' ἀρετῆς, live for ever (ζῆν εἰς ἀεί), κἂν τῆς πρὸς σῶμα κοινωνίας διαζευχθῶσι (Fug. 55), [233] and in this sense Philo calls the ζωή (or βίος) of the wise ἀθάνατος, [234] or ἀίδιος, [235] αἰώνιος, [236] ἄφθαρτος, [237] though one could not always say whether this is a real eternity or an ideal in the Gk. sense, [238] just as ἀποθνήσκειν τὸν μετὰ σωμάτων βίον does not have to be physical death but can also mean philosophical life. [239] 2. On the other hand, ἀθάνατος καὶ μακαρία ζωή, which has left the θνητὸς βίος, is in Vit. Conf., 12 f. rapturous vision and therefore also the λογικῶν καὶ εὐδαιμόνων ψυχῶν βίος θεῖος, Ebr., 99 f. [240]

God is called ἀεὶ ζῶν in Decal., 67, but ζωή is never predicated of Him. He is ζωῆς αἴτιος (Op. Mund., 30; cf. Aet. Mund., 106) both in the sense of physical and of spiritual ζωή (Fug., 198); but ἡ μὲν γὰρ ὕλη νεκρόν, ὁ δὲ θεὸς πλέον τι ἢ ζωή, πηγὴ τοῦ ζῆν, ὡς αὐτὸς εἶπεν (Jer. 2:13), ἀέναος (ibid.). Philo can speak of His βίος when He describes Him as τὸ ἀρχέτυπον τοῦ χρόνου καὶ παράδειγμα αἰών (Deus Imm., 32).

E. The Concept of Life in the NT.

1. Natural Life.

In the NT ζωή (and ζῆν) is first used of the natural life of man. [241] Its opposite and end are to be found in natural death. [242] It is corruptible. [243] It has limited

σῶμα, Migr. Abr., 21; Som., II, 237; ibid., I, 148 : ταῖς δὲ τῶν ἔτι ἀπολουομένων (sc. ψυχαῖς), μήπω δὲ κατὰ τὸ παντελὲς ἐκνιψαμένων τὴν ῥυπῶσαν καὶ κεκηλιδωμένην (sullied) <ἐν> σώμασι βαρέσι ζωήν. The σῶμα and its ἐπιθυμίαι hinder the ἀνάληψις and χρῆσις of ἀρετή; it is thus ἀλλοτριοῦσθαι, Leg. All., I, 103 f.; Ebr., 71. For the σῶμα does not merely suffer physical death; it also threatens the ψυχή with the death of κακία, Leg. All., I, 105-108. Cf. also Spec. Leg., IV, 114 f.: ἡ μὲν γὰρ τοῦ σώματος ὁλκὴ (drag) φύσει βρίθουσα, → θάνατος. The same thought occurs in Jos. Bell., 7, 344.

233 Plant., 37: ἡ μὲν πρὸς ἀρετὴν ὁδὸς αὕτη ζωὴν καὶ ἀθανασίαν ἔχουσα τὸ τέλος. Conf. Ling., 161; Vit. Mos., II, 288. Cf. E. Bréhier, Les Idées philosophiques et religieuses de Philon d'Alexandrie (1907), 240-242; H. Windisch, Die Frömmigkeit Philos (1909), 6.

234 Op. Mund., 155 f.; Poster. C., 39 and 68 f. (λογικὴ καὶ ἀθάνατος ζωή); Plant., 44; Fug., 55; Spec. Leg., I, 31 and 345.

235 Fug., 97.

236 Ibid., 78.

237 Det. Pot. Ins., 49; Gig., 14; Fug., 59.

238 Both are found expressly in Spec. Leg., II, 262 : ἀρετή is promised ἀθανασία διὰ πολυχρονίου ζωῆς καὶ βίου μακραίωνος, ὃν καὶ μετὰ σώματος θρέψεις ψυχῆ κεκαθαρμένη τελείᾳ καθάρσει βιῶν. Philo can even speak in true Gk. fashion of the eternal continuation of life through immortal acts, ibid., IV, 169.

239 Gig., 14, → θάνατος.

240 Cf. Mut. Nom., 209 f.; Som., II, 250. This ἀνάκλησις τοῦ προφήτου is characterised in Quaest. in Ex., II, 46 as a second birth, cf. Bréhier, op. cit., 242, also 203-205. The text and the related passages from Quaest. in Ex. are to be found in R. Reitzenstein, Die Vorgeschichte der christl. Taufe (1929), 107-119. On the influence of the mysteries, cf. Bréhier, 242-246. The notions of entry into life at death and of entry into rapture are combined in a distinctive way in Vit. Mos., II, 291.

241 As in the OT the natural man or Adam can be called a ψυχὴ ζῶσα at 1 C. 15:45; all living creatures can be called πᾶσα ψυχὴ ζωῆς at Rev. 16:3; ψυχὴ can be used synon. with ζωή at Mk. 8:35 etc.; cf. esp. Lk. 12:15 and 20.

242 Phil. 1:20 : εἴτε διὰ ζωῆς εἴτε διὰ θανάτου; 2 Tm. 1:10 etc.

243 Jm. 4:14, also the par. in Dib. Jk. and Wnd. Jk.

extension in time. [244] It stirs and moves. [245] It is actual in the ability of what is alive to do things. Thus "to live," as in the OT, can sometimes mean "to live in health" (Mk. 5:23; Jn. 4:50). [246] Similarly, we have the opposite expressions in which something which is not active can be called νεκρόν, e.g., ἁμαρτία in R. 7:8, ἔργα which do not reach their goal, [247] inactive πίστις [248] and false gods. [249] Reference should also be made to the figurative use according to which an attitude or action which is sure of its power and efficacy can be called "living," e.g., words, [250] hope (1 Pt. 1:3), sacrifice (R. 12:1). In the strict sense, this use is not metaphorical, [251] since operative power is of the very essence of life itself. This life is a good, indeed, it is the supreme good (Mk. 8:36 f.). Hence the miraculous power of Jesus is invoked to save life which is threatened (Mk. 5:23; Jn. 4:47 ff. etc.) or to restore it when it has gone (Mt. 9:18 etc.). The transgressor may no longer live (Ac. 22:22; 25:24; 28:4), and the greatest affliction is : ἐξαπορηθῆναι καὶ τοῦ ζῆν (2 C. 1:8), → θάνατος.

Human life is sustained by nourishment, [252] but it is not assured thereby, [253] since it does not rest on it but on the πνεῦμα (ζωῆς), which signifies, not vital cosmic force in the Stoic sense, but the power given by God in the OT sense. [254] For ζωή is proper to God as the ζῶν, [255] i.e., as not only the One who has life originally in Himself (Jn. 5:26), who lives eternally [256] and who alone has ἀθανασία (1 Tm. 6:16), but above all as the One who can both make alive and kill. [257] Since He makes alive through His Spirit, the Spirit, too, can be called ζωοποιοῦν. [258] Thus God is Lord of life and death, [259] as He is also Judge of the quick and the dead. [260]

---

[244] R. 7:1-3 : ... ἐφ' ὅσον χρόνον ζῇ ..., 1 C. 7:39; Hb. 2:15 : διὰ παντὸς τοῦ ζῆν, 9:17; Lk. 1:75; 2:36; 1 Cl., 25, 2; Barn., 4, 9; 10, 6 etc. Similarly βιοῦν and βίος in 1 Pt. 4:2, 3 (א). As in the OT ζωή and ἡμέραι are synon. at Hb. 7:3, "days of life" in Herm. v., 4, 2, 5; 5, 2 etc.

[245] Ac. 17:28 : ζῶμεν καὶ κινούμεθα.

[246] The aor. of ζῆν for "to get better," Mk. 5:23 etc.

[247] Hb. 9:14; Herm. s., 9, 21, 2.

[248] Jm. 2:17, 20 (vl.), 26; cf. Rev. 3:1 f.

[249] Did., 6, 3; 2 Cl., 3, 1.

[250] Ac. 7:38; Hb. 4:12; Jn. 6:63, 68; Herm. s., 9, 21, 2.

[251] → 833. One might speak of a figur. use where the subst. characterised as living is itself used figur., e.g., ὁδὸς ζῶσα (Hb. 10:20); λίθος ζῶν (1 Pt. 2:4 f.). But this is not true of the use of living water for running water as in the OT, cf. Did., 7, 1 f.

[252] Mt. 4:4 par.; Lk. 12:15; 1 C. 9:14 (ἐκ τοῦ εὐαγγελίου ζῆν); Barn., 6, 17. Thus βίος is used of the support of life in Mk. 12:44; Lk. 8:43; 15:12, 30, and ζωή in Herm. s., 9, 26, 2. βιωτικός denotes things or thoughts relating to the maintenance of life, 1 C. 6:3 f.; Lk. 21:34 : μερίμναις βιωτικαῖς, cf. Philo Vit. Mos., II, 158 : βιωτικαί χρεῖαι, → n. 28. Death and famine belong together, Rev. 6:8; 18:8.

[253] Mt. 4:4 par.; Lk. 12:15.

[254] Rev. 11:11. At Ac. 17:25 : διδοὺς πᾶσιν ζωὴν καὶ πνοήν, → πνεῦμα, there is approximation to the Gk. but also allusion to Is. 42:5.

[255] God as ζῶν after the OT pattern, R. 9:26; Mt. 16:16; 26:63; Ac. 14:15; Ign. Phld., 1, 2; 2 Cl., 20, 2; Herm. v., 2, 3, 2 etc.; cf. the widespread oath, 1 Cl., 58, 2; on R. 14:11 cf. Is. 49:18.

[256] Rev. 4:9 f.: τῷ ζῶντι εἰς τοὺς αἰῶνας τῶν αἰώνων; ibid., 10:6; 15:7; cf. Sir. 18:1.

[257] R. 4:17: τοῦ ζωοποιοῦντος τοὺς νεκρούς· (→ 833, n. 7 and cf. 2 C. 1:9); 1 Tm. 6:13 : τοῦ ζωογονοῦντος (vl. ζωοποιοῦντος) τὰ πάντα; Jn. 5:21; 6:57. God as ἀποκτείνων καὶ ζῆν ποιῶν, 1 Cl., 59, 3 (cf. Kn. Cl., ad loc.); cf. Mt. 10:28 par.

[258] 1 C. 15:45; Jn. 6:63; cf. Herm. s., 9, 14, 3.

[259] Lk. 12:20; 2 C. 1:9; Jm. 4:15 (cf. Dib. Jk. and Wnd. Jk.).

[260] 1 Pt. 4:5; of Christ (R. 14:9;) Ac. 10:42; 2 Tm. 4:1; Barn., 7, 2; 2 Cl., 1, 1; Pol. 2, 1.

Nevertheless, this derivation of ζωή from God is not primitive mythology in which ζωή as a natural phenomenon is traced back to a metaphysical αἰτία. On the contrary, it expresses the absolute dependence of man on God and the transcendence of God's existence. Thus ζωή is never regarded or investigated as an observable phenomenon. But it is perceived, as among the Greeks, that human life is fulfilled in the manner of leading it. Hence ζωή can be characterised by adverbs and adverbial expressions as a manner of life.[261] In this sense βίος can be used instead of ζωή.[262] But there is no development of the distinctive Greek concept of βίος (→ 835). The reason for this is that ζωή does not take on its meaningful content in a βίος; it is rather responsible before God the Judge (→ 862). Man, and specifically the believer, is not to live his life for himself, but for God, for the κύριος.[263] If he tries to live for himself, he lives for sin and death.[264] His life stands under the question of its whence and whither.

2. True Life according to the General NT View.

Death (→ θάνατος) is no more understood as a natural phenomenon than ζωή. It is neither self-evident nor necessary. It is a punishment for sin. This means, however, that in NT thinking indestructibility is part of the concept of life. In this sense ζωή belongs to God (→ 862), and this ζωή is true ζωή in comparison with which the ζωή which is subject to death cannot be regarded as true ζωή but is distinguished from it as provisional ζωή[265] or as ζῆν ἐν σαρκί.[266] Of a piece with this is the fact that men who are bound to natural life can be called dead in spite of their natural vitality.[267] True and proper ζωή[268] is in the first instance the

---

261 ζῆν ἀσώτως, Lk. 15:13; ἐθνικῶς or 'Ιουδαϊκῶς, Gl. 2:14; εὐσεβῶς, 2 Tm. 3:12; Tt. 2:12; πανούργως, Herm. m., 3, 3. Ac. 26:5 : κατὰ τὴν ἀκριβεστάτην αἵρεσιν τῆς ἡμετέρας θρησκείας ἔζησα Φαρισαῖος. So in Ign. ζῆν κατὰ 'Ιουδαϊσμόν, Mg., 8, 1; κατὰ Χριστιανισμόν, Mg., 10, 1; κατὰ κυριακήν (opp. σαββατίζειν), Mg., 9, 1; κατὰ Χριστόν 'Ιησοῦν, Mg., 8, 2; Phld., 3, 2; κατὰ ἄνθρωπον or ἀνθρώπους, Tr., 2, 1; R., 8, 1: κατὰ θεόν; Eph., 8, 1; Ditt. Syll.³, 910 AB ; κατὰ σάρκα, R. 8:12 f. (also Dg., 5, 8); κατὰ ἀλήθειαν, Ign. Eph., 6, 2. ζῆν ἐν αὐτῇ (τῇ ἁμαρτίᾳ), R., 6, 2; ἐν αὐτοῖς (vices), Col. 3:7; ἐν κόσμῳ, Col. 2:20; ἐν πίστει, Gl. 2:20.
262 1 Tm. 2:2 : ἵνα ἤρεμον καὶ ἡσύχιον βίον διάγωμεν. βίος seems to suggest "manner of life" without adv. or adj. definition at Lk. 8:14; 2 Tm. 2:4 (?); 1 Jn. 2:16; βίωσις is found in this sense at Ac. 26:4, and cf. ζωή in Herm. m., 11, 7 and 16.
263 R. 14:7 f.; 2 C. 5:15; Gl. 2:19; cf. 1 Pt. 2:24 (τῇ δικαιοσύνῃ). ζῆν τῷ θεῷ, which is common in Hermes (e.g., s., 8, 11, 1 ff.), does not refer to conduct but to having life with God (→ n. 278).
264 2 C. 5:15; R. 6:2.
265 1 C. 15:19 : εἰ ἐν τῇ ζωῇ ταύτῃ ἐν Χριστῷ ἠλπικότες ἐσμὲν μόνον; 1 Tm. 4:8 : ἐπαγγελίαν ἔχουσα ζωῆς τῆς νῦν καὶ τῆς μελλούσης.
266 Gl. 2:20; Phil. 1:22.
267 Mt. 8:22 par.; Lk. 15:24, 32; Col. 2:13 and Eph. 2:1, 5 : ὑμᾶς νεκροὺς ὄντας τοῖς παραπτώμασιν ..., Eph. 5:14 : ἀνάστα ἐκ τῶν νεκρῶν; Rev. 3:1: ὅτι ζῇς καὶ νεκρὸς εἶ, 1 Tm. 5:6 : ζῶσα τέθνηκε, esp. Jn. 5:21, 25. Cf. also 2 Cl., 1, 6 : ὁ βίος ἡμῶν ὅλος ἄλλο οὐδὲν ἦν εἰ μὴ θάνατος. Acc. to Herm. s., 9, 16, 1 ff. man is dead before baptism. Here there is a formal par. to the later Greek Stoic usage, but with the material difference that true ζωή is not understood in the ideal sense. Cf. Eph. 4:18 (ἀπηλλοτριωμένοι τῆς ζωῆς τοῦ θεοῦ) with Philo Poster. C., 29 (ἀνάγκη τὸν ἀλόγως βιοῦντα τῆς τοῦ θεοῦ ζωῆς ἀπεσχοινίσθαι). The influence of Gk. usage may be seen at Did., 4, 8 : εἰ γὰρ ἐν τῷ ἀθανάτῳ κοινωνοί ἐστε, πόσῳ μᾶλλον ἐν τοῖς θνητοῖς (i.e., in earthly goods, though cf. R. 15:27; 1 C. 9:11; Barn., 19, 8); cf. also Dg., 7, 1: θνητὴ ἐπίνοια; 1 Cl., 36, 2 : ἀθάνατος γνῶσις.
268 ζωὴ ἀληθινή, Ign. Eph., 7, 2; τὸ ἀληθινὸν ζῆν, ibid., 11, 1; Tr., 9, 2; Sm., 4, 1; τὸ ἀληθῶς ζῆν, Dg., 10, 7. In Jn. ἀληθινός is never an attribute of ζωή, but the same thought is present in the combination of → ἀλήθεια and ζωή, cf. the combination of ζῶν and

future life after death, the μέλλουσα. [269] Because the future ζωή is the true one, it can simply be called ζωή without attribute, as already in Judaism (n. 197; 859). [270] The simple ζῆν can also be used in this sense. [271] Since it is indestructible it is often called αἰώνιος, [272] and as deliverance from death it is sometimes linked with σωτηρία. [273] It will be inherited, [274] received, [275] attained, [276] entered into. [277] Man may be worthy of ζωή by his present conduct, [278] so that the NT, like Judaism, can speak of the way of life [279] and of the repentance which leads to life. [280] But man has as little control over this life as over natural life. As the latter is given to him by the creative act of God, so ζωή is given to him at the resurrection when God raises him. The idea of the immortality of the soul is quite alien. [281] The sovereignty of God is expressed in OT phrases like ὅσοι ἦσαν τεταγμένοι εἰς ζωὴν αἰώνιον, Ac. 13:48 [282] and also by originally deterministic ideas like that of the book or books of life in which those predestined to life are inscribed, [283] though the element of determinism is now removed. [284]

ἀληθινός as divine predicates in 1 Th. 1:9. We once have the Gk. concept of ὄντως ζωή (1 Tm. 6:19), to which the ὄντως θάνατος of Dg., 10, 7 corresponds.

[269] 1 Tm. 4:8; τὸ προκείμενον ζῆν, Ign. Eph., 17, 1.

[270] Mk. 9:43, 45; Mt. 7:14; 18:8 f.; 1 Pt. 3:7, 10; 2 Pt. 1:3; Did., 9, 3; Barn., 2,10; Herm. v., 1, 1, 9; Dg., 9, 6; ἀνάστασις ζωῆς, Jn. 5:29; Mart. Pol., 4, 2, → n. 214. In this sense we can also have the phrases στέφανος τῆς ζωῆς, Rev. 2:10; Jm. 1:12 → n. 204, and ξύλον τῆς ζωῆς, Rev. 2:7; 22:2, 14, 19, → n. 201.

[271] R. 1:17; 8:13; 1 Th. 5:10; Lk. 10:28; Hb. 12:9; Barn., 6, 17 etc. So of Christians: ἡμεῖς οἱ ζῶντες, 2 Cl., 3, 1. Perhaps οἱ ζῶντες came into use as an early designation for Christians, F. J. Dölger, Ἰχθύς, I (1910), 167 f.; E. Peterson, Εἷς θεός (1926), 18 f.

[272] Mk. 10:17; Mt. 19:16, 29; 25:46; R. 2:7; 5:21; 6:22 f.; Gl. 6:8; 1 Tm. 1:16; 6:12; Tt. 1:2; 3:7; Jd. 21; Ac. 13:46, 48; Jn. 3:15 f.; 4:14; 6:27; Herm. v., 2, 3, 2; Mart. Pol., 14, 2 etc.; → n. 56, → n. 197, → 859; ζῆν εἰς τὸν αἰῶνα, Barn., 8, 5; 9, 2; 11, 10 f.; καινότης ἀϊδίου ζωῆς; Ign. Eph., 19, 3; ἐπουράνιος ζωή, 2 Cl., 20, 5.

[273] Ign. Eph., 18, 1; 2 Cl., 19, 1; (ζῆν and σωθῆναι of restoration to health in Mk. 5:23); cf. R. 5:10. The combination of ζωή and → ἀφθαρσία, 2 Tm. 1:10; Ign. Pol., 2, 3; cf. R. 2:7; Mart. Pol., 14, 2; 2 Cl., 14, 5. The first of God's δῶρα acc. to 1 Cl., 35, 2 is ζωὴ ἐν ἀφθαρσίᾳ.

[274] κληρονομεῖν, Mk. 10:17; Mt. 19:29; Lk. 10:25; Tt. 3:7; 1 Pt. 3:7; Herm. v., 3, 8, 4 etc.

[275] (ἀπο)λαμβάνειν, Mk. 10:30; Lk. 18:30; 2 Cl., 8, 6; cf. Mt. 19:16.

[276] περιποιεῖσθαι, Herm. m., 3, 5; s., 6, 5, 7.

[277] εἰσελθεῖν εἰς τὴν ζωήν, Mk. 9:43 ff.; Mt. 18:8 f.; 19:17.

[278] Mk. 10:17 par., 30 par.; Mt. 25:46; R. 2:7; 6:22 f.; Gl. 6:8; Jn. 5:29; 12:25; 2 Cl., 8, 4; 10, 1 etc. Lk. 10:28 : τοῦτο ποίει καὶ ζήσῃ, and many instances in Herm., usually with the addition τῷ θεῷ, e.g., v., 3, 8, 5; m., 4, 2, 3 f. → n. 263; cf. Mart. Pol., 14, 1: τῶν δικαίων, οἳ ζῶσιν ἐνώπιόν σου (God).

[279] Mt. 7:13 f. (cf. Kl. Mt., Schl. Mt. → 851; → n. 182); Did., 1, 1 f.; 4, 14; Barn., 19, 1 f.; 20, 1; Herm. s., 5, 6, 3 (αἱ τρίβοι τῆς ζωῆς), though cf. Ac. 2:28 on the basis of ψ 15:11.

[280] Ac. 11:18; Herm. s., 6, 2, 3; 8, 6, 6.

[281] The idea of the immortality of the soul is first found along with dualistic Hellenistic psychology in Dg., 6. Since we can see from 1 C. 15 and Ac. 17:18, 32 that the Christian belief in resurrection is alien to Gk. hearers, the defence of this belief (cf. 1 Cl., 24-27) is one of the main concerns of the Apologists, J. Geffcken, Zwei griech. Apologeten (1907), 235 ff., 244 f. For the Apologists the ψυχή is certainly ἀθάνατος in itself, but through sin it has fallen victim to death (Just. Dial., 124, 4; Tat. 13, 1; 15, 4) and can really become ἀθάνατος only through the resurrection (Just. Dial., 46, 7; 69, 7; 117, 3; Tat., 13, 1; 15, 4). But Justin is unable to make a clear distinction from the Gk. belief in the immortality of the soul (Dial., 4, 5; Apol., 44, 9). Cf. L. Atzberger, Geschichte der christl. Eschatologie innerhalb der vornicänischen Zeit (1896), 116-121.

[282] Cf. Herm. v., 4, 3, 5 : οἱ ἐκλελεγμένοι εἰς ζωὴν αἰώνιον.

[283] Rev. 13:8; 17:8; 1 Cl., 53, 4 (Ex. 32:31 f.); Herm. v., 1, 3, 2; s., 2, 9, → βίβλος.

[284] Cf. Rev. 3:5; 20:12, 15; 21:27.

3. The Grounding of Life in Jesus Christ.

Thus far the early Christian view corresponds to the Jewish both in matter and expression. The decisive distinction, however, is that according to NT belief God's future act of awakening is grounded in the resurrection of Jesus Christ from the dead. That He who was dead now lives is the Easter message [285] and the heart of the Christian *kerygma*, [286] and this life is eternal and indestructible. [287] Death is thus deprived of its force (→ θάνατος).

Hence faith in the possibility of a future ζωή does not rest on the concept of God in general, although this can provide a motive for the concept of resurrection (Mk. 12:27 par.). In practice this means that the concept of God is taken more radically, that the gulf between God and man as a result of sin is seen to be deeper, and that man's claim is more radically negated. If God gives new and true life, it is on the basis of His free, unexpected and gracious act of salvation, without which we should be lost. [288] Hope (→ 531) rests, therefore, on faith in this act of salvation: ὁ δίκαιος ἐκ πίστεως ζήσεται. [289] He who believes in Jesus will have life. [290] Jesus Christ, then, is the One who has brought ζωή and ἀφθαρσία to light (2 Tm. 1:10). He is the ἀρχηγὸς τῆς ζωῆς (Ac. 3:15). It is by His life, which has overcome death, that we shall be saved (R. 5:10). [291] He is our life, and, inasmuch as this is now imparted to us, it is now hidden with Him in God (Col. 3:3 f.). In Him is life. [292] He is the ἀνάστασις and the ζωή (Jn. 11:25), the ὁδός, ἀλήθεια and ζωή (14:6), so that it can be said of Him in 1 Jn. 5:20: οὗτός ἐστιν ὁ ἀληθινὸς θεὸς καὶ ζωὴ αἰώνιος. [293]

4. Life Future and Present.

This involves a further development. For if future ζωή is established by the event of salvation already enacted in the death and resurrection of Christ, the decisive thing has already taken place and the future resurrection of the dead is simply the consummation of the event of the replacement of the old aeon by the new which has already commenced in Christ. This development is expressed with varying degrees of clarity and consistency, and in varied forms, in the different NT writings, so that ζωή bears to some degree the character of something for which we still hope, and to some degree it is a present possession.

---

[285] Lk. 24:9, 23; Ac. 1:3.

[286] R. 6:10; 14:9; 2 C. 13:4; Ac. 25:19; 7:8, 25; Rev. 1:18; 2:8; cf. also R. 10:9; 1 C. 15:3 ff. etc.; also Ign. Mg., 9, 1; Tr., 9, 2.

[287] εἰς τοὺς αἰῶνας τῶν αἰώνων, Rev. 1:18; ἀκατάλυτος, Hb. 7:16. Cf. R. 6:10: ὃ γὰρ ἀπέθανεν, τῇ ἁμαρτίᾳ ἀπέθανεν ἐφάπαξ, ὃ δὲ ζῇ, ζῇ τῷ θεῷ and the comm. *ad loc.*

[288] God's → χάρις (R. 5:15, 17; 1 Pt. 3:7), or Christ's ἔλεος → 483 (Jd. 21) imparts life.

[289] Quoting Hab. 2:4: R. 1:17; Gl. 3:11; Hb. 10:38. Cf. Tt. 1:1 f.; Barn., 1, 6: ζωῆς ἐλπίς as ἀρχὴ καὶ τέλος πίστεως ἡμῶν (v. Wnd. Barn.); 8, 5: οἱ ἐλπίζοντες ἐπ' αὐτὸν ζήσονται εἰς τὸν αἰῶνα. Ign. Eph., 14, 1: πίστις and ἀγάπη as ἀρχὴ ζωῆς καὶ τέλος.

[290] R. 6:8 ff.; 1 Tm. 1:16; Jn. 3:15 f.; cf. Ac. 11:18 with 15:7-9; 13:48; also R. 10:9. Only the believer is ἄξιος τῆς αἰωνίου ζωῆς, Ac. 13:46.

[291] Cf. also Did., 9, 3: εὐχαριστοῦμεν ... ὑπὲρ τῆς ζωῆς καὶ γνώσεως, ἧς ἐγνώρισας ἡμῖν διὰ Ἰησοῦ τοῦ παιδός σου. Barn., 1, 4: ἐπ' ἐλπίδι ζωῆς αὐτοῦ, 12, 5: καὶ αὐτὸς (Jesus) ζωοποιήσει. Ign. Mg., 9, 2: πῶς ἡμεῖς δυνησόμεθα ζῆσαι χωρὶς αὐτοῦ, Tr., 9, 2: οὗ χωρὶς τὸ ἀληθινὸν ζῆν οὐκ ἔχομεν.

[292] R. 8:2; 2 Tm. 1:1; 1 Jn. 5:11.

[293] In Ign. Christ is described as τὸ ἀδιάκριτον ἡμῶν ζῆν, Eph., 3, 2; as ἐν θανάτῳ ζωὴ ἀληθινή, Eph., 7, 2; as τὸ διὰ παντὸς ἡμῶν ζῆν, Mg., 1, 2; as τὸ ἀληθινὸν ἡμῶν ζῆν, Sm., 4, 1.

It is natural that in the Synoptic preaching of Jesus there should be reference only to future ζωή, [294] since this preaching does not yet look back to the death and resurrection as events which determine the present. It is also natural that all the NT writings should speak of future ζωή. The question is to what extent the present is already understood in the light of this ζωή. This is true to the extent that the present stands under a hope which is sure of its goal because it is grounded in the event of salvation (→ ἐλπίς). For this reason ἐλπίς can be described as ζῶσα (→ 862), since God has begotten us again to it through the resurrection of Christ (1 Pt. 1:3). Hence Rev. speaks only of future life (e.g., 2:7, 10; 20:4 f.), and yet the present is sustained by the certainty of this future. [295] In Col. 3:3 f. the certainty finds expression in the fact that the ζωή is understood to be already present but for the time being hidden until it shall be ultimately manifested. [296] The same thought is present in the statement that ζωή is given in Jesus Christ (2 Tm. 1:1, → n. 292). Similarly there is the exhortation in 1 Tm. 6:12 to lay hold of this ζωή, though it is also future, 1 Tm. 6:19. Indeed, the Past. can say that the ζωή is already revealed, being present in the proclamation of the Gospel (→ 732). [297]

In such cases it is hard to say how far the concept of ζωή itself is deepened by the more or less radical relationship to the present, i.e., whether and how ζωή is conceived of as genuinely otherworldly and not more or less as a resumption of the present ζωή after its interruption by death. It is obviously thought of as a life without suffering or corruption; [298] it will be in χαρά; [299] it will consist in δόξα, [300] so that ζωή and δόξα can be more or less synonymous. [301] But none of this differs from the Jewish concept of life, nor is this modified by the express statement in Mk. 12:25 par. that earthly conditions of life will no longer apply (→ 857).

5. Paul's View of Life as Present.

a. The terms used to describe life as present. It is Paul who first gives radical expression to the thought that life is present. He can use for this purpose not only the Jewish eschatological conception of the replacement of the old aeon by the new, which has already taken place for Paul, but also the terminology of the Gnostic *anthropos* myth, [302] according to which Christ has become by His re-

---

[294] Dalman WJ, I, 132.

[295] Cf. also Ac. 11:18; 13:46-48; 1 Pt. 3:7, 10; Jd. 21.

[296] → n. 289 on the connection between ζωή and ἐλπίς.

[297] 2 Tm. 1:10, copied in 2 Cl., 20, 5; Tt. 1:2 f. Without this relationship Ign. Mg., 9, 1: ἐν ᾗ (the κυριακὴ ἡμέρα) καὶ ἡ ζωὴ ἡμῶν ἀνέτειλεν δι' αὐτοῦ καὶ τοῦ θανάτου αὐτοῦ. In Ign., for whom the Lord's Supper is φάρμακον ἀθανασίας (Eph., 20, 2), the idea of the presence of ζωή is influenced by the sacramental conceptions of the mysteries (H. Schlier, *Religionsgeschichtl. Untersuchungen zu den Ignatiusbriefen* [1929], 165 ff.). In respect of the Lord's Supper it is said in Did., 10, 3: ἡμῖν δὲ ἐχαρίσω πνευματικὴν τροφὴν καὶ ποτὸν καὶ ζωὴν αἰώνιον διὰ τοῦ παιδός σου. In Herm. ζωή is a present possession through baptism (v., 3, 3, 5; s., 9, 16, 2-7) in so far as one may speak of life as present for him.

[298] Rev. 21:4 etc.

[299] Mt. 25:21, 23; 1 Th. 2:19 f.; 1 Pt. 1:8 → χαρά.

[300] 2 Tm. 2:10; 1 Pt. 5:1, 4, 10 etc. → δόξα.

[301] Cf. 1 Pt. 5:4 with Jm. 1:12; Rev. 2:10 and the connection between δόξα and ζωή in 2 C. 3:6-11.

[302] So far as we can see, Jewish apocal. had adopted other aspects of the *anthropos* myth as early as Da. 7, → υἱὸς τοῦ ἀνθρώπου.

surrection the second Adam, the author of a new humanity to which believers in Him belong, the → ἀπαρχὴ τῶν κεκοιμημένων (1 C. 15:20, 23), the πρωτότοκος (ἐκ τῶν νεκρῶν) (R. 8:29, cf. Col. 1:18). In his use of this terminology Paul can sometimes think of the future fulfilment (1 Cor. 15:20-22, 44-49) and sometimes of the decisive renewal of the present (R. 5:12-21). He can also employ the πνεῦμα conception of the mysteries and Gnosticism (→ πνεῦμα) to express the same thought. The πνεῦμα given to the believer in baptism is an earnest of the future. [303] Paul can even use Hellenistic expressions as though the πνεῦμα were a wonderful something, a possession, which guarantees the future resurrection (R. 8:11). [304] In fact, however, the πνεῦμα has for him the sense of the manner of the life of faith in its relationship (→ πίστις) to God's act of salvation in Christ. It is just because this relationship is achieved in the manner of a present existence that he can adopt the Hellenistic conception of πνεῦμα (modified, of course, by the OT view of the Spirit) and that, to bring out the fact that Christ is present and active, he can link Christ with the πνεῦμα so closely that he refers to Christ what is said of the Spirit in the OT (2 C. 3:17). As Christ is not for him an idea or a cosmic force (as in Gnosticism), so ζωή for him is not an idea or hyperphysical state, but the present historical actuality of the believer. For the πνεῦμα ζωοποιοῦν, [305] expressly distinguished by him from the power of purely natural life, the ψυχὴ ζῶσα (1 C. 15:45), is indeed present. [306] If, then, the resurrection life can come to its full development only in the future, so that ζωή is to this extent an object of hope, [307] in some sense it is still present already, just as the future → δόξα is already anticipated in faith (R. 8:30; 2 C. 3:6-18).

b. Life present in the Word and in faith. This presence of ζωή is to be understood neither in the idealistic sense of Stoicism (→ 837) as though it consisted in the timeless validity of a βίος κατ᾽ ἀρετήν, nor in the sense of Gnosticism as though it were a mysterious substance guaranteeing ἀφθαρσία, a possession of the believer rising to consciousness in isolated moments which interrupt the stream of life (→ 842), nor in the sense of Philo who combines these two possibilities (→ 860). The view of Paul is differentiated from that of the Stoics (and Philo) by the fact that the πνεῦμα is not the νοῦς in the philosophical sense but the supernatural power of God which is not proper to man as such and which cannot be developed, like the νοῦς, through the βίος. It differs again from that of the Gnostics in the fact that, although formally the πνεῦμα is represented in Gnostic fashion as a mysterious substance or fluid, materially it is understood very differently. The presupposition of reception of πνεῦμα and ζωή is on the one side the preached Word, which proclaims, not timeless truths in the garb of myth, but a historical event, and which as such is not the simple mediation of what is knowable, so that it can be readily detached from it as proclamation, but which itself belongs to the saving event, continually allotting to the individual the grace of God active in this event. Hence the presence of life can be seen in this preached Word as a historical happening. It dispenses life (2 C. 2:16; 3:6-18; 5:18-20), it is the δύναμις θεοῦ εἰς σωτηρίαν (R. 1:16), it is the λόγος ζωῆς (Phil. 2:16), [308]

---

303 ἀπαρχή, R. 8:23; → ἀρραβών, 2 C. 1:22; 5:5; cf. Gl. 4:6 f.; 5:5.
304 K. Deissner, Auferstehungshoffnung und Pneumagedanke bei Pls. (1912).
305 1 C. 15:45; 2 C. 3:6; R. 8:6.
306 Sickb. K., 80.
307 R. 5:1-11; 8:12-39; 1 C. 15; 2 C. 5:1-5.
308 Cf. ῥήματα ζωῆς, Ac. 5:20; Jn. 6:63, 68.

so that it can be said in the sense of Paul that the Gospel destroys death and manifests life (2 Tm. 1:10; cf. Tt. 1:2 f.). The presupposition of the reception of life is on the other hand faith, which grasps the act of God and the order of salvation established thereby (→ σταυρός) as obedience (→ πίστις). As death is seen to be the consequence of sin, so the presupposition of ζωή is the forgiveness of sin, the δικαιοσύνη (ἐκ) θεοῦ, [309] which comes to man in the Word of proclamation (→ κήρυγμα). As, then, the ultimate meaning of the act of salvation is forgiveness, so the ζωή present in the πνεῦμα implies a presence of remission with all the possibilities thereby given to believers. Hence the πνεῦμα is not a possession of man in either the Stoic or the Gnostic sense. On the contrary, the πνεῦμα implies that man cannot possibly live of himself, or by what he himself possesses, but only by the act of God, his → δικαιοσύνη being the δικαιοσύνη θεοῦ. It is for this reason that Paul can say that the life which he now has is not his own, but that Christ lives in him (Gl. 2:19 f.; R. 8:10), that His ζωή is in us (2 C. 4:10 f.), or that we live in Christ (R. 6:11), that we shall live in Him (2 C. 13:4), and that in Christ is our life (R. 8:2). [310] Nor does this refer to a Christ myth. It refers to the fact that we have life only in relation to the divine act of salvation accomplished in Christ.

c. The concrete possibilities of life. If in Stoicism the moment which encounters man will be destroyed by reduction to the general (→ 838), and if in Gnosticism the concrete possibilities of life are neutralised by asceticism or indifference (→ 842), the pneumatic ζωή of Paul is true ζωή in the very fact that it is active every moment in the concrete possibilities of life which the believer nevertheless confronts with the reservation of the ὡς μή (1 C. 7:29-31). It is freedom from death, for the believer has made his own the death which is still ahead of him by dying with Christ (→ σύν), has accepted the cross by which the world is crucified with its possibilities, and has thus attained to life from out of this death. [311] But this freedom from death (2 C. 3:16-18 etc.) is displayed precisely in the fact that the believer puts to use the concrete possibilities of death and thus manifests the ζωή τοῦ Ἰησοῦ in constant dying (2 C. 4:8-16). "Dying, and, behold we live" (2 C. 6:4-10). The concrete possibilities of earthly living and dying are swallowed up by Christ ; by living and dying Paul glorifies Him alone, and, as dying is a κέρδος, so ζῆν ἐν σαρκί can only be καρπὸς ἔργου, i.e., a work in the service of Christ (Phil. 1:20-22). [312] As his ζωή is a life from God (Christ), so it is only for God (Christ). [313] Thus living and dying (like waking and sleeping) are relativised and neutralised, not in the Stoic sense, but simply because the believer belongs to Christ and God (1 C. 3:22 f.), serves Him (2 C. 5:9) and is indissolubly bound to God's ἀγάπη imparted in Christ (R. 8:38 f.), so that the concrete possibilities of existence

---

[309] Cf. the relation of R. 5-8 to 3:21-4:25. R. Bultmann, *Imago Dei* (1932), 53-62.

[310] The Pauline formulae concerning life in Christ are found again in Ign. Eph., 11, 1; 20, 2; Ep. Pol., 8, 1; and concerning His life in us, Ign. Mg., 5, 2. Materially we have the same thought in the concept of the → σῶμα Χριστοῦ, and this recurs in 2 Cl. when there is reference in 14, 1 to the ἐκκλησία τῆς ζωῆς and when in 14, 2 the ἐκκλησία ζῶσα is defined as the σῶμα Χριστοῦ.

[311] Gl. 2:19 f.; 6:14; R. 6:1-11, → θάνατος.

[312] On Phil. 1:21 cf. the comm. I cannot quite accept the explanation of O. Schmitz, *Nt.liche Studien für Heinrici* (1914), 155-169. τὸ ζῆν in v. 21 cannot be different from ζωή in v. 20 and ζῆν ἐν σαρκί in v. 22, i.e., earthly, corporeal life. This life now means Christ, i.e., it has been truly realised in Him and therefore in itself it has become indifferent.

[313] R. 6:11, 13; Gl. 2:19 f.; 2 C. 5:15.

are only mediately through faith and not directly the possibilities of his existence, and must remain so as long as the believer does not walk by sight. The ζῆν πνεύματι is a στοιχεῖν πνεύματι (Gl. 5:25; cf. R. 8:12 ff.) whose first fruit is ἀγάπη (Gl. 5:22 f.); dying and rising again with Christ is a περιπατεῖν ἐν καινότητι ζωῆς (R. 6:4) which stands under an imperative and which, as life raised from the dead, must show itself to be a walk in righteousness (R. 6:12-23). That this walk as such, however, is not ζωή in the ideal sense is seen not only in the fact that it rests on the prior gift of justification but also in the fact that it is not self-enclosed as individual ζωή. For 1. ζωή propagates itself in the word of preaching, i.e., the believer does not have ζωή for himself alone in the inwardness of his spiritual life, but stands in the history established by the act of salvation, in which this ζωή is for those who obey the will to save (2 C. 2:16; 4:12), and 2. ζωή is not limited in time, since the τέλος or fruit of this pneumatic life is again ζωή (R. 6:22 f.; Gl. 6:8; Phil. 3:8-14). The old conception that only conduct corresponding to the will of God makes worthy of αἰώνιος ζωή is maintained (→ 864), but it is given a new foundation, for this conduct springs only from ζωή already given. Without this foundation the intention to fulfil the will of God set forth in the Law [314] leads to death, so that the ζωή of the believer is the freedom from the → νόμος (2 C. 3:17; Gl. 5:1) which, because it is also freedom from sin (R. 6:18, 22; 8:2), is also a new attachment to the will of God (R. 6:2, 12-14; 8:2-10). In virtue of this twofold nature of the ζωή concept, the Pauline statements have a twofold reference. Sometimes (αἰώνιος) ζωή means the future blessing, [315] sometimes it means the present life (R. 6:4, 11, 13; 8:2-10), and often it means both in an inseparable relationship. [316] Paul did not attempt to harmonise the two concepts. One might suppose that there is a movement in this direction in the idea of a gradual transformation of mortal life which seems to be suggested in 2 C. 3:18; 4:16. But this transformation is not to be understood as a natural process, for Paul seems to understand the natural process of growth from the standpoint of the miraculous in 1 C. 15:36-38. Furthermore, Paul followed Jewish apocalyptic in linking miraculous transformation (1 C. 15:51) with a dramatic cosmic event (1 Th. 4:13-18; 1 C. 15). At the core of this eschatological hope is surely the fact that not merely is natural dying indifferent in face of the true ζωή given by God but even death already accomplished is reversed by the resurrection, so that mortality is overcome. [317]

d. Future life. If it is natural that true ζωή should be otherworldly even though it is now present, it is obvious that it defies conception as future ζωή. If in traditional terminology it can be negatively described as a σωθῆναι, [318] it can also be described positively as → δόξα. [319] Though earthly possibilities of life are no longer present in this life (R. 14:17), it is still somatic life, [320] since a non-somatic life is inconceivable to Paul (→ σῶμα). But no description is given. It is not even

---

[314] In the hope that this will lead to ζωή, R. 7:10; 10:5; Gl. 3:12.
[315] R. 1:17; 2:7; 5:17 f., 21; 8:13, 18-39; 2 C. 5:1-10; Gl. 6:8.
[316] Cf. R. 6; 8:2-10, 11-13; 2 C. 4:7-16 and 4:17-5:10.
[317] 1 C. 15:23-26, 50-57; 2 C. 5:1-5; Phil. 3:20 f.
[318] R. 5:10, cf. → σωτηρία as the goal of faith, R. 1:16 f.; 10:9 f. etc.
[319] Cf. esp. 2 C. 3:6-11, where the superiority of the new διακονία to the old is described in terms of the antitheses θάνατος / πνεῦμα ζωοποιοῦν, κατάκρισις / δικαιοσύνη, τὸ καταργούμενον / τὸ μένον.
[320] 1 C. 15:35-54; 2 C. 5:1-5; Phil. 3:21.

suggested that the soul is given a place among the cosmic powers (→ 842). We merely have such hints as δικαιοσύνη καὶ εἰρήνη καὶ χαρὰ ἐν πνεύματι ἁγίῳ (R. 14:17), a βλέπειν πρόσωπον πρὸς πρόσωπον (1 C. 13:12; cf. 2 C. 5:7), perfect knowledge, the abiding of πίστις, ἐλπίς, ἀγάπη, and being with Christ. [321]

6. John's View of Life as Present.

a. Life and the Revealer. John's conception of ζωή as present is even more radical. This is connected with the fact that he traces the resurrection of Jesus to the fact that as the λόγος of God and the eternal Son of God He is life and has life in Himself, [322] not merely as the power of His life as a living creature, but as the creative power of God. As a living creature He has a ψυχή and He gives it up to death (10:11, 15, 17), but His ζωή is not interrupted by death. [323] His ζωή is described as the φῶς τῶν ἀνθρώπων even before the incarnation (1:4), for in the dependence of the whole of creation on Him there lies the possibility that man may have life by an apperceptive return to his origin in Him as the revelation of God (→ φῶς). If He is called ζωή, this is not in the sense of a cosmic power open to speculation, but as the Revealer of God for whom, fulfilling the divine commission, the ἐντολή of God is ζωὴ αἰώνιος (12:50), and who as such gives the possibility of true life to faith. In this sense He calls Himself the ζωή (11:25; 14:6), the ἄρτος τῆς ζωῆς (6:35, 48), [324] the φῶς τῆς ζωῆς (8:12), the One who dispenses ὕδωρ ζῶν (4:10 f.; 7:38) or ἄρτος ζῶν (6:51), i.e., the Revealer. His words are πνεῦμα καὶ ζωή (6:63), the ῥήματα ζωῆς αἰωνίου (6:68). He has come to give life to the world (6:33; 10:10; 1 Jn. 4:9).

b. Life present in faith. Since He is and gives ζωή as the Revealer, and since ζωή is manifested with His coming (1 Jn. 1:1 f.), believers already have ζωή in faith. [325] The paradox of this assertion is intentionally heightened. He who believes has already passed from death to life (5:24; 1 Jn. 3:14). Now that He speaks, and on John's view this means also when His Word is proclaimed, the eschatological hour is present (5:25). As the One who speaks He is the ἀνάστασις and the ζωή, so that he who believes in Him lives though he dies, and in the true sense will not die (11:25). With His revelation He has already given δόξα to His own (17:22). Hence the promises in the future tense do not refer to a later eschatological future but to the moment of decision when confronted by the Word. He who will believe, will live. [326] Yet this ζωή is not understood in the timeless, ideal sense. It is a ζωή which has an eternal future (4:14; 6:27; 12:25), and His own, to whom He has given His δόξα, are promised a future vision of δόξα along with the glorified Son (17:24). Yet in the Gospel there are no express references to an eschatological future in the sense of Jewish and early Christian eschatology and of Pauline teaching until we come to 5:28 f. (the future ἀνάστασις) and 6:51b-56 (participation in the Lord's Supper as a guarantee of ἀνάστασις at the ἐσχάτῃ ἡμέρα, cf. also what is said about the ἐσχάτη ἡμέρα in 6:39, 40, 44; 12:48). If we do not regard it as possible to interpret these passages in harmony with the others, and thus to achieve the union of both streams in a common view, we shall have

---

[321] 1 Th. 4:17; 2 C. 5:8; Phil. 1:23.
[322] Jn. 1:4; 5:26; 6:57; 1 Jn. 1:1 f.; 5:11, 20.
[323] Cf. esp. 14:19, the pres. ὅτι ἐγὼ ζῶ, but καὶ ὑμεῖς ζήσετε.
[324] V. E. Janot, "Le Pain de Vie," Gregorianum, XI (1930), 161-170.
[325] 3:15 f., 36; 6:40, 47; 20:31; 1 Jn. 3:15; 5:11 f., 13.
[326] 4:14; 5:25; 6:51, 58; 14:19; 1 Jn. 4:9 and ἵνα sentences like 5:40; 6:40.

to ascribe the second group to a redaction of the Gospel which tries to bring it into line with traditional eschatology, cf. also 1 Jn. 2:28 f.; 3:2; 4:17.

c. Life present in love and joy. The essential point is to understand the manner in which life is present. As it is not an ideal magnitude, so it does not consist in the inwardness of the life of the soul after the fashion of mysticism. For John has not spiritualised and thereby dissolved early Christian eschatology. Like Jesus and Paul, he has radicalised it, i.e., taken it with such radical seriousness that the coming of Jesus as Revealer is the decisive eschatological event, the κρίσις. [327] Life is attained, not in relation to an idea or to a supra-historical, metaphysical being, but in believing commitment to a historical fact and a historical person. It thus consists in the manner of a historical existence, in determination by the Word of revelation, which constantly teaches us to understand the moment in a new way as free from the past and open to the future. It is both way and goal at the same time. In the parting discourses as in 1 John this is brought out in the fact that the life of the believer is shown to stand under the ἐντολή, and indeed under that of ἀγάπη. For abiding in Him (15:1-8) is abiding in love (15:9-17). And that this means life is indicated by the fact that love is grounded in being loved (13:34; 15:12; 1 Jn. 4:7-10). Along with faith is the reception of revelation, i.e., life. For this reason brotherly love is the criterion for μεταβεβηκέναι ἐκ τοῦ θανάτου εἰς τὴν ζωήν (1 Jn. 3:14 f.). If ζωή manifests itself outwardly in ἀγάπη, it does so inwardly in → παρρησία (1 Jn. 3:21; 5:14), in which φόβος is overcome (1 Jn. 4:18) and there is the joy of prayer, [328] in the → χαρά [329] in which all λύπη is conquered (16:20-22). Nor does this involve a διάθεσις of soul, for it takes place in relation to revelation, in which there is a clarity (παρρησία) before which every question and every riddle disperses (16:23, 25, 29). For this reason ζωή can be defined as the knowledge of God and of the One whom He has sent (17:3). He who has this ζωή has all things (10:10 : ἵνα ζωὴν καὶ περισσὸν ἔχωσιν).

d. The relation to the Hellenistic concept of life. In this view John comes close to the philosophical and mythological view of Hellenistic religion and he makes use of its terminology. [330] Nevertheless, we misunderstand the historical relationship if we speak of mere dependence. For in fact this is a completely different view. As John radicalises the Jewish and Christian view of life and the related eschatology, so in some sense he radicalises both the popular and the Gnostic conception of life in the Hellenistic world. If for him ζωή and φῶς imply revelation, there is surely some conscious antithesis to Gnosticism (→ 841), though not polemical opposition. For when he adopts for his Christology the framework of the Gnostic myth of redemption, [331] he makes it plain that he is recognising, refashioning and answering the urgent Gnostic question concerning ζωή. This is equally apparent in his understanding of the terms ἀλήθεια (→ I, 245) and γνῶσις (→ I, 712), so that if we cannot prove any direct literary connections with half mythological and half religious speculations, there can be no doubt as to the historical connection

[327] 3:18 f.; 5:27; 12:31; cf. 12:46-48 and the μένειν of ὀργή (3:36) and ἁμαρτία (9:41); R. Bultmann, ZdZ, 6 (1928), 4-22.
[328] 14:13 f.; 15:7, 16; 16:23 f.; 1 Jn. 5:15.
[329] 15:11; 16:20-24; 17:13; 1 Jn. 1:4.
[330] In this respect I prefer the understanding of John found in, e.g., W. Bousset, *Kyrios Christos*² (1921) and Bau. J. to that of F. Büchsel, *Joh. u. der hellen. Synkretismus* (1928).
[331] Cf. Bau. J.; R. Bultmann, ZNW, 24 (1925), 100-146; H. Odeberg, *The Fourth Gospel*, I (1929).

with ideas formulated already by Philo and later in Plotinus and the Corp. Herm. The statement that ζωή is the knowledge of God and of Jesus Christ (17:3) is to be regarded as an antithesis to these. He who seeks life is guided away from speculation and mysticism to revelation. [332] Hence full weight is to be attached to the sayings which begin ἐγώ εἰμι. What is everywhere sought is here actuality. This means that the seeking or questioning is not wrong ; it has a positive meaning. The saying in 1:4 : ἡ ζωὴ ἦν τὸ φῶς τῶν ἀνθρώπων, also takes on full significance. The fact that the ζωή of creation has the character of light is not an outdated fact. It is an actual fact even though the κόσμος has closed itself against the φῶς of this ζωή (1:5). The φῶς of the λόγος is still active even in the σκοτία, i.e., in the fact that the question of ζωή is still an urgent one in the σκοτία. For σκοτία is what it is only in antithesis to φῶς, and there is no reversal of the fact that all things owe their being to the λόγος. The question itself may lead to self-deception, i.e., to the supposed finding of life where it is not (5:39 f.). But the question, the ἐραυνᾶν, is present, as shown in the fact that the κόσμος has the concept of ζωή, and that revelation adopts the term to lead from false ζωή to true. This concrete significance of the concepts found in the κόσμος, and historically this means in Gnostic piety, is expressed by John in his description of revelation as ὕδωρ ζῶν or ἄρτος ζῶν (τῆς ζωῆς). He here adopts the widespread yearnings for and fables concerning a water of life or food of life (→ n. 63). Hunger and thirst do not seek only momentary satisfaction. At root they do not just demand something specific. In them is reflected the quest for life generally. What is not true or genuine points in the form of a question to what is. For this reason both the Samaritans and the Jews have some understanding of Jesus when He offers ὕδωρ ζῶν and ἄρτος ζῶν, and they ask for it. [333]

† ἀναζάω.

ἀναζῆν "to become alive again," "to rise again," a rare and late word. [1] It is found neither in the LXX nor elsewhere in Hell. Jewish literature. [2]

It is used of the resurrection of the dead in Rev. 20:5 (ἀνέζησαν vl. for ἔζησαν), and of Christ's resurrection in R. 14:9 (vl. with ἀνέστη for ἔζησεν). In the same sense, but figur., it also occurs at Lk. 15:24 : οὗτος ὁ υἱός μου νεκρὸς ἦν καὶ ἀνέζησεν (vl. ἔζησεν; this is the better attested reading in v. 32). Though with

---

[332] Cf. on Jn. 5:24 the quotation from Plotinus in → n. 52.

[333] If under Gnostic influence the Alexandrians later use Johannine terminology very largely in the original Gnostic sense, the related terminology of Ign. shows us the sphere from which John drew his concepts, namely, that of mythological sacramental thinking. For Ign. Jesus Christ is the ἐν θανάτῳ ζωὴ ἀληθινή, Eph., 7, 2. He is manifested εἰς καινότητα ἀϊδίου ζωῆς, Eph., 19, 3. In virtue of his participation in the sacraments, Ign. can say : ὕδωρ δὲ ζῶν καὶ λαλοῦν ἐν ἐμοί, R., 7, 2. Ign. similarly applies Pauline terminology, under whose influence he stands, along the lines of Gnostic thinking, → n. 297. Formally, Gnostic and Johannine descriptions of the Redeemer (ἰατρός, νοῦς! φῶς, ζωή) are applied to God in Dg., 9, 6, and we also find the combination of ζωή and γνῶσις in Dg., 12, 2-7.

ἀναζάω. [1] Nägeli, 47; Deissmann LO, 75 f. From the Attic ζῶ — ἐβίων one would expect the Attic ἀναζῶ — ἀνεβίων. But "to become alive again" is a typical aor. concept. The pres. "gradually to come to life again" would be less usual and is thus rare, the inchoative ἀναβιώσκεσθαι being used instead. In place of ἀναβιῶναι (ἀναβιῶσαι) we find the Ionic Hellenistic ἀναζῆσαι.

[2] At LXX Gn. 45:27 F² reads : ἀνέζησεν τὸ πνεῦμα Ἰακώβ. Joseph. uses ἀναβιοῦν and ἀναβιῶσαι → ζωή, n. 206.

no emphasis on the ἀνα- ("again"), we read in R. 7:9 : (χωρὶς γὰρ νόμου ἡ ἁμαρτία νεκρά ...) ἐλθούσης δὲ τῆς ἐντολῆς ἡ ἁμαρτία ἀνέζησεν, ἐγὼ δὲ ἀπέθανον.

The word does not occur in the post-apost. fathers or the Apologists.

ζῷον (→ ζωή, 833).

ζῷον means in Gk. a "living creature." It is used of both men and animals, the latter being for the Stoics ἄλογα ζῷα as compared with λογικὰ ζῷα. Normally, however, ζῷον is used for "animal," as in the LXX at Gn. 1:21; ψ 67:11; 103:25; Ez. 47:9 (for חַיָּה); Wis. 7:20;11:15 etc. and in the NT at Hb. 13:11. [1] Only where there is express emphasis on the animal level to which heretical teachers have sunk do we have ἄλογα ζῷα, Jd. 10; 2 Pt. 2:12. [2]

As the four marvellous heavenly creatures, the cherubim, are called ζῷα (חַיּוֹת) in Ez. 1:5, 13 ff., so are the four creatures around the throne of God in Rev. 4:6 ff.; 5:6 ff.

This is in keeping with the usage found on inscr. and in the pap., where the wonderful divine animals of the Egyptians are called ζῷα. [3] Similarly the phoenix is a ζῷον in 1 Cl., 25, 3. Men and animals are grouped as ζῷα in 1 Cl., 20, 4. [4]

† ζωογονέω.

ζωογονεῖν [1] is attested in Greece from the time of Aristot. and Theophrast. in the sense of "to make alive," "to beget." It is normally used of φύσις, of animals and plants, and only rarely of men. [2] That nature has the power of giving life is expressly traced back to the deity. Thus Aphrodite is invoked as the ἱερὰ τῶν ὅλων φύσις, who πᾶν ἐζωογόνησεν ἔμψυχον, in Luc. Amores, 19, and in the Paris magic pap. the deity is invoked as ὁ ζωογονῶν (Preis. Zaub., IV, 1162) or as τὸν ... εἰς τὰς ψυχὰς πάσας ζωογόνον ἐμπνέοντα λογισμόν (ibid., 1754). At the command of Helios ἐζωογόνησε τὰ ζῷα (ibid., 1614 f.), and Helios is invoked as ὁ τὰ ὅλα συνέχων καὶ ζωογονῶν καὶ συγκρατῶν τὸν κόσμον (ibid., VII, 529 f.). Similarly Corp. Herm., IX, 6 says of the (divine) κόσμος : οὐκ ἔστιν ὃ μὴ ζωογονεῖ, and acc. to Jul. Or., V, p. 169b the mother of the gods is the προγονικὴ καὶ ζωογόνος.

In the LXX ζωογονεῖν is often used for the pi and hi of חיה. In Lv. 11:47 animals (הַחַיָה) are called τὰ ζωογονοῦντα. It is said of God in 1 Βασ. 2:6 : κύριος θανατοῖ καὶ ζωογονεῖ. [3] In deviation from Gk. usage [4] ζωογονεῖν is often used in the sense of

---

ζ ῷ ο ν. [1] Cf. 1 Cl., 20, 4 and 10; 33, 3; Barn., 10, 7 f. and often in the Apol., Just. Ap., 55, 4; Dial., 3, 6; 4, 4.
[2] So also Just. Ap., 24, 1; 55, 4; Dial., 107, 2 etc.; λογικὸν ζῷον is also found in Just. Dial., 93, 3.
[3] Cf. Preisigke Wört. and Pr.-Bauer ; also Athenag. Suppl., 18, 3. On the ζῷα of Rev. cf. the comm., also H. Gunkel, Zum religionsgeschichtlichen Verständnis des NT² (1910), 43-47; F. Boll, Aus der Offenbarung Joh. (1914), 36-38.
[4] This usage is naturally found in the Apol., e.g., Just. Dial., 3, 7; 4, 2; 107, 2.
ζ ω ο γ ο ν έ ω. [1] ζωογονεῖν (from ζωός, ζῶς) "to bring forth what is living," rather than ζωογονεῖν, "to bring forth living creatures (ζῷα)."
[2] Theophr. De Causis Plantarum, IV, 15, 4 (ζωογονεῖσθαι of plants): Athen., VII, 52 (p. 298c) (ζωογονεῖσθαι of the seed of the eel in the mud); Luc. Dialogi Deorum, 8 (παρθένον ζωογονῶν of Zeus).
[3] Cf. ζωοποιεῖν in 4 Βασ. 5:7 and ζῆν ποιεῖν in Dt. 32:39.
[4] Though cf. Diod. S., I, 23, 4, where ζωογονεῖσθαι is used of the growing up, i.e., the remaining alive, of the children of Semele.

"to leave alive" (subj. always men, and the opp. always "to kill"): Ex. 1:17 f., 22; Ju. 8:19; 1 Βασ. 27:9, 11; 3 Βασ. 21(20):31; 4 Βασ. 7:4.

In the NT ζωογονεῖν is found at 1 Tm. 6:13 as a predication of God, as in Gk. usage: τοῦ θεοῦ τοῦ ζωογονοῦντος (vl. ζωοποιοῦντος) τὰ πάντα. ζωογονεῖν is not used in a specifically Christological (soteriological) sense, like → ζωοποιεῖν. Yet it is found in the non-Greek LXX sense at Ac. 7:19 (cf. Ex. 1:17 f.) and Lk. 17:33: ὃς ἂν ἀπολέσει (τὴν ψυχὴν) ζωογονήσει αὐτήν. [5]

ζωογονεῖν does not occur in the post-apostolic fathers, and it is found only once in the Apologists in Tat. Or. Graec., 12, 2: The heaven and the stars consist of ὕλη: καὶ ἡ γῆ δὲ καὶ πᾶν τὸ ἀπ' (ὑπ'?) αὐτῆς ζωογονούμενον τὴν ὁμοίαν ἔχει σύστασιν. Here again we have the original Gk. sense.

† ζωοποιέω.

In Gk. ζωοποιεῖν, like → ζωογονεῖν, is used from the time of Aristot. and Theophrast. in the sense of "to make alive," usually of the birth of animals or in the med. of the growth of plants. In this sense it is also used of the Godhead. Thus in Corp. Herm., IX, 6 of the (divine) κόσμος: φερόμενος πάντα ζωοποιεῖ, and in XI, 4 of the ψυχή which fills the κόσμος: ζωοποιοῦσα τὸ πᾶν. According to XI, 17 the ζωή and κίνησις of God consist in this: κινεῖν τὰ πάντα καὶ ζωοποιεῖν. In XII, 22 it is through God that ζωοποιεῖται τὰ πάντα, and in XVI, 8 God is characterised as ζωοποιῶν and ἀνακινῶν. Similarly, in the Hermetic Fr., 29 in Cyril Contra Julianum (W. Scott, Hermetica, I [1924], 544), it is said of the Logos: δημιουργεῖ καὶ ζωοποιεῖ. [1]

The LXX uses ζωοποιεῖν for the pi and hi of חיה. God is almost always the subj. of ζωοποιεῖν. God is a God τοῦ θανατῶσαι καὶ ζωοποιῆσαι (4 Βασ. 5:7 → ζωογονέω, n. 3). The delivered can confess: ἐζωοποίησάς με (ψ 70:20). God gives ζωοποίησις (2 Ἐσδρ. 9:8 f.), and it is confessed of Him in prayer: σὺ ζωοποιεῖς τὰ πάντα (2 Ἐσδρ. 19:6). It is said of wisdom in Qoh. 7:13: ζωοποιήσει τὸν παρ' αὐτῆς. [2] The usage here is not non-Greek, but the life of which God is the Creator is not primarily the life of nature; it is the salvation of the people and of the righteous, → ζωή, 850. In Ju. 21:14; Job 36:6, however, ζωοποιεῖν is used like → ζωογονεῖν in the sense of "to keep alive" (opp. "to kill").

In the NT and post-apostolic fathers ζωοποιεῖν always means "to make alive" in the soteriological sense. The subj. is naturally God or Christ or the πνεῦμα. [3] It is expressly said of the Law that it cannot make alive (Gl. 3:21). As in the predication of R. 4:17 God is described as ζωοποιῶν τοὺς νεκροὺς καὶ καλῶν τὰ μὴ ὄντα ὡς ὄντα, so ζωοποιοῦν is used generally of the eschatological raising of the dead: R. 8:11: ὁ ἐγείρας ἐκ νεκρῶν Χριστὸν Ἰησοῦν ζωοποιήσει καὶ τὰ θνητὰ σώματα ὑμῶν; also 1 C. 15:22: ὥσπερ γὰρ ἐν τῷ Ἀδὰμ πάντες ἀποθνήσκουσιν, οὕτως καὶ ἐν τῷ Χριστῷ πάντες ζωοποιηθήσονται. [4] ζωοποιεῖν thus means the same as ἐγείρειν (cf. 2 C. 1:9 with R. 4:17), and in Jn. 5:21, as in

---

[5] This is not good Gk. (as against Schl. Lk., 555) but LXX Gk. In the par. we have περιποιεῖσθαι, which in the LXX also is sometimes used for the pi of חיה (Gn. 12:12; Ex. 22:18), as the σῴζειν in the variant at Mk. 8:35 can also be used for the pi (ψ 29:4) and hi (Gn. 47:25).

ζωοποιέω. [1] Diog. L., VIII, 27 with ref. to Pythagorean teaching: ζωοποιεῖν πάντα, of the sun.

[2] Ep. Ar., 16 of God: δι' ὃν ζωοποιοῦνται τὰ πάντα καὶ γίνεται.

[3] Once of the water of baptism, Herm. s., 9, 16, 2 and 7.

[4] Cf. also Barn., 6, 17 (pass.); 7, 2; 12, 5 and 7 (Christ or His πληγή subj.).

R. 8:11, the two words occur together : ὥσπερ γὰρ ὁ πατὴρ ἐγείρει τοὺς νεκροὺς καὶ ζωοποιεῖ, οὕτως καὶ ὁ υἱὸς οὓς θέλει ζωοποιεῖ. ζωοποιεῖν is used in the same sense of Christ's resurrection in 1 Pt. 3:18 : θανατωθεὶς μὲν σαρκί, ζωοποιηθεὶς δὲ πνεύματι. [5] As eschatological ζωή is in some sense present (→ ζωή, 865), so the divine ζωοποιεῖν can also refer to the present. We see this in Jn. 5:21, in Col. 2:13, in Eph. 2:5 (→ n. 5), and with reference to the ζωοποιεῖν of the πνεῦμα in 1 C. 15:45; 2 C. 3:6; Jn. 6:63. [6]

In this sense it is said of Christians in Dg., 5, 12 : θανατοῦνται καὶ ζωοποιοῦνται, and ibid., 16 : κολαζόμενοι χαίρουσιν ὡς ζωοποιούμενοι. [7]

Bultmann

ζέω, ζεστός
(χλιαρός, ψυχρός)

† ζέω.

In the NT this is only used figur. of being stirred by the Holy Spirit : R. 12:11: τῷ πνεύματι ζέοντες; Ac. 18:25 : ζέων τῷ πνεύματι.

Etymology gives the basic sense of "to well up," "to bubble." [1] The meaning "to boil" is old, but is a secondary specialisation, so that in the first instance it is used only intr. [2] Lexical study gives wide support to the sense of stormy movement (Hdt., VII, 188 : of the raging sea ; Diosc. Mat. Med., V, 8 : of fermenting wine). What causes the movement, or appears with it, is put in the gen. (λίμνη ζέουσα ὕδατος καὶ πηλοῦ, Plat. Phaed., 113a) or more rarely the dat. (θάλασσα αἵματι καὶ ῥοθίῳ (burning) ζέουσα, Ael. Arist., XIII [I, 230, 11 f. Dindorf]). Both constructions are found in Luc. of vermin (Alex., 59 : σκωλήκων [worms] ζέσας, Saturnalia, 26 : φθειρί). In isolated cases at first, then increasingly, the idea of heat comes to be associated with the term. Thus ζέω can mean "to glow" in relation to solid objects (Hes. Theog., 695; 847). This change of sense particularly affects the figur. usage (ἔζει θυμός, Soph. Oed. Col., 434; cf. Plat. Resp., IV, 440c; burning desire opp. κατασβέννυται, Plut. Suav. Viv. Epic., 4 [II, 1088 f.]). The Lexicon Vindobonense [3] shows a good grasp of the facts in spite of the disputable order : ζέει οὐ μόνον ἐπὶ τῶν βραζομένων (boiling) ὑδάτων λέγεται, ἀλλὰ καὶ ἐπὶ θυμοῦ ... καὶ ἐπὶ θαλάσσης. In the LXX the word is used in the strict sense of the manna going bad (Ex. 16:20 : [ἐξ]έζεσεν σκώληκας, on the constr. cf. the HT), of fermenting wine as the figure of a stormy spirit (Job 32:19) and of a

---

[5] For this reason the NT can use for the resurrection of believers on the basis of Christ's resurrection the term συζωοποιεῖν, which is not previously attested and which does not occur in the post-apostolic fathers or apologists : Col. 2:13 : ὑμᾶς νεκροὺς ὄντας τοῖς παραπτώμασιν ... συνεζωοποίησεν σὺν αὐτῷ, χαρισάμενος ἡμῖν πάντα τὰ παραπτώματα ... ; Eph. 2:5.

[6] V. Sickb. K., 80.

[7] In the Gk. sense ζωοποιεῖσθαι is used of the seed in 1 C. 15:36, and figur. in Herm. m., 4, 3, 7: ἐζωοποιήθην ταῦτα παρὰ σοῦ ἀκούσας οὕτως ἀκριβῶς.

ζέω. [1] Prellwitz Etym. Wört., 168; Walde-Pok., I, 208; Indo-germ. i̯esō; Sansk. √ yas- "to boil," "to well up," "to bubble" ; Old High Germ. jesan "to ferment," "to bubble up"; cf. Germ. *Gischt,* Eng. yeast, Low Germ. *Gest.*

[2] The trans. occurs only in later lyrics and the pap., where it is common in medical prescriptions (P. Lond., I, 121, 170; P. Oxy., XI, 1384, 36).

[3] Ed. A. Nauck (1867), 95, 1 ff.

seething pot representing judgment on Jerusalem (Ez. 24:5). It is also used figur. of boiling rage in 4 Macc. 18:20. Philo seems to know only the sense of "to boil," and except in Som., I, 19 (hot springs) he always uses it figur. of anger : Vit. Mos., II (III), 280 : ζέων καὶ πεπυρωμένος ὑπὸ τῆς νομίμου διαγανακτήσεως; cf. Migr. Abr., 210; Rer. Div. Her., 64; Sacr. AC, 15 : θυμοὺς ζέοντας καὶ πεπυρωμένας ἐπιθυμίας ἀναφλέγον. Josephus, too, finds in the term the idea of heat (Bell., 5, 479 : of glowing iron). Yet he does not use it figur., though he often uses θερμός and θερμότης of inner dispositions (Ant., 8, 209; Bell. 1, 109 etc.).

The combination τῷ πνεύματι ζέειν seems to be peculiar to the NT and was perhaps coined by Paul. Though we cannot overlook the ideas of welling up or fermenting (cf. Mk. 2:22 and par.), the sense is primarily in terms of "to boil" as used figuratively (cf. 1 Th. 5:19). In R. 12:11, in a sequence which becomes increasingly imperative, the readers are told that it is their duty fully to develop their energy as Christians. In the first instance this is human energy. But then attention is drawn to the impelling power of God, i.e., to the Spirit. And finally all things are subjected to obedience to the Lord. [4] In Ac. 18:25 the predicate ζέων τῷ πνεύματι applied to Apollos is explained by most modern exegetes in terms of his fiery spirit and eloquence. [5] But his natural gifts are emphasised in v. 24 : ἀνὴρ λόγιος, and the context of v. 25 is purely religious. Pre-Christian possession of the Spirit is not unknown elsewhere (→ I, 543, n. 68). We thus seem to have a similar use to that of R. 12:11.

† ζεστός († χλιαρός, † ψυχρός).

Except for ψυχρός in Mt. 10:42, these three terms are found only in Rev. 3:15 f.: οἶδά σου τὰ ἔργα, ὅτι οὔτε ψυχρός εἶ οὔτε ζεστός. ὄφελον ψυχρὸς ἦς ἢ ζεστός. οὕτως ὅτι χλιαρὸς εἶ, καὶ οὔτε ζεστὸς οὔτε ψυχρός, μέλλω σε ἐμέσαι ἐκ τοῦ στόματός μου.

ζεστός, a rare verbal adj. from ζέω trans., which is not found in the LXX, Philo, Jos. or the pap., is sometimes uses of "cooked" meat (Appian Rom. Hist. Hisp., 85) or "glowing" sand (Diog. L., VI, 2, 3), but mostly of "boiling" water (Diosc. Mat. Med., I, 33 etc.), opp. χλιαρός (Sext. Emp. Pyrrh. Hyp., I, 101). There is no known inst. of metaph. usage in secular Gk. The Rabbis make a figur. distinction between the "hot" (רוֹתְחִין) and the "tepid" (פּוֹשְׁרִין : Gn. r., 86 on 39:3), as also between wholehearted transgressors(רְשָׁעִים גְּמוּרִין) or righteous (צַדִּיקִים גְּמוּרִין) and the lukewarm (בֵּינוֹנִיִּים). Judgement of death or life is pronounced at New Year on the first two classes, but those who belong to the third are kept in suspense until the day of atonement or purified for a period in Gehinnom, the purgatorial fire (RH, 16b; jRH, 1, 57a, line 49; cf. AbRNat., 32 [8c]). [1]

In the rebuke to the church of Laodicaea there is evidence of an unparalleled clash between early Christian enthusiasm and the world. If allusion is made to the

---

[4] On the text cf. Ltzm., Sickb. R., ad loc.
[5] Pr. Ag.; Zn. Ag.: "fiery in spirit as he was." Cf. also Wdt. Ag., ad loc., where the human spirit is regarded as the centre of his zeal; also Steinmann Ag. (1934), ad loc.; R. Schumacher, Der Alexandriner Apollos (1916/18). On the other hand. M. Dibelius, "Die urchristl. Überlieferung von Johannes dem Täufer," FRL, 15 (1911), 95 rightly refers to Ac. 6:3, 10. On the question of the baptism of Apollos → I, 539, n. 47. H. W. Beyer (NT Deutsch, ad loc.) has "set on fire by the Spirit," but this does not amount to much more than "with glowing inspiration or enthusiasm," and this reflects modern conceptions.
ζεστός. R. H. Charles in ICC (1920); Bss., Zn., Loh., Had. Apk., ad loc.
[1] Str.-B., I, 50 f.; II, 170; III, 95.

fact that the hot springs of Hierapolis are only lukewarm at Laodicaea,[2] this is not the important point. Nor does the use of → ζέω in the NT justify us in laying too much stress on inner warmth generated by the Spirit.[3] What is really at issue is the glow of unconditional self-offering, if necessary even to death, to the Lord who is even now knocking at the door (v. 20). The charge is not so much one of "not yet" as of "no longer" (2:4 f.; 3:19). Featureless lukewarmness is worse, and more difficult to overcome, than complete alienation from or hostility to Christ. The Judge will reject the half-hearted with distaste as one spews out a tepid and tasteless drink. Now is the time for repentance and conversion.

Oepke

ζῆλος, ζηλόω, ζηλωτής,
παραζηλόω [1]

---

† ζῆλος.

A. ζῆλος in Greek Usage.

ὁ ζῆλος, and occasionally τὸ ζῆλος, is usually translated "zeal." The original scope of the term in this sense cannot be fixed with certainty. Its general character fits it for varied use, and its immediate sense must be determined either by a directly related gen. or from the context. a. ζῆλος as the capacity or state of passionate committal to a person or cause is essentially *vox media*: ὁ δὲ ζῆλος, ὅταν περὶ ἀρετῆς γένηται, ἀγαθός, καὶ συγγενὴς τοῦ ἀγαθοῦ ἔρωτος· ὅταν δὲ περί τι τῶν ἐκτός, φαῦλος, καὶ τῷ φθόνῳ συντεταγμένος, Simplicius in Epict., 19, 2 (p. 57, Dübner). Thus the word in found in Plato in a list with partly good and partly bad emotions, Phileb., 47e and 50b (in both cases between ἔρως and φθόνος). It is also found in the plur. in a biographical and anthropological sense as a comprehensive word to denote the forces which motivate a personality, ἀγωγαὶ καὶ ζῆλοι (used interchangeably with ἀγωγαὶ καὶ φύσεις); Polyb., 10, 21, 2; 3; 7. Cf. also the sense of "taste" or "interest," Pseudo-Longinus De Sublimitate, 7, 4 (ed. Photiados); Theophr. Char. prooem., 4 and ὁ περὶ τὰ στρατιωτικὰ ζῆλος "the warlike spirit (of a tribe)," Strabo Geographica, XIV, 2, 27 (ed. Kramer). Occasionally it can mean "style" in the literary sense, Plut. Anton, 2 (I, 916d); Strabo Geographica, XIV, 1, 41. b. ζῆλος as orientation to a worthy goal (ζῆλος τῶν ἀρίστων: Luc. Indoct., 17; ἀνδραγαθίας: Plut. De Marco Coriolano, 4 [I, 215b]) can have the sense of the "zeal of imitation," Plut. Pericl., 2 (I, 153a); Herodian Hist., II, 4, 2, and this may take on the heightened sense of "passionate rivalry," Plut. Thes., 6 (I, 3 f.) or, with only a slight shift of meaning, "zealous recognition," "praise" or "fame," Soph. Ai., 503; Demosth., 23, 64, or even "enthusiasm," Demosth., 18, 217. The word here serves to denote a noble ethical impulse towards the development of character, and to this degree it is to be distinguished from (→ c.) envy or jealousy. This genuinely Gk. thought comprehended in ζῆλος is given its finest expression in the definition of Aristot.: Εἰ γάρ ἐστιν ζῆλος λύπη τις ἐπὶ φαινομένη παρουσίᾳ ἀγαθῶν ἐντίμων καὶ ἐνδεχομένων αὐτῷ λαβεῖν περὶ τοὺς ὁμοίους τῇ φύσει, οὐχ ὅτι

---

[2] W. M. Ramsay, *The Cities and Bishoprics of Phrygia*, II (1897), 85 f.
[3] Zn. Apk., *ad loc.*

ζ ῆ λ ο ς κτλ. Apart from the dictionaries, Ammonius Grammaticus (ed. L. C. Valckenaer, 1822), *s.v.*; Trench, s.v.; Wettstein on 1 C. 12:31; J. B. Lightfoot, *Notes on Epistles of St. Paul* (1895) on 1 C. 3:3; F. Küchler, "Der Gedanke des Eifers Jahwes im AT," ZAW, 28 (1908), 42 ff.
[1] → 881.

ἄλλῳ ἀλλ᾽ ὅτι οὐχὶ καὶ αὐτῷ ἐστιν· διὸ καὶ ἐπιεικής ἐστιν ὁ ζῆλος καὶ ἐπιεικῶν, τὸ δὲ φθονεῖν φαῦλον καὶ φαύλων· ὁ μὲν γὰρ αὐτὸν παρασκευάζει διὰ τὸν ζῆλον τυγχάνειν τῶν ἀγαθῶν, ὁ δὲ τὸν πλησίον μὴ ἔχειν διὰ τὸν φθόνον· ἀνάγκη δὴ ζηλωτικοὺς μὲν εἶναι τοὺς ἀξιοῦντας αὑτοὺς ἀγαθῶν ὧν μὴ ἔχουσιν· οὐδεὶς γὰρ ἀξιοῖ τὰ φαινόμενα ἀδύνατα. Διὸ οἱ νέοι καὶ οἱ μεγαλόψυχοι τοιοῦτοι Rhet., II, 11, p. 1388a, 32 ff. c. Zeal can also take a less reputable form : ζῆλος δὲ οὐ καλός, ὅταν τις σπεύδῃ ἐκβαλεῖν τῆς ἀρετῆς τὸν κατορθοῦντα, Theophylact on Gl. 4:17 f. (MPG, 124, 1001d). Hesiod in his description of the iron age uses the term in this sense for a "passion which poisons human society" : βλάψει δ᾽ ὁ κακὸς τὸν ἀρείονα φῶτα μύθοισιν σκολιοῖς ἐνέπων, ἐπὶ δ᾽ ὅρκον ὀμεῖται. ζῆλος δ᾽ ἀνθρώποισιν ὀιζυροῖσιν (miserable, pitiable) ἅπασι δυσκέλαδος (shrieking discordantly, spreading evil rumours), κακόχαρτος ὁμαρτήσει (go along with), στυγερώτης, Op., 193 ff. (→ 883). To denote the different forms of reprehensible zeal, Plato used ζῆλοι along with ὕβρις, ἀδικία φθόνοι, Leg., III, 679c. Thus ζῆλος can mean "contention" (with ἀγών), Plut. Artaxerxes, 4 (I, 1013a); "jealousy" (with φθόνος), Lys., 2, 48; Herodian Hist., III, 2, 8; and (with ἔρις) Herodian Hist., III, 2, 7. In classical Gk. I have not found any instances of the sense of "jealousy" with special reference to husbands or wives. Eur. Hec., 352 has the term for the stage prior to marriage in the sense of "competition." Yet the idea of jealousy is not far off. Luc. Symp., 39 : κατὰ τὰ Πλάτωνι δοκοῦντα κοινὰς εἶναι ἐχρῆν τὰς γυναῖκας, ὡς ἔξω ζήλου εἴημεν. Cf. Scholion, ad loc. (p. 34, Rabe).

B. Zeal in the OT and Judaism.

A review of the use of ζῆλος in the LXX shows us first that there are no instances of the Gk. sense of zealous striving to ennoble personality (→ 877). This sense is alien to the Heb. קִנְאָה which underlies all [2] uses of ζῆλος in the LXX.

1. ζῆλος as a human emotion is almost completely restricted to the later parts of the OT.

a. The term is used in a purely descriptive sense, as a characteristic of the living, in Qoh. 9:6 : καί γε ἀγάπη αὐτῶν (sc. the dead) καί γε μῖσος αὐτῶν καί γε ζῆλος αὐτῶν ἤδη ἀπώλετο. In Sir. 30:24 it is used in a derogatory sense, λύπη, θυμός and ζῆλος being dispositions of spirit which ἐλαττοῦσιν ἡμέρας. The same (non-Jewish) view is found in Sir. 40:5. In Prv. 27:4 it is a "hostile and disruptive passion" which is even worse than θυμὸς καὶ ὀξεῖα ὀργή (cf. Job 5:2). Possibly Qoh. 4:4 has the same implication. In all these passages we have judgments on general human relations. Occasionally ζῆλος is used to describe specific individual phenomena, as in 1 Macc. 8:16, where it is said of the Romans : οὐκ ἔστιν φθόνος οὔτε ζῆλος ἐν αὐτοῖς. Here it may be seen that the presence or absence of ζῆλος in a man or group is clearly manifested in their conduct. ζῆλος as a vl. in Is. 11:13 (Ephraim and Judah) denotes the discord between peoples, or rather the inner tension and feeling which gives rise to it ; cf. Ez. 35:11 (Edom and Israel). b. In two passages ζῆλος means jealousy in married life, Prv. 6:34; Cant. 8:6. c. ζῆλος can also have a special meaning not found in secular Gk. : ὁ ζῆλος τοῦ οἴκου σου καταφάγεταί με, ψ 68:9; cf. ψ 118:139. The sense here is a passionate, consuming zeal focused on God, or rather on the doing of His will and the maintaining of His honour in face of the ungodly acts of men and nations. Phinehas, Elijah and Jehu are particular examples of this zeal : Φινεὲς ὁ πατὴρ ἡμῶν ἐν τῷ ζηλῶσαι ζῆλον (cf. Nu. 25:6-13) ἔλαβεν διαθήκην ἱερωσύνης ἁγίας, 1 Macc. 2:54, and Ἠλίας ἐν τῷ ζηλῶσαι ζῆλον νόμου (cf. 3 Βασ. 19) ἀνελήμφθη ὡς εἰς τὸν οὐρανόν, 1 Macc. 2:58, cf. Sir. 48:2 (→ 884).

---

[2] Acc. to Hatch-Redpath. The Heb. קִנְאָה is usually translated ζῆλος in the LXX. The only exceptions are Ez. 36:5 (θυμός) and Prv. 14:30 (καρδία αἰσθητική) [Bertram].

2. In about half the instances of ζῆλος in the LXX the word denotes a specific intensity in the divine action. In this sense the word is comparatively common in Ezekiel, though there are many earlier examples within the OT.[3] The divine action thus accomplished with ζῆλος may mean either good or ill, either salvation or perdition, for the men or nations concerned. The term may be listed with ὀργή (Dt. 29:20) or θυμός (Nu. 25:11; Ez. 16:38, 42; 36:6; 38:19; cf. 5:13). As a consuming force, it is linked with πῦρ: ἐν πυρὶ ζήλους, Zeph. 1:18; 3:8; cf. ψ 78:5; Is. 26:11. Yet cf. Is. 63:15: ποῦ ἐστιν ὁ ζῆλός σου καὶ ἡ ἰσχύς σου, ποῦ ἐστιν τὸ πλῆθος τοῦ ἐλέους σου καὶ οἰκτειρμῶν σου, ὅτι ἀνέσχου ἡμῶν;

In the OT the zeal of Yahweh is more comprehensive than the term ζῆλος, which is not found, e.g., in Hosea or Jeremiah. Linguistic analysis[4] has yielded the following results in relation to the OT קִנְאַת יהוה. When the reference is to Yahweh, it is almost always a question of His relations to His people Israel. Yahweh's zeal is provoked when Israel worships idols and thus transgresses the commandment which has as its basis Ex. 20:5: ἐγὼ γάρ εἰμι κύριος ὁ θεός σου, θεὸς ζηλωτής. Following Hosea, Ezekiel describes this apostasy as adultery, and in him ζῆλος can thus mean jealousy in the special sense of marital jealousy[5] (Ez. 16:38; 23:25; cf. 5:13). In this connection ζῆλος is an expression of the holiness of Yahweh, cf. Ez. 39:25. The same is true of ζῆλος in passages in which Yahweh is the God operative in history. If the nations think they can disrupt God's plan for Israel, the ζῆλος of God intervenes for His people. It is a matter of each historical situation, and cannot easily be decided, whether this ζῆλος is put forth in a segment of history or at the end of the age (cf. 4 Βασ. 19:31; Ez. 36:6; 38:19;[6] Is. 9:7; 37:32; 42:13; 63:15; Zech. 1:14). The reference is plainly eschatological in Is. 26:11 and Zeph. 1:18; 3:8, this being a feature of the יום יהוה in Zephaniah. The combinations ζῆλος κυρίου Σαβαώθ (Is. 9:7; 37:32) and ζῆλος κυρίου τῶν δυνάμεων (4 Βασ. 19:31, cf. Is. 42:13) make it plain (cf. also Is. 26:11 and the whole context of Wis. 5:17) that ζῆλος in this sense is strictly related to the concept of Yahweh as the only true Lord of history.

On the connection of the zeal of Yahweh with His self-revelation, which is implicit in what we have already said, cf. → 883 f.

3. Philo uses ζῆλος exclusively in connection with praiseworthy qualities, in the sense of "striving after things."[7] He thus belongs to the sphere of Gk. ethics. How far he thinks of ζῆλος as a concept linked with the nature of man and not suitable to the understanding of God may be seen clearly when he refers to the ζῆλος of Yahweh in the OT: τίνος οὖν ἕνεκα Μωυσῆς βάσεις, χεῖρας, εἰσόδους, ἐξόδους, φησὶν εἶναι περὶ τὸ ἀγένητον, τίνος δὲ χάριν ὅπλισιν τὴν πρὸς ἐχθρῶν ἄμυναν (defence, help); ... πρὸς δὲ ἔτι ζῆλον, θυμόν, ὀργάς, ὅσα τούτοις ὅμοια ἀνθρωπολογῶν

---

[3] How far the examples adduced are later than the context from which they derive must be decided in detail by literary criticism. The question is not of decisive importance in relation to the meaning of the term.

[4] Cf. also the various OT theologies.

[5] We cannot agree with Küchler, op. cit., 43 that this is the original sense of קִנְאָה/ζῆλος.

[6] Küchler, 49 (with some commentators) perceives in Ezekiel "a sharp turn (sc. in the use of קִנְאָה) at the moment when judgment is fully executed on Judah with the fall of Jerusalem and the destruction of the temple. In all the later instances the קִנְאָה of Yahweh has a completely different reference. It is now directed, not against unfaithful Israel-Judah, but against its enemies."

[7] There are many clear examples in Leisegang's Index, s.v.

διεξέρχεται; Deus Imm., 60 f. In an express answer Philo develops the statement : τῷ ἄριστα νομοθετήσαντι τέλος ἓν δεῖ προκεῖσθαι, πάντας ὠφελῆσαι τοὺς ἐντυγχάνοντας, ibid., 61, and he shows that God must be depicted in human traits in order that those who are not in possession of full intellectual capacities may still be able to grasp something of God.

4. Painful fear of any kind of anthropomorphising of the thought of God makes it impossible for the Rabbis to incorporate the concept of the ζῆλος of Yahweh into their theology. [8] Their evasions may best be seen in two examples [9] of the exposition of אל קנא in Ex. 20:5 : M. Ex., 6 on 20:5 (ed. Horovitz-Rabin [1928 ff.], 226, 1 ff.) : " 'For I the Lord thy God am a jealous God' : How, then, am I a God of קנאה (jealousy, envy)? I rule over קנאה, and not קנאה over me ... Another explanation : I punish idolatry with קנאה (zeal), but I am merciful and gracious in other things." And then Mek. R. Sim (ed. Hoffmann [1905], 105) : " 'For I am the Lord thy God.' This shows that the prophets viewed God [10] as the One who will give rewards in the future ... 'A jealous God.' This teaches that the prophets viewed God [10] as the One who will punish the wicked in the future. [11] 'A jealous God,' i.e., a God of judgment, a hard God, a fearful God." In this connection the two passages also deal with the question raised by the preceding prohibition of idolatry : I am קנא אל. This cannot mean that God is jealous or envious [12] of idols. One can be envious only of rivals or competitors, but idols have no real existence. The Rabbinic answer to the problem is that God is jealous that idolaters should put these non-existent things in His place and thus do serious despite to His honour (cf. also → 884).

C. ζῆλος in the NT.

1. In the NT ζῆλος is always in the sing. except in R. 13:13 vl. and Gl. 5:20 vl. It is not found in the Synoptic Gospels and occurs only once in Jn. at 2:17 in a quotation from Ps. 69, which was quickly interpreted in a Messianic sense in Christianity. [13] Nevertheless the Evangelist does not attribute to Jesus Himself, but to His disciples, a recollection of the zeal of the OT righteous for maintaining the honour of God and His house as this is kindled by the incident of the cleansing of the temple (→ 884). The same OT sense is undoubtedly present when Acts speaks of the ζῆλος manifested by the Jews in opposition to the proclamation of the Christian message in word and act, Ac. 5:17. Even in Ac. 13:45 this rendering must be considered along with the more usual "envy," cf. Ac. 17:5 (→ 887). Paul uses the term most clearly in its specific Jewish sense in R. 10:2, where he says of the Israelites : ζῆλον θεοῦ ἔχουσιν. Here what we learn from linguistic investigation takes on special theological significance in the thought of Paul. A zeal for God (θεοῦ is an obj. gen., for though this is not in keeping with OT usage [14] it

---

[8] Cf. in this connection the fact that among the many phrases used instead of the divine name in Rabb. lit. there is none deriving from Ex. 20:5; 34:14. V. the collection in A. Marmorstein, The Old Rabbinic Doctrine of God, I : The Names and Attributes of God (1927).

[9] I owe this reference to K. G. Kuhn.

[10] Lit. "the face (of God)."

[11] The explanation is similar to that of S. Nu., 115 on 15:41 with reference to the twofold "I am the Lord your God" : "I am the Lord your God" : "I am He who rewards." "I am the Lord your God" : "I am He who punishes."

[12] This is the meaning of the root קנא in Rabb. usage.

[13] Bau. J., ad loc.

[14] Philo in a similar connection has the formulae ζηλώσας τὸν θεοῦ τοῦ πρώτου καὶ μόνου ζῆλον in Poster. C., 183 and ζηλώσας τὸν ὑπὲρ θεοῦ ζῆλον in Leg. All., III, 242.

agrees with the order of the words [cf. 2 C. 11:2 → *infra*] and the context) may be very good, but it may also be misplaced or perverted. [15] Paul is convinced that this is so in the present instance. A zeal for God's glory has in reality become something very different : ἀγνοοῦντες γὰρ τὴν τοῦ θεοῦ δικαιοσύνην καὶ τὴν ἰδίαν ζητοῦντες στῆσαι ... Paul uses the word in exactly the same sense in Phil. 3:6 when speaking of his own past : κατὰ ζῆλος διώκων τὴν ἐκκλησίαν. (On Gl. 1:14; Ac. 21:20; 22:3 → ζηλόω, 887.)

2. What, then, is the meaning of the ζῆλος of Paul in relation to the Corinthian community : ζηλῶ γὰρ ὑμᾶς θεοῦ ζήλῳ (2 C. 11:2)?

If, like most commentators, we take the θεοῦ here as a subj. gen., [16] the usage and conception are the same as we find in the OT (→ 883 f.). There are no other instances of this in the NT, except perhaps for 1 C. 10:22 : ἢ παραζηλοῦμεν τὸν κύριον, where in a very similar situation to that of the OT Paul is possibly quoting Dt. 32:21 to remind his readers of the wrathful zeal of God.

Since the immediate continuation in 2 C. 11:2 is : ἡρμοσάμην γὰρ ὑμᾶς ἑνὶ ἀνδρὶ παρθένον ἁγνὴν παραστῆσαι τῷ Χριστῷ, we come very near to the sense of jealousy. Paul is watching over the church with jealous interest lest it should be persuaded to follow a different and erroneous preaching. He describes this jealousy as God's jealousy in terms of the OT conception of God as One who with holy zeal seeks to keep His people from adultery with idols (→ 879). On this understanding the NT community has taken the place of God's ancient people. It can hardly be adduced against this view [17] that Paul as an → ἀπόστολος makes himself the bearer of this divine ζῆλος. [18]

3. In all other cases where it occurs in the NT ζῆλος has the ordinary Gk. sense of "zeal" with no direct religious associations. a. It is true that there is no clear instance of the sense of "striving after a moral ideal" (→ 877), but in 2 C. 9:2 it denotes the active enthusiasm with which the Corinthians have made the collection, and it is hoped that this ζῆλος will stir (ἐρεθίζειν) others, i.e., kindle a similar zeal in them. Elsewhere Paul expresses the same thought in the word παραζηλοῦν, which is not found in secular Gk. (R. 11:11, 14; cf. 1 C. 10:22 → *supra*). In 2 C. ζῆλος is also found at 7:7, 11, where the reference is to the personal relationship between the community and the apostle (τὸν ὑμῶν ζῆλον ὑπὲρ ἐμοῦ, 7:7) which the congregation is now anxiously concerned to restore (perhaps the context suggests a new attitude which has only recently been adopted). b. In R. 13:13; 1 C. 3:3; 2 C. 12:20; Gl. 5:20; Jm. 3:14, 16 ζῆλος is linked with terms which express passions and faults, ἔρις, ἐριθεία, θυμός etc. Similar lists are found outside the NT and it is doubtful whether in relation to them we can or should try to fix with precision the meaning of each individual word. ζῆλος here denotes

---

[15] Str.-B., *ad loc.*: "Every page of the Rabb. writings reminds us of this saying of Paul. There is a zeal for God and a readiness to serve Him to the last breath, and yet they do not know God's way and go astray."

[16] "Zeal which derives from God," Ltzm., *ad loc.*; "zeal such as God has," H. A. W. Meyer⁵ (1870), *ad loc.*

[17] Heinr. Sendschr., II and 2 K., *ad loc.* One is almost tempted to urge against Heinrici the full powers of the later Jewish קִנְאָה, → I, 415.

[18] Reitzenstein suggests that in this use of ζῆλος Paul has in view a Corinthian objection that by his ζῆλος the apostle shows that he, too, is "only a man," Hell. Myst.³, 365 f. But this specialised usage would be unique. Cf. also Ltzm., *ad loc.*

the kind of zeal which does not try to help others but rather to harm them, the predominant concern being for personal advancement. [19] In relation to the occurrence of the word in such contexts one should perhaps observe that any direct zeal in the character and walk of individuals has to bear its share of responsibility for the free development of the καρπὸς τοῦ πνεύματος (Gl. 5:22) in the community, cf. 1 C. 3:1, 3 : σαρκικοί — πνευματικοί. c. Hb. 10:27: πυρὸς ζῆλος. In spite of the reminiscence of Is. 26:11 LXX, we are forced to link ζῆλος with πῦρ in the sense of the consuming ardour of (personified) fire.

When we turn to the early fathers, we find that ζῆλος is an important word in 1 Cl., 4-6. The author finds the motive for the murder of Abel in ζῆλος καὶ φθόνος, and he traces the vicious role of human ζῆλος (here negatively estimated as passionate illwill, jealousy and envy) through the biblical history to the martyrdom of Peter and Paul, with additional illustrations from general history. Similarly Cyprian in his treatise De Zelo ac Livore sees in human *zelus* the most dangerous and often secret evil in the life of Christians (MPL, 4, 665 B): ... *quoniam frequentiora sunt tela eius* (sc. diaboli) *quae latenter obrepunt, magisque occulta et clandestina iaculatio quo minus perspicitur hoc et gravius et crebrius in vulnera nostra grassatur, ad haec quoque intelligenda et depellenda vigilemus. ex quibus est zeli et livoris malum. Quod si quis penitus inspiciat, inveniet nihil magis Christiano cavendum, nihil cautius providendum quam ne quis invidia et livore capiatur ; ne quis fallentis inimici caecis laqueis implicatus, dum zelo frater in fratris odia convertitur, gladio suo nescius ipse perimatur, ibid., 3.* On the other hand, Chrysostom in a homily on 1 C. 12:21, although he sees the dangers in a divisive ζῆλος, can see high ethical value in ζῆλος in the secular Gk. sense of the zeal of imitation : ζήλωσον, ἀλλ' ἵνα κατ' ἐκεῖνον γένῃ τὸν εὐδοκιμοῦντα· μὴ ἵνα αὐτὸν καταβιβάσῃς, ἀλλ' ἵνα πρὸς τὴν αὐτὴν φθάσῃς κορυφήν, ἵνα τὴν αὐτὴν ἀρετὴν ἐπιδείξῃ. Τοῦτο ζῆλος καλός, τὸ μιμεῖσθαι καὶ μὴ πολεμεῖν, τὸ μὴ ἀλγεῖν ἐπὶ τοῖς ἑτέρων ἀγαθοῖς, ἀλλὰ δάκνεσθαι ἐπὶ τοῖς οἰκείοις κακοῖς ... (MPG, 61, 262 f.).

† ζηλόω, † ζηλωτής.

A. The Gk. Usage.

In secular Gk. this word is mostly used in the act. (→ n. 23) and its most common sense is "to admire or commend someone," [1] usually with a pers. obj. in the acc., the cause of admiration, if given, being put in the gen., e.g., Plat. Resp., VIII, 561e; Isoc., 9, 43, and often in the tragic dramatists. The personal emotion expressed in the admiration is the true and probably the original core of the meaning, namely, "to be stirred" — ζηλοῦν is sometimes used in the abs. — usually in a friendly or hostile way either for or against someone or something. Thus a. "to be enthusiastic" for something, Plat. Prot., 326a (with μιμεῖσθαι and ὀρέγεσθαι); Ps.-Plat. Theag., 121d; Polyb., 10, 21, 4; "to admire," Ps.-Plat. Alc., II, 148b; Isoc., 12, 260, and this not merely as a spectator but with a view to emulation, hence "to concern oneself with something, to take up a matter, to make it the goal of one's striving," Eur. Hec., 255; Demosth., 14, 1; 20, 154; Thuc., II, 64; Theophr. Char. prooem., 4; Epic. Ep., 2, 113; P. Greci e Latini, 94, 9 (elsewhere the word is rare in the pap.), or with a pers. obj. "zealously to seek to imitate," Plat. Gorg., 468e; 469a; Resp., VIII, 553a; Thuc., II, 37 (νόμους); Isoc., 1, 36. Cf. also Eur. Or., 521; Aristoph. Eq., 837; Plat. Ion, 530b c; Phaedr., 232a; Isoc., 9, 43, where it

[19] Cf. Herm. s., 8, 7, 4. Lightfoot in his Comm.[4] on Gl. 5:20 (1874) is suggestive, though he perhaps goes a little too far (→ 887 f.): "ζῆλος — not necessarily, like φθόνος, in a bad sense, and in fact with classical writers it is generally used otherwise. But as it is the tendency of Christian teaching to exalt the gentler qualities and to depress their opposites, ζῆλος falls in the scale of Christian ethics — while ταπεινότης for instance rises."

ζ η λ ό ω κ τ λ. [1] There are many examples in the dictionaries.

might be translated "to envy" in the good sense of an impulse towards the higher development of character (→ 877). b. It can also mean "to envy" in the more hostile sense of not wanting others to have things. This sense is less common than a., but it occurs in all the older writings in which the word is used. Cf. Hesiod. Op., 23: ζηλοῖ δέ τε γείτονα γείτων εἰς ἄφενον (riches) σπεύδοντ᾽ ... with ἔρις (rivalry, ibid., 24), κοτέει, 25, φθονέει, 26; cf. εἰς ἕτερον ... ἰδών, 21. Similarly ζῆλος, Op., 195 (→ 878). Also ῥεῖά κέ τίς σε ἰδοῦσα γυναικῶν θηλυτεράων ζηλώσαι, Hom. Hymn. Cer., 168.² A late example is, e.g., Isoc., 4, 91; cf. 12, 16. c. Very rarely ζηλοῦν can mean "to be jealous" in the special sphere of the marital relationship, Theocr. Idyll., 6, 27, cf. 3, 50.

B. The Usage in the OT and LXX.

In the LXX ζηλόω is almost always used for קנא in both the kal and the piel forms.³ The word is comparatively rare (LXX 45 [47] times),⁴ and it would therefore be rash to try to trace a historical development of its meaning. From the concordances we may group the various senses as follows.

1. a. It is used most consistently in Prv. Here, in accordance with the moralistic spirit of the book, it means "to strive after" on the basis of preceding approval or admiration. To this degree there is close approximation to the Gk. usage. But it should be noted that usually there is warning against this striving; the projected goal causes a μή to be put before ζηλοῦν, Prv. 3:31; 4:14; 23:17; 24:1, 19; cf. also Sir. 9:11. The only exception is the well-known Prv. 6:6: ἴσθι πρὸς τὸν μύρμηκα, ὦ ὀκνηρέ, καὶ ζήλωσον ἰδὼν τὰς ὁδοὺς αὐτοῦ. The classical sense is found in Sir. 51:18: ἐζήλωσα τὸ ἀγαθόν, also 2 Macc. 4:16, where the ζηλοῦν τὰς ἀγωγάς (sc. of the Greeks), "zealous interest with the desire to emulate," refers to doubtful aspects of the Hellenising policy of Jason. Probably Wis. 1:12 should also be cited in this connection. b. We come closer to the original sense in other passages. Thus, when Mattathias sees a Jew offering sacrifice to an idol, we read in 1 Macc. 2:24: ἐζήλωσεν (on v. 26: ἐζήλωσεν τῷ νόμῳ, → 2. b.), καὶ ἐτρόμησαν οἱ νεφροὶ αὐτοῦ. The same wrathful indignation, in a direct and involuntary outburst which can involve the human physis too in an accompanying passion, is also to be seen in ψ 72:3: ἐζήλωσα ἐπὶ τοῖς ἀνόμοις, εἰρήνην ἁμαρτωλῶν θεωρῶν, cf. also v. 21 and 22: "Thus my heart was grieved, and I was pricked in my reins. So foolish was I and ignorant: I was as a beast before thee." Cf. again, though less specifically, ψ 36:1. The ζηλοῦν of Joseph's brethren in Gn. 37:11 (cf. Ac. 7:9) introduces the thought of illwill and therefore leads to the sense of "to envy," Gn. 26:14; 30:1; Ez. 31:9; Sir. 37:10; 45:18. On the other hand ζηλοῦν in 2 Βασ. 21:2 means "to strive in the interests of someone," "zealously to exert oneself on behalf of someone." c. Only in Nu. 5:14, 30 does ζηλοῦν means marital jealousy in connection with the so-called jealousy offering.⁵

2. ζηλόω has a specific religious content when used either of God or of man in relation to God. For material reasons there is no parallel to this usage in non-Jewish literature. The ζηλοῦν of God is very closely linked with His holiness and power (→ 879), which belong to Him alone.

---

² Cf. ζηλοσύνη, "jealousy," Hom. Hymn. Ap., 100 and ζηλήμων, "jealous," the only word in the family found in Homer [Debrunner].

³ V. Hatch-Redpath, s.v. The Heb. קנא is almost always rendered ζηλοῦν (4 times παραζηλοῦν) in the LXX. The only exceptions are Dt. 32:16: παροξύνειν (᾽Α ζηλοῦν) and Ps. 105:16 παροργίζειν (vl. παραζηλοῦν) [Bertram].

⁴ V. Hatch-Redpath, s.v. ζηλόω, 4 Βασ. 10:18; Is. 11:11 rests on a mistranslation.

⁵ For further details v. the OT theologies.

a. Our starting-point must be the expression θεὸς ζηλωτής in Ex. 20:5; 34:14. The construction ζηλωτής (first attested in Isoc., 1, 11) corresponds to the Heb. קַנָּא and expresses the fact that the ζηλοῦν of God is not regarded as a passing mood but belongs to the very essence of God, as in Ex. 34:14 : יְהוָה קַנָּא שְׁמוֹ אֵל קַנָּא הוּא. The jealous zeal of God is directed against Israel if it breaks the commandments (Dt. 32:19; Jos. 24:19) or does not listen to the prophets (Zech. 8:2). In this case it is closely related to His punitive ὀργή (cf. Dt. 32:19). But it also operates on behalf of Israel when enemies threaten to destroy it (cf. the later period of Ez. [→ 879, n. 6], Ez. 39:25; also Jl. 2:18; Zech. 1:14). It is worth noting that in both Ez. and Jl. the ζηλοῦν of Yahweh leads to a manifestation of His omnipotent reality. Israel is to experience the fact that "I, the Lord, am your God," Ez. 39:28; Jl. 2:27. b. That men too may in some sense representatively be filled by this holy zeal for the maintaining of the divine glory and therefore for the Law, esp. against idolatry, is something which occurs only later in relation to a distinct group of persons (1 Macc. 2:27, 50). At first, according to the evidence, it has this sense only in respect of a few individuals who are highly valued for this reason, e.g., Phinehas in Nu. 25:11, 13, whose ζηλοῦν is extolled in Sir. 45:23 and 1 Macc. 2:26, 54, above all Elijah in 3 Βασ. 19:10, 14, who is mentioned in 1 Macc. 2:58, and finally Jehu in 4 Βασ. 10:16. Mattathias takes his place in the same line at a time when the situation summons all genuine Jews to ζηλοῦν for the Law of the God of Israel, 1 Macc. 2:24, 26, 27, 50; cf. Jdt. 9:4. In all these cases ζηλοῦν is characterised by direct action on behalf of God, just as God's zeal is no mere mood but always leads to action or finds expression in it.

C. Zelotism.

1. If the concept of ζῆλος is lacking in the Rabb. view of God (→ 880), the trait of zeal for God and His Law and honour, which is found in the OT figures mentioned, corresponds to the basic orientation of Pharisaism. The judgments of the Rabbis on this pious zeal for God cannot, of course, be separated from the historical background. The concept personified, e.g., in Phinehas, [6] had evoked a movement which played a significant role in Jewish history in the first century A.D., namely, Zelotism. [7] The Zealot makes active zeal for God the determinative feature of his whole conduct; he proudly calls himself ζηλωτής, Joseph. Bell., 4, 161.

2. The origin of the Zealot movement has not been fully explained. It is almost certain that it has its source in Pharisaism. [8] It is usually assumed [9] that it emerged as a historical magnitude when Judas of Galilee joined the Pharisee Zadok, who had separated himself from Pharisaism, in resistance against Roman rule on the occasion of the census under Quirinius. [10] But the possibility has also to be considered [11] that the Zealots

---

[6] Or Elijah — both being later equated as "zealots," Tg. J. I on Ex. 6:18; Pirke R. Eliezer, 29; 47.

[7] On the history and significance of Zelotism cf. F. Sieffert, Art. "Zeloten" in RE³, XXI, 655 ff.; of the lit. there mentioned cf. esp. J. Wellhausen, *Die Pharisäer u. d. Sadduzäer* (1874), 22 f.; Schürer, I, 486 f., 617 ff.; cf. also K. Kohler, Art. "Zealots" in Jew. Enc., XII (1906), 639 ff.; J. Klausner, *Jesus von Nazareth²* (1934), 272 ff.; K. G. Kuhn, *Sifre Numeri* (1933 ff.), 519 ff. on S. Nu., 131 (on Nu. 25:5 ff.); Comm. on Mt. 10:4; finally Schl., *Gesch. d. Chr.*, 304 ff.; *Gesch. d. erst. Chr.*, Index s.v. *Zeloten*; *Theol. d. Judt.*, 214 ff.

[8] Wellhausen, *op. cit.*, 22; Klausner, *op. cit.*, 272, 275; cf. Sieffert, *op. cit.*, who part. emphasises the close relationship to the radical school of the Shammaites; Schl., *Theol. d. Judt.*, 215.

[9] Mainly on the basis of Jos. Ant., 18, 1 ff. (cf. Ac. 5:37).

[10] That the Zealot party is brought into being by this event perhaps indicates that it is marked by a distinctive social attitude. For obvious reasons the wealthy are in general friendly towards the Romans, so that the patriotism of the Zealots easily brings them into opposition to this upper stratum. May it be that the regard for social distinctions in Lk. owes something to this?

[11] Cf. the careful account in Volz Esch., 184. This view is strongly favoured by K. Kohler in Jew. Enc., XII, esp. 640.

largely consisted of the "robber bands" (→ λῃστής) [12] which even before Judas, under the leadership of his father Hezekiah, had pursued their way as fanatical patriots with originally religious motives. Be that as it may, Pharisaism did what was essential to prepare the ground for Zelotism. [13] And in practice it sided with the Zealots, granting them the right of summary jurisdiction and punishment in cases where a Jew entered into the marriage bond with a non-Jew, Sanh., 9, 6. This was the practical side of the high praise accorded to the zeal of Phinehas, a zealot and the son of a zealot, S. Nu. § 131 on 25:5-11. This midrash on the story of Phinehas, with its recognition of the act which transcended normal justice but which contended for the divine honour by punishing transgressors, is "in its true orientation ... a magnifying of Zelotism, of which Phinehas is the prototype." [14] In this connection reference should be made to the inscription on the temple wall prescribing instant death for non-Jews entering the sacred precincts. [15]

The two older Rabb. passages (Sanh., 9, 6; S. Nu. § 131 on 25:5-11) are particularly important for the judgment of Pharisaism on the Zealots, for in later utterances the zeal of Phinehas and Elijah receives more negative appraisal. [16] Historical development had meantime brought Zelotism to a point where the social, revolutionary and anarchical aspect came strongly to the forefront, and this necessarily led to its complete separation from Pharisaism.

3. There are close connections between Zelotism and the story of Palestinian Christianity. The historical relationship, most concretely expressed in the fact that the first band of disciples included a Zealot (→ 886 f.), [17] rests mainly on the convictions common to the theology of both groups. (This is not to say that the conclusions drawn as to practical conduct took the same channels on the Christian side as among the Zealots.) [18]

In Ac. 5:34 ff. the Christian movement is evaluated by Pharisaism in the person of Gamaliel according to the same principle of waiting neutrally as was followed in relation to Zelotism (cf. the significant if chronologically inaccurate comparison with the revolt of Theudas). Again in Ac. 23:12 ff. the Zealots initiate a plot to murder the imprisoned Paul. Whatever their historical value in detail, these records both bring out the tension in the situation. The principle of the sole sovereignty of God is a self-evident part of Pharisaic theology. It finds a concrete and activist expression in Zelotism. The rule of God is to be set up by the overthrow of Roman domination. Instead of hopeful patience there is to be resolute action with passionate trust that God will intervene miraculously to make possible the impossible. A constant readiness to fight is thus no less intrinsic in Zelotism than a reckless readiness to suffer. Both express an untamable love of freedom. This gives point to a saying like Mt. 11:12 : ἡ βασιλεία τῶν οὐρανῶν → βιάζεται, καὶ βιασταὶ

---

[12] This well-known designation used by Josephus (e.g., Bell., 2, 253 f.; Ant., 20 [160,] 161, 167) naturally reflects the personal attitude of a friend of the Romans towards patriotic movements which resisted their alien rule. The sharpest criticism of this biased presentation is to be found in Kohler, op. cit.

[13] Cf. the presentation in Schlatter, *Theol. d. Judt.*, 195 ff.

[14] K. G. Kuhn, op. cit., 519, n. 113.

[15] Schürer, II³, 273, n. 55; cf. Jos. Bell., 6, 124 ff.

[16] Seder Eliahu rabba and Seder Eliahu zuta, ed. M. Friedmann (1902), 186; Jalkut Shim'oni on K. § 217; Cant. r., 1, 6; Agadoth Shir ha-shirim, p. 45 (acc. to S. Schechter, *Some Aspects of Rabbinic Theol.* [1909], 204 f.).

[17] Cf. Schl. Mt. on 10:4.

[18] What follows is a brief summary of the important conclusions of Schlatter (→ n. 7).

ἁρπάζουσιν αὐτήν. Similarly, the sayings about taking up the cross and readiness to lose one's life (Mk. 8:34 f. and par.) would be immediately understood and accepted by those committed to Zelotism. Again, since those who paid taxes acknowledged themselves to be subjects of the government which imposed them, the question of Mk. 12:13-17 and par.: ἔξεστιν δοῦναι κῆνσον Καίσαρι ἢ οὔ; was answered by Zealots, as distinct from the Pharisees, in the negative. This whole question is set, therefore, against the background of tension created by Zelotism, and the religious as well as the social and political conduct of the individual is directly involved. Schlatter thinks that there are traits in John the son of Zebedee in particular which bear evidence of close contact with Zealot views, e.g., the name Βοανηργές which is given to the two brothers (Mk. 3:17), their idea of calling down fire from heaven to destroy the Samaritan village which would not receive Jesus (Lk. 9:54) and their readiness for martyrdom (Mk. 10:38 f. and par.). [19] Furthermore, Rev. 13:4-8 is in full agreement with the radical Zealot repudiation of the current deification of men. A particularly interesting question is how far Zealot exegesis may have influenced Christian theology. The religio-political attitude of the Zealots towards the Roman Empire led to an application to Rome of the OT prophecies concerning Edom and Babylon. We can see this in Rev., e.g., 18:2 f., 9-19; cf. 14:8-20. The passionate demand for national freedom also led the Zealots to see in leaders of the movement divinely sent liberators. Thus a kind of Messianic prophecy developed out of Zelotism. The desert also played a constant role (→ ἔρημος, 658) as the place where the coming salvation would be manifested (cf. Rev. 12:6).

In spite of these by no means inconsiderable connections between Zelotism and early Christian thinking, the historical relationship of the two movements was already sharply antithetical even at the time of the outbreak of the Jewish War. Christians could not stay in Jerusalem once the rule of the Zealots had been established. Nor was this due merely to the fact that the Zealots increasingly became a party of revolutionary fanaticism (→ 885). The truth is that the preaching of Jesus contained from the very first principles which were completely incompatible with the practical conduct of the Zealots, e.g., the command to love one's enemies (Mt. 5:43 ff.) or the injunction to patient renunciation of the law of retribution (Mt. 5:38 ff.). The contrast in the conception of crucifixion — for the Zealots "a hard and inexplicable disposition of God ... before which man can only bow," [20] but for Jesus the ultimate fulfilment of His divine commission — is brought to expression in the two malefactors (→ λῃστής) crucified with Jesus.

D. ζηλόω/ζηλωτής in the NT.

ζηλόω can still bear many different meanings in the NT both on the positive side and on the negative. The NT usage is in keeping with the assumption that the word is originally *vox media* (→ 882), signifying a human emotion which leads to action. In the NT, too, ζηλοῦν is determined either by an obj. or by the context when used abstr. Against the background of secular and OT usage a review of the NT data yields the following results.

1. ζηλόω, including ζηλωτής, in the sense of "to be zealous for God" (→ 884) can a. refer to the historical background of the NT. Thus one of the disciples,

---

[19] Schl. also points to biographical details in Jn. 1:37-41; 18:15 f.; 19:26; 21:19 (*Gesch. d. erst. Chr.*, 65).

[20] Schl., *Gesch. d. Chr.*, 307.

Simon, undoubtedly belonged to the Zealot party. Luke calls him ζηλωτής (Lk. 6:15; Ac. 1:13), and this is a correct translation of קַנְאָן or קַנְאָנָא, the Aram. term for Zealot. In Mt. 10:4 this appears in the form of ὁ Καναναῖος (vl. Κανανίτης), which has given rise to the mistake[21] that we have here the name of his race or city.

b. More particularly, however, Lk. uses ζηλόω/ζηλωτής in this sense to denote the attitude of the Jews towards Christian preaching, Ac. 17:5; cf. 5:17; 13:45. The zeal of the Jews against the message of the Christian missionaries, i.e., their personal concern for the fulfilment of the Law, even though this be misunderstood (R. 10:2 → 880), is to be estimated positively from the subjective angle. This is obvious when Paul in relation to his own past ranks himself with these zealous Jews: ζηλωτὴς τῶν πατρικῶν μου παραδόσεων, Gl. 1:14; cf. Phil. 3:6, and ζηλωτὴς ὑπάρχων τοῦ θεοῦ, Ac. 22:3. Finally, Lk. has preserved an important historical and theological record in Ac. 21:20, where Paul in Jerusalem has to wrestle with the fact that μυριάδες εἰσὶν ἐν τοῖς Ἰουδαίοις τῶν πεπιστευκότων, καὶ πάντες ζηλωταὶ τοῦ νόμου ὑπάρχουσιν. Could this ζηλοῦν be a legitimate trait in the NT community?

2. In 2 C. 11:2 ζηλοῦν is used of the personal attitude of the apostle towards a particular congregation. What is at issue is the zealous wooing of the congregation, not for their favour, but for their obedience to the Gospel preached by Paul. The emphasis is on the strong personal concern. The usage reflects the OT use of ζηλοῦν for God's zeal for His people (→ 880; on this whole passage → ζῆλος, 881). The word occurs in a similar context, thought not in the same sense, at Gl. 4:17, 18: ζηλοῦσιν ὑμᾶς οὐ καλῶς, ἀλλὰ ἐκκλεῖσαι ὑμᾶς θέλουσιν, ἵνα αὐτοὺς ζηλοῦτε. καλὸν δὲ ζηλοῦσθαι ἐν καλῷ πάντοτε.

There are difficulties in this passage. The first is ζηλοῦσιν, ἵνα αὐτοὺς ζηλοῦτε.[22] Most probably ζηλοῦν is used in the same sense in both cases. But in view of the ἵνα clause it cannot have exactly the same meaning as in 2 C. 11:2 (→ supra). This is strengthened and explained by οὐ καλῶς. A ζηλοῦν which has a self-centred purpose is not apostolic. It is ordinary human striving or concern for someone. This sense also satisfies the ἵνα clause. To be sure, there are no direct instances of this in secular Gk. But there is an exact parallel in Pauline usage at 2 C. 7:7: τὸν ὑμῶν ζῆλον ὑπὲρ ἐμοῦ (→ 881). Hence, with most commentators, we must take ζηλοῦσθαι (vl. ζηλοῦσθε) as a passive form.[23] There can be no doubt that the ἐν καλῷ is closely related to it, the ζηλοῦσθαι being thus differentiated from the preceding ζηλοῦν οὐ καλῶς in v. 17. The meaning is thus that the Galatian community is encircled (pres.) by the true (= ἐν καλῷ) apostolic zeal of Paul (cf. 2 C. 11:2). The sudden change of subject assumed on this interpretation avoids the difficulties of trying to link the second part of the verse (18b) to the first (18a).

3. The predominant Gk. use of ζηλόω or ζηλωτής for an ethical attitude (in the special sense) also occurs sometimes in the NT with the sense of "to strive

---

21 It is not very likely that this is an intentional change; cf. Klausner, op. cit., 277: "When Jesus had declared that His kingdom was not of this world, it was hard to understand how a Zealot, a Jewish nationalist and fiery patriot, could have found a place among the disciples of Jesus."

22 On the form ζηλοῦτε after ἵνα cf. Bl.-Debr.[6] § 91.

23 E.g., H. A. W. Meyer[4] (1862); F. Sieffert[9] (1899); R. A. Lipsius[2] (1892); Zn. Gl., ad loc. The pass. is very rare in secular Gk. (cf. Lys., 2, 26) and it does not occur elsewhere in the LXX or NT.

after something." Thus ζηλωτὴς καλῶν ἔργων in Tt. 2:14 and τοῦ ἀγαθοῦ ζηλωταί in 1 Pt. 3:13 both have a good Gk. ring, denoting the consistent and zealous orientation of action to a moral ideal. That this is not to be understood along the lines of an idealistic individual ethics, which would be contrary to the basic position of the NT, may be seen from Paul's similar usage in 1 C. 12:31; 14:1, 12, 39. Here χαρίσματα are the goal of ζηλοῦν, and these are certainly not ideals, but gifts which God gives to the community for its true edification. In this sense ζηλοῦν as a striving kindled by and directed towards these gifts is a constituent part of the ethics of the Christian community. On the other hand, in the two remaining passages at 1 C. 13:4 and Jm. 4:2 we may deduce from the context that ζηλοῦν is not so much directed towards the edification of the community but is rather an uncontrolled outburst. Thus in 1 C. 13:4 it has the general sense of "to envy," "to be passionate," while in Jm. 4:2 the ensuing καὶ οὐ δύνασθε ἐπιτυχεῖν suggests the translation: "to strive with envious greed" (i.e., for the goods of others) (→ 878).

Stumpff

---

† ζημία, † ζημιόω

ζημία[1] originally[2] means "disadvantage;" ζημιόω[3] "to set someone in a disadvantageous position," "to do someone hurt;" ζημιόομαι pass. "to be set at a disadvantage."[4]

1. As the word "disadvantage" carries some measure of comparison with a preceding advantage, so it is with ζημία/ζημιόω in Gk. As the following passage from Aristot. shows, it is contrasted with κέρδος/κερδαίνειν, the middle point to which the two antitheses relate being the relation or state of μέσον or ἴσον: τούτῳ ἄρα γνωριοῦμεν τί τε ἀφελεῖν δεῖ ἀπὸ τοῦ πλέον ἔχοντος, καὶ τί προσθεῖναι τῷ ἔλαττον ἔχοντι· ᾧ μὲν γὰρ τὸ μέσον ὑπερέχει, τοῦτο προσθεῖναι δεῖ τῷ ἔλαττον ἔχοντι, ᾧ δ' ὑπερέχεται, ἀφελεῖν ἀπὸ τοῦ μεγίστου ... (there follows an example of mathematical subtraction and addition) — ἔστι δὲ καὶ ἐπὶ τῶν ἄλλων τεχνῶν τοῦτο· ἀνῃροῦντο γὰρ ἄν, εἰ μὴ ἐποίει τὸ ποιοῦν καὶ ὅσον καὶ οἷον, καὶ τὸ πάσχον ἔπασχε τοῦτο καὶ τοσοῦτον καὶ τοιοῦτον. ἐλήλυθε δὲ τὰ ὀνόματα ταῦτα, ἥ τε ζημία καὶ τὸ κέρδος, ἐκ τῆς ἑκουσίου ἀλλαγῆς· τὸ μὲν γὰρ πλέον ἔχειν ἢ τὰ ἑαυτοῦ κερδαίνειν λέγεται, τὸ δ' ἔλαττον τῶν ἐξ ἀρχῆς ζημιοῦσθαι, οἷον ἐν τῷ ὠνεῖσθαι καὶ πωλεῖν καὶ ἐν ὅσοις ἄλλοις ἄδειαν (leave, amnesty) ἔδωκεν ὁ νόμος. ὅταν δὲ μήτε πλέον μήτ' ἔλαττον ἀλλ' αὐτὰ δι' αὐτῶν γένηται, τὰ αὐτῶν φασὶν ἔχειν

ζ η μ ί α κτλ. [1] In the NT as in secular Gk. ζημία is mostly used without a dependent subst., but as in Ac. 27:10 there may be added a *gen. obj.* (P. Flor., 142, 8 f.) or (→ l.c.) a *gen. criminis* (Plat. Theaet., 176d). The verb occurs only in the pass. in the NT; on the constr. *v.* Bl.-Debr.[6] § 159, 2.

[2] The Indo-Germ. etymology is uncertain. It is perhaps related to δίζημαι, "strive," "seek"; ζητέω, "seek"; ζῆλος, "zeal"; cf. Boisacq, 309; Walde-Pok., I, 775 [Debrunner]. Cf. also Moult.-Mill., *s.v.* ζημιόω and H. J. Schmidt, *Synonymik d. griech. Sprache* (1876 ff.), IV, No. 167, 4.

[3] Cf. Debr. Gr. Wortb. for verbs in -οῦν §§ 198 and 204.

[4] Too great stress should not be laid on the formally pass. character of ζημιωθῆναι. It can often be used interchangeably with ζημίαν λαβεῖν (Phot. Lex., *s.v.*). Nor does secular Gk. usage necessitate Klostermann's unsupported attempt to derive the ζημιωθῆναι of Mk. 8:36 from an Aram. act. (Kl. Mk., *ad loc.*).

καὶ οὔτε ζημιοῦσθαι οὔτε κερδαίνειν· ὥστε κέρδους τινὸς καὶ ζημίας μέσον τὸ δίκαιόν ἐστι τῶν παρὰ τὸ ἑκούσιον, τὸ ἴσον ἔχειν καὶ πρότερον καὶ ὕστερον (Eth. Nic., V, 7, p. 1132b, 2 ff.).

a. Already in the preceding quotation commercial life is mentioned as a setting for ζημία/ζημιόω/ζημιόομαι. Here disadvantage takes the form of "loss" (opp. κέρδος, "gain") or "damage" (synon. βλάβη/βλάπτω,[5] opp. "profit") in money or material goods in the broadest sense. For this meaning both literature [6] and esp. the pap. [7] provide rich attestation. [8] ζημία is used in this sense in Ac. 27:10, 21. It is here used with → ὕβρις for the loss in goods and lives caused by unfavourable conditions at sea : μετὰ ὕβρεως καὶ πολλῆς ζημίας οὐ μόνον τοῦ φορτίου καὶ τοῦ πλοίου ἀλλὰ καὶ τῶν ψυχῶν ἡμῶν, v. 10 and also v. 21. b. The word can also denote "disadvantage" in the moral and spiritual as well as the material sense. Philo esp. likes to use ζημία/ζημιόω in this way with the sense of "hurt" or "ruin." Thus he speaks of the harmful effects of homosexuality : λυμηνάμενος δὲ τὴν παιδικὴν ἡλικίαν καὶ εἰς ἐρωμένης τάξιν καὶ διάθεσιν ἀγαγὼν ἐζημίωσε καὶ τοὺς ἐραστὰς περὶ τὰ ἀναγκαιότατα σῶμα καὶ ψυχὴν καὶ οὐσίαν, Vit. Cont., 61; λύμη καὶ ζημία καὶ κοινὸν μίασμα, Spec. Leg., III, 51; βαρύταται ζημίαι σώματός τε καὶ ψυχῆς, Virt., 182; οἷς μὲν ἂν ἐθελήσῃ (sc. ἡ ἡδονή) τῶν ἰδίων ἀγαθῶν μεταδοῦναι, τούτους εὐθὺς ἐζημίωσεν, οὓς δ᾽ ἂν ἀφελέσθαι, τὰ μέγιστα ὤνησε· βλάπτει μὲν γὰρ ὅταν διδῷ, χαρίζεται δ᾽ ὅταν ἀφαιρῆται, Gig., 43; cf. also Vit. Mos., II, 53; Migr. Abr., 61; 172; Mut. Nom., 173; Deus Imm., 113. Cf. also in this connection Prv. 22:3; 27:12. With a subj. nuance ζημία can mean "unpleasantness" as opp. to ἡδύ, Aristot. Rhet., I, 12, p. 1372b, 14. c. The relations denoted by ζημία/κέρδος (→ supra) can be seen from the standpoint of law : τὸ ἄδικον ... ἄνισον ὂν ἰσάζειν πειρᾶται ὁ δικαστής· καὶ γὰρ ὅταν ὁ μὲν πληγῇ ὁ δὲ πατάξῃ, ἢ καὶ κτείνῃ ὁ δ᾽ ἀποθάνῃ, διῄρηται τὸ πάθος καὶ ἡ πρᾶξις εἰς ἄνισα· ἀλλὰ πειρᾶται τῇ ζημίᾳ ἰσάζειν, ἀφαιρῶν τοῦ κέρδους, Aristot. Eth. Nic., V, 4, p. 1132a, 6 ff. (cf. the whole section). The "disadvantage" (ζημία) on the one side is weighed against the "advantage" (κέρδος — "κἂν εἰ μή τισιν οἰκεῖον ὄνομα εἴη") on the other, and the one who has the advantage is forced to suffer loss (ζημία) to the extent of his advantage. Thus ζημία can take on the sense of "penalty," ζημιόω "to punish" and ζημιόομαι "to be punished." This sense is attested quite early [9] and it is very common, esp. in inscr. [10]

2. a. Sense 1. b. underlies the statement of Pl. at 2 C. 7:9 : ἐλυπήθητε (sc. through the stern letter of the apostle) ... ἵνα ἐν μηδενὶ ζημιωθῆτε ἐξ ἡμῶν, i.e., "that at no point (in your Christian lives) should you suffer injury through our fault." The saying gives evidence of apostolic responsibility for the σωτηρία (v. 10) of the community, or, in other words, of awareness of the claim of the community to the unreserved and in no way attenuated proclamation which the apostle has here exercised in the form of a sharp, uncompromising and merited

---

[5] Cf. Poll. Onom., VIII, 147.

[6] V. the dict., s.v.

[7] V. Preisigke Wört. and Moult.-Mill., s.v.

[8] The comparative aspect is not consistently maintained, so that occasionally ζημία can simply mean "fee," "expense," Ditt. Syll.³, 717, 81; P. Lond., V, 1674, 23 (c. 570 A.D.); cf. Hesych., s.v. ζημία : θυσία τις ἀποδιδομένη ὑπὲρ τῶν γινομένων ἐν θεσμοφορίοις.

[9] E.g., Epicharmus, 148 (CGF, I, 118). ζημία is also found in the tragic and comic dramatists, though not very frequently.

[10] Plutarch, e.g., uses the word almost exclusively in this sense. The legal sense also predominates in the inscr. collected by Dittenberger (Ditt. Syll.³ and Ditt. Or.). Schl. Mt. on 16:26 gives some examples from Joseph. There are even examples in Philo (e.g., Spec. Leg., IV, 34), though he leans heavily to → 1. b. Examples in the LXX are Ex. 21:22; Dt. 22:19; 1 Ἔσδρ. 8:24; 2 Macc. 4:48.

rebuke.[11] It is probable that the usage in 1 C. 3:15 also rests on 1. b. According to 1 C. 3:14 the apostle will receive a reward (→ μισθός) if his work survives the fire on the day of testing : εἴ τινος τὸ ἔργον μενεῖ ὃ ἐποικοδόμησεν, μισθὸν λήμψεται. There is a precise antithesis in v. 15 : εἴ τινος τὸ ἔργον κατακαήσεται, ζημιωθήσεται. The natural opposite of "to receive a reward" would seem to be "to suffer punishment" (→ l.c.), but it is doubtful from the context whether the word should be taken in its juridical sense.[12] The thought of a δικαιοσύνη worked out in punishment is not in keeping with the passage (in spite of ἡ → ἡμέρα). Nor can we link the phrase directly with the αὐτὸς δὲ σωθήσεται which follows.[13] Hence we probably give the sense more correctly if we render ζημιωθῆναι by "to suffer loss," filling it out from the preceding τὸν μισθόν construed as an accus. of relation.[14]

That there is a reward for the apostle's work is a conviction plainly expressed by Paul (→ μισθός). Loss, or the missing of the reward, is the result, or even more directly the experience, of the κατακαυσθῆναι of his work. As Paul does not give any material description of the reward, so we cannot depict the ζημιωθῆναι in detail. The context gives us only one hint, namely, that the salvation of the ζημιωθείς takes place οὕτως ὡς διὰ πυρός, i.e., by the same way as his work is consumed. If we remember how essentially the apostle and his work are related in Paul's eyes (→ 733), it is evident how seriously and concretely Paul understands the loss, the missing of the μισθός, when this work is destroyed as wood, hay or stubble in the fire of testing.

The particular difficulty of ζημία/ζημιόομαι in Phil. 3:7, 8 is that Paul here describes the natural and historical presuppositions of his life as ζημία, and therefore things which in fact one cannot lose. (Similarly → κέρδος in the same context cannot be "gain" in the sense of "what is above a given norm.") The repeated ἡγεῖσθαι in v. 7, 8 provides a correct solution to the difficulty. ζημία is not the objective loss of the thing itself. It is the subjective loss of its value. The verses thus mean that everything that was once valuable has now in my estimation lost its value for me. I now regard it all as definitively deprived of value in virtue of the superiority of the knowledge of Jesus Christ for the sake of which I have experienced this comprehensive devaluation. There is here no philosophical discussion of religious values. Rather, a man's conduct is determined by his estimation of a thing (Mt. 6:21). The whole attitude and conduct of Paul are determined by the fact that absolutely all value is now enclosed in Christ and none at all in the presuppositions (v. 5) and attainments (v. 6) of his own δικαιοσύνη, which is incontestably the highest value in the eyes of pious Jews. If Paul had been thinking of the given factors of his life as actually prejudicial to his Christian life,

---

[11] Cf. on the whole passage : ἐπειδὴ ... ἔλαβες ἰσχὺν παρὰ τοῦ δυνατωτάτου, μετάδος ἄλλοις ἰσχύος διαθεὶς ὃ ἔπαθες, ἵνα μιμήσῃ θεὸν τῷ παραπλήσια χαρίζεσθαι. κοινωφελεῖς γὰρ αἱ τοῦ πρώτου ἡγεμόνος δωρεαί, ἃς δίδωσιν ἐνίοις, οὐχ ἵν' ἐκεῖνοι λαβόντες ἀποκρύψωσιν ἢ καταχρήσωνται πρὸς ζημίαν ἑτέρων, ἀλλ' ἵν' εἰς μέσον προενεγκόντες ὥσπερ ἐν δημοθοινίᾳ (popular feast) πάντας ὅσους οἷόν τε καλέσωσιν ἐπὶ τὴν χρῆσιν καὶ ἀπόλαυσιν αὐτῶν. Phil. Virt., 168 f.

[12] So Ltzm. K., Schl. K., ad loc.; cf. Pr.-Bauer, s.v. ζημιόω. (On the antithesis ζημία/μισθός, v. Aristot. Pol., IV, 9, p. 1294a, 38 f.; ibid., 13, p. 1297a, 18 etc.).

[13] P. W. Schmiedel[2] (1892), ad loc.; also A. Robertson-A. Plummer in ICC[2] (1929), ad loc.

[14] So (with Luther, Calvin, Bengel) Bchm. K., ad loc.; on the constr. cf. Plato Leg., XI, 916e; Ael. Nat. An., 10, 1; Philo Spec. Leg., III, 143; also H. A. W. Meyer[6] (1881), Robertson-Plummer, ad loc. and J. B. Lightfoot, Notes on Epistles of St. Paul (1895), ad loc. Lightfoot refers to 2 Jn. 8 for a correct interpretation.

he could not have used the expression ἡγοῦμαι σκύβαλα, nor in v. 13 could he have stated his complete break with the past in terms of τὰ ὀπίσω ἐπιλανθανό-μενος. Both expressions indicate that ζημία refers to a personal experience of devaluation in which he had to lose, to renounce (ἐζημιώθην), what had pre-viously been of supreme value to him. Only thus does the statement agree with what he says elsewhere concerning his Jewish past.[15]

> The meaning "punishment" (→ l.c.) is quite impossible here. It has no basis in the context, it does not agree with the supporting σκύβαλα or the antithetical κέρδος/κερδαίνειν, and it is made completely impossible by the subjective ἡγεῖσθαι and the ἐπιλανθανόμενος which follows later.

b. Since ζημιόομαι occurs in only one sentence in the Synpt. at Mt. 16:26 (par. Mk. 8:36; Lk. 9:25), we must deduce the meaning from the context of this single passage. The familiar antithesis κερδαίνειν/ζημιοῦσθαι (→ 888) tells in favour of the sense "to lose;"[16] to the gain consisting in the ὅλος κόσμος there corre-sponds as the price to be paid, the payment to be forfeited, the → ψυχή, the "self," if Lk. is right in his paraphrase[17] ἑαυτὸν δὲ ἀπολέσας ἢ ζημιωθείς.[18] Further aspects of this commercial figure may be found under ἀντάλλαγμα (→ I, 252). Values are compared, and we are therefore in the true sphere of ζημιόω. But, as the context shows, they are values which cannot really be com-pared. The loss of the → ψυχή is in no way compensated by the winning of the → κόσμος. If the reference of κερδαίνειν τὸν κόσμον is to the missionary work of the disciples,[19] the loss is one which can be incurred in and with their activity. In this case the danger of ζημιωθῆναι τὴν ψυχήν is integrally linked with the discharge of their mission. The ἀπέχουσιν τὸν μισθὸν αὐτῶν of Mt. 6 carries the same message, though with a broader reference. But even if we understand by κερδαίνειν τὸν κόσμον the attaining of earthly goods in the traditional sense, and are thus reminded of the story of the temptation in Mt. 4:8 f.,[20] ζημιωθῆναι certainly refers to something which takes place in this age. On the other hand, there is a reference in all three Synpt. to the coming of the Son of Man to

---

[15] The translation of Luther ("I regarded as of no advantage") must not be taken to mean that Paul is describing his natural religious and national inheritance as a harmful obstacle to becoming or being a Christian. In his use of ζημία he does not estimate these natural factors negatively, but simply denies to them the particular religious value (→ κέρδος) which they had for the Jews.

[16] → n. 4. The statement: τί δὲ κερδανοῦμεν ἅπασαν τὴν Περσίδα ... προσλαμβά-νοντες, τὰς δὲ ψυχὰς ἐζημιωμένοι; is not an instance supporting the NT usage, since it only belongs to the 6th cent. A.D. (Agathias Scholasticus Historiae, III, 12 [ed. Dindorf in Historici Graeci Minores, II, 1871]).

[17] So H. J. Holtzmann Synpt.³ (1901), ad loc.; a different view is taken in Schl. Lk., 99.

[18] Luther's rendering "to suffer loss in" for ζημιωθῆναι with the acc. is without support. In content we find the idea of inner loss or damage in Philo, e.g., Omn. Prob. Lib., 55: ζημία γὰρ χρημάτων ἢ ἀτιμία ἢ φυγαὶ ἢ αἱ διὰ πληγῶν ὕβρεις ἢ ὅσα ὁμοιότροπα βραχέα καὶ τὸ μηδὲν ἀντιτιθέμενα κακίαις, καὶ ὧν αἱ κακίαι δημιουργοί. τοὺς δὲ πολλούς, οὐ συνορῶντας τὰς ψυχῆς βλάβας διὰ λογισμοῦ πήρωσιν (extenuation), ἐπὶ μόναις ταῖς ἐκτὸς συμβέβηκεν ἄχθεσθαι, τὸ κριτήριον ἀφῃρημένους, ᾧ μόνῳ καταλαβεῖν ἔστι διανοίας ζημίαν. Cf. Deus Imm., 113; Virt., 182; Poster. C., 184. It is another question whether the distinction here presumed between the outer and the inner man is quite in keeping with the Synpt. and whether we thus have material support for Luther's translation; → ψυχή.

[19] Schl. Mt., ad loc. on the basis of Mt.

[20] Cf. also F. Kattenbusch, "Das Wort vom unersetzlichen Wert der Seele," ZNW, 10 (1909), 329 ff.

judgment, and therefore we have to consider the possibility that ζημιωθῆναι is part of the judgment and will take place, not in the present age, but only at the end. [21] In this case we are reminded of the legal sense of ζημιόω (→ l.c.) and we should thus translate: [22] "to be punished for ..." It is true that when ζημιωθῆναι is used in the sense of punishment the dat. is more usual, but there are instances of the accusative. [23]

Stumpff

| ζητέω, ζήτησις, |
| ἐκζητέω, ἐπιζητέω |

ζητέω.

1. When used in a religious sense this word first denotes the "seeking" of what is lost which is undertaken by the Son of Man with a view to saving it (Lk. 19:10), as a shepherd looks for the lost sheep (Mt. 18:12) or a woman for the lost coin (Lk. 15:8). But the same term can also be used of the holy "demand" of God who requires much from him to whom much is given (Lk. 12:48), and who expects fruit from the tree (Lk. 13:6 f.), faithfulness from the steward (1 C. 4:2) [1] and worship in spirit and in truth by the true righteous (Jn. 4:23). It is obvious that there are different nuances in the two uses. But the fact that the word is the same must be brought out so far as possible in translation. Thus the seeking of Jesus is accompanied by and grounded in a claim to what belongs to Him, while on the other side ζητεῖν as requirement does not have the ring of pitiless rigour but rather of patient and hopeful expectation, as may be seen in the parable of the unfruitful fig-tree (Lk. 13:6 ff.). [2]

Difficulties arise in relation to Jn. 8:50: ἐγὼ δὲ οὐ ζητῶ τὴν δόξαν μου· ἔστιν ὁ ζητῶν καὶ κρίνων. Bauer [3] thinks that ζητῶν (in combination with κρίνων) has here a legal sense: "who investigates and judges." But since in v. 50b Jesus is giving the reason (an ἔστιν is assumed) why He does not seek, and does not need to seek, His own glory, it is hard to think that there is a change in meaning between ζητῶ in 50a and ζητῶν in 50b. The object of investigation is also left indefinite. On the other hand the thought of the passage is convincingly developed if we take it that ὁ ζητῶν describes God as the One who sees to the δόξα of the One whom He has sent, maintaining His δόξα by judging and condemning those who will not recognise Him (cf. Jn. 1:14).

---

[21] H. J. Holtzmann, *Die Synpt.*[3] (1901), on Mk. 8:36; Kl. Mk. on 8:36; J. Weiss in *Schr. NT*[3] on Mt. 16:26.

[22] *V.* esp. Schl. Mt. on 16:26; ζημία in the non-legal sense occurs in Josephus, e.g., Ant., 4, 274: ἐὰν δέ τις χρυσίον ἢ ἀργύριον εὕρῃ καθ᾽ ὁδόν, ... ἀποδότω, τὴν ἐκ τῆς ἑτέρου ζημίας ὠφέλειαν οὐκ ἀγαθὴν ὑπολαμβάνων.

[23] E.g., Plato Leg., VI, 774b (though cf. a); the passage from Hdt., VII, 39 which has been much quoted since adduced by Wettstein: σὲ μὲν (γὰρ) καὶ τοὺς τέσσερας τῶν παίδων ῥύεται τὰ ξείνια· τοῦ δὲ ἑνός, τοῦ περιέχεαι μάλιστα, τὴν ψυχὴν ζημιώσεαι, can hardly be regarded as an instance, since the best MSS have τῇ ψυχῇ rather than τὴν ψυχήν.

ζ η τ έ ω. Liddell-Scott, 756; Bl.-Debr.[6] § 392, 1a; 400, 5; Dalman WJ, I, 99 f.

[1] On the pass. ζητεῖται cf. Str.-B., I, 443.

[2] Luther Lk. 12:48; 1 C. 4:2 etc.: "*suchen.*"

[3] Bau. J., *ad loc.*; Pr.-Bauer, *s.v.* ζητέω 1. e.

2. In most cases the subject of ζητέω is man. If we restrict our enquiry to passages with a religious reference, we find that in these instances the term denotes man's general philosophical search or quest. The root of this concept is to be found in the frequent LXX use of ζητεῖν for בִּקֵּשׁ and also in the use of the term in secular literature, where it is a technical term for philosophical investigation. There is a hint of the latter in the saying concerning the Greek search after wisdom in 1 C. 1:22. In Ac. 17:27, too, Paul uses an almost completely Greek mode of expression.[4] The OT tradition[5] emerges at R. 10:20 in a quotation from Isaiah: εὑρέθην τοῖς ἐμὲ μὴ ζητοῦσιν. ζητεῖν here denotes the total attitude towards God (cf. v. 20b and on this → 687). Also based on the OT (ζητεῖν τὸ πρόσωπον τοῦ θεοῦ, ψ 23:6; 26:8; cf. 39:16) are passages in which ζητέω is used in the absol. in relation to the hearing of prayer: ζητεῖτε, καὶ εὑρήσετε ..., ὁ ζητῶν εὑρίσκει (Mt. 7:7-11). For prayer is seeking God if it is to be successful prayer, to open the door and to give access to God. Thus ζητεῖν covers the seeking of man and the orientation of his will in the widest sense. If the heathen are primarily concerned about food and clothes, Christians are to seek first the kingdom of God and His righteousness (Mt. 6:32 f.; cf. Lk. 13:24). They are to seek those things which are above (Col. 3:1). This kind of life will be directed towards the attainment of δόξα, τιμή and ἀφθαρσία (R. 2:7). As the merchant in his search for fine pearls (Mt. 13:45) one day finds a jewel for which he will sell all the rest, so man is to direct everything towards the one great goal. In Pauline terms, he is to seek to be justified (Gl. 2:17). Seeking after God can be perverted in the demand for a sign with which a morally corrupt generation hopes to find an easier way to God than that indicated by the call to repentance (Mk. 8:11 f. and par.).[6]

On other uses of ζητέω in the NT and on the constr. cf. Pr.-Bauer, s.v. Examples need hardly be given of the class. ζητεῖν "to investigate" and τὸ ζητούμενον "the object of enquiry." The striking par. to Mt. 7:7: ζήτει καὶ εὑρήσεις, in Epict. Diss., I, 28, 20; IV, 1, 51 has reference in both passages to philosophical investigation. So, too, does Jos. Ant., 12, 99: πρὸς τὴν τῶν ζητουμένων θεωρίαν ἀκριβῶς ἐκείνων ... διασαφούντων ... In Philo the philosophical enquiry of the mind is combined in a unique way with the heart's seeking after God: οἱ γὰρ ζητοῦντες καὶ ἐπιποθοῦντες θεὸν ἀνευρεῖν τὴν φίλην αὐτῷ μόνωσιν (solitariness) ἀγαπῶσι ... Abr., 87; ὅταν οὖν φιλόθεος ψυχὴ τὸ τί ἐστι τὸ ὂν κατὰ τὴν οὐσίαν ζητῇ, Poster. C., 15; cf. also → 894. There appears to be a par. to R. 10:20 in Deus Imm., 93: συμβαίνει δὲ πολλάκις τοῖς μὲν ἐπιπόνως ζητοῦσιν ἀποτυγχάνειν τοῦ ζητουμένου, τοῖς δ' ἄνευ φροντίδος ῥᾷστα καὶ ἃ μὴ διενοήθησαν εὑρίσκειν. But here the reference is to philosophical seeking and finding.

† ζήτησις.

On the basis of the Greek technical term for philosophical enquiry (→ ζητέω), ζήτησις is used in the NT as a nomen actionis in the sense of "debate," or "dispute."[1] But here the accent does not lie on the activity of seeking after a goal,

---

[4] D gig Iren ClAl go much further, reading τὸ θεῖον for τὸν θεόν. On this whole question cf. E. Norden, Agnostos Theos (1913), 14-18.

[5] ζητεῖν θεόν or ζητεῖν κύριον is constantly used in the OT to describe man's voluntary turning to God, so that it almost becomes a technical term. In 2 Ch. ζητεῖν is used almost exclusively in this sense [Bertram].

[6] Cf. Schl. Mt. on 12:39; Schl. also refers here to Ex. r., 9 on 7:9 and Tanch. Lv. 18:10. ζ ή τ η σ ι ς. Liddell-Scott, 756; Pr.-Bauer, 529; Preisigke Wört., 647.

[1] → συ(ν)ζήτησις is found in many MSS.

which is still primary, e.g., in Philo. It is shifted to the manner in which this is done, and therefore a degree of specialisation is introduced. Possibly the fact that dialogue and later the diatribe were well-known literary forms of philosophical investigation exercised some influence in this respect. The strife between the disciples of John and the Jews in Jn. 3:25, the clash of Paul and Barnabas with the Judaizers in Antioch in Ac. 15:2, the similar event in Jerusalem in Ac. 15:7 and the combination of ζητήσεις καὶ λογομαχίας in 1 Tm. 6:4 all indicate an exchange of words rather than a true search. In other passages in the Past. this is the most obvious sense. General disputing must be presumed in 2 Tm. 2:23, since otherwise it is hard to see how "unlearned questions"[2] would give rise to conflict. In Tt. 3:9 ζητήσεις is used with γενεαλογίαι, ἔρις (ACKLP lat sy: ἔρεις) and μάχαι νομικαί.[3] The last of these reminds us forcibly of the two previous passages from the Past. and seems to suggest the same or a very similar meaning for ζητήσεις. As the author sees it, these disputations are not merely useless and foolish and of no instructional value; they cannot be reconciled with a confident faith and they have all kinds of evil results (cf. esp. 1 Tm. 6:4 f.). The only occasion when it seems from the context that ζήτησις must be understood as a legal term for "enquiry" is in Ac. 25:20, though the object of investigation obviously does not belong to the legal sphere.

ζήτησις is not found in the LXX or the post-apost. fathers. Secular Gk. uses it in several senses corresponding to those of ζητέω. As a technical term for philosophical enquiry and investigation it is found from the time of Plato (e.g., Ap., 29c; Crat., 406a).[4] It is always found in Epict. (Diss., I, 22, 17; II, 11, 13; III, 14, 10) either in, or in direct proximity to, definitions of philosophy or the philosopher. In Philo its technical use is easily the most common (e.g., Spec. Leg., I, 345: τὴν τοῦ ὄντος ζήτησιν οὐ μεθησό-μεθα [release], τὴν ἐπιστήμην αὐτοῦ τέλος εὐδαιμονίας εἶναι νομίζοντες καὶ ζωὴν ἀκραίωνα), though in several passages it can also mean the gaining of a livelihood (e.g., ζήτησις βίου καὶ τροφῆς, Op. Mund., 167; cf. also 128; Vit. Mos., II [III], 211 and 219). There are no clear instances of the specialised sense of a "clash of opinions" or "disputation" (Jn. 3:25; Ac. 15:2) in the pre-Christian era.[5]

† ἐκζητέω.

The meaning of ἐκζητέω is essentially the same as that of the simple form. The fact that they are used almost indiscriminately alongside one another is due to the increasing popularity of compounds.[1] In verbal (Ac. 15:17; R. 3:11) or material (Hb. 11:6) dependence on the LXX ἐκζητεῖν τὸν κύριον denotes the attitude of the righteous as they ask after God and are concerned about His grace. There is more of the element of search (→ ζητέω, 893) in 1 Pt. 1:10: περὶ ἧς σωτηρίας ἐξεζήτησαν καὶ ἐξηρεύνησαν προφῆται; cf. Barn., 4, 1: δεῖ οὖν ἡμᾶς περὶ τῶν ἐνεστώτων ἐπὶ πολὺ ἐραυνῶντας ἐκζητεῖν τὰ δυνάμενα ἡμᾶς σῴζειν. On the

---

[2] So Dib. Past., ad loc.

[3] Similarly in 1 Tm. 1:4 the ζητήσεις of DGKLP pl are opposed to the ἀγάπη of v. 5. The ἐκζητήσεις forbidden by ℵ A are perhaps to be understood as "contentious discussions"; cf. Wbg. Past. on 1 Tm. 1:4.

[4] Cf. Liddell-Scott, s.v.

[5] Dion. Hal. Ant. Rom., VIII, 89, 4 (cf. Pr.-Bauer, s.v.) does not demand more than "search" or "investigation."

ἐ κ ζ η τ έ ω. Pr.-Bauer, 372 f.; Moult.-Mill., 194.

[1] Cf. Radermacher, 31. Sophocles Lex.: ζητέω strengthened. So, too, Rgg. Hb. on 11:6; 12:17, though it is difficult to sustain this view.

other hand, the word implies more general seeking and striving in Hb. 12:17: μετὰ δακρύων ἐκζητήσας αὐτήν (sc. τὴν μετάνοιαν). The term has a certain independence in relation to ζητέω as the consistent translation of the Heb. בִּקֵּשׁ דָּם or דָּרַשׁ דָּם, e.g., 2 Βασ. 4:11; ψ 9:12; Ez. 33:6, 8, though in the NT this sense is found only at Lk. 11:50 f.: ἵνα ἐκζητηθῇ τὸ αἷμα πάντων τῶν προφητῶν ... ἀπὸ τῆς γενεᾶς ταύτης ... ναὶ λέγω ὑμῖν· ἐκζητηθήσεται ... The obvious eschatological orientation of this demand for justice for the blood of the slain distinguishes the understanding of the Greek phrase in the NT from the Hebrew usage in at least the older strata of the OT, where, in the absence of a doctrine of final judgment, the only possibility is an immanent conception of divine retribution. It is an open question whether the Greek translators of the OT already linked eschatological notions with their phraseology.

In the LXX both ζητέω and ἐκζητέω are used for בָּקַשׁ and דָּרַשׁ, though ζητέω more frequently for the former and ἐκζητέω for the latter. ἐκζητεῖν occurs in secular Gk. from the 1st cent. B.C., with instances in the pap.: περὶ δὲ τῆς σκιᾶς φανερόν μοι ἐγενήθη ἐκζητήσαντι ἠλλάχθαι μὲν τὴν πορφυρᾶν ... BGU, IV, 1141, 40 ff. (14 B.C.). For further examples v. Pr.-Bauer and Moult.-Mill. In the Gk. sense of "to investigate," "to discover," the word is found on an expiatory inscr. from Lydia (Ath. Mitt., VI, 373, No. 23 [2nd cent. A.D.], where the deity seeks out and punishes unknown transgressors. [2]

ἐπιζητέω.

ἐπιζητέω, too, has almost identically the same meaning as ζητέω (→ ἐκζητέω) in the NT, with which it is sometimes interchangeable in Synpt. par. and textual history. Like the simple form, it denotes the striving of man, the deployment of his will and desire. If it is a mark of the Gentile way of life that earthly things claim supreme attention (Mt. 6:32 and par.), Paul bears witness of the Jews, the people of God, that their search is for δικαιοσύνη, even though this can never reach its goal (R. 11:17; cf. 9:31). It is approvingly reported of the pro-consul Sergius Paulus: προσκαλεσάμενος Βαρναβᾶν καὶ Σαῦλον ἐπεζήτησεν ἀκοῦσαι τὸν λόγον τοῦ θεοῦ (Ac. 13:7). A distinctive feature of Hebrews is that it does not merely understand the Christian life as a way or pilgrimage to the future eternal city (Hb. 13:14), [1] but also represents the faith of OT saints as seeking and striving after the heavenly home (11:14). [2]

In law the word is a technical term for "to search for someone," "to seek out someone," or "to collect debts or deposits." [3] Technical use might seem to be suggested in Ac. 12:19 and 19:39, but none of these senses is suitable and therefore the more general meanings "to look for" (12:19) and "to desire" (19:39) are to be accepted. The LXX uses ἐπιζητέω in the same senses as ζητέω, but much less frequently. In Philo the word hovers, like → ζητέω, 893, between the enquiry of the mind and the yearning of the heart: ἐπιζητήσειε δ' ἄν τις τὴν αἰτίαν, Op. Mund., 77; ψυχῆς ... ἀνδρὸς ὄντως φρονήμασιν ἐπιζητούσης εὔδιον (calm) κατάστασιν, Abr., 26. Cf. also Epict. Diss., I, 17, 16 and IV, 8, 33. Joseph. uses ἐπιζητέω like ζητέω for "to seek" in the general

[2] Cf. Steinleitner Beicht, 33, 105; J. Zingerle, "Heiliges Recht," Oestr. Jhft., 23 (1926), Beiblatt, 42 [I owe this reference to Joseph Keil].
ἐ π ι ζ η τ έ ω. Liddell-Scott, 633; Preisigke Wört., 553; Bl.-Debr.[6] § 392, 1a.
[1] Cf. Dg., 12, 6: ὁ δὲ ... ζωὴν ἐπιζητῶν ἐπ' ἐλπίδι φυτεύει.
[2] On the request for signs in Mt. 12:39; 16:4 → 893.
[3] Cf. Preisigke Wört., s.v. and Zingerle (→ ἐκζητέω, n. 2), 37 ff.

sense : (Saul) κλήρῳ τὸν ἡμαρτηκότα μαθεῖν ἐπεζήτησε, Ant., 6, 125; (Elisha) ἐπηρώτησε τίνα ἐπιζητοῦντες ἦλθον, Ant., 9, 56, cf. 54. In Herm. m., 10, 1, 4 we have ἐπιζητέω along with ἐρευνάω (→ 894). In 1 Cl., 1, 1 περὶ τῶν ἐπιζητουμένων παρ' ὑμῖν πραγμάτων is used for a clash of opinions : "the things contested among you," στάσις being parallel to it in the same context ; cf. Ac. 15:2.

Greeven

ζυγός, ἑτεροζυγέω

† ζυγός.

A. ζυγός in the LXX.

1. In the LXX the term is used at 3 Macc. 4:9 for the cross-beam between the sides of a ship which served as a bench for rowers, but normally ζυγός or ζυγόν means either "scales" or "yoke," and in both senses it occurs mostly in ethical or religious contexts. For "scales" the only instances of secular use are at Ez. 5:1 (a means of division), Is. 46:6 (of measuring) and Jer. 39(32):10 (for weighing gold). [1] In Is. 40:12 the balance is an instrument in the hands of the architect of the universe. Similarly, in Eth. En. 43:2 it is an instrument of cosmic measure to fix the nature of the stars, their strength, their courses and their periods. The demand for just weights in the Bible is often given a religious basis, as in Lv. 19:35, 36; Ez. 45:10; Hos. 12:7; Am. 8:5; Prv. 11:1; 20:23; Sir. 42:4 (cf. also Mi. 6:11 Mas.: "Shall I pardon in spite of ungodly weights ?"). [2] LXX also understands ψ 61:9 along these lines : "The sons of men are liars with the weights to do wrong" (so also Θ, but not the Mas. → 897). The religious basis is most explicit in Prv. 16:11 Mas.: "The weights and balances are the Lord's," though the LXX understands this figur. of the righteous weighing of judgment as a gift which God gives to the king. Here the scales are a symbol of justice. Similarly, the sign of scales is allotted to Dan, the son of Jacob, in accordance with the significance of his name as a representative of justice. [3] This line of understanding continues into the Christian era, unites with similar ideas of antiquity and leads to mediaeval portrayals of *justitia* with scales as one of the four cardinal virtues. [4] In the moral sphere we also have a figur. use in Sir. 21:25 : The words of prudent men can be weighed. Cf. also the admonition in Sir. 28:25 : Measure your words with scales and weights.

2. More important, however, is the figur. use with regard to the destiny and worth of man, which, though it is not found in the NT, strongly influenced the eschatological conceptions of Christian piety. Thus Job thinks that when his sufferings are weighed they will be heavier than the sand of the sea (Job 6:2). In other words, his sufferings cannot be weighed. This contradicts the view which even in this passage is the normative one, namely, that man's destiny is weighed out by God so that none can add to it (Ps. Sol. 5:4). In other passages man himself is said to be weighed. Thus we read in Job 31:6 'A : (God) σταθμίσει ("weigh") με ἐν ζυγῷ δικαίῳ (also the Mas.), LXX : ἔσταμαι γὰρ ἐν ζυγῷ δικαίῳ, "I am valued with correct balances." In keeping with this is the question in Mi. 6:11 LXX (on the Mas. → *supra*): εἰ δικαιωθήσεται ἐν ζυγῷ ἄνομος ("Will he prove to be of full weight on the scales of the unright-

---

ζυγός κτλ. Moult.-Mill., *s.v.*; Pr.-Bauer, *s.v.*; Str.-B., I, 608 ff.; Dalman WJ, I, 80; A. Büchler, *Studies in Sin and Atonement in the Rabbinic Literature of the First Century* (1928), 52 ff.; A. Steinmann, *Die Apostelgeschichte*[4] (1934), 158 ff. (on 15:10).

[1] Cf. I. Benzinger, *Hebräische Archäologie*[3] (1927), 198.
[2] Acc. to H. Guthe in Kautzsch, *ad loc.*
[3] Benzinger, *op. cit.*, 257.
[4] W. Molsdorf, *Christliche Symbolik der mittelalterlichen Kunst* (1926), 215 ff.

eous ?"). The saying in Ps. 62(61):9 is generally true of all men: "A breath ... an illusion are the children of men; they flee away on the balances ..." [5] It is also said of the nations in Is. 40:15: πάντα τὰ ἔθνη ... ὡς ῥοπὴ ζυγοῦ ἐλογίσθησαν, "All the nations do not count as more than a quiver of the scales." The best known passage in relation to the balances is the Tekel of Da. 5:27, which Θ, like the Mas., interprets as follows: ἐστάθη ἐν ζυγῷ καὶ εὑρέθη ὑστεροῦσα. It is here that the image takes on its most significant form in relation to the last judgment, though perhaps even the Mas. does not construe correctly the original sense of the magic writing, which is possibly depicting the value of worldly kingdoms in terms of different kinds of money. [6] The LXX adopts another interpretation with its συντέτμηται καὶ συντετέλεσται, and in so doing it shows that the idea of the scales as an instrument of world judgment was not widespread in the biblical sphere.

Yet there are many apocryphal texts which use the figure in this sense. [7] Here again the application varies. Sometimes good and bad acts are weighed according to their frequency or significance. Sometimes man himself is weighed. Thus we find the prayer in 4 Esr. 3:34: "Weigh our sins and those of the inhabitants of the world in the scales, that it may be seen which way the balance tips." The scales are an instrument of eschatological judgment in Slav. En. 49:2: [8] "Before a man was in his mother's womb, I prepared a place of judgment for each soul, and a measure and a scales, so far as he shall live in this aeon, that man may be proved therein" (cf. 44:5; 52:15, 16 in the shorter redaction). The good and the bad will be weighed in the last judgment, Apc. Eliae 13:4. Similarly, according to Eth. En. 41:1 the acts of men will be weighed in the scales, and in 61:8 the Messianic Judge has the task of weighing in the balances the acts of the saints, cf. 89:63; S. Bar. 41:6. The image is also common in the Rabb. tradition, cf. jPea., 1, 16b; 37: "If merits and transgressions are equal in the scales, God will take off a debt so that the merits cause the scales to sink." [9]

The same or similar ideas are found in Christian apocalyptic up to the mediaeval and Reformation period. Thus in the pamphlets of the Reformation Luther and the pope are set against each other on two scales. The weight of sins pulls the latter and his supporters down into hell, while the side of the righteous rises up into the light — a figurative concept which to some degree is in contradiction with that of the balances, though it is perhaps found already in Slav. En. 52:16: "Keep your hearts from all unrighteousness, that you may inherit the balance of light in eternity."

3. The image of the yoke [10] is relatively common in the LXX. It occurs in the political sphere for domestic tyranny — cf. Rehoboam in 2 Ch. 10:4 ff., and also the relation of Esau to Jacob acc. to Gn. 27:40 — and for the rule of alien nations (Dt. 28:48 'A), esp. the great empires. Thus it is used of Egypt in Is. 19:10 LXX (not the Mas.), of Assyria in Is. 14:29, of Babylon in Is. 47:6; 'Ιερ. 35(28):14; Lam. 5:5 Σ, of Syria in Da. 8:25 Θ (not the LXX or Mas.). Liberation from this kind of dominion is the corresponding content of the message of deliverance. Thus the yoke is taken away from Israel in Is. 9:3; 10:27; 11:13 A; 14:25; or God breaks it in Lv. 26:13; Is. 14:5; 'Ιερ. 27(34):8 (cf. the false prophecy in 'Ιερ. 34[27]:6[8]; 35[28]:2, 4, 11); Ez. 34:27.

The image is also significant in many different connections in relation to the development of morality. The yoke is for slaves whose self-will must be broken, Sir. 30:35 (33:27). Care must be taken not to fall under the power of garrulity (the yoke of the

---

[5] Cf. the comm., ad loc.

[6] Cf. A. Bertholet, Daniel u. d. griech. Gefahr (1907), 34.

[7] Volz Esch., 293.

[8] G. N. Bonwetsch, Die Bücher der Geheimnisse Henochs: Das sogenannte slavische Henochbuch (1922).

[9] Str.-B. on R. 2:6, where other passages are given, as in Volz, op. cit.

[10] The Gk. translators often use terms like "shoulder," "staff," "stick" or "bands" for "yoke" with no basic alteration in sense.

tongue), Sir. 28:19, 20. On the other hand, it is good to accept the yoke of wisdom, Sir. 51:26. In Lam. 3:27 we find the pedagogic insight that it is good for a man to bear the yoke in youth. In Job 16:8 Σ the fate of Job is called a heavy yoke. The Heb., which is correctly rendered in the LXX, has לְעֵד, "for a witness," which Σ seems to have misread as עֹל. The same sense is found in Sir. 40:1 with reference to human destiny : ζυγὸς βαρὺς ἐπὶ υἱοὺς 'Αδάμ. [11]

The figure acquires a theological sense when the reference is to God's yoke. Men want to break this yoke (Jer. 2:20; 5:5) or to throw it off (ψ 2:3, Mas. "bands"); Slav. En. 34:1. They do not want to bear any yoke (Hos. 7:16 Σ and E', which are both independent of the obscure Mas., much emended in the LXX). On the other hand, cf. Zeph. 3:9 : τοῦ δουλεύειν αὐτῷ ὑπὸ ζυγὸν ἕνα. Those who bear the yoke are called blessed in Slav. En. 48:9, the yoke here being that of written revelation. It is commonly accepted that "we stand always under thy yoke and under the rod of thy discipline," the reference being to the suffering of the righteous. [12] This is important in relation to Mt. 11:29 f. and it is plainly reflected in 1 Cl., 16, 17, where the humiliation of the Lord is set forth as an example to those who stand under the yoke of His grace. In formulation there is even greater stress on the relation to the suffering of the righteous in Just. Dial., 53, 1: καὶ τὸν ζυγὸν τοῦ λόγου αὐτοῦ βαστάσαντες τὸν νῶτον ὑπέθηκαν πρὸς τὸ πάντα ὑπομένειν.

Bertram

B. ζυγός in the NT.

Of the meanings which derive from the basic sense of "yoke" and which are found in the usage of classical Greek, Hellenism and the Gk. Bible, we find in the vocabulary of the NT only two, namely, ζυγός [13] in the sense of "scales" [14] and in the sense of the "yoke" borne by the beast or the slave.

1. In Rev. 6:5 the third of the horsemen of the Apocalypse, the rider on a black horse, is described as ἔχων ζυγὸν ἐν τῇ χειρὶ αὐτοῦ. As may be seen expressly from v. 6, he is a representative of scarcity and hunger as preliminary signs of the impending judgment. Models for the use of scales as a symbol of dearth are perhaps to be found in Lv. 26:26; Ez. 4:16, [15] though the word ζυγός is not used in these passages. [16] It cannot be decided with certainty whether or not the author here stands in the apocalyptic tradition and applies the idea that a year standing under the sign of the scales will be one of disaster, [17] but this is not very likely.

It is not clear whether the word is masc. or neuter in Rev. 6:5. Older Gk. usually has τὸ ζυγόν for "scales" (though cf. Plat. Tim., 63b : αἴρων τὸν ζυγόν), whereas the Gk. Bible obviously inclines to ὁ ζυγός [18] and in this follows the process of development. This suggests that ὁ ζυγός is also more likely than τὸ ζυγόν at Rev. 6:5.

---

[11] Cf. the hymn of J. H. Schroeder which speaks of one thing alone as necessary and of all the rest as a heavy yoke. For other material from Protestant hymns, esp. with reference to the yoke of Christ, v. G. Brock, *Evangelische Liederkonkordanz* (1926), 233.

[12] Cf. G. Bertram, *Der Begriff der Erziehung in der griech. Bibel* (1932), 41 f.

[13] On the gender → *infra*.

[14] What is meant is in the first instance the beam, but this gives its name to the whole scales

[15] Cf. the comm., *ad loc.*

[16] The original has מִשְׁקָל; the LXX σταθμός.

[17] So F. Boll, *Aus der Offenbarung Johannis* (1914), 84 ff.

[18] Cf. H. St. J. Thackeray, *A Grammar of the OT in Greek*, I (1909), 154.

2. In other NT passages where ζυγός occurs the sense is that of "yoke." It is used only figuratively. As in older and contemporary Greek usage, and as also in contemporary Jewish usage, the word expresses a relation of absolute dependence. Though there are differences in detail, the general sense is unmistakably the same.

a. At 1 Tm. 6:1 Paul uses the expression ὅσοι εἰσὶν ὑπὸ ζυγὸν δοῦλοι in his admonition to show full respect to masters. Here the words ὑπὸ ζυγόν admirably express the situation of the slave, who cannot do as he pleases but stands under an imposed order and must bow to it.

We cannot, therefore, speak of a special burden resting on those whom Paul addresses. On the other hand, the words do take account of their situation to the degree that from the context they refer to the Christian slaves of non-Christian masters who stand under Jesus' law of love in respect of their own conduct but who will not be treated in accordance with it. [19] When the master is a Christian, the legal position of the slave is not essentially altered (v. 2; cf. Phlm. 10 ff.), but their mutual personal relationship is no longer determined by formal law, which imposes the ζυγός, but by the law of love under which they are both placed as ἀδελφοί (cf. v. 2; Phlm. 16). [20]

b. The combination of ζυγός and δουλεῖα can also describe bondage in the moral and spiritual sense. In Gl. 5:1 Paul warns the Galatians, who have been released by the Gospel from slavery to the → στοιχεῖα τοῦ κόσμου (cf. 4:8 ff.), not to rob themselves of this divinely effected and established freedom by subjecting themselves to the Jewish Law, for in so doing they will again be reduced to the position of the δοῦλος who lives under the ζυγός : μὴ πάλιν ζυγῷ δουλείας ἐνέχεσθε.

The essential point is that the νόμος is here on the same level as the στοιχεῖα τοῦ κόσμου. Both rob man of his freedom, and therefore both Jews and Gentiles need Christ, who alone can lead them to freedom, i.e., to a relationship to God which corresponds, not to that of a slave to his master, but to that of a child to its father (→ υἱοθεσία).

Ac. 15:10 speaks similarly of the νόμος and refuses to make it binding on Gentile Christians : νῦν οὖν τί πειράζετε τὸν θεόν, ἐπιθεῖναι ζυγὸν ἐπὶ τὸν τράχηλον τῶν μαθητῶν, ὃν οὔτε οἱ πατέρες ἡμῶν οὔτε ἡμεῖς ἰσχύσαμεν βαστάσαι;

There is here a formal dependence on Jewish usage which will be discussed under c.

c. In Mt. 11:29 f. Jesus invites the κοπιῶντες καὶ πεφορτισμένοι to take upon them His ζυγός : ἄρατε τὸν ζυγόν μου ἐφ᾽ ὑμᾶς καὶ μάθετε ἀπ᾽ ἐμοῦ, ὅτι πραΰς εἰμι καὶ ταπεινὸς τῇ καρδίᾳ, καὶ εὑρήσετε ἀνάπαυσιν ταῖς ψυχαῖς ὑμῶν· ὁ γὰρ ζυγός μου χρηστὸς καὶ τὸ φορτίον μου ἐλαφρόν ἐστιν. [21] The saying, which

---

[19] It makes no difference here whether the treatment is good or bad. What matters is whether the slave is for his master a brother or only a slave. Cf. also Wbg. Past., ad loc.

[20] The combination of ζυγός and δοῦλος is old. In Soph. Ai., 944 δουλείας ζυγά is used of the feared lot of the slave (cf. also Plat. Ep., 8, 354d : δούλειος ζυγός). ζυγός and δουλεία are also used of lost freedom in, e.g., 1 Macc. 8:17 f.: Ἰούδας ... ἀπέστειλεν αὐτοὺς εἰς Ῥώμην, στῆσαι φιλίαν καὶ συμμαχίαν καὶ τοῦ ἆραι τὸν ζυγὸν ἀπ᾽ αὐτῶν, ὅτι εἶδον τὴν βασιλείαν τῶν Ἑλλήνων καταδουλουμένους τὸν Ἰσραὴλ δουλείᾳ. Cf. also 8:31 and 13:41.

[21] On Mt. 11:28-30 as a whole cf. T. Haering in Aus Schrift und Geschichte, Festschr. f. A. Schlatter (1922), 3-15.

formally belongs to the larger context of wisdom sayings, [22] is obviously formulated as a conscious paradox. How can a ζυγός be easy? But the paradox evaporates when we remember who is speaking and to whom. Jesus is clearly speaking to those who already bear a ζυγός, for He refers expressly to His ζυγός, to the ζυγός of the Messiah, contrasting this with another ζυγός, with *the* other ζυγός. But this other ζυγός can only be that of worship under the Law, which involves the oppressive labour and attitude of the slave. This is clear from Mt. 23:4, where we find the image of the burden used. [23] In this saying, therefore, a contrast is drawn between the Messianic ζυγός of Jesus and the ζυγός of legalism. Jesus is thus contrasted with the νόμος, as in John's Gospel and sometimes in Paul. Thus the ζυγός which Jesus lays on those who accept it is the new worship of God in the free access to the Father which is the portion of all who bow obediently to the Word of Jesus and receive from Him the revelation of the will of God. This access is not the result of human attainment; it is the gift of Jesus in His Word and person. For this reason acceptance of His ζυγός is possible only in faith in Him as the Christ. Hence only to those who believe in Him is His yoke a ζυγὸς χρηστός and His burden a φορτίον ἐλαφρόν.

The formula ὁ ζυγός μου obviously stands in conscious correspondence to the expression עוֹל תּוֹרָה. This for its part is par. to such expressions as עוֹל מַלְכוּת שָׁמַיִם, "yoke of the kingdom of heaven" (→ I, 572), עוֹל מִצְוֹת, "yoke of the commandments," עוֹל שֶׁל הַקָּדוֹשׁ בָּרוּךְ הוּא, "yoke of the Holy One, blessed be He," עוֹל שָׁמַיִם, "yoke of heaven, i.e., God" (→ οὐρανός), עוֹל שֶׁל ה׳, "yoke of God," [24] which all express the idea of subordination to the will of God. At Sir. 51:17 we have in the Heb. the עֹל of σοφία. The Rabbis also speak in the same way of the עוֹל מַלְכוּת, "the yoke of (earthly) government," the עוֹל דֶּרֶךְ אֶרֶץ, "the yoke of earthly conduct," and also the עוֹל בָּשָׂר וָדָם, "the human yoke." [25] The two groups are sometimes contrasted. Thus Ab., 3, 5: "He who accepts the yoke of the Torah, from him they take off [26] the yoke of government and the yoke of earthly conduct." What is meant is that where the will of God is alone accepted, and where His dominion is present, there is no place for political or economic care. The statement is thus near to the message of Jesus (Mt. 6:10 f.), but with the basic distinction that it presupposes human achievement prior to the dawn of the divine kingdom (→ 525). Similarly, we read in T. Sota, 14, 4 that he who breaks the yoke of heaven, i.e., he who wickedly transgresses the will of God revealed and definitively established in the Torah, brings himself under the yoke of an earthly king, [27] i.e., becomes a servant of man instead of a servant of God. [28]

It is essential to the Jewish world to stand under the עוֹל תּוֹרָה. Yet this is not felt to be a burden; it is a privilege. It rests on God's dealings with Israel. By the deliverance from Egypt Israel became an elect people ordained to fulfil God's will. The Rabbis interpreted the law-giving at Sinai in this sense, [29] and thus made the service of God

[22] Wisdom issues a demand and invitation to come to it (Prv. 8:1 ff.; 9:5 f.; Σιρ. 24:19 ff.; 51:23); it has a yoke (Σιρ. 51:26) and gives peace (Σιρ. 51:27).
[23] Cf. Schl. Mt., 385.
[24] Cf. the passages in Str.-B., I, 608 f.; Schl. Mt., 386; Büchler, 52 ff.
[25] V. the examples in Str.-B., I, 609 f.
[26] A cautious way of referring to God, as in Lk. 6:38; cf. Dalman WJ, I, 183 ff.
[27] In the first instance the reference is obviously to the Roman emperor.
[28] The text makes it plain that the primary reference of קִבֵּל עוֹל is to the proof of obedience. Cf. merely the most instructive passage in Midr. Ps. 59:4 (Buber, p. 152a), from which we learn that to accept the yoke of one's earthly father is to subject oneself without reservation to his will.
[29] Cf. the comprehensive material in Büchler, 52 ff.

the meaning of the existence of the Jews. In this light we can understand that the recitation of the sch^ema (Dt. 6:4-9; 11:13-21; Nu. 15:37-41), i.e., the confession of the one God of heaven and earth, who is the God of the Jewish people, is equivalent to bowing beneath the yoke of the kingdom of heaven. [30] We can see why the texts say that the proselyte takes upon him the מַלְכוּת שָׁמַיִם עֹל, [31] and why it is also recorded that the dying Aqiba recited the sch^ema when he breathed his last, tortured to death by the Romans because of his part in the Zealot uprising (bBer., 61b). And when Jesus was asked whether it was lawful to pay taxes to Caesar (Mt. 22:15 ff. and par.) there stood in the background those eager souls who were not prepared to tolerate for themselves or for the people any other yoke or will than that of God, the real question being whether Jesus would give the same answer as they did, and therefore take His stand with them, on the question as to the nature of the מַלְכוּת שָׁמַיִם. Here is the point where with perfect clarity the yoke of Jesus and the yoke of a divine dominion conceived in human terms divide with all the sharpness with which the Gospel is distinct from the Law.

d. The Jewish use of the "yoke" passes over from the NT into the early Church. In Did., 6, 2 we read : εἰ μὲν γὰρ δύνασαι βαστάσαι ὅλον τὸν ζυγὸν τοῦ κυρίου, τέλειος ἔσῃ. εἰ δ᾽ οὐ δύνασαι, ὃ δύνῃ τοῦτο ποίει. Since the following verses deal with abstention from certain foods and from meat offered to idols, as with the general folly of idolatry, it seems fairly certain that ὅλος ὁ ζυγὸς τοῦ κυρίου implies sexual asceticism. [32] If so, the admonition as a whole (v. 2-3) renews the so-called apostolic decree of Ac. 15:29, except that now → πορνεία embraces also the marital relationship — a sign that the Didache is already moving in a different direction from the NT (cf. 1 C. 7:5). Here, as in Barn., 2, 6, the idea of the ζυγός is linked with the Word of Jesus. In Barn., however, there is clear differentiation from Judaism. The description of the Word of Jesus as ὁ καινὸς νόμος ... ἄνευ ζυγοῦ ἀνάγκης ὤν is designed, according to the context, to express the fact that the νόμος of Jesus is more gift than obligation, so that it excludes the deployment of human works in the service of God.

† ἑτεροζυγέω.

The word is a further construction from ἑτερόζυγος, "unequally yoked" (so Lv. 19:19; Philo Spec. Leg., IV, 203 in the prohibition of mating animals under a different yoke, i.e., of a different species, like the ass and the ox), and is not found prior to 2 C. 6:14. ἑτερόζυγος gives us the meaning of the verb, namely, "to go under one and the same yoke with someone else even though one does not have the requisite presuppositions."

In 2 C. 6:14 the word describes figur. the abnormal situation which results when Christians in their conduct follow the rules of the world, which knows nothing of what is given to the community : μὴ γίνεσθε ἑτεροζυγοῦντες ἀπίστοις· τίς γὰρ μετοχὴ δικαιοσύνῃ καὶ ἀνομίᾳ, ἢ τίς κοινωνία φωτὶ πρὸς σκότος; ... τίς μερὶς πιστῷ μετὰ ἀπίστου; Paul leaves us in no doubt that when this happens the community ceases to exist as such, even though it continues to do so in outward form (cf. v. 15 ff.).

Rengstorf

---

[30] Cf. Ber., 2, 2 and the passages in Str.-B., I, 177. → I, 572.

[31] Tanchuma לֵךְ לְךָ § 6 (Str.-B., I, 176).

[32] Cf. Kn. Did., 21, *ad loc.* → τέλειος.

ἑτεροζυγέω. Pr.-Bauer, *s.v.*; cf. the comm. on 2 C. 6:14.

| † ζύμη, ζυμόω, ἄζυμος | → ἄρτος, πάσχα.

1. The NT usage rests on the OT feast of unleavened bread with the rules prescribed for it in Ex. 12:18 : ἐναρχομένου τῇ τεσσαρεσκαιδεκάτῃ ἡμέρᾳ τοῦ μηνὸς τοῦ πρώτου (Nisan) ἀφ᾿ ἑσπέρας ἔδεσθε ἄζυμα ἕως ἡμέρας μιᾶς καὶ εἰκάδος τοῦ μηνὸς ἕως ἑσπέρας· ἑπτὰ ἡμέρας ζύμη οὐχ εὑρεθήσεται ἐν ταῖς οἰκίαις ὑμῶν ..., v. 20 : πᾶν ζυμωτὸν οὐκ ἔδεσθε, ἐν παντὶ δὲ κατοικητηρίῳ ὑμῶν ἔδεσθε ἄζυμα, cf. 13:6 f.; Nu. 28:16 f.; Dt. 16:3 f.

While the true Passover feast (→ πάσχα), which lasts only a single day, undoubtedly derives from the nomadic and pre-Canaanite period, many scholars believe that the seven day Mazzot feast was an agrarian festival which was adopted by Israel only in Canaan. If this is so, there is no original connection between the two. In favour of this is the ancient calendar in Ex. 23:14 f., which does not mention the connection. In Dt. 16:1-8, too, the interrelationship seems to be very external. It is now impossible to determine the original religious meaning of the Mazzot feast, and the etymology of מַצָּה is obscure. Israel early read into it historical significance, connecting it with the Exodus. It may be seen from the earliest aetiological explanation in Ex. 12:34, 39 that this historicisation must have taken place prior to the interfusion with the true Passover. [1]

2. The feast [2] is mentioned twice at the commencement of the passion narrative in the Synoptic Gospels : Mk. 14:1 = Lk. 22:1 and Mk. 14:2 = Mt. 26:17 = Lk. 22:7. It is also mentioned twice in Acts at 12:3 : ἦσαν δὲ ἡμέραι τῶν ἀζύμων and 20:6 : μετὰ τὰς ἡμέρας τῶν ἀζύμων.

Mk. 14:1: ἦν δὲ τὸ πάσχα καὶ τὰ ἄζυμα μετὰ δύο ἡμέρας, is the most accurate version. The ἄζυμα are the seven days which follow the evening of the Passover (14th Nisan); cf. 2 Ch. 35:17; 1 ῎Εσδρ. 1:17(19) LXX : καὶ ἠγάγοσαν ... τὸ πάσχα καὶ τὴν ἑορτὴν τῶν ἀζύμων ἡμέρας ἑπτά. The name is an abbreviation of ἡ ἑορτὴ τῶν ἀζύμων (cf. Ex. 23:15 etc.; Jos. Ant., 2, 317; 3, 249) and is in keeping with other Gk. forms of the names of festivals (cf. τὰ ἐγκαίνια at Jn. 10:22). Luke's ἡ ἑορτὴ τῶν ἀζύμων ἡ λεγομένη πάσχα equates the two feasts (cf. also 22:7), as is customary in Judaism, [3] Jos. Bell., 2, 10 : τῆς τῶν ἀζύμων ἐνστάσης ἑορτῆς, ἣ πάσχα παρὰ ᾿Ιουδαίοις καλεῖται. [4] Mt. 26:2 has only τὸ πάσχα.

Mk. in 14:12 introduces the story of the preparation of the Passover by fixing the time as follows : καὶ τῇ πρώτῃ ἡμέρᾳ τῶν ἀζύμων, ὅτε τὸ πάσχα ἔθυον. He is thus reckoning the 14th Nisan as the first day of the eight day feast of the ἄζυμα. Strictly the 15th Nisan, the day after the Passover, is the first day of unleavened bread. Yet even in the Rabbis the 14th Nisan is sometimes called the first day of the ἄζυμα. [5] The varying usage is to be explained by the fact that already on the evening of the 14th Nisan only unleavened bread was to be eaten according to Ex. 12:18. The setting aside of what was leavened took place during the course of the 14th Nisan. [6]

In 26:17 Mt. has the shorter τῇ δὲ πρώτῃ τῶν ἀζύμων, but it may be seen clearly from 26:17b that the evening of the Passover still lay ahead. Lk. paraphrases : ἦλθεν

ζ ύ μ η. Calwer Bibellexikon⁴ (1924), 654; Cr.-Kö., 477 f.; S. Krauss, *Talmudische Archäologie*, I (1910), 99 f., 458 f.; G. Beer, *Pesachim* (1912), 18 ff.

[1] This par. is by v. Rad. Cf. J. Pedersen, ZAW, NF, 11 (1934), 161 ff.

[2] Kl. Mk.², 156 f.

[3] Kl. Lk.², 205; Str.-B., I, 987 f.

[4] For further examples cf. Ant., 18, 29; 14, 21; 10, 70 (text uncertain).

[5] Str.-B., II, 813 f.

[6] Pes., I, 1-4, and cf. Beer, 110 ff.

δὲ ἡ ἡμέρα τῶν ἀζύμων, ἐν ᾗ ἔδει θύεσθαι τὸ πάσχα, as though the 14th Nisan were called ἡ ἡμέρα τῶν ἀζύμων (22:7). [7]

It is perhaps surprising that in the accounts of the Last Supper we nowhere find the common LXX expression ἐσθίειν ἄζυμα, [8] for on the evening of the Passover ἄζυμα alone were eaten and not ordinary bread (ἄρτος). This implies either that the meal presupposed in the story (Mk., Mt., 1 C. 11) was not the Passover but took place the evening before (cf. Jn. 13:1, 4; 18:28) [9] or that ἄρτος is used in these accounts for ἄζυμα. [10]

3. The ritual of the ἄζυμα also underlies the brief exhortation in 1 C. 5:6-8. This is true even though the assumption that Paul was writing during the Passover season (cf. 16:8 : ἕως τῆς πεντηκοστῆς) is neither certain nor perhaps correct. [11] A brief summons is issued to the festival of the ἄζυμα = πάσχα, [12] but the cultic command has now become a moral injunction — an important example of the translation of cultic concepts into ethical. [13]

The following phrases may be singled out as formulae of priestly and cultic admonition : ἐκκαθάρατε τὴν ... ζύμην ..., καὶ γὰρ τὸ πάσχα ... ἐτύθη ...· ὥστε ἑορτάζωμεν μὴ ἐν ζύμῃ ..., ἀλλ' ἐν ἀζύμοις ("with what is unleavened," = "with unleavened bread" = either "with mazza" or "with unleavened dough"). We also have the proverbial οὐκ οἴδατε, ὅτι μικρὰ ζύμη ὅλον τὸ φύραμα ζυμοῖ; [14] 1 C. 5:6 = Gl. 5:9, which in this context might mean that even the smallest bit of ζύμη is to be set aside. [15]

The moral application, i.e., the translation of the cultic ordinance into an exhortation to conversion and the relating of ζύμη to the wickedness and impurity

---

[7] Zn. Lk., 665-667, n. 21 and 25.

[8] Ex. 12:8, 15 etc.; Ez. 45:21. In the Gospels we have only φαγεῖν τὸ πάσχα at Mk. 14:14, 16; Lk. 22:7 f. In the LXX this is found only at 2 Ἔσδρ. 6:21. From this it may be seen that the Gospels are not dependent on the usage of the LXX but go back to Aram. and Heb. usage. The Rabbis also have אכל הפסח or עשה הפסח, like the Mas. (cf. K. G. Kuhn, S. Nu. [1933 ff.], 178, n. 36). On the other hand, אֲכָל מַצּוֹת never seems to occur in Rabb. lit. as a distinctive expression for this festival (Kuhn). A rather different question is raised, of course, by the surprising fact noted above that in the accounts of the Last Supper the reference is always to ἄρτος (לחם) rather than to ἄζυμα (מצות).

[9] J. Wellhausen, ZNW, 7 (1906), 182.

[10] P. Fiebig, ThLZ, 59 (1934), 416. ἄρτος ἄζυμος = מַצָּה at LXX Ju. 6:20 A (B : ἄζυμα) shows that the term ἄρτος does not exclude ἄζυμος, but that in certain circumstances, e.g., in description of the Passover, it may mean this. Hence the occurrence of ἄρτος at the Last Supper is no proof that this was not really the Passover [Bertram]. Cf. also Philo Spec. Leg., II, 158. At Dt. 16:3 the mazza are called ἄρτος κακώσεως (לֶחֶם עֹנִי). Jos. in Ant., II, 316 describes the mazza, which are kneaded from meal and baked over a slow fire, as τοῖς ἀπ' αὐτῶν ἄρτοις. The loaves of the show-bread, which were unleavened (Jos. Ant., III, 255 : ἄρτος ὀπτὸς ζύμης ἄμοιρος), were regularly called ἄρτοι, Jos. Ant., III, 142 : ἄρτους τε δώδεκα ἀζύμους. Cf. also Joach. Jeremias, Die Abendmahlsworte Jesu (1935), 27 ff.

[11] Zn. Einleitung, I, 192; Joh. W. 1 K., 137; Schl. K., 182 f.

[12] This is the original setting of the passage.

[13] H. Wenschkewitz, "Die Spiritualisierung der Kultusbegriffe" in Angelos, 4 (1932), 180 f. (Beiheft, IV [1932], 116), though there is here no detailed examination of the spiritualising of the ζύμη ordinance.

[14] On the secondary variant δολοῖ, cf. Ltzm. K., ad loc.

[15] On the debated Rabbinical question how much leaven of Chullin or Teruma must fall into the dough to give effect to the prohibition, we have a judgment of the elder Gamaliel, the teacher of Paul (Orla, 2, 12). Paul's interest in these questions might thus derive from his Rabbinic training.

of the unconverted man, now follows in the phrases: παλαιάν ..., ἵνα ἦτε νέον φύραμα, καθώς ἐστε ἄζυμοι and ... παλαιᾳ̃ ..., μηδὲ ἐν ζύμῃ κακίας καὶ πονηρίας, ... εἰλικρινείας (→ 397) καὶ ἀληθείας. ζύμη for Paul is the old, the bad, the impure, the false. ἄζυμα, on the other hand, means freedom from ζύμη, i.e., freedom from everything bad, from moral defilement, and therefore newness, **purity and truthfulness** (→ 397; I, 243). [16] This symbolism, as may be seen from similar expressions in Philo (→ infra), is suggested by the ordinance and is wholly appropriate. Less self-evident is the description of ζύμη as old and the designation of the unleavened dough as a νέον φύραμα, i.e., the idea that the dough itself is unleavened. This application of the figure is to be explained by the introduction of the antithesis of old and new (R. 7:6; Col. 3:9 f.; Eph. 4:22 f.) [17] as suggested by the admonition to conversion. There is also a degree of allegorising. Man (Christian), or better the community, is the dough, [18] sin is the bad element in it, the leaven, and conversion and mortification are the introduction of a new and pure dough. [19] The combination opens up new vistas. The converted are themselves the ἄζυμοι, the pure festal community; the new life is the feast; Christ, who both demands renewal and makes it possible, is the paschal lamb. The little sentence καθώς ἐστε ἄζυμοι is a good example of the combined indicative and imperative in Paul's theology of conversion: ἐκκαθάρατε τὴν ζύμην ..., καθώς ἐστε ἄζυμοι, i.e., "become what you are." [20]

Philo has given us various allegorical interpretations of ἄζυμα and ζύμη. In Congr., 161 f. he takes it that the ἄρτος κακώσεως (bread of affliction) of Dt. 16:3 is ἄζυμα, and he notes concerning it: τὰ γὰρ πλεῖστα καὶ μέγιστα τῶν ἀγαθῶν ἀσκητικαῖς ᾿ἀθλήσεσι καὶ ἡβῶσι πόνοις εἴωθε περιγίνεσθαι. Thus the eating of ἄζυμα here symbolises asceticism. Logically, therefore, ζύμη might be a symbol of luxury, but Philo does not draw this conclusion from the passage. What is lacking here is found in rather a different form in Quaest. in Ex., I, 15 (on Ex. 12:8) (*Bibliotheca Sacra Patrum Ecclesiae Graecorum, Pars II : Philonis Judaei Opera Omnia* VII [1830], 274), where it is said of the leavened and unleavened: *utrumque symbolum est animarum status : unum superbi elati ob fastum, alterum modesti et demissi atque praeeligentis media prius quam summitates ad aemulationem aequitatis.* τὰ ἄζυμα, then, are a symbol of humility and ζύμη of pride. Cf. also the exposition of Ex. 23:18 : οὐ θύσεις ἐπὶ ζύμῃ αἷμα θυμιάματός μου (*ibid.*, II, 14). [21] The prohibition implies symbolically : καταφρονεῖν ἡδονῆς — ζύμη γὰρ ἥδυσμα τροφῆς, οὐ τροφή — καὶ τὸ μὴ δεῖν ὑπὸ κενῆς φυσωμένους οἰήσεως αἴρεσθαι. Here ζύμη is a symbol of sinful lust and vain pretension. These interpretations are related to that of Paul in 1 C. 5:8, though Philo does not apply

---

[16] "Let us therefore keep the feast ... with the sweet dough (unleavened dough, or *mazza*) of sincerity and truth."

[17] Possibly ζύμη itself also suggests dough which is old, i.e., sour and bad.

[18] Cf. the remarks of O. Holtzmann NT, II, 523 on this equation.

[19] Cf. the admonition in Ign. Mg., 10, 2 (which is based on 1 C. 5): ὑπέρθεσθε οὖν τὴν κακὴν ζύμην, τὴν παλαιωθεῖσαν καὶ ἐνοξίσασαν (become sour), καὶ μεταβάλεσθε εἰς νέαν ζύμην, ὅ ἐστιν Ἰησοῦς Χριστός. Ign. thus distinguishes between bad ζύμη and good (i.e., new). Cf. also Just. Dial., 14, 2 and 3 : τοῦτο γάρ ἐστιν τὸ σύμβολον τῶν ἀζύμων, ἵνα μὴ τὰ παλαιὰ τῆς κακῆς ζύμης ἔργα πράττητε ... διὸ καὶ μετὰ τὰς ἑπτὰ ἡμέρας τῶν ἀζυμοφαγιῶν νέαν ζύμην φυρᾶσαι ἑαυτοῖς ὁ θεὸς παρήγγειλε ... In Ps.-Clem. Hom., 8, 17 the generation of the flood is κακὴ ζύμη which is destroyed by God.

[20] H. Windisch, "Das Problem des paul. Imperativs," ZNW, 23 (1924), 265 ff. Cf. on this whole passage the comm. on 1 C., esp. Joh. W., Bchm., Ltzm., Sickb. and Schl.

[21] The Gk. text is to be found in P. Wendland, *Neuentdeckte Fragmente Philos* (1891), 96 f.

the command to cleanse the house from all ζύμη, i.e., he has no powerful injunction to cleanse out all the evil represented by ζύμη. For a very different interpretation of ζύμη as the legitimate elevation of the soul, cf. Spec. Leg., II, 185 (→ infra).[22] There are no similar allegorical interpretations in Jos. or Ep. Ar.

An important tradition from Graeco-Roman culture is to be found in Plut. Quaest. Rom., 109 (II, 289, F). It is here explained why the flamen Dialis is forbidden to touch ἄλευρον and ζύμη, and it is said of ζύμη : ἡ δὲ ζύμη καὶ γέγονεν ἐκ φθορᾶς αὐτὴ καὶ φθείρει τὸ φύραμα μιγνυμένη· γίνεται γὰρ ἄτονον (slack) καὶ ἀδρανὲς (powerless) καὶ ὅλως ἔοικε σῆψις ἡ ζύμωσις εἶναι· πλεονάσασα γοῦν ἀποξύνει παντάπασι καὶ φθείρει τὸ ἄλευρον. Here ζύμη is something unclean and corrupt. The process of leavening is compared with that of defilement.[23] The thinking of Paul is along similar lines, for in this respect the Hebrew and the Roman prohibitions of ζύμη derive from much the same view.[24]

4. The proverbial saying in 1 C. 5:6 = Gl. 5:9 goes rather beyond the thought and usage of the Jewish festival. It is a generally valid saying, an illustration of the truth of experience that little causes can have great effects; cf. Jm. 3:3-5.[25] The point of the saying is elaborated by Jesus in the parable of the leaven in Mt. 13:33 = Lk. 13:21. To be sure, we do not have the emphatic μικρὰ ζύμη, but the result : εἰς ἀλεύρου σάτα τρία, and the conclusion : ἕως οὗ ἐζυμώθη ὅλον, make it clear that only a small amount of ζύμη is presumed, but that this is so powerful that it can leaven three whole measures of meal.

The text of both versions of the parable compares the βασιλεία τῶν οὐρανῶν (τοῦ θεοῦ) with ζύμη. Here we are a long way from the Passover ordinance, which regards ζύμη as something evil and disruptive. The view is more like that of the housewife or the baker who hopes that a small amount of ζύμη will be able to leaven the whole lump, and who is gratified that it can do this. The βασιλεία, or the Word concerning it, is regarded, on a strict exegesis, as a kind of δύναμις which, although present only in a small measure (restricted to Jesus and His followers or to Jesus Himself and His small sphere of possible operation), is ordained and able to penetrate the whole earth (→ I, 585), cf. Mt. 5:13 : ὑμεῖς ἐστε τὸ → ἅλας τῆς γῆς, i.e., "you are to work like salt on the earth."[26]

Here, as distinct from 1 C. 5, ζύμη represents something good. In this respect we may compare the two interpretations espoused by Philo in Spec. Leg., II, 184 f. under the influence of Cynic-Stoic traditions. ζύμη is now 1. (σύμβολον) ἐντελεστάτης καὶ ὁλοκλήρου τροφῆς and 2. the symbol of a joyous inner exaltation (πᾶν τὸ ἐζυμωμένον ἐπαίρεται, χαρὰ δὲ ψυχῆς ἐστιν εὔλογος ἔπαρσις). The typical feature of the parable, namely, that of power to penetrate the dough, is not present in Philo. In spite of all the various analogies, the parable bears the stamp of originality. In

---

[22] On this whole subject cf. J. Heinemann, Philons griech. u. jüd. Bildung (1932), 122 ff., 129 f.

[23] Cf. Plut. Convivalium Disputationum, III, 10, 3 (II, 659 B): ἡ γὰρ ζύμωσις ὀλίγον ἀποδεὴς εἶναι κἂν ἀπολάβῃ τὸ μέτρον, ἐπὶ τὴν αὐτὴν φθορὰν ἀραιοῦσα (loosening) καὶ προβάλλουσα τὸ φύραμα προήγαγεν.

[24] Cf. G. Beer, op. cit., 16.

[25] Wnd. Kath. Br., 23. Herm. m., 5, 1, 5; cf. Dib. Herm., 515. There is a Buddhist par. in Dīghanikāya, II, 75, 76 (H. W. Schomerus, Buddha u. Christus [1931], 76).

[26] Though cf. J. Weiss in Schr. NT³, I, 323, where reference is made to the contrast between a modest beginning and the final comprehensive success. Cf. also Jülicher Gl. J., II, 579 f., Zn. Mt., 495 f., Bultmann Trad., 217, R. Otto, Reich Gottes u. Menschensohn (1934), 98 f.

contrast to the Plutarch tradition Jesus views the process of leavening as something healthy. [27]

5. Figurative, too, is our Lord's saying in Mk. 8:15; Mt. 16:6; Lk. 12:1. This is a warning against the ζύμη of the Pharisees (Lk.), of the Pharisees and Herodians (Mk.), or of the Pharisees and Sadducees (Mt.). In Mk. it is delivered without commentary, though it is (artificially) connected with the negative commentary in vv. 16-21 lest it should be referred to the fact that the disciples forgot to take bread with them. In Lk. there is the explanatory gloss : ἥτις ἐστὶν ὑπόκρισις, while Mt., after the much shortened teaching concerning ἄρτοι in 11 f., repeats the warning : προσέχετε ἀπὸ τῆς ζύμης τῶν Φαρισαίων καὶ Σαδδουκαίων, and then adds independently : τότε συνῆκαν, ὅτι οὐκ εἶπεν προσέχειν ἀπὸ τῆς ζύμης κτλ. In this way the possible literal understanding that the disciples should not buy ἄρτοι from the Pharisees and Sadducees is set aside [28] and the ζύμη is linked with διδαχή.

In this case one might see a reference to the cultic prohibition, for ζύμη is at least seen as something corruptible which also brings corruption. Perhaps the best analogy, however, is offered by the common Rabbinic designation of the יֵצֶר הָרָע as leaven. [29] In this case the warning is one of the sharpest attacks on the teachers of the Jews. But even here the concept of ζύμη may be neutral. For the idea is that every man has a leaven. That is to say, every man or teacher exerts an influence, whether for good or for bad. The emphasis, then, is not on the ζύμη but on the genitive : τῶν Φαρισαίων κτλ. [30]

In the LXX ζύμη is used only in regulations for the feasts and sacrifices : Ex. 12:15, 19; 13:3, 7; 23:18; 34:25; Dt. 16:3 f.; Lv. 2:11, where it is the rendering of חָמֵץ and שְׂאֹר. The verb ζυμοῦσθαι is found in Ex. 12:34, 39; Lv. 6:10; 23:17 and Hos. 7:4. ἄζυμος occurs almost exclusively in the form τὰ ἄζυμα = הַמַּצּוֹת, e.g., Ex. 12:8, 15 ff.; 13:6 f.; 23:15; Lv. 2:4 f. and ἑορτὴ τῶν ἀζύμων (חַג הַמַּצּוֹת), Ex. 34:18; 2 Ch. 8:13; 30:13, 21 f.; 1 Ἔσδρ. 1:17 (19); 7:14,; 2 Ἔσδρ. 6:22. ζυμόω is not found in Joseph.; for ζύμη cf. Ant., 3, 252 and 255. [31]

Windisch

ζωή, ζωογονέω, ζῷον, ζωοποιέω → ζάω.

---

[27] The fact that Jesus expressly uses this image for the growth of the kingdom of God in man shows His strong inner independence of Jewish religious tradition acc. to O. Holtzmann NT, I, 150.

[28] As, e.g., the Rabbis might say : "Beware of the leaven or meat of the Samaritans" (cf. Str.-B., I, 541 f.).

[29] bBer., 17a; Str.-B., I, 728 f., IV, 466 ff., Schl. Mt., 499. On the designation of διδαχή as ζύμη, cf. the statement of R. Chijja b. Ba (jChag., 2, 76c, 37) concerning the leaven in the Torah which has the power to lead Israelites who observe the Torah back to God (Str.-B., I, 728). On the equation of ζύμη and ὑπόκρισις, cf. Philo, where ζύμη is pride or arrogance (→ 904). In Philo, however, the basic idea is that of an actual quality of leaven, whereas in the Evangelist the connecting thought is simply the general idea that ζύμη represents something bad.

[30] In exposition cf. Schl. Mt., 499; J. Wellhausen, *Das Ev. Marci*[2] (1909), 61; M. Dibelius, *Die Formgeschichte des Evangeliums*[2] (1933), 230; F. Vogel in *Bayr. Blätter f. d. Gymnasial-Schulwesen*, 60 (1924), 361 f.

[31] On non-biblical usage, cf. for ζύμη Plut. → 905, Preisigke Wört., 648; Moult.-Mill., 274; for ζυμόω Plut. Convivalium Disputationum, III, 10, 3 (II, 659 B); for ἄζυμος Pass. (-Cr.), 128; Pr.-Bauer, 29; Liddell-Scott, *s.v.* Etymologically ζύμη is not to be derived from → ζέω but from an Indo-germ. root *jūs*, "soup" (e.g., Lat. *jūs, jūris*, "soup"); cf. Boisacq, 311 and 309; Walde-Pok., I, 199.

ἡγέομαι, ἐξηγέομαι,
προηγέομαι, διήγησις

ἡγέομαι.

1. ἡγέομαι means a. "to lead"; b. "to think," "to believe," "to regard as."[1] Sense a. occurs in the NT only in the pres. part. (→ 2.). In sense b. we find the word in Acts, Paul, the Past., Hebrews, James and Peter, but not in the Johannine writings (including Rev.).[2]

In 1 Th. 5:13: ἡγεῖσθαι αὐτοὺς ὑπερεκπερισσῶς ἐν ἀγάπῃ, ἡγεῖσθαι ὑπερεκπερισσῶς is best understood as in Thuc., II, 89, 9: κόσμον καὶ σιγὴν περὶ πλείστου ἡγεῖσθε, "to regard as particularly important," "to esteem." It is not necessary to see here a shift in meaning of the *vox media* "to judge" *in bonam partem,* "to value highly," though support for this might be found in the analogous εἰδέναι of the preceding verse (v. 12). The combination ἡγεῖσθαι ἐν ἀγάπῃ runs contrary to the order.[3]

2. a. ἡγούμενοι,[4] mostly in the plural, is used for the leaders of the community in Hb. 13:7, 17, 24. In the greeting in 13:24 the ἡγούμενοι are mentioned before the ἅγιοι. The community is obviously divided into those who lead and those who are led. In 13:17 they are pastors responsible to God. God has entrusted the other members of the community to them, and therefore these owe them obedience. The founders of the community, who have died (as martyrs?), are also among the ἡγούμενοι, and they are set up as examples of faith (13:7). The community here is not, as in Paul, the pneumatic organism in which each is assured that he is moved by the Spirit of God.[5] Reverent subjection to human officers with divinely given pastoral authority is now integral to Christian piety. This high estimation of office implies transition to early Catholicism, unless it can be explained from an early regard for office.[6] Similarly in 1 Cl., 1, 3 the ἡγούμενοι are leaders of the community who must be distinguished from the πρεσβύτεροι as the elders (cf. νέοι). Subjection and respect for them belong essentially to Christian piety, cf. the exact par. in 1 Cl., 21, 6, though here we have προηγούμενοι. In Hermas, too, there is reference to ἡγούμενοι as leaders of the community (v., 2, 2, 6; 3, 9, 7), though the prophet does not treat them as authorities, but asserts his own autonomy in relation to them. We find the same usage in Luke's writings. In Lk. 22:26 the ἡγούμενος is contrasted with the διακονῶν and is parallel to the μείζων ἐν ὑμῖν. He is admonished to be humble. Ac. 15:22 calls Judas Barsabbas and Silas ἡγουμένους ἐν τοῖς ἀδελφοῖς, i.e., leading men among the brethren.

ἡ γ έ ο μ α ι. [1] Cf. Pape, Pr.-Bauer, *s.v.*

[2] On the constr. with the inf., acc. and infin. and double acc., cf. Pr.-Bauer, who also gives par. from the pap.

[3] Cf. Dob. Th., 217.

[4] Rgg. Hb. [2], [3], 433, n. 81, 448, 456; Kn. Cl., 45; Pr.-Bauer, *s.v.* ἡγέομαι.

[5] Cf. F. Büchsel, *Der Geist Gottes im NT* (1926), 344 ff.

[6] Cf. K. Holl, *Gesammelte Aufsätze,* II (1928), 54. Whether these are elected by the community or appointed by their predecessors, whether they are charismatics or in what way they are related to charismatics, whether they have the title ἐπίσκοποι or πρεσβύτεροι — all these matters are obscure. The interest of Hb. in the ἡγούμενοι is ethical and religious rather than ecclesiastical.

b. The word ἡγούμενοι can also be used of non-Christian leaders, great men, officials and princes : 1 Cl., 5, 7; 32, 2; 37, 2 and 3; 51, 5; 55, 1. It is used similarly in the LXX of military leaders, 1 Macc. 9:30; 2 Macc. 14:16; of leaders of the people, Ez. 43:7; Sir. 17:17; 30:27; 41:17. In Sir. 33:19 the ἡγούμενοι ἐκκλησίας alongside the μεγιστᾶνες λαοῦ can hardly be priests. We find a similar use of ἡγούμενος in free quotations from the OT at Mt. 2:6 (Mi. 5:1-3) and Ac. 7:10 (Joseph). Among heathen priests there are ἡγούμενοι ἱερέων, P. Lond., II, 281, 2 (66 A.D.); cf. P. Tebt., II, 525 : Παεῦς ἡγ[ούμενος] ἱερέων. This usage may also be seen in Soph. Phil., 386, Polyb. passim, Diod. S., I, 4, 6 f., Luc. Alex., 44. It thus seems to have been taken over by Christians from non-Christian sources.

Ac. 14:12, where Paul as the ἡγούμενος τοῦ λόγου is taken for Hermes, is to be explained in terms of Iambl. Myst., 1, 1, where Hermes is called θεὸς ὁ τῶν λόγων ἡγεμών — a traditional predicate of the god used already at the time of Luke. The constr. ἡγέομαί τινος is common, cf. Pape, s.v. No par. have been adduced for λόγου ἡγεῖσθαι.

† ἐξηγέομαι.

Of the two meanings, a. "to introduce," "to adduce," "to be the introducer or cause," and b. "to expound," "to present," "to recount," [1] only b. is found in the NT (Jn. 1:18; Lk. 24:35; Ac. 10:8; 15:12, 14; 21:19). ἐξηγεῖσθαι is a technical term for the exposition of poets (Plat. Crat., 407a), of laws (Demosth. Or., 47, 69; Plat. Leg., VII, 802c); for the religious teaching of priests etc., Lys., 6, 10; Xenoph. Cyrop., VIII, 3, 11: οἱ μάγοι ἐξηγοῦντο; and for revelations of the gods, Plat. Resp., V, 469a; IV, 427c, where the Delphic Apollo is called ἐξηγητής. Poll. Onom., VIII, 124 : ἐξηγηταὶ δ' ἐκαλοῦντο οἱ τὰ περὶ τῶν διοσημιῶν (signs of the gods) καὶ τὰ τῶν ἄλλων ἱερῶν διδάσκοντες. [2] In accordance with this usage Josephus calls two rabbis ἐξηγούμενοι τοὺς νόμους, Bell., 1, 649, or ἐξηγηταὶ τῶν πατρίων νόμων, Ant., 17, 149, and the Pharisees μετὰ ἀκριβείας δοκοῦντες ἐξηγεῖσθαι τὰ νόμιμα, cf. also Ant., 18, 81. Philo speaks of ἐξήγησις τῶν ἱερῶν γραμμάτων, Vit. Cont., 78, of the ἐξηγητής of the same, Spec. Leg., II, 159, and of his ἐξηγεῖσθαι in relation to the OT, Leg. All., III, 21. There is a clear affinity between Jn. 1:18 and Sir. 43:31(35): τίς ἑόρακεν αὐτὸν (God) καὶ ἐκδιηγήσεται. [3]

Jn. 1:18 is like an intentional answer to this question. Thus the Heb. equivalent would be ספר. Schlatter suggests פרש. but the fact that ἐξηγήσατο is without object [4] does not permit the rendering "to explain." In accordance with Gk. religious usage it must be given the sense of "to reveal."

† προηγέομαι.

This is found in the NT only at R. 12:10. The most obvious understanding is by analogy with Phil. 2:3 : τῇ ταπεινοφροσύνῃ ἀλλήλους ἡγούμενοι ὑπερέχοντας

ἐ ξ η γ έ ο μ α ι. Pape, s.v.; Bau. J.; B. Weiss, Erklärung des Joh.-Ev.⁹ (1902); Schl. J. on Jn. 1:18.
[1] Cf. Pape, s.v.
[2] Cf. Rohde ⁵, ⁶, I, 259, n. 2. M. P. Nilsson in A. Bertholet-E. Lehmann, Lehrbuch der Religionsgeschichte⁴, II (1925), 359; Liddell-Scott, s.v.
[3] Cf. Zn. J., ad loc. The fact that Jn., who must have read Sir. in the Heb., has ἐξηγεῖσθαι rather than ἐκδιηγεῖσθαι (recount in full) implies only a slight difference from the Heb.
[4] One can hardly supply θεόν as obj. from v. 18a, since God is not an obj. of explanation.
π ρ ο η γ έ ο μ α ι. Pr.-Bauer, s.v.; Zn. R., 548, n. 41; B. Weiss, R.⁹ (1899), 521 on 12:10.

ἑαυτῶν, "each esteeming others more highly than himself." The Lat., however, has *invicem praevenientes*. But, while προηγεῖσθαι can mean "to precede" in the sense of "to introduce," it cannot mean "to take the lead."[1] Nor can we translate "to go before, inviting others to follow,"[2] since there is nothing about inviting others to follow in the text. The obvious sense of "to prefer," "to esteem more highly" seems to find adequate enough support in 2 Macc. 10:12 (τὸ δίκαιον συντηρεῖν προηγούμενος, "he preferred to observe righteousness").

† διήγησις.

In his preface to the Gospel in 1:1, Lk. describes the labours of his predecessors as attempts διήγησιν ἀνατάξασθαι. In the efforts to solve the problem of the origins of our canonical Gospels, the struggle against Eichhorn's theory of an original written gospel led to the conjecture that our present Gospels developed out of written records which did not present the whole of the material but more or less random extracts from it, e.g., miracle stories, the sayings of Jesus, the passion narrative or the story of the resurrection. The term *diegesis* was taken from Lk. 1:1 to denote this kind of record.[1] This raises the question what Lk. himself really meant by it. The answer can only be, not something special, but a narrative. The word could not have been used for a literary or semi-literary product or other magnitude along the lines of form criticism. The usage thus provides no help towards solving the problem of the origin of the Gospels or towards the understanding of Lk. 1:1-4. The word is found from the time of Plato[2] and simply denotes an oral or written record as such.[3]

Büchsel

† ἡδονή, † φιλήδονος

In the NT ἡδονή represents one of the many forces which belong to the world of unsanctified carnality, which strive against the work of God and His Spirit and which drag man back again into the kingdom of evil. The concept of ἡδονή, like many others, is first set in the light of the relationship to God by the NT. But it has an important previous history which shows it to be a vital issue in discussions both by Gk. philosophers and Hellenistic Jewish authors.

---

[1] Zn., *op. cit.* Several examples may be found in Pape.

[2] B. Weiss, *op. cit.*

διήγησις. [1] This conjecture was made in relation to Lk. by Schleiermacher in his treatise : *Über die Schriften des Lukas, ein kritischer Versuch* (1817) (= *Sämtl. Werke*, 1, II [1836], 10 ff.). Schleiermacher appeals to H. E. G. Paulus, who in his exegetical manual on the first three Gospels, 1, 1 (1830), 64, uses the term *Diegesen*, which Schleiermacher does not do.

[2] Resp., III, 392d; Phaedr., 266e.

[3] Gk. Sir. often uses the word for narrative in conversation, cf. 6:35; 9:15; 22:6; 27:11, 13; 38:25; 39:2. Ep. Ar. uses it of a written account, 322; cf. also 1 and 8, and 2 Macc. 2:32; 6:17. Paulus appeals to Eus. Hist. Eccl., II, 25, 2; III, 24, 7; 39, 9 and 14, but in these passages διήγησις has the usual sense of record or account.

ἡδονή. Pr.-Bauer, 537; Moult.-Mill., 278. Art. "lust" in Hastings DB, 173 f.; Art. "pleasure" in DCG, II, 371 f.; Dib. Jk., 198 ff.; Hck. Jk., 188 f., 193; Meinertz Kath. Br., 42 f.; Meinertz Past., 93; Stenzel, Art. *Kyrenaiker* in Pauly-W., XII, 1 (1924), 137-150 (esp. on ἡδονή in Plat. Prot.).

A. General Greek Usage.

1. Semasiological Development.

a. The word ἡδονή derives from the same root as ἡδύς, "sweet," "pleasant," "delightful" (Lat. *suavis*), and it shares with this adj. the original sense of what is pleasant to the senses, namely, to the sense of taste. [1]

It means sensual pleasure, e.g., in Hdt., II, 137: ἡδονὴ ἰδέσθαι; Aesch. Prom., 493 ff.: ... χροιὰν τίνα ἔχουσ᾽ ἂν εἴη δαίμοσιν πρὸς ἡδονὴν χολή ..., "what colour the gall must be to please the gods." Cf. also Aristoph. Nu., 1072 f.: ὄψεις, πότοι, κιχλισμοί (feasting) as ἡδοναί, also Plat. Resp., III, 389e : ... τῶν περὶ πότους καὶ ἀφροδίσια καὶ περὶ ἐδωδὰς (foods) ἡδονῶν; Thuc., III, 38, 7; ἀκοῆς ἡδονή, III, 40, 2 : ἡδονὴ λόγων (→ n. 15) of superficial "pleasure in rhetoric" (feasting the ears).

The narrower basic meaning, which relates to what tastes good, was accompanied for many centuries by a subsidiary semasiological strand according to which ἡδονή denotes that which causes pleasure to the senses. The specific sense of "pleasant taste" in first found in Ionic nature philosophy (Anaxagoras; Diogenes of Apollonia) and in the peripatetics (Arist. Part. An., II, 17, p. 660b, 9; Theophr.; Eudemos), [2] and it is then found in later Hell. liter. (cf. the quotations in Athen., VIII, 55 [p. 357 f.]; XIV, 60 [p. 649a]): ἡδοναὶ τραγημάτων (sweet-meats), in the LXX (Wis. 16:20; → 916) and early Christian writings (Herm. m., 10, 3, 3; 12, 5, 3 : ἡ ἡδονὴ τοῦ οἴνου).

Already in its earliest use, [3] however, the term ἡδονή bears the broader sense of a general "feeling of pleasure" or "enjoyment." The development from the sensual to the psychical and then to the ethical, which we can trace in ἡδονή, is often to be noted in the evolution of words and their meanings. Already at an early period the rise of a feeling of pleasure is both restricted to sensual perceptions but is linked with enjoyable experiences of all kinds, and esp. with desired communications. The multiplicity of the nature of ἡδονή, of its causes and objects, is reflected in the prepositional constructions ἡδονὴ ἀπό τινος, ἐπί τινι, διά τι, κατά τι and περί τι. [4]

ἡδονή is often found in this general sense in inscr. of the Roman period, [5] as also in the NT: 2 Pt. 2:13: ἡδονὴν ἡγεῖσθαί τι, "to regard something as a pleasure" (→ 918 f.).

b. Instead of the "sense of pleasure" ἡδονή can sometimes denote the "desire" for it, e.g., Xenoph. Mem., I, 2, 23. In this group we should reckon instances in which it is par. to ἐπιθυμία and thus denotes "passionate yearning," as in the Stoics (Diog. L., VII, 110) and Philo (Migr. Abr., 60) or in which it is equivalent to "desire," as in Philo Spec. Leg., III, 8, but esp. Decal., 143 : τοῦ παρόντος καὶ νομισθέντος ἀγαθοῦ φαντασία διεγείρει καὶ διανίστησι τὴν ψυχὴν ἠρεμοῦσαν καὶ σφόδρα μετέωρον ἐξαίρει καθάπερ ὀφθαλμοὺς φῶς ἀναστράψαν· καλεῖται δὲ τουτὶ τὸ πάθος

---

[1] Cf. Walde-Pok., II, 516 f.

[2] Examples may be found in Liddell-Scott, *s.v.*, II.

[3] Instead of ἡδονή, which does not fit the hexameter, Homer uses the genetically older form ἦδος. ἡδονή is first found in Simonides of Ceos, 57 (Diehl, II, 83).

[4] ἀπό: Aristot. Poet., 14, p. 1453b, 12 : ἡ ἀπὸ ἐλέου καὶ φόβου ἡδονή; Plat.Resp., IX, 582b : ἡδονὴ ἀπὸ τοῦ εἰδέναι. ἐπί : Demosth. Or., 18, 138 : ἡ ἐπὶ ταῖς λοιδορίαις ἡδονή. R. Cagnat, *Inscriptiones Graecae ad Res Romanas Pertinentes*, IV, 1 (1908), 566, 12 (c. 200 A.D.): ἡδονὴν ἐπὶ τοῖς κατωρθωμένοις ἔχειν. διά : 4 Macc. 9:31: αἱ διὰ τὴν ἀρετὴν ἡδοναί. Inscr. Priene, 105, 20 (c. 9 B.C.; illustr. in Deissmann LO, 316): ἰδία τις διὰ τὴν ἀρχὴν ἡδονή, "some pleasure for oneself in connection with the New Year" (in addition to joy on the emperor's birthday), cf. Moult.-Mill., *s.v.* ἥδιστα. κατά, περί : Xenoph. Hist. Graec., VI, 1, 16 : αἱ περὶ τὸ σῶμα ἡδοναί; Plat. Resp., I, 328d : αἱ κατὰ τὸ σῶμα ἡδοναί ... αἱ περὶ τοὺς λόγους ... ἡδοναί. Cf. also Liddell-Scott, Pape, Pass. etc. for examples of the prepositional phrases μεθ᾽, πρὸς, ὑφ᾽, ἡδονῆς — ἐν ἡδονῇ — καθ᾽, πρὸς ἡδονήν.

[5] → n. 4, *s.v.* ἐπί, διά; also Inscr. Priene, 113, 64 (84 B.C.) → ἀπάτη (→ I, 385): τὰ πρὸς ἡδονήν is obviously a technical term for "the usual pleasures" on festive occasions.

αὐτῆς ἡδονή. It is probably in this sense that ἡδονή is used at Jm. 4:1 [6] and perhaps also Tt. 3:3.

c. In a further shift of meaning for which there are many par. ἡδονή can also denote "that which kindles the feeling of desire" or "that which gives pleasure" (cf. the special sense of "pleasant taste" already noted, → 910). Thus ἡδονή, e.g., in Soph. El., 873 (ἡδονὰς φέρειν) means "good news," [7] and in Aristoph. Nu., 1072 (ἡδονῶν ἀποστερεῖσθαι) it means "pleasure," with an enumeration in v. 1073 of the pleasures envisaged, namely, παῖδες (love for boys), γυναῖκες, κότταβοι (carousing), ὄψεις κτλ. (→ 910). There is here already a restriction or declension of meaning which is common in the NT period, ἡδονή coming to signify "sensual lust or enjoyment" (→ 919).

2. Ethical Evaluation.

For the Greeks ἡδονή, which affects life in so many ways, is from the time of the poems of Solon and Mimnermos a problem, since on the one side it is something which is necessarily integrated into the totality of bios and which essentially enriches it, while on the other it often seems to threaten and even to dissolve the true meaning and purpose of life. [8]

ἡδονή is originally always vox media and is adapted to denote the noblest of joys. Plato, e.g., deals with it in his teaching on values, and ἡδονή is for him pleasure in the good, the true and the beautiful (cf. Resp., IX, 583 ff.; Phileb., 51 ff.). Aristotle has a similar estimate esp. of the ἡδονή which consists in the exercise of ἀρετή and in pleasure in beautiful works of art (Eth. Nic., VII, 14, p. 1153b, 1 ff.; X, 5, p. 1175a, 18 ff. etc.). In keeping with this is the fact that here — in contrast to the NT — ἡδονή and χαρά, ἥδεσθαι [9] and χαίρειν, are interchangeable concepts (cf., e.g., the usage in Aristot. Poet. and Eth. Nic., also in Plat. Prot., 354c etc. and Diog. L., II, 89). Even in the Shepherd of Hermas (s., 6, 5, 7), in a passage full of pointed antitheses, ἡδονή can still be used for "pleasure in the good."

But already in the class. period ἡδονή suffers a change in malam partem, being used not merely for pleasures of the senses (→ 910) but for "sensual pleasure" in the narrower sense, [10] as in stock expressions like αἱ σωματικαὶ ἡδοναί (Aristot. Eth. Nic., VII, 9, p. 1151a, 13), or αἱ τοῦ σώματος ἡδοναί (Xenoph. Hist. Graec., IV, 8, 22), or ἡ τῶν σωμάτων ἡδονή (Phil. Op. Mund., 152). [11] A clear reference to "sexual desire" is to be found in the oldest of the passages relevant in this connection, Soph. Ant., 648 f.: μὴ ... τὰς φρένας ὑφ' ἡδονῆς γυναικὸς εἵνεκ' ἐκβάλῃς; cf. later Muson., p. 89,

---

[6] Cf. Dib. Jk., 198, n. 3.
[7] Cf. also Eur. Hel., 700 f.:
    Μενέλαε, κἀμοὶ πρόσδοτέ τι τῆς ἡδονῆς,
    ἣν μανθάνω μὲν καὐτός, οὐ σαφῶς δ' ἔχω.
    "Menelaus, give me a share in that which makes you glad,
    I know it indeed, but I do not truly understand it."
[8] For a comprehensive survey to the time of Aristotle cf. W. Jaeger, Paideia, I (1934), 178 ff.
[9] On the other hand Prodicos in Plat. Prot., 337c distinguishes between εὐφραίνεσθαι and ἥδεσθαι as terms for spiritual enjoyment on the one side and corporeal on the other.
[10] In this respect ἡδονή has much in common with ἀπάτη and ἐπιθυμία in their shifts of meaning. As in the case of → ἀπάτη (I, 385) the sense of "deception" is probably secondary and the meaning "delight" asserts itself (again) in Hellenistic usage (Moult.-Mill., s.v.; cf. Deissmann, NJbch. Kl. Alt., 6 [1903], 165, n. 5), so in the case of ἡδονή the meaning "sensual desire" is predominant in the NT period, but the sense of "delight" or "enjoyment" still lingers. Similarly → ἐπιθυμία is originally vox media and is still found as such in the NT (cf. Lk. 22:15; Phil. 1:23; 1 Th. 2:17), but it is used in malam partem by the Stoics (Cr.-Kö., 501, s.v.) and it normally means the "desire of sinful lust" in the NT.
[11] → n. 4 s.v. περί.

16 f. [12] and Luc. Vit. Auct., 8, where there is reference to a struggle against ἡδοναί like that of Heracles. Vettius Valens (p. 76, 1) goes even further in this direction when he links πάθη ἀκάθαρτα with παρὰ φύσιν ἡδοναί. The most explicit passages are two from the Jewish world (→ 916), Jos. Ant., 2, 51: (Joseph to Potiphar's wife) νέμειν ... ἢ τῇ προσκαίρῳ τῆς ἐπιθυμίας ἡδονῇ, [13] and esp. Wis. 7:2 : (of man) παγεὶς ἐν αἵματι ἐκ σπέρματος ἀνδρὸς καὶ ἡδονῆς ὕπνῳ συνελθούσης.

In a broader sense we should also mention ἡδονοκρασία in this connection in the sense of "giving oneself up to a life of enjoyment" (Ep. Ar., 278).

This restriction of meaning, which makes the word a very definite ethical term instead of one which is psychological and ethically neutral, finds reflection a. in the fact that, to the degree that the term narrows in sense, it also declines in estimation. [14]

Already Demosth. (Or., 1, 15) speaks disapprovingly of ἅπαντα πρὸς ἡδονὴν ζητοῦντες; earlier Herodot. (VII, 101) contrasts ἀλήθεια and ἡδονή, and Arrian (Anabasis [ed. A. G. Roos, 1907], V, 27, 3) sets τὰ καθ' ἡδονήν in antithesis to ἃ νομίζω σύμφορα. [15] The end of the process is reached when later Stoicism on the one side (→ 914) and the NT on the other (→ 918) pass definite moral verdicts on ἡδονή.

The restriction of sense also finds reflection b. in the way in which the antonyms change.

In Aesch. (Prom., 261) we find ἄλγος, in Plato (Prot., 351e ff.) and Aristot. (Eth. Nic., II, p. 1105b, 23) λύπη, in Aristipp. (Diog. L., II, 86 etc.) and Epicurus (ibid., X, 137 etc.) πόνος. [16] On the other hand the Stoic Musonius has ἀρετή (p. 89, 16 f.), Philo (Leg. All., III, 116) and Maximus of Tyre (Or., 33, 7a) λόγος and the NT χαρά (in the sense of R. 14:7 as a καρπός of the πνεῦμα ἅγιον, while ἡδονή is an ἴδιον σαρκῶν [Max. Tyr., loc. cit.]).

The shifting content of ἡδονή and its progressive ethical devaluation gave rise to the problem which provoked such intense and radical discussion in Greek philosophy.

B. ἡδονή in Greek Philosophy.

The term ἡδονή plays an important role both in the anthropology of Greek philosophy and in the ethics of the various schools. [17]

1. ἡδονή in philosophical anthropology. Amongst other things the nature of man includes πάθη, [18] which imply more than "feelings" (→ 910) and more than "emotions"

---

[12] V. Moult.-Mill., s.v. βιόω.

[13] ἐπιθυμία underwent a similar restriction to "sexual desire" as ἡδονή, cf. Kn. Pt., 164.

[14] The same downward tendency in the understanding of the term is to be seen in other developments, e.g., ἡδονή in the sense of "malicious joy" (Aesch. Suppl., 1008; Soph. Ai., 382; El., 1153: ὑφ' ἡδονῆς, "full of malicious joy"; Plat. Phileb., 50a: ἡδονὴ ἐπὶ τοῖς τῶν φίλων κακοῖς); "pleasure in flatteries" (Thuc., II, 65, 8 : πρὸς ἡδονήν τι λέγειν; cf. also Isoc., 12, 271), or "in fine (rhetorical) speech" (Thuc., III, 40, 2 → n. 15; III, 38, 7: ἀκοῆς ἡδονῇ ἡσσώμενοι); or "of capricious preference" (Heracl. Fr., 67 [I, 91, 3, Diels]; Thuc., II, 37, 2 : καθ' ἡδονήν).

[15] Cf. also Thuc., III, 40, 2 : μηδὲ τρισὶ τοῖς ἀξυμφορωτάτοις τῇ ἀρχῇ, οἴκτῳ καὶ ἡδονῇ λόγων καὶ ἐπιεικείᾳ ἁμαρτάνειν.

[16] Similarly 4 Macc. 1:20 ff. → 916.

[17] Cf. the histories of Gk. philosophy (E. Zeller⁵ [1922]; F. Überweg-K. Praechter¹¹ [1920] etc.) and of ancient ethics (T. Ziegler [1881 ff.]; M. Wundt [1908 ff.]; also W. Gass, Geschichte der christl. Ethik [1881 ff.]; O. Dittrich, Geschichte der Ethik [1926 ff.] etc.). ἡδονή also has a specific role in the Poet. of Arist., cf. → n. 37.

[18] Plato and Aristot. diverge as to its seat in human nature. For the latter it is the lower ψυχή (An., I, 1, p. 402a, 1 ff.) whereas for the former the πάθη come from the σῶμα and play their part in the harmful effect of the body on the soul ; cf. Phaed., 81b: (ἡ ψυχὴ) γοητευομένη ὑπ' αὐτοῦ (sc. τοῦ σώματος) ὑπό τε τῶν ἐπιθυμιῶν καὶ ἡδονῶν κτλ.

(" 'suffering' states of the soul"). One of these basic feelings is ἡδονή, "pleasure" and another λύπη or πόνος, "pain" or "grief," cf. esp. Aristot. (An., III, 7, p. 431a, 9 ff.; Eth. Nic., II, 4, p. 1105b, 23, → 914) and the Cyrenaics (Diog. L., II, 86 : δύο πάθη ὑφίσταντο, πόνον καὶ ἡδονήν (cf. II, 87). [19] If on the other hand we interpret the πάθη as "emotions" (as Aristot. sometimes does), then ἡδονή is either understood to be a result of the πάθη (e.g., Aristot. Eth. Nic., II, 4, p. 1105b, 23 : [20] ὅλως οἷς ἕπεται ἡδονὴ ἢ λύπη) or it is itself one of the πάθη as in Stoicism (Diog. L., VII, 110 : τῶν δὲ παθῶν τὰ ἀνωτάτω, καθά φησιν ... Ζήνων ἐν τῷ περὶ παθῶν, εἶναι γένη τέτταρα, λύπην, φόβον, ἐπιθυμίαν, ἡδονήν). [21]

2. ἡδονή in Philosophical Ethics.

The estimation of ἡδονή is one of the basic questions in philosophical ethics and the doctrine of values. Is ἡδονή an ἀγαθόν [22] or a κακόν? Is it a τέλος, a supreme goal, or not? How is it related to εὐδαιμονία as the true goal of all endeavour? [23] Is it conformable with reason and nature? Does it advance virtue? The various schools of post-Socratic philosophy give different answers to these questions.

For Socrates himself, the founder of philosophical ethics, they are not primary questions. The felicity of which virtue is the basic presupposition includes pleasure and enjoyment in so far as they remain within the limits of self-control ; ἡδύ is a common term in his teaching on virtue. Similarly Plato (Phileb., 60 ff.) can reckon ἡδονή [24] amongst that which is good. He can say (Prot., 357a): ἡδονῆς τε καὶ λύπης ἐν ὀρθῇ τῇ αἱρέσει ἐφάνη ἡμῖν ἡ σωτηρία τοῦ βίου οὖσα, and on the other hand (354c): οὐκοῦν τὴν μὲν ἡδονὴν διώκετε ὡς ἀγαθὸν ὄν, τὴν δὲ λύπην φεύγετε ὡς κακόν κτλ. But this applies with distinct qualifications only to the pleasure which can co-exist with other basic forms of the good, which is moderate, harmonious and judicious, i.e., which is not inordinate or passionate (Phileb., 51-53, 63). To this degree it is with φρόνησις a part of true felicity (Phileb., 21c). On the other hand, pleasure or desire cannot be described absolutely as an ἀγαθόν, since in its sensual form especially it belongs to the sphere of the ἄπειρον by virtue of the fact that it is immoderate and inconstant (Phileb., 24; 28; 52). [25] The evil consequences of things which cause it often mean that we must reckon it among the κακά (Prot., 353d e).

Aristot. makes a similar distinction between φαῦλαι ἡδοναί and τὶς ἡδονή, i.e., that which necessarily springs out of a virtuous life. [26] This ἡδονή is an ἀγαθόν without which εὐδαιμονία would not be felicity and God Himself, the Blessed, could not be conceived (Eth. Nic., X, 5-7, p. 1175a, 18 ff.). [27]

When we turn to the schools, instead of these wise distinctions of the masters we find onesided and generalised approval or disparagement of ἡδονή. Already Plato's immediate pupil, Speusippus, would no longer accept ἡδονή as an ἀγαθόν (Cic. Tusc., V, 10, 30), and Antisthenes, who declared virtue itself to be the only good quite apart

---

[19] In Porphyr. Abst., I, 33, too, ἡδονή and λύπη are described as the two πάθη which derive from αἴσθησις.

[20] Acc. to a list of 11 πάθη : ἐπιθυμία, ὀργή, φόβος etc.

[21] This distinction is essential, for the widespread development in malam partem during the Hellen. period is linked with this second understanding of the term (→ 911).

[22] E.g., Plat. Prot., 351e : τὴν ἡδονὴν αὐτὴν ἐρωτῶν εἰ οὐκ ἀγαθόν ἐστιν.

[23] Cf. M. Heinze, Der Eudämonismus in der griech. Philosophie (1883).

[24] Along with 1. μέτρον, 2. σύμμετρον καὶ τέλειον καὶ ἱκανόν, 3. νοῦς καὶ φρόνησις, 4. ἐπιστῆμαί τε καὶ τέχναι καὶ δόξαι ὀρθαί.

[25] Cf. Resp., I, 328d : Cephalos to Socrates : ὡς εὖ ἴσθι ὅτι ἔμοιγε ὅσον αἱ ἄλλαι αἱ κατὰ τὸ σῶμα ἡδοναὶ ἀπομαραίνονται (withered), τοσοῦτον αὔξονται αἱ περὶ τοὺς λόγους ἐπιθυμίαι τε καὶ ἡδοναί.

[26] Eth. Nic., VII, 14, p. 1153b, 12 f.: ὥστε εἴη ἄν τις ἡδονὴ τὸ ἄριστον, τῶν πολλῶν ἡδονῶν φαύλων οὐσῶν.

[27] Cf. already Simonides, 57 (Diehl, II, 83): τᾶσδ' (sc. ἀδονᾶς) ἄτερ οὐδὲ θεῶν ζαλωτὸς αἰών.

from its consequences, regarded ἡδονή as a κακόν (Sext. Emp. Math., XI, 73); he is credited with the saying : μανείην μᾶλλον ἢ ἡσθείην (ibid.; Diog. L., VI, 3). On the other hand Aristippus and the other Cyrenaics regarded ἡδονή as the epitome of the good and the quintessence of happiness [28] and therefore as the supreme goal in life, [29] no matter what the object of enjoyment and pleasure may be, [30] since all that counts is simply pleasure as such and the strength of the feeling of gratification. [31]

This philosophy [32] gave to its representatives the equivocal title of ἡδονικοί (Athen., VII, 91 [p. 312 f.]; XIII, 53 [p. 588a]). With some modification their teaching was adopted by Epicurus. For him, too, ἡδονή is the πρῶτον ἀγαθόν (Diog. L., X, 129), the τέλος of life, because true εὐδαιμονία is attained only in undisturbed ἡδονή (X, 128). In contrast to this treatment of ἡδονή as the central term by the Cyrenaics and Epicureans, the Stoics consciously set it on the periphery and declared it to be ἀδιάφορον καὶ οὐ προηγμένον ("not of pre-eminent value"; Sext. Emp. Math., XI, 73; cf. Stob. Ecl., II, 80, 22 ff.). Pleasure has value only in so far as it springs out of a virtuous life, but the pleasurable accompaniments or results of this (ἐπιγεννήματα) are better described as χαρά and εὐφροσύνη etc. (Diog. L., VII, 116; 94), whereas ἡδονή is merely an ἐπιγέννημα in the satisfaction of natural requirements (ibid., 86).

3. The criteria for answering the question of the value of ἡδονή are sought primarily in its relation to what is conformable to nature, to reason and to virtue.

Already Aristot. had stated : πάντες τὸν εὐδαίμονα ἡδὺν οἴονται βίον εἶναι, καὶ ἐμπλέκουσι τὴν ἡδονὴν εἰς εὐδαιμονίαν, and among the presuppositions laid down by him he included εὐλόγως (Eth. Nic., VII, 14, p. 1153b, 14 f.). The Cyrenaics [33] and Epicureans (Diog. L., X, 137) supported their central estimation of ἡδονή by maintaining that the demand for pleasure and aversion to pain is the πρώτη ὁρμή, the basic impulse, in human life. The Stoics explicitly contested this view [34] and instead raised and vigorously discussed the question whether ἡδονή is really in accordance with nature at all. [35]

Discussion of the relation of ἡδονή to reason follows similar lines. While the Stoics described ἡδονή as an ἄλογος ἔπαρσις ἐφ' αἱρετῷ δοκοῦντι ὑπάρχειν (Diog. L., VII, 114) and therefore rejected all desire for enjoyment as contrary to reason (Stob. Ecl., II, 96 f.), and while the Cynics, repudiating ἡδονή, regarded insight and know-

---

[28] Eus. Praep. Ev. (ed. W. Dindorf, 1867), 14, 18, 31: δυνάμει (according to the sense) δὲ τῆς εὐδαιμονίας τὴν ὑπόστασιν ἔλεγεν (sc. Aristippus) ἐν ἡδοναῖς κεῖσθαι.
[29] Sext. Emp. Math., VII, 199 : τὰ ἡδέα (φασὶν εἶναι) ἀγαθά, ὧν τέλος ἐστὶν ἀδιάψευστος ἡδονή. Cf. Diog. L., II, 88; Cl. Al. Strom., II, 127, 2.
[30] Diog. L., II, 87: μὴ διαφέρειν τε ἡδονὴν ἡδονῆς, μηδὲ ἥδιόν τι εἶναι.
[31] Ibid., 88 : εἶναι δὲ τὴν ἡδονὴν ἀγαθόν, κἂν ἀπὸ τῶν ἀσχημοτάτων γένηται ... εἰ γὰρ καὶ ἡ πρᾶξις ἄτοπος εἴη, ἀλλ' οὖν ἡ ἡδονὴ δι' αὐτὴν αἱρετὴ καὶ ἀγαθόν.
[32] Cf. on this pt. Stenzel, op. cit.; Natorp, Art. "Aristippos" in Pauly-W., II (1896), 902-906; and for further references E. Zeller, op. cit., II, 1⁵ (1922), 336, n. 2 ff.; F. Überweg-K. Praechter, Grundriss der Gesch. d. Philosophie, I¹² (1926), 170 ff.
[33] Diog. L., II, 87: καὶ τὴν μὲν (sc. ἡδονὴν) εὐδοκητὴν πᾶσι ζῷοις, τὸν δ' (sc. πόνον) ἀποκρουστικόν ... 88 : πίστιν (proof) δ' εἶναι τοῦ τέλος εἶναι τὴν ἡδονὴν τὸ ἀπροαιρέτως ἡμᾶς ἐκ παίδων ᾠκειῶσθαι πρὸς αὐτήν, καὶ τυχόντας αὐτῆς μηθὲν ἐπιζητεῖν· μηθέν τε οὕτω φεύγειν ὡς τὴν ἐναντίαν αὐτῇ ἀλγηδόνα.
[34] Ibid., VII, 85: ὃ δὲ λέγουσί τινες, πρὸς ἡδονὴν γίγνεσθαι τὴν πρώτην ὁρμὴν τοῖς ζῷοις, ψεῦδος ἀποφαίνουσιν (sc. the Stoics).
[35] Sext. Emp. Math., XI, 73 (continuation of the passage quoted → supra): Κλεάνθης μὲν μήτε κατὰ φύσιν αὐτὴν (sc. τὴν ἡδονὴν) εἶναι μήτε ἀξίαν ἔχειν ἐν τῷ βίῳ. ὁ δὲ Ἀρχέδημος κατὰ φύσιν μὲν εἶναι ὡς τὰς ἐν μασχάλῃ (armpit) τρίχας, οὐχὶ δὲ καὶ ἀξίαν ἔχειν. Παναίτιος δὲ τινὰ μὲν κατὰ φύσιν ὑπάρχειν, τινὰ δὲ παρὰ φύσιν. If later Musonius (p. 89, 16 f.) denies that a life ἐν ἡδονῇ is κατὰ φύσιν βιοῦν, this assertion is much less radical and surprising than that of Cleanthes, because it is based on the restricted concept of "sensual pleasure" (→ 915), as when Vettius Valens (p. 76, 1) speaks f παρὰ φύσιν ἡδοναί.

ledge as alone essential to the philosopher, the other main schools tried to find a formula which would unite the two values. In accordance with the order of values which they espoused, the Hedonists treated φρόνησις as a mere means to the right use of ἡδονή; it is not δι' ἑαυτὴν αἱρετή (Diog. L., II, 91). Plato and Aristotle take a different view. Insight and rational activities are the chief value, but they carry with them a high sense of well-being (cf. Plat. Phileb., 21). Indeed, Aristot. solves the problem by declaring that true pleasure and rational activity are essentially identical. True ἡδονή is the consummation of all rational activity. [36]

Particularly important and characteristic is the way in which ἡδονή is related to the leading ethical concept of → ἀρετή.

For Aristot., as we have seen, true pleasure is related very closely to true ethos. Of this it may be said: ἔχει τὴν ἡδονὴν ἐν ἑαυτῷ (Eth. Nic., I, 9, p. 1099a, 16), and conversely it receives from the ἡδονή proper to it a further impulsion. [37] Thus ἀρετή and ἡδονή belong inseparably together, though ἀρετή always has the last word, all ἡδοναί finding their measure and limit in virtue and in the good which is its vehicle. [38]

The Cyrenaics and Epicureans reverse these basic principles in the light of their presuppositions. For them ἀρετή is at root the capacity for enjoyment. [39] Thus, whereas for Aristot. ἀρετή is the norm of ἡδονή, for the Cyrenaics [40] as for the Epicureans (Diog. L., X, 129) ἡδονή is finally the norm of all things. And whereas Aristot. at root values ἡδονή because it kindles striving after virtue, Epicurus commends striving after virtue because it promotes and enriches happiness (Diog. L., X, 138; cf. Cic. Fin., 14, 47).

For the further development of the concept it is essential that already in the classical period a definite line should be drawn between the higher and lower ἡδοναί.

Aristot., as we have seen, distinguished between ἡδοναί which spring from virtue and those which are merely asscciated with it, and he further distinguished these two groups together (his ἀνθρώπου ἡδοναί, "true human joys") from sub-human ἡδοναί (Eth. Nic., X, 5, p. 1176a, 5 f.; VII, 13, p. 1152b, 25 ff.). [41] We also find in him the tech. term σωματικαὶ ἡδοναί (ibid., VII, 7, p. 1149b, 26). Cf. Plato's disparagement of αἱ κατὰ τὸ σῶμα ἡδοναί in Resp., I, 328d. On the other hand, Aristippus and Epicurus ask which are of more value, ψυχικαὶ ἡδοναί or σωματικαὶ ἡδοναί. The former answers (Diog. L., II, 90): πολὺ μέντοι τῶν ψυχικῶν (ἡδονῶν) τὰς σωματικὰς ἀμείνους εἶναι, while the latter comes to the opposite result (ibid., X, 137): μείζονας ἡδονὰς εἶναι (τῶν σωματικῶν τὰς) τῆς ψυχῆς. At any rate bodily pleasure is for

---

[36] Eth. Nic., X, 4, p. 1174b, 31 ff.: τελειοῖ δὲ τὴν ἐνέργειαν ἡ ἡδονή ... ὡς ἐπιγιγνόμενόν τι τέλος οἷον τοῖς ἀκμαίοις ἡ ὥρα.

[37] Eth. Nic., X, 5, p. 1175a, 30 ff.: συναύξει γὰρ τὴν ἐνέργειαν ἡ οἰκεία ἡδονή· μᾶλλον γὰρ ἕκαστα κρίνουσι καὶ ἐξακριβοῦσιν οἱ μεθ' ἡδονῆς ἐνεργοῦντες. This is true of virtuous action as of any other ἐνέργεια. Each has its οἰκεία ἡδονή, even including, e.g., tragic poetry; cf. Poet., 14, p. 1453b, 12 f.: τὴν ἀπὸ ἐλέου καὶ φόβου διὰ μιμήσεως δεῖ ἡδονὴν παρασκευάζειν τὸν ποιητήν. ἡδονή is indeed quoted as one of the ends of all art, cf. Pol., VIII, 5, 7, p. 1339a, 11 ff., p. 1341b, 19 ff.

[38] Eth. Nic., X, 5, p. 1176a, 17 ff.: ἔστιν ἑκάστου μέτρον ἡ ἀρετὴ καὶ ὁ ἀγαθός ... καὶ ἡδοναὶ εἶεν ἂν αἱ τούτῳ φαινόμεναι καὶ ἡδέα οἷς οὗτος χαίρει. From this definition it may be concluded that for Aristot. only noble pleasure deserves the name ἡδονή in the true sense, or that only this deserves the name of "true human pleasure," as he himself puts it in Eth. Nic., X, 5 (→ supra).

[39] W. Windelband, Lehrbuch der Geschichte der Philosophie[3] (1903), 68.

[40] Cf. what Cl. Al. (Strom., II, 130, 7) tells us concerning the Ἀννικέρειοι καλούμενοι ἐκ τῆς Κυρηναϊκῆς διαδοχῆς.

[41] Cf. Eth. Nic., VII, p. 1153b, 8: φαῦλαι ἡδοναί; Andronici Rhodii qui fertur libelli Περὶ Παθῶν, Pars altera de Virtutibus et Vitiis (ed. C. Schuchhardt, 1883), p. 24, 19-25, 1: κατέχειν τὴν ἐπιθυμίαν ὁρμῶσαν ἐπὶ φαύλας ἡδονάς, or ἐπὶ τὰς φαύλας ἀπολαύσεις ἡδονῶν.

him the original seat of all spiritual joy as well, [42] the adverse saying being reported of him (Athen., XII, 67, p. 546 f.): ἀρχὴ καὶ ῥίζα παντὸς ἀγαθοῦ ἡ τῆς γαστρὸς ἡδονή. If this is genuine, it is simply a dramatic expression of his common belief that supreme pleasure is the joy of soul which derives from corporal well-being. Certainly Epicurus was very far from proclaiming sensual pleasure to be the goal of life. We can see this, e.g., in the letter preserved in Diog. L., X, 122 ff., which tells us a great deal about his conception of ἡδονή.

It may be said in conclusion that Greek philosophy developed a noble view of ἡδονή and with greater or lesser reservations ascribed to it great significance for the ideal of human life. Only the Cynic and Stoic schools took a more strongly critical or even radically negative attitude. But these schools exercised great influence on later popular philosophy, and in alliance with the growing pessimism of later antiquity they helped to produce a predominantly negative evaluation of ἡδονή.

C. ἡδονή in Jewish Literature.

1. The use of ἡδονή in the LXX is striking. Except in 4 Macc. (→ infra) it is very rare, occurring only twice in the transl. of the canonical writings (Nu. 11:8; Prv. 17:1). In only one case can we fix the Heb. equivalent and this is טעם. The ancient specialised sense of "pleasant taste" (→ 910) is predominant except in 4 Macc.: Nu. 11:8 : καὶ ἦν ἡ ἡδονὴ αὐτοῦ ὡσεὶ γεῦμα ἐγκρὶς ἐξ ἐλαίου; [43] Wis. 16:20 ... ἄρτον (manna) ... πᾶσαν ἡδονὴν ("every kind of pleasant taste") [44] ἰσχύοντα καὶ πρὸς πᾶσαν ἁρμόνιον γεῦσιν. The nearest to the usual sense is Prv. 17:1, where μεθ' ἡδονῆς corresponds to ἐν εἰρήνῃ and is contrasted with οἶκος ... ἀδίκων θυμάτων μετὰ μάχης (cf. Prv. 15:16 f.; 16:8; Tob., 12:8).

In Wis. 7:2 (→ 912) ἡδονή is used for "sexual desire." The LXX usage displays connections neither with Gk. thought nor with the NT. Apart from works which are strongly influenced in content by Hellenism (e.g., 4 Macc., Philo), the word does not seem to have been current in Jewish writings in its main senses. We have no examples at all of its use in Aquila, Symmachus or Theodotion.

2. To some degree 4 Macc. forms a bridge from the Gk. world to the biblical. As presented in the introduction, the ἡδονή concept is here strongly dependent on the definitions of Gk. philosophy. On the one side the author takes from Gk. anthropology the pair ἡδονή/πόνος — the terminology shows a strikingly exact agreement with that of Aristippus and Epicurus — as the two most embracing πάθη [45] with which a whole series of others is linked (1:21, 28). To this degree ἡδονή merely denotes the ethically neutral emotion of joy or pleasure. But the superficial eclecticism of the author at once integrates this concept into a conception which reminds us of Stoicism. ἡδονή is described as the seat of all evil impulses [46] and is thus opposed to ἀρετή as in later

---

[42] In this the Hedonists were less onesided. Their teaching was (Diog. L., II, 89): οὐ πάσας μέντοι τὰς ψυχικὰς ἡδονὰς καὶ ἀλγηδόνας ἐπὶ σωματικαῖς ἡδοναῖς καὶ ἀλγηδόσι γίνεσθαι. καὶ γὰρ ἐπὶ ψιλῇ τῇ τῆς πατρίδος εὐημερίᾳ ἥπερ τῇ ἰδίᾳ χαρὰν ἐγγίνεσθαι.

[43] γεῦμα, with which ἡδονή is here synon. (Mas. טעם for both), is also found in the same specialised sense for "pleasant taste" at Job 6:6 LXX.

[44] The legend that manna satisfied every favourite taste is also found in Ex. r., 25 on 16:4; Philo Det. Pot. Ins., 115 ff.

[45] 1:20 : παθῶν ... φύσεις εἰσὶν αἱ περιεκτικώταται (comprehensive) δύο, ἡδονή τε καὶ πόνος.

[46] 1:25 : ἐν δὲ τῇ ἡδονῇ ἐστιν καὶ ἡ κακοήθης διάθεσις πολυτροπωτάτη πάντων τῶν παθῶν οὖσα, cf. the Stoic definition of ἀρετή as a διάθεσις ὁμολογουμένη (Diog. L., VII, 89), "a state corresponding to nature."

Stoicism (Musonius). [47] From the same sphere of the Cynic-Stoic diatribe derives also the demand which is the main theme of the book, namely, that reason should be mistress of the emotions [48] (1:30 ff.) and that it should thus rule the ἡδοναί in particular (5:23; 6:35).

In the main, however, this philosophical veneer cannot really conceal the obviously Jewish thinking of the author. The reference of ἡδονή (and πόνος) to both body and soul [49] is enough of itself to betray a non-Greek anthropology, and in addition we have the understanding of λογισμός as the pious mind schooled by and unconditionally obedient to the Torah, εὐσεβὴς λογισμός being a normative slogan throughout the book. [50]

3. In several respects Philo is close to 4 Macc. He, too, mixes anthropological and ethical principles in relation to ἡδονή, and he, too, conceals his Jewish ethos by Greek pathos. But in ἡδονή, as in other matters, the Greek varnish is much stronger and more durable in Philo.

As in Plato the seat of ἡδονή is the body, and indeed the στῆθος καὶ κοιλία (Leg. All., III, 116). This is the dwelling-place of τὸ ἄλογον, to which the πάθη also belong, whereas τὸ λογιστικόν or ὁ λόγος has its seat in the head. On the other hand, ἡδονή, like the other πάθη, finds its sphere of operation in the soul (Migr. Abr., 60).

Ethical and religious definitions go hand in hand with the anthropological. The desire for pleasure is the root of many evils, e.g., war (Decal., 151 ff.). But the reason for repudiating ἡδονή lies deeper in Philo. For him ἡδονή is very closely related in sense to ἐπιθυμία, and it can denote the impulse (→ 910) which provokes to transgression of the commandments. In particular ἡδονή is the basic sin of the 10th commandment (Decal., 143). This reveals its ungodly character. But this is brought out even more clearly by its association with ἀφροσύνη (which is an explicitly religious term in the light of ψ 13:1 and Mk. 7:22) and ἀδικία, also ἐπιθυμία, λύπη and φόβος. A striking mixture of psychological and religious aspects is hereby disclosed (Migr. Abr., 60). The decisive point, however, is the fact that ἡδονή is set in consistent antithesis to λόγος. [51] Its undisciplined hosts are at war with the orderly ranks of the λόγος (ibid.). There is here a formal resemblance to Stoicism (ἡδονή = ἄλογος, → 914). But as in the case of the λογισμός of 4 Macc., λόγος has for Philo a religious orientation. On the other hand, it is a material as well as a formal legacy of the Stoics, and esp. of Panaitios (→ n. 35), that Philo, even though he obviously distinguishes ἡ κατὰ φύσιν ἡδονή from an unspecified unnatural lust (Spec. Leg., III, 9), is nevertheless thinking of ἡδονή primarily as sensual pleasure (III, 8, with reference to the 7th commandment).

If in his definition and ethical evaluation of ἡδονή Philo approximates to Stoicism, he is biblical and theocentric in his religious appraisal. This position between two worlds finds typical expression in Agric., 88: φιλήδονον καὶ φιλοπαθῆ μᾶλλον ἢ φιλάρετον καὶ φιλόθεον ἀνὰ κράτος ἐργάσηται. Here Philo fuses the secular (Stoic) antithesis ἡδονή/ἀρετή with the biblical (2 Tm. 3:4) ἡδονή/θεός.

4. In Rabb. literature there is no exact equivalent for ἡδονή. But the doctrine of the

---

[47] 1:30: ὁ γὰρ λογισμὸς τῶν μὲν ἀρετῶν ἐστιν ἡγεμών, τῶν δὲ παθῶν αὐτοκράτωρ (ibid., αὐτοδέσποτος), this being also a fine example of the difference between a leader and a despot. But the author can also refer on occasion (9:31) to the joys which spring from virtue (ταῖς διὰ τὴν ἀρετὴν ἡδοναῖς) after the manner of Aristot. (→ 915).

[48] Cf. E. Norden, Die antike Kunstprosa vom 6. Jhdt. v. Chr. bis in die Zeit der Renaissance, I (1898), 417.

[49] 1:28: δυοῖν τοῦ σώματος καὶ τῆς ψυχῆς φυτῶν (plant, shoot) ὄντων, ἡδονῆς τε καὶ πόνου.

[50] A. Deissmann in Kautzsch Apkr. u. Pseudepigr., 151.

[51] Cf. Leg. All., III, 116 μάχεται ὁ λόγος τῷ πάθει (ἡδονή is meant) καὶ ἐν ταὐτῷ μένειν οὐ δύναται.

evil impulse (יצר הרע)[52] offers striking parallels to many ideas connected with ἡδονή. The parallel obtains only to the degree that the element of desire (→ 910) is contained in ἡδονή and that the primary characteristic of ἡδονή, the experience of pleasure, is particularly emphasised in evil impulse, e.g., when it is called "sweet" in Lv. r., 16 on 14:4 (cf. ἡδύς, which derives from the same root as ἡδονή, and Ign. Tr., 6, 2). Nevertheless, it occupies much the same position as ἡδονή and → ἐπιθυμία. The essential point is that from the very first it has the defect of ethical perversity (→ 924). It dwells in the heart of man (on the right side),[53] thought there are passages which seem to localise it, as do the Greeks, in corporeality (e.g., Gn. r., 34 on 8:21 in Weber, 211). It is true, of course,[54] that the Rabbinic world links *yezer*, as does 4 Macc. πάθη (→ 917), with the whole man. Individual resemblances between the NT idea of ἡδονή and the Rabbinic *yezer* teaching will be discussed later (E., *passim*).

D. The Non-Biblical Use of φιλήδονος.[55]

φιλήδονος, a Hellenistic construction, follows the same course of development as ἡδονή even in detail.

1. In relation to persons it means "intent on pleasure." In antithesis to φυγόπονος (Polyb., 39, 1, 10) it reflects the ἡδονή/πόνος of philosophical anthropology. Together with ἐπιθυμία (Cl. Al. Strom., V, 51, 3) it speaks of the common demand for ἡδονή; φιλήδονως ζῆν (*ibid.*, III, 30, 1) denotes an orientation of life in virtue of which Aristippus is called φιλήδονος (Eus. Praep. Ev., 14; 18; 31). Like ἡδονή, it is used *in malam partem* when combined with φιλοσώματος (Plut. Amat., 20 [II, 766b]; Cl. Al. Strom., IV, 12, 4) and given the sense of "abandoned to sensual pleasure." A further step is taken in Plut. Lib. Educ., 9 [II, 6b]: ὁρῶ ... τοὺς τοῖς συρφετώδεσιν (common, vulgar) ὄχλοις ἀρεστῶς καὶ κεχαρισμένως ἐπιτηδεύοντας λέγειν καὶ τὸν βίον ... ἀσώτους καὶ φιληδόνους ἀποβαίνοντας, "I observe that those who are wont to speak in a way which is agreeable and desirable to the vulgar mob themselves become corrupt in their manner of life and the slaves of pleasure."

In the sphere of biblical religion a religious light falls on φιλήδονος. As ἡδονή is contrasted with the divine λόγος in Philo, so the attitude of the φιλήδονος is contrasted with that of the φιλόθεος (Agric., 88 → 918; cf. 2 Tm. 3:4).

In striking contrast, Epictetus sets the φιλήδονος in antithesis to the φιλάνθρωπος (Gnom. Stob., 46). Philosophy thinks anthropocentrically, the Bible theocentrically.

2. In respect of objects it means "bringing joy," Anth. Pal., X, 118: ἀλλ' ἄγε μοι Βάκχοιο φιλήδονον ἔντυε νᾶμα. ‖ τοῦτο γάρ ἐστι κακῶν φάρμακον ἀντίδοτον. Cl. Al. Strom., II, 119, 5 φιλήδονος λιχνεία (dainties), where it possibly means "tasty" (from ἡδονή in the sense of "pleasant taste").

E. ἡδονή in the NT.

Of the senses found in secular usage (→ 910) the following are to be noted in the NT: a. "pleasure," "joy," "delight"[56] (in general), 2 Pt. 2:13;[57] b. "desire for joy,"

---

[52] Cf. Weber, 211, 213, 219-239, 240, 243; Bousset-Gressm., 402-405; Cr.-Kö., 501 f. F. C. Porter, "The Yeçer Harâ" in *Biblical and Semitic Studies of Yale Univ.* (1902), 91-210; Str.-B., IV, 466-483 (Excursus 19).
[53] Cf. the examples in Str.-B., IV, 467; III, 94 f.
[54] Porter, *op. cit.*, 98 ff. in Bousset-Gressm., 405.
[55] On φιλήδονος cf. Pr.-Bauer, 1371; Moult.-Mill., 670.
[56] There are examples of this ethically neutral use of ἡδονή (→ n. 11 on ἐπιθυμία) in early Christian literature, cf. Ign. Tr., 6, 2; Phld., 2, 2, where ἡδονή is qualified by the addition of κακή (cf. ἐπιθυμία κακή in Col. 3:5); Act. Thom., 120: τί σοι πρὸς ἡδονήν

"lust for pleasure," Jm. 4:1 [58] and perhaps Tt. 3:3; c. "worldly joy," "sensual pleasure" [59] (though not unequivocally restricted to sexual lust [60] as, e.g., in Jos. Ant., 2, 51; Wis. 7:2), Lk. 8:14; Jm. 4:3; Tt. 3:3 (→ 911).

These slight shades of difference in meaning, however, are insignificant compared with the consistent use of ἡδονή throughout the NT.

1. The Origin and Nature of ἡδονή.

ἡδονή is one of the marks of a definite orientation of life [61] opposed to the Christian. As such it has its place in the antitheses on which the world of NT thinking is based. It belongs to the sphere ruled by ungodly forces, as may be seen from the way in which it is related to αἰὼν οὗτος and the σάρξ. The ἡδοναί belong to βίος (Lk. 8:14), i.e., (cf. Ign. R., 7, 3) to βίος οὗτος [62] (in contrast to

ἐστιν γενέσθαι; and indirectly Herm. s., 6, 5, 5-7. As with a rigorous Stoic, πᾶσα πρᾶξις ... ὃ ἐὰν ἡδέως ποιῇ is here described as τρυφή. Thus ἡδονή falls in the most general sense under an ethical verdict. But this judgment is limited as in § 7. There is also a good ἡδονή (→ 911) to which a very different τρυφή corresponds. On the dualistic scheme of Hermas, thus introduced into a new field, cf. Dib. Herm., 520, 584.

[57] Only in this sense and in this one passage do we find the sing. of ἡδονή in the NT.

[58] Cf. Hugonis Grotii Annotationes in NT (ed. C. E. de Windheim, 1757), ad loc.: cupiditates rerum voluptariarum; J. H. Thayer, Grimm's Wilke's Clavis Novi Testamenti translated, revised and enlarged² (1899), s.v. ἡδονή; "desires for pleasure"; esp. Dib. Jk., 198, n. 3. The expressions used in Jm. 4:1 ff. bring out the intensity of the desire.

[59] For the same deflection in malam partem (→ 911) cf. the early Christian writings, Ign. Rom., 7, 3 (cf. Lk. 8:14); Hermas s., 8, 8, 5; 8, 9, 4: ἐπιμένειν ταῖς ἡδοναῖς; Diog., 6, 5: σάρξ ... ταῖς ἡδοναῖς κωλύεται χρῆσθαι; ibid.: (Χριστιανοὶ) ταῖς ἡδοναῖς ἀντιτάσσονται; 9, 1: ἡδοναῖς καὶ ἐπιθυμίαις ἀπαγομένους. On the other hand, there may also be distinguished a line of understanding a parte potiore in post-NT literature, as in Gk. philosophy from the time of Plato and Aristot. (→ 911); cf. Herm. s., 6, 5, 7: πολλοὶ ... ἀγαθὸν ἐργαζόμενοι τρυφῶσι τῇ ἑαυτῶν ἡδονῇ φερόμενοι "impelled by their joy in the good" (cf. m., 12, 2, 4; 5: ἐπιθυμία τῆς δικαιοσύνης = ἐπιθυμία ἀγαθή). There are traces of a similar use in Jewish literature, e.g., 4 Macc. 9:31: ταῖς διὰ τὴν ἀρετὴν ἡδοναῖς τὸν πόνον ἐπικουφίζομαι, "through the joys which derive from faithfulness to the Law, or from the display of faithfulness in martyrdom (→ ἀρετή, I, 459), I feel alleviation in my torment." Here one might almost speak of the heavenly bliss which is the portion of God's hero. We are to think of a similar joy when 2 Cl., 15, 5 contrasts ἡδονή and κατάκρισις in the eschatological sense: ὅσην γὰρ ἡδονὴν ἔχει τὰ ῥήματα ταῦτα τοῖς ποιήσασιν αὐτά, τοσαύτην κατάκρισιν ἔχει τοῖς παρακούσασιν. For in ἡδονή there is taken up again the thought of 14, 5, which refers to the ineffable things that God has prepared for His elect. Cf. the LXX use of τρυφή, which in 2 Pt. 2:13 and elsewhere (Herm. s., 6, 5, 5 ff.) is so closely linked with ἡδονή, e.g., ψ 35:8: χειμάρρουν τῆς τρυφῆς (עֵדֶן) σου, "the river of thy (God's) pleasures." It is used in the same sense for the proper name עֵדֶן Ez. 28:13; 31:9: παράδεισος τῆς τρυφῆς τοῦ θεοῦ; 36:35; Jl. 2:3. Hermas again offers a counterpart to this special use of τρυφή with his paradoxical expression τρυφαὶ σώζουσαι (s., 6, 5, 7).

[60] This might seem to be suggested, e.g., in Jm. 4:3, since those addressed are expressly called μοιχαλίδες (v. 4); but here is the same figur. use of μοιχαλίς as in the saying of Jesus concerning the γενεὰ μοιχαλίς (Mk. 8:38 etc.), and cf. also the πορνεία and πορνεύω of Rev. On the other hand, the μοιχαλίς which immediately follows, and which is to be taken literally, throws a distinctive light, not on the meaning of ἡδονή itself, but on the τρυφή described as ἡδονή.

[61] Cf. Diog. L., V, 31: βίος ἡδονικός; Cl. Al. Strom., III, 30, 1: φιλήδονως ζῆν.

[62] The expositions which take as their starting-point such senses as support of life (B. Weiss⁹ [1901], ad loc.) or means of life (H. J. Holtzmann³ [1901], ad loc.) are refuted by the oldest and authentic interpretation in Ign. R., 7, 3.

the ἄλλος βίος, Ign. Eph., 9, 2), [63] and therefore to αἰὼν οὗτος (cf. Mt. 13:22 and par.). Hence what is true of this applies to them also (→ αἰών, I, 205). [64]

Similarly we learn from James (4:1) that τὰ μέλη are the seat of the ἡδοναί and the sphere of their operation. If, like those addressed in Jm. 4:1 ff., we live κατὰ σάρκα, then τὰ μέλη are completely in the service of ἁμαρτία (cf. R. 6:13, 19; 7:5, 23), and the ἡδοναί are orientated accordingly. They are sinful impulses of the σάρξ and they thus stand in absolute contrast to χαρά, the fruit of the Holy Ghost (Gl. 5:22). [65]

> Whereas the Gks. either affirm ἡδονή because of its naturalness (→ 914) or deny it because it belongs to the material world (→ 911, cf. n. 18), the NT sets ἡδονή under the same judgment as fallen human nature. This approximates closely to the judgment on the *yezer hara'* in Judaism. Man went forth from the Creator's hand furnished with the יצר הרע [66] and the יצר הטוב. The evil impulse was at first weak. It amounted to little more than an indifferent natural impulse. [67] Only through sin did it become evil and powerful, [68] cf. Tanch. Gn. 4b (Str.-B., IV, 469): "If anyone were to say: Why has He (God) created the evil impulse ... then reply: It is evil, who will make it good? But know that God says: You make it evil. Why does not a child of 5, 6, 7, 8, 9 years sin, but only from 10 years and upwards? It itself, then, brings up the wicked enemy."

2. ἡδονή and Man's Relationship to God.

a. ἡδονή is a magnitude which is opposed to God. [69] It is the other side of the alternative with which man is confronted by the question of God. For this reason a decisive word is uttered concerning men when in 2 Tm. 3:4 they are called φιλήδονοι μᾶλλον ἢ φιλόθεοι as disturbers of the early Christian community. Yielding to ἡδοναί in Jm. 4:1 ff. (cf. especially the ἵνα of v. 3) is unfaithfulness [70] to God (v. 4 μοιχαλίδες) and as φιλία τοῦ κόσμου [71] it is enmity against God [72] and of Satanic origin [73] (cf. Jm. 4:7: ἀντίστητε τῷ διαβόλῳ).

---

[63] I prefer the reading ἄλλος to Zn.'s conjectured ὅλος; cf. Bau. Ign., 209.

[64] On the connection of ἡδονή with this αἰών cf. also Cl. Al. Strom., VI, 68, 1: σοφία τοῦ αἰῶνος τούτου ἡ φιλήδονος καὶ φίλαυτος. Cf. also the many Rabb. passages which relate the evil impulse to this aeon, e.g., Sukka, 52b : "The evil impulse seduces man in this world" etc. (Str.-B., IV, 847, cf. also the other passages, 847 f.).

[65] Outside the NT the two terms are related if not identified (→ 911), cf. esp. 4 Macc. 1:22 : πρὸ μὲν ... τῆς ἡδονῆς ἐστιν ἐπιθυμία, μετὰ δὲ τὴν ἡδονὴν χαρά: χαρά is one of the ἀκολουθίαι (v. 21) of ἡδονή, the gratification which follows when desire is satisfied. The Greeks differentiate along rather different lines. For Stoicism → 914 : in the wise man χαρά, a by-product of experienced ἀρετή, takes the place of ἡδονή, which results from the satisfaction of natural desires, e.g., Diog. L., VII, 116. The Cyrenaic Theodore ὁ ἄθεος regards χαρά as a permanent cheerful disposition based on rational enjoyment (χαρὰ ἐπὶ φρονήσει), whereas ἡδονή is only momentary pleasure (Diog. L., II, 98).

[66] Cf. the examples in Str.-B., IV, 469 f.

[67] Cf. Gn. r., 9 on 1:31 in Str.-B., IV, 467: "If it were not for the evil impulse no one would build a house or take a wife or beget children or engage in trade" (it thus falls under the verdict of Gn. 1:31: "It was very good").

[68] Cf. Weber, 211; Str.-B., IV, 468 f.

[69] Cf. the statements of Cl. Al. concerning the divine nature, which has no connections with ἡδονή, Strom., VII, 15, 1: οὐ φιλήδονον τὸ θεῖον; Paed., III, 37, 2 : ἀλλοτριώτατον τῆς θείας φύσεως ἡ φιληδονία. Aristot. seems to say the very opposite (→ 913; also n. 27).

[70] Hence Cl. Al. Strom., VII, 75, 3 can describe φιληδονία (with φιλαργυρία and εἰδωλολατρεία) as a form of πορνεία.

[71] Cf. what the NT says concerning → κόσμος and → ἐπιθυμία (Tt. 2:12; 1 Jn. 2:16 f.; 2 Pt. 1:4).

[72] The same point is made in Jd. 18 by the linking of ἐπιθυμίαι and ἀσέβειαι.

[73] Cf. Herm. m., 12, 2, 2 : ἡ ἐπιθυμία ἡ πονηρὰ τοῦ διαβόλου θυγάτηρ ἐστίν.

The evil impulse is described as the enemy of God. It is given seven names in Sukka, 52a : the evil one, the uncircumcised. the impure, the enemy etc. It is thus opposed to God.[74] Its ultimate aim is apostasy from God ; Shab., 105b, Bar (Str.-B., IV, 475): ". . . This is the trick of the evil impulse : to-day it says to a man : Do this ; to-morrow it says : Do that ; and finally it says : worship idols" (cf. also Sanh., 64 in Weber, 235);[75] Shab., 105b: "The evil impulse is itself a strange god in man" (cf. Str.-B., III, 331). It is indeed identified with Satan in BB, 16a (Str.-B., III, 468): "One and the same are Satan, the evil impulse and the angel of death" (i.e., the three are identical). Chag., 16a (Str.-B., IV, 474): "The evil one is no other than the evil impulse."[76]

ἡδονή influences all aspects of man's relations with God, his attitude to the divine will, to the divine Word and to prayer.

b. ἡδονή in man is opposed to the will of God. Man lives either according to his own desires or according to God's will (cf. 1 Pt. 4:2 : εἰς τὸ μηκέτι ἀνθρώπων ἐπιθυμίαις[77] ἀλλὰ θελήματι θεοῦ ... βιῶσαι). The ἴδιαι ἐπιθυμίαι etc. (R. 1:24; 2 Tm. 4:3; Jm. 1:14; 2 Pt. 3:3; Jd. 16; 18) as a goal in life denote rejection of God's will in an impotent attempt at revolt. Persistence in lusts (Herm. s., 8, 8, 5; 8, 9, 4 : ἐπιμένειν ταῖς ἡδοναῖς) is the state which follows decision against God.

The evil impulse as an enemy of the will of God is again a τόπος in Rabb. doctrine : cf. jBer. 7d, 52 (Str.-B., IV, 235): "For this reason hast Thou created us, that we should do Thy will, and we are under obligation to do Thy will. Thou dost will it, and we will it, and who hinders it ? The leaven in the lump (the evil impulse in our body)." Cf. also Ber., 17a (Str.-B., IV, 474 etc.).

c. So long as no decision is taken against God, ἡδονή struggles bitterly against the Word of God in man (Lk. 8:14) to try to hamper its work. Indeed, we even read in Mk. 4:19 that ἐπιθυμίαι choke the Word.

Similarly, the evil impulse is said to fight against the Torah, since it interrupts study of the Torah : M. Ex. on 18:27 (Str.-B., IV, 473): ". . . that the evil impulse does not disturb me so that I do not engage in study of the Torah." It raises objections against the Word of God ; cf. S. Lv., 18, 3 f.; Pesikt., 38b (Str.-B., IV, 473 f.). It hinders fulfilment of the Law : Ber., 17a; Nu. r., 17 on 15:38; S. Dt., 43 on 11:16; Str.-B., IV, 474 : "Be on guard lest the evil impulse seduce you and separate you from the Torah" etc.

d. In Christians who find a place for ἡδονή in their lives, however, it is not only what is said by God, the Word, but also what is said to God, i.e., prayer, that is affected by the destructive operation of ἡδονή. Jm. 4:3 : αἰτεῖσθε ἵνα ἐν ταῖς ἡδοναῖς ὑμῶν δαπανήσητε. To make the satisfaction of carnal ἡδοναί the object of prayer is κακῶς αἰτεῖσθαι. To use what is requested from God in accordance with ungodly principles is a complete perversion of the relationship to God. It is the hypocritical misuse which Ignatius calls λαλεῖν Ἰησοῦν Χριστόν, κόσμον δὲ ἐπιθυμεῖν (R., 7, 1).

Thus prayer, too, is brought into the attitude which Jm. (4:1) calls the conflict of ἡδοναί and which he describes in 4:2 f.,[78] the attitude of unbridled earthly desire, of a greedy lust to possess, which derives from the σάρξ rather than the Spirit and which is orientated to the carnal, to ἡδονή, rather than to the spiritual. This attitude is completely opposed to that of prayer for what can be asked in the name of Jesus and of true waiting on God (cf. Jm. 4:2 : διὰ τὸ μὴ αἰτεῖσθαι ὑμᾶς).

---

[74] Cf. Weber, 234.

[75] The *yezer hara'* is also called the source of idolatry in Sanh., 64a; Ex. r., 41 on 32:6 (Weber, 235).

[76] Cf. also Weber, 237 f.; Str.-B., I, 139.

[77] Cf. the ἀνθρώπου ἡδοναί of Aristot., his phrase for noble joys (→ 915).

[78] On what follows cf. esp. Hck. Jk., 187 ff.; Meinertz Kath. Br., 42 f.

It relies on one's own efforts (μάχεσθαι, πολεμεῖν, ζηλοῦν), and if it inconsistently (cf. μὴ αἰτεῖσθαι — αἰτεῖτε) seeks the help of prayer, prayer is made to serve this false basic attitude, and it is orientated to earthly desires rather than to God. Hence it is not real prayer. [79]

But prayer which is not inspired by God nor directed to Him shares the fate of ἡδοναί; it is in vain. The βίος ἡδονικός is a vicious circle in the literal sense. Its starting-point is ἡδονή (Jm. 4:1) and its goals are ἡδοναί (Jm. 4:3), which simply give rise to new desire. It never reaches its goal [80] and ends only in death.

3. ἡδοναί and Man.

ἡδοναί are not merely the enemies of God; they are the enemies of man too. [81] We can see this from three images which are at least suggested in the Bible to describe the way in which ἡδοναί work: that of conflict; that of slavery; and that of thorns in the field. All three express the same paradox that the pleasures themselves are hard and terrible, hostile and destructive.

a. Those who belong to Christ have peace. This is peace with God (R. 5:1) and peace of soul (R. 15:13). But it is also εἰρήνη in the comprehensive sense of the salvation which is given (→ εἰρήνη, F., 2b; 3; 5 [→ 414; 415; 417]; cf. esp. Jm. 3:18). In those who live to ἡδονή, however, there rules a constant state of war. Jm. 4:1 ... τῶν ἡδονῶν ὑμῶν τῶν στρατευομένων ἐν τοῖς μέλεσιν ὑμῶν. With whom do ἡδοναί strive? [82] With God? This we read in v. 4. Against men? The first words of v. 1 speak of this. Against themselves? In favour of this we might refer to the dualistic conceptions of Hermas concerning the twofold ἐπιθυμία (m., 12, 1, 1 to 12, 3, 1, with allusion to the conflict in 2, 4 f.) or concerning the twofold ἡδονή or τρυφή (s., 6, 5, 5-7). We might also allude to the conflict of the two impulses in Rabbinic theory. [83] Materially this comes to the same thing as when we are told in Gl. 5:17 that the σάρξ and the πνεῦμα ἀλλήλοις ἀντίκειται, or in Dg., 6, 5: μισεῖ τὴν ψυχὴν ἡ σάρξ καὶ πολεμεῖ. One might ask, therefore, whether ἡδοναί do not war against the soul which is orientated to God, as in the undoubtedly analogous passage in 1 Pt. 2:11: ἀπέχεσθαι τῶν σαρκικῶν ἐπιθυμιῶν, αἵτινες στρατεύονται κατὰ τῆς ψυχῆς. In other words, is not the same thought expressed in R. 7:23 in the image of the conflict (ἀντιστρατεύεσθαι) of the two νόμοι, the νόμος τοῦ νοός μου and the νόμος τῆς ἁμαρτίας ὁ ὢν ἐν τοῖς μελεσίν μου? Perhaps there is something of all this in the στρατεύεσθαι of Jm. 4:1, which has no object. Undoubtedly the equally figurative μάχεσθε καὶ πολεμεῖτε of v. 2 refers back to it, though here the reference is to wild and uncontrolled passions which war against one another no less than against God's will, and which finally do most harm to man himself. A "hedonistic" attitude of life implies a life of constant unrest and conflict in the sense of Is. 57:20 f.; 48:22: "There is no peace unto the wicked."

Thucydides (III, 38, 7) and Plato (Prot., 352d; 355b) also speak of man's conflict against ἡδοναί and his defeat (ἡσσᾶσθαι) by them. Nearer in time and content is the

---

[79] Bengel on Jm. 4:2: *neque enim cupidus, homicida, pugnax homo orare potest.*

[80] Teles, p. 35: ἐπιθυμοῦντες οὐδενὸς γεύονται.

[81] Cf. the continuation of Sukka, 52a (→ 921), where the further names of the *yezer* are offence, the stone, the hidden one. All these indicate that it is the enemy of man. The impulse is often compared to a hard and inflexible stone, e.g., Lv. r., 35 on 26:3 (Str.-B., IV, 477); Tanch. B יצר § 1 (95a) (*ibid.*, IV, 481).

[82] This question must be raised even though no final answer can be given (as against Hck. Jk., 189).

[83] V. Str.-B., III, 95; IV, 471.

use of the same image in Jewish writings. Philo describes in a way not unlike R. 7:23; Gl. 5:17; 1 Pt. 2:11 the war of the logos against lust or pleasure ; Leg. All., III, 116 : μάχεται ὁ λόγος τῷ πάθει (sc. ἡδονῇ) ... κρατοῦντος μὲν γὰρ λόγου φροῦδος (gone away) ἡ ἡδονή, νικώσης δὲ ἡδονῆς φυγὰς ὁ λόγος. Similarly he speaks in Migr. Abr., 60 of πολλαὶ τάξεις ἀκοσμοῦσαι ὧν ἡδοναί ... ταξιαρχοῦσι which in the soul confront the μία εὖ διακεκοσμημένη (τάξις) ἧς ὁ ὀρθὸς λόγος ἀφηγεῖται. Test. A. 6:2 speaks of spirits of seduction which war against man (cf. Dg., 9, 1 → n. 59).

The Rabbis, too, speak of the artful assaults of the evil impulse, cf. Sukka 52b : "The (evil) impulse of man rises up daily with great force against him and seeks to kill him, as it is written : 'The wicked watcheth the righteous, and seeketh to slay him' (Ps. 37:32)." For this reason it is called the robber in Gn. r., 54 on 21:22 etc.

In the NT (apart from Gl. 5:17) ἡδοναί (or ἐπιθυμίαι or the σάρξ) are called the aggressor, the main thought being that of defence (cf. Eph. 6:11 ff.). In Philo, however, the logos takes the offensive (→ 922). For active warfare against ἡδοναί cf. also Luc. Vit. Auct., 8 : στρατεύομαι δὲ ὥσπερ ἐκεῖνος (Heracles) ἐπὶ τὰς ἡδονάς. Cf. Dg., 6, 5 : → n. 59. Hermes writes similarly of the conflict against ἐπιθυμίαι in m., 12, 2, 4 f. Admonitions to fight against the evil impulse are particularly common in the Rabb. writings, e.g., Ber., 5a (Str.-B., I, 994): "Man should always stir up the good impulse against the bad ... if he overcomes it, it is good, but if not he should study the Torah ... If he overcomes it, it is good, but if not he should recite the schᵉma ... If he overcomes it, it is good, but if not he should think of the day of death." The main allies and weapons in the struggle are the good impulse (cf., e.g., Midr. Qoh., 9, 15 [45a]; Str.-B., IV, 472), the Torah, [84] prayer, especially the recitation of the name of God, the thought of the end (including judgment), also the worship of the synagogue, since this combines study of the Torah and prayer [85] (cf. Qid., 30b : "If he encounters thee, this despoiler, go into the house of instruction ; he will be shattered"), fasting, [86] works of charity (Str.-B., IV, 564), visiting the sick (ibid., 573 ff.) and especially exorcism by the name of God (ibid., 477 f.).

In James the emphasis is not so much, perhaps, on the inner conflict, but rather on its results, on conflict with others. For ἡδοναί disrupt not merely the relationship with God and man's εἰρήνη, but also relationships with other men. As Bengel says (ad loc.), ἡδοναί are the prima sedes belli [87] and of all that follows. [88]

b. Closely related to the image of conflict is that of slavery, for if we are defeated by ἡδοναί, or refuse to fight them, we become their servants. Tt. 3:3 : ἦμεν γάρ ποτε καὶ ἡμεῖς ... δουλεύοντες ἐπιθυμίαις καὶ ἡδοναῖς ποικίλαις. Even more clearly than in the previous image ἡδονή is here personified, as such concepts commonly are in Paul (cf. esp. ἁμαρτία in R. 7, but also, e.g., ἐπιθυμία in Jm. 1:13-15), particularly in terms of the image of slavery (→ ἁμαρτία, R. 6:6 ff. etc.). ἡδοναί are masters which rule men instead of God the Lord. In the pre-Christian and non-Christian life the service of ἡδονή takes the place of the service of God. [89]

---

[84] For further examples cf. Str.-B., IV, 476 f.

[85] Weber, 238.

[86] Cf. Str.-B., IV, 108.

[87] For this thought, which is common also in non-Christian antiquity, cf. the many examples given in Dib. Jk., 199, n. 1, also 4 Macc. 1:26 (φιλονεικία), Tanch., 15a : "God said : In this world my creatures were of divided opinions because of the evil impulse."

[88] If the ἐκ τῶν ἡδονῶν of Jm. 4:1 denotes the place where strife originates, 4 Macc. 1:25 uses the image rather differently, finding the seat of conflict ἐν τῇ ἡδονῇ.

[89] Cf. Meinertz Past., 93; also Cl. Al. Strom., IV, 12, 4 : δούλους ... τοὺς φιληδόνους καὶ φιλοσωμάτους οἶδεν ἡ γραφή; cf. also Philo Virt., 36 : ἡδονῇ ἁλωτὸν ἄνθρωπος; Andronici Rhodii qui fertur libelli Περὶ Παθῶν Pars altera de Virtutibus et Vitiis (ed. C. Schuchhardt, 1883), p. 24, 3 : ἐγκράτεια ἕξις ἀήττητος ὑφ' ἡδονῶν.

Both Greeks and Jews speak reprovingly of the dominion of ἡδονή : Plat. Prot., 352b : ἐνούσης πολλάκις ἀνθρώπῳ ἐπιστήμης οὐ τὴν ἐπιστήμην αὐτοῦ ἄρχειν ἀλλ' ἄλλο τι, τοτὲ μὲν θυμόν, τοτὲ δὲ ἡδονήν κτλ. Philo Spec. Leg., III, 8 : πανταχοῦ τῆς οἰκουμένης μέγα πνεῖ ἡ ἡδονή καὶ οὐδὲν μέρος τὴν δυναστείαν αὐτῆς ἐκπέφευγεν ... πάντα ... τοῖς ἐπιτάγμασιν αὐτῆς ὑπείκει πρός τι βλέμμα καὶ νεῦμα ἀφορῶντα κτλ.

This theme is particularly explicit in Rabb. lit. Suk., 52b speaks plainly of the growth of the *yezer hara*ʿ : "The evil impulse is first a wanderer (who passes by), then a guest and finally master of the house who gives orders." Ab. R. Nat., 16 (5d): "The evil impulse within is king over the 248 members in man." The designation "king" is common elsewhere, e.g., Ned., 32d. S. Dt. § 45 on 11:18 : "So long as you occupy yourself with it (sc. the Torah), it (sc. the evil impulse) does not reign in you ... but if you do not occupy yourself with it, you are delivered up into its hands." Cf. also Qid., 40a; Gn. r., 22 on 4:7 (Str.-B., IV, 481).

In the figure of slavery and service, as in that of conflict, the reversal of the relationship plays an important role. In both the Gk. and the Semitic world control of ἡδονή [90] is demanded instead of slavish submission. Plat. Resp., III, 389 d e : σωφροσύνης ... οὐ τὰ τοιάδε μέγιστα, ἀρχόντων μὲν ὑπηκόους εἶναι, αὐτούς δὲ ἄρχοντας τῶν περὶ πότους καὶ ἀφροδίσια καὶ περὶ ἐδωδὰς (foods) ἡδονῶν; 4 Macc. 1:30 : λογισμός = παθῶν (sc. ἡδονή καὶ λύπη) αὐτοκράτωρ (αὐτοδέσποτος); 5:23 (similarly 6:35): ... πασῶν τῶν ἡδονῶν καὶ ἐπιθυμιῶν κρατεῖν.

There is again explicit teaching in the Rabbis concerning the subjugation and guidance of the evil impulse. Ab., 4, 1: "Who is a hero ? He who subdues his evil impulse" (cf. Cant. r., 16a). "It is part of the heroism of the wise man to keep himself against the *yezer*." [91] Midr. Ps. 86 § 5 (187b): "If it (sc. a cow) will not accept the yoke, we force it to do so against its will and lead it where we want. And should you not lead the evil impulse (sc. by forcing it along with the good impulse as a refractory cow is forced along with a willing one)?" [92]

To subdue desire the means commended by the Greeks is φρόνησις, by 4 Macc. (εὐσεβής) λογισμός, by the Rabbis the study of the Torah, the use of the name of God etc. (→ 923), and by the NT (Jm. 4:1 ff.) prayer, seeking the presence of God and submission to Him.

c. The third image speaks most clearly of the destructive operation of ἡδονή. Lk. 8:14 : As thorns choke the seed, so after a long struggle [93] ἡδοναί choke those who yield to them. The two other figures eventually produce the same result. The wages of the master sin are death (R. 6:23) and the fight against ἡδονή, if not waged in the power of God, ends with defeat and death (cf. also Herm. s., 8, 8, 5; 8, 9, 4).

Death is also the ultimate end of the evil impulse. Ab., 2, 11: "The envious eye, the evil impulse and hatred remove a man from the world." Tanch. (ed. Buber) קדושים § 14 (40a): "Because the evil impulse is in you in this world, you sin and your children die" (cf. Dt. r., 2 on 3:41; Str.-B., IV, 848). Cf. also the fine comparison in Ab. R. Nat., 16 (6a) (Str.-B., IV, 482) and the equation of the evil impulse with the angel of death in BB, 16a.

---

[90] Though we do not find this image in the NT, we find the same thought expressed in even stronger figures, cf. esp. Col. 3:5 (νεκρώσατε οὖν τὰ μέλη τὰ ἐπὶ τῆς γῆς ... πάθος, ἐπιθυμίαν κακήν) and Gl. 5:24 (τὴν σάρκα ἐσταύρωσαν σὺν τοῖς παθήμασιν καὶ ταῖς ἐπιθυμίαις).

[91] Weber, 238 f.

[92] For more details v. Str.-B., IV, 476.

[93] Schl. Mt., 437.

4. The Bearers and Victims of ἡδονή.

In the NT three groups of men are bearers or victims of ἡδονή as a decisive power in their lives, a. the heathen, or Christians prior to baptism, b. the δίψυχοι among Christians, and c. false teachers.

a. Tt. 3:3 : ἦμεν γάρ ποτε καὶ ἡμεῖς δουλεύοντες ἐπιθυμίαις καὶ ἡδοναῖς ποικίλαις. Descriptions of the pre-Christian state and references to it with a view to warning against relapse and emphasising the glory of the new life are amongst the most common τόποι in early Christian and especially in Pauline preaching. [94] The numerous passages in this connection (→ n. 94) cover the whole range of correlative concepts which in ever new variations illustrate and depict this state without God (ἀπείθεια, ἄγνοια, ἐχθροί, τέκνα ὀργῆς, ἄθεοι ἐν τῷ κόσμῳ, χωρὶς Χριστοῦ, without ἐλπίς etc.). For the ἡδοναὶ ποικίλαι (cf. 2 Tm. 3:6; 1 Tm. 6:9) which characterise the heathen world one may refer to the lists of vices in the NT. [95] ἡδοναί (or ἐπιθυμίαι, cf. Tt. 3:3, also Eph. 2:3; 4:22; 1 Pt. 1:14) and ἔθνη are correlative terms (cf. also, e.g., Herm. s., 8, 9, 1 ff.). This is also the meaning of βούλημα τῶν ἐθνῶν (1 Pt. 4:3) in antithesis to the θέλημα τοῦ θεοῦ (v. 2).

b. The clearest depiction of the way in which the life of the δίψυχοι among Christians (Jm. 4:8) is determined by ἡδονή, both in its totality and especially in its relationship to God, is to be found in Jm. 4:1 ff. (→ 922). There is a parallel in the description of the third group in the parable of the Sower (Lk. 8:14): τὸ δὲ εἰς τὰς ἀκάνθας πεσόν, οὗτοί εἰσιν οἱ ἀκούσαντες, καὶ ὑπὸ μεριμνῶν καὶ πλούτου καὶ ἡδονῶν τοῦ βίου πορευόμενοι συμπνίγονται καὶ οὐ τελεσφοροῦσιν. These are men who for a period are open to the operation of the Word but who at the same time (συμφυεῖσαι, v. 7) and in increasing measure (cf. ἀνέβησαν, Mk. 4:7 and par.) give themselves up to an attitude which is the reverse of faith. [96] As distinct from the second group, who fall because of the afflictions which necessarily follow the obedience of faith, [97] these men fall because they yield voluntarily to the forces which separate from God and make it difficult to maintain an attitude of faith.

c. The term ἡδονή is linked particularly with false teachers, whose ethical characterisation is almost always far more comprehensive in the NT than their theological. Thus we find the phrase φιλήδονοι μᾶλλον ἢ φιλόθεοι (2 Tm. 3:4) in a long list of vices which is partly a concrete description of the false teachers against whom Paul is contesting and partly a dogmatic depiction of the final pre-

---

[94] Usually Eph., Col. and 1 Pt., where most of the passages are found, speak in the 2nd person of exhortation (Eph. 2:2, 11-13; 4:22; 5:8; Col. 1:21; 3:7; 1 Pt. 1:14; 4:3; also R. 11:30). But Paul can sometimes include himself with his readers (Tt. 3:3, also Eph. 2:3 and R. 7:5), as the author of Dg. does in a passage (9, 1) similar to Tt. 3:3 : (God) εἴασεν ἡμᾶς ... ἀτάκτοις φοραῖς φέρεσθαι, ἡδοναῖς καὶ ἐπιθυμίαις ἀπαγομένους.

[95] Cf. also the lists of πάθη κατὰ ψυχήν and κατὰ σῶμα in 4 Macc. 1:26 f., of τρυφαὶ βλαβεραί in Herm. s., 6, 5, 5 and of the works of πονηρὰ ἐπιθυμία, ibid., m., 12, 2 etc.

[96] This attitude is characterised not only by ἡδοναί or ἐπιθυμίαι (Mk. 4:19) and μέριμναι (cf. Mt. 6:25 ff.) but also by the ἀπάτη τοῦ πλούτου (Mt. 13:22; Mk. 4:19). This is either a synpt. equivalent to ἡδοναί in the sense of "pleasure," or else, in view of the corresponding αἱ περὶ τὰ λοιπὰ ἐπιθυμίαι in Mk., we are to take it in the usual sense of the deceitfulness of the demon wealth (cf. Mt. 6:24). Even in the latter case we still have the mark of a corrupt outlook, since the deception victimises only those who lack the divine wisdom which is given directly with faith.

[97] Cf. G. Stählin, Skandalon (1930), 220.

eschatological period which Paul believes has already come (cf. Jd. 18). ἡδονή or φιληδονία is thus a mark of the godless situation prior to the second coming of Jesus, as before His first coming (→ 925). There is a more exact delineation of the ἡδονή of false teachers in 2 Pt. 2:13 : ἡδονὴν ἡγούμενοι τὴν ἐν ἡμέρᾳ τροφήν, σπίλοι καὶ μῶμοι, ἐντρυφῶντες ἐν ταῖς ἀπάταις αὐτῶν ... κτλ.

Although ἡδονή has here the general meaning of "pleasure," it is used in a particularly pregnant sense. These teachers regard τρυφή [98] as the epitome of joy and the supreme goal in life. In the precise expression of Bengel, *voluptatem illam, quam homo summe debeat appetere*. It is thus used in the sense of the Cyrenaics and Epicureans (→ 914). The object of ἡδονή is ἡ ἐν ἡμέρᾳ [99] τρυφή [100] which according to the expositions that follow consists in carousing (συνευωχούμενοι ὑμῖν) and intemperance (v. 14 : ὀφθαλμοὺς ἔχοντες μεστοὺς μοιχαλίδος, → n. 60). The same type is described in Phil. 3:19.

The connection of false doctrine with ἡδονή is to be found also in Ign. In Phld., 2, 2 ἡδονὴ κακή is a means used by false teachers to take souls captive (αἰχμαλωτίζειν, as in 2 Tm. 3:6). In Tr., 6, 2 we have the image of poison (false doctrine) in the honey-wine (Christ).

Happiness and enjoyment have always been a goal of human desire and striving, whether in the noble form of Socratic εὐδαιμονία or the cruder form of heretical τρυφή. The NT, too, can speak of joy as the final and supreme thing both in this life and the next. But NT joy shares in the transvaluation of all concepts and values and thus comes to have in this world a paradoxical content. Not ἡδοναὶ ποικίλαι (Tt. 3:3), but πειρασμοὶ ποικίλοι are its object, as in the fine counterpart to 2 Pt. 2:13 in Jm. 1:2 : πᾶσαν χαρὰν ἡγήσασθε ... ὅταν πειρασμοῖς περιπέσητε ποικίλοις. Suffering and martyrdom in following Christ and in fellowship with Him are supreme bliss for the disciple, both in themselves, and because πειρασμοί are the way to τελειότης (Jm. 1:4) and to the eternal χαρά in which there is no more paradox (Mt. 25:21, 23).

Stählin

ἥκω

Attested from the time of Homer, though not common. It is formally a present (imp. class. ἧκε, ἡκέτω) but denotes a state and thus has the force of a perf. to ἐρχ-, ἐλθ- (cf. κεῖμαι to τίθημι, κάθημαι to καθίζω). In the Hell. period it was thus made into a formal perf. [1] On the other hand it is also used in the pres. sense of "to come," and an aor. ἧξα (Paus.,Gal.) is constructed in the Hell. period. ἥξω is class., but first means "I will be there." [2] In the pap. [3] it means a. "to come to," "to reach"; b. "to turn

---

[98] On the combination of ἡδονή and τρυφή cf. also Herm. s., 6, 5, 7 (→ n. 59).

[99] The meaning of this phrase is contested (cf. Kn. Pt., *ad loc.*; Vrede Kath. Br., 132). Does ἐν ἡμέρᾳ denote the transitory aspect of this enjoyment ? Cf. Aristipp. : ἡ κατὰ μέρος ἡδονή, "momentary enjoyment" (Diog. L., II, 87) and Plat. Prot., 355b : ... διὰ τὰς παραχρῆμα ἡδονάς (also 353d e).

[100] In the phrase ἐντρυφῶντες ἐν ταῖς ἀπάταις αὐτῶν, ἀπάτη can only mean "pleasure," since ἐντρυφάω so near to τρυφή must be taken literally (not : "they enjoy the fruit of their deceptions"). Kn. Pt., 299 argues not very convincingly for a different view. The combination τρυφή καὶ ἀπάτη is common in Herm. s., 6, 4, 1-6, 5, 4. That the two words are practically synon. is proved by 6, 5, 6, where τρυφαί is immediately followed by ἀπάται, cf. also m., 11, 12.

ἥ κ ω. [1] Bl.-Debr.[6] § 101.
[2] Following Debrunner.
[3] For examples cf. Preisigke Wört., *s.v.*

to someone with a request"; c. "to resolve on something"; and d. "to attain something" (e.g., old age).

The term is esp. important in the cultic and sacral sphere. It denotes the coming of the deity to men, primarily to those participating in the cult. The deity solemnly appears. In the 2nd prologue of the pap. text of Ghoran col. II (BCH, 30 [1906], 141) Cypris says: ἥκω φράσουσα δεῦρο (cf. the self-declaration of Eros in the 1st prologue col. I : ἐλήλυθ[α ἀ]γγελῶν τοιοῦτο πρᾶγμά τι· πρᾶγμ[ά] τι τοιοῦτον [ἀγ]γελῶν [ἐλ]ήλυθα). In P. Giess, I, 3, 2 we have a depiction of the coming of the god Phoebus (at the coronation of Hadrian). The god comes and says:

ἥκω σοι, ὦ δῆμ[ε,
οὐκ ἄγνωστος Φοῖβος θεὸς ἄνα-
κτα καινὸν Ἀδριανὸν ἀγγελῶ[ν.

In the same connection we may refer to the use of ἥκω as an entrance formula in the prologues of Eur. (Hec., Ion, Ba., 1 ff.). In the form of a self-declaration the cultic word attests the presence of the god. The god says who he is and declares why he has come. In this sense ἥκω is parallel to the common ἐγώ εἰμι or ἐγὼ ὁ θεός εἰμι. [4] V. also Sib., III, 49 f.: ἥξει δ' ἁγνὸς ἄναξ, πάσης γῆς σκῆπτρα κρατήσων ‖ εἰς αἰῶνας ἅπαντας ἐπειγομένοιο χρόνοιο, and III, 63 f.: ἐκ δὲ Σεβαστηνῶν ἥξει Βελίαρ μετόπισθεν ‖ καὶ στήσει ὀρέων ὕψος, στήσει δὲ θάλασσαν.

The term can also denote the coming of men, of cultic participants, to the deity (Ditt. Or., I, 186, 6 ff.: ἥκω πρὸς τὴν κ[υ]ρίαν ⸗Ισιν καὶ πεποίηκα τὸ προσκύνημα τοῦ κυρίου βασιλ[έ]ος; ibid., 184, 4 ff.: ἥκω καὶ προσκεκύνηκα τὴν μεγίστην θεὰν κυρίαν Σώτειραν ⸗Ισιν; ibid., 196, 2 ff.: ἥκω<ι> καὶ προσκεκύνηκα τὴν κυρίαν ⸗Ισιν. Cf. also P. Par., 48, 9 ff.: ἥκαμεν εἰς τὸ Σεραπεῖον βολάμενοι συνμίξαι σοι, and P. Oxy., VI, 933, 13 : μεγ[ά]λην ἑορτὴν ἥξα).

Particular mention should be made of the proskynemata of which we have many examples in Preis. Sammelbuch, I (e.g., I, 146 : Μενεκράτης ἥκω; I, 1046 : Σεραπίων ἥκω πρὸς Σέραπι[ν] πατέρ[α] ; I, 1059 : Παύρων Φιλοπίου Σόλιος ἥκω προσκυ-νῆσαι θε[οὺς] μεγάλους ⸗Ισιν καὶ Σάραπιν). [5] Finally, reference may be made to the ancient call to prayer ἧκέ μοι (κύριε), Preis. Zaub., XIII, 89; 604; XIV, 25.

In the Septuagint it is used for 14 Heb. words. The cultic use is found as well as the local. It mostly signifies man's coming to God (to sacrifice, to prayer, 1 Βασ. 16:2, 5; 3 Βασ. 8:42 etc.). But it can also denote the coming of God to men (Dt. 33:2; cf. 1 Βασ. 4:7 etc.; in ψ 100:2 the righteous prays : πότε ἥξεις πρός με;). In the prophets ἥξει is used of the eschatological coming of God, cf. esp. Is. 45:24 : δικαιοσύνη καὶ δόξα πρὸς αὐτὸν ἥξει, and Is. 60:1 : ἥκει γάρ σου τὸ φῶς. God will come as the Redeemer of His people (ἥξει ὁ ῥυόμενος, Is. 59:20; ἥξει ὁ ἀνασῳζόμενος; Ez. 24:26; ἥξει καὶ σώσει ἡμᾶς, Is. 35:4). But God also comes to judgment at the end of the age (Is. 3:14 and esp. Da. 4:20[23]: ἥξει ἡ κρίσις τοῦ θεοῦ; 9:26 : ἡ συντέλεια αὐτοῦ μετ' ὀργῆς; cf. also Da. 11:45). There is a collection of judgment sayings in Ez. 7:2 ff., in which the expressions τὸ πέρας ἥκει, ἥκει ὁ καιρός, constantly recur. In the age of salvation the Gentiles (Hag. 2:7: τὰ ἐκλεκτὰ πάντων τῶν ἐθνῶν) will also come and see the glory of God (Ps. and prophets, esp. Is., Jer., Ez.).

It is often used with → καιρός to denote the coming of the eschatological age (e.g., Ez. 7:7, 12 : ἥκει ὁ καιρός).

Heavy things come upon men in their lives (στεναγμός, πόνος, καταστροφή, θλῖψις, συντριβή, ἀπώλεια, ὄλεθρος etc.), but also good things. Yet the heavy blows of fate predominate (as in statements with ἔρχεσθαι).

---

[4] Cf. O. Weinreich, ARW, 18 (1915): De Dis Ignotis Quaestiones Selectae, 28 f., esp. 39 ff. Cf. E. Norden, Agnostos Theos (1913), 188 ff., 194, 300 and Reitzenstein Poim., 222 f. (quotation from Orig. Cels., VII, 9 : ἐγὼ ὁ θεός εἰμι ἢ θεοῦ παῖς ἢ πνεῦμα θεῖον· ἥκω δέ).

[5] Cf. the list of proskynemata in Preis. Sammelbuch, II, 2, 406, s.v. On προσκυνεῖν cf. J. Horst, Proskynein (1932).

In Jos. Bell., 7, 323 there is reference to the coming of a specific point in time : ἥκει νῦν καιρός. In Test. XII we find both the local use and also cultic and eschatological statements (the divine epiphany): S. 6:5(a): κύριος ὁ θεὸς φαινόμενος ἐπὶ τῆς γῆς ἥξει; L. 18:6 : οἱ οὐρανοὶ ἀνοιγήσονται καὶ ἐκ τοῦ ναοῦ τῆς δόξης ἥξει ἐπ' αὐτὸν ἁγίασμα.

In the NT the word is used predominantly of the eschatological coming to salvation and judgment. Jesus looks forward (Mt. 8:11; Lk. 13:29) to the future of the kingdom of God and sees the Gentiles too having a share in it. In the same sense Mt. 24:14 contains a reference to the progress of eschatological events. First the Gospel will be preached in all the world and then the end will come. Rev. attests to the return of Christ in the word of the exalted Lord : ἥξω (Rev. 2:25; 3:3). In 2 Pt. 3:10 the coming day of the Lord is announced with the terrible cosmic events which accompany it. The fall of Babylon intimated in Rev. also stands under the saying : ἥξουσιν αἱ πληγαὶ αὐτῆς (Rev. 18:8). The saying of Jesus concerning the destruction of Jerusalem in Lk. 19:43 is introduced by the words : ἥξουσιν ἡμέραι ἐπὶ σέ (cf. Mt. 23:36; Lk. 13:35).

In John's Gospel ἥκειν is used like ἔρχεσθαι (→ 671) to express the epiphany. The Messianic self-witness of Jesus can run : ἐκ τοῦ θεοῦ ἐξῆλθον καὶ ἥκω (Jn. 8:42). [6] The saying concerning the coming of the hour of Jesus can take the form : οὔπω ἥκει ἡ ὥρα μου (2:4). The coming of men to Jesus can be formulated as follows : πᾶν ὃ δίδωσίν μοι ὁ πατὴρ πρὸς ἐμὲ ἥξει (6:37). In 1 Jn. 5:20 the confession of the community is : οἴδαμεν δὲ ὅτι ὁ υἱὸς τοῦ θεοῦ ἥκει.

Ac. 28:23 vl. speaks of the coming of men who sought salvation to the preaching of the divine Word. The term has an explicit cultic ring when combined with → προσκυνεῖν (Rev. 3:9; cf. 15:4). [7]

Schneider

---

† Ἠλ(ε)ίας [1]

A. Elijah in Later Judaism.

No biblical figure so exercised the religious thinking of post-biblical Judaism as that of the prophet Elijah who in the reign of Ahab (1st half of the 9th cent. B.C.) saved Yahweh religion from destruction by the cult of Baal (1 K. 17:1—2 K. 2:12).

---

[6] On this pt. see the comm., also O. Weinreich, *op. cit.*, 42 and E. Norden, *op. cit.*, 189.

[7] Grammatically significant is Mk. 8:3 vl. : ἥκασιν. Because of its meaning and "under the influence of the κ" (Helbing) ἥκω takes the form of a perf. Helbing gives examples from the LXX (104), Mayser from the pap. (372) and G. Schmidt from Joseph. (*Jbch. f. klass. Philol. Suppl.*, XX (1894), 470 (plup. ἥκεσαν).

Ἠλ(ε)ίας. A.: J. Lightfoot, *Opera Omnia*, II (1686) on Mt. 17:10; Lk. 4:25; J. A. Eisenmenger, *Entdecktes Judenthum* (1700), I, 11, II, 212, 402-407; J. A. Fabricius, *Codex Pseudepigraphicus Veteris Testamenti* (1713), 1070 ff.; C. Schöttgen, *Horae Hebraicae*, II (1742), 533 ff.; L. Bertholdt, *Christologia Judaeorum* (1811), 58-68; A. F. Gfrörer, *Das Jahrhundert des Heils* (1838), II, 227-229; S. K(ohn), "Der Prophet Elia in der Legende," MGWJ, 12 (1863), 241-255, 281-296; D. Castelli, *Il Messia secondo gli Ebrei* (1874), 196-201; J. Drummond, *The Jewish Messiah* (1877), 222-225; J. Derenbourg, "Le prophète Élie dans le rituel," REJ, 2 (1881), 290-293; A. Edersheim, *The Life and Times of Jesus the Messiah*, II (1884), 706-709; G. Dalman, *Der leidende und der sterbende Messias der Synagoge* (1888), 8 f., 28 ff., 78, 83 f.; Bacher, *Tannaiten*, II, Index ; W. Bousset, *Der Antichrist* (1895), 134-139; Weber, 352-354; M. Friedmann, *Seder Eliahu* (1902), Intro. 2-44; Volz. Esch.², 195-197, 200 f.; L. Ginzberg, *Jew. Enc.*, V (1903), 121-7; J. Klausner, *Die mes-*

The following are the sources for the later Jewish conception : 2 Ch. 21:12-19; Mal. 3:23 f.; Sir. 48:1-12a; Eth. En. 89:52; 90:31; 93:8; 1 Macc. 2:58; Damasc. (→ 932); Philo only at Deus Imm., 136-139; Joseph. a repetition of the biblical narrative augmented from Menander, Ant., 8, 324; 4 Esr. 6:26; 7:109; S. Bar. 77:24; Sib., II, 187-189; Mart. Is. 2:14-16; Just. Dial., 8, 4; 49, 1; Rabb. material in Str.-B., bin Gorion, Levinsohn, Zion → Lit. A. *Tanna d^ebē Eliahu* (= *Seder Eliahu Rabba* and *Seder Eliahu zuṭa*) contains ethical teaching, legal enactments and narratives which are traced back to Elijah (ed. M. Friedmann [1900, 1902]), composed in the 5th cent.[2] Later Elijah apocalypses:[3] 1. There is a pre-Pauline Jewish apocalypse which is extant only in a short fragment[4] depicting the torments of the sinner in the next life and from which Paul is stated by Origen (Commentarorium Series on Mt. 27:9 [GCS, Orig., XI, 250, Klostermann]), Ambrosiaster (Commentaria in XIII Epistolas Pauli on 1 C. 2:9, MPL, 17, 205) etc. to have taken the quotation in 1 C. 2:9. Acc. to Epiph. Haer., 42, 12, 3 (II, 179 f., Holl)

---

sianischen Vorstellungen des jüd. Volks (1903), 58-63; M. J. Lagrange, *Le Messianisme chez les Juifs* (1909), 210-213; Schürer, II, 407, 592, 610 ff., III, 361-366; L. Ginzberg, *The Legends of the Jews,* IV (1913), 195-235; M. J. bin Gorion (= Mika Josef Berdyczewski), *Der Born Judas* (1917 f.); *Die Sagen der Juden,* V (1927), 219-232; P. Billerbeck, "Der Prophet Elias nach seiner Entrückung aus dem Diesseits," *Nathanael,* 30 (1914), 43 ff., 93 ff., 112 ff.; "Der wiederkehrende Elias," *ibid.* 31 (1915), 18 ff.; 32 (1916), 33 ff.; G. Kittel, *Rabbinica* (1920), 31-35; Kittel *Probleme,* 53, 59; G. Dalman, *Jesus-Jeschua* (1922), 48, 185 f.; *Ergänzungen u. Verbesserungen zu Jesus-Jeschua* (1929), 5, 10-12; L. Ginzberg, *Eine unbekannte jüd. Sekte* (1922), 299 ff.; W. Staerk, *Die jüd. Gemeinde des Neuen Bundes in Damaskus* (1922), 92 ff.; R. Scott, "The Expectation of Elijah," *Canadian Journal of Religious Thought* (1926), 3 ff.; A. v. Gall, Βασιλεια του θεου (1926), 378 ff.; V. Aptowitzer, Malkizedek, MGWJ, 70 (1926), 93 ff.; Bousset-Gressm., 232 f., 261 f., 513; Moore, II, 357 ff.; V. Aptowitzer, *Parteipolitik der Hasmonäer* (1927), 96-104, 244 f.; J. Klausner, *Ha-ra'jon Ha-meschichi bejisrael*[2] (1927), 291 ff.; *Jesus von Nazareth* (1930), 109, 333 ff.; B. Murmelstein, "Adam," WZKM, 35 (1928), 242 ff.; 36 (1929), 51 ff., esp. 65-70; M. W. Levinsohn, *Der Prophet Elia* (Diss. Zürich, 1929); J. Jeremias, "Der Erlösungsgedanke" in *Deutsche Theol.,* II (1929), 114 f.; *Jesus als Weltvollender* (1930), 9 f.; R. Zion, *Beiträge zur Gesch. u. Legende des Propheten Elia* (Diss. Würzburg, 1931); EJ, VI (1930), 481-496; J. Schur, *Profeten Elijahu (Elia) enligt Bibeln, Talmud och Midrasch* (1932); W. Staerk, *Soter,* I (1933), 59 ff. Local Palestinian Traditions concerning Elijah : J. P. van Kasteren, ZDPV, 13 (1890), 207-211; P. Geyer, "Itinera Hierosolymitana Saeculi," IV-VIII, CSEL, 39 (1898), Index ; E. v. Mülinen, ZDPV, 30 (1907), 117 ff.; Schürer, II, 47; G. Dalman, PJB, 10 (1914), 37 ff.; 18/19 (1923), 20 ff., 26 f.; A. Alt, ZDPV, 48 (1925), 393 ff.; C. Kopp, "Elias und Christentum auf dem Karmel," *Collectanea Hierosolymitana,* 3 (1929). On B. : A. Schweitzer, *Das Messianitäts- und Leidensgeheimnis* (1901), 44-48; *Geschichte der Leben-Jesu-Forschung* (1913), 417-421; *Die Mystik des Apost. Pls.* (1930), 160 ff.; M. Dibelius, *Die urchristliche Überlieferung von Joh. dem Täufer* (1911); E. Lohmeyer, ZNW, 21 (1922), 188 ff.; *Das Urchristentum,* I (1932); W. Michaelis, "Das Sendungsbewusstsein Joh. des Täufers," *Der Kirchenfreund* (publ. by the Schweizerischer ev.-kirchl. Verein), 66 (1932), 52 ff., 72 ff., 83 ff.); the comm. On Elijah in early Christian legend, cf. S. K(ohn), MGWJ, 12 (1863), 293 ff.; K. M. Ittameier, "Die Eliassage," *Zeitschrift f. kirchl. Wiss. u. kirchl. Leben,* 4 (1883), 416-430, 476-493.

[1] The spelling vacillates between -είας (consistently in B*, 14 times in א, 8 in A, 19 in D, 3 in L, twice in HΔ, once each in FGPU[2] 057) and -ίας (consistently in C, 15 times in א, 14 in A, 7 in D and most Gk. MSS). The oldest MSS (apart from B* and C) thus vacillate arbitrarily between ει and ι, and only in the 6th cent. does ι come to predominate. There is similar vacillation (often in the same MSS) between the breathings, as is frequently the case with Semitic words in NT MSS (for examples cf. C. Tischendorf-C. R. Gregory, *NT Graece,* III [1884], 106 ff.); the rough breathing is much the more common, as also attested in it and vg (Helias, only occasionally Elias), possibly under the influence of ἥλιος [Debrunner]. On the declension cf. Bl.-Debr.[6] § 55, 1.

[2] J. Mann, *Hebrew Union Coll. Annual,* 4 (1927); only written in the 10th cent. acc. to L. Zunz, *Die gottesdienstlichen Vorträge der Juden*[2] (1892), 119.

[3] Schürer, III, 361-366.

[4] Ed. D. de Bruyne, *Revue Bénédictine,* 25 (1908), 153 f.

Eph. 5:14 was also taken from Elijah, though this is most unlikely.[5] 2. There is also a Jewish Elijah apoc. from the 3rd cent. A.D.[6] published by A. Jellinek, *Beth ha-midrasch*, III (1855), 65-68; cf. also A. Wünsche, *Aus Israels Lehrhallen*, II (1908), 33-38; M. Buttenwieser, *Die hbr. Elias-Apokalypse* (1897); P. Riessler, *Altjüd. Schrifttum* (1928), 234-240. This depicts the wars of the last time, the victory of the Messiah, resurrection and judgment and the new Jerusalem. 3. We may also refer to a Copt. Elijah apoc. published by G. Steindorff, TU, 17, 3a (NF, 2) (1899), with Germ. transl., 114-125. This apocalypse, which bears in Akhmimic script the subscription "The Apocalypse of Elijah," is basically Jewish, but was thoroughly worked over by Christians at the beginning of the 4th cent. It consists in the main of prophecies of the troubles which indicate the coming end. Most important (→ 940) are the passages on the conflict of Elijah and Enoch with the Antichrist (Sah., 7-8; Akhm., 35 and 42 f.).

The reason for the prominence of Elijah in popular legend, in theological discussion and in eschatological expectation is twofold: 1. his mysterious rapture (2 K. 2:11; cf. Sir. 48:9, 12; Eth. En. 89:52; 93:8; Jos. Ant., 9, 28), in which was seen the reward of his zeal for the Law (1 Macc. 2:58) and which gave rise to the idea of his sinlessness;[7] and 2. the prophecy of his return as in Mal. 4:5 f. (= LXX 4:4 f.): "Behold, I will send you Elijah the prophet before the coming of the great and dreadful day of the Lord: and he shall turn the heart of the fathers to the children, and the heart of the children to their fathers, lest I come and smite the earth with a curse." These words are perhaps an addition to the book to show that the messenger and precursor of Yahweh[8] mentioned in 3:1 is the returning Elijah.

1. The Elijah of history in later Judaism. The miracles of Elijah provided rich material for legend, and the obscurity of his origin gave opportunity for lively discussion of his descent, the three main theories being that he was a Gadite (→ 931), a Benjamite (→ n. 20) or a Levite (→ 932).[9]

2. Elijah as a helper in time of need. After his rapture Elijah ranks with the angels.[10] This is first attested in Mal. 4:5 f., where he is the angelic messenger mentioned in 3:1. Up to the last time he stays in Paradise (Eth. En. 89:52; cf. 87:3) and assists his people (the oldest attestation is Mk. 15:35 f.), being magnified in many legends in this capacity.[11] He flies down to earth and appears in various forms. No place is too distant nor is any means left unused for the protection of innocence, the saving of the righteous, the healing of the sick, the establishment of peace and the giving of consolation and admonition.[12]

---

[5] Schürer, III, 362.

[6] P. Riessler, *Altjüd. Schrifttum ausserhalb der Bibel* (1928), 1279 f.

[7] Pesikt., 9 (76a) and many par.

[8] This figure is perhaps related to the Persian Saošyant-Astvatereta (Bousset-Gressm., 232, 513, n. 1; v. Gall, 252, 379 even thinks Zarathustra himself was a model). A Samaritan analogy is the *Taheb* (= the one who comes again, the Samaritan term for the Messiah) (→ I, 388).

[9] Str.-B., IV, 781 ff.; Levinsohn, 6 ff.; Zion, 9 ff. For critical material cf. Levinsohn, 35 ff.

[10] Acc. to Eth. En. 90:31 Elijah will appear at the end with Enoch and three angels. Rabb. lit. also links Elijah with the archangels, Ber., 4b etc.

[11] Str.-B., IV, 769 ff.; S. K(ohn), 251 f.; *Jew. Enc.*, V, 124 f.; bin Gorion, *Born Judas*, II, 210-222, 247-252, 333-335; Dalman, *Jesus-Jeschua*, 186; Levinsohn, 13 ff. The roots of the idea of Elijah as helper in time of need are to be found in the Zarephath story in 1 K. 17:8 ff.

[12] Rabb. lit. likes to depict Elijah in the company of the learned and pious. He teaches and instructs them, listens in the house of instruction and reveals the mysteries of the higher world (S. K[ohn], 281 ff.; Str.-B., 773 ff.). But he ceases to visit his friends if they do even the slightest wrong (S. K[ohn], 252 ff.; Str.-B., IV, 775 ff.).

In the inter-test. period [13] Elijah was also allotted functions in the heavenly world. a. He is the heavenly scribe who enters men's deeds in a book, esp. the matrimonial connections of the Israelites (→ 934). [14] b. He is also psychopompos. [15] c. He is Israel's intercessor. [16]

3. The Return of Elijah.

a. The oldest passage which refers to the return of Elijah (Mal. 4:5 f.) sees in him a Messianic figure. He prepares the divine way for the heavenly King (3:1) by purifying the priesthood (3:2-4) and establishing peace (4:6). Sir. 48:10 adds to the twofold task of Mal., i.e., mitigating the wrath of Yahweh before the judgment (= Mal. 4:5, 6b) and turning the heart of the father to the son (= 4:6a), the third task of restoring the tribes of Israel (להכין שבטי ישראל). There is thus attributed to the returning Elijah a task which Dt. Is. ascribes to the Servant of the Lord (Is. 49:6). Since Sir. makes no other reference to the Messiah, he, too, seems to have expected Elijah as the Messiah. [17] The same view is found in later Rabbis who think of Elijah as a Gadite and see in him the military deliverer who will overcome the world powers. [18]

b. Far more widespread, however, was a second view which saw in Elijah the forerunner of the Messiah rather than of God. This is prepared in the pseudepigrapha inasmuch as Elijah here comes with Enoch before the *parousia* of the Messiah (Eth. En. 90:31; cf. 89:52; 4 Esr. 6:26). [19] That Elijah alone was also expected as the forerunner of the Messiah is attested in Just. Dial., 8, 4; 49, 1 (→ 934), several Rabb. passages [20] and the ancient blessing of the wine [21] at the New Year feast as preserved in Soph., 19, 9 : "Elijah the prophet, come to us soon ; may the King Messiah sprout forth in our days." We know from the NT how widespread this view was in popular eschatology (→ 936).

It is an open question whether the Damascus document, [22] which belongs to much the same time as Jesus, represents the expectation that Elijah will come again as the forerunner of the Messiah, though this is the common interpretation under the influence of L. Ginzberg. [23] What the document has to say about the figures of the last time is

---

[13] Works on Elijah in later Judaism (→ 928, Bibl.) almost all fail to distinguish between pre- and post-NT material, so that it is difficult to use them in NT exegesis.

[14] Weber, 282; Str.-B., IV, 766 f.

[15] *Jew. Enc.* (1903), V, 128; Str.-B., IV, 766 f. This view is perhaps present in Sir. 48:11.

[16] Str.-B., IV, 768 f. The passage from Qoh. r., 11, 2 quoted in Volz Esch.², 195 refers to the historical and not the translated Elijah.

[17] Dalman, *Der leidende Messiah,* 28; Str.-B., IV, 780; Staerk, *Soter,* I, 69. If the Taxo of the Ass. Mos. is identical with Elijah (→ 933), Elijah is here, too, the Messiah, since there is no other mention of the Messiah.

[18] Str.-B., IV, 782-784. Elijah as redeemer, Aptowitzer, *Parteipolitik,* 96-104, 244 f.; Murmelstein, 65-70. On the related Samaritan expectation of the *Taheb,* the returning one, → I, 388.

[19] 4 Esr. 6:26 : "And the men will appear who were translated, who did not taste death from their birth, and the hearts of those who dwell on the earth will be changed and they will be turned to a new mind." In the OT, translation is recounted only of Enoch and Elijah (Gn. 5:24; 2 K. 2:11, and, in spite of the account of the rapture of Ezra in 14:9, 14, 49, the original reference in 4 Esr. 6:26 was simply to these two (so E. B. Allo, *Saint Jean. L'Apocalypse*³ [1933], 160), since the final return of these two holy men was a constituent part of the apocalyptic depiction of the end (938 ff.). The later period increased the number, so that there are 9 or 10 in *Derekh 'Ereç zuṭa,* 1 (20c) (Str.-B., IV, 766).

[20] Rabb. examples may be found in Str.-B., IV, 748-789 : "Elias of the tribe of Benjamin, the forerunner of the Messiah." But the passages quoted in Billerbeck, IV, 792-798 mostly belong to this group, though Billerbeck puts them all amongst those which regard Elijah as the high-priest of the last days (→ 932).

[21] P. Fiebig, RH (1914), 29; J. Elbogen, *Der jüd. Gottesdienst in seiner geschichtl. Entwicklung*² (1924), 123; v. Gall, 378.

[22] Cf. L. Rost, Kl. T., 167 (1933). The following references are to the pages and lines in the MS.

[23] *Sekte,* 303 ff.

obscure and its interpretation uncertain. The main results are as follows : a. The founder of the community is called in 1, 11 "the teacher of truth," מורה צדק ;20, 28 : מורה ; 20, 32 — ‎הוחיד =| and ‎מורה צדק = "the excellent one"; 20, 1: מורה היחיד ; 20, 14 : יוריה היחיד = "the excellent teacher." He is taken away, i.e., taken from the community by death (19, 35; 20, 14). b. Looking to the future, the community expects the יורה הצדק (lit. "he will teach the truth" used as a title) who will come at the end of the days, 6, 11. Now the expression יורה צדק, which is borrowed from Hos. 10:12 : "until he comes and teaches the truth," and which is first used in post-Talmudic lit., though perhaps already in bBek., 24a (R. Johanan, c. 250), is a consistent term for the coming of Elijah. [24] There can also be no doubt that even in the pre-Christian period it was expected that Elijah would decide disputed questions of the Law (→ 933 f.). Hence many scholars have concluded that the expected "teacher of truth" is Elijah. [25] Comparison of the findings under a. and b. suggests that the community expected the return of their own teacher as Elijah. If so, the Damascus community was a precursor community and the document gives an impression of the liveliness of expectation of the forerunner of the Messiah in the NT period.

The document also speaks of the Messiah. In two passages it envisages Him as belonging to the past (2, 12 : משיחו ; 6, 1: משיחו הקודש). [26] In the future the community expects the Messiah of Aaron and of Israel (12, 23/13, 1: משוח אהרן וישראל ; 14, 19 [corrupt]: ‎ח אהרן וישראל ...; 19, 10 f.: משיח אהרן וישראל ; 20, 1: משיח מאהרן ומישראל). [27] We thus have the past and coming teacher on the one hand and the past and coming Messiah on the other, and the question arises whether the teacher and the Messiah are not one and the same. [28] If so, [29] Elijah cannot be the "teacher of truth."

c. Quite early expectation of the return of Elijah took a further form of which there are indications already in the pre-Christian period. On this view Elijah is the high-priest of the last time. We know from the Test. XII that already in the 2nd cent. B.C. an eschatological high-priest was expected as well as the Messiah. [30] This expectation,

---

[24] Ginzberg, Sekte, 303 ff. From the 9th cent. Elijah is also called מורה צדק (306 ff.), this being used of pre-eminent scholars from the 11th cent. (311 ff.).

[25] Ginzberg, 316; Staerk, Damask., 95 etc.

[26] In 6, 1 the refer. of the "holy anointed one" is perhaps to Aaron.

[27] The meaning of the phrase "Messiah of Aaron and of Israel" is disputed. Ginzberg's suggestion (Sekte, 324 ff., 342 ff. and esp. 351 ff.) that the ref. is to two figures, the high-priest and the king of the last days, is not acceptable on linguistic grounds, for the document always speaks of the "anointed one" in the sing. The phrase is rather to be explained, as Staerk saw (Damask., 96) in terms of 6, 2 f., where the members of the Damascus community describe themselves as the "percipient ones of Aaron and the clever ones of Israel" (cf. 1, 7). Thus, if the Messiah is of Aaron and Israel, this hardly means that he is of the priesthood and laity as distinct from the dynastic ideal of the Messiah (so Staerk), but it rather expresses the certainty that He will come from the community, which obviously uses the phrase Aaron and Israel of itself as the true priestly people of God (4, 12 ff.; 12, 8).

[28] So S. Schechter, Documents of Jewish Sectaries, I (1910), 211, n. 11 in the first edit. of the document; H. Odeberg, The Fourth Gospel (1929), 154, who in relation to the Messianic title "teacher of truth" refers to Jn. 4:25.

[29] The decisive passage is 7, 18-21. Here the prophecy of the star of Jacob and the comet of Israel in Nu. 24:17 is expounded as follows. The star of Jacob refers to the founder of the community and the comet of Israel to the prince of the whole community (i.e., the Messiah). It is an open question whether these are two different figures or whether we simply have the historical and the eschatological forms of the founder of the community. If the second theory is correct, then the document bears testimony that in the time of Jesus there might be expectation of the return of one already dead as the Messiah.

[30] Test. R. 6; S. 7; L. 2; 8; 18; Jud. 21; D. 5; N. 8; G. 8; Jos. 19. Some of these passages have been worked over by Christians, but the eschatological high-priest who stands alongside the Messianic King belongs to the basic material. For how could a Christian have invented this figure in plain contradiction of Hb. ?

which has its roots in Zech. 4:1 ff., is common in the Talmudic lit. [31] How vigorous it was may be seen from coins of the early period of the revolt of Bar Cochba, which are inscribed "El'azar the priest" as well as "Simon prince of Israel." [32] Expectation of Elijah grew with this expectation of the Messianic high-priest, probably on the basis of a combination of Mal. 3:1; 4:5 f. (Elijah the angel of the covenant) with 2:4-5 (the covenant with Levi). This combination caused priestly descent to be ascribed to Elijah, so that he came to be identified with the high-priest of the Messianic period. [33] The Targumim show how popular was this conception. [34]

As regards the dating of this idea of Elijah as priest and as eschatological high-priest, we may first refer to Ass. Mos. 9:1-7, where immediately before the end (10:1) there is expected the coming of a man of the tribe of Levi whose name Taxo (= Τάξων = [future] orderer) is possibly connected with the task of the returning Elijah as the restorer (→ infra). [35] Reference may then be made to Rev. 11:3 ff., where Elijah and Moses appear before the end and on the basis of Zech. 4:3, 11-14 are called "the two olive trees and the two candlesticks standing before the God of the earth." In Rabb. lit., in accordance with the original, the two olive trees are usually expounded as representatives of the priesthood and the monarchy. [36] We learn from Jn. 1:21 that the priestly descent of John the Baptist was no obstacle to his identification with Elijah. Finally there is the report of Justin (→ 934) that Elijah will anoint the Messiah, it being presumed that he possesses high-priestly dignity. On the other hand, the equation of Elijah with the priestly zealot Pinᵉhas [37] belongs to the post-Christian era. [38]

4. The Task of the Returning Elijah.

The coming of Elijah announces the time of salvation. His task is that of apokatastasis (LXX Mal. 4:5: ἀποκαταστήσει; cf. Mk. 9:12; Mt. 17:11; → I, 387 ff.), the restitutio in integrum of the people of God separated from its God by sin. He prepares the community of salvation for the reception of salvation (Lk. 1:17: ἑτοιμάσαι κυρίῳ λαὸν κατεσκευασμένον). a. The inner restitution of the people of God. In Mal. 4:6 it is said that the returning Elijah will restore peace in families. In LXX Mal. 4:5 (= 4:6) the restoration of peace is extended to the mutual relations of all members of the people. [39] In succeeding periods this was variously expounded. One interpretation is that he preaches repentance. He will "turn the disobedient to the wisdom of the just" (Lk. 1:17) and will wear the garments of mourning in token of his ministry of repentance (Rev. 11:3). "Without repentance Israel will not be redeemed ... They will do great penance

---

[31] Str.-B., III, 696, 812; IV, 457, 460 ff., 789 ff., Ginzberg, Sekte, 330, 342 ff.; Dalman, Der leidende Messias, 8 f.

[32] Schürer, I, 684, 767 ff.; Schl. Gesch. Isr., 374 f.

[33] Str.-B., IV, 462 f., 789-792.

[34] Tg. J., I, Ex. 40:10; Dt. 30:4; Tg. Lam. 4:22.

[35] The figure of Taxo seems to have been influenced by legends of the Maccabean period. The seven martyr brothers of 4 Macc. (1:8 etc.) may be compared with his seven sons (unless we refer to the account in Jos. Ant., 14, 429 of the "robber" who himself killed his seven sons). This does not alter the fact that Taxo is an eschatological figure in Ass. Mos., cf. C. Clemen in Kautzsch Apkr. u. Pseudepigr., II, 326, n. d ; Bousset-Gressm., 232; Schl. Gesch. Isr., 267, 434; v. Gall, 381.

[36] Examples may be found in Str.-B., III, 811 f.

[37] Str.-B., IV, 462 f., 789-792. This equation of the zealot Elijah (1 K. 19:10) with the zealot Pinᵉhas (Nu. 25:11) — cf. Pirqe R. Eli'ezer, 29 — was due to the recurrence of the words "my covenant ... of peace" (Mal. 2:5) in Nu. 25:12 (cf. Nu. r., 21 on 25:12, Str.-B., IV, 791b).

[38] It is first found in Tg. J., I (Ex. 4:13; 6:18; Nu. 25:12) and in post-Tann. lit. (e.g., Pirqe R. Eli'ezer, 29), but it is already familiar to Origen (Comm. in Jn. 1:21 [IV, 123, Preuschen]).

[39] ὃς ἀποκαταστήσει καρδίαν πατρὸς πρὸς υἱὸν καὶ καρδίαν ἀνθρώπου πρὸς τὸν πλησίον αὐτοῦ.

תשובה גדולה only when Elijah comes." [40] Another interpretation of the restoration of peace which reaches back into the pre-Christian period [41] is that Elijah will solve all disputed issues in the sphere of biblical exposition, ritual and law. [42] b. The outer restitution of the people of God. Already in Sir. 48:10 Elijah is given the further task of restoring the tribes of Israel (→ 931). This is usually taken to mean that Elijah will expel illegitimate Israelites and bring back the legitimate to the redeemed people, [43] purity of blood being the only claim to participation in final bliss. But sometimes reference is seen to the regathering of the scattered people, [44] and this is perhaps the original sense of Sir. 48:10. [45] c. Proclamation of the time of salvation. War with Antichrist. Introduction of the Messiah. i. It is repeatedly stated (first in the 4th benediction of the grace after a meal) [46] that Elijah will announce the coming of the time of salvation. [47] ii. On the other hand, the tradition that Elijah will fight Antichrist (first found in Rev. 11:7) and finally kill him (Apc. Eliae, Steindorff, 169) is found only in apoc. lit. → 940. [48] iii. Only outside the older Rabb. lit. do we find the tradition that Elijah will identify (Just. Dial., 8, 4, cf. Test. L. 2) [49] and anoint the Messiah (Just. Dial., 8, 4; 49, 1); there is perhaps a trace of the tradition of the anointing of the Messiah by Elijah in the Rabb. doctrine that Elijah will set up again the three bowls with the manna, the water of purification and the oil of anointing. [50]

Thus Elijah prepares the people of God for the last time. When peace has been restored, the community reconstituted, Antichrist overcome and killed and the Messiah anointed for His kingly office, then the great final age of grace begins.

B. Elijah in the NT.

After Moses (80 times), Abraham (73) and David (59), Elijah is the most frequently mentioned OT figure in the NT (29 + vl. Lk. 9:54).

1. The Historical Elijah in the NT.

Four events from the life of the prophet are mentioned in the NT. The first is a. that he proclaimed the drought (1 K. 17:1) and the associated famine (cf. Lk. 4:25; Jm. 5:17; Rev. 11:6). In all three NT passages the time of the drought is 3½ years, unlike 1 K. 18:1; [51] this is probably a distinctive Palestinian tradition. [52] In Jm. 5:17 f. the drought and its end [53] are both attributed to Elijah's efficacy in

---

[40] Pirqe R. Eli'ezer, 43. Cf. 4 Esr. 6:26, as in → n. 19.

[41] bPes., 70b Bar.; jPes., 3, 30b, 25 (Str.-B., IV, 795, 788 f.).

[42] Str.-B., IV, 794 ff.; Ginzberg, Sekte, 304, n. 1 (a full collection of passages).

[43] Str.-B., IV, 792 ff., cf. 767.

[44] Tg. J., I, Dt. 30:4; Ex. 6:18.

[45] The idea that Elijah will bring about the raising of the dead is occasionally found very much later (Drummond, 224; Str.-B., I, 194; Dalman, Ergänzungen, 11).

[46] This benediction belongs to the 1st cent. A.D. (Str.-B., IV, 634).

[47] Str.-B., III, 8 f. → 716. Cf. Sib., 2, 187-189 (→ n. 50).

[48] → n. 106 for references.

[49] For a late Rabb. statement to this effect cf. Str.-B., IV, 798.

[50] M. Ex. on 16:33 (Str.-B., 797). When we read in Sib., II, 187-189 that the Tishbite will come from heaven in his chariot and give a threefold sign to the whole earth, we are not to think of his bringing back the three bowls but of the eschatological signs which will shake the whole earth (after the manner of the three signs of the truth in Did., 16, 6-7). The silence of Rabb. lit. regarding ii. and iii. may be due to polemical reasons.

[51] "In the third year."

[52] Lightfoot on Lk. 4:25; Kittel, Rabbinica, 31 ff., 35; Kittel Probleme, 53, 59, 150; Dalman, Jesus-Jeschua, 48; Str.-B., III, 761. Like seven elsewhere, the half-seven is a round figure for a long time. Its use in the Elijah tradition has no connection with its use as an apocalyptic number from Da. onwards (Da. 7:25; 12:7; cf. 8:14; 12:11-12; Rev. 11:2, 3, 9, 11; 12:6, 14; 13:5).

[53] For the end of the drought cf. 4 Esr. 7:109. The reference is to 1 K. 18:42, where the fact that Elijah put his face between his knees is — probably correctly — taken to be a

prayer and thus illustrate and prove the statement: πολὺ ἰσχύει δέησις δικαίου ἐνεργουμένη (Jm. 5:16). Elijah did not owe his power to move heaven and earth by prayer to any supernatural endowment (Jm. 5:17 f.). He was "subject to like passions as we are" (5:17). His prayer was effective because he was a δίκαιος (→ 190; Jm. 5:16).

The miraculous nourishment of the heavenly woman in the wilderness (Rev. 12:6, 14), which is represented as accomplished through an angel, is probably modelled on the feeding of Elijah at the brook Cherith (1 K. 17:2 ff.), [54] though there might also be allusion to the provision of manna in the wilderness (Ex. 16:13 ff.; Ps. 78:24; 105:40).

b. The fact that God sent Elijah to a widow of Sidon during the 3½ year drought [55] is used by Jesus in Lk. 4:25 f. to show from Scripture that it may please God to offer salvation to the Gentiles to the exclusion of the salvation people. c. The special Lucan material in the story of Gethsemane (Lk. 22:43, cf. 1 K. 19:5, 7) is reminiscent of the story of the flight of Elijah in 1 K. 19:1 ff. [56] The assurance given on this occasion to the despairing prophet that God has reserved 7000 in Israel who have not bowed the knee to Baal (19:18) [57] makes Paul quite certain that there is present in Israel in his day a sacred remnant according to the election of grace (R. 11:2-5). [58] d. Lk. 9:54 (cf. Rev. 11:5) refers to the divine judgment which Elijah executes on his enemies when he destroys them by fire from heaven (2 K. 1:10, 12; Sir. 48:3). Jesus sharply rebukes the sons of Zebedee for their question whether they should call down fire from heaven on the Samaritan village which would not receive them (Lk. 9:54; vl. attested from the time of Marcion [59] adds ὡς καὶ Ἠλίας ἐποίησεν). For, as additions to the text rightly point out, such a miracle of judgment would be incompatible with the spirit of the Gospel [60] and the saving work of Jesus. [61]

2. The Later Jewish Conception of Elijah in the NT.

a. Elijah as helper in time of need. This is recognised only as a popular Jewish belief in the NT (Mk. 15:35 f.; Mt. 27:47, 49). Through misunderstanding or wilful misinterpretation, the cry of the Crucified 'Eli, 'Eli (Ps. 22:1) [62] is mockingly construed by bystanders as a cry for help to the helper Elijah. "The Messianic claim of Jesus was shattered in Jewish eyes when Elijah failed to help." [63] The Christian

---

gesture of prayer. On the other hand, the OT does not attribute the drought itself to his prayer.

[54] H. Gressmann, Der Messias (1929), 398.

[55] In the ἐπέμφθη of Lk. 4:26 the divine name is contained in the pass.

[56] Perhaps Lk. 22:38b (ἱκανόν ἐστιν) is also to be linked with the Gethsemane narrative and to be interpreted in the light of 1 K. 19:4.

[57] The fem. art. before Βάαλ in R. 11:4 (τῇ Βάαλ) is an indication that we should read τῇ αἰσχύνη (= הַבֹּשֶׁת) (A. Dillmann, Monatsberichte der Berliner Akademie der Wissenschaften, 1881 (601-620); Βάαλ is thus Kᵉthib, αἰσχύνη Kᵉrē.

[58] ἐν Ἠλείᾳ in R. 11:2 means "in Elijah," i.e., "in the Elijah story" (Str.-B., III, 288).

[59] Zn. Lk. ³, ⁴, ad loc. and exc. VIII regards the variants of Lk. 9:54-56 (→ n. 60, 61) as original.

[60] vl. on Lk. 9:55.

[61] vl. on Lk. 9:56.

[62] The misunderstanding shows that Mt. (Heb. address ἠλεί and Aram. question, 27:46) is original rather than Mk. (Aram. address ἐλωΐ [= אֱלָהִי with an obscure articulation of the ā, Dalman, WJ, I, 43, n. 1] and Aram. question), since only the Mt. form explains how there could be the impression that Jesus was calling on Elijah for help. Tg. Ps. 22:2 has the same mixed form as Mt., the Heb. address 'ēlī and the Aram. question, so that this is not at all unusual, but rather to be expected.

[63] Schl. Mt., 783.

community did not adopt the conception of Elijah as helper; it knew only one Helper in time of need, namely, Christ.

b. The return of Elijah. The expectation that Elijah would return prior to the end is assumed to be generally known and recognised in the Gospels (Mk. 9:11; Mt. 17:10 etc.). How tense was the expectation may be seen from the report that the people thought it possible John the Baptist might be Elijah (Jn. 1:21, 25) and that there were circles which were convinced that Jesus was Elijah (Mk. 6:15 [64] par. Lk. 9:8; Mk. 8:28 par. Mt. 16:14; Lk. 9:19). According to Lk. 9:7 f. it seems to have been the miracles of Jesus especially (τὰ γινόμενα πάντα, 9:7) which gave rise to His equation with Elijah. It also appears from Mk. 9:11 that Elijah was expected as the forerunner of the Messiah rather than the Messiah Himself (→ 931). [65] Mk. 9:12 and par. shows that his task was seen to be that of ἀπο-κατάστασις (→ 933), and Rev. 11:3 that this would be brought about through the preaching of repentance (→ 933). The δεῖ of Mk. 9:11 and par. (→ 23 f.) shows finally that there was awareness that this expectation rested on Scripture. On the basis of this δεῖ the scribes tried to dispute the Messiahship of Jesus on the ground that Elijah had not yet come, and the disciples themselves questioned Jesus' announcement of His passion (Mk. 9:11).

c. Elijah's war against Antichrist (→ 940).

3. The NT Understanding of Expectation of Elijah and its Fulfilment in John the Baptist.

a. The Baptist's sense of mission and Elijah expectation. The question whether John related himself to Elijah expectation is difficult to answer in view of the paucity of source material. It certainly cannot be shown that he thought of himself as the forerunner of Elijah. [66] Quite apart from the fact that a forerunner of the forerunner is an ad hoc invention, the description which the Baptist gives of the ἐρχόμενος does not fit the returning Elijah, who is nowhere expected as the One who baptises with the Spirit (Mk. 1:8 and par.) or as the Judge (Mt. 3:12 and par.). [67] More worthy of consideration is the thesis that the Baptist thought of himself as the returning Elijah. [68] There is much to be said for this. Thus he preaches repentance and announces the time of salvation (→ 933; 934). His clothing (a mantle and undergarment of camel's hair and a leather girdle over the undergarment, Mk. 1:6, Mt. 3:4) [69] bears some resemblance to that of Elijah. [70] Finally,

---

[64] On the constr. of Mk. 6:14 cf. H. Ljungvik, ZNW, 33 (1934), 90-92: καὶ ἔλεγον takes the place of an object of ἤκουσεν with ὅτι, so that 14b., like 15, represents the judgment of the people, not the view of Herod.

[65] The reference of Mal. 3:1 to the forerunner of the Messiah, which Mk. 1:2; Mt. 11:10; Lk. 7:27 establish by reading LXX Ex. 23:20: πρὸ προσώπου σου instead of LXX Mal. 3:1: πρὸ προσώπου μου, is not, therefore, a purely Christian theologoumenon.

[66] A. Schweitzer has consistently maintained this thesis (→ Bibl.), also F. Kattenbusch, ZNW, 12 (1911), 283 and more cautiously C. A. Bernoulli, Joh. d. Täufer und die Urgemeinde (1918), 78 f.

[67] W. Michaelis, 55 f., 72 ff.

[68] J. Klausner, Jesus von Nazareth, 333 ff.; W. Michaelis, 74; 84, n. 15; 86.

[69] Not dressed in camel skins and a leather apron etc. The true explanation of Mk. 1:6, in agreement with ancient exegesis, is provided by acquaintance with Palestinian dress, D. Buzy, "Pagne ou Ceinture?" Recherches de Science Religieuse, 23 (1933), 589-598. The special features in the clothing of the Baptist are a. that the undergarment as well as the mantle is woven of rough camel's hair and b. that the girdle is not of linen but (in nomadic style) of leather.

[70] The fact that Elijah wore a mantle (1 K. 19:13, 19; 2 K. 2:8, 13, 14) is in no way distinctive apart from the leather girdle (2 K. 1:8). It would be more significant if בַּעַל שֵׂעָר

Lk. 1:14-17 — assuming that these verses and their context come from circles which followed the Baptist — supports the conclusion that in these circles John was regarded as the returned Elijah, and according to the wording of 1:17 (ἐνώπιον αὐτοῦ = God according to v. 16) [71] Elijah was even seen to be the forerunner who prepares the way for God, and therefore a Messianic figure. [72] Can we deduce from all this that John thought of himself as Elijah? Hardly. The hairy mantle was a common prophetic garment according to Zech. 13:4, so that no important conclusions can be deduced from it, [73] and the fact that John was regarded as a Messianic figure by his followers, and that this corresponded to a widespread popular judgment (Lk. 3:15; Jn. 1:20; Ac. 13:25), does not mean that his own judgment of himself follows the same lines. Above all, caution is enjoined by the silence of the sources. For the only account in the Gospels concerning the Baptist's sense of mission in relation to Elijah expectation tells us (Jn. 1:21, 25) that he repudiated the idea that he was Elijah *redivivus* with an emphatic οὐκ εἰμί. Even though this passage may reflect a trend hostile to the Baptist, it rings true, since it deviates from the common early Christian conception which saw Elijah in John. The most probable view is that the Baptist, who announced the One who was to come without naming Him (Mt. 3:11; 11:3), desired to be himself only the anonymous voice in the wilderness (Jn. 1:23 = Is. 40:3) and no more. [74]

b. The judgment of Jesus concerning John. The fact that Elijah has not returned seems to the scribes to negate the possibility that Jesus is the Messiah and it also seems to have been advanced by the disciples as an argument against the necessity of the passion (Mk. 9:11 and par.). This objection is met by Jesus with the judgment, expressed in veiled form in Mk. 9:13 par. Mt. 17:12 (cf. esp. 17:13) and Mt. 11:10 par. Lk. 7:27 (referring Mal. 3:1 to the Baptist), [75] and in open form in Mt. 11:14, that the Malachi prophecy regarding the return of Elijah has been fulfilled in John the Baptist. The εἰ θέλετε δέξασθαι of Mt. 11:14 seems to be designed to indicate that this interpretation of the figure of the Baptist is new and that the fulfilment of the Elijah prophecy does not take place in the form of a reincarnation. If the sayings mentioned are genuine — and those who deny the Messianic consciousness of Jesus will necessarily dispute them — they are significant because they show how Jesus places Himself under Scripture. No promise of Scripture will fail, and this includes Mal. 4:5 f. [76] It also shows that Jesus understands the ἀποκατάστασις of Mal. 4:5 f., not as a political, but as a religious renewal of the people through repentance and forgiveness. It shows again how close the end is for Jesus, since Elijah is already present as the forerunner of the

---

(2 K. 1:8) meant that Elijah wore clothing of hair, but the LXX and Tg. both take it to mean that he was a hairy man. It is possible that Mk. mentions the leather girdle in ref. to Elijah (2 K. 1:8), cf. E. Lohmeyer, *Das Urchristentum*, I, (1932), 50, n. 2. J. Wellhausen, *Das Ev. Marci*[2] (1909), 4 and H. Peter, *Joh. d. Täufer* (1911), 12 f. find in Mt. 3:4 a reference to Elijah.

[71] Cf. Lk. 1:76 : ἐνώπιον κυρίου is perhaps originally meant in this way.

[72] Bultmann Trad., 178, 320; Kl. Lk. on 1:17; E. Lohmeyer, *op. cit.*, I, 23; F. Hauck, *Das Ev. des Lks.* (1934) on 1:17.

[73] So the majority of scholars, cf. H. Windisch, "Die Notiz über Tracht und Speise des Täufers Joh.," ZNW, 32 (1933), 77.

[74] Cf. Lohmeyer, *op. cit.*, I, 171.

[75] The comparison of John with a burning and shining light (Jn. 5:35) is perhaps to be grouped with the veiled declarations, cf. Midr. Ps. 43 § 1 (134a): " 'Thy light' (Ps. 43:3), that is, the prophet Elijah."

[76] Schl. Mt., 371.

Messiah, and how clearly He sees His passion before Him, since the fate of the Baptist is already known (Mk. 9:13). When the early community takes up this judgment that Elijah expectation is fulfilled in the Baptist (Mk. 1:2; Lk. 1:16 f., 76), it does so with full awareness that it is thus confessing the Messiahship of Jesus.

4. Elijah's Appearance on the Mount of Transfiguration.

It is recorded in Mk. 9:4-5 (par. Mt. 17:3-4; Lk. 9:30, 33) that Elijah and Moses appeared on the Mount of Transfiguration and talked with Jesus. The report is a remarkable one since nowhere in older Rabbinic literature do we find either 1. the idea of two forerunners of the Messiah [77] or 2. the idea that Moses and Elijah will appear together in the last days. [78]

In addition to this twofold difficulty it may be noted that the attempts to expound Mk. 9:4-5 are extraordinarily varied. It has been suggested a. that they represent the Law and prophecy doing homage to Him who is greater (cf. Mk. 9:7); [79] b. that the appearance of the two heavenly figures represents the unveiling of the heavenly world which Jesus experienced in prayer; [80] c. that Elijah appears as the harbinger and Moses as the immediate predecessor[81] of the Messiah; [82] d. that we have here the two escorts of an oriental king, [83] i.e., two heavenly figures who complete the tableau and who, though nameless at first, are later identified and differentiated; [84] e. that the background is to be sought in a Persian conception which has crept into Judaism, namely, that of the two messengers who bring the soul its heavenly garment, [85] or of the two deities, Vaê the wind god and Bahrâm the god of victory, who support Sraosha, the conductor of souls, [86] or of the two precursors [87] or companions [88] of the Persian Saoshyant.

Difficulties arise, in fact, if we maintain that alongside the popular expectation of a single forerunner, which is echoed in Rabb. lit., there was also in the pre-Christian apocalyptic tradition a second form of eschatological expectation which taught the coming of two forerunners of the Messiah. The oldest passage which can be cited is Eth. En. 90:31 (→ 931), then Rev. 11:3 ff. (→ 939), 4 Esr. 6:26 (→ n. 19), Apc. Pt. 2, Copt. Apc. El. (Steindorff [TU, NF, Heft 3a, 1899], 163 f., 169, → 940) etc. [89] This tradition of

---

[77] The few passages which put the Messiah b. Joseph and the eschatological high-priest alongside Elijah (or the Messiah ben Manasse) (Str.-B., IV, 786d, 463-465, esp. 463, n. 2; II, 296c) are all post-Tannaitic.

[78] Str.-B., I, 756-758. We need to correct older presentations (e.g., Volz Esch.², 197; Bousset-Gressm., 233; v. Gall, 378) which appeal to Dt. r., 3 on 10:1, since this is post-Talmudic.

[79] So the usual interpretation of older exegesis and more recently O. Holtzmann, Das NT (1926), 39.

[80] L. Brun, ZNW, 32 (1933), 271.

[81] Cf. Dt. 18:15, 18 and Jn. 6:14; 7:40; Ac. 3:22; 7:37; Midr. Ps. 43 § 1 (Str.-B., I, 87).

[82] A. v. Harnack, SAB, 1922, 76; Kl. Mk. on 9:4. This view is perhaps supported by the conception of Elijah in Mk. 9:4, where the historical order is reversed. This order is restored in Mt. 17:3-4 and Lk. 9:30, 33, also Mk. 9:5 and syˢ 9:4 and Apc. Pt. 16 f. But this involves correction, since Elijah comes first in Rev. 11:3 ff. and the Copt. Elijah Apc. (→ 940). The surprising precedence of Elijah raises the question whether it is imposed by an eschatological order of expectation in which Elijah redivivus will come first and then Moses redivivus.

[83] A. Meyer, Die Auferstehung Christi (1905), 57, 342 f.

[84] Bultmann Trad., 279.

[85] A. Meyer in Festgabe f. H. Blümner (1914), 45 f.

[86] K. G. Goetz, "Petrus als Gründer und Oberhaupt der Kirche und Schauer von Gesichten nach den altchristlichen Berichten und Legenden" in UNT, 13 (1927), 86.

[87] v. Gall, 377 ff. — but the two forerunners come one or two millennia before Saoshyant.

[88] Bousset-Gressmann, 233.

[89] For full materials from early Christian tradition, which is essentially independent of Mk. 9:4 f. and Rev. 11:3 ff. (→ 940), cf. W. Bousset, Der Antichrist (1895), 134-139; K. M. Ittameier, 420 ff.

two forerunners is also present in Mk. 9:4 f. Outside the NT and in passages not influenced by Mk. 9:4 f. and Rev. 11:3 ff. the forerunners are almost always [90] Enoch and Elijah, the link between them being that they were both translated alive according to the witness of the OT. [91] If Mk. 9:4 f. and independently Rev. 11:3 ff. substitute Moses for Enoch, this is obviously because of a tradition which taught a translation of Moses similar to that of Enoch and Elijah. [92]

Elijah and Moses thus appear on the Mount of Transfiguration as the precursors of Jesus. As in Rev. 11:3 ff. their appearance has eschatological significance. [93] It proclaims the inauguration of the last time. Probably we should take a further step. In Rev. 11:3 ff., in the Elijah Apc. and in other traditions of Antichrist, Elijah and his companion are suffering figures of the last time (→ *infra*). Thus their appearance in the story of the transfiguration implies an intimation of the passion of Jesus, confirming the prophecy of Mk. 8:31 ff. Certainly, this is how it is understood in the special Lucan tradition: [94] "They spake of his decease [95] which he should accomplish at Jerusalem" (Lk. 9:31).

5. The Suffering Elijah.

In only one NT passage (Rev. 11:3 ff.) is the expectation that Elijah *redivivus* has still to come in the future plainly [96] advanced as a doctrine of the early Christian community. Here the two preachers of repentance in the last time, who are killed by the beast and who are raised again after 3½ days, are Elijah and Moses. [97] This may be seen from 11:6, where the power to close heaven for 3½ years (→ 934) comes from the Elijah story (1 K. 17:1) and the changing of water into blood from the Moses story (Ex. 7:17, 19, 20). [98]

Since the conception of Elijah in Rev. 11, which expects his coming in the future, conflicts with that of the Gospels, according to which he has already come in the

---

[90] There are very few exceptions. In 5 Esr. 2:18 (P. Riessler, *Altjüd. Schrifttum* [1928]) the mission of Isaiah and Jeremiah is promised, but it is not said that they are forerunners of the Messiah.

[91] Enoch: Gn. 5:24; cf. Sir. 44:16; 49:14; Jub. 4:23; Eth. En. 70:1 ff.; Slav. En. 36:2; Wis. 4:10 f.; Hb. 11:5; Jos. Ant., 9, 28; Elijah: 2 K. 2:11; cf. Sir. 48:9, 12; Eth. En. 89:52; 93:8; Jos. Ant., 9, 28.

[92] The dominant Rabb. tradition teaches the death of Moses (Str.-B., I, 753-756), as also Jd. 9 (the strife concerning his body) and Philo Vit. Mos., II (III), 291. Jos. Ant., 4, 326 is, perhaps intentionally, ambiguous: "A cloud suddenly stood over him, and he was withdrawn from view into a valley. He wrote in the sacred books that he died for fear lest some should dare to maintain, by reason of his outstanding virtues, that he ascended up to the Godhead." The tradition of a rapture of Moses is clearly found in a Bar. preserved in S. Dt. § 357 on 34:5 and bSota, 13b: "Some say that Moses did not die but stands and serves above" (Str.-B., I, 754). It was perhaps contained also in the lost ending of the Ass. Mos. (so Schürer, III, 298, 301; J. Wellhausen, *Das Ev. Marci²* [1909], 69; Bousset-Gressm., 122; P. L. Couchoud, "Les deux Messies," *Mercure de France*, 199 [1927], 580; Loh. Apk., 91; but cf. C. Clemen in Kautzsch Apkr. u. Pseudepigr., II, 312; Str.-B., I, 754).

[93] E. Lohmeyer, ZNW, 21 (1922), 185-215.

[94] Schl. Lk., 100.

[95] On the constr. ἤν = ὅτι αὐτήν (the obj. of the subordinate clause being presupposed in the main clause), cf. J. Wellhausen, *Einl. in die drei ersten Evangelien²* (1911), 12, who rightly perceives Semitic influence.

[96] In Mk. 9:4 f. this expectation is implicitly present.

[97] So Loh. Apk., Had. Apk. and the comm. of W. Bousset⁶ (1906), J. Weiss (*Schr. NT*), J. Behm (*NT Deutsch,* 1935), ad loc.; also Clemen, 144; P. L. Couchoud, *L'Apocalypse* (1930), 149; E. B. Allo, *St. Jean. L'Apocalypse³* (1933), ad loc.

[98] On the combination Elijah and Moses → *supra*.

Baptist, [99] it may be supposed that Rev. 11 borrows from pre-Christian apocalyptic material which treats of the return of Elijah and Moses (or Enoch, → 939) (11:3-6), of their execution (11:7), of the shaming of their corpses (11:8-10), of their resurrection (11:11) and of their ascent to heaven (11:12). This conjecture is supported by Mk. 9:12 f., where Jesus prophesies the suffering of the Son of Man and of Elijah (which is already fulfilled in the execution of the Baptist), since this suggests an extra-canonical tradition which was perhaps expunged from later Jewish lit. for polemical reasons. [100] Reference also seems to be made to this tradition in Lk. 9:31 (→ 939). In fact, this lost later Jewish tradition of the martyrdom of the returned Elijah and his companion in the last days is preserved in several examples of the early Christian Antichrist tradition. [101] Particularly important is the testimony of the Coptic Elijah Apc. edited in 1899 by G. Steindorff. [102]

In connection with the description of the coming of Antichrist we are here told: "When, therefore, Elijah and Enoch hear that the shameless one has displayed himself on the holy place, they come down and fight with him, saying ... The shameless one will hear it and become angry and will fight with them in the market place of the great city and will make war with them for seven days and they will lie dead for three and a half days on the market place in view of the whole people. But on the fourth day they will rise again (163) ... On that day they will rejoice to high heaven as they shine forth and the whole people and the whole world sees them" (164). Elijah and Enoch appear again directly before the *parousia* of the Messiah: "They lay aside the flesh of this world and put on their heavenly flesh; they prosecute the son of lawlessness and kill him" (169). That we have here a similar tradition to that of Rev. 11:3 ff. is shown by the following important points of agreement: the precedence of Elijah; the martyrdom of the two witnesses; the shaming of the corpses for 3½ days; the resurrection and the ascension. The differences are thus the more noteworthy, since they make it plain that Copt. El. is using an independent tradition in which we have Enoch, not Moses, the appearance of Antichrist prior to rather than during the ministry of the two witnesses, a coming specifically to fight Antichrist rather than to preach repentance etc. This conclusion is confirmed by the fact that the features which are independent of Rev. 11:3 ff. recur with "astonishing continuity" [103] in the early Christian Antichrist tradition. [104]

If in the Elijah Apc. we have an independent form of the later Jewish tradition of the martyrdom of the returned Elijah in his struggle with Antichrist, as this is also used in Rev. 11:3 ff., then one feature which takes on great significance is that in the Elijah Apc. the account concludes by telling us that Elijah and Enoch return after their resurrection and kill Antichrist. It is quite possible that this is the original conclusion of the martyrdom of the returned Elijah even though it is not preserved in Rev. 11:3 ff., [105] since Tertullian speaks of Enoch and Elijah being

---

[99] Is this the reason for the fact that the witnesses are not named in Rev.? Or is this part of the secrecy of apocal. style? The early Church was acutely aware of the contradiction, since it is dealt with already by Justin, who suggests that the spirit which was in Elijah reveals himself in John, while Elijah will reveal himself in person at the *parousia* (Dial., 49, 3). This explanation became normative (Tertullian, Origen etc.; cf. K. M. Ittameier, 416 ff.) and is still upheld by L. van den Eerenbeemt, "Elias Profeta in novissimis Diebus," *Verbum Domini*, 4 (1924), 259-263.

[100] I have given further examples of this kind of anti-Christian polemics in ZNW, 25 (1926), 128.

[101] W. Bousset, *Der Antichrist* (1895), 134-139.

[102] → 930. The conclusion of the Copt. Elijah Apc. was not known to Bousset when he wrote the work mentioned in n. 101.

[103] Bousset, *Antichrist*, 138.

[104] For numerous examples cf. *ibid.*, 134-139; Ittameier, 416 ff.

[105] The reason for the omission might be that for the Christian apocalyptist Christ is the One who overcomes Antichrist (2 Th. 2:8; Rev. 19:17 ff.).

"reserved for martyrdom that they might destroy Antichrist by their blood." [106]

It is worth noting that recollection of the suffering Elijah has come down in altered form in the Germanic sagas. The High German poem Muspilli [107] gives us in vv. 37-62 two versions of the battle between Elijah and Antichrist. According to the first, the description by "exalted wise men of the world," Elijah overcomes Antichrist (vv. 37-47), whereas according to the second, the description of "many men of God," he is wounded by Antichrist and when his blood flows to the earth [108] the cosmic fire bursts into flame (vv. 48 ff.). [109]

From the standpoint of biblical theology the establishment of the date of the apocalyptic tradition of the martyrdom of the returning Elijah is of great importance. For it enables us to see that Mk. 9:12 f. is right when it assumes that the idea of a suffering forerunner is not strange to the contemporaries of Jesus. Strong support is thus given to the historicity of Jesus prophecy of His passion and of His statements concerning the atoning power of His death.

J. Jeremias

---

† ἡλικία

This word means in class. Gk. [1] 1. "age," esp. the age of physical maturity, also the age of discretion, of adult life. ἡλικίαν ἔχειν = "to be of age" (e.g., Plat. Euthyd., 306d; Theaet., 142d : εἰς ἡλικίαν ἐλθεῖν); it is often used also of old age (e.g., Hom. Il., 22, 419; Plat. La., 180d; Pind. Pyth., 4, 279 f.: γηραιὸν μέρος ἀλικίας). Collectively οἱ ἥλικες means "contemporaries," "those of the same generation," esp. young men capable of bearing arms (e.g., Hom. Il., 16, 808; Thuc., III, 67, 3; VIII, 1, 2 etc.). 2. "Age" or "generation" (Demosth. Or., 60, 11: ἡ νῦν ζῶσα ἡλικία, "the present generation"; cf. also Isoc., 4, 167: ἡ νῦν ἡλικία; Dinarch. Or., 1, 38 : ἡ ἡμετέρα ἡλικία; Plut. Pericl., 27 [I, 167a]: πολλαῖς ἔμπροσθεν ἡλικίαις); 3. "Physical size" or "growth" as the sign of a particular age (e.g., Hdt., 3, 16; Plat. Euthyd., 271b; Plut. Philop., 11 [I, 362c]; Luc. Historiae Verae, I, 40). The word is also used of the height of pillars in Pseud.-Luc. Syr. Dea, 28.

In the pap. it usually means "age," denoting the various stages of life according to the context. [2] In P. Oxy., III, 437, 7 it means the young men of the gymnasium. In Preisigke Sammelbuch, III, 6611 the gen. τῶν ἡλεικειῶν in the phrase κτίστου τῆς [πό]λεως κα[ὶ] τῶν ἡ[λ]εικειῶν denotes "all the citizens organised by ages." The sense of "size" or "growth" or "stature" is not found in the pap. [3] The fragment of a lost apcr. Gospel in P. Oxy., IV, 655 is no exception. We read here in 14 ff.: τίς ἂν προσθ<εί>η

---

[106] *De Anima*, 50 (CSEL, 20, I, p. 382): *morituri reservantur, ut antichristum sanguine suo extinguant.* Cf. the following Rabb. traditions. Acc. to Jalqut Schim'oni וישלח 32 § 133 (ed. Zolkiew [1858], 154, 1-2) Elijah is killed by the national genius of Edom (= Rome). In Seder 'Olam Rabba, 17 he "was hidden and did not show himself again until Messiah comes ; then he will show himself and be hidden a second time, not showing himself until Gog and Magog come."

[107] W. Braune, *Althochdeutsches Lesebuch*[7] (1911), 83; G. Ehrismann, *Gesch. der deutschen Lit.*, I (1918), 141-150; A. Olrik, *Ragnarök* (1922), 358 f. [I owe this reference to Elisabeth Kittel].

[108] → *supra*.

[109] The same theme is to be found in a Tartar song of the end of the world, which derives from the Elijah saga : "Of the blood of Mai-Tärä the earth will burn in fire" (A. Olrik, *op. cit.*, 364 f.).

ἡ λ ι κ ί α. [1] On this pt. cf. esp. Liddell-Scott, 768, *s.v.* ἡλικία.
[2] V. the examples in Preisigke Wört., *s.v.* ἡλικία.
[3] Cf. also Moult.-Mill., III, 279, *s.v.* ἡλικία.

ἐπὶ τὴν ἡλικίαν ὑμῶν; The saying follows the Synpt. tradition (or Q?) and as in Mt. 6:27 = Lk. 12:25 ἡλικία refers to length of life rather than to physical stature. [4] ἡλικία is often used legally in the pap. for "majority." At 14 (or 20?) [5] the ἀφῆλιξ or minor becomes an ἐνῆλιξ or major. [6] Here are some distinctive expressions. P. Ryl., II, 256, 4 : νυ<ν>ὶ δ' ἐμοῦ ἐν ἡλικίᾳ γεγονότος. It is said of a daughter in P. Oxy., II, 273, 13 : οὐδέπω οὔσῃ ἐν ἡλικίᾳ, and of children in P. Oxy., III, 496, 12 : τέκνων παρὰ τῇ μητρὶ διαιτ[ο]υμένων ἕως ἡλικίας γέ[ν]ωντ[α]ι, cf. BGU, I, 168, 5 : τοῖς ἀτελέσι ἔχουσι τὴν ἡλικίαν. [7] ἡ ἔννομος ἡλικία is a t.t. for legal age, i.e., the age when minority ceases and majority begins. [8]

Philo uses the term in the general sense of "age." Unless specifically defined, the context shows which age is meant. The word acquires a specific nuance when linked with ἀκμή. ἡ ἀκμάζουσα ἡλικία (Aet. Mund., 73) is the age of full maturity and vigour. At this time man is λογικός. In Op. Mund., 104 f. Philo follows Hippocrates in dividing human life into seven ages, and he also quotes approvingly the 10 'weeks' of Solon.

The meaning "age" is also predominant in the Sept. The word is particularly common in 2, 3, 4 Macc. The four ages of youth, [9] maturity, [10] advancing years [11] and old age [12] are distinguished. The sense of "size" occurs at Sir. 26:17. At Cant. 7:7(8) Σ has ἡλικία ("growth") for קוֹמָה, whereas LXX has μέγεθος and 'A the meaningless ἀνάστασις. At Ez. 13:18 Σ and Θ have ἐπὶ πᾶσαν κεφαλὴν πάσης ἡλικίας for the Heb. עַל־רֹאשׁ כָּל־קוֹמָה. Here ἡλικία can mean "age," but "stature" or "shape" is more likely.

In the NT Lk. 19:3 (Ζακχαῖος τῇ ἡλικίᾳ μικρὸς ἦν) is the only passage where the word indisputably means "stature." Mt. 6:27 = Lk. 12:25 (προσθεῖναι ἐπὶ τὴν ἡλικίαν αὐτοῦ πῆχυν ἕνα) has always been debated. ἡλικία might refer to "size," as also πῆχυς. But the context demands that ἡλικία should mean "span of life" [13] and that πῆχυς should be a measure of time. Jesus is saying that anxious care is futile. No one can thereby add even a fraction of time to his life. [14] This is even plainer in Lk. The addition ἐλάχιστον in v. 26 only makes sense if ἡλικία refers to length of days rather than to length of body. The term means maturity in Jn. 9:21, 23. In Hb. 11:11 ἡλικία means age of virility (used of Sarah). There is an interesting par. to Lk. 2:52 ('Ιησοῦς προέκοπτεν ἐν ἡλικίᾳ, "Jesus grew in age") in an inscr. in honour of a young citizen of Istropolis, Ditt. Syll.[3], 708, 18 : [τῇ] τε ἡλικίᾳ προκόπτων καὶ προαγόμενος εἰς τὸ θεοσεβεῖν ὡς ἔπρεπεν αὐτῷ πρῶτον μὲν ἐτείμησεν τοὺς θεούς.

Of theological significance is Eph. 4:13 : μέχρι καταντήσωμεν οἱ πάντες ... εἰς ἄνδρα τέλειον, εἰς μέτρον ἡλικίας τοῦ πληρώματος τοῦ Χριστοῦ. The sentence states the final goal of Christian faith and the Christian life. It makes little difference whether we understand by ἡλικία mature age or full physical

[4] So also Pr.-Bauer, 539. Grenfell and Hunt, the editors of the Oxyr. Pap., take a different view, translating : "Who could add to your stature?" They are followed by Moult.-Mill., III, 279.

[5] Acc. to Preisigke Fachw., 37 the precise age is not known.

[6] V. on ἀφῆλιξ and ἐνῆλιξ Preisigke Fachw., 37 and 76, with bibl.

[7] For further examples cf. Preisigke Wört., s.v. ἡλικία.

[8] Preisigke Fachw., 98, s.v., with bibl. on legal questions. For examples cf. P. Ryl., II, 153, 19 : [ἄχ]ρι οὗ γένη[ται τῇ]ς ἐννό[μο]υ [ἡ]λικίας; P. Oxy., II, 247, 13 : προστρέχοντι τῇ ἐννόμῳ ἡλικίᾳ. Cf. also BGU, I, 86, 19 : μέχρι ἐὰν ἐν τῇ νόμῳ (Preisigke : ἐν τῇ [ἐν-]νόμῳ) ἡλικείᾳ γένο[νται].

[9] 2 Macc. 7:27; 3 Macc. 4:8; 4 Macc. 8:10, 20.

[10] 2 Macc. 5:24.

[11] 2 Macc. 4:40; 6:18 (ἀνὴρ ἤδη προβεβηκὼς τὴν ἡλικίαν); 6:23, 24; 4 Macc. 5:4.

[12] 3 Macc. 6:1; 4 Macc. 5:7, 1, 36; cf. also Wis. 4:9.

[13] So also Wettstein, 334 (on Mt. 6:27): ἡλικία ergo hic significat aetatem, vel tempus vitae. ἡλικία est cursus vitae.

[14] So also Kl. Mt., 63 and Zn. Mt., 294. Zn. gives a short history of exposition, 294, n. 206.

maturity. [15] Since the statement applies to the Church, the meaning is that the work of apostles, prophets, evangelists, pastors and teachers serves the edification of the Church. Its aim is the perfect form of the Church. This perfect form is achieved when all who are appointed to it by the divine plan of salvation belong to the Church. The emphasis is on the words οἱ πάντες. The Church, which is the body of Christ, represents in its perfected form the *pleroma* of Christ. [16]

Schlier takes another view. [17] He expounds Ephesians in terms of the concepts of Persian Gnosticism, and sees in the τέλειος ἀνήρ the heavenly *anthropos,* i.e., Christ, "the supreme point of His own *pleroma.*" Thus Eph. 4:13 means that Christ is in the heavens. He has given the charismatic leaders and teachers for the upbuilding of His body until all believers finally come to Him in the heavenly world. But the words εἰς μέτρον ἡλικίας κτλ. do not allow of this interpretation. We must insist that through the ministry of the apostles, prophets, evangelists, pastors and teachers the Church is to be brought to the perfect form of the σῶμα which represents the fulness of Christ. The fulness of Christ (τὸ πλήρωμα τοῦ Χριστοῦ) is represented in the Church when it has actually achieved its divinely ordained form, i.e., when all the men appointed thereto have been incorporated into the σῶμα Χριστοῦ. The conceptions which Schlier takes over from the *anthropos* myth do not clarify the material situation. Indeed, they obscure the profound but basically simple thoughts of the text.

Schneider

ἡμέρα

A. "Day" in the OT.

1. The ancient Hebrew day consisted of day and night, and according to the cultus it officially began in the evening (Ex. 12:18; Lv. 23:32). The P. creation narrative harmonises well with this cultic usage : the creation of light ; the separation of light and the darkness of chaos, i.e., the creation of daylight ; and then comprehensively : "Thus it was evening and it was morning, one day" (Gn. 1:5). It also worth noting that by creation day and night are in no sense on the same plane or of the same value according to Gn. 1. Day is an effect of specially created light, whereas night is part of the chaotic darkness which intrudes into the cosmic order and separates itself from light. Thus the fact that God recognises day and night as such is on the ancient Israelite view an expression of the ultimate actualisation of their creation and the author thus distinguishes himself theologically from all the mythical and speculative ideas of the surrounding heathen world. Time and

---

[15] Dib. Gefbr., 62 on Eph. 4:13 starts with the words εἰς ἄνδρα τέλειον and is inclined to take τέλειος in the mystical Gnostic sense of the "perfect one." He thinks that the idea of space is suggested by πλήρωμα and μέτρον and that ἡλικία is thus to be related to physical stature. Ew. Gefbr., 197 translates ἡλικία τοῦ πληρώματος as "full age" or "maturity." Schl. Erl., *ad loc.* does not seem to take the gen. τοῦ πληρώματος τοῦ Χριστοῦ too strictly. He translates : "to the full man, to the measure of age which secures for us the fulness of Christ."

[16] Bengel, 490 : ἡλικία *statura spiritualis est plenitudo Christi.*

[17] H. Schlier, *Christus und die Kirche im Epheserbrief* (1930), 28.

ἡ μ έ ρ α. G. Bilfinger, *Der bürgerl. Tag* (1888); M. P. Nilsson, *Die Entstehung u. religiöse Bedeutung des gr. Kalenders* (1918), 12 ff.; Roscher, I, 2031 f., *s.v.*; G.Weicker in Pauly-W., VIII (1913), 230 f., *s.v.*; H. Gressmann, *Der Ursprung der isr.-jüd. Eschatologie* (1905), 141 ff.; L. Dürr, *Die Stellung des Propheten Ezechiel in der isr.-jüd. Apocalyptik* (1923), 75 ff.; S. Mowinckel, *Psalmenstudien,* II (1922), 229 ff.; Volz Esch.[2], 32 : "Der Tag Gottes"; R. Kabisch, *Die Eschatologie des Pls.* (1893), 228-266.

its elementary rhythm are a creation of God, and the whole of the OT bears testimony to the fact that absolutely everything that takes place within the bounds of temporality, i.e., of creatureliness, is under the control of God (Ps. 31:15 : בְּיָדְךָ עִתֹּתָי).

2. Vital though this belief was, the secular nature of life demanded the conception that certain days belong in a special way to God. This is particularly true of set days in the cultic calendar. It is said not merely of the Sabbath (→ σάββα-τον) but also of other cultic feast-days that they are holy to Yahweh (Neh. 8:9). Yet the idea of certain days being specially related to Yahweh is not limited to the cultic life. Thus the day of Midian (Is. 9:3) referred to a day in history whose commemoration was indissolubly linked with Yahweh. Even more widely the day of Yahweh was not a day of the present or the past but a day of the future, and since the terse *status constructus* combination יוֹם יְהוָֹה is not in fact used for present days, and very seldom (→ *infra*) for past, but very frequently for an expected future day, it leads us into a comparatively self-enclosed circle of ideas. This is supported by the constant הַיּוֹם הַהוּא, "where the demonstrative pronoun cannot be explained from the context." [1] It is to-day generally admitted that this circle of ideas was not created by the writing prophets, but was already present in popular belief. How it arose we cannot tell. [2] It is taken for granted in the polemics of pre-exilic prophets, and is obviously deeply embedded in popular belief. The expectation of a day of Yahweh rests on the important presupposition that Yahweh is confessed, i.e., that there is knowledge of His might, of His readiness to save and of His judicial power. Israel knew that with the Gentiles it was in the hands of a God who could be expected in all circumstances to fulfil His promises and threats, so that this expectation was an act of faith.

Nevertheless, expectation of a day of Yahweh should not be too hastily related to the more comprehensive problem of Israelite eschatology. In the interests of linguistic sobriety only that should be called eschatological which really relates to the ἔσχατον, to the final activity of God either for or against Israel. Now there can be no doubt that the day of Yahweh is often to be taken in this sense. Yet from time to time the possibility has to be considered that expectation of a day of Yahweh applies to an event in Israel's history which, though it is of supreme importance, does not imply the inauguration of the last time. In these cases the prophet is simply prophesying a catastrophe or a deliverance which will take place in conceivable time. There is an instructive example in Lam. 1:21: "Thou hast brought the day which thou didst proclaim." The overthrow of Jerusalem was a day of Yahweh. It is now past, history rolls on and one can look back upon it. Ezekiel speaks similarly (34:12) of the day of Yahweh as one which belongs to history, and he here uses the same expression from nature mythology as that used by Zephaniah (1:15) and Joel (2:2) in relation to the "coming" day.

---

[1] Gressmann, *Eschatologie*, 142.

[2] Mowinckel's thesis that the day of Yahweh is the day of His coronation is improbable. It is rendered impossible by Mowinckel's own late dating of the festival (ZAW, NF, 7 [1930], 267). Expectation of the day of Yahweh is older. It was naturally possible that Yahweh's kingship did play some part in the יוֹם יְהוָֹה and that the two circles of religious ideas thus intersected. On the other hand, it must be insisted that the idea of the day of the Yahweh developed in striking alienation from the world of the cultus. The cultus, when followed seriously, seeks constantly to overcome tension in the relationship to God. Only to some degree outside cultic experience and activity do hopes and fears combine to create great tension.

The *locus classicus* for יוֹם יְהֹוָה in Amos 5:18 ff. does seem, of course, to refer to an eschatological hope : "Woe to those who desire the day of the Lord ! What will the day of the Lord be for you ? It is darkness and not light." There is popular longing for a great day of salvation, and the express statement of Amos that it will not be light (אֲפֵל וְלֹא נֹגַהּ, חֹשֶׁךְ וְלֹא אוֹר, v. 18, 20) shows that this hope included cosmic changes (cf. Zech. 14:7). Indeed, an obscure mixture of purely historical and political events on the one side and cosmic changes on the other characterises this expectation as far back as we can trace it. [3] The first time we meet it, it does not have the simple form of an early stage in evolution. It is already a complicated construct. A particular complication is the expectation of natural catastrophes and judgments on the Gentiles on the one hand, and of salvation for Israel on the other. The new thing contributed by the writing prophets is the radical transformation of this hope into a message of judgment. [4] So far as the evidence goes, its content in the pre-prophetic period was one of unequivocal salvation for Israel. Expectation of a day of Yahweh as such is not disputed by the prophets. Even mythological forms of presentation are taken over by them. The new and unheard of feature in their proclamation is that the judgment of this day will not fall on Israel's enemies, as previously believed, but on Israel itself. Alongside the powerful depiction of the day of Yahweh in Isaiah, Zephaniah contains the most comprehensive proclamation of this day of judgment. [5]

3. It is impossible to discern any regular development in the expectation of a day of Yahweh. The ideas of judgment, of mythological natural events and of political catastrophes remain strikingly similar. [6] It has also to be considered that prophesying the day of Yahweh is not the dominant content of every prophetic declaration of the future. It is only one of the forms of such declaration. In Hosea, e.g., it is very subsidiary, and we often have prophesies of judgments, natural disasters etc. with no mention of the day of Yahweh. [7] The fall of Jerusalem and the exile are an important turning-point in prophetic proclamation. After this, prophecy becomes prophecy of salvation and the prophesied day of Yahweh means deliverance, restoration and ultimate salvation for the deeply humiliated people. The very day and hour of this change can be dated in Ez. (33:21 f.). To be sure, he does not speak of the day of Yahweh as a day of salvation. For him the concept יוֹם יְהֹוָה had too negative an orientation to be used in this way. Materially, however, there is the change to prophecy of salvation, [8] and in the post-exilic prophets [9] we have full-blooded prophecies of the day of Yahweh which will bring judgment and destruction to the Gentiles but protection (Zech. 12:1 ff.), purification (Mal. 3:2), cleansing (Zech. 13:1 f.), the endowment of the Spirit (Jl. 3; Zech. 12:10) and paradisean waters (Jl. 4:18; Zech. 14:8) to Jerusalem. The ancient

---

[3] Am. 8:9; Is. 2:6 ff.; Mi. 1:2 ff.; Zeph. 1; Jl. 3:4; Zech. 14:1 ff.; Is. 24:21.

[4] Am. 5:18 ff.; 6:3; 9:10; Ez. 7:7.

[5] Is. 2:6 ff.; 13 (non-Isaianic); Zeph. 1.

[6] Cf. the common catchwords : יוֹם עָנָן וַעֲרָפֶל, Zeph. 1:15; Ez. 34:12; Jl. 2:2; יוֹם עֶבְרָה, Nah. 1:7; Hab. 3:16; Zeph. 1:15; Jer. 16:19; Ob. 12, 14; Zech. 10:11; יוֹם נָקָם, Is. 34:8; 63:4; Jer. 46:10.

[7] E.g., Is. 28:14 ff.; Mi. 1:2 ff.; Jer. 4.

[8] Ez. 34; 36. The Gog Magog passages (38 f.) seem to be an exception with their occasional references to "that day," but, if these are genuine, they probably belong to another phase of his prophecy. H. Gressmann, *Der Messias* (1929), 123 f.

[9] Prophecy of the day of Yahweh has a very minor role in Dt. Is.

popular expectations of salvation now pour into prophetic proclamation in full
flood, and here for the first time the reference seems to be to express eschatological
events, as in the powerful depictions of Joel (3 f.) or Zech. (12 ff.). [10]

This specifically eschatological prospect is sometimes called the end of days,
אַחֲרִית הַיָּמִים. [11] Whether all the examples can be attributed to the authors named is
open to question. On the other hand, there is no reason to exclude this concept
from the pre-exilic period. [12] In relation to OT religion as a whole it is significant
that this emphatically eschatological idea is firmly embedded in it and that in
essentials it is identical with the day of Yahweh as prophesied in the post-exilic
period.

4. If the day of Yahweh is not to be interpreted narrowly as a calendar day,
the fact that this term is used signifies the occurrence of an event which is rich
in content and marks it off from a divinely inaugurated period of time, which the
prophets denote by "the days come," [13] or "in those days," [14] or "at that time." [15]
When Yahweh hides His face, when He visits Jerusalem, when He brings hunger
or paradisean plenty on the land, when all know Him in the new covenant [16] etc.,
the reference is to a state and therefore the authors speak of "that time" or of
"those days" rather than of "that day." Nevertheless, it has also to be remembered
that the time indicated in this way is not always to be understood as an eschatological era. It may also denote specific conditions which will come upon the
contemporaries of the prophet in the more or less immediate future. This is a
possibility which has to be taken into account especially in the case of Jeremiah,
who makes considerable use of these expressions. We must also remember that
there are individual differences in the use of the expressions by different prophets.
Thus Jeremiah, e.g., never speaks of the day of Yahweh, but he frequently refers
to "that time" or "those days" (→ n. 13-15), and in Jeremiah this seems to have
essentially the same meaning as יוֹם יְהוָה in other prophets. On one occasion Ez.
uses עֵת and הַיּוֹם together (7:12; cf. 30:3). This was the more possible the more
eschatological the conception of the day of Yahweh, for eschatologically it signified
in any case the inauguration of a new era.

It is understandable that Daniel did not prophesy the day of Yahweh, which
denoted only an acute crisis, but preferred expressions more in keeping with his
apocalyptic belief. Once he calls the new aeon הָעֵת הַהִיא (12:1). In relation to the
end of the old aeon he speaks of קֵץ (Da. 9:26; 11:27; 12:13), עֵת קֵץ (Da. 8:17;
11:35, 40; 12:4, 9), קֵץ יָמִים (Da. 12:13), אַחֲרִית הַיָּמִים (Da. 10:14). [17] But the concept
behind these expressions is complex. קֵץ, קֵץ יָמִים is the end, עֵת קֵץ the time of afflic-

---

[10] Amos can already prophesy the restoration of the fallen tabernacle of David in "that
day," unless 9:11 is not regarded as genuine. But the main content of his proclamation was
judgment on Israel in the day of Yahweh, and this element now retreated almost completely
into the background.

[11] Is. 2:2; Jer. 23:20; 30:24; 48:47; 49:39; Ez. 38:16; Hos. 3:5; Mi. 4:1; Da. 10:14.

[12] W. Staerk, ZAW, 11 (1891), 247 ff.

[13] Am. 4:2; 8:11; 9:13; Jer. 7:32; 9:24; 16:14; 19:6; 23:5, 7; 31:27, 31, 38; 33:14; 48:12;
51:47, 52.

[14] Jer. 3:16, 18; 5:18; 31:29; 33:15 f.; 50:4, 20; Ez. 38:17; Jl. 3:2; 4:1; Zech. 8:6, 23.

[15] Am. 5:13; Is. 18:7; Mi. 3:4; Zeph. 1:12; 3:19 f.; Jer. 3:17; 4:11; 8:1; 31:1; Ez. 7:7, 12;
Da. 12:1.

[16] Mi. 3:4; Zeph. 1:12; Am. 8:11; 9:13; Jer. 31:31.

[17] Though cf. the Is. apocalypse : בַּיּוֹם הַהוּא, Is. 24:21; 25:9; 26:1; 27:1 f., 12 f.

tion which precedes the end. אַחֲרִית הַיָּמִים has also changed its meaning. In this new complexity of the concept of the end lay the seeds of new shoots which later sprouted in profusion on the stem of earlier expectation of the day of Yahweh.

v. Rad

B. General Greek Usage.

1. "Day": a. "daylight," "light" as distinct from night (historically this is earlier; → νύξ), then of varying lengths; [18] b. "full day," [19] i.e., a period of 24 hours; c. "day" of the week or month etc., hence a fixed day in law. [20]

2. "Time" (not common): a. obj. acc. to its course (in the life of the individual): πρώτη ἡμέρα "time of youth," τελευταία ἡμέρα, "time of old age": Aristot. Rhet., II, 12 (p. 1389a, 24); II, 13 (p. 1389b, 33); cf. Eur. Ion, 720; μακραὶ ἀμέραι, "long lifetime," Soph. Oed. Col., 1216; b. subj. as it is determined by external events and inward experiences or by the resultant situation or disposition of soul (Heracl., I, 75, 9 f., Diels): ὁποίην Ζεὺς ἐφ' ἡμέρην ἄγει, so men think and feel; Soph. El., 266: ποίας ἡμέρας δοκεῖς μ' ἄγειν. Here the sense of "day" sometimes shines through, the concept of time being characterised by its content.

3. Very rarely it is personified in religion and art [21] (e.g., daughter of Helios) in sense 1. a.

C. LXX Usage.

1. It is often used in the LXX as in 1. a. (*v.* esp. Gn. 1:5; ἐγένετο ἡμέρα, 4 Βασ. 4:8, 11; Ju. 19:8: κλῖναι); 1. b. with attrib. (gen.) ἡμέρα καθαρισμοῦ, Ex. 29:36; ἐξιλασμοῦ, Lv. 23:27 f.; also with → πιμπλάναι and → πληροῦν, Gn. 25:24; Lv. 12:4; 2 Βασ. 7:12; sometimes in transition to 2. b. (e.g., ἡμέρα θλίψεως, Gn. 35:3).

2. The use of ἡμέρα in sense 2., which is not common in non-bibl. Gk., is far more widespread in the LXX under the undoubted influence of יוֹם.

a. (i) In what are for us purely temporal definitions, esp. in the plur.: either "lifetime," Gn. 5:17 etc., cf. esp. Gn. 25:7: ἔτη ἡμερῶν ζωῆς Ἀβραάμ; Gn. 18:11: προβεβηκότες ἡμερῶν; infinitely prolonged in Da. 7:9, 13, 22: παλαιὸς ἡμερῶν; or "times" in relative chronological reference to a historical epoch when there is no current means of reckoning. Hence it is used gen. for historical periods, ἡμέραι πρότεραι, Dt. 4:32, ἡμέραι τοῦ αἰῶνος (former time), Mi. 7:14 etc., ἀρχαῖαι, Is. 37:26 etc. → ἔσχαται (αἱ) ἡμέραι, which is strictly eschatological, in Is. 2:2; Ez. 38:16; Da. (LXX, sometimes Θ) 2:28, 45; 10:14; 11:20 = συντέλεια ἡμερῶν, Da. 12:13; sometimes first understood in this way in the LXX, Gn. 49:1; Dt. 32:20; cf. Hos. 3:5; Mi. 4:1; cf. ἔσχατον τῶν ἡμερῶν, Nu. 24:14; Dt. 4:30; Jer. 23:20 etc.; cf. also Jer. 16:14; 23:5, 7 etc. ἡμέραι ἔρχονται. In reality the Jew does not take these as primarily temporal statements; they rather characterise the material context of the event. (ii) In emphatic material and temporal definitions, esp. in connection with expectations of the future, predominantly in the prophets and the Ps., e.g., the day of God (→ n. 2-4) as the time of God's destructive and reconstructive action, ἡμέρα (τοῦ) κυρίου: Am. 5:18, 20; Jl. 2:1; 3:14 (LXX 4:14); Ob. 1, 15; Zeph. 1:7; Is. 13:6, 9; Ἰερ. 32:19 (25:33); Ez. 7:10; 13:5; ἡμέρα (τοῦ) κυρίου ἡ μεγάλη, Zeph. 1:14; Mal. 4:3; ἡμέρα αὐτοῦ, ψ 36:13. [22] It is likely that this action is felt to be much more definitive in the LXX than in the

---

[18] ἡμέρη and εὐφρόνη (night) are one acc. to Heraclitus and are comprehended in God, Fr., 57; 67 (I, 88, 15 f.; 90, 13, Diels).

[19] Nilsson, 12.

[20] Examples may be found in Preisigke Wört., *s.v.* On the naming of days after the emperors (dates of birth, accession etc.), cf. Fritz Blumenthal, "Der ägypt. Kaiserkult," *Archiv f. Papyrusforschung,* V (1913), 336-344.

[21] Cf. G. Weicker in Pauly-W., VIII (1913), 230 f.

[22] On ἡμέρα in the absol. for the day of judgment, though not, or not wholly, in the eschatological sense, cf. Ἰερ. 31:16 (48:16); Ob. 12 [Bertram].

OT (κυρίου is added to the Heb. at ᾿Ιερ. 32:33). [23] ἡμέρα ὀργῆς (αὐτοῦ, κυρίου), ψ 109:5; Ez. 22:24; Zeph. 2:3; Lam. 1:12; 2:21 f. ἡμέρα κρίσεως, Is. 34:8. ἡμέρα ἀντα-ποδόσεως, Is. 61:2; Jdt. 16:17 (20); ἡμέρα τῆς δυνάμεώς σου: ψ 109:3. [24] ἐκείνη ἡ ἡμέρα, predominantly in Is. and Zech. for the day of God's decisive intervention, though naturally in other senses too. The fact that an eschatological signification is often possible but not certain in all these combinations is linked with the fact that םוֹי means generally the time of God's intervention.

b. The subj. use is naturally common in the book which contains the most personal confessions in the OT: ἡμέρα κακῶν μου, ψ 26:5; ἡμέρα τοῦ πειρασμοῦ, ψ 94:8; ἡμέρα θλίψεως, frequently in ψ.

D. NT Usage.

1. ἡμέρα, day.

a. From sunrise to sunset, [25] the time of "sunlight" or "sunlight" itself, hence ἡμέρα μέση, "mid-day," Ac. 26:13; with γίνεσθαι of dawn (only Lk. Ac.; Jos. Ant., 10, 202; Vit., 405); with κλίνειν of sunset (only Lk. 9:12; 24:29); βάρος ἡμέρας, the burden of the sun's heat, Mt. 20:12. As distinct from night, cf. νύκτα καὶ ἡμέραν (also in the plur.) and ἡ ἐν ἡμέρᾳ τρυφή, rioting in "broad daylight," 2 Pt. 2:13. In the new Jerusalem it is always ἡμέρα, i.e., daylight, Rev. 21:25. [26] The degree of brightness is restricted in intensity to a third in Rev. 8:12 [27] as a sign of imminent judgment on the nations. [28] In Rev. 18:8 ἡμέρα denotes, if possible, an even shorter measure of time. [29]

b. The day as a measure of time, from sunset to sunset or from sunrise to sunrise, either ἐν τῇ ἑξῆς ἡμέρᾳ, Lk. 9:37; τῇ ἐχομένῃ ἡμέρᾳ, Ac. 21:26 (Jos. Ant., 5, 327: ταῖς ἐχομέναις ἡμέραις) or with a precise number, μετὰ δύο ἡμέρας, Mt. 26:2 (= "on the second day," cf. Jos. Bell., 6, 68). In connection with the resurrection of Jesus (Mk. 8:31 and par.; 9:31 and par.; 10:34 and par.; 14:58 and par. [?]; 15:29 and par. [?]; Mt. 12:40; 27:63 f.; Lk. 24:7 [21]; Jn. 2:19 f.; 1 C. 15:4): μετὰ τρεῖς ἡμέρας = τῇ τρίτῃ = "on the third day." [30]

As regards the significance and origin of the number three in relation to the day of the resurrection (→ τρεῖς), it is a crucial question whether the Christian community might or might not have had an interest of faith in the length of time between the death and the resurrection. If not, the possibility cannot be rejected outright that the number has intruded into the NT from the myth of dying and rising gods, e.g., Osiris or Attis. [31] This is not at all likely, however, since the doctrine of the resurrection of Jesus on the third day must have been present in the Jerusalem community shortly after the death of Jesus if 1 C. 15:3 is to be taken strictly and to be referred to this original community, and it is highly improbable that the mystery religions could have had any influence here in the short space

---

[23] ἐπ᾿ ἐσχάτων τῶν ἡμερῶν is added in the sense of the eschatological period of salvation at Dt. 8:16, and more clearly as the time of judgment at 32:20 (B) [Bertram].

[24] ψ 109 was expounded eschatologically in early Christianity, Mt. 22:44.

[25] Cf. Str.-B. on Jn. 11:9.

[26] Materially cf. Eth. En. 58:6: "There will be unceasing light."

[27] πλήττεσθαι is a t.t. for darkness of the sun or moon, like the Rabb. הֶקְל, cf. bSukka, 29a: "Darkness of the sun is a bad sign for the nations, darkness of the moon a bad sign for Israel," etc.; cf. M. Ex., 12, 2.

[28] bSukka, 29a: "Thou hast no nation which is smitten whose deity is not also smitten."

[29] Cf. the vl. and Loh. Apk., ad loc.

[30] Cf. Jos. Ant., 7, 280 f.: μεθ᾿ ἡμέρας τρεῖς — τῇ τρίτῃ τῶν ἡμερῶν, also 8, 214/218: obviously meant in full by Jos., without counting the opening day; cf. Ant., 5, 17: δύο ... ἡμέραι for Joshua 3:2: τρεῖς.

[31] J. Leipoldt, Sterbende und auferstehende Götter (1923), 77. For bibl. cf. Kl. Mk. on 8:31; cf. also G. Kittel, Rabbinica (1920), 35-38.

of time available. The simpler solution that "the number three is used as an obvious instance of a small number"[32] would leave open the possibility that the relevant Synoptic passages are not *vaticinia ex eventu*. The fact that the prophecies and the actual span of time agree is no more remarkable than the fulfilment of other prophecies in the NT. But considerations of this nature do not really bring us to the heart of the matter.

What interest of faith, however, could the community have in the resurrection on the third day? It could hardly be an external concern to emphasise the completeness of the death of Jesus by the separation of the soul from the body, since on the Jewish view this separation did not take place for certain until the fourth day.[33] The κατὰ τὰς γραφάς of 1 C. 15:4 (cf. also Lk. 24:7: δεῖ ...) points in a different direction. Scripture proof for the resurrection on the third day might be found in Hos. 6:2: "After two days will he revive us (the nation); in the third day he will raise us up," this being rendered in the LXX: ὑγιάσει ἡμᾶς μετὰ δύο ἡμέρας· ἐν τῇ ἡμέρᾳ τῇ τρίτῃ καὶ ἀναστησόμεθα καὶ ζησόμεθα ἐνώπιον αὐτοῦ. The Targum, of course, alters the decisive point: "He will revive us in the days of consolation[34] which shall come in the future; on the day of the resurrection of the dead he will raise us up that we may live before him." But this alteration is strange and makes us wonder why it is made. When we note that in Rabbinic exegesis the number three in Hos. 6:2 Mas. is referred to the final resurrection, there must have been some good reason for the suppression of the two numbers in the Targum. In view of the revision of the Ebed Yahweh songs in the Targum, which seems to be according to the same principles,[35] the most probable explanation is that it was thought to be necessary to undermine the Christian reference of Hos. 6:2 to the resurrection of the Messiah by altering the plain text at these two difficult points. To the same end there is a change of the days into millennia where the Heb. text is retained in Rabbinic exegesis (Sanh., 97a). Thus the passage is proof of "the resurrection of the dead on the third day after the end of the world"[36] according to Pirqe R. Eliezer, 51, while elsewhere in Rabbinic literature Hosea 6:2 is regarded as a basis for the hope of the resurrection.

It is probable, therefore, that the resurrection of Jesus on the third day was regarded by the early community as grounded in Scripture, and when we remember that Jesus related OT passages to His own destiny to give a detailed picture of the future development of His course, and that His whole Messianic consciousness is inconceivable apart from selected parts of the OT, there is every reason to suppose that He Himself, being certain of the resurrection in accordance with an inner necessity,[37] found the relative day of His resurrection in the OT, namely, in the בַּיּוֹם הַשְּׁלִישִׁי of Hos. 6:2.

The difficulty has often been advanced that there is a discrepancy between the τῇ ... τρίτῃ of Mt., Lk. and Pl. and the usual μετὰ τρεῖς ἡμέρας of Mk. But in this connection it has to be remembered that difficulties always arise in the reckoning of days according to Jewish usage. Thus "in Halachic statements part

---

[32] Leipoldt, 79. Examples in the NT are Lk. 13:32 f. (Leipoldt, 79), perhaps also Mk. 14:58 and par.; 15:29 and par.; Jn. 2:19 f.

[33] Leipoldt, 78 f.; in the NT Jn. 11:39 (*ibid.*, 79).

[34] An eschatol. term; cf. Levy Chald. Wört., *s.v.* נחמתא and Levy Wört., *s.v.* נחמה.

[35] Cf. Str.-B., I, 482 f.

[36] *Ibid.*, I, 747. Pirqe R. Eliezer, 51: "All inhabitants of the earth will taste of death ... And on the third day he will requicken them and set them before him, cf. Hos. 6:2."

[37] Cf. Clemen, 98; Kittel, *op. cit.*, 37.

of a day is reckoned as a whole day" [38] and already in the first century A.D. we read: "A day and a night constitute a עונה (a full day), and part of a עונה counts as a whole עונה" (jShab., 12a, 15, 17; it is in this light that we are to understand Mt. 12:40). Thus the Marcan narrative means that Friday and the night up to the resurrection are each counted as a day, while Mt., Lk. and Pl. (perhaps unintentionally) use a mode of expression which would be regarded as more correct by Greeks. Both forms are found in close proximity in Mt. 27:63 f.; → n. 30.

ἐκείνη ἡ ἡμέρα (→ infra) is often used to fix definite points of time (individual days) in a narrative (also in the plur.) with ἐν (though Jos. probably feels this to be a Semitism and avoids it).

ἡμέρα is relativised into something inconceivable in 2 Pt. 3:8 (following ψ 89:4). For (τὸ) [39] καθ᾽ ἡμέραν cf. esp. 1 C. 15:31; 2 C. 11:28; Lk. 9:23; 11:3; for ἡμέρα καὶ ἡμέρα, 2 C. 4:16. [40]

c. Day of the week etc., μία τῶν σαββάτων (the first, cf. ἐν ἡμέρᾳ μιᾷ τοῦ μηνός: Ex. 40:2; 2 Ἐσδρ. 3:6; cf. 10:17); Mk. 16:2 and par. (obviously Lk. 24:1) etc. Date, Rev. 9:15. "Day of judgment," 1 C. 4:3 (→ n. 22, but not strictly). "Religious fast or feast day," Rom. 14:5 f.; Gl. 4:10; Christian, ἡμέρα κυριακή, Rev. 1:10; Jewish: ἡμέρα τῶν σαββάτων (τοῦ σαββάτου), Lk. 4:16; 13:14, 16; 14:5 (Jos. Ant., 14, 264; 12, 259; 7, 305; יום הַשַּׁבָּת: Tanch. B נשא, 43-44), ἡμέρα τῶν ἀζύμων, Lk. 22:7; ἡμέρα παρασκευῆς, Lk. 23:54 (jPes., 30d: יומָא דַ עֲרוּבְתָּא).

2. ἡμέρα, Time.

This usage of ἡμέρα has par. in the OT, in Aram., and in the LXX. It is thus influenced by Semitic modes of thought [41] (cf. Tg. Is. 9:5: יומוהי [as in the OT: בְּיָמָיו] = αἱ ἡμέραι αὐτοῦ = "the time of His [Messiah's] rule").

a. Obj. in the plur. "lifetime," Hb. 5:7; "time of existence," Hb. 7:3; "space (of years)," Hb. 12:10. ἡμέραι τινός, like בִּימֵי פְלוֹנִי in the OT (and the corresponding LXX) [42] of past epochs of Jewish history (cf. Tanch. B בלק, 14 [p. 140]: מִימֵי נֹחַ); for fixing historical events with greater chronological exactitude; [43] thus also ἐκεῖναι (the Gospels passim, like the OT הַיָּמִים הָהֵם, → 947). Of future events, Rev. 10:7 and the Mt. and Mk. Apc. ἡμέραι ἀρχαῖαι (= time of the early community), Ac. 15:7 (corresponding to πρότερον ἡμέραι in Hb. 10:32). Eschatologically: → ἔσχαται ἡμέραι (like the OT אחרית הימים, but in the same sense as the LXX), either (imprecisely) the time just before the last judgment, 2 Pt. 3:3; of the present, Ac. 2:17; Jm. 5:3 (this is why the guilt of the wealthy is so heavy); or the time of judgment

---

[38] Str.-B., I, 649. מקצת היום ככולו, "part of a day counts as a whole day," e.g., bNazir, 5b; Pes., 4, 2.

[39] Cf. Lk. 19:47; Jos. Ant., 19, 70: τὸ καθ᾽ ἡμέραν; 18, 242: τοῦ ἐφ᾽ ἡμέρας.

[40] On the syntax, cf. Pr.-Bauer, 540 f.

[41] There is here neither a mere dependence on the OT nor a derivation from similar Rabb. usage. The Rabb. par. simply illustrate the distinctive elements in the Semitic conception of time. As in the LXX ἡμέρα is a linguistic but not a material translation of יום, so the Semites who wrote the NT translated verbally but retained the OT content. They thus used the Gk. terms within the Jewish concept of time.

[42] Particularly striking is the echo of Hebraisms (such as we find in the LXX) in the opening chapters of Ac., esp. in the speeches. But this is even more striking in Lk. 1 f. (1:7, 18; 2:36: προβεβηκυῖα ἐν ἡμέραις, "lifetime"; "accomplishment" of time, 1:23; 2:6, 21 f., 43; cf. Ac. 9:23; 21:27; cf. also Lk. 1:24 f., 80) in contrast to the later chapters.

[43] On Mt. 2:1 cf. the linguistic par. in Lv. r., 35 on 26:3: בִּימֵי הוֹרְדוֹס הַמֶּלֶךְ; on Hb. 1:2: αὗται αἱ ἡμέραι, "the present time," cf. Jer. 23:20. Everywhere there is the same Semitic linguistic sense.

itself, 2 Tm. 3:1 (cf. ἡμέραι ἐκδικήσεως, Lk. 21:22). ἐλεύσονται ἡμέραι (non-
eschatol., after the death of Jesus), Mk. 2:20 and par.; ἔρχονται ἡμέραι (time before the
judgment), Lk. 23:29, though cf. Hb. 8:8, quoting Jer. 31:31; ἥξουσιν ἡμέραι (destruction of Jerusalem), Lk. 19:43 (= ἐλεύσονται ἡμέραι, 21:6). Lk. 17:22 : the "days of
the Messiah," (a stock term in Rabb. theology, [44] e.g., Ber., 1, 5 : יְמוֹת הַמָּשִׁיחַ). [45]

In the singular, the term can mean the eschatological time of judgment and
salvation. In connection with the development of later Jewish apocalyptic, in which
predominantly political and temporal expectation changes decisively into a nationally restricted but genuinely definitive or eschatological hope for the renewal of
the world, sometimes with a strong transcendental character, the concept of the day
undergoes a parallel transformation. The term is clarified to the degree that it
refers unequivocally to the divine action in the last days. But it can be used in
very different ways as regards its content and its temporal extension. Where it
embraces the final tribulation, one may read : ἔσσεται ἦμαρ ἐκεῖνο χρόνον πολύν
(Sib., 5, 351), and since this may also be described as κρίσις (ibid., 3, 55 f.), the
expression "day of judgment," which is the most frequent in occurrence, must
also be taken to include generally the time of final affliction. Here may be seen
the influence of the OT hope of the future according to the later Jewish understanding. Nevertheless, it is more exactly in accordance with the sense of Jewish
apocalyptic when the term is used for the day of the great final judgment of the
world. It is noteworthy that in most cases the "day" is furnished with an attribute
which defines its content, usually the "day of judgment," esp. 4 Esr. and Eth. En.,
Slav. En.; the "day of the great judgment," esp. Eth. En., Slav. En.; more rarely
the "day of God" ("thy day," S. Bar. 48:47; 49:2) or the "day of the Messiah"
(4 Esr. 13:52 : the "day of the Servant"); Eth. En. 61:5 : the "day of the Elect").
It is perhaps in keeping that the "day of God" does not appear in the brief
allusions of Josephus. Certainly the Rabbis use this expression very sparingly :
עַד שֶׁיָּבֹא הַיּוֹם שֶׁל ה" (Cant. r. on 7:3; the plur. יְמוֹת הַמָּשִׁיחַ is to be construed differently,
→ supra). The special expression "day of God" or "day of the Messiah" is always
interpreted as the day of judgment.

If the "day of God" or the ἡμέρα κυρίου plays a more important part in the
NT, this, too, may be traced back directly to the usage of the OT (or the LXX).
Materially, especially in the non-Pauline literature, the influence of the apocalyptic
circle of ideas is not to be underrated. It is of truly decisive importance in relation
to the world of thought of Jesus Himself, though naturally only to one specific
part of it. It seems highly probable that in His Messianic terminology Jesus was
influenced, if not by the imagery of Enoch (Eth. En. 37-71), at least by a group
dependent on it. If instead of the "day of the Elect" of Eth. En. 61:5, Lk. 17:24
has the "day of the Son of Man," this implies a mere shift in terminology by
Jesus on the basis of the equation of the Son of Man and the Elect in Enoch itself.
At the decisive point, namely, the referring of the day to the Messiah rather than
to God, the content is the same. In Lk. 17:24 Jesus describes as the day of the Son
of Man that point in time when He shall appear in the glory of the kingdom. In
Jn. 8:56, too, His day is the day of the definitive revelation of His glory (cf.
4 Esr. 13:52, which is perhaps post-Christian).

There is, however, a return to pre-Christian thinking in the use of ἡμέρα θεοῦ,
and also of ἡμέρα κυρίου with reference to God, in non-Pauline literature,

---

[44] Cf. also Str.-B., IV, 816; Excursus 29.
[45] On other uses of ἡμέρα cf. Pr.-Bauer, s.v., 542 f.

although here, too, we may discern a similar and materially perhaps even stronger influence of Jewish apocalyptic. In 2 Pt. 3:12, as in Jewish conceptions, the ἡμέρα θεοῦ, which is an alternative for ἡμέρα κυρίου in v. 10, is the time of the cosmic conflagration (cf. Sib., 3, 54). It may also be the time of the war of the true Ruler of the world against the kings of the earth (Rev. 16:14 : ἡμέρα ἡ μεγάλη τοῦ θεοῦ; cf. Ac. 2:20, quoting Jl. 3:4).

In Paul, [46] on the other hand, the "day" plays an essential part as the day of world judgment for the community (1 C. 1:8; Phil. 1:6, 10 [1 C. 5:5 ?]), for the apostle himself (2 C. 1:14; Phil. 2:16) and also, of course, for non-Christians. In the passages mentioned its main importance is as an ethical incentive. In 1 Th. 5:2; 2 Th. 2:2 the primary concern is the *parousia* of Christ and therefore the definitive manifestation of His glory. Obviously in Paul, as in the Gospels, Christ is the Lord of this ἡμέρα. It is true that in Th. we find only ἡμέρα κυρίου, but in 1 and 2 C. this is sometimes enlarged to ἡμέρα τοῦ κυρίου ἡμῶν Ἰησοῦ, while in Phil. we have the simpler ἡμέρα Χριστοῦ [Ἰησοῦ].

The absolute use of ἡμέρα (without genitival attribute) is used for the day of judgment at 1 Th. 5:5; 1 C. 3:13 and Hb. 10:25. This is to be explained in terms of OT terminology (cf. Mal. 3:19 : הַיּוֹם). The same is true of the formula ἐκείνη ἡ ἡμέρα, which denotes the all-embracing day of judgment (Mt. 7:22; Lk. 10:12; 2 Tm. 1:12, 18 [4:8]). [47] In this use of ἡμέρα we can see the tendency of Semitic languages to evaluate temporal terms from the standpoint of their content, and even to understand them as essentially charged with content. This is true of the designation of the day of judgment as ἡμέρα μεγάλη (Jd. 6; Rev. 6:17; 16:14), for which there are models in the LXX.

The difference in the material filling out of ἡμέρα is thus partly present under OT and later Jewish linguistic influence, but it is kept down to a minimum. For the day of the manifestation of the glory of Christ is very closely linked with the day of world judgment. Thus the "day" acquires a more fixed content through the concentration of expectation of the future on the person of Jesus. Herein lies the distinction from the OT and also the greater precision as compared with later Jewish apocalyptic except in so far as this exerted particularly strong influence, e.g., on Rev. and 2 Pt.

Occasionally the content of the "day" is denoted by such phrases as ἡμέρα κρίσεως (cf. LXX; e.g., jChag., 77a, M : יוֹם הַדִּין Ex. r., 23 on 15:1), [48] Mt. 11:22, 24; 12:36 (cf. S. Nu., 112 on 15:31; Nu. r., 14 on 7:54); 1 Jn. 4:17; 2 Pt. 2:9; for 3:7 → *supra* on 3:12 (cf. R. 2:16; Ac. 17:31); ὀργῆς κτλ., R. 2:5 (cf. ψ 109:5), cf. Rev. 6:17; also in the positive sense ἀπολυτρώσεως, Eph. 4:30.

In relation to the eschatological awareness of early Christianity it is important to affirm that in these passages ἡμέρα is a purely future and eschatological concept. Nowhere [49] is there any suggestion that this "day," which is not only a day

---

[46] It is hard to understand why Kabisch, 266 sees an equation of the "day" and the millennium in Pl. Certainly no passage gives grounds for the assumption that Pl. understood the day of judgment as also "day as the time of light in antithesis to night" (Kabisch, 236).
[47] Perhaps this more specific sense is also present in Mt. 24:36; Lk. 21:34; 2 Th. 1:10 (2 Tm. 4:8). On the other hand ἐκείνη ἡ ἡμέρα means generally the time after the death of Jesus in Mk. 2:20; Jn. 14:20; 16:23, 26.
[48] For similar passages, cf. Str.-B., IV, 1093 f. (b).
[49] In Hb. 4:7 ἡμέρα is the future time of rest which is now (σήμερον) promised as the Sabbath of the new covenant (on → ὁρίζειν, cf. Jos. Ant., 6, 103). 2 C. 6:2 is not relevant in this connection; it simply tells us that the time of salvation promised to the fathers is now present.

of judgment, is already present or even reaches into the present. It will dawn with the revelation of the glory of Jesus at His *parousia*. In other passages the day fixed for the resurrection (of the righteous) is called the ἐσχάτη ἡμέρα (Jn. 6:39 f., 44, 54; 11:24). It brings temporal being in the present aeon to an end and is thus the last day.

It can also be used in the general sense of a point of time in Col. 1:6, 9 etc. This can sometimes be meant by day, cf. Mt. 24:38, 42; 26:29; Lk. 17:30; Jm. 5:5; 1 Pt. 2:12. The two last passages are not meant eschatologically. In Jm. 5:5 ἡμέρα σφαγῆς is the time of an unrecognised need (of the poor), and in 1 Pt. 2:12 ἡμέρα ἐπισκοπῆς is the time of your earthly rehabilitation (through God). The sense in Lk. 19:42 is the (decisive) time (→ καιρός).

b. Subj. we have in the sing. ἡμέρα πονηρά, Eph. 6:13, the time of the μεθοδεῖαι τοῦ διαβόλου, v. 11, = ἡμέρα τοῦ πειρασμοῦ, Hb. 3:8 (quoting ψ 94:8). ἡμέρα εὔκαιρος, Mk. 6:21. In the plur. "the course of time," Eph. 5:16; ἰδεῖν ἡμέρας ἀγαθάς, 1 Pt. 3:10 (quoting ψ 33:13; cf. Eth. En. 102:9 : "Ye sinners, it suffices you ... to see good days").

3. ἡμέρα in the sing. is used figuratively at Rev. 11:9, 11 in the sense of year. It is also used figuratively in the sense of 2. a at Jn. 9:4; 11:9a (the lifetime which God has appointed for man), and in the sense of 1. a. at Jn. 11:9b (the light which illuminates Jesus in His decisions, cf. v. 10). According to R. 13:12 f. the epoch since the resurrection of Jesus Christ is the time of daylight whose brightness is shunned by the world of demons (σκότος), so that Christians are under obligation not only to keep themselves from the immoral influences of this world but also from all inner possibilities in this direction. For Christians are children of this age of light. That is to say, they share in its brightness, their whole existence being illumined by it (1 Th. 5:5, 8). [50] In 2 Pt. 1:19 faith, which is propagated by the OT Word, is the brightness of day before which the powers of darkness cannot stand.

Delling

---

† Ἠσαῦ

1. The rejection of Esau is applied typologically by Paul in R. 9:13. Paul is seeking to prove that God's counsel is dependent neither on the privilege of birth nor on merits. Esau is no less the son of Abraham than the elect Jacob. Thus the privilege of birth belongs equally to the descendants of Esau and to the descendants of Jacob, i.e., Israel, who call themselves the sons of Abraham. Nor is it a matter of merits or the reverse, "for the children being not yet born, neither having done any good or evil, that the purpose of God according to election might stand, not of works, but of him that calleth, it was said unto her (Rebekah), The elder shall serve the younger" (R. 9:11 f.). This typological use of the story of Esau's rejection is peculiar to Paul. There are no parallels to it in contemporary Jewish writings.

One may not appeal at this point to general ideas of predestination in Judaism. On the contrary, in their handling of the rejection of Esau Jewish writings start with the basic continuation of his privilege of birth. Solution to the problem is sought and found

---

[50] ἡμέρα cannot have eschatological significance here (H. E. Weber, *Eschatologie und Mystik im NT* [1930], 48), → νύξ; ἡμέρα as the day of judgment is always future in the NT. The material understanding of ἡμέρα in Kabisch, 249 is also impossible.

along the lines that the privilege was invalidated by his evil works. In this respect future works, both his own and his descendants', were foreseen and taken into account. At the very most, therefore, we have here only a *praedestinatio de praeviso*. The Jewish standpoint is typically expressed in Jub. 35:13 : (Isaac says) "... I once loved Esau more than Jacob because he was born first. But I now love Jacob more than Esau because the latter has done many wicked works and there is no righteousness in him, but all his ways are unrighteousness and violence, and there is no righteousness about him ... He and his seed cannot be saved but are such as will perish from the earth ... for he has forsaken the God of Abraham ... he and his children." Esau and his people have by their own choice separated themselves from the children of Abraham. "They (the descendants of Esau) became estranged to God, since they did not become children among those who feared the Lord." [1] There is an apparent — but only apparent — similarity to Paul's train of thought in 4 Esr. 3:16 : "And thou didst choose Isaac for thyself, but didst reject Esau." Esau, who is here a type of worldly power (Rome), is rejected because of his wickedness. Thus Esau is consistently called "the wicked one." In Rabbinic writings Ishmael and Esau are represented as belonging originally to the children of Abraham but as later excluded because of their uncleanness. "For three generations uncleanness (זוהמא) did not disappear from our fathers : Abraham begat Ishmael, Isaac begat Esau and only Jacob begat the twelve tribes in whom was no spot (דופי)". [2] In Jewish writings Esau signifies Edom, [3] then Rome and the Christian Church. [4] The starting-point of Philo's allegorical use of the name of Esau is the tradition which represents Esau as "the wicked one." For him, therefore, Esau can represent allegorically τὸ φαῦλον καὶ ἄλογον etc. [5]

2. In Hb. 11:20 Isaac blessed Esau concerning things to come. The current view of contemporary Judaism was that God caused Isaac unconsciously in the act of blessing to subordinate Esau to his brother because He foresaw the wickedness of Esau. Only later did Isaac see the reason for this divine action. [6]

3. On the other hand, Hb. 12:16 is at one with general Jewish tradition when it calls Esau a βέβηλος (→ I, 605). So, too, is 1 Cl., 4, 8 when it represents Esau as a type of the jealous man and illustrates the evil effects of jealousy from the story of Esau and Jacob : "... rivalry and envy are responsible for fratricide. Because of rivalry our forefather Jacob fled from the presence of his brother Esau..." (→ Ἰακώβ).

Odeberg

---

† ἠχέω

a. Intr. "to sound," "to ring," "to peal," "to boom." b. Trans. "to cause to sound." The med. also in the sense of "to sing" (e.g., Pind. Fr., 75, 18 f.: ἀχεῖ τ' ... Σεμέλαν). The word is used with χαλκός or χαλκεῖον in Hdt., IV, 200 : ἠχέεσκε ὁ χαλκὸς τῆς ἀσπίδος; Plat. Prot., 329a : χαλκεῖα πληγέντα μακρὸν ἠχεῖ; Theocr. Idyll., 2, 36 : χαλκίον ἀχεῖ.

It occurs in different connections in the Septuagint. Thus it may be used for the "sounding of a zither" (Is. 16:11; Σ reads : ἡ κοιλία μου ὡς ψαλτήριον ἠχήσει);

Ἡ σ α ῦ. [1] Test. B., X, 10.
[2] bShab, 146a; cf. Jub. 15:30 (God does not choose Ishmael and Esau, even though they are children of Abraham, because He knows them).
[3] Jub. 24:6; 38:8, 14 etc.
[4] 4 Esr. 6:7-10; bGit., 56b, 57b; jAZ, 1, 2; bPes., 5a.
[5] Philo Leg. All., III, 29 etc.
[6] Cf. Jub. 35:13; Gn. r., 67 on 27:33 f.; 78 on 33:8 f.

of the "roaring of the sea or its waves" (Is. 51:15; Ἰερ. 27:42; ΣΘ ψ 95:11; Σ ψ 97:7; Θ Is. 24:14); of the "ringing of the earth" (1 Βασ. 4:5; cf. also 3 Macc. 1:29 : τὰ τείχη καὶ τὸ πᾶν ἔδαφος ἠχεῖν); of the "tumult of enemies" (ψ 82:2); even of the "howling of a dog," Θ ψ 58:6 : καὶ ἠχήσουσιν ὡς κύων; LXX : λιμώξουσιν (λιμώσσω = "to be hungry") ὡς κύων. It is used figur. at Ju. 1:19 : ἤχησεν πᾶσα ἡ πόλις, "the whole city was in an uproar" ; cf. also 3 Βασ. 1:45; Ἰερ. 31:20 Ἀ : ἤχησεν ἡ κοιλία μου αὐτῷ, "my heart beats for him" (Σ : ἐταράχθη τὰ ἐντός μου ἐπ᾽ αὐτῷ). Cultic use is found at Sir. 45:9 : The little bells on Aaron's robe give out a sweet sound (ἠχῆσαι φωνήν); Sir. 50:16(18), in the description of the high-priestly ministry of Simon : The sons of Aaron blow on the trumpets (ἐν σάλπιγξιν ἐλαταῖς ἤχησαν); Sir. 47:10 : The sanctuary resounds with jubilation (ἠχεῖν τὸ ἁγίασμα).

In Philo Cher., 7: ἠχεῖ μὲν γὰρ ὁ γεγωνὸς λόγος, πατὴρ δὲ τούτου ὁ νοῦς, "the loudly spoken word resounds ; its father, however, is the spirit."

In the NT the word occurs only at 1 C. 13:1. [1] Paul compares *glossolalia* without love to the resounding of a brass cymbal. It is empty noise without clarity, meaning or deep significance. Above all, such ecstatic speech has no moral worth, however brilliant and perfect its execution. If spiritual utterance of this kind cannot be brought into combination with love, i.e., if it cannot be made to serve the edification of the community, then it is a mere clanging which may draw attention and intoxicate the hearers but which cannot produce any decisive spiritual or moral results. [2]

The χαλκὸς ἠχῶν (= χαλκεῖον) is usually taken to be the gong which was hung in temples or on sacred trees and on which long and booming notes were struck in orgiastic cults to induce a state of ecstasy. [3]

Schneider

ἠ χ έ ω. [1] At Lk. 21:25 the *textus receptus,* with D ℜ al, has ἠχούσης θαλάσσης (instead of ἤχους θαλάσσης).

[2] Joh. W. 1 K., 313 takes rather a different view. For him love is the full inner emotion which impels to self-forgetful self-giving. Cf. Bengel, 425 : *sine vita et sensu.* For the view represented above, cf. Bchm. 1 K., 298.

[3] Cf. esp. Joh. W. 1 K., 313.